ALTITUDE CORRECTION TABLES 0°-10°—SUN, STARS, PLANETS A3

App. Alt.	OCT.—MAR. SUN Lower Limb	OCT.—MAR. SUN Upper Limb	APR.—SEPT. SUN Lower Limb	APR.—SEPT. SUN Upper Limb	STARS PLANETS
° ′	′	′	′	′	′
0 00	−17·5	−49·8	−17·8	−49·6	−33·8
0 03	16·9	49·2	17·2	49·0	33·2
0 06	16·3	48·6	16·6	48·4	32·6
0 09	15·7	48·0	16·0	47·8	32·0
0 12	15·2	47·5	15·4	47·2	31·5
0 15	14·6	46·9	14·8	46·6	30·9
0 18	−14·1	−46·4	−14·3	−46·1	−30·4
0 21	13·5	45·8	13·8	45·6	29·8
0 24	13·0	45·3	13·3	45·1	29·3
0 27	12·5	44·8	12·8	44·6	28·8
0 30	12·0	44·3	12·3	44·1	28·3
0 33	11·6	43·9	11·8	43·6	27·9
0 36	−11·1	−43·4	−11·3	−43·1	−27·4
0 39	10·6	42·9	10·9	42·7	26·9
0 42	10·2	42·5	10·5	42·3	26·5
0 45	9·8	42·1	10·0	41·8	26·1
0 48	9·4	41·7	9·6	41·4	25·7
0 51	9·0	41·3	9·2	41·0	25·3
0 54	− 8·6	−40·9	− 8·8	−40·6	−24·9
0 57	8·2	40·5	8·4	40·2	24·5
1 00	7·8	40·1	8·0	39·8	24·1
1 03	7·4	39·7	7·7	39·5	23·7
1 06	7·1	39·4	7·3	39·1	23·4
1 09	6·7	39·0	7·0	38·8	23·0
1 12	− 6·4	−38·7	− 6·6	−38·4	−22·7
1 15	6·0	38·3	6·3	38·1	22·3
1 18	5·7	38·0	6·0	37·8	22·0
1 21	5·4	37·7	5·7	37·5	21·7
1 24	5·1	37·4	5·3	37·1	21·4
1 27	4·8	37·1	5·0	36·8	21·1
1 30	− 4·5	−36·8	− 4·7	−36·5	−20·8
1 35	4·0	36·3	4·3	36·1	20·3
1 40	3·6	35·9	3·8	35·6	19·9
1 45	3·1	35·4	3·4	35·2	19·4
1 50	2·7	35·0	2·9	34·7	19·0
1 55	2·3	34·6	2·5	34·3	18·6
2 00	− 1·9	−34·2	− 2·1	−33·9	−18·2
2 05	1·5	33·8	1·7	33·5	17·8
2 10	1·1	33·4	1·4	33·2	17·4
2 15	0·8	33·1	1·0	32·8	17·1
2 20	0·4	32·7	0·7	32·5	16·7
2 25	− 0·1	32·4	− 0·3	32·1	16·4
2 30	+ 0·2	−32·1	0·0	−31·8	−16·1
2 35	0·5	31·8	+ 0·3	31·5	15·8
2 40	0·8	31·5	0·6	31·2	15·4
2 45	1·1	31·2	0·9	30·9	15·2
2 50	1·4	30·9	1·2	30·6	14·9
2 55	1·7	30·6	1·4	30·4	14·6
3 00	+ 2·0	−30·3	+ 1·7	−30·1	−14·3
3 05	2·2	30·1	2·0	29·8	14·1
3 10	2·5	29·8	2·2	29·6	13·8
3 15	2·7	29·6	2·5	29·3	13·6
3 20	2·9	29·4	2·7	29·1	13·4
3 25	3·2	29·1	2·9	28·9	13·1
3 30	+ 3·4	−28·9	+ 3·1	−28·7	−12·9

App. Alt.	OCT.—MAR. SUN Lower Limb	OCT.—MAR. SUN Upper Limb	APR.—SEPT. SUN Lower Limb	APR.—SEPT. SUN Upper Limb	STARS PLANETS
° ′	′	′	′	′	′
[illegible]	+ 3·4	−28·9	+ 3·1	−28·7	−12·9
[illegible]	[illegible]	[illegible]	3·3	28·5	12·7
[illegible]	[illegible]	[illegible]	[illegible]	28·2	12·5
[illegible]	[illegible]	[illegible]	[illegible]	28·0	12·3
[illegible]	[illegible]	[illegible]	[illegible]	27·8	12·1
[illegible]	[illegible]	[illegible]	[illegible]	27·7	11·9
[illegible]	[illegible]	[illegible]	[illegible]	−27·5	−11·7
[illegible]	[illegible]	[illegible]	[illegible]	27·3	11·5
[illegible]	[illegible]	[illegible]	[illegible]	27·1	11·4
4 15	[illegible]	[illegible]	[illegible]	26·9	11·2
4 20	5·3	27·0	[illegible]	26·8	11·0
4 25	5·4	26·9	5·2	26·6	10·9
4 30	+ 5·6	−26·7	+ 5·3	−26·5	−10·7
4 35	5·7	26·6	5·5	26·3	10·6
4 40	5·9	26·4	5·6	26·2	10·4
4 45	6·0	26·3	5·8	26·0	10·3
4 50	6·2	26·1	5·9	25·9	10·1
4 55	6·3	26·0	6·1	25·7	10·0
5 00	+ 6·4	−25·9	+ 6·2	−25·6	− 9·8
5 05	6·6	25·7	6·3	25·5	9·7
5 10	6·7	25·6	6·5	25·3	9·6
5 15	6·8	25·5	6·6	25·2	9·5
5 20	7·0	25·3	6·7	25·1	9·3
5 25	7·1	25·2	6·8	25·0	9·2
5 30	+ 7·2	−25·1	+ 6·9	−24·9	− 9·1
5 35	7·3	25·0	7·1	24·7	9·0
5 40	7·4	24·9	7·2	24·6	8·9
5 45	7·5	24·8	7·3	24·5	8·8
5 50	7·6	24·7	7·4	24·4	8·7
5 55	7·7	24·6	7·5	24·3	8·6
6 00	+ 7·8	−24·5	+ 7·6	−24·2	− 8·5
6 10	8·0	24·3	7·8	24·0	8·3
6 20	8·2	24·1	8·0	23·8	8·1
6 30	8·4	23·9	8·2	23·6	7·9
6 40	8·6	23·7	8·3	23·5	7·7
6 50	8·7	23·6	8·5	23·3	7·6
7 00	+ 8·9	−23·4	+ 8·7	−23·1	− 7·4
7 10	9·1	23·2	8·8	23·0	7·2
7 20	9·2	23·1	9·0	22·8	7·1
7 30	9·3	23·0	9·1	22·7	6·9
7 40	9·5	22·8	9·2	22·6	6·8
7 50	9·6	22·7	9·4	22·4	6·7
8 00	+ 9·7	−22·6	+ 9·5	−22·3	− 6·6
8 10	9·9	22·4	9·6	22·2	6·4
8 20	10·0	22·3	9·7	22·1	6·3
8 30	10·1	22·2	9·9	21·9	6·2
8 40	10·2	22·1	10·0	21·8	6·1
8 50	10·3	22·0	10·1	21·7	6·0
9 00	+10·4	−21·9	+10·2	−21·6	− 5·9
9 10	10·5	21·8	10·3	21·5	5·8
9 20	10·6	21·7	10·4	21·4	5·7
9 30	10·7	21·6	10·5	21·3	5·6
9 40	10·8	21·5	10·6	21·2	5·5
9 50	10·9	21·4	10·6	21·2	5·4
10 00	+11·0	−21·3	+10·7	−21·1	− 5·3

Additional corrections for temperature and pressure are given on the following page.

For bubble sextant observations ignore dip and use the star corrections for Sun, planets and stars.

A4 ALTITUDE CORRECTION TABLES—ADDITIONAL CORRECTIONS

ADDITIONAL REFRACTION CORRECTIONS FOR NON-STANDARD CONDITIONS

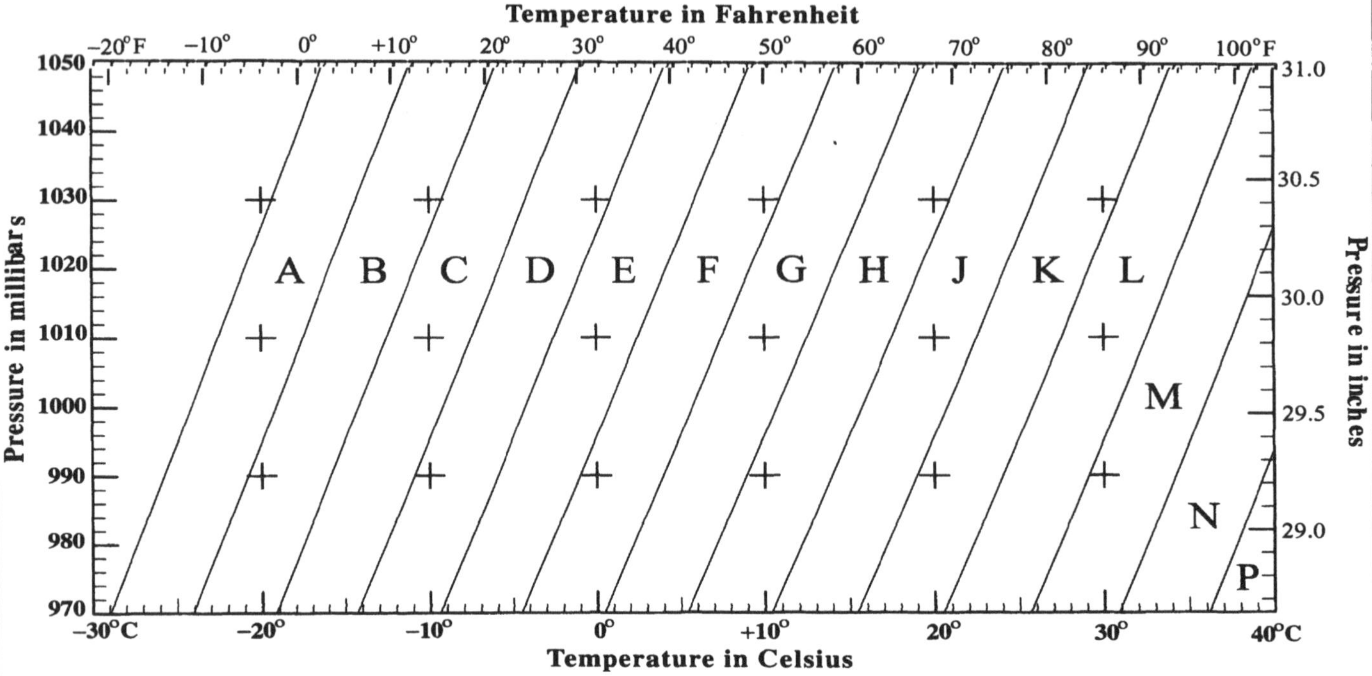

App. Alt.	A	B	C	D	E	F	G	H	J	K	L	M	N	P	App. Alt.
° ′	′	′	′	′	′	′	′	′	′	′	′	′	′	′	° ′
00 00	−7·3	−5·9	−4·6	−3·4	−2·2	−1·1	0·0	+1·0	+2·0	+3·0	+4·0	+4·9	+5·9	+6·9	00 00
00 30	5·5	4·5	3·5	2·6	1·7	0·8	0·0	0·8	1·6	2·3	3·1	3·8	4·5	5·3	00 30
01 00	4·4	3·5	2·8	2·0	1·3	0·7	0·0	0·6	1·2	1·8	2·4	3·0	3·6	4·2	01 00
01 30	3·5	2·9	2·2	1·7	1·1	0·5	0·0	0·5	1·0	1·5	2·0	2·5	2·9	3·4	01 30
02 00	2·9	2·4	1·9	1·4	0·9	0·4	0·0	0·4	0·8	1·3	1·7	2·0	2·4	2·8	02 00
02 30	−2·5	−2·0	−1·6	−1·2	−0·8	−0·4	0·0	+0·4	+0·7	+1·1	+1·4	+1·7	+2·1	+2·4	02 30
03 00	2·1	1·7	1·4	1·0	0·7	0·3	0·0	0·3	0·6	0·9	1·2	1·5	1·8	2·1	03 00
03 30	1·9	1·5	1·2	0·9	0·6	0·3	0·0	0·3	0·5	0·8	1·1	1·3	1·6	1·8	03 30
04 00	1·6	1·3	1·1	0·8	0·5	0·3	0·0	0·2	0·5	0·7	0·9	1·2	1·4	1·6	04 00
04 30	1·5	1·2	0·9	0·7	0·5	0·2	0·0	0·2	0·4	0·6	0·8	1·0	1·3	1·5	04 30
05 00	−1·3	−1·1	−0·9	−0·6	−0·4	−0·2	0·0	+0·2	+0·4	+0·6	+0·8	+0·9	+1·1	+1·3	05 00
06	1·1	0·9	0·7	0·5	0·3	0·2	0·0	0·2	0·3	0·5	0·6	0·8	0·9	1·1	06
07	1·0	0·8	0·6	0·5	0·3	0·1	0·0	0·1	0·3	0·4	0·5	0·7	0·8	0·9	07
08	0·8	0·7	0·5	0·4	0·3	0·1	0·0	0·1	0·2	0·4	0·5	0·6	0·7	0·8	08
09	0·7	0·6	0·5	0·4	0·2	0·1	0·0	0·1	0·2	0·3	0·4	0·5	0·6	0·7	09
10 00	−0·7	−0·5	−0·4	−0·3	−0·2	−0·1	0·0	+0·1	+0·2	+0·3	+0·4	+0·5	+0·6	+0·7	10 00
12	0·6	0·5	0·4	0·3	0·2	0·1	0·0	0·1	0·2	0·2	0·3	0·4	0·5	0·5	12
14	0·5	0·4	0·3	0·2	0·1	0·1	0·0	0·1	0·1	0·2	0·3	0·3	0·4	0·5	14
16	0·4	0·3	0·3	0·2	0·1	0·1	0·0	0·1	0·1	0·2	0·2	0·3	0·3	0·4	16
18	0·4	0·3	0·2	0·2	0·1	−0·1	0·0	+0·1	0·1	0·2	0·2	0·3	0·3	0·4	18
20 00	−0·3	−0·3	−0·2	−0·2	−0·1	0·0	0·0	0·0	+0·1	+0·1	+0·2	+0·2	+0·3	+0·3	20 00
25	0·3	0·2	0·2	0·1	0·1	0·0	0·0	0·0	0·1	0·1	0·1	0·2	0·2	0·2	25
30	0·2	0·2	0·1	0·1	0·1	0·0	0·0	0·0	+0·1	0·1	0·1	0·1	0·2	0·2	30
35	0·2	0·1	0·1	0·1	−0·1	0·0	0·0	0·0	0·0	0·1	0·1	0·1	0·1	0·2	35
40	0·1	0·1	0·1	−0·1	0·0	0·0	0·0	0·0	0·0	+0·1	0·1	0·1	0·1	0·1	40
50 00	−0·1	−0·1	−0·1	0·0	0·0	0·0	0·0	0·0	0·0	0·0	+0·1	+0·1	+0·1	+0·1	50 00

The graph is entered with arguments temperature and pressure to find a zone letter; using as arguments this zone letter and apparent altitude (sextant altitude corrected for index error and dip), a correction is taken from the table. This correction is to be applied to the sextant altitude in addition to the corrections for standard conditions (for the Sun, stars and planets from page A2-A3 and for the Moon from pages xxxiv and xxxv).

2026
Nautical Almanac
COMMERCIAL EDITION

NOTE

Every care is taken to prevent errors in the production of this publication. As a final precaution it is recommended that the sequence of pages in this copy be examined on receipt. If faulty, it should be returned for replacement.

staxltd@outlook.com

THE NAUTICAL ALMANAC 2026

LIST OF CONTENTS

Pages	
A2 — A3	Altitude correction tables for Sun, stars, planets
A4	Additional refraction corrections for non-standard conditions
1 — 3	Title page, preface, etc.
4	Phases of the Moon
4 — 5	Calendars
5 — 7	Eclipses
8 — 9	Planet notes and diagram
10 — 253	Daily pages: Ephemerides of Sun, Moon, Aries and planets; sunrise, sunset, twilights, moonrise, moonset, etc.
254 — 261	Explanation
262 — 265	Standard times
266 — 267	Star charts
268 — 273	Stars: SHA and Dec of 173 stars, in order of SHA (accuracy 0′.1)
274 — 276	*Polaris* (Pole Star) tables
277 — 283	Sight reduction procedures; direct computation
284 — 318	Concise sight reduction tables
319	Form for use with concise sight reduction tables
320 — 321	Polar Phenomena
322	Semi-duration of sunlight and twilight
323 — 325	Semi-duration of moonlight
i	Conversion of arc to time
ii — xxxi	Tables of increments and corrections for Sun, planets, Aries, Moon
xxxii	Tables for interpolating sunrise, sunset, twilights, moonrise, moonset, Moon's meridian passage
xxxiii	Index to selected stars
xxxiv — xxxv	Altitude correction tables for the Moon
Bookmark	Same as pages A2 and xxxiii

RELIGIOUS CALENDARS

Epiphany	Jan. 6	Low Sunday	Apr. 12
Septuagesima Sunday	Feb. 1	Rogation Sunday	May 10
Quinquagesima Sunday	Feb. 15	Ascension Day—Holy Thursday	May 14
Ash Wednesday	Feb. 18	Whit Sunday—Pentecost	May 24
Quadragesima Sunday	Feb. 22	Trinity Sunday	May 31
Palm Sunday	Mar. 29	Corpus Christi	June 4
Good Friday	Apr. 3	First Sunday in Advent	Nov. 29
Easter Day	Apr. 5	Christmas Day (Friday)	Dec. 25

First Day of Passover (Pesach)	Apr. 2	Day of Atonement (Yom Kippur)	Sept. 21
Feast of Weeks (Shavuot)	May 22	First day of Tabernacles (Succoth)	Sept. 26
Jewish New Year 5787 (Rosh Hashanah)	Sept. 12		

Ramadân, First day of (tabular)	Feb. 18	Islamic New Year (1448)	June 17

The Jewish and Islamic dates above are tabular dates, which begin at sunset on the previous evening and end at sunset on the date tabulated. In practice, the dates of Islamic fasts and festivals are determined by an actual sighting of the appropriate new moon.

CIVIL CALENDAR—UNITED KINGDOM

St David (Wales)	Mar. 1	Birthday of the Prince of Wales	June 21
Commonwealth Day	Mar. 9	Birthday of Camilla, Queen Consort	July 17
St Patrick (Ireland)	Mar. 17	Accession of King Charles III	Sept. 8
St George (England)	Apr. 23	Remembrance Sunday	Nov. 8
Coronation Day	May 6	Birthday of King Charles III	Nov. 14
The King's Official Birthday†	June 13	St Andrew (Scotland)	Nov. 30

PUBLIC HOLIDAYS

England and Wales—Jan. 1, Apr. 3, Apr. 6, May 4, May 25, Aug. 31, Dec. 25, Dec. 28
Northern Ireland—Jan. 1, Mar. 17, Apr. 3, Apr. 6, May 4, May 25, July 13, Aug. 31, Dec. 25, Dec. 28
Scotland—Jan. 1, Jan. 2, Apr. 3, May 4, May 25, Aug. 3, Dec. 25, Dec. 28

CIVIL CALENDAR—UNITED STATES OF AMERICA

New Year's Day	Jan. 1	Labor Day	Sept. 7
Martin Luther King's Birthday	Jan. 19	Columbus Day	Oct. 12
Washington's Birthday	Feb. 16	General Election Day	Nov. 3
Memorial Day	May 25	Veterans Day	Nov. 11
Juneteenth National Independence Day	June 19	Thanksgiving Day	Nov. 26
Independence Day	July 4		

†Date subject to confirmation

PHASES OF THE MOON

New Moon	d h m	First Quarter	d h m	Full Moon	d h m	Last Quarter	d h m
				Jan.	3 10 03	Jan.	10 15 48
Jan.	18 19 52	Jan.	26 04 47	Feb.	1 22 09	Feb.	9 12 43
Feb.	17 12 01	Feb.	24 12 28	Mar.	3 11 38	Mar.	11 09 39
Mar.	19 01 23	Mar.	25 19 18	Apr.	2 02 12	Apr.	10 04 52
Apr.	17 11 52	Apr.	24 02 32	May	1 17 23	May	9 21 10
May	16 20 01	May	23 11 11	May	31 08 45	June	8 10 01
June	15 02 54	June	21 21 55	June	29 23 57	July	7 19 29
July	14 09 44	July	21 11 06	July	29 14 36	Aug.	6 02 21
Aug.	12 17 37	Aug.	20 02 46	Aug.	28 04 19	Sept.	4 07 51
Sept.	11 03 27	Sept.	18 20 44	Sept.	26 16 49	Oct.	3 13 25
Oct.	10 15 50	Oct.	18 16 13	Oct.	26 04 12	Nov.	1 20 28
Nov.	9 07 02	Nov.	17 11 48	Nov.	24 14 54	Dec.	1 06 09
Dec.	9 00 52	Dec.	17 05 43	Dec.	24 01 28	Dec.	30 18 59

DAYS OF THE WEEK AND DAYS OF THE YEAR

	JAN.	FEB.	MAR.	APR.	MAY	JUNE	JULY	AUG.	SEPT.	OCT.	NOV.	DEC.
Day	Wk Yr	Wk Yr	Wk Yr	Wk Yr	Wk Yr	Wk Yr	Wk Yr	Wk Yr	Wk Yr	Wk Yr	Wk Yr	Wk Yr
1	Th. 1	Su. 32	Su. 60	W. 91	F. 121	M. 152	W. 182	Sa. 213	Tu. 244	Th. 274	Su. 305	Tu. 335
2	F. 2	M. 33	M. 61	Th. 92	Sa. 122	Tu. 153	Th. 183	Su. 214	W. 245	F. 275	M. 306	W. 336
3	Sa. 3	Tu. 34	Tu. 62	F. 93	Su. 123	W. 154	F. 184	M. 215	Th. 246	Sa. 276	Tu. 307	Th. 337
4	Su. 4	W. 35	W. 63	Sa. 94	M. 124	Th. 155	Sa. 185	Tu. 216	F. 247	Su. 277	W. 308	F. 338
5	M. 5	Th. 36	Th. 64	Su. 95	Tu. 125	F. 156	Su. 186	W. 217	Sa. 248	M. 278	Th. 309	Sa. 339
6	Tu. 6	F. 37	F. 65	M. 96	W. 126	Sa. 157	M. 187	Th. 218	Su. 249	Tu. 279	F. 310	Su. 340
7	W. 7	Sa. 38	Sa. 66	Tu. 97	Th. 127	Su. 158	Tu. 188	F. 219	M. 250	W. 280	Sa. 311	M. 341
8	Th. 8	Su. 39	Su. 67	W. 98	F. 128	M. 159	W. 189	Sa. 220	Tu. 251	Th. 281	Su. 312	Tu. 342
9	F. 9	M. 40	M. 68	Th. 99	Sa. 129	Tu. 160	Th. 190	Su. 221	W. 252	F. 282	M. 313	W. 343
10	Sa. 10	Tu. 41	Tu. 69	F. 100	Su. 130	W. 161	F. 191	M. 222	Th. 253	Sa. 283	Tu. 314	Th. 344
11	Su. 11	W. 42	W. 70	Sa. 101	M. 131	Th. 162	Sa. 192	Tu. 223	F. 254	Su. 284	W. 315	F. 345
12	M. 12	Th. 43	Th. 71	Su. 102	Tu. 132	F. 163	Su. 193	W. 224	Sa. 255	M. 285	Th. 316	Sa. 346
13	Tu. 13	F. 44	F. 72	M. 103	W. 133	Sa. 164	M. 194	Th. 225	Su. 256	Tu. 286	F. 317	Su. 347
14	W. 14	Sa. 45	Sa. 73	Tu. 104	Th. 134	Su. 165	Tu. 195	F. 226	M. 257	W. 287	Sa. 318	M. 348
15	Th. 15	Su. 46	Su. 74	W. 105	F. 135	M. 166	W. 196	Sa. 227	Tu. 258	Th. 288	Su. 319	Tu. 349
16	F. 16	M. 47	M. 75	Th. 106	Sa. 136	Tu. 167	Th. 197	Su. 228	W. 259	F. 289	M. 320	W. 350
17	Sa. 17	Tu. 48	Tu. 76	F. 107	Su. 137	W. 168	F. 198	M. 229	Th. 260	Sa. 290	Tu. 321	Th. 351
18	Su. 18	W. 49	W. 77	Sa. 108	M. 138	Th. 169	Sa. 199	Tu. 230	F. 261	Su. 291	W. 322	F. 352
19	M. 19	Th. 50	Th. 78	Su. 109	Tu. 139	F. 170	Su. 200	W. 231	Sa. 262	M. 292	Th. 323	Sa. 353
20	Tu. 20	F. 51	F. 79	M. 110	W. 140	Sa. 171	M. 201	Th. 232	Su. 263	Tu. 293	F. 324	Su. 354
21	W. 21	Sa. 52	Sa. 80	Tu. 111	Th. 141	Su. 172	Tu. 202	F. 233	M. 264	W. 294	Sa. 325	M. 355
22	Th. 22	Su. 53	Su. 81	W. 112	F. 142	M. 173	W. 203	Sa. 234	Tu. 265	Th. 295	Su. 326	Tu. 356
23	F. 23	M. 54	M. 82	Th. 113	Sa. 143	Tu. 174	Th. 204	Su. 235	W. 266	F. 296	M. 327	W. 357
24	Sa. 24	Tu. 55	Tu. 83	F. 114	Su. 144	W. 175	F. 205	M. 236	Th. 267	Sa. 297	Tu. 328	Th. 358
25	Su. 25	W. 56	W. 84	Sa. 115	M. 145	Th. 176	Sa. 206	Tu. 237	F. 268	Su. 298	W. 329	F. 359
26	M. 26	Th. 57	Th. 85	Su. 116	Tu. 146	F. 177	Su. 207	W. 238	Sa. 269	M. 299	Th. 330	Sa. 360
27	Tu. 27	F. 58	F. 86	M. 117	W. 147	Sa. 178	M. 208	Th. 239	Su. 270	Tu. 300	F. 331	Su. 361
28	W. 28	Sa. 59	Sa. 87	Tu. 118	Th. 148	Su. 179	Tu. 209	F. 240	M. 271	W. 301	Sa. 332	M. 362
29	Th. 29		Su. 88	W. 119	F. 149	M. 180	W. 210	Sa. 241	Tu. 272	Th. 302	Su. 333	Tu. 363
30	F. 30		M. 89	Th. 120	Sa. 150	Tu. 181	Th. 211	Su. 242	W. 273	F. 303	M. 334	W. 364
31	Sa. 31		Tu. 90		Su. 151		F. 212	M. 243		Sa. 304		Th. 365

ECLIPSES

There are two eclipses of the Sun.

1. *An annular eclipse of the Sun,* February 17. See map page 6. The eclipse begins at $09^h\ 56^m$ and ends at $14^h\ 28^m$; the annular phase begins at $11^h 43^m$ and ends at $12^h 41^m$. The maximum duration of annularity is $2^m\ 18^s$.

2. *A total eclipse of the Sun,* August 12. See map on page 7. The eclipse begins at $15^h\ 34^m$ and ends at $19^h\ 59^m$. The total phase begins at $16^h 58^m$ and ends at $18^h 34^m$. The maximum duration of totality is $2^m\ 21^s$.

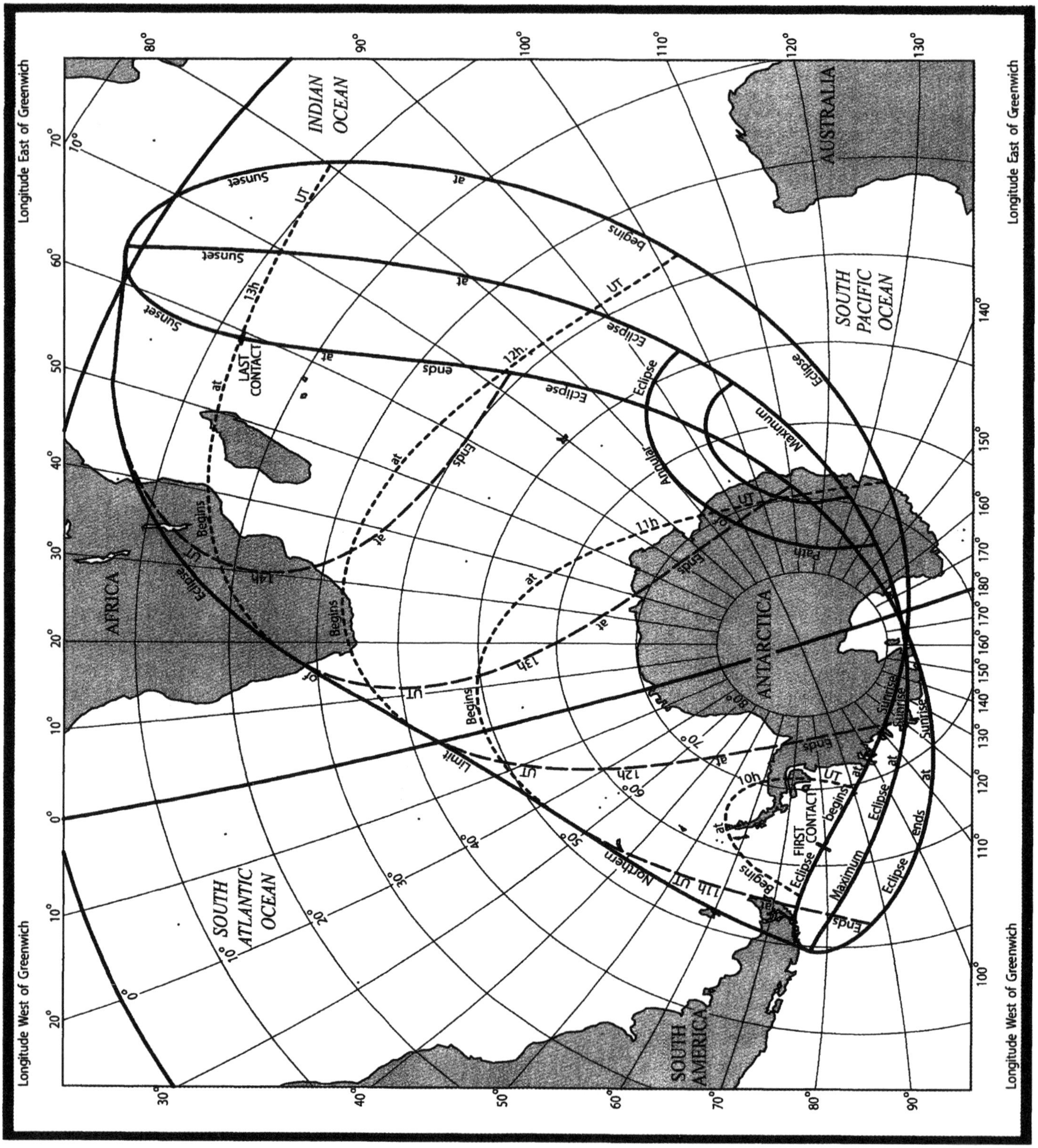

SOLAR ECLIPSE DIAGRAMS

The principal features shown on the above diagrams are: the paths of total and annular eclipses; the northern and southern limits of partial eclipse; the sunrise and sunset curves; dashed lines which show the times of beginning and end of partial eclipse at hourly intervals.

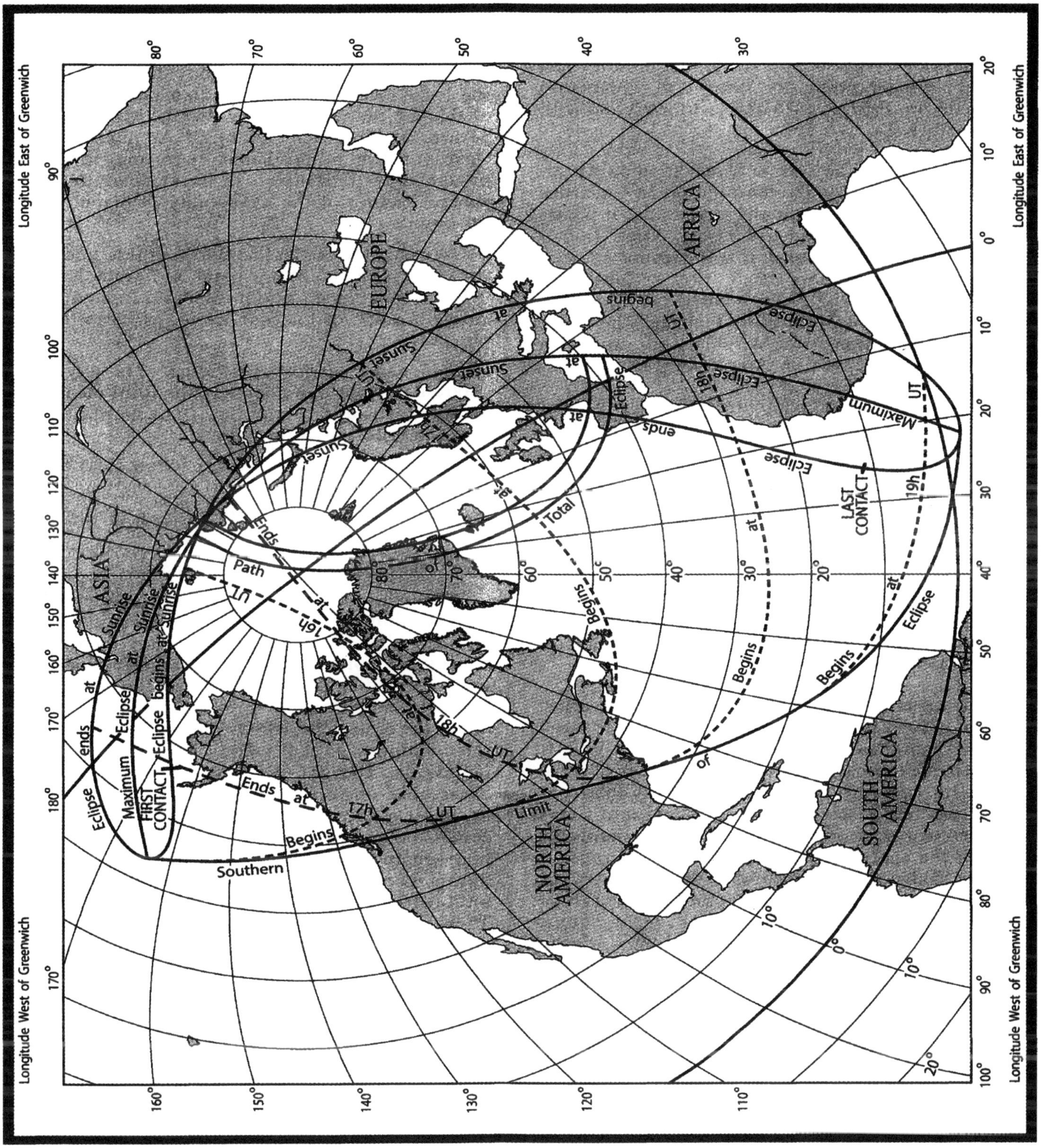

SOLAR ECLIPSE DIAGRAMS

Further details of the paths and times of central eclipse are given in *The Astronomical Almanac.*

VISIBILITY OF PLANETS

VENUS is too close to the Sun for observation until mid-February when it appears as a brilliant object in the evening sky. In mid-October it again becomes too close to the Sun for observation until late in that month when it reappears in the morning sky. Venus is in conjunction with Mercury on February 26 and October 5 and with Jupiter on June 9.

MARS is too close to the Sun for observation until mid-March when it appears in the morning sky in Aquarius. Its westward elongation gradually increases as it passes through Pisces, Cetus, again into Pisces, Aries, Taurus (passing 5° N of *Aldebaran* on July 14), Gemini (passing 6° S of *Pollux* on September 19), Cancer and into Leo (passing 1.8° N of *Regulus* on November 24). From late November it can be seen for more than half the night. Mars is in conjunction with Mercury and Saturn on April 20 and with Jupiter on November 15.

JUPITER can be seen in Gemini from the beginning of the year for most of the night. It is at opposition on January 10 when it can be seen throughout the night. Its eastward elongation then gradually decreases and from mid-April it can only be seen in the evening sky (passing 6° S of *Pollux* on June 4) and moves into Cancer in late June. In mid-July it becomes too close to the Sun for observation until mid-August when it reappears in the morning sky. It passes into Leo in late September and from late November can be seen for more than half the night. Jupiter is in conjunction with Venus on June 9, with Mercury on August 15 and with Mars on November 15.

SATURN can be seen in the evening sky in Aquarius, passing into Pisces from mid-January until early March when it becomes too close to the Sun for observation. It reappears in the morning sky in the second week of April in Cetus. Its westward elongation gradually increases passing again into Pisces in early June and into Cetus in early September in which constellation it remains for the rest of the year. It is at opposition on October 4 when it is visible throughout the night. Its eastward elongation then gradually decreases and for the rest of the year can be seen for more than half the night. Saturn is in conjunction with Mercury and Mars on April 20.

MERCURY can only be seen low in the east before sunrise, or low in the west after sunset (about the time of beginning or end of civil twilight). It is visible in the mornings between the following approximate dates: January 1 (−0·6) to January 6 (−0·7), March 15 (+2·3) to May 7 (−1·3), July 22 (+2·5) to August 19 (−1·5) and November 11 (+1·2) to December 15 (−0·7); the planet is brighter at the end of each period. It is visible in the evenings between the following approximate dates: February 3 (−1·2) to February 28 (+1·5), May 2 (−1·5) to July 4 (+3·0) and September 7 (−0·9) to October 30 (+2·0); the planet is brighter at the beginning of each period. The figures in parentheses are the magnitudes.

CONFIGURATIONS: (1) Mercury, Mars and Venus in alignment with separations of 6°5 and 1°26 on January 10. (2) Mercury, Saturn and Mars in alignment with separations 0°5 and 1°2 on April 20. (3) Mercury, Mars and Saturn in a grouping on April 21 with a minimum diameter of 1°65.

PLANET DIAGRAM

General Description. The diagram on the opposite page shows, in graphical form for any date during the year, the local mean time of meridian passage of the Sun, of the five planets Mercury, Venus, Mars, Jupiter, and Saturn, and of each 30° of SHA; intermediate lines corresponding to particular stars, may be drawn in by the user if desired. It is intended to provide a general picture of the availability of planets and stars for observation.

On each side of the line marking the time of meridian passage of the Sun a band, 45^m wide, is shaded to indicate that planets and most stars crossing the meridian within 45^m of the Sun are too close to the Sun for observation.

Method of use and interpretation. For any date, the diagram provides immediately the local mean times of meridian passage of the Sun, planets and stars, and thus the following information:

(a) whether a planet or star is too close to the Sun for observation;

(b) some indication of its position in the sky, especially during twilight;

(c) the proximity of other planets.

When the meridian passage of an outer planet occurs at midnight, the body is in opposition to the Sun and is visible all night; a planet may then be observable during both morning and evening twilights. As the time of meridian passage decreases, the body eventually ceases to be observable in the morning, but its altitude above the eastern horizon at sunset gradually increases; this continues until the body is on the meridian during evening twilight. From then onwards, the body is observable above the western horizon and its altitude at sunset gradually decreases; eventually the body becomes too close to the Sun for observation. When the body again becomes visible it is seen low in the east during morning twilight; its altitude at sunrise increases until meridian passage occurs during morning twilight. Then, as the time of meridian passage decreases to 0^h, the body is observable in the west during morning twilight with a gradually decreasing altitude, until it once again reaches opposition.

DO NOT CONFUSE

Venus with Mercury in late February, with Saturn in early March and with Jupiter in the first half of June; on all occasions Venus is the brighter object.

Mars with Mercury in mid-March when Mars is the brighter object.

Saturn with Mars in the second half of April when Saturn is the brighter object.

Mercury with Mars and Mercury with Saturn both in the second half of April with Mercury the brighter object.

Jupiter with Mercury from mid-June to the start of July and again in mid-August, with Mars in November; on all occasions Jupiter is the brighter object.

LOCAL MEAN TIME OF MERIDIAN PASSAGE

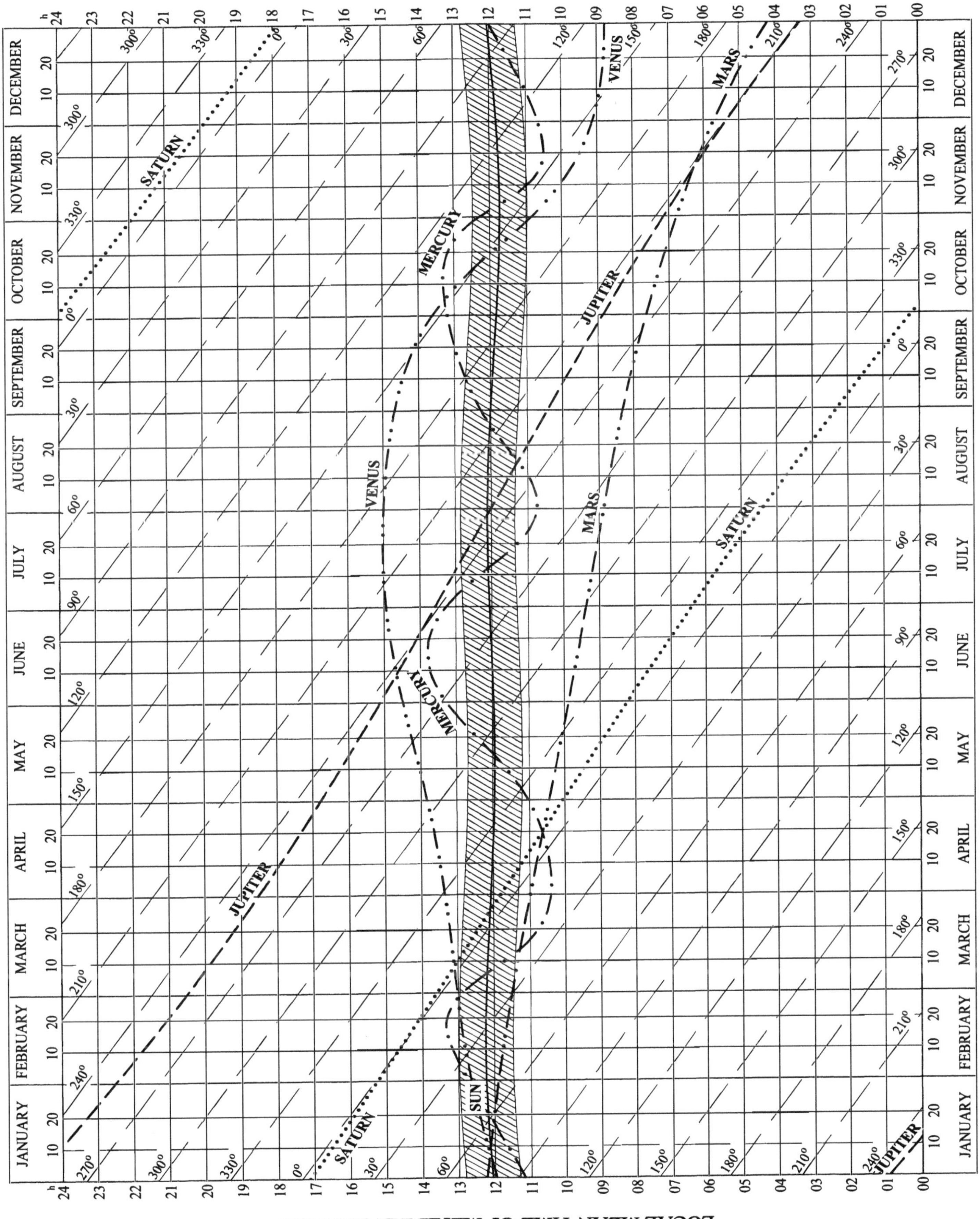

LOCAL MEAN TIME OF MERIDIAN PASSAGE

UT d	h	ARIES GHA	VENUS −3·9 GHA	VENUS Dec	MARS +1·1 GHA	MARS Dec	JUPITER −2·7 GHA	JUPITER Dec	SATURN +1·0 GHA	SATURN Dec
		° ′	° ′	° ′	° ′	° ′	° ′	° ′	° ′	° ′
1 THURSDAY	00	100 39.7	180 36.3	S23 37.3	176 47.0	S23 43.2	347 32.3	N21 58.7	103 16.9	S 3 35.8
	01	115 42.2	195 35.4	37.2	191 47.3	43.0	2 35.1	58.8	118 19.2	35.7
	02	130 44.7	210 34.4	37.1	206 47.7	42.9	17 37.9	58.9	133 21.5	35.7
	03	145 47.1	225 33.4	. . 37.0	221 48.1	. . 42.7	32 40.7	. . 58.9	148 23.9	. . 35.6
	04	160 49.6	240 32.5	36.8	236 48.5	42.5	47 43.5	59.0	163 26.2	35.5
	05	175 52.1	255 31.5	36.7	251 48.9	42.4	62 46.3	59.0	178 28.5	35.5
	06	190 54.5	270 30.5	S23 36.6	266 49.2	S23 42.2	77 49.1	N21 59.1	193 30.9	S 3 35.4
	07	205 57.0	285 29.6	36.4	281 49.6	42.0	92 52.0	59.1	208 33.2	35.3
	08	220 59.4	300 28.6	36.3	296 50.0	41.8	107 54.8	59.2	223 35.5	35.3
	09	236 01.9	315 27.6	. . 36.2	311 50.4	. . 41.7	122 57.6	. . 59.3	238 37.9	. . 35.2
	10	251 04.4	330 26.7	36.0	326 50.8	41.5	138 00.4	59.3	253 40.2	35.1
	11	266 06.8	345 25.7	35.9	341 51.1	41.3	153 03.2	59.4	268 42.5	35.1
	12	281 09.3	0 24.7	S23 35.7	356 51.5	S23 41.2	168 06.0	N21 59.4	283 44.9	S 3 35.0
	13	296 11.8	15 23.8	35.6	11 51.9	41.0	183 08.8	59.5	298 47.2	34.9
	14	311 14.2	30 22.8	35.5	26 52.3	40.8	198 11.6	59.5	313 49.5	34.9
	15	326 16.7	45 21.8	. . 35.3	41 52.7	. . 40.6	213 14.4	. . 59.6	328 51.9	. . 34.8
	16	341 19.2	60 20.9	35.2	56 53.0	40.5	228 17.3	59.7	343 54.2	34.7
	17	356 21.6	75 19.9	35.0	71 53.4	40.3	243 20.1	59.7	358 56.5	34.7
	18	11 24.1	90 18.9	S23 34.9	86 53.8	S23 40.1	258 22.9	N21 59.8	13 58.9	S 3 34.6
	19	26 26.6	105 18.0	34.7	101 54.2	39.9	273 25.7	59.8	29 01.2	34.5
	20	41 29.0	120 17.0	34.6	116 54.6	39.8	288 28.5	59.9	44 03.5	34.5
	21	56 31.5	135 16.0	. . 34.4	131 54.9	. . 39.6	303 31.3	21 59.9	59 05.8	. . 34.4
	22	71 33.9	150 15.1	34.3	146 55.3	39.4	318 34.1	22 00.0	74 08.2	34.3
	23	86 36.4	165 14.1	34.1	161 55.7	39.2	333 37.0	00.1	89 10.5	34.3
2 FRIDAY	00	101 38.9	180 13.2	S23 34.0	176 56.1	S23 39.1	348 39.8	N22 00.1	104 12.8	S 3 34.2
	01	116 41.3	195 12.2	33.8	191 56.5	38.9	3 42.6	00.2	119 15.2	34.1
	02	131 43.8	210 11.2	33.7	206 56.8	38.7	18 45.4	00.2	134 17.5	34.1
	03	146 46.3	225 10.3	. . 33.5	221 57.2	. . 38.5	33 48.2	. . 00.3	149 19.8	. . 34.0
	04	161 48.7	240 09.3	33.3	236 57.6	38.3	48 51.0	00.3	164 22.2	33.9
	05	176 51.2	255 08.3	33.2	251 58.0	38.2	63 53.8	00.4	179 24.5	33.9
	06	191 53.7	270 07.4	S23 33.0	266 58.4	S23 38.0	78 56.6	N22 00.5	194 26.8	S 3 33.8
	07	206 56.1	285 06.4	32.8	281 58.7	37.8	93 59.5	00.5	209 29.1	33.7
	08	221 58.6	300 05.4	32.7	296 59.1	37.6	109 02.3	00.6	224 31.5	33.7
	09	237 01.1	315 04.5	. . 32.5	311 59.5	. . 37.4	124 05.1	. . 00.6	239 33.8	. . 33.6
	10	252 03.5	330 03.5	32.3	326 59.9	37.2	139 07.9	00.7	254 36.1	33.5
	11	267 06.0	345 02.5	32.2	342 00.3	37.1	154 10.7	00.7	269 38.5	33.5
	12	282 08.4	0 01.6	S23 32.0	357 00.6	S23 36.9	169 13.5	N22 00.8	284 40.8	S 3 33.4
	13	297 10.9	15 00.6	31.8	12 01.0	36.7	184 16.3	00.9	299 43.1	33.3
	14	312 13.4	29 59.7	31.7	27 01.4	36.5	199 19.2	00.9	314 45.4	33.3
	15	327 15.8	44 58.7	. . 31.5	42 01.8	. . 36.3	214 22.0	. . 01.0	329 47.8	. . 33.2
	16	342 18.3	59 57.7	31.3	57 02.2	36.1	229 24.8	01.0	344 50.1	33.1
	17	357 20.8	74 56.8	31.1	72 02.5	36.0	244 27.6	01.1	359 52.4	33.0
	18	12 23.2	89 55.8	S23 31.0	87 02.9	S23 35.8	259 30.4	N22 01.1	14 54.8	S 3 33.0
	19	27 25.7	104 54.8	30.8	102 03.3	35.6	274 33.2	01.2	29 57.1	32.9
	20	42 28.2	119 53.9	30.6	117 03.7	35.4	289 36.0	01.3	44 59.4	32.8
	21	57 30.6	134 52.9	. . 30.4	132 04.1	. . 35.2	304 38.9	. . 01.3	60 01.7	. . 32.8
	22	72 33.1	149 52.0	30.2	147 04.4	35.0	319 41.7	01.4	75 04.1	32.7
	23	87 35.6	164 51.0	30.1	162 04.8	34.8	334 44.5	01.4	90 06.4	32.6
3 SATURDAY	00	102 38.0	179 50.0	S23 29.9	177 05.2	S23 34.6	349 47.3	N22 01.5	105 08.7	S 3 32.6
	01	117 40.5	194 49.1	29.7	192 05.6	34.4	4 50.1	01.5	120 11.0	32.5
	02	132 42.9	209 48.1	29.5	207 06.0	34.3	19 52.9	01.6	135 13.4	32.4
	03	147 45.4	224 47.2	. . 29.3	222 06.3	. . 34.1	34 55.8	. . 01.7	150 15.7	. . 32.4
	04	162 47.9	239 46.2	29.1	237 06.7	33.9	49 58.6	01.7	165 18.0	32.3
	05	177 50.3	254 45.2	28.9	252 07.1	33.7	65 01.4	01.8	180 20.3	32.2
	06	192 52.8	269 44.3	S23 28.7	267 07.5	S23 33.5	80 04.2	N22 01.8	195 22.7	S 3 32.2
	07	207 55.3	284 43.3	28.5	282 07.9	33.3	95 07.0	01.9	210 25.0	32.1
	08	222 57.7	299 42.4	28.3	297 08.2	33.1	110 09.8	01.9	225 27.3	32.0
	09	238 00.2	314 41.4	. . 28.1	312 08.6	. . 32.9	125 12.7	. . 02.0	240 29.6	. . 32.0
	10	253 02.7	329 40.4	27.9	327 09.0	32.7	140 15.5	02.1	255 32.0	31.9
	11	268 05.1	344 39.5	27.7	342 09.4	32.5	155 18.3	02.1	270 34.3	31.8
	12	283 07.6	359 38.5	S23 27.5	357 09.8	S23 32.3	170 21.1	N22 02.2	285 36.6	S 3 31.7
	13	298 10.1	14 37.6	27.3	12 10.2	32.1	185 23.9	02.2	300 38.9	31.7
	14	313 12.5	29 36.6	27.1	27 10.5	31.9	200 26.7	02.3	315 41.3	31.6
	15	328 15.0	44 35.6	. . 26.9	42 10.9	. . 31.7	215 29.6	. . 02.3	330 43.6	. . 31.5
	16	343 17.4	59 34.7	26.7	57 11.3	31.5	230 32.4	02.4	345 45.9	31.5
	17	358 19.9	74 33.7	26.5	72 11.7	31.4	245 35.2	02.5	0 48.2	31.4
	18	13 22.4	89 32.8	S23 26.3	87 12.1	S23 31.2	260 38.0	N22 02.5	15 50.6	S 3 31.3
	19	28 24.8	104 31.8	26.1	102 12.4	31.0	275 40.8	02.6	30 52.9	31.3
	20	43 27.3	119 30.9	25.9	117 12.8	30.8	290 43.6	02.6	45 55.2	31.2
	21	58 29.8	134 29.9	. . 25.7	132 13.2	. . 30.6	305 46.5	. . 02.7	60 57.5	. . 31.1
	22	73 32.2	149 28.9	25.5	147 13.6	30.4	320 49.3	02.7	75 59.9	31.1
	23	88 34.7	164 28.0	25.3	162 14.0	30.2	335 52.1	02.8	91 02.2	31.0
Mer. Pass.		h m 17 10.6	v −1.0	d 0.2	v 0.4	d 0.2	v 2.8	d 0.1	v 2.3	d 0.1

STARS

Name	SHA	Dec
	° ′	° ′
Acamar	315 10.9	S40 12.2
Achernar	335 19.4	S57 06.5
Acrux	172 59.1	S63 14.3
Adhara	255 04.8	S29 00.4
Aldebaran	290 38.4	N16 33.7
Alioth	166 12.3	N55 48.8
Alkaid	152 51.5	N49 10.7
Alnair	27 32.2	S46 50.3
Alnilam	275 36.6	S 1 11.1
Alphard	217 46.7	S 8 46.3
Alphecca	126 03.3	N26 37.4
Alpheratz	357 34.0	N29 14.2
Altair	61 59.5	N 8 56.2
Ankaa	353 06.4	S42 10.1
Antares	112 15.1	S26 29.3
Arcturus	145 47.3	N19 02.6
Atria	107 09.1	S69 04.3
Avior	234 13.8	S59 35.4
Bellatrix	278 21.7	N 6 22.4
Betelgeuse	270 50.9	N 7 24.7
Canopus	263 51.5	S52 42.6
Capella	280 20.2	N46 01.5
Deneb	49 25.7	N45 22.5
Denebola	182 24.0	N14 25.5
Diphda	348 46.5	S17 50.7
Dubhe	193 39.7	N61 36.3
Elnath	278 00.5	N28 37.8
Eltanin	90 42.3	N51 29.0
Enif	33 38.2	N 9 59.7
Fomalhaut	15 13.8	S29 29.2
Gacrux	171 50.7	S57 15.3
Gienah	175 42.7	S17 41.1
Hadar	148 35.1	S60 29.7
Hamal	327 50.1	N23 35.3
Kaus Aust.	83 31.8	S34 22.3
Kochab	137 20.5	N74 02.5
Markab	13 29.2	N15 20.8
Menkar	314 05.1	N 4 11.5
Menkent	147 56.8	S36 29.7
Miaplacidus	221 37.3	S69 49.2
Mirfak	308 26.7	N49 57.4
Nunki	75 47.1	S26 15.9
Peacock	53 05.0	S56 39.2
Pollux	243 15.9	N27 57.7
Procyon	244 49.6	N 5 09.4
Rasalhague	95 58.1	N12 32.4
Regulus	207 33.4	N11 50.3
Rigel	281 02.8	S 8 10.3
Rigil Kent.	139 39.5	S60 56.3
Sabik	102 02.2	S15 45.4
Schedar	349 30.1	N56 41.1
Shaula	96 09.7	S37 07.3
Sirius	258 25.2	S16 45.1
Spica	158 21.5	S11 17.8
Suhail	222 45.3	S43 32.1
Vega	80 33.1	N38 48.4
Zuben'ubi	136 55.3	S16 09.0

	SHA	Mer. Pass.
	° ′	h m
Venus	78 34.3	12 00
Mars	75 17.2	12 12
Jupiter	247 00.9	0 45
Saturn	2 34.0	17 01

UT d h		SUN GHA ° ′	SUN Dec ° ′	MOON GHA ° ′	MOON v ′	MOON Dec ° ′	MOON d ′	MOON HP ′
1 00	THURSDAY	179 09.9	S23 01.0	36 44.5	2.5	N26 24.2	6.7	60.7
01		194 09.6	00.8	51 06.0	2.3	26 30.9	6.5	60.7
02		209 09.3	00.6	65 27.3	2.3	26 37.4	6.3	60.8
03		224 09.0	. . 00.4	79 48.6	2.1	26 43.7	6.1	60.8
04		239 08.7	00.2	94 09.7	2.1	26 49.8	5.9	60.8
05		254 08.4	23 00.0	108 30.8	2.0	26 55.7	5.8	60.8
06		269 08.1	S22 59.8	122 51.8	1.9	N27 01.5	5.5	60.8
07		284 07.8	59.6	137 12.7	1.8	27 07.0	5.3	60.8
08		299 07.6	59.4	151 33.5	1.8	27 12.3	5.1	60.8
09		314 07.3	. . 59.2	165 54.3	1.6	27 17.4	4.9	60.8
10		329 07.0	59.0	180 14.9	1.7	27 22.3	4.7	60.8
11		344 06.7	58.8	194 35.6	1.5	27 27.0	4.4	60.8
12		359 06.4	S22 58.6	208 56.1	1.5	N27 31.4	4.3	60.8
13		14 06.1	58.3	223 16.6	1.4	27 35.7	4.1	60.8
14		29 05.8	58.1	237 37.0	1.3	27 39.8	3.8	60.8
15		44 05.5	. . 57.9	251 57.3	1.3	27 43.6	3.7	60.8
16		59 05.2	57.7	266 17.6	1.3	27 47.3	3.4	60.8
17		74 04.9	57.5	280 37.9	1.2	27 50.7	3.2	60.8
18		89 04.6	S22 57.3	294 58.1	1.1	N27 53.9	3.0	60.8
19		104 04.3	57.1	309 18.2	1.1	27 56.9	2.8	60.8
20		119 04.0	56.8	323 38.3	1.1	27 59.7	2.5	60.9
21		134 03.8	. . 56.6	337 58.4	1.1	28 02.2	2.4	60.9
22		149 03.5	56.4	352 18.5	1.0	28 04.6	2.1	60.9
23		164 03.2	56.2	6 38.5	0.9	28 06.7	1.9	60.9
2 00	FRIDAY	179 02.9	S22 56.0	20 58.4	1.0	N28 08.6	1.7	60.8
01		194 02.6	55.7	35 18.4	0.9	28 10.3	1.5	60.8
02		209 02.3	55.5	49 38.3	0.9	28 11.8	1.2	60.8
03		224 02.0	. . 55.3	63 58.2	1.0	28 13.0	1.1	60.8
04		239 01.7	55.1	78 18.2	0.8	28 14.1	0.8	60.8
05		254 01.4	54.8	92 38.0	0.9	28 14.9	0.6	60.8
06		269 01.1	S22 54.6	106 57.9	0.9	N28 15.5	0.3	60.8
07		284 00.8	54.4	121 17.8	0.9	28 15.8	0.2	60.8
08		299 00.6	54.2	135 37.7	0.9	28 16.0	0.1	60.8
09		314 00.3	. . 53.9	149 57.6	0.9	28 15.9	0.3	60.8
10		329 00.0	53.7	164 17.5	0.9	28 15.6	0.5	60.8
11		343 59.7	53.5	178 37.4	0.9	28 15.1	0.7	60.8
12		358 59.4	S22 53.3	192 57.3	1.0	N28 14.4	1.0	60.8
13		13 59.1	53.0	207 17.3	1.0	28 13.4	1.1	60.8
14		28 58.8	52.8	221 37.3	1.0	28 12.3	1.4	60.8
15		43 58.5	. . 52.6	235 57.3	1.0	28 10.9	1.6	60.8
16		58 58.2	52.3	250 17.3	1.1	28 09.3	1.9	60.8
17		73 58.0	52.1	264 37.4	1.1	28 07.4	2.0	60.8
18		88 57.7	S22 51.9	278 57.5	1.1	N28 05.4	2.3	60.7
19		103 57.4	51.6	293 17.6	1.2	28 03.1	2.4	60.7
20		118 57.1	51.4	307 37.8	1.2	28 00.7	2.7	60.7
21		133 56.8	. . 51.1	321 58.0	1.3	27 58.0	2.9	60.7
22		148 56.5	50.9	336 18.3	1.4	27 55.1	3.1	60.7
23		163 56.2	50.7	350 38.7	1.4	27 52.0	3.4	60.7
3 00	SATURDAY	178 55.9	S22 50.4	4 59.1	1.4	N27 48.6	3.5	60.7
01		193 55.7	50.2	19 19.5	1.6	27 45.1	3.7	60.7
02		208 55.4	49.9	33 40.1	1.6	27 41.4	4.0	60.7
03		223 55.1	. . 49.7	48 00.7	1.6	27 37.4	4.2	60.6
04		238 54.8	49.5	62 21.3	1.8	27 33.2	4.3	60.6
05		253 54.5	49.2	76 42.1	1.8	27 28.9	4.6	60.6
06		268 54.2	S22 49.0	91 02.9	1.9	N27 24.3	4.8	60.6
07		283 53.9	48.7	105 23.8	2.0	27 19.5	5.0	60.6
08		298 53.6	48.5	119 44.8	2.1	27 14.5	5.2	60.6
09		313 53.4	. . 48.2	134 05.9	2.1	27 09.3	5.3	60.5
10		328 53.1	48.0	148 27.0	2.3	27 04.0	5.6	60.5
11		343 52.8	47.7	162 48.3	2.3	26 58.4	5.8	60.5
12		358 52.5	S22 47.5	177 09.6	2.5	N26 52.6	6.0	60.5
13		13 52.2	47.2	191 31.1	2.5	26 46.6	6.1	60.5
14		28 51.9	47.0	205 52.6	2.7	26 40.5	6.4	60.4
15		43 51.6	. . 46.7	220 14.3	2.7	26 34.1	6.5	60.4
16		58 51.4	46.5	234 36.0	2.9	26 27.6	6.8	60.4
17		73 51.1	46.2	248 57.9	2.9	26 20.8	6.9	60.4
18		88 50.8	S22 46.0	263 19.8	3.1	N26 13.9	7.1	60.4
19		103 50.5	45.7	277 41.9	3.2	26 06.8	7.3	60.3
20		118 50.2	45.5	292 04.1	3.3	25 59.5	7.4	60.3
21		133 49.9	. . 45.2	306 26.4	3.4	25 52.1	7.7	60.3
22		148 49.7	45.0	320 48.8	3.6	25 44.4	7.8	60.3
23		163 49.4	44.7	335 11.4	3.6	N25 36.6	8.0	60.3
		SD 16.3	*d* 0.2	SD	16.6	16.6		16.5

Lat. °	Twilight Naut. h m	Twilight Civil h m	Sunrise h m	Moonrise 1 h m	Moonrise 2 h m	Moonrise 3 h m	Moonrise 4 h m
N 72	08 23	10 39	■	□	□	□	□
N 70	08 04	09 48	■	□	□	□	□
68	07 49	09 16	■	□	□	□	□
66	07 37	08 52	10 26	□	□	□	14 23
64	07 26	08 34	09 48	□	□	□	15 18
62	07 17	08 18	09 22	10 58	□	13 35	15 50
60	07 09	08 05	09 02	11 50	12 40	14 19	16 14
N 58	07 02	07 54	08 45	12 21	13 18	14 48	16 33
56	06 55	07 44	08 31	12 45	13 44	15 10	16 49
54	06 50	07 35	08 19	13 05	14 05	15 28	17 03
52	06 44	07 27	08 08	13 21	14 23	15 44	17 15
50	06 39	07 20	07 58	13 36	14 38	15 57	17 25
45	06 28	07 05	07 38	14 05	15 08	16 25	17 47
N 40	06 18	06 52	07 22	14 27	15 32	16 46	18 04
35	06 09	06 40	07 08	14 46	15 51	17 04	18 19
30	06 00	06 30	06 56	15 03	16 08	17 19	18 32
20	05 44	06 11	06 35	15 30	16 36	17 45	18 53
N 10	05 28	05 55	06 17	15 54	17 01	18 08	19 12
0	05 12	05 38	06 00	16 16	17 23	18 29	19 29
S 10	04 53	05 20	05 43	16 39	17 46	18 49	19 46
20	04 31	05 00	05 25	17 03	18 10	19 12	20 05
30	04 03	04 36	05 03	17 31	18 39	19 37	20 26
35	03 44	04 21	04 50	17 48	18 55	19 52	20 38
40	03 22	04 03	04 36	18 07	19 15	20 10	20 52
45	02 52	03 41	04 18	18 31	19 38	20 31	21 09
S 50	02 09	03 12	03 56	19 01	20 09	20 57	21 29
52	01 43	02 58	03 46	19 16	20 24	21 09	21 39
54	01 03	02 41	03 34	19 34	20 41	21 24	21 50
56	////	02 19	03 20	19 55	21 02	21 41	22 02
58	////	01 52	03 04	20 23	21 29	22 01	22 16
S 60	////	01 09	02 45	21 01	22 05	22 26	22 33

Lat. °	Sunset h m	Twilight Civil h m	Twilight Naut. h m	Moonset 1 h m	Moonset 2 h m	Moonset 3 h m	Moonset 4 h m
N 72	■	13 29	15 46	□	□	□	□
N 70	■	14 21	16 04	□	□	□	□
68	■	14 53	16 19	□	□	□	□
66	13 43	15 16	16 32	□	□	□	12 20
64	14 20	15 35	16 42	□	□	□	11 24
62	14 46	15 50	16 51	08 53	□	10 56	10 51
60	15 07	16 03	16 59	08 02	09 32	10 12	10 26
N 58	15 23	16 14	17 06	07 31	08 55	09 43	10 06
56	15 37	16 24	17 13	07 07	08 28	09 20	09 49
54	15 50	16 33	17 19	06 48	08 07	09 01	09 35
52	16 00	16 41	17 24	06 32	07 49	08 46	09 23
50	16 10	16 48	17 29	06 18	07 34	08 32	09 12
45	16 30	17 04	17 41	05 49	07 04	08 04	08 49
N 40	16 46	17 17	17 51	05 27	06 40	07 42	08 30
35	17 00	17 28	18 00	05 09	06 20	07 23	08 15
30	17 12	17 38	18 08	04 53	06 04	07 07	08 01
20	17 33	17 57	18 24	04 26	05 35	06 40	07 38
N 10	17 51	18 14	18 40	04 03	05 11	06 17	07 17
0	18 08	18 30	18 56	03 42	04 48	05 55	06 58
S 10	18 25	18 48	19 15	03 20	04 25	05 33	06 39
20	18 43	19 08	19 37	02 58	04 01	05 09	06 18
30	19 05	19 32	20 05	02 31	03 32	04 42	05 54
35	19 17	19 47	20 23	02 16	03 16	04 25	05 40
40	19 32	20 05	20 46	01 58	02 56	04 06	05 23
45	19 50	20 27	21 15	01 36	02 32	03 43	05 03
S 50	20 11	20 55	21 58	01 08	02 01	03 13	04 38
52	20 22	21 10	22 24	00 55	01 46	02 58	04 26
54	20 34	21 27	23 02	00 40	01 28	02 41	04 12
56	20 47	21 48	////	00 22	01 06	02 20	03 55
58	21 03	22 15	////	00 00	00 39	01 54	03 36
S 60	21 23	22 56	////	24 00	00 00	01 17	03 11

Day	SUN Eqn. of Time 00^h	SUN Eqn. of Time 12^h	SUN Mer. Pass.	MOON Mer. Pass. Upper	MOON Mer. Pass. Lower	MOON Age	MOON Phase
d	m s	m s	h m	h m	h m	d %	
1	03 20	03 34	12 04	22 32	09 59	12 94	○
2	03 48	04 02	12 04	23 39	11 06	13 99	
3	04 16	04 29	12 04	24 44	12 12	14 100	

	UT	ARIES	VENUS −3·9		MARS +1·1		JUPITER −2·7		SATURN +1·0	
	d h	GHA ° ′	GHA ° ′	Dec ° ′	GHA ° ′	Dec ° ′	GHA ° ′	Dec ° ′	GHA ° ′	Dec ° ′
	4 00	103 37.2	179 27.0	S23 25.0	177 14.3	S23 30.0	350 54.9	N22 02.9	106 04.5	S 3 30.9
	01	118 39.6	194 26.1	24.8	192 14.7	29.8	5 57.7	02.9	121 06.8	30.8
	02	133 42.1	209 25.1	24.6	207 15.1	29.6	21 00.5	03.0	136 09.2	30.8
	03	148 44.6	224 24.2	. . 24.4	222 15.5	. . 29.4	36 03.4	. . 03.0	151 11.5	. . 30.7
	04	163 47.0	239 23.2	24.2	237 15.9	29.2	51 06.2	03.1	166 13.8	30.6
	05	178 49.5	254 22.3	23.9	252 16.3	29.0	66 09.0	03.1	181 16.1	30.6
	06	193 51.9	269 21.3	S23 23.7	267 16.6	S23 28.7	81 11.8	N22 03.2	196 18.4	S 3 30.5
	07	208 54.4	284 20.3	23.5	282 17.0	28.5	96 14.6	03.3	211 20.8	30.4
	08	223 56.9	299 19.4	23.3	297 17.4	28.3	111 17.4	03.3	226 23.1	30.4
S	09	238 59.3	314 18.4	. . 23.0	312 17.8	. . 28.1	126 20.3	. . 03.4	241 25.4	. . 30.3
U	10	254 01.8	329 17.5	22.8	327 18.2	27.9	141 23.1	03.4	256 27.7	30.2
N	11	269 04.3	344 16.5	22.6	342 18.5	27.7	156 25.9	03.5	271 30.1	30.1
D	12	284 06.7	359 15.6	S23 22.3	357 18.9	S23 27.5	171 28.7	N22 03.5	286 32.4	S 3 30.1
A	13	299 09.2	14 14.6	22.1	12 19.3	27.3	186 31.5	03.6	301 34.7	30.0
Y	14	314 11.7	29 13.7	21.9	27 19.7	27.1	201 34.4	03.6	316 37.0	29.9
	15	329 14.1	44 12.7	. . 21.6	42 20.1	. . 26.9	216 37.2	. . 03.7	331 39.3	. . 29.9
	16	344 16.6	59 11.8	21.4	57 20.5	26.7	231 40.0	03.8	346 41.7	29.8
	17	359 19.1	74 10.8	21.2	72 20.8	26.5	246 42.8	03.8	1 44.0	29.7
	18	14 21.5	89 09.8	S23 20.9	87 21.2	S23 26.3	261 45.6	N22 03.9	16 46.3	S 3 29.6
	19	29 24.0	104 08.9	20.7	102 21.6	26.1	276 48.4	03.9	31 48.6	29.6
	20	44 26.4	119 07.9	20.5	117 22.0	25.9	291 51.3	04.0	46 50.9	29.5
	21	59 28.9	134 07.0	. . 20.2	132 22.4	. . 25.6	306 54.1	. . 04.0	61 53.3	. . 29.4
	22	74 31.4	149 06.0	20.0	147 22.7	25.4	321 56.9	04.1	76 55.6	29.4
	23	89 33.8	164 05.1	19.7	162 23.1	25.2	336 59.7	04.2	91 57.9	29.3
	5 00	104 36.3	179 04.1	S23 19.5	177 23.5	S23 25.0	352 02.5	N22 04.2	107 00.2	S 3 29.2
	01	119 38.8	194 03.2	19.2	192 23.9	24.8	7 05.4	04.3	122 02.5	29.2
	02	134 41.2	209 02.2	19.0	207 24.3	24.6	22 08.2	04.3	137 04.9	29.1
	03	149 43.7	224 01.3	. . 18.7	222 24.7	. . 24.4	37 11.0	. . 04.4	152 07.2	. . 29.0
	04	164 46.2	239 00.3	18.5	237 25.0	24.2	52 13.8	04.4	167 09.5	28.9
	05	179 48.6	253 59.4	18.2	252 25.4	24.0	67 16.6	04.5	182 11.8	28.9
	06	194 51.1	268 58.4	S23 18.0	267 25.8	S23 23.7	82 19.5	N22 04.6	197 14.1	S 3 28.8
	07	209 53.6	283 57.5	17.7	282 26.2	23.5	97 22.3	04.6	212 16.5	28.7
	08	224 56.0	298 56.5	17.5	297 26.6	23.3	112 25.1	04.7	227 18.8	28.6
M	09	239 58.5	313 55.6	. . 17.2	312 26.9	. . 23.1	127 27.9	. . 04.7	242 21.1	. . 28.6
O	10	255 00.9	328 54.6	17.0	327 27.3	22.9	142 30.7	04.8	257 23.4	28.5
N	11	270 03.4	343 53.7	16.7	342 27.7	22.7	157 33.6	04.8	272 25.7	28.4
D	12	285 05.9	358 52.7	S23 16.4	357 28.1	S23 22.4	172 36.4	N22 04.9	287 28.0	S 3 28.4
A	13	300 08.3	13 51.8	16.2	12 28.5	22.2	187 39.2	05.0	302 30.4	28.3
Y	14	315 10.8	28 50.8	15.9	27 28.9	22.0	202 42.0	05.0	317 32.7	28.2
	15	330 13.3	43 49.9	. . 15.6	42 29.2	. . 21.8	217 44.8	. . 05.1	332 35.0	. . 28.1
	16	345 15.7	58 48.9	15.4	57 29.6	21.6	232 47.7	05.1	347 37.3	28.1
	17	0 18.2	73 48.0	15.1	72 30.0	21.4	247 50.5	05.2	2 39.6	28.0
	18	15 20.7	88 47.0	S23 14.8	87 30.4	S23 21.1	262 53.3	N22 05.2	17 41.9	S 3 27.9
	19	30 23.1	103 46.1	14.6	102 30.8	20.9	277 56.1	05.3	32 44.3	27.9
	20	45 25.6	118 45.1	14.3	117 31.2	20.7	292 58.9	05.4	47 46.6	27.8
	21	60 28.0	133 44.2	. . 14.0	132 31.5	. . 20.5	308 01.8	. . 05.4	62 48.9	. . 27.7
	22	75 30.5	148 43.3	13.8	147 31.9	20.3	323 04.6	05.5	77 51.2	27.6
	23	90 33.0	163 42.3	13.5	162 32.3	20.0	338 07.4	05.5	92 53.5	27.6
	6 00	105 35.4	178 41.4	S23 13.2	177 32.7	S23 19.8	353 10.2	N22 05.6	107 55.8	S 3 27.5
	01	120 37.9	193 40.4	12.9	192 33.1	19.6	8 13.0	05.6	122 58.2	27.4
	02	135 40.4	208 39.5	12.7	207 33.5	19.4	23 15.9	05.7	138 00.5	27.4
	03	150 42.8	223 38.5	. . 12.4	222 33.8	. . 19.1	38 18.7	. . 05.8	153 02.8	. . 27.3
	04	165 45.3	238 37.6	12.1	237 34.2	18.9	53 21.5	05.8	168 05.1	27.2
	05	180 47.8	253 36.6	11.8	252 34.6	18.7	68 24.3	05.9	183 07.4	27.1
	06	195 50.2	268 35.7	S23 11.5	267 35.0	S23 18.5	83 27.1	N22 05.9	198 09.7	S 3 27.1
	07	210 52.7	283 34.7	11.2	282 35.4	18.2	98 30.0	06.0	213 12.1	27.0
T	08	225 55.2	298 33.8	11.0	297 35.8	18.0	113 32.8	06.0	228 14.4	26.9
U	09	240 57.6	313 32.9	. . 10.7	312 36.1	. . 17.8	128 35.6	. . 06.1	243 16.7	. . 26.8
E	10	256 00.1	328 31.9	10.4	327 36.5	17.6	143 38.4	06.1	258 19.0	26.8
S	11	271 02.5	343 31.0	10.1	342 36.9	17.3	158 41.2	06.2	273 21.3	26.7
D	12	286 05.0	358 30.0	S23 09.8	357 37.3	S23 17.1	173 44.1	N22 06.3	288 23.6	S 3 26.6
A	13	301 07.5	13 29.1	09.5	12 37.7	16.9	188 46.9	06.3	303 25.9	26.5
Y	14	316 09.9	28 28.1	09.2	27 38.1	16.7	203 49.7	06.4	318 28.3	26.5
	15	331 12.4	43 27.2	. . 08.9	42 38.4	. . 16.4	218 52.5	. . 06.4	333 30.6	. . 26.4
	16	346 14.9	58 26.3	08.6	57 38.8	16.2	233 55.4	06.5	348 32.9	26.3
	17	1 17.3	73 25.3	08.3	72 39.2	16.0	248 58.2	06.5	3 35.2	26.3
	18	16 19.8	88 24.4	S23 08.0	87 39.6	S23 15.7	264 01.0	N22 06.6	18 37.5	S 3 26.2
	19	31 22.3	103 23.4	07.7	102 40.0	15.5	279 03.8	06.7	33 39.8	26.1
	20	46 24.7	118 22.5	07.4	117 40.4	15.3	294 06.6	06.7	48 42.1	26.0
	21	61 27.2	133 21.5	. . 07.1	132 40.7	. . 15.0	309 09.5	. . 06.8	63 44.5	. . 26.0
	22	76 29.7	148 20.6	06.8	147 41.1	14.8	324 12.3	06.8	78 46.8	25.9
	23	91 32.1	163 19.7	06.5	162 41.5	14.6	339 15.1	06.9	93 49.1	25.8
	Mer. Pass.	h m 16 58.8	*v* −0.9	*d* 0.3	*v* 0.4	*d* 0.2	*v* 2.8	*d* 0.1	*v* 2.3	*d* 0.1

STARS

Name	SHA ° ′	Dec ° ′
Acamar	315 10.9	S40 12.2
Achernar	335 19.4	S57 06.5
Acrux	172 59.0	S63 14.4
Adhara	255 04.8	S29 00.4
Aldebaran	290 38.4	N16 33.7
Alioth	166 12.2	N55 48.8
Alkaid	152 51.5	N49 10.7
Alnair	27 32.2	S46 50.3
Alnilam	275 36.6	S 1 11.1
Alphard	217 46.7	S 8 46.3
Alphecca	126 03.3	N26 37.4
Alpheratz	357 34.0	N29 14.2
Altair	61 59.5	N 8 56.2
Ankaa	353 06.4	S42 10.1
Antares	112 15.1	S26 29.3
Arcturus	145 47.3	N19 02.6
Atria	107 09.1	S69 04.3
Avior	234 13.8	S59 35.4
Bellatrix	278 21.7	N 6 22.4
Betelgeuse	270 50.8	N 7 24.7
Canopus	263 51.5	S52 42.6
Capella	280 20.2	N46 01.5
Deneb	49 25.7	N45 22.5
Denebola	182 24.0	N14 25.4
Diphda	348 46.5	S17 50.7
Dubhe	193 39.6	N61 36.3
Elnath	278 00.4	N28 37.8
Eltanin	90 42.3	N51 29.0
Enif	33 38.2	N 9 59.7
Fomalhaut	15 13.8	S29 29.2
Gacrux	171 50.7	S57 15.3
Gienah	175 42.7	S17 41.2
Hadar	148 35.0	S60 29.7
Hamal	327 50.1	N23 35.3
Kaus Aust.	83 31.8	S34 22.3
Kochab	137 20.4	N74 02.5
Markab	13 29.2	N15 20.8
Menkar	314 05.1	N 4 11.5
Menkent	147 56.8	S36 29.7
Miaplacidus	221 37.3	S69 49.2
Mirfak	308 26.7	N49 57.4
Nunki	75 47.1	S26 15.9
Peacock	53 05.0	S56 39.2
Pollux	243 15.9	N27 57.7
Procyon	244 49.6	N 5 09.4
Rasalhague	95 58.1	N12 32.4
Regulus	207 33.3	N11 50.3
Rigel	281 02.8	S 8 10.3
Rigil Kent.	139 39.4	S60 56.3
Sabik	102 02.1	S15 45.4
Schedar	349 30.1	N56 41.1
Shaula	96 09.6	S37 07.3
Sirius	258 25.1	S16 45.1
Spica	158 21.5	S11 17.8
Suhail	222 45.3	S43 32.1
Vega	80 33.1	N38 48.4
Zuben'ubi	136 55.3	S16 09.0

	SHA ° ′	Mer. Pass. h m
Venus	74 27.8	12 04
Mars	72 47.2	12 10
Jupiter	247 26.2	0 32
Saturn	2 23.9	16 49

	UT	SUN GHA	SUN Dec	MOON GHA	v	MOON Dec	d	HP
	d h	° ′	° ′	° ′	′	° ′	′	′
	4 00	178 49.1	S22 44.4	349 34.0	3.8	N25 28.6	8.1	60.2
	01	193 48.8	44.2	3 56.8	3.9	25 20.5	8.4	60.2
	02	208 48.5	43.9	18 19.7	4.0	25 12.1	8.5	60.2
	03	223 48.2	. . 43.7	32 42.7	4.2	25 03.6	8.6	60.2
	04	238 48.0	43.4	47 05.9	4.3	24 55.0	8.9	60.1
	05	253 47.7	43.1	61 29.2	4.4	24 46.1	9.0	60.1
	06	268 47.4	S22 42.9	75 52.6	4.5	N24 37.1	9.1	60.1
	07	283 47.1	42.6	90 16.1	4.7	24 28.0	9.3	60.0
	08	298 46.8	42.4	104 39.8	4.8	24 18.7	9.5	60.0
S	09	313 46.6	. . 42.1	119 03.6	4.9	24 09.2	9.6	60.0
U	10	328 46.3	41.8	133 27.5	5.1	23 59.6	9.8	60.0
N	11	343 46.0	41.6	147 51.6	5.2	23 49.8	9.9	59.9
D	12	358 45.7	S22 41.3	162 15.8	5.4	N23 39.9	10.1	59.9
A	13	13 45.4	41.0	176 40.2	5.4	23 29.8	10.2	59.9
Y	14	28 45.1	40.7	191 04.6	5.6	23 19.6	10.3	59.9
	15	43 44.9	. . 40.5	205 29.2	5.8	23 09.3	10.5	59.8
	16	58 44.6	40.2	219 54.0	5.9	22 58.8	10.6	59.8
	17	73 44.3	39.9	234 18.9	6.0	22 48.2	10.8	59.8
	18	88 44.0	S22 39.7	248 43.9	6.2	N22 37.4	10.9	59.7
	19	103 43.7	39.4	263 09.1	6.3	22 26.5	11.0	59.7
	20	118 43.5	39.1	277 34.4	6.4	22 15.5	11.2	59.7
	21	133 43.2	. . 38.8	291 59.8	6.6	22 04.3	11.3	59.6
	22	148 42.9	38.6	306 25.4	6.7	21 53.0	11.4	59.6
	23	163 42.6	38.3	320 51.1	6.9	21 41.6	11.5	59.6
	5 00	178 42.3	S22 38.0	335 17.0	7.0	N21 30.1	11.6	59.5
	01	193 42.1	37.7	349 43.0	7.1	21 18.5	11.8	59.5
	02	208 41.8	37.5	4 09.1	7.3	21 06.7	11.9	59.5
	03	223 41.5	. . 37.2	18 35.4	7.4	20 54.8	12.0	59.4
	04	238 41.2	36.9	33 01.8	7.5	20 42.8	12.1	59.4
	05	253 41.0	36.6	47 28.3	7.7	20 30.7	12.2	59.4
	06	268 40.7	S22 36.3	61 55.0	7.9	N20 18.5	12.3	59.3
	07	283 40.4	36.1	76 21.9	7.9	20 06.2	12.4	59.3
	08	298 40.1	35.8	90 48.8	8.1	19 53.8	12.6	59.3
M	09	313 39.8	. . 35.5	105 15.9	8.3	19 41.2	12.6	59.2
O	10	328 39.6	35.2	119 43.2	8.3	19 28.6	12.7	59.2
N	11	343 39.3	34.9	134 10.5	8.5	19 15.9	12.8	59.2
D	12	358 39.0	S22 34.6	148 38.0	8.7	N19 03.1	12.9	59.1
A	13	13 38.7	34.3	163 05.7	8.8	18 50.2	13.0	59.1
Y	14	28 38.5	34.1	177 33.5	8.9	18 37.2	13.1	59.1
	15	43 38.2	. . 33.8	192 01.4	9.0	18 24.1	13.2	59.0
	16	58 37.9	33.5	206 29.4	9.2	18 10.9	13.3	59.0
	17	73 37.6	33.2	220 57.6	9.3	17 57.6	13.3	59.0
	18	88 37.4	S22 32.9	235 25.9	9.4	N17 44.3	13.4	58.9
	19	103 37.1	32.6	249 54.3	9.6	17 30.9	13.5	58.9
	20	118 36.8	32.3	264 22.9	9.7	17 17.4	13.6	58.8
	21	133 36.5	. . 32.0	278 51.6	9.8	17 03.8	13.7	58.8
	22	148 36.3	31.7	293 20.4	9.9	16 50.1	13.7	58.8
	23	163 36.0	31.4	307 49.3	10.1	16 36.4	13.8	58.7
	6 00	178 35.7	S22 31.1	322 18.4	10.2	N16 22.6	13.9	58.7
	01	193 35.4	30.8	336 47.6	10.3	16 08.7	13.9	58.7
	02	208 35.2	30.5	351 16.9	10.4	15 54.8	14.0	58.6
	03	223 34.9	. . 30.2	5 46.3	10.6	15 40.8	14.1	58.6
	04	238 34.6	29.9	20 15.9	10.6	15 26.7	14.1	58.5
	05	253 34.3	29.6	34 45.5	10.8	15 12.6	14.2	58.5
	06	268 34.1	S22 29.3	49 15.3	10.9	N14 58.4	14.3	58.5
	07	283 33.8	29.0	63 45.2	11.1	14 44.1	14.3	58.4
T	08	298 33.5	28.7	78 15.3	11.1	14 29.8	14.3	58.4
U	09	313 33.2	. . 28.4	92 45.4	11.3	14 15.5	14.4	58.4
E	10	328 33.0	28.1	107 15.7	11.3	14 01.1	14.5	58.3
S	11	343 32.7	27.8	121 46.0	11.5	13 46.6	14.5	58.3
D	12	358 32.4	S22 27.5	136 16.5	11.6	N13 32.1	14.6	58.2
A	13	13 32.2	27.2	150 47.1	11.7	13 17.5	14.6	58.2
Y	14	28 31.9	26.9	165 17.8	11.8	13 02.9	14.6	58.2
	15	43 31.6	. . 26.6	179 48.6	11.9	12 48.3	14.7	58.1
	16	58 31.3	26.3	194 19.5	12.0	12 33.6	14.7	58.1
	17	73 31.1	26.0	208 50.5	12.1	12 18.9	14.8	58.0
	18	88 30.8	S22 25.7	223 21.6	12.3	N12 04.1	14.8	58.0
	19	103 30.5	25.4	237 52.9	12.3	11 49.3	14.8	58.0
	20	118 30.3	25.1	252 24.2	12.4	11 34.5	14.9	57.9
	21	133 30.0	. . 24.7	266 55.6	12.5	11 19.6	14.9	57.9
	22	148 29.7	24.4	281 27.1	12.6	11 04.7	15.0	57.9
	23	163 29.4	24.1	295 58.7	12.7	N10 49.7	14.9	57.8
		SD 16.3	*d* 0.3	SD 16.3		16.1		15.9

Lat.	Twilight Naut.	Twilight Civil	Sunrise	Moonrise 4	Moonrise 5	Moonrise 6	Moonrise 7
°	h m	h m	h m	h m	h m	h m	h m
N 72	08 19	10 29	■	□	□	18 27	20 51
N 70	08 01	09 43	■	□	16 00	18 49	20 59
68	07 47	09 12	11 29	□	16 44	19 06	21 05
66	07 35	08 49	10 20	14 23	17 13	19 19	21 10
64	07 25	08 31	09 44	15 18	17 34	19 30	21 15
62	07 16	08 16	09 19	15 50	17 51	19 40	21 19
60	07 08	08 04	09 00	16 14	18 06	19 48	21 22
N 58	07 01	07 53	08 43	16 33	18 18	19 55	21 25
56	06 55	07 43	08 30	16 49	18 28	20 01	21 27
54	06 49	07 35	08 18	17 03	18 37	20 06	21 30
52	06 44	07 27	08 07	17 15	18 45	20 11	21 32
50	06 39	07 20	07 58	17 25	18 53	20 16	21 34
45	06 28	07 05	07 38	17 47	19 08	20 25	21 38
N 40	06 18	06 52	07 22	18 04	19 21	20 33	21 41
35	06 09	06 41	07 08	18 19	19 32	20 40	21 44
30	06 01	06 30	06 57	18 32	19 41	20 46	21 46
20	05 45	06 12	06 36	18 53	19 57	20 56	21 51
N 10	05 30	05 56	06 18	19 12	20 11	21 05	21 55
0	05 13	05 39	06 02	19 29	20 24	21 13	21 59
S 10	04 55	05 22	05 45	19 46	20 37	21 22	22 02
20	04 33	05 02	05 27	20 05	20 51	21 30	22 06
30	04 05	04 38	05 05	20 26	21 06	21 40	22 10
35	03 47	04 23	04 53	20 38	21 15	21 46	22 13
40	03 25	04 06	04 38	20 52	21 26	21 53	22 16
45	02 56	03 44	04 21	21 09	21 38	22 00	22 19
S 50	02 14	03 16	04 00	21 29	21 52	22 09	22 23
52	01 49	03 02	03 49	21 39	21 59	22 13	22 25
54	01 13	02 45	03 38	21 50	22 06	22 18	22 27
56	////	02 25	03 24	22 02	22 15	22 23	22 29
58	////	01 58	03 09	22 16	22 24	22 28	22 31
S 60	////	01 19	02 50	22 33	22 35	22 35	22 34

Lat.	Sunset	Twilight Civil	Twilight Naut.	Moonset 4	Moonset 5	Moonset 6	Moonset 7
°	h m	h m	h m	h m	h m	h m	h m
N 72	■	13 42	15 52	□	□	12 03	11 16
N 70	■	14 29	16 10	□	12 42	11 39	11 05
68	12 43	14 59	16 24	□	11 57	11 20	10 56
66	13 52	15 22	16 36	12 20	11 27	11 05	10 49
64	14 27	15 40	16 46	11 24	11 04	10 52	10 43
62	14 52	15 55	16 55	10 51	10 46	10 41	10 37
60	15 12	16 07	17 03	10 26	10 31	10 32	10 32
N 58	15 28	16 18	17 10	10 06	10 18	10 24	10 28
56	15 41	16 28	17 16	09 49	10 06	10 17	10 24
54	15 53	16 36	17 22	09 35	09 56	10 10	10 21
52	16 04	16 44	17 27	09 23	09 47	10 05	10 18
50	16 13	16 51	17 32	09 12	09 39	09 59	10 15
45	16 33	17 06	17 43	08 49	09 22	09 48	10 08
N 40	16 49	17 19	17 53	08 30	09 08	09 38	10 03
35	17 02	17 30	18 02	08 15	08 56	09 30	09 59
30	17 14	17 40	18 10	08 01	08 45	09 23	09 55
20	17 35	17 58	18 26	07 38	08 27	09 10	09 47
N 10	17 52	18 15	18 41	07 17	08 11	08 59	09 41
0	18 09	18 32	18 58	06 58	07 56	08 48	09 35
S 10	18 26	18 49	19 16	06 39	07 41	08 37	09 29
20	18 44	19 09	19 38	06 18	07 24	08 26	09 23
30	19 05	19 32	20 05	05 54	07 05	08 12	09 15
35	19 18	19 47	20 23	05 40	06 54	08 05	09 11
40	19 32	20 04	20 45	05 23	06 41	07 56	09 06
45	19 49	20 26	21 14	05 03	06 26	07 45	09 00
S 50	20 11	20 54	21 56	04 38	06 07	07 33	08 53
52	20 21	21 08	22 20	04 26	05 58	07 27	08 50
54	20 32	21 25	22 56	04 12	05 48	07 20	08 47
56	20 46	21 45	////	03 55	05 36	07 13	08 43
58	21 01	22 11	////	03 36	05 23	07 04	08 38
S 60	21 20	22 49	////	03 11	05 07	06 55	08 33

Day	SUN Eqn. of Time 00^h	SUN Eqn. of Time 12^h	SUN Mer. Pass.	MOON Mer. Pass. Upper	MOON Mer. Pass. Lower	Age	Phase
d	m s	m s	h m	h m	h m	d %	
4	04 43	04 57	12 05	00 44	13 14	15 98	○
5	05 10	05 23	12 05	01 43	14 10	16 94	
6	05 37	05 50	12 06	02 36	15 01	17 88	

Day	UT d h	ARIES GHA ° ′	VENUS −3·9 GHA ° ′	VENUS Dec ° ′	MARS +1·1 GHA ° ′	MARS Dec ° ′	JUPITER −2·7 GHA ° ′	JUPITER Dec ° ′	SATURN +1·0 GHA ° ′	SATURN Dec ° ′
WEDNESDAY	7 00	106 34.6	178 18.7	S23 06.2	177 41.9	S23 14.3	354 17.9	N22 06.9	108 51.4	S 3 25.7
	01	121 37.0	193 17.8	05.9	192 42.3	14.1	9 20.7	07.0	123 53.7	25.7
	02	136 39.5	208 16.8	05.6	207 42.7	13.9	24 23.6	07.1	138 56.0	25.6
	03	151 42.0	223 15.9	. . 05.3	222 43.0	. . 13.6	39 26.4	. . 07.1	153 58.3	. . 25.5
	04	166 44.4	238 15.0	05.0	237 43.4	13.4	54 29.2	07.2	169 00.6	25.4
	05	181 46.9	253 14.0	04.7	252 43.8	13.2	69 32.0	07.2	184 03.0	25.4
	06	196 49.4	268 13.1	S23 04.4	267 44.2	S23 12.9	84 34.9	N22 07.3	199 05.3	S 3 25.3
	07	211 51.8	283 12.2	04.0	282 44.6	12.7	99 37.7	07.3	214 07.6	25.2
	08	226 54.3	298 11.2	03.7	297 45.0	12.5	114 40.5	07.4	229 09.9	25.1
	09	241 56.8	313 10.3	. . 03.4	312 45.4	. . 12.2	129 43.3	. . 07.4	244 12.2	. . 25.1
	10	256 59.2	328 09.3	03.1	327 45.7	12.0	144 46.1	07.5	259 14.5	25.0
	11	272 01.7	343 08.4	02.8	342 46.1	11.7	159 49.0	07.6	274 16.8	24.9
	12	287 04.1	358 07.5	S23 02.5	357 46.5	S23 11.5	174 51.8	N22 07.6	289 19.1	S 3 24.8
	13	302 06.6	13 06.5	02.1	12 46.9	11.3	189 54.6	07.7	304 21.4	24.8
	14	317 09.1	28 05.6	01.8	27 47.3	11.0	204 57.4	07.7	319 23.8	24.7
	15	332 11.5	43 04.7	. . 01.5	42 47.7	. . 10.8	220 00.3	. . 07.8	334 26.1	. . 24.6
	16	347 14.0	58 03.7	01.2	57 48.0	10.5	235 03.1	07.8	349 28.4	24.5
	17	2 16.5	73 02.8	00.8	72 48.4	10.3	250 05.9	07.9	4 30.7	24.5
	18	17 18.9	88 01.9	S23 00.5	87 48.8	S23 10.1	265 08.7	N22 08.0	19 33.0	S 3 24.4
	19	32 21.4	103 00.9	23 00.2	102 49.2	09.8	280 11.5	08.0	34 35.3	24.3
	20	47 23.9	118 00.0	22 59.8	117 49.6	09.6	295 14.4	08.1	49 37.6	24.2
	21	62 26.3	132 59.0	. . 59.5	132 50.0	. . 09.3	310 17.2	. . 08.1	64 39.9	. . 24.2
	22	77 28.8	147 58.1	59.2	147 50.4	09.1	325 20.0	08.2	79 42.2	24.1
	23	92 31.3	162 57.2	58.8	162 50.7	08.8	340 22.8	08.2	94 44.5	24.0
THURSDAY	8 00	107 33.7	177 56.2	S22 58.5	177 51.1	S23 08.6	355 25.7	N22 08.3	109 46.9	S 3 23.9
	01	122 36.2	192 55.3	58.2	192 51.5	08.4	10 28.5	08.3	124 49.2	23.9
	02	137 38.6	207 54.4	57.8	207 51.9	08.1	25 31.3	08.4	139 51.5	23.8
	03	152 41.1	222 53.4	. . 57.5	222 52.3	. . 07.9	40 34.1	. . 08.5	154 53.8	. . 23.7
	04	167 43.6	237 52.5	57.2	237 52.7	07.6	55 36.9	08.5	169 56.1	23.6
	05	182 46.0	252 51.6	56.8	252 53.1	07.4	70 39.8	08.6	184 58.4	23.6
	06	197 48.5	267 50.7	S22 56.5	267 53.4	S23 07.1	85 42.6	N22 08.6	200 00.7	S 3 23.5
	07	212 51.0	282 49.7	56.1	282 53.8	06.9	100 45.4	08.7	215 03.0	23.4
	08	227 53.4	297 48.8	55.8	297 54.2	06.6	115 48.2	08.7	230 05.3	23.3
	09	242 55.9	312 47.9	. . 55.4	312 54.6	. . 06.4	130 51.1	. . 08.8	245 07.6	. . 23.3
	10	257 58.4	327 46.9	55.1	327 55.0	06.1	145 53.9	08.9	260 09.9	23.2
	11	273 00.8	342 46.0	54.7	342 55.4	05.9	160 56.7	08.9	275 12.3	23.1
	12	288 03.3	357 45.1	S22 54.4	357 55.8	S23 05.6	175 59.5	N22 09.0	290 14.6	S 3 23.0
	13	303 05.8	12 44.1	54.0	12 56.1	05.4	191 02.4	09.0	305 16.9	23.0
	14	318 08.2	27 43.2	53.7	27 56.5	05.1	206 05.2	09.1	320 19.2	22.9
	15	333 10.7	42 42.3	. . 53.3	42 56.9	. . 04.9	221 08.0	. . 09.1	335 21.5	. . 22.8
	16	348 13.1	57 41.4	53.0	57 57.3	04.6	236 10.8	09.2	350 23.8	22.7
	17	3 15.6	72 40.4	52.6	72 57.7	04.4	251 13.6	09.2	5 26.1	22.7
	18	18 18.1	87 39.5	S22 52.3	87 58.1	S23 04.1	266 16.5	N22 09.3	20 28.4	S 3 22.6
	19	33 20.5	102 38.6	51.9	102 58.5	03.9	281 19.3	09.4	35 30.7	22.5
	20	48 23.0	117 37.6	51.5	117 58.8	03.6	296 22.1	09.4	50 33.0	22.4
	21	63 25.5	132 36.7	. . 51.2	132 59.2	. . 03.4	311 24.9	. . 09.5	65 35.3	. . 22.4
	22	78 27.9	147 35.8	50.8	147 59.6	03.1	326 27.8	09.5	80 37.6	22.3
	23	93 30.4	162 34.9	50.5	163 00.0	02.9	341 30.6	09.6	95 39.9	22.2
FRIDAY	9 00	108 32.9	177 33.9	S22 50.1	178 00.4	S23 02.6	356 33.4	N22 09.6	110 42.2	S 3 22.1
	01	123 35.3	192 33.0	49.7	193 00.8	02.4	11 36.2	09.7	125 44.5	22.0
	02	138 37.8	207 32.1	49.4	208 01.2	02.1	26 39.1	09.7	140 46.9	22.0
	03	153 40.2	222 31.2	. . 49.0	223 01.6	. . 01.8	41 41.9	. . 09.8	155 49.2	. . 21.9
	04	168 42.7	237 30.2	48.6	238 01.9	01.6	56 44.7	09.9	170 51.5	21.8
	05	183 45.2	252 29.3	48.3	253 02.3	01.3	71 47.5	09.9	185 53.8	21.7
	06	198 47.6	267 28.4	S22 47.9	268 02.7	S23 01.1	86 50.3	N22 10.0	200 56.1	S 3 21.7
	07	213 50.1	282 27.5	47.5	283 03.1	00.8	101 53.2	10.0	215 58.4	21.6
	08	228 52.6	297 26.5	47.1	298 03.5	00.6	116 56.0	10.1	231 00.7	21.5
	09	243 55.0	312 25.6	. . 46.8	313 03.9	. . 00.3	131 58.8	. . 10.1	246 03.0	. . 21.4
	10	258 57.5	327 24.7	46.4	328 04.3	23 00.0	147 01.6	10.2	261 05.3	21.4
	11	274 00.0	342 23.8	46.0	343 04.7	22 59.8	162 04.5	10.3	276 07.6	21.3
	12	289 02.4	357 22.8	S22 45.6	358 05.0	S22 59.5	177 07.3	N22 10.3	291 09.9	S 3 21.2
	13	304 04.9	12 21.9	45.2	13 05.4	59.3	192 10.1	10.4	306 12.2	21.1
	14	319 07.4	27 21.0	44.9	28 05.8	59.0	207 12.9	10.4	321 14.5	21.0
	15	334 09.8	42 20.1	. . 44.5	43 06.2	. . 58.7	222 15.8	. . 10.5	336 16.8	. . 21.0
	16	349 12.3	57 19.2	44.1	58 06.6	58.5	237 18.6	10.5	351 19.1	20.9
	17	4 14.7	72 18.2	43.7	73 07.0	58.2	252 21.4	10.6	6 21.4	20.8
	18	19 17.2	87 17.3	S22 43.3	88 07.4	S22 57.9	267 24.2	N22 10.6	21 23.7	S 3 20.7
	19	34 19.7	102 16.4	42.9	103 07.8	57.7	282 27.1	10.7	36 26.0	20.7
	20	49 22.1	117 15.5	42.6	118 08.1	57.4	297 29.9	10.8	51 28.3	20.6
	21	64 24.6	132 14.6	. . 42.2	133 08.5	. . 57.1	312 32.7	. . 10.8	66 30.6	. . 20.5
	22	79 27.1	147 13.6	41.8	148 08.9	56.9	327 35.5	10.9	81 32.9	20.4
	23	94 29.5	162 12.7	41.4	163 09.3	56.6	342 38.3	10.9	96 35.2	20.3
	Mer. Pass. (h m)	16 47.0	*v* −0.9	*d* 0.4	*v* 0.4	*d* 0.2	*v* 2.8	*d* 0.1	*v* 2.3	*d* 0.1

STARS

Name	SHA ° ′	Dec ° ′
Acamar	315 10.9	S40 12.2
Achernar	335 19.5	S57 06.5
Acrux	172 59.0	S63 14.4
Adhara	255 04.8	S29 00.5
Aldebaran	290 38.4	N16 33.7
Alioth	166 12.2	N55 48.8
Alkaid	152 51.4	N49 10.7
Alnair	27 32.2	S46 50.3
Alnilam	275 36.6	S 1 11.1
Alphard	217 46.7	S 8 46.3
Alphecca	126 03.3	N26 37.4
Alpheratz	357 34.0	N29 14.2
Altair	61 59.5	N 8 56.2
Ankaa	353 06.4	S42 10.1
Antares	112 15.1	S26 29.3
Arcturus	145 47.2	N19 02.6
Atria	107 09.1	S69 04.3
Avior	234 13.8	S59 35.5
Bellatrix	278 21.7	N 6 22.4
Betelgeuse	270 50.8	N 7 24.7
Canopus	263 51.5	S52 42.6
Capella	280 20.2	N46 01.5
Deneb	49 25.7	N45 22.5
Denebola	182 24.0	N14 25.4
Diphda	348 46.5	S17 50.7
Dubhe	193 39.6	N61 36.3
Elnath	278 00.5	N28 37.8
Eltanin	90 42.3	N51 29.0
Enif	33 38.2	N 9 59.7
Fomalhaut	15 13.8	S29 29.2
Gacrux	171 50.6	S57 15.3
Gienah	175 42.6	S17 41.2
Hadar	148 35.0	S60 29.7
Hamal	327 50.1	N23 35.3
Kaus Aust.	83 31.8	S34 22.3
Kochab	137 20.3	N74 02.5
Markab	13 29.2	N15 20.8
Menkar	314 05.1	N 4 11.5
Menkent	147 56.7	S36 29.7
Miaplacidus	221 37.3	S69 49.3
Mirfak	308 26.7	N49 57.4
Nunki	75 47.1	S26 15.9
Peacock	53 05.0	S56 39.2
Pollux	243 15.9	N27 57.7
Procyon	244 49.6	N 5 09.4
Rasalhague	95 58.1	N12 32.4
Regulus	207 33.3	N11 50.3
Rigel	281 02.8	S 8 10.3
Rigil Kent.	139 39.4	S60 56.3
Sabik	102 02.1	S15 45.4
Schedar	349 30.2	N56 41.1
Shaula	96 09.6	S37 07.3
Sirius	258 25.1	S16 45.1
Spica	158 21.4	S11 17.8
Suhail	222 45.3	S43 32.2
Vega	80 33.1	N38 48.4
Zuben'ubi	136 55.2	S16 09.0

	SHA ° ′	Mer. Pass. h m
Venus	70 22.5	12 09
Mars	70 17.4	12 08
Jupiter	247 51.9	0 18
Saturn	2 13.1	16 38

UT d h	SUN GHA ° ′	SUN Dec ° ′	MOON GHA ° ′	v ′	MOON Dec ° ′	d ′	HP ′
7 00	178 29.2	S22 23.8	310 30.4	12.9	N10 34.8	15.0	57.8
01	193 28.9	23.5	325 02.3	12.8	10 19.8	15.1	57.7
02	208 28.6	23.2	339 34.1	13.0	10 04.7	15.0	57.7
03	223 28.4	. . 22.9	354 06.1	13.1	9 49.7	15.1	57.7
04	238 28.1	22.5	8 38.2	13.2	9 34.6	15.1	57.6
05	253 27.8	22.2	23 10.4	13.2	9 19.5	15.1	57.6
06	268 27.6	S22 21.9	37 42.6	13.4	N 9 04.4	15.1	57.5
WEDNESDAY 07	283 27.3	21.6	52 15.0	13.4	8 49.3	15.2	57.5
08	298 27.0	21.3	66 47.4	13.5	8 34.1	15.2	57.5
09	313 26.8	. . 20.9	81 19.9	13.6	8 18.9	15.2	57.4
10	328 26.5	20.6	95 52.5	13.6	8 03.7	15.2	57.4
11	343 26.2	20.3	110 25.1	13.8	7 48.5	15.2	57.4
12	358 26.0	S22 20.0	124 57.9	13.8	N 7 33.3	15.2	57.3
13	13 25.7	19.7	139 30.7	13.9	7 18.1	15.3	57.3
14	28 25.4	19.3	154 03.6	14.0	7 02.8	15.2	57.2
15	43 25.2	. . 19.0	168 36.6	14.0	6 47.6	15.3	57.2
16	58 24.9	18.7	183 09.6	14.1	6 32.3	15.2	57.2
17	73 24.6	18.4	197 42.7	14.2	6 17.1	15.3	57.1
18	88 24.4	S22 18.0	212 15.9	14.3	N 6 01.8	15.3	57.1
19	103 24.1	17.7	226 49.2	14.3	5 46.5	15.3	57.0
20	118 23.8	17.4	241 22.5	14.4	5 31.2	15.3	57.0
21	133 23.6	. . 17.0	255 55.9	14.4	5 15.9	15.2	57.0
22	148 23.3	16.7	270 29.3	14.5	5 00.7	15.3	56.9
23	163 23.0	16.4	285 02.8	14.6	4 45.4	15.3	56.9
8 00	178 22.8	S22 16.0	299 36.4	14.6	N 4 30.1	15.3	56.9
01	193 22.5	15.7	314 10.0	14.7	4 14.8	15.3	56.8
02	208 22.2	15.4	328 43.7	14.8	3 59.5	15.3	56.8
03	223 22.0	. . 15.0	343 17.5	14.8	3 44.2	15.2	56.8
04	238 21.7	14.7	357 51.3	14.8	3 29.0	15.3	56.7
05	253 21.4	14.4	12 25.1	14.9	3 13.7	15.3	56.7
06	268 21.2	S22 14.0	26 59.0	15.0	N 2 58.4	15.2	56.6
THURSDAY 07	283 20.9	13.7	41 33.0	15.0	2 43.2	15.3	56.6
08	298 20.7	13.4	56 07.0	15.1	2 27.9	15.2	56.6
09	313 20.4	. . 13.0	70 41.1	15.1	2 12.7	15.2	56.5
10	328 20.1	12.7	85 15.2	15.1	1 57.5	15.2	56.5
11	343 19.9	12.3	99 49.3	15.2	1 42.3	15.2	56.5
12	358 19.6	S22 12.0	114 23.5	15.3	N 1 27.1	15.2	56.4
13	13 19.3	11.7	128 57.8	15.2	1 11.9	15.2	56.4
14	28 19.1	11.3	143 32.0	15.4	0 56.7	15.1	56.4
15	43 18.8	. . 11.0	158 06.4	15.3	0 41.6	15.1	56.3
16	58 18.6	10.6	172 40.7	15.4	0 26.5	15.2	56.3
17	73 18.3	10.3	187 15.1	15.5	N 0 11.3	15.1	56.3
18	88 18.0	S22 09.9	201 49.6	15.4	S 0 03.8	15.0	56.2
19	103 17.8	09.6	216 24.0	15.6	0 18.8	15.1	56.2
20	118 17.5	09.2	230 58.6	15.5	0 33.9	15.0	56.2
21	133 17.3	. . 08.9	245 33.1	15.6	0 48.9	15.1	56.1
22	148 17.0	08.5	260 07.7	15.6	1 04.0	15.0	56.1
23	163 16.7	08.2	274 42.3	15.6	1 19.0	14.9	56.1
9 00	178 16.5	S22 07.8	289 16.9	15.7	S 1 33.9	15.0	56.0
01	193 16.2	07.5	303 51.6	15.6	1 48.9	14.9	56.0
02	208 16.0	07.1	318 26.2	15.7	2 03.8	14.9	56.0
03	223 15.7	. . 06.8	333 00.9	15.8	2 18.7	14.9	55.9
04	238 15.4	06.4	347 35.7	15.7	2 33.6	14.8	55.9
05	253 15.2	06.1	2 10.4	15.8	2 48.4	14.8	55.9
06	268 14.9	S22 05.7	16 45.2	15.8	S 3 03.2	14.8	55.8
07	283 14.7	05.4	31 20.0	15.8	3 18.0	14.8	55.8
08	298 14.4	05.0	45 54.8	15.8	3 32.8	14.7	55.8
FRIDAY 09	313 14.1	. . 04.6	60 29.6	15.9	3 47.5	14.7	55.7
10	328 13.9	04.3	75 04.5	15.8	4 02.2	14.6	55.7
11	343 13.6	03.9	89 39.3	15.9	4 16.8	14.7	55.7
12	358 13.4	S22 03.6	104 14.2	15.9	S 4 31.5	14.6	55.6
13	13 13.1	03.2	118 49.1	15.9	4 46.1	14.5	55.6
14	28 12.9	02.9	133 24.0	15.9	5 00.6	14.5	55.6
15	43 12.6	. . 02.5	147 58.9	15.9	5 15.1	14.5	55.6
16	58 12.4	02.1	162 33.8	15.9	5 29.6	14.5	55.5
17	73 12.1	01.8	177 08.7	16.0	5 44.1	14.4	55.5
18	88 11.8	S22 01.4	191 43.7	15.9	S 5 58.5	14.4	55.5
19	103 11.6	01.0	206 18.6	15.9	6 12.9	14.3	55.4
20	118 11.3	00.7	220 53.5	16.0	6 27.2	14.3	55.4
21	133 11.1	22 00.3	235 28.5	15.9	6 41.5	14.3	55.4
22	148 10.8	21 59.9	250 03.4	16.0	6 55.8	14.2	55.4
23	163 10.6	S21 59.6	264 38.4	15.9	S 7 10.0	14.2	55.3
	SD 16.3	*d* 0.3	SD		15.6	15.4	15.2

Lat.	Twilight Naut.	Twilight Civil	Sunrise	Moonrise 7	Moonrise 8	Moonrise 9	Moonrise 10
°	h m	h m	h m	h m	h m	h m	h m
N 72	08 15	10 19	▬	20 51	22 59	25 04	01 04
N 70	07 58	09 36	▬	20 59	22 57	24 52	00 52
68	07 44	09 07	11 09	21 05	22 55	24 42	00 42
66	07 32	08 46	10 12	21 10	22 54	24 34	00 34
64	07 23	08 28	09 40	21 15	22 53	24 28	00 28
62	07 14	08 14	09 16	21 19	22 52	24 22	00 22
60	07 07	08 02	08 57	21 22	22 51	24 17	00 17
N 58	07 00	07 51	08 41	21 25	22 50	24 13	00 13
56	06 54	07 42	08 28	21 27	22 49	24 09	00 09
54	06 48	07 34	08 16	21 30	22 49	24 05	00 05
52	06 43	07 26	08 06	21 32	22 48	24 02	00 02
50	06 38	07 19	07 57	21 34	22 48	23 59	25 10
45	06 27	07 04	07 38	21 38	22 46	23 53	24 59
N 40	06 18	06 52	07 22	21 41	22 46	23 48	24 50
35	06 09	06 41	07 09	21 44	22 45	23 44	24 42
30	06 01	06 31	06 57	21 46	22 44	23 40	24 35
20	05 46	06 13	06 37	21 51	22 43	23 34	24 24
N 10	05 31	05 57	06 19	21 55	22 42	23 28	24 13
0	05 15	05 41	06 03	21 59	22 41	23 22	24 04
S 10	04 57	05 24	05 46	22 02	22 40	23 17	23 54
20	04 35	05 04	05 28	22 06	22 39	23 12	23 44
30	04 08	04 41	05 08	22 10	22 38	23 05	23 33
35	03 50	04 26	04 55	22 13	22 38	23 02	23 27
40	03 28	04 09	04 41	22 16	22 37	22 58	23 19
45	03 00	03 48	04 24	22 19	22 36	22 53	23 11
S 50	02 19	03 20	04 03	22 23	22 35	22 48	23 00
52	01 56	03 07	03 53	22 25	22 35	22 45	22 56
54	01 22	02 50	03 42	22 27	22 35	22 42	22 51
56	////	02 31	03 29	22 29	22 34	22 39	22 45
58	////	02 06	03 14	22 31	22 34	22 36	22 39
S 60	////	01 30	02 56	22 34	22 33	22 32	22 31

Lat.	Sunset	Twilight Civil	Twilight Naut.	Moonset 7	Moonset 8	Moonset 9	Moonset 10
°	h m	h m	h m	h m	h m	h m	h m
N 72	▬	13 55	15 59	11 16	10 41	10 08	09 32
N 70	▬	14 38	16 16	11 05	10 38	10 13	09 46
68	13 05	15 07	16 30	10 56	10 37	10 18	09 58
66	14 01	15 28	16 42	10 49	10 35	10 22	10 08
64	14 34	15 45	16 51	10 43	10 34	10 25	10 16
62	14 58	16 00	17 00	10 37	10 33	10 28	10 24
60	15 17	16 12	17 07	10 32	10 32	10 31	10 30
N 58	15 33	16 23	17 14	10 28	10 31	10 33	10 35
56	15 46	16 32	17 20	10 24	10 30	10 35	10 40
54	15 58	16 40	17 26	10 21	10 29	10 37	10 45
52	16 08	16 48	17 31	10 18	10 28	10 39	10 49
50	16 17	16 55	17 35	10 15	10 28	10 40	10 53
45	16 36	17 09	17 46	10 08	10 26	10 43	11 01
N 40	16 52	17 22	17 56	10 03	10 25	10 46	11 07
35	17 05	17 33	18 04	09 59	10 24	10 49	11 13
30	17 17	17 43	18 12	09 55	10 23	10 51	11 18
20	17 37	18 00	18 28	09 47	10 22	10 55	11 27
N 10	17 54	18 17	18 43	09 41	10 20	10 58	11 35
0	18 10	18 33	18 59	09 35	10 19	11 01	11 42
S 10	18 27	18 50	19 17	09 29	10 18	11 04	11 50
20	18 45	19 09	19 38	09 23	10 16	11 07	11 58
30	19 05	19 33	20 05	09 15	10 14	11 11	12 07
35	19 18	19 47	20 23	09 11	10 13	11 13	12 12
40	19 32	20 04	20 44	09 06	10 12	11 16	12 18
45	19 49	20 25	21 13	09 00	10 11	11 19	12 25
S 50	20 09	20 52	21 53	08 53	10 09	11 22	12 34
52	20 19	21 06	22 16	08 50	10 09	11 24	12 37
54	20 31	21 22	22 48	08 47	10 08	11 26	12 42
56	20 44	21 41	////	08 43	10 07	11 28	12 47
58	20 59	22 06	////	08 38	10 06	11 30	12 52
S 60	21 17	22 41	////	08 33	10 05	11 32	12 58

Day	SUN Eqn. of Time 00^h	SUN Eqn. of Time 12^h	SUN Mer. Pass.	MOON Mer. Pass. Upper	MOON Mer. Pass. Lower	MOON Age	MOON Phase
d	m s	m s	h m	h m	h m	d %	
7	06 03	06 16	12 06	03 24	15 47	18 80	
8	06 28	06 41	12 07	04 09	16 30	19 71	
9	06 54	07 06	12 07	04 51	17 12	20 61	

UT	ARIES	VENUS −3·9		MARS +1·1		JUPITER −2·7		SATURN +1·0	
	GHA	GHA	Dec	GHA	Dec	GHA	Dec	GHA	Dec
d h	° ′	° ′	° ′	° ′	° ′	° ′	° ′	° ′	° ′
SATURDAY 10 00	109 32.0	177 11.8	S22 41.0	178 09.7	S22 56.4	357 41.2	N22 11.0	111 37.5	S 3 20.3
01	124 34.5	192 10.9	40.6	193 10.1	56.1	12 44.0	11.0	126 39.8	20.2
02	139 36.9	207 10.0	40.2	208 10.5	55.8	27 46.8	11.1	141 42.2	20.1
03	154 39.4	222 09.1	. . 39.8	223 10.9	. . 55.6	42 49.6	. . 11.1	156 44.5	. . 20.0
04	169 41.9	237 08.1	39.4	238 11.2	55.3	57 52.5	11.2	171 46.8	20.0
05	184 44.3	252 07.2	39.0	253 11.6	55.0	72 55.3	11.3	186 49.1	19.9
06	199 46.8	267 06.3	S22 38.6	268 12.0	S22 54.7	87 58.1	N22 11.3	201 51.4	S 3 19.8
07	214 49.2	282 05.4	38.2	283 12.4	54.5	103 00.9	11.4	216 53.7	19.7
08	229 51.7	297 04.5	37.8	298 12.8	54.2	118 03.8	11.4	231 56.0	19.6
09	244 54.2	312 03.6	. . 37.4	313 13.2	. . 53.9	133 06.6	. . 11.5	246 58.3	. . 19.6
10	259 56.6	327 02.6	37.0	328 13.6	53.7	148 09.4	11.5	262 00.6	19.5
11	274 59.1	342 01.7	36.6	343 14.0	53.4	163 12.2	11.6	277 02.9	19.4
12	290 01.6	357 00.8	S22 36.2	358 14.4	S22 53.1	178 15.1	N22 11.6	292 05.2	S 3 19.3
13	305 04.0	11 59.9	35.8	13 14.7	52.9	193 17.9	11.7	307 07.5	19.2
14	320 06.5	26 59.0	35.3	28 15.1	52.6	208 20.7	11.8	322 09.8	19.2
15	335 09.0	41 58.1	. . 34.9	43 15.5	. . 52.3	223 23.5	. . 11.8	337 12.1	. . 19.1
16	350 11.4	56 57.2	34.5	58 15.9	52.0	238 26.3	11.9	352 14.4	19.0
17	5 13.9	71 56.2	34.1	73 16.3	51.8	253 29.2	11.9	7 16.7	18.9
18	20 16.3	86 55.3	S22 33.7	88 16.7	S22 51.5	268 32.0	N22 12.0	22 19.0	S 3 18.9
19	35 18.8	101 54.4	33.3	103 17.1	51.2	283 34.8	12.0	37 21.3	18.8
20	50 21.3	116 53.5	32.9	118 17.5	50.9	298 37.6	12.1	52 23.6	18.7
21	65 23.7	131 52.6	. . 32.4	133 17.9	. . 50.7	313 40.5	. . 12.1	67 25.9	. . 18.6
22	80 26.2	146 51.7	32.0	148 18.3	50.4	328 43.3	12.2	82 28.2	18.5
23	95 28.7	161 50.8	31.6	163 18.6	50.1	343 46.1	12.3	97 30.5	18.5
SUNDAY 11 00	110 31.1	176 49.9	S22 31.2	178 19.0	S22 49.8	358 48.9	N22 12.3	112 32.8	S 3 18.4
01	125 33.6	191 49.0	30.8	193 19.4	49.6	13 51.8	12.4	127 35.1	18.3
02	140 36.1	206 48.0	30.3	208 19.8	49.3	28 54.6	12.4	142 37.4	18.2
03	155 38.5	221 47.1	. . 29.9	223 20.2	. . 49.0	43 57.4	. . 12.5	157 39.7	. . 18.1
04	170 41.0	236 46.2	29.5	238 20.6	48.7	59 00.2	12.5	172 42.0	18.1
05	185 43.5	251 45.3	29.0	253 21.0	48.4	74 03.1	12.6	187 44.3	18.0
06	200 45.9	266 44.4	S22 28.6	268 21.4	S22 48.2	89 05.9	N22 12.6	202 46.6	S 3 17.9
07	215 48.4	281 43.5	28.2	283 21.8	47.9	104 08.7	12.7	217 48.9	17.8
08	230 50.8	296 42.6	27.8	298 22.2	47.6	119 11.5	12.7	232 51.2	17.7
09	245 53.3	311 41.7	. . 27.3	313 22.5	. . 47.3	134 14.4	. . 12.8	247 53.5	. . 17.7
10	260 55.8	326 40.8	26.9	328 22.9	47.0	149 17.2	12.9	262 55.8	17.6
11	275 58.2	341 39.9	26.5	343 23.3	46.8	164 20.0	12.9	277 58.1	17.5
12	291 00.7	356 39.0	S22 26.0	358 23.7	S22 46.5	179 22.8	N22 13.0	293 00.4	S 3 17.4
13	306 03.2	11 38.1	25.6	13 24.1	46.2	194 25.6	13.0	308 02.7	17.3
14	321 05.6	26 37.2	25.1	28 24.5	45.9	209 28.5	13.1	323 05.0	17.3
15	336 08.1	41 36.3	. . 24.7	43 24.9	. . 45.6	224 31.3	. . 13.1	338 07.2	. . 17.2
16	351 10.6	56 35.4	24.3	58 25.3	45.3	239 34.1	13.2	353 09.5	17.1
17	6 13.0	71 34.5	23.8	73 25.7	45.1	254 36.9	13.2	8 11.8	17.0
18	21 15.5	86 33.5	S22 23.4	88 26.1	S22 44.8	269 39.8	N22 13.3	23 14.1	S 3 16.9
19	36 18.0	101 32.6	22.9	103 26.4	44.5	284 42.6	13.4	38 16.4	16.9
20	51 20.4	116 31.7	22.5	118 26.8	44.2	299 45.4	13.4	53 18.7	16.8
21	66 22.9	131 30.8	. . 22.0	133 27.2	. . 43.9	314 48.2	. . 13.5	68 21.0	. . 16.7
22	81 25.3	146 29.9	21.6	148 27.6	43.6	329 51.1	13.5	83 23.3	16.6
23	96 27.8	161 29.0	21.1	163 28.0	43.3	344 53.9	13.6	98 25.6	16.5
MONDAY 12 00	111 30.3	176 28.1	S22 20.7	178 28.4	S22 43.1	359 56.7	N22 13.6	113 27.9	S 3 16.5
01	126 32.7	191 27.2	20.2	193 28.8	42.8	14 59.5	13.7	128 30.2	16.4
02	141 35.2	206 26.3	19.8	208 29.2	42.5	30 02.4	13.7	143 32.5	16.3
03	156 37.7	221 25.4	. . 19.3	223 29.6	. . 42.2	45 05.2	. . 13.8	158 34.8	. . 16.2
04	171 40.1	236 24.5	18.9	238 30.0	41.9	60 08.0	13.8	173 37.1	16.1
05	186 42.6	251 23.6	18.4	253 30.4	41.6	75 10.8	13.9	188 39.4	16.1
06	201 45.1	266 22.7	S22 18.0	268 30.8	S22 41.3	90 13.6	N22 14.0	203 41.7	S 3 16.0
07	216 47.5	281 21.8	17.5	283 31.1	41.0	105 16.5	14.0	218 44.0	15.9
08	231 50.0	296 20.9	17.0	298 31.5	40.7	120 19.3	14.1	233 46.3	15.8
09	246 52.4	311 20.0	. . 16.6	313 31.9	. . 40.4	135 22.1	. . 14.1	248 48.6	. . 15.7
10	261 54.9	326 19.1	16.1	328 32.3	40.2	150 24.9	14.2	263 50.9	15.6
11	276 57.4	341 18.2	15.6	343 32.7	39.9	165 27.8	14.2	278 53.2	15.6
12	291 59.8	356 17.3	S22 15.2	358 33.1	S22 39.6	180 30.6	N22 14.3	293 55.5	S 3 15.5
13	307 02.3	11 16.5	14.7	13 33.5	39.3	195 33.4	14.3	308 57.8	15.4
14	322 04.8	26 15.6	14.2	28 33.9	39.0	210 36.2	14.4	324 00.1	15.3
15	337 07.2	41 14.7	. . 13.8	43 34.3	. . 38.7	225 39.1	. . 14.4	339 02.3	. . 15.2
16	352 09.7	56 13.8	13.3	58 34.7	38.4	240 41.9	14.5	354 04.6	15.2
17	7 12.2	71 12.9	12.8	73 35.1	38.1	255 44.7	14.6	9 06.9	15.1
18	22 14.6	86 12.0	S22 12.4	88 35.5	S22 37.8	270 47.5	N22 14.6	24 09.2	S 3 15.0
19	37 17.1	101 11.1	11.9	103 35.9	37.5	285 50.3	14.7	39 11.5	14.9
20	52 19.6	116 10.2	11.4	118 36.3	37.2	300 53.2	14.7	54 13.8	14.8
21	67 22.0	131 09.3	. . 10.9	133 36.6	. . 36.9	315 56.0	. . 14.8	69 16.1	. . 14.7
22	82 24.5	146 08.4	10.5	148 37.0	36.6	330 58.8	14.8	84 18.4	14.7
23	97 26.9	161 07.5	10.0	163 37.4	36.3	346 01.6	14.9	99 20.7	14.6
Mer. Pass. (h m)	16 35.2	v −0.9	d 0.4	v 0.4	d 0.3	v 2.8	d 0.1	v 2.3	d 0.1

STARS Name	SHA	Dec
	° ′	° ′
Acamar	315 10.9	S40 12.2
Achernar	335 19.5	S57 06.5
Acrux	172 59.0	S63 14.4
Adhara	255 04.8	S29 00.5
Aldebaran	290 38.4	N16 33.7
Alioth	166 12.2	N55 48.8
Alkaid	152 51.4	N49 10.7
Alnair	27 32.2	S46 50.3
Alnilam	275 36.6	S 1 11.2
Alphard	217 46.6	S 8 46.3
Alphecca	126 03.2	N26 37.4
Alpheratz	357 34.0	N29 14.2
Altair	61 59.5	N 8 56.2
Ankaa	353 06.4	S42 10.1
Antares	112 15.1	S26 29.3
Arcturus	145 47.2	N19 02.6
Atria	107 09.0	S69 04.3
Avior	234 13.8	S59 35.5
Bellatrix	278 21.7	N 6 22.4
Betelgeuse	270 50.8	N 7 24.7
Canopus	263 51.5	S52 42.6
Capella	280 20.2	N46 01.5
Deneb	49 25.7	N45 22.4
Denebola	182 24.0	N14 25.4
Diphda	348 46.5	S17 50.7
Dubhe	193 39.6	N61 36.3
Elnath	278 00.5	N28 37.8
Eltanin	90 42.3	N51 28.9
Enif	33 38.2	N 9 59.7
Fomalhaut	15 13.8	S29 29.2
Gacrux	171 50.6	S57 15.3
Gienah	175 42.6	S17 41.2
Hadar	148 35.0	S60 29.7
Hamal	327 50.2	N23 35.3
Kaus Aust.	83 31.8	S34 22.3
Kochab	137 20.3	N74 02.5
Markab	13 29.3	N15 20.8
Menkar	314 05.1	N 4 11.5
Menkent	147 56.7	S36 29.8
Miaplacidus	221 37.3	S69 49.3
Mirfak	308 26.8	N49 57.4
Nunki	75 47.1	S26 15.9
Peacock	53 05.0	S56 39.2
Pollux	243 15.9	N27 57.7
Procyon	244 49.6	N 5 09.4
Rasalhague	95 58.1	N12 32.4
Regulus	207 33.3	N11 50.3
Rigel	281 02.8	S 8 10.3
Rigil Kent.	139 39.3	S60 56.3
Sabik	102 02.1	S15 45.4
Schedar	349 30.2	N56 41.1
Shaula	96 09.6	S37 07.3
Sirius	258 25.1	S16 45.2
Spica	158 21.4	S11 17.9
Suhail	222 45.3	S43 32.2
Vega	80 33.1	N38 48.4
Zuben'ubi	136 55.2	S16 09.0

	SHA	Mer. Pass.
	° ′	h m
Venus	66 18.7	12 13
Mars	67 47.9	12 06
Jupiter	248 17.8	0 05
Saturn	2 01.6	16 27

Day	UT (d h)	SUN GHA (° ′)	SUN Dec (° ′)	MOON GHA (° ′)	MOON v (′)	MOON Dec (° ′)	MOON d (′)	MOON HP (′)
SATURDAY	10 00	178 10.3	S21 59.2	279 13.3	15.9	S 7 24.2	14.1	55.3
	01	193 10.1	58.8	293 48.2	16.0	7 38.3	14.1	55.3
	02	208 09.8	58.5	308 23.2	15.9	7 52.4	14.1	55.3
	03	223 09.6	. . 58.1	322 58.1	15.9	8 06.5	14.0	55.2
	04	238 09.3	57.7	337 33.0	15.9	8 20.5	13.9	55.2
	05	253 09.0	57.3	352 07.9	15.9	8 34.4	13.9	55.2
	06	268 08.8	S21 57.0	6 42.8	15.9	S 8 48.3	13.9	55.2
	07	283 08.5	56.6	21 17.7	15.9	9 02.2	13.8	55.1
	08	298 08.3	56.2	35 52.6	15.9	9 16.0	13.8	55.1
	09	313 08.0	. . 55.8	50 27.5	15.9	9 29.8	13.7	55.1
	10	328 07.8	55.5	65 02.4	15.8	9 43.5	13.7	55.1
	11	343 07.5	55.1	79 37.2	15.9	9 57.2	13.6	55.0
	12	358 07.3	S21 54.7	94 12.1	15.8	S10 10.8	13.6	55.0
	13	13 07.0	54.3	108 46.9	15.8	10 24.4	13.5	55.0
	14	28 06.8	54.0	123 21.7	15.8	10 37.9	13.5	55.0
	15	43 06.5	. . 53.6	137 56.5	15.8	10 51.4	13.4	54.9
	16	58 06.3	53.2	152 31.3	15.7	11 04.8	13.4	54.9
	17	73 06.0	52.8	167 06.0	15.7	11 18.2	13.3	54.9
	18	88 05.8	S21 52.4	181 40.7	15.7	S11 31.5	13.3	54.9
	19	103 05.5	52.1	196 15.4	15.7	11 44.8	13.2	54.9
	20	118 05.3	51.7	210 50.1	15.7	11 58.0	13.1	54.8
	21	133 05.0	. . 51.3	225 24.8	15.6	12 11.1	13.1	54.8
	22	148 04.8	50.9	239 59.4	15.6	12 24.2	13.1	54.8
	23	163 04.5	50.5	254 34.0	15.6	12 37.3	13.0	54.8
SUNDAY	11 00	178 04.3	S21 50.1	269 08.6	15.5	S12 50.3	12.9	54.8
	01	193 04.0	49.7	283 43.1	15.6	13 03.2	12.8	54.7
	02	208 03.8	49.4	298 17.7	15.5	13 16.0	12.9	54.7
	03	223 03.5	. . 49.0	312 52.2	15.4	13 28.9	12.7	54.7
	04	238 03.3	48.6	327 26.6	15.5	13 41.6	12.7	54.7
	05	253 03.0	48.2	342 01.1	15.4	13 54.3	12.6	54.7
	06	268 02.8	S21 47.8	356 35.5	15.3	S14 06.9	12.6	54.6
	07	283 02.6	47.4	11 09.8	15.3	14 19.5	12.5	54.6
	08	298 02.3	47.0	25 44.1	15.3	14 32.0	12.4	54.6
	09	313 02.1	. . 46.6	40 18.4	15.3	14 44.4	12.3	54.6
	10	328 01.8	46.2	54 52.7	15.2	14 56.7	12.4	54.6
	11	343 01.6	45.8	69 26.9	15.2	15 09.1	12.2	54.6
	12	358 01.3	S21 45.4	84 01.1	15.1	S15 21.3	12.2	54.5
	13	13 01.1	45.0	98 35.2	15.1	15 33.5	12.1	54.5
	14	28 00.8	44.6	113 09.3	15.1	15 45.6	12.0	54.5
	15	43 00.6	. . 44.2	127 43.4	15.0	15 57.6	12.0	54.5
	16	58 00.3	43.8	142 17.4	15.0	16 09.6	11.9	54.5
	17	73 00.1	43.4	156 51.4	14.9	16 21.5	11.8	54.5
	18	87 59.9	S21 43.0	171 25.3	14.9	S16 33.3	11.7	54.4
	19	102 59.6	42.6	185 59.2	14.9	16 45.0	11.7	54.4
	20	117 59.4	42.2	200 33.1	14.8	16 56.7	11.6	54.4
	21	132 59.1	. . 41.8	215 06.9	14.7	17 08.3	11.6	54.4
	22	147 58.9	41.4	229 40.6	14.7	17 19.9	11.4	54.4
	23	162 58.6	41.0	244 14.3	14.7	17 31.3	11.4	54.4
MONDAY	12 00	177 58.4	S21 40.6	258 48.0	14.6	S17 42.7	11.4	54.4
	01	192 58.2	40.2	273 21.6	14.6	17 54.1	11.2	54.3
	02	207 57.9	39.8	287 55.2	14.5	18 05.3	11.2	54.3
	03	222 57.7	. . 39.4	302 28.7	14.4	18 16.5	11.1	54.3
	04	237 57.4	39.0	317 02.1	14.4	18 27.6	11.0	54.3
	05	252 57.2	38.6	331 35.5	14.4	18 38.6	10.9	54.3
	06	267 57.0	S21 38.2	346 08.9	14.3	S18 49.5	10.8	54.3
	07	282 56.7	37.8	0 42.2	14.2	19 00.3	10.8	54.3
	08	297 56.5	37.4	15 15.4	14.2	19 11.1	10.7	54.3
	09	312 56.2	. . 37.0	29 48.6	14.2	19 21.8	10.6	54.3
	10	327 56.0	36.6	44 21.8	14.0	19 32.4	10.5	54.2
	11	342 55.8	36.1	58 54.8	14.1	19 42.9	10.5	54.2
	12	357 55.5	S21 35.7	73 27.9	13.9	S19 53.4	10.4	54.2
	13	12 55.3	35.3	88 00.8	14.0	20 03.8	10.2	54.2
	14	27 55.0	34.9	102 33.8	13.8	20 14.0	10.2	54.2
	15	42 54.8	. . 34.5	117 06.6	13.8	20 24.2	10.1	54.2
	16	57 54.6	34.1	131 39.4	13.8	20 34.3	10.0	54.2
	17	72 54.3	33.7	146 12.2	13.6	20 44.3	10.0	54.2
	18	87 54.1	S21 33.2	160 44.8	13.7	S20 54.3	9.8	54.2
	19	102 53.8	32.8	175 17.5	13.5	21 04.1	9.8	54.2
	20	117 53.6	32.4	189 50.0	13.5	21 13.9	9.6	54.2
	21	132 53.4	. . 32.0	204 22.5	13.5	21 23.5	9.6	54.2
	22	147 53.1	31.6	218 55.0	13.3	21 33.1	9.5	54.2
	23	162 52.9	31.1	233 27.3	13.4	S21 42.6	9.4	54.1
		SD 16.3	*d* 0.4	SD	15.0	14.9		14.8

Lat.	Twilight Naut. (h m)	Twilight Civil (h m)	Sunrise (h m)	Moonrise 10 (h m)	Moonrise 11 (h m)	Moonrise 12 (h m)	Moonrise 13 (h m)
N 72	08 09	10 07	■	01 04	03 23	■	■
N 70	07 53	09 29	■	00 52	02 54	05 33	■
68	07 40	09 02	10 52	00 42	02 33	04 40	■
66	07 29	08 41	10 04	00 34	02 17	04 08	06 27
64	07 20	08 25	09 34	00 28	02 04	03 45	05 37
62	07 12	08 11	09 11	00 22	01 53	03 26	05 05
60	07 04	07 59	08 53	00 17	01 43	03 11	04 42
N 58	06 58	07 49	08 38	00 13	01 35	02 58	04 24
56	06 52	07 40	08 25	00 09	01 28	02 47	04 08
54	06 47	07 32	08 14	00 05	01 21	02 38	03 55
52	06 42	07 25	08 04	00 02	01 16	02 29	03 43
50	06 37	07 18	07 55	25 10	01 10	02 22	03 33
45	06 27	07 04	07 37	24 59	00 59	02 05	03 12
N 40	06 18	06 51	07 21	24 50	00 50	01 52	02 55
35	06 09	06 41	07 08	24 42	00 42	01 41	02 40
30	06 01	06 31	06 57	24 35	00 35	01 31	02 28
20	05 47	06 14	06 37	24 24	00 24	01 14	02 06
N 10	05 32	05 58	06 20	24 13	00 13	01 00	01 48
0	05 16	05 42	06 04	24 04	00 04	00 47	01 31
S 10	04 58	05 25	05 48	23 54	24 33	00 33	01 14
20	04 37	05 06	05 30	23 44	24 19	00 19	00 56
30	04 11	04 43	05 10	23 33	24 03	00 03	00 36
35	03 53	04 29	04 58	23 27	23 53	24 24	00 24
40	03 32	04 12	04 44	23 19	23 43	24 10	00 10
45	03 05	03 52	04 28	23 11	23 30	23 54	24 23
S 50	02 25	03 25	04 07	23 00	23 15	23 34	23 58
52	02 03	03 12	03 58	22 56	23 08	23 25	23 47
54	01 33	02 56	03 47	22 51	23 01	23 14	23 33
56	00 32	02 37	03 34	22 45	22 52	23 02	23 18
58	////	02 13	03 19	22 39	22 42	22 49	23 00
S 60	////	01 41	03 02	22 31	22 31	22 33	22 37

Lat.	Sunset (h m)	Twilight Civil (h m)	Twilight Naut. (h m)	Moonset 10 (h m)	Moonset 11 (h m)	Moonset 12 (h m)	Moonset 13 (h m)
N 72	■	14 09	16 07	09 32	08 41	■	■
N 70	■	14 48	16 23	09 46	09 12	08 03	■
68	13 24	15 15	16 36	09 58	09 34	08 57	■
66	14 12	15 35	16 47	10 08	09 52	09 30	08 45
64	14 42	15 52	16 57	10 16	10 07	09 55	09 36
62	15 05	16 05	17 05	10 24	10 19	10 14	10 08
60	15 23	16 17	17 12	10 30	10 29	10 30	10 32
N 58	15 38	16 27	17 18	10 35	10 39	10 43	10 51
56	15 51	16 36	17 24	10 40	10 47	10 55	11 07
54	16 02	16 44	17 29	10 45	10 54	11 05	11 21
52	16 12	16 52	17 34	10 49	11 00	11 15	11 33
50	16 21	16 58	17 39	10 53	11 06	11 23	11 44
45	16 40	17 13	17 49	11 01	11 19	11 40	12 06
N 40	16 55	17 25	17 58	11 07	11 30	11 55	12 24
35	17 08	17 35	18 07	11 13	11 39	12 07	12 40
30	17 19	17 45	18 15	11 18	11 47	12 18	12 53
20	17 39	18 02	18 29	11 27	12 01	12 36	13 16
N 10	17 56	18 18	18 44	11 35	12 13	12 53	13 35
0	18 12	18 34	19 00	11 42	12 24	13 08	13 54
S 10	18 28	18 51	19 17	11 50	12 36	13 23	14 12
20	18 45	19 09	19 38	11 58	12 48	13 39	14 32
30	19 05	19 32	20 05	12 07	13 02	13 58	14 55
35	19 17	19 46	20 22	12 12	13 11	14 09	15 09
40	19 31	20 03	20 43	12 18	13 20	14 22	15 25
45	19 47	20 23	21 10	12 25	13 31	14 37	15 43
S 50	20 08	20 50	21 49	12 34	13 45	14 56	16 07
52	20 17	21 03	22 11	12 37	13 51	15 05	16 18
54	20 28	21 19	22 41	12 42	13 58	15 15	16 31
56	20 41	21 37	23 35	12 47	14 06	15 26	16 46
58	20 55	22 00	////	12 52	14 15	15 39	17 04
S 60	21 12	22 32	////	12 58	14 25	15 54	17 26

Day	SUN Eqn. of Time 00^h (m s)	SUN Eqn. of Time 12^h (m s)	SUN Mer. Pass. (h m)	MOON Mer. Pass. Upper (h m)	MOON Mer. Pass. Lower (h m)	MOON Age (d)	MOON Age (%)	Phase
10	07 18	07 30	12 08	05 32	17 53	21	52	
11	07 42	07 54	12 08	06 14	18 35	22	42	
12	08 06	08 17	12 08	06 57	19 19	23	33	

UT d	h	ARIES GHA ° ′	VENUS −3·9 GHA ° ′	VENUS Dec ° ′	MARS +1·1 GHA ° ′	MARS Dec ° ′	JUPITER −2·7 GHA ° ′	JUPITER Dec ° ′	SATURN +1·0 GHA ° ′	SATURN Dec ° ′
13 (TUESDAY)	00	112 29.4	176 06.6	S22 09.5	178 37.8	S22 36.0	1 04.5	N22 14.9	114 23.0	S 3 14.5
	01	127 31.9	191 05.7	09.0	193 38.2	35.7	16 07.3	15.0	129 25.3	14.4
	02	142 34.3	206 04.8	08.5	208 38.6	35.4	31 10.1	15.0	144 27.6	14.3
	03	157 36.8	221 03.9	. . 08.1	223 39.0	. . 35.1	46 12.9	. . 15.1	159 29.9	. . 14.3
	04	172 39.3	236 03.1	07.6	238 39.4	34.8	61 15.8	15.2	174 32.2	14.2
	05	187 41.7	251 02.2	07.1	253 39.8	34.5	76 18.6	15.2	189 34.5	14.1
	06	202 44.2	266 01.3	S22 06.6	268 40.2	S22 34.2	91 21.4	N22 15.3	204 36.7	S 3 14.0
	07	217 46.7	281 00.4	06.1	283 40.6	33.9	106 24.2	15.3	219 39.0	13.9
	08	232 49.1	295 59.5	05.6	298 41.0	33.6	121 27.0	15.4	234 41.3	13.8
	09	247 51.6	310 58.6	. . 05.1	313 41.4	. . 33.3	136 29.9	. . 15.4	249 43.6	. . 13.8
	10	262 54.1	325 57.7	04.7	328 41.8	33.0	151 32.7	15.5	264 45.9	13.7
	11	277 56.5	340 56.8	04.2	343 42.2	32.7	166 35.5	15.5	279 48.2	13.6
	12	292 59.0	355 55.9	S22 03.7	358 42.6	S22 32.4	181 38.3	N22 15.6	294 50.5	S 3 13.5
	13	308 01.4	10 55.1	03.2	13 42.9	32.1	196 41.2	15.6	309 52.8	13.4
	14	323 03.9	25 54.2	02.7	28 43.3	31.8	211 44.0	15.7	324 55.1	13.3
	15	338 06.4	40 53.3	. . 02.2	43 43.7	. . 31.5	226 46.8	. . 15.7	339 57.4	. . 13.3
	16	353 08.8	55 52.4	01.7	58 44.1	31.2	241 49.6	15.8	354 59.7	13.2
	17	8 11.3	70 51.5	01.2	73 44.5	30.9	256 52.5	15.9	10 02.0	13.1
	18	23 13.8	85 50.6	S22 00.7	88 44.9	S22 30.6	271 55.3	N22 15.9	25 04.2	S 3 13.0
	19	38 16.2	100 49.7	22 00.2	103 45.3	30.3	286 58.1	16.0	40 06.5	12.9
	20	53 18.7	115 48.9	21 59.7	118 45.7	30.0	302 00.9	16.0	55 08.8	12.9
	21	68 21.2	130 48.0	. . 59.2	133 46.1	. . 29.7	317 03.7	. . 16.1	70 11.1	. . 12.8
	22	83 23.6	145 47.1	58.7	148 46.5	29.3	332 06.6	16.1	85 13.4	12.7
	23	98 26.1	160 46.2	58.2	163 46.9	29.0	347 09.4	16.2	100 15.7	12.6
14 (WEDNESDAY)	00	113 28.5	175 45.3	S21 57.7	178 47.3	S22 28.7	2 12.2	N22 16.2	115 18.0	S 3 12.5
	01	128 31.0	190 44.4	57.2	193 47.7	28.4	17 15.0	16.3	130 20.3	12.4
	02	143 33.5	205 43.6	56.6	208 48.1	28.1	32 17.9	16.3	145 22.6	12.4
	03	158 35.9	220 42.7	. . 56.1	223 48.5	. . 27.8	47 20.7	. . 16.4	160 24.9	. . 12.3
	04	173 38.4	235 41.8	55.6	238 48.9	27.5	62 23.5	16.4	175 27.1	12.2
	05	188 40.9	250 40.9	55.1	253 49.3	27.2	77 26.3	16.5	190 29.4	12.1
	06	203 43.3	265 40.0	S21 54.6	268 49.7	S22 26.9	92 29.1	N22 16.6	205 31.7	S 3 12.0
	07	218 45.8	280 39.2	54.1	283 50.1	26.6	107 32.0	16.6	220 34.0	11.9
	08	233 48.3	295 38.3	53.6	298 50.5	26.2	122 34.8	16.7	235 36.3	11.9
	09	248 50.7	310 37.4	. . 53.0	313 50.9	. . 25.9	137 37.6	. . 16.7	250 38.6	. . 11.8
	10	263 53.2	325 36.5	52.5	328 51.3	25.6	152 40.4	16.8	265 40.9	11.7
	11	278 55.7	340 35.6	52.0	343 51.6	25.3	167 43.2	16.8	280 43.2	11.6
	12	293 58.1	355 34.8	S21 51.5	358 52.0	S22 25.0	182 46.1	N22 16.9	295 45.5	S 3 11.5
	13	309 00.6	10 33.9	51.0	13 52.4	24.7	197 48.9	16.9	310 47.7	11.4
	14	324 03.0	25 33.0	50.4	28 52.8	24.4	212 51.7	17.0	325 50.0	11.3
	15	339 05.5	40 32.1	. . 49.9	43 53.2	. . 24.0	227 54.5	. . 17.0	340 52.3	. . 11.3
	16	354 08.0	55 31.3	49.4	58 53.6	23.7	242 57.4	17.1	355 54.6	11.2
	17	9 10.4	70 30.4	48.9	73 54.0	23.4	258 00.2	17.1	10 56.9	11.1
	18	24 12.9	85 29.5	S21 48.3	88 54.4	S22 23.1	273 03.0	N22 17.2	25 59.2	S 3 11.0
	19	39 15.4	100 28.6	47.8	103 54.8	22.8	288 05.8	17.3	41 01.5	10.9
	20	54 17.8	115 27.8	47.3	118 55.2	22.5	303 08.6	17.3	56 03.8	10.8
	21	69 20.3	130 26.9	. . 46.8	133 55.6	. . 22.1	318 11.5	. . 17.4	71 06.0	. . 10.8
	22	84 22.8	145 26.0	46.2	148 56.0	21.8	333 14.3	17.4	86 08.3	10.7
	23	99 25.2	160 25.1	45.7	163 56.4	21.5	348 17.1	17.5	101 10.6	10.6
15 (THURSDAY)	00	114 27.7	175 24.3	S21 45.2	178 56.8	S22 21.2	3 19.9	N22 17.5	116 12.9	S 3 10.5
	01	129 30.2	190 23.4	44.6	193 57.2	20.9	18 22.8	17.6	131 15.2	10.4
	02	144 32.6	205 22.5	44.1	208 57.6	20.5	33 25.6	17.6	146 17.5	10.3
	03	159 35.1	220 21.7	. . 43.5	223 58.0	. . 20.2	48 28.4	. . 17.7	161 19.8	. . 10.3
	04	174 37.5	235 20.8	43.0	238 58.4	19.9	63 31.2	17.7	176 22.1	10.2
	05	189 40.0	250 19.9	42.5	253 58.8	19.6	78 34.0	17.8	191 24.3	10.1
	06	204 42.5	265 19.0	S21 41.9	268 59.2	S22 19.3	93 36.9	N22 17.8	206 26.6	S 3 10.0
	07	219 44.9	280 18.2	41.4	283 59.6	18.9	108 39.7	17.9	221 28.9	09.9
	08	234 47.4	295 17.3	40.8	299 00.0	18.6	123 42.5	17.9	236 31.2	09.8
	09	249 49.9	310 16.4	. . 40.3	314 00.4	. . 18.3	138 45.3	. . 18.0	251 33.5	. . 09.7
	10	264 52.3	325 15.6	39.7	329 00.8	18.0	153 48.1	18.1	266 35.8	09.7
	11	279 54.8	340 14.7	39.2	344 01.2	17.6	168 51.0	18.1	281 38.1	09.6
	12	294 57.3	355 13.8	S21 38.6	359 01.6	S22 17.3	183 53.8	N22 18.2	296 40.3	S 3 09.5
	13	309 59.7	10 13.0	38.1	14 02.0	17.0	198 56.6	18.2	311 42.6	09.4
	14	325 02.2	25 12.1	37.5	29 02.4	16.7	213 59.4	18.3	326 44.9	09.3
	15	340 04.7	40 11.2	. . 37.0	44 02.8	. . 16.3	229 02.2	. . 18.3	341 47.2	. . 09.2
	16	355 07.1	55 10.4	36.4	59 03.2	16.0	244 05.1	18.4	356 49.5	09.1
	17	10 09.6	70 09.5	35.9	74 03.6	15.7	259 07.9	18.4	11 51.8	09.1
	18	25 12.0	85 08.6	S21 35.3	89 04.0	S22 15.4	274 10.7	N22 18.5	26 54.0	S 3 09.0
	19	40 14.5	100 07.8	34.8	104 04.4	15.0	289 13.5	18.5	41 56.3	08.9
	20	55 17.0	115 06.9	34.2	119 04.8	14.7	304 16.3	18.6	56 58.6	08.8
	21	70 19.4	130 06.1	. . 33.7	134 05.2	. . 14.4	319 19.2	. . 18.6	72 00.9	. . 08.7
	22	85 21.9	145 05.2	33.1	149 05.6	14.0	334 22.0	18.7	87 03.2	08.6
	23	100 24.4	160 04.3	32.5	164 06.0	13.7	349 24.8	18.7	102 05.5	08.5
Mer. Pass.		h m 16 23.4	v −0.9	d 0.5	v 0.4	d 0.3	v 2.8	d 0.1	v 2.3	d 0.1

STARS

Name	SHA ° ′	Dec ° ′
Acamar	315 10.9	S40 12.2
Achernar	335 19.5	S57 06.5
Acrux	172 58.9	S63 14.4
Adhara	255 04.8	S29 00.5
Aldebaran	290 38.4	N16 33.7
Alioth	166 12.1	N55 48.8
Alkaid	152 51.4	N49 10.6
Alnair	27 32.2	S46 50.3
Alnilam	275 36.6	S 1 11.2
Alphard	217 46.6	S 8 46.3
Alphecca	126 03.2	N26 37.4
Alpheratz	357 34.0	N29 14.2
Altair	61 59.5	N 8 56.2
Ankaa	353 06.4	S42 10.1
Antares	112 15.1	S26 29.3
Arcturus	145 47.2	N19 02.6
Atria	107 09.0	S69 04.2
Avior	234 13.8	S59 35.5
Bellatrix	278 21.7	N 6 22.4
Betelgeuse	270 50.8	N 7 24.7
Canopus	263 51.5	S52 42.6
Capella	280 20.2	N46 01.5
Deneb	49 25.7	N45 22.4
Denebola	182 23.9	N14 25.4
Diphda	348 46.5	S17 50.7
Dubhe	193 39.5	N61 36.3
Elnath	278 00.5	N28 37.8
Eltanin	90 42.3	N51 28.9
Enif	33 38.2	N 9 59.7
Fomalhaut	15 13.8	S29 29.2
Gacrux	171 50.6	S57 15.3
Gienah	175 42.6	S17 41.2
Hadar	148 34.9	S60 29.7
Hamal	327 50.2	N23 35.2
Kaus Aust.	83 31.8	S34 22.3
Kochab	137 20.2	N74 02.5
Markab	13 29.3	N15 20.8
Menkar	314 05.1	N 4 11.5
Menkent	147 56.7	S36 29.8
Miaplacidus	221 37.2	S69 49.3
Mirfak	308 26.8	N49 57.4
Nunki	75 47.1	S26 15.9
Peacock	53 05.0	S56 39.1
Pollux	243 15.9	N27 57.7
Procyon	244 49.6	N 5 09.4
Rasalhague	95 58.1	N12 32.3
Regulus	207 33.3	N11 50.3
Rigel	281 02.8	S 8 10.3
Rigil Kent.	139 39.3	S60 56.3
Sabik	102 02.1	S15 45.4
Schedar	349 30.2	N56 41.1
Shaula	96 09.6	S37 07.3
Sirius	258 25.1	S16 45.2
Spica	158 21.4	S11 17.9
Suhail	222 45.3	S43 32.2
Vega	80 33.1	N38 48.3
Zuben'ubi	136 55.2	S16 09.0

	SHA ° ′	Mer. Pass. h m
Venus	62 16.8	12 18
Mars	65 18.7	12 05
Jupiter	248 43.7	23 47
Saturn	1 49.4	16 16

UT		SUN GHA	SUN Dec	MOON GHA	v	MOON Dec	d	HP
d	h	° ′	° ′	° ′	′	° ′	′	′
13	00	177 52.7	S21 30.7	247 59.7	13.2	S21 52.0	9.3	54.1
	01	192 52.4	30.3	262 31.9	13.2	22 01.3	9.2	54.1
	02	207 52.2	29.9	277 04.1	13.2	22 10.5	9.1	54.1
	03	222 52.0	. . 29.4	291 36.3	13.0	22 19.6	9.0	54.1
	04	237 51.7	29.0	306 08.3	13.0	22 28.6	8.9	54.1
	05	252 51.5	28.6	320 40.3	13.0	22 37.5	8.8	54.1
	06	267 51.3	S21 28.2	335 12.3	12.9	S22 46.3	8.8	54.1
	07	282 51.0	27.7	349 44.2	12.8	22 55.1	8.6	54.1
T	08	297 50.8	27.3	4 16.0	12.7	23 03.7	8.5	54.1
U	09	312 50.6	. . 26.9	18 47.7	12.7	23 12.2	8.4	54.1
E	10	327 50.3	26.5	33 19.4	12.6	23 20.6	8.4	54.1
S	11	342 50.1	26.0	47 51.0	12.6	23 29.0	8.2	54.1
D	12	357 49.9	S21 25.6	62 22.6	12.5	S23 37.2	8.1	54.1
A	13	12 49.6	25.2	76 54.1	12.4	23 45.3	8.0	54.1
Y	14	27 49.4	24.7	91 25.5	12.4	23 53.3	7.9	54.1
	15	42 49.2	. . 24.3	105 56.9	12.3	24 01.2	7.8	54.1
	16	57 48.9	23.9	120 28.2	12.2	24 09.0	7.7	54.1
	17	72 48.7	23.4	134 59.4	12.2	24 16.7	7.6	54.1
	18	87 48.5	S21 23.0	149 30.6	12.1	S24 24.3	7.5	54.1
	19	102 48.2	22.6	164 01.7	12.1	24 31.8	7.4	54.1
	20	117 48.0	22.1	178 32.8	11.9	24 39.2	7.3	54.1
	21	132 47.8	. . 21.7	193 03.7	12.0	24 46.5	7.1	54.1
	22	147 47.5	21.3	207 34.7	11.8	24 53.6	7.1	54.1
	23	162 47.3	20.8	222 05.5	11.8	25 00.7	6.9	54.1
14	00	177 47.1	S21 20.4	236 36.3	11.7	S25 07.6	6.9	54.1
	01	192 46.9	19.9	251 07.0	11.7	25 14.5	6.7	54.1
	02	207 46.6	19.5	265 37.7	11.6	25 21.2	6.6	54.1
	03	222 46.4	. . 19.1	280 08.3	11.5	25 27.8	6.5	54.1
	04	237 46.2	18.6	294 38.8	11.5	25 34.3	6.3	54.1
	05	252 45.9	18.2	309 09.3	11.4	25 40.6	6.3	54.1
	06	267 45.7	S21 17.7	323 39.7	11.4	S25 46.9	6.1	54.1
W	07	282 45.5	17.3	338 10.1	11.3	25 53.0	6.1	54.1
E	08	297 45.3	16.8	352 40.4	11.2	25 59.1	5.9	54.1
D	09	312 45.0	. . 16.4	7 10.6	11.2	26 05.0	5.8	54.1
N	10	327 44.8	16.0	21 40.8	11.1	26 10.8	5.6	54.1
E	11	342 44.6	15.5	36 10.9	11.0	26 16.4	5.6	54.1
S	12	357 44.3	S21 15.1	50 40.9	11.0	S26 22.0	5.4	54.1
D	13	12 44.1	14.6	65 10.9	11.0	26 27.4	5.3	54.1
A	14	27 43.9	14.2	79 40.9	10.8	26 32.7	5.2	54.1
Y	15	42 43.7	. . 13.7	94 10.7	10.8	26 37.9	5.1	54.1
	16	57 43.4	13.3	108 40.5	10.8	26 43.0	4.9	54.1
	17	72 43.2	12.8	123 10.3	10.7	26 47.9	4.8	54.1
	18	87 43.0	S21 12.4	137 40.0	10.7	S26 52.7	4.7	54.1
	19	102 42.8	11.9	152 09.7	10.6	26 57.4	4.6	54.1
	20	117 42.5	11.5	166 39.3	10.5	27 02.0	4.4	54.1
	21	132 42.3	. . 11.0	181 08.8	10.5	27 06.4	4.3	54.2
	22	147 42.1	10.5	195 38.3	10.4	27 10.7	4.2	54.2
	23	162 41.9	10.1	210 07.7	10.4	27 14.9	4.1	54.2
15	00	177 41.7	S21 09.6	224 37.1	10.3	S27 19.0	3.9	54.2
	01	192 41.4	09.2	239 06.4	10.3	27 22.9	3.8	54.2
	02	207 41.2	08.7	253 35.7	10.3	27 26.7	3.6	54.2
	03	222 41.0	. . 08.3	268 05.0	10.1	27 30.3	3.6	54.2
	04	237 40.8	07.8	282 34.1	10.2	27 33.9	3.4	54.2
	05	252 40.5	07.3	297 03.3	10.1	27 37.3	3.2	54.2
	06	267 40.3	S21 06.9	311 32.4	10.0	S27 40.5	3.2	54.2
	07	282 40.1	06.4	326 01.4	10.0	27 43.7	3.0	54.2
T	08	297 39.9	06.0	340 30.4	10.0	27 46.7	2.9	54.2
H	09	312 39.7	. . 05.5	354 59.4	9.9	27 49.6	2.7	54.2
U	10	327 39.4	05.0	9 28.3	9.9	27 52.3	2.6	54.2
R	11	342 39.2	04.6	23 57.2	9.8	27 54.9	2.5	54.3
S	12	357 39.0	S21 04.1	38 26.0	9.8	S27 57.4	2.3	54.3
D	13	12 38.8	03.6	52 54.8	9.8	27 59.7	2.2	54.3
A	14	27 38.6	03.2	67 23.6	9.7	28 01.9	2.1	54.3
Y	15	42 38.3	. . 02.7	81 52.3	9.7	28 04.0	1.9	54.3
	16	57 38.1	02.2	96 21.0	9.6	28 05.9	1.8	54.3
	17	72 37.9	01.8	110 49.6	9.6	28 07.7	1.6	54.3
	18	87 37.7	S21 01.3	125 18.2	9.6	S28 09.3	1.5	54.3
	19	102 37.5	00.8	139 46.8	9.6	28 10.8	1.4	54.3
	20	117 37.3	21 00.4	154 15.4	9.5	28 12.2	1.2	54.3
	21	132 37.0	20 59.9	168 43.9	9.5	28 13.4	1.1	54.4
	22	147 36.8	59.4	183 12.4	9.5	28 14.5	1.0	54.4
	23	162 36.6	59.0	197 40.9	9.4	S28 15.5	0.8	54.4
		SD 16.3	d 0.4	SD 14.7		14.7		14.8

Lat.	Twilight Naut.	Twilight Civil	Sunrise	Moonrise 13	Moonrise 14	Moonrise 15	Moonrise 16
°	h m	h m	h m	h m	h m	h m	h m
N 72	08 03	09 55	■	■	■	■	■
N 70	07 48	09 20	■	■	■	■	■
68	07 35	08 55	10 38	■	■	■	■
66	07 25	08 36	09 56	06 27	■	■	■
64	07 16	08 20	09 28	05 37	■	■	■
62	07 09	08 07	09 06	05 05	06 52	09 01	■
60	07 02	07 56	08 49	04 42	06 15	07 42	08 47
N 58	06 56	07 46	08 35	04 24	05 48	07 07	08 08
56	06 50	07 38	08 22	04 08	05 28	06 41	07 41
54	06 45	07 30	08 12	03 55	05 11	06 21	07 19
52	06 40	07 23	08 02	03 43	04 56	06 04	07 01
50	06 36	07 16	07 53	03 33	04 43	05 49	06 46
45	06 26	07 02	07 35	03 12	04 17	05 19	06 16
N 40	06 17	06 51	07 20	02 55	03 57	04 56	05 52
35	06 09	06 40	07 08	02 40	03 39	04 37	05 32
30	06 01	06 31	06 57	02 28	03 25	04 21	05 15
20	05 47	06 14	06 38	02 06	03 00	03 54	04 47
N 10	05 33	05 59	06 21	01 48	02 38	03 30	04 23
0	05 17	05 43	06 05	01 31	02 18	03 08	04 00
S 10	05 00	05 27	05 50	01 14	01 59	02 47	03 38
20	04 40	05 08	05 32	00 56	01 38	02 23	03 13
30	04 13	04 46	05 13	00 36	01 13	01 56	02 45
35	03 57	04 32	05 01	00 24	00 59	01 40	02 29
40	03 36	04 16	04 48	00 10	00 42	01 22	02 09
45	03 09	03 56	04 32	24 23	00 23	00 59	01 46
S 50	02 32	03 30	04 12	23 58	24 31	00 31	01 15
52	02 11	03 17	04 02	23 47	24 17	00 17	01 00
54	01 43	03 02	03 52	23 33	24 01	00 01	00 43
56	00 57	02 44	03 40	23 18	23 42	24 22	00 22
58	////	02 22	03 26	23 00	23 19	23 55	24 55
S 60	////	01 52	03 09	22 37	22 49	23 18	24 20

Lat.	Sunset	Twilight Civil	Twilight Naut.	Moonset 13	Moonset 14	Moonset 15	Moonset 16
°	h m	h m	h m	h m	h m	h m	h m
N 72	■	14 23	16 16	■	■	■	■
N 70	■	14 58	16 31	■	■	■	■
68	13 41	15 23	16 43	■	■	■	■
66	14 23	15 43	16 54	08 45	■	■	■
64	14 51	15 58	17 02	09 36	■	■	■
62	15 12	16 11	17 10	10 08	10 01	09 37	■
60	15 29	16 23	17 17	10 32	10 39	10 56	11 39
N 58	15 44	16 32	17 23	10 51	11 05	11 32	12 19
56	15 56	16 41	17 28	11 07	11 26	11 57	12 46
54	16 07	16 49	17 34	11 21	11 44	12 18	13 07
52	16 17	16 56	17 38	11 33	11 59	12 35	13 25
50	16 25	17 02	17 43	11 44	12 12	12 50	13 40
45	16 43	17 16	17 52	12 06	12 39	13 20	14 11
N 40	16 58	17 28	18 01	12 24	13 00	13 43	14 35
35	17 11	17 38	18 09	12 40	13 18	14 02	14 54
30	17 22	17 47	18 17	12 53	13 33	14 19	15 11
20	17 40	18 04	18 31	13 16	13 59	14 47	15 39
N 10	17 57	18 20	18 46	13 35	14 21	15 11	16 03
0	18 13	18 35	19 01	13 54	14 42	15 33	16 26
S 10	18 28	18 51	19 18	14 12	15 03	15 56	16 48
20	18 45	19 10	19 38	14 32	15 26	16 20	17 12
30	19 05	19 32	20 04	14 55	15 52	16 48	17 40
35	19 17	19 46	20 21	15 09	16 08	17 04	17 57
40	19 30	20 02	20 41	15 25	16 26	17 24	18 16
45	19 46	20 22	21 08	15 43	16 47	17 47	18 39
S 50	20 06	20 47	21 45	16 07	17 15	18 17	19 09
52	20 15	21 00	22 06	16 18	17 29	18 32	19 24
54	20 25	21 15	22 33	16 31	17 45	18 49	19 41
56	20 37	21 32	23 16	16 46	18 03	19 10	20 01
58	20 51	21 54	////	17 04	18 26	19 37	20 27
S 60	21 08	22 23	////	17 26	18 56	20 14	21 02

Day	SUN Eqn. of Time 00^h	SUN Eqn. of Time 12^h	SUN Mer. Pass.	MOON Mer. Pass. Upper	MOON Mer. Pass. Lower	MOON Age	MOON Phase
d	m s	m s	h m	h m	h m	d %	
13	08 29	08 40	12 09	07 42	20 06	24 24	
14	08 51	09 02	12 09	08 30	20 55	25 17	
15	09 13	09 24	12 09	09 21	21 47	26 10	

UT (d h)	ARIES GHA	VENUS −3·9 GHA	VENUS Dec	MARS +1·1 GHA	MARS Dec	JUPITER −2·7 GHA	JUPITER Dec	SATURN +1·0 GHA	SATURN Dec
	° ′	° ′	° ′	° ′	° ′	° ′	° ′	° ′	° ′
16 00	115 26.8	175 03.5	S21 32.0	179 06.4	S22 13.4	4 27.6	N22 18.8	117 07.8	S 3 08.5
01	130 29.3	190 02.6	31.4	194 06.8	13.1	19 30.4	18.8	132 10.0	08.4
02	145 31.8	205 01.7	30.9	209 07.2	12.7	34 33.3	18.9	147 12.3	08.3
03	160 34.2	220 00.9	. . 30.3	224 07.6	. . 12.4	49 36.1	. . 19.0	162 14.6	. . 08.2
04	175 36.7	235 00.0	29.7	239 08.0	12.1	64 38.9	19.0	177 16.9	08.1
05	190 39.2	249 59.2	29.2	254 08.4	11.7	79 41.7	19.1	192 19.2	08.0
06	205 41.6	264 58.3	S21 28.6	269 08.8	S22 11.4	94 44.5	N22 19.1	207 21.5	S 3 07.9
07	220 44.1	279 57.4	28.0	284 09.2	11.1	109 47.4	19.2	222 23.7	07.9
F 08	235 46.5	294 56.6	27.5	299 09.6	10.7	124 50.2	19.2	237 26.0	07.8
R 09	250 49.0	309 55.7	. . 26.9	314 10.0	. . 10.4	139 53.0	. . 19.3	252 28.3	. . 07.7
I 10	265 51.5	324 54.9	26.3	329 10.4	10.1	154 55.8	19.3	267 30.6	07.6
D 11	280 53.9	339 54.0	25.7	344 10.8	09.7	169 58.6	19.4	282 32.9	07.5
A 12	295 56.4	354 53.2	S21 25.2	359 11.2	S22 09.4	185 01.5	N22 19.4	297 35.1	S 3 07.4
Y 13	310 58.9	9 52.3	24.6	14 11.6	09.1	200 04.3	19.5	312 37.4	07.3
14	326 01.3	24 51.5	24.0	29 12.0	08.7	215 07.1	19.5	327 39.7	07.3
15	341 03.8	39 50.6	. . 23.4	44 12.4	. . 08.4	230 09.9	. . 19.6	342 42.0	. . 07.2
16	356 06.3	54 49.7	22.8	59 12.8	08.1	245 12.7	19.6	357 44.3	07.1
17	11 08.7	69 48.9	22.3	74 13.2	07.7	260 15.6	19.7	12 46.6	07.0
18	26 11.2	84 48.0	S21 21.7	89 13.6	S22 07.4	275 18.4	N22 19.7	27 48.8	S 3 06.9
19	41 13.7	99 47.2	21.1	104 14.0	07.0	290 21.2	19.8	42 51.1	06.8
20	56 16.1	114 46.3	20.5	119 14.4	06.7	305 24.0	19.8	57 53.4	06.7
21	71 18.6	129 45.5	. . 19.9	134 14.8	. . 06.4	320 26.8	. . 19.9	72 55.7	. . 06.6
22	86 21.0	144 44.6	19.3	149 15.2	06.0	335 29.6	20.0	87 58.0	06.6
23	101 23.5	159 43.8	18.8	164 15.6	05.7	350 32.5	20.0	103 00.2	06.5
17 00	116 26.0	174 42.9	S21 18.2	179 16.0	S22 05.3	5 35.3	N22 20.1	118 02.5	S 3 06.4
01	131 28.4	189 42.1	17.6	194 16.4	05.0	20 38.1	20.1	133 04.8	06.3
02	146 30.9	204 41.2	17.0	209 16.8	04.7	35 40.9	20.2	148 07.1	06.2
03	161 33.4	219 40.4	. . 16.4	224 17.2	. . 04.3	50 43.7	. . 20.2	163 09.4	. . 06.1
04	176 35.8	234 39.5	15.8	239 17.6	04.0	65 46.6	20.3	178 11.6	06.0
05	191 38.3	249 38.7	15.2	254 18.0	03.6	80 49.4	20.3	193 13.9	06.0
06	206 40.8	264 37.8	S21 14.6	269 18.4	S22 03.3	95 52.2	N22 20.4	208 16.2	S 3 05.9
S 07	221 43.2	279 37.0	14.0	284 18.8	02.9	110 55.0	20.4	223 18.5	05.8
A 08	236 45.7	294 36.1	13.4	299 19.2	02.6	125 57.8	20.5	238 20.8	05.7
T 09	251 48.1	309 35.3	. . 12.8	314 19.6	. . 02.3	141 00.6	. . 20.5	253 23.0	. . 05.6
U 10	266 50.6	324 34.4	12.2	329 20.0	01.9	156 03.5	20.6	268 25.3	05.5
R 11	281 53.1	339 33.6	11.6	344 20.4	01.6	171 06.3	20.6	283 27.6	05.4
D 12	296 55.5	354 32.7	S21 11.0	359 20.8	S22 01.2	186 09.1	N22 20.7	298 29.9	S 3 05.3
A 13	311 58.0	9 31.9	10.4	14 21.2	00.9	201 11.9	20.7	313 32.2	05.3
Y 14	327 00.5	24 31.1	09.8	29 21.7	00.5	216 14.7	20.8	328 34.4	05.2
15	342 02.9	39 30.2	. . 09.2	44 22.1	22 00.2	231 17.5	. . 20.8	343 36.7	. . 05.1
16	357 05.4	54 29.4	08.6	59 22.5	21 59.8	246 20.4	20.9	358 39.0	05.0
17	12 07.9	69 28.5	08.0	74 22.9	59.5	261 23.2	20.9	13 41.3	04.9
18	27 10.3	84 27.7	S21 07.4	89 23.3	S21 59.1	276 26.0	N22 21.0	28 43.6	S 3 04.8
19	42 12.8	99 26.8	06.8	104 23.7	58.8	291 28.8	21.0	43 45.8	04.7
20	57 15.3	114 26.0	06.2	119 24.1	58.4	306 31.6	21.1	58 48.1	04.6
21	72 17.7	129 25.2	. . 05.6	134 24.5	. . 58.1	321 34.5	. . 21.1	73 50.4	. . 04.5
22	87 20.2	144 24.3	05.0	149 24.9	57.7	336 37.3	21.2	88 52.7	04.5
23	102 22.6	159 23.5	04.3	164 25.3	57.4	351 40.1	21.3	103 54.9	04.4
18 00	117 25.1	174 22.6	S21 03.7	179 25.7	S21 57.0	6 42.9	N22 21.3	118 57.2	S 3 04.3
01	132 27.6	189 21.8	03.1	194 26.1	56.7	21 45.7	21.4	133 59.5	04.2
02	147 30.0	204 21.0	02.5	209 26.5	56.3	36 48.5	21.4	149 01.8	04.1
03	162 32.5	219 20.1	. . 01.9	224 26.9	. . 56.0	51 51.3	. . 21.5	164 04.1	. . 04.0
04	177 35.0	234 19.3	01.3	239 27.3	55.6	66 54.2	21.5	179 06.3	03.9
05	192 37.4	249 18.4	00.6	254 27.7	55.3	81 57.0	21.6	194 08.6	03.8
06	207 39.9	264 17.6	S21 00.0	269 28.1	S21 54.9	96 59.8	N22 21.6	209 10.9	S 3 03.8
07	222 42.4	279 16.8	20 59.4	284 28.5	54.6	112 02.6	21.7	224 13.2	03.7
08	237 44.8	294 15.9	58.8	299 28.9	54.2	127 05.4	21.7	239 15.4	03.6
S 09	252 47.3	309 15.1	. . 58.1	314 29.3	. . 53.9	142 08.2	. . 21.8	254 17.7	. . 03.5
U 10	267 49.8	324 14.3	57.5	329 29.8	53.5	157 11.1	21.8	269 20.0	03.4
N 11	282 52.2	339 13.4	56.9	344 30.2	53.2	172 13.9	21.9	284 22.3	03.3
D 12	297 54.7	354 12.6	S20 56.3	359 30.6	S21 52.8	187 16.7	N22 21.9	299 24.5	S 3 03.2
A 13	312 57.1	9 11.8	55.6	14 31.0	52.4	202 19.5	22.0	314 26.8	03.1
Y 14	327 59.6	24 10.9	55.0	29 31.4	52.1	217 22.3	22.0	329 29.1	03.0
15	343 02.1	39 10.1	. . 54.4	44 31.8	. . 51.7	232 25.1	. . 22.1	344 31.4	. . 03.0
16	358 04.5	54 09.3	53.7	59 32.2	51.4	247 28.0	22.1	359 33.7	02.9
17	13 07.0	69 08.4	53.1	74 32.6	51.0	262 30.8	22.2	14 35.9	02.8
18	28 09.5	84 07.6	S20 52.5	89 33.0	S21 50.7	277 33.6	N22 22.2	29 38.2	S 3 02.7
19	43 11.9	99 06.8	51.8	104 33.4	50.3	292 36.4	22.3	44 40.5	02.6
20	58 14.4	114 05.9	51.2	119 33.8	49.9	307 39.2	22.3	59 42.8	02.5
21	73 16.9	129 05.1	. . 50.6	134 34.2	. . 49.6	322 42.0	. . 22.4	74 45.0	. . 02.4
22	88 19.3	144 04.3	49.9	149 34.6	49.2	337 44.8	22.4	89 47.3	02.3
23	103 21.8	159 03.5	49.3	164 35.0	48.9	352 47.7	22.5	104 49.6	02.2
Mer. Pass.	h m 16 11.6	v −0.8	d 0.6	v 0.4	d 0.3	v 2.8	d 0.1	v 2.3	d 0.1

STARS

Name	SHA	Dec
	° ′	° ′
Acamar	315 11.0	S40 12.2
Achernar	335 19.5	S57 06.5
Acrux	172 58.9	S63 14.4
Adhara	255 04.8	S29 00.5
Aldebaran	290 38.4	N16 33.7
Alioth	166 12.1	N55 48.7
Alkaid	152 51.3	N49 10.6
Alnair	27 32.2	S46 50.2
Alnilam	275 36.6	S 1 11.2
Alphard	217 46.6	S 8 46.4
Alphecca	126 03.2	N26 37.4
Alpheratz	357 34.0	N29 14.2
Altair	61 59.5	N 8 56.2
Ankaa	353 06.4	S42 10.1
Antares	112 15.0	S26 29.3
Arcturus	145 47.2	N19 02.6
Atria	107 08.9	S69 04.2
Avior	234 13.7	S59 35.5
Bellatrix	278 21.7	N 6 22.4
Betelgeuse	270 50.8	N 7 24.7
Canopus	263 51.5	S52 42.6
Capella	280 20.2	N46 01.5
Deneb	49 25.7	N45 22.4
Denebola	182 23.9	N14 25.4
Diphda	348 46.5	S17 50.7
Dubhe	193 39.5	N61 36.3
Elnath	278 00.5	N28 37.8
Eltanin	90 42.3	N51 28.9
Enif	33 38.2	N 9 59.7
Fomalhaut	15 13.8	S29 29.2
Gacrux	171 50.5	S57 15.3
Gienah	175 42.6	S17 41.2
Hadar	148 34.9	S60 29.7
Hamal	327 50.2	N23 35.2
Kaus Aust.	83 31.8	S34 22.3
Kochab	137 20.2	N74 02.5
Markab	13 29.3	N15 20.8
Menkar	314 05.1	N 4 11.5
Menkent	147 56.6	S36 29.8
Miaplacidus	221 37.2	S69 49.3
Mirfak	308 26.8	N49 57.4
Nunki	75 47.1	S26 15.9
Peacock	53 05.0	S56 39.1
Pollux	243 15.9	N27 57.7
Procyon	244 49.6	N 5 09.4
Rasalhague	95 58.0	N12 32.3
Regulus	207 33.2	N11 50.3
Rigel	281 02.8	S 8 10.4
Rigil Kent.	139 39.3	S60 56.3
Sabik	102 02.1	S15 45.4
Schedar	349 30.2	N56 41.1
Shaula	96 09.6	S37 07.3
Sirius	258 25.1	S16 45.2
Spica	158 21.4	S11 17.9
Suhail	222 45.3	S43 32.2
Vega	80 33.1	N38 48.3
Zuben'ubi	136 55.2	S16 09.0

	SHA	Mer. Pass.
	° ′	h m
Venus	58 16.9	12 22
Mars	62 50.0	12 03
Jupiter	249 09.3	23 33
Saturn	1 36.6	16 05

UT	SUN GHA	SUN Dec	MOON GHA	v	MOON Dec	d	HP
d h	° ′	° ′	° ′	′	° ′	′	′
16 00	177 36.4	S20 58.5	212 09.3	9.4	S28 16.3	0.7	54.4
01	192 36.2	58.0	226 37.7	9.4	28 17.0	0.5	54.4
02	207 36.0	57.5	241 06.1	9.4	28 17.5	0.4	54.4
03	222 35.7	. . 57.1	255 34.5	9.3	28 17.9	0.2	54.4
04	237 35.5	56.6	270 02.8	9.4	28 18.1	0.1	54.4
05	252 35.3	56.1	284 31.2	9.3	28 18.2	0.0	54.4
06	267 35.1	S20 55.6	298 59.5	9.3	S28 18.2	0.2	54.5
07	282 34.9	55.2	313 27.8	9.3	28 18.0	0.3	54.5
08	297 34.7	54.7	327 56.1	9.2	28 17.7	0.4	54.5
F 09	312 34.5	. . 54.2	342 24.3	9.3	28 17.3	0.7	54.5
R 10	327 34.2	53.7	356 52.6	9.2	28 16.6	0.7	54.5
I 11	342 34.0	53.2	11 20.8	9.3	28 15.9	0.9	54.5
D 12	357 33.8	S20 52.8	25 49.1	9.2	S28 15.0	1.0	54.5
A 13	12 33.6	52.3	40 17.3	9.2	28 14.0	1.2	54.5
Y 14	27 33.4	51.8	54 45.5	9.2	28 12.8	1.3	54.6
15	42 33.2	. . 51.3	69 13.7	9.2	28 11.5	1.5	54.6
16	57 33.0	50.8	83 41.9	9.2	28 10.0	1.6	54.6
17	72 32.8	50.3	98 10.1	9.2	28 08.4	1.7	54.6
18	87 32.6	S20 49.9	112 38.3	9.2	S28 06.7	1.9	54.6
19	102 32.3	49.4	127 06.5	9.2	28 04.8	2.1	54.6
20	117 32.1	48.9	141 34.7	9.2	28 02.7	2.1	54.6
21	132 31.9	. . 48.4	156 02.9	9.2	28 00.6	2.4	54.7
22	147 31.7	47.9	170 31.1	9.2	27 58.2	2.4	54.7
23	162 31.5	47.4	184 59.3	9.3	27 55.8	2.6	54.7
17 00	177 31.3	S20 46.9	199 27.6	9.2	S27 53.2	2.8	54.7
01	192 31.1	46.4	213 55.8	9.2	27 50.4	2.9	54.7
02	207 30.9	45.9	228 24.0	9.3	27 47.5	3.0	54.7
03	222 30.7	. . 45.5	242 52.3	9.2	27 44.5	3.2	54.7
04	237 30.5	45.0	257 20.5	9.3	27 41.3	3.3	54.8
05	252 30.3	44.5	271 48.8	9.3	27 38.0	3.5	54.8
06	267 30.0	S20 44.0	286 17.1	9.3	S27 34.5	3.6	54.8
07	282 29.8	43.5	300 45.4	9.3	27 30.9	3.7	54.8
S 08	297 29.6	43.0	315 13.7	9.3	27 27.2	3.9	54.8
A 09	312 29.4	. . 42.5	329 42.0	9.4	27 23.3	4.1	54.8
T 10	327 29.2	42.0	344 10.4	9.3	27 19.2	4.1	54.9
U 11	342 29.0	41.5	358 38.7	9.4	27 15.1	4.3	54.9
R 12	357 28.8	S20 41.0	13 07.1	9.5	S27 10.8	4.5	54.9
D 13	12 28.6	40.5	27 35.6	9.4	27 06.3	4.6	54.9
A 14	27 28.4	40.0	42 04.0	9.5	27 01.7	4.7	54.9
Y 15	42 28.2	. . 39.5	56 32.5	9.5	26 57.0	4.9	54.9
16	57 28.0	39.0	71 01.0	9.5	26 52.1	5.0	55.0
17	72 27.8	38.5	85 29.5	9.5	26 47.1	5.1	55.0
18	87 27.6	S20 38.0	99 58.0	9.6	S26 42.0	5.3	55.0
19	102 27.4	37.5	114 26.6	9.6	26 36.7	5.4	55.0
20	117 27.2	37.0	128 55.2	9.7	26 31.3	5.6	55.0
21	132 27.0	. . 36.5	143 23.9	9.6	26 25.7	5.7	55.0
22	147 26.8	36.0	157 52.5	9.7	26 20.0	5.8	55.1
23	162 26.6	35.5	172 21.2	9.8	26 14.2	6.0	55.1
18 00	177 26.4	S20 35.0	186 50.0	9.8	S26 08.2	6.1	55.1
01	192 26.2	34.5	201 18.8	9.8	26 02.1	6.2	55.1
02	207 26.0	34.0	215 47.6	9.8	25 55.9	6.4	55.1
03	222 25.8	. . 33.5	230 16.4	9.9	25 49.5	6.5	55.1
04	237 25.6	32.9	244 45.3	10.0	25 43.0	6.6	55.2
05	252 25.4	32.4	259 14.3	9.9	25 36.4	6.8	55.2
06	267 25.2	S20 31.9	273 43.2	10.0	S25 29.6	6.9	55.2
07	282 25.0	31.4	288 12.2	10.1	25 22.7	7.0	55.2
08	297 24.8	30.9	302 41.3	10.1	25 15.7	7.2	55.2
S 09	312 24.6	. . 30.4	317 10.4	10.1	25 08.5	7.3	55.3
U 10	327 24.4	29.9	331 39.5	10.2	25 01.2	7.4	55.3
N 11	342 24.2	29.4	346 08.7	10.3	24 53.8	7.6	55.3
D 12	357 24.0	S20 28.9	0 38.0	10.2	S24 46.2	7.6	55.3
A 13	12 23.8	28.3	15 07.2	10.4	24 38.6	7.8	55.3
Y 14	27 23.6	27.8	29 36.6	10.3	24 30.8	8.0	55.3
15	42 23.4	. . 27.3	44 05.9	10.4	24 22.8	8.0	55.4
16	57 23.2	26.8	58 35.3	10.5	24 14.8	8.2	55.4
17	72 23.0	26.3	73 04.8	10.5	24 06.6	8.3	55.4
18	87 22.8	S20 25.8	87 34.3	10.6	S23 58.3	8.4	55.4
19	102 22.6	25.2	102 03.9	10.6	23 49.9	8.6	55.4
20	117 22.4	24.7	116 33.5	10.6	23 41.3	8.6	55.5
21	132 22.2	. . 24.2	131 03.1	10.8	23 32.7	8.8	55.5
22	147 22.0	23.7	145 32.9	10.7	23 23.9	8.9	55.5
23	162 21.8	23.2	160 02.6	10.8	S23 15.0	9.1	55.5
	SD 16.3	*d* 0.5	SD 14.9		15.0		15.1

Lat.	Twilight Naut.	Twilight Civil	Sunrise	Moonrise 16	17	18	19
°	h m	h m	h m	h m	h m	h m	h m
N 72	07 56	09 43	■	■	■	■	■
N 70	07 42	09 12	11 41	■	■	■	■
68	07 30	08 48	10 23	■	■	■	11 44
66	07 21	08 30	09 47	■	■	■	10 51
64	07 12	08 15	09 21	■	■	10 48	10 19
62	07 05	08 03	09 01	■	10 13	10 01	09 54
60	06 59	07 52	08 44	08 47	09 19	09 31	09 35
N 58	06 53	07 43	08 31	08 08	08 46	09 07	09 19
56	06 48	07 35	08 19	07 41	08 22	08 49	09 05
54	06 43	07 27	08 08	07 19	08 03	08 33	08 53
52	06 38	07 20	07 59	07 01	07 46	08 19	08 43
50	06 34	07 14	07 51	06 46	07 32	08 07	08 33
45	06 25	07 01	07 33	06 16	07 03	07 42	08 13
N 40	06 16	06 50	07 19	05 52	06 41	07 22	07 57
35	06 09	06 40	07 07	05 32	06 22	07 06	07 43
30	06 01	06 31	06 56	05 15	06 06	06 51	07 31
20	05 47	06 14	06 38	04 47	05 38	06 26	07 10
N 10	05 33	05 59	06 22	04 23	05 15	06 05	06 52
0	05 19	05 44	06 06	04 00	04 53	05 45	06 35
S 10	05 02	05 28	05 51	03 38	04 31	05 25	06 19
20	04 42	05 10	05 34	03 13	04 07	05 03	06 00
30	04 16	04 49	05 15	02 45	03 40	04 38	05 39
35	04 00	04 35	05 04	02 29	03 24	04 24	05 27
40	03 40	04 19	04 51	02 09	03 05	04 07	05 12
45	03 14	04 00	04 35	01 46	02 42	03 46	04 55
S 50	02 38	03 35	04 16	01 15	02 12	03 20	04 34
52	02 19	03 23	04 07	01 00	01 58	03 07	04 24
54	01 53	03 08	03 57	00 43	01 41	02 52	04 13
56	01 15	02 51	03 45	00 22	01 20	02 35	04 00
58	////	02 31	03 32	24 55	00 55	02 15	03 44
S 60	////	02 03	03 16	24 20	00 20	01 48	03 26

Lat.	Sunset	Twilight Civil	Twilight Naut.	Moonset 16	17	18	19
°	h m	h m	h m	h m	h m	h m	h m
N 72	■	14 38	16 26	■	■	■	■
N 70	12 40	15 09	16 39	■	■	■	■
68	13 58	15 33	16 51	■	■	■	14 07
66	14 34	15 51	17 00	■	■	■	14 59
64	15 00	16 05	17 09	■	■	13 18	15 30
62	15 20	16 18	17 16	■	12 04	14 04	15 54
60	15 36	16 28	17 22	11 39	12 58	14 34	16 12
N 58	15 50	16 38	17 28	12 19	13 30	14 56	16 28
56	16 02	16 46	17 33	12 46	13 54	15 14	16 41
54	16 12	16 53	17 38	13 07	14 13	15 30	16 52
52	16 21	17 00	17 42	13 25	14 29	15 43	17 02
50	16 30	17 06	17 46	13 40	14 43	15 55	17 11
45	16 47	17 20	17 56	14 11	15 11	16 19	17 30
N 40	17 01	17 31	18 04	14 35	15 34	16 38	17 45
35	17 13	17 41	18 12	14 54	15 52	16 54	17 57
30	17 24	17 50	18 19	15 11	16 08	17 08	18 09
20	17 42	18 06	18 33	15 39	16 34	17 31	18 27
N 10	17 59	18 21	18 47	16 03	16 57	17 51	18 44
0	18 14	18 36	19 02	16 26	17 18	18 10	18 59
S 10	18 29	18 52	19 18	16 48	17 39	18 28	19 14
20	18 45	19 09	19 38	17 12	18 02	18 48	19 30
30	19 05	19 31	20 03	17 40	18 28	19 11	19 48
35	19 16	19 44	20 19	17 57	18 43	19 24	19 59
40	19 29	20 00	20 39	18 16	19 01	19 39	20 11
45	19 44	20 19	21 05	18 39	19 22	19 57	20 25
S 50	20 03	20 44	21 40	19 09	19 49	20 19	20 42
52	20 12	20 56	22 00	19 24	20 02	20 30	20 50
54	20 22	21 10	22 24	19 41	20 17	20 42	20 59
56	20 34	21 27	23 01	20 01	20 35	20 56	21 09
58	20 47	21 47	////	20 27	20 56	21 12	21 20
S 60	21 02	22 14	////	21 02	21 23	21 30	21 34

Day	SUN Eqn. of Time 00^h	SUN Eqn. of Time 12^h	SUN Mer. Pass.	MOON Mer. Pass. Upper	MOON Mer. Pass. Lower	Age	Phase
d	m s	m s	h m	h m	h m	d	%
16	09 34	09 44	12 10	10 13	22 39	27	5
17	09 54	10 04	12 10	11 06	23 32	28	2 ●
18	10 14	10 24	12 10	11 57	24 23	29	0

2026 JANUARY 19, 20, 21 (MON., TUES., WED.)

UT d h	ARIES GHA ° ′	VENUS −3·9 GHA ° ′	VENUS Dec ° ′	MARS +1·1 GHA ° ′	MARS Dec ° ′	JUPITER −2·7 GHA ° ′	JUPITER Dec ° ′	SATURN +1·0 GHA ° ′	SATURN Dec ° ′
19 00 MONDAY	118 24.3	174 02.6	S20 48.6	179 35.4	S21 48.5	7 50.5	N22 22.5	119 51.9	S 3 02.2
01	133 26.7	189 01.8	48.0	194 35.9	48.1	22 53.3	22.6	134 54.1	02.1
02	148 29.2	204 01.0	47.4	209 36.3	47.8	37 56.1	22.6	149 56.4	02.0
03	163 31.6	219 00.2	. . 46.7	224 36.7	. . 47.4	52 58.9	. . 22.7	164 58.7	. . 01.9
04	178 34.1	233 59.3	46.1	239 37.1	47.1	68 01.7	22.7	180 00.9	01.8
05	193 36.6	248 58.5	45.4	254 37.5	46.7	83 04.5	22.8	195 03.2	01.7
06	208 39.0	263 57.7	S20 44.8	269 37.9	S21 46.3	98 07.4	N22 22.8	210 05.5	S 3 01.6
07	223 41.5	278 56.8	44.1	284 38.3	46.0	113 10.2	22.9	225 07.8	01.5
08	238 44.0	293 56.0	43.5	299 38.7	45.6	128 13.0	22.9	240 10.0	01.4
09	253 46.4	308 55.2	. . 42.8	314 39.1	. . 45.2	143 15.8	. . 23.0	255 12.3	. . 01.3
10	268 48.9	323 54.4	42.2	329 39.5	44.9	158 18.6	23.0	270 14.6	01.3
11	283 51.4	338 53.6	41.5	344 39.9	44.5	173 21.4	23.1	285 16.9	01.2
12	298 53.8	353 52.7	S20 40.9	359 40.3	S21 44.1	188 24.2	N22 23.1	300 19.1	S 3 01.1
13	313 56.3	8 51.9	40.2	14 40.8	43.8	203 27.0	23.2	315 21.4	01.0
14	328 58.8	23 51.1	39.6	29 41.2	43.4	218 29.9	23.2	330 23.7	00.9
15	344 01.2	38 50.3	. . 38.9	44 41.6	. . 43.0	233 32.7	. . 23.3	345 26.0	. . 00.8
16	359 03.7	53 49.5	38.3	59 42.0	42.7	248 35.5	23.3	0 28.2	00.7
17	14 06.1	68 48.6	37.6	74 42.4	42.3	263 38.3	23.4	15 30.5	00.6
18	29 08.6	83 47.8	S20 36.9	89 42.8	S21 41.9	278 41.1	N22 23.4	30 32.8	S 3 00.5
19	44 11.1	98 47.0	36.3	104 43.2	41.6	293 43.9	23.5	45 35.0	00.4
20	59 13.5	113 46.2	35.6	119 43.6	41.2	308 46.7	23.5	60 37.3	00.4
21	74 16.0	128 45.4	. . 34.9	134 44.0	. . 40.8	323 49.5	. . 23.6	75 39.6	. . 00.3
22	89 18.5	143 44.5	34.3	149 44.4	40.5	338 52.4	23.7	90 41.9	00.2
23	104 20.9	158 43.7	33.6	164 44.9	40.1	353 55.2	23.7	105 44.1	00.1
20 00 TUESDAY	119 23.4	173 42.9	S20 33.0	179 45.3	S21 39.7	8 58.0	N22 23.8	120 46.4	S 3 00.0
01	134 25.9	188 42.1	32.3	194 45.7	39.3	24 00.8	23.8	135 48.7	2 59.9
02	149 28.3	203 41.3	31.6	209 46.1	39.0	39 03.6	23.9	150 51.0	59.8
03	164 30.8	218 40.5	. . 30.9	224 46.5	. . 38.6	54 06.4	. . 23.9	165 53.2	. . 59.7
04	179 33.2	233 39.6	30.3	239 46.9	38.2	69 09.2	24.0	180 55.5	59.6
05	194 35.7	248 38.8	29.6	254 47.3	37.9	84 12.0	24.0	195 57.8	59.5
06	209 38.2	263 38.0	S20 28.9	269 47.7	S21 37.5	99 14.9	N22 24.1	211 00.0	S 2 59.4
07	224 40.6	278 37.2	28.3	284 48.1	37.1	114 17.7	24.1	226 02.3	59.4
08	239 43.1	293 36.4	27.6	299 48.6	36.7	129 20.5	24.2	241 04.6	59.3
09	254 45.6	308 35.6	. . 26.9	314 49.0	. . 36.4	144 23.3	. . 24.2	256 06.9	. . 59.2
10	269 48.0	323 34.8	26.2	329 49.4	36.0	159 26.1	24.3	271 09.1	59.1
11	284 50.5	338 34.0	25.6	344 49.8	35.6	174 28.9	24.3	286 11.4	59.0
12	299 53.0	353 33.2	S20 24.9	359 50.2	S21 35.2	189 31.7	N22 24.4	301 13.7	S 2 58.9
13	314 55.4	8 32.3	24.2	14 50.6	34.9	204 34.5	24.4	316 15.9	58.8
14	329 57.9	23 31.5	23.5	29 51.0	34.5	219 37.3	24.5	331 18.2	58.7
15	345 00.4	38 30.7	. . 22.8	44 51.4	. . 34.1	234 40.1	. . 24.5	346 20.5	. . 58.6
16	0 02.8	53 29.9	22.2	59 51.8	33.7	249 43.0	24.6	1 22.7	58.5
17	15 05.3	68 29.1	21.5	74 52.3	33.3	264 45.8	24.6	16 25.0	58.4
18	30 07.7	83 28.3	S20 20.8	89 52.7	S21 33.0	279 48.6	N22 24.7	31 27.3	S 2 58.4
19	45 10.2	98 27.5	20.1	104 53.1	32.6	294 51.4	24.7	46 29.6	58.3
20	60 12.7	113 26.7	19.4	119 53.5	32.2	309 54.2	24.8	61 31.8	58.2
21	75 15.1	128 25.9	. . 18.7	134 53.9	. . 31.8	324 57.0	. . 24.8	76 34.1	. . 58.1
22	90 17.6	143 25.1	18.0	149 54.3	31.4	339 59.8	24.9	91 36.4	58.0
23	105 20.1	158 24.3	17.3	164 54.7	31.1	355 02.6	24.9	106 38.6	57.9
21 00 WEDNESDAY	120 22.5	173 23.5	S20 16.7	179 55.2	S21 30.7	10 05.4	N22 25.0	121 40.9	S 2 57.8
01	135 25.0	188 22.7	16.0	194 55.6	30.3	25 08.2	25.0	136 43.2	57.7
02	150 27.5	203 21.9	15.3	209 56.0	29.9	40 11.1	25.0	151 45.4	57.6
03	165 29.9	218 21.1	. . 14.6	224 56.4	. . 29.5	55 13.9	. . 25.1	166 47.7	. . 57.5
04	180 32.4	233 20.3	13.9	239 56.8	29.2	70 16.7	25.1	181 50.0	57.4
05	195 34.9	248 19.5	13.2	254 57.2	28.8	85 19.5	25.2	196 52.2	57.3
06	210 37.3	263 18.7	S20 12.5	269 57.6	S21 28.4	100 22.3	N22 25.2	211 54.5	S 2 57.3
07	225 39.8	278 17.9	11.8	284 58.1	28.0	115 25.1	25.3	226 56.8	57.2
08	240 42.2	293 17.1	11.1	299 58.5	27.6	130 27.9	25.3	241 59.0	57.1
09	255 44.7	308 16.3	. . 10.4	314 58.9	. . 27.2	145 30.7	. . 25.4	257 01.3	. . 57.0
10	270 47.2	323 15.5	09.7	329 59.3	26.9	160 33.5	25.4	272 03.6	56.9
11	285 49.6	338 14.7	09.0	344 59.7	26.5	175 36.3	25.5	287 05.8	56.8
12	300 52.1	353 13.9	S20 08.3	0 00.1	S21 26.1	190 39.1	N22 25.5	302 08.1	S 2 56.7
13	315 54.6	8 13.1	07.6	15 00.5	25.7	205 41.9	25.6	317 10.4	56.6
14	330 57.0	23 12.3	06.9	30 01.0	25.3	220 44.8	25.6	332 12.7	56.5
15	345 59.5	38 11.5	. . 06.2	45 01.4	. . 24.9	235 47.6	. . 25.7	347 14.9	. . 56.4
16	1 02.0	53 10.7	05.5	60 01.8	24.5	250 50.4	25.7	2 17.2	56.3
17	16 04.4	68 09.9	04.7	75 02.2	24.1	265 53.2	25.8	17 19.5	56.2
18	31 06.9	83 09.1	S20 04.0	90 02.6	S21 23.8	280 56.0	N22 25.8	32 21.7	S 2 56.1
19	46 09.3	98 08.3	03.3	105 03.0	23.4	295 58.8	25.9	47 24.0	56.1
20	61 11.8	113 07.5	02.6	120 03.4	23.0	311 01.6	25.9	62 26.3	56.0
21	76 14.3	128 06.7	. . 01.9	135 03.9	. . 22.6	326 04.4	. . 26.0	77 28.5	. . 55.9
22	91 16.7	143 05.9	01.2	150 04.3	22.2	341 07.2	26.0	92 30.8	55.8
23	106 19.2	158 05.1	00.5	165 04.7	21.8	356 10.0	26.1	107 33.1	55.7
Mer. Pass.	h m 15 59.8	*v* −0.8	*d* 0.7	*v* 0.4	*d* 0.4	*v* 2.8	*d* 0.0	*v* 2.3	*d* 0.1

STARS Name	SHA ° ′	Dec ° ′
Acamar	315 11.0	S40 12.2
Achernar	335 19.6	S57 06.5
Acrux	172 58.8	S63 14.4
Adhara	255 04.8	S29 00.5
Aldebaran	290 38.4	N16 33.7
Alioth	166 12.0	N55 48.7
Alkaid	152 51.3	N49 10.6
Alnair	27 32.2	S46 50.2
Alnilam	275 36.6	S 1 11.2
Alphard	217 46.6	S 8 46.4
Alphecca	126 03.2	N26 37.4
Alpheratz	357 34.0	N29 14.2
Altair	61 59.4	N 8 56.2
Ankaa	353 06.4	S42 10.1
Antares	112 15.0	S26 29.3
Arcturus	145 47.1	N19 02.6
Atria	107 08.9	S69 04.2
Avior	234 13.7	S59 35.5
Bellatrix	278 21.7	N 6 22.4
Betelgeuse	270 50.8	N 7 24.7
Canopus	263 51.5	S52 42.7
Capella	280 20.2	N46 01.5
Deneb	49 25.7	N45 22.4
Denebola	182 23.9	N14 25.4
Diphda	348 46.5	S17 50.7
Dubhe	193 39.5	N61 36.3
Elnath	278 00.5	N28 37.8
Eltanin	90 42.2	N51 28.9
Enif	33 38.2	N 9 59.7
Fomalhaut	15 13.8	S29 29.2
Gacrux	171 50.5	S57 15.4
Gienah	175 42.5	S17 41.2
Hadar	148 34.8	S60 29.7
Hamal	327 50.2	N23 35.2
Kaus Aust.	83 31.7	S34 22.3
Kochab	137 20.1	N74 02.5
Markab	13 29.3	N15 20.8
Menkar	314 05.1	N 4 11.5
Menkent	147 56.6	S36 29.8
Miaplacidus	221 37.2	S69 49.3
Mirfak	308 26.8	N49 57.4
Nunki	75 47.0	S26 15.9
Peacock	53 05.0	S56 39.1
Pollux	243 15.9	N27 57.7
Procyon	244 49.6	N 5 09.4
Rasalhague	95 58.0	N12 32.3
Regulus	207 33.2	N11 50.2
Rigel	281 02.8	S 8 10.4
Rigil Kent.	139 39.2	S60 56.3
Sabik	102 02.0	S15 45.4
Schedar	349 30.2	N56 41.1
Shaula	96 09.5	S37 07.3
Sirius	258 25.1	S16 45.2
Spica	158 21.3	S11 17.9
Suhail	222 45.2	S43 32.2
Vega	80 33.0	N38 48.3
Zuben'ubi	136 55.1	S16 09.0

	SHA ° ′	Mer. Pass. h m
Venus	54 19.5	12 26
Mars	60 21.9	12 01
Jupiter	249 34.6	23 20
Saturn	1 23.0	15 54

UT d	h	SUN GHA ° ′	SUN Dec ° ′	MOON GHA ° ′	v ′	MOON Dec ° ′	d ′	HP ′
19 MONDAY	00	177 21.6	S20 22.6	174 32.4	10.9	S23 05.9	9.1	55.5
	01	192 21.4	22.1	189 02.3	10.9	22 56.8	9.3	55.6
	02	207 21.2	21.6	203 32.2	11.0	22 47.5	9.4	55.6
	03	222 21.1	. . 21.1	218 02.2	11.0	22 38.1	9.5	55.6
	04	237 20.9	20.5	232 32.2	11.1	22 28.6	9.6	55.6
	05	252 20.7	20.0	247 02.3	11.1	22 19.0	9.7	55.6
	06	267 20.5	S20 19.5	261 32.4	11.2	S22 09.3	9.8	55.6
	07	282 20.3	19.0	276 02.6	11.2	21 59.5	10.0	55.7
	08	297 20.1	18.4	290 32.8	11.3	21 49.5	10.1	55.7
	09	312 19.9	. . 17.9	305 03.1	11.3	21 39.4	10.1	55.7
	10	327 19.7	17.4	319 33.4	11.4	21 29.3	10.3	55.7
	11	342 19.5	16.9	334 03.8	11.5	21 19.0	10.4	55.7
	12	357 19.3	S20 16.3	348 34.3	11.5	S21 08.6	10.5	55.8
	13	12 19.1	15.8	3 04.8	11.5	20 58.1	10.6	55.8
	14	27 18.9	15.3	17 35.3	11.6	20 47.5	10.7	55.8
	15	42 18.8	. . 14.7	32 05.9	11.7	20 36.8	10.8	55.8
	16	57 18.6	14.2	46 36.6	11.7	20 26.0	10.9	55.8
	17	72 18.4	13.7	61 07.3	11.8	20 15.1	11.1	55.9
	18	87 18.2	S20 13.1	75 38.1	11.8	S20 04.0	11.1	55.9
	19	102 18.0	12.6	90 08.9	11.9	19 52.9	11.2	55.9
	20	117 17.8	12.1	104 39.8	11.9	19 41.7	11.3	55.9
	21	132 17.6	. . 11.5	119 10.7	12.0	19 30.4	11.5	55.9
	22	147 17.4	11.0	133 41.7	12.0	19 18.9	11.5	56.0
	23	162 17.3	10.5	148 12.7	12.1	19 07.4	11.6	56.0
20 TUESDAY	00	177 17.1	S20 09.9	162 43.8	12.1	S18 55.8	11.7	56.0
	01	192 16.9	09.4	177 14.9	12.2	18 44.1	11.8	56.0
	02	207 16.7	08.8	191 46.1	12.3	18 32.3	11.9	56.0
	03	222 16.5	. . 08.3	206 17.4	12.2	18 20.4	12.0	56.1
	04	237 16.3	07.8	220 48.6	12.4	18 08.4	12.1	56.1
	05	252 16.1	07.2	235 20.0	12.4	17 56.3	12.2	56.1
	06	267 16.0	S20 06.7	249 51.4	12.4	S17 44.1	12.2	56.1
	07	282 15.8	06.1	264 22.8	12.5	17 31.9	12.4	56.1
	08	297 15.6	05.6	278 54.3	12.5	17 19.5	12.4	56.2
	09	312 15.4	. . 05.0	293 25.8	12.6	17 07.1	12.6	56.2
	10	327 15.2	04.5	307 57.4	12.7	16 54.5	12.6	56.2
	11	342 15.0	04.0	322 29.1	12.7	16 41.9	12.7	56.2
	12	357 14.9	S20 03.4	337 00.8	12.7	S16 29.2	12.8	56.2
	13	12 14.7	02.9	351 32.5	12.8	16 16.4	12.8	56.3
	14	27 14.5	02.3	6 04.3	12.8	16 03.6	13.0	56.3
	15	42 14.3	. . 01.8	20 36.1	12.9	15 50.6	13.0	56.3
	16	57 14.1	01.2	35 08.0	12.9	15 37.6	13.1	56.3
	17	72 14.0	00.7	49 39.9	12.9	15 24.5	13.2	56.3
	18	87 13.8	S20 00.1	64 11.8	13.0	S15 11.3	13.3	56.4
	19	102 13.6	19 59.6	78 43.8	13.1	14 58.0	13.3	56.4
	20	117 13.4	59.0	93 15.9	13.1	14 44.7	13.4	56.4
	21	132 13.2	. . 58.5	107 48.0	13.1	14 31.3	13.5	56.4
	22	147 13.1	57.9	122 20.1	13.2	14 17.8	13.6	56.4
	23	162 12.9	57.4	136 52.3	13.2	14 04.2	13.6	56.5
21 WEDNESDAY	00	177 12.7	S19 56.8	151 24.5	13.3	S13 50.6	13.7	56.5
	01	192 12.5	56.3	165 56.8	13.2	13 36.9	13.8	56.5
	02	207 12.3	55.7	180 29.0	13.4	13 23.1	13.8	56.5
	03	222 12.2	. . 55.1	195 01.4	13.3	13 09.3	13.9	56.5
	04	237 12.0	54.6	209 33.7	13.4	12 55.4	14.0	56.6
	05	252 11.8	54.0	224 06.1	13.5	12 41.4	14.1	56.6
	06	267 11.6	S19 53.5	238 38.6	13.5	S12 27.3	14.1	56.6
	07	282 11.5	52.9	253 11.1	13.5	12 13.2	14.2	56.6
	08	297 11.3	52.4	267 43.6	13.5	11 59.0	14.2	56.6
	09	312 11.1	. . 51.8	282 16.1	13.6	11 44.8	14.3	56.7
	10	327 10.9	51.2	296 48.7	13.6	11 30.5	14.3	56.7
	11	342 10.8	50.7	311 21.3	13.6	11 16.2	14.5	56.7
	12	357 10.6	S19 50.1	325 53.9	13.7	S11 01.7	14.4	56.7
	13	12 10.4	49.6	340 26.6	13.7	10 47.3	14.6	56.7
	14	27 10.2	49.0	354 59.3	13.7	10 32.7	14.5	56.8
	15	42 10.1	. . 48.4	9 32.0	13.8	10 18.2	14.7	56.8
	16	57 09.9	47.9	24 04.8	13.7	10 03.5	14.7	56.8
	17	72 09.7	47.3	38 37.5	13.8	9 48.8	14.7	56.8
	18	87 09.5	S19 46.7	53 10.3	13.9	S 9 34.1	14.8	56.8
	19	102 09.4	46.2	67 43.2	13.8	9 19.3	14.9	56.9
	20	117 09.2	45.6	82 16.0	13.9	9 04.4	14.9	56.9
	21	132 09.0	. . 45.0	96 48.9	13.9	8 49.5	14.9	56.9
	22	147 08.9	44.5	111 21.8	13.9	8 34.6	15.0	56.9
	23	162 08.7	43.9	125 54.7	13.9	S 8 19.6	15.0	57.0
		SD 16.3	*d* 0.5	SD	15.2	15.3		15.5

Lat.	Twilight Naut. h m	Twilight Civil h m	Sunrise h m	Moonrise 19 h m	Moonrise 20 h m	Moonrise 21 h m	Moonrise 22 h m
N 72	07 48	09 31	▬	▬	11 58	10 48	10 07
N 70	07 35	09 02	11 05	▬	11 14	10 30	09 59
68	07 24	08 41	10 10	11 44	10 44	10 15	09 53
66	07 15	08 24	09 37	10 51	10 22	10 03	09 48
64	07 08	08 10	09 13	10 19	10 04	09 53	09 43
62	07 01	07 58	08 55	09 54	09 49	09 44	09 39
60	06 55	07 48	08 39	09 35	09 36	09 36	09 36
N 58	06 50	07 39	08 26	09 19	09 26	09 30	09 33
56	06 45	07 31	08 15	09 05	09 16	09 24	09 30
54	06 40	07 24	08 05	08 53	09 08	09 18	09 27
52	06 36	07 18	07 56	08 43	09 00	09 14	09 25
50	06 32	07 12	07 48	08 33	08 53	09 09	09 23
45	06 23	06 59	07 31	08 13	08 38	09 00	09 19
N 40	06 15	06 48	07 18	07 57	08 26	08 52	09 15
35	06 08	06 39	07 06	07 43	08 16	08 45	09 11
30	06 01	06 30	06 56	07 31	08 07	08 39	09 09
20	05 47	06 14	06 38	07 10	07 51	08 28	09 03
N 10	05 34	06 00	06 22	06 52	07 37	08 19	08 59
0	05 20	05 45	06 07	06 35	07 24	08 10	08 55
S 10	05 04	05 30	05 53	06 19	07 11	08 01	08 50
20	04 44	05 13	05 36	06 00	06 56	07 52	08 46
30	04 19	04 51	05 18	05 39	06 40	07 41	08 41
35	04 04	04 38	05 07	05 27	06 31	07 34	08 38
40	03 44	04 23	04 54	05 12	06 20	07 27	08 34
45	03 20	04 05	04 40	04 55	06 07	07 19	08 30
S 50	02 45	03 41	04 21	04 34	05 51	07 09	08 26
52	02 27	03 29	04 12	04 24	05 44	07 04	08 23
54	02 03	03 15	04 03	04 13	05 36	06 59	08 21
56	01 31	02 59	03 52	04 00	05 26	06 53	08 18
58	////	02 39	03 39	03 44	05 16	06 46	08 15
S 60	////	02 14	03 24	03 26	05 04	06 39	08 12

Lat.	Sunset h m	Twilight Civil h m	Twilight Naut. h m	Moonset 19 h m	Moonset 20 h m	Moonset 21 h m	Moonset 22 h m
N 72	▬	14 52	16 35	▬	15 36	18 22	20 39
N 70	13 18	15 21	16 48	▬	16 18	18 38	20 44
68	14 13	15 42	16 59	14 07	16 46	18 51	20 47
66	14 46	15 59	17 07	14 59	17 07	19 01	20 50
64	15 09	16 13	17 15	15 30	17 24	19 10	20 52
62	15 28	16 25	17 22	15 54	17 38	19 17	20 54
60	15 44	16 35	17 28	16 12	17 49	19 23	20 56
N 58	15 57	16 43	17 33	16 28	17 59	19 29	20 58
56	16 08	16 51	17 38	16 41	18 08	19 34	20 59
54	16 18	16 58	17 42	16 52	18 15	19 38	21 00
52	16 26	17 05	17 47	17 02	18 22	19 42	21 01
50	16 34	17 11	17 51	17 11	18 28	19 46	21 02
45	16 51	17 23	17 59	17 30	18 41	19 53	21 05
N 40	17 05	17 34	18 07	17 45	18 52	19 59	21 07
35	17 16	17 44	18 15	17 57	19 01	20 05	21 08
30	17 27	17 52	18 21	18 09	19 09	20 10	21 10
20	17 44	18 08	18 35	18 27	19 23	20 18	21 12
N 10	18 00	18 22	18 48	18 44	19 35	20 25	21 14
0	18 15	18 37	19 02	18 59	19 46	20 31	21 16
S 10	18 29	18 52	19 18	19 14	19 57	20 38	21 18
20	18 45	19 09	19 37	19 30	20 09	20 45	21 20
30	19 04	19 30	20 02	19 48	20 22	20 53	21 22
35	19 15	19 43	20 18	19 59	20 29	20 57	21 23
40	19 27	19 58	20 37	20 11	20 38	21 02	21 25
45	19 42	20 17	21 01	20 25	20 48	21 08	21 26
S 50	20 00	20 40	21 35	20 42	21 00	21 15	21 28
52	20 09	20 52	21 53	20 50	21 05	21 18	21 29
54	20 18	21 05	22 16	20 59	21 12	21 21	21 30
56	20 29	21 21	22 47	21 09	21 18	21 25	21 31
58	20 42	21 40	23 57	21 20	21 26	21 29	21 32
S 60	20 56	22 05	////	21 34	21 34	21 34	21 33

Day	SUN Eqn. of Time 00^h m s	SUN Eqn. of Time 12^h m s	SUN Mer. Pass. h m	MOON Mer. Pass. Upper h m	MOON Mer. Pass. Lower h m	MOON Age d	MOON Phase %
19	10 33	10 42	12 11	12 47	00 23	01	1
20	10 51	11 00	12 11	13 35	01 11	02	3 ●
21	11 09	11 17	12 11	14 21	01 58	03	7

2026 JANUARY 22, 23, 24 (THURS., FRI., SAT.)

	UT	ARIES	VENUS −3·9		MARS +1·1		JUPITER −2·7		SATURN +1·0	
	d h	GHA ° ′	GHA ° ′	Dec ° ′	GHA ° ′	Dec ° ′	GHA ° ′	Dec ° ′	GHA ° ′	Dec ° ′
	22 00	121 21.7	173 04.3	S19 59.8	180 05.1	S21 21.4	11 12.8	N22 26.1	122 35.3	S 2 55.6
	01	136 24.1	188 03.5	59.0	195 05.5	21.0	26 15.6	26.2	137 37.6	55.5
	02	151 26.6	203 02.7	58.3	210 05.9	20.6	41 18.4	26.2	152 39.8	55.4
	03	166 29.1	218 02.0	. . 57.6	225 06.4	. . 20.2	56 21.2	. . 26.3	167 42.1	. . 55.3
	04	181 31.5	233 01.2	56.9	240 06.8	19.8	71 24.0	26.3	182 44.4	55.2
	05	196 34.0	248 00.4	56.2	255 07.2	19.5	86 26.8	26.4	197 46.6	55.1
	06	211 36.5	262 59.6	S19 55.4	270 07.6	S21 19.1	101 29.7	N22 26.4	212 48.9	S 2 55.0
	07	226 38.9	277 58.8	54.7	285 08.0	18.7	116 32.5	26.5	227 51.2	54.9
T	08	241 41.4	292 58.0	54.0	300 08.5	18.3	131 35.3	26.5	242 53.4	54.8
H	09	256 43.8	307 57.2	. . 53.3	315 08.9	. . 17.9	146 38.1	. . 26.6	257 55.7	. . 54.8
U	10	271 46.3	322 56.4	52.5	330 09.3	17.5	161 40.9	26.6	272 58.0	54.7
R	11	286 48.8	337 55.7	51.8	345 09.7	17.1	176 43.7	26.7	288 00.2	54.6
S	12	301 51.2	352 54.9	S19 51.1	0 10.1	S21 16.7	191 46.5	N22 26.7	303 02.5	S 2 54.5
D	13	316 53.7	7 54.1	50.4	15 10.5	16.3	206 49.3	26.8	318 04.8	54.4
A	14	331 56.2	22 53.3	49.6	30 11.0	15.9	221 52.1	26.8	333 07.0	54.3
Y	15	346 58.6	37 52.5	. . 48.9	45 11.4	. . 15.5	236 54.9	. . 26.9	348 09.3	. . 54.2
	16	2 01.1	52 51.7	48.2	60 11.8	15.1	251 57.7	26.9	3 11.6	54.1
	17	17 03.6	67 51.0	47.4	75 12.2	14.7	267 00.5	27.0	18 13.8	54.0
	18	32 06.0	82 50.2	S19 46.7	90 12.6	S21 14.3	282 03.3	N22 27.0	33 16.1	S 2 53.9
	19	47 08.5	97 49.4	46.0	105 13.1	13.9	297 06.1	27.1	48 18.4	53.8
	20	62 11.0	112 48.6	45.2	120 13.5	13.5	312 08.9	27.1	63 20.6	53.7
	21	77 13.4	127 47.8	. . 44.5	135 13.9	. . 13.1	327 11.7	. . 27.2	78 22.9	. . 53.6
	22	92 15.9	142 47.0	43.8	150 14.3	12.7	342 14.5	27.2	93 25.1	53.5
	23	107 18.3	157 46.3	43.0	165 14.7	12.3	357 17.3	27.2	108 27.4	53.4
	23 00	122 20.8	172 45.5	S19 42.3	180 15.2	S21 11.9	12 20.1	N22 27.3	123 29.7	S 2 53.4
	01	137 23.3	187 44.7	41.5	195 15.6	11.5	27 22.9	27.3	138 31.9	53.3
	02	152 25.7	202 43.9	40.8	210 16.0	11.1	42 25.7	27.4	153 34.2	53.2
	03	167 28.2	217 43.2	. . 40.1	225 16.4	. . 10.7	57 28.5	. . 27.4	168 36.5	. . 53.1
	04	182 30.7	232 42.4	39.3	240 16.8	10.3	72 31.3	27.5	183 38.7	53.0
	05	197 33.1	247 41.6	38.6	255 17.3	09.9	87 34.1	27.5	198 41.0	52.9
	06	212 35.6	262 40.8	S19 37.8	270 17.7	S21 09.5	102 36.9	N22 27.6	213 43.2	S 2 52.8
	07	227 38.1	277 40.0	37.1	285 18.1	09.1	117 39.7	27.6	228 45.5	52.7
	08	242 40.5	292 39.3	36.3	300 18.5	08.7	132 42.5	27.7	243 47.8	52.6
F	09	257 43.0	307 38.5	. . 35.6	315 18.9	. . 08.3	147 45.3	. . 27.7	258 50.0	. . 52.5
R	10	272 45.4	322 37.7	34.8	330 19.4	07.9	162 48.1	27.8	273 52.3	52.4
I	11	287 47.9	337 37.0	34.1	345 19.8	07.5	177 51.0	27.8	288 54.6	52.3
D	12	302 50.4	352 36.2	S19 33.3	0 20.2	S21 07.1	192 53.8	N22 27.9	303 56.8	S 2 52.2
A	13	317 52.8	7 35.4	32.6	15 20.6	06.7	207 56.6	27.9	318 59.1	52.1
Y	14	332 55.3	22 34.6	31.8	30 21.0	06.2	222 59.4	28.0	334 01.3	52.0
	15	347 57.8	37 33.9	. . 31.1	45 21.5	. . 05.8	238 02.2	. . 28.0	349 03.6	. . 51.9
	16	3 00.2	52 33.1	30.3	60 21.9	05.4	253 05.0	28.1	4 05.9	51.8
	17	18 02.7	67 32.3	29.5	75 22.3	05.0	268 07.8	28.1	19 08.1	51.7
	18	33 05.2	82 31.6	S19 28.8	90 22.7	S21 04.6	283 10.6	N22 28.2	34 10.4	S 2 51.7
	19	48 07.6	97 30.8	28.0	105 23.2	04.2	298 13.4	28.2	49 12.7	51.6
	20	63 10.1	112 30.0	27.3	120 23.6	03.8	313 16.2	28.3	64 14.9	51.5
	21	78 12.6	127 29.3	. . 26.5	135 24.0	. . 03.4	328 19.0	. . 28.3	79 17.2	. . 51.4
	22	93 15.0	142 28.5	25.8	150 24.4	03.0	343 21.8	28.3	94 19.4	51.3
	23	108 17.5	157 27.7	25.0	165 24.8	02.6	358 24.6	28.4	109 21.7	51.2
	24 00	123 19.9	172 27.0	S19 24.2	180 25.3	S21 02.2	13 27.4	N22 28.4	124 24.0	S 2 51.1
	01	138 22.4	187 26.2	23.5	195 25.7	01.7	28 30.2	28.5	139 26.2	51.0
	02	153 24.9	202 25.4	22.7	210 26.1	01.3	43 33.0	28.5	154 28.5	50.9
	03	168 27.3	217 24.7	. . 21.9	225 26.5	. . 00.9	58 35.8	. . 28.6	169 30.7	. . 50.8
	04	183 29.8	232 23.9	21.2	240 27.0	00.5	73 38.6	28.6	184 33.0	50.7
	05	198 32.3	247 23.1	20.4	255 27.4	21 00.1	88 41.4	28.7	199 35.3	50.6
	06	213 34.7	262 22.4	S19 19.6	270 27.8	S20 59.7	103 44.1	N22 28.7	214 37.5	S 2 50.5
	07	228 37.2	277 21.6	18.9	285 28.2	59.3	118 46.9	28.8	229 39.8	50.4
S	08	243 39.7	292 20.8	18.1	300 28.7	58.9	133 49.7	28.8	244 42.0	50.3
A	09	258 42.1	307 20.1	. . 17.3	315 29.1	. . 58.4	148 52.5	. . 28.9	259 44.3	. . 50.2
T	10	273 44.6	322 19.3	16.5	330 29.5	58.0	163 55.3	28.9	274 46.6	50.1
U	11	288 47.1	337 18.6	15.8	345 29.9	57.6	178 58.1	29.0	289 48.8	50.0
R	12	303 49.5	352 17.8	S19 15.0	0 30.4	S20 57.2	194 00.9	N22 29.0	304 51.1	S 2 49.9
D	13	318 52.0	7 17.0	14.2	15 30.8	56.8	209 03.7	29.1	319 53.3	49.8
A	14	333 54.4	22 16.3	13.4	30 31.2	56.4	224 06.5	29.1	334 55.6	49.8
Y	15	348 56.9	37 15.5	. . 12.7	45 31.6	. . 55.9	239 09.3	. . 29.1	349 57.9	. . 49.7
	16	3 59.4	52 14.8	11.9	60 32.1	55.5	254 12.1	29.2	5 00.1	49.6
	17	19 01.8	67 14.0	11.1	75 32.5	55.1	269 14.9	29.2	20 02.4	49.5
	18	34 04.3	82 13.3	S19 10.3	90 32.9	S20 54.7	284 17.7	N22 29.3	35 04.6	S 2 49.4
	19	49 06.8	97 12.5	09.5	105 33.3	54.3	299 20.5	29.3	50 06.9	49.3
	20	64 09.2	112 11.7	08.8	120 33.8	53.9	314 23.3	29.4	65 09.1	49.2
	21	79 11.7	127 11.0	. . 08.0	135 34.2	. . 53.4	329 26.1	. . 29.4	80 11.4	. . 49.1
	22	94 14.2	142 10.2	07.2	150 34.6	53.0	344 28.9	29.5	95 13.7	49.0
	23	109 16.6	157 09.5	06.4	165 35.0	52.6	359 31.7	29.5	110 15.9	48.9
	Mer. Pass.	h m 15 48.0	*v* −0.8	*d* 0.8	*v* 0.4	*d* 0.4	*v* 2.8	*d* 0.0	*v* 2.3	*d* 0.1

STARS Name	SHA ° ′	Dec ° ′
Acamar	315 11.0	S40 12.2
Achernar	335 19.6	S57 06.5
Acrux	172 58.8	S63 14.4
Adhara	255 04.8	S29 00.5
Aldebaran	290 38.4	N16 33.7
Alioth	166 12.0	N55 48.7
Alkaid	152 51.3	N49 10.6
Alnair	27 32.2	S46 50.2
Alnilam	275 36.6	S 1 11.2
Alphard	217 46.6	S 8 46.4
Alphecca	126 03.1	N26 37.4
Alpheratz	357 34.1	N29 14.2
Altair	61 59.4	N 8 56.2
Ankaa	353 06.5	S42 10.1
Antares	112 15.0	S26 29.3
Arcturus	145 47.1	N19 02.6
Atria	107 08.8	S69 04.2
Avior	234 13.7	S59 35.6
Bellatrix	278 21.7	N 6 22.4
Betelgeuse	270 50.8	N 7 24.7
Canopus	263 51.5	S52 42.7
Capella	280 20.2	N46 01.5
Deneb	49 25.7	N45 22.4
Denebola	182 23.9	N14 25.4
Diphda	348 46.5	S17 50.7
Dubhe	193 39.4	N61 36.3
Elnath	278 00.5	N28 37.8
Eltanin	90 42.2	N51 28.9
Enif	33 38.2	N 9 59.6
Fomalhaut	15 13.8	S29 29.2
Gacrux	171 50.4	S57 15.4
Gienah	175 42.5	S17 41.2
Hadar	148 34.8	S60 29.7
Hamal	327 50.2	N23 35.2
Kaus Aust.	83 31.7	S34 22.3
Kochab	137 20.0	N74 02.5
Markab	13 29.3	N15 20.8
Menkar	314 05.1	N 4 11.5
Menkent	147 56.6	S36 29.8
Miaplacidus	221 37.2	S69 49.4
Mirfak	308 26.8	N49 57.4
Nunki	75 47.0	S26 15.9
Peacock	53 04.9	S56 39.1
Pollux	243 15.9	N27 57.7
Procyon	244 49.6	N 5 09.4
Rasalhague	95 58.0	N12 32.3
Regulus	207 33.2	N11 50.2
Rigel	281 02.8	S 8 10.4
Rigil Kent.	139 39.2	S60 56.3
Sabik	102 02.0	S15 45.5
Schedar	349 30.3	N56 41.1
Shaula	96 09.5	S37 07.3
Sirius	258 25.1	S16 45.2
Spica	158 21.3	S11 17.9
Suhail	222 45.2	S43 32.3
Vega	80 33.0	N38 48.3
Zuben'ubi	136 55.1	S16 09.0

	SHA ° ′	Mer. Pass. h m
Venus	50 24.7	12 30
Mars	57 54.3	11 59
Jupiter	249 59.3	23 06
Saturn	1 08.9	15 44

UT d h	SUN GHA ° ′	SUN Dec ° ′	MOON GHA ° ′	MOON v ′	MOON Dec ° ′	MOON d ′	MOON HP ′
22 THURSDAY 00	177 08.5	S19 43.3	140 27.6	14.0	S 8 04.6	15.1	57.0
01	192 08.3	42.8	155 00.6	13.9	7 49.5	15.2	57.0
02	207 08.2	42.2	169 33.5	14.0	7 34.3	15.1	57.0
03	222 08.0	. . 41.6	184 06.5	14.0	7 19.2	15.2	57.0
04	237 07.8	41.1	198 39.5	14.0	7 04.0	15.3	57.1
05	252 07.7	40.5	213 12.5	14.1	6 48.7	15.3	57.1
06	267 07.5	S19 39.9	227 45.6	14.0	S 6 33.4	15.3	57.1
07	282 07.3	39.3	242 18.6	14.0	6 18.1	15.4	57.1
08	297 07.2	38.8	256 51.6	14.1	6 02.7	15.4	57.1
09	312 07.0	. . 38.2	271 24.7	14.1	5 47.3	15.4	57.2
10	327 06.8	37.6	285 57.8	14.0	5 31.9	15.5	57.2
11	342 06.7	37.0	300 30.8	14.1	5 16.4	15.5	57.2
12	357 06.5	S19 36.5	315 03.9	14.1	S 5 00.9	15.6	57.2
13	12 06.3	35.9	329 37.0	14.1	4 45.3	15.5	57.2
14	27 06.2	35.3	344 10.1	14.1	4 29.8	15.6	57.3
15	42 06.0	. . 34.7	358 43.2	14.1	4 14.2	15.7	57.3
16	57 05.8	34.1	13 16.3	14.0	3 58.5	15.6	57.3
17	72 05.7	33.6	27 49.3	14.1	3 42.9	15.7	57.3
18	87 05.5	S19 33.0	42 22.4	14.1	S 3 27.2	15.7	57.3
19	102 05.3	32.4	56 55.5	14.1	3 11.5	15.7	57.4
20	117 05.2	31.8	71 28.6	14.1	2 55.8	15.8	57.4
21	132 05.0	. . 31.2	86 01.7	14.1	2 40.0	15.8	57.4
22	147 04.9	30.7	100 34.8	14.0	2 24.2	15.8	57.4
23	162 04.7	30.1	115 07.8	14.1	2 08.4	15.8	57.4
23 FRIDAY 00	177 04.5	S19 29.5	129 40.9	14.0	S 1 52.6	15.8	57.5
01	192 04.4	28.9	144 13.9	14.1	1 36.8	15.9	57.5
02	207 04.2	28.3	158 47.0	14.0	1 20.9	15.8	57.5
03	222 04.0	. . 27.7	173 20.0	14.0	1 05.1	15.9	57.5
04	237 03.9	27.1	187 53.0	14.0	0 49.2	15.9	57.5
05	252 03.7	26.6	202 26.0	14.0	0 33.3	15.9	57.6
06	267 03.6	S19 26.0	216 59.0	14.0	S 0 17.4	15.9	57.6
07	282 03.4	25.4	231 32.0	13.9	S 0 01.5	16.0	57.6
08	297 03.2	24.8	246 04.9	14.0	N 0 14.5	15.9	57.6
09	312 03.1	. . 24.2	260 37.9	13.9	0 30.4	15.9	57.6
10	327 02.9	23.6	275 10.8	13.9	0 46.3	16.0	57.7
11	342 02.8	23.0	289 43.7	13.8	1 02.3	16.0	57.7
12	357 02.6	S19 22.4	304 16.5	13.9	N 1 18.3	15.9	57.7
13	12 02.5	21.8	318 49.4	13.8	1 34.2	16.0	57.7
14	27 02.3	21.2	333 22.2	13.8	1 50.2	15.9	57.7
15	42 02.1	. . 20.7	347 55.0	13.7	2 06.1	16.0	57.8
16	57 02.0	20.1	2 27.7	13.7	2 22.1	16.0	57.8
17	72 01.8	19.5	17 00.4	13.7	2 38.1	16.0	57.8
18	87 01.7	S19 18.9	31 33.1	13.7	N 2 54.1	15.9	57.8
19	102 01.5	18.3	46 05.8	13.6	3 10.0	16.0	57.8
20	117 01.4	17.7	60 38.4	13.6	3 26.0	15.9	57.9
21	132 01.2	. . 17.1	75 11.0	13.6	3 41.9	16.0	57.9
22	147 01.1	16.5	89 43.6	13.5	3 57.9	15.9	57.9
23	162 00.9	15.9	104 16.1	13.5	4 13.8	15.9	57.9
24 SATURDAY 00	177 00.7	S19 15.3	118 48.6	13.4	N 4 29.7	16.0	57.9
01	192 00.6	14.7	133 21.0	13.4	4 45.7	15.9	58.0
02	207 00.4	14.1	147 53.4	13.4	5 01.6	15.9	58.0
03	222 00.3	. . 13.5	162 25.8	13.3	5 17.5	15.8	58.0
04	237 00.1	12.9	176 58.1	13.3	5 33.3	15.9	58.0
05	252 00.0	12.3	191 30.4	13.2	5 49.2	15.9	58.0
06	266 59.8	S19 11.7	206 02.6	13.1	N 6 05.1	15.8	58.1
07	281 59.7	11.1	220 34.7	13.2	6 20.9	15.8	58.1
08	296 59.5	10.5	235 06.9	13.0	6 36.7	15.8	58.1
09	311 59.4	. . 09.9	249 38.9	13.0	6 52.5	15.8	58.1
10	326 59.2	09.3	264 10.9	13.0	7 08.3	15.7	58.1
11	341 59.1	08.7	278 42.9	12.9	7 24.0	15.7	58.2
12	356 58.9	S19 08.1	293 14.8	12.9	N 7 39.7	15.7	58.2
13	11 58.8	07.4	307 46.7	12.7	7 55.4	15.7	58.2
14	26 58.6	06.8	322 18.4	12.8	8 11.1	15.6	58.2
15	41 58.5	. . 06.2	336 50.2	12.6	8 26.7	15.6	58.2
16	56 58.3	05.6	351 21.8	12.7	8 42.3	15.6	58.3
17	71 58.2	05.0	5 53.5	12.5	8 57.9	15.6	58.3
18	86 58.0	S19 04.4	20 25.0	12.5	N 9 13.5	15.5	58.3
19	101 57.9	03.8	34 56.5	12.4	9 29.0	15.4	58.3
20	116 57.7	03.2	49 27.9	12.3	9 44.4	15.5	58.3
21	131 57.6	. . 02.6	63 59.2	12.3	9 59.9	15.4	58.4
22	146 57.5	02.0	78 30.5	12.2	10 15.3	15.3	58.4
23	161 57.3	01.3	93 01.7	12.2	N10 30.6	15.4	58.4
	SD 16.3	*d* 0.6	SD 15.6		15.7		15.9

Lat. °	Twilight Naut. h m	Twilight Civil h m	Sunrise h m	Moonrise 22 h m	Moonrise 23 h m	Moonrise 24 h m	Moonrise 25 h m
N 72	07 39	09 18	▬	10 07	09 32	08 56	08 10
N 70	07 27	08 52	10 41	09 59	09 33	09 06	08 32
68	07 18	08 33	09 56	09 53	09 33	09 13	08 50
66	07 10	08 17	09 27	09 48	09 34	09 20	09 04
64	07 03	08 04	09 05	09 43	09 34	09 25	09 15
62	06 56	07 53	08 48	09 39	09 35	09 30	09 25
60	06 51	07 43	08 33	09 36	09 35	09 34	09 34
N 58	06 46	07 35	08 21	09 33	09 35	09 38	09 42
56	06 41	07 27	08 10	09 30	09 36	09 41	09 48
54	06 37	07 21	08 01	09 27	09 36	09 44	09 55
52	06 33	07 15	07 53	09 25	09 36	09 47	10 00
50	06 30	07 09	07 45	09 23	09 36	09 50	10 05
45	06 21	06 57	07 29	09 19	09 37	09 55	10 16
N 40	06 14	06 47	07 16	09 15	09 37	10 00	10 25
35	06 07	06 37	07 05	09 11	09 37	10 04	10 33
30	06 00	06 29	06 55	09 09	09 38	10 07	10 40
20	05 47	06 14	06 37	09 03	09 38	10 14	10 52
N 10	05 35	06 00	06 22	08 59	09 39	10 19	11 02
0	05 21	05 46	06 08	08 55	09 39	10 25	11 12
S 10	05 05	05 31	05 54	08 50	09 40	10 30	11 22
20	04 47	05 15	05 38	08 46	09 40	10 36	11 33
30	04 23	04 54	05 21	08 41	09 41	10 42	11 46
35	04 07	04 42	05 10	08 38	09 41	10 46	11 53
40	03 49	04 27	04 58	08 34	09 42	10 50	12 02
45	03 25	04 09	04 44	08 30	09 42	10 56	12 11
S 50	02 52	03 46	04 26	08 26	09 43	11 02	12 23
52	02 35	03 35	04 18	08 23	09 43	11 05	12 29
54	02 14	03 22	04 08	08 21	09 44	11 08	12 35
56	01 45	03 07	03 58	08 18	09 44	11 11	12 42
58	00 55	02 49	03 46	08 15	09 44	11 15	12 50
S 60	////	02 26	03 32	08 12	09 45	11 20	12 59

Lat. °	Sunset h m	Twilight Civil h m	Twilight Naut. h m	Moonset 22 h m	Moonset 23 h m	Moonset 24 h m	Moonset 25 h m
N 72	▬	15 07	16 46	20 39	22 53	25 19	01 19
N 70	13 44	15 33	16 57	20 44	22 47	24 59	00 59
68	14 28	15 52	17 07	20 47	22 42	24 44	00 44
66	14 57	16 08	17 15	20 50	22 38	24 32	00 32
64	15 19	16 21	17 22	20 52	22 35	24 22	00 22
62	15 36	16 32	17 28	20 54	22 32	24 13	00 13
60	15 51	16 41	17 34	20 56	22 29	24 06	00 06
N 58	16 03	16 49	17 38	20 58	22 27	23 59	25 37
56	16 14	16 57	17 43	20 59	22 25	23 54	25 27
54	16 23	17 03	17 47	21 00	22 23	23 49	25 18
52	16 32	17 09	17 51	21 01	22 22	23 44	25 10
50	16 39	17 15	17 55	21 02	22 20	23 40	25 04
45	16 55	17 27	18 03	21 05	22 17	23 31	24 49
N 40	17 08	17 37	18 10	21 07	22 14	23 24	24 37
35	17 19	17 47	18 17	21 08	22 12	23 18	24 26
30	17 29	17 55	18 24	21 10	22 10	23 12	24 17
20	17 46	18 10	18 36	21 12	22 07	23 03	24 02
N 10	18 01	18 24	18 49	21 14	22 03	22 55	23 49
0	18 15	18 37	19 03	21 16	22 01	22 47	23 36
S 10	18 30	18 52	19 18	21 18	21 58	22 39	23 24
20	18 45	19 09	19 37	21 20	21 55	22 31	23 11
30	19 03	19 29	20 01	21 22	21 51	22 22	22 56
35	19 13	19 41	20 16	21 23	21 49	22 16	22 47
40	19 25	19 56	20 34	21 25	21 47	22 10	22 37
45	19 39	20 14	20 58	21 26	21 44	22 04	22 26
S 50	19 57	20 36	21 30	21 28	21 41	21 55	22 12
52	20 05	20 47	21 47	21 29	21 40	21 51	22 05
54	20 14	21 00	22 07	21 30	21 38	21 47	21 58
56	20 24	21 15	22 35	21 31	21 36	21 43	21 51
58	20 36	21 33	23 20	21 32	21 35	21 37	21 42
S 60	20 50	21 55	////	21 33	21 32	21 32	21 32

Day	SUN Eqn. of Time 00^h	SUN Eqn. of Time 12^h	SUN Mer. Pass.	MOON Mer. Pass Upper	MOON Mer. Pass Lower	MOON Age	MOON Phase
d	m s	m s	h m	h m	h m	d %	
22	11 26	11 34	12 12	15 05	02 43	04 14	
23	11 42	11 49	12 12	15 50	03 27	05 22	
24	11 57	12 04	12 12	16 36	04 13	06 32	

UT d h	ARIES GHA ° ′	VENUS −3·9 GHA ° ′	VENUS Dec ° ′	MARS +1·1 GHA ° ′	MARS Dec ° ′	JUPITER −2·6 GHA ° ′	JUPITER Dec ° ′	SATURN +1·0 GHA ° ′	SATURN Dec ° ′
SUNDAY 25 00	124 19.1	172 08.7	S19 05.6	180 35.5	S20 52.2	14 34.5	N22 29.6	125 18.2	S 2 48.8
01	139 21.5	187 08.0	04.8	195 35.9	51.8	29 37.3	29.6	140 20.4	48.7
02	154 24.0	202 07.2	04.0	210 36.3	51.3	44 40.1	29.7	155 22.7	48.6
03	169 26.5	217 06.5	. . 03.2	225 36.7	. . 50.9	59 42.9	. . 29.7	170 25.0	. . 48.5
04	184 28.9	232 05.7	02.5	240 37.2	50.5	74 45.7	29.7	185 27.2	48.4
05	199 31.4	247 05.0	01.7	255 37.6	50.1	89 48.5	29.8	200 29.5	48.3
06	214 33.9	262 04.2	S19 00.9	270 38.0	S20 49.6	104 51.3	N22 29.8	215 31.7	S 2 48.2
07	229 36.3	277 03.5	19 00.1	285 38.4	49.2	119 54.1	29.9	230 34.0	48.1
08	244 38.8	292 02.7	18 59.3	300 38.9	48.8	134 56.9	29.9	245 36.2	48.0
09	259 41.3	307 02.0	. . 58.5	315 39.3	. . 48.4	149 59.7	. . 30.0	260 38.5	. . 47.9
10	274 43.7	322 01.2	57.7	330 39.7	47.9	165 02.4	30.0	275 40.8	47.8
11	289 46.2	337 00.5	56.9	345 40.2	47.5	180 05.2	30.1	290 43.0	47.7
12	304 48.7	351 59.7	S18 56.1	0 40.6	S20 47.1	195 08.0	N22 30.1	305 45.3	S 2 47.6
13	319 51.1	6 59.0	55.3	15 41.0	46.7	210 10.8	30.2	320 47.5	47.5
14	334 53.6	21 58.2	54.5	30 41.4	46.2	225 13.6	30.2	335 49.8	47.4
15	349 56.0	36 57.5	. . 53.7	45 41.9	. . 45.8	240 16.4	. . 30.3	350 52.0	. . 47.3
16	4 58.5	51 56.7	52.9	60 42.3	45.4	255 19.2	30.3	5 54.3	47.2
17	20 01.0	66 56.0	52.1	75 42.7	45.0	270 22.0	30.3	20 56.5	47.2
18	35 03.4	81 55.3	S18 51.3	90 43.2	S20 44.5	285 24.8	N22 30.4	35 58.8	S 2 47.1
19	50 05.9	96 54.5	50.5	105 43.6	44.1	300 27.6	30.4	51 01.1	47.0
20	65 08.4	111 53.8	49.7	120 44.0	43.7	315 30.4	30.5	66 03.3	46.9
21	80 10.8	126 53.0	. . 48.9	135 44.4	. . 43.3	330 33.2	. . 30.5	81 05.6	. . 46.8
22	95 13.3	141 52.3	48.1	150 44.9	42.8	345 36.0	30.6	96 07.8	46.7
23	110 15.8	156 51.5	47.3	165 45.3	42.4	0 38.8	30.6	111 10.1	46.6
MONDAY 26 00	125 18.2	171 50.8	S18 46.4	180 45.7	S20 42.0	15 41.5	N22 30.7	126 12.3	S 2 46.5
01	140 20.7	186 50.1	45.6	195 46.2	41.5	30 44.3	30.7	141 14.6	46.4
02	155 23.1	201 49.3	44.8	210 46.6	41.1	45 47.1	30.8	156 16.8	46.3
03	170 25.6	216 48.6	. . 44.0	225 47.0	. . 40.7	60 49.9	. . 30.8	171 19.1	. . 46.2
04	185 28.1	231 47.9	43.2	240 47.5	40.2	75 52.7	30.8	186 21.4	46.1
05	200 30.5	246 47.1	42.4	255 47.9	39.8	90 55.5	30.9	201 23.6	46.0
06	215 33.0	261 46.4	S18 41.6	270 48.3	S20 39.4	105 58.3	N22 30.9	216 25.9	S 2 45.9
07	230 35.5	276 45.6	40.8	285 48.8	38.9	121 01.1	31.0	231 28.1	45.8
08	245 37.9	291 44.9	39.9	300 49.2	38.5	136 03.9	31.0	246 30.4	45.7
09	260 40.4	306 44.2	. . 39.1	315 49.6	. . 38.1	151 06.7	. . 31.1	261 32.6	. . 45.6
10	275 42.9	321 43.4	38.3	330 50.0	37.6	166 09.5	31.1	276 34.9	45.5
11	290 45.3	336 42.7	37.5	345 50.5	37.2	181 12.2	31.2	291 37.1	45.4
12	305 47.8	351 42.0	S18 36.7	0 50.9	S20 36.8	196 15.0	N22 31.2	306 39.4	S 2 45.3
13	320 50.3	6 41.2	35.8	15 51.3	36.3	211 17.8	31.3	321 41.6	45.2
14	335 52.7	21 40.5	35.0	30 51.8	35.9	226 20.6	31.3	336 43.9	45.1
15	350 55.2	36 39.8	. . 34.2	45 52.2	. . 35.5	241 23.4	. . 31.3	351 46.2	. . 45.0
16	5 57.6	51 39.0	33.4	60 52.6	35.0	256 26.2	31.4	6 48.4	44.9
17	21 00.1	66 38.3	32.5	75 53.1	34.6	271 29.0	31.4	21 50.7	44.8
18	36 02.6	81 37.6	S18 31.7	90 53.5	S20 34.2	286 31.8	N22 31.5	36 52.9	S 2 44.7
19	51 05.0	96 36.9	30.9	105 53.9	33.7	301 34.6	31.5	51 55.2	44.6
20	66 07.5	111 36.1	30.1	120 54.4	33.3	316 37.3	31.6	66 57.4	44.5
21	81 10.0	126 35.4	. . 29.2	135 54.8	. . 32.8	331 40.1	. . 31.6	81 59.7	. . 44.4
22	96 12.4	141 34.7	28.4	150 55.2	32.4	346 42.9	31.7	97 01.9	44.3
23	111 14.9	156 33.9	27.6	165 55.7	32.0	1 45.7	31.7	112 04.2	44.2
TUESDAY 27 00	126 17.4	171 33.2	S18 26.7	180 56.1	S20 31.5	16 48.5	N22 31.8	127 06.4	S 2 44.1
01	141 19.8	186 32.5	25.9	195 56.5	31.1	31 51.3	31.8	142 08.7	44.0
02	156 22.3	201 31.8	25.1	210 57.0	30.6	46 54.1	31.8	157 10.9	43.9
03	171 24.8	216 31.0	. . 24.2	225 57.4	. . 30.2	61 56.9	. . 31.9	172 13.2	. . 43.8
04	186 27.2	231 30.3	23.4	240 57.8	29.8	76 59.6	31.9	187 15.4	43.7
05	201 29.7	246 29.6	22.6	255 58.3	29.3	92 02.4	32.0	202 17.7	43.6
06	216 32.1	261 28.9	S18 21.7	270 58.7	S20 28.9	107 05.2	N22 32.0	217 19.9	S 2 43.5
07	231 34.6	276 28.1	20.9	285 59.1	28.4	122 08.0	32.1	232 22.2	43.4
08	246 37.1	291 27.4	20.1	300 59.6	28.0	137 10.8	32.1	247 24.4	43.3
09	261 39.5	306 26.7	. . 19.2	316 00.0	. . 27.5	152 13.6	. . 32.2	262 26.7	. . 43.2
10	276 42.0	321 26.0	18.4	331 00.4	27.1	167 16.4	32.2	277 29.0	43.1
11	291 44.5	336 25.2	17.5	346 00.9	26.7	182 19.1	32.2	292 31.2	43.1
12	306 46.9	351 24.5	S18 16.7	1 01.3	S20 26.2	197 21.9	N22 32.3	307 33.5	S 2 43.0
13	321 49.4	6 23.8	15.8	16 01.8	25.8	212 24.7	32.3	322 35.7	42.9
14	336 51.9	21 23.1	15.0	31 02.2	25.3	227 27.5	32.4	337 38.0	42.8
15	351 54.3	36 22.4	. . 14.2	46 02.6	. . 24.9	242 30.3	. . 32.4	352 40.2	. . 42.7
16	6 56.8	51 21.7	13.3	61 03.1	24.4	257 33.1	32.5	7 42.5	42.6
17	21 59.3	66 20.9	12.5	76 03.5	24.0	272 35.9	32.5	22 44.7	42.5
18	37 01.7	81 20.2	S18 11.6	91 03.9	S20 23.5	287 38.6	N22 32.5	37 47.0	S 2 42.4
19	52 04.2	96 19.5	10.8	106 04.4	23.1	302 41.4	32.6	52 49.2	42.3
20	67 06.6	111 18.8	09.9	121 04.8	22.6	317 44.2	32.6	67 51.5	42.2
21	82 09.1	126 18.1	. . 09.1	136 05.2	. . 22.2	332 47.0	. . 32.7	82 53.7	. . 42.1
22	97 11.6	141 17.4	08.2	151 05.7	21.8	347 49.8	32.7	97 56.0	42.0
23	112 14.0	156 16.6	07.4	166 06.1	21.3	2 52.6	32.8	112 58.2	41.9
Mer. Pass.	h m 15 36.2	*v* −0.7	*d* 0.8	*v* 0.4	*d* 0.4	*v* 2.8	*d* 0.0	*v* 2.3	*d* 0.1

STARS

Name	SHA ° ′	Dec ° ′
Acamar	315 11.0	S40 12.2
Achernar	335 19.6	S57 06.5
Acrux	172 58.7	S63 14.4
Adhara	255 04.8	S29 00.5
Aldebaran	290 38.4	N16 33.7
Alioth	166 12.0	N55 48.7
Alkaid	152 51.2	N49 10.6
Alnair	27 32.2	S46 50.2
Alnilam	275 36.6	S 1 11.2
Alphard	217 46.6	S 8 46.4
Alphecca	126 03.1	N26 37.3
Alpheratz	357 34.1	N29 14.2
Altair	61 59.4	N 8 56.1
Ankaa	353 06.5	S42 10.1
Antares	112 15.0	S26 29.4
Arcturus	145 47.1	N19 02.6
Atria	107 08.8	S69 04.2
Avior	234 13.7	S59 35.6
Bellatrix	278 21.7	N 6 22.4
Betelgeuse	270 50.9	N 7 24.7
Canopus	263 51.5	S52 42.7
Capella	280 20.2	N46 01.6
Deneb	49 25.7	N45 22.4
Denebola	182 23.8	N14 25.4
Diphda	348 46.5	S17 50.7
Dubhe	193 39.4	N61 36.3
Elnath	278 00.5	N28 37.8
Eltanin	90 42.2	N51 28.9
Enif	33 38.2	N 9 59.6
Fomalhaut	15 13.8	S29 29.2
Gacrux	171 50.4	S57 15.4
Gienah	175 42.5	S17 41.2
Hadar	148 34.7	S60 29.7
Hamal	327 50.2	N23 35.2
Kaus Aust.	83 31.7	S34 22.3
Kochab	137 20.0	N74 02.5
Markab	13 29.3	N15 20.7
Menkar	314 05.2	N 4 11.5
Menkent	147 56.6	S36 29.8
Miaplacidus	221 37.2	S69 49.4
Mirfak	308 26.8	N49 57.4
Nunki	75 47.0	S26 15.9
Peacock	53 04.9	S56 39.1
Pollux	243 15.9	N27 57.7
Procyon	244 49.6	N 5 09.4
Rasalhague	95 58.0	N12 32.3
Regulus	207 33.2	N11 50.2
Rigel	281 02.8	S 8 10.4
Rigil Kent.	139 39.1	S60 56.3
Sabik	102 02.0	S15 45.5
Schedar	349 30.3	N56 41.1
Shaula	96 09.5	S37 07.3
Sirius	258 25.1	S16 45.2
Spica	158 21.3	S11 17.9
Suhail	222 45.2	S43 32.3
Vega	80 33.0	N38 48.3
Zuben'ubi	136 55.1	S16 09.0

	SHA ° ′	Mer. Pass. h m
Venus	46 32.6	12 33
Mars	55 27.5	11 57
Jupiter	250 23.3	22 53
Saturn	0 54.1	15 33

	UT	SUN GHA	SUN Dec	MOON GHA	MOON v	MOON Dec	MOON d	MOON HP
	d h	° ′	° ′	° ′	′	° ′	′	′
	25 00	176 57.2	S19 00.7	107 32.9	12.0	N10 46.0	15.2	58.4
	01	191 57.0	19 00.1	122 03.9	12.0	11 01.2	15.3	58.4
	02	206 56.9	18 59.5	136 34.9	11.9	11 16.5	15.1	58.5
	03	221 56.7	. . 58.9	151 05.8	11.9	11 31.6	15.2	58.5
	04	236 56.6	58.3	165 36.7	11.7	11 46.8	15.1	58.5
	05	251 56.4	57.7	180 07.4	11.7	12 01.9	15.0	58.5
	06	266 56.3	S18 57.0	194 38.1	11.6	N12 16.9	15.0	58.5
	07	281 56.2	56.4	209 08.7	11.5	12 31.9	14.9	58.6
	08	296 56.0	55.8	223 39.2	11.4	12 46.8	14.9	58.6
S	09	311 55.9	. . 55.2	238 09.6	11.4	13 01.7	14.8	58.6
U	10	326 55.7	54.6	252 40.0	11.3	13 16.5	14.8	58.6
N	11	341 55.6	53.9	267 10.3	11.1	13 31.3	14.7	58.6
D	12	356 55.4	S18 53.3	281 40.4	11.1	N13 46.0	14.6	58.7
A	13	11 55.3	52.7	296 10.5	11.0	14 00.6	14.6	58.7
Y	14	26 55.2	52.1	310 40.5	10.9	14 15.2	14.5	58.7
	15	41 55.0	. . 51.5	325 10.4	10.9	14 29.7	14.5	58.7
	16	56 54.9	50.8	339 40.3	10.7	14 44.2	14.4	58.7
	17	71 54.7	50.2	354 10.0	10.6	14 58.6	14.3	58.7
	18	86 54.6	S18 49.6	8 39.6	10.6	N15 12.9	14.2	58.8
	19	101 54.5	49.0	23 09.2	10.4	15 27.1	14.2	58.8
	20	116 54.3	48.3	37 38.6	10.4	15 41.3	14.1	58.8
	21	131 54.2	. . 47.7	52 08.0	10.2	15 55.4	14.0	58.8
	22	146 54.1	47.1	66 37.2	10.2	16 09.4	14.0	58.8
	23	161 53.9	46.5	81 06.4	10.0	16 23.4	13.8	58.9
	26 00	176 53.8	S18 45.8	95 35.4	10.0	N16 37.2	13.8	58.9
	01	191 53.6	45.2	110 04.4	9.8	16 51.0	13.7	58.9
	02	206 53.5	44.6	124 33.2	9.8	17 04.7	13.6	58.9
	03	221 53.4	. . 43.9	139 02.0	9.6	17 18.3	13.6	58.9
	04	236 53.2	43.3	153 30.6	9.5	17 31.9	13.4	59.0
	05	251 53.1	42.7	167 59.1	9.5	17 45.3	13.4	59.0
	06	266 53.0	S18 42.0	182 27.6	9.3	N17 58.7	13.2	59.0
	07	281 52.8	41.4	196 55.9	9.2	18 11.9	13.2	59.0
	08	296 52.7	40.8	211 24.1	9.1	18 25.1	13.1	59.0
M	09	311 52.6	. . 40.2	225 52.2	9.0	18 38.2	12.9	59.0
O	10	326 52.4	39.5	240 20.2	8.9	18 51.1	12.9	59.1
N	11	341 52.3	38.9	254 48.1	8.8	19 04.0	12.8	59.1
D	12	356 52.2	S18 38.2	269 15.9	8.7	N19 16.8	12.7	59.1
A	13	11 52.0	37.6	283 43.6	8.5	19 29.5	12.6	59.1
Y	14	26 51.9	37.0	298 11.1	8.5	19 42.1	12.4	59.1
	15	41 51.8	. . 36.3	312 38.6	8.3	19 54.5	12.4	59.1
	16	56 51.6	35.7	327 05.9	8.2	20 06.9	12.2	59.2
	17	71 51.5	35.1	341 33.1	8.1	20 19.1	12.2	59.2
	18	86 51.4	S18 34.4	356 00.2	8.0	N20 31.3	12.0	59.2
	19	101 51.2	33.8	10 27.2	7.9	20 43.3	11.9	59.2
	20	116 51.1	33.1	24 54.1	7.8	20 55.2	11.8	59.2
	21	131 51.0	. . 32.5	39 20.9	7.6	21 07.0	11.7	59.2
	22	146 50.9	31.9	53 47.5	7.5	21 18.7	11.6	59.3
	23	161 50.7	31.2	68 14.0	7.5	21 30.3	11.4	59.3
	27 00	176 50.6	S18 30.6	82 40.5	7.3	N21 41.7	11.3	59.3
	01	191 50.5	29.9	97 06.8	7.2	21 53.0	11.2	59.3
	02	206 50.3	29.3	111 33.0	7.0	22 04.2	11.1	59.3
	03	221 50.2	. . 28.7	125 59.0	7.0	22 15.3	10.9	59.3
	04	236 50.1	28.0	140 25.0	6.8	22 26.2	10.8	59.4
	05	251 50.0	27.4	154 50.8	6.8	22 37.0	10.7	59.4
	06	266 49.8	S18 26.7	169 16.6	6.6	N22 47.7	10.5	59.4
	07	281 49.7	26.1	183 42.2	6.5	22 58.2	10.4	59.4
T	08	296 49.6	25.4	198 07.7	6.3	23 08.6	10.3	59.4
U	09	311 49.5	. . 24.8	212 33.0	6.3	23 18.9	10.1	59.4
E	10	326 49.3	24.1	226 58.3	6.2	23 29.0	10.0	59.4
S	11	341 49.2	23.5	241 23.5	6.0	23 39.0	9.8	59.5
D	12	356 49.1	S18 22.8	255 48.5	5.9	N23 48.8	9.7	59.5
A	13	11 49.0	22.2	270 13.4	5.8	23 58.5	9.5	59.5
Y	14	26 48.8	21.5	284 38.2	5.7	24 08.0	9.4	59.5
	15	41 48.7	. . 20.9	299 02.9	5.6	24 17.4	9.2	59.5
	16	56 48.6	20.2	313 27.5	5.5	24 26.6	9.1	59.5
	17	71 48.5	19.6	327 52.0	5.3	24 35.7	8.9	59.5
	18	86 48.4	S18 18.9	342 16.3	5.3	N24 44.6	8.8	59.6
	19	101 48.2	18.3	356 40.6	5.1	24 53.4	8.6	59.6
	20	116 48.1	17.6	11 04.7	5.1	25 02.0	8.5	59.6
	21	131 48.0	. . 17.0	25 28.8	4.9	25 10.5	8.3	59.6
	22	146 47.9	16.3	39 52.7	4.8	25 18.8	8.1	59.6
	23	161 47.7	15.7	54 16.5	4.8	N25 26.9	8.0	59.6
		SD 16.3	d 0.6	SD 16.0		16.1		16.2

Lat.	Twilight Naut.	Twilight Civil	Sunrise	Moonrise 25	Moonrise 26	Moonrise 27	Moonrise 28
°	h m	h m	h m	h m	h m	h m	h m
N 72	07 30	09 05	11 38	08 10	06 17	▭	▭
N 70	07 19	08 42	10 20	08 32	07 36	▭	▭
68	07 11	08 24	09 43	08 50	08 15	▭	▭
66	07 03	08 09	09 17	09 04	08 42	07 58	▭
64	06 57	07 57	08 57	09 15	09 03	08 45	▭
62	06 51	07 47	08 41	09 25	09 21	09 16	09 09
60	06 46	07 38	08 27	09 34	09 35	09 39	09 49
N 58	06 42	07 30	08 16	09 42	09 48	09 58	10 17
56	06 38	07 23	08 06	09 48	09 58	10 13	10 39
54	06 34	07 17	07 57	09 55	10 08	10 27	10 57
52	06 30	07 11	07 49	10 00	10 16	10 39	11 13
50	06 27	07 06	07 42	10 05	10 24	10 50	11 26
45	06 19	06 54	07 26	10 16	10 40	11 12	11 54
N 40	06 12	06 45	07 14	10 25	10 54	11 30	12 15
35	06 05	06 36	07 03	10 33	11 06	11 45	12 34
30	05 59	06 28	06 53	10 40	11 16	11 58	12 49
20	05 47	06 14	06 37	10 52	11 34	12 21	13 16
N 10	05 35	06 00	06 23	11 02	11 49	12 41	13 39
0	05 22	05 47	06 09	11 12	12 04	13 00	14 01
S 10	05 07	05 33	05 55	11 22	12 18	13 19	14 22
20	04 49	05 17	05 40	11 33	12 34	13 39	14 46
30	04 26	04 57	05 23	11 46	12 53	14 02	15 13
35	04 11	04 45	05 13	11 53	13 03	14 16	15 29
40	03 53	04 31	05 02	12 02	13 16	14 32	15 48
45	03 30	04 14	04 48	12 11	13 31	14 52	16 11
S 50	03 00	03 52	04 31	12 23	13 49	15 16	16 40
52	02 43	03 41	04 23	12 29	13 57	15 28	16 55
54	02 24	03 29	04 14	12 35	14 07	15 41	17 12
56	01 58	03 15	04 04	12 42	14 18	15 57	17 32
58	01 19	02 58	03 53	12 50	14 31	16 16	17 57
S 60	////	02 37	03 40	12 59	14 45	16 39	18 32

Lat.	Sunset	Twilight Civil	Twilight Naut.	Moonset 25	Moonset 26	Moonset 27	Moonset 28
°	h m	h m	h m	h m	h m	h m	h m
N 72	12 48	15 21	16 57	01 19	04 58	▭	▭
N 70	14 06	15 44	17 07	00 59	03 41	▭	▭
68	14 43	16 02	17 15	00 44	03 04	▭	▭
66	15 09	16 17	17 23	00 32	02 37	05 15	▭
64	15 29	16 29	17 29	00 22	02 18	04 30	▭
62	15 45	16 39	17 35	00 13	02 01	04 00	06 11
60	15 59	16 48	17 40	00 06	01 48	03 37	05 31
N 58	16 10	16 55	17 44	25 37	01 37	03 19	05 03
56	16 20	17 02	17 48	25 27	01 27	03 04	04 42
54	16 29	17 09	17 52	25 18	01 18	02 51	04 24
52	16 37	17 14	17 56	25 10	01 10	02 40	04 09
50	16 44	17 20	17 59	25 04	01 04	02 30	03 56
45	16 59	17 31	18 07	24 49	00 49	02 09	03 30
N 40	17 12	17 41	18 14	24 37	00 37	01 52	03 09
35	17 23	17 49	18 20	24 26	00 26	01 38	02 51
30	17 32	17 57	18 26	24 17	00 17	01 26	02 36
20	17 48	18 11	18 38	24 02	00 02	01 05	02 11
N 10	18 03	18 25	18 50	23 49	24 47	00 47	01 49
0	18 16	18 38	19 03	23 36	24 30	00 30	01 28
S 10	18 30	18 52	19 18	23 24	24 13	00 13	01 08
20	18 44	19 08	19 36	23 11	23 55	24 46	00 46
30	19 01	19 28	19 59	22 56	23 35	24 21	00 21
35	19 11	19 39	20 13	22 47	23 23	24 06	00 06
40	19 23	19 53	20 31	22 37	23 09	23 49	24 40
45	19 36	20 10	20 53	22 26	22 53	23 29	24 17
S 50	19 53	20 32	21 24	22 12	22 33	23 03	23 47
52	20 01	20 43	21 40	22 05	22 24	22 51	23 32
54	20 09	20 55	21 59	21 58	22 14	22 37	23 15
56	20 19	21 09	22 24	21 51	22 02	22 21	22 55
58	20 30	21 25	23 00	21 42	21 49	22 02	22 29
S 60	20 43	21 46	////	21 32	21 33	21 38	21 54

Day	SUN Eqn. of Time 00^h	SUN Eqn. of Time 12^h	SUN Mer. Pass.	MOON Mer. Pass. Upper	MOON Mer. Pass. Lower	MOON Age	MOON Phase
d	m s	m s	h m	h m	h m	d %	
25	12 11	12 18	12 12	17 24	04 59	07 42	◐
26	12 25	12 31	12 13	18 17	05 50	08 54	
27	12 37	12 43	12 13	19 14	06 45	09 65	

UT d h	ARIES GHA	VENUS −3·9 GHA	VENUS Dec	MARS +1·1 GHA	MARS Dec	JUPITER −2·6 GHA	JUPITER Dec	SATURN +1·0 GHA	SATURN Dec
	° ′	° ′	° ′	° ′	° ′	° ′	° ′	° ′	° ′
28 00	127 16.5	171 15.9	S18 06.5	181 06.6	S20 20.9	17 55.3	N22 32.8	128 00.5	S 2 41.8
01	142 19.0	186 15.2	05.7	196 07.0	20.4	32 58.1	32.9	143 02.7	41.7
02	157 21.4	201 14.5	04.8	211 07.4	20.0	48 00.9	32.9	158 05.0	41.6
03	172 23.9	216 13.8	. . 03.9	226 07.9	. . 19.5	63 03.7	. . 32.9	173 07.2	. . 41.5
04	187 26.4	231 13.1	03.1	241 08.3	19.1	78 06.5	33.0	188 09.5	41.4
05	202 28.8	246 12.4	02.2	256 08.7	18.6	93 09.2	33.0	203 11.7	41.3
06	217 31.3	261 11.7	S18 01.4	271 09.2	S20 18.2	108 12.0	N22 33.1	218 14.0	S 2 41.2
W 07	232 33.8	276 10.9	18 00.5	286 09.6	17.7	123 14.8	33.1	233 16.2	41.1
E 08	247 36.2	291 10.2	17 59.6	301 10.1	17.2	138 17.6	33.2	248 18.5	41.0
D 09	262 38.7	306 09.5	. . 58.8	316 10.5	. . 16.8	153 20.4	. . 33.2	263 20.7	. . 40.9
N 10	277 41.1	321 08.8	57.9	331 10.9	16.3	168 23.2	33.2	278 23.0	40.8
E 11	292 43.6	336 08.1	57.1	346 11.4	15.9	183 25.9	33.3	293 25.2	40.7
S 12	307 46.1	351 07.4	S17 56.2	1 11.8	S20 15.4	198 28.7	N22 33.3	308 27.5	S 2 40.6
D 13	322 48.5	6 06.7	55.3	16 12.3	15.0	213 31.5	33.4	323 29.7	40.5
A 14	337 51.0	21 06.0	54.5	31 12.7	14.5	228 34.3	33.4	338 32.0	40.4
Y 15	352 53.5	36 05.3	. . 53.6	46 13.1	. . 14.1	243 37.1	. . 33.5	353 34.2	. . 40.3
16	7 55.9	51 04.6	52.7	61 13.6	13.6	258 39.8	33.5	8 36.5	40.2
17	22 58.4	66 03.9	51.9	76 14.0	13.2	273 42.6	33.6	23 38.7	40.1
18	38 00.9	81 03.2	S17 51.0	91 14.4	S20 12.7	288 45.4	N22 33.6	38 40.9	S 2 40.0
19	53 03.3	96 02.5	50.1	106 14.9	12.2	303 48.2	33.6	53 43.2	39.9
20	68 05.8	111 01.8	49.3	121 15.3	11.8	318 51.0	33.7	68 45.4	39.8
21	83 08.2	126 01.1	. . 48.4	136 15.8	. . 11.3	333 53.7	. . 33.7	83 47.7	. . 39.7
22	98 10.7	141 00.4	47.5	151 16.2	10.9	348 56.5	33.8	98 49.9	39.6
23	113 13.2	155 59.7	46.6	166 16.7	10.4	3 59.3	33.8	113 52.2	39.5
29 00	128 15.6	170 59.0	S17 45.8	181 17.1	S20 10.0	19 02.1	N22 33.9	128 54.4	S 2 39.4
01	143 18.1	185 58.3	44.9	196 17.5	09.5	34 04.8	33.9	143 56.7	39.3
02	158 20.6	200 57.6	44.0	211 18.0	09.0	49 07.6	33.9	158 58.9	39.2
03	173 23.0	215 56.9	. . 43.1	226 18.4	. . 08.6	64 10.4	. . 34.0	174 01.2	. . 39.1
04	188 25.5	230 56.2	42.3	241 18.9	08.1	79 13.2	34.0	189 03.4	39.0
05	203 28.0	245 55.5	41.4	256 19.3	07.7	94 16.0	34.1	204 05.7	38.9
06	218 30.4	260 54.8	S17 40.5	271 19.7	S20 07.2	109 18.7	N22 34.1	219 07.9	S 2 38.8
T 07	233 32.9	275 54.1	39.6	286 20.2	06.7	124 21.5	34.2	234 10.2	38.7
H 08	248 35.4	290 53.4	38.7	301 20.6	06.3	139 24.3	34.2	249 12.4	38.6
U 09	263 37.8	305 52.7	. . 37.9	316 21.1	. . 05.8	154 27.1	. . 34.2	264 14.7	. . 38.5
R 10	278 40.3	320 52.0	37.0	331 21.5	05.4	169 29.8	34.3	279 16.9	38.4
S 11	293 42.7	335 51.3	36.1	346 22.0	04.9	184 32.6	34.3	294 19.2	38.3
D 12	308 45.2	350 50.6	S17 35.2	1 22.4	S20 04.4	199 35.4	N22 34.4	309 21.4	S 2 38.2
A 13	323 47.7	5 49.9	34.3	16 22.8	04.0	214 38.2	34.4	324 23.6	38.1
Y 14	338 50.1	20 49.2	33.4	31 23.3	03.5	229 40.9	34.5	339 25.9	38.0
15	353 52.6	35 48.5	. . 32.5	46 23.7	. . 03.0	244 43.7	. . 34.5	354 28.1	. . 37.9
16	8 55.1	50 47.8	31.7	61 24.2	02.6	259 46.5	34.5	9 30.4	37.8
17	23 57.5	65 47.1	30.8	76 24.6	02.1	274 49.3	34.6	24 32.6	37.7
18	39 00.0	80 46.4	S17 29.9	91 25.1	S20 01.6	289 52.0	N22 34.6	39 34.9	S 2 37.6
19	54 02.5	95 45.8	29.0	106 25.5	01.2	304 54.8	34.7	54 37.1	37.5
20	69 04.9	110 45.1	28.1	121 25.9	00.7	319 57.6	34.7	69 39.4	37.4
21	84 07.4	125 44.4	. . 27.2	136 26.4	20 00.2	335 00.4	. . 34.7	84 41.6	. . 37.3
22	99 09.9	140 43.7	26.3	151 26.8	19 59.8	350 03.1	34.8	99 43.9	37.2
23	114 12.3	155 43.0	25.4	166 27.3	59.3	5 05.9	34.8	114 46.1	37.1
30 00	129 14.8	170 42.3	S17 24.5	181 27.7	S19 58.8	20 08.7	N22 34.9	129 48.4	S 2 37.0
01	144 17.2	185 41.6	23.6	196 28.2	58.4	35 11.5	34.9	144 50.6	36.9
02	159 19.7	200 40.9	22.7	211 28.6	57.9	50 14.2	35.0	159 52.8	36.8
03	174 22.2	215 40.3	. . 21.8	226 29.1	. . 57.4	65 17.0	. . 35.0	174 55.1	. . 36.7
04	189 24.6	230 39.6	20.9	241 29.5	57.0	80 19.8	35.0	189 57.3	36.6
05	204 27.1	245 38.9	20.0	256 29.9	56.5	95 22.6	35.1	204 59.6	36.5
06	219 29.6	260 38.2	S17 19.1	271 30.4	S19 56.0	110 25.3	N22 35.1	220 01.8	S 2 36.4
07	234 32.0	275 37.5	18.2	286 30.8	55.6	125 28.1	35.2	235 04.1	36.3
08	249 34.5	290 36.8	17.3	301 31.3	55.1	140 30.9	35.2	250 06.3	36.2
F 09	264 37.0	305 36.2	. . 16.4	316 31.7	. . 54.6	155 33.6	. . 35.2	265 08.6	. . 36.0
R 10	279 39.4	320 35.5	15.5	331 32.2	54.2	170 36.4	35.3	280 10.8	35.9
I 11	294 41.9	335 34.8	14.6	346 32.6	53.7	185 39.2	35.3	295 13.0	35.8
D 12	309 44.4	350 34.1	S17 13.7	1 33.1	S19 53.2	200 42.0	N22 35.4	310 15.3	S 2 35.7
A 13	324 46.8	5 33.4	12.8	16 33.5	52.7	215 44.7	35.4	325 17.5	35.6
Y 14	339 49.3	20 32.7	11.9	31 34.0	52.3	230 47.5	35.5	340 19.8	35.5
15	354 51.7	35 32.1	. . 11.0	46 34.4	. . 51.8	245 50.3	. . 35.5	355 22.0	. . 35.4
16	9 54.2	50 31.4	10.1	61 34.9	51.3	260 53.0	35.5	10 24.3	35.3
17	24 56.7	65 30.7	09.2	76 35.3	50.8	275 55.8	35.6	25 26.5	35.2
18	39 59.1	80 30.0	S17 08.3	91 35.8	S19 50.4	290 58.6	N22 35.6	40 28.7	S 2 35.1
19	55 01.6	95 29.4	07.3	106 36.2	49.9	306 01.3	35.7	55 31.0	35.0
20	70 04.1	110 28.7	06.4	121 36.6	49.4	321 04.1	35.7	70 33.2	34.9
21	85 06.5	125 28.0	. . 05.5	136 37.1	. . 48.9	336 06.9	. . 35.7	85 35.5	. . 34.8
22	100 09.0	140 27.3	04.6	151 37.5	48.5	351 09.7	35.8	100 37.7	34.7
23	115 11.5	155 26.7	03.7	166 38.0	48.0	6 12.4	35.8	115 40.0	34.6
Mer. Pass.	h m 15 24.4	*v* −0.7	*d* 0.9	*v* 0.4	*d* 0.5	*v* 2.8	*d* 0.0	*v* 2.2	*d* 0.1

STARS

Name	SHA ° ′	Dec ° ′
Acamar	315 11.0	S40 12.2
Achernar	335 19.6	S57 06.5
Acrux	172 58.7	S63 14.5
Adhara	255 04.8	S29 00.6
Aldebaran	290 38.4	N16 33.7
Alioth	166 11.9	N55 48.7
Alkaid	152 51.2	N49 10.6
Alnair	27 32.2	S46 50.2
Alnilam	275 36.6	S 1 11.2
Alphard	217 46.6	S 8 46.4
Alphecca	126 03.1	N26 37.3
Alpheratz	357 34.1	N29 14.2
Altair	61 59.4	N 8 56.1
Ankaa	353 06.5	S42 10.1
Antares	112 14.9	S26 29.4
Arcturus	145 47.1	N19 02.6
Atria	107 08.7	S69 04.2
Avior	234 13.7	S59 35.6
Bellatrix	278 21.7	N 6 22.4
Betelgeuse	270 50.9	N 7 24.7
Canopus	263 51.5	S52 42.7
Capella	280 20.2	N46 01.6
Deneb	49 25.7	N45 22.4
Denebola	182 23.8	N14 25.4
Diphda	348 46.5	S17 50.7
Dubhe	193 39.4	N61 36.4
Elnath	278 00.5	N28 37.8
Eltanin	90 42.2	N51 28.9
Enif	33 38.2	N 9 59.6
Fomalhaut	15 13.8	S29 29.2
Gacrux	171 50.4	S57 15.4
Gienah	175 42.5	S17 41.2
Hadar	148 34.7	S60 29.7
Hamal	327 50.2	N23 35.2
Kaus Aust.	83 31.7	S34 22.3
Kochab	137 19.9	N74 02.5
Markab	13 29.3	N15 20.7
Menkar	314 05.2	N 4 11.5
Menkent	147 56.5	S36 29.8
Miaplacidus	221 37.2	S69 49.4
Mirfak	308 26.8	N49 57.4
Nunki	75 47.0	S26 15.9
Peacock	53 04.9	S56 39.1
Pollux	243 15.8	N27 57.7
Procyon	244 49.6	N 5 09.4
Rasalhague	95 58.0	N12 32.3
Regulus	207 33.2	N11 50.2
Rigel	281 02.8	S 8 10.4
Rigil Kent.	139 39.1	S60 56.3
Sabik	102 02.0	S15 45.5
Schedar	349 30.3	N56 41.1
Shaula	96 09.5	S37 07.3
Sirius	258 25.1	S16 45.2
Spica	158 21.3	S11 17.9
Suhail	222 45.2	S43 32.3
Vega	80 33.0	N38 48.3
Zuben'ubi	136 55.1	S16 09.0

	SHA ° ′	Mer. Pass. h m
Venus	42 43.3	12 37
Mars	53 01.5	11 55
Jupiter	250 46.4	22 40
Saturn	0 38.8	15 22

UT	SUN GHA	SUN Dec	MOON GHA	v	MOON Dec	d	HP
d h	° ′	° ′	° ′	′	° ′	′	′
28 00	176 47.6	S18 15.0	68 40.3	4.6	N25 34.9	7.8	59.6
01	191 47.5	14.4	83 03.9	4.5	25 42.7	7.6	59.6
02	206 47.4	13.7	97 27.4	4.4	25 50.3	7.4	59.7
03	221 47.3	. . 13.0	111 50.8	4.3	25 57.7	7.3	59.7
04	236 47.2	12.4	126 14.1	4.3	26 05.0	7.1	59.7
05	251 47.0	11.7	140 37.4	4.1	26 12.1	7.0	59.7
06	266 46.9	S18 11.1	155 00.5	4.0	N26 19.1	6.7	59.7
W 07	281 46.8	10.4	169 23.5	3.9	26 25.8	6.6	59.7
E 08	296 46.7	09.7	183 46.4	3.9	26 32.4	6.4	59.7
D 09	311 46.6	. . 09.1	198 09.3	3.8	26 38.8	6.2	59.7
N 10	326 46.5	08.4	212 32.1	3.6	26 45.0	6.1	59.7
E 11	341 46.3	07.8	226 54.7	3.6	26 51.1	5.8	59.8
S 12	356 46.2	S18 07.1	241 17.3	3.5	N26 56.9	5.7	59.8
D 13	11 46.1	06.4	255 39.8	3.4	27 02.6	5.5	59.8
A 14	26 46.0	05.8	270 02.2	3.4	27 08.1	5.3	59.8
Y 15	41 45.9	. . 05.1	284 24.6	3.2	27 13.4	5.1	59.8
16	56 45.8	04.4	298 46.8	3.2	27 18.5	4.9	59.8
17	71 45.6	03.8	313 09.0	3.1	27 23.4	4.7	59.8
18	86 45.5	S18 03.1	327 31.1	3.1	N27 28.1	4.6	59.8
19	101 45.4	02.4	341 53.2	3.0	27 32.7	4.3	59.8
20	116 45.3	01.8	356 15.2	2.9	27 37.0	4.1	59.8
21	131 45.2	. . 01.1	10 37.1	2.8	27 41.1	4.0	59.8
22	146 45.1	18 00.4	24 58.9	2.8	27 45.1	3.7	59.8
23	161 45.0	17 59.8	39 20.7	2.7	27 48.8	3.6	59.9
29 00	176 44.9	S17 59.1	53 42.4	2.7	N27 52.4	3.3	59.9
01	191 44.8	58.4	68 04.1	2.6	27 55.7	3.2	59.9
02	206 44.6	57.8	82 25.7	2.6	27 58.9	2.9	59.9
03	221 44.5	. . 57.1	96 47.3	2.5	28 01.8	2.8	59.9
04	236 44.4	56.4	111 08.8	2.5	28 04.6	2.5	59.9
05	251 44.3	55.7	125 30.3	2.5	28 07.1	2.4	59.9
06	266 44.2	S17 55.1	139 51.8	2.4	N28 09.5	2.1	59.9
T 07	281 44.1	54.4	154 13.2	2.3	28 11.6	2.0	59.9
H 08	296 44.0	53.7	168 34.5	2.4	28 13.6	1.7	59.9
U 09	311 43.9	. . 53.1	182 55.9	2.3	28 15.3	1.5	59.9
R 10	326 43.8	52.4	197 17.2	2.2	28 16.8	1.4	59.9
S 11	341 43.7	51.7	211 38.4	2.3	28 18.2	1.1	59.9
D 12	356 43.6	S17 51.0	225 59.7	2.2	N28 19.3	0.9	59.9
A 13	11 43.5	50.4	240 20.9	2.2	28 20.2	0.7	59.9
Y 14	26 43.3	49.7	254 42.1	2.2	28 20.9	0.5	59.9
15	41 43.2	. . 49.0	269 03.3	2.2	28 21.4	0.3	59.9
16	56 43.1	48.3	283 24.5	2.2	28 21.7	0.1	59.9
17	71 43.0	47.6	297 45.7	2.2	28 21.8	0.2	59.9
18	86 42.9	S17 47.0	312 06.9	2.2	N28 21.6	0.3	59.9
19	101 42.8	46.3	326 28.1	2.2	28 21.3	0.5	59.9
20	116 42.7	45.6	340 49.3	2.1	28 20.8	0.8	59.9
21	131 42.6	. . 44.9	355 10.4	2.2	28 20.0	0.9	59.9
22	146 42.5	44.2	9 31.6	2.2	28 19.1	1.2	59.9
23	161 42.4	43.6	23 52.8	2.2	28 17.9	1.4	59.9
30 00	176 42.3	S17 42.9	38 14.0	2.3	N28 16.5	1.6	59.9
01	191 42.2	42.2	52 35.3	2.2	28 14.9	1.7	59.9
02	206 42.1	41.5	66 56.5	2.3	28 13.2	2.0	59.9
03	221 42.0	. . 40.8	81 17.8	2.3	28 11.2	2.2	59.9
04	236 41.9	40.1	95 39.1	2.3	28 09.0	2.4	59.9
05	251 41.8	39.5	110 00.4	2.4	28 06.6	2.6	59.9
06	266 41.7	S17 38.8	124 21.8	2.4	N28 04.0	2.8	59.9
07	281 41.6	38.1	138 43.2	2.4	28 01.2	3.0	59.9
08	296 41.5	37.4	153 04.6	2.5	27 58.2	3.2	59.9
F 09	311 41.4	. . 36.7	167 26.1	2.5	27 55.0	3.5	59.9
R 10	326 41.3	36.0	181 47.6	2.6	27 51.5	3.6	59.9
I 11	341 41.2	35.3	196 09.2	2.6	27 47.9	3.8	59.9
D 12	356 41.1	S17 34.6	210 30.8	2.7	N27 44.1	4.0	59.9
A 13	11 41.0	34.0	224 52.5	2.7	27 40.1	4.2	59.9
Y 14	26 40.9	33.3	239 14.2	2.8	27 35.9	4.4	59.9
15	41 40.8	. . 32.6	253 36.0	2.8	27 31.5	4.6	59.9
16	56 40.7	31.9	267 57.8	3.0	27 26.9	4.8	59.9
17	71 40.6	31.2	282 19.8	2.9	27 22.1	5.0	59.9
18	86 40.5	S17 30.5	296 41.7	3.1	N27 17.1	5.2	59.9
19	101 40.4	29.8	311 03.8	3.1	27 11.9	5.4	59.9
20	116 40.3	29.1	325 25.9	3.2	27 06.5	5.6	59.8
21	131 40.2	. . 28.4	339 48.1	3.2	27 00.9	5.8	59.8
22	146 40.1	27.7	354 10.3	3.4	26 55.1	5.9	59.8
23	161 40.1	27.0	8 32.7	3.4	N26 49.2	6.2	59.8
	SD 16.3	*d* 0.7	SD 16.3		16.3		16.3

Lat.	Twilight Naut.	Twilight Civil	Sunrise	Moonrise 28	Moonrise 29	Moonrise 30	Moonrise 31
°	h m	h m	h m	h m	h m	h m	h m
N 72	07 20	08 52	10 55	□	□	□	□
N 70	07 11	08 31	10 02	□	□	□	□
68	07 03	08 15	09 30	□	□	□	□
66	06 57	08 01	09 07	□	□	□	□
64	06 51	07 50	08 48	□	□	□	12 03
62	06 46	07 41	08 33	09 09	□	10 33	12 56
60	06 41	07 33	08 21	09 49	10 21	11 38	13 28
N 58	06 37	07 25	08 10	10 17	10 58	12 12	13 51
56	06 33	07 19	08 00	10 39	11 25	12 37	14 10
54	06 30	07 13	07 52	10 57	11 46	12 57	14 26
52	06 27	07 07	07 45	11 13	12 03	13 14	14 40
50	06 23	07 03	07 38	11 26	12 18	13 29	14 52
45	06 16	06 52	07 23	11 54	12 49	13 58	15 17
N 40	06 10	06 42	07 11	12 15	13 13	14 21	15 37
35	06 04	06 34	07 01	12 34	13 32	14 40	15 53
30	05 58	06 27	06 52	12 49	13 49	14 56	16 07
20	05 47	06 13	06 36	13 16	14 17	15 24	16 31
N 10	05 35	06 01	06 23	13 39	14 42	15 47	16 52
0	05 23	05 48	06 10	14 01	15 05	16 09	17 11
S 10	05 08	05 34	05 56	14 22	15 28	16 31	17 30
20	04 51	05 19	05 42	14 46	15 52	16 55	17 51
30	04 29	05 00	05 26	15 13	16 21	17 22	18 14
35	04 15	04 48	05 16	15 29	16 38	17 38	18 28
40	03 58	04 35	05 05	15 48	16 58	17 57	18 44
45	03 36	04 19	04 52	16 11	17 22	18 19	19 03
S 50	03 07	03 58	04 36	16 40	17 53	18 48	19 26
52	02 52	03 48	04 29	16 55	18 08	19 02	19 37
54	02 34	03 36	04 21	17 12	18 26	19 18	19 50
56	02 11	03 23	04 11	17 32	18 48	19 37	20 05
58	01 38	03 07	04 00	17 57	19 16	20 01	20 22
S 60	00 21	02 48	03 48	18 32	19 57	20 32	20 42

Lat.	Sunset	Twilight Civil	Twilight Naut.	Moonset 28	Moonset 29	Moonset 30	Moonset 31
°	h m	h m	h m	h m	h m	h m	h m
N 72	13 32	15 36	17 08	□	□	□	□
N 70	14 25	15 56	17 17	□	□	□	□
68	14 57	16 13	17 24	□	□	□	□
66	15 20	16 26	17 31	□	□	□	□
64	15 39	16 37	17 36	□	□	□	09 59
62	15 54	16 46	17 41	06 11	□	09 17	09 06
60	16 06	16 55	17 46	05 31	07 13	08 12	08 33
N 58	16 17	17 02	17 50	05 03	06 36	07 37	08 09
56	16 26	17 08	17 54	04 42	06 09	07 12	07 49
54	16 35	17 14	17 57	04 24	05 48	06 51	07 33
52	16 42	17 19	18 00	04 09	05 31	06 34	07 19
50	16 49	17 24	18 03	03 56	05 16	06 20	07 06
45	17 03	17 35	18 10	03 30	04 45	05 50	06 40
N 40	17 15	17 44	18 17	03 09	04 22	05 26	06 20
35	17 26	17 52	18 23	02 51	04 02	05 07	06 02
30	17 35	18 00	18 29	02 36	03 46	04 51	05 47
20	17 50	18 13	18 40	02 11	03 18	04 22	05 22
N 10	18 04	18 26	18 51	01 49	02 53	03 58	05 00
0	18 17	18 38	19 04	01 28	02 31	03 36	04 39
S 10	18 30	18 52	19 18	01 08	02 08	03 13	04 18
20	18 44	19 07	19 35	00 46	01 44	02 49	03 56
30	19 00	19 26	19 57	00 21	01 16	02 20	03 30
35	19 09	19 37	20 11	00 06	01 00	02 03	03 14
40	19 20	19 50	20 28	24 40	00 40	01 43	02 56
45	19 33	20 07	20 49	24 17	00 17	01 19	02 34
S 50	19 49	20 27	21 18	23 47	24 48	00 48	02 06
52	19 56	20 37	21 32	23 32	24 33	00 33	01 53
54	20 04	20 49	21 50	23 15	24 15	00 15	01 37
56	20 14	21 02	22 12	22 55	23 53	25 18	01 18
58	20 24	21 17	22 43	22 29	23 25	24 55	00 55
S 60	20 36	21 36	00 05	21 54	22 44	24 25	00 25

Day	SUN Eqn. of Time 00^h	SUN Eqn. of Time 12^h	SUN Mer. Pass.	MOON Mer. Pass. Upper	MOON Mer. Pass. Lower	MOON Age	MOON Phase
d	m s	m s	h m	h m	h m	d %	
28	12 49	12 55	12 13	20 16	07 44	10 75	
29	13 00	13 06	12 13	21 20	08 48	11 85	
30	13 11	13 15	12 13	22 24	09 53	12 92	

UT	ARIES	VENUS −3·9		MARS +1·1		JUPITER −2·6		SATURN +1·0		STARS		
	GHA	GHA	Dec	GHA	Dec	GHA	Dec	GHA	Dec	Name	SHA	Dec
d h	° ′	° ′	° ′	° ′	° ′	° ′	° ′	° ′	° ′		° ′	° ′
31 00	130 13.9	170 26.0	S17 02.8	181 38.4	S19 47.5	21 15.2	N22 35.9	130 42.2	S 2 34.5	Acamar	315 11.0	S40 12.2
01	145 16.4	185 25.3	01.9	196 38.9	47.0	36 18.0	35.9	145 44.4	34.4	Achernar	335 19.7	S57 06.5
02	160 18.9	200 24.6	00.9	211 39.3	46.6	51 20.7	36.0	160 46.7	34.3	Acrux	172 58.7	S63 14.5
03	175 21.3	215 24.0	17 00.0	226 39.8	. . 46.1	66 23.5	. . 36.0	175 48.9	. . 34.2	Adhara	255 04.8	S29 00.6
04	190 23.8	230 23.3	16 59.1	241 40.2	45.6	81 26.3	36.0	190 51.2	34.1	Aldebaran	290 38.4	N16 33.7
05	205 26.2	245 22.6	58.2	256 40.7	45.1	96 29.0	36.1	205 53.4	34.0			
06	220 28.7	260 21.9	S16 57.3	271 41.1	S19 44.6	111 31.8	N22 36.1	220 55.7	S 2 33.9	Alioth	166 11.9	N55 48.7
07	235 31.2	275 21.3	56.4	286 41.6	44.2	126 34.6	36.2	235 57.9	33.8	Alkaid	152 51.2	N49 10.6
S 08	250 33.6	290 20.6	55.4	301 42.0	43.7	141 37.3	36.2	251 00.1	33.7	Alnair	27 32.2	S46 50.2
A 09	265 36.1	305 19.9	. . 54.5	316 42.5	. . 43.2	156 40.1	. . 36.2	266 02.4	. . 33.6	Alnilam	275 36.6	S 1 11.2
T 10	280 38.6	320 19.3	53.6	331 42.9	42.7	171 42.9	36.3	281 04.6	33.5	Alphard	217 46.5	S 8 46.4
U 11	295 41.0	335 18.6	52.7	346 43.4	42.2	186 45.6	36.3	296 06.9	33.4			
R 12	310 43.5	350 17.9	S16 51.7	1 43.8	S19 41.8	201 48.4	N22 36.4	311 09.1	S 2 33.3	Alphecca	126 03.1	N26 37.3
D 13	325 46.0	5 17.3	50.8	16 44.3	41.3	216 51.2	36.4	326 11.4	33.2	Alpheratz	357 34.1	N29 14.2
A 14	340 48.4	20 16.6	49.9	31 44.7	40.8	231 53.9	36.4	341 13.6	33.1	Altair	61 59.4	N 8 56.1
Y 15	355 50.9	35 15.9	. . 49.0	46 45.2	. . 40.3	246 56.7	. . 36.5	356 15.8	. . 33.0	Ankaa	353 06.5	S42 10.1
16	10 53.4	50 15.3	48.0	61 45.6	39.8	261 59.5	36.5	11 18.1	32.9	Antares	112 14.9	S26 29.4
17	25 55.8	65 14.6	47.1	76 46.1	39.4	277 02.2	36.6	26 20.3	32.8			
18	40 58.3	80 13.9	S16 46.2	91 46.5	S19 38.9	292 05.0	N22 36.6	41 22.6	S 2 32.7	Arcturus	145 47.0	N19 02.5
19	56 00.7	95 13.3	45.2	106 47.0	38.4	307 07.7	36.6	56 24.8	32.6	Atria	107 08.6	S69 04.2
20	71 03.2	110 12.6	44.3	121 47.4	37.9	322 10.5	36.7	71 27.0	32.5	Avior	234 13.7	S59 35.6
21	86 05.7	125 12.0	. . 43.4	136 47.9	. . 37.4	337 13.3	. . 36.7	86 29.3	. . 32.4	Bellatrix	278 21.7	N 6 22.4
22	101 08.1	140 11.3	42.4	151 48.4	36.9	352 16.0	36.8	101 31.5	32.3	Betelgeuse	270 50.9	N 7 24.7
23	116 10.6	155 10.6	41.5	166 48.8	36.4	7 18.8	36.8	116 33.8	32.2			
1 00	131 13.1	170 10.0	S16 40.6	181 49.3	S19 36.0	22 21.6	N22 36.8	131 36.0	S 2 32.1	Canopus	263 51.5	S52 42.7
01	146 15.5	185 09.3	39.6	196 49.7	35.5	37 24.3	36.9	146 38.2	32.0	Capella	280 20.2	N46 01.6
02	161 18.0	200 08.6	38.7	211 50.2	35.0	52 27.1	36.9	161 40.5	31.9	Deneb	49 25.7	N45 22.3
03	176 20.5	215 08.0	. . 37.8	226 50.6	. . 34.5	67 29.9	. . 37.0	176 42.7	. . 31.8	Denebola	182 23.8	N14 25.4
04	191 22.9	230 07.3	36.8	241 51.1	34.0	82 32.6	37.0	191 45.0	31.7	Diphda	348 46.6	S17 50.7
05	206 25.4	245 06.7	35.9	256 51.5	33.5	97 35.4	37.0	206 47.2	31.6			
06	221 27.9	260 06.0	S16 34.9	271 52.0	S19 33.0	112 38.1	N22 37.1	221 49.4	S 2 31.4	Dubhe	193 39.3	N61 36.4
07	236 30.3	275 05.4	34.0	286 52.4	32.6	127 40.9	37.1	236 51.7	31.3	Elnath	278 00.5	N28 37.8
08	251 32.8	290 04.7	33.1	301 52.9	32.1	142 43.7	37.2	251 53.9	31.2	Eltanin	90 42.2	N51 28.8
S 09	266 35.2	305 04.0	. . 32.1	316 53.3	. . 31.6	157 46.4	. . 37.2	266 56.2	. . 31.1	Enif	33 38.2	N 9 59.6
U 10	281 37.7	320 03.4	31.2	331 53.8	31.1	172 49.2	37.2	281 58.4	31.0	Fomalhaut	15 13.8	S29 29.2
N 11	296 40.2	335 02.7	30.2	346 54.2	30.6	187 51.9	37.3	297 00.6	30.9			
D 12	311 42.6	350 02.1	S16 29.3	1 54.7	S19 30.1	202 54.7	N22 37.3	312 02.9	S 2 30.8	Gacrux	171 50.3	S57 15.4
A 13	326 45.1	5 01.4	28.3	16 55.2	29.6	217 57.5	37.4	327 05.1	30.7	Gienah	175 42.5	S17 41.3
Y 14	341 47.6	20 00.8	27.4	31 55.6	29.1	233 00.2	37.4	342 07.4	30.6	Hadar	148 34.6	S60 29.7
15	356 50.0	35 00.1	. . 26.4	46 56.1	. . 28.6	248 03.0	. . 37.4	357 09.6	. . 30.5	Hamal	327 50.2	N23 35.2
16	11 52.5	49 59.5	25.5	61 56.5	28.1	263 05.7	37.5	12 11.8	30.4	Kaus Aust.	83 31.6	S34 22.3
17	26 55.0	64 58.8	24.6	76 57.0	27.7	278 08.5	37.5	27 14.1	30.3			
18	41 57.4	79 58.2	S16 23.6	91 57.4	S19 27.2	293 11.3	N22 37.6	42 16.3	S 2 30.2	Kochab	137 19.8	N74 02.5
19	56 59.9	94 57.5	22.7	106 57.9	26.7	308 14.0	37.6	57 18.6	30.1	Markab	13 29.3	N15 20.7
20	72 02.3	109 56.9	21.7	121 58.3	26.2	323 16.8	37.6	72 20.8	30.0	Menkar	314 05.2	N 4 11.5
21	87 04.8	124 56.2	. . 20.8	136 58.8	. . 25.7	338 19.5	. . 37.7	87 23.0	. . 29.9	Menkent	147 56.5	S36 29.8
22	102 07.3	139 55.6	19.8	151 59.2	25.2	353 22.3	37.7	102 25.3	29.8	Miaplacidus	221 37.2	S69 49.4
23	117 09.7	154 54.9	18.8	166 59.7	24.7	8 25.0	37.8	117 27.5	29.7			
2 00	132 12.2	169 54.3	S16 17.9	182 00.2	S19 24.2	23 27.8	N22 37.8	132 29.7	S 2 29.6	Mirfak	308 26.8	N49 57.4
01	147 14.7	184 53.6	16.9	197 00.6	23.7	38 30.6	37.8	147 32.0	29.5	Nunki	75 47.0	S26 15.9
02	162 17.1	199 53.0	16.0	212 01.1	23.2	53 33.3	37.9	162 34.2	29.4	Peacock	53 04.9	S56 39.1
03	177 19.6	214 52.3	. . 15.0	227 01.5	. . 22.7	68 36.1	. . 37.9	177 36.5	. . 29.3	Pollux	243 15.8	N27 57.7
04	192 22.1	229 51.7	14.1	242 02.0	22.2	83 38.8	38.0	192 38.7	29.2	Procyon	244 49.6	N 5 09.4
05	207 24.5	244 51.0	13.1	257 02.4	21.7	98 41.6	38.0	207 40.9	29.1			
06	222 27.0	259 50.4	S16 12.2	272 02.9	S19 21.2	113 44.3	N22 38.0	222 43.2	S 2 29.0	Rasalhague	95 57.9	N12 32.3
07	237 29.5	274 49.7	11.2	287 03.4	20.7	128 47.1	38.1	237 45.4	28.9	Regulus	207 33.2	N11 50.2
08	252 31.9	289 49.1	10.2	302 03.8	20.2	143 49.9	38.1	252 47.6	28.8	Rigel	281 02.8	S 8 10.4
M 09	267 34.4	304 48.5	. . 09.3	317 04.3	. . 19.7	158 52.6	. . 38.2	267 49.9	. . 28.7	Rigil Kent.	139 39.0	S60 56.3
O 10	282 36.8	319 47.8	08.3	332 04.7	19.2	173 55.4	38.2	282 52.1	28.5	Sabik	102 02.0	S15 45.5
N 11	297 39.3	334 47.2	07.3	347 05.2	18.7	188 58.1	38.2	297 54.4	28.4			
D 12	312 41.8	349 46.5	S16 06.4	2 05.6	S19 18.2	204 00.9	N22 38.3	312 56.6	S 2 28.3	Schedar	349 30.3	N56 41.1
A 13	327 44.2	4 45.9	05.4	17 06.1	17.7	219 03.6	38.3	327 58.8	28.2	Shaula	96 09.4	S37 07.3
Y 14	342 46.7	19 45.2	04.5	32 06.6	17.2	234 06.4	38.3	343 01.1	28.1	Sirius	258 25.1	S16 45.2
15	357 49.2	34 44.6	. . 03.5	47 07.0	. . 16.7	249 09.1	. . 38.4	358 03.3	. . 28.0	Spica	158 21.2	S11 17.9
16	12 51.6	49 44.0	02.5	62 07.5	16.2	264 11.9	38.4	13 05.5	27.9	Suhail	222 45.2	S43 32.3
17	27 54.1	64 43.3	01.6	77 07.9	15.7	279 14.6	38.5	28 07.8	27.8			
18	42 56.6	79 42.7	S16 00.6	92 08.4	S19 15.2	294 17.4	N22 38.5	43 10.0	S 2 27.7	Vega	80 33.0	N38 48.3
19	57 59.0	94 42.1	15 59.6	107 08.9	14.7	309 20.2	38.5	58 12.3	27.6	Zuben'ubi	136 55.0	S16 09.0
20	73 01.5	109 41.4	58.6	122 09.3	14.2	324 22.9	38.6	73 14.5	27.5		SHA	Mer. Pass.
21	88 04.0	124 40.8	. . 57.7	137 09.8	. . 13.7	339 25.7	. . 38.6	88 16.7	. . 27.4		° ′	h m
22	103 06.4	139 40.1	56.7	152 10.2	13.2	354 28.4	38.7	103 19.0	27.3	Venus	38 56.9	12 40
23	118 08.9	154 39.5	55.7	167 10.7	12.7	9 31.2	38.7	118 21.2	27.2	Mars	50 36.2	11 52
Mer. Pass.	h m 15 12.6	*v* −0.7	*d* 0.9	*v* 0.5	*d* 0.5	*v* 2.8	*d* 0.0	*v* 2.2	*d* 0.1	Jupiter	251 08.5	22 26
										Saturn	0 22.9	15 11

	UT	SUN GHA	SUN Dec	MOON GHA	v	MOON Dec	d	HP
	d h	° ′	° ′	° ′	′	° ′	′	′
	31 00	176 40.0	S17 26.3	22 55.1	3.5	N26 43.0	6.3	59.8
	01	191 39.9	25.6	37 17.6	3.6	26 36.7	6.5	59.8
	02	206 39.8	24.9	51 40.2	3.7	26 30.2	6.7	59.8
	03	221 39.7	. . 24.3	66 02.9	3.7	26 23.5	6.9	59.8
	04	236 39.6	23.6	80 25.6	3.9	26 16.6	7.0	59.8
	05	251 39.5	22.9	94 48.5	3.9	26 09.6	7.2	59.8
	06	266 39.4	S17 22.2	109 11.4	4.1	N26 02.4	7.5	59.8
	07	281 39.3	21.5	123 34.5	4.1	25 54.9	7.5	59.7
S	08	296 39.2	20.8	137 57.6	4.3	25 47.4	7.8	59.7
A	09	311 39.1	. . 20.1	152 20.9	4.3	25 39.6	7.9	59.7
T	10	326 39.0	19.4	166 44.2	4.4	25 31.7	8.1	59.7
U	11	341 38.9	18.7	181 07.6	4.6	25 23.6	8.3	59.7
R	12	356 38.9	S17 18.0	195 31.2	4.6	N25 15.3	8.4	59.7
D	13	11 38.8	17.3	209 54.8	4.8	25 06.9	8.6	59.7
A	14	26 38.7	16.6	224 18.6	4.8	24 58.3	8.8	59.7
Y	15	41 38.6	. . 15.8	238 42.4	5.0	24 49.5	8.9	59.6
	16	56 38.5	15.1	253 06.4	5.1	24 40.6	9.1	59.6
	17	71 38.4	14.4	267 30.5	5.2	24 31.5	9.2	59.6
	18	86 38.3	S17 13.7	281 54.7	5.3	N24 22.3	9.4	59.6
	19	101 38.2	13.0	296 19.0	5.4	24 12.9	9.6	59.6
	20	116 38.2	12.3	310 43.4	5.5	24 03.3	9.7	59.6
	21	131 38.1	. . 11.6	325 07.9	5.7	23 53.6	9.8	59.6
	22	146 38.0	10.9	339 32.6	5.7	23 43.8	10.0	59.5
	23	161 37.9	10.2	353 57.3	5.9	23 33.8	10.2	59.5
	1 00	176 37.8	S17 09.5	8 22.2	6.0	N23 23.6	10.3	59.5
	01	191 37.7	08.8	22 47.2	6.1	23 13.3	10.4	59.5
	02	206 37.6	08.1	37 12.3	6.2	23 02.9	10.5	59.5
	03	221 37.6	. . 07.4	51 37.5	6.4	22 52.4	10.8	59.4
	04	236 37.5	06.7	66 02.9	6.4	22 41.6	10.8	59.4
	05	251 37.4	05.9	80 28.3	6.6	22 30.8	11.0	59.4
	06	266 37.3	S17 05.2	94 53.9	6.7	N22 19.8	11.1	59.4
	07	281 37.2	04.5	109 19.6	6.8	22 08.7	11.2	59.4
	08	296 37.1	03.8	123 45.4	7.0	21 57.5	11.4	59.4
S	09	311 37.1	. . 03.1	138 11.4	7.1	21 46.1	11.5	59.3
U	10	326 37.0	02.4	152 37.5	7.1	21 34.6	11.6	59.3
N	11	341 36.9	01.7	167 03.6	7.4	21 23.0	11.7	59.3
D	12	356 36.8	S17 01.0	181 30.0	7.4	N21 11.3	11.9	59.3
A	13	11 36.7	17 00.2	195 56.4	7.5	20 59.4	12.0	59.3
Y	14	26 36.7	16 59.5	210 22.9	7.7	20 47.4	12.1	59.2
	15	41 36.6	. . 58.8	224 49.6	7.8	20 35.3	12.2	59.2
	16	56 36.5	58.1	239 16.4	7.9	20 23.1	12.3	59.2
	17	71 36.4	57.4	253 43.3	8.1	20 10.8	12.4	59.2
	18	86 36.3	S16 56.7	268 10.4	8.1	N19 58.4	12.5	59.1
	19	101 36.3	55.9	282 37.5	8.3	19 45.9	12.7	59.1
	20	116 36.2	55.2	297 04.8	8.4	19 33.2	12.7	59.1
	21	131 36.1	. . 54.5	311 32.2	8.5	19 20.5	12.9	59.1
	22	146 36.0	53.8	325 59.7	8.6	19 07.6	12.9	59.0
	23	161 36.0	53.1	340 27.3	8.8	18 54.7	13.1	59.0
	2 00	176 35.9	S16 52.3	354 55.1	8.9	N18 41.6	13.1	59.0
	01	191 35.8	51.6	9 23.0	9.0	18 28.5	13.2	59.0
	02	206 35.7	50.9	23 51.0	9.1	18 15.3	13.3	58.9
	03	221 35.6	. . 50.2	38 19.1	9.2	18 02.0	13.5	58.9
	04	236 35.6	49.5	52 47.3	9.3	17 48.5	13.4	58.9
	05	251 35.5	48.7	67 15.6	9.5	17 35.1	13.6	58.9
	06	266 35.4	S16 48.0	81 44.1	9.5	N17 21.5	13.7	58.8
	07	281 35.3	47.3	96 12.6	9.7	17 07.8	13.7	58.8
	08	296 35.3	46.6	110 41.3	9.8	16 54.1	13.9	58.8
M	09	311 35.2	. . 45.8	125 10.1	9.9	16 40.2	13.9	58.8
O	10	326 35.1	45.1	139 39.0	10.1	16 26.3	14.0	58.7
N	11	341 35.1	44.4	154 08.1	10.1	16 12.3	14.0	58.7
D	12	356 35.0	S16 43.7	168 37.2	10.2	N15 58.3	14.1	58.7
A	13	11 34.9	42.9	183 06.4	10.4	15 44.2	14.2	58.7
Y	14	26 34.8	42.2	197 35.8	10.4	15 30.0	14.3	58.6
	15	41 34.8	. . 41.5	212 05.2	10.6	15 15.7	14.3	58.6
	16	56 34.7	40.8	226 34.8	10.7	15 01.4	14.4	58.6
	17	71 34.6	40.0	241 04.5	10.8	14 47.0	14.5	58.5
	18	86 34.6	S16 39.3	255 34.3	10.8	N14 32.5	14.5	58.5
	19	101 34.5	38.6	270 04.1	11.0	14 18.0	14.6	58.5
	20	116 34.4	37.8	284 34.1	11.1	14 03.4	14.6	58.5
	21	131 34.3	. . 37.1	299 04.2	11.2	13 48.8	14.7	58.4
	22	146 34.3	36.4	313 34.4	11.3	13 34.1	14.8	58.4
	23	161 34.2	35.6	328 04.7	11.4	N13 19.3	14.8	58.4
		SD 16.3	*d* 0.7	SD 16.3		16.1		16.0

Lat.	Twilight Naut.	Twilight Civil	Sunrise	Moonrise 31	Moonrise 1	Moonrise 2	Moonrise 3
°	h m	h m	h m	h m	h m	h m	h m
N 72	07 09	08 38	10 27	▭	▭	15 08	17 56
N 70	07 02	08 20	09 45	▭	▭	15 45	18 09
68	06 55	08 05	09 17	▭	13 17	16 10	18 20
66	06 49	07 53	08 56	▭	14 08	16 30	18 29
64	06 44	07 43	08 39	12 03	14 40	16 45	18 36
62	06 40	07 34	08 26	12 56	15 03	16 58	18 43
60	06 36	07 27	08 14	13 28	15 22	17 09	18 48
N 58	06 32	07 20	08 04	13 51	15 37	17 18	18 53
56	06 29	07 14	07 55	14 10	15 50	17 26	18 57
54	06 26	07 08	07 47	14 26	16 01	17 34	19 01
52	06 23	07 03	07 40	14 40	16 11	17 40	19 04
50	06 20	06 59	07 34	14 52	16 20	17 46	19 07
45	06 13	06 49	07 20	15 17	16 39	17 58	19 14
N 40	06 08	06 40	07 09	15 37	16 54	18 09	19 20
35	06 02	06 32	06 59	15 53	17 07	18 17	19 24
30	05 57	06 25	06 50	16 07	17 18	18 25	19 29
20	05 46	06 12	06 35	16 31	17 37	18 38	19 36
N 10	05 35	06 00	06 22	16 52	17 53	18 50	19 42
0	05 23	05 48	06 10	17 11	18 08	19 00	19 48
S 10	05 10	05 35	05 58	17 30	18 23	19 11	19 54
20	04 53	05 21	05 44	17 51	18 40	19 22	20 00
30	04 32	05 03	05 29	18 14	18 58	19 35	20 07
35	04 18	04 52	05 19	18 28	19 09	19 42	20 11
40	04 02	04 39	05 09	18 44	19 21	19 51	20 16
45	03 42	04 23	04 57	19 03	19 35	20 01	20 21
S 50	03 14	04 04	04 42	19 26	19 53	20 12	20 28
52	03 00	03 54	04 35	19 37	20 01	20 18	20 31
54	02 43	03 43	04 27	19 50	20 10	20 24	20 34
56	02 22	03 31	04 18	20 05	20 20	20 30	20 37
58	01 55	03 16	04 08	20 22	20 32	20 38	20 41
S 60	01 10	02 58	03 56	20 42	20 45	20 46	20 45

Lat.	Sunset	Twilight Civil	Twilight Naut.	Moonset 31	Moonset 1	Moonset 2	Moonset 3
°	h m	h m	h m	h m	h m	h m	h m
N 72	14 01	15 50	17 19	▭	▭	10 53	09 47
N 70	14 43	16 09	17 27	▭	▭	10 14	09 31
68	15 11	16 23	17 33	▭	10 49	09 47	09 18
66	15 32	16 35	17 39	▭	09 57	09 26	09 07
64	15 49	16 45	17 44	09 59	09 24	09 09	08 58
62	16 02	16 54	17 48	09 06	09 00	08 55	08 50
60	16 14	17 01	17 52	08 33	08 40	08 43	08 43
N 58	16 24	17 08	17 56	08 09	08 24	08 32	08 37
56	16 33	17 14	17 59	07 49	08 10	08 23	08 32
54	16 41	17 20	18 02	07 33	07 58	08 15	08 27
52	16 48	17 24	18 05	07 19	07 48	08 08	08 23
50	16 54	17 29	18 08	07 06	07 38	08 01	08 18
45	17 08	17 39	18 14	06 40	07 18	07 47	08 10
N 40	17 19	17 48	18 20	06 20	07 02	07 35	08 02
35	17 29	17 55	18 26	06 02	06 48	07 25	07 56
30	17 37	18 02	18 31	05 47	06 36	07 16	07 50
20	17 52	18 15	18 41	05 22	06 15	07 00	07 40
N 10	18 05	18 27	18 52	05 00	05 56	06 47	07 32
0	18 17	18 39	19 04	04 39	05 39	06 34	07 23
S 10	18 29	18 51	19 17	04 18	05 22	06 21	07 15
20	18 43	19 06	19 34	03 56	05 03	06 07	07 06
30	18 58	19 24	19 55	03 30	04 41	05 50	06 56
35	19 07	19 35	20 08	03 14	04 28	05 41	06 50
40	19 17	19 47	20 24	02 56	04 13	05 30	06 43
45	19 30	20 03	20 44	02 34	03 56	05 17	06 35
S 50	19 44	20 22	21 11	02 06	03 34	05 01	06 25
52	19 51	20 32	21 25	01 53	03 23	04 54	06 21
54	19 59	20 42	21 42	01 37	03 11	04 45	06 16
56	20 08	20 55	22 02	01 18	02 57	04 36	06 10
58	20 18	21 09	22 28	00 55	02 41	04 25	06 04
S 60	20 29	21 26	23 09	00 25	02 21	04 13	05 57

Day	SUN Eqn. of Time 00^h	SUN Eqn. of Time 12^h	SUN Mer. Pass.	MOON Mer. Pass. Upper	MOON Mer. Pass. Lower	MOON Age	MOON Phase
d	m s	m s	h m	h m	h m	d %	
31	13 20	13 24	12 13	23 25	10 55	13 97	
1	13 29	13 33	12 14	24 21	11 54	14 100	○
2	13 36	13 40	12 14	00 21	12 47	15 100	

UT d	h	ARIES GHA	VENUS −3·9 GHA	VENUS Dec	MARS +1·1 GHA	MARS Dec	JUPITER −2·6 GHA	JUPITER Dec	SATURN +1·0 GHA	SATURN Dec
		° ′	° ′	° ′	° ′	° ′	° ′	° ′	° ′	° ′
3 TUESDAY	00	133 11.3	169 38.9	S15 54.8	182 11.2	S19 12.2	24 33.9	N22 38.7	133 23.4	S 2 27.1
	01	148 13.8	184 38.2	53.8	197 11.6	11.7	39 36.7	38.8	148 25.7	27.0
	02	163 16.3	199 37.6	52.8	212 12.1	11.2	54 39.4	38.8	163 27.9	26.9
	03	178 18.7	214 37.0	. . 51.8	227 12.5	. . 10.7	69 42.2	. . 38.8	178 30.1	. . 26.8
	04	193 21.2	229 36.3	50.9	242 13.0	10.2	84 44.9	38.9	193 32.4	26.7
	05	208 23.7	244 35.7	49.9	257 13.5	09.7	99 47.7	38.9	208 34.6	26.6
	06	223 26.1	259 35.1	S15 48.9	272 13.9	S19 09.2	114 50.4	N22 39.0	223 36.8	S 2 26.5
	07	238 28.6	274 34.4	47.9	287 14.4	08.7	129 53.2	39.0	238 39.1	26.4
	08	253 31.1	289 33.8	47.0	302 14.8	08.2	144 55.9	39.0	253 41.3	26.2
	09	268 33.5	304 33.2	. . 46.0	317 15.3	. . 07.7	159 58.7	. . 39.1	268 43.6	. . 26.1
	10	283 36.0	319 32.6	45.0	332 15.8	07.2	175 01.4	39.1	283 45.8	26.0
	11	298 38.4	334 31.9	44.0	347 16.2	06.7	190 04.2	39.2	298 48.0	25.9
	12	313 40.9	349 31.3	S15 43.0	2 16.7	S19 06.2	205 06.9	N22 39.2	313 50.3	S 2 25.8
	13	328 43.4	4 30.7	42.0	17 17.2	05.7	220 09.7	39.2	328 52.5	25.7
	14	343 45.8	19 30.0	41.1	32 17.6	05.1	235 12.4	39.3	343 54.7	25.6
	15	358 48.3	34 29.4	. . 40.1	47 18.1	. . 04.6	250 15.2	. . 39.3	358 57.0	. . 25.5
	16	13 50.8	49 28.8	39.1	62 18.5	04.1	265 17.9	39.3	13 59.2	25.4
	17	28 53.2	64 28.2	38.1	77 19.0	03.6	280 20.7	39.4	29 01.4	25.3
	18	43 55.7	79 27.5	S15 37.1	92 19.5	S19 03.1	295 23.4	N22 39.4	44 03.7	S 2 25.2
	19	58 58.2	94 26.9	36.1	107 19.9	02.6	310 26.2	39.5	59 05.9	25.1
	20	74 00.6	109 26.3	35.2	122 20.4	02.1	325 28.9	39.5	74 08.1	25.0
	21	89 03.1	124 25.7	. . 34.2	137 20.9	. . 01.6	340 31.7	. . 39.5	89 10.4	. . 24.9
	22	104 05.6	139 25.0	33.2	152 21.3	01.1	355 34.4	39.6	104 12.6	24.8
	23	119 08.0	154 24.4	32.2	167 21.8	00.6	10 37.1	39.6	119 14.8	24.7
4 WEDNESDAY	00	134 10.5	169 23.8	S15 31.2	182 22.3	S19 00.0	25 39.9	N22 39.6	134 17.1	S 2 24.6
	01	149 12.9	184 23.2	30.2	197 22.7	18 59.5	40 42.6	39.7	149 19.3	24.5
	02	164 15.4	199 22.5	29.2	212 23.2	59.0	55 45.4	39.7	164 21.6	24.4
	03	179 17.9	214 21.9	. . 28.2	227 23.7	. . 58.5	70 48.1	. . 39.8	179 23.8	. . 24.3
	04	194 20.3	229 21.3	27.2	242 24.1	58.0	85 50.9	39.8	194 26.0	24.1
	05	209 22.8	244 20.7	26.2	257 24.6	57.5	100 53.6	39.8	209 28.2	24.0
	06	224 25.3	259 20.1	S15 25.2	272 25.0	S18 57.0	115 56.4	N22 39.9	224 30.5	S 2 23.9
	07	239 27.7	274 19.4	24.2	287 25.5	56.4	130 59.1	39.9	239 32.7	23.8
	08	254 30.2	289 18.8	23.2	302 26.0	55.9	146 01.8	39.9	254 34.9	23.7
	09	269 32.7	304 18.2	. . 22.2	317 26.4	. . 55.4	161 04.6	. . 40.0	269 37.2	. . 23.6
	10	284 35.1	319 17.6	21.2	332 26.9	54.9	176 07.3	40.0	284 39.4	23.5
	11	299 37.6	334 17.0	20.2	347 27.4	54.4	191 10.1	40.0	299 41.6	23.4
	12	314 40.1	349 16.4	S15 19.2	2 27.8	S18 53.9	206 12.8	N22 40.1	314 43.9	S 2 23.3
	13	329 42.5	4 15.7	18.2	17 28.3	53.4	221 15.6	40.1	329 46.1	23.2
	14	344 45.0	19 15.1	17.2	32 28.8	52.8	236 18.3	40.2	344 48.3	23.1
	15	359 47.4	34 14.5	. . 16.2	47 29.2	. . 52.3	251 21.1	. . 40.2	359 50.6	. . 23.0
	16	14 49.9	49 13.9	15.2	62 29.7	51.8	266 23.8	40.2	14 52.8	22.9
	17	29 52.4	64 13.3	14.2	77 30.2	51.3	281 26.5	40.3	29 55.0	22.8
	18	44 54.8	79 12.7	S15 13.2	92 30.6	S18 50.8	296 29.3	N22 40.3	44 57.3	S 2 22.7
	19	59 57.3	94 12.1	12.2	107 31.1	50.2	311 32.0	40.3	59 59.5	22.6
	20	74 59.8	109 11.5	11.2	122 31.6	49.7	326 34.8	40.4	75 01.7	22.5
	21	90 02.2	124 10.8	. . 10.2	137 32.0	. . 49.2	341 37.5	. . 40.4	90 03.9	. . 22.3
	22	105 04.7	139 10.2	09.2	152 32.5	48.7	356 40.2	40.5	105 06.2	22.2
	23	120 07.2	154 09.6	08.2	167 33.0	48.2	11 43.0	40.5	120 08.4	22.1
5 THURSDAY	00	135 09.6	169 09.0	S15 07.2	182 33.4	S18 47.7	26 45.7	N22 40.5	135 10.6	S 2 22.0
	01	150 12.1	184 08.4	06.2	197 33.9	47.1	41 48.5	40.6	150 12.9	21.9
	02	165 14.5	199 07.8	05.2	212 34.4	46.6	56 51.2	40.6	165 15.1	21.8
	03	180 17.0	214 07.2	. . 04.2	227 34.9	. . 46.1	71 53.9	. . 40.6	180 17.3	. . 21.7
	04	195 19.5	229 06.6	03.2	242 35.3	45.6	86 56.7	40.7	195 19.6	21.6
	05	210 21.9	244 06.0	02.1	257 35.8	45.0	101 59.4	40.7	210 21.8	21.5
	06	225 24.4	259 05.4	S15 01.1	272 36.3	S18 44.5	117 02.2	N22 40.7	225 24.0	S 2 21.4
	07	240 26.9	274 04.8	15 00.1	287 36.7	44.0	132 04.9	40.8	240 26.3	21.3
	08	255 29.3	289 04.2	14 59.1	302 37.2	43.5	147 07.6	40.8	255 28.5	21.2
	09	270 31.8	304 03.5	. . 58.1	317 37.7	. . 43.0	162 10.4	. . 40.8	270 30.7	. . 21.1
	10	285 34.3	319 02.9	57.1	332 38.1	42.4	177 13.1	40.9	285 33.0	21.0
	11	300 36.7	334 02.3	56.1	347 38.6	41.9	192 15.8	40.9	300 35.2	20.9
	12	315 39.2	349 01.7	S14 55.0	2 39.1	S18 41.4	207 18.6	N22 41.0	315 37.4	S 2 20.7
	13	330 41.7	4 01.1	54.0	17 39.6	40.9	222 21.3	41.0	330 39.6	20.6
	14	345 44.1	19 00.5	53.0	32 40.0	40.3	237 24.1	41.0	345 41.9	20.5
	15	0 46.6	33 59.9	. . 52.0	47 40.5	. . 39.8	252 26.8	. . 41.1	0 44.1	. . 20.4
	16	15 49.0	48 59.3	51.0	62 41.0	39.3	267 29.5	41.1	15 46.3	20.3
	17	30 51.5	63 58.7	49.9	77 41.4	38.8	282 32.3	41.1	30 48.6	20.2
	18	45 54.0	78 58.1	S14 48.9	92 41.9	S18 38.2	297 35.0	N22 41.2	45 50.8	S 2 20.1
	19	60 56.4	93 57.5	47.9	107 42.4	37.7	312 37.7	41.2	60 53.0	20.0
	20	75 58.9	108 56.9	46.9	122 42.8	37.2	327 40.5	41.2	75 55.3	19.9
	21	91 01.4	123 56.3	. . 45.9	137 43.3	. . 36.6	342 43.2	. . 41.3	90 57.5	. . 19.8
	22	106 03.8	138 55.7	44.8	152 43.8	36.1	357 45.9	41.3	105 59.7	19.7
	23	121 06.3	153 55.1	43.8	167 44.3	35.6	12 48.7	41.3	121 01.9	19.6
Mer. Pass.	h m	15 00.8	v −0.6	d 1.0	v 0.5	d 0.5	v 2.7	d 0.0	v 2.2	d 0.1

STARS

Name	SHA	Dec
	° ′	° ′
Acamar	315 11.1	S40 12.2
Achernar	335 19.7	S57 06.5
Acrux	172 58.6	S63 14.5
Adhara	255 04.8	S29 00.6
Aldebaran	290 38.4	N16 33.7
Alioth	166 11.9	N55 48.7
Alkaid	152 51.1	N49 10.6
Alnair	27 32.2	S46 50.2
Alnilam	275 36.6	S 1 11.2
Alphard	217 46.5	S 8 46.4
Alphecca	126 03.0	N26 37.3
Alpheratz	357 34.1	N29 14.2
Altair	61 59.4	N 8 56.1
Ankaa	353 06.5	S42 10.0
Antares	112 14.9	S26 29.4
Arcturus	145 47.0	N19 02.5
Atria	107 08.6	S69 04.2
Avior	234 13.7	S59 35.6
Bellatrix	278 21.7	N 6 22.4
Betelgeuse	270 50.9	N 7 24.7
Canopus	263 51.6	S52 42.7
Capella	280 20.3	N46 01.6
Deneb	49 25.7	N45 22.3
Denebola	182 23.8	N14 25.4
Diphda	348 46.6	S17 50.7
Dubhe	193 39.3	N61 36.4
Elnath	278 00.5	N28 37.8
Eltanin	90 42.1	N51 28.8
Enif	33 38.2	N 9 59.6
Fomalhaut	15 13.8	S29 29.2
Gacrux	171 50.3	S57 15.4
Gienah	175 42.4	S17 41.3
Hadar	148 34.6	S60 29.7
Hamal	327 50.2	N23 35.2
Kaus Aust.	83 31.6	S34 22.3
Kochab	137 19.8	N74 02.4
Markab	13 29.3	N15 20.7
Menkar	314 05.2	N 4 11.5
Menkent	147 56.5	S36 29.8
Miaplacidus	221 37.2	S69 49.4
Mirfak	308 26.9	N49 57.4
Nunki	75 46.9	S26 15.9
Peacock	53 04.9	S56 39.1
Pollux	243 15.8	N27 57.7
Procyon	244 49.6	N 5 09.4
Rasalhague	95 57.9	N12 32.3
Regulus	207 33.2	N11 50.2
Rigel	281 02.8	S 8 10.4
Rigil Kent.	139 39.0	S60 56.4
Sabik	102 01.9	S15 45.5
Schedar	349 30.3	N56 41.1
Shaula	96 09.4	S37 07.3
Sirius	258 25.1	S16 45.2
Spica	158 21.2	S11 17.9
Suhail	222 45.2	S43 32.3
Vega	80 33.0	N38 48.2
Zuben'ubi	136 55.0	S16 09.1

	SHA	Mer. Pass.
	° ′	h m
Venus	35 13.3	12 43
Mars	48 11.8	11 50
Jupiter	251 29.4	22 13
Saturn	0 06.6	15 01

UT (d h)		SUN GHA	SUN Dec	MOON GHA	v	MOON Dec	d	HP
		° ′	° ′	° ′	′	° ′	′	′
3 00	TUESDAY	176 34.1	S16 34.9	342 35.1	11.5	N13 04.5	14.8	58.3
01		191 34.1	34.2	357 05.6	11.5	12 49.7	14.9	58.3
02		206 34.0	33.4	11 36.1	11.7	12 34.8	14.9	58.3
03		221 33.9	. . 32.7	26 06.8	11.8	12 19.9	15.0	58.3
04		236 33.9	32.0	40 37.6	11.9	12 04.9	15.1	58.2
05		251 33.8	31.2	55 08.5	11.9	11 49.8	15.0	58.2
06		266 33.7	S16 30.5	69 39.4	12.1	N11 34.8	15.1	58.2
07		281 33.7	29.8	84 10.5	12.1	11 19.7	15.2	58.1
08		296 33.6	29.0	98 41.6	12.3	11 04.5	15.2	58.1
09		311 33.5	. . 28.3	113 12.9	12.3	10 49.3	15.2	58.1
10		326 33.5	27.6	127 44.2	12.4	10 34.1	15.3	58.0
11		341 33.4	26.8	142 15.6	12.5	10 18.8	15.3	58.0
12		356 33.3	S16 26.1	156 47.1	12.5	N10 03.5	15.3	58.0
13		11 33.3	25.3	171 18.6	12.7	9 48.2	15.3	57.9
14		26 33.2	24.6	185 50.3	12.7	9 32.9	15.4	57.9
15		41 33.2	. . 23.9	200 22.0	12.9	9 17.5	15.4	57.9
16		56 33.1	23.1	214 53.9	12.9	9 02.1	15.4	57.8
17		71 33.0	22.4	229 25.8	12.9	8 46.7	15.5	57.8
18		86 33.0	S16 21.6	243 57.7	13.1	N 8 31.2	15.5	57.8
19		101 32.9	20.9	258 29.8	13.1	8 15.7	15.4	57.8
20		116 32.8	20.2	273 01.9	13.2	8 00.3	15.6	57.7
21		131 32.8	. . 19.4	287 34.1	13.3	7 44.7	15.5	57.7
22		146 32.7	18.7	302 06.4	13.3	7 29.2	15.5	57.7
23		161 32.7	17.9	316 38.7	13.5	7 13.7	15.6	57.6
4 00	WEDNESDAY	176 32.6	S16 17.2	331 11.2	13.4	N 6 58.1	15.6	57.6
01		191 32.5	16.4	345 43.6	13.6	6 42.5	15.5	57.6
02		206 32.5	15.7	0 16.2	13.6	6 27.0	15.6	57.5
03		221 32.4	. . 14.9	14 48.8	13.7	6 11.4	15.6	57.5
04		236 32.4	14.2	29 21.5	13.8	5 55.8	15.7	57.5
05		251 32.3	13.4	43 54.3	13.8	5 40.1	15.6	57.4
06		266 32.3	S16 12.7	58 27.1	13.8	N 5 24.5	15.6	57.4
07		281 32.2	12.0	72 59.9	14.0	5 08.9	15.6	57.4
08		296 32.1	11.2	87 32.9	14.0	4 53.3	15.7	57.3
09		311 32.1	. . 10.5	102 05.9	14.0	4 37.6	15.6	57.3
10		326 32.0	09.7	116 38.9	14.1	4 22.0	15.6	57.3
11		341 32.0	09.0	131 12.0	14.2	4 06.4	15.6	57.2
12		356 31.9	S16 08.2	145 45.2	14.2	N 3 50.8	15.7	57.2
13		11 31.9	07.5	160 18.4	14.3	3 35.1	15.6	57.2
14		26 31.8	06.7	174 51.7	14.3	3 19.5	15.6	57.1
15		41 31.8	. . 05.9	189 25.0	14.4	3 03.9	15.6	57.1
16		56 31.7	05.2	203 58.4	14.4	2 48.3	15.6	57.1
17		71 31.6	04.4	218 31.8	14.5	2 32.7	15.6	57.0
18		86 31.6	S16 03.7	233 05.3	14.5	N 2 17.1	15.6	57.0
19		101 31.5	02.9	247 38.8	14.5	2 01.5	15.6	57.0
20		116 31.5	02.2	262 12.3	14.6	1 45.9	15.6	56.9
21		131 31.4	. . 01.4	276 45.9	14.7	1 30.3	15.5	56.9
22		146 31.4	16 00.7	291 19.6	14.7	1 14.8	15.6	56.9
23		161 31.3	15 59.9	305 53.3	14.7	0 59.2	15.5	56.8
5 00	THURSDAY	176 31.3	S15 59.2	320 27.0	14.8	N 0 43.7	15.5	56.8
01		191 31.2	58.4	335 00.8	14.8	0 28.2	15.5	56.8
02		206 31.2	57.6	349 34.6	14.8	N 0 12.7	15.5	56.7
03		221 31.1	. . 56.9	4 08.4	14.9	S 0 02.8	15.4	56.7
04		236 31.1	56.1	18 42.3	14.9	0 18.2	15.5	56.7
05		251 31.0	55.4	33 16.2	14.9	0 33.7	15.4	56.6
06		266 31.0	S15 54.6	47 50.1	15.0	S 0 49.1	15.4	56.6
07		281 30.9	53.9	62 24.1	15.0	1 04.5	15.3	56.6
08		296 30.9	53.1	76 58.1	15.0	1 19.8	15.4	56.5
09		311 30.8	. . 52.3	91 32.1	15.0	1 35.2	15.3	56.5
10		326 30.8	51.6	106 06.1	15.1	1 50.5	15.3	56.5
11		341 30.7	50.8	120 40.2	15.1	2 05.8	15.3	56.5
12		356 30.7	S15 50.1	135 14.3	15.2	S 2 21.1	15.2	56.4
13		11 30.6	49.3	149 48.5	15.1	2 36.3	15.2	56.4
14		26 30.6	48.5	164 22.6	15.2	2 51.5	15.2	56.4
15		41 30.5	. . 47.8	178 56.8	15.2	3 06.7	15.2	56.3
16		56 30.5	47.0	193 31.0	15.2	3 21.9	15.1	56.3
17		71 30.5	46.2	208 05.2	15.2	3 37.0	15.1	56.3
18		86 30.4	S15 45.5	222 39.4	15.3	S 3 52.1	15.0	56.2
19		101 30.4	44.7	237 13.7	15.2	4 07.1	15.0	56.2
20		116 30.3	43.9	251 47.9	15.3	4 22.1	15.0	56.2
21		131 30.3	. . 43.2	266 22.2	15.3	4 37.1	15.0	56.1
22		146 30.2	42.4	280 56.5	15.3	4 52.1	14.9	56.1
23		161 30.2	41.6	295 30.8	15.3	S 5 07.0	14.9	56.1
		SD 16.3	*d* 0.8	SD 15.8		15.6		15.4

Lat.	Twilight Naut.	Twilight Civil	Sunrise	Moonrise 3	Moonrise 4	Moonrise 5	Moonrise 6
°	h m	h m	h m	h m	h m	h m	h m
N 72	06 58	08 25	10 04	17 56	20 12	22 20	24 34
N 70	06 52	08 08	09 29	18 09	20 14	22 13	24 14
68	06 46	07 55	09 04	18 20	20 16	22 07	23 58
66	06 41	07 44	08 45	18 29	20 18	22 02	23 45
64	06 37	07 35	08 30	18 36	20 19	21 57	23 35
62	06 33	07 27	08 17	18 43	20 20	21 54	23 26
60	06 30	07 20	08 07	18 48	20 21	21 51	23 19
N 58	06 27	07 14	07 57	18 53	20 22	21 48	23 12
56	06 24	07 08	07 49	18 57	20 23	21 45	23 06
54	06 21	07 03	07 42	19 01	20 24	21 43	23 01
52	06 19	06 59	07 35	19 04	20 24	21 41	22 56
50	06 16	06 55	07 29	19 07	20 25	21 39	22 52
45	06 10	06 45	07 16	19 14	20 26	21 35	22 43
N 40	06 05	06 37	07 06	19 20	20 27	21 32	22 36
35	06 00	06 30	06 56	19 24	20 28	21 29	22 29
30	05 55	06 24	06 48	19 29	20 29	21 27	22 24
20	05 45	06 12	06 34	19 36	20 30	21 23	22 14
N 10	05 35	06 00	06 22	19 42	20 31	21 19	22 05
0	05 24	05 49	06 10	19 48	20 33	21 15	21 58
S 10	05 11	05 37	05 59	19 54	20 34	21 12	21 50
20	04 55	05 23	05 46	20 00	20 35	21 08	21 42
30	04 35	05 06	05 31	20 07	20 37	21 04	21 32
35	04 22	04 55	05 22	20 11	20 37	21 02	21 27
40	04 07	04 43	05 13	20 16	20 38	21 00	21 21
45	03 47	04 28	05 01	20 21	20 39	20 57	21 14
S 50	03 21	04 09	04 47	20 28	20 41	20 53	21 06
52	03 08	04 00	04 40	20 31	20 41	20 51	21 02
54	02 53	03 50	04 33	20 34	20 42	20 50	20 58
56	02 34	03 39	04 25	20 37	20 43	20 48	20 53
58	02 09	03 25	04 15	20 41	20 44	20 46	20 48
S 60	01 35	03 09	04 05	20 45	20 44	20 43	20 42

Lat.	Sunset	Twilight Civil	Twilight Naut.	Moonset 3	Moonset 4	Moonset 5	Moonset 6
°	h m	h m	h m	h m	h m	h m	h m
N 72	14 25	16 04	17 31	09 47	09 07	08 33	07 59
N 70	15 00	16 21	17 37	09 31	09 01	08 35	08 09
68	15 24	16 34	17 43	09 18	08 56	08 37	08 18
66	15 43	16 45	17 48	09 07	08 52	08 39	08 25
64	15 59	16 54	17 52	08 58	08 49	08 40	08 31
62	16 11	17 02	17 55	08 50	08 46	08 41	08 36
60	16 22	17 08	17 59	08 43	08 43	08 42	08 41
N 58	16 31	17 15	18 02	08 37	08 40	08 43	08 45
56	16 40	17 20	18 05	08 32	08 38	08 44	08 49
54	16 47	17 25	18 07	08 27	08 36	08 44	08 52
52	16 53	17 30	18 10	08 23	08 34	08 45	08 55
50	16 59	17 34	18 12	08 18	08 33	08 45	08 58
45	17 12	17 43	18 18	08 10	08 29	08 47	09 04
N 40	17 23	17 51	18 23	08 02	08 26	08 48	09 09
35	17 32	17 58	18 28	07 56	08 23	08 49	09 13
30	17 40	18 05	18 33	07 50	08 21	08 49	09 17
20	17 54	18 16	18 43	07 40	08 17	08 51	09 24
N 10	18 06	18 28	18 53	07 32	08 13	08 52	09 30
0	18 17	18 39	19 04	07 23	08 10	08 53	09 36
S 10	18 29	18 51	19 17	07 15	08 06	08 54	09 41
20	18 42	19 05	19 32	07 06	08 02	08 56	09 47
30	18 56	19 22	19 52	06 56	07 58	08 57	09 54
35	19 05	19 32	20 05	06 50	07 55	08 58	09 58
40	19 14	19 44	20 20	06 43	07 52	08 58	10 03
45	19 26	19 59	20 39	06 35	07 49	09 00	10 08
S 50	19 40	20 17	21 05	06 25	07 45	09 01	10 14
52	19 46	20 26	21 18	06 21	07 43	09 01	10 17
54	19 54	20 36	21 33	06 16	07 41	09 02	10 21
56	20 02	20 47	21 51	06 10	07 39	09 03	10 24
58	20 11	21 01	22 14	06 04	07 36	09 03	10 28
S 60	20 21	21 16	22 47	05 57	07 33	09 04	10 33

Day	SUN Eqn. of Time 00^h	SUN Eqn. of Time 12^h	SUN Mer. Pass.	MOON Mer. Pass. Upper	MOON Mer. Pass. Lower	Age	%	Phase
d	m s	m s	h m	h m	h m	d	%	
3	13 43	13 46	12 14	01 12	13 36	16	97	
4	13 49	13 52	12 14	01 59	14 21	17	92	
5	13 55	13 57	12 14	02 43	15 04	18	86	

UT	ARIES	VENUS −3·9		MARS +1·1		JUPITER −2·6		SATURN +1·0	
	GHA	GHA	Dec	GHA	Dec	GHA	Dec	GHA	Dec
d h	° ′	° ′	° ′	° ′	° ′	° ′	° ′	° ′	° ′
6 00	136 08.8	168 54.5	S14 42.8	182 44.7	S18 35.1	27 51.4	N22 41.4	136 04.2	S 2 19.5
01	151 11.2	183 53.9	41.8	197 45.2	34.5	42 54.1	41.4	151 06.4	19.4
02	166 13.7	198 53.3	40.7	212 45.7	34.0	57 56.9	41.5	166 08.6	19.3
03	181 16.1	213 52.7	. . 39.7	227 46.2	. . 33.5	72 59.6	. . 41.5	181 10.9	. . 19.1
04	196 18.6	228 52.1	38.7	242 46.6	32.9	88 02.3	41.5	196 13.1	19.0
05	211 21.1	243 51.6	37.6	257 47.1	32.4	103 05.1	41.6	211 15.3	18.9
06	226 23.5	258 51.0	S14 36.6	272 47.6	S18 31.9	118 07.8	N22 41.6	226 17.5	S 2 18.8
07	241 26.0	273 50.4	35.6	287 48.0	31.3	133 10.5	41.6	241 19.8	18.7
08	256 28.5	288 49.8	34.6	302 48.5	30.8	148 13.3	41.7	256 22.0	18.6
F 09	271 30.9	303 49.2	. . 33.5	317 49.0	. . 30.3	163 16.0	. . 41.7	271 24.2	. . 18.5
R 10	286 33.4	318 48.6	32.5	332 49.5	29.7	178 18.7	41.7	286 26.5	18.4
I 11	301 35.9	333 48.0	31.5	347 49.9	29.2	193 21.5	41.8	301 28.7	18.3
D 12	316 38.3	348 47.4	S14 30.4	2 50.4	S18 28.7	208 24.2	N22 41.8	316 30.9	S 2 18.2
A 13	331 40.8	3 46.8	29.4	17 50.9	28.2	223 26.9	41.8	331 33.1	18.1
Y 14	346 43.3	18 46.2	28.4	32 51.4	27.6	238 29.6	41.9	346 35.4	18.0
15	1 45.7	33 45.6	. . 27.3	47 51.8	. . 27.1	253 32.4	. . 41.9	1 37.6	. . 17.9
16	16 48.2	48 45.0	26.3	62 52.3	26.5	268 35.1	41.9	16 39.8	17.7
17	31 50.6	63 44.5	25.2	77 52.8	26.0	283 37.8	42.0	31 42.1	17.6
18	46 53.1	78 43.9	S14 24.2	92 53.3	S18 25.5	298 40.6	N22 42.0	46 44.3	S 2 17.5
19	61 55.6	93 43.3	23.2	107 53.7	24.9	313 43.3	42.0	61 46.5	17.4
20	76 58.0	108 42.7	22.1	122 54.2	24.4	328 46.0	42.1	76 48.7	17.3
21	92 00.5	123 42.1	. . 21.1	137 54.7	. . 23.9	343 48.7	. . 42.1	91 51.0	. . 17.2
22	107 03.0	138 41.5	20.1	152 55.2	23.3	358 51.5	42.2	106 53.2	17.1
23	122 05.4	153 40.9	19.0	167 55.6	22.8	13 54.2	42.2	121 55.4	17.0
7 00	137 07.9	168 40.4	S14 18.0	182 56.1	S18 22.3	28 56.9	N22 42.2	136 57.6	S 2 16.9
01	152 10.4	183 39.8	16.9	197 56.6	21.7	43 59.7	42.3	151 59.9	16.8
02	167 12.8	198 39.2	15.9	212 57.1	21.2	59 02.4	42.3	167 02.1	16.7
03	182 15.3	213 38.6	. . 14.8	227 57.6	. . 20.6	74 05.1	. . 42.3	182 04.3	. . 16.6
04	197 17.8	228 38.0	13.8	242 58.0	20.1	89 07.8	42.4	197 06.6	16.5
05	212 20.2	243 37.4	12.7	257 58.5	19.6	104 10.6	42.4	212 08.8	16.3
06	227 22.7	258 36.9	S14 11.7	272 59.0	S18 19.0	119 13.3	N22 42.4	227 11.0	S 2 16.2
S 07	242 25.1	273 36.3	10.7	287 59.5	18.5	134 16.0	42.5	242 13.2	16.1
A 08	257 27.6	288 35.7	09.6	302 59.9	18.0	149 18.7	42.5	257 15.5	16.0
T 09	272 30.1	303 35.1	. . 08.6	318 00.4	. . 17.4	164 21.5	. . 42.5	272 17.7	. . 15.9
U 10	287 32.5	318 34.5	07.5	333 00.9	16.9	179 24.2	42.6	287 19.9	15.8
R 11	302 35.0	333 33.9	06.5	348 01.4	16.3	194 26.9	42.6	302 22.1	15.7
D 12	317 37.5	348 33.4	S14 05.4	3 01.9	S18 15.8	209 29.6	N22 42.6	317 24.4	S 2 15.6
A 13	332 39.9	3 32.8	04.4	18 02.3	15.2	224 32.4	42.7	332 26.6	15.5
Y 14	347 42.4	18 32.2	03.3	33 02.8	14.7	239 35.1	42.7	347 28.8	15.4
15	2 44.9	33 31.6	. . 02.3	48 03.3	. . 14.2	254 37.8	. . 42.7	2 31.0	. . 15.3
16	17 47.3	48 31.1	01.2	63 03.8	13.6	269 40.5	42.8	17 33.3	15.2
17	32 49.8	63 30.5	14 00.2	78 04.2	13.1	284 43.3	42.8	32 35.5	15.0
18	47 52.2	78 29.9	S13 59.1	93 04.7	S18 12.5	299 46.0	N22 42.8	47 37.7	S 2 14.9
19	62 54.7	93 29.3	58.0	108 05.2	12.0	314 48.7	42.9	62 39.9	14.8
20	77 57.2	108 28.8	57.0	123 05.7	11.4	329 51.4	42.9	77 42.2	14.7
21	92 59.6	123 28.2	. . 55.9	138 06.2	. . 10.9	344 54.1	. . 42.9	92 44.4	. . 14.6
22	108 02.1	138 27.6	54.9	153 06.6	10.4	359 56.9	43.0	107 46.6	14.5
23	123 04.6	153 27.0	53.8	168 07.1	09.8	14 59.6	43.0	122 48.8	14.4
8 00	138 07.0	168 26.5	S13 52.8	183 07.6	S18 09.3	30 02.3	N22 43.0	137 51.1	S 2 14.3
01	153 09.5	183 25.9	51.7	198 08.1	08.7	45 05.0	43.1	152 53.3	14.2
02	168 12.0	198 25.3	50.6	213 08.6	08.2	60 07.7	43.1	167 55.5	14.1
03	183 14.4	213 24.7	. . 49.6	228 09.0	. . 07.6	75 10.5	. . 43.1	182 57.7	. . 14.0
04	198 16.9	228 24.2	48.5	243 09.5	07.1	90 13.2	43.2	198 00.0	13.9
05	213 19.4	243 23.6	47.5	258 10.0	06.5	105 15.9	43.2	213 02.2	13.7
06	228 21.8	258 23.0	S13 46.4	273 10.5	S18 06.0	120 18.6	N22 43.2	228 04.4	S 2 13.6
07	243 24.3	273 22.5	45.3	288 11.0	05.4	135 21.3	43.3	243 06.6	13.5
08	258 26.7	288 21.9	44.3	303 11.5	04.9	150 24.1	43.3	258 08.9	13.4
S 09	273 29.2	303 21.3	. . 43.2	318 11.9	. . 04.3	165 26.8	. . 43.3	273 11.1	. . 13.3
U 10	288 31.7	318 20.8	42.2	333 12.4	03.8	180 29.5	43.4	288 13.3	13.2
N 11	303 34.1	333 20.2	41.1	348 12.9	03.2	195 32.2	43.4	303 15.5	13.1
D 12	318 36.6	348 19.6	S13 40.0	3 13.4	S18 02.7	210 34.9	N22 43.4	318 17.8	S 2 13.0
A 13	333 39.1	3 19.1	39.0	18 13.9	02.1	225 37.7	43.5	333 20.0	12.9
Y 14	348 41.5	18 18.5	37.9	33 14.3	01.6	240 40.4	43.5	348 22.2	12.8
15	3 44.0	33 17.9	. . 36.8	48 14.8	. . 01.0	255 43.1	. . 43.5	3 24.4	. . 12.7
16	18 46.5	48 17.4	35.8	63 15.3	18 00.5	270 45.8	43.6	18 26.7	12.5
17	33 48.9	63 16.8	34.7	78 15.8	17 59.9	285 48.5	43.6	33 28.9	12.4
18	48 51.4	78 16.2	S13 33.6	93 16.3	S17 59.4	300 51.2	N22 43.6	48 31.1	S 2 12.3
19	63 53.9	93 15.7	32.5	108 16.8	58.8	315 53.9	43.7	63 33.3	12.2
20	78 56.3	108 15.1	31.5	123 17.3	58.3	330 56.7	43.7	78 35.6	12.1
21	93 58.8	123 14.5	. . 30.4	138 17.7	. . 57.7	345 59.4	. . 43.7	93 37.8	. . 12.0
22	109 01.2	138 14.0	29.3	153 18.2	57.2	1 02.1	43.8	108 40.0	11.9
23	124 03.7	153 13.4	28.3	168 18.7	56.6	16 04.8	43.8	123 42.2	11.8
Mer. Pass.	h m 14 49.0	*v* −0.6	*d* 1.1	*v* 0.5	*d* 0.5	*v* 2.7	*d* 0.0	*v* 2.2	*d* 0.1

STARS Name	SHA	Dec
	° ′	° ′
Acamar	315 11.1	S40 12.2
Achernar	335 19.7	S57 06.5
Acrux	172 58.6	S63 14.5
Adhara	255 04.8	S29 00.6
Aldebaran	290 38.4	N16 33.7
Alioth	166 11.8	N55 48.7
Alkaid	152 51.1	N49 10.6
Alnair	27 32.2	S46 50.2
Alnilam	275 36.6	S 1 11.2
Alphard	217 46.5	S 8 46.4
Alphecca	126 03.0	N26 37.3
Alpheratz	357 34.1	N29 14.1
Altair	61 59.4	N 8 56.1
Ankaa	353 06.5	S42 10.0
Antares	112 14.9	S26 29.4
Arcturus	145 47.0	N19 02.5
Atria	107 08.5	S69 04.2
Avior	234 13.7	S59 35.7
Bellatrix	278 21.7	N 6 22.3
Betelgeuse	270 50.9	N 7 24.7
Canopus	263 51.6	S52 42.7
Capella	280 20.3	N46 01.6
Deneb	49 25.7	N45 22.3
Denebola	182 23.8	N14 25.4
Diphda	348 46.6	S17 50.7
Dubhe	193 39.3	N61 36.4
Elnath	278 00.5	N28 37.8
Eltanin	90 42.1	N51 28.8
Enif	33 38.2	N 9 59.6
Fomalhaut	15 13.8	S29 29.2
Gacrux	171 50.3	S57 15.4
Gienah	175 42.4	S17 41.3
Hadar	148 34.6	S60 29.7
Hamal	327 50.3	N23 35.2
Kaus Aust.	83 31.6	S34 22.3
Kochab	137 19.7	N74 02.4
Markab	13 29.3	N15 20.7
Menkar	314 05.2	N 4 11.5
Menkent	147 56.4	S36 29.8
Miaplacidus	221 37.2	S69 49.5
Mirfak	308 26.9	N49 57.4
Nunki	75 46.9	S26 15.9
Peacock	53 04.9	S56 39.0
Pollux	243 15.8	N27 57.7
Procyon	244 49.6	N 5 09.4
Rasalhague	95 57.9	N12 32.3
Regulus	207 33.1	N11 50.2
Rigel	281 02.8	S 8 10.4
Rigil Kent.	139 38.9	S60 56.4
Sabik	102 01.9	S15 45.5
Schedar	349 30.4	N56 41.0
Shaula	96 09.4	S37 07.3
Sirius	258 25.2	S16 45.2
Spica	158 21.2	S11 17.9
Suhail	222 45.2	S43 32.3
Vega	80 32.9	N38 48.2
Zuben'ubi	136 55.0	S16 09.1

	SHA	Mer. Pass.
	° ′	h m
Venus	31 32.5	12 46
Mars	45 48.2	11 48
Jupiter	251 49.0	22 00
Saturn	359 49.8	14 50

UT	SUN GHA	SUN Dec	MOON GHA	v	MOON Dec	d	HP
d h	° ′	° ′	° ′	′	° ′	′	′
6 00	176 30.1	S15 40.9	310 05.1	15.3	S 5 21.9	14.8	56.0
01	191 30.1	40.1	324 39.4	15.4	5 36.7	14.8	56.0
02	206 30.1	39.3	339 13.8	15.3	5 51.5	14.8	56.0
03	221 30.0	. . 38.6	353 48.1	15.4	6 06.3	14.7	56.0
04	236 30.0	37.8	8 22.5	15.3	6 21.0	14.7	55.9
05	251 29.9	37.0	22 56.8	15.4	6 35.7	14.6	55.9
06	266 29.9	S15 36.3	37 31.2	15.3	S 6 50.3	14.6	55.9
07	281 29.8	35.5	52 05.5	15.4	7 04.9	14.5	55.8
08	296 29.8	34.7	66 39.9	15.4	7 19.4	14.5	55.8
F 09	311 29.8	. . 33.9	81 14.3	15.3	7 33.9	14.5	55.8
R 10	326 29.7	33.2	95 48.6	15.4	7 48.4	14.4	55.8
I 11	341 29.7	32.4	110 23.0	15.3	8 02.8	14.3	55.7
D 12	356 29.6	S15 31.6	124 57.3	15.4	S 8 17.1	14.3	55.7
A 13	11 29.6	30.9	139 31.7	15.3	8 31.4	14.3	55.7
Y 14	26 29.6	30.1	154 06.0	15.4	8 45.7	14.2	55.6
15	41 29.5	. . 29.3	168 40.4	15.3	8 59.9	14.2	55.6
16	56 29.5	28.5	183 14.7	15.3	9 14.1	14.1	55.6
17	71 29.5	27.8	197 49.0	15.4	9 28.2	14.0	55.6
18	86 29.4	S15 27.0	212 23.4	15.3	S 9 42.2	14.1	55.5
19	101 29.4	26.2	226 57.7	15.3	9 56.3	13.9	55.5
20	116 29.3	25.4	241 32.0	15.2	10 10.2	13.9	55.5
21	131 29.3	. . 24.6	256 06.2	15.3	10 24.1	13.8	55.5
22	146 29.3	23.9	270 40.5	15.3	10 37.9	13.8	55.4
23	161 29.2	23.1	285 14.8	15.2	10 51.7	13.8	55.4
7 00	176 29.2	S15 22.3	299 49.0	15.2	S11 05.5	13.6	55.4
01	191 29.2	21.5	314 23.2	15.3	11 19.1	13.6	55.4
02	206 29.1	20.8	328 57.5	15.2	11 32.7	13.6	55.3
03	221 29.1	. . 20.0	343 31.7	15.1	11 46.3	13.5	55.3
04	236 29.1	19.2	358 05.8	15.2	11 59.8	13.4	55.3
05	251 29.0	18.4	12 40.0	15.1	12 13.2	13.4	55.3
06	266 29.0	S15 17.6	27 14.1	15.1	S12 26.6	13.3	55.2
07	281 29.0	16.8	41 48.2	15.1	12 39.9	13.3	55.2
S 08	296 28.9	16.1	56 22.3	15.1	12 53.2	13.2	55.2
A 09	311 28.9	. . 15.3	70 56.4	15.0	13 06.4	13.1	55.2
T 10	326 28.9	14.5	85 30.4	15.0	13 19.5	13.0	55.1
U 11	341 28.8	13.7	100 04.4	15.0	13 32.5	13.0	55.1
R 12	356 28.8	S15 12.9	114 38.4	15.0	S13 45.5	13.0	55.1
D 13	11 28.8	12.1	129 12.4	14.9	13 58.5	12.8	55.1
A 14	26 28.7	11.4	143 46.3	14.9	14 11.3	12.8	55.0
Y 15	41 28.7	. . 10.6	158 20.2	14.9	14 24.1	12.7	55.0
16	56 28.7	09.8	172 54.1	14.8	14 36.8	12.7	55.0
17	71 28.7	09.0	187 27.9	14.8	14 49.5	12.6	55.0
18	86 28.6	S15 08.2	202 01.7	14.8	S15 02.1	12.5	55.0
19	101 28.6	07.4	216 35.5	14.8	15 14.6	12.5	54.9
20	116 28.6	06.6	231 09.3	14.7	15 27.1	12.3	54.9
21	131 28.5	. . 05.9	245 43.0	14.6	15 39.4	12.3	54.9
22	146 28.5	05.1	260 16.6	14.7	15 51.7	12.3	54.9
23	161 28.5	04.3	274 50.3	14.6	16 04.0	12.1	54.9
8 00	176 28.5	S15 03.5	289 23.9	14.6	S16 16.1	12.1	54.8
01	191 28.4	02.7	303 57.5	14.5	16 28.2	12.0	54.8
02	206 28.4	01.9	318 31.0	14.5	16 40.2	11.9	54.8
03	221 28.4	. . 01.1	333 04.5	14.4	16 52.1	11.9	54.8
04	236 28.4	15 00.3	347 37.9	14.4	17 04.0	11.8	54.8
05	251 28.3	14 59.5	2 11.3	14.4	17 15.8	11.7	54.7
06	266 28.3	S14 58.7	16 44.7	14.3	S17 27.5	11.6	54.7
07	281 28.3	58.0	31 18.0	14.3	17 39.1	11.5	54.7
08	296 28.3	57.2	45 51.3	14.2	17 50.6	11.5	54.7
S 09	311 28.2	. . 56.4	60 24.5	14.2	18 02.1	11.4	54.7
U 10	326 28.2	55.6	74 57.7	14.2	18 13.5	11.3	54.7
N 11	341 28.2	54.8	89 30.9	14.1	18 24.8	11.2	54.6
D 12	356 28.2	S14 54.0	104 04.0	14.0	S18 36.0	11.1	54.6
A 13	11 28.1	53.2	118 37.0	14.1	18 47.1	11.1	54.6
Y 14	26 28.1	52.4	133 10.1	13.9	18 58.2	10.9	54.6
15	41 28.1	. . 51.6	147 43.0	13.9	19 09.1	10.9	54.6
16	56 28.1	50.8	162 15.9	13.9	19 20.0	10.8	54.6
17	71 28.1	50.0	176 48.8	13.8	19 30.8	10.7	54.5
18	86 28.0	S14 49.2	191 21.6	13.8	S19 41.5	10.6	54.5
19	101 28.0	48.4	205 54.4	13.7	19 52.1	10.6	54.5
20	116 28.0	47.6	220 27.1	13.7	20 02.7	10.4	54.5
21	131 28.0	. . 46.8	234 59.8	13.6	20 13.1	10.4	54.5
22	146 28.0	46.0	249 32.4	13.6	20 23.5	10.3	54.5
23	161 27.9	45.2	264 05.0	13.5	S20 33.8	10.1	54.5
	SD 16.2	*d* 0.8	SD 15.2		15.0		14.9

Lat.	Twilight Naut.	Twilight Civil	Sunrise	Moonrise 6	Moonrise 7	Moonrise 8	Moonrise 9
°	h m	h m	h m	h m	h m	h m	h m
N 72	06 47	08 11	09 43	24 34	00 34	03 33	▬
N 70	06 42	07 57	09 13	24 14	00 14	02 33	▬
68	06 37	07 45	08 52	23 58	25 59	01 59	04 50
66	06 33	07 35	08 35	23 45	25 34	01 34	03 40
64	06 30	07 27	08 21	23 35	25 16	01 16	03 04
62	06 27	07 20	08 09	23 26	25 00	01 00	02 39
60	06 24	07 13	07 59	23 19	24 48	00 48	02 19
N 58	06 21	07 08	07 50	23 12	24 37	00 37	02 03
56	06 19	07 03	07 43	23 06	24 27	00 27	01 49
54	06 16	06 58	07 36	23 01	24 19	00 19	01 37
52	06 14	06 54	07 30	22 56	24 11	00 11	01 26
50	06 12	06 50	07 24	22 52	24 05	00 05	01 17
45	06 07	06 42	07 12	22 43	23 50	24 58	00 58
N 40	06 02	06 34	07 02	22 36	23 39	24 42	00 42
35	05 58	06 28	06 54	22 29	23 29	24 29	00 29
30	05 53	06 22	06 46	22 24	23 20	24 17	00 17
20	05 44	06 10	06 33	22 14	23 05	23 58	24 51
N 10	05 35	06 00	06 22	22 05	22 52	23 41	24 30
0	05 24	05 49	06 11	21 58	22 40	23 25	24 11
S 10	05 12	05 38	05 59	21 50	22 29	23 09	23 52
20	04 57	05 24	05 48	21 42	22 16	22 53	23 32
30	04 38	05 08	05 34	21 32	22 02	22 34	23 09
35	04 26	04 58	05 26	21 27	21 53	22 22	22 56
40	04 11	04 47	05 16	21 21	21 44	22 10	22 40
45	03 53	04 33	05 05	21 14	21 33	21 55	22 22
S 50	03 28	04 15	04 52	21 06	21 20	21 37	21 59
52	03 16	04 07	04 46	21 02	21 14	21 29	21 48
54	03 02	03 57	04 39	20 58	21 07	21 19	21 36
56	02 45	03 47	04 31	20 53	21 00	21 09	21 22
58	02 23	03 34	04 23	20 48	20 51	20 56	21 05
S 60	01 54	03 19	04 13	20 42	20 42	20 43	20 45

Lat.	Sunset	Twilight Civil	Twilight Naut.	Moonset 6	Moonset 7	Moonset 8	Moonset 9
°	h m	h m	h m	h m	h m	h m	h m
N 72	14 47	16 18	17 43	07 59	07 15	05 48	▬
N 70	15 16	16 33	17 48	08 09	07 38	06 49	▬
68	15 38	16 44	17 52	08 18	07 55	07 24	06 07
66	15 55	16 54	17 56	08 25	08 09	07 50	07 18
64	16 08	17 02	18 00	08 31	08 21	08 10	07 54
62	16 20	17 09	18 03	08 36	08 31	08 26	08 21
60	16 30	17 16	18 05	08 41	08 40	08 40	08 41
N 58	16 39	17 21	18 08	08 45	08 48	08 52	08 58
56	16 46	17 26	18 10	08 49	08 55	09 02	09 13
54	16 53	17 31	18 13	08 52	09 01	09 11	09 25
52	16 59	17 35	18 15	08 55	09 06	09 19	09 36
50	17 04	17 39	18 17	08 58	09 11	09 27	09 46
45	17 16	17 47	18 22	09 04	09 22	09 42	10 06
N 40	17 26	17 54	18 27	09 09	09 31	09 55	10 23
35	17 35	18 01	18 31	09 13	09 39	10 06	10 37
30	17 42	18 07	18 35	09 17	09 46	10 16	10 50
20	17 55	18 18	18 44	09 24	09 58	10 33	11 11
N 10	18 07	18 28	18 53	09 30	10 08	10 48	11 30
0	18 18	18 39	19 04	09 36	10 18	11 02	11 47
S 10	18 29	18 50	19 16	09 41	10 28	11 15	12 04
20	18 40	19 03	19 31	09 47	10 39	11 30	12 23
30	18 54	19 19	19 50	09 54	10 51	11 48	12 45
35	19 02	19 29	20 02	09 58	10 58	11 58	12 57
40	19 11	19 40	20 16	10 03	11 06	12 09	13 12
45	19 22	19 54	20 34	10 08	11 16	12 23	13 30
S 50	19 35	20 12	20 58	10 14	11 27	12 40	13 52
52	19 41	20 20	21 10	10 17	11 32	12 47	14 02
54	19 48	20 29	21 24	10 21	11 38	12 56	14 14
56	19 55	20 40	21 41	10 24	11 45	13 06	14 28
58	20 04	20 52	22 02	10 28	11 52	13 18	14 44
S 60	20 13	21 07	22 29	10 33	12 01	13 31	15 03

Day	SUN Eqn. of Time 00^h	SUN Eqn. of Time 12^h	SUN Mer. Pass.	MOON Mer. Pass. Upper	MOON Mer. Pass. Lower	MOON Age	MOON Phase
d	m s	m s	h m	h m	h m	d	%
6	13 59	14 01	12 14	03 26	15 47	19	78
7	14 03	14 05	12 14	04 08	16 29	20	69
8	14 06	14 07	12 14	04 51	17 13	21	60

Day	UT d h	ARIES GHA ° ′	VENUS −3·9 GHA ° ′	VENUS Dec ° ′	MARS +1·1 GHA ° ′	MARS Dec ° ′	JUPITER −2·6 GHA ° ′	JUPITER Dec ° ′	SATURN +1·0 GHA ° ′	SATURN Dec ° ′
MONDAY	9 00	139 06.2	168 12.9	S13 27.2	183 19.2	S17 56.1	31 07.5	N22 43.8	138 44.4	S 2 11.7
	01	154 08.6	183 12.3	26.1	198 19.7	55.5	46 10.2	43.9	153 46.7	11.6
	02	169 11.1	198 11.7	25.0	213 20.2	55.0	61 12.9	43.9	168 48.9	11.5
	03	184 13.6	213 11.2	. . 24.0	228 20.6	. . 54.4	76 15.7	. . 43.9	183 51.1	. . 11.3
	04	199 16.0	228 10.6	22.9	243 21.1	53.9	91 18.4	44.0	198 53.3	11.2
	05	214 18.5	243 10.1	21.8	258 21.6	53.3	106 21.1	44.0	213 55.6	11.1
	06	229 21.0	258 09.5	S13 20.7	273 22.1	S17 52.7	121 23.8	N22 44.0	228 57.8	S 2 11.0
	07	244 23.4	273 08.9	19.7	288 22.6	52.2	136 26.5	44.0	244 00.0	10.9
	08	259 25.9	288 08.4	18.6	303 23.1	51.6	151 29.2	44.1	259 02.2	10.8
	09	274 28.3	303 07.8	. . 17.5	318 23.6	. . 51.1	166 31.9	. . 44.1	274 04.4	. . 10.7
	10	289 30.8	318 07.3	16.4	333 24.0	50.5	181 34.6	44.1	289 06.7	10.6
	11	304 33.3	333 06.7	15.3	348 24.5	50.0	196 37.4	44.2	304 08.9	10.5
	12	319 35.7	348 06.2	S13 14.3	3 25.0	S17 49.4	211 40.1	N22 44.2	319 11.1	S 2 10.4
	13	334 38.2	3 05.6	13.2	18 25.5	48.9	226 42.8	44.2	334 13.3	10.2
	14	349 40.7	18 05.1	12.1	33 26.0	48.3	241 45.5	44.3	349 15.6	10.1
	15	4 43.1	33 04.5	. . 11.0	48 26.5	. . 47.7	256 48.2	. . 44.3	4 17.8	. . 10.0
	16	19 45.6	48 03.9	09.9	63 27.0	47.2	271 50.9	44.3	19 20.0	09.9
	17	34 48.1	63 03.4	08.8	78 27.5	46.6	286 53.6	44.4	34 22.2	09.8
	18	49 50.5	78 02.8	S13 07.8	93 27.9	S17 46.1	301 56.3	N22 44.4	49 24.4	S 2 09.7
	19	64 53.0	93 02.3	06.7	108 28.4	45.5	316 59.0	44.4	64 26.7	09.6
	20	79 55.5	108 01.7	05.6	123 28.9	44.9	332 01.7	44.5	79 28.9	09.5
	21	94 57.9	123 01.2	. . 04.5	138 29.4	. . 44.4	347 04.4	. . 44.5	94 31.1	. . 09.4
	22	110 00.4	138 00.6	03.4	153 29.9	43.8	2 07.2	44.5	109 33.3	09.3
	23	125 02.8	153 00.1	02.3	168 30.4	43.3	17 09.9	44.6	124 35.6	09.1
TUESDAY	10 00	140 05.3	167 59.5	S13 01.2	183 30.9	S17 42.7	32 12.6	N22 44.6	139 37.8	S 2 09.0
	01	155 07.8	182 59.0	13 00.2	198 31.4	42.1	47 15.3	44.6	154 40.0	08.9
	02	170 10.2	197 58.4	12 59.1	213 31.8	41.6	62 18.0	44.6	169 42.2	08.8
	03	185 12.7	212 57.9	. . 58.0	228 32.3	. . 41.0	77 20.7	. . 44.7	184 44.4	. . 08.7
	04	200 15.2	227 57.3	56.9	243 32.8	40.4	92 23.4	44.7	199 46.7	08.6
	05	215 17.6	242 56.8	55.8	258 33.3	39.9	107 26.1	44.7	214 48.9	08.5
	06	230 20.1	257 56.2	S12 54.7	273 33.8	S17 39.3	122 28.8	N22 44.8	229 51.1	S 2 08.4
	07	245 22.6	272 55.7	53.6	288 34.3	38.8	137 31.5	44.8	244 53.3	08.3
	08	260 25.0	287 55.2	52.5	303 34.8	38.2	152 34.2	44.8	259 55.5	08.2
	09	275 27.5	302 54.6	. . 51.4	318 35.3	. . 37.6	167 36.9	. . 44.9	274 57.8	. . 08.0
	10	290 30.0	317 54.1	50.3	333 35.8	37.1	182 39.6	44.9	290 00.0	07.9
	11	305 32.4	332 53.5	49.2	348 36.3	36.5	197 42.3	44.9	305 02.2	07.8
	12	320 34.9	347 53.0	S12 48.1	3 36.7	S17 35.9	212 45.0	N22 45.0	320 04.4	S 2 07.7
	13	335 37.3	2 52.4	47.0	18 37.2	35.4	227 47.7	45.0	335 06.6	07.6
	14	350 39.8	17 51.9	45.9	33 37.7	34.8	242 50.4	45.0	350 08.9	07.5
	15	5 42.3	32 51.3	. . 44.8	48 38.2	. . 34.2	257 53.1	. . 45.1	5 11.1	. . 07.4
	16	20 44.7	47 50.8	43.7	63 38.7	33.7	272 55.8	45.1	20 13.3	07.3
	17	35 47.2	62 50.3	42.6	78 39.2	33.1	287 58.5	45.1	35 15.5	07.2
	18	50 49.7	77 49.7	S12 41.5	93 39.7	S17 32.5	303 01.2	N22 45.1	50 17.7	S 2 07.0
	19	65 52.1	92 49.2	40.4	108 40.2	32.0	318 04.0	45.2	65 20.0	06.9
	20	80 54.6	107 48.6	39.3	123 40.7	31.4	333 06.7	45.2	80 22.2	06.8
	21	95 57.1	122 48.1	. . 38.2	138 41.2	. . 30.8	348 09.4	. . 45.2	95 24.4	. . 06.7
	22	110 59.5	137 47.6	37.1	153 41.7	30.3	3 12.1	45.3	110 26.6	06.6
	23	126 02.0	152 47.0	36.0	168 42.2	29.7	18 14.8	45.3	125 28.8	06.5
WEDNESDAY	11 00	141 04.4	167 46.5	S12 34.9	183 42.7	S17 29.1	33 17.5	N22 45.3	140 31.1	S 2 06.4
	01	156 06.9	182 45.9	33.8	198 43.1	28.6	48 20.2	45.4	155 33.3	06.3
	02	171 09.4	197 45.4	32.7	213 43.6	28.0	63 22.9	45.4	170 35.5	06.2
	03	186 11.8	212 44.9	. . 31.6	228 44.1	. . 27.4	78 25.6	. . 45.4	185 37.7	. . 06.0
	04	201 14.3	227 44.3	30.5	243 44.6	26.8	93 28.3	45.4	200 39.9	05.9
	05	216 16.8	242 43.8	29.4	258 45.1	26.3	108 30.9	45.5	215 42.1	05.8
	06	231 19.2	257 43.3	S12 28.3	273 45.6	S17 25.7	123 33.6	N22 45.5	230 44.4	S 2 05.7
	07	246 21.7	272 42.7	27.2	288 46.1	25.1	138 36.3	45.5	245 46.6	05.6
	08	261 24.2	287 42.2	26.1	303 46.6	24.6	153 39.0	45.6	260 48.8	05.5
	09	276 26.6	302 41.7	. . 25.0	318 47.1	. . 24.0	168 41.7	. . 45.6	275 51.0	. . 05.4
	10	291 29.1	317 41.1	23.9	333 47.6	23.4	183 44.4	45.6	290 53.2	05.3
	11	306 31.6	332 40.6	22.8	348 48.1	22.8	198 47.1	45.7	305 55.5	05.2
	12	321 34.0	347 40.1	S12 21.7	3 48.6	S17 22.3	213 49.8	N22 45.7	320 57.7	S 2 05.0
	13	336 36.5	2 39.5	20.6	18 49.1	21.7	228 52.5	45.7	335 59.9	04.9
	14	351 38.9	17 39.0	19.4	33 49.6	21.1	243 55.2	45.7	351 02.1	04.8
	15	6 41.4	32 38.5	. . 18.3	48 50.1	. . 20.5	258 57.9	. . 45.8	6 04.3	. . 04.7
	16	21 43.9	47 37.9	17.2	63 50.6	20.0	274 00.6	45.8	21 06.5	04.6
	17	36 46.3	62 37.4	16.1	78 51.1	19.4	289 03.3	45.8	36 08.8	04.5
	18	51 48.8	77 36.9	S12 15.0	93 51.6	S17 18.8	304 06.0	N22 45.9	51 11.0	S 2 04.4
	19	66 51.3	92 36.3	13.9	108 52.0	18.2	319 08.7	45.9	66 13.2	04.3
	20	81 53.7	107 35.8	12.8	123 52.5	17.7	334 11.4	45.9	81 15.4	04.2
	21	96 56.2	122 35.3	. . 11.7	138 53.0	. . 17.1	349 14.1	. . 46.0	96 17.6	. . 04.0
	22	111 58.7	137 34.8	10.5	153 53.5	16.5	4 16.8	46.0	111 19.8	03.9
	23	127 01.1	152 34.2	09.4	168 54.0	15.9	19 19.5	46.0	126 22.1	03.8
	Mer. Pass. (h m)	14 37.2	v −0.5	d 1.1	v 0.5	d 0.6	v 2.7	d 0.0	v 2.2	d 0.1

STARS

Name	SHA ° ′	Dec ° ′
Acamar	315 11.1	S40 12.2
Achernar	335 19.7	S57 06.5
Acrux	172 58.6	S63 14.5
Adhara	255 04.8	S29 00.6
Aldebaran	290 38.4	N16 33.7
Alioth	166 11.8	N55 48.7
Alkaid	152 51.1	N49 10.6
Alnair	27 32.2	S46 50.2
Alnilam	275 36.6	S 1 11.2
Alphard	217 46.5	S 8 46.4
Alphecca	126 03.0	N26 37.3
Alpheratz	357 34.1	N29 14.1
Altair	61 59.4	N 8 56.1
Ankaa	353 06.5	S42 10.0
Antares	112 14.8	S26 29.4
Arcturus	145 47.0	N19 02.5
Atria	107 08.5	S69 04.2
Avior	234 13.8	S59 35.7
Bellatrix	278 21.7	N 6 22.3
Betelgeuse	270 50.9	N 7 24.7
Canopus	263 51.6	S52 42.8
Capella	280 20.3	N46 01.6
Deneb	49 25.6	N45 22.3
Denebola	182 23.7	N14 25.4
Diphda	348 46.6	S17 50.7
Dubhe	193 39.3	N61 36.4
Elnath	278 00.5	N28 37.8
Eltanin	90 42.1	N51 28.8
Enif	33 38.2	N 9 59.6
Fomalhaut	15 13.8	S29 29.2
Gacrux	171 50.2	S57 15.5
Gienah	175 42.4	S17 41.3
Hadar	148 34.5	S60 29.7
Hamal	327 50.3	N23 35.2
Kaus Aust.	83 31.6	S34 22.3
Kochab	137 19.7	N74 02.4
Markab	13 29.3	N15 20.7
Menkar	314 05.2	N 4 11.5
Menkent	147 56.4	S36 29.8
Miaplacidus	221 37.2	S69 49.5
Mirfak	308 26.9	N49 57.4
Nunki	75 46.9	S26 15.9
Peacock	53 04.9	S56 39.0
Pollux	243 15.8	N27 57.7
Procyon	244 49.6	N 5 09.4
Rasalhague	95 57.9	N12 32.3
Regulus	207 33.1	N11 50.2
Rigel	281 02.8	S 8 10.4
Rigil Kent.	139 38.9	S60 56.4
Sabik	102 01.9	S15 45.5
Schedar	349 30.4	N56 41.0
Shaula	96 09.4	S37 07.3
Sirius	258 25.2	S16 45.3
Spica	158 21.2	S11 18.0
Suhail	222 45.2	S43 32.4
Vega	80 32.9	N38 48.2
Zuben'ubi	136 55.0	S16 09.1

	SHA ° ′	Mer. Pass. h m
Venus	27 54.2	12 48
Mars	43 25.6	11 46
Jupiter	252 07.3	21 47
Saturn	359 32.5	14 39

UT	SUN GHA	SUN Dec	MOON GHA	v	MOON Dec	d	HP
d h	° ′	° ′	° ′	′	° ′	′	′
9 00	176 27.9	S14 44.4	278 37.5	13.4	S20 43.9	10.1	54.5
01	191 27.9	43.6	293 09.9	13.5	20 54.0	10.0	54.4
02	206 27.9	42.8	307 42.4	13.3	21 04.0	9.9	54.4
03	221 27.9	. . 42.0	322 14.7	13.3	21 13.9	9.8	54.4
04	236 27.8	41.2	336 47.0	13.3	21 23.7	9.7	54.4
05	251 27.8	40.4	351 19.3	13.2	21 33.4	9.6	54.4
06	266 27.8	S14 39.6	5 51.5	13.1	S21 43.0	9.6	54.4
07	281 27.8	38.8	20 23.6	13.1	21 52.6	9.4	54.4
08	296 27.8	38.0	34 55.7	13.0	22 02.0	9.3	54.4
M 09	311 27.8	. . 37.2	49 27.7	13.0	22 11.3	9.2	54.4
O 10	326 27.7	36.4	63 59.7	12.9	22 20.5	9.2	54.3
N 11	341 27.7	35.6	78 31.6	12.8	22 29.7	9.0	54.3
D 12	356 27.7	S14 34.8	93 03.4	12.8	S22 38.7	8.9	54.3
A 13	11 27.7	34.0	107 35.2	12.8	22 47.6	8.9	54.3
Y 14	26 27.7	33.2	122 07.0	12.7	22 56.5	8.7	54.3
15	41 27.7	. . 32.4	136 38.7	12.6	23 05.2	8.6	54.3
16	56 27.7	31.6	151 10.3	12.6	23 13.8	8.6	54.3
17	71 27.6	30.7	165 41.9	12.5	23 22.4	8.4	54.3
18	86 27.6	S14 29.9	180 13.4	12.5	S23 30.8	8.3	54.3
19	101 27.6	29.1	194 44.9	12.4	23 39.1	8.2	54.3
20	116 27.6	28.3	209 16.3	12.3	23 47.3	8.1	54.3
21	131 27.6	. . 27.5	223 47.6	12.3	23 55.4	8.0	54.3
22	146 27.6	26.7	238 18.9	12.2	24 03.4	7.9	54.3
23	161 27.6	25.9	252 50.1	12.2	24 11.3	7.8	54.2
10 00	176 27.6	S14 25.1	267 21.3	12.1	S24 19.1	7.7	54.2
01	191 27.5	24.3	281 52.4	12.0	24 26.8	7.5	54.2
02	206 27.5	23.5	296 23.4	12.0	24 34.3	7.5	54.2
03	221 27.5	. . 22.6	310 54.4	12.0	24 41.8	7.4	54.2
04	236 27.5	21.8	325 25.4	11.8	24 49.2	7.2	54.2
05	251 27.5	21.0	339 56.2	11.8	24 56.4	7.1	54.2
06	266 27.5	S14 20.2	354 27.0	11.8	S25 03.5	7.0	54.2
07	281 27.5	19.4	8 57.8	11.7	25 10.5	6.9	54.2
T 08	296 27.5	18.6	23 28.5	11.7	25 17.4	6.8	54.2
U 09	311 27.5	. . 17.8	37 59.2	11.5	25 24.2	6.7	54.2
E 10	326 27.5	17.0	52 29.7	11.6	25 30.9	6.5	54.2
S 11	341 27.5	16.1	67 00.3	11.4	25 37.4	6.5	54.2
D 12	356 27.5	S14 15.3	81 30.7	11.5	S25 43.9	6.3	54.2
A 13	11 27.4	14.5	96 01.2	11.3	25 50.2	6.2	54.2
Y 14	26 27.4	13.7	110 31.5	11.3	25 56.4	6.1	54.2
15	41 27.4	. . 12.9	125 01.8	11.3	26 02.5	6.0	54.2
16	56 27.4	12.1	139 32.1	11.2	26 08.5	5.8	54.2
17	71 27.4	11.2	154 02.3	11.1	26 14.3	5.7	54.2
18	86 27.4	S14 10.4	168 32.4	11.1	S26 20.0	5.6	54.2
19	101 27.4	09.6	183 02.5	11.0	26 25.6	5.5	54.2
20	116 27.4	08.8	197 32.5	11.0	26 31.1	5.4	54.2
21	131 27.4	. . 08.0	212 02.5	10.9	26 36.5	5.2	54.2
22	146 27.4	07.2	226 32.4	10.9	26 41.7	5.1	54.2
23	161 27.4	06.3	241 02.3	10.8	26 46.8	5.0	54.2
11 00	176 27.4	S14 05.5	255 32.1	10.8	S26 51.8	4.9	54.2
01	191 27.4	04.7	270 01.9	10.7	26 56.7	4.7	54.2
02	206 27.4	03.9	284 31.6	10.7	27 01.4	4.7	54.2
03	221 27.4	. . 03.0	299 01.3	10.6	27 06.1	4.5	54.2
04	236 27.4	02.2	313 30.9	10.5	27 10.6	4.3	54.2
05	251 27.4	01.4	328 00.4	10.6	27 14.9	4.3	54.2
06	266 27.4	S14 00.6	342 30.0	10.4	S27 19.2	4.1	54.2
W 07	281 27.4	13 59.8	356 59.4	10.4	27 23.3	3.9	54.2
E 08	296 27.4	58.9	11 28.8	10.4	27 27.2	3.9	54.2
D 09	311 27.4	. . 58.1	25 58.2	10.3	27 31.1	3.7	54.2
N 10	326 27.4	57.3	40 27.5	10.3	27 34.8	3.6	54.2
E 11	341 27.4	56.5	54 56.8	10.3	27 38.4	3.5	54.2
S 12	356 27.4	S13 55.6	69 26.1	10.2	S27 41.9	3.3	54.3
D 13	11 27.4	54.8	83 55.3	10.1	27 45.2	3.2	54.3
A 14	26 27.4	54.0	98 24.4	10.1	27 48.4	3.0	54.3
Y 15	41 27.4	. . 53.2	112 53.5	10.1	27 51.4	3.0	54.3
16	56 27.4	52.3	127 22.6	10.0	27 54.4	2.8	54.3
17	71 27.4	51.5	141 51.6	10.0	27 57.2	2.6	54.3
18	86 27.4	S13 50.7	156 20.6	10.0	S27 59.8	2.6	54.3
19	101 27.4	49.9	170 49.6	9.9	28 02.4	2.4	54.3
20	116 27.4	49.0	185 18.5	9.9	28 04.8	2.2	54.3
21	131 27.4	. . 48.2	199 47.4	9.8	28 07.0	2.1	54.3
22	146 27.4	47.4	214 16.2	9.8	28 09.1	2.0	54.3
23	161 27.4	46.5	228 45.0	9.8	S28 11.1	1.9	54.3
	SD 16.2	d 0.8	SD	14.8	14.8		14.8

Lat.	Twilight Naut.	Twilight Civil	Sunrise	Moonrise 9	Moonrise 10	Moonrise 11	Moonrise 12
°	h m	h m	h m	h m	h m	h m	h m
N 72	06 35	07 58	09 24	■	■	■	■
N 70	06 31	07 45	08 58	■	■	■	■
68	06 28	07 35	08 39	04 50	■	■	■
66	06 25	07 26	08 24	03 40	■	■	■
64	06 22	07 19	08 11	03 04	05 15	■	■
62	06 20	07 12	08 01	02 39	04 23	06 21	■
60	06 17	07 07	07 51	02 19	03 52	05 24	06 40
N 58	06 15	07 01	07 44	02 03	03 29	04 51	06 00
56	06 13	06 57	07 36	01 49	03 10	04 27	05 32
54	06 11	06 53	07 30	01 37	02 54	04 07	05 11
52	06 09	06 49	07 25	01 26	02 40	03 51	04 53
50	06 07	06 46	07 19	01 17	02 29	03 37	04 38
45	06 03	06 38	07 08	00 58	02 04	03 08	04 07
N 40	05 59	06 31	06 59	00 42	01 45	02 46	03 43
35	05 55	06 25	06 51	00 29	01 28	02 27	03 23
30	05 51	06 19	06 44	00 17	01 14	02 11	03 07
20	05 43	06 09	06 32	24 51	00 51	01 45	02 38
N 10	05 34	05 59	06 21	24 30	00 30	01 22	02 14
0	05 25	05 49	06 11	24 11	00 11	01 00	01 51
S 10	05 13	05 39	06 00	23 52	24 39	00 39	01 29
20	04 59	05 26	05 49	23 32	24 16	00 16	01 05
30	04 41	05 11	05 36	23 09	23 50	24 37	00 37
35	04 29	05 02	05 29	22 56	23 35	24 20	00 20
40	04 15	04 51	05 20	22 40	23 17	24 01	00 01
45	03 58	04 38	05 10	22 22	22 55	23 37	24 29
S 50	03 35	04 21	04 58	21 59	22 28	23 07	23 59
52	03 24	04 13	04 52	21 48	22 15	22 52	23 44
54	03 11	04 05	04 45	21 36	22 00	22 35	23 26
56	02 55	03 54	04 38	21 22	21 42	22 15	23 05
58	02 36	03 43	04 30	21 05	21 20	21 48	22 38
S 60	02 11	03 29	04 21	20 45	20 53	21 12	22 00

Lat.	Sunset	Twilight Civil	Twilight Naut.	Moonset 9	Moonset 10	Moonset 11	Moonset 12
°	h m	h m	h m	h m	h m	h m	h m
N 72	15 06	16 32	17 55	■	■	■	■
N 70	15 31	16 45	17 59	■	■	■	■
68	15 51	16 55	18 02	06 07	■	■	■
66	16 06	17 04	18 05	07 18	■	■	■
64	16 18	17 11	18 08	07 54	07 22	■	■
62	16 29	17 17	18 10	08 21	08 13	07 59	■
60	16 38	17 23	18 12	08 41	08 45	08 56	09 27
N 58	16 46	17 28	18 14	08 58	09 09	09 29	10 07
56	16 53	17 32	18 16	09 13	09 28	09 54	10 35
54	16 59	17 36	18 18	09 25	09 45	10 14	10 56
52	17 05	17 40	18 20	09 36	09 59	10 30	11 14
50	17 10	17 44	18 22	09 46	10 11	10 45	11 30
45	17 21	17 51	18 26	10 06	10 36	11 14	12 01
N 40	17 30	17 58	18 30	10 23	10 56	11 36	12 24
35	17 38	18 04	18 34	10 37	11 13	11 55	12 44
30	17 45	18 09	18 38	10 50	11 28	12 12	13 01
20	17 57	18 19	18 46	11 11	11 53	12 39	13 29
N 10	18 07	18 29	18 54	11 30	12 14	13 03	13 54
0	18 18	18 39	19 04	11 47	12 35	13 25	14 17
S 10	18 28	18 50	19 15	12 04	12 55	13 47	14 39
20	18 39	19 02	19 29	12 23	13 17	14 11	15 04
30	18 52	19 17	19 47	12 45	13 42	14 38	15 32
35	18 59	19 26	19 58	12 57	13 57	14 55	15 49
40	19 08	19 37	20 12	13 12	14 14	15 14	16 08
45	19 18	19 50	20 29	13 30	14 35	15 37	16 32
S 50	19 30	20 06	20 51	13 52	15 02	16 06	17 02
52	19 35	20 14	21 03	14 02	15 15	16 21	17 17
54	19 42	20 22	21 16	14 14	15 29	16 38	17 35
56	19 49	20 32	21 31	14 28	15 47	16 59	17 56
58	19 56	20 44	21 49	14 44	16 08	17 25	18 23
S 60	20 05	20 57	22 13	15 03	16 35	18 01	19 02

Day	SUN Eqn. of Time 00^h	SUN Eqn. of Time 12^h	SUN Mer. Pass.	MOON Mer. Pass. Upper	MOON Mer. Pass. Lower	MOON Age	MOON Phase
d	m s	m s	h m	h m	h m	d %	
9	14 08	14 09	12 14	05 36	17 59	22 50	◐
10	14 10	14 10	12 14	06 23	18 47	23 41	
11	14 10	14 10	12 14	07 12	19 38	24 32	

2026 FEBRUARY 12, 13, 14 (THURS., FRI., SAT.)

UT d	UT h	ARIES GHA	VENUS −3·9 GHA	VENUS Dec	MARS +1·1 GHA	MARS Dec	JUPITER −2·6 GHA	JUPITER Dec	SATURN +1·0 GHA	SATURN Dec
		° ′	° ′	° ′	° ′	° ′	° ′	° ′	° ′	° ′
12	00	142 03.6	167 33.7	S12 08.3	183 54.5	S17 15.4	34 22.2	N22 46.0	141 24.3	S 2 03.7
	01	157 06.1	182 33.2	07.2	198 55.0	14.8	49 24.9	46.1	156 26.5	03.6
	02	172 08.5	197 32.7	06.1	213 55.5	14.2	64 27.5	46.1	171 28.7	03.5
	03	187 11.0	212 32.1	. . 05.0	228 56.0	. . 13.6	79 30.2	. . 46.1	186 30.9	. . 03.4
	04	202 13.4	227 31.6	03.8	243 56.5	13.1	94 32.9	46.2	201 33.2	03.3
	05	217 15.9	242 31.1	02.7	258 57.0	12.5	109 35.6	46.2	216 35.4	03.1
	06	232 18.4	257 30.6	S12 01.6	273 57.5	S17 11.9	124 38.3	N22 46.2	231 37.6	S 2 03.0
	07	247 20.8	272 30.0	12 00.5	288 58.0	11.3	139 41.0	46.2	246 39.8	02.9
T	08	262 23.3	287 29.5	11 59.4	303 58.5	10.7	154 43.7	46.3	261 42.0	02.8
H	09	277 25.8	302 29.0	. . 58.2	318 59.0	. . 10.2	169 46.4	. . 46.3	276 44.2	. . 02.7
U	10	292 28.2	317 28.5	57.1	333 59.5	09.6	184 49.1	46.3	291 46.5	02.6
R	11	307 30.7	332 27.9	56.0	349 00.0	09.0	199 51.8	46.4	306 48.7	02.5
S	12	322 33.2	347 27.4	S11 54.9	4 00.5	S17 08.4	214 54.5	N22 46.4	321 50.9	S 2 02.4
D	13	337 35.6	2 26.9	53.7	19 01.0	07.8	229 57.1	46.4	336 53.1	02.3
A	14	352 38.1	17 26.4	52.6	34 01.5	07.3	244 59.8	46.5	351 55.3	02.1
Y	15	7 40.6	32 25.9	. . 51.5	49 02.0	. . 06.7	260 02.5	. . 46.5	6 57.5	. . 02.0
	16	22 43.0	47 25.3	50.4	64 02.5	06.1	275 05.2	46.5	21 59.7	01.9
	17	37 45.5	62 24.8	49.2	79 03.0	05.5	290 07.9	46.5	37 02.0	01.8
	18	52 47.9	77 24.3	S11 48.1	94 03.5	S17 04.9	305 10.6	N22 46.6	52 04.2	S 2 01.7
	19	67 50.4	92 23.8	47.0	109 04.0	04.3	320 13.3	46.6	67 06.4	01.6
	20	82 52.9	107 23.3	45.9	124 04.5	03.8	335 16.0	46.6	82 08.6	01.5
	21	97 55.3	122 22.7	. . 44.7	139 05.0	. . 03.2	350 18.6	. . 46.7	97 10.8	. . 01.4
	22	112 57.8	137 22.2	43.6	154 05.5	02.6	5 21.3	46.7	112 13.0	01.2
	23	128 00.3	152 21.7	42.5	169 06.0	02.0	20 24.0	46.7	127 15.3	01.1
13	00	143 02.7	167 21.2	S11 41.4	184 06.5	S17 01.4	35 26.7	N22 46.7	142 17.5	S 2 01.0
	01	158 05.2	182 20.7	40.2	199 07.0	00.8	50 29.4	46.8	157 19.7	00.9
	02	173 07.7	197 20.2	39.1	214 07.5	17 00.3	65 32.1	46.8	172 21.9	00.8
	03	188 10.1	212 19.6	. . 38.0	229 08.0	16 59.7	80 34.8	. . 46.8	187 24.1	. . 00.7
	04	203 12.6	227 19.1	36.8	244 08.5	59.1	95 37.4	46.9	202 26.3	00.6
	05	218 15.1	242 18.6	35.7	259 09.0	58.5	110 40.1	46.9	217 28.5	00.5
	06	233 17.5	257 18.1	S11 34.6	274 09.5	S16 57.9	125 42.8	N22 46.9	232 30.8	S 2 00.3
	07	248 20.0	272 17.6	33.4	289 10.0	57.3	140 45.5	46.9	247 33.0	00.2
	08	263 22.4	287 17.1	32.3	304 10.5	56.7	155 48.2	47.0	262 35.2	00.1
F	09	278 24.9	302 16.6	. . 31.2	319 11.0	. . 56.1	170 50.9	. . 47.0	277 37.4	2 00.0
R	10	293 27.4	317 16.1	30.0	334 11.5	55.6	185 53.5	47.0	292 39.6	1 59.9
I	11	308 29.8	332 15.5	28.9	349 12.0	55.0	200 56.2	47.0	307 41.8	59.8
D	12	323 32.3	347 15.0	S11 27.8	4 12.5	S16 54.4	215 58.9	N22 47.1	322 44.0	S 1 59.7
A	13	338 34.8	2 14.5	26.6	19 13.0	53.8	231 01.6	47.1	337 46.3	59.6
Y	14	353 37.2	17 14.0	25.5	34 13.6	53.2	246 04.3	47.1	352 48.5	59.4
	15	8 39.7	32 13.5	. . 24.3	49 14.1	. . 52.6	261 06.9	. . 47.2	7 50.7	. . 59.3
	16	23 42.2	47 13.0	23.2	64 14.6	52.0	276 09.6	47.2	22 52.9	59.2
	17	38 44.6	62 12.5	22.1	79 15.1	51.4	291 12.3	47.2	37 55.1	59.1
	18	53 47.1	77 12.0	S11 20.9	94 15.6	S16 50.8	306 15.0	N22 47.2	52 57.3	S 1 59.0
	19	68 49.5	92 11.5	19.8	109 16.1	50.3	321 17.7	47.3	67 59.5	58.9
	20	83 52.0	107 11.0	18.6	124 16.6	49.7	336 20.3	47.3	83 01.8	58.8
	21	98 54.5	122 10.5	. . 17.5	139 17.1	. . 49.1	351 23.0	. . 47.3	98 04.0	. . 58.7
	22	113 56.9	137 09.9	16.4	154 17.6	48.5	6 25.7	47.4	113 06.2	58.5
	23	128 59.4	152 09.4	15.2	169 18.1	47.9	21 28.4	47.4	128 08.4	58.4
14	00	144 01.9	167 08.9	S11 14.1	184 18.6	S16 47.3	36 31.1	N22 47.4	143 10.6	S 1 58.3
	01	159 04.3	182 08.4	12.9	199 19.1	46.7	51 33.7	47.4	158 12.8	58.2
	02	174 06.8	197 07.9	11.8	214 19.6	46.1	66 36.4	47.5	173 15.0	58.1
	03	189 09.3	212 07.4	. . 10.7	229 20.1	. . 45.5	81 39.1	. . 47.5	188 17.3	. . 58.0
	04	204 11.7	227 06.9	09.5	244 20.6	44.9	96 41.8	47.5	203 19.5	57.9
	05	219 14.2	242 06.4	08.4	259 21.1	44.3	111 44.4	47.5	218 21.7	57.7
	06	234 16.7	257 05.9	S11 07.2	274 21.6	S16 43.7	126 47.1	N22 47.6	233 23.9	S 1 57.6
	07	249 19.1	272 05.4	06.1	289 22.1	43.1	141 49.8	47.6	248 26.1	57.5
S	08	264 21.6	287 04.9	04.9	304 22.7	42.6	156 52.5	47.6	263 28.3	57.4
A	09	279 24.0	302 04.4	. . 03.8	319 23.2	. . 42.0	171 55.1	. . 47.7	278 30.5	. . 57.3
T	10	294 26.5	317 03.9	02.6	334 23.7	41.4	186 57.8	47.7	293 32.7	57.2
U	11	309 29.0	332 03.4	01.5	349 24.2	40.8	202 00.5	47.7	308 35.0	57.1
R	12	324 31.4	347 02.9	S11 00.3	4 24.7	S16 40.2	217 03.2	N22 47.7	323 37.2	S 1 57.0
D	13	339 33.9	2 02.4	10 59.2	19 25.2	39.6	232 05.8	47.8	338 39.4	56.8
A	14	354 36.4	17 01.9	58.0	34 25.7	39.0	247 08.5	47.8	353 41.6	56.7
Y	15	9 38.8	32 01.4	. . 56.9	49 26.2	. . 38.4	262 11.2	. . 47.8	8 43.8	. . 56.6
	16	24 41.3	47 00.9	55.7	64 26.7	37.8	277 13.9	47.8	23 46.0	56.5
	17	39 43.8	62 00.4	54.6	79 27.2	37.2	292 16.5	47.9	38 48.2	56.4
	18	54 46.2	76 59.9	S10 53.4	94 27.7	S16 36.6	307 19.2	N22 47.9	53 50.4	S 1 56.3
	19	69 48.7	91 59.4	52.3	109 28.2	36.0	322 21.9	47.9	68 52.7	56.2
	20	84 51.2	106 58.9	51.1	124 28.7	35.4	337 24.5	47.9	83 54.9	56.0
	21	99 53.6	121 58.4	. . 50.0	139 29.3	. . 34.8	352 27.2	. . 48.0	98 57.1	. . 55.9
	22	114 56.1	136 57.9	48.8	154 29.8	34.2	7 29.9	48.0	113 59.3	55.8
	23	129 58.5	151 57.4	47.7	169 30.3	33.6	22 32.6	48.0	129 01.5	55.7
Mer. Pass.		h m 14 25.4	v −0.5	d 1.1	v 0.5	d 0.6	v 2.7	d 0.0	v 2.2	d 0.1

STARS

Name	SHA	Dec
	° ′	° ′
Acamar	315 11.1	S40 12.2
Achernar	335 19.7	S57 06.5
Acrux	172 58.5	S63 14.5
Adhara	255 04.8	S29 00.6
Aldebaran	290 38.5	N16 33.7
Alioth	166 11.8	N55 48.8
Alkaid	152 51.0	N49 10.6
Alnair	27 32.2	S46 50.1
Alnilam	275 36.6	S 1 11.2
Alphard	217 46.5	S 8 46.4
Alphecca	126 03.0	N26 37.3
Alpheratz	357 34.1	N29 14.1
Altair	61 59.4	N 8 56.1
Ankaa	353 06.5	S42 10.0
Antares	112 14.8	S26 29.4
Arcturus	145 47.0	N19 02.5
Atria	107 08.4	S69 04.2
Avior	234 13.8	S59 35.7
Bellatrix	278 21.7	N 6 22.3
Betelgeuse	270 50.9	N 7 24.7
Canopus	263 51.6	S52 42.8
Capella	280 20.3	N46 01.6
Deneb	49 25.6	N45 22.3
Denebola	182 23.7	N14 25.4
Diphda	348 46.6	S17 50.7
Dubhe	193 39.2	N61 36.4
Elnath	278 00.5	N28 37.8
Eltanin	90 42.1	N51 28.8
Enif	33 38.2	N 9 59.6
Fomalhaut	15 13.8	S29 29.1
Gacrux	171 50.2	S57 15.5
Gienah	175 42.4	S17 41.3
Hadar	148 34.5	S60 29.8
Hamal	327 50.3	N23 35.2
Kaus Aust.	83 31.6	S34 22.3
Kochab	137 19.6	N74 02.4
Markab	13 29.3	N15 20.7
Menkar	314 05.2	N 4 11.5
Menkent	147 56.4	S36 29.9
Miaplacidus	221 37.2	S69 49.5
Mirfak	308 26.9	N49 57.4
Nunki	75 46.9	S26 15.9
Peacock	53 04.8	S56 39.0
Pollux	243 15.8	N27 57.7
Procyon	244 49.6	N 5 09.4
Rasalhague	95 57.9	N12 32.3
Regulus	207 33.1	N11 50.2
Rigel	281 02.8	S 8 10.4
Rigil Kent.	139 38.9	S60 56.4
Sabik	102 01.9	S15 45.5
Schedar	349 30.4	N56 41.0
Shaula	96 09.3	S37 07.3
Sirius	258 25.2	S16 45.3
Spica	158 21.2	S11 18.0
Suhail	222 45.2	S43 32.4
Vega	80 32.9	N38 48.2
Zuben'ubi	136 54.9	S16 09.1

	SHA	Mer. Pass.
	° ′	h m
Venus	24 18.5	12 51
Mars	41 03.8	11 43
Jupiter	252 24.0	21 34
Saturn	359 14.7	14 29

UT		SUN GHA	SUN Dec	MOON GHA	v	MOON Dec	d	HP
d	h	° ′	° ′	° ′	′	° ′	′	′
12 THURSDAY	00	176 27.4	S13 45.7	243 13.8	9.8	S28 13.0	1.7	54.3
	01	191 27.4	44.9	257 42.6	9.7	28 14.7	1.6	54.3
	02	206 27.4	44.0	272 11.3	9.7	28 16.3	1.4	54.4
	03	221 27.4	. . 43.2	286 40.0	9.6	28 17.7	1.3	54.4
	04	236 27.4	42.4	301 08.6	9.6	28 19.0	1.2	54.4
	05	251 27.4	41.5	315 37.2	9.6	28 20.2	1.0	54.4
	06	266 27.4	S13 40.7	330 05.8	9.6	S28 21.2	0.9	54.4
	07	281 27.5	39.9	344 34.4	9.6	28 22.1	0.7	54.4
	08	296 27.5	39.1	359 03.0	9.5	28 22.8	0.6	54.4
	09	311 27.5	. . 38.2	13 31.5	9.5	28 23.4	0.5	54.4
	10	326 27.5	37.4	28 00.0	9.5	28 23.9	0.3	54.4
	11	341 27.5	36.6	42 28.5	9.4	28 24.2	0.2	54.5
	12	356 27.5	S13 35.7	56 56.9	9.5	S28 24.4	0.0	54.5
	13	11 27.5	34.9	71 25.4	9.4	28 24.4	0.1	54.5
	14	26 27.5	34.0	85 53.8	9.4	28 24.3	0.2	54.5
	15	41 27.5	. . 33.2	100 22.2	9.4	28 24.1	0.4	54.5
	16	56 27.5	32.4	114 50.6	9.4	28 23.7	0.5	54.5
	17	71 27.5	31.5	129 19.0	9.3	28 23.2	0.7	54.5
	18	86 27.6	S13 30.7	143 47.3	9.4	S28 22.5	0.8	54.5
	19	101 27.6	29.9	158 15.7	9.3	28 21.7	0.9	54.6
	20	116 27.6	29.0	172 44.0	9.3	28 20.8	1.1	54.6
	21	131 27.6	. . 28.2	187 12.3	9.4	28 19.7	1.3	54.6
	22	146 27.6	27.3	201 40.7	9.3	28 18.4	1.3	54.6
	23	161 27.6	26.5	216 09.0	9.3	28 17.1	1.6	54.6
13 FRIDAY	00	176 27.6	S13 25.7	230 37.3	9.3	S28 15.5	1.6	54.6
	01	191 27.6	24.8	245 05.6	9.3	28 13.9	1.8	54.6
	02	206 27.6	24.0	259 33.9	9.3	28 12.1	2.0	54.7
	03	221 27.7	. . 23.2	274 02.2	9.3	28 10.1	2.1	54.7
	04	236 27.7	22.3	288 30.5	9.3	28 08.0	2.2	54.7
	05	251 27.7	21.5	302 58.8	9.3	28 05.8	2.4	54.7
	06	266 27.7	S13 20.6	317 27.1	9.3	S28 03.4	2.5	54.7
	07	281 27.7	19.8	331 55.4	9.3	28 00.9	2.6	54.7
	08	296 27.7	18.9	346 23.7	9.3	27 58.3	2.9	54.8
	09	311 27.7	. . 18.1	0 52.0	9.3	27 55.4	2.9	54.8
	10	326 27.8	17.3	15 20.3	9.3	27 52.5	3.1	54.8
	11	341 27.8	16.4	29 48.6	9.4	27 49.4	3.2	54.8
	12	356 27.8	S13 15.6	44 17.0	9.3	S27 46.2	3.4	54.8
	13	11 27.8	14.7	58 45.3	9.4	27 42.8	3.5	54.8
	14	26 27.8	13.9	73 13.7	9.3	27 39.3	3.7	54.9
	15	41 27.8	. . 13.0	87 42.0	9.4	27 35.6	3.8	54.9
	16	56 27.9	12.2	102 10.4	9.4	27 31.8	3.9	54.9
	17	71 27.9	11.3	116 38.8	9.4	27 27.9	4.1	54.9
	18	86 27.9	S13 10.5	131 07.2	9.4	S27 23.8	4.2	54.9
	19	101 27.9	09.7	145 35.6	9.5	27 19.6	4.4	55.0
	20	116 27.9	08.8	160 04.1	9.4	27 15.2	4.5	55.0
	21	131 28.0	. . 08.0	174 32.5	9.5	27 10.7	4.6	55.0
	22	146 28.0	07.1	189 01.0	9.5	27 06.1	4.8	55.0
	23	161 28.0	06.3	203 29.5	9.5	27 01.3	4.9	55.0
14 SATURDAY	00	176 28.0	S13 05.4	217 58.0	9.6	S26 56.4	5.1	55.0
	01	191 28.0	04.6	232 26.6	9.5	26 51.3	5.2	55.1
	02	206 28.1	03.7	246 55.1	9.6	26 46.1	5.3	55.1
	03	221 28.1	. . 02.9	261 23.7	9.6	26 40.8	5.5	55.1
	04	236 28.1	02.0	275 52.3	9.7	26 35.3	5.6	55.1
	05	251 28.1	01.2	290 21.0	9.7	26 29.7	5.8	55.1
	06	266 28.1	S13 00.3	304 49.7	9.7	S26 23.9	5.9	55.2
	07	281 28.2	12 59.5	319 18.4	9.7	26 18.0	6.0	55.2
	08	296 28.2	58.6	333 47.1	9.7	26 12.0	6.2	55.2
	09	311 28.2	. . 57.8	348 15.8	9.8	26 05.8	6.3	55.2
	10	326 28.2	56.9	2 44.6	9.9	25 59.5	6.4	55.3
	11	341 28.2	56.1	17 13.5	9.8	25 53.1	6.6	55.3
	12	356 28.3	S12 55.2	31 42.3	9.9	S25 46.5	6.7	55.3
	13	11 28.3	54.4	46 11.2	9.9	25 39.8	6.8	55.3
	14	26 28.3	53.5	60 40.1	10.0	25 33.0	7.0	55.3
	15	41 28.3	. . 52.6	75 09.1	10.0	25 26.0	7.1	55.4
	16	56 28.4	51.8	89 38.1	10.0	25 18.9	7.2	55.4
	17	71 28.4	50.9	104 07.1	10.1	25 11.7	7.4	55.4
	18	86 28.4	S12 50.1	118 36.2	10.1	S25 04.3	7.5	55.4
	19	101 28.4	49.2	133 05.3	10.1	24 56.8	7.6	55.5
	20	116 28.5	48.4	147 34.4	10.2	24 49.2	7.8	55.5
	21	131 28.5	. . 47.5	162 03.6	10.2	24 41.4	7.9	55.5
	22	146 28.5	46.7	176 32.8	10.3	24 33.5	8.0	55.5
	23	161 28.6	45.8	191 02.1	10.3	S24 25.5	8.1	55.5
		SD 16.2	*d* 0.8	SD 14.8		14.9		15.1

Lat.	Twilight Naut.	Twilight Civil	Sunrise	Moonrise 12	Moonrise 13	Moonrise 14	Moonrise 15
°	h m	h m	h m	h m	h m	h m	h m
N 72	06 23	07 44	09 05	■	■	■	■
N 70	06 20	07 33	08 43	■	■	■	■
68	06 18	07 24	08 26	■	■	■	■
66	06 16	07 16	08 13	■	■	■	09 27
64	06 14	07 10	08 01	■	■	■	08 40
62	06 12	07 04	07 52	■	■	08 18	08 10
60	06 10	06 59	07 44	06 40	07 24	07 40	07 46
N 58	06 09	06 55	07 36	06 00	06 47	07 13	07 28
56	06 07	06 51	07 30	05 32	06 21	06 52	07 12
54	06 06	06 47	07 24	05 11	06 00	06 35	06 58
52	06 04	06 44	07 19	04 53	05 43	06 20	06 47
50	06 03	06 41	07 14	04 38	05 28	06 07	06 36
45	05 59	06 34	07 04	04 07	04 58	05 40	06 14
N 40	05 56	06 28	06 55	03 43	04 34	05 19	05 56
35	05 52	06 22	06 48	03 23	04 15	05 01	05 41
30	05 49	06 17	06 42	03 07	03 58	04 46	05 28
20	05 42	06 08	06 30	02 38	03 30	04 20	05 05
N 10	05 34	05 59	06 20	02 14	03 06	03 57	04 46
0	05 25	05 49	06 11	01 51	02 44	03 36	04 27
S 10	05 14	05 39	06 01	01 29	02 21	03 15	04 09
20	05 01	05 28	05 51	01 05	01 57	02 52	03 49
30	04 44	05 14	05 39	00 37	01 29	02 26	03 26
35	04 33	05 05	05 32	00 20	01 12	02 11	03 13
40	04 20	04 55	05 24	00 01	00 53	01 53	02 57
45	04 03	04 42	05 14	24 29	00 29	01 31	02 39
S 50	03 42	04 27	05 03	23 59	25 03	01 03	02 15
52	03 32	04 20	04 58	23 44	24 49	00 49	02 04
54	03 19	04 12	04 52	23 26	24 33	00 33	01 51
56	03 05	04 02	04 45	23 05	24 15	00 15	01 36
58	02 48	03 51	04 38	22 38	23 51	25 19	01 19
S 60	02 26	03 39	04 29	22 00	23 21	24 57	00 57

Lat.	Sunset	Twilight Civil	Twilight Naut.	Moonset 12	Moonset 13	Moonset 14	Moonset 15
°	h m	h m	h m	h m	h m	h m	h m
N 72	15 25	16 46	18 07	■	■	■	■
N 70	15 46	16 57	18 10	■	■	■	■
68	16 03	17 06	18 12	■	■	■	■
66	16 17	17 13	18 14	■	■	■	12 06
64	16 28	17 20	18 16	■	■	■	12 52
62	16 38	17 25	18 18	■	■	11 27	13 22
60	16 46	17 30	18 19	09 27	10 33	12 05	13 44
N 58	16 53	17 34	18 21	10 07	11 09	12 31	14 02
56	16 59	17 38	18 22	10 35	11 35	12 52	14 17
54	17 05	17 42	18 24	10 56	11 56	13 09	14 30
52	17 10	17 45	18 25	11 14	12 13	13 24	14 42
50	17 15	17 48	18 26	11 30	12 28	13 36	14 52
45	17 25	17 55	18 30	12 01	12 57	14 02	15 13
N 40	17 33	18 01	18 33	12 24	13 21	14 23	15 30
35	17 41	18 07	18 36	12 44	13 40	14 40	15 44
30	17 47	18 12	18 40	13 01	13 56	14 55	15 56
20	17 58	18 21	18 47	13 29	14 23	15 20	16 17
N 10	18 08	18 30	18 55	13 54	14 47	15 41	16 35
0	18 18	18 39	19 03	14 17	15 09	16 01	16 51
S 10	18 27	18 49	19 14	14 39	15 31	16 21	17 08
20	18 37	19 00	19 27	15 04	15 54	16 42	17 26
30	18 49	19 14	19 44	15 32	16 21	17 06	17 46
35	18 56	19 23	19 55	15 49	16 38	17 20	17 58
40	19 04	19 33	20 07	16 08	16 56	17 37	18 11
45	19 13	19 45	20 24	16 32	17 18	17 56	18 27
S 50	19 24	20 00	20 45	17 02	17 47	18 21	18 46
52	19 30	20 07	20 55	17 17	18 01	18 32	18 55
54	19 35	20 15	21 07	17 35	18 17	18 46	19 05
56	19 42	20 24	21 21	17 56	18 36	19 01	19 17
58	19 49	20 35	21 38	18 23	18 59	19 19	19 30
S 60	19 57	20 47	21 59	19 02	19 30	19 41	19 45

Day	SUN Eqn. of Time 00^h	SUN Eqn. of Time 12^h	SUN Mer. Pass.	MOON Mer. Pass. Upper	MOON Mer. Pass. Lower	MOON Age	MOON Phase
d	m s	m s	h m	h m	h m	d	%
12	14 10	14 10	12 14	08 04	20 30	25	23
13	14 10	14 09	12 14	08 56	21 23	26	16
14	14 08	14 07	12 14	09 49	22 14	27	9

UT d	UT h	ARIES GHA	VENUS −3·9 GHA	VENUS Dec	MARS +1·1 GHA	MARS Dec	JUPITER −2·5 GHA	JUPITER Dec	SATURN +1·0 GHA	SATURN Dec
		° ′	° ′	° ′	° ′	° ′	° ′	° ′	° ′	° ′
15 SUNDAY	00	145 01.0	166 56.9	S10 46.5	184 30.8	S16 33.0	37 35.2	N22 48.1	144 03.7	S 1 55.6
	01	160 03.5	181 56.4	45.4	199 31.3	32.4	52 37.9	48.1	159 05.9	55.5
	02	175 05.9	196 55.9	44.2	214 31.8	31.8	67 40.6	48.1	174 08.1	55.4
	03	190 08.4	211 55.4	43.0	229 32.3	31.2	82 43.2	48.1	189 10.3	55.3
	04	205 10.9	226 54.9	41.9	244 32.8	30.6	97 45.9	48.2	204 12.6	55.1
	05	220 13.3	241 54.4	40.7	259 33.3	30.0	112 48.6	48.2	219 14.8	55.0
	06	235 15.8	256 54.0	S10 39.6	274 33.9	S16 29.4	127 51.2	N22 48.2	234 17.0	S 1 54.9
	07	250 18.3	271 53.5	38.4	289 34.4	28.8	142 53.9	48.2	249 19.2	54.8
	08	265 20.7	286 53.0	37.3	304 34.9	28.2	157 56.6	48.3	264 21.4	54.7
	09	280 23.2	301 52.5	36.1	319 35.4	27.6	172 59.2	48.3	279 23.6	54.6
	10	295 25.7	316 52.0	34.9	334 35.9	27.0	188 01.9	48.3	294 25.8	54.5
	11	310 28.1	331 51.5	33.8	349 36.4	26.4	203 04.6	48.3	309 28.0	54.3
	12	325 30.6	346 51.0	S10 32.6	4 36.9	S16 25.8	218 07.2	N22 48.4	324 30.2	S 1 54.2
	13	340 33.0	1 50.5	31.5	19 37.4	25.2	233 09.9	48.4	339 32.5	54.1
	14	355 35.5	16 50.0	30.3	34 37.9	24.6	248 12.6	48.4	354 34.7	54.0
	15	10 38.0	31 49.5	29.1	49 38.5	24.0	263 15.2	48.4	9 36.9	53.9
	16	25 40.4	46 49.0	28.0	64 39.0	23.4	278 17.9	48.5	24 39.1	53.8
	17	40 42.9	61 48.6	26.8	79 39.5	22.8	293 20.6	48.5	39 41.3	53.7
	18	55 45.4	76 48.1	S10 25.6	94 40.0	S16 22.2	308 23.2	N22 48.5	54 43.5	S 1 53.5
	19	70 47.8	91 47.6	24.5	109 40.5	21.6	323 25.9	48.5	69 45.7	53.4
	20	85 50.3	106 47.1	23.3	124 41.0	21.0	338 28.6	48.6	84 47.9	53.3
	21	100 52.8	121 46.6	22.2	139 41.5	20.4	353 31.2	48.6	99 50.1	53.2
	22	115 55.2	136 46.1	21.0	154 42.1	19.7	8 33.9	48.6	114 52.4	53.1
	23	130 57.7	151 45.6	19.8	169 42.6	19.1	23 36.6	48.6	129 54.6	53.0
16 MONDAY	00	146 00.1	166 45.2	S10 18.7	184 43.1	S16 18.5	38 39.2	N22 48.7	144 56.8	S 1 52.9
	01	161 02.6	181 44.7	17.5	199 43.6	17.9	53 41.9	48.7	159 59.0	52.7
	02	176 05.1	196 44.2	16.3	214 44.1	17.3	68 44.5	48.7	175 01.2	52.6
	03	191 07.5	211 43.7	15.2	229 44.6	16.7	83 47.2	48.7	190 03.4	52.5
	04	206 10.0	226 43.2	14.0	244 45.1	16.1	98 49.9	48.8	205 05.6	52.4
	05	221 12.5	241 42.7	12.8	259 45.7	15.5	113 52.5	48.8	220 07.8	52.3
	06	236 14.9	256 42.2	S10 11.7	274 46.2	S16 14.9	128 55.2	N22 48.8	235 10.0	S 1 52.2
	07	251 17.4	271 41.8	10.5	289 46.7	14.3	143 57.8	48.8	250 12.2	52.1
	08	266 19.9	286 41.3	09.3	304 47.2	13.7	159 00.5	48.9	265 14.4	51.9
	09	281 22.3	301 40.8	08.1	319 47.7	13.1	174 03.2	48.9	280 16.7	51.8
	10	296 24.8	316 40.3	07.0	334 48.2	12.5	189 05.8	48.9	295 18.9	51.7
	11	311 27.3	331 39.8	05.8	349 48.7	11.8	204 08.5	48.9	310 21.1	51.6
	12	326 29.7	346 39.4	S10 04.6	4 49.3	S16 11.2	219 11.1	N22 49.0	325 23.3	S 1 51.5
	13	341 32.2	1 38.9	03.5	19 49.8	10.6	234 13.8	49.0	340 25.5	51.4
	14	356 34.6	16 38.4	02.3	34 50.3	10.0	249 16.5	49.0	355 27.7	51.3
	15	11 37.1	31 37.9	10 01.1	49 50.8	09.4	264 19.1	49.0	10 29.9	51.1
	16	26 39.6	46 37.4	9 59.9	64 51.3	08.8	279 21.8	49.1	25 32.1	51.0
	17	41 42.0	61 37.0	58.8	79 51.8	08.2	294 24.4	49.1	40 34.3	50.9
	18	56 44.5	76 36.5	S 9 57.6	94 52.4	S16 07.6	309 27.1	N22 49.1	55 36.5	S 1 50.8
	19	71 47.0	91 36.0	56.4	109 52.9	07.0	324 29.7	49.1	70 38.7	50.7
	20	86 49.4	106 35.5	55.2	124 53.4	06.3	339 32.4	49.2	85 41.0	50.6
	21	101 51.9	121 35.0	54.1	139 53.9	05.7	354 35.1	49.2	100 43.2	50.5
	22	116 54.4	136 34.6	52.9	154 54.4	05.1	9 37.7	49.2	115 45.4	50.3
	23	131 56.8	151 34.1	51.7	169 55.0	04.5	24 40.4	49.2	130 47.6	50.2
17 TUESDAY	00	146 59.3	166 33.6	S 9 50.5	184 55.5	S16 03.9	39 43.0	N22 49.3	145 49.8	S 1 50.1
	01	162 01.8	181 33.1	49.4	199 56.0	03.3	54 45.7	49.3	160 52.0	50.0
	02	177 04.2	196 32.7	48.2	214 56.5	02.7	69 48.3	49.3	175 54.2	49.9
	03	192 06.7	211 32.2	47.0	229 57.0	02.1	84 51.0	49.3	190 56.4	49.8
	04	207 09.1	226 31.7	45.8	244 57.5	01.4	99 53.6	49.4	205 58.6	49.6
	05	222 11.6	241 31.2	44.6	259 58.1	00.8	114 56.3	49.4	221 00.8	49.5
	06	237 14.1	256 30.8	S 9 43.5	274 58.6	S16 00.2	129 58.9	N22 49.4	236 03.0	S 1 49.4
	07	252 16.5	271 30.3	42.3	289 59.1	15 59.6	145 01.6	49.4	251 05.2	49.3
	08	267 19.0	286 29.8	41.1	304 59.6	59.0	160 04.2	49.5	266 07.5	49.2
	09	282 21.5	301 29.4	39.9	320 00.1	58.4	175 06.9	49.5	281 09.7	49.1
	10	297 23.9	316 28.9	38.7	335 00.7	57.7	190 09.5	49.5	296 11.9	49.0
	11	312 26.4	331 28.4	37.6	350 01.2	57.1	205 12.2	49.5	311 14.1	48.8
	12	327 28.9	346 27.9	S 9 36.4	5 01.7	S15 56.5	220 14.8	N22 49.6	326 16.3	S 1 48.7
	13	342 31.3	1 27.5	35.2	20 02.2	55.9	235 17.5	49.6	341 18.5	48.6
	14	357 33.8	16 27.0	34.0	35 02.8	55.3	250 20.1	49.6	356 20.7	48.5
	15	12 36.2	31 26.5	32.8	50 03.3	54.7	265 22.8	49.6	11 22.9	48.4
	16	27 38.7	46 26.1	31.6	65 03.8	54.0	280 25.4	49.7	26 25.1	48.3
	17	42 41.2	61 25.6	30.5	80 04.3	53.4	295 28.1	49.7	41 27.3	48.2
	18	57 43.6	76 25.1	S 9 29.3	95 04.8	S15 52.8	310 30.7	N22 49.7	56 29.5	S 1 48.0
	19	72 46.1	91 24.6	28.1	110 05.4	52.2	325 33.4	49.7	71 31.7	47.9
	20	87 48.6	106 24.2	26.9	125 05.9	51.6	340 36.0	49.7	86 33.9	47.8
	21	102 51.0	121 23.7	25.7	140 06.4	50.9	355 38.7	49.8	101 36.1	47.7
	22	117 53.5	136 23.2	24.5	155 06.9	50.3	10 41.3	49.8	116 38.4	47.6
	23	132 56.0	151 22.8	23.3	170 07.4	49.7	25 44.0	49.8	131 40.6	47.5
Mer. Pass.		h m 14 13.7	v −0.5	d 1.2	v 0.5	d 0.6	v 2.7	d 0.0	v 2.2	d 0.1

STARS

Name	SHA ° ′	Dec ° ′
Acamar	315 11.1	S40 12.2
Achernar	335 19.8	S57 06.5
Acrux	172 58.5	S63 14.5
Adhara	255 04.9	S29 00.6
Aldebaran	290 38.5	N16 33.7
Alioth	166 11.7	N55 48.8
Alkaid	152 51.0	N49 10.6
Alnair	27 32.2	S46 50.1
Alnilam	275 36.6	S 1 11.2
Alphard	217 46.5	S 8 46.4
Alphecca	126 02.9	N26 37.3
Alpheratz	357 34.1	N29 14.1
Altair	61 59.3	N 8 56.1
Ankaa	353 06.5	S42 10.0
Antares	112 14.8	S26 29.4
Arcturus	145 46.9	N19 02.5
Atria	107 08.3	S69 04.2
Avior	234 13.8	S59 35.7
Bellatrix	278 21.7	N 6 22.3
Betelgeuse	270 50.9	N 7 24.7
Canopus	263 51.6	S52 42.8
Capella	280 20.3	N46 01.6
Deneb	49 25.6	N45 22.3
Denebola	182 23.7	N14 25.4
Diphda	348 46.6	S17 50.7
Dubhe	193 39.2	N61 36.4
Elnath	278 00.5	N28 37.8
Eltanin	90 42.0	N51 28.8
Enif	33 38.2	N 9 59.6
Fomalhaut	15 13.8	S29 29.1
Gacrux	171 50.2	S57 15.5
Gienah	175 42.4	S17 41.3
Hadar	148 34.4	S60 29.8
Hamal	327 50.3	N23 35.2
Kaus Aust.	83 31.5	S34 22.3
Kochab	137 19.5	N74 02.4
Markab	13 29.3	N15 20.7
Menkar	314 05.2	N 4 11.5
Menkent	147 56.4	S36 29.9
Miaplacidus	221 37.2	S69 49.5
Mirfak	308 26.9	N49 57.4
Nunki	75 46.9	S26 15.9
Peacock	53 04.8	S56 39.0
Pollux	243 15.8	N27 57.7
Procyon	244 49.6	N 5 09.4
Rasalhague	95 57.8	N12 32.2
Regulus	207 33.1	N11 50.2
Rigel	281 02.8	S 8 10.4
Rigil Kent.	139 38.8	S60 56.4
Sabik	102 01.8	S15 45.5
Schedar	349 30.4	N56 41.0
Shaula	96 09.3	S37 07.3
Sirius	258 25.2	S16 45.3
Spica	158 21.1	S11 18.0
Suhail	222 45.2	S43 32.4
Vega	80 32.9	N38 48.2
Zuben'ubi	136 54.9	S16 09.1

	SHA ° ′	Mer. Pass. h m
Venus	20 45.0	12 53
Mars	38 42.9	11 41
Jupiter	252 39.1	21 22
Saturn	358 56.6	14 18

Day	UT d h	SUN GHA ° ′	SUN Dec ° ′	MOON GHA ° ′	v ′	MOON Dec ° ′	d ′	HP ′
SUNDAY	15 00	176 28.6	S12 44.9	205 31.4	10.4	S24 17.4	8.3	55.6
	01	191 28.6	44.1	220 00.8	10.4	24 09.1	8.4	55.6
	02	206 28.6	43.2	234 30.2	10.4	24 00.7	8.5	55.6
	03	221 28.7	. . 42.4	248 59.6	10.5	23 52.2	8.7	55.6
	04	236 28.7	41.5	263 29.1	10.5	23 43.5	8.8	55.7
	05	251 28.7	40.7	277 58.6	10.5	23 34.7	8.9	55.7
	06	266 28.8	S12 39.8	292 28.1	10.7	S23 25.8	9.0	55.7
	07	281 28.8	38.9	306 57.8	10.6	23 16.8	9.1	55.7
	08	296 28.8	38.1	321 27.4	10.7	23 07.7	9.3	55.8
	09	311 28.8	. . 37.2	335 57.1	10.7	22 58.4	9.4	55.8
	10	326 28.9	36.4	350 26.8	10.8	22 49.0	9.5	55.8
	11	341 28.9	35.5	4 56.6	10.9	22 39.5	9.6	55.8
	12	356 28.9	S12 34.6	19 26.5	10.8	S22 29.9	9.8	55.8
	13	11 29.0	33.8	33 56.3	11.0	22 20.1	9.8	55.9
	14	26 29.0	32.9	48 26.3	10.9	22 10.3	10.0	55.9
	15	41 29.0	. . 32.0	62 56.2	11.0	22 00.3	10.1	55.9
	16	56 29.1	31.2	77 26.2	11.1	21 50.2	10.2	55.9
	17	71 29.1	30.3	91 56.3	11.1	21 40.0	10.3	56.0
	18	86 29.1	S12 29.5	106 26.4	11.2	S21 29.7	10.5	56.0
	19	101 29.2	28.6	120 56.6	11.2	21 19.2	10.5	56.0
	20	116 29.2	27.7	135 26.8	11.2	21 08.7	10.7	56.0
	21	131 29.2	. . 26.9	149 57.0	11.3	20 58.0	10.7	56.1
	22	146 29.3	26.0	164 27.3	11.4	20 47.3	10.9	56.1
	23	161 29.3	25.1	178 57.7	11.4	20 36.4	11.0	56.1
MONDAY	16 00	176 29.3	S12 24.3	193 28.1	11.4	S20 25.4	11.1	56.1
	01	191 29.4	23.4	207 58.5	11.5	20 14.3	11.2	56.2
	02	206 29.4	22.5	222 29.0	11.5	20 03.1	11.3	56.2
	03	221 29.4	. . 21.7	236 59.5	11.6	19 51.8	11.5	56.2
	04	236 29.5	20.8	251 30.1	11.6	19 40.3	11.5	56.2
	05	251 29.5	19.9	266 00.7	11.7	19 28.8	11.6	56.3
	06	266 29.5	S12 19.1	280 31.4	11.7	S19 17.2	11.7	56.3
	07	281 29.6	18.2	295 02.1	11.8	19 05.5	11.9	56.3
	08	296 29.6	17.3	309 32.9	11.8	18 53.6	11.9	56.3
	09	311 29.7	. . 16.5	324 03.7	11.8	18 41.7	12.0	56.4
	10	326 29.7	15.6	338 34.5	11.9	18 29.7	12.2	56.4
	11	341 29.7	14.7	353 05.4	12.0	18 17.5	12.2	56.4
	12	356 29.8	S12 13.9	7 36.4	12.0	S18 05.3	12.3	56.4
	13	11 29.8	13.0	22 07.4	12.0	17 53.0	12.4	56.5
	14	26 29.9	12.1	36 38.4	12.1	17 40.6	12.5	56.5
	15	41 29.9	. . 11.2	51 09.5	12.1	17 28.1	12.6	56.5
	16	56 29.9	10.4	65 40.6	12.2	17 15.5	12.7	56.5
	17	71 30.0	09.5	80 11.8	12.2	17 02.8	12.8	56.6
	18	86 30.0	S12 08.6	94 43.0	12.2	S16 50.0	12.9	56.6
	19	101 30.1	07.8	109 14.2	12.3	16 37.1	13.0	56.6
	20	116 30.1	06.9	123 45.5	12.3	16 24.1	13.0	56.6
	21	131 30.1	. . 06.0	138 16.8	12.4	16 11.1	13.2	56.7
	22	146 30.2	05.1	152 48.2	12.4	15 57.9	13.2	56.7
	23	161 30.2	04.3	167 19.6	12.5	15 44.7	13.3	56.7
TUESDAY	17 00	176 30.3	S12 03.4	181 51.1	12.5	S15 31.4	13.4	56.7
	01	191 30.3	02.5	196 22.6	12.5	15 18.0	13.5	56.8
	02	206 30.3	01.6	210 54.1	12.6	15 04.5	13.6	56.8
	03	221 30.4	12 00.8	225 25.7	12.6	14 50.9	13.6	56.8
	04	236 30.4	11 59.9	239 57.3	12.6	14 37.3	13.8	56.8
	05	251 30.5	59.0	254 28.9	12.7	14 23.5	13.8	56.9
	06	266 30.5	S11 58.1	269 00.6	12.7	S14 09.7	13.8	56.9
	07	281 30.6	57.3	283 32.3	12.8	13 55.9	14.0	56.9
	08	296 30.6	56.4	298 04.1	12.8	13 41.9	14.0	56.9
	09	311 30.7	. . 55.5	312 35.9	12.8	13 27.9	14.1	57.0
	10	326 30.7	54.6	327 07.7	12.9	13 13.8	14.2	57.0
	11	341 30.7	53.8	341 39.6	12.9	S12 59.6	14.3	57.0
	12	356 30.8	S11 52.9					
	13	11 30.8	52.0					
	14	26 30.9	51.1					
	15	41 30.9	. . 50.2					
	16	56 31.0	49.4					
	17	71 31.0	48.5					
	18	86 31.1	S11 47.6	83 23.4	13.1	S11 18.4	14.7	57.2
	19	101 31.1	46.7	97 55.5	13.1	11 03.7	14.8	57.2
	20	116 31.2	45.8	112 27.6	13.2	10 48.9	14.9	57.2
	21	131 31.2	. . 45.0	126 59.8	13.2	10 34.0	14.9	57.2
	22	146 31.3	44.1	141 32.0	13.2	10 19.1	14.9	57.3
	23	161 31.3	43.2	156 04.2	13.2	S10 04.2	15.1	57.3
		SD 16.2	*d* 0.9	SD 15.2		15.4		15.5

An annular eclipse of the Sun occurs on this date. See page 5.

Lat.	Twilight Naut.	Twilight Civil	Sunrise	Moonrise 15	Moonrise 16	Moonrise 17	Moonrise 18
°	h m	h m	h m	h m	h m	h m	h m
N 72	06 10	07 30	08 48	■	■	09 21	08 33
N 70	06 09	07 21	08 29	■	09 57	08 56	08 22
68	06 08	07 13	08 14	■	09 13	08 37	08 13
66	06 07	07 06	08 02	09 27	08 44	08 22	08 05
64	06 05	07 01	07 52	08 40	08 21	08 09	07 59
62	06 04	06 56	07 43	08 10	08 03	07 58	07 53
60	06 03	06 52	07 35	07 46	07 48	07 49	07 48
N 58	06 02	06 48	07 29	07 28	07 36	07 41	07 44
56	06 01	06 44	07 23	07 12	07 25	07 33	07 40
54	06 00	06 41	07 18	06 58	07 15	07 27	07 36
52	05 59	06 38	07 13	06 47	07 06	07 21	07 33
50	05 58	06 36	07 09	06 36	06 58	07 16	07 30
45	05 55	06 29	06 59	06 14	06 41	07 04	07 24
N 40	05 52	06 24	06 52	05 56	06 27	06 54	07 19
35	05 49	06 19	06 45	05 41	06 16	06 46	07 14
30	05 47	06 15	06 39	05 28	06 05	06 39	07 10
20	05 40	06 06	06 29	05 05	05 47	06 26	07 03
N 10	05 33	05 58	06 19	04 46	05 32	06 15	06 57
0	05 25	05 49	06 11	04 27	05 17	06 05	06 51
S 10	05 15	05 40	06 02	04 09	05 02	05 54	06 45
20	05 03	05 29	05 52	03 49	04 46	05 43	06 38
30	04 47	05 16	05 41	03 26	04 28	05 30	06 31
35	04 36	05 08	05 35	03 13	04 17	05 22	06 27
40	04 24	04 59	05 27	02 57	04 05	05 14	06 22
45	04 09	04 47	05 19	02 39	03 50	05 04	06 17
S 50	03 49	04 33	05 08	02 15	03 33	04 51	06 10
52	03 39	04 26	05 03	02 04	03 24	04 45	06 07
54	03 28	04 18	04 58	01 51	03 15	04 39	06 03
56	03 15	04 10	04 52	01 36	03 04	04 32	06 00
58	02 59	04 00	04 45	01 19	02 51	04 24	05 55
S 60	02 39	03 48	04 38	00 57	02 37	04 15	05 51

Lat.	Sunset	Twilight Civil	Twilight Naut.	Moonset 15	Moonset 16	Moonset 17	Moonset 18
°	h m	h m	h m	h m	h m	h m	h m
N 72	15 42	17 00	18 20	■	■	15 38	18 05
N 70	16 01	17 09	18 21	■	13 21	16 01	18 13
68	16 16	17 17	18 22	■	14 03	16 18	18 19
66	16 28	17 23	18 23	12 06	14 31	16 32	18 24
64	16 38	17 28	18 24	12 52	14 53	16 43	18 29
62	16 46	17 33	18 25	13 22	15 10	16 52	18 32
60	16 54	17 37	18 26	13 44	15 24	17 01	18 36
N 58	17 00	17 41	18 27	14 02	15 35	17 08	18 39
56	17 06	17 45	18 28	14 17	15 46	17 14	18 41
54	17 11	17 48	18 29	14 30	15 55	17 19	18 44
52	17 16	17 51	18 30	14 42	16 03	17 24	18 46
50	17 20	17 53	18 31	14 52	16 10	17 29	18 48
45	17 29	17 59	18 34	15 13	16 25	17 39	18 52
N 40	17 37	18 05	18 36	15 30	16 38	17 47	18 55
35	17 44	18 09	18 39	15 44	16 49	17 53	18 58
30	17 49	18 14	18 42	15 56	16 58	17 59	19 01
20	18 00	18 22	18 48	16 17	17 14	18 10	19 05
N 10	18 09	18 30	18 55	16 35	17 27	18 18	19 09
0	18 17	18 39	19 03	16 51	17 40	18 27	19 12
S 10	18 26	18 48	19 13	17 08	17 53	18 35	19 16
20	18 36	18 58	19 25	17 26	18 06	18 44	19 20
30	18 46	19 11	19 41	17 46	18 21	18 53	19 24
35	18 53	19 19	19 51	17 58	18 30	18 59	19 26
40	19 00	19 29	20 03	18 11	18 40	19 05	19 29
45	19 09	19 40	20 18	18 27	18 52	19 13	19 32
S 50	19 19	19 54	20 38	18 46	19 06	19 22	19 36
52	19 24	20 01	20 47	18 55	19 12	19 26	19 37
54	19 29	20 08	20 58	19 05	19 19	19 30	19 39
56	19 35	20 16	21 11	19 17	19 27	19 35	19 41
58	19 41	20 26	21 26	19 30	19 36	19 40	19 43
S 60	19 49	20 37	21 45	19 45	19 46	19 46	19 46

Day	SUN Eqn. of Time 00^h	SUN Eqn. of Time 12^h	SUN Mer. Pass.	MOON Mer. Pass. Upper	MOON Mer. Pass. Lower	Age	Phase
d	m s	m s	h m	h m	h m	d	%
15	14 06	14 04	12 14	10 40	23 04	28	4
16	14 03	14 01	12 14	11 29	23 52	29	1
17	13 59	13 57	12 14	12 16	24 39	30	0

UT	ARIES	VENUS −3·9		MARS +1·1		JUPITER −2·5		SATURN +1·0		STARS		
	GHA	GHA	Dec	GHA	Dec	GHA	Dec	GHA	Dec	Name	SHA	Dec
d h	° ′	° ′	° ′	° ′	° ′	° ′	° ′	° ′	° ′		° ′	° ′
18 00	147 58.4	166 22.3	S 9 22.1	185 08.0	S15 49.1	40 46.6	N22 49.8	146 42.8	S 1 47.3	Acamar	315 11.1	S40 12.2
01	163 00.9	181 21.8	21.0	200 08.5	48.5	55 49.3	49.9	161 45.0	47.2	Achernar	335 19.8	S57 06.5
02	178 03.4	196 21.4	19.8	215 09.0	47.8	70 51.9	49.9	176 47.2	47.1	Acrux	172 58.5	S63 14.6
03	193 05.8	211 20.9	. . 18.6	230 09.5	. . 47.2	85 54.6	. . 49.9	191 49.4	. . 47.0	Adhara	255 04.9	S29 00.6
04	208 08.3	226 20.4	17.4	245 10.1	46.6	100 57.2	49.9	206 51.6	46.9	Aldebaran	290 38.5	N16 33.7
05	223 10.7	241 20.0	16.2	260 10.6	46.0	115 59.9	50.0	221 53.8	46.8			
W 06	238 13.2	256 19.5	S 9 15.0	275 11.1	S15 45.4	131 02.5	N22 50.0	236 56.0	S 1 46.7	Alioth	166 11.7	N55 48.8
E 07	253 15.7	271 19.1	13.8	290 11.6	44.7	146 05.1	50.0	251 58.2	46.5	Alkaid	152 51.0	N49 10.6
D 08	268 18.1	286 18.6	12.6	305 12.2	44.1	161 07.8	50.0	267 00.4	46.4	Alnair	27 32.2	S46 50.1
N 09	283 20.6	301 18.1	. . 11.4	320 12.7	. . 43.5	176 10.4	. . 50.0	282 02.6	. . 46.3	Alnilam	275 36.6	S 1 11.2
E 10	298 23.1	316 17.7	10.2	335 13.2	42.9	191 13.1	50.1	297 04.8	46.2	Alphard	217 46.5	S 8 46.5
S 11	313 25.5	331 17.2	09.1	350 13.7	42.2	206 15.7	50.1	312 07.0	46.1			
D 12	328 28.0	346 16.7	S 9 07.9	5 14.3	S15 41.6	221 18.4	N22 50.1	327 09.2	S 1 46.0	Alphecca	126 02.9	N26 37.3
A 13	343 30.5	1 16.3	06.7	20 14.8	41.0	236 21.0	50.1	342 11.4	45.8	Alpheratz	357 34.1	N29 14.1
Y 14	358 32.9	16 15.8	05.5	35 15.3	40.4	251 23.6	50.2	357 13.6	45.7	Altair	61 59.3	N 8 56.1
15	13 35.4	31 15.4	. . 04.3	50 15.8	. . 39.8	266 26.3	. . 50.2	12 15.9	. . 45.6	Ankaa	353 06.5	S42 10.0
16	28 37.9	46 14.9	03.1	65 16.4	39.1	281 28.9	50.2	27 18.1	45.5	Antares	112 14.7	S26 29.4
17	43 40.3	61 14.4	01.9	80 16.9	38.5	296 31.6	50.2	42 20.3	45.4			
18	58 42.8	76 14.0	S 9 00.7	95 17.4	S15 37.9	311 34.2	N22 50.3	57 22.5	S 1 45.3	Arcturus	145 46.9	N19 02.5
19	73 45.2	91 13.5	8 59.5	110 17.9	37.3	326 36.8	50.3	72 24.7	45.1	Atria	107 08.3	S69 04.2
20	88 47.7	106 13.1	58.3	125 18.5	36.6	341 39.5	50.3	87 26.9	45.0	Avior	234 13.8	S59 35.7
21	103 50.2	121 12.6	. . 57.1	140 19.0	. . 36.0	356 42.1	. . 50.3	102 29.1	. . 44.9	Bellatrix	278 21.7	N 6 22.3
22	118 52.6	136 12.1	55.9	155 19.5	35.4	11 44.8	50.3	117 31.3	44.8	Betelgeuse	270 50.9	N 7 24.7
23	133 55.1	151 11.7	54.7	170 20.0	34.7	26 47.4	50.4	132 33.5	44.7			
19 00	148 57.6	166 11.2	S 8 53.5	185 20.6	S15 34.1	41 50.0	N22 50.4	147 35.7	S 1 44.6	Canopus	263 51.7	S52 42.8
01	164 00.0	181 10.8	52.3	200 21.1	33.5	56 52.7	50.4	162 37.9	44.5	Capella	280 20.3	N46 01.6
02	179 02.5	196 10.3	51.1	215 21.6	32.9	71 55.3	50.4	177 40.1	44.3	Deneb	49 25.6	N45 22.3
03	194 05.0	211 09.8	. . 49.9	230 22.2	. . 32.2	86 58.0	. . 50.5	192 42.3	. . 44.2	Denebola	182 23.7	N14 25.4
04	209 07.4	226 09.4	48.7	245 22.7	31.6	102 00.6	50.5	207 44.5	44.1	Diphda	348 46.6	S17 50.7
05	224 09.9	241 08.9	47.5	260 23.2	31.0	117 03.2	50.5	222 46.7	44.0			
06	239 12.3	256 08.5	S 8 46.3	275 23.7	S15 30.4	132 05.9	N22 50.5	237 48.9	S 1 43.9	Dubhe	193 39.2	N61 36.4
T 07	254 14.8	271 08.0	45.1	290 24.3	29.7	147 08.5	50.5	252 51.1	43.8	Elnath	278 00.5	N28 37.8
H 08	269 17.3	286 07.6	43.9	305 24.8	29.1	162 11.1	50.6	267 53.3	43.6	Eltanin	90 42.0	N51 28.8
U 09	284 19.7	301 07.1	. . 42.7	320 25.3	. . 28.5	177 13.8	. . 50.6	282 55.5	. . 43.5	Enif	33 38.2	N 9 59.6
R 10	299 22.2	316 06.7	41.5	335 25.9	27.8	192 16.4	50.6	297 57.7	43.4	Fomalhaut	15 13.8	S29 29.1
S 11	314 24.7	331 06.2	40.3	350 26.4	27.2	207 19.0	50.6	313 00.0	43.3			
D 12	329 27.1	346 05.8	S 8 39.1	5 26.9	S15 26.6	222 21.7	N22 50.6	328 02.2	S 1 43.2	Gacrux	171 50.2	S57 15.5
A 13	344 29.6	1 05.3	37.9	20 27.4	25.9	237 24.3	50.7	343 04.4	43.1	Gienah	175 42.4	S17 41.3
Y 14	359 32.1	16 04.8	36.7	35 28.0	25.3	252 26.9	50.7	358 06.6	42.9	Hadar	148 34.4	S60 29.8
15	14 34.5	31 04.4	. . 35.5	50 28.5	. . 24.7	267 29.6	. . 50.7	13 08.8	. . 42.8	Hamal	327 50.3	N23 35.2
16	29 37.0	46 03.9	34.3	65 29.0	24.0	282 32.2	50.7	28 11.0	42.7	Kaus Aust.	83 31.5	S34 22.3
17	44 39.5	61 03.5	33.1	80 29.6	23.4	297 34.8	50.8	43 13.2	42.6			
18	59 41.9	76 03.0	S 8 31.9	95 30.1	S15 22.8	312 37.5	N22 50.8	58 15.4	S 1 42.5	Kochab	137 19.5	N74 02.4
19	74 44.4	91 02.6	30.7	110 30.6	22.2	327 40.1	50.8	73 17.6	42.4	Markab	13 29.3	N15 20.7
20	89 46.8	106 02.1	29.5	125 31.2	21.5	342 42.7	50.8	88 19.8	42.2	Menkar	314 05.2	N 4 11.5
21	104 49.3	121 01.7	. . 28.3	140 31.7	. . 20.9	357 45.4	. . 50.8	103 22.0	. . 42.1	Menkent	147 56.3	S36 29.9
22	119 51.8	136 01.2	27.1	155 32.2	20.3	12 48.0	50.9	118 24.2	42.0	Miaplacidus	221 37.2	S69 49.5
23	134 54.2	151 00.8	25.9	170 32.7	19.6	27 50.6	50.9	133 26.4	41.9			
20 00	149 56.7	166 00.3	S 8 24.6	185 33.3	S15 19.0	42 53.3	N22 50.9	148 28.6	S 1 41.8	Mirfak	308 27.0	N49 57.4
01	164 59.2	180 59.9	23.4	200 33.8	18.4	57 55.9	50.9	163 30.8	41.7	Nunki	75 46.8	S26 15.9
02	180 01.6	195 59.4	22.2	215 34.3	17.7	72 58.5	50.9	178 33.0	41.5	Peacock	53 04.8	S56 39.0
03	195 04.1	210 59.0	. . 21.0	230 34.9	. . 17.1	88 01.2	. . 51.0	193 35.2	. . 41.4	Pollux	243 15.8	N27 57.7
04	210 06.6	225 58.5	19.8	245 35.4	16.5	103 03.8	51.0	208 37.4	41.3	Procyon	244 49.6	N 5 09.4
05	225 09.0	240 58.1	18.6	260 35.9	15.8	118 06.4	51.0	223 39.6	41.2			
06	240 11.5	255 57.7	S 8 17.4	275 36.5	S15 15.2	133 09.0	N22 51.0	238 41.8	S 1 41.1	Rasalhague	95 57.8	N12 32.2
07	255 13.9	270 57.2	16.2	290 37.0	14.5	148 11.7	51.1	253 44.0	41.0	Regulus	207 33.1	N11 50.2
08	270 16.4	285 56.8	15.0	305 37.5	13.9	163 14.3	51.1	268 46.2	40.8	Rigel	281 02.8	S 8 10.4
F 09	285 18.9	300 56.3	. . 13.8	320 38.1	. . 13.3	178 16.9	. . 51.1	283 48.4	. . 40.7	Rigil Kent.	139 38.8	S60 56.4
R 10	300 21.3	315 55.9	12.6	335 38.6	12.6	193 19.5	51.1	298 50.6	40.6	Sabik	102 01.8	S15 45.5
I 11	315 23.8	330 55.4	11.3	350 39.1	12.0	208 22.2	51.1	313 52.8	40.5			
D 12	330 26.3	345 55.0	S 8 10.1	5 39.7	S15 11.4	223 24.8	N22 51.2	328 55.0	S 1 40.4	Schedar	349 30.4	N56 41.0
A 13	345 28.7	0 54.5	08.9	20 40.2	10.7	238 27.4	51.2	343 57.2	40.3	Shaula	96 09.3	S37 07.3
Y 14	0 31.2	15 54.1	07.7	35 40.7	10.1	253 30.0	51.2	358 59.4	40.1	Sirius	258 25.2	S16 45.3
15	15 33.7	30 53.6	. . 06.5	50 41.3	. . 09.5	268 32.7	. . 51.2	14 01.6	. . 40.0	Spica	158 21.1	S11 18.0
16	30 36.1	45 53.2	05.3	65 41.8	08.8	283 35.3	51.2	29 03.8	39.9	Suhail	222 45.2	S43 32.4
17	45 38.6	60 52.8	04.1	80 42.3	08.2	298 37.9	51.3	44 06.0	39.8			
18	60 41.1	75 52.3	S 8 02.9	95 42.9	S15 07.5	313 40.5	N22 51.3	59 08.3	S 1 39.7	Vega	80 32.9	N38 48.2
19	75 43.5	90 51.9	01.6	110 43.4	06.9	328 43.2	51.3	74 10.5	39.6	Zuben'ubi	136 54.9	S16 09.1
20	90 46.0	105 51.4	8 00.4	125 43.9	06.3	343 45.8	51.3	89 12.7	39.4		SHA	Mer. Pass.
21	105 48.4	120 51.0	7 59.2	140 44.5	. . 05.6	358 48.4	. . 51.3	104 14.9	. . 39.3		° ′	h m
22	120 50.9	135 50.5	58.0	155 45.0	05.0	13 51.0	51.4	119 17.1	39.2	Venus	17 13.7	12 56
23	135 53.4	150 50.1	56.8	170 45.6	04.3	28 53.7	51.4	134 19.3	39.1	Mars	36 23.0	11 38
Mer. Pass.	h m 14 01.9	*v* −0.5	*d* 1.2	*v* 0.5	*d* 0.6	*v* 2.6	*d* 0.0	*v* 2.2	*d* 0.1	Jupiter	252 52.5	21 09
										Saturn	358 38.1	14 08

UT d	h	SUN GHA ° ′	SUN Dec ° ′	MOON GHA ° ′	v ′	Dec ° ′	d ′	HP ′
18	00	176 31.4	S11 42.3	170 36.4	13.2	S 9 49.1	15.0	57.3
	01	191 31.4	41.4	185 08.6	13.3	9 34.1	15.2	57.3
	02	206 31.5	40.6	199 40.9	13.2	9 18.9	15.2	57.4
	03	221 31.5	. . 39.7	214 13.1	13.3	9 03.7	15.2	57.4
	04	236 31.6	38.8	228 45.4	13.4	8 48.5	15.3	57.4
	05	251 31.6	37.9	243 17.8	13.3	8 33.2	15.3	57.4
	06	266 31.7	S11 37.0	257 50.1	13.4	S 8 17.9	15.4	57.4
W	07	281 31.7	36.1	272 22.5	13.3	8 02.5	15.5	57.5
E	08	296 31.8	35.3	286 54.8	13.4	7 47.0	15.5	57.5
D	09	311 31.8	. . 34.4	301 27.2	13.4	7 31.5	15.5	57.5
N	10	326 31.9	33.5	315 59.6	13.4	7 16.0	15.6	57.5
E	11	341 31.9	32.6	330 32.0	13.4	7 00.4	15.6	57.6
S	12	356 32.0	S11 31.7	345 04.4	13.5	S 6 44.8	15.7	57.6
D	13	11 32.0	30.8	359 36.9	13.4	6 29.1	15.7	57.6
A	14	26 32.1	29.9	14 09.3	13.5	6 13.4	15.7	57.6
Y	15	41 32.1	. . 29.1	28 41.8	13.4	5 57.7	15.8	57.6
	16	56 32.2	28.2	43 14.2	13.5	5 41.9	15.8	57.7
	17	71 32.3	27.3	57 46.7	13.4	5 26.1	15.9	57.7
	18	86 32.3	S11 26.4	72 19.1	13.5	S 5 10.2	15.8	57.7
	19	101 32.4	25.5	86 51.6	13.5	4 54.4	16.0	57.7
	20	116 32.4	24.6	101 24.1	13.5	4 38.4	15.9	57.8
	21	131 32.5	. . 23.7	115 56.6	13.5	4 22.5	16.0	57.8
	22	146 32.5	22.8	130 29.1	13.4	4 06.5	16.0	57.8
	23	161 32.6	22.0	145 01.5	13.5	3 50.5	16.1	57.8
19	00	176 32.6	S11 21.1	159 34.0	13.5	S 3 34.4	16.0	57.8
	01	191 32.7	20.2	174 06.5	13.5	3 18.4	16.1	57.9
	02	206 32.8	19.3	188 39.0	13.4	3 02.3	16.2	57.9
	03	221 32.8	. . 18.4	203 11.4	13.5	2 46.1	16.1	57.9
	04	236 32.9	17.5	217 43.9	13.5	2 30.0	16.2	57.9
	05	251 32.9	16.6	232 16.4	13.4	2 13.8	16.1	57.9
	06	266 33.0	S11 15.7	246 48.8	13.5	S 1 57.7	16.2	58.0
	07	281 33.0	14.8	261 21.3	13.4	1 41.5	16.3	58.0
T	08	296 33.1	13.9	275 53.7	13.4	1 25.2	16.2	58.0
H	09	311 33.2	. . 13.1	290 26.1	13.4	1 09.0	16.3	58.0
U	10	326 33.2	12.2	304 58.5	13.4	0 52.7	16.2	58.0
R	11	341 33.3	11.3	319 30.9	13.4	0 36.5	16.3	58.1
S	12	356 33.3	S11 10.4	334 03.3	13.4	S 0 20.2	16.3	58.1
D	13	11 33.4	09.5	348 35.7	13.3	S 0 03.9	16.3	58.1
A	14	26 33.5	08.6	3 08.0	13.3	N 0 12.4	16.3	58.1
Y	15	41 33.5	. . 07.7	17 40.3	13.3	0 28.7	16.3	58.1
	16	56 33.6	06.8	32 12.6	13.3	0 45.0	16.3	58.1
	17	71 33.6	05.9	46 44.9	13.3	1 01.3	16.4	58.2
	18	86 33.7	S11 05.0	61 17.2	13.2	N 1 17.7	16.3	58.2
	19	101 33.8	04.1	75 49.4	13.3	1 34.0	16.3	58.2
	20	116 33.8	03.2	90 21.7	13.2	1 50.3	16.4	58.2
	21	131 33.9	. . 02.3	104 53.9	13.1	2 06.7	16.3	58.2
	22	146 34.0	01.4	119 26.0	13.2	2 23.0	16.3	58.2
	23	161 34.0	11 00.5	133 58.2	13.1	2 39.3	16.3	58.3
20	00	176 34.1	S10 59.6	148 30.3	13.1	N 2 55.6	16.3	58.3
	01	191 34.2	58.7	163 02.4	13.0	3 11.9	16.4	58.3
	02	206 34.2	57.8	177 34.4	13.0	3 28.3	16.3	58.3
	03	221 34.3	. . 56.9	192 06.4	13.0	3 44.6	16.2	58.3
	04	236 34.3	56.0	206 38.4	13.0	4 00.8	16.3	58.3
	05	251 34.4	55.1	221 10.4	12.9	4 17.1	16.3	58.4
	06	266 34.5	S10 54.3	235 42.3	12.9	N 4 33.4	16.3	58.4
	07	281 34.5	53.4	250 14.2	12.8	4 49.7	16.2	58.4
	08	296 34.6	52.5	264 46.0	12.8	5 05.9	16.2	58.4
F	09	311 34.7	. . 51.6	279 17.8	12.8	5 22.1	16.2	58.4
R	10	326 34.7	50.7	293 49.6	12.7	5 38.3	16.2	58.4
I	11	341 34.8	49.8	308 21.3	12.6	5 54.5	16.2	58.5
D	12	356 34.9	S10 48.9	322 52.9	12.7	N 6 10.7	16.1	58.5
A	13	11 34.9	48.0	337 24.6	12.5	6 26.8	16.1	58.5
Y	14	26 35.0	47.1	351 56.1	12.6	6 42.9	16.1	58.5
	15	41 35.1	. . 46.2	6 27.7	12.5	6 59.0	16.1	58.5
	16	56 35.1	45.3	20 59.2	12.4	7 15.1	16.0	58.5
	17	71 35.2	44.4	35 30.6	12.4	7 31.1	16.0	58.5
	18	86 35.3	S10 43.4	50 02.0	12.3	N 7 47.1	16.0	58.6
	19	101 35.4	42.5	64 33.3	12.3	8 03.1	16.0	58.6
	20	116 35.4	41.6	79 04.6	12.2	8 19.1	15.9	58.6
	21	131 35.5	. . 40.7	93 35.8	12.2	8 35.0	15.8	58.6
	22	146 35.6	39.8	108 07.0	12.1	8 50.8	15.9	58.6
	23	161 35.6	38.9	122 38.1	12.1	N 9 06.7	15.8	58.6
		SD 16.2	*d* 0.9	SD	15.7		15.8	15.9

Lat.	Twilight Naut.	Twilight Civil	Sunrise	Moonrise 18	Moonrise 19	Moonrise 20	Moonrise 21
°	h m	h m	h m	h m	h m	h m	h m
N 72	05 57	07 16	08 31	08 33	07 56	07 20	06 38
N 70	05 57	07 08	08 14	08 22	07 54	07 27	06 55
68	05 57	07 02	08 01	08 13	07 52	07 32	07 09
66	05 57	06 56	07 51	08 05	07 51	07 36	07 21
64	05 57	06 52	07 42	07 59	07 49	07 40	07 30
62	05 56	06 48	07 34	07 53	07 48	07 44	07 39
60	05 56	06 44	07 27	07 48	07 47	07 47	07 46
N 58	05 55	06 41	07 21	07 44	07 47	07 49	07 52
56	05 55	06 38	07 16	07 40	07 46	07 52	07 58
54	05 54	06 35	07 11	07 36	07 45	07 54	08 03
52	05 53	06 33	07 07	07 33	07 44	07 56	08 08
50	05 53	06 30	07 03	07 30	07 44	07 57	08 12
45	05 51	06 25	06 55	07 24	07 43	08 01	08 21
N 40	05 49	06 20	06 48	07 19	07 42	08 05	08 29
35	05 46	06 16	06 42	07 14	07 41	08 07	08 36
30	05 44	06 12	06 36	07 10	07 40	08 10	08 42
20	05 39	06 04	06 27	07 03	07 39	08 14	08 52
N 10	05 32	05 57	06 18	06 57	07 37	08 18	09 01
0	05 25	05 49	06 10	06 51	07 36	08 22	09 10
S 10	05 16	05 41	06 02	06 45	07 35	08 26	09 19
20	05 04	05 31	05 54	06 38	07 34	08 30	09 28
30	04 49	05 19	05 43	06 31	07 33	08 35	09 39
35	04 40	05 11	05 38	06 27	07 32	08 38	09 45
40	04 28	05 02	05 31	06 22	07 31	08 41	09 52
45	04 14	04 52	05 23	06 17	07 30	08 44	10 01
S 50	03 55	04 39	05 13	06 10	07 29	08 49	10 11
52	03 46	04 32	05 09	06 07	07 28	08 51	10 16
54	03 36	04 25	05 01	06 03	07 28	08 53	10 21
56	03 24	04 17	04 59	06 00	07 27	08 56	10 27
58	03 10	04 08	04 53	05 55	07 26	08 58	10 34
S 60	02 52	03 58	04 46	05 51	07 26	09 02	10 41

Lat.	Sunset	Twilight Civil	Twilight Naut.	Moonset 18	Moonset 19	Moonset 20	Moonset 21
°	h m	h m	h m	h m	h m	h m	h m
N 72	15 58	17 14	18 33	18 05	20 21	22 44	25 42
N 70	16 15	17 21	18 32	18 13	20 19	22 29	25 00
68	16 28	17 27	18 32	18 19	20 17	22 18	24 32
66	16 38	17 33	18 32	18 24	20 15	22 08	24 11
64	16 47	17 37	18 33	18 29	20 13	22 01	23 55
62	16 55	17 41	18 33	18 32	20 12	21 54	23 41
60	17 01	17 45	18 33	18 36	20 11	21 48	23 30
N 58	17 07	17 48	18 34	18 39	20 10	21 43	23 20
56	17 12	17 51	18 34	18 41	20 09	21 39	23 11
54	17 17	17 53	18 35	18 44	20 08	21 35	23 04
52	17 21	17 56	18 35	18 46	20 07	21 31	22 57
50	17 25	17 58	18 36	18 48	20 07	21 28	22 51
45	17 33	18 03	18 38	18 52	20 05	21 21	22 38
N 40	17 40	18 08	18 40	18 55	20 04	21 15	22 27
35	17 46	18 12	18 42	18 58	20 03	21 10	22 18
30	17 52	18 16	18 44	19 01	20 02	21 05	22 10
20	18 01	18 23	18 49	19 05	20 01	20 57	21 56
N 10	18 09	18 31	18 55	19 09	19 59	20 51	21 45
0	18 17	18 38	19 03	19 12	19 58	20 45	21 33
S 10	18 25	18 47	19 12	19 16	19 57	20 38	21 22
20	18 34	18 56	19 23	19 20	19 55	20 32	21 11
30	18 44	19 08	19 38	19 24	19 54	20 24	20 57
35	18 49	19 16	19 47	19 26	19 53	20 20	20 50
40	18 56	19 24	19 58	19 29	19 52	20 15	20 41
45	19 04	19 35	20 12	19 32	19 50	20 09	20 31
S 50	19 13	19 48	20 31	19 36	19 49	20 03	20 19
52	19 17	19 54	20 39	19 37	19 48	20 00	20 13
54	19 22	20 01	20 50	19 39	19 47	19 56	20 07
56	19 28	20 08	21 01	19 41	19 47	19 53	20 00
58	19 33	20 17	21 15	19 43	19 46	19 48	19 52
S 60	19 40	20 28	21 32	19 46	19 45	19 44	19 43

Day	SUN Eqn. of Time 00^h	SUN Eqn. of Time 12^h	SUN Mer. Pass.	MOON Mer. Pass. Upper	MOON Mer. Pass. Lower	MOON Age	MOON Phase
d	m s	m s	h m	h m	h m	d %	
18	13 55	13 52	12 14	13 02	00 39	01 1	
19	13 50	13 47	12 14	13 47	01 24	02 5	●
20	13 44	13 41	12 14	14 33	02 10	03 10	

2026 FEBRUARY 21, 22, 23 (SAT., SUN., MON.)

	UT	ARIES	VENUS −3·9		MARS +1·1		JUPITER −2·5		SATURN +1·0	
		GHA	GHA	Dec	GHA	Dec	GHA	Dec	GHA	Dec
	d h	° ′	° ′	° ′	° ′	° ′	° ′	° ′	° ′	° ′
	21 00	150 55.8	165 49.7	S 7 55.6	185 46.1	S15 03.7	43 56.3	N22 51.4	149 21.5	S 1 39.0
	01	165 58.3	180 49.2	54.3	200 46.6	03.1	58 58.9	51.4	164 23.7	38.9
	02	181 00.8	195 48.8	53.1	215 47.2	02.4	74 01.5	51.4	179 25.9	38.7
	03	196 03.2	210 48.3	. . 51.9	230 47.7	. . 01.8	89 04.1	. . 51.5	194 28.1	. . 38.6
	04	211 05.7	225 47.9	50.7	245 48.2	01.1	104 06.8	51.5	209 30.3	38.5
	05	226 08.2	240 47.5	49.5	260 48.8	15 00.5	119 09.4	51.5	224 32.5	38.4
	06	241 10.6	255 47.0	S 7 48.3	275 49.3	S14 59.9	134 12.0	N22 51.5	239 34.7	S 1 38.3
	07	256 13.1	270 46.6	47.0	290 49.8	59.2	149 14.6	51.5	254 36.9	38.2
S	08	271 15.5	285 46.2	45.8	305 50.4	58.6	164 17.2	51.6	269 39.1	38.0
A	09	286 18.0	300 45.7	. . 44.6	320 50.9	. . 57.9	179 19.9	. . 51.6	284 41.3	. . 37.9
T	10	301 20.5	315 45.3	43.4	335 51.5	57.3	194 22.5	51.6	299 43.5	37.8
U	11	316 22.9	330 44.8	42.2	350 52.0	56.6	209 25.1	51.6	314 45.7	37.7
R	12	331 25.4	345 44.4	S 7 40.9	5 52.5	S14 56.0	224 27.7	N22 51.6	329 47.9	S 1 37.6
D	13	346 27.9	0 44.0	39.7	20 53.1	55.4	239 30.3	51.7	344 50.1	37.5
A	14	1 30.3	15 43.5	38.5	35 53.6	54.7	254 33.0	51.7	359 52.3	37.3
Y	15	16 32.8	30 43.1	. . 37.3	50 54.1	. . 54.1	269 35.6	. . 51.7	14 54.5	. . 37.2
	16	31 35.3	45 42.7	36.1	65 54.7	53.4	284 38.2	51.7	29 56.7	37.1
	17	46 37.7	60 42.2	34.8	80 55.2	52.8	299 40.8	51.7	44 58.9	37.0
	18	61 40.2	75 41.8	S 7 33.6	95 55.8	S14 52.1	314 43.4	N22 51.8	60 01.1	S 1 36.9
	19	76 42.7	90 41.4	32.4	110 56.3	51.5	329 46.0	51.8	75 03.3	36.7
	20	91 45.1	105 40.9	31.2	125 56.8	50.8	344 48.6	51.8	90 05.5	36.6
	21	106 47.6	120 40.5	. . 29.9	140 57.4	. . 50.2	359 51.3	. . 51.8	105 07.7	. . 36.5
	22	121 50.0	135 40.0	28.7	155 57.9	49.6	14 53.9	51.8	120 09.9	36.4
	23	136 52.5	150 39.6	27.5	170 58.5	48.9	29 56.5	51.9	135 12.1	36.3
	22 00	151 55.0	165 39.2	S 7 26.3	185 59.0	S14 48.3	44 59.1	N22 51.9	150 14.3	S 1 36.2
	01	166 57.4	180 38.8	25.0	200 59.5	47.6	60 01.7	51.9	165 16.5	36.0
	02	181 59.9	195 38.3	23.8	216 00.1	47.0	75 04.3	51.9	180 18.7	35.9
	03	197 02.4	210 37.9	. . 22.6	231 00.6	. . 46.3	90 06.9	. . 51.9	195 20.9	. . 35.8
	04	212 04.8	225 37.5	21.4	246 01.2	45.7	105 09.6	52.0	210 23.1	35.7
	05	227 07.3	240 37.0	20.1	261 01.7	45.0	120 12.2	52.0	225 25.3	35.6
	06	242 09.8	255 36.6	S 7 18.9	276 02.2	S14 44.4	135 14.8	N22 52.0	240 27.5	S 1 35.5
	07	257 12.2	270 36.2	17.7	291 02.8	43.7	150 17.4	52.0	255 29.7	35.3
	08	272 14.7	285 35.7	16.5	306 03.3	43.1	165 20.0	52.0	270 31.9	35.2
S	09	287 17.2	300 35.3	. . 15.2	321 03.9	. . 42.4	180 22.6	. . 52.0	285 34.1	. . 35.1
U	10	302 19.6	315 34.9	14.0	336 04.4	41.8	195 25.2	52.1	300 36.3	35.0
N	11	317 22.1	330 34.4	12.8	351 05.0	41.1	210 27.8	52.1	315 38.5	34.9
D	12	332 24.5	345 34.0	S 7 11.6	6 05.5	S14 40.5	225 30.4	N22 52.1	330 40.7	S 1 34.8
A	13	347 27.0	0 33.6	10.3	21 06.0	39.8	240 33.0	52.1	345 42.9	34.6
Y	14	2 29.5	15 33.2	09.1	36 06.6	39.2	255 35.7	52.1	0 45.1	34.5
	15	17 31.9	30 32.7	. . 07.9	51 07.1	. . 38.5	270 38.3	. . 52.2	15 47.3	. . 34.4
	16	32 34.4	45 32.3	06.6	66 07.7	37.9	285 40.9	52.2	30 49.5	34.3
	17	47 36.9	60 31.9	05.4	81 08.2	37.2	300 43.5	52.2	45 51.7	34.2
	18	62 39.3	75 31.4	S 7 04.2	96 08.8	S14 36.6	315 46.1	N22 52.2	60 53.9	S 1 34.0
	19	77 41.8	90 31.0	02.9	111 09.3	35.9	330 48.7	52.2	75 56.1	33.9
	20	92 44.3	105 30.6	01.7	126 09.8	35.3	345 51.3	52.2	90 58.3	33.8
	21	107 46.7	120 30.2	7 00.5	141 10.4	. . 34.6	0 53.9	. . 52.3	106 00.5	. . 33.7
	22	122 49.2	135 29.7	6 59.2	156 10.9	34.0	15 56.5	52.3	121 02.7	33.6
	23	137 51.6	150 29.3	58.0	171 11.5	33.3	30 59.1	52.3	136 04.9	33.5
	23 00	152 54.1	165 28.9	S 6 56.8	186 12.0	S14 32.7	46 01.7	N22 52.3	151 07.1	S 1 33.3
	01	167 56.6	180 28.5	55.6	201 12.6	32.0	61 04.3	52.3	166 09.3	33.2
	02	182 59.0	195 28.0	54.3	216 13.1	31.4	76 06.9	52.4	181 11.5	33.1
	03	198 01.5	210 27.6	. . 53.1	231 13.7	. . 30.7	91 09.5	. . 52.4	196 13.7	. . 33.0
	04	213 04.0	225 27.2	51.9	246 14.2	30.1	106 12.1	52.4	211 15.9	32.9
	05	228 06.4	240 26.8	50.6	261 14.7	29.4	121 14.7	52.4	226 18.1	32.7
	06	243 08.9	255 26.3	S 6 49.4	276 15.3	S14 28.8	136 17.3	N22 52.4	241 20.3	S 1 32.6
	07	258 11.4	270 25.9	48.1	291 15.8	28.1	151 19.9	52.4	256 22.5	32.5
	08	273 13.8	285 25.5	46.9	306 16.4	27.4	166 22.5	52.5	271 24.7	32.4
M	09	288 16.3	300 25.1	. . 45.7	321 16.9	. . 26.8	181 25.1	. . 52.5	286 26.9	. . 32.3
O	10	303 18.8	315 24.6	44.4	336 17.5	26.1	196 27.8	52.5	301 29.1	32.2
N	11	318 21.2	330 24.2	43.2	351 18.0	25.5	211 30.4	52.5	316 31.3	32.0
D	12	333 23.7	345 23.8	S 6 42.0	6 18.6	S14 24.8	226 33.0	N22 52.5	331 33.5	S 1 31.9
A	13	348 26.1	0 23.4	40.7	21 19.1	24.2	241 35.6	52.6	346 35.7	31.8
Y	14	3 28.6	15 23.0	39.5	36 19.7	23.5	256 38.2	52.6	1 37.9	31.7
	15	18 31.1	30 22.5	. . 38.3	51 20.2	. . 22.9	271 40.8	. . 52.6	16 40.1	. . 31.6
	16	33 33.5	45 22.1	37.0	66 20.8	22.2	286 43.4	52.6	31 42.3	31.4
	17	48 36.0	60 21.7	35.8	81 21.3	21.5	301 46.0	52.6	46 44.5	31.3
	18	63 38.5	75 21.3	S 6 34.5	96 21.9	S14 20.9	316 48.5	N22 52.6	61 46.7	S 1 31.2
	19	78 40.9	90 20.9	33.3	111 22.4	20.2	331 51.1	52.7	76 48.9	31.1
	20	93 43.4	105 20.4	32.1	126 23.0	19.6	346 53.7	52.7	91 51.1	31.0
	21	108 45.9	120 20.0	. . 30.8	141 23.5	. . 18.9	1 56.3	. . 52.7	106 53.3	. . 30.9
	22	123 48.3	135 19.6	29.6	156 24.1	18.3	16 58.9	52.7	121 55.5	30.7
	23	138 50.8	150 19.2	28.4	171 24.6	17.6	32 01.5	52.7	136 57.7	30.6
	Mer. Pass.	h m 13 50.1	v −0.4	d 1.2	v 0.5	d 0.6	v 2.6	d 0.0	v 2.2	d 0.1

STARS

Name	SHA	Dec
	° ′	° ′
Acamar	315 11.2	S40 12.2
Achernar	335 19.8	S57 06.5
Acrux	172 58.5	S63 14.6
Adhara	255 04.9	S29 00.6
Aldebaran	290 38.5	N16 33.7
Alioth	166 11.7	N55 48.8
Alkaid	152 51.0	N49 10.6
Alnair	27 32.2	S46 50.1
Alnilam	275 36.6	S 1 11.2
Alphard	217 46.5	S 8 46.5
Alphecca	126 02.9	N26 37.3
Alpheratz	357 34.1	N29 14.1
Altair	61 59.3	N 8 56.1
Ankaa	353 06.6	S42 10.0
Antares	112 14.7	S26 29.4
Arcturus	145 46.9	N19 02.5
Atria	107 08.2	S69 04.2
Avior	234 13.8	S59 35.7
Bellatrix	278 21.8	N 6 22.3
Betelgeuse	270 50.9	N 7 24.6
Canopus	263 51.7	S52 42.8
Capella	280 20.4	N46 01.6
Deneb	49 25.6	N45 22.2
Denebola	182 23.7	N14 25.4
Diphda	348 46.6	S17 50.7
Dubhe	193 39.2	N61 36.4
Elnath	278 00.5	N28 37.8
Eltanin	90 42.0	N51 28.8
Enif	33 38.2	N 9 59.6
Fomalhaut	15 13.8	S29 29.1
Gacrux	171 50.1	S57 15.5
Gienah	175 42.3	S17 41.3
Hadar	148 34.4	S60 29.8
Hamal	327 50.3	N23 35.2
Kaus Aust.	83 31.5	S34 22.3
Kochab	137 19.4	N74 02.5
Markab	13 29.3	N15 20.7
Menkar	314 05.2	N 4 11.5
Menkent	147 56.3	S36 29.9
Miaplacidus	221 37.2	S69 49.6
Mirfak	308 27.0	N49 57.4
Nunki	75 46.8	S26 15.8
Peacock	53 04.8	S56 39.0
Pollux	243 15.9	N27 57.7
Procyon	244 49.6	N 5 09.4
Rasalhague	95 57.8	N12 32.2
Regulus	207 33.1	N11 50.2
Rigel	281 02.9	S 8 10.4
Rigil Kent.	139 38.7	S60 56.4
Sabik	102 01.8	S15 45.5
Schedar	349 30.4	N56 41.0
Shaula	96 09.2	S37 07.3
Sirius	258 25.2	S16 45.3
Spica	158 21.1	S11 18.0
Suhail	222 45.2	S43 32.4
Vega	80 32.8	N38 48.2
Zuben'ubi	136 54.9	S16 09.1

	SHA	Mer. Pass.
	° ′	h m
Venus	13 44.2	12 58
Mars	34 04.0	11 36
Jupiter	253 04.1	20 56
Saturn	358 19.3	13 57

UT d	h	SUN GHA ° ′	SUN Dec ° ′	MOON GHA ° ′	v ′	MOON Dec ° ′	d ′	HP ′
21	00	176 35.7	S10 38.0	137 09.2	11.9	N 9 22.5	15.7	58.6
	01	191 35.8	37.1	151 40.1	12.0	9 38.2	15.7	58.7
	02	206 35.8	36.2	166 11.1	11.9	9 53.9	15.7	58.7
	03	221 35.9	. . 35.3	180 42.0	11.8	10 09.6	15.6	58.7
	04	236 36.0	34.4	195 12.8	11.7	10 25.2	15.6	58.7
	05	251 36.1	33.5	209 43.5	11.7	10 40.8	15.5	58.7
	06	266 36.1	S10 32.6	224 14.2	11.6	N10 56.3	15.5	58.7
	07	281 36.2	31.7	238 44.8	11.6	11 11.8	15.5	58.7
SATURDAY	08	296 36.3	30.8	253 15.4	11.4	11 27.3	15.3	58.7
	09	311 36.3	. . 29.9	267 45.8	11.4	11 42.6	15.4	58.8
	10	326 36.4	29.0	282 16.2	11.4	11 58.0	15.2	58.8
	11	341 36.5	28.1	296 46.6	11.3	12 13.2	15.2	58.8
	12	356 36.6	S10 27.2	311 16.9	11.1	N12 28.4	15.2	58.8
	13	11 36.6	26.3	325 47.0	11.2	12 43.6	15.1	58.8
	14	26 36.7	25.4	340 17.2	11.0	12 58.7	15.0	58.8
	15	41 36.8	. . 24.4	354 47.2	11.0	13 13.7	15.0	58.8
	16	56 36.9	23.5	9 17.2	10.9	13 28.7	14.9	58.8
	17	71 36.9	22.6	23 47.1	10.8	13 43.6	14.8	58.8
	18	86 37.0	S10 21.7	38 16.9	10.7	N13 58.4	14.8	58.9
	19	101 37.1	20.8	52 46.6	10.7	14 13.2	14.7	58.9
	20	116 37.2	19.9	67 16.3	10.6	14 27.9	14.6	58.9
	21	131 37.2	. . 19.0	81 45.9	10.5	14 42.5	14.5	58.9
	22	146 37.3	18.1	96 15.4	10.4	14 57.0	14.5	58.9
	23	161 37.4	17.2	110 44.8	10.3	15 11.5	14.4	58.9
22	00	176 37.5	S10 16.3	125 14.1	10.2	N15 25.9	14.3	58.9
	01	191 37.6	15.4	139 43.3	10.2	15 40.2	14.3	58.9
	02	206 37.6	14.4	154 12.5	10.1	15 54.5	14.1	58.9
	03	221 37.7	. . 13.5	168 41.6	9.9	16 08.6	14.1	58.9
	04	236 37.8	12.6	183 10.5	9.9	16 22.7	14.0	58.9
	05	251 37.9	11.7	197 39.4	9.8	16 36.7	13.9	59.0
	06	266 37.9	S10 10.8	212 08.2	9.7	N16 50.6	13.8	59.0
	07	281 38.0	09.9	226 36.9	9.7	17 04.4	13.7	59.0
	08	296 38.1	09.0	241 05.6	9.5	17 18.1	13.6	59.0
SUNDAY	09	311 38.2	. . 08.1	255 34.1	9.4	17 31.7	13.6	59.0
	10	326 38.3	07.2	270 02.5	9.4	17 45.3	13.4	59.0
	11	341 38.3	06.2	284 30.9	9.2	17 58.7	13.3	59.0
	12	356 38.4	S10 05.3	298 59.1	9.2	N18 12.0	13.3	59.0
	13	11 38.5	04.4	313 27.3	9.1	18 25.3	13.1	59.0
	14	26 38.6	03.5	327 55.4	8.9	18 38.4	13.1	59.0
	15	41 38.7	. . 02.6	342 23.3	8.9	18 51.5	12.9	59.0
	16	56 38.8	01.7	356 51.2	8.8	19 04.4	12.8	59.0
	17	71 38.8	10 00.8	11 19.0	8.7	19 17.2	12.8	59.1
	18	86 38.9	S 9 59.8	25 46.7	8.6	N19 30.0	12.6	59.1
	19	101 39.0	58.9	40 14.3	8.4	19 42.6	12.5	59.1
	20	116 39.1	58.0	54 41.7	8.4	19 55.1	12.4	59.1
	21	131 39.2	. . 57.1	69 09.1	8.3	20 07.5	12.3	59.1
	22	146 39.3	56.2	83 36.4	8.2	20 19.8	12.1	59.1
	23	161 39.3	55.3	98 03.6	8.1	20 31.9	12.1	59.1
23	00	176 39.4	S 9 54.3	112 30.7	8.0	N20 44.0	11.9	59.1
	01	191 39.5	53.4	126 57.7	7.9	20 55.9	11.8	59.1
	02	206 39.6	52.5	141 24.6	7.8	21 07.7	11.7	59.1
	03	221 39.7	. . 51.6	155 51.4	7.7	21 19.4	11.6	59.1
	04	236 39.8	50.7	170 18.1	7.6	21 31.0	11.4	59.1
	05	251 39.8	49.8	184 44.7	7.5	21 42.4	11.3	59.1
	06	266 39.9	S 9 48.8	199 11.2	7.4	N21 53.7	11.2	59.1
	07	281 40.0	47.9	213 37.6	7.3	22 04.9	11.1	59.1
	08	296 40.1	47.0	228 03.9	7.2	22 16.0	10.9	59.1
MONDAY	09	311 40.2	. . 46.1	242 30.1	7.1	22 26.9	10.8	59.1
	10	326 40.3	45.2	256 56.2	7.0	22 37.7	10.6	59.2
	11	341 40.4	44.2	271 22.2	6.9	22 48.3	10.5	59.2
	12	356 40.4	S 9 43.3	285 48.1	6.8	N22 58.8	10.4	59.2
	13	11 40.5	42.4	300 13.9	6.7	23 09.2	10.2	59.2
	14	26 40.6	41.5	314 39.6	6.6	23 19.4	10.1	59.2
	15	41 40.7	. . 40.6	329 05.2	6.5	23 29.5	9.9	59.2
	16	56 40.8	39.6	343 30.7	6.4	23 39.4	9.8	59.2
	17	71 40.9	38.7	357 56.1	6.3	23 49.2	9.7	59.2
	18	86 41.0	S 9 37.8	12 21.4	6.3	N23 58.9	9.5	59.2
	19	101 41.1	36.9	26 46.7	6.1	24 08.4	9.4	59.2
	20	116 41.2	36.0	41 11.8	6.0	24 17.8	9.2	59.2
	21	131 41.2	. . 35.0	55 36.8	5.9	24 27.0	9.0	59.2
	22	146 41.3	34.1	70 01.7	5.9	24 36.0	8.9	59.2
	23	161 41.4	33.2	84 26.6	5.7	N24 44.9	8.7	59.2
		SD 16.2	*d* 0.9	SD 16.0		16.1		16.1

Lat.	Twilight Naut.	Twilight Civil	Sunrise	Moonrise 21	Moonrise 22	Moonrise 23	Moonrise 24
°	h m	h m	h m	h m	h m	h m	h m
N 72	05 43	07 02	08 14	06 38	05 25	▭	▭
N 70	05 45	06 55	08 00	06 55	06 09	▭	▭
68	05 46	06 50	07 49	07 09	06 39	05 26	▭
66	05 47	06 46	07 39	07 21	07 01	06 28	▭
64	05 47	06 42	07 31	07 30	07 19	07 03	06 22
62	05 48	06 39	07 25	07 39	07 34	07 29	07 22
60	05 48	06 36	07 19	07 46	07 46	07 49	07 56
N 58	05 48	06 33	07 13	07 52	07 57	08 06	08 21
56	05 48	06 31	07 09	07 58	08 07	08 20	08 41
54	05 48	06 29	07 05	08 03	08 15	08 32	08 58
52	05 47	06 27	07 01	08 08	08 23	08 43	09 12
50	05 47	06 25	06 57	08 12	08 30	08 53	09 25
45	05 46	06 20	06 50	08 21	08 45	09 14	09 51
N 40	05 45	06 16	06 44	08 29	08 57	09 31	10 12
35	05 43	06 13	06 38	08 36	09 08	09 45	10 30
30	05 41	06 09	06 33	08 42	09 17	09 57	10 45
20	05 37	06 03	06 25	08 52	09 33	10 19	11 10
N 10	05 31	05 56	06 17	09 01	09 47	10 37	11 33
0	05 25	05 49	06 10	09 10	10 00	10 55	11 54
S 10	05 16	05 41	06 03	09 19	10 14	11 13	12 15
20	05 06	05 32	05 55	09 28	10 28	11 32	12 37
30	04 52	05 21	05 46	09 39	10 45	11 54	13 04
35	04 43	05 14	05 40	09 45	10 55	12 07	13 19
40	04 32	05 06	05 34	09 52	11 06	12 22	13 38
45	04 19	04 56	05 27	10 01	11 20	12 40	14 00
S 50	04 02	04 44	05 19	10 11	11 36	13 03	14 28
52	03 53	04 38	05 15	10 16	11 44	13 14	14 42
54	03 44	04 32	05 10	10 21	11 52	13 26	14 58
56	03 33	04 25	05 05	10 27	12 02	13 41	15 17
58	03 20	04 16	05 00	10 34	12 13	13 57	15 40
S 60	03 04	04 07	04 54	10 41	12 26	14 18	16 12

Lat.	Sunset	Twilight Civil	Twilight Naut.	Moonset 21	Moonset 22	Moonset 23	Moonset 24
°	h m	h m	h m	h m	h m	h m	h m
N 72	16 14	17 27	18 46	25 42	01 42	▭	▭
N 70	16 28	17 33	18 44	25 00	01 00	▭	▭
68	16 40	17 38	18 43	24 32	00 32	03 37	▭
66	16 49	17 42	18 42	24 11	00 11	02 36	▭
64	16 57	17 46	18 41	23 55	26 02	02 02	04 43
62	17 03	17 49	18 41	23 41	25 37	01 37	03 44
60	17 09	17 52	18 40	23 30	25 18	01 18	03 10
N 58	17 14	17 55	18 40	23 20	25 02	01 02	02 46
56	17 19	17 57	18 40	23 11	24 48	00 48	02 26
54	17 23	17 59	18 40	23 04	24 37	00 37	02 10
52	17 27	18 01	18 40	22 57	24 26	00 26	01 56
50	17 30	18 03	18 41	22 51	24 17	00 17	01 43
45	17 38	18 07	18 42	22 38	23 58	25 18	01 18
N 40	17 44	18 11	18 43	22 27	23 42	24 58	00 58
35	17 49	18 15	18 44	22 18	23 29	24 42	00 42
30	17 54	18 18	18 46	22 10	23 18	24 27	00 27
20	18 02	18 25	18 50	21 56	22 58	24 03	00 03
N 10	18 10	18 31	18 56	21 45	22 42	23 42	24 45
0	18 17	18 38	19 02	21 33	22 26	23 22	24 23
S 10	18 24	18 45	19 10	21 22	22 10	23 03	24 01
20	18 32	18 54	19 21	21 11	21 54	22 42	23 37
30	18 41	19 05	19 34	20 57	21 35	22 18	23 10
35	18 46	19 12	19 43	20 50	21 24	22 04	22 54
40	18 52	19 20	19 54	20 41	21 11	21 48	22 35
45	18 59	19 29	20 07	20 31	20 56	21 29	22 12
S 50	19 07	19 41	20 24	20 19	20 38	21 05	21 43
52	19 11	19 47	20 32	20 13	20 30	20 54	21 29
54	19 15	19 53	20 41	20 07	20 21	20 41	21 13
56	19 20	20 00	20 52	20 00	20 10	20 26	20 53
58	19 25	20 09	21 04	19 52	19 58	20 08	20 29
S 60	19 31	20 18	21 20	19 43	19 44	19 47	19 58

Day	SUN Eqn. of Time 00h	SUN Eqn. of Time 12h	SUN Mer. Pass.	MOON Mer. Pass. Upper	MOON Mer. Pass. Lower	MOON Age	Phase
d	m s	m s	h m	h m	h m	d %	
21	13 37	13 34	12 14	15 22	02 57	04 18	
22	13 30	13 26	12 13	16 13	03 47	05 28	
23	13 22	13 18	12 13	17 09	04 40	06 39	

UT d	UT h	ARIES GHA	VENUS −3·9 GHA	VENUS Dec	MARS +1·1 GHA	MARS Dec	JUPITER −2·5 GHA	JUPITER Dec	SATURN +1·0 GHA	SATURN Dec
d	h	° ′	° ′	° ′	° ′	° ′	° ′	° ′	° ′	° ′
24 TUESDAY	00	153 53.3	165 18.8	S 6 27.1	186 25.1	S14 16.9	47 04.1	N22 52.7	151 59.8	S 1 30.5
	01	168 55.7	180 18.3	25.9	201 25.7	16.3	62 06.7	52.8	167 02.0	30.4
	02	183 58.2	195 17.9	24.6	216 26.2	15.6	77 09.3	52.8	182 04.2	30.3
	03	199 00.6	210 17.5	23.4	231 26.8	15.0	92 11.9	52.8	197 06.4	30.1
	04	214 03.1	225 17.1	22.2	246 27.3	14.3	107 14.5	52.8	212 08.6	30.0
	05	229 05.6	240 16.7	20.9	261 27.9	13.6	122 17.1	52.8	227 10.8	29.9
	06	244 08.0	255 16.3	S 6 19.7	276 28.4	S14 13.0	137 19.7	N22 52.8	242 13.0	S 1 29.8
	07	259 10.5	270 15.8	18.4	291 29.0	12.3	152 22.3	52.9	257 15.2	29.7
	08	274 13.0	285 15.4	17.2	306 29.5	11.7	167 24.9	52.9	272 17.4	29.6
	09	289 15.4	300 15.0	15.9	321 30.1	11.0	182 27.5	52.9	287 19.6	29.4
	10	304 17.9	315 14.6	14.7	336 30.6	10.3	197 30.1	52.9	302 21.8	29.3
	11	319 20.4	330 14.2	13.5	351 31.2	09.7	212 32.7	52.9	317 24.0	29.2
	12	334 22.8	345 13.8	S 6 12.2	6 31.7	S14 09.0	227 35.3	N22 52.9	332 26.2	S 1 29.1
	13	349 25.3	0 13.4	11.0	21 32.3	08.4	242 37.9	53.0	347 28.4	29.0
	14	4 27.8	15 12.9	09.7	36 32.9	07.7	257 40.4	53.0	2 30.6	28.8
	15	19 30.2	30 12.5	08.5	51 33.4	07.0	272 43.0	53.0	17 32.8	28.7
	16	34 32.7	45 12.1	07.2	66 34.0	06.4	287 45.6	53.0	32 35.0	28.6
	17	49 35.1	60 11.7	06.0	81 34.5	05.7	302 48.2	53.0	47 37.2	28.5
	18	64 37.6	75 11.3	S 6 04.8	96 35.1	S14 05.0	317 50.8	N22 53.0	62 39.4	S 1 28.4
	19	79 40.1	90 10.9	03.5	111 35.6	04.4	332 53.4	53.1	77 41.6	28.2
	20	94 42.5	105 10.5	02.3	126 36.2	03.7	347 56.0	53.1	92 43.8	28.1
	21	109 45.0	120 10.0	6 01.0	141 36.7	03.1	2 58.6	53.1	107 46.0	28.0
	22	124 47.5	135 09.6	5 59.8	156 37.3	02.4	18 01.2	53.1	122 48.2	27.9
	23	139 49.9	150 09.2	58.5	171 37.8	01.7	33 03.8	53.1	137 50.4	27.8
25 WEDNESDAY	00	154 52.4	165 08.8	S 5 57.3	186 38.4	S14 01.1	48 06.3	N22 53.1	152 52.6	S 1 27.7
	01	169 54.9	180 08.4	56.0	201 38.9	14 00.4	63 08.9	53.2	167 54.8	27.5
	02	184 57.3	195 08.0	54.8	216 39.5	13 59.7	78 11.5	53.2	182 57.0	27.4
	03	199 59.8	210 07.6	53.5	231 40.0	59.1	93 14.1	53.2	197 59.2	27.3
	04	215 02.2	225 07.2	52.3	246 40.6	58.4	108 16.7	53.2	213 01.4	27.2
	05	230 04.7	240 06.8	51.0	261 41.1	57.7	123 19.3	53.2	228 03.6	27.1
	06	245 07.2	255 06.3	S 5 49.8	276 41.7	S13 57.1	138 21.9	N22 53.2	243 05.8	S 1 26.9
	07	260 09.6	270 05.9	48.5	291 42.3	56.4	153 24.4	53.3	258 08.0	26.8
	08	275 12.1	285 05.5	47.3	306 42.8	55.7	168 27.0	53.3	273 10.1	26.7
	09	290 14.6	300 05.1	46.0	321 43.4	55.1	183 29.6	53.3	288 12.3	26.6
	10	305 17.0	315 04.7	44.8	336 43.9	54.4	198 32.2	53.3	303 14.5	26.5
	11	320 19.5	330 04.3	43.5	351 44.5	53.7	213 34.8	53.3	318 16.7	26.3
	12	335 22.0	345 03.9	S 5 42.3	6 45.0	S13 53.1	228 37.4	N22 53.3	333 18.9	S 1 26.2
	13	350 24.4	0 03.5	41.0	21 45.6	52.4	243 39.9	53.3	348 21.1	26.1
	14	5 26.9	15 03.1	39.8	36 46.1	51.7	258 42.5	53.4	3 23.3	26.0
	15	20 29.4	30 02.7	38.5	51 46.7	51.1	273 45.1	53.4	18 25.5	25.9
	16	35 31.8	45 02.3	37.3	66 47.3	50.4	288 47.7	53.4	33 27.7	25.7
	17	50 34.3	60 01.9	36.0	81 47.8	49.7	303 50.3	53.4	48 29.9	25.6
	18	65 36.7	75 01.4	S 5 34.8	96 48.4	S13 49.1	318 52.9	N22 53.4	63 32.1	S 1 25.5
	19	80 39.2	90 01.0	33.5	111 48.9	48.4	333 55.4	53.4	78 34.3	25.4
	20	95 41.7	105 00.6	32.3	126 49.5	47.7	348 58.0	53.5	93 36.5	25.3
	21	110 44.1	120 00.2	31.0	141 50.0	47.1	4 00.6	53.5	108 38.7	25.2
	22	125 46.6	134 59.8	29.8	156 50.6	46.4	19 03.2	53.5	123 40.9	25.0
	23	140 49.1	149 59.4	28.5	171 51.1	45.7	34 05.8	53.5	138 43.1	24.9
26 THURSDAY	00	155 51.5	164 59.0	S 5 27.3	186 51.7	S13 45.0	49 08.3	N22 53.5	153 45.3	S 1 24.8
	01	170 54.0	179 58.6	26.0	201 52.3	44.4	64 10.9	53.5	168 47.5	24.7
	02	185 56.5	194 58.2	24.8	216 52.8	43.7	79 13.5	53.5	183 49.7	24.6
	03	200 58.9	209 57.8	23.5	231 53.4	43.0	94 16.1	53.6	198 51.9	24.4
	04	216 01.4	224 57.4	22.3	246 53.9	42.4	109 18.7	53.6	213 54.1	24.3
	05	231 03.9	239 57.0	21.0	261 54.5	41.7	124 21.2	53.6	228 56.3	24.2
	06	246 06.3	254 56.6	S 5 19.8	276 55.1	S13 41.0	139 23.8	N22 53.6	243 58.4	S 1 24.1
	07	261 08.8	269 56.2	18.5	291 55.6	40.3	154 26.4	53.6	259 00.6	24.0
	08	276 11.2	284 55.8	17.3	306 56.2	39.7	169 29.0	53.6	274 02.8	23.8
	09	291 13.7	299 55.4	16.0	321 56.7	39.0	184 31.5	53.6	289 05.0	23.7
	10	306 16.2	314 55.0	14.7	336 57.3	38.3	199 34.1	53.7	304 07.2	23.6
	11	321 18.6	329 54.6	13.5	351 57.8	37.7	214 36.7	53.7	319 09.4	23.5
	12	336 21.1	344 54.2	S 5 12.2	6 58.4	S13 37.0	229 39.3	N22 53.7	334 11.6	S 1 23.4
	13	351 23.6	359 53.8	11.0	21 59.0	36.3	244 41.8	53.7	349 13.8	23.2
	14	6 26.0	14 53.4	09.7	36 59.5	35.6	259 44.4	53.7	4 16.0	23.1
	15	21 28.5	29 53.0	08.5	52 00.1	35.0	274 47.0	53.7	19 18.2	23.0
	16	36 31.0	44 52.6	07.2	67 00.6	34.3	289 49.6	53.7	34 20.4	22.9
	17	51 33.4	59 52.2	05.9	82 01.2	33.6	304 52.1	53.8	49 22.6	22.8
	18	66 35.9	74 51.8	S 5 04.7	97 01.8	S13 32.9	319 54.7	N22 53.8	64 24.8	S 1 22.6
	19	81 38.4	89 51.4	03.4	112 02.3	32.3	334 57.3	53.8	79 27.0	22.5
	20	96 40.8	104 51.0	02.2	127 02.9	31.6	349 59.8	53.8	94 29.2	22.4
	21	111 43.3	119 50.6	5 00.9	142 03.5	30.9	5 02.4	53.8	109 31.4	22.3
	22	126 45.7	134 50.2	4 59.7	157 04.0	30.2	20 05.0	53.8	124 33.6	22.2
	23	141 48.2	149 49.8	S 4 58.4	172 04.6	29.6	35 07.6	53.8	139 35.8	22.0
Mer. Pass.		h m 13 38.3	v −0.4	d 1.2	v 0.6	d 0.7	v 2.6	d 0.0	v 2.2	d 0.1

STARS

Name	SHA	Dec
	° ′	° ′
Acamar	315 11.2	S40 12.2
Achernar	335 19.8	S57 06.5
Acrux	172 58.4	S63 14.6
Adhara	255 04.9	S29 00.7
Aldebaran	290 38.5	N16 33.7
Alioth	166 11.7	N55 48.8
Alkaid	152 50.9	N49 10.6
Alnair	27 32.2	S46 50.1
Alnilam	275 36.7	S 1 11.2
Alphard	217 46.5	S 8 46.5
Alphecca	126 02.9	N26 37.3
Alpheratz	357 34.1	N29 14.1
Altair	61 59.3	N 8 56.1
Ankaa	353 06.6	S42 10.0
Antares	112 14.7	S26 29.4
Arcturus	145 46.9	N19 02.5
Atria	107 08.2	S69 04.2
Avior	234 13.8	S59 35.8
Bellatrix	278 21.8	N 6 22.3
Betelgeuse	270 50.9	N 7 24.6
Canopus	263 51.7	S52 42.8
Capella	280 20.4	N46 01.6
Deneb	49 25.6	N45 22.2
Denebola	182 23.7	N14 25.4
Diphda	348 46.6	S17 50.7
Dubhe	193 39.2	N61 36.4
Elnath	278 00.6	N28 37.8
Eltanin	90 42.0	N51 28.8
Enif	33 38.2	N 9 59.6
Fomalhaut	15 13.8	S29 29.1
Gacrux	171 50.1	S57 15.5
Gienah	175 42.3	S17 41.3
Hadar	148 34.3	S60 29.8
Hamal	327 50.3	N23 35.2
Kaus Aust.	83 31.5	S34 22.3
Kochab	137 19.3	N74 02.5
Markab	13 29.3	N15 20.7
Menkar	314 05.3	N 4 11.5
Menkent	147 56.3	S36 29.9
Miaplacidus	221 37.2	S69 49.6
Mirfak	308 27.0	N49 57.4
Nunki	75 46.8	S26 15.8
Peacock	53 04.7	S56 39.0
Pollux	243 15.9	N27 57.7
Procyon	244 49.6	N 5 09.4
Rasalhague	95 57.8	N12 32.2
Regulus	207 33.1	N11 50.2
Rigel	281 02.9	S 8 10.4
Rigil Kent.	139 38.7	S60 56.4
Sabik	102 01.8	S15 45.5
Schedar	349 30.4	N56 41.0
Shaula	96 09.2	S37 07.3
Sirius	258 25.2	S16 45.3
Spica	158 21.1	S11 18.0
Suhail	222 45.2	S43 32.4
Vega	80 32.8	N38 48.2
Zuben'ubi	136 54.8	S16 09.1

	SHA	Mer. Pass.
	° ′	h m
Venus	10 16.4	13 00
Mars	31 46.0	11 33
Jupiter	253 13.9	20 44
Saturn	358 00.2	13 46

UT d	UT h	SUN GHA ° ′	SUN Dec ° ′	MOON GHA ° ′	MOON *v* ′	MOON Dec ° ′	MOON *d* ′	MOON HP ′
24 TUESDAY	00	176 41.5	S 9 32.3	98 51.3	5.7	N24 53.6	8.6	59.2
	01	191 41.6	31.4	113 16.0	5.6	25 02.2	8.4	59.2
	02	206 41.7	30.4	127 40.6	5.4	25 10.6	8.3	59.2
	03	221 41.8	. . 29.5	142 05.0	5.4	25 18.9	8.1	59.2
	04	236 41.9	28.6	156 29.4	5.3	25 27.0	7.9	59.2
	05	251 42.0	27.7	170 53.7	5.3	25 34.9	7.8	59.2
	06	266 42.1	S 9 26.7	185 18.0	5.1	N25 42.7	7.6	59.2
	07	281 42.2	25.8	199 42.1	5.0	25 50.3	7.5	59.2
	08	296 42.2	24.9	214 06.1	5.0	25 57.8	7.2	59.2
	09	311 42.3	. . 24.0	228 30.1	4.9	26 05.0	7.1	59.2
	10	326 42.4	23.0	242 54.0	4.8	26 12.1	7.0	59.2
	11	341 42.5	22.1	257 17.8	4.7	26 19.1	6.7	59.2
	12	356 42.6	S 9 21.2	271 41.5	4.7	N26 25.8	6.6	59.2
	13	11 42.7	20.3	286 05.2	4.5	26 32.4	6.4	59.2
	14	26 42.8	19.3	300 28.7	4.5	26 38.8	6.2	59.2
	15	41 42.9	. . 18.4	314 52.2	4.5	26 45.0	6.1	59.2
	16	56 43.0	17.5	329 15.7	4.3	26 51.1	5.8	59.2
	17	71 43.1	16.6	343 39.0	4.3	26 56.9	5.7	59.2
	18	86 43.2	S 9 15.6	358 02.3	4.2	N27 02.6	5.5	59.2
	19	101 43.3	14.7	12 25.5	4.2	27 08.1	5.4	59.2
	20	116 43.4	13.8	26 48.7	4.1	27 13.5	5.1	59.2
	21	131 43.5	. . 12.8	41 11.8	4.0	27 18.6	5.0	59.2
	22	146 43.6	11.9	55 34.8	4.0	27 23.6	4.8	59.2
	23	161 43.7	11.0	69 57.8	3.9	27 28.4	4.6	59.2
25 WEDNESDAY	00	176 43.8	S 9 10.1	84 20.7	3.9	N27 33.0	4.4	59.2
	01	191 43.9	09.1	98 43.6	3.8	27 37.4	4.2	59.2
	02	206 44.0	08.2	113 06.4	3.8	27 41.6	4.0	59.2
	03	221 44.1	. . 07.3	127 29.2	3.7	27 45.6	3.8	59.2
	04	236 44.2	06.3	141 51.9	3.7	27 49.4	3.7	59.2
	05	251 44.3	05.4	156 14.6	3.6	27 53.1	3.5	59.2
	06	266 44.4	S 9 04.5	170 37.2	3.6	N27 56.6	3.2	59.2
	07	281 44.5	03.6	184 59.8	3.5	27 59.8	3.1	59.2
	08	296 44.6	02.6	199 22.3	3.5	28 02.9	2.9	59.2
	09	311 44.6	. . 01.7	213 44.8	3.5	28 05.8	2.7	59.2
	10	326 44.7	9 00.8	228 07.3	3.5	28 08.5	2.5	59.2
	11	341 44.8	8 59.8	242 29.8	3.4	28 11.0	2.3	59.2
	12	356 44.9	S 8 58.9	256 52.2	3.4	N28 13.3	2.1	59.2
	13	11 45.0	58.0	271 14.6	3.3	28 15.4	1.9	59.2
	14	26 45.1	57.0	285 36.9	3.4	28 17.3	1.7	59.2
	15	41 45.2	. . 56.1	299 59.3	3.3	28 19.0	1.5	59.2
	16	56 45.4	55.2	314 21.6	3.3	28 20.5	1.4	59.2
	17	71 45.5	54.2	328 43.9	3.3	28 21.9	1.1	59.2
	18	86 45.6	S 8 53.3	343 06.2	3.3	N28 23.0	0.9	59.2
	19	101 45.7	52.4	357 28.5	3.3	28 23.9	0.8	59.2
	20	116 45.8	51.4	11 50.8	3.2	28 24.7	0.5	59.2
	21	131 45.9	. . 50.5	26 13.0	3.3	28 25.2	0.3	59.2
	22	146 46.0	49.6	40 35.3	3.3	28 25.5	0.2	59.2
	23	161 46.1	48.6	54 57.6	3.2	28 25.7	0.1	59.2
26 THURSDAY	00	176 46.2	S 8 47.7	69 19.8	3.3	N28 25.6	0.2	59.2
	01	191 46.3	46.8	83 42.1	3.3	28 25.4	0.5	59.2
	02	206 46.4	45.8	98 04.4	3.3	28 24.9	0.6	59.2
	03	221 46.5	. . 44.9	112 26.7	3.3	28 24.3	0.8	59.2
	04	236 46.6	44.0	126 49.0	3.3	28 23.5	1.1	59.2
	05	251 46.7	43.0	141 11.3	3.3	28 22.4	1.2	59.2
	06	266 46.8	S 8 42.1	155 33.6	3.4	N28 21.2	1.4	59.2
	07	281 46.9	41.2	169 56.0	3.3	28 19.8	1.6	59.2
	08	296 47.0	40.2	184 18.3	3.4	28 18.2	1.8	59.2
	09	311 47.1	. . 39.3	198 40.7	3.5	28 16.4	2.1	59.2
	10	326 47.2	38.4	213 03.2	3.4	28 14.3	2.2	59.2
	11	341 47.3	37.4	227 25.6	3.5	28 12.1	2.4	59.2
	12	356 47.4	S 8 36.5	241 48.1	3.6	N28 09.7	2.5	59.1
	13	11 47.5	35.6	256 10.7	3.5	28 07.2	2.8	59.1
	14	26 47.6	34.6	270 33.2	3.6	28 04.4	3.0	59.1
	15	41 47.7	. . 33.7	284 55.8	3.7	28 01.4	3.2	59.1
	16	56 47.8	32.7	299 18.5	3.7	27 58.2	3.3	59.1
	17	71 48.0	31.8	313 41.2	3.7	27 54.9	3.6	59.1
	18	86 48.1	S 8 30.9	328 03.9	3.8	N27 51.3	3.7	59.1
	19	101 48.2	29.9	342 26.7	3.9	27 47.6	3.9	59.1
	20	116 48.3	29.0	356 49.6	3.9	27 43.7	4.1	59.1
	21	131 48.4	. . 28.1	11 12.5	3.9	27 39.6	4.3	59.1
	22	146 48.5	27.1	25 35.4	4.0	27 35.3	4.5	59.1
	23	161 48.6	26.2	39 58.4	4.1	N27 30.8	4.7	59.1
		SD 16.2	*d* 0.9	SD	16.1	16.1		16.1

Lat. °	Twilight Naut. h m	Twilight Civil h m	Sunrise h m	Moonrise 24 h m	Moonrise 25 h m	Moonrise 26 h m	Moonrise 27 h m
N 72	05 29	06 47	07 58	□	□	□	□
N 70	05 32	06 43	07 46	□	□	□	□
68	05 35	06 39	07 36	□	□	□	□
66	05 37	06 36	07 28	□	□	□	□
64	05 38	06 33	07 21	06 22	□	□	□
62	05 39	06 30	07 15	07 22	07 06	□	10 14
60	05 40	06 28	07 10	07 56	08 17	09 15	10 55
N 58	05 40	06 26	07 06	08 21	08 53	09 53	11 23
56	05 41	06 24	07 02	08 41	09 18	10 20	11 44
54	05 41	06 22	06 58	08 58	09 39	10 41	12 02
52	05 41	06 20	06 55	09 12	09 56	10 58	12 17
50	05 42	06 19	06 52	09 25	10 11	11 13	12 31
45	05 41	06 15	06 45	09 51	10 41	11 44	12 57
N 40	05 41	06 12	06 39	10 12	11 04	12 07	13 19
35	05 40	06 09	06 35	10 30	11 24	12 27	13 36
30	05 38	06 06	06 30	10 45	11 40	12 44	13 51
20	05 35	06 01	06 23	11 10	12 09	13 12	14 17
N 10	05 30	05 55	06 16	11 33	12 33	13 36	14 39
0	05 24	05 49	06 10	11 54	12 56	13 58	15 00
S 10	05 17	05 42	06 03	12 15	13 18	14 21	15 20
20	05 07	05 34	05 56	12 37	13 43	14 45	15 42
30	04 55	05 23	05 48	13 04	14 11	15 13	16 07
35	04 46	05 17	05 43	13 19	14 28	15 30	16 22
40	04 36	05 10	05 38	13 38	14 48	15 49	16 39
45	04 24	05 01	05 31	14 00	15 12	16 13	17 00
S 50	04 08	04 50	05 24	14 28	15 43	16 43	17 25
52	04 00	04 45	05 20	14 42	15 59	16 57	17 38
54	03 52	04 39	05 16	14 58	16 17	17 15	17 52
56	03 41	04 32	05 12	15 17	16 39	17 35	18 08
58	03 30	04 25	05 07	15 40	17 07	18 01	18 28
S 60	03 16	04 16	05 02	16 12	17 48	18 37	18 52

Lat. °	Sunset h m	Twilight Civil h m	Twilight Naut. h m	Moonset 24 h m	Moonset 25 h m	Moonset 26 h m	Moonset 27 h m
N 72	16 30	17 41	18 59	□	□	□	□
N 70	16 42	17 45	18 56	□	□	□	□
68	16 51	17 49	18 53	□	□	□	□
66	16 59	17 52	18 51	□	□	□	□
64	17 06	17 55	18 50	04 43	□	□	□
62	17 12	17 57	18 49	03 44	06 08	□	07 22
60	17 17	17 59	18 48	03 10	04 57	06 11	06 41
N 58	17 21	18 01	18 47	02 46	04 22	05 33	06 13
56	17 25	18 03	18 46	02 26	03 56	05 06	05 50
54	17 29	18 05	18 46	02 10	03 36	04 45	05 32
52	17 32	18 06	18 46	01 56	03 19	04 27	05 17
50	17 35	18 08	18 45	01 43	03 04	04 12	05 03
45	17 42	18 11	18 45	01 18	02 35	03 42	04 35
N 40	17 47	18 15	18 46	00 58	02 12	03 18	04 14
35	17 52	18 17	18 47	00 42	01 53	02 58	03 55
30	17 56	18 20	18 48	00 27	01 36	02 41	03 40
20	18 04	18 26	18 51	00 03	01 09	02 13	03 13
N 10	18 10	18 31	18 56	24 45	00 45	01 48	02 50
0	18 16	18 37	19 02	24 23	00 23	01 26	02 28
S 10	18 23	18 44	19 09	24 01	00 01	01 03	02 06
20	18 30	18 52	19 18	23 37	24 38	00 38	01 43
30	18 38	19 02	19 31	23 10	24 09	00 09	01 15
35	18 42	19 08	19 39	22 54	23 52	24 59	00 59
40	18 48	19 15	19 49	22 35	23 32	24 40	00 40
45	18 54	19 24	20 01	22 12	23 08	24 17	00 17
S 50	19 01	19 35	20 16	21 43	22 37	23 48	25 10
52	19 05	19 40	20 24	21 29	22 22	23 33	24 58
54	19 08	19 46	20 33	21 13	22 03	23 16	24 44
56	19 13	19 52	20 42	20 53	21 41	22 56	24 28
58	19 17	20 00	20 54	20 29	21 13	22 30	24 09
S 60	19 23	20 08	21 08	19 58	20 32	21 55	23 46

Day d	SUN Eqn. of Time 00^h m s	SUN Eqn. of Time 12^h m s	SUN Mer. Pass. h m	MOON Mer. Pass. Upper h m	MOON Mer. Pass. Lower h m	MOON Age d	MOON %	Phase
24	13 14	13 10	12 13	18 08	05 38	07	50	
25	13 05	13 00	12 13	19 11	06 39	08	61	
26	12 56	12 51	12 13	20 13	07 42	09	72	

UT d	h	ARIES GHA	VENUS −3·9 GHA	VENUS Dec	MARS +1·1 GHA	MARS Dec	JUPITER −2·4 GHA	JUPITER Dec	SATURN +1·0 GHA	SATURN Dec
		° ′	° ′	° ′	° ′	° ′	° ′	° ′	° ′	° ′
27 FRIDAY	00	156 50.7	164 49.4	S 4 57.1	187 05.1	S13 28.9	50 10.1	N22 53.9	154 37.9	S 1 21.9
	01	171 53.1	179 49.0	55.9	202 05.7	28.2	65 12.7	53.9	169 40.1	21.8
	02	186 55.6	194 48.6	54.6	217 06.3	27.5	80 15.3	53.9	184 42.3	21.7
	03	201 58.1	209 48.2	. . 53.4	232 06.8	. . 26.9	95 17.8	. . 53.9	199 44.5	. . 21.6
	04	217 00.5	224 47.8	52.1	247 07.4	26.2	110 20.4	53.9	214 46.7	21.4
	05	232 03.0	239 47.4	50.9	262 07.9	25.5	125 23.0	53.9	229 48.9	21.3
	06	247 05.5	254 47.0	S 4 49.6	277 08.5	S13 24.8	140 25.5	N22 53.9	244 51.1	S 1 21.2
	07	262 07.9	269 46.6	48.3	292 09.1	24.2	155 28.1	54.0	259 53.3	21.1
	08	277 10.4	284 46.2	47.1	307 09.6	23.5	170 30.7	54.0	274 55.5	21.0
	09	292 12.9	299 45.8	. . 45.8	322 10.2	. . 22.8	185 33.3	. . 54.0	289 57.7	. . 20.8
	10	307 15.3	314 45.4	44.5	337 10.8	22.1	200 35.8	54.0	304 59.9	20.7
	11	322 17.8	329 45.0	43.3	352 11.3	21.4	215 38.4	54.0	320 02.1	20.6
	12	337 20.2	344 44.6	S 4 42.0	7 11.9	S13 20.8	230 41.0	N22 54.0	335 04.3	S 1 20.5
	13	352 22.7	359 44.2	40.8	22 12.5	20.1	245 43.5	54.0	350 06.5	20.4
	14	7 25.2	14 43.8	39.5	37 13.0	19.4	260 46.1	54.1	5 08.7	20.2
	15	22 27.6	29 43.4	. . 38.2	52 13.6	. . 18.7	275 48.6	. . 54.1	20 10.9	. . 20.1
	16	37 30.1	44 43.0	37.0	67 14.1	18.1	290 51.2	54.1	35 13.0	20.0
	17	52 32.6	59 42.6	35.7	82 14.7	17.4	305 53.8	54.1	50 15.2	19.9
	18	67 35.0	74 42.2	S 4 34.5	97 15.3	S13 16.7	320 56.3	N22 54.1	65 17.4	S 1 19.8
	19	82 37.5	89 41.8	33.2	112 15.8	16.0	335 58.9	54.1	80 19.6	19.6
	20	97 40.0	104 41.4	31.9	127 16.4	15.3	351 01.5	54.1	95 21.8	19.5
	21	112 42.4	119 41.0	. . 30.7	142 17.0	. . 14.7	6 04.0	. . 54.2	110 24.0	. . 19.4
	22	127 44.9	134 40.6	29.4	157 17.5	14.0	21 06.6	54.2	125 26.2	19.3
	23	142 47.4	149 40.2	28.1	172 18.1	13.3	36 09.2	54.2	140 28.4	19.2
28 SATURDAY	00	157 49.8	164 39.9	S 4 26.9	187 18.7	S13 12.6	51 11.7	N22 54.2	155 30.6	S 1 19.0
	01	172 52.3	179 39.5	25.6	202 19.2	11.9	66 14.3	54.2	170 32.8	18.9
	02	187 54.7	194 39.1	24.4	217 19.8	11.2	81 16.8	54.2	185 35.0	18.8
	03	202 57.2	209 38.7	. . 23.1	232 20.4	. . 10.6	96 19.4	. . 54.2	200 37.2	. . 18.7
	04	217 59.7	224 38.3	21.8	247 20.9	09.9	111 22.0	54.2	215 39.4	18.6
	05	233 02.1	239 37.9	20.6	262 21.5	09.2	126 24.5	54.3	230 41.6	18.4
	06	248 04.6	254 37.5	S 4 19.3	277 22.1	S13 08.5	141 27.1	N22 54.3	245 43.7	S 1 18.3
	07	263 07.1	269 37.1	18.0	292 22.6	07.8	156 29.6	54.3	260 45.9	18.2
	08	278 09.5	284 36.7	16.8	307 23.2	07.2	171 32.2	54.3	275 48.1	18.1
	09	293 12.0	299 36.3	. . 15.5	322 23.8	. . 06.5	186 34.8	. . 54.3	290 50.3	. . 18.0
	10	308 14.5	314 35.9	14.2	337 24.3	05.8	201 37.3	54.3	305 52.5	17.8
	11	323 16.9	329 35.5	13.0	352 24.9	05.1	216 39.9	54.3	320 54.7	17.7
	12	338 19.4	344 35.1	S 4 11.7	7 25.5	S13 04.4	231 42.4	N22 54.3	335 56.9	S 1 17.6
	13	353 21.8	359 34.8	10.4	22 26.0	03.7	246 45.0	54.4	350 59.1	17.5
	14	8 24.3	14 34.4	09.2	37 26.6	03.1	261 47.5	54.4	6 01.3	17.4
	15	23 26.8	29 34.0	. . 07.9	52 27.2	. . 02.4	276 50.1	. . 54.4	21 03.5	. . 17.2
	16	38 29.2	44 33.6	06.6	67 27.7	01.7	291 52.7	54.4	36 05.7	17.1
	17	53 31.7	59 33.2	05.4	82 28.3	01.0	306 55.2	54.4	51 07.9	17.0
	18	68 34.2	74 32.8	S 4 04.1	97 28.9	S13 00.3	321 57.8	N22 54.4	66 10.1	S 1 16.9
	19	83 36.6	89 32.4	02.8	112 29.5	12 59.6	337 00.3	54.4	81 12.2	16.8
	20	98 39.1	104 32.0	01.6	127 30.0	58.9	352 02.9	54.4	96 14.4	16.6
	21	113 41.6	119 31.6	4 00.3	142 30.6	. . 58.3	7 05.4	. . 54.5	111 16.6	. . 16.5
	22	128 44.0	134 31.2	3 59.0	157 31.2	57.6	22 08.0	54.5	126 18.8	16.4
	23	143 46.5	149 30.9	57.8	172 31.7	56.9	37 10.5	54.5	141 21.0	16.3
1 SUNDAY	00	158 49.0	164 30.5	S 3 56.5	187 32.3	S12 56.2	52 13.1	N22 54.5	156 23.2	S 1 16.2
	01	173 51.4	179 30.1	55.2	202 32.9	55.5	67 15.6	54.5	171 25.4	16.0
	02	188 53.9	194 29.7	54.0	217 33.4	54.8	82 18.2	54.5	186 27.6	15.9
	03	203 56.3	209 29.3	. . 52.7	232 34.0	. . 54.1	97 20.8	. . 54.5	201 29.8	. . 15.8
	04	218 58.8	224 28.9	51.4	247 34.6	53.4	112 23.3	54.5	216 32.0	15.7
	05	234 01.3	239 28.5	50.1	262 35.2	52.8	127 25.9	54.6	231 34.2	15.6
	06	249 03.7	254 28.1	S 3 48.9	277 35.7	S12 52.1	142 28.4	N22 54.6	246 36.4	S 1 15.4
	07	264 06.2	269 27.7	47.6	292 36.3	51.4	157 31.0	54.6	261 38.5	15.3
	08	279 08.7	284 27.4	46.3	307 36.9	50.7	172 33.5	54.6	276 40.7	15.2
	09	294 11.1	299 27.0	. . 45.1	322 37.4	. . 50.0	187 36.1	. . 54.6	291 42.9	. . 15.1
	10	309 13.6	314 26.6	43.8	337 38.0	49.3	202 38.6	54.6	306 45.1	15.0
	11	324 16.1	329 26.2	42.5	352 38.6	48.6	217 41.2	54.6	321 47.3	14.8
	12	339 18.5	344 25.8	S 3 41.3	7 39.2	S12 47.9	232 43.7	N22 54.6	336 49.5	S 1 14.7
	13	354 21.0	359 25.4	40.0	22 39.7	47.3	247 46.3	54.6	351 51.7	14.6
	14	9 23.5	14 25.0	38.7	37 40.3	46.6	262 48.8	54.7	6 53.9	14.5
	15	24 25.9	29 24.7	. . 37.4	52 40.9	. . 45.9	277 51.3	. . 54.7	21 56.1	. . 14.4
	16	39 28.4	44 24.3	36.2	67 41.4	45.2	292 53.9	54.7	36 58.3	14.2
	17	54 30.8	59 23.9	34.9	82 42.0	44.5	307 56.4	54.7	52 00.5	14.1
	18	69 33.3	74 23.5	S 3 33.6	97 42.6	S12 43.8	322 59.0	N22 54.7	67 02.6	S 1 14.0
	19	84 35.8	89 23.1	32.4	112 43.2	43.1	338 01.5	54.7	82 04.8	13.9
	20	99 38.2	104 22.7	31.1	127 43.7	42.4	353 04.1	54.7	97 07.0	13.8
	21	114 40.7	119 22.3	. . 29.8	142 44.3	. . 41.7	8 06.6	. . 54.7	112 09.2	. . 13.6
	22	129 43.2	134 22.0	28.5	157 44.9	41.0	23 09.2	54.8	127 11.4	13.5
	23	144 45.6	149 21.6	27.3	172 45.5	40.4	38 11.7	54.8	142 13.6	13.4
Mer. Pass.		h m 13 26.5	*v* −0.4	*d* 1.3	*v* 0.6	*d* 0.7	*v* 2.6	*d* 0.0	*v* 2.2	*d* 0.1

STARS

Name	SHA	Dec
	° ′	° ′
Acamar	315 11.2	S40 12.2
Achernar	335 19.8	S57 06.4
Acrux	172 58.4	S63 14.6
Adhara	255 04.9	S29 00.7
Aldebaran	290 38.5	N16 33.7
Alioth	166 11.6	N55 48.8
Alkaid	152 50.9	N49 10.6
Alnair	27 32.2	S46 50.1
Alnilam	275 36.7	S 1 11.2
Alphard	217 46.5	S 8 46.5
Alphecca	126 02.8	N26 37.3
Alpheratz	357 34.1	N29 14.1
Altair	61 59.3	N 8 56.1
Ankaa	353 06.6	S42 10.0
Antares	112 14.7	S26 29.4
Arcturus	145 46.8	N19 02.5
Atria	107 08.1	S69 04.2
Avior	234 13.8	S59 35.8
Bellatrix	278 21.8	N 6 22.3
Betelgeuse	270 50.9	N 7 24.6
Canopus	263 51.7	S52 42.8
Capella	280 20.4	N46 01.6
Deneb	49 25.6	N45 22.2
Denebola	182 23.7	N14 25.4
Diphda	348 46.6	S17 50.7
Dubhe	193 39.1	N61 36.4
Elnath	278 00.6	N28 37.8
Eltanin	90 41.9	N51 28.7
Enif	33 38.2	N 9 59.6
Fomalhaut	15 13.8	S29 29.1
Gacrux	171 50.1	S57 15.6
Gienah	175 42.3	S17 41.4
Hadar	148 34.3	S60 29.8
Hamal	327 50.3	N23 35.2
Kaus Aust.	83 31.4	S34 22.3
Kochab	137 19.3	N74 02.5
Markab	13 29.3	N15 20.7
Menkar	314 05.3	N 4 11.5
Menkent	147 56.3	S36 29.9
Miaplacidus	221 37.3	S69 49.6
Mirfak	308 27.0	N49 57.4
Nunki	75 46.8	S26 15.8
Peacock	53 04.7	S56 38.9
Pollux	243 15.9	N27 57.7
Procyon	244 49.6	N 5 09.4
Rasalhague	95 57.7	N12 32.2
Regulus	207 33.1	N11 50.2
Rigel	281 02.9	S 8 10.4
Rigil Kent.	139 38.6	S60 56.4
Sabik	102 01.7	S15 45.5
Schedar	349 30.5	N56 41.0
Shaula	96 09.2	S37 07.3
Sirius	258 25.2	S16 45.3
Spica	158 21.1	S11 18.0
Suhail	222 45.2	S43 32.5
Vega	80 32.8	N38 48.2
Zuben'ubi	136 54.8	S16 09.1

	SHA	Mer. Pass.
	° ′	h m
Venus	6 50.0	13 02
Mars	29 28.9	11 30
Jupiter	253 21.9	20 32
Saturn	357 40.8	13 36

Day	UT d h	SUN GHA ° ′	SUN Dec ° ′	MOON GHA ° ′	v ′	MOON Dec ° ′	d ′	HP ′
	27 00	176 48.7	S 8 25.2	54 21.5	4.2	N27 26.1	4.8	59.1
	01	191 48.8	24.3	68 44.7	4.2	27 21.3	5.0	59.1
	02	206 48.9	23.4	83 07.9	4.2	27 16.3	5.2	59.1
	03	221 49.0	22.4	97 31.1	4.4	27 11.1	5.4	59.1
	04	236 49.2	21.5	111 54.5	4.4	27 05.7	5.6	59.0
	05	251 49.3	20.5	126 17.9	4.5	27 00.1	5.8	59.0
	06	266 49.4	S 8 19.6	140 41.4	4.6	N26 54.3	5.9	59.0
	07	281 49.5	18.7	155 05.0	4.6	26 48.4	6.1	59.0
	08	296 49.6	17.7	169 28.6	4.7	26 42.3	6.3	59.0
FRIDAY	09	311 49.7	16.8	183 52.3	4.8	26 36.0	6.4	59.0
	10	326 49.8	15.8	198 16.1	4.9	26 29.6	6.6	59.0
	11	341 49.9	14.9	212 40.0	5.0	26 23.0	6.8	59.0
	12	356 50.0	S 8 14.0	227 04.0	5.0	N26 16.2	7.0	59.0
	13	11 50.2	13.0	241 28.0	5.1	26 09.2	7.1	59.0
	14	26 50.3	12.1	255 52.1	5.3	26 02.1	7.3	59.0
	15	41 50.4	11.1	270 16.4	5.3	25 54.8	7.5	58.9
	16	56 50.5	10.2	284 40.7	5.4	25 47.3	7.6	58.9
	17	71 50.6	09.2	299 05.1	5.5	25 39.7	7.8	58.9
	18	86 50.7	S 8 08.3	313 29.6	5.6	N25 31.9	7.9	58.9
	19	101 50.8	07.4	327 54.2	5.6	25 24.0	8.1	58.9
	20	116 50.9	06.4	342 18.8	5.8	25 15.9	8.3	58.9
	21	131 51.1	05.5	356 43.6	5.9	25 07.6	8.4	58.9
	22	146 51.2	04.5	11 08.5	6.0	24 59.2	8.6	58.9
	23	161 51.3	03.6	25 33.5	6.0	24 50.6	8.7	58.9
	28 00	176 51.4	S 8 02.6	39 58.5	6.2	N24 41.9	8.9	58.9
	01	191 51.5	01.7	54 23.7	6.3	24 33.0	9.0	58.8
	02	206 51.6	8 00.8	68 49.0	6.4	24 24.0	9.2	58.8
	03	221 51.7	7 59.8	83 14.4	6.4	24 14.8	9.3	58.8
	04	236 51.9	58.9	97 39.8	6.6	24 05.5	9.4	58.8
	05	251 52.0	57.9	112 05.4	6.7	23 56.1	9.7	58.8
	06	266 52.1	S 7 57.0	126 31.1	6.8	N23 46.4	9.7	58.8
	07	281 52.2	56.0	140 56.9	6.8	23 36.7	9.9	58.8
SATURDAY	08	296 52.3	55.1	155 22.7	7.0	23 26.8	10.0	58.8
	09	311 52.4	54.1	169 48.7	7.1	23 16.8	10.2	58.7
	10	326 52.6	53.2	184 14.8	7.2	23 06.6	10.3	58.7
	11	341 52.7	52.2	198 41.0	7.3	22 56.3	10.4	58.7
	12	356 52.8	S 7 51.3	213 07.3	7.5	N22 45.9	10.6	58.7
	13	11 52.9	50.4	227 33.8	7.5	22 35.3	10.7	58.7
	14	26 53.0	49.4	242 00.3	7.6	22 24.6	10.8	58.7
	15	41 53.1	48.5	256 26.9	7.7	22 13.8	10.9	58.7
	16	56 53.3	47.5	270 53.6	7.9	22 02.9	11.1	58.6
	17	71 53.4	46.6	285 20.5	7.9	21 51.8	11.2	58.6
	18	86 53.5	S 7 45.6	299 47.4	8.1	N21 40.6	11.3	58.6
	19	101 53.6	44.7	314 14.5	8.2	21 29.3	11.5	58.6
	20	116 53.7	43.7	328 41.7	8.2	21 17.8	11.5	58.6
	21	131 53.9	42.8	343 08.9	8.4	21 06.3	11.7	58.6
	22	146 54.0	41.8	357 36.3	8.5	20 54.6	11.7	58.6
	23	161 54.1	40.9	12 03.8	8.6	20 42.9	11.9	58.5
	1 00	176 54.2	S 7 39.9	26 31.4	8.7	N20 31.0	12.0	58.5
	01	191 54.3	39.0	40 59.1	8.8	20 19.0	12.1	58.5
	02	206 54.5	38.0	55 26.9	8.9	20 06.9	12.3	58.5
	03	221 54.6	37.1	69 54.8	9.0	19 54.6	12.3	58.5
	04	236 54.7	36.1	84 22.8	9.2	19 42.3	12.4	58.5
	05	251 54.8	35.2	98 51.0	9.2	19 29.9	12.5	58.4
	06	266 54.9	S 7 34.2	113 19.2	9.3	N19 17.4	12.7	58.4
	07	281 55.1	33.3	127 47.5	9.5	19 04.7	12.7	58.4
	08	296 55.2	32.3	142 16.0	9.5	18 52.0	12.8	58.4
SUNDAY	09	311 55.3	31.4	156 44.5	9.6	18 39.2	12.9	58.4
	10	326 55.4	30.4	171 13.1	9.8	18 26.3	13.0	58.4
	11	341 55.6	29.5	185 41.9	9.8	18 13.3	13.1	58.3
	12	356 55.7	S 7 28.5	200 10.7	10.0	N18 00.2	13.2	58.3
	13	11 55.8	27.6	214 39.7	10.1	17 47.0	13.3	58.3
	14	26 55.9	26.6	229 08.8	10.1	17 33.7	13.3	58.3
	15	41 56.1	25.7	243 37.9	10.3	17 20.4	13.5	58.3
	16	56 56.2	24.7	258 07.2	10.3	17 06.9	13.5	58.3
	17	71 56.3	23.8	272 36.5	10.5	16 53.4	13.6	58.2
	18	86 56.4	S 7 22.8	287 06.0	10.5	N16 39.8	13.7	58.2
	19	101 56.5	21.9	301 35.5	10.7	16 26.1	13.8	58.2
	20	116 56.7	20.9	316 05.2	10.7	16 12.3	13.8	58.2
	21	131 56.8	20.0	330 34.9	10.9	15 58.5	13.9	58.2
	22	146 56.9	19.0	345 04.8	10.9	15 44.6	14.0	58.1
	23	161 57.0	18.1	359 34.7	11.0	N15 30.6	14.0	58.1
		SD 16.2	*d* 0.9	SD	16.1	16.0		15.9

Lat. °	Twilight Naut. h m	Twilight Civil h m	Sunrise h m	Moonrise 27 h m	Moonrise 28 h m	Moonrise 1 h m	Moonrise 2 h m
N 72	05 15	06 33	07 42	▭	▭	▭	14 58
N 70	05 19	06 30	07 32	▭	▭	12 35	15 19
68	05 23	06 27	07 24	▭	▭	13 15	15 35
66	05 26	06 25	07 17	▭	11 03	13 43	15 48
64	05 28	06 23	07 11	▭	11 52	14 04	15 59
62	05 30	06 21	07 06	10 14	12 23	14 20	16 08
60	05 32	06 20	07 01	10 55	12 46	14 34	16 15
N 58	05 33	06 18	06 58	11 23	13 05	14 46	16 22
56	05 34	06 17	06 54	11 44	13 20	14 56	16 28
54	05 35	06 15	06 51	12 02	13 33	15 05	16 33
52	05 35	06 14	06 48	12 17	13 45	15 13	16 38
50	05 36	06 13	06 45	12 31	13 55	15 20	16 42
45	05 36	06 10	06 40	12 57	14 16	15 35	16 52
N 40	05 36	06 08	06 35	13 19	14 34	15 48	16 59
35	05 36	06 05	06 31	13 36	14 48	15 58	17 06
30	05 35	06 03	06 27	13 51	15 00	16 08	17 12
20	05 33	05 58	06 21	14 17	15 22	16 23	17 22
N 10	05 29	05 54	06 15	14 39	15 40	16 37	17 30
0	05 24	05 48	06 09	15 00	15 57	16 50	17 39
S 10	05 18	05 42	06 03	15 20	16 14	17 03	17 47
20	05 09	05 35	05 57	15 42	16 32	17 16	17 55
30	04 57	05 26	05 50	16 07	16 53	17 31	18 05
35	04 50	05 20	05 46	16 22	17 05	17 40	18 11
40	04 40	05 13	05 41	16 39	17 19	17 50	18 17
45	04 29	05 05	05 36	17 00	17 35	18 02	18 24
S 50	04 14	04 55	05 29	17 25	17 55	18 16	18 33
52	04 07	04 50	05 26	17 38	18 04	18 23	18 37
54	03 59	04 45	05 22	17 52	18 15	18 30	18 41
56	03 50	04 39	05 19	18 08	18 27	18 38	18 46
58	03 39	04 32	05 14	18 28	18 41	18 48	18 52
S 60	03 26	04 25	05 09	18 52	18 57	18 58	18 58

Lat. °	Sunset h m	Twilight Civil h m	Twilight Naut. h m	Moonset 27 h m	Moonset 28 h m	Moonset 1 h m	Moonset 2 h m
N 72	16 45	17 55	19 13	▭	▭	▭	08 24
N 70	16 55	17 57	19 08	▭	▭	09 01	08 00
68	17 03	18 00	19 04	▭	▭	08 18	07 42
66	17 10	18 02	19 01	▭	08 37	07 49	07 27
64	17 15	18 04	18 59	▭	07 47	07 27	07 15
62	17 20	18 05	18 57	07 22	07 15	07 09	07 04
60	17 25	18 07	18 55	06 41	06 51	06 55	06 55
N 58	17 28	18 08	18 54	06 13	06 32	06 42	06 47
56	17 32	18 09	18 52	05 50	06 16	06 31	06 40
54	17 35	18 11	18 52	05 32	06 02	06 21	06 34
52	17 38	18 12	18 51	05 17	05 50	06 12	06 28
50	17 40	18 13	18 50	05 03	05 39	06 04	06 23
45	17 46	18 15	18 49	04 35	05 16	05 48	06 12
N 40	17 51	18 18	18 49	04 14	04 58	05 34	06 03
35	17 55	18 20	18 49	03 55	04 43	05 22	05 54
30	17 58	18 22	18 50	03 40	04 29	05 11	05 47
20	18 05	18 27	18 52	03 13	04 06	04 53	05 35
N 10	18 10	18 32	18 56	02 50	03 46	04 38	05 24
0	18 16	18 37	19 01	02 28	03 27	04 23	05 13
S 10	18 21	18 43	19 07	02 06	03 09	04 08	05 03
20	18 27	18 50	19 16	01 43	02 48	03 52	04 52
30	18 34	18 59	19 27	01 15	02 24	03 33	04 39
35	18 38	19 04	19 35	00 59	02 10	03 22	04 31
40	18 43	19 11	19 44	00 40	01 54	03 09	04 22
45	18 49	19 19	19 55	00 17	01 34	02 54	04 12
S 50	18 55	19 29	20 09	25 10	01 10	02 36	04 00
52	18 58	19 33	20 16	24 58	00 58	02 27	03 54
54	19 01	19 38	20 24	24 44	00 44	02 17	03 48
56	19 05	19 44	20 33	24 28	00 28	02 06	03 40
58	19 09	19 51	20 44	24 09	00 09	01 53	03 32
S 60	19 14	19 58	20 56	23 46	25 38	01 38	03 23

Day	SUN Eqn. of Time 00^h	SUN Eqn. of Time 12^h	SUN Mer. Pass.	MOON Mer. Pass. Upper	MOON Mer. Pass. Lower	MOON Age	MOON Phase
d	m s	m s	h m	h m	h m	d	%
27	12 45	12 40	12 13	21 14	08 44	10	82
28	12 35	12 29	12 12	22 10	09 42	11	90
1	12 23	12 18	12 12	23 02	10 36	12	95

UT		ARIES	VENUS −3·9		MARS +1·1		JUPITER −2·4		SATURN +1·0	
		GHA	GHA	Dec	GHA	Dec	GHA	Dec	GHA	Dec
d h		° ′	° ′	° ′	° ′	° ′	° ′	° ′	° ′	° ′
2 00	MONDAY	159 48.1	164 21.2	S 3 26.0	187 46.0	S12 39.7	53 14.3	N22 54.8	157 15.8	S 1 13.3
01		174 50.6	179 20.8	24.7	202 46.6	39.0	68 16.8	54.8	172 18.0	13.2
02		189 53.0	194 20.4	23.5	217 47.2	38.3	83 19.3	54.8	187 20.2	13.0
03		204 55.5	209 20.0	. . 22.2	232 47.8	. . 37.6	98 21.9	. . 54.8	202 22.4	. . 12.9
04		219 57.9	224 19.7	20.9	247 48.3	36.9	113 24.4	54.8	217 24.6	12.8
05		235 00.4	239 19.3	19.6	262 48.9	36.2	128 27.0	54.8	232 26.7	12.7
06		250 02.9	254 18.9	S 3 18.4	277 49.5	S12 35.5	143 29.5	N22 54.8	247 28.9	S 1 12.5
07		265 05.3	269 18.5	17.1	292 50.1	34.8	158 32.1	54.8	262 31.1	12.4
08		280 07.8	284 18.1	15.8	307 50.6	34.1	173 34.6	54.9	277 33.3	12.3
09		295 10.3	299 17.7	. . 14.5	322 51.2	. . 33.4	188 37.1	. . 54.9	292 35.5	. . 12.2
10		310 12.7	314 17.4	13.3	337 51.8	32.7	203 39.7	54.9	307 37.7	12.1
11		325 15.2	329 17.0	12.0	352 52.4	32.0	218 42.2	54.9	322 39.9	11.9
12		340 17.7	344 16.6	S 3 10.7	7 52.9	S12 31.3	233 44.8	N22 54.9	337 42.1	S 1 11.8
13		355 20.1	359 16.2	09.4	22 53.5	30.6	248 47.3	54.9	352 44.3	11.7
14		10 22.6	14 15.8	08.2	37 54.1	30.0	263 49.8	54.9	7 46.5	11.6
15		25 25.1	29 15.5	. . 06.9	52 54.7	. . 29.3	278 52.4	. . 54.9	22 48.6	. . 11.5
16		40 27.5	44 15.1	05.6	67 55.2	28.6	293 54.9	54.9	37 50.8	11.3
17		55 30.0	59 14.7	04.3	82 55.8	27.9	308 57.5	55.0	52 53.0	11.2
18		70 32.4	74 14.3	S 3 03.1	97 56.4	S12 27.2	324 00.0	N22 55.0	67 55.2	S 1 11.1
19		85 34.9	89 13.9	01.8	112 57.0	26.5	339 02.5	55.0	82 57.4	11.0
20		100 37.4	104 13.5	3 00.5	127 57.5	25.8	354 05.1	55.0	97 59.6	10.9
21		115 39.8	119 13.2	2 59.2	142 58.1	. . 25.1	9 07.6	. . 55.0	113 01.8	. . 10.7
22		130 42.3	134 12.8	58.0	157 58.7	24.4	24 10.1	55.0	128 04.0	10.6
23		145 44.8	149 12.4	56.7	172 59.3	23.7	39 12.7	55.0	143 06.2	10.5
3 00	TUESDAY	160 47.2	164 12.0	S 2 55.4	187 59.9	S12 23.0	54 15.2	N22 55.0	158 08.4	S 1 10.4
01		175 49.7	179 11.6	54.1	203 00.4	22.3	69 17.8	55.0	173 10.5	10.3
02		190 52.2	194 11.3	52.9	218 01.0	21.6	84 20.3	55.0	188 12.7	10.1
03		205 54.6	209 10.9	. . 51.6	233 01.6	. . 20.9	99 22.8	. . 55.1	203 14.9	. . 10.0
04		220 57.1	224 10.5	50.3	248 02.2	20.2	114 25.4	55.1	218 17.1	09.9
05		235 59.6	239 10.1	49.0	263 02.7	19.5	129 27.9	55.1	233 19.3	09.8
06		251 02.0	254 09.8	S 2 47.8	278 03.3	S12 18.8	144 30.4	N22 55.1	248 21.5	S 1 09.6
07		266 04.5	269 09.4	46.5	293 03.9	18.1	159 33.0	55.1	263 23.7	09.5
08		281 06.9	284 09.0	45.2	308 04.5	17.4	174 35.5	55.1	278 25.9	09.4
09		296 09.4	299 08.6	. . 43.9	323 05.1	. . 16.7	189 38.0	. . 55.1	293 28.1	. . 09.3
10		311 11.9	314 08.2	42.6	338 05.6	16.0	204 40.6	55.1	308 30.2	09.2
11		326 14.3	329 07.9	41.4	353 06.2	15.3	219 43.1	55.1	323 32.4	09.0
12		341 16.8	344 07.5	S 2 40.1	8 06.8	S12 14.6	234 45.6	N22 55.1	338 34.6	S 1 08.9
13		356 19.3	359 07.1	38.8	23 07.4	13.9	249 48.1	55.2	353 36.8	08.8
14		11 21.7	14 06.7	37.5	38 08.0	13.2	264 50.7	55.2	8 39.0	08.7
15		26 24.2	29 06.3	. . 36.3	53 08.5	. . 12.5	279 53.2	. . 55.2	23 41.2	. . 08.6
16		41 26.7	44 06.0	35.0	68 09.1	11.8	294 55.7	55.2	38 43.4	08.4
17		56 29.1	59 05.6	33.7	83 09.7	11.1	309 58.3	55.2	53 45.6	08.3
18		71 31.6	74 05.2	S 2 32.4	98 10.3	S12 10.4	325 00.8	N22 55.2	68 47.8	S 1 08.2
19		86 34.0	89 04.8	31.1	113 10.9	09.7	340 03.3	55.2	83 49.9	08.1
20		101 36.5	104 04.5	29.9	128 11.5	09.0	355 05.9	55.2	98 52.1	08.0
21		116 39.0	119 04.1	. . 28.6	143 12.0	. . 08.3	10 08.4	. . 55.2	113 54.3	. . 07.8
22		131 41.4	134 03.7	27.3	158 12.6	07.6	25 10.9	55.2	128 56.5	07.7
23		146 43.9	149 03.3	26.0	173 13.2	06.9	40 13.4	55.3	143 58.7	07.6
4 00	WEDNESDAY	161 46.4	164 03.0	S 2 24.7	188 13.8	S12 06.2	55 16.0	N22 55.3	159 00.9	S 1 07.5
01		176 48.8	179 02.6	23.5	203 14.4	05.5	70 18.5	55.3	174 03.1	07.3
02		191 51.3	194 02.2	· 22.2	218 14.9	04.8	85 21.0	55.3	189 05.3	07.2
03		206 53.8	209 01.8	. . 20.9	233 15.5	. . 04.1	100 23.5	. . 55.3	204 07.5	. . 07.1
04		221 56.2	224 01.5	19.6	248 16.1	03.4	115 26.1	55.3	219 09.6	07.0
05		236 58.7	239 01.1	18.4	263 16.7	02.7	130 28.6	55.3	234 11.8	06.9
06		252 01.2	254 00.7	S 2 17.1	278 17.3	S12 02.0	145 31.1	N22 55.3	249 14.0	S 1 06.7
07		267 03.6	269 00.3	15.8	293 17.9	01.3	160 33.6	55.3	264 16.2	06.6
08		282 06.1	284 00.0	14.5	308 18.4	12 00.6	175 36.2	55.3	279 18.4	06.5
09		297 08.5	298 59.6	. . 13.2	323 19.0	11 59.9	190 38.7	. . 55.3	294 20.6	. . 06.4
10		312 11.0	313 59.2	11.9	338 19.6	59.2	205 41.2	55.4	309 22.8	06.3
11		327 13.5	328 58.8	10.7	353 20.2	58.5	220 43.7	55.4	324 25.0	06.1
12		342 15.9	343 58.5	S 2 09.4	8 20.8	S11 57.8	235 46.3	N22 55.4	339 27.2	S 1 06.0
13		357 18.4	358 58.1	08.1	23 21.4	57.1	250 48.8	55.4	354 29.3	05.9
14		12 20.9	13 57.7	06.8	38 21.9	56.4	265 51.3	55.4	9 31.5	05.8
15		27 23.3	28 57.3	. . 05.5	53 22.5	. . 55.7	280 53.8	. . 55.4	24 33.7	. . 05.6
16		42 25.8	43 57.0	04.3	68 23.1	55.0	295 56.3	55.4	39 35.9	05.5
17		57 28.3	58 56.6	03.0	83 23.7	54.3	310 58.9	55.4	54 38.1	05.4
18		72 30.7	73 56.2	S 2 01.7	98 24.3	S11 53.6	326 01.4	N22 55.4	69 40.3	S 1 05.3
19		87 33.2	88 55.8	2 00.4	113 24.9	52.8	341 03.9	55.4	84 42.5	05.2
20		102 35.6	103 55.5	1 59.1	128 25.5	52.1	356 06.4	55.4	99 44.7	05.0
21		117 38.1	118 55.1	. . 57.9	143 26.0	. . 51.4	11 08.9	. . 55.4	114 46.8	. . 04.9
22		132 40.6	133 54.7	56.6	158 26.6	50.7	26 11.5	55.5	129 49.0	04.8
23		147 43.0	148 54.3	55.3	173 27.2	50.0	41 14.0	55.5	144 51.2	04.7
Mer. Pass.		h m 13 14.7	v −0.4	d 1.3	v 0.6	d 0.7	v 2.5	d 0.0	v 2.2	d 0.1

STARS

Name	SHA	Dec
	° ′	° ′
Acamar	315 11.2	S40 12.2
Achernar	335 19.9	S57 06.4
Acrux	172 58.4	S63 14.6
Adhara	255 04.9	S29 00.7
Aldebaran	290 38.5	N16 33.7
Alioth	166 11.6	N55 48.8
Alkaid	152 50.9	N49 10.6
Alnair	27 32.1	S46 50.1
Alnilam	275 36.7	S 1 11.2
Alphard	217 46.5	S 8 46.5
Alphecca	126 02.8	N26 37.3
Alpheratz	357 34.1	N29 14.1
Altair	61 59.3	N 8 56.1
Ankaa	353 06.6	S42 10.0
Antares	112 14.6	S26 29.4
Arcturus	145 46.8	N19 02.5
Atria	107 08.0	S69 04.2
Avior	234 13.9	S59 35.8
Bellatrix	278 21.8	N 6 22.3
Betelgeuse	270 50.9	N 7 24.6
Canopus	263 51.7	S52 42.8
Capella	280 20.4	N46 01.6
Deneb	49 25.5	N45 22.2
Denebola	182 23.6	N14 25.4
Diphda	348 46.6	S17 50.7
Dubhe	193 39.1	N61 36.5
Elnath	278 00.6	N28 37.8
Eltanin	90 41.9	N51 28.7
Enif	33 38.2	N 9 59.6
Fomalhaut	15 13.8	S29 29.1
Gacrux	171 50.1	S57 15.6
Gienah	175 42.3	S17 41.4
Hadar	148 34.2	S60 29.8
Hamal	327 50.3	N23 35.2
Kaus Aust.	83 31.4	S34 22.3
Kochab	137 19.2	N74 02.5
Markab	13 29.3	N15 20.7
Menkar	314 05.3	N 4 11.5
Menkent	147 56.2	S36 29.9
Miaplacidus	221 37.3	S69 49.6
Mirfak	308 27.0	N49 57.4
Nunki	75 46.8	S26 15.8
Peacock	53 04.7	S56 38.9
Pollux	243 15.9	N27 57.8
Procyon	244 49.6	N 5 09.4
Rasalhague	95 57.7	N12 32.2
Regulus	207 33.1	N11 50.2
Rigel	281 02.9	S 8 10.4
Rigil Kent.	139 38.6	S60 56.4
Sabik	102 01.7	S15 45.5
Schedar	349 30.5	N56 41.0
Shaula	96 09.1	S37 07.3
Sirius	258 25.2	S16 45.3
Spica	158 21.0	S11 18.0
Suhail	222 45.2	S43 32.5
Vega	80 32.8	N38 48.1
Zuben'ubi	136 54.8	S16 09.1

	SHA	Mer. Pass.
	° ′	h m
Venus	3 24.8	13 04
Mars	27 12.6	11 28
Jupiter	253 28.0	20 20
Saturn	357 21.1	13 25

UT (d h)	SUN GHA (° ′)	SUN Dec (° ′)	MOON GHA (° ′)	MOON v (′)	MOON Dec (° ′)	MOON d (′)	MOON HP (′)
2 00	176 57.2	S 7 17.1	14 04.7	11.1	N15 16.6	14.2	58.1
01	191 57.3	16.2	28 34.8	11.2	15 02.4	14.1	58.1
02	206 57.4	15.2	43 05.0	11.4	14 48.3	14.3	58.1
03	221 57.6	. . 14.2	57 35.4	11.3	14 34.0	14.3	58.0
04	236 57.7	13.3	72 05.7	11.5	14 19.7	14.4	58.0
05	251 57.8	12.3	86 36.2	11.6	14 05.3	14.4	58.0
06	266 57.9	S 7 11.4	101 06.8	11.7	N13 50.9	14.5	58.0
07	281 58.1	10.4	115 37.5	11.7	13 36.4	14.6	58.0
08	296 58.2	09.5	130 08.2	11.8	13 21.8	14.6	57.9
M 09	311 58.3	. . 08.5	144 39.0	12.0	13 07.2	14.7	57.9
O 10	326 58.4	07.6	159 10.0	12.0	12 52.5	14.7	57.9
N 11	341 58.6	06.6	173 41.0	12.0	12 37.8	14.8	57.9
D 12	356 58.7	S 7 05.7	188 12.0	12.2	N12 23.0	14.8	57.9
A 13	11 58.8	04.7	202 43.2	12.3	12 08.2	14.8	57.8
Y 14	26 59.0	03.7	217 14.5	12.3	11 53.4	14.9	57.8
15	41 59.1	. . 02.8	231 45.8	12.4	11 38.5	15.0	57.8
16	56 59.2	01.8	246 17.2	12.5	11 23.5	15.0	57.8
17	71 59.3	7 00.9	260 48.7	12.5	11 08.5	15.0	57.7
18	86 59.5	S 6 59.9	275 20.2	12.7	N10 53.5	15.1	57.7
19	101 59.6	59.0	289 51.9	12.7	10 38.4	15.1	57.7
20	116 59.7	58.0	304 23.6	12.7	10 23.3	15.2	57.7
21	131 59.9	. . 57.1	318 55.3	12.9	10 08.1	15.2	57.7
22	147 00.0	56.1	333 27.2	12.9	9 52.9	15.2	57.6
23	162 00.1	55.1	347 59.1	13.0	9 37.7	15.3	57.6
3 00	177 00.2	S 6 54.2	2 31.1	13.1	N 9 22.4	15.3	57.6
01	192 00.4	53.2	17 03.2	13.1	9 07.1	15.3	57.6
02	207 00.5	52.3	31 35.3	13.2	8 51.8	15.3	57.5
03	222 00.6	. . 51.3	46 07.5	13.2	8 36.5	15.4	57.5
04	237 00.8	50.4	60 39.7	13.4	8 21.1	15.4	57.5
05	252 00.9	49.4	75 12.1	13.4	8 05.7	15.4	57.5
06	267 01.0	S 6 48.4	89 44.5	13.4	N 7 50.3	15.5	57.4
07	282 01.2	47.5	104 16.9	13.5	7 34.8	15.5	57.4
T 08	297 01.3	46.5	118 49.4	13.6	7 19.3	15.4	57.4
U 09	312 01.4	. . 45.6	133 22.0	13.6	7 03.9	15.6	57.4
E 10	327 01.6	44.6	147 54.6	13.7	6 48.3	15.5	57.3
S 11	342 01.7	43.6	162 27.3	13.7	6 32.8	15.5	57.3
D 12	357 01.8	S 6 42.7	177 00.0	13.8	N 6 17.3	15.6	57.3
A 13	12 02.0	41.7	191 32.8	13.9	6 01.7	15.5	57.3
Y 14	27 02.1	40.8	206 05.7	13.9	5 46.2	15.6	57.3
15	42 02.2	. . 39.8	220 38.6	13.9	5 30.6	15.6	57.2
16	57 02.4	38.8	235 11.5	14.0	5 15.0	15.6	57.2
17	72 02.5	37.9	249 44.5	14.1	4 59.4	15.6	57.2
18	87 02.6	S 6 36.9	264 17.6	14.1	N 4 43.8	15.6	57.2
19	102 02.8	36.0	278 50.7	14.1	4 28.2	15.7	57.1
20	117 02.9	35.0	293 23.8	14.2	4 12.5	15.6	57.1
21	132 03.0	. . 34.0	307 57.0	14.3	3 56.9	15.6	57.1
22	147 03.2	33.1	322 30.3	14.2	3 41.3	15.7	57.1
23	162 03.3	32.1	337 03.5	14.4	3 25.6	15.6	57.0
4 00	177 03.4	S 6 31.2	351 36.9	14.3	N 3 10.0	15.6	57.0
01	192 03.6	30.2	6 10.2	14.4	2 54.4	15.6	57.0
02	207 03.7	29.2	20 43.6	14.5	2 38.8	15.7	57.0
03	222 03.9	. . 28.3	35 17.1	14.5	2 23.1	15.6	56.9
04	237 04.0	27.3	49 50.6	14.5	2 07.5	15.6	56.9
05	252 04.1	26.4	64 24.1	14.5	1 51.9	15.6	56.9
06	267 04.3	S 6 25.4	78 57.6	14.6	N 1 36.3	15.6	56.8
W 07	282 04.4	24.4	93 31.2	14.6	1 20.7	15.6	56.8
E 08	297 04.5	23.5	108 04.8	14.7	1 05.1	15.6	56.8
D 09	312 04.7	. . 22.5	122 38.5	14.7	0 49.5	15.6	56.8
N 10	327 04.8	21.5	137 12.2	14.7	0 33.9	15.5	56.7
E 11	342 04.9	20.6	151 45.9	14.7	0 18.4	15.6	56.7
S 12	357 05.1	S 6 19.6	166 19.6	14.8	N 0 02.8	15.5	56.7
D 13	12 05.2	18.7	180 53.4	14.8	S 0 12.7	15.5	56.7
A 14	27 05.4	17.7	195 27.2	14.8	0 28.2	15.5	56.6
Y 15	42 05.5	. . 16.7	210 01.0	14.8	0 43.7	15.5	56.6
16	57 05.6	15.8	224 34.8	14.9	0 59.2	15.5	56.6
17	72 05.8	14.8	239 08.7	14.9	1 14.7	15.4	56.6
18	87 05.9	S 6 13.8	253 42.6	14.9	S 1 30.1	15.4	56.5
19	102 06.1	12.9	268 16.5	14.9	1 45.5	15.4	56.5
20	117 06.2	11.9	282 50.4	15.0	2 00.9	15.4	56.5
21	132 06.3	. . 10.9	297 24.4	14.9	2 16.3	15.4	56.5
22	147 06.5	10.0	311 58.3	15.0	2 31.7	15.3	56.4
23	162 06.6	09.0	326 32.3	15.0	S 2 47.0	15.3	56.4
	SD 16.2	*d* 1.0	SD 15.8		15.6		15.4

Lat. (°)	Twilight Naut. (h m)	Twilight Civil (h m)	Sunrise (h m)	Moonrise 2 (h m)	Moonrise 3 (h m)	Moonrise 4 (h m)	Moonrise 5 (h m)
N 72	05 00	06 18	07 26	14 58	17 22	19 33	21 43
N 70	05 06	06 17	07 18	15 19	17 29	19 30	21 30
68	05 11	06 15	07 11	15 35	17 35	19 28	21 19
66	05 15	06 14	07 05	15 48	17 40	19 26	21 10
64	05 18	06 13	07 01	15 59	17 44	19 24	21 02
62	05 21	06 12	06 56	16 08	17 47	19 23	20 56
60	05 23	06 11	06 53	16 15	17 50	19 21	20 51
N 58	05 25	06 10	06 49	16 22	17 53	19 20	20 46
56	05 26	06 09	06 47	16 28	17 55	19 19	20 41
54	05 28	06 09	06 44	16 33	17 57	19 18	20 38
52	05 29	06 08	06 42	16 38	17 59	19 18	20 34
50	05 30	06 07	06 39	16 42	18 01	19 17	20 31
45	05 31	06 05	06 35	16 52	18 05	19 15	20 24
N 40	05 32	06 03	06 30	16 59	18 08	19 14	20 19
35	05 32	06 02	06 27	17 06	18 11	19 13	20 14
30	05 32	06 00	06 24	17 12	18 13	19 12	20 10
20	05 31	05 56	06 18	17 22	18 17	19 10	20 02
N 10	05 28	05 52	06 13	17 30	18 21	19 09	19 56
0	05 24	05 48	06 09	17 39	18 24	19 08	19 50
S 10	05 18	05 43	06 04	17 47	18 27	19 06	19 45
20	05 10	05 36	05 58	17 55	18 31	19 05	19 38
30	04 59	05 28	05 52	18 05	18 35	19 03	19 31
35	04 53	05 23	05 49	18 11	18 37	19 03	19 28
40	04 44	05 17	05 45	18 17	18 40	19 02	19 23
45	04 34	05 10	05 40	18 24	18 43	19 01	19 18
S 50	04 20	05 01	05 34	18 33	18 47	18 59	19 12
52	04 14	04 56	05 31	18 37	18 48	18 59	19 09
54	04 06	04 51	05 28	18 41	18 50	18 58	19 06
56	03 58	04 46	05 25	18 46	18 52	18 57	19 03
58	03 48	04 40	05 21	18 52	18 54	18 57	18 59
S 60	03 37	04 33	05 17	18 58	18 57	18 56	18 55

Lat. (°)	Sunset (h m)	Twilight Civil (h m)	Twilight Naut. (h m)	Moonset 2 (h m)	Moonset 3 (h m)	Moonset 4 (h m)	Moonset 5 (h m)
N 72	16 59	18 08	19 27	08 24	07 37	07 01	06 27
N 70	17 08	18 09	19 20	08 00	07 26	06 59	06 33
68	17 14	18 10	19 15	07 42	07 18	06 58	06 39
66	17 20	18 11	19 11	07 27	07 11	06 57	06 43
64	17 25	18 12	19 07	07 15	07 05	06 56	06 47
62	17 29	18 13	19 05	07 04	07 00	06 55	06 50
60	17 32	18 14	19 02	06 55	06 55	06 54	06 53
N 58	17 35	18 15	19 00	06 47	06 51	06 54	06 56
56	17 38	18 16	18 59	06 40	06 47	06 53	06 58
54	17 41	18 16	18 57	06 34	06 44	06 52	07 00
52	17 43	18 17	18 56	06 28	06 41	06 52	07 02
50	17 45	18 18	18 55	06 23	06 38	06 51	07 04
45	17 50	18 19	18 53	06 12	06 32	06 50	07 08
N 40	17 54	18 21	18 52	06 03	06 27	06 50	07 11
35	17 57	18 23	18 52	05 54	06 23	06 49	07 14
30	18 00	18 24	18 52	05 47	06 19	06 48	07 16
20	18 06	18 28	18 53	05 35	06 12	06 47	07 21
N 10	18 11	18 32	18 56	05 24	06 06	06 46	07 24
0	18 15	18 36	19 00	05 13	06 01	06 45	07 28
S 10	18 20	18 41	19 06	05 03	05 55	06 44	07 32
20	18 25	18 47	19 13	04 52	05 49	06 43	07 35
30	18 31	18 55	19 24	04 39	05 41	06 42	07 40
35	18 35	19 00	19 30	04 31	05 37	06 41	07 42
40	18 39	19 06	19 39	04 22	05 33	06 40	07 45
45	18 43	19 13	19 49	04 12	05 27	06 39	07 49
S 50	18 49	19 22	20 02	04 00	05 20	06 38	07 53
52	18 51	19 26	20 09	03 54	05 17	06 37	07 54
54	18 54	19 31	20 16	03 48	05 14	06 36	07 56
56	18 57	19 36	20 24	03 40	05 10	06 36	07 59
58	19 01	19 42	20 33	03 32	05 06	06 35	08 01
S 60	19 05	19 49	20 45	03 23	05 01	06 34	08 04

Day (d)	SUN Eqn. of Time 00^h (m s)	SUN Eqn. of Time 12^h (m s)	SUN Mer. Pass. (h m)	MOON Mer. Pass. Upper (h m)	MOON Mer. Pass. Lower (h m)	MOON Age (d)	MOON Phase (%)
2	12 12	12 05	12 12	23 50	11 26	13	99
3	11 59	11 53	12 12	24 35	12 12	14	100
4	11 46	11 40	12 12	00 35	12 56	15	99

Day	UT (d h)	ARIES GHA	VENUS −3·9 GHA	VENUS Dec	MARS +1·1 GHA	MARS Dec	JUPITER −2·4 GHA	JUPITER Dec	SATURN +0·9 GHA	SATURN Dec	STARS Name	SHA	Dec
		° ′	° ′	° ′	° ′	° ′	° ′	° ′	° ′	° ′		° ′	° ′
THURSDAY	5 00	162 45.5	163 54.0	S 1 54.0	188 27.8	S11 49.3	56 16.5	N22 55.5	159 53.4	S 1 04.6	Acamar	315 11.2	S40 12.2
	01	177 48.0	178 53.6	52.7	203 28.4	48.6	71 19.0	55.5	174 55.6	04.4	Achernar	335 19.9	S57 06.4
	02	192 50.4	193 53.2	51.4	218 29.0	47.9	86 21.5	55.5	189 57.8	04.3	Acrux	172 58.4	S63 14.7
	03	207 52.9	208 52.9	. . 50.2	233 29.6	. . 47.2	101 24.1	. . 55.5	205 00.0	. . 04.2	Adhara	255 04.9	S29 00.7
	04	222 55.4	223 52.5	48.9	248 30.1	46.5	116 26.6	55.5	220 02.2	04.1	Aldebaran	290 38.5	N16 33.7
	05	237 57.8	238 52.1	47.6	263 30.7	45.8	131 29.1	55.5	235 04.3	03.9			
	06	253 00.3	253 51.7	S 1 46.3	278 31.3	S11 45.1	146 31.6	N22 55.5	250 06.5	S 1 03.8	Alioth	166 11.6	N55 48.8
	07	268 02.8	268 51.4	45.0	293 31.9	44.4	161 34.1	55.5	265 08.7	03.7	Alkaid	152 50.9	N49 10.6
	08	283 05.2	283 51.0	43.8	308 32.5	43.7	176 36.6	55.5	280 10.9	03.6	Alnair	27 32.1	S46 50.1
	09	298 07.7	298 50.6	. . 42.5	323 33.1	. . 43.0	191 39.1	. . 55.5	295 13.1	. . 03.5	Alnilam	275 36.7	S 1 11.2
	10	313 10.1	313 50.2	41.2	338 33.7	42.2	206 41.7	55.5	310 15.3	03.3	Alphard	217 46.5	S 8 46.5
	11	328 12.6	328 49.9	39.9	353 34.2	41.5	221 44.2	55.6	325 17.5	03.2			
	12	343 15.1	343 49.5	S 1 38.6	8 34.8	S11 40.8	236 46.7	N22 55.6	340 19.7	S 1 03.1	Alphecca	126 02.8	N26 37.3
	13	358 17.5	358 49.1	37.3	23 35.4	40.1	251 49.2	55.6	355 21.8	03.0	Alpheratz	357 34.1	N29 14.1
	14	13 20.0	13 48.8	36.1	38 36.0	39.4	266 51.7	55.6	10 24.0	02.9	Altair	61 59.2	N 8 56.1
	15	28 22.5	28 48.4	. . 34.8	53 36.6	. . 38.7	281 54.2	. . 55.6	25 26.2	. . 02.7	Ankaa	353 06.6	S42 09.9
	16	43 24.9	43 48.0	33.5	68 37.2	38.0	296 56.7	55.6	40 28.4	02.6	Antares	112 14.6	S26 29.4
	17	58 27.4	58 47.6	32.2	83 37.8	37.3	311 59.3	55.6	55 30.6	02.5			
	18	73 29.9	73 47.3	S 1 30.9	98 38.4	S11 36.6	327 01.8	N22 55.6	70 32.8	S 1 02.4	Arcturus	145 46.8	N19 02.5
	19	88 32.3	88 46.9	29.6	113 39.0	35.9	342 04.3	55.6	85 35.0	02.2	Atria	107 08.0	S69 04.2
	20	103 34.8	103 46.5	28.4	128 39.5	35.1	357 06.8	55.6	100 37.1	02.1	Avior	234 13.9	S59 35.8
	21	118 37.2	118 46.2	. . 27.1	143 40.1	. . 34.4	12 09.3	. . 55.6	115 39.3	. . 02.0	Bellatrix	278 21.8	N 6 22.3
	22	133 39.7	133 45.8	25.8	158 40.7	33.7	27 11.8	55.6	130 41.5	01.9	Betelgeuse	270 51.0	N 7 24.6
	23	148 42.2	148 45.4	24.5	173 41.3	33.0	42 14.3	55.6	145 43.7	01.8			
FRIDAY	6 00	163 44.6	163 45.1	S 1 23.2	188 41.9	S11 32.3	57 16.8	N22 55.7	160 45.9	S 1 01.6	Canopus	263 51.8	S52 42.8
	01	178 47.1	178 44.7	21.9	203 42.5	31.6	72 19.3	55.7	175 48.1	01.5	Capella	280 20.4	N46 01.6
	02	193 49.6	193 44.3	20.6	218 43.1	30.9	87 21.8	55.7	190 50.3	01.4	Deneb	49 25.5	N45 22.2
	03	208 52.0	208 43.9	. . 19.4	233 43.7	. . 30.2	102 24.4	. . 55.7	205 52.5	. . 01.3	Denebola	182 23.6	N14 25.4
	04	223 54.5	223 43.6	18.1	248 44.3	29.5	117 26.9	55.7	220 54.6	01.1	Diphda	348 46.6	S17 50.7
	05	238 57.0	238 43.2	16.8	263 44.9	28.7	132 29.4	55.7	235 56.8	01.0			
	06	253 59.4	253 42.8	S 1 15.5	278 45.4	S11 28.0	147 31.9	N22 55.7	250 59.0	S 1 00.9	Dubhe	193 39.1	N61 36.5
	07	269 01.9	268 42.5	14.2	293 46.0	27.3	162 34.4	55.7	266 01.2	00.8	Elnath	278 00.6	N28 37.8
	08	284 04.4	283 42.1	12.9	308 46.6	26.6	177 36.9	55.7	281 03.4	00.7	Eltanin	90 41.9	N51 28.7
	09	299 06.8	298 41.7	. . 11.7	323 47.2	. . 25.9	192 39.4	. . 55.7	296 05.6	. . 00.5	Enif	33 38.2	N 9 59.6
	10	314 09.3	313 41.4	10.4	338 47.8	25.2	207 41.9	55.7	311 07.8	00.4	Fomalhaut	15 13.8	S29 29.1
	11	329 11.7	328 41.0	09.1	353 48.4	24.5	222 44.4	55.7	326 09.9	00.3			
	12	344 14.2	343 40.6	S 1 07.8	8 49.0	S11 23.8	237 46.9	N22 55.7	341 12.1	S 1 00.2	Gacrux	171 50.1	S57 15.6
	13	359 16.7	358 40.2	06.5	23 49.6	23.0	252 49.4	55.7	356 14.3	1 00.1	Gienah	175 42.3	S17 41.4
	14	14 19.1	13 39.9	05.2	38 50.2	22.3	267 51.9	55.8	11 16.5	0 59.9	Hadar	148 34.2	S60 29.9
	15	29 21.6	28 39.5	. . 03.9	53 50.8	. . 21.6	282 54.4	. . 55.8	26 18.7	. . 59.8	Hamal	327 50.3	N23 35.2
	16	44 24.1	43 39.1	02.7	68 51.4	20.9	297 56.9	55.8	41 20.9	59.7	Kaus Aust.	83 31.4	S34 22.3
	17	59 26.5	58 38.8	01.4	83 52.0	20.2	312 59.4	55.8	56 23.1	59.6			
	18	74 29.0	73 38.4	S 1 00.1	98 52.5	S11 19.5	328 01.9	N22 55.8	71 25.3	S 0 59.4	Kochab	137 19.2	N74 02.5
	19	89 31.5	88 38.0	0 58.8	113 53.1	18.8	343 04.4	55.8	86 27.4	59.3	Markab	13 29.3	N15 20.7
	20	104 33.9	103 37.7	57.5	128 53.7	18.0	358 06.9	55.8	101 29.6	59.2	Menkar	314 05.3	N 4 11.5
	21	119 36.4	118 37.3	. . 56.2	143 54.3	. . 17.3	13 09.4	. . 55.8	116 31.8	. . 59.1	Menkent	147 56.2	S36 29.9
	22	134 38.8	133 36.9	54.9	158 54.9	16.6	28 11.9	55.8	131 34.0	59.0	Miaplacidus	221 37.3	S69 49.6
	23	149 41.3	148 36.6	53.7	173 55.5	15.9	43 14.4	55.8	146 36.2	58.8			
SATURDAY	7 00	164 43.8	163 36.2	S 0 52.4	188 56.1	S11 15.2	58 16.9	N22 55.8	161 38.4	S 0 58.7	Mirfak	308 27.1	N49 57.4
	01	179 46.2	178 35.8	51.1	203 56.7	14.5	73 19.4	55.8	176 40.6	58.6	Nunki	75 46.7	S26 15.8
	02	194 48.7	193 35.5	49.8	218 57.3	13.8	88 21.9	55.8	191 42.7	58.5	Peacock	53 04.6	S56 38.9
	03	209 51.2	208 35.1	. . 48.5	233 57.9	. . 13.0	103 24.4	. . 55.8	206 44.9	. . 58.3	Pollux	243 15.9	N27 57.8
	04	224 53.6	223 34.7	47.2	248 58.5	12.3	118 26.9	55.8	221 47.1	58.2	Procyon	244 49.6	N 5 09.4
	05	239 56.1	238 34.4	45.9	263 59.1	11.6	133 29.4	55.8	236 49.3	58.1			
	06	254 58.6	253 34.0	S 0 44.7	278 59.7	S11 10.9	148 31.9	N22 55.9	251 51.5	S 0 58.0	Rasalhague	95 57.7	N12 32.2
	07	270 01.0	268 33.6	43.4	294 00.3	10.2	163 34.4	55.9	266 53.7	57.9	Regulus	207 33.1	N11 50.2
	08	285 03.5	283 33.3	42.1	309 00.9	09.5	178 36.9	55.9	281 55.9	57.7	Rigel	281 02.9	S 8 10.4
	09	300 06.0	298 32.9	. . 40.8	324 01.5	. . 08.7	193 39.4	. . 55.9	296 58.0	. . 57.6	Rigil Kent.	139 38.6	S60 56.5
	10	315 08.4	313 32.5	39.5	339 02.0	08.0	208 41.9	55.9	312 00.2	57.5	Sabik	102 01.7	S15 45.5
	11	330 10.9	328 32.2	38.2	354 02.6	07.3	223 44.4	55.9	327 02.4	57.4			
	12	345 13.3	343 31.8	S 0 36.9	9 03.2	S11 06.6	238 46.9	N22 55.9	342 04.6	S 0 57.2	Schedar	349 30.5	N56 40.9
	13	0 15.8	358 31.4	35.7	24 03.8	05.9	253 49.4	55.9	357 06.8	57.1	Shaula	96 09.1	S37 07.3
	14	15 18.3	13 31.1	34.4	39 04.4	05.1	268 51.9	55.9	12 09.0	57.0	Sirius	258 25.2	S16 45.3
	15	30 20.7	28 30.7	. . 33.1	54 05.0	. . 04.4	283 54.4	. . 55.9	27 11.1	. . 56.9	Spica	158 21.0	S11 18.0
	16	45 23.2	43 30.3	31.8	69 05.6	03.7	298 56.9	55.9	42 13.3	56.8	Suhail	222 45.2	S43 32.5
	17	60 25.7	58 30.0	30.5	84 06.2	03.0	313 59.4	55.9	57 15.5	56.6			
	18	75 28.1	73 29.6	S 0 29.2	99 06.8	S11 02.3	329 01.9	N22 55.9	72 17.7	S 0 56.5	Vega	80 32.7	N38 48.1
	19	90 30.6	88 29.2	27.9	114 07.4	01.6	344 04.4	55.9	87 19.9	56.4	Zuben'ubi	136 54.8	S16 09.1
	20	105 33.1	103 28.9	26.6	129 08.0	00.8	359 06.9	55.9	102 22.1	56.3			
	21	120 35.5	118 28.5	. . 25.4	144 08.6	11 00.1	14 09.4	. . 55.9	117 24.3	. . 56.1		SHA ° ′	Mer. Pass. h m
	22	135 38.0	133 28.1	24.1	159 09.2	10 59.4	29 11.9	55.9	132 26.4	56.0	Venus	0 00.4	13 05
	23	150 40.5	148 27.8	22.8	174 09.8	S10 58.7	44 14.4	55.9	147 28.6	55.9	Mars	24 57.3	11 25
	Mer. Pass.	13 02.9 (h m)	v −0.4	d 1.3	v 0.6	d 0.7	v 2.5	d 0.0	v 2.2	d 0.1	Jupiter	253 32.2	20 08
											Saturn	357 01.3	13 15

Day	UT (d h)	SUN GHA (° ′)	SUN Dec (° ′)	MOON GHA (° ′)	v (′)	MOON Dec (° ′)	d (′)	HP (′)
THURSDAY	5 00	177 06.8	S 6 08.1	341 06.3	15.0	S 3 02.3	15.3	56.4
	01	192 06.9	07.1	355 40.3	15.0	3 17.6	15.2	56.4
	02	207 07.0	06.1	10 14.3	15.0	3 32.8	15.2	56.3
	03	222 07.2	. . 05.2	24 48.3	15.1	3 48.0	15.2	56.3
	04	237 07.3	04.2	39 22.4	15.0	4 03.2	15.2	56.3
	05	252 07.5	03.2	53 56.4	15.1	4 18.4	15.1	56.3
	06	267 07.6	S 6 02.3	68 30.5	15.1	S 4 33.5	15.1	56.2
	07	282 07.7	01.3	83 04.6	15.0	4 48.6	15.1	56.2
	08	297 07.9	6 00.3	97 38.6	15.1	5 03.7	15.0	56.2
	09	312 08.0	5 59.4	112 12.7	15.1	5 18.7	15.0	56.2
	10	327 08.2	58.4	126 46.8	15.1	5 33.7	14.9	56.1
	11	342 08.3	57.4	141 20.9	15.1	5 48.6	14.9	56.1
	12	357 08.4	S 5 56.5	155 55.0	15.1	S 6 03.5	14.9	56.1
	13	12 08.6	55.5	170 29.1	15.1	6 18.4	14.8	56.1
	14	27 08.7	54.5	185 03.2	15.0	6 33.2	14.8	56.0
	15	42 08.9	. . 53.6	199 37.2	15.1	6 48.0	14.8	56.0
	16	57 09.0	52.6	214 11.3	15.1	7 02.8	14.7	56.0
	17	72 09.2	51.6	228 45.4	15.1	7 17.5	14.6	56.0
	18	87 09.3	S 5 50.7	243 19.5	15.1	S 7 32.1	14.6	55.9
	19	102 09.4	49.7	257 53.6	15.1	7 46.7	14.6	55.9
	20	117 09.6	48.7	272 27.7	15.0	8 01.3	14.5	55.9
	21	132 09.7	. . 47.8	287 01.7	15.1	8 15.8	14.5	55.9
	22	147 09.9	46.8	301 35.8	15.0	8 30.3	14.4	55.8
	23	162 10.0	45.8	316 09.8	15.1	8 44.7	14.4	55.8
FRIDAY	6 00	177 10.2	S 5 44.9	330 43.9	15.0	S 8 59.1	14.4	55.8
	01	192 10.3	43.9	345 17.9	15.0	9 13.5	14.2	55.8
	02	207 10.5	42.9	359 51.9	15.0	9 27.7	14.3	55.7
	03	222 10.6	. . 41.9	14 25.9	15.0	9 42.0	14.1	55.7
	04	237 10.7	41.0	28 59.9	15.0	9 56.1	14.2	55.7
	05	252 10.9	40.0	43 33.9	14.9	10 10.3	14.0	55.7
	06	267 11.0	S 5 39.0	58 07.8	15.0	S10 24.3	14.0	55.6
	07	282 11.2	38.1	72 41.8	14.9	10 38.3	14.0	55.6
	08	297 11.3	37.1	87 15.7	14.9	10 52.3	13.9	55.6
	09	312 11.5	. . 36.1	101 49.6	14.9	11 06.2	13.8	55.6
	10	327 11.6	35.2	116 23.5	14.9	11 20.0	13.8	55.5
	11	342 11.8	34.2	130 57.4	14.9	11 33.8	13.7	55.5
	12	357 11.9	S 5 33.2	145 31.3	14.8	S11 47.5	13.7	55.5
	13	12 12.1	32.3	160 05.1	14.8	12 01.2	13.6	55.5
	14	27 12.2	31.3	174 38.9	14.8	12 14.8	13.6	55.4
	15	42 12.4	. . 30.3	189 12.7	14.7	12 28.4	13.4	55.4
	16	57 12.5	29.3	203 46.4	14.8	12 41.8	13.4	55.4
	17	72 12.6	28.4	218 20.2	14.7	12 55.2	13.4	55.4
	18	87 12.8	S 5 27.4	232 53.9	14.7	S13 08.6	13.3	55.4
	19	102 12.9	26.4	247 27.6	14.6	13 21.9	13.2	55.3
	20	117 13.1	25.5	262 01.2	14.7	13 35.1	13.1	55.3
	21	132 13.2	. . 24.5	276 34.9	14.6	13 48.2	13.1	55.3
	22	147 13.4	23.5	291 08.5	14.5	14 01.3	13.0	55.3
	23	162 13.5	22.5	305 42.0	14.6	14 14.3	13.0	55.2
SATURDAY	7 00	177 13.7	S 5 21.6	320 15.6	14.5	S14 27.3	12.9	55.2
	01	192 13.8	20.6	334 49.1	14.5	14 40.2	12.8	55.2
	02	207 14.0	19.6	349 22.6	14.4	14 53.0	12.7	55.2
	03	222 14.1	. . 18.7	3 56.0	14.4	15 05.7	12.7	55.2
	04	237 14.3	17.7	18 29.4	14.4	15 18.4	12.6	55.1
	05	252 14.4	16.7	33 02.8	14.3	15 31.0	12.5	55.1
	06	267 14.6	S 5 15.7	47 36.1	14.3	S15 43.5	12.4	55.1
	07	282 14.7	14.8	62 09.4	14.3	15 55.9	12.4	55.1
	08	297 14.9	13.8	76 42.7	14.2	16 08.3	12.3	55.1
	09	312 15.0	. . 12.8	91 15.9	14.2	16 20.6	12.2	55.0
	10	327 15.2	11.9	105 49.1	14.2	16 32.8	12.1	55.0
	11	342 15.3	10.9	120 22.3	14.1	16 44.9	12.1	55.0
	12	357 15.5	S 5 09.9	134 55.4	14.1	S16 57.0	11.9	55.0
	13	12 15.6	08.9	149 28.5	14.0	17 08.9	11.9	55.0
	14	27 15.8	08.0	164 01.5	14.0	17 20.8	11.8	54.9
	15	42 15.9	. . 07.0	178 34.5	14.0	17 32.6	11.8	54.9
	16	57 16.1	06.0	193 07.5	13.9	17 44.4	11.6	54.9
	17	72 16.2	05.0	207 40.4	13.9	17 56.0	11.6	54.9
	18	87 16.4	S 5 04.1	222 13.3	13.8	S18 07.6	11.5	54.9
	19	102 16.5	03.1	236 46.1	13.8	18 19.1	11.4	54.9
	20	117 16.7	02.1	251 18.9	13.7	18 30.5	11.3	54.8
	21	132 16.8	. . 01.1	265 51.6	13.7	18 41.8	11.2	54.8
	22	147 17.0	5 00.2	280 24.3	13.7	18 53.0	11.1	54.8
	23	162 17.1	S 4 59.2	294 57.0	13.6	S19 04.1	11.1	54.8
		SD 16.1	*d* 1.0	SD 15.3		15.1		15.0

Lat. (°)	Twilight Naut. (h m)	Twilight Civil (h m)	Sunrise (h m)	Moonrise 5 (h m)	Moonrise 6 (h m)	Moonrise 7 (h m)	Moonrise 8 (h m)
N 72	04 44	06 03	07 11	21 43	24 13	00 13	■
N 70	04 52	06 03	07 04	21 30	23 39	27 05	03 05
68	04 59	06 03	06 59	21 19	23 16	25 33	01 33
66	05 04	06 03	06 54	21 10	22 57	24 55	00 55
64	05 08	06 03	06 50	21 02	22 43	24 28	00 28
62	05 11	06 03	06 47	20 56	22 30	24 08	00 08
60	05 14	06 02	06 44	20 51	22 20	23 51	25 25
N 58	05 17	06 02	06 41	20 46	22 11	23 38	25 05
56	05 19	06 02	06 39	20 41	22 03	23 26	24 48
54	05 21	06 02	06 37	20 38	21 56	23 15	24 34
52	05 22	06 01	06 35	20 34	21 50	23 06	24 22
50	05 24	06 01	06 33	20 31	21 45	22 58	24 11
45	05 26	06 00	06 29	20 24	21 33	22 41	23 48
N 40	05 28	05 59	06 26	20 19	21 23	22 27	23 30
35	05 28	05 58	06 23	20 14	21 14	22 15	23 15
30	05 29	05 57	06 20	20 10	21 07	22 05	23 02
20	05 28	05 54	06 16	20 02	20 54	21 47	22 40
N 10	05 26	05 51	06 12	19 56	20 44	21 32	22 21
0	05 23	05 47	06 08	19 50	20 33	21 18	22 04
S 10	05 18	05 43	06 04	19 45	20 23	21 03	21 46
20	05 11	05 37	05 59	19 38	20 12	20 48	21 27
30	05 02	05 30	05 54	19 31	20 00	20 31	21 06
35	04 56	05 26	05 51	19 28	19 53	20 21	20 53
40	04 48	05 20	05 48	19 23	19 45	20 10	20 39
45	04 38	05 14	05 44	19 18	19 36	19 57	20 22
S 50	04 26	05 06	05 39	19 12	19 25	19 41	20 01
52	04 20	05 02	05 37	19 09	19 20	19 34	19 51
54	04 13	04 58	05 34	19 06	19 15	19 26	19 40
56	04 06	04 53	05 31	19 03	19 09	19 16	19 27
58	03 57	04 48	05 28	18 59	19 02	19 06	19 13
S 60	03 47	04 41	05 25	18 55	18 54	18 54	18 56

Lat. (°)	Sunset (h m)	Twilight Civil (h m)	Twilight Naut. (h m)	Moonset 5 (h m)	Moonset 6 (h m)	Moonset 7 (h m)	Moonset 8 (h m)
N 72	17 14	18 22	19 41	06 27	05 48	04 51	■
N 70	17 20	18 21	19 33	06 33	06 05	05 26	03 34
68	17 26	18 21	19 26	06 39	06 18	05 51	05 07
66	17 30	18 21	19 21	06 43	06 29	06 11	05 46
64	17 34	18 21	19 16	06 47	06 38	06 27	06 14
62	17 37	18 21	19 13	06 50	06 45	06 40	06 35
60	17 40	18 21	19 10	06 53	06 52	06 52	06 52
N 58	17 42	18 22	19 07	06 56	06 58	07 02	07 07
56	17 45	18 22	19 05	06 58	07 04	07 10	07 19
54	17 47	18 22	19 03	07 00	07 09	07 18	07 30
52	17 49	18 22	19 01	07 02	07 13	07 25	07 40
50	17 50	18 23	19 00	07 04	07 17	07 31	07 49
45	17 54	18 23	18 57	07 08	07 26	07 45	08 08
N 40	17 57	18 24	18 56	07 11	07 33	07 56	08 23
35	18 00	18 25	18 55	07 14	07 39	08 06	08 36
30	18 02	18 26	18 54	07 16	07 45	08 14	08 47
20	18 07	18 29	18 54	07 21	07 54	08 29	09 06
N 10	18 11	18 32	18 56	07 24	08 03	08 42	09 23
0	18 14	18 35	18 59	07 28	08 11	08 54	09 39
S 10	18 18	18 40	19 04	07 32	08 19	09 07	09 55
20	18 23	18 45	19 11	07 35	08 27	09 20	10 13
30	18 28	18 52	19 20	07 40	08 37	09 35	10 32
35	18 31	18 56	19 26	07 42	08 43	09 44	10 44
40	18 34	19 01	19 34	07 45	08 50	09 54	10 58
45	18 38	19 08	19 43	07 49	08 57	10 05	11 13
S 50	18 42	19 15	19 55	07 53	09 06	10 20	11 33
52	18 45	19 19	20 01	07 54	09 11	10 27	11 43
54	18 47	19 23	20 07	07 56	09 15	10 34	11 53
56	18 50	19 28	20 15	07 59	09 21	10 43	12 05
58	18 53	19 33	20 23	08 01	09 27	10 52	12 19
S 60	18 56	19 39	20 33	08 04	09 33	11 03	12 36

Day (d)	SUN Eqn. of Time 00^h (m s)	SUN Eqn. of Time 12^h (m s)	SUN Mer. Pass. (h m)	MOON Mer. Pass. Upper (h m)	MOON Mer. Pass. Lower (h m)	MOON Age (d)	MOON Phase (%)
5	11 33	11 26	12 11	01 18	13 39	16	96
6	11 20	11 13	12 11	02 01	14 22	17	91
7	11 06	10 58	12 11	02 44	15 06	18	84

2026 MARCH 8, 9, 10 (SUN., MON., TUES.)

UT d	h	ARIES GHA	VENUS −3·9 GHA	VENUS Dec	MARS +1·1 GHA	MARS Dec	JUPITER −2·4 GHA	JUPITER Dec	SATURN +0·9 GHA	SATURN Dec
		° ′	° ′	° ′	° ′	° ′	° ′	° ′	° ′	° ′
8 SUNDAY	00	165 42.9	163 27.4	S 0 21.5	189 10.4	S10 58.0	59 16.8	N22 56.0	162 30.8	S 0 55.8
	01	180 45.4	178 27.0	20.2	204 11.0	57.2	74 19.3	56.0	177 33.0	55.7
	02	195 47.8	193 26.7	18.9	219 11.6	56.5	89 21.8	56.0	192 35.2	55.5
	03	210 50.3	208 26.3	. . 17.6	234 12.2	. . 55.8	104 24.3	. . 56.0	207 37.4	. . 55.4
	04	225 52.8	223 25.9	16.4	249 12.8	55.1	119 26.8	56.0	222 39.6	55.3
	05	240 55.2	238 25.6	15.1	264 13.4	54.4	134 29.3	56.0	237 41.7	55.2
	06	255 57.7	253 25.2	S 0 13.8	279 14.0	S10 53.6	149 31.8	N22 56.0	252 43.9	S 0 55.0
	07	271 00.2	268 24.8	12.5	294 14.6	52.9	164 34.3	56.0	267 46.1	54.9
	08	286 02.6	283 24.5	11.2	309 15.2	52.2	179 36.8	56.0	282 48.3	54.8
	09	301 05.1	298 24.1	. . 09.9	324 15.8	. . 51.5	194 39.3	. . 56.0	297 50.5	. . 54.7
	10	316 07.6	313 23.7	08.6	339 16.4	50.7	209 41.7	56.0	312 52.7	54.6
	11	331 10.0	328 23.4	07.3	354 17.0	50.0	224 44.2	56.0	327 54.8	54.4
	12	346 12.5	343 23.0	S 0 06.1	9 17.6	S10 49.3	239 46.7	N22 56.0	342 57.0	S 0 54.3
	13	1 14.9	358 22.6	04.8	24 18.2	48.6	254 49.2	56.0	357 59.2	54.2
	14	16 17.4	13 22.3	03.5	39 18.8	47.9	269 51.7	56.0	13 01.4	54.1
	15	31 19.9	28 21.9	. . 02.2	54 19.4	. . 47.1	284 54.2	. . 56.0	28 03.6	. . 53.9
	16	46 22.3	43 21.5	S 00.9	69 20.0	46.4	299 56.7	56.0	43 05.8	53.8
	17	61 24.8	58 21.2	N 00.4	84 20.6	45.7	314 59.1	56.0	58 08.0	53.7
	18	76 27.3	73 20.8	N 0 01.7	99 21.2	S10 45.0	330 01.6	N22 56.0	73 10.1	S 0 53.6
	19	91 29.7	88 20.5	03.0	114 21.8	44.2	345 04.1	56.0	88 12.3	53.5
	20	106 32.2	103 20.1	04.2	129 22.4	43.5	0 06.6	56.0	103 14.5	53.3
	21	121 34.7	118 19.7	. . 05.5	144 23.0	. . 42.8	15 09.1	. . 56.1	118 16.7	. . 53.2
	22	136 37.1	133 19.4	06.8	159 23.6	42.1	30 11.6	56.1	133 18.9	53.1
	23	151 39.6	148 19.0	08.1	174 24.2	41.3	45 14.1	56.1	148 21.1	53.0
9 MONDAY	00	166 42.1	163 18.6	N 0 09.4	189 24.8	S10 40.6	60 16.5	N22 56.1	163 23.2	S 0 52.8
	01	181 44.5	178 18.3	10.7	204 25.4	39.9	75 19.0	56.1	178 25.4	52.7
	02	196 47.0	193 17.9	12.0	219 26.0	39.2	90 21.5	56.1	193 27.6	52.6
	03	211 49.4	208 17.5	. . 13.3	234 26.6	. . 38.4	105 24.0	. . 56.1	208 29.8	. . 52.5
	04	226 51.9	223 17.2	14.5	249 27.2	37.7	120 26.5	56.1	223 32.0	52.4
	05	241 54.4	238 16.8	15.8	264 27.8	37.0	135 28.9	56.1	238 34.2	52.2
	06	256 56.8	253 16.4	N 0 17.1	279 28.4	S10 36.3	150 31.4	N22 56.1	253 36.3	S 0 52.1
	07	271 59.3	268 16.1	18.4	294 29.0	35.5	165 33.9	56.1	268 38.5	52.0
	08	287 01.8	283 15.7	19.7	309 29.6	34.8	180 36.4	56.1	283 40.7	51.9
	09	302 04.2	298 15.3	. . 21.0	324 30.2	. . 34.1	195 38.9	. . 56.1	298 42.9	. . 51.7
	10	317 06.7	313 15.0	22.3	339 30.8	33.4	210 41.3	56.1	313 45.1	51.6
	11	332 09.2	328 14.6	23.6	354 31.4	32.6	225 43.8	56.1	328 47.3	51.5
	12	347 11.6	343 14.3	N 0 24.9	9 32.0	S10 31.9	240 46.3	N22 56.1	343 49.5	S 0 51.4
	13	2 14.1	358 13.9	26.1	24 32.6	31.2	255 48.8	56.1	358 51.6	51.3
	14	17 16.6	13 13.5	27.4	39 33.2	30.5	270 51.3	56.1	13 53.8	51.1
	15	32 19.0	28 13.2	. . 28.7	54 33.8	. . 29.7	285 53.7	. . 56.1	28 56.0	. . 51.0
	16	47 21.5	43 12.8	30.0	69 34.4	29.0	300 56.2	56.1	43 58.2	50.9
	17	62 23.9	58 12.4	31.3	84 35.0	28.3	315 58.7	56.1	59 00.4	50.8
	18	77 26.4	73 12.1	N 0 32.6	99 35.6	S10 27.6	331 01.2	N22 56.1	74 02.6	S 0 50.6
	19	92 28.9	88 11.7	33.9	114 36.2	26.8	346 03.6	56.1	89 04.7	50.5
	20	107 31.3	103 11.3	35.2	129 36.8	26.1	1 06.1	56.1	104 06.9	50.4
	21	122 33.8	118 11.0	. . 36.4	144 37.4	. . 25.4	16 08.6	. . 56.1	119 09.1	. . 50.3
	22	137 36.3	133 10.6	37.7	159 38.0	24.6	31 11.1	56.2	134 11.3	50.1
	23	152 38.7	148 10.3	39.0	174 38.6	23.9	46 13.5	56.2	149 13.5	50.0
10 TUESDAY	00	167 41.2	163 09.9	N 0 40.3	189 39.2	S10 23.2	61 16.0	N22 56.2	164 15.7	S 0 49.9
	01	182 43.7	178 09.5	41.6	204 39.8	22.5	76 18.5	56.2	179 17.8	49.8
	02	197 46.1	193 09.2	42.9	219 40.4	21.7	91 21.0	56.2	194 20.0	49.7
	03	212 48.6	208 08.8	. . 44.2	234 41.0	. . 21.0	106 23.4	. . 56.2	209 22.2	. . 49.5
	04	227 51.0	223 08.4	45.5	249 41.7	20.3	121 25.9	56.2	224 24.4	49.4
	05	242 53.5	238 08.1	46.7	264 42.3	19.5	136 28.4	56.2	239 26.6	49.3
	06	257 56.0	253 07.7	N 0 48.0	279 42.9	S10 18.8	151 30.9	N22 56.2	254 28.8	S 0 49.2
	07	272 58.4	268 07.3	49.3	294 43.5	18.1	166 33.3	56.2	269 30.9	49.0
	08	288 00.9	283 07.0	50.6	309 44.1	17.4	181 35.8	56.2	284 33.1	48.9
	09	303 03.4	298 06.6	. . 51.9	324 44.7	. . 16.6	196 38.3	. . 56.2	299 35.3	. . 48.8
	10	318 05.8	313 06.3	53.2	339 45.3	15.9	211 40.7	56.2	314 37.5	48.7
	11	333 08.3	328 05.9	54.5	354 45.9	15.2	226 43.2	56.2	329 39.7	48.6
	12	348 10.8	343 05.5	N 0 55.8	9 46.5	S10 14.4	241 45.7	N22 56.2	344 41.9	S 0 48.4
	13	3 13.2	358 05.2	57.0	24 47.1	13.7	256 48.1	56.2	359 44.0	48.3
	14	18 15.7	13 04.8	58.3	39 47.7	13.0	271 50.6	56.2	14 46.2	48.2
	15	33 18.2	28 04.4	0 59.6	54 48.3	. . 12.2	286 53.1	. . 56.2	29 48.4	. . 48.1
	16	48 20.6	43 04.1	1 00.9	69 48.9	11.5	301 55.6	56.2	44 50.6	47.9
	17	63 23.1	58 03.7	02.2	84 49.5	10.8	316 58.0	56.2	59 52.8	47.8
	18	78 25.5	73 03.3	N 1 03.5	99 50.1	S10 10.1	332 00.5	N22 56.2	74 55.0	S 0 47.7
	19	93 28.0	88 03.0	04.8	114 50.7	09.3	347 03.0	56.2	89 57.1	47.6
	20	108 30.5	103 02.6	06.1	129 51.3	08.6	2 05.4	56.2	104 59.3	47.4
	21	123 32.9	118 02.3	. . 07.3	144 52.0	. . 07.9	17 07.9	. . 56.2	120 01.5	. . 47.3
	22	138 35.4	133 01.9	08.6	159 52.6	07.1	32 10.4	56.2	135 03.7	47.2
	23	153 37.9	148 01.5	09.9	174 53.2	06.4	47 12.8	56.2	150 05.9	47.1
Mer. Pass.		h m 12 51.1	v −0.4	d 1.3	v 0.6	d 0.7	v 2.5	d 0.0	v 2.2	d 0.1

STARS

Name	SHA	Dec
	° ′	° ′
Acamar	315 11.2	S40 12.2
Achernar	335 19.9	S57 06.4
Acrux	172 58.3	S63 14.7
Adhara	255 04.9	S29 00.7
Aldebaran	290 38.6	N16 33.7
Alioth	166 11.6	N55 48.8
Alkaid	152 50.8	N49 10.6
Alnair	27 32.1	S46 50.0
Alnilam	275 36.7	S 1 11.2
Alphard	217 46.5	S 8 46.5
Alphecca	126 02.8	N26 37.3
Alpheratz	357 34.1	N29 14.1
Altair	61 59.2	N 8 56.1
Ankaa	353 06.6	S42 09.9
Antares	112 14.6	S26 29.4
Arcturus	145 46.8	N19 02.5
Atria	107 07.9	S69 04.2
Avior	234 13.9	S59 35.8
Bellatrix	278 21.8	N 6 22.3
Betelgeuse	270 51.0	N 7 24.6
Canopus	263 51.8	S52 42.8
Capella	280 20.4	N46 01.6
Deneb	49 25.5	N45 22.2
Denebola	182 23.6	N14 25.4
Diphda	348 46.6	S17 50.7
Dubhe	193 39.1	N61 36.5
Elnath	278 00.6	N28 37.8
Eltanin	90 41.8	N51 28.7
Enif	33 38.1	N 9 59.6
Fomalhaut	15 13.8	S29 29.1
Gacrux	171 50.0	S57 15.6
Gienah	175 42.3	S17 41.4
Hadar	148 34.2	S60 29.9
Hamal	327 50.4	N23 35.2
Kaus Aust.	83 31.3	S34 22.3
Kochab	137 19.1	N74 02.5
Markab	13 29.3	N15 20.7
Menkar	314 05.3	N 4 11.5
Menkent	147 56.2	S36 29.9
Miaplacidus	221 37.3	S69 49.6
Mirfak	308 27.1	N49 57.4
Nunki	75 46.7	S26 15.8
Peacock	53 04.6	S56 38.9
Pollux	243 15.9	N27 57.8
Procyon	244 49.6	N 5 09.4
Rasalhague	95 57.7	N12 32.2
Regulus	207 33.1	N11 50.2
Rigel	281 02.9	S 8 10.4
Rigil Kent.	139 38.6	S60 56.5
Sabik	102 01.7	S15 45.5
Schedar	349 30.5	N56 40.9
Shaula	96 09.1	S37 07.3
Sirius	258 25.3	S16 45.3
Spica	158 21.0	S11 18.0
Suhail	222 45.2	S43 32.5
Vega	80 32.7	N38 48.1
Zuben'ubi	136 54.8	S16 09.1

	SHA	Mer. Pass.
	° ′	h m
Venus	356 36.6	13 07
Mars	22 42.7	11 22
Jupiter	253 34.5	19 56
Saturn	356 41.2	13 05

UT	SUN GHA	SUN Dec	MOON GHA	v	MOON Dec	d	HP
d h	° ′	° ′	° ′	′	° ′	′	′
8 00	177 17.3	S 4 58.2	309 29.6	13.6	S19 15.2	10.9	54.8
01	192 17.5	57.3	324 02.2	13.5	19 26.1	10.9	54.8
02	207 17.6	56.3	338 34.7	13.5	19 37.0	10.8	54.7
03	222 17.8	. . 55.3	353 07.2	13.4	19 47.8	10.7	54.7
04	237 17.9	54.3	7 39.6	13.4	19 58.5	10.6	54.7
05	252 18.1	53.4	22 12.0	13.3	20 09.1	10.5	54.7
06	267 18.2	S 4 52.4	36 44.3	13.3	S20 19.6	10.4	54.7
07	282 18.4	51.4	51 16.6	13.2	20 30.0	10.3	54.7
08	297 18.5	50.4	65 48.8	13.2	20 40.3	10.3	54.6
SUNDAY 09	312 18.7	. . 49.5	80 21.0	13.1	20 50.6	10.1	54.6
10	327 18.8	48.5	94 53.1	13.1	21 00.7	10.0	54.6
11	342 19.0	47.5	109 25.2	13.0	21 10.7	10.0	54.6
12	357 19.1	S 4 46.5	123 57.2	13.0	S21 20.7	9.8	54.6
13	12 19.3	45.5	138 29.2	12.9	21 30.5	9.8	54.6
14	27 19.5	44.6	153 01.1	12.9	21 40.3	9.6	54.6
15	42 19.6	. . 43.6	167 33.0	12.8	21 49.9	9.5	54.5
16	57 19.8	42.6	182 04.8	12.8	21 59.4	9.5	54.5
17	72 19.9	41.6	196 36.6	12.7	22 08.9	9.3	54.5
18	87 20.1	S 4 40.7	211 08.3	12.7	S22 18.2	9.3	54.5
19	102 20.2	39.7	225 40.0	12.6	22 27.5	9.1	54.5
20	117 20.4	38.7	240 11.6	12.6	22 36.6	9.0	54.5
21	132 20.5	. . 37.7	254 43.2	12.5	22 45.6	9.0	54.5
22	147 20.7	36.8	269 14.7	12.4	22 54.6	8.8	54.5
23	162 20.8	35.8	283 46.1	12.4	23 03.4	8.7	54.4
9 00	177 21.0	S 4 34.8	298 17.5	12.4	S23 12.1	8.6	54.4
01	192 21.2	33.8	312 48.9	12.3	23 20.7	8.6	54.4
02	207 21.3	32.9	327 20.2	12.3	23 29.3	8.4	54.4
03	222 21.5	. . 31.9	341 51.5	12.2	23 37.7	8.3	54.4
04	237 21.6	30.9	356 22.7	12.1	23 46.0	8.1	54.4
05	252 21.8	29.9	10 53.8	12.1	23 54.1	8.1	54.4
06	267 21.9	S 4 28.9	25 24.9	12.0	S24 02.2	8.0	54.4
07	282 22.1	28.0	39 55.9	12.0	24 10.2	7.8	54.4
08	297 22.3	27.0	54 26.9	12.0	24 18.0	7.8	54.4
MONDAY 09	312 22.4	. . 26.0	68 57.9	11.8	24 25.8	7.6	54.3
10	327 22.6	25.0	83 28.7	11.9	24 33.4	7.5	54.3
11	342 22.7	24.1	97 59.6	11.8	24 40.9	7.4	54.3
12	357 22.9	S 4 23.1	112 30.4	11.7	S24 48.3	7.3	54.3
13	12 23.0	22.1	127 01.1	11.7	24 55.6	7.2	54.3
14	27 23.2	21.1	141 31.8	11.6	25 02.8	7.1	54.3
15	42 23.4	. . 20.1	156 02.4	11.6	25 09.9	6.9	54.3
16	57 23.5	19.2	170 33.0	11.5	25 16.8	6.9	54.3
17	72 23.7	18.2	185 03.5	11.4	25 23.7	6.7	54.3
18	87 23.8	S 4 17.2	199 33.9	11.5	S25 30.4	6.6	54.3
19	102 24.0	16.2	214 04.4	11.3	25 37.0	6.5	54.3
20	117 24.2	15.2	228 34.7	11.4	25 43.5	6.3	54.3
21	132 24.3	. . 14.3	243 05.1	11.2	25 49.8	6.3	54.3
22	147 24.5	13.3	257 35.3	11.2	25 56.1	6.1	54.3
23	162 24.6	12.3	272 05.5	11.2	26 02.2	6.0	54.3
10 00	177 24.8	S 4 11.3	286 35.7	11.1	S26 08.2	5.8	54.3
01	192 25.0	10.3	301 05.8	11.1	26 14.0	5.8	54.2
02	207 25.1	09.4	315 35.9	11.0	26 19.8	5.6	54.2
03	222 25.3	. . 08.4	330 05.9	11.0	26 25.4	5.5	54.2
04	237 25.4	07.4	344 35.9	11.0	26 30.9	5.4	54.2
05	252 25.6	06.4	359 05.9	10.9	26 36.3	5.3	54.2
06	267 25.8	S 4 05.4	13 35.8	10.8	S26 41.6	5.1	54.2
07	282 25.9	04.5	28 05.6	10.8	26 46.7	5.0	54.2
TUESDAY 08	297 26.1	03.5	42 35.4	10.7	26 51.7	4.9	54.2
09	312 26.2	. . 02.5	57 05.1	10.8	26 56.6	4.8	54.2
10	327 26.4	01.5	71 34.9	10.6	27 01.4	4.6	54.2
11	342 26.6	4 00.5	86 04.5	10.6	27 06.0	4.5	54.2
12	357 26.7	S 3 59.6	100 34.1	10.6	S27 10.5	4.4	54.2
13	12 26.9	58.6	115 03.7	10.6	27 14.9	4.3	54.2
14	27 27.0	57.6	129 33.3	10.5	27 19.2	4.1	54.2
15	42 27.2	. . 56.6	144 02.8	10.4	27 23.3	4.0	54.2
16	57 27.4	55.6	158 32.2	10.5	27 27.3	3.8	54.2
17	72 27.5	54.7	173 01.7	10.3	27 31.1	3.8	54.2
18	87 27.7	S 3 53.7	187 31.0	10.4	S27 34.9	3.6	54.2
19	102 27.9	52.7	202 00.4	10.3	27 38.5	3.4	54.2
20	117 28.0	51.7	216 29.7	10.3	27 41.9	3.4	54.2
21	132 28.2	. . 50.7	230 59.0	10.2	27 45.3	3.2	54.2
22	147 28.3	49.8	245 28.2	10.2	27 48.5	3.1	54.2
23	162 28.5	48.8	259 57.4	10.2	S27 51.6	2.9	54.2
	SD 16.1	*d* 1.0	SD 14.9		14.8		14.8

Lat.	Twilight Naut.	Twilight Civil	Sunrise	Moonrise 8	9	10	11
°	h m	h m	h m	h m	h m	h m	h m
N 72	04 28	05 48	06 55	■	■	■	■
N 70	04 38	05 50	06 50	03 05	■	■	■
68	04 46	05 51	06 46	01 33	■	■	■
66	04 52	05 52	06 43	00 55	03 45	■	■
64	04 57	05 53	06 40	00 28	02 27	■	■
62	05 02	05 53	06 37	00 08	01 51	03 42	■
60	05 05	05 54	06 35	25 25	01 25	02 59	04 24
N 58	05 08	05 54	06 33	25 05	01 05	02 30	03 46
56	05 11	05 54	06 31	24 48	00 48	02 08	03 19
54	05 13	05 54	06 30	24 34	00 34	01 50	02 58
52	05 15	05 55	06 28	24 22	00 22	01 34	02 40
50	05 17	05 55	06 27	24 11	00 11	01 21	02 25
45	05 21	05 55	06 24	23 48	24 54	00 54	01 55
N 40	05 23	05 54	06 21	23 30	24 33	00 33	01 32
35	05 24	05 54	06 19	23 15	24 15	00 15	01 13
30	05 25	05 53	06 17	23 02	24 00	00 00	00 56
20	05 26	05 51	06 14	22 40	23 34	24 28	00 28
N 10	05 25	05 49	06 10	22 21	23 12	24 04	00 04
0	05 22	05 46	06 07	22 04	22 52	23 42	24 34
S 10	05 18	05 43	06 04	21 46	22 31	23 20	24 11
20	05 13	05 38	06 00	21 27	22 10	22 56	23 47
30	05 04	05 32	05 56	21 06	21 44	22 29	23 18
35	04 58	05 28	05 54	20 53	21 30	22 12	23 02
40	04 51	05 24	05 51	20 39	21 13	21 53	22 42
45	04 43	05 18	05 48	20 22	20 52	21 31	22 18
S 50	04 32	05 11	05 44	20 01	20 27	21 02	21 48
52	04 26	05 08	05 42	19 51	20 15	20 47	21 33
54	04 20	05 04	05 40	19 40	20 00	20 31	21 15
56	04 13	05 00	05 38	19 27	19 44	20 11	20 53
58	04 05	04 55	05 35	19 13	19 25	19 47	20 26
S 60	03 56	04 50	05 33	18 56	19 01	19 14	19 47

Lat.	Sunset	Twilight Civil	Twilight Naut.	Moonset 8	9	10	11
°	h m	h m	h m	h m	h m	h m	h m
N 72	17 28	18 35	19 56	■	■	■	■
N 70	17 33	18 34	19 46	03 34	■	■	■
68	17 37	18 32	19 38	05 07	■	■	■
66	17 40	18 31	19 31	05 46	04 33	■	■
64	17 43	18 30	19 26	06 14	05 52	■	■
62	17 45	18 29	19 21	06 35	06 29	06 19	■
60	17 47	18 29	19 17	06 52	06 55	07 02	07 22
N 58	17 49	18 28	19 14	07 07	07 16	07 31	08 00
56	17 51	18 28	19 11	07 19	07 33	07 54	08 27
54	17 52	18 28	19 09	07 30	07 47	08 12	08 49
52	17 54	18 27	19 07	07 40	08 00	08 28	09 06
50	17 55	18 27	19 05	07 49	08 11	08 41	09 21
45	17 58	18 27	19 01	08 08	08 35	09 09	09 52
N 40	18 00	18 27	18 59	08 23	08 54	09 31	10 15
35	18 02	18 28	18 57	08 36	09 10	09 49	10 35
30	18 04	18 28	18 56	08 47	09 23	10 05	10 52
20	18 08	18 30	18 55	09 06	09 47	10 31	11 20
N 10	18 11	18 32	18 56	09 23	10 07	10 54	11 44
0	18 14	18 34	18 59	09 39	10 27	11 16	12 07
S 10	18 17	18 38	19 02	09 55	10 46	11 37	12 29
20	18 20	18 42	19 08	10 13	11 06	12 00	12 54
30	18 24	18 48	19 16	10 32	11 30	12 27	13 22
35	18 27	18 52	19 22	10 44	11 44	12 43	13 39
40	18 29	18 56	19 29	10 58	12 01	13 02	13 58
45	18 32	19 02	19 37	11 13	12 20	13 24	14 22
S 50	18 36	19 09	19 48	11 33	12 45	13 53	14 52
52	18 38	19 12	19 53	11 43	12 57	14 07	15 08
54	18 40	19 16	19 59	11 53	13 11	14 23	15 25
56	18 42	19 20	20 06	12 05	13 27	14 43	15 47
58	18 44	19 24	20 14	12 19	13 46	15 07	16 14
S 60	18 47	19 30	20 23	12 36	14 09	15 39	16 53

Day	SUN Eqn. of Time 00^h	12^h	Mer. Pass.	MOON Mer. Pass. Upper	Lower	Age	Phase
d	m s	m s	h m	h m	h m	d	%
8	10 51	10 44	12 11	03 28	15 51	19	76
9	10 36	10 29	12 10	04 15	16 39	20	68
10	10 21	10 13	12 10	05 04	17 29	21	59

2026 MARCH 11, 12, 13 (WED., THURS., FRI.)

UT d h	ARIES GHA	VENUS −3·9 GHA	VENUS Dec	MARS +1·2 GHA	MARS Dec	JUPITER −2·4 GHA	JUPITER Dec	SATURN +0·9 GHA	SATURN Dec
	° ′	° ′	° ′	° ′	° ′	° ′	° ′	° ′	° ′
11 00 (WEDNESDAY)	168 40.3	163 01.2	N 1 11.2	189 53.8	S10 05.7	62 15.3	N22 56.2	165 08.0	S 0 47.0
01	183 42.8	178 00.8	12.5	204 54.4	04.9	77 17.8	56.2	180 10.2	46.8
02	198 45.3	193 00.4	13.8	219 55.0	04.2	92 20.2	56.2	195 12.4	46.7
03	213 47.7	208 00.1	. . 15.1	234 55.6	. . 03.5	107 22.7	. . 56.2	210 14.6	. . 46.6
04	228 50.2	222 59.7	16.4	249 56.2	02.7	122 25.1	56.2	225 16.8	46.5
05	243 52.7	237 59.4	17.6	264 56.8	02.0	137 27.6	56.2	240 19.0	46.3
06	258 55.1	252 59.0	N 1 18.9	279 57.4	S10 01.3	152 30.1	N22 56.2	255 21.1	S 0 46.2
07	273 57.6	267 58.6	20.2	294 58.0	10 00.5	167 32.5	56.2	270 23.3	46.1
08	289 00.0	282 58.3	21.5	309 58.6	9 59.8	182 35.0	56.2	285 25.5	46.0
09	304 02.5	297 57.9	. . 22.8	324 59.3	. . 59.1	197 37.5	. . 56.2	300 27.7	. . 45.9
10	319 05.0	312 57.5	24.1	339 59.9	58.3	212 39.9	56.3	315 29.9	45.7
11	334 07.4	327 57.2	25.4	355 00.5	57.6	227 42.4	56.3	330 32.1	45.6
12	349 09.9	342 56.8	N 1 26.7	10 01.1	S 9 56.9	242 44.8	N22 56.3	345 34.2	S 0 45.5
13	4 12.4	357 56.4	27.9	25 01.7	56.1	257 47.3	56.3	0 36.4	45.4
14	19 14.8	12 56.1	29.2	40 02.3	55.4	272 49.8	56.3	15 38.6	45.2
15	34 17.3	27 55.7	. . 30.5	55 02.9	. . 54.7	287 52.2	. . 56.3	30 40.8	. . 45.1
16	49 19.8	42 55.4	31.8	70 03.5	53.9	302 54.7	56.3	45 43.0	45.0
17	64 22.2	57 55.0	33.1	85 04.1	53.2	317 57.1	56.3	60 45.2	44.9
18	79 24.7	72 54.6	N 1 34.4	100 04.7	S 9 52.5	332 59.6	N22 56.3	75 47.3	S 0 44.7
19	94 27.2	87 54.3	35.7	115 05.4	51.7	348 02.1	56.3	90 49.5	44.6
20	109 29.6	102 53.9	37.0	130 06.0	51.0	3 04.5	56.3	105 51.7	44.5
21	124 32.1	117 53.5	. . 38.2	145 06.6	. . 50.2	18 07.0	. . 56.3	120 53.9	. . 44.4
22	139 34.5	132 53.2	39.5	160 07.2	49.5	33 09.4	56.3	135 56.1	44.3
23	154 37.0	147 52.8	40.8	175 07.8	48.8	48 11.9	56.3	150 58.2	44.1
12 00 (THURSDAY)	169 39.5	162 52.5	N 1 42.1	190 08.4	S 9 48.0	63 14.3	N22 56.3	166 00.4	S 0 44.0
01	184 41.9	177 52.1	43.4	205 09.0	47.3	78 16.8	56.3	181 02.6	43.9
02	199 44.4	192 51.7	44.7	220 09.6	46.6	93 19.3	56.3	196 04.8	43.8
03	214 46.9	207 51.4	. . 46.0	235 10.2	. . 45.8	108 21.7	. . 56.3	211 07.0	. . 43.6
04	229 49.3	222 51.0	47.2	250 10.9	45.1	123 24.2	56.3	226 09.2	43.5
05	244 51.8	237 50.6	48.5	265 11.5	44.4	138 26.6	56.3	241 11.3	43.4
06	259 54.3	252 50.3	N 1 49.8	280 12.1	S 9 43.6	153 29.1	N22 56.3	256 13.5	S 0 43.3
07	274 56.7	267 49.9	51.1	295 12.7	42.9	168 31.5	56.3	271 15.7	43.1
08	289 59.2	282 49.5	52.4	310 13.3	42.1	183 34.0	56.3	286 17.9	43.0
09	305 01.6	297 49.2	. . 53.7	325 13.9	. . 41.4	198 36.4	. . 56.3	301 20.1	. . 42.9
10	320 04.1	312 48.8	55.0	340 14.5	40.7	213 38.9	56.3	316 22.2	42.8
11	335 06.6	327 48.5	56.2	355 15.1	39.9	228 41.3	56.3	331 24.4	42.7
12	350 09.0	342 48.1	N 1 57.5	10 15.8	S 9 39.2	243 43.8	N22 56.3	346 26.6	S 0 42.5
13	5 11.5	357 47.7	1 58.8	25 16.4	38.5	258 46.2	56.3	1 28.8	42.4
14	20 14.0	12 47.4	2 00.1	40 17.0	37.7	273 48.7	56.3	16 31.0	42.3
15	35 16.4	27 47.0	. . 01.4	55 17.6	. . 37.0	288 51.2	. . 56.3	31 33.2	. . 42.2
16	50 18.9	42 46.6	02.7	70 18.2	36.2	303 53.6	56.3	46 35.3	42.0
17	65 21.4	57 46.3	04.0	85 18.8	35.5	318 56.1	56.3	61 37.5	41.9
18	80 23.8	72 45.9	N 2 05.2	100 19.4	S 9 34.8	333 58.5	N22 56.3	76 39.7	S 0 41.8
19	95 26.3	87 45.6	06.5	115 20.1	34.0	349 01.0	56.3	91 41.9	41.7
20	110 28.8	102 45.2	07.8	130 20.7	33.3	4 03.4	56.3	106 44.1	41.5
21	125 31.2	117 44.8	. . 09.1	145 21.3	. . 32.5	19 05.8	. . 56.3	121 46.2	. . 41.4
22	140 33.7	132 44.5	10.4	160 21.9	31.8	34 08.3	56.3	136 48.4	41.3
23	155 36.1	147 44.1	11.7	175 22.5	31.1	49 10.7	56.3	151 50.6	41.2
13 00 (FRIDAY)	170 38.6	162 43.7	N 2 13.0	190 23.1	S 9 30.3	64 13.2	N22 56.3	166 52.8	S 0 41.1
01	185 41.1	177 43.4	14.2	205 23.7	29.6	79 15.6	56.3	181 55.0	40.9
02	200 43.5	192 43.0	15.5	220 24.4	28.8	94 18.1	56.3	196 57.1	40.8
03	215 46.0	207 42.6	. . 16.8	235 25.0	. . 28.1	109 20.5	. . 56.3	211 59.3	. . 40.7
04	230 48.5	222 42.3	18.1	250 25.6	27.4	124 23.0	56.3	227 01.5	40.6
05	245 50.9	237 41.9	19.4	265 26.2	26.6	139 25.4	56.3	242 03.7	40.4
06	260 53.4	252 41.6	N 2 20.7	280 26.8	S 9 25.9	154 27.9	N22 56.3	257 05.9	S 0 40.3
07	275 55.9	267 41.2	22.0	295 27.4	25.1	169 30.3	56.3	272 08.1	40.2
08	290 58.3	282 40.8	23.2	310 28.1	24.4	184 32.8	56.3	287 10.2	40.1
09	306 00.8	297 40.5	. . 24.5	325 28.7	. . 23.7	199 35.2	. . 56.3	302 12.4	. . 39.9
10	321 03.3	312 40.1	25.8	340 29.3	22.9	214 37.7	56.3	317 14.6	39.8
11	336 05.7	327 39.7	27.1	355 29.9	22.2	229 40.1	56.3	332 16.8	39.7
12	351 08.2	342 39.4	N 2 28.4	10 30.5	S 9 21.4	244 42.5	N22 56.3	347 19.0	S 0 39.6
13	6 10.6	357 39.0	29.7	25 31.1	20.7	259 45.0	56.3	2 21.1	39.5
14	21 13.1	12 38.6	30.9	40 31.7	20.0	274 47.4	56.3	17 23.3	39.3
15	36 15.6	27 38.3	. . 32.2	55 32.4	. . 19.2	289 49.9	. . 56.3	32 25.5	. . 39.2
16	51 18.0	42 37.9	33.5	70 33.0	18.5	304 52.3	56.3	47 27.7	39.1
17	66 20.5	57 37.6	34.8	85 33.6	17.7	319 54.7	56.3	62 29.9	39.0
18	81 23.0	72 37.2	N 2 36.1	100 34.2	S 9 17.0	334 57.2	N22 56.3	77 32.0	S 0 38.8
19	96 25.4	87 36.8	37.4	115 34.8	16.2	349 59.6	56.3	92 34.2	38.7
20	111 27.9	102 36.5	38.7	130 35.5	15.5	5 02.1	56.3	107 36.4	38.6
21	126 30.4	117 36.1	. . 39.9	145 36.1	. . 14.8	20 04.5	. . 56.3	122 38.6	. . 38.5
22	141 32.8	132 35.7	41.2	160 36.7	14.0	35 07.0	56.3	137 40.8	38.3
23	156 35.3	147 35.4	42.5	175 37.3	13.3	50 09.4	56.3	152 43.0	38.2
Mer. Pass. (h m)	12 39.3	*v* −0.4	*d* 1.3	*v* 0.6	*d* 0.7	*v* 2.5	*d* 0.0	*v* 2.2	*d* 0.1

STARS

Name	SHA ° ′	Dec ° ′
Acamar	315 11.3	S40 12.2
Achernar	335 19.9	S57 06.4
Acrux	172 58.3	S63 14.7
Adhara	255 05.0	S29 00.7
Aldebaran	290 38.6	N16 33.7
Alioth	166 11.6	N55 48.8
Alkaid	152 50.8	N49 10.7
Alnair	27 32.1	S46 50.0
Alnilam	275 36.7	S 1 11.2
Alphard	217 46.5	S 8 46.5
Alphecca	126 02.7	N26 37.3
Alpheratz	357 34.1	N29 14.1
Altair	61 59.2	N 8 56.1
Ankaa	353 06.6	S42 09.9
Antares	112 14.6	S26 29.4
Arcturus	145 46.8	N19 02.5
Atria	107 07.9	S69 04.2
Avior	234 13.9	S59 35.8
Bellatrix	278 21.8	N 6 22.3
Betelgeuse	270 51.0	N 7 24.6
Canopus	263 51.8	S52 42.8
Capella	280 20.5	N46 01.6
Deneb	49 25.5	N45 22.2
Denebola	182 23.6	N14 25.4
Diphda	348 46.6	S17 50.7
Dubhe	193 39.1	N61 36.5
Elnath	278 00.6	N28 37.8
Eltanin	90 41.8	N51 28.7
Enif	33 38.1	N 9 59.6
Fomalhaut	15 13.8	S29 29.1
Gacrux	171 50.0	S57 15.6
Gienah	175 42.3	S17 41.4
Hadar	148 34.2	S60 29.9
Hamal	327 50.4	N23 35.2
Kaus Aust.	83 31.3	S34 22.3
Kochab	137 19.1	N74 02.5
Markab	13 29.3	N15 20.7
Menkar	314 05.3	N 4 11.5
Menkent	147 56.2	S36 30.0
Miaplacidus	221 37.4	S69 49.7
Mirfak	308 27.1	N49 57.4
Nunki	75 46.7	S26 15.8
Peacock	53 04.6	S56 38.9
Pollux	243 15.9	N27 57.8
Procyon	244 49.6	N 5 09.4
Rasalhague	95 57.7	N12 32.2
Regulus	207 33.1	N11 50.2
Rigel	281 02.9	S 8 10.4
Rigil Kent.	139 38.5	S60 56.5
Sabik	102 01.6	S15 45.5
Schedar	349 30.5	N56 40.9
Shaula	96 09.1	S37 07.3
Sirius	258 25.3	S16 45.3
Spica	158 21.0	S11 18.0
Suhail	222 45.2	S43 32.5
Vega	80 32.7	N38 48.1
Zuben'ubi	136 54.7	S16 09.1

	SHA ° ′	Mer. Pass. h m
Venus	353 13.0	13 09
Mars	20 28.9	11 19
Jupiter	253 34.9	19 44
Saturn	356 21.0	12 54

UT	SUN GHA	SUN Dec	MOON GHA	v	MOON Dec	d	HP
d h	° ′	° ′	° ′	′	° ′	′	′
11 00	177 28.7	S 3 47.8	274 26.6	10.1	S27 54.5	2.8	54.2
01	192 28.8	46.8	288 55.7	10.1	27 57.3	2.7	54.2
02	207 29.0	45.8	303 24.8	10.1	28 00.0	2.5	54.2
03	222 29.2	. . 44.8	317 53.9	10.0	28 02.5	2.4	54.3
04	237 29.3	43.9	332 22.9	10.0	28 04.9	2.3	54.3
05	252 29.5	42.9	346 51.9	10.0	28 07.2	2.1	54.3
06	267 29.6	S 3 41.9	1 20.9	10.0	S28 09.3	2.0	54.3
W 07	282 29.8	40.9	15 49.9	9.9	28 11.3	1.9	54.3
E 08	297 30.0	39.9	30 18.8	9.9	28 13.2	1.7	54.3
D 09	312 30.1	. . 39.0	44 47.7	9.9	28 14.9	1.6	54.3
N 10	327 30.3	38.0	59 16.6	9.8	28 16.5	1.5	54.3
E 11	342 30.5	37.0	73 45.4	9.9	28 18.0	1.3	54.3
S 12	357 30.6	S 3 36.0	88 14.3	9.8	S28 19.3	1.2	54.3
D 13	12 30.8	35.0	102 43.1	9.8	28 20.5	1.0	54.3
A 14	27 31.0	34.0	117 11.9	9.8	28 21.5	0.9	54.3
Y 15	42 31.1	. . 33.1	131 40.7	9.7	28 22.4	0.8	54.3
16	57 31.3	32.1	146 09.4	9.7	28 23.2	0.6	54.3
17	72 31.5	31.1	160 38.1	9.8	28 23.8	0.5	54.3
18	87 31.6	S 3 30.1	175 06.9	9.7	S28 24.3	0.4	54.3
19	102 31.8	29.1	189 35.6	9.6	28 24.7	0.2	54.4
20	117 32.0	28.1	204 04.2	9.7	28 24.9	0.1	54.4
21	132 32.1	. . 27.2	218 32.9	9.7	28 25.0	0.1	54.4
22	147 32.3	26.2	233 01.6	9.6	28 24.9	0.2	54.4
23	162 32.5	25.2	247 30.2	9.7	28 24.7	0.3	54.4
12 00	177 32.6	S 3 24.2	261 58.9	9.6	S28 24.4	0.5	54.4
01	192 32.8	23.2	276 27.5	9.6	28 23.9	0.6	54.4
02	207 32.9	22.2	290 56.1	9.6	28 23.3	0.8	54.4
03	222 33.1	. . 21.3	305 24.7	9.6	28 22.5	0.9	54.4
04	237 33.3	20.3	319 53.3	9.7	28 21.6	1.0	54.4
05	252 33.4	19.3	334 22.0	9.6	28 20.6	1.2	54.5
06	267 33.6	S 3 18.3	348 50.6	9.6	S28 19.4	1.3	54.5
07	282 33.8	17.3	3 19.2	9.5	28 18.1	1.5	54.5
T 08	297 33.9	16.3	17 47.7	9.6	28 16.6	1.6	54.5
H 09	312 34.1	. . 15.4	32 16.3	9.6	28 15.0	1.7	54.5
U 10	327 34.3	14.4	46 44.9	9.6	28 13.3	1.9	54.5
R 11	342 34.5	13.4	61 13.5	9.6	28 11.4	2.0	54.5
S 12	357 34.6	S 3 12.4	75 42.1	9.6	S28 09.4	2.2	54.6
D 13	12 34.8	11.4	90 10.7	9.6	28 07.2	2.3	54.6
A 14	27 35.0	10.4	104 39.3	9.7	28 04.9	2.4	54.6
Y 15	42 35.1	. . 09.5	119 08.0	9.6	28 02.5	2.6	54.6
16	57 35.3	08.5	133 36.6	9.6	27 59.9	2.7	54.6
17	72 35.5	07.5	148 05.2	9.6	27 57.2	2.9	54.6
18	87 35.6	S 3 06.5	162 33.8	9.7	S27 54.3	3.0	54.6
19	102 35.8	05.5	177 02.5	9.6	27 51.3	3.1	54.7
20	117 36.0	04.5	191 31.1	9.7	27 48.2	3.3	54.7
21	132 36.1	. . 03.5	205 59.8	9.7	27 44.9	3.4	54.7
22	147 36.3	02.6	220 28.5	9.7	27 41.5	3.6	54.7
23	162 36.5	01.6	234 57.2	9.7	27 37.9	3.7	54.7
13 00	177 36.6	S 3 00.6	249 25.9	9.7	S27 34.2	3.8	54.7
01	192 36.8	2 59.6	263 54.6	9.7	27 30.4	4.0	54.8
02	207 37.0	58.6	278 23.3	9.8	27 26.4	4.1	54.8
03	222 37.1	. . 57.6	292 52.1	9.8	27 22.3	4.2	54.8
04	237 37.3	56.6	307 20.9	9.8	27 18.1	4.4	54.8
05	252 37.5	55.7	321 49.7	9.8	27 13.7	4.5	54.8
06	267 37.7	S 2 54.7	336 18.5	9.8	S27 09.2	4.7	54.8
07	282 37.8	53.7	350 47.3	9.9	27 04.5	4.8	54.9
08	297 38.0	52.7	5 16.2	9.8	26 59.7	4.9	54.9
F 09	312 38.2	. . 51.7	19 45.0	9.9	26 54.8	5.1	54.9
R 10	327 38.3	50.7	34 13.9	10.0	26 49.7	5.2	54.9
I 11	342 38.5	49.7	48 42.9	9.9	26 44.5	5.3	54.9
D 12	357 38.7	S 2 48.8	63 11.8	10.0	S26 39.2	5.5	55.0
A 13	12 38.8	47.8	77 40.8	10.0	26 33.7	5.6	55.0
Y 14	27 39.0	46.8	92 09.8	10.0	26 28.1	5.7	55.0
15	42 39.2	. . 45.8	106 38.8	10.1	26 22.4	5.9	55.0
16	57 39.4	44.8	121 07.9	10.1	26 16.5	6.0	55.1
17	72 39.5	43.8	135 37.0	10.1	26 10.5	6.2	55.1
18	87 39.7	S 2 42.8	150 06.1	10.1	S26 04.3	6.2	55.1
19	102 39.9	41.9	164 35.2	10.2	25 58.1	6.4	55.1
20	117 40.0	40.9	179 04.4	10.2	25 51.7	6.6	55.1
21	132 40.2	. . 39.9	193 33.6	10.3	25 45.1	6.7	55.2
22	147 40.4	38.9	208 02.9	10.2	25 38.4	6.8	55.2
23	162 40.5	37.9	222 32.1	10.3	S25 31.6	6.9	55.2
	SD 16.1	*d* 1.0	SD	14.8	14.9		15.0

Lat.	Twilight Naut.	Twilight Civil	Sunrise	Moonrise 11	Moonrise 12	Moonrise 13	Moonrise 14
°	h m	h m	h m	h m	h m	h m	h m
N 72	04 11	05 33	06 40	▬	▬	▬	▬
N 70	04 23	05 36	06 36	▬	▬	▬	▬
68	04 32	05 38	06 34	▬	▬	▬	▬
66	04 40	05 40	06 31	▬	▬	▬	▬
64	04 46	05 42	06 29	▬	▬	▬	07 07
62	04 52	05 44	06 28	▬	▬	06 37	06 25
60	04 56	05 45	06 26	04 24	05 22	05 47	05 57
N 58	05 00	05 46	06 25	03 46	04 42	05 16	05 34
56	05 03	05 46	06 23	03 19	04 15	04 53	05 16
54	05 06	05 47	06 22	02 58	03 53	04 34	05 01
52	05 09	05 48	06 21	02 40	03 35	04 17	04 48
50	05 11	05 48	06 20	02 25	03 20	04 03	04 36
45	05 15	05 49	06 18	01 55	02 49	03 35	04 12
N 40	05 18	05 50	06 16	01 32	02 26	03 13	03 52
35	05 20	05 50	06 15	01 13	02 06	02 54	03 36
30	05 22	05 50	06 14	00 56	01 49	02 38	03 22
20	05 23	05 49	06 11	00 28	01 21	02 11	02 58
N 10	05 23	05 48	06 09	00 04	00 56	01 47	02 37
0	05 22	05 46	06 06	24 34	00 34	01 26	02 17
S 10	05 19	05 43	06 04	24 11	00 11	01 04	01 57
20	05 14	05 39	06 01	23 47	24 40	00 40	01 36
30	05 06	05 34	05 58	23 18	24 13	00 13	01 12
35	05 01	05 31	05 56	23 02	23 57	24 57	00 57
40	04 55	05 27	05 54	22 42	23 38	24 40	00 40
45	04 47	05 22	05 52	22 18	23 15	24 20	00 20
S 50	04 37	05 16	05 49	21 48	22 46	23 55	25 09
52	04 32	05 13	05 47	21 33	22 32	23 42	25 00
54	04 27	05 10	05 46	21 15	22 15	23 28	24 49
56	04 21	05 06	05 44	20 53	21 55	23 11	24 36
58	04 13	05 02	05 42	20 26	21 30	22 51	24 22
S 60	04 05	04 58	05 40	19 47	20 55	22 26	24 04

Lat.	Sunset	Twilight Civil	Twilight Naut.	Moonset 11	Moonset 12	Moonset 13	Moonset 14
°	h m	h m	h m	h m	h m	h m	h m
N 72	17 42	18 49	20 12	▬	▬	▬	▬
N 70	17 45	18 46	19 59	▬	▬	▬	▬
68	17 48	18 43	19 50	▬	▬	▬	▬
66	17 50	18 41	19 42	▬	▬	▬	▬
64	17 52	18 39	19 35	▬	▬	▬	10 03
62	17 53	18 37	19 30	▬	▬	08 46	10 44
60	17 55	18 36	19 25	07 22	08 12	09 35	11 12
N 58	17 56	18 35	19 21	08 00	08 52	10 06	11 33
56	17 57	18 34	19 18	08 27	09 19	10 29	11 51
54	17 58	18 33	19 15	08 49	09 41	10 48	12 06
52	17 59	18 33	19 12	09 06	09 58	11 04	12 18
50	18 00	18 32	19 10	09 21	10 14	11 17	12 30
45	18 02	18 31	19 05	09 52	10 44	11 45	12 53
N 40	18 04	18 31	19 02	10 15	11 08	12 07	13 12
35	18 05	18 30	19 00	10 35	11 27	12 25	13 27
30	18 06	18 30	18 58	10 52	11 44	12 41	13 41
20	18 09	18 31	18 56	11 20	12 12	13 07	14 03
N 10	18 11	18 32	18 56	11 44	12 36	13 30	14 23
0	18 13	18 34	18 58	12 07	12 59	13 51	14 41
S 10	18 15	18 36	19 01	12 29	13 21	14 11	14 59
20	18 18	18 40	19 05	12 54	13 45	14 34	15 19
30	18 21	18 45	19 13	13 22	14 13	14 59	15 41
35	18 22	18 48	19 18	13 39	14 30	15 14	15 54
40	18 24	18 52	19 24	13 58	14 49	15 32	16 08
45	18 27	18 56	19 31	14 22	15 12	15 53	16 26
S 50	18 30	19 02	19 41	14 52	15 41	16 19	16 48
52	18 31	19 05	19 46	15 08	15 56	16 32	16 58
54	18 32	19 08	19 51	15 25	16 13	16 47	17 09
56	18 34	19 12	19 57	15 47	16 33	17 04	17 23
58	18 36	19 16	20 04	16 14	16 59	17 24	17 38
S 60	18 38	19 20	20 12	16 53	17 33	17 50	17 56

Day	SUN Eqn. of Time 00h	SUN Eqn. of Time 12h	SUN Mer. Pass.	MOON Mer. Pass. Upper	MOON Mer. Pass. Lower	Age	Phase
d	m s	m s	h m	h m	h m	d	%
11	10 06	09 58	12 10	05 54	18 20	22	49
12	09 50	09 42	12 10	06 46	19 12	23	40
13	09 34	09 26	12 09	07 38	20 04	24	31

	UT	ARIES	VENUS −3·9		MARS +1·2		JUPITER −2·3		SATURN +0·9	
	d h	GHA ° ′	GHA ° ′	Dec ° ′	GHA ° ′	Dec ° ′	GHA ° ′	Dec ° ′	GHA ° ′	Dec ° ′
	14 00	171 37.8	162 35.0	N 2 43.8	190 37.9	S 9 12.5	65 11.8	N22 56.3	167 45.1	S 0 38.1
	01	186 40.2	177 34.6	45.1	205 38.5	11.8	80 14.3	56.3	182 47.3	38.0
	02	201 42.7	192 34.3	46.4	220 39.2	11.0	95 16.7	56.3	197 49.5	37.9
	03	216 45.1	207 33.9	. . 47.6	235 39.8	. . 10.3	110 19.1	. . 56.3	212 51.7	. . 37.7
	04	231 47.6	222 33.5	48.9	250 40.4	09.6	125 21.6	56.3	227 53.9	37.6
	05	246 50.1	237 33.2	50.2	265 41.0	08.8	140 24.0	56.3	242 56.0	37.5
	06	261 52.5	252 32.8	N 2 51.5	280 41.6	S 9 08.1	155 26.5	N22 56.3	257 58.2	S 0 37.4
	07	276 55.0	267 32.5	52.8	295 42.3	07.3	170 28.9	56.3	273 00.4	37.2
S	08	291 57.5	282 32.1	54.0	310 42.9	06.6	185 31.3	56.3	288 02.6	37.1
A	09	306 59.9	297 31.7	. . 55.3	325 43.5	. . 05.8	200 33.8	. . 56.3	303 04.8	. . 37.0
T	10	322 02.4	312 31.4	56.6	340 44.1	05.1	215 36.2	56.3	318 06.9	36.9
U	11	337 04.9	327 31.0	57.9	355 44.7	04.3	230 38.6	56.3	333 09.1	36.7
R	12	352 07.3	342 30.6	N 2 59.2	10 45.4	S 9 03.6	245 41.1	N22 56.3	348 11.3	S 0 36.6
D	13	7 09.8	357 30.3	3 00.5	25 46.0	02.9	260 43.5	56.3	3 13.5	36.5
A	14	22 12.2	12 29.9	01.7	40 46.6	02.1	275 45.9	56.3	18 15.7	36.4
Y	15	37 14.7	27 29.5	. . 03.0	55 47.2	. . 01.4	290 48.4	. . 56.3	33 17.8	. . 36.3
	16	52 17.2	42 29.2	04.3	70 47.8	9 00.6	305 50.8	56.3	48 20.0	36.1
	17	67 19.6	57 28.8	05.6	85 48.5	8 59.9	320 53.2	56.3	63 22.2	36.0
	18	82 22.1	72 28.4	N 3 06.9	100 49.1	S 8 59.1	335 55.7	N22 56.3	78 24.4	S 0 35.9
	19	97 24.6	87 28.1	08.2	115 49.7	58.4	350 58.1	56.3	93 26.6	35.8
	20	112 27.0	102 27.7	09.4	130 50.3	57.6	6 00.5	56.3	108 28.7	35.6
	21	127 29.5	117 27.3	. . 10.7	145 50.9	. . 56.9	21 03.0	. . 56.3	123 30.9	. . 35.5
	22	142 32.0	132 27.0	12.0	160 51.6	56.1	36 05.4	56.3	138 33.1	35.4
	23	157 34.4	147 26.6	13.3	175 52.2	55.4	51 07.8	56.3	153 35.3	35.3
	15 00	172 36.9	162 26.2	N 3 14.6	190 52.8	S 8 54.6	66 10.3	N22 56.3	168 37.5	S 0 35.1
	01	187 39.4	177 25.9	15.8	205 53.4	53.9	81 12.7	56.3	183 39.6	35.0
	02	202 41.8	192 25.5	17.1	220 54.0	53.2	96 15.1	56.3	198 41.8	34.9
	03	217 44.3	207 25.1	. . 18.4	235 54.7	. . 52.4	111 17.5	. . 56.3	213 44.0	. . 34.8
	04	232 46.7	222 24.8	19.7	250 55.3	51.7	126 20.0	56.3	228 46.2	34.7
	05	247 49.2	237 24.4	21.0	265 55.9	50.9	141 22.4	56.3	243 48.4	34.5
	06	262 51.7	252 24.0	N 3 22.2	280 56.5	S 8 50.2	156 24.8	N22 56.3	258 50.5	S 0 34.4
	07	277 54.1	267 23.7	23.5	295 57.2	49.4	171 27.3	56.3	273 52.7	34.3
	08	292 56.6	282 23.3	24.8	310 57.8	48.7	186 29.7	56.3	288 54.9	34.2
S	09	307 59.1	297 23.0	. . 26.1	325 58.4	. . 47.9	201 32.1	. . 56.3	303 57.1	. . 34.0
U	10	323 01.5	312 22.6	27.4	340 59.0	47.2	216 34.5	56.3	318 59.3	33.9
N	11	338 04.0	327 22.2	28.6	355 59.6	46.4	231 37.0	56.3	334 01.4	33.8
D	12	353 06.5	342 21.9	N 3 29.9	11 00.3	S 8 45.7	246 39.4	N22 56.3	349 03.6	S 0 33.7
A	13	8 08.9	357 21.5	31.2	26 00.9	44.9	261 41.8	56.3	4 05.8	33.5
Y	14	23 11.4	12 21.1	32.5	41 01.5	44.2	276 44.2	56.3	19 08.0	33.4
	15	38 13.9	27 20.8	. . 33.8	56 02.1	. . 43.4	291 46.7	. . 56.3	34 10.2	. . 33.3
	16	53 16.3	42 20.4	35.0	71 02.8	42.7	306 49.1	56.3	49 12.3	33.2
	17	68 18.8	57 20.0	36.3	86 03.4	41.9	321 51.5	56.3	64 14.5	33.1
	18	83 21.2	72 19.7	N 3 37.6	101 04.0	S 8 41.2	336 53.9	N22 56.2	79 16.7	S 0 32.9
	19	98 23.7	87 19.3	38.9	116 04.6	40.4	351 56.4	56.2	94 18.9	32.8
	20	113 26.2	102 18.9	40.2	131 05.3	39.7	6 58.8	56.2	109 21.1	32.7
	21	128 28.6	117 18.6	. . 41.4	146 05.9	. . 38.9	22 01.2	. . 56.2	124 23.2	. . 32.6
	22	143 31.1	132 18.2	42.7	161 06.5	38.2	37 03.6	56.2	139 25.4	32.4
	23	158 33.6	147 17.8	44.0	176 07.1	37.4	52 06.1	56.2	154 27.6	32.3
	16 00	173 36.0	162 17.4	N 3 45.3	191 07.8	S 8 36.7	67 08.5	N22 56.2	169 29.8	S 0 32.2
	01	188 38.5	177 17.1	46.5	206 08.4	35.9	82 10.9	56.2	184 32.0	32.1
	02	203 41.0	192 16.7	47.8	221 09.0	35.2	97 13.3	56.2	199 34.1	31.9
	03	218 43.4	207 16.3	. . 49.1	236 09.6	. . 34.4	112 15.7	. . 56.2	214 36.3	. . 31.8
	04	233 45.9	222 16.0	50.4	251 10.3	33.7	127 18.2	56.2	229 38.5	31.7
	05	248 48.3	237 15.6	51.7	266 10.9	32.9	142 20.6	56.2	244 40.7	31.6
	06	263 50.8	252 15.2	N 3 52.9	281 11.5	S 8 32.2	157 23.0	N22 56.2	259 42.9	S 0 31.4
	07	278 53.3	267 14.9	54.2	296 12.1	31.4	172 25.4	56.2	274 45.0	31.3
	08	293 55.7	282 14.5	55.5	311 12.8	30.7	187 27.8	56.2	289 47.2	31.2
M	09	308 58.2	297 14.1	. . 56.8	326 13.4	. . 29.9	202 30.3	. . 56.2	304 49.4	. . 31.1
O	10	324 00.7	312 13.8	58.0	341 14.0	29.2	217 32.7	56.2	319 51.6	31.0
N	11	339 03.1	327 13.4	3 59.3	356 14.6	28.4	232 35.1	56.2	334 53.8	30.8
D	12	354 05.6	342 13.0	N 4 00.6	11 15.3	S 8 27.7	247 37.5	N22 56.2	349 55.9	S 0 30.7
A	13	9 08.1	357 12.7	01.9	26 15.9	26.9	262 39.9	56.2	4 58.1	30.6
Y	14	24 10.5	12 12.3	03.1	41 16.5	26.2	277 42.3	56.2	20 00.3	30.5
	15	39 13.0	27 11.9	. . 04.4	56 17.1	. . 25.4	292 44.8	. . 56.2	35 02.5	. . 30.3
	16	54 15.5	42 11.6	05.7	71 17.8	24.7	307 47.2	56.2	50 04.7	30.2
	17	69 17.9	57 11.2	07.0	86 18.4	23.9	322 49.6	56.2	65 06.8	30.1
	18	84 20.4	72 10.8	N 4 08.2	101 19.0	S 8 23.2	337 52.0	N22 56.2	80 09.0	S 0 30.0
	19	99 22.8	87 10.5	09.5	116 19.6	22.4	352 54.4	56.2	95 11.2	29.8
	20	114 25.3	102 10.1	10.8	131 20.3	21.7	7 56.8	56.2	110 13.4	29.7
	21	129 27.8	117 09.7	. . 12.1	146 20.9	. . 20.9	22 59.2	. . 56.2	125 15.6	. . 29.6
	22	144 30.2	132 09.3	13.3	161 21.5	20.2	38 01.7	56.2	140 17.7	29.5
	23	159 32.7	147 09.0	14.6	176 22.2	19.4	53 04.1	56.2	155 19.9	29.4
	Mer. Pass.	h m 12 27.5	*v* −0.4	*d* 1.3	*v* 0.6	*d* 0.7	*v* 2.4	*d* 0.0	*v* 2.2	*d* 0.1

STARS

Name	SHA ° ′	Dec ° ′
Acamar	315 11.3	S40 12.2
Achernar	335 19.9	S57 06.4
Acrux	172 58.3	S63 14.7
Adhara	255 05.0	S29 00.7
Aldebaran	290 38.6	N16 33.7
Alioth	166 11.6	N55 48.8
Alkaid	152 50.8	N49 10.7
Alnair	27 32.1	S46 50.0
Alnilam	275 36.7	S 1 11.2
Alphard	217 46.5	S 8 46.5
Alphecca	126 02.7	N26 37.3
Alpheratz	357 34.1	N29 14.1
Altair	61 59.2	N 8 56.1
Ankaa	353 06.6	S42 09.9
Antares	112 14.5	S26 29.4
Arcturus	145 46.8	N19 02.5
Atria	107 07.8	S69 04.2
Avior	234 14.0	S59 35.8
Bellatrix	278 21.8	N 6 22.3
Betelgeuse	270 51.0	N 7 24.6
Canopus	263 51.9	S52 42.8
Capella	280 20.5	N46 01.6
Deneb	49 25.5	N45 22.2
Denebola	182 23.6	N14 25.4
Diphda	348 46.6	S17 50.7
Dubhe	193 39.1	N61 36.5
Elnath	278 00.6	N28 37.8
Eltanin	90 41.8	N51 28.7
Enif	33 38.1	N 9 59.6
Fomalhaut	15 13.8	S29 29.1
Gacrux	171 50.0	S57 15.6
Gienah	175 42.3	S17 41.4
Hadar	148 34.1	S60 29.9
Hamal	327 50.4	N23 35.2
Kaus Aust.	83 31.3	S34 22.3
Kochab	137 19.0	N74 02.5
Markab	13 29.2	N15 20.7
Menkar	314 05.3	N 4 11.5
Menkent	147 56.2	S36 30.0
Miaplacidus	221 37.4	S69 49.7
Mirfak	308 27.1	N49 57.4
Nunki	75 46.7	S26 15.8
Peacock	53 04.6	S56 38.9
Pollux	243 15.9	N27 57.8
Procyon	244 49.6	N 5 09.4
Rasalhague	95 57.6	N12 32.2
Regulus	207 33.1	N11 50.2
Rigel	281 02.9	S 8 10.4
Rigil Kent.	139 38.5	S60 56.5
Sabik	102 01.6	S15 45.5
Schedar	349 30.5	N56 40.9
Shaula	96 09.0	S37 07.3
Sirius	258 25.3	S16 45.3
Spica	158 21.0	S11 18.0
Suhail	222 45.3	S43 32.5
Vega	80 32.7	N38 48.1
Zuben'ubi	136 54.7	S16 09.1

	SHA ° ′	Mer. Pass. h m
Venus	349 49.4	13 11
Mars	18 15.9	11 16
Jupiter	253 33.4	19 32
Saturn	356 00.6	12 44

	UT	SUN GHA	SUN Dec	MOON GHA	v	MOON Dec	d	HP
	d h	° ′	° ′	° ′	′	° ′	′	′
	14 00	177 40.7	S 2 36.9	237 01.4	10.4	S25 24.7	7.1	55.2
	01	192 40.9	35.9	251 30.8	10.3	25 17.6	7.2	55.3
	02	207 41.1	35.0	266 00.1	10.4	25 10.4	7.3	55.3
	03	222 41.2	. . 34.0	280 29.5	10.5	25 03.1	7.4	55.3
	04	237 41.4	33.0	294 59.0	10.5	24 55.7	7.6	55.3
	05	252 41.6	32.0	309 28.5	10.5	24 48.1	7.7	55.4
	06	267 41.8	S 2 31.0	323 58.0	10.5	S24 40.4	7.9	55.4
	07	282 41.9	30.0	338 27.5	10.6	24 32.5	7.9	55.4
S	08	297 42.1	29.0	352 57.1	10.6	24 24.6	8.1	55.4
A	09	312 42.3	. . 28.1	7 26.7	10.7	24 16.5	8.2	55.5
T	10	327 42.4	27.1	21 56.4	10.7	24 08.3	8.4	55.5
U	11	342 42.6	26.1	36 26.1	10.7	23 59.9	8.4	55.5
R	12	357 42.8	S 2 25.1	50 55.8	10.8	S23 51.5	8.6	55.5
D	13	12 43.0	24.1	65 25.6	10.8	23 42.9	8.7	55.6
A	14	27 43.1	23.1	79 55.4	10.9	23 34.2	8.9	55.6
Y	15	42 43.3	. . 22.1	94 25.3	10.9	23 25.3	8.9	55.6
	16	57 43.5	21.1	108 55.2	10.9	23 16.4	9.1	55.6
	17	72 43.7	20.2	123 25.1	11.0	23 07.3	9.2	55.7
	18	87 43.8	S 2 19.2	137 55.1	11.0	S22 58.1	9.3	55.7
	19	102 44.0	18.2	152 25.1	11.0	22 48.8	9.4	55.7
	20	117 44.2	17.2	166 55.1	11.1	22 39.4	9.6	55.7
	21	132 44.3	. . 16.2	181 25.2	11.2	22 29.8	9.7	55.8
	22	147 44.5	15.2	195 55.4	11.1	22 20.1	9.7	55.8
	23	162 44.7	14.2	210 25.5	11.2	22 10.4	9.9	55.8
	15 00	177 44.9	S 2 13.2	224 55.7	11.3	S22 00.5	10.1	55.9
	01	192 45.0	12.3	239 26.0	11.3	21 50.4	10.1	55.9
	02	207 45.2	11.3	253 56.3	11.3	21 40.3	10.3	55.9
	03	222 45.4	. . 10.3	268 26.6	11.4	21 30.0	10.3	55.9
	04	237 45.6	09.3	282 57.0	11.4	21 19.7	10.5	56.0
	05	252 45.7	08.3	297 27.4	11.5	21 09.2	10.6	56.0
	06	267 45.9	S 2 07.3	311 57.9	11.5	S20 58.6	10.7	56.0
	07	282 46.1	06.3	326 28.4	11.5	20 47.9	10.8	56.1
	08	297 46.3	05.3	340 58.9	11.6	20 37.1	10.9	56.1
S	09	312 46.4	. . 04.4	355 29.5	11.6	20 26.2	11.0	56.1
U	10	327 46.6	03.4	10 00.1	11.6	20 15.2	11.2	56.1
N	11	342 46.8	02.4	24 30.7	11.7	20 04.0	11.2	56.2
D	12	357 47.0	S 2 01.4	39 01.4	11.8	S19 52.8	11.4	56.2
A	13	12 47.1	2 00.4	53 32.2	11.7	19 41.4	11.4	56.2
Y	14	27 47.3	1 59.4	68 02.9	11.8	19 30.0	11.6	56.3
	15	42 47.5	. . 58.4	82 33.7	11.9	19 18.4	11.7	56.3
	16	57 47.7	57.4	97 04.6	11.9	19 06.7	11.7	56.3
	17	72 47.8	56.4	111 35.5	11.9	18 55.0	11.9	56.4
	18	87 48.0	S 1 55.5	126 06.4	12.0	S18 43.1	12.0	56.4
	19	102 48.2	54.5	140 37.4	12.0	18 31.1	12.1	56.4
	20	117 48.4	53.5	155 08.4	12.0	18 19.0	12.1	56.4
	21	132 48.5	. . 52.5	169 39.4	12.1	18 06.9	12.3	56.5
	22	147 48.7	51.5	184 10.5	12.1	17 54.6	12.4	56.5
	23	162 48.9	50.5	198 41.6	12.1	17 42.2	12.5	56.5
	16 00	177 49.1	S 1 49.5	213 12.7	12.2	S17 29.7	12.5	56.6
	01	192 49.2	48.5	227 43.9	12.2	17 17.2	12.7	56.6
	02	207 49.4	47.6	242 15.1	12.2	17 04.5	12.7	56.6
	03	222 49.6	. . 46.6	256 46.3	12.3	16 51.8	12.9	56.7
	04	237 49.8	45.6	271 17.6	12.3	16 38.9	12.9	56.7
	05	252 49.9	44.6	285 48.9	12.4	16 26.0	13.1	56.7
	06	267 50.1	S 1 43.6	300 20.3	12.4	S16 12.9	13.1	56.8
	07	282 50.3	42.6	314 51.7	12.4	15 59.8	13.2	56.8
	08	297 50.5	41.6	329 23.1	12.4	15 46.6	13.3	56.8
M	09	312 50.7	. . 40.6	343 54.5	12.5	15 33.3	13.4	56.8
O	10	327 50.8	39.6	358 26.0	12.5	15 19.9	13.5	56.9
N	11	342 51.0	38.7	12 57.5	12.5	15 06.4	13.5	56.9
D	12	357 51.2	S 1 37.7	27 29.0	12.6	S14 52.9	13.7	56.9
A	13	12 51.4	36.7	42 00.6	12.6	14 39.2	13.7	57.0
Y	14	27 51.5	35.7	56 32.2	12.6	14 25.5	13.8	57.0
	15	42 51.7	. . 34.7	71 03.8	12.6	14 11.7	13.9	57.0
	16	57 51.9	33.7	85 35.4	12.7	13 57.8	14.0	57.1
	17	72 52.1	32.7	100 07.1	12.7	13 43.8	14.1	57.1
	18	87 52.3	S 1 31.7	114 38.8	12.7	S13 29.7	14.1	57.1
	19	102 52.4	30.7	129 10.5	12.7	13 15.6	14.2	57.2
	20	117 52.6	29.8	143 42.2	12.8	13 01.4	14.3	57.2
	21	132 52.8	. . 28.8	158 14.0	12.8	12 47.1	14.4	57.2
	22	147 53.0	27.8	172 45.8	12.8	12 32.7	14.4	57.3
	23	162 53.1	26.8	187 17.6	12.8	S12 18.3	14.5	57.3
		SD 16.1	d 1.0	SD	15.1	15.3		15.5

Lat.	Twilight Naut.	Twilight Civil	Sunrise	Moonrise 14	Moonrise 15	Moonrise 16	Moonrise 17
°	h m	h m	h m	h m	h m	h m	h m
N 72	03 53	05 17	06 24	■	■	08 07	07 04
N 70	04 08	05 22	06 22	■	■	07 30	06 48
68	04 19	05 26	06 21	■	07 55	07 03	06 35
66	04 28	05 29	06 20	■	07 10	06 43	06 24
64	04 35	05 32	06 19	07 07	06 41	06 26	06 15
62	04 41	05 34	06 18	06 25	06 18	06 13	06 07
60	04 47	05 36	06 17	05 57	06 00	06 01	06 01
N 58	04 51	05 37	06 16	05 34	05 45	05 51	05 55
56	04 55	05 39	06 16	05 16	05 32	05 42	05 49
54	04 59	05 40	06 15	05 01	05 20	05 34	05 44
52	05 01	05 41	06 14	04 48	05 10	05 27	05 40
50	05 04	05 42	06 14	04 36	05 01	05 20	05 36
45	05 09	05 44	06 13	04 12	04 42	05 06	05 27
N 40	05 13	05 45	06 12	03 52	04 26	04 55	05 20
35	05 16	05 46	06 11	03 36	04 13	04 45	05 14
30	05 18	05 46	06 10	03 22	04 01	04 36	05 08
20	05 21	05 46	06 08	02 58	03 41	04 21	04 59
N 10	05 22	05 46	06 07	02 37	03 23	04 08	04 50
0	05 21	05 45	06 06	02 17	03 07	03 55	04 42
S 10	05 19	05 43	06 04	01 57	02 50	03 43	04 34
20	05 15	05 40	06 02	01 36	02 33	03 29	04 25
30	05 08	05 36	06 00	01 12	02 12	03 14	04 15
35	05 04	05 34	05 59	00 57	02 00	03 05	04 10
40	04 58	05 30	05 57	00 40	01 46	02 54	04 03
45	04 51	05 26	05 56	00 20	01 30	02 42	03 56
S 50	04 43	05 21	05 54	25 09	01 09	02 27	03 46
52	04 38	05 19	05 53	25 00	01 00	02 20	03 42
54	04 33	05 16	05 52	24 49	00 49	02 13	03 37
56	04 28	05 13	05 50	24 36	00 36	02 04	03 32
58	04 21	05 09	05 49	24 22	00 22	01 54	03 26
S 60	04 14	05 05	05 48	24 04	00 04	01 43	03 19

Lat.	Sunset	Twilight Civil	Twilight Naut.	Moonset 14	Moonset 15	Moonset 16	Moonset 17
°	h m	h m	h m	h m	h m	h m	h m
N 72	17 56	19 03	20 28	■	■	12 31	15 13
N 70	17 57	18 58	20 13	■	■	13 07	15 27
68	17 59	18 54	20 02	■	11 00	13 31	15 37
66	18 00	18 51	19 52	■	11 43	13 50	15 46
64	18 01	18 48	19 45	10 03	12 12	14 06	15 54
62	18 01	18 46	19 38	10 44	12 33	14 18	16 00
60	18 02	18 44	19 33	11 12	12 51	14 29	16 05
N 58	18 03	18 42	19 28	11 33	13 05	14 38	16 10
56	18 03	18 40	19 24	11 51	13 18	14 46	16 14
54	18 04	18 39	19 21	12 06	13 28	14 53	16 18
52	18 04	18 38	19 18	12 18	13 38	14 59	16 21
50	18 05	18 37	19 15	12 30	13 46	15 05	16 24
45	18 06	18 35	19 09	12 53	14 04	15 17	16 31
N 40	18 07	18 34	19 05	13 12	14 19	15 27	16 36
35	18 07	18 33	19 02	13 27	14 31	15 36	16 41
30	18 08	18 32	19 00	13 41	14 42	15 43	16 45
20	18 10	18 32	18 57	14 03	15 00	15 56	16 52
N 10	18 11	18 32	18 56	14 23	15 16	16 07	16 58
0	18 12	18 33	18 57	14 41	15 30	16 18	17 04
S 10	18 14	18 35	18 59	14 59	15 45	16 28	17 10
20	18 15	18 37	19 03	15 19	16 00	16 39	17 16
30	18 17	18 41	19 09	15 41	16 18	16 51	17 22
35	18 18	18 44	19 13	15 54	16 28	16 58	17 26
40	18 20	18 47	19 18	16 08	16 39	17 06	17 31
45	18 21	18 51	19 25	16 26	16 53	17 16	17 36
S 50	18 23	18 56	19 34	16 48	17 09	17 27	17 42
52	18 24	18 58	19 38	16 58	17 17	17 32	17 44
54	18 25	19 01	19 43	17 09	17 26	17 37	17 47
56	18 26	19 03	19 48	17 23	17 35	17 44	17 50
58	18 27	19 07	19 55	17 38	17 46	17 51	17 54
S 60	18 29	19 11	20 02	17 56	17 58	17 59	17 58

Day	SUN Eqn. of Time 00^h	SUN Eqn. of Time 12^h	SUN Mer. Pass.	MOON Mer. Pass. Upper	MOON Mer. Pass. Lower	Age	Phase
d	m s	m s	h m	h m	h m	d %	
14	09 17	09 09	12 09	08 29	20 54	25 22	
15	09 01	08 53	12 09	09 19	21 43	26 14	
16	08 44	08 36	12 09	10 06	22 30	27 8	

UT (d h)	ARIES GHA	VENUS −3·9 GHA	VENUS Dec	MARS +1·2 GHA	MARS Dec	JUPITER −2·3 GHA	JUPITER Dec	SATURN +0·9 GHA	SATURN Dec
	° ′	° ′	° ′	° ′	° ′	° ′	° ′	° ′	° ′
17 00	174 35.2	162 08.6	N 4 15.9	191 22.8	S 8 18.7	68 06.5	N22 56.2	170 22.1	S 0 29.2
01	189 37.6	177 08.2	17.2	206 23.4	17.9	83 08.9	56.2	185 24.3	29.1
02	204 40.1	192 07.9	18.4	221 24.0	17.1	98 11.3	56.2	200 26.5	29.0
03	219 42.6	207 07.5	19.7	236 24.7	16.4	113 13.7	56.2	215 28.6	28.9
04	234 45.0	222 07.1	21.0	251 25.3	15.6	128 16.1	56.2	230 30.8	28.7
05	249 47.5	237 06.8	22.3	266 25.9	14.9	143 18.5	56.2	245 33.0	28.6
06	264 50.0	252 06.4	N 4 23.5	281 26.6	S 8 14.1	158 20.9	N22 56.1	260 35.2	S 0 28.5
T 07	279 52.4	267 06.0	24.8	296 27.2	13.4	173 23.4	56.1	275 37.3	28.4
U 08	294 54.9	282 05.6	26.1	311 27.8	12.6	188 25.8	56.1	290 39.5	28.2
E 09	309 57.3	297 05.3	27.4	326 28.4	11.9	203 28.2	56.1	305 41.7	28.1
S 10	324 59.8	312 04.9	28.6	341 29.1	11.1	218 30.6	56.1	320 43.9	28.0
D 11	340 02.3	327 04.5	29.9	356 29.7	10.4	233 33.0	56.1	335 46.1	27.9
A 12	355 04.7	342 04.2	N 4 31.2	11 30.3	S 8 09.6	248 35.4	N22 56.1	350 48.2	S 0 27.7
Y 13	10 07.2	357 03.8	32.5	26 31.0	08.9	263 37.8	56.1	5 50.4	27.6
14	25 09.7	12 03.4	33.7	41 31.6	08.1	278 40.2	56.1	20 52.6	27.5
15	40 12.1	27 03.1	35.0	56 32.2	07.3	293 42.6	56.1	35 54.8	27.4
16	55 14.6	42 02.7	36.3	71 32.9	06.6	308 45.0	56.1	50 57.0	27.3
17	70 17.1	57 02.3	37.5	86 33.5	05.8	323 47.4	56.1	65 59.1	27.1
18	85 19.5	72 01.9	N 4 38.8	101 34.1	S 8 05.1	338 49.8	N22 56.1	81 01.3	S 0 27.0
19	100 22.0	87 01.6	40.1	116 34.7	04.3	353 52.3	56.1	96 03.5	26.9
20	115 24.4	102 01.2	41.4	131 35.4	03.6	8 54.7	56.1	111 05.7	26.8
21	130 26.9	117 00.8	42.6	146 36.0	02.8	23 57.1	56.1	126 07.9	26.6
22	145 29.4	132 00.5	43.9	161 36.6	02.1	38 59.5	56.1	141 10.0	26.5
23	160 31.8	147 00.1	45.2	176 37.3	01.3	54 01.9	56.1	156 12.2	26.4
18 00	175 34.3	161 59.7	N 4 46.4	191 37.9	S 8 00.5	69 04.3	N22 56.1	171 14.4	S 0 26.3
01	190 36.8	176 59.3	47.7	206 38.5	7 59.8	84 06.7	56.1	186 16.6	26.1
02	205 39.2	191 59.0	49.0	221 39.2	59.0	99 09.1	56.1	201 18.8	26.0
03	220 41.7	206 58.6	50.3	236 39.8	58.3	114 11.5	56.1	216 20.9	25.9
04	235 44.2	221 58.2	51.5	251 40.4	57.5	129 13.9	56.1	231 23.1	25.8
05	250 46.6	236 57.8	52.8	266 41.1	56.8	144 16.3	56.1	246 25.3	25.7
06	265 49.1	251 57.5	N 4 54.1	281 41.7	S 7 56.0	159 18.7	N22 56.1	261 27.5	S 0 25.5
W 07	280 51.6	266 57.1	55.3	296 42.3	55.2	174 21.1	56.1	276 29.6	25.4
E 08	295 54.0	281 56.7	56.6	311 42.9	54.5	189 23.5	56.0	291 31.8	25.3
D 09	310 56.5	296 56.4	57.9	326 43.6	53.7	204 25.9	56.0	306 34.0	25.2
N 10	325 58.9	311 56.0	4 59.1	341 44.2	53.0	219 28.3	56.0	321 36.2	25.0
E 11	341 01.4	326 55.6	5 00.4	356 44.8	52.2	234 30.7	56.0	336 38.4	24.9
S 12	356 03.9	341 55.2	N 5 01.7	11 45.5	S 7 51.5	249 33.1	N22 56.0	351 40.5	S 0 24.8
D 13	11 06.3	356 54.9	02.9	26 46.1	50.7	264 35.5	56.0	6 42.7	24.7
A 14	26 08.8	11 54.5	04.2	41 46.7	49.9	279 37.9	56.0	21 44.9	24.5
Y 15	41 11.3	26 54.1	05.5	56 47.4	49.2	294 40.3	56.0	36 47.1	24.4
16	56 13.7	41 53.7	06.7	71 48.0	48.4	309 42.7	56.0	51 49.3	24.3
17	71 16.2	56 53.4	08.0	86 48.6	47.7	324 45.1	56.0	66 51.4	24.2
18	86 18.7	71 53.0	N 5 09.3	101 49.3	S 7 46.9	339 47.5	N22 56.0	81 53.6	S 0 24.1
19	101 21.1	86 52.6	10.5	116 49.9	46.2	354 49.9	56.0	96 55.8	23.9
20	116 23.6	101 52.2	11.8	131 50.5	45.4	9 52.3	56.0	111 58.0	23.8
21	131 26.0	116 51.9	13.1	146 51.2	44.6	24 54.7	56.0	127 00.1	23.7
22	146 28.5	131 51.5	14.3	161 51.8	43.9	39 57.1	56.0	142 02.3	23.6
23	161 31.0	146 51.1	15.6	176 52.4	43.1	54 59.5	56.0	157 04.5	23.4
19 00	176 33.4	161 50.7	N 5 16.9	191 53.1	S 7 42.4	70 01.9	N22 56.0	172 06.7	S 0 23.3
01	191 35.9	176 50.4	18.1	206 53.7	41.6	85 04.3	56.0	187 08.9	23.2
02	206 38.4	191 50.0	19.4	221 54.3	40.8	100 06.7	56.0	202 11.0	23.1
03	221 40.8	206 49.6	20.7	236 55.0	40.1	115 09.1	56.0	217 13.2	22.9
04	236 43.3	221 49.2	21.9	251 55.6	39.3	130 11.4	55.9	232 15.4	22.8
05	251 45.8	236 48.9	23.2	266 56.2	38.6	145 13.8	55.9	247 17.6	22.7
06	266 48.2	251 48.5	N 5 24.5	281 56.9	S 7 37.8	160 16.2	N22 55.9	262 19.8	S 0 22.6
T 07	281 50.7	266 48.1	25.7	296 57.5	37.1	175 18.6	55.9	277 21.9	22.4
H 08	296 53.2	281 47.7	27.0	311 58.2	36.3	190 21.0	55.9	292 24.1	22.3
U 09	311 55.6	296 47.4	28.3	326 58.8	35.5	205 23.4	55.9	307 26.3	22.2
R 10	326 58.1	311 47.0	29.5	341 59.4	34.8	220 25.8	55.9	322 28.5	22.1
S 11	342 00.5	326 46.6	30.8	357 00.1	34.0	235 28.2	55.9	337 30.6	22.0
D 12	357 03.0	341 46.2	N 5 32.1	12 00.7	S 7 33.3	250 30.6	N22 55.9	352 32.8	S 0 21.8
A 13	12 05.5	356 45.9	33.3	27 01.3	32.5	265 33.0	55.9	7 35.0	21.7
Y 14	27 07.9	11 45.5	34.6	42 02.0	31.7	280 35.4	55.9	22 37.2	21.6
15	42 10.4	26 45.1	35.8	57 02.6	31.0	295 37.8	55.9	37 39.4	21.5
16	57 12.9	41 44.7	37.1	72 03.2	30.2	310 40.1	55.9	52 41.5	21.3
17	72 15.3	56 44.3	38.4	87 03.9	29.5	325 42.5	55.9	67 43.7	21.2
18	87 17.8	71 44.0	N 5 39.6	102 04.5	S 7 28.7	340 44.9	N22 55.9	82 45.9	S 0 21.1
19	102 20.3	86 43.6	40.9	117 05.1	27.9	355 47.3	55.9	97 48.1	21.0
20	117 22.7	101 43.2	42.2	132 05.8	27.2	10 49.7	55.9	112 50.2	20.8
21	132 25.2	116 42.8	43.4	147 06.4	26.4	25 52.1	55.9	127 52.4	20.7
22	147 27.6	131 42.5	44.7	162 07.1	25.6	40 54.5	55.8	142 54.6	20.6
23	162 30.1	146 42.1	45.9	177 07.7	24.9	55 56.9	55.8	157 56.8	20.5
Mer. Pass.	h m 12 15.7	v −0.4	d 1.3	v 0.6	d 0.8	v 2.4	d 0.0	v 2.2	d 0.1

STARS

Name	SHA	Dec
	° ′	° ′
Acamar	315 11.3	S40 12.2
Achernar	335 19.9	S57 06.4
Acrux	172 58.3	S63 14.7
Adhara	255 05.0	S29 00.7
Aldebaran	290 38.6	N16 33.7
Alioth	166 11.5	N55 48.8
Alkaid	152 50.8	N49 10.7
Alnair	27 32.1	S46 50.0
Alnilam	275 36.7	S 1 11.2
Alphard	217 46.5	S 8 46.5
Alphecca	126 02.7	N26 37.3
Alpheratz	357 34.1	N29 14.0
Altair	61 59.2	N 8 56.1
Ankaa	353 06.6	S42 09.9
Antares	112 14.5	S26 29.4
Arcturus	145 46.7	N19 02.5
Atria	107 07.7	S69 04.2
Avior	234 14.0	S59 35.8
Bellatrix	278 21.9	N 6 22.3
Betelgeuse	270 51.0	N 7 24.6
Canopus	263 51.9	S52 42.8
Capella	280 20.5	N46 01.6
Deneb	49 25.5	N45 22.2
Denebola	182 23.6	N14 25.4
Diphda	348 46.6	S17 50.7
Dubhe	193 39.1	N61 36.5
Elnath	278 00.7	N28 37.8
Eltanin	90 41.7	N51 28.7
Enif	33 38.1	N 9 59.6
Fomalhaut	15 13.8	S29 29.1
Gacrux	171 50.0	S57 15.7
Gienah	175 42.3	S17 41.4
Hadar	148 34.1	S60 29.9
Hamal	327 50.4	N23 35.2
Kaus Aust.	83 31.3	S34 22.3
Kochab	137 19.0	N74 02.5
Markab	13 29.2	N15 20.7
Menkar	314 05.3	N 4 11.5
Menkent	147 56.1	S36 30.0
Miaplacidus	221 37.4	S69 49.7
Mirfak	308 27.1	N49 57.4
Nunki	75 46.6	S26 15.8
Peacock	53 04.5	S56 38.9
Pollux	243 15.9	N27 57.8
Procyon	244 49.7	N 5 09.4
Rasalhague	95 57.6	N12 32.2
Regulus	207 33.1	N11 50.2
Rigel	281 03.0	S 8 10.4
Rigil Kent.	139 38.5	S60 56.5
Sabik	102 01.6	S15 45.5
Schedar	349 30.5	N56 40.9
Shaula	96 09.0	S37 07.3
Sirius	258 25.3	S16 45.3
Spica	158 21.0	S11 18.0
Suhail	222 45.3	S43 32.5
Vega	80 32.6	N38 48.1
Zuben'ubi	136 54.7	S16 09.2

	SHA	Mer. Pass.
	° ′	h m
Venus	346 25.4	13 12
Mars	16 03.6	11 13
Jupiter	253 30.0	19 21
Saturn	355 40.1	12 33

Day	UT	SUN GHA	SUN Dec	MOON GHA	v	MOON Dec	d	HP
	d h	° ′	° ′	° ′	′	° ′	′	′
17	00	177 53.3	S 1 25.8	201 49.4	12.9	S12 03.8	14.6	57.3
	01	192 53.5	24.8	216 21.3	12.8	11 49.2	14.7	57.3
	02	207 53.7	23.8	230 53.1	12.9	11 34.5	14.7	57.4
	03	222 53.9	. . 22.8	245 25.0	12.9	11 19.8	14.8	57.4
	04	237 54.0	21.8	259 56.9	12.9	11 05.0	14.9	57.4
	05	252 54.2	20.9	274 28.8	13.0	10 50.1	14.9	57.5
	06	267 54.4	S 1 19.9	289 00.8	12.9	S10 35.2	15.0	57.5
	07	282 54.6	18.9	303 32.7	13.0	10 20.2	15.1	57.5
T	08	297 54.7	17.9	318 04.7	12.9	10 05.1	15.1	57.6
U	09	312 54.9	. . 16.9	332 36.6	13.0	9 50.0	15.2	57.6
E	10	327 55.1	15.9	347 08.6	13.0	9 34.8	15.2	57.6
S	11	342 55.3	14.9	1 40.6	13.0	9 19.6	15.3	57.7
D	12	357 55.5	S 1 13.9	16 12.6	13.1	S 9 04.3	15.4	57.7
A	13	12 55.6	12.9	30 44.7	13.0	8 48.9	15.4	57.7
Y	14	27 55.8	12.0	45 16.7	13.0	8 33.5	15.5	57.7
	15	42 56.0	. . 11.0	59 48.7	13.1	8 18.0	15.6	57.8
	16	57 56.2	10.0	74 20.8	13.0	8 02.4	15.6	57.8
	17	72 56.4	09.0	88 52.8	13.1	7 46.8	15.6	57.8
	18	87 56.5	S 1 08.0	103 24.9	13.0	S 7 31.2	15.7	57.9
	19	102 56.7	07.0	117 56.9	13.1	7 15.5	15.8	57.9
	20	117 56.9	06.0	132 29.0	13.0	6 59.7	15.8	57.9
	21	132 57.1	. . 05.0	147 01.0	13.1	6 43.9	15.8	58.0
	22	147 57.3	04.0	161 33.1	13.1	6 28.1	15.9	58.0
	23	162 57.4	03.1	176 05.2	13.0	6 12.2	15.9	58.0
18	00	177 57.6	S 1 02.1	190 37.2	13.1	S 5 56.3	16.0	58.0
	01	192 57.8	01.1	205 09.3	13.0	5 40.3	16.0	58.1
	02	207 58.0	1 00.1	219 41.3	13.1	5 24.3	16.1	58.1
	03	222 58.2	0 59.1	234 13.4	13.0	5 08.2	16.1	58.1
	04	237 58.3	58.1	248 45.4	13.1	4 52.1	16.2	58.2
	05	252 58.5	57.1	263 17.5	13.0	4 35.9	16.2	58.2
	06	267 58.7	S 0 56.1	277 49.5	13.0	S 4 19.7	16.2	58.2
W	07	282 58.9	55.1	292 21.5	13.0	4 03.5	16.2	58.2
E	08	297 59.1	54.2	306 53.5	13.0	3 47.3	16.3	58.3
D	09	312 59.2	. . 53.2	321 25.5	13.0	3 31.0	16.3	58.3
N	10	327 59.4	52.2	335 57.5	13.0	3 14.7	16.4	58.3
E	11	342 59.6	51.2	350 29.5	12.9	2 58.3	16.4	58.4
S	12	357 59.8	S 0 50.2	5 01.4	13.0	S 2 41.9	16.4	58.4
D	13	13 00.0	49.2	19 33.4	12.9	2 25.5	16.4	58.4
A	14	28 00.1	48.2	34 05.3	12.9	2 09.1	16.5	58.4
Y	15	43 00.3	. . 47.2	48 37.2	12.9	1 52.6	16.5	58.5
	16	58 00.5	46.2	63 09.1	12.9	1 36.1	16.5	58.5
	17	73 00.7	45.3	77 41.0	12.8	1 19.6	16.5	58.5
	18	88 00.9	S 0 44.3	92 12.8	12.9	S 1 03.1	16.6	58.5
	19	103 01.1	43.3	106 44.7	12.8	0 46.5	16.5	58.6
	20	118 01.2	42.3	121 16.5	12.7	0 30.0	16.6	58.6
	21	133 01.4	. . 41.3	135 48.2	12.8	S 0 13.4	16.6	58.6
	22	148 01.6	40.3	150 20.0	12.7	N 0 03.2	16.7	58.7
	23	163 01.8	39.3	164 51.7	12.7	0 19.9	16.6	58.7
19	00	178 02.0	S 0 38.3	179 23.4	12.7	N 0 36.5	16.6	58.7
	01	193 02.1	37.3	193 55.1	12.6	0 53.1	16.7	58.7
	02	208 02.3	36.4	208 26.7	12.6	1 09.8	16.6	58.8
	03	223 02.5	. . 35.4	222 58.3	12.6	1 26.4	16.7	58.8
	04	238 02.7	34.4	237 29.9	12.5	1 43.1	16.7	58.8
	05	253 02.9	33.4	252 01.4	12.5	1 59.8	16.6	58.8
	06	268 03.1	S 0 32.4	266 32.9	12.5	N 2 16.4	16.7	58.8
T	07	283 03.2	31.4	281 04.4	12.4	2 33.1	16.7	58.9
H	08	298 03.4	30.4	295 35.8	12.4	2 49.8	16.7	58.9
U	09	313 03.6	. . 29.4	310 07.2	12.4	3 06.5	16.6	58.9
R	10	328 03.8	28.4	324 38.6	12.3	3 23.1	16.7	58.9
S	11	343 04.0	27.4	339 09.9	12.3	3 39.8	16.6	59.0
D	12	358 04.1	S 0 26.5	353 41.2	12.2	N 3 56.4	16.7	59.0
A	13	13 04.3	25.5	8 12.4	12.2	4 13.1	16.6	59.0
Y	14	28 04.5	24.5	22 43.6	12.1	4 29.7	16.7	59.0
	15	43 04.7	. . 23.5	37 14.7	12.1	4 46.4	16.6	59.0
	16	58 04.9	22.5	51 45.8	12.0	5 03.0	16.6	59.1
	17	73 05.1	21.5	66 16.8	12.0	5 19.6	16.6	59.1
	18	88 05.2	S 0 20.5	80 47.8	11.9	N 5 36.2	16.6	59.1
	19	103 05.4	19.5	95 18.7	11.9	5 52.8	16.5	59.1
	20	118 05.6	18.5	109 49.6	11.9	6 09.3	16.6	59.1
	21	133 05.8	. . 17.6	124 20.5	11.7	6 25.9	16.5	59.2
	22	148 06.0	16.6	138 51.2	11.8	6 42.4	16.5	59.2
	23	163 06.2	15.6	153 22.0	11.6	N 6 58.9	16.4	59.2
		SD 16.1	*d* 1.0	SD 15.7		15.9		16.1

Lat.	Twilight Naut.	Twilight Civil	Sunrise	Moonrise 17	18	19	20
°	h m	h m	h m	h m	h m	h m	h m
N 72	03 35	05 01	06 09	07 04	06 24	05 48	05 09
N 70	03 52	05 08	06 09	06 48	06 18	05 51	05 21
68	04 05	05 13	06 08	06 35	06 13	05 53	05 31
66	04 15	05 17	06 08	06 24	06 09	05 55	05 40
64	04 24	05 21	06 08	06 15	06 06	05 56	05 47
62	04 31	05 24	06 08	06 07	06 03	05 58	05 53
60	04 37	05 26	06 08	06 01	06 00	05 59	05 59
N 58	04 42	05 29	06 08	05 55	05 58	06 00	06 03
56	04 47	05 31	06 08	05 49	05 55	06 01	06 08
54	04 51	05 32	06 08	05 44	05 54	06 02	06 12
52	04 54	05 34	06 07	05 40	05 52	06 03	06 15
50	04 57	05 35	06 07	05 36	05 50	06 04	06 18
45	05 04	05 38	06 07	05 27	05 47	06 06	06 26
N 40	05 08	05 40	06 07	05 20	05 44	06 07	06 31
35	05 12	05 41	06 07	05 14	05 41	06 08	06 37
30	05 15	05 43	06 06	05 08	05 39	06 09	06 41
20	05 18	05 44	06 06	04 59	05 35	06 11	06 49
N 10	05 20	05 44	06 05	04 50	05 32	06 13	06 56
0	05 20	05 44	06 05	04 42	05 28	06 15	07 03
S 10	05 19	05 43	06 04	04 34	05 25	06 17	07 10
20	05 16	05 41	06 03	04 25	05 22	06 18	07 17
30	05 10	05 38	06 02	04 15	05 18	06 21	07 25
35	05 07	05 36	06 01	04 10	05 15	06 22	07 30
40	05 02	05 34	06 01	04 03	05 13	06 23	07 36
45	04 56	05 30	06 00	03 56	05 10	06 25	07 43
S 50	04 48	05 26	05 58	03 46	05 06	06 27	07 50
52	04 44	05 24	05 58	03 42	05 04	06 28	07 54
54	04 40	05 22	05 57	03 37	05 03	06 29	07 58
56	04 35	05 19	05 57	03 32	05 00	06 30	08 03
58	04 29	05 16	05 56	03 26	04 58	06 31	08 08
S 60	04 22	05 13	05 55	03 19	04 56	06 33	08 13

Lat.	Sunset	Twilight Civil	Twilight Naut.	Moonset 17	18	19	20
°	h m	h m	h m	h m	h m	h m	h m
N 72	18 10	19 18	20 46	15 13	17 34	19 56	22 37
N 70	18 10	19 11	20 28	15 27	17 36	19 47	22 11
68	18 10	19 05	20 15	15 37	17 37	19 39	21 51
66	18 10	19 01	20 04	15 46	17 39	19 33	21 35
64	18 10	18 57	19 55	15 54	17 40	19 28	21 22
62	18 10	18 54	19 47	16 00	17 41	19 24	21 12
60	18 10	18 51	19 41	16 05	17 42	19 20	21 03
N 58	18 10	18 49	19 35	16 10	17 42	19 17	20 55
56	18 10	18 47	19 31	16 14	17 43	19 14	20 48
54	18 10	18 45	19 27	16 18	17 43	19 11	20 42
52	18 10	18 43	19 23	16 21	17 44	19 09	20 36
50	18 10	18 42	19 20	16 24	17 44	19 06	20 31
45	18 10	18 39	19 13	16 31	17 45	19 02	20 20
N 40	18 10	18 37	19 08	16 36	17 46	18 58	20 12
35	18 10	18 35	19 05	16 41	17 47	18 54	20 04
30	18 10	18 34	19 02	16 45	17 48	18 51	19 57
20	18 10	18 32	18 58	16 52	17 49	18 46	19 46
N 10	18 11	18 32	18 56	16 58	17 49	18 42	19 36
0	18 11	18 32	18 56	17 04	17 50	18 37	19 27
S 10	18 12	18 33	18 57	17 10	17 51	18 33	19 18
20	18 13	18 35	19 00	17 16	17 52	18 29	19 08
30	18 13	18 37	19 05	17 22	17 53	18 24	18 57
35	18 14	18 39	19 09	17 26	17 53	18 21	18 50
40	18 15	18 42	19 13	17 31	17 54	18 17	18 43
45	18 16	18 45	19 19	17 36	17 54	18 14	18 35
S 50	18 17	18 49	19 27	17 42	17 55	18 09	18 25
52	18 17	18 51	19 31	17 44	17 56	18 07	18 20
54	18 18	18 53	19 35	17 47	17 56	18 05	18 15
56	18 18	18 55	19 40	17 50	17 56	18 02	18 09
58	18 19	18 58	19 45	17 54	17 57	18 00	18 03
S 60	18 20	19 01	19 52	17 58	17 57	17 56	17 56

Day	SUN Eqn. of Time 00^h	SUN Eqn. of Time 12^h	SUN Mer. Pass.	MOON Mer. Pass. Upper	MOON Mer. Pass. Lower	Age	Phase
d	m s	m s	h m	h m	h m	d %	
17	08 27	08 19	12 08	10 53	23 16	28 3	
18	08 10	08 01	12 08	11 39	24 03	29 0	●
19	07 53	07 44	12 08	12 26	00 03	00 0	

2026 MARCH 20, 21, 22 (FRI., SAT., SUN.)

UT d	UT h	ARIES GHA ° ′	VENUS −3·9 GHA ° ′	VENUS Dec ° ′	MARS +1·2 GHA ° ′	MARS Dec ° ′	JUPITER −2·3 GHA ° ′	JUPITER Dec ° ′	SATURN +0·9 GHA ° ′	SATURN Dec ° ′
20 FRIDAY	00	177 32.6	161 41.7	N 5 47.2	192 08.3	S 7 24.1	70 59.3	N22 55.8	172 59.0	S 0 20.4
	01	192 35.0	176 41.3	48.5	207 09.0	23.4	86 01.6	55.8	188 01.1	20.2
	02	207 37.5	191 40.9	49.7	222 09.6	22.6	101 04.0	55.8	203 03.3	20.1
	03	222 40.0	206 40.6	. . 51.0	237 10.2	. . 21.8	116 06.4	. . 55.8	218 05.5	. . 20.0
	04	237 42.4	221 40.2	52.3	252 10.9	21.1	131 08.8	55.8	233 07.7	19.9
	05	252 44.9	236 39.8	53.5	267 11.5	20.3	146 11.2	55.8	248 09.9	19.7
	06	267 47.4	251 39.4	N 5 54.8	282 12.2	S 7 19.6	161 13.6	N22 55.8	263 12.0	S 0 19.6
	07	282 49.8	266 39.0	56.0	297 12.8	18.8	176 16.0	55.8	278 14.2	19.5
	08	297 52.3	281 38.7	57.3	312 13.4	18.0	191 18.3	55.8	293 16.4	19.4
	09	312 54.8	296 38.3	. . 58.5	327 14.1	. . 17.3	206 20.7	. . 55.8	308 18.6	. . 19.2
	10	327 57.2	311 37.9	5 59.8	342 14.7	16.5	221 23.1	55.8	323 20.7	19.1
	11	342 59.7	326 37.5	6 01.1	357 15.3	15.7	236 25.5	55.8	338 22.9	19.0
	12	358 02.1	341 37.2	N 6 02.3	12 16.0	S 7 15.0	251 27.9	N22 55.8	353 25.1	S 0 18.9
	13	13 04.6	356 36.8	03.6	27 16.6	14.2	266 30.3	55.8	8 27.3	18.7
	14	28 07.1	11 36.4	04.8	42 17.3	13.5	281 32.6	55.7	23 29.5	18.6
	15	43 09.5	26 36.0	. . 06.1	57 17.9	. . 12.7	296 35.0	. . 55.7	38 31.6	. . 18.5
	16	58 12.0	41 35.6	07.4	72 18.5	11.9	311 37.4	55.7	53 33.8	18.4
	17	73 14.5	56 35.2	08.6	87 19.2	11.2	326 39.8	55.7	68 36.0	18.3
	18	88 16.9	71 34.9	N 6 09.9	102 19.8	S 7 10.4	341 42.2	N22 55.7	83 38.2	S 0 18.1
	19	103 19.4	86 34.5	11.1	117 20.5	09.6	356 44.5	55.7	98 40.3	18.0
	20	118 21.9	101 34.1	12.4	132 21.1	08.9	11 46.9	55.7	113 42.5	17.9
	21	133 24.3	116 33.7	. . 13.6	147 21.7	. . 08.1	26 49.3	. . 55.7	128 44.7	. . 17.8
	22	148 26.8	131 33.3	14.9	162 22.4	07.4	41 51.7	55.7	143 46.9	17.6
	23	163 29.2	146 33.0	16.2	177 23.0	06.6	56 54.1	55.7	158 49.1	17.5
21 SATURDAY	00	178 31.7	161 32.6	N 6 17.4	192 23.7	S 7 05.8	71 56.4	N22 55.7	173 51.2	S 0 17.4
	01	193 34.2	176 32.2	18.7	207 24.3	05.1	86 58.8	55.7	188 53.4	17.3
	02	208 36.6	191 31.8	19.9	222 24.9	04.3	102 01.2	55.7	203 55.6	17.1
	03	223 39.1	206 31.4	. . 21.2	237 25.6	. . 03.5	117 03.6	. . 55.7	218 57.8	. . 17.0
	04	238 41.6	221 31.0	22.4	252 26.2	02.8	132 05.9	55.6	233 59.9	16.9
	05	253 44.0	236 30.7	23.7	267 26.9	02.0	147 08.3	55.6	249 02.1	16.8
	06	268 46.5	251 30.3	N 6 24.9	282 27.5	S 7 01.2	162 10.7	N22 55.6	264 04.3	S 0 16.7
	07	283 49.0	266 29.9	26.2	297 28.1	7 00.5	177 13.1	55.6	279 06.5	16.5
	08	298 51.4	281 29.5	27.4	312 28.8	6 59.7	192 15.4	55.6	294 08.7	16.4
	09	313 53.9	296 29.1	. . 28.7	327 29.4	. . 58.9	207 17.8	. . 55.6	309 10.8	. . 16.3
	10	328 56.4	311 28.7	30.0	342 30.1	58.2	222 20.2	55.6	324 13.0	16.2
	11	343 58.8	326 28.4	31.2	357 30.7	57.4	237 22.6	55.6	339 15.2	16.0
	12	359 01.3	341 28.0	N 6 32.5	12 31.4	S 6 56.7	252 24.9	N22 55.6	354 17.4	S 0 15.9
	13	14 03.7	356 27.6	33.7	27 32.0	55.9	267 27.3	55.6	9 19.5	15.8
	14	29 06.2	11 27.2	35.0	42 32.6	55.1	282 29.7	55.6	24 21.7	15.7
	15	44 08.7	26 26.8	. . 36.2	57 33.3	. . 54.4	297 32.1	. . 55.6	39 23.9	. . 15.5
	16	59 11.1	41 26.4	37.5	72 33.9	53.6	312 34.4	55.6	54 26.1	15.4
	17	74 13.6	56 26.1	38.7	87 34.6	52.8	327 36.8	55.5	69 28.3	15.3
	18	89 16.1	71 25.7	N 6 40.0	102 35.2	S 6 52.1	342 39.2	N22 55.5	84 30.4	S 0 15.2
	19	104 18.5	86 25.3	41.2	117 35.8	51.3	357 41.6	55.5	99 32.6	15.1
	20	119 21.0	101 24.9	42.5	132 36.5	50.5	12 43.9	55.5	114 34.8	14.9
	21	134 23.5	116 24.5	. . 43.7	147 37.1	. . 49.8	27 46.3	. . 55.5	129 37.0	. . 14.8
	22	149 25.9	131 24.1	45.0	162 37.8	49.0	42 48.7	55.5	144 39.1	14.7
	23	164 28.4	146 23.7	46.2	177 38.4	48.2	57 51.0	55.5	159 41.3	14.6
22 SUNDAY	00	179 30.9	161 23.4	N 6 47.5	192 39.1	S 6 47.5	72 53.4	N22 55.5	174 43.5	S 0 14.4
	01	194 33.3	176 23.0	48.7	207 39.7	46.7	87 55.8	55.5	189 45.7	14.3
	02	209 35.8	191 22.6	50.0	222 40.3	45.9	102 58.1	55.5	204 47.9	14.2
	03	224 38.2	206 22.2	. . 51.2	237 41.0	. . 45.2	118 00.5	. . 55.5	219 50.0	. . 14.1
	04	239 40.7	221 21.8	52.5	252 41.6	44.4	133 02.9	55.5	234 52.2	13.9
	05	254 43.2	236 21.4	53.7	267 42.3	43.6	148 05.2	55.5	249 54.4	13.8
	06	269 45.6	251 21.0	N 6 55.0	282 42.9	S 6 42.9	163 07.6	N22 55.4	264 56.6	S 0 13.7
	07	284 48.1	266 20.6	56.2	297 43.6	42.1	178 10.0	55.4	279 58.7	13.6
	08	299 50.6	281 20.3	57.5	312 44.2	41.3	193 12.3	55.4	295 00.9	13.5
	09	314 53.0	296 19.9	6 58.7	327 44.9	. . 40.6	208 14.7	. . 55.4	310 03.1	. . 13.3
	10	329 55.5	311 19.5	7 00.0	342 45.5	39.8	223 17.1	55.4	325 05.3	13.2
	11	344 58.0	326 19.1	01.2	357 46.1	39.0	238 19.4	55.4	340 07.5	13.1
	12	0 00.4	341 18.7	N 7 02.4	12 46.8	S 6 38.3	253 21.8	N22 55.4	355 09.6	S 0 13.0
	13	15 02.9	356 18.3	03.7	27 47.4	37.5	268 24.2	55.4	10 11.8	12.8
	14	30 05.3	11 17.9	04.9	42 48.1	36.7	283 26.5	55.4	25 14.0	12.7
	15	45 07.8	26 17.5	. . 06.2	57 48.7	. . 36.0	298 28.9	. . 55.4	40 16.2	. . 12.6
	16	60 10.3	41 17.1	07.4	72 49.4	35.2	313 31.3	55.4	55 18.3	12.5
	17	75 12.7	56 16.8	08.7	87 50.0	34.4	328 33.6	55.4	70 20.5	12.3
	18	90 15.2	71 16.4	N 7 09.9	102 50.7	S 6 33.7	343 36.0	N22 55.3	85 22.7	S 0 12.2
	19	105 17.7	86 16.0	11.2	117 51.3	32.9	358 38.4	55.3	100 24.9	12.1
	20	120 20.1	101 15.6	12.4	132 51.9	32.1	13 40.7	55.3	115 27.1	12.0
	21	135 22.6	116 15.2	. . 13.7	147 52.6	. . 31.4	28 43.1	. . 55.3	130 29.2	. . 11.9
	22	150 25.1	131 14.8	14.9	162 53.2	30.6	43 45.5	55.3	145 31.4	11.7
	23	165 27.5	146 14.4	16.1	177 53.9	29.8	58 47.8	55.3	160 33.6	11.6
Mer. Pass.		h m 12 03.9	*v* −0.4	*d* 1.3	*v* 0.6	*d* 0.8	*v* 2.4	*d* 0.0	*v* 2.2	*d* 0.1

STARS

Name	SHA ° ′	Dec ° ′
Acamar	315 11.3	S40 12.2
Achernar	335 19.9	S57 06.3
Acrux	172 58.3	S63 14.7
Adhara	255 05.0	S29 00.7
Aldebaran	290 38.6	N16 33.7
Alioth	166 11.5	N55 48.9
Alkaid	152 50.8	N49 10.7
Alnair	27 32.1	S46 50.0
Alnilam	275 36.8	S 1 11.2
Alphard	217 46.5	S 8 46.5
Alphecca	126 02.7	N26 37.3
Alpheratz	357 34.1	N29 14.0
Altair	61 59.1	N 8 56.1
Ankaa	353 06.6	S42 09.9
Antares	112 14.5	S26 29.4
Arcturus	145 46.7	N19 02.5
Atria	107 07.7	S69 04.2
Avior	234 14.0	S59 35.9
Bellatrix	278 21.9	N 6 22.3
Betelgeuse	270 51.0	N 7 24.6
Canopus	263 51.9	S52 42.8
Capella	280 20.5	N46 01.6
Deneb	49 25.4	N45 22.2
Denebola	182 23.6	N14 25.4
Diphda	348 46.6	S17 50.7
Dubhe	193 39.1	N61 36.5
Elnath	278 00.7	N28 37.8
Eltanin	90 41.7	N51 28.7
Enif	33 38.1	N 9 59.6
Fomalhaut	15 13.8	S29 29.0
Gacrux	171 50.0	S57 15.7
Gienah	175 42.2	S17 41.4
Hadar	148 34.1	S60 29.9
Hamal	327 50.4	N23 35.2
Kaus Aust.	83 31.2	S34 22.3
Kochab	137 18.9	N74 02.5
Markab	13 29.2	N15 20.7
Menkar	314 05.3	N 4 11.5
Menkent	147 56.1	S36 30.0
Miaplacidus	221 37.5	S69 49.7
Mirfak	308 27.2	N49 57.4
Nunki	75 46.6	S26 15.8
Peacock	53 04.5	S56 38.9
Pollux	243 15.9	N27 57.8
Procyon	244 49.7	N 5 09.4
Rasalhague	95 57.6	N12 32.2
Regulus	207 33.1	N11 50.2
Rigel	281 03.0	S 8 10.4
Rigil Kent.	139 38.4	S60 56.5
Sabik	102 01.6	S15 45.5
Schedar	349 30.5	N56 40.9
Shaula	96 09.0	S37 07.3
Sirius	258 25.3	S16 45.3
Spica	158 21.0	S11 18.0
Suhail	222 45.3	S43 32.5
Vega	80 32.6	N38 48.1
Zuben'ubi	136 54.7	S16 09.2

	SHA ° ′	Mer. Pass. h m
Venus	343 00.9	13 14
Mars	13 51.9	11 10
Jupiter	253 24.7	19 09
Saturn	355 19.5	12 23

	UT	SUN GHA	SUN Dec	MOON GHA	v	MOON Dec	d	HP
	d h	° ′	° ′	° ′	′	° ′	′	′
	20 00	178 06.3	S 0 14.6	167 52.6	11.6	N 7 15.3	16.5	59.2
	01	193 06.5	13.6	182 23.2	11.6	7 31.8	16.4	59.2
	02	208 06.7	12.6	196 53.8	11.5	7 48.2	16.3	59.3
	03	223 06.9	. . 11.6	211 24.3	11.4	8 04.5	16.4	59.3
	04	238 07.1	10.6	225 54.7	11.4	8 20.9	16.3	59.3
	05	253 07.3	09.6	240 25.1	11.3	8 37.2	16.3	59.3
	06	268 07.4	S 0 08.7	254 55.4	11.2	N 8 53.5	16.2	59.3
	07	283 07.6	07.7	269 25.6	11.2	9 09.7	16.2	59.3
	08	298 07.8	06.7	283 55.8	11.1	9 25.9	16.1	59.4
F	09	313 08.0	. . 05.7	298 25.9	11.1	9 42.0	16.1	59.4
R	10	328 08.2	04.7	312 56.0	10.9	9 58.1	16.1	59.4
I	11	343 08.4	03.7	327 25.9	10.9	10 14.2	16.0	59.4
D	12	358 08.5	S 0 02.7	341 55.8	10.9	N10 30.2	16.0	59.4
A	13	13 08.7	01.7	356 25.7	10.7	10 46.2	15.9	59.4
Y	14	28 08.9	S 00.8	10 55.4	10.7	11 02.1	15.9	59.5
	15	43 09.1	N 00.2	25 25.1	10.6	11 18.0	15.8	59.5
	16	58 09.3	01.2	39 54.7	10.5	11 33.8	15.8	59.5
	17	73 09.5	02.2	54 24.2	10.5	11 49.6	15.7	59.5
	18	88 09.7	N 0 03.2	68 53.7	10.4	N12 05.3	15.6	59.5
	19	103 09.8	04.2	83 23.1	10.3	12 20.9	15.6	59.5
	20	118 10.0	05.2	97 52.4	10.2	12 36.5	15.5	59.5
	21	133 10.2	. . 06.2	112 21.6	10.2	12 52.0	15.5	59.5
	22	148 10.4	07.2	126 50.8	10.0	13 07.5	15.4	59.6
	23	163 10.6	08.1	141 19.8	10.0	13 22.9	15.3	59.6
	21 00	178 10.8	N 0 09.1	155 48.8	9.9	N13 38.2	15.2	59.6
	01	193 10.9	10.1	170 17.7	9.8	13 53.4	15.2	59.6
	02	208 11.1	11.1	184 46.5	9.7	14 08.6	15.1	59.6
	03	223 11.3	. . 12.1	199 15.2	9.7	14 23.7	15.0	59.6
	04	238 11.5	13.1	213 43.9	9.6	14 38.7	15.0	59.6
	05	253 11.7	14.1	228 12.5	9.4	14 53.7	14.9	59.6
	06	268 11.9	N 0 15.1	242 40.9	9.4	N15 08.6	14.7	59.6
	07	283 12.1	16.0	257 09.3	9.3	15 23.3	14.7	59.6
S	08	298 12.2	17.0	271 37.6	9.2	15 38.0	14.7	59.7
A	09	313 12.4	. . 18.0	286 05.8	9.1	15 52.7	14.5	59.7
T	10	328 12.6	19.0	300 33.9	9.1	16 07.2	14.4	59.7
U	11	343 12.8	20.0	315 02.0	8.9	16 21.6	14.4	59.7
R	12	358 13.0	N 0 21.0	329 29.9	8.8	N16 36.0	14.3	59.7
D	13	13 13.2	22.0	343 57.7	8.8	16 50.3	14.1	59.7
A	14	28 13.3	23.0	358 25.5	8.6	17 04.4	14.1	59.7
Y	15	43 13.5	. . 24.0	12 53.1	8.6	17 18.5	14.0	59.7
	16	58 13.7	24.9	27 20.7	8.5	17 32.5	13.8	59.7
	17	73 13.9	25.9	41 48.2	8.4	17 46.3	13.8	59.7
	18	88 14.1	N 0 26.9	56 15.6	8.2	N18 00.1	13.7	59.7
	19	103 14.3	27.9	70 42.8	8.2	18 13.8	13.5	59.7
	20	118 14.5	28.9	85 10.0	8.1	18 27.3	13.5	59.7
	21	133 14.6	. . 29.9	99 37.1	8.0	18 40.8	13.3	59.7
	22	148 14.8	30.9	114 04.1	7.9	18 54.1	13.2	59.7
	23	163 15.0	31.9	128 31.0	7.8	19 07.3	13.1	59.7
	22 00	178 15.2	N 0 32.8	142 57.8	7.7	N19 20.4	13.0	59.8
	01	193 15.4	33.8	157 24.5	7.6	19 33.4	12.9	59.8
	02	208 15.6	34.8	171 51.1	7.5	19 46.3	12.8	59.8
	03	223 15.8	. . 35.8	186 17.6	7.4	19 59.1	12.6	59.8
	04	238 15.9	36.8	200 44.0	7.4	20 11.7	12.5	59.8
	05	253 16.1	37.8	215 10.4	7.2	20 24.2	12.4	59.8
	06	268 16.3	N 0 38.8	229 36.6	7.1	N20 36.6	12.3	59.8
	07	283 16.5	39.8	244 02.7	7.0	20 48.9	12.1	59.8
	08	298 16.7	40.7	258 28.7	6.9	21 01.0	12.0	59.8
S	09	313 16.9	. . 41.7	272 54.6	6.9	21 13.0	11.9	59.8
U	10	328 17.1	42.7	287 20.5	6.7	21 24.9	11.7	59.8
N	11	343 17.3	43.7	301 46.2	6.6	21 36.6	11.7	59.8
D	12	358 17.4	N 0 44.7	316 11.8	6.6	N21 48.3	11.4	59.8
A	13	13 17.6	45.7	330 37.4	6.4	21 59.7	11.3	59.8
Y	14	28 17.8	46.7	345 02.8	6.4	22 11.0	11.2	59.8
	15	43 18.0	. . 47.6	359 28.2	6.2	22 22.2	11.1	59.8
	16	58 18.2	48.6	13 53.4	6.2	22 33.3	10.9	59.8
	17	73 18.4	49.6	28 18.6	6.1	22 44.2	10.7	59.8
	18	88 18.6	N 0 50.6	42 43.7	5.9	N22 54.9	10.6	59.8
	19	103 18.7	51.6	57 08.6	5.9	23 05.5	10.5	59.8
	20	118 18.9	52.6	71 33.5	5.8	23 16.0	10.3	59.8
	21	133 19.1	. . 53.6	85 58.3	5.7	23 26.3	10.2	59.8
	22	148 19.3	54.6	100 23.0	5.6	23 36.5	10.0	59.8
	23	163 19.5	55.5	114 47.6	5.5	N23 46.5	9.8	59.8
		SD 16.1	*d* 1.0	SD		16.2	16.3	16.3

Lat.	Twilight Naut.	Twilight Civil	Sunrise	Moonrise 20	Moonrise 21	Moonrise 22	Moonrise 23
°	h m	h m	h m	h m	h m	h m	h m
N 72	03 15	04 45	05 53	05 09	04 14	▭	▭
N 70	03 35	04 53	05 55	05 21	04 43	03 05	▭
68	03 50	05 00	05 56	05 31	05 05	04 18	▭
66	04 02	05 05	05 57	05 40	05 22	04 56	▭
64	04 12	05 10	05 58	05 47	05 36	05 23	04 57
62	04 20	05 14	05 58	05 53	05 48	05 44	05 38
60	04 27	05 17	05 59	05 59	05 59	06 01	06 06
N 58	04 33	05 20	05 59	06 03	06 08	06 15	06 28
56	04 38	05 23	06 00	06 08	06 16	06 28	06 46
54	04 43	05 25	06 00	06 12	06 23	06 39	07 02
52	04 47	05 27	06 01	06 15	06 30	06 48	07 15
50	04 51	05 29	06 01	06 18	06 36	06 57	07 27
45	04 58	05 32	06 01	06 26	06 48	07 16	07 51
N 40	05 03	05 35	06 02	06 31	06 59	07 31	08 11
35	05 08	05 37	06 02	06 37	07 08	07 44	08 27
30	05 11	05 39	06 03	06 41	07 16	07 55	08 42
20	05 16	05 41	06 03	06 49	07 30	08 15	09 06
N 10	05 18	05 43	06 04	06 56	07 42	08 32	09 27
0	05 19	05 43	06 04	07 03	07 54	08 49	09 47
S 10	05 19	05 43	06 04	07 10	08 06	09 05	10 07
20	05 16	05 42	06 04	07 17	08 18	09 23	10 29
30	05 12	05 40	06 04	07 25	08 33	09 43	10 54
35	05 09	05 39	06 04	07 30	08 41	09 55	11 09
40	05 05	05 37	06 04	07 36	08 51	10 09	11 27
45	05 00	05 34	06 04	07 43	09 03	10 25	11 48
S 50	04 53	05 31	06 03	07 50	09 17	10 46	12 14
52	04 50	05 29	06 03	07 54	09 24	10 56	12 27
54	04 46	05 28	06 03	07 58	09 31	11 07	12 42
56	04 41	05 26	06 03	08 03	09 39	11 20	13 00
58	04 36	05 23	06 03	08 08	09 49	11 34	13 21
S 60	04 31	05 21	06 02	08 13	09 59	11 52	13 48

Lat.	Sunset	Twilight Civil	Twilight Naut.	Moonset 20	Moonset 21	Moonset 22	Moonset 23
°	h m	h m	h m	h m	h m	h m	h m
N 72	18 23	19 32	21 05	22 37	▭	▭	▭
N 70	18 22	19 24	20 44	22 11	25 41	01 41	▭
68	18 20	19 17	20 28	21 51	24 29	00 29	▭
66	18 19	19 11	20 15	21 35	23 53	▭	▭
64	18 18	19 06	20 05	21 22	23 27	25 53	01 53
62	18 18	19 02	19 56	21 12	23 07	25 13	01 13
60	18 17	18 59	19 49	21 03	22 51	24 45	00 45
N 58	18 16	18 56	19 43	20 55	22 38	24 24	00 24
56	18 16	18 53	19 37	20 48	22 26	24 07	00 07
54	18 15	18 51	19 33	20 42	22 16	23 52	25 23
52	18 15	18 49	19 29	20 36	22 07	23 39	25 07
50	18 14	18 47	19 25	20 31	21 59	23 28	24 53
45	18 14	18 43	19 17	20 20	21 42	23 05	24 24
N 40	18 13	18 40	19 12	20 12	21 28	22 46	24 02
35	18 12	18 38	19 07	20 04	21 16	22 30	23 44
30	18 12	18 36	19 04	19 57	21 06	22 17	23 28
20	18 11	18 33	18 59	19 46	20 49	21 54	23 01
N 10	18 11	18 32	18 56	19 36	20 33	21 34	22 38
0	18 10	18 31	18 55	19 27	20 19	21 16	22 17
S 10	18 10	18 31	18 55	19 18	20 05	20 58	21 55
20	18 10	18 32	18 57	19 08	19 50	20 38	21 32
30	18 10	18 34	19 02	18 57	19 33	20 16	21 06
35	18 10	18 35	19 05	18 50	19 24	20 03	20 50
40	18 10	18 37	19 08	18 43	19 12	19 48	20 32
45	18 10	18 39	19 13	18 35	18 59	19 30	20 10
S 50	18 10	18 42	19 20	18 25	18 43	19 08	19 43
52	18 10	18 44	19 23	18 20	18 36	18 58	19 30
54	18 10	18 45	19 27	18 15	18 28	18 46	19 14
56	18 10	18 47	19 31	18 09	18 19	18 33	18 56
58	18 10	18 50	19 36	18 03	18 08	18 17	18 34
S 60	18 11	18 52	19 42	17 56	17 56	17 59	18 07

Day	SUN Eqn. of Time 00^h	SUN Eqn. of Time 12^h	SUN Mer. Pass.	MOON Mer. Pass. Upper	MOON Mer. Pass. Lower	Age	Phase
d	m s	m s	h m	h m	h m	d %	
20	07 35	07 26	12 07	13 15	00 50	01 3	
21	07 17	07 08	12 07	14 07	01 40	02 8	
22	07 00	06 51	12 07	15 02	02 34	03 15	

UT	ARIES	VENUS −3·9		MARS +1·2		JUPITER −2·3		SATURN +0·9	
	GHA	GHA	Dec	GHA	Dec	GHA	Dec	GHA	Dec
d h	° ′	° ′	° ′	° ′	° ′	° ′	° ′	° ′	° ′
23 00 (MONDAY)	180 30.0	161 14.0	N 7 17.4	192 54.5	S 6 29.0	73 50.2	N22 55.3	175 35.8	S 0 11.5
01	195 32.5	176 13.6	18.6	207 55.2	28.3	88 52.5	55.3	190 37.9	11.4
02	210 34.9	191 13.2	19.9	222 55.8	27.5	103 54.9	55.3	205 40.1	11.2
03	225 37.4	206 12.9	. . 21.1	237 56.5	. . 26.7	118 57.3	. . 55.3	220 42.3	. . 11.1
04	240 39.8	221 12.5	22.4	252 57.1	26.0	133 59.6	55.3	235 44.5	11.0
05	255 42.3	236 12.1	23.6	267 57.8	25.2	149 02.0	55.2	250 46.7	10.9
06	270 44.8	251 11.7	N 7 24.8	282 58.4	S 6 24.4	164 04.3	N22 55.2	265 48.8	S 0 10.7
07	285 47.2	266 11.3	26.1	297 59.1	23.7	179 06.7	55.2	280 51.0	10.6
08	300 49.7	281 10.9	27.3	312 59.7	22.9	194 09.1	55.2	295 53.2	10.5
09	315 52.2	296 10.5	. . 28.6	328 00.3	. . 22.1	209 11.4	. . 55.2	310 55.4	. . 10.4
10	330 54.6	311 10.1	29.8	343 01.0	21.4	224 13.8	55.2	325 57.5	10.3
11	345 57.1	326 09.7	31.0	358 01.6	20.6	239 16.1	55.2	340 59.7	10.1
12	0 59.6	341 09.3	N 7 32.3	13 02.3	S 6 19.8	254 18.5	N22 55.2	356 01.9	S 0 10.0
13	16 02.0	356 08.9	33.5	28 02.9	19.1	269 20.8	55.2	11 04.1	09.9
14	31 04.5	11 08.5	34.8	43 03.6	18.3	284 23.2	55.2	26 06.3	09.8
15	46 07.0	26 08.1	. . 36.0	58 04.2	. . 17.5	299 25.6	. . 55.2	41 08.4	. . 09.6
16	61 09.4	41 07.7	37.2	73 04.9	16.7	314 27.9	55.1	56 10.6	09.5
17	76 11.9	56 07.4	38.5	88 05.5	16.0	329 30.3	55.1	71 12.8	09.4
18	91 14.3	71 07.0	N 7 39.7	103 06.2	S 6 15.2	344 32.6	N22 55.1	86 15.0	S 0 09.3
19	106 16.8	86 06.6	40.9	118 06.8	14.4	359 35.0	55.1	101 17.1	09.1
20	121 19.3	101 06.2	42.2	133 07.5	13.7	14 37.3	55.1	116 19.3	09.0
21	136 21.7	116 05.8	. . 43.4	148 08.1	. . 12.9	29 39.7	. . 55.1	131 21.5	. . 08.9
22	151 24.2	131 05.4	44.7	163 08.8	12.1	44 42.0	55.1	146 23.7	08.8
23	166 26.7	146 05.0	45.9	178 09.4	11.4	59 44.4	55.1	161 25.8	08.7
24 00 (TUESDAY)	181 29.1	161 04.6	N 7 47.1	193 10.1	S 6 10.6	74 46.7	N22 55.1	176 28.0	S 0 08.5
01	196 31.6	176 04.2	48.4	208 10.7	09.8	89 49.1	55.1	191 30.2	08.4
02	211 34.1	191 03.8	49.6	223 11.4	09.0	104 51.4	55.0	206 32.4	08.3
03	226 36.5	206 03.4	. . 50.8	238 12.0	. . 08.3	119 53.8	. . 55.0	221 34.6	. . 08.2
04	241 39.0	221 03.0	52.1	253 12.7	07.5	134 56.1	55.0	236 36.7	08.0
05	256 41.5	236 02.6	53.3	268 13.3	06.7	149 58.5	55.0	251 38.9	07.9
06	271 43.9	251 02.2	N 7 54.5	283 14.0	S 6 06.0	165 00.9	N22 55.0	266 41.1	S 0 07.8
07	286 46.4	266 01.8	55.8	298 14.6	05.2	180 03.2	55.0	281 43.3	07.7
08	301 48.8	281 01.4	57.0	313 15.3	04.4	195 05.6	55.0	296 45.4	07.5
09	316 51.3	296 01.0	. . 58.2	328 15.9	. . 03.6	210 07.9	. . 55.0	311 47.6	. . 07.4
10	331 53.8	311 00.6	7 59.5	343 16.6	02.9	225 10.3	55.0	326 49.8	07.3
11	346 56.2	326 00.2	8 00.7	358 17.2	02.1	240 12.6	55.0	341 52.0	07.2
12	1 58.7	340 59.8	N 8 01.9	13 17.9	S 6 01.3	255 14.9	N22 54.9	356 54.2	S 0 07.1
13	17 01.2	355 59.4	03.2	28 18.5	6 00.6	270 17.3	54.9	11 56.3	06.9
14	32 03.6	10 59.0	04.4	43 19.2	5 59.8	285 19.6	54.9	26 58.5	06.8
15	47 06.1	25 58.6	. . 05.6	58 19.8	. . 59.0	300 22.0	. . 54.9	42 00.7	. . 06.7
16	62 08.6	40 58.2	06.9	73 20.5	58.2	315 24.3	54.9	57 02.9	06.6
17	77 11.0	55 57.8	08.1	88 21.1	57.5	330 26.7	54.9	72 05.0	06.4
18	92 13.5	70 57.4	N 8 09.3	103 21.8	S 5 56.7	345 29.0	N22 54.9	87 07.2	S 0 06.3
19	107 15.9	85 57.0	10.6	118 22.4	55.9	0 31.4	54.9	102 09.4	06.2
20	122 18.4	100 56.6	11.8	133 23.1	55.2	15 33.7	54.9	117 11.6	06.1
21	137 20.9	115 56.2	. . 13.0	148 23.7	. . 54.4	30 36.1	. . 54.8	132 13.8	. . 05.9
22	152 23.3	130 55.8	14.2	163 24.4	53.6	45 38.4	54.8	147 15.9	05.8
23	167 25.8	145 55.4	15.5	178 25.0	52.8	60 40.8	54.8	162 18.1	05.7
25 00 (WEDNESDAY)	182 28.3	160 55.0	N 8 16.7	193 25.7	S 5 52.1	75 43.1	N22 54.8	177 20.3	S 0 05.6
01	197 30.7	175 54.6	17.9	208 26.3	51.3	90 45.5	54.8	192 22.5	05.5
02	212 33.2	190 54.2	19.2	223 27.0	50.5	105 47.8	54.8	207 24.6	05.3
03	227 35.7	205 53.8	. . 20.4	238 27.6	. . 49.8	120 50.1	. . 54.8	222 26.8	. . 05.2
04	242 38.1	220 53.4	21.6	253 28.3	49.0	135 52.5	54.8	237 29.0	05.1
05	257 40.6	235 53.0	22.8	268 28.9	48.2	150 54.8	54.8	252 31.2	05.0
06	272 43.1	250 52.6	N 8 24.1	283 29.6	S 5 47.4	165 57.2	N22 54.7	267 33.3	S 0 04.8
07	287 45.5	265 52.2	25.3	298 30.2	46.7	180 59.5	54.7	282 35.5	04.7
08	302 48.0	280 51.8	26.5	313 30.9	45.9	196 01.9	54.7	297 37.7	04.6
09	317 50.4	295 51.4	. . 27.7	328 31.5	. . 45.1	211 04.2	. . 54.7	312 39.9	. . 04.5
10	332 52.9	310 51.0	29.0	343 32.2	44.3	226 06.5	54.7	327 42.1	04.3
11	347 55.4	325 50.6	30.2	358 32.8	43.6	241 08.9	54.7	342 44.2	04.2
12	2 57.8	340 50.2	N 8 31.4	13 33.5	S 5 42.8	256 11.2	N22 54.7	357 46.4	S 0 04.1
13	18 00.3	355 49.8	32.6	28 34.1	42.0	271 13.6	54.7	12 48.6	04.0
14	33 02.8	10 49.4	33.9	43 34.8	41.3	286 15.9	54.7	27 50.8	03.9
15	48 05.2	25 49.0	. . 35.1	58 35.5	. . 40.5	301 18.2	. . 54.6	42 52.9	. . 03.7
16	63 07.7	40 48.6	36.3	73 36.1	39.7	316 20.6	54.6	57 55.1	03.6
17	78 10.2	55 48.2	37.5	88 36.8	38.9	331 22.9	54.6	72 57.3	03.5
18	93 12.6	70 47.8	N 8 38.8	103 37.4	S 5 38.2	346 25.3	N22 54.6	87 59.5	S 0 03.4
19	108 15.1	85 47.4	40.0	118 38.1	37.4	1 27.6	54.6	103 01.7	03.2
20	123 17.6	100 47.0	41.2	133 38.7	36.6	16 29.9	54.6	118 03.8	03.1
21	138 20.0	115 46.6	. . 42.4	148 39.4	. . 35.8	31 32.3	. . 54.6	133 06.0	. . 03.0
22	153 22.5	130 46.1	43.6	163 40.0	35.1	46 34.6	54.6	148 08.2	02.9
23	168 24.9	145 45.7	44.9	178 40.7	34.3	61 36.9	54.6	163 10.4	02.8
Mer. Pass. (h m)	11 52.1	*v* −0.4	*d* 1.2	*v* 0.7	*d* 0.8	*v* 2.3	*d* 0.0	*v* 2.2	*d* 0.1

STARS

Name	SHA	Dec
	° ′	° ′
Acamar	315 11.3	S40 12.1
Achernar	335 20.0	S57 06.3
Acrux	172 58.3	S63 14.8
Adhara	255 05.0	S29 00.7
Aldebaran	290 38.6	N16 33.7
Alioth	166 11.5	N55 48.9
Alkaid	152 50.8	N49 10.7
Alnair	27 32.0	S46 50.0
Alnilam	275 36.8	S 1 11.2
Alphard	217 46.5	S 8 46.5
Alphecca	126 02.7	N26 37.3
Alpheratz	357 34.1	N29 14.0
Altair	61 59.1	N 8 56.1
Ankaa	353 06.6	S42 09.9
Antares	112 14.5	S26 29.4
Arcturus	145 46.7	N19 02.5
Atria	107 07.6	S69 04.2
Avior	234 14.0	S59 35.9
Bellatrix	278 21.9	N 6 22.3
Betelgeuse	270 51.0	N 7 24.6
Canopus	263 51.9	S52 42.8
Capella	280 20.5	N46 01.6
Deneb	49 25.4	N45 22.1
Denebola	182 23.6	N14 25.4
Diphda	348 46.6	S17 50.7
Dubhe	193 39.1	N61 36.6
Elnath	278 00.7	N28 37.8
Eltanin	90 41.7	N51 28.7
Enif	33 38.1	N 9 59.6
Fomalhaut	15 13.8	S29 29.0
Gacrux	171 50.0	S57 15.7
Gienah	175 42.2	S17 41.4
Hadar	148 34.0	S60 29.9
Hamal	327 50.4	N23 35.2
Kaus Aust.	83 31.2	S34 22.3
Kochab	137 18.9	N74 02.5
Markab	13 29.2	N15 20.7
Menkar	314 05.3	N 4 11.5
Menkent	147 56.1	S36 30.0
Miaplacidus	221 37.5	S69 49.7
Mirfak	308 27.2	N49 57.4
Nunki	75 46.6	S26 15.8
Peacock	53 04.5	S56 38.9
Pollux	243 16.0	N27 57.8
Procyon	244 49.7	N 5 09.4
Rasalhague	95 57.6	N12 32.2
Regulus	207 33.1	N11 50.2
Rigel	281 03.0	S 8 10.4
Rigil Kent.	139 38.4	S60 56.5
Sabik	102 01.6	S15 45.5
Schedar	349 30.5	N56 40.9
Shaula	96 08.9	S37 07.3
Sirius	258 25.3	S16 45.3
Spica	158 21.0	S11 18.1
Suhail	222 45.3	S43 32.6
Vega	80 32.6	N38 48.1
Zuben'ubi	136 54.7	S16 09.2

	SHA	Mer. Pass.
	° ′	h m
Venus	339 35.5	13 16
Mars	11 40.9	11 07
Jupiter	253 17.6	18 58
Saturn	354 58.9	12 12

UT (d h)	SUN GHA	SUN Dec	MOON GHA	v	MOON Dec	d	HP
	° ′	° ′	° ′	′	° ′	′	′
23 MONDAY 00	178 19.7	N 0 56.5	129 12.1	5.4	N23 56.3	9.7	59.8
01	193 19.9	57.5	143 36.5	5.4	24 06.0	9.5	59.7
02	208 20.1	58.5	158 00.9	5.2	24 15.5	9.4	59.7
03	223 20.2	0 59.5	172 25.1	5.2	24 24.9	9.2	59.7
04	238 20.4	1 00.5	186 49.3	5.1	24 34.1	9.0	59.7
05	253 20.6	01.5	201 13.4	5.0	24 43.1	8.9	59.7
06	268 20.8	N 1 02.4	215 37.4	4.9	N24 52.0	8.7	59.7
07	283 21.0	03.4	230 01.3	4.8	25 00.7	8.5	59.7
08	298 21.2	04.4	244 25.1	4.8	25 09.2	8.4	59.7
09	313 21.4	. . 05.4	258 48.9	4.7	25 17.6	8.2	59.7
10	328 21.5	06.4	273 12.6	4.6	25 25.8	8.0	59.7
11	343 21.7	07.4	287 36.2	4.5	25 33.8	7.9	59.7
12	358 21.9	N 1 08.4	301 59.7	4.4	N25 41.7	7.7	59.7
13	13 22.1	09.3	316 23.1	4.4	25 49.4	7.5	59.7
14	28 22.3	10.3	330 46.5	4.3	25 56.9	7.3	59.7
15	43 22.5	. . 11.3	345 09.8	4.3	26 04.2	7.1	59.7
16	58 22.7	12.3	359 33.1	4.1	26 11.3	7.0	59.7
17	73 22.9	13.3	13 56.2	4.1	26 18.3	6.8	59.7
18	88 23.0	N 1 14.3	28 19.3	4.1	N26 25.1	6.6	59.7
19	103 23.2	15.3	42 42.4	3.9	26 31.7	6.4	59.6
20	118 23.4	16.2	57 05.3	4.0	26 38.1	6.2	59.6
21	133 23.6	. . 17.2	71 28.3	3.8	26 44.3	6.1	59.6
22	148 23.8	18.2	85 51.1	3.8	26 50.4	5.9	59.6
23	163 24.0	19.2	100 13.9	3.8	26 56.3	5.6	59.6
24 TUESDAY 00	178 24.2	N 1 20.2	114 36.7	3.7	N27 01.9	5.5	59.6
01	193 24.4	21.2	128 59.4	3.6	27 07.4	5.3	59.6
02	208 24.5	22.2	143 22.0	3.6	27 12.7	5.1	59.6
03	223 24.7	. . 23.1	157 44.6	3.6	27 17.8	4.9	59.6
04	238 24.9	24.1	172 07.2	3.5	27 22.7	4.8	59.6
05	253 25.1	25.1	186 29.7	3.5	27 27.5	4.5	59.6
06	268 25.3	N 1 26.1	200 52.2	3.4	N27 32.0	4.4	59.5
07	283 25.5	27.1	215 14.6	3.4	27 36.4	4.1	59.5
08	298 25.7	28.1	229 37.0	3.4	27 40.5	4.0	59.5
09	313 25.9	. . 29.0	243 59.4	3.3	27 44.5	3.7	59.5
10	328 26.0	30.0	258 21.7	3.3	27 48.2	3.6	59.5
11	343 26.2	31.0	272 44.0	3.3	27 51.8	3.4	59.5
12	358 26.4	N 1 32.0	287 06.3	3.2	N27 55.2	3.1	59.5
13	13 26.6	33.0	301 28.5	3.3	27 58.3	3.0	59.5
14	28 26.8	34.0	315 50.8	3.2	28 01.3	2.8	59.5
15	43 27.0	. . 34.9	330 13.0	3.2	28 04.1	2.6	59.4
16	58 27.2	35.9	344 35.2	3.2	28 06.7	2.4	59.4
17	73 27.4	36.9	358 57.4	3.1	28 09.1	2.2	59.4
18	88 27.6	N 1 37.9	13 19.5	3.2	N28 11.3	2.0	59.4
19	103 27.7	38.9	27 41.7	3.2	28 13.3	1.8	59.4
20	118 27.9	39.9	42 03.9	3.1	28 15.1	1.6	59.4
21	133 28.1	. . 40.9	56 26.0	3.2	28 16.7	1.4	59.4
22	148 28.3	41.8	70 48.2	3.1	28 18.1	1.2	59.4
23	163 28.5	42.8	85 10.3	3.2	28 19.3	1.0	59.3
25 WEDNESDAY 00	178 28.7	N 1 43.8	99 32.5	3.2	N28 20.3	0.8	59.3
01	193 28.9	44.8	113 54.7	3.1	28 21.1	0.6	59.3
02	208 29.1	45.8	128 16.8	3.2	28 21.7	0.4	59.3
03	223 29.2	. . 46.8	142 39.0	3.2	28 22.1	0.2	59.3
04	238 29.4	47.7	157 01.2	3.2	28 22.3	0.0	59.3
05	253 29.6	48.7	171 23.4	3.3	28 22.3	0.2	59.3
06	268 29.8	N 1 49.7	185 45.7	3.3	N28 22.1	0.3	59.3
07	283 30.0	50.7	200 08.0	3.3	28 21.8	0.6	59.2
08	298 30.2	51.7	214 30.3	3.3	28 21.2	0.8	59.2
09	313 30.4	. . 52.7	228 52.6	3.3	28 20.4	0.9	59.2
10	328 30.6	53.6	243 14.9	3.4	28 19.5	1.2	59.2
11	343 30.8	54.6	257 37.3	3.4	28 18.3	1.4	59.2
12	358 30.9	N 1 55.6	271 59.7	3.5	N28 16.9	1.5	59.2
13	13 31.1	56.6	286 22.2	3.5	28 15.4	1.7	59.2
14	28 31.3	57.6	300 44.7	3.5	28 13.7	2.0	59.1
15	43 31.5	. . 58.5	315 07.2	3.6	28 11.7	2.1	59.1
16	58 31.7	1 59.5	329 29.8	3.6	28 09.6	2.3	59.1
17	73 31.9	2 00.5	343 52.4	3.7	28 07.3	2.5	59.1
18	88 32.1	N 2 01.5	358 15.1	3.8	N28 04.8	2.7	59.1
19	103 32.3	02.5	12 37.9	3.7	28 02.1	2.9	59.1
20	118 32.5	03.5	27 00.6	3.9	27 59.2	3.1	59.1
21	133 32.6	. . 04.4	41 23.5	3.9	27 56.1	3.2	59.0
22	148 32.8	05.4	55 46.4	4.0	27 52.9	3.5	59.0
23	163 33.0	06.4	70 09.4	4.0	N27 49.4	3.6	59.0
	SD 16.1	*d* 1.0	SD 16.3		16.2		16.1

Lat.	Twilight Naut.	Twilight Civil	Sunrise	Moonrise 23	Moonrise 24	Moonrise 25	Moonrise 26
°	h m	h m	h m	h m	h m	h m	h m
N 72	02 53	04 28	05 38	▭	▭	▭	▭
N 70	03 17	04 39	05 41	▭	▭	▭	▭
68	03 34	04 47	05 43	▭	▭	▭	▭
66	03 48	04 53	05 45	▭	▭	▭	▭
64	04 00	04 59	05 47	04 57	▭	▭	▭
62	04 09	05 04	05 48	05 38	05 29	▭	07 46
60	04 17	05 08	05 50	06 06	06 22	07 07	08 36
N 58	04 24	05 11	05 51	06 28	06 54	07 45	09 07
56	04 30	05 15	05 52	06 46	07 18	08 12	09 30
54	04 35	05 17	05 53	07 02	07 38	08 33	09 49
52	04 40	05 20	05 54	07 15	07 54	08 51	10 05
50	04 44	05 22	05 54	07 27	08 08	09 06	10 19
45	04 52	05 27	05 56	07 51	08 37	09 37	10 47
N 40	04 58	05 30	05 57	08 11	09 00	10 00	11 09
35	05 03	05 33	05 58	08 27	09 19	10 20	11 28
30	05 07	05 35	05 59	08 42	09 36	10 37	11 43
20	05 13	05 39	06 01	09 06	10 03	11 05	12 10
N 10	05 17	05 41	06 02	09 27	10 27	11 30	12 33
0	05 18	05 42	06 03	09 47	10 49	11 52	12 54
S 10	05 19	05 43	06 04	10 07	11 12	12 15	13 15
20	05 17	05 43	06 05	10 29	11 36	12 40	13 38
30	05 14	05 42	06 06	10 54	12 04	13 08	14 04
35	05 12	05 41	06 06	11 09	12 21	13 25	14 19
40	05 08	05 40	06 07	11 27	12 40	13 44	14 37
45	05 04	05 38	06 07	11 48	13 04	14 08	14 59
S 50	04 58	05 36	06 08	12 14	13 34	14 39	15 26
52	04 55	05 35	06 08	12 27	13 49	14 54	15 39
54	04 52	05 33	06 09	12 42	14 07	15 12	15 54
56	04 48	05 32	06 09	13 00	14 29	15 33	16 12
58	04 44	05 30	06 09	13 21	14 56	16 00	16 33
S 60	04 39	05 28	06 10	13 48	15 35	16 39	17 01

Lat.	Sunset	Twilight Civil	Twilight Naut.	Moonset 23	Moonset 24	Moonset 25	Moonset 26
°	h m	h m	h m	h m	h m	h m	h m
N 72	18 37	19 47	21 25	▭	▭	▭	▭
N 70	18 34	19 37	21 00	▭	▭	▭	▭
68	18 31	19 28	20 42	▭	▭	▭	▭
66	18 29	19 21	20 27	▭	▭	▭	▭
64	18 27	19 15	20 15	01 53	▭	▭	▭
62	18 26	19 10	20 06	01 13	03 30	▭	05 37
60	18 24	19 06	19 57	00 45	02 38	04 05	04 47
N 58	18 23	19 03	19 50	00 24	02 06	03 27	04 15
56	18 22	18 59	19 44	00 07	01 42	03 00	03 51
54	18 21	18 56	19 39	25 23	01 23	02 39	03 32
52	18 20	18 54	19 34	25 07	01 07	02 21	03 16
50	18 19	18 52	19 30	24 53	00 53	02 06	03 02
45	18 17	18 47	19 22	24 24	00 24	01 35	02 33
N 40	18 16	18 43	19 15	24 02	00 02	01 12	02 10
35	18 15	18 40	19 10	23 44	24 52	00 52	01 52
30	18 14	18 38	19 06	23 28	24 35	00 35	01 35
20	18 12	18 34	19 00	23 01	24 07	00 07	01 08
N 10	18 11	18 32	18 56	22 38	23 42	24 44	00 44
0	18 10	18 30	18 54	22 17	23 19	24 22	00 22
S 10	18 08	18 29	18 54	21 55	22 57	24 00	00 00
20	18 07	18 29	18 55	21 32	22 32	23 36	24 41
30	18 06	18 30	18 58	21 06	22 04	23 08	24 16
35	18 06	18 31	19 00	20 50	21 47	22 51	24 01
40	18 05	18 32	19 03	20 32	21 27	22 32	23 44
45	18 04	18 34	19 08	20 10	21 03	22 08	23 23
S 50	18 04	18 36	19 13	19 43	20 32	21 38	22 57
52	18 03	18 37	19 16	19 30	20 17	21 23	22 44
54	18 03	18 38	19 19	19 14	19 59	21 06	22 29
56	18 02	18 39	19 23	18 56	19 38	20 44	22 12
58	18 02	18 41	19 27	18 34	19 10	20 17	21 51
S 60	18 02	18 43	19 32	18 07	18 31	19 39	21 24

Day	SUN Eqn. of Time 00^h	SUN Eqn. of Time 12^h	SUN Mer. Pass.	MOON Mer. Pass. Upper	MOON Mer. Pass. Lower	MOON Age	MOON Phase
d	m s	m s	h m	h m	h m	d %	
23	06 42	06 33	12 07	16 02	03 32	04 25	
24	06 24	06 15	12 06	17 04	04 33	05 35	
25	06 06	05 57	12 06	18 07	05 36	06 47	

2026 MARCH 26, 27, 28 (THURS., FRI., SAT.)

UT		ARIES	VENUS −3·9		MARS +1·2		JUPITER −2·2		SATURN +0·9	
		GHA	GHA	Dec	GHA	Dec	GHA	Dec	GHA	Dec
d h		° ′	° ′	° ′	° ′	° ′	° ′	° ′	° ′	° ′
26 00		183 27.4	160 45.3	N 8 46.1	193 41.3	S 5 33.5	76 39.3	N22 54.5	178 12.5	S 0 02.6
01		198 29.9	175 44.9	47.3	208 42.0	32.7	91 41.6	54.5	193 14.7	02.5
02		213 32.3	190 44.5	48.5	223 42.6	32.0	106 43.9	54.5	208 16.9	02.4
03		228 34.8	205 44.1	. . 49.7	238 43.3	. . 31.2	121 46.3	. . 54.5	223 19.1	. . 02.3
04		243 37.3	220 43.7	51.0	253 44.0	30.4	136 48.6	54.5	238 21.3	02.1
05		258 39.7	235 43.3	52.2	268 44.6	29.6	151 51.0	54.5	253 23.4	02.0
06		273 42.2	250 42.9	N 8 53.4	283 45.3	S 5 28.9	166 53.3	N22 54.5	268 25.6	S 0 01.9
07		288 44.7	265 42.5	54.6	298 45.9	28.1	181 55.6	54.5	283 27.8	01.8
08	T	303 47.1	280 42.1	55.8	313 46.6	27.3	196 58.0	54.4	298 30.0	01.6
09	H	318 49.6	295 41.7	. . 57.0	328 47.2	. . 26.5	212 00.3	. . 54.4	313 32.1	. . 01.5
10	U	333 52.1	310 41.3	58.3	343 47.9	25.8	227 02.6	54.4	328 34.3	01.4
11	R	348 54.5	325 40.8	8 59.5	358 48.5	25.0	242 05.0	54.4	343 36.5	01.3
12	S	3 57.0	340 40.4	N 9 00.7	13 49.2	S 5 24.2	257 07.3	N22 54.4	358 38.7	S 0 01.2
13	D	18 59.4	355 40.0	01.9	28 49.8	23.4	272 09.6	54.4	13 40.8	01.0
14	A	34 01.9	10 39.6	03.1	43 50.5	22.7	287 11.9	54.4	28 43.0	00.9
15	Y	49 04.4	25 39.2	. . 04.3	58 51.2	. . 21.9	302 14.3	. . 54.4	43 45.2	. . 00.8
16		64 06.8	40 38.8	05.6	73 51.8	21.1	317 16.6	54.3	58 47.4	00.7
17		79 09.3	55 38.4	06.8	88 52.5	20.3	332 18.9	54.3	73 49.6	00.5
18		94 11.8	70 38.0	N 9 08.0	103 53.1	S 5 19.6	347 21.3	N22 54.3	88 51.7	S 0 00.4
19		109 14.2	85 37.6	09.2	118 53.8	18.8	2 23.6	54.3	103 53.9	00.3
20		124 16.7	100 37.1	10.4	133 54.4	18.0	17 25.9	54.3	118 56.1	00.2
21		139 19.2	115 36.7	. . 11.6	148 55.1	. . 17.2	32 28.3	. . 54.3	133 58.3	S 00.1
22		154 21.6	130 36.3	12.8	163 55.8	16.5	47 30.6	54.3	149 00.4	N 00.1
23		169 24.1	145 35.9	14.0	178 56.4	15.7	62 32.9	54.3	164 02.6	00.2
27 00		184 26.6	160 35.5	N 9 15.3	193 57.1	S 5 14.9	77 35.2	N22 54.2	179 04.8	N 0 00.3
01		199 29.0	175 35.1	16.5	208 57.7	14.1	92 37.6	54.2	194 07.0	00.4
02		214 31.5	190 34.7	17.7	223 58.4	13.4	107 39.9	54.2	209 09.2	00.6
03		229 33.9	205 34.3	. . 18.9	238 59.0	. . 12.6	122 42.2	. . 54.2	224 11.3	. . 00.7
04		244 36.4	220 33.8	20.1	253 59.7	11.8	137 44.6	54.2	239 13.5	00.8
05		259 38.9	235 33.4	21.3	269 00.4	11.0	152 46.9	54.2	254 15.7	00.9
06		274 41.3	250 33.0	N 9 22.5	284 01.0	S 5 10.3	167 49.2	N22 54.2	269 17.9	N 0 01.0
07		289 43.8	265 32.6	23.7	299 01.7	09.5	182 51.5	54.2	284 20.0	01.2
08		304 46.3	280 32.2	24.9	314 02.3	08.7	197 53.9	54.1	299 22.2	01.3
09	F	319 48.7	295 31.8	. . 26.1	329 03.0	. . 07.9	212 56.2	. . 54.1	314 24.4	. . 01.4
10	R	334 51.2	310 31.4	27.4	344 03.6	07.2	227 58.5	54.1	329 26.6	01.5
11	I	349 53.7	325 30.9	28.6	359 04.3	06.4	243 00.8	54.1	344 28.7	01.7
12	D	4 56.1	340 30.5	N 9 29.8	14 05.0	S 5 05.6	258 03.2	N22 54.1	359 30.9	N 0 01.8
13	A	19 58.6	355 30.1	31.0	29 05.6	04.8	273 05.5	54.1	14 33.1	01.9
14	Y	35 01.0	10 29.7	32.2	44 06.3	04.1	288 07.8	54.1	29 35.3	02.0
15		50 03.5	25 29.3	. . 33.4	59 06.9	. . 03.3	303 10.1	. . 54.1	44 37.5	. . 02.2
16		65 06.0	40 28.9	34.6	74 07.6	02.5	318 12.4	54.0	59 39.6	02.3
17		80 08.4	55 28.4	35.8	89 08.2	01.7	333 14.8	54.0	74 41.8	02.4
18		95 10.9	70 28.0	N 9 37.0	104 08.9	S 5 00.9	348 17.1	N22 54.0	89 44.0	N 0 02.5
19		110 13.4	85 27.6	38.2	119 09.6	5 00.2	3 19.4	54.0	104 46.2	02.6
20		125 15.8	100 27.2	39.4	134 10.2	4 59.4	18 21.7	54.0	119 48.3	02.8
21		140 18.3	115 26.8	. . 40.6	149 10.9	. . 58.6	33 24.1	. . 54.0	134 50.5	. . 02.9
22		155 20.8	130 26.4	41.8	164 11.5	57.8	48 26.4	54.0	149 52.7	03.0
23		170 23.2	145 25.9	43.0	179 12.2	57.1	63 28.7	53.9	164 54.9	03.1
28 00		185 25.7	160 25.5	N 9 44.2	194 12.9	S 4 56.3	78 31.0	N22 53.9	179 57.1	N 0 03.3
01		200 28.2	175 25.1	45.4	209 13.5	55.5	93 33.3	53.9	194 59.2	03.4
02		215 30.6	190 24.7	46.6	224 14.2	54.7	108 35.7	53.9	210 01.4	03.5
03		230 33.1	205 24.3	. . 47.8	239 14.8	. . 54.0	123 38.0	. . 53.9	225 03.6	. . 03.6
04		245 35.5	220 23.8	49.0	254 15.5	53.2	138 40.3	53.9	240 05.8	03.7
05		260 38.0	235 23.4	50.2	269 16.2	52.4	153 42.6	53.9	255 07.9	03.9
06		275 40.5	250 23.0	N 9 51.4	284 16.8	S 4 51.6	168 44.9	N22 53.8	270 10.1	N 0 04.0
07		290 42.9	265 22.6	52.6	299 17.5	50.8	183 47.2	53.8	285 12.3	04.1
08	S	305 45.4	280 22.2	53.8	314 18.1	50.1	198 49.6	53.8	300 14.5	04.2
09	A	320 47.9	295 21.7	. . 55.0	329 18.8	. . 49.3	213 51.9	. . 53.8	315 16.7	. . 04.4
10	T	335 50.3	310 21.3	56.2	344 19.5	48.5	228 54.2	53.8	330 18.8	04.5
11	U	350 52.8	325 20.9	57.4	359 20.1	47.7	243 56.5	53.8	345 21.0	04.6
12	R	5 55.3	340 20.5	N 9 58.6	14 20.8	S 4 47.0	258 58.8	N22 53.8	0 23.2	N 0 04.7
13	D	20 57.7	355 20.0	9 59.8	29 21.4	46.2	274 01.1	53.8	15 25.4	04.8
14	A	36 00.2	10 19.6	10 01.0	44 22.1	45.4	289 03.5	53.7	30 27.5	05.0
15	Y	51 02.7	25 19.2	. . 02.2	59 22.8	. . 44.6	304 05.8	. . 53.7	45 29.7	. . 05.1
16		66 05.1	40 18.8	03.4	74 23.4	43.8	319 08.1	53.7	60 31.9	05.2
17		81 07.6	55 18.4	04.6	89 24.1	43.1	334 10.4	53.7	75 34.1	05.3
18		96 10.0	70 17.9	N10 05.8	104 24.7	S 4 42.3	349 12.7	N22 53.7	90 36.2	N 0 05.5
19		111 12.5	85 17.5	07.0	119 25.4	41.5	4 15.0	53.7	105 38.4	05.6
20		126 15.0	100 17.1	08.2	134 26.1	40.7	19 17.4	53.7	120 40.6	05.7
21		141 17.4	115 16.7	. . 09.4	149 26.7	. . 40.0	34 19.7	. . 53.6	135 42.8	. . 05.8
22		156 19.9	130 16.2	10.6	164 27.4	39.2	49 22.0	53.6	150 45.0	05.9
23		171 22.4	145 15.8	11.8	179 28.0	38.4	64 24.3	53.6	165 47.1	06.1
Mer. Pass.		h m 11 40.3	v −0.4	d 1.2	v 0.7	d 0.8	v 2.3	d 0.0	v 2.2	d 0.1

STARS

Name	SHA	Dec
	° ′	° ′
Acamar	315 11.3	S40 12.1
Achernar	335 20.0	S57 06.3
Acrux	172 58.3	S63 14.8
Adhara	255 05.0	S29 00.7
Aldebaran	290 38.6	N16 33.7
Alioth	166 11.5	N55 48.9
Alkaid	152 50.7	N49 10.7
Alnair	27 32.0	S46 50.0
Alnilam	275 36.8	S 1 11.2
Alphard	217 46.5	S 8 46.5
Alphecca	126 02.6	N26 37.3
Alpheratz	357 34.1	N29 14.0
Altair	61 59.1	N 8 56.1
Ankaa	353 06.6	S42 09.9
Antares	112 14.4	S26 29.4
Arcturus	145 46.7	N19 02.5
Atria	107 07.6	S69 04.2
Avior	234 14.1	S59 35.9
Bellatrix	278 21.9	N 6 22.3
Betelgeuse	270 51.0	N 7 24.6
Canopus	263 52.0	S52 42.8
Capella	280 20.5	N46 01.6
Deneb	49 25.4	N45 22.1
Denebola	182 23.6	N14 25.4
Diphda	348 46.6	S17 50.6
Dubhe	193 39.1	N61 36.6
Elnath	278 00.7	N28 37.8
Eltanin	90 41.6	N51 28.7
Enif	33 38.1	N 9 59.6
Fomalhaut	15 13.7	S29 29.0
Gacrux	171 50.0	S57 15.7
Gienah	175 42.2	S17 41.4
Hadar	148 34.0	S60 30.0
Hamal	327 50.4	N23 35.2
Kaus Aust.	83 31.2	S34 22.3
Kochab	137 18.8	N74 02.5
Markab	13 29.2	N15 20.7
Menkar	314 05.3	N 4 11.5
Menkent	147 56.1	S36 30.0
Miaplacidus	221 37.5	S69 49.7
Mirfak	308 27.2	N49 57.4
Nunki	75 46.6	S26 15.8
Peacock	53 04.4	S56 38.9
Pollux	243 16.0	N27 57.8
Procyon	244 49.7	N 5 09.4
Rasalhague	95 57.5	N12 32.2
Regulus	207 33.1	N11 50.2
Rigel	281 03.0	S 8 10.4
Rigil Kent.	139 38.4	S60 56.5
Sabik	102 01.5	S15 45.5
Schedar	349 30.5	N56 40.9
Shaula	96 08.9	S37 07.3
Sirius	258 25.3	S16 45.3
Spica	158 20.9	S11 18.1
Suhail	222 45.3	S43 32.6
Vega	80 32.6	N38 48.1
Zuben'ubi	136 54.6	S16 09.2

	SHA	Mer. Pass.
	° ′	h m
Venus	336 08.9	13 18
Mars	9 30.5	11 04
Jupiter	253 08.7	18 47
Saturn	354 38.2	12 02

UT		SUN GHA	SUN Dec	MOON GHA	v	MOON Dec	d	HP
d	h	° ′	° ′	° ′	′	° ′	′	′
26	00	178 33.2	N 2 07.4	84 32.4	4.1	N27 45.8	3.8	59.0
	01	193 33.4	08.4	98 55.5	4.2	27 42.0	4.0	59.0
	02	208 33.6	09.3	113 18.7	4.2	27 38.0	4.2	59.0
	03	223 33.8	. . 10.3	127 41.9	4.3	27 33.8	4.4	58.9
	04	238 34.0	11.3	142 05.2	4.4	27 29.4	4.5	58.9
	05	253 34.2	12.3	156 28.6	4.4	27 24.9	4.7	58.9
	06	268 34.3	N 2 13.3	170 52.0	4.6	N27 20.2	4.9	58.9
	07	283 34.5	14.2	185 15.6	4.6	27 15.3	5.1	58.9
T	08	298 34.7	15.2	199 39.2	4.7	27 10.2	5.2	58.9
H	09	313 34.9	. . 16.2	214 02.9	4.8	27 05.0	5.5	58.8
U	10	328 35.1	17.2	228 26.7	4.8	26 59.5	5.6	58.8
R	11	343 35.3	18.2	242 50.5	5.0	26 53.9	5.7	58.8
S	12	358 35.5	N 2 19.2	257 14.5	5.0	N26 48.2	6.0	58.8
D	13	13 35.7	20.1	271 38.5	5.1	26 42.2	6.1	58.8
A	14	28 35.9	21.1	286 02.6	5.2	26 36.1	6.2	58.8
Y	15	43 36.0	. . 22.1	300 26.8	5.3	26 29.9	6.5	58.7
	16	58 36.2	23.1	314 51.1	5.4	26 23.4	6.6	58.7
	17	73 36.4	24.1	329 15.5	5.5	26 16.8	6.8	58.7
	18	88 36.6	N 2 25.0	343 40.0	5.6	N26 10.0	6.9	58.7
	19	103 36.8	26.0	358 04.6	5.7	26 03.1	7.1	58.7
	20	118 37.0	27.0	12 29.3	5.7	25 56.0	7.2	58.7
	21	133 37.2	. . 28.0	26 54.0	5.9	25 48.8	7.4	58.6
	22	148 37.4	29.0	41 18.9	6.0	25 41.4	7.6	58.6
	23	163 37.6	29.9	55 43.9	6.1	25 33.8	7.7	58.6
27	00	178 37.7	N 2 30.9	70 09.0	6.1	N25 26.1	7.9	58.6
	01	193 37.9	31.9	84 34.1	6.3	25 18.2	8.0	58.6
	02	208 38.1	32.9	98 59.4	6.4	25 10.2	8.2	58.6
	03	223 38.3	. . 33.8	113 24.8	6.5	25 02.0	8.3	58.5
	04	238 38.5	34.8	127 50.3	6.6	24 53.7	8.4	58.5
	05	253 38.7	35.8	142 15.9	6.6	24 45.3	8.7	58.5
	06	268 38.9	N 2 36.8	156 41.5	6.8	N24 36.6	8.7	58.5
	07	283 39.1	37.8	171 07.3	6.9	24 27.9	8.9	58.5
	08	298 39.3	38.7	185 33.2	7.1	24 19.0	9.0	58.5
F	09	313 39.4	. . 39.7	199 59.3	7.1	24 10.0	9.2	58.4
R	10	328 39.6	40.7	214 25.4	7.2	24 00.8	9.3	58.4
I	11	343 39.8	41.7	228 51.6	7.3	23 51.5	9.5	58.4
D	12	358 40.0	N 2 42.7	243 17.9	7.5	N23 42.0	9.6	58.4
A	13	13 40.2	43.6	257 44.4	7.5	23 32.4	9.7	58.4
Y	14	28 40.4	44.6	272 10.9	7.7	23 22.7	9.8	58.3
	15	43 40.6	. . 45.6	286 37.6	7.8	23 12.9	10.0	58.3
	16	58 40.8	46.6	301 04.4	7.8	23 02.9	10.1	58.3
	17	73 41.0	47.5	315 31.2	8.0	22 52.8	10.2	58.3
	18	88 41.1	N 2 48.5	329 58.2	8.1	N22 42.6	10.4	58.3
	19	103 41.3	49.5	344 25.3	8.2	22 32.2	10.4	58.3
	20	118 41.5	50.5	358 52.5	8.3	22 21.8	10.6	58.2
	21	133 41.7	. . 51.5	13 19.8	8.4	22 11.2	10.8	58.2
	22	148 41.9	52.4	27 47.2	8.6	22 00.4	10.8	58.2
	23	163 42.1	53.4	42 14.8	8.6	21 49.6	10.9	58.2
28	00	178 42.3	N 2 54.4	56 42.4	8.7	N21 38.7	11.1	58.2
	01	193 42.5	55.4	71 10.1	8.9	21 27.6	11.2	58.1
	02	208 42.7	56.3	85 38.0	9.0	21 16.4	11.2	58.1
	03	223 42.8	. . 57.3	100 06.0	9.0	21 05.2	11.4	58.1
	04	238 43.0	58.3	114 34.0	9.2	20 53.8	11.5	58.1
	05	253 43.2	2 59.3	129 02.2	9.3	20 42.3	11.6	58.1
	06	268 43.4	N 3 00.2	143 30.5	9.4	N20 30.7	11.8	58.0
	07	283 43.6	01.2	157 58.9	9.5	20 18.9	11.8	58.0
S	08	298 43.8	02.2	172 27.4	9.6	20 07.1	11.9	58.0
A	09	313 44.0	. . 03.2	186 56.0	9.7	19 55.2	12.0	58.0
T	10	328 44.2	04.2	201 24.7	9.8	19 43.2	12.1	58.0
U	11	343 44.4	05.1	215 53.5	9.9	19 31.1	12.2	58.0
R	12	358 44.5	N 3 06.1	230 22.4	10.0	N19 18.9	12.3	57.9
D	13	13 44.7	07.1	244 51.4	10.1	19 06.6	12.4	57.9
A	14	28 44.9	08.1	259 20.5	10.2	18 54.2	12.5	57.9
Y	15	43 45.1	. . 09.0	273 49.7	10.4	18 41.7	12.6	57.9
	16	58 45.3	10.0	288 19.1	10.4	18 29.1	12.6	57.9
	17	73 45.5	11.0	302 48.5	10.5	18 16.5	12.8	57.8
	18	88 45.7	N 3 12.0	317 18.0	10.6	N18 03.7	12.8	57.8
	19	103 45.9	12.9	331 47.6	10.8	17 50.9	13.0	57.8
	20	118 46.1	13.9	346 17.4	10.8	17 37.9	13.0	57.8
	21	133 46.2	. . 14.9	0 47.2	10.9	17 24.9	13.0	57.8
	22	148 46.4	15.9	15 17.1	11.0	17 11.9	13.2	57.7
	23	163 46.6	16.8	29 47.1	11.1	N16 58.7	13.2	57.7
		SD 16.1	*d* 1.0	SD 16.0		15.9		15.8

Lat.	Twilight Naut.	Twilight Civil	Sunrise	Moonrise 26	Moonrise 27	Moonrise 28	Moonrise 29
°	h m	h m	h m	h m	h m	h m	h m
N 72	02 29	04 11	05 22	▭	▭	▭	12 09
N 70	02 57	04 24	05 27	▭	▭	09 11	12 39
68	03 18	04 33	05 31	▭	▭	10 31	13 00
66	03 34	04 41	05 34	▭	▭	11 08	13 17
64	03 47	04 48	05 36	▭	09 18	11 35	13 31
62	03 58	04 54	05 39	07 46	09 57	11 55	13 42
60	04 07	04 59	05 41	08 36	10 24	12 11	13 52
N 58	04 15	05 03	05 42	09 07	10 45	12 25	14 01
56	04 21	05 06	05 44	09 30	11 02	12 37	14 08
54	04 27	05 10	05 45	09 49	11 17	12 47	14 14
52	04 32	05 13	05 47	10 05	11 30	12 56	14 20
50	04 37	05 15	05 48	10 19	11 41	13 04	14 26
45	04 46	05 21	05 50	10 47	12 04	13 21	14 37
N 40	04 53	05 25	05 52	11 09	12 22	13 35	14 46
35	04 59	05 29	05 54	11 28	12 38	13 47	14 54
30	05 04	05 32	05 56	11 43	12 51	13 58	15 01
20	05 10	05 36	05 58	12 10	13 14	14 15	15 13
N 10	05 15	05 39	06 00	12 33	13 33	14 30	15 24
0	05 17	05 41	06 02	12 54	13 52	14 45	15 34
S 10	05 18	05 43	06 04	13 15	14 10	14 59	15 43
20	05 18	05 44	06 06	13 38	14 29	15 14	15 54
30	05 16	05 44	06 08	14 04	14 51	15 31	16 05
35	05 14	05 43	06 09	14 19	15 04	15 41	16 12
40	05 11	05 43	06 10	14 37	15 19	15 53	16 20
45	05 08	05 42	06 11	14 59	15 37	16 06	16 29
S 50	05 03	05 41	06 13	15 26	15 59	16 22	16 39
52	05 00	05 40	06 13	15 39	16 09	16 29	16 44
54	04 58	05 39	06 14	15 54	16 21	16 38	16 50
56	04 54	05 38	06 15	16 12	16 34	16 47	16 56
58	04 51	05 37	06 16	16 33	16 49	16 58	17 02
S 60	04 46	05 35	06 17	17 01	17 08	17 10	17 10

Lat.	Sunset	Twilight Civil	Twilight Naut.	Moonset 26	Moonset 27	Moonset 28	Moonset 29
°	h m	h m	h m	h m	h m	h m	h m
N 72	18 51	20 03	21 49	▭	▭	▭	07 00
N 70	18 46	19 50	21 18	▭	▭	08 12	06 28
68	18 42	19 40	20 56	▭	▭	06 50	06 05
66	18 39	19 32	20 40	▭	▭	06 12	05 46
64	18 36	19 25	20 26	▭	06 08	05 44	05 31
62	18 34	19 19	20 15	05 37	05 29	05 23	05 18
60	18 32	19 14	20 06	04 47	05 01	05 06	05 07
N 58	18 30	19 09	19 58	04 15	04 39	04 51	04 58
56	18 28	19 06	19 51	03 51	04 21	04 39	04 50
54	18 26	19 02	19 45	03 32	04 06	04 28	04 42
52	18 25	18 59	19 40	03 16	03 53	04 18	04 35
50	18 24	18 56	19 35	03 02	03 41	04 09	04 29
45	18 21	18 51	19 26	02 33	03 17	03 50	04 16
N 40	18 19	18 46	19 18	02 10	02 58	03 35	04 05
35	18 17	18 43	19 12	01 52	02 41	03 22	03 56
30	18 16	18 40	19 08	01 35	02 27	03 11	03 48
20	18 13	18 35	19 01	01 08	02 03	02 51	03 33
N 10	18 11	18 32	18 56	00 44	01 42	02 34	03 21
0	18 09	18 29	18 53	00 22	01 22	02 17	03 09
S 10	18 07	18 28	18 52	00 00	01 02	02 01	02 56
20	18 05	18 27	18 52	24 41	00 41	01 44	02 43
30	18 03	18 26	18 54	24 16	00 16	01 23	02 28
35	18 01	18 27	18 56	24 01	00 01	01 11	02 20
40	18 00	18 27	18 59	23 44	24 57	00 57	02 10
45	17 59	18 28	19 02	23 23	24 41	00 41	01 58
S 50	17 57	18 29	19 07	22 57	24 20	00 20	01 43
52	17 56	18 30	19 09	22 44	24 11	00 11	01 37
54	17 55	18 31	19 12	22 29	24 00	00 00	01 29
56	17 55	18 31	19 15	22 12	23 47	25 21	01 21
58	17 54	18 33	19 18	21 51	23 32	25 11	01 11
S 60	17 52	18 34	19 22	21 24	23 15	25 00	01 00

Day	SUN Eqn. of Time 00^h	SUN Eqn. of Time 12^h	SUN Mer. Pass.	MOON Mer. Pass. Upper	MOON Mer. Pass. Lower	MOON Age	MOON %	Phase
d	m s	m s	h m	h m	h m	d	%	
26	05 48	05 38	12 06	19 08	06 38	07	58	
27	05 29	05 20	12 05	20 05	07 37	08	69	
28	05 11	05 02	12 05	20 57	08 31	09	78	

UT	ARIES	VENUS −3·9		MARS +1·2		JUPITER −2·2		SATURN +0·9	
	GHA	GHA	Dec	GHA	Dec	GHA	Dec	GHA	Dec
d h	° ′	° ′	° ′	° ′	° ′	° ′	° ′	° ′	° ′
29 00	186 24.8	160 15.4	N10 13.0	194 28.7	S 4 37.6	79 26.6	N22 53.6	180 49.3	N 0 06.2
01	201 27.3	175 15.0	14.2	209 29.4	36.8	94 28.9	53.6	195 51.5	06.3
02	216 29.8	190 14.5	15.3	224 30.0	36.1	109 31.2	53.6	210 53.7	06.4
03	231 32.2	205 14.1	. . 16.5	239 30.7	. . 35.3	124 33.5	. . 53.5	225 55.8	. . 06.6
04	246 34.7	220 13.7	17.7	254 31.4	34.5	139 35.8	53.5	240 58.0	06.7
05	261 37.2	235 13.2	18.9	269 32.0	33.7	154 38.2	53.5	256 00.2	06.8
06	276 39.6	250 12.8	N10 20.1	284 32.7	S 4 32.9	169 40.5	N22 53.5	271 02.4	N 0 06.9
07	291 42.1	265 12.4	21.3	299 33.3	32.2	184 42.8	53.5	286 04.6	07.0
S 08	306 44.5	280 12.0	22.5	314 34.0	31.4	199 45.1	53.5	301 06.7	07.2
U 09	321 47.0	295 11.5	. . 23.7	329 34.7	. . 30.6	214 47.4	. . 53.5	316 08.9	. . 07.3
N 10	336 49.5	310 11.1	24.9	344 35.3	29.8	229 49.7	53.4	331 11.1	07.4
D 11	351 51.9	325 10.7	26.1	359 36.0	29.1	244 52.0	53.4	346 13.3	07.5
A 12	6 54.4	340 10.2	N10 27.2	14 36.6	S 4 28.3	259 54.3	N22 53.4	1 15.4	N 0 07.7
Y 13	21 56.9	355 09.8	28.4	29 37.3	27.5	274 56.6	53.4	16 17.6	07.8
14	36 59.3	10 09.4	29.6	44 38.0	26.7	289 58.9	53.4	31 19.8	07.9
15	52 01.8	25 09.0	. . 30.8	59 38.6	. . 25.9	305 01.2	. . 53.4	46 22.0	. . 08.0
16	67 04.3	40 08.5	32.0	74 39.3	25.2	320 03.5	53.4	61 24.2	08.1
17	82 06.7	55 08.1	33.2	89 40.0	24.4	335 05.9	53.3	76 26.3	08.3
18	97 09.2	70 07.7	N10 34.4	104 40.6	S 4 23.6	350 08.2	N22 53.3	91 28.5	N 0 08.4
19	112 11.6	85 07.2	35.5	119 41.3	22.8	5 10.5	53.3	106 30.7	08.5
20	127 14.1	100 06.8	36.7	134 42.0	22.0	20 12.8	53.3	121 32.9	08.6
21	142 16.6	115 06.4	. . 37.9	149 42.6	. . 21.3	35 15.1	. . 53.3	136 35.0	. . 08.8
22	157 19.0	130 05.9	39.1	164 43.3	20.5	50 17.4	53.3	151 37.2	08.9
23	172 21.5	145 05.5	40.3	179 43.9	19.7	65 19.7	53.2	166 39.4	09.0
30 00	187 24.0	160 05.1	N10 41.5	194 44.6	S 4 18.9	80 22.0	N22 53.2	181 41.6	N 0 09.1
01	202 26.4	175 04.6	42.6	209 45.3	18.1	95 24.3	53.2	196 43.8	09.2
02	217 28.9	190 04.2	43.8	224 45.9	17.4	110 26.6	53.2	211 45.9	09.4
03	232 31.4	205 03.8	. . 45.0	239 46.6	. . 16.6	125 28.9	. . 53.2	226 48.1	. . 09.5
04	247 33.8	220 03.3	46.2	254 47.3	15.8	140 31.2	53.2	241 50.3	09.6
05	262 36.3	235 02.9	47.4	269 47.9	15.0	155 33.5	53.2	256 52.5	09.7
06	277 38.8	250 02.5	N10 48.6	284 48.6	S 4 14.2	170 35.8	N22 53.1	271 54.6	N 0 09.8
07	292 41.2	265 02.0	49.7	299 49.3	13.5	185 38.1	53.1	286 56.8	10.0
08	307 43.7	280 01.6	50.9	314 49.9	12.7	200 40.4	53.1	301 59.0	10.1
M 09	322 46.1	295 01.2	. . 52.1	329 50.6	. . 11.9	215 42.7	. . 53.1	317 01.2	. . 10.2
O 10	337 48.6	310 00.7	53.3	344 51.3	11.1	230 45.0	53.1	332 03.4	10.3
N 11	352 51.1	325 00.3	54.4	359 51.9	10.3	245 47.3	53.1	347 05.5	10.5
D 12	7 53.5	339 59.9	N10 55.6	14 52.6	S 4 09.6	260 49.6	N22 53.0	2 07.7	N 0 10.6
A 13	22 56.0	354 59.4	56.8	29 53.2	08.8	275 51.9	53.0	17 09.9	10.7
Y 14	37 58.5	9 59.0	58.0	44 53.9	08.0	290 54.2	53.0	32 12.1	10.8
15	53 00.9	24 58.5	10 59.2	59 54.6	. . 07.2	305 56.5	. . 53.0	47 14.2	. . 10.9
16	68 03.4	39 58.1	11 00.3	74 55.2	06.4	320 58.8	53.0	62 16.4	11.1
17	83 05.9	54 57.7	01.5	89 55.9	05.7	336 01.1	53.0	77 18.6	11.2
18	98 08.3	69 57.2	N11 02.7	104 56.6	S 4 04.9	351 03.4	N22 52.9	92 20.8	N 0 11.3
19	113 10.8	84 56.8	03.9	119 57.2	04.1	6 05.7	52.9	107 22.9	11.4
20	128 13.2	99 56.4	05.0	134 57.9	03.3	21 08.0	52.9	122 25.1	11.6
21	143 15.7	114 55.9	. . 06.2	149 58.6	. . 02.5	36 10.3	. . 52.9	137 27.3	. . 11.7
22	158 18.2	129 55.5	07.4	164 59.2	01.8	51 12.6	52.9	152 29.5	11.8
23	173 20.6	144 55.0	08.5	179 59.9	01.0	66 14.9	52.9	167 31.7	11.9
31 00	188 23.1	159 54.6	N11 09.7	195 00.6	S 4 00.2	81 17.2	N22 52.8	182 33.8	N 0 12.0
01	203 25.6	174 54.2	10.9	210 01.2	3 59.4	96 19.5	52.8	197 36.0	12.2
02	218 28.0	189 53.7	12.1	225 01.9	58.6	111 21.8	52.8	212 38.2	12.3
03	233 30.5	204 53.3	. . 13.2	240 02.6	. . 57.9	126 24.1	. . 52.8	227 40.4	. . 12.4
04	248 33.0	219 52.8	14.4	255 03.2	57.1	141 26.4	52.8	242 42.5	12.5
05	263 35.4	234 52.4	15.6	270 03.9	56.3	156 28.7	52.8	257 44.7	12.6
06	278 37.9	249 51.9	N11 16.7	285 04.6	S 3 55.5	171 31.0	N22 52.7	272 46.9	N 0 12.8
07	293 40.4	264 51.5	17.9	300 05.2	54.7	186 33.3	52.7	287 49.1	12.9
T 08	308 42.8	279 51.1	19.1	315 05.9	53.9	201 35.5	52.7	302 51.3	13.0
U 09	323 45.3	294 50.6	. . 20.2	330 06.6	. . 53.2	216 37.8	. . 52.7	317 53.4	. . 13.1
E 10	338 47.7	309 50.2	21.4	345 07.2	52.4	231 40.1	52.7	332 55.6	13.3
S 11	353 50.2	324 49.7	22.6	0 07.9	51.6	246 42.4	52.7	347 57.8	13.4
D 12	8 52.7	339 49.3	N11 23.7	15 08.6	S 3 50.8	261 44.7	N22 52.6	3 00.0	N 0 13.5
A 13	23 55.1	354 48.8	24.9	30 09.2	50.0	276 47.0	52.6	18 02.1	13.6
Y 14	38 57.6	9 48.4	26.1	45 09.9	49.3	291 49.3	52.6	33 04.3	13.7
15	54 00.1	24 48.0	. . 27.2	60 10.6	. . 48.5	306 51.6	. . 52.6	48 06.5	. . 13.9
16	69 02.5	39 47.5	28.4	75 11.2	47.7	321 53.9	52.6	63 08.7	14.0
17	84 05.0	54 47.1	29.6	90 11.9	46.9	336 56.2	52.6	78 10.9	14.1
18	99 07.5	69 46.6	N11 30.7	105 12.6	S 3 46.1	351 58.5	N22 52.5	93 13.0	N 0 14.2
19	114 09.9	84 46.2	31.9	120 13.2	45.4	7 00.8	52.5	108 15.2	14.4
20	129 12.4	99 45.7	33.1	135 13.9	44.6	22 03.0	52.5	123 17.4	14.5
21	144 14.8	114 45.3	. . 34.2	150 14.6	. . 43.8	37 05.3	. . 52.5	138 19.6	. . 14.6
22	159 17.3	129 44.8	35.4	165 15.2	43.0	52 07.6	52.5	153 21.8	14.7
23	174 19.8	144 44.4	36.5	180 15.9	42.2	67 09.9	52.5	168 23.9	14.8
Mer. Pass.	h m 11 28.5	v −0.4	d 1.2	v 0.7	d 0.8	v 2.3	d 0.0	v 2.2	d 0.1

STARS		
Name	SHA	Dec
	° ′	° ′
Acamar	315 11.3	S40 12.1
Achernar	335 20.0	S57 06.3
Acrux	172 58.3	S63 14.8
Adhara	255 05.0	S29 00.7
Aldebaran	290 38.6	N16 33.7
Alioth	166 11.5	N55 48.9
Alkaid	152 50.7	N49 10.7
Alnair	27 32.0	S46 50.0
Alnilam	275 36.8	S 1 11.2
Alphard	217 46.6	S 8 46.5
Alphecca	126 02.6	N26 37.3
Alpheratz	357 34.1	N29 14.0
Altair	61 59.1	N 8 56.1
Ankaa	353 06.6	S42 09.8
Antares	112 14.4	S26 29.4
Arcturus	145 46.7	N19 02.5
Atria	107 07.5	S69 04.3
Avior	234 14.1	S59 35.9
Bellatrix	278 21.9	N 6 22.3
Betelgeuse	270 51.1	N 7 24.6
Canopus	263 52.0	S52 42.8
Capella	280 20.6	N46 01.6
Deneb	49 25.4	N45 22.1
Denebola	182 23.6	N14 25.4
Diphda	348 46.6	S17 50.6
Dubhe	193 39.1	N61 36.6
Elnath	278 00.7	N28 37.8
Eltanin	90 41.6	N51 28.7
Enif	33 38.0	N 9 59.6
Fomalhaut	15 13.7	S29 29.0
Gacrux	171 50.0	S57 15.7
Gienah	175 42.2	S17 41.4
Hadar	148 34.0	S60 30.0
Hamal	327 50.4	N23 35.2
Kaus Aust.	83 31.1	S34 22.3
Kochab	137 18.8	N74 02.6
Markab	13 29.2	N15 20.7
Menkar	314 05.3	N 4 11.5
Menkent	147 56.1	S36 30.0
Miaplacidus	221 37.6	S69 49.7
Mirfak	308 27.2	N49 57.4
Nunki	75 46.5	S26 15.8
Peacock	53 04.4	S56 38.8
Pollux	243 16.0	N27 57.8
Procyon	244 49.7	N 5 09.4
Rasalhague	95 57.5	N12 32.2
Regulus	207 33.1	N11 50.2
Rigel	281 03.0	S 8 10.4
Rigil Kent.	139 38.3	S60 56.6
Sabik	102 01.5	S15 45.5
Schedar	349 30.5	N56 40.8
Shaula	96 08.9	S37 07.3
Sirius	258 25.3	S16 45.3
Spica	158 20.9	S11 18.1
Suhail	222 45.3	S43 32.6
Vega	80 32.5	N38 48.1
Zuben'ubi	136 54.6	S16 09.2

	SHA	Mer. Pass.
	° ′	h m
Venus	332 41.1	13 20
Mars	7 20.6	11 01
Jupiter	252 58.0	18 36
Saturn	354 17.6	11 52

UT d	UT h	SUN GHA	SUN Dec	MOON GHA	v	MOON Dec	d	HP
		° ′	° ′	° ′	′	° ′	′	′
29	00	178 46.8	N 3 17.8	44 17.2	11.2	N16 45.5	13.4	57.7
	01	193 47.0	18.8	58 47.4	11.3	16 32.1	13.3	57.7
	02	208 47.2	19.8	73 17.7	11.4	16 18.8	13.5	57.7
	03	223 47.4	. . 20.7	87 48.1	11.5	16 05.3	13.5	57.6
	04	238 47.6	21.7	102 18.6	11.5	15 51.8	13.6	57.6
	05	253 47.8	22.7	116 49.1	11.7	15 38.2	13.7	57.6
	06	268 47.9	N 3 23.6	131 19.8	11.7	N15 24.5	13.7	57.6
	07	283 48.1	24.6	145 50.5	11.9	15 10.8	13.9	57.6
	08	298 48.3	25.6	160 21.4	11.9	14 56.9	13.8	57.5
S	09	313 48.5	. . 26.6	174 52.3	12.0	14 43.1	13.9	57.5
U	10	328 48.7	27.5	189 23.3	12.1	14 29.2	14.0	57.5
N	11	343 48.9	28.5	203 54.4	12.2	14 15.2	14.1	57.5
D	12	358 49.1	N 3 29.5	218 25.6	12.2	N14 01.1	14.1	57.5
A	13	13 49.3	30.5	232 56.8	12.4	13 47.0	14.2	57.4
Y	14	28 49.5	31.4	247 28.2	12.4	13 32.8	14.2	57.4
	15	43 49.6	. . 32.4	261 59.6	12.5	13 18.6	14.2	57.4
	16	58 49.8	33.4	276 31.1	12.6	13 04.4	14.4	57.4
	17	73 50.0	34.4	291 02.7	12.6	12 50.0	14.3	57.4
	18	88 50.2	N 3 35.3	305 34.3	12.8	N12 35.7	14.5	57.3
	19	103 50.4	36.3	320 06.1	12.8	12 21.2	14.4	57.3
	20	118 50.6	37.3	334 37.9	12.9	12 06.8	14.6	57.3
	21	133 50.8	. . 38.2	349 09.8	12.9	11 52.2	14.5	57.3
	22	148 51.0	39.2	3 41.7	13.1	11 37.7	14.6	57.3
	23	163 51.1	40.2	18 13.8	13.1	11 23.1	14.7	57.2
30	00	178 51.3	N 3 41.2	32 45.9	13.1	N11 08.4	14.7	57.2
	01	193 51.5	42.1	47 18.0	13.3	10 53.7	14.7	57.2
	02	208 51.7	43.1	61 50.3	13.3	10 39.0	14.8	57.2
	03	223 51.9	. . 44.1	76 22.6	13.4	10 24.2	14.8	57.2
	04	238 52.1	45.0	90 55.0	13.4	10 09.4	14.9	57.1
	05	253 52.3	46.0	105 27.4	13.5	9 54.5	14.8	57.1
	06	268 52.5	N 3 47.0	119 59.9	13.6	N 9 39.7	14.9	57.1
	07	283 52.7	48.0	134 32.5	13.6	9 24.8	15.0	57.1
	08	298 52.8	48.9	149 05.1	13.7	9 09.8	15.0	57.1
M	09	313 53.0	. . 49.9	163 37.8	13.7	8 54.8	15.0	57.0
O	10	328 53.2	50.9	178 10.5	13.8	8 39.8	15.0	57.0
N	11	343 53.4	51.8	192 43.3	13.9	8 24.8	15.1	57.0
D	12	358 53.6	N 3 52.8	207 16.2	13.9	N 8 09.7	15.1	57.0
A	13	13 53.8	53.8	221 49.1	14.0	7 54.6	15.1	57.0
Y	14	28 54.0	54.7	236 22.1	14.0	7 39.5	15.1	56.9
	15	43 54.2	. . 55.7	250 55.1	14.1	7 24.4	15.2	56.9
	16	58 54.3	56.7	265 28.2	14.1	7 09.2	15.2	56.9
	17	73 54.5	57.7	280 01.3	14.2	6 54.0	15.2	56.9
	18	88 54.7	N 3 58.6	294 34.5	14.3	N 6 38.8	15.2	56.9
	19	103 54.9	3 59.6	309 07.8	14.2	6 23.6	15.2	56.8
	20	118 55.1	4 00.6	323 41.0	14.4	6 08.4	15.3	56.8
	21	133 55.3	. . 01.5	338 14.4	14.3	5 53.1	15.2	56.8
	22	148 55.5	02.5	352 47.7	14.5	5 37.9	15.3	56.8
	23	163 55.7	03.5	7 21.2	14.4	5 22.6	15.3	56.8
31	00	178 55.8	N 4 04.4	21 54.6	14.5	N 5 07.3	15.3	56.7
	01	193 56.0	05.4	36 28.1	14.6	4 52.0	15.3	56.7
	02	208 56.2	06.4	51 01.7	14.6	4 36.7	15.3	56.7
	03	223 56.4	. . 07.3	65 35.3	14.6	4 21.4	15.4	56.7
	04	238 56.6	08.3	80 08.9	14.6	4 06.0	15.3	56.7
	05	253 56.8	09.3	94 42.5	14.7	3 50.7	15.3	56.6
	06	268 57.0	N 4 10.2	109 16.2	14.8	N 3 35.4	15.4	56.6
T	07	283 57.2	11.2	123 50.0	14.7	3 20.0	15.3	56.6
U	08	298 57.3	12.2	138 23.7	14.8	3 04.7	15.4	56.6
E	09	313 57.5	. . 13.1	152 57.5	14.9	2 49.3	15.3	56.6
S	10	328 57.7	14.1	167 31.4	14.8	2 34.0	15.4	56.5
D	11	343 57.9	15.1	182 05.2	14.9	2 18.6	15.4	56.5
A	12	358 58.1	N 4 16.0	196 39.1	15.0	N 2 03.2	15.3	56.5
Y	13	13 58.3	17.0	211 13.1	14.9	1 47.9	15.4	56.5
	14	28 58.5	18.0	225 47.0	15.0	1 32.5	15.3	56.4
	15	43 58.7	. . 18.9	240 21.0	15.0	1 17.2	15.3	56.4
	16	58 58.8	19.9	254 55.0	15.0	1 01.9	15.4	56.4
	17	73 59.0	20.9	269 29.0	15.1	0 46.5	15.3	56.4
	18	88 59.2	N 4 21.8	284 03.1	15.0	N 0 31.2	15.3	56.4
	19	103 59.4	22.8	298 37.1	15.1	0 15.9	15.3	56.3
	20	118 59.6	23.8	313 11.2	15.1	N 0 00.6	15.3	56.3
	21	133 59.8	. . 24.7	327 45.3	15.1	S 0 14.7	15.3	56.3
	22	149 00.0	25.7	342 19.4	15.2	0 30.0	15.3	56.3
	23	164 00.2	26.7	356 53.6	15.2	S 0 45.3	15.2	56.3
		SD 16.0	d 1.0	SD 15.7		15.5		15.4

Lat.	Twilight Naut.	Twilight Civil	Sunrise	Moonrise 29	Moonrise 30	Moonrise 31	Moonrise 1
°	h m	h m	h m	h m	h m	h m	h m
N 72	02 01	03 54	05 07	12 09	14 42	16 53	19 01
N 70	02 36	04 08	05 13	12 39	14 54	16 54	18 52
68	03 01	04 20	05 18	13 00	15 03	16 55	18 45
66	03 20	04 29	05 22	13 17	15 10	16 56	18 39
64	03 34	04 37	05 26	13 31	15 17	16 57	18 34
62	03 46	04 43	05 29	13 42	15 22	16 57	18 30
60	03 56	04 49	05 32	13 52	15 27	16 57	18 26
N 58	04 05	04 54	05 34	14 01	15 31	16 58	18 23
56	04 12	04 58	05 36	14 08	15 35	16 58	18 20
54	04 19	05 02	05 38	14 14	15 38	16 59	18 17
52	04 25	05 06	05 40	14 20	15 41	16 59	18 15
50	04 30	05 09	05 41	14 26	15 44	16 59	18 13
45	04 40	05 15	05 45	14 37	15 49	17 00	18 08
N 40	04 48	05 20	05 47	14 46	15 54	17 00	18 04
35	04 55	05 24	05 50	14 54	15 58	17 00	18 01
30	05 00	05 28	05 52	15 01	16 02	17 01	17 58
20	05 08	05 33	05 55	15 13	16 08	17 01	17 53
N 10	05 13	05 37	05 58	15 24	16 14	17 02	17 49
0	05 16	05 40	06 01	15 34	16 19	17 03	17 45
S 10	05 18	05 43	06 04	15 43	16 24	17 03	17 41
20	05 19	05 44	06 06	15 54	16 30	17 04	17 37
30	05 18	05 46	06 09	16 05	16 36	17 04	17 32
35	05 16	05 46	06 11	16 12	16 40	17 05	17 30
40	05 14	05 46	06 13	16 20	16 44	17 05	17 27
45	05 12	05 46	06 15	16 29	16 48	17 06	17 23
S 50	05 08	05 45	06 17	16 39	16 54	17 07	17 19
52	05 06	05 45	06 19	16 44	16 56	17 07	17 17
54	05 03	05 44	06 20	16 50	16 59	17 07	17 15
56	05 01	05 44	06 21	16 56	17 02	17 08	17 13
58	04 58	05 43	06 23	17 02	17 06	17 08	17 10
S 60	04 54	05 43	06 24	17 10	17 09	17 08	17 07

Lat.	Sunset	Twilight Civil	Twilight Naut.	Moonset 29	Moonset 30	Moonset 31	Moonset 1
°	h m	h m	h m	h m	h m	h m	h m
N 72	19 05	20 19	22 17	07 00	06 04	05 27	04 53
N 70	18 59	20 04	21 38	06 28	05 50	05 22	04 56
68	18 53	19 52	21 12	06 05	05 38	05 18	04 59
66	18 49	19 42	20 53	05 46	05 29	05 15	05 01
64	18 45	19 34	20 37	05 31	05 21	05 12	05 03
62	18 42	19 27	20 25	05 18	05 14	05 09	05 05
60	18 39	19 22	20 15	05 07	05 08	05 07	05 06
N 58	18 36	19 16	20 06	04 58	05 02	05 05	05 07
56	18 34	19 12	19 58	04 50	04 57	05 03	05 08
54	18 32	19 08	19 52	04 42	04 53	05 02	05 09
52	18 30	19 05	19 46	04 35	04 49	05 00	05 10
50	18 29	19 01	19 41	04 29	04 45	04 59	05 11
45	18 25	18 55	19 30	04 16	04 37	04 56	05 13
N 40	18 22	18 49	19 22	04 05	04 31	04 53	05 15
35	18 20	18 45	19 15	03 56	04 25	04 51	05 16
30	18 17	18 41	19 10	03 48	04 20	04 49	05 17
20	18 14	18 36	19 02	03 33	04 11	04 46	05 19
N 10	18 11	18 32	18 56	03 21	04 03	04 43	05 21
0	18 08	18 28	18 52	03 09	03 56	04 40	05 23
S 10	18 05	18 26	18 50	02 56	03 48	04 37	05 25
20	18 02	18 24	18 50	02 43	03 40	04 34	05 26
30	17 59	18 23	18 51	02 28	03 31	04 31	05 29
35	17 57	18 23	18 52	02 20	03 25	04 28	05 30
40	17 55	18 22	18 54	02 10	03 19	04 26	05 31
45	17 53	18 22	18 56	01 58	03 12	04 23	05 33
S 50	17 51	18 23	19 00	01 43	03 03	04 20	05 35
52	17 49	18 23	19 02	01 37	02 59	04 19	05 35
54	17 48	18 23	19 04	01 29	02 55	04 17	05 36
56	17 47	18 24	19 07	01 21	02 50	04 15	05 37
58	17 45	18 24	19 10	01 11	02 44	04 13	05 39
S 60	17 43	18 25	19 13	01 00	02 38	04 11	05 40

Day	SUN Eqn. of Time 00^h	SUN Eqn. of Time 12^h	SUN Mer. Pass.	MOON Mer. Pass. Upper	MOON Mer. Pass. Lower	MOON Age	MOON Phase
d	m s	m s	h m	h m	h m	d %	
29	04 53	04 44	12 05	21 45	09 21	10 87	
30	04 35	04 26	12 04	22 30	10 08	11 93	
31	04 17	04 08	12 04	23 13	10 51	12 97	

UT		ARIES	VENUS −3·9		MARS +1·2		JUPITER −2·2		SATURN +0·9	
	d h	GHA ° ′	GHA ° ′	Dec ° ′	GHA ° ′	Dec ° ′	GHA ° ′	Dec ° ′	GHA ° ′	Dec ° ′
	1 00	189 22.2	159 43.9	N11 37.7	195 16.6	S 3 41.4	82 12.2	N22 52.4	183 26.1	N 0 15.0
	01	204 24.7	174 43.5	38.9	210 17.2	40.7	97 14.5	52.4	198 28.3	15.1
	02	219 27.2	189 43.0	40.0	225 17.9	39.9	112 16.8	52.4	213 30.5	15.2
	03	234 29.6	204 42.6	. . 41.2	240 18.6	. . 39.1	127 19.1	. . 52.4	228 32.6	. . 15.3
	04	249 32.1	219 42.1	42.3	255 19.2	38.3	142 21.4	52.4	243 34.8	15.4
	05	264 34.6	234 41.7	43.5	270 19.9	37.5	157 23.6	52.4	258 37.0	15.6
	06	279 37.0	249 41.2	N11 44.7	285 20.6	S 3 36.8	172 25.9	N22 52.3	273 39.2	N 0 15.7
W	07	294 39.5	264 40.8	45.8	300 21.3	36.0	187 28.2	52.3	288 41.4	15.8
E	08	309 42.0	279 40.3	47.0	315 21.9	35.2	202 30.5	52.3	303 43.5	15.9
D	09	324 44.4	294 39.9	. . 48.1	330 22.6	. . 34.4	217 32.8	. . 52.3	318 45.7	. . 16.1
N	10	339 46.9	309 39.4	49.3	345 23.3	33.6	232 35.1	52.3	333 47.9	16.2
E	11	354 49.3	324 39.0	50.4	0 23.9	32.8	247 37.4	52.2	348 50.1	16.3
S	12	9 51.8	339 38.5	N11 51.6	15 24.6	S 3 32.1	262 39.6	N22 52.2	3 52.2	N 0 16.4
D	13	24 54.3	354 38.1	52.7	30 25.3	31.3	277 41.9	52.2	18 54.4	16.5
A	14	39 56.7	9 37.6	53.9	45 25.9	30.5	292 44.2	52.2	33 56.6	16.7
Y	15	54 59.2	24 37.2	. . 55.1	60 26.6	. . 29.7	307 46.5	. . 52.2	48 58.8	. . 16.8
	16	70 01.7	39 36.7	56.2	75 27.3	28.9	322 48.8	52.2	64 01.0	16.9
	17	85 04.1	54 36.3	57.4	90 27.9	28.1	337 51.1	52.1	79 03.1	17.0
	18	100 06.6	69 35.8	N11 58.5	105 28.6	S 3 27.4	352 53.3	N22 52.1	94 05.3	N 0 17.1
	19	115 09.1	84 35.4	11 59.7	120 29.3	26.6	7 55.6	52.1	109 07.5	17.3
	20	130 11.5	99 34.9	12 00.8	135 30.0	25.8	22 57.9	52.1	124 09.7	17.4
	21	145 14.0	114 34.4	. . 02.0	150 30.6	. . 25.0	38 00.2	. . 52.1	139 11.8	. . 17.5
	22	160 16.4	129 34.0	03.1	165 31.3	24.2	53 02.5	52.0	154 14.0	17.6
	23	175 18.9	144 33.5	04.3	180 32.0	23.5	68 04.8	52.0	169 16.2	17.7
	2 00	190 21.4	159 33.1	N12 05.4	195 32.6	S 3 22.7	83 07.0	N22 52.0	184 18.4	N 0 17.9
	01	205 23.8	174 32.6	06.6	210 33.3	21.9	98 09.3	52.0	199 20.6	18.0
	02	220 26.3	189 32.2	07.7	225 34.0	21.1	113 11.6	52.0	214 22.7	18.1
	03	235 28.8	204 31.7	. . 08.9	240 34.6	. . 20.3	128 13.9	. . 52.0	229 24.9	. . 18.2
	04	250 31.2	219 31.2	10.0	255 35.3	19.5	143 16.2	51.9	244 27.1	18.4
	05	265 33.7	234 30.8	11.1	270 36.0	18.8	158 18.4	51.9	259 29.3	18.5
	06	280 36.2	249 30.3	N12 12.3	285 36.7	S 3 18.0	173 20.7	N22 51.9	274 31.4	N 0 18.6
	07	295 38.6	264 29.9	13.4	300 37.3	17.2	188 23.0	51.9	289 33.6	18.7
T	08	310 41.1	279 29.4	14.6	315 38.0	16.4	203 25.3	51.9	304 35.8	18.8
H	09	325 43.6	294 29.0	. . 15.7	330 38.7	. . 15.6	218 27.5	. . 51.8	319 38.0	. . 19.0
U	10	340 46.0	309 28.5	16.9	345 39.3	14.8	233 29.8	51.8	334 40.2	19.1
R	11	355 48.5	324 28.0	18.0	0 40.0	14.1	248 32.1	51.8	349 42.3	19.2
S	12	10 50.9	339 27.6	N12 19.2	15 40.7	S 3 13.3	263 34.4	N22 51.8	4 44.5	N 0 19.3
D	13	25 53.4	354 27.1	20.3	30 41.3	12.5	278 36.7	51.8	19 46.7	19.4
A	14	40 55.9	9 26.7	21.4	45 42.0	11.7	293 38.9	51.8	34 48.9	19.6
Y	15	55 58.3	24 26.2	. . 22.6	60 42.7	. . 10.9	308 41.2	. . 51.7	49 51.1	. . 19.7
	16	71 00.8	39 25.7	23.7	75 43.4	10.1	323 43.5	51.7	64 53.2	19.8
	17	86 03.3	54 25.3	24.9	90 44.0	09.4	338 45.8	51.7	79 55.4	19.9
	18	101 05.7	69 24.8	N12 26.0	105 44.7	S 3 08.6	353 48.0	N22 51.7	94 57.6	N 0 20.0
	19	116 08.2	84 24.3	27.1	120 45.4	07.8	8 50.3	51.7	109 59.8	20.2
	20	131 10.7	99 23.9	28.3	135 46.0	07.0	23 52.6	51.6	125 01.9	20.3
	21	146 13.1	114 23.4	. . 29.4	150 46.7	. . 06.2	38 54.9	. . 51.6	140 04.1	. . 20.4
	22	161 15.6	129 23.0	30.6	165 47.4	05.4	53 57.1	51.6	155 06.3	20.5
	23	176 18.1	144 22.5	31.7	180 48.1	04.7	68 59.4	51.6	170 08.5	20.7
	3 00	191 20.5	159 22.0	N12 32.8	195 48.7	S 3 03.9	84 01.7	N22 51.6	185 10.7	N 0 20.8
	01	206 23.0	174 21.6	34.0	210 49.4	03.1	99 03.9	51.5	200 12.8	20.9
	02	221 25.4	189 21.1	35.1	225 50.1	02.3	114 06.2	51.5	215 15.0	21.0
	03	236 27.9	204 20.6	. . 36.2	240 50.8	. . 01.5	129 08.5	. . 51.5	230 17.2	. . 21.1
	04	251 30.4	219 20.2	37.4	255 51.4	00.7	144 10.8	51.5	245 19.4	21.3
	05	266 32.8	234 19.7	38.5	270 52.1	3 00.0	159 13.0	51.5	260 21.6	21.4
	06	281 35.3	249 19.2	N12 39.6	285 52.8	S 2 59.2	174 15.3	N22 51.4	275 23.7	N 0 21.5
	07	296 37.8	264 18.8	40.8	300 53.4	58.4	189 17.6	51.4	290 25.9	21.6
	08	311 40.2	279 18.3	41.9	315 54.1	57.6	204 19.8	51.4	305 28.1	21.7
F	09	326 42.7	294 17.8	. . 43.0	330 54.8	. . 56.8	219 22.1	. . 51.4	320 30.3	. . 21.9
R	10	341 45.2	309 17.4	44.2	345 55.5	56.0	234 24.4	51.4	335 32.4	22.0
I	11	356 47.6	324 16.9	45.3	0 56.1	55.3	249 26.7	51.3	350 34.6	22.1
D	12	11 50.1	339 16.4	N12 46.4	15 56.8	S 2 54.5	264 28.9	N22 51.3	5 36.8	N 0 22.2
A	13	26 52.5	354 15.9	47.6	30 57.5	53.7	279 31.2	51.3	20 39.0	22.3
Y	14	41 55.0	9 15.5	48.7	45 58.2	52.9	294 33.5	51.3	35 41.2	22.5
	15	56 57.5	24 15.0	. . 49.8	60 58.8	. . 52.1	309 35.7	. . 51.3	50 43.3	. . 22.6
	16	71 59.9	39 14.5	51.0	75 59.5	51.3	324 38.0	51.2	65 45.5	22.7
	17	87 02.4	54 14.1	52.1	91 00.2	50.6	339 40.3	51.2	80 47.7	22.8
	18	102 04.9	69 13.6	N12 53.2	106 00.8	S 2 49.8	354 42.5	N22 51.2	95 49.9	N 0 22.9
	19	117 07.3	84 13.1	54.3	121 01.5	49.0	9 44.8	51.2	110 52.1	23.1
	20	132 09.8	99 12.7	55.5	136 02.2	48.2	24 47.1	51.2	125 54.2	23.2
	21	147 12.3	114 12.2	. . 56.6	151 02.9	. . 47.4	39 49.3	. . 51.1	140 56.4	. . 23.3
	22	162 14.7	129 11.7	57.7	166 03.5	46.6	54 51.6	51.1	155 58.6	23.4
	23	177 17.2	144 11.2	58.8	181 04.2	45.9	69 53.9	51.1	171 00.8	23.6
	Mer. Pass.	h m 11 16.7	v −0.5	d 1.1	v 0.7	d 0.8	v 2.3	d 0.0	v 2.2	d 0.1

STARS

Name	SHA ° ′	Dec ° ′
Acamar	315 11.3	S40 12.1
Achernar	335 20.0	S57 06.3
Acrux	172 58.3	S63 14.8
Adhara	255 05.1	S29 00.7
Aldebaran	290 38.6	N16 33.7
Alioth	166 11.5	N55 48.9
Alkaid	152 50.7	N49 10.7
Alnair	27 32.0	S46 49.9
Alnilam	275 36.8	S 1 11.2
Alphard	217 46.6	S 8 46.5
Alphecca	126 02.6	N26 37.3
Alpheratz	357 34.1	N29 14.0
Altair	61 59.1	N 8 56.1
Ankaa	353 06.6	S42 09.8
Antares	112 14.4	S26 29.4
Arcturus	145 46.7	N19 02.5
Atria	107 07.5	S69 04.3
Avior	234 14.1	S59 35.9
Bellatrix	278 21.9	N 6 22.3
Betelgeuse	270 51.1	N 7 24.6
Canopus	263 52.0	S52 42.8
Capella	280 20.6	N46 01.6
Deneb	49 25.3	N45 22.1
Denebola	182 23.6	N14 25.4
Diphda	348 46.6	S17 50.6
Dubhe	193 39.2	N61 36.6
Elnath	278 00.7	N28 37.8
Eltanin	90 41.6	N51 28.7
Enif	33 38.0	N 9 59.6
Fomalhaut	15 13.7	S29 29.0
Gacrux	171 50.0	S57 15.7
Gienah	175 42.2	S17 41.4
Hadar	148 34.0	S60 30.0
Hamal	327 50.4	N23 35.2
Kaus Aust.	83 31.1	S34 22.3
Kochab	137 18.8	N74 02.6
Markab	13 29.2	N15 20.7
Menkar	314 05.4	N 4 11.5
Menkent	147 56.1	S36 30.0
Miaplacidus	221 37.6	S69 49.8
Mirfak	308 27.2	N49 57.3
Nunki	75 46.5	S26 15.8
Peacock	53 04.4	S56 38.8
Pollux	243 16.0	N27 57.8
Procyon	244 49.7	N 5 09.4
Rasalhague	95 57.5	N12 32.2
Regulus	207 33.1	N11 50.2
Rigel	281 03.0	S 8 10.4
Rigil Kent.	139 38.3	S60 56.6
Sabik	102 01.5	S15 45.5
Schedar	349 30.5	N56 40.8
Shaula	96 08.9	S37 07.3
Sirius	258 25.4	S16 45.3
Spica	158 20.9	S11 18.1
Suhail	222 45.3	S43 32.6
Vega	80 32.5	N38 48.1
Zuben'ubi	136 54.6	S16 09.2

	SHA ° ′	Mer. Pass. h m
Venus	329 11.7	13 22
Mars	5 11.3	10 57
Jupiter	252 45.7	18 25
Saturn	353 57.0	11 41

UT	SUN GHA	SUN Dec	MOON GHA	v	MOON Dec	d	HP
d h	° ′	° ′	° ′	′	° ′	′	′
1 00	179 00.3	N 4 27.6	11 27.8	15.1	S 1 00.5	15.3	56.2
01	194 00.5	28.6	26 01.9	15.2	1 15.8	15.2	56.2
02	209 00.7	29.6	40 36.1	15.2	1 31.0	15.2	56.2
03	224 00.9	. . 30.5	55 10.3	15.2	1 46.2	15.2	56.2
04	239 01.1	31.5	69 44.5	15.3	2 01.4	15.2	56.2
05	254 01.3	32.5	84 18.8	15.2	2 16.6	15.1	56.1
06	269 01.5	N 4 33.4	98 53.0	15.2	S 2 31.7	15.1	56.1
W 07	284 01.6	34.4	113 27.2	15.3	2 46.8	15.1	56.1
E 08	299 01.8	35.4	128 01.5	15.3	3 01.9	15.1	56.1
D 09	314 02.0	. . 36.3	142 35.8	15.2	3 17.0	15.1	56.1
N 10	329 02.2	37.3	157 10.0	15.3	3 32.1	15.0	56.0
E 11	344 02.4	38.2	171 44.3	15.3	3 47.1	15.0	56.0
S 12	359 02.6	N 4 39.2	186 18.6	15.2	S 4 02.1	15.0	56.0
D 13	14 02.8	40.2	200 52.8	15.3	4 17.1	15.0	56.0
A 14	29 02.9	41.1	215 27.1	15.3	4 32.1	14.9	56.0
Y 15	44 03.1	. . 42.1	230 01.4	15.3	4 47.0	14.9	55.9
16	59 03.3	43.1	244 35.7	15.2	5 01.9	14.9	55.9
17	74 03.5	44.0	259 09.9	15.3	5 16.8	14.8	55.9
18	89 03.7	N 4 45.0	273 44.2	15.3	S 5 31.6	14.8	55.9
19	104 03.9	46.0	288 18.5	15.2	5 46.4	14.8	55.9
20	119 04.1	46.9	302 52.7	15.3	6 01.2	14.7	55.8
21	134 04.2	. . 47.9	317 27.0	15.3	6 15.9	14.7	55.8
22	149 04.4	48.8	332 01.3	15.2	6 30.6	14.6	55.8
23	164 04.6	49.8	346 35.5	15.2	6 45.2	14.7	55.8
2 00	179 04.8	N 4 50.8	1 09.7	15.3	S 6 59.9	14.5	55.8
01	194 05.0	51.7	15 44.0	15.2	7 14.4	14.6	55.7
02	209 05.2	52.7	30 18.2	15.2	7 29.0	14.5	55.7
03	224 05.4	. . 53.6	44 52.4	15.2	7 43.5	14.4	55.7
04	239 05.5	54.6	59 26.6	15.2	7 57.9	14.5	55.7
05	254 05.7	55.6	74 00.8	15.1	8 12.4	14.3	55.7
06	269 05.9	N 4 56.5	88 34.9	15.2	S 8 26.7	14.4	55.6
T 07	284 06.1	57.5	103 09.1	15.1	8 41.1	14.2	55.6
H 08	299 06.3	58.5	117 43.2	15.1	8 55.3	14.3	55.6
U 09	314 06.5	4 59.4	132 17.3	15.1	9 09.6	14.2	55.6
R 10	329 06.7	5 00.4	146 51.4	15.1	9 23.8	14.1	55.6
S 11	344 06.8	01.3	161 25.5	15.1	9 37.9	14.1	55.5
D 12	359 07.0	N 5 02.3	175 59.6	15.0	S 9 52.0	14.0	55.5
A 13	14 07.2	03.3	190 33.6	15.1	10 06.0	14.0	55.5
Y 14	29 07.4	04.2	205 07.7	15.0	10 20.0	14.0	55.5
15	44 07.6	. . 05.2	219 41.7	14.9	10 34.0	13.9	55.5
16	59 07.8	06.1	234 15.6	15.0	10 47.9	13.8	55.4
17	74 07.9	07.1	248 49.6	14.9	11 01.7	13.8	55.4
18	89 08.1	N 5 08.1	263 23.5	14.9	S11 15.5	13.7	55.4
19	104 08.3	09.0	277 57.4	14.9	11 29.2	13.7	55.4
20	119 08.5	10.0	292 31.3	14.8	11 42.9	13.6	55.4
21	134 08.7	. . 10.9	307 05.1	14.9	11 56.5	13.5	55.3
22	149 08.9	11.9	321 39.0	14.8	12 10.0	13.5	55.3
23	164 09.1	12.8	336 12.8	14.7	12 23.5	13.5	55.3
3 00	179 09.2	N 5 13.8	350 46.5	14.8	S12 37.0	13.3	55.3
01	194 09.4	14.8	5 20.3	14.7	12 50.3	13.4	55.3
02	209 09.6	15.7	19 54.0	14.6	13 03.7	13.2	55.3
03	224 09.8	. . 16.7	34 27.6	14.7	13 16.9	13.2	55.2
04	239 10.0	17.6	49 01.3	14.6	13 30.1	13.1	55.2
05	254 10.2	18.6	63 34.9	14.6	13 43.2	13.1	55.2
06	269 10.3	N 5 19.5	78 08.5	14.5	S13 56.3	13.0	55.2
07	284 10.5	20.5	92 42.0	14.5	14 09.3	12.9	55.2
08	299 10.7	21.5	107 15.5	14.5	14 22.2	12.8	55.1
F 09	314 10.9	. . 22.4	121 49.0	14.4	14 35.0	12.8	55.1
R 10	329 11.1	23.4	136 22.4	14.4	14 47.8	12.7	55.1
I 11	344 11.3	24.3	150 55.8	14.4	15 00.5	12.7	55.1
D 12	359 11.4	N 5 25.3	165 29.2	14.3	S15 13.2	12.6	55.1
A 13	14 11.6	26.2	180 02.5	14.3	15 25.8	12.5	55.1
Y 14	29 11.8	27.2	194 35.8	14.2	15 38.3	12.4	55.0
15	44 12.0	. . 28.2	209 09.0	14.2	15 50.7	12.4	55.0
16	59 12.2	29.1	223 42.2	14.2	16 03.1	12.2	55.0
17	74 12.4	30.1	238 15.4	14.1	16 15.3	12.2	55.0
18	89 12.5	N 5 31.0	252 48.5	14.0	S16 27.5	12.2	55.0
19	104 12.7	32.0	267 21.5	14.1	16 39.7	12.0	55.0
20	119 12.9	32.9	281 54.6	14.0	16 51.7	12.0	54.9
21	134 13.1	. . 33.9	296 27.6	13.9	17 03.7	11.9	54.9
22	149 13.3	34.8	311 00.5	13.9	17 15.6	11.8	54.9
23	164 13.5	35.8	325 33.4	13.9	S17 27.4	11.7	54.9
	SD 16.0	*d* 1.0	SD 15.3		15.1		15.0

Lat.	Twilight Naut.	Twilight Civil	Sunrise	Moonrise 1	Moonrise 2	Moonrise 3	Moonrise 4
°	h m	h m	h m	h m	h m	h m	h m
N 72	01 25	03 35	04 51	19 01	21 18	25 10	01 10
N 70	02 13	03 52	04 59	18 52	20 55	23 22	■
68	02 43	04 06	05 05	18 45	20 38	22 42	■
66	03 04	04 16	05 11	18 39	20 24	22 16	24 27
64	03 21	04 25	05 15	18 34	20 12	21 55	23 47
62	03 34	04 33	05 19	18 30	20 03	21 39	23 19
60	03 46	04 39	05 22	18 26	19 55	21 25	22 58
N 58	03 55	04 45	05 25	18 23	19 48	21 13	22 41
56	04 03	04 50	05 28	18 20	19 41	21 03	22 26
54	04 11	04 54	05 31	18 17	19 36	20 55	22 14
52	04 17	04 58	05 33	18 15	19 31	20 47	22 03
50	04 22	05 02	05 35	18 13	19 26	20 40	21 53
45	04 34	05 09	05 39	18 08	19 16	20 25	21 33
N 40	04 43	05 15	05 43	18 04	19 08	20 12	21 16
35	04 50	05 20	05 46	18 01	19 01	20 02	21 03
30	04 56	05 24	05 48	17 58	18 55	19 53	20 51
20	05 05	05 31	05 53	17 53	18 45	19 37	20 31
N 10	05 11	05 36	05 57	17 49	18 36	19 24	20 13
0	05 15	05 40	06 00	17 45	18 28	19 11	19 57
S 10	05 18	05 43	06 04	17 41	18 19	18 59	19 41
20	05 20	05 45	06 07	17 37	18 11	18 46	19 23
30	05 20	05 47	06 11	17 32	18 01	18 31	19 04
35	05 19	05 48	06 13	17 30	17 55	18 22	18 52
40	05 17	05 49	06 16	17 27	17 48	18 12	18 39
45	05 15	05 49	06 19	17 23	17 41	18 01	18 24
S 50	05 12	05 50	06 22	17 19	17 32	17 47	18 05
52	05 11	05 50	06 24	17 17	17 28	17 40	17 56
54	05 09	05 50	06 25	17 15	17 23	17 33	17 46
56	05 07	05 50	06 27	17 13	17 18	17 26	17 35
58	05 04	05 50	06 29	17 10	17 13	17 17	17 23
S 60	05 01	05 50	06 31	17 07	17 07	17 07	17 08

Lat.	Sunset	Twilight Civil	Twilight Naut.	Moonset 1	Moonset 2	Moonset 3	Moonset 4
°	h m	h m	h m	h m	h m	h m	h m
N 72	19 19	20 36	22 55	04 53	04 18	03 32	01 13
N 70	19 11	20 18	22 01	04 56	04 30	03 57	03 03
68	19 04	20 04	21 29	04 59	04 39	04 16	03 43
66	18 59	19 53	21 07	05 01	04 47	04 32	04 11
64	18 54	19 44	20 49	05 03	04 54	04 44	04 33
62	18 50	19 36	20 35	05 05	05 00	04 55	04 50
60	18 46	19 29	20 24	05 06	05 05	05 05	05 05
N 58	18 43	19 24	20 14	05 07	05 10	05 13	05 17
56	18 40	19 18	20 05	05 08	05 14	05 20	05 28
54	18 38	19 14	19 58	05 09	05 17	05 27	05 38
52	18 35	19 10	19 52	05 10	05 21	05 32	05 46
50	18 33	19 06	19 46	05 11	05 24	05 38	05 54
45	18 29	18 59	19 34	05 13	05 31	05 49	06 10
N 40	18 25	18 53	19 25	05 15	05 36	05 59	06 24
35	18 22	18 48	19 18	05 16	05 41	06 07	06 36
30	18 19	18 43	19 12	05 17	05 45	06 14	06 46
20	18 15	18 37	19 03	05 19	05 53	06 27	07 03
N 10	18 10	18 32	18 56	05 21	05 59	06 38	07 19
0	18 07	18 28	18 52	05 23	06 05	06 48	07 33
S 10	18 03	18 24	18 49	05 25	06 12	06 59	07 47
20	18 00	18 22	18 47	05 26	06 18	07 10	08 03
30	17 55	18 19	18 47	05 29	06 26	07 23	08 21
35	17 53	18 18	18 48	05 30	06 30	07 31	08 31
40	17 51	18 18	18 49	05 31	06 35	07 39	08 43
45	17 48	18 17	18 51	05 33	06 41	07 49	08 58
S 50	17 44	18 16	18 54	05 35	06 48	08 01	09 15
52	17 43	18 16	18 55	05 35	06 51	08 07	09 23
54	17 41	18 16	18 57	05 36	06 55	08 13	09 33
56	17 39	18 16	18 59	05 37	06 59	08 21	09 43
58	17 37	18 16	19 01	05 39	07 03	08 29	09 55
S 60	17 34	18 16	19 04	05 40	07 08	08 38	10 09

Day	SUN Eqn. of Time 00^h	SUN Eqn. of Time 12^h	SUN Mer. Pass.	MOON Mer. Pass. Upper	MOON Mer. Pass. Lower	MOON Age	MOON %	Phase
d	m s	m s	h m	h m	h m	d	%	
1	03 59	03 50	12 04	23 55	11 34	13	100	○
2	03 41	03 32	12 04	24 38	12 17	14	100	
3	03 23	03 15	12 03	00 38	13 00	15	98	

	UT (d h)	ARIES GHA	VENUS −3·9 GHA	VENUS Dec	MARS +1·2 GHA	MARS Dec	JUPITER −2·2 GHA	JUPITER Dec	SATURN +0·9 GHA	SATURN Dec
		° ′	° ′	° ′	° ′	° ′	° ′	° ′	° ′	° ′
	4 00	192 19.7	159 10.8	N13 00.0	196 04.9	S 2 45.1	84 56.1	N22 51.1	186 02.9	N 0 23.7
	01	207 22.1	174 10.3	01.1	211 05.6	44.3	99 58.4	51.1	201 05.1	23.8
	02	222 24.6	189 09.8	02.2	226 06.2	43.5	115 00.7	51.0	216 07.3	23.9
	03	237 27.0	204 09.3	. . 03.3	241 06.9	. . 42.7	130 02.9	. . 51.0	231 09.5	. . 24.0
	04	252 29.5	219 08.9	04.4	256 07.6	41.9	145 05.2	51.0	246 11.7	24.2
	05	267 32.0	234 08.4	05.6	271 08.3	41.1	160 07.5	51.0	261 13.8	24.3
	06	282 34.4	249 07.9	N13 06.7	286 08.9	S 2 40.4	175 09.7	N22 51.0	276 16.0	N 0 24.4
	07	297 36.9	264 07.4	07.8	301 09.6	39.6	190 12.0	50.9	291 18.2	24.5
S	08	312 39.4	279 07.0	08.9	316 10.3	38.8	205 14.2	50.9	306 20.4	24.6
A	09	327 41.8	294 06.5	. . 10.1	331 11.0	. . 38.0	220 16.5	. . 50.9	321 22.6	. . 24.8
T	10	342 44.3	309 06.0	11.2	346 11.6	37.2	235 18.8	50.9	336 24.7	24.9
U	11	357 46.8	324 05.5	12.3	1 12.3	36.4	250 21.0	50.9	351 26.9	25.0
R	12	12 49.2	339 05.0	N13 13.4	16 13.0	S 2 35.7	265 23.3	N22 50.8	6 29.1	N 0 25.1
D	13	27 51.7	354 04.6	14.5	31 13.6	34.9	280 25.6	50.8	21 31.3	25.2
A	14	42 54.1	9 04.1	15.6	46 14.3	34.1	295 27.8	50.8	36 33.4	25.4
Y	15	57 56.6	24 03.6	. . 16.8	61 15.0	. . 33.3	310 30.1	. . 50.8	51 35.6	. . 25.5
	16	72 59.1	39 03.1	17.9	76 15.7	32.5	325 32.3	50.8	66 37.8	25.6
	17	88 01.5	54 02.7	19.0	91 16.3	31.7	340 34.6	50.7	81 40.0	25.7
	18	103 04.0	69 02.2	N13 20.1	106 17.0	S 2 31.0	355 36.9	N22 50.7	96 42.2	N 0 25.8
	19	118 06.5	84 01.7	21.2	121 17.7	30.2	10 39.1	50.7	111 44.3	26.0
	20	133 08.9	99 01.2	22.3	136 18.4	29.4	25 41.4	50.7	126 46.5	26.1
	21	148 11.4	114 00.7	. . 23.4	151 19.0	. . 28.6	40 43.6	. . 50.7	141 48.7	. . 26.2
	22	163 13.9	129 00.2	24.5	166 19.7	27.8	55 45.9	50.6	156 50.9	26.3
	23	178 16.3	143 59.8	25.7	181 20.4	27.0	70 48.2	50.6	171 53.1	26.4
	5 00	193 18.8	158 59.3	N13 26.8	196 21.1	S 2 26.2	85 50.4	N22 50.6	186 55.2	N 0 26.6
	01	208 21.3	173 58.8	27.9	211 21.8	25.5	100 52.7	50.6	201 57.4	26.7
	02	223 23.7	188 58.3	29.0	226 22.4	24.7	115 54.9	50.5	216 59.6	26.8
	03	238 26.2	203 57.8	. . 30.1	241 23.1	. . 23.9	130 57.2	. . 50.5	232 01.8	. . 26.9
	04	253 28.6	218 57.4	31.2	256 23.8	23.1	145 59.4	50.5	247 04.0	27.0
	05	268 31.1	233 56.9	32.3	271 24.5	22.3	161 01.7	50.5	262 06.1	27.2
	06	283 33.6	248 56.4	N13 33.4	286 25.1	S 2 21.5	176 04.0	N22 50.5	277 08.3	N 0 27.3
	07	298 36.0	263 55.9	34.5	301 25.8	20.8	191 06.2	50.4	292 10.5	27.4
	08	313 38.5	278 55.4	35.6	316 26.5	20.0	206 08.5	50.4	307 12.7	27.5
S	09	328 41.0	293 54.9	. . 36.7	331 27.2	. . 19.2	221 10.7	. . 50.4	322 14.9	. . 27.6
U	10	343 43.4	308 54.4	37.8	346 27.8	18.4	236 13.0	50.4	337 17.0	27.8
N	11	358 45.9	323 54.0	39.0	1 28.5	17.6	251 15.2	50.4	352 19.2	27.9
D	12	13 48.4	338 53.5	N13 40.1	16 29.2	S 2 16.8	266 17.5	N22 50.3	7 21.4	N 0 28.0
A	13	28 50.8	353 53.0	41.2	31 29.9	16.0	281 19.7	50.3	22 23.6	28.1
Y	14	43 53.3	8 52.5	42.3	46 30.5	15.3	296 22.0	50.3	37 25.7	28.2
	15	58 55.8	23 52.0	. . 43.4	61 31.2	. . 14.5	311 24.2	. . 50.3	52 27.9	. . 28.4
	16	73 58.2	38 51.5	44.5	76 31.9	13.7	326 26.5	50.2	67 30.1	28.5
	17	89 00.7	53 51.0	45.6	91 32.6	12.9	341 28.8	50.2	82 32.3	28.6
	18	104 03.1	68 50.5	N13 46.7	106 33.2	S 2 12.1	356 31.0	N22 50.2	97 34.5	N 0 28.7
	19	119 05.6	83 50.0	47.8	121 33.9	11.3	11 33.3	50.2	112 36.6	28.8
	20	134 08.1	98 49.6	48.9	136 34.6	10.6	26 35.5	50.2	127 38.8	29.0
	21	149 10.5	113 49.1	. . 50.0	151 35.3	. . 09.8	41 37.8	. . 50.1	142 41.0	. . 29.1
	22	164 13.0	128 48.6	51.1	166 36.0	09.0	56 40.0	50.1	157 43.2	29.2
	23	179 15.5	143 48.1	52.2	181 36.6	08.2	71 42.3	50.1	172 45.4	29.3
	6 00	194 17.9	158 47.6	N13 53.3	196 37.3	S 2 07.4	86 44.5	N22 50.1	187 47.5	N 0 29.4
	01	209 20.4	173 47.1	54.4	211 38.0	06.6	101 46.8	50.0	202 49.7	29.6
	02	224 22.9	188 46.6	55.5	226 38.7	05.8	116 49.0	50.0	217 51.9	29.7
	03	239 25.3	203 46.1	. . 56.5	241 39.3	. . 05.1	131 51.3	. . 50.0	232 54.1	. . 29.8
	04	254 27.8	218 45.6	57.6	256 40.0	04.3	146 53.5	50.0	247 56.3	29.9
	05	269 30.2	233 45.1	58.7	271 40.7	03.5	161 55.8	50.0	262 58.4	30.0
	06	284 32.7	248 44.6	N13 59.8	286 41.4	S 2 02.7	176 58.0	N22 49.9	278 00.6	N 0 30.2
	07	299 35.2	263 44.1	14 00.9	301 42.0	01.9	192 00.3	49.9	293 02.8	30.3
	08	314 37.6	278 43.6	02.0	316 42.7	01.1	207 02.5	49.9	308 05.0	30.4
M	09	329 40.1	293 43.1	. . 03.1	331 43.4	2 00.4	222 04.8	. . 49.9	323 07.2	. . 30.5
O	10	344 42.6	308 42.6	04.2	346 44.1	1 59.6	237 07.0	49.8	338 09.3	30.6
N	11	359 45.0	323 42.2	05.3	1 44.8	58.8	252 09.2	49.8	353 11.5	30.8
D	12	14 47.5	338 41.7	N14 06.4	16 45.4	S 1 58.0	267 11.5	N22 49.8	8 13.7	N 0 30.9
A	13	29 50.0	353 41.2	07.5	31 46.1	57.2	282 13.7	49.8	23 15.9	31.0
Y	14	44 52.4	8 40.7	08.6	46 46.8	56.4	297 16.0	49.8	38 18.1	31.1
	15	59 54.9	23 40.2	. . 09.6	61 47.5	. . 55.6	312 18.2	. . 49.7	53 20.2	. . 31.2
	16	74 57.4	38 39.7	10.7	76 48.1	54.9	327 20.5	49.7	68 22.4	31.4
	17	89 59.8	53 39.2	11.8	91 48.8	54.1	342 22.7	49.7	83 24.6	31.5
	18	105 02.3	68 38.7	N14 12.9	106 49.5	S 1 53.3	357 25.0	N22 49.7	98 26.8	N 0 31.6
	19	120 04.7	83 38.2	14.0	121 50.2	52.5	12 27.2	49.6	113 29.0	31.7
	20	135 07.2	98 37.7	15.1	136 50.9	51.7	27 29.5	49.6	128 31.1	31.8
	21	150 09.7	113 37.2	. . 16.2	151 51.5	. . 50.9	42 31.7	. . 49.6	143 33.3	. . 32.0
	22	165 12.1	128 36.7	17.2	166 52.2	50.1	57 33.9	49.6	158 35.5	32.1
	23	180 14.6	143 36.2	18.3	181 52.9	49.4	72 36.2	49.5	173 37.7	32.2
	Mer. Pass. (h m)	11 04.9	v −0.5	d 1.1	v 0.7	d 0.8	v 2.3	d 0.0	v 2.2	d 0.1

STARS

Name	SHA	Dec
	° ′	° ′
Acamar	315 11.4	S40 12.1
Achernar	335 20.0	S57 06.3
Acrux	172 58.3	S63 14.8
Adhara	255 05.1	S29 00.7
Aldebaran	290 38.7	N16 33.7
Alioth	166 11.5	N55 48.9
Alkaid	152 50.7	N49 10.7
Alnair	27 32.0	S46 49.9
Alnilam	275 36.8	S 1 11.2
Alphard	217 46.6	S 8 46.5
Alphecca	126 02.6	N26 37.3
Alpheratz	357 34.1	N29 14.0
Altair	61 59.0	N 8 56.1
Ankaa	353 06.5	S42 09.8
Antares	112 14.4	S26 29.4
Arcturus	145 46.7	N19 02.5
Atria	107 07.4	S69 04.3
Avior	234 14.1	S59 35.9
Bellatrix	278 21.9	N 6 22.3
Betelgeuse	270 51.1	N 7 24.6
Canopus	263 52.0	S52 42.8
Capella	280 20.6	N46 01.6
Deneb	49 25.3	N45 22.1
Denebola	182 23.6	N14 25.4
Diphda	348 46.6	S17 50.6
Dubhe	193 39.2	N61 36.6
Elnath	278 00.7	N28 37.8
Eltanin	90 41.6	N51 28.7
Enif	33 38.0	N 9 59.6
Fomalhaut	15 13.7	S29 29.0
Gacrux	171 50.0	S57 15.8
Gienah	175 42.2	S17 41.4
Hadar	148 34.0	S60 30.0
Hamal	327 50.4	N23 35.1
Kaus Aust.	83 31.1	S34 22.3
Kochab	137 18.8	N74 02.6
Markab	13 29.2	N15 20.7
Menkar	314 05.4	N 4 11.5
Menkent	147 56.1	S36 30.0
Miaplacidus	221 37.6	S69 49.8
Mirfak	308 27.2	N49 57.3
Nunki	75 46.5	S26 15.8
Peacock	53 04.3	S56 38.8
Pollux	243 16.0	N27 57.8
Procyon	244 49.7	N 5 09.4
Rasalhague	95 57.5	N12 32.2
Regulus	207 33.1	N11 50.2
Rigel	281 03.0	S 8 10.4
Rigil Kent.	139 38.3	S60 56.6
Sabik	102 01.5	S15 45.5
Schedar	349 30.5	N56 40.8
Shaula	96 08.8	S37 07.3
Sirius	258 25.4	S16 45.3
Spica	158 20.9	S11 18.1
Suhail	222 45.4	S43 32.6
Vega	80 32.5	N38 48.1
Zuben'ubi	136 54.6	S16 09.2

	SHA	Mer. Pass.
	° ′	h m
Venus	325 40.5	13 24
Mars	3 02.3	10 54
Jupiter	252 31.6	18 14
Saturn	353 36.4	11 31

UT (d h)	SUN GHA	SUN Dec	MOON GHA	v	MOON Dec	d	HP
	° ′	° ′	° ′	′	° ′	′	′
4 00 SATURDAY	179 13.6	N 5 36.7	340 06.3	13.8	S17 39.1	11.7	54.9
01	194 13.8	37.7	354 39.1	13.8	17 50.8	11.6	54.9
02	209 14.0	38.7	9 11.9	13.7	18 02.4	11.4	54.8
03	224 14.2	. . 39.6	23 44.6	13.7	18 13.8	11.4	54.8
04	239 14.4	40.6	38 17.3	13.6	18 25.2	11.4	54.8
05	254 14.6	41.5	52 49.9	13.6	18 36.6	11.2	54.8
06	269 14.7	N 5 42.5	67 22.5	13.5	S18 47.8	11.1	54.8
07	284 14.9	43.4	81 55.0	13.5	18 58.9	11.1	54.8
08	299 15.1	44.4	96 27.5	13.4	19 10.0	11.0	54.7
09	314 15.3	. . 45.3	110 59.9	13.4	19 21.0	10.8	54.7
10	329 15.5	46.3	125 32.3	13.3	19 31.8	10.8	54.7
11	344 15.6	47.2	140 04.6	13.3	19 42.6	10.7	54.7
12	359 15.8	N 5 48.2	154 36.9	13.3	S19 53.3	10.6	54.7
13	14 16.0	49.1	169 09.2	13.2	20 03.9	10.6	54.7
14	29 16.2	50.1	183 41.4	13.1	20 14.5	10.4	54.7
15	44 16.4	. . 51.0	198 13.5	13.1	20 24.9	10.3	54.6
16	59 16.5	52.0	212 45.6	13.0	20 35.2	10.2	54.6
17	74 16.7	52.9	227 17.6	13.0	20 45.4	10.2	54.6
18	89 16.9	N 5 53.9	241 49.6	13.0	S20 55.6	10.0	54.6
19	104 17.1	54.8	256 21.6	12.8	21 05.6	10.0	54.6
20	119 17.3	55.8	270 53.4	12.9	21 15.6	9.8	54.6
21	134 17.5	. . 56.7	285 25.3	12.8	21 25.4	9.8	54.6
22	149 17.6	57.7	299 57.1	12.7	21 35.2	9.6	54.5
23	164 17.8	58.6	314 28.8	12.7	21 44.8	9.6	54.5
5 00 SUNDAY	179 18.0	N 5 59.6	329 00.5	12.6	S21 54.4	9.4	54.5
01	194 18.2	6 00.5	343 32.1	12.6	22 03.8	9.4	54.5
02	209 18.4	01.5	358 03.7	12.5	22 13.2	9.2	54.5
03	224 18.5	. . 02.4	12 35.2	12.5	22 22.4	9.1	54.5
04	239 18.7	03.4	27 06.7	12.4	22 31.5	9.1	54.5
05	254 18.9	04.3	41 38.1	12.3	22 40.6	8.9	54.5
06	269 19.1	N 6 05.3	56 09.4	12.4	S22 49.5	8.8	54.5
07	284 19.3	06.2	70 40.8	12.2	22 58.3	8.8	54.4
08	299 19.4	07.2	85 12.0	12.2	23 07.1	8.6	54.4
09	314 19.6	. . 08.1	99 43.2	12.2	23 15.7	8.5	54.4
10	329 19.8	09.1	114 14.4	12.1	23 24.2	8.4	54.4
11	344 20.0	10.0	128 45.5	12.0	23 32.6	8.3	54.4
12	359 20.2	N 6 11.0	143 16.5	12.0	S23 40.9	8.1	54.4
13	14 20.3	11.9	157 47.5	12.0	23 49.0	8.1	54.4
14	29 20.5	12.9	172 18.5	11.9	23 57.1	8.0	54.4
15	44 20.7	. . 13.8	186 49.4	11.9	24 05.1	7.8	54.4
16	59 20.9	14.8	201 20.3	11.7	24 12.9	7.8	54.3
17	74 21.1	15.7	215 51.0	11.8	24 20.7	7.6	54.3
18	89 21.2	N 6 16.7	230 21.8	11.7	S24 28.3	7.5	54.3
19	104 21.4	17.6	244 52.5	11.6	24 35.8	7.4	54.3
20	119 21.6	18.6	259 23.1	11.6	24 43.2	7.2	54.3
21	134 21.8	. . 19.5	273 53.7	11.6	24 50.4	7.2	54.3
22	149 21.9	20.5	288 24.3	11.5	24 57.6	7.0	54.3
23	164 22.1	21.4	302 54.8	11.4	25 04.6	7.0	54.3
6 00 MONDAY	179 22.3	N 6 22.3	317 25.2	11.5	S25 11.6	6.8	54.3
01	194 22.5	23.3	331 55.7	11.3	25 18.4	6.7	54.3
02	209 22.7	24.2	346 26.0	11.3	25 25.1	6.5	54.3
03	224 22.8	. . 25.2	0 56.3	11.3	25 31.6	6.5	54.3
04	239 23.0	26.1	15 26.6	11.2	25 38.1	6.3	54.2
05	254 23.2	27.1	29 56.8	11.2	25 44.4	6.2	54.2
06	269 23.4	N 6 28.0	44 27.0	11.1	S25 50.6	6.1	54.2
07	284 23.6	29.0	58 57.1	11.1	25 56.7	6.0	54.2
08	299 23.7	29.9	73 27.2	11.0	26 02.7	5.8	54.2
09	314 23.9	. . 30.8	87 57.2	11.0	26 08.5	5.8	54.2
10	329 24.1	31.8	102 27.2	11.0	26 14.3	5.6	54.2
11	344 24.3	32.7	116 57.2	10.9	26 19.9	5.4	54.2
12	359 24.4	N 6 33.7	131 27.1	10.8	S26 25.3	5.4	54.2
13	14 24.6	34.6	145 56.9	10.8	26 30.7	5.2	54.2
14	29 24.8	35.6	160 26.7	10.8	26 35.9	5.1	54.2
15	44 25.0	. . 36.5	174 56.5	10.8	26 41.0	5.0	54.2
16	59 25.2	37.5	189 26.3	10.7	26 46.0	4.8	54.2
17	74 25.3	38.4	203 56.0	10.6	26 50.8	4.7	54.2
18	89 25.5	N 6 39.3	218 25.6	10.7	S26 55.5	4.6	54.2
19	104 25.7	40.3	232 55.3	10.6	27 00.1	4.5	54.2
20	119 25.9	41.2	247 24.9	10.5	27 04.6	4.3	54.2
21	134 26.0	. . 42.2	261 54.4	10.5	27 08.9	4.2	54.2
22	149 26.2	43.1	276 23.9	10.5	27 13.1	4.1	54.2
23	164 26.4	44.0	290 53.4	10.5	S27 17.2	3.9	54.2
	SD 16.0	d 0.9	SD 14.9		14.8		14.8

Lat.	Twilight Naut.	Twilight Civil	Sunrise	Moonrise 4	Moonrise 5	Moonrise 6	Moonrise 7
°	h m	h m	h m	h m	h m	h m	h m
N 72	00 08	03 16	04 35	01 10	▬	▬	▬
N 70	01 46	03 36	04 44	▬	▬	▬	▬
68	02 23	03 51	04 52	▬	▬	▬	▬
66	02 48	04 04	04 59	24 27	00 27	▬	▬
64	03 07	04 14	05 04	23 47	26 07	02 07	▬
62	03 22	04 22	05 09	23 19	25 06	01 06	03 04
60	03 35	04 30	05 13	22 58	24 32	00 32	02 02
N 58	03 45	04 36	05 17	22 41	24 07	00 07	01 28
56	03 54	04 42	05 20	22 26	23 48	25 03	01 03
54	04 02	04 47	05 23	22 14	23 31	24 43	00 43
52	04 09	04 51	05 26	22 03	23 17	24 26	00 26
50	04 15	04 55	05 28	21 53	23 05	24 12	00 12
45	04 28	05 04	05 34	21 33	22 40	23 43	24 40
N 40	04 38	05 10	05 38	21 16	22 20	23 20	24 16
35	04 46	05 16	05 42	21 03	22 03	23 02	23 57
30	04 52	05 21	05 45	20 51	21 49	22 46	23 40
20	05 02	05 28	05 50	20 31	21 25	22 19	23 12
N 10	05 09	05 34	05 55	20 13	21 04	21 55	22 48
0	05 14	05 39	05 59	19 57	20 44	21 34	22 25
S 10	05 18	05 43	06 04	19 41	20 25	21 12	22 03
20	05 20	05 46	06 08	19 23	20 04	20 49	21 38
30	05 21	05 49	06 13	19 04	19 41	20 23	21 10
35	05 21	05 50	06 16	18 52	19 27	20 07	20 54
40	05 20	05 52	06 19	18 39	19 11	19 49	20 34
45	05 19	05 53	06 22	18 24	18 52	19 27	20 11
S 50	05 17	05 54	06 27	18 05	18 28	19 00	19 41
52	05 16	05 55	06 29	17 56	18 17	18 46	19 26
54	05 14	05 55	06 31	17 46	18 04	18 31	19 09
56	05 13	05 56	06 33	17 35	17 50	18 12	18 48
58	05 11	05 56	06 36	17 23	17 32	17 50	18 22
S 60	05 09	05 57	06 39	17 08	17 12	17 21	17 45

Lat.	Sunset	Twilight Civil	Twilight Naut.	Moonset 4	Moonset 5	Moonset 6	Moonset 7
°	h m	h m	h m	h m	h m	h m	h m
N 72	19 34	20 54	////	01 13	▬	▬	▬
N 70	19 24	20 33	22 29	03 03	▬	▬	▬
68	19 15	20 17	21 48	03 43	▬	▬	▬
66	19 09	20 04	21 22	04 11	03 35	▬	▬
64	19 03	19 54	21 02	04 33	04 17	03 36	▬
62	18 58	19 45	20 46	04 50	04 45	04 38	04 23
60	18 53	19 37	20 33	05 05	05 07	05 12	05 27
N 58	18 50	19 31	20 22	05 17	05 25	05 37	06 01
56	18 46	19 25	20 13	05 28	05 40	05 58	06 26
54	18 43	19 20	20 05	05 38	05 53	06 14	06 46
52	18 41	19 15	19 58	05 46	06 04	06 29	07 03
50	18 38	19 11	19 51	05 54	06 14	06 41	07 17
45	18 33	19 03	19 38	06 10	06 36	07 07	07 46
N 40	18 28	18 56	19 28	06 24	06 53	07 28	08 10
35	18 24	18 50	19 20	06 36	07 08	07 45	08 29
30	18 21	18 45	19 14	06 46	07 21	08 00	08 45
20	18 15	18 38	19 04	07 03	07 43	08 26	09 13
N 10	18 10	18 32	18 56	07 19	08 02	08 48	09 36
0	18 06	18 27	18 51	07 33	08 19	09 08	09 58
S 10	18 02	18 23	18 47	07 47	08 37	09 29	10 21
20	17 57	18 19	18 45	08 03	08 57	09 51	10 45
30	17 52	18 16	18 44	08 21	09 19	10 16	11 12
35	17 49	18 14	18 44	08 31	09 32	10 32	11 29
40	17 46	18 13	18 44	08 43	09 47	10 49	11 48
45	17 42	18 11	18 45	08 58	10 05	11 11	12 11
S 50	17 38	18 10	18 47	09 15	10 28	11 38	12 41
52	17 36	18 09	18 48	09 23	10 39	11 51	12 56
54	17 34	18 09	18 50	09 33	10 51	12 06	13 13
56	17 31	18 08	18 51	09 43	11 05	12 24	13 34
58	17 29	18 08	18 53	09 55	11 22	12 46	14 00
S 60	17 26	18 07	18 55	10 09	11 42	13 15	14 36

Day	SUN Eqn. of Time 00^h	SUN Eqn. of Time 12^h	SUN Mer. Pass.	MOON Mer. Pass. Upper	MOON Mer. Pass. Lower	Age	%	Phase
d	m s	m s	h m	h m	h m	d	%	
4	03 06	02 57	12 03	01 22	13 45	16	94	
5	02 48	02 40	12 03	02 08	14 32	17	89	
6	02 31	02 23	12 02	02 56	15 21	18	82	

Day	UT (d h)	ARIES GHA	VENUS −3·9 GHA	VENUS Dec	MARS +1·2 GHA	MARS Dec	JUPITER −2·1 GHA	JUPITER Dec	SATURN +0·9 GHA	SATURN Dec	STARS Name	SHA	Dec
		° ′	° ′	° ′	° ′	° ′	° ′	° ′	° ′	° ′		° ′	° ′
TUESDAY	7 00	195 17.1	158 35.7	N14 19.4	196 53.6	S 1 48.6	87 38.4	N22 49.5	188 39.9	N 0 32.3	Acamar	315 11.4	S40 12.1
	01	210 19.5	173 35.2	20.5	211 54.3	47.8	102 40.7	49.5	203 42.0	32.4	Achernar	335 20.0	S57 06.2
	02	225 22.0	188 34.7	21.6	226 54.9	47.0	117 42.9	49.5	218 44.2	32.6	Acrux	172 58.3	S63 14.8
	03	240 24.5	203 34.2	. . 22.7	241 55.6	. . 46.2	132 45.2	. . 49.5	233 46.4	. . 32.7	Adhara	255 05.1	S29 00.7
	04	255 26.9	218 33.7	23.7	256 56.3	45.4	147 47.4	49.4	248 48.6	32.8	Aldebaran	290 38.7	N16 33.7
	05	270 29.4	233 33.2	24.8	271 57.0	44.7	162 49.6	49.4	263 50.8	32.9			
	06	285 31.9	248 32.6	N14 25.9	286 57.6	S 1 43.9	177 51.9	N22 49.4	278 52.9	N 0 33.0	Alioth	166 11.5	N55 48.9
	07	300 34.3	263 32.1	27.0	301 58.3	43.1	192 54.1	49.4	293 55.1	33.2	Alkaid	152 50.7	N49 10.8
	08	315 36.8	278 31.6	28.1	316 59.0	42.3	207 56.4	49.3	308 57.3	33.3	Alnair	27 31.9	S46 49.9
	09	330 39.2	293 31.1	. . 29.1	331 59.7	. . 41.5	222 58.6	. . 49.3	323 59.5	. . 33.4	Alnilam	275 36.8	S 1 11.2
	10	345 41.7	308 30.6	30.2	347 00.4	40.7	238 00.8	49.3	339 01.7	33.5	Alphard	217 46.6	S 8 46.5
	11	0 44.2	323 30.1	31.3	2 01.0	39.9	253 03.1	49.3	354 03.8	33.6			
	12	15 46.6	338 29.6	N14 32.4	17 01.7	S 1 39.2	268 05.3	N22 49.2	9 06.0	N 0 33.8	Alphecca	126 02.6	N26 37.3
	13	30 49.1	353 29.1	33.4	32 02.4	38.4	283 07.6	49.2	24 08.2	33.9	Alpheratz	357 34.1	N29 14.0
	14	45 51.6	8 28.6	34.5	47 03.1	37.6	298 09.8	49.2	39 10.4	34.0	Altair	61 59.0	N 8 56.1
	15	60 54.0	23 28.1	. . 35.6	62 03.8	. . 36.8	313 12.0	. . 49.2	54 12.6	. . 34.1	Ankaa	353 06.5	S42 09.8
	16	75 56.5	38 27.6	36.7	77 04.4	36.0	328 14.3	49.1	69 14.7	34.2	Antares	112 14.3	S26 29.4
	17	90 59.0	53 27.1	37.7	92 05.1	35.2	343 16.5	49.1	84 16.9	34.4			
	18	106 01.4	68 26.6	N14 38.8	107 05.8	S 1 34.4	358 18.8	N22 49.1	99 19.1	N 0 34.5	Arcturus	145 46.7	N19 02.5
	19	121 03.9	83 26.1	39.9	122 06.5	33.7	13 21.0	49.1	114 21.3	34.6	Atria	107 07.4	S69 04.3
	20	136 06.4	98 25.5	40.9	137 07.2	32.9	28 23.2	49.1	129 23.5	34.7	Avior	234 14.2	S59 35.9
	21	151 08.8	113 25.0	. . 42.0	152 07.8	. . 32.1	43 25.5	. . 49.0	144 25.6	. . 34.8	Bellatrix	278 21.9	N 6 22.3
	22	166 11.3	128 24.5	43.1	167 08.5	31.3	58 27.7	49.0	159 27.8	34.9	Betelgeuse	270 51.1	N 7 24.6
	23	181 13.7	143 24.0	44.1	182 09.2	30.5	73 29.9	49.0	174 30.0	35.1			
WEDNESDAY	8 00	196 16.2	158 23.5	N14 45.2	197 09.9	S 1 29.7	88 32.2	N22 49.0	189 32.2	N 0 35.2	Canopus	263 52.1	S52 42.8
	01	211 18.7	173 23.0	46.3	212 10.6	29.0	103 34.4	48.9	204 34.4	35.3	Capella	280 20.6	N46 01.6
	02	226 21.1	188 22.5	47.3	227 11.2	28.2	118 36.6	48.9	219 36.5	35.4	Deneb	49 25.3	N45 22.1
	03	241 23.6	203 22.0	. . 48.4	242 11.9	. . 27.4	133 38.9	. . 48.9	234 38.7	. . 35.5	Denebola	182 23.6	N14 25.4
	04	256 26.1	218 21.5	49.5	257 12.6	26.6	148 41.1	48.9	249 40.9	35.7	Diphda	348 46.6	S17 50.6
	05	271 28.5	233 20.9	50.5	272 13.3	25.8	163 43.4	48.8	264 43.1	35.8			
	06	286 31.0	248 20.4	N14 51.6	287 14.0	S 1 25.0	178 45.6	N22 48.8	279 45.3	N 0 35.9	Dubhe	193 39.2	N61 36.6
	07	301 33.5	263 19.9	52.7	302 14.6	24.2	193 47.8	48.8	294 47.4	36.0	Elnath	278 00.7	N28 37.8
	08	316 35.9	278 19.4	53.7	317 15.3	23.5	208 50.1	48.8	309 49.6	36.1	Eltanin	90 41.5	N51 28.7
	09	331 38.4	293 18.9	. . 54.8	332 16.0	. . 22.7	223 52.3	. . 48.7	324 51.8	. . 36.3	Enif	33 38.0	N 9 59.6
	10	346 40.8	308 18.4	55.9	347 16.7	21.9	238 54.5	48.7	339 54.0	36.4	Fomalhaut	15 13.7	S29 29.0
	11	1 43.3	323 17.9	56.9	2 17.4	21.1	253 56.8	48.7	354 56.2	36.5			
	12	16 45.8	338 17.3	N14 58.0	17 18.0	S 1 20.3	268 59.0	N22 48.7	9 58.3	N 0 36.6	Gacrux	171 50.0	S57 15.8
	13	31 48.2	353 16.8	14 59.0	32 18.7	19.5	284 01.2	48.6	25 00.5	36.7	Gienah	175 42.2	S17 41.5
	14	46 50.7	8 16.3	15 00.1	47 19.4	18.7	299 03.4	48.6	40 02.7	36.9	Hadar	148 33.9	S60 30.0
	15	61 53.2	23 15.8	. . 01.2	62 20.1	. . 18.0	314 05.7	. . 48.6	55 04.9	. . 37.0	Hamal	327 50.4	N23 35.1
	16	76 55.6	38 15.3	02.2	77 20.8	17.2	329 07.9	48.6	70 07.1	37.1	Kaus Aust.	83 31.1	S34 22.2
	17	91 58.1	53 14.7	03.3	92 21.4	16.4	344 10.1	48.5	85 09.3	37.2			
	18	107 00.6	68 14.2	N15 04.3	107 22.1	S 1 15.6	359 12.4	N22 48.5	100 11.4	N 0 37.3	Kochab	137 18.7	N74 02.6
	19	122 03.0	83 13.7	05.4	122 22.8	14.8	14 14.6	48.5	115 13.6	37.4	Markab	13 29.2	N15 20.7
	20	137 05.5	98 13.2	06.4	137 23.5	14.0	29 16.8	48.5	130 15.8	37.6	Menkar	314 05.4	N 4 11.5
	21	152 08.0	113 12.7	. . 07.5	152 24.2	. . 13.3	44 19.1	. . 48.4	145 18.0	. . 37.7	Menkent	147 56.0	S36 30.0
	22	167 10.4	128 12.1	08.6	167 24.9	12.5	59 21.3	48.4	160 20.2	37.8	Miaplacidus	221 37.7	S69 49.8
	23	182 12.9	143 11.6	09.6	182 25.5	11.7	74 23.5	48.4	175 22.3	37.9			
THURSDAY	9 00	197 15.3	158 11.1	N15 10.7	197 26.2	S 1 10.9	89 25.7	N22 48.4	190 24.5	N 0 38.0	Mirfak	308 27.2	N49 57.3
	01	212 17.8	173 10.6	11.7	212 26.9	10.1	104 28.0	48.3	205 26.7	38.2	Nunki	75 46.5	S26 15.8
	02	227 20.3	188 10.1	12.8	227 27.6	09.3	119 30.2	48.3	220 28.9	38.3	Peacock	53 04.3	S56 38.8
	03	242 22.7	203 09.5	. . 13.8	242 28.3	. . 08.5	134 32.4	. . 48.3	235 31.1	. . 38.4	Pollux	243 16.0	N27 57.8
	04	257 25.2	218 09.0	14.9	257 28.9	07.8	149 34.7	48.3	250 33.2	38.5	Procyon	244 49.7	N 5 09.4
	05	272 27.7	233 08.5	15.9	272 29.6	07.0	164 36.9	48.2	265 35.4	38.6			
	06	287 30.1	248 08.0	N15 17.0	287 30.3	S 1 06.2	179 39.1	N22 48.2	280 37.6	N 0 38.8	Rasalhague	95 57.5	N12 32.2
	07	302 32.6	263 07.4	18.0	302 31.0	05.4	194 41.3	48.2	295 39.8	38.9	Regulus	207 33.1	N11 50.2
	08	317 35.1	278 06.9	19.1	317 31.7	04.6	209 43.6	48.2	310 42.0	39.0	Rigel	281 03.0	S 8 10.4
	09	332 37.5	293 06.4	. . 20.1	332 32.4	. . 03.8	224 45.8	. . 48.1	325 44.1	. . 39.1	Rigil Kent.	139 38.3	S60 56.6
	10	347 40.0	308 05.9	21.1	347 33.0	03.0	239 48.0	48.1	340 46.3	39.2	Sabik	102 01.4	S15 45.5
	11	2 42.5	323 05.3	22.2	2 33.7	02.3	254 50.2	48.1	355 48.5	39.4			
	12	17 44.9	338 04.8	N15 23.2	17 34.4	S 1 01.5	269 52.5	N22 48.1	10 50.7	N 0 39.5	Schedar	349 30.5	N56 40.8
	13	32 47.4	353 04.3	24.3	32 35.1	1 00.7	284 54.7	48.0	25 52.9	39.6	Shaula	96 08.8	S37 07.3
	14	47 49.8	8 03.8	25.3	47 35.8	0 59.9	299 56.9	48.0	40 55.1	39.7	Sirius	258 25.4	S16 45.3
	15	62 52.3	23 03.2	. . 26.4	62 36.4	. . 59.1	314 59.1	. . 48.0	55 57.2	. . 39.8	Spica	158 20.9	S11 18.1
	16	77 54.8	38 02.7	27.4	77 37.1	58.3	330 01.4	48.0	70 59.4	39.9	Suhail	222 45.4	S43 32.6
	17	92 57.2	53 02.2	28.5	92 37.8	57.6	345 03.6	47.9	86 01.6	40.1			
	18	107 59.7	68 01.6	N15 29.5	107 38.5	S 0 56.8	0 05.8	N22 47.9	101 03.8	N 0 40.2	Vega	80 32.5	N38 48.1
	19	123 02.2	83 01.1	30.5	122 39.2	56.0	15 08.0	47.9	116 06.0	40.3	Zuben'ubi	136 54.6	S16 09.2
	20	138 04.6	98 00.6	31.6	137 39.9	55.2	30 10.3	47.9	131 08.1	40.4			
	21	153 07.1	113 00.1	. . 32.6	152 40.5	. . 54.4	45 12.5	. . 47.8	146 10.3	. . 40.5			
	22	168 09.6	127 59.5	33.7	167 41.2	53.6	60 14.7	47.8	161 12.5	40.7			
	23	183 12.0	142 59.0	34.7	182 41.9	52.8	75 16.9	47.8	176 14.7	40.8			
	Mer. Pass.	10 53.1 (h m)	*v* −0.5	*d* 1.1	*v* 0.7	*d* 0.8	*v* 2.2	*d* 0.0	*v* 2.2	*d* 0.1			

	SHA (° ′)	Mer. Pass. (h m)
Venus	322 07.3	13 27
Mars	0 53.7	10 51
Jupiter	252 16.0	18 03
Saturn	353 16.0	11 20

	UT	SUN GHA	SUN Dec	MOON GHA	v	MOON Dec	d	HP
	d h	° ′	° ′	° ′	′	° ′	′	′
TUESDAY	7 00	179 26.6	N 6 45.0	305 22.9	10.4	S27 21.1	3.9	54.2
	01	194 26.7	45.9	319 52.3	10.4	27 25.0	3.6	54.2
	02	209 26.9	46.9	334 21.7	10.3	27 28.6	3.6	54.2
	03	224 27.1	. . 47.8	348 51.0	10.3	27 32.2	3.4	54.1
	04	239 27.3	48.7	3 20.3	10.3	27 35.6	3.3	54.1
	05	254 27.4	49.7	17 49.6	10.3	27 38.9	3.2	54.1
	06	269 27.6	N 6 50.6	32 18.9	10.2	S27 42.1	3.0	54.1
	07	284 27.8	51.6	46 48.1	10.2	27 45.1	2.9	54.1
	08	299 28.0	52.5	61 17.3	10.2	27 48.0	2.7	54.1
	09	314 28.1	. . 53.4	75 46.5	10.2	27 50.7	2.7	54.1
	10	329 28.3	54.4	90 15.7	10.1	27 53.4	2.4	54.1
	11	344 28.5	55.3	104 44.8	10.1	27 55.8	2.4	54.1
	12	359 28.7	N 6 56.3	119 13.9	10.1	S27 58.2	2.2	54.1
	13	14 28.8	57.2	133 43.0	10.1	28 00.4	2.1	54.1
	14	29 29.0	58.1	148 12.1	10.0	28 02.5	2.0	54.1
	15	44 29.2	6 59.1	162 41.1	10.0	28 04.5	1.8	54.2
	16	59 29.4	7 00.0	177 10.1	10.0	28 06.3	1.7	54.2
	17	74 29.5	01.0	191 39.1	10.0	28 08.0	1.5	54.2
	18	89 29.7	N 7 01.9	206 08.1	10.0	S28 09.5	1.4	54.2
	19	104 29.9	02.8	220 37.1	10.0	28 10.9	1.3	54.2
	20	119 30.1	03.8	235 06.1	9.9	28 12.2	1.1	54.2
	21	134 30.2	. . 04.7	249 35.0	9.9	28 13.3	1.0	54.2
	22	149 30.4	05.6	264 03.9	10.0	28 14.3	0.9	54.2
	23	164 30.6	06.6	278 32.9	9.9	28 15.2	0.7	54.2
WEDNESDAY	8 00	179 30.8	N 7 07.5	293 01.8	9.9	S28 15.9	0.6	54.2
	01	194 30.9	08.4	307 30.7	9.9	28 16.5	0.5	54.2
	02	209 31.1	09.4	321 59.6	9.8	28 17.0	0.3	54.2
	03	224 31.3	. . 10.3	336 28.4	9.9	28 17.3	0.2	54.2
	04	239 31.5	11.3	350 57.3	9.9	28 17.5	0.0	54.2
	05	254 31.6	12.2	5 26.2	9.8	28 17.5	0.1	54.2
	06	269 31.8	N 7 13.1	19 55.0	9.9	S28 17.4	0.2	54.2
	07	284 32.0	14.1	34 23.9	9.9	28 17.2	0.4	54.2
	08	299 32.2	15.0	48 52.8	9.8	28 16.8	0.5	54.2
	09	314 32.3	. . 15.9	63 21.6	9.9	28 16.3	0.6	54.2
	10	329 32.5	16.9	77 50.5	9.8	28 15.7	0.8	54.2
	11	344 32.7	17.8	92 19.3	9.9	28 14.9	0.9	54.2
	12	359 32.8	N 7 18.7	106 48.2	9.9	S28 14.0	1.1	54.2
	13	14 33.0	19.7	121 17.1	9.8	28 12.9	1.1	54.3
	14	29 33.2	20.6	135 45.9	9.9	28 11.8	1.4	54.3
	15	44 33.4	. . 21.5	150 14.8	9.9	28 10.4	1.4	54.3
	16	59 33.5	22.5	164 43.7	9.9	28 09.0	1.6	54.3
	17	74 33.7	23.4	179 12.6	9.9	28 07.4	1.8	54.3
	18	89 33.9	N 7 24.3	193 41.5	9.9	S28 05.6	1.8	54.3
	19	104 34.0	25.3	208 10.4	9.9	28 03.8	2.1	54.3
	20	119 34.2	26.2	222 39.3	9.9	28 01.7	2.1	54.3
	21	134 34.4	. . 27.1	237 08.2	9.9	27 59.6	2.3	54.3
	22	149 34.6	28.1	251 37.1	10.0	27 57.3	2.4	54.3
	23	164 34.7	29.0	266 06.1	9.9	27 54.9	2.6	54.4
THURSDAY	9 00	179 34.9	N 7 29.9	280 35.0	10.0	S27 52.3	2.7	54.4
	01	194 35.1	30.8	295 04.0	10.0	27 49.6	2.8	54.4
	02	209 35.2	31.8	309 33.0	10.0	27 46.8	3.0	54.4
	03	224 35.4	. . 32.7	324 02.0	10.0	27 43.8	3.1	54.4
	04	239 35.6	33.6	338 31.0	10.0	27 40.7	3.2	54.4
	05	254 35.8	34.6	353 00.0	10.1	27 37.5	3.4	54.4
	06	269 35.9	N 7 35.5	7 29.1	10.1	S27 34.1	3.5	54.4
	07	284 36.1	36.4	21 58.2	10.1	27 30.6	3.6	54.4
	08	299 36.3	37.4	36 27.3	10.1	27 27.0	3.8	54.5
	09	314 36.4	. . 38.3	50 56.4	10.2	27 23.2	3.9	54.5
	10	329 36.6	39.2	65 25.6	10.1	27 19.3	4.0	54.5
	11	344 36.8	40.1	79 54.7	10.2	27 15.3	4.2	54.5
	12	359 36.9	N 7 41.1	94 23.9	10.2	S27 11.1	4.3	54.5
	13	14 37.1	42.0	108 53.1	10.3	27 06.8	4.4	54.5
	14	29 37.3	42.9	123 22.4	10.3	27 02.4	4.6	54.5
	15	44 37.5	. . 43.9	137 51.7	10.2	26 57.8	4.7	54.6
	16	59 37.6	44.8	152 20.9	10.4	26 53.1	4.9	54.6
	17	74 37.8	45.7	166 50.3	10.3	26 48.2	4.9	54.6
	18	89 38.0	N 7 46.6	181 19.6	10.4	S26 43.3	5.1	54.6
	19	104 38.1	47.6	195 49.0	10.4	26 38.2	5.3	54.6
	20	119 38.3	48.5	210 18.4	10.5	26 32.9	5.3	54.6
	21	134 38.5	. . 49.4	224 47.9	10.4	26 27.6	5.5	54.7
	22	149 38.6	50.3	239 17.3	10.6	26 22.1	5.6	54.7
	23	164 38.8	51.3	253 46.9	10.5	S26 16.5	5.8	54.7
		SD 16.0	d 0.9	SD 14.8		14.8		14.9

Lat.	Twilight Naut.	Twilight Civil	Sunrise	Moonrise 7	Moonrise 8	Moonrise 9	Moonrise 10
°	h m	h m	h m	h m	h m	h m	h m
N 72	////	02 55	04 19	■	■	■	■
N 70	01 09	03 19	04 30	■	■	■	■
68	02 00	03 36	04 40	■	■	■	■
66	02 30	03 51	04 47	■	■	■	■
64	02 52	04 02	04 54	■	■	■	05 41
62	03 10	04 12	04 59	03 04	■	04 53	04 38
60	03 24	04 20	05 04	02 02	03 12	03 49	04 04
N 58	03 35	04 27	05 09	01 28	02 32	03 15	03 38
56	03 45	04 34	05 13	01 03	02 05	02 50	03 18
54	03 54	04 39	05 16	00 43	01 44	02 30	03 02
52	04 01	04 44	05 19	00 26	01 26	02 13	02 47
50	04 08	04 49	05 22	00 12	01 11	01 58	02 35
45	04 22	04 58	05 28	24 40	00 40	01 29	02 09
N 40	04 33	05 05	05 33	24 16	00 16	01 06	01 48
35	04 41	05 12	05 37	23 57	24 47	00 47	01 31
30	04 48	05 17	05 41	23 40	24 30	00 30	01 16
20	04 59	05 25	05 48	23 12	24 03	00 03	00 50
N 10	05 08	05 32	05 53	22 48	23 39	24 28	00 28
0	05 14	05 38	05 59	22 25	23 17	24 08	00 08
S 10	05 18	05 42	06 04	22 03	22 54	23 47	24 39
20	05 21	05 47	06 09	21 38	22 31	23 25	24 20
30	05 23	05 51	06 15	21 10	22 03	22 59	23 58
35	05 23	05 53	06 18	20 54	21 46	22 44	23 45
40	05 23	05 55	06 22	20 34	21 27	22 26	23 30
45	05 23	05 57	06 26	20 11	21 04	22 05	23 12
S 50	05 22	05 59	06 31	19 41	20 34	21 38	22 49
52	05 21	06 00	06 34	19 26	20 19	21 25	22 38
54	05 20	06 01	06 36	19 09	20 02	21 09	22 26
56	05 19	06 02	06 39	18 48	19 41	20 51	22 12
58	05 17	06 03	06 42	18 22	19 15	20 29	21 55
S 60	05 16	06 04	06 46	17 45	18 39	20 01	21 35

Lat.	Sunset	Twilight Civil	Twilight Naut.	Moonset 7	Moonset 8	Moonset 9	Moonset 10
°	h m	h m	h m	h m	h m	h m	h m
N 72	19 48	21 14	////	■	■	■	■
N 70	19 36	20 49	23 09	■	■	■	■
68	19 27	20 31	22 10	■	■	■	■
66	19 19	20 16	21 38	■	■	■	■
64	19 12	20 04	21 15	■	■	■	07 08
62	19 06	19 54	20 57	04 23	■	06 10	08 10
60	19 01	19 45	20 43	05 27	06 03	07 13	08 44
N 58	18 56	19 38	20 31	06 01	06 42	07 47	09 09
56	18 52	19 32	20 20	06 26	07 10	08 12	09 28
54	18 49	19 26	20 11	06 46	07 31	08 32	09 45
52	18 46	19 21	20 04	07 03	07 49	08 49	09 59
50	18 43	19 16	19 57	07 17	08 04	09 03	10 11
45	18 36	19 07	19 43	07 46	08 35	09 32	10 36
N 40	18 31	18 59	19 32	08 10	08 59	09 55	10 56
35	18 27	18 53	19 23	08 29	09 18	10 13	11 13
30	18 23	18 47	19 16	08 45	09 35	10 29	11 27
20	18 16	18 38	19 05	09 13	10 03	10 57	11 51
N 10	18 10	18 32	18 56	09 36	10 27	11 20	12 12
0	18 05	18 26	18 50	09 58	10 50	11 41	12 32
S 10	18 00	18 21	18 46	10 21	11 12	12 03	12 51
20	17 54	18 17	18 42	10 45	11 37	12 26	13 12
30	17 48	18 12	18 40	11 12	12 05	12 52	13 35
35	17 45	18 10	18 40	11 29	12 21	13 08	13 49
40	17 41	18 08	18 40	11 48	12 41	13 26	14 05
45	17 37	18 06	18 40	12 11	13 04	13 48	14 24
S 50	17 31	18 04	18 41	12 41	13 34	14 16	14 48
52	17 29	18 03	18 42	12 56	13 49	14 29	14 59
54	17 26	18 02	18 43	13 13	14 06	14 45	15 12
56	17 23	18 01	18 44	13 34	14 27	15 03	15 26
58	17 20	18 00	18 45	14 00	14 53	15 26	15 43
S 60	17 17	17 58	18 46	14 36	15 30	15 54	16 04

Day	SUN Eqn. of Time 00^h	SUN Eqn. of Time 12^h	SUN Mer. Pass.	MOON Mer. Pass. Upper	MOON Mer. Pass. Lower	MOON Age	MOON %	Phase
d	m s	m s	h m	h m	h m	d	%	
7	02 14	02 06	12 02	03 46	16 12	19	75	
8	01 57	01 49	12 02	04 37	17 03	20	66	
9	01 41	01 33	12 02	05 29	17 54	21	57	

2026 APRIL 10, 11, 12 (FRI., SAT., SUN.)

UT		ARIES	VENUS −3·9		MARS +1·2		JUPITER −2·1		SATURN +0·9	
d	h	GHA ° ′	GHA ° ′	Dec ° ′	GHA ° ′	Dec ° ′	GHA ° ′	Dec ° ′	GHA ° ′	Dec ° ′
10 FRIDAY	00	198 14.5	157 58.5	N15 35.7	197 42.6	S 0 52.1	90 19.1	N22 47.8	191 16.9	N 0 40.9
	01	213 17.0	172 57.9	36.8	212 43.3	51.3	105 21.4	47.7	206 19.0	41.0
	02	228 19.4	187 57.4	37.8	227 44.0	50.5	120 23.6	47.7	221 21.2	41.1
	03	243 21.9	202 56.9	. . 38.8	242 44.6	. . 49.7	135 25.8	. . 47.7	236 23.4	. . 41.2
	04	258 24.3	217 56.3	39.9	257 45.3	48.9	150 28.0	47.7	251 25.6	41.4
	05	273 26.8	232 55.8	40.9	272 46.0	48.1	165 30.3	47.6	266 27.8	41.5
	06	288 29.3	247 55.3	N15 41.9	287 46.7	S 0 47.3	180 32.5	N22 47.6	281 30.0	N 0 41.6
	07	303 31.7	262 54.7	43.0	302 47.4	46.6	195 34.7	47.6	296 32.1	41.7
	08	318 34.2	277 54.2	44.0	317 48.0	45.8	210 36.9	47.5	311 34.3	41.8
	09	333 36.7	292 53.7	. . 45.0	332 48.7	. . 45.0	225 39.1	. . 47.5	326 36.5	. . 42.0
	10	348 39.1	307 53.1	46.1	347 49.4	44.2	240 41.3	47.5	341 38.7	42.1
	11	3 41.6	322 52.6	47.1	2 50.1	43.4	255 43.6	47.5	356 40.9	42.2
	12	18 44.1	337 52.0	N15 48.1	17 50.8	S 0 42.6	270 45.8	N22 47.4	11 43.0	N 0 42.3
	13	33 46.5	352 51.5	49.1	32 51.5	41.9	285 48.0	47.4	26 45.2	42.4
	14	48 49.0	7 51.0	50.2	47 52.1	41.1	300 50.2	47.4	41 47.4	42.5
	15	63 51.4	22 50.4	. . 51.2	62 52.8	. . 40.3	315 52.4	. . 47.4	56 49.6	. . 42.7
	16	78 53.9	37 49.9	52.2	77 53.5	39.5	330 54.7	47.3	71 51.8	42.8
	17	93 56.4	52 49.4	53.3	92 54.2	38.7	345 56.9	47.3	86 54.0	42.9
	18	108 58.8	67 48.8	N15 54.3	107 54.9	S 0 37.9	0 59.1	N22 47.3	101 56.1	N 0 43.0
	19	124 01.3	82 48.3	55.3	122 55.6	37.1	16 01.3	47.3	116 58.3	43.1
	20	139 03.8	97 47.7	56.3	137 56.3	36.4	31 03.5	47.2	132 00.5	43.3
	21	154 06.2	112 47.2	. . 57.3	152 56.9	. . 35.6	46 05.7	. . 47.2	147 02.7	. . 43.4
	22	169 08.7	127 46.7	58.4	167 57.6	34.8	61 07.9	47.2	162 04.9	43.5
	23	184 11.2	142 46.1	15 59.4	182 58.3	34.0	76 10.2	47.2	177 07.0	43.6
11 SATURDAY	00	199 13.6	157 45.6	N16 00.4	197 59.0	S 0 33.2	91 12.4	N22 47.1	192 09.2	N 0 43.7
	01	214 16.1	172 45.0	01.4	212 59.7	32.4	106 14.6	47.1	207 11.4	43.8
	02	229 18.6	187 44.5	02.5	228 00.4	31.7	121 16.8	47.1	222 13.6	44.0
	03	244 21.0	202 43.9	. . 03.5	243 01.0	. . 30.9	136 19.0	. . 47.0	237 15.8	. . 44.1
	04	259 23.5	217 43.4	04.5	258 01.7	30.1	151 21.2	47.0	252 18.0	44.2
	05	274 25.9	232 42.9	05.5	273 02.4	29.3	166 23.4	47.0	267 20.1	44.3
	06	289 28.4	247 42.3	N16 06.5	288 03.1	S 0 28.5	181 25.7	N22 47.0	282 22.3	N 0 44.4
	07	304 30.9	262 41.8	07.5	303 03.8	27.7	196 27.9	46.9	297 24.5	44.6
	08	319 33.3	277 41.2	08.6	318 04.5	26.9	211 30.1	46.9	312 26.7	44.7
	09	334 35.8	292 40.7	. . 09.6	333 05.1	. . 26.2	226 32.3	. . 46.9	327 28.9	. . 44.8
	10	349 38.3	307 40.1	10.6	348 05.8	25.4	241 34.5	46.9	342 31.0	44.9
	11	4 40.7	322 39.6	11.6	3 06.5	24.6	256 36.7	46.8	357 33.2	45.0
	12	19 43.2	337 39.0	N16 12.6	18 07.2	S 0 23.8	271 38.9	N22 46.8	12 35.4	N 0 45.1
	13	34 45.7	352 38.5	13.6	33 07.9	23.0	286 41.1	46.8	27 37.6	45.3
	14	49 48.1	7 37.9	14.6	48 08.6	22.2	301 43.3	46.7	42 39.8	45.4
	15	64 50.6	22 37.4	. . 15.6	63 09.2	. . 21.5	316 45.6	. . 46.7	57 42.0	. . 45.5
	16	79 53.1	37 36.8	16.6	78 09.9	20.7	331 47.8	46.7	72 44.1	45.6
	17	94 55.5	52 36.3	17.7	93 10.6	19.9	346 50.0	46.7	87 46.3	45.7
	18	109 58.0	67 35.7	N16 18.7	108 11.3	S 0 19.1	1 52.2	N22 46.6	102 48.5	N 0 45.9
	19	125 00.4	82 35.2	19.7	123 12.0	18.3	16 54.4	46.6	117 50.7	46.0
	20	140 02.9	97 34.6	20.7	138 12.7	17.5	31 56.6	46.6	132 52.9	46.1
	21	155 05.4	112 34.1	. . 21.7	153 13.4	. . 16.8	46 58.8	. . 46.6	147 55.1	. . 46.2
	22	170 07.8	127 33.5	22.7	168 14.0	16.0	62 01.0	46.5	162 57.2	46.3
	23	185 10.3	142 33.0	23.7	183 14.7	15.2	77 03.2	46.5	177 59.4	46.4
12 SUNDAY	00	200 12.8	157 32.4	N16 24.7	198 15.4	S 0 14.4	92 05.4	N22 46.5	193 01.6	N 0 46.6
	01	215 15.2	172 31.9	25.7	213 16.1	13.6	107 07.6	46.4	208 03.8	46.7
	02	230 17.7	187 31.3	26.7	228 16.8	12.8	122 09.9	46.4	223 06.0	46.8
	03	245 20.2	202 30.8	. . 27.7	243 17.5	. . 12.0	137 12.1	. . 46.4	238 08.2	. . 46.9
	04	260 22.6	217 30.2	28.7	258 18.2	11.3	152 14.3	46.4	253 10.3	47.0
	05	275 25.1	232 29.7	29.7	273 18.8	10.5	167 16.5	46.3	268 12.5	47.1
	06	290 27.6	247 29.1	N16 30.7	288 19.5	S 0 09.7	182 18.7	N22 46.3	283 14.7	N 0 47.3
	07	305 30.0	262 28.5	31.7	303 20.2	08.9	197 20.9	46.3	298 16.9	47.4
	08	320 32.5	277 28.0	32.7	318 20.9	08.1	212 23.1	46.2	313 19.1	47.5
	09	335 34.9	292 27.4	. . 33.7	333 21.6	. . 07.3	227 25.3	. . 46.2	328 21.2	. . 47.6
	10	350 37.4	307 26.9	34.7	348 22.3	06.6	242 27.5	46.2	343 23.4	47.7
	11	5 39.9	322 26.3	35.7	3 23.0	05.8	257 29.7	46.2	358 25.6	47.9
	12	20 42.3	337 25.8	N16 36.7	18 23.6	S 0 05.0	272 31.9	N22 46.1	13 27.8	N 0 48.0
	13	35 44.8	352 25.2	37.7	33 24.3	04.2	287 34.1	46.1	28 30.0	48.1
	14	50 47.3	7 24.6	38.7	48 25.0	03.4	302 36.3	46.1	43 32.2	48.2
	15	65 49.7	22 24.1	. . 39.7	63 25.7	. . 02.6	317 38.5	. . 46.0	58 34.3	. . 48.3
	16	80 52.2	37 23.5	40.7	78 26.4	01.9	332 40.7	46.0	73 36.5	48.4
	17	95 54.7	52 23.0	41.7	93 27.1	01.1	347 42.9	46.0	88 38.7	48.6
	18	110 57.1	67 22.4	N16 42.6	108 27.8	S 0 00.3	2 45.1	N22 46.0	103 40.9	N 0 48.7
	19	125 59.6	82 21.8	43.6	123 28.4	N 00.5	17 47.3	45.9	118 43.1	48.8
	20	141 02.0	97 21.3	44.6	138 29.1	01.3	32 49.5	45.9	133 45.3	48.9
	21	156 04.5	112 20.7	. . 45.6	153 29.8	. . 02.1	47 51.7	. . 45.9	148 47.4	. . 49.0
	22	171 07.0	127 20.1	46.6	168 30.5	02.8	62 53.9	45.8	163 49.6	49.1
	23	186 09.4	142 19.6	47.6	183 31.2	03.6	77 56.1	45.8	178 51.8	49.3
Mer. Pass.	h m	10 41.3	*v* −0.5	*d* 1.0	*v* 0.7	*d* 0.8	*v* 2.2	*d* 0.0	*v* 2.2	*d* 0.1

STARS

Name	SHA ° ′	Dec ° ′
Acamar	315 11.4	S40 12.1
Achernar	335 20.0	S57 06.2
Acrux	172 58.3	S63 14.9
Adhara	255 05.1	S29 00.7
Aldebaran	290 38.7	N16 33.7
Alioth	166 11.5	N55 49.0
Alkaid	152 50.7	N49 10.8
Alnair	27 31.9	S46 49.9
Alnilam	275 36.8	S 1 11.2
Alphard	217 46.6	S 8 46.5
Alphecca	126 02.6	N26 37.3
Alpheratz	357 34.1	N29 14.0
Altair	61 59.0	N 8 56.1
Ankaa	353 06.5	S42 09.8
Antares	112 14.3	S26 29.4
Arcturus	145 46.6	N19 02.5
Atria	107 07.3	S69 04.3
Avior	234 14.2	S59 35.9
Bellatrix	278 21.9	N 6 22.3
Betelgeuse	270 51.1	N 7 24.6
Canopus	263 52.1	S52 42.8
Capella	280 20.6	N46 01.6
Deneb	49 25.2	N45 22.1
Denebola	182 23.6	N14 25.4
Diphda	348 46.6	S17 50.6
Dubhe	193 39.2	N61 36.6
Elnath	278 00.8	N28 37.8
Eltanin	90 41.5	N51 28.8
Enif	33 38.0	N 9 59.6
Fomalhaut	15 13.7	S29 29.0
Gacrux	171 50.0	S57 15.8
Gienah	175 42.2	S17 41.5
Hadar	148 33.9	S60 30.0
Hamal	327 50.4	N23 35.1
Kaus Aust.	83 31.0	S34 22.2
Kochab	137 18.7	N74 02.6
Markab	13 29.1	N15 20.7
Menkar	314 05.4	N 4 11.5
Menkent	147 56.0	S36 30.1
Miaplacidus	221 37.7	S69 49.8
Mirfak	308 27.2	N49 57.3
Nunki	75 46.4	S26 15.8
Peacock	53 04.2	S56 38.8
Pollux	243 16.0	N27 57.8
Procyon	244 49.8	N 5 09.4
Rasalhague	95 57.4	N12 32.2
Regulus	207 33.1	N11 50.2
Rigel	281 03.1	S 8 10.4
Rigil Kent.	139 38.2	S60 56.6
Sabik	102 01.4	S15 45.5
Schedar	349 30.4	N56 40.8
Shaula	96 08.8	S37 07.3
Sirius	258 25.4	S16 45.3
Spica	158 20.9	S11 18.1
Suhail	222 45.4	S43 32.6
Vega	80 32.4	N38 48.1
Zuben'ubi	136 54.6	S16 09.2

	SHA ° ′	Mer. Pass. h m
Venus	318 31.9	13 29
Mars	358 45.4	10 48
Jupiter	251 58.7	17 53
Saturn	352 55.6	11 10

	UT	SUN GHA	SUN Dec	MOON GHA	MOON *v*	MOON Dec	MOON *d*	MOON HP
	d h	° ′	° ′	° ′	′	° ′	′	′
	10 00	179 39.0	N 7 52.2	268 16.4	10.6	S26 10.7	5.8	54.7
	01	194 39.1	53.1	282 46.0	10.6	26 04.9	6.0	54.7
	02	209 39.3	54.1	297 15.6	10.6	25 58.9	6.2	54.8
	03	224 39.5	. . 55.0	311 45.2	10.7	25 52.7	6.2	54.8
	04	239 39.6	55.9	326 14.9	10.7	25 46.5	6.4	54.8
	05	254 39.8	56.8	340 44.6	10.7	25 40.1	6.5	54.8
	06	269 40.0	N 7 57.8	355 14.3	10.8	S25 33.6	6.7	54.8
	07	284 40.1	58.7	9 44.1	10.8	25 26.9	6.7	54.8
	08	299 40.3	7 59.6	24 13.9	10.9	25 20.2	6.9	54.9
F	09	314 40.5	8 00.5	38 43.8	10.9	25 13.3	7.0	54.9
R	10	329 40.7	01.4	53 13.7	10.9	25 06.3	7.2	54.9
I	11	344 40.8	02.4	67 43.6	11.0	24 59.1	7.2	54.9
D	12	359 41.0	N 8 03.3	82 13.6	11.0	S24 51.9	7.4	55.0
A	13	14 41.2	04.2	96 43.6	11.0	24 44.5	7.5	55.0
Y	14	29 41.3	05.1	111 13.6	11.1	24 37.0	7.6	55.0
	15	44 41.5	. . 06.1	125 43.7	11.1	24 29.4	7.8	55.0
	16	59 41.6	07.0	140 13.8	11.2	24 21.6	7.9	55.0
	17	74 41.8	07.9	154 44.0	11.2	24 13.7	7.9	55.1
	18	89 42.0	N 8 08.8	169 14.2	11.2	S24 05.8	8.1	55.1
	19	104 42.1	09.7	183 44.4	11.3	23 57.7	8.3	55.1
	20	119 42.3	10.7	198 14.7	11.3	23 49.4	8.3	55.1
	21	134 42.5	. . 11.6	212 45.0	11.4	23 41.1	8.5	55.2
	22	149 42.6	12.5	227 15.4	11.4	23 32.6	8.6	55.2
	23	164 42.8	13.4	241 45.8	11.4	23 24.0	8.7	55.2
	11 00	179 43.0	N 8 14.4	256 16.2	11.5	S23 15.3	8.8	55.2
	01	194 43.1	15.3	270 46.7	11.5	23 06.5	8.9	55.3
	02	209 43.3	16.2	285 17.2	11.6	22 57.6	9.1	55.3
	03	224 43.5	. . 17.1	299 47.8	11.6	22 48.5	9.1	55.3
	04	239 43.6	18.0	314 18.4	11.6	22 39.4	9.3	55.3
	05	254 43.8	19.0	328 49.0	11.7	22 30.1	9.4	55.4
	06	269 44.0	N 8 19.9	343 19.7	11.7	S22 20.7	9.5	55.4
S	07	284 44.1	20.8	357 50.4	11.8	22 11.2	9.6	55.4
A	08	299 44.3	21.7	12 21.2	11.8	22 01.6	9.7	55.4
T	09	314 44.5	. . 22.6	26 52.0	11.8	21 51.9	9.8	55.5
U	10	329 44.6	23.5	41 22.8	11.9	21 42.1	10.0	55.5
R	11	344 44.8	24.5	55 53.7	11.9	21 32.1	10.0	55.5
D	12	359 44.9	N 8 25.4	70 24.6	12.0	S21 22.1	10.2	55.6
A	13	14 45.1	26.3	84 55.6	12.0	21 11.9	10.3	55.6
Y	14	29 45.3	27.2	99 26.6	12.0	21 01.6	10.3	55.6
	15	44 45.4	. . 28.1	113 57.6	12.1	20 51.3	10.5	55.6
	16	59 45.6	29.0	128 28.7	12.1	20 40.8	10.6	55.7
	17	74 45.8	30.0	142 59.8	12.2	20 30.2	10.7	55.7
	18	89 45.9	N 8 30.9	157 31.0	12.2	S20 19.5	10.8	55.7
	19	104 46.1	31.8	172 02.2	12.2	20 08.7	10.9	55.8
	20	119 46.3	32.7	186 33.4	12.3	19 57.8	11.0	55.8
	21	134 46.4	. . 33.6	201 04.7	12.3	19 46.8	11.1	55.8
	22	149 46.6	34.5	215 36.0	12.3	19 35.7	11.2	55.8
	23	164 46.7	35.5	230 07.3	12.4	19 24.5	11.3	55.9
	12 00	179 46.9	N 8 36.4	244 38.7	12.4	S19 13.2	11.4	55.9
	01	194 47.1	37.3	259 10.1	12.5	19 01.8	11.5	55.9
	02	209 47.2	38.2	273 41.6	12.4	18 50.3	11.6	56.0
	03	224 47.4	. . 39.1	288 13.0	12.6	18 38.7	11.8	56.0
	04	239 47.5	40.0	302 44.6	12.5	18 26.9	11.8	56.0
	05	254 47.7	40.9	317 16.1	12.6	18 15.1	11.9	56.1
	06	269 47.9	N 8 41.9	331 47.7	12.6	S18 03.2	12.0	56.1
	07	284 48.0	42.8	346 19.3	12.6	17 51.2	12.0	56.1
	08	299 48.2	43.7	0 50.9	12.7	17 39.2	12.2	56.2
S	09	314 48.4	. . 44.6	15 22.6	12.7	17 27.0	12.3	56.2
U	10	329 48.5	45.5	29 54.3	12.8	17 14.7	12.4	56.2
N	11	344 48.7	46.4	44 26.1	12.7	17 02.3	12.5	56.3
D	12	359 48.8	N 8 47.3	58 57.8	12.8	S16 49.8	12.5	56.3
A	13	14 49.0	48.2	73 29.6	12.9	16 37.3	12.7	56.3
Y	14	29 49.2	49.1	88 01.5	12.8	16 24.6	12.7	56.4
	15	44 49.3	. . 50.1	102 33.3	12.9	16 11.9	12.8	56.4
	16	59 49.5	51.0	117 05.2	12.9	15 59.1	12.9	56.4
	17	74 49.6	51.9	131 37.1	13.0	15 46.2	13.0	56.5
	18	89 49.8	N 8 52.8	146 09.1	12.9	S15 33.2	13.1	56.5
	19	104 50.0	53.7	160 41.0	13.0	15 20.1	13.2	56.5
	20	119 50.1	54.6	175 13.0	13.0	15 06.9	13.2	56.6
	21	134 50.3	. . 55.5	189 45.0	13.1	14 53.7	13.4	56.6
	22	149 50.4	56.4	204 17.1	13.0	14 40.3	13.4	56.6
	23	164 50.6	57.3	218 49.1	13.1	S14 26.9	13.5	56.7
		SD 16.0	*d* 0.9	SD		15.0	15.1	15.3

Lat.	Twilight Naut.	Twilight Civil	Sunrise	Moonrise 10	Moonrise 11	Moonrise 12	Moonrise 13
°	h m	h m	h m	h m	h m	h m	h m
N 72	////	02 33	04 02	▬	▬	07 28	05 39
N 70	////	03 01	04 16	▬	▬	06 10	05 16
68	01 33	03 21	04 27	▬	▬	05 31	04 58
66	02 11	03 37	04 36	▬	05 40	05 04	04 43
64	02 37	03 50	04 43	05 41	04 59	04 43	04 31
62	02 56	04 01	04 50	04 38	04 31	04 26	04 21
60	03 12	04 10	04 55	04 04	04 09	04 11	04 12
N 58	03 25	04 18	05 00	03 38	03 52	03 59	04 04
56	03 36	04 25	05 05	03 18	03 36	03 48	03 57
54	03 45	04 32	05 09	03 02	03 24	03 39	03 51
52	03 54	04 37	05 12	02 47	03 12	03 31	03 45
50	04 01	04 42	05 16	02 35	03 02	03 23	03 40
45	04 16	04 52	05 23	02 09	02 41	03 07	03 29
N 40	04 28	05 01	05 28	01 48	02 23	02 53	03 20
35	04 37	05 08	05 33	01 31	02 09	02 42	03 12
30	04 45	05 13	05 38	01 16	01 56	02 32	03 05
20	04 57	05 23	05 45	00 50	01 34	02 15	02 53
N 10	05 06	05 30	05 52	00 28	01 15	01 59	02 42
0	05 13	05 37	05 58	00 08	00 57	01 45	02 32
S 10	05 18	05 42	06 04	24 39	00 39	01 31	02 22
20	05 22	05 48	06 10	24 20	00 20	01 16	02 11
30	05 25	05 52	06 17	23 58	24 58	00 58	01 58
35	05 26	05 55	06 20	23 45	24 47	00 47	01 51
40	05 26	05 58	06 25	23 30	24 36	00 36	01 43
45	05 26	06 00	06 30	23 12	24 22	00 22	01 33
S 50	05 26	06 03	06 36	22 49	24 04	00 04	01 21
52	05 26	06 05	06 39	22 38	23 56	25 16	01 16
54	05 25	06 06	06 42	22 26	23 47	25 10	01 10
56	05 25	06 08	06 45	22 12	23 37	25 03	01 03
58	05 24	06 09	06 49	21 55	23 25	24 55	00 55
S 60	05 23	06 11	06 53	21 35	23 11	24 46	00 46

Lat.	Sunset	Twilight Civil	Twilight Naut.	Moonset 10	Moonset 11	Moonset 12	Moonset 13
°	h m	h m	h m	h m	h m	h m	h m
N 72	20 04	21 36	////	▬	▬	08 48	12 14
N 70	19 49	21 06	////	▬	▬	10 04	12 35
68	19 38	20 44	22 38	▬	▬	10 41	12 51
66	19 29	20 28	21 56	▬	08 52	11 07	13 04
64	19 21	20 14	21 29	07 08	09 32	11 27	13 15
62	19 14	20 03	21 09	08 10	09 59	11 43	13 24
60	19 08	19 53	20 53	08 44	10 20	11 56	13 31
N 58	19 03	19 45	20 39	09 09	10 37	12 08	13 38
56	18 59	19 38	20 28	09 28	10 52	12 18	13 44
54	18 54	19 32	20 18	09 45	11 04	12 26	13 49
52	18 51	19 26	20 10	09 59	11 15	12 34	13 54
50	18 47	19 21	20 03	10 11	11 25	12 41	13 58
45	18 40	19 11	19 47	10 36	11 45	12 56	14 08
N 40	18 34	19 02	19 35	10 56	12 01	13 08	14 15
35	18 29	18 55	19 26	11 13	12 15	13 18	14 22
30	18 25	18 49	19 18	11 27	12 27	13 27	14 27
20	18 17	18 39	19 06	11 51	12 47	13 42	14 37
N 10	18 10	18 32	18 56	12 12	13 04	13 55	14 46
0	18 04	18 25	18 49	12 32	13 20	14 08	14 54
S 10	17 58	18 20	18 44	12 51	13 37	14 20	15 02
20	17 52	18 14	18 40	13 12	13 54	14 33	15 10
30	17 45	18 09	18 37	13 35	14 13	14 48	15 19
35	17 41	18 06	18 36	13 49	14 25	14 56	15 25
40	17 37	18 04	18 35	14 05	14 38	15 06	15 31
45	17 31	18 01	18 35	14 24	14 53	15 17	15 38
S 50	17 25	17 58	18 35	14 48	15 12	15 30	15 46
52	17 22	17 56	18 35	14 59	15 20	15 37	15 50
54	17 19	17 55	18 36	15 12	15 30	15 44	15 54
56	17 16	17 53	18 36	15 26	15 41	15 51	15 59
58	17 12	17 52	18 37	15 43	15 54	16 00	16 04
S 60	17 08	17 50	18 38	16 04	16 08	16 10	16 10

Day	SUN Eqn. of Time 00ʰ	SUN Eqn. of Time 12ʰ	SUN Mer. Pass.	MOON Mer. Pass. Upper	MOON Mer. Pass. Lower	MOON Age	MOON Phase
d	m s	m s	h m	h m	h m	d %	
10	01 24	01 16	12 01	06 20	18 45	22 47	
11	01 08	01 01	12 01	07 09	19 33	23 38	◐
12	00 53	00 45	12 01	07 56	20 20	24 28	

UT (d h)	Day	ARIES GHA ° ′	VENUS −3·9 GHA ° ′	VENUS Dec ° ′	MARS +1·2 GHA ° ′	MARS Dec ° ′	JUPITER −2·1 GHA ° ′	JUPITER Dec ° ′	SATURN +0·9 GHA ° ′	SATURN Dec ° ′
13 00	MONDAY	201 11.9	157 19.0	N16 48.6	198 31.9	N 0 04.4	92 58.3	N22 45.8	193 54.0	N 0 49.4
01		216 14.4	172 18.5	49.6	213 32.6	05.2	108 00.5	45.8	208 56.2	49.5
02		231 16.8	187 17.9	50.5	228 33.2	06.0	123 02.7	45.7	223 58.4	49.6
03		246 19.3	202 17.3	. . 51.5	243 33.9	. . 06.8	138 04.9	. . 45.7	239 00.5	. . 49.7
04		261 21.8	217 16.8	52.5	258 34.6	07.5	153 07.1	45.7	254 02.7	49.8
05		276 24.2	232 16.2	53.5	273 35.3	08.3	168 09.3	45.6	269 04.9	50.0
06		291 26.7	247 15.6	N16 54.5	288 36.0	N 0 09.1	183 11.5	N22 45.6	284 07.1	N 0 50.1
07		306 29.2	262 15.1	55.5	303 36.7	09.9	198 13.7	45.6	299 09.3	50.2
08		321 31.6	277 14.5	56.4	318 37.4	10.7	213 15.9	45.6	314 11.5	50.3
09		336 34.1	292 13.9	. . 57.4	333 38.0	. . 11.5	228 18.1	. . 45.5	329 13.6	. . 50.4
10		351 36.5	307 13.4	58.4	348 38.7	12.2	243 20.3	45.5	344 15.8	50.5
11		6 39.0	322 12.8	16 59.4	3 39.4	13.0	258 22.5	45.5	359 18.0	50.7
12		21 41.5	337 12.2	N17 00.4	18 40.1	N 0 13.8	273 24.7	N22 45.4	14 20.2	N 0 50.8
13		36 43.9	352 11.7	01.3	33 40.8	14.6	288 26.9	45.4	29 22.4	50.9
14		51 46.4	7 11.1	02.3	48 41.5	15.4	303 29.1	45.4	44 24.6	51.0
15		66 48.9	22 10.5	. . 03.3	63 42.2	. . 16.2	318 31.3	. . 45.3	59 26.7	. . 51.1
16		81 51.3	37 09.9	04.3	78 42.8	16.9	333 33.5	45.3	74 28.9	51.2
17		96 53.8	52 09.4	05.2	93 43.5	17.7	348 35.7	45.3	89 31.1	51.4
18		111 56.3	67 08.8	N17 06.2	108 44.2	N 0 18.5	3 37.9	N22 45.3	104 33.3	N 0 51.5
19		126 58.7	82 08.2	07.2	123 44.9	19.3	18 40.1	45.2	119 35.5	51.6
20		142 01.2	97 07.7	08.1	138 45.6	20.1	33 42.3	45.2	134 37.7	51.7
21		157 03.6	112 07.1	. . 09.1	153 46.3	. . 20.9	48 44.5	. . 45.2	149 39.9	. . 51.8
22		172 06.1	127 06.5	10.1	168 47.0	21.6	63 46.7	45.1	164 42.0	51.9
23		187 08.6	142 05.9	11.1	183 47.7	22.4	78 48.9	45.1	179 44.2	52.1
14 00	TUESDAY	202 11.0	157 05.4	N17 12.0	198 48.3	N 0 23.2	93 51.1	N22 45.1	194 46.4	N 0 52.2
01		217 13.5	172 04.8	13.0	213 49.0	24.0	108 53.2	45.1	209 48.6	52.3
02		232 16.0	187 04.2	14.0	228 49.7	24.8	123 55.4	45.0	224 50.8	52.4
03		247 18.4	202 03.6	. . 14.9	243 50.4	. . 25.5	138 57.6	. . 45.0	239 53.0	. . 52.5
04		262 20.9	217 03.1	15.9	258 51.1	26.3	153 59.8	45.0	254 55.1	52.6
05		277 23.4	232 02.5	16.9	273 51.8	27.1	169 02.0	44.9	269 57.3	52.8
06		292 25.8	247 01.9	N17 17.8	288 52.5	N 0 27.9	184 04.2	N22 44.9	284 59.5	N 0 52.9
07		307 28.3	262 01.3	18.8	303 53.2	28.7	199 06.4	44.9	300 01.7	53.0
08		322 30.8	277 00.7	19.7	318 53.8	29.5	214 08.6	44.8	315 03.9	53.1
09		337 33.2	292 00.2	. . 20.7	333 54.5	. . 30.2	229 10.8	. . 44.8	330 06.1	. . 53.2
10		352 35.7	306 59.6	21.7	348 55.2	31.0	244 13.0	44.8	345 08.2	53.3
11		7 38.1	321 59.0	22.6	3 55.9	31.8	259 15.2	44.8	0 10.4	53.5
12		22 40.6	336 58.4	N17 23.6	18 56.6	N 0 32.6	274 17.4	N22 44.7	15 12.6	N 0 53.6
13		37 43.1	351 57.8	24.5	33 57.3	33.4	289 19.5	44.7	30 14.8	53.7
14		52 45.5	6 57.3	25.5	48 58.0	34.2	304 21.7	44.7	45 17.0	53.8
15		67 48.0	21 56.7	. . 26.5	63 58.7	. . 34.9	319 23.9	. . 44.6	60 19.2	. . 53.9
16		82 50.5	36 56.1	27.4	78 59.3	35.7	334 26.1	44.6	75 21.4	54.0
17		97 52.9	51 55.5	28.4	94 00.0	36.5	349 28.3	44.6	90 23.5	54.2
18		112 55.4	66 54.9	N17 29.3	109 00.7	N 0 37.3	4 30.5	N22 44.5	105 25.7	N 0 54.3
19		127 57.9	81 54.3	30.3	124 01.4	38.1	19 32.7	44.5	120 27.9	54.4
20		143 00.3	96 53.8	31.2	139 02.1	38.8	34 34.9	44.5	135 30.1	54.5
21		158 02.8	111 53.2	. . 32.2	154 02.8	. . 39.6	49 37.1	. . 44.4	150 32.3	. . 54.6
22		173 05.3	126 52.6	33.1	169 03.5	40.4	64 39.2	44.4	165 34.5	54.7
23		188 07.7	141 52.0	34.1	184 04.2	41.2	79 41.4	44.4	180 36.6	54.9
15 00	WEDNESDAY	203 10.2	156 51.4	N17 35.0	199 04.8	N 0 42.0	94 43.6	N22 44.4	195 38.8	N 0 55.0
01		218 12.6	171 50.8	36.0	214 05.5	42.8	109 45.8	44.3	210 41.0	55.1
02		233 15.1	186 50.3	36.9	229 06.2	43.5	124 48.0	44.3	225 43.2	55.2
03		248 17.6	201 49.7	. . 37.9	244 06.9	. . 44.3	139 50.2	. . 44.3	240 45.4	. . 55.3
04		263 20.0	216 49.1	38.8	259 07.6	45.1	154 52.4	44.2	255 47.6	55.4
05		278 22.5	231 48.5	39.8	274 08.3	45.9	169 54.6	44.2	270 49.8	55.6
06		293 25.0	246 47.9	N17 40.7	289 09.0	N 0 46.7	184 56.7	N22 44.2	285 51.9	N 0 55.7
07		308 27.4	261 47.3	41.7	304 09.7	47.4	199 58.9	44.1	300 54.1	55.8
08		323 29.9	276 46.7	42.6	319 10.3	48.2	215 01.1	44.1	315 56.3	55.9
09		338 32.4	291 46.1	. . 43.6	334 11.0	. . 49.0	230 03.3	. . 44.1	330 58.5	. . 56.0
10		353 34.8	306 45.5	44.5	349 11.7	49.8	245 05.5	44.0	346 00.7	56.1
11		8 37.3	321 45.0	45.4	4 12.4	50.6	260 07.7	44.0	1 02.9	56.2
12		23 39.7	336 44.4	N17 46.4	19 13.1	N 0 51.4	275 09.8	N22 44.0	16 05.1	N 0 56.4
13		38 42.2	351 43.8	47.3	34 13.8	52.1	290 12.0	44.0	31 07.2	56.5
14		53 44.7	6 43.2	48.3	49 14.5	52.9	305 14.2	43.9	46 09.4	56.6
15		68 47.1	21 42.6	. . 49.2	64 15.2	. . 53.7	320 16.4	. . 43.9	61 11.6	. . 56.7
16		83 49.6	36 42.0	50.1	79 15.9	54.5	335 18.6	43.9	76 13.8	56.8
17		98 52.1	51 41.4	51.1	94 16.5	55.3	350 20.8	43.8	91 16.0	56.9
18		113 54.5	66 40.8	N17 52.0	109 17.2	N 0 56.0	5 22.9	N22 43.8	106 18.2	N 0 57.1
19		128 57.0	81 40.2	52.9	124 17.9	56.8	20 25.1	43.8	121 20.3	57.2
20		143 59.5	96 39.6	53.9	139 18.6	57.6	35 27.3	43.7	136 22.5	57.3
21		159 01.9	111 39.0	. . 54.8	154 19.3	. . 58.4	50 29.5	. . 43.7	151 24.7	. . 57.4
22		174 04.4	126 38.4	55.7	169 20.0	59.2	65 31.7	43.7	166 26.9	57.5
23		189 06.9	141 37.8	56.7	184 20.7	59.9	80 33.8	43.6	181 29.1	57.6
Mer. Pass.		h m 10 29.5	v −0.6	d 1.0	v 0.7	d 0.8	v 2.2	d 0.0	v 2.2	d 0.1

STARS

Name	SHA ° ′	Dec ° ′
Acamar	315 11.4	S40 12.1
Achernar	335 20.0	S57 06.2
Acrux	172 58.3	S63 14.9
Adhara	255 05.1	S29 00.7
Aldebaran	290 38.7	N16 33.7
Alioth	166 11.5	N55 49.0
Alkaid	152 50.7	N49 10.8
Alnair	27 31.9	S46 49.9
Alnilam	275 36.8	S 1 11.2
Alphard	217 46.6	S 8 46.5
Alphecca	126 02.5	N26 37.3
Alpheratz	357 34.0	N29 14.0
Altair	61 59.0	N 8 56.1
Ankaa	353 06.5	S42 09.8
Antares	112 14.3	S26 29.4
Arcturus	145 46.6	N19 02.5
Atria	107 07.3	S69 04.3
Avior	234 14.2	S59 35.9
Bellatrix	278 22.0	N 6 22.3
Betelgeuse	270 51.1	N 7 24.6
Canopus	263 52.1	S52 42.8
Capella	280 20.6	N46 01.6
Deneb	49 25.2	N45 22.1
Denebola	182 23.6	N14 25.4
Diphda	348 46.6	S17 50.6
Dubhe	193 39.2	N61 36.6
Elnath	278 00.8	N28 37.8
Eltanin	90 41.5	N51 28.8
Enif	33 37.9	N 9 59.6
Fomalhaut	15 13.6	S29 28.9
Gacrux	171 50.0	S57 15.8
Gienah	175 42.2	S17 41.5
Hadar	148 33.9	S60 30.0
Hamal	327 50.4	N23 35.1
Kaus Aust.	83 31.0	S34 22.2
Kochab	137 18.7	N74 02.6
Markab	13 29.1	N15 20.7
Menkar	314 05.4	N 4 11.5
Menkent	147 56.0	S36 30.1
Miaplacidus	221 37.8	S69 49.8
Mirfak	308 27.2	N49 57.3
Nunki	75 46.4	S26 15.8
Peacock	53 04.2	S56 38.8
Pollux	243 16.0	N27 57.8
Procyon	244 49.8	N 5 09.4
Rasalhague	95 57.4	N12 32.2
Regulus	207 33.2	N11 50.2
Rigel	281 03.1	S 8 10.4
Rigil Kent.	139 38.2	S60 56.6
Sabik	102 01.4	S15 45.5
Schedar	349 30.4	N56 40.8
Shaula	96 08.8	S37 07.3
Sirius	258 25.4	S16 45.3
Spica	158 20.9	S11 18.1
Suhail	222 45.4	S43 32.6
Vega	80 32.4	N38 48.1
Zuben'ubi	136 54.6	S16 09.2

	SHA ° ′	Mer. Pass. h m
Venus	314 54.3	13 32
Mars	356 37.3	10 44
Jupiter	251 40.0	17 42
Saturn	352 35.4	10 59

Day	UT	SUN GHA	SUN Dec	MOON GHA	v	MOON Dec	d	HP
	d h	° ′	° ′	° ′	′	° ′	′	′
13 MONDAY	00	179 50.7	N 8 58.2	233 21.2	13.1	S14 13.4	13.6	56.7
	01	194 50.9	8 59.2	247 53.3	13.1	13 59.8	13.7	56.7
	02	209 51.1	9 00.1	262 25.4	13.1	13 46.1	13.7	56.8
	03	224 51.2	. . 01.0	276 57.5	13.2	13 32.4	13.9	56.8
	04	239 51.4	01.9	291 29.7	13.2	13 18.5	13.9	56.8
	05	254 51.5	02.8	306 01.9	13.2	13 04.6	13.9	56.9
	06	269 51.7	N 9 03.7	320 34.1	13.2	S12 50.7	14.1	56.9
	07	284 51.9	04.6	335 06.3	13.2	12 36.6	14.1	56.9
	08	299 52.0	05.5	349 38.5	13.2	12 22.5	14.3	57.0
	09	314 52.2	. . 06.4	4 10.7	13.3	12 08.2	14.2	57.0
	10	329 52.3	07.3	18 43.0	13.2	11 54.0	14.4	57.1
	11	344 52.5	08.2	33 15.2	13.3	11 39.6	14.4	57.1
	12	359 52.6	N 9 09.1	47 47.5	13.3	S11 25.2	14.5	57.1
	13	14 52.8	10.0	62 19.8	13.3	11 10.7	14.6	57.2
	14	29 53.0	10.9	76 52.1	13.3	10 56.1	14.6	57.2
	15	44 53.1	. . 11.8	91 24.4	13.3	10 41.5	14.7	57.2
	16	59 53.3	12.7	105 56.7	13.3	10 26.8	14.8	57.3
	17	74 53.4	13.6	120 29.0	13.3	10 12.0	14.8	57.3
	18	89 53.6	N 9 14.6	135 01.3	13.4	S 9 57.2	14.9	57.3
	19	104 53.7	15.5	149 33.7	13.3	9 42.3	15.0	57.4
	20	119 53.9	16.4	164 06.0	13.3	9 27.3	15.0	57.4
	21	134 54.0	. . 17.3	178 38.3	13.4	9 12.3	15.1	57.5
	22	149 54.2	18.2	193 10.7	13.3	8 57.2	15.2	57.5
	23	164 54.4	19.1	207 43.0	13.3	8 42.0	15.2	57.5
14 TUESDAY	00	179 54.5	N 9 20.0	222 15.3	13.4	S 8 26.8	15.3	57.6
	01	194 54.7	20.9	236 47.7	13.3	8 11.5	15.3	57.6
	02	209 54.8	21.8	251 20.0	13.3	7 56.2	15.4	57.6
	03	224 55.0	. . 22.7	265 52.3	13.3	7 40.8	15.4	57.7
	04	239 55.1	23.6	280 24.6	13.3	7 25.4	15.5	57.7
	05	254 55.3	24.5	294 56.9	13.4	7 09.9	15.6	57.8
	06	269 55.4	N 9 25.4	309 29.3	13.3	S 6 54.3	15.6	57.8
	07	284 55.6	26.3	324 01.6	13.2	6 38.7	15.6	57.8
	08	299 55.7	27.2	338 33.8	13.3	6 23.1	15.7	57.9
	09	314 55.9	. . 28.1	353 06.1	13.3	6 07.4	15.8	57.9
	10	329 56.0	29.0	7 38.4	13.3	5 51.6	15.8	57.9
	11	344 56.2	29.9	22 10.7	13.2	5 35.8	15.8	58.0
	12	359 56.4	N 9 30.8	36 42.9	13.2	S 5 20.0	15.9	58.0
	13	14 56.5	31.7	51 15.1	13.2	5 04.1	16.0	58.1
	14	29 56.7	32.6	65 47.3	13.2	4 48.1	16.0	58.1
	15	44 56.8	. . 33.5	80 19.5	13.2	4 32.1	16.0	58.1
	16	59 57.0	34.4	94 51.7	13.2	4 16.1	16.1	58.2
	17	74 57.1	35.3	109 23.9	13.1	4 00.0	16.1	58.2
	18	89 57.3	N 9 36.2	123 56.0	13.1	S 3 43.9	16.1	58.2
	19	104 57.4	37.1	138 28.1	13.1	3 27.8	16.2	58.3
	20	119 57.6	38.0	153 00.2	13.1	3 11.6	16.2	58.3
	21	134 57.7	. . 38.9	167 32.3	13.0	2 55.4	16.3	58.3
	22	149 57.9	39.7	182 04.3	13.0	2 39.1	16.2	58.4
	23	164 58.0	40.6	196 36.3	13.0	2 22.9	16.4	58.4
15 WEDNESDAY	00	179 58.2	N 9 41.5	211 08.3	13.0	S 2 06.5	16.3	58.5
	01	194 58.3	42.4	225 40.3	12.9	1 50.2	16.4	58.5
	02	209 58.5	43.3	240 12.2	12.9	1 33.8	16.4	58.5
	03	224 58.6	. . 44.2	254 44.1	12.9	1 17.4	16.4	58.6
	04	239 58.8	45.1	269 16.0	12.8	1 01.0	16.5	58.6
	05	254 58.9	46.0	283 47.8	12.8	0 44.5	16.5	58.6
	06	269 59.1	N 9 46.9	298 19.6	12.7	S 0 28.0	16.5	58.7
	07	284 59.2	47.8	312 51.3	12.8	S 0 11.5	16.5	58.7
	08	299 59.4	48.7	327 23.1	12.6	N 0 05.0	16.6	58.7
	09	314 59.5	. . 49.6	341 54.7	12.7	0 21.6	16.5	58.8
	10	329 59.7	50.5	356 26.4	12.6	0 38.1	16.6	58.8
	11	344 59.8	51.4	10 58.0	12.5	0 54.7	16.6	58.8
	12	0 00.0	N 9 52.3	25 29.5	12.6	N 1 11.3	16.6	58.9
	13	15 00.1	53.2	40 01.1	12.4	1 27.9	16.7	58.9
	14	30 00.3	54.1	54 32.5	12.4	1 44.6	16.6	58.9
	15	45 00.4	. . 54.9	69 03.9	12.4	2 01.2	16.6	59.0
	16	60 00.6	55.8	83 35.3	12.3	2 17.8	16.7	59.0
	17	75 00.7	56.7	98 06.6	12.3	2 34.5	16.7	59.0
	18	90 00.9	N 9 57.6	112 37.9	12.2	N 2 51.2	16.6	59.1
	19	105 01.0	58.5	127 09.1	12.2	3 07.8	16.7	59.1
	20	120 01.2	9 59.4	141 40.3	12.1	3 24.5	16.7	59.1
	21	135 01.3	10 00.3	156 11.4	12.0	3 41.2	16.7	59.2
	22	150 01.5	01.2	170 42.4	12.0	3 57.9	16.6	59.2
	23	165 01.6	02.1	185 13.4	12.0	N 4 14.5	16.7	59.2
		SD 16.0	*d* 0.9	SD 15.6		15.8		16.0

Lat.	Twilight Naut.	Twilight Civil	Sunrise	Moonrise 13	Moonrise 14	Moonrise 15	Moonrise 16
°	h m	h m	h m	h m	h m	h m	h m
N 72	////	02 07	03 45	05 39	04 53	04 17	03 41
N 70	////	02 41	04 01	05 16	04 43	04 15	03 48
68	00 57	03 05	04 14	04 58	04 35	04 14	03 54
66	01 50	03 24	04 24	04 43	04 27	04 13	03 59
64	02 20	03 38	04 33	04 31	04 21	04 12	04 04
62	02 43	03 50	04 40	04 21	04 16	04 12	04 07
60	03 00	04 01	04 47	04 12	04 12	04 11	04 11
N 58	03 15	04 10	04 52	04 04	04 08	04 11	04 14
56	03 27	04 17	04 57	03 57	04 04	04 10	04 16
54	03 37	04 24	05 02	03 51	04 01	04 10	04 19
52	03 46	04 30	05 06	03 45	03 58	04 09	04 21
50	03 54	04 35	05 09	03 40	03 55	04 09	04 23
45	04 10	04 47	05 17	03 29	03 49	04 08	04 27
N 40	04 23	04 56	05 24	03 20	03 44	04 07	04 31
35	04 33	05 04	05 29	03 12	03 40	04 07	04 34
30	04 41	05 10	05 34	03 05	03 36	04 06	04 37
20	04 54	05 20	05 43	02 53	03 29	04 05	04 42
N 10	05 04	05 29	05 50	02 42	03 23	04 04	04 47
0	05 12	05 36	05 57	02 32	03 18	04 04	04 51
S 10	05 18	05 42	06 04	02 22	03 12	04 03	04 55
20	05 23	05 48	06 11	02 11	03 06	04 02	05 00
30	05 26	05 54	06 18	01 58	02 59	04 01	05 05
35	05 28	05 57	06 23	01 51	02 55	04 01	05 09
40	05 29	06 01	06 28	01 43	02 51	04 00	05 12
45	05 30	06 04	06 34	01 33	02 46	04 00	05 16
S 50	05 30	06 08	06 41	01 21	02 39	03 59	05 21
52	05 30	06 10	06 44	01 16	02 36	03 59	05 24
54	05 30	06 11	06 47	01 10	02 33	03 58	05 26
56	05 30	06 13	06 51	01 03	02 30	03 58	05 29
58	05 30	06 15	06 55	00 55	02 26	03 57	05 32
S 60	05 29	06 18	07 00	00 46	02 21	03 57	05 36

Lat.	Sunset	Twilight Civil	Twilight Naut.	Moonset 13	Moonset 14	Moonset 15	Moonset 16
°	h m	h m	h m	h m	h m	h m	h m
N 72	20 19	22 01	////	12 14	14 38	16 57	19 27
N 70	20 03	21 24	////	12 35	14 45	16 54	19 10
68	19 50	20 59	23 21	12 51	14 51	16 51	18 57
66	19 39	20 40	22 17	13 04	14 56	16 48	18 47
64	19 30	20 25	21 45	13 15	15 00	16 46	18 38
62	19 22	20 12	21 21	13 24	15 03	16 45	18 31
60	19 16	20 02	21 03	13 31	15 06	16 43	18 24
N 58	19 10	19 53	20 48	13 38	15 09	16 42	18 19
56	19 05	19 45	20 36	13 44	15 11	16 41	18 14
54	19 00	19 38	20 26	13 49	15 13	16 40	18 09
52	18 56	19 32	20 16	13 54	15 15	16 39	18 05
50	18 52	19 26	20 08	13 58	15 17	16 38	18 02
45	18 44	19 15	19 52	14 08	15 21	16 36	17 54
N 40	18 37	19 05	19 39	14 15	15 24	16 34	17 47
35	18 32	18 58	19 29	14 22	15 26	16 33	17 42
30	18 27	18 51	19 20	14 27	15 29	16 32	17 37
20	18 18	18 40	19 07	14 37	15 33	16 30	17 29
N 10	18 10	18 32	18 57	14 46	15 36	16 28	17 21
0	18 04	18 25	18 49	14 54	15 39	16 26	17 15
S 10	17 57	18 18	18 43	15 02	15 43	16 24	17 08
20	17 50	18 12	18 38	15 10	15 46	16 22	17 00
30	17 42	18 06	18 34	15 19	15 50	16 20	16 52
35	17 37	18 03	18 32	15 25	15 52	16 19	16 48
40	17 32	17 59	18 31	15 31	15 54	16 17	16 42
45	17 26	17 56	18 30	15 38	15 57	16 16	16 36
S 50	17 19	17 52	18 29	15 46	16 00	16 14	16 29
52	17 16	17 50	18 29	15 50	16 02	16 13	16 25
54	17 12	17 48	18 29	15 54	16 03	16 12	16 22
56	17 08	17 46	18 29	15 59	16 05	16 11	16 18
58	17 04	17 44	18 29	16 04	16 07	16 10	16 13
S 60	16 59	17 42	18 30	16 10	16 09	16 09	16 08

Day	SUN Eqn. of Time 00^h	SUN Eqn. of Time 12^h	SUN Mer. Pass.	MOON Mer. Pass. Upper	MOON Mer. Pass. Lower	Age	Phase
d	m s	m s	h m	h m	h m	d %	
13	00 37	00 30	12 00	08 43	21 06	25 19	
14	00 22	00 15	12 00	09 28	21 51	26 11	
15	00 08	00 00	12 00	10 15	22 38	27 5	

UT d	UT h	ARIES GHA ° ′	VENUS −3·9 GHA ° ′	VENUS Dec ° ′	MARS +1·2 GHA ° ′	MARS Dec ° ′	JUPITER −2·1 GHA ° ′	JUPITER Dec ° ′	SATURN +0·9 GHA ° ′	SATURN Dec ° ′
16	00	204 09.3	156 37.2	N17 57.6	199 21.4	N 1 00.7	95 36.0	N22 43.6	196 31.3	N 0 57.8
	01	219 11.8	171 36.6	58.5	214 22.1	01.5	110 38.2	43.6	211 33.5	57.9
	02	234 14.2	186 36.0	17 59.5	229 22.7	02.3	125 40.4	43.5	226 35.6	58.0
	03	249 16.7	201 35.4	18 00.4	244 23.4	. . 03.1	140 42.6	. . 43.5	241 37.8	. . 58.1
	04	264 19.2	216 34.8	01.3	259 24.1	03.9	155 44.7	43.5	256 40.0	58.2
	05	279 21.6	231 34.2	02.3	274 24.8	04.6	170 46.9	43.4	271 42.2	58.3
	06	294 24.1	246 33.6	N18 03.2	289 25.5	N 1 05.4	185 49.1	N22 43.4	286 44.4	N 0 58.4
	07	309 26.6	261 33.0	04.1	304 26.2	06.2	200 51.3	43.4	301 46.6	58.6
T	08	324 29.0	276 32.4	05.0	319 26.9	07.0	215 53.5	43.3	316 48.8	58.7
H	09	339 31.5	291 31.8	. . 06.0	334 27.6	. . 07.8	230 55.6	. . 43.3	331 50.9	. . 58.8
U	10	354 34.0	306 31.2	06.9	349 28.3	08.5	245 57.8	43.3	346 53.1	58.9
R	11	9 36.4	321 30.6	07.8	4 28.9	09.3	261 00.0	43.3	1 55.3	59.0
S	12	24 38.9	336 30.0	N18 08.7	19 29.6	N 1 10.1	276 02.2	N22 43.2	16 57.5	N 0 59.1
D	13	39 41.3	351 29.4	09.6	34 30.3	10.9	291 04.3	43.2	31 59.7	59.3
A	14	54 43.8	6 28.8	10.6	49 31.0	11.7	306 06.5	43.2	47 01.9	59.4
Y	15	69 46.3	21 28.2	. . 11.5	64 31.7	. . 12.4	321 08.7	. . 43.1	62 04.1	. . 59.5
	16	84 48.7	36 27.6	12.4	79 32.4	13.2	336 10.9	43.1	77 06.3	59.6
	17	99 51.2	51 27.0	13.3	94 33.1	14.0	351 13.0	43.1	92 08.4	59.7
	18	114 53.7	66 26.4	N18 14.2	109 33.8	N 1 14.8	6 15.2	N22 43.0	107 10.6	N 0 59.8
	19	129 56.1	81 25.8	15.1	124 34.5	15.6	21 17.4	43.0	122 12.8	0 59.9
	20	144 58.6	96 25.2	16.1	139 35.1	16.3	36 19.6	43.0	137 15.0	1 00.1
	21	160 01.1	111 24.6	. . 17.0	154 35.8	. . 17.1	51 21.7	. . 42.9	152 17.2	. . 00.2
	22	175 03.5	126 24.0	17.9	169 36.5	17.9	66 23.9	42.9	167 19.4	00.3
	23	190 06.0	141 23.4	18.8	184 37.2	18.7	81 26.1	42.9	182 21.6	00.4
17	00	205 08.5	156 22.8	N18 19.7	199 37.9	N 1 19.5	96 28.3	N22 42.8	197 23.7	N 1 00.5
	01	220 10.9	171 22.2	20.6	214 38.6	20.2	111 30.4	42.8	212 25.9	00.6
	02	235 13.4	186 21.6	21.5	229 39.3	21.0	126 32.6	42.8	227 28.1	00.7
	03	250 15.8	201 20.9	. . 22.4	244 40.0	. . 21.8	141 34.8	. . 42.7	242 30.3	. . 00.9
	04	265 18.3	216 20.3	23.4	259 40.7	22.6	156 37.0	42.7	257 32.5	01.0
	05	280 20.8	231 19.7	24.3	274 41.4	23.4	171 39.1	42.7	272 34.7	01.1
	06	295 23.2	246 19.1	N18 25.2	289 42.0	N 1 24.1	186 41.3	N22 42.6	287 36.9	N 1 01.2
	07	310 25.7	261 18.5	26.1	304 42.7	24.9	201 43.5	42.6	302 39.0	01.3
	08	325 28.2	276 17.9	27.0	319 43.4	25.7	216 45.6	42.6	317 41.2	01.4
F	09	340 30.6	291 17.3	. . 27.9	334 44.1	. . 26.5	231 47.8	. . 42.5	332 43.4	. . 01.6
R	10	355 33.1	306 16.7	28.8	349 44.8	27.2	246 50.0	42.5	347 45.6	01.7
I	11	10 35.6	321 16.1	29.7	4 45.5	28.0	261 52.2	42.5	2 47.8	01.8
D	12	25 38.0	336 15.4	N18 30.6	19 46.2	N 1 28.8	276 54.3	N22 42.4	17 50.0	N 1 01.9
A	13	40 40.5	351 14.8	31.5	34 46.9	29.6	291 56.5	42.4	32 52.2	02.0
Y	14	55 42.9	6 14.2	32.4	49 47.6	30.4	306 58.7	42.4	47 54.4	02.1
	15	70 45.4	21 13.6	. . 33.3	64 48.3	. . 31.1	322 00.8	. . 42.3	62 56.5	. . 02.2
	16	85 47.9	36 13.0	34.2	79 48.9	31.9	337 03.0	42.3	77 58.7	02.4
	17	100 50.3	51 12.4	35.1	94 49.6	32.7	352 05.2	42.3	93 00.9	02.5
	18	115 52.8	66 11.7	N18 36.0	109 50.3	N 1 33.5	7 07.3	N22 42.2	108 03.1	N 1 02.6
	19	130 55.3	81 11.1	36.9	124 51.0	34.3	22 09.5	42.2	123 05.3	02.7
	20	145 57.7	96 10.5	37.8	139 51.7	35.0	37 11.7	42.2	138 07.5	02.8
	21	161 00.2	111 09.9	. . 38.7	154 52.4	. . 35.8	52 13.8	. . 42.1	153 09.7	. . 02.9
	22	176 02.7	126 09.3	39.6	169 53.1	36.6	67 16.0	42.1	168 11.9	03.0
	23	191 05.1	141 08.7	40.5	184 53.8	37.4	82 18.2	42.1	183 14.0	03.2
18	00	206 07.6	156 08.0	N18 41.4	199 54.5	N 1 38.2	97 20.3	N22 42.0	198 16.2	N 1 03.3
	01	221 10.1	171 07.4	42.2	214 55.2	38.9	112 22.5	42.0	213 18.4	03.4
	02	236 12.5	186 06.8	43.1	229 55.8	39.7	127 24.7	42.0	228 20.6	03.5
	03	251 15.0	201 06.2	. . 44.0	244 56.5	. . 40.5	142 26.8	. . 41.9	243 22.8	. . 03.6
	04	266 17.4	216 05.6	44.9	259 57.2	41.3	157 29.0	41.9	258 25.0	03.7
	05	281 19.9	231 04.9	45.8	274 57.9	42.0	172 31.2	41.9	273 27.2	03.8
	06	296 22.4	246 04.3	N18 46.7	289 58.6	N 1 42.8	187 33.3	N22 41.8	288 29.4	N 1 04.0
	07	311 24.8	261 03.7	47.6	304 59.3	43.6	202 35.5	41.8	303 31.5	04.1
S	08	326 27.3	276 03.1	48.5	320 00.0	44.4	217 37.7	41.8	318 33.7	04.2
A	09	341 29.8	291 02.4	. . 49.3	335 00.7	. . 45.2	232 39.8	. . 41.7	333 35.9	. . 04.3
T	10	356 32.2	306 01.8	50.2	350 01.4	45.9	247 42.0	41.7	348 38.1	04.4
U	11	11 34.7	321 01.2	51.1	5 02.1	46.7	262 44.2	41.7	3 40.3	04.5
R	12	26 37.2	336 00.6	N18 52.0	20 02.8	N 1 47.5	277 46.3	N22 41.6	18 42.5	N 1 04.6
D	13	41 39.6	351 00.0	52.9	35 03.4	48.3	292 48.5	41.6	33 44.7	04.8
A	14	56 42.1	5 59.3	53.8	50 04.1	49.0	307 50.7	41.5	48 46.9	04.9
Y	15	71 44.6	20 58.7	. . 54.6	65 04.8	. . 49.8	322 52.8	. . 41.5	63 49.0	. . 05.0
	16	86 47.0	35 58.1	55.5	80 05.5	50.6	337 55.0	41.5	78 51.2	05.1
	17	101 49.5	50 57.4	56.4	95 06.2	51.4	352 57.1	41.4	93 53.4	05.2
	18	116 51.9	65 56.8	N18 57.3	110 06.9	N 1 52.2	7 59.3	N22 41.4	108 55.6	N 1 05.3
	19	131 54.4	80 56.2	58.1	125 07.6	52.9	23 01.5	41.4	123 57.8	05.4
	20	146 56.9	95 55.6	59.0	140 08.3	53.7	38 03.6	41.3	139 00.0	05.6
	21	161 59.3	110 54.9	18 59.9	155 09.0	. . 54.5	53 05.8	. . 41.3	154 02.2	. . 05.7
	22	177 01.8	125 54.3	19 00.8	170 09.7	55.3	68 08.0	41.3	169 04.4	05.8
	23	192 04.3	140 53.7	N19 01.6	185 10.4	56.0	83 10.1	41.2	184 06.5	05.9
Mer. Pass.		h m 10 17.7	*v* −0.6	*d* 0.9	*v* 0.7	*d* 0.8	*v* 2.2	*d* 0.0	*v* 2.2	*d* 0.1

STARS

Name	SHA ° ′	Dec ° ′
Acamar	315 11.4	S40 12.0
Achernar	335 20.0	S57 06.2
Acrux	172 58.3	S63 14.9
Adhara	255 05.1	S29 00.7
Aldebaran	290 38.7	N16 33.7
Alioth	166 11.5	N55 49.0
Alkaid	152 50.7	N49 10.8
Alnair	27 31.9	S46 49.9
Alnilam	275 36.9	S 1 11.2
Alphard	217 46.6	S 8 46.5
Alphecca	126 02.5	N26 37.3
Alpheratz	357 34.0	N29 14.0
Altair	61 58.9	N 8 56.1
Ankaa	353 06.5	S42 09.7
Antares	112 14.3	S26 29.5
Arcturus	145 46.6	N19 02.6
Atria	107 07.2	S69 04.3
Avior	234 14.3	S59 35.9
Bellatrix	278 22.0	N 6 22.3
Betelgeuse	270 51.1	N 7 24.6
Canopus	263 52.1	S52 42.8
Capella	280 20.7	N46 01.5
Deneb	49 25.2	N45 22.1
Denebola	182 23.6	N14 25.4
Diphda	348 46.6	S17 50.6
Dubhe	193 39.2	N61 36.7
Elnath	278 00.8	N28 37.8
Eltanin	90 41.4	N51 28.8
Enif	33 37.9	N 9 59.6
Fomalhaut	15 13.6	S29 28.9
Gacrux	171 50.0	S57 15.8
Gienah	175 42.2	S17 41.5
Hadar	148 33.9	S60 30.1
Hamal	327 50.4	N23 35.1
Kaus Aust.	83 31.0	S34 22.2
Kochab	137 18.7	N74 02.6
Markab	13 29.1	N15 20.7
Menkar	314 05.4	N 4 11.5
Menkent	147 56.0	S36 30.1
Miaplacidus	221 37.8	S69 49.8
Mirfak	308 27.2	N49 57.3
Nunki	75 46.4	S26 15.8
Peacock	53 04.2	S56 38.8
Pollux	243 16.1	N27 57.8
Procyon	244 49.8	N 5 09.4
Rasalhague	95 57.4	N12 32.2
Regulus	207 33.2	N11 50.2
Rigel	281 03.1	S 8 10.4
Rigil Kent.	139 38.2	S60 56.6
Sabik	102 01.4	S15 45.5
Schedar	349 30.4	N56 40.8
Shaula	96 08.7	S37 07.3
Sirius	258 25.4	S16 45.3
Spica	158 20.9	S11 18.1
Suhail	222 45.4	S43 32.6
Vega	80 32.4	N38 48.2
Zuben'ubi	136 54.6	S16 09.2

	SHA ° ′	Mer. Pass. h m
Venus	311 14.3	13 35
Mars	354 29.5	10 41
Jupiter	251 19.8	17 32
Saturn	352 15.3	10 49

Day	UT (d h)	SUN GHA (° ′)	SUN Dec (° ′)	MOON GHA (° ′)	v (′)	MOON Dec (° ′)	d (′)	HP (′)
THURSDAY	16 00	180 01.8	N10 03.0	199 44.4	11.9	N 4 31.2	16.7	59.3
	01	195 01.9	03.8	214 15.3	11.8	4 47.9	16.6	59.3
	02	210 02.1	04.7	228 46.1	11.7	5 04.5	16.7	59.3
	03	225 02.2	. . 05.6	243 16.8	11.7	5 21.2	16.6	59.4
	04	240 02.4	06.5	257 47.5	11.7	5 37.8	16.7	59.4
	05	255 02.5	07.4	272 18.2	11.5	5 54.5	16.6	59.4
	06	270 02.6	N10 08.3	286 48.7	11.5	N 6 11.1	16.6	59.5
	07	285 02.8	09.2	301 19.2	11.5	6 27.7	16.6	59.5
	08	300 02.9	10.1	315 49.7	11.3	6 44.3	16.5	59.5
	09	315 03.1	. . 10.9	330 20.0	11.3	7 00.8	16.6	59.5
	10	330 03.2	11.8	344 50.3	11.2	7 17.4	16.5	59.6
	11	345 03.4	12.7	359 20.5	11.2	7 33.9	16.5	59.6
	12	0 03.5	N10 13.6	13 50.7	11.0	N 7 50.4	16.5	59.6
	13	15 03.7	14.5	28 20.7	11.0	8 06.9	16.5	59.7
	14	30 03.8	15.4	42 50.7	10.9	8 23.4	16.4	59.7
	15	45 04.0	. . 16.2	57 20.6	10.9	8 39.8	16.4	59.7
	16	60 04.1	17.1	71 50.5	10.7	8 56.2	16.3	59.7
	17	75 04.2	18.0	86 20.2	10.7	9 12.5	16.4	59.8
	18	90 04.4	N10 18.9	100 49.9	10.6	N 9 28.9	16.2	59.8
	19	105 04.5	19.8	115 19.5	10.5	9 45.1	16.3	59.8
	20	120 04.7	20.7	129 49.0	10.4	10 01.4	16.2	59.8
	21	135 04.8	. . 21.6	144 18.4	10.4	10 17.6	16.2	59.9
	22	150 05.0	22.4	158 47.8	10.2	10 33.8	16.1	59.9
	23	165 05.1	23.3	173 17.0	10.2	10 49.9	16.1	59.9
FRIDAY	17 00	180 05.3	N10 24.2	187 46.2	10.1	N11 06.0	16.0	59.9
	01	195 05.4	25.1	202 15.3	10.0	11 22.0	16.0	60.0
	02	210 05.5	26.0	216 44.3	9.8	11 38.0	15.9	60.0
	03	225 05.7	. . 26.8	231 13.1	9.9	11 53.9	15.9	60.0
	04	240 05.8	27.7	245 42.0	9.7	12 09.8	15.8	60.0
	05	255 06.0	28.6	260 10.7	9.6	12 25.6	15.8	60.1
	06	270 06.1	N10 29.5	274 39.3	9.5	N12 41.4	15.7	60.1
	07	285 06.3	30.4	289 07.8	9.4	12 57.1	15.6	60.1
	08	300 06.4	31.2	303 36.2	9.4	13 12.7	15.6	60.1
	09	315 06.5	. . 32.1	318 04.6	9.2	13 28.3	15.5	60.2
	10	330 06.7	33.0	332 32.8	9.1	13 43.8	15.4	60.2
	11	345 06.8	33.9	347 00.9	9.1	13 59.2	15.4	60.2
	12	0 07.0	N10 34.8	1 29.0	8.9	N14 14.6	15.3	60.2
	13	15 07.1	35.6	15 56.9	8.8	14 29.9	15.2	60.2
	14	30 07.3	36.5	30 24.7	8.8	14 45.1	15.1	60.2
	15	45 07.4	. . 37.4	44 52.5	8.6	15 00.2	15.1	60.3
	16	60 07.5	38.3	59 20.1	8.5	15 15.3	15.0	60.3
	17	75 07.7	39.1	73 47.6	8.4	15 30.3	14.9	60.3
	18	90 07.8	N10 40.0	88 15.0	8.4	N15 45.2	14.8	60.3
	19	105 08.0	40.9	102 42.4	8.2	16 00.0	14.7	60.3
	20	120 08.1	41.8	117 09.6	8.1	16 14.7	14.6	60.4
	21	135 08.2	. . 42.6	131 36.7	8.0	16 29.3	14.6	60.4
	22	150 08.4	43.5	146 03.7	7.8	16 43.9	14.4	60.4
	23	165 08.5	44.4	160 30.5	7.8	16 58.3	14.4	60.4
SATURDAY	18 00	180 08.7	N10 45.3	174 57.3	7.7	N17 12.7	14.2	60.4
	01	195 08.8	46.1	189 24.0	7.6	17 26.9	14.2	60.4
	02	210 08.9	47.0	203 50.6	7.4	17 41.1	14.0	60.4
	03	225 09.1	. . 47.9	218 17.0	7.4	17 55.1	14.0	60.5
	04	240 09.2	48.8	232 43.4	7.2	18 09.1	13.8	60.5
	05	255 09.3	49.6	247 09.6	7.1	18 22.9	13.7	60.5
	06	270 09.5	N10 50.5	261 35.7	7.0	N18 36.6	13.6	60.5
	07	285 09.6	51.4	276 01.7	6.9	18 50.2	13.5	60.5
	08	300 09.8	52.3	290 27.6	6.8	19 03.7	13.4	60.5
	09	315 09.9	. . 53.1	304 53.4	6.7	19 17.1	13.3	60.5
	10	330 10.0	54.0	319 19.1	6.6	19 30.4	13.1	60.5
	11	345 10.2	54.9	333 44.7	6.4	19 43.5	13.0	60.5
	12	0 10.3	N10 55.7	348 10.1	6.4	N19 56.5	12.9	60.6
	13	15 10.5	56.6	2 35.5	6.2	20 09.4	12.8	60.6
	14	30 10.6	57.5	17 00.7	6.1	20 22.2	12.6	60.6
	15	45 10.7	. . 58.4	31 25.8	6.1	20 34.8	12.5	60.6
	16	60 10.9	10 59.2	45 50.9	5.9	20 47.3	12.4	60.6
	17	75 11.0	11 00.1	60 15.8	5.8	20 59.7	12.2	60.6
	18	90 11.1	N11 01.0	74 40.6	5.6	N21 11.9	12.1	60.6
	19	105 11.3	01.8	89 05.2	5.6	21 24.0	12.0	60.6
	20	120 11.4	02.7	103 29.8	5.5	21 36.0	11.8	60.6
	21	135 11.5	. . 03.6	117 54.3	5.4	21 47.8	11.7	60.6
	22	150 11.7	04.4	132 18.7	5.2	21 59.5	11.5	60.6
	23	165 11.8	05.3	146 42.9	5.1	N22 11.0	11.4	60.6
		SD 16.0	*d* 0.9	SD	16.2		16.4	16.5

Lat. (°)	Twilight Naut. (h m)	Twilight Civil (h m)	Sunrise (h m)	Moonrise 16 (h m)	Moonrise 17 (h m)	Moonrise 18 (h m)	Moonrise 19 (h m)
N 72	////	01 37	03 28	03 41	02 56	01 25	▭
N 70	////	02 21	03 46	03 48	03 16	02 23	▭
68	////	02 49	04 01	03 54	03 31	02 57	▭
66	01 24	03 10	04 12	03 59	03 43	03 23	02 42
64	02 02	03 26	04 22	04 04	03 54	03 42	03 25
62	02 28	03 40	04 31	04 07	04 03	03 59	03 54
60	02 48	03 51	04 38	04 11	04 11	04 12	04 17
N 58	03 04	04 01	04 44	04 14	04 18	04 24	04 35
56	03 17	04 09	04 50	04 16	04 24	04 34	04 51
54	03 28	04 16	04 55	04 19	04 30	04 44	05 04
52	03 38	04 23	04 59	04 21	04 35	04 52	05 16
50	03 46	04 29	05 03	04 23	04 39	04 59	05 26
45	04 04	04 41	05 12	04 27	04 49	05 15	05 48
N 40	04 17	04 51	05 19	04 31	04 57	05 28	06 06
35	04 28	05 00	05 26	04 34	05 05	05 39	06 21
30	04 37	05 07	05 31	04 37	05 11	05 49	06 34
20	04 52	05 18	05 41	04 42	05 22	06 06	06 56
N 10	05 02	05 27	05 49	04 47	05 32	06 21	07 16
0	05 11	05 35	05 56	04 51	05 41	06 36	07 35
S 10	05 18	05 42	06 04	04 55	05 51	06 50	07 53
20	05 23	05 49	06 11	05 00	06 01	07 05	08 13
30	05 28	05 56	06 20	05 05	06 13	07 23	08 37
35	05 30	06 00	06 25	05 09	06 19	07 34	08 50
40	05 32	06 03	06 31	05 12	06 27	07 46	09 06
45	05 33	06 08	06 37	05 16	06 36	08 00	09 26
S 50	05 35	06 12	06 45	05 21	06 47	08 18	09 50
52	05 35	06 14	06 49	05 24	06 53	08 26	10 01
54	05 35	06 17	06 53	05 26	06 58	08 35	10 15
56	05 36	06 19	06 57	05 29	07 05	08 46	10 30
58	05 36	06 22	07 02	05 32	07 12	08 58	10 48
S 60	05 36	06 24	07 07	05 36	07 20	09 12	11 11

Lat. (°)	Sunset (h m)	Twilight Civil (h m)	Twilight Naut. (h m)	Moonset 16 (h m)	Moonset 17 (h m)	Moonset 18 (h m)	Moonset 19 (h m)
N 72	20 36	22 32	////	19 27	22 49	▭	▭
N 70	20 16	21 44	////	19 10	21 54	▭	▭
68	20 01	21 15	////	18 57	21 21	▭	▭
66	19 49	20 53	22 44	18 47	20 58	23 39	▭
64	19 39	20 36	22 02	18 38	20 39	22 57	▭
62	19 30	20 22	21 35	18 31	20 24	22 28	24 43
60	19 23	20 10	21 14	18 24	20 12	22 07	24 05
N 58	19 17	20 00	20 58	18 19	20 01	21 49	23 38
56	19 11	19 52	20 44	18 14	19 52	21 35	23 16
54	19 06	19 44	20 33	18 09	19 44	21 22	22 59
52	19 01	19 37	20 23	18 05	19 36	21 11	22 44
50	18 57	19 31	20 14	18 02	19 30	21 01	22 31
45	18 48	19 19	19 56	17 54	19 16	20 40	22 05
N 40	18 40	19 09	19 43	17 47	19 04	20 24	21 44
35	18 34	19 00	19 31	17 42	18 54	20 10	21 26
30	18 28	18 53	19 22	17 37	18 46	19 58	21 12
20	18 19	18 41	19 08	17 29	18 31	19 37	20 46
N 10	18 11	18 32	18 57	17 21	18 18	19 20	20 24
0	18 03	18 24	18 48	17 15	18 07	19 03	20 04
S 10	17 55	18 17	18 41	17 08	17 55	18 47	19 44
20	17 47	18 10	18 36	17 00	17 42	18 29	19 22
30	17 38	18 03	18 31	16 52	17 28	18 09	18 57
35	17 33	17 59	18 29	16 48	17 20	17 57	18 43
40	17 28	17 55	18 27	16 42	17 10	17 44	18 26
45	17 21	17 51	18 25	16 36	16 59	17 28	18 06
S 50	17 13	17 46	18 23	16 29	16 46	17 09	17 40
52	17 09	17 44	18 23	16 25	16 40	17 00	17 28
54	17 05	17 42	18 23	16 22	16 34	16 50	17 15
56	17 01	17 39	18 22	16 18	16 26	16 38	16 59
58	16 56	17 36	18 22	16 13	16 18	16 25	16 40
S 60	16 51	17 33	18 22	16 08	16 08	16 10	16 16

Day (d)	SUN Eqn. of Time 00^h (m s)	SUN Eqn. of Time 12^h (m s)	SUN Mer. Pass. (h m)	MOON Mer. Pass. Upper (h m)	MOON Mer. Pass. Lower (h m)	MOON Age (d)	MOON Phase (%)
16	00 07	00 14	12 00	11 03	23 28	28	1
17	00 21	00 28	12 00	11 54	24 21	00	0 ●
18	00 34	00 41	11 59	12 49	00 21	01	2

2026 APRIL 19, 20, 21 (SUN., MON., TUES.)

	UT	ARIES	VENUS −3·9		MARS +1·2		JUPITER −2·1		SATURN +0·9	
	d h	GHA ° ′	GHA ° ′	Dec ° ′	GHA ° ′	Dec ° ′	GHA ° ′	Dec ° ′	GHA ° ′	Dec ° ′
	19 00	207 06.7	155 53.0	N19 02.5	200 11.0	N 1 56.8	98 12.3	N22 41.2	199 08.7	N 1 06.0
	01	222 09.2	170 52.4	03.4	215 11.7	57.6	113 14.4	41.2	214 10.9	06.1
	02	237 11.7	185 51.8	04.2	230 12.4	58.4	128 16.6	41.1	229 13.1	06.2
	03	252 14.1	200 51.2	. . 05.1	245 13.1	. . 59.1	143 18.8	. . 41.1	244 15.3	. . 06.4
	04	267 16.6	215 50.5	06.0	260 13.8	1 59.9	158 20.9	41.1	259 17.5	06.5
	05	282 19.0	230 49.9	06.9	275 14.5	2 00.7	173 23.1	41.0	274 19.7	06.6
	06	297 21.5	245 49.3	N19 07.7	290 15.2	N 2 01.5	188 25.2	N22 41.0	289 21.9	N 1 06.7
	07	312 24.0	260 48.6	08.6	305 15.9	02.3	203 27.4	41.0	304 24.1	06.8
	08	327 26.4	275 48.0	09.4	320 16.6	03.0	218 29.6	40.9	319 26.2	06.9
S	09	342 28.9	290 47.4	. . 10.3	335 17.3	. . 03.8	233 31.7	. . 40.9	334 28.4	. . 07.0
U	10	357 31.4	305 46.7	11.2	350 18.0	04.6	248 33.9	40.9	349 30.6	07.2
N	11	12 33.8	320 46.1	12.0	5 18.6	05.4	263 36.0	40.8	4 32.8	07.3
D	12	27 36.3	335 45.4	N19 12.9	20 19.3	N 2 06.1	278 38.2	N22 40.8	19 35.0	N 1 07.4
A	13	42 38.8	350 44.8	13.8	35 20.0	06.9	293 40.3	40.7	34 37.2	07.5
Y	14	57 41.2	5 44.2	14.6	50 20.7	07.7	308 42.5	40.7	49 39.4	07.6
	15	72 43.7	20 43.5	. . 15.5	65 21.4	. . 08.5	323 44.7	. . 40.7	64 41.6	. . 07.7
	16	87 46.2	35 42.9	16.3	80 22.1	09.2	338 46.8	40.6	79 43.8	07.8
	17	102 48.6	50 42.3	17.2	95 22.8	10.0	353 49.0	40.6	94 45.9	07.9
	18	117 51.1	65 41.6	N19 18.0	110 23.5	N 2 10.8	8 51.1	N22 40.6	109 48.1	N 1 08.1
	19	132 53.5	80 41.0	18.9	125 24.2	11.6	23 53.3	40.5	124 50.3	08.2
	20	147 56.0	95 40.3	19.8	140 24.9	12.3	38 55.4	40.5	139 52.5	08.3
	21	162 58.5	110 39.7	. . 20.6	155 25.6	. . 13.1	53 57.6	. . 40.5	154 54.7	. . 08.4
	22	178 00.9	125 39.1	21.5	170 26.3	13.9	68 59.7	40.4	169 56.9	08.5
	23	193 03.4	140 38.4	22.3	185 26.9	14.7	84 01.9	40.4	184 59.1	08.6
	20 00	208 05.9	155 37.8	N19 23.2	200 27.6	N 2 15.4	99 04.1	N22 40.4	200 01.3	N 1 08.7
	01	223 08.3	170 37.1	24.0	215 28.3	16.2	114 06.2	40.3	215 03.5	08.9
	02	238 10.8	185 36.5	24.9	230 29.0	17.0	129 08.4	40.3	230 05.6	09.0
	03	253 13.3	200 35.9	. . 25.7	245 29.7	. . 17.8	144 10.5	. . 40.2	245 07.8	. . 09.1
	04	268 15.7	215 35.2	26.6	260 30.4	18.5	159 12.7	40.2	260 10.0	09.2
	05	283 18.2	230 34.6	27.4	275 31.1	19.3	174 14.8	40.2	275 12.2	09.3
	06	298 20.7	245 33.9	N19 28.2	290 31.8	N 2 20.1	189 17.0	N22 40.1	290 14.4	N 1 09.4
	07	313 23.1	260 33.3	29.1	305 32.5	20.9	204 19.1	40.1	305 16.6	09.5
	08	328 25.6	275 32.6	29.9	320 33.2	21.6	219 21.3	40.1	320 18.8	09.6
M	09	343 28.0	290 32.0	. . 30.8	335 33.9	. . 22.4	234 23.4	. . 40.0	335 21.0	. . 09.8
O	10	358 30.5	305 31.3	31.6	350 34.6	23.2	249 25.6	40.0	350 23.2	09.9
N	11	13 33.0	320 30.7	32.5	5 35.2	24.0	264 27.7	40.0	5 25.4	10.0
D	12	28 35.4	335 30.1	N19 33.3	20 35.9	N 2 24.7	279 29.9	N22 39.9	20 27.5	N 1 10.1
A	13	43 37.9	350 29.4	34.1	35 36.6	25.5	294 32.0	39.9	35 29.7	10.2
Y	14	58 40.4	5 28.8	35.0	50 37.3	26.3	309 34.2	39.8	50 31.9	10.3
	15	73 42.8	20 28.1	. . 35.8	65 38.0	. . 27.1	324 36.3	. . 39.8	65 34.1	. . 10.4
	16	88 45.3	35 27.5	36.7	80 38.7	27.8	339 38.5	39.8	80 36.3	10.6
	17	103 47.8	50 26.8	37.5	95 39.4	28.6	354 40.6	39.7	95 38.5	10.7
	18	118 50.2	65 26.2	N19 38.3	110 40.1	N 2 29.4	9 42.8	N22 39.7	110 40.7	N 1 10.8
	19	133 52.7	80 25.5	39.2	125 40.8	30.2	24 44.9	39.7	125 42.9	10.9
	20	148 55.2	95 24.9	40.0	140 41.5	30.9	39 47.1	39.6	140 45.1	11.0
	21	163 57.6	110 24.2	. . 40.8	155 42.2	. . 31.7	54 49.2	. . 39.6	155 47.3	. . 11.1
	22	179 00.1	125 23.6	41.7	170 42.9	32.5	69 51.4	39.6	170 49.4	11.2
	23	194 02.5	140 22.9	42.5	185 43.5	33.3	84 53.5	39.5	185 51.6	11.3
	21 00	209 05.0	155 22.3	N19 43.3	200 44.2	N 2 34.0	99 55.7	N22 39.5	200 53.8	N 1 11.5
	01	224 07.5	170 21.6	44.1	215 44.9	34.8	114 57.8	39.4	215 56.0	11.6
	02	239 09.9	185 21.0	45.0	230 45.6	35.6	130 00.0	39.4	230 58.2	11.7
	03	254 12.4	200 20.3	. . 45.8	245 46.3	. . 36.4	145 02.1	. . 39.4	246 00.4	. . 11.8
	04	269 14.9	215 19.6	46.6	260 47.0	37.1	160 04.3	39.3	261 02.6	11.9
	05	284 17.3	230 19.0	47.4	275 47.7	37.9	175 06.4	39.3	276 04.8	12.0
	06	299 19.8	245 18.3	N19 48.3	290 48.4	N 2 38.7	190 08.6	N22 39.3	291 07.0	N 1 12.1
	07	314 22.3	260 17.7	49.1	305 49.1	39.5	205 10.7	39.2	306 09.2	12.2
T	08	329 24.7	275 17.0	49.9	320 49.8	40.2	220 12.9	39.2	321 11.4	12.4
U	09	344 27.2	290 16.4	. . 50.7	335 50.5	. . 41.0	235 15.0	. . 39.1	336 13.5	. . 12.5
E	10	359 29.7	305 15.7	51.6	350 51.2	41.8	250 17.1	39.1	351 15.7	12.6
S	11	14 32.1	320 15.1	52.4	5 51.9	42.5	265 19.3	39.1	6 17.9	12.7
D	12	29 34.6	335 14.4	N19 53.2	20 52.5	N 2 43.3	280 21.4	N22 39.0	21 20.1	N 1 12.8
A	13	44 37.0	350 13.7	54.0	35 53.2	44.1	295 23.6	39.0	36 22.3	12.9
Y	14	59 39.5	5 13.1	54.8	50 53.9	44.9	310 25.7	39.0	51 24.5	13.0
	15	74 42.0	20 12.4	. . 55.6	65 54.6	. . 45.6	325 27.9	. . 38.9	66 26.7	. . 13.1
	16	89 44.4	35 11.8	56.5	80 55.3	46.4	340 30.0	38.9	81 28.9	13.3
	17	104 46.9	50 11.1	57.3	95 56.0	47.2	355 32.2	38.8	96 31.1	13.4
	18	119 49.4	65 10.4	N19 58.1	110 56.7	N 2 48.0	10 34.3	N22 38.8	111 33.3	N 1 13.5
	19	134 51.8	80 09.8	58.9	125 57.4	48.7	25 36.4	38.8	126 35.5	13.6
	20	149 54.3	95 09.1	19 59.7	140 58.1	49.5	40 38.6	38.7	141 37.6	13.7
	21	164 56.8	110 08.5	20 00.5	155 58.8	. . 50.3	55 40.7	. . 38.7	156 39.8	. . 13.8
	22	179 59.2	125 07.8	01.3	170 59.5	51.0	70 42.9	38.7	171 42.0	13.9
	23	195 01.7	140 07.1	02.1	186 00.2	51.8	85 45.0	38.6	186 44.2	14.0
	Mer. Pass.	h m 10 05.9	*v* −0.6	*d* 0.8	*v* 0.7	*d* 0.8	*v* 2.2	*d* 0.0	*v* 2.2	*d* 0.1

STARS

Name	SHA ° ′	Dec ° ′
Acamar	315 11.4	S40 12.0
Achernar	335 20.0	S57 06.2
Acrux	172 58.3	S63 14.9
Adhara	255 05.2	S29 00.7
Aldebaran	290 38.7	N16 33.7
Alioth	166 11.5	N55 49.0
Alkaid	152 50.7	N49 10.8
Alnair	27 31.8	S46 49.9
Alnilam	275 36.9	S 1 11.2
Alphard	217 46.6	S 8 46.5
Alphecca	126 02.5	N26 37.4
Alpheratz	357 34.0	N29 14.0
Altair	61 58.9	N 8 56.1
Ankaa	353 06.5	S42 09.7
Antares	112 14.3	S26 29.5
Arcturus	145 46.6	N19 02.6
Atria	107 07.2	S69 04.3
Avior	234 14.3	S59 35.9
Bellatrix	278 22.0	N 6 22.3
Betelgeuse	270 51.1	N 7 24.6
Canopus	263 52.2	S52 42.8
Capella	280 20.7	N46 01.5
Deneb	49 25.2	N45 22.1
Denebola	182 23.6	N14 25.4
Diphda	348 46.6	S17 50.6
Dubhe	193 39.3	N61 36.7
Elnath	278 00.8	N28 37.8
Eltanin	90 41.4	N51 28.8
Enif	33 37.9	N 9 59.6
Fomalhaut	15 13.6	S29 28.9
Gacrux	171 50.0	S57 15.8
Gienah	175 42.2	S17 41.5
Hadar	148 33.9	S60 30.1
Hamal	327 50.4	N23 35.1
Kaus Aust.	83 31.0	S34 22.2
Kochab	137 18.7	N74 02.7
Markab	13 29.1	N15 20.7
Menkar	314 05.4	N 4 11.5
Menkent	147 56.0	S36 30.1
Miaplacidus	221 37.8	S69 49.8
Mirfak	308 27.2	N49 57.3
Nunki	75 46.4	S26 15.8
Peacock	53 04.1	S56 38.8
Pollux	243 16.1	N27 57.8
Procyon	244 49.8	N 5 09.4
Rasalhague	95 57.4	N12 32.3
Regulus	207 33.2	N11 50.2
Rigel	281 03.1	S 8 10.4
Rigil Kent.	139 38.2	S60 56.7
Sabik	102 01.4	S15 45.5
Schedar	349 30.4	N56 40.8
Shaula	96 08.7	S37 07.3
Sirius	258 25.4	S16 45.3
Spica	158 20.9	S11 18.1
Suhail	222 45.4	S43 32.6
Vega	80 32.4	N38 48.2
Zuben'ubi	136 54.5	S16 09.2

	SHA ° ′	Mer. Pass. h m
Venus	307 31.9	13 38
Mars	352 21.8	10 38
Jupiter	250 58.2	17 21
Saturn	351 55.4	10 38

Day	UT d h	SUN GHA ° ′	SUN Dec ° ′	MOON GHA ° ′	v ′	MOON Dec ° ′	d ′	HP ′
	19 00	180 12.0	N11 06.2	161 07.0	5.1	N22 22.4	11.2	60.6
	01	195 12.1	07.0	175 31.1	4.9	22 33.6	11.1	60.6
	02	210 12.2	07.9	189 55.0	4.9	22 44.7	10.9	60.6
	03	225 12.4	. . 08.8	204 18.9	4.7	22 55.6	10.7	60.6
	04	240 12.5	09.6	218 42.6	4.6	23 06.3	10.6	60.6
	05	255 12.6	10.5	233 06.2	4.5	23 16.9	10.5	60.6
	06	270 12.8	N11 11.4	247 29.7	4.4	N23 27.4	10.3	60.6
	07	285 12.9	12.2	261 53.1	4.4	23 37.7	10.1	60.6
	08	300 13.0	13.1	276 16.5	4.2	23 47.8	9.9	60.6
SUNDAY	09	315 13.2	. . 14.0	290 39.7	4.1	23 57.7	9.8	60.6
	10	330 13.3	14.8	305 02.8	4.0	24 07.5	9.6	60.6
	11	345 13.4	15.7	319 25.8	4.0	24 17.1	9.5	60.6
	12	0 13.6	N11 16.5	333 48.8	3.8	N24 26.6	9.2	60.6
	13	15 13.7	17.4	348 11.6	3.8	24 35.8	9.1	60.6
	14	30 13.8	18.3	2 34.4	3.6	24 44.9	8.9	60.6
	15	45 14.0	. . 19.1	16 57.0	3.6	24 53.8	8.8	60.6
	16	60 14.1	20.0	31 19.6	3.5	25 02.6	8.5	60.6
	17	75 14.2	20.9	45 42.1	3.4	25 11.1	8.4	60.6
	18	90 14.4	N11 21.7	60 04.5	3.3	N25 19.5	8.2	60.6
	19	105 14.5	22.6	74 26.8	3.3	25 27.7	8.0	60.6
	20	120 14.6	23.4	88 49.1	3.1	25 35.7	7.9	60.6
	21	135 14.8	. . 24.3	103 11.2	3.1	25 43.6	7.6	60.6
	22	150 14.9	25.2	117 33.3	3.0	25 51.2	7.4	60.6
	23	165 15.0	26.0	131 55.3	3.0	25 58.6	7.3	60.6
	20 00	180 15.1	N11 26.9	146 17.3	2.8	N26 05.9	7.1	60.6
	01	195 15.3	27.7	160 39.1	2.8	26 13.0	6.8	60.6
	02	210 15.4	28.6	175 00.9	2.8	26 19.8	6.7	60.6
	03	225 15.5	. . 29.5	189 22.7	2.6	26 26.5	6.5	60.5
	04	240 15.7	30.3	203 44.3	2.7	26 33.0	6.3	60.5
	05	255 15.8	31.2	218 06.0	2.5	26 39.3	6.1	60.5
	06	270 15.9	N11 32.0	232 27.5	2.5	N26 45.4	5.9	60.5
	07	285 16.1	32.9	246 49.0	2.5	26 51.3	5.7	60.5
	08	300 16.2	33.7	261 10.5	2.3	26 57.0	5.4	60.5
MONDAY	09	315 16.3	. . 34.6	275 31.8	2.4	27 02.4	5.3	60.5
	10	330 16.4	35.5	289 53.2	2.3	27 07.7	5.1	60.5
	11	345 16.6	36.3	304 14.5	2.3	27 12.8	4.9	60.5
	12	0 16.7	N11 37.2	318 35.8	2.2	N27 17.7	4.7	60.5
	13	15 16.8	38.0	332 57.0	2.2	27 22.4	4.5	60.4
	14	30 17.0	38.9	347 18.2	2.1	27 26.9	4.2	60.4
	15	45 17.1	. . 39.7	1 39.3	2.1	27 31.1	4.1	60.4
	16	60 17.2	40.6	16 00.4	2.1	27 35.2	3.9	60.4
	17	75 17.3	41.4	30 21.5	2.1	27 39.1	3.6	60.4
	18	90 17.5	N11 42.3	44 42.6	2.0	N27 42.7	3.4	60.4
	19	105 17.6	43.1	59 03.6	2.0	27 46.1	3.3	60.4
	20	120 17.7	44.0	73 24.6	2.0	27 49.4	3.0	60.3
	21	135 17.9	. . 44.8	87 45.6	2.0	27 52.4	2.8	60.3
	22	150 18.0	45.7	102 06.6	2.0	27 55.2	2.6	60.3
	23	165 18.1	46.5	116 27.6	2.0	27 57.8	2.4	60.3
	21 00	180 18.2	N11 47.4	130 48.6	2.0	N28 00.2	2.2	60.3
	01	195 18.4	48.3	145 09.6	1.9	28 02.4	2.0	60.3
	02	210 18.5	49.1	159 30.5	2.0	28 04.4	1.8	60.2
	03	225 18.6	. . 50.0	173 51.5	2.0	28 06.2	1.5	60.2
	04	240 18.7	50.8	188 12.5	2.0	28 07.7	1.4	60.2
	05	255 18.9	51.7	202 33.5	2.0	28 09.1	1.1	60.2
	06	270 19.0	N11 52.5	216 54.5	2.0	N28 10.2	1.0	60.2
	07	285 19.1	53.3	231 15.5	2.0	28 11.2	0.7	60.2
	08	300 19.2	54.2	245 36.5	2.1	28 11.9	0.5	60.1
TUESDAY	09	315 19.4	. . 55.0	259 57.6	2.0	28 12.4	0.3	60.1
	10	330 19.5	55.9	274 18.6	2.1	28 12.7	0.1	60.1
	11	345 19.6	56.7	288 39.7	2.2	28 12.8	0.1	60.1
	12	0 19.7	N11 57.6	303 00.9	2.1	N28 12.7	0.3	60.1
	13	15 19.9	58.4	317 22.0	2.2	28 12.4	0.5	60.0
	14	30 20.0	11 59.3	331 43.2	2.3	28 11.9	0.8	60.0
	15	45 20.1	12 00.1	346 04.5	2.3	28 11.1	0.9	60.0
	16	60 20.2	01.0	0 25.8	2.3	28 10.2	1.1	60.0
	17	75 20.4	01.8	14 47.1	2.4	28 09.1	1.4	60.0
	18	90 20.5	N12 02.7	29 08.5	2.4	N28 07.7	1.5	59.9
	19	105 20.6	03.5	43 29.9	2.5	28 06.2	1.7	59.9
	20	120 20.7	04.4	57 51.4	2.5	28 04.5	2.0	59.9
	21	135 20.9	. . 05.2	72 12.9	2.6	28 02.5	2.1	59.9
	22	150 21.0	06.0	86 34.5	2.6	28 00.4	2.4	59.8
	23	165 21.1	06.9	100 56.1	2.7	N27 58.0	2.5	59.8
		SD 15.9	d 0.9	SD 16.5		16.5		16.4

Lat. °	Twilight Naut. h m	Twilight Civil h m	Sunrise h m	Moonrise 19 h m	Moonrise 20 h m	Moonrise 21 h m	Moonrise 22 h m
N 72	////	00 56	03 10	▭	▭	▭	▭
N 70	////	01 57	03 31	▭	▭	▭	▭
68	////	02 31	03 47	▭	▭	▭	▭
66	00 48	02 55	04 01	02 42	▭	▭	▭
64	01 42	03 14	04 12	03 25	▭	▭	▭
62	02 13	03 29	04 21	03 54	03 50	03 40	05 20
60	02 35	03 41	04 29	04 17	04 29	05 02	06 19
N 58	02 53	03 52	04 36	04 35	04 56	05 38	06 52
56	03 07	04 01	04 42	04 51	05 18	06 05	07 17
54	03 20	04 09	04 48	05 04	05 36	06 25	07 37
52	03 30	04 16	04 53	05 16	05 51	06 43	07 53
50	03 39	04 22	04 57	05 26	06 04	06 58	08 08
45	03 58	04 36	05 07	05 48	06 31	07 28	08 37
N 40	04 13	04 47	05 15	06 06	06 53	07 51	08 59
35	04 24	04 56	05 22	06 21	07 11	08 11	09 18
30	04 34	05 03	05 28	06 34	07 27	08 28	09 34
20	04 49	05 16	05 38	06 56	07 53	08 56	10 02
N 10	05 01	05 26	05 47	07 16	08 16	09 20	10 25
0	05 10	05 34	05 56	07 35	08 38	09 43	10 47
S 10	05 18	05 42	06 04	07 53	08 59	10 05	11 08
20	05 24	05 50	06 12	08 13	09 23	10 30	11 32
30	05 30	05 58	06 22	08 37	09 50	10 58	11 59
35	05 32	06 02	06 28	08 50	10 06	11 15	12 15
40	05 35	06 06	06 34	09 06	10 25	11 35	12 33
45	05 37	06 11	06 41	09 26	10 47	11 59	12 56
S 50	05 39	06 17	06 50	09 50	11 17	12 30	13 24
52	05 40	06 19	06 54	10 01	11 31	12 45	13 38
54	05 41	06 22	06 58	10 15	11 48	13 03	13 54
56	05 41	06 25	07 03	10 30	12 08	13 24	14 12
58	05 42	06 28	07 09	10 48	12 33	13 52	14 35
S 60	05 43	06 31	07 15	11 11	13 07	14 31	15 06

Lat. °	Sunset h m	Twilight Civil h m	Twilight Naut. h m	Moonset 19 h m	Moonset 20 h m	Moonset 21 h m	Moonset 22 h m
N 72	20 53	23 22	////	▭	▭	▭	▭
N 70	20 30	22 07	////	▭	▭	▭	▭
68	20 13	21 31	////	▭	▭	▭	▭
66	20 00	21 06	23 27	▭	▭	▭	▭
64	19 48	20 47	22 22	▭	▭	▭	▭
62	19 39	20 32	21 49	24 43	00 43	03 09	03 45
60	19 30	20 19	21 26	24 05	00 05	01 47	02 46
N 58	19 23	20 08	21 08	23 38	25 11	01 11	02 12
56	19 17	19 59	20 53	23 16	24 45	00 45	01 47
54	19 11	19 50	20 40	22 59	24 24	00 24	01 27
52	19 06	19 43	20 29	22 44	24 07	00 07	01 11
50	19 02	19 37	20 20	22 31	23 52	24 56	00 56
45	18 52	19 23	20 01	22 05	23 22	24 27	00 27
N 40	18 43	19 12	19 46	21 44	22 59	24 04	00 04
35	18 36	19 03	19 34	21 26	22 40	23 44	24 39
30	18 30	18 55	19 24	21 12	22 23	23 28	24 24
20	18 20	18 42	19 09	20 46	21 55	23 00	23 58
N 10	18 11	18 32	18 57	20 24	21 31	22 36	23 36
0	18 02	18 23	18 48	20 04	21 09	22 14	23 16
S 10	17 54	18 15	18 40	19 44	20 46	21 51	22 55
20	17 45	18 08	18 33	19 22	20 22	21 27	22 33
30	17 35	18 00	18 28	18 57	19 54	20 59	22 07
35	17 30	17 55	18 25	18 43	19 38	20 42	21 52
40	17 23	17 51	18 23	18 26	19 18	20 22	21 34
45	17 16	17 46	18 20	18 06	18 55	19 58	21 12
S 50	17 07	17 40	18 18	17 40	18 26	19 28	20 45
52	17 03	17 38	18 17	17 28	18 11	19 12	20 31
54	16 59	17 35	18 16	17 15	17 54	18 55	20 15
56	16 54	17 32	18 15	16 59	17 34	18 33	19 57
58	16 48	17 29	18 15	16 40	17 08	18 06	19 34
S 60	16 42	17 25	18 14	16 16	16 34	17 26	19 05

Day d	SUN Eqn. of Time 00^h m s	SUN Eqn. of Time 12^h m s	SUN Mer. Pass. h m	MOON Mer. Pass. Upper h m	MOON Mer. Pass. Lower h m	MOON Age d	MOON Phase %
19	00 48	00 54	11 59	13 49	01 19	02	6
20	01 00	01 07	11 59	14 53	02 21	03	13
21	01 13	01 19	11 59	15 58	03 26	04	22

2026 APRIL 22, 23, 24 (WED., THURS., FRI.)

UT d h	ARIES GHA	VENUS −3·9 GHA	VENUS Dec	MARS +1·2 GHA	MARS Dec	JUPITER −2·1 GHA	JUPITER Dec	SATURN +0·9 GHA	SATURN Dec
	° ′	° ′	° ′	° ′	° ′	° ′	° ′	° ′	° ′
22 00 WEDNESDAY	210 04.2	155 06.5	N20 02.9	201 00.9	N 2 52.6	100 47.2	N22 38.6	201 46.4	N 1 14.2
01	225 06.6	170 05.8	03.8	216 01.6	53.4	115 49.3	38.5	216 48.6	14.3
02	240 09.1	185 05.1	04.6	231 02.2	54.1	130 51.4	38.5	231 50.8	14.4
03	255 11.5	200 04.5	. . 05.4	246 02.9	. . 54.9	145 53.6	. . 38.5	246 53.0	. . 14.5
04	270 14.0	215 03.8	06.2	261 03.6	55.7	160 55.7	38.4	261 55.2	14.6
05	285 16.5	230 03.2	07.0	276 04.3	56.4	175 57.9	38.4	276 57.4	14.7
06	300 18.9	245 02.5	N20 07.8	291 05.0	N 2 57.2	191 00.0	N22 38.4	291 59.6	N 1 14.8
07	315 21.4	260 01.8	08.6	306 05.7	58.0	206 02.1	38.3	307 01.7	14.9
08	330 23.9	275 01.2	09.4	321 06.4	58.8	221 04.3	38.3	322 03.9	15.1
09	345 26.3	290 00.5	. . 10.2	336 07.1	2 59.5	236 06.4	. . 38.2	337 06.1	. . 15.2
10	0 28.8	304 59.8	11.0	351 07.8	3 00.3	251 08.6	38.2	352 08.3	15.3
11	15 31.3	319 59.2	11.8	6 08.5	01.1	266 10.7	38.2	7 10.5	15.4
12	30 33.7	334 58.5	N20 12.6	21 09.2	N 3 01.8	281 12.8	N22 38.1	22 12.7	N 1 15.5
13	45 36.2	349 57.8	13.4	36 09.9	02.6	296 15.0	38.1	37 14.9	15.6
14	60 38.7	4 57.1	14.2	51 10.6	03.4	311 17.1	38.0	52 17.1	15.7
15	75 41.1	19 56.5	. . 14.9	66 11.3	. . 04.2	326 19.2	. . 38.0	67 19.3	. . 15.8
16	90 43.6	34 55.8	15.7	81 11.9	04.9	341 21.4	38.0	82 21.5	15.9
17	105 46.0	49 55.1	16.5	96 12.6	05.7	356 23.5	37.9	97 23.7	16.1
18	120 48.5	64 54.5	N20 17.3	111 13.3	N 3 06.5	11 25.7	N22 37.9	112 25.9	N 1 16.2
19	135 51.0	79 53.8	18.1	126 14.0	07.2	26 27.8	37.9	127 28.1	16.3
20	150 53.4	94 53.1	18.9	141 14.7	08.0	41 29.9	37.8	142 30.2	16.4
21	165 55.9	109 52.4	. . 19.7	156 15.4	. . 08.8	56 32.1	. . 37.8	157 32.4	. . 16.5
22	180 58.4	124 51.8	20.5	171 16.1	09.5	71 34.2	37.7	172 34.6	16.6
23	196 00.8	139 51.1	21.3	186 16.8	10.3	86 36.3	37.7	187 36.8	16.7
23 00 THURSDAY	211 03.3	154 50.4	N20 22.0	201 17.5	N 3 11.1	101 38.5	N22 37.7	202 39.0	N 1 16.8
01	226 05.8	169 49.8	22.8	216 18.2	11.9	116 40.6	37.6	217 41.2	16.9
02	241 08.2	184 49.1	23.6	231 18.9	12.6	131 42.8	37.6	232 43.4	17.1
03	256 10.7	199 48.4	. . 24.4	246 19.6	. . 13.4	146 44.9	. . 37.5	247 45.6	. . 17.2
04	271 13.1	214 47.7	25.2	261 20.3	14.2	161 47.0	37.5	262 47.8	17.3
05	286 15.6	229 47.1	26.0	276 21.0	14.9	176 49.2	37.5	277 50.0	17.4
06	301 18.1	244 46.4	N20 26.7	291 21.6	N 3 15.7	191 51.3	N22 37.4	292 52.2	N 1 17.5
07	316 20.5	259 45.7	27.5	306 22.3	16.5	206 53.4	37.4	307 54.4	17.6
08	331 23.0	274 45.0	28.3	321 23.0	17.2	221 55.6	37.3	322 56.6	17.7
09	346 25.5	289 44.3	. . 29.1	336 23.7	. . 18.0	236 57.7	. . 37.3	337 58.8	. . 17.8
10	1 27.9	304 43.7	29.8	351 24.4	18.8	251 59.8	37.3	353 00.9	18.0
11	16 30.4	319 43.0	30.6	6 25.1	19.6	267 02.0	37.2	8 03.1	18.1
12	31 32.9	334 42.3	N20 31.4	21 25.8	N 3 20.3	282 04.1	N22 37.2	23 05.3	N 1 18.2
13	46 35.3	349 41.6	32.2	36 26.5	21.1	297 06.2	37.2	38 07.5	18.3
14	61 37.8	4 41.0	32.9	51 27.2	21.9	312 08.4	37.1	53 09.7	18.4
15	76 40.3	19 40.3	. . 33.7	66 27.9	. . 22.6	327 10.5	. . 37.1	68 11.9	. . 18.5
16	91 42.7	34 39.6	34.5	81 28.6	23.4	342 12.6	37.0	83 14.1	18.6
17	106 45.2	49 38.9	35.3	96 29.3	24.2	357 14.8	37.0	98 16.3	18.7
18	121 47.6	64 38.2	N20 36.0	111 30.0	N 3 24.9	12 16.9	N22 37.0	113 18.5	N 1 18.8
19	136 50.1	79 37.5	36.8	126 30.7	25.7	27 19.0	36.9	128 20.7	19.0
20	151 52.6	94 36.9	37.6	141 31.4	26.5	42 21.1	36.9	143 22.9	19.1
21	166 55.0	109 36.2	. . 38.3	156 32.0	. . 27.2	57 23.3	. . 36.8	158 25.1	. . 19.2
22	181 57.5	124 35.5	39.1	171 32.7	28.0	72 25.4	36.8	173 27.3	19.3
23	197 00.0	139 34.8	39.8	186 33.4	28.8	87 27.5	36.8	188 29.5	19.4
24 00 FRIDAY	212 02.4	154 34.1	N20 40.6	201 34.1	N 3 29.5	102 29.7	N22 36.7	203 31.7	N 1 19.5
01	227 04.9	169 33.4	41.4	216 34.8	30.3	117 31.8	36.7	218 33.8	19.6
02	242 07.4	184 32.8	42.1	231 35.5	31.1	132 33.9	36.6	233 36.0	19.7
03	257 09.8	199 32.1	. . 42.9	246 36.2	. . 31.8	147 36.1	. . 36.6	248 38.2	. . 19.8
04	272 12.3	214 31.4	43.6	261 36.9	32.6	162 38.2	36.6	263 40.4	19.9
05	287 14.8	229 30.7	44.4	276 37.6	33.4	177 40.3	36.5	278 42.6	20.1
06	302 17.2	244 30.0	N20 45.2	291 38.3	N 3 34.2	192 42.4	N22 36.5	293 44.8	N 1 20.2
07	317 19.7	259 29.3	45.9	306 39.0	34.9	207 44.6	36.4	308 47.0	20.3
08	332 22.1	274 28.6	46.7	321 39.7	35.7	222 46.7	36.4	323 49.2	20.4
09	347 24.6	289 28.0	. . 47.4	336 40.4	. . 36.5	237 48.8	. . 36.4	338 51.4	. . 20.5
10	2 27.1	304 27.3	48.2	351 41.1	37.2	252 50.9	36.3	353 53.6	20.6
11	17 29.5	319 26.6	48.9	6 41.8	38.0	267 53.1	36.3	8 55.8	20.7
12	32 32.0	334 25.9	N20 49.7	21 42.4	N 3 38.8	282 55.2	N22 36.2	23 58.0	N 1 20.8
13	47 34.5	349 25.2	50.4	36 43.1	39.5	297 57.3	36.2	39 00.2	20.9
14	62 36.9	4 24.5	51.2	51 43.8	40.3	312 59.5	36.2	54 02.4	21.1
15	77 39.4	19 23.8	. . 51.9	66 44.5	. . 41.1	328 01.6	. . 36.1	69 04.6	. . 21.2
16	92 41.9	34 23.1	52.7	81 45.2	41.8	343 03.7	36.1	84 06.8	21.3
17	107 44.3	49 22.4	53.4	96 45.9	42.6	358 05.8	36.0	99 09.0	21.4
18	122 46.8	64 21.7	N20 54.2	111 46.6	N 3 43.4	13 08.0	N22 36.0	114 11.1	N 1 21.5
19	137 49.3	79 21.0	54.9	126 47.3	44.1	28 10.1	36.0	129 13.3	21.6
20	152 51.7	94 20.4	55.7	141 48.0	44.9	43 12.2	35.9	144 15.5	21.7
21	167 54.2	109 19.7	. . 56.4	156 48.7	. . 45.7	58 14.3	. . 35.9	159 17.7	. . 21.8
22	182 56.6	124 19.0	57.1	171 49.4	46.4	73 16.5	35.8	174 19.9	21.9
23	197 59.1	139 18.3	57.9	186 50.1	47.2	88 18.6	35.8	189 22.1	22.0
Mer. Pass.	h m 9 54.2	*v* −0.7	*d* 0.8	*v* 0.7	*d* 0.8	*v* 2.1	*d* 0.0	*v* 2.2	*d* 0.1

STARS

Name	SHA	Dec
	° ′	° ′
Acamar	315 11.4	S40 12.0
Achernar	335 20.0	S57 06.1
Acrux	172 58.3	S63 14.9
Adhara	255 05.2	S29 00.7
Aldebaran	290 38.7	N16 33.7
Alioth	166 11.5	N55 49.0
Alkaid	152 50.7	N49 10.8
Alnair	27 31.8	S46 49.8
Alnilam	275 36.9	S 1 11.2
Alphard	217 46.6	S 8 46.5
Alphecca	126 02.5	N26 37.4
Alpheratz	357 34.0	N29 14.0
Altair	61 58.9	N 8 56.1
Ankaa	353 06.5	S42 09.7
Antares	112 14.2	S26 29.5
Arcturus	145 46.6	N19 02.6
Atria	107 07.1	S69 04.3
Avior	234 14.3	S59 35.9
Bellatrix	278 22.0	N 6 22.3
Betelgeuse	270 51.1	N 7 24.6
Canopus	263 52.2	S52 42.8
Capella	280 20.7	N46 01.5
Deneb	49 25.1	N45 22.1
Denebola	182 23.6	N14 25.4
Diphda	348 46.5	S17 50.6
Dubhe	193 39.3	N61 36.7
Elnath	278 00.8	N28 37.8
Eltanin	90 41.4	N51 28.8
Enif	33 37.9	N 9 59.6
Fomalhaut	15 13.6	S29 28.9
Gacrux	171 50.0	S57 15.9
Gienah	175 42.2	S17 41.5
Hadar	148 33.9	S60 30.1
Hamal	327 50.4	N23 35.1
Kaus Aust.	83 30.9	S34 22.2
Kochab	137 18.6	N74 02.7
Markab	13 29.1	N15 20.7
Menkar	314 05.4	N 4 11.5
Menkent	147 56.0	S36 30.1
Miaplacidus	221 37.9	S69 49.8
Mirfak	308 27.2	N49 57.3
Nunki	75 46.3	S26 15.8
Peacock	53 04.1	S56 38.8
Pollux	243 16.1	N27 57.8
Procyon	244 49.8	N 5 09.4
Rasalhague	95 57.4	N12 32.3
Regulus	207 33.2	N11 50.2
Rigel	281 03.1	S 8 10.4
Rigil Kent.	139 38.2	S60 56.7
Sabik	102 01.3	S15 45.5
Schedar	349 30.4	N56 40.8
Shaula	96 08.7	S37 07.3
Sirius	258 25.5	S16 45.3
Spica	158 20.9	S11 18.1
Suhail	222 45.5	S43 32.6
Vega	80 32.3	N38 48.2
Zuben'ubi	136 54.5	S16 09.2

	SHA	Mer. Pass.
	° ′	h m
Venus	303 47.1	13 41
Mars	350 14.2	10 34
Jupiter	250 35.2	17 11
Saturn	351 35.7	10 28

UT d	h	SUN GHA ° ′	SUN Dec ° ′	MOON GHA ° ′	v ′	MOON Dec ° ′	d ′	HP ′
22 Wednesday	00	180 21.2	N12 07.7	115 17.8	2.8	N27 55.5	2.8	59.8
	01	195 21.4	08.6	129 39.6	2.9	27 52.7	2.9	59.8
	02	210 21.5	09.4	144 01.5	2.9	27 49.8	3.1	59.8
	03	225 21.6	. . 10.3	158 23.4	3.0	27 46.7	3.4	59.7
	04	240 21.7	11.1	172 45.4	3.1	27 43.3	3.5	59.7
	05	255 21.8	11.9	187 07.5	3.1	27 39.8	3.7	59.7
	06	270 22.0	N12 12.8	201 29.6	3.3	N27 36.1	3.9	59.7
	07	285 22.1	13.6	215 51.9	3.3	27 32.2	4.1	59.6
	08	300 22.2	14.5	230 14.2	3.4	27 28.1	4.3	59.6
	09	315 22.3	. . 15.3	244 36.6	3.5	27 23.8	4.4	59.6
	10	330 22.4	16.1	258 59.1	3.6	27 19.4	4.7	59.6
	11	345 22.6	17.0	273 21.7	3.7	27 14.7	4.8	59.5
	12	0 22.7	N12 17.8	287 44.4	3.7	N27 09.9	5.1	59.5
	13	15 22.8	18.7	302 07.1	3.9	27 04.8	5.1	59.5
	14	30 22.9	19.5	316 30.0	3.9	26 59.7	5.4	59.5
	15	45 23.0	. . 20.3	330 52.9	4.1	26 54.3	5.6	59.4
	16	60 23.2	21.2	345 16.0	4.2	26 48.7	5.7	59.4
	17	75 23.3	22.0	359 39.2	4.2	26 43.0	5.9	59.4
	18	90 23.4	N12 22.8	14 02.4	4.4	N26 37.1	6.1	59.4
	19	105 23.5	23.7	28 25.8	4.5	26 31.0	6.3	59.3
	20	120 23.6	24.5	42 49.3	4.6	26 24.7	6.4	59.3
	21	135 23.8	. . 25.3	57 12.9	4.7	26 18.3	6.6	59.3
	22	150 23.9	26.2	71 36.6	4.8	26 11.7	6.7	59.3
	23	165 24.0	27.0	86 00.4	4.9	26 05.0	7.0	59.2
23 Thursday	00	180 24.1	N12 27.8	100 24.3	5.0	N25 58.0	7.0	59.2
	01	195 24.2	28.7	114 48.3	5.1	25 51.0	7.3	59.2
	02	210 24.3	29.5	129 12.4	5.3	25 43.7	7.4	59.2
	03	225 24.5	. . 30.4	143 36.7	5.3	25 36.3	7.6	59.1
	04	240 24.6	31.2	158 01.0	5.5	25 28.7	7.7	59.1
	05	255 24.7	32.0	172 25.5	5.6	25 21.0	7.9	59.1
	06	270 24.8	N12 32.8	186 50.1	5.7	N25 13.1	8.0	59.0
	07	285 24.9	33.7	201 14.8	5.9	25 05.1	8.2	59.0
	08	300 25.0	34.5	215 39.7	5.9	24 56.9	8.3	59.0
	09	315 25.2	. . 35.3	230 04.6	6.1	24 48.6	8.5	59.0
	10	330 25.3	36.2	244 29.7	6.2	24 40.1	8.6	58.9
	11	345 25.4	37.0	258 54.9	6.3	24 31.5	8.8	58.9
	12	0 25.5	N12 37.8	273 20.2	6.5	N24 22.7	8.9	58.9
	13	15 25.6	38.7	287 45.7	6.6	24 13.8	9.0	58.9
	14	30 25.7	39.5	302 11.3	6.6	24 04.8	9.2	58.8
	15	45 25.9	. . 40.3	316 36.9	6.8	23 55.6	9.3	58.8
	16	60 26.0	41.2	331 02.7	7.0	23 46.3	9.5	58.8
	17	75 26.1	42.0	345 28.7	7.0	23 36.8	9.6	58.7
	18	90 26.2	N12 42.8	359 54.7	7.2	N23 27.2	9.7	58.7
	19	105 26.3	43.6	14 20.9	7.3	23 17.5	9.8	58.7
	20	120 26.4	44.5	28 47.2	7.4	23 07.7	10.0	58.7
	21	135 26.5	. . 45.3	43 13.6	7.6	22 57.7	10.1	58.6
	22	150 26.7	46.1	57 40.2	7.7	22 47.6	10.3	58.6
	23	165 26.8	46.9	72 06.9	7.8	22 37.3	10.3	58.6
24 Friday	00	180 26.9	N12 47.8	86 33.7	7.9	N22 27.0	10.5	58.5
	01	195 27.0	48.6	101 00.6	8.0	22 16.5	10.6	58.5
	02	210 27.1	49.4	115 27.6	8.2	22 05.9	10.7	58.5
	03	225 27.2	. . 50.2	129 54.8	8.3	21 55.2	10.8	58.5
	04	240 27.3	51.1	144 22.1	8.4	21 44.4	10.9	58.4
	05	255 27.4	51.9	158 49.5	8.5	21 33.5	11.1	58.4
	06	270 27.6	N12 52.7	173 17.0	8.7	N21 22.4	11.1	58.4
	07	285 27.7	53.5	187 44.7	8.8	21 11.3	11.3	58.3
	08	300 27.8	54.4	202 12.5	8.9	21 00.0	11.3	58.3
	09	315 27.9	. . 55.2	216 40.4	9.0	20 48.7	11.5	58.3
	10	330 28.0	56.0	231 08.4	9.1	20 37.2	11.6	58.3
	11	345 28.1	56.8	245 36.5	9.3	20 25.6	11.7	58.2
	12	0 28.2	N12 57.6	260 04.8	9.3	N20 13.9	11.7	58.2
	13	15 28.3	58.5	274 33.1	9.5	20 02.2	11.9	58.2
	14	30 28.4	12 59.3	289 01.6	9.6	19 50.3	12.0	58.2
	15	45 28.6	13 00.1	303 30.2	9.8	19 38.3	12.0	58.1
	16	60 28.7	00.9	317 59.0	9.8	19 26.3	12.2	58.1
	17	75 28.8	01.7	332 27.8	10.0	19 14.1	12.2	58.1
	18	90 28.9	N13 02.6	346 56.8	10.0	N19 01.9	12.3	58.0
	19	105 29.0	03.4	1 25.8	10.2	18 49.6	12.5	58.0
	20	120 29.1	04.2	15 55.0	10.3	18 37.1	12.5	58.0
	21	135 29.2	. . 05.0	30 24.3	10.4	18 24.6	12.6	58.0
	22	150 29.3	05.8	44 53.7	10.5	18 12.0	12.6	57.9
	23	165 29.4	06.7	59 23.2	10.6	N17 59.4	12.8	57.9
		SD 15.9	d 0.8	SD	16.2	16.0		15.9

Lat. °	Twilight Naut. h m	Twilight Civil h m	Sunrise h m	Moonrise 22 h m	Moonrise 23 h m	Moonrise 24 h m	Moonrise 25 h m
N 72	////	////	02 51	▭	▭	▭	09 27
N 70	////	01 30	03 15	▭	▭	▭	10 08
68	////	02 12	03 34	▭	▭	07 47	10 35
66	////	02 40	03 49	▭	▭	08 40	10 55
64	01 18	03 01	04 01	▭	06 44	09 12	11 12
62	01 56	03 18	04 12	05 20	07 34	09 35	11 25
60	02 22	03 31	04 20	06 19	08 05	09 54	11 36
N 58	02 42	03 43	04 28	06 52	08 29	10 09	11 46
56	02 58	03 53	04 35	07 17	08 47	10 22	11 54
54	03 11	04 02	04 41	07 37	09 03	10 34	12 02
52	03 22	04 09	04 46	07 53	09 17	10 44	12 09
50	03 32	04 16	04 51	08 08	09 29	10 53	12 15
45	03 52	04 31	05 02	08 37	09 53	11 12	12 28
N 40	04 08	04 42	05 11	08 59	10 13	11 27	12 38
35	04 20	04 52	05 18	09 18	10 29	11 40	12 47
30	04 30	05 00	05 25	09 34	10 43	11 51	12 55
20	04 47	05 13	05 36	10 02	11 07	12 10	13 09
N 10	04 59	05 24	05 46	10 25	11 28	12 26	13 21
0	05 09	05 34	05 55	10 47	11 47	12 42	13 32
S 10	05 18	05 42	06 04	11 08	12 06	12 57	13 43
20	05 25	05 51	06 13	11 32	12 26	13 13	13 54
30	05 31	05 59	06 24	11 59	12 50	13 32	14 08
35	05 34	06 04	06 30	12 15	13 03	13 43	14 15
40	05 37	06 09	06 37	12 33	13 19	13 55	14 24
45	05 40	06 15	06 45	12 56	13 38	14 10	14 34
S 50	05 43	06 21	06 54	13 24	14 01	14 27	14 46
52	05 44	06 24	06 59	13 38	14 12	14 35	14 52
54	05 45	06 27	07 04	13 54	14 25	14 45	14 58
56	05 47	06 30	07 09	14 12	14 39	14 55	15 05
58	05 48	06 34	07 15	14 35	14 56	15 07	15 13
S 60	05 49	06 38	07 22	15 06	15 17	15 20	15 21

Lat. °	Sunset h m	Twilight Civil h m	Twilight Naut. h m	Moonset 22 h m	Moonset 23 h m	Moonset 24 h m	Moonset 25 h m
N 72	21 11	////	////	▭	▭	▭	05 36
N 70	20 45	22 36	////	▭	▭	▭	04 54
68	20 26	21 50	////	▭	▭	05 26	04 25
66	20 10	21 20	////	▭	▭	04 32	04 03
64	19 58	20 59	22 46	▭	04 30	03 59	03 45
62	19 47	20 42	22 05	03 45	03 39	03 35	03 31
60	19 38	20 27	21 38	02 46	03 08	03 15	03 18
N 58	19 30	20 16	21 18	02 12	02 44	02 59	03 08
56	19 23	20 05	21 01	01 47	02 24	02 45	02 58
54	19 17	19 57	20 48	01 27	02 08	02 33	02 50
52	19 11	19 49	20 36	01 11	01 54	02 23	02 42
50	19 06	19 42	20 26	00 56	01 42	02 13	02 35
45	18 55	19 27	20 06	00 27	01 16	01 53	02 21
N 40	18 46	19 15	19 50	00 04	00 56	01 36	02 09
35	18 39	19 05	19 37	24 39	00 39	01 22	01 58
30	18 32	18 57	19 27	24 24	00 24	01 10	01 49
20	18 21	18 44	19 10	23 58	24 49	00 49	01 33
N 10	18 11	18 32	18 58	23 36	24 31	00 31	01 19
0	18 02	18 23	18 47	23 16	24 14	00 14	01 06
S 10	17 53	18 14	18 39	22 55	23 56	24 53	00 53
20	17 43	18 06	18 32	22 33	23 38	24 39	00 39
30	17 32	17 57	18 25	22 07	23 16	24 22	00 22
35	17 26	17 52	18 22	21 52	23 03	24 12	00 12
40	17 19	17 47	18 19	21 34	22 48	24 01	00 01
45	17 11	17 41	18 16	21 12	22 31	23 48	25 03
S 50	17 01	17 35	18 13	20 45	22 08	23 32	24 52
52	16 57	17 32	18 11	20 31	21 58	23 25	24 48
54	16 52	17 29	18 10	20 15	21 46	23 16	24 42
56	16 47	17 25	18 09	19 57	21 32	23 07	24 36
58	16 41	17 22	18 08	19 34	21 16	22 56	24 30
S 60	16 34	17 18	18 06	19 05	20 56	22 43	24 22

Day	SUN Eqn. of Time 00ʰ m s	SUN Eqn. of Time 12ʰ m s	SUN Mer. Pass. h m	MOON Mer. Pass. Upper h m	MOON Mer. Pass. Lower h m	MOON Age d	MOON %	Phase
22	01 25	01 31	11 58	17 01	04 30	05	32	
23	01 36	01 42	11 58	18 00	05 32	06	43	◐
24	01 47	01 53	11 58	18 54	06 28	07	54	

2026 APRIL 25, 26, 27 (SAT., SUN., MON.)

	UT (d h)	ARIES GHA ° ′	VENUS −3·9 GHA ° ′	VENUS Dec ° ′	MARS +1·2 GHA ° ′	MARS Dec ° ′	JUPITER −2·0 GHA ° ′	JUPITER Dec ° ′	SATURN +0·9 GHA ° ′	SATURN Dec ° ′
	25 00	213 01.6	154 17.6	N20 58.6	201 50.8	N 3 48.0	103 20.7	N22 35.7	204 24.3	N 1 22.2
	01	228 04.0	169 16.9	20 59.4	216 51.5	48.7	118 22.8	35.7	219 26.5	22.3
	02	243 06.5	184 16.2	21 00.1	231 52.2	49.5	133 25.0	35.7	234 28.7	22.4
	03	258 09.0	199 15.5	. . 00.8	246 52.9	. . 50.2	148 27.1	. . 35.6	249 30.9	. . 22.5
	04	273 11.4	214 14.8	01.6	261 53.5	51.0	163 29.2	35.6	264 33.1	22.6
	05	288 13.9	229 14.1	02.3	276 54.2	51.8	178 31.3	35.5	279 35.3	22.7
	06	303 16.4	244 13.4	N21 03.0	291 54.9	N 3 52.5	193 33.4	N22 35.5	294 37.5	N 1 22.8
	07	318 18.8	259 12.7	03.8	306 55.6	53.3	208 35.6	35.5	309 39.7	22.9
S	08	333 21.3	274 12.0	04.5	321 56.3	54.1	223 37.7	35.4	324 41.9	23.0
A	09	348 23.7	289 11.3	. . 05.2	336 57.0	. . 54.8	238 39.8	. . 35.4	339 44.1	. . 23.1
T	10	3 26.2	304 10.6	06.0	351 57.7	55.6	253 41.9	35.3	354 46.3	23.3
U	11	18 28.7	319 09.9	06.7	6 58.4	56.4	268 44.1	35.3	9 48.5	23.4
R	12	33 31.1	334 09.2	N21 07.4	21 59.1	N 3 57.1	283 46.2	N22 35.3	24 50.7	N 1 23.5
D	13	48 33.6	349 08.5	08.1	36 59.8	57.9	298 48.3	35.2	39 52.9	23.6
A	14	63 36.1	4 07.8	08.9	52 00.5	58.7	313 50.4	35.2	54 55.0	23.7
Y	15	78 38.5	19 07.1	. . 09.6	67 01.2	3 59.4	328 52.5	. . 35.1	69 57.2	. . 23.8
	16	93 41.0	34 06.4	10.3	82 01.9	4 00.2	343 54.7	35.1	84 59.4	23.9
	17	108 43.5	49 05.7	11.0	97 02.6	01.0	358 56.8	35.0	100 01.6	24.0
	18	123 45.9	64 05.0	N21 11.8	112 03.3	N 4 01.7	13 58.9	N22 35.0	115 03.8	N 1 24.1
	19	138 48.4	79 04.3	12.5	127 04.0	02.5	29 01.0	35.0	130 06.0	24.2
	20	153 50.9	94 03.6	13.2	142 04.6	03.2	44 03.1	34.9	145 08.2	24.4
	21	168 53.3	109 02.9	. . 13.9	157 05.3	. . 04.0	59 05.3	. . 34.9	160 10.4	. . 24.5
	22	183 55.8	124 02.2	14.6	172 06.0	04.8	74 07.4	34.8	175 12.6	24.6
	23	198 58.2	139 01.5	15.3	187 06.7	05.5	89 09.5	34.8	190 14.8	24.7
	26 00	214 00.7	154 00.8	N21 16.1	202 07.4	N 4 06.3	104 11.6	N22 34.8	205 17.0	N 1 24.8
	01	229 03.2	169 00.1	16.8	217 08.1	07.1	119 13.7	34.7	220 19.2	24.9
	02	244 05.6	183 59.4	17.5	232 08.8	07.8	134 15.8	34.7	235 21.4	25.0
	03	259 08.1	198 58.7	. . 18.2	247 09.5	. . 08.6	149 18.0	. . 34.6	250 23.6	. . 25.1
	04	274 10.6	213 58.0	18.9	262 10.2	09.4	164 20.1	34.6	265 25.8	25.2
	05	289 13.0	228 57.3	19.6	277 10.9	10.1	179 22.2	34.5	280 28.0	25.3
	06	304 15.5	243 56.5	N21 20.3	292 11.6	N 4 10.9	194 24.3	N22 34.5	295 30.2	N 1 25.4
	07	319 18.0	258 55.8	21.0	307 12.3	11.6	209 26.4	34.5	310 32.4	25.6
	08	334 20.4	273 55.1	21.7	322 13.0	12.4	224 28.5	34.4	325 34.6	25.7
S	09	349 22.9	288 54.4	. . 22.5	337 13.7	. . 13.2	239 30.7	. . 34.4	340 36.8	. . 25.8
U	10	4 25.4	303 53.7	23.2	352 14.4	13.9	254 32.8	34.3	355 39.0	25.9
N	11	19 27.8	318 53.0	23.9	7 15.1	14.7	269 34.9	34.3	10 41.2	26.0
D	12	34 30.3	333 52.3	N21 24.6	22 15.8	N 4 15.5	284 37.0	N22 34.2	25 43.4	N 1 26.1
A	13	49 32.7	348 51.6	25.3	37 16.4	16.2	299 39.1	34.2	40 45.6	26.2
Y	14	64 35.2	3 50.9	26.0	52 17.1	17.0	314 41.2	34.2	55 47.8	26.3
	15	79 37.7	18 50.2	. . 26.7	67 17.8	. . 17.7	329 43.4	. . 34.1	70 50.0	. . 26.4
	16	94 40.1	33 49.4	27.4	82 18.5	18.5	344 45.5	34.1	85 52.2	26.5
	17	109 42.6	48 48.7	28.1	97 19.2	19.3	359 47.6	34.0	100 54.3	26.6
	18	124 45.1	63 48.0	N21 28.8	112 19.9	N 4 20.0	14 49.7	N22 34.0	115 56.5	N 1 26.8
	19	139 47.5	78 47.3	29.5	127 20.6	20.8	29 51.8	34.0	130 58.7	26.9
	20	154 50.0	93 46.6	30.2	142 21.3	21.6	44 53.9	33.9	146 00.9	27.0
	21	169 52.5	108 45.9	. . 30.9	157 22.0	. . 22.3	59 56.0	. . 33.9	161 03.1	. . 27.1
	22	184 54.9	123 45.2	31.5	172 22.7	23.1	74 58.1	33.8	176 05.3	27.2
	23	199 57.4	138 44.5	32.2	187 23.4	23.8	90 00.3	33.8	191 07.5	27.3
	27 00	214 59.8	153 43.7	N21 32.9	202 24.1	N 4 24.6	105 02.4	N22 33.7	206 09.7	N 1 27.4
	01	230 02.3	168 43.0	33.6	217 24.8	25.4	120 04.5	33.7	221 11.9	27.5
	02	245 04.8	183 42.3	34.3	232 25.5	26.1	135 06.6	33.7	236 14.1	27.6
	03	260 07.2	198 41.6	. . 35.0	247 26.2	. . 26.9	150 08.7	. . 33.6	251 16.3	. . 27.7
	04	275 09.7	213 40.9	35.7	262 26.9	27.6	165 10.8	33.6	266 18.5	27.8
	05	290 12.2	228 40.2	36.4	277 27.5	28.4	180 12.9	33.5	281 20.7	27.9
	06	305 14.6	243 39.4	N21 37.1	292 28.2	N 4 29.2	195 15.0	N22 33.5	296 22.9	N 1 28.1
	07	320 17.1	258 38.7	37.7	307 28.9	29.9	210 17.2	33.4	311 25.1	28.2
	08	335 19.6	273 38.0	38.4	322 29.6	30.7	225 19.3	33.4	326 27.3	28.3
M	09	350 22.0	288 37.3	. . 39.1	337 30.3	. . 31.4	240 21.4	. . 33.3	341 29.5	. . 28.4
O	10	5 24.5	303 36.6	39.8	352 31.0	32.2	255 23.5	33.3	356 31.7	28.5
N	11	20 27.0	318 35.9	40.5	7 31.7	33.0	270 25.6	33.3	11 33.9	28.6
D	12	35 29.4	333 35.1	N21 41.1	22 32.4	N 4 33.7	285 27.7	N22 33.2	26 36.1	N 1 28.7
A	13	50 31.9	348 34.4	41.8	37 33.1	34.5	300 29.8	33.2	41 38.3	28.8
Y	14	65 34.3	3 33.7	42.5	52 33.8	35.2	315 31.9	33.1	56 40.5	28.9
	15	80 36.8	18 33.0	. . 43.2	67 34.5	. . 36.0	330 34.0	. . 33.1	71 42.7	. . 29.0
	16	95 39.3	33 32.3	43.9	82 35.2	36.8	345 36.1	33.0	86 44.9	29.1
	17	110 41.7	48 31.5	44.5	97 35.9	37.5	0 38.3	33.0	101 47.1	29.2
	18	125 44.2	63 30.8	N21 45.2	112 36.6	N 4 38.3	15 40.4	N22 33.0	116 49.3	N 1 29.4
	19	140 46.7	78 30.1	45.9	127 37.3	39.0	30 42.5	32.9	131 51.5	29.5
	20	155 49.1	93 29.4	46.5	142 38.0	39.8	45 44.6	32.9	146 53.7	29.6
	21	170 51.6	108 28.6	. . 47.2	157 38.6	. . 40.6	60 46.7	. . 32.8	161 55.9	. . 29.7
	22	185 54.1	123 27.9	47.9	172 39.3	41.3	75 48.8	32.8	176 58.1	29.8
	23	200 56.5	138 27.2	48.5	187 40.0	42.1	90 50.9	32.7	192 00.3	29.9
	Mer. Pass.	h m 9 42.4	v −0.7	d 0.7	v 0.7	d 0.8	v 2.1	d 0.0	v 2.2	d 0.1

STARS

Name	SHA ° ′	Dec ° ′
Acamar	315 11.4	S40 12.0
Achernar	335 20.0	S57 06.1
Acrux	172 58.3	S63 14.9
Adhara	255 05.2	S29 00.7
Aldebaran	290 38.7	N16 33.7
Alioth	166 11.5	N55 49.0
Alkaid	152 50.7	N49 10.8
Alnair	27 31.8	S46 49.8
Alnilam	275 36.9	S 1 11.2
Alphard	217 46.6	S 8 46.5
Alphecca	126 02.5	N26 37.4
Alpheratz	357 34.0	N29 14.0
Altair	61 58.9	N 8 56.1
Ankaa	353 06.5	S42 09.7
Antares	112 14.2	S26 29.5
Arcturus	145 46.6	N19 02.6
Atria	107 07.1	S69 04.3
Avior	234 14.4	S59 35.9
Bellatrix	278 22.0	N 6 22.3
Betelgeuse	270 51.1	N 7 24.7
Canopus	263 52.2	S52 42.8
Capella	280 20.7	N46 01.5
Deneb	49 25.1	N45 22.1
Denebola	182 23.6	N14 25.4
Diphda	348 46.5	S17 50.5
Dubhe	193 39.3	N61 36.7
Elnath	278 00.8	N28 37.8
Eltanin	90 41.4	N51 28.8
Enif	33 37.9	N 9 59.6
Fomalhaut	15 13.6	S29 28.9
Gacrux	171 50.0	S57 15.9
Gienah	175 42.2	S17 41.5
Hadar	148 33.9	S60 30.1
Hamal	327 50.4	N23 35.1
Kaus Aust.	83 30.9	S34 22.2
Kochab	137 18.6	N74 02.7
Markab	13 29.1	N15 20.7
Menkar	314 05.4	N 4 11.5
Menkent	147 56.0	S36 30.1
Miaplacidus	221 37.9	S69 49.8
Mirfak	308 27.2	N49 57.3
Nunki	75 46.3	S26 15.8
Peacock	53 04.0	S56 38.8
Pollux	243 16.1	N27 57.8
Procyon	244 49.8	N 5 09.4
Rasalhague	95 57.3	N12 32.3
Regulus	207 33.2	N11 50.2
Rigel	281 03.1	S 8 10.4
Rigil Kent.	139 38.2	S60 56.7
Sabik	102 01.3	S15 45.5
Schedar	349 30.4	N56 40.8
Shaula	96 08.6	S37 07.3
Sirius	258 25.5	S16 45.3
Spica	158 20.9	S11 18.1
Suhail	222 45.5	S43 32.6
Vega	80 32.3	N38 48.2
Zuben'ubi	136 54.5	S16 09.2

	SHA ° ′	Mer. Pass. h m
Venus	300 00.1	13 45
Mars	348 06.7	10 31
Jupiter	250 10.9	17 01
Saturn	351 16.3	10 17

UT		SUN GHA	SUN Dec	MOON GHA	v	MOON Dec	d	HP
d	h	° ′	° ′	° ′	′	° ′	′	′
25	00	180 29.5	N13 07.5	73 52.8	10.8	N17 46.6	12.8	57.9
	01	195 29.7	08.3	88 22.6	10.8	17 33.8	12.9	57.8
	02	210 29.8	09.1	102 52.4	11.0	17 20.9	13.0	57.8
	03	225 29.9	. . 09.9	117 22.4	11.0	17 07.9	13.0	57.8
	04	240 30.0	10.7	131 52.4	11.2	16 54.9	13.2	57.8
	05	255 30.1	11.5	146 22.6	11.2	16 41.7	13.2	57.7
	06	270 30.2	N13 12.4	160 52.8	11.4	N16 28.5	13.2	57.7
	07	285 30.3	13.2	175 23.2	11.4	16 15.3	13.4	57.7
S	08	300 30.4	14.0	189 53.6	11.6	16 01.9	13.4	57.7
A	09	315 30.5	. . 14.8	204 24.2	11.7	15 48.5	13.5	57.6
T	10	330 30.6	15.6	218 54.9	11.7	15 35.0	13.5	57.6
U	11	345 30.7	16.4	233 25.6	11.9	15 21.5	13.6	57.6
R	12	0 30.8	N13 17.2	247 56.5	11.9	N15 07.9	13.6	57.5
D	13	15 30.9	18.1	262 27.4	12.1	14 54.3	13.8	57.5
A	14	30 31.0	18.9	276 58.5	12.1	14 40.5	13.7	57.5
Y	15	45 31.1	. . 19.7	291 29.6	12.3	14 26.8	13.9	57.5
	16	60 31.3	20.5	306 00.9	12.3	14 12.9	13.9	57.4
	17	75 31.4	21.3	320 32.2	12.4	13 59.0	13.9	57.4
	18	90 31.5	N13 22.1	335 03.6	12.5	N13 45.1	14.0	57.4
	19	105 31.6	22.9	349 35.1	12.6	13 31.1	14.0	57.4
	20	120 31.7	23.7	4 06.7	12.7	13 17.1	14.1	57.3
	21	135 31.8	. . 24.5	18 38.4	12.7	13 03.0	14.2	57.3
	22	150 31.9	25.3	33 10.1	12.9	12 48.8	14.1	57.3
	23	165 32.0	26.1	47 42.0	12.9	12 34.7	14.3	57.3
26	00	180 32.1	N13 27.0	62 13.9	13.0	N12 20.4	14.2	57.2
	01	195 32.2	27.8	76 45.9	13.1	12 06.2	14.4	57.2
	02	210 32.3	28.6	91 18.0	13.2	11 51.8	14.3	57.2
	03	225 32.4	. . 29.4	105 50.2	13.2	11 37.5	14.4	57.2
	04	240 32.5	30.2	120 22.4	13.4	11 23.1	14.5	57.1
	05	255 32.6	31.0	134 54.8	13.4	11 08.6	14.4	57.1
	06	270 32.7	N13 31.8	149 27.2	13.4	N10 54.2	14.6	57.1
	07	285 32.8	32.6	163 59.6	13.6	10 39.6	14.5	57.0
	08	300 32.9	33.4	178 32.2	13.6	10 25.1	14.6	57.0
S	09	315 33.0	. . 34.2	193 04.8	13.7	10 10.5	14.6	57.0
U	10	330 33.1	35.0	207 37.5	13.7	9 55.9	14.6	57.0
N	11	345 33.2	35.8	222 10.2	13.9	9 41.3	14.7	56.9
D	12	0 33.3	N13 36.6	236 43.1	13.8	N 9 26.6	14.7	56.9
A	13	15 33.4	37.4	251 15.9	14.0	9 11.9	14.8	56.9
Y	14	30 33.5	38.2	265 48.9	14.0	8 57.1	14.7	56.9
	15	45 33.6	. . 39.0	280 21.9	14.1	8 42.4	14.8	56.8
	16	60 33.7	39.8	294 55.0	14.1	8 27.6	14.8	56.8
	17	75 33.8	40.6	309 28.1	14.2	8 12.8	14.9	56.8
	18	90 33.9	N13 41.4	324 01.3	14.3	N 7 57.9	14.8	56.8
	19	105 34.0	42.2	338 34.6	14.3	7 43.1	14.9	56.7
	20	120 34.1	43.0	353 07.9	14.4	7 28.2	14.9	56.7
	21	135 34.2	. . 43.8	7 41.3	14.4	7 13.3	14.9	56.7
	22	150 34.3	44.6	22 14.7	14.5	6 58.4	14.9	56.7
	23	165 34.4	45.4	36 48.2	14.5	6 43.5	15.0	56.7
27	00	180 34.5	N13 46.2	51 21.7	14.6	N 6 28.5	15.0	56.6
	01	195 34.6	47.0	65 55.3	14.6	6 13.5	14.9	56.6
	02	210 34.7	47.8	80 28.9	14.7	5 58.6	15.0	56.6
	03	225 34.8	. . 48.6	95 02.6	14.7	5 43.6	15.0	56.6
	04	240 34.9	49.4	109 36.3	14.8	5 28.6	15.1	56.5
	05	255 35.0	50.2	124 10.1	14.8	5 13.5	15.0	56.5
	06	270 35.1	N13 51.0	138 43.9	14.9	N 4 58.5	15.0	56.5
	07	285 35.2	51.8	153 17.8	14.9	4 43.5	15.1	56.5
	08	300 35.3	52.6	167 51.7	14.9	4 28.4	15.0	56.4
M	09	315 35.4	. . 53.4	182 25.6	15.0	4 13.4	15.1	56.4
O	10	330 35.5	54.2	196 59.6	15.0	3 58.3	15.0	56.4
N	11	345 35.6	55.0	211 33.6	15.1	3 43.3	15.1	56.4
D	12	0 35.7	N13 55.8	226 07.7	15.1	N 3 28.2	15.1	56.3
A	13	15 35.8	56.6	240 41.8	15.1	3 13.1	15.0	56.3
Y	14	30 35.9	57.4	255 15.9	15.2	2 58.1	15.1	56.3
	15	45 36.0	. . 58.1	269 50.1	15.2	2 43.0	15.1	56.3
	16	60 36.1	58.9	284 24.3	15.2	2 27.9	15.0	56.3
	17	75 36.2	13 59.7	298 58.5	15.2	2 12.9	15.1	56.2
	18	90 36.3	N14 00.5	313 32.7	15.3	N 1 57.8	15.1	56.2
	19	105 36.3	01.3	328 07.0	15.3	1 42.7	15.0	56.2
	20	120 36.4	02.1	342 41.3	15.4	1 27.7	15.1	56.2
	21	135 36.5	. . 02.9	357 15.7	15.3	1 12.6	15.0	56.1
	22	150 36.6	03.7	11 50.0	15.4	0 57.6	15.1	56.1
	23	165 36.7	04.5	26 24.4	15.4	N 0 42.5	15.0	56.1
		SD 15.9	d 0.8	SD	15.7	15.5		15.4

Lat.	Twilight Naut.	Twilight Civil	Sunrise	Moonrise 25	26	27	28
°	h m	h m	h m	h m	h m	h m	h m
N 72	////	////	02 30	09 27	12 13	14 26	16 31
N 70	////	00 52	02 59	10 08	12 28	14 30	16 25
68	////	01 51	03 20	10 35	12 40	14 33	16 21
66	////	02 24	03 37	10 55	12 50	14 36	16 17
64	00 46	02 48	03 51	11 12	12 58	14 38	16 14
62	01 38	03 06	04 02	11 25	13 05	14 40	16 11
60	02 08	03 21	04 12	11 36	13 12	14 42	16 09
N 58	02 30	03 34	04 20	11 46	13 17	14 43	16 07
56	02 48	03 45	04 28	11 54	13 21	14 45	16 05
54	03 02	03 54	04 34	12 02	13 26	14 46	16 04
52	03 14	04 03	04 40	12 09	13 29	14 47	16 02
50	03 25	04 10	04 46	12 15	13 33	14 48	16 01
45	03 46	04 25	04 57	12 28	13 40	14 50	15 58
N 40	04 03	04 38	05 07	12 38	13 46	14 52	15 55
35	04 16	04 48	05 15	12 47	13 52	14 53	15 53
30	04 27	04 57	05 22	12 55	13 56	14 55	15 52
20	04 44	05 11	05 34	13 09	14 04	14 57	15 48
N 10	04 58	05 23	05 45	13 21	14 11	14 59	15 46
0	05 08	05 33	05 54	13 32	14 18	15 01	15 43
S 10	05 18	05 43	06 04	13 43	14 24	15 03	15 41
20	05 26	05 52	06 14	13 54	14 31	15 05	15 38
30	05 33	06 01	06 26	14 08	14 39	15 08	15 35
35	05 37	06 06	06 32	14 15	14 43	15 09	15 33
40	05 40	06 12	06 40	14 24	14 49	15 11	15 32
45	05 44	06 18	06 49	14 34	14 54	15 12	15 29
S 50	05 47	06 25	06 59	14 46	15 01	15 14	15 27
52	05 49	06 29	07 04	14 52	15 05	15 15	15 26
54	05 50	06 32	07 09	14 58	15 08	15 17	15 24
56	05 52	06 36	07 15	15 05	15 12	15 18	15 23
58	05 54	06 40	07 22	15 13	15 16	15 19	15 21
S 60	05 55	06 44	07 29	15 21	15 21	15 20	15 20

Lat.	Sunset	Twilight Civil	Twilight Naut.	Moonset 25	26	27	28
°	h m	h m	h m	h m	h m	h m	h m
N 72	21 31	////	////	05 36	04 29	03 49	03 16
N 70	21 00	23 22	////	04 54	04 11	03 42	03 16
68	20 38	22 11	////	04 25	03 57	03 35	03 17
66	20 21	21 36	////	04 03	03 45	03 30	03 17
64	20 07	21 11	23 26	03 45	03 35	03 26	03 18
62	19 55	20 52	22 23	03 31	03 26	03 22	03 18
60	19 45	20 36	21 51	03 18	03 19	03 19	03 18
N 58	19 37	20 23	21 28	03 08	03 13	03 16	03 18
56	19 29	20 12	21 10	02 58	03 07	03 13	03 19
54	19 22	20 03	20 56	02 50	03 02	03 11	03 19
52	19 16	19 54	20 43	02 42	02 57	03 09	03 19
50	19 11	19 47	20 32	02 35	02 52	03 07	03 19
45	18 59	19 31	20 10	02 21	02 43	03 02	03 20
N 40	18 50	19 18	19 54	02 09	02 35	02 58	03 20
35	18 41	19 08	19 40	01 58	02 29	02 55	03 20
30	18 34	18 59	19 29	01 49	02 23	02 52	03 20
20	18 22	18 45	19 12	01 33	02 12	02 47	03 21
N 10	18 11	18 33	18 58	01 19	02 03	02 43	03 21
0	18 01	18 22	18 47	01 06	01 54	02 39	03 21
S 10	17 51	18 13	18 38	00 53	01 45	02 34	03 22
20	17 41	18 04	18 30	00 39	01 36	02 30	03 22
30	17 29	17 54	18 22	00 22	01 25	02 25	03 22
35	17 23	17 49	18 19	00 12	01 19	02 22	03 22
40	17 15	17 43	18 15	00 01	01 11	02 18	03 23
45	17 06	17 37	18 11	25 03	01 03	02 14	03 23
S 50	16 56	17 30	18 08	24 52	00 52	02 09	03 23
52	16 51	17 26	18 06	24 48	00 48	02 07	03 23
54	16 46	17 23	18 04	24 42	00 42	02 04	03 23
56	16 40	17 19	18 03	24 36	00 36	02 02	03 23
58	16 33	17 15	18 01	24 30	00 30	01 58	03 24
S 60	16 26	17 10	17 59	24 22	00 22	01 55	03 24

Day	SUN Eqn. of Time 00^h	SUN Eqn. of Time 12^h	SUN Mer. Pass.	MOON Mer. Pass. Upper	MOON Mer. Pass. Lower	Age	Phase
d	m s	m s	h m	h m	h m	d %	
25	01 58	02 03	11 58	19 43	07 19	08 65	
26	02 08	02 13	11 58	20 28	08 06	09 75	
27	02 18	02 23	11 58	21 11	08 50	10 83	

2026 APRIL 28, 29, 30 (TUES., WED., THURS.)

UT	ARIES	VENUS −3·9		MARS +1·2		JUPITER −2·0		SATURN +0·9	
	GHA	GHA	Dec	GHA	Dec	GHA	Dec	GHA	Dec
d h	° ′	° ′	° ′	° ′	° ′	° ′	° ′	° ′	° ′
28 00	215 59.0	153 26.5	N21 49.2	202 40.7	N 4 42.8	105 53.0	N22 32.7	207 02.5	N 1 30.0
01	231 01.4	168 25.7	49.9	217 41.4	43.6	120 55.1	32.6	222 04.7	30.1
02	246 03.9	183 25.0	50.5	232 42.1	44.3	135 57.2	32.6	237 06.9	30.2
03	261 06.4	198 24.3	. . 51.2	247 42.8	. . 45.1	150 59.3	. . 32.6	252 09.1	. . 30.3
04	276 08.8	213 23.6	51.9	262 43.5	45.9	166 01.4	32.5	267 11.3	30.4
05	291 11.3	228 22.8	52.5	277 44.2	46.6	181 03.5	32.5	282 13.5	30.5
06	306 13.8	243 22.1	N21 53.2	292 44.9	N 4 47.4	196 05.6	N22 32.4	297 15.7	N 1 30.6
T 07	321 16.2	258 21.4	53.9	307 45.6	48.1	211 07.7	32.4	312 17.9	30.8
U 08	336 18.7	273 20.7	54.5	322 46.3	48.9	226 09.9	32.3	327 20.1	30.9
E 09	351 21.2	288 19.9	. . 55.2	337 47.0	. . 49.7	241 12.0	. . 32.3	342 22.3	. . 31.0
S 10	6 23.6	303 19.2	55.8	352 47.7	50.4	256 14.1	32.3	357 24.5	31.1
D 11	21 26.1	318 18.5	56.5	7 48.4	51.2	271 16.2	32.2	12 26.7	31.2
A 12	36 28.6	333 17.7	N21 57.1	22 49.1	N 4 51.9	286 18.3	N22 32.2	27 28.9	N 1 31.3
Y 13	51 31.0	348 17.0	57.8	37 49.8	52.7	301 20.4	32.1	42 31.1	31.4
14	66 33.5	3 16.3	58.4	52 50.4	53.4	316 22.5	32.1	57 33.3	31.5
15	81 35.9	18 15.5	. . 59.1	67 51.1	. . 54.2	331 24.6	. . 32.0	72 35.5	. . 31.6
16	96 38.4	33 14.8	21 59.7	82 51.8	55.0	346 26.7	32.0	87 37.7	31.7
17	111 40.9	48 14.1	22 00.4	97 52.5	55.7	1 28.8	31.9	102 39.9	31.8
18	126 43.3	63 13.4	N22 01.0	112 53.2	N 4 56.5	16 30.9	N22 31.9	117 42.1	N 1 31.9
19	141 45.8	78 12.6	01.7	127 53.9	57.2	31 33.0	31.9	132 44.3	32.0
20	156 48.3	93 11.9	02.3	142 54.6	58.0	46 35.1	31.8	147 46.5	32.2
21	171 50.7	108 11.2	. . 03.0	157 55.3	. . 58.7	61 37.2	. . 31.8	162 48.7	. . 32.3
22	186 53.2	123 10.4	03.6	172 56.0	4 59.5	76 39.3	31.7	177 50.9	32.4
23	201 55.7	138 09.7	04.3	187 56.7	5 00.2	91 41.4	31.7	192 53.1	32.5
29 00	216 58.1	153 09.0	N22 04.9	202 57.4	N 5 01.0	106 43.5	N22 31.6	207 55.3	N 1 32.6
01	232 00.6	168 08.2	05.5	217 58.1	01.8	121 45.6	31.6	222 57.5	32.7
02	247 03.0	183 07.5	06.2	232 58.8	02.5	136 47.7	31.5	237 59.7	32.8
03	262 05.5	198 06.8	. . 06.8	247 59.5	. . 03.3	151 49.8	. . 31.5	253 01.9	. . 32.9
04	277 08.0	213 06.0	07.5	263 00.2	04.0	166 51.9	31.4	268 04.1	33.0
05	292 10.4	228 05.3	08.1	278 00.9	04.8	181 54.0	31.4	283 06.3	33.1
06	307 12.9	243 04.5	N22 08.7	293 01.5	N 5 05.5	196 56.1	N22 31.4	298 08.5	N 1 33.2
W 07	322 15.4	258 03.8	09.4	308 02.2	06.3	211 58.2	31.3	313 10.7	33.3
E 08	337 17.8	273 03.1	10.0	323 02.9	07.0	227 00.3	31.3	328 12.9	33.4
D 09	352 20.3	288 02.3	. . 10.6	338 03.6	. . 07.8	242 02.4	. . 31.2	343 15.1	. . 33.5
N 10	7 22.8	303 01.6	11.3	353 04.3	08.6	257 04.5	31.2	358 17.3	33.7
E 11	22 25.2	318 00.9	11.9	8 05.0	09.3	272 06.6	31.1	13 19.5	33.8
S 12	37 27.7	333 00.1	N22 12.5	23 05.7	N 5 10.1	287 08.7	N22 31.1	28 21.7	N 1 33.9
D 13	52 30.2	347 59.4	13.2	38 06.4	10.8	302 10.8	31.0	43 23.9	34.0
A 14	67 32.6	2 58.6	13.8	53 07.1	11.6	317 12.9	31.0	58 26.1	34.1
Y 15	82 35.1	17 57.9	. . 14.4	68 07.8	. . 12.3	332 15.0	. . 30.9	73 28.3	. . 34.2
16	97 37.5	32 57.2	15.0	83 08.5	13.1	347 17.1	30.9	88 30.5	34.3
17	112 40.0	47 56.4	15.7	98 09.2	13.8	2 19.2	30.9	103 32.7	34.4
18	127 42.5	62 55.7	N22 16.3	113 09.9	N 5 14.6	17 21.3	N22 30.8	118 34.9	N 1 34.5
19	142 44.9	77 54.9	16.9	128 10.6	15.3	32 23.4	30.8	133 37.1	34.6
20	157 47.4	92 54.2	17.5	143 11.3	16.1	47 25.5	30.7	148 39.3	34.7
21	172 49.9	107 53.5	. . 18.1	158 12.0	. . 16.9	62 27.6	. . 30.7	163 41.5	. . 34.8
22	187 52.3	122 52.7	18.8	173 12.6	17.6	77 29.7	30.6	178 43.7	34.9
23	202 54.8	137 52.0	19.4	188 13.3	18.4	92 31.8	30.6	193 45.9	35.0
30 00	217 57.3	152 51.2	N22 20.0	203 14.0	N 5 19.1	107 33.9	N22 30.5	208 48.1	N 1 35.1
01	232 59.7	167 50.5	20.6	218 14.7	19.9	122 36.0	30.5	223 50.3	35.3
02	248 02.2	182 49.7	21.2	233 15.4	20.6	137 38.1	30.4	238 52.5	35.4
03	263 04.7	197 49.0	. . 21.8	248 16.1	. . 21.4	152 40.2	. . 30.4	253 54.7	. . 35.5
04	278 07.1	212 48.2	22.5	263 16.8	22.1	167 42.3	30.3	268 56.9	35.6
05	293 09.6	227 47.5	23.1	278 17.5	22.9	182 44.3	30.3	283 59.1	35.7
06	308 12.0	242 46.8	N22 23.7	293 18.2	N 5 23.6	197 46.4	N22 30.3	299 01.3	N 1 35.8
T 07	323 14.5	257 46.0	24.3	308 18.9	24.4	212 48.5	30.2	314 03.5	35.9
H 08	338 17.0	272 45.3	24.9	323 19.6	25.1	227 50.6	30.2	329 05.7	36.0
U 09	353 19.4	287 44.5	. . 25.5	338 20.3	. . 25.9	242 52.7	. . 30.1	344 07.9	. . 36.1
R 10	8 21.9	302 43.8	26.1	353 21.0	26.6	257 54.8	30.1	359 10.1	36.2
S 11	23 24.4	317 43.0	26.7	8 21.7	27.4	272 56.9	30.0	14 12.3	36.3
D 12	38 26.8	332 42.3	N22 27.3	23 22.4	N 5 28.1	287 59.0	N22 30.0	29 14.5	N 1 36.4
A 13	53 29.3	347 41.5	27.9	38 23.0	28.9	303 01.1	29.9	44 16.7	36.5
Y 14	68 31.8	2 40.8	28.5	53 23.7	29.6	318 03.2	29.9	59 18.9	36.6
15	83 34.2	17 40.0	. . 29.1	68 24.4	. . 30.4	333 05.3	. . 29.8	74 21.1	. . 36.7
16	98 36.7	32 39.3	29.7	83 25.1	31.2	348 07.4	29.8	89 23.3	36.8
17	113 39.1	47 38.5	30.3	98 25.8	31.9	3 09.5	29.7	104 25.5	37.0
18	128 41.6	62 37.8	N22 30.9	113 26.5	N 5 32.7	18 11.6	N22 29.7	119 27.7	N 1 37.1
19	143 44.1	77 37.0	31.5	128 27.2	33.4	33 13.7	29.7	134 29.9	37.2
20	158 46.5	92 36.3	32.1	143 27.9	34.2	48 15.7	29.6	149 32.1	37.3
21	173 49.0	107 35.5	. . 32.7	158 28.6	. . 34.9	63 17.8	. . 29.6	164 34.3	. . 37.4
22	188 51.5	122 34.8	33.3	173 29.3	35.7	78 19.9	29.5	179 36.5	37.5
23	203 53.9	137 34.0	33.9	188 30.0	36.4	93 22.0	29.5	194 38.7	37.6
Mer. Pass.	h m 9 30.6	v −0.7	d 0.6	v 0.7	d 0.8	v 2.1	d 0.0	v 2.2	d 0.1

STARS Name	SHA	Dec
	° ′	° ′
Acamar	315 11.4	S40 12.0
Achernar	335 19.9	S57 06.1
Acrux	172 58.3	S63 15.0
Adhara	255 05.2	S29 00.7
Aldebaran	290 38.7	N16 33.7
Alioth	166 11.5	N55 49.0
Alkaid	152 50.7	N49 10.8
Alnair	27 31.7	S46 49.8
Alnilam	275 36.9	S 1 11.2
Alphard	217 46.7	S 8 46.5
Alphecca	126 02.5	N26 37.4
Alpheratz	357 34.0	N29 14.0
Altair	61 58.8	N 8 56.1
Ankaa	353 06.4	S42 09.7
Antares	112 14.2	S26 29.5
Arcturus	145 46.6	N19 02.6
Atria	107 07.0	S69 04.3
Avior	234 14.4	S59 35.9
Bellatrix	278 22.0	N 6 22.3
Betelgeuse	270 51.2	N 7 24.7
Canopus	263 52.2	S52 42.8
Capella	280 20.7	N46 01.5
Deneb	49 25.1	N45 22.1
Denebola	182 23.6	N14 25.4
Diphda	348 46.5	S17 50.5
Dubhe	193 39.3	N61 36.7
Elnath	278 00.8	N28 37.8
Eltanin	90 41.3	N51 28.8
Enif	33 37.8	N 9 59.6
Fomalhaut	15 13.5	S29 28.9
Gacrux	171 50.0	S57 15.9
Gienah	175 42.2	S17 41.5
Hadar	148 33.9	S60 30.1
Hamal	327 50.3	N23 35.1
Kaus Aust.	83 30.9	S34 22.2
Kochab	137 18.6	N74 02.7
Markab	13 29.0	N15 20.7
Menkar	314 05.4	N 4 11.5
Menkent	147 56.0	S36 30.1
Miaplacidus	221 38.0	S69 49.8
Mirfak	308 27.2	N49 57.3
Nunki	75 46.3	S26 15.8
Peacock	53 04.0	S56 38.8
Pollux	243 16.1	N27 57.8
Procyon	244 49.8	N 5 09.4
Rasalhague	95 57.3	N12 32.3
Regulus	207 33.2	N11 50.2
Rigel	281 03.1	S 8 10.4
Rigil Kent.	139 38.2	S60 56.7
Sabik	102 01.3	S15 45.5
Schedar	349 30.3	N56 40.7
Shaula	96 08.6	S37 07.3
Sirius	258 25.5	S16 45.3
Spica	158 20.9	S11 18.1
Suhail	222 45.5	S43 32.6
Vega	80 32.3	N38 48.2
Zuben'ubi	136 54.5	S16 09.2

	SHA	Mer. Pass.
	° ′	h m
Venus	296 10.8	13 48
Mars	345 59.3	10 28
Jupiter	249 45.4	16 51
Saturn	350 57.1	10 07

Day	UT (d h)	SUN GHA (° ′)	SUN Dec (° ′)	MOON GHA (° ′)	*v* (′)	MOON Dec (° ′)	*d* (′)	HP (′)
TUESDAY	28 00	180 36.8	N14 05.3	40 58.8	15.4	N 0 27.5	15.1	56.1
	01	195 36.9	06.0	55 33.2	15.5	N 0 12.4	15.0	56.1
	02	210 37.0	06.8	70 07.7	15.5	S 0 02.6	15.0	56.0
	03	225 37.1	. . 07.6	84 42.2	15.4	0 17.6	15.0	56.0
	04	240 37.2	08.4	99 16.6	15.5	0 32.6	15.0	56.0
	05	255 37.3	09.2	113 51.1	15.6	0 47.6	14.9	56.0
	06	270 37.4	N14 10.0	128 25.7	15.5	S 1 02.5	15.0	55.9
	07	285 37.5	10.8	143 00.2	15.5	1 17.5	14.9	55.9
	08	300 37.6	11.5	157 34.7	15.6	1 32.4	14.9	55.9
	09	315 37.6	. . 12.3	172 09.3	15.6	1 47.3	14.9	55.9
	10	330 37.7	13.1	186 43.9	15.5	2 02.2	14.9	55.9
	11	345 37.8	13.9	201 18.4	15.6	2 17.1	14.9	55.8
	12	0 37.9	N14 14.7	215 53.0	15.6	S 2 32.0	14.8	55.8
	13	15 38.0	15.5	230 27.6	15.6	2 46.8	14.9	55.8
	14	30 38.1	16.2	245 02.2	15.6	3 01.7	14.8	55.8
	15	45 38.2	. . 17.0	259 36.8	15.6	3 16.5	14.8	55.8
	16	60 38.3	17.8	274 11.4	15.6	3 31.3	14.7	55.7
	17	75 38.4	18.6	288 46.0	15.6	3 46.0	14.7	55.7
	18	90 38.5	N14 19.4	303 20.6	15.7	S 4 00.7	14.8	55.7
	19	105 38.6	20.2	317 55.3	15.6	4 15.5	14.6	55.7
	20	120 38.6	20.9	332 29.9	15.6	4 30.1	14.7	55.7
	21	135 38.7	. . 21.7	347 04.5	15.6	4 44.8	14.6	55.6
	22	150 38.8	22.5	1 39.1	15.6	4 59.4	14.6	55.6
	23	165 38.9	23.3	16 13.7	15.6	5 14.0	14.6	55.6
WEDNESDAY	29 00	180 39.0	N14 24.1	30 48.3	15.6	S 5 28.6	14.5	55.6
	01	195 39.1	24.8	45 22.9	15.6	5 43.1	14.5	55.6
	02	210 39.2	25.6	59 57.5	15.6	5 57.6	14.5	55.5
	03	225 39.3	. . 26.4	74 32.1	15.5	6 12.1	14.4	55.5
	04	240 39.3	27.2	89 06.6	15.6	6 26.5	14.4	55.5
	05	255 39.4	27.9	103 41.2	15.6	6 40.9	14.4	55.5
	06	270 39.5	N14 28.7	118 15.8	15.5	S 6 55.3	14.3	55.5
	07	285 39.6	29.5	132 50.3	15.5	7 09.6	14.3	55.5
	08	300 39.7	30.3	147 24.8	15.6	7 23.9	14.3	55.4
	09	315 39.8	. . 31.0	161 59.4	15.5	7 38.2	14.2	55.4
	10	330 39.9	31.8	176 33.9	15.4	7 52.4	14.2	55.4
	11	345 40.0	32.6	191 08.3	15.5	8 06.6	14.1	55.4
	12	0 40.0	N14 33.4	205 42.8	15.5	S 8 20.7	14.1	55.4
	13	15 40.1	34.1	220 17.3	15.4	8 34.8	14.1	55.3
	14	30 40.2	34.9	234 51.7	15.4	8 48.9	14.0	55.3
	15	45 40.3	. . 35.7	249 26.1	15.4	9 02.9	14.0	55.3
	16	60 40.4	36.5	264 00.5	15.4	9 16.9	13.9	55.3
	17	75 40.5	37.2	278 34.9	15.3	9 30.8	13.9	55.3
	18	90 40.5	N14 38.0	293 09.2	15.4	S 9 44.7	13.8	55.3
	19	105 40.6	38.8	307 43.6	15.3	9 58.5	13.8	55.2
	20	120 40.7	39.5	322 17.9	15.3	10 12.3	13.7	55.2
	21	135 40.8	. . 40.3	336 52.2	15.2	10 26.0	13.7	55.2
	22	150 40.9	41.1	351 26.4	15.2	10 39.7	13.6	55.2
	23	165 41.0	41.8	6 00.6	15.2	10 53.3	13.6	55.2
THURSDAY	30 00	180 41.0	N14 42.6	20 34.8	15.2	S11 06.9	13.6	55.2
	01	195 41.1	43.4	35 09.0	15.2	11 20.5	13.4	55.1
	02	210 41.2	44.2	49 43.2	15.1	11 33.9	13.5	55.1
	03	225 41.3	. . 44.9	64 17.3	15.1	11 47.4	13.3	55.1
	04	240 41.4	45.7	78 51.4	15.0	12 00.7	13.4	55.1
	05	255 41.5	46.5	93 25.4	15.0	12 14.1	13.2	55.1
	06	270 41.5	N14 47.2	107 59.4	15.0	S12 27.3	13.2	55.1
	07	285 41.6	48.0	122 33.4	15.0	12 40.5	13.2	55.0
	08	300 41.7	48.8	137 07.4	14.9	12 53.7	13.0	55.0
	09	315 41.8	. . 49.5	151 41.3	14.9	13 06.7	13.1	55.0
	10	330 41.9	50.3	166 15.2	14.8	13 19.8	12.9	55.0
	11	345 41.9	51.0	180 49.0	14.8	13 32.7	12.9	55.0
	12	0 42.0	N14 51.8	195 22.8	14.8	S13 45.6	12.9	55.0
	13	15 42.1	52.6	209 56.6	14.7	13 58.5	12.8	54.9
	14	30 42.2	53.3	224 30.3	14.7	14 11.3	12.7	54.9
	15	45 42.3	. . 54.1	239 04.0	14.7	14 24.0	12.6	54.9
	16	60 42.3	54.9	253 37.7	14.6	14 36.6	12.6	54.9
	17	75 42.4	55.6	268 11.3	14.6	14 49.2	12.5	54.9
	18	90 42.5	N14 56.4	282 44.9	14.5	S15 01.7	12.5	54.9
	19	105 42.6	57.1	297 18.4	14.5	15 14.2	12.3	54.8
	20	120 42.7	57.9	311 51.9	14.4	15 26.5	12.4	54.8
	21	135 42.7	. . 58.7	326 25.3	14.4	15 38.9	12.2	54.8
	22	150 42.8	14 59.4	340 58.7	14.4	15 51.1	12.2	54.8
	23	165 42.9	N15 00.2	355 32.1	14.3	S16 03.3	12.1	54.8
		SD 15.9	*d* 0.8	SD 15.2		15.1		15.0

Lat. (°)	Twilight Naut. (h m)	Twilight Civil (h m)	Sunrise (h m)	Moonrise 28 (h m)	Moonrise 29 (h m)	Moonrise 30 (h m)	Moonrise 1 (h m)
N 72	////	////	02 09	16 31	18 40	21 17	■
N 70	////	////	02 43	16 25	18 23	20 35	■
68	////	01 27	03 07	16 21	18 10	20 07	22 33
66	////	02 07	03 25	16 17	17 59	19 46	21 46
64	////	02 35	03 40	16 14	17 50	19 30	21 16
62	01 17	02 55	03 53	16 11	17 43	19 16	20 53
60	01 53	03 12	04 04	16 09	17 36	19 05	20 36
N 58	02 18	03 25	04 13	16 07	17 30	18 55	20 21
56	02 38	03 37	04 21	16 05	17 25	18 46	20 08
54	02 53	03 47	04 28	16 04	17 21	18 38	19 57
52	03 07	03 56	04 34	16 02	17 17	18 32	19 47
50	03 18	04 04	04 40	16 01	17 13	18 26	19 38
45	03 41	04 20	04 53	15 58	17 05	18 12	19 20
N 40	03 58	04 34	05 03	15 55	16 59	18 02	19 05
35	04 12	04 45	05 11	15 53	16 53	17 53	18 53
30	04 24	04 54	05 19	15 52	16 48	17 45	18 42
20	04 42	05 09	05 32	15 48	16 39	17 31	18 23
N 10	04 56	05 22	05 43	15 46	16 32	17 19	18 07
0	05 08	05 33	05 54	15 43	16 25	17 08	17 52
S 10	05 18	05 43	06 04	15 41	16 18	16 57	17 38
20	05 26	05 53	06 15	15 38	16 11	16 45	17 22
30	05 35	06 03	06 28	15 35	16 03	16 32	17 04
35	05 39	06 09	06 35	15 33	15 58	16 24	16 53
40	05 43	06 15	06 43	15 32	15 53	16 16	16 41
45	05 47	06 22	06 52	15 29	15 47	16 06	16 28
S 50	05 51	06 30	07 04	15 27	15 40	15 54	16 11
52	05 53	06 33	07 09	15 26	15 36	15 48	16 03
54	05 55	06 37	07 15	15 24	15 33	15 42	15 54
56	05 57	06 41	07 21	15 23	15 29	15 35	15 44
58	05 59	06 46	07 28	15 21	15 24	15 28	15 33
S 60	06 01	06 51	07 36	15 20	15 19	15 19	15 20

Lat. (°)	Sunset (h m)	Twilight Civil (h m)	Twilight Naut. (h m)	Moonset 28 (h m)	Moonset 29 (h m)	Moonset 30 (h m)	Moonset 1 (h m)
N 72	21 52	////	////	03 16	02 43	02 03	00 57
N 70	21 16	////	////	03 16	02 51	02 22	01 41
68	20 51	22 36	////	03 17	02 58	02 37	02 10
66	20 32	21 52	////	03 17	03 04	02 50	02 33
64	20 16	21 24	////	03 18	03 09	03 00	02 50
62	20 04	21 02	22 45	03 18	03 14	03 09	03 05
60	19 53	20 45	22 06	03 18	03 18	03 17	03 17
N 58	19 43	20 31	21 40	03 18	03 21	03 24	03 28
56	19 35	20 19	21 20	03 19	03 24	03 30	03 38
54	19 28	20 09	21 04	03 19	03 27	03 36	03 46
52	19 21	20 00	20 50	03 19	03 29	03 40	03 54
50	19 16	19 52	20 38	03 19	03 32	03 45	04 00
45	19 03	19 35	20 15	03 20	03 37	03 55	04 15
N 40	18 53	19 22	19 57	03 20	03 41	04 03	04 27
35	18 44	19 11	19 43	03 20	03 45	04 10	04 37
30	18 36	19 01	19 31	03 20	03 48	04 16	04 47
20	18 23	18 46	19 13	03 21	03 54	04 27	05 02
N 10	18 11	18 33	18 59	03 21	03 59	04 37	05 16
0	18 01	18 22	18 47	03 21	04 03	04 45	05 29
S 10	17 50	18 12	18 37	03 22	04 08	04 54	05 42
20	17 39	18 02	18 28	03 22	04 13	05 04	05 56
30	17 27	17 51	18 20	03 22	04 19	05 15	06 12
35	17 19	17 46	18 16	03 22	04 22	05 22	06 22
40	17 11	17 39	18 11	03 23	04 26	05 29	06 32
45	17 02	17 32	18 07	03 23	04 30	05 37	06 45
S 50	16 50	17 24	18 03	03 23	04 36	05 48	07 01
52	16 45	17 21	18 01	03 23	04 38	05 53	07 08
54	16 39	17 17	17 59	03 23	04 41	05 58	07 16
56	16 33	17 13	17 57	03 23	04 44	06 04	07 25
58	16 26	17 08	17 54	03 24	04 47	06 11	07 36
S 60	16 18	17 03	17 52	03 24	04 51	06 18	07 48

Day (d)	SUN Eqn. of Time 00^h (m s)	SUN Eqn. of Time 12^h (m s)	SUN Mer. Pass. (h m)	MOON Mer. Pass. Upper (h m)	MOON Mer. Pass. Lower (h m)	MOON Age (d)	MOON Phase (%)
28	02 27	02 32	11 57	21 53	09 32	11	90
29	02 36	02 40	11 57	22 35	10 14	12	95
30	02 44	02 48	11 57	23 18	10 57	13	98

2026 MAY 1, 2, 3 (FRI., SAT., SUN.)

UT	ARIES	VENUS −3·9		MARS +1·2		JUPITER −2·0		SATURN +0·9	
	GHA	GHA	Dec	GHA	Dec	GHA	Dec	GHA	Dec
d h	° ′	° ′	° ′	° ′	° ′	° ′	° ′	° ′	° ′
1 00 FRIDAY	218 56.4	152 33.3	N22 34.5	203 30.7	N 5 37.2	108 24.1	N22 29.4	209 40.9	N 1 37.7
01	233 58.9	167 32.5	35.1	218 31.4	37.9	123 26.2	29.4	224 43.1	37.8
02	249 01.3	182 31.8	35.7	233 32.1	38.7	138 28.3	29.3	239 45.3	37.9
03	264 03.8	197 31.0	. . 36.2	248 32.8	. . 39.4	153 30.4	. . 29.3	254 47.5	. . 38.0
04	279 06.3	212 30.3	36.8	263 33.5	40.2	168 32.5	29.2	269 49.8	38.1
05	294 08.7	227 29.5	37.4	278 34.1	40.9	183 34.6	29.2	284 52.0	38.2
06	309 11.2	242 28.8	N22 38.0	293 34.8	N 5 41.7	198 36.6	N22 29.1	299 54.2	N 1 38.3
07	324 13.6	257 28.0	38.6	308 35.5	42.4	213 38.7	29.1	314 56.4	38.4
08	339 16.1	272 27.2	39.2	323 36.2	43.2	228 40.8	29.0	329 58.6	38.5
09	354 18.6	287 26.5	. . 39.7	338 36.9	. . 43.9	243 42.9	. . 29.0	345 00.8	. . 38.6
10	9 21.0	302 25.7	40.3	353 37.6	44.7	258 45.0	28.9	0 03.0	38.7
11	24 23.5	317 25.0	40.9	8 38.3	45.4	273 47.1	28.9	15 05.2	38.9
12	39 26.0	332 24.2	N22 41.5	23 39.0	N 5 46.2	288 49.2	N22 28.8	30 07.4	N 1 39.0
13	54 28.4	347 23.5	42.1	38 39.7	46.9	303 51.3	28.8	45 09.6	39.1
14	69 30.9	2 22.7	42.6	53 40.4	47.7	318 53.4	28.8	60 11.8	39.2
15	84 33.4	17 22.0	. . 43.2	68 41.1	. . 48.4	333 55.4	. . 28.7	75 14.0	. . 39.3
16	99 35.8	32 21.2	43.8	83 41.8	49.1	348 57.5	28.7	90 16.2	39.4
17	114 38.3	47 20.4	44.4	98 42.5	49.9	3 59.6	28.6	105 18.4	39.5
18	129 40.8	62 19.7	N22 44.9	113 43.2	N 5 50.6	19 01.7	N22 28.6	120 20.6	N 1 39.6
19	144 43.2	77 18.9	45.5	128 43.8	51.4	34 03.8	28.5	135 22.8	39.7
20	159 45.7	92 18.2	46.1	143 44.5	52.1	49 05.9	28.5	150 25.0	39.8
21	174 48.1	107 17.4	. . 46.6	158 45.2	. . 52.9	64 08.0	. . 28.4	165 27.2	. . 39.9
22	189 50.6	122 16.6	47.2	173 45.9	53.6	79 10.0	28.4	180 29.4	40.0
23	204 53.1	137 15.9	47.8	188 46.6	54.4	94 12.1	28.3	195 31.6	40.1
2 00 SATURDAY	219 55.5	152 15.1	N22 48.3	203 47.3	N 5 55.1	109 14.2	N22 28.3	210 33.8	N 1 40.2
01	234 58.0	167 14.4	48.9	218 48.0	55.9	124 16.3	28.2	225 36.0	40.3
02	250 00.5	182 13.6	49.5	233 48.7	56.6	139 18.4	28.2	240 38.2	40.4
03	265 02.9	197 12.8	. . 50.0	248 49.4	. . 57.4	154 20.5	. . 28.1	255 40.4	. . 40.5
04	280 05.4	212 12.1	50.6	263 50.1	58.1	169 22.6	28.1	270 42.6	40.6
05	295 07.9	227 11.3	51.1	278 50.8	58.9	184 24.6	28.0	285 44.8	40.7
06	310 10.3	242 10.5	N22 51.7	293 51.5	N 5 59.6	199 26.7	N22 28.0	300 47.1	N 1 40.8
07	325 12.8	257 09.8	52.3	308 52.2	6 00.4	214 28.8	27.9	315 49.3	40.9
08	340 15.2	272 09.0	52.8	323 52.9	01.1	229 30.9	27.9	330 51.5	41.1
09	355 17.7	287 08.3	. . 53.4	338 53.5	. . 01.9	244 33.0	. . 27.8	345 53.7	. . 41.2
10	10 20.2	302 07.5	53.9	353 54.2	02.6	259 35.1	27.8	0 55.9	41.3
11	25 22.6	317 06.7	54.5	8 54.9	03.3	274 37.1	27.7	15 58.1	41.4
12	40 25.1	332 06.0	N22 55.0	23 55.6	N 6 04.1	289 39.2	N22 27.7	31 00.3	N 1 41.5
13	55 27.6	347 05.2	55.6	38 56.3	04.8	304 41.3	27.6	46 02.5	41.6
14	70 30.0	2 04.4	56.1	53 57.0	05.6	319 43.4	27.6	61 04.7	41.7
15	85 32.5	17 03.7	. . 56.7	68 57.7	. . 06.3	334 45.5	. . 27.5	76 06.9	. . 41.8
16	100 35.0	32 02.9	57.2	83 58.4	07.1	349 47.6	27.5	91 09.1	41.9
17	115 37.4	47 02.1	57.8	98 59.1	07.8	4 49.6	27.4	106 11.3	42.0
18	130 39.9	62 01.4	N22 58.3	113 59.8	N 6 08.6	19 51.7	N22 27.4	121 13.5	N 1 42.1
19	145 42.4	77 00.6	58.9	129 00.5	09.3	34 53.8	27.4	136 15.7	42.2
20	160 44.8	91 59.8	59.4	144 01.2	10.1	49 55.9	27.3	151 17.9	42.3
21	175 47.3	106 59.1	22 59.9	159 01.9	. . 10.8	64 58.0	. . 27.3	166 20.1	. . 42.4
22	190 49.7	121 58.3	23 00.5	174 02.6	11.5	80 00.0	27.2	181 22.3	42.5
23	205 52.2	136 57.5	01.0	189 03.2	12.3	95 02.1	27.2	196 24.5	42.6
3 00 SUNDAY	220 54.7	151 56.8	N23 01.6	204 03.9	N 6 13.0	110 04.2	N22 27.1	211 26.7	N 1 42.7
01	235 57.1	166 56.0	02.1	219 04.6	13.8	125 06.3	27.1	226 29.0	42.8
02	250 59.6	181 55.2	02.6	234 05.3	14.5	140 08.4	27.0	241 31.2	42.9
03	266 02.1	196 54.4	. . 03.2	249 06.0	. . 15.3	155 10.4	. . 27.0	256 33.4	. . 43.0
04	281 04.5	211 53.7	03.7	264 06.7	16.0	170 12.5	26.9	271 35.6	43.1
05	296 07.0	226 52.9	04.2	279 07.4	16.8	185 14.6	26.9	286 37.8	43.2
06	311 09.5	241 52.1	N23 04.8	294 08.1	N 6 17.5	200 16.7	N22 26.8	301 40.0	N 1 43.3
07	326 11.9	256 51.4	05.3	309 08.8	18.2	215 18.8	26.8	316 42.2	43.5
08	341 14.4	271 50.6	05.8	324 09.5	19.0	230 20.8	26.7	331 44.4	43.6
09	356 16.9	286 49.8	. . 06.4	339 10.2	. . 19.7	245 22.9	. . 26.7	346 46.6	. . 43.7
10	11 19.3	301 49.0	06.9	354 10.9	20.5	260 25.0	26.6	1 48.8	43.8
11	26 21.8	316 48.3	07.4	9 11.6	21.2	275 27.1	26.6	16 51.0	43.9
12	41 24.2	331 47.5	N23 07.9	24 12.2	N 6 22.0	290 29.1	N22 26.5	31 53.2	N 1 44.0
13	56 26.7	346 46.7	08.5	39 12.9	22.7	305 31.2	26.5	46 55.4	44.1
14	71 29.2	1 46.0	09.0	54 13.6	23.4	320 33.3	26.4	61 57.6	44.2
15	86 31.6	16 45.2	. . 09.5	69 14.3	. . 24.2	335 35.4	. . 26.4	76 59.8	. . 44.3
16	101 34.1	31 44.4	10.0	84 15.0	24.9	350 37.5	26.3	92 02.0	44.4
17	116 36.6	46 43.6	10.5	99 15.7	25.7	5 39.5	26.3	107 04.3	44.5
18	131 39.0	61 42.9	N23 11.1	114 16.4	N 6 26.4	20 41.6	N22 26.2	122 06.5	N 1 44.6
19	146 41.5	76 42.1	11.6	129 17.1	27.2	35 43.7	26.2	137 08.7	44.7
20	161 44.0	91 41.3	12.1	144 17.8	27.9	50 45.8	26.1	152 10.9	44.8
21	176 46.4	106 40.5	. . 12.6	159 18.5	. . 28.6	65 47.8	. . 26.1	167 13.1	. . 44.9
22	191 48.9	121 39.8	13.1	174 19.2	29.4	80 49.9	26.0	182 15.3	45.0
23	206 51.3	136 39.0	13.6	189 19.9	30.1	95 52.0	26.0	197 17.5	45.1
Mer. Pass.	h m 9 18.8	v −0.8	d 0.6	v 0.7	d 0.7	v 2.1	d 0.0	v 2.2	d 0.1

STARS

Name	SHA	Dec
	° ′	° ′
Acamar	315 11.4	S40 12.0
Achernar	335 19.9	S57 06.1
Acrux	172 58.3	S63 15.0
Adhara	255 05.2	S29 00.7
Aldebaran	290 38.7	N16 33.7
Alioth	166 11.5	N55 49.0
Alkaid	152 50.7	N49 10.9
Alnair	27 31.7	S46 49.8
Alnilam	275 36.9	S 1 11.2
Alphard	217 46.7	S 8 46.5
Alphecca	126 02.5	N26 37.4
Alpheratz	357 33.9	N29 14.0
Altair	61 58.8	N 8 56.1
Ankaa	353 06.4	S42 09.7
Antares	112 14.2	S26 29.5
Arcturus	145 46.6	N19 02.6
Atria	107 07.0	S69 04.4
Avior	234 14.4	S59 35.9
Bellatrix	278 22.0	N 6 22.3
Betelgeuse	270 51.2	N 7 24.7
Canopus	263 52.3	S52 42.8
Capella	280 20.7	N46 01.5
Deneb	49 25.1	N45 22.1
Denebola	182 23.6	N14 25.4
Diphda	348 46.5	S17 50.5
Dubhe	193 39.3	N61 36.7
Elnath	278 00.8	N28 37.8
Eltanin	90 41.3	N51 28.8
Enif	33 37.8	N 9 59.6
Fomalhaut	15 13.5	S29 28.9
Gacrux	171 50.0	S57 15.9
Gienah	175 42.2	S17 41.5
Hadar	148 33.9	S60 30.1
Hamal	327 50.3	N23 35.1
Kaus Aust.	83 30.9	S34 22.2
Kochab	137 18.6	N74 02.7
Markab	13 29.0	N15 20.7
Menkar	314 05.4	N 4 11.5
Menkent	147 56.0	S36 30.1
Miaplacidus	221 38.0	S69 49.8
Mirfak	308 27.2	N49 57.3
Nunki	75 46.3	S26 15.8
Peacock	53 04.0	S56 38.8
Pollux	243 16.1	N27 57.8
Procyon	244 49.8	N 5 09.4
Rasalhague	95 57.3	N12 32.3
Regulus	207 33.2	N11 50.2
Rigel	281 03.1	S 8 10.4
Rigil Kent.	139 38.2	S60 56.7
Sabik	102 01.3	S15 45.5
Schedar	349 30.3	N56 40.7
Shaula	96 08.6	S37 07.3
Sirius	258 25.5	S16 45.3
Spica	158 20.9	S11 18.1
Suhail	222 45.5	S43 32.6
Vega	80 32.3	N38 48.2
Zuben'ubi	136 54.5	S16 09.2

	SHA	Mer. Pass.
	° ′	h m
Venus	292 19.6	13 52
Mars	343 51.8	10 24
Jupiter	249 18.7	16 41
Saturn	350 38.3	9 56

Day	UT d h	SUN GHA ° ′	SUN Dec ° ′	MOON GHA ° ′	v ′	MOON Dec ° ′	d ′	HP ′
FRIDAY	1 00	180 43.0	N15 00.9	10 05.4	14.3	S16 15.4	12.0	54.8
	01	195 43.0	01.7	24 38.7	14.2	16 27.4	11.9	54.8
	02	210 43.1	02.5	39 11.9	14.2	16 39.3	11.9	54.7
	03	225 43.2	. . 03.2	53 45.1	14.1	16 51.2	11.8	54.7
	04	240 43.3	04.0	68 18.2	14.1	17 03.0	11.7	54.7
	05	255 43.4	04.7	82 51.3	14.0	17 14.7	11.7	54.7
	06	270 43.4	N15 05.5	97 24.3	14.0	S17 26.4	11.5	54.7
	07	285 43.5	06.2	111 57.3	14.0	17 37.9	11.5	54.7
	08	300 43.6	07.0	126 30.3	13.9	17 49.4	11.4	54.7
	09	315 43.7	. . 07.7	141 03.2	13.8	18 00.8	11.4	54.7
	10	330 43.7	08.5	155 36.0	13.8	18 12.2	11.2	54.6
	11	345 43.8	09.3	170 08.8	13.7	18 23.4	11.2	54.6
	12	0 43.9	N15 10.0	184 41.5	13.7	S18 34.6	11.1	54.6
	13	15 44.0	10.8	199 14.2	13.6	18 45.7	11.0	54.6
	14	30 44.0	11.5	213 46.8	13.6	18 56.7	10.9	54.6
	15	45 44.1	. . 12.3	228 19.4	13.6	19 07.6	10.8	54.6
	16	60 44.2	13.0	242 52.0	13.4	19 18.4	10.7	54.6
	17	75 44.2	13.8	257 24.4	13.5	19 29.1	10.7	54.6
	18	90 44.3	N15 14.5	271 56.9	13.3	S19 39.8	10.6	54.5
	19	105 44.4	15.3	286 29.2	13.4	19 50.4	10.4	54.5
	20	120 44.5	16.0	301 01.6	13.2	20 00.8	10.4	54.5
	21	135 44.5	. . 16.8	315 33.8	13.2	20 11.2	10.3	54.5
	22	150 44.6	17.5	330 06.0	13.2	20 21.5	10.2	54.5
	23	165 44.7	18.3	344 38.2	13.1	20 31.7	10.1	54.5
SATURDAY	2 00	180 44.8	N15 19.0	359 10.3	13.1	S20 41.8	10.0	54.5
	01	195 44.8	19.8	13 42.4	13.0	20 51.8	10.0	54.5
	02	210 44.9	20.5	28 14.4	12.9	21 01.8	9.8	54.4
	03	225 45.0	. . 21.3	42 46.3	12.9	21 11.6	9.7	54.4
	04	240 45.0	22.0	57 18.2	12.8	21 21.3	9.6	54.4
	05	255 45.1	22.7	71 50.0	12.8	21 30.9	9.6	54.4
	06	270 45.2	N15 23.5	86 21.8	12.7	S21 40.5	9.4	54.4
	07	285 45.3	24.2	100 53.5	12.7	21 49.9	9.3	54.4
	08	300 45.3	25.0	115 25.2	12.6	21 59.2	9.3	54.4
	09	315 45.4	. . 25.7	129 56.8	12.6	22 08.5	9.1	54.4
	10	330 45.5	26.5	144 28.4	12.5	22 17.6	9.1	54.4
	11	345 45.5	27.2	158 59.9	12.4	22 26.7	8.9	54.3
	12	0 45.6	N15 28.0	173 31.3	12.4	S22 35.6	8.8	54.3
	13	15 45.7	28.7	188 02.7	12.4	22 44.4	8.7	54.3
	14	30 45.7	29.4	202 34.1	12.2	22 53.1	8.7	54.3
	15	45 45.8	. . 30.2	217 05.3	12.3	23 01.8	8.5	54.3
	16	60 45.9	30.9	231 36.6	12.1	23 10.3	8.4	54.3
	17	75 45.9	31.7	246 07.7	12.2	23 18.7	8.3	54.3
	18	90 46.0	N15 32.4	260 38.9	12.0	S23 27.0	8.2	54.3
	19	105 46.1	33.1	275 09.9	12.0	23 35.2	8.1	54.3
	20	120 46.1	33.9	289 40.9	12.0	23 43.3	7.9	54.3
	21	135 46.2	. . 34.6	304 11.9	11.9	23 51.2	7.9	54.3
	22	150 46.3	35.4	318 42.8	11.9	23 59.1	7.7	54.2
	23	165 46.3	36.1	333 13.7	11.8	24 06.8	7.7	54.2
SUNDAY	3 00	180 46.4	N15 36.8	347 44.5	11.7	S24 14.5	7.5	54.2
	01	195 46.5	37.6	2 15.2	11.7	24 22.0	7.4	54.2
	02	210 46.5	38.3	16 45.9	11.7	24 29.4	7.3	54.2
	03	225 46.6	. . 39.0	31 16.6	11.6	24 36.7	7.2	54.2
	04	240 46.7	39.8	45 47.2	11.5	24 43.9	7.1	54.2
	05	255 46.7	40.5	60 17.7	11.5	24 51.0	7.0	54.2
	06	270 46.8	N15 41.2	74 48.2	11.5	S24 58.0	6.8	54.2
	07	285 46.9	42.0	89 18.7	11.4	25 04.8	6.7	54.2
	08	300 46.9	42.7	103 49.1	11.3	25 11.5	6.6	54.2
	09	315 47.0	. . 43.4	118 19.4	11.3	25 18.1	6.5	54.2
	10	330 47.1	44.2	132 49.7	11.2	25 24.6	6.4	54.2
	11	345 47.1	44.9	147 19.9	11.3	25 31.0	6.2	54.1
	12	0 47.2	N15 45.6	161 50.2	11.1	S25 37.2	6.2	54.1
	13	15 47.2	46.4	176 20.3	11.1	25 43.4	6.0	54.1
	14	30 47.3	47.1	190 50.4	11.1	25 49.4	5.9	54.1
	15	45 47.4	. . 47.8	205 20.5	11.0	25 55.3	5.7	54.1
	16	60 47.4	48.6	219 50.5	11.0	26 01.0	5.7	54.1
	17	75 47.5	49.3	234 20.5	10.9	26 06.7	5.5	54.1
	18	90 47.6	N15 50.0	248 50.4	10.9	S26 12.2	5.4	54.1
	19	105 47.6	50.8	263 20.3	10.9	26 17.6	5.2	54.1
	20	120 47.7	51.5	277 50.2	10.8	26 22.8	5.2	54.1
	21	135 47.7	. . 52.2	292 20.0	10.7	26 28.0	5.0	54.1
	22	150 47.8	52.9	306 49.7	10.8	26 33.0	4.9	54.1
	23	165 47.9	53.7	321 19.5	10.7	S26 37.9	4.8	54.1
		SD 15.9	d 0.7	SD 14.9		14.8		14.8

Lat. °	Twilight Naut. h m	Twilight Civil h m	Sunrise h m	Moonrise 1 h m	Moonrise 2 h m	Moonrise 3 h m	Moonrise 4 h m
N 72	////	////	01 44	■	■	■	■
N 70	////	////	02 25	■	■	■	■
68	////	00 55	02 53	22 33	■	■	■
66	////	01 49	03 14	21 46	■	■	■
64	////	02 21	03 30	21 16	23 17	■	■
62	00 49	02 44	03 44	20 53	22 36	24 26	00 26
60	01 37	03 02	03 55	20 36	22 09	23 40	24 58
N 58	02 06	03 17	04 05	20 21	21 47	23 10	24 21
56	02 27	03 29	04 14	20 08	21 30	22 47	23 54
54	02 44	03 40	04 22	19 57	21 15	22 29	23 34
52	02 59	03 50	04 29	19 47	21 02	22 13	23 16
50	03 11	03 58	04 35	19 38	20 51	22 00	23 01
45	03 35	04 16	04 48	19 20	20 27	21 32	22 31
N 40	03 54	04 30	04 59	19 05	20 09	21 10	22 08
35	04 09	04 41	05 08	18 53	19 53	20 52	21 49
30	04 21	04 51	05 16	18 42	19 40	20 37	21 32
20	04 40	05 07	05 30	18 23	19 17	20 11	21 05
N 10	04 55	05 20	05 42	18 07	18 57	19 49	20 41
0	05 07	05 32	05 54	17 52	18 39	19 28	20 19
S 10	05 18	05 43	06 05	17 38	18 21	19 07	19 56
20	05 27	05 54	06 16	17 22	18 02	18 45	19 33
30	05 36	06 05	06 30	17 04	17 39	18 20	19 05
35	05 41	06 11	06 37	16 53	17 26	18 05	18 49
40	05 45	06 18	06 46	16 41	17 12	17 47	18 30
45	05 50	06 25	06 56	16 28	16 54	17 27	18 07
S 50	05 55	06 34	07 08	16 11	16 32	17 00	17 38
52	05 57	06 38	07 14	16 03	16 22	16 48	17 24
54	06 00	06 42	07 20	15 54	16 10	16 33	17 07
56	06 02	06 47	07 27	15 44	15 57	16 17	16 47
58	06 05	06 52	07 34	15 33	15 42	15 56	16 23
S 60	06 07	06 57	07 43	15 20	15 23	15 31	15 50

Lat. °	Sunset h m	Twilight Civil h m	Twilight Naut. h m	Moonset 1 h m	Moonset 2 h m	Moonset 3 h m	Moonset 4 h m
N 72	22 18	////	////	00 57	■	■	■
N 70	21 33	////	////	01 41	■	■	■
68	21 05	23 12	////	02 10	01 18	■	■
66	20 43	22 10	////	02 33	02 06	■	■
64	20 26	21 37	////	02 50	02 37	02 14	■
62	20 12	21 13	23 17	03 05	03 00	02 55	02 48
60	20 00	20 55	22 22	03 17	03 19	03 24	03 35
N 58	19 50	20 39	21 51	03 28	03 35	03 46	04 05
56	19 41	20 26	21 29	03 38	03 48	04 04	04 28
54	19 33	20 15	21 12	03 46	04 00	04 19	04 47
52	19 26	20 06	20 57	03 54	04 10	04 32	05 03
50	19 20	19 57	20 45	04 00	04 19	04 44	05 16
45	19 07	19 39	20 20	04 15	04 39	05 08	05 44
N 40	18 56	19 25	20 01	04 27	04 55	05 27	06 07
35	18 46	19 13	19 46	04 37	05 08	05 44	06 25
30	18 38	19 03	19 34	04 47	05 20	05 58	06 41
20	18 24	18 47	19 14	05 02	05 40	06 22	07 08
N 10	18 12	18 34	18 59	05 16	05 58	06 43	07 31
0	18 00	18 22	18 47	05 29	06 15	07 02	07 52
S 10	17 49	18 11	18 36	05 42	06 31	07 22	08 14
20	17 37	18 00	18 26	05 56	06 49	07 43	08 37
30	17 24	17 49	18 17	06 12	07 10	08 08	09 04
35	17 16	17 43	18 13	06 22	07 22	08 22	09 20
40	17 08	17 36	18 08	06 32	07 36	08 39	09 39
45	16 57	17 28	18 03	06 45	07 53	08 59	10 01
S 50	16 45	17 20	17 58	07 01	08 13	09 24	10 30
52	16 40	17 16	17 56	07 08	08 23	09 37	10 44
54	16 33	17 11	17 53	07 16	08 34	09 51	11 01
56	16 26	17 07	17 51	07 25	08 47	10 07	11 20
58	16 19	17 01	17 48	07 36	09 02	10 27	11 45
S 60	16 10	16 56	17 45	07 48	09 20	10 52	12 18

Day	SUN Eqn. of Time 00h m s	SUN Eqn. of Time 12h m s	SUN Mer. Pass. h m	MOON Mer. Pass. Upper h m	MOON Mer. Pass. Lower h m	MOON Age d	MOON Phase %
1	02 52	02 55	11 57	24 03	11 41	14	100
2	02 59	03 02	11 57	00 03	12 27	15	99
3	03 05	03 09	11 57	00 51	13 15	16	97

Day	UT d h	ARIES GHA	VENUS −3·9 GHA	VENUS Dec	MARS +1·2 GHA	MARS Dec	JUPITER −2·0 GHA	JUPITER Dec	SATURN +0·9 GHA	SATURN Dec
		° ′	° ′	° ′	° ′	° ′	° ′	° ′	° ′	° ′
MONDAY	4 00	221 53.8	151 38.2	N23 14.2	204 20.6	N 6 30.9	110 54.1	N22 25.9	212 19.7	N 1 45.2
	01	236 56.3	166 37.4	14.7	219 21.2	31.6	125 56.1	25.9	227 21.9	45.3
	02	251 58.7	181 36.6	15.2	234 21.9	32.3	140 58.2	25.8	242 24.1	45.4
	03	267 01.2	196 35.9	. . 15.7	249 22.6	. . 33.1	156 00.3	. . 25.8	257 26.3	. . 45.5
	04	282 03.7	211 35.1	16.2	264 23.3	33.8	171 02.4	25.7	272 28.5	45.6
	05	297 06.1	226 34.3	16.7	279 24.0	34.6	186 04.4	25.7	287 30.7	45.7
	06	312 08.6	241 33.5	N23 17.2	294 24.7	N 6 35.3	201 06.5	N22 25.6	302 32.9	N 1 45.8
	07	327 11.1	256 32.8	17.7	309 25.4	36.0	216 08.6	25.6	317 35.2	45.9
	08	342 13.5	271 32.0	18.2	324 26.1	36.8	231 10.7	25.5	332 37.4	46.0
	09	357 16.0	286 31.2	. . 18.7	339 26.8	. . 37.5	246 12.7	. . 25.5	347 39.6	. . 46.1
	10	12 18.5	301 30.4	19.2	354 27.5	38.3	261 14.8	25.4	2 41.8	46.2
	11	27 20.9	316 29.6	19.7	9 28.2	39.0	276 16.9	25.4	17 44.0	46.3
	12	42 23.4	331 28.9	N23 20.2	24 28.9	N 6 39.7	291 18.9	N22 25.3	32 46.2	N 1 46.4
	13	57 25.8	346 28.1	20.7	39 29.6	40.5	306 21.0	25.3	47 48.4	46.6
	14	72 28.3	1 27.3	21.2	54 30.2	41.2	321 23.1	25.2	62 50.6	46.7
	15	87 30.8	16 26.5	. . 21.7	69 30.9	. . 42.0	336 25.2	. . 25.2	77 52.8	. . 46.8
	16	102 33.2	31 25.7	22.2	84 31.6	42.7	351 27.2	25.1	92 55.0	46.9
	17	117 35.7	46 24.9	22.7	99 32.3	43.4	6 29.3	25.1	107 57.2	47.0
	18	132 38.2	61 24.2	N23 23.2	114 33.0	N 6 44.2	21 31.4	N22 25.0	122 59.4	N 1 47.1
	19	147 40.6	76 23.4	23.7	129 33.7	44.9	36 33.4	25.0	138 01.7	47.2
	20	162 43.1	91 22.6	24.2	144 34.4	45.7	51 35.5	24.9	153 03.9	47.3
	21	177 45.6	106 21.8	. . 24.6	159 35.1	. . 46.4	66 37.6	. . 24.8	168 06.1	. . 47.4
	22	192 48.0	121 21.0	25.1	174 35.8	47.1	81 39.7	24.8	183 08.3	47.5
	23	207 50.5	136 20.2	25.6	189 36.5	47.9	96 41.7	24.7	198 10.5	47.6
TUESDAY	5 00	222 53.0	151 19.5	N23 26.1	204 37.2	N 6 48.6	111 43.8	N22 24.7	213 12.7	N 1 47.7
	01	237 55.4	166 18.7	26.6	219 37.9	49.3	126 45.9	24.6	228 14.9	47.8
	02	252 57.9	181 17.9	27.1	234 38.5	50.1	141 47.9	24.6	243 17.1	47.9
	03	268 00.3	196 17.1	. . 27.6	249 39.2	. . 50.8	156 50.0	. . 24.5	258 19.3	. . 48.0
	04	283 02.8	211 16.3	28.0	264 39.9	51.6	171 52.1	24.5	273 21.5	48.1
	05	298 05.3	226 15.5	28.5	279 40.6	52.3	186 54.1	24.4	288 23.7	48.2
	06	313 07.7	241 14.8	N23 29.0	294 41.3	N 6 53.0	201 56.2	N22 24.4	303 26.0	N 1 48.3
	07	328 10.2	256 14.0	29.5	309 42.0	53.8	216 58.3	24.3	318 28.2	48.4
	08	343 12.7	271 13.2	29.9	324 42.7	54.5	232 00.4	24.3	333 30.4	48.5
	09	358 15.1	286 12.4	. . 30.4	339 43.4	. . 55.2	247 02.4	. . 24.2	348 32.6	. . 48.6
	10	13 17.6	301 11.6	30.9	354 44.1	56.0	262 04.5	24.2	3 34.8	48.7
	11	28 20.1	316 10.8	31.4	9 44.8	56.7	277 06.6	24.1	18 37.0	48.8
	12	43 22.5	331 10.0	N23 31.8	24 45.5	N 6 57.5	292 08.6	N22 24.1	33 39.2	N 1 48.9
	13	58 25.0	346 09.2	32.3	39 46.1	58.2	307 10.7	24.0	48 41.4	49.0
	14	73 27.5	1 08.5	32.8	54 46.8	58.9	322 12.8	24.0	63 43.6	49.1
	15	88 29.9	16 07.7	. . 33.2	69 47.5	6 59.7	337 14.8	. . 23.9	78 45.8	. . 49.2
	16	103 32.4	31 06.9	33.7	84 48.2	7 00.4	352 16.9	23.9	93 48.0	49.3
	17	118 34.8	46 06.1	34.2	99 48.9	01.1	7 19.0	23.8	108 50.3	49.4
	18	133 37.3	61 05.3	N23 34.6	114 49.6	N 7 01.9	22 21.0	N22 23.8	123 52.5	N 1 49.5
	19	148 39.8	76 04.5	35.1	129 50.3	02.6	37 23.1	23.7	138 54.7	49.6
	20	163 42.2	91 03.7	35.6	144 51.0	03.3	52 25.2	23.7	153 56.9	49.7
	21	178 44.7	106 02.9	. . 36.0	159 51.7	. . 04.1	67 27.2	. . 23.6	168 59.1	. . 49.8
	22	193 47.2	121 02.1	36.5	174 52.4	04.8	82 29.3	23.6	184 01.3	49.9
	23	208 49.6	136 01.3	36.9	189 53.1	05.5	97 31.4	23.5	199 03.5	50.0
WEDNESDAY	6 00	223 52.1	151 00.6	N23 37.4	204 53.7	N 7 06.3	112 33.4	N22 23.5	214 05.7	N 1 50.1
	01	238 54.6	165 59.8	37.9	219 54.4	07.0	127 35.5	23.4	229 07.9	50.2
	02	253 57.0	180 59.0	38.3	234 55.1	07.7	142 37.6	23.3	244 10.1	50.3
	03	268 59.5	195 58.2	. . 38.8	249 55.8	. . 08.5	157 39.6	. . 23.3	259 12.4	. . 50.4
	04	284 02.0	210 57.4	39.2	264 56.5	09.2	172 41.7	23.2	274 14.6	50.5
	05	299 04.4	225 56.6	39.7	279 57.2	09.9	187 43.7	23.2	289 16.8	50.6
	06	314 06.9	240 55.8	N23 40.1	294 57.9	N 7 10.7	202 45.8	N22 23.1	304 19.0	N 1 50.7
	07	329 09.3	255 55.0	40.6	309 58.6	11.4	217 47.9	23.1	319 21.2	50.8
	08	344 11.8	270 54.2	41.0	324 59.3	12.1	232 49.9	23.0	334 23.4	50.9
	09	359 14.3	285 53.4	. . 41.5	340 00.0	. . 12.9	247 52.0	. . 23.0	349 25.6	. . 51.0
	10	14 16.7	300 52.6	41.9	355 00.7	13.6	262 54.1	22.9	4 27.8	51.1
	11	29 19.2	315 51.8	42.4	10 01.3	14.3	277 56.1	22.9	19 30.0	51.2
	12	44 21.7	330 51.0	N23 42.8	25 02.0	N 7 15.1	292 58.2	N22 22.8	34 32.3	N 1 51.3
	13	59 24.1	345 50.2	43.2	40 02.7	15.8	308 00.3	22.8	49 34.5	51.4
	14	74 26.6	0 49.4	43.7	55 03.4	16.5	323 02.3	22.7	64 36.7	51.5
	15	89 29.1	15 48.6	. . 44.1	70 04.1	. . 17.3	338 04.4	. . 22.7	79 38.9	. . 51.6
	16	104 31.5	30 47.9	44.6	85 04.8	18.0	353 06.4	22.6	94 41.1	51.8
	17	119 34.0	45 47.1	45.0	100 05.5	18.7	8 08.5	22.6	109 43.3	51.9
	18	134 36.4	60 46.3	N23 45.4	115 06.2	N 7 19.5	23 10.6	N22 22.5	124 45.5	N 1 52.0
	19	149 38.9	75 45.5	45.9	130 06.9	20.2	38 12.6	22.5	139 47.7	52.1
	20	164 41.4	90 44.7	46.3	145 07.6	20.9	53 14.7	22.4	154 50.0	52.2
	21	179 43.8	105 43.9	. . 46.7	160 08.2	. . 21.7	68 16.7	. . 22.3	169 52.2	. . 52.3
	22	194 46.3	120 43.1	47.2	175 08.9	22.4	83 18.8	22.3	184 54.4	52.4
	23	209 48.8	135 42.3	47.6	190 09.6	23.1	98 20.9	22.2	199 56.6	52.5
	Mer. Pass.	h m 9 07.0	v −0.8	d 0.5	v 0.7	d 0.7	v 2.1	d 0.1	v 2.2	d 0.1

STARS

Name	SHA	Dec
	° ′	° ′
Acamar	315 11.4	S40 12.0
Achernar	335 19.9	S57 06.1
Acrux	172 58.3	S63 15.0
Adhara	255 05.2	S29 00.7
Aldebaran	290 38.7	N16 33.7
Alioth	166 11.5	N55 49.1
Alkaid	152 50.7	N49 10.9
Alnair	27 31.7	S46 49.8
Alnilam	275 36.9	S 1 11.2
Alphard	217 46.7	S 8 46.5
Alphecca	126 02.5	N26 37.4
Alpheratz	357 33.9	N29 14.0
Altair	61 58.8	N 8 56.1
Ankaa	353 06.4	S42 09.7
Antares	112 14.2	S26 29.5
Arcturus	145 46.6	N19 02.6
Atria	107 06.9	S69 04.4
Avior	234 14.4	S59 35.9
Bellatrix	278 22.0	N 6 22.3
Betelgeuse	270 51.2	N 7 24.7
Canopus	263 52.3	S52 42.8
Capella	280 20.7	N46 01.5
Deneb	49 25.0	N45 22.2
Denebola	182 23.6	N14 25.4
Diphda	348 46.5	S17 50.5
Dubhe	193 39.4	N61 36.7
Elnath	278 00.8	N28 37.8
Eltanin	90 41.3	N51 28.8
Enif	33 37.8	N 9 59.6
Fomalhaut	15 13.5	S29 28.9
Gacrux	171 50.0	S57 15.9
Gienah	175 42.2	S17 41.5
Hadar	148 33.8	S60 30.1
Hamal	327 50.3	N23 35.1
Kaus Aust.	83 30.8	S34 22.2
Kochab	137 18.6	N74 02.7
Markab	13 29.0	N15 20.7
Menkar	314 05.3	N 4 11.5
Menkent	147 56.0	S36 30.1
Miaplacidus	221 38.1	S69 49.8
Mirfak	308 27.2	N49 57.2
Nunki	75 46.2	S26 15.8
Peacock	53 03.9	S56 38.8
Pollux	243 16.1	N27 57.8
Procyon	244 49.8	N 5 09.4
Rasalhague	95 57.3	N12 32.3
Regulus	207 33.2	N11 50.2
Rigel	281 03.1	S 8 10.4
Rigil Kent.	139 38.1	S60 56.7
Sabik	102 01.3	S15 45.5
Schedar	349 30.3	N56 40.7
Shaula	96 08.6	S37 07.3
Sirius	258 25.5	S16 45.3
Spica	158 20.9	S11 18.1
Suhail	222 45.5	S43 32.6
Vega	80 32.2	N38 48.2
Zuben'ubi	136 54.5	S16 09.2

	SHA	Mer. Pass.
	° ′	h m
Venus	288 26.5	13 55
Mars	341 44.2	10 21
Jupiter	248 50.8	16 31
Saturn	350 19.7	9 46

UT (d h)	SUN GHA (° ′)	SUN Dec (° ′)	MOON GHA (° ′)	v (′)	MOON Dec (° ′)	d (′)	HP (′)
4 00 (MONDAY)	180 47.9	N15 54.4	335 49.2	10.6	S26 42.7	4.6	54.1
01	195 48.0	55.1	350 18.8	10.6	26 47.3	4.5	54.1
02	210 48.0	55.8	4 48.4	10.6	26 51.8	4.4	54.1
03	225 48.1	. . 56.6	19 18.0	10.6	26 56.2	4.2	54.1
04	240 48.2	57.3	33 47.6	10.5	27 00.4	4.2	54.1
05	255 48.2	58.0	48 17.1	10.4	27 04.6	4.0	54.1
06	270 48.3	N15 58.7	62 46.5	10.5	S27 08.6	3.8	54.1
07	285 48.3	15 59.5	77 16.0	10.4	27 12.4	3.8	54.1
08	300 48.4	16 00.2	91 45.4	10.4	27 16.2	3.6	54.1
09	315 48.5	. . 00.9	106 14.8	10.3	27 19.8	3.5	54.0
10	330 48.5	01.6	120 44.1	10.4	27 23.3	3.3	54.0
11	345 48.6	02.4	135 13.5	10.3	27 26.6	3.2	54.0
12	0 48.6	N16 03.1	149 42.8	10.2	S27 29.8	3.1	54.0
13	15 48.7	03.8	164 12.0	10.3	27 32.9	2.9	54.0
14	30 48.7	04.5	178 41.3	10.2	27 35.8	2.9	54.0
15	45 48.8	. . 05.2	193 10.5	10.2	27 38.7	2.6	54.0
16	60 48.9	06.0	207 39.7	10.2	27 41.3	2.6	54.0
17	75 48.9	06.7	222 08.9	10.1	27 43.9	2.4	54.0
18	90 49.0	N16 07.4	236 38.0	10.2	S27 46.3	2.3	54.0
19	105 49.0	08.1	251 07.2	10.1	27 48.6	2.1	54.0
20	120 49.1	08.8	265 36.3	10.1	27 50.7	2.0	54.0
21	135 49.1	. . 09.5	280 05.4	10.0	27 52.7	1.9	54.0
22	150 49.2	10.3	294 34.4	10.1	27 54.6	1.8	54.0
23	165 49.2	11.0	309 03.5	10.0	27 56.4	1.6	54.0
5 00 (TUESDAY)	180 49.3	N16 11.7	323 32.5	10.1	S27 58.0	1.5	54.0
01	195 49.3	12.4	338 01.6	10.0	27 59.5	1.3	54.0
02	210 49.4	13.1	352 30.6	10.0	28 00.8	1.2	54.0
03	225 49.5	. . 13.8	6 59.6	10.0	28 02.0	1.1	54.0
04	240 49.5	14.5	21 28.6	10.0	28 03.1	0.9	54.0
05	255 49.6	15.3	35 57.6	10.0	28 04.0	0.8	54.0
06	270 49.6	N16 16.0	50 26.6	10.0	S28 04.8	0.7	54.0
07	285 49.7	16.7	64 55.6	9.9	28 05.5	0.5	54.0
08	300 49.7	17.4	79 24.5	10.0	28 06.0	0.4	54.0
09	315 49.8	. . 18.1	93 53.5	10.0	28 06.4	0.2	54.0
10	330 49.8	18.8	108 22.5	9.9	28 06.6	0.2	54.0
11	345 49.9	19.5	122 51.4	10.0	28 06.8	0.1	54.0
12	0 49.9	N16 20.2	137 20.4	10.0	S28 06.7	0.1	54.0
13	15 50.0	21.0	151 49.4	9.9	28 06.6	0.3	54.1
14	30 50.0	21.7	166 18.3	10.0	28 06.3	0.4	54.1
15	45 50.1	. . 22.4	180 47.3	9.9	28 05.9	0.6	54.1
16	60 50.1	23.1	195 16.2	10.0	28 05.3	0.7	54.1
17	75 50.2	23.8	209 45.2	10.0	28 04.6	0.8	54.1
18	90 50.2	N16 24.5	224 14.2	10.0	S28 03.8	1.0	54.1
19	105 50.3	25.2	238 43.2	10.0	28 02.8	1.1	54.1
20	120 50.3	25.9	253 12.2	10.0	28 01.7	1.2	54.1
21	135 50.4	. . 26.6	267 41.2	10.0	28 00.5	1.4	54.1
22	150 50.4	27.3	282 10.2	10.0	27 59.1	1.5	54.1
23	165 50.5	28.0	296 39.2	10.1	27 57.6	1.7	54.1
6 00 (WEDNESDAY)	180 50.5	N16 28.7	311 08.3	10.0	S27 55.9	1.8	54.1
01	195 50.6	29.4	325 37.3	10.1	27 54.1	1.9	54.1
02	210 50.6	30.1	340 06.4	10.1	27 52.2	2.0	54.1
03	225 50.7	. . 30.8	354 35.5	10.1	27 50.2	2.2	54.1
04	240 50.7	31.5	9 04.6	10.1	27 48.0	2.3	54.1
05	255 50.8	32.2	23 33.7	10.1	27 45.7	2.5	54.1
06	270 50.8	N16 32.9	38 02.8	10.2	S27 43.2	2.6	54.1
07	285 50.9	33.6	52 32.0	10.1	27 40.6	2.7	54.1
08	300 50.9	34.3	67 01.1	10.2	27 37.9	2.8	54.2
09	315 51.0	. . 35.0	81 30.3	10.3	27 35.1	3.0	54.2
10	330 51.0	35.7	95 59.6	10.2	27 32.1	3.2	54.2
11	345 51.0	36.4	110 28.8	10.3	27 28.9	3.2	54.2
12	0 51.1	N16 37.1	124 58.1	10.3	S27 25.7	3.4	54.2
13	15 51.1	37.8	139 27.4	10.3	27 22.3	3.5	54.2
14	30 51.2	38.5	153 56.7	10.3	27 18.8	3.6	54.2
15	45 51.2	. . 39.2	168 26.0	10.4	27 15.2	3.8	54.2
16	60 51.3	39.9	182 55.4	10.4	27 11.4	3.9	54.2
17	75 51.3	40.6	197 24.8	10.5	27 07.5	4.1	54.2
18	90 51.4	N16 41.3	211 54.3	10.4	S27 03.4	4.1	54.2
19	105 51.4	42.0	226 23.7	10.5	26 59.3	4.3	54.2
20	120 51.4	42.7	240 53.2	10.6	26 55.0	4.5	54.3
21	135 51.5	. . 43.4	255 22.8	10.5	26 50.5	4.5	54.3
22	150 51.5	44.1	269 52.3	10.6	26 46.0	4.7	54.3
23	165 51.6	44.8	284 21.9	10.7	S26 41.3	4.8	54.3
	SD 15.9	*d* 0.7	SD	14.7	14.7		14.8

Lat. (°)	Twilight Naut. (h m)	Twilight Civil (h m)	Sunrise (h m)	Moonrise 4 (h m)	Moonrise 5 (h m)	Moonrise 6 (h m)	Moonrise 7 (h m)
N 72	////	////	01 14	■	■	■	■
N 70	////	////	02 07	■	■	■	■
68	////	////	02 39	■	■	■	■
66	////	01 29	03 02	■	■	■	■
64	////	02 06	03 20	■	■	■	■
62	////	02 32	03 35	00 26	■	03 03	02 48
60	01 19	02 52	03 47	24 58	00 58	01 47	02 08
N 58	01 53	03 08	03 58	24 21	00 21	01 11	01 41
56	02 17	03 22	04 07	23 54	24 45	00 45	01 19
54	02 36	03 33	04 16	23 34	24 25	00 25	01 01
52	02 51	03 43	04 23	23 16	24 08	00 08	00 46
50	03 04	03 52	04 30	23 01	23 53	24 33	00 33
45	03 30	04 11	04 44	22 31	23 23	24 06	00 06
N 40	03 49	04 26	04 55	22 08	23 00	23 44	24 21
35	04 05	04 38	05 05	21 49	22 41	23 26	24 06
30	04 18	04 48	05 14	21 32	22 24	23 11	23 52
20	04 38	05 05	05 29	21 05	21 56	22 45	23 29
N 10	04 54	05 19	05 41	20 41	21 32	22 22	23 09
0	05 07	05 32	05 53	20 19	21 10	22 01	22 51
S 10	05 18	05 43	06 05	19 56	20 48	21 40	22 32
20	05 28	05 54	06 17	19 33	20 24	21 17	22 11
30	05 38	06 06	06 31	19 05	19 56	20 51	21 48
35	05 43	06 13	06 40	18 49	19 39	20 35	21 34
40	05 48	06 20	06 49	18 30	19 20	20 17	21 18
45	05 53	06 28	06 59	18 07	18 57	19 55	20 59
S 50	05 59	06 38	07 12	17 38	18 27	19 27	20 35
52	06 02	06 42	07 18	17 24	18 12	19 13	20 23
54	06 04	06 47	07 25	17 07	17 55	18 57	20 10
56	06 07	06 52	07 33	16 47	17 34	18 38	19 55
58	06 10	06 57	07 41	16 23	17 08	18 15	19 36
S 60	06 13	07 04	07 50	15 50	16 32	17 44	19 14

Lat. (°)	Sunset (h m)	Twilight Civil (h m)	Twilight Naut. (h m)	Moonset 4 (h m)	Moonset 5 (h m)	Moonset 6 (h m)	Moonset 7 (h m)
N 72	22 51	////	////	■	■	■	■
N 70	21 52	////	////	■	■	■	■
68	21 18	////	////	■	■	■	■
66	20 54	22 31	////	■	■	■	■
64	20 36	21 51	////	■	■	■	■
62	20 20	21 24	////	02 48	■	03 44	05 45
60	20 08	21 04	22 41	03 35	04 03	05 01	06 25
N 58	19 57	20 47	22 04	04 05	04 40	05 36	06 52
56	19 47	20 34	21 39	04 28	05 06	06 02	07 13
54	19 39	20 22	21 20	04 47	05 27	06 22	07 31
52	19 31	20 11	21 04	05 03	05 45	06 39	07 46
50	19 25	20 02	20 51	05 16	05 59	06 54	07 58
45	19 10	19 43	20 25	05 44	06 30	07 24	08 25
N 40	18 59	19 28	20 05	06 07	06 53	07 47	08 46
35	18 49	19 16	19 49	06 25	07 12	08 06	09 03
30	18 40	19 06	19 36	06 41	07 29	08 22	09 18
20	18 25	18 48	19 16	07 08	07 57	08 49	09 43
N 10	18 12	18 34	19 00	07 31	08 21	09 13	10 05
0	18 00	18 22	18 47	07 52	08 43	09 35	10 25
S 10	17 48	18 10	18 35	08 14	09 06	09 57	10 45
20	17 36	17 59	18 25	08 37	09 30	10 20	11 07
30	17 22	17 47	18 15	09 04	09 58	10 47	11 31
35	17 13	17 40	18 10	09 20	10 14	11 03	11 46
40	17 04	17 33	18 05	09 39	10 34	11 22	12 02
45	16 53	17 24	17 59	10 01	10 57	11 44	12 22
S 50	16 40	17 15	17 54	10 30	11 27	12 12	12 47
52	16 34	17 11	17 51	10 44	11 42	12 26	12 59
54	16 28	17 06	17 48	11 01	11 59	12 43	13 13
56	16 20	17 01	17 45	11 20	12 20	13 02	13 29
58	16 12	16 55	17 42	11 45	12 46	13 25	13 48
S 60	16 02	16 49	17 39	12 18	13 22	13 56	14 11

Day (d)	SUN Eqn. of Time 00^h (m s)	SUN Eqn. of Time 12^h (m s)	SUN Mer. Pass. (h m)	MOON Mer. Pass. Upper (h m)	MOON Mer. Pass. Lower (h m)	MOON Age (d)	MOON Phase (%)
4	03 12	03 14	11 57	01 40	14 05	17	93
5	03 17	03 20	11 57	02 31	14 57	18	87
6	03 22	03 24	11 57	03 22	15 48	19	81

Day	UT d h	ARIES GHA	VENUS −3·9 GHA	VENUS Dec	MARS +1·2 GHA	MARS Dec	JUPITER −2·0 GHA	JUPITER Dec	SATURN +0·9 GHA	SATURN Dec
		° ′	° ′	° ′	° ′	° ′	° ′	° ′	° ′	° ′
THURSDAY	7 00	224 51.2	150 41.5	N23 48.0	205 10.3	N 7 23.9	113 22.9	N22 22.2	214 58.8	N 1 52.6
	01	239 53.7	165 40.7	48.5	220 11.0	24.6	128 25.0	22.1	230 01.0	52.7
	02	254 56.2	180 39.9	48.9	235 11.7	25.3	143 27.0	22.1	245 03.2	52.8
	03	269 58.6	195 39.1	. . 49.3	250 12.4	. . 26.1	158 29.1	. . 22.0	260 05.4	. . 52.9
	04	285 01.1	210 38.3	49.7	265 13.1	26.8	173 31.2	22.0	275 07.6	53.0
	05	300 03.6	225 37.5	50.2	280 13.8	27.5	188 33.2	21.9	290 09.9	53.1
	06	315 06.0	240 36.7	N23 50.6	295 14.5	N 7 28.2	203 35.3	N22 21.9	305 12.1	N 1 53.2
	07	330 08.5	255 35.9	51.0	310 15.1	29.0	218 37.3	21.8	320 14.3	53.3
	08	345 10.9	270 35.1	51.4	325 15.8	29.7	233 39.4	21.8	335 16.5	53.4
	09	0 13.4	285 34.3	. . 51.8	340 16.5	. . 30.4	248 41.5	. . 21.7	350 18.7	. . 53.5
	10	15 15.9	300 33.5	52.3	355 17.2	31.2	263 43.5	21.7	5 20.9	53.6
	11	30 18.3	315 32.7	52.7	10 17.9	31.9	278 45.6	21.6	20 23.1	53.7
	12	45 20.8	330 31.9	N23 53.1	25 18.6	N 7 32.6	293 47.6	N22 21.5	35 25.3	N 1 53.8
	13	60 23.3	345 31.1	53.5	40 19.3	33.4	308 49.7	21.5	50 27.6	53.9
	14	75 25.7	0 30.3	53.9	55 20.0	34.1	323 51.7	21.4	65 29.8	54.0
	15	90 28.2	15 29.5	. . 54.3	70 20.7	. . 34.8	338 53.8	. . 21.4	80 32.0	. . 54.1
	16	105 30.7	30 28.7	54.8	85 21.4	35.5	353 55.9	21.3	95 34.2	54.2
	17	120 33.1	45 27.9	55.2	100 22.0	36.3	8 57.9	21.3	110 36.4	54.3
	18	135 35.6	60 27.1	N23 55.6	115 22.7	N 7 37.0	24 00.0	N22 21.2	125 38.6	N 1 54.4
	19	150 38.1	75 26.3	56.0	130 23.4	37.7	39 02.0	21.2	140 40.8	54.5
	20	165 40.5	90 25.5	56.4	145 24.1	38.5	54 04.1	21.1	155 43.1	54.6
	21	180 43.0	105 24.7	. . 56.8	160 24.8	. . 39.2	69 06.1	. . 21.1	170 45.3	. . 54.7
	22	195 45.4	120 23.9	57.2	175 25.5	39.9	84 08.2	21.0	185 47.5	54.8
	23	210 47.9	135 23.1	57.6	190 26.2	40.6	99 10.3	20.9	200 49.7	54.9
FRIDAY	8 00	225 50.4	150 22.3	N23 58.0	205 26.9	N 7 41.4	114 12.3	N22 20.9	215 51.9	N 1 55.0
	01	240 52.8	165 21.4	58.4	220 27.6	42.1	129 14.4	20.8	230 54.1	55.1
	02	255 55.3	180 20.6	58.8	235 28.3	42.8	144 16.4	20.8	245 56.3	55.2
	03	270 57.8	195 19.8	. . 59.2	250 28.9	. . 43.5	159 18.5	. . 20.7	260 58.6	. . 55.3
	04	286 00.2	210 19.0	23 59.6	265 29.6	44.3	174 20.5	20.7	276 00.8	55.4
	05	301 02.7	225 18.2	24 00.0	280 30.3	45.0	189 22.6	20.6	291 03.0	55.5
	06	316 05.2	240 17.4	N24 00.4	295 31.0	N 7 45.7	204 24.6	N22 20.6	306 05.2	N 1 55.6
	07	331 07.6	255 16.6	00.8	310 31.7	46.5	219 26.7	20.5	321 07.4	55.7
	08	346 10.1	270 15.8	01.2	325 32.4	47.2	234 28.7	20.5	336 09.6	55.8
	09	1 12.6	285 15.0	. . 01.6	340 33.1	. . 47.9	249 30.8	. . 20.4	351 11.8	. . 55.9
	10	16 15.0	300 14.2	02.0	355 33.8	48.6	264 32.9	20.3	6 14.1	56.0
	11	31 17.5	315 13.4	02.3	10 34.5	49.4	279 34.9	20.3	21 16.3	56.1
	12	46 19.9	330 12.6	N24 02.7	25 35.1	N 7 50.1	294 37.0	N22 20.2	36 18.5	N 1 56.2
	13	61 22.4	345 11.8	03.1	40 35.8	50.8	309 39.0	20.2	51 20.7	56.3
	14	76 24.9	0 11.0	03.5	55 36.5	51.5	324 41.1	20.1	66 22.9	56.4
	15	91 27.3	15 10.2	. . 03.9	70 37.2	. . 52.3	339 43.1	. . 20.1	81 25.1	. . 56.5
	16	106 29.8	30 09.4	04.3	85 37.9	53.0	354 45.2	20.0	96 27.3	56.6
	17	121 32.3	45 08.5	04.7	100 38.6	53.7	9 47.2	20.0	111 29.6	56.7
	18	136 34.7	60 07.7	N24 05.0	115 39.3	N 7 54.4	24 49.3	N22 19.9	126 31.8	N 1 56.8
	19	151 37.2	75 06.9	05.4	130 40.0	55.2	39 51.3	19.9	141 34.0	56.9
	20	166 39.7	90 06.1	05.8	145 40.7	55.9	54 53.4	19.8	156 36.2	57.0
	21	181 42.1	105 05.3	. . 06.2	160 41.3	. . 56.6	69 55.4	. . 19.7	171 38.4	. . 57.1
	22	196 44.6	120 04.5	06.5	175 42.0	57.3	84 57.5	19.7	186 40.6	57.2
	23	211 47.1	135 03.7	06.9	190 42.7	58.1	99 59.5	19.6	201 42.8	57.3
SATURDAY	9 00	226 49.5	150 02.9	N24 07.3	205 43.4	N 7 58.8	115 01.6	N22 19.6	216 45.1	N 1 57.4
	01	241 52.0	165 02.1	07.7	220 44.1	7 59.5	130 03.6	19.5	231 47.3	57.4
	02	256 54.4	180 01.3	08.0	235 44.8	8 00.2	145 05.7	19.5	246 49.5	57.5
	03	271 56.9	195 00.5	. . 08.4	250 45.5	. . 00.9	160 07.7	. . 19.4	261 51.7	. . 57.6
	04	286 59.4	209 59.6	08.8	265 46.2	01.7	175 09.8	19.4	276 53.9	57.7
	05	302 01.8	224 58.8	09.1	280 46.8	02.4	190 11.8	19.3	291 56.1	57.8
	06	317 04.3	239 58.0	N24 09.5	295 47.5	N 8 03.1	205 13.9	N22 19.2	306 58.4	N 1 57.9
	07	332 06.8	254 57.2	09.9	310 48.2	03.8	220 15.9	19.2	322 00.6	58.0
	08	347 09.2	269 56.4	10.2	325 48.9	04.6	235 18.0	19.1	337 02.8	58.1
	09	2 11.7	284 55.6	. . 10.6	340 49.6	. . 05.3	250 20.0	. . 19.1	352 05.0	. . 58.2
	10	17 14.2	299 54.8	11.0	355 50.3	06.0	265 22.1	19.0	7 07.2	58.3
	11	32 16.6	314 54.0	11.3	10 51.0	06.7	280 24.1	19.0	22 09.4	58.4
	12	47 19.1	329 53.2	N24 11.7	25 51.7	N 8 07.5	295 26.2	N22 18.9	37 11.7	N 1 58.5
	13	62 21.5	344 52.3	12.0	40 52.4	08.2	310 28.2	18.9	52 13.9	58.6
	14	77 24.0	359 51.5	12.4	55 53.0	08.9	325 30.3	18.8	67 16.1	58.7
	15	92 26.5	14 50.7	. . 12.8	70 53.7	. . 09.6	340 32.3	. . 18.7	82 18.3	. . 58.8
	16	107 28.9	29 49.9	13.1	85 54.4	10.3	355 34.4	18.7	97 20.5	58.9
	17	122 31.4	44 49.1	13.5	100 55.1	11.1	10 36.4	18.6	112 22.7	59.0
	18	137 33.9	59 48.3	N24 13.8	115 55.8	N 8 11.8	25 38.5	N22 18.6	127 25.0	N 1 59.1
	19	152 36.3	74 47.5	14.2	130 56.5	12.5	40 40.5	18.5	142 27.2	59.2
	20	167 38.8	89 46.7	14.5	145 57.2	13.2	55 42.6	18.5	157 29.4	59.3
	21	182 41.3	104 45.8	. . 14.9	160 57.9	. . 13.9	70 44.6	. . 18.4	172 31.6	. . 59.4
	22	197 43.7	119 45.0	15.2	175 58.5	14.7	85 46.7	18.3	187 33.8	59.5
	23	212 46.2	134 44.2	15.6	190 59.2	15.4	100 48.7	18.3	202 36.0	59.6
	Mer. Pass. (h m)	8 55.2	v −0.8	d 0.4	v 0.7	d 0.7	v 2.1	d 0.1	v 2.2	d 0.1

STARS

Name	SHA ° ′	Dec ° ′
Acamar	315 11.4	S40 11.9
Achernar	335 19.9	S57 06.1
Acrux	172 58.3	S63 15.0
Adhara	255 05.2	S29 00.7
Aldebaran	290 38.7	N16 33.7
Alioth	166 11.5	N55 49.1
Alkaid	152 50.7	N49 10.9
Alnair	27 31.7	S46 49.8
Alnilam	275 36.9	S 1 11.2
Alphard	217 46.7	S 8 46.5
Alphecca	126 02.5	N26 37.4
Alpheratz	357 33.9	N29 14.0
Altair	61 58.8	N 8 56.1
Ankaa	353 06.4	S42 09.6
Antares	112 14.2	S26 29.5
Arcturus	145 46.6	N19 02.6
Atria	107 06.9	S69 04.4
Avior	234 14.5	S59 35.9
Bellatrix	278 22.0	N 6 22.4
Betelgeuse	270 51.2	N 7 24.7
Canopus	263 52.3	S52 42.8
Capella	280 20.7	N46 01.5
Deneb	49 25.0	N45 22.2
Denebola	182 23.6	N14 25.4
Diphda	348 46.5	S17 50.5
Dubhe	193 39.4	N61 36.7
Elnath	278 00.8	N28 37.8
Eltanin	90 41.3	N51 28.8
Enif	33 37.8	N 9 59.6
Fomalhaut	15 13.5	S29 28.9
Gacrux	171 50.0	S57 15.9
Gienah	175 42.2	S17 41.5
Hadar	148 33.8	S60 30.2
Hamal	327 50.3	N23 35.1
Kaus Aust.	83 30.8	S34 22.2
Kochab	137 18.6	N74 02.8
Markab	13 29.0	N15 20.7
Menkar	314 05.3	N 4 11.5
Menkent	147 56.0	S36 30.1
Miaplacidus	221 38.1	S69 49.8
Mirfak	308 27.2	N49 57.2
Nunki	75 46.2	S26 15.8
Peacock	53 03.9	S56 38.8
Pollux	243 16.1	N27 57.8
Procyon	244 49.8	N 5 09.4
Rasalhague	95 57.3	N12 32.3
Regulus	207 33.2	N11 50.2
Rigel	281 03.1	S 8 10.4
Rigil Kent.	139 38.1	S60 56.7
Sabik	102 01.2	S15 45.5
Schedar	349 30.3	N56 40.7
Shaula	96 08.6	S37 07.3
Sirius	258 25.5	S16 45.3
Spica	158 20.9	S11 18.1
Suhail	222 45.5	S43 32.6
Vega	80 32.2	N38 48.2
Zuben'ubi	136 54.5	S16 09.2

	SHA ° ′	Mer. Pass. h m
Venus	284 31.9	13 59
Mars	339 36.5	10 18
Jupiter	248 21.9	16 21
Saturn	350 01.5	9 35

Day	UT (d h)	SUN GHA (° ′)	SUN Dec (° ′)	MOON GHA (° ′)	*v* (′)	MOON Dec (° ′)	*d* (′)	HP (′)
THURSDAY	7 00	180 51.6	N16 45.5	298 51.6	10.6	S26 36.5	4.9	54.3
	01	195 51.7	46.2	313 21.2	10.7	26 31.6	5.1	54.3
	02	210 51.7	46.9	327 50.9	10.8	26 26.5	5.2	54.3
	03	225 51.7	. . 47.6	342 20.7	10.7	26 21.3	5.3	54.3
	04	240 51.8	48.2	356 50.4	10.9	26 16.0	5.5	54.4
	05	255 51.8	48.9	11 20.3	10.8	26 10.5	5.5	54.4
	06	270 51.9	N16 49.6	25 50.1	10.9	S26 05.0	5.7	54.4
	07	285 51.9	50.3	40 20.0	10.9	25 59.3	5.8	54.4
	08	300 51.9	51.0	54 49.9	11.0	25 53.5	6.0	54.4
	09	315 52.0	. . 51.7	69 19.9	11.0	25 47.5	6.0	54.4
	10	330 52.0	52.4	83 49.9	11.1	25 41.5	6.2	54.4
	11	345 52.1	53.1	98 20.0	11.1	25 35.3	6.3	54.4
	12	0 52.1	N16 53.8	112 50.1	11.1	S25 29.0	6.5	54.5
	13	15 52.1	54.4	127 20.2	11.2	25 22.5	6.5	54.5
	14	30 52.2	55.1	141 50.4	11.2	25 16.0	6.7	54.5
	15	45 52.2	. . 55.8	156 20.6	11.3	25 09.3	6.8	54.5
	16	60 52.3	56.5	170 50.9	11.3	25 02.5	6.9	54.5
	17	75 52.3	57.2	185 21.2	11.3	24 55.6	7.0	54.5
	18	90 52.3	N16 57.9	199 51.5	11.4	S24 48.6	7.2	54.6
	19	105 52.4	58.6	214 21.9	11.5	24 41.4	7.2	54.6
	20	120 52.4	59.2	228 52.4	11.5	24 34.2	7.4	54.6
	21	135 52.4	16 59.9	243 22.9	11.5	24 26.8	7.5	54.6
	22	150 52.5	17 00.6	257 53.4	11.6	24 19.3	7.6	54.6
	23	165 52.5	01.3	272 24.0	11.6	24 11.7	7.7	54.6
FRIDAY	8 00	180 52.6	N17 02.0	286 54.6	11.6	S24 04.0	7.9	54.7
	01	195 52.6	02.6	301 25.2	11.8	23 56.1	7.9	54.7
	02	210 52.6	03.3	315 56.0	11.7	23 48.2	8.1	54.7
	03	225 52.7	. . 04.0	330 26.7	11.8	23 40.1	8.2	54.7
	04	240 52.7	04.7	344 57.5	11.9	23 31.9	8.3	54.7
	05	255 52.7	05.4	359 28.4	11.9	23 23.6	8.4	54.8
	06	270 52.8	N17 06.0	13 59.3	11.9	S23 15.2	8.5	54.8
	07	285 52.8	06.7	28 30.2	12.0	23 06.7	8.6	54.8
	08	300 52.8	07.4	43 01.2	12.0	22 58.1	8.8	54.8
	09	315 52.9	. . 08.1	57 32.2	12.1	22 49.3	8.8	54.8
	10	330 52.9	08.7	72 03.3	12.1	22 40.5	9.0	54.9
	11	345 52.9	09.4	86 34.4	12.2	22 31.5	9.0	54.9
	12	0 53.0	N17 10.1	101 05.6	12.2	S22 22.5	9.2	54.9
	13	15 53.0	10.8	115 36.8	12.3	22 13.3	9.3	54.9
	14	30 53.0	11.4	130 08.1	12.3	22 04.0	9.3	54.9
	15	45 53.1	. . 12.1	144 39.4	12.3	21 54.7	9.5	55.0
	16	60 53.1	12.8	159 10.7	12.4	21 45.2	9.6	55.0
	17	75 53.1	13.5	173 42.1	12.5	21 35.6	9.7	55.0
	18	90 53.2	N17 14.1	188 13.6	12.4	S21 25.9	9.8	55.0
	19	105 53.2	14.8	202 45.0	12.6	21 16.1	9.9	55.0
	20	120 53.2	15.5	217 16.6	12.5	21 06.2	10.0	55.1
	21	135 53.3	. . 16.2	231 48.1	12.7	20 56.2	10.1	55.1
	22	150 53.3	16.8	246 19.8	12.6	20 46.1	10.2	55.1
	23	165 53.3	17.5	260 51.4	12.7	20 35.9	10.3	55.1
SATURDAY	9 00	180 53.4	N17 18.2	275 23.1	12.8	S20 25.6	10.4	55.2
	01	195 53.4	18.8	289 54.9	12.8	20 15.2	10.5	55.2
	02	210 53.4	19.5	304 26.7	12.8	20 04.7	10.6	55.2
	03	225 53.4	. . 20.2	318 58.5	12.9	19 54.1	10.7	55.2
	04	240 53.5	20.8	333 30.4	12.9	19 43.4	10.7	55.3
	05	255 53.5	21.5	348 02.3	12.9	19 32.7	10.9	55.3
	06	270 53.5	N17 22.2	2 34.2	13.0	S19 21.8	11.0	55.3
	07	285 53.6	22.8	17 06.2	13.0	19 10.8	11.1	55.3
	08	300 53.6	23.5	31 38.2	13.1	18 59.7	11.1	55.4
	09	315 53.6	. . 24.2	46 10.3	13.1	18 48.6	11.3	55.4
	10	330 53.6	24.8	60 42.4	13.2	18 37.3	11.3	55.4
	11	345 53.7	25.5	75 14.6	13.2	18 26.0	11.5	55.4
	12	0 53.7	N17 26.2	89 46.8	13.2	S18 14.5	11.5	55.5
	13	15 53.7	26.8	104 19.0	13.2	18 03.0	11.6	55.5
	14	30 53.8	27.5	118 51.2	13.3	17 51.4	11.7	55.5
	15	45 53.8	. . 28.1	133 23.5	13.4	17 39.7	11.8	55.6
	16	60 53.8	28.8	147 55.9	13.3	17 27.9	11.9	55.6
	17	75 53.8	29.5	162 28.2	13.4	17 16.0	12.0	55.6
	18	90 53.9	N17 30.1	177 00.6	13.5	S17 04.0	12.0	55.6
	19	105 53.9	30.8	191 33.1	13.4	16 52.0	12.2	55.7
	20	120 53.9	31.4	206 05.5	13.5	16 39.8	12.2	55.7
	21	135 53.9	. . 32.1	220 38.0	13.5	16 27.6	12.3	55.7
	22	150 54.0	32.8	235 10.5	13.6	16 15.3	12.4	55.8
	23	165 54.0	33.4	249 43.1	13.6	S16 02.9	12.5	55.8
		SD 15.9	*d* 0.7	SD	14.8	15.0		15.1

Lat. (°)	Twilight Naut. (h m)	Twilight Civil (h m)	Sunrise (h m)	Moonrise 7 (h m)	Moonrise 8 (h m)	Moonrise 9 (h m)	Moonrise 10 (h m)
N 72	////	////	00 25	■	■	■	04 14
N 70	////	////	01 46	■	■	05 03	03 42
68	////	////	02 24	■	■	03 59	03 19
66	////	01 04	02 50	■	04 16	03 23	03 00
64	////	01 51	03 10	■	03 16	02 57	02 45
62	////	02 20	03 26	02 48	02 42	02 37	02 33
60	00 57	02 42	03 40	02 08	02 17	02 20	02 22
N 58	01 39	03 00	03 51	01 41	01 57	02 06	02 12
56	02 06	03 14	04 01	01 19	01 40	01 54	02 04
54	02 27	03 27	04 10	01 01	01 26	01 44	01 57
52	02 43	03 37	04 18	00 46	01 14	01 34	01 50
50	02 57	03 47	04 25	00 33	01 03	01 26	01 44
45	03 25	04 06	04 40	00 06	00 40	01 08	01 31
N 40	03 45	04 22	04 52	24 21	00 21	00 53	01 20
35	04 02	04 35	05 02	24 06	00 06	00 40	01 11
30	04 15	04 46	05 11	23 52	24 29	00 29	01 03
20	04 36	05 04	05 27	23 29	24 10	00 10	00 48
N 10	04 53	05 18	05 41	23 09	23 54	24 36	00 36
0	05 06	05 31	05 53	22 51	23 38	24 24	00 24
S 10	05 18	05 43	06 05	22 32	23 23	24 12	00 12
20	05 29	05 55	06 18	22 11	23 06	24 00	00 00
30	05 40	06 08	06 33	21 48	22 46	23 45	24 44
35	05 45	06 15	06 42	21 34	22 35	23 37	24 39
40	05 51	06 23	06 52	21 18	22 22	23 27	24 33
45	05 56	06 32	07 03	20 59	22 06	23 16	24 26
S 50	06 03	06 42	07 17	20 35	21 47	23 02	24 17
52	06 06	06 46	07 23	20 23	21 38	22 55	24 13
54	06 09	06 51	07 30	20 10	21 28	22 48	24 09
56	06 12	06 57	07 38	19 55	21 16	22 40	24 04
58	06 15	07 03	07 47	19 36	21 03	22 31	23 58
S 60	06 19	07 10	07 57	19 14	20 47	22 20	23 52

Lat. (°)	Sunset (h m)	Twilight Civil (h m)	Twilight Naut. (h m)	Moonset 7 (h m)	Moonset 8 (h m)	Moonset 9 (h m)	Moonset 10 (h m)
N 72	□	□	□	■	■	■	09 21
N 70	22 13	////	////	■	■	06 55	09 50
68	21 33	////	////	■	■	07 57	10 12
66	21 06	22 59	////	■	06 01	08 32	10 29
64	20 45	22 07	////	■	07 00	08 56	10 43
62	20 29	21 36	////	05 45	07 33	09 16	10 54
60	20 15	21 13	23 05	06 25	07 58	09 32	11 04
N 58	20 03	20 55	22 18	06 52	08 17	09 45	11 13
56	19 53	20 41	21 50	07 13	08 33	09 56	11 20
54	19 44	20 28	21 28	07 31	08 47	10 06	11 27
52	19 36	20 17	21 11	07 46	08 59	10 15	11 32
50	19 29	20 07	20 57	07 58	09 09	10 23	11 38
45	19 14	19 47	20 29	08 25	09 31	10 40	11 49
N 40	19 02	19 32	20 09	08 46	09 49	10 53	11 58
35	18 51	19 19	19 52	09 03	10 03	11 05	12 06
30	18 42	19 08	19 39	09 18	10 16	11 15	12 13
20	18 26	18 50	19 17	09 43	10 38	11 32	12 26
N 10	18 13	18 35	19 00	10 05	10 56	11 47	12 36
0	18 00	18 22	18 47	10 25	11 14	12 00	12 46
S 10	17 47	18 09	18 35	10 45	11 31	12 14	12 55
20	17 34	17 57	18 24	11 07	11 49	12 29	13 05
30	17 19	17 44	18 13	11 31	12 10	12 45	13 17
35	17 11	17 37	18 08	11 46	12 23	12 55	13 24
40	17 01	17 29	18 02	12 02	12 37	13 06	13 31
45	16 49	17 21	17 56	12 22	12 53	13 18	13 40
S 50	16 36	17 10	17 49	12 47	13 14	13 34	13 50
52	16 29	17 06	17 46	12 59	13 23	13 41	13 55
54	16 22	17 01	17 43	13 13	13 34	13 49	14 00
56	16 14	16 55	17 40	13 29	13 46	13 58	14 06
58	16 05	16 49	17 37	13 48	14 00	14 08	14 13
S 60	15 55	16 42	17 33	14 11	14 17	14 19	14 20

Day (d)	SUN Eqn. of Time 00ʰ (m s)	SUN Eqn. of Time 12ʰ (m s)	SUN Mer. Pass. (h m)	MOON Mer. Pass. Upper (h m)	MOON Mer. Pass. Lower (h m)	MOON Age (d)	MOON Phase (%)
7	03 26	03 28	11 57	04 13	16 38	20	73
8	03 30	03 32	11 56	05 02	17 26	21	64
9	03 33	03 35	11 56	05 49	18 12	22	54

UT d h	ARIES GHA	VENUS −3·9 GHA	VENUS Dec	MARS +1·2 GHA	MARS Dec	JUPITER −2·0 GHA	JUPITER Dec	SATURN +0·9 GHA	SATURN Dec
	° ′	° ′	° ′	° ′	° ′	° ′	° ′	° ′	° ′
10 00 (SUNDAY)	227 48.7	149 43.4	N24 15.9	205 59.9	N 8 16.1	115 50.7	N22 18.2	217 38.3	N 1 59.7
01	242 51.1	164 42.6	16.3	221 00.6	16.8	130 52.8	18.2	232 40.5	59.8
02	257 53.6	179 41.8	16.6	236 01.3	17.5	145 54.8	18.1	247 42.7	1 59.9
03	272 56.0	194 40.9	. . 16.9	251 02.0	. . 18.3	160 56.9	. . 18.1	262 44.9	2 00.0
04	287 58.5	209 40.1	17.3	266 02.7	19.0	175 58.9	18.0	277 47.1	00.1
05	303 01.0	224 39.3	17.6	281 03.4	19.7	191 01.0	17.9	292 49.3	00.2
06	318 03.4	239 38.5	N24 18.0	296 04.0	N 8 20.4	206 03.0	N22 17.9	307 51.6	N 2 00.3
07	333 05.9	254 37.7	18.3	311 04.7	21.1	221 05.1	17.8	322 53.8	00.4
08	348 08.4	269 36.9	18.6	326 05.4	21.9	236 07.1	17.8	337 56.0	00.5
09	3 10.8	284 36.1	. . 19.0	341 06.1	. . 22.6	251 09.2	. . 17.7	352 58.2	. . 00.6
10	18 13.3	299 35.2	19.3	356 06.8	23.3	266 11.2	17.7	8 00.4	00.7
11	33 15.8	314 34.4	19.6	11 07.5	24.0	281 13.2	17.6	23 02.6	00.8
12	48 18.2	329 33.6	N24 20.0	26 08.2	N 8 24.7	296 15.3	N22 17.6	38 04.9	N 2 00.9
13	63 20.7	344 32.8	20.3	41 08.9	25.4	311 17.3	17.5	53 07.1	01.0
14	78 23.2	359 32.0	20.6	56 09.5	26.2	326 19.4	17.4	68 09.3	01.1
15	93 25.6	14 31.2	. . 21.0	71 10.2	. . 26.9	341 21.4	. . 17.4	83 11.5	. . 01.2
16	108 28.1	29 30.3	21.3	86 10.9	27.6	356 23.5	17.3	98 13.7	01.3
17	123 30.5	44 29.5	21.6	101 11.6	28.3	11 25.5	17.3	113 16.0	01.4
18	138 33.0	59 28.7	N24 21.9	116 12.3	N 8 29.0	26 27.5	N22 17.2	128 18.2	N 2 01.5
19	153 35.5	74 27.9	22.2	131 13.0	29.7	41 29.6	17.2	143 20.4	01.6
20	168 37.9	89 27.1	22.6	146 13.7	30.5	56 31.6	17.1	158 22.6	01.7
21	183 40.4	104 26.2	. . 22.9	161 14.3	. . 31.2	71 33.7	. . 17.0	173 24.8	. . 01.8
22	198 42.9	119 25.4	23.2	176 15.0	31.9	86 35.7	17.0	188 27.1	01.9
23	213 45.3	134 24.6	23.5	191 15.7	32.6	101 37.8	16.9	203 29.3	02.0
11 00 (MONDAY)	228 47.8	149 23.8	N24 23.8	206 16.4	N 8 33.3	116 39.8	N22 16.9	218 31.5	N 2 02.1
01	243 50.3	164 23.0	24.2	221 17.1	34.0	131 41.8	16.8	233 33.7	02.2
02	258 52.7	179 22.1	24.5	236 17.8	34.8	146 43.9	16.7	248 35.9	02.2
03	273 55.2	194 21.3	. . 24.8	251 18.5	. . 35.5	161 45.9	. . 16.7	263 38.1	. . 02.3
04	288 57.6	209 20.5	25.1	266 19.2	36.2	176 48.0	16.6	278 40.4	02.4
05	304 00.1	224 19.7	25.4	281 19.8	36.9	191 50.0	16.6	293 42.6	02.5
06	319 02.6	239 18.9	N24 25.7	296 20.5	N 8 37.6	206 52.0	N22 16.5	308 44.8	N 2 02.6
07	334 05.0	254 18.0	26.0	311 21.2	38.3	221 54.1	16.5	323 47.0	02.7
08	349 07.5	269 17.2	26.3	326 21.9	39.0	236 56.1	16.4	338 49.2	02.8
09	4 10.0	284 16.4	. . 26.6	341 22.6	. . 39.8	251 58.2	. . 16.3	353 51.5	. . 02.9
10	19 12.4	299 15.6	26.9	356 23.3	40.5	267 00.2	16.3	8 53.7	03.0
11	34 14.9	314 14.8	27.2	11 24.0	41.2	282 02.2	16.2	23 55.9	03.1
12	49 17.4	329 13.9	N24 27.6	26 24.6	N 8 41.9	297 04.3	N22 16.2	38 58.1	N 2 03.2
13	64 19.8	344 13.1	27.9	41 25.3	42.6	312 06.3	16.1	54 00.3	03.3
14	79 22.3	359 12.3	28.2	56 26.0	43.3	327 08.4	16.1	69 02.6	03.4
15	94 24.8	14 11.5	. . 28.5	71 26.7	. . 44.0	342 10.4	. . 16.0	84 04.8	. . 03.5
16	109 27.2	29 10.7	28.7	86 27.4	44.8	357 12.4	15.9	99 07.0	03.6
17	124 29.7	44 09.8	29.0	101 28.1	45.5	12 14.5	15.9	114 09.2	03.7
18	139 32.1	59 09.0	N24 29.3	116 28.8	N 8 46.2	27 16.5	N22 15.8	129 11.4	N 2 03.8
19	154 34.6	74 08.2	29.6	131 29.4	46.9	42 18.6	15.8	144 13.7	03.9
20	169 37.1	89 07.4	29.9	146 30.1	47.6	57 20.6	15.7	159 15.9	04.0
21	184 39.5	104 06.5	. . 30.2	161 30.8	. . 48.3	72 22.6	. . 15.6	174 18.1	. . 04.1
22	199 42.0	119 05.7	30.5	176 31.5	49.0	87 24.7	15.6	189 20.3	04.2
23	214 44.5	134 04.9	30.8	191 32.2	49.7	102 26.7	15.5	204 22.5	04.3
12 00 (TUESDAY)	229 46.9	149 04.1	N24 31.1	206 32.9	N 8 50.5	117 28.7	N22 15.5	219 24.8	N 2 04.4
01	244 49.4	164 03.3	31.4	221 33.6	51.2	132 30.8	15.4	234 27.0	04.5
02	259 51.9	179 02.4	31.7	236 34.2	51.9	147 32.8	15.4	249 29.2	04.6
03	274 54.3	194 01.6	. . 31.9	251 34.9	. . 52.6	162 34.8	. . 15.3	264 31.4	. . 04.7
04	289 56.8	209 00.8	32.2	266 35.6	53.3	177 36.9	15.2	279 33.7	04.8
05	304 59.2	224 00.0	32.5	281 36.3	54.0	192 38.9	15.2	294 35.9	04.9
06	320 01.7	238 59.1	N24 32.8	296 37.0	N 8 54.7	207 41.0	N22 15.1	309 38.1	N 2 04.9
07	335 04.2	253 58.3	33.1	311 37.7	55.4	222 43.0	15.1	324 40.3	05.0
08	350 06.6	268 57.5	33.3	326 38.4	56.1	237 45.0	15.0	339 42.5	05.1
09	5 09.1	283 56.7	. . 33.6	341 39.0	. . 56.9	252 47.1	. . 14.9	354 44.8	. . 05.2
10	20 11.6	298 55.8	33.9	356 39.7	57.6	267 49.1	14.9	9 47.0	05.3
11	35 14.0	313 55.0	34.2	11 40.4	58.3	282 51.1	14.8	24 49.2	05.4
12	50 16.5	328 54.2	N24 34.4	26 41.1	N 8 59.0	297 53.2	N22 14.8	39 51.4	N 2 05.5
13	65 19.0	343 53.4	34.7	41 41.8	8 59.7	312 55.2	14.7	54 53.6	05.6
14	80 21.4	358 52.5	35.0	56 42.5	9 00.4	327 57.2	14.6	69 55.9	05.7
15	95 23.9	13 51.7	. . 35.3	71 43.2	. . 01.1	342 59.3	. . 14.6	84 58.1	. . 05.8
16	110 26.4	28 50.9	35.5	86 43.8	01.8	358 01.3	14.5	100 00.3	05.9
17	125 28.8	43 50.1	35.8	101 44.5	02.5	13 03.3	14.5	115 02.5	06.0
18	140 31.3	58 49.2	N24 36.1	116 45.2	N 9 03.2	28 05.4	N22 14.4	130 04.8	N 2 06.1
19	155 33.7	73 48.4	36.3	131 45.9	03.9	43 07.4	14.3	145 07.0	06.2
20	170 36.2	88 47.6	36.6	146 46.6	04.7	58 09.4	14.3	160 09.2	06.3
21	185 38.7	103 46.8	. . 36.9	161 47.3	. . 05.4	73 11.5	. . 14.2	175 11.4	. . 06.4
22	200 41.1	118 45.9	37.1	176 48.0	06.1	88 13.5	14.2	190 13.6	06.5
23	215 43.6	133 45.1	37.4	191 48.6	06.8	103 15.5	14.1	205 15.9	06.6
Mer. Pass.	h m 8 43.4	v −0.8	d 0.3	v 0.7	d 0.7	v 2.0	d 0.1	v 2.2	d 0.1

STARS Name	SHA	Dec
	° ′	° ′
Acamar	315 11.4	S40 11.9
Achernar	335 19.9	S57 06.0
Acrux	172 58.3	S63 15.0
Adhara	255 05.2	S29 00.6
Aldebaran	290 38.7	N16 33.7
Alioth	166 11.6	N55 49.1
Alkaid	152 50.7	N49 10.9
Alnair	27 31.6	S46 49.8
Alnilam	275 36.9	S 1 11.2
Alphard	217 46.7	S 8 46.5
Alphecca	126 02.4	N26 37.4
Alpheratz	357 33.9	N29 14.0
Altair	61 58.8	N 8 56.1
Ankaa	353 06.4	S42 09.6
Antares	112 14.1	S26 29.5
Arcturus	145 46.6	N19 02.6
Atria	107 06.9	S69 04.4
Avior	234 14.5	S59 35.9
Bellatrix	278 22.0	N 6 22.4
Betelgeuse	270 51.2	N 7 24.7
Canopus	263 52.3	S52 42.8
Capella	280 20.7	N46 01.5
Deneb	49 25.0	N45 22.2
Denebola	182 23.6	N14 25.4
Diphda	348 46.5	S17 50.5
Dubhe	193 39.4	N61 36.7
Elnath	278 00.8	N28 37.8
Eltanin	90 41.2	N51 28.9
Enif	33 37.7	N 9 59.6
Fomalhaut	15 13.5	S29 28.8
Gacrux	171 50.0	S57 15.9
Gienah	175 42.2	S17 41.5
Hadar	148 33.8	S60 30.2
Hamal	327 50.3	N23 35.1
Kaus Aust.	83 30.8	S34 22.2
Kochab	137 18.6	N74 02.8
Markab	13 28.9	N15 20.7
Menkar	314 05.3	N 4 11.5
Menkent	147 56.0	S36 30.1
Miaplacidus	221 38.2	S69 49.8
Mirfak	308 27.2	N49 57.2
Nunki	75 46.2	S26 15.8
Peacock	53 03.8	S56 38.8
Pollux	243 16.1	N27 57.8
Procyon	244 49.9	N 5 09.4
Rasalhague	95 57.2	N12 32.3
Regulus	207 33.2	N11 50.3
Rigel	281 03.1	S 8 10.4
Rigil Kent.	139 38.1	S60 56.8
Sabik	102 01.2	S15 45.5
Schedar	349 30.2	N56 40.7
Shaula	96 08.5	S37 07.3
Sirius	258 25.5	S16 45.3
Spica	158 20.9	S11 18.1
Suhail	222 45.6	S43 32.6
Vega	80 32.2	N38 48.2
Zuben'ubi	136 54.5	S16 09.2

	SHA	Mer. Pass.
	° ′	h m
Venus	280 36.0	14 03
Mars	337 28.6	10 14
Jupiter	247 52.0	16 11
Saturn	349 43.7	9 25

UT d h	SUN GHA ° ′	SUN Dec ° ′	MOON GHA ° ′	v ′	MOON Dec ° ′	d ′	HP ′
10 00	180 54.0	N17 34.1	264 15.7	13.6	S15 50.4	12.5	55.8
01	195 54.0	34.7	278 48.3	13.7	15 37.9	12.7	55.9
02	210 54.1	35.4	293 21.0	13.6	15 25.2	12.7	55.9
03	225 54.1	. . 36.0	307 53.6	13.7	15 12.5	12.8	55.9
04	240 54.1	36.7	322 26.3	13.7	14 59.7	12.9	56.0
05	255 54.1	37.4	336 59.0	13.8	14 46.8	12.9	56.0
06	270 54.1	N17 38.0	351 31.8	13.8	S14 33.9	13.1	56.0
07	285 54.2	38.7	6 04.6	13.8	14 20.8	13.1	56.0
08	300 54.2	39.3	20 37.4	13.8	14 07.7	13.2	56.1
S 09	315 54.2	. . 40.0	35 10.2	13.8	13 54.5	13.2	56.1
U 10	330 54.2	40.6	49 43.0	13.9	13 41.3	13.4	56.1
N 11	345 54.3	41.3	64 15.9	13.9	13 27.9	13.4	56.2
D 12	0 54.3	N17 41.9	78 48.8	13.9	S13 14.5	13.5	56.2
A 13	15 54.3	42.6	93 21.7	13.9	13 01.0	13.5	56.2
Y 14	30 54.3	43.2	107 54.6	13.9	12 47.5	13.6	56.3
15	45 54.3	. . 43.9	122 27.5	14.0	12 33.9	13.7	56.3
16	60 54.4	44.5	137 00.5	13.9	12 20.2	13.8	56.3
17	75 54.4	45.2	151 33.4	14.0	12 06.4	13.8	56.4
18	90 54.4	N17 45.8	166 06.4	14.0	S11 52.6	13.9	56.4
19	105 54.4	46.5	180 39.4	14.0	11 38.7	14.0	56.4
20	120 54.4	47.1	195 12.4	14.0	11 24.7	14.1	56.5
21	135 54.5	. . 47.8	209 45.4	14.0	11 10.6	14.1	56.5
22	150 54.5	48.4	224 18.4	14.1	10 56.5	14.1	56.6
23	165 54.5	49.0	238 51.5	14.0	10 42.4	14.3	56.6
11 00	180 54.5	N17 49.7	253 24.5	14.1	S10 28.1	14.3	56.6
01	195 54.5	50.3	267 57.6	14.0	10 13.8	14.3	56.7
02	210 54.5	51.0	282 30.6	14.1	9 59.5	14.4	56.7
03	225 54.6	. . 51.6	297 03.7	14.1	9 45.1	14.5	56.7
04	240 54.6	52.3	311 36.8	14.0	9 30.6	14.6	56.8
05	255 54.6	52.9	326 09.8	14.1	9 16.0	14.6	56.8
06	270 54.6	N17 53.6	340 42.9	14.1	S 9 01.4	14.6	56.8
07	285 54.6	54.2	355 16.0	14.0	8 46.8	14.7	56.9
08	300 54.6	54.8	9 49.0	14.1	8 32.1	14.8	56.9
M 09	315 54.7	. . 55.5	24 22.1	14.1	8 17.3	14.8	57.0
O 10	330 54.7	56.1	38 55.2	14.0	8 02.5	14.9	57.0
N 11	345 54.7	56.8	53 28.2	14.1	7 47.6	15.0	57.0
D 12	0 54.7	N17 57.4	68 01.3	14.0	S 7 32.6	15.0	57.1
A 13	15 54.7	58.0	82 34.3	14.1	7 17.6	15.0	57.1
Y 14	30 54.7	58.7	97 07.4	14.0	7 02.6	15.1	57.1
15	45 54.7	. . 59.3	111 40.4	14.0	6 47.5	15.1	57.2
16	60 54.8	17 59.9	126 13.4	14.0	6 32.4	15.2	57.2
17	75 54.8	18 00.6	140 46.4	14.0	6 17.2	15.3	57.3
18	90 54.8	N18 01.2	155 19.4	14.0	S 6 01.9	15.3	57.3
19	105 54.8	01.8	169 52.4	14.0	5 46.6	15.3	57.3
20	120 54.8	02.5	184 25.4	13.9	5 31.3	15.4	57.4
21	135 54.8	. . 03.1	198 58.3	14.0	5 15.9	15.4	57.4
22	150 54.8	03.7	213 31.3	13.9	5 00.5	15.5	57.4
23	165 54.9	04.4	228 04.2	13.9	4 45.0	15.5	57.5
12 00	180 54.9	N18 05.0	242 37.1	13.9	S 4 29.5	15.6	57.5
01	195 54.9	05.6	257 10.0	13.8	4 13.9	15.6	57.6
02	210 54.9	06.3	271 42.8	13.8	3 58.3	15.6	57.6
03	225 54.9	. . 06.9	286 15.6	13.8	3 42.7	15.7	57.6
04	240 54.9	07.5	300 48.4	13.8	3 27.0	15.7	57.7
05	255 54.9	08.2	315 21.2	13.8	3 11.3	15.7	57.7
06	270 54.9	N18 08.8	329 54.0	13.7	S 2 55.6	15.8	57.8
T 07	285 54.9	09.4	344 26.7	13.7	2 39.8	15.8	57.8
U 08	300 54.9	10.1	358 59.4	13.7	2 24.0	15.9	57.8
E 09	315 55.0	. . 10.7	13 32.1	13.6	2 08.1	15.9	57.9
S 10	330 55.0	11.3	28 04.7	13.6	1 52.2	15.9	57.9
D 11	345 55.0	11.9	42 37.3	13.5	1 36.3	15.9	58.0
A 12	0 55.0	N18 12.6	57 09.8	13.6	S 1 20.4	16.0	58.0
Y 13	15 55.0	13.2	71 42.4	13.5	1 04.4	16.0	58.0
14	30 55.0	13.8	86 14.9	13.4	0 48.4	16.0	58.1
15	45 55.0	. . 14.4	100 47.3	13.4	0 32.4	16.1	58.1
16	60 55.0	15.1	115 19.7	13.4	0 16.3	16.1	58.2
17	75 55.0	15.7	129 52.1	13.3	S 0 00.2	16.1	58.2
18	90 55.0	N18 16.3	144 24.4	13.3	N 0 15.9	16.1	58.2
19	105 55.0	16.9	158 56.7	13.2	0 32.0	16.1	58.3
20	120 55.0	17.5	173 28.9	13.2	0 48.1	16.2	58.3
21	135 55.1	. . 18.2	188 01.1	13.1	1 04.3	16.2	58.4
22	150 55.1	18.8	202 33.2	13.1	1 20.5	16.2	58.4
23	165 55.1	19.4	217 05.3	13.0	N 1 36.7	16.2	58.4
	SD 15.9	*d* 0.6	SD	15.3		15.5	15.8

Lat. °	Twilight Naut. h m	Twilight Civil h m	Sunrise h m	Moonrise 10 h m	Moonrise 11 h m	Moonrise 12 h m	Moonrise 13 h m
N 72	▭	▭	▭	04 14	03 21	02 43	02 09
N 70	////	////	01 23	03 42	03 06	02 38	02 12
68	////	////	02 09	03 19	02 54	02 34	02 15
66	////	00 24	02 38	03 00	02 44	02 30	02 17
64	////	01 34	03 00	02 45	02 36	02 27	02 19
62	////	02 08	03 18	02 33	02 28	02 24	02 20
60	00 22	02 32	03 32	02 22	02 22	02 22	02 22
N 58	01 24	02 51	03 44	02 12	02 16	02 20	02 23
56	01 55	03 07	03 55	02 04	02 11	02 18	02 24
54	02 18	03 20	04 04	01 57	02 07	02 16	02 25
52	02 36	03 31	04 13	01 50	02 03	02 15	02 26
50	02 51	03 42	04 20	01 44	01 59	02 13	02 27
45	03 20	04 02	04 36	01 31	01 51	02 10	02 29
N 40	03 41	04 19	04 49	01 20	01 44	02 07	02 30
35	03 58	04 32	05 00	01 11	01 39	02 05	02 32
30	04 12	04 43	05 09	01 03	01 33	02 03	02 33
20	04 34	05 02	05 26	00 48	01 24	01 59	02 35
N 10	04 52	05 18	05 40	00 36	01 16	01 56	02 37
0	05 06	05 31	05 53	00 24	01 09	01 53	02 39
S 10	05 18	05 44	06 06	00 12	01 01	01 51	02 41
20	05 30	05 57	06 20	00 00	00 53	01 47	02 43
30	05 41	06 10	06 35	24 44	00 44	01 44	02 45
35	05 47	06 17	06 44	24 39	00 39	01 42	02 47
40	05 53	06 26	06 55	24 33	00 33	01 40	02 48
45	06 00	06 35	07 07	24 26	00 26	01 37	02 50
S 50	06 07	06 46	07 21	24 17	00 17	01 34	02 52
52	06 10	06 51	07 28	24 13	00 13	01 32	02 54
54	06 13	06 56	07 35	24 09	00 09	01 31	02 55
56	06 17	07 02	07 44	24 04	00 04	01 29	02 56
58	06 20	07 09	07 53	23 58	25 27	01 27	02 57
S 60	06 24	07 16	08 04	23 52	25 24	01 24	02 59

Lat. °	Sunset h m	Twilight Civil h m	Twilight Naut. h m	Moonset 10 h m	Moonset 11 h m	Moonset 12 h m	Moonset 13 h m
N 72	▭	▭	▭	09 21	11 49	14 04	16 22
N 70	22 37	////	////	09 50	12 01	14 05	16 13
68	21 48	////	////	10 12	12 11	14 06	16 05
66	21 18	////	////	10 29	12 19	14 07	15 59
64	20 55	22 24	////	10 43	12 25	14 08	15 54
62	20 37	21 48	////	10 54	12 31	14 08	15 49
60	20 22	21 23	////	11 04	12 36	14 09	15 45
N 58	20 10	21 04	22 33	11 13	12 40	14 09	15 42
56	19 59	20 48	22 00	11 20	12 44	14 10	15 39
54	19 50	20 34	21 37	11 27	12 48	14 10	15 36
52	19 41	20 23	21 19	11 32	12 51	14 11	15 34
50	19 34	20 12	21 03	11 38	12 53	14 11	15 31
45	19 18	19 51	20 34	11 49	13 00	14 12	15 26
N 40	19 05	19 35	20 12	11 58	13 05	14 12	15 22
35	18 53	19 21	19 55	12 06	13 09	14 13	15 19
30	18 44	19 10	19 41	12 13	13 13	14 13	15 16
20	18 27	18 51	19 19	12 26	13 19	14 14	15 10
N 10	18 13	18 35	19 01	12 36	13 25	14 14	15 06
0	18 00	18 22	18 47	12 46	13 30	14 15	15 01
S 10	17 47	18 09	18 34	12 55	13 35	14 15	14 57
20	17 33	17 56	18 23	13 05	13 41	14 16	14 52
30	17 17	17 42	18 11	13 17	13 47	14 17	14 47
35	17 08	17 35	18 05	13 24	13 51	14 17	14 44
40	16 58	17 27	17 59	13 31	13 55	14 17	14 41
45	16 46	17 17	17 53	13 40	13 59	14 18	14 37
S 50	16 31	17 06	17 45	13 50	14 05	14 18	14 32
52	16 24	17 01	17 42	13 55	14 07	14 18	14 30
54	16 17	16 56	17 39	14 00	14 10	14 19	14 28
56	16 08	16 50	17 35	14 06	14 13	14 19	14 25
58	15 59	16 43	17 32	14 13	14 16	14 19	14 22
S 60	15 48	16 36	17 27	14 20	14 20	14 20	14 19

Day	SUN Eqn. of Time 00^h m s	SUN Eqn. of Time 12^h m s	SUN Mer. Pass. h m	MOON Mer. Pass. Upper h m	MOON Mer. Pass. Lower h m	Age d	%	Phase
10	03 36	03 37	11 56	06 35	18 57	23	44	
11	03 38	03 39	11 56	07 20	19 42	24	34	◐
12	03 39	03 40	11 56	08 04	20 27	25	24	

2026 MAY 13, 14, 15 (WED., THURS., FRI.)

UT	ARIES	VENUS −3·9		MARS +1·2		JUPITER −1·9		SATURN +0·9		STARS		
	GHA	GHA	Dec	GHA	Dec	GHA	Dec	GHA	Dec	Name	SHA	Dec
d h	° ′	° ′	° ′	° ′	° ′	° ′	° ′	° ′	° ′		° ′	° ′
13 00	230 46.1	148 44.3	N24 37.6	206 49.3	N 9 07.5	118 17.6	N22 14.0	220 18.1	N 2 06.7	Acamar	315 11.4	S40 11.9
01	245 48.5	163 43.5	37.9	221 50.0	08.2	133 19.6	14.0	235 20.3	06.8	Achernar	335 19.9	S57 06.0
02	260 51.0	178 42.6	38.1	236 50.7	08.9	148 21.6	13.9	250 22.5	06.9	Acrux	172 58.4	S63 15.0
03	275 53.5	193 41.8	38.4	251 51.4	09.6	163 23.7	13.9	265 24.8	07.0	Adhara	255 05.3	S29 00.6
04	290 55.9	208 41.0	38.7	266 52.1	10.3	178 25.7	13.8	280 27.0	07.0	Aldebaran	290 38.7	N16 33.7
05	305 58.4	223 40.1	38.9	281 52.7	11.0	193 27.7	13.7	295 29.2	07.1			
06	321 00.9	238 39.3	N24 39.2	296 53.4	N 9 11.7	208 29.8	N22 13.7	310 31.4	N 2 07.2	Alioth	166 11.6	N55 49.1
W 07	336 03.3	253 38.5	39.4	311 54.1	12.4	223 31.8	13.6	325 33.7	07.3	Alkaid	152 50.7	N49 10.9
E 08	351 05.8	268 37.7	39.7	326 54.8	13.1	238 33.8	13.6	340 35.9	07.4	Alnair	27 31.6	S46 49.8
D 09	6 08.2	283 36.8	39.9	341 55.5	13.8	253 35.9	13.5	355 38.1	07.5	Alnilam	275 36.9	S 1 11.2
N 10	21 10.7	298 36.0	40.2	356 56.2	14.6	268 37.9	13.4	10 40.3	07.6	Alphard	217 46.7	S 8 46.5
E 11	36 13.2	313 35.2	40.4	11 56.8	15.3	283 39.9	13.4	25 42.5	07.7			
S 12	51 15.6	328 34.4	N24 40.6	26 57.5	N 9 16.0	298 41.9	N22 13.3	40 44.8	N 2 07.8	Alphecca	126 02.4	N26 37.4
D 13	66 18.1	343 33.5	40.9	41 58.2	16.7	313 44.0	13.3	55 47.0	07.9	Alpheratz	357 33.9	N29 14.0
A 14	81 20.6	358 32.7	41.1	56 58.9	17.4	328 46.0	13.2	70 49.2	08.0	Altair	61 58.7	N 8 56.2
Y 15	96 23.0	13 31.9	41.4	71 59.6	18.1	343 48.0	13.1	85 51.4	08.1	Ankaa	353 06.4	S42 09.6
16	111 25.5	28 31.0	41.6	87 00.3	18.8	358 50.1	13.1	100 53.7	08.2	Antares	112 14.1	S26 29.5
17	126 28.0	43 30.2	41.8	102 01.0	19.5	13 52.1	13.0	115 55.9	08.3			
18	141 30.4	58 29.4	N24 42.1	117 01.6	N 9 20.2	28 54.1	N22 13.0	130 58.1	N 2 08.4	Arcturus	145 46.6	N19 02.6
19	156 32.9	73 28.6	42.3	132 02.3	20.9	43 56.2	12.9	146 00.3	08.5	Atria	107 06.8	S69 04.4
20	171 35.3	88 27.7	42.6	147 03.0	21.6	58 58.2	12.8	161 02.6	08.6	Avior	234 14.5	S59 35.9
21	186 37.8	103 26.9	42.8	162 03.7	22.3	74 00.2	12.8	176 04.8	08.7	Bellatrix	278 22.0	N 6 22.4
22	201 40.3	118 26.1	43.0	177 04.4	23.0	89 02.2	12.7	191 07.0	08.8	Betelgeuse	270 51.2	N 7 24.7
23	216 42.7	133 25.2	43.2	192 05.1	23.7	104 04.3	12.7	206 09.2	08.8			
14 00	231 45.2	148 24.4	N24 43.5	207 05.7	N 9 24.4	119 06.3	N22 12.6	221 11.5	N 2 08.9	Canopus	263 52.3	S52 42.7
01	246 47.7	163 23.6	43.7	222 06.4	25.1	134 08.3	12.5	236 13.7	09.0	Capella	280 20.7	N46 01.5
02	261 50.1	178 22.8	43.9	237 07.1	25.8	149 10.4	12.5	251 15.9	09.1	Deneb	49 24.9	N45 22.2
03	276 52.6	193 21.9	44.2	252 07.8	26.5	164 12.4	12.4	266 18.1	09.2	Denebola	182 23.7	N14 25.4
04	291 55.1	208 21.1	44.4	267 08.5	27.2	179 14.4	12.4	281 20.4	09.3	Diphda	348 46.4	S17 50.5
05	306 57.5	223 20.3	44.6	282 09.2	27.9	194 16.4	12.3	296 22.6	09.4			
06	322 00.0	238 19.4	N24 44.8	297 09.8	N 9 28.6	209 18.5	N22 12.2	311 24.8	N 2 09.5	Dubhe	193 39.4	N61 36.7
T 07	337 02.5	253 18.6	45.1	312 10.5	29.3	224 20.5	12.2	326 27.0	09.6	Elnath	278 00.8	N28 37.8
H 08	352 04.9	268 17.8	45.3	327 11.2	30.0	239 22.5	12.1	341 29.3	09.7	Eltanin	90 41.2	N51 28.9
U 09	7 07.4	283 16.9	45.5	342 11.9	30.7	254 24.5	12.1	356 31.5	09.8	Enif	33 37.7	N 9 59.6
R 10	22 09.8	298 16.1	45.7	357 12.6	31.4	269 26.6	12.0	11 33.7	09.9	Fomalhaut	15 13.4	S29 28.8
S 11	37 12.3	313 15.3	45.9	12 13.3	32.1	284 28.6	11.9	26 35.9	10.0			
D 12	52 14.8	328 14.5	N24 46.1	27 13.9	N 9 32.8	299 30.6	N22 11.9	41 38.2	N 2 10.1	Gacrux	171 50.0	S57 15.9
A 13	67 17.2	343 13.6	46.4	42 14.6	33.5	314 32.7	11.8	56 40.4	10.2	Gienah	175 42.3	S17 41.5
Y 14	82 19.7	358 12.8	46.6	57 15.3	34.2	329 34.7	11.7	71 42.6	10.3	Hadar	148 33.8	S60 30.2
15	97 22.2	13 12.0	46.8	72 16.0	34.9	344 36.7	11.7	86 44.8	10.3	Hamal	327 50.3	N23 35.1
16	112 24.6	28 11.1	47.0	87 16.7	35.6	359 38.7	11.6	101 47.1	10.4	Kaus Aust.	83 30.8	S34 22.2
17	127 27.1	43 10.3	47.2	102 17.3	36.3	14 40.8	11.6	116 49.3	10.5			
18	142 29.6	58 09.5	N24 47.4	117 18.0	N 9 37.0	29 42.8	N22 11.5	131 51.5	N 2 10.6	Kochab	137 18.6	N74 02.8
19	157 32.0	73 08.6	47.6	132 18.7	37.7	44 44.8	11.4	146 53.7	10.7	Markab	13 28.9	N15 20.7
20	172 34.5	88 07.8	47.8	147 19.4	38.4	59 46.8	11.4	161 56.0	10.8	Menkar	314 05.3	N 4 11.5
21	187 36.9	103 07.0	48.0	162 20.1	39.1	74 48.9	11.3	176 58.2	10.9	Menkent	147 56.0	S36 30.2
22	202 39.4	118 06.1	48.2	177 20.8	39.8	89 50.9	11.3	192 00.4	11.0	Miaplacidus	221 38.2	S69 49.8
23	217 41.9	133 05.3	48.4	192 21.4	40.5	104 52.9	11.2	207 02.7	11.1			
15 00	232 44.3	148 04.5	N24 48.6	207 22.1	N 9 41.2	119 54.9	N22 11.1	222 04.9	N 2 11.2	Mirfak	308 27.2	N49 57.2
01	247 46.8	163 03.7	48.8	222 22.8	41.9	134 57.0	11.1	237 07.1	11.3	Nunki	75 46.2	S26 15.8
02	262 49.3	178 02.8	49.0	237 23.5	42.6	149 59.0	11.0	252 09.3	11.4	Peacock	53 03.8	S56 38.8
03	277 51.7	193 02.0	49.2	252 24.2	43.3	165 01.0	10.9	267 11.6	11.5	Pollux	243 16.2	N27 57.8
04	292 54.2	208 01.2	49.4	267 24.9	44.0	180 03.0	10.9	282 13.8	11.6	Procyon	244 49.9	N 5 09.4
05	307 56.7	223 00.3	49.6	282 25.5	44.7	195 05.0	10.8	297 16.0	11.7			
06	322 59.1	237 59.5	N24 49.8	297 26.2	N 9 45.4	210 07.1	N22 10.8	312 18.2	N 2 11.7	Rasalhague	95 57.2	N12 32.3
07	338 01.6	252 58.7	50.0	312 26.9	46.1	225 09.1	10.7	327 20.5	11.8	Regulus	207 33.2	N11 50.3
08	353 04.1	267 57.8	50.2	327 27.6	46.8	240 11.1	10.6	342 22.7	11.9	Rigel	281 03.1	S 8 10.3
F 09	8 06.5	282 57.0	50.4	342 28.3	47.5	255 13.1	10.6	357 24.9	12.0	Rigil Kent.	139 38.1	S60 56.8
R 10	23 09.0	297 56.2	50.6	357 28.9	48.2	270 15.2	10.5	12 27.2	12.1	Sabik	102 01.2	S15 45.5
I 11	38 11.4	312 55.3	50.7	12 29.6	48.9	285 17.2	10.4	27 29.4	12.2			
D 12	53 13.9	327 54.5	N24 50.9	27 30.3	N 9 49.6	300 19.2	N22 10.4	42 31.6	N 2 12.3	Schedar	349 30.2	N56 40.7
A 13	68 16.4	342 53.7	51.1	42 31.0	50.3	315 21.2	10.3	57 33.8	12.4	Shaula	96 08.5	S37 07.3
Y 14	83 18.8	357 52.8	51.3	57 31.7	51.0	330 23.2	10.3	72 36.1	12.5	Sirius	258 25.5	S16 45.3
15	98 21.3	12 52.0	51.5	72 32.4	51.7	345 25.3	10.2	87 38.3	12.6	Spica	158 20.9	S11 18.1
16	113 23.8	27 51.2	51.7	87 33.0	52.4	0 27.3	10.1	102 40.5	12.7	Suhail	222 45.6	S43 32.6
17	128 26.2	42 50.3	51.8	102 33.7	53.1	15 29.3	10.1	117 42.7	12.8			
18	143 28.7	57 49.5	N24 52.0	117 34.4	N 9 53.8	30 31.3	N22 10.0	132 45.0	N 2 12.9	Vega	80 32.2	N38 48.2
19	158 31.2	72 48.7	52.2	132 35.1	54.5	45 33.3	09.9	147 47.2	13.0	Zuben'ubi	136 54.5	S16 09.2
20	173 33.6	87 47.8	52.4	147 35.8	55.2	60 35.4	09.9	162 49.4	13.0			
21	188 36.1	102 47.0	52.5	162 36.4	55.9	75 37.4	09.8	177 51.7	13.1			
22	203 38.6	117 46.2	52.7	177 37.1	56.6	90 39.4	09.8	192 53.9	13.2			
23	218 41.0	132 45.3	52.9	192 37.8	57.3	105 41.4	09.7	207 56.1	13.3			
Mer. Pass.	h m 8 31.6	v −0.8	d 0.2	v 0.7	d 0.7	v 2.0	d 0.1	v 2.2	d 0.1			

	SHA	Mer. Pass.
	° ′	h m
Venus	276 39.2	14 07
Mars	335 20.5	10 11
Jupiter	247 21.1	16 01
Saturn	349 26.3	9 14

	UT	SUN GHA	SUN Dec	MOON GHA	v	MOON Dec	d	HP
	d h	° ′	° ′	° ′	′	° ′	′	′
	13 00	180 55.1	N18 20.0	231 37.3	13.0	N 1 52.9	16.2	58.5
	01	195 55.1	20.6	246 09.3	12.9	2 09.1	16.2	58.5
	02	210 55.1	21.3	260 41.2	12.9	2 25.3	16.3	58.6
	03	225 55.1	. . 21.9	275 13.1	12.8	2 41.6	16.3	58.6
	04	240 55.1	22.5	289 44.9	12.7	2 57.9	16.2	58.6
	05	255 55.1	23.1	304 16.6	12.7	3 14.1	16.3	58.7
	06	270 55.1	N18 23.7	318 48.3	12.7	N 3 30.4	16.3	58.7
W	07	285 55.1	24.4	333 20.0	12.5	3 46.7	16.3	58.8
E	08	300 55.1	25.0	347 51.5	12.5	4 03.0	16.3	58.8
D	09	315 55.1	. . 25.6	2 23.0	12.5	4 19.3	16.3	58.8
N	10	330 55.1	26.2	16 54.5	12.3	4 35.6	16.3	58.9
E	11	345 55.1	26.8	31 25.8	12.3	4 51.9	16.3	58.9
S	12	0 55.1	N18 27.4	45 57.1	12.3	N 5 08.2	16.2	59.0
D	13	15 55.1	28.0	60 28.4	12.1	5 24.4	16.3	59.0
A	14	30 55.1	28.6	74 59.5	12.1	5 40.7	16.3	59.0
Y	15	45 55.1	. . 29.3	89 30.6	12.0	5 57.0	16.3	59.1
	16	60 55.1	29.9	104 01.6	11.9	6 13.3	16.2	59.1
	17	75 55.1	30.5	118 32.5	11.9	6 29.5	16.3	59.1
	18	90 55.1	N18 31.1	133 03.4	11.8	N 6 45.8	16.2	59.2
	19	105 55.1	31.7	147 34.2	11.7	7 02.0	16.3	59.2
	20	120 55.1	32.3	162 04.9	11.6	7 18.3	16.2	59.3
	21	135 55.1	. . 32.9	176 35.5	11.5	7 34.5	16.2	59.3
	22	150 55.1	33.5	191 06.0	11.5	7 50.7	16.1	59.3
	23	165 55.1	34.1	205 36.5	11.3	8 06.8	16.2	59.4
	14 00	180 55.1	N18 34.7	220 06.8	11.3	N 8 23.0	16.1	59.4
	01	195 55.1	35.3	234 37.1	11.2	8 39.1	16.1	59.4
	02	210 55.1	35.9	249 07.3	11.1	8 55.2	16.1	59.5
	03	225 55.1	. . 36.6	263 37.4	11.0	9 11.3	16.1	59.5
	04	240 55.1	37.2	278 07.4	10.9	9 27.4	16.0	59.6
	05	255 55.1	37.8	292 37.3	10.8	9 43.4	16.0	59.6
	06	270 55.1	N18 38.4	307 07.1	10.8	N 9 59.4	15.9	59.6
T	07	285 55.1	39.0	321 36.9	10.6	10 15.3	16.0	59.7
H	08	300 55.1	39.6	336 06.5	10.5	10 31.3	15.8	59.7
U	09	315 55.1	. . 40.2	350 36.0	10.5	10 47.1	15.9	59.7
R	10	330 55.1	40.8	5 05.5	10.3	11 03.0	15.8	59.8
S	11	345 55.1	41.4	19 34.8	10.2	11 18.8	15.8	59.8
D	12	0 55.1	N18 42.0	34 04.0	10.1	N11 34.6	15.7	59.8
A	13	15 55.1	42.6	48 33.1	10.1	11 50.3	15.7	59.9
Y	14	30 55.1	43.2	63 02.2	9.9	12 06.0	15.6	59.9
	15	45 55.1	. . 43.8	77 31.1	9.8	12 21.6	15.5	59.9
	16	60 55.1	44.4	91 59.9	9.7	12 37.1	15.6	60.0
	17	75 55.1	45.0	106 28.6	9.6	12 52.7	15.4	60.0
	18	90 55.1	N18 45.6	120 57.2	9.5	N13 08.1	15.4	60.0
	19	105 55.1	46.2	135 25.7	9.4	13 23.5	15.4	60.1
	20	120 55.1	46.8	149 54.1	9.2	13 38.9	15.3	60.1
	21	135 55.1	. . 47.3	164 22.3	9.2	13 54.2	15.2	60.1
	22	150 55.1	47.9	178 50.5	9.0	14 09.4	15.2	60.2
	23	165 55.0	48.5	193 18.5	8.9	14 24.6	15.1	60.2
	15 00	180 55.0	N18 49.1	207 46.4	8.8	N14 39.7	15.0	60.2
	01	195 55.0	49.7	222 14.2	8.7	14 54.7	15.0	60.3
	02	210 55.0	50.3	236 41.9	8.6	15 09.7	14.8	60.3
	03	225 55.0	. . 50.9	251 09.5	8.4	15 24.5	14.8	60.3
	04	240 55.0	51.5	265 36.9	8.3	15 39.3	14.8	60.3
	05	255 55.0	52.1	280 04.2	8.2	15 54.1	14.6	60.4
	06	270 55.0	N18 52.7	294 31.4	8.1	N16 08.7	14.6	60.4
	07	285 55.0	53.3	308 58.5	8.0	16 23.3	14.4	60.4
	08	300 55.0	53.9	323 25.5	7.8	16 37.7	14.4	60.5
F	09	315 55.0	. . 54.4	337 52.3	7.7	16 52.1	14.3	60.5
R	10	330 55.0	55.0	352 19.0	7.6	17 06.4	14.2	60.5
I	11	345 55.0	55.6	6 45.6	7.5	17 20.6	14.1	60.5
D	12	0 54.9	N18 56.2	21 12.1	7.3	N17 34.7	14.1	60.6
A	13	15 54.9	56.8	35 38.4	7.2	17 48.8	13.9	60.6
Y	14	30 54.9	57.4	50 04.6	7.1	18 02.7	13.8	60.6
	15	45 54.9	. . 58.0	64 30.7	7.0	18 16.5	13.7	60.6
	16	60 54.9	58.6	78 56.7	6.8	18 30.2	13.6	60.7
	17	75 54.9	59.1	93 22.5	6.7	18 43.8	13.5	60.7
	18	90 54.9	N18 59.7	107 48.2	6.6	N18 57.3	13.4	60.7
	19	105 54.9	19 00.3	122 13.8	6.4	19 10.7	13.3	60.7
	20	120 54.9	00.9	136 39.2	6.3	19 24.0	13.1	60.8
	21	135 54.8	. . 01.5	151 04.5	6.2	19 37.1	13.1	60.8
	22	150 54.8	02.0	165 29.7	6.1	19 50.2	12.9	60.8
	23	165 54.8	02.6	179 54.8	5.9	N20 03.1	12.8	60.8
		SD 15.9	*d* 0.6	SD		16.1	16.3	16.5

Lat.	Twilight Naut.	Twilight Civil	Sunrise	Moonrise 13	Moonrise 14	Moonrise 15	Moonrise 16
°	h m	h m	h m	h m	h m	h m	h m
N 72	▭	▭	▭	02 09	01 31	00 36	▭
N 70	////	////	00 54	02 12	01 44	{01 06 / 23 19}	▭
68	////	////	01 53	02 15	01 54	01 28	00 41
66	////	////	02 26	02 17	02 03	01 46	01 20
64	////	01 15	02 50	02 19	02 10	02 00	01 47
62	////	01 56	03 09	02 20	02 16	02 12	02 09
60	////	02 22	03 25	02 22	02 22	02 23	02 26
N 58	01 07	02 43	03 38	02 23	02 27	02 32	02 41
56	01 44	03 00	03 49	02 24	02 31	02 40	02 53
54	02 09	03 14	03 59	02 25	02 35	02 47	03 04
52	02 29	03 26	04 08	02 26	02 39	02 54	03 14
50	02 45	03 36	04 16	02 27	02 42	03 00	03 23
45	03 15	03 58	04 32	02 29	02 49	03 13	03 42
N 40	03 38	04 15	04 46	02 30	02 55	03 23	03 58
35	03 55	04 29	04 57	02 32	03 00	03 32	04 11
30	04 10	04 41	05 07	02 33	03 05	03 41	04 22
20	04 33	05 01	05 24	02 35	03 13	03 55	04 42
N 10	04 51	05 17	05 39	02 37	03 20	04 07	04 59
0	05 06	05 31	05 53	02 39	03 27	04 19	05 16
S 10	05 19	05 44	06 06	02 41	03 34	04 31	05 32
20	05 31	05 58	06 21	02 43	03 41	04 44	05 50
30	05 43	06 12	06 37	02 45	03 50	04 58	06 11
35	05 49	06 20	06 47	02 47	03 55	05 07	06 23
40	05 56	06 28	06 57	02 48	04 00	05 17	06 37
45	06 03	06 38	07 10	02 50	04 07	05 29	06 54
S 50	06 10	06 50	07 25	02 52	04 15	05 43	07 15
52	06 14	06 55	07 32	02 54	04 19	05 49	07 25
54	06 17	07 01	07 40	02 55	04 23	05 57	07 36
56	06 21	07 07	07 49	02 56	04 28	06 05	07 49
58	06 25	07 14	07 59	02 57	04 33	06 15	08 04
S 60	06 30	07 22	08 11	02 59	04 38	06 26	08 22

Lat.	Sunset	Twilight Civil	Twilight Naut.	Moonset 13	Moonset 14	Moonset 15	Moonset 16
°	h m	h m	h m	h m	h m	h m	h m
N 72	▭	▭	▭	16 22	19 04	▭	▭
N 70	23 11	////	////	16 13	18 37	22 20	▭
68	22 05	////	////	16 05	18 17	20 59	▭
66	21 30	////	////	15 59	18 01	20 22	▭
64	21 05	22 44	////	15 54	17 48	19 55	22 27
62	20 45	22 01	////	15 49	17 37	19 35	21 45
60	20 30	21 33	////	15 45	17 28	19 19	21 17
N 58	20 16	21 12	22 51	15 42	17 20	19 05	20 55
56	20 05	20 55	22 12	15 39	17 13	18 53	20 37
54	19 55	20 40	21 46	15 36	17 07	18 43	20 22
52	19 46	20 28	21 26	15 34	17 01	18 34	20 10
50	19 38	20 17	21 10	15 31	16 56	18 26	19 58
45	19 21	19 55	20 39	15 26	16 45	18 09	19 35
N 40	19 07	19 38	20 16	15 22	16 36	17 55	19 16
35	18 56	19 24	19 58	15 19	16 29	17 43	19 00
30	18 46	19 12	19 43	15 16	16 22	17 32	18 46
20	18 29	18 52	19 20	15 10	16 10	17 15	18 23
N 10	18 14	18 36	19 02	15 06	16 00	16 59	18 03
0	18 00	18 22	18 47	15 01	15 51	16 45	17 45
S 10	17 46	18 08	18 34	14 57	15 42	16 31	17 26
20	17 32	17 55	18 22	14 52	15 32	16 16	17 07
30	17 15	17 41	18 09	14 47	15 21	15 59	16 44
35	17 06	17 33	18 03	14 44	15 14	15 49	16 31
40	16 55	17 24	17 57	14 41	15 07	15 38	16 16
45	16 42	17 14	17 50	14 37	14 58	15 24	15 58
S 50	16 27	17 02	17 42	14 32	14 48	15 08	15 35
52	16 20	16 57	17 38	14 30	14 44	15 01	15 25
54	16 12	16 51	17 35	14 28	14 38	14 52	15 13
56	16 03	16 45	17 31	14 25	14 33	14 43	14 59
58	15 53	16 38	17 27	14 22	14 26	14 33	14 44
S 60	15 41	16 30	17 22	14 19	14 19	14 21	14 25

Day	SUN Eqn. of Time 00^h	SUN Eqn. of Time 12^h	SUN Mer. Pass.	MOON Mer. Pass. Upper	MOON Mer. Pass. Lower	MOON Age	MOON Phase
d	m s	m s	h m	h m	h m	d %	
13	03 40	03 40	11 56	08 50	21 14	26 15	
14	03 41	03 40	11 56	09 39	22 05	27 8	
15	03 40	03 40	11 56	10 32	23 00	28 3	

UT d h		ARIES GHA	VENUS −3·9 GHA	VENUS Dec	MARS +1·3 GHA	MARS Dec	JUPITER −1·9 GHA	JUPITER Dec	SATURN +0·9 GHA	SATURN Dec	STARS Name	SHA	Dec
		° ′	° ′	° ′	° ′	° ′	° ′	° ′	° ′	° ′		° ′	° ′
16 00		233 43.5	147 44.5	N24 53.1	207 38.5	N 9 57.9	120 43.5	N22 09.6	222 58.3	N 2 13.4	Acamar	315 11.4	S40 11.9
01		248 45.9	162 43.7	53.2	222 39.2	58.6	135 45.5	09.6	238 00.6	13.5	Achernar	335 19.9	S57 06.0
02		263 48.4	177 42.8	53.4	237 39.9	9 59.3	150 47.5	09.5	253 02.8	13.6	Acrux	172 58.4	S63 15.0
03		278 50.9	192 42.0	. . 53.6	252 40.5	10 00.0	165 49.5	. . 09.4	268 05.0	. . 13.7	Adhara	255 05.3	S29 00.6
04		293 53.3	207 41.2	53.7	267 41.2	00.7	180 51.5	09.4	283 07.3	13.8	Aldebaran	290 38.7	N16 33.7
05		308 55.8	222 40.3	53.9	282 41.9	01.4	195 53.5	09.3	298 09.5	13.9			
06		323 58.3	237 39.5	N24 54.1	297 42.6	N10 02.1	210 55.6	N22 09.2	313 11.7	N 2 14.0	Alioth	166 11.6	N55 49.1
07		339 00.7	252 38.7	54.2	312 43.3	02.8	225 57.6	09.2	328 13.9	14.1	Alkaid	152 50.7	N49 10.9
08	S	354 03.2	267 37.8	54.4	327 43.9	03.5	240 59.6	09.1	343 16.2	14.1	Alnair	27 31.6	S46 49.8
09	A	9 05.7	282 37.0	. . 54.5	342 44.6	. . 04.2	256 01.6	. . 09.1	358 18.4	. . 14.2	Alnilam	275 36.9	S 1 11.2
10	T	24 08.1	297 36.2	54.7	357 45.3	04.9	271 03.6	09.0	13 20.6	14.3	Alphard	217 46.7	S 8 46.5
11	U	39 10.6	312 35.3	54.9	12 46.0	05.6	286 05.7	08.9	28 22.9	14.4			
12	R	54 13.1	327 34.5	N24 55.0	27 46.7	N10 06.3	301 07.7	N22 08.9	43 25.1	N 2 14.5	Alphecca	126 02.4	N26 37.5
13	D	69 15.5	342 33.7	55.2	42 47.3	07.0	316 09.7	08.8	58 27.3	14.6	Alpheratz	357 33.8	N29 14.0
14	A	84 18.0	357 32.8	55.3	57 48.0	07.6	331 11.7	08.7	73 29.6	14.7	Altair	61 58.7	N 8 56.2
15	Y	99 20.4	12 32.0	. . 55.5	72 48.7	. . 08.3	346 13.7	. . 08.7	88 31.8	. . 14.8	Ankaa	353 06.3	S42 09.6
16		114 22.9	27 31.2	55.6	87 49.4	09.0	1 15.7	08.6	103 34.0	14.9	Antares	112 14.1	S26 29.5
17		129 25.4	42 30.3	55.8	102 50.1	09.7	16 17.8	08.5	118 36.2	15.0			
18		144 27.8	57 29.5	N24 55.9	117 50.7	N10 10.4	31 19.8	N22 08.5	133 38.5	N 2 15.1	Arcturus	145 46.6	N19 02.6
19		159 30.3	72 28.7	56.1	132 51.4	11.1	46 21.8	08.4	148 40.7	15.2	Atria	107 06.8	S69 04.4
20		174 32.8	87 27.8	56.2	147 52.1	11.8	61 23.8	08.4	163 42.9	15.2	Avior	234 14.6	S59 35.9
21		189 35.2	102 27.0	. . 56.4	162 52.8	. . 12.5	76 25.8	. . 08.3	178 45.2	. . 15.3	Bellatrix	278 22.0	N 6 22.4
22		204 37.7	117 26.2	56.5	177 53.5	13.2	91 27.8	08.2	193 47.4	15.4	Betelgeuse	270 51.2	N 7 24.7
23		219 40.2	132 25.3	56.7	192 54.1	13.9	106 29.9	08.2	208 49.6	15.5			
17 00		234 42.6	147 24.5	N24 56.8	207 54.8	N10 14.6	121 31.9	N22 08.1	223 51.9	N 2 15.6	Canopus	263 52.3	S52 42.7
01		249 45.1	162 23.7	56.9	222 55.5	15.2	136 33.9	08.0	238 54.1	15.7	Capella	280 20.7	N46 01.5
02		264 47.5	177 22.8	57.1	237 56.2	15.9	151 35.9	08.0	253 56.3	15.8	Deneb	49 24.9	N45 22.2
03		279 50.0	192 22.0	. . 57.2	252 56.9	. . 16.6	166 37.9	. . 07.9	268 58.6	. . 15.9	Denebola	182 23.7	N14 25.4
04		294 52.5	207 21.2	57.3	267 57.5	17.3	181 39.9	07.8	284 00.8	16.0	Diphda	348 46.4	S17 50.5
05		309 54.9	222 20.3	57.5	282 58.2	18.0	196 42.0	07.8	299 03.0	16.1			
06		324 57.4	237 19.5	N24 57.6	297 58.9	N10 18.7	211 44.0	N22 07.7	314 05.2	N 2 16.2	Dubhe	193 39.5	N61 36.7
07		339 59.9	252 18.7	57.7	312 59.6	19.4	226 46.0	07.6	329 07.5	16.3	Elnath	278 00.8	N28 37.8
08		355 02.3	267 17.8	57.9	328 00.3	20.1	241 48.0	07.6	344 09.7	16.3	Eltanin	90 41.2	N51 28.9
09	S	10 04.8	282 17.0	. . 58.0	343 00.9	. . 20.8	256 50.0	. . 07.5	359 11.9	. . 16.4	Enif	33 37.7	N 9 59.6
10	U	25 07.3	297 16.2	58.1	358 01.6	21.4	271 52.0	07.5	14 14.2	16.5	Fomalhaut	15 13.4	S29 28.8
11	N	40 09.7	312 15.3	58.3	13 02.3	22.1	286 54.0	07.4	29 16.4	16.6			
12	D	55 12.2	327 14.5	N24 58.4	28 03.0	N10 22.8	301 56.0	N22 07.3	44 18.6	N 2 16.7	Gacrux	171 50.0	S57 15.9
13	A	70 14.7	342 13.7	58.5	43 03.7	23.5	316 58.1	07.3	59 20.9	16.8	Gienah	175 42.3	S17 41.5
14	Y	85 17.1	357 12.8	58.6	58 04.3	24.2	332 00.1	07.2	74 23.1	16.9	Hadar	148 33.8	S60 30.2
15		100 19.6	12 12.0	. . 58.8	73 05.0	. . 24.9	347 02.1	. . 07.1	89 25.3	. . 17.0	Hamal	327 50.3	N23 35.1
16		115 22.0	27 11.2	58.9	88 05.7	25.6	2 04.1	07.1	104 27.6	17.1	Kaus Aust.	83 30.7	S34 22.2
17		130 24.5	42 10.3	59.0	103 06.4	26.2	17 06.1	07.0	119 29.8	17.2			
18		145 27.0	57 09.5	N24 59.1	118 07.1	N10 26.9	32 08.1	N22 06.9	134 32.0	N 2 17.2	Kochab	137 18.7	N74 02.8
19		160 29.4	72 08.7	59.2	133 07.7	27.6	47 10.1	06.9	149 34.3	17.3	Markab	13 28.9	N15 20.7
20		175 31.9	87 07.8	59.4	148 08.4	28.3	62 12.2	06.8	164 36.5	17.4	Menkar	314 05.3	N 4 11.5
21		190 34.4	102 07.0	. . 59.5	163 09.1	. . 29.0	77 14.2	. . 06.7	179 38.7	. . 17.5	Menkent	147 55.9	S36 30.2
22		205 36.8	117 06.2	59.6	178 09.8	29.7	92 16.2	06.7	194 41.0	17.6	Miaplacidus	221 38.2	S69 49.8
23		220 39.3	132 05.3	59.7	193 10.5	30.4	107 18.2	06.6	209 43.2	17.7			
18 00		235 41.8	147 04.5	N24 59.8	208 11.1	N10 31.0	122 20.2	N22 06.5	224 45.4	N 2 17.8	Mirfak	308 27.2	N49 57.2
01		250 44.2	162 03.7	24 59.9	223 11.8	31.7	137 22.2	06.5	239 47.7	17.9	Nunki	75 46.1	S26 15.8
02		265 46.7	177 02.8	25 00.0	238 12.5	32.4	152 24.2	06.4	254 49.9	18.0	Peacock	53 03.8	S56 38.8
03		280 49.2	192 02.0	. . 00.1	253 13.2	. . 33.1	167 26.2	. . 06.3	269 52.1	. . 18.1	Pollux	243 16.2	N27 57.8
04		295 51.6	207 01.2	00.2	268 13.9	33.8	182 28.2	06.3	284 54.4	18.1	Procyon	244 49.9	N 5 09.4
05		310 54.1	222 00.3	00.4	283 14.5	34.5	197 30.3	06.2	299 56.6	18.2			
06		325 56.5	236 59.5	N25 00.5	298 15.2	N10 35.1	212 32.3	N22 06.2	314 58.8	N 2 18.3	Rasalhague	95 57.2	N12 32.3
07		340 59.0	251 58.7	00.6	313 15.9	35.8	227 34.3	06.1	330 01.1	18.4	Regulus	207 33.3	N11 50.3
08		356 01.5	266 57.8	00.7	328 16.6	36.5	242 36.3	06.0	345 03.3	18.5	Rigel	281 03.1	S 8 10.3
09	M	11 03.9	281 57.0	. . 00.8	343 17.2	. . 37.2	257 38.3	. . 06.0	0 05.5	. . 18.6	Rigil Kent.	139 38.1	S60 56.8
10	O	26 06.4	296 56.2	00.9	358 17.9	37.9	272 40.3	05.9	15 07.8	18.7	Sabik	102 01.2	S15 45.5
11	N	41 08.9	311 55.3	01.0	13 18.6	38.6	287 42.3	05.8	30 10.0	18.8			
12	D	56 11.3	326 54.5	N25 01.1	28 19.3	N10 39.2	302 44.3	N22 05.8	45 12.2	N 2 18.9	Schedar	349 30.2	N56 40.7
13	A	71 13.8	341 53.7	01.2	43 20.0	39.9	317 46.3	05.7	60 14.5	19.0	Shaula	96 08.5	S37 07.3
14	Y	86 16.3	356 52.8	01.2	58 20.6	40.6	332 48.3	05.6	75 16.7	19.0	Sirius	258 25.5	S16 45.3
15		101 18.7	11 52.0	. . 01.3	73 21.3	. . 41.3	347 50.4	. . 05.6	90 18.9	. . 19.1	Spica	158 20.9	S11 18.1
16		116 21.2	26 51.2	01.4	88 22.0	42.0	2 52.4	05.5	105 21.2	19.2	Suhail	222 45.6	S43 32.6
17		131 23.7	41 50.3	01.5	103 22.7	42.7	17 54.4	05.4	120 23.4	19.3			
18		146 26.1	56 49.5	N25 01.6	118 23.4	N10 43.3	32 56.4	N22 05.4	135 25.6	N 2 19.4	Vega	80 32.2	N38 48.3
19		161 28.6	71 48.7	01.7	133 24.0	44.0	47 58.4	05.3	150 27.9	19.5	Zuben'ubi	136 54.5	S16 09.2
20		176 31.0	86 47.8	01.8	148 24.7	44.7	63 00.4	05.2	165 30.1	19.6			
21		191 33.5	101 47.0	. . 01.9	163 25.4	. . 45.4	78 02.4	. . 05.2	180 32.3	. . 19.7			
22		206 36.0	116 46.2	02.0	178 26.1	46.1	93 04.4	05.1	195 34.6	19.8			
23		221 38.4	131 45.3	02.0	193 26.7	46.7	108 06.4	05.0	210 36.8	19.9			
Mer. Pass.		h m 8 19.8	v −0.8	d 0.1	v 0.7	d 0.7	v 2.0	d 0.1	v 2.2	d 0.1			

	SHA	Mer. Pass.
	° ′	h m
Venus	272 41.9	14 11
Mars	333 12.2	10 08
Jupiter	246 49.3	15 52
Saturn	349 09.2	9 03

UT		SUN GHA	SUN Dec	MOON GHA	v	MOON Dec	d	HP
d	h	° ′	° ′	° ′	′	° ′	′	′
16 SATURDAY	00	180 54.8	N19 03.2	194 19.7	5.8	N20 15.9	12.6	60.8
	01	195 54.8	03.8	208 44.5	5.7	20 28.5	12.6	60.9
	02	210 54.8	04.4	223 09.2	5.5	20 41.1	12.4	60.9
	03	225 54.8	. . 04.9	237 33.7	5.4	20 53.5	12.3	60.9
	04	240 54.8	05.5	251 58.1	5.3	21 05.8	12.1	60.9
	05	255 54.7	06.1	266 22.4	5.2	21 17.9	12.0	60.9
	06	270 54.7	N19 06.7	280 46.6	5.0	N21 29.9	11.9	61.0
	07	285 54.7	07.3	295 10.6	4.9	21 41.8	11.7	61.0
	08	300 54.7	07.8	309 34.5	4.8	21 53.5	11.6	61.0
	09	315 54.7	. . 08.4	323 58.3	4.6	22 05.1	11.4	61.0
	10	330 54.7	09.0	338 21.9	4.5	22 16.5	11.3	61.0
	11	345 54.7	09.6	352 45.4	4.4	22 27.8	11.2	61.0
	12	0 54.6	N19 10.1	7 08.8	4.3	N22 39.0	11.0	61.1
	13	15 54.6	10.7	21 32.1	4.2	22 50.0	10.8	61.1
	14	30 54.6	11.3	35 55.3	4.0	23 00.8	10.7	61.1
	15	45 54.6	. . 11.8	50 18.3	3.9	23 11.5	10.5	61.1
	16	60 54.6	12.4	64 41.2	3.8	23 22.0	10.3	61.1
	17	75 54.6	13.0	79 04.0	3.7	23 32.3	10.2	61.1
	18	90 54.5	N19 13.6	93 26.7	3.5	N23 42.5	10.0	61.1
	19	105 54.5	14.1	107 49.2	3.4	23 52.5	9.9	61.1
	20	120 54.5	14.7	122 11.6	3.4	24 02.4	9.6	61.1
	21	135 54.5	. . 15.3	136 34.0	3.2	24 12.0	9.5	61.2
	22	150 54.5	15.8	150 56.2	3.1	24 21.5	9.4	61.2
	23	165 54.5	16.4	165 18.3	2.9	24 30.9	9.1	61.2
17 SUNDAY	00	180 54.4	N19 17.0	179 40.2	2.9	N24 40.0	9.0	61.2
	01	195 54.4	17.5	194 02.1	2.8	24 49.0	8.8	61.2
	02	210 54.4	18.1	208 23.9	2.7	24 57.8	8.6	61.2
	03	225 54.4	. . 18.7	222 45.6	2.5	25 06.4	8.4	61.2
	04	240 54.4	19.2	237 07.1	2.5	25 14.8	8.2	61.2
	05	255 54.3	19.8	251 28.6	2.4	25 23.0	8.1	61.2
	06	270 54.3	N19 20.3	265 50.0	2.2	N25 31.1	7.8	61.2
	07	285 54.3	20.9	280 11.2	2.2	25 38.9	7.7	61.2
	08	300 54.3	21.5	294 32.4	2.1	25 46.6	7.4	61.2
	09	315 54.3	. . 22.0	308 53.5	2.0	25 54.0	7.3	61.2
	10	330 54.2	22.6	323 14.5	1.9	26 01.3	7.1	61.2
	11	345 54.2	23.2	337 35.4	1.8	26 08.4	6.9	61.2
	12	0 54.2	N19 23.7	351 56.2	1.7	N26 15.3	6.6	61.2
	13	15 54.2	24.3	6 16.9	1.7	26 21.9	6.5	61.2
	14	30 54.1	24.8	20 37.6	1.6	26 28.4	6.3	61.2
	15	45 54.1	. . 25.4	34 58.2	1.5	26 34.7	6.0	61.2
	16	60 54.1	25.9	49 18.7	1.4	26 40.7	5.9	61.2
	17	75 54.1	26.5	63 39.1	1.4	26 46.6	5.6	61.2
	18	90 54.1	N19 27.1	77 59.5	1.3	N26 52.2	5.5	61.2
	19	105 54.0	27.6	92 19.8	1.3	26 57.7	5.2	61.2
	20	120 54.0	28.2	106 40.1	1.2	27 02.9	5.0	61.2
	21	135 54.0	. . 28.7	121 00.3	1.1	27 07.9	4.8	61.2
	22	150 54.0	29.3	135 20.4	1.1	27 12.7	4.6	61.2
	23	165 53.9	29.8	149 40.5	1.0	27 17.3	4.4	61.2
18 MONDAY	00	180 53.9	N19 30.4	164 00.5	1.0	N27 21.7	4.1	61.2
	01	195 53.9	30.9	178 20.5	1.0	27 25.8	4.0	61.2
	02	210 53.9	31.5	192 40.5	0.9	27 29.8	3.7	61.2
	03	225 53.8	. . 32.0	207 00.4	0.9	27 33.5	3.5	61.2
	04	240 53.8	32.6	221 20.3	0.8	27 37.0	3.3	61.2
	05	255 53.8	33.1	235 40.1	0.8	27 40.3	3.1	61.2
	06	270 53.8	N19 33.7	249 59.9	0.8	N27 43.4	2.8	61.2
	07	285 53.7	34.2	264 19.7	0.8	27 46.2	2.7	61.2
	08	300 53.7	34.8	278 39.5	0.8	27 48.9	2.4	61.1
	09	315 53.7	. . 35.3	292 59.3	0.7	27 51.3	2.2	61.1
	10	330 53.7	35.9	307 19.0	0.7	27 53.5	1.9	61.1
	11	345 53.6	36.4	321 38.7	0.8	27 55.4	1.8	61.1
	12	0 53.6	N19 37.0	335 58.5	0.7	N27 57.2	1.5	61.1
	13	15 53.6	37.5	350 18.2	0.7	27 58.7	1.3	61.1
	14	30 53.6	38.1	4 37.9	0.7	28 00.0	1.1	61.1
	15	45 53.5	. . 38.6	18 57.6	0.8	28 01.1	0.9	61.1
	16	60 53.5	39.2	33 17.4	0.7	28 02.0	0.6	61.0
	17	75 53.5	39.7	47 37.1	0.8	28 02.6	0.4	61.0
	18	90 53.4	N19 40.2	61 56.9	0.8	N28 03.0	0.2	61.0
	19	105 53.4	40.8	76 16.7	0.8	28 03.2	0.0	61.0
	20	120 53.4	41.3	90 36.5	0.8	28 03.2	0.2	61.0
	21	135 53.4	. . 41.9	104 56.3	0.9	28 03.0	0.5	61.0
	22	150 53.3	42.4	119 16.2	0.9	28 02.5	0.7	61.0
	23	165 53.3	42.9	133 36.1	0.9	N28 01.8	0.9	60.9
		SD 15.8	d 0.6	SD 16.6		16.7		16.6

Lat.	Twilight Naut.	Twilight Civil	Sunrise	Moonrise 16	17	18	19
°	h m	h m	h m	h m	h m	h m	h m
N 72	▭	▭	▭	▭	▭	▭	▭
N 70	▭	▭	▭	▭	▭	▭	▭
68	////	////	01 36	00 41	▭	▭	▭
66	////	////	02 14	01 20	▭	▭	▭
64	////	00 52	02 41	01 47	01 23	▭	▭
62	////	01 43	03 01	02 09	02 05	02 04	02 47
60	////	02 13	03 18	02 26	02 34	02 57	03 56
N 58	00 47	02 35	03 32	02 41	02 57	03 29	04 31
56	01 33	02 53	03 44	02 53	03 15	03 53	04 57
54	02 01	03 08	03 54	03 04	03 31	04 13	05 17
52	02 21	03 21	04 03	03 14	03 44	04 29	05 34
50	02 38	03 32	04 11	03 23	03 56	04 44	05 49
45	03 11	03 54	04 29	03 42	04 21	05 13	06 19
N 40	03 34	04 12	04 43	03 58	04 41	05 36	06 42
35	03 53	04 27	04 55	04 11	04 57	05 54	07 01
30	04 08	04 39	05 05	04 22	05 12	06 11	07 18
20	04 31	05 00	05 23	04 42	05 37	06 38	07 46
N 10	04 50	05 16	05 39	04 59	05 58	07 02	08 09
0	05 05	05 31	05 53	05 16	06 18	07 25	08 32
S 10	05 19	05 45	06 07	05 32	06 39	07 47	08 54
20	05 32	05 59	06 22	05 50	07 00	08 11	09 18
30	05 44	06 14	06 39	06 11	07 26	08 39	09 46
35	05 51	06 22	06 49	06 23	07 41	08 56	10 02
40	05 58	06 31	07 00	06 37	07 59	09 15	10 21
45	06 05	06 41	07 13	06 54	08 20	09 39	10 44
S 50	06 14	06 53	07 29	07 15	08 47	10 09	11 14
52	06 17	06 59	07 37	07 25	09 00	10 24	11 28
54	06 21	07 05	07 45	07 36	09 15	10 42	11 45
56	06 25	07 12	07 55	07 49	09 33	11 03	12 05
58	06 30	07 19	08 05	08 04	09 55	11 30	12 30
S 60	06 35	07 27	08 18	08 22	10 23	12 08	13 04

Lat.	Sunset	Twilight Civil	Twilight Naut.	Moonset 16	17	18	19
°	h m	h m	h m	h m	h m	h m	h m
N 72	▭	▭	▭	▭	▭	▭	▭
N 70	▭	▭	▭	▭	▭	▭	▭
68	22 23	////	////	▭	▭	▭	▭
66	21 42	////	////	▭	▭	▭	▭
64	21 14	23 09	////	22 27	▭	▭	▭
62	20 53	22 14	////	21 45	24 04	00 04	01 44
60	20 37	21 43	////	21 17	23 12	24 34	00 34
N 58	20 22	21 20	23 14	20 55	22 40	23 59	24 43
56	20 10	21 02	22 24	20 37	22 16	23 33	24 21
54	20 00	20 46	21 55	20 22	21 57	23 13	24 04
52	19 50	20 33	21 33	20 10	21 40	22 55	23 49
50	19 42	20 22	21 16	19 58	21 26	22 41	23 36
45	19 25	19 59	20 43	19 35	20 58	22 11	23 08
N 40	19 10	19 41	20 19	19 16	20 35	21 47	22 47
35	18 58	19 26	20 01	19 00	20 17	21 28	22 29
30	18 48	19 14	19 46	18 46	20 01	21 11	22 13
20	18 30	18 53	19 22	18 23	19 34	20 43	21 47
N 10	18 14	18 37	19 03	18 03	19 11	20 19	21 24
0	18 00	18 22	18 47	17 45	18 49	19 57	21 03
S 10	17 46	18 08	18 34	17 26	18 28	19 34	20 41
20	17 31	17 54	18 21	17 07	18 05	19 10	20 18
30	17 14	17 39	18 08	16 44	17 38	18 41	19 51
35	17 04	17 31	18 01	16 31	17 22	18 25	19 35
40	16 52	17 22	17 54	16 16	17 04	18 05	19 16
45	16 39	17 11	17 47	15 58	16 42	17 41	18 54
S 50	16 23	16 59	17 39	15 35	16 15	17 11	18 25
52	16 15	16 53	17 35	15 25	16 01	16 56	18 11
54	16 07	16 47	17 31	15 13	15 45	16 38	17 54
56	15 58	16 41	17 27	14 59	15 27	16 17	17 34
58	15 47	16 33	17 22	14 44	15 05	15 50	17 09
S 60	15 35	16 25	17 17	14 25	14 36	15 12	16 36

Day	SUN Eqn. of Time 00^h	SUN Eqn. of Time 12^h	SUN Mer. Pass.	MOON Mer. Pass. Upper	MOON Mer. Pass. Lower	Age	Phase
d	m s	m s	h m	h m	h m	d	%
16	03 39	03 39	11 56	11 30	24 01	29	0 ●
17	03 38	03 37	11 56	12 34	00 01	01	1
18	03 36	03 34	11 56	13 41	01 07	02	4

UT d	h	ARIES GHA	VENUS −3·9 GHA	VENUS Dec	MARS +1·3 GHA	MARS Dec	JUPITER −1·9 GHA	JUPITER Dec	SATURN +0·9 GHA	SATURN Dec
		° ′	° ′	° ′	° ′	° ′	° ′	° ′	° ′	° ′
19	00	236 40.9	146 44.5	N25 02.1	208 27.4	N10 47.4	123 08.4	N22 05.0	225 39.0	N 2 19.9
	01	251 43.4	161 43.7	02.2	223 28.1	48.1	138 10.4	04.9	240 41.3	20.0
	02	266 45.8	176 42.8	02.3	238 28.8	48.8	153 12.4	04.8	255 43.5	20.1
	03	281 48.3	191 42.0	. . 02.4	253 29.5	. . 49.5	168 14.5	. . 04.8	270 45.7	. . 20.2
	04	296 50.8	206 41.2	02.4	268 30.1	50.1	183 16.5	04.7	285 48.0	20.3
	05	311 53.2	221 40.3	02.5	283 30.8	50.8	198 18.5	04.6	300 50.2	20.4
	06	326 55.7	236 39.5	N25 02.6	298 31.5	N10 51.5	213 20.5	N22 04.6	315 52.4	N 2 20.5
	07	341 58.2	251 38.7	02.7	313 32.2	52.2	228 22.5	04.5	330 54.7	20.6
TUESDAY	08	357 00.6	266 37.8	02.7	328 32.8	52.9	243 24.5	04.4	345 56.9	20.7
	09	12 03.1	281 37.0	. . 02.8	343 33.5	. . 53.5	258 26.5	. . 04.4	0 59.2	. . 20.7
	10	27 05.5	296 36.2	02.9	358 34.2	54.2	273 28.5	04.3	16 01.4	20.8
	11	42 08.0	311 35.3	02.9	13 34.9	54.9	288 30.5	04.2	31 03.6	20.9
	12	57 10.5	326 34.5	N25 03.0	28 35.5	N10 55.6	303 32.5	N22 04.2	46 05.9	N 2 21.0
	13	72 12.9	341 33.7	03.1	43 36.2	56.2	318 34.5	04.1	61 08.1	21.1
	14	87 15.4	356 32.9	03.1	58 36.9	56.9	333 36.5	04.0	76 10.3	21.2
	15	102 17.9	11 32.0	. . 03.2	73 37.6	. . 57.6	348 38.5	. . 04.0	91 12.6	. . 21.3
	16	117 20.3	26 31.2	03.3	88 38.3	58.3	3 40.5	03.9	106 14.8	21.4
	17	132 22.8	41 30.4	03.3	103 38.9	58.9	18 42.5	03.8	121 17.0	21.4
	18	147 25.3	56 29.5	N25 03.4	118 39.6	N10 59.6	33 44.5	N22 03.8	136 19.3	N 2 21.5
	19	162 27.7	71 28.7	03.4	133 40.3	11 00.3	48 46.5	03.7	151 21.5	21.6
	20	177 30.2	86 27.9	03.5	148 41.0	01.0	63 48.6	03.6	166 23.8	21.7
	21	192 32.7	101 27.0	. . 03.6	163 41.6	. . 01.6	78 50.6	. . 03.6	181 26.0	. . 21.8
	22	207 35.1	116 26.2	03.6	178 42.3	02.3	93 52.6	03.5	196 28.2	21.9
	23	222 37.6	131 25.4	03.7	193 43.0	03.0	108 54.6	03.4	211 30.5	22.0
20	00	237 40.0	146 24.5	N25 03.7	208 43.7	N11 03.7	123 56.6	N22 03.4	226 32.7	N 2 22.1
	01	252 42.5	161 23.7	03.8	223 44.3	04.3	138 58.6	03.3	241 34.9	22.2
	02	267 45.0	176 22.9	03.8	238 45.0	05.0	154 00.6	03.2	256 37.2	22.2
	03	282 47.4	191 22.0	. . 03.9	253 45.7	. . 05.7	169 02.6	. . 03.2	271 39.4	. . 22.3
	04	297 49.9	206 21.2	03.9	268 46.4	06.4	184 04.6	03.1	286 41.7	22.4
	05	312 52.4	221 20.4	04.0	283 47.1	07.0	199 06.6	03.0	301 43.9	22.5
	06	327 54.8	236 19.5	N25 04.0	298 47.7	N11 07.7	214 08.6	N22 03.0	316 46.1	N 2 22.6
	07	342 57.3	251 18.7	04.0	313 48.4	08.4	229 10.6	02.9	331 48.4	22.7
	08	357 59.8	266 17.9	04.1	328 49.1	09.1	244 12.6	02.8	346 50.6	22.8
	09	13 02.2	281 17.1	. . 04.1	343 49.8	. . 09.7	259 14.6	. . 02.8	1 52.8	. . 22.9
WEDNESDAY	10	28 04.7	296 16.2	04.2	358 50.4	10.4	274 16.6	02.7	16 55.1	22.9
	11	43 07.2	311 15.4	04.2	13 51.1	11.1	289 18.6	02.6	31 57.3	23.0
	12	58 09.6	326 14.6	N25 04.2	28 51.8	N11 11.8	304 20.6	N22 02.5	46 59.6	N 2 23.1
	13	73 12.1	341 13.7	04.3	43 52.5	12.4	319 22.6	02.5	62 01.8	23.2
	14	88 14.5	356 12.9	04.3	58 53.1	13.1	334 24.6	02.4	77 04.0	23.3
	15	103 17.0	11 12.1	. . 04.4	73 53.8	. . 13.8	349 26.6	. . 02.3	92 06.3	. . 23.4
	16	118 19.5	26 11.2	04.4	88 54.5	14.4	4 28.6	02.3	107 08.5	23.5
	17	133 21.9	41 10.4	04.4	103 55.2	15.1	19 30.6	02.2	122 10.7	23.6
	18	148 24.4	56 09.6	N25 04.4	118 55.8	N11 15.8	34 32.6	N22 02.1	137 13.0	N 2 23.6
	19	163 26.9	71 08.7	04.5	133 56.5	16.5	49 34.6	02.1	152 15.2	23.7
	20	178 29.3	86 07.9	04.5	148 57.2	17.1	64 36.6	02.0	167 17.5	23.8
	21	193 31.8	101 07.1	. . 04.5	163 57.9	. . 17.8	79 38.6	. . 01.9	182 19.7	. . 23.9
	22	208 34.3	116 06.3	04.6	178 58.5	18.5	94 40.6	01.9	197 21.9	24.0
	23	223 36.7	131 05.4	04.6	193 59.2	19.1	109 42.6	01.8	212 24.2	24.1
21	00	238 39.2	146 04.6	N25 04.6	208 59.9	N11 19.8	124 44.6	N22 01.7	227 26.4	N 2 24.2
	01	253 41.7	161 03.8	04.6	224 00.6	20.5	139 46.6	01.7	242 28.7	24.2
	02	268 44.1	176 02.9	04.6	239 01.2	21.1	154 48.6	01.6	257 30.9	24.3
	03	283 46.6	191 02.1	. . 04.7	254 01.9	. . 21.8	169 50.6	. . 01.5	272 33.1	. . 24.4
	04	298 49.0	206 01.3	04.7	269 02.6	22.5	184 52.6	01.5	287 35.4	24.5
	05	313 51.5	221 00.5	04.7	284 03.3	23.2	199 54.6	01.4	302 37.6	24.6
	06	328 54.0	235 59.6	N25 04.7	299 03.9	N11 23.8	214 56.6	N22 01.3	317 39.9	N 2 24.7
	07	343 56.4	250 58.8	04.7	314 04.6	24.5	229 58.6	01.3	332 42.1	24.8
	08	358 58.9	265 58.0	04.7	329 05.3	25.2	245 00.6	01.2	347 44.3	24.9
	09	14 01.4	280 57.1	. . 04.7	344 06.0	. . 25.8	260 02.6	. . 01.1	2 46.6	. . 24.9
	10	29 03.8	295 56.3	04.8	359 06.6	26.5	275 04.6	01.0	17 48.8	25.0
THURSDAY	11	44 06.3	310 55.5	04.8	14 07.3	27.2	290 06.6	01.0	32 51.1	25.1
	12	59 08.8	325 54.7	N25 04.8	29 08.0	N11 27.8	305 08.6	N22 00.9	47 53.3	N 2 25.2
	13	74 11.2	340 53.8	04.8	44 08.7	28.5	320 10.6	00.8	62 55.5	25.3
	14	89 13.7	355 53.0	04.8	59 09.3	29.2	335 12.6	00.8	77 57.8	25.4
	15	104 16.2	10 52.2	. . 04.8	74 10.0	. . 29.8	350 14.6	. . 00.7	93 00.0	. . 25.5
	16	119 18.6	25 51.3	04.8	89 10.7	30.5	5 16.6	00.6	108 02.3	25.5
	17	134 21.1	40 50.5	04.8	104 11.4	31.2	20 18.6	00.6	123 04.5	25.6
	18	149 23.5	55 49.7	N25 04.8	119 12.0	N11 31.8	35 20.6	N22 00.5	138 06.7	N 2 25.7
	19	164 26.0	70 48.9	04.8	134 12.7	32.5	50 22.6	00.4	153 09.0	25.8
	20	179 28.5	85 48.0	04.8	149 13.4	33.2	65 24.6	00.4	168 11.2	25.9
	21	194 30.9	100 47.2	. . 04.8	164 14.1	. . 33.8	80 26.6	. . 00.3	183 13.5	. . 26.0
	22	209 33.4	115 46.4	04.8	179 14.7	34.5	95 28.6	00.2	198 15.7	26.1
	23	224 35.9	130 45.6	04.8	194 15.4	35.2	110 30.6	00.1	213 18.0	26.1
Mer. Pass.		h m 8 08.0	v −0.8	d 0.0	v 0.7	d 0.7	v 2.0	d 0.1	v 2.2	d 0.1

STARS

Name	SHA	Dec
	° ′	° ′
Acamar	315 11.3	S40 11.9
Achernar	335 19.8	S57 06.0
Acrux	172 58.4	S63 15.0
Adhara	255 05.3	S29 00.6
Aldebaran	290 38.7	N16 33.7
Alioth	166 11.6	N55 49.1
Alkaid	152 50.7	N49 10.9
Alnair	27 31.5	S46 49.8
Alnilam	275 36.9	S 1 11.2
Alphard	217 46.7	S 8 46.5
Alphecca	126 02.4	N26 37.5
Alpheratz	357 33.8	N29 14.0
Altair	61 58.7	N 8 56.2
Ankaa	353 06.3	S42 09.6
Antares	112 14.1	S26 29.5
Arcturus	145 46.6	N19 02.6
Atria	107 06.8	S69 04.4
Avior	234 14.6	S59 35.9
Bellatrix	278 22.0	N 6 22.4
Betelgeuse	270 51.2	N 7 24.7
Canopus	263 52.4	S52 42.7
Capella	280 20.7	N46 01.5
Deneb	49 24.9	N45 22.2
Denebola	182 23.7	N14 25.4
Diphda	348 46.4	S17 50.5
Dubhe	193 39.5	N61 36.7
Elnath	278 00.8	N28 37.8
Eltanin	90 41.2	N51 28.9
Enif	33 37.7	N 9 59.7
Fomalhaut	15 13.4	S29 28.8
Gacrux	171 50.0	S57 16.0
Gienah	175 42.3	S17 41.5
Hadar	148 33.8	S60 30.2
Hamal	327 50.3	N23 35.1
Kaus Aust.	83 30.7	S34 22.2
Kochab	137 18.7	N74 02.8
Markab	13 28.9	N15 20.7
Menkar	314 05.3	N 4 11.5
Menkent	147 55.9	S36 30.2
Miaplacidus	221 38.3	S69 49.8
Mirfak	308 27.2	N49 57.2
Nunki	75 46.1	S26 15.8
Peacock	53 03.7	S56 38.7
Pollux	243 16.2	N27 57.8
Procyon	244 49.9	N 5 09.4
Rasalhague	95 57.2	N12 32.3
Regulus	207 33.3	N11 50.3
Rigel	281 03.1	S 8 10.3
Rigil Kent.	139 38.1	S60 56.8
Sabik	102 01.2	S15 45.5
Schedar	349 30.1	N56 40.7
Shaula	96 08.5	S37 07.3
Sirius	258 25.5	S16 45.3
Spica	158 20.9	S11 18.1
Suhail	222 45.6	S43 32.6
Vega	80 32.1	N38 48.3
Zuben'ubi	136 54.5	S16 09.2

	SHA	Mer. Pass.
	° ′	h m
Venus	268 44.5	14 15
Mars	331 03.6	10 05
Jupiter	246 16.5	15 42
Saturn	348 52.7	8 52

UT d	UT h	SUN GHA ° ′	SUN Dec ° ′	MOON GHA ° ′	v ′	MOON Dec ° ′	d ′	HP ′
19	00	180 53.3	N19 43.5	147 56.0	1.0	N28 00.9	1.1	60.9
	01	195 53.2	44.0	162 16.0	1.0	27 59.8	1.3	60.9
	02	210 53.2	44.6	176 36.0	1.1	27 58.5	1.5	60.9
	03	225 53.2	. . 45.1	190 56.1	1.1	27 57.0	1.8	60.9
	04	240 53.1	45.6	205 16.2	1.1	27 55.2	2.0	60.8
	05	255 53.1	46.2	219 36.3	1.3	27 53.2	2.2	60.8
	06	270 53.1	N19 46.7	233 56.6	1.3	N27 51.0	2.4	60.8
	07	285 53.1	47.2	248 16.9	1.3	27 48.6	2.6	60.8
T	08	300 53.0	47.8	262 37.2	1.4	27 46.0	2.8	60.8
U	09	315 53.0	. . 48.3	276 57.6	1.5	27 43.2	3.0	60.7
E	10	330 53.0	48.8	291 18.1	1.6	27 40.2	3.3	60.7
S	11	345 52.9	49.4	305 38.7	1.6	27 36.9	3.4	60.7
D	12	0 52.9	N19 49.9	319 59.3	1.8	N27 33.5	3.7	60.7
A	13	15 52.9	50.4	334 20.1	1.8	27 29.8	3.8	60.7
Y	14	30 52.8	51.0	348 40.9	1.9	27 26.0	4.1	60.6
	15	45 52.8	. . 51.5	3 01.8	1.9	27 21.9	4.3	60.6
	16	60 52.8	52.0	17 22.7	2.1	27 17.6	4.4	60.6
	17	75 52.7	52.6	31 43.8	2.2	27 13.2	4.7	60.6
	18	90 52.7	N19 53.1	46 05.0	2.2	N27 08.5	4.9	60.5
	19	105 52.7	53.6	60 26.2	2.4	27 03.6	5.0	60.5
	20	120 52.6	54.1	74 47.6	2.4	26 58.6	5.3	60.5
	21	135 52.6	. . 54.7	89 09.0	2.6	26 53.3	5.4	60.5
	22	150 52.6	55.2	103 30.6	2.7	26 47.9	5.6	60.4
	23	165 52.5	55.7	117 52.3	2.7	26 42.3	5.8	60.4
20	00	180 52.5	N19 56.2	132 14.0	2.9	N26 36.5	6.0	60.4
	01	195 52.4	56.8	146 35.9	3.0	26 30.5	6.2	60.3
	02	210 52.4	57.3	160 57.9	3.1	26 24.3	6.4	60.3
	03	225 52.4	. . 57.8	175 20.0	3.3	26 17.9	6.6	60.3
	04	240 52.3	58.3	189 42.3	3.3	26 11.3	6.7	60.3
	05	255 52.3	58.9	204 04.6	3.5	26 04.6	6.9	60.2
	06	270 52.3	N19 59.4	218 27.1	3.5	N25 57.7	7.1	60.2
W	07	285 52.2	19 59.9	232 49.6	3.7	25 50.6	7.3	60.2
E	08	300 52.2	20 00.4	247 12.3	3.9	25 43.3	7.4	60.1
D	09	315 52.2	. . 00.9	261 35.2	3.9	25 35.9	7.6	60.1
N	10	330 52.1	01.5	275 58.1	4.1	25 28.3	7.8	60.1
E	11	345 52.1	02.0	290 21.2	4.2	25 20.5	7.9	60.1
S	12	0 52.0	N20 02.5	304 44.4	4.3	N25 12.6	8.1	60.0
D	13	15 52.0	03.0	319 07.7	4.5	25 04.5	8.3	60.0
A	14	30 52.0	03.5	333 31.2	4.6	24 56.2	8.4	60.0
Y	15	45 51.9	. . 04.0	347 54.8	4.7	24 47.8	8.6	59.9
	16	60 51.9	04.6	2 18.5	4.9	24 39.2	8.7	59.9
	17	75 51.8	05.1	16 42.4	5.0	24 30.5	8.9	59.9
	18	90 51.8	N20 05.6	31 06.4	5.1	N24 21.6	9.0	59.8
	19	105 51.8	06.1	45 30.5	5.3	24 12.6	9.2	59.8
	20	120 51.7	06.6	59 54.8	5.4	24 03.4	9.4	59.8
	21	135 51.7	. . 07.1	74 19.2	5.5	23 54.0	9.5	59.7
	22	150 51.6	07.6	88 43.7	5.7	23 44.5	9.6	59.7
	23	165 51.6	08.1	103 08.4	5.8	23 34.9	9.7	59.7
21	00	180 51.6	N20 08.7	117 33.2	6.0	N23 25.2	9.9	59.6
	01	195 51.5	09.2	131 58.2	6.1	23 15.3	10.1	59.6
	02	210 51.5	09.7	146 23.3	6.2	23 05.2	10.2	59.6
	03	225 51.4	. . 10.2	160 48.5	6.4	22 55.0	10.3	59.5
	04	240 51.4	10.7	175 13.9	6.5	22 44.7	10.4	59.5
	05	255 51.4	11.2	189 39.4	6.6	22 34.3	10.6	59.5
	06	270 51.3	N20 11.7	204 05.0	6.8	N22 23.7	10.6	59.4
T	07	285 51.3	12.2	218 30.8	6.9	22 13.1	10.9	59.4
H	08	300 51.2	12.7	232 56.7	7.0	22 02.2	10.9	59.4
U	09	315 51.2	. . 13.2	247 22.7	7.2	21 51.3	11.0	59.3
R	10	330 51.1	13.7	261 48.9	7.4	21 40.3	11.2	59.3
S	11	345 51.1	14.2	276 15.3	7.4	21 29.1	11.3	59.3
D	12	0 51.1	N20 14.7	290 41.7	7.6	N21 17.8	11.4	59.2
A	13	15 51.0	15.2	305 08.3	7.8	21 06.4	11.5	59.2
Y	14	30 51.0	15.7	319 35.1	7.9	20 54.9	11.6	59.2
	15	45 50.9	. . 16.2	334 02.0	8.0	20 43.3	11.8	59.1
	16	60 50.9	16.7	348 29.0	8.1	20 31.5	11.8	59.1
	17	75 50.8	17.2	2 56.1	8.3	20 19.7	11.9	59.1
	18	90 50.8	N20 17.7	17 23.4	8.4	N20 07.8	12.1	59.0
	19	105 50.7	18.2	31 50.8	8.6	19 55.7	12.1	59.0
	20	120 50.7	18.7	46 18.4	8.6	19 43.6	12.2	58.9
	21	135 50.7	. . 19.2	60 46.0	8.8	19 31.4	12.4	58.9
	22	150 50.6	19.7	75 13.8	9.0	19 19.0	12.4	58.9
	23	165 50.6	20.2	89 41.8	9.1	N19 06.6	12.5	58.8
		SD 15.8	*d* 0.5	SD 16.5		16.4		16.1

Lat. °	Twilight Naut. h m	Twilight Civil h m	Sunrise h m	Moonrise 19 h m	Moonrise 20 h m	Moonrise 21 h m	Moonrise 22 h m
N 72	▭	▭	▭	▭	▭	▭	06 17
N 70	▭	▭	▭	▭	▭	▭	07 27
68	////	////	01 17	▭	▭	▭	08 03
66	////	////	02 02	▭	▭	05 57	08 29
64	////	00 13	02 32	▭	▭	06 39	08 48
62	////	01 29	02 54	02 47	05 00	07 08	09 04
60	////	02 03	03 11	03 56	05 37	07 30	09 17
N 58	00 11	02 27	03 26	04 31	06 04	07 48	09 28
56	01 20	02 46	03 39	04 57	06 25	08 02	09 38
54	01 52	03 02	03 49	05 17	06 42	08 15	09 47
52	02 15	03 16	03 59	05 34	06 57	08 26	09 54
50	02 33	03 27	04 08	05 49	07 10	08 36	10 01
45	03 06	03 51	04 26	06 19	07 36	08 57	10 16
N 40	03 31	04 09	04 41	06 42	07 57	09 13	10 28
35	03 50	04 25	04 53	07 01	08 14	09 27	10 38
30	04 06	04 37	05 04	07 18	08 29	09 40	10 47
20	04 30	04 58	05 22	07 46	08 54	10 00	11 02
N 10	04 49	05 16	05 38	08 09	09 16	10 18	11 15
0	05 05	05 31	05 53	08 32	09 36	10 35	11 28
S 10	05 20	05 45	06 08	08 54	09 56	10 51	11 40
20	05 33	06 00	06 23	09 18	10 17	11 09	11 53
30	05 46	06 15	06 41	09 46	10 42	11 29	12 08
35	05 53	06 24	06 51	10 02	10 57	11 41	12 17
40	06 00	06 33	07 03	10 21	11 14	11 54	12 26
45	06 08	06 44	07 17	10 44	11 34	12 10	12 38
S 50	06 17	06 57	07 33	11 14	11 59	12 30	12 51
52	06 21	07 03	07 41	11 28	12 11	12 39	12 58
54	06 25	07 09	07 50	11 45	12 25	12 49	13 05
56	06 30	07 16	08 00	12 05	12 41	13 01	13 13
58	06 34	07 24	08 11	12 30	12 59	13 14	13 21
S 60	06 40	07 33	08 24	13 04	13 23	13 29	13 31

Lat. °	Sunset h m	Twilight Civil h m	Twilight Naut. h m	Moonset 19 h m	Moonset 20 h m	Moonset 21 h m	Moonset 22 h m
N 72	▭	▭	▭	▭	▭	▭	04 36
N 70	▭	▭	▭	▭	▭	▭	03 24
68	22 43	////	////	▭	▭	▭	02 46
66	21 54	////	////	▭	▭	02 59	02 20
64	21 24	////	////	▭	▭	02 15	01 59
62	21 01	22 28	////	01 44	01 48	01 45	01 42
60	20 43	21 53	////	00 34	01 10	01 23	01 27
N 58	20 28	21 28	////	24 43	00 43	01 04	01 15
56	20 16	21 08	22 36	24 21	00 21	00 49	01 05
54	20 05	20 52	22 04	24 04	00 04	00 35	00 55
52	19 55	20 39	21 40	23 49	24 24	00 24	00 47
50	19 46	20 27	21 22	23 36	24 13	00 13	00 39
45	19 28	20 03	20 48	23 08	23 51	24 23	00 23
N 40	19 13	19 44	20 23	22 47	23 33	24 09	00 09
35	19 00	19 29	20 04	22 29	23 18	23 58	24 31
30	18 50	19 16	19 48	22 13	23 05	23 48	24 24
20	18 31	18 55	19 23	21 47	22 43	23 30	24 12
N 10	18 15	18 37	19 04	21 24	22 23	23 15	24 01
0	18 00	18 22	18 48	21 03	22 05	23 01	23 51
S 10	17 45	18 08	18 33	20 41	21 46	22 46	23 41
20	17 30	17 53	18 20	20 18	21 26	22 30	23 30
30	17 12	17 38	18 07	19 51	21 03	22 12	23 18
35	17 02	17 29	18 00	19 35	20 49	22 02	23 10
40	16 50	17 19	17 52	19 16	20 33	21 49	23 02
45	16 36	17 08	17 44	18 54	20 14	21 35	22 52
S 50	16 19	16 56	17 36	18 25	19 50	21 17	22 40
52	16 11	16 50	17 32	18 11	19 38	21 08	22 35
54	16 03	16 43	17 27	17 54	19 25	20 59	22 28
56	15 53	16 36	17 23	17 34	19 10	20 48	22 22
58	15 42	16 28	17 18	17 09	18 51	20 36	22 14
S 60	15 29	16 20	17 13	16 36	18 29	20 21	22 05

Day	SUN Eqn. of Time 00^h	SUN Eqn. of Time 12^h	SUN Mer. Pass.	MOON Mer. Pass. Upper	MOON Mer. Pass. Lower	MOON Age	MOON Phase
d	m s	m s	h m	h m	h m	d	%
19	03 33	03 32	11 56	14 47	02 14	03	11
20	03 30	03 28	11 57	15 50	03 19	04	19
21	03 26	03 24	11 57	16 48	04 20	05	29

UT		ARIES	VENUS −3·9		MARS +1·3		JUPITER −1·9		SATURN +0·8	
		GHA	GHA	Dec	GHA	Dec	GHA	Dec	GHA	Dec
d	h	° ′	° ′	° ′	° ′	° ′	° ′	° ′	° ′	° ′
22	00	239 38.3	145 44.7	N25 04.8	209 16.1	N11 35.8	125 32.6	N22 00.1	228 20.2	N 2 26.2
	01	254 40.8	160 43.9	04.8	224 16.8	36.5	140 34.6	22 00.0	243 22.4	26.3
	02	269 43.3	175 43.1	04.8	239 17.4	37.1	155 36.6	21 59.9	258 24.7	26.4
	03	284 45.7	190 42.2	04.7	254 18.1	37.8	170 38.6	59.9	273 26.9	26.5
	04	299 48.2	205 41.4	04.7	269 18.8	38.5	185 40.6	59.8	288 29.2	26.6
	05	314 50.6	220 40.6	04.7	284 19.5	39.1	200 42.5	59.7	303 31.4	26.7
	06	329 53.1	235 39.8	N25 04.7	299 20.1	N11 39.8	215 44.5	N21 59.7	318 33.6	N 2 26.7
	07	344 55.6	250 38.9	04.7	314 20.8	40.5	230 46.5	59.6	333 35.9	26.8
	08	359 58.0	265 38.1	04.7	329 21.5	41.1	245 48.5	59.5	348 38.1	26.9
FRIDAY	09	15 00.5	280 37.3	04.7	344 22.2	41.8	260 50.5	59.4	3 40.4	27.0
	10	30 03.0	295 36.5	04.6	359 22.8	42.5	275 52.5	59.4	18 42.6	27.1
	11	45 05.4	310 35.6	04.6	14 23.5	43.1	290 54.5	59.3	33 44.9	27.2
	12	60 07.9	325 34.8	N25 04.6	29 24.2	N11 43.8	305 56.5	N21 59.2	48 47.1	N 2 27.3
	13	75 10.4	340 34.0	04.6	44 24.8	44.4	320 58.5	59.2	63 49.3	27.3
	14	90 12.8	355 33.2	04.5	59 25.5	45.1	336 00.5	59.1	78 51.6	27.4
	15	105 15.3	10 32.3	04.5	74 26.2	45.8	351 02.5	59.0	93 53.8	27.5
	16	120 17.8	25 31.5	04.5	89 26.9	46.4	6 04.5	59.0	108 56.1	27.6
	17	135 20.2	40 30.7	04.5	104 27.5	47.1	21 06.5	58.9	123 58.3	27.7
	18	150 22.7	55 29.9	N25 04.4	119 28.2	N11 47.7	36 08.5	N21 58.8	139 00.6	N 2 27.8
	19	165 25.1	70 29.0	04.4	134 28.9	48.4	51 10.5	58.7	154 02.8	27.9
	20	180 27.6	85 28.2	04.4	149 29.6	49.1	66 12.5	58.7	169 05.0	27.9
	21	195 30.1	100 27.4	04.3	164 30.2	49.7	81 14.5	58.6	184 07.3	28.0
	22	210 32.5	115 26.6	04.3	179 30.9	50.4	96 16.5	58.5	199 09.5	28.1
	23	225 35.0	130 25.8	04.3	194 31.6	51.0	111 18.4	58.5	214 11.8	28.2
23	00	240 37.5	145 24.9	N25 04.2	209 32.2	N11 51.7	126 20.4	N21 58.4	229 14.0	N 2 28.3
	01	255 39.9	160 24.1	04.2	224 32.9	52.4	141 22.4	58.3	244 16.3	28.4
	02	270 42.4	175 23.3	04.2	239 33.6	53.0	156 24.4	58.3	259 18.5	28.4
	03	285 44.9	190 22.5	04.1	254 34.3	53.7	171 26.4	58.2	274 20.8	28.5
	04	300 47.3	205 21.6	04.1	269 34.9	54.3	186 28.4	58.1	289 23.0	28.6
	05	315 49.8	220 20.8	04.0	284 35.6	55.0	201 30.4	58.0	304 25.2	28.7
	06	330 52.3	235 20.0	N25 04.0	299 36.3	N11 55.7	216 32.4	N21 58.0	319 27.5	N 2 28.8
	07	345 54.7	250 19.2	03.9	314 37.0	56.3	231 34.4	57.9	334 29.7	28.9
	08	0 57.2	265 18.4	03.9	329 37.6	57.0	246 36.4	57.8	349 32.0	29.0
SATURDAY	09	15 59.6	280 17.5	03.8	344 38.3	57.6	261 38.4	57.8	4 34.2	29.0
	10	31 02.1	295 16.7	03.8	359 39.0	58.3	276 40.4	57.7	19 36.5	29.1
	11	46 04.6	310 15.9	03.7	14 39.6	58.9	291 42.4	57.6	34 38.7	29.2
	12	61 07.0	325 15.1	N25 03.7	29 40.3	N11 59.6	306 44.3	N21 57.5	49 41.0	N 2 29.3
	13	76 09.5	340 14.2	03.6	44 41.0	12 00.3	321 46.3	57.5	64 43.2	29.4
	14	91 12.0	355 13.4	03.6	59 41.7	00.9	336 48.3	57.4	79 45.5	29.5
	15	106 14.4	10 12.6	03.5	74 42.3	01.6	351 50.3	57.3	94 47.7	29.5
	16	121 16.9	25 11.8	03.5	89 43.0	02.2	6 52.3	57.3	109 49.9	29.6
	17	136 19.4	40 11.0	03.4	104 43.7	02.9	21 54.3	57.2	124 52.2	29.7
	18	151 21.8	55 10.1	N25 03.4	119 44.3	N12 03.5	36 56.3	N21 57.1	139 54.4	N 2 29.8
	19	166 24.3	70 09.3	03.3	134 45.0	04.2	51 58.3	57.0	154 56.7	29.9
	20	181 26.7	85 08.5	03.2	149 45.7	04.8	67 00.3	57.0	169 58.9	30.0
	21	196 29.2	100 07.7	03.2	164 46.4	05.5	82 02.3	56.9	185 01.2	30.0
	22	211 31.7	115 06.9	03.1	179 47.0	06.2	97 04.2	56.8	200 03.4	30.1
	23	226 34.1	130 06.0	03.0	194 47.7	06.8	112 06.2	56.8	215 05.7	30.2
24	00	241 36.6	145 05.2	N25 03.0	209 48.4	N12 07.5	127 08.2	N21 56.7	230 07.9	N 2 30.3
	01	256 39.1	160 04.4	02.9	224 49.0	08.1	142 10.2	56.6	245 10.2	30.4
	02	271 41.5	175 03.6	02.8	239 49.7	08.8	157 12.2	56.5	260 12.4	30.5
	03	286 44.0	190 02.8	02.8	254 50.4	09.4	172 14.2	56.5	275 14.6	30.5
	04	301 46.5	205 02.0	02.7	269 51.1	10.1	187 16.2	56.4	290 16.9	30.6
	05	316 48.9	220 01.1	02.6	284 51.7	10.7	202 18.2	56.3	305 19.1	30.7
	06	331 51.4	235 00.3	N25 02.6	299 52.4	N12 11.4	217 20.2	N21 56.3	320 21.4	N 2 30.8
	07	346 53.9	249 59.5	02.5	314 53.1	12.0	232 22.1	56.2	335 23.6	30.9
	08	1 56.3	264 58.7	02.4	329 53.7	12.7	247 24.1	56.1	350 25.9	31.0
SUNDAY	09	16 58.8	279 57.9	02.3	344 54.4	13.3	262 26.1	56.0	5 28.1	31.0
	10	32 01.2	294 57.0	02.2	359 55.1	14.0	277 28.1	56.0	20 30.4	31.1
	11	47 03.7	309 56.2	02.2	14 55.8	14.6	292 30.1	55.9	35 32.6	31.2
	12	62 06.2	324 55.4	N25 02.1	29 56.4	N12 15.3	307 32.1	N21 55.8	50 34.9	N 2 31.3
	13	77 08.6	339 54.6	02.0	44 57.1	15.9	322 34.1	55.7	65 37.1	31.4
	14	92 11.1	354 53.8	01.9	59 57.8	16.6	337 36.1	55.7	80 39.4	31.5
	15	107 13.6	9 53.0	01.8	74 58.4	17.2	352 38.0	55.6	95 41.6	31.5
	16	122 16.0	24 52.2	01.7	89 59.1	17.9	7 40.0	55.5	110 43.9	31.6
	17	137 18.5	39 51.3	01.7	104 59.8	18.5	22 42.0	55.5	125 46.1	31.7
	18	152 21.0	54 50.5	N25 01.6	120 00.5	N12 19.2	37 44.0	N21 55.4	140 48.4	N 2 31.8
	19	167 23.4	69 49.7	01.5	135 01.1	19.8	52 46.0	55.3	155 50.6	31.9
	20	182 25.9	84 48.9	01.4	150 01.8	20.5	67 48.0	55.2	170 52.9	32.0
	21	197 28.4	99 48.1	01.3	165 02.5	21.1	82 50.0	55.2	185 55.1	32.0
	22	212 30.8	114 47.3	01.2	180 03.1	21.8	97 52.0	55.1	200 57.4	32.1
	23	227 33.3	129 46.4	01.1	195 03.8	22.4	112 53.9	55.0	215 59.6	32.2
Mer. Pass.	h m	7 56.2	v −0.8	d 0.1	v 0.7	d 0.7	v 2.0	d 0.1	v 2.2	d 0.1

STARS

Name	SHA	Dec
	° ′	° ′
Acamar	315 11.3	S40 11.9
Achernar	335 19.8	S57 06.0
Acrux	172 58.4	S63 15.0
Adhara	255 05.3	S29 00.6
Aldebaran	290 38.7	N16 33.7
Alioth	166 11.6	N55 49.1
Alkaid	152 50.7	N49 10.9
Alnair	27 31.5	S46 49.7
Alnilam	275 36.9	S 1 11.2
Alphard	217 46.7	S 8 46.5
Alphecca	126 02.4	N26 37.5
Alpheratz	357 33.8	N29 14.0
Altair	61 58.7	N 8 56.2
Ankaa	353 06.3	S42 09.6
Antares	112 14.1	S26 29.5
Arcturus	145 46.6	N19 02.6
Atria	107 06.7	S69 04.4
Avior	234 14.6	S59 35.9
Bellatrix	278 22.0	N 6 22.4
Betelgeuse	270 51.2	N 7 24.7
Canopus	263 52.4	S52 42.7
Capella	280 20.7	N46 01.5
Deneb	49 24.9	N45 22.2
Denebola	182 23.7	N14 25.4
Diphda	348 46.4	S17 50.4
Dubhe	193 39.5	N61 36.7
Elnath	278 00.8	N28 37.8
Eltanin	90 41.2	N51 28.9
Enif	33 37.6	N 9 59.7
Fomalhaut	15 13.3	S29 28.8
Gacrux	171 50.1	S57 16.0
Gienah	175 42.3	S17 41.5
Hadar	148 33.8	S60 30.2
Hamal	327 50.2	N23 35.1
Kaus Aust.	83 30.7	S34 22.2
Kochab	137 18.7	N74 02.8
Markab	13 28.9	N15 20.7
Menkar	314 05.3	N 4 11.6
Menkent	147 55.9	S36 30.2
Miaplacidus	221 38.3	S69 49.8
Mirfak	308 27.1	N49 57.2
Nunki	75 46.1	S26 15.8
Peacock	53 03.7	S56 38.7
Pollux	243 16.2	N27 57.8
Procyon	244 49.9	N 5 09.4
Rasalhague	95 57.2	N12 32.3
Regulus	207 33.3	N11 50.3
Rigel	281 03.1	S 8 10.3
Rigil Kent.	139 38.1	S60 56.8
Sabik	102 01.2	S15 45.5
Schedar	349 30.1	N56 40.7
Shaula	96 08.4	S37 07.3
Sirius	258 25.5	S16 45.2
Spica	158 20.9	S11 18.1
Suhail	222 45.6	S43 32.6
Vega	80 32.1	N38 48.3
Zuben'ubi	136 54.4	S16 09.2

	SHA	Mer. Pass.
	° ′	h m
Venus	264 47.5	14 19
Mars	328 54.8	10 01
Jupiter	245 43.0	15 33
Saturn	348 36.6	8 42

UT d h	SUN GHA	SUN Dec	MOON GHA	v	MOON Dec	d	HP
	° ′	° ′	° ′	′	° ′	′	′
22 (FRIDAY) 00	180 50.5	N20 20.7	104 09.9	9.2	N18 54.1	12.6	58.8
01	195 50.5	21.2	118 38.1	9.3	18 41.5	12.7	58.8
02	210 50.4	21.7	133 06.4	9.5	18 28.8	12.8	58.7
03	225 50.4	. . 22.2	147 34.9	9.5	18 16.0	12.8	58.7
04	240 50.3	22.7	162 03.4	9.7	18 03.2	12.9	58.7
05	255 50.3	23.2	176 32.1	9.9	17 50.3	13.1	58.6
06	270 50.2	N20 23.7	191 01.0	9.9	N17 37.2	13.1	58.6
07	285 50.2	24.2	205 29.9	10.1	17 24.1	13.1	58.6
08	300 50.1	24.7	219 59.0	10.2	17 11.0	13.3	58.5
09	315 50.1	. . 25.2	234 28.2	10.3	16 57.7	13.3	58.5
10	330 50.0	25.6	248 57.5	10.5	16 44.4	13.4	58.4
11	345 50.0	26.1	263 27.0	10.5	16 31.0	13.5	58.4
12	0 49.9	N20 26.6	277 56.5	10.7	N16 17.5	13.5	58.4
13	15 49.9	27.1	292 26.2	10.8	16 04.0	13.6	58.3
14	30 49.8	27.6	306 56.0	10.9	15 50.4	13.6	58.3
15	45 49.8	. . 28.1	321 25.9	11.0	15 36.8	13.8	58.3
16	60 49.7	28.6	335 55.9	11.2	15 23.0	13.8	58.2
17	75 49.7	29.1	350 26.1	11.2	15 09.2	13.8	58.2
18	90 49.6	N20 29.5	4 56.3	11.4	N14 55.4	13.9	58.2
19	105 49.6	30.0	19 26.7	11.4	14 41.5	14.0	58.1
20	120 49.5	30.5	33 57.1	11.6	14 27.5	14.0	58.1
21	135 49.5	. . 31.0	48 27.7	11.7	14 13.5	14.0	58.0
22	150 49.4	31.5	62 58.4	11.7	13 59.5	14.1	58.0
23	165 49.4	32.0	77 29.1	11.9	13 45.4	14.2	58.0
23 (SATURDAY) 00	180 49.3	N20 32.4	92 00.0	12.0	N13 31.2	14.2	57.9
01	195 49.3	32.9	106 31.0	12.1	13 17.0	14.3	57.9
02	210 49.2	33.4	121 02.1	12.2	13 02.7	14.3	57.9
03	225 49.2	. . 33.9	135 33.3	12.2	12 48.4	14.3	57.8
04	240 49.1	34.4	150 04.5	12.4	12 34.1	14.4	57.8
05	255 49.1	34.8	164 35.9	12.5	12 19.7	14.5	57.8
06	270 49.0	N20 35.3	179 07.4	12.5	N12 05.2	14.4	57.7
07	285 49.0	35.8	193 38.9	12.7	11 50.8	14.5	57.7
08	300 48.9	36.3	208 10.6	12.7	11 36.3	14.6	57.7
09	315 48.9	. . 36.7	222 42.3	12.9	11 21.7	14.6	57.6
10	330 48.8	37.2	237 14.2	12.9	11 07.1	14.6	57.6
11	345 48.8	37.7	251 46.1	13.0	10 52.5	14.6	57.6
12	0 48.7	N20 38.2	266 18.1	13.1	N10 37.9	14.7	57.5
13	15 48.7	38.6	280 50.2	13.2	10 23.2	14.7	57.5
14	30 48.6	39.1	295 22.4	13.2	10 08.5	14.7	57.5
15	45 48.5	. . 39.6	309 54.6	13.4	9 53.8	14.8	57.4
16	60 48.5	40.1	324 27.0	13.4	9 39.0	14.8	57.4
17	75 48.4	40.5	338 59.4	13.5	9 24.2	14.8	57.4
18	90 48.4	N20 41.0	353 31.9	13.5	N 9 09.4	14.9	57.3
19	105 48.3	41.5	8 04.4	13.7	8 54.5	14.8	57.3
20	120 48.3	41.9	22 37.1	13.7	8 39.7	14.9	57.3
21	135 48.2	. . 42.4	37 09.8	13.8	8 24.8	14.9	57.2
22	150 48.2	42.9	51 42.6	13.9	8 09.9	14.9	57.2
23	165 48.1	43.3	66 15.5	13.9	7 55.0	15.0	57.2
24 (SUNDAY) 00	180 48.0	N20 43.8	80 48.4	14.0	N 7 40.0	14.9	57.1
01	195 48.0	44.3	95 21.4	14.1	7 25.1	15.0	57.1
02	210 47.9	44.7	109 54.5	14.1	7 10.1	15.0	57.1
03	225 47.9	. . 45.2	124 27.6	14.2	6 55.1	15.0	57.0
04	240 47.8	45.7	139 00.8	14.3	6 40.1	15.0	57.0
05	255 47.8	46.1	153 34.1	14.3	6 25.1	15.0	57.0
06	270 47.7	N20 46.6	168 07.4	14.4	N 6 10.1	15.0	56.9
07	285 47.6	47.1	182 40.8	14.4	5 55.1	15.1	56.9
08	300 47.6	47.5	197 14.2	14.5	5 40.0	15.0	56.9
09	315 47.5	. . 48.0	211 47.7	14.5	5 25.0	15.1	56.8
10	330 47.5	48.4	226 21.2	14.6	5 09.9	15.0	56.8
11	345 47.4	48.9	240 54.8	14.7	4 54.9	15.1	56.8
12	0 47.4	N20 49.4	255 28.5	14.7	N 4 39.8	15.1	56.7
13	15 47.3	49.8	270 02.2	14.8	4 24.7	15.0	56.7
14	30 47.2	50.3	284 36.0	14.8	4 09.7	15.1	56.7
15	45 47.2	. . 50.7	299 09.8	14.8	3 54.6	15.1	56.6
16	60 47.1	51.2	313 43.6	14.9	3 39.5	15.1	56.6
17	75 47.1	51.6	328 17.5	15.0	3 24.4	15.0	56.6
18	90 47.0	N20 52.1	342 51.5	15.0	N 3 09.4	15.1	56.6
19	105 46.9	52.5	357 25.5	15.0	2 54.3	15.1	56.5
20	120 46.9	53.0	11 59.5	15.0	2 39.2	15.0	56.5
21	135 46.8	. . 53.5	26 33.5	15.2	2 24.2	15.1	56.5
22	150 46.8	53.9	41 07.7	15.1	2 09.1	15.0	56.4
23	165 46.7	54.4	55 41.8	15.2	N 1 54.1	15.1	56.4
	SD 15.8	*d* 0.5	SD	15.9		15.7	15.5

Lat.	Twilight Naut.	Twilight Civil	Sunrise	Moonrise 22	Moonrise 23	Moonrise 24	Moonrise 25
°	h m	h m	h m	h m	h m	h m	h m
N 72	▭	▭	▭	06 17	09 43	12 02	14 08
N 70	▭	▭	▭	07 27	10 02	12 08	14 05
68	////	////	00 54	08 03	10 18	12 14	14 02
66	////	////	01 50	08 29	10 30	12 18	14 00
64	////	////	02 22	08 48	10 40	12 22	13 59
62	////	01 15	02 46	09 04	10 49	12 25	13 57
60	////	01 54	03 05	09 17	10 56	12 28	13 56
N 58	////	02 20	03 21	09 28	11 03	12 31	13 55
56	01 07	02 40	03 34	09 38	11 08	12 33	13 54
54	01 43	02 57	03 45	09 47	11 13	12 35	13 53
52	02 08	03 11	03 55	09 54	11 18	12 37	13 53
50	02 27	03 23	04 04	10 01	11 22	12 38	13 52
45	03 02	03 48	04 23	10 16	11 31	12 42	13 50
N 40	03 28	04 07	04 38	10 28	11 38	12 45	13 49
35	03 48	04 23	04 51	10 38	11 45	12 48	13 48
30	04 04	04 36	05 02	10 47	11 50	12 50	13 47
20	04 29	04 58	05 21	11 02	12 00	12 54	13 45
N 10	04 49	05 15	05 38	11 15	12 08	12 57	13 44
0	05 05	05 31	05 53	11 28	12 16	13 00	13 43
S 10	05 20	05 46	06 08	11 40	12 24	13 04	13 42
20	05 34	06 01	06 24	11 53	12 32	13 07	13 40
30	05 48	06 17	06 43	12 08	12 41	13 11	13 39
35	05 55	06 26	06 53	12 17	12 47	13 13	13 38
40	06 03	06 36	07 05	12 26	12 53	13 16	13 37
45	06 11	06 47	07 20	12 38	13 00	13 18	13 36
S 50	06 20	07 00	07 37	12 51	13 08	13 22	13 35
52	06 24	07 06	07 45	12 58	13 12	13 23	13 34
54	06 29	07 13	07 54	13 05	13 16	13 25	13 33
56	06 34	07 21	08 05	13 13	13 21	13 27	13 33
58	06 39	07 29	08 16	13 21	13 26	13 29	13 32
S 60	06 44	07 38	08 30	13 31	13 32	13 32	13 31

Lat.	Sunset	Twilight Civil	Twilight Naut.	Moonset 22	Moonset 23	Moonset 24	Moonset 25
°	h m	h m	h m	h m	h m	h m	h m
N 72	▭	▭	▭	04 36	02 53	02 09	01 36
N 70	▭	▭	▭	03 24	02 31	02 00	01 34
68	23 09	////	////	02 46	02 14	01 52	01 33
66	22 07	////	////	02 20	02 00	01 45	01 32
64	21 33	////	////	01 59	01 48	01 39	01 31
62	21 09	22 44	////	01 42	01 38	01 34	01 30
60	20 50	22 03	////	01 27	01 29	01 30	01 29
N 58	20 34	21 36	////	01 15	01 22	01 26	01 29
56	20 21	21 15	22 50	01 05	01 15	01 22	01 28
54	20 09	20 58	22 13	00 55	01 09	01 19	01 28
52	19 59	20 44	21 47	00 47	01 03	01 16	01 27
50	19 50	20 31	21 28	00 39	00 58	01 14	01 27
45	19 31	20 06	20 52	00 23	00 48	01 08	01 26
N 40	19 16	19 47	20 26	00 09	00 39	01 03	01 25
35	19 03	19 31	20 06	24 31	00 31	00 59	01 24
30	18 51	19 18	19 50	24 24	00 24	00 55	01 24
20	18 32	18 56	19 25	24 12	00 12	00 49	01 23
N 10	18 16	18 38	19 05	24 01	00 01	00 43	01 22
0	18 00	18 22	18 48	23 51	24 37	00 37	01 21
S 10	17 45	18 08	18 33	23 41	24 32	00 32	01 20
20	17 29	17 53	18 20	23 30	24 26	00 26	01 19
30	17 11	17 36	18 06	23 18	24 19	00 19	01 18
35	17 00	17 27	17 58	23 10	24 15	00 15	01 17
40	16 48	17 17	17 51	23 02	24 11	00 11	01 16
45	16 34	17 06	17 42	22 52	24 05	00 05	01 15
S 50	16 16	16 53	17 33	22 40	23 59	25 14	01 14
52	16 08	16 47	17 29	22 35	23 56	25 13	01 13
54	15 59	16 40	17 24	22 28	23 53	25 13	01 13
56	15 48	16 32	17 19	22 22	23 49	25 12	01 12
58	15 37	16 24	17 14	22 14	23 45	25 11	01 11
S 60	15 23	16 15	17 08	22 05	23 41	25 11	01 11

Day	SUN Eqn. of Time 00h	SUN Eqn. of Time 12h	SUN Mer. Pass.	MOON Mer. Pass. Upper	MOON Mer. Pass. Lower	MOON Age	%	Phase
d	m s	m s	h m	h m	h m	d	%	
22	03 22	03 20	11 57	17 40	05 14	06	40	◐
23	03 17	03 15	11 57	18 27	06 04	07	50	
24	03 12	03 10	11 57	19 11	06 49	08	61	

UT		ARIES	VENUS −3·9		MARS +1·3		JUPITER −1·9		SATURN +0·8	
d	h	GHA	GHA	Dec	GHA	Dec	GHA	Dec	GHA	Dec
		° ′	° ′	° ′	° ′	° ′	° ′	° ′	° ′	° ′
25	00	242 35.7	144 45.6	N25 01.0	210 04.5	N12 23.1	127 55.9	N21 54.9	231 01.8	N 2 32.3
	01	257 38.2	159 44.8	00.9	225 05.1	23.7	142 57.9	54.9	246 04.1	32.4
	02	272 40.7	174 44.0	00.8	240 05.8	24.4	157 59.9	54.8	261 06.3	32.4
	03	287 43.1	189 43.2	. . 00.7	255 06.5	. . 25.0	173 01.9	. . 54.7	276 08.6	. . 32.5
	04	302 45.6	204 42.4	00.6	270 07.2	25.7	188 03.9	54.7	291 10.8	32.6
	05	317 48.1	219 41.6	00.5	285 07.8	26.3	203 05.9	54.6	306 13.1	32.7
	06	332 50.5	234 40.8	N25 00.4	300 08.5	N12 27.0	218 07.8	N21 54.5	321 15.3	N 2 32.8
	07	347 53.0	249 39.9	00.3	315 09.2	27.6	233 09.8	54.4	336 17.6	32.9
	08	2 55.5	264 39.1	00.2	330 09.8	28.3	248 11.8	54.4	351 19.8	32.9
M	09	17 57.9	279 38.3	. . 00.1	345 10.5	. . 28.9	263 13.8	. . 54.3	6 22.1	. . 33.0
O	10	33 00.4	294 37.5	25 00.0	0 11.2	29.6	278 15.8	54.2	21 24.3	33.1
N	11	48 02.8	309 36.7	24 59.9	15 11.8	30.2	293 17.8	54.1	36 26.6	33.2
D	12	63 05.3	324 35.9	N24 59.8	30 12.5	N12 30.8	308 19.7	N21 54.1	51 28.8	N 2 33.3
A	13	78 07.8	339 35.1	59.7	45 13.2	31.5	323 21.7	54.0	66 31.1	33.3
Y	14	93 10.2	354 34.3	59.5	60 13.8	32.1	338 23.7	53.9	81 33.3	33.4
	15	108 12.7	9 33.5	. . 59.4	75 14.5	. . 32.8	353 25.7	. . 53.9	96 35.6	. . 33.5
	16	123 15.2	24 32.6	59.3	90 15.2	33.4	8 27.7	53.8	111 37.8	33.6
	17	138 17.6	39 31.8	59.2	105 15.9	34.1	23 29.7	53.7	126 40.1	33.7
	18	153 20.1	54 31.0	N24 59.1	120 16.5	N12 34.7	38 31.6	N21 53.6	141 42.3	N 2 33.8
	19	168 22.6	69 30.2	59.0	135 17.2	35.4	53 33.6	53.6	156 44.6	33.8
	20	183 25.0	84 29.4	58.8	150 17.9	36.0	68 35.6	53.5	171 46.8	33.9
	21	198 27.5	99 28.6	. . 58.7	165 18.5	. . 36.6	83 37.6	. . 53.4	186 49.1	. . 34.0
	22	213 30.0	114 27.8	58.6	180 19.2	37.3	98 39.6	53.3	201 51.3	34.1
	23	228 32.4	129 27.0	58.5	195 19.9	37.9	113 41.6	53.3	216 53.6	34.2
26	00	243 34.9	144 26.2	N24 58.3	210 20.5	N12 38.6	128 43.5	N21 53.2	231 55.8	N 2 34.2
	01	258 37.3	159 25.4	58.2	225 21.2	39.2	143 45.5	53.1	246 58.1	34.3
	02	273 39.8	174 24.6	58.1	240 21.9	39.9	158 47.5	53.0	262 00.3	34.4
	03	288 42.3	189 23.7	. . 58.0	255 22.5	. . 40.5	173 49.5	. . 53.0	277 02.6	. . 34.5
	04	303 44.7	204 22.9	57.8	270 23.2	41.1	188 51.5	52.9	292 04.9	34.6
	05	318 47.2	219 22.1	57.7	285 23.9	41.8	203 53.5	52.8	307 07.1	34.6
	06	333 49.7	234 21.3	N24 57.6	300 24.5	N12 42.4	218 55.4	N21 52.7	322 09.4	N 2 34.7
	07	348 52.1	249 20.5	57.4	315 25.2	43.1	233 57.4	52.7	337 11.6	34.8
T	08	3 54.6	264 19.7	57.3	330 25.9	43.7	248 59.4	52.6	352 13.9	34.9
U	09	18 57.1	279 18.9	. . 57.2	345 26.5	. . 44.3	264 01.4	. . 52.5	7 16.1	. . 35.0
E	10	33 59.5	294 18.1	57.0	0 27.2	45.0	279 03.4	52.4	22 18.4	35.1
S	11	49 02.0	309 17.3	56.9	15 27.9	45.6	294 05.3	52.4	37 20.6	35.1
D	12	64 04.4	324 16.5	N24 56.8	30 28.6	N12 46.3	309 07.3	N21 52.3	52 22.9	N 2 35.2
A	13	79 06.9	339 15.7	56.6	45 29.2	46.9	324 09.3	52.2	67 25.1	35.3
Y	14	94 09.4	354 14.9	56.5	60 29.9	47.5	339 11.3	52.1	82 27.4	35.4
	15	109 11.8	9 14.1	. . 56.3	75 30.6	. . 48.2	354 13.3	. . 52.1	97 29.6	. . 35.5
	16	124 14.3	24 13.3	56.2	90 31.2	48.8	9 15.2	52.0	112 31.9	35.5
	17	139 16.8	39 12.5	56.0	105 31.9	49.5	24 17.2	51.9	127 34.1	35.6
	18	154 19.2	54 11.7	N24 55.9	120 32.6	N12 50.1	39 19.2	N21 51.8	142 36.4	N 2 35.7
	19	169 21.7	69 10.9	55.7	135 33.2	50.7	54 21.2	51.8	157 38.6	35.8
	20	184 24.2	84 10.1	55.6	150 33.9	51.4	69 23.2	51.7	172 40.9	35.9
	21	199 26.6	99 09.3	. . 55.4	165 34.6	. . 52.0	84 25.1	. . 51.6	187 43.1	. . 35.9
	22	214 29.1	114 08.4	55.3	180 35.2	52.7	99 27.1	51.5	202 45.4	36.0
	23	229 31.6	129 07.6	55.1	195 35.9	53.3	114 29.1	51.5	217 47.6	36.1
27	00	244 34.0	144 06.8	N24 55.0	210 36.6	N12 53.9	129 31.1	N21 51.4	232 49.9	N 2 36.2
	01	259 36.5	159 06.0	54.8	225 37.2	54.6	144 33.1	51.3	247 52.2	36.3
	02	274 38.9	174 05.2	54.7	240 37.9	55.2	159 35.0	51.2	262 54.4	36.3
	03	289 41.4	189 04.4	. . 54.5	255 38.6	. . 55.8	174 37.0	. . 51.2	277 56.7	. . 36.4
	04	304 43.9	204 03.6	54.3	270 39.2	56.5	189 39.0	51.1	292 58.9	36.5
	05	319 46.3	219 02.8	54.2	285 39.9	57.1	204 41.0	51.0	308 01.2	36.6
	06	334 48.8	234 02.0	N24 54.0	300 40.6	N12 57.7	219 43.0	N21 50.9	323 03.4	N 2 36.7
W	07	349 51.3	249 01.2	53.9	315 41.2	58.4	234 44.9	50.9	338 05.7	36.7
E	08	4 53.7	264 00.4	53.7	330 41.9	59.0	249 46.9	50.8	353 07.9	36.8
D	09	19 56.2	278 59.6	. . 53.5	345 42.6	12 59.7	264 48.9	. . 50.7	8 10.2	. . 36.9
N	10	34 58.7	293 58.8	53.4	0 43.2	13 00.3	279 50.9	50.6	23 12.4	37.0
E	11	50 01.1	308 58.0	53.2	15 43.9	00.9	294 52.8	50.6	38 14.7	37.1
S	12	65 03.6	323 57.2	N24 53.0	30 44.6	N13 01.6	309 54.8	N21 50.5	53 17.0	N 2 37.1
D	13	80 06.1	338 56.4	52.9	45 45.2	02.2	324 56.8	50.4	68 19.2	37.2
A	14	95 08.5	353 55.6	52.7	60 45.9	02.8	339 58.8	50.3	83 21.5	37.3
Y	15	110 11.0	8 54.8	. . 52.5	75 46.6	. . 03.5	355 00.8	. . 50.3	98 23.7	. . 37.4
	16	125 13.4	23 54.0	52.3	90 47.2	04.1	10 02.7	50.2	113 26.0	37.4
	17	140 15.9	38 53.3	52.2	105 47.9	04.7	25 04.7	50.1	128 28.2	37.5
	18	155 18.4	53 52.5	N24 52.0	120 48.6	N13 05.4	40 06.7	N21 50.0	143 30.5	N 2 37.6
	19	170 20.8	68 51.7	51.8	135 49.2	06.0	55 08.7	50.0	158 32.7	37.7
	20	185 23.3	83 50.9	51.6	150 49.9	06.6	70 10.6	49.9	173 35.0	37.8
	21	200 25.8	98 50.1	. . 51.5	165 50.6	. . 07.3	85 12.6	. . 49.8	188 37.2	. . 37.8
	22	215 28.2	113 49.3	51.3	180 51.2	07.9	100 14.6	49.7	203 39.5	37.9
	23	230 30.7	128 48.5	51.1	195 51.9	08.5	115 16.6	49.7	218 41.8	38.0
Mer. Pass.		h m 7 44.4	*v* −0.8	*d* 0.1	*v* 0.7	*d* 0.6	*v* 2.0	*d* 0.1	*v* 2.3	*d* 0.1

STARS

Name	SHA	Dec
	° ′	° ′
Acamar	315 11.3	S40 11.8
Achernar	335 19.8	S57 06.0
Acrux	172 58.4	S63 15.1
Adhara	255 05.3	S29 00.6
Aldebaran	290 38.7	N16 33.7
Alioth	166 11.6	N55 49.1
Alkaid	152 50.7	N49 11.0
Alnair	27 31.5	S46 49.7
Alnilam	275 36.9	S 1 11.2
Alphard	217 46.7	S 8 46.5
Alphecca	126 02.4	N26 37.5
Alpheratz	357 33.8	N29 14.0
Altair	61 58.6	N 8 56.2
Ankaa	353 06.3	S42 09.6
Antares	112 14.1	S26 29.5
Arcturus	145 46.6	N19 02.7
Atria	107 06.7	S69 04.5
Avior	234 14.6	S59 35.9
Bellatrix	278 22.0	N 6 22.4
Betelgeuse	270 51.2	N 7 24.7
Canopus	263 52.4	S52 42.7
Capella	280 20.7	N46 01.5
Deneb	49 24.8	N45 22.2
Denebola	182 23.7	N14 25.5
Diphda	348 46.4	S17 50.4
Dubhe	193 39.5	N61 36.7
Elnath	278 00.8	N28 37.8
Eltanin	90 41.2	N51 28.9
Enif	33 37.6	N 9 59.7
Fomalhaut	15 13.3	S29 28.8
Gacrux	171 50.1	S57 16.0
Gienah	175 42.3	S17 41.5
Hadar	148 33.8	S60 30.2
Hamal	327 50.2	N23 35.1
Kaus Aust.	83 30.7	S34 22.3
Kochab	137 18.7	N74 02.8
Markab	13 28.8	N15 20.7
Menkar	314 05.3	N 4 11.6
Menkent	147 55.9	S36 30.2
Miaplacidus	221 38.4	S69 49.8
Mirfak	308 27.1	N49 57.2
Nunki	75 46.1	S26 15.8
Peacock	53 03.7	S56 38.7
Pollux	243 16.2	N27 57.8
Procyon	244 49.9	N 5 09.4
Rasalhague	95 57.2	N12 32.4
Regulus	207 33.3	N11 50.3
Rigel	281 03.1	S 8 10.3
Rigil Kent.	139 38.1	S60 56.8
Sabik	102 01.1	S15 45.5
Schedar	349 30.1	N56 40.7
Shaula	96 08.4	S37 07.3
Sirius	258 25.5	S16 45.2
Spica	158 20.9	S11 18.1
Suhail	222 45.6	S43 32.6
Vega	80 32.1	N38 48.3
Zuben'ubi	136 54.4	S16 09.2

	SHA	Mer. Pass.
	° ′	h m
Venus	260 51.3	14 23
Mars	326 45.7	9 58
Jupiter	245 08.7	15 23
Saturn	348 21.0	8 31

Day	UT h	SUN GHA ° ′	SUN Dec ° ′	MOON GHA ° ′	v ′	MOON Dec ° ′	d ′	HP ′
25 MONDAY	00	180 46.6	N20 54.8	70 16.0	15.2	N 1 39.0	15.0	56.4
	01	195 46.6	55.3	84 50.2	15.2	1 24.0	15.0	56.3
	02	210 46.5	55.7	99 24.4	15.3	1 09.0	15.0	56.3
	03	225 46.4	. . 56.2	113 58.7	15.3	0 54.0	15.0	56.3
	04	240 46.4	56.6	128 33.0	15.4	0 39.0	15.0	56.3
	05	255 46.3	57.1	143 07.4	15.4	0 24.0	15.0	56.2
	06	270 46.3	N20 57.5	157 41.8	15.3	N 0 09.0	14.9	56.2
	07	285 46.2	58.0	172 16.1	15.5	S 0 05.9	15.0	56.2
	08	300 46.1	58.4	186 50.6	15.4	0 20.9	14.9	56.1
	09	315 46.1	. . 58.8	201 25.0	15.5	0 35.8	14.9	56.1
	10	330 46.0	59.3	215 59.5	15.5	0 50.7	14.9	56.1
	11	345 45.9	20 59.7	230 34.0	15.5	1 05.6	14.9	56.1
	12	0 45.9	N21 00.2	245 08.5	15.5	S 1 20.5	14.9	56.0
	13	15 45.8	00.6	259 43.0	15.6	1 35.4	14.8	56.0
	14	30 45.7	01.1	274 17.6	15.6	1 50.2	14.8	56.0
	15	45 45.7	. . 01.5	288 52.2	15.5	2 05.0	14.8	56.0
	16	60 45.6	01.9	303 26.7	15.6	2 19.8	14.8	55.9
	17	75 45.6	02.4	318 01.3	15.7	2 34.6	14.8	55.9
	18	90 45.5	N21 02.8	332 36.0	15.6	S 2 49.4	14.7	55.9
	19	105 45.4	03.3	347 10.6	15.6	3 04.1	14.7	55.9
	20	120 45.4	03.7	1 45.2	15.7	3 18.8	14.7	55.8
	21	135 45.3	. . 04.1	16 19.9	15.6	3 33.5	14.6	55.8
	22	150 45.2	04.6	30 54.5	15.7	3 48.1	14.7	55.8
	23	165 45.2	05.0	45 29.2	15.6	4 02.8	14.6	55.7
26 TUESDAY	00	180 45.1	N21 05.5	60 03.8	15.7	S 4 17.4	14.5	55.7
	01	195 45.0	05.9	74 38.5	15.7	4 31.9	14.6	55.7
	02	210 45.0	06.3	89 13.2	15.7	4 46.5	14.5	55.7
	03	225 44.9	. . 06.8	103 47.9	15.7	5 01.0	14.5	55.7
	04	240 44.8	07.2	118 22.6	15.6	5 15.5	14.4	55.6
	05	255 44.8	07.6	132 57.2	15.7	5 29.9	14.4	55.6
	06	270 44.7	N21 08.1	147 31.9	15.7	S 5 44.3	14.4	55.6
	07	285 44.6	08.5	162 06.6	15.7	5 58.7	14.3	55.6
	08	300 44.6	08.9	176 41.3	15.6	6 13.0	14.4	55.5
	09	315 44.5	. . 09.4	191 15.9	15.7	6 27.4	14.2	55.5
	10	330 44.4	09.8	205 50.6	15.7	6 41.6	14.3	55.5
	11	345 44.3	10.2	220 25.3	15.6	6 55.9	14.2	55.5
	12	0 44.3	N21 10.6	234 59.9	15.7	S 7 10.1	14.1	55.4
	13	15 44.2	11.1	249 34.6	15.6	7 24.2	14.1	55.4
	14	30 44.1	11.5	264 09.2	15.6	7 38.3	14.1	55.4
	15	45 44.1	. . 11.9	278 43.8	15.6	7 52.4	14.1	55.4
	16	60 44.0	12.4	293 18.4	15.6	8 06.5	14.0	55.4
	17	75 43.9	12.8	307 53.0	15.6	8 20.5	13.9	55.3
	18	90 43.9	N21 13.2	322 27.6	15.6	S 8 34.4	13.9	55.3
	19	105 43.8	13.6	337 02.2	15.5	8 48.3	13.9	55.3
	20	120 43.7	14.0	351 36.7	15.6	9 02.2	13.8	55.3
	21	135 43.7	. . 14.5	6 11.3	15.5	9 16.0	13.8	55.2
	22	150 43.6	14.9	20 45.8	15.5	9 29.8	13.7	55.2
	23	165 43.5	15.3	35 20.3	15.5	9 43.5	13.7	55.2
27 WEDNESDAY	00	180 43.4	N21 15.7	49 54.8	15.4	S 9 57.2	13.6	55.2
	01	195 43.4	16.2	64 29.2	15.5	10 10.8	13.6	55.2
	02	210 43.3	16.6	79 03.7	15.4	10 24.4	13.6	55.1
	03	225 43.2	. . 17.0	93 38.1	15.4	10 38.0	13.4	55.1
	04	240 43.2	17.4	108 12.5	15.4	10 51.4	13.5	55.1
	05	255 43.1	17.8	122 46.9	15.3	11 04.9	13.4	55.1
	06	270 43.0	N21 18.2	137 21.2	15.3	S11 18.3	13.3	55.1
	07	285 42.9	18.7	151 55.5	15.3	11 31.6	13.3	55.0
	08	300 42.9	19.1	166 29.8	15.3	11 44.9	13.2	55.0
	09	315 42.8	. . 19.5	181 04.1	15.2	11 58.1	13.2	55.0
	10	330 42.7	19.9	195 38.3	15.2	12 11.3	13.1	55.0
	11	345 42.6	20.3	210 12.5	15.2	12 24.4	13.0	55.0
	12	0 42.6	N21 20.7	224 46.7	15.1	S12 37.4	13.0	55.0
	13	15 42.5	21.2	239 20.8	15.1	12 50.4	13.0	54.9
	14	30 42.4	21.6	253 54.9	15.1	13 03.4	12.8	54.9
	15	45 42.3	. . 22.0	268 29.0	15.0	13 16.2	12.9	54.9
	16	60 42.3	22.4	283 03.0	15.0	13 29.1	12.7	54.9
	17	75 42.2	22.8	297 37.0	15.0	13 41.8	12.7	54.9
	18	90 42.1	N21 23.2	312 11.0	14.9	S13 54.5	12.7	54.8
	19	105 42.0	23.6	326 44.9	14.9	14 07.2	12.5	54.8
	20	120 42.0	24.0	341 18.8	14.9	14 19.7	12.5	54.8
	21	135 41.9	. . 24.4	355 52.7	14.8	14 32.2	12.5	54.8
	22	150 41.8	24.8	10 26.5	14.7	14 44.7	12.4	54.8
	23	165 41.7	25.2	25 00.2	14.8	S14 57.1	12.3	54.8
		SD 15.8	*d* 0.4	SD	15.3		15.1	15.0

Lat. °	Twilight Naut. h m	Twilight Civil h m	Sunrise h m	Moonrise 25 h m	Moonrise 26 h m	Moonrise 27 h m	Moonrise 28 h m
N 72	▭	▭	▭	14 08	16 13	18 35	■
N 70	▭	▭	▭	14 05	16 00	18 05	20 54
68	////	////	00 17	14 02	15 50	17 43	19 53
66	////	////	01 38	14 00	15 41	17 25	19 18
64	////	////	02 14	13 59	15 34	17 11	18 54
62	////	00 58	02 39	13 57	15 28	17 00	18 35
60	////	01 44	02 59	13 56	15 23	16 50	18 19
N 58	////	02 13	03 16	13 55	15 18	16 41	18 06
56	00 53	02 35	03 29	13 54	15 14	16 34	17 54
54	01 35	02 52	03 41	13 53	15 10	16 27	17 44
52	02 02	03 07	03 52	13 53	15 07	16 21	17 36
50	02 22	03 19	04 01	13 52	15 04	16 16	17 28
45	02 59	03 45	04 21	13 50	14 57	16 04	17 11
N 40	03 25	04 05	04 36	13 49	14 52	15 55	16 57
35	03 46	04 21	04 50	13 48	14 47	15 46	16 46
30	04 02	04 34	05 01	13 47	14 43	15 39	16 36
20	04 28	04 57	05 21	13 45	14 36	15 27	16 19
N 10	04 49	05 15	05 38	13 44	14 30	15 17	16 04
0	05 05	05 31	05 53	13 43	14 25	15 07	15 50
S 10	05 21	05 47	06 09	13 42	14 19	14 57	15 37
20	05 35	06 02	06 26	13 40	14 13	14 46	15 22
30	05 49	06 19	06 44	13 39	14 06	14 35	15 05
35	05 57	06 28	06 55	13 38	14 02	14 28	14 56
40	06 05	06 38	07 08	13 37	13 58	14 20	14 45
45	06 13	06 50	07 23	13 36	13 53	14 11	14 32
S 50	06 23	07 04	07 41	13 35	13 47	14 01	14 17
52	06 28	07 10	07 49	13 34	13 44	13 56	14 10
54	06 32	07 17	07 59	13 33	13 41	13 51	14 02
56	06 37	07 25	08 09	13 33	13 38	13 45	13 53
58	06 43	07 33	08 22	13 32	13 35	13 38	13 43
S 60	06 49	07 43	08 36	13 31	13 31	13 31	13 31

Lat. °	Sunset h m	Twilight Civil h m	Twilight Naut. h m	Moonset 25 h m	Moonset 26 h m	Moonset 27 h m	Moonset 28 h m
N 72	▭	▭	▭	01 36	01 03	{00 27 / 23 35}	■
N 70	▭	▭	▭	01 34	01 10	00 43	{00 07 / 22 50}
68	▭	▭	▭	01 33	01 15	00 55	{00 31 / 23 53}
66	22 20	////	////	01 32	01 19	01 06	00 50
64	21 43	////	////	01 31	01 23	01 15	01 05
62	21 16	23 01	////	01 30	01 26	01 22	01 18
60	20 56	22 13	////	01 29	01 29	01 29	01 29
N 58	20 40	21 43	////	01 29	01 31	01 34	01 38
56	20 26	21 21	23 06	01 28	01 34	01 40	01 47
54	20 14	21 03	22 22	01 28	01 36	01 44	01 54
52	20 03	20 48	21 54	01 27	01 38	01 49	02 01
50	19 54	20 36	21 34	01 27	01 39	01 52	02 07
45	19 34	20 10	20 56	01 26	01 43	02 01	02 20
N 40	19 18	19 50	20 30	01 25	01 46	02 08	02 31
35	19 05	19 34	20 09	01 24	01 49	02 14	02 41
30	18 53	19 20	19 52	01 24	01 51	02 19	02 49
20	18 33	18 58	19 26	01 23	01 56	02 29	03 03
N 10	18 16	18 39	19 06	01 22	01 59	02 37	03 16
0	18 01	18 23	18 49	01 21	02 03	02 45	03 27
S 10	17 45	18 07	18 33	01 20	02 06	02 52	03 39
20	17 28	17 52	18 19	01 19	02 10	03 01	03 52
30	17 09	17 35	18 05	01 18	02 14	03 10	04 07
35	16 59	17 26	17 57	01 17	02 17	03 16	04 15
40	16 46	17 16	17 49	01 16	02 19	03 22	04 25
45	16 31	17 04	17 40	01 15	02 23	03 29	04 36
S 50	16 13	16 50	17 31	01 14	02 27	03 38	04 50
52	16 05	16 44	17 26	01 13	02 28	03 42	04 57
54	15 55	16 37	17 21	01 13	02 30	03 47	05 04
56	15 44	16 29	17 16	01 12	02 32	03 52	05 12
58	15 32	16 20	17 11	01 11	02 35	03 58	05 21
S 60	15 18	16 11	17 05	01 11	02 38	04 04	05 32

Day	SUN Eqn. of Time 00^h	SUN Eqn. of Time 12^h	SUN Mer. Pass.	MOON Mer. Pass. Upper	MOON Mer. Pass. Lower	MOON Age	MOON Phase
d	m s	m s	h m	h m	h m	d %	
25	03 07	03 04	11 57	19 53	07 32	09 71	
26	03 01	02 57	11 57	20 35	08 14	10 79	
27	02 54	02 50	11 57	21 17	08 56	11 87	

UT (d h)	ARIES GHA ° ′	VENUS −4·0 GHA ° ′	VENUS Dec ° ′	MARS +1·3 GHA ° ′	MARS Dec ° ′	JUPITER −1·9 GHA ° ′	JUPITER Dec ° ′	SATURN +0·8 GHA ° ′	SATURN Dec ° ′
28 00 (Thursday)	245 33.2	143 47.7	N24 50.9	210 52.5	N13 09.2	130 18.5	N21 49.6	233 44.0	N 2 38.1
01	260 35.6	158 46.9	50.7	225 53.2	09.8	145 20.5	49.5	248 46.3	38.2
02	275 38.1	173 46.1	50.5	240 53.9	10.4	160 22.5	49.4	263 48.5	38.2
03	290 40.5	188 45.3	. . 50.3	255 54.5	. . 11.0	175 24.5	. . 49.4	278 50.8	. . 38.3
04	305 43.0	203 44.5	50.2	270 55.2	11.7	190 26.4	49.3	293 53.0	38.4
05	320 45.5	218 43.7	50.0	285 55.9	12.3	205 28.4	49.2	308 55.3	38.5
06	335 47.9	233 42.9	N24 49.8	300 56.5	N13 12.9	220 30.4	N21 49.1	323 57.6	N 2 38.6
07	350 50.4	248 42.1	49.6	315 57.2	13.6	235 32.4	49.1	338 59.8	38.6
08	5 52.9	263 41.3	49.4	330 57.9	14.2	250 34.4	49.0	354 02.1	38.7
09	20 55.3	278 40.5	. . 49.2	345 58.5	. . 14.8	265 36.3	. . 48.9	9 04.3	. . 38.8
10	35 57.8	293 39.7	49.0	0 59.2	15.5	280 38.3	48.8	24 06.6	38.9
11	51 00.3	308 39.0	48.8	15 59.9	16.1	295 40.3	48.7	39 08.8	38.9
12	66 02.7	323 38.2	N24 48.6	31 00.5	N13 16.7	310 42.2	N21 48.7	54 11.1	N 2 39.0
13	81 05.2	338 37.4	48.4	46 01.2	17.3	325 44.2	48.6	69 13.4	39.1
14	96 07.7	353 36.6	48.2	61 01.9	18.0	340 46.2	48.5	84 15.6	39.2
15	111 10.1	8 35.8	. . 48.0	76 02.5	. . 18.6	355 48.2	. . 48.4	99 17.9	. . 39.3
16	126 12.6	23 35.0	47.8	91 03.2	19.2	10 50.1	48.4	114 20.1	39.3
17	141 15.0	38 34.2	47.6	106 03.9	19.8	25 52.1	48.3	129 22.4	39.4
18	156 17.5	53 33.4	N24 47.4	121 04.5	N13 20.5	40 54.1	N21 48.2	144 24.6	N 2 39.5
19	171 20.0	68 32.6	47.2	136 05.2	21.1	55 56.1	48.1	159 26.9	39.6
20	186 22.4	83 31.8	47.0	151 05.8	21.7	70 58.0	48.1	174 29.2	39.6
21	201 24.9	98 31.1	. . 46.8	166 06.5	. . 22.4	86 00.0	. . 48.0	189 31.4	. . 39.7
22	216 27.4	113 30.3	46.6	181 07.2	23.0	101 02.0	47.9	204 33.7	39.8
23	231 29.8	128 29.5	46.3	196 07.8	23.6	116 04.0	47.8	219 35.9	39.9
29 00 (Friday)	246 32.3	143 28.7	N24 46.1	211 08.5	N13 24.2	131 05.9	N21 47.7	234 38.2	N 2 40.0
01	261 34.8	158 27.9	45.9	226 09.2	24.9	146 07.9	47.7	249 40.4	40.0
02	276 37.2	173 27.1	45.7	241 09.8	25.5	161 09.9	47.6	264 42.7	40.1
03	291 39.7	188 26.3	. . 45.5	256 10.5	. . 26.1	176 11.9	. . 47.5	279 45.0	. . 40.2
04	306 42.2	203 25.5	45.3	271 11.2	26.7	191 13.8	47.4	294 47.2	40.3
05	321 44.6	218 24.8	45.1	286 11.8	27.4	206 15.8	47.4	309 49.5	40.3
06	336 47.1	233 24.0	N24 44.8	301 12.5	N13 28.0	221 17.8	N21 47.3	324 51.7	N 2 40.4
07	351 49.5	248 23.2	44.6	316 13.1	28.6	236 19.7	47.2	339 54.0	40.5
08	6 52.0	263 22.4	44.4	331 13.8	29.2	251 21.7	47.1	354 56.3	40.6
09	21 54.5	278 21.6	. . 44.2	346 14.5	. . 29.8	266 23.7	. . 47.0	9 58.5	. . 40.7
10	36 56.9	293 20.8	43.9	1 15.1	30.5	281 25.7	47.0	25 00.8	40.7
11	51 59.4	308 20.0	43.7	16 15.8	31.1	296 27.6	46.9	40 03.0	40.8
12	67 01.9	323 19.3	N24 43.5	31 16.5	N13 31.7	311 29.6	N21 46.8	55 05.3	N 2 40.9
13	82 04.3	338 18.5	43.3	46 17.1	32.3	326 31.6	46.7	70 07.6	41.0
14	97 06.8	353 17.7	43.0	61 17.8	33.0	341 33.5	46.7	85 09.8	41.0
15	112 09.3	8 16.9	. . 42.8	76 18.5	. . 33.6	356 35.5	. . 46.6	100 12.1	. . 41.1
16	127 11.7	23 16.1	42.6	91 19.1	34.2	11 37.5	46.5	115 14.3	41.2
17	142 14.2	38 15.3	42.3	106 19.8	34.8	26 39.5	46.4	130 16.6	41.3
18	157 16.6	53 14.6	N24 42.1	121 20.4	N13 35.4	41 41.4	N21 46.3	145 18.9	N 2 41.3
19	172 19.1	68 13.8	41.9	136 21.1	36.1	56 43.4	46.3	160 21.1	41.4
20	187 21.6	83 13.0	41.6	151 21.8	36.7	71 45.4	46.2	175 23.4	41.5
21	202 24.0	98 12.2	. . 41.4	166 22.4	. . 37.3	86 47.3	. . 46.1	190 25.6	. . 41.6
22	217 26.5	113 11.4	41.2	181 23.1	37.9	101 49.3	46.0	205 27.9	41.7
23	232 29.0	128 10.7	40.9	196 23.8	38.6	116 51.3	46.0	220 30.2	41.7
30 00 (Saturday)	247 31.4	143 09.9	N24 40.7	211 24.4	N13 39.2	131 53.2	N21 45.9	235 32.4	N 2 41.8
01	262 33.9	158 09.1	40.4	226 25.1	39.8	146 55.2	45.8	250 34.7	41.9
02	277 36.4	173 08.3	40.2	241 25.7	40.4	161 57.2	45.7	265 36.9	42.0
03	292 38.8	188 07.5	. . 39.9	256 26.4	. . 41.0	176 59.2	. . 45.6	280 39.2	. . 42.0
04	307 41.3	203 06.8	39.7	271 27.1	41.6	192 01.1	45.6	295 41.5	42.1
05	322 43.8	218 06.0	39.5	286 27.7	42.3	207 03.1	45.5	310 43.7	42.2
06	337 46.2	233 05.2	N24 39.2	301 28.4	N13 42.9	222 05.1	N21 45.4	325 46.0	N 2 42.3
07	352 48.7	248 04.4	39.0	316 29.1	43.5	237 07.0	45.3	340 48.3	42.3
08	7 51.1	263 03.7	38.7	331 29.7	44.1	252 09.0	45.2	355 50.5	42.4
09	22 53.6	278 02.9	. . 38.5	346 30.4	. . 44.7	267 11.0	. . 45.2	10 52.8	. . 42.5
10	37 56.1	293 02.1	38.2	1 31.0	45.4	282 12.9	45.1	25 55.0	42.6
11	52 58.5	308 01.3	37.9	16 31.7	46.0	297 14.9	45.0	40 57.3	42.6
12	68 01.0	323 00.6	N24 37.7	31 32.4	N13 46.6	312 16.9	N21 44.9	55 59.6	N 2 42.7
13	83 03.5	337 59.8	37.4	46 33.0	47.2	327 18.8	44.9	71 01.8	42.8
14	98 05.9	352 59.0	37.2	61 33.7	47.8	342 20.8	44.8	86 04.1	42.9
15	113 08.4	7 58.2	. . 36.9	76 34.3	. . 48.4	357 22.8	. . 44.7	101 06.4	. . 42.9
16	128 10.9	22 57.5	36.7	91 35.0	49.1	12 24.7	44.6	116 08.6	43.0
17	143 13.3	37 56.7	36.4	106 35.7	49.7	27 26.7	44.5	131 10.9	43.1
18	158 15.8	52 55.9	N24 36.1	121 36.3	N13 50.3	42 28.7	N21 44.5	146 13.1	N 2 43.2
19	173 18.3	67 55.1	35.9	136 37.0	50.9	57 30.6	44.4	161 15.4	43.2
20	188 20.7	82 54.4	35.6	151 37.6	51.5	72 32.6	44.3	176 17.7	43.3
21	203 23.2	97 53.6	. . 35.3	166 38.3	. . 52.1	87 34.6	. . 44.2	191 19.9	. . 43.4
22	218 25.6	112 52.8	35.1	181 39.0	52.7	102 36.5	44.1	206 22.2	43.5
23	233 28.1	127 52.1	34.8	196 39.6	53.4	117 38.5	44.1	221 24.5	43.5
Mer. Pass. (h m)	7 32.6	v −0.8	d 0.2	v 0.7	d 0.6	v 2.0	d 0.1	v 2.3	d 0.1

STARS

Name	SHA ° ′	Dec ° ′
Acamar	315 11.3	S40 11.8
Achernar	335 19.8	S57 05.9
Acrux	172 58.4	S63 15.1
Adhara	255 05.3	S29 00.6
Aldebaran	290 38.7	N16 33.7
Alioth	166 11.6	N55 49.1
Alkaid	152 50.7	N49 11.0
Alnair	27 31.4	S46 49.7
Alnilam	275 36.9	S 1 11.1
Alphard	217 46.7	S 8 46.5
Alphecca	126 02.4	N26 37.5
Alpheratz	357 33.7	N29 14.0
Altair	61 58.6	N 8 56.2
Ankaa	353 06.2	S42 09.5
Antares	112 14.1	S26 29.5
Arcturus	145 46.6	N19 02.7
Atria	107 06.7	S69 04.5
Avior	234 14.7	S59 35.9
Bellatrix	278 22.0	N 6 22.4
Betelgeuse	270 51.2	N 7 24.7
Canopus	263 52.4	S52 42.7
Capella	280 20.7	N46 01.5
Deneb	49 24.8	N45 22.2
Denebola	182 23.7	N14 25.5
Diphda	348 46.3	S17 50.4
Dubhe	193 39.6	N61 36.7
Elnath	278 00.8	N28 37.8
Eltanin	90 41.1	N51 29.0
Enif	33 37.6	N 9 59.7
Fomalhaut	15 13.3	S29 28.8
Gacrux	171 50.1	S57 16.0
Gienah	175 42.3	S17 41.5
Hadar	148 33.9	S60 30.2
Hamal	327 50.2	N23 35.1
Kaus Aust.	83 30.6	S34 22.3
Kochab	137 18.7	N74 02.9
Markab	13 28.8	N15 20.7
Menkar	314 05.3	N 4 11.6
Menkent	147 55.9	S36 30.2
Miaplacidus	221 38.4	S69 49.8
Mirfak	308 27.1	N49 57.2
Nunki	75 46.0	S26 15.8
Peacock	53 03.6	S56 38.7
Pollux	243 16.2	N27 57.8
Procyon	244 49.9	N 5 09.4
Rasalhague	95 57.2	N12 32.4
Regulus	207 33.3	N11 50.3
Rigel	281 03.1	S 8 10.3
Rigil Kent.	139 38.1	S60 56.8
Sabik	102 01.1	S15 45.5
Schedar	349 30.1	N56 40.7
Shaula	96 08.4	S37 07.3
Sirius	258 25.5	S16 45.2
Spica	158 20.9	S11 18.1
Suhail	222 45.7	S43 32.6
Vega	80 32.1	N38 48.3
Zuben'ubi	136 54.4	S16 09.2

	SHA ° ′	Mer. Pass. h m
Venus	256 56.4	14 27
Mars	324 36.2	9 55
Jupiter	244 33.6	15 14
Saturn	348 05.9	8 20

UT	SUN GHA	SUN Dec	MOON GHA	v	MOON Dec	d	HP
d h	° ′	° ′	° ′	′	° ′	′	′
28 00	180 41.7	N21 25.6	39 34.0	14.7	S15 09.4	12.2	54.7
01	195 41.6	26.1	54 07.7	14.6	15 21.6	12.2	54.7
02	210 41.5	26.5	68 41.3	14.6	15 33.8	12.1	54.7
03	225 41.4	. . 26.9	83 14.9	14.6	15 45.9	12.0	54.7
04	240 41.4	27.3	97 48.5	14.5	15 57.9	12.0	54.7
05	255 41.3	27.7	112 22.0	14.5	16 09.9	11.9	54.7
06	270 41.2	N21 28.1	126 55.5	14.4	S16 21.8	11.8	54.7
T 07	285 41.1	28.5	141 28.9	14.4	16 33.6	11.8	54.6
H 08	300 41.1	28.9	156 02.3	14.3	16 45.4	11.7	54.6
U 09	315 41.0	. . 29.3	170 35.6	14.3	16 57.1	11.6	54.6
R 10	330 40.9	29.7	185 08.9	14.3	17 08.7	11.5	54.6
S 11	345 40.8	30.1	199 42.2	14.2	17 20.2	11.4	54.6
D 12	0 40.7	N21 30.5	214 15.4	14.1	S17 31.6	11.4	54.6
A 13	15 40.7	30.9	228 48.5	14.1	17 43.0	11.3	54.6
Y 14	30 40.6	31.3	243 21.6	14.1	17 54.3	11.2	54.5
15	45 40.5	. . 31.7	257 54.7	14.0	18 05.5	11.2	54.5
16	60 40.4	32.1	272 27.7	13.9	18 16.7	11.0	54.5
17	75 40.3	32.4	287 00.6	13.9	18 27.7	11.0	54.5
18	90 40.3	N21 32.8	301 33.5	13.8	S18 38.7	10.9	54.5
19	105 40.2	33.2	316 06.3	13.8	18 49.6	10.8	54.5
20	120 40.1	33.6	330 39.1	13.8	19 00.4	10.7	54.5
21	135 40.0	. . 34.0	345 11.9	13.7	19 11.1	10.7	54.4
22	150 39.9	34.4	359 44.6	13.6	19 21.8	10.5	54.4
23	165 39.9	34.8	14 17.2	13.6	19 32.3	10.5	54.4
29 00	180 39.8	N21 35.2	28 49.8	13.5	S19 42.8	10.4	54.4
01	195 39.7	35.6	43 22.3	13.5	19 53.2	10.3	54.4
02	210 39.6	36.0	57 54.8	13.4	20 03.5	10.2	54.4
03	225 39.5	. . 36.4	72 27.2	13.3	20 13.7	10.1	54.4
04	240 39.5	36.7	86 59.5	13.3	20 23.8	10.0	54.4
05	255 39.4	37.1	101 31.8	13.3	20 33.8	10.0	54.4
06	270 39.3	N21 37.5	116 04.1	13.2	S20 43.8	9.8	54.3
07	285 39.2	37.9	130 36.3	13.1	20 53.6	9.8	54.3
08	300 39.1	38.3	145 08.4	13.1	21 03.4	9.6	54.3
F 09	315 39.1	. . 38.7	159 40.5	13.0	21 13.0	9.6	54.3
R 10	330 39.0	39.1	174 12.5	13.0	21 22.6	9.5	54.3
I 11	345 38.9	39.4	188 44.5	12.9	21 32.1	9.4	54.3
D 12	0 38.8	N21 39.8	203 16.4	12.9	S21 41.5	9.2	54.3
A 13	15 38.7	40.2	217 48.3	12.8	21 50.7	9.2	54.3
Y 14	30 38.6	40.6	232 20.1	12.7	21 59.9	9.1	54.3
15	45 38.6	. . 41.0	246 51.8	12.7	22 09.0	9.0	54.3
16	60 38.5	41.3	261 23.5	12.6	22 18.0	8.9	54.2
17	75 38.4	41.7	275 55.1	12.6	22 26.9	8.8	54.2
18	90 38.3	N21 42.1	290 26.7	12.5	S22 35.7	8.6	54.2
19	105 38.2	42.5	304 58.2	12.5	22 44.3	8.6	54.2
20	120 38.1	42.9	319 29.7	12.4	22 52.9	8.5	54.2
21	135 38.1	. . 43.2	334 01.1	12.3	23 01.4	8.4	54.2
22	150 38.0	43.6	348 32.4	12.3	23 09.8	8.2	54.2
23	165 37.9	44.0	3 03.7	12.3	23 18.0	8.2	54.2
30 00	180 37.8	N21 44.4	17 35.0	12.1	S23 26.2	8.1	54.2
01	195 37.7	44.7	32 06.1	12.2	23 34.3	7.9	54.2
02	210 37.6	45.1	46 37.3	12.0	23 42.2	7.8	54.2
03	225 37.5	. . 45.5	61 08.3	12.0	23 50.0	7.8	54.1
04	240 37.5	45.9	75 39.3	12.0	23 57.8	7.6	54.1
05	255 37.4	46.2	90 10.3	11.9	24 05.4	7.5	54.1
06	270 37.3	N21 46.6	104 41.2	11.8	S24 12.9	7.4	54.1
S 07	285 37.2	47.0	119 12.0	11.8	24 20.3	7.3	54.1
A 08	300 37.1	47.3	133 42.8	11.8	24 27.6	7.2	54.1
T 09	315 37.0	. . 47.7	148 13.6	11.7	24 34.8	7.1	54.1
U 10	330 36.9	48.1	162 44.3	11.6	24 41.9	6.9	54.1
R 11	345 36.8	48.4	177 14.9	11.6	24 48.8	6.8	54.1
D 12	0 36.8	N21 48.8	191 45.5	11.5	S24 55.6	6.8	54.1
A 13	15 36.7	49.2	206 16.0	11.5	25 02.4	6.6	54.1
Y 14	30 36.6	49.5	220 46.5	11.4	25 09.0	6.5	54.1
15	45 36.5	. . 49.9	235 16.9	11.4	25 15.5	6.3	54.1
16	60 36.4	50.3	249 47.3	11.3	25 21.8	6.3	54.1
17	75 36.3	50.6	264 17.6	11.3	25 28.1	6.1	54.1
18	90 36.2	N21 51.0	278 47.9	11.2	S25 34.2	6.1	54.1
19	105 36.1	51.4	293 18.1	11.2	25 40.3	5.9	54.0
20	120 36.1	51.7	307 48.3	11.1	25 46.2	5.7	54.0
21	135 36.0	. . 52.1	322 18.4	11.1	25 51.9	5.7	54.0
22	150 35.9	52.4	336 48.5	11.0	25 57.6	5.5	54.0
23	165 35.8	52.8	351 18.5	11.0	S26 03.1	5.4	54.0
	SD 15.8	d 0.4	SD 14.9		14.8		14.7

Lat.	Twilight Naut.	Twilight Civil	Sunrise	Moonrise 28	Moonrise 29	Moonrise 30	Moonrise 31
°	h m	h m	h m	h m	h m	h m	h m
N 72	□	□	□	■	■	■	■
N 70	□	□	□	20 54	■	■	■
68	□	□	□	19 53	■	■	■
66	////	////	01 25	19 18	21 43	■	■
64	////	////	02 06	18 54	20 47	■	■
62	////	00 39	02 33	18 35	20 15	22 00	23 53
60	////	01 35	02 54	18 19	19 50	21 22	22 45
N 58	////	02 06	03 11	18 06	19 31	20 55	22 10
56	00 35	02 29	03 25	17 54	19 15	20 34	21 45
54	01 27	02 48	03 38	17 44	19 02	20 17	21 25
52	01 56	03 03	03 49	17 36	18 50	20 02	21 08
50	02 17	03 16	03 58	17 28	18 40	19 50	20 54
45	02 56	03 42	04 18	17 11	18 18	19 23	20 24
N 40	03 23	04 03	04 35	16 57	18 01	19 03	20 02
35	03 44	04 19	04 48	16 46	17 46	18 45	19 43
30	04 01	04 33	05 00	16 36	17 33	18 31	19 27
20	04 27	04 56	05 20	16 19	17 12	18 06	18 59
N 10	04 48	05 15	05 38	16 04	16 53	17 44	18 36
0	05 06	05 32	05 54	15 50	16 36	17 24	18 14
S 10	05 21	05 47	06 10	15 37	16 19	17 04	17 52
20	05 36	06 03	06 27	15 22	16 01	16 43	17 29
30	05 51	06 20	06 46	15 05	15 40	16 18	17 02
35	05 58	06 30	06 57	14 56	15 27	16 04	16 46
40	06 07	06 40	07 10	14 45	15 13	15 47	16 28
45	06 16	06 52	07 25	14 32	14 57	15 28	16 06
S 50	06 26	07 07	07 44	14 17	14 37	15 03	15 37
52	06 31	07 13	07 53	14 10	14 27	14 51	15 24
54	06 35	07 20	08 03	14 02	14 17	14 37	15 08
56	06 41	07 28	08 14	13 53	14 04	14 22	14 49
58	06 46	07 37	08 26	13 43	13 50	14 03	14 26
S 60	06 53	07 47	08 41	13 31	13 34	13 40	13 55

Lat.	Sunset	Twilight Civil	Twilight Naut.	Moonset 28	Moonset 29	Moonset 30	Moonset 31
°	h m	h m	h m	h m	h m	h m	h m
N 72	□	□	□	■	■	■	■
N 70	□	□	□	{00 07 22 50}	■	■	■
68	□	□	□	{00 31 23 53}	■	■	■
66	22 34	////	////	00 50	{00 28 23 40}	■	■
64	21 51	////	////	01 05	00 54	00 36	■
62	21 23	23 24	////	01 18	01 14	01 10	01 05
60	21 02	22 22	////	01 29	01 30	01 34	01 43
N 58	20 45	21 50	////	01 38	01 44	01 54	02 10
56	20 30	21 27	23 27	01 47	01 56	02 10	02 32
54	20 18	21 08	22 31	01 54	02 07	02 24	02 49
52	20 07	20 53	22 01	02 01	02 16	02 37	03 04
50	19 57	20 40	21 39	02 07	02 25	02 47	03 17
45	19 37	20 13	21 00	02 20	02 43	03 10	03 44
N 40	19 21	19 52	20 33	02 31	02 58	03 29	04 06
35	19 07	19 36	20 11	02 41	03 10	03 44	04 23
30	18 55	19 22	19 54	02 49	03 21	03 57	04 39
20	18 35	18 59	19 28	03 03	03 40	04 20	05 05
N 10	18 17	18 40	19 07	03 16	03 56	04 40	05 27
0	18 01	18 23	18 49	03 27	04 12	04 59	05 48
S 10	17 45	18 08	18 34	03 39	04 28	05 18	06 09
20	17 28	17 52	18 19	03 52	04 44	05 38	06 32
30	17 09	17 35	18 04	04 07	05 04	06 01	06 58
35	16 57	17 25	17 56	04 15	05 15	06 15	07 13
40	16 44	17 14	17 48	04 25	05 28	06 31	07 31
45	16 29	17 02	17 39	04 36	05 43	06 50	07 53
S 50	16 11	16 48	17 28	04 50	06 02	07 14	08 21
52	16 02	16 41	17 24	04 57	06 11	07 25	08 35
54	15 52	16 34	17 19	05 04	06 22	07 38	08 50
56	15 41	16 26	17 14	05 12	06 33	07 53	09 09
58	15 28	16 17	17 08	05 21	06 47	08 12	09 32
S 60	15 13	16 07	17 02	05 32	07 02	08 34	10 02

Day	SUN Eqn. of Time 00^h	SUN Eqn. of Time 12^h	SUN Mer. Pass.	MOON Mer. Pass. Upper	MOON Mer. Pass. Lower	Age	Phase
d	m s	m s	h m	h m	h m	d %	
28	02 47	02 43	11 57	22 01	09 39	12 93	
29	02 39	02 35	11 57	22 47	10 24	13 97	○
30	02 31	02 27	11 58	23 36	11 11	14 99	

2026 MAY 31, JUNE 1, 2 (SUN., MON., TUES.)

Day	UT d h	ARIES GHA	VENUS −4·0 GHA	VENUS Dec	MARS +1·3 GHA	MARS Dec	JUPITER −1·9 GHA	JUPITER Dec	SATURN +0·8 GHA	SATURN Dec
		° ′	° ′	° ′	° ′	° ′	° ′	° ′	° ′	° ′
SUNDAY	31 00	248 30.6	142 51.3	N24 34.5	211 40.3	N13 54.0	132 40.5	N21 44.0	236 26.7	N 2 43.6
	01	263 33.0	157 50.5	34.3	226 41.0	54.6	147 42.4	43.9	251 29.0	43.7
	02	278 35.5	172 49.7	34.0	241 41.6	55.2	162 44.4	43.8	266 31.2	43.8
	03	293 38.0	187 49.0	. . 33.7	256 42.3	. . 55.8	177 46.4	. . 43.7	281 33.5	. . 43.8
	04	308 40.4	202 48.2	33.4	271 42.9	56.4	192 48.3	43.7	296 35.8	43.9
	05	323 42.9	217 47.4	33.2	286 43.6	57.0	207 50.3	43.6	311 38.0	44.0
	06	338 45.4	232 46.7	N24 32.9	301 44.3	N13 57.6	222 52.3	N21 43.5	326 40.3	N 2 44.1
	07	353 47.8	247 45.9	32.6	316 44.9	58.3	237 54.2	43.4	341 42.6	44.1
	08	8 50.3	262 45.1	32.3	331 45.6	58.9	252 56.2	43.3	356 44.8	44.2
	09	23 52.8	277 44.4	. . 32.0	346 46.2	13 59.5	267 58.2	. . 43.3	11 47.1	. . 44.3
	10	38 55.2	292 43.6	31.8	1 46.9	14 00.1	283 00.1	43.2	26 49.4	44.4
	11	53 57.7	307 42.8	31.5	16 47.6	00.7	298 02.1	43.1	41 51.6	44.4
	12	69 00.1	322 42.1	N24 31.2	31 48.2	N14 01.3	313 04.1	N21 43.0	56 53.9	N 2 44.5
	13	84 02.6	337 41.3	30.9	46 48.9	01.9	328 06.0	42.9	71 56.2	44.6
	14	99 05.1	352 40.5	30.6	61 49.5	02.5	343 08.0	42.9	86 58.4	44.7
	15	114 07.5	7 39.8	. . 30.3	76 50.2	. . 03.1	358 10.0	. . 42.8	102 00.7	. . 44.7
	16	129 10.0	22 39.0	30.1	91 50.9	03.7	13 11.9	42.7	117 03.0	44.8
	17	144 12.5	37 38.2	29.8	106 51.5	04.4	28 13.9	42.6	132 05.2	44.9
	18	159 14.9	52 37.5	N24 29.5	121 52.2	N14 05.0	43 15.9	N21 42.5	147 07.5	N 2 45.0
	19	174 17.4	67 36.7	29.2	136 52.8	05.6	58 17.8	42.5	162 09.7	45.0
	20	189 19.9	82 36.0	28.9	151 53.5	06.2	73 19.8	42.4	177 12.0	45.1
	21	204 22.3	97 35.2	. . 28.6	166 54.1	. . 06.8	88 21.8	. . 42.3	192 14.3	. . 45.2
	22	219 24.8	112 34.4	28.3	181 54.8	07.4	103 23.7	42.2	207 16.5	45.3
	23	234 27.3	127 33.7	28.0	196 55.5	08.0	118 25.7	42.1	222 18.8	45.3
MONDAY	1 00	249 29.7	142 32.9	N24 27.7	211 56.1	N14 08.6	133 27.6	N21 42.1	237 21.1	N 2 45.4
	01	264 32.2	157 32.1	27.4	226 56.8	09.2	148 29.6	42.0	252 23.3	45.5
	02	279 34.6	172 31.4	27.1	241 57.4	09.8	163 31.6	41.9	267 25.6	45.6
	03	294 37.1	187 30.6	. . 26.8	256 58.1	. . 10.4	178 33.5	. . 41.8	282 27.9	. . 45.6
	04	309 39.6	202 29.9	26.5	271 58.8	11.0	193 35.5	41.7	297 30.1	45.7
	05	324 42.0	217 29.1	26.2	286 59.4	11.7	208 37.5	41.7	312 32.4	45.8
	06	339 44.5	232 28.3	N24 25.9	302 00.1	N14 12.3	223 39.4	N21 41.6	327 34.7	N 2 45.9
	07	354 47.0	247 27.6	25.6	317 00.7	12.9	238 41.4	41.5	342 36.9	45.9
	08	9 49.4	262 26.8	25.3	332 01.4	13.5	253 43.4	41.4	357 39.2	46.0
	09	24 51.9	277 26.1	. . 25.0	347 02.1	. . 14.1	268 45.3	. . 41.3	12 41.5	. . 46.1
	10	39 54.4	292 25.3	24.7	2 02.7	14.7	283 47.3	41.3	27 43.7	46.1
	11	54 56.8	307 24.6	24.3	17 03.4	15.3	298 49.2	41.2	42 46.0	46.2
	12	69 59.3	322 23.8	N24 24.0	32 04.0	N14 15.9	313 51.2	N21 41.1	57 48.3	N 2 46.3
	13	85 01.7	337 23.0	23.7	47 04.7	16.5	328 53.2	41.0	72 50.5	46.4
	14	100 04.2	352 22.3	23.4	62 05.3	17.1	343 55.1	40.9	87 52.8	46.4
	15	115 06.7	7 21.5	. . 23.1	77 06.0	. . 17.7	358 57.1	. . 40.9	102 55.1	. . 46.5
	16	130 09.1	22 20.8	22.8	92 06.7	18.3	13 59.1	40.8	117 57.3	46.6
	17	145 11.6	37 20.0	22.5	107 07.3	18.9	29 01.0	40.7	132 59.6	46.7
	18	160 14.1	52 19.3	N24 22.1	122 08.0	N14 19.5	44 03.0	N21 40.6	148 01.9	N 2 46.7
	19	175 16.5	67 18.5	21.8	137 08.6	20.1	59 04.9	40.5	163 04.2	46.8
	20	190 19.0	82 17.8	21.5	152 09.3	20.7	74 06.9	40.4	178 06.4	46.9
	21	205 21.5	97 17.0	. . 21.2	167 09.9	. . 21.3	89 08.9	. . 40.4	193 08.7	. . 47.0
	22	220 23.9	112 16.3	20.8	182 10.6	21.9	104 10.8	40.3	208 11.0	47.0
	23	235 26.4	127 15.5	20.5	197 11.3	22.5	119 12.8	40.2	223 13.2	47.1
TUESDAY	2 00	250 28.9	142 14.8	N24 20.2	212 11.9	N14 23.1	134 14.7	N21 40.1	238 15.5	N 2 47.2
	01	265 31.3	157 14.0	19.9	227 12.6	23.7	149 16.7	40.0	253 17.8	47.2
	02	280 33.8	172 13.2	19.5	242 13.2	24.3	164 18.7	40.0	268 20.0	47.3
	03	295 36.2	187 12.5	. . 19.2	257 13.9	. . 24.9	179 20.6	. . 39.9	283 22.3	. . 47.4
	04	310 38.7	202 11.7	18.9	272 14.6	25.5	194 22.6	39.8	298 24.6	47.5
	05	325 41.2	217 11.0	18.5	287 15.2	26.1	209 24.5	39.7	313 26.8	47.5
	06	340 43.6	232 10.2	N24 18.2	302 15.9	N14 26.7	224 26.5	N21 39.6	328 29.1	N 2 47.6
	07	355 46.1	247 09.5	17.9	317 16.5	27.3	239 28.5	39.6	343 31.4	47.7
	08	10 48.6	262 08.8	17.5	332 17.2	27.9	254 30.4	39.5	358 33.7	47.8
	09	25 51.0	277 08.0	. . 17.2	347 17.8	. . 28.5	269 32.4	. . 39.4	13 35.9	. . 47.8
	10	40 53.5	292 07.3	16.9	2 18.5	29.1	284 34.4	39.3	28 38.2	47.9
	11	55 56.0	307 06.5	16.5	17 19.1	29.7	299 36.3	39.2	43 40.5	48.0
	12	70 58.4	322 05.8	N24 16.2	32 19.8	N14 30.3	314 38.3	N21 39.1	58 42.7	N 2 48.0
	13	86 00.9	337 05.0	15.9	47 20.5	30.9	329 40.2	39.1	73 45.0	48.1
	14	101 03.4	352 04.3	15.5	62 21.1	31.5	344 42.2	39.0	88 47.3	48.2
	15	116 05.8	7 03.5	. . 15.2	77 21.8	. . 32.1	359 44.1	. . 38.9	103 49.5	. . 48.3
	16	131 08.3	22 02.8	14.8	92 22.4	32.7	14 46.1	38.8	118 51.8	48.3
	17	146 10.7	37 02.0	14.5	107 23.1	33.3	29 48.1	38.7	133 54.1	48.4
	18	161 13.2	52 01.3	N24 14.1	122 23.7	N14 33.9	44 50.0	N21 38.6	148 56.4	N 2 48.5
	19	176 15.7	67 00.6	13.8	137 24.4	34.5	59 52.0	38.6	163 58.6	48.5
	20	191 18.1	81 59.8	13.4	152 25.1	35.1	74 53.9	38.5	179 00.9	48.6
	21	206 20.6	96 59.1	. . 13.1	167 25.7	. . 35.7	89 55.9	. . 38.4	194 03.2	. . 48.7
	22	221 23.1	111 58.3	12.7	182 26.4	36.3	104 57.9	38.3	209 05.4	48.8
	23	236 25.5	126 57.6	12.4	197 27.0	36.9	119 59.8	38.2	224 07.7	48.8
	Mer. Pass.	h m 7 20.8	v −0.8	d 0.3	v 0.7	d 0.6	v 2.0	d 0.1	v 2.3	d 0.1

STARS

Name	SHA	Dec
	° ′	° ′
Acamar	315 11.3	S40 11.8
Achernar	335 19.8	S57 05.9
Acrux	172 58.5	S63 15.1
Adhara	255 05.3	S29 00.6
Aldebaran	290 38.7	N16 33.7
Alioth	166 11.7	N55 49.1
Alkaid	152 50.7	N49 11.0
Alnair	27 31.4	S46 49.7
Alnilam	275 36.9	S 1 11.1
Alphard	217 46.8	S 8 46.5
Alphecca	126 02.4	N26 37.5
Alpheratz	357 33.7	N29 14.0
Altair	61 58.6	N 8 56.2
Ankaa	353 06.2	S42 09.5
Antares	112 14.1	S26 29.5
Arcturus	145 46.6	N19 02.7
Atria	107 06.7	S69 04.5
Avior	234 14.7	S59 35.9
Bellatrix	278 22.0	N 6 22.4
Betelgeuse	270 51.2	N 7 24.7
Canopus	263 52.4	S52 42.7
Capella	280 20.7	N46 01.4
Deneb	49 24.8	N45 22.2
Denebola	182 23.7	N14 25.5
Diphda	348 46.3	S17 50.4
Dubhe	193 39.6	N61 36.7
Elnath	278 00.8	N28 37.8
Eltanin	90 41.1	N51 29.0
Enif	33 37.6	N 9 59.7
Fomalhaut	15 13.3	S29 28.8
Gacrux	171 50.1	S57 16.0
Gienah	175 42.3	S17 41.5
Hadar	148 33.9	S60 30.3
Hamal	327 50.2	N23 35.1
Kaus Aust.	83 30.6	S34 22.3
Kochab	137 18.8	N74 02.9
Markab	13 28.8	N15 20.8
Menkar	314 05.3	N 4 11.6
Menkent	147 55.9	S36 30.2
Miaplacidus	221 38.4	S69 49.8
Mirfak	308 27.1	N49 57.2
Nunki	75 46.0	S26 15.8
Peacock	53 03.6	S56 38.7
Pollux	243 16.2	N27 57.8
Procyon	244 49.9	N 5 09.4
Rasalhague	95 57.2	N12 32.4
Regulus	207 33.3	N11 50.3
Rigel	281 03.1	S 8 10.3
Rigil Kent.	139 38.1	S60 56.8
Sabik	102 01.1	S15 45.5
Schedar	349 30.0	N56 40.7
Shaula	96 08.4	S37 07.3
Sirius	258 25.5	S16 45.2
Spica	158 20.9	S11 18.1
Suhail	222 45.7	S43 32.6
Vega	80 32.1	N38 48.3
Zuben'ubi	136 54.4	S16 09.2

	SHA	Mer. Pass.
	° ′	h m
Venus	253 03.2	14 31
Mars	322 26.4	9 52
Jupiter	243 57.9	15 04
Saturn	347 51.4	8 09

UT	SUN GHA	SUN Dec	MOON GHA	*v*	MOON Dec	*d*	HP
d h	° ′	° ′	° ′	′	° ′	′	′
31 00 (SUNDAY)	180 35.7	N21 53.2	5 48.5	11.0	S26 08.5	5.3	54.0
01	195 35.6	53.5	20 18.5	10.9	26 13.8	5.2	54.0
02	210 35.5	53.9	34 48.4	10.8	26 19.0	5.0	54.0
03	225 35.4	. . 54.2	49 18.2	10.8	26 24.0	5.0	54.0
04	240 35.3	54.6	63 48.0	10.8	26 29.0	4.8	54.0
05	255 35.3	54.9	78 17.8	10.7	26 33.8	4.6	54.0
06	270 35.2	N21 55.3	92 47.5	10.7	S26 38.4	4.6	54.0
07	285 35.1	55.6	107 17.2	10.7	26 43.0	4.4	54.0
08	300 35.0	56.0	121 46.9	10.6	26 47.4	4.3	54.0
09	315 34.9	. . 56.3	136 16.5	10.6	26 51.7	4.1	54.0
10	330 34.8	56.7	150 46.1	10.5	26 55.8	4.1	54.0
11	345 34.7	57.1	165 15.6	10.5	26 59.9	3.9	54.0
12	0 34.6	N21 57.4	179 45.1	10.5	S27 03.8	3.8	54.0
13	15 34.5	57.8	194 14.6	10.5	27 07.6	3.6	54.0
14	30 34.4	58.1	208 44.1	10.4	27 11.2	3.5	54.0
15	45 34.3	. . 58.5	223 13.5	10.3	27 14.7	3.4	54.0
16	60 34.2	58.8	237 42.8	10.4	27 18.1	3.3	54.0
17	75 34.2	59.1	252 12.2	10.3	27 21.4	3.1	54.0
18	90 34.1	N21 59.5	266 41.5	10.3	S27 24.5	3.0	54.0
19	105 34.0	21 59.8	281 10.8	10.2	27 27.5	2.9	54.0
20	120 33.9	22 00.2	295 40.0	10.3	27 30.4	2.7	54.0
21	135 33.8	. . 00.5	310 09.3	10.2	27 33.1	2.6	54.0
22	150 33.7	00.9	324 38.5	10.2	27 35.7	2.4	54.0
23	165 33.6	01.2	339 07.7	10.1	27 38.1	2.4	54.0
1 00 (MONDAY)	180 33.5	N22 01.6	353 36.8	10.2	S27 40.5	2.2	54.0
01	195 33.4	01.9	8 06.0	10.1	27 42.7	2.0	54.0
02	210 33.3	02.2	22 35.1	10.1	27 44.7	2.0	54.0
03	225 33.2	. . 02.6	37 04.2	10.1	27 46.7	1.8	54.0
04	240 33.1	02.9	51 33.3	10.1	27 48.5	1.6	54.0
05	255 33.0	03.3	66 02.4	10.0	27 50.1	1.6	54.0
06	270 32.9	N22 03.6	80 31.4	10.1	S27 51.7	1.4	54.0
07	285 32.8	03.9	95 00.5	10.0	27 53.1	1.2	54.0
08	300 32.7	04.3	109 29.5	10.0	27 54.3	1.1	54.0
09	315 32.6	. . 04.6	123 58.5	10.0	27 55.4	1.0	54.0
10	330 32.6	05.0	138 27.5	10.0	27 56.4	0.9	54.0
11	345 32.5	05.3	152 56.5	10.0	27 57.3	0.7	54.0
12	0 32.4	N22 05.6	167 25.5	9.9	S27 58.0	0.6	54.0
13	15 32.3	06.0	181 54.4	10.0	27 58.6	0.4	54.0
14	30 32.2	06.3	196 23.4	10.0	27 59.0	0.3	54.0
15	45 32.1	. . 06.6	210 52.4	9.9	27 59.3	0.2	54.0
16	60 32.0	07.0	225 21.3	10.0	27 59.5	0.1	54.0
17	75 31.9	07.3	239 50.3	10.0	27 59.6	0.1	54.0
18	90 31.8	N22 07.6	254 19.3	9.9	S27 59.5	0.3	54.0
19	105 31.7	07.9	268 48.2	10.0	27 59.2	0.3	54.0
20	120 31.6	08.3	283 17.2	10.0	27 58.9	0.5	54.0
21	135 31.5	. . 08.6	297 46.2	9.9	27 58.4	0.7	54.0
22	150 31.4	08.9	312 15.1	10.0	27 57.7	0.7	54.0
23	165 31.3	09.3	326 44.1	10.0	27 57.0	1.0	54.0
2 00 (TUESDAY)	180 31.2	N22 09.6	341 13.1	10.0	S27 56.0	1.0	54.0
01	195 31.1	09.9	355 42.1	10.0	27 55.0	1.2	54.0
02	210 31.0	10.2	10 11.1	10.0	27 53.8	1.3	54.0
03	225 30.9	. . 10.6	24 40.1	10.0	27 52.5	1.4	54.0
04	240 30.8	10.9	39 09.1	10.0	27 51.1	1.6	54.0
05	255 30.7	11.2	53 38.1	10.1	27 49.5	1.7	54.0
06	270 30.6	N22 11.5	68 07.2	10.0	S27 47.8	1.9	54.0
07	285 30.5	11.9	82 36.2	10.1	27 45.9	2.0	54.0
08	300 30.4	12.2	97 05.3	10.1	27 43.9	2.1	54.0
09	315 30.3	. . 12.5	111 34.4	10.1	27 41.8	2.3	54.0
10	330 30.2	12.8	126 03.5	10.2	27 39.5	2.4	54.0
11	345 30.1	13.1	140 32.7	10.1	27 37.1	2.5	54.0
12	0 30.0	N22 13.5	155 01.8	10.2	S27 34.6	2.6	54.0
13	15 29.9	13.8	169 31.0	10.2	27 32.0	2.8	54.0
14	30 29.8	14.1	184 00.2	10.2	27 29.2	3.0	54.1
15	45 29.7	. . 14.4	198 29.4	10.3	27 26.2	3.0	54.1
16	60 29.6	14.7	212 58.7	10.2	27 23.2	3.2	54.1
17	75 29.5	15.0	227 27.9	10.3	27 20.0	3.3	54.1
18	90 29.4	N22 15.4	241 57.2	10.4	S27 16.7	3.5	54.1
19	105 29.3	15.7	256 26.6	10.3	27 13.2	3.5	54.1
20	120 29.2	16.0	270 55.9	10.4	27 09.7	3.7	54.1
21	135 29.1	. . 16.3	285 25.3	10.4	27 06.0	3.9	54.1
22	150 29.0	16.6	299 54.7	10.5	27 02.1	4.0	54.1
23	165 28.9	16.9	314 24.2	10.5	S26 58.1	4.1	54.1
	SD 15.8	*d* 0.3	SD	14.7	14.7		14.7

Lat.	Twilight Naut.	Twilight Civil	Sunrise	Moonrise 31	Moonrise 1	Moonrise 2	Moonrise 3
°	h m	h m	h m	h m	h m	h m	h m
N 72	▭	▭	▭	▬	▬	▬	▬
N 70	▭	▭	▭	▬	▬	▬	▬
68	▭	▭	▭	▬	▬	▬	▬
66	////	////	01 12	▬	▬	▬	▬
64	////	////	01 58	▬	▬	▬	▬
62	////	////	02 27	23 53	25 16	01 16	00 57
60	////	01 26	02 49	22 45	23 43	24 12	00 12
N 58	////	02 00	03 07	22 10	23 07	23 43	24 02
56	////	02 25	03 22	21 45	22 41	23 20	23 45
54	01 18	02 44	03 35	21 25	22 20	23 01	23 29
52	01 50	03 00	03 46	21 08	22 03	22 45	23 16
50	02 13	03 13	03 56	20 54	21 48	22 32	23 05
45	02 53	03 40	04 17	20 24	21 19	22 04	22 41
N 40	03 21	04 01	04 33	20 02	20 55	21 42	22 21
35	03 42	04 18	04 47	19 43	20 36	21 24	22 05
30	04 00	04 32	04 59	19 27	20 19	21 08	21 51
20	04 27	04 56	05 20	18 59	19 52	20 41	21 27
N 10	04 48	05 15	05 38	18 36	19 28	20 18	21 06
0	05 06	05 32	05 54	18 14	19 05	19 57	20 47
S 10	05 22	05 48	06 11	17 52	18 43	19 35	20 27
20	05 37	06 04	06 28	17 29	18 19	19 12	20 06
30	05 52	06 22	06 48	17 02	17 51	18 45	19 42
35	06 00	06 31	06 59	16 46	17 35	18 29	19 27
40	06 09	06 42	07 12	16 28	17 16	18 11	19 11
45	06 18	06 55	07 28	16 06	16 53	17 48	18 51
S 50	06 29	07 09	07 47	15 37	16 23	17 20	18 25
52	06 33	07 16	07 56	15 24	16 08	17 06	18 13
54	06 38	07 24	08 06	15 08	15 51	16 49	17 59
56	06 44	07 32	08 18	14 49	15 31	16 30	17 43
58	06 50	07 41	08 31	14 26	15 05	16 06	17 23
S 60	06 57	07 52	08 46	13 55	14 30	15 33	16 58

Lat.	Sunset	Twilight Civil	Twilight Naut.	Moonset 31	Moonset 1	Moonset 2	Moonset 3
°	h m	h m	h m	h m	h m	h m	h m
N 72	▭	▭	▭	▬	▬	▬	▬
N 70	▭	▭	▭	▬	▬	▬	▬
68	▭	▭	▭	▬	▬	▬	▬
66	22 47	////	////	▬	▬	▬	▬
64	22 00	////	////	▬	▬	▬	▬
62	21 30	////	////	01 05	00 57	01 21	03 26
60	21 08	22 32	////	01 43	02 05	02 54	04 11
N 58	20 50	21 57	////	02 10	02 40	03 30	04 40
56	20 34	21 32	////	02 32	03 05	03 56	05 03
54	20 22	21 13	22 40	02 49	03 26	04 16	05 21
52	20 10	20 57	22 07	03 04	03 43	04 34	05 37
50	20 00	20 43	21 44	03 17	03 57	04 48	05 50
45	19 40	20 16	21 04	03 44	04 27	05 18	06 17
N 40	19 23	19 55	20 35	04 06	04 50	05 41	06 39
35	19 09	19 38	20 14	04 23	05 09	06 00	06 57
30	18 56	19 24	19 56	04 39	05 25	06 17	07 12
20	18 36	19 00	19 29	05 05	05 53	06 44	07 38
N 10	18 18	18 41	19 08	05 27	06 17	07 08	08 00
0	18 01	18 24	18 50	05 48	06 39	07 30	08 21
S 10	17 45	18 08	18 34	06 09	07 01	07 52	08 42
20	17 28	17 51	18 19	06 32	07 25	08 16	09 04
30	17 08	17 34	18 03	06 58	07 53	08 43	09 29
35	16 56	17 24	17 55	07 13	08 09	08 59	09 44
40	16 43	17 13	17 47	07 31	08 28	09 18	10 01
45	16 27	17 01	17 37	07 53	08 51	09 41	10 22
S 50	16 08	16 46	17 27	08 21	09 21	10 10	10 48
52	15 59	16 39	17 22	08 35	09 35	10 24	11 00
54	15 49	16 32	17 17	08 50	09 52	10 41	11 15
56	15 38	16 23	17 11	09 09	10 13	11 00	11 31
58	15 24	16 14	17 05	09 32	10 39	11 24	11 51
S 60	15 09	16 04	16 59	10 02	11 14	11 57	12 17

Day	SUN Eqn. of Time 00^h	SUN Eqn. of Time 12^h	SUN Mer. Pass.	MOON Mer. Pass. Upper	MOON Mer. Pass. Lower	MOON Age	MOON Phase
d	m s	m s	h m	h m	h m	d %	
31	02 23	02 19	11 58	24 26	12 01	15 100	○
1	02 14	02 10	11 58	00 26	12 52	16 99	
2	02 05	02 00	11 58	01 18	13 43	17 96	

UT d h	ARIES GHA	VENUS −4·0 GHA	VENUS Dec	MARS +1·3 GHA	MARS Dec	JUPITER −1·9 GHA	JUPITER Dec	SATURN +0·8 GHA	SATURN Dec
	° ′	° ′	° ′	° ′	° ′	° ′	° ′	° ′	° ′
3 00 (WEDNESDAY)	251 28.0	141 56.8	N24 12.0	212 27.7	N14 37.5	135 01.8	N21 38.2	239 10.0	N 2 48.9
01	266 30.5	156 56.1	11.7	227 28.3	38.1	150 03.7	38.1	254 12.3	49.0
02	281 32.9	171 55.4	11.3	242 29.0	38.7	165 05.7	38.0	269 14.5	49.0
03	296 35.4	186 54.6	. . 11.0	257 29.6	. . 39.3	180 07.6	. . 37.9	284 16.8	. . 49.1
04	311 37.9	201 53.9	10.6	272 30.3	39.9	195 09.6	37.8	299 19.1	49.2
05	326 40.3	216 53.1	10.2	287 31.0	40.4	210 11.6	37.7	314 21.3	49.3
06	341 42.8	231 52.4	N24 09.9	302 31.6	N14 41.0	225 13.5	N21 37.7	329 23.6	N 2 49.3
07	356 45.2	246 51.7	09.5	317 32.3	41.6	240 15.5	37.6	344 25.9	49.4
08	11 47.7	261 50.9	09.1	332 32.9	42.2	255 17.4	37.5	359 28.2	49.5
09	26 50.2	276 50.2	. . 08.8	347 33.6	. . 42.8	270 19.4	. . 37.4	14 30.4	. . 49.5
10	41 52.6	291 49.5	08.4	2 34.2	43.4	285 21.4	37.3	29 32.7	49.6
11	56 55.1	306 48.7	08.1	17 34.9	44.0	300 23.3	37.2	44 35.0	49.7
12	71 57.6	321 48.0	N24 07.7	32 35.5	N14 44.6	315 25.3	N21 37.2	59 37.2	N 2 49.8
13	87 00.0	336 47.2	07.3	47 36.2	45.2	330 27.2	37.1	74 39.5	49.8
14	102 02.5	351 46.5	06.9	62 36.8	45.8	345 29.2	37.0	89 41.8	49.9
15	117 05.0	6 45.8	. . 06.6	77 37.5	. . 46.4	0 31.1	. . 36.9	104 44.1	. . 50.0
16	132 07.4	21 45.0	06.2	92 38.2	47.0	15 33.1	36.8	119 46.3	50.0
17	147 09.9	36 44.3	05.8	107 38.8	47.6	30 35.0	36.7	134 48.6	50.1
18	162 12.4	51 43.6	N24 05.5	122 39.5	N14 48.1	45 37.0	N21 36.7	149 50.9	N 2 50.2
19	177 14.8	66 42.8	05.1	137 40.1	48.7	60 39.0	36.6	164 53.2	50.2
20	192 17.3	81 42.1	04.7	152 40.8	49.3	75 40.9	36.5	179 55.4	50.3
21	207 19.7	96 41.4	. . 04.3	167 41.4	. . 49.9	90 42.9	. . 36.4	194 57.7	. . 50.4
22	222 22.2	111 40.7	03.9	182 42.1	50.5	105 44.8	36.3	210 00.0	50.5
23	237 24.7	126 39.9	03.6	197 42.7	51.1	120 46.8	36.2	225 02.3	50.5
4 00 (THURSDAY)	252 27.1	141 39.2	N24 03.2	212 43.4	N14 51.7	135 48.7	N21 36.2	240 04.5	N 2 50.6
01	267 29.6	156 38.5	02.8	227 44.0	52.3	150 50.7	36.1	255 06.8	50.7
02	282 32.1	171 37.7	02.4	242 44.7	52.9	165 52.6	36.0	270 09.1	50.7
03	297 34.5	186 37.0	. . 02.0	257 45.4	. . 53.4	180 54.6	. . 35.9	285 11.4	. . 50.8
04	312 37.0	201 36.3	01.6	272 46.0	54.0	195 56.6	35.8	300 13.6	50.9
05	327 39.5	216 35.5	01.3	287 46.7	54.6	210 58.5	35.7	315 15.9	51.0
06	342 41.9	231 34.8	N24 00.9	302 47.3	N14 55.2	226 00.5	N21 35.7	330 18.2	N 2 51.0
07	357 44.4	246 34.1	00.5	317 48.0	55.8	241 02.4	35.6	345 20.5	51.1
08	12 46.9	261 33.4	24 00.1	332 48.6	56.4	256 04.4	35.5	0 22.7	51.2
09	27 49.3	276 32.6	23 59.7	347 49.3	. . 57.0	271 06.3	. . 35.4	15 25.0	. . 51.2
10	42 51.8	291 31.9	59.3	2 49.9	57.6	286 08.3	35.3	30 27.3	51.3
11	57 54.2	306 31.2	58.9	17 50.6	58.1	301 10.2	35.2	45 29.6	51.4
12	72 56.7	321 30.5	N23 58.5	32 51.2	N14 58.7	316 12.2	N21 35.1	60 31.8	N 2 51.4
13	87 59.2	336 29.7	58.1	47 51.9	59.3	331 14.1	35.1	75 34.1	51.5
14	103 01.6	351 29.0	57.7	62 52.5	14 59.9	346 16.1	35.0	90 36.4	51.6
15	118 04.1	6 28.3	. . 57.3	77 53.2	15 00.5	1 18.1	. . 34.9	105 38.7	. . 51.6
16	133 06.6	21 27.6	56.9	92 53.8	01.1	16 20.0	34.8	120 40.9	51.7
17	148 09.0	36 26.9	56.5	107 54.5	01.6	31 22.0	34.7	135 43.2	51.8
18	163 11.5	51 26.1	N23 56.1	122 55.1	N15 02.2	46 23.9	N21 34.6	150 45.5	N 2 51.9
19	178 14.0	66 25.4	55.7	137 55.8	02.8	61 25.9	34.6	165 47.8	51.9
20	193 16.4	81 24.7	55.3	152 56.5	03.4	76 27.8	34.5	180 50.0	52.0
21	208 18.9	96 24.0	. . 54.9	167 57.1	. . 04.0	91 29.8	. . 34.4	195 52.3	. . 52.1
22	223 21.3	111 23.2	54.5	182 57.8	04.6	106 31.7	34.3	210 54.6	52.1
23	238 23.8	126 22.5	54.1	197 58.4	05.1	121 33.7	34.2	225 56.9	52.2
5 00 (FRIDAY)	253 26.3	141 21.8	N23 53.7	212 59.1	N15 05.7	136 35.6	N21 34.1	240 59.1	N 2 52.3
01	268 28.7	156 21.1	53.3	227 59.7	06.3	151 37.6	34.0	256 01.4	52.3
02	283 31.2	171 20.4	52.9	243 00.4	06.9	166 39.5	34.0	271 03.7	52.4
03	298 33.7	186 19.7	. . 52.5	258 01.0	. . 07.5	181 41.5	. . 33.9	286 06.0	. . 52.5
04	313 36.1	201 18.9	52.0	273 01.7	08.1	196 43.4	33.8	301 08.3	52.5
05	328 38.6	216 18.2	51.6	288 02.3	08.6	211 45.4	33.7	316 10.5	52.6
06	343 41.1	231 17.5	N23 51.2	303 03.0	N15 09.2	226 47.3	N21 33.6	331 12.8	N 2 52.7
07	358 43.5	246 16.8	50.8	318 03.6	09.8	241 49.3	33.5	346 15.1	52.7
08	13 46.0	261 16.1	50.4	333 04.3	10.4	256 51.3	33.5	1 17.4	52.8
09	28 48.5	276 15.4	. . 50.0	348 04.9	. . 11.0	271 53.2	. . 33.4	16 19.6	. . 52.9
10	43 50.9	291 14.6	49.5	3 05.6	11.5	286 55.2	33.3	31 21.9	53.0
11	58 53.4	306 13.9	49.1	18 06.2	12.1	301 57.1	33.2	46 24.2	53.0
12	73 55.8	321 13.2	N23 48.7	33 06.9	N15 12.7	316 59.1	N21 33.1	61 26.5	N 2 53.1
13	88 58.3	336 12.5	48.3	48 07.5	13.3	332 01.0	33.0	76 28.8	53.2
14	104 00.8	351 11.8	47.8	63 08.2	13.8	347 03.0	32.9	91 31.0	53.2
15	119 03.2	6 11.1	. . 47.4	78 08.8	. . 14.4	2 04.9	. . 32.9	106 33.3	. . 53.3
16	134 05.7	21 10.4	47.0	93 09.5	15.0	17 06.9	32.8	121 35.6	53.4
17	149 08.2	36 09.7	46.6	108 10.1	15.6	32 08.8	32.7	136 37.9	53.4
18	164 10.6	51 09.0	N23 46.1	123 10.8	N15 16.2	47 10.8	N21 32.6	151 40.1	N 2 53.5
19	179 13.1	66 08.2	45.7	138 11.4	16.7	62 12.7	32.5	166 42.4	53.6
20	194 15.6	81 07.5	45.3	153 12.1	17.3	77 14.7	32.4	181 44.7	53.6
21	209 18.0	96 06.8	. . 44.8	168 12.7	. . 17.9	92 16.6	. . 32.3	196 47.0	. . 53.7
22	224 20.5	111 06.1	44.4	183 13.4	18.5	107 18.6	32.3	211 49.3	53.8
23	239 23.0	126 05.4	44.0	198 14.0	19.0	122 20.5	32.2	226 51.5	53.8
Mer. Pass.	h m 7 09.0	v −0.7	d 0.4	v 0.7	d 0.6	v 2.0	d 0.1	v 2.3	d 0.1

STARS Name	SHA	Dec
	° ′	° ′
Acamar	315 11.3	S40 11.8
Achernar	335 19.7	S57 05.9
Acrux	172 58.5	S63 15.1
Adhara	255 05.3	S29 00.6
Aldebaran	290 38.6	N16 33.7
Alioth	166 11.7	N55 49.2
Alkaid	152 50.8	N49 11.0
Alnair	27 31.4	S46 49.7
Alnilam	275 36.9	S 1 11.1
Alphard	217 46.8	S 8 46.5
Alphecca	126 02.4	N26 37.5
Alpheratz	357 33.7	N29 14.0
Altair	61 58.6	N 8 56.2
Ankaa	353 06.2	S42 09.5
Antares	112 14.0	S26 29.5
Arcturus	145 46.6	N19 02.7
Atria	107 06.6	S69 04.5
Avior	234 14.7	S59 35.9
Bellatrix	278 22.0	N 6 22.4
Betelgeuse	270 51.2	N 7 24.7
Canopus	263 52.4	S52 42.7
Capella	280 20.7	N46 01.4
Deneb	49 24.7	N45 22.3
Denebola	182 23.7	N14 25.5
Diphda	348 46.3	S17 50.4
Dubhe	193 39.6	N61 36.7
Elnath	278 00.8	N28 37.8
Eltanin	90 41.1	N51 29.0
Enif	33 37.6	N 9 59.7
Fomalhaut	15 13.2	S29 28.8
Gacrux	171 50.1	S57 16.0
Gienah	175 42.3	S17 41.5
Hadar	148 33.9	S60 30.3
Hamal	327 50.2	N23 35.1
Kaus Aust.	83 30.6	S34 22.3
Kochab	137 18.8	N74 02.9
Markab	13 28.8	N15 20.8
Menkar	314 05.2	N 4 11.6
Menkent	147 55.9	S36 30.2
Miaplacidus	221 38.5	S69 49.8
Mirfak	308 27.1	N49 57.2
Nunki	75 46.0	S26 15.8
Peacock	53 03.5	S56 38.7
Pollux	243 16.2	N27 57.8
Procyon	244 49.9	N 5 09.4
Rasalhague	95 57.1	N12 32.4
Regulus	207 33.3	N11 50.3
Rigel	281 03.1	S 8 10.3
Rigil Kent.	139 38.1	S60 56.8
Sabik	102 01.1	S15 45.5
Schedar	349 30.0	N56 40.7
Shaula	96 08.4	S37 07.4
Sirius	258 25.5	S16 45.2
Spica	158 20.9	S11 18.1
Suhail	222 45.7	S43 32.6
Vega	80 32.0	N38 48.3
Zuben'ubi	136 54.4	S16 09.2

	SHA	Mer. Pass.
	° ′	h m
Venus	249 12.1	14 34
Mars	320 16.3	9 49
Jupiter	243 21.6	14 55
Saturn	347 37.4	7 58

Day	UT (h)	SUN GHA (° ′)	SUN Dec (° ′)	MOON GHA (° ′)	v (′)	MOON Dec (° ′)	d (′)	HP (′)
3 WEDNESDAY	00	180 28.8	N22 17.2	328 53.7	10.5	S26 54.0	4.2	54.1
	01	195 28.7	17.5	343 23.2	10.5	26 49.8	4.3	54.1
	02	210 28.6	17.9	357 52.7	10.6	26 45.5	4.5	54.1
	03	225 28.5	. . 18.2	12 22.3	10.6	26 41.0	4.6	54.1
	04	240 28.4	18.5	26 51.9	10.7	26 36.4	4.8	54.1
	05	255 28.3	18.8	41 21.6	10.7	26 31.6	4.8	54.2
	06	270 28.2	N22 19.1	55 51.3	10.7	S26 26.8	5.0	54.2
	07	285 28.1	19.4	70 21.0	10.8	26 21.8	5.1	54.2
	08	300 28.0	19.7	84 50.8	10.8	26 16.7	5.3	54.2
	09	315 27.9	. . 20.0	99 20.6	10.9	26 11.4	5.4	54.2
	10	330 27.8	20.3	113 50.5	10.9	26 06.0	5.4	54.2
	11	345 27.7	20.6	128 20.4	10.9	26 00.6	5.7	54.2
	12	0 27.6	N22 20.9	142 50.3	11.0	S25 54.9	5.7	54.2
	13	15 27.5	21.2	157 20.3	11.1	25 49.2	5.8	54.2
	14	30 27.4	21.5	171 50.4	11.0	25 43.4	6.0	54.2
	15	45 27.3	. . 21.8	186 20.4	11.2	25 37.4	6.1	54.2
	16	60 27.2	22.1	200 50.6	11.1	25 31.3	6.2	54.3
	17	75 27.0	22.4	215 20.7	11.2	25 25.1	6.4	54.3
	18	90 26.9	N22 22.7	229 50.9	11.3	S25 18.7	6.4	54.3
	19	105 26.8	23.0	244 21.2	11.3	25 12.3	6.6	54.3
	20	120 26.7	23.3	258 51.5	11.4	25 05.7	6.7	54.3
	21	135 26.6	. . 23.6	273 21.9	11.4	24 59.0	6.8	54.3
	22	150 26.5	23.9	287 52.3	11.4	24 52.2	7.0	54.3
	23	165 26.4	24.2	302 22.7	11.5	24 45.2	7.0	54.3
4 THURSDAY	00	180 26.3	N22 24.5	316 53.2	11.5	S24 38.2	7.2	54.3
	01	195 26.2	24.8	331 23.7	11.6	24 31.0	7.2	54.4
	02	210 26.1	25.1	345 54.3	11.7	24 23.8	7.4	54.4
	03	225 26.0	. . 25.4	0 25.0	11.7	24 16.4	7.5	54.4
	04	240 25.9	25.7	14 55.7	11.7	24 08.9	7.6	54.4
	05	255 25.8	25.9	29 26.4	11.8	24 01.3	7.8	54.4
	06	270 25.7	N22 26.2	43 57.2	11.9	S23 53.5	7.8	54.4
	07	285 25.6	26.5	58 28.1	11.9	23 45.7	8.0	54.4
	08	300 25.5	26.8	72 59.0	11.9	23 37.7	8.0	54.5
	09	315 25.4	. . 27.1	87 29.9	12.0	23 29.7	8.2	54.5
	10	330 25.2	27.4	102 00.9	12.1	23 21.5	8.3	54.5
	11	345 25.1	27.7	116 32.0	12.1	23 13.2	8.4	54.5
	12	0 25.0	N22 28.0	131 03.1	12.1	S23 04.8	8.4	54.5
	13	15 24.9	28.3	145 34.2	12.2	22 56.4	8.6	54.5
	14	30 24.8	28.5	160 05.4	12.3	22 47.8	8.7	54.5
	15	45 24.7	. . 28.8	174 36.7	12.3	22 39.1	8.9	54.6
	16	60 24.6	29.1	189 08.0	12.4	22 30.2	8.9	54.6
	17	75 24.5	29.4	203 39.4	12.4	22 21.3	9.0	54.6
	18	90 24.4	N22 29.7	218 10.8	12.4	S22 12.3	9.1	54.6
	19	105 24.3	30.0	232 42.2	12.6	22 03.2	9.2	54.6
	20	120 24.2	30.2	247 13.8	12.5	21 54.0	9.4	54.6
	21	135 24.1	. . 30.5	261 45.3	12.6	21 44.6	9.4	54.7
	22	150 23.9	30.8	276 16.9	12.7	21 35.2	9.5	54.7
	23	165 23.8	31.1	290 48.6	12.7	21 25.7	9.6	54.7
5 FRIDAY	00	180 23.7	N22 31.3	305 20.3	12.8	S21 16.1	9.7	54.7
	01	195 23.6	31.6	319 52.1	12.8	21 06.4	9.9	54.7
	02	210 23.5	31.9	334 23.9	12.9	20 56.5	9.9	54.7
	03	225 23.4	. . 32.2	348 55.8	12.9	20 46.6	10.0	54.8
	04	240 23.3	32.5	3 27.7	13.0	20 36.6	10.1	54.8
	05	255 23.2	32.7	17 59.7	13.0	20 26.5	10.2	54.8
	06	270 23.1	N22 33.0	32 31.7	13.1	S20 16.3	10.3	54.8
	07	285 23.0	33.3	47 03.8	13.1	20 06.0	10.4	54.8
	08	300 22.8	33.5	61 35.9	13.1	19 55.6	10.5	54.8
	09	315 22.7	. . 33.8	76 08.0	13.3	19 45.1	10.5	54.9
	10	330 22.6	34.1	90 40.3	13.2	19 34.6	10.7	54.9
	11	345 22.5	34.4	105 12.5	13.3	19 23.9	10.7	54.9
	12	0 22.4	N22 34.6	119 44.8	13.4	S19 13.2	10.9	54.9
	13	15 22.3	34.9	134 17.2	13.4	19 02.3	10.9	54.9
	14	30 22.2	35.2	148 49.6	13.4	18 51.4	11.0	55.0
	15	45 22.1	. . 35.4	163 22.0	13.5	18 40.4	11.1	55.0
	16	60 22.0	35.7	177 54.5	13.6	18 29.3	11.2	55.0
	17	75 21.8	36.0	192 27.1	13.5	18 18.1	11.3	55.0
	18	90 21.7	N22 36.2	206 59.6	13.7	S18 06.8	11.4	55.0
	19	105 21.6	36.5	221 32.3	13.6	17 55.4	11.4	55.1
	20	120 21.5	36.8	236 04.9	13.7	17 44.0	11.6	55.1
	21	135 21.4	. . 37.0	250 37.6	13.8	17 32.4	11.6	55.1
	22	150 21.3	37.3	265 10.4	13.8	17 20.8	11.7	55.1
	23	165 21.2	37.6	279 43.2	13.8	S17 09.1	11.7	55.2
		SD 15.8	d 0.3	SD 14.8		14.9		15.0

Lat.	Twilight Naut.	Twilight Civil	Sunrise	Moonrise 3	Moonrise 4	Moonrise 5	Moonrise 6
°	h m	h m	h m	h m	h m	h m	h m
N 72	☐	☐	☐	■	■	■	02 51
N 70	☐	☐	☐	■	■	■	02 08
68	☐	☐	☐	■	■	02 29	01 38
66	////	////	00 59	■	■	01 42	01 16
64	////	////	01 51	■	01 33	01 11	00 58
62	////	////	02 22	00 57	00 52	00 48	00 44
60	////	01 18	02 45	00 12	00 24	00 29	00 31
N 58	////	01 55	03 04	24 02	00 02	00 14	00 21
56	////	02 20	03 19	23 45	24 01	00 01	00 11
54	01 11	02 40	03 32	23 29	23 49	24 03	00 03
52	01 45	02 57	03 44	23 16	23 39	23 56	24 09
50	02 09	03 11	03 54	23 05	23 29	23 49	24 05
45	02 50	03 39	04 15	22 41	23 10	23 34	23 55
N 40	03 19	04 00	04 32	22 21	22 54	23 22	23 47
35	03 41	04 17	04 46	22 05	22 41	23 12	23 40
30	03 59	04 32	04 59	21 51	22 29	23 03	23 34
20	04 27	04 55	05 20	21 27	22 09	22 47	23 23
N 10	04 48	05 15	05 38	21 06	21 51	22 33	23 13
0	05 06	05 32	05 55	20 47	21 34	22 20	23 05
S 10	05 22	05 49	06 11	20 27	21 18	22 07	22 56
20	05 38	06 05	06 29	20 06	21 00	21 53	22 46
30	05 53	06 23	06 49	19 42	20 39	21 37	22 35
35	06 02	06 33	07 01	19 27	20 27	21 28	22 29
40	06 10	06 44	07 14	19 11	20 13	21 17	22 21
45	06 20	06 57	07 30	18 51	19 57	21 05	22 13
S 50	06 31	07 12	07 50	18 25	19 36	20 49	22 03
52	06 36	07 19	07 59	18 13	19 26	20 42	21 58
54	06 41	07 27	08 10	17 59	19 15	20 34	21 53
56	06 47	07 35	08 21	17 43	19 03	20 25	21 47
58	06 53	07 45	08 35	17 23	18 48	20 14	21 40
S 60	07 00	07 55	08 51	16 58	18 30	20 02	21 33

Lat.	Sunset	Twilight Civil	Twilight Naut.	Moonset 3	Moonset 4	Moonset 5	Moonset 6
°	h m	h m	h m	h m	h m	h m	h m
N 72	☐	☐	☐	■	■	■	06 34
N 70	☐	☐	☐	■	■	■	07 16
68	☐	☐	☐	■	■	05 18	07 43
66	23 02	////	////	■	■	06 04	08 04
64	22 08	////	////	■	04 34	06 34	08 21
62	21 36	////	////	03 26	05 14	06 56	08 34
60	21 13	22 42	////	04 11	05 41	07 14	08 46
N 58	20 54	22 03	////	04 40	06 03	07 29	08 55
56	20 38	21 37	////	05 03	06 20	07 42	09 04
54	20 25	21 17	22 48	05 21	06 35	07 53	09 12
52	20 13	21 01	22 13	05 37	06 48	08 02	09 18
50	20 03	20 47	21 49	05 50	06 59	08 11	09 24
45	19 42	20 19	21 07	06 17	07 22	08 29	09 37
N 40	19 25	19 57	20 38	06 39	07 41	08 44	09 48
35	19 10	19 40	20 16	06 57	07 56	08 57	09 57
30	18 58	19 25	19 58	07 12	08 09	09 07	10 05
20	18 37	19 01	19 30	07 38	08 32	09 26	10 19
N 10	18 19	18 42	19 09	08 00	08 52	09 42	10 31
0	18 02	18 24	18 50	08 21	09 10	09 57	10 42
S 10	17 45	18 08	18 34	08 42	09 28	10 12	10 53
20	17 28	17 51	18 19	09 04	09 47	10 27	11 04
30	17 07	17 33	18 03	09 29	10 09	10 45	11 17
35	16 56	17 23	17 55	09 44	10 22	10 56	11 25
40	16 42	17 12	17 46	10 01	10 37	11 07	11 34
45	16 26	17 00	17 36	10 22	10 55	11 21	11 44
S 50	16 07	16 44	17 25	10 48	11 16	11 38	11 56
52	15 57	16 37	17 21	11 00	11 27	11 46	12 01
54	15 47	16 30	17 15	11 15	11 38	11 55	12 07
56	15 35	16 21	17 10	11 31	11 51	12 05	12 14
58	15 21	16 12	17 03	11 51	12 07	12 16	12 21
S 60	15 05	16 01	16 56	12 17	12 25	12 29	12 30

Day	SUN Eqn. of Time 00^h	SUN Eqn. of Time 12^h	SUN Mer. Pass.	MOON Mer. Pass. Upper	MOON Mer. Pass. Lower	MOON Age	MOON Phase
d	m s	m s	h m	h m	h m	d %	
3	01 55	01 50	11 58	02 09	14 34	18 91	
4	01 45	01 40	11 58	02 58	15 22	19 85	
5	01 35	01 30	11 59	03 46	16 09	20 78	

UT	ARIES	VENUS −4·0		MARS +1·3		JUPITER −1·9		SATURN +0·8	
	GHA	GHA	Dec	GHA	Dec	GHA	Dec	GHA	Dec
d h	° ′	° ′	° ′	° ′	° ′	° ′	° ′	° ′	° ′
SATURDAY 6 00	254 25.4	141 04.7	N23 43.5	213 14.7	N15 19.6	137 22.5	N21 32.1	241 53.8	N 2 53.9
01	269 27.9	156 04.0	43.1	228 15.3	20.2	152 24.4	32.0	256 56.1	54.0
02	284 30.3	171 03.3	42.7	243 16.0	20.8	167 26.4	31.9	271 58.4	54.0
03	299 32.8	186 02.6	. . 42.2	258 16.6	. . 21.3	182 28.3	. . 31.8	287 00.7	. . 54.1
04	314 35.3	201 01.9	41.8	273 17.3	21.9	197 30.3	31.7	302 02.9	54.2
05	329 37.7	216 01.2	41.4	288 17.9	22.5	212 32.2	31.7	317 05.2	54.2
06	344 40.2	231 00.5	N23 40.9	303 18.6	N15 23.1	227 34.2	N21 31.6	332 07.5	N 2 54.3
07	359 42.7	245 59.8	40.5	318 19.2	23.6	242 36.1	31.5	347 09.8	54.4
08	14 45.1	260 59.1	40.0	333 19.9	24.2	257 38.1	31.4	2 12.1	54.4
09	29 47.6	275 58.4	. . 39.6	348 20.5	. . 24.8	272 40.0	. . 31.3	17 14.3	. . 54.5
10	44 50.1	290 57.7	39.1	3 21.2	25.4	287 42.0	31.2	32 16.6	54.6
11	59 52.5	305 57.0	38.7	18 21.8	25.9	302 43.9	31.1	47 18.9	54.6
12	74 55.0	320 56.3	N23 38.2	33 22.5	N15 26.5	317 45.9	N21 31.1	62 21.2	N 2 54.7
13	89 57.5	335 55.6	37.8	48 23.1	27.1	332 47.8	31.0	77 23.5	54.8
14	104 59.9	350 54.9	37.3	63 23.8	27.7	347 49.8	30.9	92 25.8	54.8
15	120 02.4	5 54.2	. . 36.9	78 24.4	. . 28.2	2 51.7	. . 30.8	107 28.0	. . 54.9
16	135 04.8	20 53.5	36.4	93 25.1	28.8	17 53.7	30.7	122 30.3	55.0
17	150 07.3	35 52.8	36.0	108 25.7	29.4	32 55.6	30.6	137 32.6	55.0
18	165 09.8	50 52.1	N23 35.5	123 26.4	N15 29.9	47 57.6	N21 30.5	152 34.9	N 2 55.1
19	180 12.2	65 51.4	35.1	138 27.0	30.5	62 59.5	30.4	167 37.2	55.2
20	195 14.7	80 50.7	34.6	153 27.7	31.1	78 01.4	30.4	182 39.4	55.2
21	210 17.2	95 50.0	. . 34.1	168 28.3	. . 31.6	93 03.4	. . 30.3	197 41.7	. . 55.3
22	225 19.6	110 49.3	33.7	183 29.0	32.2	108 05.3	30.2	212 44.0	55.4
23	240 22.1	125 48.6	33.2	198 29.6	32.8	123 07.3	30.1	227 46.3	55.4
SUNDAY 7 00	255 24.6	140 47.9	N23 32.8	213 30.3	N15 33.4	138 09.2	N21 30.0	242 48.6	N 2 55.5
01	270 27.0	155 47.2	32.3	228 30.9	33.9	153 11.2	29.9	257 50.9	55.6
02	285 29.5	170 46.5	31.8	243 31.6	34.5	168 13.1	29.8	272 53.1	55.6
03	300 31.9	185 45.8	. . 31.4	258 32.2	. . 35.1	183 15.1	. . 29.8	287 55.4	. . 55.7
04	315 34.4	200 45.1	30.9	273 32.9	35.6	198 17.0	29.7	302 57.7	55.8
05	330 36.9	215 44.4	30.4	288 33.5	36.2	213 19.0	29.6	318 00.0	55.8
06	345 39.3	230 43.7	N23 30.0	303 34.2	N15 36.8	228 20.9	N21 29.5	333 02.3	N 2 55.9
07	0 41.8	245 43.1	29.5	318 34.8	37.3	243 22.9	29.4	348 04.6	56.0
08	15 44.3	260 42.4	29.0	333 35.5	37.9	258 24.8	29.3	3 06.8	56.0
09	30 46.7	275 41.7	. . 28.6	348 36.1	. . 38.5	273 26.8	. . 29.2	18 09.1	. . 56.1
10	45 49.2	290 41.0	28.1	3 36.8	39.0	288 28.7	29.1	33 11.4	56.2
11	60 51.7	305 40.3	27.6	18 37.4	39.6	303 30.7	29.1	48 13.7	56.2
12	75 54.1	320 39.6	N23 27.1	33 38.1	N15 40.2	318 32.6	N21 29.0	63 16.0	N 2 56.3
13	90 56.6	335 38.9	26.7	48 38.7	40.7	333 34.5	28.9	78 18.3	56.4
14	105 59.1	350 38.2	26.2	63 39.3	41.3	348 36.5	28.8	93 20.5	56.4
15	121 01.5	5 37.5	. . 25.7	78 40.0	. . 41.9	3 38.4	. . 28.7	108 22.8	. . 56.5
16	136 04.0	20 36.9	25.2	93 40.6	42.4	18 40.4	28.6	123 25.1	56.6
17	151 06.4	35 36.2	24.7	108 41.3	43.0	33 42.3	28.5	138 27.4	56.6
18	166 08.9	50 35.5	N23 24.3	123 41.9	N15 43.6	48 44.3	N21 28.4	153 29.7	N 2 56.7
19	181 11.4	65 34.8	23.8	138 42.6	44.1	63 46.2	28.4	168 32.0	56.8
20	196 13.8	80 34.1	23.3	153 43.2	44.7	78 48.2	28.3	183 34.2	56.8
21	211 16.3	95 33.4	. . 22.8	168 43.9	. . 45.2	93 50.1	. . 28.2	198 36.5	. . 56.9
22	226 18.8	110 32.8	22.3	183 44.5	45.8	108 52.1	28.1	213 38.8	57.0
23	241 21.2	125 32.1	21.8	198 45.2	46.4	123 54.0	28.0	228 41.1	57.0
MONDAY 8 00	256 23.7	140 31.4	N23 21.3	213 45.8	N15 46.9	138 55.9	N21 27.9	243 43.4	N 2 57.1
01	271 26.2	155 30.7	20.9	228 46.5	47.5	153 57.9	27.8	258 45.7	57.1
02	286 28.6	170 30.0	20.4	243 47.1	48.1	168 59.8	27.7	273 48.0	57.2
03	301 31.1	185 29.4	. . 19.9	258 47.8	. . 48.6	184 01.8	. . 27.7	288 50.2	. . 57.3
04	316 33.6	200 28.7	19.4	273 48.4	49.2	199 03.7	27.6	303 52.5	57.3
05	331 36.0	215 28.0	18.9	288 49.1	49.7	214 05.7	27.5	318 54.8	57.4
06	346 38.5	230 27.3	N23 18.4	303 49.7	N15 50.3	229 07.6	N21 27.4	333 57.1	N 2 57.5
07	1 40.9	245 26.6	17.9	318 50.3	50.9	244 09.6	27.3	348 59.4	57.5
08	16 43.4	260 26.0	17.4	333 51.0	51.4	259 11.5	27.2	4 01.7	57.6
09	31 45.9	275 25.3	. . 16.9	348 51.6	. . 52.0	274 13.4	. . 27.1	19 04.0	. . 57.7
10	46 48.3	290 24.6	16.4	3 52.3	52.5	289 15.4	27.0	34 06.2	57.7
11	61 50.8	305 23.9	15.9	18 52.9	53.1	304 17.3	26.9	49 08.5	57.8
12	76 53.3	320 23.3	N23 15.4	33 53.6	N15 53.7	319 19.3	N21 26.9	64 10.8	N 2 57.9
13	91 55.7	335 22.6	14.9	48 54.2	54.2	334 21.2	26.8	79 13.1	57.9
14	106 58.2	350 21.9	14.4	63 54.9	54.8	349 23.2	26.7	94 15.4	58.0
15	122 00.7	5 21.2	. . 13.9	78 55.5	. . 55.3	4 25.1	. . 26.6	109 17.7	. . 58.1
16	137 03.1	20 20.6	13.4	93 56.2	55.9	19 27.1	26.5	124 20.0	58.1
17	152 05.6	35 19.9	12.9	108 56.8	56.4	34 29.0	26.4	139 22.3	58.2
18	167 08.0	50 19.2	N23 12.4	123 57.5	N15 57.0	49 30.9	N21 26.3	154 24.5	N 2 58.2
19	182 10.5	65 18.5	11.9	138 58.1	57.6	64 32.9	26.2	169 26.8	58.3
20	197 13.0	80 17.9	11.3	153 58.7	58.1	79 34.8	26.1	184 29.1	58.4
21	212 15.4	95 17.2	. . 10.8	168 59.4	. . 58.7	94 36.8	. . 26.1	199 31.4	. . 58.4
22	227 17.9	110 16.5	10.3	184 00.0	59.2	109 38.7	26.0	214 33.7	58.5
23	242 20.4	125 15.9	09.8	199 00.7	59.8	124 40.7	25.9	229 36.0	58.6
Mer. Pass.	h m 6 57.2	*v* −0.7	*d* 0.5	*v* 0.6	*d* 0.6	*v* 1.9	*d* 0.1	*v* 2.3	*d* 0.1

STARS

Name	SHA ° ′	Dec ° ′
Acamar	315 11.3	S40 11.8
Achernar	335 19.7	S57 05.9
Acrux	172 58.5	S63 15.1
Adhara	255 05.3	S29 00.6
Aldebaran	290 38.6	N16 33.7
Alioth	166 11.7	N55 49.2
Alkaid	152 50.8	N49 11.0
Alnair	27 31.3	S46 49.7
Alnilam	275 36.9	S 1 11.1
Alphard	217 46.8	S 8 46.5
Alphecca	126 02.4	N26 37.5
Alpheratz	357 33.7	N29 14.0
Altair	61 58.6	N 8 56.2
Ankaa	353 06.2	S42 09.5
Antares	112 14.0	S26 29.5
Arcturus	145 46.6	N19 02.7
Atria	107 06.6	S69 04.5
Avior	234 14.7	S59 35.9
Bellatrix	278 22.0	N 6 22.4
Betelgeuse	270 51.2	N 7 24.7
Canopus	263 52.4	S52 42.6
Capella	280 20.7	N46 01.4
Deneb	49 24.7	N45 22.3
Denebola	182 23.7	N14 25.5
Diphda	348 46.3	S17 50.4
Dubhe	193 39.6	N61 36.7
Elnath	278 00.8	N28 37.8
Eltanin	90 41.1	N51 29.0
Enif	33 37.5	N 9 59.7
Fomalhaut	15 13.2	S29 28.7
Gacrux	171 50.1	S57 16.0
Gienah	175 42.3	S17 41.5
Hadar	148 33.9	S60 30.3
Hamal	327 50.1	N23 35.2
Kaus Aust.	83 30.6	S34 22.3
Kochab	137 18.8	N74 02.9
Markab	13 28.7	N15 20.8
Menkar	314 05.2	N 4 11.6
Menkent	147 56.0	S36 30.2
Miaplacidus	221 38.5	S69 49.8
Mirfak	308 27.1	N49 57.2
Nunki	75 46.0	S26 15.8
Peacock	53 03.5	S56 38.8
Pollux	243 16.2	N27 57.8
Procyon	244 49.9	N 5 09.4
Rasalhague	95 57.1	N12 32.4
Regulus	207 33.3	N11 50.3
Rigel	281 03.1	S 8 10.3
Rigil Kent.	139 38.1	S60 56.9
Sabik	102 01.1	S15 45.5
Schedar	349 29.9	N56 40.7
Shaula	96 08.4	S37 07.4
Sirius	258 25.5	S16 45.2
Spica	158 20.9	S11 18.1
Suhail	222 45.7	S43 32.6
Vega	80 32.0	N38 48.4
Zuben'ubi	136 54.4	S16 09.2

	SHA ° ′	Mer. Pass. h m
Venus	245 23.3	14 37
Mars	318 05.7	9 46
Jupiter	242 44.7	14 45
Saturn	347 24.0	7 48

	UT	SUN GHA	SUN Dec	MOON GHA	v	MOON Dec	d	HP
	d h	° ′	° ′	° ′	′	° ′	′	′
	6 00	180 21.1	N22 37.8	294 16.0	13.9	S16 57.4	11.9	55.2
	01	195 20.9	38.1	308 48.9	13.9	16 45.5	11.9	55.2
	02	210 20.8	38.3	323 21.8	13.9	16 33.6	12.0	55.2
	03	225 20.7	. . 38.6	337 54.7	14.0	16 21.6	12.1	55.2
	04	240 20.6	38.9	352 27.7	14.0	16 09.5	12.2	55.3
	05	255 20.5	39.1	7 00.7	14.1	15 57.3	12.2	55.3
	06	270 20.4	N22 39.4	21 33.8	14.1	S15 45.1	12.4	55.3
	07	285 20.3	39.6	36 06.9	14.1	15 32.7	12.4	55.3
S	08	300 20.2	39.9	50 40.0	14.2	15 20.3	12.4	55.4
A	09	315 20.0	. . 40.1	65 13.2	14.2	15 07.9	12.6	55.4
T	10	330 19.9	40.4	79 46.4	14.2	14 55.3	12.6	55.4
U	11	345 19.8	40.7	94 19.6	14.3	14 42.7	12.7	55.4
R	12	0 19.7	N22 40.9	108 52.9	14.3	S14 30.0	12.7	55.5
D	13	15 19.6	41.2	123 26.2	14.3	14 17.3	12.9	55.5
A	14	30 19.5	41.4	137 59.6	14.4	14 04.4	12.9	55.5
Y	15	45 19.4	. . 41.7	152 32.9	14.3	13 51.5	12.9	55.5
	16	60 19.2	41.9	167 06.2	14.5	13 38.6	13.1	55.6
	17	75 19.1	42.2	181 39.7	14.4	13 25.5	13.1	55.6
	18	90 19.0	N22 42.4	196 13.1	14.5	S13 12.4	13.1	55.6
	19	105 18.9	42.7	210 46.6	14.4	12 59.3	13.3	55.6
	20	120 18.8	42.9	225 20.0	14.6	12 46.0	13.3	55.7
	21	135 18.7	. . 43.2	239 53.6	14.5	12 32.7	13.3	55.7
	22	150 18.5	43.4	254 27.1	14.5	12 19.4	13.5	55.7
	23	165 18.4	43.6	269 00.6	14.6	12 05.9	13.4	55.8
	7 00	180 18.3	N22 43.9	283 34.2	14.6	S11 52.5	13.6	55.8
	01	195 18.2	44.1	298 07.8	14.6	11 38.9	13.6	55.8
	02	210 18.1	44.4	312 41.4	14.7	11 25.3	13.7	55.8
	03	225 18.0	. . 44.6	327 15.1	14.6	11 11.6	13.7	55.9
	04	240 17.8	44.9	341 48.7	14.7	10 57.9	13.8	55.9
	05	255 17.7	45.1	356 22.4	14.7	10 44.1	13.9	55.9
	06	270 17.6	N22 45.3	10 56.1	14.7	S10 30.2	13.9	56.0
	07	285 17.5	45.6	25 29.8	14.7	10 16.3	13.9	56.0
	08	300 17.4	45.8	40 03.5	14.7	10 02.4	14.1	56.0
S	09	315 17.3	. . 46.1	54 37.2	14.7	9 48.3	14.0	56.0
U	10	330 17.1	46.3	69 10.9	14.8	9 34.3	14.2	56.1
N	11	345 17.0	46.5	83 44.7	14.7	9 20.1	14.1	56.1
D	12	0 16.9	N22 46.8	98 18.4	14.8	S 9 06.0	14.3	56.1
A	13	15 16.8	47.0	112 52.2	14.8	8 51.7	14.3	56.2
Y	14	30 16.7	47.2	127 26.0	14.7	8 37.4	14.3	56.2
	15	45 16.6	. . 47.5	141 59.7	14.8	8 23.1	14.4	56.2
	16	60 16.4	47.7	156 33.5	14.8	8 08.7	14.4	56.3
	17	75 16.3	48.0	171 07.3	14.8	7 54.3	14.5	56.3
	18	90 16.2	N22 48.2	185 41.1	14.7	S 7 39.8	14.5	56.3
	19	105 16.1	48.4	200 14.8	14.8	7 25.3	14.6	56.4
	20	120 16.0	48.6	214 48.6	14.8	7 10.7	14.7	56.4
	21	135 15.8	. . 48.9	229 22.4	14.8	6 56.0	14.6	56.4
	22	150 15.7	49.1	243 56.2	14.7	6 41.4	14.7	56.5
	23	165 15.6	49.3	258 29.9	14.8	6 26.7	14.8	56.5
	8 00	180 15.5	N22 49.6	273 03.7	14.8	S 6 11.9	14.8	56.5
	01	195 15.4	49.8	287 37.5	14.7	5 57.1	14.8	56.6
	02	210 15.2	50.0	302 11.2	14.8	5 42.3	14.9	56.6
	03	225 15.1	. . 50.2	316 45.0	14.7	5 27.4	15.0	56.6
	04	240 15.0	50.5	331 18.7	14.7	5 12.4	14.9	56.7
	05	255 14.9	50.7	345 52.4	14.7	4 57.5	15.0	56.7
	06	270 14.8	N22 50.9	0 26.1	14.7	S 4 42.5	15.1	56.7
	07	285 14.6	51.1	14 59.8	14.7	4 27.4	15.0	56.8
	08	300 14.5	51.4	29 33.5	14.7	4 12.4	15.2	56.8
M	09	315 14.4	. . 51.6	44 07.2	14.6	3 57.2	15.1	56.8
O	10	330 14.3	51.8	58 40.8	14.7	3 42.1	15.2	56.9
N	11	345 14.2	52.0	73 14.5	14.6	3 26.9	15.2	56.9
D	12	0 14.0	N22 52.3	87 48.1	14.6	S 3 11.7	15.3	56.9
A	13	15 13.9	52.5	102 21.7	14.5	2 56.4	15.2	57.0
Y	14	30 13.8	52.7	116 55.2	14.6	2 41.2	15.3	57.0
	15	45 13.7	. . 52.9	131 28.8	14.5	2 25.9	15.4	57.0
	16	60 13.6	53.1	146 02.3	14.5	2 10.5	15.4	57.1
	17	75 13.4	53.3	160 35.8	14.5	1 55.1	15.4	57.1
	18	90 13.3	N22 53.6	175 09.3	14.4	S 1 39.7	15.4	57.1
	19	105 13.2	53.8	189 42.7	14.4	1 24.3	15.4	57.2
	20	120 13.1	54.0	204 16.1	14.4	1 08.9	15.5	57.2
	21	135 13.0	. . 54.2	218 49.5	14.3	0 53.4	15.5	57.2
	22	150 12.8	54.4	233 22.8	14.3	0 37.9	15.5	57.3
	23	165 12.7	54.6	247 56.1	14.3	S 0 22.4	15.6	57.3
		SD 15.8	d 0.2	SD 15.1		15.3		15.5

Lat.	Twilight Naut.	Twilight Civil	Sunrise	Moonrise 6	Moonrise 7	Moonrise 8	Moonrise 9
°	h m	h m	h m	h m	h m	h m	h m
N 72	▭	▭	▭	02 51	01 45	01 06	{00 32 / 23 58}
N 70	▭	▭	▭	02 08	01 26	00 58	00 32
68	▭	▭	▭	01 38	01 11	00 51	00 32
66	////	////	00 45	01 16	00 59	00 45	00 32
64	////	////	01 45	00 58	00 49	00 40	00 32
62	////	////	02 18	00 44	00 40	00 36	00 32
60	////	01 10	02 42	00 31	00 32	00 32	00 32
N 58	////	01 50	03 01	00 21	00 25	00 29	00 32
56	////	02 17	03 17	00 11	00 19	00 26	00 32
54	01 04	02 37	03 30	00 03	00 14	00 23	00 32
52	01 41	02 54	03 42	24 09	00 09	00 21	00 32
50	02 06	03 09	03 52	24 05	00 05	00 18	00 32
45	02 49	03 37	04 14	23 55	24 14	00 14	00 32
N 40	03 18	03 59	04 31	23 47	24 09	00 09	00 32
35	03 40	04 16	04 46	23 40	24 06	00 06	00 32
30	03 58	04 31	04 58	23 34	24 03	00 03	00 32
20	04 26	04 55	05 20	23 23	23 57	24 31	00 31
N 10	04 48	05 15	05 38	23 13	23 52	24 31	00 31
0	05 07	05 33	05 55	23 05	23 48	24 31	00 31
S 10	05 23	05 49	06 12	22 56	23 43	24 32	00 32
20	05 39	06 06	06 30	22 46	23 38	24 32	00 32
30	05 55	06 24	06 51	22 35	23 33	24 32	00 32
35	06 03	06 35	07 03	22 29	23 30	24 32	00 32
40	06 12	06 46	07 16	22 21	23 26	24 32	00 32
45	06 22	06 59	07 32	22 13	23 22	24 32	00 32
S 50	06 33	07 14	07 52	22 03	23 17	24 32	00 32
52	06 38	07 21	08 02	21 58	23 14	24 32	00 32
54	06 44	07 29	08 13	21 53	23 12	24 32	00 32
56	06 49	07 38	08 25	21 47	23 09	24 32	00 32
58	06 56	07 48	08 39	21 40	23 06	24 32	00 32
S 60	07 03	07 59	08 55	21 33	23 02	24 32	00 32

Lat.	Sunset	Twilight Civil	Twilight Naut.	Moonset 6	Moonset 7	Moonset 8	Moonset 9
°	h m	h m	h m	h m	h m	h m	h m
N 72	▭	▭	▭	06 34	09 12	11 25	13 35
N 70	▭	▭	▭	07 16	09 29	11 30	13 30
68	▭	▭	▭	07 43	09 42	11 34	13 27
66	23 18	////	////	08 04	09 53	11 37	13 23
64	22 15	////	////	08 21	10 01	11 40	13 21
62	21 41	////	////	08 34	10 09	11 43	13 18
60	21 17	22 50	////	08 46	10 15	11 45	13 16
N 58	20 58	22 09	////	08 55	10 21	11 47	13 14
56	20 42	21 42	////	09 04	10 26	11 48	13 13
54	20 28	21 21	22 56	09 12	10 30	11 50	13 11
52	20 16	21 04	22 18	09 18	10 34	11 51	13 10
50	20 06	20 50	21 53	09 24	10 38	11 52	13 09
45	19 44	20 21	21 10	09 37	10 46	11 55	13 06
N 40	19 27	19 59	20 40	09 48	10 52	11 57	13 04
35	19 12	19 42	20 18	09 57	10 58	11 59	13 02
30	18 59	19 27	20 00	10 05	11 03	12 01	13 00
20	18 38	19 02	19 32	10 19	11 11	12 04	12 58
N 10	18 20	18 43	19 10	10 31	11 18	12 06	12 55
0	18 03	18 25	18 51	10 42	11 25	12 09	12 53
S 10	17 46	18 08	18 35	10 53	11 32	12 11	12 50
20	17 28	17 51	18 19	11 04	11 39	12 13	12 48
30	17 07	17 33	18 03	11 17	11 47	12 16	12 45
35	16 55	17 23	17 55	11 25	11 52	12 17	12 43
40	16 41	17 12	17 46	11 34	11 57	12 19	12 41
45	16 25	16 59	17 36	11 44	12 03	12 21	12 39
S 50	16 05	16 43	17 24	11 56	12 10	12 23	12 37
52	15 56	16 36	17 19	12 01	12 13	12 25	12 36
54	15 45	16 28	17 14	12 07	12 17	12 26	12 34
56	15 33	16 19	17 08	12 14	12 21	12 27	12 33
58	15 19	16 10	17 02	12 21	12 25	12 28	12 31
S 60	15 02	15 59	16 55	12 30	12 30	12 30	12 30

Day	SUN Eqn. of Time 00^h	SUN Eqn. of Time 12^h	SUN Mer. Pass.	MOON Mer. Pass. Upper	MOON Mer. Pass. Lower	MOON Age	MOON Phase
d	m s	m s	h m	h m	h m	d %	
6	01 24	01 19	11 59	04 31	16 53	21 69	
7	01 13	01 08	11 59	05 15	17 37	22 60	◐
8	01 02	00 56	11 59	05 58	18 20	23 49	

UT d h	ARIES GHA	VENUS −4·0 GHA	VENUS Dec	MARS +1·3 GHA	MARS Dec	JUPITER −1·9 GHA	JUPITER Dec	SATURN +0·8 GHA	SATURN Dec	STARS Name	SHA	Dec
	° ′	° ′	° ′	° ′	° ′	° ′	° ′	° ′	° ′		° ′	° ′
9 00 (TUESDAY)	257 22.8	140 15.2	N23 09.3	214 01.3	N16 00.3	139 42.6	N21 25.8	244 38.3	N 2 58.6	Acamar	315 11.2	S40 11.8
01	272 25.3	155 14.5	08.8	229 02.0	00.9	154 44.5	25.7	259 40.6	58.7	Achernar	335 19.7	S57 05.9
02	287 27.8	170 13.9	08.3	244 02.6	01.5	169 46.5	25.6	274 42.8	58.8	Acrux	172 58.5	S63 15.1
03	302 30.2	185 13.2	. . 07.7	259 03.3	. . 02.0	184 48.4	. . 25.5	289 45.1	. . 58.8	Adhara	255 05.3	S29 00.6
04	317 32.7	200 12.5	07.2	274 03.9	02.6	199 50.4	25.4	304 47.4	58.9	Aldebaran	290 38.6	N16 33.7
05	332 35.2	215 11.9	06.7	289 04.5	03.1	214 52.3	25.3	319 49.7	58.9			
06	347 37.6	230 11.2	N23 06.2	304 05.2	N16 03.7	229 54.2	N21 25.3	334 52.0	N 2 59.0	Alioth	166 11.7	N55 49.2
07	2 40.1	245 10.5	05.7	319 05.8	04.2	244 56.2	25.2	349 54.3	59.1	Alkaid	152 50.8	N49 11.0
08	17 42.5	260 09.9	05.1	334 06.5	04.8	259 58.1	25.1	4 56.6	59.1	Alnair	27 31.3	S46 49.7
09	32 45.0	275 09.2	. . 04.6	349 07.1	. . 05.3	275 00.1	. . 25.0	19 58.9	. . 59.2	Alnilam	275 36.9	S 1 11.1
10	47 47.5	290 08.5	04.1	4 07.8	05.9	290 02.0	24.9	35 01.2	59.3	Alphard	217 46.8	S 8 46.5
11	62 49.9	305 07.9	03.6	19 08.4	06.4	305 04.0	24.8	50 03.5	59.3			
12	77 52.4	320 07.2	N23 03.0	34 09.1	N16 07.0	320 05.9	N21 24.7	65 05.7	N 2 59.4	Alphecca	126 02.4	N26 37.5
13	92 54.9	335 06.6	02.5	49 09.7	07.5	335 07.8	24.6	80 08.0	59.4	Alpheratz	357 33.6	N29 14.0
14	107 57.3	350 05.9	02.0	64 10.3	08.1	350 09.8	24.5	95 10.3	59.5	Altair	61 58.6	N 8 56.2
15	122 59.8	5 05.2	. . 01.5	79 11.0	. . 08.6	5 11.7	. . 24.4	110 12.6	. . 59.6	Ankaa	353 06.1	S42 09.5
16	138 02.3	20 04.6	00.9	94 11.6	09.2	20 13.7	24.4	125 14.9	59.6	Antares	112 14.0	S26 29.5
17	153 04.7	35 03.9	23 00.4	109 12.3	09.7	35 15.6	24.3	140 17.2	59.7			
18	168 07.2	50 03.3	N22 59.9	124 12.9	N16 10.3	50 17.5	N21 24.2	155 19.5	N 2 59.8	Arcturus	145 46.6	N19 02.7
19	183 09.6	65 02.6	59.3	139 13.6	10.8	65 19.5	24.1	170 21.8	59.8	Atria	107 06.6	S69 04.5
20	198 12.1	80 01.9	58.8	154 14.2	11.4	80 21.4	24.0	185 24.1	59.9	Avior	234 14.7	S59 35.9
21	213 14.6	95 01.3	. . 58.2	169 14.9	. . 11.9	95 23.4	. . 23.9	200 26.4	2 59.9	Bellatrix	278 22.0	N 6 22.4
22	228 17.0	110 00.6	57.7	184 15.5	12.5	110 25.3	23.8	215 28.6	3 00.0	Betelgeuse	270 51.2	N 7 24.7
23	243 19.5	125 00.0	57.2	199 16.1	13.0	125 27.2	23.7	230 30.9	00.1			
10 00 (WEDNESDAY)	258 22.0	139 59.3	N22 56.6	214 16.8	N16 13.6	140 29.2	N21 23.6	245 33.2	N 3 00.1	Canopus	263 52.4	S52 42.6
01	273 24.4	154 58.7	56.1	229 17.4	14.1	155 31.1	23.5	260 35.5	00.2	Capella	280 20.7	N46 01.4
02	288 26.9	169 58.0	55.5	244 18.1	14.7	170 33.1	23.5	275 37.8	00.3	Deneb	49 24.7	N45 22.3
03	303 29.4	184 57.4	. . 55.0	259 18.7	. . 15.2	185 35.0	. . 23.4	290 40.1	. . 00.3	Denebola	182 23.7	N14 25.5
04	318 31.8	199 56.7	54.5	274 19.4	15.8	200 36.9	23.3	305 42.4	00.4	Diphda	348 46.3	S17 50.4
05	333 34.3	214 56.1	53.9	289 20.0	16.3	215 38.9	23.2	320 44.7	00.4			
06	348 36.8	229 55.4	N22 53.4	304 20.6	N16 16.9	230 40.8	N21 23.1	335 47.0	N 3 00.5	Dubhe	193 39.6	N61 36.7
07	3 39.2	244 54.8	52.8	319 21.3	17.4	245 42.8	23.0	350 49.3	00.6	Elnath	278 00.8	N28 37.8
08	18 41.7	259 54.1	52.3	334 21.9	18.0	260 44.7	22.9	5 51.6	00.6	Eltanin	90 41.1	N51 29.0
09	33 44.1	274 53.5	. . 51.7	349 22.6	. . 18.5	275 46.6	. . 22.8	20 53.9	. . 00.7	Enif	33 37.5	N 9 59.7
10	48 46.6	289 52.8	51.2	4 23.2	19.1	290 48.6	22.7	35 56.1	00.8	Fomalhaut	15 13.2	S29 28.7
11	63 49.1	304 52.2	50.6	19 23.9	19.6	305 50.5	22.6	50 58.4	00.8			
12	78 51.5	319 51.5	N22 50.1	34 24.5	N16 20.2	320 52.5	N21 22.6	66 00.7	N 3 00.9	Gacrux	171 50.2	S57 16.0
13	93 54.0	334 50.9	49.5	49 25.1	20.7	335 54.4	22.5	81 03.0	00.9	Gienah	175 42.3	S17 41.5
14	108 56.5	349 50.2	49.0	64 25.8	21.2	350 56.3	22.4	96 05.3	01.0	Hadar	148 33.9	S60 30.3
15	123 58.9	4 49.6	. . 48.4	79 26.4	. . 21.8	5 58.3	. . 22.3	111 07.6	. . 01.1	Hamal	327 50.1	N23 35.2
16	139 01.4	19 48.9	47.9	94 27.1	22.3	21 00.2	22.2	126 09.9	01.1	Kaus Aust.	83 30.6	S34 22.3
17	154 03.9	34 48.3	47.3	109 27.7	22.9	36 02.2	22.1	141 12.2	01.2			
18	169 06.3	49 47.6	N22 46.7	124 28.4	N16 23.4	51 04.1	N21 22.0	156 14.5	N 3 01.2	Kochab	137 18.9	N74 02.9
19	184 08.8	64 47.0	46.2	139 29.0	24.0	66 06.0	21.9	171 16.8	01.3	Markab	13 28.7	N15 20.8
20	199 11.3	79 46.4	45.6	154 29.6	24.5	81 08.0	21.8	186 19.1	01.4	Menkar	314 05.2	N 4 11.6
21	214 13.7	94 45.7	. . 45.1	169 30.3	. . 25.0	96 09.9	. . 21.7	201 21.4	. . 01.4	Menkent	147 56.0	S36 30.2
22	229 16.2	109 45.1	44.5	184 30.9	25.6	111 11.8	21.6	216 23.7	01.5	Miaplacidus	221 38.6	S69 49.8
23	244 18.6	124 44.4	43.9	199 31.6	26.1	126 13.8	21.5	231 26.0	01.5			
11 00 (THURSDAY)	259 21.1	139 43.8	N22 43.4	214 32.2	N16 26.7	141 15.7	N21 21.5	246 28.3	N 3 01.6	Mirfak	308 27.0	N49 57.2
01	274 23.6	154 43.1	42.8	229 32.8	27.2	156 17.7	21.4	261 30.5	01.7	Nunki	75 46.0	S26 15.8
02	289 26.0	169 42.5	42.2	244 33.5	27.8	171 19.6	21.3	276 32.8	01.7	Peacock	53 03.5	S56 38.8
03	304 28.5	184 41.9	. . 41.7	259 34.1	. . 28.3	186 21.5	. . 21.2	291 35.1	. . 01.8	Pollux	243 16.2	N27 57.8
04	319 31.0	199 41.2	41.1	274 34.8	28.8	201 23.5	21.1	306 37.4	01.9	Procyon	244 49.9	N 5 09.4
05	334 33.4	214 40.6	40.5	289 35.4	29.4	216 25.4	21.0	321 39.7	01.9			
06	349 35.9	229 40.0	N22 39.9	304 36.1	N16 29.9	231 27.3	N21 20.9	336 42.0	N 3 02.0	Rasalhague	95 57.1	N12 32.4
07	4 38.4	244 39.3	39.4	319 36.7	30.5	246 29.3	20.8	351 44.3	02.0	Regulus	207 33.3	N11 50.3
08	19 40.8	259 38.7	38.8	334 37.3	31.0	261 31.2	20.7	6 46.6	02.1	Rigel	281 03.1	S 8 10.3
09	34 43.3	274 38.0	. . 38.2	349 38.0	. . 31.5	276 33.2	. . 20.6	21 48.9	. . 02.2	Rigil Kent.	139 38.2	S60 56.9
10	49 45.7	289 37.4	37.7	4 38.6	32.1	291 35.1	20.5	36 51.2	02.2	Sabik	102 01.1	S15 45.5
11	64 48.2	304 36.8	37.1	19 39.3	32.6	306 37.0	20.5	51 53.5	02.3			
12	79 50.7	319 36.1	N22 36.5	34 39.9	N16 33.1	321 39.0	N21 20.4	66 55.8	N 3 02.3	Schedar	349 29.9	N56 40.7
13	94 53.1	334 35.5	35.9	49 40.5	33.7	336 40.9	20.3	81 58.1	02.4	Shaula	96 08.4	S37 07.4
14	109 55.6	349 34.9	35.3	64 41.2	34.2	351 42.8	20.2	97 00.4	02.5	Sirius	258 25.5	S16 45.2
15	124 58.1	4 34.2	. . 34.8	79 41.8	. . 34.8	6 44.8	. . 20.1	112 02.7	. . 02.5	Spica	158 20.9	S11 18.1
16	140 00.5	19 33.6	34.2	94 42.5	35.3	21 46.7	20.0	127 05.0	02.6	Suhail	222 45.7	S43 32.6
17	155 03.0	34 33.0	33.6	109 43.1	35.8	36 48.7	19.9	142 07.3	02.6			
18	170 05.5	49 32.4	N22 33.0	124 43.7	N16 36.4	51 50.6	N21 19.8	157 09.6	N 3 02.7	Vega	80 32.0	N38 48.4
19	185 07.9	64 31.7	32.4	139 44.4	36.9	66 52.5	19.7	172 11.9	02.8	Zuben'ubi	136 54.4	S16 09.2
20	200 10.4	79 31.1	31.8	154 45.0	37.4	81 54.5	19.6	187 14.2	02.8			
21	215 12.9	94 30.5	. . 31.3	169 45.7	. . 38.0	96 56.4	. . 19.5	202 16.5	. . 02.9			
22	230 15.3	109 29.8	30.7	184 46.3	38.5	111 58.3	19.4	217 18.8	02.9			
23	245 17.8	124 29.2	30.1	199 46.9	39.0	127 00.3	19.3	232 21.1	03.0			
Mer. Pass.	h m 6 45.4	v −0.6	d 0.6	v 0.6	d 0.5	v 1.9	d 0.1	v 2.3	d 0.1			

	SHA ° ′	Mer. Pass. h m
Venus	241 37.4	14 41
Mars	315 54.8	9 42
Jupiter	242 07.2	14 36
Saturn	347 11.3	7 37

UT	SUN GHA	SUN Dec	MOON GHA	v	MOON Dec	d	HP
d h	° ′	° ′	° ′	′	° ′	′	′
9 00	180 12.6	N22 54.8	262 29.4	14.2	S 0 06.8	15.5	57.4
01	195 12.5	55.0	277 02.6	14.2	N 0 08.7	15.6	57.4
02	210 12.3	55.3	291 35.8	14.1	0 24.3	15.6	57.4
03	225 12.2	. . 55.5	306 08.9	14.1	0 39.9	15.6	57.5
04	240 12.1	55.7	320 42.0	14.1	0 55.5	15.6	57.5
05	255 12.0	55.9	335 15.1	14.0	1 11.1	15.7	57.5
06	270 11.9	N22 56.1	349 48.1	14.0	N 1 26.8	15.7	57.6
T 07	285 11.7	56.3	4 21.1	13.9	1 42.5	15.6	57.6
U 08	300 11.6	56.5	18 54.0	13.9	1 58.1	15.7	57.7
E 09	315 11.5	. . 56.7	33 26.9	13.8	2 13.8	15.7	57.7
S 10	330 11.4	56.9	47 59.7	13.8	2 29.5	15.7	57.7
D 11	345 11.2	57.1	62 32.5	13.7	2 45.2	15.8	57.8
A 12	0 11.1	N22 57.3	77 05.2	13.7	N 3 01.0	15.7	57.8
Y 13	15 11.0	57.5	91 37.9	13.6	3 16.7	15.7	57.8
14	30 10.9	57.7	106 10.5	13.6	3 32.4	15.8	57.9
15	45 10.7	. . 57.9	120 43.1	13.5	3 48.2	15.7	57.9
16	60 10.6	58.1	135 15.6	13.4	4 03.9	15.7	58.0
17	75 10.5	58.3	149 48.0	13.4	4 19.6	15.8	58.0
18	90 10.4	N22 58.5	164 20.4	13.3	N 4 35.4	15.7	58.0
19	105 10.2	58.7	178 52.7	13.2	4 51.1	15.8	58.1
20	120 10.1	58.9	193 24.9	13.2	5 06.9	15.7	58.1
21	135 10.0	. . 59.1	207 57.1	13.1	5 22.6	15.8	58.2
22	150 09.9	59.3	222 29.2	13.1	5 38.4	15.7	58.2
23	165 09.7	59.5	237 01.3	12.9	5 54.1	15.7	58.2
10 00	180 09.6	N22 59.7	251 33.2	12.9	N 6 09.8	15.8	58.3
01	195 09.5	22 59.9	266 05.1	12.9	6 25.6	15.7	58.3
02	210 09.4	23 00.1	280 37.0	12.7	6 41.3	15.7	58.3
03	225 09.2	. . 00.3	295 08.7	12.7	6 57.0	15.7	58.4
04	240 09.1	00.5	309 40.4	12.6	7 12.7	15.7	58.4
05	255 09.0	00.7	324 12.0	12.5	7 28.4	15.6	58.5
06	270 08.9	N23 00.9	338 43.5	12.4	N 7 44.0	15.7	58.5
W 07	285 08.7	01.1	353 14.9	12.4	7 59.7	15.6	58.5
E 08	300 08.6	01.2	7 46.3	12.2	8 15.3	15.6	58.6
D 09	315 08.5	. . 01.4	22 17.5	12.2	8 30.9	15.6	58.6
N 10	330 08.4	01.6	36 48.7	12.1	8 46.5	15.6	58.7
E 11	345 08.2	01.8	51 19.8	12.0	9 02.1	15.5	58.7
S 12	0 08.1	N23 02.0	65 50.8	11.9	N 9 17.6	15.5	58.7
D 13	15 08.0	02.2	80 21.7	11.9	9 33.1	15.5	58.8
A 14	30 07.9	02.4	94 52.6	11.7	9 48.6	15.5	58.8
Y 15	45 07.7	. . 02.5	109 23.3	11.6	10 04.1	15.4	58.9
16	60 07.6	02.7	123 53.9	11.6	10 19.5	15.5	58.9
17	75 07.5	02.9	138 24.5	11.4	10 35.0	15.3	58.9
18	90 07.4	N23 03.1	152 54.9	11.4	N10 50.3	15.4	59.0
19	105 07.2	03.3	167 25.3	11.2	11 05.7	15.3	59.0
20	120 07.1	03.5	181 55.5	11.2	11 21.0	15.2	59.0
21	135 07.0	. . 03.6	196 25.7	11.0	11 36.2	15.3	59.1
22	150 06.8	03.8	210 55.7	10.9	11 51.5	15.2	59.1
23	165 06.7	04.0	225 25.6	10.9	12 06.7	15.1	59.2
11 00	180 06.6	N23 04.2	239 55.5	10.7	N12 21.8	15.1	59.2
01	195 06.5	04.3	254 25.2	10.6	12 36.9	15.0	59.2
02	210 06.3	04.5	268 54.8	10.5	12 51.9	15.0	59.3
03	225 06.2	. . 04.7	283 24.3	10.4	13 06.9	15.0	59.3
04	240 06.1	04.9	297 53.7	10.3	13 21.9	14.9	59.3
05	255 06.0	05.0	312 23.0	10.2	13 36.8	14.8	59.4
06	270 05.8	N23 05.2	326 52.2	10.0	N13 51.6	14.8	59.4
T 07	285 05.7	05.4	341 21.2	10.0	14 06.4	14.8	59.5
H 08	300 05.6	05.6	355 50.2	9.8	14 21.2	14.6	59.5
U 09	315 05.4	. . 05.7	10 19.0	9.7	14 35.8	14.6	59.5
R 10	330 05.3	05.9	24 47.7	9.6	14 50.4	14.6	59.6
S 11	345 05.2	06.1	39 16.3	9.4	15 05.0	14.5	59.6
D 12	0 05.1	N23 06.3	53 44.7	9.4	N15 19.5	14.4	59.6
A 13	15 04.9	06.4	68 13.1	9.2	15 33.9	14.3	59.7
Y 14	30 04.8	06.6	82 41.3	9.1	15 48.2	14.3	59.7
15	45 04.7	. . 06.8	97 09.4	9.0	16 02.5	14.2	59.7
16	60 04.5	06.9	111 37.4	8.8	16 16.7	14.1	59.8
17	75 04.4	07.1	126 05.2	8.7	16 30.8	14.1	59.8
18	90 04.3	N23 07.3	140 32.9	8.6	N16 44.9	13.9	59.9
19	105 04.2	07.4	155 00.5	8.4	16 58.8	13.9	59.9
20	120 04.0	07.6	169 27.9	8.4	17 12.7	13.8	59.9
21	135 03.9	. . 07.7	183 55.3	8.2	17 26.5	13.7	60.0
22	150 03.8	07.9	198 22.5	8.0	17 40.2	13.6	60.0
23	165 03.6	08.1	212 49.5	8.0	N17 53.8	13.5	60.0
	SD 15.8	d 0.2	SD 15.8		16.0		16.2

Lat.	Twilight Naut.	Twilight Civil	Sunrise	Moonrise 9	Moonrise 10	Moonrise 11	Moonrise 12
°	h m	h m	h m	h m	h m	h m	h m
N 72	▭	▭	▭	{00 32 / 23 58}	23 15	21 45	▭
N 70	▭	▭	▭	00 32	{00 06 / 23 35}	22 44	▭
68	▭	▭	▭	00 32	{00 13 / 23 51}	23 19	▭
66	////	////	00 28	00 32	00 19	{00 04 / 23 44}	23 06
64	////	////	01 39	00 32	00 24	00 15	{00 04 / 23 49}
62	////	////	02 14	00 32	00 28	00 24	00 21
60	////	01 03	02 39	00 32	00 32	00 32	00 34
N 58	////	01 46	02 59	00 32	00 35	00 40	00 46
56	////	02 14	03 15	00 32	00 38	00 46	00 57
54	00 57	02 35	03 29	00 32	00 41	00 52	01 06
52	01 37	02 53	03 41	00 32	00 43	00 57	01 14
50	02 03	03 07	03 51	00 32	00 46	01 01	01 21
45	02 47	03 36	04 13	00 32	00 50	01 12	01 37
N 40	03 17	03 58	04 31	00 32	00 55	01 20	01 51
35	03 40	04 16	04 46	00 32	00 58	01 28	02 02
30	03 58	04 31	04 58	00 32	01 01	01 34	02 12
20	04 26	04 55	05 20	00 31	01 07	01 46	02 29
N 10	04 49	05 16	05 39	00 31	01 12	01 56	02 44
0	05 07	05 33	05 56	00 31	01 17	02 05	02 58
S 10	05 24	05 50	06 13	00 32	01 22	02 15	03 13
20	05 40	06 07	06 31	00 32	01 27	02 25	03 28
30	05 56	06 26	06 52	00 32	01 33	02 37	03 46
35	06 04	06 36	07 04	00 32	01 36	02 44	03 56
40	06 14	06 47	07 18	00 32	01 40	02 52	04 08
45	06 24	07 01	07 34	00 32	01 45	03 01	04 23
S 50	06 35	07 16	07 55	00 32	01 50	03 13	04 40
52	06 40	07 24	08 04	00 32	01 53	03 18	04 49
54	06 46	07 32	08 15	00 32	01 55	03 24	04 58
56	06 52	07 40	08 27	00 32	01 59	03 30	05 09
58	06 58	07 50	08 42	00 32	02 02	03 38	05 21
S 60	07 05	08 02	08 59	00 32	02 06	03 46	05 35

Lat.	Sunset	Twilight Civil	Twilight Naut.	Moonset 9	Moonset 10	Moonset 11	Moonset 12
°	h m	h m	h m	h m	h m	h m	h m
N 72	▭	▭	▭	13 35	15 58	19 17	▭
N 70	▭	▭	▭	13 30	15 41	18 20	▭
68	▭	▭	▭	13 27	15 27	17 46	▭
66	23 38	////	////	13 23	15 16	17 22	19 59
64	22 21	////	////	13 21	15 07	17 04	19 18
62	21 46	////	////	13 18	14 59	16 49	18 50
60	21 21	22 59	////	13 16	14 52	16 36	18 28
N 58	21 01	22 14	////	13 14	14 46	16 25	18 11
56	20 45	21 46	////	13 13	14 41	16 16	17 56
54	20 31	21 24	23 04	13 11	14 37	16 08	17 44
52	20 19	21 07	22 23	13 10	14 32	16 00	17 33
50	20 08	20 52	21 56	13 09	14 29	15 53	17 23
45	19 46	20 23	21 12	13 06	14 21	15 39	17 03
N 40	19 28	20 01	20 42	13 04	14 14	15 28	16 46
35	19 14	19 43	20 20	13 02	14 08	15 18	16 32
30	19 01	19 28	20 01	13 00	14 03	15 09	16 20
20	18 39	19 04	19 33	12 58	13 54	14 54	16 00
N 10	18 20	18 43	19 10	12 55	13 46	14 42	15 42
0	18 03	18 26	18 52	12 53	13 39	14 30	15 25
S 10	17 46	18 09	18 35	12 50	13 32	14 18	15 09
20	17 28	17 52	18 19	12 48	13 25	14 05	14 51
30	17 07	17 33	18 03	12 45	13 16	13 51	14 31
35	16 55	17 23	17 54	12 43	13 11	13 42	14 20
40	16 41	17 11	17 45	12 41	13 05	13 33	14 06
45	16 24	16 58	17 35	12 39	12 59	13 22	13 51
S 50	16 04	16 42	17 24	12 37	12 51	13 09	13 31
52	15 54	16 35	17 19	12 36	12 48	13 02	13 22
54	15 44	16 27	17 13	12 34	12 44	12 56	13 12
56	15 31	16 18	17 07	12 33	12 40	12 48	13 01
58	15 17	16 08	17 01	12 31	12 35	12 40	12 48
S 60	15 00	15 57	16 53	12 30	12 30	12 30	12 33

Day	SUN Eqn. of Time 00^h	SUN Eqn. of Time 12^h	SUN Mer. Pass.	MOON Mer. Pass. Upper	MOON Mer. Pass. Lower	MOON Age	MOON Phase
d	m s	m s	h m	h m	h m	d %	
9	00 51	00 45	11 59	06 42	19 05	24 39	
10	00 39	00 33	11 59	07 28	19 52	25 28	◐
11	00 27	00 20	12 00	08 17	20 44	26 19	

2026 JUNE 12, 13, 14 (FRI., SAT., SUN.)

UT d h	ARIES GHA ° ′	VENUS −4·0 GHA ° ′	VENUS Dec ° ′	MARS +1·3 GHA ° ′	MARS Dec ° ′	JUPITER −1·8 GHA ° ′	JUPITER Dec ° ′	SATURN +0·8 GHA ° ′	SATURN Dec ° ′
12 00	260 20.2	139 28.6	N22 29.5	214 47.6	N16 39.6	142 02.2	N21 19.3	247 23.3	N 3 03.1
01	275 22.7	154 28.0	28.9	229 48.2	40.1	157 04.1	19.2	262 25.6	03.1
02	290 25.2	169 27.3	28.3	244 48.9	40.7	172 06.1	19.1	277 27.9	03.2
03	305 27.6	184 26.7	. . 27.7	259 49.5	. . 41.2	187 08.0	. . 19.0	292 30.2	. . 03.2
04	320 30.1	199 26.1	27.1	274 50.1	41.7	202 09.9	18.9	307 32.5	03.3
05	335 32.6	214 25.5	26.5	289 50.8	42.3	217 11.9	18.8	322 34.8	03.3
06	350 35.0	229 24.8	N22 25.9	304 51.4	N16 42.8	232 13.8	N21 18.7	337 37.1	N 3 03.4
07	5 37.5	244 24.2	25.3	319 52.1	43.3	247 15.7	18.6	352 39.4	03.5
F 08	20 40.0	259 23.6	24.7	334 52.7	43.9	262 17.7	18.5	7 41.7	03.5
R 09	35 42.4	274 23.0	. . 24.1	349 53.3	. . 44.4	277 19.6	. . 18.4	22 44.0	. . 03.6
I 10	50 44.9	289 22.4	23.5	4 54.0	44.9	292 21.6	18.3	37 46.3	03.6
D 11	65 47.4	304 21.7	22.9	19 54.6	45.4	307 23.5	18.2	52 48.6	03.7
A 12	80 49.8	319 21.1	N22 22.3	34 55.3	N16 46.0	322 25.4	N21 18.1	67 50.9	N 3 03.8
Y 13	95 52.3	334 20.5	21.7	49 55.9	46.5	337 27.4	18.0	82 53.2	03.8
14	110 54.7	349 19.9	21.1	64 56.5	47.0	352 29.3	18.0	97 55.5	03.9
15	125 57.2	4 19.3	. . 20.5	79 57.2	. . 47.6	7 31.2	. . 17.9	112 57.8	. . 03.9
16	140 59.7	19 18.6	19.9	94 57.8	48.1	22 33.2	17.8	128 00.1	04.0
17	156 02.1	34 18.0	19.3	109 58.5	48.6	37 35.1	17.7	143 02.4	04.1
18	171 04.6	49 17.4	N22 18.7	124 59.1	N16 49.2	52 37.0	N21 17.6	158 04.7	N 3 04.1
19	186 07.1	64 16.8	18.1	139 59.7	49.7	67 39.0	17.5	173 07.0	04.2
20	201 09.5	79 16.2	17.5	155 00.4	50.2	82 40.9	17.4	188 09.3	04.2
21	216 12.0	94 15.6	. . 16.9	170 01.0	. . 50.7	97 42.8	. . 17.3	203 11.6	. . 04.3
22	231 14.5	109 15.0	16.3	185 01.6	51.3	112 44.8	17.2	218 13.9	04.3
23	246 16.9	124 14.3	15.6	200 02.3	51.8	127 46.7	17.1	233 16.2	04.4
13 00	261 19.4	139 13.7	N22 15.0	215 02.9	N16 52.3	142 48.6	N21 17.0	248 18.5	N 3 04.5
01	276 21.9	154 13.1	14.4	230 03.6	52.9	157 50.6	16.9	263 20.8	04.5
02	291 24.3	169 12.5	13.8	245 04.2	53.4	172 52.5	16.8	278 23.1	04.6
03	306 26.8	184 11.9	. . 13.2	260 04.8	. . 53.9	187 54.4	. . 16.7	293 25.4	. . 04.6
04	321 29.2	199 11.3	12.6	275 05.5	54.4	202 56.4	16.6	308 27.7	04.7
05	336 31.7	214 10.7	11.9	290 06.1	55.0	217 58.3	16.6	323 30.0	04.8
06	351 34.2	229 10.1	N22 11.3	305 06.8	N16 55.5	233 00.2	N21 16.5	338 32.3	N 3 04.8
S 07	6 36.6	244 09.5	10.7	320 07.4	56.0	248 02.2	16.4	353 34.6	04.9
A 08	21 39.1	259 08.9	10.1	335 08.0	56.5	263 04.1	16.3	8 36.9	04.9
T 09	36 41.6	274 08.3	. . 09.5	350 08.7	. . 57.1	278 06.0	. . 16.2	23 39.2	. . 05.0
U 10	51 44.0	289 07.6	08.8	5 09.3	57.6	293 08.0	16.1	38 41.5	05.0
R 11	66 46.5	304 07.0	08.2	20 09.9	58.1	308 09.9	16.0	53 43.8	05.1
D 12	81 49.0	319 06.4	N22 07.6	35 10.6	N16 58.6	323 11.8	N21 15.9	68 46.1	N 3 05.2
A 13	96 51.4	334 05.8	06.9	50 11.2	59.2	338 13.8	15.8	83 48.4	05.2
Y 14	111 53.9	349 05.2	06.3	65 11.9	16 59.7	353 15.7	15.7	98 50.7	05.3
15	126 56.4	4 04.6	. . 05.7	80 12.5	17 00.2	8 17.6	. . 15.6	113 53.0	. . 05.3
16	141 58.8	19 04.0	05.1	95 13.1	00.7	23 19.6	15.5	128 55.3	05.4
17	157 01.3	34 03.4	04.4	110 13.8	01.2	38 21.5	15.4	143 57.6	05.4
18	172 03.7	49 02.8	N22 03.8	125 14.4	N17 01.8	53 23.4	N21 15.3	158 59.9	N 3 05.5
19	187 06.2	64 02.2	03.2	140 15.0	02.3	68 25.3	15.2	174 02.2	05.6
20	202 08.7	79 01.6	02.5	155 15.7	02.8	83 27.3	15.1	189 04.6	05.6
21	217 11.1	94 01.0	. . 01.9	170 16.3	. . 03.3	98 29.2	. . 15.0	204 06.9	. . 05.7
22	232 13.6	109 00.4	01.3	185 16.9	03.9	113 31.1	15.0	219 09.2	05.7
23	247 16.1	123 59.8	00.6	200 17.6	04.4	128 33.1	14.9	234 11.5	05.8
14 00	262 18.5	138 59.2	N22 00.0	215 18.2	N17 04.9	143 35.0	N21 14.8	249 13.8	N 3 05.8
01	277 21.0	153 58.6	21 59.3	230 18.9	05.4	158 36.9	14.7	264 16.1	05.9
02	292 23.5	168 58.0	58.7	245 19.5	05.9	173 38.9	14.6	279 18.4	06.0
03	307 25.9	183 57.4	. . 58.1	260 20.1	. . 06.5	188 40.8	. . 14.5	294 20.7	. . 06.0
04	322 28.4	198 56.9	57.4	275 20.8	07.0	203 42.7	14.4	309 23.0	06.1
05	337 30.8	213 56.3	56.8	290 21.4	07.5	218 44.7	14.3	324 25.3	06.1
06	352 33.3	228 55.7	N21 56.1	305 22.0	N17 08.0	233 46.6	N21 14.2	339 27.6	N 3 06.2
07	7 35.8	243 55.1	55.5	320 22.7	08.5	248 48.5	14.1	354 29.9	06.2
08	22 38.2	258 54.5	54.8	335 23.3	09.0	263 50.4	14.0	9 32.2	06.3
S 09	37 40.7	273 53.9	. . 54.2	350 23.9	. . 09.6	278 52.4	. . 13.9	24 34.5	. . 06.3
U 10	52 43.2	288 53.3	53.5	5 24.6	10.1	293 54.3	13.8	39 36.8	06.4
N 11	67 45.6	303 52.7	52.9	20 25.2	10.6	308 56.2	13.7	54 39.1	06.5
D 12	82 48.1	318 52.1	N21 52.2	35 25.9	N17 11.1	323 58.2	N21 13.6	69 41.4	N 3 06.5
A 13	97 50.6	333 51.5	51.6	50 26.5	11.6	339 00.1	13.5	84 43.7	06.6
Y 14	112 53.0	348 50.9	50.9	65 27.1	12.2	354 02.0	13.4	99 46.0	06.6
15	127 55.5	3 50.4	. . 50.3	80 27.8	. . 12.7	9 04.0	. . 13.3	114 48.3	. . 06.7
16	142 58.0	18 49.8	49.6	95 28.4	13.2	24 05.9	13.2	129 50.6	06.7
17	158 00.4	33 49.2	49.0	110 29.0	13.7	39 07.8	13.2	144 52.9	06.8
18	173 02.9	48 48.6	N21 48.3	125 29.7	N17 14.2	54 09.7	N21 13.1	159 55.2	N 3 06.9
19	188 05.3	63 48.0	47.7	140 30.3	14.7	69 11.7	13.0	174 57.6	06.9
20	203 07.8	78 47.4	47.0	155 30.9	15.2	84 13.6	12.9	189 59.9	07.0
21	218 10.3	93 46.9	. . 46.4	170 31.6	. . 15.8	99 15.5	. . 12.8	205 02.2	. . 07.0
22	233 12.7	108 46.3	45.7	185 32.2	16.3	114 17.5	12.7	220 04.5	07.1
23	248 15.2	123 45.7	45.0	200 32.8	16.8	129 19.4	12.6	235 06.8	07.1
Mer. Pass.	h m 6 33.6	*v* −0.6	*d* 0.6	*v* 0.6	*d* 0.5	*v* 1.9	*d* 0.1	*v* 2.3	*d* 0.1

STARS

Name	SHA ° ′	Dec ° ′
Acamar	315 11.2	S40 11.7
Achernar	335 19.6	S57 05.9
Acrux	172 58.5	S63 15.1
Adhara	255 05.3	S29 00.5
Aldebaran	290 38.6	N16 33.7
Alioth	166 11.7	N55 49.2
Alkaid	152 50.8	N49 11.0
Alnair	27 31.3	S46 49.7
Alnilam	275 36.9	S 1 11.1
Alphard	217 46.8	S 8 46.5
Alphecca	126 02.4	N26 37.6
Alpheratz	357 33.6	N29 14.1
Altair	61 58.5	N 8 56.3
Ankaa	353 06.1	S42 09.5
Antares	112 14.0	S26 29.5
Arcturus	145 46.6	N19 02.7
Atria	107 06.6	S69 04.5
Avior	234 14.8	S59 35.8
Bellatrix	278 22.0	N 6 22.4
Betelgeuse	270 51.2	N 7 24.7
Canopus	263 52.4	S52 42.6
Capella	280 20.6	N46 01.4
Deneb	49 24.7	N45 22.3
Denebola	182 23.7	N14 25.5
Diphda	348 46.2	S17 50.4
Dubhe	193 39.7	N61 36.7
Elnath	278 00.8	N28 37.7
Eltanin	90 41.1	N51 29.0
Enif	33 37.5	N 9 59.7
Fomalhaut	15 13.2	S29 28.7
Gacrux	171 50.2	S57 16.0
Gienah	175 42.3	S17 41.5
Hadar	148 33.9	S60 30.3
Hamal	327 50.1	N23 35.2
Kaus Aust.	83 30.6	S34 22.3
Kochab	137 18.9	N74 02.9
Markab	13 28.7	N15 20.8
Menkar	314 05.2	N 4 11.6
Menkent	147 56.0	S36 30.2
Miaplacidus	221 38.6	S69 49.8
Mirfak	308 27.0	N49 57.2
Nunki	75 46.0	S26 15.8
Peacock	53 03.4	S56 38.8
Pollux	243 16.2	N27 57.8
Procyon	244 49.9	N 5 09.4
Rasalhague	95 57.1	N12 32.4
Regulus	207 33.3	N11 50.3
Rigel	281 03.1	S 8 10.3
Rigil Kent.	139 38.2	S60 56.9
Sabik	102 01.1	S15 45.5
Schedar	349 29.9	N56 40.7
Shaula	96 08.3	S37 07.4
Sirius	258 25.5	S16 45.2
Spica	158 20.9	S11 18.1
Suhail	222 45.7	S43 32.6
Vega	80 32.0	N38 48.4
Zuben'ubi	136 54.4	S16 09.2

	SHA ° ′	Mer. Pass. h m
Venus	237 54.3	14 44
Mars	313 43.5	9 39
Jupiter	241 29.2	14 27
Saturn	346 59.1	7 26

	UT	SUN GHA	SUN Dec	MOON GHA	v	MOON Dec	d	HP
	d h	° ′	° ′	° ′	′	° ′	′	′
	12 00	180 03.5	N23 08.2	227 16.5	7.8	N18 07.3	13.5	60.1
	01	195 03.4	08.4	241 43.3	7.6	18 20.8	13.3	60.1
	02	210 03.2	08.5	256 09.9	7.5	18 34.1	13.3	60.1
	03	225 03.1	. . 08.7	270 36.4	7.4	18 47.4	13.1	60.2
	04	240 03.0	08.9	285 02.8	7.3	19 00.5	13.0	60.2
	05	255 02.9	09.0	299 29.1	7.1	19 13.5	13.0	60.2
	06	270 02.7	N23 09.2	313 55.2	7.0	N19 26.5	12.8	60.3
	07	285 02.6	09.3	328 21.2	6.8	19 39.3	12.7	60.3
	08	300 02.5	09.5	342 47.0	6.7	19 52.0	12.6	60.3
F	09	315 02.3	. . 09.6	357 12.7	6.6	20 04.6	12.5	60.3
R	10	330 02.2	09.8	11 38.3	6.4	20 17.1	12.4	60.4
I	11	345 02.1	10.0	26 03.7	6.3	20 29.5	12.3	60.4
D	12	0 01.9	N23 10.1	40 29.0	6.2	N20 41.8	12.1	60.4
A	13	15 01.8	10.3	54 54.2	6.0	20 53.9	12.0	60.5
Y	14	30 01.7	10.4	69 19.2	5.9	21 05.9	11.9	60.5
	15	45 01.6	. . 10.6	83 44.1	5.7	21 17.8	11.8	60.5
	16	60 01.4	10.7	98 08.8	5.6	21 29.6	11.6	60.6
	17	75 01.3	10.9	112 33.4	5.5	21 41.2	11.5	60.6
	18	90 01.2	N23 11.0	126 57.9	5.3	N21 52.7	11.3	60.6
	19	105 01.0	11.2	141 22.2	5.1	22 04.0	11.3	60.6
	20	120 00.9	11.3	155 46.3	5.1	22 15.3	11.0	60.7
	21	135 00.8	. . 11.4	170 10.4	4.9	22 26.3	11.0	60.7
	22	150 00.6	11.6	184 34.3	4.8	22 37.3	10.8	60.7
	23	165 00.5	11.7	198 58.1	4.6	22 48.1	10.6	60.7
	13 00	180 00.4	N23 11.9	213 21.7	4.5	N22 58.7	10.5	60.8
	01	195 00.2	12.0	227 45.2	4.3	23 09.2	10.4	60.8
	02	210 00.1	12.2	242 08.5	4.3	23 19.6	10.2	60.8
	03	225 00.0	. . 12.3	256 31.8	4.1	23 29.8	10.0	60.8
	04	239 59.8	12.4	270 54.9	3.9	23 39.8	9.9	60.9
	05	254 59.7	12.6	285 17.8	3.8	23 49.7	9.7	60.9
	06	269 59.6	N23 12.7	299 40.6	3.7	N23 59.4	9.6	60.9
S	07	284 59.4	12.9	314 03.3	3.6	24 09.0	9.4	60.9
A	08	299 59.3	13.0	328 25.9	3.4	24 18.4	9.2	61.0
T	09	314 59.2	. . 13.1	342 48.3	3.4	24 27.6	9.1	61.0
U	10	329 59.1	13.3	357 10.7	3.1	24 36.7	8.8	61.0
R	11	344 58.9	13.4	11 32.8	3.1	24 45.5	8.7	61.0
D	12	359 58.8	N23 13.5	25 54.9	3.0	N24 54.2	8.6	61.0
A	13	14 58.7	13.7	40 16.9	2.8	25 02.8	8.3	61.1
Y	14	29 58.5	13.8	54 38.7	2.7	25 11.1	8.2	61.1
	15	44 58.4	. . 13.9	69 00.4	2.6	25 19.3	8.0	61.1
	16	59 58.3	14.1	83 22.0	2.4	25 27.3	7.8	61.1
	17	74 58.1	14.2	97 43.4	2.4	25 35.1	7.6	61.1
	18	89 58.0	N23 14.3	112 04.8	2.2	N25 42.7	7.4	61.1
	19	104 57.9	14.5	126 26.0	2.2	25 50.1	7.3	61.2
	20	119 57.7	14.6	140 47.2	2.0	25 57.4	7.0	61.2
	21	134 57.6	. . 14.7	155 08.2	1.9	26 04.4	6.9	61.2
	22	149 57.5	14.9	169 29.1	1.9	26 11.3	6.6	61.2
	23	164 57.3	15.0	183 50.0	1.7	26 17.9	6.5	61.2
	14 00	179 57.2	N23 15.1	198 10.7	1.6	N26 24.4	6.3	61.2
	01	194 57.1	15.2	212 31.3	1.5	26 30.7	6.0	61.2
	02	209 56.9	15.4	226 51.8	1.5	26 36.7	5.9	61.3
	03	224 56.8	. . 15.5	241 12.3	1.4	26 42.6	5.6	61.3
	04	239 56.7	15.6	255 32.7	1.2	26 48.2	5.5	61.3
	05	254 56.5	15.7	269 52.9	1.2	26 53.7	5.2	61.3
	06	269 56.4	N23 15.9	284 13.1	1.1	N26 58.9	5.0	61.3
	07	284 56.3	16.0	298 33.2	1.1	27 03.9	4.8	61.3
	08	299 56.1	16.1	312 53.3	0.9	27 08.7	4.7	61.3
S	09	314 56.0	. . 16.2	327 13.2	0.9	27 13.4	4.3	61.3
U	10	329 55.9	16.3	341 33.1	0.8	27 17.7	4.2	61.3
N	11	344 55.7	16.5	355 52.9	0.8	27 21.9	4.0	61.3
D	12	359 55.6	N23 16.6	10 12.7	0.7	N27 25.9	3.7	61.4
A	13	14 55.5	16.7	24 32.4	0.6	27 29.6	3.6	61.4
Y	14	29 55.3	16.8	38 52.0	0.6	27 33.2	3.3	61.4
	15	44 55.2	. . 16.9	53 11.6	0.6	27 36.5	3.0	61.4
	16	59 55.1	17.0	67 31.2	0.5	27 39.5	2.9	61.4
	17	74 54.9	17.2	81 50.7	0.4	27 42.4	2.7	61.4
	18	89 54.8	N23 17.3	96 10.1	0.4	N27 45.1	2.4	61.4
	19	104 54.6	17.4	110 29.5	0.4	27 47.5	2.2	61.4
	20	119 54.5	17.5	124 48.9	0.4	27 49.7	2.0	61.4
	21	134 54.4	. . 17.6	139 08.3	0.3	27 51.7	1.7	61.4
	22	149 54.2	17.7	153 27.6	0.3	27 53.4	1.6	61.4
	23	164 54.1	17.8	167 46.9	0.3	N27 55.0	1.3	61.4
		SD 15.8	d 0.1	SD	16.5	16.6		16.7

Lat.	Twilight Naut.	Twilight Civil	Sunrise	Moonrise 12	Moonrise 13	Moonrise 14	Moonrise 15
°	h m	h m	h m	h m	h m	h m	h m
N 72	▭	▭	▭	▭	▭	▭	▭
N 70	▭	▭	▭	▭	▭	▭	▭
68	▭	▭	▭	▭	▭	▭	▭
66	▭	▭	▭	23 06	▭	▭	▭
64	////	////	01 35	{00 04 / 23 49}	▭	▭	▭
62	////	////	02 11	00 21	00 18	00 16	00 25
60	////	00 56	02 37	00 34	00 40	00 54	01 32
N 58	////	01 43	02 57	00 46	00 58	01 21	02 07
56	////	02 12	03 14	00 57	01 13	01 42	02 33
54	00 52	02 34	03 28	01 06	01 27	02 00	02 54
52	01 35	02 51	03 40	01 14	01 38	02 15	03 11
50	02 01	03 06	03 50	01 21	01 49	02 28	03 25
45	02 46	03 35	04 13	01 37	02 11	02 55	03 55
N 40	03 16	03 58	04 31	01 51	02 28	03 17	04 19
35	03 39	04 16	04 45	02 02	02 43	03 35	04 38
30	03 58	04 31	04 58	02 12	02 57	03 51	04 54
20	04 26	04 56	05 20	02 29	03 19	04 17	05 22
N 10	04 49	05 16	05 39	02 44	03 39	04 40	05 47
0	05 08	05 34	05 56	02 58	03 57	05 01	06 09
S 10	05 25	05 51	06 14	03 13	04 16	05 23	06 32
20	05 41	06 08	06 32	03 28	04 36	05 46	06 56
30	05 57	06 27	06 53	03 46	04 59	06 13	07 24
35	06 06	06 37	07 05	03 56	05 12	06 29	07 41
40	06 15	06 49	07 19	04 08	05 28	06 48	08 00
45	06 25	07 02	07 36	04 23	05 48	07 11	08 24
S 50	06 37	07 18	07 57	04 40	06 12	07 40	08 54
52	06 42	07 25	08 06	04 49	06 23	07 54	09 09
54	06 47	07 34	08 17	04 58	06 36	08 11	09 27
56	06 54	07 43	08 30	05 09	06 52	08 30	09 48
58	07 00	07 53	08 44	05 21	07 10	08 55	10 15
S 60	07 08	08 04	09 01	05 35	07 33	09 29	10 52

Lat.	Sunset	Twilight Civil	Twilight Naut.	Moonset 12	Moonset 13	Moonset 14	Moonset 15
°	h m	h m	h m	h m	h m	h m	h m
N 72	▭	▭	▭	▭	▭	▭	▭
N 70	▭	▭	▭	▭	▭	▭	▭
68	▭	▭	▭	▭	▭	▭	▭
66	▭	▭	▭	19 59	▭	▭	▭
64	22 26	////	////	19 18	▭	▭	▭
62	21 49	////	////	18 50	21 03	23 16	23 56
60	21 24	23 06	////	18 28	20 26	22 08	23 06
N 58	21 03	22 18	////	18 11	19 59	21 33	22 35
56	20 47	21 49	////	17 56	19 38	21 08	22 11
54	20 33	21 27	23 10	17 44	19 21	20 48	21 52
52	20 21	21 09	22 26	17 33	19 06	20 30	21 35
50	20 10	20 54	21 59	17 23	18 53	20 16	21 21
45	19 48	20 25	21 14	17 03	18 27	19 46	20 52
N 40	19 30	20 03	20 44	16 46	18 06	19 23	20 30
35	19 15	19 44	20 21	16 32	17 49	19 04	20 11
30	19 02	19 29	20 03	16 20	17 34	18 47	19 55
20	18 40	19 05	19 34	16 00	17 09	18 19	19 27
N 10	18 21	18 44	19 11	15 42	16 47	17 56	19 04
0	18 04	18 26	18 52	15 25	16 27	17 33	18 41
S 10	17 46	18 09	18 36	15 09	16 07	17 11	18 19
20	17 28	17 52	18 20	14 51	15 45	16 47	17 55
30	17 07	17 33	18 03	14 31	15 20	16 19	17 27
35	16 55	17 23	17 55	14 20	15 06	16 03	17 11
40	16 41	17 11	17 45	14 06	14 49	15 44	16 51
45	16 24	16 58	17 35	13 51	14 29	15 21	16 28
S 50	16 04	16 42	17 23	13 31	14 04	14 51	15 58
52	15 54	16 35	17 18	13 22	13 52	14 37	15 43
54	15 43	16 26	17 13	13 12	13 38	14 20	15 25
56	15 30	16 17	17 06	13 01	13 22	14 00	15 04
58	15 16	16 07	17 00	12 48	13 03	13 35	14 38
S 60	14 59	15 56	16 52	12 33	12 40	13 01	14 01

Day	SUN Eqn. of Time 00^h	SUN Eqn. of Time 12^h	SUN Mer. Pass.	MOON Mer. Pass. Upper	MOON Mer. Pass. Lower	Age	Phase
d	m s	m s	h m	h m	h m	d	%
12	00 14	00 08	12 00	09 12	21 41	27	10
13	00 02	00 05	12 00	10 12	22 44	28	4 ●
14	00 31	00 17	12 00	11 17	23 51	29	1

2026 JUNE 15, 16, 17 (MON., TUES., WED.)

UT d h		ARIES GHA ° ′	VENUS −4·0 GHA ° ′	Dec ° ′	MARS +1·3 GHA ° ′	Dec ° ′	JUPITER −1·8 GHA ° ′	Dec ° ′	SATURN +0·8 GHA ° ′	Dec ° ′
15 00		263 17.7	138 45.1	N21 44.4	215 33.5	N17 17.3	144 21.3	N21 12.5	250 09.1	N 3 07.2
01		278 20.1	153 44.5	43.7	230 34.1	17.8	159 23.3	12.4	265 11.4	07.2
02		293 22.6	168 43.9	43.0	245 34.8	18.3	174 25.2	12.3	280 13.7	07.3
03		308 25.1	183 43.4	. . 42.4	260 35.4	. . 18.8	189 27.1	. . 12.2	295 16.0	. . 07.3
04		323 27.5	198 42.8	41.7	275 36.0	19.3	204 29.0	12.1	310 18.3	07.4
05		338 30.0	213 42.2	41.1	290 36.7	19.9	219 31.0	12.0	325 20.6	07.5
06		353 32.5	228 41.6	N21 40.4	305 37.3	N17 20.4	234 32.9	N21 11.9	340 22.9	N 3 07.5
07		8 34.9	243 41.1	39.7	320 37.9	20.9	249 34.8	11.8	355 25.2	07.6
08		23 37.4	258 40.5	39.0	335 38.6	21.4	264 36.8	11.7	10 27.5	07.6
09	M	38 39.8	273 39.9	. . 38.4	350 39.2	. . 21.9	279 38.7	. . 11.6	25 29.8	. . 07.7
10	O	53 42.3	288 39.3	37.7	5 39.8	22.4	294 40.6	11.5	40 32.2	07.7
11	N	68 44.8	303 38.8	37.0	20 40.5	22.9	309 42.5	11.4	55 34.5	07.8
12	D	83 47.2	318 38.2	N21 36.4	35 41.1	N17 23.4	324 44.5	N21 11.3	70 36.8	N 3 07.8
13	A	98 49.7	333 37.6	35.7	50 41.7	23.9	339 46.4	11.2	85 39.1	07.9
14	Y	113 52.2	348 37.0	35.0	65 42.4	24.4	354 48.3	11.1	100 41.4	08.0
15		128 54.6	3 36.5	. . 34.3	80 43.0	. . 25.0	9 50.3	. . 11.0	115 43.7	. . 08.0
16		143 57.1	18 35.9	33.7	95 43.6	25.5	24 52.2	10.9	130 46.0	08.1
17		158 59.6	33 35.3	33.0	110 44.3	26.0	39 54.1	10.9	145 48.3	08.1
18		174 02.0	48 34.7	N21 32.3	125 44.9	N17 26.5	54 56.0	N21 10.8	160 50.6	N 3 08.2
19		189 04.5	63 34.2	31.6	140 45.5	27.0	69 58.0	10.7	175 52.9	08.2
20		204 07.0	78 33.6	30.9	155 46.2	27.5	84 59.9	10.6	190 55.2	08.3
21		219 09.4	93 33.0	. . 30.3	170 46.8	. . 28.0	100 01.8	. . 10.5	205 57.5	. . 08.3
22		234 11.9	108 32.5	29.6	185 47.4	28.5	115 03.7	10.4	220 59.9	08.4
23		249 14.3	123 31.9	28.9	200 48.1	29.0	130 05.7	10.3	236 02.2	08.4
16 00		264 16.8	138 31.3	N21 28.2	215 48.7	N17 29.5	145 07.6	N21 10.2	251 04.5	N 3 08.5
01		279 19.3	153 30.8	27.5	230 49.3	30.0	160 09.5	10.1	266 06.8	08.5
02		294 21.7	168 30.2	26.8	245 50.0	30.5	175 11.5	10.0	281 09.1	08.6
03		309 24.2	183 29.6	. . 26.1	260 50.6	. . 31.0	190 13.4	. . 09.9	296 11.4	. . 08.7
04		324 26.7	198 29.1	25.5	275 51.2	31.5	205 15.3	09.8	311 13.7	08.7
05		339 29.1	213 28.5	24.8	290 51.9	32.0	220 17.2	09.7	326 16.0	08.8
06		354 31.6	228 28.0	N21 24.1	305 52.5	N17 32.5	235 19.2	N21 09.6	341 18.3	N 3 08.8
07		9 34.1	243 27.4	23.4	320 53.1	33.0	250 21.1	09.5	356 20.6	08.9
08	T	24 36.5	258 26.8	22.7	335 53.8	33.6	265 23.0	09.4	11 23.0	08.9
09	U	39 39.0	273 26.3	. . 22.0	350 54.4	. . 34.1	280 24.9	. . 09.3	26 25.3	. . 09.0
10	E	54 41.5	288 25.7	21.3	5 55.0	34.6	295 26.9	09.2	41 27.6	09.0
11	S	69 43.9	303 25.2	20.6	20 55.7	35.1	310 28.8	09.1	56 29.9	09.1
12	D	84 46.4	318 24.6	N21 19.9	35 56.3	N17 35.6	325 30.7	N21 09.0	71 32.2	N 3 09.1
13		99 48.8	333 24.0	19.2	50 56.9	36.1	340 32.6	08.9	86 34.5	09.2
14	A	114 51.3	348 23.5	18.5	65 57.6	36.6	355 34.6	08.8	101 36.8	09.2
15	Y	129 53.8	3 22.9	. . 17.8	80 58.2	. . 37.1	10 36.5	. . 08.7	116 39.1	. . 09.3
16		144 56.2	18 22.4	17.1	95 58.8	37.6	25 38.4	08.6	131 41.5	09.3
17		159 58.7	33 21.8	16.4	110 59.5	38.1	40 40.3	08.5	146 43.8	09.4
18		175 01.2	48 21.3	N21 15.7	126 00.1	N17 38.6	55 42.3	N21 08.4	161 46.1	N 3 09.5
19		190 03.6	63 20.7	15.0	141 00.7	39.1	70 44.2	08.3	176 48.4	09.5
20		205 06.1	78 20.2	14.3	156 01.4	39.6	85 46.1	08.2	191 50.7	09.6
21		220 08.6	93 19.6	. . 13.6	171 02.0	. . 40.1	100 48.1	. . 08.1	206 53.0	. . 09.6
22		235 11.0	108 19.1	12.9	186 02.6	40.6	115 50.0	08.0	221 55.3	09.7
23		250 13.5	123 18.5	12.2	201 03.3	41.1	130 51.9	07.9	236 57.6	09.7
17 00		265 16.0	138 18.0	N21 11.5	216 03.9	N17 41.6	145 53.8	N21 07.8	251 59.9	N 3 09.8
01		280 18.4	153 17.4	10.8	231 04.5	42.1	160 55.8	07.7	267 02.3	09.8
02		295 20.9	168 16.9	10.1	246 05.2	42.6	175 57.7	07.6	282 04.6	09.9
03		310 23.3	183 16.3	. . 09.4	261 05.8	. . 43.1	190 59.6	. . 07.6	297 06.9	. . 09.9
04		325 25.8	198 15.8	08.6	276 06.4	43.6	206 01.5	07.5	312 09.2	10.0
05		340 28.3	213 15.2	07.9	291 07.1	44.0	221 03.5	07.4	327 11.5	10.0
06		355 30.7	228 14.7	N21 07.2	306 07.7	N17 44.5	236 05.4	N21 07.3	342 13.8	N 3 10.1
07	W	10 33.2	243 14.1	06.5	321 08.3	45.0	251 07.3	07.2	357 16.1	10.1
08	E	25 35.7	258 13.6	05.8	336 09.0	45.5	266 09.2	07.1	12 18.5	10.2
09	D	40 38.1	273 13.0	. . 05.1	351 09.6	. . 46.0	281 11.2	. . 07.0	27 20.8	. . 10.2
10	N	55 40.6	288 12.5	04.4	6 10.2	46.5	296 13.1	06.9	42 23.1	10.3
11	E	70 43.1	303 12.0	03.6	21 10.9	47.0	311 15.0	06.8	57 25.4	10.3
12	S	85 45.5	318 11.4	N21 02.9	36 11.5	N17 47.5	326 16.9	N21 06.7	72 27.7	N 3 10.4
13	D	100 48.0	333 10.9	02.2	51 12.1	48.0	341 18.8	06.6	87 30.0	10.4
14	A	115 50.5	348 10.3	01.5	66 12.7	48.5	356 20.8	06.5	102 32.3	10.5
15	Y	130 52.9	3 09.8	. . 00.8	81 13.4	. . 49.0	11 22.7	. . 06.4	117 34.7	. . 10.5
16		145 55.4	18 09.3	21 00.0	96 14.0	49.5	26 24.6	06.3	132 37.0	10.6
17		160 57.8	33 08.7	20 59.3	111 14.6	50.0	41 26.5	06.2	147 39.3	10.6
18		176 00.3	48 08.2	N20 58.6	126 15.3	N17 50.5	56 28.5	N21 06.1	162 41.6	N 3 10.7
19		191 02.8	63 07.6	57.9	141 15.9	51.0	71 30.4	06.0	177 43.9	10.7
20		206 05.2	78 07.1	57.1	156 16.5	51.5	86 32.3	05.9	192 46.2	10.8
21		221 07.7	93 06.6	. . 56.4	171 17.2	. . 52.0	101 34.2	. . 05.8	207 48.5	. . 10.9
22		236 10.2	108 06.0	55.7	186 17.8	52.4	116 36.2	05.7	222 50.9	10.9
23		251 12.6	123 05.5	55.0	201 18.4	52.9	131 38.1	05.6	237 53.2	11.0
Mer. Pass.		h m 6 21.8	v −0.6	d 0.7	v 0.6	d 0.5	v 1.9	d 0.1	v 2.3	d 0.1

STARS

Name	SHA ° ′	Dec ° ′
Acamar	315 11.2	S40 11.7
Achernar	335 19.6	S57 05.8
Acrux	172 58.6	S63 15.1
Adhara	255 05.3	S29 00.5
Aldebaran	290 38.6	N16 33.7
Alioth	166 11.8	N55 49.2
Alkaid	152 50.8	N49 11.0
Alnair	27 31.2	S46 49.7
Alnilam	275 36.9	S 1 11.1
Alphard	217 46.8	S 8 46.5
Alphecca	126 02.4	N26 37.6
Alpheratz	357 33.6	N29 14.1
Altair	61 58.5	N 8 56.3
Ankaa	353 06.1	S42 09.5
Antares	112 14.0	S26 29.5
Arcturus	145 46.6	N19 02.7
Atria	107 06.6	S69 04.5
Avior	234 14.8	S59 35.8
Bellatrix	278 21.9	N 6 22.4
Betelgeuse	270 51.1	N 7 24.7
Canopus	263 52.4	S52 42.6
Capella	280 20.6	N46 01.4
Deneb	49 24.6	N45 22.3
Denebola	182 23.7	N14 25.5
Diphda	348 46.2	S17 50.3
Dubhe	193 39.7	N61 36.7
Elnath	278 00.7	N28 37.7
Eltanin	90 41.1	N51 29.1
Enif	33 37.5	N 9 59.8
Fomalhaut	15 13.1	S29 28.7
Gacrux	171 50.2	S57 16.0
Gienah	175 42.3	S17 41.5
Hadar	148 33.9	S60 30.3
Hamal	327 50.1	N23 35.2
Kaus Aust.	83 30.5	S34 22.3
Kochab	137 18.9	N74 02.9
Markab	13 28.7	N15 20.8
Menkar	314 05.2	N 4 11.6
Menkent	147 56.0	S36 30.2
Miaplacidus	221 38.6	S69 49.8
Mirfak	308 27.0	N49 57.2
Nunki	75 45.9	S26 15.8
Peacock	53 03.4	S56 38.8
Pollux	243 16.2	N27 57.8
Procyon	244 49.9	N 5 09.4
Rasalhague	95 57.1	N12 32.4
Regulus	207 33.3	N11 50.3
Rigel	281 03.1	S 8 10.3
Rigil Kent.	139 38.2	S60 56.9
Sabik	102 01.1	S15 45.5
Schedar	349 29.8	N56 40.7
Shaula	96 08.3	S37 07.4
Sirius	258 25.5	S16 45.2
Spica	158 20.9	S11 18.1
Suhail	222 45.7	S43 32.6
Vega	80 32.0	N38 48.4
Zuben'ubi	136 54.4	S16 09.2

	SHA ° ′	Mer. Pass. h m
Venus	234 14.5	14 46
Mars	311 31.9	9 36
Jupiter	240 50.8	14 18
Saturn	346 47.7	7 15

UT		SUN GHA	SUN Dec	MOON GHA	v	MOON Dec	d	HP
d	h	° ′	° ′	° ′	′	° ′	′	′
15	00	179 54.0	N23 17.9	182 06.2	0.3	N27 56.3	1.0	61.4
	01	194 53.8	18.1	196 25.5	0.2	27 57.3	0.9	61.4
	02	209 53.7	18.2	210 44.7	0.3	27 58.2	0.6	61.4
	03	224 53.6	. . 18.3	225 04.0	0.2	27 58.8	0.4	61.4
	04	239 53.4	18.4	239 23.2	0.2	27 59.2	0.2	61.4
	05	254 53.3	18.5	253 42.4	0.3	27 59.4	0.0	61.4
	06	269 53.2	N23 18.6	268 01.7	0.2	N27 59.4	0.3	61.4
	07	284 53.0	18.7	282 20.9	0.3	27 59.1	0.5	61.4
	08	299 52.9	18.8	296 40.2	0.3	27 58.6	0.7	61.4
M	09	314 52.8	. . 18.9	310 59.5	0.3	27 57.9	1.0	61.4
O	10	329 52.6	19.0	325 18.8	0.3	27 56.9	1.2	61.4
N	11	344 52.5	19.1	339 38.1	0.4	27 55.7	1.4	61.3
D	12	359 52.4	N23 19.2	353 57.5	0.3	N27 54.3	1.6	61.3
A	13	14 52.2	19.3	8 16.8	0.5	27 52.7	1.8	61.3
Y	14	29 52.1	19.4	22 36.3	0.4	27 50.9	2.1	61.3
	15	44 51.9	. . 19.5	36 55.7	0.5	27 48.8	2.3	61.3
	16	59 51.8	19.6	51 15.2	0.6	27 46.5	2.5	61.3
	17	74 51.7	19.7	65 34.8	0.6	27 44.0	2.7	61.3
	18	89 51.5	N23 19.8	79 54.4	0.6	N27 41.3	2.9	61.3
	19	104 51.4	19.9	94 14.0	0.7	27 38.4	3.2	61.3
	20	119 51.3	20.0	108 33.7	0.8	27 35.2	3.4	61.3
	21	134 51.1	. . 20.1	122 53.5	0.8	27 31.8	3.6	61.3
	22	149 51.0	20.2	137 13.3	0.9	27 28.2	3.8	61.2
	23	164 50.9	20.3	151 33.2	1.0	27 24.4	4.0	61.2
16	00	179 50.7	N23 20.4	165 53.2	1.0	N27 20.4	4.3	61.2
	01	194 50.6	20.5	180 13.2	1.1	27 16.1	4.4	61.2
	02	209 50.5	20.5	194 33.3	1.2	27 11.7	4.7	61.2
	03	224 50.3	. . 20.6	208 53.5	1.3	27 07.0	4.8	61.2
	04	239 50.2	20.7	223 13.8	1.3	27 02.2	5.1	61.2
	05	254 50.1	20.8	237 34.1	1.5	26 57.1	5.3	61.1
	06	269 49.9	N23 20.9	251 54.6	1.5	N26 51.8	5.5	61.1
	07	284 49.8	21.0	266 15.1	1.7	26 46.3	5.7	61.1
T	08	299 49.6	21.1	280 35.8	1.7	26 40.6	5.9	61.1
U	09	314 49.5	. . 21.2	294 56.5	1.8	26 34.7	6.0	61.1
E	10	329 49.4	21.2	309 17.3	2.0	26 28.7	6.3	61.0
S	11	344 49.2	21.3	323 38.3	2.0	26 22.4	6.5	61.0
D	12	359 49.1	N23 21.4	337 59.3	2.2	N26 15.9	6.7	61.0
A	13	14 49.0	21.5	352 20.5	2.2	26 09.2	6.8	61.0
Y	14	29 48.8	21.6	6 41.7	2.4	26 02.4	7.1	61.0
	15	44 48.7	. . 21.7	21 03.1	2.5	25 55.3	7.2	60.9
	16	59 48.6	21.7	35 24.6	2.6	25 48.1	7.4	60.9
	17	74 48.4	21.8	49 46.2	2.7	25 40.7	7.6	60.9
	18	89 48.3	N23 21.9	64 07.9	2.9	N25 33.1	7.8	60.9
	19	104 48.1	22.0	78 29.8	2.9	25 25.3	8.0	60.8
	20	119 48.0	22.1	92 51.7	3.1	25 17.3	8.1	60.8
	21	134 47.9	. . 22.1	107 13.8	3.2	25 09.2	8.4	60.8
	22	149 47.7	22.2	121 36.0	3.4	25 00.8	8.4	60.8
	23	164 47.6	22.3	135 58.4	3.5	24 52.4	8.7	60.8
17	00	179 47.5	N23 22.4	150 20.9	3.5	N24 43.7	8.8	60.7
	01	194 47.3	22.4	164 43.4	3.8	24 34.9	9.0	60.7
	02	209 47.2	22.5	179 06.2	3.8	24 25.9	9.2	60.7
	03	224 47.1	. . 22.6	193 29.0	4.0	24 16.7	9.3	60.6
	04	239 46.9	22.7	207 52.0	4.2	24 07.4	9.5	60.6
	05	254 46.8	22.7	222 15.2	4.2	23 57.9	9.7	60.6
	06	269 46.6	N23 22.8	236 38.4	4.4	N23 48.2	9.8	60.6
W	07	284 46.5	22.9	251 01.8	4.6	23 38.4	9.9	60.5
E	08	299 46.4	22.9	265 25.4	4.7	23 28.5	10.1	60.5
D	09	314 46.2	. . 23.0	279 49.1	4.8	23 18.4	10.3	60.5
N	10	329 46.1	23.1	294 12.9	4.9	23 08.1	10.3	60.4
E	11	344 46.0	23.1	308 36.8	5.1	22 57.8	10.6	60.4
S	12	359 45.8	N23 23.2	323 00.9	5.3	N22 47.2	10.7	60.4
D	13	14 45.7	23.3	337 25.2	5.3	22 36.5	10.8	60.4
A	14	29 45.5	23.3	351 49.5	5.6	22 25.7	10.9	60.3
Y	15	44 45.4	. . 23.4	6 14.1	5.6	22 14.8	11.1	60.3
	16	59 45.3	23.5	20 38.7	5.8	22 03.7	11.3	60.3
	17	74 45.1	23.5	35 03.5	6.0	21 52.4	11.3	60.2
	18	89 45.0	N23 23.6	49 28.5	6.1	N21 41.1	11.5	60.2
	19	104 44.9	23.7	63 53.6	6.2	21 29.6	11.6	60.2
	20	119 44.7	23.7	78 18.8	6.4	21 18.0	11.7	60.1
	21	134 44.6	. . 23.8	92 44.2	6.5	21 06.3	11.9	60.1
	22	149 44.5	23.8	107 09.7	6.6	20 54.4	11.9	60.1
	23	164 44.3	23.9	121 35.3	6.8	N20 42.5	12.1	60.0
		SD 15.8	d 0.1	SD	16.7	16.6		16.5

Lat.	Twilight Naut.	Twilight Civil	Sunrise	Moonrise 15	16	17	18
°	h m	h m	h m	h m	h m	h m	h m
N 72	▭	▭	▭	▭	▭	▭	▭
N 70	▭	▭	▭	▭	▭	▭	03 57
68	▭	▭	▭	▭	▭	▭	05 08
66	▭	▭	▭	▭	▭	▭	05 44
64	////	////	01 32	▭	▭	03 45	06 09
62	////	////	02 10	00 25	02 08	04 24	06 29
60	////	00 52	02 36	01 32	02 58	04 51	06 45
N 58	////	01 41	02 56	02 07	03 29	05 12	06 59
56	////	02 11	03 13	02 33	03 52	05 30	07 11
54	00 47	02 33	03 27	02 54	04 11	05 45	07 21
52	01 33	02 51	03 39	03 11	04 27	05 57	07 30
50	02 00	03 06	03 50	03 25	04 41	06 08	07 38
45	02 46	03 35	04 13	03 55	05 09	06 32	07 55
N 40	03 16	03 58	04 31	04 19	05 31	06 50	08 09
35	03 39	04 16	04 46	04 38	05 50	07 06	08 20
30	03 58	04 31	04 59	04 54	06 06	07 19	08 31
20	04 27	04 56	05 21	05 22	06 32	07 42	08 48
N 10	04 49	05 16	05 40	05 47	06 55	08 02	09 03
0	05 08	05 35	05 57	06 09	07 17	08 20	09 17
S 10	05 25	05 52	06 14	06 32	07 38	08 38	09 31
20	05 41	06 09	06 33	06 56	08 01	08 58	09 46
30	05 58	06 28	06 54	07 24	08 27	09 20	10 03
35	06 07	06 38	07 06	07 41	08 43	09 33	10 13
40	06 16	06 50	07 21	08 00	09 01	09 48	10 24
45	06 26	07 03	07 37	08 24	09 22	10 06	10 38
S 50	06 38	07 20	07 58	08 54	09 50	10 27	10 54
52	06 43	07 27	08 08	09 09	10 03	10 38	11 01
54	06 49	07 35	08 19	09 27	10 18	10 50	11 09
56	06 55	07 44	08 32	09 48	10 36	11 03	11 18
58	07 02	07 54	08 46	10 15	10 58	11 18	11 29
S 60	07 09	08 06	09 04	10 52	11 26	11 37	11 41

Lat.	Sunset	Twilight Civil	Twilight Naut.	Moonset 15	16	17	18
°	h m	h m	h m	h m	h m	h m	h m
N 72	▭	▭	▭	▭	▭	▭	▭
N 70	▭	▭	▭	▭	▭	▭	02 30
68	▭	▭	▭	▭	▭	▭	01 18
66	▭	▭	▭	▭	▭	▭	00 40
64	22 30	////	////	▭	▭	00 36	00 14
62	21 52	////	////	23 56	23 56	23 53	23 49
60	21 26	23 11	////	23 06	23 28	23 36	23 39
N 58	21 05	22 21	////	22 35	23 06	23 21	23 30
56	20 49	21 51	////	22 11	22 48	23 09	23 21
54	20 35	21 29	23 15	21 52	22 32	22 58	23 14
52	20 22	21 11	22 29	21 35	22 19	22 48	23 08
50	20 11	20 56	22 01	21 21	22 08	22 39	23 02
45	19 49	20 26	21 16	20 52	21 43	22 21	22 49
N 40	19 31	20 04	20 45	20 30	21 24	22 05	22 38
35	19 16	19 46	20 22	20 11	21 07	21 52	22 29
30	19 03	19 30	20 04	19 55	20 53	21 41	22 21
20	18 41	19 05	19 35	19 27	20 28	21 21	22 07
N 10	18 22	18 45	19 12	19 04	20 07	21 04	21 54
0	18 04	18 27	18 53	18 41	19 47	20 48	21 43
S 10	17 47	18 10	18 36	18 19	19 27	20 32	21 31
20	17 28	17 53	18 20	17 55	19 06	20 14	21 18
30	17 07	17 34	18 04	17 27	18 40	19 54	21 03
35	16 55	17 23	17 55	17 11	18 26	19 42	20 55
40	16 41	17 11	17 45	16 51	18 08	19 28	20 45
45	16 24	16 58	17 35	16 28	17 47	19 11	20 33
S 50	16 03	16 42	17 23	15 58	17 21	18 51	20 19
52	15 54	16 34	17 18	15 43	17 08	18 41	20 12
54	15 42	16 26	17 12	15 25	16 53	18 30	20 05
56	15 30	16 17	17 06	15 04	16 35	18 17	19 57
58	15 15	16 07	17 00	14 38	16 14	18 02	19 47
S 60	14 58	15 55	16 52	14 01	15 47	17 45	19 36

Day	SUN Eqn. of Time 00^h	SUN Eqn. of Time 12^h	SUN Mer. Pass.	MOON Mer. Pass. Upper	MOON Mer. Pass. Lower	MOON Age	MOON Phase
d	m s	m s	h m	h m	h m	d	%
15	00 24	00 30	12 01	12 25	24 59	00	0
16	00 37	00 43	12 01	13 32	00 59	01	3
17	00 50	00 56	12 01	14 34	02 04	02	8

UT d	UT h	ARIES GHA	VENUS −4·0 GHA	VENUS Dec	MARS +1·3 GHA	MARS Dec	JUPITER −1·8 GHA	JUPITER Dec	SATURN +0·8 GHA	SATURN Dec
d	h	° ′	° ′	° ′	° ′	° ′	° ′	° ′	° ′	° ′
18 THURSDAY	00	266 15.1	138 05.0	N20 54.2	216 19.1	N17 53.4	146 40.0	N21 05.5	252 55.5	N 3 11.0
	01	281 17.6	153 04.4	53.5	231 19.7	53.9	161 41.9	05.4	267 57.8	11.1
	02	296 20.0	168 03.9	52.8	246 20.3	54.4	176 43.9	05.3	283 00.1	11.1
	03	311 22.5	183 03.4	. . 52.0	261 21.0	. . 54.9	191 45.8	. . 05.2	298 02.4	. . 11.2
	04	326 25.0	198 02.8	51.3	276 21.6	55.4	206 47.7	05.1	313 04.8	11.2
	05	341 27.4	213 02.3	50.6	291 22.2	55.9	221 49.6	05.0	328 07.1	11.3
	06	356 29.9	228 01.8	N20 49.8	306 22.8	N17 56.4	236 51.5	N21 04.9	343 09.4	N 3 11.3
	07	11 32.3	243 01.2	49.1	321 23.5	56.9	251 53.5	04.8	358 11.7	11.4
	08	26 34.8	258 00.7	48.4	336 24.1	57.3	266 55.4	04.7	13 14.0	11.4
	09	41 37.3	273 00.2	. . 47.6	351 24.7	. . 57.8	281 57.3	. . 04.6	28 16.3	. . 11.5
	10	56 39.7	287 59.7	46.9	6 25.4	58.3	296 59.2	04.5	43 18.7	11.5
	11	71 42.2	302 59.1	46.1	21 26.0	58.8	312 01.2	04.4	58 21.0	11.6
	12	86 44.7	317 58.6	N20 45.4	36 26.6	N17 59.3	327 03.1	N21 04.3	73 23.3	N 3 11.6
	13	101 47.1	332 58.1	44.7	51 27.3	17 59.8	342 05.0	04.2	88 25.6	11.7
	14	116 49.6	347 57.6	43.9	66 27.9	18 00.3	357 06.9	04.1	103 27.9	11.7
	15	131 52.1	2 57.0	. . 43.2	81 28.5	. . 00.8	12 08.9	. . 04.0	118 30.3	. . 11.8
	16	146 54.5	17 56.5	42.4	96 29.1	01.2	27 10.8	03.9	133 32.6	11.8
	17	161 57.0	32 56.0	41.7	111 29.8	01.7	42 12.7	03.8	148 34.9	11.9
	18	176 59.5	47 55.5	N20 40.9	126 30.4	N18 02.2	57 14.6	N21 03.7	163 37.2	N 3 11.9
	19	192 01.9	62 55.0	40.2	141 31.0	02.7	72 16.5	03.6	178 39.5	12.0
	20	207 04.4	77 54.4	39.5	156 31.7	03.2	87 18.5	03.5	193 41.8	12.0
	21	222 06.8	92 53.9	. . 38.7	171 32.3	. . 03.7	102 20.4	. . 03.4	208 44.2	. . 12.1
	22	237 09.3	107 53.4	38.0	186 32.9	04.1	117 22.3	03.3	223 46.5	12.1
	23	252 11.8	122 52.9	37.2	201 33.6	04.6	132 24.2	03.2	238 48.8	12.2
19 FRIDAY	00	267 14.2	137 52.4	N20 36.5	216 34.2	N18 05.1	147 26.1	N21 03.1	253 51.1	N 3 12.2
	01	282 16.7	152 51.8	35.7	231 34.8	05.6	162 28.1	03.0	268 53.4	12.3
	02	297 19.2	167 51.3	34.9	246 35.4	06.1	177 30.0	02.9	283 55.8	12.3
	03	312 21.6	182 50.8	. . 34.2	261 36.1	. . 06.6	192 31.9	. . 02.8	298 58.1	. . 12.4
	04	327 24.1	197 50.3	33.4	276 36.7	07.0	207 33.8	02.7	314 00.4	12.4
	05	342 26.6	212 49.8	32.7	291 37.3	07.5	222 35.8	02.6	329 02.7	12.5
	06	357 29.0	227 49.3	N20 31.9	306 38.0	N18 08.0	237 37.7	N21 02.5	344 05.0	N 3 12.5
	07	12 31.5	242 48.8	31.2	321 38.6	08.5	252 39.6	02.4	359 07.4	12.6
	08	27 33.9	257 48.2	30.4	336 39.2	09.0	267 41.5	02.3	14 09.7	12.6
	09	42 36.4	272 47.7	. . 29.7	351 39.8	. . 09.4	282 43.4	. . 02.2	29 12.0	. . 12.6
	10	57 38.9	287 47.2	28.9	6 40.5	09.9	297 45.4	02.1	44 14.3	12.7
	11	72 41.3	302 46.7	28.1	21 41.1	10.4	312 47.3	02.0	59 16.6	12.7
	12	87 43.8	317 46.2	N20 27.4	36 41.7	N18 10.9	327 49.2	N21 01.9	74 19.0	N 3 12.8
	13	102 46.3	332 45.7	26.6	51 42.4	11.4	342 51.1	01.8	89 21.3	12.8
	14	117 48.7	347 45.2	25.8	66 43.0	11.8	357 53.0	01.7	104 23.6	12.9
	15	132 51.2	2 44.7	. . 25.1	81 43.6	. . 12.3	12 55.0	. . 01.6	119 25.9	. . 12.9
	16	147 53.7	17 44.2	24.3	96 44.2	12.8	27 56.9	01.5	134 28.3	13.0
	17	162 56.1	32 43.7	23.5	111 44.9	13.3	42 58.8	01.4	149 30.6	13.0
	18	177 58.6	47 43.2	N20 22.8	126 45.5	N18 13.8	58 00.7	N21 01.3	164 32.9	N 3 13.1
	19	193 01.1	62 42.7	22.0	141 46.1	14.2	73 02.6	01.2	179 35.2	13.1
	20	208 03.5	77 42.2	21.2	156 46.8	14.7	88 04.6	01.1	194 37.5	13.2
	21	223 06.0	92 41.7	. . 20.5	171 47.4	. . 15.2	103 06.5	. . 01.0	209 39.9	. . 13.2
	22	238 08.4	107 41.2	19.7	186 48.0	15.7	118 08.4	00.9	224 42.2	13.3
	23	253 10.9	122 40.6	18.9	201 48.6	16.1	133 10.3	00.8	239 44.5	13.3
20 SATURDAY	00	268 13.4	137 40.1	N20 18.2	216 49.3	N18 16.6	148 12.2	N21 00.7	254 46.8	N 3 13.4
	01	283 15.8	152 39.6	17.4	231 49.9	17.1	163 14.2	00.6	269 49.2	13.4
	02	298 18.3	167 39.1	16.6	246 50.5	17.6	178 16.1	00.5	284 51.5	13.5
	03	313 20.8	182 38.7	. . 15.8	261 51.2	. . 18.0	193 18.0	. . 00.4	299 53.8	. . 13.5
	04	328 23.2	197 38.2	15.1	276 51.8	18.5	208 19.9	00.3	314 56.1	13.6
	05	343 25.7	212 37.7	14.3	291 52.4	19.0	223 21.8	00.2	329 58.4	13.6
	06	358 28.2	227 37.2	N20 13.5	306 53.0	N18 19.5	238 23.8	N21 00.1	345 00.8	N 3 13.7
	07	13 30.6	242 36.7	12.7	321 53.7	19.9	253 25.7	21 00.0	0 03.1	13.7
	08	28 33.1	257 36.2	11.9	336 54.3	20.4	268 27.6	20 59.9	15 05.4	13.8
	09	43 35.6	272 35.7	. . 11.2	351 54.9	. . 20.9	283 29.5	. . 59.8	30 07.7	. . 13.8
	10	58 38.0	287 35.2	10.4	6 55.6	21.3	298 31.4	59.7	45 10.1	13.9
	11	73 40.5	302 34.7	09.6	21 56.2	21.8	313 33.4	59.6	60 12.4	13.9
	12	88 42.9	317 34.2	N20 08.8	36 56.8	N18 22.3	328 35.3	N20 59.5	75 14.7	N 3 13.9
	13	103 45.4	332 33.7	08.0	51 57.4	22.8	343 37.2	59.4	90 17.0	14.0
	14	118 47.9	347 33.2	07.3	66 58.1	23.2	358 39.1	59.3	105 19.4	14.0
	15	133 50.3	2 32.7	. . 06.5	81 58.7	. . 23.7	13 41.0	. . 59.2	120 21.7	. . 14.1
	16	148 52.8	17 32.2	05.7	96 59.3	24.2	28 43.0	59.1	135 24.0	14.1
	17	163 55.3	32 31.7	04.9	111 59.9	24.6	43 44.9	59.0	150 26.3	14.2
	18	178 57.7	47 31.3	N20 04.1	127 00.6	N18 25.1	58 46.8	N20 58.9	165 28.7	N 3 14.2
	19	194 00.2	62 30.8	03.3	142 01.2	25.6	73 48.7	58.8	180 31.0	14.3
	20	209 02.7	77 30.3	02.5	157 01.8	26.1	88 50.6	58.7	195 33.3	14.3
	21	224 05.1	92 29.8	. . 01.7	172 02.5	. . 26.5	103 52.5	. . 58.6	210 35.6	. . 14.4
	22	239 07.6	107 29.3	00.9	187 03.1	27.0	118 54.5	58.5	225 38.0	14.4
	23	254 10.0	122 28.8	00.2	202 03.7	27.5	133 56.4	58.4	240 40.3	14.5
Mer. Pass.		6 10.0 (h m)	v −0.5	d 0.8	v 0.6	d 0.5	v 1.9	d 0.1	v 2.3	d 0.0

STARS

Name	SHA ° ′	Dec ° ′
Acamar	315 11.2	S40 11.7
Achernar	335 19.6	S57 05.8
Acrux	172 58.6	S63 15.1
Adhara	255 05.3	S29 00.5
Aldebaran	290 38.6	N16 33.7
Alioth	166 11.8	N55 49.2
Alkaid	152 50.8	N49 11.0
Alnair	27 31.2	S46 49.7
Alnilam	275 36.9	S 1 11.1
Alphard	217 46.8	S 8 46.5
Alphecca	126 02.4	N26 37.6
Alpheratz	357 33.6	N29 14.1
Altair	61 58.5	N 8 56.3
Ankaa	353 06.0	S42 09.4
Antares	112 14.0	S26 29.5
Arcturus	145 46.6	N19 02.7
Atria	107 06.6	S69 04.6
Avior	234 14.8	S59 35.8
Bellatrix	278 21.9	N 6 22.4
Betelgeuse	270 51.1	N 7 24.7
Canopus	263 52.4	S52 42.6
Capella	280 20.6	N46 01.4
Deneb	49 24.6	N45 22.3
Denebola	182 23.7	N14 25.5
Diphda	348 46.2	S17 50.3
Dubhe	193 39.7	N61 36.7
Elnath	278 00.7	N28 37.7
Eltanin	90 41.1	N51 29.1
Enif	33 37.4	N 9 59.8
Fomalhaut	15 13.1	S29 28.7
Gacrux	171 50.2	S57 16.0
Gienah	175 42.3	S17 41.5
Hadar	148 33.9	S60 30.3
Hamal	327 50.0	N23 35.2
Kaus Aust.	83 30.5	S34 22.3
Kochab	137 19.0	N74 02.9
Markab	13 28.6	N15 20.8
Menkar	314 05.1	N 4 11.6
Menkent	147 56.0	S36 30.2
Miaplacidus	221 38.7	S69 49.8
Mirfak	308 26.9	N49 57.2
Nunki	75 45.9	S26 15.8
Peacock	53 03.4	S56 38.8
Pollux	243 16.2	N27 57.8
Procyon	244 49.9	N 5 09.4
Rasalhague	95 57.1	N12 32.4
Regulus	207 33.3	N11 50.3
Rigel	281 03.1	S 8 10.2
Rigil Kent.	139 38.2	S60 56.9
Sabik	102 01.1	S15 45.5
Schedar	349 29.8	N56 40.7
Shaula	96 08.3	S37 07.4
Sirius	258 25.5	S16 45.2
Spica	158 20.9	S11 18.1
Suhail	222 45.7	S43 32.6
Vega	80 32.0	N38 48.4
Zuben'ubi	136 54.4	S16 09.2

	SHA ° ′	Mer. Pass. h m
Venus	230 38.1	14 49
Mars	309 19.9	9 33
Jupiter	240 11.9	14 08
Saturn	346 36.9	7 04

UT	SUN GHA	SUN Dec	MOON GHA	v	MOON Dec	d	HP
d h	° ′	° ′	° ′	′	° ′	′	′
18 00	179 44.2	N23 24.0	136 01.1	7.0	N20 30.4	12.2	60.0
01	194 44.0	24.0	150 27.1	7.0	20 18.2	12.3	60.0
02	209 43.9	24.1	164 53.1	7.3	20 05.9	12.4	59.9
03	224 43.8	. . 24.1	179 19.4	7.3	19 53.5	12.5	59.9
04	239 43.6	24.2	193 45.7	7.5	19 41.0	12.7	59.9
05	254 43.5	24.2	208 12.2	7.7	19 28.3	12.7	59.8
06	269 43.4	N23 24.3	222 38.9	7.7	N19 15.6	12.8	59.8
T 07	284 43.2	24.3	237 05.6	7.9	19 02.8	12.9	59.7
H 08	299 43.1	24.4	251 32.5	8.1	18 49.9	13.0	59.7
U 09	314 42.9	. . 24.4	265 59.6	8.2	18 36.9	13.2	59.7
R 10	329 42.8	24.5	280 26.8	8.3	18 23.7	13.2	59.6
S 11	344 42.7	24.6	294 54.1	8.5	18 10.5	13.3	59.6
D 12	359 42.5	N23 24.6	309 21.6	8.5	N17 57.2	13.3	59.6
A 13	14 42.4	24.6	323 49.1	8.8	17 43.9	13.5	59.5
Y 14	29 42.3	24.7	338 16.9	8.8	17 30.4	13.5	59.5
15	44 42.1	. . 24.7	352 44.7	9.0	17 16.9	13.7	59.5
16	59 42.0	24.8	7 12.7	9.1	17 03.2	13.7	59.4
17	74 41.8	24.8	21 40.8	9.3	16 49.5	13.8	59.4
18	89 41.7	N23 24.9	36 09.1	9.3	N16 35.7	13.8	59.3
19	104 41.6	24.9	50 37.4	9.5	16 21.9	14.0	59.3
20	119 41.4	25.0	65 05.9	9.7	16 07.9	14.0	59.3
21	134 41.3	. . 25.0	79 34.6	9.7	15 53.9	14.0	59.2
22	149 41.2	25.1	94 03.3	9.9	15 39.9	14.2	59.2
23	164 41.0	25.1	108 32.2	10.0	15 25.7	14.2	59.2
19 00	179 40.9	N23 25.1	123 01.2	10.1	N15 11.5	14.2	59.1
01	194 40.8	25.2	137 30.3	10.2	14 57.3	14.3	59.1
02	209 40.6	25.2	151 59.5	10.4	14 43.0	14.4	59.0
03	224 40.5	. . 25.3	166 28.9	10.5	14 28.6	14.5	59.0
04	239 40.3	25.3	180 58.4	10.6	14 14.1	14.5	59.0
05	254 40.2	25.3	195 28.0	10.7	13 59.6	14.5	58.9
06	269 40.1	N23 25.4	209 57.7	10.8	N13 45.1	14.6	58.9
07	284 39.9	25.4	224 27.5	10.9	13 30.5	14.7	58.8
08	299 39.8	25.4	238 57.4	11.1	13 15.8	14.7	58.8
F 09	314 39.7	. . 25.5	253 27.5	11.1	13 01.1	14.7	58.8
R 10	329 39.5	25.5	267 57.6	11.3	12 46.4	14.8	58.7
I 11	344 39.4	25.5	282 27.9	11.3	12 31.6	14.8	58.7
D 12	359 39.2	N23 25.6	296 58.2	11.5	N12 16.8	14.9	58.6
A 13	14 39.1	25.6	311 28.7	11.6	12 01.9	14.9	58.6
Y 14	29 39.0	25.6	325 59.3	11.7	11 47.0	15.0	58.6
15	44 38.8	. . 25.7	340 30.0	11.8	11 32.0	14.9	58.5
16	59 38.7	25.7	355 00.8	11.8	11 17.1	15.1	58.5
17	74 38.6	25.7	9 31.6	12.0	11 02.0	15.0	58.4
18	89 38.4	N23 25.7	24 02.6	12.1	N10 47.0	15.1	58.4
19	104 38.3	25.8	38 33.7	12.2	10 31.9	15.1	58.4
20	119 38.1	25.8	53 04.9	12.2	10 16.8	15.2	58.3
21	134 38.0	. . 25.8	67 36.1	12.4	10 01.6	15.1	58.3
22	149 37.9	25.9	82 07.5	12.4	9 46.5	15.2	58.2
23	164 37.7	25.9	96 38.9	12.6	9 31.3	15.3	58.2
20 00	179 37.6	N23 25.9	111 10.5	12.6	N 9 16.0	15.2	58.2
01	194 37.5	25.9	125 42.1	12.7	9 00.8	15.3	58.1
02	209 37.3	25.9	140 13.8	12.8	8 45.5	15.3	58.1
03	224 37.2	. . 26.0	154 45.6	12.9	8 30.2	15.3	58.0
04	239 37.0	26.0	169 17.5	13.0	8 14.9	15.3	58.0
05	254 36.9	26.0	183 49.5	13.0	7 59.6	15.3	58.0
06	269 36.8	N23 26.0	198 21.5	13.2	N 7 44.3	15.4	57.9
S 07	284 36.6	26.0	212 53.7	13.2	7 28.9	15.3	57.9
A 08	299 36.5	26.1	227 25.9	13.3	7 13.6	15.4	57.9
T 09	314 36.4	. . 26.1	241 58.2	13.3	6 58.2	15.4	57.8
U 10	329 36.2	26.1	256 30.5	13.5	6 42.8	15.4	57.8
R 11	344 36.1	26.1	271 03.0	13.5	6 27.4	15.4	57.7
D 12	359 36.0	N23 26.1	285 35.5	13.5	N 6 12.0	15.4	57.7
A 13	14 35.8	26.1	300 08.0	13.7	5 56.6	15.4	57.7
Y 14	29 35.7	26.2	314 40.7	13.7	5 41.2	15.4	57.6
15	44 35.5	. . 26.2	329 13.4	13.8	5 25.8	15.5	57.6
16	59 35.4	26.2	343 46.2	13.8	5 10.3	15.4	57.5
17	74 35.3	26.2	358 19.0	13.9	4 54.9	15.4	57.5
18	89 35.1	N23 26.2	12 51.9	14.0	N 4 39.5	15.4	57.5
19	104 35.0	26.2	27 24.9	14.0	4 24.1	15.5	57.4
20	119 34.9	26.2	41 57.9	14.1	4 08.6	15.4	57.4
21	134 34.7	. . 26.2	56 31.0	14.2	3 53.2	15.4	57.3
22	149 34.6	26.2	71 04.2	14.2	3 37.8	15.4	57.3
23	164 34.4	26.2	85 37.4	14.2	N 3 22.4	15.4	57.3
	SD 15.8	*d* 0.0	SD	16.2	16.0		15.7

Lat.	Twilight Naut.	Twilight Civil	Sunrise	Moonrise 18	19	20	21
°	h m	h m	h m	h m	h m	h m	h m
N 72	▭	▭	▭	▭	06 54	09 28	11 40
N 70	▭	▭	▭	03 57	07 21	09 38	11 40
68	▭	▭	▭	05 08	07 42	09 47	11 40
66	▭	▭	▭	05 44	07 58	09 54	11 40
64	////	////	01 31	06 09	08 11	09 59	11 40
62	////	////	02 09	06 29	08 22	10 04	11 40
60	////	00 49	02 36	06 45	08 31	10 09	11 40
N 58	////	01 40	02 56	06 59	08 39	10 12	11 40
56	////	02 10	03 13	07 11	08 46	10 16	11 40
54	00 45	02 33	03 27	07 21	08 53	10 19	11 40
52	01 32	02 51	03 39	07 30	08 58	10 21	11 40
50	02 00	03 06	03 50	07 38	09 03	10 24	11 40
45	02 46	03 35	04 13	07 55	09 14	10 29	11 40
N 40	03 16	03 58	04 31	08 09	09 23	10 34	11 40
35	03 40	04 16	04 46	08 20	09 31	10 37	11 40
30	03 58	04 32	04 59	08 31	09 38	10 41	11 40
20	04 27	04 57	05 21	08 48	09 49	10 46	11 40
N 10	04 50	05 17	05 40	09 03	10 00	10 51	11 40
0	05 09	05 35	05 58	09 17	10 09	10 56	11 40
S 10	05 26	05 52	06 15	09 31	10 18	11 01	11 40
20	05 42	06 10	06 34	09 46	10 28	11 06	11 41
30	05 59	06 29	06 55	10 03	10 40	11 12	11 41
35	06 07	06 39	07 07	10 13	10 46	11 15	11 41
40	06 17	06 51	07 22	10 24	10 54	11 19	11 41
45	06 27	07 04	07 38	10 38	11 02	11 23	11 41
S 50	06 39	07 21	07 59	10 54	11 13	11 28	11 41
52	06 44	07 28	08 09	11 01	11 17	11 30	11 41
54	06 50	07 36	08 20	11 09	11 23	11 33	11 41
56	06 56	07 45	08 33	11 18	11 28	11 36	11 42
58	07 03	07 56	08 48	11 29	11 35	11 39	11 42
S 60	07 10	08 07	09 05	11 41	11 42	11 42	11 42

Lat.	Sunset	Twilight Civil	Twilight Naut.	Moonset 18	19	20	21
°	h m	h m	h m	h m	h m	h m	h m
N 72	▭	▭	▭	▭	01 26	{00 33 / 23 56}	23 24
N 70	▭	▭	▭	02 30	00 56	{00 20 / 23 52}	23 28
68	▭	▭	▭	01 18	00 34	{00 09 / 23 49}	23 31
66	▭	▭	▭	00 40	00 16	{00 00 / 23 46}	23 34
64	22 32	////	////	00 14	{00 02 / 23 52}	23 44	23 36
62	21 54	////	////	23 49	23 46	23 42	23 38
60	21 27	23 14	////	23 39	23 40	23 40	23 40
N 58	21 07	22 23	////	23 30	23 35	23 38	23 41
56	20 50	21 53	////	23 21	23 30	23 37	23 43
54	20 36	21 30	23 18	23 14	23 26	23 35	23 44
52	20 23	21 12	22 31	23 08	23 22	23 34	23 45
50	20 12	20 57	22 03	23 02	23 19	23 33	23 46
45	19 50	20 27	21 17	22 49	23 11	23 31	23 49
N 40	19 32	20 05	20 46	22 38	23 05	23 29	23 50
35	19 17	19 47	20 23	22 29	23 00	23 27	23 52
30	19 04	19 31	20 05	22 21	22 55	23 25	23 54
20	18 42	19 06	19 35	22 07	22 46	23 22	23 56
N 10	18 23	18 46	19 13	21 54	22 39	23 20	23 59
0	18 05	18 28	18 54	21 43	22 32	23 18	24 01
S 10	17 48	18 10	18 37	21 31	22 25	23 15	24 03
20	17 29	17 53	18 21	21 18	22 17	23 12	24 05
30	17 08	17 34	18 04	21 03	22 08	23 09	24 08
35	16 55	17 24	17 55	20 55	22 03	23 08	24 09
40	16 41	17 12	17 46	20 45	21 57	23 06	24 11
45	16 24	16 58	17 36	20 33	21 51	23 03	24 13
S 50	16 04	16 42	17 24	20 19	21 42	23 01	24 15
52	15 54	16 35	17 18	20 12	21 38	22 59	24 17
54	15 43	16 26	17 13	20 05	21 34	22 58	24 18
56	15 30	16 17	17 07	19 57	21 29	22 56	24 19
58	15 15	16 07	17 00	19 47	21 24	22 55	24 21
S 60	14 58	15 55	16 52	19 36	21 18	22 53	24 22

Day	SUN Eqn. of Time 00^h	SUN Eqn. of Time 12^h	SUN Mer. Pass.	MOON Mer. Pass. Upper	MOON Mer. Pass. Lower	Age	Phase
d	m s	m s	h m	h m	h m	d %	
18	01 03	01 10	12 01	15 30	03 03	03 16	
19	01 16	01 23	12 01	16 21	03 56	04 25	
20	01 29	01 36	12 02	17 07	04 44	05 35	

UT (d h)	ARIES GHA	VENUS −4·0 GHA	VENUS Dec	MARS +1·3 GHA	MARS Dec	JUPITER −1·8 GHA	JUPITER Dec	SATURN +0·8 GHA	SATURN Dec
	° ′	° ′	° ′	° ′	° ′	° ′	° ′	° ′	° ′
21 00 (SUNDAY)	269 12.5	137 28.3	N19 59.4	217 04.3	N18 27.9	148 58.3	N20 58.3	255 42.6	N 3 14.5
01	284 15.0	152 27.9	58.6	232 05.0	28.4	164 00.2	58.2	270 44.9	14.6
02	299 17.4	167 27.4	57.8	247 05.6	28.9	179 02.1	58.1	285 47.3	14.6
03	314 19.9	182 26.9	. . 57.0	262 06.2	. . 29.3	194 04.1	. . 58.0	300 49.6	. . 14.6
04	329 22.4	197 26.4	56.2	277 06.8	29.8	209 06.0	57.9	315 51.9	14.7
05	344 24.8	212 25.9	55.4	292 07.5	30.3	224 07.9	57.8	330 54.2	14.7
06	359 27.3	227 25.5	N19 54.6	307 08.1	N18 30.7	239 09.8	N20 57.7	345 56.6	N 3 14.8
07	14 29.8	242 25.0	53.8	322 08.7	31.2	254 11.7	57.6	0 58.9	14.8
08	29 32.2	257 24.5	53.0	337 09.3	31.7	269 13.6	57.5	16 01.2	14.9
09	44 34.7	272 24.0	. . 52.2	352 10.0	. . 32.1	284 15.6	. . 57.4	31 03.6	. . 14.9
10	59 37.2	287 23.5	51.4	7 10.6	32.6	299 17.5	57.2	46 05.9	15.0
11	74 39.6	302 23.1	50.6	22 11.2	33.1	314 19.4	57.1	61 08.2	15.0
12	89 42.1	317 22.6	N19 49.8	37 11.9	N18 33.5	329 21.3	N20 57.0	76 10.5	N 3 15.1
13	104 44.5	332 22.1	49.0	52 12.5	34.0	344 23.2	56.9	91 12.9	15.1
14	119 47.0	347 21.6	48.2	67 13.1	34.4	359 25.1	56.8	106 15.2	15.1
15	134 49.5	2 21.2	. . 47.4	82 13.7	. . 34.9	14 27.1	. . 56.7	121 17.5	. . 15.2
16	149 51.9	17 20.7	46.6	97 14.4	35.4	29 29.0	56.6	136 19.8	15.2
17	164 54.4	32 20.2	45.8	112 15.0	35.8	44 30.9	56.5	151 22.2	15.3
18	179 56.9	47 19.8	N19 44.9	127 15.6	N18 36.3	59 32.8	N20 56.4	166 24.5	N 3 15.3
19	194 59.3	62 19.3	44.1	142 16.2	36.8	74 34.7	56.3	181 26.8	15.4
20	210 01.8	77 18.8	43.3	157 16.9	37.2	89 36.7	56.2	196 29.2	15.4
21	225 04.3	92 18.3	. . 42.5	172 17.5	. . 37.7	104 38.6	. . 56.1	211 31.5	. . 15.5
22	240 06.7	107 17.9	41.7	187 18.1	38.1	119 40.5	56.0	226 33.8	15.5
23	255 09.2	122 17.4	40.9	202 18.7	38.6	134 42.4	55.9	241 36.1	15.6
22 00 (MONDAY)	270 11.7	137 16.9	N19 40.1	217 19.4	N18 39.1	149 44.3	N20 55.8	256 38.5	N 3 15.6
01	285 14.1	152 16.5	39.3	232 20.0	39.5	164 46.2	55.7	271 40.8	15.6
02	300 16.6	167 16.0	38.4	247 20.6	40.0	179 48.2	55.6	286 43.1	15.7
03	315 19.0	182 15.5	. . 37.6	262 21.2	. . 40.4	194 50.1	. . 55.5	301 45.5	. . 15.7
04	330 21.5	197 15.1	36.8	277 21.9	40.9	209 52.0	55.4	316 47.8	15.8
05	345 24.0	212 14.6	36.0	292 22.5	41.4	224 53.9	55.3	331 50.1	15.8
06	0 26.4	227 14.2	N19 35.2	307 23.1	N18 41.8	239 55.8	N20 55.2	346 52.5	N 3 15.9
07	15 28.9	242 13.7	34.4	322 23.7	42.3	254 57.7	55.1	1 54.8	15.9
08	30 31.4	257 13.2	33.5	337 24.4	42.7	269 59.6	55.0	16 57.1	16.0
09	45 33.8	272 12.8	. . 32.7	352 25.0	. . 43.2	285 01.6	. . 54.9	31 59.4	. . 16.0
10	60 36.3	287 12.3	31.9	7 25.6	43.6	300 03.5	54.8	47 01.8	16.0
11	75 38.8	302 11.9	31.1	22 26.2	44.1	315 05.4	54.7	62 04.1	16.1
12	90 41.2	317 11.4	N19 30.3	37 26.9	N18 44.6	330 07.3	N20 54.6	77 06.4	N 3 16.1
13	105 43.7	332 10.9	29.4	52 27.5	45.0	345 09.2	54.5	92 08.8	16.2
14	120 46.1	347 10.5	28.6	67 28.1	45.5	0 11.1	54.4	107 11.1	16.2
15	135 48.6	2 10.0	. . 27.8	82 28.7	. . 45.9	15 13.1	. . 54.3	122 13.4	. . 16.3
16	150 51.1	17 09.6	27.0	97 29.4	46.4	30 15.0	54.2	137 15.8	16.3
17	165 53.5	32 09.1	26.1	112 30.0	46.8	45 16.9	54.1	152 18.1	16.4
18	180 56.0	47 08.7	N19 25.3	127 30.6	N18 47.3	60 18.8	N20 54.0	167 20.4	N 3 16.4
19	195 58.5	62 08.2	24.5	142 31.2	47.7	75 20.7	53.9	182 22.8	16.4
20	211 00.9	77 07.8	23.6	157 31.9	48.2	90 22.6	53.7	197 25.1	16.5
21	226 03.4	92 07.3	. . 22.8	172 32.5	. . 48.6	105 24.6	. . 53.6	212 27.4	. . 16.5
22	241 05.9	107 06.8	22.0	187 33.1	49.1	120 26.5	53.5	227 29.8	16.6
23	256 08.3	122 06.4	21.1	202 33.7	49.5	135 28.4	53.4	242 32.1	16.6
23 00 (TUESDAY)	271 10.8	137 05.9	N19 20.3	217 34.4	N18 50.0	150 30.3	N20 53.3	257 34.4	N 3 16.7
01	286 13.3	152 05.5	19.5	232 35.0	50.5	165 32.2	53.2	272 36.8	16.7
02	301 15.7	167 05.1	18.6	247 35.6	50.9	180 34.1	53.1	287 39.1	16.7
03	316 18.2	182 04.6	. . 17.8	262 36.2	. . 51.4	195 36.0	. . 53.0	302 41.4	. . 16.8
04	331 20.6	197 04.2	17.0	277 36.9	51.8	210 38.0	52.9	317 43.8	16.8
05	346 23.1	212 03.7	16.1	292 37.5	52.3	225 39.9	52.8	332 46.1	16.9
06	1 25.6	227 03.3	N19 15.3	307 38.1	N18 52.7	240 41.8	N20 52.7	347 48.4	N 3 16.9
07	16 28.0	242 02.8	14.5	322 38.7	53.2	255 43.7	52.6	2 50.8	17.0
08	31 30.5	257 02.4	13.6	337 39.4	53.6	270 45.6	52.5	17 53.1	17.0
09	46 33.0	272 01.9	. . 12.8	352 40.0	. . 54.1	285 47.5	. . 52.4	32 55.4	. . 17.0
10	61 35.4	287 01.5	11.9	7 40.6	54.5	300 49.4	52.3	47 57.8	17.1
11	76 37.9	302 01.0	11.1	22 41.2	55.0	315 51.4	52.2	63 00.1	17.1
12	91 40.4	317 00.6	N19 10.3	37 41.8	N18 55.4	330 53.3	N20 52.1	78 02.4	N 3 17.2
13	106 42.8	332 00.2	09.4	52 42.5	55.8	345 55.2	52.0	93 04.8	17.2
14	121 45.3	346 59.7	08.6	67 43.1	56.3	0 57.1	51.9	108 07.1	17.3
15	136 47.7	1 59.3	. . 07.7	82 43.7	. . 56.7	15 59.0	. . 51.8	123 09.4	. . 17.3
16	151 50.2	16 58.8	06.9	97 44.3	57.2	31 00.9	51.7	138 11.8	17.3
17	166 52.7	31 58.4	06.0	112 45.0	57.6	46 02.8	51.6	153 14.1	17.4
18	181 55.1	46 58.0	N19 05.2	127 45.6	N18 58.1	61 04.8	N20 51.5	168 16.4	N 3 17.4
19	196 57.6	61 57.5	04.3	142 46.2	58.5	76 06.7	51.4	183 18.8	17.5
20	212 00.1	76 57.1	03.5	157 46.8	59.0	91 08.6	51.2	198 21.1	17.5
21	227 02.5	91 56.7	. . 02.6	172 47.5	. . 59.4	106 10.5	. . 51.1	213 23.4	. . 17.6
22	242 05.0	106 56.2	01.8	187 48.1	18 59.9	121 12.4	51.0	228 25.8	17.6
23	257 07.5	121 55.8	00.9	202 48.7	N19 00.3	136 14.3	50.9	243 28.1	17.6
Mer. Pass.	h m 5 58.2	v −0.5	d 0.8	v 0.6	d 0.5	v 1.9	d 0.1	v 2.3	d 0.0

STARS Name	SHA	Dec
	° ′	° ′
Acamar	315 11.2	S40 11.7
Achernar	335 19.5	S57 05.8
Acrux	172 58.6	S63 15.1
Adhara	255 05.3	S29 00.5
Aldebaran	290 38.6	N16 33.7
Alioth	166 11.8	N55 49.2
Alkaid	152 50.8	N49 11.0
Alnair	27 31.2	S46 49.7
Alnilam	275 36.8	S 1 11.1
Alphard	217 46.8	S 8 46.5
Alphecca	126 02.4	N26 37.6
Alpheratz	357 33.5	N29 14.1
Altair	61 58.5	N 8 56.3
Ankaa	353 06.0	S42 09.4
Antares	112 14.0	S26 29.5
Arcturus	145 46.6	N19 02.7
Atria	107 06.6	S69 04.6
Avior	234 14.8	S59 35.8
Bellatrix	278 21.9	N 6 22.4
Betelgeuse	270 51.1	N 7 24.7
Canopus	263 52.4	S52 42.6
Capella	280 20.6	N46 01.4
Deneb	49 24.6	N45 22.3
Denebola	182 23.7	N14 25.5
Diphda	348 46.2	S17 50.3
Dubhe	193 39.7	N61 36.7
Elnath	278 00.7	N28 37.7
Eltanin	90 41.1	N51 29.1
Enif	33 37.4	N 9 59.8
Fomalhaut	15 13.1	S29 28.7
Gacrux	171 50.2	S57 16.0
Gienah	175 42.3	S17 41.5
Hadar	148 33.9	S60 30.3
Hamal	327 50.0	N23 35.2
Kaus Aust.	83 30.5	S34 22.3
Kochab	137 19.0	N74 03.0
Markab	13 28.6	N15 20.8
Menkar	314 05.1	N 4 11.6
Menkent	147 56.0	S36 30.2
Miaplacidus	221 38.7	S69 49.8
Mirfak	308 26.9	N49 57.2
Nunki	75 45.9	S26 15.8
Peacock	53 03.3	S56 38.8
Pollux	243 16.2	N27 57.8
Procyon	244 49.9	N 5 09.4
Rasalhague	95 57.1	N12 32.4
Regulus	207 33.3	N11 50.3
Rigel	281 03.0	S 8 10.2
Rigil Kent.	139 38.2	S60 56.9
Sabik	102 01.1	S15 45.5
Schedar	349 29.8	N56 40.7
Shaula	96 08.3	S37 07.4
Sirius	258 25.5	S16 45.2
Spica	158 20.9	S11 18.1
Suhail	222 45.8	S43 32.5
Vega	80 32.0	N38 48.4
Zuben'ubi	136 54.4	S16 09.2

	SHA	Mer. Pass.
	° ′	h m
Venus	227 05.3	14 51
Mars	307 07.7	9 30
Jupiter	239 32.7	13 59
Saturn	346 26.8	6 52

UT	SUN GHA	SUN Dec	MOON GHA	v	MOON Dec	d	HP
d h	° ′	° ′	° ′	′	° ′	′	′
21 00	179 34.3	N23 26.3	100 10.6	14.3	N 3 07.0	15.4	57.2
01	194 34.2	26.3	114 43.9	14.4	2 51.6	15.4	57.2
02	209 34.0	26.3	129 17.3	14.4	2 36.2	15.4	57.2
03	224 33.9	. . 26.3	143 50.7	14.5	2 20.8	15.4	57.1
04	239 33.8	26.3	158 24.2	14.5	2 05.4	15.3	57.1
05	254 33.6	26.3	172 57.7	14.5	1 50.1	15.4	57.1
06	269 33.5	N23 26.3	187 31.2	14.6	N 1 34.7	15.3	57.0
07	284 33.4	26.3	202 04.8	14.7	1 19.4	15.3	57.0
08	299 33.2	26.3	216 38.5	14.7	1 04.1	15.3	56.9
S 09	314 33.1	. . 26.3	231 12.2	14.7	0 48.8	15.3	56.9
U 10	329 32.9	26.3	245 45.9	14.8	0 33.5	15.3	56.9
N 11	344 32.8	26.3	260 19.7	14.8	0 18.2	15.3	56.8
D 12	359 32.7	N23 26.3	274 53.5	14.8	N 0 02.9	15.2	56.8
A 13	14 32.5	26.3	289 27.3	14.9	S 0 12.3	15.2	56.8
Y 14	29 32.4	26.3	304 01.2	14.9	0 27.5	15.2	56.7
15	44 32.3	. . 26.3	318 35.1	14.9	0 42.7	15.2	56.7
16	59 32.1	26.3	333 09.0	15.0	0 57.9	15.1	56.7
17	74 32.0	26.2	347 43.0	15.0	1 13.0	15.1	56.6
18	89 31.9	N23 26.2	2 17.0	15.0	S 1 28.1	15.1	56.6
19	104 31.7	26.2	16 51.0	15.1	1 43.2	15.1	56.6
20	119 31.6	26.2	31 25.1	15.1	1 58.3	15.1	56.5
21	134 31.4	. . 26.2	45 59.2	15.1	2 13.4	15.0	56.5
22	149 31.3	26.2	60 33.3	15.1	2 28.4	15.0	56.5
23	164 31.2	26.2	75 07.4	15.2	2 43.4	15.0	56.4
22 00	179 31.0	N23 26.2	89 41.6	15.1	S 2 58.4	14.9	56.4
01	194 30.9	26.2	104 15.7	15.2	3 13.3	14.9	56.4
02	209 30.8	26.2	118 49.9	15.2	3 28.2	14.9	56.3
03	224 30.6	. . 26.2	133 24.1	15.3	3 43.1	14.8	56.3
04	239 30.5	26.1	147 58.4	15.2	3 57.9	14.8	56.3
05	254 30.4	26.1	162 32.6	15.3	4 12.7	14.8	56.2
06	269 30.2	N23 26.1	177 06.9	15.2	S 4 27.5	14.7	56.2
07	284 30.1	26.1	191 41.1	15.3	4 42.2	14.7	56.2
08	299 29.9	26.1	206 15.4	15.3	4 56.9	14.7	56.1
M 09	314 29.8	. . 26.1	220 49.7	15.3	5 11.6	14.6	56.1
O 10	329 29.7	26.0	235 24.0	15.3	5 26.2	14.6	56.1
N 11	344 29.5	26.0	249 58.3	15.3	5 40.8	14.6	56.0
D 12	359 29.4	N23 26.0	264 32.6	15.4	S 5 55.4	14.5	56.0
A 13	14 29.3	26.0	279 07.0	15.3	6 09.9	14.5	56.0
Y 14	29 29.1	26.0	293 41.3	15.3	6 24.4	14.4	55.9
15	44 29.0	. . 25.9	308 15.6	15.4	6 38.8	14.4	55.9
16	59 28.9	25.9	322 50.0	15.3	6 53.2	14.4	55.9
17	74 28.7	25.9	337 24.3	15.3	7 07.6	14.3	55.8
18	89 28.6	N23 25.9	351 58.6	15.4	S 7 21.9	14.2	55.8
19	104 28.5	25.8	6 33.0	15.3	7 36.1	14.2	55.8
20	119 28.3	25.8	21 07.3	15.3	7 50.3	14.2	55.8
21	134 28.2	. . 25.8	35 41.6	15.3	8 04.5	14.1	55.7
22	149 28.1	25.8	50 15.9	15.3	8 18.6	14.1	55.7
23	164 27.9	25.7	64 50.2	15.4	8 32.7	14.1	55.7
23 00	179 27.8	N23 25.7	79 24.6	15.3	S 8 46.8	13.9	55.6
01	194 27.6	25.7	93 58.9	15.2	9 00.7	14.0	55.6
02	209 27.5	25.7	108 33.1	15.3	9 14.7	13.9	55.6
03	224 27.4	. . 25.6	123 07.4	15.3	9 28.6	13.8	55.6
04	239 27.2	25.6	137 41.7	15.2	9 42.4	13.8	55.5
05	254 27.1	25.6	152 15.9	15.3	9 56.2	13.7	55.5
06	269 27.0	N23 25.5	166 50.2	15.2	S10 09.9	13.7	55.5
07	284 26.8	25.5	181 24.4	15.2	10 23.6	13.6	55.5
T 08	299 26.7	25.5	195 58.6	15.2	10 37.2	13.6	55.4
U 09	314 26.6	. . 25.4	210 32.8	15.2	10 50.8	13.5	55.4
E 10	329 26.4	25.4	225 07.0	15.2	11 04.3	13.4	55.4
S 11	344 26.3	25.4	239 41.2	15.1	11 17.7	13.4	55.4
D 12	359 26.2	N23 25.3	254 15.3	15.1	S11 31.1	13.4	55.3
A 13	14 26.0	25.3	268 49.4	15.1	11 44.5	13.3	55.3
Y 14	29 25.9	25.2	283 23.5	15.1	11 57.8	13.2	55.3
15	44 25.8	. . 25.2	297 57.6	15.0	12 11.0	13.2	55.3
16	59 25.6	25.2	312 31.6	15.1	12 24.2	13.1	55.2
17	74 25.5	25.1	327 05.7	15.0	12 37.3	13.0	55.2
18	89 25.4	N23 25.1	341 39.7	15.0	S12 50.3	13.0	55.2
19	104 25.2	25.0	356 13.7	14.9	13 03.3	12.9	55.2
20	119 25.1	25.0	10 47.6	14.9	13 16.2	12.9	55.1
21	134 24.9	. . 25.0	25 21.5	14.9	13 29.1	12.8	55.1
22	149 24.8	24.9	39 55.4	14.9	13 41.9	12.7	55.1
23	164 24.7	24.9	54 29.3	14.8	S13 54.6	12.7	55.1
	SD 15.8	d 0.0	SD	15.5	15.3		15.1

Lat.	Twilight Naut.	Twilight Civil	Sunrise	Moonrise 21	Moonrise 22	Moonrise 23	Moonrise 24
°	h m	h m	h m	h m	h m	h m	h m
N 72	□	□	□	11 40	13 47	16 02	■
N 70	□	□	□	11 40	13 37	15 38	18 04
68	□	□	□	11 40	13 29	15 20	17 23
66	□	□	□	11 40	13 22	15 06	16 56
64	////	////	01 31	11 40	13 17	14 54	16 35
62	////	////	02 10	11 40	13 12	14 44	16 18
60	////	00 49	02 36	11 40	13 08	14 36	16 04
N 58	////	01 41	02 57	11 40	13 04	14 28	15 52
56	////	02 11	03 13	11 40	13 01	14 22	15 42
54	00 45	02 33	03 28	11 40	12 58	14 16	15 33
52	01 33	02 51	03 40	11 40	12 56	14 11	15 25
50	02 01	03 06	03 51	11 40	12 54	14 06	15 18
45	02 46	03 36	04 13	11 40	12 48	13 56	15 03
N 40	03 17	03 59	04 32	11 40	12 44	13 47	14 50
35	03 40	04 17	04 47	11 40	12 41	13 40	14 40
30	03 59	04 32	05 00	11 40	12 38	13 34	14 31
20	04 28	04 57	05 22	11 40	12 32	13 23	14 15
N 10	04 51	05 18	05 41	11 40	12 27	13 14	14 01
0	05 10	05 36	05 58	11 40	12 23	13 05	13 49
S 10	05 27	05 53	06 16	11 40	12 19	12 57	13 36
20	05 43	06 10	06 34	11 41	12 14	12 48	13 23
30	05 59	06 29	06 56	11 41	12 09	12 37	13 07
35	06 08	06 40	07 08	11 41	12 06	12 31	12 58
40	06 18	06 52	07 22	11 41	12 02	12 25	12 48
45	06 28	07 05	07 39	11 41	11 59	12 17	12 37
S 50	06 40	07 21	08 00	11 41	11 54	12 08	12 23
52	06 45	07 29	08 10	11 41	11 52	12 03	12 16
54	06 51	07 37	08 21	11 41	11 50	11 59	12 09
56	06 57	07 46	08 34	11 42	11 47	11 53	12 01
58	07 04	07 56	08 48	11 42	11 44	11 48	11 52
S 60	07 11	08 08	09 06	11 42	11 41	11 41	11 42

Lat.	Sunset	Twilight Civil	Twilight Naut.	Moonset 21	Moonset 22	Moonset 23	Moonset 24
°	h m	h m	h m	h m	h m	h m	h m
N 72	□	□	□	23 24	22 49	22 04	■
N 70	□	□	□	23 28	23 02	22 30	21 35
68	□	□	□	23 31	23 12	22 50	22 17
66	□	□	□	23 34	23 20	23 06	22 46
64	22 33	////	////	23 36	23 28	23 19	23 08
62	21 54	////	////	23 38	23 34	23 30	23 26
60	21 28	23 14	////	23 40	23 39	23 40	23 41
N 58	21 07	22 23	////	23 41	23 44	23 48	23 53
56	20 51	21 53	////	23 43	23 49	23 55	24 04
54	20 36	21 31	23 19	23 44	23 52	24 02	00 02
52	20 24	21 13	22 31	23 45	23 56	24 08	00 08
50	20 13	20 58	22 03	23 46	23 59	24 13	00 13
45	19 51	20 28	21 18	23 49	24 06	00 06	00 25
N 40	19 33	20 05	20 47	23 50	24 12	00 12	00 35
35	19 17	19 47	20 24	23 52	24 17	00 17	00 43
30	19 04	19 32	20 05	23 54	24 22	00 22	00 51
20	18 42	19 07	19 36	23 56	24 30	00 30	01 04
N 10	18 23	18 46	19 13	23 59	24 37	00 37	01 15
0	18 06	18 28	18 54	24 01	00 01	00 43	01 26
S 10	17 48	18 11	18 37	24 03	00 03	00 50	01 37
20	17 30	17 54	18 21	24 05	00 05	00 57	01 48
30	17 08	17 35	18 05	24 08	00 08	01 05	02 01
35	16 56	17 24	17 56	24 09	00 09	01 09	02 09
40	16 42	17 12	17 47	24 11	00 11	01 15	02 18
45	16 25	16 59	17 36	24 13	00 13	01 21	02 28
S 50	16 04	16 43	17 24	24 15	00 15	01 28	02 41
52	15 54	16 35	17 19	24 17	00 17	01 32	02 46
54	15 43	16 27	17 13	24 18	00 18	01 36	02 53
56	15 30	16 18	17 07	24 19	00 19	01 40	03 00
58	15 16	16 08	17 00	24 21	00 21	01 44	03 08
S 60	14 58	15 56	16 53	24 22	00 22	01 50	03 18

Day	SUN Eqn. of Time 00^h	SUN Eqn. of Time 12^h	SUN Mer. Pass.	MOON Mer. Pass. Upper	MOON Mer. Pass. Lower	MOON Age	MOON Phase
d	m s	m s	h m	h m	h m	d %	
21	01 42	01 49	12 02	17 51	05 29	06 46	
22	01 56	02 02	12 02	18 33	06 12	07 56	◐
23	02 09	02 15	12 02	19 16	06 54	08 66	

UT	ARIES	VENUS −4·0		MARS +1·3		JUPITER −1·8		SATURN +0·7		STARS		
	GHA	GHA	Dec	GHA	Dec	GHA	Dec	GHA	Dec	Name	SHA	Dec
d h	° ′	° ′	° ′	° ′	° ′	° ′	° ′	° ′	° ′		° ′	° ′
24 00 WEDNESDAY	272 09.9	136 55.4	N19 00.1	217 49.3	N19 00.8	151 16.2	N20 50.8	258 30.4	N 3 17.7	Acamar	315 11.1	S40 11.7
01	287 12.4	151 54.9	18 59.2	232 50.0	01.2	166 18.2	50.7	273 32.8	17.7	Achernar	335 19.5	S57 05.8
02	302 14.9	166 54.5	58.4	247 50.6	01.6	181 20.1	50.6	288 35.1	17.8	Acrux	172 58.6	S63 15.1
03	317 17.3	181 54.1	. . 57.5	262 51.2	. . 02.1	196 22.0	. . 50.5	303 37.5	. . 17.8	Adhara	255 05.3	S29 00.5
04	332 19.8	196 53.6	56.7	277 51.8	02.5	211 23.9	50.4	318 39.8	17.9	Aldebaran	290 38.6	N16 33.7
05	347 22.2	211 53.2	55.8	292 52.4	03.0	226 25.8	50.3	333 42.1	17.9			
06	2 24.7	226 52.8	N18 54.9	307 53.1	N19 03.4	241 27.7	N20 50.2	348 44.5	N 3 17.9	Alioth	166 11.8	N55 49.2
07	17 27.2	241 52.4	54.1	322 53.7	03.9	256 29.6	50.1	3 46.8	18.0	Alkaid	152 50.9	N49 11.0
08	32 29.6	256 51.9	53.2	337 54.3	04.3	271 31.6	50.0	18 49.1	18.0	Alnair	27 31.2	S46 49.7
09	47 32.1	271 51.5	. . 52.4	352 54.9	. . 04.7	286 33.5	. . 49.9	33 51.5	. . 18.1	Alnilam	275 36.8	S 1 11.1
10	62 34.6	286 51.1	51.5	7 55.6	05.2	301 35.4	49.8	48 53.8	18.1	Alphard	217 46.8	S 8 46.5
11	77 37.0	301 50.7	50.6	22 56.2	05.6	316 37.3	49.7	63 56.2	18.1			
12	92 39.5	316 50.2	N18 49.8	37 56.8	N19 06.1	331 39.2	N20 49.6	78 58.5	N 3 18.2	Alphecca	126 02.4	N26 37.6
13	107 42.0	331 49.8	48.9	52 57.4	06.5	346 41.1	49.5	94 00.8	18.2	Alpheratz	357 33.5	N29 14.1
14	122 44.4	346 49.4	48.1	67 58.0	06.9	1 43.0	49.4	109 03.2	18.3	Altair	61 58.5	N 8 56.3
15	137 46.9	1 49.0	. . 47.2	82 58.7	. . 07.4	16 44.9	. . 49.2	124 05.5	. . 18.3	Ankaa	353 06.0	S42 09.4
16	152 49.4	16 48.5	46.3	97 59.3	07.8	31 46.9	49.1	139 07.8	18.3	Antares	112 14.0	S26 29.5
17	167 51.8	31 48.1	45.5	112 59.9	08.3	46 48.8	49.0	154 10.2	18.4			
18	182 54.3	46 47.7	N18 44.6	128 00.5	N19 08.7	61 50.7	N20 48.9	169 12.5	N 3 18.4	Arcturus	145 46.6	N19 02.7
19	197 56.7	61 47.3	43.7	143 01.2	09.1	76 52.6	48.8	184 14.9	18.5	Atria	107 06.6	S69 04.6
20	212 59.2	76 46.9	42.9	158 01.8	09.6	91 54.5	48.7	199 17.2	18.5	Avior	234 14.8	S59 35.8
21	228 01.7	91 46.4	. . 42.0	173 02.4	. . 10.0	106 56.4	. . 48.6	214 19.5	. . 18.6	Bellatrix	278 21.9	N 6 22.4
22	243 04.1	106 46.0	41.1	188 03.0	10.4	121 58.3	48.5	229 21.9	18.6	Betelgeuse	270 51.1	N 7 24.7
23	258 06.6	121 45.6	40.3	203 03.6	10.9	137 00.2	48.4	244 24.2	18.6			
25 00 THURSDAY	273 09.1	136 45.2	N18 39.4	218 04.3	N19 11.3	152 02.2	N20 48.3	259 26.6	N 3 18.7	Canopus	263 52.4	S52 42.5
01	288 11.5	151 44.8	38.5	233 04.9	11.8	167 04.1	48.2	274 28.9	18.7	Capella	280 20.6	N46 01.4
02	303 14.0	166 44.4	37.6	248 05.5	12.2	182 06.0	48.1	289 31.2	18.8	Deneb	49 24.6	N45 22.4
03	318 16.5	181 44.0	. . 36.8	263 06.1	. . 12.6	197 07.9	. . 48.0	304 33.6	. . 18.8	Denebola	182 23.8	N14 25.5
04	333 18.9	196 43.5	35.9	278 06.8	13.1	212 09.8	47.9	319 35.9	18.8	Diphda	348 46.1	S17 50.3
05	348 21.4	211 43.1	35.0	293 07.4	13.5	227 11.7	47.8	334 38.3	18.9			
06	3 23.9	226 42.7	N18 34.1	308 08.0	N19 13.9	242 13.6	N20 47.7	349 40.6	N 3 18.9	Dubhe	193 39.8	N61 36.7
07	18 26.3	241 42.3	33.3	323 08.6	14.4	257 15.5	47.6	4 42.9	19.0	Elnath	278 00.7	N28 37.7
08	33 28.8	256 41.9	32.4	338 09.2	14.8	272 17.5	47.4	19 45.3	19.0	Eltanin	90 41.1	N51 29.1
09	48 31.2	271 41.5	. . 31.5	353 09.9	. . 15.2	287 19.4	. . 47.3	34 47.6	. . 19.0	Enif	33 37.4	N 9 59.8
10	63 33.7	286 41.1	30.6	8 10.5	15.7	302 21.3	47.2	49 50.0	19.1	Fomalhaut	15 13.1	S29 28.7
11	78 36.2	301 40.7	29.8	23 11.1	16.1	317 23.2	47.1	64 52.3	19.1			
12	93 38.6	316 40.3	N18 28.9	38 11.7	N19 16.5	332 25.1	N20 47.0	79 54.6	N 3 19.2	Gacrux	171 50.2	S57 16.0
13	108 41.1	331 39.9	28.0	53 12.3	17.0	347 27.0	46.9	94 57.0	19.2	Gienah	175 42.3	S17 41.5
14	123 43.6	346 39.5	27.1	68 13.0	17.4	2 28.9	46.8	109 59.3	19.2	Hadar	148 34.0	S60 30.3
15	138 46.0	1 39.1	. . 26.2	83 13.6	. . 17.8	17 30.8	. . 46.7	125 01.7	. . 19.3	Hamal	327 50.0	N23 35.2
16	153 48.5	16 38.7	25.3	98 14.2	18.3	32 32.7	46.6	140 04.0	19.3	Kaus Aust.	83 30.5	S34 22.3
17	168 51.0	31 38.2	24.5	113 14.8	18.7	47 34.7	46.5	155 06.3	19.4			
18	183 53.4	46 37.8	N18 23.6	128 15.5	N19 19.1	62 36.6	N20 46.4	170 08.7	N 3 19.4	Kochab	137 19.1	N74 03.0
19	198 55.9	61 37.4	22.7	143 16.1	19.5	77 38.5	46.3	185 11.0	19.4	Markab	13 28.6	N15 20.8
20	213 58.3	76 37.0	21.8	158 16.7	20.0	92 40.4	46.2	200 13.4	19.5	Menkar	314 05.1	N 4 11.6
21	229 00.8	91 36.6	. . 20.9	173 17.3	. . 20.4	107 42.3	. . 46.1	215 15.7	. . 19.5	Menkent	147 56.0	S36 30.2
22	244 03.3	106 36.2	20.0	188 17.9	20.8	122 44.2	46.0	230 18.1	19.5	Miaplacidus	221 38.7	S69 49.8
23	259 05.7	121 35.8	19.1	203 18.6	21.3	137 46.1	45.9	245 20.4	19.6			
26 00 FRIDAY	274 08.2	136 35.4	N18 18.3	218 19.2	N19 21.7	152 48.0	N20 45.7	260 22.7	N 3 19.6	Mirfak	308 26.9	N49 57.2
01	289 10.7	151 35.1	17.4	233 19.8	22.1	167 49.9	45.6	275 25.1	19.7	Nunki	75 45.9	S26 15.8
02	304 13.1	166 34.7	16.5	248 20.4	22.6	182 51.9	45.5	290 27.4	19.7	Peacock	53 03.3	S56 38.8
03	319 15.6	181 34.3	. . 15.6	263 21.0	. . 23.0	197 53.8	. . 45.4	305 29.8	. . 19.7	Pollux	243 16.2	N27 57.8
04	334 18.1	196 33.9	14.7	278 21.7	23.4	212 55.7	45.3	320 32.1	19.8	Procyon	244 49.9	N 5 09.4
05	349 20.5	211 33.5	13.8	293 22.3	23.8	227 57.6	45.2	335 34.5	19.8			
06	4 23.0	226 33.1	N18 12.9	308 22.9	N19 24.3	242 59.5	N20 45.1	350 36.8	N 3 19.9	Rasalhague	95 57.1	N12 32.5
07	19 25.5	241 32.7	12.0	323 23.5	24.7	258 01.4	45.0	5 39.2	19.9	Regulus	207 33.3	N11 50.3
08	34 27.9	256 32.3	11.1	338 24.1	25.1	273 03.3	44.9	20 41.5	19.9	Rigel	281 03.0	S 8 10.2
09	49 30.4	271 31.9	. . 10.2	353 24.8	. . 25.5	288 05.2	. . 44.8	35 43.8	. . 20.0	Rigil Kent.	139 38.2	S60 56.9
10	64 32.8	286 31.5	09.3	8 25.4	26.0	303 07.1	44.7	50 46.2	20.0	Sabik	102 01.1	S15 45.5
11	79 35.3	301 31.1	08.4	23 26.0	26.4	318 09.0	44.6	65 48.5	20.0			
12	94 37.8	316 30.7	N18 07.5	38 26.6	N19 26.8	333 11.0	N20 44.5	80 50.9	N 3 20.1	Schedar	349 29.7	N56 40.7
13	109 40.2	331 30.3	06.6	53 27.2	27.2	348 12.9	44.4	95 53.2	20.1	Shaula	96 08.3	S37 07.4
14	124 42.7	346 30.0	05.7	68 27.9	27.7	3 14.8	44.2	110 55.6	20.2	Sirius	258 25.5	S16 45.1
15	139 45.2	1 29.6	. . 04.8	83 28.5	. . 28.1	18 16.7	. . 44.1	125 57.9	. . 20.2	Spica	158 20.9	S11 18.1
16	154 47.6	16 29.2	03.9	98 29.1	28.5	33 18.6	44.0	141 00.3	20.2	Suhail	222 45.8	S43 32.5
17	169 50.1	31 28.8	03.0	113 29.7	28.9	48 20.5	43.9	156 02.6	20.3			
18	184 52.6	46 28.4	N18 02.1	128 30.3	N19 29.3	63 22.4	N20 43.8	171 04.9	N 3 20.3	Vega	80 32.0	N38 48.5
19	199 55.0	61 28.0	01.2	143 31.0	29.8	78 24.3	43.7	186 07.3	20.4	Zuben'ubi	136 54.5	S16 09.2
20	214 57.5	76 27.6	18 00.3	158 31.6	30.2	93 26.2	43.6	201 09.6	20.4			
21	230 00.0	91 27.3	17 59.4	173 32.2	. . 30.6	108 28.1	. . 43.5	216 12.0	. . 20.4			
22	245 02.4	106 26.9	58.5	188 32.8	31.0	123 30.1	43.4	231 14.3	20.5			
23	260 04.9	121 26.5	57.6	203 33.4	31.5	138 32.0	43.3	246 16.7	20.5			
Mer. Pass.	h m 5 46.4	*v* −0.4	*d* 0.9	*v* 0.6	*d* 0.4	*v* 1.9	*d* 0.1	*v* 2.3	*d* 0.0			

	SHA	Mer. Pass.
	° ′	h m
Venus	223 36.1	14 53
Mars	304 55.2	9 27
Jupiter	238 53.1	13 50
Saturn	346 17.5	6 41

UT (d h)	SUN GHA ° ′	SUN Dec ° ′	MOON GHA ° ′	v ′	MOON Dec ° ′	d ′	HP ′
24 00 (Wednesday)	179 24.5	N23 24.8	69 03.1	14.8	S14 07.3	12.6	55.0
01	194 24.4	24.8	83 36.9	14.8	14 19.9	12.5	55.0
02	209 24.3	24.7	98 10.7	14.7	14 32.4	12.5	55.0
03	224 24.1	. . 24.7	112 44.4	14.7	14 44.9	12.4	55.0
04	239 24.0	24.6	127 18.1	14.7	14 57.3	12.3	55.0
05	254 23.9	24.6	141 51.8	14.6	15 09.6	12.3	54.9
06	269 23.7	N23 24.5	156 25.4	14.6	S15 21.9	12.2	54.9
07	284 23.6	24.5	170 59.0	14.5	15 34.1	12.1	54.9
08	299 23.5	24.4	185 32.5	14.5	15 46.2	12.0	54.9
09	314 23.3	. . 24.4	200 06.0	14.5	15 58.2	12.0	54.9
10	329 23.2	24.3	214 39.5	14.4	16 10.2	11.9	54.8
11	344 23.1	24.3	229 12.9	14.4	16 22.1	11.8	54.8
12	359 22.9	N23 24.2	243 46.3	14.4	S16 33.9	11.8	54.8
13	14 22.8	24.2	258 19.7	14.3	16 45.7	11.7	54.8
14	29 22.7	24.1	272 53.0	14.3	16 57.4	11.6	54.8
15	44 22.5	. . 24.1	287 26.3	14.2	17 09.0	11.5	54.7
16	59 22.4	24.0	301 59.5	14.2	17 20.5	11.4	54.7
17	74 22.3	23.9	316 32.7	14.1	17 31.9	11.4	54.7
18	89 22.1	N23 23.9	331 05.8	14.1	S17 43.3	11.3	54.7
19	104 22.0	23.8	345 38.9	14.1	17 54.6	11.2	54.7
20	119 21.9	23.8	0 12.0	14.0	18 05.8	11.1	54.6
21	134 21.7	. . 23.7	14 45.0	13.9	18 16.9	11.0	54.6
22	149 21.6	23.6	29 17.9	13.9	18 27.9	11.0	54.6
23	164 21.5	23.6	43 50.8	13.9	18 38.9	10.9	54.6
25 00 (Thursday)	179 21.3	N23 23.5	58 23.7	13.8	S18 49.8	10.8	54.6
01	194 21.2	23.5	72 56.5	13.8	19 00.6	10.7	54.6
02	209 21.1	23.4	87 29.3	13.7	19 11.3	10.6	54.6
03	224 20.9	. . 23.3	102 02.0	13.6	19 21.9	10.5	54.5
04	239 20.8	23.3	116 34.6	13.7	19 32.4	10.5	54.5
05	254 20.7	23.2	131 07.3	13.5	19 42.9	10.4	54.5
06	269 20.5	N23 23.1	145 39.8	13.5	S19 53.3	10.2	54.5
07	284 20.4	23.1	160 12.3	13.5	20 03.5	10.2	54.5
08	299 20.3	23.0	174 44.8	13.4	20 13.7	10.1	54.5
09	314 20.1	. . 22.9	189 17.2	13.4	20 23.8	10.0	54.4
10	329 20.0	22.9	203 49.6	13.3	20 33.8	9.9	54.4
11	344 19.9	22.8	218 21.9	13.2	20 43.7	9.9	54.4
12	359 19.8	N23 22.7	232 54.1	13.2	S20 53.6	9.7	54.4
13	14 19.6	22.6	247 26.3	13.1	21 03.3	9.6	54.4
14	29 19.5	22.6	261 58.4	13.1	21 12.9	9.6	54.4
15	44 19.4	. . 22.5	276 30.5	13.1	21 22.5	9.4	54.4
16	59 19.2	22.4	291 02.6	13.0	21 31.9	9.4	54.4
17	74 19.1	22.3	305 34.6	12.9	21 41.3	9.2	54.3
18	89 19.0	N23 22.3	320 06.5	12.9	S21 50.5	9.2	54.3
19	104 18.8	22.2	334 38.4	12.8	21 59.7	9.0	54.3
20	119 18.7	22.1	349 10.2	12.7	22 08.7	9.0	54.3
21	134 18.6	. . 22.0	3 41.9	12.7	22 17.7	8.8	54.3
22	149 18.4	22.0	18 13.6	12.7	22 26.5	8.8	54.3
23	164 18.3	21.9	32 45.3	12.6	22 35.3	8.7	54.3
26 00 (Friday)	179 18.2	N23 21.8	47 16.9	12.5	S22 44.0	8.5	54.3
01	194 18.0	21.7	61 48.4	12.5	22 52.5	8.5	54.2
02	209 17.9	21.6	76 19.9	12.5	23 01.0	8.3	54.2
03	224 17.8	. . 21.6	90 51.4	12.3	23 09.3	8.3	54.2
04	239 17.6	21.5	105 22.7	12.3	23 17.6	8.1	54.2
05	254 17.5	21.4	119 54.0	12.3	23 25.7	8.0	54.2
06	269 17.4	N23 21.3	134 25.3	12.2	S23 33.7	8.0	54.2
07	284 17.3	21.2	148 56.5	12.2	23 41.7	7.8	54.2
08	299 17.1	21.1	163 27.7	12.1	23 49.5	7.7	54.2
09	314 17.0	. . 21.1	177 58.8	12.0	23 57.2	7.6	54.2
10	329 16.9	21.0	192 29.8	12.0	24 04.8	7.5	54.2
11	344 16.7	20.9	207 00.8	12.0	24 12.3	7.4	54.2
12	359 16.6	N23 20.8	221 31.8	11.8	S24 19.7	7.3	54.1
13	14 16.5	20.7	236 02.6	11.9	24 27.0	7.1	54.1
14	29 16.3	20.6	250 33.5	11.8	24 34.1	7.1	54.1
15	44 16.2	. . 20.5	265 04.3	11.7	24 41.2	6.9	54.1
16	59 16.1	20.4	279 35.0	11.7	24 48.1	6.8	54.1
17	74 15.9	20.3	294 05.7	11.6	24 54.9	6.8	54.1
18	89 15.8	N23 20.3	308 36.3	11.5	S25 01.7	6.6	54.1
19	104 15.7	20.2	323 06.8	11.6	25 08.3	6.4	54.1
20	119 15.6	20.1	337 37.4	11.4	25 14.7	6.4	54.1
21	134 15.4	. . 20.0	352 07.8	11.4	25 21.1	6.3	54.1
22	149 15.3	19.9	6 38.2	11.4	25 27.4	6.1	54.1
23	164 15.2	19.8	21 08.6	11.3	S25 33.5	6.0	54.1
	SD 15.8	*d* 0.1	SD	14.9	14.8		14.8

Lat. °	Twilight Naut. h m	Twilight Civil h m	Sunrise h m	Moonrise 24 h m	Moonrise 25 h m	Moonrise 26 h m	Moonrise 27 h m
N 72	□	□	□	■	■	■	■
N 70	□	□	□	18 04	■	■	■
68	□	□	□	17 23	■	■	■
66	□	□	□	16 56	19 05	■	■
64	////	////	01 33	16 35	18 24	20 38	■
62	////	////	02 11	16 18	17 56	19 40	21 29
60	////	00 52	02 37	16 04	17 35	19 07	20 33
N 58	////	01 42	02 58	15 52	17 18	18 42	20 01
56	////	02 12	03 14	15 42	17 03	18 23	19 37
54	00 48	02 34	03 29	15 33	16 51	18 07	19 17
52	01 34	02 52	03 41	15 25	16 40	17 53	19 01
50	02 02	03 07	03 52	15 18	16 30	17 41	18 47
45	02 47	03 37	04 14	15 03	16 10	17 16	18 18
N 40	03 18	04 00	04 32	14 50	15 53	16 56	17 56
35	03 41	04 18	04 47	14 40	15 40	16 39	17 37
30	04 00	04 33	05 00	14 31	15 28	16 25	17 21
20	04 29	04 58	05 22	14 15	15 07	16 01	16 55
N 10	04 51	05 18	05 41	14 01	14 50	15 40	16 32
0	05 10	05 36	05 59	13 49	14 34	15 21	16 10
S 10	05 27	05 54	06 16	13 36	14 17	15 02	15 49
20	05 43	06 11	06 35	13 23	14 00	14 41	15 26
30	06 00	06 30	06 56	13 07	13 40	14 17	15 00
35	06 09	06 40	07 08	12 58	13 29	14 04	14 44
40	06 18	06 52	07 23	12 48	13 16	13 48	14 26
45	06 28	07 06	07 39	12 37	13 00	13 29	14 05
S 50	06 40	07 22	08 00	12 23	12 41	13 05	13 37
52	06 45	07 29	08 10	12 16	12 33	12 54	13 24
54	06 51	07 37	08 21	12 09	12 23	12 41	13 09
56	06 57	07 46	08 34	12 01	12 11	12 27	12 51
58	07 04	07 57	08 48	11 52	11 59	12 10	12 29
S 60	07 11	08 08	09 06	11 42	11 44	11 49	12 01

Lat. °	Sunset h m	Twilight Civil h m	Twilight Naut. h m	Moonset 24 h m	Moonset 25 h m	Moonset 26 h m	Moonset 27 h m
N 72	□	□	□	■	■	■	■
N 70	□	□	□	21 35	■	■	■
68	□	□	□	22 17	■	■	■
66	□	□	□	22 46	22 12	■	■
64	22 32	////	////	23 08	22 53	22 18	■
62	21 54	////	////	23 26	23 22	23 17	23 11
60	21 28	23 12	////	23 41	23 44	23 51	24 08
N 58	21 07	22 23	////	23 53	24 01	00 01	00 15
56	20 51	21 53	////	24 04	00 04	00 17	00 35
54	20 37	21 31	23 17	00 02	00 14	00 30	00 52
52	20 24	21 13	22 31	00 08	00 22	00 41	01 06
50	20 13	20 58	22 03	00 13	00 30	00 51	01 19
45	19 51	20 28	21 18	00 25	00 47	01 13	01 44
N 40	19 33	20 06	20 47	00 35	01 00	01 30	02 05
35	19 18	19 48	20 24	00 43	01 12	01 45	02 22
30	19 05	19 32	20 06	00 51	01 22	01 57	02 37
20	18 43	19 07	19 37	01 04	01 40	02 19	03 02
N 10	18 24	18 47	19 14	01 15	01 55	02 38	03 24
0	18 06	18 29	18 55	01 26	02 10	02 56	03 44
S 10	17 49	18 12	18 38	01 37	02 25	03 14	04 05
20	17 30	17 54	18 22	01 48	02 40	03 33	04 27
30	17 09	17 36	18 05	02 01	02 58	03 55	04 52
35	16 57	17 25	17 57	02 09	03 09	04 09	05 07
40	16 43	17 13	17 47	02 18	03 21	04 24	05 25
45	16 26	17 00	17 37	02 28	03 35	04 42	05 46
S 50	16 05	16 44	17 25	02 41	03 53	05 04	06 13
52	15 55	16 36	17 20	02 46	04 01	05 15	06 26
54	15 44	16 28	17 14	02 53	04 10	05 27	06 41
56	15 32	16 19	17 08	03 00	04 21	05 42	06 59
58	15 17	16 09	17 01	03 08	04 33	05 58	07 20
S 60	14 59	15 57	16 54	03 18	04 47	06 18	07 48

Day	SUN Eqn. of Time 00^h m s	SUN Eqn. of Time 12^h m s	SUN Mer. Pass. h m	MOON Mer. Pass. Upper h m	MOON Mer. Pass. Lower h m	MOON Age d	MOON %	Phase
24	02 22	02 28	12 02	19 59	07 37	09	75	
25	02 34	02 41	12 03	20 45	08 22	10	83	
26	02 47	02 53	12 03	21 33	09 08	11	89	

UT		ARIES	VENUS −4·1		MARS +1·3		JUPITER −1·8		SATURN +0·7	
		GHA	GHA	Dec	GHA	Dec	GHA	Dec	GHA	Dec
d	h	° ′	° ′	° ′	° ′	° ′	° ′	° ′	° ′	° ′
27	00	275 07.3	136 26.1	N17 56.7	218 34.1	N19 31.9	153 33.9	N20 43.2	261 19.0	N 3 20.5
	01	290 09.8	151 25.7	55.8	233 34.7	32.3	168 35.8	43.1	276 21.4	20.6
	02	305 12.3	166 25.4	54.9	248 35.3	32.7	183 37.7	43.0	291 23.7	20.6
	03	320 14.7	181 25.0	. . 54.0	263 35.9	. . 33.1	198 39.6	. . 42.8	306 26.1	. . 20.7
	04	335 17.2	196 24.6	53.1	278 36.5	33.6	213 41.5	42.7	321 28.4	20.7
	05	350 19.7	211 24.2	52.1	293 37.2	34.0	228 43.4	42.6	336 30.8	20.7
	06	5 22.1	226 23.8	N17 51.2	308 37.8	N19 34.4	243 45.3	N20 42.5	351 33.1	N 3 20.8
	07	20 24.6	241 23.5	50.3	323 38.4	34.8	258 47.2	42.4	6 35.4	20.8
S	08	35 27.1	256 23.1	49.4	338 39.0	35.2	273 49.2	42.3	21 37.8	20.8
A	09	50 29.5	271 22.7	. . 48.5	353 39.6	. . 35.6	288 51.1	. . 42.2	36 40.1	. . 20.9
T	10	65 32.0	286 22.3	47.6	8 40.3	36.1	303 53.0	42.1	51 42.5	20.9
U	11	80 34.5	301 22.0	46.7	23 40.9	36.5	318 54.9	42.0	66 44.8	20.9
R	12	95 36.9	316 21.6	N17 45.7	38 41.5	N19 36.9	333 56.8	N20 41.9	81 47.2	N 3 21.0
D	13	110 39.4	331 21.2	44.8	53 42.1	37.3	348 58.7	41.8	96 49.5	21.0
A	14	125 41.8	346 20.9	43.9	68 42.7	37.7	4 00.6	41.7	111 51.9	21.1
Y	15	140 44.3	1 20.5	. . 43.0	83 43.3	. . 38.1	19 02.5	. . 41.5	126 54.2	. . 21.1
	16	155 46.8	16 20.1	42.1	98 44.0	38.6	34 04.4	41.4	141 56.6	21.1
	17	170 49.2	31 19.7	41.2	113 44.6	39.0	49 06.3	41.3	156 58.9	21.2
	18	185 51.7	46 19.4	N17 40.2	128 45.2	N19 39.4	64 08.2	N20 41.2	172 01.3	N 3 21.2
	19	200 54.2	61 19.0	39.3	143 45.8	39.8	79 10.2	41.1	187 03.6	21.2
	20	215 56.6	76 18.6	38.4	158 46.4	40.2	94 12.1	41.0	202 06.0	21.3
	21	230 59.1	91 18.3	. . 37.5	173 47.1	. . 40.6	109 14.0	. . 40.9	217 08.3	. . 21.3
	22	246 01.6	106 17.9	36.6	188 47.7	41.0	124 15.9	40.8	232 10.7	21.3
	23	261 04.0	121 17.6	35.6	203 48.3	41.5	139 17.8	40.7	247 13.0	21.4
28	00	276 06.5	136 17.2	N17 34.7	218 48.9	N19 41.9	154 19.7	N20 40.6	262 15.4	N 3 21.4
	01	291 08.9	151 16.8	33.8	233 49.5	42.3	169 21.6	40.5	277 17.7	21.5
	02	306 11.4	166 16.5	32.9	248 50.2	42.7	184 23.5	40.3	292 20.1	21.5
	03	321 13.9	181 16.1	. . 31.9	263 50.8	. . 43.1	199 25.4	. . 40.2	307 22.4	. . 21.5
	04	336 16.3	196 15.7	31.0	278 51.4	43.5	214 27.3	40.1	322 24.8	21.6
	05	351 18.8	211 15.4	30.1	293 52.0	43.9	229 29.2	40.0	337 27.1	21.6
	06	6 21.3	226 15.0	N17 29.1	308 52.6	N19 44.3	244 31.1	N20 39.9	352 29.5	N 3 21.6
	07	21 23.7	241 14.7	28.2	323 53.2	44.7	259 33.1	39.8	7 31.8	21.7
	08	36 26.2	256 14.3	27.3	338 53.9	45.2	274 35.0	39.7	22 34.2	21.7
S	09	51 28.7	271 14.0	. . 26.4	353 54.5	. . 45.6	289 36.9	. . 39.6	37 36.5	. . 21.7
U	10	66 31.1	286 13.6	25.4	8 55.1	46.0	304 38.8	39.5	52 38.9	21.8
N	11	81 33.6	301 13.2	24.5	23 55.7	46.4	319 40.7	39.4	67 41.2	21.8
D	12	96 36.1	316 12.9	N17 23.6	38 56.3	N19 46.8	334 42.6	N20 39.3	82 43.6	N 3 21.8
A	13	111 38.5	331 12.5	22.6	53 57.0	47.2	349 44.5	39.1	97 45.9	21.9
Y	14	126 41.0	346 12.2	21.7	68 57.6	47.6	4 46.4	39.0	112 48.3	21.9
	15	141 43.4	1 11.8	. . 20.8	83 58.2	. . 48.0	19 48.3	. . 38.9	127 50.6	. . 21.9
	16	156 45.9	16 11.5	19.8	98 58.8	48.4	34 50.2	38.8	142 53.0	22.0
	17	171 48.4	31 11.1	18.9	113 59.4	48.8	49 52.1	38.7	157 55.3	22.0
	18	186 50.8	46 10.8	N17 17.9	129 00.0	N19 49.2	64 54.0	N20 38.6	172 57.7	N 3 22.1
	19	201 53.3	61 10.4	17.0	144 00.7	49.6	79 55.9	38.5	188 00.1	22.1
	20	216 55.8	76 10.1	16.1	159 01.3	50.0	94 57.9	38.4	203 02.4	22.1
	21	231 58.2	91 09.7	. . 15.1	174 01.9	. . 50.5	109 59.8	. . 38.3	218 04.8	. . 22.2
	22	247 00.7	106 09.4	14.2	189 02.5	50.9	125 01.7	38.2	233 07.1	22.2
	23	262 03.2	121 09.0	13.3	204 03.1	51.3	140 03.6	38.1	248 09.5	22.2
29	00	277 05.6	136 08.7	N17 12.3	219 03.7	N19 51.7	155 05.5	N20 37.9	263 11.8	N 3 22.3
	01	292 08.1	151 08.3	11.4	234 04.4	52.1	170 07.4	37.8	278 14.2	22.3
	02	307 10.6	166 08.0	10.4	249 05.0	52.5	185 09.3	37.7	293 16.5	22.3
	03	322 13.0	181 07.6	. . 09.5	264 05.6	. . 52.9	200 11.2	. . 37.6	308 18.9	. . 22.4
	04	337 15.5	196 07.3	08.5	279 06.2	53.3	215 13.1	37.5	323 21.2	22.4
	05	352 17.9	211 07.0	07.6	294 06.8	53.7	230 15.0	37.4	338 23.6	22.4
	06	7 20.4	226 06.6	N17 06.7	309 07.5	N19 54.1	245 16.9	N20 37.3	353 25.9	N 3 22.5
	07	22 22.9	241 06.3	05.7	324 08.1	54.5	260 18.8	37.2	8 28.3	22.5
	08	37 25.3	256 05.9	04.8	339 08.7	54.9	275 20.7	37.1	23 30.6	22.5
M	09	52 27.8	271 05.6	. . 03.8	354 09.3	. . 55.3	290 22.6	. . 37.0	38 33.0	. . 22.6
O	10	67 30.3	286 05.3	02.9	9 09.9	55.7	305 24.5	36.8	53 35.4	22.6
N	11	82 32.7	301 04.9	01.9	24 10.5	56.1	320 26.5	36.7	68 37.7	22.6
D	12	97 35.2	316 04.6	N17 01.0	39 11.2	N19 56.5	335 28.4	N20 36.6	83 40.1	N 3 22.7
A	13	112 37.7	331 04.2	17 00.0	54 11.8	56.9	350 30.3	36.5	98 42.4	22.7
Y	14	127 40.1	346 03.9	16 59.1	69 12.4	57.3	5 32.2	36.4	113 44.8	22.7
	15	142 42.6	1 03.6	. . 58.1	84 13.0	. . 57.7	20 34.1	. . 36.3	128 47.1	. . 22.8
	16	157 45.1	16 03.2	57.2	99 13.6	58.1	35 36.0	36.2	143 49.5	22.8
	17	172 47.5	31 02.9	56.2	114 14.2	58.5	50 37.9	36.1	158 51.8	22.8
	18	187 50.0	46 02.6	N16 55.3	129 14.9	N19 58.9	65 39.8	N20 36.0	173 54.2	N 3 22.9
	19	202 52.4	61 02.2	54.3	144 15.5	59.3	80 41.7	35.8	188 56.6	22.9
	20	217 54.9	76 01.9	53.4	159 16.1	19 59.7	95 43.6	35.7	203 58.9	22.9
	21	232 57.4	91 01.6	. . 52.4	174 16.7	20 00.1	110 45.5	. . 35.6	219 01.3	. . 23.0
	22	247 59.8	106 01.3	51.4	189 17.3	00.5	125 47.4	35.5	234 03.6	23.0
	23	263 02.3	121 00.9	50.5	204 17.9	00.9	140 49.3	35.4	249 06.0	23.0
Mer. Pass.		h m 5 34.7	v −0.4	d 0.9	v 0.6	d 0.4	v 1.9	d 0.1	v 2.4	d 0.0

STARS		
Name	SHA	Dec
	° ′	° ′
Acamar	315 11.1	S40 11.7
Achernar	335 19.5	S57 05.8
Acrux	172 58.7	S63 15.1
Adhara	255 05.3	S29 00.5
Aldebaran	290 38.5	N16 33.7
Alioth	166 11.8	N55 49.2
Alkaid	152 50.9	N49 11.1
Alnair	27 31.1	S46 49.7
Alnilam	275 36.8	S 1 11.1
Alphard	217 46.8	S 8 46.5
Alphecca	126 02.4	N26 37.6
Alpheratz	357 33.5	N29 14.1
Altair	61 58.5	N 8 56.3
Ankaa	353 06.0	S42 09.4
Antares	112 14.0	S26 29.5
Arcturus	145 46.6	N19 02.7
Atria	107 06.6	S69 04.6
Avior	234 14.8	S59 35.8
Bellatrix	278 21.9	N 6 22.4
Betelgeuse	270 51.1	N 7 24.7
Canopus	263 52.4	S52 42.5
Capella	280 20.6	N46 01.4
Deneb	49 24.6	N45 22.4
Denebola	182 23.8	N14 25.5
Diphda	348 46.1	S17 50.3
Dubhe	193 39.8	N61 36.7
Elnath	278 00.7	N28 37.7
Eltanin	90 41.1	N51 29.1
Enif	33 37.4	N 9 59.8
Fomalhaut	15 13.0	S29 28.7
Gacrux	171 50.3	S57 16.0
Gienah	175 42.3	S17 41.5
Hadar	148 34.0	S60 30.3
Hamal	327 50.0	N23 35.2
Kaus Aust.	83 30.5	S34 22.3
Kochab	137 19.1	N74 03.0
Markab	13 28.6	N15 20.8
Menkar	314 05.1	N 4 11.6
Menkent	147 56.0	S36 30.2
Miaplacidus	221 38.8	S69 49.8
Mirfak	308 26.9	N49 57.1
Nunki	75 45.9	S26 15.8
Peacock	53 03.3	S56 38.8
Pollux	243 16.2	N27 57.8
Procyon	244 49.9	N 5 09.4
Rasalhague	95 57.1	N12 32.5
Regulus	207 33.3	N11 50.3
Rigel	281 03.0	S 8 10.2
Rigil Kent.	139 38.2	S60 56.9
Sabik	102 01.0	S15 45.5
Schedar	349 29.7	N56 40.7
Shaula	96 08.3	S37 07.4
Sirius	258 25.5	S16 45.1
Spica	158 20.9	S11 18.1
Suhail	222 45.8	S43 32.5
Vega	80 32.0	N38 48.5
Zuben'ubi	136 54.5	S16 09.2

	SHA	Mer. Pass.
	° ′	h m
Venus	220 10.7	14 55
Mars	302 42.4	9 24
Jupiter	238 13.2	13 41
Saturn	346 08.9	6 30

UT	SUN GHA	SUN Dec	MOON GHA	v	MOON Dec	d	HP
d h	° ′	° ′	° ′	′	° ′	′	′
27 00 (SATURDAY)	179 15.0	N23 19.7	35 38.9	11.3	S25 39.5	5.9	54.1
01	194 14.9	19.6	50 09.2	11.2	25 45.4	5.8	54.1
02	209 14.8	19.5	64 39.4	11.2	25 51.2	5.6	54.0
03	224 14.6	. . 19.4	79 09.6	11.1	25 56.8	5.6	54.0
04	239 14.5	19.3	93 39.7	11.1	26 02.4	5.4	54.0
05	254 14.4	19.2	108 09.8	11.0	26 07.8	5.3	54.0
06	269 14.3	N23 19.1	122 39.8	11.0	S26 13.1	5.1	54.0
07	284 14.1	19.0	137 09.8	10.9	26 18.2	5.1	54.0
08	299 14.0	18.9	151 39.7	10.9	26 23.3	4.9	54.0
09	314 13.9	. . 18.8	166 09.6	10.8	26 28.2	4.8	54.0
10	329 13.7	18.7	180 39.4	10.9	26 33.0	4.7	54.0
11	344 13.6	18.6	195 09.3	10.7	26 37.7	4.5	54.0
12	359 13.5	N23 18.5	209 39.0	10.7	S26 42.2	4.5	54.0
13	14 13.4	18.4	224 08.7	10.7	26 46.7	4.3	54.0
14	29 13.2	18.3	238 38.4	10.7	26 51.0	4.1	54.0
15	44 13.1	. . 18.1	253 08.1	10.6	26 55.1	4.1	54.0
16	59 13.0	18.0	267 37.7	10.5	26 59.2	3.9	54.0
17	74 12.8	17.9	282 07.2	10.6	27 03.1	3.8	54.0
18	89 12.7	N23 17.8	296 36.8	10.5	S27 06.9	3.6	54.0
19	104 12.6	17.7	311 06.3	10.4	27 10.5	3.6	54.0
20	119 12.5	17.6	325 35.7	10.4	27 14.1	3.4	54.0
21	134 12.3	. . 17.5	340 05.1	10.4	27 17.5	3.3	54.0
22	149 12.2	17.4	354 34.5	10.4	27 20.8	3.1	54.0
23	164 12.1	17.3	9 03.9	10.3	27 23.9	3.0	54.0
28 00 (SUNDAY)	179 11.9	N23 17.1	23 33.2	10.3	S27 26.9	2.9	54.0
01	194 11.8	17.0	38 02.5	10.3	27 29.8	2.7	54.0
02	209 11.7	16.9	52 31.8	10.2	27 32.5	2.7	54.0
03	224 11.6	. . 16.8	67 01.0	10.3	27 35.2	2.4	54.0
04	239 11.4	16.7	81 30.3	10.2	27 37.6	2.4	54.0
05	254 11.3	16.6	95 59.5	10.1	27 40.0	2.2	54.0
06	269 11.2	N23 16.5	110 28.6	10.2	S27 42.2	2.1	54.0
07	284 11.1	16.3	124 57.8	10.1	27 44.3	1.9	54.0
08	299 10.9	16.2	139 26.9	10.1	27 46.2	1.9	54.0
09	314 10.8	. . 16.1	153 56.0	10.1	27 48.1	1.7	54.0
10	329 10.7	16.0	168 25.1	10.0	27 49.8	1.5	54.0
11	344 10.5	15.9	182 54.1	10.1	27 51.3	1.4	54.0
12	359 10.4	N23 15.7	197 23.2	10.0	S27 52.7	1.3	54.0
13	14 10.3	15.6	211 52.2	10.0	27 54.0	1.2	54.0
14	29 10.2	15.5	226 21.2	10.0	27 55.2	1.0	54.0
15	44 10.0	. . 15.4	240 50.2	10.0	27 56.2	0.8	54.0
16	59 09.9	15.2	255 19.2	10.0	27 57.0	0.8	54.0
17	74 09.8	15.1	269 48.2	9.9	27 57.8	0.6	54.0
18	89 09.7	N23 15.0	284 17.1	10.0	S27 58.4	0.5	54.0
19	104 09.5	14.9	298 46.1	9.9	27 58.9	0.3	54.0
20	119 09.4	14.7	313 15.0	10.0	27 59.2	0.2	54.0
21	134 09.3	. . 14.6	327 44.0	9.9	27 59.4	0.1	54.0
22	149 09.2	14.5	342 12.9	9.9	27 59.5	0.1	54.0
23	164 09.0	14.3	356 41.8	9.9	27 59.4	0.2	54.0
29 00 (MONDAY)	179 08.9	N23 14.2	11 10.7	10.0	S27 59.2	0.4	54.0
01	194 08.8	14.1	25 39.7	9.9	27 58.8	0.4	54.0
02	209 08.7	13.9	40 08.6	9.9	27 58.4	0.7	54.0
03	224 08.5	. . 13.8	54 37.5	9.9	27 57.7	0.7	54.0
04	239 08.4	13.7	69 06.4	10.0	27 57.0	0.9	54.0
05	254 08.3	13.5	83 35.4	9.9	27 56.1	1.0	54.0
06	269 08.2	N23 13.4	98 04.3	9.9	S27 55.1	1.2	54.0
07	284 08.0	13.3	112 33.2	10.0	27 53.9	1.3	54.0
08	299 07.9	13.1	127 02.2	9.9	27 52.6	1.4	54.0
09	314 07.8	. . 13.0	141 31.1	10.0	27 51.2	1.6	54.0
10	329 07.7	12.9	156 00.1	10.0	27 49.6	1.7	54.0
11	344 07.5	12.7	170 29.1	10.0	27 47.9	1.8	54.0
12	359 07.4	N23 12.6	184 58.1	10.0	S27 46.1	2.0	54.0
13	14 07.3	12.4	199 27.1	10.0	27 44.1	2.1	54.0
14	29 07.2	12.3	213 56.1	10.0	27 42.0	2.2	54.1
15	44 07.0	. . 12.2	228 25.1	10.1	27 39.8	2.4	54.1
16	59 06.9	12.0	242 54.2	10.0	27 37.4	2.5	54.1
17	74 06.8	11.9	257 23.2	10.1	27 34.9	2.7	54.1
18	89 06.7	N23 11.7	271 52.3	10.1	S27 32.2	2.7	54.1
19	104 06.5	11.6	286 21.4	10.2	27 29.5	2.9	54.1
20	119 06.4	11.4	300 50.6	10.1	27 26.6	3.1	54.1
21	134 06.3	. . 11.3	315 19.7	10.2	27 23.5	3.2	54.1
22	149 06.2	11.2	329 48.9	10.2	27 20.3	3.3	54.1
23	164 06.0	11.0	344 18.1	10.2	S27 17.0	3.4	54.1
	SD 15.8	*d* 0.1	SD 14.7		14.7		14.7

Lat.	Twilight Naut.	Twilight Civil	Sunrise	Moonrise 27	Moonrise 28	Moonrise 29	Moonrise 30
°	h m	h m	h m	h m	h m	h m	h m
N 72	□	□	□	■	■	■	■
N 70	□	□	□	■	■	■	■
68	□	□	□	■	■	■	■
66	□	□	□	■	■	■	■
64	////	////	01 36	■	■	■	23 56
62	////	////	02 13	21 29	■	23 10	23 05
60	////	00 57	02 39	20 33	21 41	22 17	22 33
N 58	////	01 45	03 00	20 01	21 04	21 45	22 09
56	////	02 14	03 16	19 37	20 37	21 21	21 49
54	00 52	02 36	03 30	19 17	20 17	21 02	21 33
52	01 36	02 54	03 42	19 01	19 59	20 45	21 19
50	02 04	03 09	03 53	18 47	19 44	20 31	21 07
45	02 49	03 38	04 16	18 18	19 14	20 03	20 42
N 40	03 19	04 01	04 33	17 56	18 51	19 40	20 21
35	03 42	04 19	04 48	17 37	18 32	19 21	20 05
30	04 01	04 34	05 01	17 21	18 15	19 05	19 50
20	04 30	04 59	05 23	16 55	17 47	18 38	19 25
N 10	04 52	05 19	05 42	16 32	17 23	18 15	19 03
0	05 11	05 37	06 00	16 10	17 01	17 53	18 43
S 10	05 28	05 54	06 17	15 49	16 39	17 31	18 23
20	05 44	06 11	06 35	15 26	16 15	17 07	18 01
30	06 00	06 30	06 56	15 00	15 47	16 40	17 36
35	06 09	06 41	07 09	14 44	15 31	16 24	17 21
40	06 18	06 52	07 23	14 26	15 12	16 05	17 04
45	06 29	07 06	07 40	14 05	14 49	15 42	16 43
S 50	06 40	07 22	08 00	13 37	14 19	15 13	16 17
52	06 45	07 29	08 10	13 24	14 05	14 59	16 04
54	06 51	07 37	08 21	13 09	13 48	14 42	15 49
56	06 57	07 46	08 33	12 51	13 28	14 22	15 32
58	07 04	07 56	08 48	12 29	13 02	13 57	15 11
S 60	07 11	08 08	09 05	12 01	12 28	13 23	14 44

Lat.	Sunset	Twilight Civil	Twilight Naut.	Moonset 27	Moonset 28	Moonset 29	Moonset 30
°	h m	h m	h m	h m	h m	h m	h m
N 72	□	□	□	■	■	■	■
N 70	□	□	□	■	■	■	■
68	□	□	□	■	■	■	■
66	□	□	□	■	■	■	■
64	22 29	////	////	■	■	■	■
62	21 53	////	////	23 11	■	■	01 05
60	21 27	23 08	////	24 08	00 08	00 47	01 57
N 58	21 07	22 21	////	00 15	00 40	01 24	02 29
56	20 50	21 52	////	00 35	01 05	01 50	02 53
54	20 36	21 30	23 13	00 52	01 24	02 11	03 12
52	20 24	21 12	22 29	01 06	01 41	02 28	03 28
50	20 13	20 58	22 02	01 19	01 55	02 43	03 42
45	19 51	20 28	21 18	01 44	02 24	03 13	04 10
N 40	19 33	20 06	20 47	02 05	02 47	03 36	04 33
35	19 18	19 48	20 24	02 22	03 06	03 56	04 51
30	19 05	19 33	20 06	02 37	03 22	04 12	05 07
20	18 43	19 08	19 37	03 02	03 49	04 40	05 33
N 10	18 24	18 47	19 15	03 24	04 13	05 04	05 56
0	18 07	18 29	18 56	03 44	04 35	05 26	06 17
S 10	17 50	18 12	18 39	04 05	04 57	05 48	06 38
20	17 31	17 55	18 23	04 27	05 20	06 12	07 01
30	17 10	17 37	18 06	04 52	05 48	06 40	07 27
35	16 58	17 26	17 58	05 07	06 04	06 56	07 43
40	16 44	17 14	17 48	05 25	06 23	07 15	08 00
45	16 27	17 01	17 38	05 46	06 46	07 38	08 22
S 50	16 07	16 45	17 27	06 13	07 15	08 08	08 49
52	15 57	16 38	17 21	06 26	07 30	08 22	09 02
54	15 46	16 30	17 16	06 41	07 47	08 39	09 17
56	15 33	16 21	17 10	06 59	08 07	08 59	09 35
58	15 19	16 10	17 03	07 20	08 32	09 24	09 56
S 60	15 02	15 59	16 56	07 48	09 06	09 58	10 23

Day	SUN Eqn. of Time 00^h	SUN Eqn. of Time 12^h	SUN Mer. Pass.	MOON Mer. Pass. Upper	MOON Mer. Pass. Lower	Age	Phase
d	m s	m s	h m	h m	h m	d %	
27	03 00	03 06	12 03	22 22	09 57	12 94	
28	03 12	03 18	12 03	23 14	10 48	13 98	○
29	03 24	03 30	12 04	24 05	11 39	14 100	

UT (d h)	ARIES GHA	VENUS −4·1 GHA	VENUS Dec	MARS +1·3 GHA	MARS Dec	JUPITER −1·8 GHA	JUPITER Dec	SATURN +0·7 GHA	SATURN Dec
	° ′	° ′	° ′	° ′	° ′	° ′	° ′	° ′	° ′
30 00 TUESDAY	278 04.8	136 00.6	N16 49.5	219 18.6	N20 01.3	155 51.2	N20 35.3	264 08.3	N 3 23.1
01	293 07.2	151 00.3	48.6	234 19.2	01.7	170 53.1	35.2	279 10.7	23.1
02	308 09.7	165 59.9	47.6	249 19.8	02.1	185 55.0	35.1	294 13.1	23.1
03	323 12.2	180 59.6	. . 46.6	264 20.4	. . 02.5	200 57.0	. . 35.0	309 15.4	. . 23.2
04	338 14.6	195 59.3	45.7	279 21.0	02.9	215 58.9	34.9	324 17.8	23.2
05	353 17.1	210 59.0	44.7	294 21.6	03.2	231 00.8	34.7	339 20.1	23.2
06	8 19.6	225 58.6	N16 43.8	309 22.3	N20 03.6	246 02.7	N20 34.6	354 22.5	N 3 23.3
07	23 22.0	240 58.3	42.8	324 22.9	04.0	261 04.6	34.5	9 24.8	23.3
08	38 24.5	255 58.0	41.8	339 23.5	04.4	276 06.5	34.4	24 27.2	23.3
09	53 26.9	270 57.7	. . 40.9	354 24.1	. . 04.8	291 08.4	. . 34.3	39 29.6	. . 23.4
10	68 29.4	285 57.3	39.9	9 24.7	05.2	306 10.3	34.2	54 31.9	23.4
11	83 31.9	300 57.0	39.0	24 25.3	05.6	321 12.2	34.1	69 34.3	23.4
12	98 34.3	315 56.7	N16 38.0	39 25.9	N20 06.0	336 14.1	N20 34.0	84 36.6	N 3 23.5
13	113 36.8	330 56.4	37.0	54 26.6	06.4	351 16.0	33.9	99 39.0	23.5
14	128 39.3	345 56.1	36.1	69 27.2	06.8	6 17.9	33.7	114 41.4	23.5
15	143 41.7	0 55.7	. . 35.1	84 27.8	. . 07.2	21 19.8	. . 33.6	129 43.7	. . 23.5
16	158 44.2	15 55.4	34.1	99 28.4	07.6	36 21.7	33.5	144 46.1	23.6
17	173 46.7	30 55.1	33.2	114 29.0	08.0	51 23.6	33.4	159 48.4	23.6
18	188 49.1	45 54.8	N16 32.2	129 29.6	N20 08.3	66 25.5	N20 33.3	174 50.8	N 3 23.6
19	203 51.6	60 54.5	31.2	144 30.3	08.7	81 27.4	33.2	189 53.2	23.7
20	218 54.1	75 54.2	30.2	159 30.9	09.1	96 29.3	33.1	204 55.5	23.7
21	233 56.5	90 53.9	. . 29.3	174 31.5	. . 09.5	111 31.3	. . 33.0	219 57.9	. . 23.7
22	248 59.0	105 53.5	28.3	189 32.1	09.9	126 33.2	32.8	235 00.2	23.8
23	264 01.4	120 53.2	27.3	204 32.7	10.3	141 35.1	32.7	250 02.6	23.8
1 00 WEDNESDAY	279 03.9	135 52.9	N16 26.4	219 33.3	N20 10.7	156 37.0	N20 32.6	265 05.0	N 3 23.8
01	294 06.4	150 52.6	25.4	234 34.0	11.1	171 38.9	32.5	280 07.3	23.9
02	309 08.8	165 52.3	24.4	249 34.6	11.5	186 40.8	32.4	295 09.7	23.9
03	324 11.3	180 52.0	. . 23.4	264 35.2	. . 11.8	201 42.7	. . 32.3	310 12.0	. . 23.9
04	339 13.8	195 51.7	22.5	279 35.8	12.2	216 44.6	32.2	325 14.4	24.0
05	354 16.2	210 51.4	21.5	294 36.4	12.6	231 46.5	32.1	340 16.8	24.0
06	9 18.7	225 51.1	N16 20.5	309 37.0	N20 13.0	246 48.4	N20 32.0	355 19.1	N 3 24.0
07	24 21.2	240 50.8	19.5	324 37.6	13.4	261 50.3	31.8	10 21.5	24.0
08	39 23.6	255 50.4	18.5	339 38.3	13.8	276 52.2	31.7	25 23.8	24.1
09	54 26.1	270 50.1	. . 17.6	354 38.9	. . 14.2	291 54.1	. . 31.6	40 26.2	. . 24.1
10	69 28.5	285 49.8	16.6	9 39.5	14.5	306 56.0	31.5	55 28.6	24.1
11	84 31.0	300 49.5	15.6	24 40.1	14.9	321 57.9	31.4	70 30.9	24.2
12	99 33.5	315 49.2	N16 14.6	39 40.7	N20 15.3	336 59.8	N20 31.3	85 33.3	N 3 24.2
13	114 35.9	330 48.9	13.6	54 41.3	15.7	352 01.7	31.2	100 35.7	24.2
14	129 38.4	345 48.6	12.7	69 41.9	16.1	7 03.6	31.1	115 38.0	24.3
15	144 40.9	0 48.3	. . 11.7	84 42.6	. . 16.5	22 05.5	. . 30.9	130 40.4	. . 24.3
16	159 43.3	15 48.0	10.7	99 43.2	16.8	37 07.4	30.8	145 42.7	24.3
17	174 45.8	30 47.7	09.7	114 43.8	17.2	52 09.3	30.7	160 45.1	24.4
18	189 48.3	45 47.4	N16 08.7	129 44.4	N20 17.6	67 11.3	N20 30.6	175 47.5	N 3 24.4
19	204 50.7	60 47.1	07.7	144 45.0	18.0	82 13.2	30.5	190 49.8	24.4
20	219 53.2	75 46.8	06.8	159 45.6	18.4	97 15.1	30.4	205 52.2	24.4
21	234 55.7	90 46.5	. . 05.8	174 46.3	. . 18.7	112 17.0	. . 30.3	220 54.6	. . 24.5
22	249 58.1	105 46.2	04.8	189 46.9	19.1	127 18.9	30.2	235 56.9	24.5
23	265 00.6	120 45.9	03.8	204 47.5	19.5	142 20.8	30.0	250 59.3	24.5
2 00 THURSDAY	280 03.0	135 45.7	N16 02.8	219 48.1	N20 19.9	157 22.7	N20 29.9	266 01.6	N 3 24.6
01	295 05.5	150 45.4	01.8	234 48.7	20.3	172 24.6	29.8	281 04.0	24.6
02	310 08.0	165 45.1	16 00.8	249 49.3	20.6	187 26.5	29.7	296 06.4	24.6
03	325 10.4	180 44.8	15 59.8	264 49.9	. . 21.0	202 28.4	. . 29.6	311 08.7	. . 24.7
04	340 12.9	195 44.5	58.9	279 50.6	21.4	217 30.3	29.5	326 11.1	24.7
05	355 15.4	210 44.2	57.9	294 51.2	21.8	232 32.2	29.4	341 13.5	24.7
06	10 17.8	225 43.9	N15 56.9	309 51.8	N20 22.2	247 34.1	N20 29.3	356 15.8	N 3 24.7
07	25 20.3	240 43.6	55.9	324 52.4	22.5	262 36.0	29.1	11 18.2	24.8
08	40 22.8	255 43.3	54.9	339 53.0	22.9	277 37.9	29.0	26 20.6	24.8
09	55 25.2	270 43.0	. . 53.9	354 53.6	. . 23.3	292 39.8	. . 28.9	41 22.9	. . 24.8
10	70 27.7	285 42.7	52.9	9 54.2	23.7	307 41.7	28.8	56 25.3	24.9
11	85 30.2	300 42.5	51.9	24 54.9	24.0	322 43.6	28.7	71 27.7	24.9
12	100 32.6	315 42.2	N15 50.9	39 55.5	N20 24.4	337 45.5	N20 28.6	86 30.0	N 3 24.9
13	115 35.1	330 41.9	49.9	54 56.1	24.8	352 47.4	28.5	101 32.4	24.9
14	130 37.5	345 41.6	48.9	69 56.7	25.2	7 49.3	28.4	116 34.8	25.0
15	145 40.0	0 41.3	. . 47.9	84 57.3	. . 25.5	22 51.2	. . 28.2	131 37.1	. . 25.0
16	160 42.5	15 41.0	46.9	99 57.9	25.9	37 53.1	28.1	146 39.5	25.0
17	175 44.9	30 40.8	45.9	114 58.5	26.3	52 55.0	28.0	161 41.9	25.1
18	190 47.4	45 40.5	N15 44.9	129 59.2	N20 26.7	67 56.9	N20 27.9	176 44.2	N 3 25.1
19	205 49.9	60 40.2	43.9	144 59.8	27.0	82 58.8	27.8	191 46.6	25.1
20	220 52.3	75 39.9	42.9	160 00.4	27.4	98 00.7	27.7	206 49.0	25.1
21	235 54.8	90 39.6	. . 41.9	175 01.0	. . 27.8	113 02.6	. . 27.6	221 51.3	. . 25.2
22	250 57.3	105 39.4	40.9	190 01.6	28.2	128 04.6	27.4	236 53.7	25.2
23	265 59.7	120 39.1	39.9	205 02.2	28.5	143 06.5	27.3	251 56.1	25.2
Mer. Pass.	h m 5 22.9	v −0.3	d 1.0	v 0.6	d 0.4	v 1.9	d 0.1	v 2.4	d 0.0

STARS

Name	SHA	Dec
	° ′	° ′
Acamar	315 11.1	S40 11.7
Achernar	335 19.4	S57 05.8
Acrux	172 58.7	S63 15.1
Adhara	255 05.3	S29 00.5
Aldebaran	290 38.5	N16 33.7
Alioth	166 11.9	N55 49.2
Alkaid	152 50.9	N49 11.1
Alnair	27 31.1	S46 49.7
Alnilam	275 36.8	S 1 11.1
Alphard	217 46.8	S 8 46.5
Alphecca	126 02.4	N26 37.6
Alpheratz	357 33.4	N29 14.1
Altair	61 58.4	N 8 56.3
Ankaa	353 05.9	S42 09.4
Antares	112 14.0	S26 29.5
Arcturus	145 46.6	N19 02.7
Atria	107 06.6	S69 04.6
Avior	234 14.8	S59 35.8
Bellatrix	278 21.9	N 6 22.4
Betelgeuse	270 51.1	N 7 24.7
Canopus	263 52.4	S52 42.5
Capella	280 20.5	N46 01.4
Deneb	49 24.6	N45 22.4
Denebola	182 23.8	N14 25.5
Diphda	348 46.1	S17 50.3
Dubhe	193 39.8	N61 36.7
Elnath	278 00.7	N28 37.7
Eltanin	90 41.1	N51 29.1
Enif	33 37.4	N 9 59.8
Fomalhaut	15 13.0	S29 28.7
Gacrux	171 50.3	S57 16.0
Gienah	175 42.3	S17 41.5
Hadar	148 34.0	S60 30.3
Hamal	327 49.9	N23 35.2
Kaus Aust.	83 30.5	S34 22.3
Kochab	137 19.2	N74 03.0
Markab	13 28.5	N15 20.9
Menkar	314 05.1	N 4 11.7
Menkent	147 56.0	S36 30.2
Miaplacidus	221 38.8	S69 49.7
Mirfak	308 26.8	N49 57.1
Nunki	75 45.9	S26 15.8
Peacock	53 03.3	S56 38.8
Pollux	243 16.2	N27 57.8
Procyon	244 49.9	N 5 09.4
Rasalhague	95 57.1	N12 32.5
Regulus	207 33.3	N11 50.3
Rigel	281 03.0	S 8 10.2
Rigil Kent.	139 38.2	S60 56.9
Sabik	102 01.0	S15 45.5
Schedar	349 29.6	N56 40.7
Shaula	96 08.3	S37 07.4
Sirius	258 25.5	S16 45.1
Spica	158 20.9	S11 18.1
Suhail	222 45.8	S43 32.5
Vega	80 32.0	N38 48.5
Zuben'ubi	136 54.5	S16 09.2

	SHA	Mer. Pass.
	° ′	h m
Venus	216 49.0	14 57
Mars	300 29.4	9 21
Jupiter	237 33.1	13 32
Saturn	346 01.0	6 19

	UT	SUN GHA	SUN Dec	MOON GHA	v	MOON Dec	d	HP
	d h	° ′	° ′	° ′	′	° ′	′	′
	30 00	179 05.9	N23 10.9	358 47.3	10.3	S27 13.6	3.6	54.1
	01	194 05.8	10.7	13 16.6	10.2	27 10.0	3.7	54.1
	02	209 05.7	10.6	27 45.8	10.4	27 06.3	3.8	54.1
	03	224 05.5	. . 10.4	42 15.2	10.3	27 02.5	4.0	54.1
	04	239 05.4	10.3	56 44.5	10.4	26 58.5	4.1	54.1
	05	254 05.3	10.1	71 13.9	10.4	26 54.4	4.2	54.1
	06	269 05.2	N23 10.0	85 43.3	10.4	S26 50.2	4.4	54.1
	07	284 05.1	09.8	100 12.7	10.5	26 45.8	4.5	54.2
T	08	299 04.9	09.7	114 42.2	10.5	26 41.3	4.6	54.2
U	09	314 04.8	. . 09.5	129 11.7	10.5	26 36.7	4.7	54.2
E	10	329 04.7	09.3	143 41.2	10.6	26 32.0	4.9	54.2
S	11	344 04.6	09.2	158 10.8	10.6	26 27.1	5.0	54.2
D	12	359 04.4	N23 09.0	172 40.4	10.7	S26 22.1	5.1	54.2
A	13	14 04.3	08.9	187 10.1	10.6	26 17.0	5.3	54.2
Y	14	29 04.2	08.7	201 39.7	10.8	26 11.7	5.3	54.2
	15	44 04.1	. . 08.6	216 09.5	10.8	26 06.4	5.5	54.2
	16	59 04.0	08.4	230 39.3	10.8	26 00.9	5.7	54.2
	17	74 03.8	08.2	245 09.1	10.8	25 55.2	5.7	54.2
	18	89 03.7	N23 08.1	259 38.9	10.9	S25 49.5	5.9	54.2
	19	104 03.6	07.9	274 08.8	11.0	25 43.6	6.0	54.3
	20	119 03.5	07.8	288 38.8	11.0	25 37.6	6.1	54.3
	21	134 03.3	. . 07.6	303 08.8	11.0	25 31.5	6.2	54.3
	22	149 03.2	07.4	317 38.8	11.1	25 25.3	6.4	54.3
	23	164 03.1	07.3	332 08.9	11.1	25 18.9	6.5	54.3
	1 00	179 03.0	N23 07.1	346 39.0	11.2	S25 12.4	6.6	54.3
	01	194 02.9	06.9	1 09.2	11.2	25 05.8	6.7	54.3
	02	209 02.7	06.8	15 39.4	11.3	24 59.1	6.8	54.3
	03	224 02.6	. . 06.6	30 09.7	11.3	24 52.3	7.0	54.3
	04	239 02.5	06.4	44 40.0	11.4	24 45.3	7.0	54.3
	05	254 02.4	06.3	59 10.4	11.4	24 38.3	7.2	54.4
	06	269 02.3	N23 06.1	73 40.8	11.4	S24 31.1	7.3	54.4
W	07	284 02.1	05.9	88 11.2	11.6	24 23.8	7.4	54.4
E	08	299 02.0	05.8	102 41.8	11.5	24 16.4	7.6	54.4
D	09	314 01.9	. . 05.6	117 12.3	11.7	24 08.8	7.6	54.4
N	10	329 01.8	05.4	131 43.0	11.6	24 01.2	7.8	54.4
E	11	344 01.7	05.3	146 13.6	11.8	23 53.4	7.8	54.4
S	12	359 01.5	N23 05.1	160 44.4	11.7	S23 45.6	8.0	54.4
D	13	14 01.4	04.9	175 15.1	11.9	23 37.6	8.1	54.4
A	14	29 01.3	04.7	189 46.0	11.8	23 29.5	8.2	54.5
Y	15	44 01.2	. . 04.6	204 16.8	12.0	23 21.3	8.3	54.5
	16	59 01.1	04.4	218 47.8	12.0	23 13.0	8.4	54.5
	17	74 00.9	04.2	233 18.8	12.0	23 04.6	8.6	54.5
	18	89 00.8	N23 04.0	247 49.8	12.1	S22 56.0	8.6	54.5
	19	104 00.7	03.9	262 20.9	12.2	22 47.4	8.7	54.5
	20	119 00.6	03.7	276 52.1	12.2	22 38.7	8.9	54.5
	21	134 00.5	. . 03.5	291 23.3	12.2	22 29.8	8.9	54.5
	22	149 00.4	03.3	305 54.5	12.3	22 20.9	9.1	54.6
	23	164 00.2	03.1	320 25.8	12.4	22 11.8	9.1	54.6
	2 00	179 00.1	N23 03.0	334 57.2	12.4	S22 02.7	9.3	54.6
	01	194 00.0	02.8	349 28.6	12.5	21 53.4	9.3	54.6
	02	208 59.9	02.6	4 00.1	12.5	21 44.1	9.5	54.6
	03	223 59.8	. . 02.4	18 31.6	12.6	21 34.6	9.6	54.6
	04	238 59.6	02.2	33 03.2	12.6	21 25.0	9.6	54.6
	05	253 59.5	02.0	47 34.8	12.7	21 15.4	9.8	54.7
	06	268 59.4	N23 01.9	62 06.5	12.8	S21 05.6	9.8	54.7
T	07	283 59.3	01.7	76 38.3	12.8	20 55.8	10.0	54.7
H	08	298 59.2	01.5	91 10.1	12.8	20 45.8	10.0	54.7
U	09	313 59.1	. . 01.3	105 41.9	12.9	20 35.8	10.1	54.7
R	10	328 58.9	01.1	120 13.8	13.0	20 25.7	10.3	54.7
S	11	343 58.8	00.9	134 45.8	13.0	20 15.4	10.3	54.7
D	12	358 58.7	N23 00.7	149 17.8	13.0	S20 05.1	10.4	54.8
A	13	13 58.6	00.5	163 49.8	13.1	19 54.7	10.5	54.8
Y	14	28 58.5	00.3	178 21.9	13.2	19 44.2	10.6	54.8
	15	43 58.4	. . 00.2	192 54.1	13.2	19 33.6	10.7	54.8
	16	58 58.2	23 00.0	207 26.3	13.3	19 22.9	10.8	54.8
	17	73 58.1	22 59.8	221 58.6	13.3	19 12.1	10.8	54.8
	18	88 58.0	N22 59.6	236 30.9	13.4	S19 01.3	11.0	54.8
	19	103 57.9	59.4	251 03.3	13.4	18 50.3	11.0	54.9
	20	118 57.8	59.2	265 35.7	13.5	18 39.3	11.2	54.9
	21	133 57.7	. . 59.0	280 08.2	13.5	18 28.1	11.2	54.9
	22	148 57.5	58.8	294 40.7	13.5	18 16.9	11.3	54.9
	23	163 57.4	58.6	309 13.2	13.7	S18 05.6	11.3	54.9
		SD 15.8	*d* 0.2	SD 14.8		14.8		14.9

Lat.	Twilight Naut.	Twilight Civil	Sunrise	Moonrise 30	Moonrise 1	Moonrise 2	Moonrise 3
°	h m	h m	h m	h m	h m	h m	h m
N 72	□	□	□	■	■	■	01 43
N 70	□	□	□	■	■	■	{00 36 / 23 47}
68	□	□	□	■	■	{01 23 / 23 59}	23 29
66	////	////	00 19	■	■	{00 04 / 23 33}	23 14
64	////	////	01 41	23 56	23 27	23 13	23 02
62	////	////	02 17	23 05	23 00	22 56	22 52
60	////	01 03	02 42	22 33	22 39	22 42	22 43
N 58	////	01 48	03 02	22 09	22 22	22 30	22 35
56	////	02 17	03 18	21 49	22 08	22 20	22 28
54	00 58	02 39	03 32	21 33	21 55	22 10	22 22
52	01 40	02 56	03 44	21 19	21 44	22 02	22 16
50	02 06	03 11	03 55	21 07	21 34	21 55	22 11
45	02 51	03 40	04 17	20 42	21 13	21 39	22 00
N 40	03 21	04 02	04 35	20 21	20 56	21 26	21 51
35	03 44	04 20	04 50	20 05	20 42	21 14	21 43
30	04 02	04 35	05 02	19 50	20 30	21 05	21 36
20	04 31	05 00	05 24	19 25	20 08	20 48	21 24
N 10	04 53	05 20	05 43	19 03	19 50	20 33	21 13
0	05 12	05 38	06 00	18 43	19 32	20 19	21 03
S 10	05 28	05 55	06 17	18 23	19 15	20 05	20 53
20	05 44	06 12	06 36	18 01	18 56	19 49	20 42
30	06 00	06 30	06 57	17 36	18 34	19 32	20 30
35	06 09	06 41	07 09	17 21	18 21	19 22	20 23
40	06 18	06 52	07 23	17 04	18 06	19 10	20 14
45	06 28	07 06	07 39	16 43	17 49	18 56	20 05
S 50	06 40	07 21	08 00	16 17	17 27	18 40	19 53
52	06 45	07 29	08 09	16 04	17 16	18 32	19 47
54	06 51	07 37	08 20	15 49	17 04	18 23	19 41
56	06 57	07 45	08 32	15 32	16 50	18 13	19 35
58	07 03	07 55	08 47	15 11	16 34	18 01	19 27
S 60	07 10	08 07	09 04	14 44	16 15	17 48	19 18

Lat.	Sunset	Twilight Civil	Twilight Naut.	Moonset 30	Moonset 1	Moonset 2	Moonset 3
°	h m	h m	h m	h m	h m	h m	h m
N 72	□	□	□	■	■	■	03 37
N 70	□	□	□	■	■	■	04 43
68	□	□	□	■	■	02 19	05 18
66	23 40	////	////	■	■	03 36	05 43
64	22 25	////	////	■	02 03	04 13	06 03
62	21 50	////	////	01 05	02 55	04 39	06 18
60	21 25	23 03	////	01 57	03 26	04 59	06 31
N 58	21 05	22 18	////	02 29	03 49	05 16	06 42
56	20 49	21 50	////	02 53	04 08	05 29	06 52
54	20 35	21 29	23 08	03 12	04 24	05 42	07 00
52	20 23	21 11	22 27	03 28	04 38	05 52	07 08
50	20 13	20 57	22 01	03 42	04 50	06 01	07 15
45	19 50	20 28	21 17	04 10	05 14	06 21	07 29
N 40	19 33	20 05	20 47	04 33	05 34	06 37	07 41
35	19 18	19 48	20 24	04 51	05 50	06 50	07 51
30	19 05	19 33	20 06	05 07	06 04	07 02	08 00
20	18 44	19 08	19 37	05 33	06 28	07 22	08 15
N 10	18 25	18 48	19 15	05 56	06 48	07 39	08 28
0	18 08	18 30	18 56	06 17	07 07	07 55	08 40
S 10	17 50	18 13	18 39	06 38	07 26	08 11	08 52
20	17 32	17 56	18 24	07 01	07 46	08 27	09 05
30	17 11	17 38	18 07	07 27	08 09	08 47	09 20
35	16 59	17 27	17 59	07 43	08 23	08 58	09 28
40	16 45	17 16	17 50	08 00	08 38	09 10	09 38
45	16 29	17 02	17 40	08 22	08 57	09 25	09 49
S 50	16 08	16 47	17 28	08 49	09 20	09 44	10 02
52	15 59	16 39	17 23	09 02	09 31	09 52	10 08
54	15 48	16 31	17 17	09 17	09 43	10 02	10 15
56	15 35	16 22	17 11	09 35	09 58	10 12	10 22
58	15 21	16 12	17 05	09 56	10 14	10 25	10 31
S 60	15 04	16 01	16 58	10 23	10 34	10 39	10 41

Day	SUN Eqn. of Time 00^h	SUN Eqn. of Time 12^h	SUN Mer. Pass.	MOON Mer. Pass. Upper	MOON Mer. Pass. Lower	MOON Age	MOON Phase
d	m s	m s	h m	h m	h m	d %	
30	03 36	03 42	12 04	00 05	12 30	15 100	○
1	03 48	03 54	12 04	00 55	13 20	16 98	
2	03 59	04 05	12 04	01 43	14 07	17 94	

Day	UT (d h)	ARIES GHA	VENUS −4·1 GHA	VENUS Dec	MARS +1·3 GHA	MARS Dec	JUPITER −1·8 GHA	JUPITER Dec	SATURN +0·7 GHA	SATURN Dec
		° ′	° ′	° ′	° ′	° ′	° ′	° ′	° ′	° ′
FRIDAY	3 00	281 02.2	135 38.8	N15 38.9	220 02.8	N20 28.9	158 08.4	N20 27.2	266 58.4	N 3 25.3
	01	296 04.7	150 38.5	37.9	235 03.4	29.3	173 10.3	27.1	282 00.8	25.3
	02	311 07.1	165 38.2	36.9	250 04.1	29.6	188 12.2	27.0	297 03.2	25.3
	03	326 09.6	180 38.0	. . 35.9	265 04.7	. . 30.0	203 14.1	. . 26.9	312 05.5	. . 25.3
	04	341 12.0	195 37.7	34.9	280 05.3	30.4	218 16.0	26.8	327 07.9	25.4
	05	356 14.5	210 37.4	33.9	295 05.9	30.8	233 17.9	26.7	342 10.3	25.4
	06	11 17.0	225 37.1	N15 32.9	310 06.5	N20 31.1	248 19.8	N20 26.5	357 12.6	N 3 25.4
	07	26 19.4	240 36.9	31.9	325 07.1	31.5	263 21.7	26.4	12 15.0	25.4
	08	41 21.9	255 36.6	30.9	340 07.7	31.9	278 23.6	26.3	27 17.4	25.5
	09	56 24.4	270 36.3	. . 29.9	355 08.4	. . 32.2	293 25.5	. . 26.2	42 19.7	. . 25.5
	10	71 26.8	285 36.1	28.8	10 09.0	32.6	308 27.4	26.1	57 22.1	25.5
	11	86 29.3	300 35.8	27.8	25 09.6	33.0	323 29.3	26.0	72 24.5	25.6
	12	101 31.8	315 35.5	N15 26.8	40 10.2	N20 33.3	338 31.2	N20 25.9	87 26.9	N 3 25.6
	13	116 34.2	330 35.3	25.8	55 10.8	33.7	353 33.1	25.7	102 29.2	25.6
	14	131 36.7	345 35.0	24.8	70 11.4	34.1	8 35.0	25.6	117 31.6	25.6
	15	146 39.1	0 34.7	. . 23.8	85 12.0	. . 34.4	23 36.9	. . 25.5	132 34.0	. . 25.7
	16	161 41.6	15 34.5	22.8	100 12.6	34.8	38 38.8	25.4	147 36.3	25.7
	17	176 44.1	30 34.2	21.8	115 13.3	35.2	53 40.7	25.3	162 38.7	25.7
	18	191 46.5	45 33.9	N15 20.7	130 13.9	N20 35.5	68 42.6	N20 25.2	177 41.1	N 3 25.7
	19	206 49.0	60 33.7	19.7	145 14.5	35.9	83 44.5	25.1	192 43.4	25.8
	20	221 51.5	75 33.4	18.7	160 15.1	36.3	98 46.4	24.9	207 45.8	25.8
	21	236 53.9	90 33.1	. . 17.7	175 15.7	. . 36.6	113 48.3	. . 24.8	222 48.2	. . 25.8
	22	251 56.4	105 32.9	16.7	190 16.3	37.0	128 50.2	24.7	237 50.6	25.9
	23	266 58.9	120 32.6	15.7	205 16.9	37.3	143 52.1	24.6	252 52.9	25.9
SATURDAY	4 00	282 01.3	135 32.4	N15 14.7	220 17.6	N20 37.7	158 54.0	N20 24.5	267 55.3	N 3 25.9
	01	297 03.8	150 32.1	13.6	235 18.2	38.1	173 55.9	24.4	282 57.7	25.9
	02	312 06.3	165 31.8	12.6	250 18.8	38.4	188 57.8	24.3	298 00.0	26.0
	03	327 08.7	180 31.6	. . 11.6	265 19.4	. . 38.8	203 59.7	. . 24.1	313 02.4	. . 26.0
	04	342 11.2	195 31.3	10.6	280 20.0	39.2	219 01.6	24.0	328 04.8	26.0
	05	357 13.6	210 31.1	09.6	295 20.6	39.5	234 03.5	23.9	343 07.2	26.0
	06	12 16.1	225 30.8	N15 08.5	310 21.2	N20 39.9	249 05.4	N20 23.8	358 09.5	N 3 26.1
	07	27 18.6	240 30.5	07.5	325 21.8	40.2	264 07.3	23.7	13 11.9	26.1
	08	42 21.0	255 30.3	06.5	340 22.5	40.6	279 09.2	23.6	28 14.3	26.1
	09	57 23.5	270 30.0	. . 05.5	355 23.1	. . 41.0	294 11.1	. . 23.4	43 16.7	. . 26.1
	10	72 26.0	285 29.8	04.4	10 23.7	41.3	309 13.0	23.3	58 19.0	26.2
	11	87 28.4	300 29.5	03.4	25 24.3	41.7	324 14.9	23.2	73 21.4	26.2
	12	102 30.9	315 29.3	N15 02.4	40 24.9	N20 42.0	339 16.8	N20 23.1	88 23.8	N 3 26.2
	13	117 33.4	330 29.0	01.4	55 25.5	42.4	354 18.7	23.0	103 26.1	26.2
	14	132 35.8	345 28.8	15 00.3	70 26.1	42.8	9 20.6	22.9	118 28.5	26.3
	15	147 38.3	0 28.5	14 59.3	85 26.7	. . 43.1	24 22.5	. . 22.8	133 30.9	. . 26.3
	16	162 40.8	15 28.3	58.3	100 27.4	43.5	39 24.4	22.6	148 33.3	26.3
	17	177 43.2	30 28.0	57.3	115 28.0	43.8	54 26.3	22.5	163 35.6	26.3
	18	192 45.7	45 27.8	N14 56.2	130 28.6	N20 44.2	69 28.2	N20 22.4	178 38.0	N 3 26.4
	19	207 48.1	60 27.5	55.2	145 29.2	44.5	84 30.1	22.3	193 40.4	26.4
	20	222 50.6	75 27.3	54.2	160 29.8	44.9	99 32.0	22.2	208 42.8	26.4
	21	237 53.1	90 27.0	. . 53.2	175 30.4	. . 45.3	114 33.9	. . 22.1	223 45.1	. . 26.4
	22	252 55.5	105 26.8	52.1	190 31.0	45.6	129 35.8	22.0	238 47.5	26.5
	23	267 58.0	120 26.6	51.1	205 31.6	46.0	144 37.7	21.8	253 49.9	26.5
SUNDAY	5 00	283 00.5	135 26.3	N14 50.1	220 32.3	N20 46.3	159 39.7	N20 21.7	268 52.3	N 3 26.5
	01	298 02.9	150 26.1	49.0	235 32.9	46.7	174 41.6	21.6	283 54.6	26.5
	02	313 05.4	165 25.8	48.0	250 33.5	47.0	189 43.5	21.5	298 57.0	26.6
	03	328 07.9	180 25.6	. . 47.0	265 34.1	. . 47.4	204 45.4	. . 21.4	313 59.4	. . 26.6
	04	343 10.3	195 25.3	45.9	280 34.7	47.7	219 47.3	21.3	329 01.8	26.6
	05	358 12.8	210 25.1	44.9	295 35.3	48.1	234 49.2	21.1	344 04.1	26.6
	06	13 15.2	225 24.9	N14 43.9	310 35.9	N20 48.4	249 51.1	N20 21.0	359 06.5	N 3 26.7
	07	28 17.7	240 24.6	42.8	325 36.5	48.8	264 53.0	20.9	14 08.9	26.7
	08	43 20.2	255 24.4	41.8	340 37.1	49.1	279 54.9	20.8	29 11.3	26.7
	09	58 22.6	270 24.1	. . 40.8	355 37.8	. . 49.5	294 56.8	. . 20.7	44 13.6	. . 26.7
	10	73 25.1	285 23.9	39.7	10 38.4	49.9	309 58.7	20.6	59 16.0	26.8
	11	88 27.6	300 23.7	38.7	25 39.0	50.2	325 00.6	20.4	74 18.4	26.8
	12	103 30.0	315 23.4	N14 37.6	40 39.6	N20 50.6	340 02.5	N20 20.3	89 20.8	N 3 26.8
	13	118 32.5	330 23.2	36.6	55 40.2	50.9	355 04.4	20.2	104 23.2	26.8
	14	133 35.0	345 23.0	35.6	70 40.8	51.3	10 06.3	20.1	119 25.5	26.9
	15	148 37.4	0 22.7	. . 34.5	85 41.4	. . 51.6	25 08.2	. . 20.0	134 27.9	. . 26.9
	16	163 39.9	15 22.5	33.5	100 42.0	52.0	40 10.1	19.9	149 30.3	26.9
	17	178 42.4	30 22.3	32.4	115 42.7	52.3	55 12.0	19.8	164 32.7	26.9
	18	193 44.8	45 22.0	N14 31.4	130 43.3	N20 52.6	70 13.9	N20 19.6	179 35.0	N 3 27.0
	19	208 47.3	60 21.8	30.4	145 43.9	53.0	85 15.8	19.5	194 37.4	27.0
	20	223 49.7	75 21.6	29.3	160 44.5	53.3	100 17.7	19.4	209 39.8	27.0
	21	238 52.2	90 21.4	. . 28.3	175 45.1	. . 53.7	115 19.6	. . 19.3	224 42.2	. . 27.0
	22	253 54.7	105 21.1	27.2	190 45.7	54.0	130 21.5	19.2	239 44.6	27.1
	23	268 57.1	120 20.9	26.2	205 46.3	54.4	145 23.4	19.1	254 46.9	27.1
	Mer. Pass. (h m)	5 11.1	*v* −0.3	*d* 1.0	*v* 0.6	*d* 0.4	*v* 1.9	*d* 0.1	*v* 2.4	*d* 0.0

STARS

Name	SHA	Dec
	° ′	° ′
Acamar	315 11.1	S40 11.6
Achernar	335 19.4	S57 05.8
Acrux	172 58.7	S63 15.1
Adhara	255 05.3	S29 00.5
Aldebaran	290 38.5	N16 33.7
Alioth	166 11.9	N55 49.2
Alkaid	152 50.9	N49 11.1
Alnair	27 31.1	S46 49.7
Alnilam	275 36.8	S 1 11.1
Alphard	217 46.8	S 8 46.5
Alphecca	126 02.4	N26 37.6
Alpheratz	357 33.4	N29 14.1
Altair	61 58.4	N 8 56.3
Ankaa	353 05.9	S42 09.4
Antares	112 14.0	S26 29.5
Arcturus	145 46.6	N19 02.7
Atria	107 06.6	S69 04.6
Avior	234 14.8	S59 35.8
Bellatrix	278 21.9	N 6 22.4
Betelgeuse	270 51.1	N 7 24.7
Canopus	263 52.4	S52 42.5
Capella	280 20.5	N46 01.4
Deneb	49 24.5	N45 22.4
Denebola	182 23.8	N14 25.5
Diphda	348 46.1	S17 50.3
Dubhe	193 39.8	N61 36.7
Elnath	278 00.7	N28 37.7
Eltanin	90 41.1	N51 29.1
Enif	33 37.3	N 9 59.8
Fomalhaut	15 13.0	S29 28.7
Gacrux	171 50.3	S57 16.0
Gienah	175 42.4	S17 41.5
Hadar	148 34.0	S60 30.3
Hamal	327 49.9	N23 35.2
Kaus Aust.	83 30.5	S34 22.3
Kochab	137 19.2	N74 03.0
Markab	13 28.5	N15 20.9
Menkar	314 05.0	N 4 11.7
Menkent	147 56.0	S36 30.2
Miaplacidus	221 38.8	S69 49.7
Mirfak	308 26.8	N49 57.1
Nunki	75 45.8	S26 15.8
Peacock	53 03.2	S56 38.8
Pollux	243 16.2	N27 57.8
Procyon	244 49.9	N 5 09.4
Rasalhague	95 57.1	N12 32.5
Regulus	207 33.3	N11 50.3
Rigel	281 03.0	S 8 10.2
Rigil Kent.	139 38.2	S60 56.9
Sabik	102 01.0	S15 45.5
Schedar	349 29.6	N56 40.7
Shaula	96 08.3	S37 07.4
Sirius	258 25.5	S16 45.1
Spica	158 20.9	S11 18.1
Suhail	222 45.8	S43 32.5
Vega	80 32.0	N38 48.5
Zuben'ubi	136 54.5	S16 09.2

	SHA (° ′)	Mer. Pass. (h m)
Venus	213 31.0	14 58
Mars	298 16.2	9 18
Jupiter	236 52.7	13 23
Saturn	345 54.0	6 07

Day	UT d h	SUN GHA ° ′	SUN Dec ° ′	MOON GHA ° ′	v ′	MOON Dec ° ′	d ′	HP ′
FRIDAY	3 00	178 57.3	N22 58.4	323 45.9	13.6	S17 54.3	11.5	54.9
	01	193 57.2	58.2	338 18.5	13.7	17 42.8	11.5	55.0
	02	208 57.1	58.0	352 51.2	13.8	17 31.3	11.6	55.0
	03	223 57.0	. . 57.8	7 24.0	13.8	17 19.7	11.7	55.0
	04	238 56.9	57.6	21 56.8	13.8	17 08.0	11.8	55.0
	05	253 56.7	57.4	36 29.6	13.9	16 56.2	11.9	55.0
	06	268 56.6	N22 57.2	51 02.5	14.0	S16 44.3	11.9	55.1
	07	283 56.5	57.0	65 35.5	14.0	16 32.4	12.0	55.1
	08	298 56.4	56.8	80 08.5	14.0	16 20.4	12.1	55.1
	09	313 56.3	. . 56.6	94 41.5	14.1	16 08.3	12.2	55.1
	10	328 56.2	56.4	109 14.6	14.1	15 56.1	12.2	55.1
	11	343 56.1	56.2	123 47.7	14.1	15 43.9	12.3	55.1
	12	358 55.9	N22 56.0	138 20.8	14.2	S15 31.6	12.4	55.2
	13	13 55.8	55.8	152 54.0	14.2	15 19.2	12.4	55.2
	14	28 55.7	55.6	167 27.2	14.3	15 06.8	12.6	55.2
	15	43 55.6	. . 55.3	182 00.5	14.3	14 54.2	12.5	55.2
	16	58 55.5	55.1	196 33.8	14.4	14 41.7	12.7	55.2
	17	73 55.4	54.9	211 07.2	14.4	14 29.0	12.7	55.3
	18	88 55.3	N22 54.7	225 40.6	14.4	S14 16.3	12.8	55.3
	19	103 55.2	54.5	240 14.0	14.5	14 03.5	12.9	55.3
	20	118 55.0	54.3	254 47.5	14.5	13 50.6	12.9	55.3
	21	133 54.9	. . 54.1	269 21.0	14.5	13 37.7	13.0	55.3
	22	148 54.8	53.9	283 54.5	14.5	13 24.7	13.0	55.4
	23	163 54.7	53.7	298 28.0	14.6	13 11.7	13.1	55.4
SATURDAY	4 00	178 54.6	N22 53.4	313 01.6	14.7	S12 58.6	13.2	55.4
	01	193 54.5	53.2	327 35.3	14.6	12 45.4	13.3	55.4
	02	208 54.4	53.0	342 08.9	14.7	12 32.1	13.3	55.4
	03	223 54.3	. . 52.8	356 42.6	14.7	12 18.8	13.3	55.5
	04	238 54.1	52.6	11 16.3	14.8	12 05.5	13.4	55.5
	05	253 54.0	52.4	25 50.1	14.8	11 52.1	13.5	55.5
	06	268 53.9	N22 52.1	40 23.9	14.7	S11 38.6	13.5	55.5
	07	283 53.8	51.9	54 57.6	14.9	11 25.1	13.6	55.5
	08	298 53.7	51.7	69 31.5	14.8	11 11.5	13.7	55.6
	09	313 53.6	. . 51.5	84 05.3	14.9	10 57.8	13.7	55.6
	10	328 53.5	51.3	98 39.2	14.9	10 44.1	13.7	55.6
	11	343 53.4	51.0	113 13.1	14.9	10 30.4	13.8	55.6
	12	358 53.3	N22 50.8	127 47.0	15.0	S10 16.6	13.9	55.7
	13	13 53.1	50.6	142 21.0	14.9	10 02.7	13.9	55.7
	14	28 53.0	50.4	156 54.9	15.0	9 48.8	13.9	55.7
	15	43 52.9	. . 50.1	171 28.9	15.0	9 34.9	14.0	55.7
	16	58 52.8	49.9	186 02.9	15.0	9 20.9	14.1	55.8
	17	73 52.7	49.7	200 36.9	15.0	9 06.8	14.1	55.8
	18	88 52.6	N22 49.5	215 10.9	15.1	S 8 52.7	14.1	55.8
	19	103 52.5	49.2	229 45.0	15.0	8 38.6	14.2	55.8
	20	118 52.4	49.0	244 19.0	15.1	8 24.4	14.3	55.8
	21	133 52.3	. . 48.8	258 53.1	15.1	8 10.1	14.3	55.9
	22	148 52.2	48.5	273 27.2	15.1	7 55.8	14.3	55.9
	23	163 52.0	48.3	288 01.3	15.1	7 41.5	14.4	55.9
SUNDAY	5 00	178 51.9	N22 48.1	302 35.4	15.1	S 7 27.1	14.4	55.9
	01	193 51.8	47.9	317 09.5	15.1	7 12.7	14.4	56.0
	02	208 51.7	47.6	331 43.6	15.1	6 58.3	14.5	56.0
	03	223 51.6	. . 47.4	346 17.7	15.1	6 43.8	14.5	56.0
	04	238 51.5	47.2	0 51.8	15.2	6 29.3	14.6	56.0
	05	253 51.4	46.9	15 26.0	15.1	6 14.7	14.6	56.1
	06	268 51.3	N22 46.7	30 00.1	15.1	S 6 00.1	14.7	56.1
	07	283 51.2	46.4	44 34.2	15.2	5 45.4	14.7	56.1
	08	298 51.1	46.2	59 08.4	15.1	5 30.7	14.7	56.1
	09	313 51.0	. . 46.0	73 42.5	15.1	5 16.0	14.7	56.2
	10	328 50.9	45.7	88 16.6	15.2	5 01.3	14.8	56.2
	11	343 50.7	45.5	102 50.8	15.1	4 46.5	14.8	56.2
	12	358 50.6	N22 45.3	117 24.9	15.1	S 4 31.7	14.9	56.2
	13	13 50.5	45.0	131 59.0	15.1	4 16.8	14.8	56.3
	14	28 50.4	44.8	146 33.1	15.2	4 02.0	14.9	56.3
	15	43 50.3	. . 44.5	161 07.3	15.1	3 47.1	15.0	56.3
	16	58 50.2	44.3	175 41.4	15.0	3 32.1	14.9	56.4
	17	73 50.1	44.0	190 15.4	15.1	3 17.2	15.0	56.4
	18	88 50.0	N22 43.8	204 49.5	15.1	S 3 02.2	15.1	56.4
	19	103 49.9	43.6	219 23.6	15.0	2 47.1	15.0	56.4
	20	118 49.8	43.3	233 57.6	15.1	2 32.1	15.1	56.5
	21	133 49.7	. . 43.1	248 31.7	15.0	2 17.0	15.1	56.5
	22	148 49.6	42.8	263 05.7	15.0	2 01.9	15.1	56.5
	23	163 49.5	42.6	277 39.7	15.0	S 1 46.8	15.1	56.5
		SD 15.8	*d* 0.2	SD 15.0		15.2		15.3

Lat. °	Twilight Naut. h m	Twilight Civil h m	Sunrise h m	Moonrise 3 h m	Moonrise 4 h m	Moonrise 5 h m	Moonrise 6 h m
N 72	▭	▭	▭	01 43	{00 10 / 23 27}	22 53	22 20
N 70	▭	▭	▭	{00 36 / 23 47}	23 16	22 51	22 26
68	▭	▭	▭	23 29	23 07	22 48	22 30
66	////	////	00 41	23 14	23 00	22 47	22 34
64	////	////	01 47	23 02	22 53	22 45	22 37
62	////	////	02 21	22 52	22 48	22 44	22 40
60	////	01 11	02 46	22 43	22 43	22 43	22 42
N 58	////	01 53	03 05	22 35	22 39	22 42	22 45
56	////	02 21	03 21	22 28	22 35	22 41	22 47
54	01 05	02 42	03 35	22 22	22 31	22 40	22 48
52	01 44	02 59	03 47	22 16	22 28	22 39	22 50
50	02 10	03 13	03 57	22 11	22 25	22 38	22 52
45	02 53	03 42	04 19	22 00	22 19	22 37	22 55
N 40	03 23	04 04	04 36	21 51	22 14	22 36	22 58
35	03 45	04 22	04 51	21 43	22 09	22 34	23 00
30	04 03	04 36	05 04	21 36	22 05	22 34	23 02
20	04 32	05 01	05 25	21 24	21 58	22 32	23 06
N 10	04 54	05 21	05 44	21 13	21 52	22 30	23 09
0	05 12	05 38	06 01	21 03	21 46	22 29	23 12
S 10	05 29	05 55	06 18	20 53	21 40	22 28	23 16
20	05 45	06 12	06 36	20 42	21 34	22 26	23 19
30	06 00	06 30	06 56	20 30	21 27	22 24	23 23
35	06 09	06 40	07 08	20 23	21 23	22 23	23 25
40	06 18	06 52	07 22	20 14	21 18	22 22	23 28
45	06 28	07 05	07 39	20 05	21 13	22 21	23 31
S 50	06 39	07 21	07 59	19 53	21 06	22 20	23 35
52	06 44	07 28	08 08	19 47	21 03	22 19	23 37
54	06 50	07 36	08 19	19 41	21 00	22 18	23 30
56	06 56	07 44	08 31	19 35	20 56	22 17	23 41
58	07 02	07 54	08 45	19 27	20 52	22 16	23 43
S 60	07 09	08 05	09 02	19 18	20 47	22 15	23 45

Lat. °	Sunset h m	Twilight Civil h m	Twilight Naut. h m	Moonset 3 h m	Moonset 4 h m	Moonset 5 h m	Moonset 6 h m
N 72	▭	▭	▭	03 37	06 43	08 57	11 05
N 70	▭	▭	▭	04 43	07 04	09 06	11 03
68	▭	▭	▭	05 18	07 20	09 12	11 02
66	23 22	////	////	05 43	07 33	09 17	11 00
64	22 20	////	////	06 03	07 44	09 22	10 59
62	21 47	////	////	06 18	07 53	09 26	10 59
60	21 22	22 56	////	06 31	08 01	09 29	10 58
N 58	21 03	22 15	////	06 42	08 08	09 32	10 57
56	20 47	21 47	////	06 52	08 14	09 35	10 57
54	20 34	21 27	23 02	07 00	08 19	09 37	10 56
52	20 22	21 10	22 24	07 08	08 24	09 39	10 56
50	20 11	20 55	21 58	07 15	08 28	09 41	10 55
45	19 50	20 27	21 15	07 29	08 37	09 45	10 54
N 40	19 32	20 05	20 46	07 41	08 45	09 49	10 54
35	19 18	19 47	20 23	07 51	08 52	09 52	10 53
30	19 05	19 32	20 05	08 00	08 57	09 55	10 52
20	18 44	19 08	19 37	08 15	09 07	09 59	10 51
N 10	18 25	18 48	19 15	08 28	09 16	10 03	10 50
0	18 08	18 31	18 57	08 40	09 24	10 07	10 49
S 10	17 51	18 14	18 40	08 52	09 32	10 10	10 49
20	17 33	17 57	18 24	09 05	09 40	10 14	10 48
30	17 13	17 39	18 09	09 20	09 50	10 18	10 47
35	17 01	17 29	18 00	09 28	09 55	10 21	10 46
40	16 47	17 17	17 51	09 38	10 01	10 24	10 45
45	16 31	17 04	17 41	09 49	10 09	10 27	10 44
S 50	16 10	16 49	17 30	10 02	10 17	10 30	10 43
52	16 01	16 41	17 25	10 08	10 21	10 32	10 43
54	15 50	16 34	17 19	10 15	10 25	10 34	10 42
56	15 38	16 25	17 13	10 22	10 30	10 36	10 42
58	15 24	16 15	17 07	10 31	10 35	10 38	10 41
S 60	15 07	16 04	17 00	10 41	10 41	10 41	10 41

Day d	SUN Eqn. of Time 00^h m s	SUN Eqn. of Time 12^h m s	SUN Mer. Pass. h m	MOON Mer. Pass. Upper h m	MOON Mer. Pass. Lower h m	Age d	%	Phase
3	04 10	04 16	12 04	02 29	14 52	18	89	
4	04 21	04 27	12 04	03 14	15 35	19	82	
5	04 32	04 37	12 05	03 56	16 18	20	74	

2026 JULY 6, 7, 8 (MON., TUES., WED.)

UT	ARIES	VENUS −4·1		MARS +1·3		JUPITER −1·8		SATURN +0·7	
	GHA	GHA	Dec	GHA	Dec	GHA	Dec	GHA	Dec
d h	° ′	° ′	° ′	° ′	° ′	° ′	° ′	° ′	° ′
6 00	283 59.6	135 20.7	N14 25.1	220 46.9	N20 54.7	160 25.3	N20 18.9	269 49.3	N 3 27.1
01	299 02.1	150 20.4	24.1	235 47.5	55.1	175 27.2	18.8	284 51.7	27.1
02	314 04.5	165 20.2	23.1	250 48.2	55.4	190 29.1	18.7	299 54.1	27.1
03	329 07.0	180 20.0	. . 22.0	265 48.8	. . 55.8	205 31.0	. . 18.6	314 56.4	. . 27.2
04	344 09.5	195 19.8	21.0	280 49.4	56.1	220 32.9	18.5	329 58.8	27.2
05	359 11.9	210 19.5	19.9	295 50.0	56.5	235 34.8	18.4	345 01.2	27.2
06	14 14.4	225 19.3	N14 18.9	310 50.6	N20 56.8	250 36.7	N20 18.2	0 03.6	N 3 27.2
M 07	29 16.9	240 19.1	17.8	325 51.2	57.1	265 38.6	18.1	15 06.0	27.3
O 08	44 19.3	255 18.9	16.8	340 51.8	57.5	280 40.5	18.0	30 08.3	27.3
N 09	59 21.8	270 18.7	. . 15.7	355 52.4	. . 57.8	295 42.4	. . 17.9	45 10.7	. . 27.3
D 10	74 24.2	285 18.4	14.7	10 53.0	58.2	310 44.3	17.8	60 13.1	27.3
A 11	89 26.7	300 18.2	13.6	25 53.7	58.5	325 46.2	17.7	75 15.5	27.4
Y 12	104 29.2	315 18.0	N14 12.6	40 54.3	N20 58.9	340 48.1	N20 17.5	90 17.9	N 3 27.4
13	119 31.6	330 17.8	11.5	55 54.9	59.2	355 50.0	17.4	105 20.2	27.4
14	134 34.1	345 17.6	10.5	70 55.5	59.5	10 51.9	17.3	120 22.6	27.4
15	149 36.6	0 17.4	. . 09.4	85 56.1	20 59.9	25 53.8	. . 17.2	135 25.0	. . 27.4
16	164 39.0	15 17.1	08.4	100 56.7	21 00.2	40 55.7	17.1	150 27.4	27.5
17	179 41.5	30 16.9	07.3	115 57.3	00.6	55 57.6	17.0	165 29.8	27.5
18	194 44.0	45 16.7	N14 06.2	130 57.9	N21 00.9	70 59.5	N20 16.8	180 32.2	N 3 27.5
19	209 46.4	60 16.5	05.2	145 58.5	01.2	86 01.4	16.7	195 34.5	27.5
20	224 48.9	75 16.3	04.1	160 59.2	01.6	101 03.3	16.6	210 36.9	27.6
21	239 51.3	90 16.1	. . 03.1	175 59.8	. . 01.9	116 05.2	. . 16.5	225 39.3	. . 27.6
22	254 53.8	105 15.9	02.0	191 00.4	02.3	131 07.1	16.4	240 41.7	27.6
23	269 56.3	120 15.6	14 01.0	206 01.0	02.6	146 09.0	16.3	255 44.1	27.6
7 00	284 58.7	135 15.4	N13 59.9	221 01.6	N21 02.9	161 10.9	N20 16.1	270 46.4	N 3 27.6
01	300 01.2	150 15.2	58.9	236 02.2	03.3	176 12.8	16.0	285 48.8	27.7
02	315 03.7	165 15.0	57.8	251 02.8	03.6	191 14.7	15.9	300 51.2	27.7
03	330 06.1	180 14.8	. . 56.7	266 03.4	. . 04.0	206 16.6	. . 15.8	315 53.6	. . 27.7
04	345 08.6	195 14.6	55.7	281 04.0	04.3	221 18.5	15.7	330 56.0	27.7
05	0 11.1	210 14.4	54.6	296 04.7	04.6	236 20.4	15.5	345 58.4	27.7
06	15 13.5	225 14.2	N13 53.6	311 05.3	N21 05.0	251 22.3	N20 15.4	1 00.7	N 3 27.8
07	30 16.0	240 14.0	52.5	326 05.9	05.3	266 24.2	15.3	16 03.1	27.8
T 08	45 18.5	255 13.8	51.4	341 06.5	05.6	281 26.1	15.2	31 05.5	27.8
U 09	60 20.9	270 13.6	. . 50.4	356 07.1	. . 06.0	296 28.0	. . 15.1	46 07.9	. . 27.8
E 10	75 23.4	285 13.4	49.3	11 07.7	06.3	311 29.9	15.0	61 10.3	27.9
S 11	90 25.8	300 13.2	48.2	26 08.3	06.6	326 31.8	14.8	76 12.7	27.9
D 12	105 28.3	315 13.0	N13 47.2	41 08.9	N21 07.0	341 33.7	N20 14.7	91 15.0	N 3 27.9
A 13	120 30.8	330 12.8	46.1	56 09.5	07.3	356 35.6	14.6	106 17.4	27.9
Y 14	135 33.2	345 12.6	45.1	71 10.2	07.6	11 37.5	14.5	121 19.8	27.9
15	150 35.7	0 12.4	. . 44.0	86 10.8	. . 08.0	26 39.4	. . 14.4	136 22.2	. . 28.0
16	165 38.2	15 12.2	42.9	101 11.4	08.3	41 41.2	14.3	151 24.6	28.0
17	180 40.6	30 12.0	41.9	116 12.0	08.6	56 43.1	14.1	166 27.0	28.0
18	195 43.1	45 11.8	N13 40.8	131 12.6	N21 09.0	71 45.0	N20 14.0	181 29.4	N 3 28.0
19	210 45.6	60 11.6	39.7	146 13.2	09.3	86 46.9	13.9	196 31.7	28.0
20	225 48.0	75 11.4	38.7	161 13.8	09.6	101 48.8	13.8	211 34.1	28.1
21	240 50.5	90 11.2	. . 37.6	176 14.4	. . 10.0	116 50.7	. . 13.7	226 36.5	. . 28.1
22	255 53.0	105 11.0	36.5	191 15.0	10.3	131 52.6	13.5	241 38.9	28.1
23	270 55.4	120 10.8	35.4	206 15.6	10.6	146 54.5	13.4	256 41.3	28.1
8 00	285 57.9	135 10.6	N13 34.4	221 16.3	N21 10.9	161 56.4	N20 13.3	271 43.7	N 3 28.1
01	301 00.3	150 10.4	33.3	236 16.9	11.3	176 58.3	13.2	286 46.1	28.2
02	316 02.8	165 10.2	32.2	251 17.5	11.6	192 00.2	13.1	301 48.4	28.2
03	331 05.3	180 10.0	. . 31.2	266 18.1	. . 11.9	207 02.1	. . 13.0	316 50.8	. . 28.2
04	346 07.7	195 09.8	30.1	281 18.7	12.3	222 04.0	12.8	331 53.2	28.2
05	1 10.2	210 09.6	29.0	296 19.3	12.6	237 05.9	12.7	346 55.6	28.2
06	16 12.7	225 09.4	N13 27.9	311 19.9	N21 12.9	252 07.8	N20 12.6	1 58.0	N 3 28.3
W 07	31 15.1	240 09.2	26.9	326 20.5	13.2	267 09.7	12.5	17 00.4	28.3
E 08	46 17.6	255 09.1	25.8	341 21.1	13.6	282 11.6	12.4	32 02.8	28.3
D 09	61 20.1	270 08.9	. . 24.7	356 21.7	. . 13.9	297 13.5	. . 12.2	47 05.2	. . 28.3
N 10	76 22.5	285 08.7	23.7	11 22.4	14.2	312 15.4	12.1	62 07.5	28.3
E 11	91 25.0	300 08.5	22.6	26 23.0	14.5	327 17.3	12.0	77 09.9	28.4
S 12	106 27.4	315 08.3	N13 21.5	41 23.6	N21 14.9	342 19.2	N20 11.9	92 12.3	N 3 28.4
D 13	121 29.9	330 08.1	20.4	56 24.2	15.2	357 21.1	11.8	107 14.7	28.4
A 14	136 32.4	345 07.9	19.3	71 24.8	15.5	12 23.0	11.6	122 17.1	28.4
Y 15	151 34.8	0 07.8	. . 18.3	86 25.4	. . 15.8	27 24.9	. . 11.5	137 19.5	. . 28.4
16	166 37.3	15 07.6	17.2	101 26.0	16.2	42 26.8	11.4	152 21.9	28.5
17	181 39.8	30 07.4	16.1	116 26.6	16.5	57 28.7	11.3	167 24.3	28.5
18	196 42.2	45 07.2	N13 15.0	131 27.2	N21 16.8	72 30.6	N20 11.2	182 26.6	N 3 28.5
19	211 44.7	60 07.0	14.0	146 27.9	17.1	87 32.5	11.1	197 29.0	28.5
20	226 47.2	75 06.9	12.9	161 28.5	17.5	102 34.4	10.9	212 31.4	28.5
21	241 49.6	90 06.7	. . 11.8	176 29.1	. . 17.8	117 36.3	. . 10.8	227 33.8	. . 28.5
22	256 52.1	105 06.5	10.7	191 29.7	18.1	132 38.2	10.7	242 36.2	28.6
23	271 54.6	120 06.3	09.6	206 30.3	18.4	147 40.1	10.6	257 38.6	28.6
Mer. Pass.	h m 4 59.3	*v* −0.2	*d* 1.1	*v* 0.6	*d* 0.3	*v* 1.9	*d* 0.1	*v* 2.4	*d* 0.0

STARS

Name	SHA	Dec
	° ′	° ′
Acamar	315 11.1	S40 11.6
Achernar	335 19.4	S57 05.8
Acrux	172 58.7	S63 15.1
Adhara	255 05.3	S29 00.4
Aldebaran	290 38.5	N16 33.7
Alioth	166 11.9	N55 49.2
Alkaid	152 50.9	N49 11.1
Alnair	27 31.0	S46 49.7
Alnilam	275 36.8	S 1 11.1
Alphard	217 46.8	S 8 46.4
Alphecca	126 02.5	N26 37.6
Alpheratz	357 33.4	N29 14.1
Altair	61 58.4	N 8 56.3
Ankaa	353 05.9	S42 09.4
Antares	112 14.0	S26 29.5
Arcturus	145 46.7	N19 02.7
Atria	107 06.6	S69 04.6
Avior	234 14.9	S59 35.7
Bellatrix	278 21.9	N 6 22.4
Betelgeuse	270 51.1	N 7 24.7
Canopus	263 52.4	S52 42.5
Capella	280 20.5	N46 01.4
Deneb	49 24.5	N45 22.4
Denebola	182 23.8	N14 25.5
Diphda	348 46.0	S17 50.3
Dubhe	193 39.8	N61 36.7
Elnath	278 00.7	N28 37.7
Eltanin	90 41.1	N51 29.2
Enif	33 37.3	N 9 59.8
Fomalhaut	15 13.0	S29 28.7
Gacrux	171 50.3	S57 16.0
Gienah	175 42.4	S17 41.5
Hadar	148 34.0	S60 30.3
Hamal	327 49.9	N23 35.2
Kaus Aust.	83 30.5	S34 22.3
Kochab	137 19.3	N74 03.0
Markab	13 28.5	N15 20.9
Menkar	314 05.0	N 4 11.7
Menkent	147 56.0	S36 30.2
Miaplacidus	221 38.8	S69 49.7
Mirfak	308 26.8	N49 57.1
Nunki	75 45.8	S26 15.8
Peacock	53 03.2	S56 38.8
Pollux	243 16.2	N27 57.8
Procyon	244 49.9	N 5 09.4
Rasalhague	95 57.1	N12 32.5
Regulus	207 33.4	N11 50.3
Rigel	281 03.0	S 8 10.2
Rigil Kent.	139 38.3	S60 56.9
Sabik	102 01.0	S15 45.5
Schedar	349 29.6	N56 40.8
Shaula	96 08.3	S37 07.4
Sirius	258 25.5	S16 45.1
Spica	158 20.9	S11 18.1
Suhail	222 45.8	S43 32.5
Vega	80 32.0	N38 48.5
Zuben'ubi	136 54.5	S16 09.2

	SHA	Mer. Pass.
	° ′	h m
Venus	210 16.7	14 59
Mars	296 02.9	9 16
Jupiter	236 12.1	13 14
Saturn	345 47.7	5 56

Day	UT (d h)	SUN GHA (° ′)	SUN Dec (° ′)	MOON GHA (° ′)	v (′)	MOON Dec (° ′)	d (′)	HP (′)
MONDAY	6 00	178 49.4	N22 42.3	292 13.7	14.9	S 1 31.7	15.2	56.6
	01	193 49.3	42.1	306 47.6	15.0	1 16.5	15.1	56.6
	02	208 49.2	41.8	321 21.6	14.9	1 01.4	15.2	56.6
	03	223 49.1	. . 41.6	335 55.5	14.9	0 46.2	15.2	56.7
	04	238 48.9	41.3	350 29.4	14.9	0 31.0	15.3	56.7
	05	253 48.8	41.1	5 03.3	14.8	0 15.7	15.2	56.7
	06	268 48.7	N22 40.8	19 37.1	14.8	S 0 00.5	15.3	56.7
	07	283 48.6	40.6	34 10.9	14.8	N 0 14.8	15.2	56.8
	08	298 48.5	40.3	48 44.7	14.8	0 30.0	15.3	56.8
	09	313 48.4	. . 40.1	63 18.5	14.7	0 45.3	15.3	56.8
	10	328 48.3	39.8	77 52.2	14.7	1 00.6	15.3	56.9
	11	343 48.2	39.6	92 25.9	14.7	1 15.9	15.3	56.9
	12	358 48.1	N22 39.3	106 59.6	14.6	N 1 31.2	15.4	56.9
	13	13 48.0	39.0	121 33.2	14.6	1 46.6	15.3	57.0
	14	28 47.9	38.8	136 06.8	14.5	2 01.9	15.4	57.0
	15	43 47.8	. . 38.5	150 40.3	14.5	2 17.3	15.3	57.0
	16	58 47.7	38.3	165 13.8	14.5	2 32.6	15.4	57.0
	17	73 47.6	38.0	179 47.3	14.4	2 48.0	15.3	57.1
	18	88 47.5	N22 37.8	194 20.7	14.4	N 3 03.3	15.4	57.1
	19	103 47.4	37.5	208 54.1	14.3	3 18.7	15.3	57.1
	20	118 47.3	37.2	223 27.4	14.3	3 34.0	15.4	57.2
	21	133 47.2	. . 37.0	238 00.7	14.2	3 49.4	15.4	57.2
	22	148 47.1	36.7	252 33.9	14.2	4 04.8	15.3	57.2
	23	163 47.0	36.4	267 07.1	14.2	4 20.1	15.4	57.3
TUESDAY	7 00	178 46.9	N22 36.2	281 40.3	14.0	N 4 35.5	15.3	57.3
	01	193 46.8	35.9	296 13.3	14.1	4 50.8	15.4	57.3
	02	208 46.7	35.6	310 46.4	14.0	5 06.2	15.3	57.4
	03	223 46.6	. . 35.4	325 19.4	13.9	5 21.5	15.4	57.4
	04	238 46.5	35.1	339 52.3	13.8	5 36.9	15.3	57.4
	05	253 46.4	34.8	354 25.1	13.8	5 52.2	15.3	57.4
	06	268 46.3	N22 34.6	8 57.9	13.8	N 6 07.5	15.3	57.5
	07	283 46.2	34.3	23 30.7	13.7	6 22.8	15.3	57.5
	08	298 46.1	34.0	38 03.4	13.6	6 38.1	15.3	57.5
	09	313 46.0	. . 33.8	52 36.0	13.5	6 53.4	15.3	57.6
	10	328 45.9	33.5	67 08.5	13.5	7 08.7	15.3	57.6
	11	343 45.8	33.2	81 41.0	13.4	7 24.0	15.2	57.6
	12	358 45.7	N22 33.0	96 13.4	13.4	N 7 39.2	15.2	57.7
	13	13 45.6	32.7	110 45.8	13.3	7 54.4	15.2	57.7
	14	28 45.5	32.4	125 18.1	13.2	8 09.6	15.2	57.7
	15	43 45.4	. . 32.1	139 50.3	13.1	8 24.8	15.2	57.8
	16	58 45.3	31.9	154 22.4	13.1	8 40.0	15.1	57.8
	17	73 45.2	31.6	168 54.5	12.9	8 55.1	15.1	57.8
	18	88 45.1	N22 31.3	183 26.4	12.9	N 9 10.2	15.1	57.9
	19	103 45.0	31.0	197 58.3	12.9	9 25.3	15.1	57.9
	20	118 44.9	30.8	212 30.2	12.7	9 40.4	15.0	57.9
	21	133 44.8	. . 30.5	227 01.9	12.7	9 55.4	15.0	58.0
	22	148 44.7	30.2	241 33.6	12.5	10 10.4	15.0	58.0
	23	163 44.6	29.9	256 05.1	12.5	10 25.4	14.9	58.0
WEDNESDAY	8 00	178 44.5	N22 29.6	270 36.6	12.4	N10 40.3	14.9	58.1
	01	193 44.4	29.4	285 08.0	12.4	10 55.2	14.9	58.1
	02	208 44.3	29.1	299 39.4	12.2	11 10.1	14.8	58.1
	03	223 44.2	. . 28.8	314 10.6	12.1	11 24.9	14.8	58.2
	04	238 44.1	28.5	328 41.7	12.1	11 39.7	14.8	58.2
	05	253 44.0	28.2	343 12.8	11.9	11 54.5	14.7	58.2
	06	268 43.9	N22 27.9	357 43.7	11.9	N12 09.2	14.7	58.3
	07	283 43.8	27.7	12 14.6	11.7	12 23.9	14.6	58.3
	08	298 43.7	27.4	26 45.3	11.7	12 38.5	14.6	58.3
	09	313 43.6	. . 27.1	41 16.0	11.6	12 53.1	14.5	58.4
	10	328 43.5	26.8	55 46.6	11.4	13 07.6	14.5	58.4
	11	343 43.4	26.5	70 17.0	11.4	13 22.1	14.5	58.4
	12	358 43.3	N22 26.2	84 47.4	11.3	N13 36.6	14.3	58.5
	13	13 43.2	25.9	99 17.7	11.1	13 50.9	14.4	58.5
	14	28 43.1	25.6	113 47.8	11.1	14 05.3	14.2	58.5
	15	43 43.0	. . 25.4	128 17.9	10.9	14 19.5	14.3	58.6
	16	58 42.9	25.1	142 47.8	10.8	14 33.8	14.1	58.6
	17	73 42.8	24.8	157 17.6	10.8	14 47.9	14.1	58.6
	18	88 42.7	N22 24.5	171 47.4	10.6	N15 02.0	14.1	58.7
	19	103 42.6	24.2	186 17.0	10.5	15 16.1	13.9	58.7
	20	118 42.6	23.9	200 46.5	10.4	15 30.0	14.0	58.7
	21	133 42.5	. . 23.6	215 15.9	10.3	15 44.0	13.8	58.8
	22	148 42.4	23.3	229 45.2	10.1	15 57.8	13.8	58.8
	23	163 42.3	23.0	244 14.3	10.1	N16 11.6	13.7	58.8
		SD 15.8	*d* 0.3	SD	15.5	15.7		15.9

Lat. (°)	Twilight Naut. (h m)	Twilight Civil (h m)	Sunrise (h m)	Moonrise 6 (h m)	Moonrise 7 (h m)	Moonrise 8 (h m)	Moonrise 9 (h m)
N 72	▭	▭	▭	22 20	21 42	20 44	▭
N 70	▭	▭	▭	22 26	21 58	21 18	▭
68	▭	▭	▭	22 30	22 10	21 43	20 53
66	////	////	00 58	22 34	22 20	22 03	21 37
64	////	////	01 54	22 37	22 29	22 19	22 06
62	////	////	02 26	22 40	22 36	22 32	22 29
60	////	01 20	02 50	22 42	22 43	22 44	22 47
N 58	////	01 58	03 09	22 45	22 48	22 54	23 02
56	////	02 25	03 24	22 47	22 53	23 02	23 15
54	01 13	02 45	03 38	22 48	22 58	23 10	23 27
52	01 49	03 02	03 49	22 50	23 02	23 17	23 37
50	02 14	03 16	04 00	22 52	23 06	23 23	23 46
45	02 56	03 44	04 21	22 55	23 14	23 37	24 06
N 40	03 25	04 06	04 38	22 58	23 21	23 48	24 22
35	03 47	04 23	04 53	23 00	23 27	23 58	24 35
30	04 05	04 38	05 05	23 02	23 33	24 07	00 07
20	04 33	05 02	05 26	23 06	23 42	24 22	00 22
N 10	04 55	05 21	05 44	23 09	23 50	24 35	00 35
0	05 13	05 39	06 01	23 12	23 58	24 47	00 47
S 10	05 29	05 55	06 18	23 16	24 06	00 06	01 00
20	05 45	06 12	06 36	23 19	24 14	00 14	01 13
30	06 00	06 30	06 56	23 23	24 24	00 24	01 29
35	06 09	06 40	07 08	23 25	24 30	00 30	01 38
40	06 18	06 51	07 22	23 28	24 36	00 36	01 49
45	06 27	07 04	07 38	23 31	24 44	00 44	02 01
S 50	06 38	07 19	07 57	23 35	24 53	00 53	02 16
52	06 43	07 26	08 07	23 37	24 57	00 57	02 23
54	06 49	07 34	08 17	23 38	25 02	01 02	02 31
56	06 54	07 43	08 29	23 41	25 07	01 07	02 40
58	07 01	07 52	08 43	23 43	25 13	01 13	02 50
S 60	07 07	08 03	08 59	23 45	25 20	01 20	03 02

Lat. (°)	Sunset (h m)	Twilight Civil (h m)	Twilight Naut. (h m)	Moonset 6 (h m)	Moonset 7 (h m)	Moonset 8 (h m)	Moonset 9 (h m)
N 72	▭	▭	▭	11 05	13 18	15 58	▭
N 70	▭	▭	▭	11 03	13 05	15 25	▭
68	▭	▭	▭	11 02	12 55	15 02	17 42
66	23 08	////	////	11 00	12 47	14 44	17 00
64	22 14	////	////	10 59	12 41	14 29	16 31
62	21 42	////	////	10 59	12 35	14 17	16 10
60	21 19	22 48	////	10 58	12 30	14 07	15 52
N 58	21 00	22 10	////	10 57	12 25	13 58	15 38
56	20 45	21 44	////	10 57	12 21	13 50	15 25
54	20 32	21 24	22 54	10 56	12 18	13 44	15 15
52	20 20	21 07	22 19	10 56	12 15	13 37	15 05
50	20 10	20 53	21 55	10 55	12 12	13 32	14 57
45	19 49	20 25	21 13	10 54	12 05	13 20	14 39
N 40	19 31	20 04	20 45	10 54	12 00	13 10	14 24
35	19 17	19 46	20 23	10 53	11 56	13 02	14 12
30	19 05	19 32	20 05	10 52	11 52	12 55	14 01
20	18 44	19 08	19 37	10 51	11 45	12 42	13 43
N 10	18 25	18 48	19 15	10 50	11 39	12 31	13 27
0	18 09	18 31	18 57	10 49	11 34	12 21	13 12
S 10	17 52	18 15	18 41	10 49	11 28	12 11	12 58
20	17 34	17 58	18 25	10 48	11 22	12 00	12 42
30	17 14	17 40	18 10	10 47	11 16	11 48	12 24
35	17 02	17 30	18 01	10 46	11 12	11 41	12 14
40	16 49	17 19	17 53	10 45	11 08	11 33	12 02
45	16 33	17 06	17 43	10 44	11 03	11 23	11 48
S 50	16 13	16 51	17 32	10 43	10 57	11 12	11 32
52	16 04	16 44	17 27	10 43	10 54	11 07	11 24
54	15 53	16 36	17 22	10 42	10 51	11 01	11 15
56	15 41	16 28	17 16	10 42	10 48	10 55	11 05
58	15 28	16 18	17 10	10 41	10 44	10 48	10 54
S 60	15 11	16 07	17 03	10 41	10 40	10 40	10 42

Day (d)	SUN Eqn. of Time 00^h (m s)	SUN Eqn. of Time 12^h (m s)	SUN Mer. Pass. (h m)	MOON Mer. Pass. Upper (h m)	MOON Mer. Pass. Lower (h m)	MOON Age (d)	MOON Phase (%)
6	04 42	04 47	12 05	04 39	17 01	21	64
7	04 52	04 57	12 05	05 23	17 46	22	54
8	05 02	05 07	12 05	06 09	18 34	23	43

UT d h	ARIES GHA ° ′	VENUS −4·1 GHA ° ′	VENUS Dec ° ′	MARS +1·3 GHA ° ′	MARS Dec ° ′	JUPITER −1·8 GHA ° ′	JUPITER Dec ° ′	SATURN +0·7 GHA ° ′	SATURN Dec ° ′
9 00 THURSDAY	286 57.0	135 06.1	N13 08.5	221 30.9	N21 18.7	162 42.0	N20 10.5	272 41.0	N 3 28.6
01	301 59.5	150 06.0	07.5	236 31.5	19.1	177 43.9	10.3	287 43.4	28.6
02	317 01.9	165 05.8	06.4	251 32.1	19.4	192 45.8	10.2	302 45.8	28.6
03	332 04.4	180 05.6	. . 05.3	266 32.7	. . 19.7	207 47.7	. . 10.1	317 48.2	. . 28.7
04	347 06.9	195 05.4	04.2	281 33.3	20.0	222 49.6	10.0	332 50.5	28.7
05	2 09.3	210 05.3	03.1	296 33.9	20.3	237 51.5	09.9	347 52.9	28.7
06	17 11.8	225 05.1	N13 02.0	311 34.6	N21 20.7	252 53.4	N20 09.7	2 55.3	N 3 28.7
07	32 14.3	240 04.9	13 01.0	326 35.2	21.0	267 55.3	09.6	17 57.7	28.7
08	47 16.7	255 04.7	12 59.9	341 35.8	21.3	282 57.2	09.5	33 00.1	28.7
09	62 19.2	270 04.6	. . 58.8	356 36.4	. . 21.6	297 59.1	. . 09.4	48 02.5	. . 28.8
10	77 21.7	285 04.4	57.7	11 37.0	21.9	313 01.0	09.3	63 04.9	28.8
11	92 24.1	300 04.2	56.6	26 37.6	22.3	328 02.9	09.1	78 07.3	28.8
12	107 26.6	315 04.1	N12 55.5	41 38.2	N21 22.6	343 04.8	N20 09.0	93 09.7	N 3 28.8
13	122 29.1	330 03.9	54.4	56 38.8	22.9	358 06.7	08.9	108 12.1	28.8
14	137 31.5	345 03.7	53.4	71 39.4	23.2	13 08.6	08.8	123 14.5	28.9
15	152 34.0	0 03.6	. . 52.3	86 40.0	. . 23.5	28 10.5	. . 08.7	138 16.9	. . 28.9
16	167 36.4	15 03.4	51.2	101 40.7	23.8	43 12.4	08.5	153 19.2	28.9
17	182 38.9	30 03.2	50.1	116 41.3	24.1	58 14.3	08.4	168 21.6	28.9
18	197 41.4	45 03.1	N12 49.0	131 41.9	N21 24.5	73 16.2	N20 08.3	183 24.0	N 3 28.9
19	212 43.8	60 02.9	47.9	146 42.5	24.8	88 18.1	08.2	198 26.4	28.9
20	227 46.3	75 02.7	46.8	161 43.1	25.1	103 20.0	08.1	213 28.8	29.0
21	242 48.8	90 02.6	. . 45.7	176 43.7	. . 25.4	118 21.9	. . 07.9	228 31.2	. . 29.0
22	257 51.2	105 02.4	44.6	191 44.3	25.7	133 23.7	07.8	243 33.6	29.0
23	272 53.7	120 02.2	43.5	206 44.9	26.0	148 25.6	07.7	258 36.0	29.0
10 00 FRIDAY	287 56.2	135 02.1	N12 42.4	221 45.5	N21 26.3	163 27.5	N20 07.6	273 38.4	N 3 29.0
01	302 58.6	150 01.9	41.3	236 46.1	26.7	178 29.4	07.5	288 40.8	29.0
02	318 01.1	165 01.8	40.3	251 46.8	27.0	193 31.3	07.3	303 43.2	29.1
03	333 03.5	180 01.6	. . 39.2	266 47.4	. . 27.3	208 33.2	. . 07.2	318 45.6	. . 29.1
04	348 06.0	195 01.4	38.1	281 48.0	27.6	223 35.1	07.1	333 48.0	29.1
05	3 08.5	210 01.3	37.0	296 48.6	27.9	238 37.0	07.0	348 50.4	29.1
06	18 10.9	225 01.1	N12 35.9	311 49.2	N21 28.2	253 38.9	N20 06.9	3 52.8	N 3 29.1
07	33 13.4	240 01.0	34.8	326 49.8	28.5	268 40.8	06.7	18 55.2	29.1
08	48 15.9	255 00.8	33.7	341 50.4	28.8	283 42.7	06.6	33 57.5	29.2
09	63 18.3	270 00.6	. . 32.6	356 51.0	. . 29.1	298 44.6	. . 06.5	48 59.9	. . 29.2
10	78 20.8	285 00.5	31.5	11 51.6	29.4	313 46.5	06.4	64 02.3	29.2
11	93 23.3	300 00.3	30.4	26 52.2	29.8	328 48.4	06.3	79 04.7	29.2
12	108 25.7	315 00.2	N12 29.3	41 52.8	N21 30.1	343 50.3	N20 06.1	94 07.1	N 3 29.2
13	123 28.2	330 00.0	28.2	56 53.5	30.4	358 52.2	06.0	109 09.5	29.2
14	138 30.7	344 59.9	27.1	71 54.1	30.7	13 54.1	05.9	124 11.9	29.3
15	153 33.1	359 59.7	. . 26.0	86 54.7	. . 31.0	28 56.0	. . 05.8	139 14.3	. . 29.3
16	168 35.6	14 59.6	24.9	101 55.3	31.3	43 57.9	05.7	154 16.7	29.3
17	183 38.0	29 59.4	23.8	116 55.9	31.6	58 59.8	05.5	169 19.1	29.3
18	198 40.5	44 59.3	N12 22.7	131 56.5	N21 31.9	74 01.7	N20 05.4	184 21.5	N 3 29.3
19	213 43.0	59 59.1	21.6	146 57.1	32.2	89 03.6	05.3	199 23.9	29.3
20	228 45.4	74 59.0	20.5	161 57.7	32.5	104 05.5	05.2	214 26.3	29.3
21	243 47.9	89 58.8	. . 19.4	176 58.3	. . 32.8	119 07.4	. . 05.1	229 28.7	. . 29.4
22	258 50.4	104 58.7	18.3	191 58.9	33.1	134 09.3	04.9	244 31.1	29.4
23	273 52.8	119 58.5	17.2	206 59.6	33.4	149 11.2	04.8	259 33.5	29.4
11 00 SATURDAY	288 55.3	134 58.4	N12 16.1	222 00.2	N21 33.7	164 13.1	N20 04.7	274 35.9	N 3 29.4
01	303 57.8	149 58.2	15.0	237 00.8	34.0	179 15.0	04.6	289 38.3	29.4
02	319 00.2	164 58.1	13.9	252 01.4	34.3	194 16.9	04.5	304 40.7	29.4
03	334 02.7	179 58.0	. . 12.7	267 02.0	. . 34.6	209 18.8	. . 04.3	319 43.1	. . 29.5
04	349 05.2	194 57.8	11.6	282 02.6	34.9	224 20.7	04.2	334 45.5	29.5
05	4 07.6	209 57.7	10.5	297 03.2	35.2	239 22.6	04.1	349 47.9	29.5
06	19 10.1	224 57.5	N12 09.4	312 03.8	N21 35.5	254 24.5	N20 04.0	4 50.3	N 3 29.5
07	34 12.5	239 57.4	08.3	327 04.4	35.9	269 26.3	03.8	19 52.7	29.5
08	49 15.0	254 57.3	07.2	342 05.0	36.2	284 28.2	03.7	34 55.1	29.5
09	64 17.5	269 57.1	. . 06.1	357 05.6	. . 36.5	299 30.1	. . 03.6	49 57.5	. . 29.5
10	79 19.9	284 57.0	05.0	12 06.3	36.8	314 32.0	03.5	64 59.9	29.6
11	94 22.4	299 56.8	03.9	27 06.9	37.1	329 33.9	03.4	80 02.3	29.6
12	109 24.9	314 56.7	N12 02.8	42 07.5	N21 37.4	344 35.8	N20 03.2	95 04.7	N 3 29.6
13	124 27.3	329 56.6	01.7	57 08.1	37.7	359 37.7	03.1	110 07.1	29.6
14	139 29.8	344 56.4	12 00.6	72 08.7	38.0	14 39.6	03.0	125 09.5	29.6
15	154 32.3	359 56.3	11 59.4	87 09.3	. . 38.2	29 41.5	. . 02.9	140 11.9	. . 29.6
16	169 34.7	14 56.2	58.3	102 09.9	38.5	44 43.4	02.8	155 14.3	29.6
17	184 37.2	29 56.0	57.2	117 10.5	38.8	59 45.3	02.6	170 16.7	29.7
18	199 39.7	44 55.9	N11 56.1	132 11.1	N21 39.1	74 47.2	N20 02.5	185 19.1	N 3 29.7
19	214 42.1	59 55.8	55.0	147 11.7	39.4	89 49.1	02.4	200 21.5	29.7
20	229 44.6	74 55.6	53.9	162 12.3	39.7	104 51.0	02.3	215 23.9	29.7
21	244 47.0	89 55.5	. . 52.8	177 13.0	. . 40.0	119 52.9	. . 02.1	230 26.3	. . 29.7
22	259 49.5	104 55.4	51.7	192 13.6	40.3	134 54.8	02.0	245 28.7	29.7
23	274 52.0	119 55.2	50.5	207 14.2	40.6	149 56.7	01.9	260 31.1	29.7
Mer. Pass.	h m 4 47.5	*v* −0.2	*d* 1.1	*v* 0.6	*d* 0.3	*v* 1.9	*d* 0.1	*v* 2.4	*d* 0.0

STARS

Name	SHA ° ′	Dec ° ′
Acamar	315 11.0	S40 11.6
Achernar	335 19.3	S57 05.8
Acrux	172 58.8	S63 15.1
Adhara	255 05.3	S29 00.4
Aldebaran	290 38.5	N16 33.7
Alioth	166 11.9	N55 49.2
Alkaid	152 50.9	N49 11.1
Alnair	27 31.0	S46 49.7
Alnilam	275 36.8	S 1 11.0
Alphard	217 46.8	S 8 46.4
Alphecca	126 02.5	N26 37.6
Alpheratz	357 33.4	N29 14.1
Altair	61 58.4	N 8 56.4
Ankaa	353 05.8	S42 09.4
Antares	112 14.0	S26 29.5
Arcturus	145 46.7	N19 02.8
Atria	107 06.6	S69 04.6
Avior	234 14.9	S59 35.7
Bellatrix	278 21.8	N 6 22.5
Betelgeuse	270 51.1	N 7 24.7
Canopus	263 52.4	S52 42.5
Capella	280 20.5	N46 01.4
Deneb	49 24.5	N45 22.4
Denebola	182 23.8	N14 25.5
Diphda	348 46.0	S17 50.3
Dubhe	193 39.9	N61 36.7
Elnath	278 00.6	N28 37.7
Eltanin	90 41.1	N51 29.2
Enif	33 37.3	N 9 59.8
Fomalhaut	15 12.9	S29 28.7
Gacrux	171 50.3	S57 16.0
Gienah	175 42.4	S17 41.5
Hadar	148 34.0	S60 30.3
Hamal	327 49.9	N23 35.2
Kaus Aust.	83 30.5	S34 22.3
Kochab	137 19.3	N74 03.0
Markab	13 28.5	N15 20.9
Menkar	314 05.0	N 4 11.7
Menkent	147 56.0	S36 30.2
Miaplacidus	221 38.9	S69 49.7
Mirfak	308 26.7	N49 57.1
Nunki	75 45.8	S26 15.8
Peacock	53 03.2	S56 38.8
Pollux	243 16.2	N27 57.7
Procyon	244 49.9	N 5 09.4
Rasalhague	95 57.1	N12 32.5
Regulus	207 33.4	N11 50.3
Rigel	281 03.0	S 8 10.2
Rigil Kent.	139 38.3	S60 56.9
Sabik	102 01.0	S15 45.5
Schedar	349 29.5	N56 40.8
Shaula	96 08.3	S37 07.4
Sirius	258 25.5	S16 45.1
Spica	158 21.0	S11 18.1
Suhail	222 45.8	S43 32.5
Vega	80 31.9	N38 48.5
Zuben'ubi	136 54.5	S16 09.2

	SHA ° ′	Mer. Pass. h m
Venus	207 05.9	15 00
Mars	293 49.4	9 13
Jupiter	235 31.4	13 05
Saturn	345 42.2	5 45

	UT	SUN GHA	SUN Dec	MOON GHA	v	MOON Dec	d	HP
	d h	° ′	° ′	° ′	′	° ′	′	′
	9 00	178 42.2	N22 22.7	258 43.4	9.9	N16 25.3	13.6	58.9
	01	193 42.1	22.4	273 12.3	9.8	16 38.9	13.6	58.9
	02	208 42.0	22.1	287 41.1	9.7	16 52.5	13.4	58.9
	03	223 41.9	. . 21.8	302 09.8	9.6	17 05.9	13.4	59.0
	04	238 41.8	21.5	316 38.4	9.4	17 19.3	13.4	59.0
	05	253 41.7	21.2	331 06.8	9.4	17 32.7	13.2	59.0
	06	268 41.6	N22 20.9	345 35.2	9.2	N17 45.9	13.2	59.1
	07	283 41.5	20.6	0 03.4	9.0	17 59.1	13.0	59.1
T	08	298 41.4	20.3	14 31.4	9.0	18 12.1	13.0	59.1
H	09	313 41.3	. . 20.0	28 59.4	8.8	18 25.1	12.9	59.2
U	10	328 41.2	19.7	43 27.2	8.7	18 38.0	12.8	59.2
R	11	343 41.1	19.4	57 54.9	8.6	18 50.8	12.7	59.2
S	12	358 41.1	N22 19.1	72 22.5	8.4	N19 03.5	12.6	59.3
D	13	13 41.0	18.8	86 49.9	8.3	19 16.1	12.5	59.3
A	14	28 40.9	18.5	101 17.2	8.2	19 28.6	12.5	59.3
Y	15	43 40.8	. . 18.2	115 44.4	8.1	19 41.1	12.3	59.4
	16	58 40.7	17.9	130 11.5	7.9	19 53.4	12.2	59.4
	17	73 40.6	17.6	144 38.4	7.8	20 05.6	12.1	59.4
	18	88 40.5	N22 17.3	159 05.2	7.6	N20 17.7	12.0	59.5
	19	103 40.4	16.9	173 31.8	7.6	20 29.7	11.9	59.5
	20	118 40.3	16.6	187 58.4	7.3	20 41.6	11.8	59.5
	21	133 40.2	. . 16.3	202 24.7	7.3	20 53.4	11.6	59.5
	22	148 40.1	16.0	216 51.0	7.1	21 05.0	11.6	59.6
	23	163 40.1	15.7	231 17.1	7.0	21 16.6	11.4	59.6
	10 00	178 40.0	N22 15.4	245 43.1	6.9	N21 28.0	11.3	59.6
	01	193 39.9	15.1	260 09.0	6.7	21 39.3	11.2	59.7
	02	208 39.8	14.8	274 34.7	6.6	21 50.5	11.1	59.7
	03	223 39.7	. . 14.4	289 00.3	6.4	22 01.6	10.9	59.7
	04	238 39.6	14.1	303 25.7	6.3	22 12.5	10.8	59.8
	05	253 39.5	13.8	317 51.0	6.2	22 23.3	10.7	59.8
	06	268 39.4	N22 13.5	332 16.2	6.0	N22 34.0	10.5	59.8
	07	283 39.3	13.2	346 41.2	5.9	22 44.5	10.4	59.8
	08	298 39.3	12.9	1 06.1	5.8	22 54.9	10.3	59.9
F	09	313 39.2	. . 12.5	15 30.9	5.6	23 05.2	10.1	59.9
R	10	328 39.1	12.2	29 55.5	5.6	23 15.3	10.0	59.9
I	11	343 39.0	11.9	44 20.1	5.3	23 25.3	9.9	60.0
D	12	358 38.9	N22 11.6	58 44.4	5.3	N23 35.2	9.7	60.0
A	13	13 38.8	11.3	73 08.7	5.1	23 44.9	9.5	60.0
Y	14	28 38.7	10.9	87 32.8	4.9	23 54.4	9.4	60.0
	15	43 38.6	. . 10.6	101 56.7	4.9	24 03.8	9.3	60.1
	16	58 38.5	10.3	116 20.6	4.7	24 13.1	9.1	60.1
	17	73 38.5	10.0	130 44.3	4.6	24 22.2	8.9	60.1
	18	88 38.4	N22 09.6	145 07.9	4.4	N24 31.1	8.8	60.2
	19	103 38.3	09.3	159 31.3	4.4	24 39.9	8.6	60.2
	20	118 38.2	09.0	173 54.7	4.2	24 48.5	8.5	60.2
	21	133 38.1	. . 08.7	188 17.9	4.0	24 57.0	8.3	60.2
	22	148 38.0	08.3	202 40.9	4.0	25 05.3	8.1	60.3
	23	163 37.9	08.0	217 03.9	3.8	25 13.4	8.0	60.3
	11 00	178 37.9	N22 07.7	231 26.7	3.7	N25 21.4	7.8	60.3
	01	193 37.8	07.4	245 49.4	3.6	25 29.2	7.6	60.3
	02	208 37.7	07.0	260 12.0	3.5	25 36.8	7.4	60.4
	03	223 37.6	. . 06.7	274 34.5	3.3	25 44.2	7.3	60.4
	04	238 37.5	06.4	288 56.8	3.2	25 51.5	7.1	60.4
	05	253 37.4	06.0	303 19.0	3.2	25 58.6	6.9	60.4
	06	268 37.3	N22 05.7	317 41.2	3.0	N26 05.5	6.7	60.5
	07	283 37.3	05.4	332 03.2	2.9	26 12.2	6.5	60.5
S	08	298 37.2	05.0	346 25.1	2.8	26 18.7	6.4	60.5
A	09	313 37.1	. . 04.7	0 46.9	2.7	26 25.1	6.2	60.5
T	10	328 37.0	04.4	15 08.6	2.5	26 31.3	5.9	60.5
U	11	343 36.9	04.0	29 30.1	2.5	26 37.2	5.8	60.6
R	12	358 36.8	N22 03.7	43 51.6	2.4	N26 43.0	5.6	60.6
D	13	13 36.8	03.3	58 13.0	2.3	26 48.6	5.4	60.6
A	14	28 36.7	03.0	72 34.3	2.2	26 54.0	5.2	60.6
Y	15	43 36.6	. . 02.7	86 55.5	2.1	26 59.2	5.0	60.6
	16	58 36.5	02.3	101 16.6	2.0	27 04.2	4.9	60.7
	17	73 36.4	02.0	115 37.6	1.9	27 09.1	4.6	60.7
	18	88 36.3	N22 01.7	129 58.5	1.8	N27 13.7	4.4	60.7
	19	103 36.3	01.3	144 19.3	1.8	27 18.1	4.2	60.7
	20	118 36.2	01.0	158 40.1	1.7	27 22.3	4.0	60.7
	21	133 36.1	. . 00.6	173 00.8	1.6	27 26.3	3.8	60.8
	22	148 36.0	22 00.3	187 21.4	1.5	27 30.1	3.5	60.8
	23	163 35.9	N21 59.9	201 41.9	1.5	N27 33.6	3.4	60.8
		SD 15.8	*d* 0.3	SD 16.1		16.3		16.5

Lat.	Twilight Naut.	Twilight Civil	Sunrise	Moonrise 9	Moonrise 10	Moonrise 11	Moonrise 12
°	h m	h m	h m	h m	h m	h m	h m
N 72	▭	▭	▭	▭	▭	▭	▭
N 70	▭	▭	▭	▭	▭	▭	▭
68	▭	▭	▭	20 53	▭	▭	▭
66	////	////	01 12	21 37	▭	▭	▭
64	////	////	02 01	22 06	21 41	▭	▭
62	////	////	02 32	22 29	22 26	22 25	23 12
60	////	01 29	02 55	22 47	22 56	23 18	24 19
N 58	////	02 05	03 13	23 02	23 18	23 51	24 54
56	////	02 30	03 28	23 15	23 37	24 15	00 15
54	01 22	02 49	03 41	23 27	23 53	24 35	00 35
52	01 55	03 05	03 52	23 37	24 06	00 06	00 51
50	02 18	03 19	04 02	23 46	24 19	00 19	01 06
45	02 59	03 47	04 23	24 06	00 06	00 44	01 35
N 40	03 27	04 08	04 40	24 22	00 22	01 04	01 58
35	03 49	04 25	04 54	24 35	00 35	01 20	02 16
30	04 07	04 39	05 06	00 07	00 47	01 35	02 33
20	04 34	05 03	05 27	00 22	01 07	02 00	03 00
N 10	04 55	05 22	05 45	00 35	01 25	02 21	03 24
0	05 13	05 39	06 02	00 47	01 42	02 42	03 47
S 10	05 29	05 56	06 18	01 00	01 59	03 02	04 09
20	05 45	06 12	06 36	01 13	02 17	03 24	04 33
30	06 00	06 30	06 56	01 29	02 38	03 50	05 01
35	06 08	06 39	07 07	01 38	02 50	04 05	05 18
40	06 17	06 50	07 21	01 49	03 05	04 22	05 37
45	06 26	07 03	07 36	02 01	03 22	04 44	06 01
S 50	06 37	07 18	07 56	02 16	03 43	05 11	06 31
52	06 42	07 25	08 05	02 23	03 53	05 24	06 46
54	06 47	07 32	08 15	02 31	04 05	05 39	07 04
56	06 52	07 41	08 26	02 40	04 18	05 57	07 25
58	06 59	07 50	08 40	02 50	04 34	06 19	07 52
S 60	07 05	08 01	08 55	03 02	04 52	06 48	08 30

Lat.	Sunset	Twilight Civil	Twilight Naut.	Moonset 9	Moonset 10	Moonset 11	Moonset 12
°	h m	h m	h m	h m	h m	h m	h m
N 72	▭	▭	▭	▭	▭	▭	▭
N 70	▭	▭	▭	▭	▭	▭	▭
68	▭	▭	▭	17 42	▭	▭	▭
66	22 54	////	////	17 00	▭	▭	▭
64	22 07	////	////	16 31	18 58	▭	▭
62	21 37	////	////	16 10	18 14	20 28	22 03
60	21 15	22 39	////	15 52	17 45	19 35	20 55
N 58	20 57	22 05	////	15 38	17 22	19 03	20 20
56	20 42	21 40	////	15 25	17 04	18 39	19 55
54	20 29	21 21	22 47	15 15	16 49	18 20	19 34
52	20 18	21 05	22 15	15 05	16 36	18 03	19 17
50	20 08	20 51	21 52	14 57	16 24	17 49	19 02
45	19 47	20 24	21 11	14 39	16 00	17 21	18 33
N 40	19 30	20 03	20 43	14 24	15 41	16 58	18 09
35	19 16	19 46	20 21	14 12	15 25	16 40	17 50
30	19 04	19 31	20 04	14 01	15 12	16 24	17 33
20	18 43	19 08	19 37	13 43	14 48	15 57	17 05
N 10	18 26	18 48	19 15	13 27	14 28	15 34	16 41
0	18 09	18 31	18 57	13 12	14 09	15 12	16 18
S 10	17 53	18 15	18 41	12 58	13 51	14 51	15 56
20	17 35	17 59	18 26	12 42	13 31	14 27	15 32
30	17 15	17 41	18 11	12 24	13 08	14 01	15 03
35	17 04	17 32	18 03	12 14	12 55	13 45	14 47
40	16 50	17 21	17 54	12 02	12 39	13 27	14 27
45	16 35	17 08	17 45	11 48	12 21	13 05	14 03
S 50	16 16	16 53	17 34	11 32	11 58	12 37	13 33
52	16 06	16 46	17 29	11 24	11 48	12 23	13 18
54	15 56	16 39	17 24	11 15	11 35	12 08	13 00
56	15 45	16 31	17 19	11 05	11 21	11 49	12 39
58	15 31	16 21	17 13	10 54	11 05	11 27	12 12
S 60	15 16	16 11	17 06	10 42	10 46	10 58	11 34

Day	SUN Eqn. of Time 00^h	SUN Eqn. of Time 12^h	SUN Mer. Pass.	MOON Mer. Pass. Upper	MOON Mer. Pass. Lower	MOON Age	MOON Phase
d	m s	m s	h m	h m	h m	d %	
9	05 11	05 16	12 05	07 00	19 27	24 32	
10	05 20	05 24	12 05	07 55	20 25	25 21	
11	05 28	05 32	12 06	08 57	21 29	26 12	

	UT	ARIES	VENUS −4·1		MARS +1·3		JUPITER −1·8		SATURN +0·7	
	d h	GHA ° ′	GHA ° ′	Dec ° ′	GHA ° ′	Dec ° ′	GHA ° ′	Dec ° ′	GHA ° ′	Dec ° ′
	12 00	289 54.4	134 55.1	N11 49.4	222 14.8	N21 40.9	164 58.6	N20 01.8	275 33.5	N 3 29.8
	01	304 56.9	149 55.0	48.3	237 15.4	41.2	180 00.5	01.7	290 35.9	29.8
	02	319 59.4	164 54.8	47.2	252 16.0	41.5	195 02.4	01.5	305 38.3	29.8
	03	335 01.8	179 54.7	. . 46.1	267 16.6	. . 41.8	210 04.3	. . 01.4	320 40.7	. . 29.8
	04	350 04.3	194 54.6	45.0	282 17.2	42.1	225 06.2	01.3	335 43.1	29.8
	05	5 06.8	209 54.5	43.8	297 17.8	42.4	240 08.1	01.2	350 45.5	29.8
	06	20 09.2	224 54.3	N11 42.7	312 18.4	N21 42.7	255 10.0	N20 01.0	5 47.9	N 3 29.8
	07	35 11.7	239 54.2	41.6	327 19.1	43.0	270 11.9	00.9	20 50.3	29.8
	08	50 14.2	254 54.1	40.5	342 19.7	43.3	285 13.8	00.8	35 52.7	29.9
S	09	65 16.6	269 54.0	. . 39.4	357 20.3	. . 43.6	300 15.6	. . 00.7	50 55.1	. . 29.9
U	10	80 19.1	284 53.8	38.3	12 20.9	43.9	315 17.5	00.6	65 57.5	29.9
N	11	95 21.5	299 53.7	37.1	27 21.5	44.1	330 19.4	00.4	80 59.9	29.9
D	12	110 24.0	314 53.6	N11 36.0	42 22.1	N21 44.4	345 21.3	N20 00.3	96 02.3	N 3 29.9
A	13	125 26.5	329 53.5	34.9	57 22.7	44.7	0 23.2	00.2	111 04.7	29.9
Y	14	140 28.9	344 53.3	33.8	72 23.3	45.0	15 25.1	20 00.1	126 07.1	29.9
	15	155 31.4	359 53.2	. . 32.7	87 23.9	. . 45.3	30 27.0	19 59.9	141 09.5	. . 30.0
	16	170 33.9	14 53.1	31.5	102 24.5	45.6	45 28.9	59.8	156 11.9	30.0
	17	185 36.3	29 53.0	30.4	117 25.1	45.9	60 30.8	59.7	171 14.3	30.0
	18	200 38.8	44 52.9	N11 29.3	132 25.8	N21 46.2	75 32.7	N19 59.6	186 16.7	N 3 30.0
	19	215 41.3	59 52.8	28.2	147 26.4	46.5	90 34.6	59.5	201 19.1	30.0
	20	230 43.7	74 52.6	27.0	162 27.0	46.7	105 36.5	59.3	216 21.5	30.0
	21	245 46.2	89 52.5	. . 25.9	177 27.6	. . 47.0	120 38.4	. . 59.2	231 23.9	. . 30.0
	22	260 48.7	104 52.4	24.8	192 28.2	47.3	135 40.3	59.1	246 26.4	30.0
	23	275 51.1	119 52.3	23.7	207 28.8	47.6	150 42.2	59.0	261 28.8	30.0
	13 00	290 53.6	134 52.2	N11 22.5	222 29.4	N21 47.9	165 44.1	N19 58.8	276 31.2	N 3 30.1
	01	305 56.0	149 52.1	21.4	237 30.0	48.2	180 46.0	58.7	291 33.6	30.1
	02	320 58.5	164 51.9	20.3	252 30.6	48.5	195 47.9	58.6	306 36.0	30.1
	03	336 01.0	179 51.8	. . 19.2	267 31.2	. . 48.8	210 49.8	. . 58.5	321 38.4	. . 30.1
	04	351 03.4	194 51.7	18.0	282 31.8	49.0	225 51.7	58.4	336 40.8	30.1
	05	6 05.9	209 51.6	16.9	297 32.5	49.3	240 53.6	58.2	351 43.2	30.1
	06	21 08.4	224 51.5	N11 15.8	312 33.1	N21 49.6	255 55.5	N19 58.1	6 45.6	N 3 30.1
	07	36 10.8	239 51.4	14.7	327 33.7	49.9	270 57.4	58.0	21 48.0	30.1
	08	51 13.3	254 51.3	13.5	342 34.3	50.2	285 59.3	57.9	36 50.4	30.2
M	09	66 15.8	269 51.2	. . 12.4	357 34.9	. . 50.5	301 01.1	. . 57.7	51 52.8	. . 30.2
O	10	81 18.2	284 51.1	11.3	12 35.5	50.7	316 03.0	57.6	66 55.2	30.2
N	11	96 20.7	299 51.0	10.1	27 36.1	51.0	331 04.9	57.5	81 57.6	30.2
D	12	111 23.2	314 50.9	N11 09.0	42 36.7	N21 51.3	346 06.8	N19 57.4	97 00.0	N 3 30.2
A	13	126 25.6	329 50.7	07.9	57 37.3	51.6	1 08.7	57.2	112 02.4	30.2
Y	14	141 28.1	344 50.6	06.8	72 37.9	51.9	16 10.6	57.1	127 04.9	30.2
	15	156 30.5	359 50.5	. . 05.6	87 38.5	. . 52.2	31 12.5	. . 57.0	142 07.3	. . 30.2
	16	171 33.0	14 50.4	04.5	102 39.2	52.4	46 14.4	56.9	157 09.7	30.2
	17	186 35.5	29 50.3	03.4	117 39.8	52.7	61 16.3	56.8	172 12.1	30.3
	18	201 37.9	44 50.2	N11 02.2	132 40.4	N21 53.0	76 18.2	N19 56.6	187 14.5	N 3 30.3
	19	216 40.4	59 50.1	01.1	147 41.0	53.3	91 20.1	56.5	202 16.9	30.3
	20	231 42.9	74 50.0	11 00.0	162 41.6	53.6	106 22.0	56.4	217 19.3	30.3
	21	246 45.3	89 49.9	10 58.8	177 42.2	. . 53.8	121 23.9	. . 56.3	232 21.7	. . 30.3
	22	261 47.8	104 49.8	57.7	192 42.8	54.1	136 25.8	56.1	247 24.1	30.3
	23	276 50.3	119 49.7	56.6	207 43.4	54.4	151 27.7	56.0	262 26.5	30.3
	14 00	291 52.7	134 49.6	N10 55.4	222 44.0	N21 54.7	166 29.6	N19 55.9	277 28.9	N 3 30.3
	01	306 55.2	149 49.5	54.3	237 44.6	54.9	181 31.5	55.8	292 31.3	30.3
	02	321 57.7	164 49.4	53.2	252 45.3	55.2	196 33.4	55.6	307 33.8	30.3
	03	337 00.1	179 49.3	. . 52.0	267 45.9	. . 55.5	211 35.3	. . 55.5	322 36.2	. . 30.4
	04	352 02.6	194 49.2	50.9	282 46.5	55.8	226 37.2	55.4	337 38.6	30.4
	05	7 05.0	209 49.1	49.8	297 47.1	56.1	241 39.1	55.3	352 41.0	30.4
	06	22 07.5	224 49.0	N10 48.6	312 47.7	N21 56.3	256 40.9	N19 55.1	7 43.4	N 3 30.4
	07	37 10.0	239 49.0	47.5	327 48.3	56.6	271 42.8	55.0	22 45.8	30.4
T	08	52 12.4	254 48.9	46.3	342 48.9	56.9	286 44.7	54.9	37 48.2	30.4
U	09	67 14.9	269 48.8	. . 45.2	357 49.5	. . 57.2	301 46.6	. . 54.8	52 50.6	. . 30.4
E	10	82 17.4	284 48.7	44.1	12 50.1	57.4	316 48.5	54.7	67 53.0	30.4
S	11	97 19.8	299 48.6	42.9	27 50.7	57.7	331 50.4	54.5	82 55.4	30.4
D	12	112 22.3	314 48.5	N10 41.8	42 51.3	N21 58.0	346 52.3	N19 54.4	97 57.9	N 3 30.4
A	13	127 24.8	329 48.4	40.6	57 52.0	58.3	1 54.2	54.3	113 00.3	30.5
Y	14	142 27.2	344 48.3	39.5	72 52.6	58.5	16 56.1	54.2	128 02.7	30.5
	15	157 29.7	359 48.2	. . 38.4	87 53.2	. . 58.8	31 58.0	. . 54.0	143 05.1	. . 30.5
	16	172 32.2	14 48.1	37.2	102 53.8	59.1	46 59.9	53.9	158 07.5	30.5
	17	187 34.6	29 48.0	36.1	117 54.4	59.3	62 01.8	53.8	173 09.9	30.5
	18	202 37.1	44 48.0	N10 34.9	132 55.0	N21 59.6	77 03.7	N19 53.7	188 12.3	N 3 30.5
	19	217 39.5	59 47.9	33.8	147 55.6	21 59.9	92 05.6	53.5	203 14.7	30.5
	20	232 42.0	74 47.8	32.7	162 56.2	22 00.2	107 07.5	53.4	218 17.2	30.5
	21	247 44.5	89 47.7	. . 31.5	177 56.8	. . 00.4	122 09.4	. . 53.3	233 19.6	. . 30.5
	22	262 46.9	104 47.6	30.4	192 57.4	00.7	137 11.3	53.2	248 22.0	30.5
	23	277 49.4	119 47.5	29.2	207 58.1	01.0	152 13.2	53.0	263 24.4	30.5
	Mer. Pass.	h m 4 35.7	v −0.1	d 1.1	v 0.6	d 0.3	v 1.9	d 0.1	v 2.4	d 0.0

STARS

Name	SHA ° ′	Dec ° ′
Acamar	315 11.0	S40 11.6
Achernar	335 19.3	S57 05.8
Acrux	172 58.8	S63 15.1
Adhara	255 05.3	S29 00.4
Aldebaran	290 38.4	N16 33.7
Alioth	166 11.9	N55 49.2
Alkaid	152 50.9	N49 11.1
Alnair	27 31.0	S46 49.7
Alnilam	275 36.8	S 1 11.0
Alphard	217 46.8	S 8 46.4
Alphecca	126 02.5	N26 37.6
Alpheratz	357 33.3	N29 14.2
Altair	61 58.4	N 8 56.4
Ankaa	353 05.8	S42 09.4
Antares	112 14.0	S26 29.5
Arcturus	145 46.7	N19 02.8
Atria	107 06.6	S69 04.6
Avior	234 14.9	S59 35.7
Bellatrix	278 21.8	N 6 22.5
Betelgeuse	270 51.0	N 7 24.7
Canopus	263 52.4	S52 42.5
Capella	280 20.4	N46 01.4
Deneb	49 24.5	N45 22.5
Denebola	182 23.8	N14 25.5
Diphda	348 46.0	S17 50.3
Dubhe	193 39.9	N61 36.7
Elnath	278 00.6	N28 37.7
Eltanin	90 41.1	N51 29.2
Enif	33 37.3	N 9 59.9
Fomalhaut	15 12.9	S29 28.7
Gacrux	171 50.4	S57 16.0
Gienah	175 42.4	S17 41.5
Hadar	148 34.1	S60 30.3
Hamal	327 49.8	N23 35.2
Kaus Aust.	83 30.4	S34 22.3
Kochab	137 19.4	N74 03.0
Markab	13 28.4	N15 20.9
Menkar	314 05.0	N 4 11.7
Menkent	147 56.0	S36 30.2
Miaplacidus	221 38.9	S69 49.7
Mirfak	308 26.7	N49 57.1
Nunki	75 45.8	S26 15.8
Peacock	53 03.2	S56 38.8
Pollux	243 16.1	N27 57.7
Procyon	244 49.9	N 5 09.4
Rasalhague	95 57.1	N12 32.5
Regulus	207 33.4	N11 50.3
Rigel	281 02.9	S 8 10.2
Rigil Kent.	139 38.3	S60 56.9
Sabik	102 01.0	S15 45.5
Schedar	349 29.5	N56 40.8
Shaula	96 08.3	S37 07.4
Sirius	258 25.5	S16 45.1
Spica	158 21.0	S11 18.1
Suhail	222 45.8	S43 32.5
Vega	80 31.9	N38 48.6
Zuben'ubi	136 54.5	S16 09.2

	SHA ° ′	Mer. Pass. h m
Venus	203 58.6	15 01
Mars	291 35.8	9 10
Jupiter	234 50.5	12 55
Saturn	345 37.6	5 33

UT		SUN GHA	SUN Dec	MOON GHA	v	MOON Dec	d	HP
d	h	° ′	° ′	° ′	′	° ′	′	′
12 SUNDAY	00	178 35.9	N21 59.6	216 02.4	1.4	N27 37.0	3.2	60.8
	01	193 35.8	59.3	230 22.8	1.3	27 40.2	2.9	60.8
	02	208 35.7	58.9	244 43.1	1.3	27 43.1	2.8	60.8
	03	223 35.6	. . 58.6	259 03.4	1.2	27 45.9	2.5	60.8
	04	238 35.5	58.2	273 23.6	1.2	27 48.4	2.3	60.9
	05	253 35.5	57.9	287 43.8	1.1	27 50.7	2.1	60.9
	06	268 35.4	N21 57.5	302 03.9	1.0	N27 52.8	1.9	60.9
	07	283 35.3	57.2	316 23.9	1.1	27 54.7	1.7	60.9
	08	298 35.2	56.8	330 44.0	0.9	27 56.4	1.5	60.9
	09	313 35.1	. . 56.5	345 03.9	1.0	27 57.9	1.2	60.9
	10	328 35.1	56.1	359 23.9	0.9	27 59.1	1.0	60.9
	11	343 35.0	55.8	13 43.8	0.9	28 00.1	0.8	60.9
	12	358 34.9	N21 55.4	28 03.7	0.9	N28 00.9	0.6	61.0
	13	13 34.8	55.1	42 23.6	0.8	28 01.5	0.4	61.0
	14	28 34.7	54.7	56 43.4	0.8	28 01.9	0.1	61.0
	15	43 34.7	. . 54.4	71 03.2	0.8	28 02.0	0.0	61.0
	16	58 34.6	54.0	85 23.0	0.8	28 02.0	0.3	61.0
	17	73 34.5	53.6	99 42.8	0.8	28 01.7	0.5	61.0
	18	88 34.4	N21 53.3	114 02.6	0.8	N28 01.2	0.8	61.0
	19	103 34.4	52.9	128 22.4	0.7	28 00.4	0.9	61.0
	20	118 34.3	52.6	142 42.1	0.8	27 59.5	1.2	61.0
	21	133 34.2	. . 52.2	157 01.9	0.8	27 58.3	1.4	61.0
	22	148 34.1	51.9	171 21.7	0.8	27 56.9	1.6	61.0
	23	163 34.0	51.5	185 41.5	0.8	27 55.3	1.9	61.0
13 MONDAY	00	178 34.0	N21 51.1	200 01.3	0.9	N27 53.4	2.0	61.0
	01	193 33.9	50.8	214 21.2	0.8	27 51.4	2.3	61.0
	02	208 33.8	50.4	228 41.0	0.9	27 49.1	2.5	61.1
	03	223 33.7	. . 50.0	243 00.9	0.9	27 46.6	2.7	61.1
	04	238 33.7	49.7	257 20.8	1.0	27 43.9	2.9	61.1
	05	253 33.6	49.3	271 40.8	0.9	27 41.0	3.1	61.1
	06	268 33.5	N21 49.0	286 00.7	1.1	N27 37.9	3.4	61.1
	07	283 33.4	48.6	300 20.8	1.0	27 34.5	3.6	61.1
	08	298 33.4	48.2	314 40.8	1.1	27 30.9	3.8	61.1
	09	313 33.3	. . 47.9	329 00.9	1.2	27 27.1	4.0	61.1
	10	328 33.2	47.5	343 21.1	1.2	27 23.1	4.2	61.1
	11	343 33.1	47.1	357 41.3	1.2	27 18.9	4.4	61.1
	12	358 33.1	N21 46.8	12 01.5	1.4	N27 14.5	4.6	61.1
	13	13 33.0	46.4	26 21.9	1.3	27 09.9	4.9	61.1
	14	28 32.9	46.0	40 42.2	1.5	27 05.0	5.0	61.1
	15	43 32.8	. . 45.7	55 02.7	1.5	27 00.0	5.3	61.0
	16	58 32.8	45.3	69 23.2	1.6	26 54.7	5.5	61.0
	17	73 32.7	44.9	83 43.8	1.7	26 49.2	5.7	61.0
	18	88 32.6	N21 44.5	98 04.5	1.7	N26 43.5	5.8	61.0
	19	103 32.6	44.2	112 25.2	1.8	26 37.7	6.1	61.0
	20	118 32.5	43.8	126 46.0	1.9	26 31.6	6.3	61.0
	21	133 32.4	. . 43.4	141 06.9	2.0	26 25.3	6.5	61.0
	22	148 32.3	43.0	155 27.9	2.1	26 18.8	6.6	61.0
	23	163 32.3	42.7	169 49.0	2.1	26 12.2	6.9	61.0
14 TUESDAY	00	178 32.2	N21 42.3	184 10.1	2.3	N26 05.3	7.1	61.0
	01	193 32.1	41.9	198 31.4	2.3	25 58.2	7.2	61.0
	02	208 32.1	41.5	212 52.7	2.5	25 51.0	7.5	61.0
	03	223 32.0	. . 41.2	227 14.2	2.5	25 43.5	7.6	61.0
	04	238 31.9	40.8	241 35.7	2.7	25 35.9	7.8	61.0
	05	253 31.8	40.4	255 57.4	2.8	25 28.1	8.0	60.9
	06	268 31.8	N21 40.0	270 19.2	2.8	N25 20.1	8.2	60.9
	07	283 31.7	39.6	284 41.0	3.0	25 11.9	8.4	60.9
	08	298 31.6	39.3	299 03.0	3.1	25 03.5	8.5	60.9
	09	313 31.6	. . 38.9	313 25.1	3.2	24 55.0	8.8	60.9
	10	328 31.5	38.5	327 47.3	3.3	24 46.2	8.9	60.9
	11	343 31.4	38.1	342 09.6	3.4	24 37.3	9.0	60.9
	12	358 31.4	N21 37.7	356 32.0	3.5	N24 28.3	9.3	60.9
	13	13 31.3	37.4	10 54.5	3.7	24 19.0	9.4	60.8
	14	28 31.2	37.0	25 17.2	3.8	24 09.6	9.6	60.8
	15	43 31.2	. . 36.6	39 40.0	3.9	24 00.0	9.7	60.8
	16	58 31.1	36.2	54 02.9	4.0	23 50.3	10.0	60.8
	17	73 31.0	35.8	68 25.9	4.1	23 40.3	10.0	60.8
	18	88 30.9	N21 35.4	82 49.0	4.3	N23 30.3	10.3	60.8
	19	103 30.9	35.0	97 12.3	4.4	23 20.0	10.3	60.7
	20	118 30.8	34.6	111 35.7	4.5	23 09.7	10.6	60.7
	21	133 30.7	. . 34.3	125 59.2	4.6	22 59.1	10.7	60.7
	22	148 30.7	33.9	140 22.8	4.8	22 48.4	10.8	60.7
	23	163 30.6	33.5	154 46.6	4.9	N22 37.6	11.0	60.7
		SD 15.8	d 0.4	SD 16.6		16.6		16.6

Lat.	Twilight Naut.	Twilight Civil	Sunrise	Moonrise 12	13	14	15
°	h m	h m	h m	h m	h m	h m	h m
N 72	▭	▭	▭	▭	▭	▭	▭
N 70	▭	▭	▭	▭	▭	▭	▭
68	▭	▭	▭	▭	▭	▭	▭
66	////	////	01 26	▭	▭	▭	02 34
64	////	////	02 10	▭	▭	00 04	03 13
62	////	00 31	02 38	23 12	25 27	01 27	03 40
60	////	01 38	03 00	24 19	00 19	02 03	04 01
N 58	////	02 11	03 17	24 54	00 54	02 29	04 18
56	00 29	02 35	03 32	00 15	01 20	02 50	04 32
54	01 30	02 54	03 45	00 35	01 40	03 07	04 44
52	02 01	03 09	03 56	00 51	01 57	03 22	04 55
50	02 23	03 23	04 05	01 06	02 12	03 34	05 05
45	03 02	03 50	04 26	01 35	02 41	04 00	05 25
N 40	03 30	04 10	04 42	01 58	03 04	04 21	05 41
35	03 51	04 27	04 56	02 16	03 24	04 38	05 55
30	04 08	04 41	05 08	02 33	03 40	04 53	06 07
20	04 35	05 04	05 28	03 00	04 08	05 18	06 27
N 10	04 56	05 23	05 46	03 24	04 32	05 39	06 44
0	05 14	05 40	06 02	03 47	04 54	05 59	07 01
S 10	05 30	05 56	06 18	04 09	05 16	06 19	07 17
20	05 45	06 12	06 35	04 33	05 40	06 41	07 34
30	05 59	06 29	06 55	05 01	06 08	07 05	07 54
35	06 07	06 39	07 06	05 18	06 24	07 20	08 05
40	06 16	06 49	07 19	05 37	06 43	07 37	08 18
45	06 25	07 02	07 35	06 01	07 06	07 56	08 34
S 50	06 35	07 16	07 53	06 31	07 35	08 21	08 53
52	06 40	07 23	08 02	06 46	07 50	08 33	09 02
54	06 45	07 30	08 12	07 04	08 07	08 47	09 11
56	06 50	07 38	08 23	07 25	08 27	09 02	09 23
58	06 56	07 47	08 36	07 52	08 51	09 21	09 35
S 60	07 03	07 57	08 51	08 30	09 25	09 43	09 50

Lat.	Sunset	Twilight Civil	Twilight Naut.	Moonset 12	13	14	15
°	h m	h m	h m	h m	h m	h m	h m
N 72	▭	▭	▭	▭	▭	▭	▭
N 70	▭	▭	▭	▭	▭	▭	23 34
68	▭	▭	▭	▭	▭	▭	23 01
66	22 41	////	////	▭	▭	23 13	22 37
64	22 00	////	////	▭	23 31	22 33	22 17
62	21 32	23 31	////	22 03	22 08	22 05	22 02
60	21 11	22 31	////	20 55	21 31	21 43	21 48
N 58	20 53	21 59	////	20 20	21 04	21 25	21 37
56	20 39	21 35	23 34	19 55	20 43	21 10	21 27
54	20 26	21 17	22 39	19 34	20 25	20 57	21 18
52	20 15	21 01	22 09	19 17	20 10	20 46	21 10
50	20 06	20 48	21 47	19 02	19 57	20 36	21 02
45	19 45	20 21	21 08	18 33	19 30	20 14	20 47
N 40	19 29	20 01	20 41	18 09	19 09	19 57	20 34
35	19 15	19 44	20 20	17 50	18 51	19 42	20 23
30	19 03	19 30	20 03	17 33	18 36	19 29	20 13
20	18 43	19 07	19 36	17 05	18 09	19 07	19 56
N 10	18 26	18 48	19 15	16 41	17 47	18 47	19 42
0	18 09	18 32	18 58	16 18	17 25	18 29	19 28
S 10	17 53	18 16	18 42	15 56	17 04	18 11	19 14
20	17 36	18 00	18 27	15 32	16 41	17 51	18 58
30	17 17	17 43	18 12	15 03	16 14	17 28	18 41
35	17 05	17 33	18 04	14 47	15 58	17 15	18 31
40	16 53	17 23	17 56	14 27	15 39	16 59	18 19
45	16 37	17 10	17 47	14 03	15 17	16 40	18 05
S 50	16 19	16 56	17 37	13 33	14 48	16 16	17 48
52	16 10	16 49	17 32	13 18	14 34	16 05	17 39
54	16 00	16 42	17 27	13 00	14 17	15 52	17 30
56	15 49	16 34	17 22	12 39	13 58	15 37	17 20
58	15 36	16 25	17 16	12 12	13 33	15 19	17 08
S 60	15 21	16 15	17 10	11 34	13 00	14 57	16 54

Day	SUN Eqn. of Time 00h	12h	Mer. Pass.	MOON Mer. Pass. Upper	Lower	Age	Phase
d	m s	m s	h m	h m	h m	d	%
12	05 36	05 40	12 06	10 03	22 36	27	6
13	05 44	05 48	12 06	11 10	23 43	28	1
14	05 51	05 54	12 06	12 14	24 45	00	0

2026 JULY 15, 16, 17 (WED., THURS., FRI.)

UT d h	ARIES GHA ° ′	VENUS −4·2 GHA ° ′	VENUS Dec ° ′	MARS +1·3 GHA ° ′	MARS Dec ° ′	JUPITER −1·8 GHA ° ′	JUPITER Dec ° ′	SATURN +0·7 GHA ° ′	SATURN Dec ° ′
15 00 (WEDNESDAY)	292 51.9	134 47.5	N10 28.1	222 58.7	N22 01.2	167 15.1	N19 52.9	278 26.8	N 3 30.6
01	307 54.3	149 47.4	26.9	237 59.3	01.5	182 17.0	52.8	293 29.2	30.6
02	322 56.8	164 47.3	25.8	252 59.9	01.8	197 18.8	52.7	308 31.6	30.6
03	337 59.3	179 47.2	. . 24.7	268 00.5	. . 02.0	212 20.7	. . 52.5	323 34.0	. . 30.6
04	353 01.7	194 47.1	23.5	283 01.1	02.3	227 22.6	52.4	338 36.5	30.6
05	8 04.2	209 47.0	22.4	298 01.7	02.6	242 24.5	52.3	353 38.9	30.6
06	23 06.6	224 47.0	N10 21.2	313 02.3	N22 02.8	257 26.4	N19 52.2	8 41.3	N 3 30.6
07	38 09.1	239 46.9	20.1	328 02.9	03.1	272 28.3	52.0	23 43.7	30.6
08	53 11.6	254 46.8	18.9	343 03.5	03.4	287 30.2	51.9	38 46.1	30.6
09	68 14.0	269 46.7	. . 17.8	358 04.2	. . 03.6	302 32.1	. . 51.8	53 48.5	. . 30.6
10	83 16.5	284 46.7	16.6	13 04.8	03.9	317 34.0	51.7	68 50.9	30.6
11	98 19.0	299 46.6	15.5	28 05.4	04.2	332 35.9	51.5	83 53.4	30.6
12	113 21.4	314 46.5	N10 14.3	43 06.0	N22 04.4	347 37.8	N19 51.4	98 55.8	N 3 30.7
13	128 23.9	329 46.4	13.2	58 06.6	04.7	2 39.7	51.3	113 58.2	30.7
14	143 26.4	344 46.4	12.0	73 07.2	05.0	17 41.6	51.2	129 00.6	30.7
15	158 28.8	359 46.3	. . 10.9	88 07.8	. . 05.2	32 43.5	. . 51.0	144 03.0	. . 30.7
16	173 31.3	14 46.2	09.7	103 08.4	05.5	47 45.4	50.9	159 05.4	30.7
17	188 33.8	29 46.1	08.6	118 09.0	05.8	62 47.3	50.8	174 07.9	30.7
18	203 36.2	44 46.1	N10 07.4	133 09.6	N22 06.0	77 49.2	N19 50.7	189 10.3	N 3 30.7
19	218 38.7	59 46.0	06.3	148 10.3	06.3	92 51.1	50.5	204 12.7	30.7
20	233 41.1	74 45.9	05.1	163 10.9	06.5	107 53.0	50.4	219 15.1	30.7
21	248 43.6	89 45.9	. . 04.0	178 11.5	. . 06.8	122 54.8	. . 50.3	234 17.5	. . 30.7
22	263 46.1	104 45.8	02.8	193 12.1	07.1	137 56.7	50.2	249 19.9	30.7
23	278 48.5	119 45.7	01.7	208 12.7	07.3	152 58.6	50.0	264 22.4	30.7
16 00 (THURSDAY)	293 51.0	134 45.6	N10 00.5	223 13.3	N22 07.6	168 00.5	N19 49.9	279 24.8	N 3 30.7
01	308 53.5	149 45.6	9 59.4	238 13.9	07.9	183 02.4	49.8	294 27.2	30.7
02	323 55.9	164 45.5	58.2	253 14.5	08.1	198 04.3	49.7	309 29.6	30.8
03	338 58.4	179 45.4	. . 57.1	268 15.1	. . 08.4	213 06.2	. . 49.5	324 32.0	. . 30.8
04	354 00.9	194 45.4	55.9	283 15.7	08.6	228 08.1	49.4	339 34.4	30.8
05	9 03.3	209 45.3	54.8	298 16.4	08.9	243 10.0	49.3	354 36.9	30.8
06	24 05.8	224 45.3	N 9 53.6	313 17.0	N22 09.2	258 11.9	N19 49.2	9 39.3	N 3 30.8
07	39 08.3	239 45.2	52.5	328 17.6	09.4	273 13.8	49.0	24 41.7	30.8
08	54 10.7	254 45.1	51.3	343 18.2	09.7	288 15.7	48.9	39 44.1	30.8
09	69 13.2	269 45.1	. . 50.2	358 18.8	. . 09.9	303 17.6	. . 48.8	54 46.5	. . 30.8
10	84 15.6	284 45.0	49.0	13 19.4	10.2	318 19.5	48.7	69 48.9	30.8
11	99 18.1	299 44.9	47.8	28 20.0	10.4	333 21.4	48.5	84 51.4	30.8
12	114 20.6	314 44.9	N 9 46.7	43 20.6	N22 10.7	348 23.3	N19 48.4	99 53.8	N 3 30.8
13	129 23.0	329 44.8	45.5	58 21.2	11.0	3 25.2	48.3	114 56.2	30.8
14	144 25.5	344 44.8	44.4	73 21.8	11.2	18 27.1	48.2	129 58.6	30.8
15	159 28.0	359 44.7	. . 43.2	88 22.5	. . 11.5	33 29.0	. . 48.0	145 01.0	. . 30.8
16	174 30.4	14 44.6	42.1	103 23.1	11.7	48 30.8	47.9	160 03.5	30.8
17	189 32.9	29 44.6	40.9	118 23.7	12.0	63 32.7	47.8	175 05.9	30.9
18	204 35.4	44 44.5	N 9 39.7	133 24.3	N22 12.2	78 34.6	N19 47.7	190 08.3	N 3 30.9
19	219 37.8	59 44.5	38.6	148 24.9	12.5	93 36.5	47.5	205 10.7	30.9
20	234 40.3	74 44.4	37.4	163 25.5	12.7	108 38.4	47.4	220 13.1	30.9
21	249 42.8	89 44.4	. . 36.3	178 26.1	. . 13.0	123 40.3	. . 47.3	235 15.6	. . 30.9
22	264 45.2	104 44.3	35.1	193 26.7	13.2	138 42.2	47.2	250 18.0	30.9
23	279 47.7	119 44.3	34.0	208 27.3	13.5	153 44.1	47.0	265 20.4	30.9
17 00 (FRIDAY)	294 50.1	134 44.2	N 9 32.8	223 28.0	N22 13.7	168 46.0	N19 46.9	280 22.8	N 3 30.9
01	309 52.6	149 44.2	31.6	238 28.6	14.0	183 47.9	46.8	295 25.2	30.9
02	324 55.1	164 44.1	30.5	253 29.2	14.2	198 49.8	46.7	310 27.7	30.9
03	339 57.5	179 44.1	. . 29.3	268 29.8	. . 14.5	213 51.7	. . 46.5	325 30.1	. . 30.9
04	355 00.0	194 44.0	28.2	283 30.4	14.7	228 53.6	46.4	340 32.5	30.9
05	10 02.5	209 44.0	27.0	298 31.0	15.0	243 55.5	46.3	355 34.9	30.9
06	25 04.9	224 43.9	N 9 25.8	313 31.6	N22 15.2	258 57.4	N19 46.2	10 37.4	N 3 30.9
07	40 07.4	239 43.9	24.7	328 32.2	15.5	273 59.3	46.0	25 39.8	30.9
08	55 09.9	254 43.8	23.5	343 32.8	15.7	289 01.2	45.9	40 42.2	30.9
09	70 12.3	269 43.8	. . 22.3	358 33.4	. . 16.0	304 03.1	. . 45.8	55 44.6	. . 30.9
10	85 14.8	284 43.7	21.2	13 34.1	16.2	319 04.9	45.6	70 47.0	30.9
11	100 17.2	299 43.7	20.0	28 34.7	16.5	334 06.8	45.5	85 49.5	30.9
12	115 19.7	314 43.6	N 9 18.8	43 35.3	N22 16.7	349 08.7	N19 45.4	100 51.9	N 3 30.9
13	130 22.2	329 43.6	17.7	58 35.9	17.0	4 10.6	45.3	115 54.3	31.0
14	145 24.6	344 43.5	16.5	73 36.5	17.2	19 12.5	45.1	130 56.7	31.0
15	160 27.1	359 43.5	. . 15.4	88 37.1	. . 17.5	34 14.4	. . 45.0	145 59.2	. . 31.0
16	175 29.6	14 43.4	14.2	103 37.7	17.7	49 16.3	44.9	161 01.6	31.0
17	190 32.0	29 43.4	13.0	118 38.3	18.0	64 18.2	44.8	176 04.0	31.0
18	205 34.5	44 43.4	N 9 11.9	133 38.9	N22 18.2	79 20.1	N19 44.6	191 06.4	N 3 31.0
19	220 37.0	59 43.3	10.7	148 39.6	18.5	94 22.0	44.5	206 08.9	31.0
20	235 39.4	74 43.3	09.5	163 40.2	18.7	109 23.9	44.4	221 11.3	31.0
21	250 41.9	89 43.2	. . 08.4	178 40.8	. . 19.0	124 25.8	. . 44.3	236 13.7	. . 31.0
22	265 44.4	104 43.2	07.2	193 41.4	19.2	139 27.7	44.1	251 16.1	31.0
23	280 46.8	119 43.2	06.0	208 42.0	19.4	154 29.6	44.0	266 18.6	31.0
Mer. Pass.	h m 4 23.9	v −0.1	d 1.2	v 0.6	d 0.3	v 1.9	d 0.1	v 2.4	d 0.0

STARS

Name	SHA ° ′	Dec ° ′
Acamar	315 11.0	S40 11.6
Achernar	335 19.3	S57 05.7
Acrux	172 58.8	S63 15.1
Adhara	255 05.2	S29 00.4
Aldebaran	290 38.4	N16 33.8
Alioth	166 11.9	N55 49.2
Alkaid	152 51.0	N49 11.1
Alnair	27 30.9	S46 49.7
Alnilam	275 36.7	S 1 11.0
Alphard	217 46.8	S 8 46.4
Alphecca	126 02.5	N26 37.6
Alpheratz	357 33.3	N29 14.2
Altair	61 58.4	N 8 56.4
Ankaa	353 05.8	S42 09.4
Antares	112 14.0	S26 29.5
Arcturus	145 46.7	N19 02.8
Atria	107 06.6	S69 04.7
Avior	234 14.9	S59 35.7
Bellatrix	278 21.8	N 6 22.5
Betelgeuse	270 51.0	N 7 24.8
Canopus	263 52.4	S52 42.4
Capella	280 20.4	N46 01.4
Deneb	49 24.5	N45 22.5
Denebola	182 23.8	N14 25.5
Diphda	348 46.0	S17 50.2
Dubhe	193 39.9	N61 36.7
Elnath	278 00.6	N28 37.7
Eltanin	90 41.1	N51 29.2
Enif	33 37.3	N 9 59.9
Fomalhaut	15 12.9	S29 28.7
Gacrux	171 50.4	S57 16.0
Gienah	175 42.4	S17 41.5
Hadar	148 34.1	S60 30.4
Hamal	327 49.8	N23 35.2
Kaus Aust.	83 30.4	S34 22.3
Kochab	137 19.4	N74 03.0
Markab	13 28.4	N15 20.9
Menkar	314 04.9	N 4 11.7
Menkent	147 56.0	S36 30.2
Miaplacidus	221 38.9	S69 49.7
Mirfak	308 26.7	N49 57.2
Nunki	75 45.8	S26 15.8
Peacock	53 03.1	S56 38.8
Pollux	243 16.1	N27 57.7
Procyon	244 49.8	N 5 09.4
Rasalhague	95 57.1	N12 32.5
Regulus	207 33.4	N11 50.3
Rigel	281 02.9	S 8 10.2
Rigil Kent.	139 38.3	S60 56.9
Sabik	102 01.0	S15 45.5
Schedar	349 29.4	N56 40.8
Shaula	96 08.3	S37 07.4
Sirius	258 25.5	S16 45.1
Spica	158 21.0	S11 18.1
Suhail	222 45.8	S43 32.5
Vega	80 31.9	N38 48.6
Zuben'ubi	136 54.5	S16 09.2

	SHA ° ′	Mer. Pass. h m
Venus	200 54.6	15 01
Mars	289 22.3	9 07
Jupiter	234 09.5	12 46
Saturn	345 33.8	5 21

UT	SUN GHA	SUN Dec	MOON GHA	v	MOON Dec	d	HP
d h	° ′	° ′	° ′	′	° ′	′	′
15 00	178 30.5	N21 33.1	169 10.5	5.0	N22 26.6	11.1	60.6
01	193 30.5	32.7	183 34.5	5.2	22 15.5	11.3	60.6
02	208 30.4	32.3	197 58.7	5.3	22 04.2	11.4	60.6
03	223 30.4	. . 31.9	212 23.0	5.4	21 52.8	11.6	60.6
04	238 30.3	31.5	226 47.4	5.5	21 41.2	11.7	60.6
05	253 30.2	31.1	241 11.9	5.7	21 29.5	11.8	60.5
06	268 30.2	N21 30.7	255 36.6	5.8	N21 17.7	11.9	60.5
W 07	283 30.1	30.3	270 01.4	6.0	21 05.8	12.1	60.5
E 08	298 30.0	29.9	284 26.4	6.1	20 53.7	12.2	60.5
D 09	313 30.0	. . 29.5	298 51.5	6.2	20 41.5	12.3	60.4
N 10	328 29.9	29.1	313 16.7	6.3	20 29.2	12.5	60.4
E 11	343 29.8	28.7	327 42.0	6.5	20 16.7	12.6	60.4
S 12	358 29.8	N21 28.3	342 07.5	6.6	N20 04.1	12.7	60.4
D 13	13 29.7	27.9	356 33.1	6.7	19 51.4	12.8	60.3
A 14	28 29.6	27.5	10 58.8	6.9	19 38.6	12.9	60.3
Y 15	43 29.6	. . 27.1	25 24.7	7.0	19 25.7	13.0	60.3
16	58 29.5	26.7	39 50.7	7.1	19 12.7	13.1	60.3
17	73 29.5	26.3	54 16.8	7.3	18 59.6	13.3	60.2
18	88 29.4	N21 25.9	68 43.1	7.4	N18 46.3	13.3	60.2
19	103 29.3	25.5	83 09.5	7.5	18 33.0	13.5	60.2
20	118 29.3	25.1	97 36.0	7.7	18 19.5	13.5	60.1
21	133 29.2	. . 24.7	112 02.7	7.7	18 06.0	13.6	60.1
22	148 29.1	24.3	126 29.4	7.9	17 52.4	13.8	60.1
23	163 29.1	23.9	140 56.3	8.1	17 38.6	13.8	60.1
16 00	178 29.0	N21 23.5	155 23.4	8.1	N17 24.8	13.9	60.0
01	193 29.0	23.1	169 50.5	8.3	17 10.9	14.0	60.0
02	208 28.9	22.7	184 17.8	8.4	16 56.9	14.1	60.0
03	223 28.8	. . 22.3	198 45.2	8.6	16 42.8	14.1	59.9
04	238 28.8	21.9	213 12.8	8.6	16 28.7	14.3	59.9
05	253 28.7	21.5	227 40.4	8.8	16 14.4	14.3	59.9
06	268 28.7	N21 21.1	242 08.2	8.9	N16 00.1	14.4	59.8
07	283 28.6	20.6	256 36.1	9.1	15 45.7	14.5	59.8
T 08	298 28.5	20.2	271 04.2	9.1	15 31.2	14.5	59.8
H 09	313 28.5	. . 19.8	285 32.3	9.3	15 16.7	14.7	59.7
U 10	328 28.4	19.4	300 00.6	9.4	15 02.0	14.6	59.7
R 11	343 28.4	19.0	314 29.0	9.5	14 47.4	14.8	59.7
S 12	358 28.3	N21 18.6	328 57.5	9.6	N14 32.6	14.8	59.6
D 13	13 28.3	18.2	343 26.1	9.7	14 17.8	14.9	59.6
A 14	28 28.2	17.8	357 54.8	9.9	14 02.9	14.9	59.6
Y 15	43 28.1	. . 17.3	12 23.7	9.9	13 48.0	15.0	59.5
16	58 28.1	16.9	26 52.6	10.1	13 33.0	15.1	59.5
17	73 28.0	16.5	41 21.7	10.2	13 17.9	15.1	59.5
18	88 28.0	N21 16.1	55 50.9	10.3	N13 02.8	15.1	59.4
19	103 27.9	15.7	70 20.2	10.4	12 47.7	15.2	59.4
20	118 27.9	15.3	84 49.6	10.5	12 32.5	15.3	59.4
21	133 27.8	. . 14.8	99 19.1	10.6	12 17.2	15.3	59.3
22	148 27.7	14.4	113 48.7	10.7	12 01.9	15.4	59.3
23	163 27.7	14.0	128 18.4	10.9	11 46.5	15.3	59.3
17 00	178 27.6	N21 13.6	142 48.3	10.9	N11 31.2	15.5	59.2
01	193 27.6	13.1	157 18.2	11.0	11 15.7	15.4	59.2
02	208 27.5	12.7	171 48.2	11.1	11 00.3	15.5	59.1
03	223 27.5	. . 12.3	186 18.3	11.3	10 44.8	15.6	59.1
04	238 27.4	11.9	200 48.6	11.3	10 29.2	15.6	59.1
05	253 27.4	11.5	215 18.9	11.4	10 13.6	15.6	59.0
06	268 27.3	N21 11.0	229 49.3	11.5	N 9 58.0	15.6	59.0
07	283 27.3	10.6	244 19.8	11.6	9 42.4	15.7	59.0
08	298 27.2	10.2	258 50.4	11.7	9 26.7	15.7	58.9
F 09	313 27.1	. . 09.7	273 21.1	11.8	9 11.0	15.7	58.9
R 10	328 27.1	09.3	287 51.9	11.9	8 55.3	15.7	58.8
I 11	343 27.0	08.9	302 22.8	11.9	8 39.6	15.8	58.8
D 12	358 27.0	N21 08.5	316 53.7	12.1	N 8 23.8	15.7	58.8
A 13	13 26.9	08.0	331 24.8	12.1	8 08.1	15.8	58.7
Y 14	28 26.9	07.6	345 55.9	12.2	7 52.3	15.9	58.7
15	43 26.8	. . 07.2	0 27.1	12.3	7 36.4	15.8	58.7
16	58 26.8	06.7	14 58.4	12.4	7 20.6	15.8	58.6
17	73 26.7	06.3	29 29.8	12.4	7 04.8	15.9	58.6
18	88 26.7	N21 05.9	44 01.2	12.6	N 6 48.9	15.9	58.5
19	103 26.6	05.4	58 32.8	12.6	6 33.0	15.8	58.5
20	118 26.6	05.0	73 04.4	12.6	6 17.2	15.9	58.5
21	133 26.5	. . 04.6	87 36.0	12.8	6 01.3	15.9	58.4
22	148 26.5	04.1	102 07.8	12.8	5 45.4	15.9	58.4
23	163 26.4	03.7	116 39.6	12.9	N 5 29.5	15.9	58.3
	SD 15.8	*d* 0.4	SD 16.4		16.3		16.0

Lat.	Twilight Naut.	Twilight Civil	Sunrise	Moonrise 15	16	17	18
°	h m	h m	h m	h m	h m	h m	h m
N 72	▭	▭	▭	▭	03 24	06 36	08 58
N 70	▭	▭	▭	▭	04 15	06 52	09 02
68	▭	▭	▭	▭	04 46	07 05	09 06
66	////	////	01 40	02 34	05 09	07 15	09 08
64	////	////	02 18	03 13	05 27	07 24	09 10
62	////	00 57	02 45	03 40	05 41	07 31	09 12
60	////	01 48	03 05	04 01	05 53	07 37	09 14
N 58	////	02 18	03 22	04 18	06 04	07 43	09 16
56	00 52	02 41	03 36	04 32	06 13	07 48	09 17
54	01 39	02 59	03 48	04 44	06 21	07 52	09 18
52	02 07	03 14	03 59	04 55	06 28	07 56	09 19
50	02 28	03 27	04 09	05 05	06 35	08 00	09 20
45	03 06	03 53	04 28	05 25	06 48	08 08	09 22
N 40	03 33	04 13	04 44	05 41	07 00	08 14	09 24
35	03 54	04 29	04 58	05 55	07 09	08 19	09 26
30	04 10	04 43	05 10	06 07	07 18	08 24	09 27
20	04 37	05 05	05 30	06 27	07 32	08 33	09 29
N 10	04 57	05 24	05 47	06 44	07 45	08 40	09 32
0	05 14	05 40	06 03	07 01	07 56	08 47	09 33
S 10	05 30	05 56	06 18	07 17	08 08	08 54	09 35
20	05 44	06 11	06 35	07 34	08 20	09 01	09 38
30	05 59	06 28	06 54	07 54	08 34	09 09	09 40
35	06 06	06 38	07 05	08 05	08 42	09 14	09 41
40	06 14	06 48	07 18	08 18	08 52	09 19	09 43
45	06 23	07 00	07 33	08 34	09 02	09 25	09 45
S 50	06 33	07 14	07 51	08 53	09 15	09 32	09 47
52	06 38	07 20	07 59	09 02	09 21	09 36	09 48
54	06 42	07 27	08 09	09 11	09 28	09 39	09 49
56	06 48	07 35	08 20	09 23	09 35	09 43	09 50
58	06 53	07 44	08 32	09 35	09 43	09 48	09 51
S 60	06 59	07 54	08 47	09 50	09 52	09 53	09 53

Lat.	Sunset	Twilight Civil	Twilight Naut.	Moonset 15	16	17	18
°	h m	h m	h m	h m	h m	h m	h m
N 72	▭	▭	▭	▭	{00 26 / 23 04}	22 21	21 47
N 70	▭	▭	▭	23 34	22 45	22 14	21 48
68	▭	▭	▭	23 01	22 30	22 08	21 49
66	22 29	////	////	22 37	22 17	22 02	21 49
64	21 52	////	////	22 17	22 07	21 58	21 50
62	21 26	23 09	////	22 02	21 58	21 54	21 50
60	21 05	22 21	////	21 48	21 50	21 51	21 50
N 58	20 49	21 52	////	21 37	21 43	21 48	21 51
56	20 35	21 30	23 15	21 27	21 37	21 45	21 51
54	20 23	21 12	22 31	21 18	21 32	21 42	21 51
52	20 12	20 57	22 03	21 10	21 27	21 40	21 52
50	20 03	20 45	21 43	21 02	21 22	21 38	21 52
45	19 43	20 19	21 05	20 47	21 12	21 33	21 52
N 40	19 27	19 59	20 39	20 34	21 04	21 30	21 53
35	19 14	19 43	20 18	20 23	20 57	21 26	21 53
30	19 02	19 29	20 01	20 13	20 51	21 23	21 53
20	18 43	19 07	19 35	19 56	20 40	21 18	21 54
N 10	18 26	18 48	19 15	19 42	20 30	21 14	21 54
0	18 10	18 32	18 58	19 28	20 21	21 09	21 55
S 10	17 54	18 17	18 42	19 14	20 11	21 05	21 55
20	17 37	18 01	18 28	18 58	20 02	21 00	21 56
30	17 18	17 44	18 14	18 41	19 50	20 55	21 56
35	17 07	17 35	18 06	18 31	19 43	20 52	21 56
40	16 55	17 25	17 58	18 19	19 36	20 48	21 57
45	16 40	17 13	17 49	18 05	19 27	20 44	21 57
S 50	16 22	16 59	17 39	17 48	19 16	20 39	21 57
52	16 13	16 52	17 35	17 39	19 11	20 36	21 57
54	16 04	16 45	17 30	17 30	19 05	20 34	21 58
56	15 53	16 38	17 25	17 20	18 59	20 31	21 58
58	15 40	16 29	17 20	17 08	18 52	20 28	21 58
S 60	15 26	16 19	17 13	16 54	18 43	20 24	21 58

Day	SUN Eqn. of Time 00^h	SUN Eqn. of Time 12^h	SUN Mer. Pass.	MOON Mer. Pass. Upper	MOON Mer. Pass. Lower	Age	Phase
d	m s	m s	h m	h m	h m	d %	
15	05 58	06 01	12 06	13 14	00 45	01 2	●
16	06 04	06 07	12 06	14 09	01 42	02 6	
17	06 09	06 12	12 06	14 58	02 34	03 13	

UT	Day	ARIES GHA	VENUS −4·2 GHA	VENUS Dec	MARS +1·3 GHA	MARS Dec	JUPITER −1·8 GHA	JUPITER Dec	SATURN +0·6 GHA	SATURN Dec	STARS Name	SHA	Dec
d h		° ′	° ′	° ′	° ′	° ′	° ′	° ′	° ′	° ′		° ′	° ′
18 00		295 49.3	134 43.1	N 9 04.9	223 42.6	N22 19.7	169 31.5	N19 43.9	281 21.0	N 3 31.0	Acamar	315 10.9	S40 11.6
01		310 51.7	149 43.1	03.7	238 43.2	19.9	184 33.4	43.7	296 23.4	31.0	Achernar	335 19.2	S57 05.7
02		325 54.2	164 43.1	02.5	253 43.8	20.2	199 35.3	43.6	311 25.8	31.0	Acrux	172 58.8	S63 15.1
03		340 56.7	179 43.0	. . 01.4	268 44.4	. . 20.4	214 37.1	. . 43.5	326 28.3	. . 31.0	Adhara	255 05.2	S29 00.4
04		355 59.1	194 43.0	9 00.2	283 45.1	20.7	229 39.0	43.4	341 30.7	31.0	Aldebaran	290 38.4	N16 33.8
05		11 01.6	209 43.0	8 59.0	298 45.7	20.9	244 40.9	43.2	356 33.1	31.0			
06		26 04.1	224 42.9	N 8 57.8	313 46.3	N22 21.1	259 42.8	N19 43.1	11 35.5	N 3 31.0	Alioth	166 12.0	N55 49.2
07		41 06.5	239 42.9	56.7	328 46.9	21.4	274 44.7	43.0	26 38.0	31.0	Alkaid	152 51.0	N49 11.1
08	S	56 09.0	254 42.9	55.5	343 47.5	21.6	289 46.6	42.9	41 40.4	31.0	Alnair	27 30.9	S46 49.7
09	A	71 11.5	269 42.8	. . 54.3	358 48.1	. . 21.9	304 48.5	. . 42.7	56 42.8	. . 31.0	Alnilam	275 36.7	S 1 11.0
10	T	86 13.9	284 42.8	53.2	13 48.7	22.1	319 50.4	42.6	71 45.2	31.0	Alphard	217 46.8	S 8 46.4
11	U	101 16.4	299 42.8	52.0	28 49.3	22.3	334 52.3	42.5	86 47.7	31.0			
12	R	116 18.9	314 42.7	N 8 50.8	43 49.9	N22 22.6	349 54.2	N19 42.4	101 50.1	N 3 31.0	Alphecca	126 02.5	N26 37.7
13	D	131 21.3	329 42.7	49.7	58 50.6	22.8	4 56.1	42.2	116 52.5	31.0	Alpheratz	357 33.3	N29 14.2
14	A	146 23.8	344 42.7	48.5	73 51.2	23.1	19 58.0	42.1	131 54.9	31.0	Altair	61 58.4	N 8 56.4
15	Y	161 26.2	359 42.6	. . 47.3	88 51.8	. . 23.3	34 59.9	. . 42.0	146 57.4	. . 31.0	Ankaa	353 05.7	S42 09.4
16		176 28.7	14 42.6	46.1	103 52.4	23.5	50 01.8	41.8	161 59.8	31.0	Antares	112 14.0	S26 29.5
17		191 31.2	29 42.6	45.0	118 53.0	23.8	65 03.7	41.7	177 02.2	31.0			
18		206 33.6	44 42.6	N 8 43.8	133 53.6	N22 24.0	80 05.6	N19 41.6	192 04.7	N 3 31.1	Arcturus	145 46.7	N19 02.8
19		221 36.1	59 42.5	42.6	148 54.2	24.2	95 07.5	41.5	207 07.1	31.1	Atria	107 06.6	S69 04.7
20		236 38.6	74 42.5	41.4	163 54.8	24.5	110 09.3	41.3	222 09.5	31.1	Avior	234 14.9	S59 35.7
21		251 41.0	89 42.5	. . 40.3	178 55.5	. . 24.7	125 11.2	. . 41.2	237 11.9	. . 31.1	Bellatrix	278 21.8	N 6 22.5
22		266 43.5	104 42.5	39.1	193 56.1	24.9	140 13.1	41.1	252 14.4	31.1	Betelgeuse	270 51.0	N 7 24.8
23		281 46.0	119 42.4	37.9	208 56.7	25.2	155 15.0	40.9	267 16.8	31.1			
19 00		296 48.4	134 42.4	N 8 36.8	223 57.3	N22 25.4	170 16.9	N19 40.8	282 19.2	N 3 31.1	Canopus	263 52.3	S52 42.4
01		311 50.9	149 42.4	35.6	238 57.9	25.6	185 18.8	40.7	297 21.6	31.1	Capella	280 20.4	N46 01.4
02		326 53.3	164 42.4	34.4	253 58.5	25.9	200 20.7	40.6	312 24.1	31.1	Deneb	49 24.5	N45 22.5
03		341 55.8	179 42.4	. . 33.2	268 59.1	. . 26.1	215 22.6	. . 40.4	327 26.5	. . 31.1	Denebola	182 23.8	N14 25.5
04		356 58.3	194 42.3	32.1	283 59.7	26.3	230 24.5	40.3	342 28.9	31.1	Diphda	348 45.9	S17 50.2
05		12 00.7	209 42.3	30.9	299 00.3	26.6	245 26.4	40.2	357 31.4	31.1			
06		27 03.2	224 42.3	N 8 29.7	314 01.0	N22 26.8	260 28.3	N19 40.1	12 33.8	N 3 31.1	Dubhe	193 39.9	N61 36.7
07		42 05.7	239 42.3	28.5	329 01.6	27.0	275 30.2	39.9	27 36.2	31.1	Elnath	278 00.6	N28 37.7
08		57 08.1	254 42.3	27.3	344 02.2	27.3	290 32.1	39.8	42 38.7	31.1	Eltanin	90 41.1	N51 29.2
09	S	72 10.6	269 42.2	. . 26.2	359 02.8	. . 27.5	305 34.0	. . 39.7	57 41.1	. . 31.1	Enif	33 37.3	N 9 59.9
10	U	87 13.1	284 42.2	25.0	14 03.4	27.7	320 35.9	39.5	72 43.5	31.1	Fomalhaut	15 12.9	S29 28.7
11	N	102 15.5	299 42.2	23.8	29 04.0	28.0	335 37.8	39.4	87 45.9	31.1			
12	D	117 18.0	314 42.2	N 8 22.6	44 04.6	N22 28.2	350 39.7	N19 39.3	102 48.4	N 3 31.1	Gacrux	171 50.4	S57 16.0
13	A	132 20.5	329 42.2	21.5	59 05.2	28.4	5 41.5	39.2	117 50.8	31.1	Gienah	175 42.4	S17 41.5
14	Y	147 22.9	344 42.2	20.3	74 05.9	28.7	20 43.4	39.0	132 53.2	31.1	Hadar	148 34.1	S60 30.4
15		162 25.4	359 42.2	. . 19.1	89 06.5	. . 28.9	35 45.3	. . 38.9	147 55.7	. . 31.1	Hamal	327 49.8	N23 35.2
16		177 27.8	14 42.1	17.9	104 07.1	29.1	50 47.2	38.8	162 58.1	31.1	Kaus Aust.	83 30.4	S34 22.3
17		192 30.3	29 42.1	16.7	119 07.7	29.3	65 49.1	38.6	178 00.5	31.1			
18		207 32.8	44 42.1	N 8 15.6	134 08.3	N22 29.6	80 51.0	N19 38.5	193 03.0	N 3 31.1	Kochab	137 19.5	N74 03.0
19		222 35.2	59 42.1	14.4	149 08.9	29.8	95 52.9	38.4	208 05.4	31.1	Markab	13 28.4	N15 20.9
20		237 37.7	74 42.1	13.2	164 09.5	30.0	110 54.8	38.3	223 07.8	31.1	Menkar	314 04.9	N 4 11.7
21		252 40.2	89 42.1	. . 12.0	179 10.1	. . 30.3	125 56.7	. . 38.1	238 10.3	. . 31.1	Menkent	147 56.1	S36 30.2
22		267 42.6	104 42.1	10.8	194 10.8	30.5	140 58.6	38.0	253 12.7	31.1	Miaplacidus	221 38.9	S69 49.7
23		282 45.1	119 42.1	09.7	209 11.4	30.7	156 00.5	37.9	268 15.1	31.1			
20 00		297 47.6	134 42.1	N 8 08.5	224 12.0	N22 30.9	171 02.4	N19 37.8	283 17.6	N 3 31.1	Mirfak	308 26.6	N49 57.2
01		312 50.0	149 42.1	07.3	239 12.6	31.2	186 04.3	37.6	298 20.0	31.1	Nunki	75 45.8	S26 15.8
02		327 52.5	164 42.0	06.1	254 13.2	31.4	201 06.2	37.5	313 22.4	31.1	Peacock	53 03.1	S56 38.8
03		342 54.9	179 42.0	. . 04.9	269 13.8	. . 31.6	216 08.1	. . 37.4	328 24.9	. . 31.1	Pollux	243 16.1	N27 57.7
04		357 57.4	194 42.0	03.8	284 14.4	31.8	231 10.0	37.2	343 27.3	31.1	Procyon	244 49.8	N 5 09.4
05		12 59.9	209 42.0	02.6	299 15.0	32.1	246 11.9	37.1	358 29.7	31.1			
06		28 02.3	224 42.0	N 8 01.4	314 15.7	N22 32.3	261 13.7	N19 37.0	13 32.2	N 3 31.1	Rasalhague	95 57.1	N12 32.5
07		43 04.8	239 42.0	8 00.2	329 16.3	32.5	276 15.6	36.9	28 34.6	31.1	Regulus	207 33.4	N11 50.3
08		58 07.3	254 42.0	7 59.0	344 16.9	32.7	291 17.5	36.7	43 37.0	31.1	Rigel	281 02.9	S 8 10.1
09	M	73 09.7	269 42.0	. . 57.8	359 17.5	. . 33.0	306 19.4	. . 36.6	58 39.5	. . 31.1	Rigil Kent.	139 38.4	S60 57.0
10	O	88 12.2	284 42.0	56.7	14 18.1	33.2	321 21.3	36.5	73 41.9	31.1	Sabik	102 01.0	S15 45.5
11	N	103 14.7	299 42.0	55.5	29 18.7	33.4	336 23.2	36.3	88 44.3	31.1			
12	D	118 17.1	314 42.0	N 7 54.3	44 19.3	N22 33.6	351 25.1	N19 36.2	103 46.8	N 3 31.1	Schedar	349 29.4	N56 40.8
13	A	133 19.6	329 42.0	53.1	59 19.9	33.8	6 27.0	36.1	118 49.2	31.1	Shaula	96 08.3	S37 07.4
14	Y	148 22.1	344 42.0	51.9	74 20.6	34.1	21 28.9	36.0	133 51.6	31.1	Sirius	258 25.4	S16 45.1
15		163 24.5	359 42.0	. . 50.7	89 21.2	. . 34.3	36 30.8	. . 35.8	148 54.1	. . 31.1	Spica	158 21.0	S11 18.1
16		178 27.0	14 42.0	49.5	104 21.8	34.5	51 32.7	35.7	163 56.5	31.1	Suhail	222 45.8	S43 32.4
17		193 29.4	29 42.0	48.4	119 22.4	34.7	66 34.6	35.6	178 58.9	31.1			
18		208 31.9	44 42.0	N 7 47.2	134 23.0	N22 34.9	81 36.5	N19 35.4	194 01.4	N 3 31.1	Vega	80 31.9	N38 48.6
19		223 34.4	59 42.0	46.0	149 23.6	35.2	96 38.4	35.3	209 03.8	31.1	Zuben'ubi	136 54.5	S16 09.2
20		238 36.8	74 42.0	44.8	164 24.2	35.4	111 40.3	35.2	224 06.2	31.1			
21		253 39.3	89 42.0	. . 43.6	179 24.9	. . 35.6	126 42.2	. . 35.0	239 08.7	. . 31.1			
22		268 41.8	104 42.1	42.4	194 25.5	35.8	141 44.0	34.9	254 11.1	31.1			
23		283 44.2	119 42.1	41.2	209 26.1	36.0	156 45.9	34.8	269 13.6	31.1			
Mer. Pass.		h m 4 12.1	*v* 0.0	*d* 1.2	*v* 0.6	*d* 0.2	*v* 1.9	*d* 0.1	*v* 2.4	*d* 0.0			

	SHA	Mer. Pass.
	° ′	h m
Venus	197 54.0	15 01
Mars	287 08.9	9 04
Jupiter	233 28.5	12 37
Saturn	345 30.8	5 10

UT	SUN GHA	SUN Dec	MOON GHA	*v*	MOON Dec	*d*	HP
d h	° ′	° ′	° ′	′	° ′	′	′
18 00	178 26.4	N21 03.3	131 11.5	13.0	N 5 13.6	15.9	58.3
01	193 26.3	02.8	145 43.5	13.0	4 57.7	15.9	58.3
02	208 26.3	02.4	160 15.5	13.1	4 41.8	15.9	58.2
03	223 26.2	. . 02.0	174 47.6	13.2	4 25.9	15.9	58.2
04	238 26.2	01.5	189 19.8	13.2	4 10.0	15.9	58.1
05	253 26.1	01.1	203 52.0	13.3	3 54.1	15.9	58.1
06	268 26.1	N21 00.6	218 24.3	13.4	N 3 38.2	15.9	58.1
S 07	283 26.0	21 00.2	232 56.7	13.4	3 22.3	15.9	58.0
A 08	298 26.0	20 59.8	247 29.1	13.4	3 06.4	15.9	58.0
T 09	313 25.9	. . 59.3	262 01.5	13.6	2 50.5	15.8	58.0
U 10	328 25.9	58.9	276 34.1	13.5	2 34.7	15.9	57.9
R 11	343 25.8	58.4	291 06.6	13.7	2 18.8	15.8	57.9
D 12	358 25.8	N20 58.0	305 39.3	13.6	N 2 03.0	15.9	57.8
A 13	13 25.8	57.5	320 11.9	13.8	1 47.1	15.8	57.8
Y 14	28 25.7	57.1	334 44.7	13.8	1 31.3	15.8	57.8
15	43 25.7	. . 56.7	349 17.5	13.8	1 15.5	15.8	57.7
16	58 25.6	56.2	3 50.3	13.9	0 59.7	15.7	57.7
17	73 25.6	55.8	18 23.2	13.9	0 44.0	15.8	57.6
18	88 25.5	N20 55.3	32 56.1	14.0	N 0 28.2	15.7	57.6
19	103 25.5	54.9	47 29.1	14.0	N 0 12.5	15.7	57.6
20	118 25.4	54.4	62 02.1	14.0	S 0 03.2	15.7	57.5
21	133 25.4	. . 54.0	76 35.1	14.1	0 18.9	15.7	57.5
22	148 25.3	53.5	91 08.2	14.2	0 34.6	15.6	57.4
23	163 25.3	53.1	105 41.4	14.1	0 50.2	15.6	57.4
19 00	178 25.3	N20 52.6	120 14.5	14.2	S 1 05.8	15.6	57.4
01	193 25.2	52.2	134 47.7	14.3	1 21.4	15.5	57.3
02	208 25.2	51.7	149 21.0	14.3	1 36.9	15.6	57.3
03	223 25.1	. . 51.3	163 54.3	14.3	1 52.5	15.5	57.3
04	238 25.1	50.8	178 27.6	14.3	2 08.0	15.4	57.2
05	253 25.0	50.4	193 00.9	14.4	2 23.4	15.5	57.2
06	268 25.0	N20 49.9	207 34.3	14.4	S 2 38.9	15.4	57.1
07	283 25.0	49.4	222 07.7	14.4	2 54.3	15.3	57.1
08	298 24.9	49.0	236 41.1	14.4	3 09.6	15.4	57.1
S 09	313 24.9	. . 48.5	251 14.5	14.5	3 25.0	15.3	57.0
U 10	328 24.8	48.1	265 48.0	14.5	3 40.3	15.2	57.0
N 11	343 24.8	47.6	280 21.5	14.5	3 55.5	15.3	57.0
D 12	358 24.8	N20 47.2	294 55.0	14.5	S 4 10.8	15.1	56.9
A 13	13 24.7	46.7	309 28.5	14.6	4 25.9	15.2	56.9
Y 14	28 24.7	46.2	324 02.1	14.6	4 41.1	15.1	56.8
15	43 24.6	. . 45.8	338 35.7	14.5	4 56.2	15.1	56.8
16	58 24.6	45.3	353 09.2	14.7	5 11.3	15.0	56.8
17	73 24.6	44.9	7 42.9	14.6	5 26.3	15.0	56.7
18	88 24.5	N20 44.4	22 16.5	14.6	S 5 41.3	14.9	56.7
19	103 24.5	43.9	36 50.1	14.6	5 56.2	14.9	56.7
20	118 24.4	43.5	51 23.7	14.7	6 11.1	14.9	56.6
21	133 24.4	. . 43.0	65 57.4	14.7	6 26.0	14.8	56.6
22	148 24.4	42.5	80 31.1	14.6	6 40.8	14.7	56.6
23	163 24.3	42.1	95 04.7	14.7	6 55.5	14.7	56.5
20 00	178 24.3	N20 41.6	109 38.4	14.7	S 7 10.2	14.7	56.5
01	193 24.2	41.1	124 12.1	14.7	7 24.9	14.6	56.5
02	208 24.2	40.7	138 45.8	14.7	7 39.5	14.6	56.4
03	223 24.2	. . 40.2	153 19.5	14.7	7 54.1	14.5	56.4
04	238 24.1	39.7	167 53.2	14.7	8 08.6	14.4	56.4
05	253 24.1	39.3	182 26.9	14.7	8 23.0	14.4	56.3
06	268 24.1	N20 38.8	197 00.6	14.7	S 8 37.4	14.4	56.3
07	283 24.0	38.3	211 34.3	14.7	8 51.8	14.3	56.2
08	298 24.0	37.9	226 08.0	14.6	9 06.1	14.2	56.2
M 09	313 24.0	. . 37.4	240 41.6	14.7	9 20.3	14.2	56.2
O 10	328 23.9	36.9	255 15.3	14.7	9 34.5	14.2	56.1
N 11	343 23.9	36.4	269 49.0	14.7	9 48.7	14.0	56.1
D 12	358 23.8	N20 36.0	284 22.7	14.6	S10 02.7	14.0	56.1
A 13	13 23.8	35.5	298 56.3	14.7	10 16.7	14.0	56.1
Y 14	28 23.8	35.0	313 30.0	14.7	10 30.7	13.9	56.0
15	43 23.7	. . 34.6	328 03.7	14.6	10 44.6	13.8	56.0
16	58 23.7	34.1	342 37.3	14.6	10 58.4	13.8	56.0
17	73 23.7	33.6	357 10.9	14.6	11 12.2	13.7	55.9
18	88 23.6	N20 33.1	11 44.5	14.6	S11 25.9	13.7	55.9
19	103 23.6	32.6	26 18.1	14.6	11 39.6	13.6	55.9
20	118 23.6	32.2	40 51.7	14.6	11 53.2	13.5	55.8
21	133 23.5	. . 31.7	55 25.3	14.5	12 06.7	13.5	55.8
22	148 23.5	31.2	69 58.8	14.6	12 20.2	13.4	55.8
23	163 23.5	30.7	84 32.4	14.5	S12 33.6	13.3	55.7
	SD 15.8	*d* 0.5	SD 15.8		15.5		15.3

Lat.	Twilight Naut.	Twilight Civil	Sunrise	Moonrise 18	Moonrise 19	Moonrise 20	Moonrise 21
°	h m	h m	h m	h m	h m	h m	h m
N 72	▭	▭	▭	08 58	11 10	13 24	16 09
N 70	▭	▭	▭	09 02	11 04	13 06	15 22
68	////	////	00 46	09 06	10 59	12 52	14 52
66	////	////	01 53	09 08	10 55	12 40	14 29
64	////	////	02 27	09 10	10 52	12 31	14 12
62	////	01 15	02 52	09 12	10 49	12 23	13 58
60	////	01 58	03 12	09 14	10 46	12 16	13 46
N 58	////	02 26	03 27	09 16	10 44	12 10	13 35
56	01 09	02 47	03 41	09 17	10 42	12 04	13 27
54	01 48	03 04	03 53	09 18	10 40	12 00	13 19
52	02 14	03 18	04 03	09 19	10 38	11 55	13 12
50	02 34	03 31	04 12	09 20	10 37	11 52	13 05
45	03 10	03 56	04 31	09 22	10 34	11 43	12 52
N 40	03 36	04 15	04 47	09 24	10 31	11 36	12 41
35	03 56	04 31	05 00	09 26	10 29	11 30	12 31
30	04 12	04 45	05 11	09 27	10 27	11 25	12 23
20	04 38	05 07	05 31	09 29	10 24	11 16	12 09
N 10	04 58	05 25	05 47	09 32	10 21	11 08	11 56
0	05 15	05 41	06 03	09 33	10 18	11 01	11 45
S 10	05 30	05 56	06 18	09 35	10 15	10 54	11 34
20	05 44	06 11	06 34	09 38	10 12	10 46	11 21
30	05 58	06 27	06 53	09 40	10 09	10 38	11 08
35	06 05	06 36	07 04	09 41	10 07	10 33	11 00
40	06 13	06 46	07 16	09 43	10 05	10 27	10 51
45	06 21	06 58	07 30	09 45	10 03	10 21	10 41
S 50	06 31	07 11	07 48	09 47	10 00	10 13	10 28
52	06 35	07 17	07 56	09 48	09 59	10 10	10 22
54	06 40	07 24	08 05	09 49	09 57	10 06	10 16
56	06 45	07 32	08 16	09 50	09 56	10 02	10 09
58	06 50	07 40	08 28	09 51	09 54	09 57	10 01
S 60	06 56	07 49	08 42	09 53	09 52	09 52	09 52

Lat.	Sunset	Twilight Civil	Twilight Naut.	Moonset 18	Moonset 19	Moonset 20	Moonset 21
°	h m	h m	h m	h m	h m	h m	h m
N 72	▭	▭	▭	21 47	21 13	20 32	19 19
N 70	▭	▭	▭	21 48	21 22	20 52	20 09
68	23 17	////	////	21 49	21 30	21 08	20 40
66	22 16	////	////	21 49	21 36	21 22	21 04
64	21 43	////	////	21 50	21 41	21 33	21 22
62	21 19	22 53	////	21 50	21 46	21 42	21 38
60	21 00	22 12	////	21 50	21 50	21 50	21 51
N 58	20 44	21 45	////	21 51	21 54	21 57	22 02
56	20 31	21 24	22 59	21 51	21 57	22 04	22 12
54	20 19	21 08	22 22	21 51	22 00	22 09	22 20
52	20 09	20 53	21 57	21 52	22 03	22 14	22 28
50	20 00	20 41	21 38	21 52	22 05	22 19	22 35
45	19 41	20 16	21 02	21 52	22 10	22 29	22 50
N 40	19 25	19 57	20 36	21 53	22 15	22 38	23 03
35	19 12	19 41	20 16	21 53	22 19	22 45	23 13
30	19 01	19 28	20 00	21 53	22 22	22 52	23 23
20	18 42	19 06	19 34	21 54	22 28	23 03	23 39
N 10	18 25	18 48	19 14	21 54	22 34	23 13	23 53
0	18 10	18 32	18 58	21 55	22 39	23 22	24 06
S 10	17 55	18 17	18 43	21 55	22 44	23 31	24 20
20	17 38	18 02	18 29	21 56	22 49	23 41	24 34
30	17 20	17 46	18 15	21 56	22 55	23 53	24 51
35	17 09	17 37	18 08	21 56	22 59	24 00	00 00
40	16 57	17 27	18 00	21 57	23 03	24 07	00 07
45	16 43	17 15	17 52	21 57	23 07	24 16	00 16
S 50	16 25	17 02	17 42	21 57	23 13	24 27	00 27
52	16 17	16 56	17 38	21 57	23 15	24 32	00 32
54	16 08	16 49	17 33	21 58	23 18	24 38	00 38
56	15 57	16 42	17 29	21 58	23 21	24 44	00 44
58	15 45	16 33	17 23	21 58	23 25	24 51	00 51
S 60	15 32	16 24	17 18	21 58	23 29	24 59	00 59

Day	SUN Eqn. of Time 00^h	SUN Eqn. of Time 12^h	SUN Mer. Pass.	MOON Mer. Pass. Upper	MOON Mer. Pass. Lower	MOON Age	MOON Phase
d	m s	m s	h m	h m	h m	d %	
18	06 14	06 17	12 06	15 44	03 21	04 21	
19	06 19	06 21	12 06	16 28	04 06	05 31	
20	06 23	06 25	12 06	17 12	04 50	06 41	

2026 JULY 21, 22, 23 (TUES., WED., THURS.)

UT		ARIES	VENUS −4·2		MARS +1·3		JUPITER −1·8		SATURN +0·6	
		GHA	GHA	Dec	GHA	Dec	GHA	Dec	GHA	Dec
d	h	° ′	° ′	° ′	° ′	° ′	° ′	° ′	° ′	° ′
21 TUESDAY	00	298 46.7	134 42.1	N 7 40.1	224 26.7	N22 36.2	171 47.8	N19 34.7	284 16.0	N 3 31.1
	01	313 49.2	149 42.1	38.9	239 27.3	36.5	186 49.7	34.5	299 18.4	31.1
	02	328 51.6	164 42.1	37.7	254 27.9	36.7	201 51.6	34.4	314 20.9	31.1
	03	343 54.1	179 42.1	. . 36.5	269 28.5	. . 36.9	216 53.5	. . 34.3	329 23.3	. . 31.1
	04	358 56.6	194 42.1	35.3	284 29.1	37.1	231 55.4	34.1	344 25.7	31.1
	05	13 59.0	209 42.1	34.1	299 29.8	37.3	246 57.3	34.0	359 28.2	31.1
	06	29 01.5	224 42.1	N 7 32.9	314 30.4	N22 37.5	261 59.2	N19 33.9	14 30.6	N 3 31.1
	07	44 03.9	239 42.1	31.7	329 31.0	37.8	277 01.1	33.8	29 33.1	31.1
	08	59 06.4	254 42.1	30.5	344 31.6	38.0	292 03.0	33.6	44 35.5	31.1
	09	74 08.9	269 42.2	. . 29.4	359 32.2	. . 38.2	307 04.9	. . 33.5	59 37.9	. . 31.1
	10	89 11.3	284 42.2	28.2	14 32.8	38.4	322 06.8	33.4	74 40.4	31.1
	11	104 13.8	299 42.2	27.0	29 33.4	38.6	337 08.7	33.2	89 42.8	31.1
	12	119 16.3	314 42.2	N 7 25.8	44 34.1	N22 38.8	352 10.6	N19 33.1	104 45.2	N 3 31.1
	13	134 18.7	329 42.2	24.6	59 34.7	39.0	7 12.5	33.0	119 47.7	31.1
	14	149 21.2	344 42.2	23.4	74 35.3	39.3	22 14.4	32.9	134 50.1	31.1
	15	164 23.7	359 42.2	. . 22.2	89 35.9	. . 39.5	37 16.2	. . 32.7	149 52.6	. . 31.1
	16	179 26.1	14 42.3	21.0	104 36.5	39.7	52 18.1	32.6	164 55.0	31.1
	17	194 28.6	29 42.3	19.8	119 37.1	39.9	67 20.0	32.5	179 57.4	31.1
	18	209 31.0	44 42.3	N 7 18.6	134 37.7	N22 40.1	82 21.9	N19 32.3	194 59.9	N 3 31.0
	19	224 33.5	59 42.3	17.5	149 38.4	40.3	97 23.8	32.2	210 02.3	31.0
	20	239 36.0	74 42.3	16.3	164 39.0	40.5	112 25.7	32.1	225 04.8	31.0
	21	254 38.4	89 42.4	. . 15.1	179 39.6	. . 40.7	127 27.6	. . 31.9	240 07.2	. . 31.0
	22	269 40.9	104 42.4	13.9	194 40.2	40.9	142 29.5	31.8	255 09.6	31.0
	23	284 43.4	119 42.4	12.7	209 40.8	41.1	157 31.4	31.7	270 12.1	31.0
22 WEDNESDAY	00	299 45.8	134 42.4	N 7 11.5	224 41.4	N22 41.4	172 33.3	N19 31.6	285 14.5	N 3 31.0
	01	314 48.3	149 42.4	10.3	239 42.0	41.6	187 35.2	31.4	300 17.0	31.0
	02	329 50.8	164 42.5	09.1	254 42.7	41.8	202 37.1	31.3	315 19.4	31.0
	03	344 53.2	179 42.5	. . 07.9	269 43.3	. . 42.0	217 39.0	. . 31.2	330 21.8	. . 31.0
	04	359 55.7	194 42.5	06.7	284 43.9	42.2	232 40.9	31.0	345 24.3	31.0
	05	14 58.2	209 42.5	05.5	299 44.5	42.4	247 42.8	30.9	0 26.7	31.0
	06	30 00.6	224 42.6	N 7 04.3	314 45.1	N22 42.6	262 44.7	N19 30.8	15 29.2	N 3 31.0
	07	45 03.1	239 42.6	03.1	329 45.7	42.8	277 46.6	30.6	30 31.6	31.0
	08	60 05.5	254 42.6	01.9	344 46.3	43.0	292 48.4	30.5	45 34.1	31.0
	09	75 08.0	269 42.6	7 00.7	359 47.0	. . 43.2	307 50.3	. . 30.4	60 36.5	. . 31.0
	10	90 10.5	284 42.7	6 59.6	14 47.6	43.4	322 52.2	30.3	75 38.9	31.0
	11	105 12.9	299 42.7	58.4	29 48.2	43.6	337 54.1	30.1	90 41.4	31.0
	12	120 15.4	314 42.7	N 6 57.2	44 48.8	N22 43.8	352 56.0	N19 30.0	105 43.8	N 3 31.0
	13	135 17.9	329 42.8	56.0	59 49.4	44.0	7 57.9	29.9	120 46.3	31.0
	14	150 20.3	344 42.8	54.8	74 50.0	44.2	22 59.8	29.7	135 48.7	31.0
	15	165 22.8	359 42.8	. . 53.6	89 50.7	. . 44.4	38 01.7	. . 29.6	150 51.2	. . 31.0
	16	180 25.3	14 42.9	52.4	104 51.3	44.6	53 03.6	29.5	165 53.6	31.0
	17	195 27.7	29 42.9	51.2	119 51.9	44.8	68 05.5	29.3	180 56.0	31.0
	18	210 30.2	44 42.9	N 6 50.0	134 52.5	N22 45.0	83 07.4	N19 29.2	195 58.5	N 3 31.0
	19	225 32.7	59 43.0	48.8	149 53.1	45.2	98 09.3	29.1	211 00.9	31.0
	20	240 35.1	74 43.0	47.6	164 53.7	45.4	113 11.2	29.0	226 03.4	31.0
	21	255 37.6	89 43.0	. . 46.4	179 54.3	. . 45.6	128 13.1	. . 28.8	241 05.8	. . 31.0
	22	270 40.0	104 43.1	45.2	194 55.0	45.8	143 15.0	28.7	256 08.3	31.0
	23	285 42.5	119 43.1	44.0	209 55.6	46.0	158 16.9	28.6	271 10.7	30.9
23 THURSDAY	00	300 45.0	134 43.1	N 6 42.8	224 56.2	N22 46.2	173 18.8	N19 28.4	286 13.1	N 3 30.9
	01	315 47.4	149 43.2	41.6	239 56.8	46.4	188 20.6	28.3	301 15.6	30.9
	02	330 49.9	164 43.2	40.4	254 57.4	46.6	203 22.5	28.2	316 18.0	30.9
	03	345 52.4	179 43.2	. . 39.2	269 58.0	. . 46.8	218 24.4	. . 28.0	331 20.5	. . 30.9
	04	0 54.8	194 43.3	38.0	284 58.7	47.0	233 26.3	27.9	346 22.9	30.9
	05	15 57.3	209 43.3	36.8	299 59.3	47.2	248 28.2	27.8	1 25.4	30.9
	06	30 59.8	224 43.4	N 6 35.6	314 59.9	N22 47.4	263 30.1	N19 27.6	16 27.8	N 3 30.9
	07	46 02.2	239 43.4	34.4	330 00.5	47.6	278 32.0	27.5	31 30.3	30.9
	08	61 04.7	254 43.4	33.2	345 01.1	47.8	293 33.9	27.4	46 32.7	30.9
	09	76 07.1	269 43.5	. . 32.0	0 01.7	. . 48.0	308 35.8	. . 27.3	61 35.2	. . 30.9
	10	91 09.6	284 43.5	30.8	15 02.3	48.2	323 37.7	27.1	76 37.6	30.9
	11	106 12.1	299 43.6	29.6	30 03.0	48.4	338 39.6	27.0	91 40.0	30.9
	12	121 14.5	314 43.6	N 6 28.4	45 03.6	N22 48.6	353 41.5	N19 26.9	106 42.5	N 3 30.9
	13	136 17.0	329 43.7	27.2	60 04.2	48.8	8 43.4	26.7	121 44.9	30.9
	14	151 19.5	344 43.7	26.0	75 04.8	49.0	23 45.3	26.6	136 47.4	30.9
	15	166 21.9	359 43.8	. . 24.8	90 05.4	. . 49.2	38 47.2	. . 26.5	151 49.8	. . 30.9
	16	181 24.4	14 43.8	23.6	105 06.0	49.4	53 49.1	26.3	166 52.3	30.9
	17	196 26.9	29 43.8	22.4	120 06.7	49.6	68 51.0	26.2	181 54.7	30.9
	18	211 29.3	44 43.9	N 6 21.2	135 07.3	N22 49.8	83 52.8	N19 26.1	196 57.2	N 3 30.9
	19	226 31.8	59 43.9	20.0	150 07.9	50.0	98 54.7	25.9	211 59.6	30.8
	20	241 34.3	74 44.0	18.8	165 08.5	50.2	113 56.6	25.8	227 02.1	30.8
	21	256 36.7	89 44.0	. . 17.6	180 09.1	. . 50.4	128 58.5	. . 25.7	242 04.5	. . 30.8
	22	271 39.2	104 44.1	16.4	195 09.7	50.6	144 00.4	25.5	257 07.0	30.8
	23	286 41.6	119 44.1	15.2	210 10.4	50.7	159 02.3	25.4	272 09.4	30.8
Mer. Pass.		h m 4 00.3	*v* 0.0	*d* 1.2	*v* 0.6	*d* 0.2	*v* 1.9	*d* 0.1	*v* 2.4	*d* 0.0

STARS

Name	SHA	Dec
	° ′	° ′
Acamar	315 10.9	S40 11.6
Achernar	335 19.2	S57 05.7
Acrux	172 58.9	S63 15.1
Adhara	255 05.2	S29 00.4
Aldebaran	290 38.4	N16 33.8
Alioth	166 12.0	N55 49.2
Alkaid	152 51.0	N49 11.1
Alnair	27 30.9	S46 49.7
Alnilam	275 36.7	S 1 11.0
Alphard	217 46.8	S 8 46.4
Alphecca	126 02.5	N26 37.7
Alpheratz	357 33.3	N29 14.2
Altair	61 58.4	N 8 56.4
Ankaa	353 05.7	S42 09.4
Antares	112 14.0	S26 29.5
Arcturus	145 46.7	N19 02.8
Atria	107 06.7	S69 04.7
Avior	234 14.9	S59 35.7
Bellatrix	278 21.8	N 6 22.5
Betelgeuse	270 51.0	N 7 24.8
Canopus	263 52.3	S52 42.4
Capella	280 20.4	N46 01.4
Deneb	49 24.5	N45 22.5
Denebola	182 23.8	N14 25.5
Diphda	348 45.9	S17 50.2
Dubhe	193 39.9	N61 36.7
Elnath	278 00.6	N28 37.7
Eltanin	90 41.1	N51 29.2
Enif	33 37.2	N 9 59.9
Fomalhaut	15 12.8	S29 28.7
Gacrux	171 50.4	S57 16.0
Gienah	175 42.4	S17 41.4
Hadar	148 34.1	S60 30.4
Hamal	327 49.8	N23 35.3
Kaus Aust.	83 30.4	S34 22.3
Kochab	137 19.5	N74 03.0
Markab	13 28.4	N15 20.9
Menkar	314 04.9	N 4 11.7
Menkent	147 56.1	S36 30.2
Miaplacidus	221 38.9	S69 49.7
Mirfak	308 26.6	N49 57.2
Nunki	75 45.8	S26 15.8
Peacock	53 03.1	S56 38.8
Pollux	243 16.1	N27 57.7
Procyon	244 49.8	N 5 09.5
Rasalhague	95 57.1	N12 32.5
Regulus	207 33.4	N11 50.3
Rigel	281 02.9	S 8 10.1
Rigil Kent.	139 38.4	S60 57.0
Sabik	102 01.0	S15 45.5
Schedar	349 29.4	N56 40.8
Shaula	96 08.3	S37 07.4
Sirius	258 25.4	S16 45.1
Spica	158 21.0	S11 18.0
Suhail	222 45.8	S43 32.4
Vega	80 32.0	N38 48.6
Zuben'ubi	136 54.5	S16 09.2

	SHA	Mer. Pass.
	° ′	h m
Venus	194 56.6	15 01
Mars	284 55.6	9 01
Jupiter	232 47.5	12 28
Saturn	345 28.7	4 58

UT d	h	SUN GHA ° ′	SUN Dec ° ′	MOON GHA ° ′	v ′	MOON Dec ° ′	d ′	HP ′
21 TUESDAY	00	178 23.4	N20 30.3	99 05.9	14.5	S12 46.9	13.2	55.7
	01	193 23.4	29.8	113 39.4	14.5	13 00.1	13.2	55.7
	02	208 23.4	29.3	128 12.9	14.4	13 13.3	13.2	55.7
	03	223 23.4	. . 28.8	142 46.3	14.5	13 26.5	13.0	55.6
	04	238 23.3	28.3	157 19.8	14.4	13 39.5	13.0	55.6
	05	253 23.3	27.8	171 53.2	14.4	13 52.5	12.9	55.6
	06	268 23.3	N20 27.4	186 26.6	14.3	S14 05.4	12.9	55.5
	07	283 23.2	26.9	200 59.9	14.3	14 18.3	12.7	55.5
	08	298 23.2	26.4	215 33.2	14.4	14 31.0	12.7	55.5
	09	313 23.2	. . 25.9	230 06.6	14.2	14 43.7	12.7	55.5
	10	328 23.1	25.4	244 39.8	14.3	14 56.4	12.5	55.4
	11	343 23.1	24.9	259 13.1	14.2	15 08.9	12.5	55.4
	12	358 23.1	N20 24.4	273 46.3	14.2	S15 21.4	12.4	55.4
	13	13 23.1	24.0	288 19.5	14.2	15 33.8	12.3	55.3
	14	28 23.0	23.5	302 52.7	14.1	15 46.1	12.3	55.3
	15	43 23.0	. . 23.0	317 25.8	14.1	15 58.4	12.1	55.3
	16	58 23.0	22.5	331 58.9	14.1	16 10.5	12.1	55.3
	17	73 22.9	22.0	346 32.0	14.0	16 22.6	12.0	55.2
	18	88 22.9	N20 21.5	1 05.0	14.0	S16 34.6	12.0	55.2
	19	103 22.9	21.0	15 38.0	13.9	16 46.6	11.8	55.2
	20	118 22.9	20.5	30 10.9	14.0	16 58.4	11.8	55.2
	21	133 22.8	. . 20.0	44 43.9	13.9	17 10.2	11.7	55.1
	22	148 22.8	19.5	59 16.8	13.8	17 21.9	11.6	55.1
	23	163 22.8	19.1	73 49.6	13.8	17 33.5	11.5	55.1
22 WEDNESDAY	00	178 22.8	N20 18.6	88 22.4	13.8	S17 45.0	11.5	55.1
	01	193 22.7	18.1	102 55.2	13.7	17 56.5	11.3	55.0
	02	208 22.7	17.6	117 27.9	13.7	18 07.8	11.3	55.0
	03	223 22.7	. . 17.1	132 00.6	13.7	18 19.1	11.2	55.0
	04	238 22.7	16.6	146 33.3	13.6	18 30.3	11.1	55.0
	05	253 22.6	16.1	161 05.9	13.6	18 41.4	11.0	55.0
	06	268 22.6	N20 15.6	175 38.5	13.5	S18 52.4	10.9	54.9
	07	283 22.6	15.1	190 11.0	13.5	19 03.3	10.8	54.9
	08	298 22.6	14.6	204 43.5	13.4	19 14.1	10.8	54.9
	09	313 22.5	. . 14.1	219 15.9	13.4	19 24.9	10.6	54.9
	10	328 22.5	13.6	233 48.3	13.4	19 35.5	10.6	54.9
	11	343 22.5	13.1	248 20.7	13.3	19 46.1	10.5	54.8
	12	358 22.5	N20 12.6	262 53.0	13.2	S19 56.6	10.4	54.8
	13	13 22.5	12.1	277 25.2	13.2	20 07.0	10.2	54.8
	14	28 22.4	11.6	291 57.4	13.2	20 17.2	10.2	54.8
	15	43 22.4	. . 11.1	306 29.6	13.1	20 27.4	10.1	54.8
	16	58 22.4	10.6	321 01.7	13.1	20 37.5	10.0	54.7
	17	73 22.4	10.1	335 33.8	13.1	20 47.5	9.9	54.7
	18	88 22.3	N20 09.6	350 05.9	12.9	S20 57.4	9.9	54.7
	19	103 22.3	09.1	4 37.8	13.0	21 07.3	9.7	54.7
	20	118 22.3	08.6	19 09.8	12.9	21 17.0	9.6	54.7
	21	133 22.3	. . 08.0	33 41.7	12.8	21 26.6	9.5	54.6
	22	148 22.3	07.5	48 13.5	12.8	21 36.1	9.4	54.6
	23	163 22.2	07.0	62 45.3	12.7	21 45.5	9.3	54.6
23 THURSDAY	00	178 22.2	N20 06.5	77 17.0	12.7	S21 54.8	9.3	54.6
	01	193 22.2	06.0	91 48.7	12.7	22 04.1	9.1	54.6
	02	208 22.2	05.5	106 20.4	12.5	22 13.2	9.0	54.6
	03	223 22.2	. . 05.0	120 51.9	12.6	22 22.2	8.9	54.5
	04	238 22.2	04.5	135 23.5	12.5	22 31.1	8.8	54.5
	05	253 22.1	04.0	149 55.0	12.4	22 39.9	8.7	54.5
	06	268 22.1	N20 03.5	164 26.4	12.4	S22 48.6	8.6	54.5
	07	283 22.1	02.9	178 57.8	12.4	22 57.2	8.5	54.5
	08	298 22.1	02.4	193 29.2	12.2	23 05.7	8.4	54.5
	09	313 22.1	. . 01.9	208 00.4	12.3	23 14.1	8.3	54.5
	10	328 22.0	01.4	222 31.7	12.2	23 22.4	8.2	54.4
	11	343 22.0	00.9	237 02.9	12.1	23 30.6	8.0	54.4
	12	358 22.0	N20 00.4	251 34.0	12.1	S23 38.6	8.0	54.4
	13	13 22.0	19 59.9	266 05.1	12.0	23 46.6	7.8	54.4
	14	28 22.0	59.3	280 36.1	12.0	23 54.4	7.8	54.4
	15	43 22.0	. . 58.8	295 07.1	12.0	24 02.2	7.6	54.4
	16	58 21.9	58.3	309 38.1	11.9	24 09.8	7.5	54.4
	17	73 21.9	57.8	324 09.0	11.8	24 17.3	7.4	54.3
	18	88 21.9	N19 57.3	338 39.8	11.8	S24 24.7	7.3	54.3
	19	103 21.9	56.8	353 10.6	11.7	24 32.0	7.2	54.3
	20	118 21.9	56.2	7 41.3	11.7	24 39.2	7.1	54.3
	21	133 21.9	. . 55.7	22 12.0	11.6	24 46.3	6.9	54.3
	22	148 21.9	55.2	36 42.6	11.6	24 53.2	6.9	54.3
	23	163 21.8	54.7	51 13.2	11.6	S25 00.1	6.7	54.3
		SD 15.8	*d* 0.5	SD	15.1	14.9		14.8

Lat. °	Twilight Naut. h m	Twilight Civil h m	Sunrise h m	Moonrise 21 h m	Moonrise 22 h m	Moonrise 23 h m	Moonrise 24 h m
N 72	□	□	□	16 09	■	■	■
N 70	□	□	□	15 22	■	■	■
68	////	////	01 14	14 52	17 24	■	■
66	////	////	02 05	14 29	16 31	■	■
64	////	////	02 37	14 12	15 59	18 02	■
62	////	01 31	03 00	13 58	15 36	17 19	19 08
60	////	02 08	03 18	13 46	15 17	16 50	18 20
N 58	////	02 33	03 33	13 35	15 02	16 28	17 49
56	01 23	02 53	03 46	13 27	14 49	16 10	17 26
54	01 57	03 09	03 57	13 19	14 37	15 55	17 08
52	02 21	03 23	04 07	13 12	14 27	15 42	16 52
50	02 39	03 35	04 16	13 05	14 18	15 30	16 38
45	03 14	03 59	04 34	12 52	14 00	15 06	16 10
N 40	03 39	04 18	04 49	12 41	13 44	14 47	15 49
35	03 59	04 34	05 02	12 31	13 32	14 32	15 31
30	04 15	04 47	05 13	12 23	13 20	14 18	15 15
20	04 40	05 08	05 32	12 09	13 01	13 55	14 49
N 10	04 59	05 25	05 48	11 56	12 45	13 35	14 26
0	05 15	05 41	06 03	11 45	12 30	13 17	14 05
S 10	05 30	05 55	06 18	11 34	12 15	12 58	13 45
20	05 43	06 10	06 34	11 21	11 59	12 39	13 22
30	05 57	06 26	06 52	11 08	11 40	12 16	12 57
35	06 04	06 35	07 02	11 00	11 29	12 03	12 42
40	06 11	06 44	07 14	10 51	11 17	11 48	12 24
45	06 19	06 55	07 28	10 41	11 03	11 30	12 03
S 50	06 28	07 08	07 45	10 28	10 46	11 08	11 37
52	06 32	07 14	07 53	10 22	10 38	10 57	11 24
54	06 37	07 21	08 02	10 16	10 29	10 45	11 09
56	06 41	07 28	08 12	10 09	10 18	10 32	10 52
58	06 46	07 36	08 23	10 01	10 07	10 16	10 32
S 60	06 52	07 45	08 36	09 52	09 54	09 57	10 06

Lat. °	Sunset h m	Twilight Civil h m	Twilight Naut. h m	Moonset 21 h m	Moonset 22 h m	Moonset 23 h m	Moonset 24 h m
N 72	□	□	□	19 19	■	■	■
N 70	□	□	□	20 09	■	■	■
68	22 52	////	////	20 40	19 42	■	■
66	22 04	////	////	21 04	20 36	■	■
64	21 34	////	////	21 22	21 09	20 44	■
62	21 12	22 38	////	21 38	21 33	21 29	21 22
60	20 54	22 03	////	21 51	21 53	21 58	22 10
N 58	20 39	21 38	////	22 02	22 09	22 20	22 41
56	20 26	21 18	22 46	22 12	22 23	22 39	23 04
54	20 15	21 02	22 14	22 20	22 35	22 54	23 23
52	20 05	20 49	21 50	22 28	22 45	23 08	23 39
50	19 56	20 37	21 32	22 35	22 55	23 20	23 53
45	19 38	20 13	20 58	22 50	23 15	23 44	24 21
N 40	19 23	19 54	20 33	23 03	23 31	24 04	00 04
35	19 11	19 39	20 14	23 13	23 45	24 20	00 20
30	19 00	19 26	19 58	23 23	23 57	24 35	00 35
20	18 41	19 05	19 33	23 39	24 17	00 17	00 59
N 10	18 25	18 47	19 14	23 53	24 35	00 35	01 20
0	18 10	18 32	18 58	24 06	00 06	00 52	01 40
S 10	17 55	18 18	18 43	24 20	00 20	01 09	02 00
20	17 40	18 03	18 30	24 34	00 34	01 27	02 21
30	17 22	17 47	18 17	24 51	00 51	01 48	02 46
35	17 11	17 39	18 10	00 00	01 00	02 01	03 00
40	17 00	17 29	18 02	00 07	01 11	02 15	03 17
45	16 46	17 18	17 54	00 16	01 24	02 32	03 38
S 50	16 29	17 05	17 45	00 27	01 40	02 53	04 03
52	16 21	16 59	17 41	00 32	01 48	03 03	04 16
54	16 12	16 53	17 37	00 38	01 56	03 14	04 30
56	16 02	16 46	17 32	00 44	02 06	03 27	04 47
58	15 51	16 38	17 27	00 51	02 17	03 43	05 07
S 60	15 37	16 29	17 22	00 59	02 29	04 01	05 32

Day	SUN Eqn. of Time 00^h	SUN Eqn. of Time 12^h	SUN Mer. Pass.	MOON Mer. Pass. Upper	MOON Mer. Pass. Lower	MOON Age	MOON Phase
d	m s	m s	h m	h m	h m	d %	
21	06 26	06 28	12 06	17 56	05 33	07 51	
22	06 29	06 30	12 07	18 41	06 18	08 60	
23	06 31	06 32	12 07	19 28	07 04	09 69	

2026 JULY 24, 25, 26 (FRI., SAT., SUN.)

UT d	h	ARIES GHA	VENUS −4·2 GHA	VENUS Dec	MARS +1·3 GHA	MARS Dec	JUPITER −1·8 GHA	JUPITER Dec	SATURN +0·6 GHA	SATURN Dec	STARS Name	SHA	Dec
		° ′	° ′	° ′	° ′	° ′	° ′	° ′	° ′	° ′		° ′	° ′
24	00	301 44.1	134 44.2	N 6 14.0	225 11.0	N22 50.9	174 04.2	N19 25.3	287 11.9	N 3 30.8	Acamar	315 10.9	S40 11.6
	01	316 46.6	149 44.2	12.8	240 11.6	51.1	189 06.1	25.2	302 14.3	30.8	Achernar	335 19.2	S57 05.7
	02	331 49.0	164 44.3	11.6	255 12.2	51.3	204 08.0	25.0	317 16.8	30.8	Acrux	172 58.9	S63 15.1
	03	346 51.5	179 44.3	. . 10.4	270 12.8	. . 51.5	219 09.9	. . 24.9	332 19.2	. . 30.8	Adhara	255 05.2	S29 00.4
	04	1 54.0	194 44.4	09.2	285 13.4	51.7	234 11.8	24.8	347 21.7	30.8	Aldebaran	290 38.3	N16 33.8
	05	16 56.4	209 44.5	08.0	300 14.1	51.9	249 13.7	24.6	2 24.1	30.8			
	06	31 58.9	224 44.5	N 6 06.8	315 14.7	N22 52.1	264 15.6	N19 24.5	17 26.6	N 3 30.8	Alioth	166 12.0	N55 49.2
	07	47 01.4	239 44.6	05.6	330 15.3	52.3	279 17.5	24.4	32 29.0	30.8	Alkaid	152 51.0	N49 11.1
	08	62 03.8	254 44.6	04.4	345 15.9	52.5	294 19.4	24.2	47 31.5	30.8	Alnair	27 30.9	S46 49.7
F	09	77 06.3	269 44.7	. . 03.2	0 16.5	. . 52.6	309 21.3	. . 24.1	62 33.9	. . 30.8	Alnilam	275 36.7	S 1 11.0
R	10	92 08.8	284 44.7	01.9	15 17.1	52.8	324 23.2	24.0	77 36.4	30.7	Alphard	217 46.8	S 8 46.4
I	11	107 11.2	299 44.8	6 00.7	30 17.8	53.0	339 25.0	23.8	92 38.8	30.7			
D	12	122 13.7	314 44.8	N 5 59.5	45 18.4	N22 53.2	354 26.9	N19 23.7	107 41.3	N 3 30.7	Alphecca	126 02.5	N26 37.7
A	13	137 16.1	329 44.9	58.3	60 19.0	53.4	9 28.8	23.6	122 43.7	30.7	Alpheratz	357 33.3	N29 14.2
Y	14	152 18.6	344 45.0	57.1	75 19.6	53.6	24 30.7	23.4	137 46.2	30.7	Altair	61 58.4	N 8 56.4
	15	167 21.1	359 45.0	. . 55.9	90 20.2	. . 53.8	39 32.6	. . 23.3	152 48.6	. . 30.7	Ankaa	353 05.7	S42 09.4
	16	182 23.5	14 45.1	54.7	105 20.8	53.9	54 34.5	23.2	167 51.1	30.7	Antares	112 14.0	S26 29.5
	17	197 26.0	29 45.1	53.5	120 21.5	54.1	69 36.4	23.1	182 53.5	30.7			
	18	212 28.5	44 45.2	N 5 52.3	135 22.1	N22 54.3	84 38.3	N19 22.9	197 56.0	N 3 30.7	Arcturus	145 46.7	N19 02.8
	19	227 30.9	59 45.3	51.1	150 22.7	54.5	99 40.2	22.8	212 58.4	30.7	Atria	107 06.7	S69 04.7
	20	242 33.4	74 45.3	49.9	165 23.3	54.7	114 42.1	22.7	228 00.9	30.7	Avior	234 14.9	S59 35.7
	21	257 35.9	89 45.4	. . 48.7	180 23.9	. . 54.9	129 44.0	. . 22.5	243 03.3	. . 30.7	Bellatrix	278 21.8	N 6 22.5
	22	272 38.3	104 45.5	47.5	195 24.5	55.0	144 45.9	22.4	258 05.8	30.7	Betelgeuse	270 51.0	N 7 24.8
	23	287 40.8	119 45.5	46.3	210 25.2	55.2	159 47.8	22.3	273 08.2	30.7			
25	00	302 43.3	134 45.6	N 5 45.1	225 25.8	N22 55.4	174 49.7	N19 22.1	288 10.7	N 3 30.6	Canopus	263 52.3	S52 42.4
	01	317 45.7	149 45.7	43.9	240 26.4	55.6	189 51.6	22.0	303 13.1	30.6	Capella	280 20.3	N46 01.4
	02	332 48.2	164 45.7	42.7	255 27.0	55.8	204 53.5	21.9	318 15.6	30.6	Deneb	49 24.5	N45 22.5
	03	347 50.6	179 45.8	. . 41.4	270 27.6	. . 56.0	219 55.4	. . 21.7	333 18.0	. . 30.6	Denebola	182 23.8	N14 25.5
	04	2 53.1	194 45.9	40.2	285 28.3	56.1	234 57.3	21.6	348 20.5	30.6	Diphda	348 45.9	S17 50.2
	05	17 55.6	209 45.9	39.0	300 28.9	56.3	249 59.1	21.5	3 22.9	30.6			
	06	32 58.0	224 46.0	N 5 37.8	315 29.5	N22 56.5	265 01.0	N19 21.3	18 25.4	N 3 30.6	Dubhe	193 39.9	N61 36.6
	07	48 00.5	239 46.1	36.6	330 30.1	56.7	280 02.9	21.2	33 27.8	30.6	Elnath	278 00.5	N28 37.7
S	08	63 03.0	254 46.1	35.4	345 30.7	56.9	295 04.8	21.1	48 30.3	30.6	Eltanin	90 41.1	N51 29.3
A	09	78 05.4	269 46.2	. . 34.2	0 31.3	. . 57.0	310 06.7	. . 20.9	63 32.8	. . 30.6	Enif	33 37.2	N 9 59.9
T	10	93 07.9	284 46.3	33.0	15 32.0	57.2	325 08.6	20.8	78 35.2	30.6	Fomalhaut	15 12.8	S29 28.7
U	11	108 10.4	299 46.4	31.8	30 32.6	57.4	340 10.5	20.7	93 37.7	30.6			
R	12	123 12.8	314 46.4	N 5 30.6	45 33.2	N22 57.6	355 12.4	N19 20.5	108 40.1	N 3 30.6	Gacrux	171 50.4	S57 16.0
D	13	138 15.3	329 46.5	29.4	60 33.8	57.8	10 14.3	20.4	123 42.6	30.5	Gienah	175 42.4	S17 41.4
A	14	153 17.8	344 46.6	28.2	75 34.4	57.9	25 16.2	20.3	138 45.0	30.5	Hadar	148 34.1	S60 30.4
Y	15	168 20.2	359 46.6	. . 26.9	90 35.1	. . 58.1	40 18.1	. . 20.1	153 47.5	. . 30.5	Hamal	327 49.7	N23 35.3
	16	183 22.7	14 46.7	25.7	105 35.7	58.3	55 20.0	20.0	168 49.9	30.5	Kaus Aust.	83 30.4	S34 22.3
	17	198 25.1	29 46.8	24.5	120 36.3	58.5	70 21.9	19.9	183 52.4	30.5			
	18	213 27.6	44 46.9	N 5 23.3	135 36.9	N22 58.6	85 23.8	N19 19.7	198 54.8	N 3 30.5	Kochab	137 19.6	N74 03.0
	19	228 30.1	59 47.0	22.1	150 37.5	58.8	100 25.7	19.6	213 57.3	30.5	Markab	13 28.4	N15 21.0
	20	243 32.5	74 47.0	20.9	165 38.2	59.0	115 27.6	19.5	228 59.8	30.5	Menkar	314 04.9	N 4 11.7
	21	258 35.0	89 47.1	. . 19.7	180 38.8	. . 59.2	130 29.5	. . 19.3	244 02.2	. . 30.5	Menkent	147 56.1	S36 30.2
	22	273 37.5	104 47.2	18.5	195 39.4	59.3	145 31.4	19.2	259 04.7	30.5	Miaplacidus	221 38.9	S69 49.6
	23	288 39.9	119 47.3	17.3	210 40.0	59.5	160 33.3	19.1	274 07.1	30.5			
26	00	303 42.4	134 47.3	N 5 16.1	225 40.6	N22 59.7	175 35.1	N19 19.0	289 09.6	N 3 30.4	Mirfak	308 26.6	N49 57.2
	01	318 44.9	149 47.4	14.8	240 41.2	22 59.9	190 37.0	18.8	304 12.0	30.4	Nunki	75 45.8	S26 15.8
	02	333 47.3	164 47.5	13.6	255 41.9	23 00.0	205 38.9	18.7	319 14.5	30.4	Peacock	53 03.1	S56 38.8
	03	348 49.8	179 47.6	. . 12.4	270 42.5	. . 00.2	220 40.8	. . 18.6	334 17.0	. . 30.4	Pollux	243 16.1	N27 57.7
	04	3 52.2	194 47.7	11.2	285 43.1	00.4	235 42.7	18.4	349 19.4	30.4	Procyon	244 49.8	N 5 09.5
	05	18 54.7	209 47.8	10.0	300 43.7	00.6	250 44.6	18.3	4 21.9	30.4			
	06	33 57.2	224 47.8	N 5 08.8	315 44.3	N23 00.7	265 46.5	N19 18.2	19 24.3	N 3 30.4	Rasalhague	95 57.1	N12 32.5
	07	48 59.6	239 47.9	07.6	330 45.0	00.9	280 48.4	18.0	34 26.8	30.4	Regulus	207 33.4	N11 50.3
	08	64 02.1	254 48.0	06.4	345 45.6	01.1	295 50.3	17.9	49 29.2	30.4	Rigel	281 02.9	S 8 10.1
S	09	79 04.6	269 48.1	. . 05.2	0 46.2	. . 01.2	310 52.2	. . 17.8	64 31.7	. . 30.4	Rigil Kent.	139 38.4	S60 57.0
U	10	94 07.0	284 48.2	03.9	15 46.8	01.4	325 54.1	17.6	79 34.2	30.3	Sabik	102 01.0	S15 45.5
N	11	109 09.5	299 48.3	02.7	30 47.4	01.6	340 56.0	17.5	94 36.6	30.3			
D	12	124 12.0	314 48.3	N 5 01.5	45 48.1	N23 01.7	355 57.9	N19 17.4	109 39.1	N 3 30.3	Schedar	349 29.3	N56 40.8
A	13	139 14.4	329 48.4	5 00.3	60 48.7	01.9	10 59.8	17.2	124 41.5	30.3	Shaula	96 08.3	S37 07.4
Y	14	154 16.9	344 48.5	4 59.1	75 49.3	02.1	26 01.7	17.1	139 44.0	30.3	Sirius	258 25.4	S16 45.0
	15	169 19.4	359 48.6	. . 57.9	90 49.9	. . 02.3	41 03.6	. . 17.0	154 46.4	. . 30.3	Spica	158 21.0	S11 18.0
	16	184 21.8	14 48.7	56.7	105 50.5	02.4	56 05.5	16.8	169 48.9	30.3	Suhail	222 45.8	S43 32.4
	17	199 24.3	29 48.8	55.5	120 51.2	02.6	71 07.4	16.7	184 51.4	30.3			
	18	214 26.7	44 48.9	N 4 54.2	135 51.8	N23 02.8	86 09.2	N19 16.6	199 53.8	N 3 30.3	Vega	80 32.0	N38 48.6
	19	229 29.2	59 49.0	53.0	150 52.4	02.9	101 11.1	16.4	214 56.3	30.3	Zuben'ubi	136 54.5	S16 09.2
	20	244 31.7	74 49.1	51.8	165 53.0	03.1	116 13.0	16.3	229 58.7	30.2			
	21	259 34.1	89 49.2	. . 50.6	180 53.6	. . 03.3	131 14.9	. . 16.2	245 01.2	. . 30.2			
	22	274 36.6	104 49.2	49.4	195 54.3	03.4	146 16.8	16.0	260 03.7	30.2			
	23	289 39.1	119 49.3	48.2	210 54.9	03.6	161 18.7	15.9	275 06.1	30.2			
Mer. Pass.		h m 3 48.5	*v* 0.1	*d* 1.2	*v* 0.6	*d* 0.2	*v* 1.9	*d* 0.1	*v* 2.5	*d* 0.0			

	SHA ° ′	Mer. Pass. h m
Venus	192 02.3	15 01
Mars	282 42.5	8 58
Jupiter	232 06.4	12 19
Saturn	345 27.4	4 47

	UT	SUN GHA	SUN Dec	MOON GHA	v	MOON Dec	d	HP
	d h	° ′	° ′	° ′	′	° ′	′	′
	24 00	178 21.8	N19 54.2	65 43.8	11.5	S25 06.8	6.6	54.3
	01	193 21.8	53.6	80 14.3	11.4	25 13.4	6.5	54.3
	02	208 21.8	53.1	94 44.7	11.4	25 19.9	6.3	54.2
	03	223 21.8	· · 52.6	109 15.1	11.4	25 26.2	6.3	54.2
	04	238 21.8	52.1	123 45.5	11.3	25 32.5	6.1	54.2
	05	253 21.8	51.5	138 15.8	11.2	25 38.6	6.0	54.2
	06	268 21.8	N19 51.0	152 46.0	11.2	S25 44.6	5.9	54.2
	07	283 21.8	50.5	167 16.2	11.2	25 50.5	5.8	54.2
	08	298 21.7	50.0	181 46.4	11.1	25 56.3	5.7	54.2
FRIDAY	09	313 21.7	· · 49.4	196 16.5	11.1	26 02.0	5.5	54.2
	10	328 21.7	48.9	210 46.6	11.0	26 07.5	5.4	54.2
	11	343 21.7	48.4	225 16.6	11.0	26 12.9	5.3	54.2
	12	358 21.7	N19 47.8	239 46.6	10.9	S26 18.2	5.2	54.2
	13	13 21.7	47.3	254 16.5	10.9	26 23.4	5.0	54.2
	14	28 21.7	46.8	268 46.4	10.9	26 28.4	4.9	54.2
	15	43 21.7	· · 46.3	283 16.3	10.8	26 33.3	4.8	54.1
	16	58 21.7	45.7	297 46.1	10.8	26 38.1	4.7	54.1
	17	73 21.7	45.2	312 15.9	10.7	26 42.8	4.5	54.1
	18	88 21.6	N19 44.7	326 45.6	10.7	S26 47.3	4.5	54.1
	19	103 21.6	44.1	341 15.3	10.7	26 51.8	4.2	54.1
	20	118 21.6	43.6	355 45.0	10.6	26 56.0	4.2	54.1
	21	133 21.6	· · 43.1	10 14.6	10.6	27 00.2	4.0	54.1
	22	148 21.6	42.5	24 44.2	10.6	27 04.2	3.9	54.1
	23	163 21.6	42.0	39 13.8	10.5	27 08.1	3.8	54.1
	25 00	178 21.6	N19 41.5	53 43.3	10.4	S27 11.9	3.7	54.1
	01	193 21.6	40.9	68 12.7	10.5	27 15.6	3.5	54.1
	02	208 21.6	40.4	82 42.2	10.4	27 19.1	3.4	54.1
	03	223 21.6	· · 39.8	97 11.6	10.4	27 22.5	3.2	54.1
	04	238 21.6	39.3	111 41.0	10.3	27 25.7	3.2	54.1
	05	253 21.6	38.8	126 10.3	10.4	27 28.9	3.0	54.1
	06	268 21.6	N19 38.2	140 39.7	10.2	S27 31.9	2.8	54.1
	07	283 21.6	37.7	155 08.9	10.3	27 34.7	2.8	54.1
	08	298 21.6	37.1	169 38.2	10.2	27 37.5	2.6	54.1
SATURDAY	09	313 21.5	· · 36.6	184 07.4	10.2	27 40.1	2.5	54.1
	10	328 21.5	36.1	198 36.6	10.2	27 42.6	2.3	54.1
	11	343 21.5	35.5	213 05.8	10.2	27 44.9	2.2	54.1
	12	358 21.5	N19 35.0	227 35.0	10.1	S27 47.1	2.1	54.1
	13	13 21.5	34.4	242 04.1	10.1	27 49.2	1.9	54.1
	14	28 21.5	33.9	256 33.2	10.1	27 51.1	1.8	54.1
	15	43 21.5	· · 33.4	271 02.3	10.1	27 52.9	1.7	54.1
	16	58 21.5	32.8	285 31.4	10.0	27 54.6	1.5	54.1
	17	73 21.5	32.3	300 00.4	10.1	27 56.1	1.4	54.1
	18	88 21.5	N19 31.7	314 29.5	10.0	S27 57.5	1.3	54.1
	19	103 21.5	31.2	328 58.5	10.0	27 58.8	1.1	54.1
	20	118 21.5	30.6	343 27.5	10.0	27 59.9	1.0	54.1
	21	133 21.5	· · 30.1	357 56.5	10.0	28 00.9	0.9	54.1
	22	148 21.5	29.5	12 25.5	9.9	28 01.8	0.7	54.1
	23	163 21.5	29.0	26 54.4	10.0	28 02.5	0.6	54.1
	26 00	178 21.5	N19 28.4	41 23.4	9.9	S28 03.1	0.5	54.1
	01	193 21.5	27.9	55 52.3	9.9	28 03.6	0.3	54.1
	02	208 21.5	27.3	70 21.2	10.0	28 03.9	0.2	54.1
	03	223 21.5	· · 26.8	84 50.2	9.9	28 04.1	0.0	54.1
	04	238 21.5	26.2	99 19.1	9.9	28 04.1	0.1	54.1
	05	253 21.5	25.7	113 48.0	9.9	28 04.0	0.2	54.1
	06	268 21.5	N19 25.1	128 16.9	9.9	S28 03.8	0.4	54.1
	07	283 21.5	24.6	142 45.8	9.9	28 03.4	0.4	54.1
	08	298 21.5	24.0	157 14.7	9.9	28 03.0	0.7	54.1
SUNDAY	09	313 21.5	· · 23.5	171 43.6	9.9	28 02.3	0.8	54.1
	10	328 21.5	22.9	186 12.5	9.9	28 01.5	0.9	54.1
	11	343 21.5	22.4	200 41.4	9.9	28 00.6	1.0	54.1
	12	358 21.5	N19 21.8	215 10.3	9.9	S27 59.6	1.2	54.1
	13	13 21.5	21.2	229 39.2	9.9	27 58.4	1.3	54.1
	14	28 21.5	20.7	244 08.1	9.9	27 57.1	1.4	54.1
	15	43 21.5	· · 20.1	258 37.0	9.9	27 55.7	1.6	54.1
	16	58 21.5	19.6	273 05.9	10.0	27 54.1	1.7	54.1
	17	73 21.5	19.0	287 34.9	9.9	27 52.4	1.9	54.1
	18	88 21.5	N19 18.4	302 03.8	10.0	S27 50.5	2.0	54.1
	19	103 21.6	17.9	316 32.8	9.9	27 48.5	2.1	54.1
	20	118 21.6	17.3	331 01.7	10.0	27 46.4	2.3	54.1
	21	133 21.6	· · 16.8	345 30.7	10.0	27 44.1	2.4	54.2
	22	148 21.6	16.2	359 59.7	10.0	27 41.7	2.5	54.2
	23	163 21.6	15.6	14 28.7	10.0	S27 39.2	2.7	54.2
		SD 15.8	*d* 0.5	SD	14.8	14.7		14.7

Lat.	Twilight Naut.	Twilight Civil	Sunrise	Moonrise 24	25	26	27
°	h m	h m	h m	h m	h m	h m	h m
N 72	□	□	□	▬	▬	▬	▬
N 70	□	□	□	▬	▬	▬	▬
68	////	////	01 35	▬	▬	▬	▬
66	////	////	02 18	▬	▬	▬	▬
64	////	00 44	02 46	▬	▬	▬	▬
62	////	01 45	03 07	19 08	▬	21 30	21 19
60	////	02 18	03 24	18 20	19 35	20 22	20 42
N 58	00 40	02 41	03 39	17 49	18 58	19 47	20 15
56	01 36	03 00	03 51	17 26	18 32	19 21	19 54
54	02 06	03 15	04 02	17 08	18 11	19 01	19 37
52	02 28	03 28	04 11	16 52	17 54	18 44	19 22
50	02 45	03 40	04 20	16 38	17 39	18 29	19 09
45	03 18	04 03	04 37	16 10	17 09	18 00	18 42
N 40	03 43	04 21	04 52	15 49	16 46	17 37	18 21
35	04 01	04 36	05 04	15 31	16 26	17 18	18 03
30	04 17	04 48	05 15	15 15	16 10	17 01	17 48
20	04 41	05 09	05 33	14 49	15 42	16 34	17 22
N 10	05 00	05 26	05 49	14 26	15 18	16 10	17 00
0	05 16	05 41	06 03	14 05	14 56	15 48	16 39
S 10	05 29	05 55	06 17	13 45	14 34	15 25	16 18
20	05 42	06 09	06 33	13 22	14 10	15 02	15 55
30	05 55	06 24	06 50	12 57	13 43	14 34	15 29
35	06 02	06 33	07 00	12 42	13 26	14 17	15 14
40	06 09	06 42	07 11	12 24	13 07	13 58	14 56
45	06 17	06 53	07 25	12 03	12 45	13 35	14 34
S 50	06 25	07 05	07 41	11 37	12 15	13 05	14 06
52	06 29	07 11	07 49	11 24	12 01	12 51	13 53
54	06 33	07 17	07 57	11 09	11 44	12 33	13 37
56	06 37	07 24	08 07	10 52	11 24	12 13	13 19
58	06 42	07 31	08 18	10 32	11 00	11 47	12 56
S 60	06 47	07 40	08 30	10 06	10 26	11 11	12 26

Lat.	Sunset	Twilight Civil	Twilight Naut.	Moonset 24	25	26	27
°	h m	h m	h m	h m	h m	h m	h m
N 72	□	□	□	▬	▬	▬	▬
N 70	□	□	□	▬	▬	▬	▬
68	22 33	////	////	▬	▬	▬	▬
66	21 52	////	////	▬	▬	▬	▬
64	21 25	23 19	////	▬	▬	▬	▬
62	21 04	22 24	////	21 22	▬	22 34	24 30
60	20 47	21 53	////	22 10	22 40	23 42	25 07
N 58	20 33	21 30	23 23	22 41	23 18	24 16	00 16
56	20 21	21 12	22 34	23 04	23 44	24 41	00 41
54	20 10	20 57	22 05	23 23	24 05	00 05	01 02
52	20 01	20 44	21 43	23 39	24 22	00 22	01 18
50	19 53	20 33	21 26	23 53	24 37	00 37	01 33
45	19 35	20 10	20 54	24 21	00 21	01 07	02 02
N 40	19 21	19 52	20 30	00 04	00 44	01 31	02 25
35	19 09	19 37	20 11	00 20	01 02	01 50	02 44
30	18 58	19 24	19 56	00 35	01 18	02 07	03 00
20	18 40	19 04	19 32	00 59	01 45	02 35	03 27
N 10	18 25	18 47	19 13	01 20	02 08	02 59	03 51
0	18 10	18 32	18 58	01 40	02 30	03 21	04 12
S 10	17 56	18 18	18 44	02 00	02 51	03 43	04 34
20	17 41	18 04	18 31	02 21	03 15	04 07	04 57
30	17 23	17 49	18 18	02 46	03 42	04 35	05 24
35	17 13	17 41	18 11	03 00	03 58	04 52	05 40
40	17 02	17 31	18 04	03 17	04 17	05 11	05 59
45	16 49	17 21	17 57	03 38	04 39	05 34	06 21
S 50	16 33	17 09	17 48	04 03	05 08	06 04	06 49
52	16 25	17 03	17 45	04 16	05 22	06 19	07 03
54	16 16	16 57	17 41	04 30	05 39	06 36	07 18
56	16 07	16 50	17 36	04 47	05 59	06 56	07 37
58	15 56	16 42	17 32	05 07	06 23	07 22	08 00
S 60	15 44	16 34	17 27	05 32	06 56	07 58	08 30

Day	SUN Eqn. of Time 00h	SUN Eqn. of Time 12h	SUN Mer. Pass.	MOON Mer. Pass. Upper	MOON Mer. Pass. Lower	Age	Phase
d	m s	m s	h m	h m	h m	d %	
24	06 33	06 33	12 07	20 18	07 53	10 78	
25	06 34	06 34	12 07	21 09	08 43	11 85	
26	06 34	06 34	12 07	22 00	09 34	12 91	

UT (d h)	ARIES GHA	VENUS −4·3 GHA	VENUS Dec	MARS +1·3 GHA	MARS Dec	JUPITER −1·8 GHA	JUPITER Dec	SATURN +0·6 GHA	SATURN Dec
	° ′	° ′	° ′	° ′	° ′	° ′	° ′	° ′	° ′
27 00 (MONDAY)	304 41.5	134 49.4	N 4 47.0	225 55.5	N23 03.8	176 20.6	N19 15.8	290 08.6	N 3 30.2
01	319 44.0	149 49.5	45.7	240 56.1	03.9	191 22.5	15.6	305 11.0	30.2
02	334 46.5	164 49.6	44.5	255 56.7	04.1	206 24.4	15.5	320 13.5	30.2
03	349 48.9	179 49.7	. . 43.3	270 57.4	. . 04.2	221 26.3	. . 15.4	335 16.0	. . 30.2
04	4 51.4	194 49.8	42.1	285 58.0	04.4	236 28.2	15.2	350 18.4	30.2
05	19 53.9	209 49.9	40.9	300 58.6	04.6	251 30.1	15.1	5 20.9	30.1
06	34 56.3	224 50.0	N 4 39.7	315 59.2	N23 04.7	266 32.0	N19 15.0	20 23.3	N 3 30.1
07	49 58.8	239 50.1	38.5	330 59.8	04.9	281 33.9	14.8	35 25.8	30.1
08	65 01.2	254 50.2	37.2	346 00.5	05.1	296 35.8	14.7	50 28.3	30.1
09	80 03.7	269 50.3	. . 36.0	1 01.1	. . 05.2	311 37.7	. . 14.6	65 30.7	. . 30.1
10	95 06.2	284 50.4	34.8	16 01.7	05.4	326 39.6	14.4	80 33.2	30.1
11	110 08.6	299 50.5	33.6	31 02.3	05.5	341 41.5	14.3	95 35.7	30.1
12	125 11.1	314 50.6	N 4 32.4	46 02.9	N23 05.7	356 43.4	N19 14.2	110 38.1	N 3 30.1
13	140 13.6	329 50.7	31.2	61 03.6	05.9	11 45.3	14.0	125 40.6	30.0
14	155 16.0	344 50.8	29.9	76 04.2	06.0	26 47.1	13.9	140 43.0	30.0
15	170 18.5	359 50.9	. . 28.7	91 04.8	. . 06.2	41 49.0	. . 13.8	155 45.5	. . 30.0
16	185 21.0	14 51.0	27.5	106 05.4	06.3	56 50.9	13.6	170 48.0	30.0
17	200 23.4	29 51.1	26.3	121 06.1	06.5	71 52.8	13.5	185 50.4	30.0
18	215 25.9	44 51.2	N 4 25.1	136 06.7	N23 06.7	86 54.7	N19 13.4	200 52.9	N 3 30.0
19	230 28.4	59 51.3	23.9	151 07.3	06.8	101 56.6	13.2	215 55.4	30.0
20	245 30.8	74 51.4	22.7	166 07.9	07.0	116 58.5	13.1	230 57.8	30.0
21	260 33.3	89 51.5	. . 21.4	181 08.5	. . 07.1	132 00.4	. . 13.0	246 00.3	. . 30.0
22	275 35.7	104 51.6	20.2	196 09.2	07.3	147 02.3	12.8	261 02.8	29.9
23	290 38.2	119 51.8	19.0	211 09.8	07.5	162 04.2	12.7	276 05.2	29.9
28 00 (TUESDAY)	305 40.7	134 51.9	N 4 17.8	226 10.4	N23 07.6	177 06.1	N19 12.6	291 07.7	N 3 29.9
01	320 43.1	149 52.0	16.6	241 11.0	07.8	192 08.0	12.4	306 10.1	29.9
02	335 45.6	164 52.1	15.4	256 11.7	07.9	207 09.9	12.3	321 12.6	29.9
03	350 48.1	179 52.2	. . 14.1	271 12.3	. . 08.1	222 11.8	. . 12.2	336 15.1	. . 29.9
04	5 50.5	194 52.3	12.9	286 12.9	08.2	237 13.7	12.0	351 17.5	29.9
05	20 53.0	209 52.4	11.7	301 13.5	08.4	252 15.6	11.9	6 20.0	29.9
06	35 55.5	224 52.5	N 4 10.5	316 14.1	N23 08.5	267 17.5	N19 11.7	21 22.5	N 3 29.8
07	50 57.9	239 52.6	09.3	331 14.8	08.7	282 19.4	11.6	36 24.9	29.8
08	66 00.4	254 52.8	08.0	346 15.4	08.8	297 21.3	11.5	51 27.4	29.8
09	81 02.9	269 52.9	. . 06.8	1 16.0	. . 09.0	312 23.2	. . 11.3	66 29.9	. . 29.8
10	96 05.3	284 53.0	05.6	16 16.6	09.2	327 25.1	11.2	81 32.3	29.8
11	111 07.8	299 53.1	04.4	31 17.3	09.3	342 26.9	11.1	96 34.8	29.8
12	126 10.2	314 53.2	N 4 03.2	46 17.9	N23 09.5	357 28.8	N19 10.9	111 37.3	N 3 29.8
13	141 12.7	329 53.3	02.0	61 18.5	09.6	12 30.7	10.8	126 39.7	29.7
14	156 15.2	344 53.4	4 00.7	76 19.1	09.8	27 32.6	10.7	141 42.2	29.7
15	171 17.6	359 53.6	3 59.5	91 19.7	. . 09.9	42 34.5	. . 10.5	156 44.7	. . 29.7
16	186 20.1	14 53.7	58.3	106 20.4	10.1	57 36.4	10.4	171 47.1	29.7
17	201 22.6	29 53.8	57.1	121 21.0	10.2	72 38.3	10.3	186 49.6	29.7
18	216 25.0	44 53.9	N 3 55.9	136 21.6	N23 10.4	87 40.2	N19 10.1	201 52.1	N 3 29.7
19	231 27.5	59 54.0	54.6	151 22.2	10.5	102 42.1	10.0	216 54.5	29.7
20	246 30.0	74 54.1	53.4	166 22.9	10.7	117 44.0	09.9	231 57.0	29.6
21	261 32.4	89 54.3	. . 52.2	181 23.5	. . 10.8	132 45.9	. . 09.7	246 59.5	. . 29.6
22	276 34.9	104 54.4	51.0	196 24.1	11.0	147 47.8	09.6	262 01.9	29.6
23	291 37.3	119 54.5	49.8	211 24.7	11.1	162 49.7	09.5	277 04.4	29.6
29 00 (WEDNESDAY)	306 39.8	134 54.6	N 3 48.5	226 25.4	N23 11.3	177 51.6	N19 09.3	292 06.9	N 3 29.6
01	321 42.3	149 54.8	47.3	241 26.0	11.4	192 53.5	09.2	307 09.3	29.6
02	336 44.7	164 54.9	46.1	256 26.6	11.6	207 55.4	09.1	322 11.8	29.6
03	351 47.2	179 55.0	. . 44.9	271 27.2	. . 11.7	222 57.3	. . 08.9	337 14.3	. . 29.6
04	6 49.7	194 55.1	43.7	286 27.8	11.8	237 59.2	08.8	352 16.7	29.5
05	21 52.1	209 55.3	42.5	301 28.5	12.0	253 01.1	08.7	7 19.2	29.5
06	36 54.6	224 55.4	N 3 41.2	316 29.1	N23 12.1	268 03.0	N19 08.5	22 21.7	N 3 29.5
07	51 57.1	239 55.5	40.0	331 29.7	12.3	283 04.9	08.4	37 24.2	29.5
08	66 59.5	254 55.6	38.8	346 30.3	12.4	298 06.8	08.3	52 26.6	29.5
09	82 02.0	269 55.8	. . 37.6	1 31.0	. . 12.6	313 08.6	. . 08.1	67 29.1	. . 29.5
10	97 04.5	284 55.9	36.4	16 31.6	12.7	328 10.5	08.0	82 31.6	29.4
11	112 06.9	299 56.0	35.1	31 32.2	12.9	343 12.4	07.9	97 34.0	29.4
12	127 09.4	314 56.1	N 3 33.9	46 32.8	N23 13.0	358 14.3	N19 07.7	112 36.5	N 3 29.4
13	142 11.8	329 56.3	32.7	61 33.5	13.1	13 16.2	07.6	127 39.0	29.4
14	157 14.3	344 56.4	31.5	76 34.1	13.3	28 18.1	07.5	142 41.4	29.4
15	172 16.8	359 56.5	. . 30.3	91 34.7	. . 13.4	43 20.0	. . 07.3	157 43.9	. . 29.4
16	187 19.2	14 56.7	29.0	106 35.3	13.6	58 21.9	07.2	172 46.4	29.4
17	202 21.7	29 56.8	27.8	121 36.0	13.7	73 23.8	07.1	187 48.9	29.3
18	217 24.2	44 56.9	N 3 26.6	136 36.6	N23 13.9	88 25.7	N19 06.9	202 51.3	N 3 29.3
19	232 26.6	59 57.1	25.4	151 37.2	14.0	103 27.6	06.8	217 53.8	29.3
20	247 29.1	74 57.2	24.1	166 37.8	14.1	118 29.5	06.6	232 56.3	29.3
21	262 31.6	89 57.3	. . 22.9	181 38.5	. . 14.3	133 31.4	. . 06.5	247 58.7	. . 29.3
22	277 34.0	104 57.5	21.7	196 39.1	14.4	148 33.3	06.4	263 01.2	29.3
23	292 36.5	119 57.6	20.5	211 39.7	14.6	163 35.2	06.2	278 03.7	29.2
Mer. Pass. (h m)	3 36.7	v 0.1	d 1.2	v 0.6	d 0.2	v 1.9	d 0.1	v 2.5	d 0.0

STARS

Name	SHA	Dec
	° ′	° ′
Acamar	315 10.9	S40 11.6
Achernar	335 19.1	S57 05.7
Acrux	172 58.9	S63 15.1
Adhara	255 05.2	S29 00.4
Aldebaran	290 38.3	N16 33.8
Alioth	166 12.0	N55 49.2
Alkaid	152 51.0	N49 11.1
Alnair	27 30.9	S46 49.7
Alnilam	275 36.7	S 1 11.0
Alphard	217 46.8	S 8 46.4
Alphecca	126 02.5	N26 37.7
Alpheratz	357 33.2	N29 14.2
Altair	61 58.4	N 8 56.4
Ankaa	353 05.7	S42 09.4
Antares	112 14.0	S26 29.5
Arcturus	145 46.7	N19 02.8
Atria	107 06.7	S69 04.7
Avior	234 14.9	S59 35.6
Bellatrix	278 21.7	N 6 22.5
Betelgeuse	270 51.0	N 7 24.8
Canopus	263 52.3	S52 42.4
Capella	280 20.3	N46 01.3
Deneb	49 24.4	N45 22.6
Denebola	182 23.8	N14 25.5
Diphda	348 45.9	S17 50.2
Dubhe	193 39.9	N61 36.6
Elnath	278 00.5	N28 37.7
Eltanin	90 41.1	N51 29.3
Enif	33 37.2	N 9 59.9
Fomalhaut	15 12.8	S29 28.7
Gacrux	171 50.5	S57 16.0
Gienah	175 42.4	S17 41.4
Hadar	148 34.2	S60 30.4
Hamal	327 49.7	N23 35.3
Kaus Aust.	83 30.4	S34 22.3
Kochab	137 19.6	N74 03.0
Markab	13 28.3	N15 21.0
Menkar	314 04.9	N 4 11.7
Menkent	147 56.1	S36 30.2
Miaplacidus	221 38.9	S69 49.6
Mirfak	308 26.5	N49 57.2
Nunki	75 45.8	S26 15.8
Peacock	53 03.1	S56 38.8
Pollux	243 16.1	N27 57.7
Procyon	244 49.8	N 5 09.5
Rasalhague	95 57.1	N12 32.5
Regulus	207 33.4	N11 50.3
Rigel	281 02.9	S 8 10.1
Rigil Kent.	139 38.4	S60 57.0
Sabik	102 01.0	S15 45.5
Schedar	349 29.3	N56 40.8
Shaula	96 08.3	S37 07.4
Sirius	258 25.4	S16 45.0
Spica	158 21.0	S11 18.0
Suhail	222 45.8	S43 32.4
Vega	80 32.0	N38 48.6
Zuben'ubi	136 54.5	S16 09.2

	SHA	Mer. Pass.
	° ′	h m
Venus	189 11.2	15 00
Mars	280 29.7	8 55
Jupiter	231 25.4	12 10
Saturn	345 27.0	4 35

UT		SUN GHA	SUN Dec	MOON GHA	v	MOON Dec	d	HP
d	h	° ′	° ′	° ′	′	° ′	′	′
27	00	178 21.6	N19 15.1	28 57.7	10.1	S27 36.5	2.8	54.2
	01	193 21.6	14.5	43 26.8	10.0	27 33.7	2.9	54.2
	02	208 21.6	14.0	57 55.8	10.1	27 30.8	3.1	54.2
	03	223 21.6	. . 13.4	72 24.9	10.1	27 27.7	3.2	54.2
	04	238 21.6	12.8	86 54.0	10.2	27 24.5	3.4	54.2
	05	253 21.6	12.3	101 23.2	10.1	27 21.1	3.4	54.2
	06	268 21.6	N19 11.7	115 52.3	10.2	S27 17.7	3.6	54.2
	07	283 21.6	11.1	130 21.5	10.2	27 14.1	3.8	54.2
	08	298 21.6	10.6	144 50.7	10.2	27 10.3	3.8	54.2
M	09	313 21.6	. . 10.0	159 19.9	10.2	27 06.5	4.0	54.2
O	10	328 21.6	09.4	173 49.1	10.3	27 02.5	4.2	54.2
N	11	343 21.7	08.9	188 18.4	10.3	26 58.3	4.2	54.3
D	12	358 21.7	N19 08.3	202 47.7	10.4	S26 54.1	4.4	54.3
A	13	13 21.7	07.7	217 17.1	10.3	26 49.7	4.6	54.3
Y	14	28 21.7	07.1	231 46.4	10.4	26 45.1	4.6	54.3
	15	43 21.7	. . 06.6	246 15.8	10.5	26 40.5	4.8	54.3
	16	58 21.7	06.0	260 45.3	10.4	26 35.7	4.9	54.3
	17	73 21.7	05.4	275 14.7	10.5	26 30.8	5.1	54.3
	18	88 21.7	N19 04.9	289 44.2	10.6	S26 25.7	5.1	54.3
	19	103 21.7	04.3	304 13.8	10.5	26 20.6	5.3	54.3
	20	118 21.7	03.7	318 43.3	10.6	26 15.3	5.4	54.3
	21	133 21.8	. . 03.1	333 12.9	10.7	26 09.9	5.6	54.3
	22	148 21.8	02.6	347 42.6	10.7	26 04.3	5.7	54.4
	23	163 21.8	02.0	2 12.3	10.7	25 58.6	5.8	54.4
28	00	178 21.8	N19 01.4	16 42.0	10.8	S25 52.8	5.9	54.4
	01	193 21.8	00.8	31 11.8	10.8	25 46.9	6.1	54.4
	02	208 21.8	19 00.3	45 41.6	10.8	25 40.8	6.1	54.4
	03	223 21.8	18 59.7	60 11.4	10.9	25 34.7	6.3	54.4
	04	238 21.8	59.1	74 41.3	10.9	25 28.4	6.5	54.4
	05	253 21.9	58.5	89 11.2	11.0	25 21.9	6.5	54.4
	06	268 21.9	N18 58.0	103 41.2	11.0	S25 15.4	6.7	54.4
	07	283 21.9	57.4	118 11.2	11.1	25 08.7	6.8	54.4
T	08	298 21.9	56.8	132 41.3	11.1	25 01.9	6.9	54.5
U	09	313 21.9	. . 56.2	147 11.4	11.2	24 55.0	7.0	54.5
E	10	328 21.9	55.6	161 41.6	11.2	24 48.0	7.1	54.5
S	11	343 21.9	55.1	176 11.8	11.2	24 40.9	7.3	54.5
D	12	358 22.0	N18 54.5	190 42.0	11.3	S24 33.6	7.4	54.5
A	13	13 22.0	53.9	205 12.3	11.4	24 26.2	7.5	54.5
Y	14	28 22.0	53.3	219 42.7	11.3	24 18.7	7.6	54.5
	15	43 22.0	. . 52.7	234 13.0	11.5	24 11.1	7.7	54.5
	16	58 22.0	52.1	248 43.5	11.5	24 03.4	7.9	54.6
	17	73 22.0	51.6	263 14.0	11.5	23 55.5	7.9	54.6
	18	88 22.1	N18 51.0	277 44.5	11.6	S23 47.6	8.1	54.6
	19	103 22.1	50.4	292 15.1	11.7	23 39.5	8.2	54.6
	20	118 22.1	49.8	306 45.8	11.6	23 31.3	8.3	54.6
	21	133 22.1	. . 49.2	321 16.4	11.8	23 23.0	8.4	54.6
	22	148 22.1	48.6	335 47.2	11.8	23 14.6	8.5	54.6
	23	163 22.1	48.0	350 18.0	11.8	23 06.1	8.7	54.6
29	00	178 22.2	N18 47.4	4 48.8	11.9	S22 57.4	8.7	54.7
	01	193 22.2	46.9	19 19.7	12.0	22 48.7	8.8	54.7
	02	208 22.2	46.3	33 50.7	12.0	22 39.9	9.0	54.7
	03	223 22.2	. . 45.7	48 21.7	12.0	22 30.9	9.0	54.7
	04	238 22.2	45.1	62 52.7	12.1	22 21.9	9.2	54.7
	05	253 22.3	44.5	77 23.8	12.2	22 12.7	9.3	54.7
	06	268 22.3	N18 43.9	91 55.0	12.2	S22 03.4	9.4	54.7
W	07	283 22.3	43.3	106 26.2	12.2	21 54.0	9.4	54.8
E	08	298 22.3	42.7	120 57.4	12.3	21 44.6	9.6	54.8
D	09	313 22.3	. . 42.1	135 28.7	12.4	21 35.0	9.7	54.8
N	10	328 22.4	41.5	150 00.1	12.4	21 25.3	9.8	54.8
E	11	343 22.4	40.9	164 31.5	12.5	21 15.5	9.9	54.8
S	12	358 22.4	N18 40.3	179 03.0	12.5	S21 05.6	10.0	54.8
D	13	13 22.4	39.7	193 34.5	12.6	20 55.6	10.0	54.8
A	14	28 22.4	39.1	208 06.1	12.6	20 45.6	10.2	54.9
Y	15	43 22.5	. . 38.6	222 37.7	12.7	20 35.4	10.3	54.9
	16	58 22.5	38.0	237 09.4	12.7	20 25.1	10.4	54.9
	17	73 22.5	37.4	251 41.1	12.8	20 14.7	10.4	54.9
	18	88 22.5	N18 36.8	266 12.9	12.8	S20 04.3	10.6	54.9
	19	103 22.6	36.2	280 44.7	12.9	19 53.7	10.6	54.9
	20	118 22.6	35.6	295 16.6	12.9	19 43.1	10.8	55.0
	21	133 22.6	. . 35.0	309 48.5	13.0	19 32.3	10.8	55.0
	22	148 22.6	34.4	324 20.5	13.0	19 21.5	11.0	55.0
	23	163 22.7	33.8	338 52.5	13.1	S19 10.5	11.0	55.0
		SD 15.8	d 0.6	SD	14.8	14.9		14.9

Lat.	Twilight Naut.	Twilight Civil	Sunrise	Moonrise 27	28	29	30
°	h m	h m	h m	h m	h m	h m	h m
N 72	□	□	□	■	■	■	22 40
N 70	////	////	00 36	■	■	23 18	22 11
68	////	////	01 53	■	■	22 26	21 49
66	////	////	02 30	■	22 37	21 53	21 31
64	////	01 13	02 55	■	21 46	21 29	21 17
62	////	01 58	03 15	21 19	21 14	21 09	21 05
60	////	02 27	03 31	20 42	20 50	20 54	20 55
N 58	01 06	02 49	03 45	20 15	20 31	20 40	20 46
56	01 48	03 06	03 56	19 54	20 15	20 28	20 38
54	02 15	03 21	04 07	19 37	20 01	20 18	20 31
52	02 35	03 33	04 16	19 22	19 49	20 09	20 24
50	02 51	03 44	04 24	19 09	19 38	20 01	20 18
45	03 23	04 06	04 41	18 42	19 16	19 43	20 06
N 40	03 46	04 24	04 55	18 21	18 58	19 29	19 56
35	04 04	04 38	05 06	18 03	18 43	19 17	19 47
30	04 19	04 50	05 17	17 48	18 29	19 06	19 39
20	04 42	05 10	05 34	17 22	18 07	18 47	19 25
N 10	05 01	05 27	05 49	17 00	17 47	18 31	19 13
0	05 16	05 41	06 03	16 39	17 28	18 16	19 02
S 10	05 29	05 55	06 17	16 18	17 10	18 01	18 50
20	05 42	06 08	06 31	15 55	16 50	17 44	18 38
30	05 54	06 23	06 48	15 29	16 27	17 26	18 24
35	06 00	06 31	06 58	15 14	16 13	17 15	18 16
40	06 07	06 40	07 09	14 56	15 58	17 02	18 07
45	06 14	06 50	07 22	14 34	15 39	16 47	17 56
S 50	06 22	07 01	07 37	14 06	15 15	16 28	17 42
52	06 26	07 07	07 44	13 53	15 04	16 19	17 36
54	06 29	07 13	07 53	13 37	14 51	16 09	17 29
56	06 33	07 19	08 02	13 19	14 36	15 58	17 21
58	06 38	07 26	08 12	12 56	14 18	15 45	17 13
S 60	06 42	07 34	08 24	12 26	13 56	15 30	17 02

Lat.	Sunset	Twilight Civil	Twilight Naut.	Moonset 27	28	29	30
°	h m	h m	h m	h m	h m	h m	h m
N 72	□	□	□	■	■	■	■
N 70	23 21	////	////	■	■	■	01 55
68	22 15	////	////	■	■	■	02 46
66	21 40	////	////	■	■	00 56	03 18
64	21 15	22 54	////	■	■	01 46	03 41
62	20 56	22 11	////	24 30	00 30	02 17	03 59
60	20 40	21 43	////	25 07	01 07	02 41	04 14
N 58	20 27	21 22	23 01	00 16	01 33	02 59	04 27
56	20 15	21 05	22 22	00 41	01 54	03 15	04 38
54	20 05	20 51	21 56	01 02	02 11	03 28	04 48
52	19 56	20 39	21 36	01 18	02 26	03 40	04 56
50	19 48	20 28	21 20	01 33	02 38	03 50	05 04
45	19 32	20 06	20 49	02 02	03 04	04 11	05 20
N 40	19 18	19 48	20 26	02 25	03 25	04 28	05 33
35	19 06	19 34	20 08	02 44	03 42	04 43	05 44
30	18 56	19 22	19 54	03 00	03 57	04 55	05 54
20	18 39	19 02	19 30	03 27	04 22	05 16	06 10
N 10	18 24	18 46	19 12	03 51	04 43	05 35	06 25
0	18 10	18 32	18 57	04 12	05 03	05 52	06 38
S 10	17 56	18 18	18 44	04 34	05 23	06 09	06 51
20	17 42	18 05	18 32	04 57	05 44	06 27	07 06
30	17 25	17 51	18 20	05 24	06 08	06 47	07 22
35	17 16	17 43	18 13	05 40	06 22	06 59	07 31
40	17 05	17 34	18 07	05 59	06 39	07 13	07 41
45	16 52	17 24	17 59	06 21	06 59	07 29	07 54
S 50	16 36	17 12	17 52	06 49	07 23	07 49	08 09
52	16 29	17 07	17 48	07 03	07 35	07 58	08 16
54	16 21	17 01	17 44	07 18	07 48	08 09	08 23
56	16 12	16 55	17 40	07 37	08 04	08 20	08 32
58	16 02	16 47	17 36	08 00	08 22	08 34	08 41
S 60	15 50	16 39	17 32	08 30	08 44	08 50	08 52

Day	SUN Eqn. of Time 00^h	SUN Eqn. of Time 12^h	SUN Mer. Pass.	MOON Mer. Pass. Upper	MOON Mer. Pass. Lower	Age	Phase
d	m s	m s	h m	h m	h m	d %	
27	06 34	06 33	12 07	22 51	10 26	13 96	
28	06 33	06 32	12 07	23 40	11 16	14 99	○
29	06 31	06 30	12 07	24 27	12 04	15 100	

UT	ARIES	VENUS −4·3		MARS +1·3		JUPITER −1·8		SATURN +0·6	
	GHA	GHA	Dec	GHA	Dec	GHA	Dec	GHA	Dec
d h	° ′	° ′	° ′	° ′	° ′	° ′	° ′	° ′	° ′
30 00	307 39.0	134 57.7	N 3 19.3	226 40.3	N23 14.7	178 37.1	N19 06.1	293 06.2	N 3 29.2
01	322 41.4	149 57.9	18.0	241 41.0	14.8	193 39.0	06.0	308 08.6	29.2
02	337 43.9	164 58.0	16.8	256 41.6	15.0	208 40.9	05.8	323 11.1	29.2
03	352 46.3	179 58.1	. . 15.6	271 42.2	. . 15.1	223 42.8	. . 05.7	338 13.6	. . 29.2
04	7 48.8	194 58.3	14.4	286 42.8	15.3	238 44.7	05.6	353 16.0	29.2
05	22 51.3	209 58.4	13.2	301 43.5	15.4	253 46.6	05.4	8 18.5	29.2
06	37 53.7	224 58.6	N 3 11.9	316 44.1	N23 15.5	268 48.5	N19 05.3	23 21.0	N 3 29.1
07	52 56.2	239 58.7	10.7	331 44.7	15.7	283 50.4	05.2	38 23.5	29.1
T 08	67 58.7	254 58.8	09.5	346 45.3	15.8	298 52.3	05.0	53 25.9	29.1
H 09	83 01.1	269 59.0	. . 08.3	1 46.0	. . 15.9	313 54.2	. . 04.9	68 28.4	. . 29.1
U 10	98 03.6	284 59.1	07.0	16 46.6	16.1	328 56.1	04.7	83 30.9	29.1
R 11	113 06.1	299 59.3	05.8	31 47.2	16.2	343 58.0	04.6	98 33.4	29.1
S 12	128 08.5	314 59.4	N 3 04.6	46 47.8	N23 16.3	358 59.9	N19 04.5	113 35.8	N 3 29.0
D 13	143 11.0	329 59.6	03.4	61 48.5	16.5	14 01.7	04.3	128 38.3	29.0
A 14	158 13.5	344 59.7	02.2	76 49.1	16.6	29 03.6	04.2	143 40.8	29.0
Y 15	173 15.9	359 59.8	3 00.9	91 49.7	. . 16.7	44 05.5	. . 04.1	158 43.3	. . 29.0
16	188 18.4	15 00.0	2 59.7	106 50.3	16.9	59 07.4	03.9	173 45.7	29.0
17	203 20.8	30 00.1	58.5	121 51.0	17.0	74 09.3	03.8	188 48.2	29.0
18	218 23.3	45 00.3	N 2 57.3	136 51.6	N23 17.1	89 11.2	N19 03.7	203 50.7	N 3 28.9
19	233 25.8	60 00.4	56.0	151 52.2	17.3	104 13.1	03.5	218 53.2	28.9
20	248 28.2	75 00.6	54.8	166 52.9	17.4	119 15.0	03.4	233 55.6	28.9
21	263 30.7	90 00.7	. . 53.6	181 53.5	. . 17.5	134 16.9	. . 03.2	248 58.1	. . 28.9
22	278 33.2	105 00.9	52.4	196 54.1	17.7	149 18.8	03.1	264 00.6	28.9
23	293 35.6	120 01.0	51.2	211 54.7	17.8	164 20.7	03.0	279 03.1	28.9
31 00	308 38.1	135 01.2	N 2 49.9	226 55.4	N23 17.9	179 22.6	N19 02.8	294 05.5	N 3 28.8
01	323 40.6	150 01.3	48.7	241 56.0	18.1	194 24.5	02.7	309 08.0	28.8
02	338 43.0	165 01.5	47.5	256 56.6	18.2	209 26.4	02.6	324 10.5	28.8
03	353 45.5	180 01.6	. . 46.3	271 57.2	. . 18.3	224 28.3	. . 02.4	339 13.0	. . 28.8
04	8 47.9	195 01.8	45.0	286 57.9	18.5	239 30.2	02.3	354 15.4	28.8
05	23 50.4	210 01.9	43.8	301 58.5	18.6	254 32.1	02.2	9 17.9	28.7
06	38 52.9	225 02.1	N 2 42.6	316 59.1	N23 18.7	269 34.0	N19 02.0	24 20.4	N 3 28.7
07	53 55.3	240 02.2	41.4	331 59.7	18.8	284 35.9	01.9	39 22.9	28.7
08	68 57.8	255 02.4	40.1	347 00.4	19.0	299 37.8	01.8	54 25.4	28.7
F 09	84 00.3	270 02.6	. . 38.9	2 01.0	. . 19.1	314 39.7	. . 01.6	69 27.8	. . 28.7
R 10	99 02.7	285 02.7	37.7	17 01.6	19.2	329 41.6	01.5	84 30.3	28.7
I 11	114 05.2	300 02.9	36.5	32 02.3	19.4	344 43.5	01.3	99 32.8	28.6
D 12	129 07.7	315 03.0	N 2 35.3	47 02.9	N23 19.5	359 45.4	N19 01.2	114 35.3	N 3 28.6
A 13	144 10.1	330 03.2	34.0	62 03.5	19.6	14 47.3	01.1	129 37.7	28.6
Y 14	159 12.6	345 03.3	32.8	77 04.1	19.7	29 49.2	00.9	144 40.2	28.6
15	174 15.1	0 03.5	. . 31.6	92 04.8	. . 19.9	44 51.1	. . 00.8	159 42.7	. . 28.6
16	189 17.5	15 03.7	30.4	107 05.4	20.0	59 53.0	00.7	174 45.2	28.5
17	204 20.0	30 03.8	29.1	122 06.0	20.1	74 54.8	00.5	189 47.7	28.5
18	219 22.4	45 04.0	N 2 27.9	137 06.7	N23 20.2	89 56.7	N19 00.4	204 50.1	N 3 28.5
19	234 24.9	60 04.1	26.7	152 07.3	20.4	104 58.6	00.3	219 52.6	28.5
20	249 27.4	75 04.3	25.5	167 07.9	20.5	120 00.5	00.1	234 55.1	28.5
21	264 29.8	90 04.5	. . 24.2	182 08.5	. . 20.6	135 02.4	19 00.0	249 57.6	. . 28.5
22	279 32.3	105 04.6	23.0	197 09.2	20.7	150 04.3	18 59.8	265 00.1	28.4
23	294 34.8	120 04.8	21.8	212 09.8	20.8	165 06.2	59.7	280 02.5	28.4
1 00	309 37.2	135 04.9	N 2 20.6	227 10.4	N23 21.0	180 08.1	N18 59.6	295 05.0	N 3 28.4
01	324 39.7	150 05.1	19.3	242 11.1	21.1	195 10.0	59.4	310 07.5	28.4
02	339 42.2	165 05.3	18.1	257 11.7	21.2	210 11.9	59.3	325 10.0	28.4
03	354 44.6	180 05.4	. . 16.9	272 12.3	. . 21.3	225 13.8	. . 59.2	340 12.5	. . 28.3
04	9 47.1	195 05.6	15.7	287 12.9	21.5	240 15.7	59.0	355 14.9	28.3
05	24 49.6	210 05.8	14.5	302 13.6	21.6	255 17.6	58.9	10 17.4	28.3
06	39 52.0	225 05.9	N 2 13.2	317 14.2	N23 21.7	270 19.5	N18 58.8	25 19.9	N 3 28.3
07	54 54.5	240 06.1	12.0	332 14.8	21.8	285 21.4	58.6	40 22.4	28.3
S 08	69 56.9	255 06.3	10.8	347 15.5	21.9	300 23.3	58.5	55 24.9	28.2
A 09	84 59.4	270 06.4	. . 09.6	2 16.1	. . 22.1	315 25.2	. . 58.3	70 27.3	. . 28.2
T 10	100 01.9	285 06.6	08.3	17 16.7	22.2	330 27.1	58.2	85 29.8	28.2
U 11	115 04.3	300 06.8	07.1	32 17.3	22.3	345 29.0	58.1	100 32.3	28.2
R 12	130 06.8	315 07.0	N 2 05.9	47 18.0	N23 22.4	0 30.9	N18 57.9	115 34.8	N 3 28.2
D 13	145 09.3	330 07.1	04.7	62 18.6	22.5	15 32.8	57.8	130 37.3	28.1
A 14	160 11.7	345 07.3	03.4	77 19.2	22.6	30 34.7	57.7	145 39.7	28.1
Y 15	175 14.2	0 07.5	. . 02.2	92 19.9	. . 22.8	45 36.6	. . 57.5	160 42.2	. . 28.1
16	190 16.7	15 07.6	2 01.0	107 20.5	22.9	60 38.5	57.4	175 44.7	28.1
17	205 19.1	30 07.8	1 59.8	122 21.1	23.0	75 40.4	57.2	190 47.2	28.1
18	220 21.6	45 08.0	N 1 58.5	137 21.8	N23 23.1	90 42.3	N18 57.1	205 49.7	N 3 28.0
19	235 24.0	60 08.2	57.3	152 22.4	23.2	105 44.2	57.0	220 52.2	28.0
20	250 26.5	75 08.3	56.1	167 23.0	23.3	120 46.1	56.8	235 54.6	28.0
21	265 29.0	90 08.5	. . 54.9	182 23.6	. . 23.5	135 48.0	. . 56.7	250 57.1	. . 28.0
22	280 31.4	105 08.7	53.6	197 24.3	23.6	150 49.9	56.6	265 59.6	28.0
23	295 33.9	120 08.9	52.4	212 24.9	23.7	165 51.8	56.4	281 02.1	27.9
Mer. Pass.	h m 3 24.9	*v* 0.2	*d* 1.2	*v* 0.6	*d* 0.1	*v* 1.9	*d* 0.1	*v* 2.5	*d* 0.0

STARS

Name	SHA	Dec
	° ′	° ′
Acamar	315 10.8	S40 11.5
Achernar	335 19.1	S57 05.7
Acrux	172 58.9	S63 15.1
Adhara	255 05.2	S29 00.3
Aldebaran	290 38.3	N16 33.8
Alioth	166 12.0	N55 49.2
Alkaid	152 51.1	N49 11.1
Alnair	27 30.8	S46 49.7
Alnilam	275 36.6	S 1 11.0
Alphard	217 46.8	S 8 46.4
Alphecca	126 02.5	N26 37.7
Alpheratz	357 33.2	N29 14.2
Altair	61 58.4	N 8 56.4
Ankaa	353 05.6	S42 09.4
Antares	112 14.0	S26 29.5
Arcturus	145 46.7	N19 02.8
Atria	107 06.7	S69 04.7
Avior	234 14.9	S59 35.6
Bellatrix	278 21.7	N 6 22.5
Betelgeuse	270 50.9	N 7 24.8
Canopus	263 52.3	S52 42.4
Capella	280 20.3	N46 01.3
Deneb	49 24.4	N45 22.6
Denebola	182 23.8	N14 25.5
Diphda	348 45.8	S17 50.2
Dubhe	193 39.9	N61 36.6
Elnath	278 00.5	N28 37.7
Eltanin	90 41.1	N51 29.3
Enif	33 37.2	N 9 59.9
Fomalhaut	15 12.8	S29 28.6
Gacrux	171 50.5	S57 16.0
Gienah	175 42.4	S17 41.4
Hadar	148 34.2	S60 30.4
Hamal	327 49.7	N23 35.3
Kaus Aust.	83 30.4	S34 22.3
Kochab	137 19.7	N74 03.0
Markab	13 28.3	N15 21.0
Menkar	314 04.8	N 4 11.7
Menkent	147 56.1	S36 30.2
Miaplacidus	221 39.0	S69 49.6
Mirfak	308 26.5	N49 57.2
Nunki	75 45.8	S26 15.8
Peacock	53 03.1	S56 38.9
Pollux	243 16.1	N27 57.7
Procyon	244 49.8	N 5 09.5
Rasalhague	95 57.1	N12 32.6
Regulus	207 33.4	N11 50.3
Rigel	281 02.8	S 8 10.1
Rigil Kent.	139 38.4	S60 57.0
Sabik	102 01.1	S15 45.5
Schedar	349 29.3	N56 40.8
Shaula	96 08.3	S37 07.4
Sirius	258 25.4	S16 45.0
Spica	158 21.0	S11 18.0
Suhail	222 45.8	S43 32.4
Vega	80 32.0	N38 48.6
Zuben'ubi	136 54.5	S16 09.2

	SHA	Mer. Pass.
	° ′	h m
Venus	186 23.1	15 00
Mars	278 17.3	8 52
Jupiter	230 44.5	12 01
Saturn	345 27.4	4 23

UT (d h)		SUN GHA (° ′)	SUN Dec (° ′)	MOON GHA (° ′)	v (′)	MOON Dec (° ′)	d (′)	HP (′)
30 00	THURSDAY	178 22.7	N18 33.2	353 24.6	13.2	S18 59.5	11.1	55.0
01		193 22.7	32.6	7 56.8	13.1	18 48.4	11.2	55.0
02		208 22.7	32.0	22 28.9	13.3	18 37.2	11.3	55.1
03		223 22.8	. . 31.4	37 01.2	13.3	18 25.9	11.3	55.1
04		238 22.8	30.7	51 33.5	13.3	18 14.6	11.5	55.1
05		253 22.8	30.1	66 05.8	13.4	18 03.1	11.5	55.1
06		268 22.8	N18 29.5	80 38.2	13.4	S17 51.6	11.7	55.1
07		283 22.9	28.9	95 10.6	13.5	17 39.9	11.7	55.1
08		298 22.9	28.3	109 43.1	13.5	17 28.2	11.8	55.1
09		313 22.9	. . 27.7	124 15.6	13.6	17 16.4	11.8	55.2
10		328 22.9	27.1	138 48.2	13.6	17 04.6	12.0	55.2
11		343 23.0	26.5	153 20.8	13.6	16 52.6	12.0	55.2
12		358 23.0	N18 25.9	167 53.4	13.7	S16 40.6	12.1	55.2
13		13 23.0	25.3	182 26.1	13.8	16 28.5	12.2	55.2
14		28 23.1	24.7	196 58.9	13.8	16 16.3	12.3	55.3
15		43 23.1	. . 24.1	211 31.7	13.8	16 04.0	12.3	55.3
16		58 23.1	23.5	226 04.5	13.9	15 51.7	12.4	55.3
17		73 23.1	22.9	240 37.4	13.9	15 39.3	12.5	55.3
18		88 23.2	N18 22.2	255 10.3	14.0	S15 26.8	12.5	55.3
19		103 23.2	21.6	269 43.3	14.0	15 14.3	12.7	55.3
20		118 23.2	21.0	284 16.3	14.0	15 01.6	12.7	55.4
21		133 23.3	. . 20.4	298 49.3	14.1	14 48.9	12.7	55.4
22		148 23.3	19.8	313 22.4	14.1	14 36.2	12.9	55.4
23		163 23.3	19.2	327 55.5	14.2	14 23.3	12.9	55.4
31 00	FRIDAY	178 23.4	N18 18.6	342 28.7	14.2	S14 10.4	13.0	55.4
01		193 23.4	18.0	357 01.9	14.2	13 57.4	13.0	55.4
02		208 23.4	17.3	11 35.1	14.3	13 44.4	13.1	55.5
03		223 23.5	. . 16.7	26 08.4	14.3	13 31.3	13.2	55.5
04		238 23.5	16.1	40 41.7	14.3	13 18.1	13.2	55.5
05		253 23.5	15.5	55 15.0	14.4	13 04.9	13.3	55.5
06		268 23.5	N18 14.9	69 48.4	14.4	S12 51.6	13.4	55.5
07		283 23.6	14.3	84 21.8	14.5	12 38.2	13.4	55.6
08		298 23.6	13.6	98 55.3	14.4	12 24.8	13.5	55.6
09		313 23.6	. . 13.0	113 28.7	14.5	12 11.3	13.5	55.6
10		328 23.7	12.4	128 02.2	14.6	11 57.8	13.6	55.6
11		343 23.7	11.8	142 35.8	14.5	11 44.2	13.7	55.6
12		358 23.8	N18 11.2	157 09.3	14.6	S11 30.5	13.7	55.7
13		13 23.8	10.5	171 42.9	14.7	11 16.8	13.8	55.7
14		28 23.8	09.9	186 16.6	14.6	11 03.0	13.8	55.7
15		43 23.9	. . 09.3	200 50.2	14.7	10 49.2	13.9	55.7
16		58 23.9	08.7	215 23.9	14.7	10 35.3	13.9	55.7
17		73 23.9	08.1	229 57.6	14.7	10 21.4	14.0	55.8
18		88 24.0	N18 07.4	244 31.3	14.7	S10 07.4	14.0	55.8
19		103 24.0	06.8	259 05.0	14.8	9 53.4	14.1	55.8
20		118 24.0	06.2	273 38.8	14.8	9 39.3	14.1	55.8
21		133 24.1	. . 05.6	288 12.6	14.8	9 25.2	14.2	55.8
22		148 24.1	04.9	302 46.4	14.9	9 11.0	14.2	55.8
23		163 24.1	04.3	317 20.3	14.8	8 56.8	14.3	55.9
1 00	SATURDAY	178 24.2	N18 03.7	331 54.1	14.9	S 8 42.5	14.3	55.9
01		193 24.2	03.1	346 28.0	14.9	8 28.2	14.3	55.9
02		208 24.3	02.4	1 01.9	14.9	8 13.9	14.4	55.9
03		223 24.3	. . 01.8	15 35.8	14.9	7 59.5	14.5	55.9
04		238 24.3	01.2	30 09.7	14.9	7 45.0	14.5	56.0
05		253 24.4	18 00.5	44 43.6	15.0	7 30.5	14.5	56.0
06		268 24.4	N17 59.9	59 17.6	14.9	S 7 16.0	14.5	56.0
07		283 24.4	59.3	73 51.5	15.0	7 01.5	14.6	56.0
08		298 24.5	58.7	88 25.5	15.0	6 46.9	14.7	56.1
09		313 24.5	. . 58.0	102 59.5	14.9	6 32.2	14.7	56.1
10		328 24.6	57.4	117 33.4	15.0	6 17.5	14.7	56.1
11		343 24.6	56.8	132 07.4	15.0	6 02.8	14.7	56.1
12		358 24.6	N17 56.1	146 41.4	15.0	S 5 48.1	14.8	56.1
13		13 24.7	55.5	161 15.4	15.1	5 33.3	14.8	56.2
14		28 24.7	54.9	175 49.5	15.0	5 18.5	14.9	56.2
15		43 24.8	. . 54.2	190 23.5	15.0	5 03.6	14.8	56.2
16		58 24.8	53.6	204 57.5	15.0	4 48.8	14.9	56.2
17		73 24.9	53.0	219 31.5	15.0	4 33.9	15.0	56.2
18		88 24.9	N17 52.3	234 05.5	15.1	S 4 18.9	14.9	56.3
19		103 24.9	51.7	248 39.6	15.0	4 04.0	15.0	56.3
20		118 25.0	51.1	263 13.6	15.0	3 49.0	15.0	56.3
21		133 25.0	. . 50.4	277 47.6	15.0	3 34.0	15.1	56.3
22		148 25.1	49.8	292 21.6	15.0	3 18.9	15.0	56.3
23		163 25.1	49.1	306 55.6	15.0	S 3 03.9	15.1	56.4
		SD 15.8	*d* 0.6	SD 15.0		15.2		15.3

Lat. (°)	Twilight Naut. (h m)	Twilight Civil (h m)	Sunrise (h m)	Moonrise 30 (h m)	Moonrise 31 (h m)	Moonrise 1 (h m)	Moonrise 2 (h m)
N 72	□	□	□	22 40	21 50	21 14	20 42
N 70	////	////	01 17	22 11	21 36	21 10	20 45
68	////	////	02 10	21 49	21 25	21 06	20 47
66	////	////	02 42	21 31	21 16	21 02	20 49
64	////	01 33	03 05	21 17	21 08	20 59	20 51
62	////	02 11	03 23	21 05	21 01	20 57	20 53
60	////	02 37	03 38	20 55	20 55	20 55	20 54
N 58	01 25	02 57	03 51	20 46	20 50	20 53	20 55
56	01 59	03 13	04 02	20 38	20 45	20 51	20 57
54	02 23	03 27	04 12	20 31	20 41	20 49	20 58
52	02 42	03 39	04 20	20 24	20 37	20 48	20 59
50	02 57	03 49	04 28	20 18	20 33	20 46	20 59
45	03 27	04 10	04 44	20 06	20 26	20 44	21 01
N 40	03 49	04 27	04 57	19 56	20 19	20 41	21 03
35	04 07	04 41	05 09	19 47	20 14	20 39	21 04
30	04 21	04 52	05 18	19 39	20 09	20 37	21 06
20	04 44	05 12	05 35	19 25	20 00	20 34	21 08
N 10	05 01	05 27	05 50	19 13	19 53	20 31	21 10
0	05 16	05 41	06 03	19 02	19 45	20 28	21 11
S 10	05 29	05 54	06 16	18 50	19 38	20 26	21 13
20	05 40	06 07	06 30	18 38	19 31	20 23	21 15
30	05 52	06 21	06 46	18 24	19 22	20 20	21 18
35	05 58	06 29	06 55	18 16	19 17	20 18	21 19
40	06 04	06 37	07 06	18 07	19 11	20 16	21 21
45	06 11	06 46	07 18	17 56	19 04	20 13	21 23
S 50	06 18	06 58	07 33	17 42	18 56	20 10	21 25
52	06 22	07 03	07 40	17 36	18 52	20 09	21 26
54	06 25	07 08	07 48	17 29	18 48	20 07	21 27
56	06 29	07 14	07 56	17 21	18 44	20 06	21 28
58	06 33	07 21	08 06	17 13	18 39	20 04	21 29
S 60	06 37	07 28	08 17	17 02	18 33	20 02	21 31

Lat. (°)	Sunset (h m)	Twilight Civil (h m)	Twilight Naut. (h m)	Moonset 30 (h m)	Moonset 31 (h m)	Moonset 1 (h m)	Moonset 2 (h m)
N 72	□	□	□	■	04 09	06 31	08 40
N 70	22 48	////	////	01 55	04 37	06 43	08 41
68	21 59	////	////	02 46	04 57	06 52	08 42
66	21 28	////	////	03 18	05 13	06 59	08 43
64	21 06	22 34	////	03 41	05 26	07 05	08 43
62	20 48	21 59	////	03 59	05 37	07 11	08 44
60	20 33	21 34	////	04 14	05 46	07 15	08 44
N 58	20 20	21 14	22 43	04 27	05 54	07 19	08 44
56	20 10	20 58	22 11	04 38	06 01	07 23	08 45
54	20 00	20 45	21 47	04 48	06 07	07 26	08 45
52	19 52	20 33	21 29	04 56	06 13	07 29	08 45
50	19 44	20 23	21 14	05 04	06 18	07 32	08 46
45	19 28	20 02	20 44	05 20	06 29	07 37	08 46
N 40	19 15	19 45	20 23	05 33	06 38	07 42	08 47
35	19 04	19 32	20 05	05 44	06 45	07 46	08 47
30	18 54	19 20	19 51	05 54	06 52	07 50	08 47
20	18 38	19 01	19 29	06 10	07 03	07 56	08 48
N 10	18 23	18 45	19 11	06 25	07 13	08 01	08 48
0	18 10	18 32	18 57	06 38	07 23	08 06	08 49
S 10	17 57	18 19	18 44	06 51	07 32	08 11	08 49
20	17 43	18 06	18 33	07 06	07 42	08 16	08 50
30	17 27	17 52	18 21	07 22	07 53	08 22	08 50
35	17 18	17 45	18 15	07 31	07 59	08 25	08 50
40	17 07	17 36	18 09	07 41	08 06	08 29	08 51
45	16 55	17 27	18 02	07 54	08 15	08 33	08 51
S 50	16 40	17 16	17 55	08 09	08 25	08 39	08 51
52	16 33	17 11	17 52	08 16	08 29	08 41	08 52
54	16 26	17 05	17 48	08 23	08 34	08 43	08 52
56	16 17	16 59	17 45	08 32	08 40	08 46	08 52
58	16 08	16 53	17 41	08 41	08 46	08 49	08 52
S 60	15 56	16 45	17 37	08 52	08 53	08 53	08 52

Day	SUN Eqn. of Time 00^h	SUN Eqn. of Time 12^h	SUN Mer. Pass.	MOON Mer. Pass. Upper	MOON Mer. Pass. Lower	MOON Age		MOON Phase
d	m s	m s	h m	h m	h m	d	%	
30	06 29	06 28	12 06	00 27	12 50	16	99	
31	06 27	06 25	12 06	01 12	13 34	17	97	○
1	06 23	06 21	12 06	01 56	14 17	18	92	

Day	UT d h	ARIES GHA ° ′	VENUS −4·3 GHA ° ′	VENUS Dec ° ′	MARS +1·3 GHA ° ′	MARS Dec ° ′	JUPITER −1·8 GHA ° ′	JUPITER Dec ° ′	SATURN +0·6 GHA ° ′	SATURN Dec ° ′
	2 00	310 36.4	135 09.0	N 1 51.2	227 25.5	N23 23.8	180 53.7	N18 56.3	296 04.6	N 3 27.9
	01	325 38.8	150 09.2	50.0	242 26.2	23.9	195 55.6	56.2	311 07.1	27.9
	02	340 41.3	165 09.4	48.7	257 26.8	24.0	210 57.5	56.0	326 09.5	27.9
	03	355 43.8	180 09.6	. . 47.5	272 27.4	. . 24.1	225 59.3	. . 55.9	341 12.0	. . 27.9
	04	10 46.2	195 09.8	46.3	287 28.1	24.2	241 01.2	55.7	356 14.5	27.8
	05	25 48.7	210 09.9	45.1	302 28.7	24.4	256 03.1	55.6	11 17.0	27.8
	06	40 51.2	225 10.1	N 1 43.8	317 29.3	N23 24.5	271 05.0	N18 55.5	26 19.5	N 3 27.8
	07	55 53.6	240 10.3	42.6	332 30.0	24.6	286 06.9	55.3	41 22.0	27.8
	08	70 56.1	255 10.5	41.4	347 30.6	24.7	301 08.8	55.2	56 24.5	27.8
S	09	85 58.5	270 10.7	. . 40.2	2 31.2	. . 24.8	316 10.7	. . 55.1	71 26.9	. . 27.7
U	10	101 01.0	285 10.9	38.9	17 31.8	24.9	331 12.6	54.9	86 29.4	27.7
N	11	116 03.5	300 11.0	37.7	32 32.5	25.0	346 14.5	54.8	101 31.9	27.7
D	12	131 05.9	315 11.2	N 1 36.5	47 33.1	N23 25.1	1 16.4	N18 54.6	116 34.4	N 3 27.7
A	13	146 08.4	330 11.4	35.3	62 33.7	25.2	16 18.3	54.5	131 36.9	27.6
Y	14	161 10.9	345 11.6	34.0	77 34.4	25.3	31 20.2	54.4	146 39.4	27.6
	15	176 13.3	0 11.8	. . 32.8	92 35.0	. . 25.5	46 22.1	. . 54.2	161 41.9	. . 27.6
	16	191 15.8	15 12.0	31.6	107 35.6	25.6	61 24.0	54.1	176 44.3	27.6
	17	206 18.3	30 12.1	30.4	122 36.3	25.7	76 25.9	54.0	191 46.8	27.6
	18	221 20.7	45 12.3	N 1 29.1	137 36.9	N23 25.8	91 27.8	N18 53.8	206 49.3	N 3 27.5
	19	236 23.2	60 12.5	27.9	152 37.5	25.9	106 29.7	53.7	221 51.8	27.5
	20	251 25.6	75 12.7	26.7	167 38.2	26.0	121 31.6	53.5	236 54.3	27.5
	21	266 28.1	90 12.9	. . 25.5	182 38.8	. . 26.1	136 33.5	. . 53.4	251 56.8	. . 27.5
	22	281 30.6	105 13.1	24.2	197 39.4	26.2	151 35.4	53.3	266 59.3	27.4
	23	296 33.0	120 13.3	23.0	212 40.1	26.3	166 37.3	53.1	282 01.8	27.4
	3 00	311 35.5	135 13.5	N 1 21.8	227 40.7	N23 26.4	181 39.2	N18 53.0	297 04.2	N 3 27.4
	01	326 38.0	150 13.7	20.6	242 41.3	26.5	196 41.1	52.9	312 06.7	27.4
	02	341 40.4	165 13.9	19.3	257 42.0	26.6	211 43.0	52.7	327 09.2	27.4
	03	356 42.9	180 14.1	. . 18.1	272 42.6	. . 26.7	226 44.9	. . 52.6	342 11.7	. . 27.3
	04	11 45.4	195 14.2	16.9	287 43.2	26.8	241 46.8	52.4	357 14.2	27.3
	05	26 47.8	210 14.4	15.7	302 43.9	26.9	256 48.7	52.3	12 16.7	27.3
	06	41 50.3	225 14.6	N 1 14.4	317 44.5	N23 27.0	271 50.6	N18 52.2	27 19.2	N 3 27.3
	07	56 52.8	240 14.8	13.2	332 45.1	27.1	286 52.5	52.0	42 21.7	27.2
	08	71 55.2	255 15.0	12.0	347 45.8	27.2	301 54.4	51.9	57 24.2	27.2
M	09	86 57.7	270 15.2	. . 10.8	2 46.4	. . 27.3	316 56.3	. . 51.8	72 26.6	. . 27.2
O	10	102 00.1	285 15.4	09.5	17 47.0	27.4	331 58.2	51.6	87 29.1	27.2
N	11	117 02.6	300 15.6	08.3	32 47.7	27.5	347 00.1	51.5	102 31.6	27.2
D	12	132 05.1	315 15.8	N 1 07.1	47 48.3	N23 27.6	2 02.0	N18 51.3	117 34.1	N 3 27.1
A	13	147 07.5	330 16.0	05.9	62 48.9	27.8	17 03.9	51.2	132 36.6	27.1
Y	14	162 10.0	345 16.2	04.6	77 49.6	27.9	32 05.8	51.1	147 39.1	27.1
	15	177 12.5	0 16.4	. . 03.4	92 50.2	. . 28.0	47 07.7	. . 50.9	162 41.6	. . 27.1
	16	192 14.9	15 16.6	02.2	107 50.8	28.0	62 09.6	50.8	177 44.1	27.0
	17	207 17.4	30 16.8	1 01.0	122 51.5	28.1	77 11.5	50.6	192 46.6	27.0
	18	222 19.9	45 17.0	N 0 59.7	137 52.1	N23 28.2	92 13.4	N18 50.5	207 49.1	N 3 27.0
	19	237 22.3	60 17.2	58.5	152 52.7	28.3	107 15.3	50.4	222 51.5	27.0
	20	252 24.8	75 17.4	57.3	167 53.4	28.4	122 17.2	50.2	237 54.0	26.9
	21	267 27.3	90 17.6	. . 56.1	182 54.0	. . 28.5	137 19.1	. . 50.1	252 56.5	. . 26.9
	22	282 29.7	105 17.8	54.8	197 54.6	28.6	152 21.0	50.0	267 59.0	26.9
	23	297 32.2	120 18.0	53.6	212 55.3	28.7	167 22.9	49.8	283 01.5	26.9
	4 00	312 34.6	135 18.2	N 0 52.4	227 55.9	N23 28.8	182 24.8	N18 49.7	298 04.0	N 3 26.9
	01	327 37.1	150 18.4	51.2	242 56.5	28.9	197 26.7	49.5	313 06.5	26.8
	02	342 39.6	165 18.6	49.9	257 57.2	29.0	212 28.6	49.4	328 09.0	26.8
	03	357 42.0	180 18.8	. . 48.7	272 57.8	. . 29.1	227 30.5	. . 49.3	343 11.5	. . 26.8
	04	12 44.5	195 19.1	47.5	287 58.4	29.2	242 32.4	49.1	358 14.0	26.8
	05	27 47.0	210 19.3	46.3	302 59.1	29.3	257 34.3	49.0	13 16.5	26.7
	06	42 49.4	225 19.5	N 0 45.0	317 59.7	N23 29.4	272 36.2	N18 48.9	28 19.0	N 3 26.7
	07	57 51.9	240 19.7	43.8	333 00.4	29.5	287 38.0	48.7	43 21.4	26.7
T	08	72 54.4	255 19.9	42.6	348 01.0	29.6	302 39.9	48.6	58 23.9	26.7
U	09	87 56.8	270 20.1	. . 41.4	3 01.6	. . 29.7	317 41.8	. . 48.4	73 26.4	. . 26.6
E	10	102 59.3	285 20.3	40.1	18 02.3	29.8	332 43.7	48.3	88 28.9	26.6
S	11	118 01.7	300 20.5	38.9	33 02.9	29.9	347 45.6	48.2	103 31.4	26.6
D	12	133 04.2	315 20.7	N 0 37.7	48 03.5	N23 30.0	2 47.5	N18 48.0	118 33.9	N 3 26.6
A	13	148 06.7	330 20.9	36.5	63 04.2	30.1	17 49.4	47.9	133 36.4	26.5
Y	14	163 09.1	345 21.2	35.2	78 04.8	30.1	32 51.3	47.7	148 38.9	26.5
	15	178 11.6	0 21.4	. . 34.0	93 05.4	. . 30.2	47 53.2	. . 47.6	163 41.4	. . 26.5
	16	193 14.1	15 21.6	32.8	108 06.1	30.3	62 55.1	47.5	178 43.9	26.5
	17	208 16.5	30 21.8	31.6	123 06.7	30.4	77 57.0	47.3	193 46.4	26.4
	18	223 19.0	45 22.0	N 0 30.4	138 07.3	N23 30.5	92 58.9	N18 47.2	208 48.9	N 3 26.4
	19	238 21.5	60 22.2	29.1	153 08.0	30.6	108 00.8	47.0	223 51.4	26.4
	20	253 23.9	75 22.4	27.9	168 08.6	30.7	123 02.7	46.9	238 53.9	26.4
	21	268 26.4	90 22.7	. . 26.7	183 09.3	. . 30.8	138 04.6	. . 46.8	253 56.4	. . 26.3
	22	283 28.9	105 22.9	25.5	198 09.9	30.9	153 06.5	46.6	268 58.9	26.3
	23	298 31.3	120 23.1	24.2	213 10.5	31.0	168 08.4	46.5	284 01.4	26.3
	Mer. Pass.	h m 3 13.1	v 0.2	d 1.2	v 0.6	d 0.1	v 1.9	d 0.1	v 2.5	d 0.0

STARS

Name	SHA ° ′	Dec ° ′
Acamar	315 10.8	S40 11.5
Achernar	335 19.1	S57 05.7
Acrux	172 59.0	S63 15.1
Adhara	255 05.2	S29 00.3
Aldebaran	290 38.3	N16 33.8
Alioth	166 12.1	N55 49.2
Alkaid	152 51.1	N49 11.1
Alnair	27 30.8	S46 49.7
Alnilam	275 36.6	S 1 11.0
Alphard	217 46.8	S 8 46.4
Alphecca	126 02.5	N26 37.7
Alpheratz	357 33.2	N29 14.2
Altair	61 58.4	N 8 56.4
Ankaa	353 05.6	S42 09.4
Antares	112 14.0	S26 29.5
Arcturus	145 46.7	N19 02.8
Atria	107 06.7	S69 04.7
Avior	234 14.9	S59 35.6
Bellatrix	278 21.7	N 6 22.5
Betelgeuse	270 50.9	N 7 24.8
Canopus	263 52.3	S52 42.3
Capella	280 20.3	N46 01.3
Deneb	49 24.4	N45 22.6
Denebola	182 23.8	N14 25.5
Diphda	348 45.8	S17 50.2
Dubhe	193 40.0	N61 36.6
Elnath	278 00.5	N28 37.7
Eltanin	90 41.2	N51 29.3
Enif	33 37.2	N 9 59.9
Fomalhaut	15 12.8	S29 28.7
Gacrux	171 50.5	S57 16.0
Gienah	175 42.4	S17 41.4
Hadar	148 34.2	S60 30.3
Hamal	327 49.7	N23 35.3
Kaus Aust.	83 30.4	S34 22.3
Kochab	137 19.8	N74 03.0
Markab	13 28.3	N15 21.0
Menkar	314 04.8	N 4 11.7
Menkent	147 56.1	S36 30.2
Miaplacidus	221 39.0	S69 49.6
Mirfak	308 26.5	N49 57.2
Nunki	75 45.8	S26 15.8
Peacock	53 03.1	S56 38.9
Pollux	243 16.1	N27 57.7
Procyon	244 49.8	N 5 09.5
Rasalhague	95 57.1	N12 32.6
Regulus	207 33.4	N11 50.3
Rigel	281 02.8	S 8 10.1
Rigil Kent.	139 38.5	S60 57.0
Sabik	102 01.1	S15 45.5
Schedar	349 29.3	N56 40.9
Shaula	96 08.3	S37 07.4
Sirius	258 25.4	S16 45.0
Spica	158 21.0	S11 18.0
Suhail	222 45.8	S43 32.4
Vega	80 32.0	N38 48.6
Zuben'ubi	136 54.5	S16 09.2

	SHA ° ′	Mer. Pass. h m
Venus	183 38.0	14 59
Mars	276 05.2	8 49
Jupiter	230 03.7	11 52
Saturn	345 28.7	4 11

UT d	UT h	SUN GHA ° ′	SUN Dec ° ′	MOON GHA ° ′	v ′	MOON Dec ° ′	d ′	HP ′
2	00	178 25.2	N17 48.5	321 29.6	15.0	S 2 48.8	15.1	56.4
	01	193 25.2	47.9	336 03.6	15.0	2 33.7	15.2	56.4
	02	208 25.2	47.2	350 37.6	15.0	2 18.5	15.1	56.4
	03	223 25.3	. . 46.6	5 11.6	14.9	2 03.4	15.2	56.5
	04	238 25.3	45.9	19 45.5	15.0	1 48.2	15.2	56.5
	05	253 25.4	45.3	34 19.5	14.9	1 33.0	15.2	56.5
	06	268 25.4	N17 44.7	48 53.4	14.9	S 1 17.8	15.2	56.5
	07	283 25.5	44.0	63 27.3	15.0	1 02.6	15.2	56.5
	08	298 25.5	43.4	78 01.3	14.8	0 47.4	15.3	56.6
SUNDAY	09	313 25.6	. . 42.7	92 35.1	14.9	0 32.1	15.3	56.6
	10	328 25.6	42.1	107 09.0	14.9	0 16.8	15.2	56.6
	11	343 25.7	41.4	121 42.9	14.8	S 0 01.6	15.3	56.6
	12	358 25.7	N17 40.8	136 16.7	14.8	N 0 13.7	15.3	56.7
	13	13 25.7	40.2	150 50.5	14.8	0 29.0	15.3	56.7
	14	28 25.8	39.5	165 24.3	14.8	0 44.3	15.3	56.7
	15	43 25.8	. . 38.9	179 58.1	14.7	0 59.6	15.3	56.7
	16	58 25.9	38.2	194 31.8	14.8	1 14.9	15.4	56.7
	17	73 25.9	37.6	209 05.6	14.7	1 30.3	15.3	56.8
	18	88 26.0	N17 36.9	223 39.3	14.6	N 1 45.6	15.3	56.8
	19	103 26.0	36.3	238 12.9	14.6	2 00.9	15.4	56.8
	20	118 26.1	35.6	252 46.5	14.6	2 16.3	15.3	56.8
	21	133 26.1	. . 35.0	267 20.1	14.6	2 31.6	15.3	56.9
	22	148 26.2	34.3	281 53.7	14.6	2 46.9	15.4	56.9
	23	163 26.2	33.7	296 27.3	14.5	3 02.3	15.3	56.9
3	00	178 26.3	N17 33.0	311 00.8	14.4	N 3 17.6	15.4	56.9
	01	193 26.3	32.4	325 34.2	14.4	3 33.0	15.3	56.9
	02	208 26.4	31.7	340 07.6	14.4	3 48.3	15.3	57.0
	03	223 26.4	. . 31.1	354 41.0	14.4	4 03.6	15.3	57.0
	04	238 26.5	30.4	9 14.4	14.3	4 18.9	15.3	57.0
	05	253 26.5	29.8	23 47.7	14.3	4 34.2	15.4	57.0
	06	268 26.6	N17 29.1	38 21.0	14.2	N 4 49.6	15.2	57.1
	07	283 26.6	28.5	52 54.2	14.2	5 04.8	15.3	57.1
	08	298 26.7	27.8	67 27.4	14.1	5 20.1	15.3	57.1
MONDAY	09	313 26.7	. . 27.2	82 00.5	14.1	5 35.4	15.3	57.1
	10	328 26.8	26.5	96 33.6	14.0	5 50.7	15.2	57.2
	11	343 26.8	25.8	111 06.6	14.0	6 05.9	15.2	57.2
	12	358 26.9	N17 25.2	125 39.6	13.9	N 6 21.1	15.3	57.2
	13	13 26.9	24.5	140 12.5	13.9	6 36.4	15.2	57.2
	14	28 27.0	23.9	154 45.4	13.8	6 51.6	15.1	57.3
	15	43 27.1	. . 23.2	169 18.2	13.8	7 06.7	15.2	57.3
	16	58 27.1	22.6	183 51.0	13.7	7 21.9	15.1	57.3
	17	73 27.2	21.9	198 23.7	13.7	7 37.0	15.1	57.3
	18	88 27.2	N17 21.2	212 56.4	13.6	N 7 52.1	15.1	57.3
	19	103 27.3	20.6	227 29.0	13.5	8 07.2	15.1	57.4
	20	118 27.3	19.9	242 01.5	13.5	8 22.3	15.0	57.4
	21	133 27.4	. . 19.3	256 34.0	13.4	8 37.3	15.1	57.4
	22	148 27.4	18.6	271 06.4	13.3	8 52.4	14.9	57.4
	23	163 27.5	17.9	285 38.7	13.3	9 07.3	15.0	57.5
4	00	178 27.5	N17 17.3	300 11.0	13.2	N 9 22.3	14.9	57.5
	01	193 27.6	16.6	314 43.2	13.2	9 37.2	14.9	57.5
	02	208 27.7	15.9	329 15.4	13.1	9 52.1	14.9	57.5
	03	223 27.7	. . 15.3	343 47.5	13.0	10 07.0	14.8	57.6
	04	238 27.8	14.6	358 19.5	12.9	10 21.8	14.8	57.6
	05	253 27.8	13.9	12 51.4	12.9	10 36.6	14.7	57.6
	06	268 27.9	N17 13.3	27 23.3	12.7	N10 51.3	14.8	57.6
	07	283 27.9	12.6	41 55.0	12.8	11 06.1	14.6	57.7
	08	298 28.0	12.0	56 26.8	12.6	11 20.7	14.7	57.7
TUESDAY	09	313 28.1	. . 11.3	70 58.4	12.5	11 35.4	14.6	57.7
	10	328 28.1	10.6	85 29.9	12.5	11 50.0	14.5	57.7
	11	343 28.2	10.0	100 01.4	12.4	12 04.5	14.5	57.8
	12	358 28.2	N17 09.3	114 32.8	12.3	N12 19.0	14.4	57.8
	13	13 28.3	08.6	129 04.1	12.3	12 33.4	14.4	57.8
	14	28 28.4	07.9	143 35.4	12.1	12 47.8	14.4	57.8
	15	43 28.4	. . 07.3	158 06.5	12.1	13 02.2	14.3	57.9
	16	58 28.5	06.6	172 37.6	11.9	13 16.5	14.3	57.9
	17	73 28.5	05.9	187 08.5	11.9	13 30.8	14.1	57.9
	18	88 28.6	N17 05.3	201 39.4	11.8	N13 44.9	14.2	57.9
	19	103 28.7	04.6	216 10.2	11.7	13 59.1	14.1	58.0
	20	118 28.7	03.9	230 40.9	11.6	14 13.2	14.0	58.0
	21	133 28.8	. . 03.2	245 11.5	11.5	14 27.2	14.0	58.0
	22	148 28.8	02.6	259 42.0	11.5	14 41.2	13.9	58.0
	23	163 28.9	01.9	274 12.5	11.3	N14 55.1	13.8	58.1
		SD 15.8	d 0.7	SD 15.4		15.6		15.7

Lat. °	Twilight Naut. h m	Twilight Civil h m	Sunrise h m	Moonrise 2 h m	Moonrise 3 h m	Moonrise 4 h m	Moonrise 5 h m
N 72	▭	▭	▭	20 42	20 06	19 17	▭
N 70	////	////	01 43	20 45	20 18	19 44	18 36
68	////	////	02 25	20 47	20 28	20 04	19 26
66	////	00 53	02 53	20 49	20 36	20 20	19 58
64	////	01 51	03 14	20 51	20 43	20 33	20 22
62	////	02 23	03 31	20 53	20 49	20 45	20 41
60	00 48	02 46	03 45	20 54	20 54	20 54	20 57
N 58	01 40	03 05	03 57	20 55	20 59	21 03	21 10
56	02 10	03 20	04 08	20 57	21 03	21 11	21 22
54	02 32	03 33	04 17	20 58	21 07	21 17	21 32
52	02 49	03 44	04 25	20 59	21 10	21 23	21 41
50	03 04	03 54	04 32	20 59	21 13	21 29	21 49
45	03 32	04 14	04 47	21 01	21 20	21 41	22 07
N 40	03 53	04 30	05 00	21 03	21 26	21 51	22 21
35	04 10	04 43	05 11	21 04	21 31	22 00	22 33
30	04 23	04 54	05 20	21 06	21 35	22 07	22 44
20	04 45	05 13	05 36	21 08	21 43	22 20	23 03
N 10	05 02	05 28	05 50	21 10	21 50	22 32	23 19
0	05 16	05 41	06 03	21 11	21 56	22 43	23 34
S 10	05 28	05 53	06 15	21 13	22 03	22 54	23 50
20	05 39	06 06	06 29	21 15	22 10	23 06	24 07
30	05 50	06 19	06 44	21 18	22 18	23 20	24 26
35	05 56	06 26	06 53	21 19	22 22	23 28	24 37
40	06 02	06 34	07 03	21 21	22 28	23 37	24 50
45	06 08	06 43	07 14	21 23	22 34	23 48	25 06
S 50	06 15	06 53	07 28	21 25	22 41	24 01	00 01
52	06 17	06 58	07 35	21 26	22 45	24 08	00 08
54	06 21	07 03	07 42	21 27	22 49	24 15	00 15
56	06 24	07 09	07 50	21 28	22 53	24 22	00 22
58	06 27	07 15	08 00	21 29	22 58	24 31	00 31
S 60	06 31	07 22	08 10	21 31	23 03	24 41	00 41

Lat. °	Sunset h m	Twilight Civil h m	Twilight Naut. h m	Moonset 2 h m	Moonset 3 h m	Moonset 4 h m	Moonset 5 h m
N 72	▭	▭	▭	08 40	10 50	13 16	▭
N 70	22 23	////	////	08 41	10 41	12 52	15 44
68	21 43	////	////	08 42	10 34	12 34	14 55
66	21 16	23 09	////	08 43	10 28	12 19	14 25
64	20 56	22 17	////	08 43	10 23	12 07	14 02
62	20 39	21 46	////	08 44	10 18	11 57	13 44
60	20 25	21 24	23 15	08 44	10 14	11 49	13 29
N 58	20 14	21 06	22 28	08 44	10 11	11 41	13 17
56	20 04	20 51	22 00	08 45	10 08	11 35	13 06
54	19 55	20 38	21 39	08 45	10 06	11 29	12 57
52	19 47	20 27	21 22	08 45	10 03	11 24	12 48
50	19 39	20 18	21 07	08 46	10 01	11 19	12 41
45	19 24	19 58	20 39	08 46	09 56	11 09	12 25
N 40	19 12	19 42	20 19	08 47	09 52	11 01	12 12
35	19 01	19 29	20 02	08 47	09 49	10 53	12 01
30	18 52	19 18	19 48	08 47	09 46	10 47	11 51
20	18 36	18 59	19 27	08 48	09 41	10 36	11 35
N 10	18 22	18 44	19 10	08 48	09 37	10 27	11 20
0	18 10	18 31	18 57	08 49	09 32	10 18	11 07
S 10	17 57	18 19	18 44	08 49	09 28	10 09	10 54
20	17 44	18 07	18 33	08 50	09 24	10 00	10 40
30	17 29	17 54	18 23	08 50	09 19	09 49	10 24
35	17 20	17 47	18 17	08 50	09 16	09 43	10 14
40	17 10	17 39	18 11	08 51	09 13	09 36	10 04
45	16 58	17 30	18 05	08 51	09 09	09 28	09 51
S 50	16 44	17 20	17 58	08 51	09 04	09 19	09 36
52	16 38	17 15	17 56	08 52	09 02	09 14	09 29
54	16 31	17 10	17 53	08 52	09 00	09 10	09 22
56	16 23	17 04	17 49	08 52	08 58	09 04	09 13
58	16 14	16 58	17 46	08 52	08 55	08 58	09 03
S 60	16 03	16 51	17 42	08 52	08 52	08 52	08 52

Day	SUN Eqn. of Time 00^h m s	SUN Eqn. of Time 12^h m s	SUN Mer. Pass. h m	MOON Mer. Pass. Upper h m	MOON Mer. Pass. Lower h m	MOON Age d	MOON Phase %
2	06 19	06 17	12 06	02 39	15 00	19	85
3	06 15	06 13	12 06	03 22	15 44	20	77
4	06 10	06 07	12 06	04 07	16 30	21	67

2026 AUGUST 5, 6, 7 (WED., THURS., FRI.)

Day	UT d h	ARIES GHA ° ′	VENUS −4·3 GHA ° ′	VENUS Dec ° ′	MARS +1·3 GHA ° ′	MARS Dec ° ′	JUPITER −1·8 GHA ° ′	JUPITER Dec ° ′	SATURN +0·5 GHA ° ′	SATURN Dec ° ′
WEDNESDAY	5 00	313 33.8	135 23.3	N 0 23.0	228 11.2	N23 31.0	183 10.3	N18 46.4	299 03.9	N 3 26.3
	01	328 36.2	150 23.5	21.8	243 11.8	31.1	198 12.2	46.2	314 06.3	26.2
	02	343 38.7	165 23.8	20.6	258 12.4	31.2	213 14.1	46.1	329 08.8	26.2
	03	358 41.2	180 24.0	. . 19.3	273 13.1	. . 31.3	228 16.0	. . 45.9	344 11.3	. . 26.2
	04	13 43.6	195 24.2	18.1	288 13.7	31.4	243 17.9	45.8	359 13.8	26.2
	05	28 46.1	210 24.4	16.9	303 14.4	31.5	258 19.8	45.7	14 16.3	26.1
	06	43 48.6	225 24.6	N 0 15.7	318 15.0	N23 31.6	273 21.7	N18 45.5	29 18.8	N 3 26.1
	07	58 51.0	240 24.9	14.4	333 15.6	31.7	288 23.6	45.4	44 21.3	26.1
	08	73 53.5	255 25.1	13.2	348 16.3	31.7	303 25.5	45.2	59 23.8	26.1
	09	88 56.0	270 25.3	. . 12.0	3 16.9	. . 31.8	318 27.4	. . 45.1	74 26.3	. . 26.0
	10	103 58.4	285 25.5	10.8	18 17.5	31.9	333 29.3	45.0	89 28.8	26.0
	11	119 00.9	300 25.8	09.5	33 18.2	32.0	348 31.2	44.8	104 31.3	26.0
	12	134 03.3	315 26.0	N 0 08.3	48 18.8	N23 32.1	3 33.1	N18 44.7	119 33.8	N 3 26.0
	13	149 05.8	330 26.2	07.1	63 19.5	32.2	18 35.0	44.5	134 36.3	25.9
	14	164 08.3	345 26.4	05.9	78 20.1	32.2	33 36.9	44.4	149 38.8	25.9
	15	179 10.7	0 26.7	. . 04.6	93 20.7	. . 32.3	48 38.8	. . 44.3	164 41.3	. . 25.9
	16	194 13.2	15 26.9	03.4	108 21.4	32.4	63 40.7	44.1	179 43.8	25.8
	17	209 15.7	30 27.1	02.2	123 22.0	32.5	78 42.6	44.0	194 46.3	25.8
	18	224 18.1	45 27.3	N 0 01.0	138 22.7	N23 32.6	93 44.5	N18 43.9	209 48.8	N 3 25.8
	19	239 20.6	60 27.6	S 00.2	153 23.3	32.7	108 46.4	43.7	224 51.3	25.8
	20	254 23.1	75 27.8	01.5	168 23.9	32.7	123 48.3	43.6	239 53.8	25.7
	21	269 25.5	90 28.0	. . 02.7	183 24.6	. . 32.8	138 50.2	. . 43.4	254 56.3	. . 25.7
	22	284 28.0	105 28.3	03.9	198 25.2	32.9	153 52.1	43.3	269 58.8	25.7
	23	299 30.5	120 28.5	05.1	213 25.8	33.0	168 54.0	43.2	285 01.3	25.7
THURSDAY	6 00	314 32.9	135 28.7	S 0 06.4	228 26.5	N23 33.1	183 55.9	N18 43.0	300 03.8	N 3 25.6
	01	329 35.4	150 29.0	07.6	243 27.1	33.1	198 57.8	42.9	315 06.3	25.6
	02	344 37.8	165 29.2	08.8	258 27.8	33.2	213 59.7	42.7	330 08.8	25.6
	03	359 40.3	180 29.4	. . 10.0	273 28.4	. . 33.3	229 01.6	. . 42.6	345 11.3	. . 25.6
	04	14 42.8	195 29.7	11.3	288 29.0	33.4	244 03.5	42.5	0 13.8	25.5
	05	29 45.2	210 29.9	12.5	303 29.7	33.4	259 05.4	42.3	15 16.3	25.5
	06	44 47.7	225 30.1	S 0 13.7	318 30.3	N23 33.5	274 07.3	N18 42.2	30 18.8	N 3 25.5
	07	59 50.2	240 30.4	14.9	333 31.0	33.6	289 09.2	42.0	45 21.3	25.4
	08	74 52.6	255 30.6	16.2	348 31.6	33.7	304 11.1	41.9	60 23.8	25.4
	09	89 55.1	270 30.8	. . 17.4	3 32.2	. . 33.8	319 13.0	. . 41.8	75 26.3	. . 25.4
	10	104 57.6	285 31.1	18.6	18 32.9	33.8	334 14.9	41.6	90 28.8	25.4
	11	120 00.0	300 31.3	19.8	33 33.5	33.9	349 16.8	41.5	105 31.3	25.3
	12	135 02.5	315 31.5	S 0 21.0	48 34.2	N23 34.0	4 18.7	N18 41.3	120 33.8	N 3 25.3
	13	150 05.0	330 31.8	22.3	63 34.8	34.1	19 20.6	41.2	135 36.3	25.3
	14	165 07.4	345 32.0	23.5	78 35.4	34.1	34 22.5	41.1	150 38.8	25.3
	15	180 09.9	0 32.3	. . 24.7	93 36.1	. . 34.2	49 24.4	. . 40.9	165 41.3	. . 25.2
	16	195 12.3	15 32.5	25.9	108 36.7	34.3	64 26.3	40.8	180 43.8	25.2
	17	210 14.8	30 32.8	27.2	123 37.4	34.4	79 28.2	40.6	195 46.3	25.2
	18	225 17.3	45 33.0	S 0 28.4	138 38.0	N23 34.4	94 30.1	N18 40.5	210 48.8	N 3 25.1
	19	240 19.7	60 33.2	29.6	153 38.7	34.5	109 32.0	40.4	225 51.3	25.1
	20	255 22.2	75 33.5	30.8	168 39.3	34.6	124 33.9	40.2	240 53.8	25.1
	21	270 24.7	90 33.7	. . 32.0	183 39.9	. . 34.6	139 35.8	. . 40.1	255 56.3	. . 25.1
	22	285 27.1	105 34.0	33.3	198 40.6	34.7	154 37.7	39.9	270 58.8	25.0
	23	300 29.6	120 34.2	34.5	213 41.2	34.8	169 39.6	39.8	286 01.3	25.0
FRIDAY	7 00	315 32.1	135 34.5	S 0 35.7	228 41.9	N23 34.9	184 41.5	N18 39.7	301 03.8	N 3 25.0
	01	330 34.5	150 34.7	36.9	243 42.5	34.9	199 43.4	39.5	316 06.3	24.9
	02	345 37.0	165 35.0	38.2	258 43.1	35.0	214 45.3	39.4	331 08.8	24.9
	03	0 39.5	180 35.2	. . 39.4	273 43.8	. . 35.1	229 47.2	. . 39.2	346 11.3	. . 24.9
	04	15 41.9	195 35.4	40.6	288 44.4	35.1	244 49.1	39.1	1 13.8	24.9
	05	30 44.4	210 35.7	41.8	303 45.1	35.2	259 51.0	39.0	16 16.4	24.8
	06	45 46.8	225 35.9	S 0 43.0	318 45.7	N23 35.3	274 52.9	N18 38.8	31 18.9	N 3 24.8
	07	60 49.3	240 36.2	44.3	333 46.4	35.3	289 54.8	38.7	46 21.4	24.8
	08	75 51.8	255 36.4	45.5	348 47.0	35.4	304 56.7	38.5	61 23.9	24.7
	09	90 54.2	270 36.7	. . 46.7	3 47.6	. . 35.5	319 58.6	. . 38.4	76 26.4	. . 24.7
	10	105 56.7	285 36.9	47.9	18 48.3	35.6	335 00.5	38.3	91 28.9	24.7
	11	120 59.2	300 37.2	49.2	33 48.9	35.6	350 02.4	38.1	106 31.4	24.7
	12	136 01.6	315 37.4	S 0 50.4	48 49.6	N23 35.7	5 04.3	N18 38.0	121 33.9	N 3 24.6
	13	151 04.1	330 37.7	51.6	63 50.2	35.8	20 06.2	37.8	136 36.4	24.6
	14	166 06.6	345 38.0	52.8	78 50.9	35.8	35 08.1	37.7	151 38.9	24.6
	15	181 09.0	0 38.2	. . 54.0	93 51.5	. . 35.9	50 10.0	. . 37.6	166 41.4	. . 24.5
	16	196 11.5	15 38.5	55.3	108 52.1	35.9	65 11.9	37.4	181 43.9	24.5
	17	211 13.9	30 38.7	56.5	123 52.8	36.0	80 13.8	37.3	196 46.4	24.5
	18	226 16.4	45 39.0	S 0 57.7	138 53.4	N23 36.1	95 15.7	N18 37.1	211 48.9	N 3 24.4
	19	241 18.9	60 39.2	0 58.9	153 54.1	36.1	110 17.6	37.0	226 51.4	24.4
	20	256 21.3	75 39.5	1 00.1	168 54.7	36.2	125 19.6	36.9	241 53.9	24.4
	21	271 23.8	90 39.7	. . 01.4	183 55.4	. . 36.3	140 21.5	. . 36.7	256 56.4	. . 24.4
	22	286 26.3	105 40.0	02.6	198 56.0	36.3	155 23.4	36.6	271 58.9	24.3
	23	301 28.7	120 40.3	03.8	213 56.7	36.4	170 25.3	36.4	287 01.5	24.3
	Mer. Pass.	h m 3 01.3	v 0.2	d 1.2	v 0.6	d 0.1	v 1.9	d 0.1	v 2.5	d 0.0

STARS

Name	SHA ° ′	Dec ° ′
Acamar	315 10.8	S40 11.5
Achernar	335 19.0	S57 05.7
Acrux	172 59.0	S63 15.1
Adhara	255 05.2	S29 00.3
Aldebaran	290 38.3	N16 33.8
Alioth	166 12.1	N55 49.2
Alkaid	152 51.1	N49 11.1
Alnair	27 30.8	S46 49.7
Alnilam	275 36.6	S 1 11.0
Alphard	217 46.8	S 8 46.4
Alphecca	126 02.6	N26 37.7
Alpheratz	357 33.2	N29 14.3
Altair	61 58.4	N 8 56.4
Ankaa	353 05.6	S42 09.4
Antares	112 14.1	S26 29.5
Arcturus	145 46.8	N19 02.8
Atria	107 06.8	S69 04.7
Avior	234 14.9	S59 35.6
Bellatrix	278 21.7	N 6 22.5
Betelgeuse	270 50.9	N 7 24.8
Canopus	263 52.2	S52 42.3
Capella	280 20.2	N46 01.3
Deneb	49 24.4	N45 22.6
Denebola	182 23.8	N14 25.5
Diphda	348 45.8	S17 50.2
Dubhe	193 40.0	N61 36.6
Elnath	278 00.4	N28 37.7
Eltanin	90 41.2	N51 29.3
Enif	33 37.2	N 9 59.9
Fomalhaut	15 12.8	S29 28.7
Gacrux	171 50.5	S57 16.0
Gienah	175 42.4	S17 41.4
Hadar	148 34.2	S60 30.3
Hamal	327 49.6	N23 35.3
Kaus Aust.	83 30.4	S34 22.3
Kochab	137 19.8	N74 03.0
Markab	13 28.3	N15 21.0
Menkar	314 04.8	N 4 11.8
Menkent	147 56.1	S36 30.2
Miaplacidus	221 39.0	S69 49.6
Mirfak	308 26.4	N49 57.2
Nunki	75 45.8	S26 15.8
Peacock	53 03.1	S56 38.9
Pollux	243 16.1	N27 57.7
Procyon	244 49.8	N 5 09.5
Rasalhague	95 57.1	N12 32.6
Regulus	207 33.4	N11 50.3
Rigel	281 02.8	S 8 10.1
Rigil Kent.	139 38.5	S60 56.9
Sabik	102 01.1	S15 45.5
Schedar	349 29.2	N56 40.9
Shaula	96 08.3	S37 07.4
Sirius	258 25.4	S16 45.0
Spica	158 21.0	S11 18.0
Suhail	222 45.8	S43 32.4
Vega	80 32.0	N38 48.7
Zuben'ubi	136 54.6	S16 09.2

	SHA ° ′	Mer. Pass. h m
Venus	180 55.8	14 58
Mars	273 53.6	8 46
Jupiter	229 23.0	11 43
Saturn	345 30.9	3 59

UT d	h	SUN GHA ° ′	SUN Dec ° ′	MOON GHA ° ′	v ′	MOON Dec ° ′	d ′	HP ′
5	00	178 29.0	N17 01.2	288 42.8	11.2	N15 08.9	13.8	58.1
	01	193 29.0	17 00.6	303 13.0	11.2	15 22.7	13.7	58.1
	02	208 29.1	16 59.9	317 43.2	11.0	15 36.4	13.6	58.1
	03	223 29.2	. . 59.2	332 13.2	10.9	15 50.0	13.6	58.2
	04	238 29.2	58.5	346 43.1	10.9	16 03.6	13.5	58.2
	05	253 29.3	57.9	1 13.0	10.7	16 17.1	13.4	58.2
	06	268 29.3	N16 57.2	15 42.7	10.6	N16 30.5	13.4	58.2
W	07	283 29.4	56.5	30 12.3	10.6	16 43.9	13.3	58.3
E	08	298 29.5	55.8	44 41.9	10.4	16 57.2	13.2	58.3
D	09	313 29.5	. . 55.1	59 11.3	10.3	17 10.4	13.1	58.3
N	10	328 29.6	54.5	73 40.6	10.2	17 23.5	13.0	58.3
E	11	343 29.7	53.8	88 09.8	10.1	17 36.5	13.0	58.4
S	12	358 29.7	N16 53.1	102 38.9	10.0	N17 49.5	12.8	58.4
D	13	13 29.8	52.4	117 07.9	9.9	18 02.3	12.8	58.4
A	14	28 29.9	51.7	131 36.8	9.8	18 15.1	12.7	58.4
Y	15	43 29.9	. . 51.1	146 05.6	9.6	18 27.8	12.7	58.5
	16	58 30.0	50.4	160 34.2	9.6	18 40.5	12.5	58.5
	17	73 30.1	49.7	175 02.8	9.4	18 53.0	12.4	58.5
	18	88 30.1	N16 49.0	189 31.2	9.4	N19 05.4	12.3	58.5
	19	103 30.2	48.3	203 59.6	9.2	19 17.7	12.3	58.6
	20	118 30.3	47.6	218 27.8	9.1	19 30.0	12.1	58.6
	21	133 30.3	. . 47.0	232 55.9	8.9	19 42.1	12.1	58.6
	22	148 30.4	46.3	247 23.8	8.9	19 54.2	11.9	58.6
	23	163 30.5	45.6	261 51.7	8.8	20 06.1	11.8	58.7
6	00	178 30.5	N16 44.9	276 19.5	8.6	N20 17.9	11.8	58.7
	01	193 30.6	44.2	290 47.1	8.5	20 29.7	11.6	58.7
	02	208 30.7	43.5	305 14.6	8.4	20 41.3	11.5	58.7
	03	223 30.7	. . 42.8	319 42.0	8.3	20 52.8	11.4	58.7
	04	238 30.8	42.2	334 09.3	8.1	21 04.2	11.3	58.8
	05	253 30.9	41.5	348 36.4	8.1	21 15.5	11.2	58.8
	06	268 30.9	N16 40.8	3 03.5	7.9	N21 26.7	11.1	58.8
T	07	283 31.0	40.1	17 30.4	7.8	21 37.8	10.9	58.8
H	08	298 31.1	39.4	31 57.2	7.7	21 48.7	10.9	58.9
U	09	313 31.2	. . 38.7	46 23.9	7.5	21 59.6	10.7	58.9
R	10	328 31.2	38.0	60 50.4	7.5	22 10.3	10.6	58.9
S	11	343 31.3	37.3	75 16.9	7.3	22 20.9	10.4	58.9
D	12	358 31.4	N16 36.6	89 43.2	7.2	N22 31.3	10.4	59.0
A	13	13 31.4	36.0	104 09.4	7.1	22 41.7	10.2	59.0
Y	14	28 31.5	35.3	118 35.5	6.9	22 51.9	10.1	59.0
	15	43 31.6	. . 34.6	133 01.4	6.9	23 02.0	9.9	59.0
	16	58 31.7	33.9	147 27.3	6.7	23 11.9	9.8	59.1
	17	73 31.7	33.2	161 53.0	6.6	23 21.7	9.7	59.1
	18	88 31.8	N16 32.5	176 18.6	6.5	N23 31.4	9.5	59.1
	19	103 31.9	31.8	190 44.1	6.3	23 40.9	9.5	59.1
	20	118 31.9	31.1	205 09.4	6.3	23 50.4	9.2	59.2
	21	133 32.0	. . 30.4	219 34.7	6.1	23 59.6	9.1	59.2
	22	148 32.1	29.7	233 59.8	6.0	24 08.7	9.0	59.2
	23	163 32.2	29.0	248 24.8	5.9	24 17.7	8.8	59.2
7	00	178 32.2	N16 28.3	262 49.7	5.8	N24 26.5	8.7	59.2
	01	193 32.3	27.6	277 14.5	5.6	24 35.2	8.5	59.3
	02	208 32.4	26.9	291 39.1	5.5	24 43.7	8.4	59.3
	03	223 32.5	. . 26.2	306 03.6	5.5	24 52.1	8.2	59.3
	04	238 32.5	25.5	320 28.1	5.3	25 00.3	8.1	59.3
	05	253 32.6	24.8	334 52.4	5.2	25 08.4	7.9	59.4
	06	268 32.7	N16 24.1	349 16.6	5.1	N25 16.3	7.8	59.4
	07	283 32.8	23.4	3 40.7	4.9	25 24.1	7.6	59.4
	08	298 32.8	22.7	18 04.6	4.9	25 31.7	7.4	59.4
F	09	313 32.9	. . 22.0	32 28.5	4.7	25 39.1	7.2	59.4
R	10	328 33.0	21.3	46 52.2	4.7	25 46.3	7.1	59.5
I	11	343 33.1	20.6	61 15.9	4.5	25 53.4	7.0	59.5
D	12	358 33.1	N16 19.9	75 39.4	4.5	N26 00.4	6.7	59.5
A	13	13 33.2	19.2	90 02.9	4.3	26 07.1	6.6	59.5
Y	14	28 33.3	18.5	104 26.2	4.2	26 13.7	6.4	59.5
	15	43 33.4	. . 17.8	118 49.4	4.1	26 20.1	6.3	59.6
	16	58 33.5	17.1	133 12.5	4.1	26 26.4	6.1	59.6
	17	73 33.5	16.4	147 35.6	3.9	26 32.5	5.9	59.6
	18	88 33.6	N16 15.7	161 58.5	3.8	N26 38.4	5.7	59.6
	19	103 33.7	15.0	176 21.3	3.8	26 44.1	5.5	59.6
	20	118 33.8	14.3	190 44.1	3.6	26 49.6	5.4	59.7
	21	133 33.8	. . 13.6	205 06.7	3.6	26 55.0	5.1	59.7
	22	148 33.9	12.9	219 29.3	3.5	27 00.1	5.0	59.7
	23	163 34.0	12.2	233 51.8	3.4	N27 05.1	4.8	59.7
		SD 15.8	*d* 0.7	SD	15.9	16.1		16.2

Lat. °	Twilight Naut. h m	Twilight Civil h m	Sunrise h m	Moonrise 5 h m	Moonrise 6 h m	Moonrise 7 h m	Moonrise 8 h m
N 72	////	////	00 58	▭	▭	▭	▭
N 70	////	////	02 04	18 36	▭	▭	▭
68	////	////	02 39	19 26	▭	▭	▭
66	////	01 23	03 04	19 58	19 05	▭	▭
64	////	02 06	03 24	20 22	20 03	▭	▭
62	////	02 34	03 39	20 41	20 37	20 34	20 37
60	01 15	02 56	03 52	20 57	21 02	21 17	21 56
N 58	01 54	03 13	04 04	21 10	21 22	21 45	22 32
56	02 20	03 27	04 13	21 22	21 39	22 08	22 59
54	02 40	03 39	04 22	21 32	21 53	22 26	23 19
52	02 56	03 49	04 29	21 41	22 05	22 42	23 37
50	03 10	03 59	04 36	21 49	22 16	22 56	23 52
45	03 36	04 18	04 51	22 07	22 40	23 23	24 22
N 40	03 57	04 33	05 03	22 21	22 58	23 46	24 45
35	04 12	04 46	05 13	22 33	23 14	24 04	00 04
30	04 26	04 56	05 22	22 44	23 28	24 20	00 20
20	04 46	05 14	05 37	23 03	23 51	24 47	00 47
N 10	05 03	05 28	05 50	23 19	24 11	00 11	01 10
0	05 16	05 41	06 02	23 34	24 31	00 31	01 32
S 10	05 27	05 53	06 15	23 50	24 50	00 50	01 53
20	05 38	06 04	06 27	24 07	00 07	01 11	02 17
30	05 48	06 17	06 42	24 26	00 26	01 35	02 44
35	05 53	06 23	06 50	24 37	00 37	01 49	03 01
40	05 59	06 31	06 59	24 50	00 50	02 06	03 20
45	06 04	06 39	07 10	25 06	01 06	02 26	03 43
S 50	06 10	06 49	07 24	00 01	01 25	02 51	04 12
52	06 13	06 53	07 30	00 08	01 34	03 03	04 27
54	06 16	06 58	07 37	00 15	01 45	03 17	04 44
56	06 19	07 04	07 44	00 22	01 56	03 33	05 04
58	06 22	07 09	07 53	00 31	02 10	03 53	05 30
S 60	06 25	07 16	08 03	00 41	02 26	04 17	06 05

Lat. °	Sunset h m	Twilight Civil h m	Twilight Naut. h m	Moonset 5 h m	Moonset 6 h m	Moonset 7 h m	Moonset 8 h m
N 72	23 01	////	////	▭	▭	▭	▭
N 70	22 02	////	////	15 44	▭	▭	▭
68	21 29	////	////	14 55	▭	▭	▭
66	21 04	22 41	////	14 25	17 12	▭	▭
64	20 46	22 01	////	14 02	16 14	▭	▭
62	20 30	21 34	////	13 44	15 41	17 49	20 00
60	20 18	21 14	22 50	13 29	15 17	17 07	18 41
N 58	20 07	20 57	22 14	13 17	14 58	16 38	18 05
56	19 57	20 43	21 49	13 06	14 42	16 16	17 39
54	19 49	20 31	21 30	12 57	14 28	15 58	17 18
52	19 41	20 21	21 14	12 48	14 16	15 43	17 01
50	19 35	20 12	21 01	12 41	14 05	15 30	16 46
45	19 20	19 53	20 34	12 25	13 44	15 02	16 16
N 40	19 08	19 38	20 14	12 12	13 26	14 41	15 52
35	18 58	19 26	19 59	12 01	13 11	14 23	15 33
30	18 49	19 15	19 46	11 51	12 58	14 08	15 17
20	18 34	18 58	19 25	11 35	12 37	13 42	14 49
N 10	18 21	18 43	19 09	11 20	12 18	13 20	14 24
0	18 09	18 31	18 56	11 07	12 00	12 59	14 02
S 10	17 57	18 19	18 45	10 54	11 43	12 38	13 40
20	17 45	18 08	18 34	10 40	11 25	12 16	13 15
30	17 30	17 55	18 24	10 24	11 03	11 51	12 47
35	17 22	17 49	18 19	10 14	10 51	11 36	12 31
40	17 13	17 41	18 14	10 04	10 37	11 18	12 12
45	17 02	17 33	18 08	09 51	10 20	10 58	11 48
S 50	16 49	17 23	18 02	09 36	09 59	10 32	11 18
52	16 43	17 19	17 59	09 29	09 49	10 19	11 03
54	16 36	17 14	17 57	09 22	09 39	10 04	10 46
56	16 28	17 09	17 54	09 13	09 26	09 48	10 26
58	16 20	17 03	17 51	09 03	09 12	09 28	10 00
S 60	16 10	16 57	17 47	08 52	08 55	09 02	09 24

Day	SUN Eqn. of Time 00h	SUN Eqn. of Time 12h	SUN Mer. Pass.	MOON Mer. Pass. Upper	MOON Mer. Pass. Lower	MOON Age	MOON Phase
d	m s	m s	h m	h m	h m	d %	
5	06 04	06 01	12 06	04 55	17 21	22 57	
6	05 58	05 55	12 06	05 47	18 15	23 46	◐
7	05 51	05 48	12 06	06 45	19 15	24 34	

UT	ARIES	VENUS −4·4		MARS +1·3		JUPITER −1·8		SATURN +0·5	
d h	GHA ° ′	GHA ° ′	Dec ° ′	GHA ° ′	Dec ° ′	GHA ° ′	Dec ° ′	GHA ° ′	Dec ° ′
8 00 SATURDAY	316 31.2	135 40.5	S 1 05.0	228 57.3	N23 36.5	185 27.2	N18 36.3	302 04.0	N 3 24.3
01	331 33.7	150 40.8	06.2	243 57.9	36.5	200 29.1	36.2	317 06.5	24.2
02	346 36.1	165 41.0	07.5	258 58.6	36.6	215 31.0	36.0	332 09.0	24.2
03	1 38.6	180 41.3	. . 08.7	273 59.2	. . 36.6	230 32.9	. . 35.9	347 11.5	. . 24.2
04	16 41.1	195 41.6	09.9	288 59.9	36.7	245 34.8	35.7	2 14.0	24.1
05	31 43.5	210 41.8	11.1	304 00.5	36.8	260 36.7	35.6	17 16.5	24.1
06	46 46.0	225 42.1	S 1 12.3	319 01.2	N23 36.8	275 38.6	N18 35.5	32 19.0	N 3 24.1
07	61 48.4	240 42.4	13.6	334 01.8	36.9	290 40.5	35.3	47 21.5	24.1
08	76 50.9	255 42.6	14.8	349 02.5	37.0	305 42.4	35.2	62 24.0	24.0
09	91 53.4	270 42.9	. . 16.0	4 03.1	. . 37.0	320 44.3	. . 35.0	77 26.5	. . 24.0
10	106 55.8	285 43.1	17.2	19 03.8	37.1	335 46.2	34.9	92 29.0	24.0
11	121 58.3	300 43.4	18.4	34 04.4	37.1	350 48.1	34.8	107 31.6	23.9
12	137 00.8	315 43.7	S 1 19.7	49 05.0	N23 37.2	5 50.0	N18 34.6	122 34.1	N 3 23.9
13	152 03.2	330 43.9	20.9	64 05.7	37.2	20 51.9	34.5	137 36.6	23.9
14	167 05.7	345 44.2	22.1	79 06.3	37.3	35 53.8	34.3	152 39.1	23.8
15	182 08.2	0 44.5	. . 23.3	94 07.0	. . 37.4	50 55.7	. . 34.2	167 41.6	. . 23.8
16	197 10.6	15 44.7	24.5	109 07.6	37.4	65 57.6	34.1	182 44.1	23.8
17	212 13.1	30 45.0	25.8	124 08.3	37.5	80 59.5	33.9	197 46.6	23.7
18	227 15.6	45 45.3	S 1 27.0	139 08.9	N23 37.5	96 01.4	N18 33.8	212 49.1	N 3 23.7
19	242 18.0	60 45.6	28.2	154 09.6	37.6	111 03.3	33.6	227 51.6	23.7
20	257 20.5	75 45.8	29.4	169 10.2	37.6	126 05.2	33.5	242 54.1	23.7
21	272 22.9	90 46.1	. . 30.6	184 10.9	. . 37.7	141 07.1	. . 33.3	257 56.7	. . 23.6
22	287 25.4	105 46.4	31.8	199 11.5	37.8	156 09.0	33.2	272 59.2	23.6
23	302 27.9	120 46.6	33.1	214 12.2	37.8	171 10.9	33.1	288 01.7	23.6
9 00 SUNDAY	317 30.3	135 46.9	S 1 34.3	229 12.8	N23 37.9	186 12.8	N18 32.9	303 04.2	N 3 23.5
01	332 32.8	150 47.2	35.5	244 13.5	37.9	201 14.7	32.8	318 06.7	23.5
02	347 35.3	165 47.5	36.7	259 14.1	38.0	216 16.6	32.6	333 09.2	23.5
03	2 37.7	180 47.7	. . 37.9	274 14.7	. . 38.0	231 18.5	. . 32.5	348 11.7	. . 23.4
04	17 40.2	195 48.0	39.2	289 15.4	38.1	246 20.4	32.4	3 14.2	23.4
05	32 42.7	210 48.3	40.4	304 16.0	38.1	261 22.3	32.2	18 16.7	23.4
06	47 45.1	225 48.6	S 1 41.6	319 16.7	N23 38.2	276 24.2	N18 32.1	33 19.3	N 3 23.3
07	62 47.6	240 48.8	42.8	334 17.3	38.2	291 26.1	31.9	48 21.8	23.3
08	77 50.1	255 49.1	44.0	349 18.0	38.3	306 28.0	31.8	63 24.3	23.3
09	92 52.5	270 49.4	. . 45.2	4 18.6	. . 38.3	321 29.9	. . 31.7	78 26.8	. . 23.2
10	107 55.0	285 49.7	46.5	19 19.3	38.4	336 31.8	31.5	93 29.3	23.2
11	122 57.4	300 50.0	47.7	34 19.9	38.4	351 33.7	31.4	108 31.8	23.2
12	137 59.9	315 50.2	S 1 48.9	49 20.6	N23 38.5	6 35.6	N18 31.2	123 34.3	N 3 23.1
13	153 02.4	330 50.5	50.1	64 21.2	38.5	21 37.5	31.1	138 36.8	23.1
14	168 04.8	345 50.8	51.3	79 21.9	38.6	36 39.4	31.0	153 39.4	23.1
15	183 07.3	0 51.1	. . 52.5	94 22.5	. . 38.6	51 41.3	. . 30.8	168 41.9	. . 23.0
16	198 09.8	15 51.4	53.8	109 23.2	38.7	66 43.2	30.7	183 44.4	23.0
17	213 12.2	30 51.6	55.0	124 23.8	38.7	81 45.1	30.5	198 46.9	23.0
18	228 14.7	45 51.9	S 1 56.2	139 24.5	N23 38.8	96 47.0	N18 30.4	213 49.4	N 3 23.0
19	243 17.2	60 52.2	57.4	154 25.1	38.8	111 49.0	30.2	228 51.9	22.9
20	258 19.6	75 52.5	58.6	169 25.8	38.9	126 50.9	30.1	243 54.4	22.9
21	273 22.1	90 52.8	1 59.8	184 26.4	. . 38.9	141 52.8	. . 30.0	258 57.0	. . 22.9
22	288 24.6	105 53.1	2 01.1	199 27.1	39.0	156 54.7	29.8	273 59.5	22.8
23	303 27.0	120 53.3	02.3	214 27.7	39.0	171 56.6	29.7	289 02.0	22.8
10 00 MONDAY	318 29.5	135 53.6	S 2 03.5	229 28.4	N23 39.1	186 58.5	N18 29.5	304 04.5	N 3 22.8
01	333 31.9	150 53.9	04.7	244 29.0	39.1	202 00.4	29.4	319 07.0	22.7
02	348 34.4	165 54.2	05.9	259 29.7	39.2	217 02.3	29.3	334 09.5	22.7
03	3 36.9	180 54.5	. . 07.1	274 30.3	. . 39.2	232 04.2	. . 29.1	349 12.1	. . 22.7
04	18 39.3	195 54.8	08.3	289 31.0	39.3	247 06.1	29.0	4 14.6	22.6
05	33 41.8	210 55.1	09.6	304 31.6	39.3	262 08.0	28.8	19 17.1	22.6
06	48 44.3	225 55.4	S 2 10.8	319 32.3	N23 39.3	277 09.9	N18 28.7	34 19.6	N 3 22.6
07	63 46.7	240 55.7	12.0	334 32.9	39.4	292 11.8	28.5	49 22.1	22.5
08	78 49.2	255 55.9	13.2	349 33.6	39.4	307 13.7	28.4	64 24.6	22.5
09	93 51.7	270 56.2	. . 14.4	4 34.2	. . 39.5	322 15.6	. . 28.3	79 27.1	. . 22.5
10	108 54.1	285 56.5	15.6	19 34.9	39.5	337 17.5	28.1	94 29.7	22.4
11	123 56.6	300 56.8	16.8	34 35.5	39.6	352 19.4	28.0	109 32.2	22.4
12	138 59.1	315 57.1	S 2 18.1	49 36.2	N23 39.6	7 21.3	N18 27.8	124 34.7	N 3 22.4
13	154 01.5	330 57.4	19.3	64 36.8	39.6	22 23.2	27.7	139 37.2	22.3
14	169 04.0	345 57.7	20.5	79 37.5	39.7	37 25.1	27.6	154 39.7	22.3
15	184 06.4	0 58.0	. . 21.7	94 38.1	. . 39.7	52 27.0	. . 27.4	169 42.3	. . 22.3
16	199 08.9	15 58.3	22.9	109 38.8	39.8	67 28.9	27.3	184 44.8	22.2
17	214 11.4	30 58.6	24.1	124 39.5	39.8	82 30.8	27.1	199 47.3	22.2
18	229 13.8	45 58.9	S 2 25.3	139 40.1	N23 39.8	97 32.7	N18 27.0	214 49.8	N 3 22.1
19	244 16.3	60 59.2	26.6	154 40.8	39.9	112 34.6	26.8	229 52.3	22.1
20	259 18.8	75 59.5	27.8	169 41.4	39.9	127 36.5	26.7	244 54.8	22.1
21	274 21.2	90 59.8	. . 29.0	184 42.1	. . 40.0	142 38.4	. . 26.6	259 57.4	. . 22.0
22	289 23.7	106 00.1	30.2	199 42.7	40.0	157 40.3	26.4	274 59.9	22.0
23	304 26.2	121 00.4	31.4	214 43.4	40.0	172 42.3	26.3	290 02.4	22.0
Mer. Pass. (h m)	2 49.5	v 0.3	d 1.2	v 0.6	d 0.1	v 1.9	d 0.1	v 2.5	d 0.0

STARS

Name	SHA ° ′	Dec ° ′
Acamar	315 10.8	S40 11.5
Achernar	335 19.0	S57 05.7
Acrux	172 59.0	S63 15.0
Adhara	255 05.1	S29 00.3
Aldebaran	290 38.2	N16 33.8
Alioth	166 12.1	N55 49.1
Alkaid	152 51.1	N49 11.1
Alnair	27 30.8	S46 49.7
Alnilam	275 36.6	S 1 11.0
Alphard	217 46.8	S 8 46.4
Alphecca	126 02.6	N26 37.7
Alpheratz	357 33.1	N29 14.3
Altair	61 58.4	N 8 56.5
Ankaa	353 05.6	S42 09.4
Antares	112 14.1	S26 29.5
Arcturus	145 46.8	N19 02.8
Atria	107 06.8	S69 04.7
Avior	234 14.8	S59 35.6
Bellatrix	278 21.6	N 6 22.5
Betelgeuse	270 50.9	N 7 24.8
Canopus	263 52.2	S52 42.3
Capella	280 20.2	N46 01.3
Deneb	49 24.4	N45 22.6
Denebola	182 23.8	N14 25.5
Diphda	348 45.8	S17 50.2
Dubhe	193 40.0	N61 36.6
Elnath	278 00.4	N28 37.7
Eltanin	90 41.2	N51 29.3
Enif	33 37.2	N10 00.0
Fomalhaut	15 12.7	S29 28.6
Gacrux	171 50.5	S57 16.0
Gienah	175 42.4	S17 41.4
Hadar	148 34.3	S60 30.3
Hamal	327 49.6	N23 35.3
Kaus Aust.	83 30.4	S34 22.3
Kochab	137 19.9	N74 03.0
Markab	13 28.3	N15 21.0
Menkar	314 04.8	N 4 11.8
Menkent	147 56.1	S36 30.2
Miaplacidus	221 39.0	S69 49.6
Mirfak	308 26.4	N49 57.2
Nunki	75 45.8	S26 15.8
Peacock	53 03.1	S56 38.9
Pollux	243 16.0	N27 57.7
Procyon	244 49.8	N 5 09.5
Rasalhague	95 57.1	N12 32.6
Regulus	207 33.3	N11 50.3
Rigel	281 02.8	S 8 10.1
Rigil Kent.	139 38.5	S60 56.9
Sabik	102 01.1	S15 45.5
Schedar	349 29.2	N56 40.9
Shaula	96 08.3	S37 07.4
Sirius	258 25.3	S16 45.0
Spica	158 21.0	S11 18.0
Suhail	222 45.8	S43 32.4
Vega	80 32.0	N38 48.7
Zuben'ubi	136 54.6	S16 09.2

	SHA ° ′	Mer. Pass. h m
Venus	178 16.6	14 57
Mars	271 42.5	8 43
Jupiter	228 42.5	11 34
Saturn	345 33.8	3 47

UT	SUN GHA	SUN Dec	MOON GHA	v	MOON Dec	d	HP
d h	° ′	° ′	° ′	′	° ′	′	′
8 00 (SATURDAY)	178 34.1	N16 11.5	248 14.2	3.3	N27 09.9	4.6	59.7
01	193 34.2	10.8	262 36.5	3.2	27 14.5	4.4	59.8
02	208 34.2	10.0	276 58.7	3.1	27 18.9	4.3	59.8
03	223 34.3	. . 09.3	291 20.8	3.1	27 23.2	4.0	59.8
04	238 34.4	08.6	305 42.9	3.0	27 27.2	3.9	59.8
05	253 34.5	07.9	320 04.9	2.9	27 31.1	3.6	59.8
06	268 34.6	N16 07.2	334 26.8	2.9	N27 34.7	3.5	59.9
07	283 34.7	06.5	348 48.7	2.8	27 38.2	3.3	59.9
08	298 34.7	05.8	3 10.5	2.7	27 41.5	3.0	59.9
09	313 34.8	. . 05.1	17 32.2	2.6	27 44.5	2.9	59.9
10	328 34.9	04.4	31 53.8	2.6	27 47.4	2.7	59.9
11	343 35.0	03.6	46 15.4	2.6	27 50.1	2.5	59.9
12	358 35.1	N16 02.9	60 37.0	2.4	N27 52.6	2.2	60.0
13	13 35.1	02.2	74 58.4	2.5	27 54.8	2.1	60.0
14	28 35.2	01.5	89 19.9	2.4	27 56.9	1.9	60.0
15	43 35.3	. . 00.8	103 41.3	2.3	27 58.8	1.7	60.0
16	58 35.4	16 00.1	118 02.6	2.3	28 00.5	1.4	60.0
17	73 35.5	15 59.4	132 23.9	2.2	28 01.9	1.3	60.0
18	88 35.6	N15 58.6	146 45.1	2.3	N28 03.2	1.1	60.0
19	103 35.7	57.9	161 06.4	2.1	28 04.3	0.8	60.1
20	118 35.7	57.2	175 27.5	2.2	28 05.1	0.7	60.1
21	133 35.8	. . 56.5	189 48.7	2.1	28 05.8	0.4	60.1
22	148 35.9	55.8	204 09.8	2.1	28 06.2	0.2	60.1
23	163 36.0	55.1	218 30.9	2.1	28 06.4	0.1	60.1
9 00 (SUNDAY)	178 36.1	N15 54.3	232 52.0	2.0	N28 06.5	0.2	60.1
01	193 36.2	53.6	247 13.0	2.1	28 06.3	0.4	60.1
02	208 36.3	52.9	261 34.1	2.0	28 05.9	0.6	60.2
03	223 36.3	. . 52.2	275 55.1	2.0	28 05.3	0.8	60.2
04	238 36.4	51.5	290 16.1	2.0	28 04.5	1.0	60.2
05	253 36.5	50.7	304 37.1	2.0	28 03.5	1.2	60.2
06	268 36.6	N15 50.0	318 58.1	2.0	N28 02.3	1.4	60.2
07	283 36.7	49.3	333 19.1	2.1	28 00.9	1.7	60.2
08	298 36.8	48.6	347 40.2	2.0	27 59.2	1.8	60.2
09	313 36.9	. . 47.9	2 01.2	2.0	27 57.4	2.1	60.2
10	328 37.0	47.1	16 22.2	2.0	27 55.3	2.2	60.2
11	343 37.0	46.4	30 43.2	2.1	27 53.1	2.5	60.2
12	358 37.1	N15 45.7	45 04.3	2.0	N27 50.6	2.7	60.3
13	13 37.2	45.0	59 25.3	2.1	27 47.9	2.8	60.3
14	28 37.3	44.2	73 46.4	2.1	27 45.1	3.1	60.3
15	43 37.4	. . 43.5	88 07.5	2.2	27 42.0	3.3	60.3
16	58 37.5	42.8	102 28.7	2.1	27 38.7	3.5	60.3
17	73 37.6	42.1	116 49.8	2.2	27 35.2	3.7	60.3
18	88 37.7	N15 41.3	131 11.0	2.3	N27 31.5	3.9	60.3
19	103 37.8	40.6	145 32.3	2.2	27 27.6	4.1	60.3
20	118 37.8	39.9	159 53.5	2.4	27 23.5	4.3	60.3
21	133 37.9	. . 39.1	174 14.9	2.3	27 19.2	4.5	60.3
22	148 38.0	38.4	188 36.2	2.4	27 14.7	4.8	60.3
23	163 38.1	37.7	202 57.6	2.5	27 09.9	4.9	60.3
10 00 (MONDAY)	178 38.2	N15 37.0	217 19.1	2.5	N27 05.0	5.1	60.3
01	193 38.3	36.2	231 40.6	2.6	26 59.9	5.3	60.3
02	208 38.4	35.5	246 02.2	2.6	26 54.6	5.5	60.3
03	223 38.5	. . 34.8	260 23.8	2.7	26 49.1	5.7	60.3
04	238 38.6	34.0	274 45.5	2.7	26 43.4	5.9	60.3
05	253 38.7	33.3	289 07.2	2.8	26 37.5	6.1	60.4
06	268 38.8	N15 32.6	303 29.0	2.9	N26 31.4	6.3	60.4
07	283 38.9	31.8	317 50.9	2.9	26 25.1	6.5	60.4
08	298 39.0	31.1	332 12.8	3.1	26 18.6	6.6	60.4
09	313 39.0	. . 30.4	346 34.9	3.0	26 12.0	6.9	60.4
10	328 39.1	29.6	0 56.9	3.2	26 05.1	7.0	60.4
11	343 39.2	28.9	15 19.1	3.3	25 58.1	7.3	60.4
12	358 39.3	N15 28.2	29 41.4	3.3	N25 50.8	7.4	60.4
13	13 39.4	27.4	44 03.7	3.4	25 43.4	7.6	60.4
14	28 39.5	26.7	58 26.1	3.5	25 35.8	7.7	60.4
15	43 39.6	. . 26.0	72 48.6	3.6	25 28.1	8.0	60.4
16	58 39.7	25.2	87 11.2	3.7	25 20.1	8.1	60.4
17	73 39.8	24.5	101 33.9	3.7	25 12.0	8.4	60.4
18	88 39.9	N15 23.8	115 56.6	3.9	N25 03.6	8.4	60.4
19	103 40.0	23.0	130 19.5	3.9	24 55.2	8.7	60.3
20	118 40.1	22.3	144 42.4	4.1	24 46.5	8.8	60.3
21	133 40.2	. . 21.6	159 05.5	4.1	24 37.7	9.1	60.3
22	148 40.3	20.8	173 28.6	4.2	24 28.6	9.1	60.3
23	163 40.4	20.1	187 51.8	4.4	N24 19.5	9.4	60.3
	SD 15.8	*d* 0.7	SD	16.3	16.4		16.4

Lat.	Twilight Naut.	Twilight Civil	Sunrise	Moonrise 8	9	10	11
°	h m	h m	h m	h m	h m	h m	h m
N 72	////	////	01 35	☐	☐	☐	☐
N 70	////	////	02 23	☐	☐	☐	☐
68	////	00 28	02 53	☐	☐	☐	☐
66	////	01 46	03 16	☐	☐	☐	☐
64	////	02 21	03 33	☐	☐	☐	00 08
62	00 25	02 46	03 48	20 37	22 32	24 48	00 48
60	01 35	03 05	04 00	21 56	23 22	25 15	01 15
N 58	02 07	03 20	04 10	22 32	23 53	25 36	01 36
56	02 30	03 34	04 19	22 59	24 17	00 17	01 53
54	02 48	03 45	04 27	23 19	24 36	00 36	02 08
52	03 03	03 55	04 34	23 37	24 52	00 52	02 21
50	03 16	04 04	04 41	23 52	25 06	01 06	02 32
45	03 41	04 22	04 54	24 22	00 22	01 34	02 55
N 40	04 00	04 36	05 06	24 45	00 45	01 56	03 14
35	04 15	04 48	05 15	00 04	01 04	02 14	03 29
30	04 28	04 58	05 24	00 20	01 21	02 30	03 43
20	04 48	05 15	05 38	00 47	01 49	02 57	04 05
N 10	05 03	05 29	05 51	01 10	02 13	03 20	04 25
0	05 16	05 41	06 02	01 32	02 36	03 41	04 43
S 10	05 27	05 52	06 14	01 53	02 59	04 02	05 01
20	05 36	06 03	06 26	02 17	03 23	04 25	05 21
30	05 46	06 14	06 39	02 44	03 51	04 51	05 43
35	05 51	06 21	06 47	03 01	04 08	05 07	05 56
40	05 55	06 28	06 56	03 20	04 28	05 25	06 11
45	06 01	06 35	07 06	03 43	04 51	05 47	06 29
S 50	06 06	06 44	07 19	04 12	05 22	06 14	06 51
52	06 08	06 49	07 25	04 27	05 37	06 27	07 01
54	06 11	06 53	07 31	04 44	05 54	06 42	07 13
56	06 13	06 58	07 38	05 04	06 15	07 00	07 26
58	06 16	07 03	07 46	05 30	06 42	07 22	07 41
S 60	06 19	07 09	07 55	06 05	07 20	07 50	08 00

Lat.	Sunset	Twilight Civil	Twilight Naut.	Moonset 8	9	10	11
°	h m	h m	h m	h m	h m	h m	h m
N 72	22 28	////	////	☐	☐	☐	☐
N 70	21 43	////	////	☐	☐	☐	22 49
68	21 14	23 22	////	☐	☐	☐	21 40
66	20 53	22 20	////	☐	☐	☐	21 03
64	20 36	21 47	////	☐	☐	20 59	20 36
62	20 22	21 23	23 27	20 00	20 22	20 19	20 15
60	20 10	21 04	22 31	18 41	19 32	19 51	19 58
N 58	20 00	20 49	22 01	18 05	19 00	19 29	19 44
56	19 51	20 36	21 38	17 39	18 37	19 11	19 31
54	19 43	20 25	21 21	17 18	18 17	18 56	19 21
52	19 36	20 15	21 06	17 01	18 01	18 43	19 11
50	19 29	20 06	20 54	16 46	17 47	18 31	19 02
45	19 16	19 48	20 29	16 16	17 18	18 07	18 44
N 40	19 05	19 34	20 10	15 52	16 55	17 47	18 28
35	18 55	19 22	19 55	15 33	16 37	17 31	18 15
30	18 47	19 12	19 43	15 17	16 20	17 16	18 04
20	18 33	18 56	19 23	14 49	15 53	16 52	17 45
N 10	18 20	18 42	19 08	14 24	15 29	16 31	17 27
0	18 09	18 30	18 55	14 02	15 07	16 11	17 11
S 10	17 58	18 19	18 45	13 40	14 45	15 51	16 55
20	17 46	18 09	18 35	13 15	14 21	15 29	16 37
30	17 32	17 57	18 26	12 47	13 53	15 04	16 17
35	17 24	17 51	18 21	12 31	13 36	14 49	16 05
40	17 16	17 44	18 16	12 12	13 17	14 32	15 51
45	17 05	17 36	18 11	11 48	12 53	14 11	15 35
S 50	16 53	17 27	18 06	11 18	12 23	13 45	15 14
52	16 47	17 23	18 03	11 03	12 08	13 32	15 04
54	16 41	17 19	18 01	10 46	11 51	13 17	14 53
56	16 34	17 14	17 59	10 26	11 30	13 00	14 41
58	16 26	17 09	17 56	10 00	11 03	12 38	14 26
S 60	16 17	17 03	17 53	09 24	10 26	12 11	14 09

Day	SUN Eqn. of Time 00^h	SUN Eqn. of Time 12^h	SUN Mer. Pass.	MOON Mer. Pass. Upper	MOON Mer. Pass. Lower	Age	Phase
d	m s	m s	h m	h m	h m	d %	
8	05 44	05 40	12 06	07 47	20 19	25 24	
9	05 36	05 32	12 06	08 52	21 24	26 14	
10	05 27	05 23	12 05	09 56	22 27	27 7	

2026 AUGUST 11, 12, 13 (TUES., WED., THURS.)

UT	ARIES	VENUS −4·4		MARS +1·3		JUPITER −1·8		SATURN +0·5	
d h	GHA	GHA	Dec	GHA	Dec	GHA	Dec	GHA	Dec
	° ′	° ′	° ′	° ′	° ′	° ′	° ′	° ′	° ′
11 00 (TUESDAY)	319 28.6	136 00.7	S 2 32.6	229 44.0	N23 40.1	187 44.2	N18 26.1	305 04.9	N 3 21.9
01	334 31.1	151 01.0	33.8	244 44.7	40.1	202 46.1	26.0	320 07.4	21.9
02	349 33.6	166 01.3	35.0	259 45.3	40.2	217 48.0	25.9	335 10.0	21.9
03	4 36.0	181 01.6	. . 36.3	274 46.0	. . 40.2	232 49.9	. . 25.7	350 12.5	. . 21.8
04	19 38.5	196 01.9	37.5	289 46.6	40.2	247 51.8	25.6	5 15.0	21.8
05	34 40.9	211 02.2	38.7	304 47.3	40.3	262 53.7	25.4	20 17.5	21.8
06	49 43.4	226 02.5	S 2 39.9	319 47.9	N23 40.3	277 55.6	N18 25.3	35 20.0	N 3 21.7
07	64 45.9	241 02.8	41.1	334 48.6	40.3	292 57.5	25.1	50 22.6	21.7
08	79 48.3	256 03.1	42.3	349 49.3	40.4	307 59.4	25.0	65 25.1	21.7
09	94 50.8	271 03.4	. . 43.5	4 49.9	. . 40.4	323 01.3	. . 24.9	80 27.6	. . 21.6
10	109 53.3	286 03.7	44.7	19 50.6	40.4	338 03.2	24.7	95 30.1	21.6
11	124 55.7	301 04.0	45.9	34 51.2	40.5	353 05.1	24.6	110 32.6	21.6
12	139 58.2	316 04.3	S 2 47.2	49 51.9	N23 40.5	8 07.0	N18 24.4	125 35.2	N 3 21.5
13	155 00.7	331 04.6	48.4	64 52.5	40.5	23 08.9	24.3	140 37.7	21.5
14	170 03.1	346 05.0	49.6	79 53.2	40.6	38 10.8	24.2	155 40.2	21.5
15	185 05.6	1 05.3	. . 50.8	94 53.8	. . 40.6	53 12.7	. . 24.0	170 42.7	. . 21.4
16	200 08.0	16 05.6	52.0	109 54.5	40.6	68 14.6	23.9	185 45.2	21.4
17	215 10.5	31 05.9	53.2	124 55.2	40.7	83 16.5	23.7	200 47.8	21.3
18	230 13.0	46 06.2	S 2 54.4	139 55.8	N23 40.7	98 18.4	N18 23.6	215 50.3	N 3 21.3
19	245 15.4	61 06.5	55.6	154 56.5	40.7	113 20.3	23.4	230 52.8	21.3
20	260 17.9	76 06.8	56.8	169 57.1	40.8	128 22.2	23.3	245 55.3	21.2
21	275 20.4	91 07.1	. . 58.0	184 57.8	. . 40.8	143 24.2	. . 23.2	260 57.8	. . 21.2
22	290 22.8	106 07.5	2 59.3	199 58.4	40.8	158 26.1	23.0	276 00.4	21.2
23	305 25.3	121 07.8	3 00.5	214 59.1	40.9	173 28.0	22.9	291 02.9	21.1
12 00 (WEDNESDAY)	320 27.8	136 08.1	S 3 01.7	229 59.7	N23 40.9	188 29.9	N18 22.7	306 05.4	N 3 21.1
01	335 30.2	151 08.4	02.9	245 00.4	40.9	203 31.8	22.6	321 07.9	21.1
02	350 32.7	166 08.7	04.1	260 01.1	40.9	218 33.7	22.4	336 10.5	21.0
03	5 35.2	181 09.0	. . 05.3	275 01.7	. . 41.0	233 35.6	. . 22.3	351 13.0	. . 21.0
04	20 37.6	196 09.3	06.5	290 02.4	41.0	248 37.5	22.2	6 15.5	21.0
05	35 40.1	211 09.7	07.7	305 03.0	41.0	263 39.4	22.0	21 18.0	20.9
06	50 42.5	226 10.0	S 3 08.9	320 03.7	N23 41.1	278 41.3	N18 21.9	36 20.6	N 3 20.9
07	65 45.0	241 10.3	10.1	335 04.3	41.1	293 43.2	21.7	51 23.1	20.8
08	80 47.5	256 10.6	11.3	350 05.0	41.1	308 45.1	21.6	66 25.6	20.8
09	95 49.9	271 10.9	. . 12.6	5 05.7	. . 41.1	323 47.0	. . 21.5	81 28.1	. . 20.8
10	110 52.4	286 11.3	13.8	20 06.3	41.2	338 48.9	21.3	96 30.7	20.7
11	125 54.9	301 11.6	15.0	35 07.0	41.2	353 50.8	21.2	111 33.2	20.7
12	140 57.3	316 11.9	S 3 16.2	50 07.6	N23 41.2	8 52.7	N18 21.0	126 35.7	N 3 20.7
13	155 59.8	331 12.2	17.4	65 08.3	41.2	23 54.6	20.9	141 38.2	20.6
14	171 02.3	346 12.5	18.6	80 09.0	41.3	38 56.5	20.7	156 40.7	20.6
15	186 04.7	1 12.9	. . 19.8	95 09.6	. . 41.3	53 58.5	. . 20.6	171 43.3	. . 20.5
16	201 07.2	16 13.2	21.0	110 10.3	41.3	69 00.4	20.5	186 45.8	20.5
17	216 09.7	31 13.5	22.2	125 10.9	41.3	84 02.3	20.3	201 48.3	20.5
18	231 12.1	46 13.8	S 3 23.4	140 11.6	N23 41.4	99 04.2	N18 20.2	216 50.9	N 3 20.4
19	246 14.6	61 14.2	24.6	155 12.2	41.4	114 06.1	20.0	231 53.4	20.4
20	261 17.0	76 14.5	25.8	170 12.9	41.4	129 08.0	19.9	246 55.9	20.4
21	276 19.5	91 14.8	. . 27.0	185 13.6	. . 41.4	144 09.9	. . 19.7	261 58.4	. . 20.3
22	291 22.0	106 15.2	28.2	200 14.2	41.5	159 11.8	19.6	277 01.0	20.3
23	306 24.4	121 15.5	29.4	215 14.9	41.5	174 13.7	19.5	292 03.5	20.2
13 00 (THURSDAY)	321 26.9	136 15.8	S 3 30.6	230 15.5	N23 41.5	189 15.6	N18 19.3	307 06.0	N 3 20.2
01	336 29.4	151 16.1	31.8	245 16.2	41.5	204 17.5	19.2	322 08.5	20.2
02	351 31.8	166 16.5	33.1	260 16.9	41.5	219 19.4	19.0	337 11.1	20.1
03	6 34.3	181 16.8	. . 34.3	275 17.5	. . 41.6	234 21.3	. . 18.9	352 13.6	. . 20.1
04	21 36.8	196 17.1	35.5	290 18.2	41.6	249 23.2	18.7	7 16.1	20.1
05	36 39.2	211 17.5	36.7	305 18.8	41.6	264 25.1	18.6	22 18.6	20.0
06	51 41.7	226 17.8	S 3 37.9	320 19.5	N23 41.6	279 27.0	N18 18.5	37 21.2	N 3 20.0
07	66 44.2	241 18.1	39.1	335 20.2	41.6	294 29.0	18.3	52 23.7	19.9
08	81 46.6	256 18.5	40.3	350 20.8	41.7	309 30.9	18.2	67 26.2	19.9
09	96 49.1	271 18.8	. . 41.5	5 21.5	. . 41.7	324 32.8	. . 18.0	82 28.8	. . 19.9
10	111 51.5	286 19.1	42.7	20 22.2	41.7	339 34.7	17.9	97 31.3	19.8
11	126 54.0	301 19.5	43.9	35 22.8	41.7	354 36.6	17.7	112 33.8	19.8
12	141 56.5	316 19.8	S 3 45.1	50 23.5	N23 41.7	9 38.5	N18 17.6	127 36.3	N 3 19.8
13	156 58.9	331 20.1	46.3	65 24.1	41.8	24 40.4	17.5	142 38.9	19.7
14	172 01.4	346 20.5	47.5	80 24.8	41.8	39 42.3	17.3	157 41.4	19.7
15	187 03.9	1 20.8	. . 48.7	95 25.5	. . 41.8	54 44.2	. . 17.2	172 43.9	. . 19.6
16	202 06.3	16 21.2	49.9	110 26.1	41.8	69 46.1	17.0	187 46.5	19.6
17	217 08.8	31 21.5	51.1	125 26.8	41.8	84 48.0	16.9	202 49.0	19.6
18	232 11.3	46 21.8	S 3 52.3	140 27.5	N23 41.8	99 49.9	N18 16.7	217 51.5	N 3 19.5
19	247 13.7	61 22.2	53.5	155 28.1	41.8	114 51.8	16.6	232 54.0	19.5
20	262 16.2	76 22.5	54.7	170 28.8	41.9	129 53.7	16.5	247 56.6	19.4
21	277 18.6	91 22.9	. . 55.9	185 29.4	. . 41.9	144 55.6	. . 16.3	262 59.1	. . 19.4
22	292 21.1	106 23.2	57.1	200 30.1	41.9	159 57.6	16.2	278 01.6	19.4
23	307 23.6	121 23.6	58.3	215 30.8	41.9	174 59.5	16.0	293 04.2	19.3
Mer. Pass.	h m 2 37.7	*v* 0.3	*d* 1.2	*v* 0.7	*d* 0.0	*v* 1.9	*d* 0.1	*v* 2.5	*d* 0.0

STARS

Name	SHA	Dec
	° ′	° ′
Acamar	315 10.7	S40 11.5
Achernar	335 19.0	S57 05.7
Acrux	172 59.0	S63 15.0
Adhara	255 05.1	S29 00.3
Aldebaran	290 38.2	N16 33.8
Alioth	166 12.1	N55 49.1
Alkaid	152 51.1	N49 11.0
Alnair	27 30.8	S46 49.7
Alnilam	275 36.6	S 1 11.0
Alphard	217 46.8	S 8 46.4
Alphecca	126 02.6	N26 37.7
Alpheratz	357 33.1	N29 14.3
Altair	61 58.3	N 8 56.5
Ankaa	353 05.5	S42 09.4
Antares	112 14.1	S26 29.5
Arcturus	145 46.8	N19 02.8
Atria	107 06.8	S69 04.7
Avior	234 14.8	S59 35.6
Bellatrix	278 21.6	N 6 22.5
Betelgeuse	270 50.9	N 7 24.8
Canopus	263 52.2	S52 42.3
Capella	280 20.2	N46 01.3
Deneb	49 24.4	N45 22.6
Denebola	182 23.8	N14 25.5
Diphda	348 45.8	S17 50.2
Dubhe	193 40.0	N61 36.6
Elnath	278 00.4	N28 37.7
Eltanin	90 41.2	N51 29.3
Enif	33 37.2	N10 00.0
Fomalhaut	15 12.7	S29 28.6
Gacrux	171 50.5	S57 15.9
Gienah	175 42.4	S17 41.4
Hadar	148 34.3	S60 30.3
Hamal	327 49.6	N23 35.3
Kaus Aust.	83 30.4	S34 22.3
Kochab	137 19.9	N74 03.0
Markab	13 28.3	N15 21.0
Menkar	314 04.7	N 4 11.8
Menkent	147 56.1	S36 30.2
Miaplacidus	221 39.0	S69 49.5
Mirfak	308 26.4	N49 57.2
Nunki	75 45.8	S26 15.8
Peacock	53 03.0	S56 38.9
Pollux	243 16.0	N27 57.7
Procyon	244 49.7	N 5 09.5
Rasalhague	95 57.1	N12 32.6
Regulus	207 33.3	N11 50.3
Rigel	281 02.7	S 8 10.1
Rigil Kent.	139 38.5	S60 56.9
Sabik	102 01.1	S15 45.5
Schedar	349 29.2	N56 40.9
Shaula	96 08.3	S37 07.4
Sirius	258 25.3	S16 45.0
Spica	158 21.0	S11 18.0
Suhail	222 45.8	S43 32.3
Vega	80 32.0	N38 48.7
Zuben'ubi	136 54.6	S16 09.2

	SHA	Mer. Pass.
	° ′	h m
Venus	175 40.3	14 55
Mars	269 32.0	8 40
Jupiter	228 02.1	11 25
Saturn	345 37.7	3 35

Day	UT d h	SUN GHA ° ′	SUN Dec ° ′	MOON GHA ° ′	v ′	MOON Dec ° ′	d ′	HP ′
TUESDAY	11 00	178 40.5	N15 19.3	202 15.2	4.4	N24 10.1	9.5	60.3
	01	193 40.6	18.6	216 38.6	4.6	24 00.6	9.6	60.3
	02	208 40.7	17.9	231 02.2	4.6	23 51.0	9.9	60.3
	03	223 40.8	. . 17.1	245 25.8	4.8	23 41.1	10.0	60.3
	04	238 40.9	16.4	259 49.6	4.8	23 31.1	10.1	60.3
	05	253 41.0	15.6	274 13.4	5.0	23 21.0	10.3	60.3
	06	268 41.1	N15 14.9	288 37.4	5.0	N23 10.7	10.5	60.3
	07	283 41.2	14.1	303 01.4	5.2	23 00.2	10.6	60.3
	08	298 41.3	13.4	317 25.6	5.3	22 49.6	10.7	60.3
	09	313 41.4	. . 12.7	331 49.9	5.4	22 38.9	10.9	60.3
	10	328 41.5	11.9	346 14.3	5.5	22 28.0	11.1	60.3
	11	343 41.6	11.2	0 38.8	5.6	22 16.9	11.2	60.2
	12	358 41.7	N15 10.4	15 03.4	5.8	N22 05.7	11.3	60.2
	13	13 41.8	09.7	29 28.2	5.8	21 54.4	11.5	60.2
	14	28 41.9	08.9	43 53.0	6.0	21 42.9	11.6	60.2
	15	43 42.0	. . 08.2	58 18.0	6.0	21 31.3	11.7	60.2
	16	58 42.1	07.4	72 43.0	6.2	21 19.6	11.9	60.2
	17	73 42.2	06.7	87 08.2	6.3	21 07.7	12.0	60.2
	18	88 42.3	N15 06.0	101 33.5	6.4	N20 55.7	12.2	60.2
	19	103 42.4	05.2	115 58.9	6.5	20 43.5	12.2	60.2
	20	118 42.5	04.5	130 24.4	6.7	20 31.3	12.4	60.1
	21	133 42.6	. . 03.7	144 50.1	6.7	20 18.9	12.5	60.1
	22	148 42.7	03.0	159 15.8	6.9	20 06.4	12.7	60.1
	23	163 42.8	02.2	173 41.7	7.0	19 53.7	12.7	60.1
WEDNESDAY	12 00	178 42.9	N15 01.5	188 07.7	7.1	N19 41.0	12.9	60.1
	01	193 43.0	00.7	202 33.8	7.2	19 28.1	13.0	60.1
	02	208 43.1	15 00.0	217 00.0	7.3	19 15.1	13.1	60.1
	03	223 43.2	14 59.2	231 26.3	7.5	19 02.0	13.2	60.0
	04	238 43.3	58.5	245 52.8	7.5	18 48.8	13.3	60.0
	05	253 43.4	57.7	260 19.3	7.7	18 35.5	13.4	60.0
	06	268 43.5	N14 57.0	274 46.0	7.8	N18 22.1	13.5	60.0
	07	283 43.6	56.2	289 12.8	7.9	18 08.6	13.7	60.0
	08	298 43.7	55.4	303 39.7	8.0	17 54.9	13.7	59.9
	09	313 43.8	. . 54.7	318 06.7	8.1	17 41.2	13.8	59.9
	10	328 43.9	53.9	332 33.8	8.2	17 27.4	13.9	59.9
	11	343 44.1	53.2	347 01.0	8.4	17 13.5	14.0	59.9
	12	358 44.2	N14 52.4	1 28.4	8.4	N16 59.5	14.1	59.9
	13	13 44.3	51.7	15 55.8	8.6	16 45.4	14.2	59.9
	14	28 44.4	50.9	30 23.4	8.7	16 31.2	14.3	59.8
	15	43 44.5	. . 50.2	44 51.1	8.7	16 16.9	14.4	59.8
	16	58 44.6	49.4	59 18.8	8.9	16 02.5	14.4	59.8
	17	73 44.7	48.7	73 46.7	9.0	N15 48.1	14.5	59.8
	18	88 44.8	N14 47.9	A total eclipse of the Sun occurs on this date. See page 5.				
	19	103 44.9	47.1					
	20	118 45.0	46.4					
	21	133 45.1	. . 45.6					
	22	148 45.2	44.9					
	23	163 45.3	44.1					
THURSDAY	13 00	178 45.5	N14 43.3	175 04.9	9.7	N14 04.9	15.1	59.6
	01	193 45.6	42.6	189 33.6	9.8	13 49.8	15.1	59.6
	02	208 45.7	41.8	204 02.4	10.0	13 34.7	15.1	59.6
	03	223 45.8	. . 41.1	218 31.4	10.0	13 19.6	15.2	59.5
	04	238 45.9	40.3	233 00.4	10.1	13 04.4	15.3	59.5
	05	253 46.0	39.5	247 29.5	10.2	12 49.1	15.3	59.5
	06	268 46.1	N14 38.8	261 58.7	10.3	N12 33.8	15.4	59.5
	07	283 46.2	38.0	276 28.0	10.4	12 18.4	15.5	59.4
	08	298 46.3	37.3	290 57.4	10.5	12 02.9	15.5	59.4
	09	313 46.5	. . 36.5	305 26.9	10.6	11 47.4	15.5	59.4
	10	328 46.6	35.7	319 56.5	10.7	11 31.9	15.6	59.4
	11	343 46.7	35.0	334 26.2	10.8	11 16.3	15.6	59.3
	12	358 46.8	N14 34.2	348 56.0	10.9	N11 00.7	15.7	59.3
	13	13 46.9	33.4	3 25.9	10.9	10 45.0	15.7	59.3
	14	28 47.0	32.7	17 55.8	11.1	10 29.3	15.8	59.3
	15	43 47.1	. . 31.9	32 25.9	11.1	10 13.5	15.7	59.2
	16	58 47.2	31.1	46 56.0	11.2	9 57.8	15.9	59.2
	17	73 47.4	30.4	61 26.2	11.3	9 41.9	15.8	59.2
	18	88 47.5	N14 29.6	75 56.5	11.3	N 9 26.1	15.9	59.1
	19	103 47.6	28.8	90 26.8	11.5	9 10.2	16.0	59.1
	20	118 47.7	28.1	104 57.3	11.5	8 54.2	15.9	59.1
	21	133 47.8	. . 27.3	119 27.8	11.7	8 38.3	16.0	59.0
	22	148 47.9	26.5	133 58.5	11.6	8 22.3	16.0	59.0
	23	163 48.0	25.8	148 29.1	11.8	N 8 06.3	16.0	59.0
		SD 15.8	d 0.8	SD	16.4	16.3		16.2

Lat. °	Twilight Naut. h m	Twilight Civil h m	Sunrise h m	Moonrise 11 h m	Moonrise 12 h m	Moonrise 13 h m	Moonrise 14 h m
N 72	////	////	02 02	▭	▭	03 25	06 03
N 70	////	////	02 40	▭	00 26	03 51	06 13
68	////	01 16	03 07	▭	01 33	04 11	06 20
66	////	02 04	03 27	▭	02 09	04 26	06 26
64	////	02 34	03 43	00 08	02 34	04 39	06 31
62	01 08	02 56	03 56	00 48	02 54	04 49	06 36
60	01 51	03 14	04 07	01 15	03 10	04 58	06 40
N 58	02 19	03 28	04 17	01 36	03 23	05 06	06 43
56	02 39	03 40	04 25	01 53	03 35	05 13	06 46
54	02 56	03 51	04 32	02 08	03 45	05 19	06 49
52	03 10	04 00	04 39	02 21	03 54	05 25	06 51
50	03 22	04 09	04 45	02 32	04 02	05 30	06 54
45	03 46	04 26	04 58	02 55	04 19	05 40	06 58
N 40	04 04	04 39	05 09	03 14	04 33	05 49	07 02
35	04 18	04 51	05 18	03 29	04 44	05 57	07 06
30	04 30	05 00	05 26	03 43	04 54	06 03	07 09
20	04 49	05 16	05 39	04 05	05 12	06 15	07 14
N 10	05 03	05 29	05 51	04 25	05 27	06 25	07 19
0	05 15	05 40	06 02	04 43	05 41	06 34	07 23
S 10	05 26	05 51	06 12	05 01	05 55	06 43	07 27
20	05 35	06 01	06 24	05 21	06 10	06 53	07 32
30	05 43	06 12	06 37	05 43	06 27	07 04	07 37
35	05 48	06 18	06 44	05 56	06 36	07 10	07 40
40	05 52	06 24	06 52	06 11	06 48	07 17	07 43
45	05 57	06 31	07 02	06 29	07 01	07 26	07 47
S 50	06 01	06 40	07 14	06 51	07 16	07 36	07 52
52	06 03	06 43	07 19	07 01	07 24	07 40	07 54
54	06 05	06 47	07 25	07 13	07 32	07 45	07 56
56	06 08	06 52	07 32	07 26	07 41	07 51	07 58
58	06 10	06 57	07 39	07 41	07 51	07 57	08 01
S 60	06 12	07 02	07 47	08 00	08 03	08 04	08 04

Lat. °	Sunset h m	Twilight Civil h m	Twilight Naut. h m	Moonset 11 h m	Moonset 12 h m	Moonset 13 h m	Moonset 14 h m
N 72	22 02	////	////	▭	21 46	20 52	20 14
N 70	21 26	////	////	22 49	21 17	20 39	20 11
68	21 00	22 45	////	21 40	20 55	20 29	20 09
66	20 41	22 01	////	21 03	20 38	20 21	20 07
64	20 25	21 32	////	20 36	20 23	20 14	20 05
62	20 12	21 11	22 54	20 15	20 11	20 07	20 03
60	20 02	20 54	22 14	19 58	20 01	20 02	20 02
N 58	19 52	20 40	21 48	19 44	19 52	19 57	20 01
56	19 44	20 28	21 28	19 31	19 44	19 53	20 00
54	19 36	20 18	21 12	19 21	19 37	19 49	19 59
52	19 30	20 08	20 58	19 11	19 30	19 45	19 58
50	19 24	20 00	20 47	19 02	19 25	19 42	19 57
45	19 11	19 43	20 23	18 44	19 12	19 35	19 55
N 40	19 01	19 30	20 06	18 28	19 01	19 29	19 53
35	18 52	19 19	19 51	18 15	18 52	19 24	19 52
30	18 44	19 09	19 39	18 04	18 44	19 19	19 51
20	18 31	18 54	19 21	17 45	18 30	19 11	19 49
N 10	18 19	18 41	19 06	17 27	18 18	19 04	19 47
0	18 08	18 30	18 55	17 11	18 07	18 58	19 45
S 10	17 58	18 20	18 45	16 55	17 55	18 51	19 43
20	17 47	18 09	18 36	16 37	17 42	18 43	19 41
30	17 34	17 59	18 27	16 17	17 28	18 35	19 39
35	17 27	17 53	18 23	16 05	17 19	18 30	19 38
40	17 18	17 47	18 19	15 51	17 10	18 25	19 36
45	17 09	17 39	18 14	15 35	16 58	18 18	19 34
S 50	16 57	17 31	18 10	15 14	16 44	18 10	19 32
52	16 52	17 28	18 08	15 04	16 37	18 06	19 31
54	16 46	17 24	18 06	14 53	16 30	18 02	19 30
56	16 39	17 19	18 03	14 41	16 22	17 58	19 29
58	16 32	17 14	18 01	14 26	16 13	17 53	19 27
S 60	16 24	17 09	17 59	14 09	16 02	17 47	19 26

Day d	SUN Eqn. of Time 00^h m s	SUN Eqn. of Time 12^h m s	SUN Mer. Pass. h m	MOON Mer. Pass. Upper h m	MOON Mer. Pass. Lower h m	MOON Age d	MOON Phase %
11	05 18	05 13	12 05	10 57	23 26	28	2
12	05 09	05 04	12 05	11 54	24 20	29	0 ●
13	04 58	04 53	12 05	12 46	00 20	01	1

UT	ARIES	VENUS −4·4		MARS +1·3		JUPITER −1·8		SATURN +0·5	
d h	GHA ° ′	GHA ° ′	Dec ° ′	GHA ° ′	Dec ° ′	GHA ° ′	Dec ° ′	GHA ° ′	Dec ° ′
14 00	322 26.0	136 23.9	S 3 59.5	230 31.4	N23 41.9	190 01.4	N18 15.9	308 06.7	N 3 19.3
01	337 28.5	151 24.2	4 00.7	245 32.1	41.9	205 03.3	15.7	323 09.2	19.3
02	352 31.0	166 24.6	01.9	260 32.8	41.9	220 05.2	15.6	338 11.8	19.2
03	7 33.4	181 24.9	. . 03.1	275 33.4	. . 42.0	235 07.1	. . 15.5	353 14.3	. . 19.2
04	22 35.9	196 25.3	04.3	290 34.1	42.0	250 09.0	15.3	8 16.8	19.1
05	37 38.4	211 25.6	05.5	305 34.7	42.0	265 10.9	15.2	23 19.3	19.1
06	52 40.8	226 26.0	S 4 06.7	320 35.4	N23 42.0	280 12.8	N18 15.0	38 21.9	N 3 19.1
07	67 43.3	241 26.3	07.9	335 36.1	42.0	295 14.7	14.9	53 24.4	19.0
F 08	82 45.8	256 26.7	09.1	350 36.7	42.0	310 16.6	14.7	68 26.9	19.0
R 09	97 48.2	271 27.0	. . 10.3	5 37.4	. . 42.0	325 18.5	. . 14.6	83 29.5	. . 18.9
I 10	112 50.7	286 27.4	11.5	20 38.1	42.0	340 20.4	14.5	98 32.0	18.9
D 11	127 53.1	301 27.7	12.7	35 38.7	42.0	355 22.4	14.3	113 34.5	18.9
A 12	142 55.6	316 28.1	S 4 13.9	50 39.4	N23 42.1	10 24.3	N18 14.2	128 37.1	N 3 18.8
Y 13	157 58.1	331 28.4	15.1	65 40.1	42.1	25 26.2	14.0	143 39.6	18.8
14	173 00.5	346 28.8	16.3	80 40.7	42.1	40 28.1	13.9	158 42.1	18.7
15	188 03.0	1 29.1	. . 17.5	95 41.4	. . 42.1	55 30.0	. . 13.7	173 44.7	. . 18.7
16	203 05.5	16 29.5	18.7	110 42.1	42.1	70 31.9	13.6	188 47.2	18.7
17	218 07.9	31 29.8	19.9	125 42.7	42.1	85 33.8	13.5	203 49.7	18.6
18	233 10.4	46 30.2	S 4 21.1	140 43.4	N23 42.1	100 35.7	N18 13.3	218 52.3	N 3 18.6
19	248 12.9	61 30.5	22.3	155 44.1	42.1	115 37.6	13.2	233 54.8	18.5
20	263 15.3	76 30.9	23.5	170 44.7	42.1	130 39.5	13.0	248 57.3	18.5
21	278 17.8	91 31.3	. . 24.7	185 45.4	. . 42.1	145 41.4	. . 12.9	263 59.9	. . 18.5
22	293 20.2	106 31.6	25.9	200 46.1	42.1	160 43.3	12.7	279 02.4	18.4
23	308 22.7	121 32.0	27.1	215 46.7	42.1	175 45.3	12.6	294 04.9	18.4
15 00	323 25.2	136 32.3	S 4 28.3	230 47.4	N23 42.1	190 47.2	N18 12.5	309 07.5	N 3 18.3
01	338 27.6	151 32.7	29.5	245 48.1	42.1	205 49.1	12.3	324 10.0	18.3
02	353 30.1	166 33.1	30.7	260 48.7	42.2	220 51.0	12.2	339 12.5	18.3
03	8 32.6	181 33.4	. . 31.8	275 49.4	. . 42.2	235 52.9	. . 12.0	354 15.1	. . 18.2
04	23 35.0	196 33.8	33.0	290 50.1	42.2	250 54.8	11.9	9 17.6	18.2
05	38 37.5	211 34.1	34.2	305 50.7	42.2	265 56.7	11.7	24 20.1	18.1
06	53 40.0	226 34.5	S 4 35.4	320 51.4	N23 42.2	280 58.6	N18 11.6	39 22.7	N 3 18.1
S 07	68 42.4	241 34.9	36.6	335 52.1	42.2	296 00.5	11.5	54 25.2	18.0
A 08	83 44.9	256 35.2	37.8	350 52.7	42.2	311 02.4	11.3	69 27.7	18.0
T 09	98 47.4	271 35.6	. . 39.0	5 53.4	. . 42.2	326 04.3	. . 11.2	84 30.3	. . 18.0
U 10	113 49.8	286 36.0	40.2	20 54.1	42.2	341 06.3	11.0	99 32.8	17.9
R 11	128 52.3	301 36.3	41.4	35 54.7	42.2	356 08.2	10.9	114 35.3	17.9
D 12	143 54.7	316 36.7	S 4 42.6	50 55.4	N23 42.2	11 10.1	N18 10.7	129 37.9	N 3 17.8
A 13	158 57.2	331 37.1	43.8	65 56.1	42.2	26 12.0	10.6	144 40.4	17.8
Y 14	173 59.7	346 37.4	45.0	80 56.8	42.2	41 13.9	10.4	159 43.0	17.8
15	189 02.1	1 37.8	. . 46.2	95 57.4	. . 42.2	56 15.8	. . 10.3	174 45.5	. . 17.7
16	204 04.6	16 38.2	47.4	110 58.1	42.2	71 17.7	10.2	189 48.0	17.7
17	219 07.1	31 38.5	48.6	125 58.8	42.2	86 19.6	10.0	204 50.6	17.6
18	234 09.5	46 38.9	S 4 49.7	140 59.4	N23 42.2	101 21.5	N18 09.9	219 53.1	N 3 17.6
19	249 12.0	61 39.3	50.9	156 00.1	42.2	116 23.4	09.7	234 55.6	17.6
20	264 14.5	76 39.6	52.1	171 00.8	42.2	131 25.3	09.6	249 58.2	17.5
21	279 16.9	91 40.0	. . 53.3	186 01.4	. . 42.2	146 27.3	. . 09.4	265 00.7	. . 17.5
22	294 19.4	106 40.4	54.5	201 02.1	42.2	161 29.2	09.3	280 03.2	17.4
23	309 21.8	121 40.8	55.7	216 02.8	42.2	176 31.1	09.2	295 05.8	17.4
16 00	324 24.3	136 41.1	S 4 56.9	231 03.5	N23 42.2	191 33.0	N18 09.0	310 08.3	N 3 17.3
01	339 26.8	151 41.5	58.1	246 04.1	42.2	206 34.9	08.9	325 10.9	17.3
02	354 29.2	166 41.9	4 59.3	261 04.8	42.2	221 36.8	08.7	340 13.4	17.3
03	9 31.7	181 42.3	5 00.5	276 05.5	. . 42.2	236 38.7	. . 08.6	355 15.9	. . 17.2
04	24 34.2	196 42.6	01.6	291 06.1	42.2	251 40.6	08.4	10 18.5	17.2
05	39 36.6	211 43.0	02.8	306 06.8	42.2	266 42.5	08.3	25 21.0	17.1
06	54 39.1	226 43.4	S 5 04.0	321 07.5	N23 42.2	281 44.4	N18 08.1	40 23.6	N 3 17.1
07	69 41.6	241 43.8	05.2	336 08.2	42.1	296 46.4	08.0	55 26.1	17.0
08	84 44.0	256 44.2	06.4	351 08.8	42.1	311 48.3	07.9	70 28.6	17.0
S 09	99 46.5	271 44.5	. . 07.6	6 09.5	. . 42.1	326 50.2	. . 07.7	85 31.2	. . 17.0
U 10	114 49.0	286 44.9	08.8	21 10.2	42.1	341 52.1	07.6	100 33.7	16.9
N 11	129 51.4	301 45.3	10.0	36 10.8	42.1	356 54.0	07.4	115 36.2	16.9
D 12	144 53.9	316 45.7	S 5 11.2	51 11.5	N23 42.1	11 55.9	N18 07.3	130 38.8	N 3 16.8
A 13	159 56.3	331 46.1	12.3	66 12.2	42.1	26 57.8	07.1	145 41.3	16.8
Y 14	174 58.8	346 46.4	13.5	81 12.9	42.1	41 59.7	07.0	160 43.9	16.8
15	190 01.3	1 46.8	. . 14.7	96 13.5	. . 42.1	57 01.6	. . 06.9	175 46.4	. . 16.7
16	205 03.7	16 47.2	15.9	111 14.2	42.1	72 03.5	06.7	190 48.9	16.7
17	220 06.2	31 47.6	17.1	126 14.9	42.1	87 05.5	06.6	205 51.5	16.6
18	235 08.7	46 48.0	S 5 18.3	141 15.6	N23 42.1	102 07.4	N18 06.4	220 54.0	N 3 16.6
19	250 11.1	61 48.4	19.5	156 16.2	42.1	117 09.3	06.3	235 56.6	16.5
20	265 13.6	76 48.8	20.6	171 16.9	42.1	132 11.2	06.1	250 59.1	16.5
21	280 16.1	91 49.1	. . 21.8	186 17.6	. . 42.0	147 13.1	. . 06.0	266 01.6	. . 16.5
22	295 18.5	106 49.5	23.0	201 18.3	42.0	162 15.0	05.8	281 04.2	16.4
23	310 21.0	121 49.9	24.2	216 18.9	42.0	177 16.9	05.7	296 06.7	16.4
Mer. Pass.	h m 2 25.9	*v* 0.4	*d* 1.2	*v* 0.7	*d* 0.0	*v* 1.9	*d* 0.1	*v* 2.5	*d* 0.0

STARS

Name	SHA ° ′	Dec ° ′
Acamar	315 10.7	S40 11.5
Achernar	335 18.9	S57 05.7
Acrux	172 59.1	S63 15.0
Adhara	255 05.1	S29 00.3
Aldebaran	290 38.2	N16 33.8
Alioth	166 12.1	N55 49.1
Alkaid	152 51.1	N49 11.0
Alnair	27 30.8	S46 49.7
Alnilam	275 36.5	S 1 11.0
Alphard	217 46.8	S 8 46.4
Alphecca	126 02.6	N26 37.7
Alpheratz	357 33.1	N29 14.3
Altair	61 58.4	N 8 56.5
Ankaa	353 05.5	S42 09.4
Antares	112 14.1	S26 29.5
Arcturus	145 46.8	N19 02.8
Atria	107 06.9	S69 04.7
Avior	234 14.8	S59 35.5
Bellatrix	278 21.6	N 6 22.5
Betelgeuse	270 50.8	N 7 24.8
Canopus	263 52.2	S52 42.3
Capella	280 20.1	N46 01.3
Deneb	49 24.4	N45 22.6
Denebola	182 23.8	N14 25.5
Diphda	348 45.7	S17 50.2
Dubhe	193 40.0	N61 36.6
Elnath	278 00.4	N28 37.7
Eltanin	90 41.2	N51 29.3
Enif	33 37.2	N10 00.0
Fomalhaut	15 12.7	S29 28.7
Gacrux	171 50.6	S57 15.9
Gienah	175 42.5	S17 41.4
Hadar	148 34.3	S60 30.3
Hamal	327 49.6	N23 35.3
Kaus Aust.	83 30.5	S34 22.3
Kochab	137 20.0	N74 03.0
Markab	13 28.3	N15 21.0
Menkar	314 04.7	N 4 11.8
Menkent	147 56.2	S36 30.2
Miaplacidus	221 39.0	S69 49.5
Mirfak	308 26.3	N49 57.2
Nunki	75 45.8	S26 15.8
Peacock	53 03.0	S56 38.9
Pollux	243 16.0	N27 57.7
Procyon	244 49.7	N 5 09.5
Rasalhague	95 57.1	N12 32.6
Regulus	207 33.3	N11 50.3
Rigel	281 02.7	S 8 10.1
Rigil Kent.	139 38.6	S60 56.9
Sabik	102 01.1	S15 45.5
Schedar	349 29.1	N56 40.9
Shaula	96 08.3	S37 07.4
Sirius	258 25.3	S16 45.0
Spica	158 21.0	S11 18.0
Suhail	222 45.8	S43 32.3
Vega	80 32.0	N38 48.7
Zuben'ubi	136 54.6	S16 09.2

	SHA ° ′	Mer. Pass. h m
Venus	173 07.2	14 53
Mars	267 22.2	8 36
Jupiter	227 22.0	11 15
Saturn	345 42.3	3 23

	UT	SUN GHA	SUN Dec	MOON GHA	v	MOON Dec	d	HP
	d h	° ′	° ′	° ′	′	° ′	′	′
	14 00	178 48.2	N14 25.0	162 59.9	11.8	N 7 50.3	16.1	58.9
	01	193 48.3	24.2	177 30.7	12.0	7 34.2	16.0	58.9
	02	208 48.4	23.5	192 01.7	12.0	7 18.2	16.1	58.9
	03	223 48.5	. . 22.7	206 32.7	12.0	7 02.1	16.1	58.9
	04	238 48.6	21.9	221 03.7	12.1	6 46.0	16.2	58.8
	05	253 48.7	21.1	235 34.8	12.2	6 29.8	16.1	58.8
	06	268 48.8	N14 20.4	250 06.0	12.3	N 6 13.7	16.2	58.8
	07	283 49.0	19.6	264 37.3	12.3	5 57.5	16.1	58.7
	08	298 49.1	18.8	279 08.6	12.4	5 41.4	16.2	58.7
F	09	313 49.2	. . 18.1	293 40.0	12.5	5 25.2	16.2	58.7
R	10	328 49.3	17.3	308 11.5	12.5	5 09.0	16.2	58.6
I	11	343 49.4	16.5	322 43.0	12.6	4 52.8	16.1	58.6
D	12	358 49.5	N14 15.7	337 14.6	12.6	N 4 36.7	16.2	58.6
A	13	13 49.7	15.0	351 46.2	12.7	4 20.5	16.2	58.5
Y	14	28 49.8	14.2	6 17.9	12.8	4 04.3	16.2	58.5
	15	43 49.9	. . 13.4	20 49.7	12.8	3 48.1	16.2	58.5
	16	58 50.0	12.6	35 21.5	12.9	3 31.9	16.2	58.4
	17	73 50.1	11.9	49 53.4	12.9	3 15.7	16.2	58.4
	18	88 50.3	N14 11.1	64 25.3	13.0	N 2 59.5	16.2	58.4
	19	103 50.4	10.3	78 57.3	13.0	2 43.3	16.2	58.3
	20	118 50.5	09.5	93 29.3	13.1	2 27.1	16.1	58.3
	21	133 50.6	. . 08.8	108 01.4	13.1	2 11.0	16.2	58.3
	22	148 50.7	08.0	122 33.5	13.2	1 54.8	16.1	58.2
	23	163 50.9	07.2	137 05.7	13.2	1 38.7	16.2	58.2
	15 00	178 51.0	N14 06.4	151 37.9	13.2	N 1 22.5	16.1	58.2
	01	193 51.1	05.6	166 10.1	13.3	1 06.4	16.1	58.1
	02	208 51.2	04.9	180 42.4	13.4	0 50.3	16.1	58.1
	03	223 51.3	. . 04.1	195 14.8	13.4	0 34.2	16.0	58.1
	04	238 51.5	03.3	209 47.2	13.4	0 18.2	16.1	58.0
	05	253 51.6	02.5	224 19.6	13.5	N 0 02.1	16.0	58.0
	06	268 51.7	N14 01.7	238 52.1	13.5	S 0 13.9	16.0	58.0
S	07	283 51.8	01.0	253 24.6	13.5	0 29.9	16.0	57.9
A	08	298 52.0	14 00.2	267 57.1	13.6	0 45.9	16.0	57.9
T	09	313 52.1	13 59.4	282 29.7	13.6	1 01.9	15.9	57.8
U	10	328 52.2	58.6	297 02.3	13.6	1 17.8	15.9	57.8
R	11	343 52.3	57.8	311 34.9	13.7	1 33.7	15.9	57.8
D	12	358 52.4	N13 57.1	326 07.6	13.7	S 1 49.6	15.9	57.7
A	13	13 52.6	56.3	340 40.3	13.7	2 05.5	15.8	57.7
Y	14	28 52.7	55.5	355 13.0	13.8	2 21.3	15.8	57.7
	15	43 52.8	. . 54.7	9 45.8	13.7	2 37.1	15.8	57.6
	16	58 52.9	53.9	24 18.5	13.8	2 52.9	15.7	57.6
	17	73 53.1	53.1	38 51.3	13.9	3 08.6	15.7	57.6
	18	88 53.2	N13 52.3	53 24.2	13.8	S 3 24.3	15.6	57.5
	19	103 53.3	51.6	67 57.0	13.9	3 39.9	15.7	57.5
	20	118 53.4	50.8	82 29.9	13.9	3 55.6	15.6	57.5
	21	133 53.6	. . 50.0	97 02.8	13.9	4 11.2	15.5	57.4
	22	148 53.7	49.2	111 35.7	13.9	4 26.7	15.5	57.4
	23	163 53.8	48.4	126 08.6	14.0	4 42.2	15.5	57.4
	16 00	178 53.9	N13 47.6	140 41.6	13.9	S 4 57.7	15.4	57.3
	01	193 54.1	46.8	155 14.5	14.0	5 13.1	15.4	57.3
	02	208 54.2	46.0	169 47.5	14.0	5 28.5	15.3	57.3
	03	223 54.3	. . 45.3	184 20.5	14.0	5 43.8	15.3	57.2
	04	238 54.5	44.5	198 53.5	14.0	5 59.1	15.3	57.2
	05	253 54.6	43.7	213 26.5	14.0	6 14.4	15.2	57.1
	06	268 54.7	N13 42.9	227 59.5	14.0	S 6 29.6	15.1	57.1
	07	283 54.8	42.1	242 32.5	14.1	6 44.7	15.1	57.1
	08	298 55.0	41.3	257 05.6	14.0	6 59.8	15.1	57.0
S	09	313 55.1	. . 40.5	271 38.6	14.1	7 14.9	15.0	57.0
U	10	328 55.2	39.7	286 11.7	14.0	7 29.9	14.9	57.0
N	11	343 55.4	38.9	300 44.7	14.1	7 44.8	14.9	56.9
D	12	358 55.5	N13 38.1	315 17.8	14.0	S 7 59.7	14.9	56.9
A	13	13 55.6	37.3	329 50.8	14.1	8 14.6	14.7	56.9
Y	14	28 55.7	36.6	344 23.9	14.0	8 29.3	14.8	56.8
	15	43 55.9	. . 35.8	358 56.9	14.1	8 44.1	14.7	56.8
	16	58 56.0	35.0	13 30.0	14.1	8 58.8	14.6	56.8
	17	73 56.1	34.2	28 03.1	14.0	9 13.4	14.5	56.7
	18	88 56.3	N13 33.4	42 36.1	14.1	S 9 27.9	14.5	56.7
	19	103 56.4	32.6	57 09.2	14.0	9 42.4	14.5	56.7
	20	118 56.5	31.8	71 42.2	14.0	9 56.9	14.4	56.6
	21	133 56.7	. . 31.0	86 15.2	14.1	10 11.3	14.3	56.6
	22	148 56.8	30.2	100 48.3	14.0	10 25.6	14.2	56.6
	23	163 56.9	29.4	115 21.3	14.0	S10 39.8	14.2	56.5
		SD 15.8	*d* 0.8	SD 16.0		15.7		15.5

Lat.	Twilight Naut.	Twilight Civil	Sunrise	Moonrise 14	Moonrise 15	Moonrise 16	Moonrise 17
°	h m	h m	h m	h m	h m	h m	h m
N 72	////	////	02 24	06 03	08 21	10 36	13 05
N 70	////	////	02 56	06 13	08 20	10 23	12 34
68	////	01 43	03 19	06 20	08 19	10 14	12 12
66	////	02 21	03 37	06 26	08 18	10 06	11 55
64	////	02 47	03 52	06 31	08 17	09 59	11 41
62	01 32	03 07	04 04	06 36	08 16	09 53	11 30
60	02 06	03 23	04 14	06 40	08 16	09 48	11 20
N 58	02 30	03 36	04 23	06 43	08 15	09 44	11 12
56	02 49	03 47	04 31	06 46	08 15	09 40	11 04
54	03 04	03 57	04 38	06 49	08 14	09 37	10 58
52	03 17	04 06	04 44	06 51	08 14	09 33	10 52
50	03 28	04 13	04 50	06 54	08 13	09 31	10 46
45	03 50	04 30	05 02	06 58	08 13	09 25	10 35
N 40	04 07	04 42	05 12	07 02	08 12	09 19	10 26
35	04 21	04 53	05 20	07 06	08 11	09 15	10 18
30	04 32	05 02	05 27	07 09	08 11	09 11	10 11
20	04 50	05 17	05 40	07 14	08 10	09 05	09 58
N 10	05 04	05 29	05 51	07 19	08 10	08 59	09 48
0	05 15	05 40	06 01	07 23	08 09	08 54	09 38
S 10	05 25	05 50	06 11	07 27	08 08	08 48	09 29
20	05 33	05 59	06 22	07 32	08 08	08 43	09 18
30	05 41	06 09	06 34	07 37	08 07	08 37	09 07
35	05 45	06 15	06 41	07 40	08 07	08 33	09 00
40	05 48	06 20	06 48	07 43	08 06	08 29	08 53
45	05 52	06 27	06 57	07 47	08 06	08 24	08 44
S 50	05 56	06 34	07 08	07 52	08 05	08 19	08 33
52	05 58	06 38	07 13	07 54	08 05	08 16	08 28
54	06 00	06 41	07 19	07 56	08 05	08 14	08 23
56	06 02	06 45	07 25	07 58	08 05	08 11	08 17
58	06 04	06 50	07 32	08 01	08 04	08 07	08 11
S 60	06 06	06 55	07 39	08 04	08 04	08 04	08 03

Lat.	Sunset	Twilight Civil	Twilight Naut.	Moonset 14	Moonset 15	Moonset 16	Moonset 17
°	h m	h m	h m	h m	h m	h m	h m
N 72	21 39	////	////	20 14	19 40	19 02	18 09
N 70	21 09	23 31	////	20 11	19 45	19 17	18 41
68	20 46	22 19	////	20 09	19 50	19 29	19 04
66	20 29	21 44	////	20 07	19 53	19 39	19 23
64	20 15	21 19	23 35	20 05	19 56	19 48	19 38
62	20 03	21 00	22 31	20 03	19 59	19 55	19 51
60	19 53	20 44	21 59	20 02	20 02	20 01	20 02
N 58	19 44	20 31	21 36	20 01	20 04	20 07	20 11
56	19 37	20 20	21 18	20 00	20 06	20 12	20 19
54	19 30	20 10	21 03	19 59	20 07	20 17	20 27
52	19 24	20 02	20 51	19 58	20 09	20 21	20 34
50	19 18	19 54	20 40	19 57	20 11	20 24	20 40
45	19 07	19 38	20 18	19 55	20 14	20 33	20 53
N 40	18 57	19 26	20 01	19 53	20 16	20 39	21 04
35	18 49	19 15	19 47	19 52	20 19	20 45	21 13
30	18 41	19 06	19 36	19 51	20 21	20 50	21 21
20	18 29	18 52	19 19	19 49	20 24	20 59	21 35
N 10	18 18	18 40	19 05	19 47	20 27	21 07	21 48
0	18 08	18 29	18 54	19 45	20 30	21 15	22 00
S 10	17 58	18 20	18 45	19 43	20 33	21 22	22 12
20	17 47	18 10	18 36	19 41	20 37	21 31	22 24
30	17 36	18 00	18 29	19 39	20 40	21 40	22 39
35	17 29	17 55	18 25	19 38	20 42	21 45	22 47
40	17 21	17 49	18 21	19 36	20 45	21 51	22 57
45	17 12	17 43	18 17	19 34	20 47	21 58	23 09
S 50	17 02	17 35	18 13	19 32	20 51	22 07	23 22
52	16 57	17 32	18 12	19 31	20 52	22 11	23 29
54	16 51	17 28	18 10	19 30	20 54	22 15	23 36
56	16 45	17 24	18 08	19 29	20 56	22 20	23 44
58	16 38	17 20	18 07	19 27	20 58	22 26	23 54
S 60	16 31	17 15	18 05	19 26	21 00	22 32	24 04

Day	SUN Eqn. of Time 00^h	SUN Eqn. of Time 12^h	SUN Mer. Pass.	MOON Mer. Pass. Upper	MOON Mer. Pass. Lower	MOON Age	MOON Phase
d	m s	m s	h m	h m	h m	d %	
14	04 48	04 42	12 05	13 34	01 10	02 4	
15	04 36	04 30	12 05	14 20	01 57	03 10	
16	04 24	04 18	12 04	15 04	02 42	04 17	

UT	ARIES	VENUS −4·5		MARS +1·3		JUPITER −1·8		SATURN +0·5		STARS		
	GHA	GHA	Dec	GHA	Dec	GHA	Dec	GHA	Dec	Name	SHA	Dec
d h	° ′	° ′	° ′	° ′	° ′	° ′	° ′	° ′	° ′		° ′	° ′
17 00 MONDAY	325 23.5	136 50.3	S 5 25.4	231 19.6	N23 42.0	192 18.8	N18 05.6	311 09.3	N 3 16.3	Acamar	315 10.7	S40 11.5
01	340 25.9	151 50.7	26.6	246 20.3	42.0	207 20.7	05.4	326 11.8	16.3	Achernar	335 18.9	S57 05.7
02	355 28.4	166 51.1	27.8	261 20.9	42.0	222 22.7	05.3	341 14.4	16.2	Acrux	172 59.1	S63 15.0
03	10 30.8	181 51.5	. . 28.9	276 21.6	. . 42.0	237 24.6	. . 05.1	356 16.9	. . 16.2	Adhara	255 05.1	S29 00.3
04	25 33.3	196 51.9	30.1	291 22.3	42.0	252 26.5	05.0	11 19.4	16.1	Aldebaran	290 38.2	N16 33.8
05	40 35.8	211 52.3	31.3	306 23.0	42.0	267 28.4	04.8	26 22.0	16.1			
06	55 38.2	226 52.7	S 5 32.5	321 23.7	N23 41.9	282 30.3	N18 04.7	41 24.5	N 3 16.1	Alioth	166 12.2	N55 49.1
07	70 40.7	241 53.1	33.7	336 24.3	41.9	297 32.2	04.5	56 27.1	16.0	Alkaid	152 51.2	N49 11.0
08	85 43.2	256 53.5	34.9	351 25.0	41.9	312 34.1	04.4	71 29.6	16.0	Alnair	27 30.8	S46 49.7
09	100 45.6	271 53.9	. . 36.0	6 25.7	. . 41.9	327 36.0	. . 04.3	86 32.1	. . 15.9	Alnilam	275 36.5	S 1 11.0
10	115 48.1	286 54.2	37.2	21 26.4	41.9	342 37.9	04.1	101 34.7	15.9	Alphard	217 46.8	S 8 46.4
11	130 50.6	301 54.6	38.4	36 27.0	41.9	357 39.9	04.0	116 37.2	15.8			
12	145 53.0	316 55.0	S 5 39.6	51 27.7	N23 41.9	12 41.8	N18 03.8	131 39.8	N 3 15.8	Alphecca	126 02.6	N26 37.7
13	160 55.5	331 55.4	40.8	66 28.4	41.9	27 43.7	03.7	146 42.3	15.8	Alpheratz	357 33.1	N29 14.3
14	175 57.9	346 55.8	41.9	81 29.1	41.8	42 45.6	03.5	161 44.9	15.7	Altair	61 58.4	N 8 56.5
15	191 00.4	1 56.2	. . 43.1	96 29.7	. . 41.8	57 47.5	. . 03.4	176 47.4	. . 15.7	Ankaa	353 05.5	S42 09.4
16	206 02.9	16 56.6	44.3	111 30.4	41.8	72 49.4	03.3	191 50.0	15.6	Antares	112 14.1	S26 29.5
17	221 05.3	31 57.0	45.5	126 31.1	41.8	87 51.3	03.1	206 52.5	15.6			
18	236 07.8	46 57.4	S 5 46.7	141 31.8	N23 41.8	102 53.2	N18 03.0	221 55.0	N 3 15.5	Arcturus	145 46.8	N19 02.8
19	251 10.3	61 57.8	47.8	156 32.4	41.8	117 55.2	02.8	236 57.6	15.5	Atria	107 06.9	S69 04.7
20	266 12.7	76 58.3	49.0	171 33.1	41.7	132 57.1	02.7	252 00.1	15.4	Avior	234 14.8	S59 35.5
21	281 15.2	91 58.7	. . 50.2	186 33.8	. . 41.7	147 59.0	. . 02.5	267 02.7	. . 15.4	Bellatrix	278 21.6	N 6 22.5
22	296 17.7	106 59.1	51.4	201 34.5	41.7	163 00.9	02.4	282 05.2	15.4	Betelgeuse	270 50.8	N 7 24.8
23	311 20.1	121 59.5	52.6	216 35.2	41.7	178 02.8	02.2	297 07.8	15.3			
18 00 TUESDAY	326 22.6	136 59.9	S 5 53.7	231 35.8	N23 41.7	193 04.7	N18 02.1	312 10.3	N 3 15.3	Canopus	263 52.2	S52 42.3
01	341 25.1	152 00.3	54.9	246 36.5	41.6	208 06.6	02.0	327 12.9	15.2	Capella	280 20.1	N46 01.3
02	356 27.5	167 00.7	56.1	261 37.2	41.6	223 08.5	01.8	342 15.4	15.2	Deneb	49 24.4	N45 22.7
03	11 30.0	182 01.1	. . 57.3	276 37.9	. . 41.6	238 10.5	. . 01.7	357 17.9	. . 15.1	Denebola	182 23.9	N14 25.5
04	26 32.4	197 01.5	58.4	291 38.6	41.6	253 12.4	01.5	12 20.5	15.1	Diphda	348 45.7	S17 50.2
05	41 34.9	212 01.9	5 59.6	306 39.2	41.6	268 14.3	01.4	27 23.0	15.0			
06	56 37.4	227 02.3	S 6 00.8	321 39.9	N23 41.5	283 16.2	N18 01.2	42 25.6	N 3 15.0	Dubhe	193 40.0	N61 36.5
07	71 39.8	242 02.7	02.0	336 40.6	41.5	298 18.1	01.1	57 28.1	14.9	Elnath	278 00.3	N28 37.7
08	86 42.3	257 03.1	03.1	351 41.3	41.5	313 20.0	00.9	72 30.7	14.9	Eltanin	90 41.3	N51 29.3
09	101 44.8	272 03.6	. . 04.3	6 42.0	. . 41.5	328 21.9	. . 00.8	87 33.2	. . 14.9	Enif	33 37.2	N10 00.0
10	116 47.2	287 04.0	05.5	21 42.6	41.5	343 23.8	00.7	102 35.8	14.8	Fomalhaut	15 12.7	S29 28.7
11	131 49.7	302 04.4	06.7	36 43.3	41.4	358 25.8	00.5	117 38.3	14.8			
12	146 52.2	317 04.8	S 6 07.8	51 44.0	N23 41.4	13 27.7	N18 00.4	132 40.9	N 3 14.7	Gacrux	171 50.6	S57 15.9
13	161 54.6	332 05.2	09.0	66 44.7	41.4	28 29.6	00.2	147 43.4	14.7	Gienah	175 42.5	S17 41.4
14	176 57.1	347 05.6	10.2	81 45.4	41.4	43 31.5	18 00.1	162 45.9	14.6	Hadar	148 34.3	S60 30.3
15	191 59.6	2 06.0	. . 11.4	96 46.0	. . 41.4	58 33.4	17 59.9	177 48.5	. . 14.6	Hamal	327 49.5	N23 35.3
16	207 02.0	17 06.5	12.5	111 46.7	41.3	73 35.3	59.8	192 51.0	14.5	Kaus Aust.	83 30.5	S34 22.3
17	222 04.5	32 06.9	13.7	126 47.4	41.3	88 37.2	59.6	207 53.6	14.5			
18	237 06.9	47 07.3	S 6 14.9	141 48.1	N23 41.3	103 39.2	N17 59.5	222 56.1	N 3 14.4	Kochab	137 20.0	N74 03.0
19	252 09.4	62 07.7	16.1	156 48.8	41.3	118 41.1	59.4	237 58.7	14.4	Markab	13 28.3	N15 21.0
20	267 11.9	77 08.1	17.2	171 49.4	41.2	133 43.0	59.2	253 01.2	14.4	Menkar	314 04.7	N 4 11.8
21	282 14.3	92 08.6	. . 18.4	186 50.1	. . 41.2	148 44.9	. . 59.1	268 03.8	. . 14.3	Menkent	147 56.2	S36 30.2
22	297 16.8	107 09.0	19.6	201 50.8	41.2	163 46.8	58.9	283 06.3	14.3	Miaplacidus	221 38.9	S69 49.5
23	312 19.3	122 09.4	20.8	216 51.5	41.2	178 48.7	58.8	298 08.9	14.2			
19 00 WEDNESDAY	327 21.7	137 09.8	S 6 21.9	231 52.2	N23 41.1	193 50.6	N17 58.6	313 11.4	N 3 14.2	Mirfak	308 26.3	N49 57.2
01	342 24.2	152 10.2	23.1	246 52.9	41.1	208 52.5	58.5	328 14.0	14.1	Nunki	75 45.8	S26 15.8
02	357 26.7	167 10.7	24.3	261 53.5	41.1	223 54.5	58.3	343 16.5	14.1	Peacock	53 03.1	S56 38.9
03	12 29.1	182 11.1	. . 25.4	276 54.2	. . 41.0	238 56.4	. . 58.2	358 19.1	. . 14.0	Pollux	243 16.0	N27 57.7
04	27 31.6	197 11.5	26.6	291 54.9	41.0	253 58.3	58.1	13 21.6	14.0	Procyon	244 49.7	N 5 09.5
05	42 34.0	212 11.9	27.8	306 55.6	41.0	269 00.2	57.9	28 24.2	13.9			
06	57 36.5	227 12.4	S 6 28.9	321 56.3	N23 41.0	284 02.1	N17 57.8	43 26.7	N 3 13.9	Rasalhague	95 57.1	N12 32.6
07	72 39.0	242 12.8	30.1	336 57.0	40.9	299 04.0	57.6	58 29.3	13.8	Regulus	207 33.3	N11 50.3
08	87 41.4	257 13.2	31.3	351 57.6	40.9	314 05.9	57.5	73 31.8	13.8	Rigel	281 02.7	S 8 10.1
09	102 43.9	272 13.7	. . 32.5	6 58.3	. . 40.9	329 07.9	. . 57.3	88 34.4	. . 13.8	Rigil Kent.	139 38.6	S60 56.9
10	117 46.4	287 14.1	33.6	21 59.0	40.8	344 09.8	57.2	103 36.9	13.7	Sabik	102 01.1	S15 45.4
11	132 48.8	302 14.5	34.8	36 59.7	40.8	359 11.7	57.0	118 39.5	13.7			
12	147 51.3	317 14.9	S 6 36.0	52 00.4	N23 40.8	14 13.6	N17 56.9	133 42.0	N 3 13.6	Schedar	349 29.1	N56 40.9
13	162 53.8	332 15.4	37.1	67 01.1	40.8	29 15.5	56.7	148 44.6	13.6	Shaula	96 08.3	S37 07.4
14	177 56.2	347 15.8	38.3	82 01.7	40.7	44 17.4	56.6	163 47.1	13.5	Sirius	258 25.3	S16 45.0
15	192 58.7	2 16.2	. . 39.5	97 02.4	. . 40.7	59 19.4	. . 56.5	178 49.7	. . 13.5	Spica	158 21.1	S11 18.0
16	208 01.2	17 16.7	40.6	112 03.1	40.7	74 21.3	56.3	193 52.2	13.4	Suhail	222 45.8	S43 32.3
17	223 03.6	32 17.1	41.8	127 03.8	40.6	89 23.2	56.2	208 54.8	13.4			
18	238 06.1	47 17.5	S 6 43.0	142 04.5	N23 40.6	104 25.1	N17 56.0	223 57.3	N 3 13.3	Vega	80 32.0	N38 48.7
19	253 08.5	62 18.0	44.1	157 05.2	40.6	119 27.0	55.9	238 59.9	13.3	Zuben'ubi	136 54.6	S16 09.2
20	268 11.0	77 18.4	45.3	172 05.9	40.5	134 28.9	55.7	254 02.4	13.2			
21	283 13.5	92 18.9	. . 46.5	187 06.5	. . 40.5	149 30.8	. . 55.6	269 05.0	. . 13.2			
22	298 15.9	107 19.3	47.6	202 07.2	40.5	164 32.8	55.4	284 07.5	13.1			
23	313 18.4	122 19.7	48.8	217 07.9	40.4	179 34.7	55.3	299 10.1	13.1			
Mer. Pass. (h m)	2 14.1	*v* 0.4	*d* 1.2	*v* 0.7	*d* 0.0	*v* 1.9	*d* 0.1	*v* 2.5	*d* 0.0			

	SHA	Mer. Pass.
	° ′	h m
Venus	170 37.3	14 52
Mars	265 13.3	8 33
Jupiter	226 42.1	11 06
Saturn	345 47.7	3 11

Day	UT d h	SUN GHA ° ′	SUN Dec ° ′	MOON GHA ° ′	v ′	MOON Dec ° ′	d ′	HP ′
	17 00	178 57.1	N13 28.6	129 54.3	14.0	S10 54.0	14.2	56.5
	01	193 57.2	27.8	144 27.3	14.0	11 08.2	14.0	56.5
	02	208 57.3	27.0	159 00.3	14.0	11 22.2	14.0	56.4
	03	223 57.4	. . 26.2	173 33.3	13.9	11 36.2	13.9	56.4
	04	238 57.6	25.4	188 06.2	14.0	11 50.1	13.9	56.4
	05	253 57.7	24.6	202 39.2	13.9	12 04.0	13.8	56.3
	06	268 57.8	N13 23.8	217 12.1	14.0	S12 17.8	13.7	56.3
	07	283 58.0	23.0	231 45.1	13.9	12 31.5	13.7	56.3
	08	298 58.1	22.2	246 18.0	13.9	12 45.2	13.6	56.2
MONDAY	09	313 58.2	. . 21.4	260 50.9	13.8	12 58.8	13.5	56.2
	10	328 58.4	20.6	275 23.7	13.9	13 12.3	13.4	56.2
	11	343 58.5	19.8	289 56.6	13.8	13 25.7	13.4	56.1
	12	358 58.7	N13 19.0	304 29.4	13.8	S13 39.1	13.3	56.1
	13	13 58.8	18.2	319 02.2	13.8	13 52.4	13.2	56.1
	14	28 58.9	17.4	333 35.0	13.8	14 05.6	13.1	56.0
	15	43 59.1	. . 16.6	348 07.8	13.7	14 18.7	13.1	56.0
	16	58 59.2	15.8	2 40.5	13.7	14 31.8	12.9	56.0
	17	73 59.3	15.0	17 13.2	13.7	14 44.7	13.0	56.0
	18	88 59.5	N13 14.2	31 45.9	13.7	S14 57.7	12.8	55.9
	19	103 59.6	13.4	46 18.6	13.7	15 10.5	12.7	55.9
	20	118 59.7	12.6	60 51.3	13.6	15 23.2	12.7	55.9
	21	133 59.9	. . 11.8	75 23.9	13.6	15 35.9	12.6	55.8
	22	149 00.0	11.0	89 56.5	13.5	15 48.5	12.5	55.8
	23	164 00.1	10.2	104 29.0	13.6	16 01.0	12.4	55.8
	18 00	179 00.3	N13 09.4	119 01.6	13.5	S16 13.4	12.3	55.8
	01	194 00.4	08.6	133 34.1	13.4	16 25.7	12.3	55.7
	02	209 00.6	07.8	148 06.5	13.5	16 38.0	12.2	55.7
	03	224 00.7	. . 07.0	162 39.0	13.4	16 50.2	12.0	55.7
	04	239 00.8	06.2	177 11.4	13.3	17 02.2	12.0	55.6
	05	254 01.0	05.3	191 43.7	13.4	17 14.2	11.9	55.6
	06	269 01.1	N13 04.5	206 16.1	13.3	S17 26.1	11.9	55.6
	07	284 01.3	03.7	220 48.4	13.3	17 38.0	11.7	55.6
	08	299 01.4	02.9	235 20.7	13.2	17 49.7	11.6	55.5
TUESDAY	09	314 01.5	. . 02.1	249 52.9	13.2	18 01.3	11.6	55.5
	10	329 01.7	01.3	264 25.1	13.2	18 12.9	11.4	55.5
	11	344 01.8	13 00.5	278 57.3	13.1	18 24.3	11.4	55.4
	12	359 01.9	N12 59.7	293 29.4	13.1	S18 35.7	11.3	55.4
	13	14 02.1	58.9	308 01.5	13.1	18 47.0	11.2	55.4
	14	29 02.2	58.1	322 33.6	13.0	18 58.2	11.1	55.4
	15	44 02.4	. . 57.3	337 05.6	13.0	19 09.3	11.0	55.3
	16	59 02.5	56.4	351 37.6	12.9	19 20.3	10.9	55.3
	17	74 02.7	55.6	6 09.5	12.9	19 31.2	10.8	55.3
	18	89 02.8	N12 54.8	20 41.4	12.9	S19 42.0	10.7	55.3
	19	104 02.9	54.0	35 13.3	12.8	19 52.7	10.6	55.2
	20	119 03.1	53.2	49 45.1	12.8	20 03.3	10.5	55.2
	21	134 03.2	. . 52.4	64 16.9	12.7	20 13.8	10.4	55.2
	22	149 03.4	51.6	78 48.6	12.7	20 24.2	10.3	55.2
	23	164 03.5	50.8	93 20.3	12.6	20 34.5	10.2	55.1
	19 00	179 03.6	N12 49.9	107 51.9	12.7	S20 44.7	10.2	55.1
	01	194 03.8	49.1	122 23.6	12.5	20 54.9	10.0	55.1
	02	209 03.9	48.3	136 55.1	12.6	21 04.9	9.9	55.1
	03	224 04.1	. . 47.5	151 26.7	12.4	21 14.8	9.8	55.1
	04	239 04.2	46.7	165 58.1	12.5	21 24.6	9.7	55.0
	05	254 04.4	45.9	180 29.6	12.4	21 34.3	9.6	55.0
	06	269 04.5	N12 45.0	195 01.0	12.3	S21 43.9	9.5	55.0
	07	284 04.7	44.2	209 32.3	12.3	21 53.4	9.4	55.0
	08	299 04.8	43.4	224 03.6	12.3	22 02.8	9.3	54.9
WEDNESDAY	09	314 04.9	. . 42.6	238 34.9	12.2	22 12.1	9.2	54.9
	10	329 05.1	41.8	253 06.1	12.2	22 21.3	9.1	54.9
	11	344 05.2	41.0	267 37.3	12.1	22 30.4	8.9	54.9
	12	359 05.4	N12 40.1	282 08.4	12.1	S22 39.3	8.9	54.9
	13	14 05.5	39.3	296 39.5	12.1	22 48.2	8.7	54.8
	14	29 05.7	38.5	311 10.6	12.0	22 56.9	8.7	54.8
	15	44 05.8	. . 37.7	325 41.6	11.9	23 05.6	8.5	54.8
	16	59 06.0	36.9	340 12.5	11.9	23 14.1	8.4	54.8
	17	74 06.1	36.1	354 43.4	11.9	23 22.5	8.3	54.8
	18	89 06.3	N12 35.2	9 14.3	11.8	S23 30.8	8.2	54.8
	19	104 06.4	34.4	23 45.1	11.8	23 39.0	8.1	54.7
	20	119 06.5	33.6	38 15.9	11.7	23 47.1	8.0	54.7
	21	134 06.7	. . 32.8	52 46.6	11.7	23 55.1	7.8	54.7
	22	149 06.8	31.9	67 17.3	11.7	24 02.9	7.8	54.7
	23	164 07.0	31.1	81 48.0	11.6	S24 10.7	7.6	54.7
		SD 15.8	*d* 0.8	SD 15.3		15.1		14.9

Lat. °	Twilight Naut. h m	Twilight Civil h m	Sunrise h m	Moonrise 17 h m	Moonrise 18 h m	Moonrise 19 h m	Moonrise 20 h m
N 72	////	////	02 44	13 05	▬	▬	▬
N 70	////	01 13	03 11	12 34	15 32	▬	▬
68	////	02 05	03 32	12 12	14 28	▬	▬
66	////	02 36	03 48	11 55	13 53	16 25	▬
64	01 04	02 59	04 01	11 41	13 28	15 25	▬
62	01 51	03 17	04 12	11 30	13 09	14 51	16 39
60	02 19	03 31	04 21	11 20	12 53	14 27	16 00
N 58	02 40	03 44	04 30	11 12	12 40	14 07	15 32
56	02 57	03 54	04 37	11 04	12 28	13 51	15 11
54	03 11	04 03	04 43	10 58	12 18	13 38	14 54
52	03 23	04 11	04 49	10 52	12 09	13 26	14 39
50	03 34	04 18	04 54	10 46	12 01	13 15	14 26
45	03 55	04 34	05 05	10 35	11 45	12 53	13 59
N 40	04 11	04 46	05 14	10 26	11 31	12 36	13 38
35	04 24	04 56	05 22	10 18	11 19	12 21	13 21
30	04 34	05 04	05 29	10 11	11 09	12 08	13 06
20	04 51	05 18	05 41	09 58	10 52	11 46	12 41
N 10	05 04	05 29	05 51	09 48	10 37	11 28	12 19
0	05 15	05 39	06 01	09 38	10 23	11 10	11 59
S 10	05 23	05 48	06 10	09 29	10 10	10 53	11 39
20	05 31	05 57	06 20	09 18	09 55	10 35	11 17
30	05 38	06 06	06 31	09 07	09 39	10 13	10 53
35	05 41	06 11	06 37	09 00	09 29	10 01	10 38
40	05 45	06 16	06 44	08 53	09 18	09 47	10 21
45	05 48	06 22	06 53	08 44	09 05	09 31	10 01
S 50	05 51	06 29	07 03	08 33	08 50	09 10	09 36
52	05 53	06 32	07 07	08 28	08 43	09 01	09 24
54	05 54	06 35	07 12	08 23	08 35	08 50	09 11
56	05 55	06 39	07 18	08 17	08 26	08 37	08 55
58	05 57	06 43	07 24	08 11	08 16	08 23	08 36
S 60	05 58	06 47	07 31	08 03	08 04	08 07	08 13

Lat. °	Sunset h m	Twilight Civil h m	Twilight Naut. h m	Moonset 17 h m	Moonset 18 h m	Moonset 19 h m	Moonset 20 h m
N 72	21 19	////	////	18 09	▬	▬	▬
N 70	20 53	22 44	////	18 41	17 19	▬	▬
68	20 33	21 57	////	19 04	18 24	▬	▬
66	20 17	21 28	////	19 23	19 00	18 06	▬
64	20 05	21 06	22 54	19 38	19 26	19 07	▬
62	19 54	20 48	22 12	19 51	19 46	19 41	19 35
60	19 45	20 34	21 45	20 02	20 03	20 07	20 15
N 58	19 37	20 22	21 24	20 11	20 17	20 27	20 43
56	19 30	20 12	21 08	20 19	20 29	20 43	21 05
54	19 23	20 03	20 54	20 27	20 40	20 57	21 23
52	19 18	19 55	20 43	20 34	20 49	21 10	21 38
50	19 13	19 48	20 33	20 40	20 58	21 21	21 51
45	19 02	19 33	20 12	20 53	21 16	21 44	22 18
N 40	18 53	19 21	19 56	21 04	21 31	22 02	22 40
35	18 45	19 12	19 43	21 13	21 43	22 18	22 58
30	18 38	19 03	19 33	21 21	21 55	22 31	23 13
20	18 27	18 49	19 16	21 35	22 14	22 55	23 39
N 10	18 17	18 38	19 03	21 48	22 30	23 15	24 02
0	18 07	18 28	18 53	22 00	22 46	23 33	24 23
S 10	17 58	18 20	18 44	22 12	23 01	23 52	24 44
20	17 48	18 11	18 37	22 24	23 18	24 13	00 13
30	17 37	18 02	18 30	22 39	23 38	24 36	00 36
35	17 31	17 57	18 27	22 47	23 49	24 50	00 50
40	17 24	17 52	18 24	22 57	24 02	00 02	01 06
45	17 16	17 46	18 20	23 09	24 18	00 18	01 25
S 50	17 06	17 39	18 17	23 22	24 37	00 37	01 49
52	17 01	17 36	18 16	23 29	24 46	00 46	02 01
54	16 56	17 33	18 15	23 36	24 56	00 56	02 14
56	16 51	17 30	18 13	23 44	25 08	01 08	02 30
58	16 45	17 26	18 12	23 54	25 21	01 21	02 48
S 60	16 37	17 22	18 11	24 04	00 04	01 37	03 11

Day	SUN Eqn. of Time 00^h	SUN Eqn. of Time 12^h	SUN Mer. Pass.	MOON Mer. Pass. Upper	MOON Mer. Pass. Lower	MOON Age	MOON Phase
d	m s	m s	h m	h m	h m	d	%
17	04 12	04 06	12 04	15 49	03 27	05	25
18	03 59	03 52	12 04	16 35	04 12	06	35
19	03 46	03 39	12 04	17 22	04 58	07	44

2026 AUGUST 20, 21, 22 (THURS., FRI., SAT.)

UT d h	ARIES GHA ° ′	VENUS −4·5 GHA ° ′	Dec ° ′	MARS +1·3 GHA ° ′	Dec ° ′	JUPITER −1·8 GHA ° ′	Dec ° ′	SATURN +0·5 GHA ° ′	Dec ° ′
20 00	328 20.9	137 20.2	S 6 49.9	232 08.6	N23 40.4	194 36.6	N17 55.2	314 12.6	N 3 13.0
01	343 23.3	152 20.6	51.1	247 09.3	40.4	209 38.5	55.0	329 15.2	13.0
02	358 25.8	167 21.1	52.3	262 10.0	40.3	224 40.4	54.9	344 17.7	13.0
03	13 28.3	182 21.5	. . 53.4	277 10.7	. . 40.3	239 42.3	. . 54.7	359 20.3	. . 12.9
04	28 30.7	197 21.9	54.6	292 11.4	40.3	254 44.2	54.6	14 22.8	12.9
05	43 33.2	212 22.4	55.8	307 12.0	40.2	269 46.2	54.4	29 25.4	12.8
06	58 35.7	227 22.8	S 6 56.9	322 12.7	N23 40.2	284 48.1	N17 54.3	44 27.9	N 3 12.8
07	73 38.1	242 23.3	58.1	337 13.4	40.2	299 50.0	54.1	59 30.5	12.7
T 08	88 40.6	257 23.7	6 59.2	352 14.1	40.1	314 51.9	54.0	74 33.1	12.7
H 09	103 43.0	272 24.2	7 00.4	7 14.8	. . 40.1	329 53.8	. . 53.9	89 35.6	. . 12.6
U 10	118 45.5	287 24.6	01.6	22 15.5	40.0	344 55.7	53.7	104 38.2	12.6
R 11	133 48.0	302 25.1	02.7	37 16.2	40.0	359 57.7	53.6	119 40.7	12.5
S 12	148 50.4	317 25.5	S 7 03.9	52 16.9	N23 40.0	14 59.6	N17 53.4	134 43.3	N 3 12.5
D 13	163 52.9	332 26.0	05.1	67 17.5	39.9	30 01.5	53.3	149 45.8	12.4
A 14	178 55.4	347 26.4	06.2	82 18.2	39.9	45 03.4	53.1	164 48.4	12.4
Y 15	193 57.8	2 26.9	. . 07.4	97 18.9	. . 39.9	60 05.3	. . 53.0	179 50.9	. . 12.3
16	209 00.3	17 27.3	08.5	112 19.6	39.8	75 07.2	52.8	194 53.5	12.3
17	224 02.8	32 27.8	09.7	127 20.3	39.8	90 09.2	52.7	209 56.0	12.2
18	239 05.2	47 28.2	S 7 10.8	142 21.0	N23 39.7	105 11.1	N17 52.5	224 58.6	N 3 12.2
19	254 07.7	62 28.7	12.0	157 21.7	39.7	120 13.0	52.4	240 01.1	12.1
20	269 10.1	77 29.1	13.2	172 22.4	39.7	135 14.9	52.3	255 03.7	12.1
21	284 12.6	92 29.6	. . 14.3	187 23.1	. . 39.6	150 16.8	. . 52.1	270 06.3	. . 12.0
22	299 15.1	107 30.0	15.5	202 23.8	39.6	165 18.7	52.0	285 08.8	12.0
23	314 17.5	122 30.5	16.6	217 24.4	39.5	180 20.7	51.8	300 11.4	11.9
21 00	329 20.0	137 30.9	S 7 17.8	232 25.1	N23 39.5	195 22.6	N17 51.7	315 13.9	N 3 11.9
01	344 22.5	152 31.4	18.9	247 25.8	39.5	210 24.5	51.5	330 16.5	11.8
02	359 24.9	167 31.9	20.1	262 26.5	39.4	225 26.4	51.4	345 19.0	11.8
03	14 27.4	182 32.3	. . 21.3	277 27.2	. . 39.4	240 28.3	. . 51.2	0 21.6	. . 11.7
04	29 29.9	197 32.8	22.4	292 27.9	39.3	255 30.2	51.1	15 24.1	11.7
05	44 32.3	212 33.2	23.6	307 28.6	39.3	270 32.2	51.0	30 26.7	11.7
06	59 34.8	227 33.7	S 7 24.7	322 29.3	N23 39.2	285 34.1	N17 50.8	45 29.3	N 3 11.6
07	74 37.3	242 34.2	25.9	337 30.0	39.2	300 36.0	50.7	60 31.8	11.6
08	89 39.7	257 34.6	27.0	352 30.7	39.2	315 37.9	50.5	75 34.4	11.5
F 09	104 42.2	272 35.1	. . 28.2	7 31.4	. . 39.1	330 39.8	. . 50.4	90 36.9	. . 11.5
R 10	119 44.6	287 35.6	29.3	22 32.1	39.1	345 41.7	50.2	105 39.5	11.4
I 11	134 47.1	302 36.0	30.5	37 32.7	39.0	0 43.7	50.1	120 42.0	11.4
D 12	149 49.6	317 36.5	S 7 31.6	52 33.4	N23 39.0	15 45.6	N17 49.9	135 44.6	N 3 11.3
A 13	164 52.0	332 37.0	32.8	67 34.1	38.9	30 47.5	49.8	150 47.2	11.3
Y 14	179 54.5	347 37.4	33.9	82 34.8	38.9	45 49.4	49.6	165 49.7	11.2
15	194 57.0	2 37.9	. . 35.1	97 35.5	. . 38.8	60 51.3	. . 49.5	180 52.3	. . 11.2
16	209 59.4	17 38.4	36.2	112 36.2	38.8	75 53.2	49.4	195 54.8	11.1
17	225 01.9	32 38.8	37.4	127 36.9	38.7	90 55.2	49.2	210 57.4	11.1
18	240 04.4	47 39.3	S 7 38.5	142 37.6	N23 38.7	105 57.1	N17 49.1	225 59.9	N 3 11.0
19	255 06.8	62 39.8	39.7	157 38.3	38.6	120 59.0	48.9	241 02.5	11.0
20	270 09.3	77 40.2	40.8	172 39.0	38.6	136 00.9	48.8	256 05.1	10.9
21	285 11.8	92 40.7	. . 42.0	187 39.7	. . 38.6	151 02.8	. . 48.6	271 07.6	. . 10.9
22	300 14.2	107 41.2	43.1	202 40.4	38.5	166 04.8	48.5	286 10.2	10.8
23	315 16.7	122 41.7	44.3	217 41.1	38.5	181 06.7	48.3	301 12.7	10.8
22 00	330 19.1	137 42.1	S 7 45.4	232 41.8	N23 38.4	196 08.6	N17 48.2	316 15.3	N 3 10.7
01	345 21.6	152 42.6	46.6	247 42.5	38.4	211 10.5	48.0	331 17.9	10.7
02	0 24.1	167 43.1	47.7	262 43.2	38.3	226 12.4	47.9	346 20.4	10.6
03	15 26.5	182 43.6	. . 48.9	277 43.9	. . 38.3	241 14.3	. . 47.8	1 23.0	. . 10.6
04	30 29.0	197 44.0	50.0	292 44.6	38.2	256 16.3	47.6	16 25.5	10.5
05	45 31.5	212 44.5	51.2	307 45.2	38.2	271 18.2	47.5	31 28.1	10.5
06	60 33.9	227 45.0	S 7 52.3	322 45.9	N23 38.1	286 20.1	N17 47.3	46 30.7	N 3 10.4
07	75 36.4	242 45.5	53.5	337 46.6	38.1	301 22.0	47.2	61 33.2	10.4
S 08	90 38.9	257 46.0	54.6	352 47.3	38.0	316 23.9	47.0	76 35.8	10.3
A 09	105 41.3	272 46.5	. . 55.8	7 48.0	. . 37.9	331 25.9	. . 46.9	91 38.3	. . 10.3
T 10	120 43.8	287 46.9	56.9	22 48.7	37.9	346 27.8	46.7	106 40.9	10.2
U 11	135 46.3	302 47.4	58.1	37 49.4	37.8	1 29.7	46.6	121 43.5	10.2
R 12	150 48.7	317 47.9	S 7 59.2	52 50.1	N23 37.8	16 31.6	N17 46.4	136 46.0	N 3 10.1
D 13	165 51.2	332 48.4	8 00.3	67 50.8	37.7	31 33.5	46.3	151 48.6	10.1
A 14	180 53.6	347 48.9	01.5	82 51.5	37.7	46 35.5	46.2	166 51.1	10.0
Y 15	195 56.1	2 49.4	. . 02.6	97 52.2	. . 37.6	61 37.4	. . 46.0	181 53.7	. . 10.0
16	210 58.6	17 49.8	03.8	112 52.9	37.6	76 39.3	45.9	196 56.3	09.9
17	226 01.0	32 50.3	04.9	127 53.6	37.5	91 41.2	45.7	211 58.8	09.9
18	241 03.5	47 50.8	S 8 06.1	142 54.3	N23 37.5	106 43.1	N17 45.6	227 01.4	N 3 09.8
19	256 06.0	62 51.3	07.2	157 55.0	37.4	121 45.1	45.4	242 03.9	09.7
20	271 08.4	77 51.8	08.3	172 55.7	37.4	136 47.0	45.3	257 06.5	09.7
21	286 10.9	92 52.3	. . 09.5	187 56.4	. . 37.3	151 48.9	. . 45.1	272 09.1	. . 09.6
22	301 13.4	107 52.8	10.6	202 57.1	37.2	166 50.8	45.0	287 11.6	09.6
23	316 15.8	122 53.3	11.8	217 57.8	37.2	181 52.7	44.8	302 14.2	09.5
Mer. Pass.	h m 2 02.3	v 0.5	d 1.2	v 0.7	d 0.0	v 1.9	d 0.1	v 2.6	d 0.0

STARS

Name	SHA ° ′	Dec ° ′
Acamar	315 10.7	S40 11.5
Achernar	335 18.9	S57 05.7
Acrux	172 59.1	S63 15.0
Adhara	255 05.1	S29 00.3
Aldebaran	290 38.1	N16 33.8
Alioth	166 12.2	N55 49.1
Alkaid	152 51.2	N49 11.0
Alnair	27 30.8	S46 49.8
Alnilam	275 36.5	S 1 11.0
Alphard	217 46.8	S 8 46.4
Alphecca	126 02.6	N26 37.7
Alpheratz	357 33.1	N29 14.3
Altair	61 58.4	N 8 56.5
Ankaa	353 05.5	S42 09.4
Antares	112 14.1	S26 29.5
Arcturus	145 46.8	N19 02.8
Atria	107 06.9	S69 04.7
Avior	234 14.8	S59 35.5
Bellatrix	278 21.6	N 6 22.5
Betelgeuse	270 50.8	N 7 24.8
Canopus	263 52.1	S52 42.3
Capella	280 20.1	N46 01.3
Deneb	49 24.4	N45 22.7
Denebola	182 23.9	N14 25.5
Diphda	348 45.7	S17 50.2
Dubhe	193 40.0	N61 36.5
Elnath	278 00.3	N28 37.7
Eltanin	90 41.3	N51 29.4
Enif	33 37.1	N10 00.0
Fomalhaut	15 12.7	S29 28.7
Gacrux	171 50.6	S57 15.9
Gienah	175 42.5	S17 41.4
Hadar	148 34.4	S60 30.3
Hamal	327 49.5	N23 35.3
Kaus Aust.	83 30.5	S34 22.3
Kochab	137 20.1	N74 03.0
Markab	13 28.2	N15 21.1
Menkar	314 04.7	N 4 11.8
Menkent	147 56.2	S36 30.2
Miaplacidus	221 38.9	S69 49.5
Mirfak	308 26.3	N49 57.2
Nunki	75 45.8	S26 15.8
Peacock	53 03.1	S56 38.9
Pollux	243 16.0	N27 57.7
Procyon	244 49.7	N 5 09.5
Rasalhague	95 57.1	N12 32.6
Regulus	207 33.3	N11 50.3
Rigel	281 02.7	S 8 10.1
Rigil Kent.	139 38.6	S60 56.9
Sabik	102 01.1	S15 45.4
Schedar	349 29.1	N56 40.9
Shaula	96 08.3	S37 07.4
Sirius	258 25.3	S16 45.0
Spica	158 21.1	S11 18.0
Suhail	222 45.8	S43 32.3
Vega	80 32.0	N38 48.7
Zuben'ubi	136 54.6	S16 09.2

	SHA ° ′	Mer. Pass. h m
Venus	168 10.9	14 49
Mars	263 05.1	8 30
Jupiter	226 02.6	10 57
Saturn	345 53.9	2 59

UT	SUN GHA	SUN Dec	MOON GHA	v	MOON Dec	d	HP
d h	° ′	° ′	° ′	′	° ′	′	′
20 00	179 07.1	N12 30.3	96 18.6	11.5	S24 18.3	7.5	54.6
01	194 07.3	29.5	110 49.1	11.5	24 25.8	7.4	54.6
02	209 07.4	28.7	125 19.6	11.5	24 33.2	7.3	54.6
03	224 07.6	. . 27.8	139 50.1	11.4	24 40.5	7.2	54.6
04	239 07.7	27.0	154 20.5	11.4	24 47.7	7.0	54.6
05	254 07.9	26.2	168 50.9	11.3	24 54.7	6.9	54.6
06	269 08.0	N12 25.4	183 21.2	11.3	S25 01.6	6.8	54.6
T 07	284 08.2	24.5	197 51.5	11.3	25 08.4	6.7	54.5
H 08	299 08.3	23.7	212 21.8	11.2	25 15.1	6.6	54.5
U 09	314 08.5	. . 22.9	226 52.0	11.2	25 21.7	6.4	54.5
R 10	329 08.6	22.1	241 22.2	11.1	25 28.1	6.4	54.5
S 11	344 08.8	21.2	255 52.3	11.1	25 34.5	6.2	54.5
D 12	359 08.9	N12 20.4	270 22.4	11.0	S25 40.7	6.1	54.5
A 13	14 09.1	19.6	284 52.4	11.0	25 46.8	5.9	54.5
Y 14	29 09.2	18.8	299 22.4	11.0	25 52.7	5.9	54.4
15	44 09.4	. . 17.9	313 52.4	10.9	25 58.6	5.7	54.4
16	59 09.5	17.1	328 22.3	10.9	26 04.3	5.6	54.4
17	74 09.7	16.3	342 52.2	10.8	26 09.9	5.4	54.4
18	89 09.8	N12 15.4	357 22.0	10.8	S26 15.3	5.4	54.4
19	104 10.0	14.6	11 51.8	10.8	26 20.7	5.2	54.4
20	119 10.1	13.8	26 21.6	10.7	26 25.9	5.1	54.4
21	134 10.3	. . 13.0	40 51.3	10.7	26 31.0	4.9	54.4
22	149 10.4	12.1	55 21.0	10.7	26 35.9	4.9	54.4
23	164 10.6	11.3	69 50.7	10.6	26 40.8	4.7	54.3
21 00	179 10.8	N12 10.5	84 20.3	10.6	S26 45.5	4.6	54.3
01	194 10.9	09.6	98 49.9	10.6	26 50.1	4.4	54.3
02	209 11.1	08.8	113 19.5	10.5	26 54.5	4.3	54.3
03	224 11.2	. . 08.0	127 49.0	10.5	26 58.8	4.2	54.3
04	239 11.4	07.1	142 18.5	10.5	27 03.0	4.1	54.3
05	254 11.5	06.3	156 48.0	10.4	27 07.1	3.9	54.3
06	269 11.7	N12 05.5	171 17.4	10.4	S27 11.0	3.8	54.3
07	284 11.8	04.6	185 46.8	10.4	27 14.8	3.7	54.3
08	299 12.0	03.8	200 16.2	10.3	27 18.5	3.5	54.3
F 09	314 12.1	. . 03.0	214 45.5	10.3	27 22.0	3.5	54.3
R 10	329 12.3	02.1	229 14.8	10.3	27 25.5	3.2	54.3
I 11	344 12.4	01.3	243 44.1	10.3	27 28.7	3.2	54.3
D 12	359 12.6	N12 00.5	258 13.4	10.2	S27 31.9	3.0	54.2
A 13	14 12.8	11 59.6	272 42.6	10.2	27 34.9	2.9	54.2
Y 14	29 12.9	58.8	287 11.8	10.2	27 37.8	2.7	54.2
15	44 13.1	. . 58.0	301 41.0	10.2	27 40.5	2.7	54.2
16	59 13.2	57.1	316 10.2	10.1	27 43.2	2.5	54.2
17	74 13.4	56.3	330 39.3	10.1	27 45.7	2.3	54.2
18	89 13.5	N11 55.5	345 08.4	10.1	S27 48.0	2.2	54.2
19	104 13.7	54.6	359 37.5	10.1	27 50.2	2.1	54.2
20	119 13.9	53.8	14 06.6	10.1	27 52.3	2.0	54.2
21	134 14.0	. . 53.0	28 35.7	10.0	27 54.3	1.8	54.2
22	149 14.2	52.1	43 04.7	10.1	27 56.1	1.7	54.2
23	164 14.3	51.3	57 33.8	10.0	27 57.8	1.5	54.2
22 00	179 14.5	N11 50.4	72 02.8	10.0	S27 59.3	1.4	54.2
01	194 14.6	49.6	86 31.8	10.0	28 00.7	1.3	54.2
02	209 14.8	48.8	101 00.8	9.9	28 02.0	1.1	54.2
03	224 15.0	. . 47.9	115 29.7	10.0	28 03.1	1.1	54.2
04	239 15.1	47.1	129 58.7	10.0	28 04.2	0.8	54.2
05	254 15.3	46.2	144 27.7	9.9	28 05.0	0.8	54.2
06	269 15.4	N11 45.4	158 56.6	10.0	S28 05.8	0.6	54.2
S 07	284 15.6	44.6	173 25.6	9.9	28 06.4	0.4	54.2
A 08	299 15.8	43.7	187 54.5	9.9	28 06.8	0.4	54.2
T 09	314 15.9	. . 42.9	202 23.4	9.9	28 07.2	0.1	54.2
U 10	329 16.1	42.0	216 52.3	9.9	28 07.3	0.1	54.2
R 11	344 16.2	41.2	231 21.2	9.9	28 07.4	0.1	54.2
D 12	359 16.4	N11 40.4	245 50.1	10.0	S28 07.3	0.2	54.2
A 13	14 16.6	39.5	260 19.1	9.9	28 07.1	0.4	54.2
Y 14	29 16.7	38.7	274 48.0	9.9	28 06.7	0.4	54.2
15	44 16.9	. . 37.8	289 16.9	9.9	28 06.3	0.7	54.2
16	59 17.0	37.0	303 45.8	9.9	28 05.6	0.7	54.2
17	74 17.2	36.1	318 14.7	9.9	28 04.9	0.9	54.2
18	89 17.4	N11 35.3	332 43.6	9.9	S28 04.0	1.1	54.2
19	104 17.5	34.5	347 12.5	10.0	28 02.9	1.1	54.2
20	119 17.7	33.6	1 41.5	9.9	28 01.8	1.3	54.2
21	134 17.9	. . 32.8	16 10.4	9.9	28 00.5	1.5	54.2
22	149 18.0	31.9	30 39.3	10.0	27 59.0	1.5	54.2
23	164 18.2	31.1	45 08.3	9.9	S27 57.5	1.8	54.2
	SD 15.8	*d* 0.8	SD	14.8	14.8		14.8

Lat.	Twilight Naut.	Twilight Civil	Sunrise	Moonrise 20	Moonrise 21	Moonrise 22	Moonrise 23
°	h m	h m	h m	h m	h m	h m	h m
N 72	////	////	03 02	■	■	■	■
N 70	////	01 44	03 26	■	■	■	■
68	////	02 24	03 44	■	■	■	■
66	////	02 50	03 58	■	■	■	■
64	01 32	03 10	04 10	■	■	■	■
62	02 07	03 27	04 20	16 39	18 42	■	19 36
60	02 32	03 40	04 29	16 00	17 23	18 22	18 49
N 58	02 50	03 51	04 36	15 32	16 48	17 44	18 19
56	03 06	04 01	04 43	15 11	16 22	17 18	17 56
54	03 19	04 09	04 48	14 54	16 02	16 57	17 38
52	03 30	04 17	04 54	14 39	15 45	16 40	17 22
50	03 40	04 23	04 58	14 26	15 30	16 25	17 08
45	03 59	04 37	05 09	13 59	15 00	15 55	16 40
N 40	04 14	04 49	05 17	13 38	14 37	15 31	16 18
35	04 26	04 58	05 24	13 21	14 18	15 12	15 59
30	04 37	05 06	05 31	13 06	14 02	14 55	15 43
20	04 52	05 19	05 42	12 41	13 35	14 27	15 17
N 10	05 04	05 30	05 51	12 19	13 11	14 03	14 53
0	05 14	05 39	06 00	11 59	12 49	13 41	14 32
S 10	05 22	05 47	06 08	11 39	12 27	13 18	14 10
20	05 29	05 55	06 17	11 17	12 04	12 54	13 47
30	05 35	06 03	06 28	10 53	11 37	12 26	13 20
35	05 38	06 08	06 34	10 38	11 21	12 10	13 04
40	05 41	06 12	06 40	10 21	11 02	11 50	12 45
45	05 43	06 18	06 48	10 01	10 40	11 27	12 23
S 50	05 46	06 24	06 57	09 36	10 11	10 57	11 54
52	05 47	06 26	07 01	09 24	09 57	10 42	11 40
54	05 48	06 29	07 06	09 11	09 41	10 25	11 24
56	05 49	06 32	07 11	08 55	09 22	10 04	11 04
58	05 50	06 36	07 16	08 36	08 59	09 38	10 39
S 60	05 51	06 39	07 23	08 13	08 27	09 02	10 07

Lat.	Sunset	Twilight Civil	Twilight Naut.	Moonset 20	Moonset 21	Moonset 22	Moonset 23
°	h m	h m	h m	h m	h m	h m	h m
N 72	20 59	23 33	////	■	■	■	■
N 70	20 37	22 14	////	■	■	■	■
68	20 20	21 38	////	■	■	■	■
66	20 06	21 12	23 37	■	■	■	■
64	19 54	20 53	22 28	■	■	■	■
62	19 44	20 37	21 55	19 35	19 19	■	21 58
60	19 36	20 24	21 31	20 15	20 37	21 26	22 45
N 58	19 29	20 13	21 13	20 43	21 13	22 03	23 14
56	19 22	20 04	20 58	21 05	21 39	22 29	23 37
54	19 17	19 56	20 46	21 23	21 59	22 50	23 56
52	19 11	19 48	20 35	21 38	22 16	23 08	24 11
50	19 07	19 42	20 25	21 51	22 31	23 23	24 25
45	18 57	19 28	20 06	22 18	23 01	23 52	24 52
N 40	18 48	19 17	19 51	22 40	23 24	24 16	00 16
35	18 41	19 08	19 39	22 58	23 43	24 35	00 35
30	18 35	19 00	19 29	23 13	24 00	00 00	00 52
20	18 24	18 47	19 14	23 39	24 28	00 28	01 19
N 10	18 15	18 37	19 02	24 02	00 02	00 52	01 43
0	18 07	18 28	18 52	24 23	00 23	01 14	02 05
S 10	17 58	18 19	18 44	24 44	00 44	01 36	02 28
20	17 49	18 12	18 37	00 13	01 07	02 00	02 51
30	17 39	18 03	18 31	00 36	01 33	02 28	03 19
35	17 33	17 59	18 29	00 50	01 49	02 45	03 35
40	17 27	17 54	18 26	01 06	02 07	03 04	03 54
45	17 19	17 49	18 24	01 25	02 29	03 27	04 17
S 50	17 10	17 43	18 21	01 49	02 57	03 57	04 46
52	17 06	17 41	18 20	02 01	03 11	04 12	05 00
54	17 01	17 38	18 19	02 14	03 27	04 29	05 17
56	16 56	17 35	18 18	02 30	03 46	04 50	05 37
58	16 51	17 32	18 18	02 48	04 09	05 16	06 01
S 60	16 44	17 28	18 17	03 11	04 40	05 52	06 34

Day	SUN Eqn. of Time 00^h	SUN Eqn. of Time 12^h	SUN Mer. Pass.	MOON Mer. Pass. Upper	MOON Mer. Pass. Lower	Age	Phase
d	m s	m s	h m	h m	h m	d	%
20	03 32	03 25	12 03	18 11	05 46	08	54
21	03 17	03 10	12 03	19 02	06 36	09	63
22	03 02	02 55	12 03	19 53	07 27	10	72

UT	ARIES	VENUS −4·5		MARS +1·3		JUPITER −1·8		SATURN +0·5	
d h	GHA ° ′	GHA ° ′	Dec ° ′	GHA ° ′	Dec ° ′	GHA ° ′	Dec ° ′	GHA ° ′	Dec ° ′
23 00 SUNDAY	331 18.3	137 53.8	S 8 12.9	232 58.5	N23 37.1	196 54.7	N17 44.7	317 16.8	N 3 09.5
01	346 20.7	152 54.3	14.0	247 59.2	37.1	211 56.6	44.6	332 19.3	09.4
02	1 23.2	167 54.8	15.2	262 59.9	37.0	226 58.5	44.4	347 21.9	09.4
03	16 25.7	182 55.3	. . 16.3	278 00.6	. . 37.0	242 00.4	. . 44.3	2 24.4	. . 09.3
04	31 28.1	197 55.8	17.4	293 01.3	36.9	257 02.3	44.1	17 27.0	09.3
05	46 30.6	212 56.3	18.6	308 02.0	36.8	272 04.3	44.0	32 29.6	09.2
06	61 33.1	227 56.8	S 8 19.7	323 02.7	N23 36.8	287 06.2	N17 43.8	47 32.1	N 3 09.2
07	76 35.5	242 57.3	20.9	338 03.4	36.7	302 08.1	43.7	62 34.7	09.1
08	91 38.0	257 57.8	22.0	353 04.1	36.7	317 10.0	43.5	77 37.3	09.1
09	106 40.5	272 58.3	. . 23.1	8 04.8	. . 36.6	332 11.9	. . 43.4	92 39.8	. . 09.0
10	121 42.9	287 58.8	24.3	23 05.5	36.5	347 13.9	43.2	107 42.4	09.0
11	136 45.4	302 59.3	25.4	38 06.2	36.5	2 15.8	43.1	122 44.9	08.9
12	151 47.9	317 59.8	S 8 26.5	53 06.9	N23 36.4	17 17.7	N17 43.0	137 47.5	N 3 08.9
13	166 50.3	333 00.3	27.7	68 07.6	36.4	32 19.6	42.8	152 50.1	08.8
14	181 52.8	348 00.8	28.8	83 08.3	36.3	47 21.5	42.7	167 52.6	08.8
15	196 55.2	3 01.3	. . 29.9	98 09.0	. . 36.2	62 23.5	. . 42.5	182 55.2	. . 08.7
16	211 57.7	18 01.8	31.1	113 09.7	36.2	77 25.4	42.4	197 57.8	08.7
17	227 00.2	33 02.3	32.2	128 10.4	36.1	92 27.3	42.2	213 00.3	08.6
18	242 02.6	48 02.8	S 8 33.3	143 11.1	N23 36.1	107 29.2	N17 42.1	228 02.9	N 3 08.6
19	257 05.1	63 03.3	34.5	158 11.8	36.0	122 31.1	41.9	243 05.5	08.5
20	272 07.6	78 03.8	35.6	173 12.5	35.9	137 33.1	41.8	258 08.0	08.5
21	287 10.0	93 04.3	. . 36.7	188 13.2	. . 35.9	152 35.0	. . 41.6	273 10.6	. . 08.4
22	302 12.5	108 04.8	37.9	203 13.9	35.8	167 36.9	41.5	288 13.2	08.4
23	317 15.0	123 05.4	39.0	218 14.6	35.7	182 38.8	41.4	303 15.7	08.3
24 00 MONDAY	332 17.4	138 05.9	S 8 40.1	233 15.3	N23 35.7	197 40.8	N17 41.2	318 18.3	N 3 08.2
01	347 19.9	153 06.4	41.3	248 16.0	35.6	212 42.7	41.1	333 20.9	08.2
02	2 22.4	168 06.9	42.4	263 16.8	35.5	227 44.6	40.9	348 23.4	08.1
03	17 24.8	183 07.4	. . 43.5	278 17.5	. . 35.5	242 46.5	. . 40.8	3 26.0	. . 08.1
04	32 27.3	198 07.9	44.6	293 18.2	35.4	257 48.4	40.6	18 28.6	08.0
05	47 29.7	213 08.5	45.8	308 18.9	35.4	272 50.4	40.5	33 31.1	08.0
06	62 32.2	228 09.0	S 8 46.9	323 19.6	N23 35.3	287 52.3	N17 40.3	48 33.7	N 3 07.9
07	77 34.7	243 09.5	48.0	338 20.3	35.2	302 54.2	40.2	63 36.3	07.9
08	92 37.1	258 10.0	49.2	353 21.0	35.2	317 56.1	40.0	78 38.8	07.8
09	107 39.6	273 10.5	. . 50.3	8 21.7	. . 35.1	332 58.0	. . 39.9	93 41.4	. . 07.8
10	122 42.1	288 11.1	51.4	23 22.4	35.0	348 00.0	39.8	108 44.0	07.7
11	137 44.5	303 11.6	52.5	38 23.1	35.0	3 01.9	39.6	123 46.5	07.7
12	152 47.0	318 12.1	S 8 53.7	53 23.8	N23 34.9	18 03.8	N17 39.5	138 49.1	N 3 07.6
13	167 49.5	333 12.6	54.8	68 24.5	34.8	33 05.7	39.3	153 51.7	07.6
14	182 51.9	348 13.1	55.9	83 25.2	34.7	48 07.7	39.2	168 54.2	07.5
15	197 54.4	3 13.7	. . 57.0	98 25.9	. . 34.7	63 09.6	. . 39.0	183 56.8	. . 07.5
16	212 56.9	18 14.2	58.2	113 26.6	34.6	78 11.5	38.9	198 59.4	07.4
17	227 59.3	33 14.7	8 59.3	128 27.3	34.5	93 13.4	38.7	214 01.9	07.3
18	243 01.8	48 15.3	S 9 00.4	143 28.0	N23 34.5	108 15.3	N17 38.6	229 04.5	N 3 07.3
19	258 04.2	63 15.8	01.5	158 28.8	34.4	123 17.3	38.4	244 07.1	07.2
20	273 06.7	78 16.3	02.7	173 29.5	34.3	138 19.2	38.3	259 09.6	07.2
21	288 09.2	93 16.8	. . 03.8	188 30.2	. . 34.3	153 21.1	. . 38.1	274 12.2	. . 07.1
22	303 11.6	108 17.4	04.9	203 30.9	34.2	168 23.0	38.0	289 14.8	07.1
23	318 14.1	123 17.9	06.0	218 31.6	34.1	183 25.0	37.9	304 17.3	07.0
25 00 TUESDAY	333 16.6	138 18.4	S 9 07.1	233 32.3	N23 34.0	198 26.9	N17 37.7	319 19.9	N 3 07.0
01	348 19.0	153 19.0	08.3	248 33.0	34.0	213 28.8	37.6	334 22.5	06.9
02	3 21.5	168 19.5	09.4	263 33.7	33.9	228 30.7	37.4	349 25.0	06.9
03	18 24.0	183 20.0	. . 10.5	278 34.4	. . 33.8	243 32.7	. . 37.3	4 27.6	. . 06.8
04	33 26.4	198 20.6	11.6	293 35.1	33.8	258 34.6	37.1	19 30.2	06.8
05	48 28.9	213 21.1	12.7	308 35.8	33.7	273 36.5	37.0	34 32.7	06.7
06	63 31.3	228 21.7	S 9 13.9	323 36.5	N23 33.6	288 38.4	N17 36.8	49 35.3	N 3 06.6
07	78 33.8	243 22.2	15.0	338 37.3	33.5	303 40.4	36.7	64 37.9	06.6
08	93 36.3	258 22.7	16.1	353 38.0	33.5	318 42.3	36.5	79 40.5	06.5
09	108 38.7	273 23.3	. . 17.2	8 38.7	. . 33.4	333 44.2	. . 36.4	94 43.0	. . 06.5
10	123 41.2	288 23.8	18.3	23 39.4	33.3	348 46.1	36.3	109 45.6	06.4
11	138 43.7	303 24.4	19.4	38 40.1	33.2	3 48.0	36.1	124 48.2	06.4
12	153 46.1	318 24.9	S 9 20.6	53 40.8	N23 33.2	18 50.0	N17 36.0	139 50.7	N 3 06.3
13	168 48.6	333 25.5	21.7	68 41.5	33.1	33 51.9	35.8	154 53.3	06.3
14	183 51.1	348 26.0	22.8	83 42.2	33.0	48 53.8	35.7	169 55.9	06.2
15	198 53.5	3 26.5	. . 23.9	98 42.9	. . 32.9	63 55.7	. . 35.5	184 58.5	. . 06.2
16	213 56.0	18 27.1	25.0	113 43.7	32.9	78 57.7	35.4	200 01.0	06.1
17	228 58.5	33 27.6	26.1	128 44.4	32.8	93 59.6	35.2	215 03.6	06.0
18	244 00.9	48 28.2	S 9 27.2	143 45.1	N23 32.7	109 01.5	N17 35.1	230 06.2	N 3 06.0
19	259 03.4	63 28.7	28.4	158 45.8	32.6	124 03.4	34.9	245 08.7	05.9
20	274 05.8	78 29.3	29.5	173 46.5	32.5	139 05.4	34.8	260 11.3	05.9
21	289 08.3	93 29.8	. . 30.6	188 47.2	. . 32.5	154 07.3	. . 34.6	275 13.9	. . 05.8
22	304 10.8	108 30.4	31.7	203 47.9	32.4	169 09.2	34.5	290 16.5	05.8
23	319 13.2	123 30.9	32.8	218 48.6	32.3	184 11.1	34.4	305 19.0	05.7
Mer. Pass. (h m)	1 50.5	*v* 0.5	*d* 1.1	*v* 0.7	*d* 0.1	*v* 1.9	*d* 0.1	*v* 2.6	*d* 0.1

STARS

Name	SHA ° ′	Dec ° ′
Acamar	315 10.6	S40 11.5
Achernar	335 18.8	S57 05.7
Acrux	172 59.1	S63 15.0
Adhara	255 05.1	S29 00.3
Aldebaran	290 38.1	N16 33.8
Alioth	166 12.2	N55 49.1
Alkaid	152 51.2	N49 11.0
Alnair	27 30.7	S46 49.8
Alnilam	275 36.5	S 1 11.0
Alphard	217 46.7	S 8 46.4
Alphecca	126 02.6	N26 37.7
Alpheratz	357 33.1	N29 14.3
Altair	61 58.4	N 8 56.5
Ankaa	353 05.5	S42 09.4
Antares	112 14.1	S26 29.5
Arcturus	145 46.8	N19 02.8
Atria	107 06.9	S69 04.7
Avior	234 14.8	S59 35.5
Bellatrix	278 21.5	N 6 22.5
Betelgeuse	270 50.8	N 7 24.8
Canopus	263 52.1	S52 42.3
Capella	280 20.0	N46 01.3
Deneb	49 24.5	N45 22.7
Denebola	182 23.9	N14 25.5
Diphda	348 45.7	S17 50.2
Dubhe	193 40.0	N61 36.5
Elnath	278 00.3	N28 37.7
Eltanin	90 41.3	N51 29.4
Enif	33 37.1	N10 00.0
Fomalhaut	15 12.7	S29 28.7
Gacrux	171 50.6	S57 15.9
Gienah	175 42.5	S17 41.4
Hadar	148 34.4	S60 30.3
Hamal	327 49.5	N23 35.4
Kaus Aust.	83 30.5	S34 22.3
Kochab	137 20.2	N74 03.0
Markab	13 28.2	N15 21.1
Menkar	314 04.6	N 4 11.8
Menkent	147 56.2	S36 30.2
Miaplacidus	221 38.9	S69 49.5
Mirfak	308 26.2	N49 57.2
Nunki	75 45.8	S26 15.8
Peacock	53 03.1	S56 38.9
Pollux	243 16.0	N27 57.7
Procyon	244 49.7	N 5 09.5
Rasalhague	95 57.2	N12 32.6
Regulus	207 33.3	N11 50.3
Rigel	281 02.7	S 8 10.1
Rigil Kent.	139 38.6	S60 56.9
Sabik	102 01.1	S15 45.4
Schedar	349 29.0	N56 41.0
Shaula	96 08.4	S37 07.5
Sirius	258 25.3	S16 45.0
Spica	158 21.1	S11 18.0
Suhail	222 45.7	S43 32.3
Vega	80 32.0	N38 48.7
Zuben'ubi	136 54.6	S16 09.2

	SHA ° ′	Mer. Pass. h m
Venus	165 48.4	14 47
Mars	260 57.9	8 27
Jupiter	225 23.3	10 48
Saturn	346 00.9	2 46

	UT	SUN GHA	SUN Dec	MOON GHA	*v*	MOON Dec	*d*	HP
	d h	° ′	° ′	° ′	′	° ′	′	′
23	00	179 18.3	N11 30.2	59 37.2	10.0	S27 55.7	1.8	54.2
	01	194 18.5	29.4	74 06.2	10.0	27 53.9	2.0	54.2
	02	209 18.7	28.5	88 35.2	10.0	27 51.9	2.1	54.2
	03	224 18.8	. . 27.7	103 04.2	10.0	27 49.8	2.3	54.2
	04	239 19.0	26.8	117 33.2	10.0	27 47.5	2.4	54.2
	05	254 19.2	26.0	132 02.2	10.0	27 45.1	2.5	54.2
	06	269 19.3	N11 25.2	146 31.2	10.1	S27 42.6	2.6	54.3
	07	284 19.5	24.3	161 00.3	10.0	27 40.0	2.8	54.3
	08	299 19.6	23.5	175 29.3	10.1	27 37.2	3.0	54.3
S	09	314 19.8	. . 22.6	189 58.4	10.1	27 34.2	3.0	54.3
U	10	329 20.0	21.8	204 27.5	10.2	27 31.2	3.2	54.3
N	11	344 20.1	20.9	218 56.7	10.1	27 28.0	3.3	54.3
D	12	359 20.3	N11 20.1	233 25.8	10.2	S27 24.7	3.5	54.3
A	13	14 20.5	19.2	247 55.0	10.2	27 21.2	3.6	54.3
Y	14	29 20.6	18.4	262 24.2	10.2	27 17.6	3.7	54.3
	15	44 20.8	. . 17.5	276 53.4	10.3	27 13.9	3.9	54.3
	16	59 21.0	16.7	291 22.7	10.2	27 10.0	4.0	54.3
	17	74 21.1	15.8	305 51.9	10.3	27 06.0	4.1	54.3
	18	89 21.3	N11 15.0	320 21.2	10.4	S27 01.9	4.2	54.3
	19	104 21.5	14.1	334 50.6	10.3	26 57.7	4.4	54.3
	20	119 21.6	13.3	349 19.9	10.4	26 53.3	4.5	54.4
	21	134 21.8	. . 12.4	3 49.3	10.4	26 48.8	4.7	54.4
	22	149 22.0	11.6	18 18.7	10.5	26 44.1	4.7	54.4
	23	164 22.1	10.7	32 48.2	10.5	26 39.4	4.9	54.4
24	00	179 22.3	N11 09.8	47 17.7	10.5	S26 34.5	5.1	54.4
	01	194 22.5	09.0	61 47.2	10.5	26 29.4	5.1	54.4
	02	209 22.6	08.1	76 16.7	10.6	26 24.3	5.3	54.4
	03	224 22.8	. . 07.3	90 46.3	10.6	26 19.0	5.4	54.4
	04	239 23.0	06.4	105 15.9	10.7	26 13.6	5.6	54.4
	05	254 23.1	05.6	119 45.6	10.6	26 08.0	5.6	54.4
	06	269 23.3	N11 04.7	134 15.2	10.8	S26 02.4	5.8	54.5
	07	284 23.5	03.9	148 45.0	10.7	25 56.6	5.9	54.5
	08	299 23.7	03.0	163 14.7	10.8	25 50.7	6.1	54.5
M	09	314 23.8	. . 02.2	177 44.5	10.9	25 44.6	6.2	54.5
O	10	329 24.0	01.3	192 14.4	10.8	25 38.4	6.3	54.5
N	11	344 24.2	11 00.4	206 44.2	11.0	25 32.1	6.4	54.5
D	12	359 24.3	N10 59.6	221 14.2	10.9	S25 25.7	6.5	54.5
A	13	14 24.5	58.7	235 44.1	11.0	25 19.2	6.7	54.5
Y	14	29 24.7	57.9	250 14.1	11.1	25 12.5	6.7	54.6
	15	44 24.8	. . 57.0	264 44.2	11.0	25 05.8	6.9	54.6
	16	59 25.0	56.2	279 14.2	11.2	24 58.9	7.1	54.6
	17	74 25.2	55.3	293 44.4	11.1	24 51.8	7.1	54.6
	18	89 25.3	N10 54.4	308 14.5	11.3	S24 44.7	7.3	54.6
	19	104 25.5	53.6	322 44.8	11.2	24 37.4	7.4	54.6
	20	119 25.7	52.7	337 15.0	11.3	24 30.0	7.5	54.6
	21	134 25.9	. . 51.9	351 45.3	11.4	24 22.5	7.6	54.7
	22	149 26.0	51.0	6 15.7	11.3	24 14.9	7.7	54.7
	23	164 26.2	50.1	20 46.0	11.5	24 07.2	7.9	54.7
25	00	179 26.4	N10 49.3	35 16.5	11.5	S23 59.3	7.9	54.7
	01	194 26.6	48.4	49 47.0	11.5	23 51.4	8.1	54.7
	02	209 26.7	47.6	64 17.5	11.6	23 43.3	8.2	54.7
	03	224 26.9	. . 46.7	78 48.1	11.6	23 35.1	8.3	54.7
	04	239 27.1	45.8	93 18.7	11.7	23 26.8	8.4	54.8
	05	254 27.2	45.0	107 49.4	11.7	23 18.4	8.6	54.8
	06	269 27.4	N10 44.1	122 20.1	11.7	S23 09.8	8.6	54.8
	07	284 27.6	43.3	136 50.8	11.8	23 01.2	8.8	54.8
T	08	299 27.8	42.4	151 21.6	11.9	22 52.4	8.8	54.8
U	09	314 27.9	. . 41.5	165 52.5	11.9	22 43.6	9.0	54.8
E	10	329 28.1	40.7	180 23.4	11.9	22 34.6	9.1	54.8
S	11	344 28.3	39.8	194 54.3	12.0	22 25.5	9.2	54.9
D	12	359 28.5	N10 38.9	209 25.3	12.1	S22 16.3	9.3	54.9
A	13	14 28.6	38.1	223 56.4	12.1	22 07.0	9.4	54.9
Y	14	29 28.8	37.2	238 27.5	12.1	21 57.6	9.5	54.9
	15	44 29.0	. . 36.3	252 58.6	12.2	21 48.1	9.6	54.9
	16	59 29.2	35.5	267 29.8	12.3	21 38.5	9.7	55.0
	17	74 29.3	34.6	282 01.1	12.2	21 28.8	9.9	55.0
	18	89 29.5	N10 33.7	296 32.3	12.4	S21 18.9	9.9	55.0
	19	104 29.7	32.9	311 03.7	12.4	21 09.0	10.0	55.0
	20	119 29.9	32.0	325 35.1	12.4	20 59.0	10.1	55.0
	21	134 30.0	. . 31.1	340 06.5	12.5	20 48.9	10.3	55.0
	22	149 30.2	30.3	354 38.0	12.5	20 38.6	10.3	55.1
	23	164 30.4	29.4	9 09.5	12.6	S20 28.3	10.4	55.1
		SD 15.8	*d* 0.9	SD	14.8	14.9		15.0

Lat.	Twilight Naut.	Twilight Civil	Sunrise	Moonrise 23	Moonrise 24	Moonrise 25	Moonrise 26
°	h m	h m	h m	h m	h m	h m	h m
N 72	////	01 14	03 19	▬	▬	▬	21 22
N 70	////	02 09	03 40	▬	▬	▬	20 41
68	////	02 41	03 56	▬	▬	21 04	20 13
66	01 04	03 04	04 08	▬	▬	20 17	19 51
64	01 52	03 22	04 19	▬	20 10	19 47	19 34
62	02 22	03 36	04 28	19 36	19 29	19 24	19 19
60	02 43	03 48	04 36	18 49	19 01	19 05	19 07
N 58	03 00	03 58	04 43	18 19	18 39	18 50	18 56
56	03 14	04 07	04 48	17 56	18 21	18 36	18 47
54	03 26	04 15	04 54	17 38	18 06	18 25	18 39
52	03 36	04 22	04 59	17 22	17 52	18 15	18 32
50	03 45	04 28	05 03	17 08	17 41	18 06	18 25
45	04 04	04 41	05 12	16 40	17 17	17 46	18 10
N 40	04 18	04 52	05 20	16 18	16 57	17 30	17 59
35	04 29	05 00	05 27	15 59	16 41	17 17	17 48
30	04 39	05 08	05 33	15 43	16 27	17 05	17 39
20	04 53	05 20	05 42	15 17	16 03	16 45	17 24
N 10	05 05	05 30	05 51	14 53	15 42	16 27	17 10
0	05 14	05 38	05 59	14 32	15 22	16 11	16 57
S 10	05 21	05 46	06 07	14 10	15 03	15 54	16 45
20	05 27	05 53	06 15	13 47	14 42	15 36	16 31
30	05 32	06 00	06 24	13 20	14 17	15 16	16 15
35	05 35	06 04	06 30	13 04	14 03	15 04	16 06
40	05 37	06 08	06 36	12 45	13 46	14 50	15 55
45	05 39	06 13	06 43	12 23	13 26	14 33	15 42
S 50	05 40	06 18	06 51	11 54	13 01	14 13	15 27
52	05 41	06 20	06 55	11 40	12 48	14 03	15 20
54	05 42	06 23	06 59	11 24	12 34	13 52	15 12
56	05 42	06 25	07 04	11 04	12 18	13 39	15 03
58	05 43	06 28	07 09	10 39	11 58	13 24	14 53
S 60	05 43	06 31	07 14	10 07	11 33	13 07	14 41

Lat.	Sunset	Twilight Civil	Twilight Naut.	Moonset 23	Moonset 24	Moonset 25	Moonset 26
°	h m	h m	h m	h m	h m	h m	h m
N 72	20 41	22 38	////	▬	▬	▬	▬
N 70	20 22	21 50	////	▬	▬	▬	▬
68	20 06	21 20	////	▬	▬	23 57	26 24
66	19 54	20 58	22 50	▬	▬	▬	00 42
64	19 44	20 40	22 07	▬	23 09	25 12	01 12
62	19 35	20 26	21 39	21 58	23 49	25 34	01 34
60	19 27	20 15	21 19	22 45	24 17	00 17	01 52
N 58	19 21	20 05	21 02	23 14	24 38	00 38	02 06
56	19 15	19 56	20 48	23 37	24 56	00 56	02 19
54	19 10	19 48	20 37	23 56	25 11	01 11	02 30
52	19 05	19 41	20 27	24 11	00 11	01 23	02 40
50	19 01	19 35	20 18	24 25	00 25	01 35	02 48
45	18 52	19 23	20 00	24 52	00 52	01 58	03 06
N 40	18 44	19 12	19 46	00 16	01 14	02 16	03 21
35	18 37	19 04	19 35	00 35	01 32	02 32	03 33
30	18 32	18 56	19 26	00 52	01 47	02 45	03 44
20	18 22	18 45	19 11	01 19	02 13	03 08	04 03
N 10	18 14	18 35	19 00	01 43	02 36	03 28	04 19
0	18 06	18 27	18 51	02 05	02 56	03 46	04 33
S 10	17 58	18 19	18 44	02 28	03 17	04 04	04 48
20	17 50	18 12	18 38	02 51	03 39	04 23	05 04
30	17 41	18 05	18 33	03 19	04 05	04 45	05 22
35	17 35	18 01	18 31	03 35	04 20	04 58	05 32
40	17 30	17 57	18 29	03 54	04 37	05 13	05 44
45	17 23	17 53	18 27	04 17	04 58	05 31	05 57
S 50	17 15	17 48	18 25	04 46	05 24	05 52	06 14
52	17 11	17 45	18 25	05 00	05 36	06 03	06 22
54	17 07	17 43	18 24	05 17	05 51	06 14	06 31
56	17 02	17 40	18 24	05 37	06 08	06 27	06 40
58	16 57	17 38	18 23	06 01	06 28	06 43	06 51
S 60	16 51	17 35	18 23	06 34	06 53	07 01	07 04

Day	SUN Eqn. of Time 00^h	SUN Eqn. of Time 12^h	SUN Mer. Pass.	MOON Mer. Pass. Upper	MOON Mer. Pass. Lower	Age	%	Phase
d	m s	m s	h m	h m	h m	d	%	
23	02 47	02 39	12 03	20 44	08 19	11	80	
24	02 31	02 23	12 02	21 34	09 09	12	87	◐
25	02 15	02 07	12 02	22 22	09 58	13	93	

UT d	UT h	ARIES GHA	VENUS −4·6 GHA	VENUS Dec	MARS +1·3 GHA	MARS Dec	JUPITER −1·8 GHA	JUPITER Dec	SATURN +0·4 GHA	SATURN Dec
		° ′	° ′	° ′	° ′	° ′	° ′	° ′	° ′	° ′
26	00	334 15.7	138 31.5	S 9 33.9	233 49.4	N23 32.2	199 13.1	N17 34.2	320 21.6	N 3 05.7
	01	349 18.2	153 32.1	35.0	248 50.1	32.2	214 15.0	34.1	335 24.2	05.6
	02	4 20.6	168 32.6	36.1	263 50.8	32.1	229 16.9	33.9	350 26.7	05.6
	03	19 23.1	183 33.2	. . 37.2	278 51.5	. . 32.0	244 18.8	. . 33.8	5 29.3	. . 05.5
	04	34 25.6	198 33.7	38.4	293 52.2	31.9	259 20.8	33.6	20 31.9	05.4
	05	49 28.0	213 34.3	39.5	308 52.9	31.8	274 22.7	33.5	35 34.5	05.4
	06	64 30.5	228 34.8	S 9 40.6	323 53.6	N23 31.8	289 24.6	N17 33.3	50 37.0	N 3 05.3
W	07	79 33.0	243 35.4	41.7	338 54.3	31.7	304 26.5	33.2	65 39.6	05.3
E	08	94 35.4	258 36.0	42.8	353 55.1	31.6	319 28.5	33.0	80 42.2	05.2
D	09	109 37.9	273 36.5	. . 43.9	8 55.8	. . 31.5	334 30.4	. . 32.9	95 44.8	. . 05.2
N	10	124 40.3	288 37.1	45.0	23 56.5	31.4	349 32.3	32.7	110 47.3	05.1
E	11	139 42.8	303 37.7	46.1	38 57.2	31.3	4 34.2	32.6	125 49.9	05.1
S	12	154 45.3	318 38.2	S 9 47.2	53 57.9	N23 31.3	19 36.2	N17 32.5	140 52.5	N 3 05.0
D	13	169 47.7	333 38.8	48.3	68 58.6	31.2	34 38.1	32.3	155 55.0	04.9
A	14	184 50.2	348 39.4	49.4	83 59.4	31.1	49 40.0	32.2	170 57.6	04.9
Y	15	199 52.7	3 39.9	. . 50.5	99 00.1	. . 31.0	64 41.9	. . 32.0	186 00.2	. . 04.8
	16	214 55.1	18 40.5	51.6	114 00.8	30.9	79 43.9	31.9	201 02.8	04.8
	17	229 57.6	33 41.1	52.7	129 01.5	30.8	94 45.8	31.7	216 05.3	04.7
	18	245 00.1	48 41.6	S 9 53.8	144 02.2	N23 30.8	109 47.7	N17 31.6	231 07.9	N 3 04.7
	19	260 02.5	63 42.2	54.9	159 02.9	30.7	124 49.7	31.4	246 10.5	04.6
	20	275 05.0	78 42.8	56.0	174 03.7	30.6	139 51.6	31.3	261 13.1	04.5
	21	290 07.5	93 43.3	. . 57.1	189 04.4	. . 30.5	154 53.5	. . 31.1	276 15.6	. . 04.5
	22	305 09.9	108 43.9	58.2	204 05.1	30.4	169 55.4	31.0	291 18.2	04.4
	23	320 12.4	123 44.5	9 59.3	219 05.8	30.3	184 57.4	30.8	306 20.8	04.4
27	00	335 14.8	138 45.1	S10 00.4	234 06.5	N23 30.3	199 59.3	N17 30.7	321 23.4	N 3 04.3
	01	350 17.3	153 45.6	01.5	249 07.2	30.2	215 01.2	30.6	336 25.9	04.3
	02	5 19.8	168 46.2	02.6	264 08.0	30.1	230 03.1	30.4	351 28.5	04.2
	03	20 22.2	183 46.8	. . 03.7	279 08.7	. . 30.0	245 05.1	. . 30.3	6 31.1	. . 04.2
	04	35 24.7	198 47.4	04.8	294 09.4	29.9	260 07.0	30.1	21 33.7	04.1
	05	50 27.2	213 48.0	05.9	309 10.1	29.8	275 08.9	30.0	36 36.2	04.0
	06	65 29.6	228 48.5	S10 07.0	324 10.8	N23 29.7	290 10.8	N17 29.8	51 38.8	N 3 04.0
T	07	80 32.1	243 49.1	08.1	339 11.6	29.6	305 12.8	29.7	66 41.4	03.9
H	08	95 34.6	258 49.7	09.2	354 12.3	29.6	320 14.7	29.5	81 44.0	03.9
U	09	110 37.0	273 50.3	. . 10.3	9 13.0	. . 29.5	335 16.6	. . 29.4	96 46.6	. . 03.8
R	10	125 39.5	288 50.9	11.4	24 13.7	29.4	350 18.6	29.2	111 49.1	03.8
S	11	140 41.9	303 51.5	12.5	39 14.4	29.3	5 20.5	29.1	126 51.7	03.7
D	12	155 44.4	318 52.0	S10 13.6	54 15.1	N23 29.2	20 22.4	N17 29.0	141 54.3	N 3 03.6
A	13	170 46.9	333 52.6	14.7	69 15.9	29.1	35 24.3	28.8	156 56.9	03.6
Y	14	185 49.3	348 53.2	15.8	84 16.6	29.0	50 26.3	28.7	171 59.4	03.5
	15	200 51.8	3 53.8	. . 16.9	99 17.3	. . 28.9	65 28.2	. . 28.5	187 02.0	. . 03.5
	16	215 54.3	18 54.4	18.0	114 18.0	28.8	80 30.1	28.4	202 04.6	03.4
	17	230 56.7	33 55.0	19.1	129 18.8	28.7	95 32.0	28.2	217 07.2	03.4
	18	245 59.2	48 55.6	S10 20.2	144 19.5	N23 28.6	110 34.0	N17 28.1	232 09.7	N 3 03.3
	19	261 01.7	63 56.2	21.3	159 20.2	28.6	125 35.9	27.9	247 12.3	03.2
	20	276 04.1	78 56.8	22.3	174 20.9	28.5	140 37.8	27.8	262 14.9	03.2
	21	291 06.6	93 57.4	. . 23.4	189 21.6	. . 28.4	155 39.8	. . 27.6	277 17.5	. . 03.1
	22	306 09.1	108 58.0	24.5	204 22.4	28.3	170 41.7	27.5	292 20.1	03.1
	23	321 11.5	123 58.6	25.6	219 23.1	28.2	185 43.6	27.3	307 22.6	03.0
28	00	336 14.0	138 59.2	S10 26.7	234 23.8	N23 28.1	200 45.5	N17 27.2	322 25.2	N 3 03.0
	01	351 16.4	153 59.8	27.8	249 24.5	28.0	215 47.5	27.1	337 27.8	02.9
	02	6 18.9	169 00.4	28.9	264 25.2	27.9	230 49.4	26.9	352 30.4	02.8
	03	21 21.4	184 01.0	. . 30.0	279 26.0	. . 27.8	245 51.3	. . 26.8	7 33.0	. . 02.8
	04	36 23.8	199 01.6	31.1	294 26.7	27.7	260 53.3	26.6	22 35.5	02.7
	05	51 26.3	214 02.2	32.1	309 27.4	27.6	275 55.2	26.5	37 38.1	02.7
	06	66 28.8	229 02.8	S10 33.2	324 28.1	N23 27.5	290 57.1	N17 26.3	52 40.7	N 3 02.6
	07	81 31.2	244 03.4	34.3	339 28.9	27.4	305 59.0	26.2	67 43.3	02.6
	08	96 33.7	259 04.0	35.4	354 29.6	27.3	321 01.0	26.0	82 45.8	02.5
F	09	111 36.2	274 04.6	. . 36.5	9 30.3	. . 27.2	336 02.9	. . 25.9	97 48.4	. . 02.4
R	10	126 38.6	289 05.2	37.6	24 31.0	27.1	351 04.8	25.7	112 51.0	02.4
I	11	141 41.1	304 05.8	38.7	39 31.8	27.0	6 06.8	25.6	127 53.6	02.3
D	12	156 43.5	319 06.4	S10 39.7	54 32.5	N23 26.9	21 08.7	N17 25.4	142 56.2	N 3 02.3
A	13	171 46.0	334 07.0	40.8	69 33.2	26.9	36 10.6	25.3	157 58.7	02.2
Y	14	186 48.5	349 07.6	41.9	84 33.9	26.8	51 12.6	25.2	173 01.3	02.2
	15	201 50.9	4 08.2	. . 43.0	99 34.7	. . 26.7	66 14.5	. . 25.0	188 03.9	. . 02.1
	16	216 53.4	19 08.9	44.1	114 35.4	26.6	81 16.4	24.9	203 06.5	02.0
	17	231 55.9	34 09.5	45.1	129 36.1	26.5	96 18.3	24.7	218 09.1	02.0
	18	246 58.3	49 10.1	S10 46.2	144 36.8	N23 26.4	111 20.3	N17 24.6	233 11.7	N 3 01.9
	19	262 00.8	64 10.7	47.3	159 37.6	26.3	126 22.2	24.4	248 14.2	01.9
	20	277 03.3	79 11.3	48.4	174 38.3	26.2	141 24.1	24.3	263 16.8	01.8
	21	292 05.7	94 11.9	. . 49.5	189 39.0	. . 26.1	156 26.1	. . 24.1	278 19.4	. . 01.7
	22	307 08.2	109 12.6	50.5	204 39.7	26.0	171 28.0	24.0	293 22.0	01.7
	23	322 10.7	124 13.2	51.6	219 40.5	25.9	186 29.9	23.8	308 24.6	01.6
Mer. Pass.		h m 1 38.7	*v* 0.6	*d* 1.1	*v* 0.7	*d* 0.1	*v* 1.9	*d* 0.1	*v* 2.6	*d* 0.1

STARS

Name	SHA	Dec
	° ′	° ′
Acamar	315 10.6	S40 11.5
Achernar	335 18.8	S57 05.7
Acrux	172 59.1	S63 15.0
Adhara	255 05.0	S29 00.3
Aldebaran	290 38.1	N16 33.8
Alioth	166 12.2	N55 49.1
Alkaid	152 51.2	N49 11.0
Alnair	27 30.7	S46 49.8
Alnilam	275 36.5	S 1 10.9
Alphard	217 46.7	S 8 46.4
Alphecca	126 02.6	N26 37.7
Alpheratz	357 33.0	N29 14.3
Altair	61 58.4	N 8 56.5
Ankaa	353 05.4	S42 09.4
Antares	112 14.1	S26 29.5
Arcturus	145 46.8	N19 02.8
Atria	107 07.0	S69 04.7
Avior	234 14.8	S59 35.5
Bellatrix	278 21.5	N 6 22.5
Betelgeuse	270 50.7	N 7 24.8
Canopus	263 52.1	S52 42.3
Capella	280 20.0	N46 01.3
Deneb	49 24.5	N45 22.7
Denebola	182 23.9	N14 25.5
Diphda	348 45.7	S17 50.2
Dubhe	193 40.0	N61 36.5
Elnath	278 00.3	N28 37.8
Eltanin	90 41.3	N51 29.4
Enif	33 37.1	N10 00.0
Fomalhaut	15 12.7	S29 28.7
Gacrux	171 50.6	S57 15.9
Gienah	175 42.5	S17 41.4
Hadar	148 34.4	S60 30.3
Hamal	327 49.5	N23 35.4
Kaus Aust.	83 30.5	S34 22.3
Kochab	137 20.2	N74 03.0
Markab	13 28.2	N15 21.1
Menkar	314 04.6	N 4 11.8
Menkent	147 56.2	S36 30.2
Miaplacidus	221 38.9	S69 49.5
Mirfak	308 26.2	N49 57.2
Nunki	75 45.8	S26 15.8
Peacock	53 03.1	S56 38.9
Pollux	243 15.9	N27 57.7
Procyon	244 49.7	N 5 09.5
Rasalhague	95 57.2	N12 32.6
Regulus	207 33.3	N11 50.3
Rigel	281 02.6	S 8 10.1
Rigil Kent.	139 38.7	S60 56.9
Sabik	102 01.1	S15 45.4
Schedar	349 29.0	N56 41.0
Shaula	96 08.4	S37 07.5
Sirius	258 25.2	S16 45.0
Spica	158 21.1	S11 18.0
Suhail	222 45.7	S43 32.3
Vega	80 32.1	N38 48.7
Zuben'ubi	136 54.6	S16 09.2

	SHA	Mer. Pass.
	° ′	h m
Venus	163 30.2	14 44
Mars	258 51.7	8 23
Jupiter	224 44.4	10 39
Saturn	346 08.5	2 34

UT		SUN GHA	SUN Dec	MOON GHA	v	MOON Dec	d	HP
d h		° ′	° ′	° ′	′	° ′	′	′
26 00		179 30.6	N10 28.5	23 41.1	12.6	S20 17.9	10.6	55.1
01		194 30.7	27.7	38 12.7	12.6	20 07.3	10.6	55.1
02		209 30.9	26.8	52 44.3	12.8	19 56.7	10.7	55.1
03		224 31.1	. . 25.9	67 16.1	12.7	19 46.0	10.8	55.1
04		239 31.3	25.1	81 47.8	12.8	19 35.2	10.9	55.2
05		254 31.4	24.2	96 19.6	12.9	19 24.3	11.0	55.2
06		269 31.6	N10 23.3	110 51.5	12.9	S19 13.3	11.1	55.2
07	WEDNESDAY	284 31.8	22.5	125 23.4	12.9	19 02.2	11.2	55.2
08		299 32.0	21.6	139 55.3	13.0	18 51.0	11.3	55.2
09		314 32.2	. . 20.7	154 27.3	13.0	18 39.7	11.3	55.3
10		329 32.3	19.9	168 59.3	13.1	18 28.4	11.5	55.3
11		344 32.5	19.0	183 31.4	13.1	18 16.9	11.6	55.3
12		359 32.7	N10 18.1	198 03.5	13.2	S18 05.3	11.6	55.3
13		14 32.9	17.2	212 35.7	13.2	17 53.7	11.7	55.3
14		29 33.0	16.4	227 07.9	13.3	17 42.0	11.8	55.4
15		44 33.2	. . 15.5	241 40.2	13.2	17 30.2	11.9	55.4
16		59 33.4	14.6	256 12.4	13.4	17 18.3	12.0	55.4
17		74 33.6	13.8	270 44.8	13.4	17 06.3	12.0	55.4
18		89 33.8	N10 12.9	285 17.2	13.4	S16 54.3	12.2	55.4
19		104 33.9	12.0	299 49.6	13.4	16 42.1	12.2	55.5
20		119 34.1	11.1	314 22.0	13.5	16 29.9	12.3	55.5
21		134 34.3	. . 10.3	328 54.5	13.6	16 17.6	12.4	55.5
22		149 34.5	09.4	343 27.1	13.5	16 05.2	12.5	55.5
23		164 34.7	08.5	357 59.6	13.7	15 52.7	12.5	55.5
27 00		179 34.8	N10 07.7	12 32.3	13.6	S15 40.2	12.6	55.6
01		194 35.0	06.8	27 04.9	13.7	15 27.6	12.7	55.6
02		209 35.2	05.9	41 37.6	13.7	15 14.9	12.8	55.6
03		224 35.4	. . 05.0	56 10.3	13.8	15 02.1	12.8	55.6
04		239 35.6	04.2	70 43.1	13.8	14 49.3	12.9	55.6
05		254 35.7	03.3	85 15.9	13.8	14 36.4	13.0	55.7
06		269 35.9	N10 02.4	99 48.7	13.9	S14 23.4	13.1	55.7
07	THURSDAY	284 36.1	01.5	114 21.6	13.9	14 10.3	13.1	55.7
08		299 36.3	10 00.6	128 54.5	13.9	13 57.2	13.2	55.7
09		314 36.5	9 59.8	143 27.4	14.0	13 44.0	13.3	55.8
10		329 36.7	58.9	158 00.4	14.0	13 30.7	13.3	55.8
11		344 36.8	58.0	172 33.4	14.0	13 17.4	13.4	55.8
12		359 37.0	N 9 57.1	187 06.4	14.1	S13 04.0	13.5	55.8
13		14 37.2	56.3	201 39.5	14.1	12 50.5	13.5	55.8
14		29 37.4	55.4	216 12.6	14.1	12 37.0	13.6	55.9
15		44 37.6	. . 54.5	230 45.7	14.1	12 23.4	13.7	55.9
16		59 37.7	53.6	245 18.8	14.2	12 09.7	13.7	55.9
17		74 37.9	52.8	259 52.0	14.2	11 56.0	13.8	55.9
18		89 38.1	N 9 51.9	274 25.2	14.2	S11 42.2	13.9	55.9
19		104 38.3	51.0	288 58.4	14.3	11 28.3	13.9	56.0
20		119 38.5	50.1	303 31.7	14.3	11 14.4	13.9	56.0
21		134 38.7	. . 49.2	318 05.0	14.3	11 00.5	14.1	56.0
22		149 38.8	48.4	332 38.3	14.3	10 46.4	14.0	56.0
23		164 39.0	47.5	347 11.6	14.3	10 32.4	14.2	56.1
28 00		179 39.2	N 9 46.6	1 44.9	14.4	S10 18.2	14.2	56.1
01		194 39.4	45.7	16 18.3	14.4	10 04.0	14.2	56.1
02		209 39.6	44.8	30 51.7	14.4	9 49.8	14.3	56.1
03		224 39.8	. . 43.9	45 25.1	14.4	9 35.5	14.3	56.1
04		239 40.0	43.1	59 58.5	14.4	9 21.2	14.4	56.2
05		254 40.1	42.2	74 31.9	14.5	9 06.8	14.5	56.2
06		269 40.3	N 9 41.3	89 05.4	14.5	S 8 52.3	14.5	56.2
07	FRIDAY	284 40.5	40.4	103 38.9	14.5	8 37.8	14.5	56.2
08		299 40.7	39.5	118 12.4	14.5	8 23.3	14.6	56.2
09		314 40.9	. . 38.7	132 45.9	14.5	8 08.7	14.6	56.3
10		329 41.1	37.8	147 19.4	14.5	7 54.1	14.7	56.3
11		344 41.3	36.9	161 52.9	14.5	7 39.4	14.7	56.3
12		359 41.4	N 9 36.0	176 26.4	14.6	S 7 24.7	14.8	56.3
13		14 41.6	35.1	191 00.0	14.5	7 09.9	14.8	56.4
14		29 41.8	34.2	205 33.5	14.6	6 55.1	14.9	56.4
15		44 42.0	. . 33.4	220 07.1	14.6	6 40.2	14.8	56.4
16		59 42.2	32.5	234 40.7	14.5	6 25.4	15.0	56.4
17		74 42.4	31.6	249 14.2	14.6	6 10.4	14.9	56.4
18		89 42.6	N 9 30.7	263 47.8	14.6	S 5 55.5	15.0	56.5
19		104 42.7	29.8	278 21.4	14.6	5 40.5	15.0	56.5
20		119 42.9	28.9	292 55.0	14.6	5 25.5	15.1	56.5
21		134 43.1	. . 28.0	307 28.6	14.6	5 10.4	15.1	56.5
22		149 43.3	27.2	322 02.2	14.6	4 55.3	15.1	56.6
23		164 43.5	26.3	336 35.8	14.6	S 4 40.2	15.2	56.6
		SD 15.9	*d* 0.9	SD 15.1		15.2		15.3

Lat.	Twilight Naut.	Twilight Civil	Sunrise	Moonrise 26	Moonrise 27	Moonrise 28	Moonrise 29
°	h m	h m	h m	h m	h m	h m	h m
N 72	////	01 49	03 36	21 22	20 18	19 38	19 05
N 70	////	02 29	03 53	20 41	20 00	19 31	19 05
68	////	02 56	04 07	20 13	19 45	19 25	19 06
66	01 34	03 16	04 18	19 51	19 34	19 19	19 06
64	02 10	03 32	04 28	19 34	19 23	19 15	19 06
62	02 35	03 45	04 36	19 19	19 15	19 11	19 07
60	02 54	03 56	04 43	19 07	19 07	19 07	19 07
N 58	03 09	04 06	04 49	18 56	19 01	19 04	19 07
56	03 22	04 14	04 54	18 47	18 55	19 01	19 07
54	03 33	04 21	04 59	18 39	18 50	18 59	19 07
52	03 43	04 27	05 03	18 32	18 45	18 57	19 07
50	03 51	04 33	05 07	18 25	18 41	18 54	19 08
45	04 08	04 45	05 16	18 10	18 31	18 50	19 08
N 40	04 21	04 55	05 23	17 59	18 23	18 46	19 08
35	04 32	05 03	05 29	17 48	18 17	18 43	19 08
30	04 41	05 10	05 34	17 39	18 11	18 40	19 09
20	04 54	05 21	05 43	17 24	18 00	18 35	19 09
N 10	05 05	05 30	05 51	17 10	17 51	18 30	19 09
0	05 13	05 37	05 58	16 57	17 42	18 26	19 10
S 10	05 19	05 44	06 05	16 45	17 34	18 22	19 10
20	05 25	05 50	06 13	16 31	17 24	18 17	19 11
30	05 29	05 57	06 21	16 15	17 14	18 12	19 11
35	05 31	06 00	06 26	16 06	17 07	18 09	19 11
40	05 32	06 04	06 31	15 55	17 00	18 06	19 12
45	05 34	06 08	06 38	15 42	16 52	18 02	19 12
S 50	05 35	06 12	06 45	15 27	16 42	17 57	19 13
52	05 35	06 14	06 48	15 20	16 37	17 55	19 13
54	05 35	06 16	06 52	15 12	16 32	17 52	19 13
56	05 35	06 18	06 56	15 03	16 27	17 50	19 13
58	05 35	06 21	07 01	14 53	16 20	17 47	19 14
S 60	05 35	06 23	07 06	14 41	16 13	17 43	19 14

Lat.	Sunset	Twilight Civil	Twilight Naut.	Moonset 26	Moonset 27	Moonset 28	Moonset 29
°	h m	h m	h m	h m	h m	h m	h m
N 72	20 24	22 06	////	■	01 18	03 56	06 09
N 70	20 07	21 28	////	■	01 57	04 12	06 14
68	19 53	21 03	23 29	26 24	02 24	04 24	06 17
66	19 42	20 44	22 22	00 42	02 44	04 34	06 20
64	19 33	20 28	21 48	01 12	03 00	04 43	06 23
62	19 25	20 15	21 25	01 34	03 14	04 50	06 25
60	19 19	20 05	21 06	01 52	03 25	04 56	06 26
N 58	19 13	19 56	20 51	02 06	03 35	05 02	06 28
56	19 07	19 48	20 39	02 19	03 43	05 06	06 30
54	19 03	19 41	20 28	02 30	03 50	05 11	06 31
52	18 58	19 34	20 19	02 40	03 57	05 14	06 32
50	18 55	19 29	20 11	02 48	04 03	05 18	06 33
45	18 46	19 17	19 54	03 06	04 16	05 25	06 35
N 40	18 39	19 07	19 41	03 21	04 26	05 32	06 37
35	18 34	19 00	19 31	03 33	04 35	05 37	06 39
30	18 28	18 53	19 22	03 44	04 43	05 42	06 40
20	18 20	18 42	19 08	04 03	04 57	05 50	06 43
N 10	18 12	18 33	18 58	04 19	05 08	05 57	06 45
0	18 05	18 26	18 50	04 33	05 19	06 03	06 47
S 10	17 58	18 19	18 44	04 48	05 30	06 10	06 49
20	17 51	18 13	18 39	05 04	05 41	06 17	06 51
30	17 42	18 07	18 34	05 22	05 54	06 24	06 53
35	17 38	18 03	18 33	05 32	06 02	06 29	06 54
40	17 32	18 00	18 31	05 44	06 10	06 34	06 56
45	17 26	17 56	18 30	05 57	06 20	06 39	06 58
S 50	17 19	17 52	18 29	06 14	06 32	06 46	07 00
52	17 16	17 50	18 29	06 22	06 37	06 49	07 00
54	17 12	17 48	18 29	06 31	06 43	06 53	07 01
56	17 08	17 46	18 29	06 40	06 50	06 57	07 02
58	17 03	17 44	18 29	06 51	06 57	07 01	07 04
S 60	16 58	17 41	18 29	07 04	07 05	07 05	07 05

Day	SUN Eqn. of Time 00^h	SUN Eqn. of Time 12^h	SUN Mer. Pass.	MOON Mer. Pass. Upper	MOON Mer. Pass. Lower	MOON Age	Phase
d	m s	m s	h m	h m	h m	d %	
26	01 58	01 50	12 02	23 08	10 45	14 97	
27	01 41	01 32	12 02	23 53	11 31	15 100	○
28	01 24	01 15	12 01	24 36	12 15	16 100	

UT (d h)	ARIES GHA	VENUS −4·6 GHA	VENUS Dec	MARS +1·3 GHA	MARS Dec	JUPITER −1·8 GHA	JUPITER Dec	SATURN +0·4 GHA	SATURN Dec	STARS Name	SHA	Dec
	° ′	° ′	° ′	° ′	° ′	° ′	° ′	° ′	° ′		° ′	° ′
29 SATURDAY 00	337 13.1	139 13.8	S10 52.7	234 41.2	N23 25.8	201 31.9	N17 23.7	323 27.1	N 3 01.6	Acamar	315 10.6	S40 11.5
01	352 15.6	154 14.4	53.8	249 41.9	25.7	216 33.8	23.5	338 29.7	01.5	Achernar	335 18.8	S57 05.7
02	7 18.0	169 15.0	54.9	264 42.7	25.6	231 35.7	23.4	353 32.3	01.5	Acrux	172 59.1	S63 15.0
03	22 20.5	184 15.7	. . 55.9	279 43.4	. . 25.5	246 37.6	. . 23.2	8 34.9	. . 01.4	Adhara	255 05.0	S29 00.2
04	37 23.0	199 16.3	57.0	294 44.1	25.4	261 39.6	23.1	23 37.5	01.3	Aldebaran	290 38.1	N16 33.8
05	52 25.4	214 16.9	58.1	309 44.8	25.3	276 41.5	23.0	38 40.0	01.3			
06	67 27.9	229 17.5	S10 59.2	324 45.6	N23 25.2	291 43.4	N17 22.8	53 42.6	N 3 01.2	Alioth	166 12.2	N55 49.1
07	82 30.4	244 18.2	11 00.2	339 46.3	25.1	306 45.4	22.7	68 45.2	01.2	Alkaid	152 51.2	N49 11.0
08	97 32.8	259 18.8	01.3	354 47.0	24.9	321 47.3	22.5	83 47.8	01.1	Alnair	27 30.7	S46 49.8
09	112 35.3	274 19.4	. . 02.4	9 47.8	. . 24.8	336 49.2	. . 22.4	98 50.4	. . 01.0	Alnilam	275 36.4	S 1 10.9
10	127 37.8	289 20.1	03.4	24 48.5	24.7	351 51.2	22.2	113 53.0	01.0	Alphard	217 46.7	S 8 46.4
11	142 40.2	304 20.7	04.5	39 49.2	24.6	6 53.1	22.1	128 55.5	00.9			
12	157 42.7	319 21.3	S11 05.6	54 49.9	N23 24.5	21 55.0	N17 21.9	143 58.1	N 3 00.9	Alphecca	126 02.7	N26 37.7
13	172 45.1	334 22.0	06.7	69 50.7	24.4	36 57.0	21.8	159 00.7	00.8	Alpheratz	357 33.0	N29 14.4
14	187 47.6	349 22.6	07.7	84 51.4	24.3	51 58.9	21.6	174 03.3	00.7	Altair	61 58.4	N 8 56.5
15	202 50.1	4 23.2	. . 08.8	99 52.1	. . 24.2	67 00.8	. . 21.5	189 05.9	. . 00.7	Ankaa	353 05.4	S42 09.4
16	217 52.5	19 23.9	09.9	114 52.9	24.1	82 02.7	21.3	204 08.5	00.6	Antares	112 14.1	S26 29.5
17	232 55.0	34 24.5	10.9	129 53.6	24.0	97 04.7	21.2	219 11.0	00.6			
18	247 57.5	49 25.1	S11 12.0	144 54.3	N23 23.9	112 06.6	N17 21.1	234 13.6	N 3 00.5	Arcturus	145 46.8	N19 02.8
19	262 59.9	64 25.8	13.1	159 55.1	23.8	127 08.5	20.9	249 16.2	00.4	Atria	107 07.0	S69 04.8
20	278 02.4	79 26.4	14.1	174 55.8	23.7	142 10.5	20.8	264 18.8	00.4	Avior	234 14.7	S59 35.5
21	293 04.9	94 27.1	. . 15.2	189 56.5	. . 23.6	157 12.4	. . 20.6	279 21.4	. . 00.3	Bellatrix	278 21.5	N 6 22.5
22	308 07.3	109 27.7	16.3	204 57.3	23.5	172 14.3	20.5	294 24.0	00.3	Betelgeuse	270 50.7	N 7 24.8
23	323 09.8	124 28.4	17.3	219 58.0	23.4	187 16.3	20.3	309 26.6	00.2			
30 SUNDAY 00	338 12.3	139 29.0	S11 18.4	234 58.7	N23 23.3	202 18.2	N17 20.2	324 29.1	N 3 00.1	Canopus	263 52.1	S52 42.2
01	353 14.7	154 29.7	19.5	249 59.4	23.2	217 20.1	20.0	339 31.7	00.1	Capella	280 20.0	N46 01.3
02	8 17.2	169 30.3	20.5	265 00.2	23.0	232 22.1	19.9	354 34.3	00.0	Deneb	49 24.5	N45 22.7
03	23 19.6	184 30.9	. . 21.6	280 00.9	. . 22.9	247 24.0	. . 19.7	9 36.9	3 00.0	Denebola	182 23.9	N14 25.5
04	38 22.1	199 31.6	22.7	295 01.6	22.8	262 25.9	19.6	24 39.5	2 59.9	Diphda	348 45.7	S17 50.2
05	53 24.6	214 32.2	23.7	310 02.4	22.7	277 27.9	19.4	39 42.1	59.8			
06	68 27.0	229 32.9	S11 24.8	325 03.1	N23 22.6	292 29.8	N17 19.3	54 44.6	N 2 59.8	Dubhe	193 40.0	N61 36.5
07	83 29.5	244 33.5	25.9	340 03.8	22.5	307 31.7	19.2	69 47.2	59.7	Elnath	278 00.2	N28 37.8
08	98 32.0	259 34.2	26.9	355 04.6	22.4	322 33.7	19.0	84 49.8	59.7	Eltanin	90 41.3	N51 29.4
09	113 34.4	274 34.9	. . 28.0	10 05.3	. . 22.3	337 35.6	. . 18.9	99 52.4	. . 59.6	Enif	33 37.1	N10 00.0
10	128 36.9	289 35.5	29.0	25 06.0	22.2	352 37.5	18.7	114 55.0	59.5	Fomalhaut	15 12.6	S29 28.7
11	143 39.4	304 36.2	30.1	40 06.8	22.1	7 39.5	18.6	129 57.6	59.5			
12	158 41.8	319 36.8	S11 31.2	55 07.5	N23 21.9	22 41.4	N17 18.4	145 00.2	N 2 59.4	Gacrux	171 50.6	S57 15.9
13	173 44.3	334 37.5	32.2	70 08.3	21.8	37 43.3	18.3	160 02.7	59.4	Gienah	175 42.5	S17 41.4
14	188 46.8	349 38.1	33.3	85 09.0	21.7	52 45.3	18.1	175 05.3	59.3	Hadar	148 34.4	S60 30.3
15	203 49.2	4 38.8	. . 34.3	100 09.7	. . 21.6	67 47.2	. . 18.0	190 07.9	. . 59.2	Hamal	327 49.5	N23 35.4
16	218 51.7	19 39.5	35.4	115 10.5	21.5	82 49.1	17.8	205 10.5	59.2	Kaus Aust.	83 30.5	S34 22.3
17	233 54.1	34 40.1	36.4	130 11.2	21.4	97 51.1	17.7	220 13.1	59.1			
18	248 56.6	49 40.8	S11 37.5	145 11.9	N23 21.3	112 53.0	N17 17.5	235 15.7	N 2 59.1	Kochab	137 20.3	N74 03.0
19	263 59.1	64 41.5	38.6	160 12.7	21.2	127 54.9	17.4	250 18.3	59.0	Markab	13 28.2	N15 21.1
20	279 01.5	79 42.1	39.6	175 13.4	21.0	142 56.9	17.3	265 20.9	58.9	Menkar	314 04.6	N 4 11.8
21	294 04.0	94 42.8	. . 40.7	190 14.1	. . 20.9	157 58.8	. . 17.1	280 23.4	. . 58.9	Menkent	147 56.2	S36 30.2
22	309 06.5	109 43.5	41.7	205 14.9	20.8	173 00.7	17.0	295 26.0	58.8	Miaplacidus	221 38.9	S69 49.5
23	324 08.9	124 44.1	42.8	220 15.6	20.7	188 02.7	16.8	310 28.6	58.8			
31 MONDAY 00	339 11.4	139 44.8	S11 43.8	235 16.3	N23 20.6	203 04.6	N17 16.7	325 31.2	N 2 58.7	Mirfak	308 26.2	N49 57.2
01	354 13.9	154 45.5	44.9	250 17.1	20.5	218 06.5	16.5	340 33.8	58.6	Nunki	75 45.8	S26 15.8
02	9 16.3	169 46.1	45.9	265 17.8	20.4	233 08.5	16.4	355 36.4	58.6	Peacock	53 03.1	S56 39.0
03	24 18.8	184 46.8	. . 47.0	280 18.6	. . 20.2	248 10.4	. . 16.2	10 39.0	. . 58.5	Pollux	243 15.9	N27 57.7
04	39 21.2	199 47.5	48.0	295 19.3	20.1	263 12.3	16.1	25 41.6	58.5	Procyon	244 49.6	N 5 09.5
05	54 23.7	214 48.2	49.1	310 20.0	20.0	278 14.3	15.9	40 44.1	58.4			
06	69 26.2	229 48.8	S11 50.1	325 20.8	N23 19.9	293 16.2	N17 15.8	55 46.7	N 2 58.3	Rasalhague	95 57.2	N12 32.6
07	84 28.6	244 49.5	51.2	340 21.5	19.8	308 18.1	15.6	70 49.3	58.3	Regulus	207 33.3	N11 50.3
08	99 31.1	259 50.2	52.2	355 22.3	19.7	323 20.1	15.5	85 51.9	58.2	Rigel	281 02.6	S 8 10.1
09	114 33.6	274 50.9	. . 53.3	10 23.0	. . 19.5	338 22.0	. . 15.3	100 54.5	. . 58.2	Rigil Kent.	139 38.7	S60 56.9
10	129 36.0	289 51.6	54.3	25 23.7	19.4	353 23.9	15.2	115 57.1	58.1	Sabik	102 01.1	S15 45.4
11	144 38.5	304 52.2	55.4	40 24.5	19.3	8 25.9	15.1	130 59.7	58.0			
12	159 41.0	319 52.9	S11 56.4	55 25.2	N23 19.2	23 27.8	N17 14.9	146 02.3	N 2 58.0	Schedar	349 29.0	N56 41.0
13	174 43.4	334 53.6	57.5	70 26.0	19.1	38 29.7	14.8	161 04.9	57.9	Shaula	96 08.4	S37 07.5
14	189 45.9	349 54.3	58.5	85 26.7	19.0	53 31.7	14.6	176 07.4	57.8	Sirius	258 25.2	S16 45.0
15	204 48.4	4 55.0	11 59.6	100 27.4	. . 18.8	68 33.6	. . 14.5	191 10.0	. . 57.8	Spica	158 21.1	S11 18.0
16	219 50.8	19 55.7	12 00.6	115 28.2	18.7	83 35.6	14.3	206 12.6	57.7	Suhail	222 45.7	S43 32.3
17	234 53.3	34 56.4	01.6	130 28.9	18.6	98 37.5	14.2	221 15.2	57.7			
18	249 55.7	49 57.0	S12 02.7	145 29.7	N23 18.5	113 39.4	N17 14.0	236 17.8	N 2 57.6	Vega	80 32.1	N38 48.7
19	264 58.2	64 57.7	03.7	160 30.4	18.4	128 41.4	13.9	251 20.4	57.5	Zuben'ubi	136 54.6	S16 09.2
20	280 00.7	79 58.4	04.8	175 31.1	18.2	143 43.3	13.7	266 23.0	57.5			
21	295 03.1	94 59.1	. . 05.8	190 31.9	. . 18.1	158 45.2	. . 13.6	281 25.6	. . 57.4			
22	310 05.6	109 59.8	06.9	205 32.6	18.0	173 47.2	13.4	296 28.2	57.4			
23	325 08.1	125 00.5	07.9	220 33.4	17.9	188 49.1	13.3	311 30.8	57.3			
Mer. Pass. (h m)	1 26.9	*v* 0.7	*d* 1.1	*v* 0.7	*d* 0.1	*v* 1.9	*d* 0.1	*v* 2.6	*d* 0.1			

	SHA (° ′)	Mer. Pass. (h m)
Venus	161 16.8	14 41
Mars	256 46.5	8 20
Jupiter	224 05.9	10 29
Saturn	346 16.9	2 22

2026 AUGUST 29, 30, 31 (SAT., SUN., MON.)

Day	UT	SUN GHA	SUN Dec	MOON GHA	v	MOON Dec	d	HP
	d h	° ′	° ′	° ′	′	° ′	′	′
SATURDAY	29 00	179 43.7	N 9 25.4	351 09.4	14.6	S 4 25.0	15.2	56.6
	01	194 43.9	24.5	5 43.0	14.5	4 09.8	15.2	56.6
	02	209 44.1	23.6	20 16.5	14.6	3 54.6	15.3	56.6
	03	224 44.3	. . 22.7	34 50.1	14.6	3 39.3	15.2	56.7
	04	239 44.4	21.8	49 23.7	14.6	3 24.1	15.3	56.7
	05	254 44.6	20.9	63 57.3	14.5	3 08.8	15.3	56.7
	06	269 44.8	N 9 20.1	78 30.8	14.6	S 2 53.5	15.4	56.7
	07	284 45.0	19.2	93 04.4	14.6	2 38.1	15.4	56.7
	08	299 45.2	18.3	107 38.0	14.5	2 22.7	15.4	56.8
	09	314 45.4	. . 17.4	122 11.5	14.5	2 07.3	15.4	56.8
	10	329 45.6	16.5	136 45.0	14.5	1 51.9	15.4	56.8
	11	344 45.8	15.6	151 18.5	14.5	1 36.5	15.4	56.8
	12	359 46.0	N 9 14.7	165 52.0	14.5	S 1 21.1	15.5	56.9
	13	14 46.1	13.8	180 25.5	14.5	1 05.6	15.5	56.9
	14	29 46.3	12.9	194 59.0	14.5	0 50.1	15.5	56.9
	15	44 46.5	. . 12.0	209 32.5	14.4	0 34.6	15.5	56.9
	16	59 46.7	11.2	224 05.9	14.4	0 19.1	15.5	56.9
	17	74 46.9	10.3	238 39.3	14.4	S 0 03.6	15.5	57.0
	18	89 47.1	N 9 09.4	253 12.7	14.4	N 0 11.9	15.6	57.0
	19	104 47.3	08.5	267 46.1	14.4	0 27.5	15.5	57.0
	20	119 47.5	07.6	282 19.5	14.3	0 43.0	15.6	57.0
	21	134 47.7	. . 06.7	296 52.8	14.3	0 58.6	15.5	57.0
	22	149 47.9	05.8	311 26.1	14.3	1 14.1	15.6	57.1
	23	164 48.1	04.9	325 59.4	14.2	1 29.7	15.6	57.1
SUNDAY	30 00	179 48.2	N 9 04.0	340 32.6	14.3	N 1 45.3	15.6	57.1
	01	194 48.4	03.1	355 05.9	14.2	2 00.9	15.5	57.1
	02	209 48.6	02.2	9 39.1	14.1	2 16.4	15.6	57.2
	03	224 48.8	. . 01.3	24 12.2	14.2	2 32.0	15.6	57.2
	04	239 49.0	9 00.4	38 45.4	14.1	2 47.6	15.6	57.2
	05	254 49.2	8 59.5	53 18.5	14.0	3 03.2	15.5	57.2
	06	269 49.4	N 8 58.7	67 51.5	14.1	N 3 18.7	15.6	57.2
	07	284 49.6	57.8	82 24.6	14.0	3 34.3	15.6	57.3
	08	299 49.8	56.9	96 57.6	13.9	3 49.9	15.5	57.3
	09	314 50.0	. . 56.0	111 30.5	14.0	4 05.4	15.6	57.3
	10	329 50.2	55.1	126 03.5	13.8	4 21.0	15.5	57.3
	11	344 50.4	54.2	140 36.3	13.9	4 36.5	15.5	57.3
	12	359 50.6	N 8 53.3	155 09.2	13.8	N 4 52.0	15.5	57.4
	13	14 50.7	52.4	169 42.0	13.8	5 07.5	15.5	57.4
	14	29 50.9	51.5	184 14.8	13.7	5 23.0	15.5	57.4
	15	44 51.1	. . 50.6	198 47.5	13.6	5 38.5	15.5	57.4
	16	59 51.3	49.7	213 20.1	13.7	5 54.0	15.5	57.4
	17	74 51.5	48.8	227 52.8	13.5	6 09.5	15.4	57.5
	18	89 51.7	N 8 47.9	242 25.3	13.6	N 6 24.9	15.4	57.5
	19	104 51.9	47.0	256 57.9	13.4	6 40.3	15.4	57.5
	20	119 52.1	46.1	271 30.3	13.5	6 55.7	15.4	57.5
	21	134 52.3	. . 45.2	286 02.8	13.3	7 11.1	15.4	57.5
	22	149 52.5	44.3	300 35.1	13.4	7 26.5	15.3	57.6
	23	164 52.7	43.4	315 07.5	13.2	7 41.8	15.3	57.6
MONDAY	31 00	179 52.9	N 8 42.5	329 39.7	13.2	N 7 57.1	15.3	57.6
	01	194 53.1	41.6	344 11.9	13.2	8 12.4	15.2	57.6
	02	209 53.3	40.7	358 44.1	13.1	8 27.6	15.2	57.6
	03	224 53.5	. . 39.8	13 16.2	13.0	8 42.8	15.2	57.7
	04	239 53.7	38.9	27 48.2	13.0	8 58.0	15.2	57.7
	05	254 53.9	38.0	42 20.2	12.9	9 13.2	15.1	57.7
	06	269 54.1	N 8 37.1	56 52.1	12.8	N 9 28.3	15.1	57.7
	07	284 54.2	36.2	71 23.9	12.8	9 43.4	15.0	57.7
	08	299 54.4	35.3	85 55.7	12.8	9 58.4	15.0	57.7
	09	314 54.6	. . 34.4	100 27.5	12.6	10 13.4	15.0	57.8
	10	329 54.8	33.5	114 59.1	12.6	10 28.4	14.9	57.8
	11	344 55.0	32.6	129 30.7	12.5	10 43.3	14.9	57.8
	12	359 55.2	N 8 31.7	144 02.2	12.5	N10 58.2	14.9	57.8
	13	14 55.4	30.8	158 33.7	12.3	11 13.1	14.8	57.8
	14	29 55.6	29.9	173 05.0	12.3	11 27.9	14.7	57.9
	15	44 55.8	. . 29.0	187 36.3	12.3	11 42.6	14.7	57.9
	16	59 56.0	28.1	202 07.6	12.1	11 57.3	14.7	57.9
	17	74 56.2	27.2	216 38.7	12.1	12 12.0	14.6	57.9
	18	89 56.4	N 8 26.3	231 09.8	12.0	N12 26.6	14.5	57.9
	19	104 56.6	25.4	245 40.8	12.0	12 41.1	14.5	58.0
	20	119 56.8	24.5	260 11.8	11.8	12 55.6	14.4	58.0
	21	134 57.0	. . 23.6	274 42.6	11.8	13 10.0	14.4	58.0
	22	149 57.2	22.7	289 13.4	11.7	13 24.4	14.4	58.0
	23	164 57.4	21.8	303 44.1	11.6	N13 38.8	14.2	58.0
		SD 15.9	*d* 0.9	SD	15.5		15.6	15.8

Lat.	Twilight Naut.	Twilight Civil	Sunrise	Moonrise 29	Moonrise 30	Moonrise 31	Moonrise 1
°	h m	h m	h m	h m	h m	h m	h m
N 72	////	02 16	03 51	19 05	18 30	17 47	16 18
N 70	////	02 48	04 06	19 05	18 39	18 08	17 18
68	01 09	03 11	04 18	19 06	18 47	18 24	17 53
66	01 57	03 28	04 28	19 06	18 53	18 38	18 18
64	02 26	03 43	04 37	19 06	18 58	18 49	18 38
62	02 47	03 54	04 44	19 07	19 02	18 58	18 54
60	03 04	04 04	04 50	19 07	19 06	19 07	19 08
N 58	03 18	04 13	04 55	19 07	19 10	19 14	19 20
56	03 30	04 20	05 00	19 07	19 13	19 21	19 30
54	03 40	04 27	05 05	19 07	19 16	19 26	19 39
52	03 49	04 33	05 08	19 07	19 19	19 32	19 48
50	03 56	04 38	05 12	19 08	19 21	19 36	19 55
45	04 12	04 49	05 19	19 08	19 26	19 47	20 11
N 40	04 24	04 58	05 26	19 08	19 31	19 55	20 24
35	04 34	05 05	05 31	19 08	19 35	20 03	20 35
30	04 43	05 11	05 36	19 09	19 38	20 10	20 45
20	04 55	05 22	05 44	19 09	19 44	20 21	21 02
N 10	05 05	05 30	05 51	19 09	19 49	20 31	21 17
0	05 12	05 36	05 57	19 10	19 54	20 41	21 31
S 10	05 18	05 42	06 04	19 10	19 59	20 51	21 45
20	05 22	05 48	06 10	19 11	20 05	21 01	22 01
30	05 26	05 54	06 18	19 11	20 11	21 13	22 19
35	05 27	05 56	06 22	19 11	20 15	21 20	22 29
40	05 28	05 59	06 27	19 12	20 19	21 29	22 41
45	05 29	06 03	06 32	19 12	20 24	21 38	22 55
S 50	05 29	06 06	06 39	19 13	20 30	21 49	23 12
52	05 29	06 08	06 42	19 13	20 32	21 55	23 21
54	05 28	06 09	06 45	19 13	20 35	22 01	23 30
56	05 28	06 11	06 49	19 13	20 39	22 07	23 40
58	05 28	06 13	06 53	19 14	20 42	22 15	23 52
S 60	05 27	06 15	06 57	19 14	20 47	22 23	24 06

Lat.	Sunset	Twilight Civil	Twilight Naut.	Moonset 29	Moonset 30	Moonset 31	Moonset 1
°	h m	h m	h m	h m	h m	h m	h m
N 72	20 06	21 39	////	06 09	08 20	10 41	13 53
N 70	19 52	21 09	////	06 14	08 14	10 22	12 55
68	19 40	20 47	22 42	06 17	08 10	10 08	12 22
66	19 31	20 30	21 59	06 20	08 06	09 56	11 58
64	19 23	20 16	21 31	06 23	08 03	09 47	11 39
62	19 16	20 05	21 11	06 25	08 00	09 39	11 24
60	19 10	19 55	20 54	06 26	07 58	09 32	11 11
N 58	19 04	19 47	20 41	06 28	07 56	09 26	11 00
56	19 00	19 39	20 29	06 30	07 54	09 20	10 51
54	18 56	19 33	20 20	06 31	07 52	09 16	10 43
52	18 52	19 27	20 11	06 32	07 50	09 11	10 35
50	18 48	19 22	20 03	06 33	07 49	09 07	10 29
45	18 41	19 11	19 48	06 35	07 46	08 59	10 14
N 40	18 35	19 03	19 36	06 37	07 44	08 52	10 03
35	18 30	18 55	19 26	06 39	07 42	08 46	09 53
30	18 25	18 49	19 18	06 40	07 40	08 41	09 44
20	18 17	18 39	19 06	06 43	07 36	08 32	09 29
N 10	18 10	18 32	18 56	06 45	07 33	08 24	09 16
0	18 04	18 25	18 49	06 47	07 31	08 16	09 04
S 10	17 58	18 19	18 44	06 49	07 28	08 09	08 53
20	17 51	18 13	18 39	06 51	07 25	08 01	08 40
30	17 44	18 08	18 36	06 53	07 22	07 52	08 25
35	17 40	18 05	18 35	06 54	07 20	07 47	08 17
40	17 35	18 02	18 34	06 56	07 18	07 41	08 08
45	17 30	17 59	18 33	06 58	07 16	07 35	07 56
S 50	17 23	17 56	18 33	07 00	07 13	07 27	07 43
52	17 20	17 55	18 34	07 00	07 11	07 23	07 37
54	17 17	17 53	18 34	07 01	07 10	07 19	07 30
56	17 14	17 51	18 34	07 02	07 08	07 15	07 23
58	17 10	17 50	18 35	07 04	07 06	07 10	07 14
S 60	17 05	17 48	18 36	07 05	07 04	07 04	07 05

Day	SUN Eqn. of Time 00h	SUN Eqn. of Time 12h	SUN Mer. Pass.	MOON Mer. Pass. Upper	MOON Mer. Pass. Lower	MOON Age	MOON Phase
d	m s	m s	h m	h m	h m	d %	
29	01 06	00 57	12 01	00 36	12 58	17 98	
30	00 47	00 38	12 01	01 20	13 42	18 94	○
31	00 29	00 19	12 00	02 05	14 29	19 88	

2026 SEPTEMBER 1, 2, 3 (TUES., WED., THURS.)

UT d h	ARIES GHA ° ′	VENUS −4·6 GHA ° ′	VENUS Dec ° ′	MARS +1·2 GHA ° ′	MARS Dec ° ′	JUPITER −1·8 GHA ° ′	JUPITER Dec ° ′	SATURN +0·4 GHA ° ′	SATURN Dec ° ′
1 00 (TUESDAY)	340 10.5	140 01.2	S12 08.9	235 34.1	N23 17.8	203 51.0	N17 13.2	326 33.3	N 2 57.2
01	355 13.0	155 01.9	10.0	250 34.8	17.6	218 53.0	13.0	341 35.9	57.2
02	10 15.5	170 02.6	11.0	265 35.6	17.5	233 54.9	12.9	356 38.5	57.1
03	25 17.9	185 03.3	. . 12.1	280 36.3	. . 17.4	248 56.8	. . 12.7	11 41.1	. . 57.0
04	40 20.4	200 04.0	13.1	295 37.1	17.3	263 58.8	12.6	26 43.7	57.0
05	55 22.8	215 04.7	14.1	310 37.8	17.1	279 00.7	12.4	41 46.3	56.9
06	70 25.3	230 05.4	S12 15.2	325 38.6	N23 17.0	294 02.7	N17 12.3	56 48.9	N 2 56.9
07	85 27.8	245 06.1	16.2	340 39.3	16.9	309 04.6	12.1	71 51.5	56.8
08	100 30.2	260 06.8	17.2	355 40.0	16.8	324 06.5	12.0	86 54.1	56.7
09	115 32.7	275 07.5	. . 18.3	10 40.8	. . 16.7	339 08.5	. . 11.8	101 56.7	. . 56.7
10	130 35.2	290 08.2	19.3	25 41.5	16.5	354 10.4	11.7	116 59.3	56.6
11	145 37.6	305 08.9	20.3	40 42.3	16.4	9 12.3	11.5	132 01.9	56.5
12	160 40.1	320 09.6	S12 21.4	55 43.0	N23 16.3	24 14.3	N17 11.4	147 04.4	N 2 56.5
13	175 42.6	335 10.4	22.4	70 43.8	16.2	39 16.2	11.2	162 07.0	56.4
14	190 45.0	350 11.1	23.4	85 44.5	16.0	54 18.2	11.1	177 09.6	56.4
15	205 47.5	5 11.8	. . 24.5	100 45.3	. . 15.9	69 20.1	. . 11.0	192 12.2	. . 56.3
16	220 50.0	20 12.5	25.5	115 46.0	15.8	84 22.0	10.8	207 14.8	56.2
17	235 52.4	35 13.2	26.5	130 46.8	15.6	99 24.0	10.7	222 17.4	56.2
18	250 54.9	50 13.9	S12 27.6	145 47.5	N23 15.5	114 25.9	N17 10.5	237 20.0	N 2 56.1
19	265 57.3	65 14.6	28.6	160 48.2	15.4	129 27.8	10.4	252 22.6	56.0
20	280 59.8	80 15.4	29.6	175 49.0	15.3	144 29.8	10.2	267 25.2	56.0
21	296 02.3	95 16.1	. . 30.6	190 49.7	. . 15.1	159 31.7	. . 10.1	282 27.8	. . 55.9
22	311 04.7	110 16.8	31.7	205 50.5	15.0	174 33.7	09.9	297 30.4	55.9
23	326 07.2	125 17.5	32.7	220 51.2	14.9	189 35.6	09.8	312 33.0	55.8
2 00 (WEDNESDAY)	341 09.7	140 18.2	S12 33.7	235 52.0	N23 14.8	204 37.5	N17 09.6	327 35.6	N 2 55.7
01	356 12.1	155 19.0	34.8	250 52.7	14.6	219 39.5	09.5	342 38.1	55.7
02	11 14.6	170 19.7	35.8	265 53.5	14.5	234 41.4	09.3	357 40.7	55.6
03	26 17.1	185 20.4	. . 36.8	280 54.2	. . 14.4	249 43.3	. . 09.2	12 43.3	. . 55.5
04	41 19.5	200 21.1	37.8	295 55.0	14.2	264 45.3	09.1	27 45.9	55.5
05	56 22.0	215 21.9	38.8	310 55.7	14.1	279 47.2	08.9	42 48.5	55.4
06	71 24.5	230 22.6	S12 39.9	325 56.5	N23 14.0	294 49.2	N17 08.8	57 51.1	N 2 55.4
07	86 26.9	245 23.3	40.9	340 57.2	13.8	309 51.1	08.6	72 53.7	55.3
08	101 29.4	260 24.1	41.9	355 58.0	13.7	324 53.0	08.5	87 56.3	55.2
09	116 31.8	275 24.8	. . 42.9	10 58.7	. . 13.6	339 55.0	. . 08.3	102 58.9	. . 55.2
10	131 34.3	290 25.5	44.0	25 59.5	13.5	354 56.9	08.2	118 01.5	55.1
11	146 36.8	305 26.3	45.0	41 00.2	13.3	9 58.9	08.0	133 04.1	55.0
12	161 39.2	320 27.0	S12 46.0	56 01.0	N23 13.2	25 00.8	N17 07.9	148 06.7	N 2 55.0
13	176 41.7	335 27.7	47.0	71 01.7	13.1	40 02.7	07.7	163 09.3	54.9
14	191 44.2	350 28.5	48.0	86 02.5	12.9	55 04.7	07.6	178 11.9	54.8
15	206 46.6	5 29.2	. . 49.1	101 03.2	. . 12.8	70 06.6	. . 07.4	193 14.5	. . 54.8
16	221 49.1	20 30.0	50.1	116 04.0	12.7	85 08.6	07.3	208 17.1	54.7
17	236 51.6	35 30.7	51.1	131 04.7	12.5	100 10.5	07.1	223 19.7	54.7
18	251 54.0	50 31.5	S12 52.1	146 05.5	N23 12.4	115 12.4	N17 07.0	238 22.3	N 2 54.6
19	266 56.5	65 32.2	53.1	161 06.2	12.3	130 14.4	06.9	253 24.9	54.5
20	281 58.9	80 32.9	54.1	176 07.0	12.1	145 16.3	06.7	268 27.5	54.5
21	297 01.4	95 33.7	. . 55.1	191 07.7	. . 12.0	160 18.2	. . 06.6	283 30.0	. . 54.4
22	312 03.9	110 34.4	56.2	206 08.5	11.9	175 20.2	06.4	298 32.6	54.3
23	327 06.3	125 35.2	57.2	221 09.2	11.7	190 22.1	06.3	313 35.2	54.3
3 00 (THURSDAY)	342 08.8	140 35.9	S12 58.2	236 10.0	N23 11.6	205 24.1	N17 06.1	328 37.8	N 2 54.2
01	357 11.3	155 36.7	12 59.2	251 10.7	11.5	220 26.0	06.0	343 40.4	54.1
02	12 13.7	170 37.5	13 00.2	266 11.5	11.3	235 28.0	05.8	358 43.0	54.1
03	27 16.2	185 38.2	. . 01.2	281 12.2	. . 11.2	250 29.9	. . 05.7	13 45.6	. . 54.0
04	42 18.7	200 39.0	02.2	296 13.0	11.0	265 31.8	05.5	28 48.2	54.0
05	57 21.1	215 39.7	03.2	311 13.7	10.9	280 33.8	05.4	43 50.8	53.9
06	72 23.6	230 40.5	S13 04.2	326 14.5	N23 10.8	295 35.7	N17 05.2	58 53.4	N 2 53.8
07	87 26.1	245 41.2	05.3	341 15.3	10.6	310 37.7	05.1	73 56.0	53.8
08	102 28.5	260 42.0	06.3	356 16.0	10.5	325 39.6	05.0	88 58.6	53.7
09	117 31.0	275 42.8	. . 07.3	11 16.8	. . 10.4	340 41.5	. . 04.8	104 01.2	. . 53.6
10	132 33.4	290 43.5	08.3	26 17.5	10.2	355 43.5	04.7	119 03.8	53.6
11	147 35.9	305 44.3	09.3	41 18.3	10.1	10 45.4	04.5	134 06.4	53.5
12	162 38.4	320 45.1	S13 10.3	56 19.0	N23 09.9	25 47.4	N17 04.4	149 09.0	N 2 53.4
13	177 40.8	335 45.8	11.3	71 19.8	09.8	40 49.3	04.2	164 11.6	53.4
14	192 43.3	350 46.6	12.3	86 20.5	09.7	55 51.2	04.1	179 14.2	53.3
15	207 45.8	5 47.4	. . 13.3	101 21.3	. . 09.5	70 53.2	. . 03.9	194 16.8	. . 53.2
16	222 48.2	20 48.1	14.3	116 22.1	09.4	85 55.1	03.8	209 19.4	53.2
17	237 50.7	35 48.9	15.3	131 22.8	09.3	100 57.1	03.6	224 22.0	53.1
18	252 53.2	50 49.7	S13 16.3	146 23.6	N23 09.1	115 59.0	N17 03.5	239 24.6	N 2 53.1
19	267 55.6	65 50.4	17.3	161 24.3	09.0	131 00.9	03.3	254 27.2	53.0
20	282 58.1	80 51.2	18.3	176 25.1	08.8	146 02.9	03.2	269 29.8	52.9
21	298 00.6	95 52.0	. . 19.3	191 25.8	. . 08.7	161 04.8	. . 03.1	284 32.4	. . 52.9
22	313 03.0	110 52.8	20.3	206 26.6	08.5	176 06.8	02.9	299 35.0	52.8
23	328 05.5	125 53.6	21.3	221 27.4	08.4	191 08.7	02.8	314 37.6	52.7
Mer. Pass. (h m)	1 15.1	v 0.7	d 1.0	v 0.8	d 0.1	v 1.9	d 0.1	v 2.6	d 0.1

STARS

Name	SHA ° ′	Dec ° ′
Acamar	315 10.6	S40 11.5
Achernar	335 18.8	S57 05.8
Acrux	172 59.1	S63 15.0
Adhara	255 05.0	S29 00.2
Aldebaran	290 38.0	N16 33.8
Alioth	166 12.2	N55 49.1
Alkaid	152 51.2	N49 11.0
Alnair	27 30.7	S46 49.8
Alnilam	275 36.4	S 1 10.9
Alphard	217 46.7	S 8 46.3
Alphecca	126 02.7	N26 37.7
Alpheratz	357 33.0	N29 14.4
Altair	61 58.4	N 8 56.5
Ankaa	353 05.4	S42 09.4
Antares	112 14.2	S26 29.5
Arcturus	145 46.8	N19 02.8
Atria	107 07.1	S69 04.7
Avior	234 14.7	S59 35.5
Bellatrix	278 21.5	N 6 22.5
Betelgeuse	270 50.7	N 7 24.8
Canopus	263 52.0	S52 42.2
Capella	280 19.9	N46 01.3
Deneb	49 24.5	N45 22.7
Denebola	182 23.9	N14 25.5
Diphda	348 45.6	S17 50.2
Dubhe	193 40.0	N61 36.5
Elnath	278 00.2	N28 37.8
Eltanin	90 41.4	N51 29.4
Enif	33 37.1	N10 00.0
Fomalhaut	15 12.6	S29 28.7
Gacrux	171 50.6	S57 15.9
Gienah	175 42.5	S17 41.4
Hadar	148 34.4	S60 30.3
Hamal	327 49.4	N23 35.4
Kaus Aust.	83 30.5	S34 22.3
Kochab	137 20.3	N74 03.0
Markab	13 28.2	N15 21.1
Menkar	314 04.6	N 4 11.8
Menkent	147 56.2	S36 30.2
Miaplacidus	221 38.9	S69 49.4
Mirfak	308 26.1	N49 57.2
Nunki	75 45.9	S26 15.8
Peacock	53 03.1	S56 39.0
Pollux	243 15.9	N27 57.7
Procyon	244 49.6	N 5 09.5
Rasalhague	95 57.2	N12 32.6
Regulus	207 33.3	N11 50.3
Rigel	281 02.6	S 8 10.1
Rigil Kent.	139 38.7	S60 56.9
Sabik	102 01.2	S15 45.4
Schedar	349 29.0	N56 41.0
Shaula	96 08.4	S37 07.5
Sirius	258 25.2	S16 45.0
Spica	158 21.1	S11 18.0
Suhail	222 45.7	S43 32.3
Vega	80 32.1	N38 48.7
Zuben'ubi	136 54.6	S16 09.2

	SHA ° ′	Mer. Pass. h m
Venus	159 08.6	14 38
Mars	254 42.3	8 16
Jupiter	223 27.9	10 20
Saturn	346 25.9	2 09

Day	UT (d h)	SUN GHA (° ′)	SUN Dec (° ′)	MOON GHA (° ′)	v (′)	MOON Dec (° ′)	d (′)	HP (′)
TUESDAY	1 00	179 57.6	N 8 20.9	318 14.7	11.5	N13 53.0	14.2	58.0
	01	194 57.8	20.0	332 45.2	11.5	14 07.2	14.2	58.1
	02	209 58.0	19.0	347 15.7	11.3	14 21.4	14.1	58.1
	03	224 58.2	. . 18.1	1 46.0	11.3	14 35.5	14.0	58.1
	04	239 58.4	17.2	16 16.3	11.2	14 49.5	13.9	58.1
	05	254 58.6	16.3	30 46.5	11.1	15 03.4	13.9	58.1
	06	269 58.8	N 8 15.4	45 16.6	11.0	N15 17.3	13.8	58.1
	07	284 59.0	14.5	59 46.6	10.9	15 31.1	13.7	58.2
	08	299 59.2	13.6	74 16.5	10.9	15 44.8	13.7	58.2
	09	314 59.4	. . 12.7	88 46.4	10.7	15 58.5	13.6	58.2
	10	329 59.6	11.8	103 16.1	10.6	16 12.1	13.5	58.2
	11	344 59.8	10.9	117 45.7	10.6	16 25.6	13.4	58.2
	12	0 00.0	N 8 10.0	132 15.3	10.5	N16 39.0	13.3	58.2
	13	15 00.2	09.1	146 44.8	10.3	16 52.3	13.3	58.3
	14	30 00.4	08.2	161 14.1	10.3	17 05.6	13.2	58.3
	15	45 00.6	. . 07.3	175 43.4	10.2	17 18.8	13.1	58.3
	16	60 00.8	06.4	190 12.6	10.1	17 31.9	13.0	58.3
	17	75 01.0	05.4	204 41.7	10.0	17 44.9	12.9	58.3
	18	90 01.2	N 8 04.5	219 10.7	9.9	N17 57.8	12.9	58.3
	19	105 01.4	03.6	233 39.6	9.7	18 10.7	12.7	58.4
	20	120 01.6	02.7	248 08.3	9.7	18 23.4	12.7	58.4
	21	135 01.8	. . 01.8	262 37.0	9.6	18 36.1	12.5	58.4
	22	150 02.0	00.9	277 05.6	9.5	18 48.6	12.5	58.4
	23	165 02.2	8 00.0	291 34.1	9.4	19 01.1	12.3	58.4
WEDNESDAY	2 00	180 02.4	N 7 59.1	306 02.5	9.3	N19 13.4	12.3	58.4
	01	195 02.6	58.2	320 30.8	9.2	19 25.7	12.2	58.5
	02	210 02.8	57.3	334 59.0	9.0	19 37.9	12.0	58.5
	03	225 03.0	. . 56.3	349 27.0	9.0	19 49.9	12.0	58.5
	04	240 03.2	55.4	3 55.0	8.9	20 01.9	11.8	58.5
	05	255 03.4	54.5	18 22.9	8.8	20 13.7	11.8	58.5
	06	270 03.6	N 7 53.6	32 50.7	8.6	N20 25.5	11.6	58.5
	07	285 03.8	52.7	47 18.3	8.6	20 37.1	11.5	58.6
	08	300 04.0	51.8	61 45.9	8.5	20 48.6	11.4	58.6
	09	315 04.2	. . 50.9	76 13.4	8.3	21 00.0	11.3	58.6
	10	330 04.4	50.0	90 40.7	8.3	21 11.3	11.2	58.6
	11	345 04.6	49.0	105 08.0	8.1	21 22.5	11.1	58.6
	12	0 04.8	N 7 48.1	119 35.1	8.0	N21 33.6	10.9	58.6
	13	15 05.0	47.2	134 02.1	8.0	21 44.5	10.8	58.6
	14	30 05.2	46.3	148 29.1	7.8	21 55.3	10.7	58.7
	15	45 05.4	. . 45.4	162 55.9	7.7	22 06.0	10.6	58.7
	16	60 05.6	44.5	177 22.6	7.6	22 16.6	10.4	58.7
	17	75 05.8	43.6	191 49.2	7.5	22 27.0	10.4	58.7
	18	90 06.0	N 7 42.6	206 15.7	7.4	N22 37.4	10.1	58.7
	19	105 06.2	41.7	220 42.1	7.3	22 47.5	10.1	58.7
	20	120 06.4	40.8	235 08.4	7.2	22 57.6	9.9	58.7
	21	135 06.6	. . 39.9	249 34.6	7.1	23 07.5	9.8	58.8
	22	150 06.8	39.0	264 00.7	7.0	23 17.3	9.7	58.8
	23	165 07.0	38.1	278 26.7	6.9	23 27.0	9.5	58.8
THURSDAY	3 00	180 07.2	N 7 37.2	292 52.6	6.8	N23 36.5	9.4	58.8
	01	195 07.4	36.2	307 18.4	6.6	23 45.9	9.2	58.8
	02	210 07.6	35.3	321 44.0	6.6	23 55.1	9.1	58.8
	03	225 07.9	. . 34.4	336 09.6	6.5	24 04.2	8.9	58.8
	04	240 08.1	33.5	350 35.1	6.3	24 13.1	8.9	58.9
	05	255 08.3	32.6	5 00.4	6.3	24 22.0	8.6	58.9
	06	270 08.5	N 7 31.7	19 25.7	6.2	N24 30.6	8.5	58.9
	07	285 08.7	30.7	33 50.9	6.0	24 39.1	8.4	58.9
	08	300 08.9	29.8	48 15.9	6.0	24 47.5	8.2	58.9
	09	315 09.1	. . 28.9	62 40.9	5.9	24 55.7	8.0	58.9
	10	330 09.3	28.0	77 05.8	5.7	25 03.7	7.9	58.9
	11	345 09.5	27.1	91 30.5	5.7	25 11.6	7.8	59.0
	12	0 09.7	N 7 26.2	105 55.2	5.6	N25 19.4	7.6	59.0
	13	15 09.9	25.2	120 19.8	5.5	25 27.0	7.4	59.0
	14	30 10.1	24.3	134 44.3	5.4	25 34.4	7.2	59.0
	15	45 10.3	. . 23.4	149 08.7	5.3	25 41.6	7.1	59.0
	16	60 10.5	22.5	163 33.0	5.2	25 48.7	7.0	59.0
	17	75 10.7	21.6	177 57.2	5.1	25 55.7	6.8	59.0
	18	90 10.9	N 7 20.6	192 21.3	5.1	N26 02.5	6.6	59.0
	19	105 11.1	19.7	206 45.4	4.9	26 09.1	6.4	59.0
	20	120 11.3	18.8	221 09.3	4.9	26 15.5	6.3	59.1
	21	135 11.5	. . 17.9	235 33.2	4.7	26 21.8	6.1	59.1
	22	150 11.7	17.0	249 56.9	4.7	26 27.9	5.9	59.1
	23	165 12.0	16.0	264 20.6	4.7	N26 33.8	5.7	59.1
		SD 15.9	*d* 0.9	SD	15.9	16.0		16.1

Lat.	Twilight Naut.	Twilight Civil	Sunrise	Moonrise 1	Moonrise 2	Moonrise 3	Moonrise 4
°	h m	h m	h m	h m	h m	h m	h m
N 72	////	02 38	04 06	16 18	▭	▭	▭
N 70	00 10	03 05	04 19	17 18	▭	▭	▭
68	01 40	03 25	04 30	17 53	▭	▭	▭
66	02 16	03 40	04 38	18 18	17 43	▭	▭
64	02 40	03 53	04 46	18 38	18 23	17 36	▭
62	02 59	04 03	04 52	18 54	18 51	18 47	18 45
60	03 14	04 12	04 57	19 08	19 12	19 23	19 51
N 58	03 27	04 20	05 02	19 20	19 30	19 49	20 25
56	03 37	04 27	05 06	19 30	19 45	20 09	20 51
54	03 47	04 33	05 10	19 39	19 58	20 27	21 11
52	03 55	04 38	05 13	19 48	20 09	20 41	21 28
50	04 02	04 43	05 16	19 55	20 20	20 54	21 43
45	04 16	04 53	05 23	20 11	20 41	21 21	22 13
N 40	04 28	05 01	05 29	20 24	20 59	21 42	22 36
35	04 37	05 08	05 33	20 35	21 13	21 59	22 55
30	04 44	05 13	05 37	20 45	21 26	22 15	23 12
20	04 56	05 22	05 45	21 02	21 48	22 41	23 40
N 10	05 05	05 30	05 51	21 17	22 07	23 03	24 04
0	05 11	05 36	05 56	21 31	22 26	23 24	24 26
S 10	05 16	05 41	06 02	21 45	22 44	23 45	24 49
20	05 20	05 46	06 08	22 01	23 03	24 08	00 08
30	05 22	05 50	06 14	22 19	23 26	24 35	00 35
35	05 23	05 52	06 18	22 29	23 40	24 51	00 51
40	05 24	05 55	06 22	22 41	23 55	25 09	01 09
45	05 23	05 57	06 27	22 55	24 14	00 14	01 31
S 50	05 23	06 00	06 32	23 12	24 37	00 37	02 00
52	05 22	06 01	06 35	23 21	24 49	00 49	02 14
54	05 22	06 02	06 38	23 30	25 01	01 01	02 30
56	05 21	06 04	06 41	23 40	25 16	01 16	02 49
58	05 20	06 05	06 44	23 52	25 34	01 34	03 13
S 60	05 18	06 06	06 48	24 06	00 06	01 56	03 45

Lat.	Sunset	Twilight Civil	Twilight Naut.	Moonset 1	Moonset 2	Moonset 3	Moonset 4
°	h m	h m	h m	h m	h m	h m	h m
N 72	19 50	21 16	////	13 53	▭	▭	▭
N 70	19 37	20 50	23 15	12 55	▭	▭	▭
68	19 27	20 31	22 12	12 22	▭	▭	▭
66	19 19	20 16	21 39	11 58	14 24	▭	▭
64	19 12	20 04	21 15	11 39	13 45	16 31	▭
62	19 06	19 54	20 57	11 24	13 18	15 21	17 32
60	19 01	19 45	20 43	11 11	12 57	14 46	16 26
N 58	18 56	19 38	20 30	11 00	12 40	14 20	15 52
56	18 52	19 31	20 20	10 51	12 25	14 00	15 26
54	18 48	19 25	20 11	10 43	12 13	13 43	15 06
52	18 45	19 20	20 03	10 35	12 02	13 29	14 49
50	18 42	19 15	19 56	10 29	11 53	13 17	14 35
45	18 35	19 06	19 42	10 14	11 32	12 51	14 05
N 40	18 30	18 58	19 31	10 03	11 16	12 30	13 42
35	18 25	18 51	19 22	09 53	11 02	12 14	13 23
30	18 21	18 46	19 14	09 44	10 51	11 59	13 07
20	18 14	18 37	19 03	09 29	10 30	11 34	12 39
N 10	18 08	18 30	18 54	09 16	10 13	11 13	12 16
0	18 03	18 24	18 48	09 04	09 57	10 53	11 54
S 10	17 58	18 19	18 43	08 53	09 40	10 33	11 32
20	17 52	18 14	18 40	08 40	09 23	10 12	11 08
30	17 46	18 10	18 37	08 25	09 03	09 48	10 40
35	17 42	18 07	18 37	08 17	08 52	09 33	10 24
40	17 38	18 05	18 37	08 08	08 39	09 17	10 05
45	17 33	18 03	18 37	07 56	08 23	08 57	09 43
S 50	17 28	18 00	18 38	07 43	08 04	08 33	09 14
52	17 25	17 59	18 38	07 37	07 55	08 21	08 59
54	17 22	17 58	18 39	07 30	07 45	08 08	08 43
56	17 19	17 57	18 40	07 23	07 34	07 52	08 23
58	17 16	17 56	18 41	07 14	07 21	07 34	07 59
S 60	17 12	17 54	18 42	07 05	07 06	07 12	07 27

Day	SUN Eqn. of Time 00^h	SUN Eqn. of Time 12^h	SUN Mer. Pass.	MOON Mer. Pass. Upper	MOON Mer. Pass. Lower	Age	Phase
d	m s	m s	h m	h m	h m	d	%
1	00 10	00 00	12 00	02 53	15 18	20	80
2	00 09	00 19	12 00	03 44	16 11	21	70
3	00 29	00 38	11 59	04 39	17 09	22	60

	UT	ARIES	VENUS −4·7		MARS +1·2		JUPITER −1·8		SATURN +0·4	
	d h	GHA ° ′	GHA ° ′	Dec ° ′	GHA ° ′	Dec ° ′	GHA ° ′	Dec ° ′	GHA ° ′	Dec ° ′
	4 00	343 07.9	140 54.3	S13 22.3	236 28.1	N23 08.3	206 10.7	N17 02.6	329 40.2	N 2 52.7
	01	358 10.4	155 55.1	23.3	251 28.9	08.1	221 12.6	02.5	344 42.8	52.6
	02	13 12.9	170 55.9	24.3	266 29.6	08.0	236 14.5	02.3	359 45.4	52.5
	03	28 15.3	185 56.7	. . 25.3	281 30.4	. . 07.8	251 16.5	. . 02.2	14 48.0	. . 52.5
	04	43 17.8	200 57.5	26.3	296 31.1	07.7	266 18.4	02.0	29 50.6	52.4
	05	58 20.3	215 58.3	27.3	311 31.9	07.6	281 20.4	01.9	44 53.2	52.3
	06	73 22.7	230 59.0	S13 28.3	326 32.7	N23 07.4	296 22.3	N17 01.7	59 55.8	N 2 52.3
	07	88 25.2	245 59.8	29.3	341 33.4	07.3	311 24.3	01.6	74 58.4	52.2
	08	103 27.7	261 00.6	30.3	356 34.2	07.1	326 26.2	01.4	90 01.0	52.1
F	09	118 30.1	276 01.4	. . 31.3	11 34.9	. . 07.0	341 28.1	. . 01.3	105 03.6	. . 52.1
R	10	133 32.6	291 02.2	32.3	26 35.7	06.8	356 30.1	01.1	120 06.2	52.0
I	11	148 35.1	306 03.0	33.2	41 36.5	06.7	11 32.0	01.0	135 08.8	51.9
D	12	163 37.5	321 03.8	S13 34.2	56 37.2	N23 06.5	26 34.0	N17 00.9	150 11.4	N 2 51.9
A	13	178 40.0	336 04.6	35.2	71 38.0	06.4	41 35.9	00.7	165 14.0	51.8
Y	14	193 42.4	351 05.4	36.2	86 38.7	06.3	56 37.9	00.6	180 16.6	51.8
	15	208 44.9	6 06.2	. . 37.2	101 39.5	. . 06.1	71 39.8	. . 00.4	195 19.2	. . 51.7
	16	223 47.4	21 07.0	38.2	116 40.3	06.0	86 41.7	00.3	210 21.8	51.6
	17	238 49.8	36 07.8	39.2	131 41.0	05.8	101 43.7	00.1	225 24.4	51.6
	18	253 52.3	51 08.6	S13 40.2	146 41.8	N23 05.7	116 45.6	N17 00.0	240 27.0	N 2 51.5
	19	268 54.8	66 09.4	41.1	161 42.6	05.5	131 47.6	16 59.8	255 29.6	51.4
	20	283 57.2	81 10.2	42.1	176 43.3	05.4	146 49.5	59.7	270 32.2	51.4
	21	298 59.7	96 11.0	. . 43.1	191 44.1	. . 05.2	161 51.5	. . 59.5	285 34.8	. . 51.3
	22	314 02.2	111 11.8	44.1	206 44.8	05.1	176 53.4	59.4	300 37.4	51.2
	23	329 04.6	126 12.6	45.1	221 45.6	04.9	191 55.4	59.2	315 40.0	51.2
	5 00	344 07.1	141 13.5	S13 46.1	236 46.4	N23 04.8	206 57.3	N16 59.1	330 42.6	N 2 51.1
	01	359 09.5	156 14.3	47.1	251 47.1	04.6	221 59.2	59.0	345 45.2	51.0
	02	14 12.0	171 15.1	48.0	266 47.9	04.5	237 01.2	58.8	0 47.8	51.0
	03	29 14.5	186 15.9	. . 49.0	281 48.7	. . 04.3	252 03.1	. . 58.7	15 50.4	. . 50.9
	04	44 16.9	201 16.7	50.0	296 49.4	04.2	267 05.1	58.5	30 53.0	50.8
	05	59 19.4	216 17.5	51.0	311 50.2	04.0	282 07.0	58.4	45 55.6	50.8
	06	74 21.9	231 18.3	S13 52.0	326 51.0	N23 03.9	297 09.0	N16 58.2	60 58.2	N 2 50.7
	07	89 24.3	246 19.2	52.9	341 51.7	03.7	312 10.9	58.1	76 00.8	50.6
S	08	104 26.8	261 20.0	53.9	356 52.5	03.6	327 12.9	57.9	91 03.4	50.6
A	09	119 29.3	276 20.8	. . 54.9	11 53.3	. . 03.4	342 14.8	. . 57.8	106 06.0	. . 50.5
T	10	134 31.7	291 21.6	55.9	26 54.0	03.3	357 16.7	57.6	121 08.6	50.4
U	11	149 34.2	306 22.5	56.8	41 54.8	03.1	12 18.7	57.5	136 11.2	50.4
R	12	164 36.7	321 23.3	S13 57.8	56 55.5	N23 03.0	27 20.6	N16 57.3	151 13.8	N 2 50.3
D	13	179 39.1	336 24.1	58.8	71 56.3	02.8	42 22.6	57.2	166 16.4	50.2
A	14	194 41.6	351 24.9	13 59.8	86 57.1	02.7	57 24.5	57.1	181 19.0	50.2
Y	15	209 44.0	6 25.8	14 00.7	101 57.8	. . 02.5	72 26.5	. . 56.9	196 21.6	. . 50.1
	16	224 46.5	21 26.6	01.7	116 58.6	02.4	87 28.4	56.8	211 24.2	50.0
	17	239 49.0	36 27.4	02.7	131 59.4	02.2	102 30.4	56.6	226 26.8	50.0
	18	254 51.4	51 28.3	S14 03.6	147 00.2	N23 02.1	117 32.3	N16 56.5	241 29.4	N 2 49.9
	19	269 53.9	66 29.1	04.6	162 00.9	01.9	132 34.3	56.3	256 32.0	49.8
	20	284 56.4	81 29.9	05.6	177 01.7	01.8	147 36.2	56.2	271 34.7	49.8
	21	299 58.8	96 30.8	. . 06.6	192 02.5	. . 01.6	162 38.2	. . 56.0	286 37.3	. . 49.7
	22	315 01.3	111 31.6	07.5	207 03.2	01.5	177 40.1	55.9	301 39.9	49.6
	23	330 03.8	126 32.5	08.5	222 04.0	01.3	192 42.0	55.7	316 42.5	49.6
	6 00	345 06.2	141 33.3	S14 09.5	237 04.8	N23 01.1	207 44.0	N16 55.6	331 45.1	N 2 49.5
	01	0 08.7	156 34.2	10.4	252 05.5	01.0	222 45.9	55.4	346 47.7	49.4
	02	15 11.2	171 35.0	11.4	267 06.3	00.8	237 47.9	55.3	1 50.3	49.4
	03	30 13.6	186 35.8	. . 12.4	282 07.1	. . 00.7	252 49.8	. . 55.2	16 52.9	. . 49.3
	04	45 16.1	201 36.7	13.3	297 07.8	00.5	267 51.8	55.0	31 55.5	49.2
	05	60 18.5	216 37.5	14.3	312 08.6	00.4	282 53.7	54.9	46 58.1	49.2
	06	75 21.0	231 38.4	S14 15.3	327 09.4	N23 00.2	297 55.7	N16 54.7	62 00.7	N 2 49.1
	07	90 23.5	246 39.2	16.2	342 10.2	23 00.1	312 57.6	54.6	77 03.3	49.0
	08	105 25.9	261 40.1	17.2	357 10.9	22 59.9	327 59.6	54.4	92 05.9	49.0
S	09	120 28.4	276 41.0	. . 18.1	12 11.7	. . 59.7	343 01.5	. . 54.3	107 08.5	. . 48.9
U	10	135 30.9	291 41.8	19.1	27 12.5	59.6	358 03.5	54.1	122 11.1	48.8
N	11	150 33.3	306 42.7	20.1	42 13.2	59.4	13 05.4	54.0	137 13.7	48.8
D	12	165 35.8	321 43.5	S14 21.0	57 14.0	N22 59.3	28 07.4	N16 53.8	152 16.3	N 2 48.7
A	13	180 38.3	336 44.4	22.0	72 14.8	59.1	43 09.3	53.7	167 18.9	48.6
Y	14	195 40.7	351 45.3	22.9	87 15.6	58.9	58 11.3	53.5	182 21.5	48.6
	15	210 43.2	6 46.1	. . 23.9	102 16.3	. . 58.8	73 13.2	. . 53.4	197 24.2	. . 48.5
	16	225 45.7	21 47.0	24.8	117 17.1	58.6	88 15.2	53.3	212 26.8	48.4
	17	240 48.1	36 47.9	25.8	132 17.9	58.5	103 17.1	53.1	227 29.4	48.4
	18	255 50.6	51 48.7	S14 26.8	147 18.6	N22 58.3	118 19.0	N16 53.0	242 32.0	N 2 48.3
	19	270 53.0	66 49.6	27.7	162 19.4	58.2	133 21.0	52.8	257 34.6	48.2
	20	285 55.5	81 50.5	28.7	177 20.2	58.0	148 22.9	52.7	272 37.2	48.2
	21	300 58.0	96 51.3	. . 29.6	192 21.0	. . 57.8	163 24.9	. . 52.5	287 39.8	. . 48.1
	22	316 00.4	111 52.2	30.6	207 21.7	57.7	178 26.8	52.4	302 42.4	48.0
	23	331 02.9	126 53.1	31.5	222 22.5	57.5	193 28.8	52.2	317 45.0	48.0
	Mer. Pass.	h m 1 03.4	v 0.8	d 1.0	v 0.8	d 0.2	v 1.9	d 0.1	v 2.6	d 0.1

STARS Name	SHA ° ′	Dec ° ′
Acamar	315 10.5	S40 11.5
Achernar	335 18.7	S57 05.8
Acrux	172 59.1	S63 14.9
Adhara	255 05.0	S29 00.2
Aldebaran	290 38.0	N16 33.8
Alioth	166 12.2	N55 49.0
Alkaid	152 51.3	N49 11.0
Alnair	27 30.7	S46 49.8
Alnilam	275 36.4	S 1 10.9
Alphard	217 46.7	S 8 46.3
Alphecca	126 02.7	N26 37.7
Alpheratz	357 33.0	N29 14.4
Altair	61 58.4	N 8 56.5
Ankaa	353 05.4	S42 09.4
Antares	112 14.2	S26 29.5
Arcturus	145 46.9	N19 02.7
Atria	107 07.1	S69 04.7
Avior	234 14.7	S59 35.5
Bellatrix	278 21.5	N 6 22.5
Betelgeuse	270 50.7	N 7 24.8
Canopus	263 52.0	S52 42.2
Capella	280 19.9	N46 01.3
Deneb	49 24.5	N45 22.7
Denebola	182 23.9	N14 25.5
Diphda	348 45.6	S17 50.2
Dubhe	193 40.0	N61 36.4
Elnath	278 00.2	N28 37.8
Eltanin	90 41.4	N51 29.4
Enif	33 37.1	N10 00.0
Fomalhaut	15 12.6	S29 28.7
Gacrux	171 50.6	S57 15.9
Gienah	175 42.5	S17 41.4
Hadar	148 34.5	S60 30.3
Hamal	327 49.4	N23 35.4
Kaus Aust.	83 30.5	S34 22.3
Kochab	137 20.4	N74 02.9
Markab	13 28.2	N15 21.1
Menkar	314 04.6	N 4 11.8
Menkent	147 56.2	S36 30.2
Miaplacidus	221 38.9	S69 49.4
Mirfak	308 26.1	N49 57.2
Nunki	75 45.9	S26 15.8
Peacock	53 03.1	S56 39.0
Pollux	243 15.9	N27 57.7
Procyon	244 49.6	N 5 09.5
Rasalhague	95 57.2	N12 32.6
Regulus	207 33.3	N11 50.3
Rigel	281 02.6	S 8 10.0
Rigil Kent.	139 38.7	S60 56.9
Sabik	102 01.2	S15 45.4
Schedar	349 29.0	N56 41.0
Shaula	96 08.4	S37 07.5
Sirius	258 25.2	S16 45.0
Spica	158 21.1	S11 18.0
Suhail	222 45.7	S43 32.2
Vega	80 32.1	N38 48.7
Zuben'ubi	136 54.6	S16 09.2

	SHA ° ′	Mer. Pass. h m
Venus	157 06.4	14 34
Mars	252 39.3	8 12
Jupiter	222 50.2	10 11
Saturn	346 35.5	1 57

UT d h	SUN GHA	SUN Dec	MOON GHA	v	MOON Dec	d	HP
	° ′	° ′	° ′	′	° ′	′	′
4 00 Friday	180 12.2	N 7 15.1	278 44.3	4.5	N26 39.5	5.6	59.1
01	195 12.4	14.2	293 07.8	4.5	26 45.1	5.4	59.1
02	210 12.6	13.3	307 31.3	4.3	26 50.5	5.3	59.1
03	225 12.8	. . 12.4	321 54.6	4.4	26 55.8	5.0	59.1
04	240 13.0	11.4	336 18.0	4.2	27 00.8	4.9	59.2
05	255 13.2	10.5	350 41.2	4.2	27 05.7	4.7	59.2
06	270 13.4	N 7 09.6	5 04.4	4.1	N27 10.4	4.5	59.2
07	285 13.6	08.7	19 27.5	4.0	27 14.9	4.3	59.2
08	300 13.8	07.7	33 50.5	4.0	27 19.2	4.1	59.2
09	315 14.0	. . 06.8	48 13.5	3.9	27 23.3	4.0	59.2
10	330 14.2	05.9	62 36.4	3.8	27 27.3	3.8	59.2
11	345 14.4	05.0	76 59.2	3.8	27 31.1	3.6	59.2
12	0 14.6	N 7 04.1	91 22.0	3.8	N27 34.7	3.4	59.2
13	15 14.8	03.1	105 44.8	3.6	27 38.1	3.2	59.2
14	30 15.1	02.2	120 07.4	3.7	27 41.3	3.0	59.3
15	45 15.3	. . 01.3	134 30.1	3.6	27 44.3	2.8	59.3
16	60 15.5	7 00.4	148 52.7	3.5	27 47.1	2.7	59.3
17	75 15.7	6 59.4	163 15.2	3.5	27 49.8	2.4	59.3
18	90 15.9	N 6 58.5	177 37.7	3.4	N27 52.2	2.3	59.3
19	105 16.1	57.6	192 00.1	3.4	27 54.5	2.1	59.3
20	120 16.3	56.7	206 22.5	3.4	27 56.6	1.8	59.3
21	135 16.5	. . 55.7	220 44.9	3.4	27 58.4	1.7	59.3
22	150 16.7	54.8	235 07.3	3.3	28 00.1	1.5	59.3
23	165 16.9	53.9	249 29.6	3.2	28 01.6	1.3	59.3
5 00 Saturday	180 17.1	N 6 53.0	263 51.8	3.3	N28 02.9	1.1	59.3
01	195 17.3	52.0	278 14.1	3.2	28 04.0	0.9	59.4
02	210 17.5	51.1	292 36.3	3.2	28 04.9	0.7	59.4
03	225 17.8	. . 50.2	306 58.5	3.2	28 05.6	0.6	59.4
04	240 18.0	49.3	321 20.7	3.2	28 06.2	0.3	59.4
05	255 18.2	48.3	335 42.9	3.1	28 06.5	0.1	59.4
06	270 18.4	N 6 47.4	350 05.0	3.2	N28 06.6	0.1	59.4
07	285 18.6	46.5	4 27.2	3.1	28 06.5	0.2	59.4
08	300 18.8	45.5	18 49.3	3.1	28 06.3	0.5	59.4
09	315 19.0	. . 44.6	33 11.4	3.1	28 05.8	0.7	59.4
10	330 19.2	43.7	47 33.5	3.2	28 05.1	0.8	59.4
11	345 19.4	42.8	61 55.7	3.1	28 04.3	1.1	59.4
12	0 19.6	N 6 41.8	76 17.8	3.1	N28 03.2	1.3	59.4
13	15 19.8	40.9	90 39.9	3.1	28 01.9	1.4	59.4
14	30 20.1	40.0	105 02.0	3.2	28 00.5	1.6	59.4
15	45 20.3	. . 39.0	119 24.2	3.1	27 58.9	1.9	59.5
16	60 20.5	38.1	133 46.3	3.2	27 57.0	2.0	59.5
17	75 20.7	37.2	148 08.5	3.2	27 55.0	2.3	59.5
18	90 20.9	N 6 36.3	162 30.7	3.2	N27 52.7	2.4	59.5
19	105 21.1	35.3	176 52.9	3.2	27 50.3	2.6	59.5
20	120 21.3	34.4	191 15.1	3.3	27 47.7	2.8	59.5
21	135 21.5	. . 33.5	205 37.4	3.3	27 44.9	3.1	59.5
22	150 21.7	32.5	219 59.7	3.3	27 41.8	3.2	59.5
23	165 22.0	31.6	234 22.0	3.3	27 38.6	3.4	59.5
6 00 Sunday	180 22.2	N 6 30.7	248 44.3	3.4	N27 35.2	3.6	59.5
01	195 22.4	29.7	263 06.7	3.4	27 31.6	3.7	59.5
02	210 22.6	28.8	277 29.1	3.5	27 27.9	4.0	59.5
03	225 22.8	. . 27.9	291 51.6	3.5	27 23.9	4.2	59.5
04	240 23.0	27.0	306 14.1	3.5	27 19.7	4.3	59.5
05	255 23.2	26.0	320 36.6	3.6	27 15.4	4.6	59.5
06	270 23.4	N 6 25.1	334 59.2	3.6	N27 10.8	4.7	59.5
07	285 23.6	24.2	349 21.8	3.7	27 06.1	5.0	59.5
08	300 23.8	23.2	3 44.5	3.8	27 01.1	5.1	59.5
09	315 24.1	. . 22.3	18 07.3	3.8	26 56.0	5.3	59.5
10	330 24.3	21.4	32 30.1	3.8	26 50.7	5.4	59.5
11	345 24.5	20.4	46 52.9	3.9	26 45.3	5.7	59.5
12	0 24.7	N 6 19.5	61 15.8	4.0	N26 39.6	5.9	59.5
13	15 24.9	18.6	75 38.8	4.1	26 33.7	6.0	59.5
14	30 25.1	17.6	90 01.9	4.1	26 27.7	6.2	59.5
15	45 25.3	. . 16.7	104 25.0	4.1	26 21.5	6.4	59.5
16	60 25.5	15.8	118 48.1	4.3	26 15.1	6.6	59.5
17	75 25.8	14.8	133 11.4	4.3	26 08.5	6.7	59.5
18	90 26.0	N 6 13.9	147 34.7	4.4	N26 01.8	6.9	59.5
19	105 26.2	13.0	161 58.1	4.4	25 54.9	7.1	59.5
20	120 26.4	12.0	176 21.5	4.6	25 47.8	7.3	59.5
21	135 26.6	. . 11.1	190 45.1	4.6	25 40.5	7.4	59.5
22	150 26.8	10.2	205 08.7	4.7	25 33.1	7.6	59.5
23	165 27.0	09.2	219 32.4	4.7	N25 25.5	7.8	59.5
	SD 15.9	*d* 0.9	SD	16.1	16.2		16.2

Lat.	Twilight Naut.	Twilight Civil	Sunrise	Moonrise 4	Moonrise 5	Moonrise 6	Moonrise 7
°	h m	h m	h m	h m	h m	h m	h m
N 72	////	02 58	04 21	▭	▭	▭	▭
N 70	01 17	03 21	04 32	▭	▭	▭	▭
68	02 03	03 38	04 41	▭	▭	▭	22 01
66	02 32	03 51	04 48	▭	▭	▭	23 12
64	02 53	04 03	04 54	▭	▭	21 05	23 48
62	03 10	04 12	05 00	18 45	19 54	22 07	24 14
60	03 24	04 20	05 04	19 51	20 58	22 41	24 34
N 58	03 35	04 27	05 08	20 25	21 32	23 06	24 50
56	03 45	04 33	05 12	20 51	21 57	23 26	25 04
54	03 53	04 38	05 15	21 11	22 18	23 42	25 16
52	04 01	04 43	05 18	21 28	22 34	23 57	25 26
50	04 07	04 48	05 21	21 43	22 49	24 09	00 09
45	04 21	04 57	05 27	22 13	23 18	24 34	00 34
N 40	04 31	05 04	05 31	22 36	23 41	24 55	00 55
35	04 39	05 10	05 36	22 55	24 00	00 00	01 11
30	04 46	05 15	05 39	23 12	24 16	00 16	01 26
20	04 57	05 23	05 45	23 40	24 44	00 44	01 50
N 10	05 05	05 29	05 51	24 04	00 04	01 08	02 11
0	05 10	05 35	05 55	24 26	00 26	01 29	02 31
S 10	05 15	05 39	06 00	24 49	00 49	01 51	02 51
20	05 17	05 43	06 05	00 08	01 13	02 15	03 12
30	05 19	05 47	06 11	00 35	01 41	02 42	03 36
35	05 19	05 48	06 14	00 51	01 58	02 59	03 50
40	05 19	05 50	06 17	01 09	02 18	03 17	04 06
45	05 18	05 52	06 21	01 31	02 42	03 40	04 25
S 50	05 16	05 54	06 26	02 00	03 12	04 09	04 50
52	05 16	05 55	06 28	02 14	03 27	04 23	05 01
54	05 14	05 55	06 31	02 30	03 45	04 39	05 14
56	05 13	05 56	06 33	02 49	04 06	04 59	05 29
58	05 12	05 57	06 36	03 13	04 34	05 23	05 47
S 60	05 10	05 58	06 39	03 45	05 12	05 54	06 09

Lat.	Sunset	Twilight Civil	Twilight Naut.	Moonset 4	Moonset 5	Moonset 6	Moonset 7
°	h m	h m	h m	h m	h m	h m	h m
N 72	19 34	20 54	////	▭	▭	▭	▭
N 70	19 23	20 33	22 30	▭	▭	▭	▭
68	19 14	20 16	21 48	▭	▭	▭	20 45
66	19 07	20 03	21 21	▭	▭	▭	19 33
64	19 01	19 52	21 01	▭	▭	19 36	18 56
62	18 56	19 43	20 44	17 32	18 35	18 33	18 29
60	18 52	19 35	20 31	16 26	17 31	17 58	18 08
N 58	18 48	19 29	20 20	15 52	16 57	17 33	17 51
56	18 44	19 23	20 11	15 26	16 31	17 12	17 37
54	18 41	19 18	20 02	15 06	16 11	16 56	17 24
52	18 38	19 13	19 55	14 49	15 54	16 41	17 13
50	18 36	19 09	19 49	14 35	15 40	16 28	17 03
45	18 30	19 00	19 36	14 05	15 10	16 02	16 42
N 40	18 25	18 53	19 25	13 42	14 47	15 41	16 25
35	18 21	18 47	19 17	13 23	14 28	15 23	16 10
30	18 18	18 42	19 10	13 07	14 11	15 08	15 58
20	18 12	18 34	19 00	12 39	13 43	14 42	15 36
N 10	18 07	18 28	18 52	12 16	13 19	14 20	15 17
0	18 02	18 23	18 47	11 54	12 56	13 59	14 59
S 10	17 57	18 18	18 43	11 32	12 34	13 38	14 41
20	17 53	18 15	18 40	11 08	12 10	13 15	14 22
30	17 47	18 11	18 39	10 40	11 41	12 49	13 59
35	17 44	18 09	18 39	10 24	11 25	12 33	13 46
40	17 41	18 08	18 39	10 05	11 05	12 15	13 31
45	17 37	18 06	18 40	09 43	10 41	11 53	13 12
S 50	17 32	18 05	18 42	09 14	10 11	11 25	12 49
52	17 30	18 04	18 43	08 59	09 56	11 11	12 38
54	17 28	18 03	18 44	08 43	09 38	10 55	12 26
56	17 25	18 02	18 45	08 23	09 17	10 36	12 11
58	17 22	18 02	18 47	07 59	08 49	10 12	11 54
S 60	17 19	18 01	18 49	07 27	08 11	09 41	11 33

Day	SUN Eqn. of Time 00^h	SUN Eqn. of Time 12^h	SUN Mer. Pass.	MOON Mer. Pass. Upper	MOON Mer. Pass. Lower	MOON Age	Phase
d	m s	m s	h m	h m	h m	d %	
4	00 48	00 58	11 59	05 39	18 10	23 48	
5	01 08	01 18	11 59	06 41	19 13	24 37	◐
6	01 28	01 38	11 58	07 44	20 15	25 26	

UT d h	ARIES GHA ° ′	VENUS −4·7 GHA ° ′	VENUS Dec ° ′	MARS +1·2 GHA ° ′	MARS Dec ° ′	JUPITER −1·8 GHA ° ′	JUPITER Dec ° ′	SATURN +0·4 GHA ° ′	SATURN Dec ° ′
7 00 MONDAY	346 05.4	141 54.0	S14 32.5	237 23.3	N22 57.3	208 30.7	N16 52.1	332 47.6	N 2 47.9
01	1 07.8	156 54.8	33.4	252 24.1	57.2	223 32.7	51.9	347 50.2	47.8
02	16 10.3	171 55.7	34.4	267 24.8	57.0	238 34.6	51.8	2 52.8	47.8
03	31 12.8	186 56.6	. . 35.3	282 25.6	. . 56.9	253 36.6	. . 51.6	17 55.4	. . 47.7
04	46 15.2	201 57.5	36.3	297 26.4	56.7	268 38.5	51.5	32 58.0	47.6
05	61 17.7	216 58.4	37.2	312 27.2	56.5	283 40.5	51.4	48 00.6	47.6
06	76 20.2	231 59.2	S14 38.2	327 27.9	N22 56.4	298 42.4	N16 51.2	63 03.3	N 2 47.5
07	91 22.6	247 00.1	39.1	342 28.7	56.2	313 44.4	51.1	78 05.9	47.4
08	106 25.1	262 01.0	40.1	357 29.5	56.1	328 46.3	50.9	93 08.5	47.4
09	121 27.5	277 01.9	. . 41.0	12 30.3	. . 55.9	343 48.3	. . 50.8	108 11.1	. . 47.3
10	136 30.0	292 02.8	41.9	27 31.1	55.7	358 50.2	50.6	123 13.7	47.2
11	151 32.5	307 03.7	42.9	42 31.8	55.6	13 52.2	50.5	138 16.3	47.1
12	166 34.9	322 04.6	S14 43.8	57 32.6	N22 55.4	28 54.1	N16 50.3	153 18.9	N 2 47.1
13	181 37.4	337 05.5	44.8	72 33.4	55.2	43 56.1	50.2	168 21.5	47.0
14	196 39.9	352 06.4	45.7	87 34.2	55.1	58 58.0	50.0	183 24.1	46.9
15	211 42.3	7 07.3	. . 46.7	102 34.9	. . 54.9	74 00.0	. . 49.9	198 26.7	. . 46.9
16	226 44.8	22 08.2	47.6	117 35.7	54.7	89 01.9	49.7	213 29.3	46.8
17	241 47.3	37 09.1	48.5	132 36.5	54.6	104 03.9	49.6	228 31.9	46.7
18	256 49.7	52 10.0	S14 49.5	147 37.3	N22 54.4	119 05.8	N16 49.5	243 34.6	N 2 46.7
19	271 52.2	67 10.9	50.4	162 38.1	54.2	134 07.8	49.3	258 37.2	46.6
20	286 54.6	82 11.8	51.3	177 38.8	54.1	149 09.7	49.2	273 39.8	46.5
21	301 57.1	97 12.7	. . 52.3	192 39.6	. . 53.9	164 11.7	. . 49.0	288 42.4	. . 46.5
22	316 59.6	112 13.6	53.2	207 40.4	53.7	179 13.6	48.9	303 45.0	46.4
23	332 02.0	127 14.5	54.2	222 41.2	53.6	194 15.6	48.7	318 47.6	46.3
8 00 TUESDAY	347 04.5	142 15.4	S14 55.1	237 42.0	N22 53.4	209 17.5	N16 48.6	333 50.2	N 2 46.3
01	2 07.0	157 16.3	56.0	252 42.7	53.2	224 19.5	48.4	348 52.8	46.2
02	17 09.4	172 17.2	57.0	267 43.5	53.1	239 21.4	48.3	3 55.4	46.1
03	32 11.9	187 18.2	. . 57.9	282 44.3	. . 52.9	254 23.4	. . 48.1	18 58.0	. . 46.1
04	47 14.4	202 19.1	58.8	297 45.1	52.7	269 25.4	48.0	34 00.6	46.0
05	62 16.8	217 20.0	14 59.7	312 45.9	52.6	284 27.3	47.9	49 03.3	45.9
06	77 19.3	232 20.9	S15 00.7	327 46.6	N22 52.4	299 29.3	N16 47.7	64 05.9	N 2 45.8
07	92 21.8	247 21.8	01.6	342 47.4	52.2	314 31.2	47.6	79 08.5	45.8
08	107 24.2	262 22.8	02.5	357 48.2	52.1	329 33.2	47.4	94 11.1	45.7
09	122 26.7	277 23.7	. . 03.5	12 49.0	. . 51.9	344 35.1	. . 47.3	109 13.7	. . 45.6
10	137 29.1	292 24.6	04.4	27 49.8	51.7	359 37.1	47.1	124 16.3	45.6
11	152 31.6	307 25.5	05.3	42 50.6	51.5	14 39.0	47.0	139 18.9	45.5
12	167 34.1	322 26.5	S15 06.2	57 51.3	N22 51.4	29 41.0	N16 46.8	154 21.5	N 2 45.4
13	182 36.5	337 27.4	07.2	72 52.1	51.2	44 42.9	46.7	169 24.1	45.4
14	197 39.0	352 28.3	08.1	87 52.9	51.0	59 44.9	46.5	184 26.8	45.3
15	212 41.5	7 29.3	. . 09.0	102 53.7	. . 50.9	74 46.8	. . 46.4	199 29.4	. . 45.2
16	227 43.9	22 30.2	09.9	117 54.5	50.7	89 48.8	46.2	214 32.0	45.2
17	242 46.4	37 31.1	10.9	132 55.3	50.5	104 50.7	46.1	229 34.6	45.1
18	257 48.9	52 32.1	S15 11.8	147 56.0	N22 50.3	119 52.7	N16 46.0	244 37.2	N 2 45.0
19	272 51.3	67 33.0	12.7	162 56.8	50.2	134 54.6	45.8	259 39.8	45.0
20	287 53.8	82 34.0	13.6	177 57.6	50.0	149 56.6	45.7	274 42.4	44.9
21	302 56.3	97 34.9	. . 14.5	192 58.4	. . 49.8	164 58.5	. . 45.5	289 45.0	. . 44.8
22	317 58.7	112 35.8	15.5	207 59.2	49.7	180 00.5	45.4	304 47.6	44.7
23	333 01.2	127 36.8	16.4	223 00.0	49.5	195 02.5	45.2	319 50.3	44.7
9 00 WEDNESDAY	348 03.6	142 37.7	S15 17.3	238 00.8	N22 49.3	210 04.4	N16 45.1	334 52.9	N 2 44.6
01	3 06.1	157 38.7	18.2	253 01.6	49.1	225 06.4	44.9	349 55.5	44.5
02	18 08.6	172 39.6	19.1	268 02.3	49.0	240 08.3	44.8	4 58.1	44.5
03	33 11.0	187 40.6	. . 20.0	283 03.1	. . 48.8	255 10.3	. . 44.6	20 00.7	. . 44.4
04	48 13.5	202 41.5	20.9	298 03.9	48.6	270 12.2	44.5	35 03.3	44.3
05	63 16.0	217 42.5	21.9	313 04.7	48.4	285 14.2	44.4	50 05.9	44.3
06	78 18.4	232 43.5	S15 22.8	328 05.5	N22 48.3	300 16.1	N16 44.2	65 08.5	N 2 44.2
07	93 20.9	247 44.4	23.7	343 06.3	48.1	315 18.1	44.1	80 11.2	44.1
08	108 23.4	262 45.4	24.6	358 07.1	47.9	330 20.0	43.9	95 13.8	44.0
09	123 25.8	277 46.3	. . 25.5	13 07.9	. . 47.7	345 22.0	. . 43.8	110 16.4	. . 44.0
10	138 28.3	292 47.3	26.4	28 08.6	47.6	0 23.9	43.6	125 19.0	43.9
11	153 30.7	307 48.3	27.3	43 09.4	47.4	15 25.9	43.5	140 21.6	43.8
12	168 33.2	322 49.2	S15 28.2	58 10.2	N22 47.2	30 27.9	N16 43.3	155 24.2	N 2 43.8
13	183 35.7	337 50.2	29.1	73 11.0	47.0	45 29.8	43.2	170 26.8	43.7
14	198 38.1	352 51.2	30.0	88 11.8	46.9	60 31.8	43.0	185 29.4	43.6
15	213 40.6	7 52.1	. . 30.9	103 12.6	. . 46.7	75 33.7	. . 42.9	200 32.1	. . 43.6
16	228 43.1	22 53.1	31.8	118 13.4	46.5	90 35.7	42.8	215 34.7	43.5
17	243 45.5	37 54.1	32.8	133 14.2	46.3	105 37.6	42.6	230 37.3	43.4
18	258 48.0	52 55.1	S15 33.7	148 15.0	N22 46.1	120 39.6	N16 42.5	245 39.9	N 2 43.4
19	273 50.5	67 56.0	34.6	163 15.8	46.0	135 41.5	42.3	260 42.5	43.3
20	288 52.9	82 57.0	35.5	178 16.5	45.8	150 43.5	42.2	275 45.1	43.2
21	303 55.4	97 58.0	. . 36.4	193 17.3	. . 45.6	165 45.5	. . 42.0	290 47.7	. . 43.1
22	318 57.9	112 59.0	37.3	208 18.1	45.4	180 47.4	41.9	305 50.4	43.1
23	334 00.3	128 00.0	38.2	223 18.9	45.3	195 49.4	41.7	320 53.0	43.0
Mer. Pass.	h m 0 51.6	*v* 0.9	*d* 0.9	*v* 0.8	*d* 0.2	*v* 2.0	*d* 0.1	*v* 2.6	*d* 0.1

STARS

Name	SHA ° ′	Dec ° ′
Acamar	315 10.5	S40 11.5
Achernar	335 18.7	S57 05.8
Acrux	172 59.2	S63 14.9
Adhara	255 05.0	S29 00.2
Aldebaran	290 38.0	N16 33.8
Alioth	166 12.2	N55 49.0
Alkaid	152 51.3	N49 11.0
Alnair	27 30.7	S46 49.8
Alnilam	275 36.4	S 1 10.9
Alphard	217 46.7	S 8 46.3
Alphecca	126 02.7	N26 37.7
Alpheratz	357 33.0	N29 14.4
Altair	61 58.4	N 8 56.5
Ankaa	353 05.4	S42 09.4
Antares	112 14.2	S26 29.5
Arcturus	145 46.9	N19 02.7
Atria	107 07.1	S69 04.8
Avior	234 14.7	S59 35.4
Bellatrix	278 21.4	N 6 22.5
Betelgeuse	270 50.7	N 7 24.8
Canopus	263 52.0	S52 42.2
Capella	280 19.9	N46 01.3
Deneb	49 24.5	N45 22.8
Denebola	182 23.9	N14 25.5
Diphda	348 45.6	S17 50.2
Dubhe	193 40.0	N61 36.4
Elnath	278 00.2	N28 37.8
Eltanin	90 41.4	N51 29.4
Enif	33 37.1	N10 00.0
Fomalhaut	15 12.6	S29 28.7
Gacrux	171 50.6	S57 15.8
Gienah	175 42.5	S17 41.4
Hadar	148 34.5	S60 30.3
Hamal	327 49.4	N23 35.4
Kaus Aust.	83 30.5	S34 22.3
Kochab	137 20.4	N74 02.9
Markab	13 28.2	N15 21.1
Menkar	314 04.5	N 4 11.8
Menkent	147 56.2	S36 30.2
Miaplacidus	221 38.8	S69 49.4
Mirfak	308 26.1	N49 57.2
Nunki	75 45.9	S26 15.8
Peacock	53 03.1	S56 39.0
Pollux	243 15.8	N27 57.7
Procyon	244 49.6	N 5 09.5
Rasalhague	95 57.2	N12 32.6
Regulus	207 33.3	N11 50.3
Rigel	281 02.6	S 8 10.0
Rigil Kent.	139 38.8	S60 56.9
Sabik	102 01.2	S15 45.4
Schedar	349 28.9	N56 41.0
Shaula	96 08.4	S37 07.5
Sirius	258 25.2	S16 44.9
Spica	158 21.1	S11 18.0
Suhail	222 45.7	S43 32.2
Vega	80 32.1	N38 48.8
Zuben'ubi	136 54.7	S16 09.2

	SHA ° ′	Mer. Pass. h m
Venus	155 10.9	14 30
Mars	250 37.5	8 09
Jupiter	222 13.0	10 02
Saturn	346 45.7	1 44

UT		SUN GHA	SUN Dec	MOON GHA	v	MOON Dec	d	HP
d h		° ′	° ′	° ′	′	° ′	′	′
7 00	MONDAY	180 27.2	N 6 08.3	233 56.1	4.9	N25 17.7	8.0	59.5
01		195 27.5	07.4	248 20.0	4.9	25 09.7	8.1	59.5
02		210 27.7	06.4	262 43.9	5.1	25 01.6	8.3	59.5
03		225 27.9	. . 05.5	277 08.0	5.1	24 53.3	8.4	59.5
04		240 28.1	04.6	291 32.1	5.2	24 44.9	8.6	59.5
05		255 28.3	03.6	305 56.3	5.2	24 36.3	8.8	59.5
06		270 28.5	N 6 02.7	320 20.5	5.4	N24 27.5	8.9	59.5
07		285 28.7	01.7	334 44.9	5.5	24 18.6	9.1	59.5
08		300 28.9	6 00.8	349 09.4	5.5	24 09.5	9.2	59.5
09		315 29.2	5 59.9	3 33.9	5.7	24 00.3	9.4	59.5
10		330 29.4	58.9	17 58.6	5.7	23 50.9	9.6	59.5
11		345 29.6	58.0	32 23.3	5.8	23 41.3	9.7	59.5
12		0 29.8	N 5 57.1	46 48.1	6.0	N23 31.6	9.9	59.5
13		15 30.0	56.1	61 13.1	6.0	23 21.7	10.0	59.5
14		30 30.2	55.2	75 38.1	6.1	23 11.7	10.1	59.5
15		45 30.4	. . 54.2	90 03.2	6.2	23 01.6	10.3	59.5
16		60 30.6	53.3	104 28.4	6.4	22 51.3	10.4	59.5
17		75 30.9	52.4	118 53.8	6.4	22 40.9	10.6	59.5
18		90 31.1	N 5 51.4	133 19.2	6.5	N22 30.3	10.7	59.5
19		105 31.3	50.5	147 44.7	6.6	22 19.6	10.9	59.5
20		120 31.5	49.6	162 10.3	6.7	22 08.7	11.0	59.5
21		135 31.7	. . 48.6	176 36.0	6.8	21 57.7	11.1	59.5
22		150 31.9	47.7	191 01.8	6.9	21 46.6	11.2	59.5
23		165 32.1	46.7	205 27.7	7.0	21 35.4	11.4	59.5
8 00	TUESDAY	180 32.4	N 5 45.8	219 53.7	7.1	N21 24.0	11.5	59.5
01		195 32.6	44.9	234 19.8	7.2	21 12.5	11.7	59.4
02		210 32.8	43.9	248 46.0	7.4	21 00.8	11.8	59.4
03		225 33.0	. . 43.0	263 12.4	7.4	20 49.0	11.8	59.4
04		240 33.2	42.0	277 38.8	7.5	20 37.2	12.1	59.4
05		255 33.4	41.1	292 05.3	7.6	20 25.1	12.1	59.4
06		270 33.6	N 5 40.2	306 31.9	7.7	N20 13.0	12.3	59.4
07		285 33.9	39.2	320 58.6	7.8	20 00.7	12.3	59.4
08		300 34.1	38.3	335 25.4	8.0	19 48.4	12.5	59.4
09		315 34.3	. . 37.3	349 52.4	8.0	19 35.9	12.6	59.4
10		330 34.5	36.4	4 19.4	8.1	19 23.3	12.7	59.4
11		345 34.7	35.5	18 46.5	8.2	19 10.6	12.8	59.4
12		0 34.9	N 5 34.5	33 13.7	8.3	N18 57.8	13.0	59.4
13		15 35.2	33.6	47 41.0	8.5	18 44.8	13.0	59.3
14		30 35.4	32.6	62 08.5	8.5	18 31.8	13.1	59.3
15		45 35.6	. . 31.7	76 36.0	8.6	18 18.7	13.3	59.3
16		60 35.8	30.8	91 03.6	8.7	18 05.4	13.3	59.3
17		75 36.0	29.8	105 31.3	8.8	17 52.1	13.4	59.3
18		90 36.2	N 5 28.9	119 59.1	8.9	N17 38.7	13.5	59.3
19		105 36.4	27.9	134 27.0	9.0	17 25.2	13.7	59.3
20		120 36.7	27.0	148 55.0	9.1	17 11.5	13.7	59.3
21		135 36.9	. . 26.0	163 23.1	9.2	16 57.8	13.8	59.3
22		150 37.1	25.1	177 51.3	9.3	16 44.0	13.9	59.2
23		165 37.3	24.2	192 19.6	9.4	16 30.1	14.0	59.2
9 00	WEDNESDAY	180 37.5	N 5 23.2	206 48.0	9.5	N16 16.1	14.0	59.2
01		195 37.7	22.3	221 16.5	9.6	16 02.1	14.2	59.2
02		210 38.0	21.3	235 45.1	9.6	15 47.9	14.2	59.2
03		225 38.2	. . 20.4	250 13.7	9.8	15 33.7	14.3	59.2
04		240 38.4	19.4	264 42.5	9.9	15 19.4	14.4	59.2
05		255 38.6	18.5	279 11.4	9.9	15 05.0	14.5	59.1
06		270 38.8	N 5 17.6	293 40.3	10.0	N14 50.5	14.5	59.1
07		285 39.0	16.6	308 09.3	10.1	14 36.0	14.6	59.1
08		300 39.3	15.7	322 38.4	10.3	14 21.4	14.7	59.1
09		315 39.5	. . 14.7	337 07.7	10.2	14 06.7	14.8	59.1
10		330 39.7	13.8	351 36.9	10.4	13 51.9	14.8	59.1
11		345 39.9	12.8	6 06.3	10.5	13 37.1	14.9	59.1
12		0 40.1	N 5 11.9	20 35.8	10.5	N13 22.2	14.9	59.0
13		15 40.3	10.9	35 05.3	10.7	13 07.3	15.0	59.0
14		30 40.6	10.0	49 35.0	10.7	12 52.3	15.1	59.0
15		45 40.8	. . 09.1	64 04.7	10.8	12 37.2	15.1	59.0
16		60 41.0	08.1	78 34.5	10.9	12 22.1	15.2	59.0
17		75 41.2	07.2	93 04.4	10.9	12 06.9	15.3	59.0
18		90 41.4	N 5 06.2	107 34.3	11.1	N11 51.6	15.2	58.9
19		105 41.6	05.3	122 04.4	11.1	11 36.4	15.4	58.9
20		120 41.9	04.3	136 34.5	11.2	11 21.0	15.4	58.9
21		135 42.1	. . 03.4	151 04.7	11.2	11 05.6	15.4	58.9
22		150 42.3	02.4	165 34.9	11.4	10 50.2	15.5	58.9
23		165 42.5	01.5	180 05.3	11.4	N10 34.7	15.5	58.8
		SD 15.9	*d* 0.9	SD 16.2		16.2		16.1

Lat.	Twilight Naut.	Twilight Civil	Sunrise	Moonrise 7	Moonrise 8	Moonrise 9	Moonrise 10
°	h m	h m	h m	h m	h m	h m	h m
N 72	00 36	03 16	04 35	▭	▭	00 02	03 06
N 70	01 48	03 36	04 44	▭	▭	00 48	03 21
68	02 23	03 50	04 51	22 01	25 18	01 18	03 34
66	02 47	04 02	04 58	23 12	25 39	01 39	03 44
64	03 06	04 12	05 03	23 48	25 57	01 57	03 52
62	03 21	04 21	05 07	24 14	00 14	02 11	03 59
60	03 33	04 28	05 11	24 34	00 34	02 23	04 05
N 58	03 43	04 34	05 15	24 50	00 50	02 33	04 11
56	03 52	04 39	05 18	25 04	01 04	02 42	04 15
54	04 00	04 44	05 21	25 16	01 16	02 49	04 20
52	04 06	04 48	05 23	25 26	01 26	02 56	04 23
50	04 12	04 52	05 25	00 09	01 36	03 03	04 27
45	04 25	05 00	05 30	00 34	01 55	03 16	04 34
N 40	04 34	05 07	05 34	00 55	02 11	03 27	04 41
35	04 42	05 12	05 38	01 11	02 25	03 37	04 46
30	04 48	05 17	05 41	01 26	02 36	03 45	04 51
20	04 58	05 24	05 46	01 50	02 56	03 59	04 59
N 10	05 05	05 29	05 50	02 11	03 13	04 11	05 06
0	05 10	05 34	05 54	02 31	03 29	04 23	05 12
S 10	05 13	05 37	05 58	02 51	03 45	04 34	05 19
20	05 15	05 40	06 02	03 12	04 02	04 46	05 26
30	05 15	05 43	06 07	03 36	04 21	05 00	05 34
35	05 15	05 44	06 10	03 50	04 32	05 08	05 38
40	05 14	05 45	06 12	04 06	04 45	05 17	05 44
45	05 13	05 46	06 16	04 25	05 00	05 27	05 49
S 50	05 10	05 47	06 20	04 50	05 18	05 40	05 57
52	05 09	05 48	06 21	05 01	05 27	05 46	06 00
54	05 07	05 48	06 23	05 14	05 37	05 52	06 03
56	05 06	05 48	06 26	05 29	05 47	05 59	06 07
58	05 03	05 49	06 28	05 47	06 00	06 07	06 12
S 60	05 01	05 49	06 31	06 09	06 14	06 16	06 16

Lat.	Sunset	Twilight Civil	Twilight Naut.	Moonset 7	Moonset 8	Moonset 9	Moonset 10
°	h m	h m	h m	h m	h m	h m	h m
N 72	19 17	20 35	22 58	▭	20 42	19 25	18 43
N 70	19 09	20 16	22 00	▭	19 54	19 07	18 36
68	19 02	20 02	21 27	20 45	19 23	18 52	18 30
66	18 56	19 50	21 04	19 33	18 59	18 40	18 25
64	18 51	19 41	20 46	18 56	18 41	18 30	18 21
62	18 46	19 33	20 32	18 29	18 25	18 21	18 17
60	18 43	19 26	20 20	18 08	18 12	18 14	18 14
N 58	18 39	19 20	20 10	17 51	18 01	18 07	18 11
56	18 36	19 15	20 02	17 37	17 51	18 01	18 09
54	18 34	19 10	19 54	17 24	17 43	17 56	18 06
52	18 31	19 06	19 47	17 13	17 35	17 51	18 04
50	18 29	19 02	19 42	17 03	17 28	17 47	18 02
45	18 24	18 54	19 30	16 42	17 12	17 37	17 58
N 40	18 20	18 48	19 20	16 25	17 00	17 29	17 54
35	18 17	18 43	19 13	16 10	16 49	17 22	17 51
30	18 14	18 38	19 07	15 58	16 40	17 16	17 48
20	18 09	18 31	18 57	15 36	16 23	17 05	17 43
N 10	18 05	18 26	18 51	15 17	16 09	16 56	17 39
0	18 01	18 22	18 46	14 59	15 55	16 47	17 35
S 10	17 57	18 18	18 43	14 41	15 41	16 38	17 31
20	17 53	18 15	18 41	14 22	15 26	16 28	17 26
30	17 49	18 13	18 40	13 59	15 09	16 17	17 21
35	17 46	18 12	18 41	13 46	14 59	16 10	17 18
40	17 43	18 11	18 42	13 31	14 48	16 03	17 15
45	17 40	18 10	18 44	13 12	14 34	15 54	17 11
S 50	17 37	18 09	18 46	12 49	14 17	15 43	17 06
52	17 35	18 09	18 48	12 38	14 09	15 38	17 04
54	17 33	18 08	18 49	12 26	14 00	15 33	17 01
56	17 31	18 08	18 51	12 11	13 50	15 27	16 58
58	17 29	18 08	18 53	11 54	13 39	15 20	16 55
S 60	17 26	18 08	18 56	11 33	13 25	15 12	16 52

Day	SUN Eqn. of Time 00^h	SUN Eqn. of Time 12^h	SUN Mer. Pass.	MOON Mer. Pass. Upper	MOON Mer. Pass. Lower	MOON Age	MOON Phase
d	m s	m s	h m	h m	h m	d %	
7	01 49	01 59	11 58	08 45	21 14	26 17	
8	02 09	02 19	11 58	09 42	22 09	27 9	
9	02 30	02 40	11 57	10 35	23 00	28 3	

2026 SEPTEMBER 10, 11, 12 (THURS., FRI., SAT.)

UT	ARIES	VENUS −4·7		MARS +1·2		JUPITER −1·8		SATURN +0·4	
d h	GHA	GHA	Dec	GHA	Dec	GHA	Dec	GHA	Dec
	° ′	° ′	° ′	° ′	° ′	° ′	° ′	° ′	° ′
10 00 (THURSDAY)	349 02.8	143 00.9	S15 39.1	238 19.7	N22 45.1	210 51.3	N16 41.6	335 55.6	N 2 42.9
01	4 05.2	158 01.9	40.0	253 20.5	44.9	225 53.3	41.4	350 58.2	42.9
02	19 07.7	173 02.9	40.8	268 21.3	44.7	240 55.2	41.3	6 00.8	42.8
03	34 10.2	188 03.9	. . 41.7	283 22.1	. . 44.5	255 57.2	. . 41.2	21 03.4	. . 42.7
04	49 12.6	203 04.9	42.6	298 22.9	44.4	270 59.2	41.0	36 06.0	42.6
05	64 15.1	218 05.9	43.5	313 23.7	44.2	286 01.1	40.9	51 08.7	42.6
06	79 17.6	233 06.9	S15 44.4	328 24.5	N22 44.0	301 03.1	N16 40.7	66 11.3	N 2 42.5
07	94 20.0	248 07.9	45.3	343 25.3	43.8	316 05.0	40.6	81 13.9	42.4
08	109 22.5	263 08.9	46.2	358 26.1	43.6	331 07.0	40.4	96 16.5	42.4
09	124 25.0	278 09.9	. . 47.1	13 26.9	. . 43.4	346 08.9	. . 40.3	111 19.1	. . 42.3
10	139 27.4	293 10.9	48.0	28 27.7	43.3	1 10.9	40.1	126 21.7	42.2
11	154 29.9	308 11.9	48.9	43 28.5	43.1	16 12.9	40.0	141 24.4	42.2
12	169 32.4	323 12.9	S15 49.8	58 29.2	N22 42.9	31 14.8	N16 39.8	156 27.0	N 2 42.1
13	184 34.8	338 13.9	50.7	73 30.0	42.7	46 16.8	39.7	171 29.6	42.0
14	199 37.3	353 14.9	51.5	88 30.8	42.5	61 18.7	39.6	186 32.2	41.9
15	214 39.7	8 15.9	. . 52.4	103 31.6	. . 42.3	76 20.7	. . 39.4	201 34.8	. . 41.9
16	229 42.2	23 16.9	53.3	118 32.4	42.2	91 22.6	39.3	216 37.4	41.8
17	244 44.7	38 18.0	54.2	133 33.2	42.0	106 24.6	39.1	231 40.0	41.7
18	259 47.1	53 19.0	S15 55.1	148 34.0	N22 41.8	121 26.6	N16 39.0	246 42.7	N 2 41.7
19	274 49.6	68 20.0	56.0	163 34.8	41.6	136 28.5	38.8	261 45.3	41.6
20	289 52.1	83 21.0	56.9	178 35.6	41.4	151 30.5	38.7	276 47.9	41.5
21	304 54.5	98 22.0	. . 57.7	193 36.4	. . 41.2	166 32.4	. . 38.5	291 50.5	. . 41.5
22	319 57.0	113 23.1	58.6	208 37.2	41.1	181 34.4	38.4	306 53.1	41.4
23	334 59.5	128 24.1	15 59.5	223 38.0	40.9	196 36.3	38.2	321 55.7	41.3
11 00 (FRIDAY)	350 01.9	143 25.1	S16 00.4	238 38.8	N22 40.7	211 38.3	N16 38.1	336 58.4	N 2 41.2
01	5 04.4	158 26.1	01.3	253 39.6	40.5	226 40.3	38.0	352 01.0	41.2
02	20 06.8	173 27.2	02.1	268 40.4	40.3	241 42.2	37.8	7 03.6	41.1
03	35 09.3	188 28.2	. . 03.0	283 41.2	. . 40.1	256 44.2	. . 37.7	22 06.2	. . 41.0
04	50 11.8	203 29.2	03.9	298 42.0	39.9	271 46.1	37.5	37 08.8	41.0
05	65 14.2	218 30.3	04.8	313 42.8	39.8	286 48.1	37.4	52 11.4	40.9
06	80 16.7	233 31.3	S16 05.6	328 43.6	N22 39.6	301 50.1	N16 37.2	67 14.1	N 2 40.8
07	95 19.2	248 32.3	06.5	343 44.4	39.4	316 52.0	37.1	82 16.7	40.7
08	110 21.6	263 33.4	07.4	358 45.2	39.2	331 54.0	36.9	97 19.3	40.7
09	125 24.1	278 34.4	. . 08.3	13 46.0	. . 39.0	346 55.9	. . 36.8	112 21.9	. . 40.6
10	140 26.6	293 35.5	09.1	28 46.8	38.8	1 57.9	36.7	127 24.5	40.5
11	155 29.0	308 36.5	10.0	43 47.6	38.6	16 59.9	36.5	142 27.2	40.5
12	170 31.5	323 37.6	S16 10.9	58 48.4	N22 38.4	32 01.8	N16 36.4	157 29.8	N 2 40.4
13	185 34.0	338 38.6	11.7	73 49.2	38.3	47 03.8	36.2	172 32.4	40.3
14	200 36.4	353 39.6	12.6	88 50.0	38.1	62 05.7	36.1	187 35.0	40.2
15	215 38.9	8 40.7	. . 13.5	103 50.8	. . 37.9	77 07.7	. . 35.9	202 37.6	. . 40.2
16	230 41.3	23 41.8	14.3	118 51.6	37.7	92 09.7	35.8	217 40.2	40.1
17	245 43.8	38 42.8	15.2	133 52.4	37.5	107 11.6	35.6	232 42.9	40.0
18	260 46.3	53 43.9	S16 16.1	148 53.2	N22 37.3	122 13.6	N16 35.5	247 45.5	N 2 40.0
19	275 48.7	68 44.9	16.9	163 54.0	37.1	137 15.5	35.3	262 48.1	39.9
20	290 51.2	83 46.0	17.8	178 54.8	36.9	152 17.5	35.2	277 50.7	39.8
21	305 53.7	98 47.0	. . 18.7	193 55.7	. . 36.7	167 19.5	. . 35.1	292 53.3	. . 39.7
22	320 56.1	113 48.1	19.5	208 56.5	36.5	182 21.4	34.9	307 56.0	39.7
23	335 58.6	128 49.2	20.4	223 57.3	36.3	197 23.4	34.8	322 58.6	39.6
12 00 (SATURDAY)	351 01.1	143 50.2	S16 21.2	238 58.1	N22 36.2	212 25.3	N16 34.6	338 01.2	N 2 39.5
01	6 03.5	158 51.3	22.1	253 58.9	36.0	227 27.3	34.5	353 03.8	39.5
02	21 06.0	173 52.4	23.0	268 59.7	35.8	242 29.3	34.3	8 06.4	39.4
03	36 08.4	188 53.5	. . 23.8	284 00.5	. . 35.6	257 31.2	. . 34.2	23 09.0	. . 39.3
04	51 10.9	203 54.5	24.7	299 01.3	35.4	272 33.2	34.0	38 11.7	39.2
05	66 13.4	218 55.6	25.5	314 02.1	35.2	287 35.2	33.9	53 14.3	39.2
06	81 15.8	233 56.7	S16 26.4	329 02.9	N22 35.0	302 37.1	N16 33.8	68 16.9	N 2 39.1
07	96 18.3	248 57.8	27.2	344 03.7	34.8	317 39.1	33.6	83 19.5	39.0
08	111 20.8	263 58.9	28.1	359 04.5	34.6	332 41.0	33.5	98 22.1	39.0
09	126 23.2	278 59.9	. . 28.9	14 05.3	. . 34.4	347 43.0	. . 33.3	113 24.8	. . 38.9
10	141 25.7	294 01.0	29.8	29 06.1	34.2	2 45.0	33.2	128 27.4	38.8
11	156 28.2	309 02.1	30.6	44 06.9	34.0	17 46.9	33.0	143 30.0	38.7
12	171 30.6	324 03.2	S16 31.5	59 07.7	N22 33.8	32 48.9	N16 32.9	158 32.6	N 2 38.7
13	186 33.1	339 04.3	32.3	74 08.6	33.6	47 50.9	32.7	173 35.2	38.6
14	201 35.6	354 05.4	33.2	89 09.4	33.5	62 52.8	32.6	188 37.9	38.5
15	216 38.0	9 06.5	. . 34.0	104 10.2	. . 33.3	77 54.8	. . 32.5	203 40.5	. . 38.4
16	231 40.5	24 07.6	34.9	119 11.0	33.1	92 56.7	32.3	218 43.1	38.4
17	246 42.9	39 08.7	35.7	134 11.8	32.9	107 58.7	32.2	233 45.7	38.3
18	261 45.4	54 09.8	S16 36.6	149 12.6	N22 32.7	123 00.7	N16 32.0	248 48.3	N 2 38.2
19	276 47.9	69 10.9	37.4	164 13.4	32.5	138 02.6	31.9	263 51.0	38.2
20	291 50.3	84 12.0	38.2	179 14.2	32.3	153 04.6	31.7	278 53.6	38.1
21	306 52.8	99 13.1	. . 39.1	194 15.0	. . 32.1	168 06.6	. . 31.6	293 56.2	. . 38.0
22	321 55.3	114 14.2	39.9	209 15.8	31.9	183 08.5	31.4	308 58.8	37.9
23	336 57.7	129 15.3	40.8	224 16.7	31.7	198 10.5	31.3	324 01.4	37.9
Mer. Pass.	h m 0 39.8	v 1.0	d 0.9	v 0.8	d 0.2	v 2.0	d 0.1	v 2.6	d 0.1

STARS

Name	SHA	Dec
	° ′	° ′
Acamar	315 10.5	S40 11.5
Achernar	335 18.7	S57 05.8
Acrux	172 59.2	S63 14.9
Adhara	255 04.9	S29 00.2
Aldebaran	290 38.0	N16 33.8
Alioth	166 12.2	N55 49.0
Alkaid	152 51.3	N49 11.0
Alnair	27 30.7	S46 49.8
Alnilam	275 36.4	S 1 10.9
Alphard	217 46.7	S 8 46.3
Alphecca	126 02.7	N26 37.7
Alpheratz	357 33.0	N29 14.4
Altair	61 58.4	N 8 56.5
Ankaa	353 05.4	S42 09.4
Antares	112 14.2	S26 29.5
Arcturus	145 46.9	N19 02.7
Atria	107 07.2	S69 04.8
Avior	234 14.6	S59 35.4
Bellatrix	278 21.4	N 6 22.5
Betelgeuse	270 50.6	N 7 24.8
Canopus	263 51.9	S52 42.2
Capella	280 19.8	N46 01.3
Deneb	49 24.5	N45 22.8
Denebola	182 23.9	N14 25.5
Diphda	348 45.6	S17 50.2
Dubhe	193 40.0	N61 36.4
Elnath	278 00.1	N28 37.8
Eltanin	90 41.4	N51 29.4
Enif	33 37.1	N10 00.0
Fomalhaut	15 12.6	S29 28.7
Gacrux	171 50.7	S57 15.8
Gienah	175 42.5	S17 41.4
Hadar	148 34.5	S60 30.3
Hamal	327 49.4	N23 35.4
Kaus Aust.	83 30.5	S34 22.4
Kochab	137 20.5	N74 02.9
Markab	13 28.2	N15 21.1
Menkar	314 04.5	N 4 11.8
Menkent	147 56.3	S36 30.1
Miaplacidus	221 38.8	S69 49.4
Mirfak	308 26.0	N49 57.3
Nunki	75 45.9	S26 15.8
Peacock	53 03.1	S56 39.0
Pollux	243 15.8	N27 57.7
Procyon	244 49.6	N 5 09.5
Rasalhague	95 57.2	N12 32.6
Regulus	207 33.3	N11 50.3
Rigel	281 02.5	S 8 10.0
Rigil Kent.	139 38.8	S60 56.9
Sabik	102 01.2	S15 45.4
Schedar	349 28.9	N56 41.1
Shaula	96 08.4	S37 07.5
Sirius	258 25.1	S16 44.9
Spica	158 21.1	S11 18.0
Suhail	222 45.7	S43 32.2
Vega	80 32.1	N38 48.8
Zuben'ubi	136 54.7	S16 09.2

	SHA	Mer. Pass.
	° ′	h m
Venus	153 23.2	14 25
Mars	248 36.9	8 05
Jupiter	221 36.4	9 52
Saturn	346 56.4	1 32

UT	SUN GHA	SUN Dec	MOON GHA	v	MOON Dec	d	HP
d h	° ′	° ′	° ′	′	° ′	′	′
10 00 THURSDAY	180 42.7	N 5 00.5	194 35.7	11.5	N10 19.2	15.6	58.8
01	195 42.9	4 59.6	209 06.2	11.6	10 03.6	15.6	58.8
02	210 43.2	58.6	223 36.8	11.6	9 48.0	15.7	58.8
03	225 43.4	. . 57.7	238 07.4	11.7	9 32.3	15.7	58.8
04	240 43.6	56.8	252 38.1	11.7	9 16.6	15.7	58.8
05	255 43.8	55.8	267 08.8	11.9	9 00.9	15.8	58.7
06	270 44.0	N 4 54.9	281 39.7	11.9	N 8 45.1	15.8	58.7
07	285 44.2	53.9	296 10.6	11.9	8 29.3	15.8	58.7
08	300 44.5	53.0	310 41.5	12.1	8 13.5	15.9	58.7
09	315 44.7	. . 52.0	325 12.6	12.1	7 57.6	15.8	58.6
10	330 44.9	51.1	339 43.7	12.1	7 41.8	15.9	58.6
11	345 45.1	50.1	354 14.8	12.2	7 25.9	16.0	58.6
12	0 45.3	N 4 49.2	8 46.0	12.3	N 7 09.9	15.9	58.6
13	15 45.6	48.2	23 17.3	12.3	6 54.0	16.0	58.6
14	30 45.8	47.3	37 48.6	12.4	6 38.0	16.0	58.5
15	45 46.0	. . 46.3	52 20.0	12.5	6 22.0	16.0	58.5
16	60 46.2	45.4	66 51.5	12.5	6 06.0	16.1	58.5
17	75 46.4	44.4	81 23.0	12.5	5 49.9	16.0	58.5
18	90 46.6	N 4 43.5	95 54.5	12.6	N 5 33.9	16.1	58.4
19	105 46.9	42.5	110 26.1	12.7	5 17.8	16.1	58.4
20	120 47.1	41.6	124 57.8	12.7	5 01.7	16.1	58.4
21	135 47.3	. . 40.6	139 29.5	12.7	4 45.6	16.1	58.4
22	150 47.5	39.7	154 01.2	12.8	4 29.5	16.1	58.4
23	165 47.7	38.7	168 33.0	12.9	4 13.4	16.1	58.3
11 00 FRIDAY	180 48.0	N 4 37.8	183 04.9	12.9	N 3 57.3	16.1	58.3
01	195 48.2	36.8	197 36.8	12.9	3 41.2	16.1	58.3
02	210 48.4	35.9	212 08.7	13.0	3 25.1	16.2	58.3
03	225 48.6	. . 34.9	226 40.7	13.0	3 08.9	16.1	58.2
04	240 48.8	34.0	241 12.7	13.1	2 52.8	16.1	58.2
05	255 49.1	33.0	255 44.8	13.1	2 36.7	16.1	58.2
06	270 49.3	N 4 32.1	270 16.9	13.1	N 2 20.6	16.2	58.2
07	285 49.5	31.1	284 49.0	13.2	2 04.4	16.1	58.1
08	300 49.7	30.2	299 21.2	13.2	1 48.3	16.1	58.1
09	315 49.9	. . 29.2	313 53.4	13.2	1 32.2	16.1	58.1
10	330 50.2	28.3	328 25.6	13.3	1 16.1	16.1	58.0
11	345 50.4	27.3	342 57.9	13.3	1 00.0	16.1	58.0
12	0 50.6	N 4 26.4	357 30.2	13.4	N 0 43.9	16.0	58.0
13	15 50.8	25.4	12 02.6	13.3	0 27.9	16.1	58.0
14	30 51.0	24.5	26 34.9	13.4	N 0 11.8	16.0	57.9
15	45 51.2	. . 23.5	41 07.3	13.5	S 0 04.2	16.1	57.9
16	60 51.5	22.6	55 39.8	13.4	0 20.3	16.0	57.9
17	75 51.7	21.6	70 12.2	13.5	0 36.3	16.0	57.9
18	90 51.9	N 4 20.7	84 44.7	13.5	S 0 52.3	16.0	57.8
19	105 52.1	19.7	99 17.2	13.6	1 08.3	15.9	57.8
20	120 52.3	18.7	113 49.8	13.5	1 24.2	15.9	57.8
21	135 52.6	. . 17.8	128 22.3	13.6	1 40.1	16.0	57.8
22	150 52.8	16.8	142 54.9	13.6	1 56.1	15.8	57.7
23	165 53.0	15.9	157 27.5	13.6	2 11.9	15.9	57.7
12 00 SATURDAY	180 53.2	N 4 14.9	172 00.1	13.6	S 2 27.8	15.8	57.7
01	195 53.4	14.0	186 32.7	13.7	2 43.6	15.8	57.6
02	210 53.7	13.0	201 05.4	13.6	2 59.4	15.8	57.6
03	225 53.9	. . 12.1	215 38.0	13.7	3 15.2	15.7	57.6
04	240 54.1	11.1	230 10.7	13.7	3 30.9	15.8	57.6
05	255 54.3	10.2	244 43.4	13.7	3 46.7	15.6	57.5
06	270 54.5	N 4 09.2	259 16.1	13.7	S 4 02.3	15.7	57.5
07	285 54.8	08.3	273 48.8	13.8	4 18.0	15.6	57.5
08	300 55.0	07.3	288 21.6	13.7	4 33.6	15.6	57.4
09	315 55.2	. . 06.4	302 54.3	13.7	4 49.2	15.5	57.4
10	330 55.4	05.4	317 27.0	13.8	5 04.7	15.5	57.4
11	345 55.6	04.4	331 59.8	13.7	5 20.2	15.4	57.4
12	0 55.9	N 4 03.5	346 32.5	13.8	S 5 35.6	15.4	57.3
13	15 56.1	02.5	1 05.3	13.8	5 51.0	15.4	57.3
14	30 56.3	01.6	15 38.1	13.7	6 06.4	15.3	57.3
15	45 56.5	4 00.6	30 10.8	13.8	6 21.7	15.3	57.2
16	60 56.8	3 59.7	44 43.6	13.8	6 37.0	15.3	57.2
17	75 57.0	58.7	59 16.4	13.8	6 52.3	15.1	57.2
18	90 57.2	N 3 57.8	73 49.2	13.7	S 7 07.4	15.2	57.2
19	105 57.4	56.8	88 21.9	13.8	7 22.6	15.1	57.1
20	120 57.6	55.8	102 54.7	13.8	7 37.7	15.0	57.1
21	135 57.9	. . 54.9	117 27.5	13.7	7 52.7	15.0	57.1
22	150 58.1	53.9	132 00.2	13.8	8 07.7	15.0	57.0
23	165 58.3	53.0	146 33.0	13.7	S 8 22.7	14.8	57.0
	SD 15.9	*d* 1.0	SD 16.0		15.8		15.6

Lat.	Twilight Naut.	Twilight Civil	Sunrise	Moonrise 10	Moonrise 11	Moonrise 12	Moonrise 13
°	h m	h m	h m	h m	h m	h m	h m
N 72	01 27	03 33	04 49	03 06	05 29	07 44	10 04
N 70	02 12	03 50	04 56	03 21	05 32	07 37	09 44
68	02 41	04 03	05 02	03 34	05 35	07 31	09 29
66	03 01	04 13	05 07	03 44	05 38	07 27	09 16
64	03 18	04 22	05 11	03 52	05 40	07 23	09 06
62	03 31	04 29	05 15	03 59	05 41	07 20	08 57
60	03 42	04 35	05 18	04 05	05 43	07 17	08 50
N 58	03 51	04 41	05 21	04 11	05 44	07 14	08 43
56	03 59	04 46	05 24	04 15	05 45	07 12	08 37
54	04 06	04 50	05 26	04 20	05 46	07 10	08 32
52	04 12	04 54	05 28	04 23	05 47	07 08	08 28
50	04 18	04 57	05 30	04 27	05 48	07 06	08 24
45	04 29	05 04	05 34	04 34	05 50	07 03	08 15
N 40	04 37	05 10	05 37	04 41	05 51	07 00	08 07
35	04 44	05 14	05 40	04 46	05 53	06 57	08 01
30	04 50	05 18	05 42	04 51	05 54	06 55	07 55
20	04 59	05 24	05 47	04 59	05 56	06 51	07 46
N 10	05 05	05 29	05 50	05 06	05 58	06 48	07 37
0	05 09	05 33	05 53	05 12	05 59	06 45	07 30
S 10	05 11	05 36	05 57	05 19	06 01	06 42	07 22
20	05 12	05 38	06 00	05 26	06 03	06 39	07 14
30	05 12	05 39	06 03	05 34	06 05	06 35	07 05
35	05 11	05 40	06 05	05 38	06 06	06 33	07 00
40	05 09	05 41	06 08	05 44	06 08	06 30	06 54
45	05 07	05 41	06 10	05 49	06 09	06 28	06 47
S 50	05 04	05 41	06 13	05 57	06 11	06 25	06 39
52	05 02	05 41	06 15	06 00	06 12	06 23	06 35
54	05 00	05 41	06 16	06 03	06 13	06 22	06 31
56	04 58	05 41	06 18	06 07	06 14	06 20	06 26
58	04 55	05 40	06 20	06 12	06 15	06 18	06 21
S 60	04 52	05 40	06 22	06 16	06 16	06 16	06 16

Lat.	Sunset	Twilight Civil	Twilight Naut.	Moonset 10	Moonset 11	Moonset 12	Moonset 13
°	h m	h m	h m	h m	h m	h m	h m
N 72	19 02	20 16	22 16	18 43	18 08	17 33	16 49
N 70	18 55	20 00	21 35	18 36	18 10	17 43	17 12
68	18 49	19 48	21 08	18 30	18 11	17 51	17 29
66	18 44	19 38	20 48	18 25	18 12	17 58	17 43
64	18 40	19 29	20 33	18 21	18 13	18 04	17 55
62	18 37	19 22	20 20	18 17	18 13	18 09	18 05
60	18 33	19 16	20 09	18 14	18 14	18 14	18 14
N 58	18 31	19 11	20 00	18 11	18 14	18 18	18 21
56	18 28	19 06	19 52	18 09	18 15	18 21	18 28
54	18 26	19 02	19 46	18 06	18 15	18 24	18 34
52	18 24	18 59	19 40	18 04	18 16	18 27	18 40
50	18 23	18 55	19 34	18 02	18 16	18 30	18 45
45	18 19	18 48	19 23	17 58	18 17	18 36	18 55
N 40	18 16	18 43	19 15	17 54	18 18	18 41	19 05
35	18 13	18 38	19 08	17 51	18 18	18 45	19 12
30	18 10	18 34	19 03	17 48	18 19	18 49	19 19
20	18 06	18 29	18 54	17 43	18 20	18 55	19 31
N 10	18 03	18 24	18 49	17 39	18 20	19 01	19 42
0	18 00	18 21	18 45	17 35	18 21	19 06	19 51
S 10	17 57	18 18	18 42	17 31	18 22	19 12	20 01
20	17 54	18 16	18 41	17 26	18 23	19 17	20 12
30	17 50	18 14	18 42	17 21	18 23	19 24	20 24
35	17 48	18 14	18 43	17 18	18 24	19 28	20 31
40	17 46	18 13	18 45	17 15	18 24	19 32	20 39
45	17 44	18 13	18 47	17 11	18 25	19 37	20 49
S 50	17 41	18 13	18 51	17 06	18 26	19 43	21 00
52	17 40	18 13	18 52	17 04	18 26	19 46	21 06
54	17 38	18 13	18 55	17 01	18 26	19 49	21 12
56	17 37	18 14	18 57	16 58	18 27	19 53	21 18
58	17 35	18 14	19 00	16 55	18 27	19 57	21 26
S 60	17 33	18 14	19 03	16 52	18 28	20 01	21 34

Day	SUN Eqn. of Time 00^h	SUN Eqn. of Time 12^h	SUN Mer. Pass.	MOON Mer. Pass. Upper	MOON Mer. Pass. Lower	MOON Age	MOON Phase
d	m s	m s	h m	h m	h m	d %	
10	02 50	03 01	11 57	11 24	23 47	29 1	●
11	03 11	03 22	11 57	12 10	24 33	00 0	
12	03 32	03 43	11 56	12 56	00 33	01 2	

UT d	h	ARIES GHA	VENUS −4·8 GHA	VENUS Dec	MARS +1·2 GHA	MARS Dec	JUPITER −1·8 GHA	JUPITER Dec	SATURN +0·4 GHA	SATURN Dec
		° ′	° ′	° ′	° ′	° ′	° ′	° ′	° ′	° ′
13 SUNDAY	00	352 00.2	144 16.4	S16 41.6	239 17.5	N22 31.5	213 12.5	N16 31.1	339 04.1	N 2 37.8
	01	7 02.7	159 17.5	42.4	254 18.3	31.3	228 14.4	31.0	354 06.7	37.7
	02	22 05.1	174 18.7	43.3	269 19.1	31.1	243 16.4	30.9	9 09.3	37.7
	03	37 07.6	189 19.8	44.1	284 19.9	30.9	258 18.3	30.7	24 11.9	37.6
	04	52 10.0	204 20.9	45.0	299 20.7	30.7	273 20.3	30.6	39 14.6	37.5
	05	67 12.5	219 22.0	45.8	314 21.5	30.5	288 22.3	30.4	54 17.2	37.4
	06	82 15.0	234 23.1	S16 46.6	329 22.3	N22 30.3	303 24.2	N16 30.3	69 19.8	N 2 37.4
	07	97 17.4	249 24.3	47.5	344 23.2	30.1	318 26.2	30.1	84 22.4	37.3
	08	112 19.9	264 25.4	48.3	359 24.0	29.9	333 28.2	30.0	99 25.0	37.2
	09	127 22.4	279 26.5	49.1	14 24.8	29.7	348 30.1	29.8	114 27.7	37.1
	10	142 24.8	294 27.6	50.0	29 25.6	29.5	3 32.1	29.7	129 30.3	37.1
	11	157 27.3	309 28.8	50.8	44 26.4	29.3	18 34.1	29.6	144 32.9	37.0
	12	172 29.8	324 29.9	S16 51.6	59 27.2	N22 29.1	33 36.0	N16 29.4	159 35.5	N 2 36.9
	13	187 32.2	339 31.1	52.4	74 28.0	28.9	48 38.0	29.3	174 38.1	36.9
	14	202 34.7	354 32.2	53.3	89 28.9	28.7	63 40.0	29.1	189 40.8	36.8
	15	217 37.2	9 33.3	54.1	104 29.7	28.5	78 41.9	29.0	204 43.4	36.7
	16	232 39.6	24 34.5	54.9	119 30.5	28.3	93 43.9	28.8	219 46.0	36.6
	17	247 42.1	39 35.6	55.7	134 31.3	28.1	108 45.9	28.7	234 48.6	36.6
	18	262 44.5	54 36.8	S16 56.6	149 32.1	N22 27.9	123 47.8	N16 28.5	249 51.3	N 2 36.5
	19	277 47.0	69 37.9	57.4	164 32.9	27.7	138 49.8	28.4	264 53.9	36.4
	20	292 49.5	84 39.1	58.2	179 33.7	27.5	153 51.8	28.3	279 56.5	36.3
	21	307 51.9	99 40.2	59.0	194 34.6	27.3	168 53.7	28.1	294 59.1	36.3
	22	322 54.4	114 41.4	16 59.8	209 35.4	27.1	183 55.7	28.0	310 01.7	36.2
	23	337 56.9	129 42.5	17 00.7	224 36.2	26.9	198 57.7	27.8	325 04.4	36.1
14 MONDAY	00	352 59.3	144 43.7	S17 01.5	239 37.0	N22 26.7	213 59.6	N16 27.7	340 07.0	N 2 36.1
	01	8 01.8	159 44.8	02.3	254 37.8	26.5	229 01.6	27.5	355 09.6	36.0
	02	23 04.3	174 46.0	03.1	269 38.7	26.3	244 03.6	27.4	10 12.2	35.9
	03	38 06.7	189 47.2	03.9	284 39.5	26.1	259 05.5	27.2	25 14.9	35.8
	04	53 09.2	204 48.3	04.7	299 40.3	25.9	274 07.5	27.1	40 17.5	35.8
	05	68 11.7	219 49.5	05.6	314 41.1	25.7	289 09.5	27.0	55 20.1	35.7
	06	83 14.1	234 50.7	S17 06.4	329 41.9	N22 25.5	304 11.4	N16 26.8	70 22.7	N 2 35.6
	07	98 16.6	249 51.9	07.2	344 42.7	25.3	319 13.4	26.7	85 25.4	35.5
	08	113 19.0	264 53.0	08.0	359 43.6	25.1	334 15.4	26.5	100 28.0	35.5
	09	128 21.5	279 54.2	08.8	14 44.4	24.8	349 17.3	26.4	115 30.6	35.4
	10	143 24.0	294 55.4	09.6	29 45.2	24.6	4 19.3	26.2	130 33.2	35.3
	11	158 26.4	309 56.6	10.4	44 46.0	24.4	19 21.3	26.1	145 35.9	35.3
	12	173 28.9	324 57.7	S17 11.2	59 46.9	N22 24.2	34 23.2	N16 26.0	160 38.5	N 2 35.2
	13	188 31.4	339 58.9	12.0	74 47.7	24.0	49 25.2	25.8	175 41.1	35.1
	14	203 33.8	355 00.1	12.8	89 48.5	23.8	64 27.2	25.7	190 43.7	35.0
	15	218 36.3	10 01.3	13.6	104 49.3	23.6	79 29.1	25.5	205 46.3	35.0
	16	233 38.8	25 02.5	14.4	119 50.1	23.4	94 31.1	25.4	220 49.0	34.9
	17	248 41.2	40 03.7	15.2	134 51.0	23.2	109 33.1	25.2	235 51.6	34.8
	18	263 43.7	55 04.9	S17 16.0	149 51.8	N22 23.0	124 35.0	N16 25.1	250 54.2	N 2 34.7
	19	278 46.1	70 06.1	16.8	164 52.6	22.8	139 37.0	24.9	265 56.8	34.7
	20	293 48.6	85 07.3	17.6	179 53.4	22.6	154 39.0	24.8	280 59.5	34.6
	21	308 51.1	100 08.5	18.4	194 54.3	22.4	169 40.9	24.7	296 02.1	34.5
	22	323 53.5	115 09.7	19.2	209 55.1	22.2	184 42.9	24.5	311 04.7	34.4
	23	338 56.0	130 10.9	20.0	224 55.9	22.0	199 44.9	24.4	326 07.3	34.4
15 TUESDAY	00	353 58.5	145 12.1	S17 20.8	239 56.7	N22 21.7	214 46.9	N16 24.2	341 10.0	N 2 34.3
	01	9 00.9	160 13.3	21.6	254 57.5	21.5	229 48.8	24.1	356 12.6	34.2
	02	24 03.4	175 14.5	22.4	269 58.4	21.3	244 50.8	23.9	11 15.2	34.1
	03	39 05.9	190 15.7	23.2	284 59.2	21.1	259 52.8	23.8	26 17.8	34.1
	04	54 08.3	205 16.9	24.0	300 00.0	20.9	274 54.7	23.6	41 20.5	34.0
	05	69 10.8	220 18.2	24.8	315 00.8	20.7	289 56.7	23.5	56 23.1	33.9
	06	84 13.3	235 19.4	S17 25.6	330 01.7	N22 20.5	304 58.7	N16 23.4	71 25.7	N 2 33.9
	07	99 15.7	250 20.6	26.4	345 02.5	20.3	320 00.6	23.2	86 28.3	33.8
	08	114 18.2	265 21.8	27.2	0 03.3	20.1	335 02.6	23.1	101 31.0	33.7
	09	129 20.6	280 23.0	27.9	15 04.2	19.9	350 04.6	22.9	116 33.6	33.6
	10	144 23.1	295 24.3	28.7	30 05.0	19.6	5 06.6	22.8	131 36.2	33.6
	11	159 25.6	310 25.5	29.5	45 05.8	19.4	20 08.5	22.6	146 38.8	33.5
	12	174 28.0	325 26.7	S17 30.3	60 06.6	N22 19.2	35 10.5	N16 22.5	161 41.5	N 2 33.4
	13	189 30.5	340 28.0	31.1	75 07.5	19.0	50 12.5	22.4	176 44.1	33.3
	14	204 33.0	355 29.2	31.9	90 08.3	18.8	65 14.4	22.2	191 46.7	33.3
	15	219 35.4	10 30.4	32.6	105 09.1	18.6	80 16.4	22.1	206 49.4	33.2
	16	234 37.9	25 31.7	33.4	120 09.9	18.4	95 18.4	21.9	221 52.0	33.1
	17	249 40.4	40 32.9	34.2	135 10.8	18.2	110 20.4	21.8	236 54.6	33.0
	18	264 42.8	55 34.2	S17 35.0	150 11.6	N22 18.0	125 22.3	N16 21.6	251 57.2	N 2 33.0
	19	279 45.3	70 35.4	35.8	165 12.4	17.7	140 24.3	21.5	266 59.9	32.9
	20	294 47.7	85 36.7	36.5	180 13.3	17.5	155 26.3	21.3	282 02.5	32.8
	21	309 50.2	100 37.9	37.3	195 14.1	17.3	170 28.2	21.2	297 05.1	32.7
	22	324 52.7	115 39.2	38.1	210 14.9	17.1	185 30.2	21.1	312 07.7	32.7
	23	339 55.1	130 40.4	38.9	225 15.8	16.9	200 32.2	20.9	327 10.4	32.6
Mer. Pass.		h m 0 28.0	*v* 1.2	*d* 0.8	*v* 0.8	*d* 0.2	*v* 2.0	*d* 0.1	*v* 2.6	*d* 0.1

STARS

Name	SHA	Dec
	° ′	° ′
Acamar	315 10.5	S40 11.5
Achernar	335 18.7	S57 05.8
Acrux	172 59.2	S63 14.9
Adhara	255 04.9	S29 00.2
Aldebaran	290 38.0	N16 33.8
Alioth	166 12.3	N55 49.0
Alkaid	152 51.3	N49 11.0
Alnair	27 30.7	S46 49.8
Alnilam	275 36.3	S 1 10.9
Alphard	217 46.7	S 8 46.3
Alphecca	126 02.7	N26 37.7
Alpheratz	357 33.0	N29 14.4
Altair	61 58.4	N 8 56.5
Ankaa	353 05.4	S42 09.4
Antares	112 14.2	S26 29.5
Arcturus	145 46.9	N19 02.7
Atria	107 07.2	S69 04.7
Avior	234 14.6	S59 35.4
Bellatrix	278 21.4	N 6 22.5
Betelgeuse	270 50.6	N 7 24.8
Canopus	263 51.9	S52 42.2
Capella	280 19.8	N46 01.3
Deneb	49 24.5	N45 22.8
Denebola	182 23.9	N14 25.4
Diphda	348 45.6	S17 50.2
Dubhe	193 40.0	N61 36.4
Elnath	278 00.1	N28 37.8
Eltanin	90 41.5	N51 29.4
Enif	33 37.1	N10 00.0
Fomalhaut	15 12.6	S29 28.7
Gacrux	171 50.7	S57 15.8
Gienah	175 42.5	S17 41.4
Hadar	148 34.5	S60 30.3
Hamal	327 49.4	N23 35.4
Kaus Aust.	83 30.6	S34 22.4
Kochab	137 20.5	N74 02.9
Markab	13 28.2	N15 21.1
Menkar	314 04.5	N 4 11.8
Menkent	147 56.3	S36 30.1
Miaplacidus	221 38.8	S69 49.4
Mirfak	308 26.0	N49 57.3
Nunki	75 45.9	S26 15.8
Peacock	53 03.1	S56 39.0
Pollux	243 15.8	N27 57.7
Procyon	244 49.6	N 5 09.5
Rasalhague	95 57.2	N12 32.6
Regulus	207 33.3	N11 50.3
Rigel	281 02.5	S 8 10.0
Rigil Kent.	139 38.8	S60 56.9
Sabik	102 01.2	S15 45.4
Schedar	349 28.9	N56 41.1
Shaula	96 08.5	S37 07.5
Sirius	258 25.1	S16 44.9
Spica	158 21.1	S11 18.0
Suhail	222 45.7	S43 32.2
Vega	80 32.2	N38 48.8
Zuben'ubi	136 54.7	S16 09.1

	SHA	Mer. Pass.
	° ′	h m
Venus	151 44.4	14 20
Mars	246 37.7	8 01
Jupiter	221 00.3	9 43
Saturn	347 07.7	1 19

UT	SUN GHA	SUN Dec	MOON GHA	v	MOON Dec	d	HP
d h	° ′	° ′	° ′	′	° ′	′	′
13 00 SUNDAY	180 58.5	N 3 52.0	161 05.7	13.8	S 8 37.5	14.9	57.0
01	195 58.7	51.1	175 38.5	13.7	8 52.4	14.7	56.9
02	210 59.0	50.1	190 11.2	13.7	9 07.1	14.8	56.9
03	225 59.2	. . 49.2	204 43.9	13.8	9 21.9	14.6	56.9
04	240 59.4	48.2	219 16.7	13.7	9 36.5	14.6	56.9
05	255 59.6	47.2	233 49.4	13.7	9 51.1	14.6	56.8
06	270 59.8	N 3 46.3	248 22.1	13.7	S10 05.7	14.5	56.8
07	286 00.1	45.3	262 54.8	13.6	10 20.2	14.4	56.8
08	301 00.3	44.4	277 27.4	13.7	10 34.6	14.3	56.7
09	316 00.5	. . 43.4	292 00.1	13.6	10 48.9	14.3	56.7
10	331 00.7	42.5	306 32.7	13.7	11 03.2	14.3	56.7
11	346 00.9	41.5	321 05.4	13.6	11 17.5	14.1	56.7
12	1 01.2	N 3 40.5	335 38.0	13.6	S11 31.6	14.1	56.6
13	16 01.4	39.6	350 10.6	13.5	11 45.7	14.1	56.6
14	31 01.6	38.6	4 43.1	13.6	11 59.8	13.9	56.6
15	46 01.8	. . 37.7	19 15.7	13.5	12 13.7	13.9	56.5
16	61 02.1	36.7	33 48.2	13.5	12 27.6	13.8	56.5
17	76 02.3	35.7	48 20.7	13.5	12 41.4	13.8	56.5
18	91 02.5	N 3 34.8	62 53.2	13.5	S12 55.2	13.7	56.5
19	106 02.7	33.8	77 25.7	13.5	13 08.9	13.6	56.4
20	121 02.9	32.9	91 58.2	13.4	13 22.5	13.5	56.4
21	136 03.2	. . 31.9	106 30.6	13.4	13 36.0	13.5	56.4
22	151 03.4	31.0	121 03.0	13.4	13 49.5	13.4	56.3
23	166 03.6	30.0	135 35.4	13.3	14 02.9	13.3	56.3
14 00 MONDAY	181 03.8	N 3 29.0	150 07.7	13.4	S14 16.2	13.2	56.3
01	196 04.1	28.1	164 40.1	13.3	14 29.4	13.1	56.3
02	211 04.3	27.1	179 12.4	13.2	14 42.5	13.1	56.2
03	226 04.5	. . 26.2	193 44.6	13.3	14 55.6	13.0	56.2
04	241 04.7	25.2	208 16.9	13.2	15 08.6	12.9	56.2
05	256 04.9	24.2	222 49.1	13.2	15 21.5	12.8	56.1
06	271 05.2	N 3 23.3	237 21.3	13.1	S15 34.3	12.8	56.1
07	286 05.4	22.3	251 53.4	13.1	15 47.1	12.6	56.1
08	301 05.6	21.4	266 25.5	13.1	15 59.7	12.6	56.1
09	316 05.8	. . 20.4	280 57.6	13.1	16 12.3	12.5	56.0
10	331 06.0	19.4	295 29.7	13.0	16 24.8	12.4	56.0
11	346 06.3	18.5	310 01.7	13.0	16 37.2	12.3	56.0
12	1 06.5	N 3 17.5	324 33.7	13.0	S16 49.5	12.3	55.9
13	16 06.7	16.6	339 05.7	12.9	17 01.8	12.1	55.9
14	31 06.9	15.6	353 37.6	12.9	17 13.9	12.0	55.9
15	46 07.2	. . 14.6	8 09.5	12.8	17 25.9	12.0	55.9
16	61 07.4	13.7	22 41.3	12.9	17 37.9	11.9	55.8
17	76 07.6	12.7	37 13.2	12.7	17 49.8	11.7	55.8
18	91 07.8	N 3 11.8	51 44.9	12.8	S18 01.5	11.7	55.8
19	106 08.0	10.8	66 16.7	12.7	18 13.2	11.6	55.8
20	121 08.3	09.8	80 48.4	12.7	18 24.8	11.5	55.7
21	136 08.5	. . 08.9	95 20.1	12.6	18 36.3	11.4	55.7
22	151 08.7	07.9	109 51.7	12.6	18 47.7	11.3	55.7
23	166 08.9	07.0	124 23.3	12.6	18 59.0	11.2	55.7
15 00 TUESDAY	181 09.2	N 3 06.0	138 54.9	12.5	S19 10.2	11.1	55.6
01	196 09.4	05.0	153 26.4	12.5	19 21.3	11.0	55.6
02	211 09.6	04.1	167 57.9	12.4	19 32.3	11.0	55.6
03	226 09.8	. . 03.1	182 29.3	12.4	19 43.3	10.8	55.6
04	241 10.1	02.1	197 00.7	12.4	19 54.1	10.7	55.5
05	256 10.3	01.2	211 32.1	12.3	20 04.8	10.6	55.5
06	271 10.5	N 3 00.2	226 03.4	12.3	S20 15.4	10.5	55.5
07	286 10.7	2 59.3	240 34.7	12.2	20 25.9	10.4	55.5
08	301 10.9	58.3	255 05.9	12.2	20 36.3	10.3	55.4
09	316 11.2	. . 57.3	269 37.1	12.2	20 46.6	10.2	55.4
10	331 11.4	56.4	284 08.3	12.1	20 56.8	10.1	55.4
11	346 11.6	55.4	298 39.4	12.1	21 06.9	10.0	55.4
12	1 11.8	N 2 54.4	313 10.5	12.0	S21 16.9	9.9	55.3
13	16 12.1	53.5	327 41.5	12.0	21 26.8	9.7	55.3
14	31 12.3	52.5	342 12.5	11.9	21 36.5	9.7	55.3
15	46 12.5	. . 51.6	356 43.4	11.9	21 46.2	9.6	55.3
16	61 12.7	50.6	11 14.3	11.9	21 55.8	9.4	55.2
17	76 12.9	49.6	25 45.2	11.8	22 05.2	9.3	55.2
18	91 13.2	N 2 48.7	40 16.0	11.8	S22 14.5	9.3	55.2
19	106 13.4	47.7	54 46.8	11.7	22 23.8	9.1	55.2
20	121 13.6	46.7	69 17.5	11.7	22 32.9	9.0	55.2
21	136 13.8	. . 45.8	83 48.2	11.7	22 41.9	8.9	55.1
22	151 14.1	44.8	98 18.9	11.6	22 50.8	8.8	55.1
23	166 14.3	43.9	112 49.5	11.6	S22 59.6	8.6	55.1
	SD 15.9	*d* 1.0	SD	15.4	15.2		15.1

Lat.	Twilight Naut.	Twilight Civil	Sunrise	Moonrise 13	Moonrise 14	Moonrise 15	Moonrise 16
°	h m	h m	h m	h m	h m	h m	h m
N 72	01 59	03 50	05 02	10 04	13 12	■	■
N 70	02 33	04 03	05 08	09 44	12 10	■	■
68	02 56	04 15	05 13	09 29	11 35	14 42	■
66	03 15	04 24	05 17	09 16	11 11	13 21	■
64	03 29	04 31	05 20	09 06	10 52	12 44	14 58
62	03 41	04 37	05 23	08 57	10 36	12 18	14 05
60	03 50	04 43	05 25	08 50	10 23	11 58	13 33
N 58	03 59	04 48	05 28	08 43	10 12	11 42	13 09
56	04 06	04 52	05 29	08 37	10 03	11 28	12 50
54	04 12	04 55	05 31	08 32	09 54	11 16	12 34
52	04 18	04 59	05 33	08 28	09 47	11 05	12 21
50	04 23	05 02	05 34	08 24	09 40	10 56	12 09
45	04 33	05 08	05 37	08 15	09 26	10 36	11 44
N 40	04 41	05 13	05 40	08 07	09 14	10 20	11 24
35	04 47	05 17	05 42	08 01	09 04	10 06	11 08
30	04 52	05 20	05 44	07 55	08 55	09 55	10 54
20	04 59	05 25	05 47	07 46	08 40	09 35	10 30
N 10	05 04	05 29	05 50	07 37	08 27	09 18	10 10
0	05 08	05 32	05 52	07 30	08 15	09 02	09 51
S 10	05 09	05 34	05 55	07 22	08 03	08 46	09 32
20	05 10	05 35	05 57	07 14	07 51	08 29	09 11
30	05 08	05 36	06 00	07 05	07 36	08 10	08 48
35	05 07	05 36	06 01	07 00	07 28	07 59	08 34
40	05 04	05 36	06 03	06 54	07 19	07 46	08 19
45	05 01	05 35	06 05	06 47	07 08	07 31	08 00
S 50	04 57	05 35	06 07	06 39	06 54	07 13	07 37
52	04 55	05 34	06 08	06 35	06 48	07 05	07 26
54	04 52	05 34	06 09	06 31	06 42	06 55	07 14
56	04 50	05 33	06 10	06 26	06 34	06 44	06 59
58	04 46	05 32	06 11	06 21	06 26	06 32	06 43
S 60	04 43	05 31	06 12	06 16	06 16	06 18	06 23

Lat.	Sunset	Twilight Civil	Twilight Naut.	Moonset 13	Moonset 14	Moonset 15	Moonset 16
°	h m	h m	h m	h m	h m	h m	h m
N 72	18 46	19 58	21 45	16 49	15 18	■	■
N 70	18 41	19 45	21 13	17 12	16 22	■	■
68	18 36	19 34	20 51	17 29	16 58	15 30	■
66	18 33	19 25	20 33	17 43	17 24	16 52	■
64	18 29	19 18	20 20	17 55	17 44	17 30	16 58
62	18 27	19 12	20 08	18 05	18 01	17 56	17 51
60	18 24	19 07	19 59	18 14	18 15	18 17	18 24
N 58	18 22	19 02	19 51	18 21	18 27	18 35	18 48
56	18 20	18 58	19 44	18 28	18 37	18 49	19 07
54	18 19	18 54	19 37	18 34	18 46	19 02	19 24
52	18 17	18 51	19 32	18 40	18 54	19 13	19 38
50	18 16	18 48	19 27	18 45	19 02	19 23	19 50
45	18 13	18 42	19 17	18 55	19 18	19 44	20 16
N 40	18 11	18 38	19 10	19 05	19 31	20 01	20 36
35	18 09	18 34	19 04	19 12	19 42	20 15	20 53
30	18 07	18 31	18 59	19 19	19 52	20 28	21 08
20	18 04	18 26	18 51	19 31	20 09	20 49	21 33
N 10	18 01	18 22	18 47	19 42	20 24	21 08	21 54
0	17 59	18 20	18 44	19 51	20 37	21 25	22 15
S 10	17 57	18 18	18 42	20 01	20 52	21 43	22 35
20	17 54	18 16	18 42	20 12	21 07	22 02	22 57
30	17 52	18 16	18 44	20 24	21 24	22 23	23 22
35	17 51	18 16	18 45	20 31	21 34	22 36	23 37
40	17 49	18 16	18 48	20 39	21 46	22 51	23 54
45	17 47	18 17	18 51	20 49	21 59	23 09	24 15
S 50	17 45	18 18	18 55	21 00	22 16	23 31	24 42
52	17 45	18 18	18 57	21 06	22 24	23 42	24 55
54	17 44	18 19	19 00	21 12	22 33	23 53	25 10
56	17 42	18 19	19 03	21 18	22 43	24 07	00 07
58	17 41	18 20	19 06	21 26	22 55	24 23	00 23
S 60	17 40	18 21	19 10	21 34	23 08	24 43	00 43

Day	SUN Eqn. of Time 00^h	SUN Eqn. of Time 12^h	SUN Mer. Pass.	MOON Mer. Pass. Upper	MOON Mer. Pass. Lower	Age	Phase
d	m s	m s	h m	h m	h m	d	%
13	03 54	04 04	11 56	13 41	01 18	02	7
14	04 15	04 26	11 56	14 26	02 03	03	13
15	04 36	04 47	11 55	15 14	02 50	04	20

Day	UT (d h)	ARIES GHA	VENUS −4·8 GHA	VENUS Dec	MARS +1·2 GHA	MARS Dec	JUPITER −1·8 GHA	JUPITER Dec	SATURN +0·4 GHA	SATURN Dec
		° ′	° ′	° ′	° ′	° ′	° ′	° ′	° ′	° ′
WEDNESDAY	16 00	354 57.6	145 41.7	S17 39.6	240 16.6	N22 16.7	215 34.2	N16 20.8	342 13.0	N 2 32.5
	01	10 00.1	160 42.9	40.4	255 17.4	16.5	230 36.1	20.6	357 15.6	32.5
	02	25 02.5	175 44.2	41.2	270 18.3	16.2	245 38.1	20.5	12 18.2	32.4
	03	40 05.0	190 45.5	. . 41.9	285 19.1	. . 16.0	260 40.1	. . 20.3	27 20.9	. . 32.3
	04	55 07.5	205 46.7	42.7	300 19.9	15.8	275 42.0	20.2	42 23.5	32.2
	05	70 09.9	220 48.0	43.5	315 20.7	15.6	290 44.0	20.1	57 26.1	32.2
	06	85 12.4	235 49.3	S17 44.2	330 21.6	N22 15.4	305 46.0	N16 19.9	72 28.8	N 2 32.1
	07	100 14.9	250 50.5	45.0	345 22.4	15.2	320 48.0	19.8	87 31.4	32.0
	08	115 17.3	265 51.8	45.8	0 23.2	15.0	335 49.9	19.6	102 34.0	31.9
	09	130 19.8	280 53.1	. . 46.5	15 24.1	. . 14.7	350 51.9	. . 19.5	117 36.6	. . 31.9
	10	145 22.2	295 54.4	47.3	30 24.9	14.5	5 53.9	19.3	132 39.3	31.8
	11	160 24.7	310 55.7	48.1	45 25.7	14.3	20 55.9	19.2	147 41.9	31.7
	12	175 27.2	325 56.9	S17 48.8	60 26.6	N22 14.1	35 57.8	N16 19.1	162 44.5	N 2 31.6
	13	190 29.6	340 58.2	49.6	75 27.4	13.9	50 59.8	18.9	177 47.1	31.6
	14	205 32.1	355 59.5	50.3	90 28.2	13.7	66 01.8	18.8	192 49.8	31.5
	15	220 34.6	11 00.8	. . 51.1	105 29.1	. . 13.4	81 03.8	. . 18.6	207 52.4	. . 31.4
	16	235 37.0	26 02.1	51.9	120 29.9	13.2	96 05.7	18.5	222 55.0	31.3
	17	250 39.5	41 03.4	52.6	135 30.8	13.0	111 07.7	18.3	237 57.7	31.3
	18	265 42.0	56 04.7	S17 53.4	150 31.6	N22 12.8	126 09.7	N16 18.2	253 00.3	N 2 31.2
	19	280 44.4	71 06.0	54.1	165 32.4	12.6	141 11.7	18.0	268 02.9	31.1
	20	295 46.9	86 07.3	54.9	180 33.3	12.3	156 13.6	17.9	283 05.5	31.0
	21	310 49.4	101 08.6	. . 55.6	195 34.1	. . 12.1	171 15.6	. . 17.8	298 08.2	. . 31.0
	22	325 51.8	116 09.9	56.4	210 34.9	11.9	186 17.6	17.6	313 10.8	30.9
	23	340 54.3	131 11.2	57.1	225 35.8	11.7	201 19.6	17.5	328 13.4	30.8
THURSDAY	17 00	355 56.7	146 12.5	S17 57.9	240 36.6	N22 11.5	216 21.5	N16 17.3	343 16.1	N 2 30.7
	01	10 59.2	161 13.8	58.6	255 37.4	11.2	231 23.5	17.2	358 18.7	30.7
	02	26 01.7	176 15.2	17 59.4	270 38.3	11.0	246 25.5	17.0	13 21.3	30.6
	03	41 04.1	191 16.5	18 00.1	285 39.1	. . 10.8	261 27.5	. . 16.9	28 23.9	. . 30.5
	04	56 06.6	206 17.8	00.8	300 40.0	10.6	276 29.4	16.8	43 26.6	30.4
	05	71 09.1	221 19.1	01.6	315 40.8	10.4	291 31.4	16.6	58 29.2	30.4
	06	86 11.5	236 20.4	S18 02.3	330 41.6	N22 10.1	306 33.4	N16 16.5	73 31.8	N 2 30.3
	07	101 14.0	251 21.8	03.1	345 42.5	09.9	321 35.4	16.3	88 34.5	30.2
	08	116 16.5	266 23.1	03.8	0 43.3	09.7	336 37.3	16.2	103 37.1	30.1
	09	131 18.9	281 24.4	. . 04.6	15 44.2	. . 09.5	351 39.3	. . 16.0	118 39.7	. . 30.1
	10	146 21.4	296 25.8	05.3	30 45.0	09.3	6 41.3	15.9	133 42.3	30.0
	11	161 23.9	311 27.1	06.0	45 45.8	09.0	21 43.3	15.8	148 45.0	29.9
	12	176 26.3	326 28.4	S18 06.8	60 46.7	N22 08.8	36 45.2	N16 15.6	163 47.6	N 2 29.8
	13	191 28.8	341 29.8	07.5	75 47.5	08.6	51 47.2	15.5	178 50.2	29.8
	14	206 31.2	356 31.1	08.2	90 48.4	08.4	66 49.2	15.3	193 52.9	29.7
	15	221 33.7	11 32.5	. . 09.0	105 49.2	. . 08.2	81 51.2	. . 15.2	208 55.5	. . 29.6
	16	236 36.2	26 33.8	09.7	120 50.0	07.9	96 53.1	15.0	223 58.1	29.5
	17	251 38.6	41 35.2	10.4	135 50.9	07.7	111 55.1	14.9	239 00.7	29.5
	18	266 41.1	56 36.5	S18 11.2	150 51.7	N22 07.5	126 57.1	N16 14.8	254 03.4	N 2 29.4
	19	281 43.6	71 37.9	11.9	165 52.6	07.3	141 59.1	14.6	269 06.0	29.3
	20	296 46.0	86 39.2	12.6	180 53.4	07.0	157 01.1	14.5	284 08.6	29.2
	21	311 48.5	101 40.6	. . 13.3	195 54.3	. . 06.8	172 03.0	. . 14.3	299 11.3	. . 29.2
	22	326 51.0	116 41.9	14.1	210 55.1	06.6	187 05.0	14.2	314 13.9	29.1
	23	341 53.4	131 43.3	14.8	225 55.9	06.4	202 07.0	14.0	329 16.5	29.0
FRIDAY	18 00	356 55.9	146 44.7	S18 15.5	240 56.8	N22 06.1	217 09.0	N16 13.9	344 19.2	N 2 28.9
	01	11 58.3	161 46.0	16.2	255 57.6	05.9	232 10.9	13.8	359 21.8	28.9
	02	27 00.8	176 47.4	17.0	270 58.5	05.7	247 12.9	13.6	14 24.4	28.8
	03	42 03.3	191 48.8	. . 17.7	285 59.3	. . 05.5	262 14.9	. . 13.5	29 27.0	. . 28.7
	04	57 05.7	206 50.2	18.4	301 00.2	05.2	277 16.9	13.3	44 29.7	28.6
	05	72 08.2	221 51.5	19.1	316 01.0	05.0	292 18.9	13.2	59 32.3	28.6
	06	87 10.7	236 52.9	S18 19.8	331 01.9	N22 04.8	307 20.8	N16 13.0	74 34.9	N 2 28.5
	07	102 13.1	251 54.3	20.5	346 02.7	04.6	322 22.8	12.9	89 37.6	28.4
	08	117 15.6	266 55.7	21.3	1 03.6	04.3	337 24.8	12.8	104 40.2	28.3
	09	132 18.1	281 57.1	. . 22.0	16 04.4	. . 04.1	352 26.8	. . 12.6	119 42.8	. . 28.3
	10	147 20.5	296 58.5	22.7	31 05.2	03.9	7 28.8	12.5	134 45.5	28.2
	11	162 23.0	311 59.9	23.4	46 06.1	03.7	22 30.7	12.3	149 48.1	28.1
	12	177 25.5	327 01.3	S18 24.1	61 06.9	N22 03.4	37 32.7	N16 12.2	164 50.7	N 2 28.0
	13	192 27.9	342 02.7	24.8	76 07.8	03.2	52 34.7	12.0	179 53.4	28.0
	14	207 30.4	357 04.1	25.5	91 08.6	03.0	67 36.7	11.9	194 56.0	27.9
	15	222 32.8	12 05.5	. . 26.2	106 09.5	. . 02.7	82 38.7	. . 11.8	209 58.6	. . 27.8
	16	237 35.3	27 06.9	26.9	121 10.3	02.5	97 40.6	11.6	225 01.3	27.7
	17	252 37.8	42 08.3	27.6	136 11.2	02.3	112 42.6	11.5	240 03.9	27.7
	18	267 40.2	57 09.7	S18 28.3	151 12.0	N22 02.1	127 44.6	N16 11.3	255 06.5	N 2 27.6
	19	282 42.7	72 11.1	29.0	166 12.9	01.8	142 46.6	11.2	270 09.1	27.5
	20	297 45.2	87 12.5	29.7	181 13.7	01.6	157 48.6	11.0	285 11.8	27.4
	21	312 47.6	102 13.9	. . 30.4	196 14.6	. . 01.4	172 50.5	. . 10.9	300 14.4	. . 27.4
	22	327 50.1	117 15.3	31.1	211 15.4	01.1	187 52.5	10.8	315 17.0	27.3
	23	342 52.6	132 16.8	31.8	226 16.3	00.9	202 54.5	10.6	330 19.7	27.2
	Mer. Pass.	h m 0 16.2	v 1.3	d 0.7	v 0.8	d 0.2	v 2.0	d 0.1	v 2.6	d 0.1

STARS

Name	SHA	Dec
	° ′	° ′
Acamar	315 10.4	S40 11.5
Achernar	335 18.6	S57 05.8
Acrux	172 59.2	S63 14.9
Adhara	255 04.9	S29 00.2
Aldebaran	290 37.9	N16 33.8
Alioth	166 12.3	N55 49.0
Alkaid	152 51.3	N49 10.9
Alnair	27 30.7	S46 49.8
Alnilam	275 36.3	S 1 10.9
Alphard	217 46.7	S 8 46.3
Alphecca	126 02.7	N26 37.7
Alpheratz	357 33.0	N29 14.4
Altair	61 58.4	N 8 56.5
Ankaa	353 05.3	S42 09.4
Antares	112 14.2	S26 29.5
Arcturus	145 46.9	N19 02.7
Atria	107 07.3	S69 04.7
Avior	234 14.6	S59 35.4
Bellatrix	278 21.4	N 6 22.5
Betelgeuse	270 50.6	N 7 24.8
Canopus	263 51.9	S52 42.2
Capella	280 19.8	N46 01.3
Deneb	49 24.5	N45 22.8
Denebola	182 23.8	N14 25.4
Diphda	348 45.6	S17 50.2
Dubhe	193 40.0	N61 36.4
Elnath	278 00.1	N28 37.8
Eltanin	90 41.5	N51 29.4
Enif	33 37.1	N10 00.0
Fomalhaut	15 12.6	S29 28.7
Gacrux	171 50.7	S57 15.8
Gienah	175 42.5	S17 41.4
Hadar	148 34.5	S60 30.2
Hamal	327 49.3	N23 35.4
Kaus Aust.	83 30.6	S34 22.4
Kochab	137 20.6	N74 02.9
Markab	13 28.2	N15 21.1
Menkar	314 04.5	N 4 11.8
Menkent	147 56.3	S36 30.1
Miaplacidus	221 38.7	S69 49.4
Mirfak	308 26.0	N49 57.3
Nunki	75 45.9	S26 15.8
Peacock	53 03.1	S56 39.0
Pollux	243 15.8	N27 57.7
Procyon	244 49.5	N 5 09.5
Rasalhague	95 57.3	N12 32.6
Regulus	207 33.3	N11 50.3
Rigel	281 02.5	S 8 10.0
Rigil Kent.	139 38.8	S60 56.9
Sabik	102 01.2	S15 45.4
Schedar	349 28.9	N56 41.1
Shaula	96 08.5	S37 07.5
Sirius	258 25.1	S16 44.9
Spica	158 21.1	S11 18.0
Suhail	222 45.6	S43 32.2
Vega	80 32.2	N38 48.8
Zuben'ubi	136 54.7	S16 09.1

	SHA	Mer. Pass.
	° ′	h m
Venus	150 15.8	14 14
Mars	244 39.9	7 57
Jupiter	220 24.8	9 33
Saturn	347 19.3	1 07

UT	SUN GHA	SUN Dec	MOON GHA	v	MOON Dec	d	HP
d h	° ′	° ′	° ′	′	° ′	′	′
16 00 (WEDNESDAY)	181 14.5	N 2 42.9	127 20.1	11.5	S23 08.2	8.6	55.1
01	196 14.7	41.9	141 50.6	11.5	23 16.8	8.4	55.0
02	211 15.0	41.0	156 21.1	11.5	23 25.2	8.3	55.0
03	226 15.2	. . 40.0	170 51.6	11.4	23 33.5	8.2	55.0
04	241 15.4	39.0	185 22.0	11.3	23 41.7	8.1	55.0
05	256 15.6	38.1	199 52.3	11.4	23 49.8	8.0	55.0
06	271 15.8	N 2 37.1	214 22.7	11.2	S23 57.8	7.9	54.9
07	286 16.1	36.1	228 52.9	11.3	24 05.7	7.7	54.9
08	301 16.3	35.2	243 23.2	11.2	24 13.4	7.6	54.9
09	316 16.5	. . 34.2	257 53.4	11.2	24 21.0	7.5	54.9
10	331 16.7	33.3	272 23.6	11.1	24 28.5	7.4	54.9
11	346 17.0	32.3	286 53.7	11.1	24 35.9	7.2	54.9
12	1 17.2	N 2 31.3	301 23.8	11.0	S24 43.1	7.2	54.8
13	16 17.4	30.4	315 53.8	11.0	24 50.3	7.0	54.8
14	31 17.6	29.4	330 23.8	11.0	24 57.3	6.9	54.8
15	46 17.8	. . 28.4	344 53.8	10.9	25 04.2	6.7	54.8
16	61 18.1	27.5	359 23.7	10.9	25 10.9	6.7	54.8
17	76 18.3	26.5	13 53.6	10.9	25 17.6	6.5	54.7
18	91 18.5	N 2 25.5	28 23.5	10.8	S25 24.1	6.4	54.7
19	106 18.7	24.6	42 53.3	10.8	25 30.5	6.2	54.7
20	121 19.0	23.6	57 23.1	10.7	25 36.7	6.2	54.7
21	136 19.2	. . 22.6	71 52.8	10.7	25 42.9	6.0	54.7
22	151 19.4	21.7	86 22.5	10.7	25 48.9	5.9	54.7
23	166 19.6	20.7	100 52.2	10.7	25 54.8	5.8	54.6
17 00 (THURSDAY)	181 19.9	N 2 19.7	115 21.9	10.6	S26 00.6	5.6	54.6
01	196 20.1	18.8	129 51.5	10.6	26 06.2	5.5	54.6
02	211 20.3	17.8	144 21.1	10.5	26 11.7	5.4	54.6
03	226 20.5	. . 16.8	158 50.6	10.5	26 17.1	5.3	54.6
04	241 20.8	15.9	173 20.1	10.5	26 22.4	5.1	54.6
05	256 21.0	14.9	187 49.6	10.5	26 27.5	5.0	54.6
06	271 21.2	N 2 13.9	202 19.1	10.4	S26 32.5	4.8	54.5
07	286 21.4	13.0	216 48.5	10.4	26 37.3	4.8	54.5
08	301 21.6	12.0	231 17.9	10.4	26 42.1	4.6	54.5
09	316 21.9	. . 11.0	245 47.3	10.3	26 46.7	4.5	54.5
10	331 22.1	10.1	260 16.6	10.3	26 51.2	4.3	54.5
11	346 22.3	09.1	274 45.9	10.3	26 55.5	4.2	54.5
12	1 22.5	N 2 08.1	289 15.2	10.3	S26 59.7	4.1	54.5
13	16 22.8	07.2	303 44.5	10.2	27 03.8	4.0	54.5
14	31 23.0	06.2	318 13.7	10.2	27 07.8	3.8	54.5
15	46 23.2	. . 05.2	332 42.9	10.2	27 11.6	3.7	54.4
16	61 23.4	04.3	347 12.1	10.2	27 15.3	3.5	54.4
17	76 23.7	03.3	1 41.3	10.1	27 18.8	3.4	54.4
18	91 23.9	N 2 02.3	16 10.4	10.2	S27 22.2	3.3	54.4
19	106 24.1	01.4	30 39.6	10.1	27 25.5	3.2	54.4
20	121 24.3	2 00.4	45 08.7	10.1	27 28.7	3.0	54.4
21	136 24.5	1 59.4	59 37.8	10.0	27 31.7	2.9	54.4
22	151 24.8	58.5	74 06.8	10.1	27 34.6	2.7	54.4
23	166 25.0	57.5	88 35.9	10.0	27 37.3	2.6	54.4
18 00 (FRIDAY)	181 25.2	N 1 56.5	103 04.9	10.1	S27 39.9	2.5	54.4
01	196 25.4	55.6	117 34.0	10.0	27 42.4	2.4	54.3
02	211 25.7	54.6	132 03.0	10.0	27 44.8	2.2	54.3
03	226 25.9	. . 53.6	146 32.0	10.0	27 47.0	2.1	54.3
04	241 26.1	52.7	161 01.0	9.9	27 49.1	1.9	54.3
05	256 26.3	51.7	175 29.9	10.0	27 51.0	1.8	54.3
06	271 26.6	N 1 50.7	189 58.9	10.0	S27 52.8	1.7	54.3
07	286 26.8	49.8	204 27.9	9.9	27 54.5	1.5	54.3
08	301 27.0	48.8	218 56.8	9.9	27 56.0	1.4	54.3
09	316 27.2	. . 47.8	233 25.7	10.0	27 57.4	1.3	54.3
10	331 27.4	46.9	247 54.7	9.9	27 58.7	1.1	54.3
11	346 27.7	45.9	262 23.6	9.9	27 59.8	1.0	54.3
12	1 27.9	N 1 44.9	276 52.5	9.9	S28 00.8	0.9	54.3
13	16 28.1	44.0	291 21.4	10.0	28 01.7	0.7	54.3
14	31 28.3	43.0	305 50.4	9.9	28 02.4	0.6	54.3
15	46 28.6	. . 42.0	320 19.3	9.9	28 03.0	0.4	54.3
16	61 28.8	41.1	334 48.2	9.9	28 03.4	0.3	54.3
17	76 29.0	40.1	349 17.1	9.9	28 03.7	0.2	54.3
18	91 29.2	N 1 39.1	3 46.0	9.9	S28 03.9	0.1	54.3
19	106 29.5	38.1	18 14.9	10.0	28 04.0	0.1	54.3
20	121 29.7	37.2	32 43.9	9.9	28 03.9	0.3	54.3
21	136 29.9	. . 36.2	47 12.8	9.9	28 03.6	0.3	54.3
22	151 30.1	35.2	61 41.7	9.9	28 03.3	0.5	54.2
23	166 30.3	34.3	76 10.6	10.0	S28 02.8	0.7	54.2
	SD 15.9	*d* 1.0	SD	14.9	14.8		14.8

Lat.	Twilight Naut.	Twilight Civil	Sunrise	Moonrise 16	Moonrise 17	Moonrise 18	Moonrise 19
°	h m	h m	h m	h m	h m	h m	h m
N 72	02 23	04 05	05 16	▬▬	▬▬	▬▬	▬▬
N 70	02 51	04 17	05 20	▬▬	▬▬	▬▬	▬▬
68	03 11	04 26	05 23	▬▬	▬▬	▬▬	▬▬
66	03 27	04 34	05 26	▬▬	▬▬	▬▬	▬▬
64	03 40	04 40	05 29	14 58	▬▬	▬▬	▬▬
62	03 50	04 46	05 31	14 05	15 57	▬▬	17 50
60	03 59	04 50	05 32	13 33	15 03	16 13	16 52
N 58	04 06	04 54	05 34	13 09	14 30	15 36	16 19
56	04 13	04 58	05 35	12 50	14 06	15 09	15 54
54	04 18	05 01	05 37	12 34	13 47	14 48	15 34
52	04 23	05 04	05 38	12 21	13 31	14 31	15 18
50	04 28	05 06	05 39	12 09	13 17	14 16	15 03
45	04 37	05 11	05 41	11 44	12 48	13 46	14 34
N 40	04 44	05 16	05 43	11 24	12 26	13 22	14 12
35	04 49	05 19	05 44	11 08	12 07	13 03	13 53
30	04 54	05 22	05 46	10 54	11 52	12 46	13 36
20	05 00	05 26	05 48	10 30	11 25	12 18	13 09
N 10	05 04	05 29	05 50	10 10	11 02	11 54	12 45
0	05 07	05 31	05 51	09 51	10 41	11 32	12 23
S 10	05 07	05 32	05 53	09 32	10 19	11 10	12 01
20	05 07	05 32	05 54	09 11	09 57	10 46	11 38
30	05 04	05 32	05 56	08 48	09 31	10 18	11 10
35	05 02	05 32	05 57	08 34	09 15	10 02	10 54
40	04 59	05 31	05 58	08 19	08 57	09 43	10 35
45	04 56	05 30	05 59	08 00	08 36	09 19	10 12
S 50	04 50	05 28	06 00	07 37	08 09	08 50	09 42
52	04 48	05 27	06 01	07 26	07 55	08 35	09 28
54	04 45	05 26	06 01	07 14	07 40	08 18	09 11
56	04 41	05 25	06 02	06 59	07 22	07 58	08 51
58	04 38	05 24	06 03	06 43	07 01	07 33	08 25
S 60	04 33	05 22	06 03	06 23	06 33	06 58	07 50

Lat.	Sunset	Twilight Civil	Twilight Naut.	Moonset 16	Moonset 17	Moonset 18	Moonset 19
°	h m	h m	h m	h m	h m	h m	h m
N 72	18 30	19 40	21 19	▬▬	▬▬	▬▬	▬▬
N 70	18 27	19 29	20 53	▬▬	▬▬	▬▬	▬▬
68	18 24	19 20	20 34	▬▬	▬▬	▬▬	▬▬
66	18 21	19 13	20 19	▬▬	▬▬	▬▬	▬▬
64	18 19	19 07	20 07	16 58	▬▬	▬▬	▬▬
62	18 17	19 02	19 57	17 51	17 44	▬▬	19 25
60	18 15	18 57	19 48	18 24	18 39	19 16	20 23
N 58	18 14	18 53	19 41	18 48	19 12	19 53	20 56
56	18 12	18 50	19 35	19 07	19 36	20 20	21 21
54	18 11	18 47	19 29	19 24	19 55	20 41	21 40
52	18 10	18 44	19 24	19 38	20 12	20 58	21 57
50	18 09	18 42	19 20	19 50	20 26	21 13	22 11
45	18 07	18 37	19 11	20 16	20 55	21 43	22 40
N 40	18 06	18 33	19 05	20 36	21 18	22 07	23 02
35	18 04	18 29	18 59	20 53	21 36	22 26	23 21
30	18 03	18 27	18 55	21 08	21 53	22 43	23 37
20	18 01	18 23	18 49	21 33	22 20	23 10	24 03
N 10	17 59	18 20	18 45	21 54	22 43	23 35	24 27
0	17 58	18 18	18 42	22 15	23 05	23 57	24 48
S 10	17 56	18 17	18 42	22 35	23 27	24 19	00 19
20	17 55	18 17	18 43	22 57	23 51	24 43	00 43
30	17 54	18 17	18 45	23 22	24 18	00 18	01 11
35	17 53	18 18	18 47	23 37	24 35	00 35	01 27
40	17 52	18 19	18 50	23 54	24 53	00 53	01 46
45	17 51	18 20	18 54	24 15	00 15	01 16	02 10
S 50	17 50	18 22	19 00	24 42	00 42	01 46	02 39
52	17 49	18 23	19 02	24 55	00 55	02 00	02 54
54	17 49	18 24	19 06	25 10	01 10	02 17	03 11
56	17 48	18 25	19 09	00 07	01 27	02 37	03 31
58	17 48	18 27	19 13	00 23	01 48	03 02	03 57
S 60	17 47	18 28	19 18	00 43	02 16	03 37	04 32

Day	SUN Eqn. of Time 00^h	SUN Eqn. of Time 12^h	SUN Mer. Pass.	MOON Mer. Pass. Upper	MOON Mer. Pass. Lower	Age	Phase
d	m s	m s	h m	h m	h m	d %	
16	04 58	05 08	11 55	16 02	03 38	05 28	
17	05 19	05 30	11 55	16 53	04 28	06 37	
18	05 40	05 51	11 54	17 44	05 19	07 47	

UT d	UT h	ARIES GHA ° ′	VENUS −4·8 GHA ° ′	VENUS Dec ° ′	MARS +1·2 GHA ° ′	MARS Dec ° ′	JUPITER −1·8 GHA ° ′	JUPITER Dec ° ′	SATURN +0·3 GHA ° ′	SATURN Dec ° ′
19	00	357 55.0	147 18.2	S18 32.5	241 17.1	N22 00.7	217 56.5	N16 10.5	345 22.3	N 2 27.1
	01	12 57.5	162 19.6	33.2	256 18.0	00.5	232 58.5	10.3	0 24.9	27.1
	02	28 00.0	177 21.0	33.9	271 18.8	00.2	248 00.4	10.2	15 27.6	27.0
	03	43 02.4	192 22.5	. . 34.6	286 19.7	22 00.0	263 02.4	. . 10.1	30 30.2	. . 26.9
	04	58 04.9	207 23.9	35.3	301 20.5	21 59.8	278 04.4	09.9	45 32.8	26.8
	05	73 07.3	222 25.4	36.0	316 21.4	59.5	293 06.4	09.8	60 35.5	26.8
	06	88 09.8	237 26.8	S18 36.7	331 22.2	N21 59.3	308 08.4	N16 09.6	75 38.1	N 2 26.7
	07	103 12.3	252 28.2	37.4	346 23.1	59.1	323 10.3	09.5	90 40.7	26.6
S	08	118 14.7	267 29.7	38.1	1 23.9	58.8	338 12.3	09.3	105 43.4	26.5
A	09	133 17.2	282 31.1	. . 38.8	16 24.8	. . 58.6	353 14.3	. . 09.2	120 46.0	. . 26.5
T	10	148 19.7	297 32.6	39.4	31 25.7	58.4	8 16.3	09.1	135 48.6	26.4
U	11	163 22.1	312 34.0	40.1	46 26.5	58.1	23 18.3	08.9	150 51.3	26.3
R	12	178 24.6	327 35.5	S18 40.8	61 27.4	N21 57.9	38 20.3	N16 08.8	165 53.9	N 2 26.2
D	13	193 27.1	342 36.9	41.5	76 28.2	57.7	53 22.2	08.6	180 56.5	26.2
A	14	208 29.5	357 38.4	42.2	91 29.1	57.4	68 24.2	08.5	195 59.2	26.1
Y	15	223 32.0	12 39.9	. . 42.9	106 29.9	. . 57.2	83 26.2	. . 08.3	211 01.8	. . 26.0
	16	238 34.5	27 41.3	43.5	121 30.8	57.0	98 28.2	08.2	226 04.4	25.9
	17	253 36.9	42 42.8	44.2	136 31.6	56.7	113 30.2	08.1	241 07.1	25.9
	18	268 39.4	57 44.3	S18 44.9	151 32.5	N21 56.5	128 32.2	N16 07.9	256 09.7	N 2 25.8
	19	283 41.8	72 45.7	45.6	166 33.3	56.3	143 34.1	07.8	271 12.3	25.7
	20	298 44.3	87 47.2	46.2	181 34.2	56.0	158 36.1	07.6	286 15.0	25.6
	21	313 46.8	102 48.7	. . 46.9	196 35.1	. . 55.8	173 38.1	. . 07.5	301 17.6	. . 25.5
	22	328 49.2	117 50.2	47.6	211 35.9	55.6	188 40.1	07.4	316 20.2	25.5
	23	343 51.7	132 51.7	48.3	226 36.8	55.3	203 42.1	07.2	331 22.9	25.4
20	00	358 54.2	147 53.1	S18 48.9	241 37.6	N21 55.1	218 44.1	N16 07.1	346 25.5	N 2 25.3
	01	13 56.6	162 54.6	49.6	256 38.5	54.9	233 46.0	06.9	1 28.1	25.2
	02	28 59.1	177 56.1	50.3	271 39.3	54.6	248 48.0	06.8	16 30.8	25.2
	03	44 01.6	192 57.6	. . 50.9	286 40.2	. . 54.4	263 50.0	. . 06.6	31 33.4	. . 25.1
	04	59 04.0	207 59.1	51.6	301 41.1	54.2	278 52.0	06.5	46 36.0	25.0
	05	74 06.5	223 00.6	52.3	316 41.9	53.9	293 54.0	06.4	61 38.7	24.9
	06	89 08.9	238 02.1	S18 52.9	331 42.8	N21 53.7	308 56.0	N16 06.2	76 41.3	N 2 24.9
	07	104 11.4	253 03.6	53.6	346 43.6	53.5	323 58.0	06.1	91 43.9	24.8
	08	119 13.9	268 05.1	54.2	1 44.5	53.2	338 59.9	05.9	106 46.6	24.7
S	09	134 16.3	283 06.6	. . 54.9	16 45.4	. . 53.0	354 01.9	. . 05.8	121 49.2	. . 24.6
U	10	149 18.8	298 08.1	55.6	31 46.2	52.7	9 03.9	05.7	136 51.8	24.6
N	11	164 21.3	313 09.6	56.2	46 47.1	52.5	24 05.9	05.5	151 54.5	24.5
D	12	179 23.7	328 11.2	S18 56.9	61 47.9	N21 52.3	39 07.9	N16 05.4	166 57.1	N 2 24.4
A	13	194 26.2	343 12.7	57.5	76 48.8	52.0	54 09.9	05.2	181 59.7	24.3
Y	14	209 28.7	358 14.2	58.2	91 49.7	51.8	69 11.9	05.1	197 02.4	24.3
	15	224 31.1	13 15.7	. . 58.8	106 50.5	. . 51.6	84 13.8	. . 04.9	212 05.0	. . 24.2
	16	239 33.6	28 17.3	18 59.5	121 51.4	51.3	99 15.8	04.8	227 07.6	24.1
	17	254 36.1	43 18.8	19 00.1	136 52.3	51.1	114 17.8	04.7	242 10.3	24.0
	18	269 38.5	58 20.3	S19 00.8	151 53.1	N21 50.8	129 19.8	N16 04.5	257 12.9	N 2 24.0
	19	284 41.0	73 21.9	01.4	166 54.0	50.6	144 21.8	04.4	272 15.5	23.9
	20	299 43.4	88 23.4	02.1	181 54.8	50.4	159 23.8	04.2	287 18.2	23.8
	21	314 45.9	103 24.9	. . 02.7	196 55.7	. . 50.1	174 25.8	. . 04.1	302 20.8	. . 23.7
	22	329 48.4	118 26.5	03.4	211 56.6	49.9	189 27.7	04.0	317 23.4	23.6
	23	344 50.8	133 28.0	04.0	226 57.4	49.7	204 29.7	03.8	332 26.1	23.6
21	00	359 53.3	148 29.6	S19 04.6	241 58.3	N21 49.4	219 31.7	N16 03.7	347 28.7	N 2 23.5
	01	14 55.8	163 31.1	05.3	256 59.2	49.2	234 33.7	03.5	2 31.3	23.4
	02	29 58.2	178 32.7	05.9	272 00.0	48.9	249 35.7	03.4	17 34.0	23.3
	03	45 00.7	193 34.2	. . 06.6	287 00.9	. . 48.7	264 37.7	. . 03.3	32 36.6	. . 23.3
	04	60 03.2	208 35.8	07.2	302 01.8	48.4	279 39.7	03.1	47 39.2	23.2
	05	75 05.6	223 37.4	07.8	317 02.6	48.2	294 41.7	03.0	62 41.9	23.1
	06	90 08.1	238 38.9	S19 08.5	332 03.5	N21 48.0	309 43.6	N16 02.8	77 44.5	N 2 23.0
	07	105 10.6	253 40.5	09.1	347 04.4	47.7	324 45.6	02.7	92 47.1	23.0
	08	120 13.0	268 42.1	09.7	2 05.2	47.5	339 47.6	02.5	107 49.8	22.9
M	09	135 15.5	283 43.6	. . 10.4	17 06.1	. . 47.2	354 49.6	. . 02.4	122 52.4	. . 22.8
O	10	150 17.9	298 45.2	11.0	32 07.0	47.0	9 51.6	02.3	137 55.0	22.7
N	11	165 20.4	313 46.8	11.6	47 07.8	46.8	24 53.6	02.1	152 57.7	22.7
D	12	180 22.9	328 48.4	S19 12.2	62 08.7	N21 46.5	39 55.6	N16 02.0	168 00.3	N 2 22.6
A	13	195 25.3	343 50.0	12.9	77 09.6	46.3	54 57.6	01.8	183 03.0	22.5
Y	14	210 27.8	358 51.5	13.5	92 10.4	46.0	69 59.6	01.7	198 05.6	22.4
	15	225 30.3	13 53.1	. . 14.1	107 11.3	. . 45.8	85 01.5	. . 01.6	213 08.2	. . 22.3
	16	240 32.7	28 54.7	14.7	122 12.2	45.5	100 03.5	01.4	228 10.9	22.3
	17	255 35.2	43 56.3	15.4	137 13.0	45.3	115 05.5	01.3	243 13.5	22.2
	18	270 37.7	58 57.9	S19 16.0	152 13.9	N21 45.1	130 07.5	N16 01.1	258 16.1	N 2 22.1
	19	285 40.1	73 59.5	16.6	167 14.8	44.8	145 09.5	01.0	273 18.8	22.0
	20	300 42.6	89 01.1	17.2	182 15.6	44.6	160 11.5	00.9	288 21.4	22.0
	21	315 45.0	104 02.7	. . 17.8	197 16.5	. . 44.3	175 13.5	. . 00.7	303 24.0	. . 21.9
	22	330 47.5	119 04.3	18.4	212 17.4	44.1	190 15.5	00.6	318 26.7	21.8
	23	345 50.0	134 06.0	19.1	227 18.3	43.8	205 17.5	00.4	333 29.3	21.7
Mer. Pass.		h m 0 04.4	v 1.5	d 0.7	v 0.9	d 0.2	v 2.0	d 0.1	v 2.6	d 0.1

STARS

Name	SHA ° ′	Dec ° ′
Acamar	315 10.4	S40 11.5
Achernar	335 18.6	S57 05.8
Acrux	172 59.2	S63 14.9
Adhara	255 04.9	S29 00.2
Aldebaran	290 37.9	N16 33.8
Alioth	166 12.3	N55 49.0
Alkaid	152 51.3	N49 10.9
Alnair	27 30.7	S46 49.8
Alnilam	275 36.3	S 1 10.9
Alphard	217 46.6	S 8 46.3
Alphecca	126 02.7	N26 37.7
Alpheratz	357 33.0	N29 14.4
Altair	61 58.4	N 8 56.5
Ankaa	353 05.3	S42 09.4
Antares	112 14.2	S26 29.5
Arcturus	145 46.9	N19 02.7
Atria	107 07.3	S69 04.7
Avior	234 14.6	S59 35.4
Bellatrix	278 21.3	N 6 22.5
Betelgeuse	270 50.6	N 7 24.8
Canopus	263 51.8	S52 42.2
Capella	280 19.7	N46 01.3
Deneb	49 24.5	N45 22.8
Denebola	182 23.8	N14 25.4
Diphda	348 45.6	S17 50.2
Dubhe	193 39.9	N61 36.4
Elnath	278 00.1	N28 37.8
Eltanin	90 41.5	N51 29.4
Enif	33 37.1	N10 00.1
Fomalhaut	15 12.6	S29 28.7
Gacrux	171 50.7	S57 15.8
Gienah	175 42.5	S17 41.4
Hadar	148 34.5	S60 30.2
Hamal	327 49.3	N23 35.4
Kaus Aust.	83 30.6	S34 22.4
Kochab	137 20.6	N74 02.9
Markab	13 28.2	N15 21.1
Menkar	314 04.5	N 4 11.8
Menkent	147 56.3	S36 30.1
Miaplacidus	221 38.7	S69 49.4
Mirfak	308 25.9	N49 57.3
Nunki	75 45.9	S26 15.8
Peacock	53 03.2	S56 39.0
Pollux	243 15.8	N27 57.7
Procyon	244 49.5	N 5 09.5
Rasalhague	95 57.3	N12 32.6
Regulus	207 33.2	N11 50.3
Rigel	281 02.5	S 8 10.0
Rigil Kent.	139 38.8	S60 56.9
Sabik	102 01.2	S15 45.4
Schedar	349 28.9	N56 41.1
Shaula	96 08.5	S37 07.5
Sirius	258 25.1	S16 44.9
Spica	158 21.1	S11 18.0
Suhail	222 45.6	S43 32.2
Vega	80 32.2	N38 48.8
Zuben'ubi	136 54.7	S16 09.1

	SHA ° ′	Mer. Pass. h m
Venus	148 59.0	14 07
Mars	242 43.5	7 53
Jupiter	219 49.9	9 24
Saturn	347 31.3	0 54

Day	UT d h	SUN GHA ° ′	SUN Dec ° ′	MOON GHA ° ′	v ′	MOON Dec ° ′	d ′	HP ′
SATURDAY	19 00	181 30.6	N 1 33.3	90 39.6	9.9	S28 02.1	0.7	54.2
	01	196 30.8	32.3	105 08.5	10.0	28 01.4	0.9	54.2
	02	211 31.0	31.4	119 37.5	10.0	28 00.5	1.1	54.2
	03	226 31.2	. . 30.4	134 06.5	10.0	27 59.4	1.2	54.2
	04	241 31.5	29.4	148 35.5	10.0	27 58.2	1.3	54.2
	05	256 31.7	28.5	163 04.5	10.0	27 56.9	1.4	54.2
	06	271 31.9	N 1 27.5	177 33.5	10.0	S27 55.5	1.6	54.2
	07	286 32.1	26.5	192 02.5	10.0	27 53.9	1.7	54.2
	08	301 32.4	25.6	206 31.5	10.1	27 52.2	1.9	54.2
	09	316 32.6	. . 24.6	221 00.6	10.1	27 50.3	2.0	54.3
	10	331 32.8	23.6	235 29.7	10.0	27 48.3	2.1	54.3
	11	346 33.0	22.6	249 58.7	10.1	27 46.2	2.2	54.3
	12	1 33.2	N 1 21.7	264 27.8	10.2	S27 44.0	2.4	54.3
	13	16 33.5	20.7	278 57.0	10.1	27 41.6	2.6	54.3
	14	31 33.7	19.7	293 26.1	10.2	27 39.0	2.6	54.3
	15	46 33.9	. . 18.8	307 55.3	10.2	27 36.4	2.8	54.3
	16	61 34.1	17.8	322 24.5	10.2	27 33.6	2.9	54.3
	17	76 34.4	16.8	336 53.7	10.2	27 30.7	3.1	54.3
	18	91 34.6	N 1 15.9	351 22.9	10.3	S27 27.6	3.1	54.3
	19	106 34.8	14.9	5 52.2	10.3	27 24.5	3.4	54.3
	20	121 35.0	13.9	20 21.5	10.3	27 21.1	3.4	54.3
	21	136 35.3	. . 12.9	34 50.8	10.3	27 17.7	3.6	54.3
	22	151 35.5	12.0	49 20.1	10.4	27 14.1	3.7	54.3
	23	166 35.7	11.0	63 49.5	10.4	27 10.4	3.8	54.3
SUNDAY	20 00	181 35.9	N 1 10.0	78 18.9	10.4	S27 06.6	4.0	54.3
	01	196 36.1	09.1	92 48.3	10.5	27 02.6	4.1	54.3
	02	211 36.4	08.1	107 17.8	10.5	26 58.5	4.2	54.3
	03	226 36.6	. . 07.1	121 47.3	10.5	26 54.3	4.4	54.3
	04	241 36.8	06.2	136 16.8	10.6	26 49.9	4.5	54.3
	05	256 37.0	05.2	150 46.4	10.5	26 45.4	4.6	54.3
	06	271 37.3	N 1 04.2	165 15.9	10.7	S26 40.8	4.7	54.4
	07	286 37.5	03.2	179 45.6	10.6	26 36.1	4.9	54.4
	08	301 37.7	02.3	194 15.2	10.7	26 31.2	5.0	54.4
	09	316 37.9	. . 01.3	208 44.9	10.7	26 26.2	5.1	54.4
	10	331 38.1	1 00.3	223 14.6	10.8	26 21.1	5.2	54.4
	11	346 38.4	0 59.4	237 44.4	10.8	26 15.9	5.4	54.4
	12	1 38.6	N 0 58.4	252 14.2	10.8	S26 10.5	5.5	54.4
	13	16 38.8	57.4	266 44.0	10.9	26 05.0	5.6	54.4
	14	31 39.0	56.4	281 13.9	10.9	25 59.4	5.8	54.4
	15	46 39.3	. . 55.5	295 43.8	11.0	25 53.6	5.8	54.4
	16	61 39.5	54.5	310 13.8	11.0	25 47.8	6.0	54.4
	17	76 39.7	53.5	324 43.8	11.0	25 41.8	6.1	54.5
	18	91 39.9	N 0 52.6	339 13.8	11.1	S25 35.7	6.3	54.5
	19	106 40.1	51.6	353 43.9	11.1	25 29.4	6.3	54.5
	20	121 40.4	50.6	8 14.0	11.1	25 23.1	6.5	54.5
	21	136 40.6	. . 49.7	22 44.1	11.2	25 16.6	6.6	54.5
	22	151 40.8	48.7	37 14.3	11.3	25 10.0	6.7	54.5
	23	166 41.0	47.7	51 44.6	11.2	25 03.3	6.8	54.5
MONDAY	21 00	181 41.3	N 0 46.7	66 14.8	11.4	S24 56.5	7.0	54.5
	01	196 41.5	45.8	80 45.2	11.3	24 49.5	7.1	54.6
	02	211 41.7	44.8	95 15.5	11.4	24 42.4	7.2	54.6
	03	226 41.9	. . 43.8	109 45.9	11.5	24 35.2	7.3	54.6
	04	241 42.1	42.9	124 16.4	11.5	24 27.9	7.4	54.6
	05	256 42.4	41.9	138 46.9	11.5	24 20.5	7.5	54.6
	06	271 42.6	N 0 40.9	153 17.4	11.6	S24 13.0	7.7	54.6
	07	286 42.8	39.9	167 48.0	11.6	24 05.3	7.7	54.6
	08	301 43.0	39.0	182 18.6	11.7	23 57.6	7.9	54.7
	09	316 43.3	. . 38.0	196 49.3	11.7	23 49.7	8.0	54.7
	10	331 43.5	37.0	211 20.0	11.8	23 41.7	8.1	54.7
	11	346 43.7	36.1	225 50.8	11.8	23 33.6	8.3	54.7
	12	1 43.9	N 0 35.1	240 21.6	11.8	S23 25.3	8.3	54.7
	13	16 44.1	34.1	254 52.4	11.9	23 17.0	8.4	54.7
	14	31 44.4	33.1	269 23.3	12.0	23 08.6	8.6	54.8
	15	46 44.6	. . 32.2	283 54.3	11.9	23 00.0	8.7	54.8
	16	61 44.8	31.2	298 25.2	12.1	22 51.3	8.7	54.8
	17	76 45.0	30.2	312 56.3	12.0	22 42.6	8.9	54.8
	18	91 45.3	N 0 29.3	327 27.3	12.2	S22 33.7	9.0	54.8
	19	106 45.5	28.3	341 58.5	12.1	22 24.7	9.1	54.8
	20	121 45.7	27.3	356 29.6	12.2	22 15.6	9.2	54.9
	21	136 45.9	. . 26.3	11 00.8	12.3	22 06.4	9.3	54.9
	22	151 46.1	25.4	25 32.1	12.3	21 57.1	9.4	54.9
	23	166 46.4	24.4	40 03.4	12.3	S21 47.7	9.5	54.9
		SD 16.0	*d* 1.0	SD 14.8		14.8		14.9

Lat. °	Twilight Naut. h m	Twilight Civil h m	Sunrise h m	Moonrise 19 h m	Moonrise 20 h m	Moonrise 21 h m	Moonrise 22 h m
N 72	02 45	04 20	05 29	▬	▬	▬	▬
N 70	03 08	04 30	05 32	▬	▬	▬	19 21
68	03 25	04 37	05 34	▬	▬	▬	18 40
66	03 39	04 44	05 36	▬	▬	18 47	18 12
64	03 50	04 49	05 37	▬	18 42	18 06	17 50
62	03 59	04 54	05 38	17 50	17 42	17 37	17 33
60	04 07	04 58	05 39	16 52	17 08	17 15	17 18
N 58	04 13	05 01	05 40	16 19	16 44	16 58	17 06
56	04 19	05 04	05 41	15 54	16 24	16 42	16 55
54	04 24	05 06	05 42	15 34	16 07	16 29	16 45
52	04 29	05 09	05 43	15 18	15 53	16 18	16 37
50	04 33	05 11	05 43	15 03	15 40	16 08	16 29
45	04 41	05 15	05 45	14 34	15 14	15 46	16 13
N 40	04 47	05 18	05 46	14 12	14 54	15 29	15 59
35	04 52	05 21	05 46	13 53	14 36	15 14	15 48
30	04 55	05 23	05 47	13 36	14 22	15 02	15 37
20	05 01	05 26	05 48	13 09	13 56	14 40	15 20
N 10	05 04	05 28	05 49	12 45	13 34	14 21	15 05
0	05 06	05 30	05 50	12 23	13 14	14 03	14 50
S 10	05 06	05 30	05 51	12 01	12 53	13 45	14 36
20	05 04	05 30	05 52	11 38	12 31	13 26	14 20
30	05 01	05 28	05 52	11 10	12 06	13 04	14 02
35	04 58	05 27	05 52	10 54	11 51	12 51	13 52
40	04 54	05 26	05 53	10 35	11 33	12 35	13 40
45	04 50	05 24	05 53	10 12	11 12	12 17	13 25
S 50	04 44	05 21	05 53	09 42	10 45	11 55	13 08
52	04 40	05 20	05 54	09 28	10 32	11 44	13 00
54	04 37	05 19	05 54	09 11	10 17	11 32	12 50
56	04 33	05 17	05 54	08 51	09 59	11 17	12 40
58	04 29	05 15	05 54	08 25	09 37	11 01	12 28
S 60	04 24	05 13	05 54	07 50	09 09	10 41	12 14

Lat. °	Sunset h m	Twilight Civil h m	Twilight Naut. h m	Moonset 19 h m	Moonset 20 h m	Moonset 21 h m	Moonset 22 h m
N 72	18 15	19 24	20 57	▬	▬	▬	▬
N 70	18 13	19 14	20 35	▬	▬	▬	23 01
68	18 11	19 07	20 18	▬	▬	▬	23 41
66	18 09	19 01	20 05	▬	▬	21 55	24 08
64	18 08	18 56	19 55	▬	20 18	22 36	24 28
62	18 07	18 51	19 46	19 25	21 18	23 04	24 45
60	18 06	18 48	19 38	20 23	21 51	23 25	24 58
N 58	18 05	18 45	19 32	20 56	22 16	23 42	25 10
56	18 04	18 42	19 26	21 21	22 35	23 56	25 20
54	18 04	18 39	19 21	21 40	22 51	24 09	00 09
52	18 03	18 37	19 17	21 57	23 05	24 20	00 20
50	18 03	18 35	19 13	22 11	23 18	24 30	00 30
45	18 02	18 31	19 05	22 40	23 43	24 50	00 50
N 40	18 01	18 28	18 59	23 02	24 03	00 03	01 06
35	18 00	18 25	18 55	23 21	24 19	00 19	01 20
30	17 59	18 23	18 51	23 37	24 34	00 34	01 32
20	17 58	18 20	18 46	24 03	00 03	00 58	01 52
N 10	17 57	18 18	18 43	24 27	00 27	01 18	02 10
0	17 57	18 17	18 41	24 48	00 48	01 38	02 26
S 10	17 56	18 17	18 41	00 19	01 09	01 57	02 42
20	17 56	18 18	18 43	00 43	01 32	02 18	02 59
30	17 55	18 19	18 47	01 11	01 59	02 41	03 19
35	17 55	18 20	18 50	01 27	02 14	02 55	03 30
40	17 55	18 22	18 53	01 46	02 32	03 11	03 43
45	17 55	18 24	18 58	02 10	02 54	03 30	03 59
S 50	17 54	18 27	19 05	02 39	03 21	03 53	04 18
52	17 54	18 28	19 08	02 54	03 35	04 05	04 26
54	17 54	18 29	19 11	03 11	03 50	04 17	04 36
56	17 54	18 31	19 15	03 31	04 08	04 32	04 47
58	17 54	18 33	19 20	03 57	04 30	04 49	05 00
S 60	17 54	18 35	19 25	04 32	04 59	05 10	05 15

Day d	SUN Eqn. of Time 00^h m s	SUN Eqn. of Time 12^h m s	SUN Mer. Pass. h m	MOON Mer. Pass. Upper h m	MOON Mer. Pass. Lower h m	MOON Age d	MOON Phase %
19	06 02	06 13	11 54	18 36	06 10	08	56
20	06 23	06 34	11 53	19 26	07 01	09	65
21	06 45	06 55	11 53	20 14	07 50	10	74

2026 SEPTEMBER 22, 23, 24 (TUES., WED., THURS.)

UT	ARIES	VENUS −4·8		MARS +1·2		JUPITER −1·8		SATURN +0·3	
d h	GHA ° ′	GHA ° ′	Dec ° ′	GHA ° ′	Dec ° ′	GHA ° ′	Dec ° ′	GHA ° ′	Dec ° ′
22 00 TUESDAY	0 52.4	149 07.6	S19 19.7	242 19.1	N21 43.6	220 19.4	N16 00.3	348 31.9	N 2 21.7
01	15 54.9	164 09.2	20.3	257 20.0	43.4	235 21.4	00.2	3 34.6	21.6
02	30 57.4	179 10.8	20.9	272 20.9	43.1	250 23.4	16 00.0	18 37.2	21.5
03	45 59.8	194 12.4	. . 21.5	287 21.7	. . 42.9	265 25.4	15 59.9	33 39.9	. . 21.4
04	61 02.3	209 14.1	22.1	302 22.6	42.6	280 27.4	59.7	48 42.5	21.4
05	76 04.8	224 15.7	22.7	317 23.5	42.4	295 29.4	59.6	63 45.1	21.3
06	91 07.2	239 17.3	S19 23.3	332 24.4	N21 42.1	310 31.4	N15 59.5	78 47.8	N 2 21.2
07	106 09.7	254 19.0	23.9	347 25.2	41.9	325 33.4	59.3	93 50.4	21.1
08	121 12.2	269 20.6	24.5	2 26.1	41.6	340 35.4	59.2	108 53.0	21.0
09	136 14.6	284 22.2	. . 25.1	17 27.0	. . 41.4	355 37.4	. . 59.0	123 55.7	. . 21.0
10	151 17.1	299 23.9	25.7	32 27.9	41.1	10 39.4	58.9	138 58.3	20.9
11	166 19.5	314 25.5	26.3	47 28.7	40.9	25 41.4	58.7	154 00.9	20.8
12	181 22.0	329 27.2	S19 26.9	62 29.6	N21 40.6	40 43.3	N15 58.6	169 03.6	N 2 20.7
13	196 24.5	344 28.8	27.5	77 30.5	40.4	55 45.3	58.5	184 06.2	20.7
14	211 26.9	359 30.5	28.1	92 31.4	40.2	70 47.3	58.3	199 08.9	20.6
15	226 29.4	14 32.1	. . 28.7	107 32.2	. . 39.9	85 49.3	. . 58.2	214 11.5	. . 20.5
16	241 31.9	29 33.8	29.3	122 33.1	39.7	100 51.3	58.0	229 14.1	20.4
17	256 34.3	44 35.5	29.9	137 34.0	39.4	115 53.3	57.9	244 16.8	20.4
18	271 36.8	59 37.1	S19 30.5	152 34.9	N21 39.2	130 55.3	N15 57.8	259 19.4	N 2 20.3
19	286 39.3	74 38.8	31.1	167 35.7	38.9	145 57.3	57.6	274 22.0	20.2
20	301 41.7	89 40.5	31.6	182 36.6	38.7	160 59.3	57.5	289 24.7	20.1
21	316 44.2	104 42.1	. . 32.2	197 37.5	. . 38.4	176 01.3	. . 57.3	304 27.3	. . 20.0
22	331 46.7	119 43.8	32.8	212 38.4	38.2	191 03.3	57.2	319 30.0	20.0
23	346 49.1	134 45.5	33.4	227 39.2	37.9	206 05.3	57.1	334 32.6	19.9
23 00 WEDNESDAY	1 51.6	149 47.2	S19 34.0	242 40.1	N21 37.7	221 07.3	N15 56.9	349 35.2	N 2 19.8
01	16 54.0	164 48.9	34.5	257 41.0	37.4	236 09.3	56.8	4 37.9	19.7
02	31 56.5	179 50.6	35.1	272 41.9	37.2	251 11.2	56.6	19 40.5	19.7
03	46 59.0	194 52.3	. . 35.7	287 42.8	. . 36.9	266 13.2	. . 56.5	34 43.1	. . 19.6
04	62 01.4	209 53.9	36.3	302 43.6	36.7	281 15.2	56.4	49 45.8	19.5
05	77 03.9	224 55.6	36.9	317 44.5	36.4	296 17.2	56.2	64 48.4	19.4
06	92 06.4	239 57.3	S19 37.4	332 45.4	N21 36.2	311 19.2	N15 56.1	79 51.1	N 2 19.4
07	107 08.8	254 59.0	38.0	347 46.3	35.9	326 21.2	55.9	94 53.7	19.3
08	122 11.3	270 00.8	38.6	2 47.2	35.7	341 23.2	55.8	109 56.3	19.2
09	137 13.8	285 02.5	. . 39.1	17 48.0	. . 35.4	356 25.2	. . 55.7	124 59.0	. . 19.1
10	152 16.2	300 04.2	39.7	32 48.9	35.2	11 27.2	55.5	140 01.6	19.0
11	167 18.7	315 05.9	40.3	47 49.8	34.9	26 29.2	55.4	155 04.2	19.0
12	182 21.1	330 07.6	S19 40.8	62 50.7	N21 34.7	41 31.2	N15 55.2	170 06.9	N 2 18.9
13	197 23.6	345 09.3	41.4	77 51.6	34.4	56 33.2	55.1	185 09.5	18.8
14	212 26.1	0 11.1	42.0	92 52.4	34.2	71 35.2	55.0	200 12.2	18.7
15	227 28.5	15 12.8	. . 42.5	107 53.3	. . 33.9	86 37.2	. . 54.8	215 14.8	. . 18.7
16	242 31.0	30 14.5	43.1	122 54.2	33.7	101 39.2	54.7	230 17.4	18.6
17	257 33.5	45 16.3	43.6	137 55.1	33.4	116 41.2	54.5	245 20.1	18.5
18	272 35.9	60 18.0	S19 44.2	152 56.0	N21 33.1	131 43.2	N15 54.4	260 22.7	N 2 18.4
19	287 38.4	75 19.7	44.8	167 56.9	32.9	146 45.2	54.3	275 25.3	18.4
20	302 40.9	90 21.5	45.3	182 57.7	32.6	161 47.2	54.1	290 28.0	18.3
21	317 43.3	105 23.2	. . 45.9	197 58.6	. . 32.4	176 49.2	. . 54.0	305 30.6	. . 18.2
22	332 45.8	120 25.0	46.4	212 59.5	32.1	191 51.1	53.9	320 33.3	18.1
23	347 48.3	135 26.7	47.0	228 00.4	31.9	206 53.1	53.7	335 35.9	18.0
24 00 THURSDAY	2 50.7	150 28.5	S19 47.5	243 01.3	N21 31.6	221 55.1	N15 53.6	350 38.5	N 2 18.0
01	17 53.2	165 30.2	48.1	258 02.2	31.4	236 57.1	53.4	5 41.2	17.9
02	32 55.6	180 32.0	48.6	273 03.1	31.1	251 59.1	53.3	20 43.8	17.8
03	47 58.1	195 33.8	. . 49.1	288 03.9	. . 30.9	267 01.1	. . 53.2	35 46.4	. . 17.7
04	63 00.6	210 35.5	49.7	303 04.8	30.6	282 03.1	53.0	50 49.1	17.7
05	78 03.0	225 37.3	50.2	318 05.7	30.4	297 05.1	52.9	65 51.7	17.6
06	93 05.5	240 39.1	S19 50.8	333 06.6	N21 30.1	312 07.1	N15 52.7	80 54.4	N 2 17.5
07	108 08.0	255 40.8	51.3	348 07.5	29.8	327 09.1	52.6	95 57.0	17.4
08	123 10.4	270 42.6	51.8	3 08.4	29.6	342 11.1	52.5	110 59.6	17.4
09	138 12.9	285 44.4	. . 52.4	18 09.3	. . 29.3	357 13.1	. . 52.3	126 02.3	. . 17.3
10	153 15.4	300 46.2	52.9	33 10.1	29.1	12 15.1	52.2	141 04.9	17.2
11	168 17.8	315 48.0	53.5	48 11.0	28.8	27 17.1	52.0	156 07.6	17.1
12	183 20.3	330 49.8	S19 54.0	63 11.9	N21 28.6	42 19.1	N15 51.9	171 10.2	N 2 17.0
13	198 22.8	345 51.6	54.5	78 12.8	28.3	57 21.1	51.8	186 12.8	17.0
14	213 25.2	0 53.4	55.0	93 13.7	28.0	72 23.1	51.6	201 15.5	16.9
15	228 27.7	15 55.2	. . 55.6	108 14.6	. . 27.8	87 25.1	. . 51.5	216 18.1	. . 16.8
16	243 30.1	30 57.0	56.1	123 15.5	27.5	102 27.1	51.3	231 20.8	16.7
17	258 32.6	45 58.8	56.6	138 16.4	27.3	117 29.1	51.2	246 23.4	16.7
18	273 35.1	61 00.6	S19 57.1	153 17.3	N21 27.0	132 31.1	N15 51.1	261 26.0	N 2 16.6
19	288 37.5	76 02.4	57.7	168 18.2	26.8	147 33.1	50.9	276 28.7	16.5
20	303 40.0	91 04.2	58.2	183 19.0	26.5	162 35.1	50.8	291 31.3	16.4
21	318 42.5	106 06.0	. . 58.7	198 19.9	. . 26.2	177 37.1	. . 50.6	306 33.9	. . 16.3
22	333 44.9	121 07.9	59.2	213 20.8	26.0	192 39.1	50.5	321 36.6	16.3
23	348 47.4	136 09.7	59.7	228 21.7	25.7	207 41.1	50.4	336 39.2	16.2
Mer. Pass.	h m 23 48.6	v 1.7	d 0.6	v 0.9	d 0.3	v 2.0	d 0.1	v 2.6	d 0.1

STARS

Name	SHA ° ′	Dec ° ′
Acamar	315 10.4	S40 11.5
Achernar	335 18.6	S57 05.8
Acrux	172 59.2	S63 14.9
Adhara	255 04.8	S29 00.2
Aldebaran	290 37.9	N16 33.8
Alioth	166 12.3	N55 49.0
Alkaid	152 51.3	N49 10.9
Alnair	27 30.7	S46 49.9
Alnilam	275 36.3	S 1 10.9
Alphard	217 46.6	S 8 46.3
Alphecca	126 02.8	N26 37.7
Alpheratz	357 33.0	N29 14.5
Altair	61 58.4	N 8 56.5
Ankaa	353 05.3	S42 09.5
Antares	112 14.2	S26 29.5
Arcturus	145 46.9	N19 02.7
Atria	107 07.3	S69 04.7
Avior	234 14.5	S59 35.4
Bellatrix	278 21.3	N 6 22.5
Betelgeuse	270 50.5	N 7 24.8
Canopus	263 51.8	S52 42.2
Capella	280 19.7	N46 01.4
Deneb	49 24.6	N45 22.8
Denebola	182 23.8	N14 25.4
Diphda	348 45.6	S17 50.2
Dubhe	193 39.9	N61 36.3
Elnath	278 00.0	N28 37.8
Eltanin	90 41.5	N51 29.4
Enif	33 37.2	N10 00.1
Fomalhaut	15 12.6	S29 28.7
Gacrux	171 50.7	S57 15.8
Gienah	175 42.5	S17 41.4
Hadar	148 34.6	S60 30.2
Hamal	327 49.3	N23 35.4
Kaus Aust.	83 30.6	S34 22.4
Kochab	137 20.7	N74 02.9
Markab	13 28.2	N15 21.1
Menkar	314 04.4	N 4 11.8
Menkent	147 56.3	S36 30.1
Miaplacidus	221 38.7	S69 49.4
Mirfak	308 25.9	N49 57.3
Nunki	75 45.9	S26 15.8
Peacock	53 03.2	S56 39.0
Pollux	243 15.7	N27 57.6
Procyon	244 49.5	N 5 09.5
Rasalhague	95 57.3	N12 32.6
Regulus	207 33.2	N11 50.2
Rigel	281 02.4	S 8 10.0
Rigil Kent.	139 38.9	S60 56.8
Sabik	102 01.2	S15 45.4
Schedar	349 28.9	N56 41.1
Shaula	96 08.5	S37 07.5
Sirius	258 25.0	S16 44.9
Spica	158 21.1	S11 18.0
Suhail	222 45.6	S43 32.2
Vega	80 32.2	N38 48.8
Zuben'ubi	136 54.7	S16 09.1

	SHA ° ′	Mer. Pass. h m
Venus	147 55.6	13 59
Mars	240 48.5	7 49
Jupiter	219 15.7	9 14
Saturn	347 43.6	0 42

UT d	UT h	SUN GHA ° ′	SUN Dec ° ′	MOON GHA ° ′	MOON v ′	MOON Dec ° ′	MOON d ′	MOON HP ′
22 TUESDAY	00	181 46.6	N 0 23.4	54 34.7	12.4	S21 38.2	9.7	54.9
	01	196 46.8	22.4	69 06.1	12.5	21 28.5	9.7	55.0
	02	211 47.0	21.5	83 37.6	12.5	21 18.8	9.8	55.0
	03	226 47.2	. . 20.5	98 09.1	12.5	21 09.0	9.9	55.0
	04	241 47.5	19.5	112 40.6	12.5	20 59.1	10.1	55.0
	05	256 47.7	18.6	127 12.1	12.7	20 49.0	10.1	55.0
	06	271 47.9	N 0 17.6	141 43.8	12.6	S20 38.9	10.2	55.0
	07	286 48.1	16.6	156 15.4	12.7	20 28.7	10.4	55.1
	08	301 48.4	15.6	170 47.1	12.8	20 18.3	10.4	55.1
	09	316 48.6	. . 14.7	185 18.9	12.7	20 07.9	10.5	55.1
	10	331 48.8	13.7	199 50.6	12.9	19 57.4	10.6	55.1
	11	346 49.0	12.7	214 22.5	12.8	19 46.8	10.7	55.2
	12	1 49.2	N 0 11.8	228 54.3	12.9	S19 36.1	10.8	55.2
	13	16 49.5	10.8	243 26.2	13.0	19 25.3	10.9	55.2
	14	31 49.7	09.8	257 58.2	13.0	19 14.4	11.0	55.2
	15	46 49.9	. . 08.8	272 30.2	13.0	19 03.4	11.1	55.2
	16	61 50.1	07.9	287 02.2	13.1	18 52.3	11.2	55.3
	17	76 50.3	06.9	301 34.3	13.1	18 41.1	11.3	55.3
	18	91 50.6	N 0 05.9	316 06.4	13.2	S18 29.8	11.4	55.3
	19	106 50.8	04.9	330 38.6	13.2	18 18.4	11.4	55.3
	20	121 51.0	04.0	345 10.8	13.2	18 07.0	11.6	55.4
	21	136 51.2	. . 03.0	359 43.0	13.3	17 55.4	11.6	55.4
	22	151 51.4	02.0	14 15.3	13.3	17 43.8	11.7	55.4
	23	166 51.7	01.1	28 47.6	13.3	17 32.1	11.8	55.4
23 WEDNESDAY	00	181 51.9	N 0 00.1	43 19.9	13.4	S17 20.3	11.9	55.4
	01	196 52.1	S 00.9	57 52.3	13.4	17 08.4	12.0	55.5
	02	211 52.3	01.9	72 24.7	13.5	16 56.4	12.0	55.5
	03	226 52.5	. . 02.8	86 57.2	13.5	16 44.4	12.2	55.5
	04	241 52.8	03.8	101 29.7	13.5	16 32.2	12.2	55.5
	05	256 53.0	04.8	116 02.2	13.5	16 20.0	12.3	55.6
	06	271 53.2	S 0 05.8	130 34.7	13.6	S16 07.7	12.4	55.6
	07	286 53.4	06.7	145 07.3	13.6	15 55.3	12.5	55.6
	08	301 53.6	07.7	159 39.9	13.7	15 42.8	12.5	55.6
	09	316 53.9	. . 08.7	174 12.6	13.7	15 30.3	12.7	55.7
	10	331 54.1	09.6	188 45.3	13.7	15 17.6	12.7	55.7
	11	346 54.3	10.6	203 18.0	13.7	15 04.9	12.7	55.7
	12	1 54.5	S 0 11.6	217 50.7	13.8	S14 52.2	12.9	55.7
	13	16 54.7	12.6	232 23.5	13.8	14 39.3	12.9	55.8
	14	31 55.0	13.5	246 56.3	13.9	14 26.4	13.0	55.8
	15	46 55.2	. . 14.5	261 29.2	13.8	14 13.4	13.1	55.8
	16	61 55.4	15.5	276 02.0	13.9	14 00.3	13.2	55.8
	17	76 55.6	16.5	290 34.9	13.9	13 47.1	13.2	55.9
	18	91 55.8	S 0 17.4	305 07.8	14.0	S13 33.9	13.3	55.9
	19	106 56.1	18.4	319 40.8	13.9	13 20.6	13.4	55.9
	20	121 56.3	19.4	334 13.7	14.0	13 07.2	13.4	55.9
	21	136 56.5	. . 20.3	348 46.7	14.0	12 53.8	13.5	56.0
	22	151 56.7	21.3	3 19.7	14.0	12 40.3	13.6	56.0
	23	166 56.9	22.3	17 52.7	14.1	12 26.7	13.6	56.0
24 THURSDAY	00	181 57.2	S 0 23.3	32 25.8	14.1	S12 13.1	13.7	56.0
	01	196 57.4	24.2	46 58.9	14.1	11 59.4	13.8	56.1
	02	211 57.6	25.2	61 32.0	14.1	11 45.6	13.8	56.1
	03	226 57.8	. . 26.2	76 05.1	14.1	11 31.8	13.9	56.1
	04	241 58.0	27.2	90 38.2	14.1	11 17.9	14.0	56.2
	05	256 58.3	28.1	105 11.3	14.2	11 03.9	14.0	56.2
	06	271 58.5	S 0 29.1	119 44.5	14.2	S10 49.9	14.1	56.2
	07	286 58.7	30.1	134 17.7	14.2	10 35.8	14.1	56.2
	08	301 58.9	31.0	148 50.9	14.2	10 21.7	14.2	56.3
	09	316 59.1	. . 32.0	163 24.1	14.2	10 07.5	14.3	56.3
	10	331 59.3	33.0	177 57.3	14.2	9 53.2	14.3	56.3
	11	346 59.6	34.0	192 30.5	14.3	9 38.9	14.4	56.3
	12	1 59.8	S 0 34.9	207 03.8	14.2	S 9 24.5	14.4	56.4
	13	17 00.0	35.9	221 37.0	14.3	9 10.1	14.5	56.4
	14	32 00.2	36.9	236 10.3	14.3	8 55.6	14.5	56.4
	15	47 00.4	. . 37.9	250 43.6	14.3	8 41.1	14.6	56.5
	16	62 00.7	38.8	265 16.9	14.2	8 26.5	14.6	56.5
	17	77 00.9	39.8	279 50.1	14.3	8 11.9	14.7	56.5
	18	92 01.1	S 0 40.8	294 23.4	14.3	S 7 57.2	14.7	56.5
	19	107 01.3	41.8	308 56.7	14.3	7 42.5	14.8	56.6
	20	122 01.5	42.7	323 30.0	14.3	7 27.7	14.9	56.6
	21	137 01.7	. . 43.7	338 03.3	14.3	7 12.8	14.8	56.6
	22	152 02.0	44.7	352 36.6	14.3	6 58.0	14.9	56.6
	23	167 02.2	45.6	7 09.9	14.3	S 6 43.1	15.0	56.7
		SD 16.0	*d* 1.0	SD	15.0		15.2	15.4

Lat. °	Twilight Naut. h m	Twilight Civil h m	Sunrise h m	Moonrise 22 h m	Moonrise 23 h m	Moonrise 24 h m	Moonrise 25 h m
N 72	03 04	04 34	05 43	▬	18 51	18 06	17 31
N 70	03 23	04 42	05 44	19 21	18 27	17 54	17 28
68	03 38	04 48	05 44	18 40	18 08	17 45	17 26
66	03 50	04 54	05 45	18 12	17 52	17 37	17 24
64	04 00	04 58	05 46	17 50	17 39	17 30	17 22
62	04 08	05 02	05 46	17 33	17 29	17 25	17 21
60	04 15	05 05	05 46	17 18	17 19	17 19	17 19
N 58	04 21	05 08	05 47	17 06	17 11	17 15	17 18
56	04 26	05 10	05 47	16 55	17 04	17 11	17 17
54	04 30	05 12	05 47	16 45	16 57	17 07	17 16
52	04 34	05 14	05 48	16 37	16 52	17 04	17 15
50	04 37	05 15	05 48	16 29	16 46	17 01	17 15
45	04 44	05 19	05 48	16 13	16 35	16 54	17 13
N 40	04 50	05 21	05 48	15 59	16 25	16 49	17 11
35	04 54	05 23	05 49	15 48	16 17	16 44	17 10
30	04 57	05 25	05 49	15 37	16 10	16 40	17 09
20	05 01	05 27	05 49	15 20	15 57	16 33	17 07
N 10	05 04	05 28	05 49	15 05	15 46	16 26	17 06
0	05 04	05 28	05 49	14 50	15 36	16 20	17 04
S 10	05 04	05 28	05 49	14 36	15 25	16 14	17 03
20	05 01	05 27	05 49	14 20	15 14	16 07	17 01
30	04 57	05 25	05 48	14 02	15 01	16 00	16 59
35	04 53	05 23	05 48	13 52	14 53	15 55	16 58
40	04 49	05 21	05 48	13 40	14 45	15 50	16 57
45	04 44	05 18	05 47	13 25	14 35	15 45	16 55
S 50	04 37	05 15	05 47	13 08	14 23	15 38	16 54
52	04 33	05 13	05 47	13 00	14 17	15 35	16 53
54	04 29	05 11	05 46	12 50	14 11	15 31	16 52
56	04 25	05 09	05 46	12 40	14 04	15 27	16 51
58	04 20	05 06	05 46	12 28	13 56	15 23	16 50
S 60	04 14	05 04	05 45	12 14	13 47	15 18	16 49

Lat. °	Sunset h m	Twilight Civil h m	Twilight Naut. h m	Moonset 22 h m	Moonset 23 h m	Moonset 24 h m	Moonset 25 h m
N 72	17 59	19 07	20 36	▬	▬	01 08	03 27
N 70	17 59	19 00	20 18	23 01	25 30	01 30	03 36
68	17 58	18 54	20 03	23 41	25 47	01 47	03 43
66	17 58	18 49	19 52	24 08	00 08	02 01	03 49
64	17 58	18 45	19 43	24 28	00 28	02 12	03 53
62	17 57	18 41	19 35	24 45	00 45	02 22	03 58
60	17 57	18 38	19 28	24 58	00 58	02 30	04 01
N 58	17 57	18 36	19 22	25 10	01 10	02 37	04 04
56	17 57	18 34	19 18	25 20	01 20	02 43	04 07
54	17 56	18 32	19 13	00 09	01 29	02 49	04 10
52	17 56	18 30	19 10	00 20	01 37	02 54	04 12
50	17 56	18 28	19 06	00 30	01 44	02 59	04 14
45	17 56	18 25	18 59	00 50	01 59	03 08	04 18
N 40	17 56	18 23	18 54	01 06	02 11	03 16	04 22
35	17 56	18 21	18 50	01 20	02 21	03 23	04 25
30	17 55	18 19	18 47	01 32	02 31	03 29	04 28
20	17 55	18 17	18 43	01 52	02 46	03 40	04 33
N 10	17 55	18 16	18 41	02 10	03 00	03 49	04 37
0	17 56	18 16	18 40	02 26	03 12	03 57	04 41
S 10	17 56	18 17	18 41	02 42	03 25	04 05	04 45
20	17 56	18 18	18 44	02 59	03 38	04 14	04 49
30	17 57	18 21	18 49	03 19	03 53	04 24	04 53
35	17 57	18 22	18 52	03 30	04 01	04 30	04 56
40	17 58	18 25	18 56	03 43	04 11	04 36	04 59
45	17 58	18 27	19 02	03 59	04 23	04 43	05 02
S 50	17 59	18 31	19 09	04 18	04 37	04 52	05 06
52	17 59	18 33	19 13	04 26	04 43	04 56	05 08
54	18 00	18 35	19 17	04 36	04 50	05 01	05 10
56	18 00	18 37	19 22	04 47	04 58	05 06	05 12
58	18 00	18 40	19 27	05 00	05 07	05 11	05 15
S 60	18 01	18 43	19 33	05 15	05 17	05 17	05 17

Day d	SUN Eqn. of Time 00^h m s	SUN Eqn. of Time 12^h m s	SUN Mer. Pass. h m	MOON Mer. Pass. Upper h m	MOON Mer. Pass. Lower h m	MOON Age d	MOON %	Phase
22	07 06	07 17	11 53	21 01	08 38	11	82	
23	07 27	07 38	11 52	21 46	09 24	12	89	
24	07 48	07 59	11 52	22 30	10 08	13	95	

2026 SEPTEMBER 25, 26, 27 (FRI., SAT., SUN.)

UT d	h	ARIES GHA	VENUS −4·8 GHA	Dec	MARS +1·1 GHA	Dec	JUPITER −1·9 GHA	Dec	SATURN +0·3 GHA	Dec
		° ′	° ′	° ′	° ′	° ′	° ′	° ′	° ′	° ′
25	00	3 49.9	151 11.5	S20 00.3	243 22.6	N21 25.5	222 43.1	N15 50.2	351 41.9	N 2 16.1
	01	18 52.3	166 13.3	00.8	258 23.5	25.2	237 45.1	50.1	6 44.5	16.0
	02	33 54.8	181 15.2	01.3	273 24.4	25.0	252 47.1	50.0	21 47.1	16.0
	03	48 57.2	196 17.0	. . 01.8	288 25.3	. . 24.7	267 49.1	. . 49.8	36 49.8	. . 15.9
	04	63 59.7	211 18.9	02.3	303 26.2	24.4	282 51.1	49.7	51 52.4	15.8
	05	79 02.2	226 20.7	02.8	318 27.1	24.2	297 53.1	49.5	66 55.1	15.7
	06	94 04.6	241 22.6	S20 03.3	333 28.0	N21 23.9	312 55.1	N15 49.4	81 57.7	N 2 15.6
	07	109 07.1	256 24.4	03.8	348 28.9	23.7	327 57.1	49.3	97 00.3	15.6
F	08	124 09.6	271 26.3	04.3	3 29.8	23.4	342 59.1	49.1	112 03.0	15.5
R	09	139 12.0	286 28.1	. . 04.8	18 30.6	. . 23.1	358 01.1	. . 49.0	127 05.6	. . 15.4
I	10	154 14.5	301 30.0	05.3	33 31.5	22.9	13 03.1	48.8	142 08.3	15.3
D	11	169 17.0	316 31.8	05.8	48 32.4	22.6	28 05.1	48.7	157 10.9	15.3
A	12	184 19.4	331 33.7	S20 06.3	63 33.3	N21 22.4	43 07.1	N15 48.6	172 13.5	N 2 15.2
Y	13	199 21.9	346 35.6	06.8	78 34.2	22.1	58 09.1	48.4	187 16.2	15.1
	14	214 24.4	1 37.5	07.3	93 35.1	21.8	73 11.1	48.3	202 18.8	15.0
	15	229 26.8	16 39.3	. . 07.8	108 36.0	. . 21.6	88 13.1	. . 48.2	217 21.5	. . 15.0
	16	244 29.3	31 41.2	08.3	123 36.9	21.3	103 15.1	48.0	232 24.1	14.9
	17	259 31.7	46 43.1	08.8	138 37.8	21.0	118 17.1	47.9	247 26.7	14.8
	18	274 34.2	61 45.0	S20 09.3	153 38.7	N21 20.8	133 19.1	N15 47.7	262 29.4	N 2 14.7
	19	289 36.7	76 46.9	09.8	168 39.6	20.5	148 21.1	47.6	277 32.0	14.6
	20	304 39.1	91 48.8	10.3	183 40.5	20.3	163 23.1	47.5	292 34.7	14.6
	21	319 41.6	106 50.7	. . 10.7	198 41.4	. . 20.0	178 25.1	. . 47.3	307 37.3	. . 14.5
	22	334 44.1	121 52.6	11.2	213 42.3	19.7	193 27.1	47.2	322 39.9	14.4
	23	349 46.5	136 54.5	11.7	228 43.2	19.5	208 29.1	47.0	337 42.6	14.3
26	00	4 49.0	151 56.4	S20 12.2	243 44.1	N21 19.2	223 31.1	N15 46.9	352 45.2	N 2 14.3
	01	19 51.5	166 58.3	12.7	258 45.0	18.9	238 33.2	46.8	7 47.9	14.2
	02	34 53.9	182 00.2	13.1	273 45.9	18.7	253 35.2	46.6	22 50.5	14.1
	03	49 56.4	197 02.1	. . 13.6	288 46.8	. . 18.4	268 37.2	. . 46.5	37 53.1	. . 14.0
	04	64 58.8	212 04.0	14.1	303 47.7	18.2	283 39.2	46.4	52 55.8	13.9
	05	80 01.3	227 05.9	14.6	318 48.6	17.9	298 41.2	46.2	67 58.4	13.9
	06	95 03.8	242 07.9	S20 15.0	333 49.5	N21 17.6	313 43.2	N15 46.1	83 01.1	N 2 13.8
S	07	110 06.2	257 09.8	15.5	348 50.4	17.4	328 45.2	45.9	98 03.7	13.7
A	08	125 08.7	272 11.7	16.0	3 51.3	17.1	343 47.2	45.8	113 06.3	13.6
T	09	140 11.2	287 13.7	. . 16.4	18 52.2	. . 16.8	358 49.2	. . 45.7	128 09.0	. . 13.6
U	10	155 13.6	302 15.6	16.9	33 53.1	16.6	13 51.2	45.5	143 11.6	13.5
R	11	170 16.1	317 17.5	17.4	48 54.0	16.3	28 53.2	45.4	158 14.3	13.4
D	12	185 18.6	332 19.5	S20 17.8	63 54.9	N21 16.0	43 55.2	N15 45.3	173 16.9	N 2 13.3
A	13	200 21.0	347 21.4	18.3	78 55.8	15.8	58 57.2	45.1	188 19.6	13.2
Y	14	215 23.5	2 23.4	18.7	93 56.7	15.5	73 59.2	45.0	203 22.2	13.2
	15	230 26.0	17 25.3	. . 19.2	108 57.6	. . 15.2	89 01.2	. . 44.8	218 24.8	. . 13.1
	16	245 28.4	32 27.3	19.7	123 58.5	15.0	104 03.2	44.7	233 27.5	13.0
	17	260 30.9	47 29.3	20.1	138 59.4	14.7	119 05.2	44.6	248 30.1	12.9
	18	275 33.3	62 31.2	S20 20.6	154 00.3	N21 14.4	134 07.2	N15 44.4	263 32.8	N 2 12.9
	19	290 35.8	77 33.2	21.0	169 01.2	14.2	149 09.2	44.3	278 35.4	12.8
	20	305 38.3	92 35.2	21.5	184 02.1	13.9	164 11.2	44.2	293 38.0	12.7
	21	320 40.7	107 37.1	. . 21.9	199 03.1	. . 13.6	179 13.3	. . 44.0	308 40.7	. . 12.6
	22	335 43.2	122 39.1	22.4	214 04.0	13.4	194 15.3	43.9	323 43.3	12.5
	23	350 45.7	137 41.1	22.8	229 04.9	13.1	209 17.3	43.7	338 46.0	12.5
27	00	5 48.1	152 43.1	S20 23.2	244 05.8	N21 12.8	224 19.3	N15 43.6	353 48.6	N 2 12.4
	01	20 50.6	167 45.1	23.7	259 06.7	12.6	239 21.3	43.5	8 51.2	12.3
	02	35 53.1	182 47.1	24.1	274 07.6	12.3	254 23.3	43.3	23 53.9	12.2
	03	50 55.5	197 49.1	. . 24.6	289 08.5	. . 12.0	269 25.3	. . 43.2	38 56.5	. . 12.2
	04	65 58.0	212 51.1	25.0	304 09.4	11.8	284 27.3	43.1	53 59.2	12.1
	05	81 00.4	227 53.1	25.4	319 10.3	11.5	299 29.3	42.9	69 01.8	12.0
	06	96 02.9	242 55.1	S20 25.9	334 11.2	N21 11.2	314 31.3	N15 42.8	84 04.5	N 2 11.9
	07	111 05.4	257 57.1	26.3	349 12.1	11.0	329 33.3	42.6	99 07.1	11.8
	08	126 07.8	272 59.1	26.7	4 13.0	10.7	344 35.3	42.5	114 09.7	11.8
S	09	141 10.3	288 01.1	. . 27.2	19 13.9	. . 10.4	359 37.3	. . 42.4	129 12.4	. . 11.7
U	10	156 12.8	303 03.1	27.6	34 14.8	10.2	14 39.3	42.2	144 15.0	11.6
N	11	171 15.2	318 05.1	28.0	49 15.8	09.9	29 41.4	42.1	159 17.7	11.5
D	12	186 17.7	333 07.2	S20 28.4	64 16.7	N21 09.6	44 43.4	N15 42.0	174 20.3	N 2 11.5
A	13	201 20.2	348 09.2	28.9	79 17.6	09.4	59 45.4	41.8	189 22.9	11.4
Y	14	216 22.6	3 11.2	29.3	94 18.5	09.1	74 47.4	41.7	204 25.6	11.3
	15	231 25.1	18 13.3	. . 29.7	109 19.4	. . 08.8	89 49.4	. . 41.5	219 28.2	. . 11.2
	16	246 27.6	33 15.3	30.1	124 20.3	08.5	104 51.4	41.4	234 30.9	11.1
	17	261 30.0	48 17.3	30.5	139 21.2	08.3	119 53.4	41.3	249 33.5	11.1
	18	276 32.5	63 19.4	S20 31.0	154 22.1	N21 08.0	134 55.4	N15 41.1	264 36.2	N 2 11.0
	19	291 34.9	78 21.4	31.4	169 23.0	07.7	149 57.4	41.0	279 38.8	10.9
	20	306 37.4	93 23.5	31.8	184 24.0	07.5	164 59.4	40.9	294 41.4	10.8
	21	321 39.9	108 25.5	. . 32.2	199 24.9	. . 07.2	180 01.4	. . 40.7	309 44.1	. . 10.8
	22	336 42.3	123 27.6	32.6	214 25.8	06.9	195 03.5	40.6	324 46.7	10.7
	23	351 44.8	138 29.7	33.0	229 26.7	06.6	210 05.5	40.4	339 49.4	10.6
Mer. Pass.		h m 23 36.9	*v* 1.9	*d* 0.5	*v* 0.9	*d* 0.3	*v* 2.0	*d* 0.1	*v* 2.6	*d* 0.1

STARS

Name	SHA	Dec
	° ′	° ′
Acamar	315 10.4	S40 11.5
Achernar	335 18.6	S57 05.8
Acrux	172 59.2	S63 14.9
Adhara	255 04.8	S29 00.2
Aldebaran	290 37.9	N16 33.8
Alioth	166 12.3	N55 48.9
Alkaid	152 51.3	N49 10.9
Alnair	27 30.8	S46 49.9
Alnilam	275 36.2	S 1 10.9
Alphard	217 46.6	S 8 46.3
Alphecca	126 02.8	N26 37.6
Alpheratz	357 33.0	N29 14.5
Altair	61 58.5	N 8 56.5
Ankaa	353 05.3	S42 09.5
Antares	112 14.3	S26 29.5
Arcturus	145 46.9	N19 02.7
Atria	107 07.4	S69 04.7
Avior	234 14.5	S59 35.4
Bellatrix	278 21.3	N 6 22.5
Betelgeuse	270 50.5	N 7 24.8
Canopus	263 51.8	S52 42.2
Capella	280 19.7	N46 01.4
Deneb	49 24.6	N45 22.8
Denebola	182 23.8	N14 25.4
Diphda	348 45.6	S17 50.2
Dubhe	193 39.9	N61 36.3
Elnath	278 00.0	N28 37.8
Eltanin	90 41.6	N51 29.4
Enif	33 37.2	N10 00.1
Fomalhaut	15 12.6	S29 28.7
Gacrux	171 50.7	S57 15.8
Gienah	175 42.5	S17 41.4
Hadar	148 34.6	S60 30.2
Hamal	327 49.3	N23 35.4
Kaus Aust.	83 30.6	S34 22.4
Kochab	137 20.7	N74 02.9
Markab	13 28.2	N15 21.2
Menkar	314 04.4	N 4 11.8
Menkent	147 56.3	S36 30.1
Miaplacidus	221 38.6	S69 49.3
Mirfak	308 25.9	N49 57.3
Nunki	75 45.9	S26 15.8
Peacock	53 03.2	S56 39.0
Pollux	243 15.7	N27 57.6
Procyon	244 49.5	N 5 09.5
Rasalhague	95 57.3	N12 32.6
Regulus	207 33.2	N11 50.2
Rigel	281 02.4	S 8 10.0
Rigil Kent.	139 38.9	S60 56.8
Sabik	102 01.3	S15 45.4
Schedar	349 28.9	N56 41.1
Shaula	96 08.5	S37 07.5
Sirius	258 25.0	S16 44.9
Spica	158 21.1	S11 18.0
Suhail	222 45.6	S43 32.2
Vega	80 32.2	N38 48.8
Zuben'ubi	136 54.7	S16 09.1

	SHA	Mer. Pass.
	° ′	h m
Venus	147 07.4	13 50
Mars	238 55.1	7 45
Jupiter	218 42.2	9 05
Saturn	347 56.2	0 29

UT d	h	SUN GHA	SUN Dec	MOON GHA	v	MOON Dec	d	HP
d	h	° ′	° ′	° ′	′	° ′	′	′
25 FRIDAY	00	182 02.4	S 0 46.6	21 43.2	14.3	S 6 28.1	15.0	56.7
	01	197 02.6	47.6	36 16.5	14.3	6 13.1	15.1	56.7
	02	212 02.8	48.6	50 49.8	14.3	5 58.0	15.0	56.8
	03	227 03.1	. . 49.5	65 23.1	14.3	5 43.0	15.2	56.8
	04	242 03.3	50.5	79 56.4	14.3	5 27.8	15.1	56.8
	05	257 03.5	51.5	94 29.7	14.3	5 12.7	15.2	56.8
	06	272 03.7	S 0 52.5	109 03.0	14.3	S 4 57.5	15.3	56.9
	07	287 03.9	53.4	123 36.3	14.3	4 42.2	15.3	56.9
	08	302 04.1	54.4	138 09.6	14.2	4 26.9	15.3	56.9
	09	317 04.4	. . 55.4	152 42.8	14.3	4 11.6	15.3	56.9
	10	332 04.6	56.3	167 16.1	14.2	3 56.3	15.4	57.0
	11	347 04.8	57.3	181 49.3	14.2	3 40.9	15.4	57.0
	12	2 05.0	S 0 58.3	196 22.5	14.2	S 3 25.5	15.4	57.0
	13	17 05.2	0 59.3	210 55.7	14.2	3 10.1	15.5	57.1
	14	32 05.4	1 00.2	225 28.9	14.2	2 54.6	15.5	57.1
	15	47 05.7	. . 01.2	240 02.1	14.2	2 39.1	15.5	57.1
	16	62 05.9	02.2	254 35.3	14.1	2 23.6	15.5	57.1
	17	77 06.1	03.2	269 08.4	14.1	2 08.1	15.6	57.2
	18	92 06.3	S 1 04.1	283 41.5	14.1	S 1 52.5	15.6	57.2
	19	107 06.5	05.1	298 14.6	14.1	1 36.9	15.6	57.2
	20	122 06.7	06.1	312 47.7	14.1	1 21.3	15.7	57.2
	21	137 07.0	. . 07.1	327 20.8	14.0	1 05.6	15.6	57.3
	22	152 07.2	08.0	341 53.8	14.0	0 50.0	15.7	57.3
	23	167 07.4	09.0	356 26.8	14.0	0 34.3	15.7	57.3
26 SATURDAY	00	182 07.6	S 1 10.0	10 59.8	14.0	S 0 18.6	15.7	57.4
	01	197 07.8	10.9	25 32.8	13.9	S 0 02.9	15.7	57.4
	02	212 08.0	11.9	40 05.7	13.9	N 0 12.8	15.7	57.4
	03	227 08.3	. . 12.9	54 38.6	13.9	0 28.5	15.8	57.4
	04	242 08.5	13.9	69 11.5	13.8	0 44.3	15.7	57.5
	05	257 08.7	14.8	83 44.3	13.9	1 00.0	15.8	57.5
	06	272 08.9	S 1 15.8	98 17.2	13.7	N 1 15.8	15.8	57.5
	07	287 09.1	16.8	112 49.9	13.8	1 31.6	15.8	57.5
	08	302 09.3	17.8	127 22.7	13.7	1 47.4	15.8	57.6
	09	317 09.5	. . 18.7	141 55.4	13.6	2 03.2	15.8	57.6
	10	332 09.8	19.7	156 28.0	13.7	2 19.0	15.8	57.6
	11	347 10.0	20.7	171 00.7	13.6	2 34.8	15.8	57.6
	12	2 10.2	S 1 21.6	185 33.3	13.5	N 2 50.6	15.8	57.7
	13	17 10.4	22.6	200 05.8	13.5	3 06.4	15.8	57.7
	14	32 10.6	23.6	214 38.3	13.5	3 22.2	15.8	57.7
	15	47 10.8	. . 24.6	229 10.8	13.4	3 38.0	15.8	57.7
	16	62 11.1	25.5	243 43.2	13.4	3 53.8	15.8	57.8
	17	77 11.3	26.5	258 15.6	13.3	4 09.6	15.7	57.8
	18	92 11.5	S 1 27.5	272 47.9	13.3	N 4 25.3	15.8	57.8
	19	107 11.7	28.5	287 20.2	13.3	4 41.1	15.8	57.8
	20	122 11.9	29.4	301 52.5	13.2	4 56.9	15.8	57.9
	21	137 12.1	. . 30.4	316 24.7	13.1	5 12.7	15.7	57.9
	22	152 12.3	31.4	330 56.8	13.1	5 28.4	15.7	57.9
	23	167 12.6	32.3	345 28.9	13.0	5 44.1	15.8	57.9
27 SUNDAY	00	182 12.8	S 1 33.3	0 00.9	13.0	N 5 59.9	15.7	58.0
	01	197 13.0	34.3	14 32.9	12.9	6 15.6	15.7	58.0
	02	212 13.2	35.3	29 04.8	12.9	6 31.3	15.6	58.0
	03	227 13.4	. . 36.2	43 36.7	12.8	6 46.9	15.7	58.0
	04	242 13.6	37.2	58 08.5	12.8	7 02.6	15.6	58.1
	05	257 13.8	38.2	72 40.3	12.6	7 18.2	15.6	58.1
	06	272 14.0	S 1 39.2	87 11.9	12.7	N 7 33.8	15.6	58.1
	07	287 14.3	40.1	101 43.6	12.5	7 49.4	15.6	58.1
	08	302 14.5	41.1	116 15.1	12.5	8 05.0	15.5	58.2
	09	317 14.7	. . 42.1	130 46.6	12.5	8 20.5	15.5	58.2
	10	332 14.9	43.0	145 18.1	12.4	8 36.0	15.5	58.2
	11	347 15.1	44.0	159 49.5	12.3	8 51.5	15.4	58.2
	12	2 15.3	S 1 45.0	174 20.8	12.2	N 9 06.9	15.4	58.2
	13	17 15.5	46.0	188 52.0	12.2	9 22.3	15.4	58.3
	14	32 15.8	46.9	203 23.2	12.1	9 37.7	15.3	58.3
	15	47 16.0	. . 47.9	217 54.3	12.0	9 53.0	15.3	58.3
	16	62 16.2	48.9	232 25.3	12.0	10 08.3	15.3	58.3
	17	77 16.4	49.9	246 56.3	11.9	10 23.6	15.2	58.3
	18	92 16.6	S 1 50.8	261 27.2	11.8	N10 38.8	15.2	58.4
	19	107 16.8	51.8	275 58.0	11.7	10 54.0	15.1	58.4
	20	122 17.0	52.8	290 28.7	11.7	11 09.1	15.1	58.4
	21	137 17.2	. . 53.7	304 59.4	11.6	11 24.2	15.0	58.4
	22	152 17.5	54.7	319 30.0	11.5	11 39.2	15.0	58.4
	23	167 17.7	55.7	334 00.5	11.4	N11 54.2	15.0	58.5
		SD 16.0	*d* 1.0	SD 15.5		15.7		15.9

Lat.	Twilight Naut.	Twilight Civil	Sunrise	Moonrise 25	Moonrise 26	Moonrise 27	Moonrise 28
°	h m	h m	h m	h m	h m	h m	h m
N 72	03 22	04 48	05 56	17 31	16 57	16 18	15 18
N 70	03 38	04 54	05 56	17 28	17 02	16 34	15 54
68	03 51	04 59	05 55	17 26	17 07	16 46	16 19
66	04 01	05 03	05 55	17 24	17 11	16 57	16 39
64	04 10	05 07	05 54	17 22	17 14	17 05	16 56
62	04 17	05 10	05 54	17 21	17 17	17 13	17 09
60	04 22	05 12	05 53	17 19	17 19	17 19	17 21
N 58	04 28	05 14	05 53	17 18	17 21	17 25	17 31
56	04 32	05 16	05 53	17 17	17 23	17 30	17 40
54	04 36	05 17	05 53	17 16	17 25	17 35	17 47
52	04 39	05 19	05 52	17 15	17 27	17 39	17 55
50	04 42	05 20	05 52	17 15	17 28	17 43	18 01
45	04 48	05 22	05 52	17 13	17 31	17 52	18 15
N 40	04 53	05 24	05 51	17 11	17 34	17 59	18 26
35	04 56	05 26	05 51	17 10	17 37	18 05	18 36
30	04 59	05 27	05 50	17 09	17 39	18 10	18 45
20	05 02	05 28	05 50	17 07	17 43	18 20	19 00
N 10	05 04	05 28	05 49	17 06	17 46	18 28	19 13
0	05 03	05 27	05 48	17 04	17 49	18 36	19 26
S 10	05 02	05 26	05 47	17 03	17 52	18 44	19 39
20	04 58	05 24	05 46	17 01	17 56	18 53	19 52
30	04 53	05 21	05 45	16 59	18 00	19 02	20 08
35	04 49	05 19	05 44	16 58	18 02	19 08	20 17
40	04 44	05 16	05 43	16 57	18 05	19 15	20 28
45	04 38	05 12	05 42	16 55	18 08	19 23	20 40
S 50	04 30	05 08	05 40	16 54	18 11	19 32	20 56
52	04 26	05 06	05 40	16 53	18 13	19 36	21 03
54	04 21	05 03	05 39	16 52	18 15	19 41	21 11
56	04 16	05 01	05 38	16 51	18 17	19 46	21 20
58	04 10	04 58	05 37	16 50	18 19	19 52	21 30
S 60	04 04	04 54	05 36	16 49	18 22	19 59	21 42

Lat.	Sunset	Twilight Civil	Twilight Naut.	Moonset 25	Moonset 26	Moonset 27	Moonset 28
°	h m	h m	h m	h m	h m	h m	h m
N 72	17 44	18 51	20 17	03 27	05 39	07 56	10 41
N 70	17 45	18 46	20 01	03 36	05 37	07 44	10 07
68	17 46	18 41	19 49	03 43	05 36	07 34	09 43
66	17 46	18 37	19 39	03 49	05 35	07 25	09 24
64	17 47	18 34	19 31	03 53	05 34	07 19	09 10
62	17 47	18 31	19 24	03 58	05 34	07 13	08 57
60	17 48	18 29	19 18	04 01	05 33	07 08	08 47
N 58	17 48	18 27	19 13	04 04	05 32	07 03	08 38
56	17 49	18 26	19 09	04 07	05 32	06 59	08 30
54	17 49	18 24	19 05	04 10	05 31	06 55	08 23
52	17 49	18 23	19 02	04 12	05 31	06 52	08 17
50	17 49	18 22	18 59	04 14	05 31	06 49	08 11
45	17 50	18 19	18 54	04 18	05 30	06 43	07 59
N 40	17 51	18 18	18 49	04 22	05 29	06 38	07 49
35	17 51	18 16	18 46	04 25	05 28	06 33	07 41
30	17 52	18 16	18 43	04 28	05 28	06 29	07 33
20	17 53	18 15	18 40	04 33	05 27	06 23	07 21
N 10	17 54	18 15	18 39	04 37	05 26	06 17	07 10
0	17 55	18 15	18 39	04 41	05 25	06 11	06 59
S 10	17 56	18 17	18 41	04 45	05 24	06 05	06 49
20	17 57	18 19	18 45	04 49	05 24	06 00	06 38
30	17 58	18 22	18 50	04 53	05 23	05 53	06 26
35	17 59	18 25	18 54	04 56	05 22	05 49	06 18
40	18 00	18 28	18 59	04 59	05 21	05 45	06 10
45	18 02	18 31	19 06	05 02	05 21	05 40	06 01
S 50	18 03	18 36	19 14	05 06	05 20	05 34	05 50
52	18 04	18 38	19 18	05 08	05 19	05 31	05 44
54	18 05	18 40	19 23	05 10	05 19	05 28	05 39
56	18 06	18 43	19 28	05 12	05 18	05 25	05 32
58	18 07	18 46	19 34	05 15	05 18	05 21	05 25
S 60	18 08	18 50	19 41	05 17	05 17	05 17	05 17

Day	SUN Eqn. of Time 00^h	SUN Eqn. of Time 12^h	SUN Mer. Pass.	MOON Mer. Pass. Upper	MOON Mer. Pass. Lower	MOON Age	MOON Phase
d	m s	m s	h m	h m	h m	d %	
25	08 09	08 20	11 52	23 15	10 52	14 98	○
26	08 30	08 40	11 51	24 00	11 37	15 100	
27	08 51	09 01	11 51	00 00	12 23	16 99	

UT	ARIES	VENUS −4·8		MARS +1·1		JUPITER −1·9		SATURN +0·3	
	GHA	GHA	Dec	GHA	Dec	GHA	Dec	GHA	Dec
d h	° ′	° ′	° ′	° ′	° ′	° ′	° ′	° ′	° ′
28 00	6 47.3	153 31.7	S20 33.4	244 27.6	N21 06.4	225 07.5	N15 40.3	354 52.0	N 2 10.5
01	21 49.7	168 33.8	33.8	259 28.5	06.1	240 09.5	40.2	9 54.6	10.4
02	36 52.2	183 35.9	34.2	274 29.4	05.8	255 11.5	40.0	24 57.3	10.4
03	51 54.7	198 37.9	. . 34.6	289 30.3	. . 05.6	270 13.5	. . 39.9	39 59.9	. . 10.3
04	66 57.1	213 40.0	35.0	304 31.3	05.3	285 15.5	39.8	55 02.6	10.2
05	81 59.6	228 42.1	35.4	319 32.2	05.0	300 17.5	39.6	70 05.2	10.1
06	97 02.0	243 44.2	S20 35.8	334 33.1	N21 04.7	315 19.5	N15 39.5	85 07.9	N 2 10.1
07	112 04.5	258 46.3	36.2	349 34.0	04.5	330 21.6	39.4	100 10.5	10.0
08	127 07.0	273 48.4	36.6	4 34.9	04.2	345 23.6	39.2	115 13.1	09.9
M 09	142 09.4	288 50.5	. . 37.0	19 35.8	. . 03.9	0 25.6	. . 39.1	130 15.8	. . 09.8
O 10	157 11.9	303 52.6	37.4	34 36.8	03.7	15 27.6	38.9	145 18.4	09.7
N 11	172 14.4	318 54.7	37.8	49 37.7	03.4	30 29.6	38.8	160 21.1	09.7
D 12	187 16.8	333 56.8	S20 38.2	64 38.6	N21 03.1	45 31.6	N15 38.7	175 23.7	N 2 09.6
A 13	202 19.3	348 58.9	38.5	79 39.5	02.8	60 33.6	38.5	190 26.4	09.5
Y 14	217 21.8	4 01.0	38.9	94 40.4	02.6	75 35.6	38.4	205 29.0	09.4
15	232 24.2	19 03.1	. . 39.3	109 41.3	. . 02.3	90 37.6	. . 38.3	220 31.6	. . 09.4
16	247 26.7	34 05.2	39.7	124 42.3	02.0	105 39.7	38.1	235 34.3	09.3
17	262 29.2	49 07.4	40.1	139 43.2	01.7	120 41.7	38.0	250 36.9	09.2
18	277 31.6	64 09.5	S20 40.4	154 44.1	N21 01.5	135 43.7	N15 37.9	265 39.6	N 2 09.1
19	292 34.1	79 11.6	40.8	169 45.0	01.2	150 45.7	37.7	280 42.2	09.0
20	307 36.5	94 13.8	41.2	184 45.9	00.9	165 47.7	37.6	295 44.8	09.0
21	322 39.0	109 15.9	. . 41.6	199 46.9	. . 00.6	180 49.7	. . 37.4	310 47.5	. . 08.9
22	337 41.5	124 18.0	41.9	214 47.8	00.4	195 51.7	37.3	325 50.1	08.8
23	352 43.9	139 20.2	42.3	229 48.7	21 00.1	210 53.8	37.2	340 52.8	08.7
29 00	7 46.4	154 22.3	S20 42.7	244 49.6	N20 59.8	225 55.8	N15 37.0	355 55.4	N 2 08.7
01	22 48.9	169 24.5	43.0	259 50.5	59.5	240 57.8	36.9	10 58.1	08.6
02	37 51.3	184 26.7	43.4	274 51.5	59.3	255 59.8	36.8	26 00.7	08.5
03	52 53.8	199 28.8	. . 43.7	289 52.4	. . 59.0	271 01.8	. . 36.6	41 03.3	. . 08.4
04	67 56.3	214 31.0	44.1	304 53.3	58.7	286 03.8	36.5	56 06.0	08.3
05	82 58.7	229 33.1	44.5	319 54.2	58.4	301 05.8	36.4	71 08.6	08.3
06	98 01.2	244 35.3	S20 44.8	334 55.1	N20 58.1	316 07.9	N15 36.2	86 11.3	N 2 08.2
07	113 03.7	259 37.5	45.2	349 56.1	57.9	331 09.9	36.1	101 13.9	08.1
T 08	128 06.1	274 39.7	45.5	4 57.0	57.6	346 11.9	35.9	116 16.6	08.0
U 09	143 08.6	289 41.8	. . 45.9	19 57.9	. . 57.3	1 13.9	. . 35.8	131 19.2	. . 08.0
E 10	158 11.0	304 44.0	46.2	34 58.8	57.0	16 15.9	35.7	146 21.8	07.9
S 11	173 13.5	319 46.2	46.6	49 59.8	56.8	31 17.9	35.5	161 24.5	07.8
D 12	188 16.0	334 48.4	S20 46.9	65 00.7	N20 56.5	46 19.9	N15 35.4	176 27.1	N 2 07.7
A 13	203 18.4	349 50.6	47.3	80 01.6	56.2	61 22.0	35.3	191 29.8	07.6
Y 14	218 20.9	4 52.8	47.6	95 02.5	55.9	76 24.0	35.1	206 32.4	07.6
15	233 23.4	19 55.0	. . 47.9	110 03.5	. . 55.6	91 26.0	. . 35.0	221 35.1	. . 07.5
16	248 25.8	34 57.2	48.3	125 04.4	55.4	106 28.0	34.9	236 37.7	07.4
17	263 28.3	49 59.4	48.6	140 05.3	55.1	121 30.0	34.7	251 40.3	07.3
18	278 30.8	65 01.6	S20 48.9	155 06.2	N20 54.8	136 32.0	N15 34.6	266 43.0	N 2 07.3
19	293 33.2	80 03.9	49.3	170 07.2	54.5	151 34.1	34.5	281 45.6	07.2
20	308 35.7	95 06.1	49.6	185 08.1	54.3	166 36.1	34.3	296 48.3	07.1
21	323 38.1	110 08.3	. . 49.9	200 09.0	. . 54.0	181 38.1	. . 34.2	311 50.9	. . 07.0
22	338 40.6	125 10.5	50.3	215 09.9	53.7	196 40.1	34.0	326 53.6	06.9
23	353 43.1	140 12.8	50.6	230 10.9	53.4	211 42.1	33.9	341 56.2	06.9
30 00	8 45.5	155 15.0	S20 50.9	245 11.8	N20 53.1	226 44.1	N15 33.8	356 58.9	N 2 06.8
01	23 48.0	170 17.2	51.2	260 12.7	52.9	241 46.2	33.6	12 01.5	06.7
02	38 50.5	185 19.5	51.6	275 13.6	52.6	256 48.2	33.5	27 04.1	06.6
03	53 52.9	200 21.7	. . 51.9	290 14.6	. . 52.3	271 50.2	. . 33.4	42 06.8	. . 06.6
04	68 55.4	215 24.0	52.2	305 15.5	52.0	286 52.2	33.2	57 09.4	06.5
05	83 57.9	230 26.2	52.5	320 16.4	51.7	301 54.2	33.1	72 12.1	06.4
06	99 00.3	245 28.5	S20 52.8	335 17.4	N20 51.5	316 56.2	N15 33.0	87 14.7	N 2 06.3
W 07	114 02.8	260 30.7	53.1	350 18.3	51.2	331 58.3	32.8	102 17.4	06.2
E 08	129 05.3	275 33.0	53.4	5 19.2	50.9	347 00.3	32.7	117 20.0	06.2
D 09	144 07.7	290 35.3	. . 53.8	20 20.2	. . 50.6	2 02.3	. . 32.6	132 22.6	. . 06.1
N 10	159 10.2	305 37.5	54.1	35 21.1	50.3	17 04.3	32.4	147 25.3	06.0
E 11	174 12.6	320 39.8	54.4	50 22.0	50.0	32 06.3	32.3	162 27.9	05.9
S 12	189 15.1	335 42.1	S20 54.7	65 22.9	N20 49.8	47 08.4	N15 32.2	177 30.6	N 2 05.9
D 13	204 17.6	350 44.4	55.0	80 23.9	49.5	62 10.4	32.0	192 33.2	05.8
A 14	219 20.0	5 46.7	55.3	95 24.8	49.2	77 12.4	31.9	207 35.9	05.7
Y 15	234 22.5	20 49.0	. . 55.6	110 25.7	. . 48.9	92 14.4	. . 31.7	222 38.5	. . 05.6
16	249 25.0	35 51.2	55.9	125 26.7	48.6	107 16.4	31.6	237 41.1	05.5
17	264 27.4	50 53.5	56.2	140 27.6	48.4	122 18.5	31.5	252 43.8	05.5
18	279 29.9	65 55.8	S20 56.5	155 28.5	N20 48.1	137 20.5	N15 31.3	267 46.4	N 2 05.4
19	294 32.4	80 58.1	56.7	170 29.5	47.8	152 22.5	31.2	282 49.1	05.3
20	309 34.8	96 00.5	57.0	185 30.4	47.5	167 24.5	31.1	297 51.7	05.2
21	324 37.3	111 02.8	. . 57.3	200 31.3	. . 47.2	182 26.5	. . 30.9	312 54.4	. . 05.2
22	339 39.8	126 05.1	57.6	215 32.3	46.9	197 28.6	30.8	327 57.0	05.1
23	354 42.2	141 07.4	57.9	230 33.2	46.7	212 30.6	30.7	342 59.7	05.0
Mer. Pass.	h m 23 25.1	*v* 2.2	*d* 0.3	*v* 0.9	*d* 0.3	*v* 2.0	*d* 0.1	*v* 2.6	*d* 0.1

STARS

Name	SHA	Dec
	° ′	° ′
Acamar	315 10.4	S40 11.6
Achernar	335 18.6	S57 05.8
Acrux	172 59.2	S63 14.8
Adhara	255 04.8	S29 00.2
Aldebaran	290 37.8	N16 33.8
Alioth	166 12.3	N55 48.9
Alkaid	152 51.3	N49 10.9
Alnair	27 30.8	S46 49.9
Alnilam	275 36.2	S 1 10.9
Alphard	217 46.6	S 8 46.3
Alphecca	126 02.8	N26 37.6
Alpheratz	357 33.0	N29 14.5
Altair	61 58.5	N 8 56.5
Ankaa	353 05.3	S42 09.5
Antares	112 14.3	S26 29.5
Arcturus	145 46.9	N19 02.7
Atria	107 07.4	S69 04.7
Avior	234 14.5	S59 35.4
Bellatrix	278 21.3	N 6 22.5
Betelgeuse	270 50.5	N 7 24.8
Canopus	263 51.8	S52 42.2
Capella	280 19.7	N46 01.4
Deneb	49 24.6	N45 22.8
Denebola	182 23.8	N14 25.4
Diphda	348 45.5	S17 50.2
Dubhe	193 39.9	N61 36.3
Elnath	278 00.0	N28 37.8
Eltanin	90 41.6	N51 29.4
Enif	33 37.2	N10 00.1
Fomalhaut	15 12.6	S29 28.7
Gacrux	171 50.7	S57 15.8
Gienah	175 42.5	S17 41.3
Hadar	148 34.6	S60 30.2
Hamal	327 49.3	N23 35.4
Kaus Aust.	83 30.6	S34 22.4
Kochab	137 20.8	N74 02.8
Markab	13 28.2	N15 21.2
Menkar	314 04.4	N 4 11.8
Menkent	147 56.3	S36 30.1
Miaplacidus	221 38.6	S69 49.3
Mirfak	308 25.9	N49 57.3
Nunki	75 46.0	S26 15.8
Peacock	53 03.2	S56 39.0
Pollux	243 15.7	N27 57.6
Procyon	244 49.5	N 5 09.5
Rasalhague	95 57.3	N12 32.6
Regulus	207 33.2	N11 50.2
Rigel	281 02.4	S 8 10.0
Rigil Kent.	139 38.9	S60 56.8
Sabik	102 01.3	S15 45.4
Schedar	349 28.9	N56 41.2
Shaula	96 08.5	S37 07.5
Sirius	258 25.0	S16 44.9
Spica	158 21.1	S11 18.0
Suhail	222 45.6	S43 32.2
Vega	80 32.3	N38 48.8
Zuben'ubi	136 54.7	S16 09.1

	SHA	Mer. Pass.
	° ′	h m
Venus	146 35.9	13 41
Mars	237 03.2	7 40
Jupiter	218 09.4	8 55
Saturn	348 09.0	0 16

UT	SUN GHA	SUN Dec	MOON GHA	v	MOON Dec	d	HP
d h	° ′	° ′	° ′	′	° ′	′	′
28 00	182 17.9	S 1 56.7	348 30.9	11.4	N12 09.2	14.8	58.5
01	197 18.1	57.6	3 01.3	11.2	12 24.0	14.9	58.5
02	212 18.3	58.6	17 31.5	11.2	12 38.9	14.8	58.5
03	227 18.5	1 59.6	32 01.7	11.1	12 53.7	14.7	58.5
04	242 18.7	2 00.5	46 31.8	11.0	13 08.4	14.6	58.6
05	257 18.9	01.5	61 01.8	11.0	13 23.0	14.6	58.6
06	272 19.1	S 2 02.5	75 31.8	10.8	N13 37.6	14.6	58.6
07	287 19.4	03.5	90 01.6	10.8	13 52.2	14.4	58.6
08	302 19.6	04.4	104 31.4	10.6	14 06.6	14.4	58.6
M 09	317 19.8	. . 05.4	119 01.0	10.6	14 21.0	14.4	58.7
O 10	332 20.0	06.4	133 30.6	10.5	14 35.4	14.2	58.7
N 11	347 20.2	07.4	148 00.1	10.4	14 49.6	14.2	58.7
D 12	2 20.4	S 2 08.3	162 29.5	10.3	N15 03.8	14.2	58.7
A 13	17 20.6	09.3	176 58.8	10.3	15 18.0	14.0	58.7
Y 14	32 20.8	10.3	191 28.1	10.1	15 32.0	14.0	58.7
15	47 21.0	. . 11.2	205 57.2	10.0	15 46.0	13.9	58.8
16	62 21.2	12.2	220 26.2	10.0	15 59.9	13.8	58.8
17	77 21.5	13.2	234 55.2	9.8	16 13.7	13.7	58.8
18	92 21.7	S 2 14.2	249 24.0	9.8	N16 27.4	13.7	58.8
19	107 21.9	15.1	263 52.8	9.6	16 41.1	13.5	58.8
20	122 22.1	16.1	278 21.4	9.6	16 54.6	13.5	58.8
21	137 22.3	. . 17.1	292 50.0	9.5	17 08.1	13.4	58.9
22	152 22.5	18.0	307 18.5	9.3	17 21.5	13.3	58.9
23	167 22.7	19.0	321 46.8	9.3	17 34.8	13.2	58.9
29 00	182 22.9	S 2 20.0	336 15.1	9.2	N17 48.0	13.1	58.9
01	197 23.1	21.0	350 43.3	9.0	18 01.1	13.0	58.9
02	212 23.3	21.9	5 11.3	9.0	18 14.1	13.0	58.9
03	227 23.6	. . 22.9	19 39.3	8.9	18 27.1	12.8	58.9
04	242 23.8	23.9	34 07.2	8.7	18 39.9	12.7	59.0
05	257 24.0	24.8	48 34.9	8.7	18 52.6	12.6	59.0
06	272 24.2	S 2 25.8	63 02.6	8.6	N19 05.2	12.5	59.0
07	287 24.4	26.8	77 30.2	8.4	19 17.7	12.4	59.0
T 08	302 24.6	27.8	91 57.6	8.4	19 30.1	12.3	59.0
U 09	317 24.8	. . 28.7	106 25.0	8.3	19 42.4	12.2	59.0
E 10	332 25.0	29.7	120 52.3	8.1	19 54.6	12.1	59.0
S 11	347 25.2	30.7	135 19.4	8.1	20 06.7	11.9	59.0
D 12	2 25.4	S 2 31.6	149 46.5	7.9	N20 18.6	11.9	59.1
A 13	17 25.6	32.6	164 13.4	7.9	20 30.5	11.7	59.1
Y 14	32 25.8	33.6	178 40.3	7.7	20 42.2	11.6	59.1
15	47 26.1	. . 34.6	193 07.0	7.7	20 53.8	11.5	59.1
16	62 26.3	35.5	207 33.7	7.5	21 05.3	11.4	59.1
17	77 26.5	36.5	222 00.2	7.4	21 16.7	11.2	59.1
18	92 26.7	S 2 37.5	236 26.6	7.4	N21 27.9	11.1	59.1
19	107 26.9	38.4	250 53.0	7.2	21 39.0	11.0	59.1
20	122 27.1	39.4	265 19.2	7.2	21 50.0	10.9	59.1
21	137 27.3	. . 40.4	279 45.4	7.0	22 00.9	10.7	59.1
22	152 27.5	41.4	294 11.4	6.9	22 11.6	10.6	59.2
23	167 27.7	42.3	308 37.3	6.8	22 22.2	10.5	59.2
30 00	182 27.9	S 2 43.3	323 03.1	6.8	N22 32.7	10.3	59.2
01	197 28.1	44.3	337 28.9	6.6	22 43.0	10.2	59.2
02	212 28.3	45.2	351 54.5	6.5	22 53.2	10.0	59.2
03	227 28.5	. . 46.2	6 20.0	6.5	23 03.2	9.9	59.2
04	242 28.7	47.2	20 45.5	6.3	23 13.1	9.8	59.2
05	257 28.9	48.1	35 10.8	6.2	23 22.9	9.6	59.2
06	272 29.2	S 2 49.1	49 36.0	6.2	N23 32.5	9.5	59.2
W 07	287 29.4	50.1	64 01.2	6.0	23 42.0	9.3	59.2
E 08	302 29.6	51.1	78 26.2	6.0	23 51.3	9.2	59.2
D 09	317 29.8	. . 52.0	92 51.2	5.8	24 00.5	9.0	59.2
N 10	332 30.0	53.0	107 16.0	5.8	24 09.5	8.9	59.3
E 11	347 30.2	54.0	121 40.8	5.6	24 18.4	8.7	59.3
S 12	2 30.4	S 2 54.9	136 05.4	5.6	N24 27.1	8.5	59.3
D 13	17 30.6	55.9	150 30.0	5.5	24 35.6	8.4	59.3
A 14	32 30.8	56.9	164 54.5	5.4	24 44.0	8.3	59.3
Y 15	47 31.0	. . 57.8	179 18.9	5.3	24 52.3	8.1	59.3
16	62 31.2	58.8	193 43.2	5.2	25 00.4	7.9	59.3
17	77 31.4	2 59.8	208 07.4	5.1	25 08.3	7.7	59.3
18	92 31.6	S 3 00.8	222 31.5	5.1	N25 16.0	7.6	59.3
19	107 31.8	01.7	236 55.6	4.9	25 23.6	7.5	59.3
20	122 32.0	02.7	251 19.5	4.9	25 31.1	7.2	59.3
21	137 32.2	. . 03.7	265 43.4	4.8	25 38.3	7.1	59.3
22	152 32.4	04.6	280 07.2	4.7	25 45.4	6.9	59.3
23	167 32.6	05.6	294 30.9	4.7	N25 52.3	6.8	59.3
	SD 16.0	*d* 1.0	SD	16.0	16.1		16.1

Lat.	Twilight Naut.	Twilight Civil	Sunrise	Moonrise 28	Moonrise 29	Moonrise 30	Moonrise 1
°	h m	h m	h m	h m	h m	h m	h m
N 72	03 38	05 02	06 10	15 18	□	□	□
N 70	03 52	05 07	06 07	15 54	□	□	□
68	04 03	05 10	06 06	16 19	15 27	□	□
66	04 12	05 13	06 04	16 39	16 13	□	□
64	04 19	05 15	06 03	16 56	16 43	16 18	□
62	04 25	05 17	06 02	17 09	17 06	17 03	17 02
60	04 30	05 19	06 01	17 21	17 24	17 33	17 54
N 58	04 34	05 21	06 00	17 31	17 40	17 56	18 26
56	04 38	05 22	05 59	17 40	17 53	18 14	18 50
54	04 42	05 23	05 58	17 47	18 05	18 30	19 10
52	04 44	05 24	05 57	17 55	18 15	18 44	19 26
50	04 47	05 25	05 57	18 01	18 24	18 56	19 40
45	04 52	05 26	05 55	18 15	18 44	19 21	20 09
N 40	04 56	05 27	05 54	18 26	19 00	19 41	20 32
35	04 59	05 28	05 53	18 36	19 13	19 57	20 51
30	05 01	05 28	05 52	18 45	19 25	20 12	21 07
20	05 03	05 28	05 50	19 00	19 45	20 37	21 34
N 10	05 03	05 28	05 49	19 13	20 03	20 58	21 58
0	05 02	05 26	05 47	19 26	20 20	21 19	22 20
S 10	05 00	05 24	05 45	19 39	20 37	21 39	22 42
20	04 56	05 21	05 43	19 52	20 55	22 01	23 06
30	04 49	05 17	05 41	20 08	21 16	22 26	23 34
35	04 45	05 14	05 40	20 17	21 29	22 41	23 51
40	04 39	05 11	05 38	20 28	21 43	22 59	24 10
45	04 32	05 07	05 36	20 40	22 01	23 20	24 34
S 50	04 23	05 01	05 34	20 56	22 22	23 47	25 04
52	04 18	04 59	05 33	21 03	22 32	24 00	00 00
54	04 13	04 56	05 31	21 11	22 44	24 15	00 15
56	04 07	04 53	05 30	21 20	22 57	24 33	00 33
58	04 01	04 49	05 29	21 30	23 13	24 55	00 55
S 60	03 53	04 45	05 27	21 42	23 32	25 23	01 23

Lat.	Sunset	Twilight Civil	Twilight Naut.	Moonset 28	Moonset 29	Moonset 30	Moonset 1
°	h m	h m	h m	h m	h m	h m	h m
N 72	17 29	18 36	19 58	10 41	□	□	□
N 70	17 31	18 32	19 45	10 07	□	□	□
68	17 33	18 28	19 35	09 43	12 25	□	□
66	17 35	18 26	19 26	09 24	11 41	□	□
64	17 36	18 23	19 20	09 10	11 12	13 37	□
62	17 38	18 22	19 14	08 57	10 50	12 52	15 00
60	17 39	18 20	19 09	08 47	10 33	12 23	14 09
N 58	17 40	18 19	19 05	08 38	10 18	12 01	13 37
56	17 41	18 18	19 01	08 30	10 05	11 42	13 13
54	17 41	18 17	18 58	08 23	09 55	11 27	12 54
52	17 42	18 16	18 55	08 17	09 45	11 14	12 38
50	17 43	18 15	18 53	08 11	09 36	11 02	12 24
45	17 44	18 14	18 48	07 59	09 18	10 39	11 56
N 40	17 46	18 13	18 44	07 49	09 04	10 19	11 33
35	17 47	18 12	18 41	07 41	08 51	10 03	11 15
30	17 48	18 12	18 40	07 33	08 40	09 50	10 59
20	17 50	18 12	18 37	07 21	08 22	09 26	10 32
N 10	17 52	18 13	18 37	07 10	08 06	09 06	10 09
0	17 54	18 14	18 38	06 59	07 51	08 47	09 48
S 10	17 55	18 16	18 41	06 49	07 36	08 29	09 26
20	17 58	18 20	18 45	06 38	07 21	08 09	09 03
30	18 00	18 24	18 52	06 26	07 03	07 46	08 37
35	18 02	18 27	18 57	06 18	06 52	07 32	08 21
40	18 03	18 31	19 03	06 10	06 40	07 17	08 03
45	18 05	18 35	19 10	06 01	06 26	06 59	07 41
S 50	18 08	18 41	19 19	05 50	06 09	06 36	07 13
52	18 09	18 43	19 24	05 44	06 02	06 25	07 00
54	18 10	18 46	19 29	05 39	05 53	06 13	06 44
56	18 12	18 49	19 35	05 32	05 43	05 59	06 26
58	18 13	18 53	19 42	05 25	05 32	05 43	06 04
S 60	18 15	18 57	19 49	05 17	05 19	05 23	05 35

Day	SUN Eqn. of Time 00^h	SUN Eqn. of Time 12^h	SUN Mer. Pass.	MOON Mer. Pass. Upper	MOON Mer. Pass. Lower	Age	Phase
d	m s	m s	h m	h m	h m	d	%
28	09 11	09 21	11 51	00 48	13 13	17	96
29	09 31	09 41	11 50	01 38	14 06	18	90
30	09 51	10 01	11 50	02 34	15 03	19	82

Day	UT d h	ARIES GHA ° ′	VENUS −4·7 GHA ° ′	VENUS Dec ° ′	MARS +1·1 GHA ° ′	MARS Dec ° ′	JUPITER −1·9 GHA ° ′	JUPITER Dec ° ′	SATURN +0·3 GHA ° ′	SATURN Dec ° ′
THURSDAY	1 00	9 44.7	156 09.7	S20 58.2	245 34.1	N20 46.4	227 32.6	N15 30.5	358 02.3	N 2 04.9
	01	24 47.1	171 12.0	58.4	260 35.1	46.1	242 34.6	30.4	13 04.9	04.8
	02	39 49.6	186 14.4	58.7	275 36.0	45.8	257 36.6	30.3	28 07.6	04.8
	03	54 52.1	201 16.7	. . 59.0	290 37.0	. . 45.5	272 38.7	. . 30.1	43 10.2	. . 04.7
	04	69 54.5	216 19.0	59.3	305 37.9	45.2	287 40.7	30.0	58 12.9	04.6
	05	84 57.0	231 21.4	59.5	320 38.8	45.0	302 42.7	29.9	73 15.5	04.5
	06	99 59.5	246 23.7	S20 59.8	335 39.8	N20 44.7	317 44.7	N15 29.7	88 18.2	N 2 04.5
	07	115 01.9	261 26.1	21 00.1	350 40.7	44.4	332 46.7	29.6	103 20.8	04.4
	08	130 04.4	276 28.4	00.4	5 41.6	44.1	347 48.8	29.5	118 23.4	04.3
	09	145 06.9	291 30.8	. . 00.6	20 42.6	. . 43.8	2 50.8	. . 29.3	133 26.1	. . 04.2
	10	160 09.3	306 33.1	00.9	35 43.5	43.5	17 52.8	29.2	148 28.7	04.1
	11	175 11.8	321 35.5	01.1	50 44.4	43.2	32 54.8	29.1	163 31.4	04.1
	12	190 14.3	336 37.9	S21 01.4	65 45.4	N20 43.0	47 56.9	N15 28.9	178 34.0	N 2 04.0
	13	205 16.7	351 40.2	01.7	80 46.3	42.7	62 58.9	28.8	193 36.7	03.9
	14	220 19.2	6 42.6	01.9	95 47.3	42.4	78 00.9	28.7	208 39.3	03.8
	15	235 21.6	21 45.0	. . 02.2	110 48.2	. . 42.1	93 02.9	. . 28.5	223 42.0	. . 03.8
	16	250 24.1	36 47.4	02.4	125 49.1	41.8	108 05.0	28.4	238 44.6	03.7
	17	265 26.6	51 49.8	02.7	140 50.1	41.5	123 07.0	28.3	253 47.2	03.6
	18	280 29.0	66 52.2	S21 02.9	155 51.0	N20 41.2	138 09.0	N15 28.1	268 49.9	N 2 03.5
	19	295 31.5	81 54.5	03.2	170 52.0	41.0	153 11.0	28.0	283 52.5	03.5
	20	310 34.0	96 56.9	03.4	185 52.9	40.7	168 13.0	27.9	298 55.2	03.4
	21	325 36.4	111 59.3	. . 03.7	200 53.8	. . 40.4	183 15.1	. . 27.7	313 57.8	. . 03.3
	22	340 38.9	127 01.7	03.9	215 54.8	40.1	198 17.1	27.6	329 00.5	03.2
	23	355 41.4	142 04.2	04.1	230 55.7	39.8	213 19.1	27.5	344 03.1	03.1
FRIDAY	2 00	10 43.8	157 06.6	S21 04.4	245 56.7	N20 39.5	228 21.1	N15 27.3	359 05.8	N 2 03.1
	01	25 46.3	172 09.0	04.6	260 57.6	39.2	243 23.2	27.2	14 08.4	03.0
	02	40 48.7	187 11.4	04.8	275 58.6	38.9	258 25.2	27.0	29 11.0	02.9
	03	55 51.2	202 13.8	. . 05.1	290 59.5	. . 38.7	273 27.2	. . 26.9	44 13.7	. . 02.8
	04	70 53.7	217 16.2	05.3	306 00.4	38.4	288 29.2	26.8	59 16.3	02.8
	05	85 56.1	232 18.7	05.5	321 01.4	38.1	303 31.3	26.6	74 19.0	02.7
	06	100 58.6	247 21.1	S21 05.8	336 02.3	N20 37.8	318 33.3	N15 26.5	89 21.6	N 2 02.6
	07	116 01.1	262 23.6	06.0	351 03.3	37.5	333 35.3	26.4	104 24.3	02.5
	08	131 03.5	277 26.0	06.2	6 04.2	37.2	348 37.3	26.2	119 26.9	02.4
	09	146 06.0	292 28.4	. . 06.4	21 05.2	. . 36.9	3 39.4	. . 26.1	134 29.5	. . 02.4
	10	161 08.5	307 30.9	06.6	36 06.1	36.6	18 41.4	26.0	149 32.2	02.3
	11	176 10.9	322 33.3	06.8	51 07.1	36.3	33 43.4	25.8	164 34.8	02.2
	12	191 13.4	337 35.8	S21 07.1	66 08.0	N20 36.1	48 45.5	N15 25.7	179 37.5	N 2 02.1
	13	206 15.9	352 38.3	07.3	81 09.0	35.8	63 47.5	25.6	194 40.1	02.1
	14	221 18.3	7 40.7	07.5	96 09.9	35.5	78 49.5	25.4	209 42.8	02.0
	15	236 20.8	22 43.2	. . 07.7	111 10.8	. . 35.2	93 51.5	. . 25.3	224 45.4	. . 01.9
	16	251 23.2	37 45.7	07.9	126 11.8	34.9	108 53.6	25.2	239 48.1	01.8
	17	266 25.7	52 48.1	08.1	141 12.7	34.6	123 55.6	25.0	254 50.7	01.7
	18	281 28.2	67 50.6	S21 08.3	156 13.7	N20 34.3	138 57.6	N15 24.9	269 53.3	N 2 01.7
	19	296 30.6	82 53.1	08.5	171 14.6	34.0	153 59.6	24.8	284 56.0	01.6
	20	311 33.1	97 55.6	08.7	186 15.6	33.7	169 01.7	24.6	299 58.6	01.5
	21	326 35.6	112 58.1	. . 08.9	201 16.5	. . 33.4	184 03.7	. . 24.5	315 01.3	. . 01.4
	22	341 38.0	128 00.6	09.1	216 17.5	33.2	199 05.7	24.4	330 03.9	01.4
	23	356 40.5	143 03.1	09.3	231 18.4	32.9	214 07.8	24.3	345 06.6	01.3
SATURDAY	3 00	11 43.0	158 05.6	S21 09.5	246 19.4	N20 32.6	229 09.8	N15 24.1	0 09.2	N 2 01.2
	01	26 45.4	173 08.1	09.7	261 20.3	32.3	244 11.8	24.0	15 11.9	01.1
	02	41 47.9	188 10.6	09.8	276 21.3	32.0	259 13.8	23.9	30 14.5	01.0
	03	56 50.4	203 13.1	. . 10.0	291 22.2	. . 31.7	274 15.9	. . 23.7	45 17.1	. . 01.0
	04	71 52.8	218 15.6	10.2	306 23.2	31.4	289 17.9	23.6	60 19.8	00.9
	05	86 55.3	233 18.1	10.4	321 24.1	31.1	304 19.9	23.5	75 22.4	00.8
	06	101 57.7	248 20.7	S21 10.6	336 25.1	N20 30.8	319 22.0	N15 23.3	90 25.1	N 2 00.7
	07	117 00.2	263 23.2	10.8	351 26.0	30.5	334 24.0	23.2	105 27.7	00.7
	08	132 02.7	278 25.7	10.9	6 27.0	30.2	349 26.0	23.1	120 30.4	00.6
	09	147 05.1	293 28.2	. . 11.1	21 27.9	. . 29.9	4 28.0	. . 22.9	135 33.0	. . 00.5
	10	162 07.6	308 30.8	11.3	36 28.9	29.7	19 30.1	22.8	150 35.7	00.4
	11	177 10.1	323 33.3	11.4	51 29.8	29.4	34 32.1	22.7	165 38.3	00.3
	12	192 12.5	338 35.9	S21 11.6	66 30.8	N20 29.1	49 34.1	N15 22.5	180 40.9	N 2 00.3
	13	207 15.0	353 38.4	11.8	81 31.8	28.8	64 36.2	22.4	195 43.6	00.2
	14	222 17.5	8 41.0	11.9	96 32.7	28.5	79 38.2	22.3	210 46.2	00.1
	15	237 19.9	23 43.5	. . 12.1	111 33.7	. . 28.2	94 40.2	. . 22.1	225 48.9	. . 00.0
	16	252 22.4	38 46.1	12.2	126 34.6	27.9	109 42.3	22.0	240 51.5	2 00.0
	17	267 24.9	53 48.7	12.4	141 35.6	27.6	124 44.3	21.9	255 54.2	1 59.9
	18	282 27.3	68 51.2	S21 12.6	156 36.5	N20 27.3	139 46.3	N15 21.7	270 56.8	N 1 59.8
	19	297 29.8	83 53.8	12.7	171 37.5	27.0	154 48.3	21.6	285 59.5	59.7
	20	312 32.2	98 56.4	12.9	186 38.4	26.7	169 50.4	21.5	301 02.1	59.6
	21	327 34.7	113 59.0	. . 13.0	201 39.4	. . 26.4	184 52.4	. . 21.3	316 04.8	. . 59.6
	22	342 37.2	129 01.6	13.2	216 40.4	26.1	199 54.4	21.2	331 07.4	59.5
	23	357 39.6	144 04.1	13.3	231 41.3	25.8	214 56.5	21.1	346 10.0	59.4
	Mer. Pass. (h m)	23 13.3	*v* 2.5	*d* 0.2	*v* 0.9	*d* 0.3	*v* 2.0	*d* 0.1	*v* 2.6	*d* 0.1

STARS

Name	SHA ° ′	Dec ° ′
Acamar	315 10.3	S40 11.6
Achernar	335 18.6	S57 05.9
Acrux	172 59.2	S63 14.8
Adhara	255 04.8	S29 00.2
Aldebaran	290 37.8	N16 33.8
Alioth	166 12.3	N55 48.9
Alkaid	152 51.3	N49 10.9
Alnair	27 30.8	S46 49.9
Alnilam	275 36.2	S 1 10.9
Alphard	217 46.6	S 8 46.3
Alphecca	126 02.8	N26 37.6
Alpheratz	357 32.9	N29 14.5
Altair	61 58.5	N 8 56.5
Ankaa	353 05.3	S42 09.5
Antares	112 14.3	S26 29.5
Arcturus	145 46.9	N19 02.7
Atria	107 07.4	S69 04.7
Avior	234 14.4	S59 35.4
Bellatrix	278 21.2	N 6 22.5
Betelgeuse	270 50.5	N 7 24.8
Canopus	263 51.7	S52 42.2
Capella	280 19.6	N46 01.4
Deneb	49 24.6	N45 22.8
Denebola	182 23.8	N14 25.4
Diphda	348 45.5	S17 50.2
Dubhe	193 39.9	N61 36.3
Elnath	278 00.0	N28 37.8
Eltanin	90 41.6	N51 29.4
Enif	33 37.2	N10 00.1
Fomalhaut	15 12.6	S29 28.7
Gacrux	171 50.6	S57 15.7
Gienah	175 42.5	S17 41.3
Hadar	148 34.6	S60 30.2
Hamal	327 49.3	N23 35.5
Kaus Aust.	83 30.7	S34 22.4
Kochab	137 20.8	N74 02.8
Markab	13 28.2	N15 21.2
Menkar	314 04.4	N 4 11.8
Menkent	147 56.3	S36 30.1
Miaplacidus	221 38.6	S69 49.3
Mirfak	308 25.8	N49 57.3
Nunki	75 46.0	S26 15.8
Peacock	53 03.2	S56 39.0
Pollux	243 15.7	N27 57.6
Procyon	244 49.4	N 5 09.5
Rasalhague	95 57.3	N12 32.6
Regulus	207 33.2	N11 50.2
Rigel	281 02.4	S 8 10.0
Rigil Kent.	139 38.9	S60 56.8
Sabik	102 01.3	S15 45.4
Schedar	349 28.8	N56 41.2
Shaula	96 08.5	S37 07.4
Sirius	258 25.0	S16 44.9
Spica	158 21.1	S11 18.0
Suhail	222 45.5	S43 32.2
Vega	80 32.3	N38 48.8
Zuben'ubi	136 54.7	S16 09.1

	SHA ° ′	Mer. Pass. h m
Venus	146 22.7	13 29
Mars	235 12.9	7 36
Jupiter	217 37.3	8 45
Saturn	348 21.9	0 04

	UT	SUN GHA	SUN Dec	MOON GHA	v	MOON Dec	d	HP
	d h	° ′	° ′	° ′	′	° ′	′	′
	1 00	182 32.8	S 3 06.6	308 54.6	4.5	N25 59.1	6.5	59.3
	01	197 33.0	07.5	323 18.1	4.5	26 05.6	6.4	59.3
	02	212 33.2	08.5	337 41.6	4.4	26 12.0	6.3	59.3
	03	227 33.4	. . 09.5	352 05.0	4.4	26 18.3	6.0	59.3
	04	242 33.6	10.5	6 28.4	4.3	26 24.3	5.9	59.3
	05	257 33.8	11.4	20 51.7	4.2	26 30.2	5.7	59.3
	06	272 34.1	S 3 12.4	35 14.9	4.1	N26 35.9	5.5	59.4
	07	287 34.3	13.4	49 38.0	4.1	26 41.4	5.3	59.4
T	08	302 34.5	14.3	64 01.1	4.0	26 46.7	5.2	59.4
H	09	317 34.7	. . 15.3	78 24.1	4.0	26 51.9	4.9	59.4
U	10	332 34.9	16.3	92 47.1	3.9	26 56.8	4.8	59.4
R	11	347 35.1	17.2	107 10.0	3.9	27 01.6	4.6	59.4
S	12	2 35.3	S 3 18.2	121 32.9	3.8	N27 06.2	4.4	59.4
D	13	17 35.5	19.2	135 55.7	3.7	27 10.6	4.3	59.4
A	14	32 35.7	20.1	150 18.4	3.7	27 14.9	4.0	59.4
Y	15	47 35.9	. . 21.1	164 41.1	3.7	27 18.9	3.8	59.4
	16	62 36.1	22.1	179 03.8	3.6	27 22.7	3.7	59.4
	17	77 36.3	23.0	193 26.4	3.5	27 26.4	3.5	59.4
	18	92 36.5	S 3 24.0	207 48.9	3.6	N27 29.9	3.3	59.4
	19	107 36.7	25.0	222 11.5	3.5	27 33.2	3.1	59.4
	20	122 36.9	26.0	236 34.0	3.4	27 36.3	2.9	59.4
	21	137 37.1	. . 26.9	250 56.4	3.4	27 39.2	2.7	59.4
	22	152 37.3	27.9	265 18.8	3.4	27 41.9	2.5	59.4
	23	167 37.5	28.9	279 41.2	3.4	27 44.4	2.3	59.4
	2 00	182 37.7	S 3 29.8	294 03.6	3.3	N27 46.7	2.1	59.4
	01	197 37.9	30.8	308 25.9	3.4	27 48.8	2.0	59.4
	02	212 38.1	31.8	322 48.3	3.3	27 50.8	1.7	59.4
	03	227 38.3	. . 32.7	337 10.6	3.2	27 52.5	1.6	59.4
	04	242 38.5	33.7	351 32.8	3.3	27 54.1	1.3	59.4
	05	257 38.7	34.7	5 55.1	3.3	27 55.4	1.2	59.4
	06	272 38.9	S 3 35.6	20 17.4	3.2	N27 56.6	1.0	59.4
	07	287 39.1	36.6	34 39.6	3.3	27 57.6	0.7	59.4
	08	302 39.3	37.6	49 01.9	3.2	27 58.3	0.6	59.4
F	09	317 39.5	. . 38.5	63 24.1	3.2	27 58.9	0.4	59.4
R	10	332 39.7	39.5	77 46.3	3.3	27 59.3	0.2	59.4
I	11	347 39.9	40.5	92 08.6	3.2	27 59.5	0.0	59.4
D	12	2 40.1	S 3 41.4	106 30.8	3.2	N27 59.5	0.3	59.4
A	13	17 40.3	42.4	120 53.0	3.3	27 59.2	0.4	59.3
Y	14	32 40.5	43.4	135 15.3	3.3	27 58.8	0.6	59.3
	15	47 40.7	. . 44.3	149 37.6	3.2	27 58.2	0.7	59.3
	16	62 40.9	45.3	163 59.8	3.3	27 57.5	1.0	59.3
	17	77 41.1	46.3	178 22.1	3.4	27 56.5	1.2	59.3
	18	92 41.3	S 3 47.2	192 44.5	3.3	N27 55.3	1.4	59.3
	19	107 41.5	48.2	207 06.8	3.3	27 53.9	1.5	59.3
	20	122 41.7	49.2	221 29.1	3.4	27 52.4	1.8	59.3
	21	137 41.9	. . 50.1	235 51.5	3.4	27 50.6	2.0	59.3
	22	152 42.1	51.1	250 13.9	3.5	27 48.6	2.1	59.3
	23	167 42.2	52.1	264 36.4	3.5	27 46.5	2.3	59.3
	3 00	182 42.4	S 3 53.0	278 58.9	3.5	N27 44.2	2.6	59.3
	01	197 42.6	54.0	293 21.4	3.5	27 41.6	2.7	59.3
	02	212 42.8	55.0	307 43.9	3.6	27 38.9	2.9	59.3
	03	227 43.0	. . 55.9	322 06.5	3.7	27 36.0	3.1	59.3
	04	242 43.2	56.9	336 29.2	3.7	27 32.9	3.3	59.3
	05	257 43.4	57.9	350 51.9	3.7	27 29.6	3.4	59.3
	06	272 43.6	S 3 58.8	5 14.6	3.8	N27 26.2	3.7	59.3
	07	287 43.8	3 59.8	19 37.4	3.8	27 22.5	3.8	59.3
S	08	302 44.0	4 00.8	34 00.2	3.9	27 18.7	4.1	59.3
A	09	317 44.2	. . 01.7	48 23.1	4.0	27 14.6	4.2	59.3
T	10	332 44.4	02.7	62 46.1	4.0	27 10.4	4.4	59.3
U	11	347 44.6	03.7	77 09.1	4.0	27 06.0	4.6	59.3
R	12	2 44.8	S 4 04.6	91 32.1	4.2	N27 01.4	4.7	59.2
D	13	17 45.0	05.6	105 55.3	4.1	26 56.7	5.0	59.2
A	14	32 45.2	06.6	120 18.4	4.3	26 51.7	5.1	59.2
Y	15	47 45.4	. . 07.5	134 41.7	4.3	26 46.6	5.3	59.2
	16	62 45.6	08.5	149 05.0	4.4	26 41.3	5.5	59.2
	17	77 45.8	09.5	163 28.4	4.5	26 35.8	5.6	59.2
	18	92 46.0	S 4 10.4	177 51.9	4.5	N26 30.2	5.8	59.2
	19	107 46.2	11.4	192 15.4	4.7	26 24.4	6.0	59.2
	20	122 46.3	12.4	206 39.1	4.6	26 18.4	6.2	59.2
	21	137 46.5	. . 13.3	221 02.7	4.8	26 12.2	6.4	59.2
	22	152 46.7	14.3	235 26.5	4.9	26 05.8	6.5	59.2
	23	167 46.9	15.2	249 50.4	4.9	N25 59.3	6.7	59.2
		SD 16.0	*d* 1.0	SD 16.2		16.2		16.1

Lat.	Twilight Naut.	Twilight Civil	Sunrise	Moonrise 1	Moonrise 2	Moonrise 3	Moonrise 4
°	h m	h m	h m	h m	h m	h m	h m
N 72	03 54	05 16	06 23	▭	▭	▭	▭
N 70	04 06	05 19	06 19	▭	▭	▭	▭
68	04 15	05 21	06 16	▭	▭	▭	▭
66	04 22	05 23	06 14	▭	▭	▭	20 25
64	04 28	05 24	06 11	▭	▭	▭	21 16
62	04 33	05 25	06 09	17 02	17 40	19 42	21 47
60	04 38	05 26	06 08	17 54	18 48	20 22	22 11
N 58	04 41	05 27	06 06	18 26	19 23	20 49	22 29
56	04 44	05 28	06 05	18 50	19 49	21 11	22 45
54	04 47	05 28	06 04	19 10	20 09	21 28	22 58
52	04 50	05 29	06 02	19 26	20 26	21 43	23 10
50	04 52	05 29	06 01	19 40	20 41	21 56	23 20
45	04 56	05 30	05 59	20 09	21 11	22 23	23 41
N 40	04 59	05 30	05 57	20 32	21 34	22 44	23 59
35	05 01	05 30	05 55	20 51	21 53	23 02	24 13
30	05 02	05 30	05 54	21 07	22 09	23 17	24 26
20	05 04	05 29	05 51	21 34	22 37	23 42	24 47
N 10	05 03	05 28	05 49	21 58	23 01	24 04	00 04
0	05 01	05 25	05 46	22 20	23 23	24 25	00 25
S 10	04 58	05 22	05 43	22 42	23 45	24 45	00 45
20	04 53	05 19	05 41	23 06	24 09	00 09	01 07
30	04 45	05 13	05 37	23 34	24 37	00 37	01 32
35	04 40	05 10	05 35	23 51	24 53	00 53	01 47
40	04 34	05 06	05 33	24 10	00 10	01 13	02 04
45	04 26	05 01	05 30	24 34	00 34	01 36	02 24
S 50	04 16	04 54	05 27	25 04	01 04	02 05	02 50
52	04 11	04 51	05 26	00 00	01 19	02 20	03 02
54	04 05	04 48	05 24	00 15	01 36	02 37	03 16
56	03 59	04 44	05 22	00 33	01 57	02 57	03 33
58	03 51	04 40	05 20	00 55	02 23	03 22	03 52
S 60	03 43	04 35	05 18	01 23	03 00	03 56	04 16

Lat.	Sunset	Twilight Civil	Twilight Naut.	Moonset 1	Moonset 2	Moonset 3	Moonset 4
°	h m	h m	h m	h m	h m	h m	h m
N 72	17 13	18 20	19 41	▭	▭	▭	▭
N 70	17 17	18 18	19 30	▭	▭	▭	▭
68	17 21	18 16	19 21	▭	▭	▭	▭
66	17 23	18 14	19 14	▭	▭	▭	18 05
64	17 26	18 13	19 08	▭	▭	▭	17 13
62	17 28	18 12	19 04	15 00	16 35	16 43	16 41
60	17 30	18 11	18 59	14 09	15 27	16 03	16 17
N 58	17 31	18 10	18 56	13 37	14 51	15 35	15 58
56	17 33	18 10	18 53	13 13	14 26	15 13	15 42
54	17 34	18 09	18 50	12 54	14 05	14 55	15 28
52	17 35	18 09	18 48	12 38	13 48	14 40	15 16
50	17 36	18 09	18 46	12 24	13 34	14 27	15 05
45	17 39	18 08	18 42	11 56	13 04	13 59	14 42
N 40	17 41	18 08	18 39	11 33	12 41	13 38	14 24
35	17 43	18 08	18 37	11 15	12 21	13 20	14 08
30	17 44	18 08	18 36	10 59	12 05	13 04	13 55
20	17 47	18 09	18 35	10 32	11 37	12 37	13 32
N 10	17 50	18 11	18 35	10 09	11 13	12 14	13 12
0	17 53	18 13	18 37	09 48	10 50	11 53	12 53
S 10	17 55	18 16	18 41	09 26	10 28	11 31	12 34
20	17 58	18 20	18 46	09 03	10 04	11 08	12 13
30	18 02	18 26	18 54	08 37	09 36	10 41	11 50
35	18 04	18 29	18 59	08 21	09 19	10 25	11 36
40	18 06	18 34	19 06	08 03	08 59	10 06	11 19
45	18 09	18 39	19 14	07 41	08 36	09 43	11 00
S 50	18 13	18 45	19 24	07 13	08 06	09 14	10 35
52	18 14	18 48	19 30	07 00	07 51	09 00	10 23
54	18 16	18 52	19 35	06 44	07 33	08 43	10 10
56	18 18	18 56	19 42	06 26	07 12	08 24	09 54
58	18 20	19 00	19 49	06 04	06 46	07 59	09 35
S 60	18 22	19 05	19 58	05 35	06 09	07 25	09 11

Day	SUN Eqn. of Time 00^h	SUN Eqn. of Time 12^h	SUN Mer. Pass.	MOON Mer. Pass. Upper	MOON Mer. Pass. Lower	MOON Age	MOON %	MOON Phase
d	m s	m s	h m	h m	h m	d	%	
1	10 11	10 21	11 50	03 33	16 04	20	73	◑
2	10 30	10 40	11 49	04 35	17 07	21	62	
3	10 49	10 59	11 49	05 38	18 09	22	51	

UT d	h	ARIES GHA	VENUS −4·7 GHA	Dec	MARS +1·1 GHA	Dec	JUPITER −1·9 GHA	Dec	SATURN +0·3 GHA	Dec	STARS Name	SHA	Dec
		° ′	° ′	° ′	° ′	° ′	° ′	° ′	° ′	° ′		° ′	° ′
4	00	12 42.1	159 06.7	S21 13.4	246 42.3	N20 25.5	229 58.5	N15 20.9	1 12.7	N 1 59.3	Acamar	315 10.3	S40 11.6
	01	27 44.6	174 09.3	13.6	261 43.2	25.2	245 00.5	20.8	16 15.3	59.3	Achernar	335 18.5	S57 05.9
	02	42 47.0	189 11.9	13.7	276 44.2	25.0	260 02.6	20.7	31 18.0	59.2	Acrux	172 59.2	S63 14.8
	03	57 49.5	204 14.5	. . 13.9	291 45.1	. . 24.7	275 04.6	. . 20.5	46 20.6	. . 59.1	Adhara	255 04.7	S29 00.2
	04	72 52.0	219 17.1	14.0	306 46.1	24.4	290 06.6	20.4	61 23.3	59.0	Aldebaran	290 37.8	N16 33.9
	05	87 54.4	234 19.8	14.1	321 47.1	24.1	305 08.7	20.3	76 25.9	59.0			
	06	102 56.9	249 22.4	S21 14.3	336 48.0	N20 23.8	320 10.7	N15 20.1	91 28.6	N 1 58.9	Alioth	166 12.3	N55 48.9
	07	117 59.4	264 25.0	14.4	351 49.0	23.5	335 12.7	20.0	106 31.2	58.8	Alkaid	152 51.3	N49 10.9
	08	133 01.8	279 27.6	14.5	6 49.9	23.2	350 14.8	19.9	121 33.8	58.7	Alnair	27 30.8	S46 49.9
S	09	148 04.3	294 30.2	. . 14.6	21 50.9	. . 22.9	5 16.8	. . 19.8	136 36.5	. . 58.6	Alnilam	275 36.2	S 1 10.9
U	10	163 06.7	309 32.9	14.7	36 51.9	22.6	20 18.8	19.6	151 39.1	58.6	Alphard	217 46.6	S 8 46.3
N	11	178 09.2	324 35.5	14.9	51 52.8	22.3	35 20.9	19.5	166 41.8	58.5			
D	12	193 11.7	339 38.2	S21 15.0	66 53.8	N20 22.0	50 22.9	N15 19.4	181 44.4	N 1 58.4	Alphecca	126 02.8	N26 37.6
A	13	208 14.1	354 40.8	15.1	81 54.7	21.7	65 24.9	19.2	196 47.1	58.3	Alpheratz	357 32.9	N29 14.5
Y	14	223 16.6	9 43.4	15.2	96 55.7	21.4	80 27.0	19.1	211 49.7	58.3	Altair	61 58.5	N 8 56.5
	15	238 19.1	24 46.1	. . 15.3	111 56.7	. . 21.1	95 29.0	. . 19.0	226 52.4	. . 58.2	Ankaa	353 05.3	S42 09.5
	16	253 21.5	39 48.7	15.4	126 57.6	20.8	110 31.0	18.8	241 55.0	58.1	Antares	112 14.3	S26 29.5
	17	268 24.0	54 51.4	15.5	141 58.6	20.5	125 33.1	18.7	256 57.6	58.0			
	18	283 26.5	69 54.1	S21 15.6	156 59.6	N20 20.2	140 35.1	N15 18.6	272 00.3	N 1 57.9	Arcturus	145 46.9	N19 02.7
	19	298 28.9	84 56.7	15.7	172 00.5	19.9	155 37.1	18.4	287 02.9	57.9	Atria	107 07.5	S69 04.7
	20	313 31.4	99 59.4	15.8	187 01.5	19.6	170 39.2	18.3	302 05.6	57.8	Avior	234 14.4	S59 35.4
	21	328 33.8	115 02.1	. . 15.9	202 02.4	. . 19.3	185 41.2	. . 18.2	317 08.2	. . 57.7	Bellatrix	278 21.2	N 6 22.5
	22	343 36.3	130 04.7	16.0	217 03.4	19.0	200 43.3	18.0	332 10.9	57.6	Betelgeuse	270 50.5	N 7 24.8
	23	358 38.8	145 07.4	16.1	232 04.4	18.7	215 45.3	17.9	347 13.5	57.6			
5	00	13 41.2	160 10.1	S21 16.2	247 05.3	N20 18.4	230 47.3	N15 17.8	2 16.2	N 1 57.5	Canopus	263 51.7	S52 42.2
	01	28 43.7	175 12.8	16.3	262 06.3	18.1	245 49.4	17.7	17 18.8	57.4	Capella	280 19.6	N46 01.4
	02	43 46.2	190 15.5	16.4	277 07.3	17.8	260 51.4	17.5	32 21.5	57.3	Deneb	49 24.6	N45 22.8
	03	58 48.6	205 18.2	. . 16.5	292 08.2	. . 17.5	275 53.4	. . 17.4	47 24.1	. . 57.3	Denebola	182 23.8	N14 25.4
	04	73 51.1	220 20.9	16.6	307 09.2	17.2	290 55.5	17.3	62 26.7	57.2	Diphda	348 45.5	S17 50.2
	05	88 53.6	235 23.6	16.7	322 10.2	16.9	305 57.5	17.1	77 29.4	57.1			
	06	103 56.0	250 26.3	S21 16.7	337 11.1	N20 16.6	320 59.5	N15 17.0	92 32.0	N 1 57.0	Dubhe	193 39.8	N61 36.3
	07	118 58.5	265 29.0	16.8	352 12.1	16.3	336 01.6	16.9	107 34.7	56.9	Elnath	277 59.9	N28 37.8
	08	134 01.0	280 31.7	16.9	7 13.1	16.0	351 03.6	16.7	122 37.3	56.9	Eltanin	90 41.6	N51 29.4
M	09	149 03.4	295 34.4	. . 17.0	22 14.0	. . 15.7	6 05.7	. . 16.6	137 40.0	. . 56.8	Enif	33 37.2	N10 00.1
O	10	164 05.9	310 37.2	17.0	37 15.0	15.4	21 07.7	16.5	152 42.6	56.7	Fomalhaut	15 12.6	S29 28.7
N	11	179 08.3	325 39.9	17.1	52 16.0	15.1	36 09.7	16.3	167 45.3	56.6			
D	12	194 10.8	340 42.6	S21 17.2	67 16.9	N20 14.8	51 11.8	N15 16.2	182 47.9	N 1 56.6	Gacrux	171 50.6	S57 15.7
A	13	209 13.3	355 45.4	17.2	82 17.9	14.5	66 13.8	16.1	197 50.5	56.5	Gienah	175 42.4	S17 41.3
Y	14	224 15.7	10 48.1	17.3	97 18.9	14.2	81 15.8	16.0	212 53.2	56.4	Hadar	148 34.6	S60 30.2
	15	239 18.2	25 50.8	. . 17.4	112 19.9	. . 13.9	96 17.9	. . 15.8	227 55.8	. . 56.3	Hamal	327 49.2	N23 35.5
	16	254 20.7	40 53.6	17.4	127 20.8	13.6	111 19.9	15.7	242 58.5	56.3	Kaus Aust.	83 30.7	S34 22.4
	17	269 23.1	55 56.3	17.5	142 21.8	13.3	126 22.0	15.6	258 01.1	56.2			
	18	284 25.6	70 59.1	S21 17.5	157 22.8	N20 13.0	141 24.0	N15 15.4	273 03.8	N 1 56.1	Kochab	137 20.8	N74 02.8
	19	299 28.1	86 01.9	17.6	172 23.7	12.7	156 26.0	15.3	288 06.4	56.0	Markab	13 28.2	N15 21.2
	20	314 30.5	101 04.6	17.6	187 24.7	12.4	171 28.1	15.2	303 09.1	55.9	Menkar	314 04.4	N 4 11.8
	21	329 33.0	116 07.4	. . 17.7	202 25.7	. . 12.1	186 30.1	. . 15.0	318 11.7	. . 55.9	Menkent	147 56.3	S36 30.1
	22	344 35.5	131 10.1	17.7	217 26.7	11.8	201 32.2	14.9	333 14.3	55.8	Miaplacidus	221 38.5	S69 49.3
	23	359 37.9	146 12.9	17.8	232 27.6	11.5	216 34.2	14.8	348 17.0	55.7			
6	00	14 40.4	161 15.7	S21 17.8	247 28.6	N20 11.2	231 36.2	N15 14.7	3 19.6	N 1 55.6	Mirfak	308 25.8	N49 57.3
	01	29 42.8	176 18.5	17.8	262 29.6	10.9	246 38.3	14.5	18 22.3	55.6	Nunki	75 46.0	S26 15.8
	02	44 45.3	191 21.3	17.9	277 30.5	10.6	261 40.3	14.4	33 24.9	55.5	Peacock	53 03.3	S56 39.1
	03	59 47.8	206 24.1	. . 17.9	292 31.5	. . 10.3	276 42.4	. . 14.3	48 27.6	. . 55.4	Pollux	243 15.6	N27 57.6
	04	74 50.2	221 26.8	17.9	307 32.5	10.0	291 44.4	14.1	63 30.2	55.3	Procyon	244 49.4	N 5 09.5
	05	89 52.7	236 29.6	18.0	322 33.5	09.7	306 46.4	14.0	78 32.9	55.2			
	06	104 55.2	251 32.4	S21 18.0	337 34.4	N20 09.4	321 48.5	N15 13.9	93 35.5	N 1 55.2	Rasalhague	95 57.3	N12 32.6
	07	119 57.6	266 35.2	18.0	352 35.4	09.1	336 50.5	13.7	108 38.2	55.1	Regulus	207 33.2	N11 50.2
T	08	135 00.1	281 38.1	18.0	7 36.4	08.8	351 52.6	13.6	123 40.8	55.0	Rigel	281 02.4	S 8 10.0
U	09	150 02.6	296 40.9	. . 18.1	22 37.4	. . 08.5	6 54.6	. . 13.5	138 43.4	. . 54.9	Rigil Kent.	139 38.9	S60 56.8
E	10	165 05.0	311 43.7	18.1	37 38.3	08.2	21 56.6	13.4	153 46.1	54.9	Sabik	102 01.3	S15 45.4
S	11	180 07.5	326 46.5	18.1	52 39.3	07.9	36 58.7	13.2	168 48.7	54.8			
D	12	195 10.0	341 49.3	S21 18.1	67 40.3	N20 07.6	52 00.7	N15 13.1	183 51.4	N 1 54.7	Schedar	349 28.8	N56 41.2
A	13	210 12.4	356 52.1	18.1	82 41.3	07.3	67 02.8	13.0	198 54.0	54.6	Shaula	96 08.6	S37 07.4
Y	14	225 14.9	11 55.0	18.1	97 42.2	07.0	82 04.8	12.8	213 56.7	54.6	Sirius	258 25.0	S16 44.9
	15	240 17.3	26 57.8	. . 18.1	112 43.2	. . 06.7	97 06.9	. . 12.7	228 59.3	. . 54.5	Spica	158 21.1	S11 18.0
	16	255 19.8	42 00.6	18.1	127 44.2	06.4	112 08.9	12.6	244 02.0	54.4	Suhail	222 45.5	S43 32.2
	17	270 22.3	57 03.5	18.1	142 45.2	06.1	127 10.9	12.4	259 04.6	54.3			
	18	285 24.7	72 06.3	S21 18.1	157 46.2	N20 05.8	142 13.0	N15 12.3	274 07.2	N 1 54.2	Vega	80 32.3	N38 48.8
	19	300 27.2	87 09.2	18.1	172 47.1	05.5	157 15.0	12.2	289 09.9	54.2	Zuben'ubi	136 54.7	S16 09.1
	20	315 29.7	102 12.0	18.1	187 48.1	05.2	172 17.1	12.1	304 12.5	54.1			
	21	330 32.1	117 14.9	. . 18.1	202 49.1	. . 04.9	187 19.1	. . 11.9	319 15.2	. . 54.0			
	22	345 34.6	132 17.8	18.1	217 50.1	04.6	202 21.2	11.8	334 17.8	53.9			
	23	0 37.1	147 20.6	18.1	232 51.1	04.3	217 23.2	11.7	349 20.5	53.9			
Mer. Pass.		23 01.5 (h m)	*v* 2.7	*d* 0.1	*v* 1.0	*d* 0.3	*v* 2.0	*d* 0.1	*v* 2.6	*d* 0.1			

	SHA	Mer. Pass.
	° ′	h m
Venus	146 28.9	13 17
Mars	233 24.1	7 31
Jupiter	217 06.1	8 36
Saturn	348 34.9	23 47

Day	UT	SUN GHA	SUN Dec	MOON GHA	v	MOON Dec	d	HP
	d h	° ′	° ′	° ′	′	° ′	′	′
SUNDAY	4 00	182 47.1	S 4 16.2	264 14.3	5.0	N25 52.6	6.8	59.2
	01	197 47.3	17.2	278 38.3	5.1	25 45.8	7.0	59.2
	02	212 47.5	18.1	293 02.4	5.2	25 38.8	7.2	59.2
	03	227 47.7	. . 19.1	307 26.6	5.3	25 31.6	7.4	59.1
	04	242 47.9	20.1	321 50.9	5.3	25 24.2	7.5	59.1
	05	257 48.1	21.0	336 15.2	5.5	25 16.7	7.7	59.1
	06	272 48.3	S 4 22.0	350 39.7	5.5	N25 09.0	7.8	59.1
	07	287 48.5	23.0	5 04.2	5.7	25 01.2	8.0	59.1
	08	302 48.7	23.9	19 28.9	5.7	24 53.2	8.1	59.1
	09	317 48.9	. . 24.9	33 53.6	5.8	24 45.1	8.3	59.1
	10	332 49.0	25.9	48 18.4	5.9	24 36.8	8.5	59.1
	11	347 49.2	26.8	62 43.3	6.0	24 28.3	8.6	59.1
	12	2 49.4	S 4 27.8	77 08.3	6.1	N24 19.7	8.7	59.1
	13	17 49.6	28.7	91 33.4	6.2	24 11.0	8.9	59.1
	14	32 49.8	29.7	105 58.6	6.3	24 02.1	9.1	59.1
	15	47 50.0	. . 30.7	120 23.9	6.4	23 53.0	9.2	59.0
	16	62 50.2	31.6	134 49.3	6.5	23 43.8	9.3	59.0
	17	77 50.4	32.6	149 14.8	6.5	23 34.5	9.5	59.0
	18	92 50.6	S 4 33.6	163 40.3	6.7	N23 25.0	9.6	59.0
	19	107 50.8	34.5	178 06.0	6.8	23 15.4	9.8	59.0
	20	122 51.0	35.5	192 31.8	6.9	23 05.6	9.9	59.0
	21	137 51.1	. . 36.4	206 57.7	7.0	22 55.7	10.0	59.0
	22	152 51.3	37.4	221 23.7	7.1	22 45.7	10.2	59.0
	23	167 51.5	38.4	235 49.8	7.1	22 35.5	10.3	59.0
MONDAY	5 00	182 51.7	S 4 39.3	250 15.9	7.3	N22 25.2	10.5	59.0
	01	197 51.9	40.3	264 42.2	7.4	22 14.7	10.5	58.9
	02	212 52.1	41.3	279 08.6	7.5	22 04.2	10.7	58.9
	03	227 52.3	. . 42.2	293 35.1	7.6	21 53.5	10.8	58.9
	04	242 52.5	43.2	308 01.7	7.7	21 42.7	11.0	58.9
	05	257 52.7	44.1	322 28.4	7.8	21 31.7	11.1	58.9
	06	272 52.8	S 4 45.1	336 55.2	7.9	N21 20.6	11.2	58.9
	07	287 53.0	46.1	351 22.1	8.0	21 09.4	11.3	58.9
	08	302 53.2	47.0	5 49.1	8.1	20 58.1	11.4	58.9
	09	317 53.4	. . 48.0	20 16.2	8.2	20 46.7	11.5	58.9
	10	332 53.6	49.0	34 43.4	8.3	20 35.2	11.7	58.8
	11	347 53.8	49.9	49 10.7	8.4	20 23.5	11.8	58.8
	12	2 54.0	S 4 50.9	63 38.1	8.5	N20 11.7	11.9	58.8
	13	17 54.2	51.8	78 05.6	8.6	19 59.8	12.0	58.8
	14	32 54.3	52.8	92 33.2	8.7	19 47.8	12.1	58.8
	15	47 54.5	. . 53.8	107 00.9	8.8	19 35.7	12.2	58.8
	16	62 54.7	54.7	121 28.7	8.9	19 23.5	12.3	58.8
	17	77 54.9	55.7	135 56.6	9.0	19 11.2	12.4	58.8
	18	92 55.1	S 4 56.6	150 24.6	9.1	N18 58.8	12.5	58.8
	19	107 55.3	57.6	164 52.7	9.2	18 46.3	12.6	58.7
	20	122 55.5	58.6	179 20.9	9.3	18 33.7	12.8	58.7
	21	137 55.6	4 59.5	193 49.2	9.4	18 20.9	12.8	58.7
	22	152 55.8	5 00.5	208 17.6	9.4	18 08.1	12.9	58.7
	23	167 56.0	01.4	222 46.0	9.6	17 55.2	13.0	58.7
TUESDAY	6 00	182 56.2	S 5 02.4	237 14.6	9.7	N17 42.2	13.1	58.7
	01	197 56.4	03.4	251 43.3	9.8	17 29.1	13.1	58.7
	02	212 56.6	04.3	266 12.1	9.8	17 16.0	13.3	58.7
	03	227 56.8	. . 05.3	280 40.9	10.0	17 02.7	13.4	58.6
	04	242 56.9	06.2	295 09.9	10.0	16 49.3	13.4	58.6
	05	257 57.1	07.2	309 38.9	10.2	16 35.9	13.5	58.6
	06	272 57.3	S 5 08.2	324 08.1	10.2	N16 22.4	13.6	58.6
	07	287 57.5	09.1	338 37.3	10.3	16 08.8	13.7	58.6
	08	302 57.7	10.1	353 06.6	10.4	15 55.1	13.8	58.6
	09	317 57.9	. . 11.0	7 36.0	10.5	15 41.3	13.8	58.6
	10	332 58.0	12.0	22 05.5	10.6	15 27.5	14.0	58.5
	11	347 58.2	13.0	36 35.1	10.6	15 13.5	13.9	58.5
	12	2 58.4	S 5 13.9	51 04.7	10.8	N14 59.6	14.1	58.5
	13	17 58.6	14.9	65 34.5	10.8	14 45.5	14.1	58.5
	14	32 58.8	15.8	80 04.3	10.9	14 31.4	14.2	58.5
	15	47 59.0	. . 16.8	94 34.2	11.0	14 17.2	14.3	58.5
	16	62 59.1	17.7	109 04.2	11.1	14 02.9	14.3	58.5
	17	77 59.3	18.7	123 34.3	11.2	13 48.6	14.4	58.4
	18	92 59.5	S 5 19.7	138 04.5	11.2	N13 34.2	14.5	58.4
	19	107 59.7	20.6	152 34.7	11.3	13 19.7	14.5	58.4
	20	122 59.9	21.6	167 05.0	11.4	13 05.2	14.6	58.4
	21	138 00.1	. . 22.5	181 35.4	11.5	12 50.6	14.6	58.4
	22	153 00.2	23.5	196 05.9	11.6	12 36.0	14.7	58.4
	23	168 00.4	24.5	210 36.5	11.6	N12 21.3	14.8	58.3
		SD 16.0	d 1.0	SD	16.1	16.0		15.9

Lat.	Twilight Naut.	Twilight Civil	Sunrise	Moonrise 4	Moonrise 5	Moonrise 6	Moonrise 7
°	h m	h m	h m	h m	h m	h m	h m
N 72	04 09	05 29	06 37	▭	▭	▭	00 19
N 70	04 18	05 30	06 31	▭	21 53	24 41	00 41
68	04 26	05 31	06 27	▭	22 37	24 58	00 58
66	04 32	05 32	06 23	20 25	23 05	25 11	01 11
64	04 37	05 33	06 20	21 16	23 27	25 23	01 23
62	04 41	05 33	06 17	21 47	23 44	25 32	01 32
60	04 45	05 33	06 15	22 11	23 58	25 40	01 40
N 58	04 48	05 34	06 13	22 29	24 10	00 10	01 47
56	04 51	05 34	06 11	22 45	24 21	00 21	01 53
54	04 53	05 34	06 09	22 58	24 30	00 30	01 59
52	04 55	05 34	06 07	23 10	24 38	00 38	02 04
50	04 56	05 34	06 06	23 20	24 45	00 45	02 08
45	04 59	05 34	06 03	23 41	25 01	01 01	02 18
N 40	05 02	05 33	06 00	23 59	25 13	01 13	02 26
35	05 03	05 32	05 58	24 13	00 13	01 24	02 32
30	05 04	05 32	05 56	24 26	00 26	01 33	02 38
20	05 04	05 30	05 52	24 47	00 47	01 49	02 49
N 10	05 03	05 27	05 48	00 04	01 06	02 03	02 58
0	05 00	05 24	05 45	00 25	01 23	02 16	03 06
S 10	04 56	05 21	05 42	00 45	01 40	02 29	03 14
20	04 50	05 16	05 38	01 07	01 58	02 43	03 23
30	04 41	05 10	05 34	01 32	02 19	02 59	03 33
35	04 36	05 06	05 31	01 47	02 31	03 08	03 39
40	04 29	05 01	05 28	02 04	02 45	03 18	03 46
45	04 20	04 55	05 25	02 24	03 01	03 30	03 53
S 50	04 08	04 48	05 21	02 50	03 22	03 45	04 02
52	04 03	04 44	05 19	03 02	03 31	03 51	04 07
54	03 57	04 41	05 17	03 16	03 42	03 59	04 11
56	03 50	04 36	05 14	03 33	03 54	04 07	04 16
58	03 42	04 31	05 12	03 52	04 08	04 16	04 22
S 60	03 32	04 26	05 09	04 16	04 24	04 27	04 28

Lat.	Sunset	Twilight Civil	Twilight Naut.	Moonset 4	Moonset 5	Moonset 6	Moonset 7
°	h m	h m	h m	h m	h m	h m	h m
N 72	16 58	18 05	19 25	▭	▭	17 57	17 10
N 70	17 04	18 04	19 16	▭	18 34	17 32	16 59
68	17 08	18 03	19 08	▭	17 49	17 13	16 50
66	17 12	18 03	19 03	18 05	17 19	16 58	16 43
64	17 15	18 03	18 58	17 13	16 56	16 45	16 36
62	17 18	18 02	18 54	16 41	16 38	16 35	16 31
60	17 21	18 02	18 50	16 17	16 23	16 25	16 26
N 58	17 23	18 02	18 47	15 58	16 10	16 17	16 22
56	17 25	18 02	18 45	15 42	15 59	16 10	16 18
54	17 27	18 02	18 43	15 28	15 49	16 03	16 14
52	17 28	18 02	18 41	15 16	15 40	15 57	16 11
50	17 30	18 02	18 39	15 05	15 32	15 52	16 08
45	17 33	18 03	18 36	14 42	15 15	15 41	16 02
N 40	17 36	18 03	18 34	14 24	15 01	15 31	15 57
35	17 39	18 04	18 33	14 08	14 49	15 23	15 52
30	17 41	18 05	18 32	13 55	14 38	15 15	15 48
20	17 45	18 07	18 32	13 32	14 20	15 02	15 41
N 10	17 48	18 09	18 34	13 12	14 04	14 51	15 35
0	17 52	18 12	18 37	12 53	13 49	14 40	15 29
S 10	17 55	18 16	18 41	12 34	13 34	14 30	15 23
20	17 59	18 21	18 47	12 13	13 17	14 18	15 16
30	18 04	18 28	18 56	11 50	12 58	14 05	15 09
35	18 06	18 32	19 02	11 36	12 47	13 57	15 04
40	18 09	18 37	19 09	11 19	12 34	13 48	14 59
45	18 13	18 43	19 18	11 00	12 19	13 38	14 54
S 50	18 17	18 50	19 30	10 35	12 00	13 25	14 47
52	18 19	18 54	19 35	10 23	11 51	13 19	14 43
54	18 21	18 58	19 42	10 10	11 41	13 12	14 40
56	18 24	19 02	19 49	09 54	11 30	13 05	14 36
58	18 27	19 07	19 57	09 35	11 17	12 57	14 31
S 60	18 30	19 13	20 07	09 11	11 01	12 47	14 26

Day	SUN Eqn. of Time 00^h	SUN Eqn. of Time 12^h	SUN Mer. Pass.	MOON Mer. Pass. Upper	MOON Mer. Pass. Lower	MOON Age	MOON Phase
d	m s	m s	h m	h m	h m	d %	
4	11 08	11 17	11 49	06 39	19 08	23 39	
5	11 26	11 36	11 48	07 36	20 03	24 29	
6	11 44	11 53	11 48	08 29	20 53	25 19	

2026 OCTOBER 7, 8, 9 (WED., THURS., FRI.)

UT (d h)	ARIES GHA	VENUS −4·6 GHA	VENUS Dec	MARS +1·1 GHA	MARS Dec	JUPITER −1·9 GHA	JUPITER Dec	SATURN +0·3 GHA	SATURN Dec
	° ′	° ′	° ′	° ′	° ′	° ′	° ′	° ′	° ′
7 00 (WEDNESDAY)	15 39.5	162 23.5	S21 18.1	247 52.0	N20 04.0	232 25.2	N15 11.5	4 23.1	N 1 53.8
01	30 42.0	177 26.4	18.1	262 53.0	03.7	247 27.3	11.4	19 25.8	53.7
02	45 44.4	192 29.2	18.1	277 54.0	03.4	262 29.3	11.3	34 28.4	53.6
03	60 46.9	207 32.1	. . 18.0	292 55.0	. . 03.0	277 31.4	. . 11.2	49 31.0	. . 53.6
04	75 49.4	222 35.0	18.0	307 56.0	02.7	292 33.4	11.0	64 33.7	53.5
05	90 51.8	237 37.9	18.0	322 56.9	02.4	307 35.5	10.9	79 36.3	53.4
06	105 54.3	252 40.8	S21 18.0	337 57.9	N20 02.1	322 37.5	N15 10.8	94 39.0	N 1 53.3
07	120 56.8	267 43.7	17.9	352 58.9	01.8	337 39.6	10.6	109 41.6	53.3
08	135 59.2	282 46.6	17.9	7 59.9	01.5	352 41.6	10.5	124 44.3	53.2
09	151 01.7	297 49.5	. . 17.9	23 00.9	. . 01.2	7 43.6	. . 10.4	139 46.9	. . 53.1
10	166 04.2	312 52.4	17.8	38 01.9	00.9	22 45.7	10.3	154 49.6	53.0
11	181 06.6	327 55.3	17.8	53 02.8	00.6	37 47.7	10.1	169 52.2	52.9
12	196 09.1	342 58.2	S21 17.8	68 03.8	N20 00.3	52 49.8	N15 10.0	184 54.8	N 1 52.9
13	211 11.6	358 01.1	17.7	83 04.8	20 00.0	67 51.8	09.9	199 57.5	52.8
14	226 14.0	13 04.1	17.7	98 05.8	19 59.7	82 53.9	09.7	215 00.1	52.7
15	241 16.5	28 07.0	. . 17.6	113 06.8	. . 59.4	97 55.9	. . 09.6	230 02.8	. . 52.6
16	256 18.9	43 09.9	17.6	128 07.8	59.1	112 58.0	09.5	245 05.4	52.6
17	271 21.4	58 12.8	17.5	143 08.8	58.8	128 00.0	09.4	260 08.1	52.5
18	286 23.9	73 15.8	S21 17.5	158 09.7	N19 58.5	143 02.1	N15 09.2	275 10.7	N 1 52.4
19	301 26.3	88 18.7	17.4	173 10.7	58.2	158 04.1	09.1	290 13.4	52.3
20	316 28.8	103 21.7	17.3	188 11.7	57.8	173 06.2	09.0	305 16.0	52.3
21	331 31.3	118 24.6	. . 17.3	203 12.7	. . 57.5	188 08.2	. . 08.8	320 18.7	. . 52.2
22	346 33.7	133 27.6	17.2	218 13.7	57.2	203 10.3	08.7	335 21.3	52.1
23	1 36.2	148 30.5	17.2	233 14.7	56.9	218 12.3	08.6	350 23.9	52.0
8 00 (THURSDAY)	16 38.7	163 33.5	S21 17.1	248 15.7	N19 56.6	233 14.3	N15 08.5	5 26.6	N 1 52.0
01	31 41.1	178 36.5	17.0	263 16.7	56.3	248 16.4	08.3	20 29.2	51.9
02	46 43.6	193 39.4	16.9	278 17.6	56.0	263 18.4	08.2	35 31.9	51.8
03	61 46.0	208 42.4	. . 16.9	293 18.6	. . 55.7	278 20.5	. . 08.1	50 34.5	. . 51.7
04	76 48.5	223 45.4	16.8	308 19.6	55.4	293 22.5	07.9	65 37.2	51.6
05	91 51.0	238 48.3	16.7	323 20.6	55.1	308 24.6	07.8	80 39.8	51.6
06	106 53.4	253 51.3	S21 16.6	338 21.6	N19 54.8	323 26.6	N15 07.7	95 42.5	N 1 51.5
07	121 55.9	268 54.3	16.5	353 22.6	54.5	338 28.7	07.6	110 45.1	51.4
08	136 58.4	283 57.3	16.5	8 23.6	54.2	353 30.7	07.4	125 47.7	51.3
09	152 00.8	299 00.3	. . 16.4	23 24.6	. . 53.8	8 32.8	. . 07.3	140 50.4	. . 51.3
10	167 03.3	314 03.3	16.3	38 25.6	53.5	23 34.8	07.2	155 53.0	51.2
11	182 05.8	329 06.3	16.2	53 26.6	53.2	38 36.9	07.1	170 55.7	51.1
12	197 08.2	344 09.3	S21 16.1	68 27.6	N19 52.9	53 38.9	N15 06.9	185 58.3	N 1 51.0
13	212 10.7	359 12.3	16.0	83 28.6	52.6	68 41.0	06.8	201 01.0	51.0
14	227 13.2	14 15.3	15.9	98 29.5	52.3	83 43.0	06.7	216 03.6	50.9
15	242 15.6	29 18.3	. . 15.8	113 30.5	. . 52.0	98 45.1	. . 06.5	231 06.3	. . 50.8
16	257 18.1	44 21.4	15.7	128 31.5	51.7	113 47.1	06.4	246 08.9	50.7
17	272 20.5	59 24.4	15.6	143 32.5	51.4	128 49.2	06.3	261 11.5	50.7
18	287 23.0	74 27.4	S21 15.5	158 33.5	N19 51.1	143 51.2	N15 06.2	276 14.2	N 1 50.6
19	302 25.5	89 30.5	15.3	173 34.5	50.8	158 53.3	06.0	291 16.8	50.5
20	317 27.9	104 33.5	15.2	188 35.5	50.4	173 55.3	05.9	306 19.5	50.4
21	332 30.4	119 36.5	. . 15.1	203 36.5	. . 50.1	188 57.4	. . 05.8	321 22.1	. . 50.4
22	347 32.9	134 39.6	15.0	218 37.5	49.8	203 59.5	05.7	336 24.8	50.3
23	2 35.3	149 42.6	14.9	233 38.5	49.5	219 01.5	05.5	351 27.4	50.2
9 00 (FRIDAY)	17 37.8	164 45.7	S21 14.7	248 39.5	N19 49.2	234 03.6	N15 05.4	6 30.1	N 1 50.1
01	32 40.3	179 48.7	14.6	263 40.5	48.9	249 05.6	05.3	21 32.7	50.0
02	47 42.7	194 51.8	14.5	278 41.5	48.6	264 07.7	05.1	36 35.3	50.0
03	62 45.2	209 54.8	. . 14.4	293 42.5	. . 48.3	279 09.7	. . 05.0	51 38.0	. . 49.9
04	77 47.6	224 57.9	14.2	308 43.5	48.0	294 11.8	04.9	66 40.6	49.8
05	92 50.1	240 01.0	14.1	323 44.5	47.6	309 13.8	04.8	81 43.3	49.7
06	107 52.6	255 04.0	S21 13.9	338 45.5	N19 47.3	324 15.9	N15 04.6	96 45.9	N 1 49.7
07	122 55.0	270 07.1	13.8	353 46.5	47.0	339 17.9	04.5	111 48.6	49.6
08	137 57.5	285 10.2	13.7	8 47.5	46.7	354 20.0	04.4	126 51.2	49.5
09	153 00.0	300 13.3	. . 13.5	23 48.5	. . 46.4	9 22.0	. . 04.3	141 53.8	. . 49.4
10	168 02.4	315 16.4	13.4	38 49.5	46.1	24 24.1	04.1	156 56.5	49.4
11	183 04.9	330 19.5	13.2	53 50.5	45.8	39 26.1	04.0	171 59.1	49.3
12	198 07.4	345 22.6	S21 13.1	68 51.5	N19 45.5	54 28.2	N15 03.9	187 01.8	N 1 49.2
13	213 09.8	0 25.7	12.9	83 52.5	45.2	69 30.2	03.8	202 04.4	49.1
14	228 12.3	15 28.8	12.7	98 53.5	44.8	84 32.3	03.6	217 07.1	49.1
15	243 14.8	30 31.9	. . 12.6	113 54.5	. . 44.5	99 34.4	. . 03.5	232 09.7	. . 49.0
16	258 17.2	45 35.0	12.4	128 55.5	44.2	114 36.4	03.4	247 12.4	48.9
17	273 19.7	60 38.1	12.2	143 56.5	43.9	129 38.5	03.2	262 15.0	48.8
18	288 22.1	75 41.2	S21 12.1	158 57.5	N19 43.6	144 40.5	N15 03.1	277 17.6	N 1 48.8
19	303 24.6	90 44.3	11.9	173 58.5	43.3	159 42.6	03.0	292 20.3	48.7
20	318 27.1	105 47.4	11.7	188 59.5	43.0	174 44.6	02.9	307 22.9	48.6
21	333 29.5	120 50.6	. . 11.6	204 00.5	. . 42.7	189 46.7	. . 02.7	322 25.6	. . 48.5
22	348 32.0	135 53.7	11.4	219 01.5	42.3	204 48.7	02.6	337 28.2	48.5
23	3 34.5	150 56.8	11.2	234 02.5	42.0	219 50.8	02.5	352 30.9	48.4
Mer. Pass.	22 49.7 (h m)	v 3.0	d 0.1	v 1.0	d 0.3	v 2.1	d 0.1	v 2.6	d 0.1

STARS

Name	SHA	Dec
	° ′	° ′
Acamar	315 10.3	S40 11.6
Achernar	335 18.5	S57 05.9
Acrux	172 59.1	S63 14.8
Adhara	255 04.7	S29 00.2
Aldebaran	290 37.8	N16 33.9
Alioth	166 12.3	N55 48.9
Alkaid	152 51.3	N49 10.8
Alnair	27 30.8	S46 49.9
Alnilam	275 36.2	S 1 10.9
Alphard	217 46.5	S 8 46.3
Alphecca	126 02.8	N26 37.6
Alpheratz	357 32.9	N29 14.5
Altair	61 58.5	N 8 56.5
Ankaa	353 05.3	S42 09.5
Antares	112 14.3	S26 29.5
Arcturus	145 46.9	N19 02.7
Atria	107 07.5	S69 04.7
Avior	234 14.4	S59 35.4
Bellatrix	278 21.2	N 6 22.5
Betelgeuse	270 50.4	N 7 24.8
Canopus	263 51.7	S52 42.2
Capella	280 19.6	N46 01.4
Deneb	49 24.7	N45 22.9
Denebola	182 23.8	N14 25.4
Diphda	348 45.5	S17 50.2
Dubhe	193 39.8	N61 36.3
Elnath	277 59.9	N28 37.8
Eltanin	90 41.7	N51 29.4
Enif	33 37.2	N10 00.1
Fomalhaut	15 12.6	S29 28.7
Gacrux	171 50.6	S57 15.7
Gienah	175 42.4	S17 41.3
Hadar	148 34.6	S60 30.2
Hamal	327 49.2	N23 35.5
Kaus Aust.	83 30.7	S34 22.4
Kochab	137 20.9	N74 02.8
Markab	13 28.2	N15 21.2
Menkar	314 04.4	N 4 11.8
Menkent	147 56.3	S36 30.1
Miaplacidus	221 38.5	S69 49.3
Mirfak	308 25.8	N49 57.3
Nunki	75 46.0	S26 15.8
Peacock	53 03.3	S56 39.1
Pollux	243 15.6	N27 57.6
Procyon	244 49.4	N 5 09.5
Rasalhague	95 57.3	N12 32.6
Regulus	207 33.1	N11 50.2
Rigel	281 02.3	S 8 10.0
Rigil Kent.	139 38.9	S60 56.8
Sabik	102 01.3	S15 45.4
Schedar	349 28.8	N56 41.2
Shaula	96 08.6	S37 07.4
Sirius	258 24.9	S16 44.9
Spica	158 21.1	S11 18.0
Suhail	222 45.5	S43 32.2
Vega	80 32.3	N38 48.8
Zuben'ubi	136 54.7	S16 09.1

	SHA (° ′)	Mer. Pass. (h m)
Venus	146 54.8	13 03
Mars	231 37.0	7 26
Jupiter	216 35.7	8 26
Saturn	348 47.9	23 34

UT		SUN GHA	SUN Dec	MOON GHA	v	MOON Dec	d	HP
d	h	° ′	° ′	° ′	′	° ′	′	′
7 WEDNESDAY	00	183 00.6	S 5 25.4	225 07.1	11.7	N12 06.5	14.8	58.3
	01	198 00.8	26.4	239 37.8	11.8	11 51.7	14.8	58.3
	02	213 01.0	27.3	254 08.6	11.8	11 36.9	14.9	58.3
	03	228 01.1	· · 28.3	268 39.4	11.9	11 22.0	15.0	58.3
	04	243 01.3	29.2	283 10.3	12.0	11 07.0	15.0	58.3
	05	258 01.5	30.2	297 41.3	12.0	10 52.0	15.0	58.3
	06	273 01.7	S 5 31.1	312 12.3	12.1	N10 37.0	15.1	58.2
	07	288 01.9	32.1	326 43.4	12.2	10 21.9	15.2	58.2
	08	303 02.0	33.1	341 14.6	12.3	10 06.7	15.2	58.2
	09	318 02.2	· · 34.0	355 45.9	12.3	9 51.5	15.2	58.2
	10	333 02.4	35.0	10 17.2	12.3	9 36.3	15.2	58.2
	11	348 02.6	35.9	24 48.5	12.5	9 21.1	15.3	58.2
	12	3 02.8	S 5 36.9	39 20.0	12.5	N 9 05.8	15.3	58.1
	13	18 02.9	37.8	53 51.5	12.5	8 50.5	15.4	58.1
	14	33 03.1	38.8	68 23.0	12.6	8 35.1	15.4	58.1
	15	48 03.3	· · 39.8	82 54.6	12.7	8 19.7	15.4	58.1
	16	63 03.5	40.7	97 26.3	12.7	8 04.3	15.5	58.1
	17	78 03.6	41.7	111 58.0	12.8	7 48.8	15.5	58.0
	18	93 03.8	S 5 42.6	126 29.8	12.8	N 7 33.3	15.5	58.0
	19	108 04.0	43.6	141 01.6	12.9	7 17.8	15.5	58.0
	20	123 04.2	44.5	155 33.5	12.9	7 02.3	15.6	58.0
	21	138 04.4	· · 45.5	170 05.4	13.0	6 46.7	15.5	58.0
	22	153 04.5	46.4	184 37.4	13.0	6 31.2	15.6	58.0
	23	168 04.7	47.4	199 09.4	13.1	6 15.6	15.7	57.9
8 THURSDAY	00	183 04.9	S 5 48.3	213 41.5	13.1	N 5 59.9	15.6	57.9
	01	198 05.1	49.3	228 13.6	13.2	5 44.3	15.7	57.9
	02	213 05.2	50.3	242 45.8	13.2	5 28.6	15.7	57.9
	03	228 05.4	· · 51.2	257 18.0	13.2	5 12.9	15.6	57.9
	04	243 05.6	52.2	271 50.2	13.3	4 57.3	15.7	57.8
	05	258 05.8	53.1	286 22.5	13.4	4 41.6	15.8	57.8
	06	273 05.9	S 5 54.1	300 54.9	13.3	N 4 25.8	15.7	57.8
	07	288 06.1	55.0	315 27.2	13.4	4 10.1	15.7	57.8
	08	303 06.3	56.0	329 59.6	13.5	3 54.4	15.8	57.8
	09	318 06.5	· · 56.9	344 32.1	13.5	3 38.6	15.7	57.8
	10	333 06.6	57.9	359 04.6	13.5	3 22.9	15.8	57.7
	11	348 06.8	58.8	13 37.1	13.5	3 07.1	15.7	57.7
	12	3 07.0	S 5 59.8	28 09.6	13.6	N 2 51.4	15.8	57.7
	13	18 07.2	6 00.7	42 42.2	13.6	2 35.6	15.8	57.7
	14	33 07.3	01.7	57 14.8	13.7	2 19.8	15.7	57.7
	15	48 07.5	· · 02.6	71 47.5	13.6	2 04.1	15.8	57.6
	16	63 07.7	03.6	86 20.1	13.7	1 48.3	15.8	57.6
	17	78 07.9	04.6	100 52.8	13.8	1 32.5	15.7	57.6
	18	93 08.0	S 6 05.5	115 25.6	13.7	N 1 16.8	15.8	57.6
	19	108 08.2	06.5	129 58.3	13.8	1 01.0	15.7	57.6
	20	123 08.4	07.4	144 31.1	13.8	0 45.3	15.8	57.5
	21	138 08.5	· · 08.4	159 03.9	13.8	0 29.5	15.7	57.5
	22	153 08.7	09.3	173 36.7	13.8	N 0 13.8	15.7	57.5
	23	168 08.9	10.3	188 09.5	13.9	S 0 01.9	15.8	57.5
9 FRIDAY	00	183 09.1	S 6 11.2	202 42.4	13.9	S 0 17.7	15.7	57.4
	01	198 09.2	12.2	217 15.3	13.9	0 33.4	15.6	57.4
	02	213 09.4	13.1	231 48.2	13.9	0 49.0	15.7	57.4
	03	228 09.6	· · 14.1	246 21.1	13.9	1 04.7	15.7	57.4
	04	243 09.8	15.0	260 54.0	13.9	1 20.4	15.6	57.4
	05	258 09.9	16.0	275 26.9	14.0	1 36.0	15.6	57.3
	06	273 10.1	S 6 16.9	289 59.9	14.0	S 1 51.6	15.6	57.3
	07	288 10.3	17.9	304 32.9	13.9	2 07.2	15.6	57.3
	08	303 10.4	18.8	319 05.8	14.0	2 22.8	15.6	57.3
	09	318 10.6	· · 19.8	333 38.8	14.0	2 38.4	15.5	57.3
	10	333 10.8	20.7	348 11.8	14.0	2 53.9	15.5	57.2
	11	348 10.9	21.7	2 44.8	14.0	3 09.4	15.5	57.2
	12	3 11.1	S 6 22.6	17 17.8	14.0	S 3 24.9	15.5	57.2
	13	18 11.3	23.6	31 50.8	14.0	3 40.4	15.4	57.2
	14	33 11.5	24.5	46 23.8	14.1	3 55.8	15.4	57.2
	15	48 11.6	· · 25.5	60 56.9	14.0	4 11.2	15.4	57.1
	16	63 11.8	26.4	75 29.9	14.0	4 26.6	15.3	57.1
	17	78 12.0	27.4	90 02.9	14.0	4 41.9	15.3	57.1
	18	93 12.1	S 6 28.3	104 35.9	14.0	S 4 57.2	15.3	57.1
	19	108 12.3	29.3	119 08.9	14.1	5 12.5	15.3	57.0
	20	123 12.5	30.2	133 42.0	14.0	5 27.8	15.2	57.0
	21	138 12.6	· · 31.2	148 15.0	14.0	5 43.0	15.1	57.0
	22	153 12.8	32.1	162 48.0	14.0	5 58.1	15.2	57.0
	23	168 13.0	33.0	177 21.0	14.0	S 6 13.3	15.1	57.0
		SD 16.0	*d* 1.0	SD 15.8		15.7		15.6

Lat.	Twilight Naut.	Twilight Civil	Sunrise	Moonrise 7	Moonrise 8	Moonrise 9	Moonrise 10
°	h m	h m	h m	h m	h m	h m	h m
N 72	04 23	05 43	06 51	00 19	02 46	05 00	07 14
N 70	04 31	05 42	06 44	00 41	02 54	04 57	07 00
68	04 37	05 42	06 38	00 58	03 00	04 55	06 49
66	04 42	05 42	06 33	01 11	03 05	04 53	06 41
64	04 46	05 41	06 29	01 23	03 10	04 52	06 33
62	04 49	05 41	06 25	01 32	03 13	04 51	06 27
60	04 52	05 40	06 22	01 40	03 17	04 50	06 22
N 58	04 55	05 40	06 19	01 47	03 19	04 49	06 17
56	04 57	05 40	06 17	01 53	03 22	04 48	06 13
54	04 58	05 39	06 15	01 59	03 24	04 47	06 09
52	05 00	05 39	06 13	02 04	03 26	04 47	06 06
50	05 01	05 38	06 11	02 08	03 28	04 46	06 03
45	05 03	05 37	06 07	02 18	03 32	04 45	05 56
N 40	05 05	05 36	06 03	02 26	03 36	04 44	05 50
35	05 05	05 35	06 00	02 32	03 38	04 43	05 46
30	05 06	05 33	05 57	02 38	03 41	04 42	05 42
20	05 05	05 31	05 53	02 49	03 45	04 40	05 34
N 10	05 03	05 27	05 48	02 58	03 49	04 39	05 28
0	04 59	05 23	05 44	03 06	03 53	04 38	05 23
S 10	04 54	05 19	05 40	03 14	03 57	04 37	05 17
20	04 47	05 13	05 35	03 23	04 00	04 36	05 11
30	04 38	05 06	05 30	03 33	04 05	04 35	05 04
35	04 31	05 01	05 27	03 39	04 07	04 34	05 00
40	04 23	04 56	05 23	03 46	04 10	04 33	04 56
45	04 14	04 49	05 19	03 53	04 13	04 32	04 51
S 50	04 01	04 41	05 14	04 02	04 17	04 31	04 45
52	03 55	04 37	05 12	04 07	04 19	04 31	04 42
54	03 48	04 33	05 09	04 11	04 21	04 30	04 39
56	03 41	04 28	05 06	04 16	04 23	04 29	04 36
58	03 32	04 22	05 03	04 22	04 26	04 29	04 32
S 60	03 21	04 16	05 00	04 28	04 28	04 28	04 28

Lat.	Sunset	Twilight Civil	Twilight Naut.	Moonset 7	Moonset 8	Moonset 9	Moonset 10
°	h m	h m	h m	h m	h m	h m	h m
N 72	16 42	17 50	19 09	17 10	16 34	16 01	15 23
N 70	16 50	17 51	19 01	16 59	16 32	16 07	15 39
68	16 56	17 51	18 56	16 50	16 31	16 12	15 52
66	17 01	17 52	18 51	16 43	16 29	16 16	16 03
64	17 05	17 52	18 47	16 36	16 28	16 20	16 12
62	17 09	17 53	18 44	16 31	16 27	16 23	16 19
60	17 12	17 53	18 41	16 26	16 26	16 26	16 26
N 58	17 15	17 54	18 39	16 22	16 25	16 29	16 32
56	17 17	17 54	18 37	16 18	16 25	16 31	16 37
54	17 20	17 55	18 36	16 14	16 24	16 33	16 42
52	17 22	17 55	18 34	16 11	16 23	16 35	16 47
50	17 24	17 56	18 33	16 08	16 23	16 36	16 51
45	17 28	17 57	18 31	16 02	16 21	16 40	16 59
N 40	17 31	17 58	18 30	15 57	16 20	16 43	17 06
35	17 34	18 00	18 29	15 52	16 19	16 46	17 13
30	17 37	18 01	18 29	15 48	16 19	16 48	17 18
20	17 42	18 04	18 30	15 41	16 17	16 52	17 28
N 10	17 47	18 08	18 32	15 35	16 16	16 56	17 36
0	17 51	18 12	18 36	15 29	16 15	16 59	17 44
S 10	17 55	18 16	18 41	15 23	16 13	17 03	17 52
20	18 00	18 22	18 48	15 16	16 12	17 06	18 00
30	18 05	18 30	18 58	15 09	16 10	17 11	18 10
35	18 09	18 34	19 05	15 04	16 09	17 13	18 16
40	18 12	18 40	19 13	14 59	16 08	17 16	18 22
45	18 17	18 47	19 22	14 54	16 07	17 19	18 30
S 50	18 22	18 55	19 35	14 47	16 06	17 23	18 39
52	18 24	18 59	19 41	14 43	16 05	17 24	18 43
54	18 27	19 04	19 48	14 40	16 04	17 26	18 48
56	18 30	19 09	19 56	14 36	16 03	17 28	18 53
58	18 33	19 14	20 05	14 31	16 02	17 31	18 59
S 60	18 37	19 21	20 16	14 26	16 01	17 34	19 06

Day	SUN Eqn. of Time 00^h	SUN Eqn. of Time 12^h	SUN Mer. Pass.	MOON Mer. Pass. Upper	MOON Mer. Pass. Lower	MOON Age	MOON Phase
d	m s	m s	h m	h m	h m	d %	
7	12 02	12 11	11 48	09 17	21 41	26 11	●
8	12 19	12 28	11 48	10 04	22 26	27 5	
9	12 36	12 44	11 47	10 49	23 11	28 2	

2026 OCTOBER 10, 11, 12 (SAT., SUN., MON.)

	UT	ARIES	VENUS −4·5		MARS +1·0		JUPITER −1·9		SATURN +0·3	
	d h	GHA ° ′	GHA ° ′	Dec ° ′	GHA ° ′	Dec ° ′	GHA ° ′	Dec ° ′	GHA ° ′	Dec ° ′
	10 00	18 36.9	166 00.0	S21 11.0	249 03.5	N19 41.7	234 52.9	N15 02.4	7 33.5	N 1 48.3
	01	33 39.4	181 03.1	10.8	264 04.5	41.4	249 54.9	02.2	22 36.2	48.2
	02	48 41.9	196 06.3	10.6	279 05.5	41.1	264 57.0	02.1	37 38.8	48.2
	03	63 44.3	211 09.4	. . 10.5	294 06.5	. . 40.8	279 59.0	. . 02.0	52 41.4	. . 48.1
	04	78 46.8	226 12.6	10.3	309 07.5	40.5	295 01.1	01.9	67 44.1	48.0
	05	93 49.2	241 15.7	10.1	324 08.5	40.2	310 03.1	01.7	82 46.7	47.9
	06	108 51.7	256 18.9	S21 09.9	339 09.5	N19 39.8	325 05.2	N15 01.6	97 49.4	N 1 47.8
	07	123 54.2	271 22.1	09.7	354 10.6	39.5	340 07.3	01.5	112 52.0	47.8
S	08	138 56.6	286 25.2	09.5	9 11.6	39.2	355 09.3	01.4	127 54.7	47.7
A	09	153 59.1	301 28.4	. . 09.3	24 12.6	. . 38.9	10 11.4	. . 01.2	142 57.3	. . 47.6
T	10	169 01.6	316 31.6	09.1	39 13.6	38.6	25 13.4	01.1	157 59.9	47.5
U	11	184 04.0	331 34.7	08.8	54 14.6	38.3	40 15.5	01.0	173 02.6	47.5
R	12	199 06.5	346 37.9	S21 08.6	69 15.6	N19 38.0	55 17.6	N15 00.9	188 05.2	N 1 47.4
D	13	214 09.0	1 41.1	08.4	84 16.6	37.6	70 19.6	00.7	203 07.9	47.3
A	14	229 11.4	16 44.3	08.2	99 17.6	37.3	85 21.7	00.6	218 10.5	47.2
Y	15	244 13.9	31 47.5	. . 08.0	114 18.6	. . 37.0	100 23.7	. . 00.5	233 13.2	. . 47.2
	16	259 16.4	46 50.7	07.8	129 19.6	36.7	115 25.8	00.4	248 15.8	47.1
	17	274 18.8	61 53.9	07.5	144 20.6	36.4	130 27.8	00.2	263 18.5	47.0
	18	289 21.3	76 57.1	S21 07.3	159 21.7	N19 36.1	145 29.9	N15 00.1	278 21.1	N 1 46.9
	19	304 23.7	92 00.3	07.1	174 22.7	35.7	160 32.0	15 00.0	293 23.7	46.9
	20	319 26.2	107 03.5	06.8	189 23.7	35.4	175 34.0	14 59.9	308 26.4	46.8
	21	334 28.7	122 06.7	. . 06.6	204 24.7	. . 35.1	190 36.1	. . 59.7	323 29.0	. . 46.7
	22	349 31.1	137 09.9	06.4	219 25.7	34.8	205 38.1	59.6	338 31.7	46.6
	23	4 33.6	152 13.2	06.1	234 26.7	34.5	220 40.2	59.5	353 34.3	46.6
	11 00	19 36.1	167 16.4	S21 05.9	249 27.7	N19 34.2	235 42.3	N14 59.4	8 37.0	N 1 46.5
	01	34 38.5	182 19.6	05.6	264 28.7	33.9	250 44.3	59.2	23 39.6	46.4
	02	49 41.0	197 22.8	05.4	279 29.8	33.5	265 46.4	59.1	38 42.2	46.3
	03	64 43.5	212 26.1	. . 05.1	294 30.8	. . 33.2	280 48.5	. . 59.0	53 44.9	. . 46.3
	04	79 45.9	227 29.3	04.9	309 31.8	32.9	295 50.5	58.9	68 47.5	46.2
	05	94 48.4	242 32.6	04.6	324 32.8	32.6	310 52.6	58.7	83 50.2	46.1
	06	109 50.9	257 35.8	S21 04.4	339 33.8	N19 32.3	325 54.6	N14 58.6	98 52.8	N 1 46.0
	07	124 53.3	272 39.1	04.1	354 34.8	32.0	340 56.7	58.5	113 55.5	46.0
	08	139 55.8	287 42.3	03.9	9 35.8	31.6	355 58.8	58.4	128 58.1	45.9
S	09	154 58.2	302 45.6	. . 03.6	24 36.9	. . 31.3	11 00.8	. . 58.2	144 00.7	. . 45.8
U	10	170 00.7	317 48.8	03.3	39 37.9	31.0	26 02.9	58.1	159 03.4	45.7
N	11	185 03.2	332 52.1	03.1	54 38.9	30.7	41 04.9	58.0	174 06.0	45.7
D	12	200 05.6	347 55.4	S21 02.8	69 39.9	N19 30.4	56 07.0	N14 57.9	189 08.7	N 1 45.6
A	13	215 08.1	2 58.6	02.5	84 40.9	30.1	71 09.1	57.7	204 11.3	45.5
Y	14	230 10.6	18 01.9	02.2	99 41.9	29.7	86 11.1	57.6	219 14.0	45.4
	15	245 13.0	33 05.2	. . 02.0	114 43.0	. . 29.4	101 13.2	. . 57.5	234 16.6	. . 45.4
	16	260 15.5	48 08.5	01.7	129 44.0	29.1	116 15.3	57.4	249 19.2	45.3
	17	275 18.0	63 11.7	01.4	144 45.0	28.8	131 17.3	57.2	264 21.9	45.2
	18	290 20.4	78 15.0	S21 01.1	159 46.0	N19 28.5	146 19.4	N14 57.1	279 24.5	N 1 45.1
	19	305 22.9	93 18.3	00.8	174 47.0	28.1	161 21.5	57.0	294 27.2	45.1
	20	320 25.3	108 21.6	00.5	189 48.1	27.8	176 23.5	56.9	309 29.8	45.0
	21	335 27.8	123 24.9	21 00.2	204 49.1	. . 27.5	191 25.6	. . 56.8	324 32.5	. . 44.9
	22	350 30.3	138 28.2	20 59.9	219 50.1	27.2	206 27.7	56.6	339 35.1	44.8
	23	5 32.7	153 31.5	59.6	234 51.1	26.9	221 29.7	56.5	354 37.7	44.8
	12 00	20 35.2	168 34.8	S20 59.3	249 52.1	N19 26.6	236 31.8	N14 56.4	9 40.4	N 1 44.7
	01	35 37.7	183 38.1	59.0	264 53.2	26.2	251 33.8	56.3	24 43.0	44.6
	02	50 40.1	198 41.4	58.7	279 54.2	25.9	266 35.9	56.1	39 45.7	44.5
	03	65 42.6	213 44.8	. . 58.4	294 55.2	. . 25.6	281 38.0	. . 56.0	54 48.3	. . 44.5
	04	80 45.1	228 48.1	58.1	309 56.2	25.3	296 40.0	55.9	69 51.0	44.4
	05	95 47.5	243 51.4	57.8	324 57.2	25.0	311 42.1	55.8	84 53.6	44.3
	06	110 50.0	258 54.7	S20 57.5	339 58.3	N19 24.6	326 44.2	N14 55.6	99 56.2	N 1 44.2
	07	125 52.5	273 58.1	57.1	354 59.3	24.3	341 46.2	55.5	114 58.9	44.2
	08	140 54.9	289 01.4	56.8	10 00.3	24.0	356 48.3	55.4	130 01.5	44.1
M	09	155 57.4	304 04.7	. . 56.5	25 01.3	. . 23.7	11 50.4	. . 55.3	145 04.2	. . 44.0
O	10	170 59.8	319 08.1	56.2	40 02.4	23.4	26 52.4	55.1	160 06.8	43.9
N	11	186 02.3	334 11.4	55.8	55 03.4	23.0	41 54.5	55.0	175 09.5	43.9
D	12	201 04.8	349 14.8	S20 55.5	70 04.4	N19 22.7	56 56.6	N14 54.9	190 12.1	N 1 43.8
A	13	216 07.2	4 18.1	55.2	85 05.4	22.4	71 58.6	54.8	205 14.7	43.7
Y	14	231 09.7	19 21.5	54.8	100 06.5	22.1	87 00.7	54.7	220 17.4	43.7
	15	246 12.2	34 24.8	. . 54.5	115 07.5	. . 21.8	102 02.8	. . 54.5	235 20.0	. . 43.6
	16	261 14.6	49 28.2	54.1	130 08.5	21.5	117 04.8	54.4	250 22.7	43.5
	17	276 17.1	64 31.5	53.8	145 09.5	21.1	132 06.9	54.3	265 25.3	43.4
	18	291 19.6	79 34.9	S20 53.5	160 10.6	N19 20.8	147 09.0	N14 54.2	280 28.0	N 1 43.4
	19	306 22.0	94 38.3	53.1	175 11.6	20.5	162 11.1	54.0	295 30.6	43.3
	20	321 24.5	109 41.7	52.8	190 12.6	20.2	177 13.1	53.9	310 33.2	43.2
	21	336 27.0	124 45.0	. . 52.4	205 13.7	. . 19.8	192 15.2	. . 53.8	325 35.9	. . 43.1
	22	351 29.4	139 48.4	52.0	220 14.7	19.5	207 17.3	53.7	340 38.5	43.1
	23	6 31.9	154 51.8	51.7	235 15.7	19.2	222 19.3	53.6	355 41.2	43.0
	Mer. Pass.	h m 22 37.9	*v* 3.3	*d* 0.3	*v* 1.0	*d* 0.3	*v* 2.1	*d* 0.1	*v* 2.6	*d* 0.1

STARS

Name	SHA ° ′	Dec ° ′
Acamar	315 10.3	S40 11.6
Achernar	335 18.5	S57 05.9
Acrux	172 59.1	S63 14.8
Adhara	255 04.7	S29 00.2
Aldebaran	290 37.8	N16 33.9
Alioth	166 12.3	N55 48.9
Alkaid	152 51.3	N49 10.8
Alnair	27 30.8	S46 49.9
Alnilam	275 36.1	S 1 10.9
Alphard	217 46.5	S 8 46.3
Alphecca	126 02.8	N26 37.6
Alpheratz	357 32.9	N29 14.5
Altair	61 58.5	N 8 56.5
Ankaa	353 05.3	S42 09.5
Antares	112 14.3	S26 29.5
Arcturus	145 46.9	N19 02.7
Atria	107 07.5	S69 04.7
Avior	234 14.3	S59 35.4
Bellatrix	278 21.2	N 6 22.5
Betelgeuse	270 50.4	N 7 24.8
Canopus	263 51.6	S52 42.2
Capella	280 19.5	N46 01.4
Deneb	49 24.7	N45 22.9
Denebola	182 23.8	N14 25.4
Diphda	348 45.5	S17 50.2
Dubhe	193 39.8	N61 36.2
Elnath	277 59.9	N28 37.8
Eltanin	90 41.7	N51 29.4
Enif	33 37.2	N10 00.1
Fomalhaut	15 12.6	S29 28.8
Gacrux	171 50.6	S57 15.7
Gienah	175 42.4	S17 41.3
Hadar	148 34.6	S60 30.1
Hamal	327 49.2	N23 35.5
Kaus Aust.	83 30.7	S34 22.4
Kochab	137 20.9	N74 02.8
Markab	13 28.2	N15 21.2
Menkar	314 04.4	N 4 11.8
Menkent	147 56.3	S36 30.1
Miaplacidus	221 38.4	S69 49.3
Mirfak	308 25.8	N49 57.3
Nunki	75 46.0	S26 15.8
Peacock	53 03.3	S56 39.1
Pollux	243 15.6	N27 57.6
Procyon	244 49.4	N 5 09.5
Rasalhague	95 57.4	N12 32.6
Regulus	207 33.1	N11 50.2
Rigel	281 02.3	S 8 10.1
Rigil Kent.	139 38.9	S60 56.8
Sabik	102 01.3	S15 45.4
Schedar	349 28.8	N56 41.2
Shaula	96 08.6	S37 07.4
Sirius	258 24.9	S16 44.9
Spica	158 21.1	S11 18.0
Suhail	222 45.5	S43 32.2
Vega	80 32.3	N38 48.8
Zuben'ubi	136 54.7	S16 09.1

	SHA ° ′	Mer. Pass. h m
Venus	147 40.3	12 48
Mars	229 51.7	7 22
Jupiter	216 06.2	8 16
Saturn	349 00.9	23 21

2026 OCTOBER 10, 11, 12 (SAT., SUN., MON.)

UT d h	SUN GHA ° ′	SUN Dec ° ′	MOON GHA ° ′	v ′	MOON Dec ° ′	d ′	HP ′
10 00	183 13.1	S 6 34.0	191 54.0	14.0	S 6 28.4	15.0	56.9
01	198 13.3	34.9	206 27.0	14.0	6 43.4	15.0	56.9
02	213 13.5	35.9	221 00.0	14.0	6 58.4	15.0	56.9
03	228 13.6	. . 36.8	235 33.0	13.9	7 13.4	14.9	56.9
04	243 13.8	37.8	250 05.9	14.0	7 28.3	14.9	56.8
05	258 14.0	38.7	264 38.9	13.9	7 43.2	14.8	56.8
06	273 14.1	S 6 39.7	279 11.8	14.0	S 7 58.0	14.8	56.8
07	288 14.3	40.6	293 44.8	13.9	8 12.8	14.8	56.8
S 08	303 14.5	41.6	308 17.7	13.9	8 27.6	14.7	56.7
A 09	318 14.6	. . 42.5	322 50.6	13.9	8 42.3	14.6	56.7
T 10	333 14.8	43.5	337 23.5	13.9	8 56.9	14.6	56.7
U 11	348 15.0	44.4	351 56.4	13.8	9 11.5	14.5	56.7
R 12	3 15.1	S 6 45.4	6 29.2	13.9	S 9 26.0	14.5	56.7
D 13	18 15.3	46.3	21 02.1	13.8	9 40.5	14.5	56.6
A 14	33 15.5	47.2	35 34.9	13.8	9 55.0	14.3	56.6
Y 15	48 15.6	. . 48.2	50 07.7	13.8	10 09.3	14.4	56.6
16	63 15.8	49.1	64 40.5	13.7	10 23.7	14.2	56.6
17	78 15.9	50.1	79 13.2	13.8	10 37.9	14.2	56.5
18	93 16.1	S 6 51.0	93 46.0	13.7	S10 52.1	14.2	56.5
19	108 16.3	52.0	108 18.7	13.7	11 06.3	14.0	56.5
20	123 16.4	52.9	122 51.4	13.7	11 20.3	14.1	56.5
21	138 16.6	. . 53.9	137 24.1	13.6	11 34.4	13.9	56.4
22	153 16.8	54.8	151 56.7	13.6	11 48.3	13.9	56.4
23	168 16.9	55.7	166 29.3	13.6	12 02.2	13.8	56.4
11 00	183 17.1	S 6 56.7	181 01.9	13.6	S12 16.0	13.8	56.4
01	198 17.2	57.6	195 34.5	13.5	12 29.8	13.7	56.4
02	213 17.4	58.6	210 07.0	13.5	12 43.5	13.6	56.3
03	228 17.6	6 59.5	224 39.5	13.5	12 57.1	13.6	56.3
04	243 17.7	7 00.5	239 12.0	13.5	13 10.7	13.5	56.3
05	258 17.9	01.4	253 44.5	13.4	13 24.2	13.4	56.3
06	273 18.1	S 7 02.3	268 16.9	13.4	S13 37.6	13.4	56.2
07	288 18.2	03.3	282 49.3	13.3	13 51.0	13.2	56.2
08	303 18.4	04.2	297 21.6	13.3	14 04.2	13.2	56.2
S 09	318 18.5	. . 05.2	311 53.9	13.3	14 17.4	13.2	56.2
U 10	333 18.7	06.1	326 26.2	13.3	14 30.6	13.0	56.1
N 11	348 18.9	07.1	340 58.5	13.2	14 43.6	13.0	56.1
D 12	3 19.0	S 7 08.0	355 30.7	13.2	S14 56.6	12.9	56.1
A 13	18 19.2	08.9	10 02.9	13.1	15 09.5	12.8	56.1
Y 14	33 19.3	09.9	24 35.0	13.1	15 22.3	12.7	56.1
15	48 19.5	. . 10.8	39 07.1	13.1	15 35.0	12.7	56.0
16	63 19.7	11.8	53 39.2	13.0	15 47.7	12.6	56.0
17	78 19.8	12.7	68 11.2	13.0	16 00.3	12.5	56.0
18	93 20.0	S 7 13.7	82 43.2	13.0	S16 12.8	12.4	56.0
19	108 20.1	14.6	97 15.2	12.9	16 25.2	12.3	55.9
20	123 20.3	15.5	111 47.1	12.9	16 37.5	12.2	55.9
21	138 20.4	. . 16.5	126 19.0	12.9	16 49.7	12.2	55.9
22	153 20.6	17.4	140 50.9	12.8	17 01.9	12.1	55.9
23	168 20.8	18.4	155 22.7	12.7	17 14.0	11.9	55.8
12 00	183 20.9	S 7 19.3	169 54.4	12.7	S17 25.9	11.9	55.8
01	198 21.1	20.2	184 26.1	12.7	17 37.8	11.8	55.8
02	213 21.2	21.2	198 57.8	12.7	17 49.6	11.7	55.8
03	228 21.4	. . 22.1	213 29.5	12.6	18 01.3	11.7	55.8
04	243 21.5	23.0	228 01.1	12.5	18 13.0	11.5	55.7
05	258 21.7	24.0	242 32.6	12.5	18 24.5	11.4	55.7
06	273 21.9	S 7 24.9	257 04.1	12.5	S18 35.9	11.3	55.7
07	288 22.0	25.9	271 35.6	12.4	18 47.2	11.3	55.7
08	303 22.2	26.8	286 07.0	12.4	18 58.5	11.1	55.6
M 09	318 22.3	. . 27.7	300 38.4	12.4	19 09.6	11.1	55.6
O 10	333 22.5	28.7	315 09.8	12.3	19 20.7	10.9	55.6
N 11	348 22.6	29.6	329 41.1	12.2	19 31.6	10.9	55.6
D 12	3 22.8	S 7 30.6	344 12.3	12.2	S19 42.5	10.7	55.6
A 13	18 22.9	31.5	358 43.5	12.2	19 53.2	10.7	55.5
Y 14	33 23.1	32.4	13 14.7	12.1	20 03.9	10.5	55.5
15	48 23.2	. . 33.4	27 45.8	12.1	20 14.4	10.5	55.5
16	63 23.4	34.3	42 16.9	12.0	20 24.9	10.3	55.5
17	78 23.6	35.2	56 47.9	12.0	20 35.2	10.3	55.4
18	93 23.7	S 7 36.2	71 18.9	11.9	S20 45.5	10.1	55.4
19	108 23.9	37.1	85 49.8	11.9	20 55.6	10.0	55.4
20	123 24.0	38.1	100 20.7	11.9	21 05.6	10.0	55.4
21	138 24.2	. . 39.0	114 51.6	11.8	21 15.6	9.8	55.4
22	153 24.3	39.9	129 22.4	11.8	21 25.4	9.7	55.3
23	168 24.5	40.9	143 53.2	11.7	S21 35.1	9.6	55.3
	SD 16.0	*d* 0.9	SD	15.4	15.3		15.1

Lat. °	Twilight Naut. h m	Twilight Civil h m	Sunrise h m	Moonrise 10 h m	Moonrise 11 h m	Moonrise 12 h m	Moonrise 13 h m
N 72	04 37	05 56	07 05	07 14	09 46	▬	▬
N 70	04 43	05 54	06 56	07 00	09 13	12 51	▬
68	04 48	05 52	06 49	06 49	08 50	11 10	▬
66	04 52	05 51	06 43	06 41	08 31	10 32	13 22
64	04 55	05 50	06 38	06 33	08 17	10 05	12 05
62	04 57	05 49	06 33	06 27	08 04	09 45	11 29
60	04 59	05 48	06 29	06 22	07 54	09 28	11 04
N 58	05 01	05 47	06 26	06 17	07 45	09 14	10 43
56	05 03	05 46	06 23	06 13	07 37	09 03	10 27
54	05 04	05 45	06 20	06 09	07 31	08 52	10 13
52	05 05	05 44	06 18	06 06	07 24	08 43	10 00
50	05 06	05 43	06 15	06 03	07 19	08 35	09 50
45	05 07	05 41	06 10	05 56	07 07	08 17	09 27
N 40	05 08	05 39	06 06	05 50	06 57	08 03	09 09
35	05 08	05 37	06 03	05 46	06 49	07 51	08 54
30	05 07	05 35	05 59	05 42	06 41	07 41	08 41
20	05 06	05 31	05 54	05 34	06 29	07 23	08 19
N 10	05 03	05 27	05 48	05 28	06 18	07 08	08 00
0	04 58	05 23	05 43	05 23	06 08	06 54	07 42
S 10	04 53	05 17	05 38	05 17	05 57	06 40	07 24
20	04 45	05 11	05 33	05 11	05 47	06 25	07 06
30	04 34	05 02	05 27	05 04	05 35	06 08	06 44
35	04 27	04 57	05 23	05 00	05 28	05 58	06 32
40	04 18	04 51	05 19	04 56	05 20	05 46	06 17
45	04 08	04 44	05 14	04 51	05 11	05 33	06 00
S 50	03 54	04 34	05 08	04 45	05 00	05 17	05 39
52	03 47	04 30	05 05	04 42	04 55	05 10	05 29
54	03 40	04 25	05 02	04 39	04 49	05 02	05 18
56	03 32	04 20	04 59	04 36	04 43	04 52	05 06
58	03 22	04 14	04 55	04 32	04 36	04 42	04 51
S 60	03 10	04 07	04 51	04 28	04 29	04 30	04 34

Lat. °	Sunset h m	Twilight Civil h m	Twilight Naut. h m	Moonset 10 h m	Moonset 11 h m	Moonset 12 h m	Moonset 13 h m
N 72	16 27	17 35	18 53	15 23	14 26	▬	▬
N 70	16 36	17 37	18 48	15 39	15 01	13 01	▬
68	16 43	17 39	18 43	15 52	15 27	14 43	▬
66	16 49	17 41	18 40	16 03	15 46	15 23	14 14
64	16 54	17 42	18 37	16 12	16 02	15 50	15 31
62	16 59	17 43	18 35	16 19	16 16	16 12	16 08
60	17 03	17 45	18 33	16 26	16 27	16 29	16 34
N 58	17 06	17 46	18 31	16 32	16 37	16 44	16 55
56	17 10	17 47	18 30	16 37	16 46	16 56	17 12
54	17 12	17 48	18 29	16 42	16 53	17 07	17 27
52	17 15	17 49	18 28	16 47	17 00	17 17	17 40
50	17 17	17 50	18 27	16 51	17 07	17 26	17 51
45	17 22	17 52	18 26	16 59	17 20	17 45	18 14
N 40	17 27	17 54	18 25	17 06	17 31	18 00	18 33
35	17 30	17 56	18 25	17 13	17 41	18 13	18 49
30	17 34	17 58	18 26	17 18	17 50	18 24	19 03
20	17 40	18 02	18 27	17 28	18 04	18 44	19 26
N 10	17 45	18 06	18 31	17 36	18 17	19 01	19 47
0	17 50	18 11	18 35	17 44	18 30	19 17	20 06
S 10	17 55	18 16	18 41	17 52	18 42	19 33	20 25
20	18 01	18 23	18 49	18 00	18 55	19 50	20 46
30	18 07	18 32	19 00	18 10	19 10	20 10	21 09
35	18 11	18 37	19 07	18 16	19 19	20 22	21 23
40	18 16	18 43	19 16	18 22	19 29	20 35	21 40
45	18 21	18 51	19 27	18 30	19 41	20 51	21 59
S 50	18 27	19 00	19 41	18 39	19 55	21 11	22 24
52	18 30	19 05	19 48	18 43	20 02	21 20	22 36
54	18 33	19 10	19 55	18 48	20 10	21 31	22 49
56	18 36	19 15	20 04	18 53	20 18	21 43	23 05
58	18 40	19 22	20 14	18 59	20 28	21 57	23 24
S 60	18 44	19 29	20 26	19 06	20 39	22 13	23 48

Day d	SUN Eqn. of Time 00h m s	SUN Eqn. of Time 12h m s	SUN Mer. Pass. h m	MOON Mer. Pass. Upper h m	MOON Mer. Pass. Lower h m	MOON Age d	MOON Age %	MOON Phase
10	12 52	13 00	11 47	11 33	23 56	29	0	
11	13 08	13 16	11 47	12 19	24 42	01	1	●
12	13 23	13 31	11 46	13 05	00 42	02	4	

UT		ARIES	VENUS −4·3		MARS +1·0		JUPITER −1·9		SATURN +0·3	
		GHA	GHA	Dec	GHA	Dec	GHA	Dec	GHA	Dec
d	h	° ′	° ′	° ′	° ′	° ′	° ′	° ′	° ′	° ′
13	00	21 34.3	169 55.2	S20 51.3	250 16.7	N19 18.9	237 21.4	N14 53.4	10 43.8	N 1 42.9
	01	36 36.8	184 58.6	51.0	265 17.8	18.6	252 23.5	53.3	25 46.5	42.8
	02	51 39.3	200 02.0	50.6	280 18.8	18.2	267 25.5	53.2	40 49.1	42.8
	03	66 41.7	215 05.4	. . 50.2	295 19.8	. . 17.9	282 27.6	. . 53.1	55 51.7	. . 42.7
	04	81 44.2	230 08.8	49.8	310 20.9	17.6	297 29.7	52.9	70 54.4	42.6
	05	96 46.7	245 12.2	49.5	325 21.9	17.3	312 31.7	52.8	85 57.0	42.5
	06	111 49.1	260 15.6	S20 49.1	340 22.9	N19 17.0	327 33.8	N14 52.7	100 59.7	N 1 42.5
	07	126 51.6	275 19.0	48.7	355 24.0	16.6	342 35.9	52.6	116 02.3	42.4
T	08	141 54.1	290 22.4	48.3	10 25.0	16.3	357 38.0	52.5	131 04.9	42.3
U	09	156 56.5	305 25.8	. . 47.9	25 26.0	. . 16.0	12 40.0	. . 52.3	146 07.6	. . 42.2
E	10	171 59.0	320 29.2	47.5	40 27.1	15.7	27 42.1	52.2	161 10.2	42.2
S	11	187 01.4	335 32.6	47.2	55 28.1	15.4	42 44.2	52.1	176 12.9	42.1
D	12	202 03.9	350 36.1	S20 46.8	70 29.1	N19 15.0	57 46.2	N14 52.0	191 15.5	N 1 42.0
A	13	217 06.4	5 39.5	46.4	85 30.2	14.7	72 48.3	51.8	206 18.2	41.9
Y	14	232 08.8	20 42.9	46.0	100 31.2	14.4	87 50.4	51.7	221 20.8	41.9
	15	247 11.3	35 46.3	. . 45.6	115 32.2	. . 14.1	102 52.5	. . 51.6	236 23.4	. . 41.8
	16	262 13.8	50 49.8	45.2	130 33.3	13.7	117 54.5	51.5	251 26.1	41.7
	17	277 16.2	65 53.2	44.8	145 34.3	13.4	132 56.6	51.4	266 28.7	41.7
	18	292 18.7	80 56.7	S20 44.4	160 35.3	N19 13.1	147 58.7	N14 51.2	281 31.4	N 1 41.6
	19	307 21.2	96 00.1	43.9	175 36.4	12.8	163 00.8	51.1	296 34.0	41.5
	20	322 23.6	111 03.6	43.5	190 37.4	12.5	178 02.8	51.0	311 36.6	41.4
	21	337 26.1	126 07.0	. . 43.1	205 38.4	. . 12.1	193 04.9	. . 50.9	326 39.3	. . 41.4
	22	352 28.6	141 10.5	42.7	220 39.5	11.8	208 07.0	50.8	341 41.9	41.3
	23	7 31.0	156 13.9	42.3	235 40.5	11.5	223 09.0	50.6	356 44.6	41.2
14	00	22 33.5	171 17.4	S20 41.8	250 41.6	N19 11.2	238 11.1	N14 50.5	11 47.2	N 1 41.1
	01	37 35.9	186 20.8	41.4	265 42.6	10.8	253 13.2	50.4	26 49.9	41.1
	02	52 38.4	201 24.3	41.0	280 43.6	10.5	268 15.3	50.3	41 52.5	41.0
	03	67 40.9	216 27.8	. . 40.6	295 44.7	. . 10.2	283 17.3	. . 50.1	56 55.1	. . 40.9
	04	82 43.3	231 31.2	40.1	310 45.7	09.9	298 19.4	50.0	71 57.8	40.8
	05	97 45.8	246 34.7	39.7	325 46.7	09.5	313 21.5	49.9	87 00.4	40.8
	06	112 48.3	261 38.2	S20 39.3	340 47.8	N19 09.2	328 23.6	N14 49.8	102 03.1	N 1 40.7
W	07	127 50.7	276 41.7	38.8	355 48.8	08.9	343 25.6	49.7	117 05.7	40.6
E	08	142 53.2	291 45.2	38.4	10 49.9	08.6	358 27.7	49.5	132 08.3	40.6
D	09	157 55.7	306 48.7	. . 37.9	25 50.9	. . 08.3	13 29.8	. . 49.4	147 11.0	. . 40.5
N	10	172 58.1	321 52.1	37.5	40 52.0	07.9	28 31.9	49.3	162 13.6	40.4
E	11	188 00.6	336 55.6	37.0	55 53.0	07.6	43 34.0	49.2	177 16.3	40.3
S	12	203 03.1	351 59.1	S20 36.6	70 54.0	N19 07.3	58 36.0	N14 49.1	192 18.9	N 1 40.3
D	13	218 05.5	7 02.6	36.1	85 55.1	07.0	73 38.1	48.9	207 21.5	40.2
A	14	233 08.0	22 06.1	35.7	100 56.1	06.6	88 40.2	48.8	222 24.2	40.1
Y	15	248 10.4	37 09.6	. . 35.2	115 57.2	. . 06.3	103 42.3	. . 48.7	237 26.8	. . 40.0
	16	263 12.9	52 13.1	34.7	130 58.2	06.0	118 44.3	48.6	252 29.5	40.0
	17	278 15.4	67 16.6	34.3	145 59.2	05.7	133 46.4	48.5	267 32.1	39.9
	18	293 17.8	82 20.2	S20 33.8	161 00.3	N19 05.3	148 48.5	N14 48.3	282 34.7	N 1 39.8
	19	308 20.3	97 23.7	33.3	176 01.3	05.0	163 50.6	48.2	297 37.4	39.7
	20	323 22.8	112 27.2	32.8	191 02.4	04.7	178 52.6	48.1	312 40.0	39.7
	21	338 25.2	127 30.7	. . 32.4	206 03.4	. . 04.4	193 54.7	. . 48.0	327 42.7	. . 39.6
	22	353 27.7	142 34.2	31.9	221 04.5	04.0	208 56.8	47.9	342 45.3	39.5
	23	8 30.2	157 37.8	31.4	236 05.5	03.7	223 58.9	47.7	357 48.0	39.5
15	00	23 32.6	172 41.3	S20 30.9	251 06.6	N19 03.4	239 01.0	N14 47.6	12 50.6	N 1 39.4
	01	38 35.1	187 44.8	30.4	266 07.6	03.1	254 03.0	47.5	27 53.2	39.3
	02	53 37.5	202 48.4	29.9	281 08.7	02.7	269 05.1	47.4	42 55.9	39.2
	03	68 40.0	217 51.9	. . 29.5	296 09.7	. . 02.4	284 07.2	. . 47.3	57 58.5	. . 39.2
	04	83 42.5	232 55.4	29.0	311 10.8	02.1	299 09.3	47.1	73 01.2	39.1
	05	98 44.9	247 59.0	28.5	326 11.8	01.8	314 11.4	47.0	88 03.8	39.0
	06	113 47.4	263 02.5	S20 28.0	341 12.8	N19 01.4	329 13.4	N14 46.9	103 06.4	N 1 38.9
T	07	128 49.9	278 06.1	27.5	356 13.9	01.1	344 15.5	46.8	118 09.1	38.9
H	08	143 52.3	293 09.6	27.0	11 14.9	00.8	359 17.6	46.7	133 11.7	38.8
U	09	158 54.8	308 13.2	. . 26.5	26 16.0	. . 00.5	14 19.7	. . 46.5	148 14.4	. . 38.7
R	10	173 57.3	323 16.7	25.9	41 17.0	19 00.1	29 21.8	46.4	163 17.0	38.7
S	11	188 59.7	338 20.3	25.4	56 18.1	18 59.8	44 23.8	46.3	178 19.6	38.6
D	12	204 02.2	353 23.8	S20 24.9	71 19.1	N18 59.5	59 25.9	N14 46.2	193 22.3	N 1 38.5
A	13	219 04.7	8 27.4	24.4	86 20.2	59.1	74 28.0	46.1	208 24.9	38.4
Y	14	234 07.1	23 31.0	23.9	101 21.2	58.8	89 30.1	45.9	223 27.6	38.4
	15	249 09.6	38 34.5	. . 23.4	116 22.3	. . 58.5	104 32.2	. . 45.8	238 30.2	. . 38.3
	16	264 12.0	53 38.1	22.8	131 23.4	58.2	119 34.2	45.7	253 32.8	38.2
	17	279 14.5	68 41.7	22.3	146 24.4	57.8	134 36.3	45.6	268 35.5	38.1
	18	294 17.0	83 45.3	S20 21.8	161 25.5	N18 57.5	149 38.4	N14 45.5	283 38.1	N 1 38.1
	19	309 19.4	98 48.8	21.2	176 26.5	57.2	164 40.5	45.4	298 40.8	38.0
	20	324 21.9	113 52.4	20.7	191 27.6	56.9	179 42.6	45.2	313 43.4	37.9
	21	339 24.4	128 56.0	. . 20.2	206 28.6	. . 56.5	194 44.7	. . 45.1	328 46.0	. . 37.9
	22	354 26.8	143 59.6	19.6	221 29.7	56.2	209 46.7	45.0	343 48.7	37.8
	23	9 29.3	159 03.2	19.1	236 30.7	55.9	224 48.8	44.9	358 51.3	37.7
Mer. Pass.		h m 22 26.1	*v* 3.5	*d* 0.5	*v* 1.0	*d* 0.3	*v* 2.1	*d* 0.1	*v* 2.6	*d* 0.1

STARS Name	SHA	Dec
	° ′	° ′
Acamar	315 10.3	S40 11.6
Achernar	335 18.5	S57 05.9
Acrux	172 59.1	S63 14.8
Adhara	255 04.7	S29 00.2
Aldebaran	290 37.7	N16 33.9
Alioth	166 12.3	N55 48.8
Alkaid	152 51.4	N49 10.8
Alnair	27 30.8	S46 49.9
Alnilam	275 36.1	S 1 10.9
Alphard	217 46.5	S 8 46.3
Alphecca	126 02.8	N26 37.6
Alpheratz	357 32.9	N29 14.5
Altair	61 58.5	N 8 56.5
Ankaa	353 05.3	S42 09.5
Antares	112 14.3	S26 29.5
Arcturus	145 46.9	N19 02.7
Atria	107 07.6	S69 04.7
Avior	234 14.3	S59 35.4
Bellatrix	278 21.2	N 6 22.5
Betelgeuse	270 50.4	N 7 24.8
Canopus	263 51.6	S52 42.2
Capella	280 19.5	N46 01.4
Deneb	49 24.7	N45 22.9
Denebola	182 23.8	N14 25.4
Diphda	348 45.5	S17 50.2
Dubhe	193 39.8	N61 36.2
Elnath	277 59.9	N28 37.8
Eltanin	90 41.7	N51 29.4
Enif	33 37.2	N10 00.1
Fomalhaut	15 12.6	S29 28.8
Gacrux	171 50.6	S57 15.7
Gienah	175 42.4	S17 41.3
Hadar	148 34.6	S60 30.1
Hamal	327 49.2	N23 35.5
Kaus Aust.	83 30.7	S34 22.4
Kochab	137 20.9	N74 02.8
Markab	13 28.2	N15 21.2
Menkar	314 04.3	N 4 11.8
Menkent	147 56.3	S36 30.1
Miaplacidus	221 38.4	S69 49.3
Mirfak	308 25.7	N49 57.4
Nunki	75 46.0	S26 15.8
Peacock	53 03.3	S56 39.1
Pollux	243 15.6	N27 57.6
Procyon	244 49.3	N 5 09.5
Rasalhague	95 57.4	N12 32.6
Regulus	207 33.1	N11 50.2
Rigel	281 02.3	S 8 10.1
Rigil Kent.	139 38.9	S60 56.8
Sabik	102 01.3	S15 45.4
Schedar	349 28.8	N56 41.2
Shaula	96 08.6	S37 07.4
Sirius	258 24.9	S16 45.0
Spica	158 21.1	S11 18.0
Suhail	222 45.4	S43 32.2
Vega	80 32.3	N38 48.8
Zuben'ubi	136 54.7	S16 09.1

	SHA	Mer. Pass.
	° ′	h m
Venus	148 43.9	12 32
Mars	228 08.1	7 17
Jupiter	215 37.6	8 06
Saturn	349 13.7	23 09

UT (d h)	Day	SUN GHA	SUN Dec	MOON GHA	v	MOON Dec	d	HP
		° ′	° ′	° ′	′	° ′	′	′
13 00	TUESDAY	183 24.6	S 7 41.8	158 23.9	11.7	S21 44.7	9.5	55.3
01		198 24.8	42.7	172 54.6	11.6	21 54.2	9.4	55.3
02		213 24.9	43.7	187 25.2	11.6	22 03.6	9.3	55.3
03		228 25.1	. . 44.6	201 55.8	11.5	22 12.9	9.1	55.2
04		243 25.2	45.5	216 26.3	11.5	22 22.0	9.1	55.2
05		258 25.4	46.5	230 56.8	11.5	22 31.1	8.9	55.2
06		273 25.5	S 7 47.4	245 27.3	11.4	S22 40.0	8.8	55.2
07		288 25.7	48.3	259 57.7	11.3	22 48.8	8.7	55.2
08		303 25.8	49.3	274 28.0	11.4	22 57.5	8.6	55.1
09		318 26.0	. . 50.2	288 58.4	11.2	23 06.1	8.5	55.1
10		333 26.1	51.1	303 28.6	11.3	23 14.6	8.4	55.1
11		348 26.3	52.1	317 58.9	11.2	23 23.0	8.2	55.1
12		3 26.4	S 7 53.0	332 29.1	11.1	S23 31.2	8.2	55.1
13		18 26.6	53.9	346 59.2	11.1	23 39.4	8.0	55.0
14		33 26.7	54.9	1 29.3	11.1	23 47.4	7.9	55.0
15		48 26.9	. . 55.8	15 59.4	11.0	23 55.3	7.7	55.0
16		63 27.0	56.7	30 29.4	11.0	24 03.0	7.7	55.0
17		78 27.2	57.7	44 59.4	11.0	24 10.7	7.5	55.0
18		93 27.3	S 7 58.6	59 29.4	10.9	S24 18.2	7.4	55.0
19		108 27.5	7 59.5	73 59.3	10.8	24 25.6	7.3	54.9
20		123 27.6	8 00.5	88 29.1	10.9	24 32.9	7.2	54.9
21		138 27.8	. . 01.4	102 59.0	10.8	24 40.1	7.0	54.9
22		153 27.9	02.3	117 28.8	10.7	24 47.1	6.9	54.9
23		168 28.1	03.3	131 58.5	10.7	24 54.0	6.8	54.9
14 00	WEDNESDAY	183 28.2	S 8 04.2	146 28.2	10.7	S25 00.8	6.7	54.8
01		198 28.3	05.1	160 57.9	10.7	25 07.5	6.6	54.8
02		213 28.5	06.0	175 27.6	10.6	25 14.1	6.4	54.8
03		228 28.6	. . 07.0	189 57.2	10.5	25 20.5	6.3	54.8
04		243 28.8	07.9	204 26.7	10.6	25 26.8	6.1	54.8
05		258 28.9	08.8	218 56.3	10.5	25 32.9	6.1	54.8
06		273 29.1	S 8 09.8	233 25.8	10.4	S25 39.0	5.9	54.7
07		288 29.2	10.7	247 55.2	10.5	25 44.9	5.8	54.7
08		303 29.4	11.6	262 24.7	10.4	25 50.7	5.6	54.7
09		318 29.5	. . 12.6	276 54.1	10.4	25 56.3	5.5	54.7
10		333 29.7	13.5	291 23.5	10.3	26 01.8	5.4	54.7
11		348 29.8	14.4	305 52.8	10.3	26 07.2	5.3	54.7
12		3 29.9	S 8 15.3	320 22.1	10.3	S26 12.5	5.1	54.7
13		18 30.1	16.3	334 51.4	10.3	26 17.6	5.0	54.6
14		33 30.2	17.2	349 20.7	10.2	26 22.6	4.9	54.6
15		48 30.4	. . 18.1	3 49.9	10.2	26 27.5	4.8	54.6
16		63 30.5	19.1	18 19.1	10.2	26 32.3	4.6	54.6
17		78 30.7	20.0	32 48.3	10.2	26 36.9	4.4	54.6
18		93 30.8	S 8 20.9	47 17.5	10.1	S26 41.3	4.4	54.6
19		108 30.9	21.8	61 46.6	10.1	26 45.7	4.2	54.6
20		123 31.1	22.8	76 15.7	10.1	26 49.9	4.1	54.5
21		138 31.2	. . 23.7	90 44.8	10.1	26 54.0	3.9	54.5
22		153 31.4	24.6	105 13.9	10.0	26 57.9	3.8	54.5
23		168 31.5	25.5	119 42.9	10.1	27 01.7	3.7	54.5
15 00	THURSDAY	183 31.6	S 8 26.5	134 12.0	10.0	S27 05.4	3.6	54.5
01		198 31.8	27.4	148 41.0	10.0	27 09.0	3.4	54.5
02		213 31.9	28.3	163 10.0	10.0	27 12.4	3.3	54.5
03		228 32.1	. . 29.2	177 39.0	9.9	27 15.7	3.1	54.5
04		243 32.2	30.2	192 07.9	10.0	27 18.8	3.0	54.4
05		258 32.4	31.1	206 36.9	9.9	27 21.8	2.9	54.4
06		273 32.5	S 8 32.0	221 05.8	10.0	S27 24.7	2.7	54.4
07		288 32.6	32.9	235 34.8	9.9	27 27.4	2.6	54.4
08		303 32.8	33.9	250 03.7	9.9	27 30.0	2.5	54.4
09		318 32.9	. . 34.8	264 32.6	9.9	27 32.5	2.3	54.4
10		333 33.0	35.7	279 01.5	9.9	27 34.8	2.2	54.4
11		348 33.2	36.6	293 30.4	9.8	27 37.0	2.1	54.4
12		3 33.3	S 8 37.6	307 59.2	9.9	S27 39.1	1.9	54.4
13		18 33.5	38.5	322 28.1	9.9	27 41.0	1.8	54.4
14		33 33.6	39.4	336 57.0	9.9	27 42.8	1.6	54.3
15		48 33.7	. . 40.3	351 25.9	9.8	27 44.4	1.5	54.3
16		63 33.9	41.3	5 54.7	9.9	27 45.9	1.4	54.3
17		78 34.0	42.2	20 23.6	9.9	27 47.3	1.3	54.3
18		93 34.1	S 8 43.1	34 52.5	9.8	S27 48.6	1.1	54.3
19		108 34.3	44.0	49 21.3	9.9	27 49.7	0.9	54.3
20		123 34.4	44.9	63 50.2	9.9	27 50.6	0.9	54.3
21		138 34.6	. . 45.9	78 19.1	9.8	27 51.5	0.7	54.3
22		153 34.7	46.8	92 47.9	9.9	27 52.2	0.5	54.3
23		168 34.8	47.7	107 16.8	9.9	S27 52.7	0.4	54.3
		SD 16.1	*d* 0.9	SD 15.0		14.9		14.8

Lat.	Twilight Naut.	Twilight Civil	Sunrise	Moonrise 13	14	15	16
°	h m	h m	h m	h m	h m	h m	h m
N 72	04 51	06 09	07 19	▬	▬	▬	▬
N 70	04 55	06 06	07 08	▬	▬	▬	▬
68	04 58	06 03	07 00	▬	▬	▬	▬
66	05 01	06 00	06 53	13 22	▬	▬	▬
64	05 03	05 58	06 47	12 05	▬	▬	▬
62	05 05	05 56	06 41	11 29	13 18	15 08	15 55
60	05 06	05 55	06 37	11 04	12 36	13 56	14 48
N 58	05 08	05 53	06 33	10 43	12 08	13 21	14 13
56	05 08	05 52	06 29	10 27	11 46	12 55	13 48
54	05 09	05 50	06 26	10 13	11 29	12 35	13 28
52	05 10	05 49	06 23	10 00	11 13	12 18	13 11
50	05 10	05 48	06 20	09 50	11 00	12 04	12 56
45	05 11	05 45	06 14	09 27	10 34	11 34	12 27
N 40	05 11	05 42	06 09	09 09	10 12	11 11	12 04
35	05 10	05 40	06 05	08 54	09 55	10 52	11 44
30	05 09	05 37	06 01	08 41	09 40	10 36	11 28
20	05 07	05 32	05 54	08 19	09 14	10 09	11 00
N 10	05 03	05 27	05 48	08 00	08 52	09 45	10 37
0	04 58	05 22	05 43	07 42	08 32	09 23	10 15
S 10	04 51	05 16	05 37	07 24	08 12	09 01	09 52
20	04 42	05 08	05 31	07 06	07 50	08 38	09 29
30	04 30	04 59	05 23	06 44	07 25	08 11	09 01
35	04 23	04 53	05 19	06 32	07 10	07 55	08 45
40	04 13	04 46	05 14	06 17	06 53	07 36	08 26
45	04 02	04 38	05 08	06 00	06 33	07 14	08 03
S 50	03 47	04 28	05 01	05 39	06 08	06 45	07 33
52	03 40	04 23	04 58	05 29	05 55	06 31	07 19
54	03 32	04 18	04 55	05 18	05 41	06 15	07 02
56	03 22	04 12	04 51	05 06	05 25	05 56	06 41
58	03 11	04 05	04 47	04 51	05 06	05 32	06 16
S 60	02 59	03 57	04 42	04 34	04 42	05 01	05 41

Lat.	Sunset	Twilight Civil	Twilight Naut.	Moonset 13	14	15	16
°	h m	h m	h m	h m	h m	h m	h m
N 72	16 11	17 21	18 39	▬	▬	▬	▬
N 70	16 22	17 24	18 35	▬	▬	▬	▬
68	16 31	17 27	18 31	▬	▬	▬	▬
66	16 38	17 30	18 29	14 14	▬	▬	▬
64	16 44	17 32	18 27	15 31	▬	▬	▬
62	16 49	17 34	18 25	16 08	16 04	16 01	17 01
60	16 54	17 36	18 24	16 34	16 46	17 13	18 08
N 58	16 58	17 38	18 23	16 55	17 14	17 48	18 43
56	17 02	17 39	18 22	17 12	17 36	18 14	19 08
54	17 05	17 41	18 22	17 27	17 55	18 34	19 28
52	17 08	17 42	18 21	17 40	18 10	18 51	19 45
50	17 11	17 44	18 21	17 51	18 23	19 06	20 00
45	17 17	17 47	18 21	18 14	18 51	19 36	20 29
N 40	17 22	17 49	18 21	18 33	19 13	19 59	20 52
35	17 27	17 52	18 21	18 49	19 31	20 18	21 11
30	17 30	17 54	18 22	19 03	19 46	20 34	21 27
20	17 37	17 59	18 25	19 26	20 12	21 02	21 54
N 10	17 43	18 05	18 29	19 47	20 35	21 26	22 18
0	17 49	18 10	18 34	20 06	20 56	21 48	22 39
S 10	17 55	18 17	18 41	20 25	21 18	22 10	23 01
20	18 02	18 24	18 50	20 46	21 41	22 34	23 24
30	18 09	18 34	19 02	21 09	22 07	23 02	23 51
35	18 14	18 40	19 10	21 23	22 23	23 18	24 07
40	18 19	18 47	19 20	21 40	22 41	23 37	24 26
45	18 25	18 55	19 31	21 59	23 03	24 00	00 00
S 50	18 32	19 05	19 47	22 24	23 31	24 30	00 30
52	18 35	19 10	19 54	22 36	23 45	24 44	00 44
54	18 38	19 16	20 02	22 49	24 01	00 01	01 01
56	18 42	19 22	20 12	23 05	24 20	00 20	01 21
58	18 47	19 29	20 23	23 24	24 44	00 44	01 47
S 60	18 52	19 37	20 36	23 48	25 15	01 15	02 22

Day	SUN Eqn. of Time 00^h	SUN Eqn. of Time 12^h	SUN Mer. Pass.	MOON Mer. Pass. Upper	MOON Mer. Pass. Lower	MOON Age	%	Phase
d	m s	m s	h m	h m	h m	d	%	
13	13 38	13 45	11 46	13 54	01 29	03	8	
14	13 53	13 59	11 46	14 44	02 19	04	14	
15	14 06	14 13	11 46	15 35	03 10	05	22	

2026 OCTOBER 16, 17, 18 (FRI., SAT., SUN.)

UT d	h	ARIES GHA	VENUS −4·1 GHA	VENUS Dec	MARS +1·0 GHA	MARS Dec	JUPITER −1·9 GHA	JUPITER Dec	SATURN +0·3 GHA	SATURN Dec
		° ′	° ′	° ′	° ′	° ′	° ′	° ′	° ′	° ′
16	00	24 31.8	174 06.8	S20 18.5	251 31.8	N18 55.6	239 50.9	N14 44.8	13 53.9	N 1 37.6
	01	39 34.2	189 10.4	18.0	266 32.8	55.2	254 53.0	44.6	28 56.6	37.6
	02	54 36.7	204 14.0	17.5	281 33.9	54.9	269 55.1	44.5	43 59.2	37.5
	03	69 39.2	219 17.6	16.9	296 34.9	54.6	284 57.2	44.4	59 01.9	37.4
	04	84 41.6	234 21.2	16.3	311 36.0	54.2	299 59.2	44.3	74 04.5	37.4
	05	99 44.1	249 24.8	15.8	326 37.1	53.9	315 01.3	44.2	89 07.1	37.3
	06	114 46.5	264 28.4	S20 15.2	341 38.1	N18 53.6	330 03.4	N14 44.1	104 09.8	N 1 37.2
	07	129 49.0	279 32.0	14.7	356 39.2	53.3	345 05.5	43.9	119 12.4	37.1
	08	144 51.5	294 35.6	14.1	11 40.2	52.9	0 07.6	43.8	134 15.1	37.1
F	09	159 53.9	309 39.2	13.5	26 41.3	52.6	15 09.7	43.7	149 17.7	37.0
R	10	174 56.4	324 42.8	13.0	41 42.3	52.3	30 11.7	43.6	164 20.3	36.9
I	11	189 58.9	339 46.4	12.4	56 43.4	52.0	45 13.8	43.5	179 23.0	36.9
D	12	205 01.3	354 50.1	S20 11.8	71 44.5	N18 51.6	60 15.9	N14 43.3	194 25.6	N 1 36.8
A	13	220 03.8	9 53.7	11.2	86 45.5	51.3	75 18.0	43.2	209 28.3	36.7
Y	14	235 06.3	24 57.3	10.7	101 46.6	51.0	90 20.1	43.1	224 30.9	36.6
	15	250 08.7	40 00.9	10.1	116 47.6	50.6	105 22.2	43.0	239 33.5	36.6
	16	265 11.2	55 04.6	09.5	131 48.7	50.3	120 24.3	42.9	254 36.2	36.5
	17	280 13.7	70 08.2	08.9	146 49.8	50.0	135 26.3	42.8	269 38.8	36.4
	18	295 16.1	85 11.8	S20 08.3	161 50.8	N18 49.7	150 28.4	N14 42.6	284 41.4	N 1 36.4
	19	310 18.6	100 15.5	07.7	176 51.9	49.3	165 30.5	42.5	299 44.1	36.3
	20	325 21.0	115 19.1	07.1	191 52.9	49.0	180 32.6	42.4	314 46.7	36.2
	21	340 23.5	130 22.7	06.5	206 54.0	48.7	195 34.7	42.3	329 49.4	36.1
	22	355 26.0	145 26.4	05.9	221 55.1	48.3	210 36.8	42.2	344 52.0	36.1
	23	10 28.4	160 30.0	05.3	236 56.1	48.0	225 38.9	42.0	359 54.6	36.0
17	00	25 30.9	175 33.7	S20 04.7	251 57.2	N18 47.7	240 41.0	N14 41.9	14 57.3	N 1 35.9
	01	40 33.4	190 37.3	04.1	266 58.3	47.4	255 43.0	41.8	29 59.9	35.8
	02	55 35.8	205 41.0	03.5	281 59.3	47.0	270 45.1	41.7	45 02.6	35.8
	03	70 38.3	220 44.6	02.9	297 00.4	46.7	285 47.2	41.6	60 05.2	35.7
	04	85 40.8	235 48.3	02.3	312 01.5	46.4	300 49.3	41.5	75 07.8	35.6
	05	100 43.2	250 51.9	01.7	327 02.5	46.0	315 51.4	41.3	90 10.5	35.6
	06	115 45.7	265 55.6	S20 01.1	342 03.6	N18 45.7	330 53.5	N14 41.2	105 13.1	N 1 35.5
	07	130 48.1	280 59.3	20 00.5	357 04.6	45.4	345 55.6	41.1	120 15.7	35.4
S	08	145 50.6	296 02.9	19 59.8	12 05.7	45.0	0 57.7	41.0	135 18.4	35.4
A	09	160 53.1	311 06.6	59.2	27 06.8	44.7	15 59.8	40.9	150 21.0	35.3
T	10	175 55.5	326 10.3	58.6	42 07.8	44.4	31 01.8	40.8	165 23.7	35.2
U	11	190 58.0	341 13.9	57.9	57 08.9	44.1	46 03.9	40.6	180 26.3	35.1
R	12	206 00.5	356 17.6	S19 57.3	72 10.0	N18 43.7	61 06.0	N14 40.5	195 28.9	N 1 35.1
D	13	221 02.9	11 21.3	56.7	87 11.0	43.4	76 08.1	40.4	210 31.6	35.0
A	14	236 05.4	26 24.9	56.0	102 12.1	43.1	91 10.2	40.3	225 34.2	34.9
Y	15	251 07.9	41 28.6	55.4	117 13.2	42.7	106 12.3	40.2	240 36.8	34.9
	16	266 10.3	56 32.3	54.8	132 14.3	42.4	121 14.4	40.1	255 39.5	34.8
	17	281 12.8	71 36.0	54.1	147 15.3	42.1	136 16.5	39.9	270 42.1	34.7
	18	296 15.3	86 39.7	S19 53.5	162 16.4	N18 41.7	151 18.6	N14 39.8	285 44.8	N 1 34.6
	19	311 17.7	101 43.4	52.8	177 17.5	41.4	166 20.7	39.7	300 47.4	34.6
	20	326 20.2	116 47.0	52.2	192 18.5	41.1	181 22.8	39.6	315 50.0	34.5
	21	341 22.6	131 50.7	51.5	207 19.6	40.8	196 24.9	39.5	330 52.7	34.4
	22	356 25.1	146 54.4	50.9	222 20.7	40.4	211 26.9	39.4	345 55.3	34.4
	23	11 27.6	161 58.1	50.2	237 21.7	40.1	226 29.0	39.3	0 57.9	34.3
18	00	26 30.0	177 01.8	S19 49.5	252 22.8	N18 39.8	241 31.1	N14 39.1	16 00.6	N 1 34.2
	01	41 32.5	192 05.5	48.9	267 23.9	39.4	256 33.2	39.0	31 03.2	34.1
	02	56 35.0	207 09.2	48.2	282 25.0	39.1	271 35.3	38.9	46 05.9	34.1
	03	71 37.4	222 12.9	47.5	297 26.0	38.8	286 37.4	38.8	61 08.5	34.0
	04	86 39.9	237 16.6	46.9	312 27.1	38.4	301 39.5	38.7	76 11.1	33.9
	05	101 42.4	252 20.3	46.2	327 28.2	38.1	316 41.6	38.6	91 13.8	33.9
	06	116 44.8	267 24.0	S19 45.5	342 29.3	N18 37.8	331 43.7	N14 38.4	106 16.4	N 1 33.8
	07	131 47.3	282 27.7	44.9	357 30.3	37.4	346 45.8	38.3	121 19.0	33.7
	08	146 49.8	297 31.4	44.2	12 31.4	37.1	1 47.9	38.2	136 21.7	33.7
S	09	161 52.2	312 35.1	43.5	27 32.5	36.8	16 50.0	38.1	151 24.3	33.6
U	10	176 54.7	327 38.9	42.8	42 33.6	36.4	31 52.1	38.0	166 26.9	33.5
N	11	191 57.1	342 42.6	42.1	57 34.6	36.1	46 54.2	37.9	181 29.6	33.4
D	12	206 59.6	357 46.3	S19 41.4	72 35.7	N18 35.8	61 56.3	N14 37.8	196 32.2	N 1 33.4
A	13	222 02.1	12 50.0	40.7	87 36.8	35.5	76 58.4	37.6	211 34.9	33.3
Y	14	237 04.5	27 53.7	40.1	102 37.9	35.1	92 00.4	37.5	226 37.5	33.2
	15	252 07.0	42 57.4	39.4	117 38.9	34.8	107 02.5	37.4	241 40.1	33.2
	16	267 09.5	58 01.2	38.7	132 40.0	34.5	122 04.6	37.3	256 42.8	33.1
	17	282 11.9	73 04.9	38.0	147 41.1	34.1	137 06.7	37.2	271 45.4	33.0
	18	297 14.4	88 08.6	S19 37.3	162 42.2	N18 33.8	152 08.8	N14 37.1	286 48.0	N 1 32.9
	19	312 16.9	103 12.3	36.6	177 43.2	33.5	167 10.9	36.9	301 50.7	32.9
	20	327 19.3	118 16.1	35.8	192 44.3	33.1	182 13.0	36.8	316 53.3	32.8
	21	342 21.8	133 19.8	35.1	207 45.4	32.8	197 15.1	36.7	331 55.9	32.7
	22	357 24.3	148 23.5	34.4	222 46.5	32.5	212 17.2	36.6	346 58.6	32.7
	23	12 26.7	163 27.3	33.7	237 47.6	32.1	227 19.3	36.5	2 01.2	32.6
Mer. Pass.		h m 22 14.3	v 3.7	d 0.6	v 1.1	d 0.3	v 2.1	d 0.1	v 2.6	d 0.1

STARS

Name	SHA	Dec
	° ′	° ′
Acamar	315 10.3	S40 11.6
Achernar	335 18.5	S57 05.9
Acrux	172 59.1	S63 14.8
Adhara	255 04.7	S29 00.2
Aldebaran	290 37.7	N16 33.9
Alioth	166 12.3	N55 48.8
Alkaid	152 51.3	N49 10.8
Alnair	27 30.8	S46 49.9
Alnilam	275 36.1	S 1 10.9
Alphard	217 46.5	S 8 46.4
Alphecca	126 02.8	N26 37.6
Alpheratz	357 32.9	N29 14.5
Altair	61 58.5	N 8 56.5
Ankaa	353 05.3	S42 09.5
Antares	112 14.3	S26 29.5
Arcturus	145 46.9	N19 02.6
Atria	107 07.6	S69 04.7
Avior	234 14.3	S59 35.4
Bellatrix	278 21.1	N 6 22.5
Betelgeuse	270 50.4	N 7 24.8
Canopus	263 51.6	S52 42.2
Capella	280 19.5	N46 01.4
Deneb	49 24.7	N45 22.9
Denebola	182 23.8	N14 25.4
Diphda	348 45.5	S17 50.2
Dubhe	193 39.8	N61 36.2
Elnath	277 59.8	N28 37.8
Eltanin	90 41.7	N51 29.4
Enif	33 37.2	N10 00.1
Fomalhaut	15 12.6	S29 28.8
Gacrux	171 50.6	S57 15.7
Gienah	175 42.4	S17 41.3
Hadar	148 34.6	S60 30.1
Hamal	327 49.2	N23 35.5
Kaus Aust.	83 30.7	S34 22.3
Kochab	137 21.0	N74 02.7
Markab	13 28.2	N15 21.2
Menkar	314 04.3	N 4 11.8
Menkent	147 56.3	S36 30.1
Miaplacidus	221 38.3	S69 49.3
Mirfak	308 25.7	N49 57.4
Nunki	75 46.0	S26 15.8
Peacock	53 03.3	S56 39.1
Pollux	243 15.5	N27 57.6
Procyon	244 49.3	N 5 09.4
Rasalhague	95 57.4	N12 32.6
Regulus	207 33.1	N11 50.2
Rigel	281 02.3	S 8 10.1
Rigil Kent.	139 38.9	S60 56.8
Sabik	102 01.3	S15 45.4
Schedar	349 28.8	N56 41.3
Shaula	96 08.6	S37 07.4
Sirius	258 24.9	S16 45.0
Spica	158 21.1	S11 18.0
Suhail	222 45.4	S43 32.2
Vega	80 32.4	N38 48.8
Zuben'ubi	136 54.7	S16 09.1

	SHA	Mer. Pass.
	° ′	h m
Venus	150 02.8	12 15
Mars	226 26.3	7 12
Jupiter	215 10.1	7 56
Saturn	349 26.4	22 56

2026 OCTOBER 16, 17, 18 (FRI., SAT., SUN.)

UT		SUN GHA	SUN Dec	MOON GHA	v	MOON Dec	d	HP
d h		° ′	° ′	° ′	′	° ′	′	′
16 00	FRIDAY	183 35.0	S 8 48.6	121 45.7	9.9	S27 53.1	0.3	54.3
01		198 35.1	49.5	136 14.6	9.9	27 53.4	0.2	54.3
02		213 35.2	50.5	150 43.5	9.9	27 53.6	0.0	54.3
03		228 35.4	. . 51.4	165 12.4	9.9	27 53.6	0.1	54.2
04		243 35.5	52.3	179 41.3	9.9	27 53.5	0.3	54.2
05		258 35.6	53.2	194 10.2	10.0	27 53.2	0.4	54.2
06		273 35.8	S 8 54.1	208 39.2	9.9	S27 52.8	0.5	54.2
07		288 35.9	55.1	223 08.1	10.0	27 52.3	0.6	54.2
08		303 36.0	56.0	237 37.1	9.9	27 51.7	0.8	54.2
09		318 36.2	. . 56.9	252 06.0	10.0	27 50.9	1.0	54.2
10		333 36.3	57.8	266 35.0	10.1	27 49.9	1.0	54.2
11		348 36.4	58.7	281 04.1	10.0	27 48.9	1.2	54.2
12		3 36.6	S 8 59.7	295 33.1	10.0	S27 47.7	1.3	54.2
13		18 36.7	9 00.6	310 02.1	10.1	27 46.4	1.5	54.2
14		33 36.8	01.5	324 31.2	10.1	27 44.9	1.6	54.2
15		48 37.0	. . 02.4	339 00.3	10.1	27 43.3	1.7	54.2
16		63 37.1	03.3	353 29.4	10.1	27 41.6	1.9	54.2
17		78 37.2	04.2	7 58.5	10.2	27 39.7	2.0	54.2
18		93 37.4	S 9 05.2	22 27.7	10.2	S27 37.7	2.1	54.2
19		108 37.5	06.1	36 56.9	10.2	27 35.6	2.3	54.2
20		123 37.6	07.0	51 26.1	10.2	27 33.3	2.4	54.2
21		138 37.7	. . 07.9	65 55.3	10.3	27 30.9	2.5	54.2
22		153 37.9	08.8	80 24.6	10.3	27 28.4	2.7	54.2
23		168 38.0	09.7	94 53.9	10.3	27 25.7	2.8	54.2
17 00	SATURDAY	183 38.1	S 9 10.7	109 23.2	10.4	S27 22.9	2.9	54.2
01		198 38.3	11.6	123 52.6	10.3	27 20.0	3.0	54.2
02		213 38.4	12.5	138 21.9	10.5	27 17.0	3.2	54.2
03		228 38.5	. . 13.4	152 51.4	10.4	27 13.8	3.3	54.2
04		243 38.6	14.3	167 20.8	10.5	27 10.5	3.4	54.2
05		258 38.8	15.2	181 50.3	10.5	27 07.1	3.6	54.2
06		273 38.9	S 9 16.2	196 19.8	10.5	S27 03.5	3.7	54.2
07		288 39.0	17.1	210 49.3	10.6	26 59.8	3.8	54.2
08		303 39.2	18.0	225 18.9	10.6	26 56.0	3.9	54.2
09		318 39.3	. . 18.9	239 48.5	10.7	26 52.1	4.1	54.2
10		333 39.4	19.8	254 18.2	10.7	26 48.0	4.2	54.2
11		348 39.5	20.7	268 47.9	10.7	26 43.8	4.3	54.2
12		3 39.7	S 9 21.6	283 17.6	10.8	S26 39.5	4.5	54.2
13		18 39.8	22.5	297 47.4	10.8	26 35.0	4.6	54.2
14		33 39.9	23.5	312 17.2	10.8	26 30.4	4.7	54.2
15		48 40.0	. . 24.4	326 47.0	10.9	26 25.7	4.8	54.2
16		63 40.2	25.3	341 16.9	11.0	26 20.9	4.9	54.2
17		78 40.3	26.2	355 46.9	10.9	26 16.0	5.1	54.2
18		93 40.4	S 9 27.1	10 16.8	11.0	S26 10.9	5.2	54.2
19		108 40.5	28.0	24 46.8	11.1	26 05.7	5.3	54.2
20		123 40.7	28.9	39 16.9	11.1	26 00.4	5.4	54.3
21		138 40.8	. . 29.8	53 47.0	11.1	25 55.0	5.6	54.3
22		153 40.9	30.7	68 17.1	11.2	25 49.4	5.7	54.3
23		168 41.0	31.7	82 47.3	11.2	25 43.7	5.8	54.3
18 00	SUNDAY	183 41.2	S 9 32.6	97 17.5	11.3	S25 37.9	5.9	54.3
01		198 41.3	33.5	111 47.8	11.3	25 32.0	6.0	54.3
02		213 41.4	34.4	126 18.1	11.4	25 26.0	6.2	54.3
03		228 41.5	. . 35.3	140 48.5	11.4	25 19.8	6.2	54.3
04		243 41.7	36.2	155 18.9	11.4	25 13.6	6.4	54.3
05		258 41.8	37.1	169 49.3	11.5	25 07.2	6.5	54.3
06		273 41.9	S 9 38.0	184 19.8	11.6	S25 00.7	6.7	54.3
07		288 42.0	38.9	198 50.4	11.6	24 54.0	6.7	54.3
08		303 42.1	39.8	213 21.0	11.6	24 47.3	6.8	54.4
09		318 42.3	. . 40.7	227 51.6	11.7	24 40.5	7.0	54.4
10		333 42.4	41.6	242 22.3	11.7	24 33.5	7.1	54.4
11		348 42.5	42.6	256 53.0	11.8	24 26.4	7.2	54.4
12		3 42.6	S 9 43.5	271 23.8	11.9	S24 19.2	7.3	54.4
13		18 42.7	44.4	285 54.7	11.8	24 11.9	7.4	54.4
14		33 42.9	45.3	300 25.5	12.0	24 04.5	7.5	54.4
15		48 43.0	. . 46.2	314 56.5	11.9	23 57.0	7.7	54.4
16		63 43.1	47.1	329 27.4	12.1	23 49.3	7.7	54.4
17		78 43.2	48.0	343 58.5	12.0	23 41.6	7.9	54.5
18		93 43.3	S 9 48.9	358 29.5	12.1	S23 33.7	7.9	54.5
19		108 43.5	49.8	13 00.6	12.2	23 25.8	8.1	54.5
20		123 43.6	50.7	27 31.8	12.2	23 17.7	8.2	54.5
21		138 43.7	. . 51.6	42 03.0	12.3	23 09.5	8.3	54.5
22		153 43.8	52.5	56 34.3	12.3	23 01.2	8.3	54.5
23		168 43.9	53.4	71 05.6	12.3	S22 52.9	8.5	54.5
		SD 16.1	*d* 0.9	SD 14.8		14.8		14.8

Lat.	Twilight Naut.	Twilight Civil	Sunrise	Moonrise 16	Moonrise 17	Moonrise 18	Moonrise 19
°	h m	h m	h m	h m	h m	h m	h m
N 72	05 04	06 22	07 34	▬	▬	▬	▬
N 70	05 07	06 17	07 21	▬	▬	▬	18 30
68	05 09	06 13	07 11	▬	▬	▬	17 11
66	05 10	06 10	07 03	▬	▬	17 28	16 33
64	05 12	06 07	06 56	▬	▬	16 23	16 06
62	05 13	06 04	06 49	15 55	15 52	15 48	15 45
60	05 13	06 02	06 44	14 48	15 12	15 23	15 27
N 58	05 14	05 59	06 39	14 13	14 45	15 03	15 13
56	05 14	05 57	06 35	13 48	14 23	14 46	15 01
54	05 15	05 56	06 31	13 28	14 05	14 31	14 50
52	05 15	05 54	06 28	13 11	13 50	14 19	14 40
50	05 15	05 52	06 25	12 56	13 37	14 08	14 31
45	05 14	05 48	06 18	12 27	13 10	13 45	14 13
N 40	05 14	05 45	06 12	12 04	12 48	13 26	13 58
35	05 13	05 42	06 08	11 44	12 31	13 11	13 45
30	05 11	05 39	06 03	11 28	12 15	12 57	13 34
20	05 07	05 33	05 55	11 00	11 49	12 34	13 15
N 10	05 03	05 27	05 49	10 37	11 26	12 14	12 58
0	04 57	05 21	05 42	10 15	11 05	11 55	12 42
S 10	04 49	05 14	05 35	09 52	10 44	11 36	12 26
20	04 40	05 06	05 28	09 29	10 22	11 15	12 09
30	04 27	04 55	05 20	09 01	09 55	10 52	11 49
35	04 18	04 49	05 15	08 45	09 40	10 38	11 38
40	04 08	04 42	05 10	08 26	09 22	10 22	11 25
45	03 56	04 33	05 03	08 03	09 00	10 03	11 09
S 50	03 40	04 21	04 55	07 33	08 32	09 38	10 49
52	03 32	04 16	04 52	07 19	08 18	09 27	10 40
54	03 23	04 10	04 48	07 02	08 02	09 13	10 30
56	03 13	04 03	04 43	06 41	07 44	08 58	10 18
58	03 01	03 56	04 38	06 16	07 21	08 39	10 04
S 60	02 47	03 47	04 33	05 41	06 50	08 16	09 48

Lat.	Sunset	Twilight Civil	Twilight Naut.	Moonset 16	Moonset 17	Moonset 18	Moonset 19
°	h m	h m	h m	h m	h m	h m	h m
N 72	15 55	17 06	18 24	▬	▬	▬	▬
N 70	16 08	17 12	18 22	▬	▬	▬	19 33
68	16 18	17 16	18 20	▬	▬	▬	20 52
66	16 27	17 19	18 18	▬	▬	18 56	21 29
64	16 34	17 23	18 17	▬	▬	20 00	21 55
62	16 40	17 25	18 17	17 01	18 49	20 34	22 15
60	16 45	17 28	18 16	18 08	19 29	20 59	22 31
N 58	16 50	17 30	18 15	18 43	19 56	21 19	22 45
56	16 54	17 32	18 15	19 08	20 17	21 35	22 57
54	16 58	17 34	18 15	19 28	20 35	21 49	23 07
52	17 02	17 36	18 15	19 45	20 50	22 01	23 16
50	17 05	17 38	18 15	20 00	21 03	22 12	23 24
45	17 12	17 42	18 16	20 29	21 29	22 34	23 41
N 40	17 18	17 45	18 16	20 52	21 50	22 52	23 55
35	17 23	17 48	18 18	21 11	22 07	23 07	24 07
30	17 27	17 51	18 19	21 27	22 22	23 19	24 17
20	17 35	17 57	18 23	21 54	22 48	23 41	24 35
N 10	17 42	18 03	18 28	22 18	23 09	24 00	00 00
0	17 49	18 10	18 34	22 39	23 29	24 18	00 18
S 10	17 55	18 17	18 42	23 01	23 49	24 35	00 35
20	18 03	18 25	18 52	23 24	24 11	00 11	00 54
30	18 11	18 36	19 05	23 51	24 36	00 36	01 15
35	18 16	18 42	19 13	24 07	00 07	00 50	01 27
40	18 22	18 50	19 23	24 26	00 26	01 07	01 42
45	18 29	18 59	19 36	00 00	00 48	01 27	01 58
S 50	18 37	19 11	19 52	00 30	01 16	01 52	02 19
52	18 40	19 16	20 00	00 44	01 30	02 04	02 29
54	18 44	19 22	20 10	01 01	01 46	02 18	02 40
56	18 49	19 29	20 20	01 21	02 05	02 34	02 52
58	18 54	19 37	20 32	01 47	02 28	02 52	03 06
S 60	19 00	19 46	20 47	02 22	02 59	03 16	03 23

Day	SUN Eqn. of Time 00^h	SUN Eqn. of Time 12^h	SUN Mer. Pass.	MOON Mer. Pass. Upper	MOON Mer. Pass. Lower	MOON Age	MOON Phase
d	m s	m s	h m	h m	h m	d %	
16	14 20	14 26	11 46	16 27	04 01	06 30	◐
17	14 32	14 38	11 45	17 17	04 52	07 39	
18	14 44	14 50	11 45	18 06	05 42	08 48	

2026 OCTOBER 19, 20, 21 (MON., TUES., WED.)

UT		ARIES	VENUS −4·2		MARS +1·0		JUPITER −1·9		SATURN +0·4	
		GHA	GHA	Dec	GHA	Dec	GHA	Dec	GHA	Dec
d h		° ′	° ′	° ′	° ′	° ′	° ′	° ′	° ′	° ′
19 00	MONDAY	27 29.2	178 31.0	S19 33.0	252 48.6	N18 31.8	242 21.4	N14 36.4	17 03.9	N 1 32.5
01		42 31.6	193 34.7	32.3	267 49.7	31.5	257 23.5	36.3	32 06.5	32.5
02		57 34.1	208 38.5	31.6	282 50.8	31.1	272 25.6	36.1	47 09.1	32.4
03		72 36.6	223 42.2	. . 30.8	297 51.9	. . 30.8	287 27.7	. . 36.0	62 11.8	. . 32.3
04		87 39.0	238 45.9	30.1	312 53.0	30.5	302 29.8	35.9	77 14.4	32.2
05		102 41.5	253 49.7	29.4	327 54.1	30.1	317 31.9	35.8	92 17.0	32.2
06		117 44.0	268 53.4	S19 28.7	342 55.1	N18 29.8	332 34.0	N14 35.7	107 19.7	N 1 32.1
07		132 46.4	283 57.2	27.9	357 56.2	29.5	347 36.1	35.6	122 22.3	32.0
08		147 48.9	299 00.9	27.2	12 57.3	29.1	2 38.2	35.5	137 24.9	32.0
09		162 51.4	314 04.7	. . 26.5	27 58.4	. . 28.8	17 40.3	. . 35.3	152 27.6	. . 31.9
10		177 53.8	329 08.4	25.7	42 59.5	28.5	32 42.4	35.2	167 30.2	31.8
11		192 56.3	344 12.2	25.0	58 00.6	28.1	47 44.5	35.1	182 32.8	31.8
12		207 58.7	359 15.9	S19 24.2	73 01.6	N18 27.8	62 46.6	N14 35.0	197 35.5	N 1 31.7
13		223 01.2	14 19.7	23.5	88 02.7	27.5	77 48.7	34.9	212 38.1	31.6
14		238 03.7	29 23.4	22.7	103 03.8	27.1	92 50.8	34.8	227 40.8	31.6
15		253 06.1	44 27.2	. . 22.0	118 04.9	. . 26.8	107 52.9	. . 34.7	242 43.4	. . 31.5
16		268 08.6	59 30.9	21.3	133 06.0	26.5	122 55.0	34.6	257 46.0	31.4
17		283 11.1	74 34.7	20.5	148 07.1	26.1	137 57.1	34.4	272 48.7	31.3
18		298 13.5	89 38.4	S19 19.7	163 08.2	N18 25.8	152 59.2	N14 34.3	287 51.3	N 1 31.3
19		313 16.0	104 42.2	19.0	178 09.2	25.5	168 01.3	34.2	302 53.9	31.2
20		328 18.5	119 46.0	18.2	193 10.3	25.1	183 03.4	34.1	317 56.6	31.1
21		343 20.9	134 49.7	. . 17.5	208 11.4	. . 24.8	198 05.5	. . 34.0	332 59.2	. . 31.1
22		358 23.4	149 53.5	16.7	223 12.5	24.5	213 07.6	33.9	348 01.8	31.0
23		13 25.9	164 57.3	15.9	238 13.6	24.1	228 09.7	33.8	3 04.5	30.9
20 00	TUESDAY	28 28.3	180 01.0	S19 15.2	253 14.7	N18 23.8	243 11.8	N14 33.6	18 07.1	N 1 30.9
01		43 30.8	195 04.8	14.4	268 15.8	23.5	258 13.9	33.5	33 09.7	30.8
02		58 33.2	210 08.6	13.6	283 16.9	23.1	273 16.0	33.4	48 12.4	30.7
03		73 35.7	225 12.3	. . 12.9	298 18.0	. . 22.8	288 18.1	. . 33.3	63 15.0	. . 30.7
04		88 38.2	240 16.1	12.1	313 19.0	22.5	303 20.2	33.2	78 17.6	30.6
05		103 40.6	255 19.9	11.3	328 20.1	22.1	318 22.3	33.1	93 20.3	30.5
06		118 43.1	270 23.6	S19 10.5	343 21.2	N18 21.8	333 24.4	N14 33.0	108 22.9	N 1 30.4
07		133 45.6	285 27.4	09.7	358 22.3	21.5	348 26.5	32.9	123 25.5	30.4
08		148 48.0	300 31.2	09.0	13 23.4	21.1	3 28.6	32.7	138 28.2	30.3
09		163 50.5	315 35.0	. . 08.2	28 24.5	. . 20.8	18 30.7	. . 32.6	153 30.8	. . 30.2
10		178 53.0	330 38.7	07.4	43 25.6	20.5	33 32.8	32.5	168 33.4	30.2
11		193 55.4	345 42.5	06.6	58 26.7	20.1	48 35.0	32.4	183 36.1	30.1
12		208 57.9	0 46.3	S19 05.8	73 27.8	N18 19.8	63 37.1	N14 32.3	198 38.7	N 1 30.0
13		224 00.4	15 50.1	05.0	88 28.9	19.5	78 39.2	32.2	213 41.3	30.0
14		239 02.8	30 53.8	04.2	103 30.0	19.1	93 41.3	32.1	228 44.0	29.9
15		254 05.3	45 57.6	. . 03.4	118 31.1	. . 18.8	108 43.4	. . 32.0	243 46.6	. . 29.8
16		269 07.7	61 01.4	02.6	133 32.2	18.5	123 45.5	31.9	258 49.2	29.8
17		284 10.2	76 05.2	01.8	148 33.3	18.1	138 47.6	31.7	273 51.9	29.7
18		299 12.7	91 09.0	S19 01.0	163 34.3	N18 17.8	153 49.7	N14 31.6	288 54.5	N 1 29.6
19		314 15.1	106 12.7	19 00.2	178 35.4	17.4	168 51.8	31.5	303 57.1	29.6
20		329 17.6	121 16.5	18 59.4	193 36.5	17.1	183 53.9	31.4	318 59.8	29.5
21		344 20.1	136 20.3	. . 58.6	208 37.6	. . 16.8	198 56.0	. . 31.3	334 02.4	. . 29.4
22		359 22.5	151 24.1	57.8	223 38.7	16.4	213 58.1	31.2	349 05.0	29.4
23		14 25.0	166 27.9	56.9	238 39.8	16.1	229 00.2	31.1	4 07.7	29.3
21 00	WEDNESDAY	29 27.5	181 31.7	S18 56.1	253 40.9	N18 15.8	244 02.3	N14 31.0	19 10.3	N 1 29.2
01		44 29.9	196 35.5	55.3	268 42.0	15.4	259 04.4	30.8	34 12.9	29.1
02		59 32.4	211 39.3	54.5	283 43.1	15.1	274 06.5	30.7	49 15.6	29.1
03		74 34.8	226 43.0	. . 53.7	298 44.2	. . 14.8	289 08.7	. . 30.6	64 18.2	. . 29.0
04		89 37.3	241 46.8	52.8	313 45.3	14.4	304 10.8	30.5	79 20.8	28.9
05		104 39.8	256 50.6	52.0	328 46.4	14.1	319 12.9	30.4	94 23.5	28.9
06		119 42.2	271 54.4	S18 51.2	343 47.5	N18 13.8	334 15.0	N14 30.3	109 26.1	N 1 28.8
07		134 44.7	286 58.2	50.4	358 48.6	13.4	349 17.1	30.2	124 28.7	28.7
08		149 47.2	302 02.0	49.5	13 49.7	13.1	4 19.2	30.1	139 31.4	28.7
09		164 49.6	317 05.8	. . 48.7	28 50.8	. . 12.8	19 21.3	. . 30.0	154 34.0	. . 28.6
10		179 52.1	332 09.6	47.9	43 51.9	12.4	34 23.4	29.8	169 36.6	28.5
11		194 54.6	347 13.4	47.0	58 53.0	12.1	49 25.5	29.7	184 39.3	28.5
12		209 57.0	2 17.2	S18 46.2	73 54.1	N18 11.7	64 27.6	N14 29.6	199 41.9	N 1 28.4
13		224 59.5	17 21.0	45.3	88 55.2	11.4	79 29.7	29.5	214 44.5	28.3
14		240 02.0	32 24.8	44.5	103 56.3	11.1	94 31.9	29.4	229 47.2	28.3
15		255 04.4	47 28.5	. . 43.7	118 57.4	. . 10.7	109 34.0	. . 29.3	244 49.8	. . 28.2
16		270 06.9	62 32.3	42.8	133 58.5	10.4	124 36.1	29.2	259 52.4	28.1
17		285 09.3	77 36.1	42.0	148 59.6	10.1	139 38.2	29.1	274 55.1	28.1
18		300 11.8	92 39.9	S18 41.1	164 00.8	N18 09.7	154 40.3	N14 29.0	289 57.7	N 1 28.0
19		315 14.3	107 43.7	40.3	179 01.9	09.4	169 42.4	28.9	305 00.3	27.9
20		330 16.7	122 47.5	39.4	194 03.0	09.1	184 44.5	28.7	320 02.9	27.9
21		345 19.2	137 51.3	. . 38.5	209 04.1	. . 08.7	199 46.6	. . 28.6	335 05.6	. . 27.8
22		0 21.7	152 55.1	37.7	224 05.2	08.4	214 48.7	28.5	350 08.2	27.7
23		15 24.1	167 58.9	36.8	239 06.3	08.0	229 50.9	28.4	5 10.8	27.7
Mer. Pass.		h m 22 02.5	*v* 3.8	*d* 0.8	*v* 1.1	*d* 0.3	*v* 2.1	*d* 0.1	*v* 2.6	*d* 0.1

STARS

Name	SHA	Dec
	° ′	° ′
Acamar	315 10.3	S40 11.6
Achernar	335 18.5	S57 05.9
Acrux	172 59.1	S63 14.8
Adhara	255 04.6	S29 00.2
Aldebaran	290 37.7	N16 33.9
Alioth	166 12.2	N55 48.8
Alkaid	152 51.3	N49 10.8
Alnair	27 30.8	S46 49.9
Alnilam	275 36.1	S 1 11.0
Alphard	217 46.5	S 8 46.4
Alphecca	126 02.8	N26 37.6
Alpheratz	357 32.9	N29 14.5
Altair	61 58.6	N 8 56.5
Ankaa	353 05.3	S42 09.6
Antares	112 14.3	S26 29.5
Arcturus	145 46.9	N19 02.6
Atria	107 07.6	S69 04.7
Avior	234 14.2	S59 35.4
Bellatrix	278 21.1	N 6 22.5
Betelgeuse	270 50.3	N 7 24.8
Canopus	263 51.5	S52 42.2
Capella	280 19.4	N46 01.4
Deneb	49 24.7	N45 22.9
Denebola	182 23.7	N14 25.4
Diphda	348 45.5	S17 50.2
Dubhe	193 39.7	N61 36.2
Elnath	277 59.8	N28 37.8
Eltanin	90 41.8	N51 29.4
Enif	33 37.2	N10 00.1
Fomalhaut	15 12.7	S29 28.8
Gacrux	171 50.6	S57 15.7
Gienah	175 42.4	S17 41.3
Hadar	148 34.6	S60 30.1
Hamal	327 49.2	N23 35.5
Kaus Aust.	83 30.7	S34 22.3
Kochab	137 21.0	N74 02.7
Markab	13 28.2	N15 21.2
Menkar	314 04.3	N 4 11.8
Menkent	147 56.3	S36 30.1
Miaplacidus	221 38.3	S69 49.3
Mirfak	308 25.7	N49 57.4
Nunki	75 46.1	S26 15.8
Peacock	53 03.4	S56 39.1
Pollux	243 15.5	N27 57.6
Procyon	244 49.3	N 5 09.4
Rasalhague	95 57.4	N12 32.6
Regulus	207 33.1	N11 50.2
Rigel	281 02.3	S 8 10.1
Rigil Kent.	139 38.9	S60 56.7
Sabik	102 01.3	S15 45.4
Schedar	349 28.8	N56 41.3
Shaula	96 08.6	S37 07.4
Sirius	258 24.8	S16 45.0
Spica	158 21.1	S11 18.0
Suhail	222 45.4	S43 32.2
Vega	80 32.4	N38 48.8
Zuben'ubi	136 54.7	S16 09.1

	SHA	Mer. Pass.
	° ′	h m
Venus	151 32.7	11 57
Mars	224 46.4	7 07
Jupiter	214 43.5	7 46
Saturn	349 38.8	22 44

Day	UT	SUN GHA	SUN Dec	MOON GHA	v	MOON Dec	d	HP
	d h	° ′	° ′	° ′	′	° ′	′	′
MONDAY	19 00	183 44.0	S 9 54.3	85 36.9	12.4	S22 44.4	8.6	54.5
	01	198 44.2	55.2	100 08.3	12.5	22 35.8	8.8	54.6
	02	213 44.3	56.1	114 39.8	12.5	22 27.0	8.8	54.6
	03	228 44.4	. . 57.0	129 11.3	12.5	22 18.2	8.9	54.6
	04	243 44.5	57.9	143 42.8	12.6	22 09.3	9.0	54.6
	05	258 44.6	58.8	158 14.4	12.7	22 00.3	9.1	54.6
	06	273 44.7	S 9 59.7	172 46.1	12.6	S21 51.2	9.2	54.6
	07	288 44.9	10 00.6	187 17.7	12.8	21 42.0	9.4	54.7
	08	303 45.0	01.5	201 49.5	12.8	21 32.6	9.4	54.7
	09	318 45.1	. . 02.4	216 21.3	12.8	21 23.2	9.5	54.7
	10	333 45.2	03.3	230 53.1	12.9	21 13.7	9.6	54.7
	11	348 45.3	04.2	245 25.0	12.9	21 04.1	9.7	54.7
	12	3 45.4	S10 05.1	259 56.9	12.9	S20 54.4	9.8	54.7
	13	18 45.5	06.1	274 28.8	13.0	20 44.6	9.9	54.8
	14	33 45.7	07.0	289 00.8	13.1	20 34.7	10.0	54.8
	15	48 45.8	. . 07.9	303 32.9	13.1	20 24.7	10.1	54.8
	16	63 45.9	08.8	318 05.0	13.1	20 14.6	10.2	54.8
	17	78 46.0	09.6	332 37.1	13.2	20 04.4	10.3	54.8
	18	93 46.1	S10 10.5	347 09.3	13.2	S19 54.1	10.4	54.9
	19	108 46.2	11.4	1 41.5	13.3	19 43.7	10.5	54.9
	20	123 46.3	12.3	16 13.8	13.3	19 33.2	10.5	54.9
	21	138 46.4	. . 13.2	30 46.1	13.3	19 22.7	10.7	54.9
	22	153 46.5	14.1	45 18.4	13.4	19 12.0	10.7	54.9
	23	168 46.7	15.0	59 50.8	13.5	19 01.3	10.9	55.0
TUESDAY	20 00	183 46.8	S10 15.9	74 23.3	13.4	S18 50.4	10.9	55.0
	01	198 46.9	16.8	88 55.7	13.5	18 39.5	11.0	55.0
	02	213 47.0	17.7	103 28.2	13.6	18 28.5	11.1	55.0
	03	228 47.1	. . 18.6	118 00.8	13.6	18 17.4	11.2	55.1
	04	243 47.2	19.5	132 33.4	13.6	18 06.2	11.3	55.1
	05	258 47.3	20.4	147 06.0	13.7	17 54.9	11.3	55.1
	06	273 47.4	S10 21.3	161 38.7	13.7	S17 43.6	11.5	55.1
	07	288 47.5	22.2	176 11.4	13.7	17 32.1	11.5	55.1
	08	303 47.6	23.1	190 44.1	13.8	17 20.6	11.6	55.2
	09	318 47.8	. . 24.0	205 16.9	13.8	17 09.0	11.7	55.2
	10	333 47.9	24.9	219 49.7	13.8	16 57.3	11.8	55.2
	11	348 48.0	25.8	234 22.5	13.9	16 45.5	11.8	55.2
	12	3 48.1	S10 26.7	248 55.4	13.9	S16 33.7	12.0	55.3
	13	18 48.2	27.6	263 28.3	13.9	16 21.7	12.0	55.3
	14	33 48.3	28.5	278 01.2	14.0	16 09.7	12.1	55.3
	15	48 48.4	. . 29.4	292 34.2	14.0	15 57.6	12.2	55.3
	16	63 48.5	30.3	307 07.2	14.0	15 45.4	12.2	55.4
	17	78 48.6	31.2	321 40.2	14.1	15 33.2	12.3	55.4
	18	93 48.7	S10 32.0	336 13.3	14.0	S15 20.9	12.4	55.4
	19	108 48.8	32.9	350 46.3	14.2	15 08.5	12.5	55.4
	20	123 48.9	33.8	5 19.5	14.1	14 56.0	12.6	55.5
	21	138 49.0	. . 34.7	19 52.6	14.2	14 43.4	12.6	55.5
	22	153 49.1	35.6	34 25.8	14.2	14 30.8	12.7	55.5
	23	168 49.2	36.5	48 59.0	14.2	14 18.1	12.8	55.6
WEDNESDAY	21 00	183 49.3	S10 37.4	63 32.2	14.2	S14 05.3	12.8	55.6
	01	198 49.4	38.3	78 05.4	14.3	13 52.5	13.0	55.6
	02	213 49.6	39.2	92 38.7	14.3	13 39.5	13.0	55.6
	03	228 49.7	. . 40.1	107 12.0	14.3	13 26.5	13.0	55.7
	04	243 49.8	41.0	121 45.3	14.3	13 13.5	13.2	55.7
	05	258 49.9	41.9	136 18.6	14.3	13 00.3	13.2	55.7
	06	273 50.0	S10 42.7	150 51.9	14.4	S12 47.1	13.2	55.7
	07	288 50.1	43.6	165 25.3	14.4	12 33.9	13.4	55.8
	08	303 50.2	44.5	179 58.7	14.4	12 20.5	13.4	55.8
	09	318 50.3	. . 45.4	194 32.1	14.4	12 07.1	13.4	55.8
	10	333 50.4	46.3	209 05.5	14.4	11 53.7	13.6	55.9
	11	348 50.5	47.2	223 38.9	14.5	11 40.1	13.5	55.9
	12	3 50.6	S10 48.1	238 12.4	14.4	S11 26.6	13.7	55.9
	13	18 50.7	49.0	252 45.8	14.5	11 12.9	13.7	56.0
	14	33 50.8	49.8	267 19.3	14.5	10 59.2	13.8	56.0
	15	48 50.9	. . 50.7	281 52.8	14.5	10 45.4	13.8	56.0
	16	63 51.0	51.6	296 26.3	14.5	10 31.6	13.9	56.0
	17	78 51.1	52.5	310 59.8	14.5	10 17.7	14.0	56.1
	18	93 51.2	S10 53.4	325 33.3	14.5	S10 03.7	14.0	56.1
	19	108 51.3	54.3	340 06.8	14.5	9 49.7	14.1	56.1
	20	123 51.4	55.2	354 40.3	14.6	9 35.6	14.1	56.2
	21	138 51.5	. . 56.0	9 13.9	14.5	9 21.5	14.2	56.2
	22	153 51.6	56.9	23 47.4	14.5	9 07.3	14.3	56.2
	23	168 51.7	57.8	38 20.9	14.6	S 8 53.0	14.3	56.3
		SD 16.1	*d* 0.9	SD	14.9	15.1		15.2

Lat.	Twilight Naut.	Twilight Civil	Sunrise	Moonrise 19	Moonrise 20	Moonrise 21	Moonrise 22
°	h m	h m	h m	h m	h m	h m	h m
N 72	05 17	06 35	07 49	■■■■	17 30	16 35	15 57
N 70	05 18	06 29	07 34	18 30	16 55	16 18	15 51
68	05 19	06 24	07 23	17 11	16 30	16 05	15 45
66	05 20	06 19	07 13	16 33	16 10	15 54	15 41
64	05 20	06 15	07 05	16 06	15 54	15 45	15 37
62	05 20	06 12	06 58	15 45	15 41	15 37	15 34
60	05 20	06 09	06 52	15 27	15 30	15 30	15 31
N 58	05 20	06 06	06 46	15 13	15 20	15 24	15 28
56	05 20	06 03	06 42	15 01	15 11	15 19	15 26
54	05 20	06 01	06 37	14 50	15 03	15 14	15 23
52	05 20	05 59	06 33	14 40	14 56	15 10	15 21
50	05 19	05 57	06 30	14 31	14 50	15 06	15 20
45	05 18	05 52	06 22	14 13	14 36	14 57	15 16
N 40	05 17	05 48	06 16	13 58	14 25	14 50	15 12
35	05 15	05 44	06 10	13 45	14 16	14 43	15 10
30	05 13	05 41	06 05	13 34	14 07	14 38	15 07
20	05 08	05 34	05 56	13 15	13 52	14 28	15 03
N 10	05 03	05 27	05 49	12 58	13 40	14 20	14 59
0	04 56	05 20	05 41	12 42	13 27	14 12	14 55
S 10	04 48	05 13	05 34	12 26	13 15	14 03	14 52
20	04 37	05 03	05 26	12 09	13 02	13 55	14 48
30	04 23	04 52	05 17	11 49	12 47	13 45	14 43
35	04 14	04 45	05 11	11 38	12 38	13 39	14 41
40	04 03	04 37	05 05	11 25	12 28	13 33	14 38
45	03 50	04 27	04 58	11 09	12 16	13 25	14 34
S 50	03 33	04 15	04 49	10 49	12 02	13 16	14 30
52	03 24	04 09	04 45	10 40	11 55	13 11	14 28
54	03 15	04 03	04 41	10 30	11 48	13 07	14 26
56	03 03	03 55	04 36	10 18	11 39	13 01	14 24
58	02 50	03 47	04 30	10 04	11 30	12 56	14 22
S 60	02 35	03 37	04 24	09 48	11 19	12 49	14 19

Lat.	Sunset	Twilight Civil	Twilight Naut.	Moonset 19	Moonset 20	Moonset 21	Moonset 22
°	h m	h m	h m	h m	h m	h m	h m
N 72	15 39	16 52	18 10	■■■■	22 10	24 38	00 38
N 70	15 54	16 59	18 09	19 33	22 43	24 52	00 52
68	16 06	17 04	18 09	20 52	23 07	25 03	01 03
66	16 15	17 09	18 08	21 29	23 25	25 12	01 12
64	16 24	17 13	18 08	21 55	23 39	25 20	01 20
62	16 31	17 17	18 08	22 15	23 52	25 26	01 26
60	16 37	17 20	18 08	22 31	24 02	00 02	01 32
N 58	16 42	17 23	18 08	22 45	24 11	00 11	01 37
56	16 47	17 25	18 08	22 57	24 19	00 19	01 41
54	16 51	17 28	18 09	23 07	24 26	00 26	01 45
52	16 55	17 30	18 09	23 16	24 32	00 32	01 48
50	16 59	17 32	18 09	23 24	24 37	00 37	01 51
45	17 07	17 37	18 11	23 41	24 49	00 49	01 58
N 40	17 13	17 41	18 12	23 55	24 59	00 59	02 04
35	17 19	17 45	18 14	24 07	00 07	01 08	02 09
30	17 24	17 48	18 16	24 17	00 17	01 15	02 13
20	17 33	17 55	18 21	24 35	00 35	01 28	02 20
N 10	17 41	18 02	18 27	00 00	00 50	01 38	02 26
0	17 48	18 09	18 34	00 18	01 04	01 49	02 32
S 10	17 56	18 17	18 42	00 35	01 18	01 59	02 38
20	18 04	18 26	18 53	00 54	01 33	02 09	02 44
30	18 13	18 38	19 07	01 15	01 50	02 22	02 51
35	18 19	18 45	19 16	01 27	02 00	02 29	02 55
40	18 25	18 53	19 27	01 42	02 11	02 36	03 00
45	18 33	19 03	19 41	01 58	02 24	02 46	03 05
S 50	18 41	19 16	19 59	02 19	02 40	02 57	03 11
52	18 46	19 22	20 07	02 29	02 47	03 02	03 14
54	18 50	19 28	20 17	02 40	02 55	03 07	03 17
56	18 55	19 36	20 28	02 52	03 04	03 13	03 21
58	19 01	19 44	20 42	03 06	03 15	03 20	03 24
S 60	19 07	19 54	20 58	03 23	03 27	03 28	03 28

Day	SUN Eqn. of Time 00^h	SUN Eqn. of Time 12^h	SUN Mer. Pass.	MOON Mer. Pass. Upper	MOON Mer. Pass. Lower	Age	Phase
d	m s	m s	h m	h m	h m	d %	
19	14 56	15 01	11 45	18 53	06 30	09 58	
20	15 07	15 12	11 45	19 38	07 16	10 67	
21	15 17	15 22	11 45	20 22	08 00	11 76	

2026 OCTOBER 22, 23, 24 (THURS., FRI., SAT.)

UT	ARIES	VENUS −4·2		MARS +0·9		JUPITER −2·0		SATURN +0·4	
d h	GHA	GHA	Dec	GHA	Dec	GHA	Dec	GHA	Dec
	° ′	° ′	° ′	° ′	° ′	° ′	° ′	° ′	° ′
22 00	30 26.6	183 02.7	S18 36.0	254 07.4	N18 07.7	244 53.0	N14 28.3	20 13.5	N 1 27.6
01	45 29.1	198 06.5	35.1	269 08.5	07.4	259 55.1	28.2	35 16.1	27.5
02	60 31.5	213 10.3	34.2	284 09.6	07.0	274 57.2	28.1	50 18.7	27.5
03	75 34.0	228 14.1	. . 33.4	299 10.7	. . 06.7	289 59.3	. . 28.0	65 21.4	. . 27.4
04	90 36.5	243 17.9	32.5	314 11.8	06.4	305 01.4	27.9	80 24.0	27.3
05	105 38.9	258 21.7	31.6	329 12.9	06.0	320 03.5	27.8	95 26.6	27.3
06	120 41.4	273 25.5	S18 30.8	344 14.0	N18 05.7	335 05.6	N14 27.6	110 29.3	N 1 27.2
07	135 43.8	288 29.3	29.9	359 15.1	05.3	350 07.8	27.5	125 31.9	27.1
T 08	150 46.3	303 33.1	29.0	14 16.3	05.0	5 09.9	27.4	140 34.5	27.1
H 09	165 48.8	318 36.9	. . 28.1	29 17.4	. . 04.7	20 12.0	. . 27.3	155 37.2	. . 27.0
U 10	180 51.2	333 40.7	27.3	44 18.5	04.3	35 14.1	27.2	170 39.8	26.9
R 11	195 53.7	348 44.5	26.4	59 19.6	04.0	50 16.2	27.1	185 42.4	26.8
S 12	210 56.2	3 48.3	S18 25.5	74 20.7	N18 03.7	65 18.3	N14 27.0	200 45.0	N 1 26.8
D 13	225 58.6	18 52.1	24.6	89 21.8	03.3	80 20.4	26.9	215 47.7	26.7
A 14	241 01.1	33 55.9	23.7	104 22.9	03.0	95 22.6	26.8	230 50.3	26.6
Y 15	256 03.6	48 59.7	. . 22.8	119 24.0	. . 02.7	110 24.7	. . 26.7	245 52.9	. . 26.6
16	271 06.0	64 03.5	22.0	134 25.1	02.3	125 26.8	26.6	260 55.6	26.5
17	286 08.5	79 07.3	21.1	149 26.3	02.0	140 28.9	26.4	275 58.2	26.4
18	301 10.9	94 11.1	S18 20.2	164 27.4	N18 01.6	155 31.0	N14 26.3	291 00.8	N 1 26.4
19	316 13.4	109 14.9	19.3	179 28.5	01.3	170 33.1	26.2	306 03.5	26.3
20	331 15.9	124 18.7	18.4	194 29.6	01.0	185 35.3	26.1	321 06.1	26.2
21	346 18.3	139 22.5	. . 17.5	209 30.7	. . 00.6	200 37.4	. . 26.0	336 08.7	. . 26.2
22	1 20.8	154 26.3	16.6	224 31.8	18 00.3	215 39.5	25.9	351 11.3	26.1
23	16 23.3	169 30.1	15.7	239 32.9	17 59.9	230 41.6	25.8	6 14.0	26.0
23 00	31 25.7	184 33.9	S18 14.8	254 34.1	N17 59.6	245 43.7	N14 25.7	21 16.6	N 1 26.0
01	46 28.2	199 37.7	13.9	269 35.2	59.3	260 45.8	25.6	36 19.2	25.9
02	61 30.7	214 41.5	13.0	284 36.3	58.9	275 48.0	25.5	51 21.9	25.9
03	76 33.1	229 45.3	. . 12.1	299 37.4	. . 58.6	290 50.1	. . 25.4	66 24.5	. . 25.8
04	91 35.6	244 49.1	11.2	314 38.5	58.3	305 52.2	25.2	81 27.1	25.7
05	106 38.1	259 52.9	10.3	329 39.6	57.9	320 54.3	25.1	96 29.8	25.7
06	121 40.5	274 56.7	S18 09.4	344 40.8	N17 57.6	335 56.4	N14 25.0	111 32.4	N 1 25.6
07	136 43.0	290 00.5	08.4	359 41.9	57.2	350 58.6	24.9	126 35.0	25.5
08	151 45.4	305 04.3	07.5	14 43.0	56.9	6 00.7	24.8	141 37.6	25.5
F 09	166 47.9	320 08.1	. . 06.6	29 44.1	. . 56.6	21 02.8	. . 24.7	156 40.3	. . 25.4
R 10	181 50.4	335 11.9	05.7	44 45.2	56.2	36 04.9	24.6	171 42.9	25.3
I 11	196 52.8	350 15.7	04.8	59 46.3	55.9	51 07.0	24.5	186 45.5	25.3
D 12	211 55.3	5 19.5	S18 03.9	74 47.5	N17 55.6	66 09.2	N14 24.4	201 48.2	N 1 25.2
A 13	226 57.8	20 23.3	02.9	89 48.6	55.2	81 11.3	24.3	216 50.8	25.1
Y 14	242 00.2	35 27.1	02.0	104 49.7	54.9	96 13.4	24.2	231 53.4	25.1
15	257 02.7	50 30.9	. . 01.1	119 50.8	. . 54.5	111 15.5	. . 24.1	246 56.0	. . 25.0
16	272 05.2	65 34.7	18 00.2	134 51.9	54.2	126 17.6	24.0	261 58.7	24.9
17	287 07.6	80 38.5	17 59.2	149 53.1	53.9	141 19.8	23.8	277 01.3	24.9
18	302 10.1	95 42.3	S17 58.3	164 54.2	N17 53.5	156 21.9	N14 23.7	292 03.9	N 1 24.8
19	317 12.5	110 46.1	57.4	179 55.3	53.2	171 24.0	23.6	307 06.6	24.7
20	332 15.0	125 49.9	56.5	194 56.4	52.8	186 26.1	23.5	322 09.2	24.7
21	347 17.5	140 53.7	. . 55.5	209 57.6	. . 52.5	201 28.2	. . 23.4	337 11.8	. . 24.6
22	2 19.9	155 57.5	54.6	224 58.7	52.2	216 30.4	23.3	352 14.4	24.5
23	17 22.4	171 01.3	53.7	239 59.8	51.8	231 32.5	23.2	7 17.1	24.5
24 00	32 24.9	186 05.1	S17 52.7	255 00.9	N17 51.5	246 34.6	N14 23.1	22 19.7	N 1 24.4
01	47 27.3	201 08.9	51.8	270 02.1	51.2	261 36.7	23.0	37 22.3	24.3
02	62 29.8	216 12.7	50.9	285 03.2	50.8	276 38.9	22.9	52 24.9	24.3
03	77 32.3	231 16.5	. . 49.9	300 04.3	. . 50.5	291 41.0	. . 22.8	67 27.6	. . 24.2
04	92 34.7	246 20.3	49.0	315 05.4	50.1	306 43.1	22.7	82 30.2	24.1
05	107 37.2	261 24.1	48.0	330 06.6	49.8	321 45.2	22.6	97 32.8	24.1
06	122 39.7	276 27.8	S17 47.1	345 07.7	N17 49.5	336 47.3	N14 22.5	112 35.5	N 1 24.0
07	137 42.1	291 31.6	46.1	0 08.8	49.1	351 49.5	22.4	127 38.1	23.9
S 08	152 44.6	306 35.4	45.2	15 09.9	48.8	6 51.6	22.2	142 40.7	23.9
A 09	167 47.0	321 39.2	. . 44.3	30 11.1	. . 48.4	21 53.7	. . 22.1	157 43.3	. . 23.8
T 10	182 49.5	336 43.0	43.3	45 12.2	48.1	36 55.8	22.0	172 46.0	23.7
U 11	197 52.0	351 46.8	42.4	60 13.3	47.8	51 58.0	21.9	187 48.6	23.7
R 12	212 54.4	6 50.6	S17 41.4	75 14.5	N17 47.4	67 00.1	N14 21.8	202 51.2	N 1 23.6
D 13	227 56.9	21 54.4	40.5	90 15.6	47.1	82 02.2	21.7	217 53.8	23.6
A 14	242 59.4	36 58.1	39.5	105 16.7	46.7	97 04.3	21.6	232 56.5	23.5
Y 15	258 01.8	52 01.9	. . 38.5	120 17.8	. . 46.4	112 06.5	. . 21.5	247 59.1	. . 23.4
16	273 04.3	67 05.7	37.6	135 19.0	46.1	127 08.6	21.4	263 01.7	23.4
17	288 06.8	82 09.5	36.6	150 20.1	45.7	142 10.7	21.3	278 04.4	23.3
18	303 09.2	97 13.3	S17 35.7	165 21.2	N17 45.4	157 12.9	N14 21.2	293 07.0	N 1 23.2
19	318 11.7	112 17.1	34.7	180 22.4	45.0	172 15.0	21.1	308 09.6	23.2
20	333 14.1	127 20.8	33.8	195 23.5	44.7	187 17.1	21.0	323 12.2	23.1
21	348 16.6	142 24.6	. . 32.8	210 24.6	. . 44.4	202 19.2	. . 20.9	338 14.9	. . 23.0
22	3 19.1	157 28.4	31.8	225 25.8	44.0	217 21.4	20.8	353 17.5	23.0
23	18 21.5	172 32.2	30.9	240 26.9	43.7	232 23.5	20.7	8 20.1	22.9
Mer. Pass.	h m 21 50.7	v 3.8	d 0.9	v 1.1	d 0.3	v 2.1	d 0.1	v 2.6	d 0.1

STARS

Name	SHA	Dec
	° ′	° ′
Acamar	315 10.3	S40 11.6
Achernar	335 18.5	S57 06.0
Acrux	172 59.1	S63 14.7
Adhara	255 04.6	S29 00.2
Aldebaran	290 37.7	N16 33.9
Alioth	166 12.2	N55 48.8
Alkaid	152 51.3	N49 10.8
Alnair	27 30.9	S46 49.9
Alnilam	275 36.0	S 1 11.0
Alphard	217 46.4	S 8 46.4
Alphecca	126 02.8	N26 37.6
Alpheratz	357 32.9	N29 14.5
Altair	61 58.6	N 8 56.5
Ankaa	353 05.3	S42 09.6
Antares	112 14.3	S26 29.5
Arcturus	145 46.9	N19 02.6
Atria	107 07.6	S69 04.7
Avior	234 14.2	S59 35.4
Bellatrix	278 21.1	N 6 22.5
Betelgeuse	270 50.3	N 7 24.8
Canopus	263 51.5	S52 42.2
Capella	280 19.4	N46 01.4
Deneb	49 24.7	N45 22.9
Denebola	182 23.7	N14 25.3
Diphda	348 45.5	S17 50.2
Dubhe	193 39.7	N61 36.2
Elnath	277 59.8	N28 37.8
Eltanin	90 41.8	N51 29.4
Enif	33 37.2	N10 00.1
Fomalhaut	15 12.7	S29 28.8
Gacrux	171 50.6	S57 15.7
Gienah	175 42.4	S17 41.3
Hadar	148 34.6	S60 30.1
Hamal	327 49.2	N23 35.5
Kaus Aust.	83 30.8	S34 22.3
Kochab	137 21.0	N74 02.7
Markab	13 28.2	N15 21.2
Menkar	314 04.3	N 4 11.8
Menkent	147 56.3	S36 30.1
Miaplacidus	221 38.2	S69 49.3
Mirfak	308 25.7	N49 57.4
Nunki	75 46.1	S26 15.8
Peacock	53 03.4	S56 39.1
Pollux	243 15.5	N27 57.6
Procyon	244 49.3	N 5 09.4
Rasalhague	95 57.4	N12 32.6
Regulus	207 33.1	N11 50.2
Rigel	281 02.2	S 8 10.1
Rigil Kent.	139 38.9	S60 56.7
Sabik	102 01.3	S15 45.4
Schedar	349 28.8	N56 41.3
Shaula	96 08.6	S37 07.4
Sirius	258 24.8	S16 45.0
Spica	158 21.1	S11 18.0
Suhail	222 45.4	S43 32.2
Vega	80 32.4	N38 48.8
Zuben'ubi	136 54.7	S16 09.1

	SHA	Mer. Pass.
	° ′	h m
Venus	153 08.2	11 39
Mars	223 08.3	7 01
Jupiter	214 18.0	7 36
Saturn	349 50.9	22 31

UT		SUN GHA	SUN Dec	MOON GHA	v	MOON Dec	d	HP
d	h	° ′	° ′	° ′	′	° ′	′	′
22	00	183 51.8	S10 58.7	52 54.5	14.5	S 8 38.7	14.3	56.3
	01	198 51.9	10 59.6	67 28.0	14.6	8 24.4	14.4	56.3
	02	213 51.9	11 00.5	82 01.6	14.5	8 10.0	14.5	56.4
	03	228 52.0	. . 01.4	96 35.1	14.6	7 55.5	14.5	56.4
	04	243 52.1	02.2	111 08.7	14.5	7 41.0	14.5	56.4
	05	258 52.2	03.1	125 42.2	14.5	7 26.5	14.6	56.5
	06	273 52.3	S11 04.0	140 15.7	14.6	S 7 11.9	14.7	56.5
T	07	288 52.4	04.9	154 49.3	14.5	6 57.2	14.7	56.5
H	08	303 52.5	05.8	169 22.8	14.5	6 42.5	14.7	56.6
U	09	318 52.6	. . 06.6	183 56.3	14.5	6 27.8	14.8	56.6
R	10	333 52.7	07.5	198 29.8	14.5	6 13.0	14.9	56.6
S	11	348 52.8	08.4	213 03.3	14.5	5 58.1	14.8	56.7
D	12	3 52.9	S11 09.3	227 36.8	14.5	S 5 43.3	15.0	56.7
A	13	18 53.0	10.2	242 10.3	14.4	5 28.3	14.9	56.7
Y	14	33 53.1	11.1	256 43.7	14.5	5 13.4	15.0	56.8
	15	48 53.2	. . 11.9	271 17.2	14.4	4 58.4	15.1	56.8
	16	63 53.3	12.8	285 50.6	14.4	4 43.3	15.1	56.8
	17	78 53.4	13.7	300 24.0	14.4	4 28.2	15.1	56.9
	18	93 53.5	S11 14.6	314 57.4	14.4	S 4 13.1	15.1	56.9
	19	108 53.6	15.5	329 30.8	14.4	3 58.0	15.2	56.9
	20	123 53.6	16.3	344 04.2	14.3	3 42.8	15.3	57.0
	21	138 53.7	. . 17.2	358 37.5	14.4	3 27.5	15.2	57.0
	22	153 53.8	18.1	13 10.9	14.3	3 12.3	15.3	57.0
	23	168 53.9	19.0	27 44.2	14.2	2 57.0	15.4	57.1
23	00	183 54.0	S11 19.8	42 17.4	14.3	S 2 41.6	15.3	57.1
	01	198 54.1	20.7	56 50.7	14.2	2 26.3	15.4	57.1
	02	213 54.2	21.6	71 23.9	14.2	2 10.9	15.4	57.2
	03	228 54.3	. . 22.5	85 57.1	14.2	1 55.5	15.5	57.2
	04	243 54.4	23.3	100 30.3	14.1	1 40.0	15.4	57.2
	05	258 54.5	24.2	115 03.4	14.1	1 24.6	15.5	57.3
	06	273 54.5	S11 25.1	129 36.5	14.1	S 1 09.1	15.6	57.3
	07	288 54.6	26.0	144 09.6	14.1	0 53.5	15.5	57.3
	08	303 54.7	26.8	158 42.7	14.0	0 38.0	15.6	57.4
F	09	318 54.8	. . 27.7	173 15.7	13.9	0 22.4	15.6	57.4
R	10	333 54.9	28.6	187 48.6	14.0	S 0 06.8	15.6	57.4
I	11	348 55.0	29.5	202 21.6	13.9	N 0 08.8	15.6	57.5
D	12	3 55.1	S11 30.3	216 54.5	13.8	N 0 24.4	15.6	57.5
A	13	18 55.2	31.2	231 27.3	13.8	0 40.0	15.7	57.5
Y	14	33 55.2	32.1	246 00.1	13.8	0 55.7	15.7	57.6
	15	48 55.3	. . 33.0	260 32.9	13.7	1 11.4	15.7	57.6
	16	63 55.4	33.8	275 05.6	13.7	1 27.1	15.7	57.6
	17	78 55.5	34.7	289 38.3	13.7	1 42.8	15.7	57.7
	18	93 55.6	S11 35.6	304 11.0	13.6	N 1 58.5	15.7	57.7
	19	108 55.7	36.5	318 43.6	13.5	2 14.2	15.8	57.7
	20	123 55.8	37.3	333 16.1	13.5	2 30.0	15.7	57.8
	21	138 55.8	. . 38.2	347 48.6	13.5	2 45.7	15.8	57.8
	22	153 55.9	39.1	2 21.1	13.4	3 01.5	15.7	57.8
	23	168 56.0	39.9	16 53.5	13.3	3 17.2	15.8	57.9
24	00	183 56.1	S11 40.8	31 25.8	13.3	N 3 33.0	15.7	57.9
	01	198 56.2	41.7	45 58.1	13.2	3 48.7	15.8	57.9
	02	213 56.3	42.5	60 30.3	13.2	4 04.5	15.8	58.0
	03	228 56.3	. . 43.4	75 02.5	13.1	4 20.3	15.7	58.0
	04	243 56.4	44.3	89 34.6	13.1	4 36.0	15.8	58.0
	05	258 56.5	45.2	104 06.7	13.0	4 51.8	15.7	58.1
	06	273 56.6	S11 46.0	118 38.7	12.9	N 5 07.5	15.8	58.1
S	07	288 56.7	46.9	133 10.6	12.9	5 23.3	15.7	58.1
A	08	303 56.7	47.8	147 42.5	12.8	5 39.0	15.8	58.2
T	09	318 56.8	. . 48.6	162 14.3	12.7	5 54.8	15.7	58.2
U	10	333 56.9	49.5	176 46.0	12.7	6 10.5	15.7	58.2
R	11	348 57.0	50.4	191 17.7	12.6	6 26.2	15.7	58.3
D	12	3 57.1	S11 51.2	205 49.3	12.5	N 6 41.9	15.7	58.3
A	13	18 57.1	52.1	220 20.8	12.5	6 57.6	15.7	58.3
Y	14	33 57.2	53.0	234 52.3	12.4	7 13.3	15.6	58.4
	15	48 57.3	. . 53.8	249 23.7	12.3	7 28.9	15.7	58.4
	16	63 57.4	54.7	263 55.0	12.3	7 44.6	15.6	58.4
	17	78 57.5	55.6	278 26.3	12.1	8 00.2	15.6	58.5
	18	93 57.5	S11 56.4	292 57.4	12.1	N 8 15.8	15.5	58.5
	19	108 57.6	57.3	307 28.5	12.1	8 31.3	15.6	58.5
	20	123 57.7	58.1	321 59.6	11.9	8 46.9	15.5	58.6
	21	138 57.8	. . 59.0	336 30.5	11.9	9 02.4	15.5	58.6
	22	153 57.8	11 59.9	351 01.4	11.7	9 17.9	15.4	58.6
	23	168 57.9	S12 00.7	5 32.1	11.7	N 9 33.3	15.5	58.7
		SD 16.1	*d* 0.9	SD 15.4		15.7		15.9

Lat.	Twilight Naut.	Twilight Civil	Sunrise	Moonrise 22	Moonrise 23	Moonrise 24	Moonrise 25
°	h m	h m	h m	h m	h m	h m	h m
N 72	05 29	06 49	08 05	15 57	15 24	14 49	14 03
N 70	05 29	06 41	07 48	15 51	15 26	15 00	14 27
68	05 29	06 34	07 34	15 45	15 27	15 08	14 45
66	05 29	06 29	07 23	15 41	15 28	15 15	15 00
64	05 28	06 24	07 14	15 37	15 29	15 21	15 13
62	05 28	06 20	07 06	15 34	15 30	15 26	15 23
60	05 27	06 16	06 59	15 31	15 31	15 31	15 32
N 58	05 27	06 12	06 53	15 28	15 31	15 35	15 40
56	05 26	06 09	06 48	15 26	15 32	15 39	15 47
54	05 25	06 07	06 43	15 23	15 32	15 42	15 54
52	05 25	06 04	06 39	15 21	15 33	15 45	15 59
50	05 24	06 02	06 35	15 20	15 33	15 48	16 05
45	05 22	05 56	06 26	15 16	15 34	15 54	16 16
N 40	05 20	05 51	06 19	15 12	15 35	15 59	16 26
35	05 17	05 47	06 13	15 10	15 36	16 03	16 34
30	05 15	05 43	06 07	15 07	15 36	16 07	16 41
20	05 09	05 35	05 58	15 03	15 38	16 14	16 53
N 10	05 03	05 28	05 49	14 59	15 39	16 20	17 05
0	04 55	05 20	05 41	14 55	15 40	16 26	17 15
S 10	04 46	05 11	05 33	14 52	15 41	16 32	17 26
20	04 35	05 01	05 24	14 48	15 42	16 38	17 37
30	04 20	04 49	05 14	14 43	15 43	16 45	17 50
35	04 10	04 41	05 08	14 41	15 44	16 49	17 58
40	03 58	04 33	05 01	14 38	15 44	16 54	18 07
45	03 44	04 22	04 53	14 34	15 45	16 59	18 17
S 50	03 25	04 09	04 43	14 30	15 47	17 06	18 30
52	03 16	04 02	04 39	14 28	15 47	17 09	18 35
54	03 06	03 55	04 34	14 26	15 48	17 13	18 42
56	02 54	03 47	04 28	14 24	15 49	17 16	18 49
58	02 40	03 38	04 22	14 22	15 49	17 21	18 57
S 60	02 22	03 28	04 15	14 19	15 50	17 25	19 07

Lat.	Sunset	Twilight Civil	Twilight Naut.	Moonset 22	Moonset 23	Moonset 24	Moonset 25
°	h m	h m	h m	h m	h m	h m	h m
N 72	15 22	16 38	17 57	00 38	02 50	05 03	07 31
N 70	15 39	16 46	17 57	00 52	02 53	04 56	07 10
68	15 53	16 53	17 58	01 03	02 55	04 50	06 53
66	16 04	16 59	17 58	01 12	02 57	04 45	06 40
64	16 14	17 04	17 59	01 20	02 59	04 41	06 29
62	16 22	17 08	17 59	01 26	03 01	04 38	06 20
60	16 28	17 12	18 00	01 32	03 02	04 35	06 13
N 58	16 35	17 15	18 01	01 37	03 03	04 32	06 06
56	16 40	17 18	18 02	01 41	03 04	04 30	06 00
54	16 45	17 21	18 02	01 45	03 05	04 28	05 54
52	16 49	17 24	18 03	01 48	03 06	04 26	05 50
50	16 53	17 26	18 04	01 51	03 07	04 24	05 45
45	17 02	17 32	18 06	01 58	03 08	04 20	05 36
N 40	17 09	17 37	18 08	02 04	03 09	04 17	05 28
35	17 15	17 41	18 11	02 09	03 11	04 15	05 21
30	17 21	17 45	18 13	02 13	03 12	04 12	05 16
20	17 31	17 53	18 19	02 20	03 13	04 08	05 06
N 10	17 39	18 01	18 26	02 26	03 15	04 05	04 57
0	17 48	18 09	18 33	02 32	03 16	04 01	04 49
S 10	17 56	18 18	18 43	02 38	03 17	03 58	04 41
20	18 05	18 28	18 54	02 44	03 19	03 54	04 32
30	18 15	18 40	19 10	02 51	03 20	03 50	04 22
35	18 22	18 48	19 19	02 55	03 21	03 48	04 16
40	18 28	18 57	19 31	03 00	03 22	03 45	04 10
45	18 37	19 08	19 46	03 05	03 23	03 42	04 03
S 50	18 46	19 21	20 05	03 11	03 25	03 39	03 54
52	18 51	19 28	20 14	03 14	03 25	03 37	03 50
54	18 56	19 35	20 25	03 17	03 26	03 35	03 45
56	19 02	19 43	20 37	03 21	03 27	03 33	03 40
58	19 08	19 52	20 52	03 24	03 28	03 31	03 35
S 60	19 15	20 03	21 10	03 28	03 28	03 29	03 29

Day	SUN Eqn. of Time 00^h	SUN Eqn. of Time 12^h	SUN Mer. Pass.	MOON Mer. Pass. Upper	MOON Mer. Pass. Lower	MOON Age	MOON Phase
d	m s	m s	h m	h m	h m	d %	
22	15 27	15 31	11 44	21 06	08 44	12 84	
23	15 36	15 40	11 44	21 50	09 28	13 91	
24	15 44	15 48	11 44	22 37	10 13	14 96	

	UT (d h)	ARIES GHA	VENUS −4·2 GHA	VENUS Dec	MARS +0·9 GHA	MARS Dec	JUPITER −2·0 GHA	JUPITER Dec	SATURN +0·4 GHA	SATURN Dec
		° ′	° ′	° ′	° ′	° ′	° ′	° ′	° ′	° ′
	25 00	33 24.0	187 36.0	S17 29.9	255 28.0	N17 43.3	247 25.6	N14 20.6	23 22.7	N 1 22.8
	01	48 26.5	202 39.7	28.9	270 29.2	43.0	262 27.7	20.4	38 25.4	22.8
	02	63 28.9	217 43.5	28.0	285 30.3	42.7	277 29.9	20.3	53 28.0	22.7
	03	78 31.4	232 47.3	. . 27.0	300 31.4	. . 42.3	292 32.0	. . 20.2	68 30.6	. . 22.7
	04	93 33.9	247 51.1	26.0	315 32.6	42.0	307 34.1	20.1	83 33.2	22.6
	05	108 36.3	262 54.8	25.1	330 33.7	41.6	322 36.3	20.0	98 35.9	22.5
	06	123 38.8	277 58.6	S17 24.1	345 34.8	N17 41.3	337 38.4	N14 19.9	113 38.5	N 1 22.5
	07	138 41.3	293 02.4	23.1	0 36.0	41.0	352 40.5	19.8	128 41.1	22.4
	08	153 43.7	308 06.2	22.1	15 37.1	40.6	7 42.6	19.7	143 43.7	22.3
S	09	168 46.2	323 09.9	. . 21.2	30 38.2	. . 40.3	22 44.8	. . 19.6	158 46.4	. . 22.3
U	10	183 48.6	338 13.7	20.2	45 39.4	39.9	37 46.9	19.5	173 49.0	22.2
N	11	198 51.1	353 17.5	19.2	60 40.5	39.6	52 49.0	19.4	188 51.6	22.1
D	12	213 53.6	8 21.2	S17 18.2	75 41.7	N17 39.3	67 51.2	N14 19.3	203 54.2	N 1 22.1
A	13	228 56.0	23 25.0	17.3	90 42.8	38.9	82 53.3	19.2	218 56.9	22.0
Y	14	243 58.5	38 28.8	16.3	105 43.9	38.6	97 55.4	19.1	233 59.5	21.9
	15	259 01.0	53 32.5	. . 15.3	120 45.1	. . 38.2	112 57.6	. . 19.0	249 02.1	. . 21.9
	16	274 03.4	68 36.3	14.3	135 46.2	37.9	127 59.7	18.9	264 04.7	21.8
	17	289 05.9	83 40.0	13.3	150 47.3	37.6	143 01.8	18.8	279 07.4	21.8
	18	304 08.4	98 43.8	S17 12.4	165 48.5	N17 37.2	158 03.9	N14 18.7	294 10.0	N 1 21.7
	19	319 10.8	113 47.6	11.4	180 49.6	36.9	173 06.1	18.6	309 12.6	21.6
	20	334 13.3	128 51.3	10.4	195 50.8	36.5	188 08.2	18.5	324 15.2	21.6
	21	349 15.8	143 55.1	. . 09.4	210 51.9	. . 36.2	203 10.3	. . 18.4	339 17.9	. . 21.5
	22	4 18.2	158 58.8	08.4	225 53.1	35.9	218 12.5	18.3	354 20.5	21.4
	23	19 20.7	174 02.6	07.4	240 54.2	35.5	233 14.6	18.2	9 23.1	21.4
	26 00	34 23.1	189 06.3	S17 06.4	255 55.3	N17 35.2	248 16.7	N14 18.0	24 25.7	N 1 21.3
	01	49 25.6	204 10.1	05.5	270 56.5	34.8	263 18.9	17.9	39 28.4	21.2
	02	64 28.1	219 13.8	04.5	285 57.6	34.5	278 21.0	17.8	54 31.0	21.2
	03	79 30.5	234 17.6	. . 03.5	300 58.8	. . 34.2	293 23.1	. . 17.7	69 33.6	. . 21.1
	04	94 33.0	249 21.3	02.5	315 59.9	33.8	308 25.3	17.6	84 36.2	21.1
	05	109 35.5	264 25.1	01.5	331 01.1	33.5	323 27.4	17.5	99 38.9	21.0
	06	124 37.9	279 28.8	S17 00.5	346 02.2	N17 33.1	338 29.5	N14 17.4	114 41.5	N 1 20.9
	07	139 40.4	294 32.6	16 59.5	1 03.3	32.8	353 31.7	17.3	129 44.1	20.9
	08	154 42.9	309 36.3	58.5	16 04.5	32.5	8 33.8	17.2	144 46.7	20.8
M	09	169 45.3	324 40.1	. . 57.5	31 05.6	. . 32.1	23 35.9	. . 17.1	159 49.4	. . 20.7
O	10	184 47.8	339 43.8	56.5	46 06.8	31.8	38 38.1	17.0	174 52.0	20.7
N	11	199 50.2	354 47.5	55.5	61 07.9	31.4	53 40.2	16.9	189 54.6	20.6
D	12	214 52.7	9 51.3	S16 54.5	76 09.1	N17 31.1	68 42.4	N14 16.8	204 57.2	N 1 20.6
A	13	229 55.2	24 55.0	53.5	91 10.2	30.7	83 44.5	16.7	219 59.9	20.5
Y	14	244 57.6	39 58.7	52.5	106 11.4	30.4	98 46.6	16.6	235 02.5	20.4
	15	260 00.1	55 02.5	. . 51.5	121 12.5	. . 30.1	113 48.8	. . 16.5	250 05.1	. . 20.4
	16	275 02.6	70 06.2	50.5	136 13.7	29.7	128 50.9	16.4	265 07.7	20.3
	17	290 05.0	85 09.9	49.5	151 14.8	29.4	143 53.0	16.3	280 10.3	20.2
	18	305 07.5	100 13.7	S16 48.5	166 16.0	N17 29.0	158 55.2	N14 16.2	295 13.0	N 1 20.2
	19	320 10.0	115 17.4	47.5	181 17.1	28.7	173 57.3	16.1	310 15.6	20.1
	20	335 12.4	130 21.1	46.5	196 18.3	28.4	188 59.4	16.0	325 18.2	20.1
	21	350 14.9	145 24.8	. . 45.5	211 19.4	. . 28.0	204 01.6	. . 15.9	340 20.8	. . 20.0
	22	5 17.4	160 28.6	44.5	226 20.6	27.7	219 03.7	15.8	355 23.5	19.9
	23	20 19.8	175 32.3	43.5	241 21.7	27.3	234 05.9	15.7	10 26.1	19.9
	27 00	35 22.3	190 36.0	S16 42.5	256 22.9	N17 27.0	249 08.0	N14 15.6	25 28.7	N 1 19.8
	01	50 24.7	205 39.7	41.5	271 24.0	26.7	264 10.1	15.5	40 31.3	19.7
	02	65 27.2	220 43.4	40.4	286 25.2	26.3	279 12.3	15.4	55 33.9	19.7
	03	80 29.7	235 47.1	. . 39.4	301 26.3	. . 26.0	294 14.4	. . 15.3	70 36.6	. . 19.6
	04	95 32.1	250 50.9	38.4	316 27.5	25.6	309 16.6	15.2	85 39.2	19.6
	05	110 34.6	265 54.6	37.4	331 28.6	25.3	324 18.7	15.1	100 41.8	19.5
	06	125 37.1	280 58.3	S16 36.4	346 29.8	N17 24.9	339 20.8	N14 15.0	115 44.4	N 1 19.4
	07	140 39.5	296 02.0	35.4	1 30.9	24.6	354 23.0	14.9	130 47.1	19.4
T	08	155 42.0	311 05.7	34.4	16 32.1	24.3	9 25.1	14.8	145 49.7	19.3
U	09	170 44.5	326 09.4	. . 33.4	31 33.2	. . 23.9	24 27.3	. . 14.7	160 52.3	. . 19.2
E	10	185 46.9	341 13.1	32.4	46 34.4	23.6	39 29.4	14.6	175 54.9	19.2
S	11	200 49.4	356 16.8	31.3	61 35.5	23.2	54 31.5	14.5	190 57.5	19.1
D	12	215 51.9	11 20.5	S16 30.3	76 36.7	N17 22.9	69 33.7	N14 14.4	206 00.2	N 1 19.1
A	13	230 54.3	26 24.2	29.3	91 37.9	22.6	84 35.8	14.3	221 02.8	19.0
Y	14	245 56.8	41 27.9	28.3	106 39.0	22.2	99 38.0	14.2	236 05.4	18.9
	15	260 59.2	56 31.6	. . 27.3	121 40.2	. . 21.9	114 40.1	. . 14.1	251 08.0	. . 18.9
	16	276 01.7	71 35.3	26.3	136 41.3	21.5	129 42.2	14.0	266 10.6	18.8
	17	291 04.2	86 39.0	25.2	151 42.5	21.2	144 44.4	13.9	281 13.3	18.8
	18	306 06.6	101 42.6	S16 24.2	166 43.6	N17 20.8	159 46.5	N14 13.8	296 15.9	N 1 18.7
	19	321 09.1	116 46.3	23.2	181 44.8	20.5	174 48.7	13.7	311 18.5	18.6
	20	336 11.6	131 50.0	22.2	196 46.0	20.2	189 50.8	13.6	326 21.1	18.6
	21	351 14.0	146 53.7	. . 21.2	211 47.1	. . 19.8	204 53.0	. . 13.5	341 23.7	. . 18.5
	22	6 16.5	161 57.4	20.1	226 48.3	19.5	219 55.1	13.4	356 26.4	18.4
	23	21 19.0	177 01.1	19.1	241 49.4	19.1	234 57.2	13.3	11 29.0	18.4
	Mer. Pass.	h m 21 38.9	v 3.7	d 1.0	v 1.1	d 0.3	v 2.1	d 0.1	v 2.6	d 0.1

STARS

Name	SHA	Dec
	° ′	° ′
Acamar	315 10.2	S40 11.7
Achernar	335 18.5	S57 06.0
Acrux	172 59.0	S63 14.7
Adhara	255 04.6	S29 00.3
Aldebaran	290 37.7	N16 33.9
Alioth	166 12.2	N55 48.8
Alkaid	152 51.3	N49 10.7
Alnair	27 30.9	S46 49.9
Alnilam	275 36.0	S 1 11.0
Alphard	217 46.4	S 8 46.4
Alphecca	126 02.8	N26 37.6
Alpheratz	357 32.9	N29 14.5
Altair	61 58.6	N 8 56.5
Ankaa	353 05.3	S42 09.6
Antares	112 14.3	S26 29.5
Arcturus	145 46.9	N19 02.6
Atria	107 07.7	S69 04.6
Avior	234 14.2	S59 35.4
Bellatrix	278 21.1	N 6 22.5
Betelgeuse	270 50.3	N 7 24.8
Canopus	263 51.5	S52 42.3
Capella	280 19.4	N46 01.4
Deneb	49 24.8	N45 22.9
Denebola	182 23.7	N14 25.3
Diphda	348 45.5	S17 50.3
Dubhe	193 39.7	N61 36.2
Elnath	277 59.8	N28 37.8
Eltanin	90 41.8	N51 29.3
Enif	33 37.2	N10 00.1
Fomalhaut	15 12.7	S29 28.8
Gacrux	171 50.5	S57 15.7
Gienah	175 42.4	S17 41.3
Hadar	148 34.6	S60 30.1
Hamal	327 49.2	N23 35.5
Kaus Aust.	83 30.8	S34 22.3
Kochab	137 21.0	N74 02.7
Markab	13 28.2	N15 21.2
Menkar	314 04.3	N 4 11.8
Menkent	147 56.3	S36 30.0
Miaplacidus	221 38.2	S69 49.3
Mirfak	308 25.7	N49 57.4
Nunki	75 46.1	S26 15.8
Peacock	53 03.4	S56 39.1
Pollux	243 15.5	N27 57.6
Procyon	244 49.2	N 5 09.4
Rasalhague	95 57.4	N12 32.6
Regulus	207 33.0	N11 50.2
Rigel	281 02.2	S 8 10.1
Rigil Kent.	139 38.9	S60 56.7
Sabik	102 01.4	S15 45.4
Schedar	349 28.8	N56 41.3
Shaula	96 08.7	S37 07.4
Sirius	258 24.8	S16 45.0
Spica	158 21.1	S11 18.0
Suhail	222 45.3	S43 32.2
Vega	80 32.4	N38 48.8
Zuben'ubi	136 54.7	S16 09.1

	SHA	Mer. Pass.
	° ′	h m
Venus	154 43.2	11 21
Mars	221 32.2	6 56
Jupiter	213 53.6	7 26
Saturn	350 02.6	22 18

Day	UT (d h)	SUN GHA	SUN Dec	MOON GHA	v	MOON Dec	d	HP
	d h	° ′	° ′	° ′	′	° ′	′	′
SUNDAY	25 00	183 58.0	S12 01.6	20 02.8	11.6	N 9 48.8	15.4	58.7
	01	198 58.1	02.5	34 33.4	11.6	10 04.2	15.3	58.7
	02	213 58.1	03.3	49 04.0	11.4	10 19.5	15.4	58.7
	03	228 58.2	. . 04.2	63 34.4	11.4	10 34.9	15.2	58.8
	04	243 58.3	05.0	78 04.8	11.2	10 50.1	15.3	58.8
	05	258 58.4	05.9	92 35.0	11.2	11 05.4	15.2	58.8
	06	273 58.4	S12 06.8	107 05.2	11.1	N11 20.6	15.1	58.9
	07	288 58.5	07.6	121 35.3	11.0	11 35.7	15.2	58.9
	08	303 58.6	08.5	136 05.3	10.9	11 50.9	15.0	58.9
	09	318 58.7	. . 09.3	150 35.2	10.8	12 05.9	15.0	58.9
	10	333 58.7	10.2	165 05.0	10.7	12 20.9	15.0	59.0
	11	348 58.8	11.1	179 34.7	10.6	12 35.9	14.9	59.0
	12	3 58.9	S12 11.9	194 04.3	10.6	N12 50.8	14.9	59.0
	13	18 59.0	12.8	208 33.9	10.4	13 05.7	14.8	59.1
	14	33 59.0	13.6	223 03.3	10.3	13 20.5	14.7	59.1
	15	48 59.1	. . 14.5	237 32.6	10.2	13 35.2	14.7	59.1
	16	63 59.2	15.4	252 01.8	10.2	13 49.9	14.7	59.1
	17	78 59.2	16.2	266 31.0	10.0	14 04.6	14.5	59.2
	18	93 59.3	S12 17.1	281 00.0	9.9	N14 19.1	14.5	59.2
	19	108 59.4	17.9	295 28.9	9.8	14 33.6	14.4	59.2
	20	123 59.4	18.8	309 57.7	9.7	14 48.0	14.4	59.2
	21	138 59.5	. . 19.6	324 26.4	9.6	15 02.4	14.3	59.3
	22	153 59.6	20.5	338 55.0	9.5	15 16.7	14.2	59.3
	23	168 59.7	21.3	353 23.5	9.4	15 30.9	14.1	59.3
MONDAY	26 00	183 59.7	S12 22.2	7 51.9	9.3	N15 45.0	14.1	59.3
	01	198 59.8	23.1	22 20.2	9.2	15 59.1	14.0	59.4
	02	213 59.9	23.9	36 48.4	9.1	16 13.1	13.9	59.4
	03	228 59.9	. . 24.8	51 16.5	8.9	16 27.0	13.8	59.4
	04	244 00.0	25.6	65 44.4	8.9	16 40.8	13.7	59.4
	05	259 00.1	26.5	80 12.3	8.7	16 54.5	13.7	59.5
	06	274 00.1	S12 27.3	94 40.0	8.7	N17 08.2	13.5	59.5
	07	289 00.2	28.2	109 07.7	8.5	17 21.7	13.5	59.5
	08	304 00.3	29.0	123 35.2	8.4	17 35.2	13.4	59.5
	09	319 00.3	. . 29.9	138 02.6	8.3	17 48.6	13.2	59.6
	10	334 00.4	30.7	152 29.9	8.2	18 01.8	13.2	59.6
	11	349 00.5	31.6	166 57.1	8.0	18 15.0	13.1	59.6
	12	4 00.5	S12 32.4	181 24.1	8.0	N18 28.1	13.0	59.6
	13	19 00.6	33.3	195 51.1	7.8	18 41.1	12.9	59.6
	14	34 00.7	34.1	210 17.9	7.8	18 54.0	12.7	59.7
	15	49 00.7	. . 35.0	224 44.7	7.6	19 06.7	12.7	59.7
	16	64 00.8	35.8	239 11.3	7.5	19 19.4	12.5	59.7
	17	79 00.8	36.7	253 37.8	7.3	19 31.9	12.5	59.7
	18	94 00.9	S12 37.5	268 04.1	7.3	N19 44.4	12.3	59.7
	19	109 01.0	38.4	282 30.4	7.2	19 56.7	12.2	59.7
	20	124 01.0	39.2	296 56.6	7.0	20 08.9	12.1	59.8
	21	139 01.1	. . 40.1	311 22.6	6.9	20 21.0	12.0	59.8
	22	154 01.2	40.9	325 48.5	6.8	20 33.0	11.8	59.8
	23	169 01.2	41.8	340 14.3	6.7	20 44.8	11.8	59.8
TUESDAY	27 00	184 01.3	S12 42.6	354 40.0	6.6	N20 56.6	11.6	59.8
	01	199 01.3	43.5	9 05.6	6.5	21 08.2	11.4	59.8
	02	214 01.4	44.3	23 31.1	6.3	21 19.6	11.4	59.9
	03	229 01.5	. . 45.2	37 56.4	6.2	21 31.0	11.2	59.9
	04	244 01.5	46.0	52 21.6	6.2	21 42.2	11.1	59.9
	05	259 01.6	46.8	66 46.8	6.0	21 53.3	10.9	59.9
	06	274 01.6	S12 47.7	81 11.8	5.9	N22 04.2	10.8	59.9
	07	289 01.7	48.5	95 36.7	5.7	22 15.0	10.7	59.9
	08	304 01.7	49.4	110 01.4	5.7	22 25.7	10.5	60.0
	09	319 01.8	. . 50.2	124 26.1	5.6	22 36.2	10.3	60.0
	10	334 01.9	51.1	138 50.7	5.4	22 46.5	10.3	60.0
	11	349 01.9	51.9	153 15.1	5.4	22 56.8	10.1	60.0
	12	4 02.0	S12 52.8	167 39.5	5.2	N23 06.9	9.9	60.0
	13	19 02.0	53.6	182 03.7	5.1	23 16.8	9.8	60.0
	14	34 02.1	54.4	196 27.8	5.1	23 26.6	9.6	60.0
	15	49 02.1	. . 55.3	210 51.9	4.9	23 36.2	9.4	60.0
	16	64 02.2	56.1	225 15.8	4.8	23 45.6	9.4	60.0
	17	79 02.3	57.0	239 39.6	4.7	23 55.0	9.1	60.1
	18	94 02.3	S12 57.8	254 03.3	4.6	N24 04.1	9.0	60.1
	19	109 02.4	58.6	268 26.9	4.5	24 13.1	8.8	60.1
	20	124 02.4	12 59.5	282 50.4	4.4	24 21.9	8.7	60.1
	21	139 02.5	13 00.3	297 13.8	4.4	24 30.6	8.5	60.1
	22	154 02.5	01.2	311 37.2	4.2	24 39.1	8.3	60.1
	23	169 02.6	02.0	326 00.4	4.1	N24 47.4	8.2	60.1
		SD 16.1	*d* 0.9	SD	16.1		16.2	16.3

Lat.	Twilight Naut.	Twilight Civil	Sunrise	Moonrise 25	26	27	28
°	h m	h m	h m	h m	h m	h m	h m
N 72	05 42	07 02	08 21	14 03	▭	▭	▭
N 70	05 40	06 52	08 02	14 27	13 26	▭	▭
68	05 39	06 45	07 46	14 45	14 10	▭	▭
66	05 38	06 38	07 34	15 00	14 40	13 54	▭
64	05 36	06 32	07 23	15 13	15 02	14 46	▭
62	05 35	06 27	07 14	15 23	15 20	15 18	15 19
60	05 34	06 23	07 07	15 32	15 35	15 42	15 59
N 58	05 33	06 19	07 00	15 40	15 48	16 02	16 27
56	05 32	06 15	06 54	15 47	15 59	16 18	16 49
54	05 31	06 12	06 49	15 54	16 09	16 32	17 07
52	05 29	06 09	06 44	15 59	16 18	16 44	17 22
50	05 28	06 06	06 40	16 05	16 26	16 55	17 36
45	05 26	06 00	06 30	16 16	16 43	17 18	18 03
N 40	05 23	05 54	06 22	16 26	16 57	17 36	18 25
35	05 20	05 49	06 15	16 34	17 09	17 52	18 43
30	05 17	05 45	06 09	16 41	17 20	18 05	18 59
20	05 10	05 36	05 59	16 53	17 38	18 28	19 25
N 10	05 03	05 28	05 49	17 05	17 54	18 48	19 48
0	04 55	05 19	05 41	17 15	18 09	19 07	20 10
S 10	04 45	05 10	05 32	17 26	18 24	19 26	20 31
20	04 33	04 59	05 22	17 37	18 40	19 47	20 55
30	04 16	04 46	05 11	17 50	18 59	20 11	21 22
35	04 06	04 38	05 04	17 58	19 10	20 25	21 38
40	03 54	04 28	04 57	18 07	19 23	20 41	21 57
45	03 38	04 17	04 48	18 17	19 38	21 01	22 19
S 50	03 18	04 02	04 38	18 30	19 57	21 25	22 48
52	03 09	03 56	04 33	18 35	20 06	21 37	23 03
54	02 57	03 48	04 27	18 42	20 16	21 51	23 19
56	02 44	03 39	04 21	18 49	20 27	22 07	23 39
58	02 28	03 29	04 14	18 57	20 40	22 26	24 04
S 60	02 09	03 18	04 07	19 07	20 56	22 50	24 38

Lat.	Sunset	Twilight Civil	Twilight Naut.	Moonset 25	26	27	28
°	h m	h m	h m	h m	h m	h m	h m
N 72	15 05	16 24	17 44	07 31	▭	▭	▭
N 70	15 25	16 34	17 46	07 10	09 59	▭	▭
68	15 40	16 42	17 47	06 53	09 17	▭	▭
66	15 53	16 49	17 49	06 40	08 49	11 34	▭
64	16 04	16 54	17 50	06 29	08 28	10 43	▭
62	16 12	17 00	17 51	06 20	08 11	10 12	12 20
60	16 20	17 04	17 53	06 13	07 57	09 48	11 40
N 58	16 27	17 08	17 54	06 06	07 45	09 30	11 13
56	16 33	17 12	17 55	06 00	07 35	09 14	10 51
54	16 38	17 15	17 56	05 54	07 26	09 01	10 33
52	16 43	17 18	17 58	05 50	07 18	08 49	10 18
50	16 48	17 21	17 59	05 45	07 11	08 39	10 05
45	16 57	17 27	18 02	05 36	06 55	08 17	09 39
N 40	17 05	17 33	18 05	05 28	06 43	08 00	09 17
35	17 12	17 38	18 08	05 21	06 32	07 46	09 00
30	17 18	17 43	18 11	05 16	06 23	07 33	08 45
20	17 29	17 51	18 17	05 06	06 07	07 12	08 19
N 10	17 38	18 00	18 25	04 57	05 53	06 53	07 57
0	17 47	18 09	18 33	04 49	05 40	06 36	07 37
S 10	17 56	18 18	18 43	04 41	05 27	06 19	07 16
20	18 06	18 29	18 56	04 32	05 13	06 01	06 54
30	18 18	18 43	19 12	04 22	04 58	05 40	06 29
35	18 24	18 51	19 23	04 16	04 49	05 27	06 14
40	18 32	19 01	19 35	04 10	04 39	05 13	05 57
45	18 41	19 12	19 51	04 03	04 27	04 57	05 36
S 50	18 51	19 27	20 11	03 54	04 12	04 37	05 11
52	18 56	19 34	20 21	03 50	04 06	04 27	04 58
54	19 02	19 42	20 33	03 45	03 58	04 17	04 44
56	19 08	19 50	20 46	03 40	03 50	04 04	04 28
58	19 15	20 01	21 02	03 35	03 41	03 51	04 08
S 60	19 23	20 12	21 23	03 29	03 30	03 34	03 44

Day	SUN Eqn. of Time 00^h	SUN Eqn. of Time 12^h	SUN Mer. Pass.	MOON Mer. Pass. Upper	MOON Mer. Pass. Lower	Age	Phase
d	m s	m s	h m	h m	h m	d %	
25	15 52	15 55	11 44	23 27	11 02	15 99	○
26	15 59	16 02	11 44	24 22	11 54	16 100	
27	16 05	16 08	11 44	00 22	12 51	17 97	

UT	ARIES GHA	VENUS −4·2 GHA	VENUS Dec	MARS +0·9 GHA	MARS Dec	JUPITER −2·0 GHA	JUPITER Dec	SATURN +0·4 GHA	SATURN Dec
d h	° ′	° ′	° ′	° ′	° ′	° ′	° ′	° ′	° ′
28 00 WEDNESDAY	36 21.4	192 04.7	S16 18.1	256 50.6	N17 18.8	249 59.4	N14 13.1	26 31.6	N 1 18.3
01	51 23.9	207 08.4	17.1	271 51.8	18.5	265 01.5	13.0	41 34.2	18.3
02	66 26.3	222 12.1	16.1	286 52.9	18.1	280 03.7	12.9	56 36.8	18.2
03	81 28.8	237 15.7	. . 15.0	301 54.1	. . 17.8	295 05.8	. . 12.8	71 39.5	. . 18.1
04	96 31.3	252 19.4	14.0	316 55.2	17.4	310 08.0	12.7	86 42.1	18.1
05	111 33.7	267 23.1	13.0	331 56.4	17.1	325 10.1	12.6	101 44.7	18.0
06	126 36.2	282 26.7	S16 12.0	346 57.6	N17 16.7	340 12.2	N14 12.5	116 47.3	N 1 18.0
07	141 38.7	297 30.4	10.9	1 58.7	16.4	355 14.4	12.4	131 49.9	17.9
08	156 41.1	312 34.1	09.9	16 59.9	16.1	10 16.5	12.3	146 52.6	17.8
09	171 43.6	327 37.7	. . 08.9	32 01.1	. . 15.7	25 18.7	. . 12.2	161 55.2	. . 17.8
10	186 46.1	342 41.4	07.9	47 02.2	15.4	40 20.8	12.1	176 57.8	17.7
11	201 48.5	357 45.0	06.8	62 03.4	15.0	55 23.0	12.1	192 00.4	17.7
12	216 51.0	12 48.7	S16 05.8	77 04.6	N17 14.7	70 25.1	N14 12.0	207 03.0	N 1 17.6
13	231 53.5	27 52.3	04.8	92 05.7	14.3	85 27.3	11.9	222 05.7	17.5
14	246 55.9	42 56.0	03.8	107 06.9	14.0	100 29.4	11.8	237 08.3	17.5
15	261 58.4	57 59.6	. . 02.7	122 08.1	. . 13.7	115 31.6	. . 11.7	252 10.9	. . 17.4
16	277 00.8	73 03.3	01.7	137 09.2	13.3	130 33.7	11.6	267 13.5	17.3
17	292 03.3	88 06.9	16 00.7	152 10.4	13.0	145 35.9	11.5	282 16.1	17.3
18	307 05.8	103 10.5	S15 59.7	167 11.6	N17 12.6	160 38.0	N14 11.4	297 18.8	N 1 17.2
19	322 08.2	118 14.2	58.6	182 12.7	12.3	175 40.2	11.3	312 21.4	17.2
20	337 10.7	133 17.8	57.6	197 13.9	11.9	190 42.3	11.2	327 24.0	17.1
21	352 13.2	148 21.4	. . 56.6	212 15.1	. . 11.6	205 44.5	. . 11.1	342 26.6	. . 17.0
22	7 15.6	163 25.1	55.6	227 16.2	11.3	220 46.6	11.0	357 29.2	17.0
23	22 18.1	178 28.7	54.5	242 17.4	10.9	235 48.7	10.9	12 31.8	16.9
29 00 THURSDAY	37 20.6	193 32.3	S15 53.5	257 18.6	N17 10.6	250 50.9	N14 10.8	27 34.5	N 1 16.9
01	52 23.0	208 35.9	52.5	272 19.7	10.2	265 53.0	10.7	42 37.1	16.8
02	67 25.5	223 39.6	51.4	287 20.9	09.9	280 55.2	10.6	57 39.7	16.7
03	82 28.0	238 43.2	. . 50.4	302 22.1	. . 09.6	295 57.3	. . 10.5	72 42.3	. . 16.7
04	97 30.4	253 46.8	49.4	317 23.2	09.2	310 59.5	10.4	87 44.9	16.6
05	112 32.9	268 50.4	48.4	332 24.4	08.9	326 01.6	10.3	102 47.5	16.6
06	127 35.3	283 54.0	S15 47.3	347 25.6	N17 08.5	341 03.8	N14 10.2	117 50.2	N 1 16.5
07	142 37.8	298 57.6	46.3	2 26.8	08.2	356 05.9	10.1	132 52.8	16.4
08	157 40.3	314 01.2	45.3	17 27.9	07.8	11 08.1	10.0	147 55.4	16.4
09	172 42.7	329 04.8	. . 44.2	32 29.1	. . 07.5	26 10.2	. . 09.9	162 58.0	. . 16.3
10	187 45.2	344 08.4	43.2	47 30.3	07.2	41 12.4	09.8	178 00.6	16.3
11	202 47.7	359 12.0	42.2	62 31.5	06.8	56 14.6	09.7	193 03.3	16.2
12	217 50.1	14 15.6	S15 41.2	77 32.6	N17 06.5	71 16.7	N14 09.6	208 05.9	N 1 16.2
13	232 52.6	29 19.2	40.1	92 33.8	06.1	86 18.9	09.5	223 08.5	16.1
14	247 55.1	44 22.8	39.1	107 35.0	05.8	101 21.0	09.4	238 11.1	16.0
15	262 57.5	59 26.4	. . 38.1	122 36.2	. . 05.4	116 23.2	. . 09.3	253 13.7	. . 16.0
16	278 00.0	74 30.0	37.0	137 37.3	05.1	131 25.3	09.2	268 16.3	15.9
17	293 02.5	89 33.5	36.0	152 38.5	04.8	146 27.5	09.1	283 19.0	15.9
18	308 04.9	104 37.1	S15 35.0	167 39.7	N17 04.4	161 29.6	N14 09.0	298 21.6	N 1 15.8
19	323 07.4	119 40.7	33.9	182 40.9	04.1	176 31.8	08.9	313 24.2	15.7
20	338 09.8	134 44.3	32.9	197 42.0	03.7	191 33.9	08.8	328 26.8	15.7
21	353 12.3	149 47.9	. . 31.9	212 43.2	. . 03.4	206 36.1	. . 08.7	343 29.4	. . 15.6
22	8 14.8	164 51.4	30.9	227 44.4	03.0	221 38.2	08.6	358 32.0	15.6
23	23 17.2	179 55.0	29.8	242 45.6	02.7	236 40.4	08.5	13 34.6	15.5
30 00 FRIDAY	38 19.7	194 58.6	S15 28.8	257 46.7	N17 02.4	251 42.5	N14 08.4	28 37.3	N 1 15.4
01	53 22.2	210 02.1	27.8	272 47.9	02.0	266 44.7	08.3	43 39.9	15.4
02	68 24.6	225 05.7	26.7	287 49.1	01.7	281 46.9	08.2	58 42.5	15.3
03	83 27.1	240 09.2	. . 25.7	302 50.3	. . 01.3	296 49.0	. . 08.1	73 45.1	. . 15.3
04	98 29.6	255 12.8	24.7	317 51.5	01.0	311 51.2	08.0	88 47.7	15.2
05	113 32.0	270 16.3	23.7	332 52.6	00.6	326 53.3	07.9	103 50.3	15.1
06	128 34.5	285 19.9	S15 22.6	347 53.8	N17 00.3	341 55.5	N14 07.8	118 53.0	N 1 15.1
07	143 37.0	300 23.4	21.6	2 55.0	17 00.0	356 57.6	07.7	133 55.6	15.0
08	158 39.4	315 27.0	20.6	17 56.2	16 59.6	11 59.8	07.6	148 58.2	15.0
09	173 41.9	330 30.5	. . 19.5	32 57.4	. . 59.3	27 01.9	. . 07.5	164 00.8	. . 14.9
10	188 44.3	345 34.0	18.5	47 58.6	58.9	42 04.1	07.5	179 03.4	14.9
11	203 46.8	0 37.6	17.5	62 59.7	58.6	57 06.3	07.4	194 06.0	14.8
12	218 49.3	15 41.1	S15 16.5	78 00.9	N16 58.2	72 08.4	N14 07.3	209 08.6	N 1 14.7
13	233 51.7	30 44.6	15.4	93 02.1	57.9	87 10.6	07.2	224 11.3	14.7
14	248 54.2	45 48.2	14.4	108 03.3	57.6	102 12.7	07.1	239 13.9	14.6
15	263 56.7	60 51.7	. . 13.4	123 04.5	. . 57.2	117 14.9	. . 07.0	254 16.5	. . 14.6
16	278 59.1	75 55.2	12.4	138 05.7	56.9	132 17.0	06.9	269 19.1	14.5
17	294 01.6	90 58.7	11.3	153 06.9	56.5	147 19.2	06.8	284 21.7	14.4
18	309 04.1	106 02.2	S15 10.3	168 08.0	N16 56.2	162 21.4	N14 06.7	299 24.3	N 1 14.4
19	324 06.5	121 05.8	09.3	183 09.2	55.8	177 23.5	06.6	314 26.9	14.3
20	339 09.0	136 09.3	08.3	198 10.4	55.5	192 25.7	06.5	329 29.6	14.3
21	354 11.5	151 12.8	. . 07.2	213 11.6	. . 55.2	207 27.8	. . 06.4	344 32.2	. . 14.2
22	9 13.9	166 16.3	06.2	228 12.8	54.8	222 30.0	06.3	359 34.8	14.2
23	24 16.4	181 19.8	05.2	243 14.0	54.5	237 32.2	06.2	14 37.4	14.1
Mer. Pass.	h m 21 27.1	v 3.6	d 1.0	v 1.2	d 0.3	v 2.2	d 0.1	v 2.6	d 0.1

STARS

Name	SHA ° ′	Dec ° ′
Acamar	315 10.2	S40 11.7
Achernar	335 18.5	S57 06.0
Acrux	172 59.0	S63 14.7
Adhara	255 04.6	S29 00.3
Aldebaran	290 37.6	N16 33.9
Alioth	166 12.2	N55 48.7
Alkaid	152 51.3	N49 10.7
Alnair	27 30.9	S46 50.0
Alnilam	275 36.0	S 1 11.0
Alphard	217 46.4	S 8 46.4
Alphecca	126 02.8	N26 37.6
Alpheratz	357 32.9	N29 14.6
Altair	61 58.6	N 8 56.5
Ankaa	353 05.3	S42 09.6
Antares	112 14.3	S26 29.5
Arcturus	145 46.9	N19 02.6
Atria	107 07.7	S69 04.6
Avior	234 14.1	S59 35.4
Bellatrix	278 21.1	N 6 22.5
Betelgeuse	270 50.3	N 7 24.8
Canopus	263 51.5	S52 42.3
Capella	280 19.4	N46 01.4
Deneb	49 24.8	N45 22.9
Denebola	182 23.7	N14 25.3
Diphda	348 45.5	S17 50.3
Dubhe	193 39.6	N61 36.1
Elnath	277 59.7	N28 37.8
Eltanin	90 41.8	N51 29.3
Enif	33 37.3	N10 00.1
Fomalhaut	15 12.7	S29 28.8
Gacrux	171 50.5	S57 15.7
Gienah	175 42.4	S17 41.3
Hadar	148 34.6	S60 30.1
Hamal	327 49.2	N23 35.5
Kaus Aust.	83 30.8	S34 22.3
Kochab	137 21.0	N74 02.7
Markab	13 28.2	N15 21.2
Menkar	314 04.3	N 4 11.8
Menkent	147 56.3	S36 30.0
Miaplacidus	221 38.1	S69 49.3
Mirfak	308 25.6	N49 57.4
Nunki	75 46.1	S26 15.8
Peacock	53 03.4	S56 39.1
Pollux	243 15.4	N27 57.6
Procyon	244 49.2	N 5 09.4
Rasalhague	95 57.4	N12 32.6
Regulus	207 30.4	N11 50.2
Rigel	281 02.2	S 8 10.1
Rigil Kent.	139 38.9	S60 56.7
Sabik	102 01.4	S15 45.4
Schedar	349 28.8	N56 41.3
Shaula	96 08.7	S37 07.4
Sirius	258 24.8	S16 45.0
Spica	158 21.1	S11 18.0
Suhail	222 45.3	S43 32.2
Vega	80 32.4	N38 48.7
Zuben'ubi	136 54.7	S16 09.1

	SHA ° ′	Mer. Pass. h m
Venus	156 11.8	11 03
Mars	219 58.0	6 50
Jupiter	213 30.3	7 16
Saturn	350 13.9	22 06

UT		SUN GHA	SUN Dec	MOON GHA	v	MOON Dec	d	HP
d	h	° ′	° ′	° ′	′	° ′	′	′
28	00	184 02.6	S13 02.8	340 23.5	4.0	N24 55.6	8.0	60.1
	01	199 02.7	03.7	354 46.5	4.0	25 03.6	7.8	60.1
	02	214 02.7	04.5	9 09.5	3.8	25 11.4	7.6	60.1
	03	229 02.8	. . 05.4	23 32.3	3.8	25 19.0	7.5	60.1
	04	244 02.8	06.2	37 55.1	3.6	25 26.5	7.3	60.1
	05	259 02.9	07.0	52 17.7	3.6	25 33.8	7.1	60.1
	06	274 02.9	S13 07.9	66 40.3	3.5	N25 40.9	6.9	60.1
W	07	289 03.0	08.7	81 02.8	3.5	25 47.8	6.7	60.2
E	08	304 03.1	09.5	95 25.3	3.3	25 54.5	6.6	60.2
D	09	319 03.1	. . 10.4	109 47.6	3.3	26 01.1	6.4	60.2
N	10	334 03.2	11.2	124 09.9	3.2	26 07.5	6.2	60.2
E	11	349 03.2	12.0	138 32.1	3.1	26 13.7	6.0	60.2
S	12	4 03.2	S13 12.9	152 54.2	3.1	N26 19.7	5.8	60.2
D	13	19 03.3	13.7	167 16.3	3.0	26 25.5	5.6	60.2
A	14	34 03.3	14.5	181 38.3	2.9	26 31.1	5.4	60.2
Y	15	49 03.4	. . 15.4	196 00.2	2.9	26 36.5	5.3	60.2
	16	64 03.4	16.2	210 22.1	2.8	26 41.8	5.0	60.2
	17	79 03.5	17.0	224 43.9	2.7	26 46.8	4.8	60.2
	18	94 03.5	S13 17.9	239 05.6	2.7	N26 51.6	4.7	60.2
	19	109 03.6	18.7	253 27.3	2.7	26 56.3	4.5	60.2
	20	124 03.6	19.5	267 49.0	2.6	27 00.8	4.2	60.2
	21	139 03.7	. . 20.4	282 10.6	2.5	27 05.0	4.1	60.2
	22	154 03.7	21.2	296 32.1	2.5	27 09.1	3.9	60.2
	23	169 03.8	22.0	310 53.6	2.5	27 13.0	3.6	60.2
29	00	184 03.8	S13 22.9	325 15.1	2.4	N27 16.6	3.5	60.2
	01	199 03.9	23.7	339 36.5	2.4	27 20.1	3.3	60.2
	02	214 03.9	24.5	353 57.9	2.4	27 23.4	3.0	60.2
	03	229 03.9	. . 25.3	8 19.3	2.3	27 26.4	2.9	60.2
	04	244 04.0	26.2	22 40.6	2.3	27 29.3	2.6	60.2
	05	259 04.0	27.0	37 01.9	2.3	27 31.9	2.5	60.2
	06	274 04.1	S13 27.8	51 23.2	2.2	N27 34.1	2.2	60.1
	07	289 04.1	28.7	65 44.4	2.3	27 36.6	2.1	60.1
T	08	304 04.2	29.5	80 05.7	2.2	27 38.7	1.8	60.1
H	09	319 04.2	. . 30.3	94 26.9	2.2	27 40.5	1.7	60.1
U	10	334 04.2	31.1	108 48.1	2.2	27 42.2	1.4	60.1
R	11	349 04.3	32.0	123 09.3	2.2	27 43.6	1.2	60.1
S	12	4 04.3	S13 32.8	137 30.5	2.2	N27 44.8	1.1	60.1
D	13	19 04.4	33.6	151 51.7	2.2	27 45.9	0.8	60.1
A	14	34 04.4	34.4	166 12.9	2.2	27 46.7	0.6	60.1
Y	15	49 04.4	. . 35.3	180 34.1	2.2	27 47.3	0.4	60.1
	16	64 04.5	36.1	194 55.3	2.3	27 47.7	0.2	60.1
	17	79 04.5	36.9	209 16.6	2.2	27 47.9	0.0	60.1
	18	94 04.6	S13 37.7	223 37.8	2.2	N27 47.9	0.2	60.1
	19	109 04.6	38.6	237 59.0	2.3	27 47.7	0.4	60.1
	20	124 04.6	39.4	252 20.3	2.3	27 47.3	0.6	60.1
	21	139 04.7	. . 40.2	266 41.6	2.3	27 46.7	0.8	60.0
	22	154 04.7	41.0	281 02.9	2.3	27 45.9	1.0	60.0
	23	169 04.8	41.8	295 24.2	2.4	27 44.9	1.2	60.0
30	00	184 04.8	S13 42.7	309 45.6	2.4	N27 43.7	1.4	60.0
	01	199 04.8	43.5	324 07.0	2.4	27 42.3	1.7	60.0
	02	214 04.9	44.3	338 28.4	2.5	27 40.6	1.8	60.0
	03	229 04.9	. . 45.1	352 49.9	2.5	27 38.8	2.0	60.0
	04	244 04.9	45.9	7 11.4	2.6	27 36.8	2.2	60.0
	05	259 05.0	46.8	21 33.0	2.6	27 34.6	2.4	60.0
	06	274 05.0	S13 47.6	35 54.6	2.7	N27 32.2	2.7	60.0
	07	289 05.0	48.4	50 16.3	2.7	27 29.5	2.8	59.9
	08	304 05.1	49.2	64 38.0	2.7	27 26.7	3.0	59.9
F	09	319 05.1	. . 50.0	78 59.7	2.9	27 23.7	3.2	59.9
R	10	334 05.1	50.9	93 21.6	2.8	27 20.5	3.4	59.9
I	11	349 05.2	51.7	107 43.4	3.0	27 17.1	3.6	59.9
D	12	4 05.2	S13 52.5	122 05.4	3.0	N27 13.5	3.8	59.9
A	13	19 05.2	53.3	136 27.4	3.1	27 09.7	3.9	59.9
Y	14	34 05.3	54.1	150 49.5	3.1	27 05.8	4.2	59.9
	15	49 05.3	. . 54.9	165 11.6	3.2	27 01.6	4.4	59.8
	16	64 05.3	55.8	179 33.8	3.3	26 57.2	4.5	59.8
	17	79 05.4	56.6	193 56.1	3.4	26 52.7	4.7	59.8
	18	94 05.4	S13 57.4	208 18.5	3.5	N26 48.0	5.0	59.8
	19	109 05.4	58.2	222 41.0	3.5	26 43.0	5.1	59.8
	20	124 05.5	59.0	237 03.5	3.6	26 37.9	5.2	59.8
	21	139 05.5	13 59.8	251 26.1	3.7	26 32.7	5.5	59.8
	22	154 05.5	14 00.6	265 48.8	3.8	26 27.2	5.6	59.7
	23	169 05.5	S14 01.5	280 11.6	3.9	N26 21.6	5.9	59.7
		SD 16.1	*d* 0.8	SD	16.4	16.4		16.3

Lat.	Twilight Naut.	Twilight Civil	Sunrise	Moonrise 28	Moonrise 29	Moonrise 30	Moonrise 31
°	h m	h m	h m	h m	h m	h m	h m
N 72	05 54	07 16	08 38	▭	▭	▭	▭
N 70	05 51	07 04	08 16	▭	▭	▭	▭
68	05 49	06 55	07 58	▭	▭	▭	▭
66	05 46	06 47	07 44	▭	▭	▭	▭
64	05 44	06 41	07 33	▭	▭	▭	18 49
62	05 43	06 35	07 23	15 19	15 40	17 21	19 26
60	05 41	06 30	07 14	15 59	16 42	18 06	19 53
N 58	05 39	06 25	07 07	16 27	17 16	18 35	20 14
56	05 37	06 21	07 00	16 49	17 41	18 58	20 31
54	05 36	06 17	06 55	17 07	18 01	19 16	20 45
52	05 34	06 14	06 49	17 22	18 18	19 32	20 57
50	05 33	06 11	06 45	17 36	18 33	19 46	21 08
45	05 29	06 04	06 34	18 03	19 02	20 13	21 31
N 40	05 26	05 58	06 26	18 25	19 25	20 35	21 50
35	05 22	05 52	06 18	18 43	19 44	20 53	22 05
30	05 19	05 47	06 12	18 59	20 01	21 08	22 18
20	05 11	05 37	06 00	19 25	20 28	21 35	22 41
N 10	05 03	05 28	05 50	19 48	20 52	21 57	23 00
0	04 54	05 19	05 40	20 10	21 15	22 18	23 18
S 10	04 44	05 09	05 31	20 31	21 37	22 39	23 36
20	04 30	04 57	05 20	20 55	22 01	23 02	23 55
30	04 13	04 43	05 08	21 22	22 29	23 28	24 17
35	04 02	04 34	05 01	21 38	22 45	23 43	24 30
40	03 49	04 24	04 53	21 57	23 04	24 01	00 01
45	03 33	04 12	04 43	22 19	23 28	24 22	00 22
S 50	03 11	03 56	04 32	22 48	23 57	24 49	00 49
52	03 01	03 49	04 27	23 03	24 12	00 12	01 02
54	02 49	03 41	04 21	23 19	24 29	00 29	01 16
56	02 34	03 31	04 14	23 39	24 50	00 50	01 34
58	02 17	03 21	04 07	24 04	00 04	01 15	01 55
S 60	01 55	03 08	03 58	24 38	00 38	01 51	02 21

Lat.	Sunset	Twilight Civil	Twilight Naut.	Moonset 28	Moonset 29	Moonset 30	Moonset 31
°	h m	h m	h m	h m	h m	h m	h m
N 72	14 48	16 10	17 31	▭	▭	▭	▭
N 70	15 10	16 22	17 34	▭	▭	▭	▭
68	15 28	16 31	17 37	▭	▭	▭	▭
66	15 42	16 39	17 39	▭	▭	▭	▭
64	15 54	16 46	17 42	▭	▭	▭	15 29
62	16 04	16 51	17 44	12 20	14 15	14 48	14 51
60	16 12	16 57	17 46	11 40	13 13	14 03	14 24
N 58	16 20	17 01	17 47	11 13	12 39	13 34	14 02
56	16 26	17 05	17 49	10 51	12 14	13 11	13 45
54	16 32	17 09	17 51	10 33	11 53	12 52	13 30
52	16 37	17 13	17 52	10 18	11 37	12 36	13 17
50	16 42	17 16	17 54	10 05	11 22	12 22	13 05
45	16 53	17 23	17 57	09 39	10 53	11 54	12 41
N 40	17 01	17 29	18 01	09 17	10 30	11 32	12 22
35	17 09	17 35	18 05	09 00	10 11	11 13	12 06
30	17 16	17 40	18 08	08 45	09 54	10 57	11 52
20	17 27	17 50	18 16	08 19	09 27	10 30	11 28
N 10	17 37	17 59	18 24	07 57	09 03	10 07	11 07
0	17 47	18 08	18 33	07 37	08 41	09 45	10 47
S 10	17 57	18 19	18 44	07 16	08 18	09 23	10 28
20	18 08	18 30	18 57	06 54	07 55	09 00	10 06
30	18 20	18 45	19 15	06 29	07 27	08 32	09 42
35	18 27	18 54	19 26	06 14	07 11	08 16	09 27
40	18 35	19 04	19 39	05 57	06 52	07 57	09 10
45	18 45	19 17	19 56	05 36	06 28	07 34	08 49
S 50	18 57	19 32	20 18	05 11	05 59	07 04	08 24
52	19 02	19 40	20 28	04 58	05 45	06 50	08 11
54	19 08	19 48	20 41	04 44	05 28	06 33	07 56
56	19 15	19 58	20 56	04 28	05 08	06 13	07 40
58	19 22	20 09	21 14	04 08	04 43	05 47	07 19
S 60	19 31	20 22	21 36	03 44	04 09	05 12	06 53

Day	SUN Eqn. of Time 00^h	SUN Eqn. of Time 12^h	SUN Mer. Pass.	MOON Mer. Pass. Upper	MOON Mer. Pass. Lower	MOON Age	MOON Phase
d	m s	m s	h m	h m	h m	d %	
28	16 10	16 13	11 44	01 22	13 53	18 92	
29	16 15	16 17	11 44	02 25	14 58	19 85	
30	16 19	16 21	11 44	03 30	16 02	20 76	

2026 OCT. 31, NOV. 1, 2 (SAT., SUN., MON.)

UT (d h)	ARIES GHA ° ′	VENUS −4·2 GHA ° ′	VENUS Dec ° ′	MARS +0·9 GHA ° ′	MARS Dec ° ′	JUPITER −2·0 GHA ° ′	JUPITER Dec ° ′	SATURN +0·4 GHA ° ′	SATURN Dec ° ′
31 00 (SATURDAY)	39 18.8	196 23.3	S15 04.2	258 15.2	N16 54.1	252 34.3	N14 06.1	29 40.0	N 1 14.0
01	54 21.3	211 26.8	03.1	273 16.3	53.8	267 36.5	06.0	44 42.6	14.0
02	69 23.8	226 30.3	02.1	288 17.5	53.4	282 38.6	05.9	59 45.2	13.9
03	84 26.2	241 33.7	. . 01.1	303 18.7	. . 53.1	297 40.8	. . 05.8	74 47.9	. . 13.9
04	99 28.7	256 37.2	15 00.1	318 19.9	52.8	312 43.0	05.7	89 50.5	13.8
05	114 31.2	271 40.7	14 59.0	333 21.1	52.4	327 45.1	05.6	104 53.1	13.8
06	129 33.6	286 44.2	S14 58.0	348 22.3	N16 52.1	342 47.3	N14 05.5	119 55.7	N 1 13.7
07	144 36.1	301 47.7	57.0	3 23.5	51.7	357 49.4	05.4	134 58.3	13.6
08	159 38.6	316 51.1	56.0	18 24.7	51.4	12 51.6	05.4	150 00.9	13.6
09	174 41.0	331 54.6	. . 55.0	33 25.9	. . 51.1	27 53.8	. . 05.3	165 03.5	. . 13.5
10	189 43.5	346 58.1	53.9	48 27.1	50.7	42 55.9	05.2	180 06.1	13.5
11	204 46.0	2 01.5	52.9	63 28.3	50.4	57 58.1	05.1	195 08.8	13.4
12	219 48.4	17 05.0	S14 51.9	78 29.5	N16 50.0	73 00.3	N14 05.0	210 11.4	N 1 13.4
13	234 50.9	32 08.5	50.9	93 30.6	49.7	88 02.4	04.9	225 14.0	13.3
14	249 53.3	47 11.9	49.9	108 31.8	49.3	103 04.6	04.8	240 16.6	13.2
15	264 55.8	62 15.4	. . 48.8	123 33.0	. . 49.0	118 06.7	. . 04.7	255 19.2	. . 13.2
16	279 58.3	77 18.8	47.8	138 34.2	48.7	133 08.9	04.6	270 21.8	13.1
17	295 00.7	92 22.3	46.8	153 35.4	48.3	148 11.1	04.5	285 24.4	13.1
18	310 03.2	107 25.7	S14 45.8	168 36.6	N16 48.0	163 13.2	N14 04.4	300 27.0	N 1 13.0
19	325 05.7	122 29.2	44.8	183 37.8	47.6	178 15.4	04.3	315 29.6	13.0
20	340 08.1	137 32.6	43.8	198 39.0	47.3	193 17.6	04.2	330 32.3	12.9
21	355 10.6	152 36.0	. . 42.7	213 40.2	. . 46.9	208 19.7	. . 04.1	345 34.9	. . 12.8
22	10 13.1	167 39.5	41.7	228 41.4	46.6	223 21.9	04.0	0 37.5	12.8
23	25 15.5	182 42.9	40.7	243 42.6	46.3	238 24.1	03.9	15 40.1	12.7
1 00 (SUNDAY)	40 18.0	197 46.3	S14 39.7	258 43.8	N16 45.9	253 26.2	N14 03.9	30 42.7	N 1 12.7
01	55 20.4	212 49.7	38.7	273 45.0	45.6	268 28.4	03.8	45 45.3	12.6
02	70 22.9	227 53.2	37.7	288 46.2	45.2	283 30.6	03.7	60 47.9	12.6
03	85 25.4	242 56.6	. . 36.7	303 47.4	. . 44.9	298 32.7	. . 03.6	75 50.5	. . 12.5
04	100 27.8	258 00.0	35.6	318 48.6	44.5	313 34.9	03.5	90 53.1	12.4
05	115 30.3	273 03.4	34.6	333 49.8	44.2	328 37.1	03.4	105 55.8	12.4
06	130 32.8	288 06.8	S14 33.6	348 51.0	N16 43.9	343 39.2	N14 03.3	120 58.4	N 1 12.3
07	145 35.2	303 10.2	32.6	3 52.2	43.5	358 41.4	03.2	136 01.0	12.3
08	160 37.7	318 13.6	31.6	18 53.4	43.2	13 43.6	03.1	151 03.6	12.2
09	175 40.2	333 17.0	. . 30.6	33 54.6	. . 42.8	28 45.7	. . 03.0	166 06.2	. . 12.2
10	190 42.6	348 20.4	29.6	48 55.8	42.5	43 47.9	02.9	181 08.8	12.1
11	205 45.1	3 23.8	28.6	63 57.0	42.1	58 50.1	02.8	196 11.4	12.1
12	220 47.6	18 27.2	S14 27.6	78 58.2	N16 41.8	73 52.2	N14 02.7	211 14.0	N 1 12.0
13	235 50.0	33 30.5	26.6	93 59.4	41.5	88 54.4	02.6	226 16.6	11.9
14	250 52.5	48 33.9	25.6	109 00.6	41.1	103 56.6	02.6	241 19.2	11.9
15	265 54.9	63 37.3	. . 24.6	124 01.8	. . 40.8	118 58.7	. . 02.5	256 21.9	. . 11.8
16	280 57.4	78 40.7	23.6	139 03.0	40.4	134 00.9	02.4	271 24.5	11.8
17	295 59.9	93 44.0	22.6	154 04.2	40.1	149 03.1	02.3	286 27.1	11.7
18	311 02.3	108 47.4	S14 21.6	169 05.4	N16 39.7	164 05.3	N14 02.2	301 29.7	N 1 11.7
19	326 04.8	123 50.8	20.6	184 06.6	39.4	179 07.4	02.1	316 32.3	11.6
20	341 07.3	138 54.1	19.6	199 07.8	39.1	194 09.6	02.0	331 34.9	11.6
21	356 09.7	153 57.5	. . 18.6	214 09.0	. . 38.7	209 11.8	. . 01.9	346 37.5	. . 11.5
22	11 12.2	169 00.8	17.6	229 10.3	38.4	224 13.9	01.8	1 40.1	11.4
23	26 14.7	184 04.2	16.6	244 11.5	38.0	239 16.1	01.7	16 42.7	11.4
2 00 (MONDAY)	41 17.1	199 07.5	S14 15.6	259 12.7	N16 37.7	254 18.3	N14 01.6	31 45.3	N 1 11.3
01	56 19.6	214 10.9	14.6	274 13.9	37.3	269 20.5	01.5	46 47.9	11.3
02	71 22.1	229 14.2	13.6	289 15.1	37.0	284 22.6	01.5	61 50.6	11.2
03	86 24.5	244 17.6	. . 12.6	304 16.3	. . 36.7	299 24.8	. . 01.4	76 53.2	. . 11.2
04	101 27.0	259 20.9	11.6	319 17.5	36.3	314 27.0	01.3	91 55.8	11.1
05	116 29.4	274 24.2	10.6	334 18.7	36.0	329 29.1	01.2	106 58.4	11.1
06	131 31.9	289 27.5	S14 09.6	349 19.9	N16 35.6	344 31.3	N14 01.1	122 01.0	N 1 11.0
07	146 34.4	304 30.9	08.6	4 21.1	35.3	359 33.5	01.0	137 03.6	10.9
08	161 36.8	319 34.2	07.6	19 22.3	34.9	14 35.7	00.9	152 06.2	10.9
09	176 39.3	334 37.5	. . 06.6	34 23.6	. . 34.6	29 37.8	. . 00.8	167 08.8	. . 10.8
10	191 41.8	349 40.8	05.6	49 24.8	34.3	44 40.0	00.7	182 11.4	10.8
11	206 44.2	4 44.1	04.6	64 26.0	33.9	59 42.2	00.6	197 14.0	10.7
12	221 46.7	19 47.4	S14 03.6	79 27.2	N16 33.6	74 44.4	N14 00.5	212 16.6	N 1 10.7
13	236 49.2	34 50.7	02.7	94 28.4	33.2	89 46.5	00.5	227 19.2	10.6
14	251 51.6	49 54.0	01.7	109 29.6	32.9	104 48.7	00.4	242 21.8	10.6
15	266 54.1	64 57.3	14 00.7	124 30.8	. . 32.6	119 50.9	. . 00.3	257 24.5	. . 10.5
16	281 56.6	80 00.6	13 59.7	139 32.0	32.2	134 53.1	00.2	272 27.1	10.5
17	296 59.0	95 03.9	58.7	154 33.3	31.9	149 55.2	00.1	287 29.7	10.4
18	312 01.5	110 07.2	S13 57.7	169 34.5	N16 31.5	164 57.4	N14 00.0	302 32.3	N 1 10.3
19	327 03.9	125 10.5	56.8	184 35.7	31.2	179 59.6	13 59.9	317 34.9	10.3
20	342 06.4	140 13.8	55.8	199 36.9	30.8	195 01.8	59.8	332 37.5	10.2
21	357 08.9	155 17.0	. . 54.8	214 38.1	. . 30.5	210 03.9	. . 59.7	347 40.1	. . 10.2
22	12 11.3	170 20.3	53.8	229 39.3	30.2	225 06.1	59.6	2 42.7	10.1
23	27 13.8	185 23.6	52.8	244 40.6	29.8	240 08.3	59.6	17 45.3	10.1
Mer. Pass. (h m)	21 15.3	*v* 3.4	*d* 1.0	*v* 1.2	*d* 0.3	*v* 2.2	*d* 0.1	*v* 2.6	*d* 0.1

STARS

Name	SHA ° ′	Dec ° ′
Acamar	315 10.2	S40 11.7
Achernar	335 18.5	S57 06.0
Acrux	172 59.0	S63 14.7
Adhara	255 04.5	S29 00.3
Aldebaran	290 37.6	N16 33.9
Alioth	166 12.2	N55 48.7
Alkaid	152 51.3	N49 10.7
Alnair	27 30.9	S46 50.0
Alnilam	275 36.0	S 1 11.0
Alphard	217 46.4	S 8 46.4
Alphecca	126 02.8	N26 37.5
Alpheratz	357 32.9	N29 14.6
Altair	61 58.6	N 8 56.5
Ankaa	353 05.3	S42 09.6
Antares	112 14.3	S26 29.5
Arcturus	145 46.9	N19 02.6
Atria	107 07.7	S69 04.6
Avior	234 14.1	S59 35.4
Bellatrix	278 21.0	N 6 22.5
Betelgeuse	270 50.3	N 7 24.8
Canopus	263 51.4	S52 42.3
Capella	280 19.3	N46 01.4
Deneb	49 24.8	N45 22.9
Denebola	182 23.7	N14 25.3
Diphda	348 45.5	S17 50.3
Dubhe	193 39.6	N61 36.1
Elnath	277 59.7	N28 37.8
Eltanin	90 41.8	N51 29.3
Enif	33 37.3	N10 00.1
Fomalhaut	15 12.7	S29 28.8
Gacrux	171 50.5	S57 15.6
Gienah	175 42.3	S17 41.3
Hadar	148 34.5	S60 30.1
Hamal	327 49.2	N23 35.5
Kaus Aust.	83 30.8	S34 22.3
Kochab	137 21.0	N74 02.6
Markab	13 28.2	N15 21.2
Menkar	314 04.3	N 4 11.8
Menkent	147 56.3	S36 30.0
Miaplacidus	221 38.1	S69 49.3
Mirfak	308 25.6	N49 57.4
Nunki	75 46.1	S26 15.8
Peacock	53 03.5	S56 39.1
Pollux	243 15.4	N27 57.6
Procyon	244 49.2	N 5 09.4
Rasalhague	95 57.4	N12 32.6
Regulus	207 33.0	N11 50.2
Rigel	281 02.2	S 8 10.1
Rigil Kent.	139 38.9	S60 56.7
Sabik	102 01.4	S15 45.4
Schedar	349 28.8	N56 41.3
Shaula	96 08.7	S37 07.4
Sirius	258 24.8	S16 45.0
Spica	158 21.1	S11 18.0
Suhail	222 45.3	S43 32.2
Vega	80 32.4	N38 48.7
Zuben'ubi	136 54.7	S16 09.1

	SHA ° ′	Mer. Pass. h m
Venus	157 28.3	10 46
Mars	218 25.8	6 45
Jupiter	213 08.2	7 05
Saturn	350 24.7	21 53

Day	UT d h	SUN GHA ° ′	SUN Dec ° ′	MOON GHA ° ′	MOON v ′	MOON Dec ° ′	MOON d ′	MOON HP ′
SATURDAY	31 00	184 05.6	S14 02.3	294 34.5	3.9	N26 15.7	6.0	59.7
	01	199 05.6	03.1	308 57.4	4.1	26 09.7	6.1	59.7
	02	214 05.6	03.9	323 20.5	4.2	26 03.6	6.4	59.7
	03	229 05.7	. . 04.7	337 43.7	4.2	25 57.2	6.5	59.7
	04	244 05.7	05.5	352 06.9	4.3	25 50.7	6.7	59.6
	05	259 05.7	06.3	6 30.2	4.5	25 44.0	6.9	59.6
	06	274 05.7	S14 07.1	20 53.7	4.5	N25 37.1	7.0	59.6
	07	289 05.8	07.9	35 17.2	4.7	25 30.1	7.2	59.6
	08	304 05.8	08.7	49 40.9	4.7	25 22.9	7.4	59.6
	09	319 05.8	. . 09.6	64 04.6	4.9	25 15.5	7.5	59.6
	10	334 05.8	10.4	78 28.5	4.9	25 08.0	7.7	59.5
	11	349 05.9	11.2	92 52.4	5.1	25 00.3	7.8	59.5
	12	4 05.9	S14 12.0	107 16.5	5.1	N24 52.5	8.0	59.5
	13	19 05.9	12.8	121 40.6	5.3	24 44.5	8.2	59.5
	14	34 05.9	13.6	136 04.9	5.4	24 36.3	8.3	59.5
	15	49 06.0	. . 14.4	150 29.3	5.5	24 28.0	8.5	59.4
	16	64 06.0	15.2	164 53.8	5.6	24 19.5	8.6	59.4
	17	79 06.0	16.0	179 18.4	5.7	24 10.9	8.8	59.4
	18	94 06.0	S14 16.8	193 43.1	5.9	N24 02.1	8.9	59.4
	19	109 06.0	17.6	208 08.0	5.9	23 53.2	9.1	59.4
	20	124 06.1	18.4	222 32.9	6.0	23 44.1	9.2	59.4
	21	139 06.1	. . 19.2	236 57.9	6.2	23 34.9	9.3	59.3
	22	154 06.1	20.0	251 23.1	6.3	23 25.6	9.5	59.3
	23	169 06.1	20.8	265 48.4	6.4	23 16.1	9.7	59.3
SUNDAY	1 00	184 06.2	S14 21.6	280 13.8	6.5	N23 06.4	9.7	59.3
	01	199 06.2	22.4	294 39.3	6.6	22 56.7	9.9	59.3
	02	214 06.2	23.2	309 04.9	6.8	22 46.8	10.1	59.2
	03	229 06.2	. . 24.0	323 30.7	6.8	22 36.7	10.1	59.2
	04	244 06.2	24.8	337 56.5	7.0	22 26.6	10.3	59.2
	05	259 06.2	25.6	352 22.5	7.1	22 16.3	10.5	59.2
	06	274 06.3	S14 26.4	6 48.6	7.2	N22 05.8	10.5	59.2
	07	289 06.3	27.2	21 14.8	7.3	21 55.3	10.7	59.1
	08	304 06.3	28.0	35 41.1	7.4	21 44.6	10.8	59.1
	09	319 06.3	. . 28.8	50 07.5	7.6	21 33.8	10.9	59.1
	10	334 06.3	29.6	64 34.1	7.7	21 22.9	11.1	59.1
	11	349 06.3	30.4	79 00.8	7.7	21 11.8	11.1	59.0
	12	4 06.4	S14 31.2	93 27.5	7.9	N21 00.7	11.3	59.0
	13	19 06.4	32.0	107 54.4	8.1	20 49.4	11.4	59.0
	14	34 06.4	32.8	122 21.5	8.1	20 38.0	11.5	59.0
	15	49 06.4	. . 33.6	136 48.6	8.2	20 26.5	11.6	59.0
	16	64 06.4	34.4	151 15.8	8.4	20 14.9	11.7	58.9
	17	79 06.4	35.2	165 43.2	8.4	20 03.2	11.8	58.9
	18	94 06.5	S14 36.0	180 10.6	8.6	N19 51.4	12.0	58.9
	19	109 06.5	36.8	194 38.2	8.7	19 39.4	12.0	58.9
	20	124 06.5	37.6	209 05.9	8.8	19 27.4	12.1	58.9
	21	139 06.5	. . 38.4	223 33.7	8.9	19 15.3	12.3	58.8
	22	154 06.5	39.2	238 01.6	9.1	19 03.0	12.3	58.8
	23	169 06.5	40.0	252 29.7	9.1	18 50.7	12.4	58.8
MONDAY	2 00	184 06.5	S14 40.8	266 57.8	9.2	N18 38.3	12.5	58.8
	01	199 06.5	41.6	281 26.0	9.4	18 25.8	12.7	58.7
	02	214 06.6	42.4	295 54.4	9.5	18 13.1	12.7	58.7
	03	229 06.6	. . 43.2	310 22.9	9.5	18 00.4	12.8	58.7
	04	244 06.6	44.0	324 51.4	9.7	17 47.6	12.8	58.7
	05	259 06.6	44.7	339 20.1	9.8	17 34.8	13.0	58.7
	06	274 06.6	S14 45.5	353 48.9	9.9	N17 21.8	13.1	58.6
	07	289 06.6	46.3	8 17.8	9.9	17 08.7	13.1	58.6
	08	304 06.6	47.1	22 46.7	10.1	16 55.6	13.2	58.6
	09	319 06.6	. . 47.9	37 15.8	10.2	16 42.4	13.3	58.6
	10	334 06.6	48.7	51 45.0	10.3	16 29.1	13.4	58.6
	11	349 06.6	49.5	66 14.3	10.4	16 15.7	13.4	58.5
	12	4 06.6	S14 50.3	80 43.7	10.5	N16 02.3	13.5	58.5
	13	19 06.6	51.1	95 13.2	10.6	15 48.8	13.6	58.5
	14	34 06.7	51.8	109 42.8	10.7	15 35.2	13.7	58.5
	15	49 06.7	. . 52.6	124 12.5	10.8	15 21.5	13.7	58.4
	16	64 06.7	53.4	138 42.3	10.8	15 07.8	13.8	58.4
	17	79 06.7	54.2	153 12.1	11.0	14 54.0	13.9	58.4
	18	94 06.7	S14 55.0	167 42.1	11.1	N14 40.1	13.9	58.4
	19	109 06.7	55.8	182 12.2	11.1	14 26.2	14.0	58.3
	20	124 06.7	56.6	196 42.3	11.3	14 12.2	14.1	58.3
	21	139 06.7	. . 57.3	211 12.6	11.3	13 58.1	14.1	58.3
	22	154 06.7	58.1	225 42.9	11.4	13 44.0	14.2	58.3
	23	169 06.7	58.9	240 13.3	11.5	N13 29.8	14.2	58.3
		SD 16.1	*d* 0.8	SD	16.2	16.1		15.9

Lat. °	Twilight Naut. h m	Twilight Civil h m	Sunrise h m	Moonrise 31 h m	Moonrise 1 h m	Moonrise 2 h m	Moonrise 3 h m
N 72	06 06	07 29	08 57	▭	▭	21 43	24 17
N 70	06 02	07 16	08 30	▭	18 53	22 12	24 28
68	05 58	07 06	08 11	▭	20 03	22 33	24 37
66	05 55	06 57	07 55	▭	20 40	22 49	24 44
64	05 52	06 49	07 42	18 49	21 05	23 03	24 50
62	05 50	06 43	07 31	19 26	21 25	23 14	24 55
60	05 47	06 37	07 22	19 53	21 41	23 24	25 00
N 58	05 45	06 32	07 14	20 14	21 55	23 32	25 04
56	05 43	06 27	07 07	20 31	22 06	23 39	25 07
54	05 41	06 23	07 00	20 45	22 17	23 46	25 11
52	05 39	06 19	06 55	20 57	22 26	23 51	25 14
50	05 37	06 16	06 50	21 08	22 34	23 57	25 16
45	05 33	06 08	06 38	21 31	22 51	24 08	00 08
N 40	05 29	06 01	06 29	21 50	23 05	24 17	00 17
35	05 25	05 55	06 21	22 05	23 16	24 25	00 25
30	05 21	05 49	06 14	22 18	23 26	24 32	00 32
20	05 13	05 39	06 01	22 41	23 44	24 44	00 44
N 10	05 04	05 29	05 50	23 00	23 59	24 54	00 54
0	04 54	05 19	05 40	23 18	24 13	00 13	01 04
S 10	04 43	05 08	05 30	23 36	24 27	00 27	01 13
20	04 28	04 55	05 18	23 55	24 42	00 42	01 24
30	04 10	04 40	05 05	24 17	00 17	00 59	01 35
35	03 59	04 31	04 58	24 30	00 30	01 09	01 42
40	03 45	04 20	04 49	00 01	00 45	01 20	01 49
45	03 27	04 07	04 39	00 22	01 03	01 34	01 58
S 50	03 04	03 50	04 27	00 49	01 24	01 50	02 09
52	02 53	03 42	04 21	01 02	01 35	01 57	02 14
54	02 40	03 34	04 14	01 16	01 46	02 05	02 19
56	02 24	03 24	04 07	01 34	01 59	02 15	02 25
58	02 05	03 12	03 59	01 55	02 14	02 25	02 31
S 60	01 40	02 58	03 50	02 21	02 32	02 37	02 39

Lat. °	Sunset h m	Twilight Civil h m	Twilight Naut. h m	Moonset 31 h m	Moonset 1 h m	Moonset 2 h m	Moonset 3 h m
N 72	14 29	15 56	17 19	▭	▭	16 26	15 32
N 70	14 55	16 10	17 24	▭	17 26	15 55	15 19
68	15 15	16 20	17 27	▭	16 14	15 32	15 07
66	15 31	16 29	17 31	▭	15 37	15 14	14 58
64	15 44	16 37	17 34	15 29	15 10	14 59	14 50
62	15 55	16 43	17 36	14 51	14 49	14 46	14 43
60	16 04	16 49	17 39	14 24	14 32	14 35	14 37
N 58	16 12	16 54	17 41	14 02	14 17	14 26	14 32
56	16 19	16 59	17 43	13 45	14 05	14 18	14 27
54	16 26	17 03	17 45	13 30	13 54	14 10	14 23
52	16 32	17 07	17 47	13 17	13 44	14 04	14 19
50	16 37	17 11	17 49	13 05	13 36	13 58	14 15
45	16 48	17 19	17 54	12 41	13 17	13 45	14 07
N 40	16 58	17 26	17 58	12 22	13 02	13 34	14 01
35	17 06	17 32	18 02	12 06	12 49	13 25	13 55
30	17 13	17 38	18 06	11 52	12 38	13 16	13 50
20	17 26	17 48	18 14	11 28	12 18	13 02	13 41
N 10	17 37	17 58	18 23	11 07	12 01	12 50	13 34
0	17 47	18 08	18 33	10 47	11 45	12 38	13 26
S 10	17 58	18 19	18 45	10 28	11 29	12 26	13 19
20	18 09	18 32	18 59	10 06	11 11	12 13	13 11
30	18 22	18 47	19 18	09 42	10 51	11 58	13 02
35	18 30	18 57	19 29	09 27	10 39	11 49	12 57
40	18 39	19 08	19 43	09 10	10 25	11 39	12 51
45	18 49	19 21	20 01	08 49	10 09	11 28	12 43
S 50	19 02	19 38	20 24	08 24	09 49	11 13	12 35
52	19 08	19 46	20 36	08 11	09 39	11 07	12 31
54	19 14	19 55	20 49	07 56	09 28	10 59	12 27
56	19 21	20 05	21 06	07 40	09 16	10 51	12 22
58	19 29	20 17	21 25	07 19	09 01	10 41	12 16
S 60	19 39	20 31	21 51	06 53	08 44	10 30	12 10

Day	SUN Eqn. of Time 00^h	SUN Eqn. of Time 12^h	SUN Mer. Pass.	MOON Mer. Pass. Upper	MOON Mer. Pass. Lower	MOON Age	MOON Phase
d	m s	m s	h m	h m	h m	d %	
31	16 22	16 23	11 44	04 33	17 03	21 65	◑
1	16 25	16 25	11 44	05 32	17 59	22 54	
2	16 26	16 27	11 44	06 26	18 51	23 43	

UT	ARIES	VENUS −4·4		MARS +0·8		JUPITER −2·0		SATURN +0·4		STARS		
d h	GHA	GHA	Dec	GHA	Dec	GHA	Dec	GHA	Dec	Name	SHA	Dec
	° ′	° ′	° ′	° ′	° ′	° ′	° ′	° ′	° ′		° ′	° ′
3 00	42 16.3	200 26.8	S13 51.9	259 41.8	N16 29.5	255 10.5	N13 59.5	32 47.9	N 1 10.0	Acamar	315 10.2	S40 11.7
01	57 18.7	215 30.1	50.9	274 43.0	29.1	270 12.6	59.4	47 50.5	10.0	Achernar	335 18.5	S57 06.0
02	72 21.2	230 33.4	49.9	289 44.2	28.8	285 14.8	59.3	62 53.1	09.9	Acrux	172 59.0	S63 14.7
03	87 23.7	245 36.6	. . 48.9	304 45.4	. . 28.4	300 17.0	. . 59.2	77 55.7	. . 09.9	Adhara	255 04.5	S29 00.3
04	102 26.1	260 39.9	48.0	319 46.6	28.1	315 19.2	59.1	92 58.3	09.8	Aldebaran	290 37.6	N16 33.9
05	117 28.6	275 43.1	47.0	334 47.9	27.8	330 21.4	59.0	108 00.9	09.8			
06	132 31.0	290 46.3	S13 46.0	349 49.1	N16 27.4	345 23.5	N13 58.9	123 03.5	N 1 09.7	Alioth	166 12.2	N55 48.7
07	147 33.5	305 49.6	45.0	4 50.3	27.1	0 25.7	58.8	138 06.2	09.6	Alkaid	152 51.3	N49 10.7
T 08	162 36.0	320 52.8	44.1	19 51.5	26.7	15 27.9	58.8	153 08.8	09.6	Alnair	27 30.9	S46 50.0
U 09	177 38.4	335 56.1	. . 43.1	34 52.8	. . 26.4	30 30.1	. . 58.7	168 11.4	. . 09.5	Alnilam	275 36.0	S 1 11.0
E 10	192 40.9	350 59.3	42.1	49 54.0	26.0	45 32.3	58.6	183 14.0	09.5	Alphard	217 46.3	S 8 46.4
S 11	207 43.4	6 02.5	41.2	64 55.2	25.7	60 34.4	58.5	198 16.6	09.4			
D 12	222 45.8	21 05.7	S13 40.2	79 56.4	N16 25.4	75 36.6	N13 58.4	213 19.2	N 1 09.4	Alphecca	126 02.8	N26 37.5
A 13	237 48.3	36 08.9	39.3	94 57.6	25.0	90 38.8	58.3	228 21.8	09.3	Alpheratz	357 33.0	N29 14.6
Y 14	252 50.8	51 12.2	38.3	109 58.9	24.7	105 41.0	58.2	243 24.4	09.3	Altair	61 58.6	N 8 56.5
15	267 53.2	66 15.4	. . 37.3	125 00.1	. . 24.3	120 43.2	. . 58.1	258 27.0	. . 09.2	Ankaa	353 05.3	S42 09.6
16	282 55.7	81 18.6	36.4	140 01.3	24.0	135 45.3	58.0	273 29.6	09.2	Antares	112 14.3	S26 29.5
17	297 58.2	96 21.8	35.4	155 02.5	23.7	150 47.5	58.0	288 32.2	09.1			
18	313 00.6	111 25.0	S13 34.5	170 03.8	N16 23.3	165 49.7	N13 57.9	303 34.8	N 1 09.1	Arcturus	145 46.9	N19 02.6
19	328 03.1	126 28.2	33.5	185 05.0	23.0	180 51.9	57.8	318 37.4	09.0	Atria	107 07.7	S69 04.6
20	343 05.5	141 31.4	32.5	200 06.2	22.6	195 54.1	57.7	333 40.0	09.0	Avior	234 14.0	S59 35.4
21	358 08.0	156 34.6	. . 31.6	215 07.4	. . 22.3	210 56.2	. . 57.6	348 42.6	. . 08.9	Bellatrix	278 21.0	N 6 22.5
22	13 10.5	171 37.7	30.6	230 08.7	21.9	225 58.4	57.5	3 45.2	08.9	Betelgeuse	270 50.2	N 7 24.8
23	28 12.9	186 40.9	29.7	245 09.9	21.6	241 00.6	57.4	18 47.8	08.8			
4 00	43 15.4	201 44.1	S13 28.7	260 11.1	N16 21.3	256 02.8	N13 57.3	33 50.4	N 1 08.7	Canopus	263 51.4	S52 42.3
01	58 17.9	216 47.3	27.8	275 12.3	20.9	271 05.0	57.3	48 53.0	08.7	Capella	280 19.3	N46 01.4
02	73 20.3	231 50.4	26.8	290 13.6	20.6	286 07.2	57.2	63 55.6	08.6	Deneb	49 24.8	N45 22.9
03	88 22.8	246 53.6	. . 25.9	305 14.8	. . 20.2	301 09.3	. . 57.1	78 58.2	. . 08.6	Denebola	182 23.7	N14 25.3
04	103 25.3	261 56.8	24.9	320 16.0	19.9	316 11.5	57.0	94 00.8	08.5	Diphda	348 45.5	S17 50.3
05	118 27.7	276 59.9	24.0	335 17.3	19.6	331 13.7	56.9	109 03.4	08.5			
06	133 30.2	292 03.1	S13 23.0	350 18.5	N16 19.2	346 15.9	N13 56.8	124 06.0	N 1 08.4	Dubhe	193 39.6	N61 36.1
W 07	148 32.6	307 06.2	22.1	5 19.7	18.9	1 18.1	56.7	139 08.6	08.4	Elnath	277 59.7	N28 37.8
E 08	163 35.1	322 09.4	21.2	20 21.0	18.5	16 20.3	56.6	154 11.2	08.3	Eltanin	90 41.9	N51 29.3
D 09	178 37.6	337 12.5	. . 20.2	35 22.2	. . 18.2	31 22.5	. . 56.6	169 13.9	. . 08.3	Enif	33 37.3	N10 00.1
N 10	193 40.0	352 15.7	19.3	50 23.4	17.8	46 24.6	56.5	184 16.5	08.2	Fomalhaut	15 12.7	S29 28.8
E 11	208 42.5	7 18.8	18.3	65 24.6	17.5	61 26.8	56.4	199 19.1	08.2			
S 12	223 45.0	22 21.9	S13 17.4	80 25.9	N16 17.2	76 29.0	N13 56.3	214 21.7	N 1 08.1	Gacrux	171 50.5	S57 15.6
D 13	238 47.4	37 25.1	16.5	95 27.1	16.8	91 31.2	56.2	229 24.3	08.1	Gienah	175 42.3	S17 41.4
A 14	253 49.9	52 28.2	15.5	110 28.3	16.5	106 33.4	56.1	244 26.9	08.0	Hadar	148 34.5	S60 30.1
Y 15	268 52.4	67 31.3	. . 14.6	125 29.6	. . 16.1	121 35.6	. . 56.0	259 29.5	. . 08.0	Hamal	327 49.2	N23 35.5
16	283 54.8	82 34.4	13.7	140 30.8	15.8	136 37.8	56.0	274 32.1	07.9	Kaus Aust.	83 30.8	S34 22.3
17	298 57.3	97 37.6	12.7	155 32.0	15.5	151 40.0	55.9	289 34.7	07.9			
18	313 59.8	112 40.7	S13 11.8	170 33.3	N16 15.1	166 42.1	N13 55.8	304 37.3	N 1 07.8	Kochab	137 21.0	N74 02.6
19	329 02.2	127 43.8	10.9	185 34.5	14.8	181 44.3	55.7	319 39.9	07.8	Markab	13 28.2	N15 21.2
20	344 04.7	142 46.9	10.0	200 35.8	14.4	196 46.5	55.6	334 42.5	07.7	Menkar	314 04.3	N 4 11.8
21	359 07.1	157 50.0	. . 09.0	215 37.0	. . 14.1	211 48.7	. . 55.5	349 45.1	. . 07.7	Menkent	147 56.3	S36 30.0
22	14 09.6	172 53.1	08.1	230 38.2	13.8	226 50.9	55.4	4 47.7	07.6	Miaplacidus	221 38.0	S69 49.3
23	29 12.1	187 56.2	07.2	245 39.5	13.4	241 53.1	55.4	19 50.3	07.6			
5 00	44 14.5	202 59.2	S13 06.3	260 40.7	N16 13.1	256 55.3	N13 55.3	34 52.9	N 1 07.5	Mirfak	308 25.6	N49 57.4
01	59 17.0	218 02.3	05.3	275 41.9	12.7	271 57.5	55.2	49 55.5	07.4	Nunki	75 46.1	S26 15.8
02	74 19.5	233 05.4	04.4	290 43.2	12.4	286 59.6	55.1	64 58.1	07.4	Peacock	53 03.5	S56 39.1
03	89 21.9	248 08.5	. . 03.5	305 44.4	. . 12.0	302 01.8	. . 55.0	80 00.7	. . 07.3	Pollux	243 15.4	N27 57.6
04	104 24.4	263 11.6	02.6	320 45.7	11.7	317 04.0	54.9	95 03.3	07.3	Procyon	244 49.2	N 5 09.4
05	119 26.9	278 14.6	01.7	335 46.9	11.4	332 06.2	54.8	110 05.9	07.2			
06	134 29.3	293 17.7	S13 00.8	350 48.1	N16 11.0	347 08.4	N13 54.8	125 08.5	N 1 07.2	Rasalhague	95 57.4	N12 32.6
07	149 31.8	308 20.8	12 59.8	5 49.4	10.7	2 10.6	54.7	140 11.1	07.1	Regulus	207 33.0	N11 50.1
T 08	164 34.3	323 23.8	58.9	20 50.6	10.3	17 12.8	54.6	155 13.7	07.1	Rigel	281 02.2	S 8 10.1
H 09	179 36.7	338 26.9	. . 58.0	35 51.9	. . 10.0	32 15.0	. . 54.5	170 16.3	. . 07.0	Rigil Kent.	139 38.9	S60 56.7
U 10	194 39.2	353 29.9	57.1	50 53.1	09.7	47 17.2	54.4	185 18.9	07.0	Sabik	102 01.4	S15 45.4
R 11	209 41.6	8 33.0	56.2	65 54.3	09.3	62 19.4	54.3	200 21.5	06.9			
S 12	224 44.1	23 36.0	S12 55.3	80 55.6	N16 09.0	77 21.6	N13 54.3	215 24.1	N 1 06.9	Schedar	349 28.8	N56 41.3
D 13	239 46.6	38 39.1	54.4	95 56.8	08.6	92 23.8	54.2	230 26.7	06.8	Shaula	96 08.7	S37 07.4
A 14	254 49.0	53 42.1	53.5	110 58.1	08.3	107 25.9	54.1	245 29.3	06.8	Sirius	258 24.7	S16 45.0
Y 15	269 51.5	68 45.1	. . 52.6	125 59.3	. . 08.0	122 28.1	. . 54.0	260 31.9	. . 06.7	Spica	158 21.0	S11 18.0
16	284 54.0	83 48.1	51.7	141 00.6	07.6	137 30.3	53.9	275 34.5	06.7	Suhail	222 45.2	S43 32.2
17	299 56.4	98 51.2	50.8	156 01.8	07.3	152 32.5	53.8	290 37.1	06.6			
18	314 58.9	113 54.2	S12 49.9	171 03.1	N16 06.9	167 34.7	N13 53.7	305 39.7	N 1 06.6	Vega	80 32.5	N38 48.7
19	330 01.4	128 57.2	49.0	186 04.3	06.6	182 36.9	53.7	320 42.3	06.5	Zuben'ubi	136 54.7	S16 09.1
20	345 03.8	144 00.2	48.1	201 05.5	06.3	197 39.1	53.6	335 44.9	06.5		SHA	Mer. Pass.
21	0 06.3	159 03.2	. . 47.2	216 06.8	. . 05.9	212 41.3	. . 53.5	350 47.5	. . 06.4		° ′	h m
22	15 08.7	174 06.2	46.3	231 08.0	05.6	227 43.5	53.4	5 50.1	06.4	Venus	158 28.7	10 31
23	30 11.2	189 09.2	45.4	246 09.3	05.2	242 45.7	53.3	20 52.7	06.3	Mars	216 55.7	6 39
	h m											
Mer. Pass.	21 03.5	*v* 3.1	*d* 0.9	*v* 1.2	*d* 0.3	*v* 2.2	*d* 0.1	*v* 2.6	*d* 0.1	Jupiter	212 47.4	6 55
										Saturn	350 35.0	21 41

Day	UT (d h)	SUN GHA (° ′)	SUN Dec (° ′)	MOON GHA (° ′)	MOON v (′)	MOON Dec (° ′)	MOON d (′)	MOON HP (′)
TUESDAY	3 00	184 06.7	S14 59.7	254 43.8	11.6	N13 15.6	14.3	58.2
	01	199 06.7	15 00.5	269 14.4	11.7	13 01.3	14.3	58.2
	02	214 06.7	01.3	283 45.1	11.8	12 47.0	14.4	58.2
	03	229 06.7	. . 02.0	298 15.9	11.8	12 32.6	14.5	58.2
	04	244 06.7	02.8	312 46.7	11.9	12 18.1	14.5	58.1
	05	259 06.7	03.6	327 17.6	12.1	12 03.6	14.5	58.1
	06	274 06.7	S15 04.4	341 48.7	12.0	N11 49.1	14.6	58.1
	07	289 06.7	05.2	356 19.7	12.2	11 34.5	14.6	58.1
	08	304 06.7	05.9	10 50.9	12.2	11 19.9	14.7	58.1
	09	319 06.7	. . 06.7	25 22.1	12.3	11 05.2	14.8	58.0
	10	334 06.7	07.5	39 53.4	12.4	10 50.4	14.7	58.0
	11	349 06.7	08.3	54 24.8	12.5	10 35.7	14.8	58.0
	12	4 06.7	S15 09.1	68 56.3	12.5	N10 20.9	14.9	58.0
	13	19 06.7	09.8	83 27.8	12.6	10 06.0	14.8	57.9
	14	34 06.7	10.6	97 59.4	12.7	9 51.2	15.0	57.9
	15	49 06.7	. . 11.4	112 31.1	12.7	9 36.2	14.9	57.9
	16	64 06.7	12.2	127 02.8	12.8	9 21.3	15.0	57.9
	17	79 06.7	12.9	141 34.6	12.9	9 06.3	15.0	57.9
	18	94 06.7	S15 13.7	156 06.5	12.9	N 8 51.3	15.0	57.8
	19	109 06.7	14.5	170 38.4	13.0	8 36.3	15.1	57.8
	20	124 06.7	15.3	185 10.4	13.1	8 21.2	15.1	57.8
	21	139 06.7	. . 16.0	199 42.5	13.1	8 06.1	15.1	57.8
	22	154 06.7	16.8	214 14.6	13.2	7 51.0	15.2	57.7
	23	169 06.7	17.6	228 46.8	13.2	7 35.8	15.2	57.7
WEDNESDAY	4 00	184 06.7	S15 18.4	243 19.0	13.3	N 7 20.6	15.2	57.7
	01	199 06.7	19.1	257 51.3	13.3	7 05.4	15.2	57.7
	02	214 06.6	19.9	272 23.6	13.4	6 50.2	15.2	57.7
	03	229 06.6	. . 20.7	286 56.0	13.4	6 35.0	15.3	57.6
	04	244 06.6	21.4	301 28.4	13.5	6 19.7	15.3	57.6
	05	259 06.6	22.2	316 00.9	13.6	6 04.4	15.3	57.6
	06	274 06.6	S15 23.0	330 33.5	13.6	N 5 49.1	15.3	57.6
	07	289 06.6	23.8	345 06.1	13.6	5 33.8	15.3	57.5
	08	304 06.6	24.5	359 38.7	13.7	5 18.5	15.3	57.5
	09	319 06.6	. . 25.3	14 11.4	13.7	5 03.2	15.4	57.5
	10	334 06.6	26.1	28 44.1	13.8	4 47.8	15.3	57.5
	11	349 06.6	26.8	43 16.9	13.8	4 32.5	15.4	57.5
	12	4 06.6	S15 27.6	57 49.7	13.9	N 4 17.1	15.4	57.4
	13	19 06.6	28.4	72 22.6	13.9	4 01.7	15.4	57.4
	14	34 06.5	29.1	86 55.5	13.9	3 46.3	15.4	57.4
	15	49 06.5	. . 29.9	101 28.4	14.0	3 30.9	15.4	57.4
	16	64 06.5	30.7	116 01.4	14.0	3 15.5	15.3	57.3
	17	79 06.5	31.4	130 34.4	14.0	3 00.2	15.4	57.3
	18	94 06.5	S15 32.2	145 07.4	14.1	N 2 44.8	15.4	57.3
	19	109 06.5	33.0	159 40.5	14.1	2 29.4	15.4	57.3
	20	124 06.5	33.7	174 13.6	14.1	2 14.0	15.4	57.3
	21	139 06.5	. . 34.5	188 46.7	14.2	1 58.6	15.4	57.2
	22	154 06.4	35.3	203 19.9	14.1	1 43.2	15.4	57.2
	23	169 06.4	36.0	217 53.0	14.3	1 27.8	15.4	57.2
THURSDAY	5 00	184 06.4	S15 36.8	232 26.3	14.2	N 1 12.4	15.4	57.2
	01	199 06.4	37.5	246 59.5	14.3	0 57.0	15.4	57.1
	02	214 06.4	38.3	261 32.8	14.2	0 41.6	15.4	57.1
	03	229 06.4	. . 39.1	276 06.0	14.4	0 26.2	15.3	57.1
	04	244 06.3	39.8	290 39.4	14.3	N 0 10.9	15.4	57.1
	05	259 06.3	40.6	305 12.7	14.3	S 0 04.5	15.3	57.1
	06	274 06.3	S15 41.3	319 46.0	14.4	S 0 19.8	15.3	57.0
	07	289 06.3	42.1	334 19.4	14.4	0 35.1	15.3	57.0
	08	304 06.3	42.9	348 52.8	14.4	0 50.4	15.3	57.0
	09	319 06.3	. . 43.6	3 26.2	14.4	1 05.7	15.3	57.0
	10	334 06.2	44.4	17 59.6	14.4	1 21.0	15.3	56.9
	11	349 06.2	45.1	32 33.0	14.5	1 36.3	15.3	56.9
	12	4 06.2	S15 45.9	47 06.5	14.4	S 1 51.6	15.2	56.9
	13	19 06.2	46.6	61 39.9	14.5	2 06.8	15.2	56.9
	14	34 06.2	47.4	76 13.4	14.4	2 22.0	15.2	56.9
	15	49 06.1	. . 48.2	90 46.8	14.5	2 37.2	15.2	56.8
	16	64 06.1	48.9	105 20.3	14.5	2 52.4	15.1	56.8
	17	79 06.1	49.7	119 53.8	14.5	3 07.5	15.1	56.8
	18	94 06.1	S15 50.4	134 27.3	14.5	S 3 22.6	15.1	56.8
	19	109 06.1	51.2	149 00.8	14.5	3 37.7	15.1	56.8
	20	124 06.0	51.9	163 34.3	14.4	3 52.8	15.1	56.7
	21	139 06.0	. . 52.7	178 07.7	14.5	4 07.9	15.0	56.7
	22	154 06.0	53.4	192 41.2	14.5	4 22.9	15.0	56.7
	23	169 06.0	54.2	207 14.7	14.5	S 4 37.9	14.9	56.7
		SD 16.2	*d* 0.8	SD 15.8		15.6		15.5

Lat. (°)	Twilight Naut. (h m)	Twilight Civil (h m)	Sunrise (h m)	Moonrise 3 (h m)	Moonrise 4 (h m)	Moonrise 5 (h m)	Moonrise 6 (h m)
N 72	06 18	07 43	09 16	24 17	00 17	02 29	04 39
N 70	06 12	07 28	08 46	24 28	00 28	02 30	04 29
68	06 08	07 16	08 23	24 37	00 37	02 30	04 22
66	06 04	07 06	08 06	24 44	00 44	02 31	04 16
64	06 00	06 58	07 52	24 50	00 50	02 31	04 10
62	05 57	06 50	07 40	24 55	00 55	02 32	04 06
60	05 54	06 44	07 30	25 00	01 00	02 32	04 02
N 58	05 51	06 38	07 21	25 04	01 04	02 32	03 59
56	05 49	06 33	07 13	25 07	01 07	02 32	03 56
54	05 46	06 28	07 06	25 11	01 11	02 33	03 53
52	05 44	06 24	07 00	25 14	01 14	02 33	03 50
50	05 42	06 20	06 55	25 16	01 16	02 33	03 48
45	05 37	06 12	06 42	00 08	01 22	02 33	03 43
N 40	05 32	06 04	06 32	00 17	01 27	02 34	03 39
35	05 27	05 57	06 24	00 25	01 31	02 34	03 36
30	05 23	05 51	06 16	00 32	01 34	02 34	03 33
20	05 14	05 40	06 03	00 44	01 40	02 35	03 28
N 10	05 04	05 29	05 51	00 54	01 46	02 35	03 23
0	04 54	05 19	05 40	01 04	01 51	02 35	03 19
S 10	04 42	05 07	05 29	01 13	01 56	02 36	03 15
20	04 27	04 54	05 17	01 24	02 01	02 36	03 11
30	04 07	04 38	05 03	01 35	02 07	02 37	03 06
35	03 55	04 28	04 55	01 42	02 11	02 37	03 03
40	03 40	04 16	04 46	01 49	02 14	02 37	03 00
45	03 22	04 02	04 35	01 58	02 19	02 38	02 56
S 50	02 58	03 45	04 21	02 09	02 24	02 38	02 52
52	02 45	03 36	04 15	02 14	02 27	02 38	02 50
54	02 31	03 27	04 08	02 19	02 30	02 39	02 48
56	02 14	03 16	04 01	02 25	02 32	02 39	02 45
58	01 53	03 03	03 52	02 31	02 36	02 39	02 43
S 60	01 24	02 48	03 42	02 39	02 39	02 40	02 40

Lat. (°)	Sunset (h m)	Twilight Civil (h m)	Twilight Naut. (h m)	Moonset 3 (h m)	Moonset 4 (h m)	Moonset 5 (h m)	Moonset 6 (h m)
N 72	14 10	15 43	17 08	15 32	14 56	14 24	13 49
N 70	14 40	15 58	17 13	15 19	14 52	14 27	14 01
68	15 03	16 10	17 18	15 07	14 48	14 30	14 11
66	15 20	16 20	17 22	14 58	14 45	14 32	14 20
64	15 34	16 28	17 26	14 50	14 42	14 34	14 27
62	15 46	16 36	17 29	14 43	14 40	14 36	14 33
60	15 56	16 42	17 32	14 37	14 38	14 38	14 38
N 58	16 05	16 48	17 35	14 32	14 36	14 39	14 43
56	16 13	16 53	17 38	14 27	14 34	14 40	14 47
54	16 20	16 58	17 40	14 23	14 32	14 41	14 51
52	16 26	17 02	17 42	14 19	14 31	14 43	14 54
50	16 32	17 06	17 45	14 15	14 30	14 43	14 57
45	16 44	17 15	17 50	14 07	14 27	14 46	15 04
N 40	16 54	17 23	17 55	14 01	14 25	14 47	15 10
35	17 03	17 29	17 59	13 55	14 23	14 49	15 15
30	17 11	17 36	18 04	13 50	14 21	14 50	15 19
20	17 24	17 47	18 13	13 41	14 18	14 52	15 27
N 10	17 36	17 58	18 23	13 34	14 15	14 54	15 34
0	17 47	18 08	18 33	13 26	14 12	14 56	15 40
S 10	17 58	18 20	18 46	13 19	14 09	14 58	15 46
20	18 11	18 34	19 01	13 11	14 06	15 00	15 53
30	18 25	18 50	19 20	13 02	14 03	15 02	16 01
35	18 33	19 00	19 33	12 57	14 01	15 04	16 06
40	18 42	19 12	19 48	12 51	13 59	15 05	16 11
45	18 53	19 26	20 06	12 43	13 56	15 07	16 17
S 50	19 07	19 44	20 31	12 35	13 53	15 09	16 24
52	19 13	19 52	20 44	12 31	13 52	15 10	16 27
54	19 20	20 02	20 58	12 27	13 50	15 11	16 31
56	19 28	20 13	21 16	12 22	13 48	15 12	16 35
58	19 37	20 26	21 38	12 16	13 46	15 14	16 40
S 60	19 47	20 41	22 08	12 10	13 44	15 15	16 45

Day (d)	SUN Eqn. of Time 00^h (m s)	SUN Eqn. of Time 12^h (m s)	SUN Mer. Pass. (h m)	MOON Mer. Pass. Upper (h m)	MOON Mer. Pass. Lower (h m)	MOON Age (d)	MOON Phase (%)
3	16 27	16 27	11 44	07 15	19 39	24	32
4	16 27	16 26	11 44	08 01	20 24	25	23
5	16 26	16 25	11 44	08 46	21 08	26	14

UT d h	ARIES GHA	VENUS −4·6 GHA	VENUS Dec	MARS +0·8 GHA	MARS Dec	JUPITER −2·0 GHA	JUPITER Dec	SATURN +0·4 GHA	SATURN Dec
	° ′	° ′	° ′	° ′	° ′	° ′	° ′	° ′	° ′
6 00 (FRIDAY)	45 13.7	204 12.2	S12 44.5	261 10.5	N16 04.9	257 47.9	N13 53.2	35 55.3	N 1 06.3
01	60 16.1	219 15.2	43.7	276 11.8	04.6	272 50.1	53.2	50 57.9	06.2
02	75 18.6	234 18.2	42.8	291 13.0	04.2	287 52.3	53.1	66 00.4	06.2
03	90 21.1	249 21.2	. . 41.9	306 14.3	. . 03.9	302 54.5	. . 53.0	81 03.0	. . 06.1
04	105 23.5	264 24.2	41.0	321 15.5	03.5	317 56.7	52.9	96 05.6	06.1
05	120 26.0	279 27.2	40.1	336 16.8	03.2	332 58.9	52.8	111 08.2	06.0
06	135 28.5	294 30.1	S12 39.2	351 18.0	N16 02.9	348 01.1	N13 52.7	126 10.8	N 1 06.0
07	150 30.9	309 33.1	38.4	6 19.3	02.5	3 03.3	52.7	141 13.4	05.9
08	165 33.4	324 36.1	37.5	21 20.5	02.2	18 05.5	52.6	156 16.0	05.9
09	180 35.9	339 39.0	. . 36.6	36 21.8	. . 01.8	33 07.7	. . 52.5	171 18.6	. . 05.8
10	195 38.3	354 42.0	35.7	51 23.0	01.5	48 09.9	52.4	186 21.2	05.8
11	210 40.8	9 44.9	34.9	66 24.3	01.2	63 12.0	52.3	201 23.8	05.7
12	225 43.2	24 47.9	S12 34.0	81 25.5	N16 00.8	78 14.2	N13 52.2	216 26.4	N 1 05.7
13	240 45.7	39 50.8	33.1	96 26.8	00.5	93 16.4	52.2	231 29.0	05.6
14	255 48.2	54 53.8	32.3	111 28.0	16 00.1	108 18.6	52.1	246 31.6	05.6
15	270 50.6	69 56.7	. . 31.4	126 29.3	15 59.8	123 20.8	. . 52.0	261 34.2	. . 05.5
16	285 53.1	84 59.6	30.5	141 30.6	59.5	138 23.0	51.9	276 36.8	05.5
17	300 55.6	100 02.6	29.7	156 31.8	59.1	153 25.2	51.8	291 39.4	05.4
18	315 58.0	115 05.5	S12 28.8	171 33.1	N15 58.8	168 27.4	N13 51.8	306 42.0	N 1 05.4
19	331 00.5	130 08.4	28.0	186 34.3	58.4	183 29.6	51.7	321 44.6	05.4
20	346 03.0	145 11.3	27.1	201 35.6	58.1	198 31.8	51.6	336 47.2	05.3
21	1 05.4	160 14.3	. . 26.2	216 36.8	. . 57.8	213 34.0	. . 51.5	351 49.8	. . 05.3
22	16 07.9	175 17.2	25.4	231 38.1	57.4	228 36.2	51.4	6 52.4	05.2
23	31 10.3	190 20.1	24.5	246 39.4	57.1	243 38.4	51.3	21 55.0	05.2
7 00 (SATURDAY)	46 12.8	205 23.0	S12 23.7	261 40.6	N15 56.7	258 40.6	N13 51.3	36 57.6	N 1 05.1
01	61 15.3	220 25.9	22.8	276 41.9	56.4	273 42.8	51.2	52 00.2	05.1
02	76 17.7	235 28.8	22.0	291 43.1	56.1	288 45.1	51.1	67 02.8	05.0
03	91 20.2	250 31.7	. . 21.1	306 44.4	. . 55.7	303 47.3	. . 51.0	82 05.4	. . 05.0
04	106 22.7	265 34.6	20.3	321 45.6	55.4	318 49.5	50.9	97 07.9	04.9
05	121 25.1	280 37.4	19.4	336 46.9	55.0	333 51.7	50.9	112 10.5	04.9
06	136 27.6	295 40.3	S12 18.6	351 48.2	N15 54.7	348 53.9	N13 50.8	127 13.1	N 1 04.8
07	151 30.1	310 43.2	17.8	6 49.4	54.4	3 56.1	50.7	142 15.7	04.8
08	166 32.5	325 46.1	16.9	21 50.7	54.0	18 58.3	50.6	157 18.3	04.7
09	181 35.0	340 48.9	. . 16.1	36 52.0	. . 53.7	34 00.5	. . 50.5	172 20.9	. . 04.7
10	196 37.5	355 51.8	15.3	51 53.2	53.4	49 02.7	50.5	187 23.5	04.6
11	211 39.9	10 54.7	14.4	66 54.5	53.0	64 04.9	50.4	202 26.1	04.6
12	226 42.4	25 57.5	S12 13.6	81 55.7	N15 52.7	79 07.1	N13 50.3	217 28.7	N 1 04.5
13	241 44.8	41 00.4	12.8	96 57.0	52.3	94 09.3	50.2	232 31.3	04.5
14	256 47.3	56 03.2	11.9	111 58.3	52.0	109 11.5	50.1	247 33.9	04.4
15	271 49.8	71 06.1	. . 11.1	126 59.5	. . 51.7	124 13.7	. . 50.1	262 36.5	. . 04.4
16	286 52.2	86 08.9	10.3	142 00.8	51.3	139 15.9	50.0	277 39.1	04.3
17	301 54.7	101 11.7	09.5	157 02.1	51.0	154 18.1	49.9	292 41.7	04.3
18	316 57.2	116 14.6	S12 08.6	172 03.3	N15 50.6	169 20.3	N13 49.8	307 44.3	N 1 04.2
19	331 59.6	131 17.4	07.8	187 04.6	50.3	184 22.5	49.7	322 46.8	04.2
20	347 02.1	146 20.2	07.0	202 05.9	50.0	199 24.7	49.7	337 49.4	04.2
21	2 04.6	161 23.1	. . 06.2	217 07.1	. . 49.6	214 26.9	. . 49.6	352 52.0	. . 04.1
22	17 07.0	176 25.9	05.4	232 08.4	49.3	229 29.1	49.5	7 54.6	04.1
23	32 09.5	191 28.7	04.5	247 09.7	49.0	244 31.3	49.4	22 57.2	04.0
8 00 (SUNDAY)	47 12.0	206 31.5	S12 03.7	262 10.9	N15 48.6	259 33.6	N13 49.3	37 59.8	N 1 04.0
01	62 14.4	221 34.3	02.9	277 12.2	48.3	274 35.8	49.3	53 02.4	03.9
02	77 16.9	236 37.1	02.1	292 13.5	47.9	289 38.0	49.2	68 05.0	03.9
03	92 19.3	251 39.9	. . 01.3	307 14.7	. . 47.6	304 40.2	. . 49.1	83 07.6	. . 03.8
04	107 21.8	266 42.7	12 00.5	322 16.0	47.3	319 42.4	49.0	98 10.2	03.8
05	122 24.3	281 45.5	11 59.7	337 17.3	46.9	334 44.6	48.9	113 12.8	03.7
06	137 26.7	296 48.3	S11 58.9	352 18.6	N15 46.6	349 46.8	N13 48.9	128 15.4	N 1 03.7
07	152 29.2	311 51.0	58.1	7 19.8	46.2	4 49.0	48.8	143 18.0	03.6
08	167 31.7	326 53.8	57.3	22 21.1	45.9	19 51.2	48.7	158 20.5	03.6
09	182 34.1	341 56.6	. . 56.5	37 22.4	. . 45.6	34 53.4	. . 48.6	173 23.1	. . 03.5
10	197 36.6	356 59.4	55.7	52 23.7	45.2	49 55.6	48.5	188 25.7	03.5
11	212 39.1	12 02.1	54.9	67 24.9	44.9	64 57.9	48.5	203 28.3	03.4
12	227 41.5	27 04.9	S11 54.1	82 26.2	N15 44.6	80 00.1	N13 48.4	218 30.9	N 1 03.4
13	242 44.0	42 07.7	53.3	97 27.5	44.2	95 02.3	48.3	233 33.5	03.4
14	257 46.4	57 10.4	52.5	112 28.7	43.9	110 04.5	48.2	248 36.1	03.3
15	272 48.9	72 13.2	. . 51.8	127 30.0	. . 43.5	125 06.7	. . 48.2	263 38.7	. . 03.3
16	287 51.4	87 15.9	51.0	142 31.3	43.2	140 08.9	48.1	278 41.3	03.2
17	302 53.8	102 18.6	50.2	157 32.6	42.9	155 11.1	48.0	293 43.9	03.2
18	317 56.3	117 21.4	S11 49.4	172 33.9	N15 42.5	170 13.3	N13 47.9	308 46.4	N 1 03.1
19	332 58.8	132 24.1	48.6	187 35.1	42.2	185 15.6	47.8	323 49.0	03.1
20	348 01.2	147 26.8	47.9	202 36.4	41.9	200 17.8	47.8	338 51.6	03.0
21	3 03.7	162 29.6	. . 47.1	217 37.7	. . 41.5	215 20.0	. . 47.7	353 54.2	. . 03.0
22	18 06.2	177 32.3	46.3	232 39.0	41.2	230 22.2	47.6	8 56.8	02.9
23	33 08.6	192 35.0	45.5	247 40.2	40.8	245 24.4	47.5	23 59.4	02.9
Mer. Pass.	h m 20 51.7	*v* 2.9	*d* 0.8	*v* 1.3	*d* 0.3	*v* 2.2	*d* 0.1	*v* 2.6	*d* 0.0

STARS

Name	SHA	Dec
	° ′	° ′
Acamar	315 10.2	S40 11.7
Achernar	335 18.5	S57 06.0
Acrux	172 58.9	S63 14.7
Adhara	255 04.5	S29 00.3
Aldebaran	290 37.6	N16 33.9
Alioth	166 12.2	N55 48.7
Alkaid	152 51.3	N49 10.7
Alnair	27 30.9	S46 50.0
Alnilam	275 36.0	S 1 11.0
Alphard	217 46.3	S 8 46.4
Alphecca	126 02.8	N26 37.5
Alpheratz	357 33.0	N29 14.6
Altair	61 58.6	N 8 56.5
Ankaa	353 05.3	S42 09.6
Antares	112 14.4	S26 29.5
Arcturus	145 46.9	N19 02.6
Atria	107 07.7	S69 04.6
Avior	234 14.0	S59 35.4
Bellatrix	278 21.0	N 6 22.5
Betelgeuse	270 50.2	N 7 24.8
Canopus	263 51.4	S52 42.3
Capella	280 19.3	N46 01.4
Deneb	49 24.8	N45 22.9
Denebola	182 23.7	N14 25.3
Diphda	348 45.5	S17 50.3
Dubhe	193 39.5	N61 36.1
Elnath	277 59.7	N28 37.8
Eltanin	90 41.9	N51 29.3
Enif	33 37.3	N10 00.1
Fomalhaut	15 12.7	S29 28.8
Gacrux	171 50.4	S57 15.6
Gienah	175 42.3	S17 41.4
Hadar	148 34.5	S60 30.0
Hamal	327 49.2	N23 35.5
Kaus Aust.	83 30.8	S34 22.3
Kochab	137 21.0	N74 02.6
Markab	13 28.2	N15 21.2
Menkar	314 04.3	N 4 11.8
Menkent	147 56.2	S36 30.0
Miaplacidus	221 38.0	S69 49.3
Mirfak	308 25.6	N49 57.4
Nunki	75 46.1	S26 15.8
Peacock	53 03.5	S56 39.1
Pollux	243 15.4	N27 57.6
Procyon	244 49.1	N 5 09.4
Rasalhague	95 57.4	N12 32.6
Regulus	207 32.9	N11 50.1
Rigel	281 02.2	S 8 10.1
Rigil Kent.	139 38.9	S60 56.7
Sabik	102 01.4	S15 45.4
Schedar	349 28.8	N56 41.3
Shaula	96 08.7	S37 07.4
Sirius	258 24.7	S16 45.0
Spica	158 21.0	S11 18.0
Suhail	222 45.2	S43 32.2
Vega	80 32.5	N38 48.7
Zuben'ubi	136 54.7	S16 09.1
	SHA ° ′	**Mer. Pass.** h m
Venus	159 10.2	10 16
Mars	215 27.8	6 33
Jupiter	212 27.8	6 44
Saturn	350 44.8	21 28

UT	SUN GHA	SUN Dec	MOON GHA	v	MOON Dec	d	HP
d h	° ′	° ′	° ′	′	° ′	′	′
6 00	184 06.0	S15 54.9	221 48.2	14.5	S 4 52.8	15.0	56.7
01	199 05.9	55.7	236 21.7	14.5	5 07.8	14.9	56.6
02	214 05.9	56.4	250 55.2	14.5	5 22.7	14.8	56.6
03	229 05.9	. . 57.2	265 28.7	14.5	5 37.5	14.8	56.6
04	244 05.9	57.9	280 02.2	14.5	5 52.3	14.8	56.6
05	259 05.8	58.7	294 35.7	14.4	6 07.1	14.8	56.5
06	274 05.8	S15 59.4	309 09.1	14.5	S 6 21.9	14.7	56.5
07	289 05.8	16 00.2	323 42.6	14.4	6 36.6	14.7	56.5
F 08	304 05.8	00.9	338 16.0	14.4	6 51.3	14.7	56.5
R 09	319 05.7	. . 01.7	352 49.4	14.5	7 06.0	14.6	56.5
I 10	334 05.7	02.4	7 22.9	14.4	7 20.6	14.5	56.4
D 11	349 05.7	03.2	21 56.3	14.4	7 35.1	14.6	56.4
A 12	4 05.6	S16 03.9	36 29.7	14.4	S 7 49.7	14.4	56.4
Y 13	19 05.6	04.7	51 03.1	14.3	8 04.1	14.5	56.4
14	34 05.6	05.4	65 36.4	14.4	8 18.6	14.4	56.4
15	49 05.6	. . 06.2	80 09.8	14.3	8 33.0	14.3	56.3
16	64 05.5	06.9	94 43.1	14.3	8 47.3	14.3	56.3
17	79 05.5	07.6	109 16.4	14.3	9 01.6	14.2	56.3
18	94 05.5	S16 08.4	123 49.7	14.3	S 9 15.8	14.2	56.3
19	109 05.4	09.1	138 23.0	14.2	9 30.0	14.2	56.3
20	124 05.4	09.9	152 56.2	14.2	9 44.2	14.1	56.2
21	139 05.4	. . 10.6	167 29.4	14.3	9 58.3	14.0	56.2
22	154 05.3	11.4	182 02.7	14.1	10 12.3	14.0	56.2
23	169 05.3	12.1	196 35.8	14.2	10 26.3	14.0	56.2
7 00	184 05.3	S16 12.8	211 09.0	14.1	S10 40.3	13.9	56.2
01	199 05.2	13.6	225 42.1	14.1	10 54.2	13.8	56.1
02	214 05.2	14.3	240 15.2	14.1	11 08.0	13.8	56.1
03	229 05.2	. . 15.1	254 48.3	14.0	11 21.8	13.7	56.1
04	244 05.1	15.8	269 21.3	14.1	11 35.5	13.6	56.1
05	259 05.1	16.5	283 54.4	13.9	11 49.1	13.6	56.1
06	274 05.1	S16 17.3	298 27.3	14.0	S12 02.7	13.6	56.0
S 07	289 05.0	18.0	313 00.3	13.9	12 16.3	13.5	56.0
A 08	304 05.0	18.7	327 33.2	13.9	12 29.8	13.4	56.0
T 09	319 05.0	. . 19.5	342 06.1	13.9	12 43.2	13.3	56.0
U 10	334 04.9	20.2	356 39.0	13.8	12 56.5	13.3	56.0
R 11	349 04.9	20.9	11 11.8	13.8	13 09.8	13.2	55.9
D 12	4 04.9	S16 21.7	25 44.6	13.7	S13 23.0	13.2	55.9
A 13	19 04.8	22.4	40 17.3	13.8	13 36.2	13.0	55.9
Y 14	34 04.8	23.1	54 50.1	13.7	13 49.2	13.1	55.9
15	49 04.8	. . 23.9	69 22.8	13.6	14 02.3	12.9	55.9
16	64 04.7	24.6	83 55.4	13.6	14 15.2	12.9	55.8
17	79 04.7	25.3	98 28.0	13.6	14 28.1	12.8	55.8
18	94 04.6	S16 26.1	113 00.6	13.5	S14 40.9	12.7	55.8
19	109 04.6	26.8	127 33.1	13.5	14 53.6	12.7	55.8
20	124 04.6	27.5	142 05.6	13.4	15 06.3	12.6	55.8
21	139 04.5	. . 28.3	156 38.0	13.5	15 18.9	12.5	55.7
22	154 04.5	29.0	171 10.5	13.3	15 31.4	12.4	55.7
23	169 04.4	29.7	185 42.8	13.4	15 43.8	12.3	55.7
8 00	184 04.4	S16 30.5	200 15.2	13.2	S15 56.1	12.3	55.7
01	199 04.4	31.2	214 47.4	13.3	16 08.4	12.2	55.7
02	214 04.3	31.9	229 19.7	13.2	16 20.6	12.1	55.6
03	229 04.3	. . 32.6	243 51.9	13.1	16 32.7	12.1	55.6
04	244 04.2	33.4	258 24.0	13.1	16 44.8	11.9	55.6
05	259 04.2	34.1	272 56.1	13.1	16 56.7	11.9	55.6
06	274 04.1	S16 34.8	287 28.2	13.0	S17 08.6	11.8	55.6
07	289 04.1	35.5	302 00.2	13.0	17 20.4	11.7	55.6
08	304 04.1	36.3	316 32.2	12.9	17 32.1	11.6	55.5
S 09	319 04.0	. . 37.0	331 04.1	12.9	17 43.7	11.5	55.5
U 10	334 04.0	37.7	345 36.0	12.8	17 55.2	11.5	55.5
N 11	349 03.9	38.4	0 07.8	12.8	18 06.7	11.3	55.5
D 12	4 03.9	S16 39.2	14 39.6	12.7	S18 18.0	11.3	55.5
A 13	19 03.8	39.9	29 11.3	12.7	18 29.3	11.2	55.4
Y 14	34 03.8	40.6	43 43.0	12.7	18 40.5	11.1	55.4
15	49 03.7	. . 41.3	58 14.7	12.6	18 51.6	10.9	55.4
16	64 03.7	42.1	72 46.3	12.5	19 02.5	10.9	55.4
17	79 03.6	42.8	87 17.8	12.5	19 13.4	10.8	55.4
18	94 03.6	S16 43.5	101 49.3	12.5	S19 24.2	10.8	55.4
19	109 03.6	44.2	116 20.8	12.4	19 35.0	10.6	55.3
20	124 03.5	44.9	130 52.2	12.3	19 45.6	10.5	55.3
21	139 03.5	. . 45.7	145 23.5	12.3	19 56.1	10.4	55.3
22	154 03.4	46.4	159 54.8	12.3	20 06.5	10.3	55.3
23	169 03.4	47.1	174 26.1	12.2	S20 16.8	10.3	55.3
	SD 16.2	*d* 0.7	SD 15.4		15.2		15.1

Lat.	Twilight Naut.	Twilight Civil	Sunrise	Moonrise 6	Moonrise 7	Moonrise 8	Moonrise 9
°	h m	h m	h m	h m	h m	h m	h m
N 72	06 29	07 57	09 38	04 39	06 58	▬	▬
N 70	06 23	07 40	09 02	04 29	06 34	09 05	▬
68	06 17	07 26	08 36	04 22	06 16	08 24	▬
66	06 12	07 15	08 17	04 16	06 02	07 56	10 09
64	06 08	07 06	08 01	04 10	05 51	07 35	09 28
62	06 04	06 58	07 48	04 06	05 41	07 18	09 00
60	06 00	06 51	07 37	04 02	05 32	07 04	08 38
N 58	05 57	06 45	07 28	03 59	05 25	06 52	08 21
56	05 54	06 39	07 20	03 56	05 19	06 42	08 06
54	05 51	06 34	07 12	03 53	05 13	06 33	07 53
52	05 49	06 29	07 06	03 50	05 08	06 25	07 42
50	05 46	06 25	07 00	03 48	05 03	06 18	07 33
45	05 40	06 15	06 47	03 43	04 53	06 03	07 12
N 40	05 35	06 07	06 36	03 39	04 45	05 50	06 56
35	05 30	06 00	06 27	03 36	04 38	05 40	06 42
30	05 25	05 54	06 18	03 33	04 32	05 31	06 30
20	05 15	05 41	06 04	03 28	04 21	05 15	06 09
N 10	05 05	05 30	05 52	03 23	04 12	05 01	05 52
0	04 54	05 19	05 40	03 19	04 03	04 48	05 35
S 10	04 41	05 06	05 28	03 15	03 55	04 36	05 19
20	04 25	04 52	05 16	03 11	03 46	04 22	05 02
30	04 05	04 35	05 01	03 06	03 35	04 07	04 42
35	03 52	04 25	04 52	03 03	03 30	03 58	04 30
40	03 36	04 13	04 42	03 00	03 23	03 48	04 17
45	03 17	03 58	04 31	02 56	03 15	03 37	04 02
S 50	02 51	03 39	04 16	02 52	03 06	03 23	03 43
52	02 38	03 30	04 10	02 50	03 02	03 16	03 34
54	02 22	03 20	04 02	02 48	02 57	03 09	03 24
56	02 04	03 08	03 54	02 45	02 52	03 01	03 13
58	01 40	02 55	03 45	02 43	02 47	02 52	03 00
S 60	01 05	02 39	03 34	02 40	02 40	02 42	02 45

Lat.	Sunset	Twilight Civil	Twilight Naut.	Moonset 6	Moonset 7	Moonset 8	Moonset 9
°	h m	h m	h m	h m	h m	h m	h m
N 72	13 48	15 29	16 56	13 49	13 04	▬	▬
N 70	14 24	15 46	17 03	14 01	13 30	12 35	▬
68	14 50	16 00	17 09	14 11	13 49	13 17	▬
66	15 09	16 11	17 14	14 20	14 05	13 46	13 12
64	15 25	16 20	17 18	14 27	14 18	14 08	13 54
62	15 38	16 29	17 22	14 33	14 29	14 26	14 23
60	15 49	16 36	17 26	14 38	14 39	14 41	14 45
N 58	15 59	16 42	17 29	14 43	14 47	14 53	15 03
56	16 07	16 48	17 32	14 47	14 55	15 04	15 18
54	16 14	16 53	17 35	14 51	15 01	15 14	15 32
52	16 21	16 57	17 38	14 54	15 07	15 23	15 43
50	16 27	17 02	17 40	14 57	15 13	15 31	15 53
45	16 40	17 11	17 46	15 04	15 24	15 47	16 15
N 40	16 51	17 20	17 52	15 10	15 34	16 01	16 32
35	17 00	17 27	17 57	15 15	15 42	16 13	16 47
30	17 09	17 34	18 02	15 19	15 50	16 23	17 00
20	17 23	17 46	18 12	15 27	16 03	16 41	17 22
N 10	17 35	17 57	18 22	15 34	16 14	16 56	17 41
0	17 47	18 09	18 34	15 40	16 25	17 11	17 59
S 10	17 59	18 21	18 47	15 46	16 35	17 25	18 17
20	18 12	18 35	19 03	15 53	16 47	17 41	18 36
30	18 27	18 53	19 23	16 01	17 00	17 59	18 58
35	18 36	19 03	19 36	16 06	17 08	18 10	19 12
40	18 46	19 16	19 52	16 11	17 16	18 22	19 27
45	18 58	19 31	20 12	16 17	17 26	18 36	19 45
S 50	19 12	19 49	20 38	16 24	17 39	18 54	20 08
52	19 19	19 59	20 51	16 27	17 45	19 02	20 19
54	19 26	20 09	21 07	16 31	17 51	19 12	20 31
56	19 35	20 21	21 27	16 35	17 58	19 22	20 45
58	19 44	20 35	21 52	16 40	18 07	19 34	21 02
S 60	19 55	20 51	22 28	16 45	18 16	19 49	21 22

Day	SUN Eqn. of Time 00^h	SUN Eqn. of Time 12^h	SUN Mer. Pass.	MOON Mer. Pass. Upper	MOON Mer. Pass. Lower	MOON Age	MOON Phase
d	m s	m s	h m	h m	h m	d %	
6	16 24	16 23	11 44	09 30	21 52	27 8	●
7	16 21	16 20	11 44	10 14	22 36	28 3	
8	16 18	16 16	11 44	10 59	23 23	29 1	

2026 NOVEMBER 9, 10, 11 (MON., TUES., WED.)

	UT d h	ARIES GHA ° ′	VENUS −4·7 GHA ° ′	VENUS Dec ° ′	MARS +0·8 GHA ° ′	MARS Dec ° ′	JUPITER −2·1 GHA ° ′	JUPITER Dec ° ′	SATURN +0·5 GHA ° ′	SATURN Dec ° ′
	9 00	48 11.1	207 37.7	S11 44.8	262 41.5	N15 40.5	260 26.6	N13 47.5	39 02.0	N 1 02.9
	01	63 13.6	222 40.4	44.0	277 42.8	40.2	275 28.8	47.4	54 04.6	02.8
	02	78 16.0	237 43.1	43.2	292 44.1	39.8	290 31.0	47.3	69 07.2	02.8
	03	93 18.5	252 45.9	. . 42.5	307 45.4	. . 39.5	305 33.3	. . 47.2	84 09.7	. . 02.7
	04	108 20.9	267 48.6	41.7	322 46.6	39.2	320 35.5	47.1	99 12.3	02.7
	05	123 23.4	282 51.2	40.9	337 47.9	38.8	335 37.7	47.1	114 14.9	02.6
	06	138 25.9	297 53.9	S11 40.2	352 49.2	N15 38.5	350 39.9	N13 47.0	129 17.5	N 1 02.6
	07	153 28.3	312 56.6	39.4	7 50.5	38.2	5 42.1	46.9	144 20.1	02.5
	08	168 30.8	327 59.3	38.7	22 51.8	37.8	20 44.3	46.8	159 22.7	02.5
M	09	183 33.3	343 02.0	. . 37.9	37 53.1	. . 37.5	35 46.6	. . 46.8	174 25.3	. . 02.4
O	10	198 35.7	358 04.7	37.2	52 54.3	37.1	50 48.8	46.7	189 27.9	02.4
N	11	213 38.2	13 07.3	36.4	67 55.6	36.8	65 51.0	46.6	204 30.5	02.4
D	12	228 40.7	28 10.0	S11 35.7	82 56.9	N15 36.5	80 53.2	N13 46.5	219 33.0	N 1 02.3
A	13	243 43.1	43 12.7	34.9	97 58.2	36.1	95 55.4	46.5	234 35.6	02.3
Y	14	258 45.6	58 15.3	34.2	112 59.5	35.8	110 57.6	46.4	249 38.2	02.2
	15	273 48.1	73 18.0	. . 33.4	128 00.8	. . 35.5	125 59.9	. . 46.3	264 40.8	. . 02.2
	16	288 50.5	88 20.6	32.7	143 02.1	35.1	141 02.1	46.2	279 43.4	02.1
	17	303 53.0	103 23.3	32.0	158 03.3	34.8	156 04.3	46.2	294 46.0	02.1
	18	318 55.4	118 25.9	S11 31.2	173 04.6	N15 34.5	171 06.5	N13 46.1	309 48.6	N 1 02.0
	19	333 57.9	133 28.6	30.5	188 05.9	34.1	186 08.7	46.0	324 51.2	02.0
	20	349 00.4	148 31.2	29.8	203 07.2	33.8	201 10.9	45.9	339 53.7	02.0
	21	4 02.8	163 33.8	. . 29.0	218 08.5	. . 33.4	216 13.2	. . 45.9	354 56.3	. . 01.9
	22	19 05.3	178 36.5	28.3	233 09.8	33.1	231 15.4	45.8	9 58.9	01.9
	23	34 07.8	193 39.1	27.6	248 11.1	32.8	246 17.6	45.7	25 01.5	01.8
	10 00	49 10.2	208 41.7	S11 26.8	263 12.4	N15 32.4	261 19.8	N13 45.6	40 04.1	N 1 01.8
	01	64 12.7	223 44.3	26.1	278 13.7	32.1	276 22.0	45.6	55 06.7	01.7
	02	79 15.2	238 46.9	25.4	293 14.9	31.8	291 24.3	45.5	70 09.3	01.7
	03	94 17.6	253 49.5	. . 24.7	308 16.2	. . 31.4	306 26.5	. . 45.4	85 11.8	. . 01.6
	04	109 20.1	268 52.1	23.9	323 17.5	31.1	321 28.7	45.3	100 14.4	01.6
	05	124 22.5	283 54.7	23.2	338 18.8	30.8	336 30.9	45.3	115 17.0	01.6
	06	139 25.0	298 57.3	S11 22.5	353 20.1	N15 30.4	351 33.2	N13 45.2	130 19.6	N 1 01.5
	07	154 27.5	313 59.9	21.8	8 21.4	30.1	6 35.4	45.1	145 22.2	01.5
T	08	169 29.9	329 02.5	21.1	23 22.7	29.8	21 37.6	45.0	160 24.8	01.4
U	09	184 32.4	344 05.1	. . 20.4	38 24.0	. . 29.4	36 39.8	. . 45.0	175 27.3	. . 01.4
E	10	199 34.9	359 07.7	19.7	53 25.3	29.1	51 42.0	44.9	190 29.9	01.3
S	11	214 37.3	14 10.3	19.0	68 26.6	28.8	66 44.3	44.8	205 32.5	01.3
D	12	229 39.8	29 12.8	S11 18.3	83 27.9	N15 28.4	81 46.5	N13 44.7	220 35.1	N 1 01.3
A	13	244 42.3	44 15.4	17.6	98 29.2	28.1	96 48.7	44.7	235 37.7	01.2
Y	14	259 44.7	59 18.0	16.9	113 30.5	27.7	111 50.9	44.6	250 40.3	01.2
	15	274 47.2	74 20.5	. . 16.2	128 31.8	. . 27.4	126 53.2	. . 44.5	265 42.9	. . 01.1
	16	289 49.7	89 23.1	15.5	143 33.1	27.1	141 55.4	44.4	280 45.4	01.1
	17	304 52.1	104 25.6	14.8	158 34.4	26.7	156 57.6	44.4	295 48.0	01.0
	18	319 54.6	119 28.2	S11 14.1	173 35.7	N15 26.4	171 59.8	N13 44.3	310 50.6	N 1 01.0
	19	334 57.0	134 30.7	13.4	188 37.0	26.1	187 02.1	44.2	325 53.2	01.0
	20	349 59.5	149 33.3	12.7	203 38.3	25.7	202 04.3	44.1	340 55.8	00.9
	21	5 02.0	164 35.8	. . 12.0	218 39.6	. . 25.4	217 06.5	. . 44.1	355 58.4	. . 00.9
	22	20 04.4	179 38.3	11.3	233 40.9	25.1	232 08.7	44.0	11 00.9	00.8
	23	35 06.9	194 40.9	10.7	248 42.2	24.7	247 11.0	43.9	26 03.5	00.8
	11 00	50 09.4	209 43.4	S11 10.0	263 43.5	N15 24.4	262 13.2	N13 43.8	41 06.1	N 1 00.7
	01	65 11.8	224 45.9	09.3	278 44.8	24.1	277 15.4	43.8	56 08.7	00.7
	02	80 14.3	239 48.4	08.6	293 46.1	23.7	292 17.6	43.7	71 11.3	00.7
	03	95 16.8	254 51.0	. . 07.9	308 47.4	. . 23.4	307 19.9	. . 43.6	86 13.9	. . 00.6
	04	110 19.2	269 53.5	07.3	323 48.7	23.1	322 22.1	43.6	101 16.4	00.6
	05	125 21.7	284 56.0	06.6	338 50.0	22.7	337 24.3	43.5	116 19.0	00.5
	06	140 24.2	299 58.5	S11 05.9	353 51.3	N15 22.4	352 26.6	N13 43.4	131 21.6	N 1 00.5
W	07	155 26.6	315 01.0	05.3	8 52.6	22.1	7 28.8	43.3	146 24.2	00.4
E	08	170 29.1	330 03.5	04.6	23 53.9	21.7	22 31.0	43.3	161 26.8	00.4
D	09	185 31.5	345 06.0	. . 03.9	38 55.2	. . 21.4	37 33.2	. . 43.2	176 29.3	. . 00.4
N	10	200 34.0	0 08.4	03.3	53 56.5	21.1	52 35.5	43.1	191 31.9	00.3
E	11	215 36.5	15 10.9	02.6	68 57.8	20.7	67 37.7	43.1	206 34.5	00.3
S	12	230 38.9	30 13.4	S11 02.0	83 59.1	N15 20.4	82 39.9	N13 43.0	221 37.1	N 1 00.2
D	13	245 41.4	45 15.9	01.3	99 00.4	20.1	97 42.2	42.9	236 39.7	00.2
A	14	260 43.9	60 18.3	00.6	114 01.7	19.7	112 44.4	42.8	251 42.3	00.2
Y	15	275 46.3	75 20.8	11 00.0	129 03.0	. . 19.4	127 46.6	. . 42.8	266 44.8	. . 00.1
	16	290 48.8	90 23.3	10 59.3	144 04.3	19.1	142 48.9	42.7	281 47.4	00.1
	17	305 51.3	105 25.7	58.7	159 05.7	18.7	157 51.1	42.6	296 50.0	00.0
	18	320 53.7	120 28.2	S10 58.1	174 07.0	N15 18.4	172 53.3	N13 42.6	311 52.6	N 1 00.0
	19	335 56.2	135 30.6	57.4	189 08.3	18.1	187 55.5	42.5	326 55.2	0 59.9
	20	350 58.7	150 33.1	56.8	204 09.6	17.7	202 57.8	42.4	341 57.7	59.9
	21	6 01.1	165 35.5	. . 56.1	219 10.9	. . 17.4	218 00.0	. . 42.3	357 00.3	. . 59.9
	22	21 03.6	180 38.0	55.5	234 12.2	17.1	233 02.2	42.3	12 02.9	59.8
	23	36 06.0	195 40.4	54.9	249 13.5	16.7	248 04.5	42.2	27 05.5	59.8
	Mer. Pass. h m	20 39.9	v 2.6	d 0.7	v 1.3	d 0.3	v 2.2	d 0.1	v 2.6	d 0.0

STARS

Name	SHA ° ′	Dec ° ′
Acamar	315 10.2	S40 11.7
Achernar	335 18.5	S57 06.0
Acrux	172 58.9	S63 14.7
Adhara	255 04.5	S29 00.3
Aldebaran	290 37.6	N16 33.9
Alioth	166 12.1	N55 48.7
Alkaid	152 51.3	N49 10.6
Alnair	27 31.0	S46 50.0
Alnilam	275 35.9	S 1 11.0
Alphard	217 46.3	S 8 46.4
Alphecca	126 02.8	N26 37.5
Alpheratz	357 33.0	N29 14.6
Altair	61 58.6	N 8 56.5
Ankaa	353 05.4	S42 09.6
Antares	112 14.3	S26 29.5
Arcturus	145 46.9	N19 02.6
Atria	107 07.7	S69 04.6
Avior	234 14.0	S59 35.4
Bellatrix	278 21.0	N 6 22.5
Betelgeuse	270 50.2	N 7 24.8
Canopus	263 51.3	S52 42.3
Capella	280 19.3	N46 01.4
Deneb	49 24.9	N45 22.9
Denebola	182 23.6	N14 25.3
Diphda	348 45.5	S17 50.3
Dubhe	193 39.5	N61 36.1
Elnath	277 59.7	N28 37.8
Eltanin	90 41.9	N51 29.3
Enif	33 37.3	N10 00.1
Fomalhaut	15 12.7	S29 28.8
Gacrux	171 50.4	S57 15.6
Gienah	175 42.3	S17 41.4
Hadar	148 34.5	S60 30.0
Hamal	327 49.2	N23 35.5
Kaus Aust.	83 30.8	S34 22.3
Kochab	137 21.1	N74 02.6
Markab	13 28.3	N15 21.2
Menkar	314 04.2	N 4 11.8
Menkent	147 56.2	S36 30.0
Miaplacidus	221 37.9	S69 49.3
Mirfak	308 25.6	N49 57.5
Nunki	75 46.1	S26 15.8
Peacock	53 03.5	S56 39.1
Pollux	243 15.3	N27 57.6
Procyon	244 49.1	N 5 09.4
Rasalhague	95 57.4	N12 32.5
Regulus	207 32.9	N11 50.1
Rigel	281 02.1	S 8 10.1
Rigil Kent.	139 38.9	S60 56.7
Sabik	102 01.4	S15 45.4
Schedar	349 28.9	N56 41.4
Shaula	96 08.7	S37 07.4
Sirius	258 24.7	S16 45.0
Spica	158 21.0	S11 18.0
Suhail	222 45.2	S43 32.2
Vega	80 32.5	N38 48.7
Zuben'ubi	136 54.7	S16 09.1

	SHA ° ′	Mer. Pass. h m
Venus	159 31.5	10 03
Mars	214 02.1	6 27
Jupiter	212 09.6	6 34
Saturn	350 53.9	21 16

UT d h	SUN GHA ° ′	SUN Dec ° ′	MOON GHA ° ′	v ′	MOON Dec ° ′	d ′	HP ′
9 00	184 03.3	S16 47.8	188 57.3	12.1	S20 27.1	10.1	55.2
01	199 03.3	48.5	203 28.4	12.1	20 37.2	10.0	55.2
02	214 03.2	49.2	217 59.5	12.1	20 47.2	9.9	55.2
03	229 03.2	. . 50.0	232 30.6	12.0	20 57.1	9.8	55.2
04	244 03.1	50.7	247 01.6	11.9	21 06.9	9.7	55.2
05	259 03.0	51.4	261 32.5	11.9	21 16.6	9.7	55.2
06	274 03.0	S16 52.1	276 03.4	11.9	S21 26.3	9.5	55.1
07	289 02.9	52.8	290 34.3	11.8	21 35.8	9.4	55.1
08	304 02.9	53.5	305 05.1	11.7	21 45.2	9.3	55.1
MONDAY 09	319 02.8	. . 54.2	319 35.8	11.7	21 54.5	9.1	55.1
10	334 02.8	55.0	334 06.5	11.7	22 03.6	9.1	55.1
11	349 02.7	55.7	348 37.2	11.6	22 12.7	9.0	55.1
12	4 02.7	S16 56.4	3 07.8	11.6	S22 21.7	8.8	55.0
13	19 02.6	57.1	17 38.4	11.5	22 30.5	8.8	55.0
14	34 02.6	57.8	32 08.9	11.4	22 39.3	8.6	55.0
15	49 02.5	. . 58.5	46 39.3	11.4	22 47.9	8.5	55.0
16	64 02.5	59.2	61 09.7	11.4	22 56.4	8.5	55.0
17	79 02.4	16 59.9	75 40.1	11.3	23 04.9	8.2	55.0
18	94 02.3	S17 00.6	90 10.4	11.3	S23 13.1	8.2	54.9
19	109 02.3	01.3	104 40.7	11.2	23 21.3	8.1	54.9
20	124 02.2	02.0	119 10.9	11.2	23 29.4	7.9	54.9
21	139 02.2	. . 02.8	133 41.1	11.1	23 37.3	7.9	54.9
22	154 02.1	03.5	148 11.2	11.1	23 45.2	7.7	54.9
23	169 02.1	04.2	162 41.3	11.1	23 52.9	7.6	54.9
10 00	184 02.0	S17 04.9	177 11.4	11.0	S24 00.5	7.5	54.8
01	199 01.9	05.6	191 41.4	10.9	24 08.0	7.3	54.8
02	214 01.9	06.3	206 11.3	10.9	24 15.3	7.3	54.8
03	229 01.8	. . 07.0	220 41.2	10.9	24 22.6	7.1	54.8
04	244 01.8	07.7	235 11.1	10.8	24 29.7	7.0	54.8
05	259 01.7	08.4	249 40.9	10.8	24 36.7	6.9	54.8
06	274 01.6	S17 09.1	264 10.7	10.7	S24 43.6	6.7	54.8
07	289 01.6	09.8	278 40.4	10.7	24 50.3	6.7	54.7
08	304 01.5	10.5	293 10.1	10.7	24 57.0	6.5	54.7
TUESDAY 09	319 01.5	. . 11.2	307 39.8	10.6	25 03.5	6.3	54.7
10	334 01.4	11.9	322 09.4	10.6	25 09.8	6.3	54.7
11	349 01.3	12.6	336 39.0	10.6	25 16.1	6.1	54.7
12	4 01.3	S17 13.3	351 08.6	10.5	S25 22.2	6.0	54.7
13	19 01.2	14.0	5 38.1	10.4	25 28.2	5.9	54.7
14	34 01.1	14.7	20 07.5	10.5	25 34.1	5.8	54.6
15	49 01.1	. . 15.4	34 37.0	10.4	25 39.9	5.6	54.6
16	64 01.0	16.1	49 06.4	10.4	25 45.5	5.5	54.6
17	79 00.9	16.8	63 35.8	10.3	25 51.0	5.4	54.6
18	94 00.9	S17 17.5	78 05.1	10.3	S25 56.4	5.2	54.6
19	109 00.8	18.2	92 34.4	10.3	26 01.6	5.1	54.6
20	124 00.7	18.9	107 03.7	10.2	26 06.7	5.0	54.6
21	139 00.7	. . 19.6	121 32.9	10.2	26 11.7	4.8	54.6
22	154 00.6	20.3	136 02.1	10.2	26 16.5	4.8	54.5
23	169 00.5	20.9	150 31.3	10.2	26 21.3	4.6	54.5
11 00	184 00.5	S17 21.6	165 00.5	10.1	S26 25.9	4.4	54.5
01	199 00.4	22.3	179 29.6	10.1	26 30.3	4.3	54.5
02	214 00.3	23.0	193 58.7	10.1	26 34.6	4.2	54.5
03	229 00.3	. . 23.7	208 27.8	10.1	26 38.8	4.1	54.5
04	244 00.2	24.4	222 56.9	10.0	26 42.9	3.9	54.5
05	259 00.1	25.1	237 25.9	10.0	26 46.8	3.8	54.5
06	274 00.1	S17 25.8	251 54.9	10.0	S26 50.6	3.7	54.4
07	289 00.0	26.5	266 23.9	10.0	26 54.3	3.5	54.4
08	303 59.9	27.2	280 52.9	10.0	26 57.8	3.4	54.4
WEDNESDAY 09	318 59.9	. . 27.9	295 21.9	9.9	27 01.2	3.2	54.4
10	333 59.8	28.5	309 50.8	9.9	27 04.4	3.2	54.4
11	348 59.7	29.2	324 19.7	9.9	27 07.6	3.0	54.4
12	3 59.6	S17 29.9	338 48.6	9.9	S27 10.6	2.8	54.4
13	18 59.6	30.6	353 17.5	9.9	27 13.4	2.7	54.4
14	33 59.5	31.3	7 46.4	9.9	27 16.1	2.6	54.3
15	48 59.4	. . 32.0	22 15.3	9.9	27 18.7	2.5	54.3
16	63 59.3	32.7	36 44.2	9.8	27 21.2	2.3	54.3
17	78 59.3	33.3	51 13.0	9.9	27 23.5	2.2	54.3
18	93 59.2	S17 34.0	65 41.9	9.8	S27 25.7	2.0	54.3
19	108 59.1	34.7	80 10.7	9.8	27 27.7	1.9	54.3
20	123 59.1	35.4	94 39.5	9.9	27 29.6	1.8	54.3
21	138 59.0	. . 36.1	109 08.4	9.8	27 31.4	1.6	54.3
22	153 58.9	36.8	123 37.2	9.8	27 33.0	1.5	54.3
23	168 58.8	37.4	138 06.0	9.8	S27 34.5	1.4	54.3
	SD 16.2	*d* 0.7	SD 15.0		14.9		14.8

Lat. °	Twilight Naut. h m	Twilight Civil h m	Sunrise h m	Moonrise 9 h m	Moonrise 10 h m	Moonrise 11 h m	Moonrise 12 h m
N 72	06 41	08 11	10 02	■	■	■	■
N 70	06 33	07 52	09 19	■	■	■	■
68	06 26	07 37	08 50	■	■	■	■
66	06 20	07 24	08 28	10 09	■	■	■
64	06 15	07 14	08 11	09 28	11 44	■	■
62	06 11	07 05	07 57	09 00	10 45	12 30	13 46
60	06 07	06 58	07 45	08 38	10 11	11 37	12 39
N 58	06 03	06 51	07 35	08 21	09 47	11 05	12 05
56	06 00	06 45	07 26	08 06	09 27	10 41	11 39
54	05 56	06 39	07 18	07 53	09 11	10 21	11 19
52	05 53	06 34	07 11	07 42	08 57	10 05	11 02
50	05 51	06 30	07 04	07 33	08 45	09 51	10 48
45	05 44	06 19	06 51	07 12	08 20	09 23	10 18
N 40	05 38	06 11	06 39	06 56	08 00	09 01	09 55
35	05 33	06 03	06 29	06 42	07 43	08 42	09 36
30	05 27	05 56	06 21	06 30	07 29	08 26	09 20
20	05 16	05 43	06 06	06 09	07 05	08 00	08 53
N 10	05 06	05 31	05 53	05 52	06 44	07 37	08 29
0	04 54	05 19	05 40	05 35	06 25	07 15	08 07
S 10	04 40	05 06	05 28	05 19	06 05	06 54	07 45
20	04 23	04 51	05 14	05 02	05 45	06 31	07 21
30	04 02	04 33	04 59	04 42	05 21	06 05	06 54
35	03 49	04 22	04 50	04 30	05 07	05 50	06 38
40	03 32	04 09	04 39	04 17	04 51	05 32	06 19
45	03 12	03 54	04 27	04 02	04 32	05 10	05 56
S 50	02 44	03 34	04 12	03 43	04 09	04 43	05 27
52	02 30	03 24	04 05	03 34	03 57	04 29	05 13
54	02 14	03 14	03 57	03 24	03 45	04 14	04 56
56	01 53	03 01	03 48	03 13	03 30	03 56	04 36
58	01 26	02 46	03 38	03 00	03 13	03 34	04 12
S 60	00 42	02 29	03 27	02 45	02 52	03 07	03 38

Lat. °	Sunset h m	Twilight Civil h m	Twilight Naut. h m	Moonset 9 h m	Moonset 10 h m	Moonset 11 h m	Moonset 12 h m
N 72	13 24	15 16	16 45	■	■	■	■
N 70	14 08	15 35	16 54	■	■	■	■
68	14 37	15 50	17 00	■	■	■	■
66	14 59	16 02	17 06	13 12	■	■	■
64	15 16	16 13	17 11	13 54	13 21	■	■
62	15 30	16 22	17 16	14 23	14 21	14 22	14 53
60	15 42	16 29	17 20	14 45	14 55	15 16	16 00
N 58	15 52	16 36	17 24	15 03	15 20	15 48	16 35
56	16 01	16 42	17 27	15 18	15 39	16 12	17 00
54	16 09	16 48	17 31	15 32	15 56	16 31	17 20
52	16 16	16 53	17 34	15 43	16 10	16 48	17 37
50	16 23	16 58	17 37	15 53	16 23	17 02	17 52
45	16 37	17 08	17 43	16 15	16 49	17 31	18 21
N 40	16 48	17 17	17 49	16 32	17 09	17 53	18 44
35	16 58	17 25	17 55	16 47	17 26	18 12	19 03
30	17 07	17 32	18 00	17 00	17 41	18 28	19 19
20	17 22	17 45	18 11	17 22	18 07	18 55	19 46
N 10	17 35	17 57	18 22	17 41	18 28	19 18	20 10
0	17 47	18 09	18 34	17 59	18 49	19 40	20 32
S 10	18 00	18 22	18 48	18 17	19 09	20 02	20 54
20	18 14	18 37	19 05	18 36	19 31	20 25	21 17
30	18 29	18 55	19 26	18 58	19 57	20 53	21 44
35	18 39	19 06	19 40	19 12	20 12	21 09	22 00
40	18 49	19 19	19 56	19 27	20 29	21 28	22 19
45	19 02	19 35	20 17	19 45	20 51	21 50	22 42
S 50	19 17	19 55	20 45	20 08	21 17	22 19	23 10
52	19 24	20 05	20 59	20 19	21 30	22 33	23 24
54	19 32	20 16	21 16	20 31	21 45	22 50	23 41
56	19 41	20 29	21 38	20 45	22 03	23 10	24 00
58	19 51	20 44	22 06	21 02	22 25	23 34	24 24
S 60	20 03	21 02	22 54	21 22	22 52	24 08	00 08

Day	SUN Eqn. of Time 00^h m s	SUN Eqn. of Time 12^h m s	SUN Mer. Pass. h m	MOON Mer. Pass. Upper h m	MOON Mer. Pass. Lower h m	MOON Age d	MOON Phase %
9	16 13	16 11	11 44	11 47	24 12	00	0
10	16 08	16 05	11 44	12 37	00 12	01	2
11	16 02	15 59	11 44	13 28	01 02	02	5

UT d h		ARIES GHA	VENUS −4·8 GHA	Dec	MARS +0·7 GHA	Dec	JUPITER −2·1 GHA	Dec	SATURN +0·5 GHA	Dec
		° ′	° ′	° ′	° ′	° ′	° ′	° ′	° ′	° ′
12 00		51 08.5	210 42.8	S10 54.2	264 14.8	N15 16.4	263 06.7	N13 42.1	42 08.1	N 0 59.7
01		66 11.0	225 45.3	53.6	279 16.1	16.1	278 08.9	42.1	57 10.6	59.7
02		81 13.4	240 47.7	53.0	294 17.5	15.7	293 11.2	42.0	72 13.2	59.7
03		96 15.9	255 50.1	52.3	309 18.8	15.4	308 13.4	41.9	87 15.8	59.6
04		111 18.4	270 52.5	51.7	324 20.1	15.1	323 15.6	41.8	102 18.4	59.6
05		126 20.8	285 54.9	51.1	339 21.4	14.8	338 17.9	41.8	117 20.9	59.5
06		141 23.3	300 57.4	S10 50.5	354 22.7	N15 14.4	353 20.1	N13 41.7	132 23.5	N 0 59.5
07		156 25.8	315 59.8	49.8	9 24.0	14.1	8 22.3	41.6	147 26.1	59.5
08	T	171 28.2	331 02.2	49.2	24 25.3	13.8	23 24.6	41.6	162 28.7	59.4
09	H	186 30.7	346 04.6	48.6	39 26.7	13.4	38 26.8	41.5	177 31.3	59.4
10	U	201 33.2	1 07.0	48.0	54 28.0	13.1	53 29.1	41.4	192 33.8	59.3
11	R	216 35.6	16 09.3	47.4	69 29.3	12.8	68 31.3	41.4	207 36.4	59.3
12	S	231 38.1	31 11.7	S10 46.8	84 30.6	N15 12.4	83 33.5	N13 41.3	222 39.0	N 0 59.3
13	D	246 40.5	46 14.1	46.2	99 31.9	12.1	98 35.8	41.2	237 41.6	59.2
14	A	261 43.0	61 16.5	45.6	114 33.3	11.8	113 38.0	41.1	252 44.2	59.2
15	Y	276 45.5	76 18.9	45.0	129 34.6	11.4	128 40.2	41.1	267 46.7	59.1
16		291 47.9	91 21.2	44.3	144 35.9	11.1	143 42.5	41.0	282 49.3	59.1
17		306 50.4	106 23.6	43.7	159 37.2	10.8	158 44.7	40.9	297 51.9	59.1
18		321 52.9	121 26.0	S10 43.2	174 38.5	N15 10.4	173 46.9	N13 40.9	312 54.5	N 0 59.0
19		336 55.3	136 28.3	42.6	189 39.9	10.1	188 49.2	40.8	327 57.0	59.0
20		351 57.8	151 30.7	42.0	204 41.2	09.8	203 51.4	40.7	342 59.6	58.9
21		7 00.3	166 33.0	41.4	219 42.5	09.5	218 53.7	40.7	358 02.2	58.9
22		22 02.7	181 35.4	40.8	234 43.8	09.1	233 55.9	40.6	13 04.8	58.9
23		37 05.2	196 37.7	40.2	249 45.1	08.8	248 58.1	40.5	28 07.3	58.8
13 00		52 07.6	211 40.1	S10 39.6	264 46.5	N15 08.5	264 00.4	N13 40.5	43 09.9	N 0 58.8
01		67 10.1	226 42.4	39.0	279 47.8	08.1	279 02.6	40.4	58 12.5	58.7
02		82 12.6	241 44.7	38.4	294 49.1	07.8	294 04.9	40.3	73 15.1	58.7
03		97 15.0	256 47.1	37.9	309 50.4	07.5	309 07.1	40.2	88 17.7	58.7
04		112 17.5	271 49.4	37.3	324 51.8	07.1	324 09.3	40.2	103 20.2	58.6
05		127 20.0	286 51.7	36.7	339 53.1	06.8	339 11.6	40.1	118 22.8	58.6
06		142 22.4	301 54.0	S10 36.1	354 54.4	N15 06.5	354 13.8	N13 40.0	133 25.4	N 0 58.5
07		157 24.9	316 56.3	35.6	9 55.7	06.1	9 16.1	40.0	148 28.0	58.5
08		172 27.4	331 58.6	35.0	24 57.1	05.8	24 18.3	39.9	163 30.5	58.5
09	F	187 29.8	347 01.0	34.4	39 58.4	05.5	39 20.6	39.8	178 33.1	58.4
10	R	202 32.3	2 03.3	33.8	54 59.7	05.2	54 22.8	39.8	193 35.7	58.4
11	I	217 34.8	17 05.6	33.3	70 01.1	04.8	69 25.0	39.7	208 38.3	58.3
12	D	232 37.2	32 07.8	S10 32.7	85 02.4	N15 04.5	84 27.3	N13 39.6	223 40.8	N 0 58.3
13	A	247 39.7	47 10.1	32.2	100 03.7	04.2	99 29.5	39.6	238 43.4	58.3
14	Y	262 42.1	62 12.4	31.6	115 05.0	03.8	114 31.8	39.5	253 46.0	58.2
15		277 44.6	77 14.7	31.0	130 06.4	03.5	129 34.0	39.4	268 48.6	58.2
16		292 47.1	92 17.0	30.5	145 07.7	03.2	144 36.3	39.4	283 51.1	58.2
17		307 49.5	107 19.3	29.9	160 09.0	02.9	159 38.5	39.3	298 53.7	58.1
18		322 52.0	122 21.5	S10 29.4	175 10.4	N15 02.5	174 40.7	N13 39.2	313 56.3	N 0 58.1
19		337 54.5	137 23.8	28.8	190 11.7	02.2	189 43.0	39.2	328 58.8	58.0
20		352 56.9	152 26.1	28.3	205 13.0	01.9	204 45.2	39.1	344 01.4	58.0
21		7 59.4	167 28.3	27.8	220 14.4	01.5	219 47.5	39.0	359 04.0	58.0
22		23 01.9	182 30.6	27.2	235 15.7	01.2	234 49.7	39.0	14 06.6	57.9
23		38 04.3	197 32.8	26.7	250 17.0	00.9	249 52.0	38.9	29 09.1	57.9
14 00		53 06.8	212 35.1	S10 26.1	265 18.4	N15 00.6	264 54.2	N13 38.8	44 11.7	N 0 57.9
01		68 09.3	227 37.3	25.6	280 19.7	15 00.2	279 56.5	38.8	59 14.3	57.8
02		83 11.7	242 39.6	25.1	295 21.0	14 59.9	294 58.7	38.7	74 16.9	57.8
03		98 14.2	257 41.8	24.5	310 22.4	59.6	310 01.0	38.6	89 19.4	57.7
04		113 16.6	272 44.0	24.0	325 23.7	59.2	325 03.2	38.6	104 22.0	57.7
05		128 19.1	287 46.3	23.5	340 25.1	58.9	340 05.4	38.5	119 24.6	57.7
06		143 21.6	302 48.5	S10 22.9	355 26.4	N14 58.6	355 07.7	N13 38.4	134 27.1	N 0 57.6
07		158 24.0	317 50.7	22.4	10 27.7	58.3	10 09.9	38.4	149 29.7	57.6
08	S	173 26.5	332 52.9	21.9	25 29.1	57.9	25 12.2	38.3	164 32.3	57.6
09	A	188 29.0	347 55.2	21.4	40 30.4	57.6	40 14.4	38.2	179 34.9	57.5
10	T	203 31.4	2 57.4	20.9	55 31.7	57.3	55 16.7	38.2	194 37.4	57.5
11	U	218 33.9	17 59.6	20.3	70 33.1	56.9	70 18.9	38.1	209 40.0	57.4
12	R	233 36.4	33 01.8	S10 19.8	85 34.4	N14 56.6	85 21.2	N13 38.1	224 42.6	N 0 57.4
13	D	248 38.8	48 04.0	19.3	100 35.8	56.3	100 23.4	38.0	239 45.1	57.4
14	A	263 41.3	63 06.2	18.8	115 37.1	56.0	115 25.7	37.9	254 47.7	57.3
15	Y	278 43.8	78 08.4	18.3	130 38.4	55.6	130 27.9	37.9	269 50.3	57.3
16		293 46.2	93 10.6	17.8	145 39.8	55.3	145 30.2	37.8	284 52.9	57.3
17		308 48.7	108 12.8	17.3	160 41.1	55.0	160 32.4	37.7	299 55.4	57.2
18		323 51.1	123 14.9	S10 16.8	175 42.5	N14 54.7	175 34.7	N13 37.7	314 58.0	N 0 57.2
19		338 53.6	138 17.1	16.3	190 43.8	54.3	190 36.9	37.6	330 00.6	57.1
20		353 56.1	153 19.3	15.8	205 45.2	54.0	205 39.2	37.5	345 03.1	57.1
21		8 58.5	168 21.5	15.3	220 46.5	53.7	220 41.4	37.5	0 05.7	57.1
22		24 01.0	183 23.6	14.8	235 47.9	53.4	235 43.7	37.4	15 08.3	57.0
23		39 03.5	198 25.8	14.3	250 49.2	53.0	250 46.0	37.3	30 10.9	57.0
Mer. Pass.		h m 20 28.1	v 2.3	d 0.6	v 1.3	d 0.3	v 2.2	d 0.1	v 2.6	d 0.0

STARS Name	SHA	Dec
	° ′	° ′
Acamar	315 10.2	S40 11.7
Achernar	335 18.5	S57 06.1
Acrux	172 58.8	S63 14.7
Adhara	255 04.4	S29 00.3
Aldebaran	290 37.6	N16 33.9
Alioth	166 12.1	N55 48.7
Alkaid	152 51.3	N49 10.6
Alnair	27 31.0	S46 50.0
Alnilam	275 35.9	S 1 11.0
Alphard	217 46.3	S 8 46.4
Alphecca	126 02.8	N26 37.5
Alpheratz	357 33.0	N29 14.6
Altair	61 58.6	N 8 56.5
Ankaa	353 05.4	S42 09.6
Antares	112 14.3	S26 29.4
Arcturus	145 46.9	N19 02.5
Atria	107 07.7	S69 04.6
Avior	234 13.9	S59 35.4
Bellatrix	278 21.0	N 6 22.5
Betelgeuse	270 50.2	N 7 24.8
Canopus	263 51.3	S52 42.3
Capella	280 19.2	N46 01.4
Deneb	49 24.9	N45 22.9
Denebola	182 23.6	N14 25.3
Diphda	348 45.5	S17 50.3
Dubhe	193 39.5	N61 36.1
Elnath	277 59.6	N28 37.8
Eltanin	90 41.9	N51 29.3
Enif	33 37.3	N10 00.1
Fomalhaut	15 12.7	S29 28.8
Gacrux	171 50.4	S57 15.6
Gienah	175 42.3	S17 41.4
Hadar	148 34.5	S60 30.0
Hamal	327 49.2	N23 35.5
Kaus Aust.	83 30.8	S34 22.3
Kochab	137 21.1	N74 02.6
Markab	13 28.3	N15 21.2
Menkar	314 04.2	N 4 11.8
Menkent	147 56.2	S36 30.0
Miaplacidus	221 37.9	S69 49.3
Mirfak	308 25.6	N49 57.5
Nunki	75 46.1	S26 15.8
Peacock	53 03.6	S56 39.1
Pollux	243 15.3	N27 57.6
Procyon	244 49.1	N 5 09.4
Rasalhague	95 57.4	N12 32.5
Regulus	207 32.9	N11 50.1
Rigel	281 02.1	S 8 10.1
Rigil Kent.	139 38.8	S60 56.7
Sabik	102 01.4	S15 45.4
Schedar	349 28.9	N56 41.4
Shaula	96 08.7	S37 07.4
Sirius	258 24.7	S16 45.0
Spica	158 21.0	S11 18.0
Suhail	222 45.2	S43 32.2
Vega	80 32.5	N38 48.7
Zuben'ubi	136 54.7	S16 09.1

	SHA	Mer. Pass.
	° ′	h m
Venus	159 32.4	9 52
Mars	212 38.8	6 20
Jupiter	211 52.7	6 23
Saturn	351 02.3	21 04

UT	SUN GHA	SUN Dec	MOON GHA	v	MOON Dec	d	HP
d h	° ′	° ′	° ′	′	° ′	′	′
12 00	183 58.7	S17 38.1	152 34.8	9.9	S27 35.9	1.2	54.3
01	198 58.7	38.8	167 03.7	9.8	27 37.1	1.1	54.2
02	213 58.6	39.5	181 32.5	9.8	27 38.2	0.9	54.2
03	228 58.5	. . 40.2	196 01.3	9.8	27 39.1	0.9	54.2
04	243 58.4	40.8	210 30.1	9.9	27 40.0	0.6	54.2
05	258 58.4	41.5	224 59.0	9.8	27 40.6	0.6	54.2
06	273 58.3	S17 42.2	239 27.8	9.9	S27 41.2	0.4	54.2
T 07	288 58.2	42.9	253 56.7	9.8	27 41.6	0.3	54.2
H 08	303 58.1	43.5	268 25.5	9.9	27 41.9	0.1	54.2
U 09	318 58.0	. . 44.2	282 54.4	9.9	27 42.0	0.0	54.2
R 10	333 58.0	44.9	297 23.3	9.9	27 42.0	0.1	54.2
S 11	348 57.9	45.6	311 52.2	9.9	27 41.9	0.3	54.2
D 12	3 57.8	S17 46.2	326 21.1	9.9	S27 41.6	0.4	54.2
A 13	18 57.7	46.9	340 50.0	9.9	27 41.2	0.5	54.2
Y 14	33 57.6	47.6	355 18.9	10.0	27 40.7	0.7	54.1
15	48 57.6	. . 48.3	9 47.9	10.0	27 40.0	0.8	54.1
16	63 57.5	48.9	24 16.9	10.0	27 39.2	0.9	54.1
17	78 57.4	49.6	38 45.9	10.0	27 38.3	1.1	54.1
18	93 57.3	S17 50.3	53 14.9	10.0	S27 37.2	1.2	54.1
19	108 57.2	50.9	67 43.9	10.1	27 36.0	1.4	54.1
20	123 57.1	51.6	82 13.0	10.0	27 34.6	1.4	54.1
21	138 57.1	. . 52.3	96 42.0	10.1	27 33.2	1.6	54.1
22	153 57.0	52.9	111 11.1	10.2	27 31.6	1.8	54.1
23	168 56.9	53.6	125 40.3	10.1	27 29.8	1.9	54.1
13 00	183 56.8	S17 54.3	140 09.4	10.2	S27 27.9	2.0	54.1
01	198 56.7	54.9	154 38.6	10.2	27 25.9	2.1	54.1
02	213 56.6	55.6	169 07.8	10.2	27 23.8	2.3	54.1
03	228 56.6	. . 56.3	183 37.0	10.3	27 21.5	2.4	54.1
04	243 56.5	56.9	198 06.3	10.3	27 19.1	2.5	54.1
05	258 56.4	57.6	212 35.6	10.3	27 16.6	2.7	54.1
06	273 56.3	S17 58.3	227 04.9	10.4	S27 13.9	2.7	54.1
07	288 56.2	58.9	241 34.3	10.4	27 11.2	3.0	54.1
08	303 56.1	17 59.6	256 03.7	10.5	27 08.2	3.0	54.1
F 09	318 56.0	18 00.3	270 33.2	10.4	27 05.2	3.2	54.1
R 10	333 55.9	00.9	285 02.6	10.5	27 02.0	3.3	54.1
I 11	348 55.9	01.6	299 32.1	10.6	26 58.7	3.4	54.1
D 12	3 55.8	S18 02.2	314 01.7	10.6	S26 55.3	3.6	54.1
A 13	18 55.7	02.9	328 31.3	10.6	26 51.7	3.6	54.1
Y 14	33 55.6	03.6	343 00.9	10.7	26 48.1	3.9	54.1
15	48 55.5	. . 04.2	357 30.6	10.7	26 44.2	3.9	54.1
16	63 55.4	04.9	12 00.3	10.7	26 40.3	4.0	54.1
17	78 55.3	05.5	26 30.0	10.8	26 36.3	4.2	54.1
18	93 55.2	S18 06.2	40 59.8	10.9	S26 32.1	4.3	54.1
19	108 55.1	06.9	55 29.7	10.8	26 27.8	4.5	54.1
20	123 55.0	07.5	69 59.5	11.0	26 23.3	4.5	54.1
21	138 54.9	. . 08.2	84 29.5	10.9	26 18.8	4.7	54.1
22	153 54.8	08.8	98 59.4	11.0	26 14.1	4.8	54.1
23	168 54.8	09.5	113 29.4	11.1	26 09.3	4.9	54.1
14 00	183 54.7	S18 10.1	127 59.5	11.1	S26 04.4	5.0	54.1
01	198 54.6	10.8	142 29.6	11.2	25 59.4	5.2	54.1
02	213 54.5	11.4	156 59.8	11.2	25 54.2	5.3	54.1
03	228 54.4	. . 12.1	171 30.0	11.2	25 48.9	5.4	54.1
04	243 54.3	12.7	186 00.2	11.3	25 43.5	5.5	54.1
05	258 54.2	13.4	200 30.5	11.4	25 38.0	5.6	54.1
06	273 54.1	S18 14.0	215 00.9	11.4	S25 32.4	5.8	54.1
07	288 54.0	14.7	229 31.3	11.4	25 26.6	5.8	54.1
S 08	303 53.9	15.4	244 01.7	11.5	25 20.8	6.0	54.1
A 09	318 53.8	. . 16.0	258 32.2	11.6	25 14.8	6.1	54.1
T 10	333 53.7	16.6	273 02.8	11.6	25 08.7	6.2	54.1
U 11	348 53.6	17.3	287 33.4	11.7	25 02.5	6.3	54.1
R 12	3 53.5	S18 17.9	302 04.1	11.7	S24 56.2	6.5	54.1
D 13	18 53.4	18.6	316 34.8	11.7	24 49.7	6.5	54.1
A 14	33 53.3	19.2	331 05.5	11.8	24 43.2	6.7	54.1
Y 15	48 53.2	. . 19.9	345 36.3	11.9	24 36.5	6.8	54.1
16	63 53.1	20.5	0 07.2	11.9	24 29.7	6.9	54.1
17	78 53.0	21.2	14 38.1	12.0	24 22.8	6.9	54.1
18	93 52.9	S18 21.8	29 09.1	12.0	S24 15.9	7.1	54.1
19	108 52.8	22.5	43 40.1	12.1	24 08.8	7.3	54.1
20	123 52.7	23.1	58 11.2	12.1	24 01.5	7.3	54.1
21	138 52.6	. . 23.7	72 42.3	12.2	23 54.2	7.4	54.2
22	153 52.5	24.4	87 13.5	12.3	23 46.8	7.5	54.2
23	168 52.4	25.0	101 44.8	12.3	S23 39.3	7.7	54.2
	SD 16.2	*d* 0.7	SD 14.8		14.7		14.7

Lat.	Twilight Naut.	Twilight Civil	Sunrise	Moonrise 12	Moonrise 13	Moonrise 14	Moonrise 15
°	h m	h m	h m	h m	h m	h m	h m
N 72	06 52	08 25	10 33	■■	■■	■■	■■
N 70	06 43	08 04	09 36	■■	■■	■■	■■
68	06 35	07 47	09 03	■■	■■	■■	15 48
66	06 28	07 34	08 39	■■	■■	■■	14 52
64	06 23	07 22	08 21	■■	■■	14 40	14 19
62	06 17	07 13	08 06	13 46	13 58	13 57	13 55
60	06 13	07 04	07 53	12 39	13 13	13 28	13 35
N 58	06 09	06 57	07 42	12 05	12 43	13 06	13 19
56	06 05	06 50	07 32	11 39	12 21	12 48	13 05
54	06 01	06 44	07 24	11 19	12 02	12 32	12 53
52	05 58	06 39	07 16	11 02	11 47	12 19	12 43
50	05 55	06 34	07 09	10 48	11 33	12 07	12 33
45	05 48	06 23	06 55	10 18	11 05	11 43	12 13
N 40	05 41	06 14	06 43	09 55	10 43	11 23	11 57
35	05 35	06 06	06 32	09 36	10 25	11 07	11 43
30	05 29	05 58	06 23	09 20	10 09	10 53	11 31
20	05 18	05 44	06 08	08 53	09 43	10 28	11 10
N 10	05 06	05 32	05 54	08 29	09 20	10 07	10 52
0	04 54	05 19	05 41	08 07	08 58	09 48	10 35
S 10	04 39	05 05	05 28	07 45	08 37	09 28	10 18
20	04 22	04 50	05 13	07 21	08 14	09 07	10 00
30	04 00	04 31	04 57	06 54	07 47	08 42	09 39
35	03 46	04 20	04 47	06 38	07 31	08 28	09 27
40	03 29	04 06	04 36	06 19	07 13	08 11	09 13
45	03 07	03 50	04 23	05 56	06 50	07 51	08 56
S 50	02 38	03 29	04 07	05 27	06 22	07 26	08 34
52	02 23	03 19	04 00	05 13	06 08	07 13	08 24
54	02 05	03 07	03 52	04 56	05 52	06 59	08 13
56	01 42	02 54	03 42	04 36	05 33	06 43	08 00
58	01 11	02 38	03 32	04 12	05 09	06 23	07 45
S 60	00 03	02 19	03 19	03 38	04 37	05 58	07 27

Lat.	Sunset	Twilight Civil	Twilight Naut.	Moonset 12	Moonset 13	Moonset 14	Moonset 15
°	h m	h m	h m	h m	h m	h m	h m
N 72	12 55	15 03	16 35	■■	■■	■■	■■
N 70	13 51	15 24	16 45	■■	■■	■■	■■
68	14 24	15 40	16 52	■■	■■	■■	18 00
66	14 48	15 54	16 59	■■	■■	■■	18 54
64	15 07	16 05	17 05	■■	■■	17 28	19 27
62	15 22	16 15	17 10	14 53	16 28	18 11	19 50
60	15 35	16 23	17 15	16 00	17 12	18 39	20 09
N 58	15 46	16 31	17 19	16 35	17 42	19 01	20 25
56	15 56	16 37	17 23	17 00	18 04	19 19	20 38
54	16 04	16 43	17 26	17 20	18 22	19 34	20 49
52	16 12	16 49	17 30	17 37	18 38	19 47	20 59
50	16 19	16 54	17 33	17 52	18 51	19 58	21 08
45	16 33	17 05	17 40	18 21	19 19	20 22	21 27
N 40	16 45	17 14	17 47	18 44	19 40	20 40	21 43
35	16 56	17 23	17 53	19 03	19 58	20 56	21 55
30	17 05	17 30	17 59	19 19	20 13	21 10	22 07
20	17 21	17 44	18 10	19 46	20 39	21 33	22 26
N 10	17 35	17 57	18 22	20 10	21 02	21 53	22 42
0	17 48	18 10	18 35	20 32	21 22	22 11	22 57
S 10	18 01	18 23	18 49	20 54	21 43	22 29	23 13
20	18 15	18 39	19 07	21 17	22 05	22 49	23 29
30	18 32	18 58	19 29	21 44	22 31	23 11	23 47
35	18 42	19 10	19 43	22 00	22 46	23 25	23 58
40	18 53	19 23	20 01	22 19	23 03	23 40	24 10
45	19 06	19 40	20 23	22 42	23 24	23 57	24 25
S 50	19 22	20 01	20 52	23 10	23 50	24 20	00 20
52	19 30	20 11	21 07	23 24	24 02	00 02	00 30
54	19 38	20 23	21 26	23 41	24 17	00 17	00 42
56	19 48	20 36	21 50	24 00	00 00	00 34	00 55
58	19 59	20 52	22 23	24 24	00 24	00 54	01 11
S 60	20 11	21 12	////	00 08	00 56	01 19	01 30

Day	SUN Eqn. of Time 00^h	SUN Eqn. of Time 12^h	SUN Mer. Pass.	MOON Mer. Pass. Upper	MOON Mer. Pass. Lower	MOON Age	MOON Phase
d	m s	m s	h m	h m	h m	d	%
12	15 55	15 51	11 44	14 19	01 54	03	10
13	15 47	15 43	11 44	15 10	02 45	04	16
14	15 39	15 34	11 44	16 00	03 35	05	23

UT	ARIES	VENUS −4·8		MARS +0·7		JUPITER −2·1		SATURN +0·5		STARS		
	GHA	GHA	Dec	GHA	Dec	GHA	Dec	GHA	Dec	Name	SHA	Dec
d h	° ′	° ′	° ′	° ′	° ′	° ′	° ′	° ′	° ′		° ′	° ′
15 00	54 05.9	213 27.9	S10 13.8	265 50.5	N14 52.7	265 48.2	N13 37.3	45 13.4	N 0 57.0	Acamar	315 10.2	S40 11.7
01	69 08.4	228 30.1	13.3	280 51.9	52.4	280 50.5	37.2	60 16.0	56.9	Achernar	335 18.5	S57 06.1
02	84 10.9	243 32.3	12.8	295 53.2	52.0	295 52.7	37.2	75 18.6	56.9	Acrux	172 58.8	S63 14.7
03	99 13.3	258 34.4	. . 12.4	310 54.6	. . 51.7	310 55.0	. . 37.1	90 21.1	. . 56.9	Adhara	255 04.4	S29 00.3
04	114 15.8	273 36.6	11.9	325 55.9	51.4	325 57.2	37.0	105 23.7	56.8	Aldebaran	290 37.5	N16 33.9
05	129 18.3	288 38.7	11.4	340 57.3	51.1	340 59.5	37.0	120 26.3	56.8			
06	144 20.7	303 40.8	S10 10.9	355 58.6	N14 50.7	356 01.7	N13 36.9	135 28.8	N 0 56.8	Alioth	166 12.1	N55 48.6
07	159 23.2	318 43.0	10.5	11 00.0	50.4	11 04.0	36.8	150 31.4	56.7	Alkaid	152 51.3	N49 10.6
08	174 25.6	333 45.1	10.0	26 01.3	50.1	26 06.2	36.8	165 34.0	56.7	Alnair	27 31.0	S46 50.0
S 09	189 28.1	348 47.2	. . 09.5	41 02.7	. . 49.8	41 08.5	. . 36.7	180 36.5	. . 56.6	Alnilam	275 35.9	S 1 11.0
U 10	204 30.6	3 49.3	09.0	56 04.0	49.4	56 10.7	36.6	195 39.1	56.6	Alphard	217 46.2	S 8 46.4
N 11	219 33.0	18 51.5	08.6	71 05.4	49.1	71 13.0	36.6	210 41.7	56.6			
D 12	234 35.5	33 53.6	S10 08.1	86 06.7	N14 48.8	86 15.3	N13 36.5	225 44.2	N 0 56.5	Alphecca	126 02.8	N26 37.5
A 13	249 38.0	48 55.7	07.6	101 08.1	48.5	101 17.5	36.5	240 46.8	56.5	Alpheratz	357 33.0	N29 14.6
Y 14	264 40.4	63 57.8	07.2	116 09.4	48.1	116 19.8	36.4	255 49.4	56.5	Altair	61 58.6	N 8 56.5
15	279 42.9	78 59.9	. . 06.7	131 10.8	. . 47.8	131 22.0	. . 36.3	270 51.9	. . 56.4	Ankaa	353 05.4	S42 09.6
16	294 45.4	94 02.0	06.3	146 12.2	47.5	146 24.3	36.3	285 54.5	56.4	Antares	112 14.3	S26 29.4
17	309 47.8	109 04.1	05.8	161 13.5	47.2	161 26.5	36.2	300 57.1	56.4			
18	324 50.3	124 06.2	S10 05.4	176 14.9	N14 46.8	176 28.8	N13 36.1	315 59.7	N 0 56.3	Arcturus	145 46.9	N19 02.5
19	339 52.7	139 08.3	04.9	191 16.2	46.5	191 31.1	36.1	331 02.2	56.3	Atria	107 07.7	S69 04.6
20	354 55.2	154 10.4	04.5	206 17.6	46.2	206 33.3	36.0	346 04.8	56.3	Avior	234 13.9	S59 35.4
21	9 57.7	169 12.5	. . 04.0	221 18.9	. . 45.9	221 35.6	. . 36.0	1 07.4	. . 56.2	Bellatrix	278 20.9	N 6 22.5
22	25 00.1	184 14.5	03.6	236 20.3	45.5	236 37.8	35.9	16 09.9	56.2	Betelgeuse	270 50.2	N 7 24.8
23	40 02.6	199 16.6	03.1	251 21.6	45.2	251 40.1	35.8	31 12.5	56.2			
16 00	55 05.1	214 18.7	S10 02.7	266 23.0	N14 44.9	266 42.4	N13 35.8	46 15.0	N 0 56.1	Canopus	263 51.3	S52 42.3
01	70 07.5	229 20.8	02.2	281 24.4	44.6	281 44.6	35.7	61 17.6	56.1	Capella	280 19.2	N46 01.4
02	85 10.0	244 22.8	01.8	296 25.7	44.2	296 46.9	35.7	76 20.2	56.1	Deneb	49 24.9	N45 22.9
03	100 12.5	259 24.9	. . 01.4	311 27.1	. . 43.9	311 49.1	. . 35.6	91 22.7	. . 56.0	Denebola	182 23.6	N14 25.3
04	115 14.9	274 26.9	00.9	326 28.4	43.6	326 51.4	35.5	106 25.3	56.0	Diphda	348 45.5	S17 50.3
05	130 17.4	289 29.0	00.5	341 29.8	43.3	341 53.7	35.5	121 27.9	55.9			
06	145 19.9	304 31.1	S10 00.1	356 31.2	N14 43.0	356 55.9	N13 35.4	136 30.4	N 0 55.9	Dubhe	193 39.4	N61 36.1
07	160 22.3	319 33.1	9 59.6	11 32.5	42.6	11 58.2	35.3	151 33.0	55.9	Elnath	277 59.6	N28 37.8
08	175 24.8	334 35.1	59.2	26 33.9	42.3	27 00.4	35.3	166 35.6	55.8	Eltanin	90 41.9	N51 29.3
M 09	190 27.2	349 37.2	. . 58.8	41 35.2	. . 42.0	42 02.7	. . 35.2	181 38.1	. . 55.8	Enif	33 37.3	N10 00.1
O 10	205 29.7	4 39.2	58.4	56 36.6	41.7	57 05.0	35.2	196 40.7	55.8	Fomalhaut	15 12.7	S29 28.8
N 11	220 32.2	19 41.3	58.0	71 38.0	41.3	72 07.2	35.1	211 43.3	55.7			
D 12	235 34.6	34 43.3	S 9 57.5	86 39.3	N14 41.0	87 09.5	N13 35.0	226 45.8	N 0 55.7	Gacrux	171 50.3	S57 15.6
A 13	250 37.1	49 45.3	57.1	101 40.7	40.7	102 11.8	35.0	241 48.4	55.7	Gienah	175 42.2	S17 41.4
Y 14	265 39.6	64 47.3	56.7	116 42.1	40.4	117 14.0	34.9	256 51.0	55.6	Hadar	148 34.4	S60 30.0
15	280 42.0	79 49.4	. . 56.3	131 43.4	. . 40.0	132 16.3	. . 34.9	271 53.5	. . 55.6	Hamal	327 49.1	N23 35.5
16	295 44.5	94 51.4	55.9	146 44.8	39.7	147 18.5	34.8	286 56.1	55.6	Kaus Aust.	83 30.8	S34 22.3
17	310 47.0	109 53.4	55.5	161 46.2	39.4	162 20.8	34.7	301 58.7	55.5			
18	325 49.4	124 55.4	S 9 55.1	176 47.5	N14 39.1	177 23.1	N13 34.7	317 01.2	N 0 55.5	Kochab	137 21.0	N74 02.6
19	340 51.9	139 57.4	54.7	191 48.9	38.8	192 25.3	34.6	332 03.8	55.5	Markab	13 28.3	N15 21.2
20	355 54.4	154 59.4	54.3	206 50.3	38.4	207 27.6	34.6	347 06.3	55.4	Menkar	314 04.2	N 4 11.8
21	10 56.8	170 01.4	. . 53.9	221 51.6	. . 38.1	222 29.9	. . 34.5	2 08.9	. . 55.4	Menkent	147 56.2	S36 30.0
22	25 59.3	185 03.4	53.5	236 53.0	37.8	237 32.1	34.4	17 11.5	55.4	Miaplacidus	221 37.8	S69 49.3
23	41 01.7	200 05.4	53.1	251 54.4	37.5	252 34.4	34.4	32 14.0	55.3			
17 00	56 04.2	215 07.4	S 9 52.7	266 55.7	N14 37.2	267 36.7	N13 34.3	47 16.6	N 0 55.3	Mirfak	308 25.5	N49 57.5
01	71 06.7	230 09.3	52.3	281 57.1	36.8	282 38.9	34.3	62 19.2	55.3	Nunki	75 46.1	S26 15.8
02	86 09.1	245 11.3	51.9	296 58.5	36.5	297 41.2	34.2	77 21.7	55.2	Peacock	53 03.6	S56 39.1
03	101 11.6	260 13.3	. . 51.5	311 59.8	. . 36.2	312 43.5	. . 34.1	92 24.3	. . 55.2	Pollux	243 15.3	N27 57.6
04	116 14.1	275 15.3	51.1	327 01.2	35.9	327 45.7	34.1	107 26.8	55.2	Procyon	244 49.1	N 5 09.4
05	131 16.5	290 17.2	50.8	342 02.6	35.5	342 48.0	34.0	122 29.4	55.1			
06	146 19.0	305 19.2	S 9 50.4	357 04.0	N14 35.2	357 50.3	N13 34.0	137 32.0	N 0 55.1	Rasalhague	95 57.4	N12 32.5
07	161 21.5	320 21.2	50.0	12 05.3	34.9	12 52.5	33.9	152 34.5	55.1	Regulus	207 32.9	N11 50.1
T 08	176 23.9	335 23.1	49.6	27 06.7	34.6	27 54.8	33.9	167 37.1	55.0	Rigel	281 02.1	S 8 10.1
U 09	191 26.4	350 25.1	. . 49.2	42 08.1	. . 34.3	42 57.1	. . 33.8	182 39.7	. . 55.0	Rigil Kent.	139 38.8	S60 56.6
E 10	206 28.8	5 27.0	48.9	57 09.5	33.9	57 59.3	33.7	197 42.2	55.0	Sabik	102 01.4	S15 45.4
S 11	221 31.3	20 29.0	48.5	72 10.8	33.6	73 01.6	33.7	212 44.8	55.0			
D 12	236 33.8	35 30.9	S 9 48.1	87 12.2	N14 33.3	88 03.9	N13 33.6	227 47.3	N 0 54.9	Schedar	349 28.9	N56 41.4
A 13	251 36.2	50 32.9	47.8	102 13.6	33.0	103 06.2	33.6	242 49.9	54.9	Shaula	96 08.7	S37 07.4
Y 14	266 38.7	65 34.8	47.4	117 15.0	32.7	118 08.4	33.5	257 52.5	54.9	Sirius	258 24.7	S16 45.0
15	281 41.2	80 36.7	. . 47.0	132 16.3	. . 32.3	133 10.7	. . 33.4	272 55.0	. . 54.8	Spica	158 21.0	S11 18.0
16	296 43.6	95 38.7	46.7	147 17.7	32.0	148 13.0	33.4	287 57.6	54.8	Suhail	222 45.1	S43 32.2
17	311 46.1	110 40.6	46.3	162 19.1	31.7	163 15.2	33.3	303 00.1	54.8			
18	326 48.6	125 42.5	S 9 46.0	177 20.5	N14 31.4	178 17.5	N13 33.3	318 02.7	N 0 54.7	Vega	80 32.5	N38 48.7
19	341 51.0	140 44.5	45.6	192 21.8	31.1	193 19.8	33.2	333 05.3	54.7	Zuben'ubi	136 54.7	S16 09.1
20	356 53.5	155 46.4	45.2	207 23.2	30.7	208 22.1	33.2	348 07.8	54.7		SHA	Mer. Pass.
21	11 56.0	170 48.3	. . 44.9	222 24.6	. . 30.4	223 24.3	. . 33.1	3 10.4	. . 54.6		° ′	h m
22	26 58.4	185 50.2	44.5	237 26.0	30.1	238 26.6	33.0	18 12.9	54.6	Venus	159 13.6	9 41
23	42 00.9	200 52.1	44.2	252 27.4	29.8	253 28.9	33.0	33 15.5	54.6	Mars	211 17.9	6 14
	h m									Jupiter	211 37.3	6 12
Mer. Pass.	20 16.3	v 2.0	d 0.4	v 1.4	d 0.3	v 2.3	d 0.1	v 2.6	d 0.0	Saturn	351 10.0	20 51

	UT	SUN GHA	SUN Dec	MOON GHA	*v*	MOON Dec	*d*	HP
	d h	° ′	° ′	° ′	′	° ′	′	′
	15 00	183 52.3	S18 25.7	116 16.1	12.3	S23 31.6	7.7	54.2
	01	198 52.2	26.3	130 47.4	12.4	23 23.9	7.9	54.2
	02	213 52.1	27.0	145 18.8	12.5	23 16.0	7.9	54.2
	03	228 52.0	. . 27.6	159 50.3	12.5	23 08.1	8.1	54.2
	04	243 51.9	28.2	174 21.8	12.6	23 00.0	8.1	54.2
	05	258 51.8	28.9	188 53.4	12.6	22 51.9	8.3	54.2
	06	273 51.7	S18 29.5	203 25.0	12.7	S22 43.6	8.3	54.2
	07	288 51.6	30.1	217 56.7	12.7	22 35.3	8.5	54.2
	08	303 51.5	30.8	232 28.4	12.8	22 26.8	8.6	54.2
S	09	318 51.4	. . 31.4	247 00.2	12.8	22 18.2	8.6	54.3
U	10	333 51.3	32.0	261 32.0	12.9	22 09.6	8.8	54.3
N	11	348 51.2	32.7	276 03.9	12.9	22 00.8	8.8	54.3
D	12	3 51.0	S18 33.3	290 35.8	13.0	S21 52.0	9.0	54.3
A	13	18 50.9	34.0	305 07.8	13.1	21 43.0	9.0	54.3
Y	14	33 50.8	34.6	319 39.9	13.1	21 34.0	9.2	54.3
	15	48 50.7	. . 35.2	334 12.0	13.1	21 24.8	9.2	54.3
	16	63 50.6	35.8	348 44.1	13.2	21 15.6	9.3	54.3
	17	78 50.5	36.5	3 16.3	13.3	21 06.3	9.5	54.3
	18	93 50.4	S18 37.1	17 48.6	13.3	S20 56.8	9.5	54.4
	19	108 50.3	37.7	32 20.9	13.3	20 47.3	9.6	54.4
	20	123 50.2	38.4	46 53.2	13.4	20 37.7	9.7	54.4
	21	138 50.1	. . 39.0	61 25.6	13.5	20 28.0	9.8	54.4
	22	153 50.0	39.6	75 58.1	13.5	20 18.2	9.9	54.4
	23	168 49.8	40.3	90 30.6	13.5	20 08.3	9.9	54.4
	16 00	183 49.7	S18 40.9	105 03.1	13.6	S19 58.4	10.1	54.4
	01	198 49.6	41.5	119 35.7	13.7	19 48.3	10.1	54.5
	02	213 49.5	42.1	134 08.4	13.7	19 38.2	10.3	54.5
	03	228 49.4	. . 42.8	148 41.1	13.7	19 27.9	10.3	54.5
	04	243 49.3	43.4	163 13.8	13.8	19 17.6	10.4	54.5
	05	258 49.2	44.0	177 46.6	13.9	19 07.2	10.5	54.5
	06	273 49.1	S18 44.6	192 19.5	13.9	S18 56.7	10.6	54.5
	07	288 49.0	45.3	206 52.4	13.9	18 46.1	10.6	54.6
	08	303 48.8	45.9	221 25.3	14.0	18 35.5	10.8	54.6
M	09	318 48.7	. . 46.5	235 58.3	14.0	18 24.7	10.8	54.6
O	10	333 48.6	47.1	250 31.3	14.0	18 13.9	10.9	54.6
N	11	348 48.5	47.7	265 04.3	14.1	18 03.0	11.0	54.6
D	12	3 48.4	S18 48.4	279 37.4	14.2	S17 52.0	11.0	54.6
A	13	18 48.3	49.0	294 10.6	14.2	17 41.0	11.2	54.7
Y	14	33 48.1	49.6	308 43.8	14.2	17 29.8	11.2	54.7
	15	48 48.0	. . 50.2	323 17.0	14.3	17 18.6	11.3	54.7
	16	63 47.9	50.8	337 50.3	14.3	17 07.3	11.4	54.7
	17	78 47.8	51.5	352 23.6	14.3	16 55.9	11.5	54.7
	18	93 47.7	S18 52.1	6 56.9	14.4	S16 44.4	11.5	54.8
	19	108 47.6	52.7	21 30.3	14.4	16 32.9	11.6	54.8
	20	123 47.4	53.3	36 03.7	14.5	16 21.3	11.7	54.8
	21	138 47.3	. . 53.9	50 37.2	14.5	16 09.6	11.7	54.8
	22	153 47.2	54.5	65 10.7	14.5	15 57.9	11.9	54.8
	23	168 47.1	55.1	79 44.2	14.6	15 46.0	11.9	54.9
	17 00	183 47.0	S18 55.8	94 17.8	14.6	S15 34.1	11.9	54.9
	01	198 46.8	56.4	108 51.4	14.6	15 22.2	12.1	54.9
	02	213 46.7	57.0	123 25.0	14.6	15 10.1	12.1	54.9
	03	228 46.6	. . 57.6	137 58.6	14.7	14 58.0	12.2	55.0
	04	243 46.5	58.2	152 32.3	14.8	14 45.8	12.3	55.0
	05	258 46.4	58.8	167 06.1	14.7	14 33.5	12.3	55.0
	06	273 46.2	S18 59.4	181 39.8	14.8	S14 21.2	12.4	55.0
	07	288 46.1	19 00.0	196 13.6	14.8	14 08.8	12.4	55.0
T	08	303 46.0	00.6	210 47.4	14.8	13 56.4	12.6	55.1
U	09	318 45.9	. . 01.3	225 21.2	14.9	13 43.8	12.6	55.1
E	10	333 45.8	01.9	239 55.1	14.9	13 31.2	12.6	55.1
S	11	348 45.6	02.5	254 29.0	14.9	13 18.6	12.7	55.1
D	12	3 45.5	S19 03.1	269 02.9	14.9	S13 05.9	12.8	55.2
	13	18 45.4	03.7	283 36.8	15.0	12 53.1	12.9	55.2
A	14	33 45.3	04.3	298 10.8	14.9	12 40.2	12.9	55.2
Y	15	48 45.1	. . 04.9	312 44.7	15.0	12 27.3	13.0	55.2
	16	63 45.0	05.5	327 18.7	15.1	12 14.3	13.0	55.3
	17	78 44.9	06.1	341 52.8	15.0	12 01.3	13.1	55.3
	18	93 44.8	S19 06.7	356 26.8	15.0	S11 48.2	13.2	55.3
	19	108 44.6	07.3	11 00.8	15.1	11 35.0	13.2	55.3
	20	123 44.5	07.9	25 34.9	15.1	11 21.8	13.2	55.4
	21	138 44.4	. . 08.5	40 09.0	15.1	11 08.6	13.4	55.4
	22	153 44.2	09.1	54 43.1	15.1	10 55.2	13.4	55.4
	23	168 44.1	09.7	69 17.2	15.1	S10 41.8	13.4	55.5
		SD 16.2	*d* 0.6	SD	14.8		14.9	15.0

Lat.	Twilight Naut.	Twilight Civil	Sunrise	Moonrise 15	Moonrise 16	Moonrise 17	Moonrise 18
°	h m	h m	h m	h m	h m	h m	h m
N 72	07 03	08 39	11 31	▬	16 17	15 02	14 22
N 70	06 52	08 15	09 56	▬	15 24	14 40	14 12
68	06 44	07 57	09 17	15 48	14 51	14 24	14 03
66	06 36	07 43	08 51	14 52	14 26	14 10	13 56
64	06 30	07 30	08 30	14 19	14 07	13 58	13 50
62	06 24	07 20	08 14	13 55	13 52	13 48	13 45
60	06 19	07 11	08 00	13 35	13 38	13 40	13 40
N 58	06 14	07 03	07 49	13 19	13 27	13 32	13 36
56	06 10	06 56	07 38	13 05	13 17	13 26	13 33
54	06 06	06 50	07 29	12 53	13 08	13 20	13 30
52	06 03	06 44	07 21	12 43	13 00	13 14	13 27
50	05 59	06 39	07 14	12 33	12 53	13 10	13 24
45	05 51	06 27	06 59	12 13	12 38	12 59	13 18
N 40	05 44	06 17	06 46	11 57	12 25	12 50	13 13
35	05 38	06 08	06 35	11 43	12 14	12 43	13 09
30	05 32	06 00	06 26	11 31	12 05	12 36	13 05
20	05 19	05 46	06 09	11 10	11 49	12 24	12 58
N 10	05 07	05 33	05 55	10 52	11 34	12 14	12 53
0	04 54	05 19	05 41	10 35	11 21	12 04	12 47
S 10	04 39	05 05	05 27	10 18	11 07	11 55	12 42
20	04 21	04 49	05 13	10 00	10 53	11 44	12 36
30	03 58	04 29	04 55	09 39	10 36	11 32	12 29
35	03 43	04 17	04 45	09 27	10 26	11 25	12 25
40	03 25	04 03	04 34	09 13	10 15	11 18	12 21
45	03 03	03 46	04 20	08 56	10 02	11 08	12 15
S 50	02 32	03 24	04 03	08 34	09 45	10 57	12 09
52	02 16	03 14	03 55	08 24	09 38	10 52	12 06
54	01 56	03 01	03 47	08 13	09 29	10 46	12 03
56	01 31	02 47	03 37	08 00	09 20	10 40	12 00
58	00 53	02 30	03 25	07 45	09 09	10 32	11 56
S 60	////	02 09	03 12	07 27	08 56	10 24	11 51

Lat.	Sunset	Twilight Civil	Twilight Naut.	Moonset 15	Moonset 16	Moonset 17	Moonset 18
°	h m	h m	h m	h m	h m	h m	h m
N 72	11 58	14 49	16 25	▬	19 07	21 53	24 04
N 70	13 32	15 13	16 36	▬	19 59	22 13	24 12
68	14 11	15 31	16 45	18 00	20 30	22 28	24 17
66	14 38	15 46	16 52	18 54	20 53	22 40	24 22
64	14 58	15 58	16 59	19 27	21 11	22 50	24 26
62	15 15	16 09	17 05	19 50	21 26	22 59	24 30
60	15 28	16 18	17 10	20 09	21 38	23 06	24 33
N 58	15 40	16 26	17 14	20 25	21 49	23 12	24 36
56	15 50	16 33	17 19	20 38	21 58	23 18	24 38
54	15 59	16 39	17 23	20 49	22 06	23 23	24 40
52	16 07	16 45	17 26	20 59	22 13	23 28	24 42
50	16 15	16 50	17 30	21 08	22 20	23 32	24 44
45	16 30	17 02	17 38	21 27	22 34	23 40	24 48
N 40	16 43	17 12	17 45	21 43	22 45	23 48	24 51
35	16 54	17 21	17 51	21 55	22 55	23 54	24 54
30	17 03	17 29	17 58	22 07	23 03	24 00	00 00
20	17 20	17 43	18 10	22 26	23 18	24 09	00 09
N 10	17 35	17 57	18 22	22 42	23 30	24 17	00 17
0	17 48	18 10	18 36	22 57	23 42	24 25	00 25
S 10	18 02	18 25	18 51	23 13	23 53	24 32	00 32
20	18 17	18 41	19 09	23 29	24 06	00 06	00 40
30	18 35	19 01	19 32	23 47	24 20	00 20	00 50
35	18 45	19 13	19 47	23 58	24 28	00 28	00 55
40	18 56	19 27	20 05	24 10	00 10	00 37	01 01
45	19 10	19 44	20 28	24 25	00 25	00 48	01 07
S 50	19 27	20 07	20 59	00 20	00 42	01 00	01 16
52	19 35	20 17	21 16	00 30	00 51	01 06	01 19
54	19 44	20 30	21 36	00 42	01 00	01 13	01 23
56	19 54	20 44	22 02	00 55	01 10	01 20	01 28
58	20 06	21 01	22 42	01 11	01 22	01 28	01 33
S 60	20 19	21 23	////	01 30	01 35	01 37	01 38

Day	SUN Eqn. of Time 00^h	SUN Eqn. of Time 12^h	SUN Mer. Pass.	MOON Mer. Pass. Upper	MOON Mer. Pass. Lower	MOON Age	MOON Phase
d	m s	m s	h m	h m	h m	d %	
15	15 29	15 24	11 45	16 46	04 23	06 32	◐
16	15 19	15 14	11 45	17 31	05 09	07 41	
17	15 08	15 02	11 45	18 15	05 53	08 50	

UT d	UT h	ARIES GHA	VENUS −4·9 GHA	VENUS Dec	MARS +0·6 GHA	MARS Dec	JUPITER −2·1 GHA	JUPITER Dec	SATURN +0·5 GHA	SATURN Dec
		° ′	° ′	° ′	° ′	° ′	° ′	° ′	° ′	° ′
18	00	57 03.3	215 54.0	S 9 43.9	267 28.7	N14 29.5	268 31.1	N13 32.9	48 18.1	N 0 54.5
	01	72 05.8	230 55.9	43.5	282 30.1	29.1	283 33.4	32.9	63 20.6	54.5
	02	87 08.3	245 57.8	43.2	297 31.5	28.8	298 35.7	32.8	78 23.2	54.5
	03	102 10.7	260 59.7	. . 42.8	312 32.9	. . 28.5	313 38.0	. . 32.8	93 25.7	. . 54.4
	04	117 13.2	276 01.6	42.5	327 34.3	28.2	328 40.2	32.7	108 28.3	54.4
	05	132 15.7	291 03.5	42.2	342 35.7	27.9	343 42.5	32.7	123 30.8	54.4
	06	147 18.1	306 05.4	S 9 41.8	357 37.0	N14 27.6	358 44.8	N13 32.6	138 33.4	N 0 54.4
W	07	162 20.6	321 07.2	41.5	12 38.4	27.2	13 47.1	32.5	153 36.0	54.3
E	08	177 23.1	336 09.1	41.2	27 39.8	26.9	28 49.3	32.5	168 38.5	54.3
D	09	192 25.5	351 11.0	. . 40.8	42 41.2	. . 26.6	43 51.6	. . 32.4	183 41.1	. . 54.3
N	10	207 28.0	6 12.9	40.5	57 42.6	26.3	58 53.9	32.4	198 43.6	54.2
E	11	222 30.5	21 14.7	40.2	72 44.0	26.0	73 56.2	32.3	213 46.2	54.2
S	12	237 32.9	36 16.6	S 9 39.9	87 45.4	N14 25.6	88 58.4	N13 32.3	228 48.8	N 0 54.2
D	13	252 35.4	51 18.4	39.5	102 46.7	25.3	104 00.7	32.2	243 51.3	54.1
A	14	267 37.8	66 20.3	39.2	117 48.1	25.0	119 03.0	32.1	258 53.9	54.1
Y	15	282 40.3	81 22.2	. . 38.9	132 49.5	. . 24.7	134 05.3	. . 32.1	273 56.4	. . 54.1
	16	297 42.8	96 24.0	38.6	147 50.9	24.4	149 07.6	32.0	288 59.0	54.1
	17	312 45.2	111 25.8	38.3	162 52.3	24.1	164 09.8	32.0	304 01.5	54.0
	18	327 47.7	126 27.7	S 9 38.0	177 53.7	N14 23.7	179 12.1	N13 31.9	319 04.1	N 0 54.0
	19	342 50.2	141 29.5	37.7	192 55.1	23.4	194 14.4	31.9	334 06.6	54.0
	20	357 52.6	156 31.4	37.4	207 56.5	23.1	209 16.7	31.8	349 09.2	53.9
	21	12 55.1	171 33.2	. . 37.1	222 57.9	. . 22.8	224 18.9	. . 31.8	4 11.8	. . 53.9
	22	27 57.6	186 35.0	36.8	237 59.3	22.5	239 21.2	31.7	19 14.3	53.9
	23	43 00.0	201 36.9	36.5	253 00.7	22.2	254 23.5	31.7	34 16.9	53.8
19	00	58 02.5	216 38.7	S 9 36.2	268 02.0	N14 21.8	269 25.8	N13 31.6	49 19.4	N 0 53.8
	01	73 04.9	231 40.5	35.9	283 03.4	21.5	284 28.1	31.5	64 22.0	53.8
	02	88 07.4	246 42.3	35.6	298 04.8	21.2	299 30.3	31.5	79 24.5	53.8
	03	103 09.9	261 44.1	. . 35.3	313 06.2	. . 20.9	314 32.6	. . 31.4	94 27.1	. . 53.7
	04	118 12.3	276 45.9	35.0	328 07.6	20.6	329 34.9	31.4	109 29.6	53.7
	05	133 14.8	291 47.7	34.7	343 09.0	20.3	344 37.2	31.3	124 32.2	53.7
	06	148 17.3	306 49.5	S 9 34.4	358 10.4	N14 20.0	359 39.5	N13 31.3	139 34.8	N 0 53.6
T	07	163 19.7	321 51.3	34.1	13 11.8	19.6	14 41.8	31.2	154 37.3	53.6
H	08	178 22.2	336 53.1	33.8	28 13.2	19.3	29 44.0	31.2	169 39.9	53.6
U	09	193 24.7	351 54.9	. . 33.6	43 14.6	. . 19.0	44 46.3	. . 31.1	184 42.4	. . 53.5
R	10	208 27.1	6 56.7	33.3	58 16.0	18.7	59 48.6	31.1	199 45.0	53.5
S	11	223 29.6	21 58.5	33.0	73 17.4	18.4	74 50.9	31.0	214 47.5	53.5
D	12	238 32.1	37 00.3	S 9 32.7	88 18.8	N14 18.1	89 53.2	N13 31.0	229 50.1	N 0 53.5
A	13	253 34.5	52 02.1	32.5	103 20.2	17.7	104 55.4	30.9	244 52.6	53.4
Y	14	268 37.0	67 03.8	32.2	118 21.6	17.4	119 57.7	30.8	259 55.2	53.4
	15	283 39.4	82 05.6	. . 31.9	133 23.0	. . 17.1	135 00.0	. . 30.8	274 57.7	. . 53.4
	16	298 41.9	97 07.4	31.7	148 24.4	16.8	150 02.3	30.7	290 00.3	53.3
	17	313 44.4	112 09.2	31.4	163 25.8	16.5	165 04.6	30.7	305 02.8	53.3
	18	328 46.8	127 10.9	S 9 31.1	178 27.2	N14 16.2	180 06.9	N13 30.6	320 05.4	N 0 53.3
	19	343 49.3	142 12.7	30.9	193 28.6	15.9	195 09.2	30.6	335 08.0	53.3
	20	358 51.8	157 14.4	30.6	208 30.0	15.5	210 11.4	30.5	350 10.5	53.2
	21	13 54.2	172 16.2	. . 30.3	223 31.4	. . 15.2	225 13.7	. . 30.5	5 13.1	. . 53.2
	22	28 56.7	187 17.9	30.1	238 32.8	14.9	240 16.0	30.4	20 15.6	53.2
	23	43 59.2	202 19.7	29.8	253 34.2	14.6	255 18.3	30.4	35 18.2	53.2
20	00	59 01.6	217 21.4	S 9 29.6	268 35.6	N14 14.3	270 20.6	N13 30.3	50 20.7	N 0 53.1
	01	74 04.1	232 23.2	29.3	283 37.0	14.0	285 22.9	30.3	65 23.3	53.1
	02	89 06.6	247 24.9	29.1	298 38.4	13.7	300 25.2	30.2	80 25.8	53.1
	03	104 09.0	262 26.6	. . 28.8	313 39.9	. . 13.4	315 27.5	. . 30.2	95 28.4	. . 53.0
	04	119 11.5	277 28.4	28.6	328 41.3	13.0	330 29.7	30.1	110 30.9	53.0
	05	134 13.9	292 30.1	28.4	343 42.7	12.7	345 32.0	30.1	125 33.5	53.0
	06	149 16.4	307 31.8	S 9 28.1	358 44.1	N14 12.4	0 34.3	N13 30.0	140 36.0	N 0 53.0
	07	164 18.9	322 33.5	27.9	13 45.5	12.1	15 36.6	30.0	155 38.6	52.9
	08	179 21.3	337 35.3	27.6	28 46.9	11.8	30 38.9	29.9	170 41.1	52.9
F	09	194 23.8	352 37.0	. . 27.4	43 48.3	. . 11.5	45 41.2	. . 29.9	185 43.7	. . 52.9
R	10	209 26.3	7 38.7	27.2	58 49.7	11.2	60 43.5	29.8	200 46.2	52.8
I	11	224 28.7	22 40.4	26.9	73 51.1	10.9	75 45.8	29.8	215 48.8	52.8
D	12	239 31.2	37 42.1	S 9 26.7	88 52.5	N14 10.5	90 48.1	N13 29.7	230 51.3	N 0 52.8
A	13	254 33.7	52 43.8	26.5	103 54.0	10.2	105 50.3	29.7	245 53.9	52.8
Y	14	269 36.1	67 45.5	26.3	118 55.4	09.9	120 52.6	29.6	260 56.4	52.7
	15	284 38.6	82 47.2	. . 26.0	133 56.8	. . 09.6	135 54.9	. . 29.6	275 59.0	. . 52.7
	16	299 41.0	97 48.9	25.8	148 58.2	09.3	150 57.2	29.5	291 01.5	52.7
	17	314 43.5	112 50.6	25.6	163 59.6	09.0	165 59.5	29.5	306 04.1	52.7
	18	329 46.0	127 52.3	S 9 25.4	179 01.0	N14 08.7	181 01.8	N13 29.4	321 06.6	N 0 52.6
	19	344 48.4	142 53.9	25.2	194 02.4	08.4	196 04.1	29.4	336 09.2	52.6
	20	359 50.9	157 55.6	25.0	209 03.9	08.1	211 06.4	29.3	351 11.7	52.6
	21	14 53.4	172 57.3	. . 24.7	224 05.3	. . 07.7	226 08.7	. . 29.3	6 14.3	. . 52.6
	22	29 55.8	187 59.0	24.5	239 06.7	07.4	241 11.0	29.2	21 16.8	52.5
	23	44 58.3	203 00.6	24.3	254 08.1	07.1	256 13.3	29.2	36 19.4	52.5
Mer. Pass.		h m 20 04.5	*v* 1.8	*d* 0.3	*v* 1.4	*d* 0.3	*v* 2.3	*d* 0.1	*v* 2.6	*d* 0.0

STARS Name	SHA ° ′	Dec ° ′
Acamar	315 10.2	S40 11.8
Achernar	335 18.6	S57 06.1
Acrux	172 58.8	S63 14.7
Adhara	255 04.4	S29 00.3
Aldebaran	290 37.5	N16 33.9
Alioth	166 12.1	N55 48.6
Alkaid	152 51.2	N49 10.6
Alnair	27 31.0	S46 50.0
Alnilam	275 35.9	S 1 11.0
Alphard	217 46.2	S 8 46.4
Alphecca	126 02.8	N26 37.5
Alpheratz	357 33.0	N29 14.6
Altair	61 58.7	N 8 56.5
Ankaa	353 05.4	S42 09.7
Antares	112 14.3	S26 29.4
Arcturus	145 46.8	N19 02.5
Atria	107 07.7	S69 04.6
Avior	234 13.8	S59 35.4
Bellatrix	278 20.9	N 6 22.5
Betelgeuse	270 50.1	N 7 24.8
Canopus	263 51.3	S52 42.4
Capella	280 19.2	N46 01.4
Deneb	49 24.9	N45 22.9
Denebola	182 23.6	N14 25.2
Diphda	348 45.5	S17 50.3
Dubhe	193 39.4	N61 36.1
Elnath	277 59.6	N28 37.8
Eltanin	90 41.9	N51 29.3
Enif	33 37.3	N10 00.1
Fomalhaut	15 12.8	S29 28.8
Gacrux	171 50.3	S57 15.6
Gienah	175 42.2	S17 41.4
Hadar	148 34.4	S60 30.0
Hamal	327 49.1	N23 35.5
Kaus Aust.	83 30.8	S34 22.3
Kochab	137 21.0	N74 02.5
Markab	13 28.3	N15 21.2
Menkar	314 04.2	N 4 11.8
Menkent	147 56.2	S36 30.0
Miaplacidus	221 37.8	S69 49.3
Mirfak	308 25.5	N49 57.5
Nunki	75 46.1	S26 15.8
Peacock	53 03.6	S56 39.1
Pollux	243 15.2	N27 57.6
Procyon	244 49.1	N 5 09.4
Rasalhague	95 57.5	N12 32.5
Regulus	207 32.8	N11 50.1
Rigel	281 02.1	S 8 10.1
Rigil Kent.	139 38.8	S60 56.6
Sabik	102 01.4	S15 45.4
Schedar	349 28.9	N56 41.4
Shaula	96 08.7	S37 07.4
Sirius	258 24.6	S16 45.1
Spica	158 21.0	S11 18.0
Suhail	222 45.1	S43 32.2
Vega	80 32.5	N38 48.7
Zuben'ubi	136 54.7	S16 09.1

	SHA ° ′	Mer. Pass. h m
Venus	158 36.2	9 32
Mars	209 59.6	6 07
Jupiter	211 23.3	6 01
Saturn	351 16.9	20 39

UT		SUN GHA	SUN Dec	MOON GHA	v	MOON Dec	d	HP
d	h	° ′	° ′	° ′	′	° ′	′	′
18	00	183 44.0	S19 10.3	83 51.3	15.2	S10 28.4	13.5	55.5
	01	198 43.9	10.9	98 25.5	15.1	10 14.9	13.6	55.5
	02	213 43.7	11.5	112 59.6	15.2	10 01.3	13.6	55.5
	03	228 43.6	. . 12.1	127 33.8	15.1	9 47.7	13.6	55.6
	04	243 43.5	12.7	142 07.9	15.2	9 34.1	13.8	55.6
	05	258 43.3	13.3	156 42.1	15.2	9 20.3	13.7	55.6
	06	273 43.2	S19 13.9	171 16.3	15.2	S 9 06.6	13.9	55.7
W	07	288 43.1	14.5	185 50.5	15.2	8 52.7	13.8	55.7
E	08	303 43.0	15.1	200 24.7	15.2	8 38.9	14.0	55.7
D	09	318 42.8	. . 15.7	214 58.9	15.2	8 24.9	13.9	55.8
N	10	333 42.7	16.3	229 33.1	15.1	8 11.0	14.0	55.8
E	11	348 42.6	16.9	244 07.2	15.2	7 57.0	14.1	55.8
S	12	3 42.4	S19 17.4	258 41.4	15.2	S 7 42.9	14.1	55.8
D	13	18 42.3	18.0	273 15.6	15.2	7 28.8	14.2	55.9
A	14	33 42.2	18.6	287 49.8	15.2	7 14.6	14.2	55.9
Y	15	48 42.0	. . 19.2	302 24.0	15.2	7 00.4	14.3	55.9
	16	63 41.9	19.8	316 58.2	15.2	6 46.1	14.2	56.0
	17	78 41.8	20.4	331 32.4	15.1	6 31.9	14.4	56.0
	18	93 41.6	S19 21.0	346 06.5	15.2	S 6 17.5	14.4	56.0
	19	108 41.5	21.6	0 40.7	15.1	6 03.1	14.4	56.1
	20	123 41.4	22.2	15 14.8	15.2	5 48.7	14.5	56.1
	21	138 41.2	. . 22.7	29 49.0	15.1	5 34.2	14.5	56.1
	22	153 41.1	23.3	44 23.1	15.1	5 19.7	14.5	56.2
	23	168 41.0	23.9	58 57.2	15.1	5 05.2	14.6	56.2
19	00	183 40.8	S19 24.5	73 31.3	15.1	S 4 50.6	14.6	56.2
	01	198 40.7	25.1	88 05.4	15.1	4 36.0	14.7	56.3
	02	213 40.5	25.7	102 39.5	15.0	4 21.3	14.7	56.3
	03	228 40.4	. . 26.3	117 13.5	15.0	4 06.6	14.7	56.3
	04	243 40.3	26.8	131 47.5	15.1	3 51.9	14.8	56.4
	05	258 40.1	27.4	146 21.6	14.9	3 37.1	14.8	56.4
	06	273 40.0	S19 28.0	160 55.5	15.0	S 3 22.3	14.8	56.4
T	07	288 39.8	28.6	175 29.5	15.0	3 07.5	14.9	56.5
H	08	303 39.7	29.2	190 03.5	14.9	2 52.6	14.9	56.5
U	09	318 39.6	. . 29.7	204 37.4	14.9	2 37.7	14.9	56.6
R	10	333 39.4	30.3	219 11.3	14.8	2 22.8	15.0	56.6
S	11	348 39.3	30.9	233 45.1	14.9	2 07.8	14.9	56.6
D	12	3 39.1	S19 31.5	248 19.0	14.8	S 1 52.9	15.1	56.7
A	13	18 39.0	32.0	262 52.8	14.7	1 37.8	15.0	56.7
Y	14	33 38.9	32.6	277 26.5	14.8	1 22.8	15.1	56.7
	15	48 38.7	. . 33.2	292 00.3	14.7	1 07.7	15.1	56.8
	16	63 38.6	33.8	306 34.0	14.6	0 52.6	15.1	56.8
	17	78 38.4	34.3	321 07.6	14.7	0 37.5	15.1	56.8
	18	93 38.3	S19 34.9	335 41.3	14.6	S 0 22.4	15.2	56.9
	19	108 38.2	35.5	350 14.9	14.5	S 0 07.2	15.2	56.9
	20	123 38.0	36.1	4 48.4	14.5	N 0 08.0	15.2	57.0
	21	138 37.9	. . 36.6	19 21.9	14.5	0 23.2	15.2	57.0
	22	153 37.7	37.2	33 55.4	14.4	0 38.4	15.2	57.0
	23	168 37.6	37.8	48 28.8	14.4	0 53.6	15.3	57.1
20	00	183 37.4	S19 38.3	63 02.2	14.3	N 1 08.9	15.3	57.1
	01	198 37.3	38.9	77 35.5	14.3	1 24.2	15.2	57.2
	02	213 37.1	39.5	92 08.8	14.3	1 39.4	15.4	57.2
	03	228 37.0	. . 40.1	106 42.1	14.2	1 54.8	15.3	57.2
	04	243 36.9	40.6	121 15.3	14.1	2 10.1	15.3	57.3
	05	258 36.7	41.2	135 48.4	14.1	2 25.4	15.3	57.3
	06	273 36.6	S19 41.8	150 21.5	14.0	N 2 40.7	15.4	57.3
	07	288 36.4	42.3	164 54.5	14.0	2 56.1	15.4	57.4
	08	303 36.3	42.9	179 27.5	13.9	3 11.5	15.3	57.4
F	09	318 36.1	. . 43.4	194 00.4	13.9	3 26.8	15.4	57.5
R	10	333 36.0	44.0	208 33.3	13.8	3 42.2	15.4	57.5
I	11	348 35.8	44.6	223 06.1	13.7	3 57.6	15.4	57.5
D	12	3 35.7	S19 45.1	237 38.8	13.7	N 4 13.0	15.3	57.6
A	13	18 35.5	45.7	252 11.5	13.6	4 28.3	15.4	57.6
Y	14	33 35.4	46.3	266 44.1	13.5	4 43.7	15.4	57.7
	15	48 35.2	. . 46.8	281 16.6	13.5	4 59.1	15.4	57.7
	16	63 35.1	47.4	295 49.1	13.4	5 14.5	15.4	57.7
	17	78 34.9	47.9	310 21.5	13.4	5 29.9	15.4	57.8
	18	93 34.8	S19 48.5	324 53.9	13.2	N 5 45.3	15.3	57.8
	19	108 34.6	49.1	339 26.1	13.2	6 00.6	15.4	57.9
	20	123 34.5	49.6	353 58.3	13.2	6 16.0	15.4	57.9
	21	138 34.3	. . 50.2	8 30.5	13.0	6 31.4	15.3	57.9
	22	153 34.2	50.7	23 02.5	13.0	6 46.7	15.4	58.0
	23	168 34.0	51.3	37 34.5	12.9	N 7 02.1	15.3	58.0
		SD 16.2	*d* 0.6	SD	15.2	15.4		15.7

Lat.	Twilight Naut.	Twilight Civil	Sunrise	Moonrise 18	Moonrise 19	Moonrise 20	Moonrise 21
°	h m	h m	h m	h m	h m	h m	h m
N 72	07 13	08 53	▬	14 22	13 49	13 17	12 39
N 70	07 02	08 27	10 18	14 12	13 47	13 23	12 55
68	06 52	08 07	09 32	14 03	13 45	13 28	13 08
66	06 44	07 51	09 02	13 56	13 44	13 32	13 19
64	06 37	07 38	08 40	13 50	13 43	13 35	13 28
62	06 30	07 27	08 22	13 45	13 42	13 38	13 35
60	06 25	07 17	08 08	13 40	13 41	13 41	13 42
N 58	06 20	07 09	07 55	13 36	13 40	13 44	13 48
56	06 15	07 01	07 45	13 33	13 39	13 46	13 54
54	06 11	06 55	07 35	13 30	13 39	13 48	13 58
52	06 07	06 49	07 27	13 27	13 38	13 50	14 03
50	06 03	06 43	07 19	13 24	13 37	13 51	14 07
45	05 55	06 31	07 03	13 18	13 36	13 55	14 15
N 40	05 47	06 20	06 50	13 13	13 35	13 58	14 23
35	05 40	06 11	06 38	13 09	13 34	14 00	14 29
30	05 34	06 03	06 28	13 05	13 33	14 03	14 34
20	05 21	05 48	06 11	12 58	13 32	14 07	14 44
N 10	05 08	05 34	05 56	12 53	13 31	14 11	14 53
0	04 54	05 20	05 42	12 47	13 30	14 14	15 01
S 10	04 39	05 05	05 27	12 42	13 29	14 18	15 09
20	04 20	04 48	05 12	12 36	13 28	14 21	15 18
30	03 56	04 28	04 54	12 29	13 26	14 26	15 28
35	03 41	04 15	04 44	12 25	13 26	14 28	15 34
40	03 22	04 01	04 32	12 21	13 25	14 31	15 41
45	02 59	03 43	04 17	12 15	13 24	14 34	15 49
S 50	02 26	03 20	04 00	12 09	13 23	14 38	15 58
52	02 09	03 09	03 51	12 06	13 22	14 40	16 03
54	01 48	02 56	03 42	12 03	13 21	14 42	16 08
56	01 19	02 41	03 32	12 00	13 21	14 45	16 13
58	00 31	02 23	03 20	11 56	13 20	14 47	16 20
S 60	////	02 00	03 06	11 51	13 19	14 50	16 27

Lat.	Sunset	Twilight Civil	Twilight Naut.	Moonset 18	Moonset 19	Moonset 20	Moonset 21
°	h m	h m	h m	h m	h m	h m	h m
N 72	▬	14 37	16 16	24 04	00 04	02 11	04 26
N 70	13 12	15 03	16 28	24 12	00 12	02 09	04 13
68	13 58	15 23	16 38	24 17	00 17	02 07	04 03
66	14 28	15 39	16 46	24 22	00 22	02 05	03 54
64	14 50	15 52	16 53	24 26	00 26	02 04	03 47
62	15 08	16 03	17 00	24 30	00 30	02 03	03 40
60	15 22	16 13	17 05	24 33	00 33	02 02	03 35
N 58	15 35	16 21	17 10	24 36	00 36	02 01	03 30
56	15 46	16 29	17 15	24 38	00 38	02 00	03 26
54	15 55	16 35	17 19	24 40	00 40	02 00	03 22
52	16 04	16 42	17 23	24 42	00 42	01 59	03 19
50	16 11	16 47	17 27	24 44	00 44	01 58	03 16
45	16 27	17 00	17 35	24 48	00 48	01 57	03 09
N 40	16 41	17 10	17 43	24 51	00 51	01 56	03 04
35	16 52	17 19	17 50	24 54	00 54	01 55	02 59
30	17 02	17 28	17 57	00 00	00 56	01 54	02 55
20	17 19	17 43	18 10	00 09	01 00	01 53	02 48
N 10	17 35	17 57	18 23	00 17	01 04	01 52	02 42
0	17 49	18 11	18 36	00 25	01 07	01 51	02 36
S 10	18 03	18 26	18 52	00 32	01 11	01 49	02 30
20	18 19	18 43	19 11	00 40	01 14	01 48	02 24
30	18 37	19 03	19 35	00 50	01 18	01 47	02 17
35	18 48	19 16	19 50	00 55	01 20	01 46	02 13
40	19 00	19 31	20 09	01 01	01 23	01 45	02 08
45	19 14	19 49	20 33	01 07	01 26	01 44	02 03
S 50	19 32	20 12	21 06	01 16	01 29	01 43	01 57
52	19 40	20 23	21 24	01 19	01 31	01 42	01 54
54	19 50	20 37	21 46	01 23	01 32	01 41	01 51
56	20 00	20 52	22 15	01 28	01 34	01 41	01 47
58	20 13	21 10	23 09	01 33	01 36	01 40	01 44
S 60	20 27	21 34	////	01 38	01 39	01 39	01 39

Day	SUN Eqn. of Time 00^h	SUN Eqn. of Time 12^h	SUN Mer. Pass.	MOON Mer. Pass. Upper	MOON Mer. Pass. Lower	MOON Age	MOON Phase
d	m s	m s	h m	h m	h m	d %	
18	14 56	14 50	11 45	18 57	06 36	09 60	
19	14 44	14 37	11 45	19 40	07 19	10 70	
20	14 30	14 23	11 46	20 25	08 02	11 79	

UT d	UT h	ARIES GHA	VENUS −4·9 GHA	VENUS Dec	MARS +0·6 GHA	MARS Dec	JUPITER −2·1 GHA	JUPITER Dec	SATURN +0·5 GHA	SATURN Dec
		° ′	° ′	° ′	° ′	° ′	° ′	° ′	° ′	° ′
21 SATURDAY	00	60 00.8	218 02.3	S 9 24.1	269 09.5	N14 06.8	271 15.6	N13 29.1	51 21.9	N 0 52.5
	01	75 03.2	233 04.0	23.9	284 10.9	06.5	286 17.9	29.1	66 24.5	52.4
	02	90 05.7	248 05.6	23.7	299 12.4	06.2	301 20.2	29.0	81 27.0	52.4
	03	105 08.2	263 07.3	23.5	314 13.8	05.9	316 22.4	29.0	96 29.6	52.4
	04	120 10.6	278 08.9	23.3	329 15.2	05.6	331 24.7	28.9	111 32.1	52.4
	05	135 13.1	293 10.6	23.1	344 16.6	05.3	346 27.0	28.9	126 34.7	52.3
	06	150 15.5	308 12.2	S 9 22.9	359 18.0	N14 04.9	1 29.3	N13 28.8	141 37.2	N 0 52.3
	07	165 18.0	323 13.9	22.7	14 19.5	04.6	16 31.6	28.8	156 39.7	52.3
	08	180 20.5	338 15.5	22.5	29 20.9	04.3	31 33.9	28.7	171 42.3	52.3
	09	195 22.9	353 17.2	22.4	44 22.3	04.0	46 36.2	28.7	186 44.8	52.2
	10	210 25.4	8 18.8	22.2	59 23.7	03.7	61 38.5	28.6	201 47.4	52.2
	11	225 27.9	23 20.4	22.0	74 25.1	03.4	76 40.8	28.6	216 49.9	52.2
	12	240 30.3	38 22.1	S 9 21.8	89 26.6	N14 03.1	91 43.1	N13 28.5	231 52.5	N 0 52.2
	13	255 32.8	53 23.7	21.6	104 28.0	02.8	106 45.4	28.5	246 55.0	52.1
	14	270 35.3	68 25.3	21.4	119 29.4	02.5	121 47.7	28.4	261 57.6	52.1
	15	285 37.7	83 26.9	21.3	134 30.8	02.2	136 50.0	28.4	277 00.1	52.1
	16	300 40.2	98 28.6	21.1	149 32.3	01.9	151 52.3	28.3	292 02.7	52.1
	17	315 42.6	113 30.2	20.9	164 33.7	01.6	166 54.6	28.3	307 05.2	52.0
	18	330 45.1	128 31.8	S 9 20.7	179 35.1	N14 01.2	181 56.9	N13 28.2	322 07.8	N 0 52.0
	19	345 47.6	143 33.4	20.6	194 36.6	00.9	196 59.2	28.2	337 10.3	52.0
	20	0 50.0	158 35.0	20.4	209 38.0	00.6	212 01.5	28.1	352 12.8	52.0
	21	15 52.5	173 36.6	20.2	224 39.4	00.3	227 03.8	28.1	7 15.4	51.9
	22	30 55.0	188 38.2	20.1	239 40.8	14 00.0	242 06.1	28.0	22 17.9	51.9
	23	45 57.4	203 39.8	19.9	254 42.3	13 59.7	257 08.4	28.0	37 20.5	51.9
22 SUNDAY	00	60 59.9	218 41.4	S 9 19.7	269 43.7	N13 59.4	272 10.7	N13 27.9	52 23.0	N 0 51.9
	01	76 02.4	233 43.0	19.6	284 45.1	59.1	287 13.0	27.9	67 25.6	51.8
	02	91 04.8	248 44.6	19.4	299 46.6	58.8	302 15.3	27.9	82 28.1	51.8
	03	106 07.3	263 46.1	19.3	314 48.0	58.5	317 17.6	27.8	97 30.7	51.8
	04	121 09.8	278 47.7	19.1	329 49.4	58.2	332 19.9	27.8	112 33.2	51.8
	05	136 12.2	293 49.3	19.0	344 50.9	57.9	347 22.2	27.7	127 35.7	51.7
	06	151 14.7	308 50.9	S 9 18.8	359 52.3	N13 57.6	2 24.5	N13 27.7	142 38.3	N 0 51.7
	07	166 17.1	323 52.4	18.7	14 53.7	57.3	17 26.8	27.6	157 40.8	51.7
	08	181 19.6	338 54.0	18.5	29 55.2	56.9	32 29.1	27.6	172 43.4	51.7
	09	196 22.1	353 55.6	18.4	44 56.6	56.6	47 31.4	27.5	187 45.9	51.6
	10	211 24.5	8 57.1	18.2	59 58.0	56.3	62 33.7	27.5	202 48.5	51.6
	11	226 27.0	23 58.7	18.1	74 59.5	56.0	77 36.0	27.4	217 51.0	51.6
	12	241 29.5	39 00.3	S 9 18.0	90 00.9	N13 55.7	92 38.3	N13 27.4	232 53.5	N 0 51.6
	13	256 31.9	54 01.8	17.8	105 02.3	55.4	107 40.6	27.3	247 56.1	51.6
	14	271 34.4	69 03.4	17.7	120 03.8	55.1	122 42.9	27.3	262 58.6	51.5
	15	286 36.9	84 04.9	17.5	135 05.2	54.8	137 45.3	27.3	278 01.2	51.5
	16	301 39.3	99 06.4	17.4	150 06.6	54.5	152 47.6	27.2	293 03.7	51.5
	17	316 41.8	114 08.0	17.3	165 08.1	54.2	167 49.9	27.2	308 06.3	51.5
	18	331 44.3	129 09.5	S 9 17.2	180 09.5	N13 53.9	182 52.2	N13 27.1	323 08.8	N 0 51.4
	19	346 46.7	144 11.1	17.0	195 11.0	53.6	197 54.5	27.1	338 11.3	51.4
	20	1 49.2	159 12.6	16.9	210 12.4	53.3	212 56.8	27.0	353 13.9	51.4
	21	16 51.6	174 14.1	16.8	225 13.9	53.0	227 59.1	27.0	8 16.4	51.4
	22	31 54.1	189 15.6	16.7	240 15.3	52.7	243 01.4	26.9	23 19.0	51.3
	23	46 56.6	204 17.2	16.5	255 16.7	52.4	258 03.7	26.9	38 21.5	51.3
23 MONDAY	00	61 59.0	219 18.7	S 9 16.4	270 18.2	N13 52.1	273 06.0	N13 26.8	53 24.0	N 0 51.3
	01	77 01.5	234 20.2	16.3	285 19.6	51.8	288 08.3	26.8	68 26.6	51.3
	02	92 04.0	249 21.7	16.2	300 21.1	51.5	303 10.6	26.8	83 29.1	51.3
	03	107 06.4	264 23.2	16.1	315 22.5	51.2	318 12.9	26.7	98 31.7	51.2
	04	122 08.9	279 24.7	16.0	330 24.0	50.9	333 15.2	26.7	113 34.2	51.2
	05	137 11.4	294 26.2	15.9	345 25.4	50.5	348 17.6	26.6	128 36.7	51.2
	06	152 13.8	309 27.7	S 9 15.8	0 26.8	N13 50.2	3 19.9	N13 26.6	143 39.3	N 0 51.2
	07	167 16.3	324 29.2	15.6	15 28.3	49.9	18 22.2	26.5	158 41.8	51.1
	08	182 18.8	339 30.7	15.5	30 29.7	49.6	33 24.5	26.5	173 44.4	51.1
	09	197 21.2	354 32.2	15.4	45 31.2	49.3	48 26.8	26.5	188 46.9	51.1
	10	212 23.7	9 33.7	15.3	60 32.6	49.0	63 29.1	26.4	203 49.4	51.1
	11	227 26.1	24 35.2	15.2	75 34.1	48.7	78 31.4	26.4	218 52.0	51.1
	12	242 28.6	39 36.7	S 9 15.1	90 35.5	N13 48.4	93 33.7	N13 26.3	233 54.5	N 0 51.0
	13	257 31.1	54 38.2	15.1	105 37.0	48.1	108 36.0	26.3	248 57.1	51.0
	14	272 33.5	69 39.7	15.0	120 38.4	47.8	123 38.4	26.2	263 59.6	51.0
	15	287 36.0	84 41.1	14.9	135 39.9	47.5	138 40.7	26.2	279 02.1	51.0
	16	302 38.5	99 42.6	14.8	150 41.3	47.2	153 43.0	26.1	294 04.7	50.9
	17	317 40.9	114 44.1	14.7	165 42.8	46.9	168 45.3	26.1	309 07.2	50.9
	18	332 43.4	129 45.5	S 9 14.6	180 44.2	N13 46.6	183 47.6	N13 26.1	324 09.8	N 0 50.9
	19	347 45.9	144 47.0	14.5	195 45.7	46.3	198 49.9	26.0	339 12.3	50.9
	20	2 48.3	159 48.5	14.4	210 47.1	46.0	213 52.2	26.0	354 14.8	50.9
	21	17 50.8	174 49.9	14.4	225 48.6	45.7	228 54.5	25.9	9 17.4	50.8
	22	32 53.2	189 51.4	14.3	240 50.0	45.4	243 56.9	25.9	24 19.9	50.8
	23	47 55.7	204 52.8	14.2	255 51.5	45.1	258 59.2	25.8	39 22.4	50.8
Mer. Pass.		h m 19 52.7	*v* 1.6	*d* 0.1	*v* 1.4	*d* 0.3	*v* 2.3	*d* 0.0	*v* 2.5	*d* 0.0

STARS

Name	SHA ° ′	Dec ° ′
Acamar	315 10.2	S40 11.8
Achernar	335 18.6	S57 06.1
Acrux	172 58.7	S63 14.7
Adhara	255 04.4	S29 00.3
Aldebaran	290 37.5	N16 33.9
Alioth	166 12.0	N55 48.6
Alkaid	152 51.2	N49 10.6
Alnair	27 31.0	S46 50.0
Alnilam	275 35.9	S 1 11.0
Alphard	217 46.2	S 8 46.4
Alphecca	126 02.8	N26 37.4
Alpheratz	357 33.0	N29 14.6
Altair	61 58.7	N 8 56.5
Ankaa	353 05.4	S42 09.7
Antares	112 14.3	S26 29.4
Arcturus	145 46.8	N19 02.5
Atria	107 07.7	S69 04.5
Avior	234 13.8	S59 35.4
Bellatrix	278 20.9	N 6 22.5
Betelgeuse	270 50.1	N 7 24.8
Canopus	263 51.3	S52 42.4
Capella	280 19.2	N46 01.4
Deneb	49 24.9	N45 22.9
Denebola	182 23.5	N14 25.2
Diphda	348 45.6	S17 50.3
Dubhe	193 39.3	N61 36.0
Elnath	277 59.6	N28 37.8
Eltanin	90 42.0	N51 29.2
Enif	33 37.3	N10 00.1
Fomalhaut	15 12.8	S29 28.8
Gacrux	171 50.3	S57 15.6
Gienah	175 42.2	S17 41.4
Hadar	148 34.4	S60 30.0
Hamal	327 49.2	N23 35.5
Kaus Aust.	83 30.8	S34 22.3
Kochab	137 21.0	N74 02.5
Markab	13 28.3	N15 21.2
Menkar	314 04.2	N 4 11.8
Menkent	147 56.2	S36 30.0
Miaplacidus	221 37.7	S69 49.3
Mirfak	308 25.5	N49 57.5
Nunki	75 46.2	S26 15.8
Peacock	53 03.6	S56 39.1
Pollux	243 15.2	N27 57.6
Procyon	244 49.0	N 5 09.4
Rasalhague	95 57.5	N12 32.5
Regulus	207 32.8	N11 50.1
Rigel	281 02.1	S 8 10.1
Rigil Kent.	139 38.8	S60 56.6
Sabik	102 01.4	S15 45.4
Schedar	349 28.9	N56 41.4
Shaula	96 08.7	S37 07.4
Sirius	258 24.6	S16 45.1
Spica	158 21.0	S11 18.0
Suhail	222 45.1	S43 32.2
Vega	80 32.5	N38 48.7
Zuben'ubi	136 54.7	S16 09.1

	SHA ° ′	Mer. Pass. h m
Venus	157 41.5	9 24
Mars	208 43.8	6 01
Jupiter	211 10.8	5 50
Saturn	351 23.1	20 27

	UT	SUN GHA	SUN Dec	MOON GHA	v	MOON Dec	d	HP
	d h	° ′	° ′	° ′	′	° ′	′	′
	21 00	183 33.9	S19 51.8	52 06.4	12.8	N 7 17.4	15.3	58.0
	01	198 33.7	52.4	66 38.2	12.7	7 32.7	15.4	58.1
	02	213 33.5	52.9	81 09.9	12.7	7 48.1	15.3	58.1
	03	228 33.4	. . 53.5	95 41.6	12.6	8 03.4	15.2	58.2
	04	243 33.2	54.1	110 13.2	12.5	8 18.6	15.3	58.2
	05	258 33.1	54.6	124 44.7	12.4	8 33.9	15.2	58.2
	06	273 32.9	S19 55.2	139 16.1	12.3	N 8 49.1	15.2	58.3
S	07	288 32.8	55.7	153 47.4	12.2	9 04.3	15.2	58.3
A	08	303 32.6	56.3	168 18.6	12.1	9 19.5	15.2	58.4
T	09	318 32.5	. . 56.8	182 49.7	12.1	9 34.7	15.2	58.4
U	10	333 32.3	57.4	197 20.8	11.9	9 49.9	15.1	58.4
R	11	348 32.2	57.9	211 51.7	11.9	10 05.0	15.1	58.5
D	12	3 32.0	S19 58.4	226 22.6	11.7	N10 20.1	15.0	58.5
A	13	18 31.8	59.0	240 53.3	11.7	10 35.1	15.1	58.6
Y	14	33 31.7	19 59.5	255 24.0	11.6	10 50.2	14.9	58.6
	15	48 31.5	20 00.1	269 54.6	11.4	11 05.1	15.0	58.6
	16	63 31.4	00.6	284 25.0	11.4	11 20.1	14.9	58.7
	17	78 31.2	01.2	298 55.4	11.3	11 35.0	14.9	58.7
	18	93 31.0	S20 01.7	313 25.7	11.1	N11 49.9	14.9	58.8
	19	108 30.9	02.3	327 55.8	11.1	12 04.8	14.8	58.8
	20	123 30.7	02.8	342 25.9	10.9	12 19.6	14.7	58.8
	21	138 30.6	. . 03.3	356 55.8	10.9	12 34.3	14.7	58.9
	22	153 30.4	03.9	11 25.7	10.7	12 49.0	14.7	58.9
	23	168 30.2	04.4	25 55.4	10.6	13 03.7	14.6	58.9
	22 00	183 30.1	S20 05.0	40 25.0	10.5	N13 18.3	14.6	59.0
	01	198 29.9	05.5	54 54.5	10.4	13 32.9	14.5	59.0
	02	213 29.8	06.0	69 23.9	10.3	13 47.4	14.4	59.1
	03	228 29.6	. . 06.6	83 53.2	10.2	14 01.8	14.4	59.1
	04	243 29.4	07.1	98 22.4	10.1	14 16.2	14.4	59.1
	05	258 29.3	07.7	112 51.5	9.9	14 30.6	14.2	59.2
	06	273 29.1	S20 08.2	127 20.4	9.8	N14 44.8	14.2	59.2
	07	288 28.9	08.7	141 49.2	9.7	14 59.0	14.2	59.2
	08	303 28.8	09.3	156 17.9	9.6	15 13.2	14.1	59.3
S	09	318 28.6	. . 09.8	170 46.5	9.5	15 27.3	14.0	59.3
U	10	333 28.5	10.3	185 15.0	9.3	15 41.3	13.9	59.4
N	11	348 28.3	10.9	199 43.3	9.3	15 55.2	13.9	59.4
D	12	3 28.1	S20 11.4	214 11.6	9.1	N16 09.1	13.8	59.4
A	13	18 28.0	11.9	228 39.7	9.0	16 22.9	13.7	59.5
Y	14	33 27.8	12.5	243 07.7	8.8	16 36.6	13.7	59.5
	15	48 27.6	. . 13.0	257 35.5	8.7	16 50.3	13.5	59.5
	16	63 27.5	13.5	272 03.2	8.6	17 03.8	13.5	59.6
	17	78 27.3	14.0	286 30.8	8.5	17 17.3	13.4	59.6
	18	93 27.1	S20 14.6	300 58.3	8.4	N17 30.7	13.3	59.6
	19	108 27.0	15.1	315 25.7	8.2	17 44.0	13.2	59.7
	20	123 26.8	15.6	329 52.9	8.1	17 57.2	13.2	59.7
	21	138 26.6	. . 16.2	344 20.0	7.9	18 10.4	13.0	59.7
	22	153 26.4	16.7	358 46.9	7.9	18 23.4	12.9	59.8
	23	168 26.3	17.2	13 13.8	7.6	18 36.3	12.9	59.8
	23 00	183 26.1	S20 17.7	27 40.4	7.6	N18 49.2	12.7	59.8
	01	198 25.9	18.3	42 07.0	7.5	19 01.9	12.7	59.9
	02	213 25.8	18.8	56 33.5	7.3	19 14.6	12.5	59.9
	03	228 25.6	. . 19.3	70 59.8	7.1	19 27.1	12.4	59.9
	04	243 25.4	19.8	85 25.9	7.1	19 39.5	12.3	60.0
	05	258 25.3	20.3	99 52.0	6.9	19 51.8	12.3	60.0
	06	273 25.1	S20 20.9	114 17.9	6.7	N20 04.1	12.0	60.0
	07	288 24.9	21.4	128 43.6	6.7	20 16.1	12.0	60.0
	08	303 24.7	21.9	143 09.3	6.5	20 28.1	11.9	60.1
M	09	318 24.6	. . 22.4	157 34.8	6.4	20 40.0	11.7	60.1
O	10	333 24.4	22.9	172 00.2	6.2	20 51.7	11.6	60.1
N	11	348 24.2	23.5	186 25.4	6.1	21 03.3	11.5	60.2
D	12	3 24.1	S20 24.0	200 50.5	6.0	N21 14.8	11.4	60.2
A	13	18 23.9	24.5	215 15.5	5.8	21 26.2	11.2	60.2
Y	14	33 23.7	25.0	229 40.3	5.7	21 37.4	11.1	60.2
	15	48 23.5	. . 25.5	244 05.0	5.6	21 48.5	11.0	60.3
	16	63 23.4	26.0	258 29.6	5.4	21 59.5	10.8	60.3
	17	78 23.2	26.5	272 54.0	5.4	22 10.3	10.7	60.3
	18	93 23.0	S20 27.1	287 18.4	5.1	N22 21.0	10.6	60.3
	19	108 22.8	27.6	301 42.5	5.1	22 31.6	10.4	60.4
	20	123 22.7	28.1	316 06.6	4.9	22 42.0	10.3	60.4
	21	138 22.5	. . 28.6	330 30.5	4.8	22 52.3	10.1	60.4
	22	153 22.3	29.1	344 54.3	4.7	23 02.4	10.0	60.4
	23	168 22.1	29.6	359 18.0	4.5	N23 12.4	9.8	60.5
		SD 16.2	*d* 0.5	SD 15.9		16.2		16.4

Lat.	Twilight Naut.	Twilight Civil	Sunrise	Moonrise 21	Moonrise 22	Moonrise 23	Moonrise 24
°	h m	h m	h m	h m	h m	h m	h m
N 72	07 24	09 07	■	12 39	11 37	□	□
N 70	07 11	08 38	10 45	12 55	12 15	□	□
68	07 00	08 17	09 47	13 08	12 42	11 47	□
66	06 51	08 00	09 14	13 19	13 02	12 36	□
64	06 43	07 46	08 49	13 28	13 19	13 07	12 44
62	06 36	07 34	08 31	13 35	13 33	13 31	13 31
60	06 30	07 24	08 15	13 42	13 45	13 50	14 02
N 58	06 25	07 15	08 02	13 48	13 55	14 06	14 25
56	06 20	07 07	07 50	13 54	14 04	14 19	14 44
54	06 15	07 00	07 40	13 58	14 12	14 31	15 00
52	06 11	06 53	07 32	14 03	14 19	14 41	15 14
50	06 07	06 47	07 24	14 07	14 26	14 51	15 26
45	05 58	06 34	07 07	14 15	14 40	15 11	15 52
N 40	05 50	06 23	06 53	14 23	14 51	15 27	16 12
35	05 43	06 14	06 41	14 29	15 02	15 41	16 29
30	05 36	06 05	06 31	14 34	15 10	15 53	16 43
20	05 23	05 49	06 13	14 44	15 26	16 13	17 09
N 10	05 09	05 35	05 57	14 53	15 39	16 32	17 30
0	04 55	05 20	05 43	15 01	15 52	16 49	17 51
S 10	04 39	05 05	05 28	15 09	16 05	17 06	18 11
20	04 19	04 48	05 12	15 18	16 19	17 24	18 33
30	03 55	04 27	04 53	15 28	16 35	17 46	18 59
35	03 39	04 14	04 42	15 34	16 44	17 59	19 14
40	03 20	03 58	04 30	15 41	16 55	18 13	19 32
45	02 55	03 40	04 15	15 49	17 08	18 31	19 53
S 50	02 21	03 16	03 56	15 58	17 23	18 52	20 21
52	02 02	03 04	03 48	16 03	17 31	19 03	20 34
54	01 39	02 50	03 38	16 08	17 39	19 15	20 49
56	01 07	02 34	03 27	16 13	17 48	19 28	21 07
58	////	02 15	03 14	16 20	17 59	19 44	21 30
S 60	////	01 50	02 59	16 27	18 11	20 04	21 58

Lat.	Sunset	Twilight Civil	Twilight Naut.	Moonset 21	Moonset 22	Moonset 23	Moonset 24
°	h m	h m	h m	h m	h m	h m	h m
N 72	■	14 24	16 08	04 26	07 13	□	□
N 70	12 47	14 53	16 21	04 13	06 37	□	□
68	13 45	15 15	16 31	04 03	06 12	09 01	□
66	14 18	15 32	16 40	03 54	05 53	08 14	□
64	14 42	15 46	16 48	03 47	05 38	07 43	10 13
62	15 01	15 58	16 55	03 40	05 25	07 21	09 27
60	15 17	16 08	17 01	03 35	05 15	07 03	08 56
N 58	15 30	16 17	17 07	03 30	05 06	06 48	08 34
56	15 41	16 25	17 12	03 26	04 57	06 35	08 15
54	15 51	16 32	17 16	03 22	04 50	06 24	07 59
52	16 00	16 39	17 20	03 19	04 44	06 14	07 46
50	16 08	16 44	17 24	03 16	04 38	06 05	07 34
45	16 25	16 57	17 33	03 09	04 26	05 47	07 10
N 40	16 39	17 08	17 42	03 04	04 16	05 32	06 51
35	16 51	17 18	17 49	02 59	04 07	05 19	06 35
30	17 01	17 27	17 56	02 55	04 00	05 08	06 21
20	17 19	17 43	18 10	02 48	03 47	04 50	05 57
N 10	17 35	17 57	18 23	02 42	03 35	04 33	05 36
0	17 50	18 12	18 37	02 36	03 25	04 18	05 18
S 10	18 05	18 27	18 54	02 30	03 14	04 03	04 59
20	18 21	18 45	19 13	02 24	03 03	03 47	04 38
30	18 40	19 06	19 38	02 17	02 50	03 29	04 15
35	18 51	19 19	19 54	02 13	02 43	03 18	04 01
40	19 03	19 34	20 13	02 08	02 35	03 06	03 46
45	19 18	19 53	20 38	02 03	02 25	02 52	03 27
S 50	19 37	20 18	21 13	01 57	02 14	02 35	03 04
52	19 46	20 29	21 32	01 54	02 08	02 27	02 53
54	19 55	20 43	21 56	01 51	02 02	02 18	02 41
56	20 07	20 59	22 29	01 47	01 56	02 08	02 27
58	20 19	21 19	////	01 44	01 49	01 56	02 10
S 60	20 35	21 45	////	01 39	01 40	01 43	01 50

Day	SUN Eqn. of Time 00^h	SUN Eqn. of Time 12^h	SUN Mer. Pass.	MOON Mer. Pass. Upper	MOON Mer. Pass. Lower	MOON Age	MOON Phase
d	m s	m s	h m	h m	h m	d %	
21	14 16	14 08	11 46	21 13	08 48	12 87	
22	14 01	13 53	11 46	22 05	09 38	13 94	○
23	13 45	13 37	11 46	23 03	10 33	14 98	

UT d	UT h	ARIES GHA	VENUS −4·9 GHA	VENUS Dec	MARS +0·6 GHA	MARS Dec	JUPITER −2·2 GHA	JUPITER Dec	SATURN +0·5 GHA	SATURN Dec
		° ′	° ′	° ′	° ′	° ′	° ′	° ′	° ′	° ′
24 TUESDAY	00	62 58.2	219 54.3	S 9 14.1	270 53.0	N13 44.8	274 01.5	N13 25.8	54 25.0	N 0 50.8
	01	78 00.6	234 55.7	14.1	285 54.4	44.5	289 03.8	25.8	69 27.5	50.8
	02	93 03.1	249 57.2	14.0	300 55.9	44.2	304 06.1	25.7	84 30.0	50.7
	03	108 05.6	264 58.6	. . 13.9	315 57.3	. . 43.9	319 08.4	. . 25.7	99 32.6	. . 50.7
	04	123 08.0	280 00.1	13.9	330 58.8	43.6	334 10.8	25.6	114 35.1	50.7
	05	138 10.5	295 01.5	13.8	346 00.2	43.3	349 13.1	25.6	129 37.7	50.7
	06	153 13.0	310 02.9	S 9 13.7	1 01.7	N13 43.0	4 15.4	N13 25.6	144 40.2	N 0 50.7
	07	168 15.4	325 04.4	13.7	16 03.2	42.7	19 17.7	25.5	159 42.7	50.6
	08	183 17.9	340 05.8	13.6	31 04.6	42.4	34 20.0	25.5	174 45.3	50.6
	09	198 20.4	355 07.2	. . 13.5	46 06.1	. . 42.1	49 22.3	. . 25.4	189 47.8	. . 50.6
	10	213 22.8	10 08.6	13.5	61 07.5	41.8	64 24.7	25.4	204 50.3	50.6
	11	228 25.3	25 10.1	13.4	76 09.0	41.5	79 27.0	25.4	219 52.9	50.5
	12	243 27.7	40 11.5	S 9 13.4	91 10.5	N13 41.2	94 29.3	N13 25.3	234 55.4	N 0 50.5
	13	258 30.2	55 12.9	13.3	106 11.9	40.9	109 31.6	25.3	249 57.9	50.5
	14	273 32.7	70 14.3	13.3	121 13.4	40.6	124 33.9	25.2	265 00.5	50.5
	15	288 35.1	85 15.7	. . 13.2	136 14.9	. . 40.3	139 36.3	. . 25.2	280 03.0	. . 50.5
	16	303 37.6	100 17.1	13.2	151 16.3	40.0	154 38.6	25.1	295 05.5	50.4
	17	318 40.1	115 18.5	13.1	166 17.8	39.7	169 40.9	25.1	310 08.1	50.4
	18	333 42.5	130 19.9	S 9 13.1	181 19.2	N13 39.4	184 43.2	N13 25.1	325 10.6	N 0 50.4
	19	348 45.0	145 21.3	13.0	196 20.7	39.1	199 45.5	25.0	340 13.1	50.4
	20	3 47.5	160 22.7	13.0	211 22.2	38.8	214 47.9	25.0	355 15.7	50.4
	21	18 49.9	175 24.1	. . 13.0	226 23.6	. . 38.5	229 50.2	. . 24.9	10 18.2	. . 50.4
	22	33 52.4	190 25.5	12.9	241 25.1	38.2	244 52.5	24.9	25 20.7	50.3
	23	48 54.9	205 26.9	12.9	256 26.6	37.9	259 54.8	24.9	40 23.3	50.3
25 WEDNESDAY	00	63 57.3	220 28.2	S 9 12.9	271 28.1	N13 37.6	274 57.1	N13 24.8	55 25.8	N 0 50.3
	01	78 59.8	235 29.6	12.8	286 29.5	37.4	289 59.5	24.8	70 28.3	50.3
	02	94 02.2	250 31.0	12.8	301 31.0	37.1	305 01.8	24.7	85 30.9	50.3
	03	109 04.7	265 32.4	. . 12.8	316 32.5	. . 36.8	320 04.1	. . 24.7	100 33.4	. . 50.2
	04	124 07.2	280 33.7	12.7	331 33.9	36.5	335 06.4	24.7	115 35.9	50.2
	05	139 09.6	295 35.1	12.7	346 35.4	36.2	350 08.8	24.6	130 38.5	50.2
	06	154 12.1	310 36.5	S 9 12.7	1 36.9	N13 35.9	5 11.1	N13 24.6	145 41.0	N 0 50.2
	07	169 14.6	325 37.8	12.7	16 38.3	35.6	20 13.4	24.6	160 43.5	50.2
	08	184 17.0	340 39.2	12.6	31 39.8	35.3	35 15.7	24.5	175 46.1	50.1
	09	199 19.5	355 40.6	. . 12.6	46 41.3	. . 35.0	50 18.1	. . 24.5	190 48.6	. . 50.1
	10	214 22.0	10 41.9	12.6	61 42.8	34.7	65 20.4	24.4	205 51.1	50.1
	11	229 24.4	25 43.3	12.6	76 44.2	34.4	80 22.7	24.4	220 53.7	50.1
	12	244 26.9	40 44.6	S 9 12.6	91 45.7	N13 34.1	95 25.0	N13 24.4	235 56.2	N 0 50.1
	13	259 29.4	55 46.0	12.6	106 47.2	33.8	110 27.4	24.3	250 58.7	50.0
	14	274 31.8	70 47.3	12.6	121 48.7	33.5	125 29.7	24.3	266 01.3	50.0
	15	289 34.3	85 48.6	. . 12.5	136 50.1	. . 33.2	140 32.0	. . 24.2	281 03.8	. . 50.0
	16	304 36.7	100 50.0	12.5	151 51.6	32.9	155 34.3	24.2	296 06.3	50.0
	17	319 39.2	115 51.3	12.5	166 53.1	32.6	170 36.7	24.2	311 08.9	50.0
	18	334 41.7	130 52.7	S 9 12.5	181 54.6	N13 32.3	185 39.0	N13 24.1	326 11.4	N 0 50.0
	19	349 44.1	145 54.0	12.5	196 56.1	32.0	200 41.3	24.1	341 13.9	49.9
	20	4 46.6	160 55.3	12.5	211 57.5	31.7	215 43.7	24.1	356 16.4	49.9
	21	19 49.1	175 56.6	. . 12.5	226 59.0	. . 31.5	230 46.0	. . 24.0	11 19.0	. . 49.9
	22	34 51.5	190 58.0	12.5	242 00.5	31.2	245 48.3	24.0	26 21.5	49.9
	23	49 54.0	205 59.3	12.5	257 02.0	30.9	260 50.6	23.9	41 24.0	49.9
26 THURSDAY	00	64 56.5	221 00.6	S 9 12.5	272 03.5	N13 30.6	275 53.0	N13 23.9	56 26.6	N 0 49.9
	01	79 58.9	236 01.9	12.6	287 04.9	30.3	290 55.3	23.9	71 29.1	49.8
	02	95 01.4	251 03.2	12.6	302 06.4	30.0	305 57.6	23.8	86 31.6	49.8
	03	110 03.9	266 04.5	. . 12.6	317 07.9	. . 29.7	321 00.0	. . 23.8	101 34.1	. . 49.8
	04	125 06.3	281 05.8	12.6	332 09.4	29.4	336 02.3	23.8	116 36.7	49.8
	05	140 08.8	296 07.1	12.6	347 10.9	29.1	351 04.6	23.7	131 39.2	49.8
	06	155 11.2	311 08.4	S 9 12.6	2 12.4	N13 28.8	6 07.0	N13 23.7	146 41.7	N 0 49.7
	07	170 13.7	326 09.7	12.6	17 13.8	28.5	21 09.3	23.7	161 44.3	49.7
	08	185 16.2	341 11.0	12.7	32 15.3	28.2	36 11.6	23.6	176 46.8	49.7
	09	200 18.6	356 12.3	. . 12.7	47 16.8	. . 27.9	51 14.0	. . 23.6	191 49.3	. . 49.7
	10	215 21.1	11 13.6	12.7	62 18.3	27.6	66 16.3	23.5	206 51.8	49.7
	11	230 23.6	26 14.9	12.7	77 19.8	27.4	81 18.6	23.5	221 54.4	49.7
	12	245 26.0	41 16.2	S 9 12.7	92 21.3	N13 27.1	96 20.9	N13 23.5	236 56.9	N 0 49.6
	13	260 28.5	56 17.5	12.8	107 22.8	26.8	111 23.3	23.4	251 59.4	49.6
	14	275 31.0	71 18.8	12.8	122 24.3	26.5	126 25.6	23.4	267 02.0	49.6
	15	290 33.4	86 20.0	. . 12.8	137 25.7	. . 26.2	141 28.0	. . 23.4	282 04.5	. . 49.6
	16	305 35.9	101 21.3	12.9	152 27.2	25.9	156 30.3	23.3	297 07.0	49.6
	17	320 38.4	116 22.6	12.9	167 28.7	25.6	171 32.6	23.3	312 09.5	49.6
	18	335 40.8	131 23.8	S 9 12.9	182 30.2	N13 25.3	186 35.0	N13 23.3	327 12.1	N 0 49.6
	19	350 43.3	146 25.1	13.0	197 31.7	25.0	201 37.3	23.2	342 14.6	49.5
	20	5 45.7	161 26.4	13.0	212 33.2	24.7	216 39.6	23.2	357 17.1	49.5
	21	20 48.2	176 27.6	. . 13.0	227 34.7	. . 24.5	231 42.0	. . 23.2	12 19.6	. . 49.5
	22	35 50.7	191 28.9	13.1	242 36.2	24.2	246 44.3	23.1	27 22.2	49.5
	23	50 53.1	206 30.1	13.1	257 37.7	23.9	261 46.6	23.1	42 24.7	49.5
Mer. Pass.	h m	19 40.9	v 1.3	d 0.0	v 1.5	d 0.3	v 2.3	d 0.0	v 2.5	d 0.0

STARS

Name	SHA	Dec
	° ′	° ′
Acamar	315 10.2	S40 11.8
Achernar	335 18.6	S57 06.1
Acrux	172 58.7	S63 14.7
Adhara	255 04.4	S29 00.4
Aldebaran	290 37.5	N16 33.8
Alioth	166 12.0	N55 48.6
Alkaid	152 51.2	N49 10.6
Alnair	27 31.0	S46 50.0
Alnilam	275 35.9	S 1 11.0
Alphard	217 46.2	S 8 46.4
Alphecca	126 02.8	N26 37.4
Alpheratz	357 33.0	N29 14.6
Altair	61 58.7	N 8 56.5
Ankaa	353 05.4	S42 09.7
Antares	112 14.3	S26 29.4
Arcturus	145 46.8	N19 02.5
Atria	107 07.7	S69 04.5
Avior	234 13.8	S59 35.5
Bellatrix	278 20.9	N 6 22.5
Betelgeuse	270 50.1	N 7 24.7
Canopus	263 51.2	S52 42.4
Capella	280 19.1	N46 01.4
Deneb	49 25.0	N45 22.9
Denebola	182 23.5	N14 25.2
Diphda	348 45.6	S17 50.3
Dubhe	193 39.3	N61 36.0
Elnath	277 59.6	N28 37.8
Eltanin	90 42.0	N51 29.2
Enif	33 37.3	N10 00.1
Fomalhaut	15 12.8	S29 28.8
Gacrux	171 50.2	S57 15.6
Gienah	175 42.2	S17 41.4
Hadar	148 34.4	S60 30.0
Hamal	327 49.1	N23 35.5
Kaus Aust.	83 30.8	S34 22.3
Kochab	137 21.0	N74 02.5
Markab	13 28.3	N15 21.2
Menkar	314 04.2	N 4 11.8
Menkent	147 56.1	S36 30.0
Miaplacidus	221 37.7	S69 49.3
Mirfak	308 25.5	N49 57.5
Nunki	75 46.2	S26 15.8
Peacock	53 03.6	S56 39.1
Pollux	243 15.2	N27 57.5
Procyon	244 49.0	N 5 09.4
Rasalhague	95 57.5	N12 32.5
Regulus	207 32.8	N11 50.1
Rigel	281 02.1	S 8 10.2
Rigil Kent.	139 38.8	S60 56.6
Sabik	102 01.4	S15 45.4
Schedar	349 28.9	N56 41.4
Shaula	96 08.7	S37 07.4
Sirius	258 24.6	S16 45.1
Spica	158 20.9	S11 18.0
Suhail	222 45.0	S43 32.2
Vega	80 32.5	N38 48.7
Zuben'ubi	136 54.6	S16 09.1

	SHA	Mer. Pass.
	° ′	h m
Venus	156 30.9	9 17
Mars	207 30.7	5 54
Jupiter	210 59.8	5 39
Saturn	351 28.5	20 15

UT d	h	SUN GHA	SUN Dec	MOON GHA	v	MOON Dec	d	HP
		° ′	° ′	° ′	′	° ′	′	′
24	00	183 21.9	S20 30.1	13 41.5	4.4	N23 22.2	9.6	60.5
	01	198 21.8	30.6	28 04.9	4.3	23 31.8	9.6	60.5
	02	213 21.6	31.1	42 28.2	4.2	23 41.4	9.3	60.5
	03	228 21.4	. . 31.6	56 51.4	4.0	23 50.7	9.2	60.6
	04	243 21.2	32.1	71 14.4	3.9	23 59.9	9.0	60.6
	05	258 21.1	32.6	85 37.3	3.8	24 08.9	8.9	60.6
	06	273 20.9	S20 33.2	100 00.1	3.7	N24 17.8	8.7	60.6
	07	288 20.7	33.7	114 22.8	3.6	24 26.5	8.5	60.6
T	08	303 20.5	34.2	128 45.4	3.4	24 35.0	8.4	60.7
U	09	318 20.3	. . 34.7	143 07.8	3.4	24 43.4	8.2	60.7
E	10	333 20.2	35.2	157 30.2	3.2	24 51.6	8.0	60.7
S	11	348 20.0	35.7	171 52.4	3.1	24 59.6	7.8	60.7
D	12	3 19.8	S20 36.2	186 14.5	3.0	N25 07.4	7.7	60.7
A	13	18 19.6	36.7	200 36.5	2.9	25 15.1	7.4	60.7
Y	14	33 19.4	37.2	214 58.4	2.8	25 22.5	7.3	60.8
	15	48 19.2	. . 37.7	229 20.2	2.7	25 29.8	7.1	60.8
	16	63 19.1	38.2	243 41.9	2.6	25 36.9	6.9	60.8
	17	78 18.9	38.7	258 03.5	2.5	25 43.8	6.8	60.8
	18	93 18.7	S20 39.2	272 25.0	2.4	N25 50.6	6.5	60.8
	19	108 18.5	39.7	286 46.4	2.3	25 57.1	6.4	60.8
	20	123 18.3	40.2	301 07.7	2.2	26 03.5	6.1	60.9
	21	138 18.1	. . 40.6	315 28.9	2.1	26 09.6	6.0	60.9
	22	153 18.0	41.1	329 50.0	2.0	26 15.6	5.8	60.9
	23	168 17.8	41.6	344 11.0	2.0	26 21.4	5.6	60.9
25	00	183 17.6	S20 42.1	358 32.0	1.9	N26 27.0	5.3	60.9
	01	198 17.4	42.6	12 52.9	1.8	26 32.3	5.2	60.9
	02	213 17.2	43.1	27 13.7	1.7	26 37.5	5.0	60.9
	03	228 17.0	. . 43.6	41 34.4	1.6	26 42.5	4.7	60.9
	04	243 16.8	44.1	55 55.0	1.6	26 47.2	4.6	60.9
	05	258 16.7	44.6	70 15.6	1.5	26 51.8	4.4	61.0
	06	273 16.5	S20 45.1	84 36.1	1.5	N26 56.2	4.1	61.0
W	07	288 16.3	45.6	98 56.6	1.4	27 00.3	4.0	61.0
E	08	303 16.1	46.0	113 17.0	1.3	27 04.3	3.7	61.0
D	09	318 15.9	. . 46.5	127 37.3	1.3	27 08.0	3.5	61.0
N	10	333 15.7	47.0	141 57.6	1.2	27 11.5	3.4	61.0
E	11	348 15.5	47.5	156 17.8	1.2	27 14.9	3.1	61.0
S	12	3 15.3	S20 48.0	170 38.0	1.1	N27 18.0	2.9	61.0
D	13	18 15.1	48.5	184 58.1	1.1	27 20.9	2.6	61.0
A	14	33 15.0	49.0	199 18.2	1.1	27 23.5	2.5	61.0
Y	15	48 14.8	. . 49.4	213 38.3	1.0	27 26.0	2.3	61.0
	16	63 14.6	49.9	227 58.3	1.0	27 28.3	2.0	61.0
	17	78 14.4	50.4	242 18.3	1.0	27 30.3	1.8	61.0
	18	93 14.2	S20 50.9	256 38.3	1.0	N27 32.1	1.6	61.0
	19	108 14.0	51.4	270 58.3	0.9	27 33.7	1.4	61.0
	20	123 13.8	51.8	285 18.2	0.9	27 35.1	1.2	61.0
	21	138 13.6	. . 52.3	299 38.1	0.9	27 36.3	0.9	61.0
	22	153 13.4	52.8	313 58.0	0.9	27 37.2	0.8	61.0
	23	168 13.2	53.3	328 17.9	0.9	27 38.0	0.5	61.0
26	00	183 13.0	S20 53.8	342 37.8	0.9	N27 38.5	0.3	61.0
	01	198 12.8	54.2	356 57.7	0.9	27 38.8	0.1	61.0
	02	213 12.7	54.7	11 17.6	0.9	27 38.9	0.1	61.0
	03	228 12.5	. . 55.2	25 37.5	0.9	27 38.8	0.4	61.0
	04	243 12.3	55.7	39 57.4	0.9	27 38.4	0.5	61.0
	05	258 12.1	56.1	54 17.3	1.0	27 37.9	0.8	61.0
	06	273 11.9	S20 56.6	68 37.3	0.9	N27 37.1	1.0	61.0
T	07	288 11.7	57.1	82 57.2	1.0	27 36.1	1.2	61.0
H	08	303 11.5	57.5	97 17.2	1.0	27 34.9	1.4	61.0
U	09	318 11.3	. . 58.0	111 37.2	1.0	27 33.5	1.7	61.0
R	10	333 11.1	58.5	125 57.2	1.1	27 31.8	1.8	61.0
S	11	348 10.9	59.0	140 17.3	1.1	27 30.0	2.1	61.0
D	12	3 10.7	S20 59.4	154 37.4	1.2	N27 27.9	2.3	61.0
A	13	18 10.5	20 59.9	168 57.6	1.2	27 25.6	2.5	61.0
Y	14	33 10.3	21 00.4	183 17.8	1.2	27 23.1	2.7	60.9
	15	48 10.1	. . 00.8	197 38.0	1.3	27 20.4	2.9	60.9
	16	63 09.9	01.3	211 58.3	1.4	27 17.5	3.1	60.9
	17	78 09.7	01.8	226 18.7	1.4	27 14.4	3.4	60.9
	18	93 09.5	S21 02.2	240 39.1	1.4	N27 11.0	3.5	60.9
	19	108 09.3	02.7	254 59.5	1.6	27 07.5	3.8	60.9
	20	123 09.1	03.1	269 20.1	1.6	27 03.7	3.9	60.9
	21	138 08.9	. . 03.6	283 40.7	1.6	26 59.8	4.2	60.9
	22	153 08.7	04.1	298 01.3	1.8	26 55.6	4.3	60.9
	23	168 08.5	04.5	312 22.1	1.8	N26 51.3	4.6	60.8
		SD 16.2	*d* 0.5	SD 16.5		16.6		16.6

Lat.	Twilight Naut.	Twilight Civil	Sunrise	Moonrise 24	Moonrise 25	Moonrise 26	Moonrise 27
°	h m	h m	h m	h m	h m	h m	h m
N 72	07 33	09 22	■	☐	☐	☐	☐
N 70	07 19	08 50	11 32	☐	☐	☐	☐
68	07 08	08 26	10 02	☐	☐	☐	☐
66	06 58	08 08	09 25	☐	☐	☐	☐
64	06 50	07 53	08 59	12 44	☐	☐	16 04
62	06 42	07 40	08 38	13 31	13 41	14 49	16 54
60	06 36	07 30	08 22	14 02	14 32	15 41	17 26
N 58	06 30	07 20	08 08	14 25	15 03	16 13	17 49
56	06 25	07 12	07 56	14 44	15 27	16 37	18 08
54	06 20	07 04	07 46	15 00	15 47	16 56	18 24
52	06 15	06 58	07 36	15 14	16 03	17 12	18 37
50	06 11	06 51	07 28	15 26	16 17	17 26	18 49
45	06 02	06 38	07 11	15 52	16 46	17 55	19 14
N 40	05 53	06 27	06 56	16 12	17 09	18 17	19 33
35	05 45	06 17	06 44	16 29	17 27	18 36	19 50
30	05 38	06 07	06 33	16 43	17 44	18 52	20 04
20	05 24	05 51	06 15	17 09	18 11	19 19	20 28
N 10	05 10	05 36	05 59	17 30	18 35	19 42	20 48
0	04 56	05 21	05 43	17 51	18 57	20 04	21 08
S 10	04 39	05 05	05 28	18 11	19 19	20 25	21 27
20	04 19	04 47	05 11	18 33	19 43	20 48	21 47
30	03 53	04 25	04 52	18 59	20 10	21 15	22 11
35	03 37	04 12	04 41	19 14	20 27	21 31	22 24
40	03 17	03 56	04 28	19 32	20 46	21 50	22 40
45	02 51	03 37	04 12	19 53	21 09	22 12	22 59
S 50	02 16	03 12	03 53	20 21	21 39	22 40	23 23
52	01 56	03 00	03 44	20 34	21 54	22 54	23 34
54	01 31	02 46	03 34	20 49	22 11	23 09	23 46
56	00 54	02 29	03 23	21 07	22 31	23 28	24 01
58	////	02 08	03 09	21 30	22 57	23 51	24 18
S 60	////	01 41	02 53	21 58	23 32	24 20	00 20

Lat.	Sunset	Twilight Civil	Twilight Naut.	Moonset 24	Moonset 25	Moonset 26	Moonset 27
°	h m	h m	h m	h m	h m	h m	h m
N 72	■	14 11	16 00	☐	☐	☐	☐
N 70	12 01	14 43	16 14	☐	☐	☐	☐
68	13 31	15 07	16 26	☐	☐	☐	☐
66	14 08	15 25	16 35	☐	☐	☐	☐
64	14 35	15 40	16 44	10 13	☐	☐	13 49
62	14 55	15 53	16 51	09 27	11 33	12 46	12 58
60	15 11	16 04	16 58	08 56	10 43	11 55	12 26
N 58	15 25	16 13	17 03	08 34	10 12	11 23	12 02
56	15 37	16 22	17 09	08 15	09 48	10 59	11 43
54	15 48	16 29	17 14	07 59	09 29	10 39	11 27
52	15 57	16 36	17 18	07 46	09 12	10 23	11 13
50	16 05	16 42	17 22	07 34	08 59	10 09	11 00
45	16 23	16 56	17 32	07 10	08 30	09 40	10 35
N 40	16 37	17 07	17 40	06 51	08 08	09 17	10 14
35	16 50	17 17	17 48	06 35	07 49	08 58	09 57
30	17 00	17 26	17 56	06 21	07 33	08 42	09 42
20	17 19	17 43	18 10	05 57	07 06	08 15	09 17
N 10	17 35	17 58	18 24	05 36	06 43	07 51	08 55
0	17 51	18 13	18 38	05 18	06 22	07 29	08 35
S 10	18 06	18 29	18 55	04 59	06 00	07 07	08 14
20	18 23	18 47	19 15	04 38	05 37	06 43	07 52
30	18 42	19 09	19 41	04 15	05 10	06 15	07 26
35	18 53	19 22	19 57	04 01	04 55	05 58	07 10
40	19 07	19 38	20 18	03 46	04 36	05 39	06 53
45	19 22	19 58	20 43	03 27	04 14	05 16	06 31
S 50	19 41	20 23	21 20	03 04	03 46	04 46	06 03
52	19 51	20 35	21 40	02 53	03 33	04 32	05 50
54	20 01	20 50	22 06	02 41	03 17	04 14	05 34
56	20 13	21 07	22 45	02 27	02 59	03 54	05 16
58	20 26	21 28	////	02 10	02 36	03 28	04 54
S 60	20 42	21 56	////	01 50	02 07	02 53	04 24

Day	SUN Eqn. of Time 00^h	SUN Eqn. of Time 12^h	SUN Mer. Pass.	MOON Mer. Pass. Upper	MOON Mer. Pass. Lower	MOON Age	MOON Phase
d	m s	m s	h m	h m	h m	d %	
24	13 28	13 20	11 47	24 06	11 34	15 100	○
25	13 11	13 02	11 47	00 06	12 39	16 99	
26	12 53	12 43	11 47	01 13	13 46	17 95	

2026 NOVEMBER 27, 28, 29 (FRI., SAT., SUN.)

Day	UT (d h)	ARIES GHA	VENUS −4·9 GHA	VENUS Dec	MARS +0·5 GHA	MARS Dec	JUPITER −2·2 GHA	JUPITER Dec	SATURN +0·5 GHA	SATURN Dec
		° ′	° ′	° ′	° ′	° ′	° ′	° ′	° ′	° ′
FRIDAY	27 00	65 55.6	221 31.4	S 9 13.2	272 39.2	N13 23.6	276 49.0	N13 23.1	57 27.2	N 0 49.5
	01	80 58.1	236 32.7	13.2	287 40.7	23.3	291 51.3	23.0	72 29.7	49.4
	02	96 00.5	251 33.9	13.3	302 42.2	23.0	306 53.6	23.0	87 32.3	49.4
	03	111 03.0	266 35.1	13.3	317 43.7	22.7	321 56.0	23.0	102 34.8	49.4
	04	126 05.5	281 36.4	13.4	332 45.2	22.4	336 58.3	22.9	117 37.3	49.4
	05	141 07.9	296 37.6	13.4	347 46.7	22.1	352 00.7	22.9	132 39.8	49.4
	06	156 10.4	311 38.9	S 9 13.5	2 48.2	N13 21.9	7 03.0	N13 22.8	147 42.4	N 0 49.4
	07	171 12.9	326 40.1	13.5	17 49.7	21.6	22 05.3	22.8	162 44.9	49.3
	08	186 15.3	341 41.3	13.6	32 51.2	21.3	37 07.7	22.8	177 47.4	49.3
	09	201 17.8	356 42.6	13.7	47 52.7	21.0	52 10.0	22.7	192 49.9	49.3
	10	216 20.2	11 43.8	13.7	62 54.2	20.7	67 12.4	22.7	207 52.5	49.3
	11	231 22.7	26 45.0	13.8	77 55.7	20.4	82 14.7	22.7	222 55.0	49.3
	12	246 25.2	41 46.2	S 9 13.8	92 57.2	N13 20.1	97 17.0	N13 22.6	237 57.5	N 0 49.3
	13	261 27.6	56 47.5	13.9	107 58.7	19.8	112 19.4	22.6	253 00.0	49.3
	14	276 30.1	71 48.7	14.0	123 00.2	19.6	127 21.7	22.6	268 02.6	49.2
	15	291 32.6	86 49.9	14.0	138 01.7	19.3	142 24.1	22.5	283 05.1	49.2
	16	306 35.0	101 51.1	14.1	153 03.2	19.0	157 26.4	22.5	298 07.6	49.2
	17	321 37.5	116 52.3	14.2	168 04.7	18.7	172 28.7	22.5	313 10.1	49.2
	18	336 40.0	131 53.5	S 9 14.3	183 06.2	N13 18.4	187 31.1	N13 22.5	328 12.6	N 0 49.2
	19	351 42.4	146 54.7	14.3	198 07.7	18.1	202 33.4	22.4	343 15.2	49.2
	20	6 44.9	161 55.9	14.4	213 09.2	17.8	217 35.8	22.4	358 17.7	49.2
	21	21 47.4	176 57.1	14.5	228 10.7	17.6	232 38.1	22.4	13 20.2	49.1
	22	36 49.8	191 58.3	14.6	243 12.2	17.3	247 40.5	22.3	28 22.7	49.1
	23	51 52.3	206 59.5	14.6	258 13.7	17.0	262 42.8	22.3	43 25.3	49.1
SATURDAY	28 00	66 54.7	222 00.7	S 9 14.7	273 15.2	N13 16.7	277 45.1	N13 22.3	58 27.8	N 0 49.1
	01	81 57.2	237 01.9	14.8	288 16.7	16.4	292 47.5	22.2	73 30.3	49.1
	02	96 59.7	252 03.1	14.9	303 18.2	16.1	307 49.8	22.2	88 32.8	49.1
	03	112 02.1	267 04.3	15.0	318 19.8	15.8	322 52.2	22.2	103 35.3	49.1
	04	127 04.6	282 05.5	15.1	333 21.3	15.6	337 54.5	22.1	118 37.9	49.0
	05	142 07.1	297 06.6	15.2	348 22.8	15.3	352 56.9	22.1	133 40.4	49.0
	06	157 09.5	312 07.8	S 9 15.3	3 24.3	N13 15.0	7 59.2	N13 22.1	148 42.9	N 0 49.0
	07	172 12.0	327 09.0	15.3	18 25.8	14.7	23 01.6	22.0	163 45.4	49.0
	08	187 14.5	342 10.2	15.4	33 27.3	14.4	38 03.9	22.0	178 47.9	49.0
	09	202 16.9	357 11.3	15.5	48 28.8	14.1	53 06.3	22.0	193 50.5	49.0
	10	217 19.4	12 12.5	15.6	63 30.3	13.9	68 08.6	21.9	208 53.0	49.0
	11	232 21.9	27 13.7	15.7	78 31.9	13.6	83 11.0	21.9	223 55.5	49.0
	12	247 24.3	42 14.8	S 9 15.8	93 33.4	N13 13.3	98 13.3	N13 21.9	238 58.0	N 0 48.9
	13	262 26.8	57 16.0	15.9	108 34.9	13.0	113 15.6	21.9	254 00.5	48.9
	14	277 29.2	72 17.1	16.0	123 36.4	12.7	128 18.0	21.8	269 03.1	48.9
	15	292 31.7	87 18.3	16.1	138 37.9	12.4	143 20.3	21.8	284 05.6	48.9
	16	307 34.2	102 19.4	16.2	153 39.4	12.2	158 22.7	21.8	299 08.1	48.9
	17	322 36.6	117 20.6	16.4	168 41.0	11.9	173 25.0	21.7	314 10.6	48.9
	18	337 39.1	132 21.7	S 9 16.5	183 42.5	N13 11.6	188 27.4	N13 21.7	329 13.1	N 0 48.9
	19	352 41.6	147 22.9	16.6	198 44.0	11.3	203 29.7	21.7	344 15.7	48.8
	20	7 44.0	162 24.0	16.7	213 45.5	11.0	218 32.1	21.6	359 18.2	48.8
	21	22 46.5	177 25.2	16.8	228 47.0	10.8	233 34.4	21.6	14 20.7	48.8
	22	37 49.0	192 26.3	16.9	243 48.6	10.5	248 36.8	21.6	29 23.2	48.8
	23	52 51.4	207 27.4	17.0	258 50.1	10.2	263 39.1	21.6	44 25.7	48.8
SUNDAY	29 00	67 53.9	222 28.6	S 9 17.2	273 51.6	N13 09.9	278 41.5	N13 21.5	59 28.2	N 0 48.8
	01	82 56.3	237 29.7	17.3	288 53.1	09.6	293 43.9	21.5	74 30.8	48.8
	02	97 58.8	252 30.8	17.4	303 54.6	09.4	308 46.2	21.5	89 33.3	48.8
	03	113 01.3	267 32.0	17.5	318 56.2	09.1	323 48.6	21.4	104 35.8	48.8
	04	128 03.7	282 33.1	17.6	333 57.7	08.8	338 50.9	21.4	119 38.3	48.7
	05	143 06.2	297 34.2	17.8	348 59.2	08.5	353 53.3	21.4	134 40.8	48.7
	06	158 08.7	312 35.3	S 9 17.9	4 00.7	N13 08.2	8 55.6	N13 21.4	149 43.3	N 0 48.7
	07	173 11.1	327 36.4	18.0	19 02.3	08.0	23 58.0	21.3	164 45.9	48.7
	08	188 13.6	342 37.6	18.1	34 03.8	07.7	39 00.3	21.3	179 48.4	48.7
	09	203 16.1	357 38.7	18.3	49 05.3	07.4	54 02.7	21.3	194 50.9	48.7
	10	218 18.5	12 39.8	18.4	64 06.9	07.1	69 05.0	21.2	209 53.4	48.7
	11	233 21.0	27 40.9	18.5	79 08.4	06.8	84 07.4	21.2	224 55.9	48.7
	12	248 23.5	42 42.0	S 9 18.7	94 09.9	N13 06.6	99 09.7	N13 21.2	239 58.4	N 0 48.6
	13	263 25.9	57 43.1	18.8	109 11.4	06.3	114 12.1	21.2	255 01.0	48.6
	14	278 28.4	72 44.2	19.0	124 13.0	06.0	129 14.5	21.1	270 03.5	48.6
	15	293 30.8	87 45.3	19.1	139 14.5	05.7	144 16.8	21.1	285 06.0	48.6
	16	308 33.3	102 46.4	19.2	154 16.0	05.5	159 19.2	21.1	300 08.5	48.6
	17	323 35.8	117 47.5	19.4	169 17.6	05.2	174 21.5	21.1	315 11.0	48.6
	18	338 38.2	132 48.6	S 9 19.5	184 19.1	N13 04.9	189 23.9	N13 21.0	330 13.5	N 0 48.6
	19	353 40.7	147 49.7	19.7	199 20.6	04.6	204 26.2	21.0	345 16.0	48.6
	20	8 43.2	162 50.7	19.8	214 22.2	04.3	219 28.6	21.0	0 18.6	48.6
	21	23 45.6	177 51.8	20.0	229 23.7	04.1	234 31.0	20.9	15 21.1	48.5
	22	38 48.1	192 52.9	20.1	244 25.2	03.8	249 33.3	20.9	30 23.6	48.5
	23	53 50.6	207 54.0	20.3	259 26.8	03.5	264 35.7	20.9	45 26.1	48.5
	Mer. Pass. (h m)	19 29.1	v 1.2	d 0.1	v 1.5	d 0.3	v 2.3	d 0.0	v 2.5	d 0.0

STARS

Name	SHA (° ′)	Dec (° ′)
Acamar	315 10.2	S40 11.8
Achernar	335 18.6	S57 06.1
Acrux	172 58.6	S63 14.7
Adhara	255 04.3	S29 00.4
Aldebaran	290 37.5	N16 33.8
Alioth	166 12.0	N55 48.6
Alkaid	152 51.2	N49 10.5
Alnair	27 31.0	S46 50.0
Alnilam	275 35.8	S 1 11.0
Alphard	217 46.1	S 8 46.5
Alphecca	126 02.8	N26 37.4
Alpheratz	357 33.0	N29 14.6
Altair	61 58.7	N 8 56.5
Ankaa	353 05.4	S42 09.7
Antares	112 14.3	S26 29.4
Arcturus	145 46.8	N19 02.5
Atria	107 07.7	S69 04.5
Avior	234 13.7	S59 35.5
Bellatrix	278 20.9	N 6 22.5
Betelgeuse	270 50.1	N 7 24.7
Canopus	263 51.2	S52 42.4
Capella	280 19.1	N46 01.5
Deneb	49 25.0	N45 22.9
Denebola	182 23.5	N14 25.2
Diphda	348 45.6	S17 50.3
Dubhe	193 39.3	N61 36.0
Elnath	277 59.5	N28 37.8
Eltanin	90 42.0	N51 29.2
Enif	33 37.3	N10 00.1
Fomalhaut	15 12.8	S29 28.8
Gacrux	171 50.2	S57 15.6
Gienah	175 42.1	S17 41.4
Hadar	148 34.3	S60 30.0
Hamal	327 49.1	N23 35.5
Kaus Aust.	83 30.8	S34 22.3
Kochab	137 21.0	N74 02.5
Markab	13 28.3	N15 21.2
Menkar	314 04.2	N 4 11.8
Menkent	147 56.1	S36 30.0
Miaplacidus	221 37.6	S69 49.3
Mirfak	308 25.5	N49 57.5
Nunki	75 46.1	S26 15.8
Peacock	53 03.6	S56 39.0
Pollux	243 15.2	N27 57.5
Procyon	244 49.0	N 5 09.3
Rasalhague	95 57.4	N12 32.5
Regulus	207 32.8	N11 50.1
Rigel	281 02.0	S 8 10.2
Rigil Kent.	139 38.7	S60 56.6
Sabik	102 01.4	S15 45.4
Schedar	349 28.9	N56 41.4
Shaula	96 08.7	S37 07.4
Sirius	258 24.6	S16 45.1
Spica	158 20.9	S11 18.1
Suhail	222 45.0	S43 32.2
Vega	80 32.5	N38 48.7
Zuben'ubi	136 54.6	S16 09.2

	SHA (° ′)	Mer. Pass. (h m)
Venus	155 06.0	9 11
Mars	206 20.5	5 46
Jupiter	210 50.4	5 28
Saturn	351 33.0	20 03

UT d	h	SUN GHA ° ′	SUN Dec ° ′	MOON GHA ° ′	v ′	MOON Dec ° ′	d ′	HP ′
27 (FRIDAY)	00	183 08.3	S21 05.0	326 42.9	1.9	N26 46.7	4.8	60.8
	01	198 08.1	05.4	341 03.8	1.9	26 41.9	4.9	60.8
	02	213 07.9	05.9	355 24.7	2.1	26 37.0	5.2	60.8
	03	228 07.7	. . 06.4	9 45.8	2.1	26 31.8	5.4	60.8
	04	243 07.5	06.8	24 06.9	2.3	26 26.4	5.5	60.8
	05	258 07.3	07.3	38 28.2	2.3	26 20.9	5.8	60.8
	06	273 07.1	S21 07.7	52 49.5	2.4	N26 15.1	5.9	60.7
	07	288 06.9	08.2	67 10.9	2.5	26 09.2	6.1	60.7
	08	303 06.7	08.6	81 32.4	2.6	26 03.1	6.3	60.7
	09	318 06.5	. . 09.1	95 54.0	2.7	25 56.8	6.5	60.7
	10	333 06.3	09.6	110 15.7	2.9	25 50.3	6.7	60.7
	11	348 06.1	10.0	124 37.6	2.9	25 43.6	6.9	60.7
	12	3 05.9	S21 10.5	138 59.5	3.0	N25 36.7	7.1	60.6
	13	18 05.7	10.9	153 21.5	3.1	25 29.6	7.2	60.6
	14	33 05.5	11.4	167 43.6	3.3	25 22.4	7.4	60.6
	15	48 05.3	. . 11.8	182 05.9	3.3	25 15.0	7.6	60.6
	16	63 05.0	12.3	196 28.2	3.5	25 07.4	7.8	60.6
	17	78 04.8	12.7	210 50.7	3.6	24 59.6	7.9	60.5
	18	93 04.6	S21 13.2	225 13.3	3.7	N24 51.7	8.1	60.5
	19	108 04.4	13.6	239 36.0	3.8	24 43.6	8.3	60.5
	20	123 04.2	14.1	253 58.8	3.9	24 35.3	8.4	60.5
	21	138 04.0	. . 14.5	268 21.7	4.1	24 26.9	8.6	60.5
	22	153 03.8	14.9	282 44.8	4.2	24 18.3	8.8	60.4
	23	168 03.6	15.4	297 08.0	4.3	24 09.5	8.9	60.4
28 (SATURDAY)	00	183 03.4	S21 15.8	311 31.3	4.4	N24 00.6	9.1	60.4
	01	198 03.2	16.3	325 54.7	4.5	23 51.5	9.2	60.4
	02	213 03.0	16.7	340 18.2	4.7	23 42.3	9.4	60.3
	03	228 02.8	. . 17.2	354 41.9	4.8	23 32.9	9.6	60.3
	04	243 02.6	17.6	9 05.7	4.9	23 23.3	9.7	60.3
	05	258 02.3	18.0	23 29.6	5.1	23 13.6	9.8	60.3
	06	273 02.1	S21 18.5	37 53.7	5.2	N23 03.8	10.0	60.3
	07	288 01.9	18.9	52 17.9	5.3	22 53.8	10.1	60.2
	08	303 01.7	19.4	66 42.2	5.4	22 43.7	10.3	60.2
	09	318 01.5	. . 19.8	81 06.6	5.6	22 33.4	10.4	60.2
	10	333 01.3	20.2	95 31.2	5.7	22 23.0	10.6	60.2
	11	348 01.1	20.7	109 55.9	5.8	22 12.4	10.7	60.1
	12	3 00.9	S21 21.1	124 20.7	6.0	N22 01.7	10.8	60.1
	13	18 00.6	21.5	138 45.7	6.1	21 50.9	10.9	60.1
	14	33 00.4	22.0	153 10.8	6.2	21 40.0	11.1	60.0
	15	48 00.2	. . 22.4	167 36.0	6.4	21 28.9	11.2	60.0
	16	63 00.0	22.8	182 01.4	6.5	21 17.7	11.3	60.0
	17	77 59.8	23.3	196 26.9	6.6	21 06.4	11.5	60.0
	18	92 59.6	S21 23.7	210 52.5	6.7	N20 54.9	11.5	59.9
	19	107 59.4	24.1	225 18.2	6.9	20 43.4	11.7	59.9
	20	122 59.2	24.6	239 44.1	7.0	20 31.7	11.8	59.9
	21	137 58.9	. . 25.0	254 10.1	7.2	20 19.9	12.0	59.9
	22	152 58.7	25.4	268 36.3	7.2	20 07.9	12.0	59.8
	23	167 58.5	25.9	283 02.5	7.4	19 55.9	12.1	59.8
29 (SUNDAY)	00	182 58.3	S21 26.3	297 28.9	7.6	N19 43.8	12.3	59.8
	01	197 58.1	26.7	311 55.5	7.6	19 31.5	12.3	59.7
	02	212 57.9	27.1	326 22.1	7.8	19 19.2	12.5	59.7
	03	227 57.6	. . 27.6	340 48.9	7.9	19 06.7	12.5	59.7
	04	242 57.4	28.0	355 15.8	8.1	18 54.2	12.7	59.6
	05	257 57.2	28.4	9 42.9	8.1	18 41.5	12.7	59.6
	06	272 57.0	S21 28.8	24 10.0	8.3	N18 28.8	12.9	59.6
	07	287 56.8	29.2	38 37.3	8.5	18 15.9	12.9	59.6
	08	302 56.5	29.7	53 04.8	8.5	18 03.0	13.0	59.5
	09	317 56.3	. . 30.1	67 32.3	8.7	17 50.0	13.2	59.5
	10	332 56.1	30.5	82 00.0	8.8	17 36.8	13.2	59.5
	11	347 55.9	30.9	96 27.8	8.9	17 23.6	13.3	59.4
	12	2 55.7	S21 31.3	110 55.7	9.0	N17 10.3	13.3	59.4
	13	17 55.5	31.8	125 23.7	9.1	16 57.0	13.5	59.4
	14	32 55.2	32.2	139 51.8	9.3	16 43.5	13.5	59.3
	15	47 55.0	. . 32.6	154 20.1	9.4	16 30.0	13.6	59.3
	16	62 54.8	33.0	168 48.5	9.5	16 16.4	13.7	59.3
	17	77 54.6	33.4	183 17.0	9.6	16 02.7	13.8	59.2
	18	92 54.3	S21 33.8	197 45.6	9.7	N15 48.9	13.8	59.2
	19	107 54.1	34.3	212 14.3	9.9	15 35.1	13.9	59.2
	20	122 53.9	34.7	226 43.2	10.0	15 21.2	14.0	59.2
	21	137 53.7	. . 35.1	241 12.2	10.0	15 07.2	14.0	59.1
	22	152 53.5	35.5	255 41.2	10.2	14 53.2	14.1	59.1
	23	167 53.2	35.9	270 10.4	10.3	N14 39.1	14.2	59.1
		SD 16.2	*d* 0.4	SD 16.5		16.4		16.2

Lat. °	Twilight Naut. h m	Twilight Civil h m	Sunrise h m	Moonrise 27 h m	Moonrise 28 h m	Moonrise 29 h m	Moonrise 30 h m
N 72	07 42	09 36	■	□	□	18 58	21 49
N 70	07 27	09 00	■	□	□	19 38	22 04
68	07 15	08 35	10 19	□	17 10	20 05	22 15
66	07 04	08 16	09 36	□	18 03	20 25	22 25
64	06 56	08 00	09 08	16 04	18 36	20 41	22 32
62	06 48	07 47	08 46	16 54	18 59	20 54	22 39
60	06 41	07 35	08 29	17 26	19 18	21 05	22 45
N 58	06 35	07 25	08 14	17 49	19 34	21 15	22 50
56	06 29	07 17	08 02	18 08	19 47	21 23	22 55
54	06 24	07 09	07 51	18 24	19 58	21 31	22 59
52	06 19	07 02	07 41	18 37	20 08	21 37	23 02
50	06 15	06 55	07 32	18 49	20 17	21 43	23 05
45	06 05	06 41	07 14	19 14	20 36	21 56	23 13
N 40	05 56	06 30	06 59	19 33	20 51	22 07	23 19
35	05 48	06 19	06 47	19 50	21 04	22 16	23 24
30	05 40	06 10	06 36	20 04	21 15	22 24	23 28
20	05 26	05 53	06 17	20 28	21 35	22 37	23 36
N 10	05 12	05 37	06 00	20 48	21 51	22 49	23 42
0	04 56	05 22	05 44	21 08	22 07	23 00	23 49
S 10	04 39	05 06	05 28	21 27	22 22	23 11	23 55
20	04 19	04 47	05 11	21 47	22 38	23 22	24 02
30	03 52	04 25	04 52	22 11	22 57	23 36	24 09
35	03 36	04 11	04 40	22 24	23 08	23 43	24 14
40	03 15	03 55	04 26	22 40	23 20	23 52	24 18
45	02 48	03 35	04 11	22 59	23 35	24 02	00 02
S 50	02 11	03 09	03 51	23 23	23 52	24 14	00 14
52	01 50	02 56	03 41	23 34	24 01	00 01	00 19
54	01 23	02 41	03 31	23 46	24 10	00 10	00 26
56	00 38	02 23	03 19	24 01	00 01	00 20	00 32
58	////	02 01	03 05	24 18	00 18	00 32	00 40
S 60	////	01 32	02 48	00 20	00 38	00 46	00 49

Lat. °	Sunset h m	Twilight Civil h m	Twilight Naut. h m	Moonset 27 h m	Moonset 28 h m	Moonset 29 h m	Moonset 30 h m
N 72	■	13 59	15 53	□	□	15 01	13 54
N 70	■	14 35	16 08	□	□	14 19	13 37
68	13 16	15 00	16 20	□	14 51	13 50	13 23
66	13 59	15 20	16 31	□	13 56	13 29	13 12
64	14 28	15 35	16 40	13 49	13 23	13 11	13 02
62	14 49	15 49	16 48	12 58	12 59	12 57	12 54
60	15 07	16 00	16 54	12 26	12 39	12 44	12 47
N 58	15 21	16 10	17 01	12 02	12 23	12 34	12 40
56	15 34	16 19	17 06	11 43	12 09	12 24	12 35
54	15 45	16 27	17 11	11 27	11 57	12 16	12 30
52	15 54	16 34	17 16	11 13	11 46	12 08	12 25
50	16 03	16 40	17 21	11 00	11 36	12 02	12 21
45	16 21	16 54	17 31	10 35	11 16	11 47	12 12
N 40	16 36	17 06	17 39	10 14	10 59	11 35	12 04
35	16 49	17 16	17 48	09 57	10 45	11 25	11 57
30	17 00	17 26	17 55	09 42	10 33	11 15	11 52
20	17 19	17 43	18 10	09 17	10 12	11 00	11 41
N 10	17 36	17 58	18 24	08 55	09 54	10 46	11 32
0	17 52	18 14	18 40	08 35	09 36	10 33	11 24
S 10	18 08	18 30	18 57	08 14	09 19	10 19	11 15
20	18 25	18 49	19 17	07 52	09 00	10 05	11 06
30	18 45	19 11	19 44	07 26	08 38	09 48	10 55
35	18 56	19 25	20 01	07 10	08 25	09 39	10 49
40	19 10	19 42	20 21	06 53	08 10	09 28	10 42
45	19 26	20 02	20 48	06 31	07 53	09 15	10 33
S 50	19 46	20 28	21 26	06 03	07 30	08 59	10 23
52	19 55	20 41	21 48	05 50	07 20	08 51	10 18
54	20 06	20 56	22 16	05 34	07 08	08 42	10 13
56	20 18	21 14	23 04	05 16	06 54	08 33	10 07
58	20 32	21 37	////	04 54	06 37	08 22	10 01
S 60	20 49	22 07	////	04 24	06 18	08 09	09 53

Day d	SUN Eqn. of Time 00^h m s	SUN Eqn. of Time 12^h m s	SUN Mer. Pass. h m	MOON Mer. Pass. Upper h m	MOON Mer. Pass. Lower h m	MOON Age d	MOON Phase %
27	12 34	12 24	11 48	02 19	14 51	18	88
28	12 14	12 04	11 48	03 22	15 52	19	79
29	11 54	11 43	11 48	04 20	16 46	20	69

2026 NOV. 30, DEC. 1, 2 (MON., TUES., WED.)

UT		ARIES	VENUS −4·9		MARS +0·5		JUPITER −2·2		SATURN +0·6	
		GHA	GHA	Dec	GHA	Dec	GHA	Dec	GHA	Dec
d h		° ′	° ′	° ′	° ′	° ′	° ′	° ′	° ′	° ′
30 00	MONDAY	68 53.0	222 55.1	S 9 20.4	274 28.3	N13 03.2	279 38.0	N13 20.9	60 28.6	N 0 48.5
01		83 55.5	237 56.1	20.6	289 29.8	03.0	294 40.4	20.8	75 31.1	48.5
02		98 58.0	252 57.2	20.7	304 31.4	02.7	309 42.8	20.8	90 33.6	48.5
03		114 00.4	267 58.3	. . 20.9	319 32.9	. . 02.4	324 45.1	. . 20.8	105 36.2	. . 48.5
04		129 02.9	282 59.3	21.0	334 34.5	02.1	339 47.5	20.8	120 38.7	48.5
05		144 05.3	298 00.4	21.2	349 36.0	01.9	354 49.8	20.7	135 41.2	48.5
06		159 07.8	313 01.5	S 9 21.4	4 37.5	N13 01.6	9 52.2	N13 20.7	150 43.7	N 0 48.5
07		174 10.3	328 02.5	21.5	19 39.1	01.3	24 54.6	20.7	165 46.2	48.4
08		189 12.7	343 03.6	21.7	34 40.6	01.0	39 56.9	20.7	180 48.7	48.4
09		204 15.2	358 04.6	. . 21.9	49 42.2	. . 00.8	54 59.3	. . 20.6	195 51.2	. . 48.4
10		219 17.7	13 05.7	22.0	64 43.7	00.5	70 01.6	20.6	210 53.7	48.4
11		234 20.1	28 06.7	22.2	79 45.3	13 00.2	85 04.0	20.6	225 56.3	48.4
12		249 22.6	43 07.8	S 9 22.4	94 46.8	N12 59.9	100 06.4	N13 20.6	240 58.8	N 0 48.4
13		264 25.1	58 08.8	22.5	109 48.3	59.7	115 08.7	20.5	256 01.3	48.4
14		279 27.5	73 09.9	22.7	124 49.9	59.4	130 11.1	20.5	271 03.8	48.4
15		294 30.0	88 10.9	. . 22.9	139 51.4	. . 59.1	145 13.5	. . 20.5	286 06.3	. . 48.4
16		309 32.5	103 12.0	23.0	154 53.0	58.9	160 15.8	20.5	301 08.8	48.4
17		324 34.9	118 13.0	23.2	169 54.5	58.6	175 18.2	20.4	316 11.3	48.4
18		339 37.4	133 14.0	S 9 23.4	184 56.1	N12 58.3	190 20.5	N13 20.4	331 13.8	N 0 48.3
19		354 39.8	148 15.1	23.6	199 57.6	58.0	205 22.9	20.4	346 16.3	48.3
20		9 42.3	163 16.1	23.8	214 59.2	57.8	220 25.3	20.4	1 18.9	48.3
21		24 44.8	178 17.1	. . 23.9	230 00.7	. . 57.5	235 27.6	. . 20.3	16 21.4	. . 48.3
22		39 47.2	193 18.1	24.1	245 02.3	57.2	250 30.0	20.3	31 23.9	48.3
23		54 49.7	208 19.2	24.3	260 03.8	57.0	265 32.4	20.3	46 26.4	48.3
1 00	TUESDAY	69 52.2	223 20.2	S 9 24.5	275 05.4	N12 56.7	280 34.7	N13 20.3	61 28.9	N 0 48.3
01		84 54.6	238 21.2	24.7	290 06.9	56.4	295 37.1	20.2	76 31.4	48.3
02		99 57.1	253 22.2	24.9	305 08.5	56.1	310 39.5	20.2	91 33.9	48.3
03		114 59.6	268 23.2	. . 25.1	320 10.0	. . 55.9	325 41.8	. . 20.2	106 36.4	. . 48.3
04		130 02.0	283 24.3	25.2	335 11.6	55.6	340 44.2	20.2	121 38.9	48.3
05		145 04.5	298 25.3	25.4	350 13.1	55.3	355 46.6	20.1	136 41.4	48.2
06		160 06.9	313 26.3	S 9 25.6	5 14.7	N12 55.1	10 48.9	N13 20.1	151 44.0	N 0 48.2
07		175 09.4	328 27.3	25.8	20 16.2	54.8	25 51.3	20.1	166 46.5	48.2
08		190 11.9	343 28.3	26.0	35 17.8	54.5	40 53.7	20.1	181 49.0	48.2
09		205 14.3	358 29.3	. . 26.2	50 19.4	. . 54.2	55 56.1	. . 20.1	196 51.5	. . 48.2
10		220 16.8	13 30.3	26.4	65 20.9	54.0	70 58.4	20.0	211 54.0	48.2
11		235 19.3	28 31.3	26.6	80 22.5	53.7	86 00.8	20.0	226 56.5	48.2
12		250 21.7	43 32.3	S 9 26.8	95 24.0	N12 53.4	101 03.2	N13 20.0	241 59.0	N 0 48.2
13		265 24.2	58 33.3	27.0	110 25.6	53.2	116 05.5	20.0	257 01.5	48.2
14		280 26.7	73 34.3	27.2	125 27.1	52.9	131 07.9	19.9	272 04.0	48.2
15		295 29.1	88 35.2	. . 27.4	140 28.7	. . 52.6	146 10.3	. . 19.9	287 06.5	. . 48.2
16		310 31.6	103 36.2	27.6	155 30.3	52.4	161 12.7	19.9	302 09.0	48.2
17		325 34.1	118 37.2	27.8	170 31.8	52.1	176 15.0	19.9	317 11.5	48.2
18		340 36.5	133 38.2	S 9 28.1	185 33.4	N12 51.8	191 17.4	N13 19.9	332 14.0	N 0 48.1
19		355 39.0	148 39.2	28.3	200 35.0	51.6	206 19.8	19.8	347 16.5	48.1
20		10 41.4	163 40.1	28.5	215 36.5	51.3	221 22.1	19.8	2 19.1	48.1
21		25 43.9	178 41.1	. . 28.7	230 38.1	. . 51.0	236 24.5	. . 19.8	17 21.6	. . 48.1
22		40 46.4	193 42.1	28.9	245 39.6	50.8	251 26.9	19.8	32 24.1	48.1
23		55 48.8	208 43.1	29.1	260 41.2	50.5	266 29.3	19.7	47 26.6	48.1
2 00	WEDNESDAY	70 51.3	223 44.0	S 9 29.3	275 42.8	N12 50.2	281 31.6	N13 19.7	62 29.1	N 0 48.1
01		85 53.8	238 45.0	29.6	290 44.3	50.0	296 34.0	19.7	77 31.6	48.1
02		100 56.2	253 46.0	29.8	305 45.9	49.7	311 36.4	19.7	92 34.1	48.1
03		115 58.7	268 46.9	. . 30.0	320 47.5	. . 49.4	326 38.8	. . 19.7	107 36.6	. . 48.1
04		131 01.2	283 47.9	30.2	335 49.0	49.2	341 41.1	19.6	122 39.1	48.1
05		146 03.6	298 48.8	30.4	350 50.6	48.9	356 43.5	19.6	137 41.6	48.1
06		161 06.1	313 49.8	S 9 30.7	5 52.2	N12 48.6	11 45.9	N13 19.6	152 44.1	N 0 48.1
07		176 08.5	328 50.8	30.9	20 53.8	48.4	26 48.3	19.6	167 46.6	48.1
08		191 11.0	343 51.7	31.1	35 55.3	48.1	41 50.6	19.6	182 49.1	48.1
09		206 13.5	358 52.7	. . 31.3	50 56.9	. . 47.8	56 53.0	. . 19.5	197 51.6	. . 48.0
10		221 15.9	13 53.6	31.6	65 58.5	47.6	71 55.4	19.5	212 54.1	48.0
11		236 18.4	28 54.5	31.8	81 00.0	47.3	86 57.8	19.5	227 56.6	48.0
12		251 20.9	43 55.5	S 9 32.0	96 01.6	N12 47.1	102 00.2	N13 19.5	242 59.1	N 0 48.0
13		266 23.3	58 56.4	32.3	111 03.2	46.8	117 02.5	19.5	258 01.6	48.0
14		281 25.8	73 57.4	32.5	126 04.8	46.5	132 04.9	19.4	273 04.1	48.0
15		296 28.3	88 58.3	. . 32.7	141 06.3	. . 46.3	147 07.3	. . 19.4	288 06.6	. . 48.0
16		311 30.7	103 59.2	33.0	156 07.9	46.0	162 09.7	19.4	303 09.1	48.0
17		326 33.2	119 00.2	33.2	171 09.5	45.7	177 12.0	19.4	318 11.6	48.0
18		341 35.7	134 01.1	S 9 33.5	186 11.1	N12 45.5	192 14.4	N13 19.4	333 14.1	N 0 48.0
19		356 38.1	149 02.0	33.7	201 12.6	45.2	207 16.8	19.3	348 16.7	48.0
20		11 40.6	164 02.9	33.9	216 14.2	45.0	222 19.2	19.3	3 19.2	48.0
21		26 43.0	179 03.9	. . 34.2	231 15.8	. . 44.7	237 21.6	. . 19.3	18 21.7	. . 48.0
22		41 45.5	194 04.8	34.4	246 17.4	44.4	252 23.9	19.3	33 24.2	48.0
23		56 48.0	209 05.7	34.7	261 19.0	44.2	267 26.3	19.3	48 26.7	48.0
Mer. Pass.		h m 19 17.4	v 1.0	d 0.2	v 1.6	d 0.3	v 2.4	d 0.0	v 2.5	d 0.0

STARS

Name	SHA	Dec
	° ′	° ′
Acamar	315 10.2	S40 11.8
Achernar	335 18.6	S57 06.1
Acrux	172 58.6	S63 14.7
Adhara	255 04.3	S29 00.4
Aldebaran	290 37.5	N16 33.9
Alioth	166 12.0	N55 48.5
Alkaid	152 51.2	N49 10.5
Alnair	27 31.1	S46 50.0
Alnilam	275 35.8	S 1 11.0
Alphard	217 46.1	S 8 46.5
Alphecca	126 02.8	N26 37.4
Alpheratz	357 33.0	N29 14.6
Altair	61 58.7	N 8 56.5
Ankaa	353 05.4	S42 09.7
Antares	112 14.3	S26 29.4
Arcturus	145 46.8	N19 02.5
Atria	107 07.7	S69 04.5
Avior	234 13.7	S59 35.5
Bellatrix	278 20.9	N 6 22.5
Betelgeuse	270 50.1	N 7 24.7
Canopus	263 51.2	S52 42.4
Capella	280 19.1	N46 01.5
Deneb	49 25.0	N45 22.8
Denebola	182 23.5	N14 25.2
Diphda	348 45.6	S17 50.3
Dubhe	193 39.2	N61 36.0
Elnath	277 59.5	N28 37.8
Eltanin	90 42.0	N51 29.2
Enif	33 37.4	N10 00.1
Fomalhaut	15 12.8	S29 28.8
Gacrux	171 50.2	S57 15.6
Gienah	175 42.1	S17 41.4
Hadar	148 34.3	S60 30.0
Hamal	327 49.1	N23 35.5
Kaus Aust.	83 30.8	S34 22.3
Kochab	137 21.0	N74 02.5
Markab	13 28.3	N15 21.2
Menkar	314 04.2	N 4 11.8
Menkent	147 56.1	S36 30.0
Miaplacidus	221 37.6	S69 49.4
Mirfak	308 25.5	N49 57.5
Nunki	75 46.2	S26 15.8
Peacock	53 03.6	S56 39.0
Pollux	243 15.1	N27 57.5
Procyon	244 49.0	N 5 09.3
Rasalhague	95 57.4	N12 32.5
Regulus	207 32.7	N11 50.1
Rigel	281 02.0	S 8 10.2
Rigil Kent.	139 38.7	S60 56.6
Sabik	102 01.3	S15 45.4
Schedar	349 28.9	N56 41.4
Shaula	96 08.7	S37 07.4
Sirius	258 24.6	S16 45.1
Spica	158 20.9	S11 18.1
Suhail	222 45.0	S43 32.3
Vega	80 32.6	N38 48.6
Zuben'ubi	136 54.6	S16 09.2

	SHA	Mer. Pass.
	° ′	h m
Venus	153 28.0	9 06
Mars	205 13.2	5 39
Jupiter	210 42.6	5 17
Saturn	351 36.7	19 51

UT		SUN GHA	SUN Dec	MOON GHA	v	MOON Dec	d	HP
d	h	° ′	° ′	° ′	′	° ′	′	′
30 (MONDAY)	00	182 53.0	S21 36.3	284 39.7	10.4	N14 24.9	14.2	59.0
	01	197 52.8	36.7	299 09.1	10.5	14 10.7	14.3	59.0
	02	212 52.6	37.1	313 38.6	10.6	13 56.4	14.3	59.0
	03	227 52.3	. . 37.5	328 08.2	10.7	13 42.1	14.4	58.9
	04	242 52.1	38.0	342 37.9	10.8	13 27.7	14.5	58.9
	05	257 51.9	38.4	357 07.7	11.0	13 13.2	14.5	58.9
	06	272 51.7	S21 38.8	11 37.7	11.0	N12 58.7	14.6	58.8
	07	287 51.4	39.2	26 07.7	11.1	12 44.1	14.6	58.8
	08	302 51.2	39.6	40 37.8	11.2	12 29.5	14.6	58.8
	09	317 51.0	. . 40.0	55 08.0	11.3	12 14.9	14.7	58.7
	10	332 50.8	40.4	69 38.3	11.4	12 00.2	14.8	58.7
	11	347 50.5	40.8	84 08.7	11.5	11 45.4	14.7	58.7
	12	2 50.3	S21 41.2	98 39.2	11.6	N11 30.7	14.9	58.6
	13	17 50.1	41.6	113 09.8	11.7	11 15.8	14.8	58.6
	14	32 49.9	42.0	127 40.5	11.8	11 01.0	14.9	58.6
	15	47 49.6	. . 42.4	142 11.3	11.8	10 46.1	15.0	58.5
	16	62 49.4	42.8	156 42.1	12.0	10 31.1	15.0	58.5
	17	77 49.2	43.2	171 13.1	12.0	10 16.1	15.0	58.5
	18	92 48.9	S21 43.6	185 44.1	12.1	N10 01.1	15.0	58.4
	19	107 48.7	44.0	200 15.2	12.2	9 46.1	15.1	58.4
	20	122 48.5	44.4	214 46.4	12.3	9 31.0	15.1	58.4
	21	137 48.3	. . 44.8	229 17.7	12.4	9 15.9	15.1	58.3
	22	152 48.0	45.2	243 49.1	12.4	9 00.8	15.2	58.3
	23	167 47.8	45.6	258 20.5	12.5	8 45.6	15.1	58.3
1 (TUESDAY)	00	182 47.6	S21 45.9	272 52.0	12.6	N 8 30.5	15.2	58.2
	01	197 47.3	46.3	287 23.6	12.7	8 15.3	15.3	58.2
	02	212 47.1	46.7	301 55.3	12.7	8 00.0	15.2	58.2
	03	227 46.9	. . 47.1	316 27.0	12.9	7 44.8	15.3	58.1
	04	242 46.6	47.5	330 58.9	12.8	7 29.5	15.3	58.1
	05	257 46.4	47.9	345 30.7	13.0	7 14.2	15.3	58.1
	06	272 46.2	S21 48.3	0 02.7	13.0	N 6 58.9	15.3	58.0
	07	287 45.9	48.7	14 34.7	13.1	6 43.6	15.3	58.0
	08	302 45.7	49.1	29 06.8	13.1	6 28.3	15.4	58.0
	09	317 45.5	. . 49.4	43 38.9	13.2	6 12.9	15.3	58.0
	10	332 45.2	49.8	58 11.1	13.3	5 57.6	15.4	57.9
	11	347 45.0	50.2	72 43.4	13.4	5 42.2	15.4	57.9
	12	2 44.8	S21 50.6	87 15.8	13.3	N 5 26.8	15.4	57.9
	13	17 44.5	51.0	101 48.1	13.5	5 11.4	15.3	57.8
	14	32 44.3	51.4	116 20.6	13.5	4 56.1	15.4	57.8
	15	47 44.1	. . 51.8	130 53.1	13.6	4 40.7	15.4	57.8
	16	62 43.8	52.1	145 25.7	13.6	4 25.3	15.4	57.7
	17	77 43.6	52.5	159 58.3	13.6	4 09.9	15.5	57.7
	18	92 43.4	S21 52.9	174 30.9	13.7	N 3 54.4	15.4	57.7
	19	107 43.1	53.3	189 03.6	13.8	3 39.0	15.4	57.6
	20	122 42.9	53.7	203 36.4	13.8	3 23.6	15.4	57.6
	21	137 42.7	. . 54.0	218 09.2	13.9	3 08.2	15.4	57.6
	22	152 42.4	54.4	232 42.1	13.9	2 52.8	15.4	57.5
	23	167 42.2	54.8	247 15.0	13.9	2 37.4	15.4	57.5
2 (WEDNESDAY)	00	182 41.9	S21 55.2	261 47.9	14.0	N 2 22.0	15.4	57.5
	01	197 41.7	55.5	276 20.9	14.0	2 06.6	15.4	57.4
	02	212 41.5	55.9	290 53.9	14.1	1 51.3	15.4	57.4
	03	227 41.2	. . 56.3	305 27.0	14.1	1 35.9	15.4	57.4
	04	242 41.0	56.7	320 00.1	14.1	1 20.5	15.3	57.4
	05	257 40.7	57.0	334 33.2	14.2	1 05.2	15.4	57.3
	06	272 40.5	S21 57.4	349 06.4	14.2	N 0 49.8	15.3	57.3
	07	287 40.3	57.8	3 39.6	14.2	0 34.5	15.3	57.3
	08	302 40.0	58.1	18 12.8	14.3	0 19.2	15.3	57.2
	09	317 39.8	. . 58.5	32 46.1	14.3	N 0 03.9	15.3	57.2
	10	332 39.6	58.9	47 19.4	14.3	S 0 11.4	15.3	57.2
	11	347 39.3	59.2	61 52.7	14.4	0 26.7	15.3	57.1
	12	2 39.1	S21 59.6	76 26.1	14.4	S 0 42.0	15.2	57.1
	13	17 38.8	22 00.0	90 59.5	14.4	0 57.2	15.2	57.1
	14	32 38.6	00.3	105 32.9	14.4	1 12.4	15.2	57.1
	15	47 38.3	. . 00.7	120 06.3	14.4	1 27.6	15.2	57.0
	16	62 38.1	01.1	134 39.7	14.5	1 42.8	15.2	57.0
	17	77 37.9	01.4	149 13.2	14.5	1 58.0	15.1	57.0
	18	92 37.6	S22 01.8	163 46.7	14.5	S 2 13.1	15.1	56.9
	19	107 37.4	02.2	178 20.2	14.5	2 28.2	15.1	56.9
	20	122 37.1	02.5	192 53.7	14.6	2 43.3	15.0	56.9
	21	137 36.9	. . 02.9	207 27.3	14.5	2 58.3	15.1	56.9
	22	152 36.6	03.2	222 00.8	14.6	3 13.4	15.0	56.8
	23	167 36.4	03.6	236 34.4	14.6	S 3 28.4	14.9	56.8
		SD 16.2	*d* 0.4	SD 16.0		15.8		15.6

Lat.	Twilight Naut.	Twilight Civil	Sunrise	Moonrise 30	Moonrise 1	Moonrise 2	Moonrise 3
°	h m	h m	h m	h m	h m	h m	h m
N 72	07 51	09 50	▬	21 49	24 06	00 06	02 14
N 70	07 35	09 11	▬	22 04	24 09	00 09	02 08
68	07 21	08 44	10 36	22 15	24 12	00 12	02 03
66	07 10	08 23	09 47	22 25	24 14	00 14	01 58
64	07 01	08 06	09 16	22 32	24 16	00 16	01 55
62	06 53	07 52	08 53	22 39	24 17	00 17	01 51
60	06 46	07 41	08 35	22 45	24 19	00 19	01 49
N 58	06 39	07 30	08 20	22 50	24 20	00 20	01 46
56	06 33	07 21	08 07	22 55	24 21	00 21	01 44
54	06 28	07 13	07 55	22 59	24 22	00 22	01 42
52	06 23	07 06	07 45	23 02	24 23	00 23	01 40
50	06 18	06 59	07 37	23 05	24 24	00 24	01 39
45	06 08	06 45	07 18	23 13	24 25	00 25	01 35
N 40	05 59	06 32	07 02	23 19	24 27	00 27	01 33
35	05 50	06 22	06 49	23 24	24 28	00 28	01 30
30	05 43	06 12	06 38	23 28	24 29	00 29	01 28
20	05 28	05 55	06 19	23 36	24 31	00 31	01 24
N 10	05 13	05 39	06 01	23 42	24 33	00 33	01 21
0	04 57	05 23	05 45	23 49	24 34	00 34	01 18
S 10	04 40	05 06	05 29	23 55	24 36	00 36	01 15
20	04 19	04 47	05 12	24 02	00 02	00 38	01 12
30	03 52	04 24	04 51	24 09	00 09	00 40	01 09
35	03 35	04 10	04 39	24 14	00 14	00 41	01 07
40	03 13	03 54	04 25	24 18	00 18	00 42	01 05
45	02 46	03 33	04 09	00 02	00 24	00 44	01 02
S 50	02 07	03 06	03 49	00 14	00 31	00 45	00 59
52	01 45	02 53	03 39	00 19	00 34	00 46	00 58
54	01 15	02 37	03 28	00 26	00 37	00 47	00 56
56	00 17	02 19	03 15	00 32	00 41	00 48	00 54
58	////	01 55	03 01	00 40	00 45	00 49	00 53
S 60	////	01 23	02 43	00 49	00 50	00 50	00 51

Lat.	Sunset	Twilight Civil	Twilight Naut.	Moonset 30	Moonset 1	Moonset 2	Moonset 3
°	h m	h m	h m	h m	h m	h m	h m
N 72	▬	13 47	15 46	13 54	13 16	12 43	12 10
N 70	▬	14 27	16 03	13 37	13 09	12 44	12 20
68	13 01	14 54	16 16	13 23	13 03	12 45	12 28
66	13 51	15 15	16 27	13 12	12 59	12 46	12 34
64	14 22	15 31	16 36	13 02	12 55	12 47	12 40
62	14 44	15 45	16 45	12 54	12 51	12 48	12 45
60	15 03	15 57	16 52	12 47	12 48	12 48	12 49
N 58	15 18	16 07	16 58	12 40	12 45	12 49	12 53
56	15 31	16 16	17 04	12 35	12 43	12 49	12 56
54	15 42	16 24	17 10	12 30	12 40	12 50	12 59
52	15 52	16 32	17 15	12 25	12 38	12 50	13 02
50	16 01	16 38	17 19	12 21	12 37	12 51	13 04
45	16 20	16 53	17 30	12 12	12 33	12 51	13 10
N 40	16 35	17 05	17 39	12 04	12 29	12 52	13 15
35	16 48	17 16	17 47	11 57	12 26	12 53	13 19
30	17 00	17 26	17 55	11 52	12 23	12 53	13 22
20	17 19	17 43	18 10	11 41	12 19	12 54	13 28
N 10	17 37	17 59	18 25	11 32	12 15	12 55	13 34
0	17 53	18 15	18 41	11 24	12 11	12 55	13 39
S 10	18 09	18 32	18 59	11 15	12 07	12 56	13 44
20	18 27	18 51	19 20	11 06	12 03	12 57	13 50
30	18 47	19 14	19 47	10 55	11 58	12 58	13 56
35	18 59	19 28	20 04	10 49	11 55	12 58	14 00
40	19 13	19 45	20 25	10 42	11 51	12 59	14 04
45	19 29	20 06	20 53	10 33	11 48	12 59	14 09
S 50	19 50	20 33	21 33	10 23	11 43	13 00	14 14
52	20 00	20 46	21 55	10 18	11 41	13 00	14 17
54	20 11	21 02	22 26	10 13	11 39	13 00	14 20
56	20 24	21 21	23 32	10 07	11 36	13 01	14 23
58	20 38	21 45	////	10 01	11 33	13 01	14 27
S 60	20 56	22 18	////	09 53	11 30	13 02	14 31

Day	SUN Eqn. of Time 00^h	SUN Eqn. of Time 12^h	SUN Mer. Pass.	MOON Mer. Pass. Upper	MOON Mer. Pass. Lower	MOON Age	MOON Phase
d	m s	m s	h m	h m	h m	d %	
30	11 32	11 22	11 49	05 12	17 36	21 58	
1	11 11	11 00	11 49	06 00	18 23	22 47	
2	10 48	10 37	11 49	06 45	19 07	23 37	

2026 DECEMBER 3, 4, 5 (THURS., FRI., SAT.)

Day	UT (d h)	ARIES GHA (° ′)	VENUS −4·8 GHA (° ′)	VENUS Dec (° ′)	MARS +0·4 GHA (° ′)	MARS Dec (° ′)	JUPITER −2·2 GHA (° ′)	JUPITER Dec (° ′)	SATURN +0·6 GHA (° ′)	SATURN Dec (° ′)
	3 00	71 50.4	224 06.6	S 9 34.9	276 20.5	N12 43.9	282 28.7	N13 19.3	63 29.2	N 0 48.0
	01	86 52.9	239 07.5	35.2	291 22.1	43.6	297 31.1	19.2	78 31.7	48.0
	02	101 55.4	254 08.5	35.4	306 23.7	43.4	312 33.5	19.2	93 34.2	48.0
	03	116 57.8	269 09.4	. . 35.7	321 25.3	. . 43.1	327 35.9	. . 19.2	108 36.7	. . 47.9
	04	132 00.3	284 10.3	35.9	336 26.9	42.9	342 38.2	19.2	123 39.2	47.9
	05	147 02.8	299 11.2	36.2	351 28.5	42.6	357 40.6	19.2	138 41.7	47.9
	06	162 05.2	314 12.1	S 9 36.4	6 30.0	N12 42.3	12 43.0	N13 19.1	153 44.2	N 0 47.9
	07	177 07.7	329 13.0	36.7	21 31.6	42.1	27 45.4	19.1	168 46.7	47.9
T	08	192 10.2	344 13.9	36.9	36 33.2	41.8	42 47.8	19.1	183 49.2	47.9
H	09	207 12.6	359 14.8	. . 37.2	51 34.8	. . 41.6	57 50.2	. . 19.1	198 51.7	. . 47.9
U	10	222 15.1	14 15.7	37.5	66 36.4	41.3	72 52.5	19.1	213 54.2	47.9
R	11	237 17.5	29 16.6	37.7	81 38.0	41.1	87 54.9	19.1	228 56.7	47.9
S	12	252 20.0	44 17.5	S 9 38.0	96 39.6	N12 40.8	102 57.3	N13 19.0	243 59.2	N 0 47.9
D	13	267 22.5	59 18.4	38.2	111 41.1	40.5	117 59.7	19.0	259 01.7	47.9
A	14	282 24.9	74 19.3	38.5	126 42.7	40.3	133 02.1	19.0	274 04.2	47.9
Y	15	297 27.4	89 20.1	. . 38.8	141 44.3	. . 40.0	148 04.5	. . 19.0	289 06.7	. . 47.9
	16	312 29.9	104 21.0	39.0	156 45.9	39.8	163 06.9	19.0	304 09.2	47.9
	17	327 32.3	119 21.9	39.3	171 47.5	39.5	178 09.3	19.0	319 11.7	47.9
	18	342 34.8	134 22.8	S 9 39.6	186 49.1	N12 39.2	193 11.6	N13 18.9	334 14.2	N 0 47.9
	19	357 37.3	149 23.7	39.8	201 50.7	39.0	208 14.0	18.9	349 16.7	47.9
	20	12 39.7	164 24.5	40.1	216 52.3	38.7	223 16.4	18.9	4 19.2	47.9
	21	27 42.2	179 25.4	. . 40.4	231 53.9	. . 38.5	238 18.8	. . 18.9	19 21.7	. . 47.9
	22	42 44.6	194 26.3	40.7	246 55.5	38.2	253 21.2	18.9	34 24.2	47.9
	23	57 47.1	209 27.2	40.9	261 57.1	38.0	268 23.6	18.9	49 26.7	47.9
	4 00	72 49.6	224 28.0	S 9 41.2	276 58.7	N12 37.7	283 26.0	N13 18.8	64 29.1	N 0 47.9
	01	87 52.0	239 28.9	41.5	292 00.3	37.5	298 28.4	18.8	79 31.6	47.9
	02	102 54.5	254 29.8	41.8	307 01.9	37.2	313 30.8	18.8	94 34.1	47.9
	03	117 57.0	269 30.6	. . 42.0	322 03.5	. . 36.9	328 33.1	. . 18.8	109 36.6	. . 47.9
	04	132 59.4	284 31.5	42.3	337 05.1	36.7	343 35.5	18.8	124 39.1	47.9
	05	148 01.9	299 32.3	42.6	352 06.7	36.4	358 37.9	18.8	139 41.6	47.8
	06	163 04.4	314 33.2	S 9 42.9	7 08.3	N12 36.2	13 40.3	N13 18.8	154 44.1	N 0 47.8
	07	178 06.8	329 34.0	43.2	22 09.9	35.9	28 42.7	18.7	169 46.6	47.8
	08	193 09.3	344 34.9	43.4	37 11.5	35.7	43 45.1	18.7	184 49.1	47.8
F	09	208 11.8	359 35.7	. . 43.7	52 13.1	. . 35.4	58 47.5	. . 18.7	199 51.6	. . 47.8
R	10	223 14.2	14 36.6	44.0	67 14.7	35.2	73 49.9	18.7	214 54.1	47.8
I	11	238 16.7	29 37.4	44.3	82 16.3	34.9	88 52.3	18.7	229 56.6	47.8
D	12	253 19.1	44 38.3	S 9 44.6	97 17.9	N12 34.7	103 54.7	N13 18.7	244 59.1	N 0 47.8
A	13	268 21.6	59 39.1	44.9	112 19.5	34.4	118 57.1	18.7	260 01.6	47.8
Y	14	283 24.1	74 40.0	45.2	127 21.1	34.2	133 59.5	18.6	275 04.1	47.8
	15	298 26.5	89 40.8	. . 45.5	142 22.7	. . 33.9	149 01.9	. . 18.6	290 06.6	. . 47.8
	16	313 29.0	104 41.6	45.8	157 24.3	33.7	164 04.2	18.6	305 09.1	47.8
	17	328 31.5	119 42.5	46.1	172 25.9	33.4	179 06.6	18.6	320 11.6	47.8
	18	343 33.9	134 43.3	S 9 46.4	187 27.5	N12 33.1	194 09.0	N13 18.6	335 14.1	N 0 47.8
	19	358 36.4	149 44.1	46.7	202 29.1	32.9	209 11.4	18.6	350 16.6	47.8
	20	13 38.9	164 45.0	47.0	217 30.7	32.6	224 13.8	18.6	5 19.1	47.8
	21	28 41.3	179 45.8	. . 47.3	232 32.3	. . 32.4	239 16.2	. . 18.5	20 21.6	. . 47.8
	22	43 43.8	194 46.6	47.6	247 33.9	32.1	254 18.6	18.5	35 24.0	47.8
	23	58 46.3	209 47.4	47.9	262 35.6	31.9	269 21.0	18.5	50 26.5	47.8
	5 00	73 48.7	224 48.3	S 9 48.2	277 37.2	N12 31.6	284 23.4	N13 18.5	65 29.0	N 0 47.8
	01	88 51.2	239 49.1	48.5	292 38.8	31.4	299 25.8	18.5	80 31.5	47.8
	02	103 53.6	254 49.9	48.8	307 40.4	31.1	314 28.2	18.5	95 34.0	47.8
	03	118 56.1	269 50.7	. . 49.1	322 42.0	. . 30.9	329 30.6	. . 18.5	110 36.5	. . 47.8
	04	133 58.6	284 51.5	49.4	337 43.6	30.6	344 33.0	18.5	125 39.0	47.8
	05	149 01.0	299 52.3	49.7	352 45.2	30.4	359 35.4	18.4	140 41.5	47.8
	06	164 03.5	314 53.1	S 9 50.0	7 46.9	N12 30.1	14 37.8	N13 18.4	155 44.0	N 0 47.8
	07	179 06.0	329 54.0	50.3	22 48.5	29.9	29 40.2	18.4	170 46.5	47.8
S	08	194 08.4	344 54.8	50.6	37 50.1	29.7	44 42.6	18.4	185 49.0	47.8
A	09	209 10.9	359 55.6	. . 50.9	52 51.7	. . 29.4	59 45.0	. . 18.4	200 51.5	. . 47.8
T	10	224 13.4	14 56.4	51.2	67 53.3	29.2	74 47.4	18.4	215 54.0	47.8
U	11	239 15.8	29 57.2	51.6	82 54.9	28.9	89 49.8	18.4	230 56.5	47.8
R	12	254 18.3	44 58.0	S 9 51.9	97 56.6	N12 28.7	104 52.2	N13 18.4	245 58.9	N 0 47.8
D	13	269 20.7	59 58.8	52.2	112 58.2	28.4	119 54.6	18.4	261 01.4	47.8
A	14	284 23.2	74 59.6	52.5	127 59.8	28.2	134 57.0	18.3	276 03.9	47.8
Y	15	299 25.7	90 00.3	. . 52.8	143 01.4	. . 27.9	149 59.4	. . 18.3	291 06.4	. . 47.8
	16	314 28.1	105 01.1	53.2	158 03.0	27.7	165 01.8	18.3	306 08.9	47.8
	17	329 30.6	120 01.9	53.5	173 04.7	27.4	180 04.2	18.3	321 11.4	47.8
	18	344 33.1	135 02.7	S 9 53.8	188 06.3	N12 27.2	195 06.6	N13 18.3	336 13.9	N 0 47.8
	19	359 35.5	150 03.5	54.1	203 07.9	26.9	210 09.0	18.3	351 16.4	47.8
	20	14 38.0	165 04.3	54.4	218 09.5	26.7	225 11.4	18.3	6 18.9	47.8
	21	29 40.5	180 05.1	. . 54.8	233 11.2	. . 26.4	240 13.8	. . 18.3	21 21.4	. . 47.8
	22	44 42.9	195 05.8	55.1	248 12.8	26.2	255 16.2	18.3	36 23.8	47.8
	23	59 45.4	210 06.6	55.4	263 14.4	26.0	270 18.6	18.2	51 26.3	47.8
	Mer. Pass.	h m 19 05.6	*v* 0.8	*d* 0.3	*v* 1.6	*d* 0.3	*v* 2.4	*d* 0.0	*v* 2.5	*d* 0.0

STARS Name	SHA (° ′)	Dec (° ′)
Acamar	315 10.2	S40 11.8
Achernar	335 18.6	S57 06.1
Acrux	172 58.6	S63 14.7
Adhara	255 04.3	S29 00.4
Aldebaran	290 37.5	N16 33.8
Alioth	166 11.9	N55 48.5
Alkaid	152 51.1	N49 10.5
Alnair	27 31.1	S46 50.0
Alnilam	275 35.8	S 1 11.0
Alphard	217 46.1	S 8 46.5
Alphecca	126 02.8	N26 37.4
Alpheratz	357 33.0	N29 14.6
Altair	61 58.7	N 8 56.5
Ankaa	353 05.4	S42 09.7
Antares	112 14.3	S26 29.4
Arcturus	145 46.8	N19 02.4
Atria	107 07.7	S69 04.5
Avior	234 13.7	S59 35.5
Bellatrix	278 20.9	N 6 22.5
Betelgeuse	270 50.1	N 7 24.7
Canopus	263 51.2	S52 42.4
Capella	280 19.1	N46 01.5
Deneb	49 25.0	N45 22.8
Denebola	182 23.4	N14 25.2
Diphda	348 45.6	S17 50.3
Dubhe	193 39.2	N61 36.0
Elnath	277 59.5	N28 37.8
Eltanin	90 42.0	N51 29.2
Enif	33 37.4	N10 00.1
Fomalhaut	15 12.8	S29 28.8
Gacrux	171 50.1	S57 15.6
Gienah	175 42.1	S17 41.4
Hadar	148 34.3	S60 30.0
Hamal	327 49.1	N23 35.5
Kaus Aust.	83 30.8	S34 22.3
Kochab	137 20.9	N74 02.4
Markab	13 28.3	N15 21.2
Menkar	314 04.2	N 4 11.8
Menkent	147 56.1	S36 30.0
Miaplacidus	221 37.5	S69 49.4
Mirfak	308 25.5	N49 57.5
Nunki	75 46.2	S26 15.8
Peacock	53 03.7	S56 39.0
Pollux	243 15.1	N27 57.5
Procyon	244 48.9	N 5 09.3
Rasalhague	95 57.4	N12 32.5
Regulus	207 32.7	N11 50.0
Rigel	281 02.0	S 8 10.2
Rigil Kent.	139 38.7	S60 56.6
Sabik	102 01.3	S15 45.4
Schedar	349 29.0	N56 41.4
Shaula	96 08.7	S37 07.4
Sirius	258 24.5	S16 45.1
Spica	158 20.9	S11 18.1
Suhail	222 44.9	S43 32.3
Vega	80 32.6	N38 48.6
Zuben'ubi	136 54.6	S16 09.2

	SHA (° ′)	Mer. Pass. (h m)
Venus	151 38.4	9 02
Mars	204 09.1	5 31
Jupiter	210 36.4	5 05
Saturn	351 39.6	19 39

UT	SUN GHA	SUN Dec	MOON GHA	v	MOON Dec	d	HP
d h	° ′	° ′	° ′	′	° ′	′	′
3 00	182 36.2	S22 04.0	251 08.0	14.5	S 3 43.3	15.0	56.8
01	197 35.9	04.3	265 41.5	14.6	3 58.3	14.9	56.7
02	212 35.7	04.7	280 15.1	14.7	4 13.2	14.9	56.7
03	227 35.4	. . 05.0	294 48.8	14.6	4 28.1	14.8	56.7
04	242 35.2	05.4	309 22.4	14.6	4 42.9	14.8	56.7
05	257 34.9	05.7	323 56.0	14.6	4 57.7	14.8	56.6
06	272 34.7	S22 06.1	338 29.6	14.6	S 5 12.5	14.8	56.6
T 07	287 34.4	06.4	353 03.2	14.7	5 27.3	14.7	56.6
H 08	302 34.2	06.8	7 36.9	14.6	5 42.0	14.7	56.6
U 09	317 33.9	. . 07.1	22 10.5	14.6	5 56.7	14.6	56.5
R 10	332 33.7	07.5	36 44.1	14.6	6 11.3	14.6	56.5
S 11	347 33.5	07.8	51 17.7	14.7	6 25.9	14.5	56.5
D 12	2 33.2	S22 08.2	65 51.4	14.6	S 6 40.4	14.6	56.4
A 13	17 33.0	08.5	80 25.0	14.6	6 55.0	14.4	56.4
Y 14	32 32.7	08.9	94 58.6	14.6	7 09.4	14.5	56.4
15	47 32.5	. . 09.2	109 32.2	14.6	7 23.9	14.4	56.4
16	62 32.2	09.6	124 05.8	14.6	7 38.3	14.3	56.3
17	77 32.0	09.9	138 39.4	14.6	7 52.6	14.3	56.3
18	92 31.7	S22 10.3	153 13.0	14.6	S 8 06.9	14.2	56.3
19	107 31.5	10.6	167 46.6	14.5	8 21.1	14.2	56.3
20	122 31.2	11.0	182 20.1	14.6	8 35.3	14.2	56.2
21	137 31.0	. . 11.3	196 53.7	14.5	8 49.5	14.1	56.2
22	152 30.7	11.6	211 27.2	14.5	9 03.6	14.1	56.2
23	167 30.5	12.0	226 00.7	14.5	9 17.7	14.0	56.2
4 00	182 30.2	S22 12.3	240 34.2	14.5	S 9 31.7	13.9	56.1
01	197 30.0	12.7	255 07.7	14.5	9 45.6	13.9	56.1
02	212 29.7	13.0	269 41.2	14.5	9 59.5	13.9	56.1
03	227 29.5	. . 13.3	284 14.7	14.4	10 13.4	13.8	56.1
04	242 29.2	13.7	298 48.1	14.4	10 27.2	13.7	56.0
05	257 29.0	14.0	313 21.5	14.4	10 40.9	13.7	56.0
06	272 28.7	S22 14.3	327 54.9	14.4	S10 54.6	13.7	56.0
07	287 28.5	14.7	342 28.3	14.3	11 08.3	13.5	56.0
08	302 28.2	15.0	357 01.6	14.3	11 21.8	13.6	55.9
F 09	317 28.0	. . 15.3	11 34.9	14.3	11 35.4	13.4	55.9
R 10	332 27.7	15.7	26 08.2	14.3	11 48.8	13.4	55.9
I 11	347 27.4	16.0	40 41.5	14.3	12 02.2	13.4	55.9
D 12	2 27.2	S22 16.3	55 14.8	14.2	S12 15.6	13.2	55.9
A 13	17 26.9	16.7	69 48.0	14.2	12 28.8	13.2	55.8
Y 14	32 26.7	17.0	84 21.2	14.1	12 42.0	13.2	55.8
15	47 26.4	. . 17.3	98 54.3	14.2	12 55.2	13.1	55.8
16	62 26.2	17.7	113 27.5	14.1	13 08.3	13.0	55.8
17	77 25.9	18.0	128 00.6	14.0	13 21.3	13.0	55.7
18	92 25.7	S22 18.3	142 33.6	14.0	S13 34.3	12.8	55.7
19	107 25.4	18.6	157 06.6	14.0	13 47.1	12.9	55.7
20	122 25.2	19.0	171 39.6	14.0	14 00.0	12.7	55.7
21	137 24.9	. . 19.3	186 12.6	13.9	14 12.7	12.7	55.7
22	152 24.6	19.6	200 45.5	13.9	14 25.4	12.6	55.6
23	167 24.4	19.9	215 18.4	13.9	14 38.0	12.5	55.6
5 00	182 24.1	S22 20.3	229 51.3	13.8	S14 50.5	12.5	55.6
01	197 23.9	20.6	244 24.1	13.8	15 03.0	12.4	55.6
02	212 23.6	20.9	258 56.9	13.7	15 15.4	12.3	55.5
03	227 23.4	. . 21.2	273 29.6	13.7	15 27.7	12.3	55.5
04	242 23.1	21.5	288 02.3	13.7	15 40.0	12.2	55.5
05	257 22.8	21.9	302 35.0	13.6	15 52.2	12.1	55.5
06	272 22.6	S22 22.2	317 07.6	13.6	S16 04.3	12.0	55.5
S 07	287 22.3	22.5	331 40.2	13.5	16 16.3	11.9	55.4
A 08	302 22.1	22.8	346 12.7	13.5	16 28.2	11.9	55.4
T 09	317 21.8	. . 23.1	0 45.2	13.5	16 40.1	11.8	55.4
U 10	332 21.6	23.4	15 17.7	13.4	16 51.9	11.7	55.4
R 11	347 21.3	23.8	29 50.1	13.4	17 03.6	11.6	55.4
D 12	2 21.0	S22 24.1	44 22.5	13.3	S17 15.2	11.5	55.3
A 13	17 20.8	24.4	58 54.8	13.3	17 26.7	11.5	55.3
Y 14	32 20.5	24.7	73 27.1	13.2	17 38.2	11.4	55.3
15	47 20.3	. . 25.0	87 59.3	13.2	17 49.6	11.2	55.3
16	62 20.0	25.3	102 31.5	13.1	18 00.8	11.2	55.3
17	77 19.7	25.6	117 03.6	13.1	18 12.0	11.2	55.3
18	92 19.5	S22 25.9	131 35.7	13.0	S18 23.2	11.0	55.2
19	107 19.2	26.2	146 07.7	13.0	18 34.2	10.9	55.2
20	122 18.9	26.5	160 39.7	13.0	18 45.1	10.9	55.2
21	137 18.7	. . 26.8	175 11.7	12.9	18 56.0	10.7	55.2
22	152 18.4	27.2	189 43.6	12.8	19 06.7	10.7	55.2
23	167 18.2	27.5	204 15.4	12.8	S19 17.4	10.6	55.1
	SD 16.3	d 0.3	SD 15.4		15.2		15.1

Lat.	Twilight Naut.	Twilight Civil	Sunrise	Moonrise 3	Moonrise 4	Moonrise 5	Moonrise 6
°	h m	h m	h m	h m	h m	h m	h m
N 72	07 59	10 04	▬	02 14	04 27	07 14	▬
N 70	07 42	09 20	▬	02 08	04 09	06 25	▬
68	07 28	08 52	10 55	02 03	03 54	05 55	08 28
66	07 16	08 30	09 57	01 58	03 43	05 32	07 35
64	07 06	08 12	09 24	01 55	03 33	05 15	07 02
62	06 58	07 58	09 00	01 51	03 25	05 00	06 39
60	06 50	07 46	08 41	01 49	03 18	04 48	06 20
N 58	06 43	07 35	08 25	01 46	03 12	04 38	06 04
56	06 37	07 26	08 11	01 44	03 06	04 29	05 51
54	06 32	07 17	08 00	01 42	03 01	04 21	05 40
52	06 27	07 10	07 50	01 40	02 57	04 13	05 30
50	06 22	07 03	07 40	01 39	02 53	04 07	05 21
45	06 11	06 48	07 21	01 35	02 45	03 53	05 02
N 40	06 02	06 35	07 05	01 33	02 37	03 42	04 47
35	05 53	06 24	06 52	01 30	02 31	03 33	04 34
30	05 45	06 14	06 40	01 28	02 26	03 24	04 23
20	05 29	05 57	06 20	01 24	02 17	03 10	04 04
N 10	05 14	05 40	06 03	01 21	02 09	02 58	03 47
0	04 58	05 24	05 46	01 18	02 02	02 46	03 32
S 10	04 40	05 07	05 30	01 15	01 54	02 35	03 17
20	04 19	04 48	05 12	01 12	01 47	02 22	03 01
30	03 51	04 24	04 51	01 09	01 38	02 09	02 42
35	03 34	04 10	04 39	01 07	01 33	02 01	02 31
40	03 12	03 53	04 25	01 05	01 27	01 52	02 19
45	02 44	03 32	04 08	01 02	01 21	01 41	02 05
S 50	02 03	03 04	03 47	00 59	01 13	01 29	01 47
52	01 40	02 50	03 37	00 58	01 09	01 23	01 39
54	01 07	02 34	03 26	00 56	01 06	01 16	01 30
56	////	02 15	03 13	00 54	01 01	01 09	01 20
58	////	01 50	02 58	00 53	00 56	01 01	01 08
S 60	////	01 14	02 39	00 51	00 51	00 52	00 55

Lat.	Sunset	Twilight Civil	Twilight Naut.	Moonset 3	Moonset 4	Moonset 5	Moonset 6
°	h m	h m	h m	h m	h m	h m	h m
N 72	▬	13 36	15 41	12 10	11 30	10 17	▬
N 70	▬	14 19	15 58	12 20	11 51	11 08	▬
68	12 45	14 48	16 12	12 28	12 07	11 40	10 43
66	13 43	15 10	16 24	12 34	12 21	12 04	11 38
64	14 16	15 28	16 34	12 40	12 32	12 23	12 11
62	14 40	15 42	16 42	12 45	12 41	12 38	12 36
60	14 59	15 54	16 50	12 49	12 50	12 51	12 55
N 58	15 15	16 05	16 57	12 53	12 57	13 03	13 11
56	15 29	16 14	17 03	12 56	13 03	13 12	13 25
54	15 40	16 23	17 08	12 59	13 09	13 21	13 37
52	15 50	16 30	17 13	13 02	13 14	13 29	13 48
50	16 00	16 37	17 18	13 04	13 19	13 36	13 57
45	16 19	16 52	17 29	13 10	13 29	13 51	14 17
N 40	16 35	17 05	17 39	13 15	13 38	14 04	14 33
35	16 48	17 16	17 47	13 19	13 45	14 15	14 47
30	17 00	17 26	17 55	13 22	13 52	14 24	14 59
20	17 20	17 44	18 11	13 28	14 03	14 40	15 20
N 10	17 37	18 00	18 26	13 34	14 13	14 54	15 38
0	17 54	18 16	18 42	13 39	14 23	15 08	15 55
S 10	18 11	18 33	19 00	13 44	14 32	15 21	16 12
20	18 29	18 53	19 22	13 50	14 42	15 36	16 30
30	18 49	19 17	19 49	13 56	14 54	15 52	16 51
35	19 02	19 31	20 07	14 00	15 01	16 02	17 03
40	19 16	19 48	20 29	14 04	15 09	16 13	17 18
45	19 33	20 09	20 57	14 09	15 18	16 26	17 35
S 50	19 54	20 37	21 38	14 14	15 29	16 42	17 56
52	20 04	20 51	22 02	14 17	15 34	16 50	18 06
54	20 15	21 07	22 36	14 20	15 39	16 58	18 17
56	20 29	21 27	////	14 23	15 46	17 08	18 30
58	20 44	21 52	////	14 27	15 53	17 19	18 45
S 60	21 02	22 29	////	14 31	16 01	17 31	19 04

Day	SUN Eqn. of Time 00^h	SUN Eqn. of Time 12^h	SUN Mer. Pass.	MOON Mer. Pass. Upper	MOON Mer. Pass. Lower	Age	Phase
d	m s	m s	h m	h m	h m	d %	
3	10 25	10 13	11 50	07 29	19 50	24 27	
4	10 01	09 49	11 50	08 12	20 34	25 19	
5	09 37	09 25	11 51	08 57	21 20	26 12	

2026 DECEMBER 6, 7, 8 (SUN., MON., TUES.)

UT	ARIES	VENUS −4·8		MARS +0·4		JUPITER −2·2		SATURN +0·6	
	GHA	GHA	Dec	GHA	Dec	GHA	Dec	GHA	Dec
d h	° ′	° ′	° ′	° ′	° ′	° ′	° ′	° ′	° ′
6 00	74 47.9	225 07.4	S 9 55.8	278 16.1	N12 25.7	285 21.0	N13 18.2	66 28.8	N 0 47.8
01	89 50.3	240 08.2	56.1	293 17.7	25.5	300 23.5	18.2	81 31.3	47.8
02	104 52.8	255 08.9	56.4	308 19.3	25.2	315 25.9	18.2	96 33.8	47.8
03	119 55.2	270 09.7	. . 56.7	323 20.9	. . 25.0	330 28.3	. . 18.2	111 36.3	. . 47.8
04	134 57.7	285 10.5	57.1	338 22.6	24.7	345 30.7	18.2	126 38.8	47.8
05	150 00.2	300 11.2	57.4	353 24.2	24.5	0 33.1	18.2	141 41.3	47.8
06	165 02.6	315 12.0	S 9 57.7	8 25.8	N12 24.3	15 35.5	N13 18.2	156 43.8	N 0 47.8
07	180 05.1	330 12.8	58.1	23 27.5	24.0	30 37.9	18.2	171 46.2	47.8
S 08	195 07.6	345 13.5	58.4	38 29.1	23.8	45 40.3	18.2	186 48.7	47.8
U 09	210 10.0	0 14.3	. . 58.8	53 30.7	. . 23.5	60 42.7	. . 18.1	201 51.2	. . 47.8
N 10	225 12.5	15 15.0	59.1	68 32.4	23.3	75 45.1	18.1	216 53.7	47.8
D 11	240 15.0	30 15.8	59.4	83 34.0	23.0	90 47.5	18.1	231 56.2	47.8
A 12	255 17.4	45 16.5	S 9 59.8	98 35.6	N12 22.8	105 49.9	N13 18.1	246 58.7	N 0 47.8
Y 13	270 19.9	60 17.3	10 00.1	113 37.3	22.6	120 52.3	18.1	262 01.2	47.8
14	285 22.4	75 18.0	00.5	128 38.9	22.3	135 54.8	18.1	277 03.7	47.8
15	300 24.8	90 18.8	. . 00.8	143 40.5	. . 22.1	150 57.2	. . 18.1	292 06.1	. . 47.8
16	315 27.3	105 19.5	01.2	158 42.2	21.8	165 59.6	18.1	307 08.6	47.8
17	330 29.7	120 20.3	01.5	173 43.8	21.6	181 02.0	18.1	322 11.1	47.8
18	345 32.2	135 21.0	S10 01.8	188 45.5	N12 21.4	196 04.4	N13 18.1	337 13.6	N 0 47.8
19	0 34.7	150 21.8	02.2	203 47.1	21.1	211 06.8	18.1	352 16.1	47.8
20	15 37.1	165 22.5	02.5	218 48.7	20.9	226 09.2	18.1	7 18.6	47.8
21	30 39.6	180 23.2	. . 02.9	233 50.4	. . 20.6	241 11.6	. . 18.1	22 21.1	. . 47.8
22	45 42.1	195 24.0	03.2	248 52.0	20.4	256 14.0	18.0	37 23.5	47.8
23	60 44.5	210 24.7	03.6	263 53.7	20.2	271 16.5	18.0	52 26.0	47.8
7 00	75 47.0	225 25.4	S10 03.9	278 55.3	N12 19.9	286 18.9	N13 18.0	67 28.5	N 0 47.8
01	90 49.5	240 26.2	04.3	293 57.0	19.7	301 21.3	18.0	82 31.0	47.8
02	105 51.9	255 26.9	04.7	308 58.6	19.4	316 23.7	18.0	97 33.5	47.8
03	120 54.4	270 27.6	. . 05.0	324 00.3	. . 19.2	331 26.1	. . 18.0	112 36.0	. . 47.8
04	135 56.9	285 28.3	05.4	339 01.9	19.0	346 28.5	18.0	127 38.5	47.8
05	150 59.3	300 29.1	05.7	354 03.5	18.7	1 30.9	18.0	142 40.9	47.8
06	166 01.8	315 29.8	S10 06.1	9 05.2	N12 18.5	16 33.3	N13 18.0	157 43.4	N 0 47.8
07	181 04.2	330 30.5	06.4	24 06.8	18.3	31 35.8	18.0	172 45.9	47.9
08	196 06.7	345 31.2	06.8	39 08.5	18.0	46 38.2	18.0	187 48.4	47.9
M 09	211 09.2	0 31.9	. . 07.2	54 10.1	. . 17.8	61 40.6	. . 18.0	202 50.9	. . 47.9
O 10	226 11.6	15 32.7	07.5	69 11.8	17.5	76 43.0	18.0	217 53.4	47.9
N 11	241 14.1	30 33.4	07.9	84 13.4	17.3	91 45.4	18.0	232 55.8	47.9
D 12	256 16.6	45 34.1	S10 08.3	99 15.1	N12 17.1	106 47.8	N13 17.9	247 58.3	N 0 47.9
A 13	271 19.0	60 34.8	08.6	114 16.8	16.8	121 50.3	17.9	263 00.8	47.9
Y 14	286 21.5	75 35.5	09.0	129 18.4	16.6	136 52.7	17.9	278 03.3	47.9
15	301 24.0	90 36.2	. . 09.4	144 20.1	. . 16.4	151 55.1	. . 17.9	293 05.8	. . 47.9
16	316 26.4	105 36.9	09.7	159 21.7	16.1	166 57.5	17.9	308 08.3	47.9
17	331 28.9	120 37.6	10.1	174 23.4	15.9	181 59.9	17.9	323 10.7	47.9
18	346 31.3	135 38.3	S10 10.5	189 25.0	N12 15.7	197 02.3	N13 17.9	338 13.2	N 0 47.9
19	1 33.8	150 39.0	10.8	204 26.7	15.4	212 04.8	17.9	353 15.7	47.9
20	16 36.3	165 39.7	11.2	219 28.3	15.2	227 07.2	17.9	8 18.2	47.9
21	31 38.7	180 40.4	. . 11.6	234 30.0	. . 15.0	242 09.6	. . 17.9	23 20.7	. . 47.9
22	46 41.2	195 41.1	12.0	249 31.7	14.7	257 12.0	17.9	38 23.1	47.9
23	61 43.7	210 41.8	12.3	264 33.3	14.5	272 14.4	17.9	53 25.6	47.9
8 00	76 46.1	225 42.4	S10 12.7	279 35.0	N12 14.3	287 16.9	N13 17.9	68 28.1	N 0 47.9
01	91 48.6	240 43.1	13.1	294 36.6	14.0	302 19.3	17.9	83 30.6	47.9
02	106 51.1	255 43.8	13.5	309 38.3	13.8	317 21.7	17.9	98 33.1	47.9
03	121 53.5	270 44.5	. . 13.9	324 40.0	. . 13.6	332 24.1	. . 17.9	113 35.5	. . 47.9
04	136 56.0	285 45.2	14.2	339 41.6	13.3	347 26.6	17.9	128 38.0	47.9
05	151 58.5	300 45.9	14.6	354 43.3	13.1	2 29.0	17.9	143 40.5	47.9
06	167 00.9	315 46.5	S10 15.0	9 45.0	N12 12.9	17 31.4	N13 17.9	158 43.0	N 0 47.9
07	182 03.4	330 47.2	15.4	24 46.6	12.7	32 33.8	17.9	173 45.5	47.9
T 08	197 05.8	345 47.9	15.8	39 48.3	12.4	47 36.2	17.9	188 47.9	47.9
U 09	212 08.3	0 48.6	. . 16.1	54 50.0	. . 12.2	62 38.7	. . 17.9	203 50.4	. . 48.0
E 10	227 10.8	15 49.2	16.5	69 51.6	12.0	77 41.1	17.8	218 52.9	48.0
S 11	242 13.2	30 49.9	16.9	84 53.3	11.7	92 43.5	17.8	233 55.4	48.0
D 12	257 15.7	45 50.6	S10 17.3	99 55.0	N12 11.5	107 45.9	N13 17.8	248 57.9	N 0 48.0
A 13	272 18.2	60 51.2	17.7	114 56.6	11.3	122 48.4	17.8	264 00.3	48.0
Y 14	287 20.6	75 51.9	18.1	129 58.3	11.0	137 50.8	17.8	279 02.8	48.0
15	302 23.1	90 52.6	. . 18.5	145 00.0	. . 10.8	152 53.2	. . 17.8	294 05.3	. . 48.0
16	317 25.6	105 53.2	18.9	160 01.6	10.6	167 55.6	17.8	309 07.8	48.0
17	332 28.0	120 53.9	19.3	175 03.3	10.4	182 58.1	17.8	324 10.3	48.0
18	347 30.5	135 54.5	S10 19.7	190 05.0	N12 10.1	198 00.5	N13 17.8	339 12.7	N 0 48.0
19	2 33.0	150 55.2	20.0	205 06.7	09.9	213 02.9	17.8	354 15.2	48.0
20	17 35.4	165 55.9	20.4	220 08.3	09.7	228 05.3	17.8	9 17.7	48.0
21	32 37.9	180 56.5	. . 20.8	235 10.0	. . 09.5	243 07.8	. . 17.8	24 20.2	. . 48.0
22	47 40.3	195 57.2	21.2	250 11.7	09.2	258 10.2	17.8	39 22.6	48.0
23	62 42.8	210 57.8	21.6	265 13.4	09.0	273 12.6	17.8	54 25.1	48.0
Mer. Pass.	h m 18 53.8	v 0.7	d 0.4	v 1.7	d 0.2	v 2.4	d 0.0	v 2.5	d 0.0

STARS

Name	SHA	Dec
	° ′	° ′
Acamar	315 10.2	S40 11.8
Achernar	335 18.7	S57 06.2
Acrux	172 58.5	S63 14.7
Adhara	255 04.3	S29 00.4
Aldebaran	290 37.5	N16 33.8
Alioth	166 11.9	N55 48.5
Alkaid	152 51.1	N49 10.5
Alnair	27 31.1	S46 50.0
Alnilam	275 35.8	S 1 11.1
Alphard	217 46.1	S 8 46.5
Alphecca	126 02.8	N26 37.4
Alpheratz	357 33.0	N29 14.6
Altair	61 58.7	N 8 56.5
Ankaa	353 05.5	S42 09.7
Antares	112 14.3	S26 29.4
Arcturus	145 46.8	N19 02.4
Atria	107 07.7	S69 04.5
Avior	234 13.6	S59 35.5
Bellatrix	278 20.9	N 6 22.5
Betelgeuse	270 50.1	N 7 24.7
Canopus	263 51.2	S52 42.5
Capella	280 19.1	N46 01.5
Deneb	49 25.0	N45 22.8
Denebola	182 23.4	N14 25.2
Diphda	348 45.6	S17 50.3
Dubhe	193 39.1	N61 36.0
Elnath	277 59.5	N28 37.8
Eltanin	90 42.0	N51 29.2
Enif	33 37.4	N10 00.1
Fomalhaut	15 12.8	S29 28.8
Gacrux	171 50.1	S57 15.6
Gienah	175 42.1	S17 41.4
Hadar	148 34.2	S60 30.0
Hamal	327 49.2	N23 35.5
Kaus Aust.	83 30.8	S34 22.3
Kochab	137 20.9	N74 02.4
Markab	13 28.3	N15 21.2
Menkar	314 04.2	N 4 11.8
Menkent	147 56.1	S36 30.0
Miaplacidus	221 37.5	S69 49.4
Mirfak	308 25.5	N49 57.5
Nunki	75 46.2	S26 15.8
Peacock	53 03.7	S56 39.0
Pollux	243 15.1	N27 57.5
Procyon	244 48.9	N 5 09.3
Rasalhague	95 57.4	N12 32.5
Regulus	207 32.7	N11 50.0
Rigel	281 02.0	S 8 10.2
Rigil Kent.	139 38.6	S60 56.6
Sabik	102 01.3	S15 45.4
Schedar	349 29.0	N56 41.4
Shaula	96 08.7	S37 07.4
Sirius	258 24.5	S16 45.1
Spica	158 20.8	S11 18.1
Suhail	222 44.9	S43 32.3
Vega	80 32.6	N38 48.6
Zuben'ubi	136 54.6	S16 09.2

	SHA	Mer. Pass.
	° ′	h m
Venus	149 38.4	8 58
Mars	203 08.3	5 24
Jupiter	210 31.9	4 54
Saturn	351 41.5	19 27

Day	UT d h	SUN GHA ° ′	SUN Dec ° ′	MOON GHA ° ′	v ′	MOON Dec ° ′	d ′	HP ′
SUNDAY	6 00	182 17.9	S22 27.8	218 47.2	12.8	S19 28.0	10.5	55.1
	01	197 17.6	28.1	233 19.0	12.7	19 38.5	10.4	55.1
	02	212 17.4	28.4	247 50.7	12.6	19 48.9	10.3	55.1
	03	227 17.1	. . 28.7	262 22.3	12.6	19 59.2	10.2	55.1
	04	242 16.8	29.0	276 53.9	12.6	20 09.4	10.1	55.1
	05	257 16.6	29.3	291 25.5	12.5	20 19.5	10.0	55.0
	06	272 16.3	S22 29.6	305 57.0	12.4	S20 29.5	9.9	55.0
	07	287 16.1	29.9	320 28.4	12.4	20 39.4	9.8	55.0
	08	302 15.8	30.2	334 59.8	12.4	20 49.2	9.8	55.0
	09	317 15.5	. . 30.5	349 31.2	12.3	20 59.0	9.6	55.0
	10	332 15.3	30.8	4 02.5	12.2	21 08.6	9.5	55.0
	11	347 15.0	31.1	18 33.7	12.2	21 18.1	9.4	54.9
	12	2 14.7	S22 31.3	33 04.9	12.2	S21 27.5	9.3	54.9
	13	17 14.5	31.6	47 36.1	12.1	21 36.8	9.2	54.9
	14	32 14.2	31.9	62 07.2	12.0	21 46.0	9.2	54.9
	15	47 13.9	. . 32.2	76 38.2	12.0	21 55.2	9.0	54.9
	16	62 13.7	32.5	91 09.2	11.9	22 04.2	8.9	54.9
	17	77 13.4	32.8	105 40.1	11.9	22 13.1	8.7	54.8
	18	92 13.1	S22 33.1	120 11.0	11.8	S22 21.8	8.7	54.8
	19	107 12.9	33.4	134 41.8	11.8	22 30.5	8.6	54.8
	20	122 12.6	33.7	149 12.6	11.8	22 39.1	8.5	54.8
	21	137 12.3	. . 34.0	163 43.4	11.6	22 47.6	8.3	54.8
	22	152 12.1	34.3	178 14.0	11.7	22 55.9	8.3	54.8
	23	167 11.8	34.5	192 44.7	11.6	23 04.2	8.1	54.8
MONDAY	7 00	182 11.5	S22 34.8	207 15.3	11.5	S23 12.3	8.1	54.7
	01	197 11.3	35.1	221 45.8	11.5	23 20.4	7.9	54.7
	02	212 11.0	35.4	236 16.3	11.4	23 28.3	7.8	54.7
	03	227 10.7	. . 35.7	250 46.7	11.4	23 36.1	7.7	54.7
	04	242 10.5	36.0	265 17.1	11.4	23 43.8	7.5	54.7
	05	257 10.2	36.2	279 47.5	11.3	23 51.3	7.5	54.7
	06	272 09.9	S22 36.5	294 17.8	11.2	S23 58.8	7.3	54.7
	07	287 09.6	36.8	308 48.0	11.2	24 06.1	7.3	54.6
	08	302 09.4	37.1	323 18.2	11.1	24 13.4	7.1	54.6
	09	317 09.1	. . 37.4	337 48.3	11.1	24 20.5	7.0	54.6
	10	332 08.8	37.6	352 18.4	11.1	24 27.5	6.9	54.6
	11	347 08.6	37.9	6 48.5	11.0	24 34.4	6.7	54.6
	12	2 08.3	S22 38.2	21 18.5	11.0	S24 41.1	6.7	54.6
	13	17 08.0	38.5	35 48.5	10.9	24 47.8	6.5	54.6
	14	32 07.8	38.7	50 18.4	10.9	24 54.3	6.4	54.5
	15	47 07.5	. . 39.0	64 48.3	10.8	25 00.7	6.2	54.5
	16	62 07.2	39.3	79 18.1	10.8	25 06.9	6.2	54.5
	17	77 06.9	39.6	93 47.9	10.8	25 13.1	6.0	54.5
	18	92 06.7	S22 39.8	108 17.7	10.7	S25 19.1	5.9	54.5
	19	107 06.4	40.1	122 47.4	10.7	25 25.0	5.8	54.5
	20	122 06.1	40.4	137 17.1	10.6	25 30.8	5.7	54.5
	21	137 05.8	. . 40.6	151 46.7	10.6	25 36.5	5.5	54.5
	22	152 05.6	40.9	166 16.3	10.6	25 42.0	5.4	54.5
	23	167 05.3	41.2	180 45.9	10.5	25 47.4	5.3	54.4
TUESDAY	8 00	182 05.0	S22 41.5	195 15.4	10.5	S25 52.7	5.1	54.4
	01	197 04.8	41.7	209 44.9	10.5	25 57.8	5.1	54.4
	02	212 04.5	42.0	224 14.4	10.4	26 02.9	4.9	54.4
	03	227 04.2	. . 42.2	238 43.8	10.4	26 07.8	4.7	54.4
	04	242 03.9	42.5	253 13.2	10.3	26 12.5	4.7	54.4
	05	257 03.7	42.8	267 42.5	10.3	26 17.2	4.5	54.4
	06	272 03.4	S22 43.0	282 11.8	10.3	S26 21.7	4.4	54.4
	07	287 03.1	43.3	296 41.1	10.3	26 26.1	4.2	54.4
	08	302 02.8	43.6	311 10.4	10.2	26 30.3	4.2	54.3
	09	317 02.6	. . 43.8	325 39.6	10.2	26 34.5	4.0	54.3
	10	332 02.3	44.1	340 08.8	10.2	26 38.5	3.8	54.3
	11	347 02.0	44.3	354 38.0	10.1	26 42.3	3.8	54.3
	12	2 01.7	S22 44.6	9 07.1	10.2	S26 46.1	3.6	54.3
	13	17 01.5	44.9	23 36.3	10.1	26 49.7	3.4	54.3
	14	32 01.2	45.1	38 05.4	10.1	26 53.1	3.4	54.3
	15	47 00.9	. . 45.4	52 34.5	10.0	26 56.5	3.2	54.3
	16	62 00.6	45.6	67 03.5	10.1	26 59.7	3.0	54.3
	17	77 00.4	45.9	81 32.6	10.0	27 02.7	3.0	54.3
	18	92 00.1	S22 46.1	96 01.6	10.0	S27 05.7	2.8	54.2
	19	106 59.8	46.4	110 30.6	10.0	27 08.5	2.7	54.2
	20	121 59.5	46.6	124 59.6	10.0	27 11.2	2.5	54.2
	21	136 59.2	. . 46.9	139 28.6	9.9	27 13.7	2.4	54.2
	22	151 59.0	47.1	153 57.5	10.0	27 16.1	2.3	54.2
	23	166 58.7	47.4	168 26.5	9.9	S27 18.4	2.1	54.2
		SD 16.3	*d* 0.3	SD 15.0		14.9		14.8

Lat.	Twilight Naut.	Twilight Civil	Sunrise	Moonrise 6	Moonrise 7	Moonrise 8	Moonrise 9
°	h m	h m	h m	h m	h m	h m	h m
N 72	08 06	10 17	▬	▬	▬	▬	▬
N 70	07 48	09 29	▬	▬	▬	▬	▬
68	07 33	08 59	11 19	08 28	▬	▬	▬
66	07 21	08 36	10 07	07 35	▬	▬	▬
64	07 11	08 18	09 31	07 02	09 04	▬	▬
62	07 02	08 03	09 06	06 39	08 21	10 05	11 35
60	06 54	07 50	08 46	06 20	07 52	09 20	10 31
N 58	06 47	07 39	08 30	06 04	07 31	08 51	09 57
56	06 41	07 29	08 16	05 51	07 13	08 28	09 32
54	06 35	07 21	08 04	05 40	06 58	08 10	09 12
52	06 30	07 13	07 53	05 30	06 45	07 55	08 55
50	06 25	07 06	07 44	05 21	06 33	07 41	08 41
45	06 14	06 51	07 24	05 02	06 10	07 14	08 12
N 40	06 04	06 38	07 08	04 47	05 51	06 52	07 49
35	05 55	06 27	06 55	04 34	05 35	06 34	07 30
30	05 47	06 17	06 43	04 23	05 21	06 19	07 14
20	05 31	05 58	06 22	04 04	04 58	05 53	06 47
N 10	05 16	05 42	06 05	03 47	04 38	05 31	06 23
0	04 59	05 25	05 48	03 32	04 20	05 10	06 01
S 10	04 41	05 08	05 31	03 17	04 02	04 49	05 39
20	04 19	04 48	05 13	03 01	03 42	04 27	05 16
30	03 51	04 24	04 51	02 42	03 19	04 02	04 49
35	03 33	04 10	04 39	02 31	03 06	03 47	04 33
40	03 11	03 52	04 24	02 19	02 51	03 29	04 14
45	02 42	03 31	04 07	02 05	02 33	03 08	03 52
S 50	02 00	03 02	03 46	01 47	02 11	02 42	03 23
52	01 36	02 48	03 36	01 39	02 01	02 30	03 09
54	01 00	02 32	03 24	01 30	01 49	02 15	02 53
56	////	02 11	03 11	01 20	01 35	01 58	02 34
58	////	01 45	02 55	01 08	01 20	01 38	02 10
S 60	////	01 06	02 36	00 55	01 01	01 13	01 38

Lat.	Sunset	Twilight Civil	Twilight Naut.	Moonset 6	Moonset 7	Moonset 8	Moonset 9
°	h m	h m	h m	h m	h m	h m	h m
N 72	▬	13 25	15 37	▬	▬	▬	▬
N 70	▬	14 13	15 55	▬	▬	▬	▬
68	12 24	14 44	16 09	10 43	▬	▬	▬
66	13 36	15 07	16 21	11 38	▬	▬	▬
64	14 11	15 25	16 32	12 11	11 50	▬	▬
62	14 37	15 40	16 40	12 36	12 34	12 35	12 52
60	14 57	15 52	16 48	12 55	13 03	13 20	13 56
N 58	15 13	16 03	16 55	13 11	13 25	13 49	14 30
56	15 27	16 13	17 02	13 25	13 43	14 12	14 55
54	15 39	16 22	17 07	13 37	13 59	14 30	15 15
52	15 49	16 29	17 13	13 48	14 12	14 46	15 32
50	15 59	16 37	17 18	13 57	14 24	15 00	15 46
45	16 18	16 52	17 29	14 17	14 49	15 28	16 15
N 40	16 35	17 05	17 39	14 33	15 08	15 50	16 38
35	16 48	17 16	17 48	14 47	15 25	16 08	16 57
30	17 00	17 26	17 56	14 59	15 39	16 24	17 13
20	17 20	17 44	18 12	15 20	16 03	16 50	17 41
N 10	17 38	18 01	18 27	15 38	16 24	17 13	18 04
0	17 55	18 18	18 44	15 55	16 44	17 35	18 26
S 10	18 12	18 35	19 02	16 12	17 04	17 56	18 48
20	18 30	18 55	19 24	16 30	17 25	18 19	19 12
30	18 52	19 19	19 52	16 51	17 49	18 46	19 39
35	19 04	19 34	20 10	17 03	18 04	19 02	19 55
40	19 19	19 51	20 32	17 18	18 21	19 20	20 14
45	19 36	20 13	21 01	17 35	18 41	19 42	20 36
S 50	19 58	20 41	21 44	17 56	19 06	20 11	21 05
52	20 08	20 55	22 09	18 06	19 19	20 25	21 19
54	20 20	21 12	22 46	18 17	19 33	20 41	21 36
56	20 33	21 33	////	18 30	19 49	21 00	21 55
58	20 49	21 59	////	18 45	20 09	21 23	22 20
S 60	21 08	22 39	////	19 04	20 34	21 55	22 52

Day	SUN Eqn. of Time 00^h	SUN Eqn. of Time 12^h	SUN Mer. Pass.	MOON Mer. Pass. Upper	MOON Mer. Pass. Lower	MOON Age	MOON Phase
d	m s	m s	h m	h m	h m	d %	
6	09 12	08 59	11 51	09 43	22 07	27 6	●
7	08 47	08 34	11 51	10 32	22 57	28 2	
8	08 21	08 07	11 52	11 22	23 48	29 0	

Day	UT (d h)	ARIES GHA	VENUS −4·8 GHA	VENUS Dec	MARS +0·3 GHA	MARS Dec	JUPITER −2·3 GHA	JUPITER Dec	SATURN +0·6 GHA	SATURN Dec
		° ′	° ′	° ′	° ′	° ′	° ′	° ′	° ′	° ′
WEDNESDAY	9 00	77 45.3	225 58.5	S10 22.0	280 15.0	N12 08.8	288 15.1	N13 17.8	69 27.6	N 0 48.0
	01	92 47.7	240 59.1	22.4	295 16.7	08.5	303 17.5	17.8	84 30.1	48.0
	02	107 50.2	255 59.7	22.8	310 18.4	08.3	318 19.9	17.8	99 32.5	48.0
	03	122 52.7	271 00.4	. . 23.2	325 20.1	. . 08.1	333 22.3	. . 17.8	114 35.0	. . 48.1
	04	137 55.1	286 01.0	23.6	340 21.8	07.9	348 24.8	17.8	129 37.5	48.1
	05	152 57.6	301 01.7	24.0	355 23.4	07.6	3 27.2	17.8	144 40.0	48.1
	06	168 00.1	316 02.3	S10 24.4	10 25.1	N12 07.4	18 29.6	N13 17.8	159 42.5	N 0 48.1
	07	183 02.5	331 02.9	24.8	25 26.8	07.2	33 32.1	17.8	174 44.9	48.1
	08	198 05.0	346 03.6	25.2	40 28.5	07.0	48 34.5	17.8	189 47.4	48.1
	09	213 07.5	1 04.2	. . 25.7	55 30.2	. . 06.8	63 36.9	. . 17.8	204 49.9	. . 48.1
	10	228 09.9	16 04.8	26.1	70 31.9	06.5	78 39.4	17.8	219 52.4	48.1
	11	243 12.4	31 05.5	26.5	85 33.5	06.3	93 41.8	17.8	234 54.8	48.1
	12	258 14.8	46 06.1	S10 26.9	100 35.2	N12 06.1	108 44.2	N13 17.8	249 57.3	N 0 48.1
	13	273 17.3	61 06.7	27.3	115 36.9	05.9	123 46.7	17.8	264 59.8	48.1
	14	288 19.8	76 07.3	27.7	130 38.6	05.6	138 49.1	17.8	280 02.3	48.1
	15	303 22.2	91 08.0	. . 28.1	145 40.3	. . 05.4	153 51.5	. . 17.8	295 04.7	. . 48.1
	16	318 24.7	106 08.6	28.5	160 42.0	05.2	168 54.0	17.8	310 07.2	48.1
	17	333 27.2	121 09.2	28.9	175 43.7	05.0	183 56.4	17.8	325 09.7	48.1
	18	348 29.6	136 09.8	S10 29.3	190 45.4	N12 04.8	198 58.8	N13 17.8	340 12.1	N 0 48.2
	19	3 32.1	151 10.4	29.8	205 47.0	04.5	214 01.3	17.8	355 14.6	48.2
	20	18 34.6	166 11.1	30.2	220 48.7	04.3	229 03.7	17.8	10 17.1	48.2
	21	33 37.0	181 11.7	. . 30.6	235 50.4	. . 04.1	244 06.1	. . 17.8	25 19.6	. . 48.2
	22	48 39.5	196 12.3	31.0	250 52.1	03.9	259 08.6	17.8	40 22.0	48.2
	23	63 42.0	211 12.9	31.4	265 53.8	03.7	274 11.0	17.8	55 24.5	48.2
THURSDAY	10 00	78 44.4	226 13.5	S10 31.8	280 55.5	N12 03.4	289 13.4	N13 17.8	70 27.0	N 0 48.2
	01	93 46.9	241 14.1	32.3	295 57.2	03.2	304 15.9	17.8	85 29.5	48.2
	02	108 49.3	256 14.7	32.7	310 58.9	03.0	319 18.3	17.8	100 31.9	48.2
	03	123 51.8	271 15.3	. . 33.1	326 00.6	. . 02.8	334 20.8	. . 17.8	115 34.4	. . 48.2
	04	138 54.3	286 15.9	33.5	341 02.3	02.6	349 23.2	17.8	130 36.9	48.2
	05	153 56.7	301 16.5	34.0	356 04.0	02.3	4 25.6	17.8	145 39.3	48.2
	06	168 59.2	316 17.1	S10 34.4	11 05.7	N12 02.1	19 28.1	N13 17.8	160 41.8	N 0 48.3
	07	184 01.7	331 17.7	34.8	26 07.4	01.9	34 30.5	17.8	175 44.3	48.3
	08	199 04.1	346 18.3	35.2	41 09.1	01.7	49 32.9	17.8	190 46.8	48.3
	09	214 06.6	1 18.9	. . 35.7	56 10.8	. . 01.5	64 35.4	. . 17.8	205 49.2	. . 48.3
	10	229 09.1	16 19.5	36.1	71 12.5	01.3	79 37.8	17.8	220 51.7	48.3
	11	244 11.5	31 20.1	36.5	86 14.2	01.0	94 40.3	17.8	235 54.2	48.3
	12	259 14.0	46 20.7	S10 36.9	101 15.9	N12 00.8	109 42.7	N13 17.8	250 56.6	N 0 48.3
	13	274 16.5	61 21.2	37.4	116 17.6	00.6	124 45.1	17.8	265 59.1	48.3
	14	289 18.9	76 21.8	37.8	131 19.3	00.4	139 47.6	17.8	281 01.6	48.3
	15	304 21.4	91 22.4	. . 38.2	146 21.0	. . 00.2	154 50.0	. . 17.8	296 04.1	. . 48.3
	16	319 23.8	106 23.0	38.7	161 22.7	12 00.0	169 52.5	17.8	311 06.5	48.3
	17	334 26.3	121 23.6	39.1	176 24.4	11 59.7	184 54.9	17.8	326 09.0	48.3
	18	349 28.8	136 24.2	S10 39.5	191 26.1	N11 59.5	199 57.4	N13 17.9	341 11.5	N 0 48.4
	19	4 31.2	151 24.7	40.0	206 27.8	59.3	214 59.8	17.9	356 13.9	48.4
	20	19 33.7	166 25.3	40.4	221 29.6	59.1	230 02.2	17.9	11 16.4	48.4
	21	34 36.2	181 25.9	. . 40.8	236 31.3	. . 58.9	245 04.7	. . 17.9	26 18.9	. . 48.4
	22	49 38.6	196 26.5	41.3	251 33.0	58.7	260 07.1	17.9	41 21.3	48.4
	23	64 41.1	211 27.0	41.7	266 34.7	58.5	275 09.6	17.9	56 23.8	48.4
FRIDAY	11 00	79 43.6	226 27.6	S10 42.1	281 36.4	N11 58.2	290 12.0	N13 17.9	71 26.3	N 0 48.4
	01	94 46.0	241 28.2	42.6	296 38.1	58.0	305 14.5	17.9	86 28.7	48.4
	02	109 48.5	256 28.7	43.0	311 39.8	57.8	320 16.9	17.9	101 31.2	48.4
	03	124 50.9	271 29.3	. . 43.5	326 41.5	. . 57.6	335 19.3	. . 17.9	116 33.7	. . 48.4
	04	139 53.4	286 29.9	43.9	341 43:2	57.4	350 21.8	17.9	131 36.1	48.5
	05	154 55.9	301 30.4	44.3	356 45.0	57.2	5 24.2	17.9	146 38.6	48.5
	06	169 58.3	316 31.0	S10 44.8	11 46.7	N11 57.0	20 26.7	N13 17.9	161 41.1	N 0 48.5
	07	185 00.8	331 31.5	45.2	26 48.4	56.8	35 29.1	17.9	176 43.5	48.5
	08	200 03.3	346 32.1	45.7	41 50.1	56.6	50 31.6	17.9	191 46.0	48.5
	09	215 05.7	1 32.7	. . 46.1	56 51.8	. . 56.3	65 34.0	. . 17.9	206 48.5	. . 48.5
	10	230 08.2	16 33.2	46.6	71 53.6	56.1	80 36.5	17.9	221 50.9	48.5
	11	245 10.7	31 33.8	47.0	86 55.3	55.9	95 38.9	17.9	236 53.4	48.5
	12	260 13.1	46 34.3	S10 47.5	101 57.0	N11 55.7	110 41.4	N13 17.9	251 55.9	N 0 48.5
	13	275 15.6	61 34.9	47.9	116 58.7	55.5	125 43.8	17.9	266 58.3	48.5
	14	290 18.1	76 35.4	48.4	132 00.4	55.3	140 46.3	17.9	282 00.8	48.6
	15	305 20.5	91 35.9	. . 48.8	147 02.2	. . 55.1	155 48.7	. . 17.9	297 03.3	. . 48.6
	16	320 23.0	106 36.5	49.3	162 03.9	54.9	170 51.2	18.0	312 05.7	48.6
	17	335 25.4	121 37.0	49.7	177 05.6	54.7	185 53.6	18.0	327 08.2	48.6
	18	350 27.9	136 37.6	S10 50.2	192 07.3	N11 54.5	200 56.1	N13 18.0	342 10.7	N 0 48.6
	19	5 30.4	151 38.1	50.6	207 09.1	54.3	215 58.5	18.0	357 13.1	48.6
	20	20 32.8	166 38.7	51.1	222 10.8	54.1	231 01.0	18.0	12 15.6	48.6
	21	35 35.3	181 39.2	. . 51.5	237 12.5	. . 53.8	246 03.4	. . 18.0	27 18.1	. . 48.6
	22	50 37.8	196 39.7	52.0	252 14.2	53.6	261 05.9	18.0	42 20.5	48.6
	23	65 40.2	211 40.3	52.4	267 16.0	53.4	276 08.3	18.0	57 23.0	48.7
	Mer. Pass.	h m 18 42.0	v 0.6	d 0.4	v 1.7	d 0.2	v 2.4	d 0.0	v 2.5	d 0.0

STARS

Name	SHA	Dec
	° ′	° ′
Acamar	315 10.2	S40 11.9
Achernar	335 18.7	S57 06.2
Acrux	172 58.5	S63 14.7
Adhara	255 04.3	S29 00.4
Aldebaran	290 37.4	N16 33.8
Alioth	166 11.9	N55 48.5
Alkaid	152 51.1	N49 10.5
Alnair	27 31.1	S46 50.0
Alnilam	275 35.8	S 1 11.1
Alphard	217 46.0	S 8 46.5
Alphecca	126 02.8	N26 37.4
Alpheratz	357 33.0	N29 14.6
Altair	61 58.7	N 8 56.5
Ankaa	353 05.5	S42 09.7
Antares	112 14.3	S26 29.4
Arcturus	145 46.7	N19 02.4
Atria	107 07.6	S69 04.5
Avior	234 13.6	S59 35.5
Bellatrix	278 20.8	N 6 22.5
Betelgeuse	270 50.0	N 7 24.7
Canopus	263 51.2	S52 42.5
Capella	280 19.1	N46 01.5
Deneb	49 25.0	N45 22.8
Denebola	182 23.4	N14 25.2
Diphda	348 45.6	S17 50.3
Dubhe	193 39.1	N61 36.0
Elnath	277 59.5	N28 37.8
Eltanin	90 42.0	N51 29.2
Enif	33 37.4	N10 00.1
Fomalhaut	15 12.8	S29 28.8
Gacrux	171 50.1	S57 15.6
Gienah	175 42.0	S17 41.4
Hadar	148 34.2	S60 30.0
Hamal	327 49.1	N23 35.6
Kaus Aust.	83 30.8	S34 22.3
Kochab	137 20.9	N74 02.4
Markab	13 28.3	N15 21.2
Menkar	314 04.2	N 4 11.8
Menkent	147 56.0	S36 30.0
Miaplacidus	221 37.4	S69 49.4
Mirfak	308 25.5	N49 57.6
Nunki	75 46.2	S26 15.8
Peacock	53 03.7	S56 39.0
Pollux	243 15.1	N27 57.5
Procyon	244 48.9	N 5 09.3
Rasalhague	95 57.4	N12 32.5
Regulus	207 32.7	N11 50.0
Rigel	281 02.0	S 8 10.2
Rigil Kent.	139 38.6	S60 56.6
Sabik	102 01.3	S15 45.4
Schedar	349 29.0	N56 41.4
Shaula	96 08.6	S37 07.4
Sirius	258 24.5	S16 45.1
Spica	158 20.8	S11 18.1
Suhail	222 44.9	S43 32.3
Vega	80 32.6	N38 48.6
Zuben'ubi	136 54.5	S16 09.2

	SHA	Mer. Pass.
	° ′	h m
Venus	147 29.1	8 55
Mars	202 11.1	5 16
Jupiter	210 29.0	4 42
Saturn	351 42.6	19 15

Day	UT (d h)	SUN GHA (° ′)	SUN Dec (° ′)	MOON GHA (° ′)	MOON v (′)	MOON Dec (° ′)	MOON d (′)	MOON HP (′)
WEDNESDAY	9 00	181 58.4	S22 47.6	182 55.4	9.9	S27 20.5	2.0	54.2
	01	196 58.1	47.9	197 24.3	9.9	27 22.5	1.9	54.2
	02	211 57.9	48.1	211 53.2	9.9	27 24.4	1.7	54.2
	03	226 57.6	. . 48.4	226 22.1	9.9	27 26.1	1.6	54.2
	04	241 57.3	48.6	240 51.0	9.9	27 27.7	1.5	54.2
	05	256 57.0	48.9	255 19.9	9.9	27 29.2	1.3	54.2
	06	271 56.7	S22 49.1	269 48.8	9.9	S27 30.5	1.2	54.1
	07	286 56.5	49.4	284 17.7	9.9	27 31.7	1.0	54.1
	08	301 56.2	49.6	298 46.6	9.9	27 32.7	1.0	54.1
	09	316 55.9	. . 49.8	313 15.5	9.8	27 33.7	0.8	54.1
	10	331 55.6	50.1	327 44.3	9.9	27 34.5	0.6	54.1
	11	346 55.3	50.3	342 13.2	9.9	27 35.1	0.5	54.1
	12	1 55.1	S22 50.6	356 42.1	9.9	S27 35.6	0.4	54.1
	13	16 54.8	50.8	11 11.0	9.9	27 36.0	0.2	54.1
	14	31 54.5	51.0	25 39.9	9.9	27 36.2	0.2	54.1
	15	46 54.2	. . 51.3	40 08.8	9.9	27 36.4	0.1	54.1
	16	61 53.9	51.5	54 37.7	9.9	27 36.3	0.1	54.1
	17	76 53.7	51.7	69 06.6	10.0	27 36.2	0.3	54.1
	18	91 53.4	S22 52.0	83 35.6	9.9	S27 35.9	0.5	54.1
	19	106 53.1	52.2	98 04.5	10.0	27 35.4	0.5	54.1
	20	121 52.8	52.4	112 33.5	9.9	27 34.9	0.7	54.1
	21	136 52.5	. . 52.7	127 02.4	10.0	27 34.2	0.8	54.0
	22	151 52.2	52.9	141 31.4	10.0	27 33.4	1.0	54.0
	23	166 52.0	53.1	156 00.4	10.0	27 32.4	1.1	54.0
THURSDAY	10 00	181 51.7	S22 53.4	170 29.4	10.1	S27 31.3	1.2	54.0
	01	196 51.4	53.6	184 58.5	10.0	27 30.1	1.4	54.0
	02	211 51.1	53.8	199 27.5	10.1	27 28.7	1.5	54.0
	03	226 50.8	. . 54.0	213 56.6	10.1	27 27.2	1.6	54.0
	04	241 50.5	54.3	228 25.7	10.2	27 25.6	1.8	54.0
	05	256 50.3	54.5	242 54.9	10.1	27 23.8	1.9	54.0
	06	271 50.0	S22 54.7	257 24.0	10.2	S27 21.9	2.0	54.0
	07	286 49.7	55.0	271 53.2	10.2	27 19.9	2.2	54.0
	08	301 49.4	55.2	286 22.4	10.2	27 17.7	2.3	54.0
	09	316 49.1	. . 55.4	300 51.6	10.3	27 15.4	2.4	54.0
	10	331 48.8	55.6	315 20.9	10.3	27 13.0	2.6	54.0
	11	346 48.6	55.8	329 50.2	10.3	27 10.4	2.6	54.0
	12	1 48.3	S22 56.1	344 19.5	10.4	S27 07.8	2.8	54.0
	13	16 48.0	56.3	358 48.9	10.4	27 05.0	3.0	54.0
	14	31 47.7	56.5	13 18.3	10.4	27 02.0	3.0	54.0
	15	46 47.4	. . 56.7	27 47.7	10.4	26 59.0	3.2	54.0
	16	61 47.1	56.9	42 17.1	10.5	26 55.8	3.4	54.0
	17	76 46.8	57.2	56 46.6	10.6	26 52.4	3.4	54.0
	18	91 46.6	S22 57.4	71 16.2	10.5	S26 49.0	3.6	54.0
	19	106 46.3	57.6	85 45.7	10.7	26 45.4	3.7	54.0
	20	121 46.0	57.8	100 15.4	10.6	26 41.7	3.8	54.0
	21	136 45.7	. . 58.0	114 45.0	10.7	26 37.9	4.0	54.0
	22	151 45.4	58.2	129 14.7	10.7	26 33.9	4.1	54.0
	23	166 45.1	58.4	143 44.4	10.8	26 29.8	4.2	54.0
FRIDAY	11 00	181 44.8	S22 58.6	158 14.2	10.9	S26 25.6	4.3	54.0
	01	196 44.6	58.9	172 44.1	10.8	26 21.3	4.5	54.0
	02	211 44.3	59.1	187 13.9	10.9	26 16.8	4.5	54.0
	03	226 44.0	. . 59.3	201 43.8	11.0	26 12.3	4.7	54.0
	04	241 43.7	59.5	216 13.8	11.0	26 07.6	4.8	54.0
	05	256 43.4	59.7	230 43.8	11.1	26 02.8	5.0	54.0
	06	271 43.1	S22 59.9	245 13.9	11.1	S25 57.8	5.0	54.0
	07	286 42.8	23 00.1	259 44.0	11.1	25 52.8	5.2	54.0
	08	301 42.5	00.3	274 14.1	11.2	25 47.6	5.3	54.0
	09	316 42.3	. . 00.5	288 44.3	11.3	25 42.3	5.4	54.0
	10	331 42.0	00.7	303 14.6	11.3	25 36.9	5.6	54.0
	11	346 41.7	00.9	317 44.9	11.3	25 31.3	5.6	54.0
	12	1 41.4	S23 01.1	332 15.2	11.4	S25 25.7	5.8	54.0
	13	16 41.1	01.3	346 45.6	11.5	25 19.9	5.8	54.0
	14	31 40.8	01.5	1 16.1	11.5	25 14.1	6.0	54.0
	15	46 40.5	. . 01.7	15 46.6	11.6	25 08.1	6.2	54.0
	16	61 40.2	01.9	30 17.2	11.6	25 01.9	6.2	54.0
	17	76 39.9	02.1	44 47.8	11.7	24 55.7	6.3	54.0
	18	91 39.7	S23 02.3	59 18.5	11.7	S24 49.4	6.5	54.0
	19	106 39.4	02.5	73 49.2	11.8	24 42.9	6.5	54.0
	20	121 39.1	02.7	88 20.0	11.8	24 36.4	6.7	54.0
	21	136 38.8	. . 02.9	102 50.8	11.9	24 29.7	6.8	54.0
	22	151 38.5	03.1	117 21.7	12.0	24 22.9	6.9	54.0
	23	166 38.2	03.3	131 52.7	12.0	S24 16.0	7.0	54.0
		SD 16.3	*d* 0.2	SD 14.7		14.7		14.7

Lat. °	Twilight Naut. h m	Twilight Civil h m	Sunrise h m	Moonrise 9 h m	Moonrise 10 h m	Moonrise 11 h m	Moonrise 12 h m
N 72	08 12	10 29	▬	▬	▬	▬	▬
N 70	07 53	09 37	▬	▬	▬	▬	▬
68	07 38	09 05	▬	▬	▬	▬	▬
66	07 26	08 41	10 15	▬	▬	▬	13 15
64	07 15	08 23	09 38	▬	▬	13 01	12 33
62	07 06	08 07	09 11	11 35	12 04	12 06	12 05
60	06 58	07 54	08 51	10 31	11 14	11 34	11 43
N 58	06 51	07 43	08 34	09 57	10 43	11 10	11 25
56	06 44	07 33	08 20	09 32	10 19	10 50	11 10
54	06 38	07 24	08 08	09 12	10 00	10 34	10 57
52	06 33	07 16	07 57	08 55	09 44	10 20	10 46
50	06 28	07 09	07 47	08 41	09 30	10 07	10 36
45	06 16	06 53	07 27	08 12	09 01	09 42	10 14
N 40	06 06	06 40	07 11	07 49	08 39	09 21	09 57
35	05 57	06 29	06 57	07 30	08 20	09 04	09 42
30	05 49	06 19	06 45	07 14	08 04	08 50	09 30
20	05 33	06 00	06 24	06 47	07 38	08 25	09 08
N 10	05 17	05 43	06 06	06 23	07 14	08 03	08 49
0	05 00	05 27	05 49	06 01	06 53	07 43	08 31
S 10	04 42	05 09	05 32	05 39	06 31	07 23	08 13
20	04 20	04 49	05 13	05 16	06 08	07 01	07 54
30	03 51	04 25	04 52	04 49	05 41	06 36	07 32
35	03 33	04 10	04 39	04 33	05 25	06 21	07 19
40	03 11	03 52	04 24	04 14	05 06	06 03	07 04
45	02 41	03 30	04 07	03 52	04 44	05 42	06 46
S 50	01 58	03 01	03 45	03 23	04 15	05 16	06 23
52	01 32	02 47	03 35	03 09	04 01	05 03	06 13
54	00 53	02 30	03 23	02 53	03 44	04 48	06 00
56	////	02 09	03 09	02 34	03 25	04 31	05 46
58	////	01 41	02 53	02 10	03 01	04 10	05 30
S 60	////	00 59	02 34	01 38	02 28	03 43	05 10

Lat. °	Sunset h m	Twilight Civil h m	Twilight Naut. h m	Moonset 9 h m	Moonset 10 h m	Moonset 11 h m	Moonset 12 h m
N 72	▬	13 16	15 33	▬	▬	▬	▬
N 70	▬	14 08	15 52	▬	▬	▬	▬
68	▬	14 40	16 07	▬	▬	▬	▬
66	13 30	15 04	16 20	▬	▬	▬	16 23
64	14 08	15 23	16 30	▬	▬	14 57	17 03
62	14 34	15 38	16 39	12 52	14 10	15 51	17 31
60	14 55	15 51	16 47	13 56	15 00	16 23	17 52
N 58	15 11	16 02	16 55	14 30	15 31	16 47	18 09
56	15 26	16 12	17 01	14 55	15 54	17 06	18 24
54	15 38	16 21	17 07	15 15	16 13	17 22	18 36
52	15 49	16 29	17 12	15 32	16 29	17 36	18 47
50	15 58	16 36	17 18	15 46	16 43	17 48	18 57
45	16 18	16 52	17 29	16 15	17 11	18 12	19 17
N 40	16 35	17 05	17 39	16 38	17 33	18 32	19 34
35	16 48	17 17	17 48	16 57	17 51	18 49	19 47
30	17 01	17 27	17 57	17 13	18 07	19 03	19 59
20	17 21	17 45	18 13	17 41	18 33	19 27	20 20
N 10	17 39	18 02	18 28	18 04	18 56	19 47	20 37
0	17 57	18 19	18 45	18 26	19 17	20 06	20 54
S 10	18 14	18 37	19 04	18 48	19 38	20 26	21 10
20	18 32	18 57	19 26	19 12	20 01	20 46	21 27
30	18 54	19 21	19 54	19 39	20 27	21 09	21 47
35	19 07	19 36	20 13	19 55	20 42	21 23	21 58
40	19 21	19 54	20 35	20 14	21 00	21 39	22 11
45	19 39	20 16	21 05	20 36	21 21	21 58	22 27
S 50	20 01	20 45	21 49	21 05	21 48	22 21	22 46
52	20 11	20 59	22 15	21 19	22 01	22 32	22 55
54	20 23	21 17	22 55	21 36	22 16	22 45	23 05
56	20 37	21 38	////	21 55	22 34	22 59	23 16
58	20 53	22 06	////	22 20	22 55	23 16	23 29
S 60	21 13	22 49	////	22 52	23 23	23 37	23 44

Day	SUN Eqn. of Time 00^h	SUN Eqn. of Time 12^h	SUN Mer. Pass.	MOON Mer. Pass. Upper	MOON Mer. Pass. Lower	MOON Age	MOON Phase
d	m s	m s	h m	h m	h m	d %	
9	07 54	07 41	11 52	12 14	24 39	00 0	●
10	07 27	07 14	11 53	13 05	00 39	01 2	
11	07 00	06 46	11 53	13 55	01 30	02 5	

	UT (d h)	ARIES GHA	VENUS −4·8 GHA	VENUS Dec	MARS +0·2 GHA	MARS Dec	JUPITER −2·3 GHA	JUPITER Dec	SATURN +0·6 GHA	SATURN Dec
		° ′	° ′	° ′	° ′	° ′	° ′	° ′	° ′	° ′
	12 00	80 42.7	226 40.8	S10 52.9	282 17.7	N11 53.2	291 10.8	N13 18.0	72 25.5	N 0 48.7
	01	95 45.2	241 41.3	53.3	297 19.4	53.0	306 13.2	18.0	87 27.9	48.7
	02	110 47.6	256 41.9	53.8	312 21.2	52.8	321 15.7	18.0	102 30.4	48.7
	03	125 50.1	271 42.4	. . 54.3	327 22.9	. . 52.6	336 18.1	. . 18.0	117 32.9	. . 48.7
	04	140 52.6	286 42.9	54.7	342 24.6	52.4	351 20.6	18.0	132 35.3	48.7
	05	155 55.0	301 43.4	55.2	357 26.4	52.2	6 23.0	18.0	147 37.8	48.7
	06	170 57.5	316 44.0	S10 55.6	12 28.1	N11 52.0	21 25.5	N13 18.0	162 40.2	N 0 48.7
	07	185 59.9	331 44.5	56.1	27 29.8	51.8	36 27.9	18.1	177 42.7	48.8
S	08	201 02.4	346 45.0	56.6	42 31.6	51.6	51 30.4	18.1	192 45.2	48.8
A	09	216 04.9	1 45.5	. . 57.0	57 33.3	. . 51.4	66 32.9	. . 18.1	207 47.6	. . 48.8
T	10	231 07.3	16 46.0	57.5	72 35.0	51.2	81 35.3	18.1	222 50.1	48.8
U	11	246 09.8	31 46.5	58.0	87 36.8	51.0	96 37.8	18.1	237 52.6	48.8
R	12	261 12.3	46 47.1	S10 58.4	102 38.5	N11 50.8	111 40.2	N13 18.1	252 55.0	N 0 48.8
D	13	276 14.7	61 47.6	58.9	117 40.3	50.6	126 42.7	18.1	267 57.5	48.8
A	14	291 17.2	76 48.1	59.4	132 42.0	50.4	141 45.1	18.1	282 59.9	48.8
Y	15	306 19.7	91 48.6	10 59.8	147 43.7	. . 50.2	156 47.6	. . 18.1	298 02.4	. . 48.9
	16	321 22.1	106 49.1	11 00.3	162 45.5	50.0	171 50.1	18.1	313 04.9	48.9
	17	336 24.6	121 49.6	00.8	177 47.2	49.8	186 52.5	18.1	328 07.3	48.9
	18	351 27.1	136 50.1	S11 01.2	192 49.0	N11 49.6	201 55.0	N13 18.1	343 09.8	N 0 48.9
	19	6 29.5	151 50.6	01.7	207 50.7	49.4	216 57.4	18.2	358 12.2	48.9
	20	21 32.0	166 51.1	02.2	222 52.5	49.2	231 59.9	18.2	13 14.7	48.9
	21	36 34.4	181 51.6	. . 02.6	237 54.2	. . 49.0	247 02.3	. . 18.2	28 17.2	. . 48.9
	22	51 36.9	196 52.1	03.1	252 55.9	48.8	262 04.8	18.2	43 19.6	48.9
	23	66 39.4	211 52.6	03.6	267 57.7	48.6	277 07.3	18.2	58 22.1	49.0
	13 00	81 41.8	226 53.1	S11 04.1	282 59.4	N11 48.4	292 09.7	N13 18.2	73 24.5	N 0 49.0
	01	96 44.3	241 53.6	04.5	298 01.2	48.2	307 12.2	18.2	88 27.0	49.0
	02	111 46.8	256 54.1	05.0	313 02.9	48.0	322 14.6	18.2	103 29.5	49.0
	03	126 49.2	271 54.6	. . 05.5	328 04.7	. . 47.8	337 17.1	. . 18.2	118 31.9	. . 49.0
	04	141 51.7	286 55.1	06.0	343 06.4	47.6	352 19.6	18.2	133 34.4	49.0
	05	156 54.2	301 55.6	06.4	358 08.2	47.4	7 22.0	18.3	148 36.8	49.0
	06	171 56.6	316 56.1	S11 06.9	13 09.9	N11 47.2	22 24.5	N13 18.3	163 39.3	N 0 49.1
	07	186 59.1	331 56.5	07.4	28 11.7	47.0	37 27.0	18.3	178 41.8	49.1
	08	202 01.6	346 57.0	07.9	43 13.5	46.8	52 29.4	18.3	193 44.2	49.1
S	09	217 04.0	1 57.5	. . 08.3	58 15.2	. . 46.6	67 31.9	. . 18.3	208 46.7	. . 49.1
U	10	232 06.5	16 58.0	08.8	73 17.0	46.4	82 34.3	18.3	223 49.1	49.1
N	11	247 08.9	31 58.5	09.3	88 18.7	46.2	97 36.8	18.3	238 51.6	49.1
D	12	262 11.4	46 58.9	S11 09.8	103 20.5	N11 46.0	112 39.3	N13 18.3	253 54.1	N 0 49.1
A	13	277 13.9	61 59.4	10.3	118 22.2	45.8	127 41.7	18.3	268 56.5	49.2
Y	14	292 16.3	76 59.9	10.8	133 24.0	45.6	142 44.2	18.3	283 59.0	49.2
	15	307 18.8	92 00.4	. . 11.2	148 25.7	. . 45.4	157 46.7	. . 18.4	299 01.4	. . 49.2
	16	322 21.3	107 00.8	11.7	163 27.5	45.2	172 49.1	18.4	314 03.9	49.2
	17	337 23.7	122 01.3	12.2	178 29.3	45.0	187 51.6	18.4	329 06.3	49.2
	18	352 26.2	137 01.8	S11 12.7	193 31.0	N11 44.8	202 54.1	N13 18.4	344 08.8	N 0 49.2
	19	7 28.7	152 02.3	13.2	208 32.8	44.7	217 56.5	18.4	359 11.3	49.2
	20	22 31.1	167 02.7	13.7	223 34.6	44.5	232 59.0	18.4	14 13.7	49.3
	21	37 33.6	182 03.2	. . 14.2	238 36.3	. . 44.3	248 01.5	. . 18.4	29 16.2	. . 49.3
	22	52 36.0	197 03.6	14.6	253 38.1	44.1	263 03.9	18.4	44 18.6	49.3
	23	67 38.5	212 04.1	15.1	268 39.9	43.9	278 06.4	18.5	59 21.1	49.3
	14 00	82 41.0	227 04.6	S11 15.6	283 41.6	N11 43.7	293 08.9	N13 18.5	74 23.5	N 0 49.3
	01	97 43.4	242 05.0	16.1	298 43.4	43.5	308 11.3	18.5	89 26.0	49.3
	02	112 45.9	257 05.5	16.6	313 45.2	43.3	323 13.8	18.5	104 28.4	49.3
	03	127 48.4	272 05.9	. . 17.1	328 46.9	. . 43.1	338 16.3	. . 18.5	119 30.9	. . 49.4
	04	142 50.8	287 06.4	17.6	343 48.7	42.9	353 18.7	18.5	134 33.4	49.4
	05	157 53.3	302 06.9	18.1	358 50.5	42.7	8 21.2	18.5	149 35.8	49.4
	06	172 55.8	317 07.3	S11 18.6	13 52.2	N11 42.5	23 23.7	N13 18.5	164 38.3	N 0 49.4
	07	187 58.2	332 07.8	19.1	28 54.0	42.4	38 26.1	18.6	179 40.7	49.4
	08	203 00.7	347 08.2	19.6	43 55.8	42.2	53 28.6	18.6	194 43.2	49.4
M	09	218 03.2	2 08.7	. . 20.0	58 57.5	. . 42.0	68 31.1	. . 18.6	209 45.6	. . 49.5
O	10	233 05.6	17 09.1	20.5	73 59.3	41.8	83 33.6	18.6	224 48.1	49.5
N	11	248 08.1	32 09.5	21.0	89 01.1	41.6	98 36.0	18.6	239 50.5	49.5
D	12	263 10.5	47 10.0	S11 21.5	104 02.9	N11 41.4	113 38.5	N13 18.6	254 53.0	N 0 49.5
A	13	278 13.0	62 10.4	22.0	119 04.6	41.2	128 41.0	18.6	269 55.4	49.5
Y	14	293 15.5	77 10.9	22.5	134 06.4	41.0	143 43.4	18.7	284 57.9	49.5
	15	308 17.9	92 11.3	. . 23.0	149 08.2	. . 40.9	158 45.9	. . 18.7	300 00.4	. . 49.5
	16	323 20.4	107 11.7	23.5	164 10.0	40.7	173 48.4	18.7	315 02.8	49.6
	17	338 22.9	122 12.2	24.0	179 11.8	40.5	188 50.9	18.7	330 05.3	49.6
	18	353 25.3	137 12.6	S11 24.5	194 13.5	N11 40.3	203 53.3	N13 18.7	345 07.7	N 0 49.6
	19	8 27.8	152 13.1	25.0	209 15.3	40.1	218 55.8	18.7	0 10.2	49.6
	20	23 30.3	167 13.5	25.5	224 17.1	39.9	233 58.3	18.7	15 12.6	49.6
	21	38 32.7	182 13.9	. . 26.0	239 18.9	. . 39.7	249 00.8	. . 18.8	30 15.1	. . 49.6
	22	53 35.2	197 14.3	26.5	254 20.7	39.6	264 03.2	18.8	45 17.5	49.7
	23	68 37.7	212 14.8	27.0	269 22.5	39.4	279 05.7	18.8	60 20.0	49.7
	Mer. Pass.	h m 18 30.2	v 0.5	d 0.5	v 1.8	d 0.2	v 2.5	d 0.0	v 2.5	d 0.0

STARS

Name	SHA	Dec
	° ′	° ′
Acamar	315 10.2	S40 11.9
Achernar	335 18.7	S57 06.2
Acrux	172 58.4	S63 14.7
Adhara	255 04.3	S29 00.4
Aldebaran	290 37.4	N16 33.8
Alioth	166 11.8	N55 48.5
Alkaid	152 51.1	N49 10.5
Alnair	27 31.1	S46 50.0
Alnilam	275 35.8	S 1 11.1
Alphard	217 46.0	S 8 46.5
Alphecca	126 02.7	N26 37.3
Alpheratz	357 33.0	N29 14.6
Altair	61 58.7	N 8 56.5
Ankaa	353 05.5	S42 09.7
Antares	112 14.3	S26 29.4
Arcturus	145 46.7	N19 02.4
Atria	107 07.6	S69 04.4
Avior	234 13.6	S59 35.5
Bellatrix	278 20.8	N 6 22.5
Betelgeuse	270 50.0	N 7 24.7
Canopus	263 51.1	S52 42.5
Capella	280 19.0	N46 01.5
Deneb	49 25.0	N45 22.8
Denebola	182 23.4	N14 25.2
Diphda	348 45.6	S17 50.3
Dubhe	193 39.0	N61 36.0
Elnath	277 59.5	N28 37.8
Eltanin	90 42.0	N51 29.1
Enif	33 37.4	N10 00.0
Fomalhaut	15 12.8	S29 28.9
Gacrux	171 50.0	S57 15.6
Gienah	175 42.0	S17 41.4
Hadar	148 34.1	S60 30.0
Hamal	327 49.2	N23 35.6
Kaus Aust.	83 30.8	S34 22.3
Kochab	137 20.8	N74 02.4
Markab	13 28.3	N15 21.2
Menkar	314 04.2	N 4 11.8
Menkent	147 56.0	S36 30.0
Miaplacidus	221 37.4	S69 49.4
Mirfak	308 25.5	N49 57.6
Nunki	75 46.1	S26 15.8
Peacock	53 03.7	S56 39.0
Pollux	243 15.1	N27 57.5
Procyon	244 48.9	N 5 09.3
Rasalhague	95 57.4	N12 32.4
Regulus	207 32.6	N11 50.0
Rigel	281 02.0	S 8 10.2
Rigil Kent.	139 38.6	S60 56.6
Sabik	102 01.3	S15 45.5
Schedar	349 29.0	N56 41.5
Shaula	96 08.6	S37 07.4
Sirius	258 24.5	S16 45.2
Spica	158 20.8	S11 18.1
Suhail	222 44.9	S43 32.3
Vega	80 32.6	N38 48.6
Zuben'ubi	136 54.5	S16 09.2

	SHA	Mer. Pass.
	° ′	h m
Venus	145 11.3	8 52
Mars	201 17.6	5 07
Jupiter	210 27.9	4 31
Saturn	351 42.7	19 03

UT d h	SUN GHA ° ′	SUN Dec ° ′	MOON GHA ° ′	v ′	MOON Dec ° ′	d ′	HP ′
12 00	181 37.9	S23 03.5	146 23.7	12.0	S24 09.0	7.1	54.0
01	196 37.6	03.7	160 54.7	12.2	24 01.9	7.2	54.0
02	211 37.3	03.8	175 25.9	12.1	23 54.7	7.3	54.0
03	226 37.0	. . 04.0	189 57.0	12.3	23 47.4	7.4	54.0
04	241 36.7	04.2	204 28.3	12.3	23 40.0	7.6	54.0
05	256 36.5	04.4	218 59.6	12.3	23 32.4	7.6	54.0
06	271 36.2	S23 04.6	233 30.9	12.4	S23 24.8	7.7	54.0
S 07	286 35.9	04.8	248 02.3	12.5	23 17.1	7.9	54.0
A 08	301 35.6	05.0	262 33.8	12.5	23 09.2	7.9	54.0
T 09	316 35.3	. . 05.2	277 05.3	12.6	23 01.3	8.1	54.0
U 10	331 35.0	05.3	291 36.9	12.7	22 53.2	8.1	54.0
R 11	346 34.7	05.5	306 08.6	12.7	22 45.1	8.2	54.0
D 12	1 34.4	S23 05.7	320 40.3	12.7	S22 36.9	8.4	54.0
A 13	16 34.1	05.9	335 12.0	12.9	22 28.5	8.4	54.0
Y 14	31 33.8	06.1	349 43.9	12.8	22 20.1	8.6	54.0
15	46 33.5	. . 06.3	4 15.7	13.0	22 11.5	8.6	54.1
16	61 33.2	06.4	18 47.7	13.0	22 02.9	8.7	54.1
17	76 32.9	06.6	33 19.7	13.0	21 54.2	8.9	54.1
18	91 32.7	S23 06.8	47 51.7	13.1	S21 45.3	8.9	54.1
19	106 32.4	07.0	62 23.8	13.2	21 36.4	9.0	54.1
20	121 32.1	07.1	76 56.0	13.2	21 27.4	9.1	54.1
21	136 31.8	. . 07.3	91 28.2	13.3	21 18.3	9.2	54.1
22	151 31.5	07.5	106 00.5	13.3	21 09.1	9.3	54.1
23	166 31.2	07.7	120 32.8	13.4	20 59.8	9.4	54.1
13 00	181 30.9	S23 07.8	135 05.2	13.5	S20 50.4	9.4	54.1
01	196 30.6	08.0	149 37.7	13.5	20 41.0	9.6	54.1
02	211 30.3	08.2	164 10.2	13.5	20 31.4	9.6	54.1
03	226 30.0	. . 08.3	178 42.7	13.7	20 21.8	9.8	54.1
04	241 29.7	08.5	193 15.4	13.6	20 12.0	9.8	54.1
05	256 29.4	08.7	207 48.0	13.8	20 02.2	9.9	54.2
06	271 29.1	S23 08.9	222 20.8	13.7	S19 52.3	10.0	54.2
07	286 28.8	09.0	236 53.5	13.9	19 42.3	10.0	54.2
08	301 28.5	09.2	251 26.4	13.9	19 32.3	10.2	54.2
S 09	316 28.2	. . 09.4	265 59.3	13.9	19 22.1	10.2	54.2
U 10	331 27.9	09.5	280 32.2	14.0	19 11.9	10.4	54.2
N 11	346 27.6	09.7	295 05.2	14.1	19 01.5	10.4	54.2
D 12	1 27.3	S23 09.8	309 38.3	14.1	S18 51.1	10.4	54.2
A 13	16 27.1	10.0	324 11.4	14.1	18 40.7	10.6	54.2
Y 14	31 26.8	10.2	338 44.5	14.2	18 30.1	10.7	54.3
15	46 26.5	. . 10.3	353 17.7	14.3	18 19.4	10.7	54.3
16	61 26.2	10.5	7 51.0	14.3	18 08.7	10.8	54.3
17	76 25.9	10.7	22 24.3	14.3	17 57.9	10.8	54.3
18	91 25.6	S23 10.8	36 57.6	14.4	S17 47.1	11.0	54.3
19	106 25.3	11.0	51 31.0	14.5	17 36.1	11.0	54.3
20	121 25.0	11.1	66 04.5	14.5	17 25.1	11.1	54.3
21	136 24.7	. . 11.3	80 38.0	14.5	17 14.0	11.2	54.3
22	151 24.4	11.4	95 11.5	14.6	17 02.8	11.2	54.4
23	166 24.1	11.6	109 45.1	14.7	16 51.6	11.3	54.4
14 00	181 23.8	S23 11.7	124 18.8	14.6	S16 40.3	11.4	54.4
01	196 23.5	11.9	138 52.4	14.8	16 28.9	11.5	54.4
02	211 23.2	12.0	153 26.2	14.7	16 17.4	11.5	54.4
03	226 22.9	. . 12.2	167 59.9	14.8	16 05.9	11.6	54.4
04	241 22.6	12.3	182 33.7	14.9	15 54.3	11.7	54.4
05	256 22.3	12.5	197 07.6	14.9	15 42.6	11.7	54.5
06	271 22.0	S23 12.6	211 41.5	14.9	S15 30.9	11.8	54.5
07	286 21.7	12.8	226 15.4	15.0	15 19.1	11.9	54.5
08	301 21.4	12.9	240 49.4	15.0	15 07.2	11.9	54.5
M 09	316 21.1	. . 13.1	255 23.4	15.1	14 55.3	12.0	54.5
O 10	331 20.8	13.2	269 57.5	15.1	14 43.3	12.1	54.5
N 11	346 20.5	13.4	284 31.6	15.1	14 31.2	12.1	54.5
D 12	1 20.2	S23 13.5	299 05.7	15.2	S14 19.1	12.2	54.6
A 13	16 19.9	13.7	313 39.9	15.2	14 06.9	12.2	54.6
Y 14	31 19.6	13.8	328 14.1	15.2	13 54.7	12.4	54.6
15	46 19.3	. . 14.0	342 48.3	15.3	13 42.3	12.3	54.6
16	61 19.0	14.1	357 22.6	15.3	13 30.0	12.5	54.6
17	76 18.7	14.2	11 56.9	15.3	13 17.5	12.4	54.7
18	91 18.4	S23 14.4	26 31.2	15.4	S13 05.1	12.6	54.7
19	106 18.1	14.5	41 05.6	15.3	12 52.5	12.6	54.7
20	121 17.8	14.6	55 39.9	15.5	12 39.9	12.7	54.7
21	136 17.5	. . 14.8	70 14.4	15.4	12 27.2	12.7	54.7
22	151 17.2	14.9	84 48.8	15.5	12 14.5	12.8	54.7
23	166 16.9	15.1	99 23.3	15.5	S12 01.7	12.8	54.8
	SD 16.3	*d* 0.2	SD 14.7		14.8		14.9

Lat. °	Twilight Naut. h m	Twilight Civil h m	Sunrise h m	Moonrise 12 h m	Moonrise 13 h m	Moonrise 14 h m	Moonrise 15 h m
N 72	08 17	10 40	■	■	■	13 29	12 44
N 70	07 58	09 44	■	■	13 56	13 02	12 31
68	07 42	09 10	■	■	13 12	12 41	12 20
66	07 30	08 46	10 23	13 15	12 43	12 24	12 11
64	07 19	08 27	09 43	12 33	12 20	12 11	12 03
62	07 09	08 11	09 16	12 05	12 02	11 59	11 56
60	07 01	07 58	08 55	11 43	11 47	11 49	11 50
N 58	06 54	07 46	08 38	11 25	11 35	11 41	11 45
56	06 47	07 36	08 23	11 10	11 24	11 33	11 41
54	06 41	07 27	08 11	10 57	11 14	11 26	11 36
52	06 36	07 19	08 00	10 46	11 05	11 20	11 33
50	06 30	07 12	07 50	10 36	10 57	11 15	11 29
45	06 19	06 56	07 30	10 14	10 41	11 03	11 22
N 40	06 09	06 43	07 13	09 57	10 27	10 53	11 15
35	05 59	06 31	06 59	09 42	10 15	10 44	11 10
30	05 51	06 21	06 47	09 30	10 05	10 36	11 05
20	05 35	06 02	06 26	09 08	09 47	10 23	10 57
N 10	05 19	05 45	06 08	08 49	09 32	10 11	10 50
0	05 02	05 28	05 50	08 31	09 17	10 01	10 43
S 10	04 43	05 10	05 33	08 13	09 02	09 50	10 36
20	04 21	04 50	05 14	07 54	08 47	09 38	10 28
30	03 52	04 25	04 53	07 32	08 28	09 24	10 20
35	03 34	04 10	04 40	07 19	08 18	09 17	10 15
40	03 11	03 52	04 25	07 04	08 06	09 08	10 09
45	02 41	03 30	04 07	06 46	07 51	08 57	10 03
S 50	01 56	03 01	03 45	06 23	07 34	08 44	09 55
52	01 30	02 46	03 34	06 13	07 25	08 38	09 51
54	00 48	02 28	03 22	06 00	07 16	08 32	09 47
56	////	02 07	03 08	05 46	07 05	08 24	09 43
58	////	01 38	02 52	05 30	06 53	08 16	09 38
S 60	////	00 53	02 32	05 10	06 39	08 06	09 32

Lat. °	Sunset h m	Twilight Civil h m	Twilight Naut. h m	Moonset 12 h m	Moonset 13 h m	Moonset 14 h m	Moonset 15 h m
N 72	■	13 08	15 31	■	■	19 16	21 30
N 70	■	14 04	15 50	■	17 18	19 42	21 41
68	■	14 38	16 06	■	18 00	20 01	21 50
66	13 25	15 02	16 19	16 23	18 28	20 16	21 57
64	14 05	15 21	16 29	17 03	18 50	20 28	22 03
62	14 32	15 37	16 39	17 31	19 07	20 39	22 08
60	14 53	15 51	16 47	17 52	19 21	20 48	22 13
N 58	15 11	16 02	16 54	18 09	19 33	20 55	22 17
56	15 25	16 12	17 01	18 24	19 43	21 02	22 20
54	15 37	16 21	17 07	18 36	19 52	21 08	22 23
52	15 48	16 29	17 13	18 47	20 00	21 13	22 26
50	15 58	16 36	17 18	18 57	20 08	21 18	22 29
45	16 19	16 52	17 29	19 17	20 23	21 29	22 34
N 40	16 35	17 06	17 40	19 34	20 36	21 37	22 39
35	16 49	17 17	17 49	19 47	20 46	21 45	22 43
30	17 01	17 28	17 57	19 59	20 56	21 51	22 46
20	17 22	17 46	18 14	20 20	21 12	22 02	22 52
N 10	17 41	18 03	18 30	20 37	21 25	22 12	22 58
0	17 58	18 20	18 47	20 54	21 38	22 21	23 03
S 10	18 15	18 38	19 05	21 10	21 51	22 30	23 07
20	18 34	18 59	19 28	21 27	22 05	22 39	23 13
30	18 56	19 23	19 57	21 47	22 20	22 50	23 18
35	19 09	19 38	20 15	21 58	22 29	22 56	23 22
40	19 24	19 56	20 38	22 11	22 39	23 03	23 25
45	19 41	20 19	21 08	22 27	22 51	23 11	23 30
S 50	20 04	20 48	21 53	22 46	23 05	23 21	23 35
52	20 14	21 03	22 20	22 55	23 12	23 25	23 37
54	20 27	21 21	23 03	23 05	23 19	23 30	23 39
56	20 41	21 42	////	23 16	23 27	23 36	23 42
58	20 57	22 11	////	23 29	23 36	23 42	23 45
S 60	21 17	22 58	////	23 44	23 47	23 48	23 49

Day d	SUN Eqn. of Time 00^h m s	SUN Eqn. of Time 12^h m s	SUN Mer. Pass. h m	MOON Mer. Pass. Upper h m	MOON Mer. Pass. Lower h m	MOON Age d	MOON Phase %
12	06 32	06 18	11 54	14 42	02 19	03	10
13	06 04	05 50	11 54	15 28	03 05	04	17
14	05 36	05 21	11 55	16 11	03 49	05	24

UT	ARIES	VENUS −4·7		MARS +0·2		JUPITER −2·3		SATURN +0·6	
	GHA	GHA	Dec	GHA	Dec	GHA	Dec	GHA	Dec
d h	° ′	° ′	° ′	° ′	° ′	° ′	° ′	° ′	° ′
15 00 (TUESDAY)	83 40.1	227 15.2	S11 27.5	284 24.2	N11 39.2	294 08.2	N13 18.8	75 22.4	N 0 49.7
01	98 42.6	242 15.6	28.0	299 26.0	39.0	309 10.7	18.8	90 24.9	49.7
02	113 45.0	257 16.1	28.6	314 27.8	38.8	324 13.1	18.8	105 27.3	49.7
03	128 47.5	272 16.5	. . 29.1	329 29.6	. . 38.6	339 15.6	. . 18.8	120 29.8	. . 49.8
04	143 50.0	287 16.9	29.6	344 31.4	38.5	354 18.1	18.9	135 32.2	49.8
05	158 52.4	302 17.3	30.1	359 33.2	38.3	9 20.6	18.9	150 34.7	49.8
06	173 54.9	317 17.7	S11 30.6	14 35.0	N11 38.1	24 23.1	N13 18.9	165 37.1	N 0 49.8
07	188 57.4	332 18.2	31.1	29 36.8	37.9	39 25.5	18.9	180 39.6	49.8
08	203 59.8	347 18.6	31.6	44 38.5	37.7	54 28.0	18.9	195 42.0	49.8
09	219 02.3	2 19.0	. . 32.1	59 40.3	. . 37.5	69 30.5	. . 18.9	210 44.5	. . 49.9
10	234 04.8	17 19.4	32.6	74 42.1	37.4	84 33.0	19.0	225 46.9	49.9
11	249 07.2	32 19.8	33.1	89 43.9	37.2	99 35.4	19.0	240 49.4	49.9
12	264 09.7	47 20.2	S11 33.6	104 45.7	N11 37.0	114 37.9	N13 19.0	255 51.8	N 0 49.9
13	279 12.1	62 20.6	34.1	119 47.5	36.8	129 40.4	19.0	270 54.3	49.9
14	294 14.6	77 21.0	34.7	134 49.3	36.6	144 42.9	19.0	285 56.7	49.9
15	309 17.1	92 21.4	. . 35.2	149 51.1	. . 36.5	159 45.4	. . 19.0	300 59.2	. . 50.0
16	324 19.5	107 21.8	35.7	164 52.9	36.3	174 47.8	19.1	316 01.6	50.0
17	339 22.0	122 22.2	36.2	179 54.7	36.1	189 50.3	19.1	331 04.1	50.0
18	354 24.5	137 22.6	S11 36.7	194 56.5	N11 35.9	204 52.8	N13 19.1	346 06.5	N 0 50.0
19	9 26.9	152 23.0	37.2	209 58.3	35.7	219 55.3	19.1	1 09.0	50.0
20	24 29.4	167 23.4	37.7	225 00.1	35.6	234 57.8	19.1	16 11.4	50.1
21	39 31.9	182 23.8	. . 38.3	240 01.9	. . 35.4	250 00.3	. . 19.1	31 13.9	. . 50.1
22	54 34.3	197 24.2	38.8	255 03.7	35.2	265 02.7	19.2	46 16.3	50.1
23	69 36.8	212 24.6	39.3	270 05.5	35.0	280 05.2	19.2	61 18.8	50.1
16 00 (WEDNESDAY)	84 39.3	227 25.0	S11 39.8	285 07.3	N11 34.9	295 07.7	N13 19.2	76 21.2	N 0 50.1
01	99 41.7	242 25.4	40.3	300 09.1	34.7	310 10.2	19.2	91 23.7	50.1
02	114 44.2	257 25.8	40.8	315 10.9	34.5	325 12.7	19.2	106 26.1	50.2
03	129 46.6	272 26.2	. . 41.4	330 12.7	. . 34.3	340 15.2	. . 19.3	121 28.5	. . 50.2
04	144 49.1	287 26.6	41.9	345 14.5	34.2	355 17.6	19.3	136 31.0	50.2
05	159 51.6	302 27.0	42.4	0 16.3	34.0	10 20.1	19.3	151 33.4	50.2
06	174 54.0	317 27.4	S11 42.9	15 18.2	N11 33.8	25 22.6	N13 19.3	166 35.9	N 0 50.2
07	189 56.5	332 27.7	43.4	30 20.0	33.6	40 25.1	19.3	181 38.3	50.3
08	204 59.0	347 28.1	44.0	45 21.8	33.5	55 27.6	19.4	196 40.8	50.3
09	220 01.4	2 28.5	. . 44.5	60 23.6	. . 33.3	70 30.1	. . 19.4	211 43.2	. . 50.3
10	235 03.9	17 28.9	45.0	75 25.4	33.1	85 32.6	19.4	226 45.7	50.3
11	250 06.4	32 29.3	45.5	90 27.2	32.9	100 35.1	19.4	241 48.1	50.3
12	265 08.8	47 29.6	S11 46.1	105 29.0	N11 32.8	115 37.5	N13 19.4	256 50.6	N 0 50.4
13	280 11.3	62 30.0	46.6	120 30.8	32.6	130 40.0	19.4	271 53.0	50.4
14	295 13.8	77 30.4	47.1	135 32.7	32.4	145 42.5	19.5	286 55.4	50.4
15	310 16.2	92 30.8	. . 47.6	150 34.5	. . 32.3	160 45.0	. . 19.5	301 57.9	. . 50.4
16	325 18.7	107 31.1	48.2	165 36.3	32.1	175 47.5	19.5	317 00.3	50.4
17	340 21.1	122 31.5	48.7	180 38.1	31.9	190 50.0	19.5	332 02.8	50.5
18	355 23.6	137 31.9	S11 49.2	195 39.9	N11 31.7	205 52.5	N13 19.5	347 05.2	N 0 50.5
19	10 26.1	152 32.3	49.7	210 41.7	31.6	220 55.0	19.6	2 07.7	50.5
20	25 28.5	167 32.6	50.3	225 43.6	31.4	235 57.5	19.6	17 10.1	50.5
21	40 31.0	182 33.0	. . 50.8	240 45.4	. . 31.2	250 59.9	. . 19.6	32 12.6	. . 50.5
22	55 33.5	197 33.3	51.3	255 47.2	31.1	266 02.4	19.6	47 15.0	50.6
23	70 35.9	212 33.7	51.9	270 49.0	30.9	281 04.9	19.7	62 17.4	50.6
17 00 (THURSDAY)	85 38.4	227 34.1	S11 52.4	285 50.9	N11 30.7	296 07.4	N13 19.7	77 19.9	N 0 50.6
01	100 40.9	242 34.4	52.9	300 52.7	30.6	311 09.9	19.7	92 22.3	50.6
02	115 43.3	257 34.8	53.4	315 54.5	30.4	326 12.4	19.7	107 24.8	50.6
03	130 45.8	272 35.2	. . 54.0	330 56.3	. . 30.2	341 14.9	. . 19.7	122 27.2	. . 50.7
04	145 48.2	287 35.5	54.5	345 58.2	30.0	356 17.4	19.8	137 29.7	50.7
05	160 50.7	302 35.9	55.0	1 00.0	29.9	11 19.9	19.8	152 32.1	50.7
06	175 53.2	317 36.2	S11 55.6	16 01.8	N11 29.7	26 22.4	N13 19.8	167 34.5	N 0 50.7
07	190 55.6	332 36.6	56.1	31 03.6	29.5	41 24.9	19.8	182 37.0	50.8
08	205 58.1	347 36.9	56.6	46 05.5	29.4	56 27.4	19.8	197 39.4	50.8
09	221 00.6	2 37.3	. . 57.2	61 07.3	. . 29.2	71 29.9	. . 19.9	212 41.9	. . 50.8
10	236 03.0	17 37.6	57.7	76 09.1	29.1	86 32.4	19.9	227 44.3	50.8
11	251 05.5	32 38.0	58.2	91 11.0	28.9	101 34.8	19.9	242 46.8	50.8
12	266 08.0	47 38.3	S11 58.8	106 12.8	N11 28.7	116 37.3	N13 19.9	257 49.2	N 0 50.9
13	281 10.4	62 38.7	59.3	121 14.6	28.6	131 39.8	20.0	272 51.6	50.9
14	296 12.9	77 39.0	11 59.9	136 16.5	28.4	146 42.3	20.0	287 54.1	50.9
15	311 15.4	92 39.3	12 00.4	151 18.3	. . 28.2	161 44.8	. . 20.0	302 56.5	. . 50.9
16	326 17.8	107 39.7	00.9	166 20.1	28.1	176 47.3	20.0	317 59.0	50.9
17	341 20.3	122 40.0	01.5	181 22.0	27.9	191 49.8	20.0	333 01.4	51.0
18	356 22.7	137 40.4	S12 02.0	196 23.8	N11 27.7	206 52.3	N13 20.1	348 03.8	N 0 51.0
19	11 25.2	152 40.7	02.5	211 25.7	27.6	221 54.8	20.1	3 06.3	51.0
20	26 27.7	167 41.0	03.1	226 27.5	27.4	236 57.3	20.1	18 08.7	51.0
21	41 30.1	182 41.4	. . 03.6	241 29.3	. . 27.3	251 59.8	. . 20.1	33 11.2	. . 51.1
22	56 32.6	197 41.7	04.2	256 31.2	27.1	267 02.3	20.2	48 13.6	51.1
23	71 35.1	212 42.0	04.7	271 33.0	26.9	282 04.8	20.2	63 16.0	51.1
Mer. Pass.	h m 18 18.4	v 0.4	d 0.5	v 1.8	d 0.2	v 2.5	d 0.0	v 2.4	d 0.0

STARS

Name	SHA	Dec
	° ′	° ′
Acamar	315 10.2	S40 11.9
Achernar	335 18.7	S57 06.2
Acrux	172 58.4	S63 14.7
Adhara	255 04.2	S29 00.5
Aldebaran	290 37.4	N16 33.8
Alioth	166 11.8	N55 48.5
Alkaid	152 51.0	N49 10.4
Alnair	27 31.1	S46 50.0
Alnilam	275 35.8	S 1 11.1
Alphard	217 46.0	S 8 46.5
Alphecca	126 02.7	N26 37.3
Alpheratz	357 33.1	N29 14.6
Altair	61 58.7	N 8 56.4
Ankaa	353 05.5	S42 09.7
Antares	112 14.2	S26 29.4
Arcturus	145 46.7	N19 02.4
Atria	107 07.6	S69 04.4
Avior	234 13.6	S59 35.6
Bellatrix	278 20.8	N 6 22.5
Betelgeuse	270 50.0	N 7 24.7
Canopus	263 51.1	S52 42.5
Capella	280 19.0	N46 01.5
Deneb	49 25.0	N45 22.8
Denebola	182 23.3	N14 25.1
Diphda	348 45.6	S17 50.4
Dubhe	193 39.0	N61 36.0
Elnath	277 59.5	N28 37.8
Eltanin	90 42.0	N51 29.1
Enif	33 37.4	N10 00.0
Fomalhaut	15 12.8	S29 28.9
Gacrux	171 50.0	S57 15.6
Gienah	175 42.0	S17 41.4
Hadar	148 34.1	S60 30.0
Hamal	327 49.2	N23 35.6
Kaus Aust.	83 30.8	S34 22.3
Kochab	137 20.8	N74 02.4
Markab	13 28.4	N15 21.2
Menkar	314 04.2	N 4 11.8
Menkent	147 56.0	S36 30.0
Miaplacidus	221 37.3	S69 49.4
Mirfak	308 25.5	N49 57.6
Nunki	75 46.1	S26 15.8
Peacock	53 03.7	S56 39.0
Pollux	243 15.0	N27 57.5
Procyon	244 48.9	N 5 09.3
Rasalhague	95 57.4	N12 32.4
Regulus	207 32.6	N11 50.0
Rigel	281 02.0	S 8 10.2
Rigil Kent.	139 38.5	S60 56.6
Sabik	102 01.3	S15 45.5
Schedar	349 29.0	N56 41.5
Shaula	96 08.6	S37 07.3
Sirius	258 24.5	S16 45.2
Spica	158 20.8	S11 18.1
Suhail	222 44.8	S43 32.3
Vega	80 32.6	N38 48.6
Zuben'ubi	136 54.5	S16 09.2

	SHA	Mer. Pass.
	° ′	h m
Venus	142 45.8	8 50
Mars	200 28.1	4 59
Jupiter	210 28.5	4 19
Saturn	351 41.9	18 52

UT		SUN GHA	SUN Dec	MOON GHA	v	MOON Dec	d	HP
d	h	° ′	° ′	° ′	′	° ′	′	′
15 TUESDAY	00	181 16.6	S23 15.2	113 57.8	15.5	S11 48.9	12.9	54.8
	01	196 16.3	15.3	128 32.3	15.6	11 36.0	12.9	54.8
	02	211 16.0	15.5	143 06.9	15.6	11 23.1	13.0	54.8
	03	226 15.7	. . 15.6	157 41.5	15.6	11 10.1	13.0	54.8
	04	241 15.4	15.7	172 16.1	15.6	10 57.1	13.1	54.9
	05	256 15.1	15.8	186 50.7	15.6	10 44.0	13.2	54.9
	06	271 14.8	S23 16.0	201 25.3	15.7	S10 30.8	13.2	54.9
	07	286 14.5	16.1	216 00.0	15.7	10 17.6	13.2	54.9
	08	301 14.2	16.2	230 34.7	15.7	10 04.4	13.3	55.0
	09	316 13.9	. . 16.4	245 09.4	15.7	9 51.1	13.3	55.0
	10	331 13.6	16.5	259 44.1	15.7	9 37.8	13.4	55.0
	11	346 13.3	16.6	274 18.8	15.8	9 24.4	13.5	55.0
	12	1 13.0	S23 16.7	288 53.6	15.7	S 9 10.9	13.4	55.0
	13	16 12.7	16.9	303 28.3	15.8	8 57.5	13.6	55.1
	14	31 12.4	17.0	318 03.1	15.8	8 43.9	13.5	55.1
	15	46 12.1	. . 17.1	332 37.9	15.8	8 30.4	13.6	55.1
	16	61 11.8	17.2	347 12.7	15.8	8 16.8	13.7	55.1
	17	76 11.5	17.3	1 47.5	15.8	8 03.1	13.7	55.2
	18	91 11.2	S23 17.5	16 22.3	15.8	S 7 49.4	13.7	55.2
	19	106 10.9	17.6	30 57.1	15.8	7 35.7	13.8	55.2
	20	121 10.6	17.7	45 31.9	15.8	7 21.9	13.8	55.2
	21	136 10.3	. . 17.8	60 06.7	15.9	7 08.1	13.9	55.3
	22	151 10.0	17.9	74 41.6	15.8	6 54.2	13.9	55.3
	23	166 09.7	18.1	89 16.4	15.8	6 40.3	13.9	55.3
16 WEDNESDAY	00	181 09.4	S23 18.2	103 51.2	15.9	S 6 26.4	14.0	55.3
	01	196 09.1	18.3	118 26.1	15.8	6 12.4	14.0	55.4
	02	211 08.8	18.4	133 00.9	15.8	5 58.4	14.1	55.4
	03	226 08.5	. . 18.5	147 35.7	15.9	5 44.3	14.1	55.4
	04	241 08.2	18.6	162 10.6	15.8	5 30.2	14.1	55.4
	05	256 07.9	18.7	176 45.4	15.8	5 16.1	14.1	55.5
	06	271 07.6	S23 18.8	191 20.2	15.8	S 5 02.0	14.2	55.5
	07	286 07.3	19.0	205 55.0	15.8	4 47.8	14.2	55.5
	08	301 07.0	19.1	220 29.8	15.8	4 33.6	14.3	55.6
	09	316 06.7	. . 19.2	235 04.6	15.8	4 19.3	14.3	55.6
	10	331 06.4	19.3	249 39.4	15.8	4 05.0	14.3	55.6
	11	346 06.1	19.4	264 14.2	15.7	3 50.7	14.3	55.6
	12	1 05.8	S23 19.5	278 48.9	15.8	S 3 36.4	14.4	55.7
	13	16 05.4	19.6	293 23.7	15.7	3 22.0	14.4	55.7
	14	31 05.1	19.7	307 58.4	15.7	3 07.6	14.4	55.7
	15	46 04.8	. . 19.8	322 33.1	15.7	2 53.2	14.5	55.8
	16	61 04.5	19.9	337 07.8	15.7	2 38.7	14.4	55.8
	17	76 04.2	20.0	351 42.5	15.7	2 24.3	14.5	55.8
	18	91 03.9	S23 20.1	6 17.2	15.6	S 2 09.8	14.6	55.9
	19	106 03.6	20.2	20 51.8	15.6	1 55.2	14.5	55.9
	20	121 03.3	20.3	35 26.4	15.6	1 40.7	14.6	55.9
	21	136 03.0	. . 20.4	50 01.0	15.6	1 26.1	14.6	55.9
	22	151 02.7	20.5	64 35.6	15.5	1 11.5	14.6	56.0
	23	166 02.4	20.6	79 10.1	15.6	0 56.9	14.6	56.0
17 THURSDAY	00	181 02.1	S23 20.7	93 44.7	15.4	S 0 42.3	14.7	56.0
	01	196 01.8	20.8	108 19.1	15.5	0 27.6	14.7	56.1
	02	211 01.5	20.9	122 53.6	15.4	S 0 12.9	14.7	56.1
	03	226 01.2	. . 21.0	137 28.0	15.4	N 0 01.8	14.7	56.1
	04	241 00.9	21.1	152 02.4	15.4	0 16.5	14.7	56.2
	05	256 00.6	21.2	166 36.8	15.3	0 31.2	14.7	56.2
	06	271 00.3	S23 21.2	181 11.1	15.3	N 0 45.9	14.8	56.2
	07	286 00.0	21.3	195 45.4	15.2	1 00.7	14.7	56.3
	08	300 59.7	21.4	210 19.6	15.2	1 15.4	14.8	56.3
	09	315 59.4	. . 21.5	224 53.8	15.2	1 30.2	14.8	56.3
	10	330 59.1	21.6	239 28.0	15.1	1 45.0	14.8	56.4
	11	345 58.7	21.7	254 02.1	15.1	1 59.8	14.8	56.4
	12	0 58.4	S23 21.8	268 36.2	15.0	N 2 14.6	14.9	56.4
	13	15 58.1	21.9	283 10.2	15.0	2 29.5	14.8	56.5
	14	30 57.8	21.9	297 44.2	14.9	2 44.3	14.8	56.5
	15	45 57.5	. . 22.0	312 18.1	14.9	2 59.1	14.9	56.5
	16	60 57.2	22.1	326 52.0	14.9	3 14.0	14.8	56.6
	17	75 56.9	22.2	341 25.9	14.8	3 28.8	14.9	56.6
	18	90 56.6	S23 22.3	355 59.7	14.7	N 3 43.7	14.9	56.7
	19	105 56.3	22.3	10 33.4	14.7	3 58.6	14.8	56.7
	20	120 56.0	22.4	25 07.1	14.6	4 13.4	14.9	56.7
	21	135 55.7	. . 22.5	39 40.7	14.6	4 28.3	14.8	56.8
	22	150 55.4	22.6	54 14.3	14.5	4 43.1	14.9	56.8
	23	165 55.1	22.7	68 47.8	14.4	N 4 58.0	14.9	56.8
		SD 16.3	*d* 0.1	SD 15.0		15.2		15.4

Lat.	Twilight Naut.	Twilight Civil	Sunrise	Moonrise 15	16	17	18
°	h m	h m	h m	h m	h m	h m	h m
N 72	08 21	10 49	▬	12 44	12 11	11 40	11 06
N 70	08 01	09 49	▬	12 31	12 06	11 43	11 18
68	07 46	09 15	▬	12 20	12 02	11 45	11 27
66	07 33	08 50	10 29	12 11	11 58	11 47	11 34
64	07 22	08 30	09 47	12 03	11 55	11 48	11 41
62	07 12	08 14	09 20	11 56	11 53	11 50	11 47
60	07 04	08 01	08 58	11 50	11 51	11 51	11 52
N 58	06 56	07 49	08 41	11 45	11 49	11 52	11 56
56	06 50	07 39	08 26	11 41	11 47	11 53	12 00
54	06 44	07 30	08 14	11 36	11 45	11 54	12 03
52	06 38	07 22	08 02	11 33	11 44	11 55	12 07
50	06 33	07 14	07 53	11 29	11 42	11 56	12 10
45	06 21	06 58	07 32	11 22	11 40	11 57	12 16
N 40	06 11	06 45	07 15	11 15	11 37	11 59	12 22
35	06 01	06 33	07 01	11 10	11 35	12 00	12 26
30	05 53	06 22	06 49	11 05	11 33	12 01	12 30
20	05 36	06 04	06 28	10 57	11 30	12 03	12 38
N 10	05 20	05 46	06 09	10 50	11 27	12 05	12 44
0	05 03	05 29	05 52	10 43	11 24	12 06	12 50
S 10	04 44	05 11	05 34	10 36	11 21	12 08	12 56
20	04 22	04 51	05 15	10 28	11 19	12 10	13 03
30	03 53	04 26	04 54	10 20	11 15	12 12	13 11
35	03 34	04 11	04 41	10 15	11 13	12 13	13 15
40	03 11	03 53	04 26	10 09	11 11	12 14	13 20
45	02 41	03 30	04 08	10 03	11 09	12 16	13 26
S 50	01 56	03 01	03 45	09 55	11 06	12 18	13 33
52	01 28	02 46	03 34	09 51	11 04	12 19	13 36
54	00 44	02 28	03 22	09 47	11 03	12 20	13 40
56	////	02 06	03 08	09 43	11 01	12 21	13 44
58	////	01 37	02 51	09 38	10 59	12 22	13 49
S 60	////	00 48	02 31	09 32	10 57	12 23	13 54

Lat.	Sunset	Twilight Civil	Twilight Naut.	Moonset 15	16	17	18
°	h m	h m	h m	h m	h m	h m	h m
N 72	▬	13 02	15 30	21 30	23 33	25 38	01 38
N 70	▬	14 02	15 50	21 41	23 34	25 30	01 30
68	▬	14 37	16 05	21 50	23 35	25 23	01 23
66	13 22	15 02	16 18	21 57	23 36	25 18	01 18
64	14 04	15 21	16 29	22 03	23 37	25 13	01 13
62	14 32	15 37	16 39	22 08	23 37	25 09	01 09
60	14 53	15 51	16 47	22 13	23 38	25 06	01 06
N 58	15 10	16 02	16 55	22 17	23 38	25 03	01 03
56	15 25	16 12	17 01	22 20	23 39	25 00	01 00
54	15 38	16 21	17 08	22 23	23 39	24 58	00 58
52	15 49	16 30	17 13	22 26	23 40	24 55	00 55
50	15 58	16 37	17 18	22 29	23 40	24 53	00 53
45	16 19	16 53	17 30	22 34	23 41	24 49	00 49
N 40	16 36	17 06	17 40	22 39	23 41	24 45	00 45
35	16 50	17 18	17 50	22 43	23 42	24 42	00 42
30	17 02	17 29	17 59	22 46	23 42	24 40	00 40
20	17 23	17 48	18 15	22 52	23 43	24 35	00 35
N 10	17 42	18 05	18 31	22 58	23 44	24 31	00 31
0	17 59	18 22	18 48	23 03	23 44	24 27	00 27
S 10	18 17	18 40	19 07	23 07	23 45	24 23	00 23
20	18 36	19 00	19 30	23 13	23 45	24 19	00 19
30	18 58	19 25	19 59	23 18	23 46	24 14	00 14
35	19 11	19 40	20 17	23 22	23 46	24 12	00 12
40	19 26	19 59	20 40	23 25	23 47	24 08	00 08
45	19 44	20 21	21 11	23 30	23 47	24 05	00 05
S 50	20 06	20 51	21 56	23 35	23 48	24 01	00 01
52	20 17	21 06	22 24	23 37	23 48	23 59	24 12
54	20 29	21 24	23 09	23 39	23 48	23 57	24 07
56	20 43	21 46	////	23 42	23 48	23 55	24 02
58	21 00	22 15	////	23 45	23 49	23 52	23 56
S 60	21 20	23 05	////	23 49	23 49	23 49	23 50

Day	SUN Eqn. of Time 00^h	SUN Eqn. of Time 12^h	SUN Mer. Pass.	MOON Mer. Pass. Upper	MOON Mer. Pass. Lower	Age	Phase
d	m s	m s	h m	h m	h m	d %	
15	05 07	04 53	11 55	16 53	04 32	06 33	◐
16	04 38	04 24	11 56	17 34	05 13	07 43	
17	04 09	03 54	11 56	18 17	05 55	08 53	

2026 DECEMBER 18, 19, 20 (FRI., SAT., SUN.)

UT d	UT h	ARIES GHA	VENUS −4·7 GHA	VENUS Dec	MARS +0·1 GHA	MARS Dec	JUPITER −2·3 GHA	JUPITER Dec	SATURN +0·6 GHA	SATURN Dec
		° ′	° ′	° ′	° ′	° ′	° ′	° ′	° ′	° ′
18	00	86 37.5	227 42.4	S12 05.2	286 34.9	N11 26.8	297 07.3	N13 20.2	78 18.5	N 0 51.1
	01	101 40.0	242 42.7	05.8	301 36.7	26.6	312 09.8	20.2	93 20.9	51.1
	02	116 42.5	257 43.0	06.3	316 38.6	26.4	327 12.3	20.3	108 23.3	51.2
	03	131 44.9	272 43.3	. . 06.9	331 40.4	. . 26.3	342 14.8	. . 20.3	123 25.8	. . 51.2
	04	146 47.4	287 43.7	07.4	346 42.2	26.1	357 17.3	20.3	138 28.2	51.2
	05	161 49.9	302 44.0	08.0	1 44.1	26.0	12 19.8	20.3	153 30.7	51.2
	06	176 52.3	317 44.3	S12 08.5	16 45.9	N11 25.8	27 22.3	N13 20.4	168 33.1	N 0 51.3
	07	191 54.8	332 44.6	09.0	31 47.8	25.7	42 24.8	20.4	183 35.5	51.3
	08	206 57.2	347 44.9	09.6	46 49.6	25.5	57 27.3	20.4	198 38.0	51.3
F	09	221 59.7	2 45.3	. . 10.1	61 51.5	. . 25.3	72 29.8	. . 20.4	213 40.4	. . 51.3
R	10	237 02.2	17 45.6	10.7	76 53.3	25.2	87 32.3	20.5	228 42.9	51.3
I	11	252 04.6	32 45.9	11.2	91 55.2	25.0	102 34.8	20.5	243 45.3	51.4
D	12	267 07.1	47 46.2	S12 11.8	106 57.0	N11 24.9	117 37.3	N13 20.5	258 47.7	N 0 51.4
A	13	282 09.6	62 46.5	12.3	121 58.9	24.7	132 39.8	20.5	273 50.2	51.4
Y	14	297 12.0	77 46.8	12.9	137 00.8	24.6	147 42.3	20.6	288 52.6	51.4
	15	312 14.5	92 47.1	. . 13.4	152 02.6	. . 24.4	162 44.8	. . 20.6	303 55.0	. . 51.5
	16	327 17.0	107 47.5	14.0	167 04.5	24.2	177 47.4	20.6	318 57.5	51.5
	17	342 19.4	122 47.8	14.5	182 06.3	24.1	192 49.9	20.6	333 59.9	51.5
	18	357 21.9	137 48.1	S12 15.1	197 08.2	N11 23.9	207 52.4	N13 20.7	349 02.3	N 0 51.5
	19	12 24.3	152 48.4	15.6	212 10.0	23.8	222 54.9	20.7	4 04.8	51.6
	20	27 26.8	167 48.7	16.2	227 11.9	23.6	237 57.4	20.7	19 07.2	51.6
	21	42 29.3	182 49.0	. . 16.7	242 13.8	. . 23.5	252 59.9	. . 20.7	34 09.6	. . 51.6
	22	57 31.7	197 49.3	17.3	257 15.6	23.3	268 02.4	20.8	49 12.1	51.6
	23	72 34.2	212 49.6	17.8	272 17.5	23.2	283 04.9	20.8	64 14.5	51.7
19	00	87 36.7	227 49.9	S12 18.4	287 19.3	N11 23.0	298 07.4	N13 20.8	79 17.0	N 0 51.7
	01	102 39.1	242 50.2	18.9	302 21.2	22.9	313 09.9	20.8	94 19.4	51.7
	02	117 41.6	257 50.5	19.5	317 23.1	22.7	328 12.4	20.9	109 21.8	51.7
	03	132 44.1	272 50.8	. . 20.0	332 24.9	. . 22.6	343 14.9	. . 20.9	124 24.3	. . 51.8
	04	147 46.5	287 51.1	20.6	347 26.8	22.4	358 17.4	20.9	139 26.7	51.8
	05	162 49.0	302 51.4	21.1	2 28.7	22.3	13 19.9	20.9	154 29.1	51.8
	06	177 51.5	317 51.7	S12 21.7	17 30.5	N11 22.1	28 22.5	N13 21.0	169 31.6	N 0 51.8
S	07	192 53.9	332 51.9	22.2	32 32.4	22.0	43 25.0	21.0	184 34.0	51.9
	08	207 56.4	347 52.2	22.8	47 34.3	21.8	58 27.5	21.0	199 36.4	51.9
A	09	222 58.8	2 52.5	. . 23.4	62 36.2	. . 21.7	73 30.0	. . 21.1	214 38.9	. . 51.9
T	10	238 01.3	17 52.8	23.9	77 38.0	21.5	88 32.5	21.1	229 41.3	51.9
U	11	253 03.8	32 53.1	24.5	92 39.9	21.4	103 35.0	21.1	244 43.7	52.0
R	12	268 06.2	47 53.4	S12 25.0	107 41.8	N11 21.2	118 37.5	N13 21.1	259 46.2	N 0 52.0
D	13	283 08.7	62 53.7	25.6	122 43.6	21.1	133 40.0	21.2	274 48.6	52.0
A	14	298 11.2	77 53.9	26.1	137 45.5	20.9	148 42.5	21.2	289 51.0	52.0
Y	15	313 13.6	92 54.2	. . 26.7	152 47.4	. . 20.8	163 45.1	. . 21.2	304 53.5	. . 52.1
	16	328 16.1	107 54.5	27.3	167 49.3	20.6	178 47.6	21.2	319 55.9	52.1
	17	343 18.6	122 54.8	27.8	182 51.2	20.5	193 50.1	21.3	334 58.3	52.1
	18	358 21.0	137 55.1	S12 28.4	197 53.0	N11 20.3	208 52.6	N13 21.3	350 00.7	N 0 52.1
	19	13 23.5	152 55.3	28.9	212 54.9	20.2	223 55.1	21.3	5 03.2	52.2
	20	28 26.0	167 55.6	29.5	227 56.8	20.0	238 57.6	21.4	20 05.6	52.2
	21	43 28.4	182 55.9	. . 30.0	242 58.7	. . 19.9	254 00.1	. . 21.4	35 08.0	. . 52.2
	22	58 30.9	197 56.2	30.6	258 00.6	19.7	269 02.6	21.4	50 10.5	52.2
	23	73 33.3	212 56.4	31.2	273 02.4	19.6	284 05.2	21.5	65 12.9	52.3
20	00	88 35.8	227 56.7	S12 31.7	288 04.3	N11 19.5	299 07.7	N13 21.5	80 15.3	N 0 52.3
	01	103 38.3	242 57.0	32.3	303 06.2	19.3	314 10.2	21.5	95 17.8	52.3
	02	118 40.7	257 57.2	32.9	318 08.1	19.2	329 12.7	21.5	110 20.2	52.3
	03	133 43.2	272 57.5	. . 33.4	333 10.0	. . 19.0	344 15.2	. . 21.6	125 22.6	. . 52.4
	04	148 45.7	287 57.8	34.0	348 11.9	18.9	359 17.7	21.6	140 25.1	52.4
	05	163 48.1	302 58.0	34.5	3 13.7	18.7	14 20.3	21.6	155 27.5	52.4
	06	178 50.6	317 58.3	S12 35.1	18 15.6	N11 18.6	29 22.8	N13 21.7	170 29.9	N 0 52.4
	07	193 53.1	332 58.5	35.7	33 17.5	18.5	44 25.3	21.7	185 32.3	52.5
	08	208 55.5	347 58.8	36.2	48 19.4	18.3	59 27.8	21.7	200 34.8	52.5
S	09	223 58.0	2 59.1	. . 36.8	63 21.3	. . 18.2	74 30.3	. . 21.7	215 37.2	. . 52.5
U	10	239 00.4	17 59.3	37.4	78 23.2	18.0	89 32.9	21.8	230 39.6	52.5
N	11	254 02.9	32 59.6	37.9	93 25.1	17.9	104 35.4	21.8	245 42.1	52.6
D	12	269 05.4	47 59.8	S12 38.5	108 27.0	N11 17.7	119 37.9	N13 21.8	260 44.5	N 0 52.6
A	13	284 07.8	63 00.1	39.1	123 28.9	17.6	134 40.4	21.9	275 46.9	52.6
Y	14	299 10.3	78 00.3	39.6	138 30.8	17.5	149 42.9	21.9	290 49.3	52.7
	15	314 12.8	93 00.6	. . 40.2	153 32.7	. . 17.3	164 45.4	. . 21.9	305 51.8	. . 52.7
	16	329 15.2	108 00.8	40.8	168 34.6	17.2	179 48.0	22.0	320 54.2	52.7
	17	344 17.7	123 01.1	41.3	183 36.5	17.1	194 50.5	22.0	335 56.6	52.7
	18	359 20.2	138 01.3	S12 41.9	198 38.4	N11 16.9	209 53.0	N13 22.0	350 59.1	N 0 52.8
	19	14 22.6	153 01.6	42.5	213 40.3	16.8	224 55.5	22.1	6 01.5	52.8
	20	29 25.1	168 01.8	43.0	228 42.2	16.6	239 58.1	22.1	21 03.9	52.8
	21	44 27.6	183 02.1	. . 43.6	243 44.1	. . 16.5	255 00.6	. . 22.1	36 06.3	. . 52.8
	22	59 30.0	198 02.3	44.2	258 46.0	16.4	270 03.1	22.2	51 08.8	52.9
	23	74 32.5	213 02.5	44.7	273 47.9	16.2	285 05.6	22.2	66 11.2	52.9
Mer. Pass.		h m 18 06.6	*v* 0.3	*d* 0.6	*v* 1.9	*d* 0.1	*v* 2.5	*d* 0.0	*v* 2.4	*d* 0.0

STARS

Name	SHA	Dec
	° ′	° ′
Acamar	315 10.2	S40 11.9
Achernar	335 18.7	S57 06.2
Acrux	172 58.3	S63 14.7
Adhara	255 04.2	S29 00.5
Aldebaran	290 37.4	N16 33.8
Alioth	166 11.8	N55 48.5
Alkaid	152 51.0	N49 10.4
Alnair	27 31.1	S46 50.0
Alnilam	275 35.8	S 1 11.1
Alphard	217 46.0	S 8 46.5
Alphecca	126 02.7	N26 37.3
Alpheratz	357 33.1	N29 14.6
Altair	61 58.7	N 8 56.4
Ankaa	353 05.5	S42 09.7
Antares	112 14.2	S26 29.4
Arcturus	145 46.7	N19 02.4
Atria	107 07.6	S69 04.4
Avior	234 13.5	S59 35.6
Bellatrix	278 20.8	N 6 22.4
Betelgeuse	270 50.0	N 7 24.7
Canopus	263 51.1	S52 42.5
Capella	280 19.0	N46 01.5
Deneb	49 25.1	N45 22.8
Denebola	182 23.3	N14 25.1
Diphda	348 45.6	S17 50.4
Dubhe	193 39.0	N61 36.0
Elnath	277 59.5	N28 37.8
Eltanin	90 42.0	N51 29.1
Enif	33 37.4	N10 00.0
Fomalhaut	15 12.9	S29 28.9
Gacrux	171 49.9	S57 15.6
Gienah	175 42.0	S17 41.5
Hadar	148 34.1	S60 30.0
Hamal	327 49.2	N23 35.6
Kaus Aust.	83 30.8	S34 22.3
Kochab	137 20.8	N74 02.4
Markab	13 28.4	N15 21.2
Menkar	314 04.2	N 4 11.8
Menkent	147 56.0	S36 30.0
Miaplacidus	221 37.3	S69 49.4
Mirfak	308 25.5	N49 57.6
Nunki	75 46.1	S26 15.8
Peacock	53 03.7	S56 39.0
Pollux	243 15.0	N27 57.5
Procyon	244 48.9	N 5 09.3
Rasalhague	95 57.4	N12 32.4
Regulus	207 32.6	N11 50.0
Rigel	281 02.0	S 8 10.2
Rigil Kent.	139 38.5	S60 56.6
Sabik	102 01.3	S15 45.5
Schedar	349 29.0	N56 41.5
Shaula	96 08.6	S37 07.3
Sirius	258 24.5	S16 45.2
Spica	158 20.8	S11 18.1
Suhail	222 44.8	S43 32.3
Vega	80 32.6	N38 48.6
Zuben'ubi	136 54.5	S16 09.2

	SHA	Mer. Pass.
	° ′	h m
Venus	140 13.2	8 48
Mars	199 42.7	4 50
Jupiter	210 30.7	4 07
Saturn	351 40.3	18 40

UT		SUN GHA	SUN Dec	MOON GHA	v	MOON Dec	d	HP
d h		° ′	° ′	° ′	′	° ′	′	′
18 00		180 54.8	S23 22.7	83 21.2	14.4	N 5 12.9	14.8	56.9
01		195 54.5	22.8	97 54.6	14.3	5 27.7	14.9	56.9
02		210 54.2	22.9	112 27.9	14.3	5 42.6	14.8	57.0
03		225 53.9	. . 23.0	127 01.2	14.2	5 57.4	14.9	57.0
04		240 53.5	23.0	141 34.4	14.1	6 12.3	14.8	57.0
05		255 53.2	23.1	156 07.5	14.1	6 27.1	14.9	57.1
06		270 52.9	S23 23.2	170 40.6	13.9	N 6 42.0	14.8	57.1
07		285 52.6	23.2	185 13.5	14.0	6 56.8	14.8	57.1
08		300 52.3	23.3	199 46.5	13.8	7 11.6	14.8	57.2
09	F	315 52.0	. . 23.4	214 19.3	13.8	7 26.4	14.8	57.2
10	R	330 51.7	23.5	228 52.1	13.7	7 41.2	14.8	57.3
11	I	345 51.4	23.5	243 24.8	13.6	7 56.0	14.7	57.3
12	D	0 51.1	S23 23.6	257 57.4	13.5	N 8 10.7	14.8	57.3
13	A	15 50.8	23.6	272 29.9	13.4	8 25.5	14.7	57.4
14	Y	30 50.5	23.7	287 02.3	13.4	8 40.2	14.7	57.4
15		45 50.2	. . 23.8	301 34.7	13.3	8 54.9	14.7	57.5
16		60 49.9	23.8	316 07.0	13.2	9 09.6	14.7	57.5
17		75 49.6	23.9	330 39.2	13.1	9 24.3	14.6	57.5
18		90 49.2	S23 24.0	345 11.3	13.1	N 9 38.9	14.7	57.6
19		105 48.9	24.0	359 43.4	12.9	9 53.6	14.6	57.6
20		120 48.6	24.1	14 15.3	12.8	10 08.2	14.5	57.7
21		135 48.3	. . 24.1	28 47.1	12.8	10 22.7	14.6	57.7
22		150 48.0	24.2	43 18.9	12.7	10 37.3	14.5	57.7
23		165 47.7	24.3	57 50.6	12.5	10 51.8	14.5	57.8
19 00		180 47.4	S23 24.3	72 22.1	12.5	N11 06.3	14.4	57.8
01		195 47.1	24.4	86 53.6	12.4	11 20.7	14.4	57.9
02		210 46.8	24.4	101 25.0	12.3	11 35.1	14.4	57.9
03		225 46.5	. . 24.5	115 56.3	12.1	11 49.5	14.4	57.9
04		240 46.2	24.5	130 27.4	12.1	12 03.9	14.3	58.0
05		255 45.9	24.6	144 58.5	12.0	12 18.2	14.3	58.0
06		270 45.6	S23 24.6	159 29.5	11.8	N12 32.5	14.2	58.1
07		285 45.2	24.7	174 00.3	11.8	12 46.7	14.2	58.1
08	S	300 44.9	24.7	188 31.1	11.7	13 00.9	14.1	58.1
09	A	315 44.6	. . 24.8	203 01.8	11.5	13 15.0	14.1	58.2
10	T	330 44.3	24.8	217 32.3	11.4	13 29.1	14.1	58.2
11	U	345 44.0	24.9	232 02.7	11.4	13 43.2	14.0	58.3
12	R	0 43.7	S23 24.9	246 33.1	11.2	N13 57.2	14.0	58.3
13	D	15 43.4	25.0	261 03.3	11.1	14 11.2	13.9	58.3
14	A	30 43.1	25.0	275 33.4	10.9	14 25.1	13.8	58.4
15	Y	45 42.8	. . 25.1	290 03.3	10.9	14 38.9	13.8	58.4
16		60 42.5	25.1	304 33.2	10.8	14 52.7	13.8	58.5
17		75 42.2	25.2	319 03.0	10.6	15 06.5	13.6	58.5
18		90 41.9	S23 25.2	333 32.6	10.5	N15 20.1	13.7	58.5
19		105 41.5	25.2	348 02.1	10.4	15 33.8	13.5	58.6
20		120 41.2	25.3	2 31.5	10.2	15 47.3	13.5	58.6
21		135 40.9	. . 25.3	17 00.7	10.2	16 00.8	13.4	58.7
22		150 40.6	25.4	31 29.9	10.0	16 14.2	13.4	58.7
23		165 40.3	25.4	45 58.9	9.9	16 27.6	13.3	58.8
20 00		180 40.0	S23 25.4	60 27.8	9.8	N16 40.9	13.2	58.8
01		195 39.7	25.5	74 56.6	9.6	16 54.1	13.2	58.8
02		210 39.4	25.5	89 25.2	9.5	17 07.3	13.0	58.9
03		225 39.1	. . 25.5	103 53.7	9.4	17 20.3	13.0	58.9
04		240 38.8	25.6	118 22.1	9.2	17 33.3	12.9	59.0
05		255 38.5	25.6	132 50.3	9.1	17 46.2	12.9	59.0
06		270 38.2	S23 25.6	147 18.4	9.0	N17 59.1	12.7	59.0
07		285 37.8	25.7	161 46.4	8.9	18 11.8	12.7	59.1
08		300 37.5	25.7	176 14.3	8.7	18 24.5	12.6	59.1
09	S	315 37.2	. . 25.7	190 42.0	8.5	18 37.1	12.5	59.2
10	U	330 36.9	25.8	205 09.5	8.5	18 49.6	12.4	59.2
11	N	345 36.6	25.8	219 37.0	8.3	19 02.0	12.3	59.2
12	D	0 36.3	S23 25.8	234 04.3	8.1	N19 14.3	12.2	59.3
13	A	15 36.0	25.8	248 31.4	8.1	19 26.5	12.1	59.3
14	Y	30 35.7	25.9	262 58.5	7.9	19 38.6	12.0	59.4
15		45 35.4	. . 25.9	277 25.4	7.7	19 50.6	11.9	59.4
16		60 35.1	25.9	291 52.1	7.6	20 02.5	11.8	59.4
17		75 34.8	25.9	306 18.7	7.5	20 14.3	11.7	59.5
18		90 34.4	S23 26.0	320 45.2	7.3	N20 26.0	11.6	59.5
19		105 34.1	26.0	335 11.5	7.2	20 37.6	11.5	59.6
20		120 33.8	26.0	349 37.7	7.0	20 49.1	11.4	59.6
21		135 33.5	. . 26.0	4 03.7	6.9	21 00.5	11.3	59.6
22		150 33.2	26.0	18 29.6	6.8	21 11.8	11.1	59.7
23		165 32.9	26.1	32 55.4	6.6	N21 22.9	11.0	59.7
		SD 16.3	d 0.0	SD 15.6		15.9		16.2

Lat.	Twilight Naut.	Twilight Civil	Sunrise	Moonrise 18	19	20	21
°	h m	h m	h m	h m	h m	h m	h m
N 72	08 24	10 56	■	11 06	10 21	▭	▭
N 70	08 04	09 53	■	11 18	10 46	09 47	▭
68	07 48	09 18	■	11 27	11 05	10 31	▭
66	07 35	08 52	10 33	11 34	11 20	11 01	10 19
64	07 24	08 33	09 51	11 41	11 33	11 23	11 09
62	07 14	08 16	09 22	11 47	11 44	11 41	11 40
60	07 06	08 03	09 01	11 52	11 53	11 57	12 04
N 58	06 59	07 51	08 43	11 56	12 01	12 09	12 24
56	06 52	07 41	08 28	12 00	12 09	12 21	12 40
54	06 46	07 32	08 16	12 03	12 15	12 31	12 54
52	06 40	07 24	08 05	12 07	12 21	12 39	13 06
50	06 35	07 16	07 55	12 10	12 26	12 47	13 16
45	06 23	07 00	07 34	12 16	12 38	13 04	13 39
N 40	06 12	06 47	07 17	12 22	12 47	13 18	13 57
35	06 03	06 35	07 03	12 26	12 56	13 30	14 13
30	05 54	06 24	06 51	12 30	13 03	13 41	14 26
20	05 38	06 05	06 29	12 38	13 16	13 59	14 49
N 10	05 22	05 48	06 11	12 44	13 27	14 15	15 09
0	05 05	05 31	05 53	12 50	13 38	14 30	15 28
S 10	04 46	05 13	05 36	12 56	13 48	14 45	15 47
20	04 23	04 52	05 17	13 03	14 00	15 01	16 07
30	03 54	04 27	04 55	13 11	14 13	15 20	16 31
35	03 35	04 12	04 42	13 15	14 21	15 31	16 45
40	03 12	03 54	04 27	13 20	14 30	15 44	17 01
45	02 41	03 31	04 09	13 26	14 40	15 59	17 21
S 50	01 56	03 01	03 46	13 33	14 53	16 18	17 45
52	01 28	02 46	03 35	13 36	14 59	16 27	17 57
54	00 41	02 28	03 23	13 40	15 06	16 37	18 11
56	////	02 06	03 09	13 44	15 13	16 48	18 27
58	////	01 36	02 52	13 49	15 21	17 01	18 46
S 60	////	00 46	02 31	13 54	15 31	17 16	19 09

Lat.	Sunset	Twilight Civil	Twilight Naut.	Moonset 18	19	20	21
°	h m	h m	h m	h m	h m	h m	h m
N 72	■	12 59	15 30	01 38	04 00	▭	▭
N 70	■	14 01	15 50	01 30	03 38	06 22	▭
68	■	14 36	16 06	01 23	03 21	05 40	▭
66	13 21	15 02	16 19	01 18	03 07	05 12	07 51
64	14 03	15 21	16 30	01 13	02 56	04 50	07 02
62	14 32	15 38	16 40	01 09	02 47	04 33	06 31
60	14 53	15 51	16 48	01 06	02 39	04 19	06 08
N 58	15 11	16 03	16 56	01 03	02 32	04 07	05 49
56	15 26	16 13	17 02	01 00	02 26	03 57	05 34
54	15 38	16 22	17 09	00 58	02 20	03 48	05 21
52	15 50	16 30	17 14	00 55	02 15	03 40	05 09
50	15 59	16 38	17 19	00 53	02 11	03 33	04 59
45	16 20	16 54	17 31	00 49	02 01	03 17	04 38
N 40	16 37	17 08	17 42	00 45	01 53	03 05	04 20
35	16 51	17 19	17 51	00 42	01 46	02 54	04 06
30	17 04	17 30	18 00	00 40	01 40	02 45	03 53
20	17 25	17 49	18 16	00 35	01 30	02 29	03 32
N 10	17 43	18 06	18 33	00 31	01 21	02 15	03 14
0	18 01	18 23	18 50	00 27	01 12	02 02	02 57
S 10	18 18	18 42	19 09	00 23	01 04	01 49	02 40
20	18 37	19 02	19 31	00 19	00 55	01 35	02 21
30	18 59	19 27	20 00	00 14	00 45	01 20	02 01
35	19 13	19 42	20 19	00 12	00 39	01 11	01 49
40	19 28	20 00	20 42	00 08	00 32	01 00	01 35
45	19 46	20 23	21 13	00 05	00 25	00 48	01 18
S 50	20 08	20 53	21 59	00 01	00 16	00 34	00 58
52	20 19	21 08	22 26	24 12	00 12	00 27	00 49
54	20 31	21 26	23 13	24 07	00 07	00 20	00 38
56	20 46	21 48	////	24 02	00 02	00 12	00 26
58	21 03	22 18	////	23 56	24 02	00 02	00 12
S 60	21 23	23 09	////	23 50	23 52	23 56	24 06

Day	SUN Eqn. of Time 00^h	12^h	Mer. Pass.	MOON Mer. Pass. Upper	Lower	Age	Phase
d	m s	m s	h m	h m	h m	d %	
18	03 40	03 25	11 57	19 01	06 38	09 63	
19	03 10	02 55	11 57	19 50	07 25	10 73	◐
20	02 41	02 26	11 58	20 43	08 16	11 82	

2026 DECEMBER 21, 22, 23 (MON., TUES., WED.)

UT d h	ARIES GHA ° ′	VENUS −4·7 GHA ° ′	VENUS Dec ° ′	MARS +0·1 GHA ° ′	MARS Dec ° ′	JUPITER −2·3 GHA ° ′	JUPITER Dec ° ′	SATURN +0·6 GHA ° ′	SATURN Dec ° ′
21 00	89 34.9	228 02.8	S12 45.3	288 49.8	N11 16.1	300 08.1	N13 22.2	81 13.6	N 0 52.9
01	104 37.4	243 03.0	45.9	303 51.7	16.0	315 10.7	22.2	96 16.0	53.0
02	119 39.9	258 03.3	46.4	318 53.6	15.8	330 13.2	22.3	111 18.5	53.0
03	134 42.3	273 03.5	. . 47.0	333 55.5	. . 15.7	345 15.7	. . 22.3	126 20.9	. . 53.0
04	149 44.8	288 03.7	47.6	348 57.4	15.6	0 18.2	22.3	141 23.3	53.0
05	164 47.3	303 04.0	48.2	3 59.3	15.4	15 20.8	22.4	156 25.7	53.1
06	179 49.7	318 04.2	S12 48.7	19 01.2	N11 15.3	30 23.3	N13 22.4	171 28.2	N 0 53.1
07	194 52.2	333 04.4	49.3	34 03.1	15.2	45 25.8	22.4	186 30.6	53.1
08	209 54.7	348 04.7	49.9	49 05.0	15.0	60 28.3	22.5	201 33.0	53.2
M 09	224 57.1	3 04.9	. . 50.4	64 07.0	. . 14.9	75 30.9	. . 22.5	216 35.4	. . 53.2
O 10	239 59.6	18 05.1	51.0	79 08.9	14.8	90 33.4	22.5	231 37.9	53.2
N 11	255 02.1	33 05.3	51.6	94 10.8	14.6	105 35.9	22.6	246 40.3	53.2
D 12	270 04.5	48 05.6	S12 52.2	109 12.7	N11 14.5	120 38.4	N13 22.6	261 42.7	N 0 53.3
A 13	285 07.0	63 05.8	52.7	124 14.6	14.4	135 41.0	22.6	276 45.1	53.3
Y 14	300 09.4	78 06.0	53.3	139 16.5	14.2	150 43.5	22.7	291 47.6	53.3
15	315 11.9	93 06.2	. . 53.9	154 18.5	. . 14.1	165 46.0	. . 22.7	306 50.0	. . 53.4
16	330 14.4	108 06.5	54.5	169 20.4	14.0	180 48.6	22.7	321 52.4	53.4
17	345 16.8	123 06.7	55.0	184 22.3	13.8	195 51.1	22.8	336 54.8	53.4
18	0 19.3	138 06.9	S12 55.6	199 24.2	N11 13.7	210 53.6	N13 22.8	351 57.3	N 0 53.4
19	15 21.8	153 07.1	56.2	214 26.1	13.6	225 56.1	22.8	6 59.7	53.5
20	30 24.2	168 07.3	56.8	229 28.1	13.5	240 58.7	22.9	22 02.1	53.5
21	45 26.7	183 07.5	. . 57.3	244 30.0	. . 13.3	256 01.2	. . 22.9	37 04.5	. . 53.5
22	60 29.2	198 07.8	57.9	259 31.9	13.2	271 03.7	22.9	52 07.0	53.6
23	75 31.6	213 08.0	58.5	274 33.8	13.1	286 06.3	23.0	67 09.4	53.6
22 00	90 34.1	228 08.2	S12 59.1	289 35.8	N11 12.9	301 08.8	N13 23.0	82 11.8	N 0 53.6
01	105 36.6	243 08.4	12 59.6	304 37.7	12.8	316 11.3	23.0	97 14.2	53.6
02	120 39.0	258 08.6	13 00.2	319 39.6	12.7	331 13.9	23.1	112 16.6	53.7
03	135 41.5	273 08.8	. . 00.8	334 41.5	. . 12.6	346 16.4	. . 23.1	127 19.1	. . 53.7
04	150 43.9	288 09.0	01.4	349 43.5	12.4	1 18.9	23.2	142 21.5	53.7
05	165 46.4	303 09.2	02.0	4 45.4	12.3	16 21.5	23.2	157 23.9	53.8
06	180 48.9	318 09.4	S13 02.5	19 47.3	N11 12.2	31 24.0	N13 23.2	172 26.3	N 0 53.8
07	195 51.3	333 09.6	03.1	34 49.3	12.1	46 26.5	23.3	187 28.8	53.8
T 08	210 53.8	348 09.8	03.7	49 51.2	11.9	61 29.1	23.3	202 31.2	53.9
U 09	225 56.3	3 10.0	. . 04.3	64 53.1	. . 11.8	76 31.6	. . 23.3	217 33.6	. . 53.9
E 10	240 58.7	18 10.2	04.9	79 55.1	11.7	91 34.1	23.4	232 36.0	53.9
S 11	256 01.2	33 10.4	05.4	94 57.0	11.6	106 36.7	23.4	247 38.4	54.0
D 12	271 03.7	48 10.6	S13 06.0	109 58.9	N11 11.4	121 39.2	N13 23.4	262 40.9	N 0 54.0
A 13	286 06.1	63 10.8	06.6	125 00.9	11.3	136 41.7	23.5	277 43.3	54.0
Y 14	301 08.6	78 11.0	07.2	140 02.8	11.2	151 44.3	23.5	292 45.7	54.0
15	316 11.1	93 11.2	. . 07.8	155 04.7	. . 11.1	166 46.8	. . 23.5	307 48.1	. . 54.1
16	331 13.5	108 11.4	08.3	170 06.7	11.0	181 49.3	23.6	322 50.5	54.1
17	346 16.0	123 11.6	08.9	185 08.6	10.8	196 51.9	23.6	337 53.0	54.1
18	1 18.4	138 11.8	S13 09.5	200 10.6	N11 10.7	211 54.4	N13 23.7	352 55.4	N 0 54.2
19	16 20.9	153 12.0	10.1	215 12.5	10.6	226 56.9	23.7	7 57.8	54.2
20	31 23.4	168 12.2	10.7	230 14.4	10.5	241 59.5	23.7	23 00.2	54.2
21	46 25.8	183 12.3	. . 11.2	245 16.4	. . 10.4	257 02.0	. . 23.8	38 02.6	. . 54.3
22	61 28.3	198 12.5	11.8	260 18.3	10.2	272 04.6	23.8	53 05.0	54.3
23	76 30.8	213 12.7	12.4	275 20.3	10.1	287 07.1	23.8	68 07.5	54.3
23 00	91 33.2	228 12.9	S13 13.0	290 22.2	N11 10.0	302 09.6	N13 23.9	83 09.9	N 0 54.4
01	106 35.7	243 13.1	13.6	305 24.2	09.9	317 12.2	23.9	98 12.3	54.4
02	121 38.2	258 13.3	14.2	320 26.1	09.8	332 14.7	24.0	113 14.7	54.4
03	136 40.6	273 13.4	. . 14.7	335 28.1	. . 09.6	347 17.3	. . 24.0	128 17.1	. . 54.4
04	151 43.1	288 13.6	15.3	350 30.0	09.5	2 19.8	24.0	143 19.6	54.5
05	166 45.6	303 13.8	15.9	5 32.0	09.4	17 22.3	24.1	158 22.0	54.5
06	181 48.0	318 14.0	S13 16.5	20 33.9	N11 09.3	32 24.9	N13 24.1	173 24.4	N 0 54.5
W 07	196 50.5	333 14.1	17.1	35 35.9	09.2	47 27.4	24.1	188 26.8	54.6
E 08	211 52.9	348 14.3	17.7	50 37.8	09.1	62 30.0	24.2	203 29.2	54.6
D 09	226 55.4	3 14.5	. . 18.3	65 39.8	. . 08.9	77 32.5	. . 24.2	218 31.6	. . 54.6
N 10	241 57.9	18 14.7	18.8	80 41.7	08.8	92 35.0	24.3	233 34.1	54.7
E 11	257 00.3	33 14.8	19.4	95 43.7	08.7	107 37.6	24.3	248 36.5	54.7
S 12	272 02.8	48 15.0	S13 20.0	110 45.7	N11 08.6	122 40.1	N13 24.3	263 38.9	N 0 54.7
D 13	287 05.3	63 15.2	20.6	125 47.6	08.5	137 42.7	24.4	278 41.3	54.8
A 14	302 07.7	78 15.3	21.2	140 49.6	08.4	152 45.2	24.4	293 43.7	54.8
Y 15	317 10.2	93 15.5	. . 21.8	155 51.5	. . 08.3	167 47.8	. . 24.5	308 46.1	. . 54.8
16	332 12.7	108 15.7	22.4	170 53.5	08.2	182 50.3	24.5	323 48.5	54.9
17	347 15.1	123 15.8	22.9	185 55.5	08.0	197 52.8	24.5	338 51.0	54.9
18	2 17.6	138 16.0	S13 23.5	200 57.4	N11 07.9	212 55.4	N13 24.6	353 53.4	N 0 54.9
19	17 20.1	153 16.2	24.1	215 59.4	07.8	227 57.9	24.6	8 55.8	55.0
20	32 22.5	168 16.3	24.7	231 01.4	07.7	243 00.5	24.6	23 58.2	55.0
21	47 25.0	183 16.5	. . 25.3	246 03.3	. . 07.6	258 03.0	. . 24.7	39 00.6	. . 55.0
22	62 27.4	198 16.6	25.9	261 05.3	07.5	273 05.6	24.7	54 03.0	55.1
23	77 29.9	213 16.8	26.5	276 07.3	07.4	288 08.1	24.8	69 05.5	55.1
Mer. Pass. h m	17 54.8	*v* 0.2	*d* 0.6	*v* 1.9	*d* 0.1	*v* 2.5	*d* 0.0	*v* 2.4	*d* 0.0

STARS

Name	SHA ° ′	Dec ° ′
Acamar	315 10.2	S40 11.9
Achernar	335 18.8	S57 06.2
Acrux	172 58.3	S63 14.7
Adhara	255 04.2	S29 00.5
Aldebaran	290 37.4	N16 33.8
Alioth	166 11.7	N55 48.5
Alkaid	152 51.0	N49 10.4
Alnair	27 31.2	S46 50.0
Alnilam	275 35.8	S 1 11.1
Alphard	217 46.0	S 8 46.6
Alphecca	126 02.7	N26 37.3
Alpheratz	357 33.1	N29 14.6
Altair	61 58.7	N 8 56.4
Ankaa	353 05.5	S42 09.7
Antares	112 14.2	S26 29.4
Arcturus	145 46.6	N19 02.4
Atria	107 07.5	S69 04.4
Avior	234 13.5	S59 35.6
Bellatrix	278 20.8	N 6 22.4
Betelgeuse	270 50.0	N 7 24.7
Canopus	263 51.1	S52 42.6
Capella	280 19.0	N46 01.5
Deneb	49 25.1	N45 22.8
Denebola	182 23.3	N14 25.1
Diphda	348 45.6	S17 50.4
Dubhe	193 38.9	N61 36.0
Elnath	277 59.4	N28 37.8
Eltanin	90 42.0	N51 29.1
Enif	33 37.4	N10 00.0
Fomalhaut	15 12.9	S29 28.9
Gacrux	171 49.9	S57 15.6
Gienah	175 41.9	S17 41.5
Hadar	148 34.0	S60 30.0
Hamal	327 49.2	N23 35.6
Kaus Aust.	83 30.8	S34 22.3
Kochab	137 20.7	N74 02.3
Markab	13 28.4	N15 21.2
Menkar	314 04.2	N 4 11.8
Menkent	147 55.9	S36 30.0
Miaplacidus	221 37.2	S69 49.4
Mirfak	308 25.5	N49 57.6
Nunki	75 46.1	S26 15.8
Peacock	53 03.7	S56 39.0
Pollux	243 15.0	N27 57.5
Procyon	244 48.8	N 5 09.3
Rasalhague	95 57.4	N12 32.4
Regulus	207 32.6	N11 50.0
Rigel	281 02.0	S 8 10.2
Rigil Kent.	139 38.5	S60 56.6
Sabik	102 01.3	S15 45.5
Schedar	349 29.1	N56 41.5
Shaula	96 08.6	S37 07.3
Sirius	258 24.5	S16 45.2
Spica	158 20.7	S11 18.1
Suhail	222 44.8	S43 32.4
Vega	80 32.6	N38 48.5
Zuben'ubi	136 54.5	S16 09.2

	SHA ° ′	Mer. Pass. h m
Venus	137 34.1	8 47
Mars	199 01.7	4 41
Jupiter	210 34.7	3 55
Saturn	351 37.7	18 28

	UT	SUN GHA	SUN Dec	MOON GHA	v	MOON Dec	d	HP
	d h	° ′	° ′	° ′	′	° ′	′	′
	21 00	180 32.6	S23 26.1	47 21.0	6.5	N21 33.9	10.9	59.7
	01	195 32.3	26.1	61 46.5	6.3	21 44.8	10.8	59.8
	02	210 32.0	26.1	76 11.8	6.2	21 55.6	10.7	59.8
	03	225 31.7	26.1	90 37.0	6.0	22 06.3	10.5	59.9
	04	240 31.4	26.1	105 02.0	5.9	22 16.8	10.4	59.9
	05	255 31.0	26.1	119 26.9	5.8	22 27.2	10.2	59.9
	06	270 30.7	S23 26.2	133 51.7	5.6	N22 37.4	10.2	60.0
	07	285 30.4	26.2	148 16.3	5.5	22 47.6	10.0	60.0
	08	300 30.1	26.2	162 40.8	5.3	22 57.6	9.8	60.0
M	09	315 29.8	26.2	177 05.1	5.2	23 07.4	9.7	60.1
O	10	330 29.5	26.2	191 29.3	5.1	23 17.1	9.6	60.1
N	11	345 29.2	26.2	205 53.4	4.9	23 26.7	9.4	60.1
D	12	0 28.9	S23 26.2	220 17.3	4.8	N23 36.1	9.3	60.2
A	13	15 28.6	26.2	234 41.1	4.6	23 45.4	9.1	60.2
Y	14	30 28.3	26.2	249 04.7	4.5	23 54.5	9.0	60.2
	15	45 27.9	26.2	263 28.2	4.4	24 03.5	8.8	60.3
	16	60 27.6	26.2	277 51.6	4.2	24 12.3	8.7	60.3
	17	75 27.3	26.2	292 14.8	4.1	24 21.0	8.5	60.3
	18	90 27.0	S23 26.2	306 37.9	4.0	N24 29.5	8.3	60.4
	19	105 26.7	26.2	321 00.9	3.8	24 37.8	8.2	60.4
	20	120 26.4	26.2	335 23.7	3.7	24 46.0	8.0	60.4
	21	135 26.1	26.2	349 46.4	3.6	24 54.0	7.8	60.5
	22	150 25.8	26.2	4 09.0	3.4	25 01.8	7.7	60.5
	23	165 25.5	26.2	18 31.4	3.3	25 09.5	7.5	60.5
	22 00	180 25.2	S23 26.2	32 53.7	3.2	N25 17.0	7.3	60.6
	01	195 24.9	26.2	47 15.9	3.1	25 24.3	7.2	60.6
	02	210 24.5	26.2	61 38.0	3.0	25 31.5	6.9	60.6
	03	225 24.2	26.2	76 00.0	2.8	25 38.4	6.8	60.7
	04	240 23.9	26.2	90 21.8	2.7	25 45.2	6.6	60.7
	05	255 23.6	26.2	104 43.5	2.6	25 51.8	6.5	60.7
	06	270 23.3	S23 26.2	119 05.1	2.5	N25 58.3	6.2	60.7
	07	285 23.0	26.2	133 26.6	2.3	26 04.5	6.1	60.8
T	08	300 22.7	26.2	147 47.9	2.3	26 10.6	5.8	60.8
U	09	315 22.4	26.2	162 09.2	2.2	26 16.4	5.7	60.8
E	10	330 22.1	26.2	176 30.4	2.0	26 22.1	5.5	60.8
S	11	345 21.8	26.2	190 51.4	2.0	26 27.6	5.3	60.9
	12	0 21.4	S23 26.2	205 12.4	1.8	N26 32.9	5.0	60.9
D	13	15 21.1	26.1	219 33.2	1.8	26 37.9	4.9	60.9
A	14	30 20.8	26.1	233 54.0	1.6	26 42.8	4.7	60.9
Y	15	45 20.5	26.1	248 14.6	1.6	26 47.5	4.5	61.0
	16	60 20.2	26.1	262 35.2	1.5	26 52.0	4.3	61.0
	17	75 19.9	26.1	276 55.7	1.4	26 56.3	4.1	61.0
	18	90 19.6	S23 26.1	291 16.1	1.3	N27 00.4	3.8	61.0
	19	105 19.3	26.0	305 36.4	1.2	27 04.2	3.7	61.1
	20	120 19.0	26.0	319 56.6	1.2	27 07.9	3.4	61.1
	21	135 18.7	26.0	334 16.8	1.1	27 11.3	3.3	61.1
	22	150 18.3	26.0	348 36.9	1.0	27 14.6	3.0	61.1
	23	165 18.0	26.0	2 56.9	1.0	27 17.6	2.8	61.1
	23 00	180 17.7	S23 25.9	17 16.9	0.8	N27 20.4	2.7	61.2
	01	195 17.4	25.9	31 36.7	0.9	27 23.1	2.3	61.2
	02	210 17.1	25.9	45 56.6	0.8	27 25.4	2.2	61.2
	03	225 16.8	25.9	60 16.4	0.7	27 27.6	2.0	61.2
	04	240 16.5	25.8	74 36.1	0.6	27 29.6	1.7	61.2
	05	255 16.2	25.8	88 55.7	0.7	27 31.3	1.6	61.3
	06	270 15.9	S23 25.8	103 15.4	0.6	N27 32.9	1.3	61.3
W	07	285 15.6	25.8	117 35.0	0.5	27 34.2	1.1	61.3
E	08	300 15.2	25.7	131 54.5	0.5	27 35.3	0.8	61.3
D	09	315 14.9	25.7	146 14.0	0.5	27 36.1	0.7	61.3
N	10	330 14.6	25.7	160 33.5	0.5	27 36.8	0.4	61.3
E	11	345 14.3	25.7	174 53.0	0.4	27 37.2	0.2	61.3
S	12	0 14.0	S23 25.6	189 12.4	0.4	N27 37.4	0.0	61.4
	13	15 13.7	25.6	203 31.8	0.4	27 37.4	0.2	61.4
D	14	30 13.4	25.6	217 51.2	0.4	27 37.2	0.5	61.4
A	15	45 13.1	25.5	232 10.6	0.4	27 36.7	0.7	61.4
Y	16	60 12.8	25.5	246 30.0	0.3	27 36.0	0.9	61.4
	17	75 12.5	25.4	260 49.3	0.4	27 35.1	1.1	61.4
	18	90 12.2	S23 25.4	275 08.7	0.4	N27 34.0	1.4	61.4
	19	105 11.8	25.4	289 28.1	0.4	27 32.6	1.5	61.4
	20	120 11.5	25.3	303 47.5	0.4	27 31.1	1.8	61.4
	21	135 11.2	25.3	318 06.9	0.4	27 29.3	2.0	61.4
	22	150 10.9	25.3	332 26.3	0.4	27 27.3	2.3	61.4
	23	165 10.6	25.2	346 45.7	0.4	N27 25.0	2.4	61.5
		SD 16.3	*d* 0.0	SD	16.4		16.6	16.7

Lat.	Twilight Naut.	Twilight Civil	Sunrise	Moonrise 21	Moonrise 22	Moonrise 23	Moonrise 24
°	h m	h m	h m	h m	h m	h m	h m
N 72	08 26	10 58	■	□	□	□	□
N 70	08 06	09 55	■	□	□	□	□
68	07 50	09 19	■	□	□	□	□
66	07 37	08 54	10 35	10 19	□	□	□
64	07 26	08 34	09 53	11 09	□	□	□
62	07 16	08 18	09 24	11 40	11 44	12 13	14 01
60	07 08	08 05	09 02	12 04	12 23	13 10	14 42
N 58	07 00	07 53	08 45	12 24	12 50	13 43	15 09
56	06 53	07 43	08 30	12 40	13 12	14 08	15 31
54	06 47	07 33	08 17	12 54	13 30	14 28	15 49
52	06 42	07 25	08 06	13 06	13 45	14 44	16 04
50	06 36	07 18	07 56	13 16	13 58	14 59	16 17
45	06 24	07 02	07 36	13 39	14 26	15 28	16 44
N 40	06 14	06 48	07 19	13 57	14 47	15 51	17 05
35	06 05	06 36	07 04	14 13	15 05	16 10	17 23
30	05 56	06 26	06 52	14 26	15 21	16 26	17 38
20	05 39	06 07	06 31	14 49	15 47	16 53	18 04
N 10	05 23	05 49	06 12	15 09	16 10	17 17	18 26
0	05 06	05 32	05 55	15 28	16 32	17 39	18 47
S 10	04 47	05 14	05 37	15 47	16 53	18 01	19 07
20	04 24	04 54	05 18	16 07	17 16	18 25	19 29
30	03 55	04 29	04 56	16 31	17 44	18 53	19 55
35	03 37	04 13	04 43	16 45	18 00	19 09	20 10
40	03 13	03 55	04 28	17 01	18 18	19 28	20 27
45	02 43	03 32	04 10	17 21	18 41	19 51	20 48
S 50	01 57	03 03	03 47	17 45	19 10	20 21	21 13
52	01 29	02 47	03 36	17 57	19 24	20 35	21 26
54	00 42	02 29	03 24	18 11	19 40	20 52	21 40
56	////	02 07	03 10	18 27	20 00	21 12	21 57
58	////	01 37	02 53	18 46	20 25	21 37	22 17
S 60	////	00 46	02 32	19 09	20 57	22 11	22 42

Lat.	Sunset	Twilight Civil	Twilight Naut.	Moonset 21	Moonset 22	Moonset 23	Moonset 24
°	h m	h m	h m	h m	h m	h m	h m
N 72	■	12 59	15 31	□	□	□	□
N 70	■	14 02	15 51	□	□	□	□
68	■	14 38	16 07	□	□	□	□
66	13 22	15 03	16 20	07 51	□	□	□
64	14 05	15 23	16 31	07 02	□	□	□
62	14 33	15 39	16 41	06 31	08 38	10 29	11 04
60	14 55	15 53	16 49	06 08	07 59	09 33	10 23
N 58	15 12	16 04	16 57	05 49	07 32	09 00	09 55
56	15 27	16 15	17 04	05 34	07 11	08 35	09 33
54	15 40	16 24	17 10	05 21	06 54	08 15	09 15
52	15 51	16 32	17 16	05 09	06 39	07 58	09 00
50	16 01	16 39	17 21	04 59	06 26	07 44	08 46
45	16 22	16 55	17 33	04 38	05 59	07 15	08 19
N 40	16 38	17 09	17 43	04 20	05 38	06 52	07 57
35	16 53	17 21	17 53	04 06	05 21	06 33	07 39
30	17 05	17 31	18 01	03 53	05 06	06 17	07 23
20	17 26	17 50	18 18	03 32	04 40	05 49	06 56
N 10	17 45	18 08	18 34	03 14	04 18	05 26	06 33
0	18 02	18 25	18 51	02 57	03 58	05 04	06 12
S 10	18 20	18 43	19 10	02 40	03 37	04 42	05 50
20	18 39	19 04	19 33	02 21	03 16	04 18	05 27
30	19 01	19 28	20 02	02 01	02 50	03 50	04 59
35	19 14	19 44	20 21	01 49	02 36	03 34	04 43
40	19 29	20 02	20 44	01 35	02 19	03 15	04 24
45	19 47	20 25	21 14	01 18	01 58	02 52	04 02
S 50	20 10	20 54	22 00	00 58	01 33	02 23	03 33
52	20 21	21 10	22 28	00 49	01 20	02 08	03 18
54	20 33	21 28	23 15	00 38	01 06	01 52	03 02
56	20 47	21 50	////	00 26	00 50	01 32	02 42
58	21 04	22 20	////	00 12	00 30	01 07	02 17
S 60	21 25	23 11	////	24 06	00 06	00 34	01 43

Day	SUN Eqn. of Time 00^h	SUN Eqn. of Time 12^h	SUN Mer. Pass.	MOON Mer. Pass. Upper	MOON Mer. Pass. Lower	Age	Phase
d	m s	m s	h m	h m	h m	d %	
21	02 11	01 56	11 58	21 43	09 12	12 90	○
22	01 41	01 26	11 59	22 48	10 15	13 96	
23	01 12	00 57	11 59	23 55	11 21	14 99	

2026 DECEMBER 24, 25, 26 (THURS., FRI., SAT.)

	UT (d h)	ARIES GHA	VENUS −4·6 GHA	VENUS Dec	MARS +0·0 GHA	MARS Dec	JUPITER −2·4 GHA	JUPITER Dec	SATURN +0·7 GHA	SATURN Dec	STARS Name	SHA	Dec
		° ′	° ′	° ′	° ′	° ′	° ′	° ′	° ′	° ′		° ′	° ′
	24 00	92 32.4	228 16.9	S13 27.1	291 09.2	N11 07.3	303 10.7	N13 24.8	84 07.9	N 0 55.1	Acamar	315 10.3	S40 11.9
	01	107 34.8	243 17.1	27.7	306 11.2	07.2	318 13.2	24.8	99 10.3	55.2	Achernar	335 18.8	S57 06.2
	02	122 37.3	258 17.2	28.2	321 13.2	07.1	333 15.8	24.9	114 12.7	55.2	Acrux	172 58.2	S63 14.7
	03	137 39.8	273 17.4	. . 28.8	336 15.1	. . 06.9	348 18.3	. . 24.9	129 15.1	. . 55.2	Adhara	255 04.2	S29 00.5
	04	152 42.2	288 17.5	29.4	351 17.1	06.8	3 20.8	25.0	144 17.5	55.3	Aldebaran	290 37.4	N16 33.8
	05	167 44.7	303 17.7	30.0	6 19.1	06.7	18 23.4	25.0	159 19.9	55.3			
	06	182 47.2	318 17.8	S13 30.6	21 21.1	N11 06.6	33 25.9	N13 25.1	174 22.3	N 0 55.3	Alioth	166 11.7	N55 48.4
	07	197 49.6	333 18.0	31.2	36 23.0	06.5	48 28.5	25.1	189 24.8	55.4	Alkaid	152 51.0	N49 10.4
T	08	212 52.1	348 18.1	31.8	51 25.0	06.4	63 31.0	25.1	204 27.2	55.4	Alnair	27 31.2	S46 50.0
H	09	227 54.6	3 18.3	. . 32.4	66 27.0	. . 06.3	78 33.6	. . 25.2	219 29.6	. . 55.4	Alnilam	275 35.7	S 1 11.1
U	10	242 57.0	18 18.4	33.0	81 29.0	06.2	93 36.1	25.2	234 32.0	55.5	Alphard	217 45.9	S 8 46.6
R	11	257 59.5	33 18.6	33.6	96 31.0	06.1	108 38.7	25.3	249 34.4	55.5			
S	12	273 01.9	48 18.7	S13 34.1	111 32.9	N11 06.0	123 41.2	N13 25.3	264 36.8	N 0 55.5	Alphecca	126 02.7	N26 37.3
D	13	288 04.4	63 18.9	34.7	126 34.9	05.9	138 43.8	25.3	279 39.2	55.6	Alpheratz	357 33.1	N29 14.6
A	14	303 06.9	78 19.0	35.3	141 36.9	05.8	153 46.3	25.4	294 41.6	55.6	Altair	61 58.7	N 8 56.4
Y	15	318 09.3	93 19.1	. . 35.9	156 38.9	. . 05.7	168 48.9	. . 25.4	309 44.1	. . 55.6	Ankaa	353 05.5	S42 09.7
	16	333 11.8	108 19.3	36.5	171 40.9	05.6	183 51.4	25.5	324 46.5	55.7	Antares	112 14.2	S26 29.4
	17	348 14.3	123 19.4	37.1	186 42.8	05.5	198 54.0	25.5	339 48.9	55.7			
	18	3 16.7	138 19.5	S13 37.7	201 44.8	N11 05.4	213 56.6	N13 25.5	354 51.3	N 0 55.7	Arcturus	145 46.6	N19 02.4
	19	18 19.2	153 19.7	38.3	216 46.8	05.3	228 59.1	25.6	9 53.7	55.8	Atria	107 07.5	S69 04.4
	20	33 21.7	168 19.8	38.9	231 48.8	05.2	244 01.7	25.6	24 56.1	55.8	Avior	234 13.5	S59 35.6
	21	48 24.1	183 19.9	. . 39.5	246 50.8	. . 05.1	259 04.2	. . 25.7	39 58.5	. . 55.8	Bellatrix	278 20.8	N 6 22.4
	22	63 26.6	198 20.1	40.1	261 52.8	05.0	274 06.8	25.7	55 00.9	55.9	Betelgeuse	270 50.0	N 7 24.7
	23	78 29.1	213 20.2	40.7	276 54.8	04.9	289 09.3	25.8	70 03.3	55.9			
	25 00	93 31.5	228 20.3	S13 41.3	291 56.8	N11 04.8	304 11.9	N13 25.8	85 05.8	N 0 55.9	Canopus	263 51.1	S52 42.6
	01	108 34.0	243 20.5	41.9	306 58.8	04.7	319 14.4	25.8	100 08.2	56.0	Capella	280 19.0	N46 01.5
	02	123 36.4	258 20.6	42.4	322 00.7	04.6	334 17.0	25.9	115 10.6	56.0	Deneb	49 25.1	N45 22.8
	03	138 38.9	273 20.7	. . 43.0	337 02.7	. . 04.5	349 19.5	. . 25.9	130 13.0	. . 56.0	Denebola	182 23.3	N14 25.1
	04	153 41.4	288 20.8	43.6	352 04.7	04.4	4 22.1	26.0	145 15.4	56.1	Diphda	348 45.6	S17 50.4
	05	168 43.8	303 20.9	44.2	7 06.7	04.3	19 24.6	26.0	160 17.8	56.1			
	06	183 46.3	318 21.1	S13 44.8	22 08.7	N11 04.2	34 27.2	N13 26.1	175 20.2	N 0 56.2	Dubhe	193 38.9	N61 36.0
	07	198 48.8	333 21.2	45.4	37 10.7	04.1	49 29.8	26.1	190 22.6	56.2	Elnath	277 59.4	N28 37.8
	08	213 51.2	348 21.3	46.0	52 12.7	04.0	64 32.3	26.1	205 25.0	56.2	Eltanin	90 42.0	N51 29.1
F	09	228 53.7	3 21.4	. . 46.6	67 14.7	. . 03.9	79 34.9	. . 26.2	220 27.4	. . 56.3	Enif	33 37.4	N10 00.0
R	10	243 56.2	18 21.5	47.2	82 16.7	03.8	94 37.4	26.2	235 29.8	56.3	Fomalhaut	15 12.9	S29 28.9
I	11	258 58.6	33 21.7	47.8	97 18.7	03.7	109 40.0	26.3	250 32.2	56.3			
D	12	274 01.1	48 21.8	S13 48.4	112 20.7	N11 03.6	124 42.5	N13 26.3	265 34.7	N 0 56.4	Gacrux	171 49.9	S57 15.6
A	13	289 03.6	63 21.9	49.0	127 22.7	03.5	139 45.1	26.4	280 37.1	56.4	Gienah	175 41.9	S17 41.5
Y	14	304 06.0	78 22.0	49.6	142 24.7	03.4	154 47.7	26.4	295 39.5	56.4	Hadar	148 34.0	S60 30.0
	15	319 08.5	93 22.1	. . 50.2	157 26.7	. . 03.3	169 50.2	. . 26.5	310 41.9	. . 56.5	Hamal	327 49.2	N23 35.6
	16	334 10.9	108 22.2	50.8	172 28.8	03.2	184 52.8	26.5	325 44.3	56.5	Kaus Aust.	83 30.8	S34 22.3
	17	349 13.4	123 22.3	51.4	187 30.8	03.1	199 55.3	26.5	340 46.7	56.5			
	18	4 15.9	138 22.4	S13 52.0	202 32.8	N11 03.0	214 57.9	N13 26.6	355 49.1	N 0 56.6	Kochab	137 20.7	N74 02.3
	19	19 18.3	153 22.5	52.6	217 34.8	02.9	230 00.5	26.6	10 51.5	56.6	Markab	13 28.4	N15 21.2
	20	34 20.8	168 22.7	53.2	232 36.8	02.8	245 03.0	26.7	25 53.9	56.7	Menkar	314 04.2	N 4 11.8
	21	49 23.3	183 22.8	. . 53.8	247 38.8	. . 02.8	260 05.6	. . 26.7	40 56.3	. . 56.7	Menkent	147 55.9	S36 30.0
	22	64 25.7	198 22.9	54.4	262 40.8	02.7	275 08.1	26.8	55 58.7	56.7	Miaplacidus	221 37.2	S69 49.5
	23	79 28.2	213 23.0	55.0	277 42.8	02.6	290 10.7	26.8	71 01.1	56.8			
	26 00	94 30.7	228 23.1	S13 55.5	292 44.8	N11 02.5	305 13.3	N13 26.9	86 03.5	N 0 56.8	Mirfak	308 25.5	N49 57.6
	01	109 33.1	243 23.2	56.1	307 46.9	02.4	320 15.8	26.9	101 05.9	56.8	Nunki	75 46.1	S26 15.8
	02	124 35.6	258 23.3	56.7	322 48.9	02.3	335 18.4	27.0	116 08.3	56.9	Peacock	53 03.7	S56 39.0
	03	139 38.0	273 23.4	. . 57.3	337 50.9	. . 02.2	350 21.0	. . 27.0	131 10.8	. . 56.9	Pollux	243 15.0	N27 57.5
	04	154 40.5	288 23.5	57.9	352 52.9	02.1	5 23.5	27.0	146 13.2	56.9	Procyon	244 48.8	N 5 09.3
	05	169 43.0	303 23.6	58.5	7 54.9	02.0	20 26.1	27.1	161 15.6	57.0			
	06	184 45.4	318 23.6	S13 59.1	22 56.9	N11 01.9	35 28.6	N13 27.1	176 18.0	N 0 57.0	Rasalhague	95 57.4	N12 32.4
	07	199 47.9	333 23.7	13 59.7	37 59.0	01.9	50 31.2	27.2	191 20.4	57.1	Regulus	207 32.5	N11 50.0
S	08	214 50.4	348 23.8	14 00.3	53 01.0	01.8	65 33.8	27.2	206 22.8	57.1	Rigel	281 02.0	S 8 10.2
A	09	229 52.8	3 23.9	. . 00.9	68 03.0	. . 01.7	80 36.3	. . 27.3	221 25.2	. . 57.1	Rigil Kent.	139 38.4	S60 56.6
T	10	244 55.3	18 24.0	01.5	83 05.0	01.6	95 38.9	27.3	236 27.6	57.2	Sabik	102 01.3	S15 45.5
U	11	259 57.8	33 24.1	02.1	98 07.1	01.5	110 41.5	27.4	251 30.0	57.2			
R	12	275 00.2	48 24.2	S14 02.7	113 09.1	N11 01.4	125 44.0	N13 27.4	266 32.4	N 0 57.2	Schedar	349 29.1	N56 41.5
D	13	290 02.7	63 24.3	03.3	128 11.1	01.3	140 46.6	27.5	281 34.8	57.3	Shaula	96 08.6	S37 07.3
A	14	305 05.2	78 24.4	03.9	143 13.1	01.3	155 49.2	27.5	296 37.2	57.3	Sirius	258 24.4	S16 45.2
Y	15	320 07.6	93 24.5	. . 04.5	158 15.2	. . 01.2	170 51.7	. . 27.6	311 39.6	. . 57.4	Spica	158 20.7	S11 18.1
	16	335 10.1	108 24.5	05.1	173 17.2	01.1	185 54.3	27.6	326 42.0	57.4	Suhail	222 44.8	S43 32.4
	17	350 12.5	123 24.6	05.7	188 19.2	01.0	200 56.9	27.7	341 44.4	57.4			
	18	5 15.0	138 24.7	S14 06.3	203 21.3	N11 00.9	215 59.4	N13 27.7	356 46.8	N 0 57.5	Vega	80 32.6	N38 48.5
	19	20 17.5	153 24.8	06.9	218 23.3	00.8	231 02.0	27.7	11 49.2	57.5	Zuben'ubi	136 54.4	S16 09.2
	20	35 19.9	168 24.9	07.5	233 25.3	00.8	246 04.6	27.8	26 51.6	57.5			
	21	50 22.4	183 24.9	. . 08.1	248 27.4	. . 00.7	261 07.1	. . 27.8	41 54.0	. . 57.6			
	22	65 24.9	198 25.0	08.7	263 29.4	00.6	276 09.7	27.9	56 56.4	57.6			
	23	80 27.3	213 25.1	09.3	278 31.4	00.5	291 12.3	27.9	71 58.8	57.7			
	Mer. Pass.	h m 17 43.0	*v* 0.1	*d* 0.6	*v* 2.0	*d* 0.1	*v* 2.6	*d* 0.0	*v* 2.4	*d* 0.0			

	SHA	Mer. Pass.
	° ′	h m
Venus	134 48.8	8 47
Mars	198 25.2	4 32
Jupiter	210 40.4	3 43
Saturn	351 34.2	18 17

UT	SUN GHA	SUN Dec	MOON GHA	v	MOON Dec	d	HP
d h	° ′	° ′	° ′	′	° ′	′	′
24 00 (Thursday)	180 10.3	S23 25.2	1 05.1	0.5	N27 22.6	2.7	61.5
01	195 10.0	25.1	15 24.6	0.5	27 19.9	2.9	61.5
02	210 09.7	25.1	29 44.1	0.6	27 17.0	3.1	61.5
03	225 09.4	. . 25.0	44 03.7	0.5	27 13.9	3.4	61.5
04	240 09.1	25.0	58 23.2	0.7	27 10.5	3.5	61.5
05	255 08.7	25.0	72 42.9	0.6	27 07.0	3.8	61.5
06	270 08.4	S23 24.9	87 02.5	0.7	N27 03.2	4.0	61.5
07	285 08.1	24.9	101 22.2	0.8	26 59.2	4.2	61.5
08	300 07.8	24.8	115 42.0	0.8	26 55.0	4.4	61.5
09	315 07.5	. . 24.8	130 01.8	0.9	26 50.6	4.6	61.5
10	330 07.2	24.7	144 21.7	0.9	26 46.0	4.9	61.5
11	345 06.9	24.7	158 41.6	1.0	26 41.1	5.0	61.5
12	0 06.6	S23 24.6	173 01.6	1.1	N26 36.1	5.3	61.5
13	15 06.3	24.6	187 21.7	1.1	26 30.8	5.4	61.5
14	30 06.0	24.5	201 41.8	1.2	26 25.4	5.7	61.5
15	45 05.7	. . 24.5	216 02.0	1.3	26 19.7	5.9	61.5
16	60 05.3	24.4	230 22.3	1.3	26 13.8	6.1	61.5
17	75 05.0	24.3	244 42.6	1.5	26 07.7	6.3	61.5
18	90 04.7	S23 24.3	259 03.1	1.5	N26 01.4	6.5	61.5
19	105 04.4	24.2	273 23.6	1.6	25 54.9	6.7	61.4
20	120 04.1	24.2	287 44.2	1.7	25 48.2	6.8	61.4
21	135 03.8	. . 24.1	302 04.9	1.8	25 41.4	7.1	61.4
22	150 03.5	24.1	316 25.7	1.9	25 34.3	7.3	61.4
23	165 03.2	24.0	330 46.6	2.0	25 27.0	7.5	61.4
25 00 (Friday)	180 02.9	S23 23.9	345 07.6	2.1	N25 19.5	7.6	61.4
01	195 02.6	23.9	359 28.7	2.2	25 11.9	7.9	61.4
02	210 02.3	23.8	13 49.9	2.3	25 04.0	8.0	61.4
03	225 01.9	. . 23.8	28 11.2	2.4	24 56.0	8.3	61.4
04	240 01.6	23.7	42 32.6	2.5	24 47.7	8.4	61.4
05	255 01.3	23.6	56 54.1	2.7	24 39.3	8.5	61.4
06	270 01.0	S23 23.6	71 15.8	2.7	N24 30.8	8.8	61.3
07	285 00.7	23.5	85 37.5	2.9	24 22.0	9.0	61.3
08	300 00.4	23.4	99 59.4	2.9	24 13.0	9.1	61.3
09	315 00.1	. . 23.4	114 21.3	3.1	24 03.9	9.3	61.3
10	329 59.8	23.3	128 43.4	3.2	23 54.6	9.4	61.3
11	344 59.5	23.2	143 05.6	3.4	23 45.2	9.7	61.3
12	359 59.2	S23 23.1	157 28.0	3.4	N23 35.5	9.7	61.3
13	14 58.9	23.1	171 50.4	3.6	23 25.8	10.0	61.2
14	29 58.6	23.0	186 13.0	3.7	23 15.8	10.1	61.2
15	44 58.2	. . 22.9	200 35.7	3.8	23 05.7	10.3	61.2
16	59 57.9	22.9	214 58.5	4.0	22 55.4	10.4	61.2
17	74 57.6	22.8	229 21.5	4.0	22 45.0	10.6	61.2
18	89 57.3	S23 22.7	243 44.5	4.2	N22 34.4	10.8	61.2
19	104 57.0	22.6	258 07.7	4.4	22 23.6	10.9	61.1
20	119 56.7	22.6	272 31.1	4.4	22 12.7	11.0	61.1
21	134 56.4	. . 22.5	286 54.5	4.6	22 01.7	11.2	61.1
22	149 56.1	22.4	301 18.1	4.8	21 50.5	11.3	61.1
23	164 55.8	22.3	315 41.9	4.8	21 39.2	11.5	61.0
26 00 (Saturday)	179 55.5	S23 22.2	330 05.7	5.0	N21 27.7	11.6	61.0
01	194 55.2	22.2	344 29.7	5.1	21 16.1	11.8	61.0
02	209 54.9	22.1	358 53.8	5.3	21 04.3	11.8	61.0
03	224 54.5	. . 22.0	13 18.1	5.4	20 52.5	12.1	61.0
04	239 54.2	21.9	27 42.5	5.5	20 40.4	12.1	60.9
05	254 53.9	21.8	42 07.0	5.7	20 28.3	12.3	60.9
06	269 53.6	S23 21.7	56 31.7	5.7	N20 16.0	12.4	60.9
07	284 53.3	21.7	70 56.4	6.0	20 03.6	12.5	60.9
08	299 53.0	21.6	85 21.4	6.0	19 51.1	12.6	60.8
09	314 52.7	. . 21.5	99 46.4	6.2	19 38.5	12.7	60.8
10	329 52.4	21.4	114 11.6	6.3	19 25.8	12.9	60.8
11	344 52.1	21.3	128 36.9	6.5	19 12.9	13.0	60.8
12	359 51.8	S23 21.2	143 02.4	6.6	N18 59.9	13.1	60.7
13	14 51.5	21.1	157 28.0	6.7	18 46.8	13.2	60.7
14	29 51.2	21.0	171 53.7	6.8	18 33.6	13.3	60.7
15	44 50.9	. . 20.9	186 19.5	7.0	18 20.3	13.4	60.6
16	59 50.5	20.8	200 45.5	7.1	18 06.9	13.5	60.6
17	74 50.2	20.7	215 11.6	7.3	17 53.4	13.6	60.6
18	89 49.9	S23 20.6	229 37.9	7.4	N17 39.8	13.6	60.5
19	104 49.6	20.6	244 04.3	7.5	17 26.2	13.8	60.5
20	119 49.3	20.5	258 30.8	7.6	17 12.4	13.9	60.5
21	134 49.0	. . 20.4	272 57.4	7.8	16 58.5	14.0	60.5
22	149 48.7	20.3	287 24.2	7.8	16 44.5	14.0	60.4
23	164 48.4	20.2	301 51.0	8.1	N16 30.5	14.2	60.4
	SD 16.3	*d* 0.1	SD	16.8	16.7		16.5

Lat.	Twilight Naut.	Twilight Civil	Sunrise	Moonrise 24	Moonrise 25	Moonrise 26	Moonrise 27
°	h m	h m	h m	h m	h m	h m	h m
N 72	08 27	10 57	▬	▭	▭	▭	19 02
N 70	08 07	09 55	▬	▭	▭	16 29	19 22
68	07 51	09 20	▬	▭	▭	17 11	19 38
66	07 38	08 55	10 35	▭	14 49	17 39	19 51
64	07 27	08 35	09 53	▭	15 41	18 01	20 02
62	07 17	08 19	09 25	14 01	16 13	18 17	20 11
60	07 09	08 06	09 03	14 42	16 37	18 31	20 19
N 58	07 01	07 54	08 46	15 09	16 56	18 43	20 25
56	06 55	07 44	08 31	15 31	17 11	18 54	20 31
54	06 48	07 35	08 19	15 49	17 25	19 03	20 36
52	06 43	07 26	08 07	16 04	17 36	19 11	20 41
50	06 37	07 19	07 58	16 17	17 47	19 18	20 45
45	06 26	07 03	07 37	16 44	18 08	19 33	20 55
N 40	06 15	06 49	07 20	17 05	18 26	19 46	21 02
35	06 06	06 38	07 06	17 23	18 40	19 57	21 09
30	05 57	06 27	06 53	17 38	18 53	20 06	21 15
20	05 41	06 08	06 32	18 04	19 14	20 22	21 25
N 10	05 25	05 51	06 14	18 26	19 33	20 36	21 33
0	05 08	05 34	05 56	18 47	19 50	20 48	21 41
S 10	04 49	05 16	05 39	19 07	20 07	21 01	21 49
20	04 26	04 55	05 20	19 29	20 26	21 15	21 58
30	03 57	04 30	04 58	19 55	20 47	21 30	22 07
35	03 38	04 15	04 45	20 10	20 59	21 39	22 13
40	03 15	03 57	04 30	20 27	21 13	21 50	22 19
45	02 44	03 34	04 12	20 48	21 30	22 01	22 27
S 50	01 59	03 04	03 49	21 13	21 50	22 16	22 35
52	01 31	02 49	03 38	21 26	22 00	22 23	22 39
54	00 45	02 31	03 26	21 40	22 10	22 30	22 44
56	////	02 09	03 12	21 57	22 23	22 38	22 48
58	////	01 39	02 55	22 17	22 37	22 47	22 54
S 60	////	00 49	02 34	22 42	22 53	22 58	23 00

Lat.	Sunset	Twilight Civil	Twilight Naut.	Moonset 24	Moonset 25	Moonset 26	Moonset 27
°	h m	h m	h m	h m	h m	h m	h m
N 72	▬	13 03	15 33	▭	▭	▭	12 24
N 70	▬	14 05	15 53	▭	▭	13 01	12 01
68	▬	14 40	16 09	▭	▭	12 17	11 43
66	13 25	15 05	16 22	▭	12 34	11 48	11 28
64	14 07	15 25	16 33	▭	11 41	11 25	11 16
62	14 35	15 41	16 43	11 04	11 08	11 07	11 05
60	14 57	15 55	16 51	10 23	10 44	10 52	10 56
N 58	15 14	16 06	16 59	09 55	10 24	10 39	10 48
56	15 29	16 16	17 06	09 33	10 08	10 28	10 41
54	15 42	16 25	17 12	09 15	09 54	10 18	10 35
52	15 53	16 34	17 17	09 00	09 41	10 09	10 29
50	16 03	16 41	17 23	08 46	09 31	10 01	10 24
45	16 23	16 57	17 34	08 19	09 08	09 44	10 13
N 40	16 40	17 11	17 45	07 57	08 49	09 30	10 03
35	16 54	17 22	17 54	07 39	08 34	09 18	09 55
30	17 07	17 33	18 03	07 23	08 20	09 08	09 48
20	17 28	17 52	18 19	06 56	07 57	08 50	09 36
N 10	17 46	18 09	18 36	06 33	07 37	08 34	09 24
0	18 04	18 26	18 53	06 12	07 17	08 19	09 14
S 10	18 21	18 44	19 12	05 50	06 58	08 03	09 04
20	18 40	19 05	19 34	05 27	06 38	07 47	08 52
30	19 02	19 30	20 03	04 59	06 14	07 28	08 39
35	19 15	19 45	20 22	04 43	05 59	07 17	08 32
40	19 30	20 03	20 45	04 24	05 43	07 04	08 23
45	19 48	20 26	21 15	04 02	05 23	06 49	08 13
S 50	20 11	20 55	22 01	03 33	04 58	06 30	08 00
52	20 22	21 11	22 29	03 18	04 46	06 21	07 54
54	20 34	21 28	23 15	03 02	04 32	06 11	07 48
56	20 48	21 51	////	02 42	04 16	06 00	07 40
58	21 05	22 20	////	02 17	03 57	05 46	07 32
S 60	21 25	23 10	////	01 43	03 33	05 31	07 23

Day	SUN Eqn. of Time 00^h	SUN Eqn. of Time 12^h	SUN Mer. Pass.	MOON Mer. Pass. Upper	MOON Mer. Pass. Lower	Age	Phase
d	m s	m s	h m	h m	h m	d %	
24	00 42	00 27	12 00	25 02	12 29	15 100	○
25	00 12	00 03	12 00	01 02	13 34	16 97	
26	00 18	00 32	12 01	02 05	14 34	17 91	

2026 DECEMBER 27, 28, 29 (SUN., MON., TUES.)

d	h	ARIES GHA	VENUS −4·6 GHA	VENUS Dec	MARS −0·1 GHA	MARS Dec	JUPITER −2·4 GHA	JUPITER Dec	SATURN +0·7 GHA	SATURN Dec
		° ′	° ′	° ′	° ′	° ′	° ′	° ′	° ′	° ′
27 SUNDAY	00	95 29.8	228 25.2	S14 09.9	293 33.5	N11 00.4	306 14.8	N13 28.0	87 01.2	N 0 57.7
	01	110 32.3	243 25.2	10.5	308 35.5	00.4	321 17.4	28.0	102 03.6	57.7
	02	125 34.7	258 25.3	11.1	323 37.5	00.3	336 20.0	28.1	117 06.0	57.8
	03	140 37.2	273 25.4	. . 11.7	338 39.6	. . 00.2	351 22.6	. . 28.1	132 08.4	. . 57.8
	04	155 39.7	288 25.5	12.3	353 41.6	00.1	6 25.1	28.2	147 10.8	57.9
	05	170 42.1	303 25.5	12.9	8 43.7	00.0	21 27.7	28.2	162 13.2	57.9
	06	185 44.6	318 25.6	S14 13.5	23 45.7	N11 00.0	36 30.3	N13 28.3	177 15.6	N 0 57.9
	07	200 47.0	333 25.7	14.1	38 47.8	10 59.9	51 32.8	28.3	192 18.0	58.0
	08	215 49.5	348 25.7	14.7	53 49.8	59.8	66 35.4	28.4	207 20.4	58.0
	09	230 52.0	3 25.8	. . 15.3	68 51.8	. . 59.7	81 38.0	. . 28.4	222 22.8	. . 58.0
	10	245 54.4	18 25.9	15.9	83 53.9	59.6	96 40.6	28.5	237 25.2	58.1
	11	260 56.9	33 25.9	16.5	98 55.9	59.6	111 43.1	28.5	252 27.6	58.1
	12	275 59.4	48 26.0	S14 17.1	113 58.0	N10 59.5	126 45.7	N13 28.6	267 30.0	N 0 58.2
	13	291 01.8	63 26.1	17.7	129 00.0	59.4	141 48.3	28.6	282 32.4	58.2
	14	306 04.3	78 26.1	18.3	144 02.1	59.3	156 50.9	28.7	297 34.8	58.2
	15	321 06.8	93 26.2	. . 18.9	159 04.1	. . 59.3	171 53.4	. . 28.7	312 37.2	. . 58.3
	16	336 09.2	108 26.2	19.5	174 06.2	59.2	186 56.0	28.8	327 39.6	58.3
	17	351 11.7	123 26.3	20.1	189 08.3	59.1	201 58.6	28.8	342 42.0	58.4
	18	6 14.2	138 26.3	S14 20.7	204 10.3	N10 59.1	217 01.2	N13 28.9	357 44.4	N 0 58.4
	19	21 16.6	153 26.4	21.3	219 12.4	59.0	232 03.7	28.9	12 46.8	58.4
	20	36 19.1	168 26.5	21.9	234 14.4	58.9	247 06.3	29.0	27 49.2	58.5
	21	51 21.5	183 26.5	. . 22.5	249 16.5	. . 58.8	262 08.9	. . 29.0	42 51.6	. . 58.5
	22	66 24.0	198 26.6	23.1	264 18.5	58.8	277 11.5	29.1	57 54.0	58.6
	23	81 26.5	213 26.6	23.7	279 20.6	58.7	292 14.0	29.1	72 56.4	58.6
28 MONDAY	00	96 28.9	228 26.7	S14 24.3	294 22.7	N10 58.6	307 16.6	N13 29.2	87 58.8	N 0 58.6
	01	111 31.4	243 26.7	24.9	309 24.7	58.6	322 19.2	29.2	103 01.2	58.7
	02	126 33.9	258 26.8	25.5	324 26.8	58.5	337 21.8	29.3	118 03.6	58.7
	03	141 36.3	273 26.8	. . 26.1	339 28.9	. . 58.4	352 24.3	. . 29.3	133 06.0	. . 58.8
	04	156 38.8	288 26.8	26.7	354 30.9	58.3	7 26.9	29.4	148 08.4	58.8
	05	171 41.3	303 26.9	27.3	9 33.0	58.3	22 29.5	29.4	163 10.8	58.8
	06	186 43.7	318 26.9	S14 27.9	24 35.0	N10 58.2	37 32.1	N13 29.5	178 13.2	N 0 58.9
	07	201 46.2	333 27.0	28.5	39 37.1	58.1	52 34.7	29.5	193 15.6	58.9
	08	216 48.6	348 27.0	29.1	54 39.2	58.1	67 37.2	29.6	208 18.0	59.0
	09	231 51.1	3 27.1	. . 29.7	69 41.3	. . 58.0	82 39.8	. . 29.6	223 20.4	. . 59.0
	10	246 53.6	18 27.1	30.3	84 43.3	57.9	97 42.4	29.7	238 22.8	59.0
	11	261 56.0	33 27.1	30.9	99 45.4	57.9	112 45.0	29.7	253 25.2	59.1
	12	276 58.5	48 27.2	S14 31.5	114 47.5	N10 57.8	127 47.6	N13 29.8	268 27.6	N 0 59.1
	13	292 01.0	63 27.2	32.1	129 49.5	57.7	142 50.1	29.8	283 30.0	59.2
	14	307 03.4	78 27.2	32.7	144 51.6	57.7	157 52.7	29.9	298 32.4	59.2
	15	322 05.9	93 27.3	. . 33.3	159 53.7	. . 57.6	172 55.3	. . 29.9	313 34.8	. . 59.2
	16	337 08.4	108 27.3	34.0	174 55.8	57.5	187 57.9	30.0	328 37.2	59.3
	17	352 10.8	123 27.3	34.6	189 57.9	57.5	203 00.5	30.1	343 39.6	59.3
	18	7 13.3	138 27.4	S14 35.2	204 59.9	N10 57.4	218 03.1	N13 30.1	358 41.9	N 0 59.4
	19	22 15.8	153 27.4	35.8	220 02.0	57.4	233 05.6	30.2	13 44.3	59.4
	20	37 18.2	168 27.4	36.4	235 04.1	57.3	248 08.2	30.2	28 46.7	59.4
	21	52 20.7	183 27.5	. . 37.0	250 06.2	. . 57.2	263 10.8	. . 30.3	43 49.1	. . 59.5
	22	67 23.1	198 27.5	37.6	265 08.3	57.2	278 13.4	30.3	58 51.5	59.5
	23	82 25.6	213 27.5	38.2	280 10.3	57.1	293 16.0	30.4	73 53.9	59.6
29 TUESDAY	00	97 28.1	228 27.5	S14 38.8	295 12.4	N10 57.0	308 18.6	N13 30.4	88 56.3	N 0 59.6
	01	112 30.5	243 27.6	39.4	310 14.5	57.0	323 21.1	30.5	103 58.7	59.7
	02	127 33.0	258 27.6	40.0	325 16.6	56.9	338 23.7	30.5	119 01.1	59.7
	03	142 35.5	273 27.6	. . 40.6	340 18.7	. . 56.9	353 26.3	. . 30.6	134 03.5	. . 59.7
	04	157 37.9	288 27.6	41.2	355 20.8	56.8	8 28.9	30.6	149 05.9	59.8
	05	172 40.4	303 27.6	41.8	10 22.9	56.8	23 31.5	30.7	164 08.3	59.8
	06	187 42.9	318 27.7	S14 42.4	25 25.0	N10 56.7	38 34.1	N13 30.7	179 10.7	N 0 59.9
	07	202 45.3	333 27.7	43.0	40 27.1	56.6	53 36.7	30.8	194 13.1	0 59.9
	08	217 47.8	348 27.7	43.6	55 29.2	56.6	68 39.2	30.9	209 15.5	1 00.0
	09	232 50.3	3 27.7	. . 44.2	70 31.2	. . 56.5	83 41.8	. . 30.9	224 17.8	. . 00.0
	10	247 52.7	18 27.7	44.8	85 33.3	56.5	98 44.4	31.0	239 20.2	00.0
	11	262 55.2	33 27.7	45.4	100 35.4	56.4	113 47.0	31.0	254 22.6	00.1
	12	277 57.6	48 27.7	S14 46.0	115 37.5	N10 56.4	128 49.6	N13 31.1	269 25.0	N 1 00.1
	13	293 00.1	63 27.8	46.6	130 39.6	56.3	143 52.2	31.1	284 27.4	00.2
	14	308 02.6	78 27.8	47.2	145 41.7	56.2	158 54.8	31.2	299 29.8	00.2
	15	323 05.0	93 27.8	. . 47.8	160 43.8	. . 56.2	173 57.4	. . 31.2	314 32.2	. . 00.2
	16	338 07.5	108 27.8	48.4	175 45.9	56.1	189 00.0	31.3	329 34.6	00.3
	17	353 10.0	123 27.8	49.0	190 48.0	56.1	204 02.5	31.3	344 37.0	00.3
	18	8 12.4	138 27.8	S14 49.6	205 50.1	N10 56.0	219 05.1	N13 31.4	359 39.4	N 1 00.4
	19	23 14.9	153 27.8	50.2	220 52.3	56.0	234 07.7	31.5	14 41.8	00.4
	20	38 17.4	168 27.8	50.8	235 54.4	55.9	249 10.3	31.5	29 44.2	00.5
	21	53 19.8	183 27.8	. . 51.4	250 56.5	. . 55.9	264 12.9	. . 31.6	44 46.5	. . 00.5
	22	68 22.3	198 27.8	52.0	265 58.6	55.8	279 15.5	31.6	59 48.9	00.5
	23	83 24.7	213 27.8	52.6	281 00.7	55.8	294 18.1	31.7	74 51.3	00.6
Mer. Pass.		h m 17 31.2	v 0.0	d 0.6	v 2.1	d 0.1	v 2.6	d 0.1	v 2.4	d 0.0

STARS

Name	SHA ° ′	Dec ° ′
Acamar	315 10.3	S40 11.9
Achernar	335 18.8	S57 06.2
Acrux	172 58.2	S63 14.7
Adhara	255 04.2	S29 00.5
Aldebaran	290 37.4	N16 33.8
Alioth	166 11.6	N55 48.4
Alkaid	152 50.9	N49 10.4
Alnair	27 31.2	S46 50.0
Alnilam	275 35.7	S 1 11.1
Alphard	217 45.9	S 8 46.6
Alphecca	126 02.6	N26 37.3
Alpheratz	357 33.1	N29 14.6
Altair	61 58.7	N 8 56.4
Ankaa	353 05.5	S42 09.7
Antares	112 14.2	S26 29.4
Arcturus	145 46.6	N19 02.3
Atria	107 07.4	S69 04.4
Avior	234 13.5	S59 35.6
Bellatrix	278 20.8	N 6 22.4
Betelgeuse	270 50.0	N 7 24.7
Canopus	263 51.1	S52 42.6
Capella	280 19.0	N46 01.5
Deneb	49 25.1	N45 22.8
Denebola	182 23.2	N14 25.1
Diphda	348 45.6	S17 50.4
Dubhe	193 38.8	N61 36.0
Elnath	277 59.4	N28 37.8
Eltanin	90 42.0	N51 29.0
Enif	33 37.4	N10 00.0
Fomalhaut	15 12.9	S29 28.9
Gacrux	171 49.8	S57 15.6
Gienah	175 41.9	S17 41.5
Hadar	148 33.9	S60 30.0
Hamal	327 49.2	N23 35.6
Kaus Aust.	83 30.8	S34 22.3
Kochab	137 20.6	N74 02.3
Markab	13 28.4	N15 21.2
Menkar	314 04.2	N 4 11.8
Menkent	147 55.9	S36 30.0
Miaplacidus	221 37.2	S69 49.5
Mirfak	308 25.5	N49 57.6
Nunki	75 46.1	S26 15.8
Peacock	53 03.7	S56 39.0
Pollux	243 15.0	N27 57.5
Procyon	244 48.8	N 5 09.3
Rasalhague	95 57.4	N12 32.4
Regulus	207 32.5	N11 50.0
Rigel	281 02.0	S 8 10.3
Rigil Kent.	139 38.4	S60 56.6
Sabik	102 01.2	S15 45.5
Schedar	349 29.1	N56 41.5
Shaula	96 08.6	S37 07.3
Sirius	258 24.4	S16 45.2
Spica	158 20.7	S11 18.1
Suhail	222 44.7	S43 32.4
Vega	80 32.6	N38 48.5
Zuben'ubi	136 54.4	S16 09.2

	SHA ° ′	Mer. Pass. h m
Venus	131 57.7	8 46
Mars	197 53.7	4 22
Jupiter	210 47.7	3 30
Saturn	351 29.9	18 05

UT		SUN GHA	SUN Dec	MOON GHA	v	MOON Dec	d	HP
d h		° ′	° ′	° ′	′	° ′	′	′
27 00	SUNDAY	179 48.1	S23 20.1	316 18.1	8.1	N16 16.3	14.2	60.4
01		194 47.8	20.0	330 45.2	8.3	16 02.1	14.3	60.3
02		209 47.5	19.9	345 12.5	8.3	15 47.8	14.4	60.3
03		224 47.2	. . 19.8	359 39.8	8.6	15 33.4	14.4	60.3
04		239 46.9	19.7	14 07.4	8.6	15 19.0	14.6	60.2
05		254 46.6	19.6	28 35.0	8.7	15 04.4	14.6	60.2
06		269 46.2	S23 19.4	43 02.7	8.9	N14 49.8	14.6	60.2
07		284 45.9	19.3	57 30.6	9.0	14 35.2	14.8	60.1
08		299 45.6	19.2	71 58.6	9.1	14 20.4	14.8	60.1
09		314 45.3	. . 19.1	86 26.7	9.2	14 05.6	14.8	60.1
10		329 45.0	19.0	100 54.9	9.4	13 50.8	14.9	60.0
11		344 44.7	18.9	115 23.3	9.4	13 35.9	15.0	60.0
12		359 44.4	S23 18.8	129 51.7	9.6	N13 20.9	15.1	60.0
13		14 44.1	18.7	144 20.3	9.7	13 05.8	15.1	59.9
14		29 43.8	18.6	158 49.0	9.7	12 50.7	15.1	59.9
15		44 43.5	. . 18.5	173 17.7	9.9	12 35.6	15.2	59.9
16		59 43.2	18.4	187 46.6	10.1	12 20.4	15.2	59.8
17		74 42.9	18.2	202 15.7	10.1	12 05.2	15.3	59.8
18		89 42.6	S23 18.1	216 44.8	10.2	N11 49.9	15.4	59.7
19		104 42.3	18.0	231 14.0	10.3	11 34.5	15.4	59.7
20		119 42.0	17.9	245 43.3	10.4	11 19.1	15.4	59.7
21		134 41.7	. . 17.8	260 12.7	10.6	11 03.7	15.4	59.6
22		149 41.3	17.7	274 42.3	10.6	10 48.3	15.5	59.6
23		164 41.0	17.5	289 11.9	10.7	10 32.8	15.6	59.6
28 00	MONDAY	179 40.7	S23 17.4	303 41.6	10.8	N10 17.2	15.5	59.5
01		194 40.4	17.3	318 11.4	10.9	10 01.7	15.6	59.5
02		209 40.1	17.2	332 41.3	11.1	9 46.1	15.7	59.5
03		224 39.8	. . 17.1	347 11.4	11.1	9 30.4	15.6	59.4
04		239 39.5	16.9	1 41.5	11.2	9 14.8	15.7	59.4
05		254 39.2	16.8	16 11.7	11.3	8 59.1	15.7	59.3
06		269 38.9	S23 16.7	30 42.0	11.3	N 8 43.4	15.8	59.3
07		284 38.6	16.6	45 12.3	11.5	8 27.6	15.7	59.3
08		299 38.3	16.4	59 42.8	11.6	8 11.9	15.8	59.2
09		314 38.0	. . 16.3	74 13.4	11.6	7 56.1	15.8	59.2
10		329 37.7	16.2	88 44.0	11.7	7 40.3	15.8	59.1
11		344 37.4	16.1	103 14.7	11.8	7 24.5	15.9	59.1
12		359 37.1	S23 15.9	117 45.5	11.9	N 7 08.6	15.8	59.1
13		14 36.8	15.8	132 16.4	12.0	6 52.8	15.9	59.0
14		29 36.5	15.7	146 47.4	12.0	6 36.9	15.8	59.0
15		44 36.2	. . 15.5	161 18.4	12.1	6 21.1	15.9	58.9
16		59 35.9	15.4	175 49.5	12.2	6 05.2	15.9	58.9
17		74 35.6	15.3	190 20.7	12.3	5 49.3	15.9	58.9
18		89 35.2	S23 15.1	204 52.0	12.3	N 5 33.4	15.9	58.8
19		104 34.9	15.0	219 23.3	12.4	5 17.5	15.9	58.8
20		119 34.6	14.9	233 54.7	12.5	5 01.6	15.9	58.8
21		134 34.3	. . 14.7	248 26.2	12.5	4 45.7	15.9	58.7
22		149 34.0	14.6	262 57.7	12.6	4 29.8	15.9	58.7
23		164 33.7	14.4	277 29.3	12.7	4 13.9	15.9	58.6
29 00	TUESDAY	179 33.4	S23 14.3	292 01.0	12.7	N 3 58.0	15.9	58.6
01		194 33.1	14.2	306 32.7	12.8	3 42.1	15.9	58.6
02		209 32.8	14.0	321 04.5	12.9	3 26.2	15.9	58.5
03		224 32.5	. . 13.9	335 36.4	12.9	3 10.3	15.9	58.5
04		239 32.2	13.7	350 08.3	13.0	2 54.4	15.9	58.4
05		254 31.9	13.6	4 40.3	13.0	2 38.5	15.8	58.4
06		269 31.6	S23 13.5	19 12.3	13.1	N 2 22.7	15.9	58.4
07		284 31.3	13.3	33 44.4	13.1	2 06.8	15.8	58.3
08		299 31.0	13.2	48 16.5	13.2	1 51.0	15.8	58.3
09		314 30.7	. . 13.0	62 48.7	13.2	1 35.2	15.9	58.2
10		329 30.4	12.9	77 20.9	13.3	1 19.3	15.7	58.2
11		344 30.1	12.7	91 53.2	13.4	1 03.6	15.8	58.2
12		359 29.8	S23 12.6	106 25.6	13.3	N 0 47.8	15.8	58.1
13		14 29.5	12.4	120 57.9	13.5	0 32.0	15.7	58.1
14		29 29.2	12.3	135 30.4	13.4	0 16.3	15.8	58.0
15		44 28.9	. . 12.1	150 02.8	13.5	N 0 00.5	15.7	58.0
16		59 28.6	12.0	164 35.3	13.6	S 0 15.2	15.6	58.0
17		74 28.3	11.8	179 07.9	13.6	0 30.8	15.7	57.9
18		89 28.0	S23 11.7	193 40.5	13.6	S 0 46.5	15.6	57.9
19		104 27.7	11.5	208 13.1	13.6	1 02.1	15.6	57.9
20		119 27.4	11.4	222 45.7	13.7	1 17.7	15.6	57.8
21		134 27.1	. . 11.2	237 18.4	13.8	1 33.3	15.5	57.8
22		149 26.8	11.1	251 51.2	13.7	1 48.8	15.6	57.7
23		164 26.5	10.9	266 23.9	13.8	S 2 04.4	15.5	57.7
		SD 16.3	*d* 0.1	SD 16.3		16.1		15.8

Lat.	Twilight Naut.	Twilight Civil	Sunrise	Moonrise 27	28	29	30
°	h m	h m	h m	h m	h m	h m	h m
N 72	08 26	10 53	▬	19 02	21 32	23 46	25 59
N 70	08 07	09 54	▬	19 22	21 38	23 42	25 44
68	07 51	09 20	▬	19 38	21 44	23 39	25 33
66	07 38	08 55	10 33	19 51	21 48	23 37	25 23
64	07 27	08 35	09 52	20 02	21 52	23 35	25 15
62	07 18	08 19	09 25	20 11	21 55	23 33	25 09
60	07 09	08 06	09 03	20 19	21 58	23 32	25 03
N 58	07 02	07 55	08 46	20 25	22 00	23 30	24 58
56	06 55	07 44	08 32	20 31	22 03	23 29	24 53
54	06 49	07 35	08 19	20 36	22 05	23 28	24 49
52	06 44	07 27	08 08	20 41	22 06	23 27	24 46
50	06 38	07 20	07 58	20 45	22 08	23 26	24 42
45	06 27	07 04	07 38	20 55	22 12	23 25	24 35
N 40	06 16	06 50	07 21	21 02	22 14	23 23	24 30
35	06 07	06 39	07 07	21 09	22 17	23 22	24 25
30	05 58	06 28	06 55	21 15	22 19	23 21	24 20
20	05 42	06 10	06 34	21 25	22 23	23 19	24 13
N 10	05 26	05 52	06 15	21 33	22 26	23 17	24 06
0	05 09	05 35	05 58	21 41	22 30	23 15	24 00
S 10	04 50	05 17	05 40	21 49	22 33	23 14	23 54
20	04 28	04 57	05 21	21 58	22 36	23 12	23 47
30	03 59	04 32	05 00	22 07	22 40	23 10	23 40
35	03 40	04 17	04 47	22 13	22 42	23 09	23 36
40	03 17	03 59	04 32	22 19	22 45	23 08	23 31
45	02 47	03 36	04 14	22 27	22 48	23 07	23 26
S 50	02 02	03 07	03 51	22 35	22 51	23 05	23 20
52	01 34	02 52	03 41	22 39	22 53	23 05	23 17
54	00 50	02 34	03 28	22 44	22 54	23 04	23 13
56	////	02 12	03 14	22 48	22 56	23 03	23 10
58	////	01 43	02 58	22 54	22 58	23 02	23 06
S 60	////	00 55	02 37	23 00	23 01	23 01	23 02

Lat.	Sunset	Twilight Civil	Twilight Naut.	Moonset 27	28	29	30
°	h m	h m	h m	h m	h m	h m	h m
N 72	▬	13 11	15 37	12 24	11 38	11 04	10 31
N 70	▬	14 09	15 57	12 01	11 28	11 02	10 38
68	▬	14 44	16 12	11 43	11 20	11 01	10 43
66	13 30	15 08	16 25	11 28	11 13	11 01	10 48
64	14 11	15 28	16 36	11 16	11 07	11 00	10 52
62	14 38	15 44	16 45	11 05	11 02	10 59	10 56
60	15 00	15 57	16 54	10 56	10 58	10 59	10 59
N 58	15 17	16 09	17 01	10 48	10 54	10 58	11 02
56	15 32	16 19	17 08	10 41	10 50	10 58	11 05
54	15 44	16 28	17 14	10 35	10 47	10 57	11 07
52	15 55	16 36	17 20	10 29	10 44	10 57	11 09
50	16 05	16 43	17 25	10 24	10 42	10 57	11 11
45	16 25	16 59	17 36	10 13	10 36	10 56	11 15
N 40	16 42	17 13	17 47	10 03	10 31	10 55	11 18
35	16 56	17 24	17 56	09 55	10 26	10 55	11 21
30	17 08	17 35	18 05	09 48	10 23	10 54	11 24
20	17 30	17 54	18 21	09 36	10 16	10 53	11 29
N 10	17 48	18 11	18 37	09 24	10 10	10 52	11 33
0	18 05	18 28	18 54	09 14	10 05	10 52	11 37
S 10	18 23	18 46	19 13	09 04	09 59	10 51	11 41
20	18 42	19 06	19 35	08 52	09 53	10 50	11 45
30	19 03	19 31	20 04	08 39	09 46	10 49	11 49
35	19 16	19 46	20 23	08 32	09 42	10 48	11 52
40	19 31	20 04	20 46	08 23	09 37	10 48	11 55
45	19 49	20 26	21 16	08 13	09 32	10 47	11 59
S 50	20 11	20 56	22 01	08 00	09 25	10 46	12 03
52	20 22	21 11	22 28	07 54	09 22	10 45	12 05
54	20 34	21 28	23 11	07 48	09 19	10 45	12 07
56	20 48	21 50	////	07 40	09 15	10 44	12 10
58	21 05	22 19	////	07 32	09 11	10 44	12 12
S 60	21 25	23 07	////	07 23	09 06	10 43	12 15

Day	SUN Eqn. of Time 00^h	SUN Eqn. of Time 12^h	SUN Mer. Pass.	MOON Mer. Pass. Upper	MOON Mer. Pass. Lower	Age	Phase
d	m s	m s	h m	h m	h m	d	%
27	00 47	01 02	12 01	03 01	15 28	18	83
28	01 16	01 31	12 02	03 53	16 17	19	74
29	01 46	02 00	12 02	04 41	17 04	20	64

UT	ARIES	VENUS −4·6		MARS −0·1		JUPITER −2·4		SATURN +0·7	
d h	GHA ° ′	GHA ° ′	Dec ° ′	GHA ° ′	Dec ° ′	GHA ° ′	Dec ° ′	GHA ° ′	Dec ° ′
30 00 (WEDNESDAY)	98 27.2	228 27.8	S14 53.2	296 02.8	N10 55.7	309 20.7	N13 31.7	89 53.7	N 1 00.6
01	113 29.7	243 27.8	53.8	311 04.9	55.7	324 23.3	31.8	104 56.1	00.7
02	128 32.1	258 27.8	54.4	326 07.0	55.6	339 25.9	31.9	119 58.5	00.7
03	143 34.6	273 27.8	. . 55.0	341 09.1	. . 55.6	354 28.5	. . 31.9	135 00.9	. . 00.8
04	158 37.1	288 27.8	55.6	356 11.2	55.5	9 31.1	32.0	150 03.3	00.8
05	173 39.5	303 27.8	56.2	11 13.4	55.5	24 33.7	32.0	165 05.7	00.9
06	188 42.0	318 27.8	S14 56.8	26 15.5	N10 55.4	39 36.2	N13 32.1	180 08.0	N 1 00.9
07	203 44.5	333 27.8	57.4	41 17.6	55.4	54 38.8	32.1	195 10.4	00.9
08	218 46.9	348 27.8	58.0	56 19.7	55.3	69 41.4	32.2	210 12.8	01.0
09	233 49.4	3 27.8	. . 58.6	71 21.8	. . 55.3	84 44.0	. . 32.2	225 15.2	. . 01.0
10	248 51.9	18 27.8	59.2	86 24.0	55.2	99 46.6	32.3	240 17.6	01.1
11	263 54.3	33 27.7	14 59.8	101 26.1	55.2	114 49.2	32.4	255 20.0	01.1
12	278 56.8	48 27.7	S15 00.4	116 28.2	N10 55.2	129 51.8	N13 32.4	270 22.4	N 1 01.2
13	293 59.2	63 27.7	01.0	131 30.3	55.1	144 54.4	32.5	285 24.8	01.2
14	309 01.7	78 27.7	01.6	146 32.4	55.1	159 57.0	32.5	300 27.1	01.2
15	324 04.2	93 27.7	. . 02.2	161 34.6	. . 55.0	174 59.6	. . 32.6	315 29.5	. . 01.3
16	339 06.6	108 27.7	02.8	176 36.7	55.0	190 02.2	32.6	330 31.9	01.3
17	354 09.1	123 27.7	03.4	191 38.8	54.9	205 04.8	32.7	345 34.3	01.4
18	9 11.6	138 27.6	S15 04.0	206 41.0	N10 54.9	220 07.4	N13 32.8	0 36.7	N 1 01.4
19	24 14.0	153 27.6	04.6	221 43.1	54.9	235 10.0	32.8	15 39.1	01.5
20	39 16.5	168 27.6	05.2	236 45.2	54.8	250 12.6	32.9	30 41.5	01.5
21	54 19.0	183 27.6	. . 05.9	251 47.4	. . 54.8	265 15.2	. . 32.9	45 43.9	. . 01.6
22	69 21.4	198 27.6	06.5	266 49.5	54.7	280 17.8	33.0	60 46.2	01.6
23	84 23.9	213 27.5	07.1	281 51.6	54.7	295 20.4	33.1	75 48.6	01.7
31 00 (THURSDAY)	99 26.4	228 27.5	S15 07.7	296 53.8	N10 54.6	310 23.0	N13 33.1	90 51.0	N 1 01.7
01	114 28.8	243 27.5	08.3	311 55.9	54.6	325 25.6	33.2	105 53.4	01.7
02	129 31.3	258 27.5	08.9	326 58.0	54.6	340 28.2	33.2	120 55.8	01.8
03	144 33.7	273 27.4	. . 09.5	342 00.2	. . 54.5	355 30.8	. . 33.3	135 58.2	. . 01.8
04	159 36.2	288 27.4	10.1	357 02.3	54.5	10 33.4	33.3	151 00.6	01.9
05	174 38.7	303 27.4	10.7	12 04.4	54.5	25 36.0	33.4	166 02.9	01.9
06	189 41.1	318 27.3	S15 11.3	27 06.6	N10 54.4	40 38.6	N13 33.5	181 05.3	N 1 02.0
07	204 43.6	333 27.3	11.9	42 08.7	54.4	55 41.2	33.5	196 07.7	02.0
08	219 46.1	348 27.3	12.5	57 10.9	54.3	70 43.8	33.6	211 10.1	02.1
09	234 48.5	3 27.3	. . 13.1	72 13.0	. . 54.3	85 46.4	. . 33.6	226 12.5	. . 02.1
10	249 51.0	18 27.2	13.7	87 15.2	54.3	100 49.0	33.7	241 14.9	02.1
11	264 53.5	33 27.2	14.3	102 17.3	54.2	115 51.6	33.8	256 17.2	02.2
12	279 55.9	48 27.1	S15 14.9	117 19.5	N10 54.2	130 54.2	N13 33.8	271 19.6	N 1 02.2
13	294 58.4	63 27.1	15.5	132 21.6	54.2	145 56.8	33.9	286 22.0	02.3
14	310 00.8	78 27.1	16.1	147 23.8	54.1	160 59.4	33.9	301 24.4	02.3
15	325 03.3	93 27.0	. . 16.7	162 25.9	. . 54.1	176 02.0	. . 34.0	316 26.8	. . 02.4
16	340 05.8	108 27.0	17.3	177 28.1	54.1	191 04.6	34.1	331 29.2	02.4
17	355 08.2	123 27.0	17.9	192 30.2	54.0	206 07.2	34.1	346 31.5	02.5
18	10 10.7	138 26.9	S15 18.5	207 32.4	N10 54.0	221 09.8	N13 34.2	1 33.9	N 1 02.5
19	25 13.2	153 26.9	19.1	222 34.5	54.0	236 12.5	34.2	16 36.3	02.6
20	40 15.6	168 26.8	19.7	237 36.7	53.9	251 15.1	34.3	31 38.7	02.6
21	55 18.1	183 26.8	. . 20.3	252 38.8	. . 53.9	266 17.7	. . 34.4	46 41.1	. . 02.7
22	70 20.6	198 26.7	20.9	267 41.0	53.9	281 20.3	34.4	61 43.4	02.7
23	85 23.0	213 26.7	21.5	282 43.2	53.9	296 22.9	34.5	76 45.8	02.8
1 00 (FRIDAY)	100 25.5	228 26.6	S15 22.1	297 45.3	N10 53.8	311 25.5	N13 34.5	91 48.2	N 1 02.8
01	115 28.0	243 26.6	22.7	312 47.5	53.8	326 28.1	34.6	106 50.6	02.8
02	130 30.4	258 26.5	23.3	327 49.7	53.8	341 30.7	34.7	121 53.0	02.9
03	145 32.9	273 26.5	. . 23.9	342 51.8	. . 53.7	356 33.3	. . 34.7	136 55.4	. . 02.9
04	160 35.3	288 26.4	24.4	357 54.0	53.7	11 35.9	34.8	151 57.7	03.0
05	175 37.8	303 26.4	25.0	12 56.2	53.7	26 38.5	34.9	167 00.1	03.0
06	190 40.3	318 26.3	S15 25.6	27 58.3	N10 53.7	41 41.1	N13 34.9	182 02.5	N 1 03.1
07	205 42.7	333 26.3	26.2	43 00.5	53.6	56 43.7	35.0	197 04.9	03.1
08	220 45.2	348 26.2	26.8	58 02.7	53.6	71 46.4	35.0	212 07.3	03.2
09	235 47.7	3 26.2	. . 27.4	73 04.8	. . 53.6	86 49.0	. . 35.1	227 09.6	. . 03.2
10	250 50.1	18 26.1	28.0	88 07.0	53.6	101 51.6	35.2	242 12.0	03.3
11	265 52.6	33 26.0	28.6	103 09.2	53.5	116 54.2	35.2	257 14.4	03.3
12	280 55.1	48 26.0	S15 29.2	118 11.3	N10 53.5	131 56.8	N13 35.3	272 16.8	N 1 03.4
13	295 57.5	63 25.9	29.8	133 13.5	53.5	146 59.4	35.4	287 19.2	03.4
14	311 00.0	78 25.9	30.4	148 15.7	53.5	162 02.0	35.4	302 21.5	03.5
15	326 02.5	93 25.8	. . 31.0	163 17.9	. . 53.5	177 04.6	. . 35.5	317 23.9	. . 03.5
16	341 04.9	108 25.7	31.6	178 20.1	53.4	192 07.2	35.5	332 26.3	03.6
17	356 07.4	123 25.7	32.2	193 22.2	53.4	207 09.9	35.6	347 28.7	03.6
18	11 09.8	138 25.6	S15 32.8	208 24.4	N10 53.4	222 12.5	N13 35.7	2 31.1	N 1 03.6
19	26 12.3	153 25.5	33.4	223 26.6	53.4	237 15.1	35.7	17 33.4	03.7
20	41 14.8	168 25.5	34.0	238 28.8	53.3	252 17.7	35.8	32 35.8	03.7
21	56 17.2	183 25.4	. . 34.6	253 31.0	. . 53.3	267 20.3	. . 35.9	47 38.2	. . 03.8
22	71 19.7	198 25.3	35.2	268 33.2	53.3	282 22.9	35.9	62 40.6	03.8
23	86 22.2	213 25.3	35.8	283 35.3	53.3	297 25.5	36.0	77 42.9	03.9
Mer. Pass.	h m 17 19.4	*v* 0.0	*d* 0.6	*v* 2.1	*d* 0.0	*v* 2.6	*d* 0.1	*v* 2.4	*d* 0.0

STARS

Name	SHA ° ′	Dec ° ′
Acamar	315 10.3	S40 11.9
Achernar	335 18.8	S57 06.2
Acrux	172 58.2	S63 14.7
Adhara	255 04.2	S29 00.5
Aldebaran	290 37.4	N16 33.8
Alioth	166 11.6	N55 48.4
Alkaid	152 50.9	N49 10.4
Alnair	27 31.2	S46 50.0
Alnilam	275 35.7	S 1 11.1
Alphard	217 45.9	S 8 46.6
Alphecca	126 02.6	N26 37.3
Alpheratz	357 33.1	N29 14.6
Altair	61 58.7	N 8 56.4
Ankaa	353 05.6	S42 09.7
Antares	112 14.1	S26 29.4
Arcturus	145 46.6	N19 02.3
Atria	107 07.4	S69 04.4
Avior	234 13.5	S59 35.6
Bellatrix	278 20.8	N 6 22.4
Betelgeuse	270 50.0	N 7 24.7
Canopus	263 51.1	S52 42.6
Capella	280 19.0	N46 01.5
Deneb	49 25.1	N45 22.7
Denebola	182 23.2	N14 25.1
Diphda	348 45.6	S17 50.4
Dubhe	193 38.8	N61 36.0
Elnath	277 59.4	N28 37.8
Eltanin	90 42.0	N51 29.0
Enif	33 37.4	N10 00.0
Fomalhaut	15 12.9	S29 28.9
Gacrux	171 49.8	S57 15.6
Gienah	175 41.9	S17 41.5
Hadar	148 33.9	S60 30.0
Hamal	327 49.2	N23 35.6
Kaus Aust.	83 30.8	S34 22.3
Kochab	137 20.6	N74 02.3
Markab	13 28.4	N15 21.2
Menkar	314 04.2	N 4 11.8
Menkent	147 55.8	S36 30.0
Miaplacidus	221 37.1	S69 49.5
Mirfak	308 25.5	N49 57.6
Nunki	75 46.1	S26 15.8
Peacock	53 03.7	S56 39.0
Pollux	243 14.9	N27 57.5
Procyon	244 48.8	N 5 09.3
Rasalhague	95 57.4	N12 32.4
Regulus	207 32.5	N11 50.0
Rigel	281 02.0	S 8 10.3
Rigil Kent.	139 38.3	S60 56.6
Sabik	102 01.2	S15 45.5
Schedar	349 29.1	N56 41.5
Shaula	96 08.6	S37 07.3
Sirius	258 24.4	S16 45.2
Spica	158 20.6	S11 18.1
Suhail	222 44.7	S43 32.4
Vega	80 32.6	N38 48.5
Zuben'ubi	136 54.4	S16 09.2

	SHA ° ′	Mer. Pass. h m
Venus	129 01.2	8 46
Mars	197 27.4	4 12
Jupiter	210 56.6	3 18
Saturn	351 24.7	17 54

UT	SUN GHA	SUN Dec	MOON GHA	v	MOON Dec	d	HP
d h	° ′	° ′	° ′	′	° ′	′	′
30 00	179 26.2	S23 10.7	280 56.7	13.8	S 2 19.9	15.4	57.7
01	194 25.9	10.6	295 29.5	13.9	2 35.3	15.4	57.6
02	209 25.6	10.4	310 02.4	13.8	2 50.7	15.4	57.6
W 03	224 25.3	. . 10.3	324 35.2	13.9	3 06.1	15.4	57.5
E 04	239 25.0	10.1	339 08.1	14.0	3 21.5	15.3	57.5
D 05	254 24.6	09.9	353 41.1	13.9	3 36.8	15.3	57.5
N 06	269 24.3	S23 09.8	8 14.0	14.0	S 3 52.1	15.2	57.4
E 07	284 24.0	09.6	22 47.0	13.9	4 07.3	15.3	57.4
S 08	299 23.7	09.4	37 19.9	14.1	4 22.6	15.1	57.4
D 09	314 23.4	. . 09.3	51 53.0	14.0	4 37.7	15.2	57.3
A 10	329 23.1	09.1	66 26.0	14.0	4 52.9	15.0	57.3
Y 11	344 22.8	08.9	80 59.0	14.1	5 07.9	15.1	57.2
12	359 22.5	S23 08.8	95 32.1	14.0	S 5 23.0	15.0	57.2
13	14 22.2	08.6	110 05.1	14.1	5 38.0	15.0	57.2
14	29 21.9	08.4	124 38.2	14.1	5 53.0	14.9	57.1
15	44 21.6	. . 08.3	139 11.3	14.1	6 07.9	14.9	57.1
16	59 21.3	08.1	153 44.4	14.1	6 22.8	14.8	57.1
17	74 21.0	07.9	168 17.5	14.1	6 37.6	14.8	57.0
18	89 20.7	S23 07.7	182 50.6	14.1	S 6 52.4	14.7	57.0
19	104 20.4	07.6	197 23.7	14.2	7 07.1	14.7	57.0
20	119 20.1	07.4	211 56.9	14.1	7 21.8	14.6	56.9
21	134 19.8	. . 07.2	226 30.0	14.1	7 36.4	14.6	56.9
22	149 19.5	07.0	241 03.1	14.2	7 51.0	14.5	56.9
23	164 19.2	06.9	255 36.3	14.1	8 05.5	14.5	56.8
31 00	179 18.9	S23 06.7	270 09.4	14.1	S 8 20.0	14.4	56.8
01	194 18.6	06.5	284 42.5	14.2	8 34.4	14.4	56.7
02	209 18.3	06.3	299 15.7	14.1	8 48.8	14.3	56.7
03	224 18.0	. . 06.2	313 48.8	14.1	9 03.1	14.2	56.7
04	239 17.7	06.0	328 21.9	14.2	9 17.3	14.2	56.6
05	254 17.4	05.8	342 55.1	14.1	9 31.5	14.2	56.6
06	269 17.2	S23 05.6	357 28.2	14.1	S 9 45.7	14.1	56.6
T 07	284 16.9	05.4	12 01.3	14.1	9 59.8	14.0	56.5
H 08	299 16.6	05.2	26 34.4	14.1	10 13.8	14.0	56.5
U 09	314 16.3	. . 05.1	41 07.5	14.1	10 27.8	13.9	56.5
R 10	329 16.0	04.9	55 40.6	14.0	10 41.7	13.8	56.4
S 11	344 15.7	04.7	70 13.6	14.1	10 55.5	13.8	56.4
D 12	359 15.4	S23 04.5	84 46.7	14.0	S11 09.3	13.7	56.4
A 13	14 15.1	04.3	99 19.7	14.1	11 23.0	13.7	56.3
Y 14	29 14.8	04.1	113 52.8	14.0	11 36.7	13.5	56.3
15	44 14.5	. . 03.9	128 25.8	14.0	11 50.2	13.6	56.3
16	59 14.2	03.7	142 58.8	14.0	12 03.8	13.4	56.3
17	74 13.9	03.6	157 31.8	13.9	12 17.2	13.4	56.2
18	89 13.6	S23 03.4	172 04.7	14.0	S12 30.6	13.3	56.2
19	104 13.3	03.2	186 37.7	13.9	12 43.9	13.3	56.2
20	119 13.0	03.0	201 10.6	13.9	12 57.2	13.2	56.1
21	134 12.7	. . 02.8	215 43.5	13.9	13 10.4	13.1	56.1
22	149 12.4	02.6	230 16.4	13.8	13 23.5	13.0	56.1
23	164 12.1	02.4	244 49.2	13.9	13 36.5	13.0	56.0
1 00	179 11.8	S23 02.2	259 22.1	13.8	S13 49.5	12.9	56.0
01	194 11.5	02.0	273 54.9	13.7	14 02.4	12.8	56.0
02	209 11.2	01.8	288 27.6	13.8	14 15.2	12.8	55.9
03	224 10.9	. . 01.6	303 00.4	13.7	14 28.0	12.6	55.9
04	239 10.6	01.4	317 33.1	13.7	14 40.6	12.6	55.9
05	254 10.3	01.2	332 05.8	13.7	14 53.2	12.6	55.9
06	269 10.0	S23 01.0	346 38.5	13.6	S15 05.8	12.4	55.8
07	284 09.7	00.8	1 11.1	13.7	15 18.2	12.4	55.8
08	299 09.4	00.6	15 43.8	13.5	15 30.6	12.3	55.8
F 09	314 09.1	. . 00.4	30 16.3	13.6	15 42.9	12.2	55.7
R 10	329 08.8	00.2	44 48.9	13.5	15 55.1	12.1	55.7
I 11	344 08.5	23 00.0	59 21.4	13.5	16 07.2	12.1	55.7
D 12	359 08.2	S22 59.8	73 53.9	13.4	S16 19.3	11.9	55.7
A 13	14 08.0	59.6	88 26.3	13.4	16 31.2	11.9	55.6
Y 14	29 07.7	59.3	102 58.7	13.4	16 43.1	11.8	55.6
15	44 07.4	. . 59.1	117 31.1	13.4	16 54.9	11.7	55.6
16	59 07.1	58.9	132 03.5	13.3	17 06.6	11.7	55.6
17	74 06.8	58.7	146 35.8	13.2	17 18.3	11.5	55.5
18	89 06.5	S22 58.5	161 08.0	13.3	S17 29.8	11.5	55.5
19	104 06.2	58.3	175 40.3	13.2	17 41.3	11.3	55.5
20	119 05.9	58.1	190 12.5	13.1	17 52.6	11.3	55.5
21	134 05.6	. . 57.9	204 44.6	13.1	18 03.9	11.2	55.4
22	149 05.3	57.7	219 16.7	13.1	18 15.1	11.1	55.4
23	164 05.0	57.4	233 48.8	13.1	S18 26.2	11.0	55.4
	SD 16.3	*d* 0.2	SD 15.6		15.4		15.2

Lat.	Twilight Naut.	Twilight Civil	Sunrise	Moonrise 30	Moonrise 31	Moonrise 1	Moonrise 2
°	h m	h m	h m	h m	h m	h m	h m
N 72	08 25	10 46	▬	25 59	01 59	04 31	▬
N 70	08 06	09 51	▬	25 44	01 44	03 55	▬
68	07 50	09 18	▬	25 33	01 33	03 31	05 49
66	07 38	08 54	10 30	25 23	01 23	03 12	05 10
64	07 27	08 35	09 51	25 15	01 15	02 57	04 43
62	07 18	08 19	09 24	25 09	01 09	02 44	04 22
60	07 09	08 06	09 03	25 03	01 03	02 34	04 05
N 58	07 02	07 54	08 46	24 58	00 58	02 24	03 51
56	06 56	07 44	08 31	24 53	00 53	02 16	03 39
54	06 50	07 36	08 19	24 49	00 49	02 09	03 29
52	06 44	07 28	08 08	24 46	00 46	02 03	03 20
50	06 39	07 20	07 59	24 42	00 42	01 57	03 11
45	06 27	07 04	07 38	24 35	00 35	01 45	02 54
N 40	06 17	06 51	07 22	24 30	00 30	01 35	02 40
35	06 08	06 40	07 08	24 25	00 25	01 26	02 28
30	05 59	06 29	06 56	24 20	00 20	01 19	02 17
20	05 43	06 11	06 35	24 13	00 13	01 06	02 00
N 10	05 27	05 54	06 16	24 06	00 06	00 55	01 44
0	05 11	05 37	05 59	24 00	00 00	00 44	01 30
S 10	04 52	05 19	05 42	23 54	24 34	00 34	01 16
20	04 30	04 59	05 23	23 47	24 23	00 23	01 00
30	04 01	04 34	05 01	23 40	24 11	00 11	00 43
35	03 43	04 19	04 49	23 36	24 03	00 03	00 33
40	03 20	04 01	04 34	23 31	23 55	24 22	00 22
45	02 50	03 39	04 16	23 26	23 46	24 09	00 09
S 50	02 05	03 10	03 54	23 20	23 35	23 53	24 15
52	01 39	02 55	03 43	23 17	23 30	23 45	24 05
54	00 57	02 38	03 31	23 13	23 24	23 37	23 54
56	////	02 16	03 17	23 10	23 18	23 27	23 41
58	////	01 48	03 01	23 06	23 11	23 17	23 26
S 60	////	01 02	02 41	23 02	23 03	23 05	23 09

Lat.	Sunset	Twilight Civil	Twilight Naut.	Moonset 30	Moonset 31	Moonset 1	Moonset 2
°	h m	h m	h m	h m	h m	h m	h m
N 72	▬	13 21	15 41	10 31	09 53	08 56	▬
N 70	▬	14 15	16 01	10 38	10 10	09 33	▬
68	▬	14 48	16 16	10 43	10 24	09 59	09 17
66	13 37	15 13	16 29	10 48	10 35	10 20	09 57
64	14 16	15 32	16 39	10 52	10 45	10 36	10 25
62	14 43	15 47	16 49	10 56	10 53	10 50	10 47
60	15 03	16 00	16 57	10 59	11 00	11 01	11 04
N 58	15 20	16 12	17 04	11 02	11 06	11 11	11 19
56	15 35	16 22	17 11	11 05	11 12	11 20	11 32
54	15 47	16 31	17 17	11 07	11 17	11 28	11 43
52	15 58	16 39	17 22	11 09	11 21	11 35	11 53
50	16 08	16 46	17 27	11 11	11 25	11 42	12 01
45	16 28	17 02	17 39	11 15	11 34	11 56	12 20
N 40	16 44	17 15	17 49	11 18	11 42	12 07	12 35
35	16 58	17 26	17 58	11 21	11 48	12 17	12 48
30	17 10	17 37	18 07	11 24	11 54	12 26	13 00
20	17 31	17 55	18 23	11 29	12 04	12 40	13 19
N 10	17 50	18 12	18 39	11 33	12 13	12 54	13 36
0	18 07	18 29	18 55	11 37	12 21	13 06	13 52
S 10	18 24	18 47	19 14	11 41	12 29	13 18	14 08
20	18 43	19 07	19 36	11 45	12 38	13 32	14 26
30	19 04	19 32	20 05	11 49	12 48	13 47	14 46
35	19 17	19 47	20 23	11 52	12 54	13 56	14 57
40	19 32	20 05	20 46	11 55	13 01	14 06	15 11
45	19 50	20 27	21 16	11 59	13 09	14 18	15 27
S 50	20 12	20 56	22 00	12 03	13 18	14 33	15 46
52	20 22	21 10	22 26	12 05	13 23	14 40	15 56
54	20 34	21 28	23 07	12 07	13 28	14 47	16 06
56	20 48	21 49	////	12 10	13 33	14 56	16 18
58	21 04	22 17	////	12 12	13 39	15 06	16 32
S 60	21 24	23 01	////	12 15	13 46	15 17	16 49

Day	SUN Eqn. of Time 00h	SUN Eqn. of Time 12h	SUN Mer. Pass.	MOON Mer. Pass. Upper	MOON Mer. Pass. Lower	Age	%	Phase
d	m s	m s	h m	h m	h m	d	%	
30	02 15	02 29	12 02	05 26	17 48	21	53	
31	02 44	02 58	12 03	06 10	18 33	22	43	
1	03 12	03 26	12 03	06 55	19 18	23	33	

EXPLANATION

PRINCIPLE AND ARRANGEMENT

1. *Object.* The object of this Almanac is to provide, in a convenient form, the data required for the practice of astronomical navigation at sea.

2. *Principle.* The main contents of the Almanac consist of data from which the *Greenwich Hour Angle* (GHA) and the *Declination* (Dec) of all the bodies used for navigation can be obtained for any instant of *Universal Time* (UT, specifically UT1, or previously Greenwich Mean Time (GMT)).

The *Local Hour Angle* (LHA) can then be obtained by means of the formula:

$$\text{LHA} = \text{GHA} \begin{smallmatrix} - \text{ west} \\ + \text{ east} \end{smallmatrix} \text{ longitude}$$

The remaining data consist of: times of rising and setting of the Sun and Moon, and times of twilight; miscellaneous calendarial and planning data and auxiliary tables, including a list of Standard Times; corrections to be applied to observed altitude.

For the Sun, Moon, and planets, the GHA and Dec are tabulated directly for each hour of UT throughout the year. For the stars, the *Sidereal Hour Angle* (SHA) is given, and the GHA is obtained from:

$$\text{GHA Star} = \text{GHA Aries} + \text{SHA Star}$$

The SHA and Dec of the stars change slowly and may be regarded as constant over periods of several days. GHA Aries, or the Greenwich Hour Angle of the first point of Aries (the Vernal Equinox), is tabulated for each hour. Permanent tables give the appropriate increments and corrections to the tabulated hourly values of GHA and Dec for the minutes and seconds of UT.

The six-volume series of *Sight Reduction Tables for Marine Navigation* (published in U.S.A. as Pub. No. 229) has been designed for the solution of the navigational triangle and is intended for use with *The Nautical Almanac*.

Two alternative procedures for sight reduction are described on pages 277–318. The first requires the use of programmable calculators or computers, while the second uses a set of concise tables that is given on pages 286–317.

The tabular accuracy is $0'.1$ throughout. The time argument on the daily pages of this Almanac is UT1 denoted throughout by UT. This scale may differ from the broadcast time signals (UTC) by an amount which, if ignored, will introduce an error of up to $0'.2$ in longitude determined from astronomical observations. The difference arises because the time argument depends on the variable rate of rotation of the Earth while the broadcast time signals are based on an atomic time-scale. Step adjustments of exactly one second are made to the time signals as required (normally at 24^h on December 31 and June 30) so that the difference between the time signals and UT, as used in this Almanac, may not exceed $0^s.9$. Those who require to reduce observations to a precision of better than 1^s must therefore obtain the correction (DUT1) to the time signals from coding in the signal, or from other sources; the required time is given by UT1=UTC+DUT1 to a precision of $0^s.1$. Alternatively, the longitude, when determined from astronomical observations, may be corrected by the corresponding amount shown in the following table:

Correction to time signals	Correction to longitude
$-0^s.9$ to $-0^s.7$	$0'.2$ to east
$-0^s.6$ to $-0^s.3$	$0'.1$ to east
$-0^s.2$ to $+0^s.2$	no correction
$+0^s.3$ to $+0^s.6$	$0'.1$ to west
$+0^s.7$ to $+0^s.9$	$0'.2$ to west

3. *Lay-out.* The ephemeral data for three days are presented on an opening of two pages: the left-hand page contains the data for the planets and stars; the right-hand page contains the data for the Sun and Moon, together with times of twilight, sunrise, sunset, moonrise and moonset.

The remaining contents are arranged as follows: for ease of reference the altitude-correction tables are given on pages A2, A3, A4, xxxiv and xxxv; calendar, Moon's phases, eclipses, and planet notes (i.e. data of general interest) precede the main tabulations. The Explanation is followed by information on standard times, star charts and list of star positions, sight reduction procedures and concise sight reduction tables, polar phenomena information and graphs, tables of increments and corrections and other auxiliary tables that are frequently used.

MAIN DATA

4. *Daily pages.* The daily pages give the GHA of Aries, the GHA and Dec of the Sun, Moon, and the four navigational planets, for each hour of UT. For the Moon, values of v and d are also tabulated for each hour to facilitate the correction of GHA and Dec to intermediate times; v and d for the Sun and planets change so slowly that they are given, at the foot of the appropriate columns, once only on the page; v is zero for Aries and negligible for the Sun, and is omitted. The SHA and Dec of the 57 selected stars, arranged in alphabetical order of proper name, are also given.

5. *Stars.* The SHA and Dec of 173 stars, including the 57 selected stars, are tabulated for each month on pages 268–273; no interpolation is required and the data can be used in precisely the same way as those for the selected stars on the daily pages. The stars are arranged in order of SHA.

The list of 173 includes all stars down to magnitude 3·0, together with a few fainter ones to fill the larger gaps. The 57 selected stars have been chosen from amongst these on account of brightness and distribution in the sky; they will suffice for the majority of observations.

The 57 selected stars are known by their proper names, but they are also numbered in descending order of SHA. In the list of 173 stars, the constellation names are always given on the left-hand page; on the facing page proper names are given where well-known names exist. Numbers for the selected stars are given in both columns.

An index to the selected stars, containing lists in both alphabetical and numerical order, is given on page xxxiii and is also reprinted on the bookmark.

6. *Increments and corrections.* The tables printed on tinted paper (pages ii–xxxi) at the back of the Almanac provide the increments and corrections for minutes and seconds to be applied to the hourly values of GHA and Dec. They consist of sixty tables, one for each minute, separated into two parts: increments to GHA for Sun and planets, Aries, and Moon for every minute and second; and, for each minute, corrections to be applied to GHA and Dec corresponding to the values of v and d given on the daily pages.

The increments are based on the following adopted hourly rates of increase of the GHA: Sun and planets, 15° precisely; Aries, 15° 02′·46; Moon, 14° 19′·0. The values of v on the daily pages are the excesses of the actual hourly motions over the adopted values; they are generally positive, except for Venus. The tabulated hourly values of the Sun's GHA have been adjusted to reduce to a minimum the error caused by treating v as negligible. The values of d on the daily pages are the hourly differences of the Dec. For the Moon, the true values of v and d are given for each hour; otherwise mean values are given for the three days on the page.

7. *Method of entry.* The UT of an observation is expressed as a day and hour, followed by a number of minutes and seconds. The tabular values of GHA and Dec, and, where necessary, the corresponding values of v and d, are taken directly from the daily pages for the day and hour of UT; this hour is always *before* the time of observation. SHA and Dec of the selected stars are also taken from the daily pages.

The table of Increments and Corrections for the minute of UT is then selected. For the GHA, the increment for minutes and seconds is taken from the appropriate column opposite the seconds of UT; the v-correction is taken from the second part of the same table opposite the value of v as given on the daily pages. Both increment and v-correction are to be added to the GHA, except for Venus when v is prefixed by a minus sign and the v-correction is to be subtracted. For the Dec there is no increment, but a d-correction is applied in the same way as the v-correction; d is given without sign on the daily pages and the sign of the correction is to be supplied by inspection of the Dec column. In many cases the correction may be applied mentally.

8. *Examples.* (a) Sun and Moon. Required the GHA and Dec of the Sun and Moon on 2026 May 26 at $15^h\ 47^m\ 13^s$ UT.

		SUN			MOON			
		GHA	Dec	d	GHA	v	Dec	d
		° ′	° ′	′	° ′	′	° ′	′
Daily page, May $26^d\ 15^h$		45 44·1	N 21 11·9	0·4	278 43·8	15·6	S 7 52·4	14·1
Increments for	$47^m\ 13^s$	11 48·3			11 16·0			
v or d corrections for	47^m		+0·3		+12·4		+11·2	
Sum for May $26^d\ 15^h\ 47^m\ 13^s$		57 32·4	N 21 12·2		290 12·2		S 8 03·6	

(b) Planets. Required the LHA and Dec of (i) Venus on 2026 May 26 at $13^h\ 22^m\ 15^s$ UT in longitude E 89° 43′; (ii) Saturn on 2026 May 26 at $9^h\ 11^m\ 59^s$ UT in longitude W 69° 41′.

		VENUS					SATURN			
		GHA	v	Dec	d		GHA	v	Dec	d
		° ′	′	° ′	′		° ′	′	° ′	′
Daily page, May 26^d	(13^h)	339 15·7	−0·8	N 24 56·6	0·1	(9^h)	7 16·1	2·3	N 2 35·0	0·1
Increments (planets)	($22^m\ 15^s$)	5 33·8				($11^m\ 59^s$)	2 59·8			
v or d corrections	(22^m)	−0·3		+0·0		(11^m)	+0·4		+0·0	
Sum = GHA and Dec.		344 49·2		N 24 56·6			10 16·3		N 2 35·0	
Longitude	(east)	+ 89 43·0				(west)	− 69 41·0			
Multiples of 360°		−360					+360			
LHA planet		74 32·2					300 35·3			

(c) Stars. Required the GHA and Dec of (i) *Pollux* on 2026 May 26 at $13^h\ 23^m\ 18^s$ UT; (ii) *Alpheratz* on 2026 May 26 at $22^h\ 35^m\ 25^s$ UT.

		Pollux			*Alpheratz*	
		GHA	Dec		GHA	Dec
		° ′	° ′		° ′	° ′
Daily page (SHA and Dec)		243 16·2	N 27 57.8		357 33·8	N 29 14.0
Daily page (GHA Aries)	(13^h)	79 06·9		(22^h)	214 29·1	
Increments (Aries)	($23^m\ 18^s$)	5 50·5		($35^m\ 25^s$)	8 52·7	
Sum = GHA star		328 13·6			580 55·6	
Multiples of 360°					−360	
GHA star		328 13·6			220 55·6	

9. *Polaris (Pole Star) tables.* The tables on pages 274–276 provide means by which the latitude can be deduced from an observed altitude of *Polaris*, and they also give its azimuth; their use is explained and illustrated on those pages. They are based on the following formula:

$$\text{Latitude} - H_O = -p\cos h + \tfrac{1}{2}p\sin p\sin^2 h\tan(\text{latitude})$$

where
H_O = Apparent altitude (corrected for refraction)
p = polar distance of *Polaris* = 90° − Dec
h = local hour angle of *Polaris* = LHA Aries + SHA

a_0, which is a function of LHA Aries only, is the value of both terms of the above formula calculated for mean values of the SHA (313° 21′) and Dec (N 89° 22′.6) of *Polaris*, for a mean latitude of 50°, and adjusted by the addition of a constant (58′.8).

a_1, which is a function of LHA Aries and latitude, is the excess of the value of the second term over its mean value for latitude 50°, increased by a constant (0′.6) to make it always positive. a_2, which is a function of LHA Aries and date, is the correction to the first term for the variation of *Polaris* from its adopted mean position; it is increased by a constant (0′.6) to make it positive. The sum of the added constants is 1°, so that:

$$\text{Latitude} = \text{Apparent altitude (corrected for refraction)} - 1^\circ + a_0 + a_1 + a_2$$

RISING AND SETTING PHENOMENA

10. *General.* On the right-hand daily pages are given the times of sunrise and sunset, of the beginning and end of civil and nautical twilights, and of moonrise and moonset for a range of latitudes from N 72° to S 60°. These times, which are given to the nearest minute, are strictly the UT of the phenomena on the Greenwich meridian; they are given for every day for moonrise and moonset, but only for the middle day of the three on each page for the solar phenomena.

They are approximately the Local Mean Times (LMT) of the corresponding phenomena on other meridians; they can be formally interpolated if desired. The UT of a phenomenon is obtained from the LMT by:

$$\text{UT} = \text{LMT} \begin{smallmatrix} +\ \text{west} \\ -\ \text{east} \end{smallmatrix} \text{ longitude}$$

in which the longitude must first be converted to time by the table on page i or otherwise. Interpolation for latitude can be done mentally or with the aid of Table I on page xxxii.

The following symbols are used to indicate the conditions under which, in high latitudes, some of the phenomena do not occur:

□ Sun or Moon remains continuously above the horizon;

■ Sun or Moon remains continuously below the horizon;

//// twilight lasts all night.

Basis of the tabulations. At sunrise and sunset 16′ is allowed for semi-diameter and 34′ for horizontal refraction, so that at the times given the Sun's upper limb is on the visible horizon; all times refer to phenomena as seen from sea level with a clear horizon.

At the times given for the beginning and end of twilight, the Sun's zenith distance is 96° for civil, and 102° for nautical twilight. The degree of illumination at the times given for civil twilight (in good conditions and in the absence of other illumination) is such that the brightest stars are visible and the horizon is clearly defined. At the times given for nautical twilight, the horizon is in general not visible, and it is too dark for observation with a marine sextant.

Times corresponding to other depressions of the Sun may be obtained by interpolation or, for depressions of more than 12°, less reliably, by extrapolation; times so obtained will be subject to considerable uncertainty near extreme conditions.

At moonrise and moonset, allowance is made for semi-diameter, parallax, and refraction (34′), so that at the times given the Moon's upper limb is on the visible horizon as seen from sea level.

Polar phenomena. Information and graphs concerning the rising and setting of the Sun and Moon and the duration of civil twilight for high latitudes are given on pages 320–325.

11. *Sunrise, sunset, twilight.* The tabulated times may be regarded, without serious error, as the LMT of the phenomena on any of the three days on the page and in any longitude. Precise times may normally be obtained by interpolating the tabular values for latitude and to the correct day and longitude, the latter being expressed as a fraction of a day by dividing it by 360°, positive for west and negative for east longitudes. In the extreme conditions near □, ■ or //// interpolation may not be possible in one direction, but accurate times are of little value in these circumstances.

Examples. Required the UT of (a) the beginning of morning twilights and sunrise on 2026 January 13 for latitude S 48° 55′, longitude E 75° 18′; (b) sunset and the end of evening twilights on 2026 January 15 for latitude N 67° 10′, longitude W 168° 05′.

	(a)	Twilight Nautical	Twilight Civil	Sunrise	(b)	Sunset	Twilight Civil	Twilight Nautical
From p. 19		d h m	d h m	d h m		d h m	d h m	d h m
LMT for Lat	S 45°	13 03 09	13 03 56	13 04 32	N 66°	15 14 23	15 15 43	15 16 54
Corr. to (p. xxxii, Table I)	S 48° 55′	−27	−20	−16	N 67° 10′	−22	−12	−6
Long (p. i)	E 75° 18′	−5 01	−5 01	−5 01	W 168° 05′	+11 12	+11 12	+11 12
UT		12 21 41	12 22 35	12 23 15		16 01 13	16 02 43	16 04 00

The LMT are strictly for January 14 (middle date on page) and 0° longitude; for more precise times it is necessary to interpolate, but rounding errors may accumulate to about 2^{m}.

(a) to January $13^{d} - 75°/360° =$ Jan. $12^{d}.8$, i.e. $\frac{1}{3}(1\cdot2) = 0\cdot4$ backwards towards the data for the same latitude interpolated similarly from page 17; the corrections are -3^{m} to nautical twilight, -2^{m} to civil twilight and -2^{m} to sunrise.

(b) to January $15^{d} + 168°/360° =$ Jan. $15^{d}.5$, i.e. $\frac{1}{3}(1\cdot5) = 0\cdot5$ forwards towards the data for the same latitude interpolated similarly from page 21; the corrections are $+7^{m}$ to sunset, $+4^{m}$ to civil twilight, and $+3^{m}$ to nautical twilight.

12. *Moonrise, moonset.* Precise times of moonrise and moonset are rarely needed; a glance at the tables will generally give sufficient indication of whether the Moon is available for observation and of the hours of rising and setting. If needed, precise times may be obtained as follows. Interpolate for latitude, using Table I on page xxxii, on the day wanted and also on the preceding day in east longitudes or the following day in west longitudes; take the difference between these times and interpolate for longitude by applying to the time for the day wanted the correction from Table II on page xxxii, so that the resulting time is between the two times used. In extreme conditions near □ or ■ interpolation for latitude or longitude may be possible only in one direction; accurate times are of little value in these circumstances.

To facilitate this interpolation, the times of moonrise and moonset are given for four days on each page; where no phenomenon occurs during a particular day (as happens once a month) the time of the phenomenon on the following day, increased by 24^{h}, is given; extra care must be taken when interpolating between two values, when one of those values exceeds 24^{h}. In practice it suffices to use the daily difference between the times for the nearest tabular latitude, and generally, to enter Table II with the nearest tabular arguments as in the examples below.

Examples. Required the UT of moonrise and moonset in latitude S 47° 10′, longitudes E 124° 00′ and W 78° 31′ on 2026 January 5.

	Longitude E 124° 00′ Moonrise	Longitude E 124° 00′ Moonset	Longitude W 78° 31′ Moonrise	Longitude W 78° 31′ Moonset
	d h m	d h m	d h m	d h m
LMT for Lat. S 45°	5 21 38	5 06 26	5 21 38	5 06 26
Lat correction (p. xxxii, Table I)	+07	−09	+07	−09
Long correction (p. xxxii, Table II)	−10	−30	+04	+18
Correct LMT	5 21 35	5 05 47	5 21 49	5 06 35
Longitude (p. i)	−8 16	−8 16	+5 14	+5 14
UT	5 13 19	4 21 31	6 03 03	5 11 49

ALTITUDE CORRECTION TABLES

13. *General.* In general, two corrections are given for application to altitudes observed with a marine sextant; additional corrections are required for Venus and Mars and also for very low altitudes.

Tables of the correction for dip of the horizon, due to height of eye above sea level, are given on pages A2 and xxxiv. Strictly this correction should be applied first and subtracted from the sextant altitude to give apparent altitude, which is the correct argument for the other tables.

Separate tables are given of the second correction for the Sun, for stars and planets (on pages A2 and A3), and for the Moon (on pages xxxiv and xxxv). For the Sun, values are given for both lower and upper limbs, for two periods of the year. The star tables are used for the planets, but additional corrections for parallax (page A2) are required for Venus and Mars. The Moon tables are in two parts: the main correction is a function of apparent altitude only and is tabulated for the lower limb (30′ must be subtracted to obtain the correction for the upper limb); the other, which is given for both lower and upper limbs, depends also on the horizontal parallax, which has to be taken from the daily pages.

An additional correction, given on page A4, is required for the change in the refraction, due to variations of pressure and temperature from the adopted standard conditions; it may generally be ignored for altitudes greater than 10°, except possibly in extreme conditions. The correction tables for the Sun, stars, and planets are in two parts; only those for altitudes greater than 10° are reprinted on the bookmark.

14. *Critical tables.* Some of the altitude correction tables are arranged as critical tables. In these, an interval of apparent altitude (or height of eye) corresponds to a single value of the correction; no interpolation is required. At a "critical" entry the upper of the two possible values of the correction is to be taken. For example, in the table of dip, a correction of −4′.1 corresponds to all values of the height of eye from 5·3 to 5·5 metres (17·5 to 18·3 feet) inclusive.

15. *Examples.* The following examples illustrate the use of the altitude correction tables; the sextant altitudes given are assumed to be taken on 2026 March 12 with a marine sextant at height 5·4 metres (18 feet), temperature −3°C and pressure 982 mb, the Moon sights being taken at about 10^h UT.

	SUN lower limb	SUN upper limb	MOON lower limb	MOON upper limb	VENUS	*Polaris*
	° ′	° ′	° ′	° ′	° ′	° ′
Sextant altitude	21 19·7	3 20·2	33 27·6	26 06·7	4 32·6	49 36·5
Dip, height 5·4 metres (18 feet)	−4·1	−4·1	−4·1	−4·1	−4·1	−4·1
Main correction ‡	+13·8	−29·6	+57·4	+60·5	−10·8	−0·8
−30′ for upper limb (Moon)	—	—	—	−30·0	—	—
L, U correction for Moon	—	—	+1·4	+1·6	—	—
Additional correction for Venus	—	—	—	—	+0·1	—
Additional refraction correction	−0·1	−0·6	−0·1	−0·1	−0·5	0·0
Corrected sextant altitude	21 29·3	2 45·9	34 22·2	26 34·6	4 17·3	49 31·6

‡ The main corrections have been taken out with apparent altitude (sextant altitude corrected for index error and dip) as argument, interpolating where possible. These refinements are rarely necessary.

16. *Composition of the Corrections.* The table for the dip of the sea horizon is based on the formula:

$$\text{Correction for dip} = -1'.76\sqrt{(\text{height of eye in metres})} = -0'.97\sqrt{(\text{height of eye in feet})}$$

The correction table for the Sun includes the effects of semi-diameter, parallax and mean refraction.

The correction tables for the stars and planets allow for the effect of mean refraction.

The phase correction for Venus has been incorporated in the tabulations for GHA and Dec, and no correction for phase is required. The additional corrections for Venus and Mars allow for parallax. Alternatively, the correction for parallax may be calculated from $p \cos H$, where p is the parallax and H is the altitude. In 2026 the values for p are:

Venus: Jan. 1 0′.1 July 9 0′.2 Aug. 27 0′.3 Sept. 19 0′.4 Oct. 5 0′.5 Nov. 14 0′.4 Nov. 29 0′.3 Dec. 23 0′.2 Dec. 31

Mars: Jan. 1 0′.1 Dec. 24 0′.2 Dec. 31

The correction table for the Moon includes the effect of semi-diameter, parallax, augmentation and mean refraction.

Mean refraction is calculated for a temperature of 10°C (50°F), a pressure of 1010 mb (29·83 inches), humidity of 80% and wavelength 0·50169 μm.

17. *Bubble sextant observations.* When observing with a bubble sextant, no correction is necessary for dip, semi-diameter, or augmentation. The altitude corrections for the stars and planets on page A2 and on the bookmark should be used for the Sun as well as for the stars and planets; for the Moon, it is easiest to take the mean of the corrections for lower and upper limbs and subtract 15′ from the altitude; the correction for dip must not be applied.

AUXILIARY AND PLANNING DATA

18. *Sun and Moon.* On the daily pages are given: hourly values of the horizontal parallax of the Moon; the semi-diameters and the times of meridian passage of both Sun and Moon over the Greenwich meridian; the equation of time; the age of the Moon, the percent (%) illuminated and a symbol indicating the phase. The times of the phases of the Moon are given in UT on page 4. For the Moon, the semi-diameters for each of the three days are given at the foot of the column; for the Sun a single value is sufficient. Table II on page xxxii may be used for interpolating the time of the Moon's meridian passage for longitude. The equation of time is given daily at 00^h and 12^h UT. The sign is *positive* for unshaded values and *negative* for shaded values. To obtain apparent time add the equation of time to mean time when the sign is *positive*. Subtract the equation of time from mean time when the sign is *negative*. At 12^h UT, when the sign is *positive*, meridian passage of the Sun occurs *before* 12^h UT, otherwise it occurs *after* 12^h UT.

19. *Planets.* The magnitudes of the planets are given immediately following their names in the headings on the daily pages; also given, for the middle day of the three on the page, are their SHA at 00^h UT and their times of meridian passage.

The planet notes and diagram on pages 8 and 9 provide descriptive information as to the suitability of the planets for observation during the year, and of their positions and movements.

20. *Stars.* The time of meridian passage of the first point of Aries over the Greenwich meridian is given on the daily pages, for the middle day of the three on the page, to $0^m\!.1$. The interval between successive meridian passages is $23^h\ 56^m\!.1$ (24^h less $3^m\!.9$), so that times for intermediate days and other meridians can readily be derived. If a precise time is required, it may be obtained by finding the UT at which LHA Aries is zero.

The meridian passage of a star occurs when its LHA is zero, that is when LHA Aries + SHA = 360°. An approximate time can be obtained from the planet diagram on page 9.

The star charts on pages 266 and 267 are intended to assist identification. They show the relative positions of the stars in the sky as seen from the Earth and include all 173 stars used in the Almanac, together with a few others to complete the main constellation configurations. The local meridian at any time may be located on the chart by means of its SHA which is 360° − LHA Aries, or west longitude − GHA Aries.

21. *Star globe.* To set a star globe on which is printed a scale of LHA Aries, first set the globe for latitude and then rotate about the polar axis until the scale under the edge of the meridian circle reads LHA Aries.

To mark the positions of the Sun, Moon, and planets on the star globe, take the difference GHA Aries − GHA body and use this along the LHA Aries scale, in conjunction with the declination, to plot the position. GHA Aries − GHA body is most conveniently found by taking the difference when the GHA of the body is small (less than 15°), which happens once a day.

22. *Calendar.* On page 4 are given lists of ecclesiastical festivals, and of the principal anniversaries and holidays in the United Kingdom and the United States of America. The calendar on page 5 includes the day of the year as well as the day of the week.

Brief particulars are given, at the foot of page 5, of the solar and lunar eclipses occurring during the year; the times given are in UT. The principal features of the more important solar eclipses are shown on the maps on pages 6 and 7.

23. *Standard times.* The lists on pages 262–265 give the standard times used in most countries. In general no attempt is made to give details of the beginning and end of summer time, since they are liable to frequent changes at short notice. For the latest information consult Admiralty List of Radio Signals Volume 2 (NP 282) corrected by Section VI of the weekly edition of Admiralty Notices to Mariners.

The Date or Calendar Line is an arbitrary line, on either side of which the date differs by one day; when crossing this line on a westerly course, the date must be advanced one day; when crossing it on an easterly course, the date must be put back one day. The line is a modification of the line of the 180th meridian, and is drawn so as to include, as far as possible, islands of any one group, etc., on the same side of the line. It may be traced by starting at the South Pole and joining up to the following positions:

	°	°	°	°	°	°	°
Lat	S 51·0	S 45·0	S 15·0	S 5·0	N 48·0	N 53·0	N 65·5
Long	180·0	W 172·5	W 172·5	180·0	180·0	E 170·0	W 169·0

thence through the middle of the Diomede Islands to Lat N 68°.0, Long W 169°.0, passing east of Ostrov Vrangelya (Wrangel Island) to Lat N 75°.0, Long 180°.0, and thence to the North Pole.

ACCURACY

24. *Main data.* The quantities tabulated in this Almanac are generally correct to the nearest 0′.1; the exception is the Sun's GHA which is deliberately adjusted by up to 0′.15 to reduce the error due to ignoring the *v*-correction. The GHA and Dec at intermediate times cannot be obtained to this precision, since at least two quantities must be added; moreover, the *v*- and *d*-corrections are based on mean values of *v* and *d* and are taken from tables for the whole minute only. The largest error that can occur in the GHA or Dec of any body other than the Sun or Moon is less than 0′.2; it may reach 0′.25 for the GHA of the Sun and 0′.3 for that of the Moon.

In practice, it may be expected that only one third of the values of GHA and Dec taken out will have errors larger than 0′.05 and less than one tenth will have errors larger than 0′.1.

25. *Altitude corrections.* The errors in the altitude corrections are nominally of the same order as those in GHA and Dec, as they result from the addition of several quantities each correctly rounded off to 0′.1. But the actual values of the dip and of the refraction at low altitudes may, in extreme atmospheric conditions, differ considerably from the mean values used in the tables.

USE OF THIS ALMANAC IN 2027

This Almanac may be used for the Sun and stars in 2027 in the following manner.

For the Sun, take out the GHA and Dec for the same date but for a time $5^h\ 48^m\ 00^s$ *earlier* than the UT of observation; add 87° 00′ to the GHA so obtained. The error, mainly due to planetary perturbations of the Earth, is unlikely to exceed 0′.4.

For the stars, calculate the GHA and Dec for the same date and the same time, but *subtract* 15′.1 from the GHA so found. The error due to incomplete correction for precession and nutation is unlikely to exceed 0′.4. If preferred, the same result can be obtained by using a time $5^h\ 48^m\ 00^s$ earlier than the UT of observation (as for the Sun) and adding 86° 59′.2 to the GHA (or adding 87° as for the Sun and subtracting 0′.8, for precession, from the SHA of the star).

The Almanac cannot be so used for the Moon or planets.

LIST I — PLACES FAST ON UTC (mainly those EAST OF GREENWICH)

The times given below should be *added* to UTC to give Standard Time / *subtracted* from Standard Time to give UTC.

Place	h	m
Admiralty Islands	10	
Afghanistan	04	30
Albania*	01	
Algeria	01	
Amirante Islands	04	
Andaman Islands	05	30
Angola	01	
Armenia	04	
Australia		
Australian Capital Territory*	10	
New South Wales *[1]	10	
Northern Territory	09	30
Queensland	10	
South Australia*	09	30
Tasmania*	10	
Victoria*	10	
Western Australia	08	
Whitsunday Islands	10	
Austria*†	01	
Azerbaijan	04	
Bahrain	03	
Balearic Islands*†	01	
Bangladesh	06	
Belarus	03	
Belgium*†	01	
Benin	01	
Bosnia and Herzegovina*	01	
Botswana, Republic of	02	
Brunei	08	
Bulgaria*†	02	
Burma (Myanmar)	06	30
Burundi	02	
Cambodia	07	
Cameroon Republic	01	
Caroline Islands [2]	10	
Central African Republic	01	
Chad	01	
Chagos Archipelago & Diego Garcia	06	
Chatham Islands*	12	45
China		
Chinese Mainland	08	
Hong Kong	08	
Macao	08	
Taiwan	08	
Christmas Island, Indian Ocean	07	
Cocos (Keeling) Islands	06	30
Comoro Islands (Comoros)	03	
Congo, Democratic Republic		
West: Kinshasa, Equateur	01	
East: Orientale, Kasai, Kivu, Shaba	02	
Congo Republic	01	
Corsica*†	01	
Crete*†	02	

Place	h	m
Croatia*†	01	
Cyprus†: Ercan*, Larnaca*	02	
Czech Republic*†	01	
Denmark*†	01	
Djibouti	03	
Egypt*, Arab Republic of	02	
Equatorial Guinea, Republic of	01	
Bioko	01	
Eritrea	03	
Estonia*†	02	
Eswatini	02	
Ethiopia	03	
Fiji	12	
Finland*†	02	
France*†	01	
Gabon	01	
Georgia	04	
Germany*†	01	
Gibraltar*	01	
Greece*†	02	
Guam	10	
Hungary*†	01	
India	05	30
Indonesia, Republic of		
Bangka, Billiton, Java, West and Central Kalimantan, Madura, Sumatra	07	
Bali, Flores, South, North and East Kalimantan, Lombok, Sulawesi, Sumba, Sumbawa, West Timor	08	
Aru, Irian Jaya, Kai, Moluccas Tanimbar	09	
Iran*	03	30
Iraq	03	
Israel*	02	
Italy*†	01	
Jan Mayen Island*	01	
Japan	09	
Jordan‡	03	
Kazakhstan		
Western: Aktau, Uralsk, Atyrau	05	
Eastern & Central: Astana	05	
Kenya	03	
Kerguelen Islands	05	
Kiribati Republic		
Gilbert Islands	12	
Phoenix Islands [3]	13	
Line Islands [3]	14	
Korea, North	09	
Korea, South	09	
Kuwait	03	
Kyrgyzstan	06	
Laccadive Islands	05	30

* Daylight-saving time may be kept in these places.
† For Summer time dates see List II footnotes.
‡ Standard time listed is permanent DST
[1] Except Broken Hill Area* which keeps $09^h 30^m$.
[2] Except Pohnpei, Pingelap and Kosrae which keep 11^h and Palau which keeps 09^h.
[3] The Line and Phoenix Is. not part of the Kiribati Republic may keep other time zones.

LIST I — (*continued*)

	h	m
Laos	07	
Latvia*†	02	
Lebanon*	02	
Lesotho	02	
Libya	02	
Liechtenstein*	01	
Lithuania*†	02	
Lord Howe Island*	10	30
Luxembourg*†	01	
Macedonia*, former Yugoslav Republic	01	
Madagascar, Democratic Republic of	03	
Malawi	02	
Malaysia, Malaya, Sabah, Sarawak	08	
Maldives, Republic of The	05	
Malta*†	01	
Mariana Islands	10	
Marshall Islands	12	
Mauritius	04	
Moldova*	02	
Monaco*	01	
Mongolia [4]	08	
Montenegro*	01	
Morocco[7]	01	
Mozambique	02	
Namibia	02	
Nauru	12	
Nepal	05	45
Netherlands, The*†	01	
New Caledonia	11	
New Zealand*	12	
Nicobar Islands	05	30
Niger	01	
Nigeria, Republic of	01	
Norfolk Island*	11	
Norway*	01	
Novaya Zemlya	03	
Okinawa	09	
Oman	04	
Pagalu (Annobon Islands)	01	
Pakistan	05	
Palau Islands	09	
Papua New Guinea[5]	10	
Pescadores Islands	08	
Philippine Republic	08	
Poland*†	01	
Qatar	03	
Reunion	04	
Romania*†	02	
Russia [6]		
Kaliningrad	02	
Moscow, St. Petersburg, Arkhangelsk, Volgograd	03	
Samara, Astrakhan, Saratov	04	
Ekaterinburg, Ufa, Perm, Novyy Port	05	
Omsk	06	
Norilsk, Krasnoyarsk, Dikson, Novosibirsk, Tomsk	07	
Irkutsk, Bratsk, Ulan-Ude	08	
Tiksi, Yakutsk, Chita	09	
Vladivostok, Khabarovsk, Okhotsk	10	
Severo-Kurilsk, Magadan, Sakhalin Island	11	
Petropavlovsk-K., Anadyr	12	
Rwanda	02	
Ryukyu Islands	09	
Samoa*	13	
Santa Cruz Islands	11	
Sardinia*†	01	
Saudi Arabia	03	
Schouten Islands	09	
Serbia*	01	
Seychelles	04	
Sicily*†	01	
Singapore	08	
Slovakia*†	01	
Slovenia*†	01	
Socotra	03	
Solomon Islands	11	
Somalia Republic	03	
South Africa, Republic of	02	
South Sudan	02	
Spain*†	01	
Spanish Possessions in North Africa*	01	
Spitsbergen (Svalbard)*	01	
Sri Lanka	0530	
Sudan, Republic of	02	
Sweden*†	01	
Switzerland*	01	
Syria (Syrian Arab Republic)‡	03	
Tajikistan	05	
Tanzania	03	
Thailand	07	
Timor-Leste	09	
Tonga	13	
Tunisia	01	
Turkey	03	
Turkmenistan	05	
Tuvalu	12	
Uganda	03	
Ukraine*	02	
United Arab Emirates	04	
Uzbekistan	05	
Vanuatu, Republic of	11	
Vietnam, Socialist Republic of	07	
Yemen	03	
Zambia, Republic of	02	
Zimbabwe	02	

* Daylight-saving time may be kept in these places. † For Summer time dates see List II footnotes.

‡ Standard time listed is permanent DST

4 Western regions of Mongolia keep 07^{h}.

5 Excluding the Autonomous Region of Bougainville which keeps 11^{h}.

6 The boundaries between the zones are irregular; listed are chief towns in each zone.

7 During Ramadan, standard time reverts to UTC

LIST II — PLACES NORMALLY KEEPING UTC

Ascension Island	Ghana	Irish Republic*†	Portugal*†	Togo Republic
Burkina-Faso	Great Britain†	Ivory Coast	Principe	Tristan da Cunha
Canary Islands*†	Guinea-Bissau	Liberia	St. Helena	
Channel Islands†	Guinea Republic	Madeira*†	São Tomé	
Faeroes*, The	Iceland	Mali	Senegal	
Gambia, The	Ireland, Northern†	Mauritania	Sierra Leone	

* Daylight-saving time may be kept in these places.

† Summer time (daylight-saving time), one hour in advance of UTC, will be kept from 2026 March 29^d 01^h to October 25^d 01^h UTC (Ninth Summer Time Directive of the European Union). Ratification by member countries has not been verified.

LIST III — PLACES SLOW ON UTC (WEST OF GREENWICH)

The times given below should be } *subtracted* from UTC to give Standard Time / *added* to Standard Time to give UTC.

Place	h	m
American Samoa	11	
Argentina	03	
Austral (Tubuai) Islands[1]	10	
Azores*†	01	
Bahamas*	05	
Barbados	04	
Belize	06	
Bermuda*	04	
Bolivia	04	
Brazil		
Fernando de Noronha I., Trindade I., Oceanic Is.	02	
N and NE coastal states, Tocantins, Minas Gerais, Goiás, Brasilia, S and E coastal states	03	
Amazonas[2], Mato Grosso do Sul, Mato Grosso, Rondônia, Roraima	04	
Acre	05	
British Antarctic Territory[3,4]	03	
Canada[4]‡		
Alberta*	07	
British Columbia*[4]	08	
Labrador*	04	
Manitoba*	06	
New Brunswick*	04	
Newfoundland*	03	30
Nunavut*		
east of long. W. 85°	05	
long. W. 85° to W. 102°	06	
west of long. W. 102°	07	
Northwest Territories*	07	
Nova Scotia*	04	
Ontario, east of long. W. 90°*	05	
Ontario, west of long. W. 90°*	06	
Canada (*continued*)		
Prince Edward Island*	04	
Quebec, east of long. W. 63°	04	
west of long. W. 63°*	05	
Saskatchewan	06	
Yukon	07	
Cape Verde Islands	01	
Cayman Islands	05	
Chile		
General*	04	
Chilean Antarctic	03	
Colombia	05	
Cook Islands	10	
Costa Rica	06	
Cuba*	05	
Curaçao Island	04	
Dominican Republic	04	
Easter Island (I. de Pascua)*	06	
Ecuador	05	
El Salvador	06	
Falkland Islands	03	
Fernando de Noronha Island	02	
French Guiana	03	
Galápagos Islands	06	
Greenland		
Danmarkshavn, Mesters Vig	00	
General*	02	
Scoresby Sound	02	
Thule*, Pituffik*	04	
Grenada	04	
Guadeloupe	04	
Guatemala	06	
Guyana, Republic of	04	

* Daylight-saving time may be kept in these places. ‡ Dates for DST are given at the end of List III.

1 This is the legal standard time, but local mean time is generally used.

2 Except the cities of Eirunepe, Benjamin Constant and Tabatinga which keep 05^h.

3 Stations may use UTC.

4 Some areas may keep another time zone.

LIST III — (*continued*)

	h	m
Haiti*	05	
Honduras	06	
Jamaica	05	
Johnston Island	10	
Juan Fernandez Islands*	04	
Leeward Islands	04	
Marquesas Islands	09	30
Martinique	04	
Mexico		
General	06	
Quintana Roo	05	
Baja California Sur* Nayarit*, Sinaloa* and Sonara	07	
Baja California Norte*	08	
Midway Islands	11	
Nicaragua	06	
Niue	11	
Panama, Republic of	05	
Paraguay	03	
Peru	05	
Pitcairn Island	08	
Puerto Rico	04	
St. Pierre and Miquelon*	03	
Society Islands	10	
South Georgia	02	
Suriname	03	
Trindade Island, South Atlantic	02	
Trinidad and Tobago	04	
Tuamotu Archipelago	10	
Tubuai (Austral) Islands	10	
Turks and Caicos Islands*	05	
United States of America‡		
Alabama	06	
Alaska	09	
Aleutian Islands, east of W. 169° 30′	09	
Aleutian Islands, west of W. 169° 30′	10	
Arizona[5]	07	
Arkansas	06	
California	08	
Colorado	07	
Connecticut	05	
Delaware	05	
District of Columbia	05	
Florida[6]	05	
Georgia	05	
Hawaii[5]	10	

	h	m
United States of America‡(*continued*)		
Idaho, southern part	07	
northern part	08	
Illinois	06	
Indiana[6]	05	
Iowa	06	
Kansas[6]	06	
Kentucky, eastern part	05	
western part	06	
Louisiana	06	
Maine	05	
Maryland	05	
Massachusetts	05	
Michigan[6]	05	
Minnesota	06	
Mississippi	06	
Missouri	06	
Montana	07	
Nebraska, eastern part	06	
western part	07	
Nevada	08	
New Hampshire	05	
New Jersey	05	
New Mexico	07	
New York	05	
North Carolina	05	
North Dakota, eastern part	06	
western part	07	
Ohio	05	
Oklahoma	06	
Oregon[6]	08	
Pennsylvania	05	
Rhode Island	05	
South Carolina	05	
South Dakota, eastern part	06	
western part	07	
Tennessee, eastern part	05	
western part	06	
Texas[6]	06	
Utah	07	
Vermont	05	
Virginia	05	
Washington D.C.	05	
Washington	08	
West Virginia	05	
Wisconsin	06	
Wyoming	07	
Uruguay	03	
Venezuela	04	
Virgin Islands	04	
Windward Islands	04	

* Daylight-saving time may be kept in these places.

‡ Daylight-saving (Summer) time, one hour fast on the time given, is kept during 2026 from March 8 (second Sunday) to November 1 (first Sunday), changing at $02^{h} 00^{m}$ local clock time.

5 Exempt from keeping daylight-saving time, except for a portion of Arizona.

6 A small portion of the state is in another time zone.

NORTHERN STARS

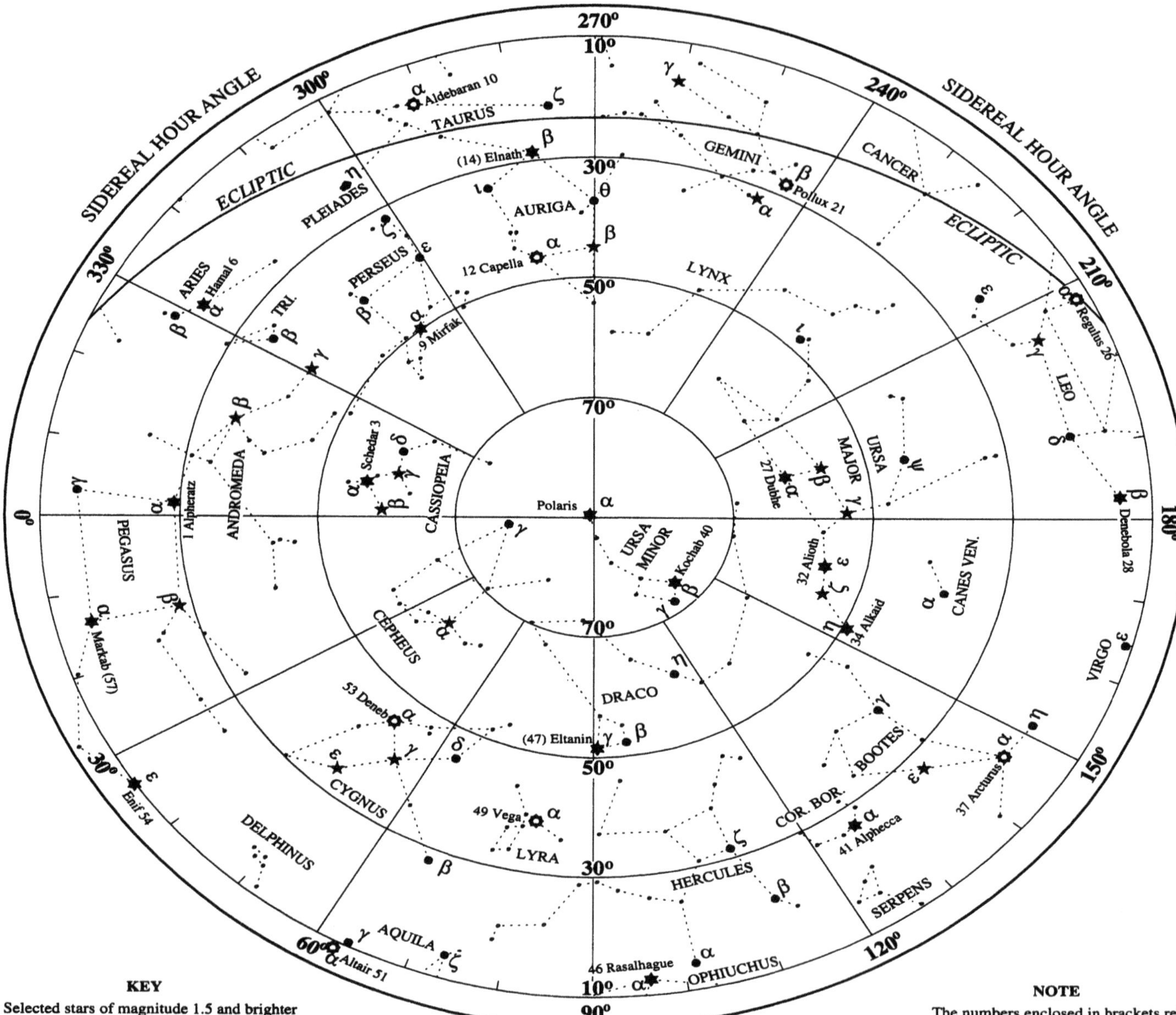

KEY

- Selected stars of magnitude 1.5 and brighter
- Selected stars of magnitude 1.6 and fainter
- Other tabulated stars of magnitude 2.5 and brighter
- Other tabulated stars of magnitude 2.6 and fainter
- Untabulated stars

NOTE

The numbers enclosed in brackets refer to those stars of the selected list which are not used in Sight Reduction Tables A.P. 3270, N.P. 303.

EQUATORIAL STARS (SHA 0° to 180°)

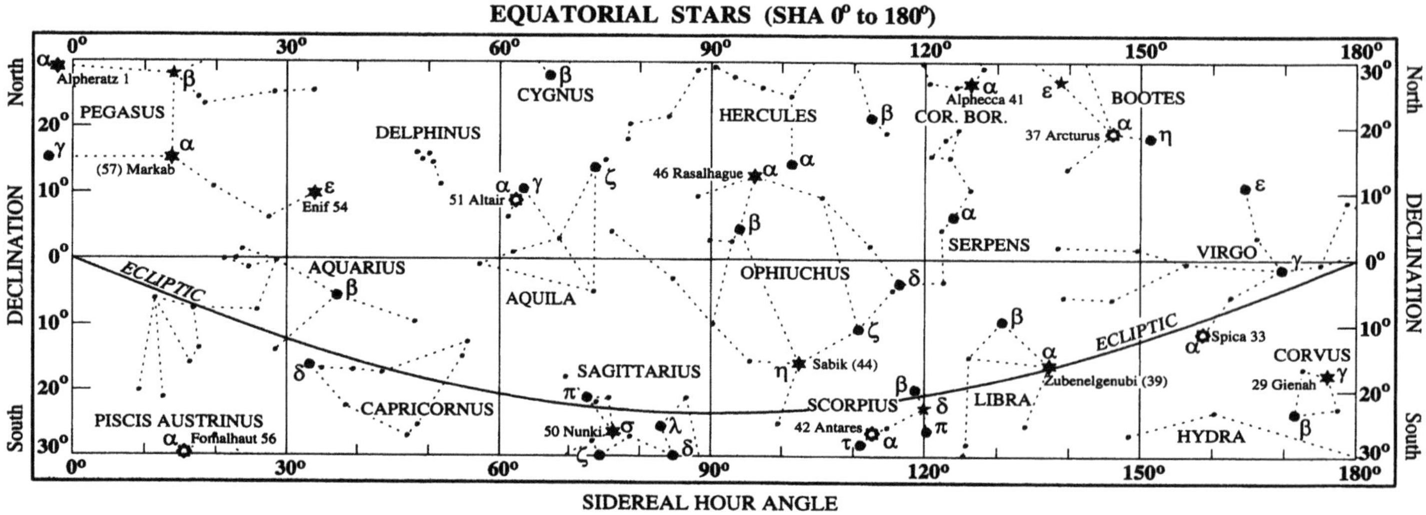

SOUTHERN STARS

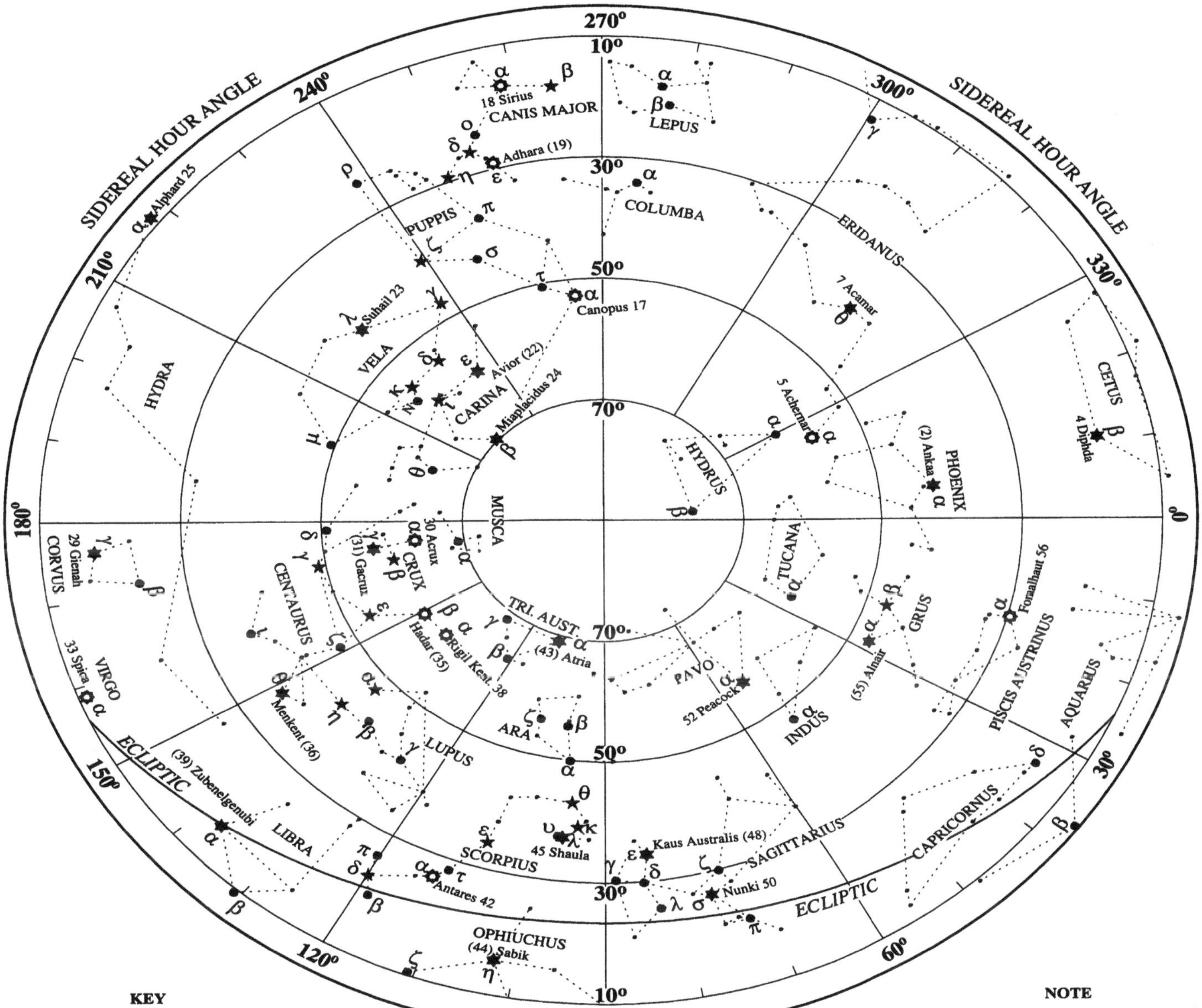

KEY

- Selected stars of magnitude 1.5 and brighter
- Selected stars of magnitude 1.6 and fainter
- Other tabulated stars of magnitude 2.5 and brighter
- Other tabulated stars of magnitude 2.6 and fainter
- Untabulated stars

NOTE

The numbers enclosed in brackets refer to those stars of the selected list which are not used in Sight Reduction Tables A.P. 3270, N.P. 303.

EQUATORIAL STARS (SHA 180° to 360°)

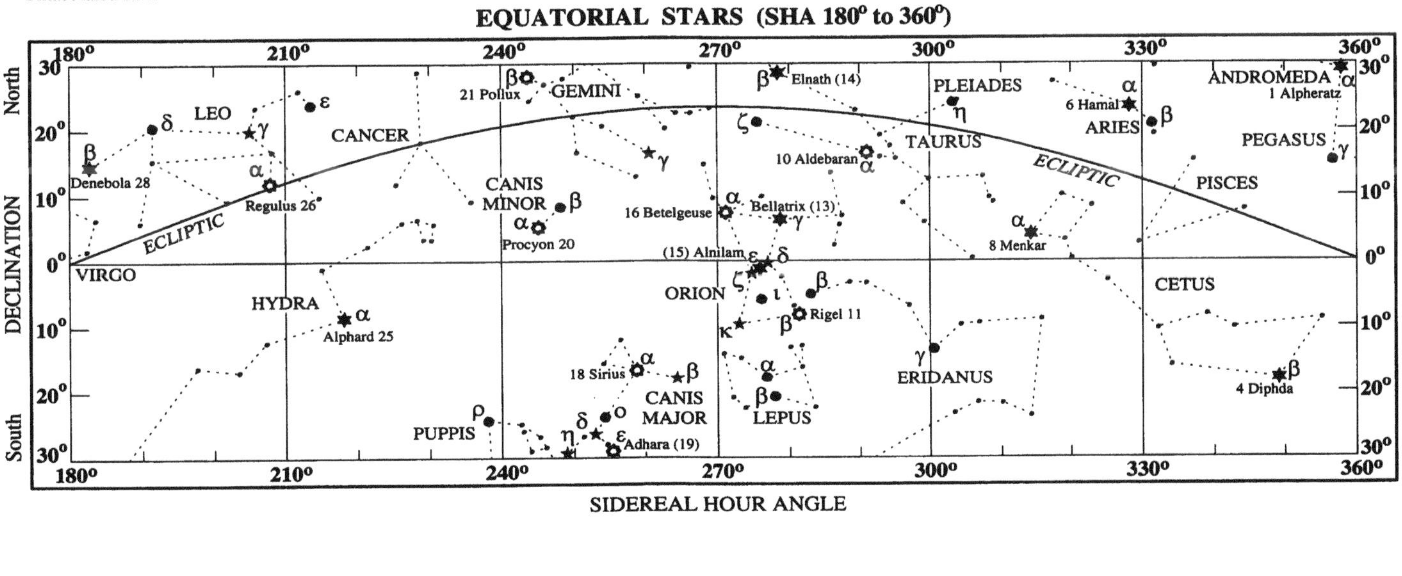

Mag.	Name and Number		SHA							Declination						
				JAN.	FEB.	MAR.	APR.	MAY	JUNE		JAN.	FEB.	MAR.	APR.	MAY	JUNE
			°	′	′	′	′	′	′	°	′	′	′	′	′	′
3·2	γ Cephei		**4**	54·7	55·2	55·4	55·1	54·5	53·6	N **77**	47·0	46·9	46·7	46·6	46·5	46·5
2·5	α Pegasi	57	**13**	29·3	29·3	29·2	29·1	28·9	28·7	N **15**	20·8	20·7	20·7	20·7	20·7	20·8
2·4	β Pegasi		**13**	44·6	44·6	44·6	44·5	44·3	44·0	N **28**	13·6	13·5	13·4	13·3	13·4	13·5
1·2	α Piscis Aust.	56	**15**	13·8	13·8	13·8	13·6	13·4	13·2	S **29**	29·2	29·1	29·1	28·9	28·8	28·7
2·1	β Gruis		**18**	56·9	57·0	56·9	56·7	56·4	56·1	S **46**	45·1	45·0	44·9	44·7	44·6	44·5
2·9	α Tucanæ		**24**	56·2	56·3	56·1	55·9	55·5	55·1	S **60**	08·0	07·8	07·7	07·5	07·4	07·3
1·7	α Gruis	55	**27**	32·2	32·2	32·1	31·9	31·6	31·3	S **46**	50·2	50·1	50·0	49·9	49·8	49·7
2·9	δ Capricorni		**32**	53·0	53·0	52·9	52·7	52·5	52·2	S **16**	00·6	00·6	00·6	00·5	00·4	00·3
2·4	ε Pegasi	54	**33**	38·2	38·2	38·1	37·9	37·7	37·5	N **9**	59·7	59·6	59·6	59·6	59·6	59·7
2·9	β Aquarii		**36**	46·3	46·2	46·1	45·9	45·7	45·5	S **5**	27·4	27·5	27·5	27·4	27·3	27·2
2·4	α Cephei		**40**	12·8	12·9	12·7	12·4	12·0	11·6	N **62**	41·8	41·7	41·6	41·5	41·5	41·6
2·5	ε Cygni		**48**	11·4	11·3	11·2	11·0	10·7	10·5	N **34**	04·1	04·0	03·9	03·8	03·9	04·0
1·3	α Cygni	53	**49**	25·7	25·6	25·5	25·2	24·9	24·7	N **45**	22·4	22·3	22·2	22·1	22·2	22·3
3·1	α Indi		**50**	09·5	09·3	09·1	08·8	08·5	08·2	S **47**	12·1	12·0	11·9	11·8	11·7	11·7
1·9	α Pavonis	52	**53**	05·0	04·8	04·6	04·2	03·8	03·4	S **56**	39·1	39·0	38·9	38·8	38·8	38·8
2·2	γ Cygni		**54**	13·0	12·9	12·7	12·5	12·2	12·0	N **40**	20·4	20·3	20·2	20·1	20·2	20·3
0·8	α Aquilæ	51	**61**	59·5	59·3	59·2	59·0	58·7	58·5	N **8**	56·2	56·1	56·1	56·1	56·2	56·3
2·7	γ Aquilæ		**63**	07·8	07·7	07·5	07·3	07·1	06·9	N **10**	40·5	40·5	40·4	40·4	40·5	40·6
2·9	δ Cygni		**63**	33·7	33·6	33·3	33·1	32·8	32·6	N **45**	11·6	11·5	11·4	11·3	11·4	11·6
3·1	β Cygni		**67**	03·8	03·6	03·5	03·2	03·0	02·8	N **28**	00·8	00·7	00·6	00·6	00·7	00·8
2·9	π Sagittarii		**72**	10·6	10·4	10·2	10·0	09·7	09·5	S **20**	59·0	59·0	58·9	58·9	58·9	58·8
3·0	ζ Aquilæ		**73**	21·2	21·0	20·8	20·6	20·4	20·2	N **13**	54·1	54·0	53·9	53·9	54·0	54·1
2·6	ζ Sagittarii		**73**	56·3	56·1	55·8	55·6	55·3	55·1	S **29**	50·6	50·5	50·5	50·5	50·5	50·4
2·0	σ Sagittarii	50	**75**	47·1	46·9	46·7	46·4	46·2	45·9	S **26**	15·9	15·9	15·8	15·8	15·8	15·8
0·0	α Lyræ	49	**80**	33·1	32·9	32·7	32·4	32·2	32·0	N **38**	48·3	48·2	48·1	48·1	48·2	48·4
2·8	λ Sagittarii		**82**	36·6	36·4	36·1	35·9	35·7	35·5	S **25**	24·4	24·4	24·4	24·4	24·4	24·4
1·9	ε Sagittarii	48	**83**	31·8	31·5	31·3	31·0	30·8	30·5	S **34**	22·3	22·3	22·3	22·2	22·2	22·3
2·7	δ Sagittarii		**84**	20·3	20·1	19·9	19·6	19·4	19·2	S **29**	49·0	49·0	49·0	49·0	49·0	49·0
3·0	γ Sagittarii		**88**	08·0	07·8	07·6	07·3	07·0	06·9	S **30**	25·4	25·4	25·4	25·4	25·4	25·4
2·2	γ Draconis	47	**90**	42·3	42·1	41·8	41·5	41·2	41·1	N **51**	28·9	28·8	28·7	28·8	28·9	29·0
2·8	β Ophiuchi		**93**	48·8	48·6	48·4	48·2	48·0	47·9	N **4**	33·3	33·2	33·2	33·2	33·3	33·4
2·4	κ Scorpii		**93**	55·9	55·6	55·4	55·1	54·8	54·6	S **39**	02·5	02·5	02·5	02·5	02·5	02·6
1·9	θ Scorpii		**95**	12·4	12·1	11·8	11·5	11·3	11·1	S **43**	00·8	00·7	00·7	00·8	00·8	00·8
2·1	α Ophiuchi	46	**95**	58·1	57·9	57·6	57·4	57·2	57·1	N **12**	32·3	32·3	32·2	32·2	32·3	32·4
1·6	λ Scorpii	45	**96**	09·6	09·3	09·0	08·7	08·5	08·3	S **37**	07·3	07·3	07·3	07·3	07·3	07·4
3·0	α Aræ		**96**	32·5	32·1	31·8	31·5	31·2	31·0	S **49**	53·7	53·6	53·6	53·7	53·7	53·8
2·7	υ Scorpii		**96**	52·2	51·9	51·7	51·4	51·1	51·0	S **37**	18·9	18·9	18·9	18·9	19·0	19·0
2·8	β Draconis		**97**	15·1	14·8	14·5	14·2	14·0	13·9	N **52**	16·7	16·5	16·5	16·5	16·7	16·8
2·8	β Aræ		**98**	08·3	08·0	07·6	07·2	06·9	06·7	S **55**	33·1	33·1	33·1	33·1	33·2	33·2
Var.‡	α Herculis		**101**	02·7	02·4	02·2	02·0	01·8	01·7	N **14**	21·5	21·4	21·4	21·4	21·5	21·6
2·4	η Ophiuchi	44	**102**	02·1	01·9	01·6	01·4	01·2	01·1	S **15**	45·4	45·5	45·5	45·5	45·5	45·5
3·1	ζ Aræ		**104**	48·6	48·2	47·8	47·5	47·2	47·0	S **56**	01·7	01·7	01·7	01·7	01·8	01·9
2·3	ε Scorpii		**107**	02·4	02·1	01·9	01·6	01·4	01·3	S **34**	20·4	20·4	20·4	20·4	20·5	20·5
1·9	α Triang. Aust.	43	**107**	09·0	08·4	07·8	07·2	06·8	06·6	S **69**	04·2	04·2	04·2	04·3	04·4	04·5
2·8	ζ Herculis		**109**	26·2	25·9	25·7	25·5	25·3	25·2	N **31**	33·1	33·0	33·0	33·0	33·1	33·3
2·6	ζ Ophiuchi		**110**	21·2	21·0	20·8	20·5	20·4	20·3	S **10**	37·2	37·3	37·3	37·3	37·3	37·3
2·8	τ Scorpii		**110**	37·6	37·3	37·0	36·8	36·6	36·5	S **28**	16·1	16·2	16·2	16·2	16·3	16·3
2·8	β Herculis		**112**	10·1	09·8	09·6	09·4	09·2	09·2	N **21**	25·8	25·7	25·7	25·7	25·8	25·9
1·0	α Scorpii	42	**112**	15·1	14·8	14·5	14·3	14·1	14·0	S **26**	29·3	29·4	29·4	29·5	29·5	29·5
2·7	η Draconis		**113**	55·1	54·8	54·4	54·1	53·9	53·9	N **61**	27·0	26·9	26·8	26·9	27·1	27·2
2·7	δ Ophiuchi		**116**	04·4	04·2	04·0	03·8	03·6	03·6	S **3**	45·7	45·8	45·9	45·9	45·8	45·8
2·6	β Scorpii		**118**	15·8	15·6	15·3	15·1	15·0	14·9	S **19**	52·6	52·6	52·7	52·7	52·7	52·7
2·3	δ Scorpii		**119**	32·0	31·7	31·5	31·3	31·1	31·0	S **22**	41·7	41·8	41·8	41·9	41·9	41·9
2·9	π Scorpii		**119**	53·7	53·4	53·1	52·9	52·8	52·7	S **26**	11·3	11·3	11·4	11·4	11·5	11·5
2·8	β Trianguli Aust.		**120**	38·5	38·0	37·6	37·2	36·9	36·8	S **63**	30·4	30·4	30·5	30·6	30·7	30·8
2·6	α Serpentis		**123**	36·8	36·6	36·3	36·2	36·0	36·0	N **6**	20·5	20·4	20·4	20·4	20·4	20·5
2·8	γ Lupi		**125**	46·9	46·6	46·3	46·1	45·9	45·8	S **41**	15·1	15·2	15·2	15·3	15·4	15·5
2·2	α Coronæ Bor.	41	**126**	03·2	03·0	02·7	02·5	02·4	02·4	N **26**	37·4	37·3	37·3	37·3	37·4	37·6

‡ 2·9 — 3·6

Mag.	Name and Number		SHA							Declination						
				JULY	AUG.	SEPT.	OCT.	NOV.	DEC.		JULY	AUG.	SEPT.	OCT.	NOV.	DEC.
			°	′	′	′	′	′	′	°	′	′	′	′	′	′
3·2	*Errai*		**4**	52·8	52·3	52·0	52·1	52·5	53·2	N **77**	46·6	46·7	46·9	47·1	47·3	47·4
2·5	*Markab*	57	**13**	28·4	28·3	28·2	28·2	28·3	28·3	N **15**	20·9	21·0	21·1	21·2	21·2	21·2
2·4	*Scheat*		**13**	43·8	43·6	43·5	43·5	43·6	43·7	N **28**	13·6	13·7	13·8	13·9	14·0	14·0
1·2	*Fomalhaut*	56	**15**	12·9	12·7	12·6	12·6	12·7	12·8	S **29**	28·7	28·7	28·7	28·8	28·8	28·9
2·1	*Tiaki*		**18**	55·8	55·6	55·5	55·6	55·7	55·9	S **46**	44·5	44·5	44·6	44·7	44·8	44·8
2·9	α Tucanæ		**24**	54·7	54·4	54·4	54·5	54·8	55·0	S **60**	07·3	07·4	07·5	07·6	07·7	07·7
1·7	*Alnair*	55	**27**	31·0	30·8	30·7	30·8	31·0	31·1	S **46**	49·7	49·7	49·8	49·9	50·0	50·0
2·9	*Deneb Algedi*		**32**	52·0	51·9	51·9	51·9	52·0	52·1	S **16**	00·3	00·2	00·2	00·3	00·3	00·3
2·4	*Enif*	54	**33**	37·3	37·2	37·1	37·2	37·3	37·4	N **9**	59·9	60·0	60·0	60·1	60·1	60·0
2·9	*Sadalsuud*		**36**	45·3	45·1	45·1	45·2	45·3	45·4	S **5**	27·1	27·1	27·1	27·1	27·1	27·1
2·4	*Alderamin*		**40**	11·3	11·2	11·3	11·6	11·9	12·2	N **62**	41·8	42·0	42·1	42·3	42·3	42·3
2·5	*Aljanah*		**48**	10·3	10·2	10·3	10·4	10·6	10·7	N **34**	04·2	04·3	04·5	04·5	04·5	04·5
1·3	*Deneb*	53	**49**	24·5	24·4	24·5	24·7	24·9	25·0	N **45**	22·5	22·6	22·8	22·9	22·9	22·8
3·1	α Indi		**50**	07·9	07·8	07·9	08·0	08·2	08·3	S **47**	11·8	11·8	11·9	12·0	12·0	11·9
1·9	*Peacock*	52	**53**	03·2	03·0	03·1	03·3	03·6	03·7	S **56**	38·8	38·9	39·0	39·1	39·1	39·0
2·2	*Sadr*		**54**	11·8	11·8	11·9	12·0	12·2	12·3	N **40**	20·5	20·6	20·8	20·8	20·8	20·8
0·8	*Altair*	51	**61**	58·4	58·4	58·4	58·5	58·6	58·7	N **8**	56·4	56·5	56·5	56·5	56·5	56·5
2·7	γ Aquilæ		**63**	06·7	06·7	06·8	06·9	07·0	07·1	N **10**	40·7	40·8	40·9	40·9	40·9	40·8
2·9	*Fawaris*		**63**	32·4	32·5	32·6	32·8	33·0	33·1	N **45**	11·7	11·9	12·0	12·1	12·0	11·9
3·1	*Albireo*		**67**	02·7	02·7	02·8	02·9	03·1	03·1	N **28**	01·0	01·1	01·2	01·2	01·2	01·1
2·9	*Albaldah*		**72**	09·4	09·4	09·4	09·6	09·7	09·7	S **20**	58·8	58·8	58·8	58·8	58·8	58·8
3·0	ζ Aquilæ		**73**	20·1	20·1	20·2	20·3	20·4	20·5	N **13**	54·2	54·3	54·4	54·4	54·4	54·3
2·6	*Ascella*		**73**	55·0	54·9	55·0	55·2	55·3	55·3	S **29**	50·5	50·5	50·5	50·5	50·5	50·5
2·0	*Nunki*	50	**75**	45·8	45·8	45·9	46·0	46·1	46·1	S **26**	15·8	15·8	15·8	15·8	15·8	15·8
0·0	*Vega*	49	**80**	31·9	32·0	32·2	32·4	32·5	32·6	N **38**	48·6	48·7	48·8	48·8	48·7	48·6
2·8	*Kaus Borealis*		**82**	35·4	35·4	35·5	35·6	35·7	35·7	S **25**	24·4	24·4	24·4	24·4	24·4	24·4
1·9	*Kaus Australis*	48	**83**	30·4	30·5	30·6	30·7	30·8	30·8	S **34**	22·3	22·3	22·4	22·3	22·3	22·3
2·7	*Kaus Media*		**84**	19·1	19·1	19·2	19·3	19·4	19·4	S **29**	49·0	49·0	49·0	49·0	49·0	49·0
3·0	*Alnasl*		**88**	06·8	06·8	06·9	07·0	07·1	07·1	S **30**	25·4	25·4	25·4	25·4	25·4	25·4
2·2	*Eltanin*	47	**90**	41·1	41·2	41·5	41·7	41·9	42·0	N **51**	29·2	29·3	29·4	29·4	29·3	29·1
2·8	*Cebalrai*		**93**	47·8	47·8	48·0	48·1	48·2	48·1	N **4**	33·4	33·5	33·5	33·5	33·5	33·4
2·4	κ Scorpii		**93**	54·6	54·6	54·7	54·9	55·0	54·9	S **39**	02·6	02·7	02·7	02·7	02·6	02·6
1·9	*Sargas*		**95**	11·0	11·1	11·2	11·4	11·5	11·4	S **43**	00·9	01·0	01·0	01·0	00·9	00·8
2·1	*Rasalhague*	46	**95**	57·1	57·1	57·2	57·4	57·4	57·4	N **12**	32·5	32·6	32·6	32·6	32·5	32·4
1·6	*Shaula*	45	**96**	08·3	08·3	08·5	08·6	08·7	08·6	S **37**	07·4	07·4	07·5	07·4	07·4	07·4
3·0	α Aræ		**96**	30·9	31·0	31·2	31·3	31·4	31·4	S **49**	53·9	53·9	53·9	53·9	53·9	53·8
2·7	*Lesath*		**96**	50·9	51·0	51·1	51·2	51·3	51·3	S **37**	19·0	19·1	19·1	19·1	19·0	19·0
2·8	*Rastaban*		**97**	13·9	14·1	14·3	14·6	14·8	14·8	N **52**	17·0	17·1	17·1	17·1	17·0	16·8
2·8	β Aræ		**98**	06·6	06·7	06·9	07·2	07·3	07·2	S **55**	33·3	33·4	33·4	33·4	33·3	33·2
Var.‡	*Rasalgethi*		**101**	01·7	01·8	01·9	02·0	02·1	02·0	N **14**	21·7	21·7	21·8	21·7	21·7	21·6
2·4	*Sabik*	44	**102**	01·0	01·1	01·2	01·3	01·4	01·3	S **15**	45·5	45·5	45·4	45·4	45·4	45·5
3·1	ζ Aræ		**104**	47·0	47·1	47·3	47·5	47·6	47·5	S **56**	02·0	02·1	02·1	02·0	01·9	01·8
2·3	*Larawag*		**107**	01·2	01·3	01·5	01·6	01·6	01·5	S **34**	20·5	20·6	20·6	20·5	20·5	20·5
1·9	*Atria*	43	**107**	06·6	06·8	07·2	07·6	07·7	07·6	S **69**	04·7	04·7	04·7	04·7	04·6	04·4
2·8	ζ Herculis		**109**	25·3	25·4	25·5	25·7	25·8	25·7	N **31**	33·4	33·4	33·5	33·4	33·3	33·1
2·6	ζ Ophiuchi		**110**	20·3	20·3	20·5	20·6	20·6	20·5	S **10**	37·3	37·2	37·2	37·2	37·2	37·3
2·8	*Paikauhale*		**110**	36·5	36·6	36·7	36·8	36·8	36·7	S **28**	16·3	16·3	16·3	16·3	16·3	16·2
2·8	*Kornephoros*		**112**	09·2	09·3	09·4	09·5	09·6	09·5	N **21**	26·0	26·1	26·1	26·0	25·9	25·8
1·0	*Antares*	42	**112**	14·0	14·1	14·2	14·3	14·3	14·2	S **26**	29·5	29·5	29·5	29·5	29·4	29·4
2·7	*Athebyne*		**113**	54·0	54·3	54·7	55·0	55·1	55·1	N **61**	27·4	27·4	27·4	27·3	27·2	27·0
2·7	*Yed Prior*		**116**	03·6	03·6	03·8	03·8	03·9	03·8	S **3**	45·7	45·7	45·7	45·7	45·7	45·8
2·6	*Acrab*		**118**	14·9	14·9	15·1	15·2	15·2	15·1	S **19**	52·7	52·7	52·7	52·7	52·7	52·7
2·3	*Dschubba*		**119**	31·0	31·1	31·2	31·3	31·3	31·2	S **22**	41·9	41·9	41·9	41·9	41·8	41·8
2·9	*Fang*		**119**	52·7	52·8	52·9	53·0	53·0	52·9	S **26**	11·5	11·5	11·5	11·5	11·4	11·4
2·8	β Trianguli Aust.		**120**	36·8	37·1	37·4	37·6	37·6	37·4	S **63**	30·9	31·0	31·0	30·9	30·8	30·6
2·6	*Unukalhai*		**123**	36·0	36·1	36·2	36·3	36·3	36·2	N **6**	20·6	20·6	20·6	20·6	20·5	20·4
2·8	γ Lupi		**125**	45·9	46·0	46·2	46·3	46·2	46·1	S **41**	15·5	15·5	15·5	15·4	15·4	15·3
2·2	*Alphecca*	41	**126**	02·5	02·6	02·7	02·8	02·8	02·7	N **26**	37·6	37·7	37·7	37·6	37·5	37·3

‡ 2·9 — 3·6

Mag.	Name and Number		SHA							Declination						
				JAN.	FEB.	MAR.	APR.	MAY	JUNE		JAN.	FEB.	MAR.	APR.	MAY	JUNE
			°	′	′	′	′	′	′	°	′	′	′	′	′	′
2·9	γ Trianguli Aust.		**129**	39·8	39·2	38·6	38·2	38·0	37·9	S **68**	46·2	46·3	46·4	46·5	46·6	46·8
3·1	γ Ursæ Minoris		**129**	49·6	49·1	48·5	48·2	48·1	48·3	N **71**	44·0	44·0	44·0	44·1	44·3	44·4
2·6	β Libræ		**130**	23·9	23·6	23·4	23·3	23·2	23·1	S **9**	28·8	28·9	28·9	28·9	28·9	28·9
2·7	β Lupi		**134**	56·4	56·1	55·8	55·6	55·5	55·4	S **43**	14·2	14·2	14·3	14·4	14·5	14·6
2·8	α Libræ	39	**136**	55·2	54·9	54·7	54·6	54·5	54·4	S **16**	09·0	09·1	09·1	09·2	09·2	09·2
2·1	β Ursæ Minoris	40	**137**	20·2	19·6	19·0	18·7	18·6	18·9	N **74**	02·5	02·4	02·5	02·6	02·8	02·9
2·4	ε Bootis		**138**	28·1	27·9	27·7	27·5	27·5	27·5	N **26**	57·7	57·6	57·6	57·6	57·7	57·9
2·3	α Lupi		**139**	05·0	04·7	04·4	04·2	04·1	04·1	S **47**	29·8	29·9	30·0	30·1	30·2	30·3
−0·3	α Centauri	38	**139**	39·3	38·8	38·5	38·2	38·1	38·2	S **60**	56·3	56·4	56·5	56·6	56·8	56·9
2·3	η Centauri		**140**	42·5	42·2	41·9	41·8	41·7	41·7	S **42**	16·2	16·3	16·4	16·5	16·6	16·6
3·0	γ Bootis		**141**	43·1	42·8	42·6	42·4	42·4	42·4	N **38**	11·4	11·3	11·3	11·4	11·5	11·6
0·0	α Bootis	37	**145**	47·2	46·9	46·8	46·6	46·6	46·6	N **19**	02·6	02·5	02·5	02·5	02·6	02·7
2·1	θ Centauri	36	**147**	56·7	56·4	56·2	56·0	56·0	56·0	S **36**	29·8	29·9	30·0	30·1	30·2	30·2
0·6	β Centauri	35	**148**	34·9	34·5	34·1	33·9	33·8	33·9	S **60**	29·7	29·8	29·9	30·0	30·2	30·3
2·6	ζ Centauri		**150**	42·4	42·1	41·8	41·7	41·6	41·6	S **47**	24·8	24·9	25·0	25·2	25·3	25·4
2·7	η Bootis		**151**	01·0	00·8	00·6	00·5	00·5	00·5	N **18**	15·8	15·8	15·7	15·8	15·9	15·9
1·9	η Ursæ Majoris	34	**152**	51·4	51·0	50·8	50·7	50·7	50·8	N **49**	10·6	10·6	10·7	10·8	10·9	11·0
2·3	ε Centauri		**154**	36·7	36·4	36·1	36·0	35·9	36·0	S **53**	35·7	35·8	36·0	36·1	36·2	36·3
1·0	α Virginis	33	**158**	21·4	21·2	21·0	20·9	20·9	20·9	S **11**	17·9	18·0	18·0	18·1	18·1	18·1
2·3	ζ Ursæ Majoris		**158**	45·2	44·8	44·6	44·5	44·5	44·7	N **54**	47·0	47·0	47·1	47·2	47·3	47·4
2·8	ι Centauri		**159**	28·9	28·6	28·5	28·4	28·3	28·4	S **36**	50·9	51·0	51·1	51·2	51·3	51·3
2·8	ε Virginis		**164**	07·7	07·5	07·4	07·3	07·3	07·3	N **10**	49·0	48·9	48·9	48·9	49·0	49·0
2·9	α Canum Venat.		**165**	41·1	40·8	40·7	40·6	40·6	40·7	N **38**	10·4	10·3	10·4	10·5	10·6	10·7
1·8	ε Ursæ Majoris	32	**166**	12·1	11·8	11·6	11·5	11·6	11·7	N **55**	48·7	48·8	48·8	49·0	49·1	49·2
1·3	β Crucis		**167**	41·1	40·7	40·5	40·4	40·4	40·6	S **59**	49·6	49·8	49·9	50·1	50·2	50·3
2·9	γ Virginis		**169**	15·1	14·9	14·8	14·7	14·7	14·8	S **1**	35·6	35·7	35·8	35·8	35·8	35·8
2·2	γ Centauri		**169**	15·5	15·2	15·0	14·9	14·9	15·0	S **49**	06·0	06·1	06·3	06·4	06·5	06·6
2·7	α Muscæ		**170**	18·5	18·0	17·8	17·7	17·8	18·1	S **69**	16·5	16·6	16·8	17·0	17·1	17·2
2·7	β Corvi		**171**	03·5	03·2	03·1	03·0	03·1	03·1	S **23**	32·4	32·5	32·6	32·7	32·8	32·8
1·6	γ Crucis	31	**171**	50·5	50·2	50·0	50·0	50·0	50·2	S **57**	15·3	15·5	15·6	15·8	15·9	16·0
1·3	α Crucis	30	**172**	58·9	58·5	58·3	58·3	58·4	58·6	S **63**	14·4	14·5	14·7	14·9	15·0	15·1
2·6	γ Corvi	29	**175**	42·6	42·4	42·3	42·2	42·3	42·3	S **17**	41·2	41·3	41·4	41·5	41·5	41·5
2·6	δ Centauri		**177**	34·1	33·8	33·7	33·7	33·7	33·9	S **50**	51·9	52·0	52·2	52·3	52·4	52·5
2·4	γ Ursæ Majoris		**181**	11·6	11·3	11·2	11·2	11·3	11·5	N **53**	32·7	32·7	32·8	32·9	33·0	33·1
2·1	β Leonis	28	**182**	23·9	23·7	23·6	23·6	23·7	23·7	N **14**	25·4	25·4	25·4	25·4	25·4	25·5
2·6	δ Leonis		**191**	07·3	07·1	07·0	07·0	07·1	07·2	N **20**	22·7	22·6	22·7	22·7	22·7	22·8
3·0	ψ Ursæ Majoris		**192**	12·7	12·5	12·4	12·4	12·6	12·7	N **44**	21·2	21·2	21·3	21·4	21·4	21·5
1·8	α Ursæ Majoris	27	**193**	39·5	39·2	39·1	39·2	39·4	39·7	N **61**	36·3	36·4	36·5	36·6	36·7	36·7
2·4	β Ursæ Majoris		**194**	08·4	08·1	08·0	08·1	08·3	08·5	N **56**	14·3	14·3	14·4	14·6	14·6	14·7
2·7	μ Velorum		**198**	01·3	01·1	01·1	01·1	01·3	01·5	S **49**	33·3	33·5	33·7	33·8	33·9	33·9
2·8	θ Carinæ		**199**	01·3	01·1	01·0	01·2	01·5	01·7	S **64**	31·7	31·9	32·0	32·2	32·3	32·3
2·3	γ Leonis		**204**	38·5	38·4	38·3	38·4	38·5	38·6	N **19**	42·4	42·4	42·4	42·4	42·5	42·5
1·4	α Leonis	26	**207**	33·3	33·1	33·1	33·2	33·2	33·3	N **11**	50·3	50·2	50·2	50·2	50·3	50·3
3·0	ε Leonis		**213**	09·7	09·5	09·5	09·6	09·7	09·8	N **23**	39·1	39·1	39·1	39·2	39·2	39·2
3·1	N Velorum		**216**	59·4	59·3	59·3	59·5	59·8	60·0	S **57**	08·8	09·0	09·2	09·3	09·4	09·3
2·0	α Hydræ	25	**217**	46·6	46·5	46·5	46·6	46·7	46·8	S **8**	46·3	46·4	46·5	46·5	46·5	46·5
2·5	κ Velorum		**219**	15·7	15·7	15·7	15·9	16·2	16·4	S **55**	07·2	07·4	07·6	07·7	07·7	07·7
2·2	ι Carinæ		**220**	32·7	32·7	32·8	33·0	33·3	33·5	S **59**	22·9	23·1	23·3	23·4	23·5	23·4
1·7	β Carinæ	24	**221**	37·2	37·2	37·4	37·8	38·2	38·6	S **69**	49·3	49·5	49·7	49·8	49·8	49·8
2·2	λ Velorum	23	**222**	45·3	45·2	45·3	45·4	45·6	45·7	S **43**	32·2	32·4	32·5	32·6	32·6	32·6
3·1	ι Ursæ Majoris		**224**	44·6	44·5	44·5	44·7	44·9	45·0	N **47**	56·2	56·3	56·4	56·4	56·4	56·4
2·0	δ Velorum		**228**	38·2	38·1	38·3	38·5	38·7	38·9	S **54**	48·2	48·4	48·5	48·6	48·6	48·6
1·9	ε Carinæ	22	**234**	13·7	13·8	13·9	14·2	14·5	14·8	S **59**	35·5	35·7	35·8	35·9	35·9	35·8
1·8	γ Velorum		**237**	24·5	24·5	24·6	24·8	25·0	25·2	S **47**	24·8	24·9	25·1	25·1	25·1	25·0
2·8	ρ Puppis		**237**	49·8	49·7	49·8	50·0	50·1	50·2	S **24**	22·8	22·9	23·0	23·0	23·0	22·9
2·3	ζ Puppis		**238**	52·1	52·0	52·2	52·3	52·5	52·6	S **40**	04·6	04·7	04·8	04·9	04·9	04·8
1·1	β Geminorum	21	**243**	15·9	15·8	15·9	16·0	16·2	16·2	N **27**	57·7	57·7	57·8	57·8	57·8	57·8
0·4	α Canis Minoris	20	**244**	49·6	49·6	49·6	49·8	49·9	49·9	N **5**	09·4	09·4	09·4	09·4	09·4	09·4

Mag.		Name and Number		SHA	JULY	AUG.	SEPT.	OCT.	NOV.	DEC.	Declination	JULY	AUG.	SEPT.	OCT.	NOV.	DEC.
				°	′	′	′	′	′	′	°	′	′	′	′	′	′
2·9	γ	Trianguli Aust.		129	38·1	38·4	38·8	39·0	39·0	38·7	S 68	46·9	46·9	46·9	46·8	46·6	46·5
3·1		*Pherkad*		129	48·6	49·1	49·7	50·0	50·2	50·1	N 71	44·5	44·5	44·5	44·4	44·2	44·0
2·6		*Zubeneschamali*		130	23·1	23·2	23·3	23·4	23·4	23·2	S 9	28·9	28·9	28·8	28·8	28·9	28·9
2·7	β	Lupi		134	55·5	55·6	55·8	55·9	55·8	55·6	S 43	14·6	14·6	14·6	14·5	14·4	14·4
2·8		*Zubenelgenubi*	39	136	54·5	54·6	54·7	54·7	54·7	54·5	S 16	09·2	09·2	09·1	09·1	09·1	09·2
2·1		*Kochab*	40	137	19·4	20·0	20·5	20·9	21·0	20·8	N 74	03·0	03·0	02·9	02·8	02·6	02·4
2·4		*Izar*		138	27·5	27·6	27·8	27·8	27·8	27·7	N 26	57·9	57·9	57·9	57·8	57·7	57·5
2·3	α	Lupi		139	04·1	04·3	04·5	04·5	04·5	04·2	S 47	30·3	30·3	30·3	30·2	30·1	30·1
−0·3		*Rigil Kent.*	38	139	38·3	38·6	38·8	38·9	38·8	38·6	S 60	56·9	56·9	56·9	56·8	56·6	56·6
2·3	η	Centauri		140	41·7	41·9	42·0	42·1	42·0	41·8	S 42	16·7	16·7	16·6	16·5	16·4	16·4
3·0		*Seginus*		141	42·5	42·6	42·8	42·9	42·8	42·7	N 38	11·7	11·7	11·7	11·5	11·4	11·2
0·0		*Arcturus*	37	145	46·7	46·8	46·9	46·9	46·9	46·7	N 19	02·8	02·8	02·7	02·7	02·5	02·4
2·1		*Menkent*	36	147	56·0	56·2	56·3	56·3	56·2	56·0	S 36	30·2	30·2	30·1	30·1	30·0	30·0
0·6		*Hadar*	35	148	34·1	34·3	34·5	34·6	34·5	34·1	S 60	30·4	30·3	30·3	30·1	30·0	30·0
2·6	ζ	Centauri		150	41·7	41·9	42·0	42·1	41·9	41·7	S 47	25·4	25·4	25·3	25·2	25·1	25·1
2·7		*Muphrid*		151	00·6	00·7	00·8	00·8	00·7	00·5	N 18	16·0	16·0	16·0	15·9	15·8	15·6
1·9		*Alkaid*	34	152	51·0	51·1	51·3	51·4	51·3	51·1	N 49	11·1	11·0	10·9	10·8	10·6	10·5
2·3	ε	Centauri		154	36·1	36·3	36·5	36·5	36·3	36·1	S 53	36·4	36·3	36·2	36·1	36·0	36·0
1·0		*Spica*	33	158	21·0	21·0	21·1	21·1	21·0	20·8	S 11	18·1	18·0	18·0	18·0	18·0	18·1
2·3		*Mizar*		158	44·9	45·1	45·2	45·3	45·2	44·9	N 54	47·4	47·4	47·3	47·1	46·9	46·8
2·8	ι	Centauri		159	28·5	28·6	28·7	28·7	28·5	28·3	S 36	51·3	51·3	51·2	51·1	51·1	51·1
2·8		*Vindemiatrix*		164	07·4	07·5	07·5	07·5	07·4	07·2	N 10	49·0	49·1	49·0	49·0	48·9	48·8
2·9		*Cor Caroli*		165	40·9	41·0	41·0	41·0	40·9	40·7	N 38	10·7	10·7	10·6	10·4	10·3	10·1
1·8		*Alioth*	32	166	11·9	12·1	12·3	12·3	12·1	11·8	N 55	49·2	49·1	49·0	48·8	48·6	48·5
1·3		*Mimosa*		167	40·8	41·0	41·1	41·1	40·9	40·5	S 59	50·3	50·3	50·2	50·0	49·9	49·9
2·9		*Porrima*		169	14·8	14·9	14·9	14·9	14·8	14·5	S 1	35·7	35·7	35·7	35·7	35·8	35·9
2·2		*Muhlifain*		169	15·2	15·3	15·4	15·4	15·2	14·9	S 49	06·6	06·5	06·4	06·3	06·3	06·3
2·7	α	Muscæ		170	18·4	18·7	18·9	18·9	18·6	18·1	S 69	17·2	17·2	17·1	16·9	16·8	16·8
2·7		*Kraz*		171	03·2	03·3	03·3	03·3	03·1	02·9	S 23	32·8	32·7	32·6	32·6	32·6	32·7
1·6		*Gacrux*	31	171	50·4	50·6	50·7	50·6	50·4	50·0	S 57	16·0	15·9	15·8	15·7	15·6	15·6
1·3		*Acrux*	30	172	58·8	59·0	59·2	59·1	58·8	58·4	S 63	15·1	15·0	14·9	14·8	14·7	14·7
2·6		*Gienah*	29	175	42·4	42·5	42·5	42·4	42·2	42·0	S 17	41·5	41·4	41·4	41·3	41·4	41·4
2·6	δ	Centauri		177	34·0	34·2	34·2	34·1	33·9	33·6	S 50	52·5	52·4	52·3	52·2	52·1	52·1
2·4		*Phecda*		181	11·7	11·8	11·8	11·8	11·5	11·2	N 53	33·1	33·0	32·8	32·7	32·5	32·4
2·1		*Denebola*	28	182	23·8	23·8	23·9	23·8	23·6	23·4	N 14	25·5	25·5	25·4	25·4	25·3	25·1
2·6		*Zosma*		191	07·3	07·3	07·3	07·2	07·0	06·7	N 20	22·8	22·8	22·7	22·6	22·5	22·4
3·0	ψ	Ursæ Majoris		192	12·8	12·9	12·8	12·7	12·5	12·1	N 44	21·4	21·4	21·2	21·1	20·9	20·8
1·8		*Dubhe*	27	193	39·9	40·0	40·0	39·8	39·4	39·0	N 61	36·7	36·6	36·4	36·2	36·1	36·0
2·4		*Merak*		194	08·6	08·7	08·7	08·5	08·2	07·8	N 56	14·6	14·5	14·3	14·2	14·0	13·9
2·7	μ	Velorum		198	01·6	01·7	01·7	01·5	01·2	00·9	S 49	33·8	33·7	33·6	33·5	33·5	33·6
2·8	θ	Carinæ		199	02·0	02·2	02·2	01·9	01·5	01·1	S 64	32·3	32·1	32·0	31·9	31·8	31·9
2·3		*Algieba*		204	38·6	38·6	38·5	38·4	38·1	37·9	N 19	42·5	42·5	42·4	42·3	42·2	42·1
1·4		*Regulus*	26	207	33·4	33·3	33·3	33·1	32·9	32·6	N 11	50·3	50·3	50·3	50·2	50·1	50·0
3·0	ε	Leonis		213	09·8	09·8	09·7	09·5	09·3	09·0	N 23	39·2	39·2	39·1	39·0	38·9	38·8
3·1	N	Velorum		216	60·2	60·2	60·1	59·8	59·5	59·1	S 57	09·2	09·1	08·9	08·9	08·9	09·0
2·0		*Alphard*	25	217	46·8	46·8	46·7	46·5	46·3	46·0	S 8	46·4	46·4	46·3	46·4	46·4	46·5
2·5		*Markeb*		219	16·5	16·5	16·4	16·2	15·8	15·5	S 55	07·6	07·4	07·3	07·2	07·2	07·3
2·2		*Aspidiske*		220	33·7	33·7	33·6	33·3	32·9	32·5	S 59	23·3	23·2	23·0	22·9	23·0	23·1
1·7		*Miaplacidus*	24	221	38·9	39·0	38·8	38·4	37·8	37·3	S 69	49·7	49·5	49·4	49·3	49·3	49·4
2·2		*Suhail*	23	222	45·8	45·8	45·7	45·4	45·1	44·9	S 43	32·5	32·3	32·2	32·2	32·2	32·3
3·1		*Talitha*		224	45·0	44·9	44·7	44·5	44·1	43·8	N 47	56·3	56·2	56·1	56·0	55·9	55·9
2·0		*Alsephina*		228	39·0	39·0	38·8	38·6	38·2	37·9	S 54	48·4	48·3	48·1	48·1	48·1	48·3
1·9		*Avior*	22	234	14·9	14·8	14·6	14·3	13·9	13·6	S 59	35·7	35·5	35·4	35·4	35·4	35·5
1·8	γ	Velorum		237	25·2	25·1	25·0	24·7	24·4	24·1	S 47	24·9	24·7	24·6	24·6	24·7	24·8
2·8		*Tureis*		237	50·2	50·1	49·9	49·7	49·4	49·2	S 24	22·8	22·7	22·7	22·7	22·7	22·8
2·3		*Naos*		238	52·6	52·5	52·4	52·1	51·8	51·6	S 40	04·7	04·5	04·4	04·4	04·5	04·6
1·1		*Pollux*	21	243	16·1	16·0	15·8	15·6	15·3	15·0	N 27	57·7	57·7	57·7	57·6	57·6	57·5
0·4		*Procyon*	20	244	49·8	49·7	49·5	49·3	49·1	48·9	N 5	09·4	09·5	09·5	09·5	09·4	09·3

Mag.	Name and Number		SHA							Declination						
				JAN.	FEB.	MAR.	APR.	MAY	JUNE		JAN.	FEB.	MAR.	APR.	MAY	JUNE
			°	′	′	′	′	′	′	°	′	′	′	′	′	′
1·6	α Geminorum		**245**	55·6	55·6	55·7	55·8	55·9	56·0	N **31**	49·8	49·8	49·8	49·9	49·9	49·8
3·3	σ Puppis		**247**	28·7	28·7	28·8	29·1	29·2	29·3	S **43**	21·3	21·4	21·5	21·5	21·5	21·4
2·9	β Canis Minoris		**247**	51·1	51·1	51·2	51·3	51·4	51·4	N **8**	14·1	14·1	14·1	14·1	14·1	14·1
2·4	η Canis Majoris		**248**	42·7	42·7	42·8	43·0	43·1	43·2	S **29**	21·3	21·4	21·5	21·5	21·5	21·4
2·7	π Puppis		**250**	28·6	28·6	28·8	28·9	29·1	29·2	S **37**	08·7	08·8	08·9	08·9	08·9	08·8
1·8	δ Canis Majoris		**252**	37·8	37·8	37·9	38·1	38·2	38·3	S **26**	26·1	26·2	26·3	26·3	26·3	26·2
3·0	ο Canis Majoris		**253**	57·9	57·9	58·0	58·2	58·3	58·3	S **23**	52·3	52·4	52·5	52·5	52·5	52·4
1·5	ε Canis Majoris	19	**255**	04·8	04·8	05·0	05·1	05·3	05·3	S **29**	00·5	00·6	00·7	00·7	00·6	00·5
2·9	τ Puppis		**257**	20·7	20·8	21·0	21·3	21·5	21·6	S **50**	38·8	38·9	39·0	39·0	38·9	38·8
−1·5	α Canis Majoris	18	**258**	25·1	25·2	25·3	25·4	25·5	25·5	S **16**	45·2	45·3	45·3	45·3	45·3	45·2
1·9	γ Geminorum		**260**	11·3	11·3	11·4	11·6	11·6	11·6	N **16**	22·6	22·6	22·6	22·6	22·6	22·6
−0·7	α Carinæ	17	**263**	51·5	51·6	51·8	52·1	52·3	52·4	S **52**	42·6	42·8	42·8	42·8	42·7	42·6
2·0	β Canis Majoris		**264**	01·9	01·9	02·0	02·2	02·3	02·3	S **17**	58·2	58·3	58·3	58·3	58·3	58·2
2·6	θ Aurigæ		**269**	37·0	37·1	37·2	37·3	37·4	37·4	N **37**	12·9	12·9	12·9	12·9	12·9	12·8
1·9	β Aurigæ		**269**	37·8	37·9	38·0	38·2	38·3	38·3	N **44**	57·0	57·1	57·1	57·1	57·0	57·0
Var.‡	α Orionis	16	**270**	50·8	50·9	51·0	51·1	51·2	51·1	N **7**	24·7	24·7	24·6	24·6	24·7	24·7
2·1	κ Orionis		**272**	44·7	44·8	44·9	45·0	45·1	45·1	S **9**	39·7	39·7	39·8	39·8	39·7	39·6
1·9	ζ Orionis		**274**	28·5	28·5	28·7	28·8	28·8	28·8	S **1**	55·8	55·8	55·8	55·8	55·8	55·7
2·6	α Columbæ		**274**	50·7	50·8	50·9	51·1	51·2	51·2	S **34**	03·7	03·8	03·8	03·8	03·7	03·6
3·0	ζ Tauri		**275**	11·5	11·6	11·7	11·8	11·9	11·8	N **21**	09·5	09·5	09·5	09·5	09·5	09·5
1·7	ε Orionis	15	**275**	36·6	36·6	36·7	36·8	36·9	36·9	S **1**	11·2	11·2	11·2	11·2	11·2	11·1
2·8	ι Orionis		**275**	49·0	49·0	49·2	49·3	49·3	49·3	S **5**	53·6	53·7	53·7	53·7	53·6	53·6
2·6	α Leporis		**276**	31·4	31·5	31·6	31·7	31·8	31·8	S **17**	48·3	48·4	48·4	48·4	48·3	48·2
2·2	δ Orionis		**276**	39·5	39·6	39·7	39·8	39·9	39·8	S **0**	16·8	16·9	16·9	16·9	16·8	16·8
2·8	β Leporis		**277**	39·2	39·2	39·4	39·5	39·6	39·6	S **20**	44·4	44·5	44·5	44·5	44·4	44·3
1·7	β Tauri	14	**278**	00·5	00·5	00·6	00·8	00·8	00·8	N **28**	37·8	37·8	37·8	37·8	37·8	37·7
1·6	γ Orionis	13	**278**	21·7	21·7	21·8	22·0	22·0	22·0	N **6**	22·4	22·3	22·3	22·3	22·4	22·4
0·1	α Aurigæ	12	**280**	20·2	20·3	20·5	20·6	20·7	20·6	N **46**	01·5	01·6	01·6	01·6	01·5	01·4
0·1	β Orionis	11	**281**	02·8	02·8	02·9	03·1	03·1	03·1	S **8**	10·4	10·4	10·4	10·4	10·3	10·3
2·8	β Eridani		**282**	42·7	42·7	42·8	43·0	43·0	42·9	S **5**	03·2	03·3	03·3	03·3	03·2	03·1
2·7	ι Aurigæ		**285**	19·2	19·3	19·4	19·5	19·6	19·5	N **33**	12·5	12·5	12·5	12·5	12·4	12·4
0·9	α Tauri	10	**290**	38·4	38·5	38·6	38·7	38·7	38·6	N **16**	33·7	33·7	33·7	33·7	33·7	33·7
2·9	ε Persei		**300**	05·5	05·6	05·8	05·9	05·9	05·7	N **40**	05·3	05·3	05·3	05·2	05·1	05·1
3·0	γ Eridani		**300**	11·0	11·1	11·2	11·3	11·3	11·2	S **13**	26·1	26·2	26·2	26·1	26·1	25·9
2·9	ζ Persei		**301**	03·1	03·2	03·3	03·4	03·4	03·2	N **31**	57·8	57·8	57·7	57·7	57·7	57·6
2·9	η Tauri		**302**	44·1	44·2	44·4	44·4	44·4	44·3	N **24**	11·2	11·2	11·2	11·2	11·1	11·1
1·8	α Persei	9	**308**	26·8	26·9	27·1	27·2	27·2	27·0	N **49**	57·4	57·4	57·4	57·3	57·2	57·2
Var.§	β Persei		**312**	31·7	31·8	31·9	32·0	32·0	31·8	N **41**	03·5	03·5	03·5	03·4	03·3	03·3
2·0	α Ursæ Minoris		**313**	24·0	37·1	49·6	57·2	56·4	48·1	N **89**	22·7	22·8	22·7	22·6	22·4	22·3
2·5	α Ceti	8	**314**	05·1	05·2	05·3	05·4	05·3	05·2	N **4**	11·5	11·5	11·5	11·5	11·5	11·6
3·2	θ Eridani	7	**315**	11·0	11·1	11·3	11·4	11·4	11·2	S **40**	12·2	12·2	12·2	12·1	11·9	11·7
3·0	β Trianguli		**327**	13·4	13·5	13·6	13·6	13·5	13·3	N **35**	06·8	06·8	06·7	06·7	06·6	06·6
2·0	α Arietis	6	**327**	50·2	50·3	50·4	50·4	50·3	50·1	N **23**	35·2	35·2	35·2	35·1	35·1	35·2
2·3	γ Andromedæ		**328**	37·3	37·4	37·5	37·6	37·5	37·2	N **42**	27·5	27·5	27·4	27·3	27·2	27·2
2·9	α Hydri		**330**	05·8	06·1	06·3	06·4	06·4	06·1	S **61**	26·9	26·8	26·7	26·5	26·3	26·2
2·6	β Arietis		**330**	58·6	58·7	58·8	58·8	58·7	58·5	N **20**	56·2	56·2	56·2	56·1	56·1	56·2
0·5	α Eridani	5	**335**	19·5	19·8	19·9	20·0	19·9	19·6	S **57**	06·5	06·5	06·4	06·2	06·0	05·9
2·7	δ Cassiopeiæ		**338**	07·0	07·2	07·4	07·4	07·2	06·8	N **60**	22·5	22·5	22·4	22·3	22·2	22·1
2·1	β Andromedæ		**342**	12·0	12·2	12·2	12·2	12·1	11·8	N **35**	45·7	45·7	45·6	45·5	45·5	45·5
Var.‖	γ Cassiopeiæ		**345**	25·7	25·9	26·1	26·0	25·8	25·4	N **60**	51·8	51·7	51·6	51·5	51·4	51·4
2·0	β Ceti	4	**348**	46·5	46·6	46·6	46·6	46·4	46·2	S **17**	50·7	50·7	50·7	50·6	50·5	50·4
2·2	α Cassiopeiæ	3	**349**	30·2	30·4	30·5	30·4	30·2	29·8	N **56**	41·1	41·0	40·9	40·8	40·7	40·7
2·4	α Phœnicis	2	**353**	06·4	06·5	06·6	06·5	06·4	06·1	S **42**	10·1	10·0	09·9	09·8	09·6	09·5
2·8	β Hydri		**353**	13·5	14·0	14·3	14·2	13·8	13·1	S **77**	06·8	06·6	06·5	06·3	06·1	06·0
2·8	γ Pegasi		**356**	21·4	21·4	21·4	21·4	21·2	21·0	N **15**	19·8	19·7	19·7	19·7	19·7	19·8
2·3	β Cassiopeiæ		**357**	21·6	21·8	21·9	21·8	21·5	21·1	N **59**	17·9	17·8	17·7	17·6	17·5	17·5
2·1	α Andromedæ	1	**357**	34·0	34·1	34·1	34·0	33·9	33·6	N **29**	14·2	14·1	14·1	14·0	14·0	14·1

‡ 0·1 — 1·2 § 2·1 — 3·4 ‖ Irregular variable; 2025 mag. 2·1

Mag.	Name and Number		SHA	JULY	AUG.	SEPT.	OCT.	NOV.	DEC.	Declination	JULY	AUG.	SEPT.	OCT.	NOV.	DEC.
			°	′	′	′	′	′	′	°	′	′	′	′	′	′
1·6	*Castor*		**245**	55·9	55·7	55·5	55·3	55·0	54·7	N **31**	49·8	49·7	49·7	49·6	49·6	49·6
3·3	σ Puppis		**247**	29·3	29·2	29·0	28·7	28·5	28·2	S **43**	21·3	21·1	21·0	21·0	21·1	21·2
2·9	*Gomeisa*		**247**	51·4	51·2	51·0	50·8	50·6	50·4	N **8**	14·2	14·2	14·2	14·2	14·1	14·0
2·4	*Aludra*		**248**	43·1	43·0	42·8	42·6	42·3	42·1	S **29**	21·2	21·1	21·0	21·0	21·1	21·3
2·7	π Puppis		**250**	29·1	29·0	28·8	28·6	28·3	28·1	S **37**	08·6	08·5	08·4	08·4	08·5	08·6
1·8	*Wezen*		**252**	38·2	38·1	37·9	37·7	37·4	37·2	S **26**	26·1	25·9	25·9	25·9	26·0	26·1
3·0	*o* Canis Majoris		**253**	58·3	58·1	57·9	57·7	57·5	57·3	S **23**	52·3	52·1	52·1	52·1	52·2	52·3
1·5	*Adhara*	19	**255**	05·2	05·1	04·9	04·7	04·4	04·2	S **29**	00·4	00·3	00·2	00·2	00·3	00·5
2·9	τ Puppis		**257**	21·6	21·4	21·2	20·9	20·6	20·4	S **50**	38·7	38·5	38·4	38·4	38·5	38·7
−1·5	*Sirius*	18	**258**	25·5	25·3	25·1	24·9	24·7	24·5	S **16**	45·1	45·0	44·9	45·0	45·0	45·2
1·9	*Alhena*		**260**	11·5	11·4	11·1	10·9	10·7	10·5	N **16**	22·6	22·6	22·6	22·6	22·5	22·5
−0·7	*Canopus*	17	**263**	52·4	52·2	51·9	51·6	51·3	51·1	S **52**	42·4	42·3	42·2	42·2	42·3	42·5
2·0	*Mirzam*		**264**	02·2	02·0	01·8	01·6	01·4	01·2	S **17**	58·1	58·0	57·9	57·9	58·0	58·1
2·6	*Mahasim*		**269**	37·2	37·0	36·7	36·4	36·2	36·0	N **37**	12·8	12·8	12·8	12·8	12·8	12·8
1·9	*Menkalinan*		**269**	38·1	37·8	37·5	37·2	36·9	36·7	N **44**	56·9	56·9	56·8	56·8	56·9	56·9
Var.‡	*Betelgeuse*	16	**270**	51·0	50·8	50·6	50·4	50·2	50·0	N **7**	24·8	24·8	24·8	24·8	24·8	24·7
2·1	*Saiph*		**272**	44·9	44·8	44·5	44·3	44·1	44·0	S **9**	39·5	39·4	39·4	39·4	39·5	39·6
1·9	*Alnitak*		**274**	28·7	28·5	28·3	28·1	27·8	27·7	S **1**	55·6	55·6	55·5	55·6	55·6	55·7
2·6	*Phact*		**274**	51·1	50·9	50·7	50·4	50·2	50·1	S **34**	03·4	03·3	03·3	03·3	03·4	03·5
3·0	*Tianguan*		**275**	11·7	11·5	11·2	11·0	10·8	10·6	N **21**	09·5	09·5	09·5	09·5	09·5	09·5
1·7	*Alnilam*	15	**275**	36·7	36·5	36·3	36·1	35·9	35·8	S **1**	11·0	11·0	10·9	10·9	11·0	11·1
2·8	*Hatysa*		**275**	49·2	49·0	48·8	48·6	48·3	48·2	S **5**	53·5	53·4	53·4	53·4	53·4	53·5
2·6	*Arneb*		**276**	31·7	31·5	31·2	31·0	30·8	30·7	S **17**	48·1	48·0	47·9	48·0	48·0	48·2
2·2	*Mintaka*		**276**	39·7	39·5	39·3	39·1	38·9	38·7	S **0**	16·7	16·6	16·6	16·6	16·7	16·7
2·8	*Nihal*		**277**	39·4	39·2	39·0	38·8	38·6	38·5	S **20**	44·2	44·1	44·0	44·0	44·1	44·3
1·7	*Elnath*	14	**277**	60·6	60·4	60·1	59·9	59·6	59·5	N **28**	37·7	37·7	37·8	37·8	37·8	37·8
1·6	*Bellatrix*	13	**278**	21·8	21·6	21·4	21·2	21·0	20·8	N **6**	22·5	22·5	22·5	22·5	22·5	22·5
0·1	*Capella*	12	**280**	20·4	20·1	19·8	19·5	19·2	19·0	N **46**	01·4	01·3	01·3	01·4	01·4	01·5
0·1	*Rigel*	11	**281**	02·9	02·7	02·5	02·3	02·1	02·0	S **8**	10·2	10·1	10·0	10·1	10·1	10·2
2·8	*Cursa*		**282**	42·8	42·6	42·4	42·2	42·0	41·9	S **5**	03·0	03·0	02·9	02·9	03·0	03·1
2·7	*Hassaleh*		**285**	19·3	19·0	18·7	18·5	18·3	18·1	N **33**	12·4	12·4	12·4	12·5	12·5	12·5
0·9	*Aldebaran*	10	**290**	38·4	38·2	37·9	37·7	37·5	37·4	N **16**	33·8	33·8	33·8	33·9	33·9	33·8
2·9	ε Persei		**300**	05·5	05·2	04·9	04·7	04·5	04·4	N **40**	05·1	05·1	05·2	05·2	05·3	05·4
3·0	*Zaurak*		**300**	11·0	10·8	10·6	10·4	10·3	10·2	S **13**	25·8	25·7	25·7	25·7	25·8	25·9
2·9	ζ Persei		**301**	03·0	02·7	02·5	02·2	02·1	02·0	N **31**	57·7	57·7	57·8	57·8	57·9	57·9
2·9	*Alcyone*		**302**	44·1	43·8	43·6	43·4	43·2	43·1	N **24**	11·2	11·2	11·3	11·3	11·4	11·4
1·8	*Mirfak*	9	**308**	26·7	26·3	26·0	25·7	25·6	25·5	N **49**	57·1	57·2	57·3	57·4	57·5	57·6
Var.§	*Algol*		**312**	31·5	31·2	30·9	30·7	30·5	30·5	N **41**	03·3	03·4	03·5	03·6	03·6	03·7
2·0	*Polaris*		**312**	94·3	78·0	62·5	50·6	44·7	47·2	N **89**	22·3	22·3	22·3	22·5	22·7	22·8
2·5	*Menkar*	8	**314**	05·0	04·7	04·5	04·3	04·2	04·2	N **4**	11·7	11·8	11·8	11·8	11·8	11·8
3·2	*Acamar*	7	**315**	11·0	10·7	10·5	10·3	10·2	10·2	S **40**	11·6	11·5	11·5	11·6	11·7	11·9
3·0	β Trianguli		**327**	13·0	12·7	12·5	12·3	12·3	12·3	N **35**	06·7	06·8	06·9	07·0	07·0	07·1
2·0	*Hamal*	6	**327**	49·8	49·6	49·4	49·2	49·1	49·2	N **23**	35·2	35·3	35·4	35·5	35·5	35·6
2·3	*Almach*		**328**	36·9	36·6	36·4	36·2	36·1	36·1	N **42**	27·3	27·4	27·5	27·6	27·7	27·8
2·9	α Hydri		**330**	05·7	05·3	05·0	04·9	04·9	05·0	S **61**	26·1	26·0	26·1	26·2	26·4	26·5
2·6	*Sheratan*		**330**	58·3	58·0	57·8	57·7	57·6	57·6	N **20**	56·2	56·3	56·4	56·5	56·5	56·5
0·5	*Achernar*	5	**335**	19·3	18·9	18·7	18·5	18·5	18·7	S **57**	05·7	05·7	05·8	05·9	06·1	06·2
2·7	*Ruchbah*		**338**	06·4	06·0	05·7	05·5	05·5	05·6	N **60**	22·2	22·3	22·4	22·6	22·7	22·8
2·1	*Mirach*		**342**	11·5	11·2	11·1	11·0	10·9	11·0	N **35**	45·6	45·7	45·8	45·9	46·0	46·1
Var.‖	γ Cassiopeiæ		**345**	25·0	24·6	24·3	24·2	24·2	24·4	N **60**	51·4	51·5	51·7	51·9	52·0	52·1
2·0	*Diphda*	4	**348**	46·0	45·7	45·6	45·5	45·5	45·6	S **17**	50·3	50·2	50·2	50·2	50·3	50·3
2·2	*Schedar*	3	**349**	29·5	29·1	28·9	28·8	28·9	29·0	N **56**	40·8	40·9	41·1	41·2	41·4	41·5
2·4	*Ankaa*	2	**353**	05·8	05·5	05·4	05·3	05·4	05·5	S **42**	09·4	09·4	09·4	09·5	09·6	09·7
2·8	β Hydri		**353**	12·4	11·6	11·2	11·2	11·5	12·1	S **77**	05·9	06·0	06·1	06·2	06·4	06·4
2·8	*Algenib*		**356**	20·7	20·5	20·4	20·3	20·3	20·4	N **15**	19·9	20·0	20·1	20·2	20·2	20·2
2·3	*Caph*		**357**	20·7	20·4	20·2	20·1	20·2	20·4	N **59**	17·6	17·7	17·9	18·1	18·2	18·3
2·1	*Alpheratz*	1	**357**	33·3	33·1	33·0	32·9	33·0	33·1	N **29**	14·2	14·3	14·4	14·5	14·6	14·6

‡ 0·1 — 1·2 § 2·1 — 3·4 ‖ Irregular variable; 2025 mag. 2·1

POLARIS (POLE STAR) TABLES, 2026

FOR DETERMINING LATITUDE FROM SEXTANT ALTITUDE AND FOR AZIMUTH

LHA ARIES	0° – 9°	10° – 19°	20° – 29°	30° – 39°	40° – 49°	50° – 59°	60° – 69°	70° – 79°	80° – 89°	90° – 99°	100° – 109°	110° – 119°
	a_0	a_0	a_0	a_0	a_0	a_0	a_0	a_0	a_0	a_0	a_0	a_0
°	° ′	° ′	° ′	° ′	° ′	° ′	° ′	° ′	° ′	° ′	° ′	° ′
0	0 33·3	0 28·9	0 25·4	0 23·0	0 21·7	0 21·5	0 22·4	0 24·5	0 27·6	0 31·7	0 36·6	0 42·2
1	32·8	28·5	25·1	22·8	21·6	21·5	22·6	24·8	28·0	32·2	37·2	42·8
2	32·3	28·1	24·9	22·6	21·5	21·6	22·8	25·0	28·4	32·6	37·7	43·4
3	31·9	27·7	24·6	22·5	21·5	21·6	22·9	25·3	28·8	33·1	38·2	44·0
4	31·4	27·4	24·3	22·3	21·4	21·7	23·1	25·6	29·2	33·6	38·8	44·6
5	0 31·0	0 27·0	0 24·1	0 22·2	0 21·4	0 21·8	0 23·3	0 25·9	0 29·6	0 34·1	0 39·4	0 45·2
6	30·5	26·7	23·8	22·1	21·4	21·9	23·5	26·3	30·0	34·6	39·9	45·8
7	30·1	26·4	23·6	21·9	21·4	22·0	23·8	26·6	30·4	35·1	40·5	46·4
8	29·7	26·0	23·4	21·8	21·4	22·1	24·0	26·9	30·8	35·6	41·1	47·1
9	29·3	25·7	23·2	21·7	21·4	22·3	24·2	27·3	31·3	36·1	41·6	47·7
10	0 28·9	0 25·4	0 23·0	0 21·7	0 21·5	0 22·4	0 24·5	0 27·6	0 31·7	0 36·6	0 42·2	0 48·3
Lat.	a_1	a_1	a_1	a_1	a_1	a_1	a_1	a_1	a_1	a_1	a_1	a_1
°	′	′	′	′	′	′	′	′	′	′	′	′
0	0·5	0·5	0·6	0·6	0·6	0·6	0·6	0·5	0·5	0·5	0·4	0·4
10	·5	·5	·6	·6	·6	·6	·6	·6	·5	·5	·5	·4
20	·5	·6	·6	·6	·6	·6	·6	·6	·5	·5	·5	·5
30	·5	·6	·6	·6	·6	·6	·6	·6	·6	·5	·5	·5
40	0·6	0·6	0·6	0·6	0·6	0·6	0·6	0·6	0·6	0·6	0·5	0·5
45	·6	·6	·6	·6	·6	·6	·6	·6	·6	·6	·6	·6
50	·6	·6	·6	·6	·6	·6	·6	·6	·6	·6	·6	·6
55	·6	·6	·6	·6	·6	·6	·6	·6	·6	·6	·6	·6
60	·6	·6	·6	·6	·6	·6	·6	·6	·6	·7	·7	·7
62	0·7	0·6	0·6	0·6	0·6	0·6	0·6	0·6	0·7	0·7	0·7	0·7
64	·7	·6	·6	·6	·6	·6	·6	·6	·7	·7	·7	·8
66	·7	·7	·6	·6	·6	·6	·6	·6	·7	·7	·8	·8
68	0·7	0·7	0·6	0·6	0·6	0·6	0·6	0·7	0·7	0·7	0·8	0·8
Month	a_2	a_2	a_2	a_2	a_2	a_2	a_2	a_2	a_2	a_2	a_2	a_2
	′	′	′	′	′	′	′	′	′	′	′	′
Jan.	0·7	0·7	0·7	0·7	0·7	0·7	0·7	0·7	0·7	0·7	0·7	0·7
Feb.	·6	·7	·7	·7	·8	·8	·8	·8	·8	·8	·8	·8
Mar.	·5	·5	·6	·6	·7	·8	·8	·8	·9	·9	·9	0·9
Apr.	0·3	0·4	0·4	0·5	0·6	0·6	0·7	0·8	0·8	0·9	0·9	1·0
May	·2	·3	·3	·4	·4	·5	·6	·6	·7	·8	·8	0·9
June	·2	·2	·2	·3	·3	·4	·4	·5	·6	·6	·7	·8
July	0·2	0·2	0·2	0·2	0·2	0·3	0·3	0·4	0·4	0·5	0·5	0·6
Aug.	·4	·3	·3	·3	·3	·3	·3	·3	·3	·4	·4	·4
Sept.	·5	·5	·4	·4	·4	·3	·3	·3	·3	·3	·3	·3
Oct.	0·7	0·7	0·6	0·6	0·5	0·4	0·4	0·3	0·3	0·3	0·3	0·3
Nov.	0·9	0·9	0·8	·8	·7	·6	·5	·5	·4	·4	·3	·3
Dec.	1·0	1·0	1·0	0·9	0·9	0·8	0·7	0·6	0·6	0·5	0·4	0·3
Lat.	AZIMUTH											
°	°	°	°	°	°	°	°	°	°	°	°	°
0	0·4	0·3	0·2	0·1	0·0	359·9	359·8	359·7	359·6	359·5	359·5	359·4
20	0·4	0·3	0·2	0·1	0·0	359·9	359·8	359·7	359·6	359·5	359·4	359·4
40	0·5	0·4	0·3	0·2	0·0	359·9	359·7	359·6	359·5	359·4	359·3	359·2
50	0·7	0·5	0·4	0·2	0·0	359·9	359·7	359·5	359·4	359·3	359·2	359·1
55	0·7	0·6	0·4	0·2	0·0	359·8	359·7	359·5	359·3	359·2	359·1	359·0
60	0·8	0·7	0·5	0·3	0·0	359·8	359·6	359·4	359·2	359·1	358·9	358·8
65	1·0	0·8	0·6	0·3	0·0	359·8	359·5	359·3	359·1	358·9	358·7	358·6

Latitude = Apparent altitude (corrected for refraction) $-1° + a_0 + a_1 + a_2$

The table is entered with LHA Aries to determine the column to be used; each column refers to a range of 10°. a_0 is taken, with mental interpolation, from the upper table with the units of LHA Aries in degrees as argument; a_1, a_2 are taken, without interpolation, from the second and third tables with arguments latitude and month respectively. a_0, a_1, a_2, are always positive. The final table gives the azimuth of *Polaris.*

POLARIS (POLE STAR) TABLES, 2026

FOR DETERMINING LATITUDE FROM SEXTANT ALTITUDE AND FOR AZIMUTH

LHA ARIES	120° – 129°	130° – 139°	140° – 149°	150° – 159°	160° – 169°	170° – 179°	180° – 189°	190° – 199°	200° – 209°	210° – 219°	220° – 229°	230° – 239°
	a_0	a_0	a_0	a_0	a_0	a_0	a_0	a_0	a_0	a_0	a_0	a_0
°	° ′	° ′	° ′	° ′	° ′	° ′	° ′	° ′	° ′	° ′	° ′	° ′
0	0 48·3	0 54·7	1 01·2	1 07·7	1 13·8	1 19·5	1 24·6	1 28·9	1 32·3	1 34·7	1 36·0	1 36·1
1	48·9	55·4	01·9	08·3	14·4	20·1	25·1	29·3	32·6	34·8	36·0	36·1
2	49·6	56·0	02·5	08·9	15·0	20·6	25·5	29·6	32·8	35·0	36·1	36·0
3	50·2	56·7	03·2	09·6	15·6	21·1	26·0	30·0	33·1	35·2	36·1	36·0
4	50·8	57·3	03·8	10·2	16·2	21·6	26·4	30·4	33·4	35·3	36·2	35·9
5	0 51·5	0 58·0	1 04·5	1 10·8	1 16·7	1 22·2	1 26·9	1 30·7	1 33·6	1 35·4	1 36·2	1 35·8
6	52·1	58·6	05·1	11·4	17·3	22·7	27·3	31·0	33·8	35·6	36·2	35·7
7	52·8	59·3	05·8	12·0	17·9	23·2	27·7	31·4	34·0	35·7	36·2	35·6
8	53·4	0 59·9	06·4	12·6	18·4	23·6	28·1	31·7	34·3	35·8	36·2	35·5
9	54·1	1 00·6	07·0	13·2	19·0	24·1	28·5	32·0	34·5	35·9	36·2	35·3
10	0 54·7	1 01·2	1 07·7	1 13·8	1 19·5	1 24·6	1 28·9	1 32·3	1 34·7	1 36·0	1 36·1	1 35·2
Lat.	a_1	a_1	a_1	a_1	a_1	a_1	a_1	a_1	a_1	a_1	a_1	a_1
°	′	′	′	′	′	′	′	′	′	′	′	′
0	0·4	0·4	0·4	0·4	0·4	0·5	0·5	0·5	0·6	0·6	0·6	0·6
10	·4	·4	·4	·4	·4	·5	·5	·5	·6	·6	·6	·6
20	·4	·4	·4	·4	·5	·5	·5	·6	·6	·6	·6	·6
30	·5	·5	·5	·5	·5	·5	·5	·6	·6	·6	·6	·6
40	0·5	0·5	0·5	0·5	0·5	0·6	0·6	0·6	0·6	0·6	0·6	0·6
45	·6	·6	·6	·6	·6	·6	·6	·6	·6	·6	·6	·6
50	·6	·6	·6	·6	·6	·6	·6	·6	·6	·6	·6	·6
55	·6	·6	·6	·6	·6	·6	·6	·6	·6	·6	·6	·6
60	·7	·7	·7	·7	·7	·7	·6	·6	·6	·6	·6	·6
62	0·7	0·7	0·7	0·7	0·7	0·7	0·7	0·6	0·6	0·6	0·6	0·6
64	·8	·8	·8	·8	·7	·7	·7	·6	·6	·6	·6	·6
66	·8	·8	·8	·8	·8	·7	·7	·7	·6	·6	·6	·6
68	0·9	0·9	0·9	0·8	0·8	0·8	0·7	0·7	0·6	0·6	0·6	0·6
Month	a_2	a_2	a_2	a_2	a_2	a_2	a_2	a_2	a_2	a_2	a_2	a_2
	′	′	′	′	′	′	′	′	′	′	′	′
Jan.	0·7	0·6	0·6	0·6	0·6	0·5	0·5	0·5	0·5	0·5	0·5	0·5
Feb.	·8	·8	·7	·7	·7	·6	·6	·5	·5	·5	·4	·4
Mar.	0·9	0·9	0·9	0·9	0·8	·8	·7	·7	·6	·6	·5	·4
Apr.	1·0	1·0	1·0	1·0	1·0	0·9	0·9	0·8	0·8	0·7	0·6	0·6
May	0·9	1·0	1·0	1·0	1·0	1·0	1·0	0·9	0·9	·8	·8	·7
June	·8	0·9	0·9	1·0	1·0	1·0	1·0	1·0	1·0	0·9	0·9	·8
July	0·7	0·7	0·8	0·8	0·9	0·9	1·0	1·0	1·0	1·0	1·0	0·9
Aug.	·5	·6	·6	·7	·7	·8	0·8	0·9	0·9	0·9	0·9	·9
Sept.	·4	·4	·4	·5	·5	·6	·7	·7	·8	·8	·8	·9
Oct.	0·3	0·3	0·3	0·3	0·4	0·4	0·5	0·5	0·6	0·6	0·7	0·8
Nov.	·2	·2	·2	·2	·2	·2	·3	·3	·4	·4	·5	·6
Dec.	0·3	0·2	0·2	0·2	0·2	0·2	0·2	0·2	0·2	0·3	0·3	0·4
Lat.	AZIMUTH											
°	°	°	°	°	°	°	°	°	°	°	°	°
0	359·4	359·4	359·4	359·4	359·5	359·5	359·6	359·7	359·8	359·9	0·0	0·1
20	359·3	359·3	359·3	359·4	359·4	359·5	359·6	359·7	359·8	359·9	0·0	0·1
40	359·2	359·2	359·2	359·2	359·3	359·4	359·5	359·6	359·7	359·8	0·0	0·1
50	359·0	359·0	359·0	359·1	359·2	359·2	359·4	359·5	359·6	359·8	0·0	0·1
55	358·9	358·9	358·9	359·0	359·1	359·2	359·3	359·4	359·6	359·8	0·0	0·2
60	358·8	358·8	358·8	358·8	358·9	359·0	359·2	359·4	359·5	359·8	0·0	0·2
65	358·5	358·5	358·5	358·6	358·7	358·9	359·0	359·2	359·5	359·7	0·0	0·2

ILLUSTRATION

On 2026 April 21 at $23^h\ 18^m\ 56^s$ UT in longitude W 37° 14′, the apparent altitude (corrected for refraction), H_O, of *Polaris* was 49° 31′.6

From the daily pages:	° ′		° ′
GHA Aries (23^h)	195 01·7	H_O	49 31·6
Increment ($18^m\ 56^s$)	4 44·8	a_0 (argument 162° 33′)	1 15·3
Longitude (west)	−37 14	a_1 (Lat 50° approx.)	0·6
		a_2 (April)	1·0
LHA Aries	162 33	Sum − 1° = Lat =	49 48·5

POLARIS (POLE STAR) TABLES, 2026

FOR DETERMINING LATITUDE FROM SEXTANT ALTITUDE AND FOR AZIMUTH

LHA ARIES	240° – 249°	250° – 259°	260° – 269°	270° – 279°	280° – 289°	290° – 299°	300° – 309°	310° – 319°	320° – 329°	330° – 339°	340° – 349°	350° – 359°
	a_0	a_0	a_0	a_0	a_0	a_0	a_0	a_0	a_0	a_0	a_0	a_0
°	° ′	° ′	° ′	° ′	° ′	° ′	° ′	° ′	° ′	° ′	° ′	° ′
0	1 35·2	1 33·2	1 30·1	1 26·1	1 21·3	1 15·8	1 09·7	1 03·4	0 56·9	0 50·4	0 44·2	0 38·4
1	35·0	32·9	29·8	25·7	20·8	15·2	09·1	02·7	56·2	49·8	43·6	37·9
2	34·9	32·6	29·4	25·2	20·2	14·6	08·5	02·1	55·6	49·1	43·0	37·3
3	34·7	32·4	29·0	24·7	19·7	14·0	07·9	01·4	54·9	48·5	42·4	36·8
4	34·5	32·1	28·6	24·3	19·1	13·4	07·2	00·8	54·3	47·9	41·8	36·3
5	1 34·3	1 31·8	1 28·2	1 23·8	1 18·6	1 12·8	1 06·6	1 00·1	0 53·6	0 47·2	0 41·2	0 35·7
6	34·1	31·5	27·8	23·3	18·0	12·2	05·9	0 59·5	53·0	46·6	40·7	35·2
7	33·9	31·1	27·4	22·8	17·5	11·6	05·3	58·8	52·3	46·0	40·1	34·7
8	33·7	30·8	27·0	22·3	16·9	11·0	04·7	58·2	51·7	45·4	39·5	34·2
9	33·4	30·5	26·6	21·8	16·3	10·4	04·0	57·5	51·0	44·8	39·0	33·7
10	1 33·2	1 30·1	1 26·1	1 21·3	1 15·8	1 09·7	1 03·4	0 56·9	0 50·4	0 44·2	0 38·4	0 33·3
Lat.	a_1	a_1	a_1	a_1	a_1	a_1	a_1	a_1	a_1	a_1	a_1	a_1
°	′	′	′	′	′	′	′	′	′	′	′	′
0	0·6	0·5	0·5	0·5	0·4	0·4	0·4	0·4	0·4	0·4	0·4	0·5
10	·6	·6	·5	·5	·5	·4	·4	·4	·4	·4	·4	·5
20	·6	·6	·5	·5	·5	·5	·4	·4	·4	·4	·5	·5
30	·6	·6	·6	·5	·5	·5	·5	·5	·5	·5	·5	·5
40	0·6	0·6	0·6	0·6	0·5	0·5	0·5	0·5	0·5	0·5	0·5	0·6
45	·6	·6	·6	·6	·6	·6	·6	·6	·6	·6	·6	·6
50	·6	·6	·6	·6	·6	·6	·6	·6	·6	·6	·6	·6
55	·6	·6	·6	·6	·6	·6	·6	·6	·6	·6	·6	·6
60	·6	·6	·6	·7	·7	·7	·7	·7	·7	·7	·7	·7
62	0·6	0·6	0·7	0·7	0·7	0·7	0·7	0·7	0·7	0·7	0·7	0·7
64	·6	·6	·7	·7	·7	·8	·8	·8	·8	·8	·7	·7
66	·6	·6	·7	·7	·8	·8	·8	·8	·8	·8	·8	·7
68	0·6	0·7	0·7	0·7	0·8	0·8	0·9	0·9	0·9	0·8	0·8	0·8
Month	a_2	a_2	a_2	a_2	a_2	a_2	a_2	a_2	a_2	a_2	a_2	a_2
	′	′	′	′	′	′	′	′	′	′	′	′
Jan.	0·5	0·5	0·5	0·5	0·5	0·5	0·5	0·6	0·6	0·6	0·6	0·7
Feb.	·4	·4	·4	·4	·4	·4	·4	·4	·5	·5	·5	·6
Mar.	·4	·4	·3	·3	·3	·3	·3	·3	·3	·3	·4	·4
Apr.	0·5	0·4	0·4	0·3	0·3	0·2	0·2	0·2	0·2	0·2	0·2	0·3
May	·6	·6	·5	·4	·4	·3	·3	·2	·2	·2	·2	·2
June	·8	·7	·6	·6	·5	·4	·4	·3	·3	·2	·2	·2
July	0·9	0·8	0·8	0·7	0·7	0·6	0·5	0·5	0·4	0·4	0·3	0·3
Aug.	·9	·9	·9	·8	·8	·8	·7	·6	·6	·5	·5	·4
Sept.	·9	·9	·9	·9	·9	·9	·8	·8	·8	·7	·7	·6
Oct.	0·8	0·9	0·9	0·9	0·9	0·9	0·9	0·9	0·9	0·9	0·8	0·8
Nov.	·7	·7	·8	·8	·9	·9	1·0	1·0	1·0	1·0	1·0	1·0
Dec.	0·5	0·6	0·6	0·7	0·8	0·9	0·9	1·0	1·0	1·0	1·0	1·0
Lat.	AZIMUTH											
°	°	°	°	°	°	°	°	°	°	°	°	°
0	0·2	0·3	0·4	0·5	0·5	0·6	0·6	0·6	0·6	0·6	0·5	0·5
20	0·2	0·3	0·4	0·5	0·6	0·6	0·6	0·7	0·7	0·6	0·6	0·5
40	0·3	0·4	0·5	0·6	0·7	0·8	0·8	0·8	0·8	0·8	0·7	0·6
50	0·3	0·5	0·6	0·7	0·8	0·9	0·9	1·0	1·0	0·9	0·9	0·8
55	0·3	0·5	0·7	0·8	0·9	1·0	1·1	1·1	1·1	1·0	1·0	0·9
60	0·4	0·6	0·8	0·9	1·1	1·2	1·2	1·2	1·2	1·2	1·1	1·0
65	0·5	0·7	0·9	1·1	1·2	1·4	1·4	1·5	1·5	1·4	1·3	1·2

$$\text{Latitude} = \text{Apparent altitude (corrected for refraction)} - 1^\circ + a_0 + a_1 + a_2$$

The table is entered with LHA Aries to determine the column to be used; each column refers to a range of 10°. a_0 is taken, with mental interpolation, from the upper table with the units of LHA Aries in degrees as argument; a_1, a_2 are taken, without interpolation, from the second and third tables with arguments latitude and month respectively. a_0, a_1, a_2, are always positive. The final table gives the azimuth of *Polaris*.

SIGHT REDUCTION PROCEDURES

METHODS AND FORMULAE FOR DIRECT COMPUTATION

1. *Introduction.* In this section, formulae and methods are provided for *calculating* position at sea from observed altitudes taken with a marine sextant using a computer or programmable calculator.

The method uses analogous concepts and similar terminology as that used in *manual* methods of astro-navigation, where position is found by plotting position lines from their intercept and azimuth on a marine chart.

The algorithms are presented in standard algebra suitable for translating into the programming language of the user's computer. The basic ephemeris data may be taken directly from the main tabular pages of a current version of *The Nautical Almanac.* Formulae are given for calculating altitude and azimuth from the *GHA* and *Dec* of a body, and the estimated position of the observer. Formulae are also given for reducing sextant observations to observed altitudes by applying the corrections for dip, refraction, parallax and semi-diameter.

The intercept and azimuth obtained from each observation determine a position line, and the observer should lie on or close to each position line. The method of least squares is used to calculate the fix by finding the position where the sum of the squares of the distances from the position lines is a minimum. The use of least squares has other advantages. For example, it is possible to improve the estimated position at the time of fix by repeating the calculation. It is also possible to include more observations in the solution and to reject doubtful ones.

2. *Notation.*

GHA = Greenwich hour angle. The range of *GHA* is from 0° to 360° starting at 0° on the Greenwich meridian increasing to the west, back to 360° on the Greenwich meridian.

SHA = sidereal hour angle. The range is 0° to 360°.

Dec = declination. The sign convention for declination is north is positive, south is negative. The range is from −90° at the south celestial pole to +90° at the north celestial pole.

Long = longitude. The sign convention is east is positive, west is negative. The range is −180° to +180°.

Lat = latitude. The sign convention is north is positive, south is negative. The range is from −90° to +90°.

LHA = *GHA* + *Long* = local hour angle. The *LHA* increases to the west from 0° on the local meridian to 360°.

H_C = calc[illegible]ed altitude. Above the horizon is positive, below the horizon is neg-[illegible]e range is from −90° in the nadir to +90° in the zenith.

H_O [illegible]titude.

[illegible]ltitude = sextant altitude corrected for instrumental error and dip.

[illegible]itude = apparent altitude corrected for refraction and, in appro-[illegible] corrected for parallax and semi-diameter.

[illegible]muth. *Z* is measured from true north through east, south, west [illegible]orth. The range is from 0° to 360°.

[illegible]rror.

[illegible]ction.

HP = horizontal parallax of the Sun, Moon, Venus or Mars.
PA = parallax in altitude of the Sun, Moon, Venus or Mars.
SD = semi-diameter of the Sun or Moon.
p = intercept $= H_O - H_C$. Towards is positive, away is negative.
T = course or track, measured as for azimuth from the north.
V = speed in knots.

3. *Entering Basic Data.* When quantities such as GHA are entered, which in *The Nautical Almanac* are given in degrees and minutes, convert them to degrees and decimals of a degree by dividing the minutes by 60 and adding to the degrees; for example, if $GHA = 123° \ 45'.6$, enter the two numbers 123 and 45·6 into the memory and set $GHA = 123 + 45{\cdot}6/60 = 123°.7600$. Although four decimal places of a degree are shown in the examples, it is assumed that full precision is maintained in the calculations.

When using a computer or programmable calculator, write a subroutine to convert degrees and minutes to degrees and decimals. Scientific calculators usually have a special key for this purpose. For quantities like Dec which require a minus sign for southern declination, change the sign from plus to minus after the value has been converted to degrees and decimals, *e.g.* $Dec = \mathrm{S}\,0° \ 12'.3 = \mathrm{S}\,0°.2050 = -0°.2050$. Other quantities which require conversion are semi-diameter, horizontal parallax, longitude and latitude.

4. *Interpolation of GHA and Dec* The GHA and Dec of the Sun, Moon and planets are interpolated to the time of observation by direct calculation as follows: If the universal time is $a^h \ b^m \ c^s$, form the interpolation factor $x = b/60 + c/3600$. Enter the tabular value GHA_0 for the preceding hour (a) and the tabular value GHA_1 for the following hour ($a + 1$) then the interpolated value GHA is given by

$$GHA = GHA_0 + x(GHA_1 - GHA_0)$$

If the GHA passes through 360° between tabular values, add 360° to GHA_1 before interpolation. If the interpolated value exceeds 360°, subtract 360° from GHA.

Similarly for declination, enter the tabular value Dec_0 for the preceding hour (a) and the tabular value Dec_1 for the following hour ($a + 1$), then the interpolated value Dec is given by

$$Dec = Dec_0 + x(Dec_1 - Dec_0)$$

5. *Example.* (a) Find the GHA and Dec of the Sun on 2026 February 7 at $11^h \ 47^m \ 13^s$ UT.

The interpolation factor $x = 47/60 + 13/3600 = 0^h.7869$

page 35 $11^h \ GHA_0 = 341° \ 28'.8 = 341°.4800$

$12^h \ GHA_1 = 356° \ 28'.8 = 356°.4800$

$11^h.7869 \ GHA = 341{\cdot}4800 + 0{\cdot}7869(356{\cdot}4800 - 341{\cdot}4800) = 353°.2842$

$11^h \ Dec_0 = \mathrm{S}\,15° \ 13'.7 = -15°.2283$

$12^h \ Dec_1 = \mathrm{S}\,15° \ 12'.9 = -15°.2150$

$11^h.7869 \ Dec = -15{\cdot}2283 + 0{\cdot}7869(-15{\cdot}2150 + 15{\cdot}2283) = -15°.2178$

GHA Aries is interpolated in the same way as GHA of a body. For a star the SHA and Dec are taken from the tabular page and do not require interpolation, then

$$GHA = GHA \text{ Aries} + SHA$$

where GHA Aries is interpolated to the time of observation.

(b) Find the *GHA* and *Dec* of *Vega* on 2026 February 7 at $14^h\ 47^m\ 13^s$ UT.

The interpolation factor $x = 0^h\!.7869$ as in the previous example

$$\text{page 34} \qquad 14^h\ GHA\ \text{Aries}_0 = 347°\ 42'\!.4 = 347°\!.7067$$
$$15^h\ GHA\ \text{Aries}_1 = 2°\ 44'\!.9 = 362°\!.7483 \quad (360°\ \text{added})$$
$$14^h\!.7869\ GHA\ \text{Aries} = 347{\cdot}7067 + 0{\cdot}7869(362{\cdot}7483 - 347{\cdot}7067) = 359°\!.5436$$
$$SHA = 80°\ 32'\!.9 = 80°\!.5483$$
$$GHA = GHA\ \text{Aries} + SHA = 80°\!.0920 \quad (\text{multiple of } 360°\ \text{removed})$$
$$Dec = \text{N}\,38°\ 48'\!.2 = +38°\!.8033$$

6. *The calculated altitude and azimuth.* The calculated altitude H_C and true azimuth Z are determined from the *GHA* and *Dec* interpolated to the time of observation and from the *Long* and *Lat* estimated at the time of observation as follows:

Step 1. Calculate the local hour angle

$$LHA = GHA + Long$$

Add or subtract multiples of 360° to set *LHA* in the range 0° to 360°.

Step 2. Calculate S, C and the altitude H_C from

$$S = \sin Dec$$
$$C = \cos Dec \cos LHA$$
$$H_C = \sin^{-1}(S \sin Lat + C \cos Lat)$$

where $\sin^{-1}$ is the inverse function of sine.

Step 3. Calculate X and A from

$$X = (S \cos Lat - C \sin Lat)/ \cos H_C$$
$$\text{If } X > +1 \quad \text{set} \quad X = +1$$
$$\text{If } X < -1 \quad \text{set} \quad X = -1$$
$$A = \cos^{-1} X$$

where $\cos^{-1}$ is the inverse function of cosine.

Step 4. Determine the azimuth Z

$$\text{If } LHA > 180° \quad \text{then} \quad Z = A$$
$$\text{Otherwise} \quad Z = 360° - A$$

7. *Example.* Find the calculated altitude H_C and azimuth Z when

$$GHA = 53° \quad Dec = \text{S}\,15° \quad Lat = \text{N}\,32° \quad Long = \text{W}\,16°$$

For the calculation

$$GHA = 53°\!.0000 \quad Dec = -15°\!.0000 \quad Lat = +32°\!.0000 \quad Long = -16°\!.0000$$

Step 1. $LHA = 53{\cdot}0000 - 16{\cdot}0000 = 37{\cdot}0000$

Step 2.

$$S = -0{\cdot}2588$$
$$C = +0{\cdot}9659 \times 0{\cdot}7986 = 0{\cdot}7714$$
$$\sin H_C = -0{\cdot}2588 \times 0{\cdot}5299 + 0{\cdot}7714 \times 0{\cdot}8480 = 0{\cdot}5171$$
$$H_C = 31°\!.1346$$

Step 3. $X = (-0{\cdot}2588 \times 0{\cdot}8480 - 0{\cdot}7714 \times 0{\cdot}5299)/0{\cdot}8560 = -0{\cdot}7340$

$A = 137^\circ\!.2239$

Step 4. Since $LHA \leq 180^\circ$ then $Z = 360^\circ - A = 222^\circ\!.7761$

8. *Reduction from sextant altitude to observed altitude.* The sextant altitude H_S is corrected for both dip and index error to produce the apparent altitude. The observed altitude H_O is calculated by applying a correction for refraction. For the Sun, Moon, Venus and Mars a correction for parallax is also applied to H, and for the Sun and Moon a further correction for semi-diameter is required. The corrections are calculated as follows:

Step 1. Calculate dip

$$D = 0^\circ\!.0293\sqrt{h}$$

where h is the height of eye above the horizon in metres.

Step 2. Calculate apparent altitude

$$H = H_S + I - D$$

where I is the sextant index error.

Step 3. Calculate refraction (R) at a standard temperature of 10° Celsius (C) and pressure of 1010 millibars (mb)

$$R_0 = 0^\circ\!.0167/\tan(H + 7{\cdot}32/(H + 4{\cdot}32))$$

If the temperature T° C and pressure P mb are known calculate the refraction from

$$R = fR_0 \qquad \text{where} \qquad f = 0{\cdot}28P/(T + 273)$$

$$\text{otherwise set} \qquad R = R_0$$

Step 4. Calculate the parallax in altitude (PA) from the horizontal parallax (HP) and the apparent altitude (H) for the Sun, Moon, Venus and Mars as follows:

$$PA = HP\cos H$$

For the Sun $HP = 0^\circ\!.0024$. This correction is very small and could be ignored.

For the Moon HP is taken for the nearest hour from the main tabular page and converted to degrees.

For Venus and Mars the HP is taken from the critical table at the bottom of page 259 and converted to degrees.

For the navigational stars and the remaining planets, Jupiter and Saturn, set $PA = 0$.

If an error of 0′.2 is significant the expression for the parallax in altitude for the Moon should include a small correction OB for the oblateness of the Earth as follows:

$$PA = HP\cos H + OB$$

$$\text{where} \quad OB = -0^\circ\!.0032\sin^2 Lat\cos H + 0^\circ\!.0032\sin(2Lat)\cos Z\sin H$$

At mid-latitudes and for altitudes of the Moon below 60° a simple approximation to OB is

$$OB = -0^\circ\!.0017\cos H$$

Step 5. Calculate the semi-diameter for the Sun and Moon as follows:

Sun: *SD* is taken from the main tabular page and converted to degrees.

Moon: $SD = 0°2724HP$ where HP is taken for the nearest hour from the main tabular page and converted to degrees.

Step 6. Calculate the observed altitude

$$H_O = H - R + PA \pm SD$$

where the plus sign is used if the lower limb of the Sun or Moon was observed and the minus sign if the upper limb was observed.

9. *Example.* The following example illustrates how to use a calculator to reduce the sextant altitude (H_S) to observed altitude (H_O); the sextant altitudes given are assumed to be taken on 2026 March 12 with a marine sextant, zero index error, at height 5·4 m, temperature −3° C and pressure 982 mb, the Moon sights are assumed to be taken at 10^h UT.

Body limb	Sun lower	Sun upper	Moon lower	Moon upper	Venus —	*Polaris* —
Sextant altitude: H_S	21·3283	3·3367	33·4600	26·1117	4·5433	49·6083
Step 1. Dip: $D = 0{\cdot}0293\sqrt{h}$	0·0681	0·0681	0·0681	0·0681	0·0681	0·0681
Step 2. Apparent altitude: $H = H_S + I - D$	21·2602	3·2686	33·3919	26·0436	4·4752	49·5402
Step 3. Refraction: R_0	0·0423	0·2256	0·0251	0·0338	0·1798	0·0142
f	1·0184	1·0184	1·0184	1·0184	1·0184	1·0184
$R = f R_0$	0·0431	0·2298	0·0256	0·0344	0·1831	0·0144
Step 4. Parallax: HP	0·0024	0·0024	(54′.5) 0·9083	(54′.5) 0·9083	(0′.1) 0·0017	—
Parallax in altitude: $PA = HP \cos H$	0·0022	0·0024	0·7584	0·8161	0·0017	—
Step 5. Semi-diameter: Sun : $SD = 16{\cdot}1/60$	0·2683	0·2683	—	—	—	—
Moon : $SD = 0{\cdot}2724HP$	—	—	0·2474	0·2474	—	—
Step 6. Observed altitude: $H_O = H - R + PA \pm SD$	21·4877	2·7729	34·3721	26·5779	4·2938	49·5258

Note that for the Moon the correction for the oblateness of the Earth of about $-0°0017 \cos H$, which equals $-0°0014$ for the lower limb and $-0°0015$ for the upper limb, has been ignored in the above calculation.

10. *Position from intercept and azimuth using a chart.* An estimate is made of the position at the adopted time of fix. The position at the time of observation is then calculated by dead reckoning from the time of fix. For example, if the course (track) T and the speed V (in knots) of the observer are constant, then *Long* and *Lat* at the time of observation are calculated from

$$Long = L_F + t\,(V/60)\sin T\,/\cos B_F$$
$$Lat = B_F + t\,(V/60)\cos T$$

where L_F and B_F are the estimated longitude and latitude at the time of fix and t is the time interval in hours from the time of fix to the time of observation, t is positive if the time of observation is after the time of fix and negative if it was before.

The position line of an observation is plotted on a chart using the intercept

$$p = H_O - H_C$$

and azimuth Z with origin at the calculated position (*Long*, *Lat*) at the time of observation, where H_C and Z are calculated using the method in section 6, page 279. Starting from this calculated position a line is drawn on the chart along the direction of the azimuth to the body. Convert p to nautical miles by multiplying by 60. The position line is drawn at right angles to the azimuth line, distance p from (*Long*, *Lat*) towards the body if p is positive and distance p away from the body if p is negative. Provided there are no gross errors, the navigator should be somewhere on or near the position line at the time of observation. Two or more position lines are required to determine a fix.

11. *Position from intercept and azimuth by calculation.* The position of the fix may be calculated from two or more sextant observations as follows.

If p_1, Z_1, are the intercept and azimuth of the first observation, p_2, Z_2, of the second observation and so on, form the summations

$$A = \cos^2 Z_1 + \cos^2 Z_2 + \cdots$$
$$B = \cos Z_1 \sin Z_1 + \cos Z_2 \sin Z_2 + \cdots$$
$$C = \sin^2 Z_1 + \sin^2 Z_2 + \cdots$$
$$D = p_1 \cos Z_1 + p_2 \cos Z_2 + \cdots$$
$$E = p_1 \sin Z_1 + p_2 \sin Z_2 + \cdots$$

where the number of terms in each summation is equal to the number of observations.

With $G = A\,C - B^2$, an improved estimate of the position at the time of fix (L_I, B_I) is given by

$$L_I = L_F + (A\,E - B\,D)/(G\cos B_F), \qquad B_I = B_F + (C\,D - B\,E)/G$$

Calculate the distance d between the initial estimated position (L_F, B_F) at the time of fix and the improved estimated position (L_I, B_I) in nautical miles from

$$d = 60\sqrt{((L_I - L_F)^2\cos^2 B_F + (B_I - B_F)^2)}$$

If d exceeds about 20 nautical miles set $L_F = L_I$, $B_F = B_I$ and repeat the calculation until d, the distance between the position at the previous estimate and the improved estimate, is less than about 20 nautical miles.

12. *Example of direct computation.* Using the method described above, calculate the position of a ship on 2026 July 4 at $21^h\,00^m\,00^s$ UT from the marine sextant observations of the three stars *Regulus* (No. 26) at $20^h\,39^m\,23^s$ UT, *Antares* (No. 42) at $20^h\,45^m\,47^s$ UT and *Kochab* (No. 40) at $21^h\,10^m\,34^s$ UT, where the observed altitudes of the three stars corrected for the effects of refraction, dip and instrumental error, are 27°0862, 25°9145 and 47°5739 respectively. The ship was travelling at a constant speed of 20 knots on a course of 325° during the period of observation, and the position of the ship at the time of fix $21^h\,00^m\,00^s$ UT is only known to the nearest whole degree W 15°, N 32°.

Intermediate values for the first iteration are shown in the table. *GHA* Aries was interpolated from the nearest tabular values on page 132. For the first iteration set $L_F = -15^\circ\!.0000$, $B_F = +32^\circ\!.0000$ at the time of fix at $21^h\ 00^m\ 00^s$ UT.

First Iteration

Body	*Regulus*	*Antares*	*Kochab*
No.	26	42	40
time of observation	$20^h\ 39^m\ 23^s$	$20^h\ 45^m\ 47^s$	$21^h\ 10^m\ 34^s$
H_O	27·0862	25·9145	47·5739
interpolation factor	0·6564	0·7631	0·1761
GHA Aries	232·7165	234·3210	240·5337
SHA (page 132)	207·5550	112·2333	137·3200
GHA	80·2715	346·5543	17·8537
Dec (page 132)	+11·8383	−26·4917	+74·0500
t	−0·3436	−0·2369	+0·1761
Long	−14·9225	−14·9466	−15·0397
Lat	+31·9062	+31·9353	+32·0481
Z	267·3224	151·8399	358·8453
H_C	27·0631	25·6087	47·9740
p	+0·0231	+0·3058	−0·4001

$$A = 1{\cdot}7791 \quad B = -0{\cdot}3896 \quad C = 1{\cdot}2209 \quad D = -0{\cdot}6707 \quad E = 0{\cdot}1293 \quad G = 2{\cdot}0204$$
$$(A\,E - B\,D)/(G \cos B_F) = -0{\cdot}0182, \qquad (C\,D - B\,E)/G = -0{\cdot}3804$$

An improved estimate of the position at the time of fix is

$$L_I = L_F - 0{\cdot}0182 = -15{\cdot}0182 \quad \text{and} \quad B_I = B_F - 0{\cdot}3804 = +31{\cdot}6196$$

Since the distance between the previous estimated position and the improved estimate is $d = 22{\cdot}8$ nautical miles, set $L_F = -15{\cdot}0182$, and $B_F = +31{\cdot}6196$ and repeat the calculation. The table shows the intermediate values of the calculation for the second iteration. In each iteration the quantities H_O, *GHA*, *Dec* and t do not change.

Second Iteration

Body	*Regulus*	*Antares*	*Kochab*
No.	26	42	40
Long	−14·9411	−14·9650	−15·0578
Lat	+31·5258	+31·5549	+31·6677
Z	267·5066	151·7367	358·8611
H_C	27·0960	25·9364	47·5940
p	−0·0098	−0·0220	−0·0201

$$A = 1{\cdot}7773 \quad B = -0{\cdot}3935 \quad C = 1{\cdot}2227 \quad D = -0{\cdot}0003 \quad E = -0{\cdot}0002 \quad G = 2{\cdot}0183$$
$$(A\,E - B\,D)/(G \cos B_F) = -0{\cdot}0003, \qquad (C\,D - B\,E)/G = -0{\cdot}0002$$

An improved estimate of the position at the time of fix is

$$L_I = L_F - 0{\cdot}0003 = -15{\cdot}0185 \quad \text{and} \quad B_I = B_F - 0{\cdot}0002 = +31{\cdot}6194$$

The distance between the previous estimated position and the improved estimated position, $d = 0{\cdot}02$ nautical miles, is so small that a third iteration would produce a negligible improvement to the estimate of the position.

USE OF CONCISE SIGHT REDUCTION TABLES

1. *Introduction.* The concise sight reduction tables given on pages 286 to 317 are intended for use when neither more extensive tables nor electronic computing aids are available. These "NAO sight reduction tables" provide for the reduction of the local hour angle and declination of a celestial object to azimuth and altitude, referred to an assumed position on the Earth, for use in the intercept method of celestial navigation which is now standard practice.

2. *Form of tables.* Entries in the reduction table are at a fixed interval of one degree for all latitudes and hour angles. A compact arrangement results from division of the navigational triangle into two right spherical triangles, so that the table has to be entered twice. Assumed latitude and local hour angle are the arguments for the first entry. The reduction table responds with the intermediate arguments A, B, and Z_1, where A is used as one of the arguments for the second entry to the table, B has to be incremented by the declination to produce the quantity F, and Z_1 is a component of the azimuth angle. The reduction table is then reentered with A and F and yields H, P, and Z_2 where H is the altitude, P is the complement of the parallactic angle, and Z_2 is the second component of the azimuth angle. It is usually necessary to adjust the tabular altitude for the fractional parts of the intermediate entering arguments to derive computed altitude, and an auxiliary table is provided for the purpose. Rules governing signs of the quantities which must be added or subtracted are given in the instructions and summarized on each tabular page. Azimuth angle is the sum of two components and is converted to true azimuth by familiar rules, repeated at the bottom of the tabular pages.

Tabular altitude and intermediate quantities are given to the nearest minute of arc, although errors of 2′ in computed altitude may accrue during adjustment for the minutes parts of entering arguments. Components of azimuth angle are stated to 0°1; for derived true azimuth, only whole degrees are warranted. Since objects near the zenith are difficult to observe with a marine sextant, they should be avoided; altitudes greater than about 80° are not suited to reduction by this method.

In many circumstances, the accuracy provided by these tables is sufficient. However, to maintain the full accuracy (0′1) of the ephemeral data in the almanac throughout their reduction to altitude and azimuth, more extensive tables or a calculator should be used.

3. *Use of Tables.*

Step 1. Determine the Greenwich hour angle (GHA) and Declination (Dec) of the body from the almanac. Select an assumed latitude (Lat) of integral degrees nearest to the estimated latitude. Choose an assumed longitude nearest to the estimated longitude such that the local hour angle

$$LHA = GHA \begin{array}{l} -\text{ west} \\ +\text{ east} \end{array} \text{longitude}$$

has integral degrees.

Step 2. Enter the reduction table with Lat and LHA as arguments. Record the quantities A, B and Z_1. Apply the rules for the sign of B and Z_1: B is minus if $90° < LHA < 270°$; Z_1 has the same sign as B. Set $A°$ = nearest whole degree of A and A' = minutes part of A. This step may be repeated for all reductions before leaving the latitude opening of the table.

Step 3. Record the declination Dec. Apply the rules for the sign of Dec: Dec is minus if the name of Dec (*i.e.* N or S) is contrary to latitude. Add B and Dec algebraically to produce F. If F is negative, the object is below the horizon (in sight reduction, this can occur when the objects are close to the horizon). Regard F as positive until step 7. Set $F°$ = nearest whole degree of F and F' = minutes part of F.

Step 4. Enter the reduction table a second time with $A°$ and $F°$ as arguments and record H, P, and Z_2. Set $P° =$ nearest whole degree of P and $Z_2° =$ nearest whole degree of Z_2.

Step 5. Enter the auxiliary table with F' and $P°$ as arguments to obtain $corr_1$ to H for F'. Apply the rule for the sign of $corr_1$: $corr_1$ is minus if $F < 90°$ and $F' > 29'$ or if $F > 90°$ and $F' < 30'$, otherwise $corr_1$ is plus.

Step 6. Enter the auxiliary table with A' and $Z_2°$ as arguments to obtain $corr_2$ to H for A'. Apply the rule for the sign of $corr_2$: $corr_2$ is minus if $A' < 30'$, otherwise $corr_2$ is plus.

Step 7. Calculate the computed altitude H_C as the sum of H, $corr_1$ and $corr_2$. Apply the rule for the sign of H_C: H_C is minus if F is negative.

Step 8. Apply the rule for the sign of Z_2: Z_2 is minus if $F > 90°$. If F is negative, replace Z_2 by $180° - Z_2$. Set the azimuth angle Z equal to the algebraic sum of Z_1 and Z_2 and ignore the resulting sign. Obtain the true azimuth Z_n from the rules

For N latitude, if	$LHA > 180°$	$Z_n = Z$
if	$LHA < 180°$	$Z_n = 360° - Z$
For S latitude, if	$LHA > 180°$	$Z_n = 180° - Z$
if	$LHA < 180°$	$Z_n = 180° + Z$

Observed altitude H_O is compared with H_C to obtain the altitude difference, which, with Z_n, is used to plot the position line.

4. *Example.* (a) Required the altitude and azimuth of *Schedar* on 2026 February 4 at UT $06^h\ 32^m$ from the estimated position N 53°, E 5°.

1. Assumed latitude	$Lat =$	53° N		
From the almanac	$GHA =$	221° 57′		
Assumed longitude		5° 03′ E		
Local hour angle	$LHA =$	227		
2. Reduction table, 1st entry $(Lat, LHA) = (53, 227)$	$A =$	26 07	$A° = 26$, $A' = 7$	
	$B =$	−27 12	$Z_1 = -49{\cdot}4$,	$90° < LHA < 270°$
3. From the almanac	$Dec =$	+56 41		*Lat* and *Dec* same
Sum $= B + Dec$	$F =$	+29 29	$F° = 29$, $F' = 29$	
4. Reduction table, 2nd entry $(A°, F°) = (26, 29)$	$H =$	25 50	$P° = 61$	
			$Z_2 = 76{\cdot}3, Z_2° = 76$	
5. Auxiliary table, 1st entry $(F', P°) = (29, 61)$	$corr_1 =$	+25		$F < 90°$, $F' < 29'$
Sum		26 15		
6. Auxiliary table, 2nd entry $(A', Z_2°) = (7, 76)$	$corr_2 =$	−2		$A' < 30'$
7. Sum = computed altitude	$H_C =$	+26° 13′		$F > 0°$
8. Azimuth, first component	$Z_1 =$	−49·4		same sign as B
second component	$Z_2 =$	+76·3		$F < 90°$, $F > 0°$
Sum = azimuth angle	$Z =$	26·9		
True azimuth	$Z_n =$	027°		N *Lat*, $LHA > 180°$

continued on page 318

SIGHT REDUCTION TABLE

B: (−) for 90° < LHA < 270°
Dec:(−) for Lat. contrary name

Z_1: same sign as B
Z_2: (−) for F > 90°

Lat. / A		0°			1°			2°			3°			4°			5°			Lat. / A	
LHA/F		A/H	B/P	Z_1/Z_2	A/H	B/P	Z_1/Z_2	A/H	B/P	Z_1/Z_2	A/H	B/P	Z_1/Z_2	A/H	B/P	Z_1/Z_2	A/H	B/P	Z_1/Z_2	LHA	
°	°	° ′	° ′	°	° ′	° ′	°	° ′	° ′	°	° ′	° ′	°	° ′	° ′	°	° ′	° ′	°	°	°
0	180	0 00	90 00	90·0	0 00	89 00	90·0	0 00	88 00	90·0	0 00	87 00	90·0	0 00	86 00	90·0	0 00	85 00	90·0	180	360
1	179	1 00	90 00	90·0	1 00	89 00	90·0	1 00	88 00	90·0	1 00	87 00	89·9	1 00	86 00	89·9	1 00	85 00	89·9	181	359
2	178	2 00	90 00	90·0	2 00	89 00	90·0	2 00	88 00	89·9	2 00	87 00	89·9	2 00	86 00	89·9	2 00	85 00	89·8	182	358
3	177	3 00	90 00	90·0	3 00	89 00	89·9	3 00	88 00	89·9	3 00	87 00	89·8	3 00	86 00	89·8	2 59	85 00	89·7	183	357
4	176	4 00	90 00	90·0	4 00	89 00	89·9	4 00	88 00	89·9	4 00	87 00	89·8	3 59	85 59	89·7	3 59	84 59	89·7	184	356
5	175	5 00	90 00	90·0	5 00	89 00	89·9	5 00	88 00	89·8	5 00	86 59	89·7	4 59	85 59	89·7	4 59	84 59	89·6	185	355
6	174	6 00	90 00	90·0	6 00	89 00	89·9	6 00	87 59	89·8	6 00	86 59	89·7	5 59	85 59	89·6	5 59	84 58	89·5	186	354
7	173	7 00	90 00	90·0	7 00	89 00	89·9	7 00	87 59	89·8	6 59	86 59	89·6	6 59	85 58	89·5	6 58	84 58	89·4	187	353
8	172	8 00	90 00	90·0	8 00	88 59	89·9	8 00	87 59	89·7	7 59	86 58	89·6	7 59	85 58	89·4	7 58	84 57	89·3	188	352
9	171	9 00	90 00	90·0	9 00	88 59	89·8	9 00	87 59	89·7	8 59	86 58	89·5	8 59	85 57	89·4	8 58	84 56	89·2	189	351
10	170	10 00	90 00	90·0	10 00	88 59	89·8	10 00	87 58	89·6	9 59	86 57	89·5	9 59	85 56	89·3	9 58	84 55	89·1	190	350
11	169	11 00	90 00	90·0	11 00	88 59	89·8	11 00	87 58	89·6	10 59	86 57	89·4	10 58	85 56	89·2	10 57	84 54	89·0	191	349
12	168	12 00	90 00	90·0	12 00	88 59	89·8	12 00	87 57	89·6	11 59	86 56	89·4	11 58	85 55	89·2	11 57	84 53	88·9	192	348
13	167	13 00	90 00	90·0	13 00	88 58	89·8	13 00	87 57	89·5	12 59	86 55	89·3	12 58	85 54	89·1	12 57	84 52	88·8	193	347
14	166	14 00	90 00	90·0	14 00	88 58	89·8	13 59	87 56	89·5	13 59	86 55	89·3	13 58	85 53	89·0	13 57	84 51	88·8	194	346
15	165	15 00	90 00	90·0	15 00	88 58	89·7	14 59	87 56	89·5	14 59	86 54	89·2	14 58	85 52	88·9	14 56	84 49	88·7	195	345
16	164	16 00	90 00	90·0	16 00	88 58	89·7	15 59	87 55	89·4	15 59	86 53	89·1	15 58	85 50	88·9	15 56	84 48	88·6	196	344
17	163	17 00	90 00	90·0	17 00	88 57	89·7	16 59	87 55	89·4	16 59	86 52	89·1	16 57	85 49	88·8	16 56	84 46	88·5	197	343
18	162	18 00	90 00	90·0	18 00	88 57	89·7	17 59	87 54	89·4	17 58	86 51	89·0	17 57	85 48	88·7	17 56	84 45	88·4	198	342
19	161	19 00	90 00	90·0	19 00	88 57	89·7	18 59	87 53	89·3	18 58	86 50	89·0	18 57	85 46	88·6	18 55	84 43	88·3	199	341
20	160	20 00	90 00	90·0	20 00	88 56	89·6	19 59	87 52	89·3	19 58	86 48	88·9	19 57	85 45	88·5	19 55	84 41	88·2	200	340
21	159	21 00	90 00	90·0	21 00	88 56	89·6	20 59	87 51	89·2	20 58	86 47	88·8	20 57	85 43	88·5	20 55	84 39	88·1	201	339
22	158	22 00	90 00	90·0	22 00	88 55	89·6	21 59	87 51	89·2	21 58	86 46	88·8	21 57	85 41	88·4	21 55	84 37	88·0	202	338
23	157	23 00	90 00	90·0	23 00	88 55	89·6	22 59	87 50	89·2	22 58	86 44	88·7	22 56	85 39	88·3	22 54	84 34	87·9	203	337
24	156	24 00	90 00	90·0	24 00	88 54	89·6	23 59	87 49	89·1	23 58	86 43	88·7	23 56	85 37	88·2	23 54	84 32	87·8	204	336
25	155	25 00	90 00	90·0	25 00	88 54	89·5	24 59	87 48	89·1	24 58	86 41	88·6	24 56	85 35	88·1	24 54	84 29	87·7	205	335
26	154	26 00	90 00	90·0	26 00	88 53	89·5	25 59	87 47	89·0	25 58	86 40	88·5	25 56	85 33	88·1	25 54	84 26	87·6	206	334
27	153	27 00	90 00	90·0	27 00	88 53	89·5	26 59	87 45	89·0	26 58	86 38	88·5	26 56	85 31	88·0	26 53	84 24	87·5	207	333
28	152	28 00	90 00	90·0	28 00	88 52	89·5	27 59	87 44	88·9	27 57	86 36	88·4	27 56	85 28	87·9	27 53	84 20	87·3	208	332
29	151	29 00	90 00	90·0	29 00	88 51	89·4	28 59	87 43	88·9	28 57	86 34	88·3	28 55	85 26	87·8	28 53	84 17	87·2	209	331
30	150	30 00	90 00	90·0	30 00	88 51	89·4	29 59	87 41	88·8	29 57	86 32	88·3	29 55	85 23	87·7	29 52	84 14	87·1	210	330
31	149	31 00	90 00	90·0	31 00	88 50	89·4	30 59	87 40	88·8	30 57	86 30	88·2	30 55	85 20	87·6	30 52	84 10	87·0	211	329
32	148	32 00	90 00	90·0	32 00	88 49	89·4	31 59	87 39	88·8	31 57	86 28	88·1	31 55	85 17	87·5	31 52	84 07	86·9	212	328
33	147	33 00	90 00	90·0	33 00	88 48	89·4	32 59	87 37	88·7	32 57	86 25	88·1	32 55	85 14	87·4	32 52	84 03	86·8	213	327
34	146	34 00	90 00	90·0	34 00	88 48	89·3	33 59	87 35	88·7	33 57	86 23	88·0	33 54	85 11	87·3	33 51	83 59	86·6	214	326
35	145	35 00	90 00	90·0	35 00	88 47	89·3	34 59	87 34	88·6	34 57	86 20	87·9	34 54	85 07	87·2	34 51	83 54	86·5	215	325
36	144	36 00	90 00	90·0	36 00	88 46	89·3	35 58	87 32	88·5	35 57	86 18	87·8	35 54	85 04	87·1	35 51	83 50	86·4	216	324
37	143	37 00	90 00	90·0	37 00	88 45	89·2	36 58	87 30	88·5	36 56	86 15	87·7	36 54	85 00	87·0	36 50	83 45	86·2	217	323
38	142	38 00	90 00	90·0	38 00	88 44	89·2	37 58	87 28	88·4	37 56	86 12	87·7	37 53	84 56	86·9	37 50	83 40	86·1	218	322
39	141	39 00	90 00	90·0	39 00	88 43	89·2	38 58	87 26	88·4	38 56	86 09	87·6	38 53	84 52	86·8	38 49	83 35	86·0	219	321
40	140	40 00	90 00	90·0	40 00	88 42	89·2	39 58	87 23	88·3	39 56	86 05	87·5	39 53	84 47	86·7	39 49	83 29	85·8	220	320
41	139	41 00	90 00	90·0	41 00	88 41	89·1	40 58	87 21	88·3	40 56	86 02	87·4	40 53	84 42	86·5	40 49	83 23	85·7	221	319
42	138	42 00	90 00	90·0	42 00	88 39	89·1	41 58	87 19	88·2	41 56	85 58	87·3	41 52	84 37	86·4	41 48	83 17	85·5	222	318
43	137	43 00	90 00	90·0	43 00	88 38	89·1	42 58	87 16	88·1	42 56	85 54	87·2	42 52	84 32	86·3	42 48	83 11	85·4	223	317
44	136	44 00	90 00	90·0	43 59	88 37	89·0	43 58	87 13	88·1	43 55	85 50	87·1	43 52	84 27	86·1	43 47	83 04	85·2	224	316
45	135	45 00	90 00	90·0	44 59	88 35	89·0	44 58	87 10	88·0	44 55	85 46	87·0	44 52	84 21	86·0	44 47	82 57	85·0	225	315

Lat. / A		0°			1°			2°			3°			4°			5°			Lat. / A	
LHA/F		A/H	B/P	Z_1/Z_2	A/H	B/P	Z_1/Z_2	A/H	B/P	Z_1/Z_2	A/H	B/P	Z_1/Z_2	A/H	B/P	Z_1/Z_2	A/H	B/P	Z_1/Z_2	LHA	
°	°	° ′	° ′	°	° ′	° ′	°	° ′	° ′	°	° ′	° ′	°	° ′	° ′	°	° ′	° ′	°	°	°
45	135	45 00	90 00	90·0	44 59	88 35	89·0	44 58	87 10	88·0	44 55	85 46	87·0	44 52	84 21	86·0	44 47	82 57	85·0	225	315
46	134	46 00	90 00	90·0	45 59	88 34	89·0	45 58	87 07	87·9	45 55	85 41	86·9	45 51	84 15	85·9	45 46	82 49	84·8	226	314
47	133	47 00	90 00	90·0	46 59	88 32	88·9	46 58	87 04	87·9	46 55	85 36	86·8	46 51	84 09	85·7	46 46	82 41	84·7	227	313
48	132	48 00	90 00	90·0	47 59	88 30	88·9	47 58	87 01	87·8	47 55	85 31	86·7	47 51	84 02	85·6	47 46	82 33	84·5	228	312
49	131	49 00	90 00	90·0	48 59	88 29	88·8	48 58	86 57	87·7	48 55	85 26	86·6	48 50	83 55	85·4	48 45	82 24	84·3	229	311
50	130	50 00	90 00	90·0	49 59	88 27	88·8	49 58	86 53	87·6	49 54	85 20	86·4	49 50	83 47	85·2	49 44	82 15	84·1	230	310
51	129	51 00	90 00	90·0	50 59	88 25	88·8	50 57	86 49	87·5	50 54	85 14	86·3	50 50	83 40	85·1	50 44	82 05	83·9	231	309
52	128	52 00	90 00	90·0	51 59	88 23	88·7	51 57	86 45	87·4	51 54	85 08	86·2	51 49	83 31	84·9	51 43	81 55	83·6	232	308
53	127	53 00	90 00	90·0	52 59	88 20	88·7	52 57	86 41	87·3	52 54	85 01	86·0	52 49	83 22	84·7	52 43	81 44	83·4	233	307
54	126	54 00	90 00	90·0	53 59	88 18	88·6	53 57	86 36	87·2	53 54	84 54	85·9	53 49	83 13	84·5	53 42	81 32	83·2	234	306
55	125	55 00	90 00	90·0	54 59	88 15	88·6	54 57	86 31	87·1	54 53	84 47	85·7	54 48	83 03	84·3	54 41	81 20	82·9	235	305
56	124	56 00	90 00	90·0	55 59	88 13	88·5	55 57	86 26	87·0	55 53	84 39	85·6	55 48	82 52	84·1	55 41	81 06	82·6	236	304
57	123	57 00	90 00	90·0	56 59	88 10	88·5	56 57	86 20	86·9	56 53	84 30	85·4	56 47	82 41	83·9	56 40	80 52	82·4	237	303
58	122	58 00	90 00	90·0	57 59	88 07	88·4	57 57	86 14	86·8	57 52	84 21	85·2	57 47	82 29	83·6	57 39	80 38	82·1	238	302
59	121	59 00	90 00	90·0	58 59	88 04	88·3	58 57	86 07	86·7	58 52	84 11	85·0	58 46	82 16	83·4	58 38	80 22	81·7	239	301
60	120	60 00	90 00	90·0	59 59	88 00	88·3	59 56	86 00	86·5	59 52	84 01	84·8	59 46	82 02	83·1	59 37	80 05	81·4	240	300
61	119	61 00	90 00	90·0	60 59	87 56	88·2	60 56	85 53	86·4	60 52	83 50	84·6	60 45	81 48	82·8	60 37	79 46	81·1	241	299
62	118	62 00	90 00	90·0	61 59	87 52	88·1	61 56	85 45	86·2	61 51	83 38	84·4	61 44	81 32	82·5	61 36	79 27	80·7	242	298
63	117	63 00	90 00	90·0	62 59	87 48	88·0	62 56	85 36	86·1	62 51	83 25	84·1	62 44	81 15	82·2	62 35	79 06	80·3	243	297
64	116	64 00	90 00	90·0	63 59	87 43	88·0	63 56	85 27	85·9	63 50	83 11	83·9	63 43	80 56	81·9	63 33	78 43	79·9	244	296
65	115	65 00	90 00	90·0	64 59	87 38	87·9	64 56	85 17	85·7	64 50	82 56	83·6	64 42	80 36	81·5	64 32	78 18	79·4	245	295
66	114	66 00	90 00	90·0	65 59	87 33	87·8	65 55	85 06	85·5	65 49	82 39	83·3	65 41	80 15	81·1	65 31	77 52	78·9	246	294
67	113	67 00	90 00	90·0	66 59	87 27	87·6	66 55	84 54	85·3	66 49	82 22	83·0	66 40	79 51	80·7	66 29	77 23	78·4	247	293
68	112	68 00	90 00	90·0	67 59	87 20	87·5	67 55	84 40	85·1	67 48	82 02	82·6	67 39	79 26	80·2	67 28	76 51	77·8	248	292
69	111	69 00	90 00	90·0	68 59	87 13	87·4	68 55	84 26	84·8	68 48	81 41	82·2	68 38	78 58	79·7	68 26	76 17	77·2	249	291
70	110	70 00	90 00	90·0	69 59	87 05	87·3	69 54	84 10	84·5	69 47	81 17	81·8	69 37	78 27	79·2	69 25	75 39	76·5	250	290
71	109	71 00	90 00	90·0	70 58	86 56	87·1	70 54	83 53	84·2	70 46	80 51	81·4	70 36	77 53	78·5	70 23	74 58	75·8	251	289
72	108	72 00	90 00	90·0	71 58	86 46	86·9	71 54	83 33	83·9	71 46	80 22	80·8	71 35	77 15	77·9	71 20	74 12	75·0	252	288
73	107	73 00	90 00	90·0	72 58	86 35	86·7	72 53	83 11	83·5	72 45	79 50	80·3	72 33	76 33	77·1	72 18	73 20	74·1	253	287
74	106	74 00	90 00	90·0	73 58	86 23	86·5	73 53	82 47	83·1	73 44	79 14	79·7	73 31	75 46	76·3	73 15	72 23	73·1	254	286
75	105	75 00	90 00	90·0	74 58	86 09	86·3	74 52	82 19	82·6	74 43	78 33	78·9	74 29	74 53	75·4	74 12	71 19	72·0	255	285
76	104	76 00	90 00	90·0	75 58	85 52	86·0	75 52	81 47	82·0	75 41	77 47	78·1	75 27	73 53	74·4	75 09	70 07	70·7	256	284
77	103	77 00	90 00	90·0	76 58	85 34	85·7	76 51	81 11	81·4	76 40	76 53	77·2	76 25	72 44	73·2	76 05	68 45	69·3	257	283
78	102	78 00	90 00	90·0	77 58	85 12	85·3	77 50	80 28	80·7	77 38	75 51	76·2	77 22	71 25	71·8	77 01	67 11	67·7	258	282
79	101	79 00	90 00	90·0	78 57	84 46	84·9	78 49	79 38	79·8	78 36	74 39	74·9	78 18	69 52	70·3	77 56	65 22	65·8	259	281
80	100	80 00	90 00	90·0	79 57	84 16	84·3	79 48	78 38	78·8	79 34	73 12	73·5	79 14	68 04	68·4	78 50	63 16	63·7	260	280
81	99	81 00	90 00	90·0	80 57	83 38	83·7	80 47	77 25	77·6	80 31	71 29	71·7	80 09	65 55	66·2	79 43	60 47	61·2	261	279
82	98	82 00	90 00	90·0	81 56	82 51	82·9	81 45	75 55	76·1	81 28	69 22	69·6	81 04	63 19	63·6	80 34	57 51	58·2	262	278
83	97	83 00	90 00	90·0	82 56	81 51	81·9	82 43	74 01	74·1	82 23	66 44	66·9	81 57	60 09	60·4	81 24	54 20	54·6	263	277
84	96	84 00	90 00	90·0	83 55	80 31	80·6	83 41	71 32	71·6	83 18	63 22	63·5	82 48	56 13	56·4	82 12	50 04	50·3	264	276
85	95	85 00	90 00	90·0	84 54	78 40	78·7	84 37	68 10	68·3	84 10	58 59	59·1	83 36	51 16	51·4	82 56	44 53	45·1	265	275
86	94	86 00	90 00	90·0	85 53	75 57	76·0	85 32	63 24	63·5	85 00	53 05	53·2	84 21	44 56	45·1	83 36	38 34	38·7	266	274
87	93	87 00	90 00	90·0	86 50	71 33	71·6	86 24	56 17	56·3	85 45	44 58	45·0	85 00	36 49	36·9	84 10	30 53	31·0	267	273
88	92	88 00	90 00	90·0	87 46	63 26	63·4	87 10	44 59	45·0	86 24	33 40	33·7	85 32	26 31	26·6	84 37	21 45	21·8	268	272
89	91	89 00	90 00	90·0	88 35	45 00	45·0	87 46	26 33	26·6	86 50	18 25	18·4	85 53	14 01	14·0	84 54	11 17	11·3	269	271
90	90	90 00	0 00	0·0	89 00	0 00	0·0	88 00	0 00	0·0	87 00	0 00	0·0	86 00	0 00	0·0	85 00	0 00	0·0	270	270

N. Lat: for LHA > 180° … $Z_n = Z$
for LHA < 180° … $Z_n = 360° - Z$

S. Lat.: for LHA > 180° … $Z_n = 180° - Z$
for LHA < 180° … $Z_n = 180° + Z$

SIGHT REDUCTION TABLE

B: (−) for 90° < LHA < 270°
Dec: (−) for Lat. contrary name

Z_1: same sign as B
Z_2: (−) for F > 90°

Lat. / A		6°			7°			8°			9°			10°			11°			Lat. / A	
LHA/F		A/H	B/P	Z_1/Z_2	A/H	B/P	Z_1/Z_2	A/H	B/P	Z_1/Z_2	A/H	B/P	Z_1/Z_2	A/H	B/P	Z_1/Z_2	A/H	B/P	Z_1/Z_2	LHA	
°	°	° ′	° ′	°	° ′	° ′	°	° ′	° ′	°	° ′	° ′	°	° ′	° ′	°	° ′	° ′	°	°	°
0	180	0 00	84 00	90·0	0 00	83 00	90·0	0 00	82 00	90·0	0 00	81 00	90·0	0 00	80 00	90·0	0 00	79 00	90·0	180	360
1	179	1 00	84 00	89·9	1 00	83 00	89·9	0 59	82 00	89·9	0 59	81 00	89·8	0 59	80 00	89·8	0 59	79 00	89·8	181	359
2	178	1 59	84 00	89·8	1 59	83 00	89·8	1 59	82 00	89·7	1 59	81 00	89·7	1 58	80 00	89·7	1 58	79 00	89·6	182	358
3	177	2 59	84 00	89·7	2 59	82 59	89·6	2 58	81 59	89·6	2 58	80 59	89·5	2 57	79 59	89·5	2 57	78 59	89·4	183	357
4	176	3 59	83 59	89·6	3 58	82 59	89·5	3 58	81 59	89·4	3 57	80 59	89·4	3 56	79 59	89·3	3 56	78 58	89·2	184	356
5	175	4 58	83 59	89·5	4 58	82 58	89·4	4 57	81 58	89·3	4 56	80 58	89·2	4 55	79 58	89·1	4 54	78 58	89·0	185	355
6	174	5 58	83 58	89·4	5 57	82 58	89·3	5 56	81 57	89·2	5 56	80 57	89·1	5 55	79 57	89·0	5 53	78 56	88·9	186	354
7	173	6 58	83 57	89·3	6 57	82 57	89·1	6 56	81 56	89·0	6 55	80 56	88·9	6 54	79 56	88·8	6 52	78 55	88·7	187	353
8	172	7 57	83 56	89·2	7 56	82 56	89·0	7 55	81 55	88·9	7 54	80 55	88·7	7 53	79 54	88·6	7 51	78 54	88·5	188	352
9	171	8 57	83 56	89·1	8 56	82 55	88·9	8 55	81 54	88·7	8 53	80 53	88·6	8 52	79 53	88·4	8 50	78 52	88·3	189	351
10	170	9 57	83 54	88·9	9 55	82 54	88·8	9 54	81 53	88·6	9 53	80 52	88·4	9 51	79 51	88·2	9 49	78 50	88·1	190	350
11	169	10 56	83 53	88·8	10 55	82 52	88·6	10 53	81 51	88·5	10 52	80 50	88·3	10 50	79 49	88·1	10 48	78 48	87·9	191	349
12	168	11 56	83 52	88·7	11 55	82 51	88·5	11 53	81 49	88·3	11 51	80 48	88·1	11 49	79 47	87·9	11 47	78 46	87·7	192	348
13	167	12 56	83 51	88·6	12 54	82 49	88·4	12 52	81 48	88·2	12 50	80 46	87·9	12 48	79 45	87·7	12 45	78 43	87·5	193	347
14	166	13 55	83 49	88·5	13 54	82 47	88·3	13 52	81 46	88·0	13 49	80 44	87·8	13 47	79 42	87·5	13 44	78 40	87·3	194	346
15	165	14 55	83 47	88·4	14 53	82 45	88·1	14 51	81 43	87·9	14 49	80 41	87·6	14 46	79 39	87·3	14 43	78 37	87·1	195	345
16	164	15 55	83 46	88·3	15 53	82 43	88·0	15 50	81 41	87·7	15 48	80 39	87·4	15 45	79 36	87·1	15 42	78 34	86·9	196	344
17	163	16 54	83 44	88·2	16 52	82 41	87·9	16 50	81 38	87·6	16 47	80 36	87·3	16 44	79 33	87·0	16 41	78 31	86·7	197	343
18	162	17 54	83 42	88·1	17 52	82 39	87·7	17 49	81 36	87·4	17 46	80 33	87·1	17 43	79 30	86·8	17 39	78 27	86·5	198	342
19	161	18 54	83 39	87·9	18 51	82 36	87·6	18 48	81 33	87·3	18 45	80 29	86·9	18 42	79 26	86·6	18 38	78 23	86·2	199	341
20	160	19 53	83 37	87·8	19 51	82 33	87·5	19 48	81 30	87·1	19 45	80 26	86·7	19 41	79 22	86·4	19 37	78 19	86·0	200	340
21	159	20 53	83 35	87·7	20 50	82 30	87·3	20 47	81 26	86·9	20 44	80 22	86·6	20 40	79 18	86·2	20 36	78 14	85·8	201	339
22	158	21 52	83 32	87·6	21 50	82 27	87·2	21 46	81 23	86·8	21 43	80 18	86·4	21 39	79 14	86·0	21 35	78 10	85·6	202	338
23	157	22 52	83 29	87·5	22 49	82 24	87·0	22 46	81 19	86·6	22 42	80 14	86·2	22 38	79 09	85·8	22 33	78 05	85·4	203	337
24	156	23 52	83 26	87·3	23 49	82 21	86·9	23 45	81 15	86·5	23 41	80 10	86·0	23 37	79 05	85·6	23 32	77 59	85·1	204	336
25	155	24 51	83 23	87·2	24 48	82 17	86·7	24 44	81 11	86·3	24 40	80 05	85·8	24 36	78 59	85·4	24 31	77 54	84·9	205	335
26	154	25 51	83 20	87·1	25 48	82 13	86·6	25 44	81 07	86·1	25 39	80 00	85·6	25 35	78 54	85·2	25 29	77 48	84·7	206	334
27	153	26 50	83 16	87·0	26 47	82 09	86·4	26 43	81 02	85·9	26 38	79 55	85·4	26 33	78 48	84·9	26 28	77 42	84·4	207	333
28	152	27 50	83 13	86·8	27 46	82 05	86·3	27 42	80 57	85·8	27 38	79 50	85·2	27 32	78 42	84·7	27 27	77 35	84·2	208	332
29	151	28 50	83 09	86·7	28 46	82 01	86·1	28 41	80 52	85·6	28 37	79 44	85·0	28 31	78 36	84·5	28 25	77 28	84·0	209	331
30	150	29 49	83 05	86·5	29 45	81 56	86·0	29 41	80 47	85·4	29 36	79 38	84·8	29 30	78 29	84·3	29 24	77 21	83·7	210	330
31	149	30 49	83 01	86·4	30 45	81 51	85·8	30 40	80 41	85·2	30 35	79 32	84·6	30 29	78 23	84·0	30 22	77 13	83·5	211	329
32	148	31 48	82 56	86·3	31 44	81 46	85·6	31 39	80 35	85·0	31 34	79 25	84·4	31 27	78 15	83·8	31 21	77 05	83·2	212	328
33	147	32 48	82 51	86·1	32 43	81 40	85·5	32 38	80 29	84·8	32 33	79 18	84·2	32 26	78 08	83·6	32 19	76 57	82·9	213	327
34	146	33 47	82 46	86·0	33 43	81 35	85·3	33 37	80 23	84·6	33 32	79 11	84·0	33 25	78 00	83·3	33 18	76 48	82·7	214	326
35	145	34 47	82 41	85·8	34 42	81 29	85·1	34 37	80 16	84·4	34 30	79 03	83·7	34 24	77 51	83·1	34 16	76 39	82·4	215	325
36	144	35 46	82 36	85·7	35 41	81 22	84·9	35 36	80 09	84·2	35 29	78 55	83·5	35 22	77 42	82·8	35 14	76 29	82·1	216	324
37	143	36 46	82 30	85·5	36 41	81 16	84·8	36 35	80 01	84·0	36 28	78 47	83·3	36 21	77 33	82·5	36 13	76 19	81·8	217	323
38	142	37 45	82 24	85·3	37 40	81 09	84·6	37 34	79 53	83·8	37 27	78 38	83·0	37 19	77 23	82·3	37 11	76 09	81·5	218	322
39	141	38 45	82 18	85·2	38 39	81 01	84·4	38 33	79 45	83·6	38 26	78 29	82·8	38 18	77 13	82·0	38 09	75 57	81·2	219	321
40	140	39 44	82 11	85·0	39 39	80 54	84·2	39 32	79 36	83·3	39 25	78 19	82·5	39 16	77 02	81·7	39 07	75 46	80·9	220	320
41	139	40 44	82 04	84·8	40 38	80 46	84·0	40 31	79 27	83·1	40 23	78 09	82·3	40 15	76 51	81·4	40 05	75 33	80·6	221	319
42	138	41 43	81 57	84·6	41 37	80 37	83·7	41 30	79 17	82·9	41 22	77 58	82·0	41 13	76 39	81·1	41 04	75 21	80·3	222	318
43	137	42 42	81 49	84·4	42 36	80 28	83·5	42 29	79 07	82·6	42 21	77 47	81·7	42 12	76 27	80·8	42 02	75 07	79·9	223	317
44	136	43 42	81 41	84·2	43 35	80 19	83·3	43 28	78 57	82·3	43 19	77 35	81·4	43 10	76 14	80·5	43 00	74 53	79·6	224	316
45	135	44 41	81 33	84·0	44 34	80 09	83·1	44 27	78 46	82·1	44 18	77 22	81·1	44 08	76 00	80·1	43 57	74 38	79·2	225	315

Lat. / A		6°			7°			8°			9°			10°			11°			Lat. / A	
LHA/F		A/H	B/P	Z_1/Z_2	A/H	B/P	Z_1/Z_2	A/H	B/P	Z_1/Z_2	A/H	B/P	Z_1/Z_2	A/H	B/P	Z_1/Z_2	A/H	B/P	Z_1/Z_2	LHA	
°	°	° ′	° ′	°	° ′	° ′	°	° ′	° ′	°	° ′	° ′	°	° ′	° ′	°	° ′	° ′	°	°	°
45	135	44 41	81 33	84·0	44 34	80 09	83·1	44 27	78 46	82·1	44 18	77 22	81·1	44 08	76 00	80·1	43 57	74 38	79·2	225	315
46	134	45 41	81 24	83·8	45 34	79 59	82·8	45 26	78 34	81·8	45 16	77 09	80·8	45 06	75 45	79·8	44 55	74 22	78·8	226	314
47	133	46 40	81 14	83·6	46 33	79 48	82·6	46 24	78 21	81·5	46 15	76 56	80·5	46 04	75 30	79·5	45 53	74 05	78·4	227	313
48	132	47 39	81 04	83·4	47 32	79 36	82·3	47 23	78 08	81·2	47 13	76 41	80·1	47 03	75 14	79·1	46 51	73 48	78·0	228	312
49	131	48 38	80 54	83·1	48 31	79 24	82·0	48 22	77 55	80·9	48 12	76 26	79·8	48 01	74 57	78·7	47 48	73 30	77·6	229	311
50	130	49 38	80 43	82·9	49 30	79 11	81·7	49 20	77 40	80·6	49 10	76 09	79·4	48 58	74 40	78·3	48 46	73 10	77·2	230	310
51	129	50 37	80 31	82·6	50 29	78 58	81·4	50 19	77 25	80·2	50 08	75 52	79·1	49 56	74 21	77·9	49 43	72 50	76·7	231	309
52	128	51 36	80 19	82·4	51 27	78 43	81·1	51 18	77 08	79·9	51 06	75 34	78·7	50 54	74 01	77·5	50 40	72 29	76·3	232	308
53	127	52 35	80 06	82·1	52 26	78 28	80·8	52 16	76 51	79·5	52 04	75 15	78·3	51 52	73 40	77·0	51 37	72 06	75·8	233	307
54	126	53 34	79 52	81·8	53 25	78 12	80·5	53 14	76 33	79·2	53 02	74 55	77·8	52 49	73 18	76·6	52 35	71 42	75·3	234	306
55	125	54 33	79 37	81·5	54 24	77 55	80·1	54 13	76 14	78·8	54 00	74 34	77·4	53 47	72 55	76·1	53 31	71 17	74·8	235	305
56	124	55 32	79 21	81·2	55 22	77 37	79·8	55 11	75 54	78·3	54 58	74 11	76·9	54 44	72 30	75·6	54 28	70 50	74·2	236	304
57	123	56 31	79 05	80·9	56 21	77 18	79·4	56 09	75 32	77·9	55 56	73 47	76·5	55 41	72 04	75·0	55 25	70 22	73·6	237	303
58	122	57 30	78 47	80·5	57 19	76 57	79·0	57 07	75 09	77·4	56 53	73 22	75·9	56 38	71 36	74·5	56 21	69 51	73·0	238	302
59	121	58 29	78 28	80·1	58 18	76 35	78·5	58 05	74 44	77·0	57 51	72 54	75·4	57 35	71 06	73·9	57 17	69 19	72·4	239	301
60	120	59 28	78 08	79·7	59 16	76 12	78·1	59 03	74 18	76·4	58 48	72 25	74·8	58 32	70 34	73·3	58 13	68 45	71·7	240	300
61	119	60 26	77 46	79·3	60 14	75 47	77·6	60 01	73 50	75·9	59 45	71 54	74·2	59 28	70 01	72·6	59 09	68 09	71·0	241	299
62	118	61 25	77 23	78·9	61 12	75 21	77·1	60 58	73 20	75·3	60 42	71 21	73·6	60 24	69 25	71·9	60 05	67 31	70·3	242	298
63	117	62 23	76 58	78·4	62 10	74 52	76·5	61 56	72 48	74·7	61 39	70 46	72·9	61 20	68 46	71·2	61 00	66 49	69·5	243	297
64	116	63 22	76 31	77·9	63 08	74 21	76·0	62 53	72 13	74·1	62 35	70 08	72·2	62 16	68 05	70·4	61 55	66 05	68·6	244	296
65	115	64 20	76 02	77·4	64 06	73 48	75·4	63 50	71 36	73·4	63 32	69 27	71·5	63 12	67 21	69·6	62 50	65 18	67·7	245	295
66	114	65 18	75 31	76·8	65 03	73 12	74·7	64 47	70 56	72·6	64 28	68 43	70·6	64 07	66 34	68·7	63 44	64 27	66·8	246	294
67	113	66 16	74 57	76·2	66 01	72 33	74·0	65 43	70 13	71·8	65 23	67 56	69·8	65 02	65 43	67·8	64 38	63 33	65·8	247	293
68	112	67 14	74 20	75·5	66 58	71 51	73·2	66 40	69 26	71·0	66 19	67 05	68·8	65 56	64 48	66·7	65 32	62 35	64·7	248	292
69	111	68 12	73 39	74·8	67 55	71 05	72·4	67 36	68 35	70·1	67 14	66 09	67·8	66 50	63 48	65·7	66 25	61 31	63·6	249	291
70	110	69 09	72 55	74·0	68 51	70 15	71·5	68 31	67 40	69·1	68 09	65 09	66·7	67 44	62 44	64·5	67 17	60 23	62·3	250	290
71	109	70 07	72 06	73·1	69 48	69 20	70·5	69 27	66 39	68·0	69 03	64 03	65·6	68 37	61 34	63·2	68 09	59 10	61·0	251	289
72	108	71 03	71 13	72·2	70 44	68 20	69·4	70 21	65 33	66·8	69 57	62 52	64·3	69 29	60 17	61·9	69 00	57 50	59·6	252	288
73	107	72 00	70 14	71·1	71 39	67 13	68·3	71 16	64 20	65·5	70 50	61 33	62·9	70 21	58 54	60·4	69 50	56 23	58·0	253	287
74	106	72 56	69 08	70·0	72 34	65 59	67·0	72 09	62 59	64·1	71 42	60 07	61·4	71 12	57 24	58·8	70 40	54 49	56·4	254	286
75	105	73 52	67 54	68·7	73 29	64 37	65·5	73 03	61 30	62·6	72 34	58 32	59·7	72 02	55 44	57·1	71 28	53 06	54·5	255	285
76	104	74 48	66 31	67·3	74 23	63 05	64·0	73 55	59 51	60·8	73 24	56 47	57·9	72 51	53 55	55·1	72 16	51 13	52·6	256	284
77	103	75 42	64 57	65·6	75 16	61 22	62·2	74 46	58 00	58·9	74 14	54 51	55·9	73 39	51 55	53·1	73 02	49 10	50·4	257	283
78	102	76 36	63 11	63·8	76 08	59 26	60·2	75 37	55 57	56·8	75 02	52 42	53·6	74 26	49 42	50·8	73 47	46 56	48·1	258	282
79	101	77 29	61 09	61·7	76 59	57 14	57·9	76 26	53 38	54·4	75 49	50 18	51·2	75 11	47 16	48·2	74 30	44 28	45·5	259	281
80	100	78 21	58 49	59·3	77 49	54 44	55·3	77 13	51 01	51·7	76 35	47 38	48·4	75 54	44 34	45·4	75 11	41 47	42·7	260	280
81	99	79 12	56 06	56·6	78 37	51 52	52·4	77 59	48 04	48·7	77 18	44 39	45·4	76 35	41 35	42·4	75 49	38 50	39·7	261	279
82	98	80 01	52 56	53·4	79 23	48 35	49·1	78 42	44 43	45·3	77 59	41 18	41·9	77 13	38 17	39·0	76 26	35 36	36·4	262	278
83	97	80 47	49 13	49·6	80 07	44 47	45·2	79 23	40 56	41·4	78 37	37 35	38·1	77 49	34 39	35·3	76 59	32 05	32·8	263	277
84	96	81 31	44 51	45·2	80 47	40 24	40·8	80 01	36 38	37·1	79 12	33 25	33·9	78 21	30 40	31·2	77 29	28 16	28·8	264	276
85	95	82 12	39 40	39·9	81 24	35 22	35·7	80 34	31 48	32·2	79 43	28 49	29·2	78 50	26 18	26·7	77 56	24 09	24·6	265	275
86	94	82 48	33 34	33·8	81 57	29 36	29·8	81 04	26 24	26·7	80 09	23 46	24·1	79 14	21 35	21·9	78 18	19 44	20·1	266	274
87	93	83 18	26 28	26·6	82 23	23 05	23·3	81 28	20 25	20·6	80 31	18 17	18·5	79 34	16 32	16·8	78 36	15 04	15·4	267	273
88	92	83 41	18 22	18·5	82 43	15 52	16·0	81 45	13 57	14·1	80 47	12 26	12·6	79 48	11 12	11·4	78 49	10 11	10·4	268	272
89	91	83 55	9 26	9·5	82 56	8 05	8·2	81 56	7 05	7·1	80 57	6 17	6·4	79 57	5 39	5·7	78 57	5 08	5·2	269	271
90	90	84 00	0 00	0·0	83 00	0 00	0·0	82 00	0 00	0·0	81 00	0 00	0·0	80 00	0 00	0·0	79 00	0 00	0·0	270	270

N. Lat: for LHA > 180° … Z_n = Z
for LHA < 180° … Z_n = 360° − Z

S. Lat.: for LHA > 180° … Z_n = 180° − Z
for LHA < 180° … Z_n = 180° + Z

SIGHT REDUCTION TABLE

B: (–) for 90° < LHA < 270°
Dec: (–) for Lat. contrary name

Z_1: same sign as B
Z_2: (–) for F > 90°

Lat. / A		12°			13°			14°			15°			16°			17°			Lat. / A	
LHA/F		A/H	B/P	Z_1/Z_2	A/H	B/P	Z_1/Z_2	A/H	B/P	Z_1/Z_2	A/H	B/P	Z_1/Z_2	A/H	B/P	Z_1/Z_2	A/H	B/P	Z_1/Z_2	LHA	
°	°	° ′	° ′	°	° ′	° ′	°	° ′	° ′	°	° ′	° ′	°	° ′	° ′	°	° ′	° ′	°	°	°
0	180	0 00	78 00	90·0	0 00	77 00	90·0	0 00	76 00	90·0	0 00	75 00	90·0	0 00	74 00	90·0	0 00	73 00	90·0	180	360
1	179	0 59	78 00	89·8	0 58	77 00	89·8	0 58	76 00	89·8	0 58	75 00	89·7	0 58	74 00	89·7	0 57	73 00	89·7	181	359
2	178	1 57	78 00	89·6	1 57	77 00	89·5	1 56	76 00	89·5	1 56	74 59	89·5	1 55	73 59	89·4	1 55	72 59	89·4	182	358
3	177	2 56	77 59	89·4	2 55	76 59	89·3	2 55	75 59	89·3	2 54	74 59	89·2	2 53	73 59	89·2	2 52	72 59	89·1	183	357
4	176	3 55	77 58	89·2	3 54	76 58	89·1	3 53	75 58	89·0	3 52	74 58	89·0	3 51	73 58	88·9	3 49	72 58	88·8	184	356
5	175	4 53	77 57	89·0	4 52	76 57	88·9	4 51	75 57	88·8	4 50	74 57	88·7	4 48	73 57	88·6	4 47	72 56	88·5	185	355
6	174	5 52	77 56	88·7	5 51	76 56	88·6	5 49	75 56	88·5	5 48	74 55	88·4	5 46	73 55	88·3	5 44	72 55	88·2	186	354
7	173	6 51	77 55	88·5	6 49	76 54	88·4	6 47	75 54	88·3	6 46	74 54	88·2	6 44	73 53	88·1	6 42	72 53	87·9	187	353
8	172	7 49	77 53	88·3	7 48	76 53	88·2	7 46	75 52	88·1	7 44	74 52	87·9	7 41	73 51	87·8	7 39	72 51	87·6	188	352
9	171	8 48	77 51	88·1	8 46	76 51	88·0	8 44	75 50	87·8	8 41	74 49	87·7	8 39	73 49	87·5	8 36	72 48	87·3	189	351
10	170	9 47	77 49	87·9	9 44	76 48	87·7	9 42	75 48	87·6	9 39	74 47	87·4	9 37	73 46	87·2	9 34	72 45	87·0	190	350
11	169	10 45	77 47	87·7	10 43	76 46	87·5	10 40	75 45	87·3	10 37	74 44	87·1	10 34	73 43	86·9	10 31	72 42	86·7	191	349
12	168	11 44	77 44	87·5	11 41	76 43	87·3	11 38	75 42	87·1	11 35	74 41	86·9	11 32	73 40	86·6	11 28	72 39	86·4	192	348
13	167	12 43	77 42	87·3	12 40	76 40	87·0	12 36	75 39	86·8	12 33	74 37	86·6	12 29	73 36	86·4	12 25	72 35	86·1	193	347
14	166	13 41	77 39	87·0	13 38	76 37	86·8	13 35	75 35	86·5	13 31	74 34	86·3	13 27	73 32	86·1	13 23	72 31	85·8	194	346
15	165	14 40	77 35	86·8	14 36	76 33	86·6	14 33	75 32	86·3	14 29	74 30	86·0	14 24	73 28	85·8	14 20	72 26	85·5	195	345
16	164	15 38	77 32	86·6	15 35	76 30	86·3	15 31	75 28	86·0	15 26	74 25	85·8	15 22	73 23	85·5	15 17	72 21	85·2	196	344
17	163	16 37	77 28	86·4	16 33	76 26	86·1	16 29	75 23	85·8	16 24	74 21	85·5	16 19	73 19	85·2	16 14	72 16	84·9	197	343
18	162	17 36	77 24	86·1	17 31	76 21	85·8	17 27	75 19	85·5	17 22	74 16	85·2	17 17	73 13	84·9	17 11	72 11	84·6	198	342
19	161	18 34	77 20	85·9	18 30	76 17	85·6	18 25	75 14	85·2	18 20	74 11	84·9	18 14	73 08	84·6	18 08	72 05	84·3	199	341
20	160	19 33	77 15	85·7	19 28	76 12	85·3	19 23	75 08	85·0	19 17	74 05	84·6	19 12	73 02	84·3	19 05	71 59	83·9	200	340
21	159	20 31	77 10	85·4	20 26	76 07	85·1	20 21	75 03	84·7	20 15	73 59	84·3	20 09	72 56	84·0	20 03	71 52	83·6	201	339
22	158	21 30	77 05	85·2	21 24	76 01	84·8	21 19	74 57	84·4	21 13	73 53	84·0	21 06	72 49	83·6	21 00	71 45	83·3	202	338
23	157	22 28	77 00	85·0	22 23	75 55	84·5	22 17	74 51	84·1	22 10	73 46	83·7	22 04	72 42	83·3	21 56	71 38	82·9	203	337
24	156	23 27	76 54	84·7	23 21	75 49	84·3	23 15	74 44	83·9	23 08	73 39	83·4	23 01	72 34	83·0	22 53	71 30	82·6	204	336
25	155	24 25	76 48	84·5	24 19	75 43	84·0	24 13	74 37	83·6	24 06	73 32	83·1	23 58	72 27	82·7	23 50	71 22	82·2	205	335
26	154	25 23	76 42	84·2	25 17	75 36	83·7	25 10	74 30	83·3	25 03	73 24	82·8	24 55	72 18	82·3	24 47	71 13	81·9	206	334
27	153	26 22	76 35	84·0	26 15	75 28	83·5	26 08	74 22	83·0	26 01	73 16	82·5	25 52	72 10	82·0	25 44	71 04	81·5	207	333
28	152	27 20	76 28	83·7	27 13	75 21	83·2	27 06	74 14	82·7	26 58	73 07	82·2	26 50	72 00	81·7	26 41	70 54	81·2	208	332
29	151	28 18	76 20	83·4	28 11	75 13	82·9	28 04	74 05	82·4	27 55	72 58	81·8	27 47	71 51	81·3	27 37	70 44	80·8	209	331
30	150	29 17	76 13	83·2	29 09	75 04	82·6	29 01	73 56	82·0	28 53	72 48	81·5	28 44	71 41	81·0	28 34	70 33	80·4	210	330
31	149	30 15	76 04	82·9	30 07	74 56	82·3	29 59	73 47	81·7	29 50	72 38	81·2	29 41	71 30	80·6	29 30	70 22	80·0	211	329
32	148	31 13	75 56	82·6	31 05	74 46	82·0	30 57	73 37	81·4	30 47	72 28	80·8	30 37	71 19	80·2	30 27	70 11	79·6	212	328
33	147	32 11	75 47	82·3	32 03	74 37	81·7	31 54	73 27	81·1	31 44	72 17	80·5	31 34	71 07	79·9	31 23	69 58	79·2	213	327
34	146	33 10	75 37	82·0	33 01	74 26	81·4	32 52	73 16	80·7	32 42	72 05	80·1	32 31	70 55	79·5	32 20	69 45	78·8	214	326
35	145	34 08	75 27	81·7	33 59	74 16	81·0	33 49	73 04	80·4	33 39	71 53	79·7	33 28	70 42	79·1	33 16	69 32	78·4	215	325
36	144	35 06	75 17	81·4	34 56	74 04	80·7	34 46	72 52	80·0	34 36	71 40	79·4	34 24	70 29	78·7	34 12	69 18	78·0	216	324
37	143	36 04	75 06	81·1	35 54	73 53	80·4	35 44	72 40	79·7	35 33	71 27	79·0	35 21	70 15	78·3	35 08	69 03	77·6	217	323
38	142	37 02	74 54	80·8	36 52	73 40	80·0	36 41	72 27	79·3	36 29	71 13	78·6	36 17	70 00	77·8	36 04	68 48	77·1	218	322
39	141	38 00	74 42	80·4	37 49	73 27	79·7	37 38	72 13	78·9	37 26	70 59	78·2	37 13	69 45	77·4	37 00	68 32	76·7	219	321
40	140	38 57	74 30	80·1	38 47	73 14	79·3	38 35	71 58	78·5	38 23	70 43	77·7	38 10	69 29	77·0	37 56	68 15	76·2	220	320
41	139	39 55	74 16	79·8	39 44	72 59	78·9	39 32	71 43	78·1	39 19	70 27	77·3	39 06	69 12	76·5	38 51	67 57	75·7	221	319
42	138	40 53	74 02	79·4	40 41	72 45	78·5	40 29	71 27	77·7	40 16	70 10	76·9	40 02	68 54	76·1	39 47	67 38	75·3	222	318
43	137	41 51	73 48	79·0	41 39	72 29	78·2	41 26	71 11	77·3	41 12	69 53	76·4	40 58	68 35	75·6	40 42	67 19	74·7	223	317
44	136	42 48	73 32	78·6	42 36	72 12	77·7	42 23	70 53	76·9	42 09	69 34	76·0	41 54	68 16	75·1	41 38	66 58	74·2	224	316
45	135	43 46	73 16	78·3	43 33	71 55	77·3	43 19	70 35	76·4	43 05	69 15	75·5	42 49	67 56	74·6	42 33	66 37	73·7	225	315

Lat. / A		12°			13°			14°			15°			16°			17°			Lat. / A	
LHA/F		A/H	B/P	Z_1/Z_2	A/H	B/P	Z_1/Z_2	A/H	B/P	Z_1/Z_2	A/H	B/P	Z_1/Z_2	A/H	B/P	Z_1/Z_2	A/H	B/P	Z_1/Z_2	LHA	
°	°	° ′	° ′	°	° ′	° ′	°	° ′	° ′	°	° ′	° ′	°	° ′	° ′	°	° ′	° ′	°	°	°
45	135	43 46	73 16	78·3	43 33	71 55	77·3	43 19	70 35	76·4	43 05	69 15	75·5	42 49	67 56	74·6	42 33	66 37	73·7	225	315
46	134	44 43	72 59	77·8	44 30	71 37	76·9	44 16	70 15	75·9	44 01	68 54	75·0	43 45	67 34	74·1	43 28	66 15	73·2	226	314
47	133	45 40	72 41	77·4	45 27	71 18	76·4	45 12	69 55	75·5	44 57	68 33	74·5	44 40	67 12	73·5	44 23	65 51	72·6	227	313
48	132	46 38	72 23	77·0	46 24	70 58	76·0	46 09	69 34	75·0	45 53	68 11	74·0	45 35	66 48	73·0	45 17	65 27	72·0	228	312
49	131	47 35	72 03	76·5	47 20	70 37	75·5	47 05	69 11	74·4	46 48	67 47	73·4	46 30	66 23	72·4	46 12	65 01	71·4	229	311
50	130	48 32	71 42	76·1	48 17	70 15	75·0	48 01	68 48	73·9	47 44	67 22	72·9	47 25	65 58	71·8	47 06	64 34	70·8	230	310
51	129	49 29	71 20	75·6	49 13	69 51	74·5	48 57	68 23	73·4	48 39	66 56	72·3	48 20	65 30	71·2	48 00	64 05	70·1	231	309
52	128	50 25	70 57	75·1	50 09	69 27	73·9	49 52	67 57	72·8	49 34	66 29	71·7	49 15	65 02	70·6	48 54	63 35	69·5	232	308
53	127	51 22	70 33	74·6	51 06	69 01	73·4	50 48	67 30	72·2	50 29	66 00	71·0	50 09	64 31	69·9	49 48	63 04	68·8	233	307
54	126	52 19	70 07	74·0	52 02	68 33	72·8	51 43	67 01	71·6	51 24	65 30	70·4	51 03	64 00	69·2	50 41	62 31	68·1	234	306
55	125	53 15	69 40	73·5	52 57	68 04	72·2	52 38	66 30	70·9	52 18	64 58	69·7	51 57	63 26	68·5	51 34	61 56	67·3	235	305
56	124	54 11	69 11	72·9	53 53	67 34	71·6	53 33	65 58	70·3	53 12	64 24	69·0	52 50	62 51	67·8	52 27	61 20	66·6	236	304
57	123	55 07	68 41	72·2	54 48	67 02	70·9	54 28	65 24	69·6	54 06	63 48	68·3	53 43	62 14	67·0	53 19	60 42	65·8	237	303
58	122	56 03	68 09	71·6	55 43	66 28	70·2	55 22	64 48	68·8	55 00	63 11	67·5	54 36	61 35	66·2	54 12	60 01	64·9	238	302
59	121	56 59	67 34	70·9	56 38	65 51	69·5	56 16	64 10	68·1	55 53	62 31	66·7	55 29	60 54	65·4	55 03	59 18	64·1	239	301
60	120	57 54	66 58	70·2	57 33	65 13	68·7	57 10	63 30	67·3	56 46	61 49	65·9	56 21	60 10	64·5	55 55	58 33	63·1	240	300
61	119	58 49	66 20	69·4	58 27	64 32	67·9	58 04	62 47	66·4	57 39	61 04	65·0	57 13	59 24	63·6	56 46	57 46	62·2	241	299
62	118	59 44	65 38	68·6	59 21	63 49	67·1	58 57	62 02	65·5	58 31	60 17	64·0	58 05	58 35	62·6	57 36	56 56	61·2	242	298
63	117	60 38	64 55	67·8	60 15	63 03	66·2	59 50	61 13	64·6	59 23	59 27	63·1	58 55	57 43	61·6	58 26	56 03	60·2	243	297
64	116	61 32	64 08	66·9	61 08	62 14	65·2	60 42	60 22	63·6	60 15	58 34	62·0	59 46	56 49	60·5	59 16	55 06	59·1	244	296
65	115	62 26	63 18	66·0	62 01	61 21	64·2	61 34	59 28	62·6	61 06	57 37	61·0	60 36	55 51	59·4	60 05	54 07	57·9	245	295
66	114	63 20	62 25	65·0	62 53	60 25	63·2	62 26	58 30	61·5	61 56	56 37	59·8	61 25	54 49	58·2	60 53	53 04	56·7	246	294
67	113	64 13	61 27	63·9	63 45	59 25	62·1	63 16	57 27	60·3	62 46	55 34	58·6	62 14	53 44	57·0	61 41	51 57	55·4	247	293
68	112	65 05	60 26	62·8	64 37	58 21	60·9	64 07	56 21	59·1	63 35	54 25	57·4	63 02	52 34	55·7	62 27	50 47	54·1	248	292
69	111	65 57	59 20	61·6	65 27	57 13	59·6	64 56	55 10	57·8	64 23	53 13	56·0	63 49	51 20	54·3	63 14	49 32	52·7	249	291
70	110	66 48	58 08	60·3	66 18	55 59	58·3	65 45	53 55	56·4	65 11	51 55	54·6	64 36	50 01	52·9	63 59	48 12	51·2	250	290
71	109	67 39	56 52	58·9	67 07	54 40	56·8	66 33	52 33	54·9	65 58	50 33	53·1	65 21	48 38	51·3	64 43	46 48	49·7	251	289
72	108	68 29	55 29	57·4	67 55	53 14	55·3	67 20	51 06	53·3	66 44	49 04	51·5	66 06	47 08	49·7	65 26	45 18	48·0	252	288
73	107	69 18	53 59	55·8	68 43	51 42	53·7	68 07	49 33	51·6	67 29	47 30	49·8	66 49	45 33	48·0	66 08	43 43	46·3	253	287
74	106	70 06	52 22	54·1	69 30	50 03	51·9	68 52	47 52	49·8	68 12	45 49	47·9	67 31	43 52	46·1	66 49	42 02	44·4	254	286
75	105	70 53	50 36	52·2	70 15	48 16	50·0	69 36	46 04	47·9	68 55	44 00	46·0	68 12	42 04	44·2	67 29	40 15	42·5	255	285
76	104	71 38	48 42	50·2	70 59	46 20	47·9	70 18	44 08	45·9	69 36	42 05	43·9	68 52	40 09	42·1	68 07	38 21	40·5	256	284
77	103	72 23	46 37	48·0	71 42	44 15	45·7	70 59	42 03	43·7	70 15	40 01	41·7	69 30	38 07	39·9	68 43	36 21	38·3	257	283
78	102	73 06	44 22	45·6	72 23	42 00	43·4	71 38	39 49	41·3	70 53	37 49	39·4	70 06	35 57	37·6	69 18	34 13	36·0	258	282
79	101	73 47	41 55	43·1	73 02	39 34	40·8	72 16	37 26	38·8	71 28	35 27	36·9	70 40	33 38	35·2	69 50	31 58	33·6	259	281
80	100	74 26	39 15	40·3	73 39	36 57	38·1	72 51	34 51	36·1	72 02	32 57	34·3	71 12	31 12	32·6	70 21	29 36	31·1	260	280
81	99	75 02	36 21	37·3	74 14	34 07	35·1	73 24	32 06	33·2	72 34	30 17	31·5	71 42	28 37	29·9	70 50	27 06	28·4	261	279
82	98	75 37	33 13	34·1	74 46	31 05	32·0	73 55	29 10	30·2	73 03	27 27	28·5	72 09	25 53	27·0	71 16	24 29	25·7	262	278
83	97	76 08	29 50	30·6	75 16	27 50	28·6	74 23	26 03	26·9	73 29	24 27	25·4	72 34	23 02	24·0	71 39	21 44	22·8	263	277
84	96	76 36	26 11	26·8	75 42	24 22	25·0	74 48	22 45	23·5	73 52	21 19	22·1	72 56	20 02	20·9	72 00	18 53	19·8	264	276
85	95	77 01	22 18	22·8	76 05	20 41	21·3	75 09	19 16	19·9	74 12	18 01	18·7	73 15	16 54	17·6	72 18	15 55	16·7	265	275
86	94	77 22	18 10	18·6	76 25	16 49	17·3	75 27	15 38	16·1	74 29	14 36	15·1	73 31	13 40	14·2	72 33	12 51	13·5	266	274
87	93	77 38	13 50	14·1	76 40	12 46	13·1	75 41	11 51	12·2	74 43	11 03	11·4	73 44	10 21	10·8	72 45	9 43	10·2	267	273
88	92	77 50	9 19	9·5	76 51	8 36	8·8	75 52	7 58	8·2	74 52	7 25	7·7	73 53	6 56	7·2	72 53	6 31	6·8	268	272
89	91	77 58	4 42	4·8	76 58	4 19	4·4	75 58	4 00	4·1	74 58	3 44	3·9	73 58	3 29	3·6	72 58	3 16	3·4	269	271
90	90	78 00	0 00	0·0	77 00	0 00	0·0	76 00	0 00	0·0	75 00	0 00	0·0	74 00	0 00	0·0	73 00	0 00	0·0	270	270

N. Lat: for LHA > 180° … $Z_n = Z$
for LHA < 180° … $Z_n = 360° - Z$

S. Lat.: for LHA > 180° … $Z_n = 180° - Z$
for LHA < 180° … $Z_n = 180° + Z$

SIGHT REDUCTION TABLE

B: (–) for 90° < LHA < 270°
Dec:(–) for Lat. contrary name

Z₁: same sign as B
Z₂: (–) for F > 90°

Lat. / A		18°			19°			20°			21°			22°			23°			Lat. / A	
LHA/F		A/H	B/P	Z_1/Z_2	A/H	B/P	Z_1/Z_2	A/H	B/P	Z_1/Z_2	A/H	B/P	Z_1/Z_2	A/H	B/P	Z_1/Z_2	A/H	B/P	Z_1/Z_2	LHA	
°	°	° ′	° ′	°	° ′	° ′	°	° ′	° ′	°	° ′	° ′	°	° ′	° ′	°	° ′	° ′	°	°	°
0	180	0 00	72 00	90·0	0 00	71 00	90·0	0 00	70 00	90·0	0 00	69 00	90·0	0 00	68 00	90·0	0 00	67 00	90·0	180	360
1	179	0 57	72 00	89·7	0 57	71 00	89·7	0 56	70 00	89·7	0 56	69 00	89·6	0 56	68 00	89·6	0 55	67 00	89·6	181	359
2	178	1 54	71 59	89·4	1 53	70 59	89·3	1 53	69 59	89·3	1 52	68 59	89·3	1 51	67 59	89·3	1 50	66 59	89·2	182	358
3	177	2 51	71 59	89·1	2 50	70 59	89·0	2 49	69 58	89·0	2 48	68 58	88·9	2 47	67 58	88·9	2 46	66 58	88·8	183	357
4	176	3 48	71 58	88·8	3 47	70 57	88·7	3 46	69 57	88·6	3 44	68 57	88·6	3 42	67 57	88·5	3 41	66 57	88·4	184	356
5	175	4 45	71 56	88·5	4 44	70 56	88·4	4 42	69 56	88·3	4 40	68 56	88·2	4 38	67 55	88·1	4 36	66 55	88·0	185	355
6	174	5 42	71 54	88·1	5 40	70 54	88·0	5 38	69 54	87·9	5 36	68 54	87·8	5 34	67 53	87·7	5 31	66 53	87·6	186	354
7	173	6 39	71 52	87·8	6 37	70 52	87·7	6 35	69 52	87·6	6 32	68 51	87·5	6 29	67 51	87·4	6 26	66 51	87·3	187	353
8	172	7 36	71 50	87·5	7 34	70 50	87·4	7 31	69 49	87·2	7 28	68 49	87·1	7 25	67 48	87·0	7 22	66 48	86·9	188	352
9	171	8 33	71 47	87·2	8 30	70 47	87·0	8 27	69 46	86·9	8 24	68 46	86·8	8 20	67 45	86·6	8 17	66 45	86·5	189	351
10	170	9 30	71 44	86·9	9 27	70 44	86·7	9 23	69 43	86·5	9 20	68 42	86·4	9 16	67 42	86·2	9 12	66 41	86·1	190	350
11	169	10 27	71 41	86·6	10 24	70 40	86·4	10 20	69 39	86·2	10 16	68 39	86·0	10 11	67 38	85·8	10 07	66 37	85·7	191	349
12	168	11 24	71 37	86·2	11 20	70 36	86·0	11 16	69 35	85·8	11 12	68 34	85·6	11 07	67 33	85·4	11 02	66 32	85·3	192	348
13	167	12 21	71 33	85·9	12 17	70 32	85·7	12 12	69 31	85·5	12 07	68 30	85·3	12 02	67 29	85·1	11 57	66 28	84·8	193	347
14	166	13 18	71 29	85·6	13 13	70 28	85·4	13 08	69 26	85·1	13 03	68 25	84·9	12 58	67 24	84·7	12 52	66 22	84·4	194	346
15	165	14 15	71 24	85·3	14 10	70 23	85·0	14 05	69 21	84·8	13 59	68 20	84·5	13 53	67 18	84·3	13 47	66 17	84·0	195	345
16	164	15 12	71 19	84·9	15 06	70 18	84·7	15 01	69 16	84·4	14 55	68 14	84·1	14 48	67 12	83·9	14 42	66 10	83·6	196	344
17	163	16 09	71 14	84·6	16 03	70 12	84·3	15 57	69 10	84·0	15 50	68 08	83·7	15 44	67 06	83·5	15 37	66 04	83·2	197	343
18	162	17 05	71 08	84·3	16 59	70 06	84·0	16 53	69 03	83·7	16 46	68 01	83·4	16 39	66 59	83·1	16 32	65 57	82·8	198	342
19	161	18 02	71 02	83·9	17 56	69 59	83·6	17 49	68 57	83·3	17 42	67 54	83·0	17 34	66 52	82·7	17 26	65 49	82·3	199	341
20	160	18 59	70 56	83·6	18 52	69 53	83·2	18 45	68 50	82·9	18 37	67 47	82·6	18 29	66 44	82·2	18 21	65 41	81·9	200	340
21	159	19 56	70 49	83·2	19 48	69 45	82·9	19 41	68 42	82·5	19 33	67 39	82·2	19 24	66 36	81·8	19 16	65 33	81·5	201	339
22	158	20 52	70 41	82·9	20 45	69 38	82·5	20 37	68 34	82·1	20 28	67 31	81·8	20 19	66 27	81·4	20 10	65 24	81·0	202	338
23	157	21 49	70 33	82·5	21 41	69 29	82·1	21 32	68 26	81·7	21 24	67 22	81·4	21 14	66 18	81·0	21 05	65 15	80·6	203	337
24	156	22 45	70 25	82·2	22 37	69 21	81·8	22 28	68 17	81·3	22 19	67 12	80·9	22 09	66 09	80·5	21 59	65 05	80·1	204	336
25	155	23 42	70 17	81·8	23 33	69 12	81·4	23 24	68 07	80·9	23 14	67 03	80·5	23 04	65 58	80·1	22 54	64 54	79·7	205	335
26	154	24 38	70 07	81·4	24 29	69 02	81·0	24 20	67 57	80·5	24 09	66 52	80·1	23 59	65 48	79·6	23 48	64 43	79·2	206	334
27	153	25 35	69 58	81·1	25 25	68 52	80·6	25 15	67 47	80·1	25 05	66 42	79·7	24 54	65 36	79·2	24 42	64 32	78·7	207	333
28	152	26 31	69 48	80·7	26 21	68 42	80·2	26 11	67 36	79·7	26 00	66 30	79·2	25 48	65 25	78·7	25 36	64 19	78·3	208	332
29	151	27 27	69 37	80·3	27 17	68 31	79·8	27 06	67 24	79·3	26 55	66 18	78·8	26 43	65 12	78·3	26 30	64 07	77·8	209	331
30	150	28 24	69 26	79·9	28 13	68 19	79·4	28 01	67 12	78·8	27 50	66 06	78·3	27 37	64 59	77·8	27 24	63 53	77·3	210	330
31	149	29 20	69 14	79·5	29 09	68 07	78·9	28 57	67 00	78·4	28 44	65 53	77·8	28 31	64 46	77·3	28 18	63 39	76·8	211	329
32	148	30 16	69 02	79·1	30 04	67 54	78·5	29 52	66 46	77·9	29 39	65 39	77·4	29 26	64 32	76·8	29 12	63 25	76·3	212	328
33	147	31 12	68 49	78·7	31 00	67 41	78·1	30 47	66 32	77·5	30 34	65 24	76·9	30 20	64 17	76·3	30 05	63 09	75·8	213	327
34	146	32 08	68 36	78·2	31 55	67 27	77·6	31 42	66 18	77·0	31 28	65 09	76·4	31 14	64 01	75·8	30 59	62 53	75·2	214	326
35	145	33 04	68 22	77·8	32 51	67 12	77·2	32 37	66 03	76·5	32 23	64 54	75·9	32 08	63 45	75·3	31 52	62 36	74·7	215	325
36	144	33 59	68 07	77·3	33 46	66 57	76·7	33 32	65 47	76·0	33 17	64 37	75·4	33 01	63 28	74·8	32 45	62 19	74·2	216	324
37	143	34 55	67 52	76·9	34 41	66 41	76·2	34 26	65 30	75·5	34 11	64 20	74·9	33 55	63 10	74·2	33 38	62 01	73·6	217	323
38	142	35 50	67 36	76·4	35 36	66 24	75·7	35 21	65 13	75·0	35 05	64 02	74·4	34 48	62 51	73·7	34 31	61 41	73·0	218	322
39	141	36 46	67 19	76·0	36 31	66 06	75·2	36 15	64 54	74·5	35 59	63 43	73·8	35 42	62 32	73·1	35 24	61 21	72·4	219	321
40	140	37 41	67 01	75·5	37 26	65 48	74·7	37 10	64 35	74·0	36 53	63 23	73·3	36 35	62 12	72·6	36 17	61 01	71·8	220	320
41	139	38 36	66 42	75·0	38 20	65 29	74·2	38 04	64 15	73·4	37 46	63 02	72·7	37 28	61 50	72·0	37 09	60 39	71·2	221	319
42	138	39 31	66 23	74·5	39 15	65 08	73·7	38 58	63 54	72·9	38 40	62 41	72·1	38 21	61 28	71·4	38 01	60 16	70·6	222	318
43	137	40 26	66 03	73·9	40 09	64 47	73·1	39 51	63 33	72·3	39 33	62 18	71·5	39 13	61 05	70·7	38 53	59 52	70·0	223	317
44	136	41 21	65 42	73·4	41 03	64 25	72·5	40 45	63 10	71·7	40 26	61 55	70·9	40 06	60 41	70·1	39 45	59 27	69·3	224	316
45	135	42 16	65 19	72·8	41 57	64 02	72·0	41 38	62 46	71·1	41 19	61 30	70·3	40 58	60 15	69·5	40 37	59 01	68·7	225	315

Lat. / A		18°			19°			20°			21°			22°			23°			Lat. / A	
LHA/F		A/H	B/P	Z₁/Z₂	A/H	B/P	Z₁/Z₂	A/H	B/P	Z₁/Z₂	A/H	B/P	Z₁/Z₂	A/H	B/P	Z₁/Z₂	A/H	B/P	Z₁/Z₂	LHA	
°	°	° ′	° ′	°	° ′	° ′	°	° ′	° ′	°	° ′	° ′	°	° ′	° ′	°	° ′	° ′	°	°	°
45	135	42 16	65 19	72·8	41 57	64 02	72·0	41 38	62 46	71·1	41 19	61 30	70·3	40 58	60 15	69·5	40 37	59 01	68·7	225	315
46	134	43 10	64 56	72·3	42 51	63 38	71·4	42 32	62 21	70·5	42 11	61 05	69·6	41 50	59 49	68·8	41 28	58 34	68·0	226	314
47	133	44 04	64 32	71·7	43 45	63 13	70·8	43 25	61 55	69·9	43 04	60 38	69·0	42 42	59 21	68·1	42 19	58 06	67·3	227	313
48	132	44 58	64 06	71·1	44 38	62 46	70·1	44 18	61 27	69·2	43 56	60 09	68·3	43 33	58 53	67·4	43 10	57 37	66·5	228	312
49	131	45 52	63 39	70·4	45 32	62 18	69·5	45 10	60 59	68·5	44 48	59 40	67·6	44 24	58 22	66·7	44 00	57 06	65·8	229	311
50	130	46 46	63 11	69·8	46 25	61 49	68·8	46 03	60 29	67·8	45 39	59 09	66·9	45 15	57 51	65·9	44 50	56 34	65·0	230	310
51	129	47 39	62 42	69·1	47 17	61 19	68·1	46 55	59 57	67·1	46 31	58 37	66·1	46 06	57 18	65·2	45 40	56 00	64·2	231	309
52	128	48 33	62 11	68·4	48 10	60 47	67·4	47 46	59 25	66·4	47 22	58 03	65·4	46 56	56 44	64·4	46 30	55 25	63·4	232	308
53	127	49 25	61 38	67·7	49 02	60 13	66·6	48 38	58 50	65·6	48 13	57 28	64·6	47 46	56 07	63·6	47 19	54 48	62·6	233	307
54	126	50 18	61 04	67·0	49 54	59 38	65·9	49 29	58 14	64·8	49 03	56 51	63·7	48 36	55 30	62·7	48 08	54 10	61·7	234	306
55	125	51 10	60 28	66·2	50 46	59 01	65·1	50 20	57 36	64·0	49 53	56 12	62·9	49 25	54 50	61·9	48 56	53 30	60·8	235	305
56	124	52 03	59 50	65·4	51 37	58 23	64·2	51 10	56 56	63·1	50 43	55 32	62·0	50 14	54 09	61·0	49 44	52 48	59·9	236	304
57	123	52 54	59 11	64·6	52 28	57 42	63·4	52 00	56 15	62·2	51 32	54 49	61·1	51 02	53 26	60·0	50 32	52 04	59·0	237	303
58	122	53 46	58 29	63·7	53 18	56 59	62·5	52 50	55 31	61·3	52 21	54 05	60·2	51 50	52 41	59·1	51 19	51 18	58·0	238	302
59	121	54 37	57 45	62·8	54 08	56 14	61·5	53 39	54 45	60·4	53 09	53 18	59·2	52 38	51 53	58·1	52 06	50 30	57·0	239	301
60	120	55 27	56 59	61·8	54 58	55 27	60·6	54 28	53 57	59·4	53 57	52 29	58·2	53 25	51 04	57·0	52 52	49 40	55·9	240	300
61	119	56 17	56 10	60·9	55 47	54 37	59·6	55 16	53 06	58·3	54 44	51 38	57·1	54 11	50 12	55·9	53 37	48 48	54·8	241	299
62	118	57 07	55 19	59·8	56 36	53 45	58·5	56 04	52 13	57·2	55 31	50 44	56·0	54 57	49 17	54·8	54 22	47 53	53·7	242	298
63	117	57 56	54 25	58·8	57 24	52 49	57·4	56 51	51 17	56·1	56 17	49 47	54·9	55 42	48 20	53·7	55 06	46 55	52·5	243	297
64	116	58 44	53 27	57·6	58 12	51 51	56·3	57 38	50 18	55·0	57 03	48 48	53·7	56 27	47 20	52·5	55 50	45 55	51·3	244	296
65	115	59 32	52 27	56·5	58 58	50 50	55·1	58 24	49 16	53·7	57 47	47 45	52·5	57 10	46 17	51·2	56 32	44 52	50·0	245	295
66	114	60 19	51 23	55·2	59 45	49 45	53·8	59 09	48 11	52·5	58 32	46 39	51·2	57 53	45 11	49·9	57 14	43 47	48·7	246	294
67	113	61 06	50 15	53·9	60 30	48 37	52·5	59 53	47 02	51·1	59 15	45 30	49·8	58 36	44 02	48·6	57 55	42 38	47·4	247	293
68	112	61 52	49 04	52·6	61 15	47 25	51·1	60 36	45 50	49·8	59 57	44 18	48·4	59 17	42 50	47·2	58 36	41 26	46·0	248	292
69	111	62 37	47 48	51·2	61 58	46 09	49·7	61 19	44 33	48·3	60 39	43 02	47·0	59 57	41 34	45·7	59 15	40 10	44·5	249	291
70	110	63 21	46 28	49·7	62 41	44 48	48·2	62 01	43 13	46·8	61 19	41 42	45·4	60 36	40 15	44·2	59 53	38 52	43·0	250	290
71	109	64 04	45 03	48·1	63 23	43 24	46·6	62 41	41 49	45·2	61 58	40 18	43·9	61 15	38 52	42·6	60 30	37 29	41·4	251	289
72	108	64 45	43 34	46·4	64 04	41 54	44·9	63 21	40 20	43·5	62 37	38 50	42·2	61 52	37 25	40·9	61 06	36 03	39·7	252	288
73	107	65 26	41 59	44·7	64 43	40 20	43·2	63 59	38 46	41·8	63 14	37 18	40·5	62 27	35 53	39·2	61 41	34 34	38·0	253	287
74	106	66 06	40 19	42·9	65 21	38 41	41·4	64 36	37 08	40·0	63 49	35 41	38·7	63 02	34 18	37·4	62 14	33 00	36·3	254	286
75	105	66 44	38 32	40·9	65 58	36 56	39·5	65 11	35 25	38·1	64 23	33 59	36·8	63 35	32 39	35·6	62 46	31 22	34·4	255	285
76	104	67 20	36 40	38·9	66 33	35 05	37·4	65 45	33 37	36·1	64 56	32 13	34·8	64 07	30 55	33·6	63 16	29 41	32·5	256	284
77	103	67 55	34 42	36·8	67 07	33 09	35·3	66 18	31 43	34·0	65 27	30 22	32·8	64 37	29 06	31·6	63 45	27 55	30·6	257	283
78	102	68 29	32 37	34·5	67 39	31 07	33·1	66 48	29 44	31·9	65 57	28 26	30·7	65 05	27 14	29·6	64 13	26 06	28·5	258	282
79	101	69 00	30 25	32·2	68 09	29 00	30·8	67 17	27 40	29·6	66 25	26 26	28·5	65 32	25 17	27·4	64 38	24 12	26·4	259	281
80	100	69 29	28 07	29·7	68 37	26 46	28·4	67 44	25 30	27·3	66 50	24 20	26·2	65 56	23 15	25·2	65 02	22 15	24·3	260	280
81	99	69 57	25 43	27·1	69 03	24 26	25·9	68 09	23 15	24·8	67 14	22 10	23·8	66 19	21 10	22·9	65 23	20 14	22·1	261	279
82	98	70 21	23 11	24·5	69 27	22 00	23·3	68 31	20 56	22·3	67 36	19 56	21·4	66 40	19 00	20·6	65 43	18 09	19·8	262	278
83	97	70 44	20 34	21·7	69 48	19 29	20·7	68 51	18 31	19·7	67 55	17 37	18·9	66 58	16 47	18·1	66 01	16 01	17·4	263	277
84	96	71 03	17 50	18·8	70 07	16 53	17·9	69 09	16 01	17·1	68 12	15 14	16·3	67 14	14 30	15·7	66 16	13 50	15·1	264	276
85	95	71 20	15 01	15·8	70 23	14 12	15·0	69 25	13 28	14·3	68 26	12 48	13·7	67 28	12 10	13·1	66 29	11 36	12·6	265	275
86	94	71 35	12 07	12·8	70 36	11 27	12·1	69 37	10 51	11·6	68 38	10 18	11·0	67 39	9 48	10·6	66 40	9 20	10·1	266	274
87	93	71 46	9 09	9·6	70 46	8 39	9·1	69 47	8 11	8·7	68 48	7 46	8·3	67 48	7 23	8·0	66 49	7 02	7·6	267	273
88	92	71 54	6 08	6·4	70 54	5 47	6·1	69 54	5 29	5·8	68 55	5 12	5·6	67 55	4 56	5·3	66 55	4 42	5·1	268	272
89	91	71 58	3 04	3·2	70 58	2 54	3·1	69 59	2 45	2·9	68 59	2 36	2·8	67 59	2 28	2·7	66 59	2 21	2·6	269	271
90	90	72 00	0 00	0·0	71 00	0 00	0·0	70 00	0 00	0·0	69 00	0 00	0·0	68 00	0 00	0·0	67 00	0 00	0·0	270	270

N. Lat: for LHA > 180° … $Z_n = Z$
for LHA < 180° … $Z_n = 360° - Z$

S. Lat.: for LHA > 180° … $Z_n = 180° - Z$
for LHA < 180° … $Z_n = 180° + Z$

SIGHT REDUCTION TABLE

B: (−) for 90° < LHA < 270°
Dec: (−) for Lat. contrary name

Z_1: same sign as B
Z_2: (−) for F > 90°

Lat. / A		24°			25°			26°			27°			28°			29°			Lat. / A	
LHA/F		A/H	B/P	Z_1/Z_2	A/H	B/P	Z_1/Z_2	A/H	B/P	Z_1/Z_2	A/H	B/P	Z_1/Z_2	A/H	B/P	Z_1/Z_2	A/H	B/P	Z_1/Z_2	LHA	
°	°	° ′	° ′	°	° ′	° ′	°	° ′	° ′	°	° ′	° ′	°	° ′	° ′	°	° ′	° ′	°	°	°
0	180	0 00	66 00	90·0	0 00	65 00	90·0	0 00	64 00	90·0	0 00	63 00	90·0	0 00	62 00	90·0	0 00	61 00	90·0	180	360
1	179	0 55	66 00	89·6	0 54	65 00	89·6	0 54	64 00	89·6	0 53	63 00	89·5	0 53	62 00	89·5	0 52	61 00	89·5	181	359
2	178	1 50	65 59	89·2	1 49	64 59	89·2	1 48	63 59	89·1	1 47	62 59	89·1	1 46	61 59	89·1	1 45	60 59	89·0	182	358
3	177	2 44	65 58	88·8	2 43	64 58	88·7	2 42	63 58	88·7	2 40	62 58	88·6	2 39	61 58	88·6	2 37	60 58	88·5	183	357
4	176	3 39	65 57	88·4	3 37	64 57	88·3	3 36	63 57	88·2	3 34	62 57	88·2	3 32	61 57	88·1	3 30	60 56	88·1	184	356
5	175	4 34	65 55	88·0	4 32	64 55	87·9	4 30	63 55	87·8	4 27	62 55	87·7	4 25	61 55	87·6	4 22	60 54	87·6	185	355
6	174	5 29	65 53	87·6	5 26	64 53	87·5	5 23	63 53	87·4	5 21	62 52	87·3	5 18	61 52	87·2	5 15	60 52	87·1	186	354
7	173	6 24	65 50	87·1	6 20	64 50	87·0	6 17	63 50	86·9	6 14	62 50	86·8	6 11	61 49	86·7	6 07	60 49	86·6	187	353
8	172	7 18	65 47	86·7	7 15	64 47	86·6	7 11	63 47	86·5	7 07	62 46	86·3	7 04	61 46	86·2	6 59	60 46	86·1	188	352
9	171	8 13	65 44	86·3	8 09	64 44	86·2	8 05	63 43	86·0	8 01	62 43	85·9	7 56	61 42	85·7	7 52	60 42	85·6	189	351
10	170	9 08	65 40	85·9	9 03	64 40	85·7	8 59	63 39	85·6	8 54	62 39	85·4	8 49	61 38	85·3	8 44	60 38	85·1	190	350
11	169	10 02	65 36	85·5	9 57	64 35	85·3	9 52	63 35	85·1	9 47	62 34	85·0	9 42	61 33	84·8	9 36	60 33	84·6	191	349
12	168	10 57	65 32	85·1	10 52	64 31	84·9	10 46	63 30	84·7	10 41	62 29	84·5	10 35	61 28	84·3	10 29	60 28	84·1	192	348
13	167	11 52	65 27	84·6	11 46	64 26	84·4	11 40	63 25	84·2	11 34	62 24	84·0	11 27	61 23	83·8	11 21	60 22	83·6	193	347
14	166	12 46	65 21	84·2	12 40	64 20	84·0	12 34	63 19	83·8	12 27	62 18	83·5	12 20	61 17	83·3	12 13	60 16	83·1	194	346
15	165	13 41	65 15	83·8	13 34	64 14	83·5	13 27	63 13	83·3	13 20	62 11	83·1	13 13	61 10	82·8	13 05	60 09	82·6	195	345
16	164	14 35	65 09	83·3	14 28	64 07	83·1	14 21	63 06	82·8	14 13	62 04	82·6	14 05	61 03	82·3	13 57	60 02	82·1	196	344
17	163	15 29	65 02	82·9	15 22	64 00	82·6	15 14	62 59	82·4	15 06	61 57	82·1	14 58	60 56	81·8	14 49	59 54	81·6	197	343
18	162	16 24	64 55	82·5	16 16	63 53	82·2	16 08	62 51	81·9	15 59	61 49	81·6	15 50	60 47	81·3	15 41	59 46	81·0	198	342
19	161	17 18	64 47	82·0	17 10	63 45	81·7	17 01	62 43	81·4	16 52	61 41	81·1	16 42	60 39	80·8	16 33	59 37	80·5	199	341
20	160	18 12	64 39	81·6	18 03	63 36	81·3	17 54	62 34	80·9	17 45	61 32	80·6	17 35	60 30	80·3	17 24	59 28	80·0	200	340
21	159	19 07	64 30	81·1	18 57	63 28	80·8	18 47	62 25	80·4	18 37	61 23	80·1	18 27	60 20	79·8	18 16	59 18	79·5	201	339
22	158	20 01	64 21	80·7	19 51	63 18	80·3	19 41	62 15	80·0	19 30	61 13	79·6	19 19	60 10	79·3	19 08	59 08	78·9	202	338
23	157	20 55	64 11	80·2	20 44	63 08	79·8	20 34	62 05	79·5	20 22	61 02	79·1	20 11	59 59	78·7	19 59	58 57	78·4	203	337
24	156	21 49	64 01	79·7	21 38	62 58	79·3	21 27	61 54	79·0	21 15	60 51	78·6	21 03	59 48	78·2	20 50	58 45	77·8	204	336
25	155	22 43	63 50	79·3	22 31	62 46	78·9	22 19	61 43	78·4	22 07	60 39	78·0	21 55	59 36	77·7	21 42	58 33	77·3	205	335
26	154	23 36	63 39	78·8	23 25	62 35	78·4	23 12	61 31	77·9	22 59	60 27	77·5	22 46	59 24	77·1	22 33	58 20	76·7	206	334
27	153	24 30	63 27	78·3	24 18	62 22	77·8	24 05	61 18	77·4	23 52	60 14	77·0	23 38	59 10	76·5	23 24	58 07	76·1	207	333
28	152	25 24	63 14	77·8	25 11	62 10	77·3	24 57	61 05	76·9	24 44	60 01	76·4	24 29	58 57	76·0	24 15	57 53	75·5	208	332
29	151	26 17	63 01	77·3	26 04	61 56	76·8	25 50	60 51	76·3	25 36	59 47	75·9	25 21	58 42	75·4	25 05	57 38	75·0	209	331
30	150	27 11	62 48	76·8	26 57	61 42	76·3	26 42	60 37	75·8	26 27	59 32	75·3	26 12	58 27	74·8	25 56	57 23	74·4	210	330
31	149	28 04	62 33	76·3	27 50	61 27	75·8	27 35	60 22	75·2	27 19	59 16	74·7	27 03	58 11	74·2	26 46	57 07	73·8	211	329
32	148	28 57	62 18	75·7	28 42	61 12	75·2	28 27	60 06	74·7	28 10	59 00	74·2	27 54	57 55	73·7	27 37	56 50	73·1	212	328
33	147	29 50	62 02	75·2	29 35	60 56	74·7	29 19	59 49	74·1	29 02	58 43	73·6	28 45	57 38	73·0	28 27	56 32	72·5	213	327
34	146	30 43	61 46	74·7	30 27	60 39	74·1	30 10	59 32	73·5	29 53	58 26	73·0	29 35	57 20	72·4	29 17	56 14	71·9	214	326
35	145	31 36	61 28	74·1	31 19	60 21	73·5	31 02	59 14	72·9	30 44	58 07	72·4	30 26	57 01	71·8	30 07	55 55	71·2	215	325
36	144	32 29	61 10	73·5	32 11	60 02	72·9	31 53	58 55	72·3	31 35	57 48	71·7	31 16	56 41	71·2	30 56	55 35	70·6	216	324
37	143	33 21	60 52	73·0	33 03	59 43	72·3	32 45	58 35	71·7	32 26	57 28	71·1	32 06	56 21	70·5	31 46	55 14	69·9	217	323
38	142	34 13	60 32	72·4	33 55	59 23	71·7	33 36	58 15	71·1	33 16	57 07	70·5	32 56	55 59	69·9	32 35	54 53	69·3	218	322
39	141	35 06	60 11	71·8	34 47	59 02	71·1	34 27	57 53	70·5	34 06	56 45	69·8	33 45	55 37	69·2	33 24	54 30	68·6	219	321
40	140	35 58	59 50	71·2	35 38	58 40	70·5	35 17	57 31	69·8	34 56	56 22	69·1	34 35	55 14	68·5	34 12	54 07	67·9	220	320
41	139	36 49	59 28	70·5	36 29	58 17	69·8	36 08	57 08	69·1	35 46	55 59	68·5	35 24	54 50	67·8	35 01	53 42	67·1	221	319
42	138	37 41	59 04	69·9	37 20	57 54	69·2	36 58	56 43	68·5	36 36	55 34	67·8	36 13	54 25	67·1	35 49	53 17	66·4	222	318
43	137	38 32	58 40	69·2	38 11	57 29	68·5	37 48	56 18	67·8	37 25	55 08	67·1	37 02	53 59	66·4	36 37	52 50	65·7	223	317
44	136	39 23	58 15	68·6	39 01	57 03	67·8	38 38	55 52	67·1	38 14	54 41	66·3	37 50	53 32	65·6	37 25	52 23	64·9	224	316
45	135	40 14	57 48	67·9	39 51	56 36	67·1	39 28	55 24	66·3	39 03	54 13	65·6	38 38	53 04	64·9	38 12	51 54	64·1	225	315

Lat. / A		24°			25°			26°			27°			28°			29°			Lat. / A	
LHA/F		A/H	B/P	Z_1/Z_2	A/H	B/P	Z_1/Z_2	A/H	B/P	Z_1/Z_2	A/H	B/P	Z_1/Z_2	A/H	B/P	Z_1/Z_2	A/H	B/P	Z_1/Z_2	LHA	
°	°	° ′	° ′	°	° ′	° ′	°	° ′	° ′	°	° ′	° ′	°	° ′	° ′	°	° ′	° ′	°	°	°
45	135	40 14	57 48	67·9	39 51	56 36	67·1	39 28	55 24	66·3	39 03	54 13	65·6	38 38	53 04	64·9	38 12	51 54	64·1	225	315
46	134	41 05	57 21	67·2	40 41	56 08	66·4	40 17	54 56	65·6	39 52	53 44	64·8	39 26	52 34	64·1	38 59	51 25	63·3	226	314
47	133	41 55	56 52	66·4	41 31	55 38	65·6	41 06	54 26	64·8	40 40	53 14	64·0	40 13	52 04	63·3	39 46	50 54	62·5	227	313
48	132	42 45	56 22	65·7	42 20	55 08	64·9	41 54	53 55	64·0	41 28	52 43	63·2	41 00	51 32	62·5	40 32	50 22	61·7	228	312
49	131	43 35	55 50	64·9	43 09	54 36	64·1	42 43	53 22	63·2	42 15	52 10	62·4	41 47	50 59	61·6	41 18	49 48	60·9	229	311
50	130	44 25	55 17	64·1	43 58	54 02	63·3	43 31	52 49	62·4	43 03	51 36	61·6	42 34	50 24	60·8	42 04	49 14	60·0	230	310
51	129	45 14	54 43	63·3	44 47	53 28	62·4	44 18	52 13	61·6	43 49	51 00	60·7	43 20	49 48	59·9	42 49	48 38	59·1	231	309
52	128	46 03	54 08	62·5	45 35	52 52	61·6	45 06	51 37	60·7	44 36	50 23	59·8	44 05	49 11	59·0	43 34	48 00	58·2	232	308
53	127	46 51	53 30	61·6	46 22	52 14	60·7	45 52	50 59	59·8	45 22	49 45	58·9	44 51	48 32	58·1	44 18	47 21	57·2	233	307
54	126	47 39	52 51	60·8	47 09	51 34	59·8	46 39	50 19	58·9	46 07	49 05	58·0	45 35	47 52	57·1	45 02	46 41	56·3	234	306
55	125	48 27	52 11	59·8	47 56	50 53	58·9	47 25	49 37	58·0	46 53	48 23	57·0	46 19	47 10	56·2	45 46	45 59	55·3	235	305
56	124	49 14	51 28	58·9	48 43	50 11	57·9	48 10	48 54	57·0	47 37	47 40	56·1	47 03	46 27	55·2	46 29	45 15	54·3	236	304
57	123	50 01	50 44	57·9	49 28	49 26	56·9	48 55	48 09	56·0	48 21	46 54	55·0	47 46	45 41	54·1	47 11	44 30	53·3	237	303
58	122	50 47	49 58	56·9	50 14	48 39	55·9	49 40	47 22	54·9	49 05	46 07	54·0	48 29	44 54	53·1	47 53	43 43	52·2	238	302
59	121	51 33	49 09	55·9	50 58	47 51	54·9	50 23	46 34	53·9	49 48	45 18	52·9	49 11	44 05	52·0	48 34	42 54	51·1	239	301
60	120	52 18	48 19	54·8	51 43	47 00	53·8	51 07	45 43	52·8	50 30	44 28	51·8	49 53	43 14	50·9	49 14	42 03	50·0	240	300
61	119	53 02	47 26	53·7	52 26	46 07	52·7	51 49	44 50	51·7	51 12	43 35	50·7	50 33	42 22	49·7	49 54	41 10	48·8	241	299
62	118	53 46	46 31	52·6	53 09	45 12	51·5	52 31	43 54	50·5	51 53	42 39	49·5	51 13	41 27	48·6	50 33	40 16	47·6	242	298
63	117	54 29	45 33	51·4	53 51	44 14	50·3	53 13	42 57	49·3	52 33	41 42	48·3	51 53	40 30	47·3	51 12	39 19	46·4	243	297
64	116	55 12	44 33	50·2	54 33	43 14	49·1	53 53	41 57	48·1	53 13	40 42	47·1	52 31	39 30	46·1	51 49	38 20	45·2	244	296
65	115	55 53	43 30	48·9	55 13	42 11	47·8	54 33	40 55	46·8	53 51	39 40	45·8	53 09	38 29	44·8	52 26	37 19	43·9	245	295
66	114	56 34	42 25	47·6	55 53	41 06	46·5	55 12	39 50	45·4	54 29	38 36	44·4	53 46	37 25	43·5	53 02	36 16	42·6	246	294
67	113	57 14	41 16	46·2	56 32	39 58	45·1	55 50	38 42	44·1	55 06	37 29	43·1	54 22	36 19	42·1	53 37	35 11	41·2	247	293
68	112	57 53	40 05	44·8	57 10	38 47	43·7	56 27	37 32	42·7	55 42	36 19	41·7	54 57	35 10	40·7	54 11	34 03	39·8	248	292
69	111	58 32	38 50	43·3	57 47	37 33	42·2	57 03	36 18	41·2	56 17	35 07	40·2	55 31	33 59	39·3	54 44	32 53	38·4	249	291
70	110	59 09	37 32	41·8	58 24	36 16	40·7	57 38	35 02	39·7	56 51	33 52	38·7	56 04	32 45	37·8	55 16	31 41	36·9	250	290
71	109	59 45	36 11	40·2	58 58	34 55	39·2	58 12	33 43	38·1	57 24	32 35	37·2	56 36	31 29	36·3	55 47	30 26	35·4	251	289
72	108	60 19	34 46	38·6	59 32	33 32	37·6	58 44	32 21	36·5	57 56	31 14	35·6	57 07	30 10	34·7	56 17	29 08	33·8	252	288
73	107	60 53	33 18	36·9	60 05	32 05	35·9	59 16	30 56	34·9	58 26	29 51	34·0	57 36	28 48	33·1	56 46	27 49	32·2	253	287
74	106	61 25	31 46	35·2	60 36	30 35	34·2	59 46	29 28	33·2	58 55	28 25	32·3	58 05	27 24	31·4	57 13	26 26	30·6	254	286
75	105	61 56	30 10	33·4	61 06	29 02	32·4	60 15	27 57	31·4	59 23	26 56	30·5	58 31	25 57	29·7	57 39	25 02	28·9	255	285
76	104	62 26	28 31	31·5	61 34	27 25	30·5	60 42	26 23	29·6	59 50	25 24	28·8	58 57	24 28	28·0	58 04	23 35	27·2	256	284
77	103	62 53	26 48	29·6	62 01	25 45	28·6	61 08	24 46	27·8	60 15	23 49	27·0	59 21	22 56	26·2	58 27	22 05	25·5	257	283
78	102	63 20	25 02	27·6	62 26	24 02	26·7	61 32	23 05	25·9	60 38	22 12	25·1	59 44	21 21	24·4	58 49	20 34	23·7	258	282
79	101	63 44	23 12	25·5	62 50	22 15	24·7	61 55	21 22	23·9	61 00	20 32	23·2	60 05	19 44	22·5	59 09	19 00	21·8	259	281
80	100	64 07	21 18	23·4	63 12	20 25	22·6	62 16	19 36	21·9	61 20	18 49	21·2	60 24	18 05	20·6	59 28	17 24	20·0	260	280
81	99	64 28	19 22	21·3	63 32	18 33	20·5	62 35	17 47	19·9	61 39	17 04	19·2	60 42	16 24	18·6	59 45	15 46	18·1	261	279
82	98	64 47	17 22	19·1	63 50	16 37	18·4	62 53	15 56	17·8	61 56	15 17	17·2	60 58	14 40	16·7	60 01	14 06	16·2	262	278
83	97	65 03	15 18	16·8	64 06	14 39	16·2	63 08	14 02	15·6	62 10	13 27	15·1	61 12	12 55	14·7	60 14	12 24	14·2	263	277
84	96	65 18	13 13	14·5	64 20	12 38	14·0	63 22	12 06	13·5	62 23	11 36	13·0	61 25	11 07	12·6	60 26	10 41	12·2	264	276
85	95	65 31	11 05	12·1	64 32	10 35	11·7	63 33	10 08	11·3	62 35	9 42	10·9	61 36	9 19	10·6	60 37	8 56	10·2	265	275
86	94	65 41	8 54	9·8	64 42	8 30	9·4	63 43	8 08	9·1	62 44	7 48	8·8	61 44	7 28	8·5	60 45	7 10	8·2	266	274
87	93	65 49	6 42	7·3	64 50	6 24	7·1	63 50	6 07	6·8	62 51	5 52	6·6	61 51	5 37	6·4	60 52	5 24	6·2	267	273
88	92	65 55	4 29	4·9	64 56	4 17	4·7	63 56	4 06	4·6	62 56	3 55	4·4	61 56	3 45	4·3	60 56	3 36	4·1	268	272
89	91	65 59	2 15	2·5	64 59	2 09	2·4	63 59	2 03	2·3	62 59	1 58	2·2	61 59	1 53	2·1	60 59	1 48	2·1	269	271
90	90	66 00	0 00	0·0	65 00	0 00	0·0	64 00	0 00	0·0	63 00	0 00	0·0	62 00	0 00	0·0	61 00	0 00	0·0	270	270

N. Lat: for LHA > 180° … $Z_n = Z$
for LHA < 180° … $Z_n = 360° - Z$

S. Lat.: for LHA > 180° … $Z_n = 180° - Z$
for LHA < 180° … $Z_n = 180° + Z$

SIGHT REDUCTION TABLE

B: (–) for 90° < LHA < 270°
Dec:(–) for Lat. contrary name

Z_1: same sign as B
Z_2: (–) for F > 90°

Lat. / A		30°			31°			32°			33°			34°			35°			Lat. / A	
LHA/F		A/H	B/P	Z_1/Z_2	A/H	B/P	Z_1/Z_2	A/H	B/P	Z_1/Z_2	A/H	B/P	Z_1/Z_2	A/H	B/P	Z_1/Z_2	A/H	B/P	Z_1/Z_2	LHA	
°	°	° ′	° ′	°	° ′	° ′	°	° ′	° ′	°	° ′	° ′	°	° ′	° ′	°	° ′	° ′	°	°	°
0	180	0 00	60 00	90·0	0 00	59 00	90·0	0 00	58 00	90·0	0 00	57 00	90·0	0 00	56 00	90·0	0 00	55 00	90·0	180	360
1	179	0 52	60 00	89·5	0 51	59 00	89·5	0 51	58 00	89·5	0 50	57 00	89·5	0 50	56 00	89·4	0 49	55 00	89·4	181	359
2	178	1 44	59 59	89·0	1 43	58 59	89·0	1 42	57 59	88·9	1 41	56 59	88·9	1 39	55 59	88·9	1 38	54 59	88·9	182	358
3	177	2 36	59 58	88·5	2 34	58 58	88·5	2 33	57 58	88·4	2 31	56 58	88·4	2 29	55 58	88·3	2 27	54 58	88·3	183	357
4	176	3 28	59 56	88·0	3 26	58 56	87·9	3 23	57 56	87·9	3 21	56 56	87·8	3 19	55 56	87·8	3 17	54 56	87·7	184	356
5	175	4 20	59 54	87·5	4 17	58 54	87·4	4 14	57 54	87·3	4 12	56 54	87·3	4 09	55 54	87·2	4 06	54 54	87·1	185	355
6	174	5 12	59 52	87·0	5 08	58 52	86·9	5 05	57 52	86·8	5 02	56 51	86·7	4 58	55 51	86·6	4 55	54 51	86·6	186	354
7	173	6 04	59 49	86·5	6 00	58 49	86·4	5 56	57 48	86·3	5 52	56 48	86·2	5 48	55 48	86·1	5 44	54 48	86·0	187	353
8	172	6 55	59 45	86·0	6 51	58 45	85·9	6 47	57 45	85·7	6 42	56 45	85·6	6 38	55 44	85·5	6 33	54 44	85·4	188	352
9	171	7 47	59 42	85·5	7 42	58 41	85·3	7 37	57 41	85·2	7 32	56 40	85·1	7 27	55 40	84·9	7 22	54 40	84·8	189	351
10	170	8 39	59 37	85·0	8 34	58 37	84·8	8 28	57 36	84·7	8 22	56 36	84·5	8 17	55 36	84·4	8 11	54 35	84·2	190	350
11	169	9 31	59 32	84·4	9 25	58 32	84·3	9 19	57 31	84·1	9 13	56 31	84·0	9 06	55 30	83·8	9 00	54 30	83·6	191	349
12	168	10 22	59 27	83·9	10 16	58 26	83·8	10 09	57 26	83·6	10 03	56 25	83·4	9 56	55 25	83·2	9 48	54 24	83·0	192	348
13	167	11 14	59 21	83·4	11 07	58 20	83·2	11 00	57 20	83·0	10 52	56 19	82·8	10 45	55 18	82·6	10 37	54 18	82·5	193	347
14	166	12 06	59 15	82·9	11 58	58 14	82·7	11 50	57 13	82·5	11 42	56 12	82·3	11 34	55 12	82·1	11 26	54 11	81·9	194	346
15	165	12 57	59 08	82·4	12 49	58 07	82·1	12 41	57 06	81·9	12 32	56 05	81·7	12 23	55 04	81·5	12 14	54 04	81·3	195	345
16	164	13 49	59 01	81·8	13 40	57 59	81·6	13 31	56 58	81·4	13 22	55 57	81·1	13 13	54 57	80·9	13 03	53 56	80·7	196	344
17	163	14 40	58 53	81·3	14 31	57 51	81·1	14 21	56 50	80·8	14 12	55 49	80·5	14 02	54 48	80·3	13 51	53 47	80·1	197	343
18	162	15 31	58 44	80·8	15 22	57 43	80·5	15 12	56 42	80·2	15 01	55 40	80·0	14 51	54 39	79·7	14 40	53 38	79·4	198	342
19	161	16 23	58 35	80·2	16 12	57 34	79·9	16 02	56 32	79·7	15 51	55 31	79·4	15 40	54 30	79·1	15 28	53 29	78·8	199	341
20	160	17 14	58 26	79·7	17 03	57 24	79·4	16 52	56 23	79·1	16 40	55 21	78·8	16 28	54 20	78·5	16 16	53 19	78·2	200	340
21	159	18 05	58 16	79·1	17 53	57 14	78·8	17 42	56 12	78·5	17 29	55 11	78·2	17 17	54 09	77·9	17 04	53 08	77·6	201	339
22	158	18 56	58 05	78·6	18 44	57 03	78·2	18 31	56 01	77·9	18 19	55 00	77·6	18 06	53 58	77·3	17 52	52 56	77·0	202	338
23	157	19 47	57 54	78·0	19 34	56 52	77·7	19 21	55 50	77·3	19 08	54 48	77·0	18 54	53 46	76·6	18 40	52 44	76·3	203	337
24	156	20 37	57 42	77·4	20 24	56 40	77·1	20 11	55 38	76·7	19 57	54 36	76·4	19 42	53 34	76·0	19 28	52 32	75·7	204	336
25	155	21 28	57 30	76·9	21 14	56 27	76·5	21 00	55 25	76·1	20 46	54 23	75·7	20 31	53 21	75·4	20 15	52 19	75·0	205	335
26	154	22 19	57 17	76·3	22 04	56 14	75·9	21 49	55 12	75·5	21 34	54 09	75·1	21 19	53 07	74·7	21 03	52 05	74·4	206	334
27	153	23 09	57 03	75·7	22 54	56 00	75·3	22 39	54 57	74·9	22 23	53 55	74·5	22 07	52 52	74·1	21 50	51 50	73·7	207	333
28	152	23 59	56 49	75·1	23 44	55 46	74·7	23 28	54 43	74·3	23 11	53 40	73·8	22 54	52 37	73·4	22 37	51 35	73·0	208	332
29	151	24 50	56 34	74·5	24 33	55 31	74·1	24 17	54 27	73·6	23 59	53 24	73·2	23 42	52 22	72·8	23 24	51 19	72·4	209	331
30	150	25 40	56 19	73·9	25 23	55 15	73·4	25 05	54 11	73·0	24 48	53 08	72·5	24 29	52 05	72·1	24 11	51 03	71·7	210	330
31	149	26 29	56 02	73·3	26 12	54 58	72·8	25 54	53 54	72·3	25 35	52 51	71·9	25 17	51 48	71·4	24 57	50 45	71·0	211	329
32	148	27 19	55 45	72·6	27 01	54 41	72·2	26 42	53 37	71·7	26 23	52 33	71·2	26 04	51 30	70·7	25 44	50 27	70·3	212	328
33	147	28 09	55 27	72·0	27 50	54 23	71·5	27 31	53 19	71·0	27 11	52 15	70·5	26 50	51 12	70·0	26 30	50 08	69·6	213	327
34	146	28 58	55 09	71·4	28 38	54 04	70·8	28 19	53 00	70·3	27 58	51 56	69·8	27 37	50 52	69·3	27 16	49 49	68·8	214	326
35	145	29 47	54 49	70·7	29 27	53 44	70·2	29 06	52 40	69·6	28 45	51 36	69·1	28 24	50 32	68·6	28 01	49 29	68·1	215	325
36	144	30 36	54 29	70·0	30 15	53 24	69·5	29 54	52 19	68·9	29 32	51 15	68·4	29 10	50 11	67·9	28 47	49 07	67·4	216	324
37	143	31 25	54 08	69·4	31 03	53 03	68·8	30 41	51 58	68·2	30 19	50 53	67·7	29 56	49 49	67·2	29 32	48 45	66·6	217	323
38	142	32 13	53 46	68·7	31 51	52 40	68·1	31 28	51 35	67·5	31 05	50 30	66·9	30 41	49 26	66·4	30 17	48 23	65·9	218	322
39	141	33 02	53 23	68·0	32 39	52 17	67·4	32 15	51 12	66·8	31 51	50 07	66·2	31 27	49 03	65·6	31 02	47 59	65·1	219	321
40	140	33 50	53 00	67·2	33 26	51 53	66·6	33 02	50 48	66·0	32 37	49 43	65·4	32 12	48 38	64·9	31 46	47 34	64·3	220	320
41	139	34 37	52 35	66·5	34 13	51 29	65·9	33 48	50 23	65·3	33 23	49 17	64·7	32 57	48 13	64·1	32 30	47 09	63·5	221	319
42	138	35 25	52 09	65·8	35 00	51 03	65·1	34 34	49 56	64·5	34 08	48 51	63·9	33 42	47 46	63·3	33 14	46 42	62·7	222	318
43	137	36 12	51 43	65·0	35 46	50 36	64·3	35 20	49 29	63·7	34 53	48 24	63·1	34 26	47 19	62·5	33 58	46 15	61·9	223	317
44	136	36 59	51 15	64·2	36 33	50 08	63·6	36 06	49 01	62·9	35 38	47 55	62·3	35 10	46 51	61·6	34 41	45 46	61·0	224	316
45	135	37 46	50 46	63·4	37 19	49 39	62·7	36 51	48 32	62·1	36 22	47 26	61·4	35 53	46 21	60·8	35 24	45 17	60·2	225	315

Lat. / A		30°			31°			32°			33°			34°			35°			Lat. / A	
LHA/F		A/H	B/P	Z_1/Z_2	A/H	B/P	Z_1/Z_2	A/H	B/P	Z_1/Z_2	A/H	B/P	Z_1/Z_2	A/H	B/P	Z_1/Z_2	A/H	B/P	Z_1/Z_2	LHA	
°	°	° ′	° ′	°	° ′	° ′	°	° ′	° ′	°	° ′	° ′	°	° ′	° ′	°	° ′	° ′	°	°	°
45	135	37 46	50 46	63·4	37 19	49 39	62·7	36 51	48 32	62·1	36 22	47 26	61·4	35 53	46 21	60·8	35 24	45 17	60·2	225	315
46	134	38 32	50 16	62·6	38 04	49 08	61·9	37 36	48 02	61·2	37 06	46 56	60·6	36 37	45 51	59·9	36 06	44 46	59·3	226	314
47	133	39 18	49 45	61·8	38 49	48 37	61·1	38 20	47 30	60·4	37 50	46 24	59·7	37 19	45 19	59·1	36 48	44 15	58·4	227	313
48	132	40 04	49 13	61·0	39 34	48 05	60·2	39 04	46 58	59·5	38 33	45 51	58·8	38 02	44 46	58·2	37 30	43 42	57·5	228	312
49	131	40 49	48 39	60·1	40 19	47 31	59·4	39 48	46 24	58·6	39 16	45 18	57·9	38 44	44 12	57·2	38 11	43 08	56·6	229	311
50	130	41 34	48 04	59·2	41 03	46 56	58·5	40 31	45 49	57·7	39 59	44 42	57·0	39 26	43 37	56·3	38 52	42 33	55·6	230	310
51	129	42 18	47 28	58·3	41 46	46 20	57·5	41 14	45 12	56·8	40 41	44 06	56·1	40 07	43 01	55·4	39 32	41 57	54·7	231	309
52	128	43 02	46 50	57·4	42 29	45 42	56·6	41 56	44 34	55·9	41 22	43 28	55·1	40 47	42 23	54·4	40 12	41 19	53·7	232	308
53	127	43 46	46 11	56·4	43 12	45 03	55·6	42 38	43 55	54·9	42 03	42 49	54·1	41 28	41 44	53·4	40 52	40 41	52·7	233	307
54	126	44 29	45 31	55·5	43 54	44 22	54·7	43 19	43 15	53·9	42 44	42 09	53·1	42 07	41 04	52·4	41 30	40 01	51·7	234	306
55	125	45 11	44 49	54·5	44 36	43 40	53·7	44 00	42 33	52·9	43 24	41 27	52·1	42 46	40 23	51·4	42 09	39 19	50·7	235	305
56	124	45 53	44 05	53·5	45 17	42 57	52·6	44 40	41 50	51·8	44 03	40 44	51·1	43 25	39 40	50·3	42 46	38 37	49·6	236	304
57	123	46 35	43 20	52·4	45 58	42 11	51·6	45 20	41 05	50·8	44 42	39 59	50·0	44 03	38 55	49·3	43 24	37 53	48·5	237	303
58	122	47 16	42 33	51·3	46 38	41 25	50·5	45 59	40 18	49·7	45 20	39 13	48·9	44 40	38 09	48·2	44 00	37 07	47·5	238	302
59	121	47 56	41 44	50·2	47 17	40 36	49·4	46 38	39 30	48·6	45 58	38 25	47·8	45 17	37 22	47·1	44 36	36 20	46·3	239	301
60	120	48 35	40 54	49·1	47 56	39 46	48·3	47 16	38 40	47·5	46 35	37 36	46·7	45 53	36 33	45·9	45 11	35 32	45·2	240	300
61	119	49 14	40 01	47·9	48 34	38 54	47·1	47 53	37 48	46·3	47 11	36 45	45·5	46 29	35 42	44·7	45 46	34 42	44·0	241	299
62	118	49 53	39 07	46·8	49 11	38 00	45·9	48 29	36 55	45·1	47 46	35 52	44·3	47 03	34 50	43·6	46 19	33 50	42·8	242	298
63	117	50 30	38 11	45·5	49 48	37 04	44·7	49 05	36 00	43·9	48 21	34 57	43·1	47 37	33 57	42·3	46 53	32 57	41·6	243	297
64	116	51 07	37 13	44·3	50 23	36 07	43·4	49 40	35 03	42·6	48 55	34 01	41·8	48 10	33 01	41·1	47 25	32 03	40·4	244	296
65	115	51 43	36 12	43·0	50 58	35 07	42·2	50 14	34 04	41·3	49 28	33 03	40·6	48 43	32 04	39·8	47 56	31 07	39·1	245	295
66	114	52 18	35 10	41·7	51 33	34 06	40·8	50 47	33 04	40·0	50 01	32 04	39·3	49 14	31 05	38·5	48 27	30 09	37·8	246	294
67	113	52 52	34 05	40·3	52 06	33 02	39·5	51 19	32 01	38·7	50 32	31 02	37·9	49 44	30 05	37·2	48 56	29 10	36·5	247	293
68	112	53 25	32 59	38·9	52 38	31 56	38·1	51 50	30 57	37·3	51 02	29 59	36·6	50 14	29 03	35·8	49 25	28 09	35·2	248	292
69	111	53 57	31 50	37·5	53 09	30 49	36·7	52 21	29 50	35·9	51 32	28 53	35·2	50 43	27 59	34·5	49 53	27 06	33·8	249	291
70	110	54 28	30 39	36·1	53 39	29 39	35·2	52 50	28 42	34·5	52 00	27 46	33·8	51 10	26 53	33·1	50 20	26 02	32·4	250	290
71	109	54 58	29 25	34·6	54 08	28 27	33·8	53 18	27 31	33·0	52 28	26 38	32·3	51 37	25 46	31·6	50 46	24 56	31·0	251	289
72	108	55 27	28 09	33·0	54 37	27 13	32·2	53 46	26 19	31·5	52 54	25 27	30·8	52 03	24 37	30·2	51 10	23 49	29·5	252	288
73	107	55 55	26 51	31·4	55 03	25 57	30·7	54 12	25 04	30·0	53 19	24 14	29·3	52 27	23 26	28·7	51 34	22 40	28·1	253	287
74	106	56 21	25 31	29·8	55 29	24 39	29·1	54 36	23 48	28·4	53 43	23 00	27·8	52 50	22 14	27·1	51 57	21 29	26·6	254	286
75	105	56 46	24 09	28·2	55 53	23 18	27·5	55 00	22 30	26·8	54 06	21 44	26·2	53 12	21 00	25·6	52 18	20 17	25·0	255	285
76	104	57 10	22 44	26·5	56 16	21 56	25·8	55 22	21 10	25·2	54 28	20 26	24·6	53 33	19 44	24·0	52 38	19 04	23·5	256	284
77	103	57 33	21 17	24·8	56 38	20 31	24·1	55 43	19 48	23·5	54 48	19 06	23·0	53 53	18 27	22·4	52 57	17 49	21·9	257	283
78	102	57 54	19 48	23·0	56 59	19 05	22·4	56 03	18 24	21·9	55 07	17 45	21·3	54 11	17 08	20·8	53 15	16 32	20·3	258	282
79	101	58 13	18 17	21·2	57 17	17 37	20·7	56 21	16 59	20·1	55 25	16 22	19·6	54 28	15 48	19·2	53 31	15 15	18·7	259	281
80	100	58 32	16 44	19·4	57 35	16 07	18·9	56 38	15 32	18·4	55 41	14 58	17·9	54 44	14 26	17·5	53 47	13 56	17·1	260	280
81	99	58 48	15 10	17·6	57 51	14 36	17·1	56 53	14 03	16·6	55 56	13 33	16·2	54 58	13 03	15·8	54 00	12 36	15·4	261	279
82	98	59 03	13 33	15·7	58 05	13 02	15·3	57 07	12 33	14·9	56 09	12 06	14·5	55 11	11 40	14·1	54 13	11 14	13·8	262	278
83	97	59 16	11 55	13·8	58 18	11 28	13·4	57 19	11 02	13·0	56 21	10 38	12·7	55 22	10 14	12·4	54 24	9 52	12·1	263	277
84	96	59 28	10 16	11·9	58 29	9 52	11·5	57 30	9 30	11·2	56 31	9 09	10·9	55 32	8 49	10·6	54 33	8 29	10·4	264	276
85	95	59 37	8 35	9·9	58 38	8 15	9·6	57 39	7 56	9·4	56 40	7 39	9·1	55 41	7 22	8·9	54 41	7 06	8·7	265	275
86	94	59 46	6 53	8·0	58 46	6 37	7·7	57 47	6 22	7·5	56 47	6 08	7·3	55 48	5 54	7·1	54 48	5 41	7·0	266	274
87	93	59 52	5 11	6·0	58 52	4 59	5·8	57 52	4 47	5·6	56 53	4 36	5·5	55 53	4 26	5·4	54 53	4 16	5·2	267	273
88	92	59 56	3 28	4·0	58 57	3 19	3·9	57 57	3 12	3·8	56 57	3 05	3·7	55 57	2 58	3·6	54 57	2 51	3·5	268	272
89	91	59 59	1 44	2·0	58 59	1 40	1·9	57 59	1 36	1·9	56 59	1 32	1·8	55 59	1 29	1·8	54 59	1 26	1·7	269	271
90	90	60 00	0 00	0·0	59 00	0 00	0·0	58 00	0 00	0·0	57 00	0 00	0·0	56 00	0 00	0·0	55 00	0 00	0·0	270	270

N. Lat: for LHA > 180° … $Z_n = Z$
for LHA < 180° … $Z_n = 360° - Z$

S. Lat.: for LHA > 180° … $Z_n = 180° - Z$
for LHA < 180° … $Z_n = 180° + Z$

SIGHT REDUCTION TABLE

B: (–) for 90° < LHA < 270°
Dec:(–) for Lat. contrary name

Z_1: same sign as B
Z_2: (–) for F > 90°

Lat. / A		36°			37°			38°			39°			40°			41°			Lat. / A	
LHA/F		A/H	B/P	Z_1/Z_2	A/H	B/P	Z_1/Z_2	A/H	B/P	Z_1/Z_2	A/H	B/P	Z_1/Z_2	A/H	B/P	Z_1/Z_2	A/H	B/P	Z_1/Z_2	LHA	
°	°	° ′	° ′	°	° ′	° ′	°	° ′	° ′	°	° ′	° ′	°	° ′	° ′	°	° ′	° ′	°	°	°
0	180	0 00	54 00	90·0	0 00	53 00	90·0	0 00	52 00	90·0	0 00	51 00	90·0	0 00	50 00	90·0	0 00	49 00	90·0	180	360
1	179	0 49	54 00	89·4	0 48	53 00	89·4	0 47	52 00	89·4	0 47	51 00	89·4	0 46	50 00	89·4	0 45	49 00	89·3	181	359
2	178	1 37	53 59	88·8	1 36	52 59	88·8	1 35	51 59	88·8	1 33	50 59	88·7	1 32	49 59	88·7	1 31	48 59	88·7	182	358
3	177	2 26	53 58	88·2	2 24	52 58	88·2	2 22	51 58	88·2	2 20	50 58	88·1	2 18	49 58	88·1	2 16	48 58	88·0	183	357
4	176	3 14	53 56	87·6	3 12	52 56	87·6	3 09	51 56	87·5	3 06	50 56	87·5	3 04	49 56	87·4	3 01	48 56	87·4	184	356
5	175	4 03	53 54	87·1	3 59	52 54	87·0	3 56	51 54	86·9	3 53	50 54	86·8	3 50	49 54	86·8	3 46	48 54	86·7	185	355
6	174	4 51	53 51	86·5	4 47	52 51	86·4	4 43	51 51	86·3	4 40	50 51	86·2	4 36	49 51	86·1	4 31	48 51	86·1	186	354
7	173	5 39	53 48	85·9	5 35	52 48	85·8	5 31	51 48	85·7	5 26	50 47	85·6	5 21	49 47	85·5	5 17	48 47	85·4	187	353
8	172	6 28	53 44	85·3	6 23	52 44	85·2	6 18	51 44	85·1	6 13	50 44	84·9	6 07	49 43	84·8	6 02	48 43	84·7	188	352
9	171	7 16	53 40	84·7	7 11	52 39	84·6	7 05	51 39	84·4	6 59	50 39	84·3	6 53	49 39	84·2	6 47	48 39	84·1	189	351
10	170	8 05	53 35	84·1	7 58	52 35	83·9	7 52	51 34	83·8	7 45	50 34	83·7	7 39	49 34	83·5	7 32	48 34	83·4	190	350
11	169	8 53	53 30	83·5	8 46	52 29	83·3	8 39	51 29	83·2	8 32	50 29	83·0	8 24	49 29	82·9	8 17	48 28	82·7	191	349
12	168	9 41	53 24	82·9	9 33	52 23	82·7	9 26	51 23	82·5	9 18	50 23	82·4	9 10	49 23	82·2	9 02	48 22	82·1	192	348
13	167	10 29	53 17	82·3	10 21	52 17	82·1	10 13	51 17	81·9	10 04	50 16	81·7	9 55	49 16	81·6	9 46	48 16	81·4	193	347
14	166	11 17	53 10	81·7	11 08	52 10	81·5	10 59	51 10	81·3	10 50	50 09	81·1	10 41	49 09	80·9	10 31	48 09	80·7	194	346
15	165	12 05	53 03	81·0	11 56	52 02	80·8	11 46	51 02	80·6	11 36	50 02	80·4	11 26	49 01	80·2	11 16	48 01	80·0	195	345
16	164	12 53	52 55	80·4	12 43	51 54	80·2	12 33	50 54	80·0	12 22	49 53	79·8	12 11	48 53	79·6	12 00	47 53	79·3	196	344
17	163	13 41	52 46	79·8	13 30	51 46	79·6	13 19	50 45	79·3	13 08	49 45	79·1	12 57	48 44	78·9	12 45	47 44	78·7	197	343
18	162	14 29	52 37	79·2	14 17	51 37	78·9	14 06	50 36	78·7	13 54	49 35	78·4	13 42	48 35	78·2	13 29	47 34	78·0	198	342
19	161	15 16	52 28	78·6	15 04	51 27	78·3	14 52	50 26	78·0	14 39	49 25	77·8	14 27	48 25	77·5	14 13	47 24	77·3	199	341
20	160	16 04	52 17	77·9	15 51	51 16	77·6	15 38	50 16	77·4	15 25	49 15	77·1	15 11	48 14	76·8	14 58	47 14	76·6	200	340
21	159	16 51	52 07	77·3	16 38	51 05	77·0	16 24	50 05	76·7	16 10	49 04	76·4	15 56	48 03	76·1	15 42	47 03	75·9	201	339
22	158	17 39	51 55	76·6	17 24	50 54	76·3	17 10	49 53	76·0	16 56	48 52	75·7	16 41	47 51	75·4	16 25	46 51	75·2	202	338
23	157	18 26	51 43	76·0	18 11	50 42	75·7	17 56	49 41	75·4	17 41	48 40	75·0	17 25	47 39	74·7	17 09	46 38	74·4	203	337
24	156	19 13	51 30	75·3	18 57	50 29	75·0	18 42	49 28	74·7	18 26	48 27	74·3	18 09	47 26	74·0	17 53	46 25	73·7	204	336
25	155	20 00	51 17	74·7	19 44	50 15	74·3	19 27	49 14	74·0	19 10	48 13	73·6	18 53	47 12	73·3	18 36	46 12	73·0	205	335
26	154	20 46	51 03	74·0	20 30	50 01	73·6	20 13	49 00	73·3	19 55	47 59	72·9	19 37	46 58	72·6	19 19	45 57	72·3	206	334
27	153	21 33	50 48	73·3	21 15	49 47	73·0	20 58	48 45	72·6	20 40	47 44	72·2	20 21	46 43	71·9	20 02	45 42	71·5	207	333
28	152	22 19	50 33	72·6	22 01	49 31	72·3	21 43	48 30	71·9	21 24	47 28	71·5	21 05	46 28	71·1	20 45	45 27	70·8	208	332
29	151	23 06	50 17	72·0	22 47	49 15	71·6	22 28	48 14	71·2	22 08	47 12	70·8	21 48	46 11	70·4	21 28	45 11	70·0	209	331
30	150	23 52	50 00	71·3	23 32	48 58	70·8	23 12	47 57	70·4	22 52	46 55	70·0	22 31	45 54	69·6	22 10	44 54	69·3	210	330
31	149	24 37	49 43	70·5	24 17	48 41	70·1	23 57	47 39	69·7	23 36	46 38	69·3	23 14	45 37	68·9	22 52	44 36	68·5	211	329
32	148	25 23	49 25	69·8	25 02	48 23	69·4	24 41	47 21	69·0	24 19	46 19	68·5	23 57	45 18	68·1	23 34	44 17	67·7	212	328
33	147	26 09	49 06	69·1	25 47	48 04	68·7	25 25	47 02	68·2	25 02	46 00	67·8	24 40	44 59	67·3	24 16	43 58	66·9	213	327
34	146	26 54	48 46	68·4	26 32	47 44	67·9	26 09	46 42	67·4	25 45	45 40	67·0	25 22	44 39	66·6	24 58	43 39	66·1	214	326
35	145	27 39	48 26	67·6	27 16	47 23	67·1	26 52	46 21	66·7	26 28	45 20	66·2	26 04	44 19	65·8	25 39	43 18	65·3	215	325
36	144	28 24	48 04	66·9	28 00	47 02	66·4	27 36	46 00	65·9	27 11	44 58	65·4	26 46	43 57	65·0	26 20	42 57	64·5	216	324
37	143	29 08	47 42	66·1	28 44	46 40	65·6	28 19	45 38	65·1	27 53	44 36	64·6	27 27	43 35	64·2	27 01	42 34	63·7	217	323
38	142	29 52	47 19	65·3	29 27	46 17	64·8	29 01	45 15	64·3	28 35	44 13	63·8	28 08	43 12	63·3	27 41	42 12	62·9	218	322
39	141	30 36	46 56	64·5	30 10	45 53	64·0	29 44	44 51	63·5	29 17	43 49	63·0	28 49	42 48	62·5	28 21	41 48	62·0	219	321
40	140	31 20	46 31	63·7	30 53	45 28	63·2	30 26	44 26	62·7	29 58	43 25	62·2	29 30	42 24	61·7	29 01	41 23	61·2	220	320
41	139	32 03	46 05	62·9	31 36	45 03	62·4	31 08	44 01	61·8	30 39	42 59	61·3	30 10	41 58	60·8	29 41	40 58	60·3	221	319
42	138	32 46	45 39	62·1	32 18	44 36	61·5	31 49	43 34	61·0	31 20	42 33	60·5	30 50	41 32	59·9	30 20	40 32	59·4	222	318
43	137	33 29	45 11	61·3	33 00	44 09	60·7	32 30	43 07	60·1	32 00	42 05	59·6	31 30	41 05	59·1	30 59	40 04	58·5	223	317
44	136	34 12	44 43	60·4	33 42	43 40	59·8	33 11	42 38	59·3	32 40	41 37	58·7	32 09	40 36	58·2	31 37	39 36	57·6	224	316
45	135	34 54	44 13	59·6	34 23	43 11	59·0	33 52	42 09	58·4	33 20	41 08	57·8	32 48	40 07	57·3	32 15	39 08	56·7	225	315

Lat. / A		36°			37°			38°			39°			40°			41°			Lat. / A	
LHA/F		A/H	B/P	Z_1/Z_2	A/H	B/P	Z_1/Z_2	A/H	B/P	Z_1/Z_2	A/H	B/P	Z_1/Z_2	A/H	B/P	Z_1/Z_2	A/H	B/P	Z_1/Z_2	LHA	
°	°	° ′	° ′	°	° ′	° ′	°	° ′	° ′	°	° ′	° ′	°	° ′	° ′	°	° ′	° ′	°	°	°
45	135	34 54	44 13	59·6	34 23	43 11	59·0	33 52	42 09	58·4	33 20	41 08	57·8	32 48	40 07	57·3	32 15	39 08	56·7	225	315
46	134	35 35	43 43	58·7	35 04	42 40	58·1	34 32	41 38	57·5	33 59	40 37	56·9	33 26	39 37	56·4	32 53	38 38	55·8	226	314
47	133	36 17	43 11	57·8	35 44	42 09	57·2	35 12	41 07	56·6	34 38	40 06	56·0	34 04	39 06	55·4	33 30	38 07	54·9	227	313
48	132	36 57	42 39	56·9	36 24	41 36	56·2	35 51	40 35	55·6	35 17	39 34	55·0	34 42	38 34	54·5	34 07	37 35	53·9	228	312
49	131	37 38	42 05	55·9	37 04	41 03	55·3	36 30	40 01	54·7	35 55	39 01	54·1	35 19	38 01	53·5	34 43	37 03	53·0	229	311
50	130	38 18	41 30	55·0	37 43	40 28	54·4	37 08	39 27	53·7	36 32	38 27	53·1	35 56	37 27	52·5	35 19	36 29	52·0	230	310
51	129	38 57	40 54	54·0	38 22	39 52	53·4	37 46	38 51	52·8	37 09	37 51	52·1	36 32	36 52	51·6	35 55	35 54	51·0	231	309
52	128	39 36	40 17	53·0	39 00	39 15	52·4	38 23	38 14	51·8	37 46	37 15	51·1	37 08	36 16	50·6	36 30	35 18	50·0	232	308
53	127	40 15	39 38	52·0	39 38	38 37	51·4	39 00	37 36	50·8	38 22	36 37	50·1	37 43	35 39	49·5	37 04	34 42	49·0	233	307
54	126	40 53	38 58	51·0	40 15	37 57	50·4	39 36	36 57	49·7	38 57	35 58	49·1	38 18	35 01	48·5	37 38	34 04	47·9	234	306
55	125	41 30	38 17	50·0	40 52	37 17	49·3	40 12	36 17	48·7	39 32	35 19	48·1	38 52	34 21	47·4	38 11	33 25	46·9	235	305
56	124	42 07	37 35	48·9	41 28	36 35	48·3	40 47	35 36	47·6	40 07	34 38	47·0	39 26	33 41	46·4	38 44	32 45	45·8	236	304
57	123	42 44	36 51	47·9	42 03	35 51	47·2	41 22	34 53	46·5	40 41	33 55	45·9	39 59	32 59	45·3	39 16	32 04	44·7	237	303
58	122	43 19	36 06	46·8	42 38	35 07	46·1	41 56	34 09	45·4	41 14	33 12	44·8	40 31	32 16	44·2	39 48	31 22	43·6	238	302
59	121	43 54	35 20	45·6	43 12	34 21	45·0	42 29	33 24	44·3	41 46	32 27	43·7	41 03	31 32	43·1	40 19	30 39	42·5	239	301
60	120	44 29	34 32	44·5	43 46	33 34	43·8	43 02	32 37	43·2	42 18	31 42	42·5	41 34	30 47	41·9	40 49	29 54	41·3	240	300
61	119	45 02	33 43	43·3	44 18	32 45	42·6	43 34	31 49	42·0	42 49	30 55	41·4	42 04	30 01	40·8	41 18	29 09	40·2	241	299
62	118	45 35	32 52	42·1	44 51	31 55	41·5	44 05	31 00	40·8	43 20	30 06	40·2	42 34	29 14	39·6	41 47	28 22	39·0	242	298
63	117	46 07	32 00	40·9	45 22	31 04	40·3	44 36	30 10	39·6	43 49	29 17	39·0	43 03	28 25	38·4	42 15	27 35	37·8	243	297
64	116	46 39	31 06	39·7	45 52	30 11	39·0	45 06	29 18	38·4	44 18	28 26	37·8	43 31	27 35	37·2	42 43	26 46	36·6	244	296
65	115	47 09	30 11	38·4	46 22	29 17	37·8	45 35	28 25	37·1	44 47	27 34	36·5	43 58	26 44	36·0	43 09	25 56	35·4	245	295
66	114	47 39	29 14	37·1	46 51	28 21	36·5	46 03	27 30	35·9	45 14	26 40	35·3	44 25	25 52	34·7	43 35	25 04	34·2	246	294
67	113	48 08	28 16	35·8	47 19	27 24	35·2	46 30	26 34	34·6	45 40	25 45	34·0	44 50	24 58	33·4	44 00	24 12	32·9	247	293
68	112	48 36	27 17	34·5	47 46	26 26	33·9	46 56	25 37	33·3	46 06	24 50	32·7	45 15	24 03	32·2	44 24	23 19	31·6	248	292
69	111	49 03	26 15	33·1	48 13	25 26	32·5	47 22	24 38	31·9	46 31	23 52	31·4	45 39	23 08	30·8	44 48	22 24	30·3	249	291
70	110	49 29	25 13	31·8	48 38	24 25	31·2	47 46	23 39	30·6	46 55	22 54	30·0	46 03	22 11	29·5	45 10	21 29	29·0	250	290
71	109	49 54	24 08	30·4	49 02	23 22	29·8	48 10	22 37	29·2	47 17	21 54	28·7	46 25	21 12	28·2	45 32	20 32	27·7	251	289
72	108	50 18	23 02	28·9	49 25	22 18	28·4	48 33	21 35	27·8	47 39	20 53	27·3	46 46	20 13	26·8	45 52	19 34	26·3	252	288
73	107	50 41	21 55	27·5	49 48	21 12	26·9	48 54	20 31	26·4	48 00	19 51	25·9	47 06	19 13	25·4	46 12	18 35	25·0	253	287
74	106	51 03	20 47	26·0	50 09	20 06	25·5	49 15	19 26	25·0	48 20	18 48	24·5	47 25	18 11	24·0	46 30	17 36	23·6	254	286
75	105	51 24	19 36	24·5	50 29	18 57	24·0	49 34	18 20	23·5	48 39	17 43	23·1	47 44	17 09	22·6	46 48	16 35	22·2	255	285
76	104	51 43	18 25	23·0	50 48	17 48	22·5	49 52	17 12	22·0	48 57	16 38	21·6	48 01	16 05	21·2	47 05	15 33	20·8	256	284
77	103	52 02	17 12	21·4	51 06	16 37	21·0	50 09	16 04	20·6	49 13	15 31	20·1	48 17	15 00	19·8	47 20	14 31	19·4	257	283
78	102	52 19	15 58	19·9	51 22	15 25	19·5	50 25	14 54	19·0	49 29	14 24	18·7	48 32	13 55	18·3	47 35	13 27	18·0	258	282
79	101	52 35	14 43	18·3	51 37	14 13	17·9	50 40	13 43	17·5	49 43	13 16	17·2	48 46	12 49	16·8	47 48	12 23	16·5	259	281
80	100	52 49	13 27	16·7	51 52	12 59	16·3	50 54	12 32	16·0	49 56	12 06	15·7	48 58	11 42	15·3	48 01	11 18	15·0	260	280
81	99	53 02	12 09	15·1	52 04	11 44	14·7	51 06	11 19	14·4	50 08	10 56	14·1	49 10	10 34	13·8	48 12	10 12	13·6	261	279
82	98	53 14	10 51	13·4	52 16	10 28	13·1	51 18	10 06	12·9	50 19	9 45	12·6	49 20	9 25	12·3	48 22	9 06	12·1	262	278
83	97	53 25	9 31	11·8	52 26	9 11	11·5	51 27	8 52	11·3	50 29	8 34	11·0	49 30	8 16	10·8	48 31	7 59	10·6	263	277
84	96	53 34	8 11	10·1	52 35	7 54	9·9	51 36	7 37	9·7	50 37	7 21	9·5	49 38	7 06	9·3	48 38	6 51	9·1	264	276
85	95	53 42	6 50	8·5	52 43	6 36	8·3	51 43	6 22	8·1	50 44	6 09	7·9	49 44	5 56	7·8	48 45	5 44	7·6	265	275
86	94	53 49	5 29	6·8	52 49	5 17	6·6	51 49	5 06	6·5	50 50	4 55	6·3	49 50	4 45	6·2	48 50	4 35	6·1	266	274
87	93	53 54	4 07	5·1	52 54	3 58	5·0	51 54	3 50	4·9	50 54	3 42	4·8	49 54	3 34	4·7	48 55	3 27	4·6	267	273
88	92	53 57	2 45	3·4	52 57	2 39	3·3	51 57	2 33	3·2	50 57	2 28	3·2	49 58	2 23	3·1	48 58	2 18	3·0	268	272
89	91	53 59	1 23	1·7	52 59	1 20	1·7	51 59	1 17	1·6	50 59	1 14	1·6	49 59	1 11	1·6	48 59	1 09	1·5	269	271
90	90	54 00	0 00	0·0	53 00	0 00	0·0	52 00	0 00	0·0	51 00	0 00	0·0	50 00	0 00	0·0	49 00	0 00	0·0	270	270

N. Lat: for LHA > 180° … $Z_n = Z$
for LHA < 180° … $Z_n = 360° - Z$

S. Lat.: for LHA > 180° … $Z_n = 180° - Z$
for LHA < 180° … $Z_n = 180° + Z$

SIGHT REDUCTION TABLE

B: (−) for 90° < LHA < 270°
Dec:(−) for Lat. contrary name

Z_1: same sign as B
Z_2: (−) for F > 90°

Lat. / A		42°			43°			44°			45°			46°			47°			Lat. / A	
LHA/F		A/H	B/P	Z_1/Z_2	A/H	B/P	Z_1/Z_2	A/H	B/P	Z_1/Z_2	A/H	B/P	Z_1/Z_2	A/H	B/P	Z_1/Z_2	A/H	B/P	Z_1/Z_2	LHA	
°	°	° ′	° ′	°	° ′	° ′	°	° ′	° ′	°	° ′	° ′	°	° ′	° ′	°	° ′	° ′	°	°	°
0	180	0 00	48 00	90·0	0 00	47 00	90·0	0 00	46 00	90·0	0 00	45 00	90·0	0 00	44 00	90·0	0 00	43 00	90·0	180	360
1	179	0 45	48 00	89·3	0 44	47 00	89·3	0 43	46 00	89·3	0 42	45 00	89·3	0 42	44 00	89·3	0 41	43 00	89·3	181	359
2	178	1 29	47 59	88·7	1 28	46 59	88·6	1 26	45 59	88·6	1 25	44 59	88·6	1 23	43 59	88·6	1 22	42 59	88·5	182	358
3	177	2 14	47 58	88·0	2 12	46 58	88·0	2 09	45 58	87·9	2 07	44 58	87·9	2 05	43 58	87·8	2 03	42 58	87·8	183	357
4	176	2 58	47 56	87·3	2 55	46 56	87·3	2 53	45 56	87·2	2 50	44 56	87·2	2 47	43 56	87·1	2 44	42 56	87·1	184	356
5	175	3 43	47 53	86·6	3 39	46 53	86·6	3 36	45 53	86·5	3 32	44 53	86·5	3 28	43 53	86·4	3 24	42 53	86·3	185	355
6	174	4 27	47 51	86·0	4 23	46 51	85·9	4 19	45 51	85·8	4 14	44 51	85·7	4 10	43 51	85·7	4 05	42 51	85·6	186	354
7	173	5 12	47 47	85·3	5 07	46 47	85·2	5 02	45 47	85·1	4 57	44 47	85·0	4 51	43 47	85·0	4 46	42 47	84·9	187	353
8	172	5 56	47 43	84·6	5 51	46 43	84·5	5 45	45 43	84·4	5 39	44 43	84·3	5 33	43 43	84·2	5 27	42 43	84·1	188	352
9	171	6 41	47 39	84·0	6 34	46 39	83·8	6 28	45 39	83·7	6 21	44 39	83·6	6 14	43 39	83·5	6 07	42 39	83·4	189	351
10	170	7 25	47 34	83·3	7 18	46 34	83·1	7 11	45 34	83·0	7 03	44 34	82·9	6 56	43 34	82·8	6 48	42 34	82·7	190	350
11	169	8 09	47 28	82·6	8 01	46 28	82·4	7 53	45 28	82·3	7 45	44 28	82·2	7 37	43 28	82·0	7 29	42 28	81·9	191	349
12	168	8 53	47 22	81·9	8 45	46 22	81·8	8 36	45 22	81·6	8 27	44 22	81·5	8 18	43 22	81·3	8 09	42 22	81·2	192	348
13	167	9 37	47 16	81·2	9 28	46 15	81·1	9 19	45 15	80·9	9 09	44 15	80·7	8 59	43 15	80·6	8 49	42 16	80·4	193	347
14	166	10 21	47 08	80·5	10 11	46 08	80·3	10 01	45 08	80·2	9 51	44 08	80·0	9 40	43 08	79·8	9 30	42 08	79·7	194	346
15	165	11 05	47 01	79·8	10 55	46 00	79·6	10 44	45 00	79·5	10 33	44 00	79·3	10 21	43 00	79·1	10 10	42 01	78·9	195	345
16	164	11 49	46 52	79·1	11 38	45 52	78·9	11 26	44 52	78·7	11 14	43 52	78·5	11 02	42 52	78·3	10 50	41 52	78·2	196	344
17	163	12 33	46 43	78·4	12 21	45 43	78·2	12 08	44 43	78·0	11 56	43 43	77·8	11 43	42 43	77·6	11 30	41 44	77·4	197	343
18	162	13 17	46 34	77·7	13 04	45 34	77·5	12 51	44 34	77·3	12 37	43 34	77·1	12 24	42 34	76·8	12 10	41 34	76·6	198	342
19	161	14 00	46 24	77·0	13 46	45 24	76·8	13 33	44 24	76·5	13 19	43 24	76·3	13 04	42 24	76·1	12 50	41 24	75·9	199	341
20	160	14 43	46 13	76·3	14 29	45 13	76·1	14 15	44 13	75·8	14 00	43 13	75·6	13 45	42 13	75·3	13 29	41 14	75·1	200	340
21	159	15 27	46 02	75·6	15 12	45 02	75·3	14 56	44 02	75·1	14 41	43 02	74·8	14 25	42 02	74·6	14 09	41 03	74·3	201	339
22	158	16 10	45 50	74·9	15 54	44 50	74·6	15 38	43 50	74·3	15 22	42 50	74·1	15 05	41 50	73·8	14 48	40 51	73·5	202	338
23	157	16 53	45 38	74·1	16 36	44 38	73·9	16 19	43 38	73·6	16 02	42 38	73·3	15 45	41 38	73·0	15 27	40 39	72·8	203	337
24	156	17 36	45 25	73·4	17 18	44 25	73·1	17 01	43 25	72·8	16 43	42 25	72·5	16 25	41 25	72·2	16 06	40 26	72·0	204	336
25	155	18 18	45 11	72·7	18 00	44 11	72·4	17 42	43 11	72·1	17 23	42 11	71·8	17 04	41 12	71·5	16 45	40 12	71·2	205	335
26	154	19 01	44 57	71·9	18 42	43 57	71·6	18 23	42 57	71·3	18 03	41 57	71·0	17 44	40 57	70·7	17 24	39 58	70·4	206	334
27	153	19 43	44 42	71·2	19 24	43 42	70·8	19 04	42 42	70·5	18 43	41 42	70·2	18 23	40 43	69·9	18 02	39 43	69·6	207	333
28	152	20 25	44 26	70·4	20 05	43 26	70·1	19 44	42 26	69·7	19 23	41 27	69·4	19 02	40 27	69·1	18 40	39 28	68·8	208	332
29	151	21 07	44 10	69·6	20 46	43 10	69·3	20 25	42 10	68·9	20 03	41 10	68·6	19 41	40 11	68·3	19 18	39 12	67·9	209	331
30	150	21 49	43 53	68·9	21 27	42 53	68·5	21 05	41 53	68·1	20 42	40 54	67·8	20 19	39 54	67·4	19 56	38 55	67·1	210	330
31	149	22 30	43 35	68·1	22 08	42 35	67·7	21 45	41 36	67·3	21 21	40 36	67·0	20 58	39 37	66·6	20 34	38 38	66·3	211	329
32	148	23 11	43 17	67·3	22 48	42 17	66·9	22 24	41 17	66·5	22 00	40 18	66·2	21 36	39 19	65·8	21 11	38 20	65·4	212	328
33	147	23 53	42 58	66·5	23 28	41 58	66·1	23 04	40 58	65·7	22 39	39 59	65·3	22 14	39 00	65·0	21 48	38 02	64·6	213	327
34	146	24 33	42 38	65·7	24 08	41 38	65·3	23 43	40 39	64·9	23 17	39 40	64·5	22 51	38 41	64·1	22 25	37 42	63·7	214	326
35	145	25 14	42 18	64·9	24 48	41 18	64·5	24 22	40 18	64·1	23 56	39 19	63·7	23 29	38 21	63·3	23 02	37 23	62·9	215	325
36	144	25 54	41 56	64·1	25 28	40 57	63·6	25 01	39 57	63·2	24 34	38 58	62·8	24 06	38 00	62·4	23 38	37 02	62·0	216	324
37	143	26 34	41 34	63·2	26 07	40 35	62·8	25 39	39 35	62·4	25 11	38 37	61·9	24 43	37 38	61·5	24 14	36 41	61·1	217	323
38	142	27 14	41 11	62·4	26 46	40 12	61·9	26 17	39 13	61·5	25 48	38 14	61·1	25 19	37 16	60·7	24 50	36 19	60·3	218	322
39	141	27 53	40 48	61·5	27 24	39 48	61·1	26 55	38 50	60·6	26 25	37 51	60·2	25 55	36 53	59·8	25 25	35 56	59·4	219	321
40	140	28 32	40 23	60·7	28 02	39 24	60·2	27 32	38 25	59·8	27 02	37 27	59·3	26 31	36 30	58·9	26 00	35 32	58·5	220	320
41	139	29 11	39 58	59·8	28 40	38 59	59·3	28 10	38 01	58·9	27 38	37 03	58·4	27 07	36 05	58·0	26 35	35 08	57·6	221	319
42	138	29 49	39 32	58·9	29 18	38 33	58·4	28 46	37 35	58·0	28 14	36 37	57·5	27 42	35 40	57·1	27 09	34 43	56·6	222	318
43	137	30 27	39 05	58·0	29 55	38 06	57·5	29 23	37 08	57·1	28 50	36 11	56·6	28 17	35 14	56·1	27 43	34 18	55·7	223	317
44	136	31 05	38 37	57·1	30 32	37 39	56·6	29 59	36 41	56·1	29 25	35 44	55·7	28 51	34 47	55·2	28 17	33 51	54·8	224	316
45	135	31 42	38 09	56·2	31 08	37 10	55·7	30 34	36 13	55·2	30 00	35 16	54·7	29 25	34 20	54·3	28 50	33 24	53·8	225	315

Lat. / A		42°			43°			44°			45°			46°			47°			Lat. / A	
LHA/F		A/H	B/P	Z_1/Z_2	A/H	B/P	Z_1/Z_2	A/H	B/P	Z_1/Z_2	A/H	B/P	Z_1/Z_2	A/H	B/P	Z_1/Z_2	A/H	B/P	Z_1/Z_2	LHA	
°	°	° ′	° ′	°	° ′	° ′	°	° ′	° ′	°	° ′	° ′	°	° ′	° ′	°	° ′	° ′	°	°	°
45	135	31 42	38 09	56·2	31 08	37 10	55·7	30 34	36 13	55·2	30 00	35 16	54·7	29 25	34 20	54·3	28 50	33 24	53·8	225	315
46	134	32 19	37 39	55·3	31 45	36 41	54·8	31 10	35 44	54·3	30 34	34 47	53·8	29 59	33 51	53·3	29 23	32 56	52·9	226	314
47	133	32 55	37 08	54·3	32 20	36 11	53·8	31 45	35 14	53·3	31 08	34 18	52·8	30 32	33 22	52·4	29 55	32 27	51·9	227	313
48	132	33 31	36 37	53·4	32 55	35 40	52·9	32 19	34 43	52·3	31 42	33 47	51·9	31 05	32 52	51·4	30 27	31 58	50·9	228	312
49	131	34 07	36 05	52·4	33 30	35 08	51·9	32 53	34 11	51·4	32 15	33 16	50·9	31 37	32 21	50·4	30 59	31 27	49·9	229	311
50	130	34 42	35 31	51·4	34 04	34 35	50·9	33 26	33 39	50·4	32 48	32 44	49·9	32 09	31 50	49·4	31 30	30 56	48·9	230	310
51	129	35 17	34 57	50·4	34 38	34 01	49·9	33 59	33 05	49·4	33 20	32 11	48·9	32 40	31 17	48·4	32 00	30 24	47·9	231	309
52	128	35 51	34 22	49·4	35 12	33 26	48·9	34 32	32 31	48·4	33 52	31 37	47·9	33 11	30 44	47·4	32 30	29 52	46·9	232	308
53	127	36 24	33 45	48·4	35 44	32 50	47·9	35 04	31 56	47·3	34 23	31 02	46·8	33 42	30 10	46·3	33 00	29 18	45·9	233	307
54	126	36 57	33 08	47·4	36 17	32 13	46·8	35 35	31 20	46·3	34 54	30 27	45·8	34 12	29 35	45·3	33 29	28 44	44·8	234	306
55	125	37 30	32 30	46·3	36 48	31 36	45·8	36 06	30 43	45·2	35 24	29 50	44·7	34 41	28 59	44·2	33 58	28 08	43·8	235	305
56	124	38 02	31 51	45·2	37 19	30 57	44·7	36 37	30 04	44·2	35 53	29 13	43·6	35 10	28 22	43·2	34 26	27 32	42·7	236	304
57	123	38 33	31 10	44·1	37 50	30 17	43·6	37 06	29 25	43·1	36 22	28 34	42·6	35 38	27 45	42·1	34 53	26 56	41·6	237	303
58	122	39 04	30 29	43·0	38 20	29 36	42·5	37 36	28 45	42·0	36 51	27 55	41·5	36 06	27 06	41·0	35 20	26 18	40·5	238	302
59	121	39 34	29 46	41·9	38 49	28 55	41·4	38 04	28 04	40·9	37 19	27 15	40·4	36 33	26 27	39·9	35 46	25 39	39·4	239	301
60	120	40 04	29 03	40·8	39 18	28 12	40·2	38 32	27 22	39·7	37 46	26 34	39·2	36 59	25 46	38·8	36 12	25 00	38·3	240	300
61	119	40 32	28 18	39·6	39 46	27 28	39·1	38 59	26 39	38·6	38 12	25 52	38·1	37 25	25 05	37·6	36 37	24 20	37·2	241	299
62	118	41 00	27 32	38·5	40 13	26 43	37·9	39 26	25 56	37·4	38 38	25 09	36·9	37 50	24 23	36·5	37 02	23 39	36·0	242	298
63	117	41 28	26 45	37·3	40 40	25 58	36·8	39 52	25 11	36·3	39 03	24 25	35·8	38 14	23 40	35·3	37 25	22 57	34·9	243	297
64	116	41 54	25 58	36·1	41 06	25 11	35·6	40 17	24 25	35·1	39 28	23 40	34·6	38 38	22 57	34·1	37 48	22 14	33·7	244	296
65	115	42 20	25 09	34·9	41 31	24 23	34·4	40 41	23 38	33·9	39 51	22 55	33·4	39 01	22 12	33·0	38 11	21 31	32·5	245	295
66	114	42 45	24 19	33·6	41 55	23 34	33·1	41 05	22 50	32·7	40 14	22 08	32·2	39 23	21 27	31·8	38 32	20 46	31·3	246	294
67	113	43 10	23 28	32·4	42 19	22 44	31·9	41 28	22 02	31·4	40 37	21 21	31·0	39 45	20 40	30·5	38 53	20 01	30·1	247	293
68	112	43 33	22 35	31·1	42 42	21 53	30·6	41 50	21 12	30·2	40 58	20 32	29·7	40 06	19 53	29·3	39 13	19 15	28·9	248	292
69	111	43 56	21 42	29·8	43 04	21 01	29·4	42 11	20 22	28·9	41 19	19 43	28·5	40 26	19 05	28·1	39 33	18 29	27·7	249	291
70	110	44 18	20 48	28·5	43 25	20 08	28·1	42 32	19 30	27·7	41 38	18 53	27·2	40 45	18 17	26·8	39 51	17 41	26·5	250	290
71	109	44 38	19 53	27·2	43 45	19 15	26·8	42 51	18 38	26·4	41 57	18 02	26·0	41 03	17 27	25·6	40 09	16 53	25·2	251	289
72	108	44 58	18 57	25·9	44 04	18 20	25·5	43 10	17 45	25·1	42 16	17 10	24·7	41 21	16 37	24·3	40 26	16 05	24·0	252	288
73	107	45 17	17 59	24·6	44 23	17 24	24·1	43 28	16 51	23·8	42 33	15 18	23·4	41 38	15 46	23·0	40 42	15 15	22·7	253	287
74	106	45 35	17 01	23·2	44 40	16 28	22·8	43 45	15 56	22·4	42 49	15 25	22·1	41 54	14 54	21·7	40 58	14 25	21·4	254	286
75	105	45 53	16 02	21·8	44 57	15 31	21·4	44 01	15 00	21·1	43 05	14 31	20·8	42 09	14 02	20·4	41 12	13 34	20·1	255	285
76	104	46 09	15 02	20·4	45 12	14 33	20·1	44 16	14 04	19·7	43 19	13 36	19·4	42 23	13 09	19·1	41 26	12 43	18·8	256	284
77	103	46 24	14 02	19·0	45 27	13 34	18·7	44 30	13 07	18·4	43 33	12 41	18·1	42 36	12 15	17·8	41 39	11 51	17·5	257	283
78	102	46 38	13 00	17·6	45 40	12 34	17·3	44 43	12 09	17·0	43 46	11 45	16·7	42 48	11 21	16·5	41 51	10 58	16·2	258	282
79	101	46 51	11 58	16·2	45 53	11 34	15·9	44 55	11 11	15·6	43 57	10 48	15·4	43 00	10 26	15·1	42 02	10 05	14·9	259	281
80	100	47 03	10 55	14·8	46 04	10 33	14·5	45 06	10 12	14·2	44 08	9 51	14·0	43 10	9 31	13·8	42 12	9 12	13·6	260	280
81	99	47 13	9 51	13·3	46 15	9 31	13·1	45 16	9 12	12·8	44 18	8 53	12·6	43 19	8 35	12·4	42 21	8 18	12·2	261	279
82	98	47 23	8 47	11·9	46 24	8 29	11·6	45 26	8 12	11·4	44 27	7 55	11·2	43 28	7 39	11·1	42 29	7 24	10·9	262	278
83	97	47 32	7 42	10·4	46 33	7 27	10·2	45 34	7 12	10·0	44 34	6 57	9·9	43 35	6 43	9·7	42 36	6 29	9·5	263	277
84	96	47 39	6 37	8·9	46 40	6 24	8·8	45 41	6 11	8·6	44 41	5 58	8·5	43 42	5 46	8·3	42 42	5 34	8·2	264	276
85	95	47 46	5 32	7·4	46 46	5 20	7·3	45 46	5 09	7·2	44 47	4 59	7·1	43 47	4 49	6·9	42 48	4 39	6·8	265	275
86	94	47 51	4 26	6·0	46 51	4 17	5·9	45 51	4 08	5·7	44 52	3 59	5·6	43 52	3 51	5·6	42 52	3 43	5·5	266	274
87	93	47 55	3 20	4·5	46 55	3 13	4·4	45 55	3 06	4·3	44 55	3 00	4·2	43 55	2 54	4·2	42 56	2 48	4·1	267	273
88	92	47 58	2 13	3·0	46 58	2 09	2·9	45 58	2 04	2·9	44 58	2 00	2·8	43 58	1 56	2·8	42 58	1 52	2·7	268	272
89	91	47 59	1 07	1·5	46 59	1 04	1·5	45 59	1 02	1·4	44 59	1 00	1·4	43 59	0 58	1·4	43 00	0 56	1·4	269	271
90	90	48 00	0 00	0·0	47 00	0 00	0·0	46 00	0 00	0·0	45 00	0 00	0·0	44 00	0 00	0·0	43 00	0 00	0·0	270	270

N. Lat: for LHA > 180° … $Z_n = Z$
for LHA < 180° … $Z_n = 360° - Z$

S. Lat.: for LHA > 180° … $Z_n = 180° - Z$
for LHA < 180° … $Z_n = 180° + Z$

SIGHT REDUCTION TABLE

B: (−) for 90° < LHA < 270°
Dec: (−) for Lat. contrary name

Z_1: same sign as B
Z_2: (−) for F > 90°

Lat. / A		48°			49°			50°			51°			52°			53°			Lat. / A	
LHA/F		A/H	B/P	Z_1/Z_2	A/H	B/P	Z_1/Z_2	A/H	B/P	Z_1/Z_2	A/H	B/P	Z_1/Z_2	A/H	B/P	Z_1/Z_2	A/H	B/P	Z_1/Z_2	LHA	
°	°	° ′	° ′	°	° ′	° ′	°	° ′	° ′	°	° ′	° ′	°	° ′	° ′	°	° ′	° ′	°	°	°
0	180	0 00	42 00	90·0	0 00	41 00	90·0	0 00	40 00	90·0	0 00	39 00	90·0	0 00	38 00	90·0	0 00	37 00	90·0	180	360
1	179	0 40	42 00	89·3	0 39	41 00	89·2	0 39	40 00	89·2	0 38	39 00	89·2	0 37	38 00	89·2	0 36	37 00	89·2	181	359
2	178	1 20	41 59	88·5	1 19	40 59	88·5	1 17	39 59	88·5	1 16	38 59	88·4	1 14	37 59	88·4	1 12	36 59	88·4	182	358
3	177	2 00	41 58	87·8	1 58	40 58	87·7	1 56	39 58	87·7	1 53	38 58	87·7	1 51	37 58	87·6	1 48	36 58	87·6	183	357
4	176	2 41	41 56	87·0	2 37	40 56	87·0	2 34	39 56	86·9	2 31	38 56	86·9	2 28	37 56	86·8	2 24	36 56	86·8	184	356
5	175	3 21	41 53	86·3	3 17	40 54	86·2	3 13	39 54	86·2	3 09	38 54	86·1	3 05	37 54	86·1	3 00	36 54	86·0	185	355
6	174	4 01	41 51	85·5	3 56	40 51	85·5	3 51	39 51	85·4	3 46	38 51	85·3	3 41	37 51	85·3	3 36	36 51	85·2	186	354
7	173	4 41	41 47	84·8	4 35	40 47	84·7	4 30	39 47	84·6	4 24	38 47	84·5	4 18	37 48	84·5	4 12	36 48	84·4	187	353
8	172	5 21	41 43	84·0	5 14	40 43	83·9	5 08	39 43	83·9	5 01	38 44	83·8	4 55	37 44	83·7	4 48	36 44	83·6	188	352
9	171	6 01	41 39	83·3	5 53	40 39	83·2	5 46	39 39	83·1	5 39	38 39	83·0	5 32	37 39	82·9	5 24	36 40	82·8	189	351
10	170	6 40	41 34	82·5	6 32	40 34	82·4	6 25	39 34	82·3	6 16	38 34	82·2	6 08	37 35	82·1	6 00	36 35	82·0	190	350
11	169	7 20	41 28	81·8	7 11	40 28	81·7	7 03	39 29	81·5	6 54	38 29	81·4	6 45	37 29	81·3	6 36	36 29	81·2	191	349
12	168	8 00	41 22	81·0	7 50	40 22	80·9	7 41	39 23	80·8	7 31	38 23	80·6	7 21	37 23	80·5	7 11	36 24	80·4	192	348
13	167	8 39	41 16	80·3	8 29	40 16	80·1	8 19	39 16	80·0	8 08	38 16	79·8	7 58	37 17	79·7	7 47	36 17	79·6	193	347
14	166	9 19	41 09	79·5	9 08	40 09	79·3	8 57	39 09	79·2	8 45	38 09	79·0	8 34	37 10	78·9	8 22	36 10	78·7	194	346
15	165	9 58	41 01	78·7	9 47	40 01	78·6	9 35	39 02	78·4	9 22	38 02	78·2	9 10	37 02	78·1	8 58	36 03	77·9	195	345
16	164	10 38	40 53	78·0	10 25	39 53	77·8	10 12	38 53	77·6	9 59	37 54	77·4	9 46	36 54	77·3	9 33	35 55	77·1	196	344
17	163	11 17	40 44	77·2	11 04	39 44	77·0	10 50	38 45	76·8	10 36	37 45	76·6	10 22	36 46	76·5	10 08	35 47	76·3	197	343
18	162	11 56	40 34	76·4	11 42	39 35	76·2	11 27	38 35	76·0	11 13	37 36	75·8	10 58	36 37	75·6	10 43	35 38	75·5	198	342
19	161	12 35	40 25	75·6	12 20	39 25	75·4	12 05	38 26	75·2	11 49	37 26	75·0	11 34	36 27	74·8	11 18	35 28	74·6	199	341
20	160	13 14	40 14	74·9	12 58	39 15	74·6	12 42	38 15	74·4	12 26	37 16	74·2	12 09	36 17	74·0	11 53	35 18	73·8	200	340
21	159	13 52	40 03	74·1	13 36	39 04	73·8	13 19	38 04	73·6	13 02	37 05	73·4	12 45	36 06	73·2	12 27	35 08	73·0	201	339
22	158	14 31	39 51	73·3	14 14	38 52	73·0	13 56	37 53	72·8	13 38	36 54	72·6	13 20	35 55	72·3	13 02	34 56	72·1	202	338
23	157	15 09	39 39	72·5	14 51	38 40	72·2	14 33	37 41	72·0	14 14	36 42	71·7	13 55	35 43	71·5	13 36	34 45	71·3	203	337
24	156	15 48	39 26	71·7	15 29	38 27	71·4	15 09	37 28	71·2	14 50	36 30	70·9	14 30	35 31	70·7	14 10	34 33	70·4	204	336
25	155	16 26	39 13	70·9	16 06	38 14	70·6	15 46	37 15	70·3	15 25	36 17	70·1	15 05	35 18	69·8	14 44	34 20	69·6	205	335
26	154	17 03	38 59	70·1	16 43	38 00	69·8	16 22	37 01	69·5	16 01	36 03	69·2	15 39	35 05	69·0	15 18	34 07	68·7	206	334
27	153	17 41	38 44	69·3	17 20	37 46	69·0	16 58	36 47	68·7	16 36	35 49	68·4	16 14	34 51	68·1	15 51	33 53	67·9	207	333
28	152	18 19	38 29	68·4	17 56	37 30	68·1	17 34	36 32	67·8	17 11	35 34	67·5	16 48	34 36	67·3	16 25	33 38	67·0	208	332
29	151	18 56	38 13	67·6	18 33	37 15	67·3	18 09	36 16	67·0	17 46	35 18	66·7	17 22	34 21	66·4	16 58	33 23	66·1	209	331
30	150	19 33	37 57	66·8	19 09	36 58	66·5	18 45	36 00	66·1	18 20	35 03	65·8	17 56	34 05	65·5	17 31	33 08	65·2	210	330
31	149	20 10	37 40	65·9	19 45	36 41	65·6	19 20	35 44	65·3	18 55	34 46	65·0	18 29	33 49	64·7	18 03	32 52	64·4	211	329
32	148	20 46	37 22	65·1	20 21	36 24	64·8	19 55	35 26	64·4	19 29	34 29	64·1	19 02	33 32	63·8	18 36	32 35	63·5	212	328
33	147	21 22	37 03	64·2	20 56	36 06	63·9	20 30	35 08	63·6	20 03	34 11	63·2	19 35	33 14	62·9	19 08	32 18	62·6	213	327
34	146	21 58	36 44	63·4	21 31	35 47	63·0	21 04	34 49	62·7	20 36	33 53	62·3	20 08	32 56	62·0	19 40	32 00	61·7	214	326
35	145	22 34	36 25	62·5	22 06	35 27	62·1	21 38	34 30	61·8	21 10	33 33	61·4	20 41	32 37	61·1	20 12	31 41	60·8	215	325
36	144	23 10	36 04	61·6	22 41	35 07	61·3	22 12	34 10	60·9	21 43	33 14	60·5	21 13	32 18	60·2	20 43	31 22	59·9	216	324
37	143	23 45	35 43	60·8	23 15	34 46	60·4	22 45	33 50	60·0	22 15	32 53	59·6	21 45	31 58	59·3	21 14	31 02	59·0	217	323
38	142	24 20	35 21	59·9	23 49	34 25	59·5	23 19	33 28	59·1	22 48	32 33	58·7	22 16	31 37	58·4	21 45	30 42	58·0	218	322
39	141	24 54	34 59	59·0	24 23	34 02	58·6	23 52	33 07	58·2	23 20	32 11	57·8	22 48	31 16	57·5	22 15	30 21	57·1	219	321
40	140	25 28	34 36	58·1	24 57	33 40	57·7	24 24	32 44	57·3	23 52	31 49	56·9	23 19	30 54	56·5	22 45	30 00	56·2	220	320
41	139	26 02	34 12	57·1	25 30	33 16	56·7	24 57	32 21	56·3	24 23	31 26	56·0	23 49	30 32	55·6	23 15	29 38	55·2	221	319
42	138	26 36	33 47	56·2	26 02	32 52	55·8	25 28	31 57	55·4	24 54	31 02	55·0	24 20	30 08	54·6	23 45	29 15	54·3	222	318
43	137	27 09	33 22	55·3	26 35	32 27	54·9	26 00	31 32	54·5	25 25	30 38	54·1	24 50	29 45	53·7	24 14	28 52	53·3	223	317
44	136	27 42	32 56	54·3	27 07	32 01	53·9	26 31	31 07	53·5	25 55	30 13	53·1	25 19	29 20	52·7	24 43	28 28	52·4	224	316
45	135	28 14	32 29	53·4	27 38	31 35	53·0	27 02	30 41	52·5	26 25	29 48	52·1	25 48	28 55	51·8	25 11	28 03	51·4	225	315

Lat. / A		48°			49°			50°			51°			52°			53°			Lat. / A	
LHA/F		A/H	B/P	Z_1/Z_2	A/H	B/P	Z_1/Z_2	A/H	B/P	Z_1/Z_2	A/H	B/P	Z_1/Z_2	A/H	B/P	Z_1/Z_2	A/H	B/P	Z_1/Z_2	LHA	
°	°	° ′	° ′	°	° ′	° ′	°	° ′	° ′	°	° ′	° ′	°	° ′	° ′	°	° ′	° ′	°	°	°
45	135	28 14	32 29	53·4	27 38	31 35	53·0	27 02	30 41	52·5	26 25	29 48	52·1	25 48	28 55	51·8	25 11	28 03	51·4	225	315
46	134	28 46	32 01	52·4	28 10	31 08	52·0	27 32	30 14	51·6	26 55	29 22	51·2	26 17	28 29	50·8	25 39	27 38	50·4	226	314
47	133	29 18	31 33	51·4	28 40	30 40	51·0	28 02	29 47	50·6	27 24	28 55	50·2	26 46	28 03	49·8	26 07	27 12	49·4	227	313
48	132	29 49	31 04	50·5	29 11	30 11	50·0	28 32	29 19	49·6	27 53	28 27	49·2	27 14	27 36	48·8	26 34	26 46	48·4	228	312
49	131	30 20	30 34	49·5	29 41	29 42	49·0	29 01	28 50	48·6	28 21	27 59	48·2	27 41	27 08	47·8	27 01	26 18	47·4	229	311
50	130	30 50	30 04	48·5	30 10	29 12	48·0	29 30	28 20	47·6	28 49	27 30	47·2	28 08	26 40	46·8	27 27	25 51	46·4	230	310
51	129	31 20	29 32	47·5	30 39	28 41	47·0	29 58	27 50	46·6	29 17	27 00	46·2	28 35	26 11	45·8	27 53	25 22	45·4	231	309
52	128	31 49	29 00	46·4	31 08	28 09	46·0	30 26	27 19	45·6	29 44	26 30	45·2	29 01	25 41	44·8	28 19	24 53	44·4	232	308
53	127	32 18	28 27	45·4	31 36	27 37	45·0	30 53	26 48	44·5	30 10	25 59	44·1	29 27	25 11	43·7	28 44	24 24	43·3	233	307
54	126	32 46	27 53	44·4	32 03	27 04	43·9	31 20	26 15	43·5	30 36	25 27	43·1	29 52	24 40	42·7	29 08	23 53	42·3	234	306
55	125	33 14	27 19	43·3	32 30	26 30	42·9	31 46	25 42	42·4	31 02	24 55	42·0	30 17	24 08	41·6	29 32	23 23	41·2	235	305
56	124	33 42	26 44	42·2	32 57	25 55	41·8	32 12	25 08	41·4	31 27	24 22	41·0	30 41	23 36	40·6	29 56	22 51	40·2	236	304
57	123	34 08	26 07	41·1	33 23	25 20	40·7	32 37	24 34	40·3	31 51	23 48	39·9	31 05	23 03	39·5	30 19	22 19	39·1	237	303
58	122	34 34	25 30	40·1	33 48	24 44	39·6	33 02	23 58	39·2	32 15	23 14	38·8	31 28	22 29	38·4	30 41	21 46	38·0	238	302
59	121	35 00	24 53	39·0	34 13	24 07	38·5	33 26	23 22	38·1	32 39	22 38	37·7	31 51	21 55	37·3	31 03	21 13	37·0	239	301
60	120	35 25	24 14	37·8	34 37	23 30	37·4	33 50	22 46	37·0	33 02	22 03	36·6	32 13	21 20	36·2	31 25	20 39	35·9	240	300
61	119	35 49	23 35	36·7	35 01	22 51	36·3	34 12	22 08	35·9	33 24	21 26	35·5	32 35	20 45	35·1	31 46	20 04	34·8	241	299
62	118	36 13	22 55	35·6	35 24	22 12	35·2	34 35	21 30	34·8	33 45	20 49	34·4	32 56	20 09	34·0	32 06	19 29	33·7	242	298
63	117	36 36	22 14	34·4	35 46	21 32	34·0	34 56	20 51	33·6	34 06	20 11	33·3	33 16	19 32	32·9	32 26	18 53	32·5	243	297
64	116	36 58	21 32	33·3	36 08	20 52	32·9	35 17	20 12	32·5	34 27	19 33	32·1	33 36	18 54	31·8	32 45	18 17	31·4	244	296
65	115	37 20	20 50	32·1	36 29	20 10	31·7	35 38	19 32	31·3	34 47	18 54	31·0	33 55	18 16	30·6	33 03	17 40	30·3	245	295
66	114	37 41	20 07	30·9	36 49	19 28	30·5	35 58	18 51	30·2	35 06	18 14	29·8	34 13	17 38	29·5	33 21	17 02	29·1	246	294
67	113	38 01	19 23	29·7	37 09	18 46	29·4	36 17	18 09	29·0	35 24	17 33	28·6	34 31	16 59	28·3	33 38	16 24	28·0	247	293
68	112	38 21	18 38	28·5	37 28	18 02	28·2	36 35	17 27	27·8	35 42	16 53	27·5	34 48	16 19	27·1	33 55	15 46	26·8	248	292
69	111	38 40	17 53	27·3	37 46	17 18	27·0	36 53	16 44	26·6	35 59	16 11	26·3	35 05	15 38	26·0	34 11	15 07	25·7	249	291
70	110	38 58	17 07	26·1	38 04	16 33	25·7	37 10	16 01	25·4	36 15	15 29	25·1	35 21	14 58	24·8	34 26	14 27	24·5	250	290
71	109	39 15	16 20	24·9	38 20	15 48	24·5	37 26	15 17	24·2	36 31	14 46	23·9	35 36	14 16	23·6	34 41	13 47	23·3	251	289
72	108	39 31	15 33	23·6	38 36	15 02	23·3	37 41	14 32	23·0	36 46	14 03	22·7	35 50	13 34	22·4	34 55	13 07	22·1	252	288
73	107	39 47	14 45	22·4	38 51	14 16	22·1	37 56	13 47	21·8	37 00	13 19	21·5	36 04	12 52	21·2	35 08	12 25	20·9	253	287
74	106	40 02	13 56	21·1	39 06	13 28	20·8	38 10	13 01	20·5	37 13	12 35	20·3	36 17	12 09	20·0	35 21	11 44	19·8	254	286
75	105	40 16	13 07	19·8	39 19	12 41	19·5	38 23	12 15	19·3	37 26	11 50	19·0	36 29	11 26	18·8	35 33	11 02	18·5	255	285
76	104	40 29	12 17	18·5	39 32	11 53	18·3	38 35	11 28	18·0	37 38	11 05	17·8	36 41	10 42	17·6	35 44	10 20	17·3	256	284
77	103	40 41	11 27	17·3	39 44	11 04	17·0	38 47	10 41	16·8	37 49	10 19	16·5	36 52	9 58	16·3	35 54	9 37	16·1	257	283
78	102	40 53	10 36	16·0	39 55	10 15	15·7	38 57	9 54	15·5	38 00	9 33	15·3	37 02	9 14	15·1	36 04	8 54	14·9	258	282
79	101	41 04	9 45	14·7	40 05	9 25	14·4	39 07	9 06	14·2	38 09	8 47	14·0	37 11	8 29	13·9	36 13	8 11	13·7	259	281
80	100	41 13	8 53	13·3	40 15	8 35	13·2	39 16	8 17	13·0	38 18	8 00	12·8	37 19	7 44	12·6	36 21	7 27	12·5	260	280
81	99	41 22	8 01	12·0	40 23	7 45	11·9	39 25	7 29	11·7	38 26	7 13	11·5	37 27	6 58	11·4	36 28	6 43	11·2	261	279
82	98	41 30	7 09	10·7	40 31	6 54	10·5	39 32	6 40	10·4	38 33	6 26	10·3	37 34	6 12	10·1	36 35	5 59	10·0	262	278
83	97	41 37	6 16	9·4	40 38	6 03	9·2	39 39	5 50	9·1	38 39	5 38	9·0	37 40	5 26	8·9	36 41	5 15	8·7	263	277
84	96	41 43	5 23	8·1	40 44	5 12	7·9	39 44	5 01	7·8	38 45	4 50	7·7	37 45	4 40	7·6	36 46	4 30	7·5	264	276
85	95	41 48	4 29	6·7	40 49	4 20	6·6	39 49	4 11	6·5	38 49	4 02	6·4	37 50	3 54	6·3	36 50	3 45	6·3	265	275
86	94	41 52	3 36	5·4	40 53	3 28	5·3	39 53	3 21	5·2	38 53	3 14	5·1	37 53	3 07	5·1	36 54	3 01	5·0	266	274
87	93	41 56	2 42	4·0	40 56	2 36	4·0	39 56	2 31	3·9	38 56	2 26	3·9	37 56	2 20	3·8	36 56	2 16	3·8	267	273
88	92	41 58	1 48	2·7	40 58	1 44	2·6	39 58	1 41	2·6	38 58	1 37	2·6	37 58	1 34	2·5	36 58	1 30	2·5	268	272
89	91	42 00	0 54	1·3	41 00	0 52	1·3	40 00	0 50	1·3	39 00	0 49	1·3	38 00	0 47	1·3	37 00	0 45	1·3	269	271
90	90	42 00	0 00	0·0	41 00	0 00	0·0	40 00	0 00	0·0	39 00	0 00	0·0	38 00	0 00	0·0	37 00	0 00	0·0	270	270

N. Lat: for LHA > 180° … $Z_n = Z$
for LHA < 180° … $Z_n = 360° - Z$

S. Lat.: for LHA > 180° … $Z_n = 180° - Z$
for LHA < 180° … $Z_n = 180° + Z$

SIGHT REDUCTION TABLE

B: (−) for 90° < LHA < 270°
Dec: (−) for Lat. contrary name

Z_1: same sign as B
Z_2: (−) for F > 90°

Lat. / A		54°			55°			56°			57°			58°			59°			Lat. / A	
LHA/F		A/H	B/P	Z_1/Z_2	A/H	B/P	Z_1/Z_2	A/H	B/P	Z_1/Z_2	A/H	B/P	Z_1/Z_2	A/H	B/P	Z_1/Z_2	A/H	B/P	Z_1/Z_2	LHA	
°	°	° ′	° ′	°	° ′	° ′	°	° ′	° ′	°	° ′	° ′	°	° ′	° ′	°	° ′	° ′	°	°	°
0	180	0 00	36 00	90·0	0 00	35 00	90·0	0 00	34 00	90·0	0 00	33 00	90·0	0 00	32 00	90·0	0 00	31 00	90·0	180	360
1	179	0 35	36 00	89·2	0 34	35 00	89·2	0 34	34 00	89·2	0 33	33 00	89·2	0 32	32 00	89·2	0 31	31 00	89·1	181	359
2	178	1 11	35 59	88·4	1 09	34 59	88·4	1 07	33 59	88·3	1 05	32 59	88·3	1 04	31 59	88·3	1 02	30 59	88·3	182	358
3	177	1 46	35 58	87·6	1 43	34 58	87·5	1 41	33 58	87·5	1 38	32 58	87·5	1 35	31 58	87·5	1 33	30 58	87·4	183	357
4	176	2 21	35 56	86·8	2 18	34 56	86·7	2 14	33 56	86·7	2 11	32 56	86·6	2 07	31 56	86·6	2 04	30 56	86·6	184	356
5	175	2 56	35 54	86·0	2 52	34 54	85·9	2 48	33 54	85·9	2 43	32 54	85·8	2 39	31 54	85·8	2 34	30 54	85·7	185	355
6	174	3 31	35 51	85·1	3 26	34 51	85·1	3 21	33 51	85·0	3 16	32 51	85·0	3 11	31 52	84·9	3 05	30 52	84·9	186	354
7	173	4 06	35 48	84·3	4 00	34 48	84·3	3 54	33 48	84·2	3 48	32 48	84·1	3 42	31 48	84·1	3 36	30 49	84·0	187	353
8	172	4 42	35 44	83·5	4 35	34 44	83·4	4 28	33 44	83·4	4 21	32 45	83·3	4 14	31 45	83·2	4 07	30 45	83·1	188	352
9	171	5 17	35 40	82·7	5 09	34 40	82·6	5 01	33 40	82·5	4 53	32 41	82·4	4 45	31 41	82·3	4 37	30 41	82·3	189	351
10	170	5 51	35 35	81·9	5 43	34 35	81·8	5 34	33 36	81·7	5 26	32 36	81·6	5 17	31 36	81·5	5 08	30 37	81·4	190	350
11	169	6 26	35 30	81·1	6 17	34 30	81·0	6 08	33 31	80·8	5 58	32 31	80·7	5 48	31 31	80·6	5 38	30 32	80·5	191	349
12	168	7 01	35 24	80·2	6 51	34 24	80·1	6 41	33 25	80·0	6 30	32 25	79·9	6 20	31 26	79·8	6 09	30 27	79·7	192	348
13	167	7 36	35 18	79·4	7 25	34 18	79·3	7 14	33 19	79·2	7 02	32 19	79·0	6 51	31 20	78·9	6 39	30 21	78·8	193	347
14	166	8 11	35 11	78·6	7 59	34 12	78·5	7 46	33 12	78·3	7 34	32 13	78·2	7 22	31 14	78·1	7 09	30 15	77·9	194	346
15	165	8 45	35 04	77·8	8 32	34 04	77·6	8 19	33 05	77·5	8 06	32 06	77·3	7 53	31 07	77·2	7 40	30 08	77·1	195	345
16	164	9 19	34 56	76·9	9 06	33 57	76·8	8 52	32 58	76·6	8 38	31 58	76·5	8 24	31 00	76·3	8 10	30 01	76·2	196	344
17	163	9 54	34 47	76·1	9 39	33 48	75·9	9 25	32 49	75·8	9 10	31 50	75·6	8 55	30 52	75·5	8 40	29 53	75·3	197	343
18	162	10 28	34 39	75·3	10 13	33 40	75·1	9 57	32 41	74·9	9 41	31 42	74·8	9 25	30 43	74·6	9 09	29 45	74·4	198	342
19	161	11 02	34 29	74·4	10 46	33 30	74·2	10 29	32 32	74·1	10 13	31 33	73·9	9 56	30 35	73·7	9 39	29 36	73·6	199	341
20	160	11 36	34 19	73·6	11 19	33 21	73·4	11 02	32 22	73·2	10 44	31 24	73·0	10 27	30 25	72·8	10 09	29 27	72·7	200	340
21	159	12 10	34 09	72·7	11 52	33 10	72·5	11 34	32 12	72·3	11 15	31 14	72·2	10 57	30 15	72·0	10 38	29 17	71·8	201	339
22	158	12 43	33 58	71·9	12 24	33 00	71·7	12 06	32 01	71·5	11 46	31 03	71·3	11 27	30 05	71·1	11 07	29 07	70·9	202	338
23	157	13 17	33 46	71·0	12 57	32 48	70·8	12 37	31 50	70·6	12 17	30 52	70·4	11 57	29 54	70·2	11 37	28 57	70·0	203	337
24	156	13 50	33 34	70·2	13 29	32 36	70·0	13 09	31 38	69·7	12 48	30 41	69·5	12 27	29 43	69·3	12 06	28 46	69·1	204	336
25	155	14 23	33 22	69·3	14 02	32 24	69·1	13 40	31 26	68·9	13 18	30 29	68·6	12 56	29 31	68·4	12 34	28 34	68·2	205	335
26	154	14 56	33 09	68·5	14 34	32 11	68·2	14 11	31 14	68·0	13 49	30 16	67·8	13 26	29 19	67·5	13 03	28 22	67·3	206	334
27	153	15 29	32 55	67·6	15 06	31 58	67·3	14 42	31 00	67·1	14 19	30 03	66·9	13 55	29 06	66·6	13 31	28 10	66·4	207	333
28	152	16 01	32 41	66·7	15 37	31 44	66·5	15 13	30 47	66·2	14 49	29 50	66·0	14 24	28 53	65·7	14 00	27 57	65·5	208	332
29	151	16 33	32 26	65·8	16 09	31 29	65·6	15 44	30 32	65·3	15 19	29 36	65·1	14 53	28 39	64·8	14 28	27 43	64·6	209	331
30	150	17 05	32 11	65·0	16 40	31 14	64·7	16 14	30 17	64·4	15 48	29 21	64·2	15 22	28 25	63·9	14 55	27 29	63·7	210	330
31	149	17 37	31 55	64·1	17 11	30 58	63·8	16 44	30 02	63·5	16 17	29 06	63·3	15 50	28 10	63·0	15 23	27 15	62·7	211	329
32	148	18 09	31 38	63·2	17 42	30 42	62·9	17 14	29 46	62·6	16 47	28 51	62·3	16 19	27 55	62·1	15 50	27 00	61·8	212	328
33	147	18 40	31 21	62·3	18 12	30 25	62·0	17 44	29 30	61·7	17 15	28 34	61·4	16 47	27 39	61·2	16 17	26 45	60·9	213	327
34	146	19 11	31 04	61·4	18 42	30 08	61·1	18 13	29 13	60·8	17 44	28 18	60·5	17 14	27 23	60·2	16 44	26 29	60·0	214	326
35	145	19 42	30 46	60·5	19 12	29 50	60·2	18 42	28 55	59·9	18 12	28 01	59·6	17 42	27 06	59·3	17 11	26 12	59·0	215	325
36	144	20 13	30 27	59·6	19 42	29 32	59·2	19 11	28 37	58·9	18 40	27 43	58·6	18 09	26 49	58·4	17 37	25 55	58·1	216	324
37	143	20 43	30 07	58·6	20 12	29 13	58·3	19 40	28 19	58·0	19 08	27 25	57·7	18 36	26 31	57·4	18 03	25 38	57·1	217	323
38	142	21 13	29 48	57·7	20 41	28 53	57·4	20 08	27 59	57·1	19 35	27 06	56·8	19 02	26 13	56·5	18 29	25 20	56·2	218	322
39	141	21 43	29 27	56·8	21 10	28 33	56·4	20 36	27 40	56·1	20 03	26 47	55·8	19 29	25 54	55·5	18 55	25 02	55·2	219	321
40	140	22 12	29 06	55·8	21 38	28 13	55·5	21 04	27 20	55·2	20 30	26 27	54·9	19 55	25 35	54·6	19 20	24 43	54·3	220	320
41	139	22 41	28 44	54·9	22 06	27 51	54·5	21 31	26 59	54·2	20 56	26 07	53·9	20 21	25 15	53·6	19 45	24 24	53·3	221	319
42	138	23 10	28 22	53·9	22 34	27 29	53·6	21 58	26 37	53·3	21 22	25 46	52·9	20 46	24 55	52·6	20 10	24 04	52·3	222	318
43	137	23 38	27 59	53·0	23 02	27 07	52·6	22 25	26 15	52·3	21 48	25 24	52·0	21 11	24 34	51·7	20 34	23 43	51·4	223	317
44	136	24 06	27 36	52·0	23 29	26 44	51·7	22 51	25 53	51·3	22 14	25 02	51·0	21 36	24 12	50·7	20 58	23 23	50·4	224	316
45	135	24 34	27 11	51·0	23 56	26 20	50·7	23 17	25 30	50·3	22 39	24 40	50·0	22 00	23 50	49·7	21 21	23 01	49·4	225	315

[illegible]		[illegible]			55°			56°			57°			58°			59°			Lat. / A	
[illegible]	[illegible]	[illegible]	[illegible]	[illegible]	[illegible]	B/P	Z_1/Z_2	A/H	B/P	Z_1/Z_2	A/H	B/P	Z_1/Z_2	A/H	B/P	Z_1/Z_2	A/H	B/P	Z_1/Z_2	LHA	
[illegible]	[illegible]	[illegible]	[illegible]	[illegible]	[illegible]	° ′	°	° ′	° ′	°	° ′	° ′	°	° ′	° ′	°	° ′	° ′	°	°	°
[illegible]	[illegible]	[illegible]	[illegible]	[illegible]	[illegible]	26 20	50·7	23 17	25 30	50·3	22 39	24 40	50·0	22 00	23 50	49·7	21 21	23 01	49·4	225	315
[illegible]	[illegible]	[illegible]	[illegible]	[illegible]	[illegible]	25 56	49·7	23 43	25 06	49·4	23 04	24 17	49·0	22 24	23 28	48·7	21 45	22 39	48·4	226	314
[illegible]	[illegible]	[illegible]	[illegible]	[illegible]	[illegible]	25 32	48·7	24 08	24 42	48·4	23 28	23 53	48·0	22 48	23 05	47·7	22 08	22 17	47·4	227	313
[illegible]	[illegible]	[illegible]	[illegible]	[illegible]	[illegible]	25 06	47·7	24 33	24 17	47·4	23 53	23 29	47·0	23 11	22 41	46·7	22 30	21 54	46·4	228	312
[illegible]	[illegible]	[illegible]	[illegible]	[illegible]	[illegible]	24 40	46·7	24 58	23 52	46·4	24 16	23 05	46·0	23 34	22 17	45·7	22 52	21 31	45·4	229	311
[illegible]	[illegible]	[illegible]	[illegible]	[illegible]	[illegible]	24 14	45·7	25 22	23 26	45·3	24 40	22 39	45·0	23 57	21 53	44·7	23 14	21 07	44·4	230	310
[illegible]	[illegible]	[illegible]	[illegible]	[illegible]	[illegible]	23 47	44·7	25 45	23 00	44·3	25 02	22 14	44·0	24 19	21 28	43·7	23 36	20 43	43·4	231	309
[illegible]	[illegible]	[illegible]	[illegible]	[illegible]	[illegible]	23 19	43·6	26 09	22 33	43·3	25 25	21 48	43·0	24 41	21 03	42·7	23 57	20 18	42·3	232	308
[illegible]	[illegible]	[illegible]	[illegible]	[illegible]	[illegible]	22 51	42·6	26 32	22 06	42·3	25 47	21 21	41·9	25 02	20 37	41·6	24 17	19 53	41·3	233	307
[illegible]	[illegible]	[illegible]	[illegible]	[illegible]	[illegible]	22 22	41·6	26 54	21 38	41·2	26 09	20 54	40·9	25 23	20 10	40·6	24 37	19 27	40·3	234	306
[illegible]	[illegible]	[illegible]	[illegible]	[illegible]	[illegible]	21 53	40·5	27 16	21 09	40·2	26 30	20 26	39·9	25 44	19 43	39·5	24 57	19 01	39·2	235	305
[illegible]	[illegible]	[illegible]	[illegible]	[illegible]	[illegible]	21 23	39·5	27 37	20 40	39·1	26 50	19 57	38·8	26 04	19 16	38·5	25 17	18 34	38·2	236	304
[illegible]	[illegible]	[illegible]	[illegible]	[illegible]	[illegible]	20 52	38·4	27 58	20 10	38·1	27 11	19 29	37·8	26 23	18 48	37·4	25 35	18 07	37·1	237	303
[illegible]	[illegible]	[illegible]	[illegible]	[illegible]	[illegible]	20 21	37·3	28 19	19 40	37·0	27 31	18 59	36·7	26 42	18 19	36·4	25 54	17 40	36·1	238	302
[illegible]	[illegible]	[illegible]	[illegible]	[illegible]	[illegible]	19 50	36·3	28 38	19 09	35·9	27 50	18 30	35·6	27 01	17 50	35·3	26 12	17 12	35·0	239	301
[illegible]	[illegible]	[illegible]	[illegible]	[illegible]	29 47	19 18	35·2	28 58	18 38	34·9	28 09	17 59	34·5	27 19	17 21	34·2	26 29	16 43	34·0	240	300
61	119	30 56	19 24	34·4	30 07	18 45	34·1	29 17	18 06	33·8	28 27	17 29	33·5	27 37	16 51	33·2	26 46	16 14	32·9	241	299
62	118	31 16	18 50	33·3	30 26	18 12	33·0	29 35	17 34	32·7	28 45	16 57	32·4	27 54	16 21	32·1	27 03	15 45	31·8	242	298
63	117	31 35	18 15	32·2	30 44	17 38	31·9	29 53	17 02	31·6	29 02	16 26	31·3	28 10	15 50	31·0	27 19	15 15	30·7	243	297
64	116	31 53	17 40	31·1	31 02	17 04	30·8	30 10	16 28	30·5	29 19	15 53	30·2	28 27	15 19	29·9	27 35	14 45	29·6	244	296
65	115	32 11	17 04	30·0	31 19	16 29	29·7	30 27	15 55	29·4	29 35	15 21	29·1	28 42	14 48	28·8	27 50	14 15	28·5	245	295
66	114	32 29	16 28	28·8	31 36	15 54	28·5	30 43	15 20	28·2	29 50	14 48	28·0	28 57	14 16	27·7	28 04	13 44	27·4	246	294
67	113	32 45	15 51	27·7	31 52	15 18	27·4	30 59	14 46	27·1	30 05	14 14	26·8	29 12	13 43	26·6	28 18	13 13	26·3	247	293
68	112	33 01	15 14	26·5	32 08	14 42	26·3	31 14	14 11	26·0	30 20	13 40	25·7	29 26	13 10	25·5	28 31	12 41	25·2	248	292
69	111	33 17	14 36	25·4	32 23	14 05	25·1	31 28	13 35	24·8	30 34	13 06	24·6	29 39	12 37	24·4	28 44	12 09	24·1	249	291
70	110	33 32	13 57	24·2	32 37	13 28	24·0	31 42	12 59	23·7	30 47	12 31	23·5	29 52	12 04	23·2	28 57	11 37	23·0	250	290
71	109	33 46	13 18	23·1	32 51	12 51	22·8	31 55	12 23	22·6	31 00	11 56	22·3	30 04	11 30	22·1	29 09	11 04	21·9	251	289
72	108	33 59	12 39	21·9	33 04	12 13	21·6	32 08	11 46	21·4	31 12	11 21	21·2	30 16	10 56	21·0	29 20	10 31	20·8	252	288
73	107	34 12	12 00	20·7	33 16	11 34	20·5	32 20	11 09	20·2	31 23	10 45	20·0	30 27	10 21	19·8	29 30	9 58	19·6	253	287
74	106	34 24	11 19	19·5	33 28	10 55	19·3	32 31	10 32	19·1	31 34	10 09	18·9	30 37	9 46	18·7	29 41	9 24	18·5	254	286
75	105	34 36	10 39	18·3	33 39	10 16	18·1	32 42	9 54	17·9	31 44	9 32	17·7	30 47	9 11	17·5	29 50	8 50	17·4	255	285
76	104	34 46	9 58	17·1	33 49	9 37	16·9	32 52	9 16	16·7	31 54	8 56	16·6	30 57	8 36	16·4	29 59	8 16	16·2	256	284
77	103	34 56	9 17	15·9	33 59	8 57	15·7	33 01	8 38	15·6	32 03	8 19	15·4	31 05	8 00	15·2	30 07	7 42	15·1	257	283
78	102	35 06	8 35	14·7	34 08	8 17	14·5	33 10	7 59	14·4	32 11	7 41	14·2	31 13	7 24	14·1	30 15	7 07	13·9	258	282
79	101	35 14	7 54	13·5	34 16	7 37	13·3	33 18	7 20	13·2	32 19	7 04	13·0	31 21	6 48	12·9	30 22	6 32	12·8	259	281
80	100	35 22	7 11	12·3	34 24	6 56	12·1	33 25	6 41	12·0	32 26	6 26	11·9	31 27	6 12	11·7	30 29	5 57	11·6	260	280
81	99	35 29	6 29	11·1	34 30	6 15	10·9	33 32	6 01	10·8	32 33	5 48	10·7	31 34	5 35	10·6	30 35	5 22	10·5	261	279
82	98	35 36	5 46	9·9	34 37	5 34	9·7	33 37	5 22	9·6	32 38	5 10	9·5	31 39	4 58	9·4	30 40	4 47	9·3	262	278
83	97	35 41	5 04	8·6	34 42	4 53	8·5	33 43	4 42	8·4	32 43	4 32	8·3	31 44	4 21	8·2	30 45	4 11	8·2	263	277
84	96	35 46	4 21	7·4	34 47	4 11	7·3	33 47	4 02	7·2	32 48	3 53	7·1	31 48	3 44	7·1	30 49	3 36	7·0	264	276
85	95	35 51	3 37	6·2	34 51	3 30	6·1	33 51	3 22	6·0	32 52	3 14	6·0	31 52	3 07	5·9	30 52	3 00	5·8	265	275
86	94	35 54	2 54	4·9	34 54	2 48	4·9	33 54	2 42	4·8	32 55	2 36	4·8	31 55	2 30	4·7	30 55	2 24	4·7	266	274
87	93	35 57	2 11	3·7	34 57	2 06	3·7	33 57	2 01	3·6	32 57	1 57	3·6	31 57	1 52	3·5	30 57	1 48	3·5	267	273
88	92	35 58	1 27	2·5	34 59	1 24	2·4	33 59	1 21	2·4	32 59	1 18	2·4	31 59	1 15	2·4	30 59	1 12	2·3	268	272
89	91	36 00	0 44	1·2	35 00	0 42	1·2	34 00	0 40	1·2	33 00	0 39	1·2	32 00	0 37	1·2	31 00	0 36	1·2	269	271
90	90	36 00	0 00	0·0	35 00	0 00	0·0	34 00	0 00	0·0	33 00	0 00	0·0	32 00	0 00	0·0	31 00	0 00	0·0	270	270

N. Lat: for LHA > 180° … $Z_n = Z$
for LHA < 180° … $Z_n = 360° - Z$

S. Lat.: for LHA > 180° … $Z_n = 180° - Z$
for LHA < 180° … $Z_n = 180° + Z$

SIGHT REDUCTION TABLE

B: (–) for 90° < LHA < 270°
Dec: (–) for Lat. contrary name

Z_1: same sign as B
Z_2: (–) for F > 90°

Lat. / A		60°			61°			62°			63°			64°			65°			Lat. / A	
LHA/F		A/H	B/P	Z_1/Z_2	A/H	B/P	Z_1/Z_2	A/H	B/P	Z_1/Z_2	A/H	B/P	Z_1/Z_2	A/H	B/P	Z_1/Z_2	A/H	B/P	Z_1/Z_2	LHA	
°	°	° ′	° ′	°	° ′	° ′	°	° ′	° ′	°	° ′	° ′	°	° ′	° ′	°	° ′	° ′	°	°	°
0	180	0 00	30 00	90·0	0 00	29 00	90·0	0 00	28 00	90·0	0 00	27 00	90·0	0 00	26 00	90·0	0 00	25 00	90·0	180	360
1	179	0 30	30 00	89·1	0 29	29 00	89·1	0 28	28 00	89·1	0 27	27 00	89·1	0 26	26 00	89·1	0 25	25 00	89·1	181	359
2	178	1 00	29 59	88·3	0 58	28 59	88·3	0 56	27 59	88·2	0 54	26 59	88·2	0 53	25 59	88·2	0 51	24 59	88·2	182	358
3	177	1 30	29 58	87·4	1 27	28 58	87·4	1 24	27 58	87·4	1 22	26 58	87·3	1 19	25 58	87·3	1 16	24 58	87·3	183	357
4	176	2 00	29 56	86·5	1 56	28 56	86·5	1 53	27 57	86·5	1 49	26 57	86·4	1 45	25 57	86·4	1 41	24 57	86·4	184	356
5	175	2 30	29 54	85·7	2 25	28 54	85·6	2 21	27 55	85·6	2 16	26 55	85·5	2 11	25 55	85·5	2 07	24 55	85·5	185	355
6	174	3 00	29 52	84·8	2 54	28 52	84·7	2 49	27 52	84·7	2 43	26 52	84·6	2 38	25 53	84·6	2 32	24 53	84·6	186	354
7	173	3 30	29 49	83·9	3 23	28 49	83·9	3 17	27 49	83·8	3 10	26 50	83·8	3 04	25 50	83·7	2 57	24 50	83·7	187	353
8	172	3 59	29 45	83·1	3 52	28 46	83·0	3 45	27 46	82·9	3 37	26 46	82·9	3 30	25 47	82·8	3 22	24 47	82·7	188	352
9	171	4 29	29 42	82·2	4 21	28 42	82·1	4 13	27 42	82·0	4 04	26 43	82·0	3 56	25 43	81·9	3 47	24 44	81·8	189	351
10	170	4 59	29 37	81·3	4 50	28 38	81·2	4 41	27 38	81·2	4 31	26 39	81·1	4 22	25 39	81·0	4 13	24 40	80·9	190	350
11	169	5 28	29 33	80·4	5 18	28 33	80·4	5 08	27 34	80·3	4 58	26 34	80·2	4 48	25 35	80·1	4 38	24 36	80·0	191	349
12	168	5 58	29 27	79·6	5 47	28 28	79·5	5 36	27 29	79·4	5 25	26 29	79·3	5 14	25 30	79·2	5 02	24 31	79·1	192	348
13	167	6 27	29 22	78·7	6 16	28 22	78·6	6 04	27 23	78·5	5 52	26 24	78·4	5 40	25 25	78·3	5 27	24 26	78·2	193	347
14	166	6 57	29 15	77·8	6 44	28 16	77·7	6 31	27 17	77·6	6 18	26 18	77·5	6 05	25 20	77·4	5 52	24 21	77·3	194	346
15	165	7 26	29 09	76·9	7 13	28 10	76·8	6 59	27 11	76·7	6 45	26 12	76·6	6 31	25 14	76·5	6 17	24 15	76·4	195	345
16	164	7 55	29 02	76·1	7 41	28 03	75·9	7 26	27 04	75·8	7 11	26 06	75·7	6 56	25 07	75·5	6 41	24 09	75·4	196	344
17	163	8 24	28 54	75·2	8 09	27 56	75·0	7 53	26 57	74·9	7 38	25 59	74·8	7 22	25 00	74·6	7 06	24 02	74·5	197	343
18	162	8 53	28 46	74·3	8 37	27 48	74·1	8 20	26 50	74·0	8 04	25 51	73·9	7 47	24 53	73·7	7 30	23 55	73·6	198	342
19	161	9 22	28 38	73·4	9 05	27 40	73·2	8 48	26 41	73·1	8 30	25 43	72·9	8 12	24 45	72·8	7 55	23 48	72·7	199	341
20	160	9 51	28 29	72·5	9 33	27 31	72·3	9 14	26 33	72·2	8 56	25 35	72·0	8 37	24 37	71·9	8 19	23 40	71·7	200	340
21	159	10 19	28 19	71·6	10 00	27 22	71·4	9 41	26 24	71·3	9 22	25 26	71·1	9 02	24 29	71·0	8 43	23 32	70·8	201	339
22	158	10 48	28 10	70·7	10 28	27 12	70·5	10 08	26 15	70·4	9 48	25 17	70·2	9 27	24 20	70·0	9 07	23 23	69·9	202	338
23	157	11 16	27 59	69·8	10 55	27 02	69·6	10 34	26 05	69·5	10 13	25 08	69·3	9 52	24 11	69·1	9 30	23 14	69·0	203	337
24	156	11 44	27 49	68·9	11 22	26 51	68·7	11 00	25 54	68·5	10 38	24 58	68·4	10 16	24 01	68·2	9 54	23 04	68·0	204	336
25	155	12 12	27 37	68·0	11 49	26 40	67·8	11 27	25 44	67·6	11 04	24 47	67·4	10 41	23 51	67·3	10 17	22 55	67·1	205	335
26	154	12 40	27 26	67·1	12 16	26 29	66·9	11 53	25 33	66·7	11 29	24 36	66·5	11 05	23 40	66·3	10 41	22 44	66·2	206	334
27	153	13 07	27 13	66·2	12 43	26 17	66·0	12 18	25 21	65·8	11 54	24 25	65·6	11 29	23 29	65·4	11 04	22 34	65·2	207	333
28	152	13 35	27 01	65·3	13 09	26 05	65·1	12 44	25 09	64·9	12 18	24 13	64·7	11 53	23 18	64·5	11 27	22 23	64·3	208	332
29	151	14 02	26 48	64·4	13 36	25 52	64·1	13 09	24 56	63·9	12 43	24 01	63·7	12 16	23 06	63·5	11 49	22 11	63·3	209	331
30	150	14 29	26 34	63·4	14 02	25 39	63·2	13 35	24 43	63·0	13 07	23 49	62·8	12 40	22 54	62·6	12 12	21 59	62·4	210	330
31	149	14 55	26 20	62·5	14 28	25 25	62·3	14 00	24 30	62·1	13 31	23 36	61·8	13 03	22 41	61·6	12 34	21 47	61·4	211	329
[illegible]	148	15 22	26 05	61·6	14 53	25 11	61·3	14 24	24 16	61·1	13 55	23 22	60·9	13 26	22 28	60·7	12 56	21 35	60·5	212	328
[illegible]	147	15 48	25 50	60·6	15 19	24 56	60·4	14 49	24 02	60·2	14 19	23 08	59·9	13 49	22 15	59·7	13 18	21 22	59·5	213	327
[illegible]	[illegible]	16 14	25 35	59·7	15 44	24 41	59·5	15 13	23 47	59·2	14 42	22 54	59·0	14 11	22 01	58·8	13 40	21 08	58·6	214	326
[illegible]	[illegible]	16 40	25 19	58·8	16 09	24 25	58·5	15 37	23 32	58·3	15 06	22 39	58·0	14 34	21 47	57·8	14 02	20 54	57·6	215	325
[illegible]	[illegible]	[illegible] 05	25 02	57·8	16 33	24 09	57·6	16 01	23 17	57·3	15 29	22 24	57·1	14 56	21 32	56·9	14 23	20 40	56·6	216	324
[illegible]	[illegible]	[illegible]	24 45	56·9	16 58	23 53	56·6	16 25	23 00	56·4	15 51	22 09	56·1	15 18	21 17	55·9	14 44	20 26	55·7	217	323
[illegible]	[illegible]	[illegible]	24 28	55·9	17 22	23 36	55·7	16 48	22 44	55·4	16 14	21 53	55·2	15 39	21 01	54·9	15 05	20 11	54·7	218	322
[illegible]	[illegible]	[illegible]	24 10	55·0	17 46	23 18	54·7	17 11	22 27	54·4	16 36	21 36	54·2	16 01	20 46	54·0	15 25	19 55	53·7	219	321
[illegible]	[illegible]	[illegible]	[illegible] 52	54·0	18 09	23 00	53·7	17 34	22 10	53·5	16 58	21 19	53·2	16 22	20 29	53·0	15 46	19 39	52·7	220	320
[illegible]	[illegible]	[illegible]	[illegible]	53·0	18 33	22 42	52·8	17 56	21 52	52·5	17 20	21 02	52·2	16 43	20 13	52·0	16 06	19 23	51·8	221	319
[illegible]	[illegible]	[illegible]	[illegible]	52·1	18 56	22 23	51·8	18 19	21 34	51·5	17 41	20 44	51·3	17 03	19 55	51·0	16 26	19 07	50·8	222	318
[illegible]	[illegible]	[illegible]	[illegible]	[illegible]	19 18	22 04	50·8	18 40	21 15	50·5	18 02	20 26	50·3	17 24	19 38	50·0	16 45	18 50	49·8	223	317
[illegible]	[illegible]	[illegible]	[illegible]	[illegible]	19 41	21 44	49·8	19 02	20 56	49·5	18 23	20 08	49·3	17 44	19 20	49·0	17 04	18 33	48·8	224	316
[illegible]	[illegible]	[illegible]	[illegible]	[illegible]	[illegible]	[illegible]	48·8	19 23	20 36	48·6	18 43	19 49	48·3	18 03	19 02	48·1	17 23	18 15	47·8	225	315

Lat. / A		60°			61°			62°			63°			64°			65°			Lat. / A	
LHA/F		A/H	B/P	Z_1/Z_2	A/H	B/P	Z_1/Z_2	A/H	B/P	Z_1/Z_2	A/H	B/P	Z_1/Z_2	A/H	B/P	Z_1/Z_2	A/H	B/P	Z_1/Z_2	LHA	
°	°	° ′	° ′	°	° ′	° ′	°	° ′	° ′	°	° ′	° ′	°	° ′	° ′	°	° ′	° ′	°	°	°
45	135	20 42	22 12	49·1	20 03	21 24	48·8	19 23	20 36	48·6	18 43	19 49	48·3	18 03	19 02	48·1	17 23	18 15	47·8	225	315
46	134	21 05	21 51	48·1	20 25	21 04	47·8	19 44	20 16	47·6	19 04	19 29	47·3	18 23	18 43	47·1	17 42	17 57	46·8	226	314
47	133	21 27	21 30	47·1	20 46	20 43	46·8	20 05	19 56	46·6	19 24	19 10	46·3	18 42	18 24	46·1	18 00	17 39	45·8	227	313
48	132	21 49	21 07	46·1	21 07	20 21	45·8	20 25	19 35	45·6	19 43	18 50	45·3	19 01	18 04	45·1	18 18	17 20	44·8	228	312
49	131	22 10	20 45	45·1	21 28	19 59	44·8	20 45	19 14	44·6	20 02	18 29	44·3	19 19	17 45	44·0	18 36	17 01	43·8	229	311
50	130	22 31	20 22	44·1	21 48	19 37	43·8	21 05	18 52	43·5	20 21	18 08	43·3	19 37	17 24	43·0	18 53	16 41	42·8	230	310
51	129	22 52	19 58	43·1	22 08	19 14	42·8	21 24	18 30	42·5	20 40	17 47	42·3	19 55	17 04	42·0	19 10	16 21	41·8	231	309
52	128	23 12	19 34	42·1	22 28	18 51	41·8	21 43	18 08	41·5	20 58	17 25	41·2	20 13	16 43	41·0	19 27	16 01	40·8	232	308
53	127	23 32	19 10	41·0	22 47	18 27	40·7	22 01	17 45	40·5	21 15	17 03	40·2	20 30	16 21	40·0	19 44	15 41	39·7	233	307
54	126	23 52	18 45	40·0	23 06	18 03	39·7	22 19	17 21	39·4	21 33	16 40	39·2	20 46	16 00	39·0	20 00	15 20	38·7	234	306
55	125	24 11	18 19	39·0	23 24	17 38	38·7	22 37	16 58	38·4	21 50	16 17	38·2	21 03	15 38	37·9	20 15	14 58	37·7	235	305
56	124	24 29	17 54	37·9	23 42	17 13	37·6	22 54	16 34	37·4	22 07	15 54	37·1	21 19	15 15	36·9	20 31	14 37	36·7	236	304
57	123	24 48	17 27	36·9	23 59	16 48	36·6	23 11	16 09	36·3	22 23	15 31	36·1	21 34	14 53	35·8	20 46	14 15	35·6	237	303
58	122	25 05	17 01	35·8	24 17	16 22	35·5	23 28	15 44	35·3	22 39	15 07	35·0	21 49	14 29	34·8	21 00	13 53	34·6	238	302
59	121	25 23	16 34	34·8	24 33	15 56	34·5	23 44	15 19	34·2	22 54	14 42	34·0	22 04	14 06	33·8	21 14	13 30	33·5	239	301
60	120	25 40	16 06	33·7	24 50	15 29	33·4	23 59	14 53	33·2	23 09	14 18	32·9	22 19	13 42	32·7	21 28	13 07	32·5	240	300
61	119	25 56	15 38	32·6	25 05	15 03	32·4	24 15	14 27	32·1	23 24	13 53	31·9	22 33	13 18	31·7	21 42	12 44	31·5	241	299
62	118	26 12	15 10	31·5	25 21	14 35	31·3	24 29	14 01	31·1	23 38	13 27	30·8	22 46	12 54	30·6	21 55	12 21	30·4	242	298
63	117	26 27	14 41	30·5	25 36	14 08	30·2	24 44	13 34	30·0	23 52	13 01	29·8	22 59	12 29	29·5	22 07	11 57	29·3	243	297
64	116	26 42	14 12	29·4	25 50	13 39	29·1	24 57	13 07	28·9	24 05	12 35	28·7	23 12	12 04	28·5	22 19	11 33	28·3	244	296
65	115	26 57	13 43	28·3	26 04	13 11	28·1	25 11	12 40	27·8	24 18	12 09	27·6	23 25	11 39	27·4	22 31	11 09	27·2	245	295
66	114	27 11	13 13	27·2	26 17	12 42	27·0	25 24	12 12	26·8	24 30	11 43	26·6	23 36	11 13	26·4	22 43	10 44	26·2	246	294
67	113	27 24	12 43	26·1	26 30	12 13	25·9	25 36	11 44	25·7	24 42	11 16	25·5	23 48	10 47	25·3	22 54	10 20	25·1	247	293
68	112	27 37	12 12	25·0	26 43	11 44	24·8	25 48	11 16	24·6	24 54	10 48	24·4	23 59	10 21	24·2	23 04	9 55	24·0	248	292
69	111	27 50	11 41	23·9	26 55	11 14	23·7	26 00	10 47	23·5	25 05	10 21	23·3	24 09	9 55	23·1	23 14	9 29	23·0	249	291
70	110	28 01	11 10	22·8	27 06	10 44	22·6	26 11	10 18	22·4	25 15	9 53	22·2	24 20	9 28	22·0	23 24	9 04	21·9	250	290
71	109	28 13	10 39	21·7	27 17	10 14	21·5	26 21	9 49	21·3	25 25	9 25	21·1	24 29	9 01	21·0	23 33	8 38	20·8	251	289
72	108	28 24	10 07	20·6	27 27	9 43	20·4	26 31	9 20	20·2	25 35	8 57	20·0	24 38	8 34	19·9	23 42	8 12	19·7	252	288
73	107	28 34	9 35	19·4	27 37	9 12	19·3	26 41	8 50	19·1	25 44	8 28	18·9	24 47	8 07	18·8	23 50	7 46	18·6	253	287
74	106	28 44	9 03	18·3	27 47	8 41	18·2	26 50	8 20	18·0	25 52	8 00	17·8	24 55	7 39	17·7	23 58	7 19	17·6	254	286
75	105	28 53	8 30	17·2	27 55	8 10	17·0	26 58	7 50	16·9	26 01	7 31	16·7	25 03	7 12	16·6	24 06	6 53	16·5	255	285
76	104	29 01	7 57	16·1	28 04	7 38	15·9	27 06	7 20	15·8	26 08	7 02	15·6	25 10	6 44	15·5	24 13	6 26	15·4	256	284
77	103	29 09	7 24	14·9	28 11	7 06	14·8	27 13	6 49	14·7	26 15	6 32	14·5	25 17	6 16	14·4	24 19	5 59	14·3	257	283
78	102	29 17	6 51	13·8	28 18	6 34	13·7	27 20	6 19	13·5	26 22	6 03	13·4	25 23	5 47	13·3	24 25	5 32	13·2	258	282
79	101	29 24	6 17	12·7	28 25	6 02	12·5	27 27	5 48	12·4	26 28	5 33	12·3	25 29	5 19	12·2	24 31	5 05	12·1	259	281
80	100	29 30	5 44	11·5	28 31	5 30	11·4	27 32	5 17	11·3	26 33	5 03	11·2	25 35	4 50	11·1	24 36	4 38	11·0	260	280
81	99	29 36	5 10	10·4	28 37	4 57	10·3	27 38	4 45	10·2	26 38	4 33	10·1	25 39	4 22	10·0	24 40	4 10	9·9	261	279
82	98	29 41	4 36	9·2	28 41	4 25	9·1	27 42	4 14	9·0	26 43	4 03	9·0	25 44	3 53	8·9	24 44	3 43	8·8	262	278
83	97	29 45	4 01	8·1	28 46	3 52	8·0	27 46	3 42	7·9	26 47	3 33	7·8	25 48	3 24	7·8	24 48	3 15	7·7	263	277
84	96	29 49	3 27	6·9	28 50	3 19	6·9	27 50	3 11	6·8	26 50	3 03	6·7	25 51	2 55	6·7	24 51	2 47	6·6	264	276
85	95	29 52	2 53	5·8	28 53	2 46	5·7	27 53	2 39	5·7	26 53	2 33	5·6	25 54	2 26	5·6	24 54	2 20	5·5	265	275
86	94	29 55	2 18	4·6	28 55	2 13	4·6	27 56	2 07	4·5	26 56	2 02	4·5	25 56	1 57	4·4	24 56	1 52	4·4	266	274
87	93	29 57	1 44	3·5	28 57	1 40	3·4	27 57	1 36	3·4	26 58	1 32	3·4	25 58	1 28	3·3	24 58	1 24	3·3	267	273
88	92	29 59	1 09	2·3	28 59	1 06	2·3	27 59	1 04	2·3	26 59	1 01	2·2	25 59	0 59	2·2	24 59	0 56	2·2	268	272
89	91	30 00	0 35	1·2	29 00	0 33	1·1	28 00	0 32	1·1	27 00	0 31	1·1	26 00	0 29	1·1	25 00	0 28	1·1	269	271
90	90	30 00	0 00	0·0	29 00	0 00	0·0	28 00	0 00	0·0	27 00	0 00	0·0	26 00	0 00	0·0	25 00	0 00	0·0	270	270

N. Lat: for LHA > 180° … $Z_n = Z$
for LHA < 180° … $Z_n = 360° - Z$

S. Lat.: for LHA > 180° … $Z_n = 180° - Z$
for LHA < 180° … $Z_n = 180° + Z$

SIGHT REDUCTION TABLE

B: (–) for 90° < LHA < 270°
Dec: (–) for Lat. contrary name

Z_1: same sign as B
Z_2: (–) for F > 90°

Lat. / A		66°			67°			68°			69°			70°			71°			Lat. / A	
LHA/F		A/H	B/P	Z_1/Z_2	A/H	B/P	Z_1/Z_2	A/H	B/P	Z_1/Z_2	A/H	B/P	Z_1/Z_2	A/H	B/P	Z_1/Z_2	A/H	B/P	Z_1/Z_2	LHA	
°	°	° ′	° ′	°	° ′	° ′	°	° ′	° ′	°	° ′	° ′	°	° ′	° ′	°	° ′	° ′	°	°	°
0	180	0 00	24 00	90·0	0 00	23 00	90·0	0 00	22 00	90·0	0 00	21 00	90·0	0 00	20 00	90·0	0 00	19 00	90·0	180	360
1	179	0 24	24 00	89·1	0 23	23 00	89·1	0 22	22 00	89·1	0 22	21 00	89·1	0 21	20 00	89·1	0 20	19 00	89·1	181	359
2	178	0 49	23 59	88·2	0 47	22 59	88·2	0 45	21 59	88·1	0 43	20 59	88·1	0 41	19 59	88·1	0 39	18 59	88·1	182	358
3	177	1 13	23 58	87·3	1 10	22 58	87·2	1 07	21 58	87·2	1 04	20 58	87·2	1 02	19 58	87·2	0 59	18 59	87·2	183	357
4	176	1 38	23 57	86·3	1 34	22 57	86·3	1 30	21 57	86·3	1 26	20 57	86·3	1 22	19 57	86·2	1 18	18 57	86·2	184	356
5	175	2 02	23 55	85·4	1 57	22 55	85·4	1 52	21 55	85·4	1 47	20 56	85·3	1 42	19 56	85·3	1 38	18 56	85·3	185	355
6	174	2 26	23 53	84·5	2 20	22 53	84·5	2 15	21 53	84·4	2 09	20 54	84·4	2 03	19 54	84·4	1 57	18 54	84·3	186	354
7	173	2 50	23 50	83·6	2 44	22 51	83·6	2 37	21 51	83·5	2 30	20 51	83·5	2 23	19 52	83·4	2 16	18 52	83·4	187	353
8	172	3 15	23 48	82·7	3 07	22 48	82·6	2 59	21 48	82·6	2 52	20 49	82·5	2 44	19 49	82·5	2 36	18 50	82·4	188	352
9	171	3 39	23 44	81·8	3 30	22 45	81·7	3 22	21 45	81·6	3 13	20 46	81·6	3 04	19 46	81·5	2 55	18 47	81·5	189	351
10	170	4 03	23 41	80·8	3 53	22 41	80·8	3 44	21 42	80·7	3 34	20 42	80·7	3 24	19 43	80·6	3 14	18 44	80·5	190	350
11	169	4 27	23 36	79·9	4 17	22 37	79·9	4 06	21 38	79·8	3 55	20 39	79·7	3 45	19 40	79·6	3 34	18 41	79·6	191	349
12	168	4 51	23 32	79·0	4 40	22 33	78·9	4 28	21 34	78·9	4 16	20 35	78·8	4 05	19 36	78·7	3 53	18 37	78·6	192	348
13	167	5 15	23 27	78·1	5 03	22 28	78·0	4 50	21 29	77·9	4 37	20 30	77·8	4 25	19 32	77·8	4 12	18 33	77·7	193	347
14	166	5 39	23 22	77·2	5 25	22 23	77·1	5 12	21 24	77·0	4 58	20 26	76·9	4 45	19 27	76·8	4 31	18 28	76·7	194	346
15	165	6 03	23 16	76·2	5 48	22 18	76·1	5 34	21 19	76·0	5 19	20 21	76·0	5 05	19 22	75·9	4 50	18 24	75·8	195	345
16	164	6 26	23 10	75·3	6 11	22 12	75·2	5 56	21 13	75·1	5 40	20 15	75·0	5 25	19 17	74·9	5 09	18 19	74·8	196	344
17	163	6 50	23 04	74·4	6 34	22 06	74·3	6 17	21 08	74·2	6 01	20 09	74·1	5 44	19 11	74·0	5 28	18 14	73·9	197	343
18	162	7 13	22 57	73·5	6 56	21 59	73·3	6 39	21 01	73·2	6 21	20 03	73·1	6 04	19 06	73·0	5 46	18 08	72·9	198	342
19	161	7 37	22 50	72·5	7 19	21 52	72·4	7 00	20 54	72·3	6 42	19 57	72·2	6 24	18 59	72·1	6 05	18 02	72·0	199	341
20	160	8 00	22 42	71·6	7 41	21 45	71·5	7 22	20 47	71·4	7 02	19 50	71·2	6 43	18 53	71·1	6 24	17 56	71·0	200	340
21	159	8 23	22 34	70·7	8 03	21 37	70·5	7 43	20 40	70·4	7 23	19 43	70·3	7 02	18 46	70·2	6 42	17 49	70·1	201	339
22	158	8 46	22 26	69·7	8 25	21 29	69·6	8 04	20 32	69·5	7 43	19 35	69·3	7 22	18 39	69·2	7 00	17 42	69·1	202	338
23	157	9 09	22 17	68·8	8 47	21 21	68·7	8 25	20 24	68·5	8 03	19 28	68·4	7 41	18 31	68·3	7 19	17 35	68·1	203	337
24	156	9 31	22 08	67·9	9 09	21 12	67·7	8 46	20 16	67·6	8 23	19 19	67·4	8 00	18 24	67·3	7 37	17 28	67·2	204	336
25	155	9 54	21 58	66·9	9 30	21 03	66·8	9 07	20 07	66·6	8 43	19 11	66·5	8 19	18 15	66·3	7 55	17 20	66·2	205	335
26	154	10 16	21 49	66·0	9 52	20 53	65·8	9 27	19 57	65·7	9 02	19 02	65·5	8 37	18 07	65·4	8 12	17 12	65·2	206	334
27	153	10 38	21 38	65·0	10 13	20 43	64·9	9 48	19 48	64·7	9 22	18 53	64·6	8 56	17 58	64·4	8 30	17 03	64·3	207	333
28	152	11 00	21 28	64·1	10 34	20 33	63·9	10 08	19 38	63·8	9 41	18 43	63·6	9 14	17 49	63·5	8 48	16 55	63·3	208	332
29	151	11 22	21 17	63·1	10 55	20 22	63·0	10 28	19 28	62·8	10 00	18 34	62·6	9 33	17 39	62·5	9 05	16 46	62·3	209	331
30	150	11 44	21 05	62·2	11 16	20 11	62·0	10 48	19 17	61·8	10 19	18 23	61·7	9 51	17 30	61·5	9 22	16 36	61·4	210	330
31	149	12 06	20 53	61·2	11 37	20 00	61·1	11 07	19 06	60·9	10 38	18 13	60·7	10 09	17 20	60·5	9 39	16 27	60·4	211	329
32	148	12 27	20 41	60·3	11 57	19 48	60·1	11 27	18 55	59·9	10 57	18 02	59·7	10 27	17 09	59·6	9 56	16 17	59·4	212	328
33	147	12 48	20 29	59·3	12 17	19 36	59·1	11 46	18 43	58·9	11 15	17 51	58·8	10 44	16 58	58·6	10 13	16 06	58·4	213	327
34	146	13 09	20 16	58·4	12 37	19 23	58·2	12 06	18 31	58·0	11 34	17 39	57·8	11 02	16 47	57·6	10 29	15 56	57·5	214	326
35	145	13 29	20 02	57·4	12 57	19 10	57·2	12 24	18 19	57·0	11 52	17 27	56·8	11 19	16 36	56·7	10 46	15 45	56·5	215	325
36	144	13 50	19 49	56·4	13 17	18 57	56·2	12 43	18 06	56·0	12 10	17 15	55·9	11 36	16 24	55·7	11 02	15 34	55·5	216	324
37	143	14 10	19 34	55·5	13 36	18 44	55·3	13 02	17 53	55·1	12 27	17 03	54·9	11 53	16 12	54·7	11 18	15 23	54·5	217	323
38	142	14 30	19 20	54·5	13 55	18 30	54·3	13 20	17 40	54·1	12 45	16 50	53·9	12 09	16 00	53·7	11 34	15 11	53·5	218	322
39	141	14 50	19 05	53·5	14 14	18 15	53·3	13 38	17 26	53·1	13 02	16 37	52·9	12 26	15 48	52·7	11 49	14 59	52·6	219	321
40	140	15 09	18 50	52·5	14 33	18 01	52·3	13 56	17 12	52·1	13 19	16 23	51·9	12 42	15 35	51·7	12 05	14 47	51·6	220	320
41	139	15 29	18 34	51·5	14 51	17 46	51·3	14 14	16 57	51·1	13 36	16 09	50·9	12 58	15 22	50·8	12 20	14 34	50·6	221	319
42	138	15 48	18 18	50·6	15 09	17 30	50·3	14 31	16 43	50·1	13 52	15 55	49·9	13 14	15 08	49·8	12 35	14 21	49·6	222	318
43	137	16 06	18 02	49·6	15 27	17 15	49·4	14 48	16 28	49·2	14 09	15 41	49·0	13 29	14 54	48·8	12 50	14 08	48·6	223	317
44	136	16 25	17 46	48·6	15 45	16 59	48·4	15 05	16 12	48·2	14 25	15 26	48·0	13 45	14 40	47·8	13 04	13 55	47·6	224	316
45	135	16 43	17 29	47·6	16 02	16 42	47·4	15 22	15 57	47·2	14 41	15 11	47·0	14 00	14 26	46·8	13 19	13 41	46·6	225	315

Lat. / A		66°			67°			68°			69°			70°			71°			Lat. / A	
LHA/F		A/H	B/P	Z_1/Z_2	A/H	B/P	Z_1/Z_2	A/H	B/P	Z_1/Z_2	A/H	B/P	Z_1/Z_2	A/H	B/P	Z_1/Z_2	A/H	B/P	Z_1/Z_2	LHA	
°	°	° ′	° ′	°	° ′	° ′	°	° ′	° ′	°	° ′	° ′	°	° ′	° ′	°	° ′	° ′	°	°	°
45	135	16 43	17 29	47·6	16 02	16 42	47·4	15 22	15 57	47·2	14 41	15 11	47·0	14 00	14 26	46·8	13 19	13 41	46·6	225	315
46	134	17 01	17 11	46·6	16 19	16 26	46·4	15 38	15 41	46·2	14 56	14 56	46·0	14 15	14 11	45·8	13 33	13 27	45·6	226	314
47	133	17 18	16 53	45·6	16 36	16 09	45·4	15 54	15 24	45·2	15 12	14 40	45·0	14 29	13 56	44·8	13 46	13 13	44·6	227	313
48	132	17 36	16 35	44·6	16 53	15 51	44·4	16 10	15 08	44·2	15 27	14 24	44·0	14 43	13 41	43·8	14 00	12 58	43·6	228	312
49	131	17 53	16 17	43·6	17 09	15 34	43·4	16 25	14 51	43·2	15 42	14 08	43·0	14 58	13 26	42·8	14 13	12 44	42·6	229	311
50	130	18 09	15 58	42·6	17 25	15 16	42·4	16 41	14 33	42·1	15 56	13 52	41·9	15 11	13 10	41·8	14 27	12 29	41·6	230	310
51	129	18 26	15 39	41·6	17 41	14 57	41·3	16 56	14 16	41·1	16 10	13 35	40·9	15 25	12 54	40·8	14 39	12 14	40·6	231	309
52	128	18 42	15 20	40·5	17 56	14 39	40·3	17 10	13 58	40·1	16 24	13 18	39·9	15 38	12 38	39·7	14 52	11 58	39·6	232	308
53	127	18 57	15 00	39·5	18 11	14 20	39·3	17 24	13 40	39·1	16 38	13 00	38·9	15 51	12 21	38·7	15 04	11 42	38·6	233	307
54	126	19 13	14 40	38·5	18 26	14 01	38·3	17 39	13 22	38·1	16 51	12 43	37·9	16 04	12 05	37·7	15 16	11 26	37·5	234	306
55	125	19 28	14 20	37·5	18 40	13 41	37·3	17 52	13 03	37·1	17 04	12 25	36·9	16 16	11 48	36·7	15 28	11 10	36·5	235	305
56	124	19 42	13 59	36·4	18 54	13 21	36·2	18 06	12 44	36·0	17 17	12 07	35·8	16 28	11 30	35·7	15 40	10 54	35·5	236	304
57	123	19 57	13 38	35·4	19 08	13 01	35·2	18 19	12 25	35·0	17 29	11 49	34·8	16 40	11 13	34·6	15 51	10 37	34·5	237	303
58	122	20 11	13 17	34·4	19 21	12 41	34·2	18 31	12 05	34·0	17 42	11 30	33·8	16 52	10 55	33·6	16 02	10 20	33·5	238	302
59	121	20 24	12 55	33·3	19 34	12 20	33·1	18 44	11 45	32·9	17 53	11 11	32·8	17 03	10 37	32·6	16 12	10 03	32·4	239	301
60	120	20 37	12 33	32·3	19 47	11 59	32·1	18 56	11 25	31·9	18 05	10 52	31·7	17 14	10 19	31·6	16 23	9 46	31·4	240	300
61	119	20 50	12 11	31·2	19 59	11 38	31·1	19 08	11 05	30·9	18 16	10 33	30·7	17 24	10 00	30·5	16 33	9 29	30·4	241	299
62	118	21 03	11 48	30·2	20 11	11 16	30·0	19 19	10 44	29·8	18 27	10 13	29·7	17 35	9 42	29·5	16 42	9 11	29·4	242	298
63	117	21 15	11 26	29·2	20 22	10 54	29·0	19 30	10 24	28·8	18 37	9 53	28·6	17 45	9 23	28·5	16 52	8 53	28·3	243	297
64	116	21 27	11 03	28·1	20 34	10 32	27·9	19 41	10 03	27·7	18 47	9 33	27·6	17 54	9 04	27·4	17 01	8 35	27·3	244	296
65	115	21 38	10 39	27·0	20 44	10 10	26·9	19 51	9 41	26·7	18 57	9 13	26·5	18 03	8 45	26·4	17 10	8 17	26·3	245	295
66	114	21 49	10 16	26·0	20 55	9 48	25·8	20 01	9 20	25·7	19 07	8 52	25·5	18 12	8 25	25·4	17 18	7 58	25·2	246	294
67	113	21 59	9 52	24·9	21 05	9 25	24·8	20 10	8 58	24·6	19 16	8 32	24·5	18 21	8 06	24·3	17 26	7 40	24·2	247	293
68	112	22 09	9 28	23·9	21 14	9 02	23·7	20 19	8 36	23·5	19 24	8 11	23·4	18 29	7 46	23·3	17 34	7 21	23·1	248	292
69	111	22 19	9 04	22·8	21 24	8 39	22·6	20 28	8 14	22·5	19 33	7 50	22·4	18 37	7 26	22·2	17 42	7 02	22·1	249	291
70	110	22 28	8 39	21·7	21 32	8 16	21·6	20 37	7 52	21·4	19 41	7 29	21·3	18 45	7 06	21·2	17 49	6 43	21·1	250	290
71	109	22 37	8 15	20·7	21 41	7 52	20·5	20 45	7 30	20·4	19 48	7 07	20·2	18 52	6 45	20·1	17 56	6 24	20·0	251	289
72	108	22 45	7 50	19·6	21 49	7 28	19·4	20 52	7 07	19·3	19 56	6 46	19·2	18 59	6 25	19·1	18 02	6 04	19·0	252	288
73	107	22 53	7 25	18·5	21 56	7 04	18·4	21 00	6 44	18·2	20 03	6 24	18·1	19 05	6 04	18·0	18 08	5 45	17·9	253	287
74	106	23 01	7 00	17·4	22 04	6 40	17·3	21 06	6 21	17·2	20 09	6 02	17·1	19 12	5 44	17·0	18 14	5 25	16·9	254	286
75	105	23 08	6 34	16·3	22 10	6 16	16·2	21 13	5 58	16·1	20 15	5 40	16·0	19 17	5 23	15·9	18 20	5 06	15·8	255	285
76	104	23 15	6 09	15·3	22 17	5 52	15·2	21 19	5 35	15·1	20 21	5 18	15·0	19 23	5 02	14·9	18 25	4 46	14·8	256	284
77	103	23 21	5 43	14·2	22 23	5 27	14·1	21 24	5 12	14·0	20 26	4 56	13·9	19 28	4 41	13·8	18 30	4 26	13·7	257	283
78	102	23 27	5 17	13·1	22 28	5 03	13·0	21 30	4 48	12·9	20 31	4 34	12·8	19 33	4 20	12·7	18 34	4 06	12·7	258	282
79	101	23 32	4 51	12·0	22 33	4 38	11·9	21 35	4 24	11·8	20 36	4 11	11·8	19 37	3 58	11·7	18 38	3 46	11·6	259	281
80	100	23 37	4 25	10·9	22 38	4 13	10·8	21 39	4 01	10·8	20 40	3 49	10·7	19 41	3 37	10·6	18 42	3 25	10·6	260	280
81	99	23 41	3 59	9·8	22 42	3 48	9·8	21 43	3 37	9·7	20 44	3 26	9·6	19 45	3 16	9·6	18 45	3 05	9·5	261	279
82	98	23 45	3 33	8·7	22 46	3 23	8·7	21 46	3 13	8·6	20 47	3 03	8·6	19 48	2 54	8·5	18 48	2 45	8·5	262	278
83	97	23 49	3 06	7·7	22 49	2 58	7·6	21 50	2 49	7·5	20 50	2 41	7·5	19 51	2 32	7·4	18 51	2 24	7·4	263	277
84	96	23 52	2 40	6·6	22 52	2 32	6·5	21 52	2 25	6·5	20 53	2 18	6·4	19 53	2 11	6·4	18 54	2 04	6·3	264	276
85	95	23 54	2 13	5·5	22 54	2 07	5·4	21 55	2 01	5·4	20 55	1 55	5·4	19 55	1 49	5·3	18 55	1 43	5·3	265	275
86	94	23 56	1 47	4·4	22 56	1 42	4·3	21 57	1 37	4·3	20 57	1 32	4·3	19 57	1 27	4·3	18 57	1 23	4·2	266	274
87	93	23 58	1 20	3·3	22 58	1 16	3·3	21 58	1 13	3·2	20 58	1 09	3·2	19 58	1 05	3·2	18 58	1 02	3·2	267	273
88	92	23 59	0 53	2·2	22 59	0 51	2·2	21 59	0 48	2·2	20 59	0 46	2·1	19 59	0 44	2·1	18 59	0 41	2·1	268	272
89	91	24 00	0 27	1·1	23 00	0 25	1·1	22 00	0 24	1·1	21 00	0 23	1·1	20 00	0 22	1·1	19 00	0 21	1·1	269	271
90	90	24 00	0 00	0·0	23 00	0 00	0·0	22 00	0 00	0·0	21 00	0 00	0·0	20 00	0 00	0·0	19 00	0 00	0·0	270	270

N. Lat: for LHA > 180° … $Z_n = Z$
for LHA < 180° … $Z_n = 360° - Z$

S. Lat.: for LHA > 180° … $Z_n = 180° - Z$
for LHA < 180° … $Z_n = 180° + Z$

SIGHT REDUCTION TABLE

B: (−) for 90° < LHA < 270°
Dec:(−) for Lat. contrary name

Z_1: same sign as B
Z_2: (−) for F > 90°

Lat. / A		72°			73°			74°			75°			76°			77°			Lat. / A	
LHA/F		A/H	B/P	Z_1/Z_2	A/H	B/P	Z_1/Z_2	A/H	B/P	Z_1/Z_2	A/H	B/P	Z_1/Z_2	A/H	B/P	Z_1/Z_2	A/H	B/P	Z_1/Z_2	LHA	
°	°	° ′	° ′	°	° ′	° ′	°	° ′	° ′	°	° ′	° ′	°	° ′	° ′	°	° ′	° ′	°	°	°
0	180	0 00	18 00	90·0	0 00	17 00	90·0	0 00	16 00	90·0	0 00	15 00	90·0	0 00	14 00	90·0	0 00	13 00	90·0	180	360
1	179	0 19	18 00	89·0	0 18	17 00	89·0	0 17	16 00	89·0	0 16	15 00	89·0	0 15	14 00	89·0	0 13	13 00	89·0	181	359
2	178	0 37	17 59	88·1	0 35	16 59	88·1	0 33	15 59	88·1	0 31	14 59	88·1	0 29	14 00	88·1	0 27	13 00	88·1	182	358
3	177	0 56	17 59	87·1	0 53	16 59	87·1	0 50	15 59	87·1	0 47	14 59	87·1	0 44	13 59	87·1	0 40	12 59	87·1	183	357
4	176	1 14	17 58	86·2	1 10	16 58	86·2	1 06	15 58	86·2	1 02	14 58	86·1	0 58	13 58	86·1	0 54	12 58	86·1	184	356
5	175	1 33	17 56	85·2	1 28	16 56	85·2	1 23	15 57	85·2	1 18	14 57	85·2	1 12	13 57	85·1	1 07	12 57	85·1	185	355
6	174	1 51	17 54	84·3	1 45	16 55	84·3	1 39	15 55	84·2	1 33	14 55	84·2	1 27	13 56	84·2	1 21	12 56	84·2	186	354
7	173	2 09	17 52	83·3	2 03	16 53	83·3	1 56	15 53	83·3	1 48	14 54	83·2	1 41	13 54	83·2	1 34	12 54	83·2	187	353
8	172	2 28	17 50	82·4	2 20	16 51	82·3	2 12	15 51	82·3	2 04	14 52	82·3	1 56	13 52	82·2	1 48	12 53	82·2	188	352
9	171	2 46	17 48	81·4	2 37	16 48	81·4	2 28	15 49	81·3	2 19	14 49	81·3	2 10	13 50	81·3	2 01	12 51	81·2	189	351
10	170	3 05	17 45	80·5	2 55	16 45	80·4	2 45	15 46	80·4	2 35	14 47	80·3	2 24	13 48	80·3	2 14	12 49	80·3	190	350
11	169	3 23	17 41	79·5	3 12	16 42	79·5	3 01	15 43	79·4	2 50	14 44	79·4	2 39	13 45	79·3	2 28	12 46	79·3	191	349
12	168	3 41	17 38	78·6	3 29	16 39	78·5	3 17	15 40	78·5	3 05	14 41	78·4	2 53	13 42	78·3	2 41	12 44	78·3	192	348
13	167	3 59	17 34	77·6	3 46	16 35	77·5	3 33	15 37	77·5	3 20	14 38	77·4	3 07	13 39	77·4	2 54	12 41	77·3	193	347
14	166	4 17	17 30	76·7	4 03	16 31	76·6	3 49	15 33	76·5	3 35	14 34	76·5	3 21	13 36	76·4	3 07	12 38	76·3	194	346
15	165	4 35	17 25	75·7	4 20	16 27	75·6	4 05	15 29	75·6	3 50	14 31	75·5	3 35	13 32	75·4	3 20	12 34	75·4	195	345
16	164	4 53	17 21	74·7	4 37	16 23	74·7	4 21	15 25	74·6	4 05	14 27	74·5	3 49	13 29	74·5	3 33	12 31	74·4	196	344
17	163	5 11	17 16	73·8	4 54	16 18	73·7	4 37	15 20	73·6	4 20	14 22	73·5	4 03	13 25	73·5	3 46	12 27	73·4	197	343
18	162	5 29	17 10	72·8	5 11	16 13	72·7	4 53	15 15	72·7	4 35	14 18	72·6	4 17	13 20	72·5	3 59	12 23	72·4	198	342
19	161	5 46	17 05	71·9	5 28	16 07	71·8	5 09	15 10	71·7	4 50	14 13	71·6	4 31	13 16	71·5	4 12	12 19	71·5	199	341
20	160	6 04	16 59	70·9	5 44	16 02	70·8	5 25	15 05	70·7	5 05	14 08	70·6	4 45	13 11	70·5	4 25	12 14	70·5	200	340
21	159	6 21	16 52	69·9	6 01	15 56	69·8	5 40	14 59	69·7	5 19	14 03	69·7	4 58	13 06	69·6	4 37	12 10	69·5	201	339
22	158	6 39	16 46	69·0	6 17	15 50	68·9	5 56	14 53	68·8	5 34	13 57	68·7	5 12	13 01	68·6	4 50	12 05	68·5	202	338
23	157	6 56	16 39	68·0	6 34	15 43	67·9	6 11	14 47	67·8	5 48	13 51	67·7	5 25	12 56	67·6	5 03	12 00	67·5	203	337
24	156	7 13	16 32	67·1	6 50	15 36	66·9	6 26	14 41	66·8	6 03	13 45	66·7	5 39	12 50	66·6	5 15	11 55	66·5	204	336
25	155	7 30	16 25	66·1	7 06	15 29	66·0	6 41	14 34	65·9	6 17	13 39	65·8	5 52	12 44	65·7	5 27	11 49	65·6	205	335
26	154	7 47	16 17	65·1	7 22	15 22	65·0	6 56	14 27	64·9	6 31	13 32	64·8	6 05	12 38	64·7	5 40	11 43	64·6	206	334
27	153	8 04	16 09	64·1	7 38	15 14	64·0	7 11	14 20	63·9	6 45	13 26	63·8	6 18	12 32	63·7	5 52	11 37	63·6	207	333
28	152	8 20	16 00	63·2	7 53	15 06	63·0	7 26	14 12	62·9	6 59	13 19	62·8	6 31	12 25	62·7	6 04	11 31	62·6	208	332
29	151	8 37	15 52	62·2	8 09	14 58	62·1	7 41	14 05	61·9	7 13	13 11	61·8	6 44	12 18	61·7	6 16	11 25	61·6	209	331
30	150	8 53	15 43	61·2	8 24	14 50	61·1	7 55	13 57	61·0	7 26	13 04	60·9	6 57	12 11	60·7	6 27	11 18	60·6	210	330
31	149	9 09	15 34	60·3	8 40	14 41	60·1	8 10	13 49	60·0	7 40	12 56	59·9	7 09	12 04	59·8	6 39	11 12	59·7	211	329
32	148	9 25	15 24	59·3	8 55	14 32	59·1	8 24	13 40	59·0	7 53	12 48	58·9	7 22	11 56	58·8	6 51	11 05	58·7	212	328
33	147	9 41	15 15	58·3	9 10	14 23	58·2	8 38	13 31	58·0	8 06	12 40	57·9	7 34	11 49	57·8	7 02	10 57	57·7	213	327
34	146	9 57	15 05	57·3	9 25	14 13	57·2	8 52	13 22	57·0	8 19	12 31	56·9	7 46	11 41	56·8	7 14	10 50	56·7	214	326
35	145	10 13	14 54	56·3	9 39	14 04	56·2	9 06	13 13	56·1	8 32	12 23	55·9	7 59	11 33	55·8	7 25	10 43	55·7	215	325
36	144	10 28	14 44	55·4	9 54	13 54	55·2	9 19	13 04	55·1	8 45	12 14	54·9	8 11	11 24	54·8	7 36	10 35	54·7	216	324
37	143	10 43	14 33	54·4	10 08	13 43	54·2	9 33	12 54	54·1	8 58	12 05	53·9	8 22	11 16	53·8	7 47	10 27	53·7	217	323
38	142	10 58	14 22	53·4	10 22	13 33	53·2	9 46	12 44	53·1	9 10	11 55	53·0	8 34	11 07	52·8	7 58	10 19	52·7	218	322
39	141	11 13	14 10	52·4	10 36	13 22	52·2	9 59	12 34	52·1	9 22	11 46	52·0	8 45	10 58	51·8	8 08	10 10	51·7	219	321
40	140	11 27	13 59	51·4	10 50	13 11	51·3	10 12	12 23	51·1	9 35	11 36	51·0	8 57	10 49	50·8	8 19	10 02	50·7	220	320
41	139	11 42	13 47	50·4	11 04	13 00	50·3	10 25	12 13	50·1	9 47	11 26	50·0	9 08	10 39	49·9	8 29	9 53	49·7	221	319
42	138	11 56	13 34	49·4	11 17	12 48	49·3	10 38	12 02	49·1	9 58	11 16	49·0	9 19	10 30	48·9	8 39	9 44	48·7	222	318
43	137	12 10	13 22	48·4	11 30	12 36	48·3	10 50	11 51	48·1	10 10	11 05	48·0	9 30	10 20	47·9	8 49	9 35	47·7	223	317
44	136	12 24	13 09	47·4	11 43	12 24	47·3	11 02	11 39	47·1	10 21	10 55	47·0	9 40	10 10	46·9	8 59	9 26	46·7	224	316
45	135	12 37	12 56	46·4	11 56	12 12	46·3	11 14	11 28	46·1	10 33	10 44	46·0	9 51	10 00	45·9	9 09	9 16	45·7	225	315

Lat. / A		72°			73°			74°			75°			76°			77°			Lat. / A	
LHA/F		A/H	B/P	Z1/Z2	A/H	B/P	Z1/Z2	A/H	B/P	Z1/Z2	A/H	B/P	Z1/Z2	A/H	B/P	Z1/Z2	A/H	B/P	Z1/Z2	LHA	
°	°	° ′	° ′	°	° ′	° ′	°	° ′	° ′	°	° ′	° ′	°	° ′	° ′	°	° ′	° ′	°	°	°
45	135	12 37	12 56	46·4	11 56	12 12	46·3	11 14	11 28	46·1	10 33	10 44	46·0	9 51	10 00	45·9	9 09	9 16	45·7	225	315
46	134	12 51	12 43	45·4	12 08	11 59	45·3	11 26	11 16	45·1	10 44	10 33	45·0	10 01	9 50	44·9	9 19	9 07	44·7	226	314
47	133	13 04	12 30	44·4	12 21	11 47	44·3	11 38	11 04	44·1	10 55	10 21	44·0	10 11	9 39	43·9	9 28	8 57	43·7	227	313
48	132	13 17	12 16	43·4	12 33	11 34	43·3	11 49	10 52	43·1	11 05	10 10	43·0	10 21	9 28	42·9	9 37	8 47	42·7	228	312
49	131	13 29	12 02	42·4	12 45	11 21	42·3	12 00	10 39	42·1	11 16	9 58	42·0	10 31	9 17	41·9	9 46	8 37	41·7	229	311
50	130	13 42	11 48	41·4	12 57	11 07	41·3	12 11	10 27	41·1	11 26	9 46	41·0	10 41	9 06	40·9	9 55	8 26	40·7	230	310
51	129	13 54	11 33	40·4	13 08	10 53	40·3	12 22	10 14	40·1	11 36	9 34	40·0	10 50	8 55	39·8	10 04	8 16	39·7	231	309
52	128	14 06	11 19	39·4	13 19	10 40	39·2	12 33	10 01	39·1	11 46	9 22	39·0	10 59	8 44	38·8	10 13	8 05	38·7	232	308
53	127	14 17	11 04	38·4	13 30	10 26	38·2	12 43	9 47	38·1	11 56	9 10	38·0	11 08	8 32	37·8	10 21	7 55	37·7	233	307
54	126	14 29	10 49	37·4	13 41	10 11	37·2	12 53	9 34	37·1	12 05	8 57	36·9	11 17	8 20	36·8	10 29	7 44	36·7	234	306
55	125	14 40	10 33	36·4	13 51	9 57	36·2	13 03	9 20	36·1	12 14	8 44	35·9	11 26	8 08	35·8	10 37	7 33	35·7	235	305
56	124	14 51	10 18	35·3	14 02	9 42	35·2	13 13	9 07	35·1	12 23	8 31	34·9	11 34	7 56	34·8	10 45	7 21	34·7	236	304
57	123	15 01	10 02	34·3	14 12	9 27	34·2	13 22	8 53	34·0	12 32	8 18	33·9	11 42	7 44	33·8	10 52	7 10	33·7	237	303
58	122	15 12	9 46	33·3	14 21	9 12	33·2	13 31	8 38	33·0	12 41	8 05	32·9	11 50	7 32	32·8	11 00	6 58	32·7	238	302
59	121	15 22	9 30	32·3	14 31	8 57	32·1	13 40	8 24	32·0	12 49	7 51	31·9	11 58	7 19	31·8	11 07	6 47	31·7	239	301
60	120	15 31	9 14	31·3	14 40	8 41	31·1	13 49	8 10	31·0	12 57	7 38	30·9	12 06	7 06	30·8	11 14	6 35	30·6	240	300
61	119	15 41	8 57	30·2	14 49	8 26	30·1	13 57	7 55	30·0	13 05	7 24	29·8	12 13	6 54	29·7	11 21	6 23	29·6	241	299
62	118	15 50	8 40	29·2	14 58	8 10	29·1	14 05	7 40	28·9	13 13	7 10	28·8	12 20	6 41	28·7	11 27	6 11	28·6	242	298
63	117	15 59	8 23	28·2	15 06	7 54	28·0	14 13	7 25	27·9	13 20	6 56	27·8	12 27	6 27	27·7	11 34	5 59	27·6	243	297
64	116	16 08	8 06	27·2	15 14	7 38	27·0	14 21	7 10	26·9	13 27	6 42	26·8	12 34	6 14	26·7	11 40	5 47	26·6	244	296
65	115	16 16	7 49	26·1	15 22	7 22	26·0	14 28	6 55	25·9	13 34	6 28	25·8	12 40	6 01	25·7	11 46	5 34	25·6	245	295
66	114	16 24	7 32	25·1	15 29	7 05	25·0	14 35	6 39	24·9	13 41	6 13	24·7	12 46	5 47	24·6	11 52	5 22	24·6	246	294
67	113	16 32	7 14	24·1	15 37	6 49	23·9	14 42	6 24	23·8	13 47	5 59	23·7	12 52	5 34	23·6	11 57	5 09	23·5	247	293
68	112	16 39	6 56	23·0	15 44	6 32	22·9	14 48	6 08	22·8	13 53	5 44	22·7	12 58	5 20	22·6	12 02	4 57	22·5	248	292
69	111	16 46	6 38	22·0	15 50	6 15	21·9	14 55	5 52	21·8	13 59	5 29	21·7	13 03	5 06	21·6	12 07	4 44	21·5	249	291
70	110	16 53	6 20	20·9	15 57	5 58	20·8	15 01	5 36	20·7	14 05	5 14	20·6	13 08	4 52	20·6	12 12	4 31	20·5	250	290
71	109	16 59	6 02	19·9	16 03	5 41	19·8	15 06	5 20	19·7	14 10	4 59	19·6	13 13	4 38	19·5	12 17	4 18	19·5	251	289
72	108	17 05	5 44	18·9	16 09	5 24	18·8	15 12	5 04	18·7	14 15	4 44	18·6	13 18	4 24	18·5	12 21	4 05	18·4	252	288
73	107	17 11	5 26	17·8	16 14	5 06	17·7	15 17	4 48	17·6	14 20	4 29	17·6	13 23	4 10	17·5	12 25	3 52	17·4	253	287
74	106	17 17	5 07	16·8	16 19	4 49	16·7	15 22	4 31	16·6	14 24	4 13	16·5	13 27	3 56	16·5	12 29	3 38	16·4	254	286
75	105	17 22	4 48	15·7	16 24	4 31	15·7	15 26	4 15	15·6	14 29	3 58	15·5	13 31	3 42	15·4	12 33	3 25	15·4	255	285
76	104	17 27	4 30	14·7	16 29	4 14	14·6	15 31	3 58	14·5	14 33	3 43	14·5	13 35	3 27	14·4	12 36	3 12	14·4	256	284
77	103	17 31	4 11	13·6	16 33	3 56	13·6	15 35	3 41	13·5	14 36	3 27	13·4	13 38	3 13	13·4	12 40	2 58	13·3	257	283
78	102	17 36	3 52	12·6	16 37	3 38	12·5	15 38	3 25	12·5	14 40	3 11	12·4	13 41	2 58	12·4	12 43	2 45	12·3	258	282
79	101	17 39	3 33	11·6	16 41	3 20	11·5	15 42	3 08	11·4	14 43	2 56	11·4	13 44	2 43	11·3	12 45	2 31	11·3	259	281
80	100	17 43	3 14	10·5	16 44	3 02	10·4	15 45	2 51	10·4	14 46	2 40	10·3	13 47	2 29	10·3	12 48	2 18	10·3	260	280
81	99	17 46	2 55	9·5	16 47	2 44	9·4	15 48	2 34	9·4	14 49	2 24	9·3	13 49	2 14	9·3	12 50	2 04	9·2	261	279
82	98	17 49	2 35	8·4	16 50	2 26	8·4	15 50	2 17	8·3	14 51	2 08	8·3	13 52	1 59	8·2	12 52	1 50	8·2	262	278
83	97	17 52	2 16	7·4	16 52	2 08	7·3	15 53	2 00	7·3	14 53	1 52	7·2	13 54	1 44	7·2	12 54	1 37	7·2	263	277
84	96	17 54	1 57	6·3	16 54	1 50	6·3	15 55	1 43	6·2	14 55	1 36	6·2	13 55	1 30	6·2	12 56	1 23	6·2	264	276
85	95	17 56	1 37	5·3	16 56	1 32	5·2	15 56	1 26	5·2	14 56	1 20	5·2	13 57	1 15	5·2	12 57	1 09	5·1	265	275
86	94	17 57	1 18	4·2	16 57	1 13	4·2	15 58	1 09	4·2	14 58	1 04	4·1	13 58	1 00	4·1	12 58	0 55	4·1	266	274
87	93	17 58	0 58	3·2	16 59	0 55	3·1	15 59	0 52	3·1	14 59	0 48	3·1	13 59	0 45	3·1	12 59	0 42	3·1	267	273
88	92	17 59	0 39	2·1	16 59	0 37	2·1	15 59	0 34	2·1	14 59	0 32	2·1	13 59	0 30	2·1	13 00	0 28	2·1	268	272
89	91	18 00	0 19	1·1	17 00	0 18	1·0	16 00	0 17	1·0	15 00	0 16	1·0	14 00	0 15	1·0	13 00	0 14	1·0	269	271
90	90	18 00	0 00	0·0	17 00	0 00	0·0	16 00	0 00	0·0	15 00	0 00	0·0	14 00	0 00	0·0	13 00	0 00	0·0	270	270

N. Lat: for LHA > 180° … $Z_n = Z$
for LHA < 180° … $Z_n = 360° - Z$

S. Lat.: for LHA > 180° … $Z_n = 180° - Z$
for LHA < 180° … $Z_n = 180° + Z$

SIGHT REDUCTION TABLE

B: (−) for 90° < LHA < 270°
Dec:(−) for Lat. contrary name

Z_1: same sign as B
Z_2: (−) for F > 90°

Lat. / A		78°			79°			80°			81°			82°			83°			Lat. / A	
LHA/F		A/H	B/P	Z_1/Z_2	A/H	B/P	Z_1/Z_2	A/H	B/P	Z_1/Z_2	A/H	B/P	Z_1/Z_2	A/H	B/P	Z_1/Z_2	A/H	B/P	Z_1/Z_2	LHA	
°	°	° ′	° ′	°	° ′	° ′	°	° ′	° ′	°	° ′	° ′	°	° ′	° ′	°	° ′	° ′	°	°	°
0	180	0 00	12 00	90·0	0 00	11 00	90·0	0 00	10 00	90·0	0 00	9 00	90·0	0 00	8 00	90·0	0 00	7 00	90·0	180	360
1	179	0 12	12 00	89·0	0 11	11 00	89·0	0 10	10 00	89·0	0 09	9 00	89·0	0 08	8 00	89·0	0 07	7 00	89·0	181	359
2	178	0 25	12 00	88·0	0 23	11 00	88·0	0 21	10 00	88·0	0 19	9 00	88·0	0 17	8 00	88·0	0 15	7 00	88·0	182	358
3	177	0 37	11 59	87·1	0 34	10 59	87·1	0 31	9 59	87·0	0 28	8 59	87·0	0 25	7 59	87·0	0 22	6 59	87·0	183	357
4	176	0 50	11 58	86·1	0 46	10 58	86·1	0 42	9 59	86·1	0 38	8 59	86·0	0 33	7 59	86·0	0 29	6 59	86·0	184	356
5	175	1 02	11 57	85·1	0 57	10 58	85·1	0 52	9 58	85·1	0 47	8 58	85·1	0 42	7 58	85·0	0 37	6 58	85·0	185	355
6	174	1 15	11 56	84·1	1 09	10 56	84·1	1 02	9 57	84·1	0 56	8 57	84·1	0 50	7 57	84·1	0 44	6 58	84·0	186	354
7	173	1 27	11 55	83·2	1 20	10 55	83·1	1 13	9 56	83·1	1 06	8 56	83·1	0 58	7 56	83·1	0 51	6 57	83·1	187	353
8	172	1 39	11 53	82·2	1 31	10 54	82·1	1 23	9 54	82·1	1 15	8 55	82·1	1 07	7 55	82·1	0 58	6 56	82·1	188	352
9	171	1 52	11 51	81·2	1 43	10 52	81·2	1 33	9 53	81·1	1 24	8 53	81·1	1 15	7 54	81·1	1 06	6 55	81·1	189	351
10	170	2 04	11 49	80·2	1 54	10 50	80·2	1 44	9 51	80·1	1 33	8 52	80·1	1 23	7 53	80·1	1 13	6 54	80·1	190	350
11	169	2 16	11 47	79·2	2 05	10 48	79·2	1 54	9 49	79·2	1 43	8 50	79·1	1 31	7 51	79·1	1 20	6 52	79·1	191	349
12	168	2 29	11 45	78·3	2 16	10 46	78·2	2 04	9 47	78·2	1 52	8 48	78·1	1 39	7 50	78·1	1 27	6 51	78·1	192	348
13	167	2 41	11 42	77·3	2 28	10 43	77·2	2 14	9 45	77·2	2 01	8 46	77·2	1 48	7 48	77·1	1 34	6 49	77·1	193	347
14	166	2 53	11 39	76·3	2 39	10 41	76·2	2 24	9 43	76·2	2 10	8 44	76·2	1 56	7 46	76·1	1 41	6 48	76·1	194	346
15	165	3 05	11 36	75·3	2 50	10 38	75·3	2 35	9 40	75·2	2 19	8 42	75·2	2 04	7 44	75·1	1 48	6 46	75·1	195	345
16	164	3 17	11 33	74·3	3 01	10 35	74·3	2 45	9 37	74·2	2 28	8 39	74·2	2 12	7 42	74·1	1 56	6 44	74·1	196	344
17	163	3 29	11 29	73·4	3 12	10 32	73·3	2 55	9 34	73·2	2 37	8 37	73·2	2 20	7 39	73·2	2 03	6 42	73·1	197	343
18	162	3 41	11 26	72·4	3 23	10 28	72·3	3 05	9 31	72·3	2 46	8 34	72·2	2 28	7 37	72·2	2 09	6 40	72·1	198	342
19	161	3 53	11 22	71·4	3 34	10 25	71·3	3 14	9 28	71·3	2 55	8 31	71·2	2 36	7 34	71·2	2 16	6 37	71·1	199	341
20	160	4 05	11 18	70·4	3 45	10 21	70·3	3 24	9 24	70·3	3 04	8 28	70·2	2 44	7 31	70·2	2 23	6 35	70·1	200	340
21	159	4 16	11 13	69·4	3 55	10 17	69·4	3 34	9 21	69·3	3 13	8 25	69·2	2 52	7 28	69·2	2 30	6 32	69·1	201	339
22	158	4 28	11 09	68·4	4 06	10 13	68·4	3 44	9 17	68·3	3 22	8 21	68·2	2 59	7 25	68·2	2 37	6 30	68·1	202	338
23	157	4 40	11 04	67·5	4 17	10 09	67·4	3 53	9 13	67·3	3 30	8 18	67·3	3 07	7 22	67·2	2 44	6 27	67·2	203	337
24	156	4 51	10 59	66·5	4 27	10 04	66·4	4 03	9 09	66·3	3 39	8 14	66·3	3 15	7 19	66·2	2 50	6 24	66·2	204	336
25	155	5 02	10 54	65·5	4 38	9 59	65·4	4 13	9 05	65·3	3 47	8 10	65·3	3 22	7 16	65·2	2 57	6 21	65·2	205	335
26	154	5 14	10 49	64·5	4 48	9 55	64·4	4 22	9 00	64·3	3 56	8 06	64·3	3 30	7 12	64·2	3 04	6 18	64·2	206	334
27	153	5 25	10 43	63·5	4 58	9 50	63·4	4 31	8 56	63·4	4 04	8 02	63·3	3 37	7 08	63·2	3 10	6 15	63·2	207	333
28	152	5 36	10 38	62·5	5 08	9 44	62·4	4 41	8 51	62·4	4 13	7 58	62·3	3 45	7 04	62·2	3 17	6 11	62·2	208	332
29	151	5 47	10 32	61·5	5 18	9 39	61·4	4 50	8 46	61·4	4 21	7 53	61·3	3 52	7 00	61·2	3 23	6 08	61·2	209	331
30	150	5 58	10 26	60·5	5 28	9 33	60·5	4 59	8 41	60·4	4 29	7 49	60·3	3 59	6 56	60·2	3 30	6 04	60·2	210	330
31	149	6 09	10 20	59·6	5 38	9 28	59·5	5 08	8 36	59·4	4 37	7 44	59·3	4 07	6 52	59·2	3 36	6 00	59·2	211	329
32	148	6 20	10 13	58·6	5 48	9 22	58·5	5 17	8 30	58·4	4 45	7 39	58·3	4 14	6 48	58·3	3 42	5 57	58·2	212	328
33	147	6 30	10 06	57·6	5 58	9 16	57·5	5 26	8 25	57·4	4 53	7 34	57·3	4 21	6 43	57·3	3 48	5 53	57·2	213	327
34	146	6 41	10 00	56·6	6 08	9 09	56·5	5 34	8 19	56·4	5 01	7 29	56·3	4 28	6 39	56·3	3 54	5 49	56·2	214	326
35	145	6 51	9 53	55·6	6 17	9 03	55·5	5 43	8 13	55·4	5 09	7 24	55·3	4 35	6 34	55·3	4 00	5 45	55·2	215	325
36	144	7 01	9 45	54·6	6 26	8 56	54·5	5 51	8 07	54·4	5 17	7 18	54·3	4 42	6 29	54·3	4 06	5 40	54·2	216	324
37	143	7 11	9 38	53·6	6 36	8 49	53·5	6 00	8 01	53·4	5 24	7 13	53·3	4 48	6 24	53·3	4 12	5 36	53·2	217	323
38	142	7 21	9 31	52·6	6 45	8 43	52·5	6 08	7 55	52·4	5 32	7 07	52·3	4 55	6 19	52·3	4 18	5 32	52·2	218	322
39	141	7 31	9 23	51·6	6 54	8 35	51·5	6 16	7 48	51·4	5 39	7 01	51·3	5 01	6 14	51·3	4 24	5 27	51·2	219	321
40	140	7 41	9 15	50·6	7 03	8 28	50·5	6 25	7 42	50·4	5 46	6 55	50·3	5 08	6 09	50·3	4 30	5 22	50·2	220	320
41	139	7 50	9 07	49·6	7 11	8 21	49·5	6 32	7 35	49·4	5 53	6 49	49·4	5 14	6 03	49·3	4 35	5 18	49·2	221	319
42	138	8 00	8 59	48·6	7 20	8 13	48·5	6 40	7 28	48·4	6 01	6 43	48·4	5 21	5 58	48·3	4 41	5 13	48·2	222	318
43	137	8 09	8 50	47·6	7 29	8 05	47·5	6 48	7 21	47·4	6 07	6 36	47·4	5 27	5 52	47·3	4 46	5 08	47·2	223	317
44	136	8 18	8 42	46·6	7 37	7 58	46·5	6 56	7 14	46·4	6 14	6 30	46·4	5 33	5 46	46·3	4 51	5 03	46·2	224	316
45	135	8 27	8 33	45·6	7 45	7 50	45·5	7 03	7 06	45·4	6 21	6 23	45·4	5 39	5 41	45·3	4 57	4 58	45·2	225	315

Lat. / A		78°			79°			80°			81°			82°			83°			Lat. / A	
LHA/F		A/H	B/P	Z_1/Z_2	A/H	B/P	Z_1/Z_2	A/H	B/P	Z_1/Z_2	A/H	B/P	Z_1/Z_2	A/H	B/P	Z_1/Z_2	A/H	B/P	Z_1/Z_2	LHA	
°	°	° ′	° ′	°	° ′	° ′	°	° ′	° ′	°	° ′	° ′	°	° ′	° ′	°	° ′	° ′	°	°	°
45	135	8 27	8 33	45·6	7 45	7 50	45·5	7 03	7 06	45·4	6 21	6 23	45·4	5 39	5 41	45·3	4 57	4 58	45·2	225	315
46	134	8 36	8 24	44·6	7 53	7 41	44·5	7 11	6 59	44·4	6 28	6 17	44·4	5 45	5 35	44·3	5 02	4 53	44·2	226	314
47	133	8 45	8 15	43·6	8 01	7 33	43·5	7 18	6 51	43·4	6 34	6 10	43·4	5 51	5 28	43·3	5 07	4 47	43·2	227	313
48	132	8 53	8 06	42·6	8 09	7 25	42·5	7 25	6 44	42·4	6 41	6 03	42·4	5 56	5 22	42·3	5 12	4 42	42·2	228	312
49	131	9 02	7 56	41·6	8 17	7 16	41·5	7 32	6 36	41·4	6 47	5 56	41·4	6 02	5 16	41·3	5 17	4 36	41·2	229	311
50	130	9 10	7 47	40·6	8 24	7 07	40·5	7 39	6 28	40·4	6 53	5 49	40·3	6 07	5 10	40·3	5 21	4 31	40·2	230	310
51	129	9 18	7 37	39·6	8 32	6 58	39·5	7 45	6 20	39·4	6 59	5 42	39·3	6 13	5 03	39·3	5 26	4 25	39·2	231	309
52	128	9 26	7 27	38·6	8 39	6 49	38·5	7 52	6 12	38·4	7 05	5 34	38·3	6 18	4 57	38·3	5 31	4 19	38·2	232	308
53	127	9 33	7 17	37·6	8 46	6 40	37·5	7 58	6 03	37·4	7 11	5 27	37·3	6 23	4 50	37·3	5 35	4 14	37·2	233	307
54	126	9 41	7 07	36·6	8 53	6 31	36·5	8 05	5 55	36·4	7 16	5 19	36·3	6 28	4 43	36·3	5 39	4 08	36·2	234	306
55	125	9 48	6 57	35·6	9 00	6 22	35·5	8 11	5 47	35·4	7 22	5 11	35·3	6 33	4 37	35·3	5 44	4 02	35·2	235	305
56	124	9 56	6 47	34·6	9 06	6 12	34·5	8 17	5 38	34·4	7 27	5 04	34·3	6 38	4 30	34·3	5 48	3 56	34·2	236	304
57	123	10 03	6 36	33·6	9 13	6 03	33·5	8 22	5 29	33·4	7 32	4 56	33·3	6 42	4 23	33·3	5 52	3 50	33·2	237	303
58	122	10 09	6 26	32·6	9 19	5 53	32·5	8 28	5 20	32·4	7 37	4 48	32·3	6 47	4 16	32·3	5 56	3 43	32·2	238	302
59	121	10 16	6 15	31·6	9 25	5 43	31·5	8 34	5 11	31·4	7 42	4 40	31·3	6 51	4 08	31·2	6 00	3 37	31·2	239	301
60	120	10 22	6 04	30·6	9 31	5 33	30·5	8 39	5 02	30·4	7 47	4 32	30·3	6 55	4 01	30·2	6 04	3 31	30·2	240	300
61	119	10 29	5 53	29·5	9 36	5 23	29·5	8 44	4 53	29·4	7 52	4 23	29·3	6 59	3 54	29·2	6 07	3 24	29·2	241	299
62	118	10 35	5 42	28·5	9 42	5 13	28·4	8 49	4 44	28·4	7 56	4 15	28·3	7 04	3 46	28·2	6 11	3 18	28·2	242	298
63	117	10 41	5 31	27·5	9 47	5 03	27·4	8 54	4 35	27·4	8 01	4 07	27·3	7 07	3 39	27·2	6 14	3 11	27·2	243	297
64	116	10 46	5 19	26·5	9 52	4 52	26·4	8 59	4 25	26·3	8 05	3 58	26·3	7 11	3 32	26·2	6 17	3 05	26·2	244	296
65	115	10 52	5 08	25·5	9 57	4 42	25·4	9 03	4 16	25·3	8 09	3 50	25·3	7 15	3 24	25·2	6 20	2 58	25·2	245	295
66	114	10 57	4 56	24·5	10 02	4 31	24·4	9 08	4 06	24·3	8 13	3 41	24·3	7 18	3 16	24·2	6 24	2 52	24·2	246	294
67	113	11 02	4 45	23·5	10 07	4 21	23·4	9 12	3 56	23·3	8 17	3 32	23·3	7 22	3 09	23·2	6 26	2 45	23·2	247	293
68	112	11 07	4 33	22·4	10 11	4 10	22·4	9 16	3 47	22·3	8 20	3 24	22·2	7 25	3 01	22·2	6 29	2 38	22·1	248	292
69	111	11 12	4 21	21·4	10 16	3 59	21·4	9 20	3 37	21·3	8 24	3 15	21·2	7 28	2 53	21·2	6 32	2 31	21·1	249	291
70	110	11 16	4 09	20·4	10 20	3 48	20·3	9 23	3 27	20·3	8 27	3 06	20·2	7 31	2 45	20·2	6 35	2 24	20·1	250	290
71	109	11 20	3 58	19·4	10 24	3 37	19·3	9 27	3 17	19·3	8 30	2 57	19·2	7 34	2 37	19·2	6 37	2 17	19·1	251	289
72	108	11 24	3 45	18·4	10 27	3 26	18·3	9 30	3 07	18·3	8 33	2 48	18·2	7 36	2 29	18·2	6 39	2 10	18·1	252	288
73	107	11 28	3 33	17·4	10 31	3 15	17·3	9 34	2 57	17·2	8 36	2 39	17·2	7 39	2 21	17·2	6 42	2 03	17·1	253	287
74	106	11 32	3 21	16·3	10 34	3 04	16·3	9 37	2 47	16·2	8 39	2 30	16·2	7 41	2 13	16·1	6 44	1 56	16·1	254	286
75	105	11 35	3 09	15·3	10 37	2 53	15·3	9 39	2 37	15·2	8 41	2 21	15·2	7 44	2 05	15·1	6 46	1 49	15·1	255	285
76	104	11 38	2 57	14·3	10 40	2 42	14·3	9 42	2 27	14·2	8 44	2 12	14·2	7 46	1 57	14·1	6 47	1 42	14·1	256	284
77	103	11 41	2 44	13·3	10 43	2 30	13·2	9 44	2 16	13·2	8 46	2 02	13·2	7 48	1 49	13·1	6 49	1 35	13·1	257	283
78	102	11 44	2 32	12·3	10 45	2 19	12·2	9 47	2 06	12·2	8 48	1 53	12·1	7 49	1 40	12·1	6 51	1 28	12·1	258	282
79	101	11 47	2 19	11·2	10 48	2 07	11·2	9 49	1 56	11·2	8 50	1 44	11·1	7 51	1 32	11·1	6 52	1 21	11·1	259	281
80	100	11 49	2 07	10·2	10 50	1 56	10·2	9 51	1 45	10·2	8 52	1 35	10·1	7 53	1 24	10·1	6 54	1 13	10·1	260	280
81	99	11 51	1 54	9·2	10 52	1 45	9·2	9 53	1 35	9·1	8 53	1 25	9·1	7 54	1 16	9·1	6 55	1 06	9·1	261	279
82	98	11 53	1 42	8·2	10 53	1 33	8·1	9 54	1 24	8·1	8 55	1 16	8·1	7 55	1 07	8·1	6 56	0 59	8·1	262	278
83	97	11 55	1 29	7·2	10 55	1 21	7·1	9 55	1 14	7·1	8 56	1 06	7·1	7 56	0 59	7·1	6 57	0 51	7·1	263	277
84	96	11 56	1 16	6·1	10 56	1 10	6·1	9 57	1 03	6·1	8 57	0 57	6·1	7 57	0 50	6·1	6 58	0 44	6·0	264	276
85	95	11 57	1 04	5·1	10 57	0 58	5·1	9 58	0 53	5·1	8 58	0 47	5·1	7 58	0 42	5·0	6 58	0 37	5·0	265	275
86	94	11 58	0 51	4·1	10 58	0 47	4·1	9 59	0 42	4·1	8 59	0 38	4·0	7 59	0 34	4·0	6 59	0 29	4·0	266	274
87	93	11 59	0 38	3·1	10 59	0 35	3·1	9 59	0 32	3·0	8 59	0 28	3·0	7 59	0 25	3·0	6 59	0 22	3·0	267	273
88	92	12 00	0 26	2·0	11 00	0 23	2·0	10 00	0 21	2·0	9 00	0 19	2·0	8 00	0 17	2·0	7 00	0 15	2·0	268	272
89	91	12 00	0 13	1·0	11 00	0 12	1·0	10 00	0 11	1·0	9 00	0 10	1·0	8 00	0 08	1·0	7 00	0 07	1·0	269	271
90	90	12 00	0 00	0·0	11 00	0 00	0·0	10 00	0 00	0·0	9 00	0 00	0·0	8 00	0 00	0·0	7 00	0 00	0·0	270	270

N. Lat: for LHA > 180° … $Z_n = Z$
for LHA < 180° … $Z_n = 360° - Z$

S. Lat.: for LHA > 180° … $Z_n = 180° - Z$
for LHA < 180° … $Z_n = 180° + Z$

SIGHT REDUCTION TABLE

B: (−) for 90° < LHA < 270°
Dec:(−) for Lat. contrary name

Z_1: same sign as B
Z_2: (−) for F > 90°

Lat. / A		84°			85°			86°			87°			88°			89°			Lat. / A	
LHA/F		A/H	B/P	Z_1/Z_2	A/H	B/P	Z_1/Z_2	A/H	B/P	Z_1/Z_2	A/H	B/P	Z_1/Z_2	A/H	B/P	Z_1/Z_2	A/H	B/P	Z_1/Z_2	LHA	
°	°	° ′	° ′	°	° ′	° ′	°	° ′	° ′	°	° ′	° ′	°	° ′	° ′	°	° ′	° ′	°	°	°
0	180	0 00	6 00	90·0	0 00	5 00	90·0	0 00	4 00	90·0	0 00	3 00	90·0	0 00	2 00	90·0	0 00	1 00	90·0	180	360
1	179	0 06	6 00	89·0	0 05	5 00	89·0	0 04	4 00	89·0	0 03	3 00	89·0	0 02	2 00	89·0	0 01	1 00	89·0	181	359
2	178	0 13	6 00	88·0	0 10	5 00	88·0	0 08	4 00	88·0	0 06	3 00	88·0	0 04	2 00	88·0	0 02	1 00	88·0	182	358
3	177	0 19	6 00	87·0	0 16	5 00	87·0	0 13	4 00	87·0	0 09	3 00	87·0	0 06	2 00	87·0	0 03	1 00	87·0	183	357
4	176	0 25	5 59	86·0	0 21	4 59	86·0	0 17	3 59	86·0	0 13	3 00	86·0	0 08	2 00	86·0	0 04	1 00	86·0	184	356
5	175	0 31	5 59	85·0	0 26	4 59	85·0	0 21	3 59	85·0	0 16	2 59	85·0	0 10	2 00	85·0	0 05	1 00	85·0	185	355
6	174	0 38	5 58	84·0	0 31	4 58	84·0	0 25	3 59	84·0	0 19	2 59	84·0	0 13	1 59	84·0	0 06	1 00	84·0	186	354
7	173	0 44	5 57	83·0	0 37	4 58	83·0	0 29	3 58	83·0	0 22	2 59	83·0	0 15	1 59	83·0	0 07	1 00	83·0	187	353
8	172	0 50	5 57	82·0	0 42	4 57	82·0	0 33	3 58	82·0	0 25	2 58	82·0	0 17	1 59	82·0	0 08	0 59	82·0	188	352
9	171	0 56	5 56	81·0	0 47	4 56	81·0	0 38	3 57	81·0	0 28	2 58	81·0	0 19	1 59	81·0	0 09	0 59	81·0	189	351
10	170	1 02	5 55	80·1	0 52	4 55	80·0	0 42	3 56	80·0	0 31	2 57	80·0	0 21	1 58	80·0	0 10	0 59	80·0	190	350
11	169	1 09	5 53	79·1	0 57	4 55	79·0	0 46	3 56	79·0	0 34	2 57	79·0	0 23	1 58	79·0	0 11	0 59	79·0	191	349
12	168	1 15	5 52	78·1	1 02	4 53	78·0	0 50	3 55	78·0	0 37	2 56	78·0	0 25	1 57	78·0	0 12	0 59	78·0	192	348
13	167	1 21	5 51	77·1	1 07	4 52	77·0	0 54	3 54	77·0	0 40	2 55	77·0	0 27	1 57	77·0	0 13	0 58	77·0	193	347
14	166	1 27	5 49	76·1	1 12	4 51	76·1	0 58	3 53	76·0	0 44	2 55	76·0	0 29	1 56	76·0	0 15	0 58	76·0	194	346
15	165	1 33	5 48	75·1	1 18	4 50	75·1	1 02	3 52	75·0	0 47	2 54	75·0	0 31	1 56	75·0	0 16	0 58	75·0	195	345
16	164	1 39	5 46	74·1	1 23	4 48	74·1	1 06	3 51	74·0	0 50	2 53	74·0	0 33	1 55	74·0	0 17	0 58	74·0	196	344
17	163	1 45	5 44	73·1	1 28	4 47	73·1	1 10	3 50	73·0	0 53	2 52	73·0	0 35	1 55	73·0	0 18	0 57	73·0	197	343
18	162	1 51	5 42	72·1	1 33	4 45	72·1	1 14	3 48	72·0	0 56	2 51	72·0	0 37	1 54	72·0	0 19	0 57	72·0	198	342
19	161	1 57	5 41	71·1	1 38	4 44	71·1	1 18	3 47	71·0	0 59	2 50	71·0	0 39	1 53	71·0	0 20	0 57	71·0	199	341
20	160	2 03	5 38	70·1	1 42	4 42	70·1	1 22	3 46	70·0	1 02	2 49	70·0	0 41	1 53	70·0	0 21	0 56	70·0	200	340
21	159	2 09	5 36	69·1	1 47	4 40	69·1	1 26	3 44	69·0	1 04	2 48	69·0	0 43	1 52	69·0	0 22	0 56	69·0	201	339
22	158	2 15	5 34	68·1	1 52	4 38	68·1	1 30	3 43	68·0	1 07	2 47	68·0	0 45	1 51	68·0	0 22	0 56	68·0	202	338
23	157	2 20	5 32	67·1	1 57	4 36	67·1	1 34	3 41	67·1	1 10	2 46	67·0	0 47	1 50	67·0	0 23	0 55	67·0	203	337
24	156	2 26	5 29	66·1	2 02	4 34	66·1	1 38	3 39	66·1	1 13	2 44	66·0	0 49	1 50	66·0	0 24	0 55	66·0	204	336
25	155	2 32	5 26	65·1	2 07	4 32	65·1	1 41	3 38	65·1	1 16	2 43	65·0	0 51	1 49	65·0	0 25	0 54	65·0	205	335
26	154	2 38	5 24	64·1	2 11	4 30	64·1	1 45	3 36	64·1	1 19	2 42	64·0	0 53	1 48	64·0	0 26	0 54	64·0	206	334
27	153	2 43	5 21	63·1	2 16	4 27	63·1	1 49	3 34	63·1	1 22	2 40	63·0	0 54	1 47	63·0	0 27	0 53	63·0	207	333
28	152	2 49	5 18	62·1	2 21	4 25	62·1	1 53	3 32	62·1	1 24	2 39	62·0	0 56	1 46	62·0	0 28	0 53	62·0	208	332
29	151	2 54	5 15	61·1	2 25	4 23	61·1	1 56	3 30	61·1	1 27	2 37	61·0	0 58	1 45	61·0	0 29	0 52	61·0	209	331
30	150	3 00	5 12	60·1	2 30	4 20	60·1	2 00	3 28	60·1	1 30	2 36	60·0	1 00	1 44	60·0	0 30	0 52	60·0	210	330
31	149	3 05	5 09	59·1	2 34	4 17	59·1	2 04	3 26	59·1	1 33	2 34	59·0	1 02	1 43	59·0	0 31	0 51	59·0	211	329
32	148	3 11	5 06	58·1	2 39	4 15	58·1	2 07	3 24	58·1	1 35	2 33	58·0	1 04	1 42	58·0	0 32	0 51	58·0	212	328
33	147	3 16	5 02	57·1	2 43	4 12	57·1	2 11	3 21	57·1	1 38	2 31	57·0	1 05	1 41	57·0	0 33	0 50	57·0	213	327
34	146	3 21	4 59	56·1	2 48	4 09	56·1	2 14	3 19	56·1	1 41	2 29	56·0	1 07	1 39	56·0	0 34	0 50	56·0	214	326
35	145	3 26	4 55	55·1	2 52	4 06	55·1	2 18	3 17	55·1	1 43	2 27	55·0	1 09	1 38	55·0	0 34	0 49	55·0	215	325
36	144	3 31	4 52	54·1	2 56	4 03	54·1	2 21	3 14	54·1	1 46	2 26	54·0	1 11	1 37	54·0	0 35	0 49	54·0	216	324
37	143	3 36	4 48	53·2	3 00	4 00	53·1	2 24	3 12	53·1	1 48	2 24	53·0	1 12	1 36	53·0	0 36	0 48	53·0	217	323
38	142	3 41	4 44	52·2	3 05	3 57	52·1	2 28	3 09	52·1	1 51	2 22	52·0	1 14	1 35	52·0	0 37	0 47	52·0	218	322
39	141	3 46	4 40	51·2	3 09	3 53	51·1	2 31	3 07	51·1	1 53	2 20	51·0	1 16	1 33	51·0	0 38	0 47	51·0	219	321
40	140	3 51	4 36	50·2	3 13	3 50	50·1	2 34	3 04	50·1	1 56	2 18	50·0	1 17	1 32	50·0	0 39	0 46	50·0	220	320
41	139	3 56	4 32	49·2	3 17	3 47	49·1	2 37	3 01	49·1	1 58	2 16	49·0	1 19	1 31	49·0	0 39	0 45	49·0	221	319
42	138	4 01	4 28	48·2	3 21	3 43	48·1	2 41	2 58	48·1	2 00	2 14	48·0	1 20	1 29	48·0	0 40	0 45	48·0	222	318
43	137	4 05	4 24	47·2	3 24	3 40	47·1	2 44	2 56	47·1	2 03	2 12	47·0	1 22	1 28	47·0	0 41	0 44	47·0	223	317
44	136	4 10	4 19	46·2	3 28	3 36	46·1	2 47	2 53	46·1	2 05	2 10	46·0	1 23	1 26	46·0	0 42	0 43	46·0	224	316
45	135	4 14	4 15	45·2	3 32	3 32	45·1	2 50	2 50	45·1	2 07	2 07	45·0	1 25	1 25	45·0	0 42	0 42	45·0	225	315

Lat. / A		84°			85°			86°			87°			88°			89°			Lat. / A	
LHA/F		A/H	B/P	Z_1/Z_2	A/H	B/P	Z_1/Z_2	A/H	B/P	Z_1/Z_2	A/H	B/P	Z_1/Z_2	A/H	B/P	Z_1/Z_2	A/H	B/P	Z_1/Z_2	LHA	
°	°	° ′	° ′	°	° ′	° ′	°	° ′	° ′	°	° ′	° ′	°	° ′	° ′	°	° ′	° ′	°	°	°
45	135	4 14	4 15	45·2	3 32	3 32	45·1	2 50	2 50	45·1	2 07	2 07	45·0	1 25	1 25	45·0	0 42	0 42	45·0	225	315
46	134	4 19	4 11	44·2	3 36	3 29	44·1	2 53	2 47	44·1	2 09	2 05	44·0	1 26	1 23	44·0	0 43	0 42	44·0	226	314
47	133	4 23	4 06	43·2	3 39	3 25	43·1	2 55	2 44	43·1	2 12	2 03	43·0	1 28	1 22	43·0	0 44	0 41	43·0	227	313
48	132	4 27	4 01	42·2	3 43	3 21	42·1	2 58	2 41	42·1	2 14	2 01	42·0	1 29	1 20	42·0	0 45	0 40	42·0	228	312
49	131	4 31	3 57	41·2	3 46	3 17	41·1	3 01	2 38	41·1	2 16	1 58	41·0	1 31	1 19	41·0	0 45	0 39	41·0	229	311
50	130	4 36	3 52	40·2	3 50	3 13	40·1	3 04	2 34	40·1	2 18	1 56	40·0	1 32	1 17	40·0	0 46	0 39	40·0	230	310
51	129	4 40	3 47	39·2	3 53	3 09	39·1	3 06	2 31	39·1	2 20	1 53	39·0	1 33	1 16	39·0	0 47	0 38	39·0	231	309
52	128	4 43	3 42	38·2	3 56	3 05	38·1	3 09	2 28	38·1	2 22	1 51	38·0	1 35	1 14	38·0	0 47	0 37	38·0	232	308
53	127	4 47	3 37	37·2	3 59	3 01	37·1	3 12	2 25	37·1	2 24	1 48	37·0	1 36	1 12	37·0	0 48	0 36	37·0	233	307
54	126	4 51	3 32	36·1	4 03	2 57	36·1	3 14	2 21	36·1	2 26	1 46	36·0	1 37	1 11	36·0	0 49	0 35	36·0	234	306
55	125	4 55	3 27	35·1	4 06	2 52	35·1	3 17	2 18	35·1	2 27	1 43	35·0	1 38	1 09	35·0	0 49	0 34	35·0	235	305
56	124	4 58	3 22	34·1	4 09	2 48	34·1	3 19	2 14	34·1	2 29	1 41	34·0	1 39	1 07	34·0	0 50	0 34	34·0	236	304
57	123	5 02	3 17	33·1	4 12	2 44	33·1	3 21	2 11	33·1	2 31	1 38	33·0	1 41	1 05	33·0	0 50	0 33	33·0	237	303
58	122	5 05	3 11	32·1	4 14	2 39	32·1	3 23	2 07	32·1	2 33	1 35	32·0	1 42	1 04	32·0	0 51	0 32	32·0	238	302
59	121	5 08	3 06	31·1	4 17	2 35	31·1	3 26	2 04	31·1	2 34	1 33	31·0	1 43	1 02	31·0	0 51	0 31	31·0	239	301
60	120	5 12	3 00	30·1	4 20	2 30	30·1	3 28	2 00	30·1	2 36	1 30	30·0	1 44	1 00	30·0	0 52	0 30	30·0	240	300
61	119	5 15	2 55	29·1	4 22	2 26	29·1	3 30	1 56	29·1	2 37	1 27	29·0	1 45	0 58	29·0	0 52	0 29	29·0	241	299
62	118	5 18	2 49	28·1	4 25	2 21	28·1	3 32	1 53	28·1	2 39	1 25	28·0	1 46	0 56	28·0	0 53	0 28	28·0	242	298
63	117	5 21	2 44	27·1	4 27	2 16	27·1	3 34	1 49	27·1	2 40	1 22	27·0	1 47	0 54	27·0	0 53	0 27	27·0	243	297
64	116	5 23	2 38	26·1	4 30	2 12	26·1	3 36	1 45	26·1	2 42	1 19	26·0	1 48	0 53	26·0	0 54	0 26	26·0	244	296
65	115	5 26	2 33	25·1	4 32	2 07	25·1	3 37	1 42	25·1	2 43	1 16	25·0	1 49	0 51	25·0	0 54	0 25	25·0	245	295
66	114	5 29	2 27	24·1	4 34	2 02	24·1	3 39	1 38	24·1	2 44	1 13	24·0	1 50	0 49	24·0	0 55	0 24	24·0	246	294
67	113	5 31	2 21	23·1	4 36	1 57	23·1	3 41	1 34	23·1	2 46	1 10	23·0	1 50	0 47	23·0	0 55	0 23	23·0	247	293
68	112	5 34	2 15	22·1	4 38	1 53	22·1	3 42	1 30	22·0	2 47	1 07	22·0	1 51	0 45	22·0	0 56	0 22	22·0	248	292
69	111	5 36	2 09	21·1	4 40	1 48	21·1	3 44	1 26	21·0	2 48	1 05	21·0	1 52	0 43	21·0	0 56	0 22	21·0	249	291
70	110	5 38	2 04	20·1	4 42	1 43	20·1	3 46	1 22	20·0	2 49	1 02	20·0	1 53	0 41	20·0	0 56	0 21	20·0	250	290
71	109	5 40	1 58	19·1	4 44	1 38	19·1	3 47	1 18	19·0	2 50	0 59	19·0	1 53	0 39	19·0	0 57	0 20	19·0	251	289
72	108	5 42	1 52	18·1	4 45	1 33	18·1	3 48	1 14	18·0	2 51	0 56	18·0	1 54	0 37	18·0	0 57	0 19	18·0	252	288
73	107	5 44	1 46	17·1	4 47	1 28	17·1	3 49	1 10	17·0	2 52	0 53	17·0	1 55	0 35	17·0	0 57	0 18	17·0	253	287
74	106	5 46	1 40	16·1	4 48	1 23	16·1	3 51	1 06	16·0	2 53	0 50	16·0	1 55	0 33	16·0	0 58	0 17	16·0	254	286
75	105	5 48	1 33	15·1	4 50	1 18	15·1	3 52	1 02	15·0	2 54	0 47	15·0	1 56	0 31	15·0	0 58	0 16	15·0	255	285
76	104	5 49	1 27	14·1	4 51	1 13	14·1	3 53	0 58	14·0	2 55	0 44	14·0	1 56	0 29	14·0	0 58	0 15	14·0	256	284
77	103	5 51	1 21	13·1	4 52	1 08	13·0	3 54	0 54	13·0	2 55	0 41	13·0	1 57	0 27	13·0	0 58	0 13	13·0	257	283
78	102	5 52	1 15	12·1	4 53	1 03	12·0	3 55	0 50	12·0	2 56	0 37	12·0	1 57	0 25	12·0	0 59	0 12	12·0	258	282
79	101	5 53	1 09	11·1	4 54	0 57	11·0	3 56	0 46	11·0	2 57	0 34	11·0	1 58	0 23	11·0	0 59	0 11	11·0	259	281
80	100	5 55	1 03	10·1	4 55	0 52	10·0	3 56	0 42	10·0	2 57	0 31	10·0	1 58	0 21	10·0	0 59	0 10	10·0	260	280
81	99	5 56	0 57	9·0	4 56	0 47	9·0	3 57	0 38	9·0	2 58	0 28	9·0	1 59	0 19	9·0	0 59	0 09	9·0	261	279
82	98	5 56	0 50	8·0	4 57	0 42	8·0	3 58	0 33	8·0	2 58	0 25	8·0	1 59	0 17	8·0	0 59	0 08	8·0	262	278
83	97	5 57	0 44	7·0	4 58	0 37	7·0	3 58	0 29	7·0	2 59	0 22	7·0	1 59	0 15	7·0	1 00	0 07	7·0	263	277
84	96	5 58	0 38	6·0	4 58	0 31	6·0	3 59	0 25	6·0	2 59	0 19	6·0	1 59	0 13	6·0	1 00	0 06	6·0	264	276
85	95	5 59	0 31	5·0	4 59	0 26	5·0	3 59	0 21	5·0	2 59	0 16	5·0	2 00	0 10	5·0	1 00	0 05	5·0	265	275
86	94	5 59	0 25	4·0	4 59	0 21	4·0	3 59	0 17	4·0	3 00	0 13	4·0	2 00	0 08	4·0	1 00	0 04	4·0	266	274
87	93	6 00	0 19	3·0	5 00	0 16	3·0	4 00	0 13	3·0	3 00	0 09	3·0	2 00	0 06	3·0	1 00	0 03	3·0	267	273
88	92	6 00	0 13	2·0	5 00	0 10	2·0	4 00	0 08	2·0	3 00	0 06	2·0	2 00	0 04	2·0	1 00	0 02	2·0	268	272
89	91	6 00	0 06	1·0	5 00	0 05	1·0	4 00	0 04	1·0	3 00	0 03	1·0	2 00	0 02	1·0	1 00	0 01	1·0	269	271
90	90	6 00	0 00	0·0	5 00	0 00	0·0	4 00	0 00	0·0	3 00	0 00	0·0	2 00	0 00	0·0	1 00	0 00	0·0	270	270

N. Lat: for LHA > 180° … $Z_n = Z$
for LHA < 180° … $Z_n = 360° - Z$

S. Lat.: for LHA > 180° … $Z_n = 180° - Z$
for LHA < 180° … $Z_n = 180° + Z$

AUXILIARY TABLE

Sign of $corr_1$ for F′. *Reverse* sign if $F > 90°$. ↓

Sign for $corr_2$ for A′. ↓

F′ +/−	1 / 59	2 / 58	3 / 57	4 / 56	5 / 55	6 / 54	7 / 53	8 / 52	9 / 51	10 / 50	11 / 49	12 / 48	13 / 47	14 / 46	15 / 45	16 / 44	17 / 43	18 / 42	19 / 41	20 / 40	21 / 39	22 / 38	23 / 37	24 / 36	25 / 35	26 / 34	27 / 33	28 / 32	29 / 31	□ / 30	−/+ A′
P°	′	′	′	′	′	′	′	′	′	′	′	′	′	′	′	′	′	′	′	′	′	′	′	′	′	′	′	′	′	′	$Z_2°$
1	0	0	0	0	0	0	0	0	0	0	0	0	0	0	0	0	0	0	0	0	0	0	0	0	0	0	0	0	1	1	89
2	0	0	0	0	0	0	0	0	0	0	0	0	0	0	1	1	1	1	1	1	1	1	1	1	1	1	1	1	1	1	88
3	0	0	0	0	0	0	0	0	0	1	1	1	1	1	1	1	1	1	1	1	1	1	1	1	1	1	1	1	2	2	87
4	0	0	0	0	0	0	0	1	1	1	1	1	1	1	1	1	1	1	1	1	1	2	2	2	2	2	2	2	2	2	86
5	0	0	0	0	0	1	1	1	1	1	1	1	1	1	1	1	1	2	2	2	2	2	2	2	2	2	2	2	3	3	85
6	0	0	0	0	1	1	1	1	1	1	1	1	1	1	2	2	2	2	2	2	2	2	2	3	3	3	3	3	3	3	84
7	0	0	0	0	1	1	1	1	1	1	1	1	2	2	2	2	2	2	2	2	3	3	3	3	3	3	3	3	4	4	83
8	0	0	0	1	1	1	1	1	1	1	2	2	2	2	2	2	2	3	3	3	3	3	3	3	3	4	4	4	4	4	82
9	0	0	0	1	1	1	1	1	1	2	2	2	2	2	2	3	3	3	3	3	3	3	4	4	4	4	4	4	5	5	81
10	0	0	1	1	1	1	1	1	2	2	2	2	2	2	3	3	3	3	3	3	4	4	4	4	4	5	5	5	5	5	80
11	0	0	1	1	1	1	1	2	2	2	2	2	2	3	3	3	3	3	4	4	4	4	4	5	5	5	5	5	6	6	79
12	0	0	1	1	1	1	1	2	2	2	2	2	3	3	3	3	4	4	4	4	4	5	5	5	5	5	6	6	6	6	78
13	0	0	1	1	1	1	2	2	2	2	2	3	3	3	3	4	4	4	4	4	5	5	5	5	6	6	6	6	7	7	77
14	0	0	1	1	1	1	2	2	2	2	3	3	3	3	4	4	4	4	5	5	5	5	6	6	6	6	7	7	7	7	76
15	0	1	1	1	1	2	2	2	2	3	3	3	3	4	4	4	4	5	5	5	5	6	6	6	6	7	7	7	8	8	75
16	0	1	1	1	1	2	2	2	2	3	3	3	4	4	4	4	5	5	5	6	6	6	6	7	7	7	7	8	8	8	74
17	0	1	1	1	1	2	2	2	3	3	3	4	4	4	4	5	5	5	6	6	6	6	7	7	7	8	8	8	8	9	73
18	0	1	1	1	2	2	2	2	3	3	3	4	4	4	5	5	5	6	6	6	6	7	7	7	8	8	8	9	9	9	72
19	0	1	1	1	2	2	2	3	3	3	4	4	4	5	5	5	6	6	6	7	7	7	7	8	8	8	9	9	9	10	71
20	0	1	1	1	2	2	2	3	3	3	4	4	4	5	5	5	6	6	6	7	7	8	8	8	9	9	9	10	10	10	70
21	0	1	1	1	2	2	3	3	3	4	4	4	5	5	5	6	6	6	7	7	8	8	8	9	9	9	10	10	10	11	69
22	0	1	1	1	2	2	3	3	3	4	4	4	5	5	6	6	6	7	7	7	8	8	9	9	9	10	10	10	11	11	68
23	0	1	1	2	2	2	3	3	4	4	4	5	5	5	6	6	7	7	7	8	8	9	9	9	10	10	11	11	11	12	67
24	0	1	1	2	2	2	3	3	4	4	4	5	5	6	6	7	7	7	8	8	9	9	9	10	10	11	11	11	12	12	66
25	0	1	1	2	2	3	3	3	4	4	5	5	5	6	6	7	7	8	8	8	9	9	10	10	11	11	11	12	12	13	65
26	0	1	1	2	2	3	3	4	4	4	5	5	6	6	7	7	7	8	8	9	9	10	10	11	11	11	12	12	13	13	64
27	0	1	1	2	2	3	3	4	4	5	5	5	6	6	7	7	8	8	9	9	10	10	10	11	11	12	12	13	13	14	63
28	0	1	1	2	2	3	3	4	4	5	5	6	6	7	7	8	8	8	9	9	10	10	11	11	12	12	13	13	14	14	62
29	0	1	1	2	2	3	3	4	4	5	5	6	6	7	7	8	8	9	9	10	10	11	11	12	12	13	13	14	14	15	61
30	0	1	1	2	2	3	3	4	4	5	5	6	6	7	7	8	8	9	9	10	10	11	11	12	12	13	13	14	14	15	60
31	1	1	2	2	3	3	4	4	5	5	6	6	7	7	8	8	9	9	10	10	11	11	12	12	13	13	14	14	15	15	59
32	1	1	2	2	3	3	4	4	5	5	6	6	7	7	8	8	9	10	10	11	11	12	12	13	13	14	14	15	15	16	58
33	1	1	2	2	3	3	4	4	5	5	6	7	7	8	8	9	9	10	10	11	11	12	13	13	14	14	15	15	16	16	57
34	1	1	2	2	3	3	4	4	5	6	6	7	7	8	8	9	10	10	11	11	12	12	13	13	14	15	15	16	16	17	56
35	1	1	2	2	3	3	4	5	5	6	6	7	7	8	9	9	10	10	11	11	12	13	13	14	14	15	15	16	17	17	55
36	1	1	2	2	3	4	4	5	5	6	6	7	8	8	9	9	10	11	11	12	12	13	14	14	15	15	16	16	17	18	54
37	1	1	2	2	3	4	4	5	5	6	7	7	8	8	9	10	10	11	11	12	13	13	14	14	15	16	16	17	17	18	53
38	1	1	2	2	3	4	4	5	6	6	7	7	8	9	9	10	10	11	12	12	13	14	14	15	15	16	17	17	18	18	52
39	1	1	2	3	3	4	4	5	6	6	7	8	8	9	9	10	11	11	12	13	13	14	14	15	16	16	17	18	18	19	51
40	1	1	2	3	3	4	4	5	6	6	7	8	8	9	10	10	11	12	12	13	13	14	15	15	16	17	17	18	19	19	50

F′ +	1	2	3	4	5	6	7	8	9	10	11	12	13	14	15	16	17	18	19	20	21	22	23	24	25	26	27	28	29	□	− A′
F′ −	59	58	57	56	55	54	53	52	51	50	49	48	47	46	45	44	43	42	41	40	39	38	37	36	35	34	33	32	31	30	+ A′
P°	′	′	′	′	′	′	′	′	′	′	′	′	′	′	′	′	′	′	′	′	′	′	′	′	′	′	′	′	′	′	Z_2°
41	1	1	2	3	3	4	5	5	6	7	7	8	9	9	10	10	11	12	12	13	14	14	15	16	16	17	18	18	19	20	49
42	1	1	2	3	3	4	5	5	6	7	7	8	9	9	10	11	11	12	13	13	14	15	15	16	17	17	18	19	19	20	48
43	1	1	2	3	3	4	5	5	6	7	8	8	9	10	10	11	12	12	13	14	14	15	16	16	17	18	18	19	20	20	47
44	1	1	2	3	3	4	5	6	6	7	8	8	9	10	10	11	12	13	13	14	15	15	16	17	17	18	19	19	20	21	46
45	1	1	2	3	4	4	5	6	6	7	8	8	9	10	11	11	12	13	13	14	15	16	16	17	18	18	19	20	21	21	45
46	1	1	2	3	4	4	5	6	6	7	8	9	9	10	11	12	12	13	14	14	15	16	17	17	18	19	19	20	21	22	44
47	1	1	2	3	4	4	5	6	7	7	8	9	10	10	11	12	12	13	14	15	15	16	17	18	18	19	20	20	21	22	43
48	1	1	2	3	4	4	5	6	7	7	8	9	10	10	11	12	13	13	14	15	16	16	17	18	19	19	20	21	22	22	42
49	1	2	2	3	4	5	5	6	7	8	8	9	10	11	11	12	13	14	14	15	16	17	17	18	19	20	20	21	22	23	41
50	1	2	2	3	4	5	5	6	7	8	8	9	10	11	11	12	13	14	15	15	16	17	18	18	19	20	21	21	22	23	40
51	1	2	2	3	4	5	5	6	7	8	9	9	10	11	12	12	13	14	15	16	16	17	18	19	19	20	21	22	23	23	39
52	1	2	2	3	4	5	6	6	7	8	9	9	10	11	12	13	13	14	15	16	17	17	18	19	20	20	21	22	23	24	38
53	1	2	2	3	4	5	6	6	7	8	9	10	10	11	12	13	14	14	15	16	17	18	18	19	20	21	22	22	23	24	37
54	1	2	2	3	4	5	6	6	7	8	9	10	11	11	12	13	14	15	15	16	17	18	19	19	20	21	22	23	23	24	36
55	1	2	2	3	4	5	6	7	7	8	9	10	11	11	12	13	14	15	16	16	17	18	19	20	20	21	22	23	24	25	35
56	1	2	2	3	4	5	6	7	7	8	9	10	11	12	12	13	14	15	16	17	17	18	19	20	21	22	22	23	24	25	34
57	1	2	3	3	4	5	6	7	8	8	9	10	11	12	13	13	14	15	16	17	18	18	19	20	21	22	23	23	24	25	33
58	1	2	3	3	4	5	6	7	8	8	9	10	11	12	13	14	14	15	16	17	18	19	20	20	21	22	23	24	25	25	32
59	1	2	3	3	4	5	6	7	8	9	9	10	11	12	13	14	15	15	16	17	18	19	20	21	21	22	23	24	25	26	31
60	1	2	3	3	4	5	6	7	8	9	10	10	11	12	13	14	15	16	16	17	18	19	20	21	22	23	23	24	25	26	30
61	1	2	3	3	4	5	6	7	8	9	10	10	11	12	13	14	15	16	17	17	18	19	20	21	22	23	24	24	25	26	29
62	1	2	3	4	4	5	6	7	8	9	10	11	11	12	13	14	15	16	17	18	19	19	20	21	22	23	24	25	26	26	28
63	1	2	3	4	4	5	6	7	8	9	10	11	12	12	13	14	15	16	17	18	19	20	20	21	22	23	24	25	26	27	27
64	1	2	3	4	4	5	6	7	8	9	10	11	12	13	13	14	15	16	17	18	19	20	21	22	22	23	24	25	26	27	26
65	1	2	3	4	5	5	6	7	8	9	10	11	12	13	14	15	15	16	17	18	19	20	21	22	23	24	24	25	26	27	25
66	1	2	3	4	5	5	6	7	8	9	10	11	12	13	14	15	16	16	17	18	19	20	21	22	23	24	25	26	26	27	24
67	1	2	3	4	5	6	6	7	8	9	10	11	12	13	14	15	16	17	17	18	19	20	21	22	23	24	25	26	27	28	23
68	1	2	3	4	5	6	6	7	8	9	10	11	12	13	14	15	16	17	18	19	19	20	21	22	23	24	25	26	27	28	22
69	1	2	3	4	5	6	7	7	8	9	10	11	12	13	14	15	16	17	18	19	20	21	21	22	23	24	25	26	27	28	21
70	1	2	3	4	5	6	7	8	8	9	10	11	12	13	14	15	16	17	18	19	20	21	22	23	23	24	25	26	27	28	20
71	1	2	3	4	5	6	7	8	9	9	10	11	12	13	14	15	16	17	18	19	20	21	22	23	24	25	26	26	27	28	19
72	1	2	3	4	5	6	7	8	9	10	10	11	12	13	14	15	16	17	18	19	20	21	22	23	24	25	26	27	28	29	18
73	1	2	3	4	5	6	7	8	9	10	11	11	12	13	14	15	16	17	18	19	20	21	22	23	24	25	26	27	28	29	17
74	1	2	3	4	5	6	7	8	9	10	11	12	12	13	14	15	16	17	18	19	20	21	22	23	24	25	26	27	28	29	16
75	1	2	3	4	5	6	7	8	9	10	11	12	13	14	14	15	16	17	18	19	20	21	22	23	24	25	26	27	28	29	15
76	1	2	3	4	5	6	7	8	9	10	11	12	13	14	15	16	16	17	18	19	20	21	22	23	24	25	26	27	28	29	14
77	1	2	3	4	5	6	7	8	9	10	11	12	13	14	15	16	17	18	19	19	20	21	22	23	24	25	26	27	28	29	13
78	1	2	3	4	5	6	7	8	9	10	11	12	13	14	15	16	17	18	19	20	21	22	22	23	24	25	26	27	28	29	12
79	1	2	3	4	5	6	7	8	9	10	11	12	13	14	15	16	17	18	19	20	21	22	23	24	25	26	27	27	28	29	11
80	1	2	3	4	5	6	7	8	9	10	11	12	13	14	15	16	17	18	19	20	21	22	23	24	25	26	27	28	29	30	10

For P > 80°, use 80°

For $Z_2 < 10°$, use 10°

USE OF CONCISE SIGHT REDUCTION TABLES (continued)

4. *Example.* (b) Required the altitude and azimuth of *Vega* on 2026 July 29 at UT 04^{h} 49^{m} from the estimated position S 15°, W 152°.

1. Assumed latitude	$Lat =$	15° S		
From the almanac	$GHA =$	99° 39′		
Assumed longitude		151° 39′ W		
Local hour angle	$LHA =$	308		
2. Reduction table, 1st entry				
$(Lat, LHA) = (15, 308)$	$A =$	49 34	$A° = 50,\ A' = 34$	
	$B =$	+66 29	$Z_1 = +71{\cdot}7,$	$LHA > 270°$
3. From the almanac	$Dec =$	−38 49		*Lat* and *Dec* contrary
Sum $= B + Dec$	$F =$	+27 40	$F° = 28,\ F' = 40$	
4. Reduction table, 2nd entry				
$(A°, F°) = (50, 28)$	$H =$	17 34	$P° = 37$	
			$Z_2 = 67{\cdot}8, Z_2° = 68$	
5. Auxiliary table, 1st entry				
$(F', P°) = (40, 37)$	$corr_1 =$	−12		$F < 90°,\ F' > 29'$
Sum		17 22		
6. Auxiliary table, 2nd entry				
$(A', Z_2°) = (34, 68)$	$corr_2 =$	+10		$A' > 30'$
7. Sum = computed altitude	$Hc =$	+17° 32′		$F > 0°$
8. Azimuth, first component	$Z_1 =$	+71·7		same sign as B
second component	$Z_2 =$	+67·8		$F < 90°,\ F > 0°$
Sum = azimuth angle	$Z =$	139·5		
True azimuth	$Zn =$	040°		S *Lat*, $LHA > 180°$

5. *Form for use with the Concise Sight Reduction Tables.* The form on the following page lays out the procedure explained on pages 284-285. Each step is shown, with notes and rules to ensure accuracy, rather than speed, throughout the calculation. The form is mainly intended for the calculation of star positions. It therefore includes the formation of the Greenwich hour of Aries (*GHA* Aries), and thus the Greenwich hour angle of the star (*GHA*) from its tabular sidereal hour angle (*SHA*). These calculations, included in step 1 of the form, can easily be replaced by the interpolation of *GHA* and *Dec* for the Sun, Moon or planets.

The form may be freely copied; however, acknowledgement of the source is requested.

Date & UT of observation h m s	**Body**	**Estimated Latitude & Longitude** ° ′ ° ′

Step	Calculate Altitude & Azimuth	Summary of Rules & Notes
Assumed latitude	*Lat* = °	Nearest estimated latitude, integral number of degrees.
Assumed longitude	*Long* = ° ′	Choose *Long* so that *LHA* has integral number of degrees.
1. From the almanac:	*Dec* = ° ′	Record the *Dec* for use in Step 3.
GHA Aries h	= ° ′	Needed if using *SHA*. Tabular value.
Increment m s	= ° ′	for minutes and seconds of time.
SHA	*SHA* = ° ′	
$GHA = GHA\ Aries + SHA$	*GHA* = ° ′	Remove multiples of 360°.
Assumed longitude	*Long* = ° ′	West longitudes are negative.
$LHA = GHA + Long$	*LHA* = °	Remove multiples of 360°.
2. Reduction table, 1st entry		
$(Lat, LHA) = (\quad °, \quad °)$	*A* = ° ′ $A° =$ °	nearest whole degree of *A*.
record *A*, *B* and Z_1.	$A' =$ ′	minutes part of *A*.
	B = ° ′	*B* is minus if $90° < LHA < 270°$.
	$Z_1 =$ °	Z_1 has the same sign as *B*.
3. From step 1	*Dec* = ° ′	*Dec* is minus if contrary to *Lat*.
$F = B + Dec$	*F* = ° ′	Regard *F* as positive until step 7.
	$F° =$ °	nearest whole degree of *F*.
	$F' =$ ′	minutes part of *F*.
4. Reduction table, 2nd entry		
$(A°, F°) = (\quad °, \quad °)$	*H* = ° ′ $P° =$ °	nearest whole degree of *P*.
record *H*, *P* and Z_2.	$Z_2 =$ °	
5. Auxiliary table, 1st entry		
$(F', P°) = (\quad ′, \quad °)$	$corr_1 =$ ′	$corr_1$ is minus if $F < 90°$ & $F' > 29'$, or if $F > 90°$ & $F' < 30'$.
record $corr_1$		
6. Auxiliary table, 2nd entry		$Z_2°$ nearest whole degree of Z_2.
$(A', Z_2°) = (\quad ′, \quad °)$	$corr_2 =$ ′	$corr_2$ is minus if $A' < 30'$.
record $corr_2$		
7. Calculated altitude = $H_C = H + corr_1 + corr_2$	$H_C =$ ° ′	H_C is minus if *F* is negative, and object is below the horizon.
8. Azimuth, 1st component	$Z_1 =$ °	Z_1 has the same sign as *B*.
2nd component	$Z_2 =$ °	Z_2 is minus if $F > 90°$. If *F* is negative, $Z_2 = 180° - Z_2$
$Z = Z_1 + Z_2$	*Z* = °	Ignore the sign of *Z*.
		N *Lat*: If $LHA > 180°$, $Z_n = Z$, or if $LHA < 180°$, $Z_n = 360° - Z$,
True azimuth	$Z_n =$ °	S *Lat*: If $LHA > 180°$, $Z_n = 180° - Z$, or if $LHA < 180°$, $Z_n = 180° + Z$.

For use with *The Nautical Almanac's* Concise Sight Reduction Tables pages 284-318.

POLAR PHENOMENA

EXPLANATION

1. *Introduction.* The graphs on pages 322-325 give data concerning the rising and setting of the Sun and Moon and the duration of civil twilight for high latitudes. Graphs are given instead of tables for high latitudes because they give a clearer picture of the phenomena and of the attainable accuracy in any given case. In the regions of the graph that are difficult to read accurately, the phenomenon itself is generally uncertain.

2. *Semiduration of sunlight.* The graphs for the semiduration of sunlight (page 322) give for latitudes north of N 65° the number of hours from sunrise to meridian passage or from meridian passage to sunset. There is continuous daylight in an area marked "Sun above horizon", and no direct sunlight in an area marked "Sun below horizon". The figures near the top indicate, for several convenient dates, the local mean times of meridian passage; with the aid of the intermediate dots the LMT on any given day may be obtained to the nearest minute. The LMT of sunrise may be found by subtracting the semiduration from the time of meridian passage, and the time of sunset by adding. The equation of time is given by subtracting the time of meridian passage from noon.

Examples. (a) Estimate the time of sunrise and sunset on 2026 March 10 at latitude N 77°. The semiduration of sunlight (page 322) is about $5^{h}00^{m}$. The time of meridian passage is $12^{h}10^{m}$, and hence the LMT of sunrise is $07^{h}10^{m}$, and of sunset $17^{h}10^{m}$. (b) Estimate the dates, for the first half of 2026, when the Sun is continuously below and above the horizon at latitude N 80°. The semiduration of sunlight graph (page 322) indicates the Sun is continuously below the horizon until about February 21, and is continuously above the horizon after April 14.

3. *Duration of civil twilight.* The graphs for the duration of twilight (page 322) give the interval from the beginning of morning civil twilight (Sun 6° below the horizon) to the time of sunrise or from the time of sunset to the end of evening civil twilight. In a region marked "No twilight or sunlight", the Sun is continuously below the horizon by more than 6°. In a region marked "Continuous twilight or sunlight", the Sun never goes lower than 6° below the horizon.

Adjacent to a region marked "No twilight or sunlight" is a region in which the Sun is continuously below the horizon, but so near to the horizon during a portion of the day that there is twilight. This area is the shaded region. The value given by the graph in this shaded region is the interval from the beginning of morning twilight to meridian passage of the Sun, or from meridian passage to the end of evening twilight, the total duration of twilight being twice the value given by the graph. The border between this shaded region and the remainder of the graph indicates that the Sun only just rises at meridian passage at the date and latitude shown. The remainder of the graph gives the total duration of civil twilight.

Examples. (a) Estimate the time of the beginning of morning civil twilight at latitude N 77° on 2026 March 10. The duration of twilight (page 322) is about $1^{h}35^{m}$. Applying this to the time of sunrise, $07^{h}10^{m}$, found in the preceding example, the beginning of morning civil twilight is $05^{h}35^{m}$ LMT. (b) Estimate, for the first half of 2026, the limiting dates of civil twilight and sunlight at latitude N 80°. The graphs (page 322) indicate there is no sunlight or twilight till about February 5, there is twilight but no sunlight from February 5 until February 21, sunlight and twilight till March 31, continuous twilight or sunlight till April 14, and then continuous sunlight. (c) Estimate the time of the beginning and end of civil twilight on 2026 February 14 at latitude N 80°. The graph (page 322) indicates there is no direct sunlight at this date and latitude, but three hours of twilight before and after meridian passage occurring at $12^{h}14^{m}$. Thus civil twilight begins at about $09^{h}14^{m}$ and ends at about $15^{h}14^{m}$ LMT.

4. *Semiduration of moonlight* The graphs, for each month, for the semiduration of moonlight give for the Moon the same data as the graphs for the semiduration of sunlight give for the Sun. The scale near the top gives the LMT of meridian passage. In addition, the phase symbols are placed on the graphs to show the day on which each phase occurs. Since the times of meridian passage and the semiduration change more rapidly from day to day for the Moon than for the Sun, special care will be required in reading the graphs accurately.

For most purposes, in these high latitudes, a rough idea of the time of moonrise or moonset is all that is required, and this may be obtained by a glance at the graph.

Example. Estimate the moon phase and the time of moonrise and moonset on 2026 February 17 at latitude N 75°. The phase is found from pages 323-325 to be near new moon, and the Moon crosses the meridian at 12^h LMT. The semiduration of moonlight taken for the time of meridian passage is 2 hours, giving moonrise at 10^h LMT on February 17 and moonset at 14^h on February 17.

If greater accuracy is required, it is necessary to read the graph for the UT of each phenomenon at the desired meridian. The dates indicated on the graph are for 00^h UT, and intermediate values of the UT may be located by estimation.

Example. Required to improve the results obtained in the preceding example, assuming the observer to be in longitude W 90° (6^h) west.

The values found previously were:

			d h				d h	
Time of meridian passage	2026	Feb.	17 12	LMT	=	Feb.	17 18	UT
Semiduration of moonlight			2					
Time of moonrise		Feb.	17 10	LMT	=	Feb.	17 16	UT
Time of moonset		Feb.	17 14	LMT	=	Feb.	17 20	UT

Returning to the graphs (pages 323-325) with these three values of the UT, the following results are obtained:

			d h m				d h m	
Time of meridian passage	2026	Feb.	17 12 10	LMT	=	Feb.	17 18 10	UT
Semiduration for moonrise			02 30					
Time of moonrise		Feb.	17 09 40	LMT	=	Feb.	17 15 40	UT
Semiduration for moonset			03 00					
Time of moonset		Feb.	17 15 10	LMT	=	Feb.	17 21 10	UT

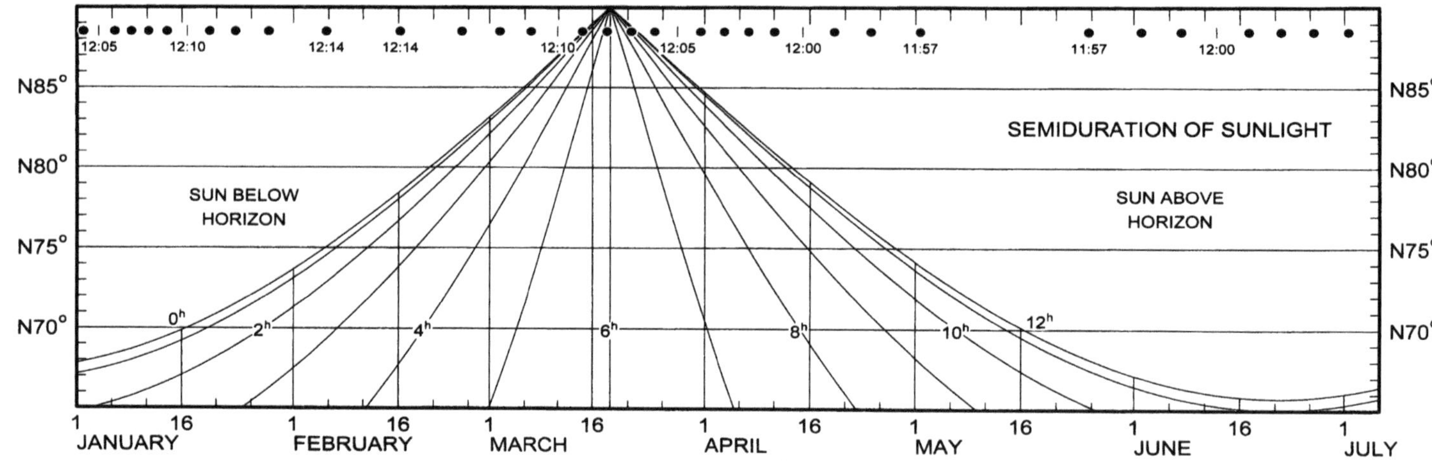
SEMIDURATION OF SUNLIGHT
SUN BELOW HORIZON
SUN ABOVE HORIZON
12:05 12:10 12:14 12:14 12:10 12:05 12:00 11:57 11:57 12:00
N85° N80° N75° N70°
0h 2h 4h 6h 8h 10h 12h
1 16 JANUARY 1 16 FEBRUARY 1 16 MARCH 1 16 APRIL 1 16 MAY 1 16 JUNE 1 JULY

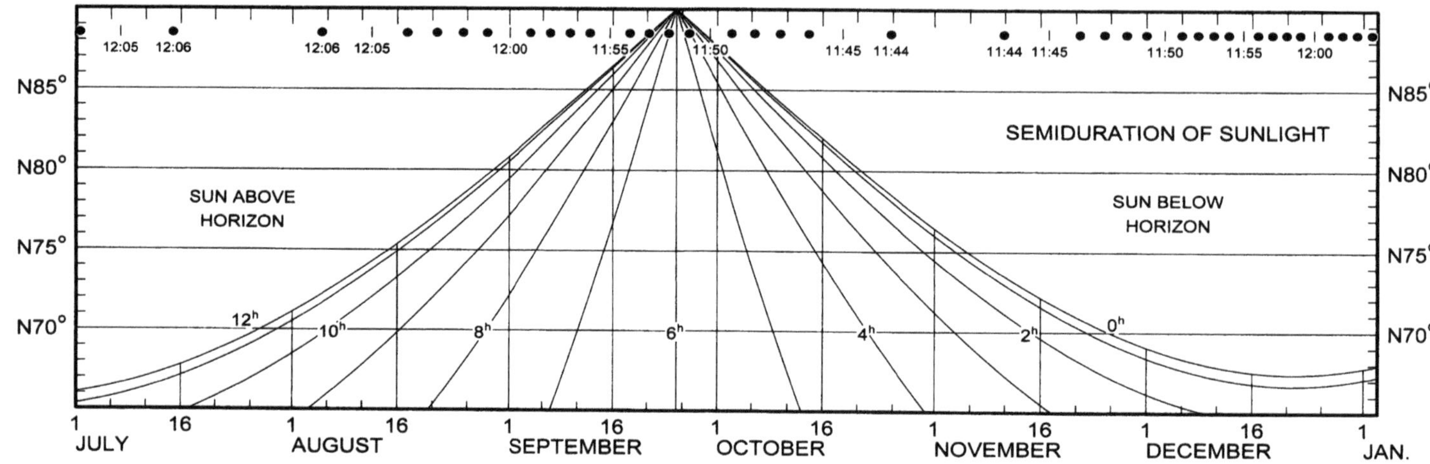
SEMIDURATION OF SUNLIGHT
SUN ABOVE HORIZON
SUN BELOW HORIZON
12:05 12:06 12:06 12:05 12:00 11:55 11:50 11:45 11:44 11:44 11:45 11:50 11:55 12:00
N85° N80° N75° N70°
12h 10h 8h 6h 4h 2h 0h
1 16 JULY 1 16 AUGUST 1 16 SEPTEMBER 1 16 OCTOBER 1 16 NOVEMBER 1 16 DECEMBER 1 JAN.

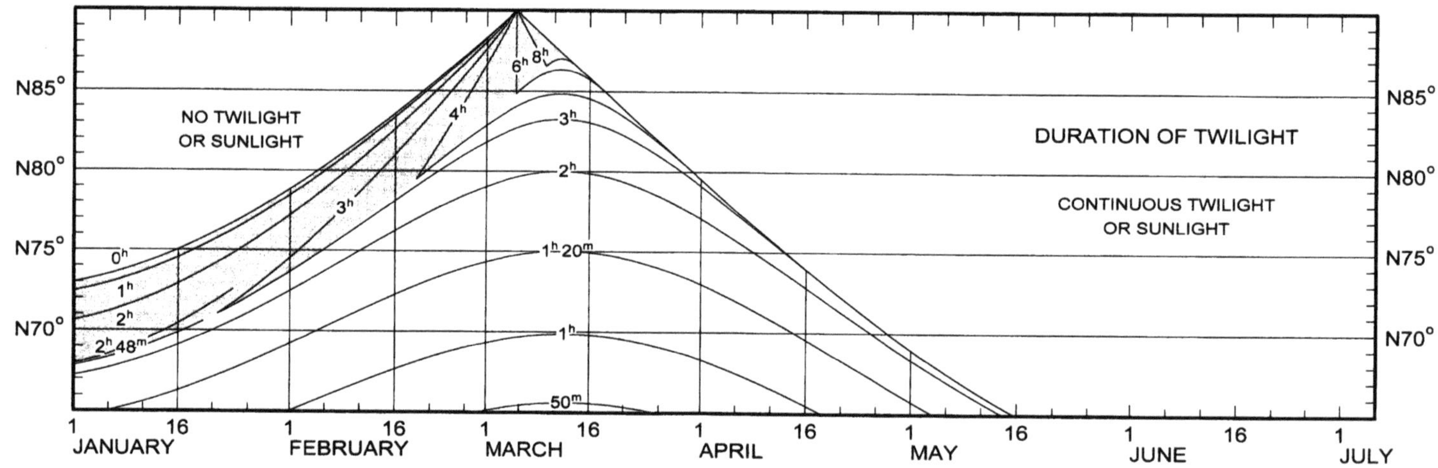
DURATION OF TWILIGHT
NO TWILIGHT OR SUNLIGHT
CONTINUOUS TWILIGHT OR SUNLIGHT
N85° N80° N75° N70°
0h 1h 2h 2h 48m 3h 4h 6h 8h 3h 2h 1h 20m 1h 50m
1 16 JANUARY 1 16 FEBRUARY 1 16 MARCH 1 16 APRIL 1 16 MAY 1 16 JUNE 1 JULY

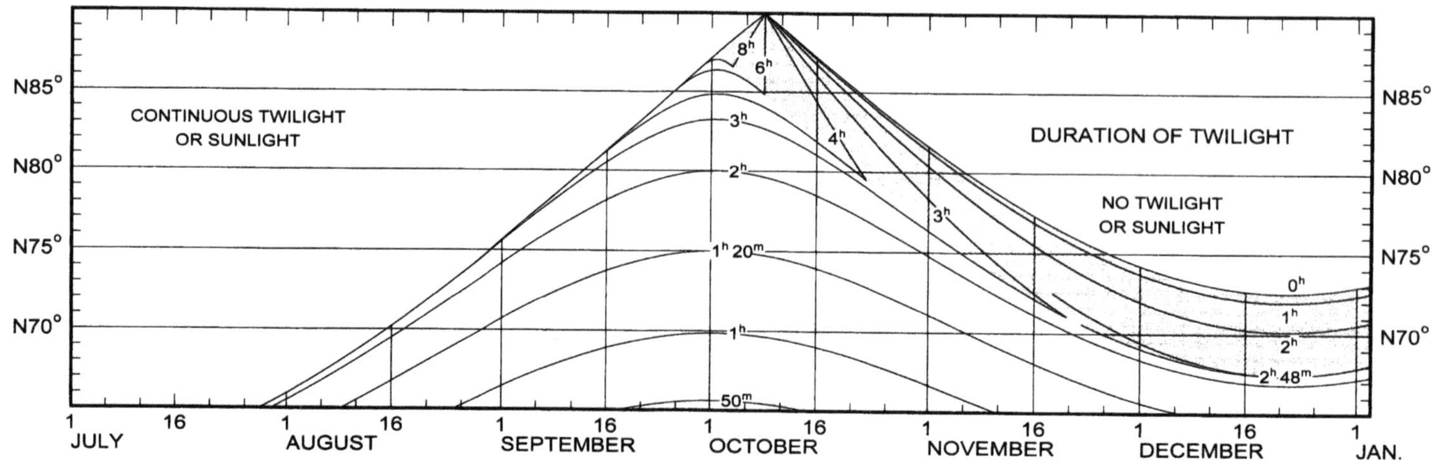
DURATION OF TWILIGHT
CONTINUOUS TWILIGHT OR SUNLIGHT
NO TWILIGHT OR SUNLIGHT
N85° N80° N75° N70°
8h 6h 3h 4h 2h 3h 1h 20m 1h 50m 0h 1h 2h 2h 48m
1 16 JULY 1 16 AUGUST 1 16 SEPTEMBER 1 16 OCTOBER 1 16 NOVEMBER 1 16 DECEMBER 1 JAN.

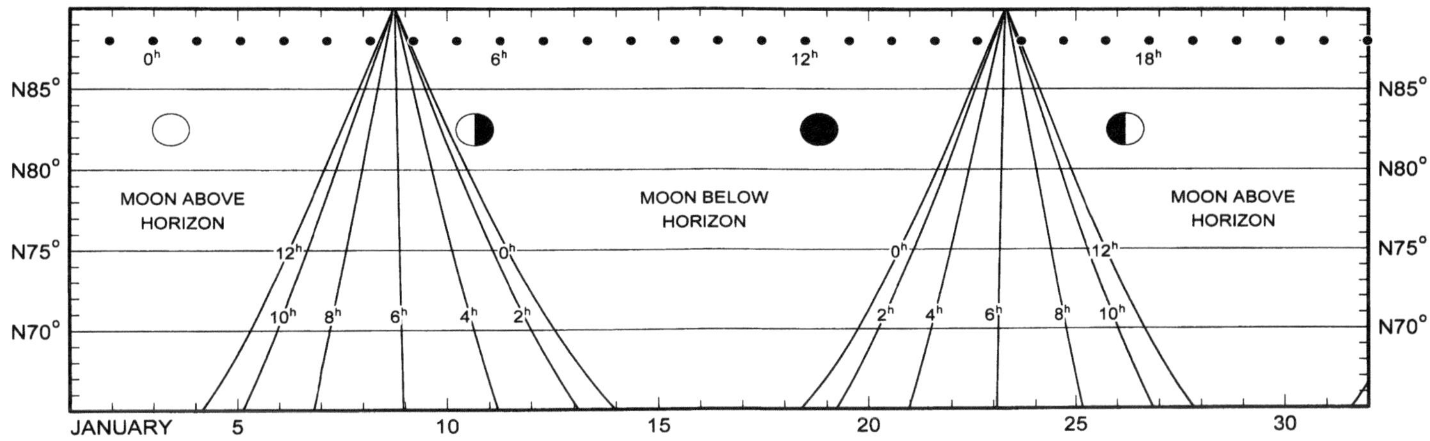
0h
6h
12h
18h
N85°
N80°
N75°
N70°
MOON ABOVE HORIZON
MOON BELOW HORIZON
MOON ABOVE HORIZON
JANUARY
5
10
15
20
25
30

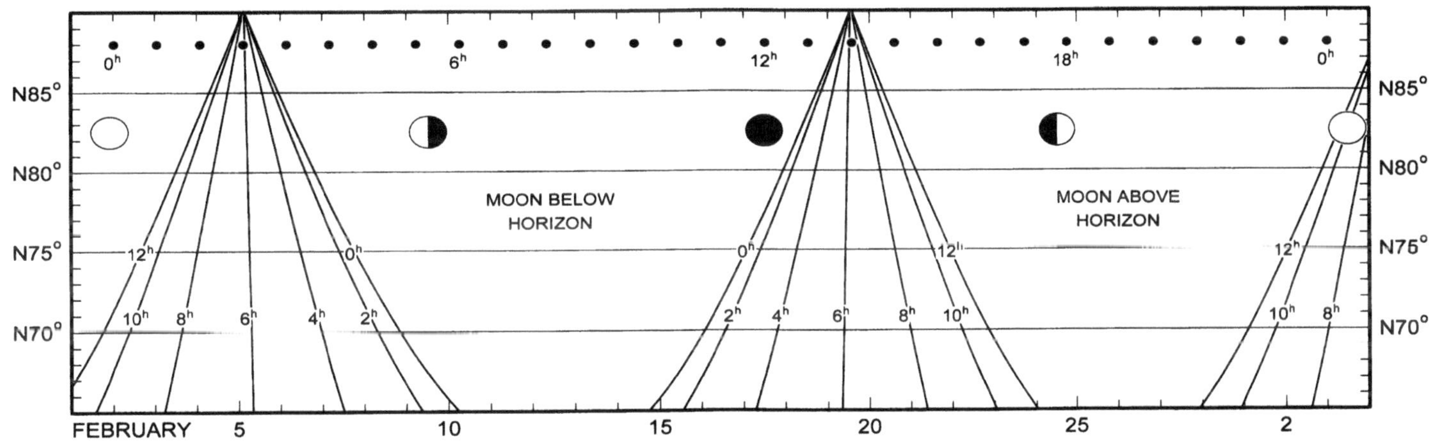
0h
6h
12h
18h
0h
N85°
N80°
N75°
N70°
MOON BELOW HORIZON
MOON ABOVE HORIZON
FEBRUARY
5
10
15
20
25
2

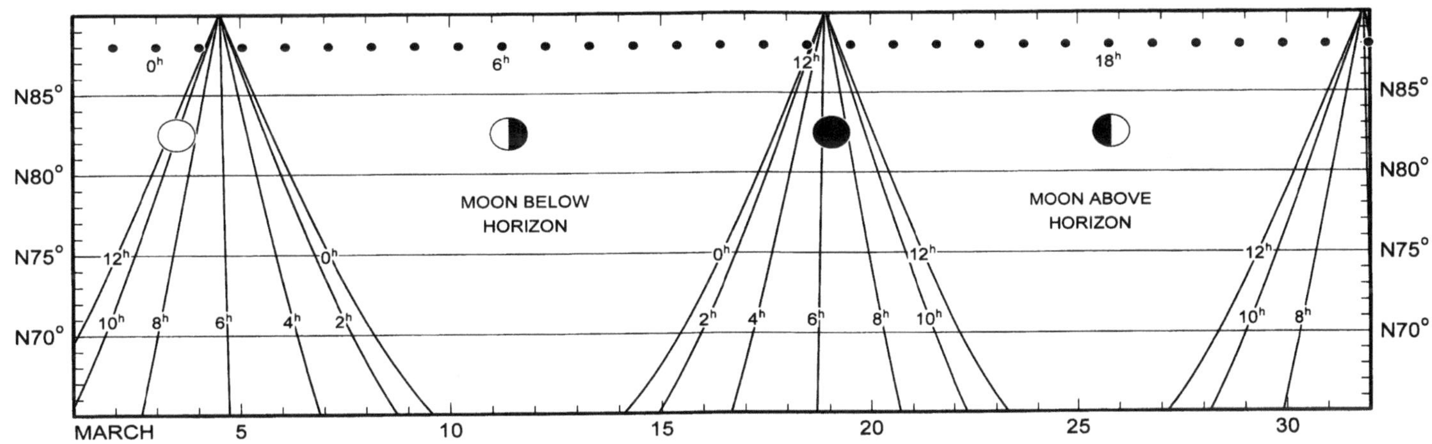
0h
6h
12h
18h
N85°
N80°
N75°
N70°
MOON BELOW HORIZON
MOON ABOVE HORIZON
MARCH
5
10
15
20
25
30

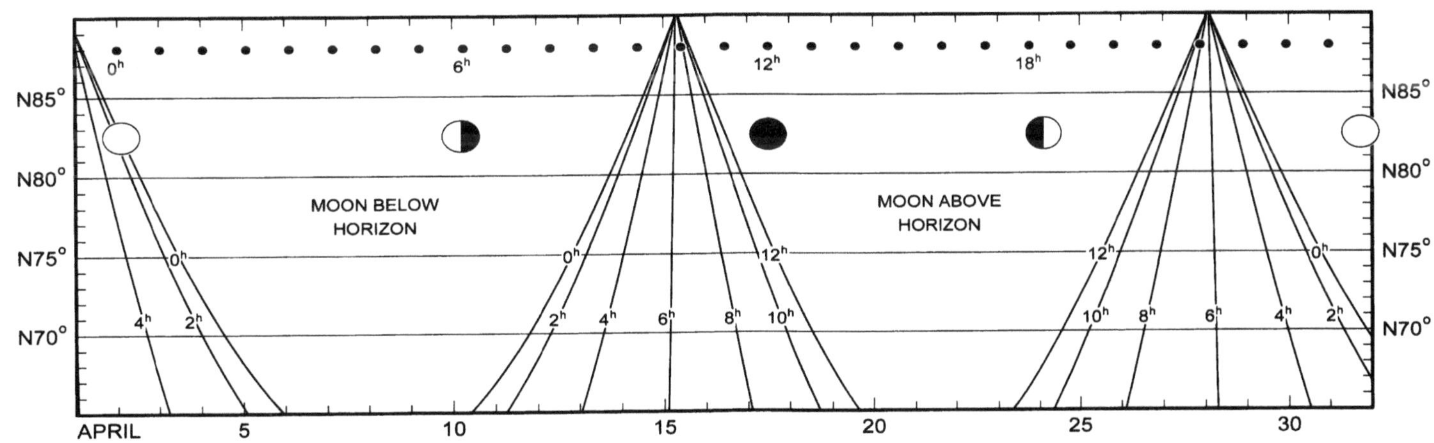
0h
6h
12h
18h
N85°
N80°
N75°
N70°
MOON BELOW HORIZON
MOON ABOVE HORIZON
APRIL
5
10
15
20
25
30

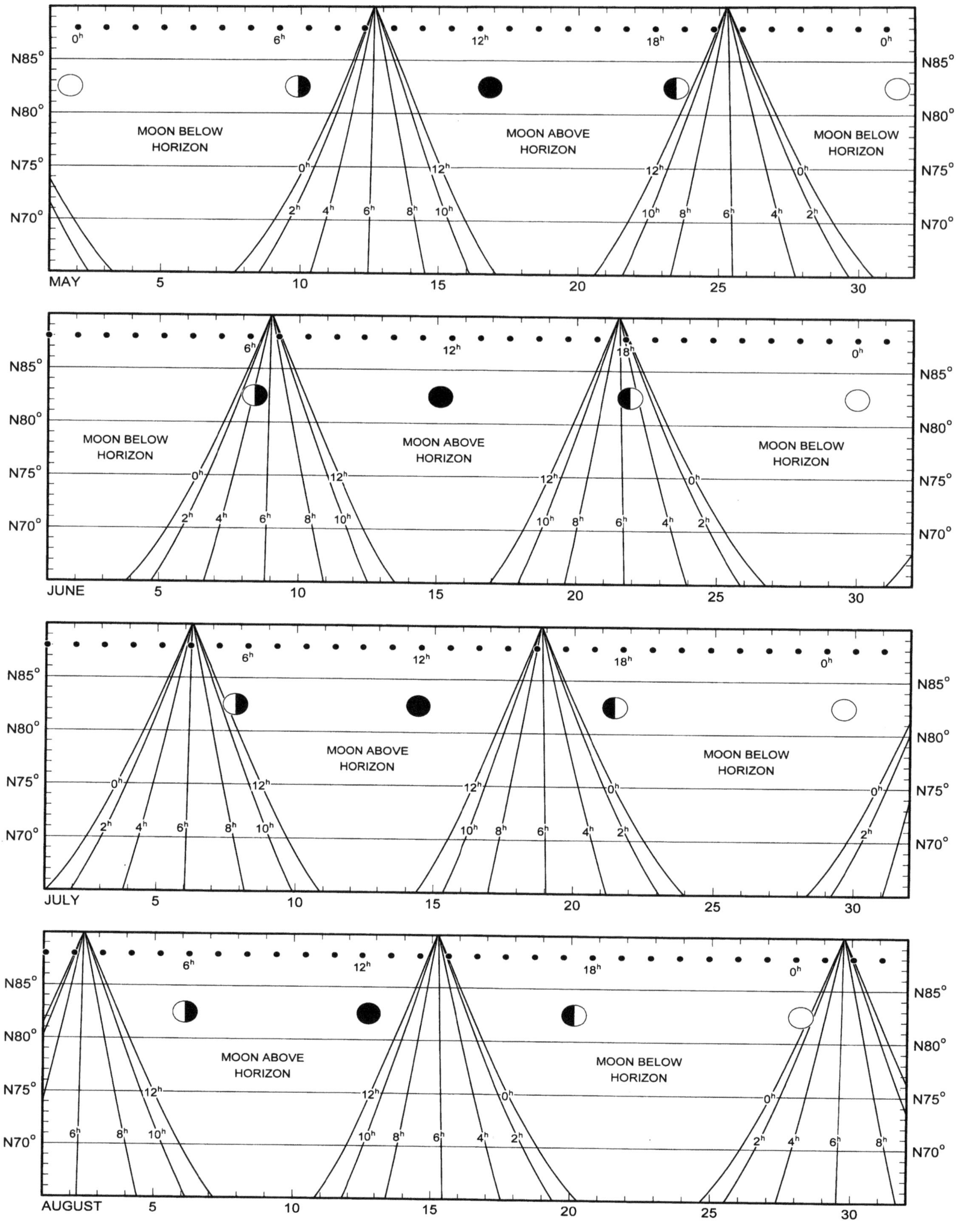
N85°
N80°
N75°
N70°
MOON BELOW HORIZON
MOON ABOVE HORIZON
MOON BELOW HORIZON
MAY 5 10 15 20 25 30
JUNE 5 10 15 20 25 30
MOON BELOW HORIZON
MOON ABOVE HORIZON
MOON BELOW HORIZON
JULY 5 10 15 20 25 30
MOON ABOVE HORIZON
MOON BELOW HORIZON
AUGUST 5 10 15 20 25 30
MOON ABOVE HORIZON
MOON BELOW HORIZON

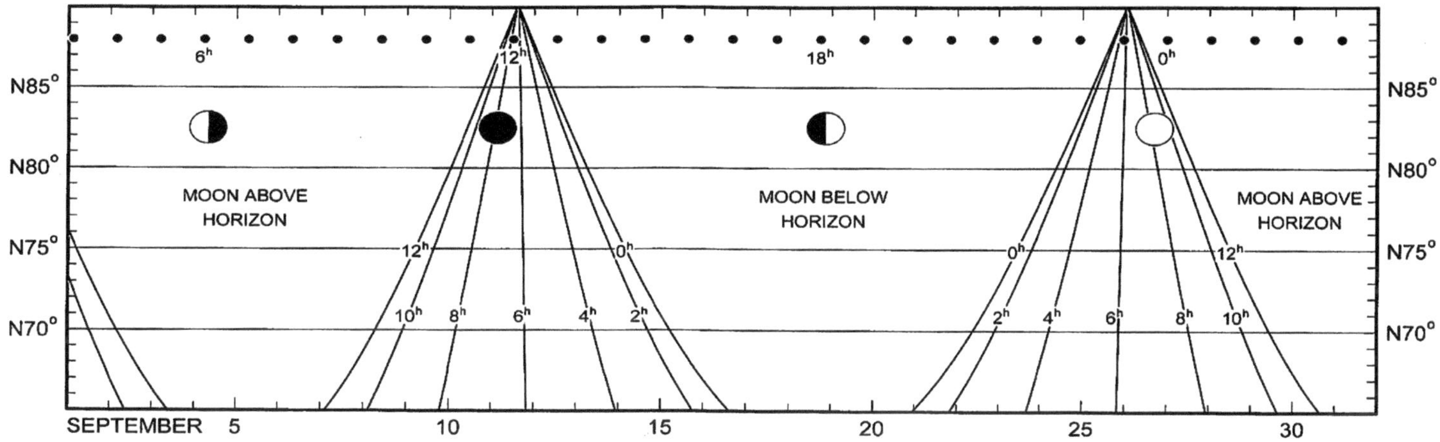
MOON ABOVE HORIZON
MOON BELOW HORIZON
MOON ABOVE HORIZON
6h 12h 18h 0h
N85° N80° N75° N70°
12h 0h 0h 12h
10h 8h 6h 4h 2h 2h 4h 6h 8h 10h
SEPTEMBER 5 10 15 20 25 30

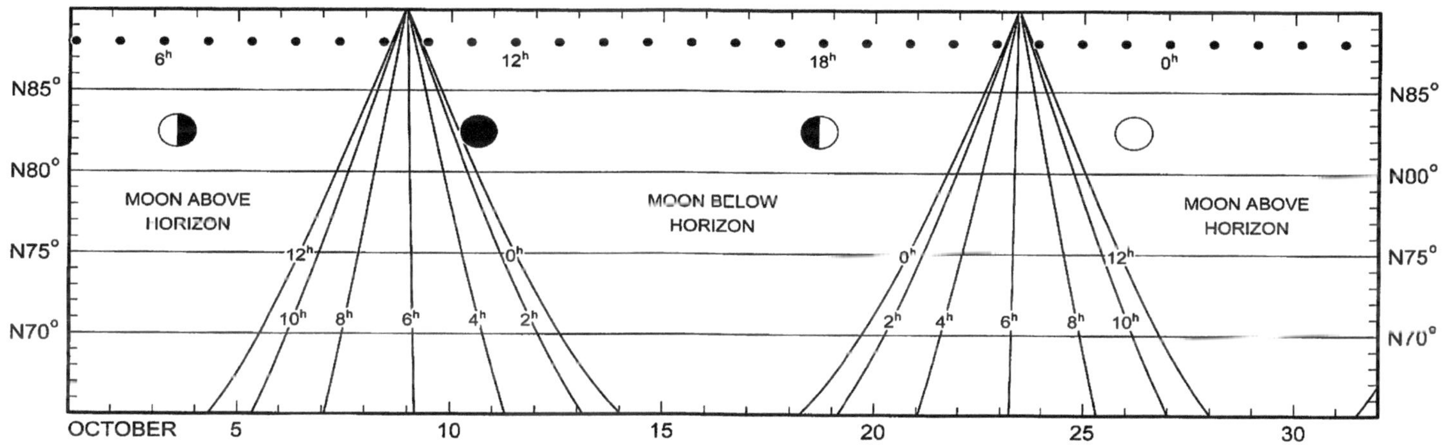
MOON ABOVE HORIZON
MOON BELOW HORIZON
MOON ABOVE HORIZON
6h 12h 18h 0h
N85° N80° N75° N70°
12h 0h 0h 12h
10h 8h 6h 4h 2h 2h 4h 6h 8h 10h
OCTOBER 5 10 15 20 25 30

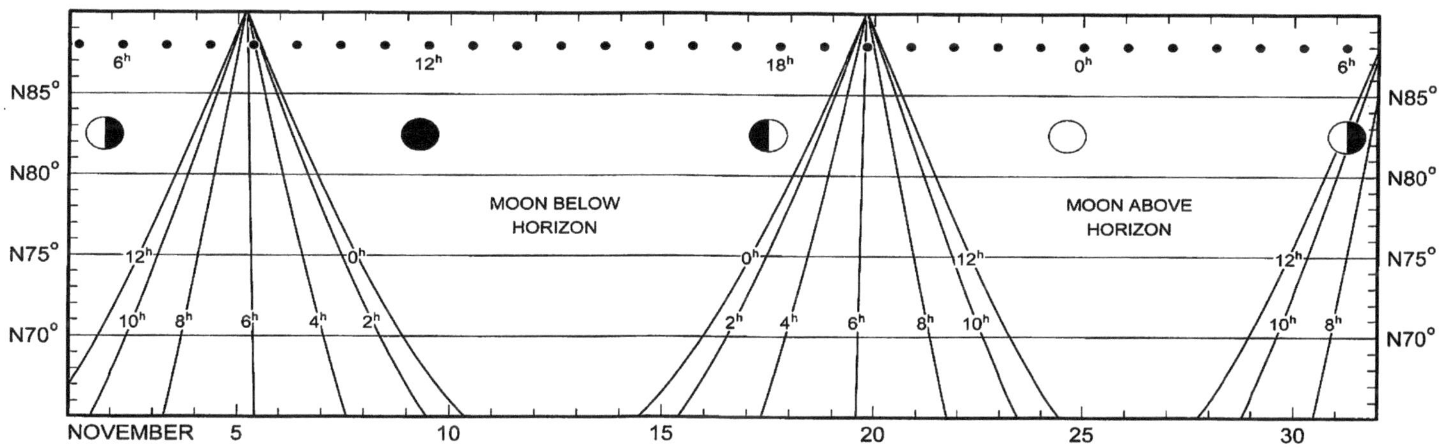
MOON BELOW HORIZON
MOON ABOVE HORIZON
6h 12h 18h 0h 6h
N85° N80° N75° N70°
12h 0h 0h 12h 12h
10h 8h 6h 4h 2h 2h 4h 6h 8h 10h 10h 8h
NOVEMBER 5 10 15 20 25 30

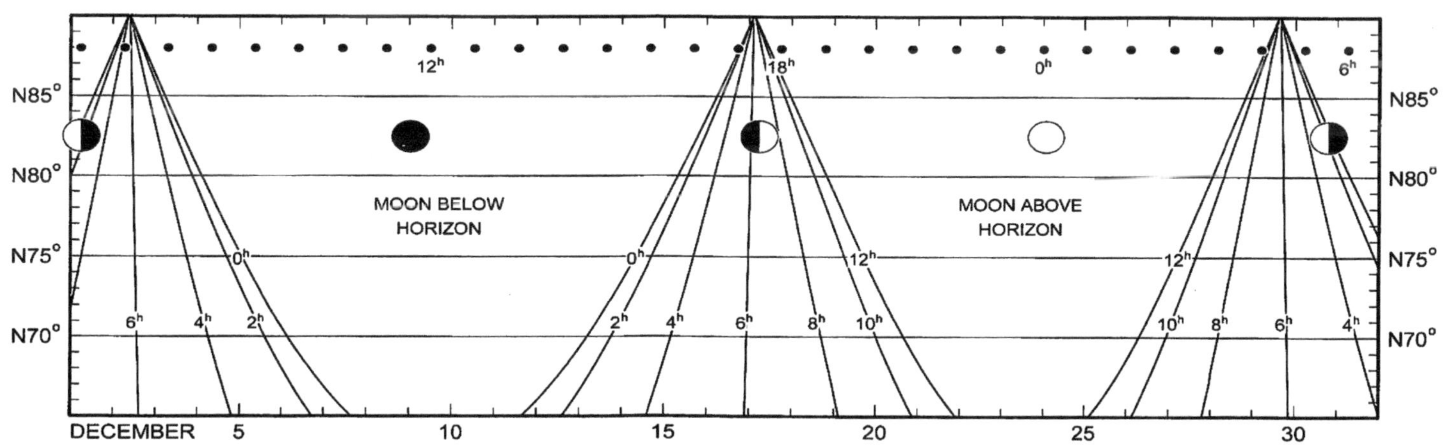
MOON BELOW HORIZON
MOON ABOVE HORIZON
12h 18h 0h 6h
N85° N80° N75° N70°
0h 0h 12h 12h
6h 4h 2h 2h 4h 6h 8h 10h 10h 8h 6h 4h
DECEMBER 5 10 15 20 25 30

NOTES

A2 ALTITUDE CORRECTION TABLES 10°–90°—SUN, STARS, PLANETS

SUN

OCT.—MAR. App. Alt.	Lower Limb	Upper Limb	APR.—SEPT. App. Alt.	Lower Limb	Upper Limb
° ′	′	′	° ′	′	′
9 33			9 39		
	+10·8	−21·5		+10·6	−21·2
9 45			9 50		
	+10·9	−21·4		+10·7	−21·1
9 56			10 02		
	+11·0	−21·3		+10·8	−21·0
10 08			10 14		
	+11·1	−21·2		+10·9	−20·9
10 20			10 27		
	+11·2	−21·1		+11·0	−20·8
10 33			10 40		
	+11·3	−21·0		+11·1	−20·7
10 46			10 53		
	+11·4	−20·9		+11·2	−20·6
11 00			11 07		
	+11·5	−20·8		+11·3	−20·5
11 15			11 22		
	+11·6	−20·7		+11·4	−20·4
11 30			11 37		
	+11·7	−20·6		+11·5	−20·3
11 45			11 53		
	+11·8	−20·5		+11·6	−20·2
12 01			12 10		
	+11·9	−20·4		+11·7	−20·1
12 18			12 27		
	+12·0	−20·3		+11·8	−20·0
12 36			12 45		
	+12·1	−20·2		+11·9	−19·9
12 54			13 04		
	+12·2	−20·1		+12·0	−19·8
13 14			13 24		
	+12·3	−20·0		+12·1	−19·7
13 34			13 44		
	+12·4	−19·9		+12·2	−19·6
13 55			14 06		
	+12·5	−19·8		+12·3	−19·5
14 17			14 29		
	+12·6	−19·7		+12·4	−19·4
14 41			14 53		
	+12·7	−19·6		+12·5	−19·3
15 05			15 18		
	+12·8	−19·5		+12·6	−19·2
15 31			15 45		
	+12·9	−19·4		+12·7	−19·1
15 59			16 13		
	+13·0	−19·3		+12·8	−19·0
16 27			16 43		
	+13·1	−19·2		+12·9	−18·9
16 58			17 14		
	+13·2	−19·1		+13·0	−18·8
17 30			17 47		
	+13·3	−19·0		+13·1	−18·7
18 05			18 23		
	+13·4	−18·9		+13·2	−18·6
18 41			19 00		
	+13·5	−18·8		+13·3	−18·5
19 20			19 41		
	+13·6	−18·7		+13·4	−18·4
20 02			20 24		
	+13·7	−18·6		+13·5	−18·3
20 46			21 10		
	+13·8	−18·5		+13·6	−18·2
21 34			21 59		
	+13·9	−18·4		+13·7	−18·1
22 25			22 52		
	+14·0	−18·3		+13·8	−18·0
23 20			23 49		
	+14·1	−18·2		+13·9	−17·9
24 20			24 51		
	+14·2	−18·1		+14·0	−17·8
25 24			25 58		
	+14·3	−18·0		+14·1	−17·7
26 34			27 11		
	+14·4	−17·9		+14·2	−17·6
27 50			28 31		
	+14·5	−17·8		+14·3	−17·5
29 13			29 58		
	+14·6	−17·7		+14·4	−17·4
30 44			31 33		
	+14·7	−17·6		+14·5	−17·3
32 24			33 18		
	+14·8	−17·5		+14·6	−17·2
34 15			35 15		
	+14·9	−17·4		+14·7	−17·1
36 17			37 24		
	+15·0	−17·3		+14·8	−17·0
38 34			39 48		
	+15·1	−17·2		+14·9	−16·9
41 06			42 28		
	+15·2	−17·1		+15·0	−16·8
43 56			45 29		
	+15·3	−17·0		+15·1	−16·7
47 07			48 52		
	+15·4	−16·9		+15·2	−16·6
50 43			52 41		
	+15·5	−16·8		+15·3	−16·5
54 46			56 59		
	+15·6	−16·7		+15·4	−16·4
59 21			61 50		
	+15·7	−16·6		+15·5	−16·3
64 28			67 15		
	+15·8	−16·5		+15·6	−16·2
70 10			73 14		
	+15·9	−16·4		+15·7	−16·1
76 24			79 42		
	+16·0	−16·3		+15·8	−16·0
83 05			86 31		
	+16·1	−16·2		+15·9	−15·9
90 00			90 00		

STARS AND PLANETS

App Alt.	Corrⁿ
° ′	′
9 55	
	−5·3
10 07	
	−5·2
10 20	
	−5·1
10 32	
	−5·0
10 46	
	−4·9
10 59	
	−4·8
11 14	
	−4·7
11 29	
	−4·6
11 44	
	−4·5
12 00	
	−4·4
12 17	
	−4·3
12 35	
	−4·2
12 53	
	−4·1
13 12	
	−4·0
13 32	
	−3·9
13 53	
	−3·8
14 16	
	−3·7
14 39	
	−3·6
15 03	
	−3·5
15 29	
	−3·4
15 56	
	−3·3
16 25	
	−3·2
16 55	
	−3·1
17 27	
	−3·0
18 01	
	−2·9
18 37	
	−2·8
19 16	
	−2·7
19 56	
	−2·6
20 40	
	−2·5
21 27	
	−2·4
22 17	
	−2·3
23 11	
	−2·2
24 09	
	−2·1
25 12	
	−2·0
26 20	
	−1·9
27 34	
	−1·8
28 54	
	−1·7
30 22	
	−1·6
31 58	
	−1·5
33 43	
	−1·4
35 38	
	−1·3
37 45	
	−1·2
40 06	
	−1·1
42 42	
	−1·0
45 34	
	−0·9
48 45	
	−0·8
52 16	
	−0·7
56 09	
	−0·6
60 26	
	−0·5
65 06	
	−0·4
70 09	
	−0·3
75 32	
	−0·2
81 12	
	−0·1
87 03	
	0·0
90 00	

App. Alt. — Additional Corrⁿ

2026

VENUS

Jan. 1–July 9

App. Alt.	Additional Corrⁿ
°	′
0	
	+0·1
60	

July 10–Aug. 27
Dec. 24–Dec. 31

App. Alt.	Additional Corrⁿ
°	′
0	
	+0·2
41	
	+0·1
76	

Aug. 28–Sept. 19
Nov. 30–Dec. 23

App. Alt.	Additional Corrⁿ
°	′
0	
	+0·3
34	
	+0·2
60	
	+0·1
80	

Sept. 20–Oct. 5
Nov. 15–Nov. 29

App. Alt.	Additional Corrⁿ
°	′
0	
	+0·4
29	
	+0·3
51	
	+0·2
68	
	+0·1
83	

Oct. 6–Nov. 14

App. Alt.	Additional Corrⁿ
°	′
0	
	+0·5
26	
	+0·4
46	
	+0·3
60	
	+0·2
73	
	+0·1
84	

MARS

Jan. 1–Dec. 24

App. Alt.	Additional Corrⁿ
°	′
0	
	+0·1
60	

Dec. 25–Dec. 31

App. Alt.	Additional Corrⁿ
°	′
0	
	+0·2
41	
	+0·1
76	

DIP

Ht. of Eye	Corrⁿ	Ht. of Eye
m	′	ft.
2·4		8·0
	−2·8	
2·6		8·6
	−2·9	
2·8		9·2
	−3·0	
3·0		9·8
	−3·1	
3·2		10·5
	−3·2	
3·4		11·2
	−3·3	
3·6		11·9
	−3·4	
3·8		12·6
	−3·5	
4·0		13·3
	−3·6	
4·3		14·1
	−3·7	
4·5		14·9
	−3·8	
4·7		15·7
	−3·9	
5·0		16·5
	−4·0	
5·2		17·4
	−4·1	
5·5		18·3
	−4·2	
5·8		19·1
	−4·3	
6·1		20·1
	−4·4	
6·3		21·0
	−4·5	
6·6		22·0
	−4·6	
6·9		22·9
	−4·7	
7·2		23·9
	−4·8	
7·5		24·9
	−4·9	
7·9		26·0
	−5·0	
8·2		27·1
	−5·1	
8·5		28·1
	−5·2	
8·8		29·2
	−5·3	
9·2		30·4
	−5·4	
9·5		31·5
	−5·5	
9·9		32·7
	−5·6	
10·3		33·9
	−5·7	
10·6		35·1
	−5·8	
11·0		36·3
	−5·9	
11·4		37·6
	−6·0	
11·8		38·9
	−6·1	
12·2		40·1
	−6·2	
12·6		41·5
	−6·3	
13·0		42·8
	−6·4	
13·4		44·2
	−6·5	
13·8		45·5
	−6·6	
14·2		46·9
	−6·7	
14·7		48·4
	−6·8	
15·1		49·8
	−6·9	
15·5		51·3
	−7·0	
16·0		52·8
	−7·1	
16·5		54·3
	−7·2	
16·9		55·8
	−7·3	
17·4		57·4
	−7·4	
17·9		58·9
	−7·5	
18·4		60·5
	−7·6	
18·8		62·1
	−7·7	
19·3		63·8
	−7·8	
19·8		65·4
	−7·9	
20·4		67·1
	−8·0	
20·9		68·8
	−8·1	
21·4		70·5

Ht. of Eye	Corrⁿ
m	′
1·0	− 1·8
1·5	− 2·2
2·0	− 2·5
2·5	− 2·8
3·0	− 3·0
See table ←	
m	′
20	− 7·9
22	− 8·3
24	− 8·6
26	− 9·0
28	− 9·3
30	− 9·6
32	− 10·0
34	− 10·3
36	− 10·6
38	− 10·8
40	− 11·1
42	− 11·4
44	− 11·7
46	− 11·9
48	− 12·2
ft.	′
2	− 1·4
4	− 1·9
6	− 2·4
8	− 2·7
10	− 3·1
See table ←	
ft.	′
70	− 8·1
75	− 8·4
80	− 8·7
85	− 8·9
90	− 9·2
95	− 9·5
100	− 9·7
105	− 9·9
110	− 10·2
115	− 10·4
120	− 10·6
125	− 10·8
130	− 11·1
135	− 11·3
140	− 11·5
145	− 11·7
150	− 11·9
155	− 12·1

App. Alt. = Apparent altitude = Sextant altitude corrected for index error and dip.

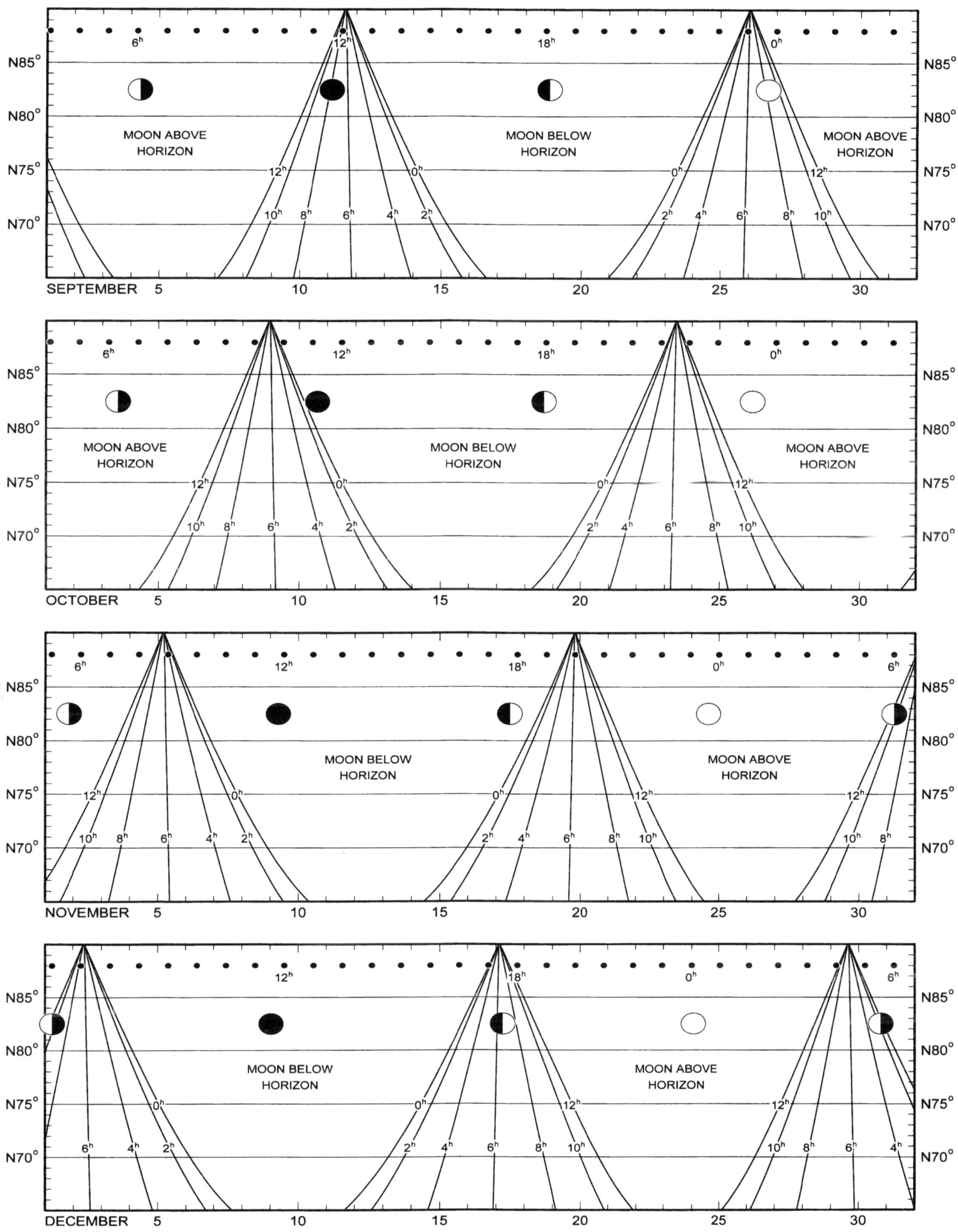
MOON ABOVE HORIZON
MOON BELOW HORIZON
N85°
N80°
N75°
N70°
SEPTEMBER
OCTOBER
NOVEMBER
DECEMBER
5
10
15
20
25
30

NOTES

CONVERSION OF ARC TO TIME

0°–59°		60°–119°		120°–179°		180°–239°		240°–299°		300°–359°			0′.00	0′.25	0′.50	0′.75
°	h m	°	h m	°	h m	°	h m	°	h m	°	h m	′	m s	m s	m s	m s
0	0 00	60	4 00	120	8 00	180	12 00	240	16 00	300	20 00	0	0 00	0 01	0 02	0 03
1	0 04	61	4 04	121	8 04	181	12 04	241	16 04	301	20 04	1	0 04	0 05	0 06	0 07
2	0 08	62	4 08	122	8 08	182	12 08	242	16 08	302	20 08	2	0 08	0 09	0 10	0 11
3	0 12	63	4 12	123	8 12	183	12 12	243	16 12	303	20 12	3	0 12	0 13	0 14	0 15
4	0 16	64	4 16	124	8 16	184	12 16	244	16 16	304	20 16	4	0 16	0 17	0 18	0 19
5	0 20	65	4 20	125	8 20	185	12 20	245	16 20	305	20 20	5	0 20	0 21	0 22	0 23
6	0 24	66	4 24	126	8 24	186	12 24	246	16 24	306	20 24	6	0 24	0 25	0 26	0 27
7	0 28	67	4 28	127	8 28	187	12 28	247	16 28	307	20 28	7	0 28	0 29	0 30	0 31
8	0 32	68	4 32	128	8 32	188	12 32	248	16 32	308	20 32	8	0 32	0 33	0 34	0 35
9	0 36	69	4 36	129	8 36	189	12 36	249	16 36	309	20 36	9	0 36	0 37	0 38	0 39
10	0 40	70	4 40	130	8 40	190	12 40	250	16 40	310	20 40	10	0 40	0 41	0 42	0 43
11	0 44	71	4 44	131	8 44	191	12 44	251	16 44	311	20 44	11	0 44	0 45	0 46	0 47
12	0 48	72	4 48	132	8 48	192	12 48	252	16 48	312	20 48	12	0 48	0 49	0 50	0 51
13	0 52	73	4 52	133	8 52	193	12 52	253	16 52	313	20 52	13	0 52	0 53	0 54	0 55
14	0 56	74	4 56	134	8 56	194	12 56	254	16 56	314	20 56	14	0 56	0 57	0 58	0 59
15	1 00	75	5 00	135	9 00	195	13 00	255	17 00	315	21 00	15	1 00	1 01	1 02	1 03
16	1 04	76	5 04	136	9 04	196	13 04	256	17 04	316	21 04	16	1 04	1 05	1 06	1 07
17	1 08	77	5 08	137	9 08	197	13 08	257	17 08	317	21 08	17	1 08	1 09	1 10	1 11
18	1 12	78	5 12	138	9 12	198	13 12	258	17 12	318	21 12	18	1 12	1 13	1 14	1 15
19	1 16	79	5 16	139	9 16	199	13 16	259	17 16	319	21 16	19	1 16	1 17	1 18	1 19
20	1 20	80	5 20	140	9 20	200	13 20	260	17 20	320	21 20	20	1 20	1 21	1 22	1 23
21	1 24	81	5 24	141	9 24	201	13 24	261	17 24	321	21 24	21	1 24	1 25	1 26	1 27
22	1 28	82	5 28	142	9 28	202	13 28	262	17 28	322	21 28	22	1 28	1 29	1 30	1 31
23	1 32	83	5 32	143	9 32	203	13 32	263	17 32	323	21 32	23	1 32	1 33	1 34	1 35
24	1 36	84	5 36	144	9 36	204	13 36	264	17 36	324	21 36	24	1 36	1 37	1 38	1 39
25	1 40	85	5 40	145	9 40	205	13 40	265	17 40	325	21 40	25	1 40	1 41	1 42	1 43
26	1 44	86	5 44	146	9 44	206	13 44	266	17 44	326	21 44	26	1 44	1 45	1 46	1 47
27	1 48	87	5 48	147	9 48	207	13 48	267	17 48	327	21 48	27	1 48	1 49	1 50	1 51
28	1 52	88	5 52	148	9 52	208	13 52	268	17 52	328	21 52	28	1 52	1 53	1 54	1 55
29	1 56	89	5 56	149	9 56	209	13 56	269	17 56	329	21 56	29	1 56	1 57	1 58	1 59
30	2 00	90	6 00	150	10 00	210	14 00	270	18 00	330	22 00	30	2 00	2 01	2 02	2 03
31	2 04	91	6 04	151	10 04	211	14 04	271	18 04	331	22 04	31	2 04	2 05	2 06	2 07
32	2 08	92	6 08	152	10 08	212	14 08	272	18 08	332	22 08	32	2 08	2 09	2 10	2 11
33	2 12	93	6 12	153	10 12	213	14 12	273	18 12	333	22 12	33	2 12	2 13	2 14	2 15
34	2 16	94	6 16	154	10 16	214	14 16	274	18 16	334	22 16	34	2 16	2 17	2 18	2 19
35	2 20	95	6 20	155	10 20	215	14 20	275	18 20	335	22 20	35	2 20	2 21	2 22	2 23
36	2 24	96	6 24	156	10 24	216	14 24	276	18 24	336	22 24	36	2 24	2 25	2 26	2 27
37	2 28	97	6 28	157	10 28	217	14 28	277	18 28	337	22 28	37	2 28	2 29	2 30	2 31
38	2 32	98	6 32	158	10 32	218	14 32	278	18 32	338	22 32	38	2 32	2 33	2 34	2 35
39	2 36	99	6 36	159	10 36	219	14 36	279	18 36	339	22 36	39	2 36	2 37	2 38	2 39
40	2 40	100	6 40	160	10 40	220	14 40	280	18 40	340	22 40	40	2 40	2 41	2 42	2 43
41	2 44	101	6 44	161	10 44	221	14 44	281	18 44	341	22 44	41	2 44	2 45	2 46	2 47
42	2 48	102	6 48	162	10 48	222	14 48	282	18 48	342	22 48	42	2 48	2 49	2 50	2 51
43	2 52	103	6 52	163	10 52	223	14 52	283	18 52	343	22 52	43	2 52	2 53	2 54	2 55
44	2 56	104	6 56	164	10 56	224	14 56	284	18 56	344	22 56	44	2 56	2 57	2 58	2 59
45	3 00	105	7 00	165	11 00	225	15 00	285	19 00	345	23 00	45	3 00	3 01	3 02	3 03
46	3 04	106	7 04	166	11 04	226	15 04	286	19 04	346	23 04	46	3 04	3 05	3 06	3 07
47	3 08	107	7 08	167	11 08	227	15 08	287	19 08	347	23 08	47	3 08	3 09	3 10	3 11
48	3 12	108	7 12	168	11 12	228	15 12	288	19 12	348	23 12	48	3 12	3 13	3 14	3 15
49	3 16	109	7 16	169	11 16	229	15 16	289	19 16	349	23 16	49	3 16	3 17	3 18	3 19
50	3 20	110	7 20	170	11 20	230	15 20	290	19 20	350	23 20	50	3 20	3 21	3 22	3 23
51	3 24	111	7 24	171	11 24	231	15 24	291	19 24	351	23 24	51	3 24	3 25	3 26	3 27
52	3 28	112	7 28	172	11 28	232	15 28	292	19 28	352	23 28	52	3 28	3 29	3 30	3 31
53	3 32	113	7 32	173	11 32	233	15 32	293	19 32	353	23 32	53	3 32	3 33	3 34	3 35
54	3 36	114	7 36	174	11 36	234	15 36	294	19 36	354	23 36	54	3 36	3 37	3 38	3 39
55	3 40	115	7 40	175	11 40	235	15 40	295	19 40	355	23 40	55	3 40	3 41	3 42	3 43
56	3 44	116	7 44	176	11 44	236	15 44	296	19 44	356	23 44	56	3 44	3 45	3 46	3 47
57	3 48	117	7 48	177	11 48	237	15 48	297	19 48	357	23 48	57	3 48	3 49	3 50	3 51
58	3 52	118	7 52	178	11 52	238	15 52	298	19 52	358	23 52	58	3 52	3 53	3 54	3 55
59	3 56	119	7 56	179	11 56	239	15 56	299	19 56	359	23 56	59	3 56	3 57	3 58	3 59

The above table is for converting expressions in arc to their equivalent in time; its main use in this Almanac is for the conversion of longitude for application to LMT (*added* if *west*, *subtracted* if *east*) to give UT or vice versa, particularly in the case of sunrise, sunset, etc.

m 0	SUN PLANETS	ARIES	MOON	v or d	Corrⁿ	v or d	Corrⁿ	v or d	Corrⁿ
s	° ′	° ′	° ′	′	′	′	′	′	′
00	0 00·0	0 00·0	0 00·0	0·0	0·0	6·0	0·1	12·0	0·1
01	0 00·3	0 00·3	0 00·2	0·1	0·0	6·1	0·1	12·1	0·1
02	0 00·5	0 00·5	0 00·5	0·2	0·0	6·2	0·1	12·2	0·1
03	0 00·8	0 00·8	0 00·7	0·3	0·0	6·3	0·1	12·3	0·1
04	0 01·0	0 01·0	0 01·0	0·4	0·0	6·4	0·1	12·4	0·1
05	0 01·3	0 01·3	0 01·2	0·5	0·0	6·5	0·1	12·5	0·1
06	0 01·5	0 01·5	0 01·4	0·6	0·0	6·6	0·1	12·6	0·1
07	0 01·8	0 01·8	0 01·7	0·7	0·0	6·7	0·1	12·7	0·1
08	0 02·0	0 02·0	0 01·9	0·8	0·0	6·8	0·1	12·8	0·1
09	0 02·3	0 02·3	0 02·1	0·9	0·0	6·9	0·1	12·9	0·1
10	0 02·5	0 02·5	0 02·4	1·0	0·0	7·0	0·1	13·0	0·1
11	0 02·8	0 02·8	0 02·6	1·1	0·0	7·1	0·1	13·1	0·1
12	0 03·0	0 03·0	0 02·9	1·2	0·0	7·2	0·1	13·2	0·1
13	0 03·3	0 03·3	0 03·1	1·3	0·0	7·3	0·1	13·3	0·1
14	0 03·5	0 03·5	0 03·3	1·4	0·0	7·4	0·1	13·4	0·1
15	0 03·8	0 03·8	0 03·6	1·5	0·0	7·5	0·1	13·5	0·1
16	0 04·0	0 04·0	0 03·8	1·6	0·0	7·6	0·1	13·6	0·1
17	0 04·3	0 04·3	0 04·1	1·7	0·0	7·7	0·1	13·7	0·1
18	0 04·5	0 04·5	0 04·3	1·8	0·0	7·8	0·1	13·8	0·1
19	0 04·8	0 04·8	0 04·5	1·9	0·0	7·9	0·1	13·9	0·1
20	0 05·0	0 05·0	0 04·8	2·0	0·0	8·0	0·1	14·0	0·1
21	0 05·3	0 05·3	0 05·0	2·1	0·0	8·1	0·1	14·1	0·1
22	0 05·5	0 05·5	0 05·2	2·2	0·0	8·2	0·1	14·2	0·1
23	0 05·8	0 05·8	0 05·5	2·3	0·0	8·3	0·1	14·3	0·1
24	0 06·0	0 06·0	0 05·7	2·4	0·0	8·4	0·1	14·4	0·1
25	0 06·3	0 06·3	0 06·0	2·5	0·0	8·5	0·1	14·5	0·1
26	0 06·5	0 06·5	0 06·2	2·6	0·0	8·6	0·1	14·6	0·1
27	0 06·8	0 06·8	0 06·4	2·7	0·0	8·7	0·1	14·7	0·1
28	0 07·0	0 07·0	0 06·7	2·8	0·0	8·8	0·1	14·8	0·1
29	0 07·3	0 07·3	0 06·9	2·9	0·0	8·9	0·1	14·9	0·1
30	0 07·5	0 07·5	0 07·2	3·0	0·0	9·0	0·1	15·0	0·1
31	0 07·8	0 07·8	0 07·4	3·1	0·0	9·1	0·1	15·1	0·1
32	0 08·0	0 08·0	0 07·6	3·2	0·0	9·2	0·1	15·2	0·1
33	0 08·3	0 08·3	0 07·9	3·3	0·0	9·3	0·1	15·3	0·1
34	0 08·5	0 08·5	0 08·1	3·4	0·0	9·4	0·1	15·4	0·1
35	0 08·8	0 08·8	0 08·4	3·5	0·0	9·5	0·1	15·5	0·1
36	0 09·0	0 09·0	0 08·6	3·6	0·0	9·6	0·1	15·6	0·1
37	0 09·3	0 09·3	0 08·8	3·7	0·0	9·7	0·1	15·7	0·1
38	0 09·5	0 09·5	0 09·1	3·8	0·0	9·8	0·1	15·8	0·1
39	0 09·8	0 09·8	0 09·3	3·9	0·0	9·9	0·1	15·9	0·1
40	0 10·0	0 10·0	0 09·5	4·0	0·0	10·0	0·1	16·0	0·1
41	0 10·3	0 10·3	0 09·8	4·1	0·0	10·1	0·1	16·1	0·1
42	0 10·5	0 10·5	0 10·0	4·2	0·0	10·2	0·1	16·2	0·1
43	0 10·8	0 10·8	0 10·3	4·3	0·0	10·3	0·1	16·3	0·1
44	0 11·0	0 11·0	0 10·5	4·4	0·0	10·4	0·1	16·4	0·1
45	0 11·3	0 11·3	0 10·7	4·5	0·0	10·5	0·1	16·5	0·1
46	0 11·5	0 11·5	0 11·0	4·6	0·0	10·6	0·1	16·6	0·1
47	0 11·8	0 11·8	0 11·2	4·7	0·0	10·7	0·1	16·7	0·1
48	0 12·0	0 12·0	0 11·5	4·8	0·0	10·8	0·1	16·8	0·1
49	0 12·3	0 12·3	0 11·7	4·9	0·0	10·9	0·1	16·9	0·1
50	0 12·5	0 12·5	0 11·9	5·0	0·0	11·0	0·1	17·0	0·1
51	0 12·8	0 12·8	0 12·2	5·1	0·0	11·1	0·1	17·1	0·1
52	0 13·0	0 13·0	0 12·4	5·2	0·0	11·2	0·1	17·2	0·1
53	0 13·3	0 13·3	0 12·6	5·3	0·0	11·3	0·1	17·3	0·1
54	0 13·5	0 13·5	0 12·9	5·4	0·0	11·4	0·1	17·4	0·1
55	0 13·8	0 13·8	0 13·1	5·5	0·0	11·5	0·1	17·5	0·1
56	0 14·0	0 14·0	0 13·4	5·6	0·0	11·6	0·1	17·6	0·1
57	0 14·3	0 14·3	0 13·6	5·7	0·0	11·7	0·1	17·7	0·1
58	0 14·5	0 14·5	0 13·8	5·8	0·0	11·8	0·1	17·8	0·1
59	0 14·8	0 14·8	0 14·1	5·9	0·0	11·9	0·1	17·9	0·1
60	0 15·0	0 15·0	0 14·3	6·0	0·1	12·0	0·1	18·0	0·2

m 1	SUN PLANETS	ARIES	MOON	v or d	Corrⁿ	v or d	Corrⁿ	v or d	Corrⁿ
s	° ′	° ′	° ′	′	′	′	′	′	′
00	0 15·0	0 15·0	0 14·3	0·0	0·0	6·0	0·2	12·0	0·3
01	0 15·3	0 15·3	0 14·6	0·1	0·0	6·1	0·2	12·1	0·3
02	0 15·5	0 15·5	0 14·8	0·2	0·0	6·2	0·2	12·2	0·3
03	0 15·8	0 15·8	0 15·0	0·3	0·0	6·3	0·2	12·3	0·3
04	0 16·0	0 16·0	0 15·3	0·4	0·0	6·4	0·2	12·4	0·3
05	0 16·3	0 16·3	0 15·5	0·5	0·0	6·5	0·2	12·5	0·3
06	0 16·5	0 16·5	0 15·7	0·6	0·0	6·6	0·2	12·6	0·3
07	0 16·8	0 16·8	0 16·0	0·7	0·0	6·7	0·2	12·7	0·3
08	0 17·0	0 17·0	0 16·2	0·8	0·0	6·8	0·2	12·8	0·3
09	0 17·3	0 17·3	0 16·5	0·9	0·0	6·9	0·2	12·9	0·3
10	0 17·5	0 17·5	0 16·7	1·0	0·0	7·0	0·2	13·0	0·3
11	0 17·8	0 17·8	0 16·9	1·1	0·0	7·1	0·2	13·1	0·3
12	0 18·0	0 18·0	0 17·2	1·2	0·0	7·2	0·2	13·2	0·3
13	0 18·3	0 18·3	0 17·4	1·3	0·0	7·3	0·2	13·3	0·3
14	0 18·5	0 18·6	0 17·7	1·4	0·0	7·4	0·2	13·4	0·3
15	0 18·8	0 18·8	0 17·9	1·5	0·0	7·5	0·2	13·5	0·3
16	0 19·0	0 19·1	0 18·1	1·6	0·0	7·6	0·2	13·6	0·3
17	0 19·3	0 19·3	0 18·4	1·7	0·0	7·7	0·2	13·7	0·3
18	0 19·5	0 19·6	0 18·6	1·8	0·0	7·8	0·2	13·8	0·3
19	0 19·8	0 19·8	0 18·9	1·9	0·0	7·9	0·2	13·9	0·3
20	0 20·0	0 20·1	0 19·1	2·0	0·1	8·0	0·2	14·0	0·4
21	0 20·3	0 20·3	0 19·3	2·1	0·1	8·1	0·2	14·1	0·4
22	0 20·5	0 20·6	0 19·6	2·2	0·1	8·2	0·2	14·2	0·4
23	0 20·8	0 20·8	0 19·8	2·3	0·1	8·3	0·2	14·3	0·4
24	0 21·0	0 21·1	0 20·0	2·4	0·1	8·4	0·2	14·4	0·4
25	0 21·3	0 21·3	0 20·3	2·5	0·1	8·5	0·2	14·5	0·4
26	0 21·5	0 21·6	0 20·5	2·6	0·1	8·6	0·2	14·6	0·4
27	0 21·8	0 21·8	0 20·8	2·7	0·1	8·7	0·2	14·7	0·4
28	0 22·0	0 22·1	0 21·0	2·8	0·1	8·8	0·2	14·8	0·4
29	0 22·3	0 22·3	0 21·2	2·9	0·1	8·9	0·2	14·9	0·4
30	0 22·5	0 22·6	0 21·5	3·0	0·1	9·0	0·2	15·0	0·4
31	0 22·8	0 22·8	0 21·7	3·1	0·1	9·1	0·2	15·1	0·4
32	0 23·0	0 23·1	0 22·0	3·2	0·1	9·2	0·2	15·2	0·4
33	0 23·3	0 23·3	0 22·2	3·3	0·1	9·3	0·2	15·3	0·4
34	0 23·5	0 23·6	0 22·4	3·4	0·1	9·4	0·2	15·4	0·4
35	0 23·8	0 23·8	0 22·7	3·5	0·1	9·5	0·2	15·5	0·4
36	0 24·0	0 24·1	0 22·9	3·6	0·1	9·6	0·2	15·6	0·4
37	0 24·3	0 24·3	0 23·1	3·7	0·1	9·7	0·2	15·7	0·4
38	0 24·5	0 24·6	0 23·4	3·8	0·1	9·8	0·2	15·8	0·4
39	0 24·8	0 24·8	0 23·6	3·9	0·1	9·9	0·2	15·9	0·4
40	0 25·0	0 25·1	0 23·9	4·0	0·1	10·0	0·3	16·0	0·4
41	0 25·3	0 25·3	0 24·1	4·1	0·1	10·1	0·3	16·1	0·4
42	0 25·5	0 25·6	0 24·3	4·2	0·1	10·2	0·3	16·2	0·4
43	0 25·8	0 25·8	0 24·6	4·3	0·1	10·3	0·3	16·3	0·4
44	0 26·0	0 26·1	0 24·8	4·4	0·1	10·4	0·3	16·4	0·4
45	0 26·3	0 26·3	0 25·1	4·5	0·1	10·5	0·3	16·5	0·4
46	0 26·5	0 26·6	0 25·3	4·6	0·1	10·6	0·3	16·6	0·4
47	0 26·8	0 26·8	0 25·5	4·7	0·1	10·7	0·3	16·7	0·4
48	0 27·0	0 27·1	0 25·8	4·8	0·1	10·8	0·3	16·8	0·4
49	0 27·3	0 27·3	0 26·0	4·9	0·1	10·9	0·3	16·9	0·4
50	0 27·5	0 27·6	0 26·2	5·0	0·1	11·0	0·3	17·0	0·4
51	0 27·8	0 27·8	0 26·5	5·1	0·1	11·1	0·3	17·1	0·4
52	0 28·0	0 28·1	0 26·7	5·2	0·1	11·2	0·3	17·2	0·4
53	0 28·3	0 28·3	0 27·0	5·3	0·1	11·3	0·3	17·3	0·4
54	0 28·5	0 28·6	0 27·2	5·4	0·1	11·4	0·3	17·4	0·4
55	0 28·8	0 28·8	0 27·4	5·5	0·1	11·5	0·3	17·5	0·4
56	0 29·0	0 29·1	0 27·7	5·6	0·1	11·6	0·3	17·6	0·4
57	0 29·3	0 29·3	0 27·9	5·7	0·1	11·7	0·3	17·7	0·4
58	0 29·5	0 29·6	0 28·2	5·8	0·1	11·8	0·3	17·8	0·4
59	0 29·8	0 29·8	0 28·4	5·9	0·1	11·9	0·3	17·9	0·4
60	0 30·0	0 30·1	0 28·6	6·0	0·2	12·0	0·3	18·0	0·5

m 2	SUN PLANETS	ARIES	MOON	v or d	Corr^n	v or d	Corr^n	v or d	Corr^n
s	° ′	° ′	° ′	′	′	′	′	′	′
00	0 30·0	0 30·1	0 28·6	0·0	0·0	6·0	0·3	12·0	0·5
01	0 30·3	0 30·3	0 28·9	0·1	0·0	6·1	0·3	12·1	0·5
02	0 30·5	0 30·6	0 29·1	0·2	0·0	6·2	0·3	12·2	0·5
03	0 30·8	0 30·8	0 29·3	0·3	0·0	6·3	0·3	12·3	0·5
04	0 31·0	0 31·1	0 29·6	0·4	0·0	6·4	0·3	12·4	0·5
05	0 31·3	0 31·3	0 29·8	0·5	0·0	6·5	0·3	12·5	0·5
06	0 31·5	0 31·6	0 30·1	0·6	0·0	6·6	0·3	12·6	0·5
07	0 31·8	0 31·8	0 30·3	0·7	0·0	6·7	0·3	12·7	0·5
08	0 32·0	0 32·1	0 30·5	0·8	0·0	6·8	0·3	12·8	0·5
09	0 32·3	0 32·3	0 30·8	0·9	0·0	6·9	0·3	12·9	0·5
10	0 32·5	0 32·6	0 31·0	1·0	0·0	7·0	0·3	13·0	0·5
11	0 32·8	0 32·8	0 31·3	1·1	0·0	7·1	0·3	13·1	0·5
12	0 33·0	0 33·1	0 31·5	1·2	0·1	7·2	0·3	13·2	0·6
13	0 33·3	0 33·3	0 31·7	1·3	0·1	7·3	0·3	13·3	0·6
14	0 33·5	0 33·6	0 32·0	1·4	0·1	7·4	0·3	13·4	0·6
15	0 33·8	0 33·8	0 32·2	1·5	0·1	7·5	0·3	13·5	0·6
16	0 34·0	0 34·1	0 32·5	1·6	0·1	7·6	0·3	13·6	0·6
17	0 34·3	0 34·3	0 32·7	1·7	0·1	7·7	0·3	13·7	0·6
18	0 34·5	0 34·6	0 32·9	1·8	0·1	7·8	0·3	13·8	0·6
19	0 34·8	0 34·8	0 33·2	1·9	0·1	7·9	0·3	13·9	0·6
20	0 35·0	0 35·1	0 33·4	2·0	0·1	8·0	0·3	14·0	0·6
21	0 35·3	0 35·3	0 33·6	2·1	0·1	8·1	0·3	14·1	0·6
22	0 35·5	0 35·6	0 33·9	2·2	0·1	8·2	0·3	14·2	0·6
23	0 35·8	0 35·8	0 34·1	2·3	0·1	8·3	0·3	14·3	0·6
24	0 36·0	0 36·1	0 34·4	2·4	0·1	8·4	0·4	14·4	0·6
25	0 36·3	0 36·3	0 34·6	2·5	0·1	8·5	0·4	14·5	0·6
26	0 36·5	0 36·6	0 34·8	2·6	0·1	8·6	0·4	14·6	0·6
27	0 36·8	0 36·9	0 35·1	2·7	0·1	8·7	0·4	14·7	0·6
28	0 37·0	0 37·1	0 35·3	2·8	0·1	8·8	0·4	14·8	0·6
29	0 37·3	0 37·4	0 35·6	2·9	0·1	8·9	0·4	14·9	0·6
30	0 37·5	0 37·6	0 35·8	3·0	0·1	9·0	0·4	15·0	0·6
31	0 37·8	0 37·9	0 36·0	3·1	0·1	9·1	0·4	15·1	0·6
32	0 38·0	0 38·1	0 36·3	3·2	0·1	9·2	0·4	15·2	0·6
33	0 38·3	0 38·4	0 36·5	3·3	0·1	9·3	0·4	15·3	0·6
34	0 38·5	0 38·6	0 36·7	3·4	0·1	9·4	0·4	15·4	0·6
35	0 38·8	0 38·9	0 37·0	3·5	0·1	9·5	0·4	15·5	0·6
36	0 39·0	0 39·1	0 37·2	3·6	0·2	9·6	0·4	15·6	0·7
37	0 39·3	0 39·4	0 37·5	3·7	0·2	9·7	0·4	15·7	0·7
38	0 39·5	0 39·6	0 37·7	3·8	0·2	9·8	0·4	15·8	0·7
39	0 39·8	0 39·9	0 37·9	3·9	0·2	9·9	0·4	15·9	0·7
40	0 40·0	0 40·1	0 38·2	4·0	0·2	10·0	0·4	16·0	0·7
41	0 40·3	0 40·4	0 38·4	4·1	0·2	10·1	0·4	16·1	0·7
42	0 40·5	0 40·6	0 38·7	4·2	0·2	10·2	0·4	16·2	0·7
43	0 40·8	0 40·9	0 38·9	4·3	0·2	10·3	0·4	16·3	0·7
44	0 41·0	0 41·1	0 39·1	4·4	0·2	10·4	0·4	16·4	0·7
45	0 41·3	0 41·4	0 39·4	4·5	0·2	10·5	0·4	16·5	0·7
46	0 41·5	0 41·6	0 39·6	4·6	0·2	10·6	0·4	16·6	0·7
47	0 41·8	0 41·9	0 39·8	4·7	0·2	10·7	0·4	16·7	0·7
48	0 42·0	0 42·1	0 40·1	4·8	0·2	10·8	0·5	16·8	0·7
49	0 42·3	0 42·4	0 40·3	4·9	0·2	10·9	0·5	16·9	0·7
50	0 42·5	0 42·6	0 40·6	5·0	0·2	11·0	0·5	17·0	0·7
51	0 42·8	0 42·9	0 40·8	5·1	0·2	11·1	0·5	17·1	0·7
52	0 43·0	0 43·1	0 41·0	5·2	0·2	11·2	0·5	17·2	0·7
53	0 43·3	0 43·4	0 41·3	5·3	0·2	11·3	0·5	17·3	0·7
54	0 43·5	0 43·6	0 41·5	5·4	0·2	11·4	0·5	17·4	0·7
55	0 43·8	0 43·9	0 41·8	5·5	0·2	11·5	0·5	17·5	0·7
56	0 44·0	0 44·1	0 42·0	5·6	0·2	11·6	0·5	17·6	0·7
57	0 44·3	0 44·4	0 42·2	5·7	0·2	11·7	0·5	17·7	0·7
58	0 44·5	0 44·6	0 42·5	5·8	0·2	11·8	0·5	17·8	0·7
59	0 44·8	0 44·9	0 42·7	5·9	0·2	11·9	0·5	17·9	0·7
60	0 45·0	0 45·1	0 43·0	6·0	0·3	12·0	0·5	18·0	0·8

m 3	SUN PLANETS	ARIES	MOON	v or d	Corr^n	v or d	Corr^n	v or d	Corr^n
s	° ′	° ′	° ′	′	′	′	′	′	′
00	0 45·0	0 45·1	0 43·0	0·0	0·0	6·0	0·4	12·0	0·7
01	0 45·3	0 45·4	0 43·2	0·1	0·0	6·1	0·4	12·1	0·7
02	0 45·5	0 45·6	0 43·4	0·2	0·0	6·2	0·4	12·2	0·7
03	0 45·8	0 45·9	0 43·7	0·3	0·0	6·3	0·4	12·3	0·7
04	0 46·0	0 46·1	0 43·9	0·4	0·0	6·4	0·4	12·4	0·7
05	0 46·3	0 46·4	0 44·1	0·5	0·0	6·5	0·4	12·5	0·7
06	0 46·5	0 46·6	0 44·4	0·6	0·0	6·6	0·4	12·6	0·7
07	0 46·8	0 46·9	0 44·6	0·7	0·0	6·7	0·4	12·7	0·7
08	0 47·0	0 47·1	0 44·9	0·8	0·0	6·8	0·4	12·8	0·7
09	0 47·3	0 47·4	0 45·1	0·9	0·1	6·9	0·4	12·9	0·8
10	0 47·5	0 47·6	0 45·3	1·0	0·1	7·0	0·4	13·0	0·8
11	0 47·8	0 47·9	0 45·6	1·1	0·1	7·1	0·4	13·1	0·8
12	0 48·0	0 48·1	0 45·8	1·2	0·1	7·2	0·4	13·2	0·8
13	0 48·3	0 48·4	0 46·1	1·3	0·1	7·3	0·4	13·3	0·8
14	0 48·5	0 48·6	0 46·3	1·4	0·1	7·4	0·4	13·4	0·8
15	0 48·8	0 48·9	0 46·5	1·5	0·1	7·5	0·4	13·5	0·8
16	0 49·0	0 49·1	0 46·8	1·6	0·1	7·6	0·4	13·6	0·8
17	0 49·3	0 49·4	0 47·0	1·7	0·1	7·7	0·4	13·7	0·8
18	0 49·5	0 49·6	0 47·2	1·8	0·1	7·8	0·5	13·8	0·8
19	0 49·8	0 49·9	0 47·5	1·9	0·1	7·9	0·5	13·9	0·8
20	0 50·0	0 50·1	0 47·7	2·0	0·1	8·0	0·5	14·0	0·8
21	0 50·3	0 50·4	0 48·0	2·1	0·1	8·1	0·5	14·1	0·8
22	0 50·5	0 50·6	0 48·2	2·2	0·1	8·2	0·5	14·2	0·8
23	0 50·8	0 50·9	0 48·4	2·3	0·1	8·3	0·5	14·3	0·8
24	0 51·0	0 51·1	0 48·7	2·4	0·1	8·4	0·5	14·4	0·8
25	0 51·3	0 51·4	0 48·9	2·5	0·1	8·5	0·5	14·5	0·8
26	0 51·5	0 51·6	0 49·2	2·6	0·2	8·6	0·5	14·6	0·9
27	0 51·8	0 51·9	0 49·4	2·7	0·2	8·7	0·5	14·7	0·9
28	0 52·0	0 52·1	0 49·6	2·8	0·2	8·8	0·5	14·8	0·9
29	0 52·3	0 52·4	0 49·9	2·9	0·2	8·9	0·5	14·9	0·9
30	0 52·5	0 52·6	0 50·1	3·0	0·2	9·0	0·5	15·0	0·9
31	0 52·8	0 52·9	0 50·3	3·1	0·2	9·1	0·5	15·1	0·9
32	0 53·0	0 53·1	0 50·6	3·2	0·2	9·2	0·5	15·2	0·9
33	0 53·3	0 53·4	0 50·8	3·3	0·2	9·3	0·5	15·3	0·9
34	0 53·5	0 53·6	0 51·1	3·4	0·2	9·4	0·5	15·4	0·9
35	0 53·8	0 53·9	0 51·3	3·5	0·2	9·5	0·6	15·5	0·9
36	0 54·0	0 54·1	0 51·5	3·6	0·2	9·6	0·6	15·6	0·9
37	0 54·3	0 54·4	0 51·8	3·7	0·2	9·7	0·6	15·7	0·9
38	0 54·5	0 54·6	0 52·0	3·8	0·2	9·8	0·6	15·8	0·9
39	0 54·8	0 54·9	0 52·3	3·9	0·2	9·9	0·6	15·9	0·9
40	0 55·0	0 55·2	0 52·5	4·0	0·2	10·0	0·6	16·0	0·9
41	0 55·3	0 55·4	0 52·7	4·1	0·2	10·1	0·6	16·1	0·9
42	0 55·5	0 55·7	0 53·0	4·2	0·2	10·2	0·6	16·2	0·9
43	0 55·8	0 55·9	0 53·2	4·3	0·3	10·3	0·6	16·3	1·0
44	0 56·0	0 56·2	0 53·4	4·4	0·3	10·4	0·6	16·4	1·0
45	0 56·3	0 56·4	0 53·7	4·5	0·3	10·5	0·6	16·5	1·0
46	0 56·5	0 56·7	0 53·9	4·6	0·3	10·6	0·6	16·6	1·0
47	0 56·8	0 56·9	0 54·2	4·7	0·3	10·7	0·6	16·7	1·0
48	0 57·0	0 57·2	0 54·4	4·8	0·3	10·8	0·6	16·8	1·0
49	0 57·3	0 57·4	0 54·6	4·9	0·3	10·9	0·6	16·9	1·0
50	0 57·5	0 57·7	0 54·9	5·0	0·3	11·0	0·6	17·0	1·0
51	0 57·8	0 57·9	0 55·1	5·1	0·3	11·1	0·6	17·1	1·0
52	0 58·0	0 58·2	0 55·4	5·2	0·3	11·2	0·7	17·2	1·0
53	0 58·3	0 58·4	0 55·6	5·3	0·3	11·3	0·7	17·3	1·0
54	0 58·5	0 58·7	0 55·8	5·4	0·3	11·4	0·7	17·4	1·0
55	0 58·8	0 58·9	0 56·1	5·5	0·3	11·5	0·7	17·5	1·0
56	0 59·0	0 59·2	0 56·3	5·6	0·3	11·6	0·7	17·6	1·0
57	0 59·3	0 59·4	0 56·6	5·7	0·3	11·7	0·7	17·7	1·0
58	0 59·5	0 59·7	0 56·8	5·8	0·3	11·8	0·7	17·8	1·0
59	0 59·8	0 59·9	0 57·0	5·9	0·3	11·9	0·7	17·9	1·0
60	1 00·0	1 00·2	0 57·3	6·0	0·4	12·0	0·7	18·0	1·1

m 4 s	SUN PLANETS ° ′	ARIES ° ′	MOON ° ′	v or d ′	Corr^n ′	v or d ′	Corr^n ′	v or d ′	Corr^n ′
00	1 00·0	1 00·2	0 57·3	0·0	0·0	6·0	0·5	12·0	0·9
01	1 00·3	1 00·4	0 57·5	0·1	0·0	6·1	0·5	12·1	0·9
02	1 00·5	1 00·7	0 57·7	0·2	0·0	6·2	0·5	12·2	0·9
03	1 00·8	1 00·9	0 58·0	0·3	0·0	6·3	0·5	12·3	0·9
04	1 01·0	1 01·2	0 58·2	0·4	0·0	6·4	0·5	12·4	0·9
05	1 01·3	1 01·4	0 58·5	0·5	0·0	6·5	0·5	12·5	0·9
06	1 01·5	1 01·7	0 58·7	0·6	0·0	6·6	0·5	12·6	0·9
07	1 01·8	1 01·9	0 58·9	0·7	0·1	6·7	0·5	12·7	1·0
08	1 02·0	1 02·2	0 59·2	0·8	0·1	6·8	0·5	12·8	1·0
09	1 02·3	1 02·4	0 59·4	0·9	0·1	6·9	0·5	12·9	1·0
10	1 02·5	1 02·7	0 59·7	1·0	0·1	7·0	0·5	13·0	1·0
11	1 02·8	1 02·9	0 59·9	1·1	0·1	7·1	0·5	13·1	1·0
12	1 03·0	1 03·2	1 00·1	1·2	0·1	7·2	0·5	13·2	1·0
13	1 03·3	1 03·4	1 00·4	1·3	0·1	7·3	0·5	13·3	1·0
14	1 03·5	1 03·7	1 00·6	1·4	0·1	7·4	0·6	13·4	1·0
15	1 03·8	1 03·9	1 00·8	1·5	0·1	7·5	0·6	13·5	1·0
16	1 04·0	1 04·2	1 01·1	1·6	0·1	7·6	0·6	13·6	1·0
17	1 04·3	1 04·4	1 01·3	1·7	0·1	7·7	0·6	13·7	1·0
18	1 04·5	1 04·7	1 01·6	1·8	0·1	7·8	0·6	13·8	1·0
19	1 04·8	1 04·9	1 01·8	1·9	0·1	7·9	0·6	13·9	1·0
20	1 05·0	1 05·2	1 02·0	2·0	0·2	8·0	0·6	14·0	1·1
21	1 05·3	1 05·4	1 02·3	2·1	0·2	8·1	0·6	14·1	1·1
22	1 05·5	1 05·7	1 02·5	2·2	0·2	8·2	0·6	14·2	1·1
23	1 05·8	1 05·9	1 02·8	2·3	0·2	8·3	0·6	14·3	1·1
24	1 06·0	1 06·2	1 03·0	2·4	0·2	8·4	0·6	14·4	1·1
25	1 06·3	1 06·4	1 03·2	2·5	0·2	8·5	0·6	14·5	1·1
26	1 06·5	1 06·7	1 03·5	2·6	0·2	8·6	0·6	14·6	1·1
27	1 06·8	1 06·9	1 03·7	2·7	0·2	8·7	0·7	14·7	1·1
28	1 07·0	1 07·2	1 03·9	2·8	0·2	8·8	0·7	14·8	1·1
29	1 07·3	1 07·4	1 04·2	2·9	0·2	8·9	0·7	14·9	1·1
30	1 07·5	1 07·7	1 04·4	3·0	0·2	9·0	0·7	15·0	1·1
31	1 07·8	1 07·9	1 04·7	3·1	0·2	9·1	0·7	15·1	1·1
32	1 08·0	1 08·2	1 04·9	3·2	0·2	9·2	0·7	15·2	1·1
33	1 08·3	1 08·4	1 05·1	3·3	0·2	9·3	0·7	15·3	1·1
34	1 08·5	1 08·7	1 05·4	3·4	0·3	9·4	0·7	15·4	1·2
35	1 08·8	1 08·9	1 05·6	3·5	0·3	9·5	0·7	15·5	1·2
36	1 09·0	1 09·2	1 05·9	3·6	0·3	9·6	0·7	15·6	1·2
37	1 09·3	1 09·4	1 06·1	3·7	0·3	9·7	0·7	15·7	1·2
38	1 09·5	1 09·7	1 06·3	3·8	0·3	9·8	0·7	15·8	1·2
39	1 09·8	1 09·9	1 06·6	3·9	0·3	9·9	0·7	15·9	1·2
40	1 10·0	1 10·2	1 06·8	4·0	0·3	10·0	0·8	16·0	1·2
41	1 10·3	1 10·4	1 07·0	4·1	0·3	10·1	0·8	16·1	1·2
42	1 10·5	1 10·7	1 07·3	4·2	0·3	10·2	0·8	16·2	1·2
43	1 10·8	1 10·9	1 07·5	4·3	0·3	10·3	0·8	16·3	1·2
44	1 11·0	1 11·2	1 07·8	4·4	0·3	10·4	0·8	16·4	1·2
45	1 11·3	1 11·4	1 08·0	4·5	0·3	10·5	0·8	16·5	1·2
46	1 11·5	1 11·7	1 08·2	4·6	0·3	10·6	0·8	16·6	1·2
47	1 11·8	1 11·9	1 08·5	4·7	0·4	10·7	0·8	16·7	1·3
48	1 12·0	1 12·2	1 08·7	4·8	0·4	10·8	0·8	16·8	1·3
49	1 12·3	1 12·4	1 09·0	4·9	0·4	10·9	0·8	16·9	1·3
50	1 12·5	1 12·7	1 09·2	5·0	0·4	11·0	0·8	17·0	1·3
51	1 12·8	1 12·9	1 09·4	5·1	0·4	11·1	0·8	17·1	1·3
52	1 13·0	1 13·2	1 09·7	5·2	0·4	11·2	0·8	17·2	1·3
53	1 13·3	1 13·5	1 09·9	5·3	0·4	11·3	0·8	17·3	1·3
54	1 13·5	1 13·7	1 10·2	5·4	0·4	11·4	0·9	17·4	1·3
55	1 13·8	1 14·0	1 10·4	5·5	0·4	11·5	0·9	17·5	1·3
56	1 14·0	1 14·2	1 10·6	5·6	0·4	11·6	0·9	17·6	1·3
57	1 14·3	1 14·5	1 10·9	5·7	0·4	11·7	0·9	17·7	1·3
58	1 14·5	1 14·7	1 11·1	5·8	0·4	11·8	0·9	17·8	1·3
59	1 14·8	1 15·0	1 11·3	5·9	0·4	11·9	0·9	17·9	1·3
60	1 15·0	1 15·2	1 11·6	6·0	0·5	12·0	0·9	18·0	1·4

m 5 s	SUN PLANETS ° ′	ARIES ° ′	MOON ° ′	v or d ′	Corr^n ′	v or d ′	Corr^n ′	v or d ′	Corr^n ′
00	1 15·0	1 15·2	1 11·6	0·0	0·0	6·0	0·6	12·0	1·1
01	1 15·3	1 15·5	1 11·8	0·1	0·0	6·1	0·6	12·1	1·1
02	1 15·5	1 15·7	1 12·1	0·2	0·0	6·2	0·6	12·2	1·1
03	1 15·8	1 16·0	1 12·3	0·3	0·0	6·3	0·6	12·3	1·1
04	1 16·0	1 16·2	1 12·5	0·4	0·0	6·4	0·6	12·4	1·1
05	1 16·3	1 16·5	1 12·8	0·5	0·0	6·5	0·6	12·5	1·1
06	1 16·5	1 16·7	1 13·0	0·6	0·1	6·6	0·6	12·6	1·2
07	1 16·8	1 17·0	1 13·3	0·7	0·1	6·7	0·6	12·7	1·2
08	1 17·0	1 17·2	1 13·5	0·8	0·1	6·8	0·6	12·8	1·2
09	1 17·3	1 17·5	1 13·7	0·9	0·1	6·9	0·6	12·9	1·2
10	1 17·5	1 17·7	1 14·0	1·0	0·1	7·0	0·6	13·0	1·2
11	1 17·8	1 18·0	1 14·2	1·1	0·1	7·1	0·7	13·1	1·2
12	1 18·0	1 18·2	1 14·4	1·2	0·1	7·2	0·7	13·2	1·2
13	1 18·3	1 18·5	1 14·7	1·3	0·1	7·3	0·7	13·3	1·2
14	1 18·5	1 18·7	1 14·9	1·4	0·1	7·4	0·7	13·4	1·2
15	1 18·8	1 19·0	1 15·2	1·5	0·1	7·5	0·7	13·5	1·2
16	1 19·0	1 19·2	1 15·4	1·6	0·1	7·6	0·7	13·6	1·2
17	1 19·3	1 19·5	1 15·6	1·7	0·2	7·7	0·7	13·7	1·3
18	1 19·5	1 19·7	1 15·9	1·8	0·2	7·8	0·7	13·8	1·3
19	1 19·8	1 20·0	1 16·1	1·9	0·2	7·9	0·7	13·9	1·3
20	1 20·0	1 20·2	1 16·4	2·0	0·2	8·0	0·7	14·0	1·3
21	1 20·3	1 20·5	1 16·6	2·1	0·2	8·1	0·7	14·1	1·3
22	1 20·5	1 20·7	1 16·8	2·2	0·2	8·2	0·8	14·2	1·3
23	1 20·8	1 21·0	1 17·1	2·3	0·2	8·3	0·8	14·3	1·3
24	1 21·0	1 21·2	1 17·3	2·4	0·2	8·4	0·8	14·4	1·3
25	1 21·3	1 21·5	1 17·5	2·5	0·2	8·5	0·8	14·5	1·3
26	1 21·5	1 21·7	1 17·8	2·6	0·2	8·6	0·8	14·6	1·3
27	1 21·8	1 22·0	1 18·0	2·7	0·2	8·7	0·8	14·7	1·3
28	1 22·0	1 22·2	1 18·3	2·8	0·3	8·8	0·8	14·8	1·4
29	1 22·3	1 22·5	1 18·5	2·9	0·3	8·9	0·8	14·9	1·4
30	1 22·5	1 22·7	1 18·7	3·0	0·3	9·0	0·8	15·0	1·4
31	1 22·8	1 23·0	1 19·0	3·1	0·3	9·1	0·8	15·1	1·4
32	1 23·0	1 23·2	1 19·2	3·2	0·3	9·2	0·8	15·2	1·4
33	1 23·3	1 23·5	1 19·5	3·3	0·3	9·3	0·9	15·3	1·4
34	1 23·5	1 23·7	1 19·7	3·4	0·3	9·4	0·9	15·4	1·4
35	1 23·8	1 24·0	1 19·9	3·5	0·3	9·5	0·9	15·5	1·4
36	1 24·0	1 24·2	1 20·2	3·6	0·3	9·6	0·9	15·6	1·4
37	1 24·3	1 24·5	1 20·4	3·7	0·3	9·7	0·9	15·7	1·4
38	1 24·5	1 24·7	1 20·7	3·8	0·3	9·8	0·9	15·8	1·4
39	1 24·8	1 25·0	1 20·9	3·9	0·4	9·9	0·9	15·9	1·5
40	1 25·0	1 25·2	1 21·1	4·0	0·4	10·0	0·9	16·0	1·5
41	1 25·3	1 25·5	1 21·4	4·1	0·4	10·1	0·9	16·1	1·5
42	1 25·5	1 25·7	1 21·6	4·2	0·4	10·2	0·9	16·2	1·5
43	1 25·8	1 26·0	1 21·8	4·3	0·4	10·3	0·9	16·3	1·5
44	1 26·0	1 26·2	1 22·1	4·4	0·4	10·4	1·0	16·4	1·5
45	1 26·3	1 26·5	1 22·3	4·5	0·4	10·5	1·0	16·5	1·5
46	1 26·5	1 26·7	1 22·6	4·6	0·4	10·6	1·0	16·6	1·5
47	1 26·8	1 27·0	1 22·8	4·7	0·4	10·7	1·0	16·7	1·5
48	1 27·0	1 27·2	1 23·0	4·8	0·4	10·8	1·0	16·8	1·5
49	1 27·3	1 27·5	1 23·3	4·9	0·4	10·9	1·0	16·9	1·5
50	1 27·5	1 27·7	1 23·5	5·0	0·5	11·0	1·0	17·0	1·6
51	1 27·8	1 28·0	1 23·8	5·1	0·5	11·1	1·0	17·1	1·6
52	1 28·0	1 28·2	1 24·0	5·2	0·5	11·2	1·0	17·2	1·6
53	1 28·3	1 28·5	1 24·2	5·3	0·5	11·3	1·0	17·3	1·6
54	1 28·5	1 28·7	1 24·5	5·4	0·5	11·4	1·0	17·4	1·6
55	1 28·8	1 29·0	1 24·7	5·5	0·5	11·5	1·1	17·5	1·6
56	1 29·0	1 29·2	1 24·9	5·6	0·5	11·6	1·1	17·6	1·6
57	1 29·3	1 29·5	1 25·2	5·7	0·5	11·7	1·1	17·7	1·6
58	1 29·5	1 29·7	1 25·4	5·8	0·5	11·8	1·1	17·8	1·6
59	1 29·8	1 30·0	1 25·7	5·9	0·5	11·9	1·1	17·9	1·6
60	1 30·0	1 30·2	1 25·9	6·0	0·6	12·0	1·1	18·0	1·7

6^m	SUN PLANETS	ARIES	MOON	v or d	Corr^n	v or d	Corr^n	v or d	Corr^n
s	° ′	° ′	° ′	′	′	′	′	′	′
00	1 30·0	1 30·2	1 25·9	0·0	0·0	6·0	0·7	12·0	1·3
01	1 30·3	1 30·5	1 26·1	0·1	0·0	6·1	0·7	12·1	1·3
02	1 30·5	1 30·7	1 26·4	0·2	0·0	6·2	0·7	12·2	1·3
03	1 30·8	1 31·0	1 26·6	0·3	0·0	6·3	0·7	12·3	1·3
04	1 31·0	1 31·2	1 26·9	0·4	0·0	6·4	0·7	12·4	1·3
05	1 31·3	1 31·5	1 27·1	0·5	0·1	6·5	0·7	12·5	1·4
06	1 31·5	1 31·8	1 27·3	0·6	0·1	6·6	0·7	12·6	1·4
07	1 31·8	1 32·0	1 27·6	0·7	0·1	6·7	0·7	12·7	1·4
08	1 32·0	1 32·3	1 27·8	0·8	0·1	6·8	0·7	12·8	1·4
09	1 32·3	1 32·5	1 28·0	0·9	0·1	6·9	0·7	12·9	1·4
10	1 32·5	1 32·8	1 28·3	1·0	0·1	7·0	0·8	13·0	1·4
11	1 32·8	1 33·0	1 28·5	1·1	0·1	7·1	0·8	13·1	1·4
12	1 33·0	1 33·3	1 28·8	1·2	0·1	7·2	0·8	13·2	1·4
13	1 33·3	1 33·5	1 29·0	1·3	0·1	7·3	0·8	13·3	1·4
14	1 33·5	1 33·8	1 29·2	1·4	0·2	7·4	0·8	13·4	1·5
15	1 33·8	1 34·0	1 29·5	1·5	0·2	7·5	0·8	13·5	1·5
16	1 34·0	1 34·3	1 29·7	1·6	0·2	7·6	0·8	13·6	1·5
17	1 34·3	1 34·5	1 30·0	1·7	0·2	7·7	0·8	13·7	1·5
18	1 34·5	1 34·8	1 30·2	1·8	0·2	7·8	0·8	13·8	1·5
19	1 34·8	1 35·0	1 30·4	1·9	0·2	7·9	0·9	13·9	1·5
20	1 35·0	1 35·3	1 30·7	2·0	0·2	8·0	0·9	14·0	1·5
21	1 35·3	1 35·5	1 30·9	2·1	0·2	8·1	0·9	14·1	1·5
22	1 35·5	1 35·8	1 31·1	2·2	0·2	8·2	0·9	14·2	1·5
23	1 35·8	1 36·0	1 31·4	2·3	0·2	8·3	0·9	14·3	1·5
24	1 36·0	1 36·3	1 31·6	2·4	0·3	8·4	0·9	14·4	1·6
25	1 36·3	1 36·5	1 31·9	2·5	0·3	8·5	0·9	14·5	1·6
26	1 36·5	1 36·8	1 32·1	2·6	0·3	8·6	0·9	14·6	1·6
27	1 36·8	1 37·0	1 32·3	2·7	0·3	8·7	0·9	14·7	1·6
28	1 37·0	1 37·3	1 32·6	2·8	0·3	8·8	1·0	14·8	1·6
29	1 37·3	1 37·5	1 32·8	2·9	0·3	8·9	1·0	14·9	1·6
30	1 37·5	1 37·8	1 33·1	3·0	0·3	9·0	1·0	15·0	1·6
31	1 37·8	1 38·0	1 33·3	3·1	0·3	9·1	1·0	15·1	1·6
32	1 38·0	1 38·3	1 33·5	3·2	0·3	9·2	1·0	15·2	1·6
33	1 38·3	1 38·5	1 33·8	3·3	0·4	9·3	1·0	15·3	1·7
34	1 38·5	1 38·8	1 34·0	3·4	0·4	9·4	1·0	15·4	1·7
35	1 38·8	1 39·0	1 34·3	3·5	0·4	9·5	1·0	15·5	1·7
36	1 39·0	1 39·3	1 34·5	3·6	0·4	9·6	1·0	15·6	1·7
37	1 39·3	1 39·5	1 34·7	3·7	0·4	9·7	1·1	15·7	1·7
38	1 39·5	1 39·8	1 35·0	3·8	0·4	9·8	1·1	15·8	1·7
39	1 39·8	1 40·0	1 35·2	3·9	0·4	9·9	1·1	15·9	1·7
40	1 40·0	1 40·3	1 35·4	4·0	0·4	10·0	1·1	16·0	1·7
41	1 40·3	1 40·5	1 35·7	4·1	0·4	10·1	1·1	16·1	1·7
42	1 40·5	1 40·8	1 35·9	4·2	0·5	10·2	1·1	16·2	1·8
43	1 40·8	1 41·0	1 36·2	4·3	0·5	10·3	1·1	16·3	1·8
44	1 41·0	1 41·3	1 36·4	4·4	0·5	10·4	1·1	16·4	1·8
45	1 41·3	1 41·5	1 36·6	4·5	0·5	10·5	1·1	16·5	1·8
46	1 41·5	1 41·8	1 36·9	4·6	0·5	10·6	1·1	16·6	1·8
47	1 41·8	1 42·0	1 37·1	4·7	0·5	10·7	1·2	16·7	1·8
48	1 42·0	1 42·3	1 37·4	4·8	0·5	10·8	1·2	16·8	1·8
49	1 42·3	1 42·5	1 37·6	4·9	0·5	10·9	1·2	16·9	1·8
50	1 42·5	1 42·8	1 37·8	5·0	0·5	11·0	1·2	17·0	1·8
51	1 42·8	1 43·0	1 38·1	5·1	0·6	11·1	1·2	17·1	1·9
52	1 43·0	1 43·3	1 38·3	5·2	0·6	11·2	1·2	17·2	1·9
53	1 43·3	1 43·5	1 38·5	5·3	0·6	11·3	1·2	17·3	1·9
54	1 43·5	1 43·8	1 38·8	5·4	0·6	11·4	1·2	17·4	1·9
55	1 43·8	1 44·0	1 39·0	5·5	0·6	11·5	1·2	17·5	1·9
56	1 44·0	1 44·3	1 39·3	5·6	0·6	11·6	1·3	17·6	1·9
57	1 44·3	1 44·5	1 39·5	5·7	0·6	11·7	1·3	17·7	1·9
58	1 44·5	1 44·8	1 39·7	5·8	0·6	11·8	1·3	17·8	1·9
59	1 44·8	1 45·0	1 40·0	5·9	0·6	11·9	1·3	17·9	1·9
60	1 45·0	1 45·3	1 40·2	6·0	0·7	12·0	1·3	18·0	2·0

7^m	SUN PLANETS	ARIES	MOON	v or d	Corr^n	v or d	Corr^n	v or d	Corr^n
s	° ′	° ′	° ′	′	′	′	′	′	′
00	1 45·0	1 45·3	1 40·2	0·0	0·0	6·0	0·8	12·0	1·5
01	1 45·3	1 45·5	1 40·5	0·1	0·0	6·1	0·8	12·1	1·5
02	1 45·5	1 45·8	1 40·7	0·2	0·0	6·2	0·8	12·2	1·5
03	1 45·8	1 46·0	1 40·9	0·3	0·0	6·3	0·8	12·3	1·5
04	1 46·0	1 46·3	1 41·2	0·4	0·1	6·4	0·8	12·4	1·6
05	1 46·3	1 46·5	1 41·4	0·5	0·1	6·5	0·8	12·5	1·6
06	1 46·5	1 46·8	1 41·6	0·6	0·1	6·6	0·8	12·6	1·6
07	1 46·8	1 47·0	1 41·9	0·7	0·1	6·7	0·8	12·7	1·6
08	1 47·0	1 47·3	1 42·1	0·8	0·1	6·8	0·9	12·8	1·6
09	1 47·3	1 47·5	1 42·4	0·9	0·1	6·9	0·9	12·9	1·6
10	1 47·5	1 47·8	1 42·6	1·0	0·1	7·0	0·9	13·0	1·6
11	1 47·8	1 48·0	1 42·8	1·1	0·1	7·1	0·9	13·1	1·6
12	1 48·0	1 48·3	1 43·1	1·2	0·2	7·2	0·9	13·2	1·7
13	1 48·3	1 48·5	1 43·3	1·3	0·2	7·3	0·9	13·3	1·7
14	1 48·5	1 48·8	1 43·6	1·4	0·2	7·4	0·9	13·4	1·7
15	1 48·8	1 49·0	1 43·8	1·5	0·2	7·5	0·9	13·5	1·7
16	1 49·0	1 49·3	1 44·0	1·6	0·2	7·6	1·0	13·6	1·7
17	1 49·3	1 49·5	1 44·3	1·7	0·2	7·7	1·0	13·7	1·7
18	1 49·5	1 49·8	1 44·5	1·8	0·2	7·8	1·0	13·8	1·7
19	1 49·8	1 50·1	1 44·8	1·9	0·2	7·9	1·0	13·9	1·7
20	1 50·0	1 50·3	1 45·0	2·0	0·3	8·0	1·0	14·0	1·8
21	1 50·3	1 50·6	1 45·2	2·1	0·3	8·1	1·0	14·1	1·8
22	1 50·5	1 50·8	1 45·5	2·2	0·3	8·2	1·0	14·2	1·8
23	1 50·8	1 51·1	1 45·7	2·3	0·3	8·3	1·0	14·3	1·8
24	1 51·0	1 51·3	1 45·9	2·4	0·3	8·4	1·1	14·4	1·8
25	1 51·3	1 51·6	1 46·2	2·5	0·3	8·5	1·1	14·5	1·8
26	1 51·5	1 51·8	1 46·4	2·6	0·3	8·6	1·1	14·6	1·8
27	1 51·8	1 52·1	1 46·7	2·7	0·3	8·7	1·1	14·7	1·8
28	1 52·0	1 52·3	1 46·9	2·8	0·4	8·8	1·1	14·8	1·9
29	1 52·3	1 52·6	1 47·1	2·9	0·4	8·9	1·1	14·9	1·9
30	1 52·5	1 52·8	1 47·4	3·0	0·4	9·0	1·1	15·0	1·9
31	1 52·8	1 53·1	1 47·6	3·1	0·4	9·1	1·1	15·1	1·9
32	1 53·0	1 53·3	1 47·9	3·2	0·4	9·2	1·2	15·2	1·9
33	1 53·3	1 53·6	1 48·1	3·3	0·4	9·3	1·2	15·3	1·9
34	1 53·5	1 53·8	1 48·3	3·4	0·4	9·4	1·2	15·4	1·9
35	1 53·8	1 54·1	1 48·6	3·5	0·4	9·5	1·2	15·5	1·9
36	1 54·0	1 54·3	1 48·8	3·6	0·5	9·6	1·2	15·6	2·0
37	1 54·3	1 54·6	1 49·0	3·7	0·5	9·7	1·2	15·7	2·0
38	1 54·5	1 54·8	1 49·3	3·8	0·5	9·8	1·2	15·8	2·0
39	1 54·8	1 55·1	1 49·5	3·9	0·5	9·9	1·2	15·9	2·0
40	1 55·0	1 55·3	1 49·8	4·0	0·5	10·0	1·3	16·0	2·0
41	1 55·3	1 55·6	1 50·0	4·1	0·5	10·1	1·3	16·1	2·0
42	1 55·5	1 55·8	1 50·2	4·2	0·5	10·2	1·3	16·2	2·0
43	1 55·8	1 56·1	1 50·5	4·3	0·5	10·3	1·3	16·3	2·0
44	1 56·0	1 56·3	1 50·7	4·4	0·6	10·4	1·3	16·4	2·1
45	1 56·3	1 56·6	1 51·0	4·5	0·6	10·5	1·3	16·5	2·1
46	1 56·5	1 56·8	1 51·2	4·6	0·6	10·6	1·3	16·6	2·1
47	1 56·8	1 57·1	1 51·4	4·7	0·6	10·7	1·3	16·7	2·1
48	1 57·0	1 57·3	1 51·7	4·8	0·6	10·8	1·4	16·8	2·1
49	1 57·3	1 57·6	1 51·9	4·9	0·6	10·9	1·4	16·9	2·1
50	1 57·5	1 57·8	1 52·1	5·0	0·6	11·0	1·4	17·0	2·1
51	1 57·8	1 58·1	1 52·4	5·1	0·6	11·1	1·4	17·1	2·1
52	1 58·0	1 58·3	1 52·6	5·2	0·7	11·2	1·4	17·2	2·2
53	1 58·3	1 58·6	1 52·9	5·3	0·7	11·3	1·4	17·3	2·2
54	1 58·5	1 58·8	1 53·1	5·4	0·7	11·4	1·4	17·4	2·2
55	1 58·8	1 59·1	1 53·3	5·5	0·7	11·5	1·4	17·5	2·2
56	1 59·0	1 59·3	1 53·6	5·6	0·7	11·6	1·5	17·6	2·2
57	1 59·3	1 59·6	1 53·8	5·7	0·7	11·7	1·5	17·7	2·2
58	1 59·5	1 59·8	1 54·1	5·8	0·7	11·8	1·5	17·8	2·2
59	1 59·8	2 00·1	1 54·3	5·9	0·7	11·9	1·5	17·9	2·2
60	2 00·0	2 00·3	1 54·5	6·0	0·8	12·0	1·5	18·0	2·3

^{m} 8	SUN PLANETS	ARIES	MOON	v or d	Corr^n	v or d	Corr^n	v or d	Corr^n
s	° ′	° ′	° ′	′	′	′	′	′	′
00	2 00·0	2 00·3	1 54·5	0·0	0·0	6·0	0·9	12·0	1·7
01	2 00·3	2 00·6	1 54·8	0·1	0·0	6·1	0·9	12·1	1·7
02	2 00·5	2 00·8	1 55·0	0·2	0·0	6·2	0·9	12·2	1·7
03	2 00·8	2 01·1	1 55·2	0·3	0·0	6·3	0·9	12·3	1·7
04	2 01·0	2 01·3	1 55·5	0·4	0·1	6·4	0·9	12·4	1·8
05	2 01·3	2 01·6	1 55·7	0·5	0·1	6·5	0·9	12·5	1·8
06	2 01·5	2 01·8	1 56·0	0·6	0·1	6·6	0·9	12·6	1·8
07	2 01·8	2 02·1	1 56·2	0·7	0·1	6·7	0·9	12·7	1·8
08	2 02·0	2 02·3	1 56·4	0·8	0·1	6·8	1·0	12·8	1·8
09	2 02·3	2 02·6	1 56·7	0·9	0·1	6·9	1·0	12·9	1·8
10	2 02·5	2 02·8	1 56·9	1·0	0·1	7·0	1·0	13·0	1·8
11	2 02·8	2 03·1	1 57·2	1·1	0·2	7·1	1·0	13·1	1·9
12	2 03·0	2 03·3	1 57·4	1·2	0·2	7·2	1·0	13·2	1·9
13	2 03·3	2 03·6	1 57·6	1·3	0·2	7·3	1·0	13·3	1·9
14	2 03·5	2 03·8	1 57·9	1·4	0·2	7·4	1·0	13·4	1·9
15	2 03·8	2 04·1	1 58·1	1·5	0·2	7·5	1·1	13·5	1·9
16	2 04·0	2 04·3	1 58·4	1·6	0·2	7·6	1·1	13·6	1·9
17	2 04·3	2 04·6	1 58·6	1·7	0·2	7·7	1·1	13·7	1·9
18	2 04·5	2 04·8	1 58·8	1·8	0·3	7·8	1·1	13·8	2·0
19	2 04·8	2 05·1	1 59·1	1·9	0·3	7·9	1·1	13·9	2·0
20	2 05·0	2 05·3	1 59·3	2·0	0·3	8·0	1·1	14·0	2·0
21	2 05·3	2 05·6	1 59·5	2·1	0·3	8·1	1·1	14·1	2·0
22	2 05·5	2 05·8	1 59·8	2·2	0·3	8·2	1·2	14·2	2·0
23	2 05·8	2 06·1	2 00·0	2·3	0·3	8·3	1·2	14·3	2·0
24	2 06·0	2 06·3	2 00·3	2·4	0·3	8·4	1·2	14·4	2·0
25	2 06·3	2 06·6	2 00·5	2·5	0·4	8·5	1·2	14·5	2·1
26	2 06·5	2 06·8	2 00·7	2·6	0·4	8·6	1·2	14·6	2·1
27	2 06·8	2 07·1	2 01·0	2·7	0·4	8·7	1·2	14·7	2·1
28	2 07·0	2 07·3	2 01·2	2·8	0·4	8·8	1·2	14·8	2·1
29	2 07·3	2 07·6	2 01·5	2·9	0·4	8·9	1·3	14·9	2·1
30	2 07·5	2 07·8	2 01·7	3·0	0·4	9·0	1·3	15·0	2·1
31	2 07·8	2 08·1	2 01·9	3·1	0·4	9·1	1·3	15·1	2·1
32	2 08·0	2 08·4	2 02·2	3·2	0·5	9·2	1·3	15·2	2·2
33	2 08·3	2 08·6	2 02·4	3·3	0·5	9·3	1·3	15·3	2·2
34	2 08·5	2 08·9	2 02·6	3·4	0·5	9·4	1·3	15·4	2·2
35	2 08·8	2 09·1	2 02·9	3·5	0·5	9·5	1·3	15·5	2·2
36	2 09·0	2 09·4	2 03·1	3·6	0·5	9·6	1·4	15·6	2·2
37	2 09·3	2 09·6	2 03·4	3·7	0·5	9·7	1·4	15·7	2·2
38	2 09·5	2 09·9	2 03·6	3·8	0·5	9·8	1·4	15·8	2·2
39	2 09·8	2 10·1	2 03·8	3·9	0·6	9·9	1·4	15·9	2·3
40	2 10·0	2 10·4	2 04·1	4·0	0·6	10·0	1·4	16·0	2·3
41	2 10·3	2 10·6	2 04·3	4·1	0·6	10·1	1·4	16·1	2·3
42	2 10·5	2 10·9	2 04·6	4·2	0·6	10·2	1·4	16·2	2·3
43	2 10·8	2 11·1	2 04·8	4·3	0·6	10·3	1·5	16·3	2·3
44	2 11·0	2 11·4	2 05·0	4·4	0·6	10·4	1·5	16·4	2·3
45	2 11·3	2 11·6	2 05·3	4·5	0·6	10·5	1·5	16·5	2·3
46	2 11·5	2 11·9	2 05·5	4·6	0·7	10·6	1·5	16·6	2·4
47	2 11·8	2 12·1	2 05·7	4·7	0·7	10·7	1·5	16·7	2·4
48	2 12·0	2 12·4	2 06·0	4·8	0·7	10·8	1·5	16·8	2·4
49	2 12·3	2 12·6	2 06·2	4·9	0·7	10·9	1·5	16·9	2·4
50	2 12·5	2 12·9	2 06·5	5·0	0·7	11·0	1·6	17·0	2·4
51	2 12·8	2 13·1	2 06·7	5·1	0·7	11·1	1·6	17·1	2·4
52	2 13·0	2 13·4	2 06·9	5·2	0·7	11·2	1·6	17·2	2·4
53	2 13·3	2 13·6	2 07·2	5·3	0·8	11·3	1·6	17·3	2·5
54	2 13·5	2 13·9	2 07·4	5·4	0·8	11·4	1·6	17·4	2·5
55	2 13·8	2 14·1	2 07·7	5·5	0·8	11·5	1·6	17·5	2·5
56	2 14·0	2 14·4	2 07·9	5·6	0·8	11·6	1·6	17·6	2·5
57	2 14·3	2 14·6	2 08·1	5·7	0·8	11·7	1·7	17·7	2·5
58	2 14·5	2 14·9	2 08·4	5·8	0·8	11·8	1·7	17·8	2·5
59	2 14·8	2 15·1	2 08·6	5·9	0·8	11·9	1·7	17·9	2·5
60	2 15·0	2 15·4	2 08·9	6·0	0·9	12·0	1·7	18·0	2·6

^{m} 9	SUN PLANETS	ARIES	MOON	v or d	Corr^n	v or d	Corr^n	v or d	Corr^n
s	° ′	° ′	° ′	′	′	′	′	′	′
00	2 15·0	2 15·4	2 08·9	0·0	0·0	6·0	1·0	12·0	1·9
01	2 15·3	2 15·6	2 09·1	0·1	0·0	6·1	1·0	12·1	1·9
02	2 15·5	2 15·9	2 09·3	0·2	0·0	6·2	1·0	12·2	1·9
03	2 15·8	2 16·1	2 09·6	0·3	0·0	6·3	1·0	12·3	1·9
04	2 16·0	2 16·4	2 09·8	0·4	0·1	6·4	1·0	12·4	2·0
05	2 16·3	2 16·6	2 10·0	0·5	0·1	6·5	1·0	12·5	2·0
06	2 16·5	2 16·9	2 10·3	0·6	0·1	6·6	1·0	12·6	2·0
07	2 16·8	2 17·1	2 10·5	0·7	0·1	6·7	1·1	12·7	2·0
08	2 17·0	2 17·4	2 10·8	0·8	0·1	6·8	1·1	12·8	2·0
09	2 17·3	2 17·6	2 11·0	0·9	0·1	6·9	1·1	12·9	2·0
10	2 17·5	2 17·9	2 11·2	1·0	0·2	7·0	1·1	13·0	2·1
11	2 17·8	2 18·1	2 11·5	1·1	0·2	7·1	1·1	13·1	2·1
12	2 18·0	2 18·4	2 11·7	1·2	0·2	7·2	1·1	13·2	2·1
13	2 18·3	2 18·6	2 12·0	1·3	0·2	7·3	1·2	13·3	2·1
14	2 18·5	2 18·9	2 12·2	1·4	0·2	7·4	1·2	13·4	2·1
15	2 18·8	2 19·1	2 12·4	1·5	0·2	7·5	1·2	13·5	2·1
16	2 19·0	2 19·4	2 12·7	1·6	0·3	7·6	1·2	13·6	2·2
17	2 19·3	2 19·6	2 12·9	1·7	0·3	7·7	1·2	13·7	2·2
18	2 19·5	2 19·9	2 13·1	1·8	0·3	7·8	1·2	13·8	2·2
19	2 19·8	2 20·1	2 13·4	1·9	0·3	7·9	1·3	13·9	2·2
20	2 20·0	2 20·4	2 13·6	2·0	0·3	8·0	1·3	14·0	2·2
21	2 20·3	2 20·6	2 13·9	2·1	0·3	8·1	1·3	14·1	2·2
22	2 20·5	2 20·9	2 14·1	2·2	0·3	8·2	1·3	14·2	2·2
23	2 20·8	2 21·1	2 14·3	2·3	0·4	8·3	1·3	14·3	2·3
24	2 21·0	2 21·4	2 14·6	2·4	0·4	8·4	1·3	14·4	2·3
25	2 21·3	2 21·6	2 14·8	2·5	0·4	8·5	1·3	14·5	2·3
26	2 21·5	2 21·9	2 15·1	2·6	0·4	8·6	1·4	14·6	2·3
27	2 21·8	2 22·1	2 15·3	2·7	0·4	8·7	1·4	14·7	2·3
28	2 22·0	2 22·4	2 15·5	2·8	0·4	8·8	1·4	14·8	2·3
29	2 22·3	2 22·6	2 15·8	2·9	0·5	8·9	1·4	14·9	2·4
30	2 22·5	2 22·9	2 16·0	3·0	0·5	9·0	1·4	15·0	2·4
31	2 22·8	2 23·1	2 16·2	3·1	0·5	9·1	1·4	15·1	2·4
32	2 23·0	2 23·4	2 16·5	3·2	0·5	9·2	1·5	15·2	2·4
33	2 23·3	2 23·6	2 16·7	3·3	0·5	9·3	1·5	15·3	2·4
34	2 23·5	2 23·9	2 17·0	3·4	0·5	9·4	1·5	15·4	2·4
35	2 23·8	2 24·1	2 17·2	3·5	0·6	9·5	1·5	15·5	2·5
36	2 24·0	2 24·4	2 17·4	3·6	0·6	9·6	1·5	15·6	2·5
37	2 24·3	2 24·6	2 17·7	3·7	0·6	9·7	1·5	15·7	2·5
38	2 24·5	2 24·9	2 17·9	3·8	0·6	9·8	1·6	15·8	2·5
39	2 24·8	2 25·1	2 18·2	3·9	0·6	9·9	1·6	15·9	2·5
40	2 25·0	2 25·4	2 18·4	4·0	0·6	10·0	1·6	16·0	2·5
41	2 25·3	2 25·6	2 18·6	4·1	0·6	10·1	1·6	16·1	2·5
42	2 25·5	2 25·9	2 18·9	4·2	0·7	10·2	1·6	16·2	2·6
43	2 25·8	2 26·1	2 19·1	4·3	0·7	10·3	1·6	16·3	2·6
44	2 26·0	2 26·4	2 19·3	4·4	0·7	10·4	1·6	16·4	2·6
45	2 26·3	2 26·7	2 19·6	4·5	0·7	10·5	1·7	16·5	2·6
46	2 26·5	2 26·9	2 19·8	4·6	0·7	10·6	1·7	16·6	2·6
47	2 26·8	2 27·2	2 20·1	4·7	0·7	10·7	1·7	16·7	2·6
48	2 27·0	2 27·4	2 20·3	4·8	0·8	10·8	1·7	16·8	2·7
49	2 27·3	2 27·7	2 20·5	4·9	0·8	10·9	1·7	16·9	2·7
50	2 27·5	2 27·9	2 20·8	5·0	0·8	11·0	1·7	17·0	2·7
51	2 27·8	2 28·2	2 21·0	5·1	0·8	11·1	1·8	17·1	2·7
52	2 28·0	2 28·4	2 21·3	5·2	0·8	11·2	1·8	17·2	2·7
53	2 28·3	2 28·7	2 21·5	5·3	0·8	11·3	1·8	17·3	2·7
54	2 28·5	2 28·9	2 21·7	5·4	0·9	11·4	1·8	17·4	2·8
55	2 28·8	2 29·2	2 22·0	5·5	0·9	11·5	1·8	17·5	2·8
56	2 29·0	2 29·4	2 22·2	5·6	0·9	11·6	1·8	17·6	2·8
57	2 29·3	2 29·7	2 22·5	5·7	0·9	11·7	1·9	17·7	2·8
58	2 29·5	2 29·9	2 22·7	5·8	0·9	11·8	1·9	17·8	2·8
59	2 29·8	2 30·2	2 22·9	5·9	0·9	11·9	1·9	17·9	2·8
60	2 30·0	2 30·4	2 23·2	6·0	1·0	12·0	1·9	18·0	2·9

10m	SUN PLANETS	ARIES	MOON	v or d	Corr^n	v or d	Corr^n	v or d	Corr^n
s	° ′	° ′	° ′	′	′	′	′	′	′
00	2 30·0	2 30·4	2 23·2	0·0	0·0	6·0	1·1	12·0	2·1
01	2 30·3	2 30·7	2 23·4	0·1	0·0	6·1	1·1	12·1	2·1
02	2 30·5	2 30·9	2 23·6	0·2	0·0	6·2	1·1	12·2	2·1
03	2 30·8	2 31·2	2 23·9	0·3	0·1	6·3	1·1	12·3	2·2
04	2 31·0	2 31·4	2 24·1	0·4	0·1	6·4	1·1	12·4	2·2
05	2 31·3	2 31·7	2 24·4	0·5	0·1	6·5	1·1	12·5	2·2
06	2 31·5	2 31·9	2 24·6	0·6	0·1	6·6	1·2	12·6	2·2
07	2 31·8	2 32·2	2 24·8	0·7	0·1	6·7	1·2	12·7	2·2
08	2 32·0	2 32·4	2 25·1	0·8	0·1	6·8	1·2	12·8	2·2
09	2 32·3	2 32·7	2 25·3	0·9	0·2	6·9	1·2	12·9	2·3
10	2 32·5	2 32·9	2 25·6	1·0	0·2	7·0	1·2	13·0	2·3
11	2 32·8	2 33·2	2 25·8	1·1	0·2	7·1	1·2	13·1	2·3
12	2 33·0	2 33·4	2 26·0	1·2	0·2	7·2	1·3	13·2	2·3
13	2 33·3	2 33·7	2 26·3	1·3	0·2	7·3	1·3	13·3	2·3
14	2 33·5	2 33·9	2 26·5	1·4	0·2	7·4	1·3	13·4	2·3
15	2 33·8	2 34·2	2 26·7	1·5	0·3	7·5	1·3	13·5	2·4
16	2 34·0	2 34·4	2 27·0	1·6	0·3	7·6	1·3	13·6	2·4
17	2 34·3	2 34·7	2 27·2	1·7	0·3	7·7	1·3	13·7	2·4
18	2 34·5	2 34·9	2 27·5	1·8	0·3	7·8	1·4	13·8	2·4
19	2 34·8	2 35·2	2 27·7	1·9	0·3	7·9	1·4	13·9	2·4
20	2 35·0	2 35·4	2 27·9	2·0	0·4	8·0	1·4	14·0	2·5
21	2 35·3	2 35·7	2 28·2	2·1	0·4	8·1	1·4	14·1	2·5
22	2 35·5	2 35·9	2 28·4	2·2	0·4	8·2	1·4	14·2	2·5
23	2 35·8	2 36·2	2 28·7	2·3	0·4	8·3	1·5	14·3	2·5
24	2 36·0	2 36·4	2 28·9	2·4	0·4	8·4	1·5	14·4	2·5
25	2 36·3	2 36·7	2 29·1	2·5	0·4	8·5	1·5	14·5	2·5
26	2 36·5	2 36·9	2 29·4	2·6	0·5	8·6	1·5	14·6	2·6
27	2 36·8	2 37·2	2 29·6	2·7	0·5	8·7	1·5	14·7	2·6
28	2 37·0	2 37·4	2 29·8	2·8	0·5	8·8	1·5	14·8	2·6
29	2 37·3	2 37·7	2 30·1	2·9	0·5	8·9	1·6	14·9	2·6
30	2 37·5	2 37·9	2 30·3	3·0	0·5	9·0	1·6	15·0	2·6
31	2 37·8	2 38·2	2 30·6	3·1	0·5	9·1	1·6	15·1	2·6
32	2 38·0	2 38·4	2 30·8	3·2	0·6	9·2	1·6	15·2	2·7
33	2 38·3	2 38·7	2 31·0	3·3	0·6	9·3	1·6	15·3	2·7
34	2 38·5	2 38·9	2 31·3	3·4	0·6	9·4	1·6	15·4	2·7
35	2 38·8	2 39·2	2 31·5	3·5	0·6	9·5	1·7	15·5	2·7
36	2 39·0	2 39·4	2 31·8	3·6	0·6	9·6	1·7	15·6	2·7
37	2 39·3	2 39·7	2 32·0	3·7	0·6	9·7	1·7	15·7	2·7
38	2 39·5	2 39·9	2 32·2	3·8	0·7	9·8	1·7	15·8	2·8
39	2 39·8	2 40·2	2 32·5	3·9	0·7	9·9	1·7	15·9	2·8
40	2 40·0	2 40·4	2 32·7	4·0	0·7	10·0	1·8	16·0	2·8
41	2 40·3	2 40·7	2 32·9	4·1	0·7	10·1	1·8	16·1	2·8
42	2 40·5	2 40·9	2 33·2	4·2	0·7	10·2	1·8	16·2	2·8
43	2 40·8	2 41·2	2 33·4	4·3	0·8	10·3	1·8	16·3	2·9
44	2 41·0	2 41·4	2 33·7	4·4	0·8	10·4	1·8	16·4	2·9
45	2 41·3	2 41·7	2 33·9	4·5	0·8	10·5	1·8	16·5	2·9
46	2 41·5	2 41·9	2 34·1	4·6	0·8	10·6	1·9	16·6	2·9
47	2 41·8	2 42·2	2 34·4	4·7	0·8	10·7	1·9	16·7	2·9
48	2 42·0	2 42·4	2 34·6	4·8	0·8	10·8	1·9	16·8	2·9
49	2 42·3	2 42·7	2 34·9	4·9	0·9	10·9	1·9	16·9	3·0
50	2 42·5	2 42·9	2 35·1	5·0	0·9	11·0	1·9	17·0	3·0
51	2 42·8	2 43·2	2 35·3	5·1	0·9	11·1	1·9	17·1	3·0
52	2 43·0	2 43·4	2 35·6	5·2	0·9	11·2	2·0	17·2	3·0
53	2 43·3	2 43·7	2 35·8	5·3	0·9	11·3	2·0	17·3	3·0
54	2 43·5	2 43·9	2 36·1	5·4	0·9	11·4	2·0	17·4	3·0
55	2 43·8	2 44·2	2 36·3	5·5	1·0	11·5	2·0	17·5	3·1
56	2 44·0	2 44·4	2 36·5	5·6	1·0	11·6	2·0	17·6	3·1
57	2 44·3	2 44·7	2 36·8	5·7	1·0	11·7	2·0	17·7	3·1
58	2 44·5	2 45·0	2 37·0	5·8	1·0	11·8	2·1	17·8	3·1
59	2 44·8	2 45·2	2 37·2	5·9	1·0	11·9	2·1	17·9	3·1
60	2 45·0	2 45·5	2 37·5	6·0	1·1	12·0	2·1	18·0	3·2

11m	SUN PLANETS	ARIES	MOON	v or d	Corr^n	v or d	Corr^n	v or d	Corr^n
s	° ′	° ′	° ′	′	′	′	′	′	′
00	2 45·0	2 45·5	2 37·5	0·0	0·0	6·0	1·2	12·0	2·3
01	2 45·3	2 45·7	2 37·7	0·1	0·0	6·1	1·2	12·1	2·3
02	2 45·5	2 46·0	2 38·0	0·2	0·0	6·2	1·2	12·2	2·3
03	2 45·8	2 46·2	2 38·2	0·3	0·1	6·3	1·2	12·3	2·4
04	2 46·0	2 46·5	2 38·4	0·4	0·1	6·4	1·2	12·4	2·4
05	2 46·3	2 46·7	2 38·7	0·5	0·1	6·5	1·2	12·5	2·4
06	2 46·5	2 47·0	2 38·9	0·6	0·1	6·6	1·3	12·6	2·4
07	2 46·8	2 47·2	2 39·2	0·7	0·1	6·7	1·3	12·7	2·4
08	2 47·0	2 47·5	2 39·4	0·8	0·2	6·8	1·3	12·8	2·5
09	2 47·3	2 47·7	2 39·6	0·9	0·2	6·9	1·3	12·9	2·5
10	2 47·5	2 48·0	2 39·9	1·0	0·2	7·0	1·3	13·0	2·5
11	2 47·8	2 48·2	2 40·1	1·1	0·2	7·1	1·4	13·1	2·5
12	2 48·0	2 48·5	2 40·3	1·2	0·2	7·2	1·4	13·2	2·5
13	2 48·3	2 48·7	2 40·6	1·3	0·2	7·3	1·4	13·3	2·5
14	2 48·5	2 49·0	2 40·8	1·4	0·3	7·4	1·4	13·4	2·6
15	2 48·8	2 49·2	2 41·1	1·5	0·3	7·5	1·4	13·5	2·6
16	2 49·0	2 49·5	2 41·3	1·6	0·3	7·6	1·5	13·6	2·6
17	2 49·3	2 49·7	2 41·5	1·7	0·3	7·7	1·5	13·7	2·6
18	2 49·5	2 50·0	2 41·8	1·8	0·3	7·8	1·5	13·8	2·6
19	2 49·8	2 50·2	2 42·0	1·9	0·4	7·9	1·5	13·9	2·7
20	2 50·0	2 50·5	2 42·3	2·0	0·4	8·0	1·5	14·0	2·7
21	2 50·3	2 50·7	2 42·5	2·1	0·4	8·1	1·6	14·1	2·7
22	2 50·5	2 51·0	2 42·7	2·2	0·4	8·2	1·6	14·2	2·7
23	2 50·8	2 51·2	2 43·0	2·3	0·4	8·3	1·6	14·3	2·7
24	2 51·0	2 51·5	2 43·2	2·4	0·5	8·4	1·6	14·4	2·8
25	2 51·3	2 51·7	2 43·4	2·5	0·5	8·5	1·6	14·5	2·8
26	2 51·5	2 52·0	2 43·7	2·6	0·5	8·6	1·6	14·6	2·8
27	2 51·8	2 52·2	2 43·9	2·7	0·5	8·7	1·7	14·7	2·8
28	2 52·0	2 52·5	2 44·2	2·8	0·5	8·8	1·7	14·8	2·8
29	2 52·3	2 52·7	2 44·4	2·9	0·6	8·9	1·7	14·9	2·9
30	2 52·5	2 53·0	2 44·6	3·0	0·6	9·0	1·7	15·0	2·9
31	2 52·8	2 53·2	2 44·9	3·1	0·6	9·1	1·7	15·1	2·9
32	2 53·0	2 53·5	2 45·1	3·2	0·6	9·2	1·8	15·2	2·9
33	2 53·3	2 53·7	2 45·4	3·3	0·6	9·3	1·8	15·3	2·9
34	2 53·5	2 54·0	2 45·6	3·4	0·7	9·4	1·8	15·4	3·0
35	2 53·8	2 54·2	2 45·8	3·5	0·7	9·5	1·8	15·5	3·0
36	2 54·0	2 54·5	2 46·1	3·6	0·7	9·6	1·8	15·6	3·0
37	2 54·3	2 54·7	2 46·3	3·7	0·7	9·7	1·9	15·7	3·0
38	2 54·5	2 55·0	2 46·6	3·8	0·7	9·8	1·9	15·8	3·0
39	2 54·8	2 55·2	2 46·8	3·9	0·7	9·9	1·9	15·9	3·0
40	2 55·0	2 55·5	2 47·0	4·0	0·8	10·0	1·9	16·0	3·1
41	2 55·3	2 55·7	2 47·3	4·1	0·8	10·1	1·9	16·1	3·1
42	2 55·5	2 56·0	2 47·5	4·2	0·8	10·2	2·0	16·2	3·1
43	2 55·8	2 56·2	2 47·7	4·3	0·8	10·3	2·0	16·3	3·1
44	2 56·0	2 56·5	2 48·0	4·4	0·8	10·4	2·0	16·4	3·1
45	2 56·3	2 56·7	2 48·2	4·5	0·9	10·5	2·0	16·5	3·2
46	2 56·5	2 57·0	2 48·5	4·6	0·9	10·6	2·0	16·6	3·2
47	2 56·8	2 57·2	2 48·7	4·7	0·9	10·7	2·1	16·7	3·2
48	2 57·0	2 57·5	2 48·9	4·8	0·9	10·8	2·1	16·8	3·2
49	2 57·3	2 57·7	2 49·2	4·9	0·9	10·9	2·1	16·9	3·2
50	2 57·5	2 58·0	2 49·4	5·0	1·0	11·0	2·1	17·0	3·3
51	2 57·8	2 58·2	2 49·7	5·1	1·0	11·1	2·1	17·1	3·3
52	2 58·0	2 58·5	2 49·9	5·2	1·0	11·2	2·1	17·2	3·3
53	2 58·3	2 58·7	2 50·1	5·3	1·0	11·3	2·2	17·3	3·3
54	2 58·5	2 59·0	2 50·4	5·4	1·0	11·4	2·2	17·4	3·3
55	2 58·8	2 59·2	2 50·6	5·5	1·1	11·5	2·2	17·5	3·4
56	2 59·0	2 59·5	2 50·8	5·6	1·1	11·6	2·2	17·6	3·4
57	2 59·3	2 59·7	2 51·1	5·7	1·1	11·7	2·2	17·7	3·4
58	2 59·5	3 00·0	2 51·3	5·8	1·1	11·8	2·3	17·8	3·4
59	2 59·8	3 00·2	2 51·6	5·9	1·1	11·9	2·3	17·9	3·4
60	3 00·0	3 00·5	2 51·8	6·0	1·2	12·0	2·3	18·0	3·5

12ᵐ	SUN PLANETS	ARIES	MOON	v or d	Corrⁿ	v or d	Corrⁿ	v or d	Corrⁿ
s	° ′	° ′	° ′	′	′	′	′	′	′
00	3 00·0	3 00·5	2 51·8	0·0	0·0	6·0	1·3	12·0	2·5
01	3 00·3	3 00·7	2 52·0	0·1	0·0	6·1	1·3	12·1	2·5
02	3 00·5	3 01·0	2 52·3	0·2	0·0	6·2	1·3	12·2	2·5
03	3 00·8	3 01·2	2 52·5	0·3	0·1	6·3	1·3	12·3	2·6
04	3 01·0	3 01·5	2 52·8	0·4	0·1	6·4	1·3	12·4	2·6
05	3 01·3	3 01·7	2 53·0	0·5	0·1	6·5	1·4	12·5	2·6
06	3 01·5	3 02·0	2 53·2	0·6	0·1	6·6	1·4	12·6	2·6
07	3 01·8	3 02·2	2 53·5	0·7	0·1	6·7	1·4	12·7	2·6
08	3 02·0	3 02·5	2 53·7	0·8	0·2	6·8	1·4	12·8	2·7
09	3 02·3	3 02·7	2 53·9	0·9	0·2	6·9	1·4	12·9	2·7
10	3 02·5	3 03·0	2 54·2	1·0	0·2	7·0	1·5	13·0	2·7
11	3 02·8	3 03·3	2 54·4	1·1	0·2	7·1	1·5	13·1	2·7
12	3 03·0	3 03·5	2 54·7	1·2	0·3	7·2	1·5	13·2	2·8
13	3 03·3	3 03·8	2 54·9	1·3	0·3	7·3	1·5	13·3	2·8
14	3 03·5	3 04·0	2 55·1	1·4	0·3	7·4	1·5	13·4	2·8
15	3 03·8	3 04·3	2 55·4	1·5	0·3	7·5	1·6	13·5	2·8
16	3 04·0	3 04·5	2 55·6	1·6	0·3	7·6	1·6	13·6	2·8
17	3 04·3	3 04·8	2 55·9	1·7	0·4	7·7	1·6	13·7	2·9
18	3 04·5	3 05·0	2 56·1	1·8	0·4	7·8	1·6	13·8	2·9
19	3 04·8	3 05·3	2 56·3	1·9	0·4	7·9	1·6	13·9	2·9
20	3 05·0	3 05·5	2 56·6	2·0	0·4	8·0	1·7	14·0	2·9
21	3 05·3	3 05·8	2 56·8	2·1	0·4	8·1	1·7	14·1	2·9
22	3 05·5	3 06·0	2 57·0	2·2	0·5	8·2	1·7	14·2	3·0
23	3 05·8	3 06·3	2 57·3	2·3	0·5	8·3	1·7	14·3	3·0
24	3 06·0	3 06·5	2 57·5	2·4	0·5	8·4	1·8	14·4	3·0
25	3 06·3	3 06·8	2 57·8	2·5	0·5	8·5	1·8	14·5	3·0
26	3 06·5	3 07·0	2 58·0	2·6	0·5	8·6	1·8	14·6	3·0
27	3 06·8	3 07·3	2 58·2	2·7	0·6	8·7	1·8	14·7	3·1
28	3 07·0	3 07·5	2 58·5	2·8	0·6	8·8	1·8	14·8	3·1
29	3 07·3	3 07·8	2 58·7	2·9	0·6	8·9	1·9	14·9	3·1
30	3 07·5	3 08·0	2 59·0	3·0	0·6	9·0	1·9	15·0	3·1
31	3 07·8	3 08·3	2 59·2	3·1	0·6	9·1	1·9	15·1	3·1
32	3 08·0	3 08·5	2 59·4	3·2	0·7	9·2	1·9	15·2	3·2
33	3 08·3	3 08·8	2 59·7	3·3	0·7	9·3	1·9	15·3	3·2
34	3 08·5	3 09·0	2 59·9	3·4	0·7	9·4	2·0	15·4	3·2
35	3 08·8	3 09·3	3 00·2	3·5	0·7	9·5	2·0	15·5	3·2
36	3 09·0	3 09·5	3 00·4	3·6	0·8	9·6	2·0	15·6	3·3
37	3 09·3	3 09·8	3 00·6	3·7	0·8	9·7	2·0	15·7	3·3
38	3 09·5	3 10·0	3 00·9	3·8	0·8	9·8	2·0	15·8	3·3
39	3 09·8	3 10·3	3 01·1	3·9	0·8	9·9	2·1	15·9	3·3
40	3 10·0	3 10·5	3 01·3	4·0	0·8	10·0	2·1	16·0	3·3
41	3 10·3	3 10·8	3 01·6	4·1	0·9	10·1	2·1	16·1	3·4
42	3 10·5	3 11·0	3 01·8	4·2	0·9	10·2	2·1	16·2	3·4
43	3 10·8	3 11·3	3 02·1	4·3	0·9	10·3	2·1	16·3	3·4
44	3 11·0	3 11·5	3 02·3	4·4	0·9	10·4	2·2	16·4	3·4
45	3 11·3	3 11·8	3 02·5	4·5	0·9	10·5	2·2	16·5	3·4
46	3 11·5	3 12·0	3 02·8	4·6	1·0	10·6	2·2	16·6	3·5
47	3 11·8	3 12·3	3 03·0	4·7	1·0	10·7	2·2	16·7	3·5
48	3 12·0	3 12·5	3 03·3	4·8	1·0	10·8	2·3	16·8	3·5
49	3 12·3	3 12·8	3 03·5	4·9	1·0	10·9	2·3	16·9	3·5
50	3 12·5	3 13·0	3 03·7	5·0	1·0	11·0	2·3	17·0	3·5
51	3 12·8	3 13·3	3 04·0	5·1	1·1	11·1	2·3	17·1	3·6
52	3 13·0	3 13·5	3 04·2	5·2	1·1	11·2	2·3	17·2	3·6
53	3 13·3	3 13·8	3 04·4	5·3	1·1	11·3	2·4	17·3	3·6
54	3 13·5	3 14·0	3 04·7	5·4	1·1	11·4	2·4	17·4	3·6
55	3 13·8	3 14·3	3 04·9	5·5	1·1	11·5	2·4	17·5	3·6
56	3 14·0	3 14·5	3 05·2	5·6	1·2	11·6	2·4	17·6	3·7
57	3 14·3	3 14·8	3 05·4	5·7	1·2	11·7	2·4	17·7	3·7
58	3 14·5	3 15·0	3 05·6	5·8	1·2	11·8	2·5	17·8	3·7
59	3 14·8	3 15·3	3 05·9	5·9	1·2	11·9	2·5	17·9	3·7
60	3 15·0	3 15·5	3 06·1	6·0	1·3	12·0	2·5	18·0	3·8

13ᵐ	SUN PLANETS	ARIES	MOON	v or d	Corrⁿ	v or d	Corrⁿ	v or d	Corrⁿ
s	° ′	° ′	° ′	′	′	′	′	′	′
00	3 15·0	3 15·5	3 06·1	0·0	0·0	6·0	1·4	12·0	2·7
01	3 15·3	3 15·8	3 06·4	0·1	0·0	6·1	1·4	12·1	2·7
02	3 15·5	3 16·0	3 06·6	0·2	0·0	6·2	1·4	12·2	2·7
03	3 15·8	3 16·3	3 06·8	0·3	0·1	6·3	1·4	12·3	2·8
04	3 16·0	3 16·5	3 07·1	0·4	0·1	6·4	1·4	12·4	2·8
05	3 16·3	3 16·8	3 07·3	0·5	0·1	6·5	1·5	12·5	2·8
06	3 16·5	3 17·0	3 07·5	0·6	0·1	6·6	1·5	12·6	2·8
07	3 16·8	3 17·3	3 07·8	0·7	0·2	6·7	1·5	12·7	2·9
08	3 17·0	3 17·5	3 08·0	0·8	0·2	6·8	1·5	12·8	2·9
09	3 17·3	3 17·8	3 08·3	0·9	0·2	6·9	1·6	12·9	2·9
10	3 17·5	3 18·0	3 08·5	1·0	0·2	7·0	1·6	13·0	2·9
11	3 17·8	3 18·3	3 08·7	1·1	0·2	7·1	1·6	13·1	2·9
12	3 18·0	3 18·5	3 09·0	1·2	0·3	7·2	1·6	13·2	3·0
13	3 18·3	3 18·8	3 09·2	1·3	0·3	7·3	1·6	13·3	3·0
14	3 18·5	3 19·0	3 09·5	1·4	0·3	7·4	1·7	13·4	3·0
15	3 18·8	3 19·3	3 09·7	1·5	0·3	7·5	1·7	13·5	3·0
16	3 19·0	3 19·5	3 09·9	1·6	0·4	7·6	1·7	13·6	3·1
17	3 19·3	3 19·8	3 10·2	1·7	0·4	7·7	1·7	13·7	3·1
18	3 19·5	3 20·0	3 10·4	1·8	0·4	7·8	1·8	13·8	3·1
19	3 19·8	3 20·3	3 10·7	1·9	0·4	7·9	1·8	13·9	3·1
20	3 20·0	3 20·5	3 10·9	2·0	0·5	8·0	1·8	14·0	3·2
21	3 20·3	3 20·8	3 11·1	2·1	0·5	8·1	1·8	14·1	3·2
22	3 20·5	3 21·0	3 11·4	2·2	0·5	8·2	1·8	14·2	3·2
23	3 20·8	3 21·3	3 11·6	2·3	0·5	8·3	1·9	14·3	3·2
24	3 21·0	3 21·6	3 11·8	2·4	0·5	8·4	1·9	14·4	3·2
25	3 21·3	3 21·8	3 12·1	2·5	0·6	8·5	1·9	14·5	3·3
26	3 21·5	3 22·1	3 12·3	2·6	0·6	8·6	1·9	14·6	3·3
27	3 21·8	3 22·3	3 12·6	2·7	0·6	8·7	2·0	14·7	3·3
28	3 22·0	3 22·6	3 12·8	2·8	0·6	8·8	2·0	14·8	3·3
29	3 22·3	3 22·8	3 13·0	2·9	0·7	8·9	2·0	14·9	3·4
30	3 22·5	3 23·1	3 13·3	3·0	0·7	9·0	2·0	15·0	3·4
31	3 22·8	3 23·3	3 13·5	3·1	0·7	9·1	2·0	15·1	3·4
32	3 23·0	3 23·6	3 13·8	3·2	0·7	9·2	2·1	15·2	3·4
33	3 23·3	3 23·8	3 14·0	3·3	0·7	9·3	2·1	15·3	3·4
34	3 23·5	3 24·1	3 14·2	3·4	0·8	9·4	2·1	15·4	3·5
35	3 23·8	3 24·3	3 14·5	3·5	0·8	9·5	2·1	15·5	3·5
36	3 24·0	3 24·6	3 14·7	3·6	0·8	9·6	2·2	15·6	3·5
37	3 24·3	3 24·8	3 14·9	3·7	0·8	9·7	2·2	15·7	3·5
38	3 24·5	3 25·1	3 15·2	3·8	0·9	9·8	2·2	15·8	3·6
39	3 24·8	3 25·3	3 15·4	3·9	0·9	9·9	2·2	15·9	3·6
40	3 25·0	3 25·6	3 15·7	4·0	0·9	10·0	2·3	16·0	3·6
41	3 25·3	3 25·8	3 15·9	4·1	0·9	10·1	2·3	16·1	3·6
42	3 25·5	3 26·1	3 16·1	4·2	0·9	10·2	2·3	16·2	3·6
43	3 25·8	3 26·3	3 16·4	4·3	1·0	10·3	2·3	16·3	3·7
44	3 26·0	3 26·6	3 16·6	4·4	1·0	10·4	2·3	16·4	3·7
45	3 26·3	3 26·8	3 16·9	4·5	1·0	10·5	2·4	16·5	3·7
46	3 26·5	3 27·1	3 17·1	4·6	1·0	10·6	2·4	16·6	3·7
47	3 26·8	3 27·3	3 17·3	4·7	1·1	10·7	2·4	16·7	3·8
48	3 27·0	3 27·6	3 17·6	4·8	1·1	10·8	2·4	16·8	3·8
49	3 27·3	3 27·8	3 17·8	4·9	1·1	10·9	2·5	16·9	3·8
50	3 27·5	3 28·1	3 18·0	5·0	1·1	11·0	2·5	17·0	3·8
51	3 27·8	3 28·3	3 18·3	5·1	1·1	11·1	2·5	17·1	3·8
52	3 28·0	3 28·6	3 18·5	5·2	1·2	11·2	2·5	17·2	3·9
53	3 28·3	3 28·8	3 18·8	5·3	1·2	11·3	2·5	17·3	3·9
54	3 28·5	3 29·1	3 19·0	5·4	1·2	11·4	2·6	17·4	3·9
55	3 28·8	3 29·3	3 19·2	5·5	1·2	11·5	2·6	17·5	3·9
56	3 29·0	3 29·6	3 19·5	5·6	1·3	11·6	2·6	17·6	4·0
57	3 29·3	3 29·8	3 19·7	5·7	1·3	11·7	2·6	17·7	4·0
58	3 29·5	3 30·1	3 20·0	5·8	1·3	11·8	2·7	17·8	4·0
59	3 29·8	3 30·3	3 20·2	5·9	1·3	11·9	2·7	17·9	4·0
60	3 30·0	3 30·6	3 20·4	6·0	1·4	12·0	2·7	18·0	4·1

14m s	SUN PLANETS ° ′	ARIES ° ′	MOON ° ′	v or d ′	Corrn ′	v or d ′	Corrn ′	v or d ′	Corrn ′
00	3 30·0	3 30·6	3 20·4	0·0	0·0	6·0	1·5	12·0	2·9
01	3 30·3	3 30·8	3 20·7	0·1	0·0	6·1	1·5	12·1	2·9
02	3 30·5	3 31·1	3 20·9	0·2	0·0	6·2	1·5	12·2	2·9
03	3 30·8	3 31·3	3 21·1	0·3	0·1	6·3	1·5	12·3	3·0
04	3 31·0	3 31·6	3 21·4	0·4	0·1	6·4	1·5	12·4	3·0
05	3 31·3	3 31·8	3 21·6	0·5	0·1	6·5	1·6	12·5	3·0
06	3 31·5	3 32·1	3 21·9	0·6	0·1	6·6	1·6	12·6	3·0
07	3 31·8	3 32·3	3 22·1	0·7	0·2	6·7	1·6	12·7	3·1
08	3 32·0	3 32·6	3 22·3	0·8	0·2	6·8	1·6	12·8	3·1
09	3 32·3	3 32·8	3 22·6	0·9	0·2	6·9	1·7	12·9	3·1
10	3 32·5	3 33·1	3 22·8	1·0	0·2	7·0	1·7	13·0	3·1
11	3 32·8	3 33·3	3 23·1	1·1	0·3	7·1	1·7	13·1	3·2
12	3 33·0	3 33·6	3 23·3	1·2	0·3	7·2	1·7	13·2	3·2
13	3 33·3	3 33·8	3 23·5	1·3	0·3	7·3	1·8	13·3	3·2
14	3 33·5	3 34·1	3 23·8	1·4	0·3	7·4	1·8	13·4	3·2
15	3 33·8	3 34·3	3 24·0	1·5	0·4	7·5	1·8	13·5	3·3
16	3 34·0	3 34·6	3 24·3	1·6	0·4	7·6	1·8	13·6	3·3
17	3 34·3	3 34·8	3 24·5	1·7	0·4	7·7	1·9	13·7	3·3
18	3 34·5	3 35·1	3 24·7	1·8	0·4	7·8	1·9	13·8	3·3
19	3 34·8	3 35·3	3 25·0	1·9	0·5	7·9	1·9	13·9	3·4
20	3 35·0	3 35·6	3 25·2	2·0	0·5	8·0	1·9	14·0	3·4
21	3 35·3	3 35·8	3 25·4	2·1	0·5	8·1	2·0	14·1	3·4
22	3 35·5	3 36·1	3 25·7	2·2	0·5	8·2	2·0	14·2	3·4
23	3 35·8	3 36·3	3 25·9	2·3	0·6	8·3	2·0	14·3	3·5
24	3 36·0	3 36·6	3 26·2	2·4	0·6	8·4	2·0	14·4	3·5
25	3 36·3	3 36·8	3 26·4	2·5	0·6	8·5	2·1	14·5	3·5
26	3 36·5	3 37·1	3 26·6	2·6	0·6	8·6	2·1	14·6	3·5
27	3 36·8	3 37·3	3 26·9	2·7	0·7	8·7	2·1	14·7	3·6
28	3 37·0	3 37·6	3 27·1	2·8	0·7	8·8	2·1	14·8	3·6
29	3 37·3	3 37·8	3 27·4	2·9	0·7	8·9	2·2	14·9	3·6
30	3 37·5	3 38·1	3 27·6	3·0	0·7	9·0	2·2	15·0	3·6
31	3 37·8	3 38·3	3 27·8	3·1	0·7	9·1	2·2	15·1	3·6
32	3 38·0	3 38·6	3 28·1	3·2	0·8	9·2	2·2	15·2	3·7
33	3 38·3	3 38·8	3 28·3	3·3	0·8	9·3	2·2	15·3	3·7
34	3 38·5	3 39·1	3 28·5	3·4	0·8	9·4	2·3	15·4	3·7
35	3 38·8	3 39·3	3 28·8	3·5	0·8	9·5	2·3	15·5	3·7
36	3 39·0	3 39·6	3 29·0	3·6	0·9	9·6	2·3	15·6	3·8
37	3 39·3	3 39·9	3 29·3	3·7	0·9	9·7	2·3	15·7	3·8
38	3 39·5	3 40·1	3 29·5	3·8	0·9	9·8	2·4	15·8	3·8
39	3 39·8	3 40·4	3 29·7	3·9	0·9	9·9	2·4	15·9	3·8
40	3 40·0	3 40·6	3 30·0	4·0	1·0	10·0	2·4	16·0	3·9
41	3 40·3	3 40·9	3 30·2	4·1	1·0	10·1	2·4	16·1	3·9
42	3 40·5	3 41·1	3 30·5	4·2	1·0	10·2	2·5	16·2	3·9
43	3 40·8	3 41·4	3 30·7	4·3	1·0	10·3	2·5	16·3	3·9
44	3 41·0	3 41·6	3 30·9	4·4	1·1	10·4	2·5	16·4	4·0
45	3 41·3	3 41·9	3 31·2	4·5	1·1	10·5	2·5	16·5	4·0
46	3 41·5	3 42·1	3 31·4	4·6	1·1	10·6	2·6	16·6	4·0
47	3 41·8	3 42·4	3 31·6	4·7	1·1	10·7	2·6	16·7	4·0
48	3 42·0	3 42·6	3 31·9	4·8	1·2	10·8	2·6	16·8	4·1
49	3 42·3	3 42·9	3 32·1	4·9	1·2	10·9	2·6	16·9	4·1
50	3 42·5	3 43·1	3 32·4	5·0	1·2	11·0	2·7	17·0	4·1
51	3 42·8	3 43·4	3 32·6	5·1	1·2	11·1	2·7	17·1	4·1
52	3 43·0	3 43·6	3 32·8	5·2	1·3	11·2	2·7	17·2	4·2
53	3 43·3	3 43·9	3 33·1	5·3	1·3	11·3	2·7	17·3	4·2
54	3 43·5	3 44·1	3 33·3	5·4	1·3	11·4	2·8	17·4	4·2
55	3 43·8	3 44·4	3 33·6	5·5	1·3	11·5	2·8	17·5	4·2
56	3 44·0	3 44·6	3 33·8	5·6	1·4	11·6	2·8	17·6	4·3
57	3 44·3	3 44·9	3 34·0	5·7	1·4	11·7	2·8	17·7	4·3
58	3 44·5	3 45·1	3 34·3	5·8	1·4	11·8	2·9	17·8	4·3
59	3 44·8	3 45·4	3 34·5	5·9	1·4	11·9	2·9	17·9	4·3
60	3 45·0	3 45·6	3 34·8	6·0	1·5	12·0	2·9	18·0	4·4

15m s	SUN PLANETS ° ′	ARIES ° ′	MOON ° ′	v or d ′	Corrn ′	v or d ′	Corrn ′	v or d ′	Corrn ′
00	3 45·0	3 45·6	3 34·8	0·0	0·0	6·0	1·6	12·0	3·1
01	3 45·3	3 45·9	3 35·0	0·1	0·0	6·1	1·6	12·1	3·1
02	3 45·5	3 46·1	3 35·2	0·2	0·1	6·2	1·6	12·2	3·2
03	3 45·8	3 46·4	3 35·5	0·3	0·1	6·3	1·6	12·3	3·2
04	3 46·0	3 46·6	3 35·7	0·4	0·1	6·4	1·7	12·4	3·2
05	3 46·3	3 46·9	3 35·9	0·5	0·1	6·5	1·7	12·5	3·2
06	3 46·5	3 47·1	3 36·2	0·6	0·2	6·6	1·7	12·6	3·3
07	3 46·8	3 47·4	3 36·4	0·7	0·2	6·7	1·7	12·7	3·3
08	3 47·0	3 47·6	3 36·7	0·8	0·2	6·8	1·8	12·8	3·3
09	3 47·3	3 47·9	3 36·9	0·9	0·2	6·9	1·8	12·9	3·3
10	3 47·5	3 48·1	3 37·1	1·0	0·3	7·0	1·8	13·0	3·4
11	3 47·8	3 48·4	3 37·4	1·1	0·3	7·1	1·8	13·1	3·4
12	3 48·0	3 48·6	3 37·6	1·2	0·3	7·2	1·9	13·2	3·4
13	3 48·3	3 48·9	3 37·9	1·3	0·3	7·3	1·9	13·3	3·4
14	3 48·5	3 49·1	3 38·1	1·4	0·4	7·4	1·9	13·4	3·5
15	3 48·8	3 49·4	3 38·3	1·5	0·4	7·5	1·9	13·5	3·5
16	3 49·0	3 49·6	3 38·6	1·6	0·4	7·6	2·0	13·6	3·5
17	3 49·3	3 49·9	3 38·8	1·7	0·4	7·7	2·0	13·7	3·5
18	3 49·5	3 50·1	3 39·0	1·8	0·5	7·8	2·0	13·8	3·6
19	3 49·8	3 50·4	3 39·3	1·9	0·5	7·9	2·0	13·9	3·6
20	3 50·0	3 50·6	3 39·5	2·0	0·5	8·0	2·1	14·0	3·6
21	3 50·3	3 50·9	3 39·8	2·1	0·5	8·1	2·1	14·1	3·6
22	3 50·5	3 51·1	3 40·0	2·2	0·6	8·2	2·1	14·2	3·7
23	3 50·8	3 51·4	3 40·2	2·3	0·6	8·3	2·1	14·3	3·7
24	3 51·0	3 51·6	3 40·5	2·4	0·6	8·4	2·2	14·4	3·7
25	3 51·3	3 51·9	3 40·7	2·5	0·6	8·5	2·2	14·5	3·7
26	3 51·5	3 52·1	3 41·0	2·6	0·7	8·6	2·2	14·6	3·8
27	3 51·8	3 52·4	3 41·2	2·7	0·7	8·7	2·2	14·7	3·8
28	3 52·0	3 52·6	3 41·4	2·8	0·7	8·8	2·3	14·8	3·8
29	3 52·3	3 52·9	3 41·7	2·9	0·7	8·9	2·3	14·9	3·8
30	3 52·5	3 53·1	3 41·9	3·0	0·8	9·0	2·3	15·0	3·9
31	3 52·8	3 53·4	3 42·1	3·1	0·8	9·1	2·4	15·1	3·9
32	3 53·0	3 53·6	3 42·4	3·2	0·8	9·2	2·4	15·2	3·9
33	3 53·3	3 53·9	3 42·6	3·3	0·9	9·3	2·4	15·3	4·0
34	3 53·5	3 54·1	3 42·9	3·4	0·9	9·4	2·4	15·4	4·0
35	3 53·8	3 54·4	3 43·1	3·5	0·9	9·5	2·5	15·5	4·0
36	3 54·0	3 54·6	3 43·3	3·6	0·9	9·6	2·5	15·6	4·0
37	3 54·3	3 54·9	3 43·6	3·7	1·0	9·7	2·5	15·7	4·1
38	3 54·5	3 55·1	3 43·8	3·8	1·0	9·8	2·5	15·8	4·1
39	3 54·8	3 55·4	3 44·1	3·9	1·0	9·9	2·6	15·9	4·1
40	3 55·0	3 55·6	3 44·3	4·0	1·0	10·0	2·6	16·0	4·1
41	3 55·3	3 55·9	3 44·5	4·1	1·1	10·1	2·6	16·1	4·2
42	3 55·5	3 56·1	3 44·8	4·2	1·1	10·2	2·6	16·2	4·2
43	3 55·8	3 56·4	3 45·0	4·3	1·1	10·3	2·7	16·3	4·2
44	3 56·0	3 56·6	3 45·2	4·4	1·1	10·4	2·7	16·4	4·2
45	3 56·3	3 56·9	3 45·5	4·5	1·2	10·5	2·7	16·5	4·3
46	3 56·5	3 57·1	3 45·7	4·6	1·2	10·6	2·7	16·6	4·3
47	3 56·8	3 57·4	3 46·0	4·7	1·2	10·7	2·8	16·7	4·3
48	3 57·0	3 57·6	3 46·2	4·8	1·2	10·8	2·8	16·8	4·3
49	3 57·3	3 57·9	3 46·4	4·9	1·3	10·9	2·8	16·9	4·4
50	3 57·5	3 58·2	3 46·7	5·0	1·3	11·0	2·8	17·0	4·4
51	3 57·8	3 58·4	3 46·9	5·1	1·3	11·1	2·9	17·1	4·4
52	3 58·0	3 58·7	3 47·2	5·2	1·3	11·2	2·9	17·2	4·4
53	3 58·3	3 58·9	3 47·4	5·3	1·4	11·3	2·9	17·3	4·5
54	3 58·5	3 59·2	3 47·6	5·4	1·4	11·4	2·9	17·4	4·5
55	3 58·8	3 59·4	3 47·9	5·5	1·4	11·5	3·0	17·5	4·5
56	3 59·0	3 59·7	3 48·1	5·6	1·4	11·6	3·0	17·6	4·5
57	3 59·3	3 59·9	3 48·4	5·7	1·5	11·7	3·0	17·7	4·6
58	3 59·5	4 00·2	3 48·6	5·8	1·5	11·8	3·0	17·8	4·6
59	3 59·8	4 00·4	3 48·8	5·9	1·5	11·9	3·1	17·9	4·6
60	4 00·0	4 00·7	3 49·1	6·0	1·6	12·0	3·1	18·0	4·7

16ᵐ	SUN PLANETS	ARIES	MOON	v or d	Corrⁿ	v or d	Corrⁿ	v or d	Corrⁿ
s	° ′	° ′	° ′	′	′	′	′	′	′
00	4 00·0	4 00·7	3 49·1	0·0	0·0	6·0	1·7	12·0	3·3
01	4 00·3	4 00·9	3 49·3	0·1	0·0	6·1	1·7	12·1	3·3
02	4 00·5	4 01·2	3 49·5	0·2	0·1	6·2	1·7	12·2	3·4
03	4 00·8	4 01·4	3 49·8	0·3	0·1	6·3	1·7	12·3	3·4
04	4 01·0	4 01·7	3 50·0	0·4	0·1	6·4	1·8	12·4	3·4
05	4 01·3	4 01·9	3 50·3	0·5	0·1	6·5	1·8	12·5	3·4
06	4 01·5	4 02·2	3 50·5	0·6	0·2	6·6	1·8	12·6	3·5
07	4 01·8	4 02·4	3 50·7	0·7	0·2	6·7	1·8	12·7	3·5
08	4 02·0	4 02·7	3 51·0	0·8	0·2	6·8	1·9	12·8	3·5
09	4 02·3	4 02·9	3 51·2	0·9	0·2	6·9	1·9	12·9	3·5
10	4 02·5	4 03·2	3 51·5	1·0	0·3	7·0	1·9	13·0	3·6
11	4 02·8	4 03·4	3 51·7	1·1	0·3	7·1	2·0	13·1	3·6
12	4 03·0	4 03·7	3 51·9	1·2	0·3	7·2	2·0	13·2	3·6
13	4 03·3	4 03·9	3 52·2	1·3	0·4	7·3	2·0	13·3	3·7
14	4 03·5	4 04·2	3 52·4	1·4	0·4	7·4	2·0	13·4	3·7
15	4 03·8	4 04·4	3 52·6	1·5	0·4	7·5	2·1	13·5	3·7
16	4 04·0	4 04·7	3 52·9	1·6	0·4	7·6	2·1	13·6	3·7
17	4 04·3	4 04·9	3 53·1	1·7	0·5	7·7	2·1	13·7	3·8
18	4 04·5	4 05·2	3 53·4	1·8	0·5	7·8	2·1	13·8	3·8
19	4 04·8	4 05·4	3 53·6	1·9	0·5	7·9	2·2	13·9	3·8
20	4 05·0	4 05·7	3 53·8	2·0	0·6	8·0	2·2	14·0	3·9
21	4 05·3	4 05·9	3 54·1	2·1	0·6	8·1	2·2	14·1	3·9
22	4 05·5	4 06·2	3 54·3	2·2	0·6	8·2	2·3	14·2	3·9
23	4 05·8	4 06·4	3 54·6	2·3	0·6	8·3	2·3	14·3	3·9
24	4 06·0	4 06·7	3 54·8	2·4	0·7	8·4	2·3	14·4	4·0
25	4 06·3	4 06·9	3 55·0	2·5	0·7	8·5	2·3	14·5	4·0
26	4 06·5	4 07·2	3 55·3	2·6	0·7	8·6	2·4	14·6	4·0
27	4 06·8	4 07·4	3 55·5	2·7	0·7	8·7	2·4	14·7	4·0
28	4 07·0	4 07·7	3 55·7	2·8	0·8	8·8	2·4	14·8	4·1
29	4 07·3	4 07·9	3 56·0	2·9	0·8	8·9	2·4	14·9	4·1
30	4 07·5	4 08·2	3 56·2	3·0	0·8	9·0	2·5	15·0	4·1
31	4 07·8	4 08·4	3 56·5	3·1	0·9	9·1	2·5	15·1	4·2
32	4 08·0	4 08·7	3 56·7	3·2	0·9	9·2	2·5	15·2	4·2
33	4 08·3	4 08·9	3 56·9	3·3	0·9	9·3	2·6	15·3	4·2
34	4 08·5	4 09·2	3 57·2	3·4	0·9	9·4	2·6	15·4	4·2
35	4 08·8	4 09·4	3 57·4	3·5	1·0	9·5	2·6	15·5	4·3
36	4 09·0	4 09·7	3 57·7	3·6	1·0	9·6	2·6	15·6	4·3
37	4 09·3	4 09·9	3 57·9	3·7	1·0	9·7	2·7	15·7	4·3
38	4 09·5	4 10·2	3 58·1	3·8	1·0	9·8	2·7	15·8	4·3
39	4 09·8	4 10·4	3 58·4	3·9	1·1	9·9	2·7	15·9	4·4
40	4 10·0	4 10·7	3 58·6	4·0	1·1	10·0	2·8	16·0	4·4
41	4 10·3	4 10·9	3 58·8	4·1	1·1	10·1	2·8	16·1	4·4
42	4 10·5	4 11·2	3 59·1	4·2	1·2	10·2	2·8	16·2	4·5
43	4 10·8	4 11·4	3 59·3	4·3	1·2	10·3	2·8	16·3	4·5
44	4 11·0	4 11·7	3 59·6	4·4	1·2	10·4	2·9	16·4	4·5
45	4 11·3	4 11·9	3 59·8	4·5	1·2	10·5	2·9	16·5	4·5
46	4 11·5	4 12·2	4 00·0	4·6	1·3	10·6	2·9	16·6	4·6
47	4 11·8	4 12·4	4 00·3	4·7	1·3	10·7	2·9	16·7	4·6
48	4 12·0	4 12·7	4 00·5	4·8	1·3	10·8	3·0	16·8	4·6
49	4 12·3	4 12·9	4 00·8	4·9	1·3	10·9	3·0	16·9	4·6
50	4 12·5	4 13·2	4 01·0	5·0	1·4	11·0	3·0	17·0	4·7
51	4 12·8	4 13·4	4 01·2	5·1	1·4	11·1	3·1	17·1	4·7
52	4 13·0	4 13·7	4 01·5	5·2	1·4	11·2	3·1	17·2	4·7
53	4 13·3	4 13·9	4 01·7	5·3	1·5	11·3	3·1	17·3	4·8
54	4 13·5	4 14·2	4 02·0	5·4	1·5	11·4	3·1	17·4	4·8
55	4 13·8	4 14·4	4 02·2	5·5	1·5	11·5	3·2	17·5	4·8
56	4 14·0	4 14·7	4 02·4	5·6	1·5	11·6	3·2	17·6	4·8
57	4 14·3	4 14·9	4 02·7	5·7	1·6	11·7	3·2	17·7	4·9
58	4 14·5	4 15·2	4 02·9	5·8	1·6	11·8	3·2	17·8	4·9
59	4 14·8	4 15·4	4 03·1	5·9	1·6	11·9	3·3	17·9	4·9
60	4 15·0	4 15·7	4 03·4	6·0	1·7	12·0	3·3	18·0	5·0

17ᵐ	SUN PLANETS	ARIES	MOON	v or d	Corrⁿ	v or d	Corrⁿ	v or d	Corrⁿ
s	° ′	° ′	° ′	′	′	′	′	′	′
00	4 15·0	4 15·7	4 03·4	0·0	0·0	6·0	1·8	12·0	3·5
01	4 15·3	4 15·9	4 03·6	0·1	0·0	6·1	1·8	12·1	3·5
02	4 15·5	4 16·2	4 03·9	0·2	0·1	6·2	1·8	12·2	3·6
03	4 15·8	4 16·5	4 04·1	0·3	0·1	6·3	1·8	12·3	3·6
04	4 16·0	4 16·7	4 04·3	0·4	0·1	6·4	1·9	12·4	3·6
05	4 16·3	4 17·0	4 04·6	0·5	0·1	6·5	1·9	12·5	3·6
06	4 16·5	4 17·2	4 04·8	0·6	0·2	6·6	1·9	12·6	3·7
07	4 16·8	4 17·5	4 05·1	0·7	0·2	6·7	2·0	12·7	3·7
08	4 17·0	4 17·7	4 05·3	0·8	0·2	6·8	2·0	12·8	3·7
09	4 17·3	4 18·0	4 05·5	0·9	0·3	6·9	2·0	12·9	3·8
10	4 17·5	4 18·2	4 05·8	1·0	0·3	7·0	2·0	13·0	3·8
11	4 17·8	4 18·5	4 06·0	1·1	0·3	7·1	2·1	13·1	3·8
12	4 18·0	4 18·7	4 06·2	1·2	0·4	7·2	2·1	13·2	3·9
13	4 18·3	4 19·0	4 06·5	1·3	0·4	7·3	2·1	13·3	3·9
14	4 18·5	4 19·2	4 06·7	1·4	0·4	7·4	2·2	13·4	3·9
15	4 18·8	4 19·5	4 07·0	1·5	0·4	7·5	2·2	13·5	3·9
16	4 19·0	4 19·7	4 07·2	1·6	0·5	7·6	2·2	13·6	4·0
17	4 19·3	4 20·0	4 07·4	1·7	0·5	7·7	2·2	13·7	4·0
18	4 19·5	4 20·2	4 07·7	1·8	0·5	7·8	2·3	13·8	4·0
19	4 19·8	4 20·5	4 07·9	1·9	0·6	7·9	2·3	13·9	4·1
20	4 20·0	4 20·7	4 08·2	2·0	0·6	8·0	2·3	14·0	4·1
21	4 20·3	4 21·0	4 08·4	2·1	0·6	8·1	2·4	14·1	4·1
22	4 20·5	4 21·2	4 08·6	2·2	0·6	8·2	2·4	14·2	4·1
23	4 20·8	4 21·5	4 08·9	2·3	0·7	8·3	2·4	14·3	4·2
24	4 21·0	4 21·7	4 09·1	2·4	0·7	8·4	2·5	14·4	4·2
25	4 21·3	4 22·0	4 09·3	2·5	0·7	8·5	2·5	14·5	4·2
26	4 21·5	4 22·2	4 09·6	2·6	0·8	8·6	2·5	14·6	4·3
27	4 21·8	4 22·5	4 09·8	2·7	0·8	8·7	2·5	14·7	4·3
28	4 22·0	4 22·7	4 10·1	2·8	0·8	8·8	2·6	14·8	4·3
29	4 22·3	4 23·0	4 10·3	2·9	0·8	8·9	2·6	14·9	4·3
30	4 22·5	4 23·2	4 10·5	3·0	0·9	9·0	2·6	15·0	4·4
31	4 22·8	4 23·5	4 10·8	3·1	0·9	9·1	2·7	15·1	4·4
32	4 23·0	4 23·7	4 11·0	3·2	0·9	9·2	2·7	15·2	4·4
33	4 23·3	4 24·0	4 11·3	3·3	1·0	9·3	2·7	15·3	4·5
34	4 23·5	4 24·2	4 11·5	3·4	1·0	9·4	2·7	15·4	4·5
35	4 23·8	4 24·5	4 11·7	3·5	1·0	9·5	2·8	15·5	4·5
36	4 24·0	4 24·7	4 12·0	3·6	1·1	9·6	2·8	15·6	4·6
37	4 24·3	4 25·0	4 12·2	3·7	1·1	9·7	2·8	15·7	4·6
38	4 24·5	4 25·2	4 12·5	3·8	1·1	9·8	2·9	15·8	4·6
39	4 24·8	4 25·5	4 12·7	3·9	1·1	9·9	2·9	15·9	4·6
40	4 25·0	4 25·7	4 12·9	4·0	1·2	10·0	2·9	16·0	4·7
41	4 25·3	4 26·0	4 13·2	4·1	1·2	10·1	2·9	16·1	4·7
42	4 25·5	4 26·2	4 13·4	4·2	1·2	10·2	3·0	16·2	4·7
43	4 25·8	4 26·5	4 13·6	4·3	1·3	10·3	3·0	16·3	4·8
44	4 26·0	4 26·7	4 13·9	4·4	1·3	10·4	3·0	16·4	4·8
45	4 26·3	4 27·0	4 14·1	4·5	1·3	10·5	3·1	16·5	4·8
46	4 26·5	4 27·2	4 14·4	4·6	1·3	10·6	3·1	16·6	4·8
47	4 26·8	4 27·5	4 14·6	4·7	1·4	10·7	3·1	16·7	4·9
48	4 27·0	4 27·7	4 14·8	4·8	1·4	10·8	3·2	16·8	4·9
49	4 27·3	4 28·0	4 15·1	4·9	1·4	10·9	3·2	16·9	4·9
50	4 27·5	4 28·2	4 15·3	5·0	1·5	11·0	3·2	17·0	5·0
51	4 27·8	4 28·5	4 15·6	5·1	1·5	11·1	3·2	17·1	5·0
52	4 28·0	4 28·7	4 15·8	5·2	1·5	11·2	3·3	17·2	5·0
53	4 28·3	4 29·0	4 16·0	5·3	1·5	11·3	3·3	17·3	5·0
54	4 28·5	4 29·2	4 16·3	5·4	1·6	11·4	3·3	17·4	5·1
55	4 28·8	4 29·5	4 16·5	5·5	1·6	11·5	3·4	17·5	5·1
56	4 29·0	4 29·7	4 16·7	5·6	1·6	11·6	3·4	17·6	5·1
57	4 29·3	4 30·0	4 17·0	5·7	1·7	11·7	3·4	17·7	5·2
58	4 29·5	4 30·2	4 17·2	5·8	1·7	11·8	3·4	17·8	5·2
59	4 29·8	4 30·5	4 17·5	5·9	1·7	11·9	3·5	17·9	5·2
60	4 30·0	4 30·7	4 17·7	6·0	1·8	12·0	3·5	18·0	5·3

18^m s	SUN PLANETS ° ′	ARIES ° ′	MOON ° ′	v or d ′	Corr^n ′	v or d ′	Corr^n ′	v or d ′	Corr^n ′
00	4 30·0	4 30·7	4 17·7	0·0	0·0	6·0	1·9	12·0	3·7
01	4 30·3	4 31·0	4 17·9	0·1	0·0	6·1	1·9	12·1	3·7
02	4 30·5	4 31·2	4 18·2	0·2	0·1	6·2	1·9	12·2	3·8
03	4 30·8	4 31·5	4 18·4	0·3	0·1	6·3	1·9	12·3	3·8
04	4 31·0	4 31·7	4 18·7	0·4	0·1	6·4	2·0	12·4	3·8
05	4 31·3	4 32·0	4 18·9	0·5	0·2	6·5	2·0	12·5	3·9
06	4 31·5	4 32·2	4 19·1	0·6	0·2	6·6	2·0	12·6	3·9
07	4 31·8	4 32·5	4 19·4	0·7	0·2	6·7	2·1	12·7	3·9
08	4 32·0	4 32·7	4 19·6	0·8	0·2	6·8	2·1	12·8	3·9
09	4 32·3	4 33·0	4 19·8	0·9	0·3	6·9	2·1	12·9	4·0
10	4 32·5	4 33·2	4 20·1	1·0	0·3	7·0	2·2	13·0	4·0
11	4 32·8	4 33·5	4 20·3	1·1	0·3	7·1	2·2	13·1	4·0
12	4 33·0	4 33·7	4 20·6	1·2	0·4	7·2	2·2	13·2	4·1
13	4 33·3	4 34·0	4 20·8	1·3	0·4	7·3	2·3	13·3	4·1
14	4 33·5	4 34·2	4 21·0	1·4	0·4	7·4	2·3	13·4	4·1
15	4 33·8	4 34·5	4 21·3	1·5	0·5	7·5	2·3	13·5	4·2
16	4 34·0	4 34·8	4 21·5	1·6	0·5	7·6	2·3	13·6	4·2
17	4 34·3	4 35·0	4 21·8	1·7	0·5	7·7	2·4	13·7	4·2
18	4 34·5	4 35·3	4 22·0	1·8	0·6	7·8	2·4	13·8	4·3
19	4 34·8	4 35·5	4 22·2	1·9	0·6	7·9	2·4	13·9	4·3
20	4 35·0	4 35·8	4 22·5	2·0	0·6	8·0	2·5	14·0	4·3
21	4 35·3	4 36·0	4 22·7	2·1	0·6	8·1	2·5	14·1	4·3
22	4 35·5	4 36·3	4 22·9	2·2	0·7	8·2	2·5	14·2	4·4
23	4 35·8	4 36·5	4 23·2	2·3	0·7	8·3	2·6	14·3	4·4
24	4 36·0	4 36·8	4 23·4	2·4	0·7	8·4	2·6	14·4	4·4
25	4 36·3	4 37·0	4 23·7	2·5	0·8	8·5	2·6	14·5	4·5
26	4 36·5	4 37·3	4 23·9	2·6	0·8	8·6	2·7	14·6	4·5
27	4 36·8	4 37·5	4 24·1	2·7	0·8	8·7	2·7	14·7	4·5
28	4 37·0	4 37·8	4 24·4	2·8	0·9	8·8	2·7	14·8	4·6
29	4 37·3	4 38·0	4 24·6	2·9	0·9	8·9	2·7	14·9	4·6
30	4 37·5	4 38·3	4 24·9	3·0	0·9	9·0	2·8	15·0	4·6
31	4 37·8	4 38·5	4 25·1	3·1	1·0	9·1	2·8	15·1	4·7
32	4 38·0	4 38·8	4 25·3	3·2	1·0	9·2	2·8	15·2	4·7
33	4 38·3	4 39·0	4 25·6	3·3	1·0	9·3	2·9	15·3	4·7
34	4 38·5	4 39·3	4 25·8	3·4	1·0	9·4	2·9	15·4	4·7
35	4 38·8	4 39·5	4 26·1	3·5	1·1	9·5	2·9	15·5	4·8
36	4 39·0	4 39·8	4 26·3	3·6	1·1	9·6	3·0	15·6	4·8
37	4 39·3	4 40·0	4 26·5	3·7	1·1	9·7	3·0	15·7	4·8
38	4 39·5	4 40·3	4 26·8	3·8	1·2	9·8	3·0	15·8	4·9
39	4 39·8	4 40·5	4 27·0	3·9	1·2	9·9	3·1	15·9	4·9
40	4 40·0	4 40·8	4 27·2	4·0	1·2	10·0	3·1	16·0	4·9
41	4 40·3	4 41·0	4 27·5	4·1	1·3	10·1	3·1	16·1	5·0
42	4 40·5	4 41·3	4 27·7	4·2	1·3	10·2	3·1	16·2	5·0
43	4 40·8	4 41·5	4 28·0	4·3	1·3	10·3	3·2	16·3	5·0
44	4 41·0	4 41·8	4 28·2	4·4	1·4	10·4	3·2	16·4	5·1
45	4 41·3	4 42·0	4 28·4	4·5	1·4	10·5	3·2	16·5	5·1
46	4 41·5	4 42·3	4 28·7	4·6	1·4	10·6	3·3	16·6	5·1
47	4 41·8	4 42·5	4 28·9	4·7	1·4	10·7	3·3	16·7	5·1
48	4 42·0	4 42·8	4 29·2	4·8	1·5	10·8	3·3	16·8	5·2
49	4 42·3	4 43·0	4 29·4	4·9	1·5	10·9	3·4	16·9	5·2
50	4 42·5	4 43·3	4 29·6	5·0	1·5	11·0	3·4	17·0	5·2
51	4 42·8	4 43·5	4 29·9	5·1	1·6	11·1	3·4	17·1	5·3
52	4 43·0	4 43·8	4 30·1	5·2	1·6	11·2	3·5	17·2	5·3
53	4 43·3	4 44·0	4 30·3	5·3	1·6	11·3	3·5	17·3	5·3
54	4 43·5	4 44·3	4 30·6	5·4	1·7	11·4	3·5	17·4	5·4
55	4 43·8	4 44·5	4 30·8	5·5	1·7	11·5	3·5	17·5	5·4
56	4 44·0	4 44·8	4 31·1	5·6	1·7	11·6	3·6	17·6	5·4
57	4 44·3	4 45·0	4 31·3	5·7	1·8	11·7	3·6	17·7	5·5
58	4 44·5	4 45·3	4 31·5	5·8	1·8	11·8	3·6	17·8	5·5
59	4 44·8	4 45·5	4 31·8	5·9	1·8	11·9	3·7	17·9	5·5
60	4 45·0	4 45·8	4 32·0	6·0	1·9	12·0	3·7	18·0	5·6

19^m s	SUN PLANETS ° ′	ARIES ° ′	MOON ° ′	v or d ′	Corr^n ′	v or d ′	Corr^n ′	v or d ′	Corr^n ′
00	4 45·0	4 45·8	4 32·0	0·0	0·0	6·0	2·0	12·0	3·9
01	4 45·3	4 46·0	4 32·3	0·1	0·0	6·1	2·0	12·1	3·9
02	4 45·5	4 46·3	4 32·5	0·2	0·1	6·2	2·0	12·2	4·0
03	4 45·8	4 46·5	4 32·7	0·3	0·1	6·3	2·0	12·3	4·0
04	4 46·0	4 46·8	4 33·0	0·4	0·1	6·4	2·1	12·4	4·0
05	4 46·3	4 47·0	4 33·2	0·5	0·2	6·5	2·1	12·5	4·1
06	4 46·5	4 47·3	4 33·4	0·6	0·2	6·6	2·1	12·6	4·1
07	4 46·8	4 47·5	4 33·7	0·7	0·2	6·7	2·2	12·7	4·1
08	4 47·0	4 47·8	4 33·9	0·8	0·3	6·8	2·2	12·8	4·2
09	4 47·3	4 48·0	4 34·2	0·9	0·3	6·9	2·2	12·9	4·2
10	4 47·5	4 48·3	4 34·4	1·0	0·3	7·0	2·3	13·0	4·2
11	4 47·8	4 48·5	4 34·6	1·1	0·4	7·1	2·3	13·1	4·3
12	4 48·0	4 48·8	4 34·9	1·2	0·4	7·2	2·3	13·2	4·3
13	4 48·3	4 49·0	4 35·1	1·3	0·4	7·3	2·4	13·3	4·3
14	4 48·5	4 49·3	4 35·4	1·4	0·5	7·4	2·4	13·4	4·4
15	4 48·8	4 49·5	4 35·6	1·5	0·5	7·5	2·4	13·5	4·4
16	4 49·0	4 49·8	4 35·8	1·6	0·5	7·6	2·5	13·6	4·4
17	4 49·3	4 50·0	4 36·1	1·7	0·6	7·7	2·5	13·7	4·5
18	4 49·5	4 50·3	4 36·3	1·8	0·6	7·8	2·5	13·8	4·5
19	4 49·8	4 50·5	4 36·6	1·9	0·6	7·9	2·6	13·9	4·5
20	4 50·0	4 50·8	4 36·8	2·0	0·7	8·0	2·6	14·0	4·6
21	4 50·3	4 51·0	4 37·0	2·1	0·7	8·1	2·6	14·1	4·6
22	4 50·5	4 51·3	4 37·3	2·2	0·7	8·2	2·7	14·2	4·6
23	4 50·8	4 51·5	4 37·5	2·3	0·7	8·3	2·7	14·3	4·6
24	4 51·0	4 51·8	4 37·7	2·4	0·8	8·4	2·7	14·4	4·7
25	4 51·3	4 52·0	4 38·0	2·5	0·8	8·5	2·8	14·5	4·7
26	4 51·5	4 52·3	4 38·2	2·6	0·8	8·6	2·8	14·6	4·7
27	4 51·8	4 52·5	4 38·5	2·7	0·9	8·7	2·8	14·7	4·8
28	4 52·0	4 52·8	4 38·7	2·8	0·9	8·8	2·9	14·8	4·8
29	4 52·3	4 53·1	4 38·9	2·9	0·9	8·9	2·9	14·9	4·8
30	4 52·5	4 53·3	4 39·2	3·0	1·0	9·0	2·9	15·0	4·9
31	4 52·8	4 53·6	4 39·4	3·1	1·0	9·1	3·0	15·1	4·9
32	4 53·0	4 53·8	4 39·7	3·2	1·0	9·2	3·0	15·2	4·9
33	4 53·3	4 54·1	4 39·9	3·3	1·1	9·3	3·0	15·3	5·0
34	4 53·5	4 54·3	4 40·1	3·4	1·1	9·4	3·1	15·4	5·0
35	4 53·8	4 54·6	4 40·4	3·5	1·1	9·5	3·1	15·5	5·0
36	4 54·0	4 54·8	4 40·6	3·6	1·2	9·6	3·1	15·6	5·1
37	4 54·3	4 55·1	4 40·8	3·7	1·2	9·7	3·2	15·7	5·1
38	4 54·5	4 55·3	4 41·1	3·8	1·2	9·8	3·2	15·8	5·1
39	4 54·8	4 55·6	4 41·3	3·9	1·3	9·9	3·2	15·9	5·2
40	4 55·0	4 55·8	4 41·6	4·0	1·3	10·0	3·3	16·0	5·2
41	4 55·3	4 56·1	4 41·8	4·1	1·3	10·1	3·3	16·1	5·2
42	4 55·5	4 56·3	4 42·0	4·2	1·4	10·2	3·3	16·2	5·3
43	4 55·8	4 56·6	4 42·3	4·3	1·4	10·3	3·3	16·3	5·3
44	4 56·0	4 56·8	4 42·5	4·4	1·4	10·4	3·4	16·4	5·3
45	4 56·3	4 57·1	4 42·8	4·5	1·5	10·5	3·4	16·5	5·4
46	4 56·5	4 57·3	4 43·0	4·6	1·5	10·6	3·4	16·6	5·4
47	4 56·8	4 57·6	4 43·2	4·7	1·5	10·7	3·5	16·7	5·4
48	4 57·0	4 57·8	4 43·5	4·8	1·6	10·8	3·5	16·8	5·5
49	4 57·3	4 58·1	4 43·7	4·9	1·6	10·9	3·5	16·9	5·5
50	4 57·5	4 58·3	4 43·9	5·0	1·6	11·0	3·6	17·0	5·5
51	4 57·8	4 58·6	4 44·2	5·1	1·7	11·1	3·6	17·1	5·6
52	4 58·0	4 58·8	4 44·4	5·2	1·7	11·2	3·6	17·2	5·6
53	4 58·3	4 59·1	4 44·7	5·3	1·7	11·3	3·7	17·3	5·6
54	4 58·5	4 59·3	4 44·9	5·4	1·8	11·4	3·7	17·4	5·7
55	4 58·8	4 59·6	4 45·1	5·5	1·8	11·5	3·7	17·5	5·7
56	4 59·0	4 59·8	4 45·4	5·6	1·8	11·6	3·8	17·6	5·7
57	4 59·3	5 00·1	4 45·6	5·7	1·9	11·7	3·8	17·7	5·8
58	4 59·5	5 00·3	4 45·9	5·8	1·9	11·8	3·8	17·8	5·8
59	4 59·8	5 00·6	4 46·1	5·9	1·9	11·9	3·9	17·9	5·8
60	5 00·0	5 00·8	4 46·3	6·0	2·0	12·0	3·9	18·0	5·9

20^m	SUN PLANETS	ARIES	MOON	*v* or *d*	Corr^n	*v* or *d*	Corr^n	*v* or *d*	Corr^n
s	° ′	° ′	° ′	′	′	′	′	′	′
00	5 00·0	5 00·8	4 46·3	0·0	0·0	6·0	2·1	12·0	4·1
01	5 00·3	5 01·1	4 46·6	0·1	0·0	6·1	2·1	12·1	4·1
02	5 00·5	5 01·3	4 46·8	0·2	0·1	6·2	2·1	12·2	4·2
03	5 00·8	5 01·6	4 47·0	0·3	0·1	6·3	2·2	12·3	4·2
04	5 01·0	5 01·8	4 47·3	0·4	0·1	6·4	2·2	12·4	4·2
05	5 01·3	5 02·1	4 47·5	0·5	0·2	6·5	2·2	12·5	4·3
06	5 01·5	5 02·3	4 47·8	0·6	0·2	6·6	2·3	12·6	4·3
07	5 01·8	5 02·6	4 48·0	0·7	0·2	6·7	2·3	12·7	4·3
08	5 02·0	5 02·8	4 48·2	0·8	0·3	6·8	2·3	12·8	4·4
09	5 02·3	5 03·1	4 48·5	0·9	0·3	6·9	2·4	12·9	4·4
10	5 02·5	5 03·3	4 48·7	1·0	0·3	7·0	2·4	13·0	4·4
11	5 02·8	5 03·6	4 49·0	1·1	0·4	7·1	2·4	13·1	4·5
12	5 03·0	5 03·8	4 49·2	1·2	0·4	7·2	2·5	13·2	4·5
13	5 03·3	5 04·1	4 49·4	1·3	0·4	7·3	2·5	13·3	4·5
14	5 03·5	5 04·3	4 49·7	1·4	0·5	7·4	2·5	13·4	4·6
15	5 03·8	5 04·6	4 49·9	1·5	0·5	7·5	2·6	13·5	4·6
16	5 04·0	5 04·8	4 50·2	1·6	0·5	7·6	2·6	13·6	4·6
17	5 04·3	5 05·1	4 50·4	1·7	0·6	7·7	2·6	13·7	4·7
18	5 04·5	5 05·3	4 50·6	1·8	0·6	7·8	2·7	13·8	4·7
19	5 04·8	5 05·6	4 50·9	1·9	0·6	7·9	2·7	13·9	4·7
20	5 05·0	5 05·8	4 51·1	2·0	0·7	8·0	2·7	14·0	4·8
21	5 05·3	5 06·1	4 51·3	2·1	0·7	8·1	2·8	14·1	4·8
22	5 05·5	5 06·3	4 51·6	2·2	0·8	8·2	2·8	14·2	4·9
23	5 05·8	5 06·6	4 51·8	2·3	0·8	8·3	2·8	14·3	4·9
24	5 06·0	5 06·8	4 52·1	2·4	0·8	8·4	2·9	14·4	4·9
25	5 06·3	5 07·1	4 52·3	2·5	0·9	8·5	2·9	14·5	5·0
26	5 06·5	5 07·3	4 52·5	2·6	0·9	8·6	2·9	14·6	5·0
27	5 06·8	5 07·6	4 52·8	2·7	0·9	8·7	3·0	14·7	5·0
28	5 07·0	5 07·8	4 53·0	2·8	1·0	8·8	3·0	14·8	5·1
29	5 07·3	5 08·1	4 53·3	2·9	1·0	8·9	3·0	14·9	5·1
30	5 07·5	5 08·3	4 53·5	3·0	1·0	9·0	3·1	15·0	5·1
31	5 07·8	5 08·6	4 53·7	3·1	1·1	9·1	3·1	15·1	5·2
32	5 08·0	5 08·8	4 54·0	3·2	1·1	9·2	3·1	15·2	5·2
33	5 08·3	5 09·1	4 54·2	3·3	1·1	9·3	3·2	15·3	5·2
34	5 08·5	5 09·3	4 54·4	3·4	1·2	9·4	3·2	15·4	5·3
35	5 08·8	5 09·6	4 54·7	3·5	1·2	9·5	3·2	15·5	5·3
36	5 09·0	5 09·8	4 54·9	3·6	1·2	9·6	3·3	15·6	5·3
37	5 09·3	5 10·1	4 55·2	3·7	1·3	9·7	3·3	15·7	5·4
38	5 09·5	5 10·3	4 55·4	3·8	1·3	9·8	3·3	15·8	5·4
39	5 09·8	5 10·6	4 55·6	3·9	1·3	9·9	3·4	15·9	5·4
40	5 10·0	5 10·8	4 55·9	4·0	1·4	10·0	3·4	16·0	5·5
41	5 10·3	5 11·1	4 56·1	4·1	1·4	10·1	3·5	16·1	5·5
42	5 10·5	5 11·4	4 56·4	4·2	1·4	10·2	3·5	16·2	5·5
43	5 10·8	5 11·6	4 56·6	4·3	1·5	10·3	3·5	16·3	5·6
44	5 11·0	5 11·9	4 56·8	4·4	1·5	10·4	3·6	16·4	5·6
45	5 11·3	5 12·1	4 57·1	4·5	1·5	10·5	3·6	16·5	5·6
46	5 11·5	5 12·4	4 57·3	4·6	1·6	10·6	3·6	16·6	5·7
47	5 11·8	5 12·6	4 57·5	4·7	1·6	10·7	3·7	16·7	5·7
48	5 12·0	5 12·9	4 57·8	4·8	1·6	10·8	3·7	16·8	5·7
49	5 12·3	5 13·1	4 58·0	4·9	1·7	10·9	3·7	16·9	5·8
50	5 12·5	5 13·4	4 58·3	5·0	1·7	11·0	3·8	17·0	5·8
51	5 12·8	5 13·6	4 58·5	5·1	1·7	11·1	3·8	17·1	5·8
52	5 13·0	5 13·9	4 58·7	5·2	1·8	11·2	3·8	17·2	5·9
53	5 13·3	5 14·1	4 59·0	5·3	1·8	11·3	3·9	17·3	5·9
54	5 13·5	5 14·4	4 59·2	5·4	1·8	11·4	3·9	17·4	5·9
55	5 13·8	5 14·6	4 59·5	5·5	1·9	11·5	3·9	17·5	6·0
56	5 14·0	5 14·9	4 59·7	5·6	1·9	11·6	4·0	17·6	6·0
57	5 14·3	5 15·1	4 59·9	5·7	1·9	11·7	4·0	17·7	6·0
58	5 14·5	5 15·4	5 00·2	5·8	2·0	11·8	4·0	17·8	6·1
59	5 14·8	5 15·6	5 00·4	5·9	2·0	11·9	4·1	17·9	6·1
60	5 15·0	5 15·9	5 00·7	6·0	2·1	12·0	4·1	18·0	6·2

21^m	SUN PLANETS	ARIES	MOON	*v* or *d*	Corr^n	*v* or *d*	Corr^n	*v* or *d*	Corr^n
s	° ′	° ′	° ′	′	′	′	′	′	′
00	5 15·0	5 15·9	5 00·7	0·0	0·0	6·0	2·2	12·0	4·3
01	5 15·3	5 16·1	5 00·9	0·1	0·0	6·1	2·2	12·1	4·3
02	5 15·5	5 16·4	5 01·1	0·2	0·1	6·2	2·2	12·2	4·4
03	5 15·8	5 16·6	5 01·4	0·3	0·1	6·3	2·3	12·3	4·4
04	5 16·0	5 16·9	5 01·6	0·4	0·1	6·4	2·3	12·4	4·4
05	5 16·3	5 17·1	5 01·8	0·5	0·2	6·5	2·3	12·5	4·5
06	5 16·5	5 17·4	5 02·1	0·6	0·2	6·6	2·4	12·6	4·5
07	5 16·8	5 17·6	5 02·3	0·7	0·3	6·7	2·4	12·7	4·6
08	5 17·0	5 17·9	5 02·6	0·8	0·3	6·8	2·4	12·8	4·6
09	5 17·3	5 18·1	5 02·8	0·9	0·3	6·9	2·5	12·9	4·6
10	5 17·5	5 18·4	5 03·0	1·0	0·4	7·0	2·5	13·0	4·7
11	5 17·8	5 18·6	5 03·3	1·1	0·4	7·1	2·5	13·1	4·7
12	5 18·0	5 18·9	5 03·5	1·2	0·4	7·2	2·6	13·2	4·7
13	5 18·3	5 19·1	5 03·8	1·3	0·5	7·3	2·6	13·3	4·8
14	5 18·5	5 19·4	5 04·0	1·4	0·5	7·4	2·7	13·4	4·8
15	5 18·8	5 19·6	5 04·2	1·5	0·5	7·5	2·7	13·5	4·8
16	5 19·0	5 19·9	5 04·5	1·6	0·6	7·6	2·7	13·6	4·9
17	5 19·3	5 20·1	5 04·7	1·7	0·6	7·7	2·8	13·7	4·9
18	5 19·5	5 20·4	5 04·9	1·8	0·6	7·8	2·8	13·8	4·9
19	5 19·8	5 20·6	5 05·2	1·9	0·7	7·9	2·8	13·9	5·0
20	5 20·0	5 20·9	5 05·4	2·0	0·7	8·0	2·9	14·0	5·0
21	5 20·3	5 21·1	5 05·7	2·1	0·8	8·1	2·9	14·1	5·1
22	5 20·5	5 21·4	5 05·9	2·2	0·8	8·2	2·9	14·2	5·1
23	5 20·8	5 21·6	5 06·1	2·3	0·8	8·3	3·0	14·3	5·1
24	5 21·0	5 21·9	5 06·4	2·4	0·9	8·4	3·0	14·4	5·2
25	5 21·3	5 22·1	5 06·6	2·5	0·9	8·5	3·0	14·5	5·2
26	5 21·5	5 22·4	5 06·9	2·6	0·9	8·6	3·1	14·6	5·2
27	5 21·8	5 22·6	5 07·1	2·7	1·0	8·7	3·1	14·7	5·3
28	5 22·0	5 22·9	5 07·3	2·8	1·0	8·8	3·2	14·8	5·3
29	5 22·3	5 23·1	5 07·6	2·9	1·0	8·9	3·2	14·9	5·3
30	5 22·5	5 23·4	5 07·8	3·0	1·1	9·0	3·2	15·0	5·4
31	5 22·8	5 23·6	5 08·0	3·1	1·1	9·1	3·3	15·1	5·4
32	5 23·0	5 23·9	5 08·3	3·2	1·1	9·2	3·3	15·2	5·4
33	5 23·3	5 24·1	5 08·5	3·3	1·2	9·3	3·3	15·3	5·5
34	5 23·5	5 24·4	5 08·8	3·4	1·2	9·4	3·4	15·4	5·5
35	5 23·8	5 24·6	5 09·0	3·5	1·3	9·5	3·4	15·5	5·6
36	5 24·0	5 24·9	5 09·2	3·6	1·3	9·6	3·4	15·6	5·6
37	5 24·3	5 25·1	5 09·5	3·7	1·3	9·7	3·5	15·7	5·6
38	5 24·5	5 25·4	5 09·7	3·8	1·4	9·8	3·5	15·8	5·7
39	5 24·8	5 25·6	5 10·0	3·9	1·4	9·9	3·5	15·9	5·7
40	5 25·0	5 25·9	5 10·2	4·0	1·4	10·0	3·6	16·0	5·7
41	5 25·3	5 26·1	5 10·4	4·1	1·5	10·1	3·6	16·1	5·8
42	5 25·5	5 26·4	5 10·7	4·2	1·5	10·2	3·7	16·2	5·8
43	5 25·8	5 26·6	5 10·9	4·3	1·5	10·3	3·7	16·3	5·8
44	5 26·0	5 26·9	5 11·1	4·4	1·6	10·4	3·7	16·4	5·9
45	5 26·3	5 27·1	5 11·4	4·5	1·6	10·5	3·8	16·5	5·9
46	5 26·5	5 27·4	5 11·6	4·6	1·6	10·6	3·8	16·6	5·9
47	5 26·8	5 27·6	5 11·9	4·7	1·7	10·7	3·8	16·7	6·0
48	5 27·0	5 27·9	5 12·1	4·8	1·7	10·8	3·9	16·8	6·0
49	5 27·3	5 28·1	5 12·3	4·9	1·8	10·9	3·9	16·9	6·1
50	5 27·5	5 28·4	5 12·6	5·0	1·8	11·0	3·9	17·0	6·1
51	5 27·8	5 28·6	5 12·8	5·1	1·8	11·1	4·0	17·1	6·1
52	5 28·0	5 28·9	5 13·1	5·2	1·9	11·2	4·0	17·2	6·2
53	5 28·3	5 29·1	5 13·3	5·3	1·9	11·3	4·0	17·3	6·2
54	5 28·5	5 29·4	5 13·5	5·4	1·9	11·4	4·1	17·4	6·2
55	5 28·8	5 29·7	5 13·8	5·5	2·0	11·5	4·1	17·5	6·3
56	5 29·0	5 29·9	5 14·0	5·6	2·0	11·6	4·2	17·6	6·3
57	5 29·3	5 30·2	5 14·3	5·7	2·0	11·7	4·2	17·7	6·3
58	5 29·5	5 30·4	5 14·5	5·8	2·1	11·8	4·2	17·8	6·4
59	5 29·8	5 30·7	5 14·7	5·9	2·1	11·9	4·3	17·9	6·4
60	5 30·0	5 30·9	5 15·0	6·0	2·2	12·0	4·3	18·0	6·5

22m s	SUN PLANETS ° ′	ARIES ° ′	MOON ° ′	v or d ′	Corrⁿ ′	v or d ′	Corrⁿ ′	v or d ′	Corrⁿ ′
00	5 30·0	5 30·9	5 15·0	0·0	0·0	6·0	2·3	12·0	4·5
01	5 30·3	5 31·2	5 15·2	0·1	0·0	6·1	2·3	12·1	4·5
02	5 30·5	5 31·4	5 15·4	0·2	0·1	6·2	2·3	12·2	4·6
03	5 30·8	5 31·7	5 15·7	0·3	0·1	6·3	2·4	12·3	4·6
04	5 31·0	5 31·9	5 15·9	0·4	0·2	6·4	2·4	12·4	4·7
05	5 31·3	5 32·2	5 16·2	0·5	0·2	6·5	2·4	12·5	4·7
06	5 31·5	5 32·4	5 16·4	0·6	0·2	6·6	2·5	12·6	4·7
07	5 31·8	5 32·7	5 16·6	0·7	0·3	6·7	2·5	12·7	4·8
08	5 32·0	5 32·9	5 16·9	0·8	0·3	6·8	2·6	12·8	4·8
09	5 32·3	5 33·2	5 17·1	0·9	0·3	6·9	2·6	12·9	4·8
10	5 32·5	5 33·4	5 17·4	1·0	0·4	7·0	2·6	13·0	4·9
11	5 32·8	5 33·7	5 17·6	1·1	0·4	7·1	2·7	13·1	4·9
12	5 33·0	5 33·9	5 17·8	1·2	0·5	7·2	2·7	13·2	5·0
13	5 33·3	5 34·2	5 18·1	1·3	0·5	7·3	2·7	13·3	5·0
14	5 33·5	5 34·4	5 18·3	1·4	0·5	7·4	2·8	13·4	5·0
15	5 33·8	5 34·7	5 18·5	1·5	0·6	7·5	2·8	13·5	5·1
16	5 34·0	5 34·9	5 18·8	1·6	0·6	7·6	2·9	13·6	5·1
17	5 34·3	5 35·2	5 19·0	1·7	0·6	7·7	2·9	13·7	5·1
18	5 34·5	5 35·4	5 19·3	1·8	0·7	7·8	2·9	13·8	5·2
19	5 34·8	5 35·7	5 19·5	1·9	0·7	7·9	3·0	13·9	5·2
20	5 35·0	5 35·9	5 19·7	2·0	0·8	8·0	3·0	14·0	5·3
21	5 35·3	5 36·2	5 20·0	2·1	0·8	8·1	3·0	14·1	5·3
22	5 35·5	5 36·4	5 20·2	2·2	0·8	8·2	3·1	14·2	5·3
23	5 35·8	5 36·7	5 20·5	2·3	0·9	8·3	3·1	14·3	5·4
24	5 36·0	5 36·9	5 20·7	2·4	0·9	8·4	3·2	14·4	5·4
25	5 36·3	5 37·2	5 20·9	2·5	0·9	8·5	3·2	14·5	5·4
26	5 36·5	5 37·4	5 21·2	2·6	1·0	8·6	3·2	14·6	5·5
27	5 36·8	5 37·7	5 21·4	2·7	1·0	8·7	3·3	14·7	5·5
28	5 37·0	5 37·9	5 21·6	2·8	1·0	8·8	3·3	14·8	5·6
29	5 37·3	5 38·2	5 21·9	2·9	1·1	8·9	3·3	14·9	5·6
30	5 37·5	5 38·4	5 22·1	3·0	1·1	9·0	3·4	15·0	5·6
31	5 37·8	5 38·7	5 22·4	3·1	1·2	9·1	3·4	15·1	5·7
32	5 38·0	5 38·9	5 22·6	3·2	1·2	9·2	3·5	15·2	5·7
33	5 38·3	5 39·2	5 22·8	3·3	1·2	9·3	3·5	15·3	5·7
34	5 38·5	5 39·4	5 23·1	3·4	1·3	9·4	3·5	15·4	5·8
35	5 38·8	5 39·7	5 23·3	3·5	1·3	9·5	3·6	15·5	5·8
36	5 39·0	5 39·9	5 23·6	3·6	1·4	9·6	3·6	15·6	5·9
37	5 39·3	5 40·2	5 23·8	3·7	1·4	9·7	3·6	15·7	5·9
38	5 39·5	5 40·4	5 24·0	3·8	1·4	9·8	3·7	15·8	5·9
39	5 39·8	5 40·7	5 24·3	3·9	1·5	9·9	3·7	15·9	6·0
40	5 40·0	5 40·9	5 24·5	4·0	1·5	10·0	3·8	16·0	6·0
41	5 40·3	5 41·2	5 24·7	4·1	1·5	10·1	3·8	16·1	6·0
42	5 40·5	5 41·4	5 25·0	4·2	1·6	10·2	3·8	16·2	6·1
43	5 40·8	5 41·7	5 25·2	4·3	1·6	10·3	3·9	16·3	6·1
44	5 41·0	5 41·9	5 25·5	4·4	1·7	10·4	3·9	16·4	6·1
45	5 41·3	5 42·2	5 25·7	4·5	1·7	10·5	3·9	16·5	6·2
46	5 41·5	5 42·4	5 25·9	4·6	1·7	10·6	4·0	16·6	6·2
47	5 41·8	5 42·7	5 26·2	4·7	1·8	10·7	4·0	16·7	6·3
48	5 42·0	5 42·9	5 26·4	4·8	1·8	10·8	4·1	16·8	6·3
49	5 42·3	5 43·2	5 26·7	4·9	1·8	10·9	4·1	16·9	6·3
50	5 42·5	5 43·4	5 26·9	5·0	1·9	11·0	4·1	17·0	6·4
51	5 42·8	5 43·7	5 27·1	5·1	1·9	11·1	4·2	17·1	6·4
52	5 43·0	5 43·9	5 27·4	5·2	2·0	11·2	4·2	17·2	6·5
53	5 43·3	5 44·2	5 27·6	5·3	2·0	11·3	4·2	17·3	6·5
54	5 43·5	5 44·4	5 27·9	5·4	2·0	11·4	4·3	17·4	6·5
55	5 43·8	5 44·7	5 28·1	5·5	2·1	11·5	4·3	17·5	6·6
56	5 44·0	5 44·9	5 28·3	5·6	2·1	11·6	4·4	17·6	6·6
57	5 44·3	5 45·2	5 28·6	5·7	2·1	11·7	4·4	17·7	6·6
58	5 44·5	5 45·4	5 28·8	5·8	2·2	11·8	4·4	17·8	6·7
59	5 44·8	5 45·7	5 29·0	5·9	2·2	11·9	4·5	17·9	6·7
60	5 45·0	5 45·9	5 29·3	6·0	2·3	12·0	4·5	18·0	6·8

23m s	SUN PLANETS ° ′	ARIES ° ′	MOON ° ′	v or d ′	Corrⁿ ′	v or d ′	Corrⁿ ′	v or d ′	Corrⁿ ′
00	5 45·0	5 45·9	5 29·3	0·0	0·0	6·0	2·4	12·0	4·7
01	5 45·3	5 46·2	5 29·5	0·1	0·0	6·1	2·4	12·1	4·7
02	5 45·5	5 46·4	5 29·8	0·2	0·1	6·2	2·4	12·2	4·8
03	5 45·8	5 46·7	5 30·0	0·3	0·1	6·3	2·5	12·3	4·8
04	5 46·0	5 46·9	5 30·2	0·4	0·2	6·4	2·5	12·4	4·9
05	5 46·3	5 47·2	5 30·5	0·5	0·2	6·5	2·5	12·5	4·9
06	5 46·5	5 47·4	5 30·7	0·6	0·2	6·6	2·6	12·6	4·9
07	5 46·8	5 47·7	5 31·0	0·7	0·3	6·7	2·6	12·7	5·0
08	5 47·0	5 48·0	5 31·2	0·8	0·3	6·8	2·7	12·8	5·0
09	5 47·3	5 48·2	5 31·4	0·9	0·4	6·9	2·7	12·9	5·1
10	5 47·5	5 48·5	5 31·7	1·0	0·4	7·0	2·7	13·0	5·1
11	5 47·8	5 48·7	5 31·9	1·1	0·4	7·1	2·8	13·1	5·1
12	5 48·0	5 49·0	5 32·1	1·2	0·5	7·2	2·8	13·2	5·2
13	5 48·3	5 49·2	5 32·4	1·3	0·5	7·3	2·9	13·3	5·2
14	5 48·5	5 49·5	5 32·6	1·4	0·5	7·4	2·9	13·4	5·2
15	5 48·8	5 49·7	5 32·9	1·5	0·6	7·5	2·9	13·5	5·3
16	5 49·0	5 50·0	5 33·1	1·6	0·6	7·6	3·0	13·6	5·3
17	5 49·3	5 50·2	5 33·3	1·7	0·7	7·7	3·0	13·7	5·4
18	5 49·5	5 50·5	5 33·6	1·8	0·7	7·8	3·1	13·8	5·4
19	5 49·8	5 50·7	5 33·8	1·9	0·7	7·9	3·1	13·9	5·4
20	5 50·0	5 51·0	5 34·1	2·0	0·8	8·0	3·1	14·0	5·5
21	5 50·3	5 51·2	5 34·3	2·1	0·8	8·1	3·2	14·1	5·5
22	5 50·5	5 51·5	5 34·5	2·2	0·9	8·2	3·2	14·2	5·6
23	5 50·8	5 51·7	5 34·8	2·3	0·9	8·3	3·3	14·3	5·6
24	5 51·0	5 52·0	5 35·0	2·4	0·9	8·4	3·3	14·4	5·6
25	5 51·3	5 52·2	5 35·2	2·5	1·0	8·5	3·3	14·5	5·7
26	5 51·5	5 52·5	5 35·5	2·6	1·0	8·6	3·4	14·6	5·7
27	5 51·8	5 52·7	5 35·7	2·7	1·1	8·7	3·4	14·7	5·8
28	5 52·0	5 53·0	5 36·0	2·8	1·1	8·8	3·4	14·8	5·8
29	5 52·3	5 53·2	5 36·2	2·9	1·1	8·9	3·5	14·9	5·8
30	5 52·5	5 53·5	5 36·4	3·0	1·2	9·0	3·5	15·0	5·9
31	5 52·8	5 53·7	5 36·7	3·1	1·2	9·1	3·6	15·1	5·9
32	5 53·0	5 54·0	5 36·9	3·2	1·3	9·2	3·6	15·2	6·0
33	5 53·3	5 54·2	5 37·2	3·3	1·3	9·3	3·6	15·3	6·0
34	5 53·5	5 54·5	5 37·4	3·4	1·3	9·4	3·7	15·4	6·0
35	5 53·8	5 54·7	5 37·6	3·5	1·4	9·5	3·7	15·5	6·1
36	5 54·0	5 55·0	5 37·9	3·6	1·4	9·6	3·8	15·6	6·1
37	5 54·3	5 55·2	5 38·1	3·7	1·4	9·7	3·8	15·7	6·1
38	5 54·5	5 55·5	5 38·4	3·8	1·5	9·8	3·8	15·8	6·2
39	5 54·8	5 55·7	5 38·6	3·9	1·5	9·9	3·9	15·9	6·2
40	5 55·0	5 56·0	5 38·8	4·0	1·6	10·0	3·9	16·0	6·3
41	5 55·3	5 56·2	5 39·1	4·1	1·6	10·1	4·0	16·1	6·3
42	5 55·5	5 56·5	5 39·3	4·2	1·6	10·2	4·0	16·2	6·3
43	5 55·8	5 56·7	5 39·5	4·3	1·7	10·3	4·0	16·3	6·4
44	5 56·0	5 57·0	5 39·8	4·4	1·7	10·4	4·1	16·4	6·4
45	5 56·3	5 57·2	5 40·0	4·5	1·8	10·5	4·1	16·5	6·5
46	5 56·5	5 57·5	5 40·3	4·6	1·8	10·6	4·2	16·6	6·5
47	5 56·8	5 57·7	5 40·5	4·7	1·8	10·7	4·2	16·7	6·5
48	5 57·0	5 58·0	5 40·7	4·8	1·9	10·8	4·2	16·8	6·6
49	5 57·3	5 58·2	5 41·0	4·9	1·9	10·9	4·3	16·9	6·6
50	5 57·5	5 58·5	5 41·2	5·0	2·0	11·0	4·3	17·0	6·7
51	5 57·8	5 58·7	5 41·5	5·1	2·0	11·1	4·3	17·1	6·7
52	5 58·0	5 59·0	5 41·7	5·2	2·0	11·2	4·4	17·2	6·7
53	5 58·3	5 59·2	5 41·9	5·3	2·1	11·3	4·4	17·3	6·8
54	5 58·5	5 59·5	5 42·2	5·4	2·1	11·4	4·5	17·4	6·8
55	5 58·8	5 59·7	5 42·4	5·5	2·2	11·5	4·5	17·5	6·9
56	5 59·0	6 00·0	5 42·6	5·6	2·2	11·6	4·5	17·6	6·9
57	5 59·3	6 00·2	5 42·9	5·7	2·2	11·7	4·6	17·7	6·9
58	5 59·5	6 00·5	5 43·1	5·8	2·3	11·8	4·6	17·8	7·0
59	5 59·8	6 00·7	5 43·4	5·9	2·3	11·9	4·7	17·9	7·0
60	6 00·0	6 01·0	5 43·6	6·0	2·4	12·0	4·7	18·0	7·1

24m s	SUN PLANETS ° ′	ARIES ° ′	MOON ° ′	v or d ′	Corrn ′	v or d ′	Corrn ′	v or d ′	Corrn ′
00	6 00·0	6 01·0	5 43·6	0·0	0·0	6·0	2·5	12·0	4·9
01	6 00·3	6 01·2	5 43·8	0·1	0·0	6·1	2·5	12·1	4·9
02	6 00·5	6 01·5	5 44·1	0·2	0·1	6·2	2·5	12·2	5·0
03	6 00·8	6 01·7	5 44·3	0·3	0·1	6·3	2·6	12·3	5·0
04	6 01·0	6 02·0	5 44·6	0·4	0·2	6·4	2·6	12·4	5·1
05	6 01·3	6 02·2	5 44·8	0·5	0·2	6·5	2·7	12·5	5·1
06	6 01·5	6 02·5	5 45·0	0·6	0·2	6·6	2·7	12·6	5·1
07	6 01·8	6 02·7	5 45·3	0·7	0·3	6·7	2·7	12·7	5·2
08	6 02·0	6 03·0	5 45·5	0·8	0·3	6·8	2·8	12·8	5·2
09	6 02·3	6 03·2	5 45·7	0·9	0·4	6·9	2·8	12·9	5·3
10	6 02·5	6 03·5	5 46·0	1·0	0·4	7·0	2·9	13·0	5·3
11	6 02·8	6 03·7	5 46·2	1·1	0·4	7·1	2·9	13·1	5·3
12	6 03·0	6 04·0	5 46·5	1·2	0·5	7·2	2·9	13·2	5·4
13	6 03·3	6 04·2	5 46·7	1·3	0·5	7·3	3·0	13·3	5·4
14	6 03·5	6 04·5	5 46·9	1·4	0·6	7·4	3·0	13·4	5·5
15	6 03·8	6 04·7	5 47·2	1·5	0·6	7·5	3·1	13·5	5·5
16	6 04·0	6 05·0	5 47·4	1·6	0·7	7·6	3·1	13·6	5·6
17	6 04·3	6 05·2	5 47·7	1·7	0·7	7·7	3·1	13·7	5·6
18	6 04·5	6 05·5	5 47·9	1·8	0·7	7·8	3·2	13·8	5·6
19	6 04·8	6 05·7	5 48·1	1·9	0·8	7·9	3·2	13·9	5·7
20	6 05·0	6 06·0	5 48·4	2·0	0·8	8·0	3·3	14·0	5·7
21	6 05·3	6 06·3	5 48·6	2·1	0·9	8·1	3·3	14·1	5·8
22	6 05·5	6 06·5	5 48·8	2·2	0·9	8·2	3·3	14·2	5·8
23	6 05·8	6 06·8	5 49·1	2·3	0·9	8·3	3·4	14·3	5·8
24	6 06·0	6 07·0	5 49·3	2·4	1·0	8·4	3·4	14·4	5·9
25	6 06·3	6 07·3	5 49·6	2·5	1·0	8·5	3·5	14·5	5·9
26	6 06·5	6 07·5	5 49·8	2·6	1·1	8·6	3·5	14·6	6·0
27	6 06·8	6 07·8	5 50·0	2·7	1·1	8·7	3·6	14·7	6·0
28	6 07·0	6 08·0	5 50·3	2·8	1·1	8·8	3·6	14·8	6·0
29	6 07·3	6 08·3	5 50·5	2·9	1·2	8·9	3·6	14·9	6·1
30	6 07·5	6 08·5	5 50·8	3·0	1·2	9·0	3·7	15·0	6·1
31	6 07·8	6 08·8	5 51·0	3·1	1·3	9·1	3·7	15·1	6·2
32	6 08·0	6 09·0	5 51·2	3·2	1·3	9·2	3·8	15·2	6·2
33	6 08·3	6 09·3	5 51·5	3·3	1·3	9·3	3·8	15·3	6·2
34	6 08·5	6 09·5	5 51·7	3·4	1·4	9·4	3·8	15·4	6·3
35	6 08·8	6 09·8	5 52·0	3·5	1·4	9·5	3·9	15·5	6·3
36	6 09·0	6 10·0	5 52·2	3·6	1·5	9·6	3·9	15·6	6·4
37	6 09·3	6 10·3	5 52·4	3·7	1·5	9·7	4·0	15·7	6·4
38	6 09·5	6 10·5	5 52·7	3·8	1·6	9·8	4·0	15·8	6·5
39	6 09·8	6 10·8	5 52·9	3·9	1·6	9·9	4·0	15·9	6·5
40	6 10·0	6 11·0	5 53·1	4·0	1·6	10·0	4·1	16·0	6·5
41	6 10·3	6 11·3	5 53·4	4·1	1·7	10·1	4·1	16·1	6·6
42	6 10·5	6 11·5	5 53·6	4·2	1·7	10·2	4·2	16·2	6·6
43	6 10·8	6 11·8	5 53·9	4·3	1·8	10·3	4·2	16·3	6·7
44	6 11·0	6 12·0	5 54·1	4·4	1·8	10·4	4·2	16·4	6·7
45	6 11·3	6 12·3	5 54·3	4·5	1·8	10·5	4·3	16·5	6·7
46	6 11·5	6 12·5	5 54·6	4·6	1·9	10·6	4·3	16·6	6·8
47	6 11·8	6 12·8	5 54·8	4·7	1·9	10·7	4·4	16·7	6·8
48	6 12·0	6 13·0	5 55·1	4·8	2·0	10·8	4·4	16·8	6·9
49	6 12·3	6 13·3	5 55·3	4·9	2·0	10·9	4·5	16·9	6·9
50	6 12·5	6 13·5	5 55·5	5·0	2·0	11·0	4·5	17·0	6·9
51	6 12·8	6 13·8	5 55·8	5·1	2·1	11·1	4·5	17·1	7·0
52	6 13·0	6 14·0	5 56·0	5·2	2·1	11·2	4·6	17·2	7·0
53	6 13·3	6 14·3	5 56·2	5·3	2·2	11·3	4·6	17·3	7·1
54	6 13·5	6 14·5	5 56·5	5·4	2·2	11·4	4·7	17·4	7·1
55	6 13·8	6 14·8	5 56·7	5·5	2·2	11·5	4·7	17·5	7·1
56	6 14·0	6 15·0	5 57·0	5·6	2·3	11·6	4·7	17·6	7·2
57	6 14·3	6 15·3	5 57·2	5·7	2·3	11·7	4·8	17·7	7·2
58	6 14·5	6 15·5	5 57·4	5·8	2·4	11·8	4·8	17·8	7·3
59	6 14·8	6 15·8	5 57·7	5·9	2·4	11·9	4·9	17·9	7·3
60	6 15·0	6 16·0	5 57·9	6·0	2·5	12·0	4·9	18·0	7·4

25m s	SUN PLANETS ° ′	ARIES ° ′	MOON ° ′	v or d ′	Corrn ′	v or d ′	Corrn ′	v or d ′	Corrn ′
00	6 15·0	6 16·0	5 57·9	0·0	0·0	6·0	2·6	12·0	5·1
01	6 15·3	6 16·3	5 58·2	0·1	0·0	6·1	2·6	12·1	5·1
02	6 15·5	6 16·5	5 58·4	0·2	0·1	6·2	2·6	12·2	5·2
03	6 15·8	6 16·8	5 58·6	0·3	0·1	6·3	2·7	12·3	5·2
04	6 16·0	6 17·0	5 58·9	0·4	0·2	6·4	2·7	12·4	5·3
05	6 16·3	6 17·3	5 59·1	0·5	0·2	6·5	2·8	12·5	5·3
06	6 16·5	6 17·5	5 59·3	0·6	0·3	6·6	2·8	12·6	5·4
07	6 16·8	6 17·8	5 59·6	0·7	0·3	6·7	2·8	12·7	5·4
08	6 17·0	6 18·0	5 59·8	0·8	0·3	6·8	2·9	12·8	5·4
09	6 17·3	6 18·3	6 00·1	0·9	0·4	6·9	2·9	12·9	5·5
10	6 17·5	6 18·5	6 00·3	1·0	0·4	7·0	3·0	13·0	5·5
11	6 17·8	6 18·8	6 00·5	1·1	0·5	7·1	3·0	13·1	5·6
12	6 18·0	6 19·0	6 00·8	1·2	0·5	7·2	3·1	13·2	5·6
13	6 18·3	6 19·3	6 01·0	1·3	0·6	7·3	3·1	13·3	5·7
14	6 18·5	6 19·5	6 01·3	1·4	0·6	7·4	3·1	13·4	5·7
15	6 18·8	6 19·8	6 01·5	1·5	0·6	7·5	3·2	13·5	5·7
16	6 19·0	6 20·0	6 01·7	1·6	0·7	7·6	3·2	13·6	5·8
17	6 19·3	6 20·3	6 02·0	1·7	0·7	7·7	3·3	13·7	5·8
18	6 19·5	6 20·5	6 02·2	1·8	0·8	7·8	3·3	13·8	5·9
19	6 19·8	6 20·8	6 02·5	1·9	0·8	7·9	3·4	13·9	5·9
20	6 20·0	6 21·0	6 02·7	2·0	0·9	8·0	3·4	14·0	6·0
21	6 20·3	6 21·3	6 02·9	2·1	0·9	8·1	3·4	14·1	6·0
22	6 20·5	6 21·5	6 03·2	2·2	0·9	8·2	3·5	14·2	6·0
23	6 20·8	6 21·8	6 03·4	2·3	1·0	8·3	3·5	14·3	6·1
24	6 21·0	6 22·0	6 03·6	2·4	1·0	8·4	3·6	14·4	6·1
25	6 21·3	6 22·3	6 03·9	2·5	1·1	8·5	3·6	14·5	6·2
26	6 21·5	6 22·5	6 04·1	2·6	1·1	8·6	3·7	14·6	6·2
27	6 21·8	6 22·8	6 04·4	2·7	1·1	8·7	3·7	14·7	6·2
28	6 22·0	6 23·0	6 04·6	2·8	1·2	8·8	3·7	14·8	6·3
29	6 22·3	6 23·3	6 04·8	2·9	1·2	8·9	3·8	14·9	6·3
30	6 22·5	6 23·5	6 05·1	3·0	1·3	9·0	3·8	15·0	6·4
31	6 22·8	6 23·8	6 05·3	3·1	1·3	9·1	3·9	15·1	6·4
32	6 23·0	6 24·0	6 05·6	3·2	1·4	9·2	3·9	15·2	6·5
33	6 23·3	6 24·3	6 05·8	3·3	1·4	9·3	4·0	15·3	6·5
34	6 23·5	6 24·5	6 06·0	3·4	1·4	9·4	4·0	15·4	6·5
35	6 23·8	6 24·8	6 06·3	3·5	1·5	9·5	4·0	15·5	6·6
36	6 24·0	6 25·1	6 06·5	3·6	1·5	9·6	4·1	15·6	6·6
37	6 24·3	6 25·3	6 06·7	3·7	1·6	9·7	4·1	15·7	6·7
38	6 24·5	6 25·6	6 07·0	3·8	1·6	9·8	4·2	15·8	6·7
39	6 24·8	6 25·8	6 07·2	3·9	1·7	9·9	4·2	15·9	6·8
40	6 25·0	6 26·1	6 07·5	4·0	1·7	10·0	4·3	16·0	6·8
41	6 25·3	6 26·3	6 07·7	4·1	1·7	10·1	4·3	16·1	6·8
42	6 25·5	6 26·6	6 07·9	4·2	1·8	10·2	4·3	16·2	6·9
43	6 25·8	6 26·8	6 08·2	4·3	1·8	10·3	4·4	16·3	6·9
44	6 26·0	6 27·1	6 08·4	4·4	1·9	10·4	4·4	16·4	7·0
45	6 26·3	6 27·3	6 08·7	4·5	1·9	10·5	4·5	16·5	7·0
46	6 26·5	6 27·6	6 08·9	4·6	2·0	10·6	4·5	16·6	7·1
47	6 26·8	6 27·8	6 09·1	4·7	2·0	10·7	4·5	16·7	7·1
48	6 27·0	6 28·1	6 09·4	4·8	2·0	10·8	4·6	16·8	7·1
49	6 27·3	6 28·3	6 09·6	4·9	2·1	10·9	4·6	16·9	7·2
50	6 27·5	6 28·6	6 09·8	5·0	2·1	11·0	4·7	17·0	7·2
51	6 27·8	6 28·8	6 10·1	5·1	2·2	11·1	4·7	17·1	7·3
52	6 28·0	6 29·1	6 10·3	5·2	2·2	11·2	4·8	17·2	7·3
53	6 28·3	6 29·3	6 10·6	5·3	2·3	11·3	4·8	17·3	7·4
54	6 28·5	6 29·6	6 10·8	5·4	2·3	11·4	4·8	17·4	7·4
55	6 28·8	6 29·8	6 11·0	5·5	2·3	11·5	4·9	17·5	7·4
56	6 29·0	6 30·1	6 11·3	5·6	2·4	11·6	4·9	17·6	7·5
57	6 29·3	6 30·3	6 11·5	5·7	2·4	11·7	5·0	17·7	7·5
58	6 29·5	6 30·6	6 11·8	5·8	2·5	11·8	5·0	17·8	7·6
59	6 29·8	6 30·8	6 12·0	5·9	2·5	11·9	5·1	17·9	7·6
60	6 30·0	6 31·1	6 12·2	6·0	2·6	12·0	5·1	18·0	7·7

26m s	SUN PLANETS ° ′	ARIES ° ′	MOON ° ′	v or d ′	Corrⁿ ′	v or d ′	Corrⁿ ′	v or d ′	Corrⁿ ′
00	6 30·0	6 31·1	6 12·2	0·0	0·0	6·0	2·7	12·0	5·3
01	6 30·3	6 31·3	6 12·5	0·1	0·0	6·1	2·7	12·1	5·3
02	6 30·5	6 31·6	6 12·7	0·2	0·1	6·2	2·7	12·2	5·4
03	6 30·8	6 31·8	6 12·9	0·3	0·1	6·3	2·8	12·3	5·4
04	6 31·0	6 32·1	6 13·2	0·4	0·2	6·4	2·8	12·4	5·5
05	6 31·3	6 32·3	6 13·4	0·5	0·2	6·5	2·9	12·5	5·5
06	6 31·5	6 32·6	6 13·7	0·6	0·3	6·6	2·9	12·6	5·6
07	6 31·8	6 32·8	6 13·9	0·7	0·3	6·7	3·0	12·7	5·6
08	6 32·0	6 33·1	6 14·1	0·8	0·4	6·8	3·0	12·8	5·7
09	6 32·3	6 33·3	6 14·4	0·9	0·4	6·9	3·0	12·9	5·7
10	6 32·5	6 33·6	6 14·6	1·0	0·4	7·0	3·1	13·0	5·7
11	6 32·8	6 33·8	6 14·9	1·1	0·5	7·1	3·1	13·1	5·8
12	6 33·0	6 34·1	6 15·1	1·2	0·5	7·2	3·2	13·2	5·8
13	6 33·3	6 34·3	6 15·3	1·3	0·6	7·3	3·2	13·3	5·9
14	6 33·5	6 34·6	6 15·6	1·4	0·6	7·4	3·3	13·4	5·9
15	6 33·8	6 34·8	6 15·8	1·5	0·7	7·5	3·3	13·5	6·0
16	6 34·0	6 35·1	6 16·1	1·6	0·7	7·6	3·4	13·6	6·0
17	6 34·3	6 35·3	6 16·3	1·7	0·8	7·7	3·4	13·7	6·1
18	6 34·5	6 35·6	6 16·5	1·8	0·8	7·8	3·4	13·8	6·1
19	6 34·8	6 35·8	6 16·8	1·9	0·8	7·9	3·5	13·9	6·1
20	6 35·0	6 36·1	6 17·0	2·0	0·9	8·0	3·5	14·0	6·2
21	6 35·3	6 36·3	6 17·2	2·1	0·9	8·1	3·6	14·1	6·2
22	6 35·5	6 36·6	6 17·5	2·2	1·0	8·2	3·6	14·2	6·3
23	6 35·8	6 36·8	6 17·7	2·3	1·0	8·3	3·7	14·3	6·3
24	6 36·0	6 37·1	6 18·0	2·4	1·1	8·4	3·7	14·4	6·4
25	6 36·3	6 37·3	6 18·2	2·5	1·1	8·5	3·8	14·5	6·4
26	6 36·5	6 37·6	6 18·4	2·6	1·1	8·6	3·8	14·6	6·4
27	6 36·8	6 37·8	6 18·7	2·7	1·2	8·7	3·8	14·7	6·5
28	6 37·0	6 38·1	6 18·9	2·8	1·2	8·8	3·9	14·8	6·5
29	6 37·3	6 38·3	6 19·2	2·9	1·3	8·9	3·9	14·9	6·6
30	6 37·5	6 38·6	6 19·4	3·0	1·3	9·0	4·0	15·0	6·6
31	6 37·8	6 38·8	6 19·6	3·1	1·4	9·1	4·0	15·1	6·7
32	6 38·0	6 39·1	6 19·9	3·2	1·4	9·2	4·1	15·2	6·7
33	6 38·3	6 39·3	6 20·1	3·3	1·5	9·3	4·1	15·3	6·8
34	6 38·5	6 39·6	6 20·3	3·4	1·5	9·4	4·2	15·4	6·8
35	6 38·8	6 39·8	6 20·6	3·5	1·5	9·5	4·2	15·5	6·8
36	6 39·0	6 40·1	6 20·8	3·6	1·6	9·6	4·2	15·6	6·9
37	6 39·3	6 40·3	6 21·1	3·7	1·6	9·7	4·3	15·7	6·9
38	6 39·5	6 40·6	6 21·3	3·8	1·7	9·8	4·3	15·8	7·0
39	6 39·8	6 40·8	6 21·5	3·9	1·7	9·9	4·4	15·9	7·0
40	6 40·0	6 41·1	6 21·8	4·0	1·8	10·0	4·4	16·0	7·1
41	6 40·3	6 41·3	6 22·0	4·1	1·8	10·1	4·5	16·1	7·1
42	6 40·5	6 41·6	6 22·3	4·2	1·9	10·2	4·5	16·2	7·2
43	6 40·8	6 41·8	6 22·5	4·3	1·9	10·3	4·5	16·3	7·2
44	6 41·0	6 42·1	6 22·7	4·4	1·9	10·4	4·6	16·4	7·2
45	6 41·3	6 42·3	6 23·0	4·5	2·0	10·5	4·6	16·5	7·3
46	6 41·5	6 42·6	6 23·2	4·6	2·0	10·6	4·7	16·6	7·3
47	6 41·8	6 42·8	6 23·4	4·7	2·1	10·7	4·7	16·7	7·4
48	6 42·0	6 43·1	6 23·7	4·8	2·1	10·8	4·8	16·8	7·4
49	6 42·3	6 43·4	6 23·9	4·9	2·2	10·9	4·8	16·9	7·5
50	6 42·5	6 43·6	6 24·2	5·0	2·2	11·0	4·9	17·0	7·5
51	6 42·8	6 43·9	6 24·4	5·1	2·3	11·1	4·9	17·1	7·6
52	6 43·0	6 44·1	6 24·6	5·2	2·3	11·2	4·9	17·2	7·6
53	6 43·3	6 44·4	6 24·9	5·3	2·3	11·3	5·0	17·3	7·6
54	6 43·5	6 44·6	6 25·1	5·4	2·4	11·4	5·0	17·4	7·7
55	6 43·8	6 44·9	6 25·4	5·5	2·4	11·5	5·1	17·5	7·7
56	6 44·0	6 45·1	6 25·6	5·6	2·5	11·6	5·1	17·6	7·8
57	6 44·3	6 45·4	6 25·8	5·7	2·5	11·7	5·2	17·7	7·8
58	6 44·5	6 45·6	6 26·1	5·8	2·6	11·8	5·2	17·8	7·9
59	6 44·8	6 45·9	6 26·3	5·9	2·6	11·9	5·3	17·9	7·9
60	6 45·0	6 46·1	6 26·6	6·0	2·7	12·0	5·3	18·0	8·0

27m s	SUN PLANETS ° ′	ARIES ° ′	MOON ° ′	v or d ′	Corrⁿ ′	v or d ′	Corrⁿ ′	v or d ′	Corrⁿ ′
00	6 45·0	6 46·1	6 26·6	0·0	0·0	6·0	2·8	12·0	5·5
01	6 45·3	6 46·4	6 26·8	0·1	0·0	6·1	2·8	12·1	5·5
02	6 45·5	6 46·6	6 27·0	0·2	0·1	6·2	2·8	12·2	5·6
03	6 45·8	6 46·9	6 27·3	0·3	0·1	6·3	2·9	12·3	5·6
04	6 46·0	6 47·1	6 27·5	0·4	0·2	6·4	2·9	12·4	5·7
05	6 46·3	6 47·4	6 27·7	0·5	0·2	6·5	3·0	12·5	5·7
06	6 46·5	6 47·6	6 28·0	0·6	0·3	6·6	3·0	12·6	5·8
07	6 46·8	6 47·9	6 28·2	0·7	0·3	6·7	3·1	12·7	5·8
08	6 47·0	6 48·1	6 28·5	0·8	0·4	6·8	3·1	12·8	5·9
09	6 47·3	6 48·4	6 28·7	0·9	0·4	6·9	3·2	12·9	5·9
10	6 47·5	6 48·6	6 28·9	1·0	0·5	7·0	3·2	13·0	6·0
11	6 47·8	6 48·9	6 29·2	1·1	0·5	7·1	3·3	13·1	6·0
12	6 48·0	6 49·1	6 29·4	1·2	0·6	7·2	3·3	13·2	6·1
13	6 48·3	6 49·4	6 29·7	1·3	0·6	7·3	3·3	13·3	6·1
14	6 48·5	6 49·6	6 29·9	1·4	0·6	7·4	3·4	13·4	6·1
15	6 48·8	6 49·9	6 30·1	1·5	0·7	7·5	3·4	13·5	6·2
16	6 49·0	6 50·1	6 30·4	1·6	0·7	7·6	3·5	13·6	6·2
17	6 49·3	6 50·4	6 30·6	1·7	0·8	7·7	3·5	13·7	6·3
18	6 49·5	6 50·6	6 30·8	1·8	0·8	7·8	3·6	13·8	6·3
19	6 49·8	6 50·9	6 31·1	1·9	0·9	7·9	3·6	13·9	6·4
20	6 50·0	6 51·1	6 31·3	2·0	0·9	8·0	3·7	14·0	6·4
21	6 50·3	6 51·4	6 31·6	2·1	1·0	8·1	3·7	14·1	6·5
22	6 50·5	6 51·6	6 31·8	2·2	1·0	8·2	3·8	14·2	6·5
23	6 50·8	6 51·9	6 32·0	2·3	1·1	8·3	3·8	14·3	6·6
24	6 51·0	6 52·1	6 32·3	2·4	1·1	8·4	3·9	14·4	6·6
25	6 51·3	6 52·4	6 32·5	2·5	1·1	8·5	3·9	14·5	6·6
26	6 51·5	6 52·6	6 32·8	2·6	1·2	8·6	3·9	14·6	6·7
27	6 51·8	6 52·9	6 33·0	2·7	1·2	8·7	4·0	14·7	6·7
28	6 52·0	6 53·1	6 33·2	2·8	1·3	8·8	4·0	14·8	6·8
29	6 52·3	6 53·4	6 33·5	2·9	1·3	8·9	4·1	14·9	6·8
30	6 52·5	6 53·6	6 33·7	3·0	1·4	9·0	4·1	15·0	6·9
31	6 52·8	6 53·9	6 33·9	3·1	1·4	9·1	4·2	15·1	6·9
32	6 53·0	6 54·1	6 34·2	3·2	1·5	9·2	4·2	15·2	7·0
33	6 53·3	6 54·4	6 34·4	3·3	1·5	9·3	4·3	15·3	7·0
34	6 53·5	6 54·6	6 34·7	3·4	1·6	9·4	4·3	15·4	7·1
35	6 53·8	6 54·9	6 34·9	3·5	1·6	9·5	4·4	15·5	7·1
36	6 54·0	6 55·1	6 35·1	3·6	1·7	9·6	4·4	15·6	7·2
37	6 54·3	6 55·4	6 35·4	3·7	1·7	9·7	4·4	15·7	7·2
38	6 54·5	6 55·6	6 35·6	3·8	1·7	9·8	4·5	15·8	7·2
39	6 54·8	6 55·9	6 35·9	3·9	1·8	9·9	4·5	15·9	7·3
40	6 55·0	6 56·1	6 36·1	4·0	1·8	10·0	4·6	16·0	7·3
41	6 55·3	6 56·4	6 36·3	4·1	1·9	10·1	4·6	16·1	7·4
42	6 55·5	6 56·6	6 36·6	4·2	1·9	10·2	4·7	16·2	7·4
43	6 55·8	6 56·9	6 36·8	4·3	2·0	10·3	4·7	16·3	7·5
44	6 56·0	6 57·1	6 37·0	4·4	2·0	10·4	4·8	16·4	7·5
45	6 56·3	6 57·4	6 37·3	4·5	2·1	10·5	4·8	16·5	7·6
46	6 56·5	6 57·6	6 37·5	4·6	2·1	10·6	4·9	16·6	7·6
47	6 56·8	6 57·9	6 37·8	4·7	2·2	10·7	4·9	16·7	7·7
48	6 57·0	6 58·1	6 38·0	4·8	2·2	10·8	5·0	16·8	7·7
49	6 57·3	6 58·4	6 38·2	4·9	2·2	10·9	5·0	16·9	7·7
50	6 57·5	6 58·6	6 38·5	5·0	2·3	11·0	5·0	17·0	7·8
51	6 57·8	6 58·9	6 38·7	5·1	2·3	11·1	5·1	17·1	7·8
52	6 58·0	6 59·1	6 39·0	5·2	2·4	11·2	5·1	17·2	7·9
53	6 58·3	6 59·4	6 39·2	5·3	2·4	11·3	5·2	17·3	7·9
54	6 58·5	6 59·6	6 39·4	5·4	2·5	11·4	5·2	17·4	8·0
55	6 58·8	6 59·9	6 39·7	5·5	2·5	11·5	5·3	17·5	8·0
56	6 59·0	7 00·1	6 39·9	5·6	2·6	11·6	5·3	17·6	8·1
57	6 59·3	7 00·4	6 40·2	5·7	2·6	11·7	5·4	17·7	8·1
58	6 59·5	7 00·6	6 40·4	5·8	2·7	11·8	5·4	17·8	8·2
59	6 59·8	7 00·9	6 40·6	5·9	2·7	11·9	5·5	17·9	8·2
60	7 00·0	7 01·1	6 40·9	6·0	2·8	12·0	5·5	18·0	8·3

28m	SUN PLANETS	ARIES	MOON	v or d	Corrn	v or d	Corrn	v or d	Corrn
s	° ′	° ′	° ′	′	′	′	′	′	′
00	7 00·0	7 01·1	6 40·9	0·0	0·0	6·0	2·9	12·0	5·7
01	7 00·3	7 01·4	6 41·1	0·1	0·0	6·1	2·9	12·1	5·7
02	7 00·5	7 01·7	6 41·3	0·2	0·1	6·2	2·9	12·2	5·8
03	7 00·8	7 01·9	6 41·6	0·3	0·1	6·3	3·0	12·3	5·8
04	7 01·0	7 02·2	6 41·8	0·4	0·2	6·4	3·0	12·4	5·9
05	7 01·3	7 02·4	6 42·1	0·5	0·2	6·5	3·1	12·5	5·9
06	7 01·5	7 02·7	6 42·3	0·6	0·3	6·6	3·1	12·6	6·0
07	7 01·8	7 02·9	6 42·5	0·7	0·3	6·7	3·2	12·7	6·0
08	7 02·0	7 03·2	6 42·8	0·8	0·4	6·8	3·2	12·8	6·1
09	7 02·3	7 03·4	6 43·0	0·9	0·4	6·9	3·3	12·9	6·1
10	7 02·5	7 03·7	6 43·3	1·0	0·5	7·0	3·3	13·0	6·2
11	7 02·8	7 03·9	6 43·5	1·1	0·5	7·1	3·4	13·1	6·2
12	7 03·0	7 04·2	6 43·7	1·2	0·6	7·2	3·4	13·2	6·3
13	7 03·3	7 04·4	6 44·0	1·3	0·6	7·3	3·5	13·3	6·3
14	7 03·5	7 04·7	6 44·2	1·4	0·7	7·4	3·5	13·4	6·4
15	7 03·8	7 04·9	6 44·4	1·5	0·7	7·5	3·6	13·5	6·4
16	7 04·0	7 05·2	6 44·7	1·6	0·8	7·6	3·6	13·6	6·5
17	7 04·3	7 05·4	6 44·9	1·7	0·8	7·7	3·7	13·7	6·5
18	7 04·5	7 05·7	6 45·2	1·8	0·9	7·8	3·7	13·8	6·6
19	7 04·8	7 05·9	6 45·4	1·9	0·9	7·9	3·8	13·9	6·6
20	7 05·0	7 06·2	6 45·6	2·0	1·0	8·0	3·8	14·0	6·7
21	7 05·3	7 06·4	6 45·9	2·1	1·0	8·1	3·8	14·1	6·7
22	7 05·5	7 06·7	6 46·1	2·2	1·0	8·2	3·9	14·2	6·7
23	7 05·8	7 06·9	6 46·4	2·3	1·1	8·3	3·9	14·3	6·8
24	7 06·0	7 07·2	6 46·6	2·4	1·1	8·4	4·0	14·4	6·8
25	7 06·3	7 07·4	6 46·8	2·5	1·2	8·5	4·0	14·5	6·9
26	7 06·5	7 07·7	6 47·1	2·6	1·2	8·6	4·1	14·6	6·9
27	7 06·8	7 07·9	6 47·3	2·7	1·3	8·7	4·1	14·7	7·0
28	7 07·0	7 08·2	6 47·5	2·8	1·3	8·8	4·2	14·8	7·0
29	7 07·3	7 08·4	6 47·8	2·9	1·4	8·9	4·2	14·9	7·1
30	7 07·5	7 08·7	6 48·0	3·0	1·4	9·0	4·3	15·0	7·1
31	7 07·8	7 08·9	6 48·3	3·1	1·5	9·1	4·3	15·1	7·2
32	7 08·0	7 09·2	6 48·5	3·2	1·5	9·2	4·4	15·2	7·2
33	7 08·3	7 09·4	6 48·7	3·3	1·6	9·3	4·4	15·3	7·3
34	7 08·5	7 09·7	6 49·0	3·4	1·6	9·4	4·5	15·4	7·3
35	7 08·8	7 09·9	6 49·2	3·5	1·7	9·5	4·5	15·5	7·4
36	7 09·0	7 10·2	6 49·5	3·6	1·7	9·6	4·6	15·6	7·4
37	7 09·3	7 10·4	6 49·7	3·7	1·8	9·7	4·6	15·7	7·5
38	7 09·5	7 10·7	6 49·9	3·8	1·8	9·8	4·7	15·8	7·5
39	7 09·8	7 10·9	6 50·2	3·9	1·9	9·9	4·7	15·9	7·6
40	7 10·0	7 11·2	6 50·4	4·0	1·9	10·0	4·8	16·0	7·6
41	7 10·3	7 11·4	6 50·6	4·1	1·9	10·1	4·8	16·1	7·6
42	7 10·5	7 11·7	6 50·9	4·2	2·0	10·2	4·8	16·2	7·7
43	7 10·8	7 11·9	6 51·1	4·3	2·0	10·3	4·9	16·3	7·7
44	7 11·0	7 12·2	6 51·4	4·4	2·1	10·4	4·9	16·4	7·8
45	7 11·3	7 12·4	6 51·6	4·5	2·1	10·5	5·0	16·5	7·8
46	7 11·5	7 12·7	6 51·8	4·6	2·2	10·6	5·0	16·6	7·9
47	7 11·8	7 12·9	6 52·1	4·7	2·2	10·7	5·1	16·7	7·9
48	7 12·0	7 13·2	6 52·3	4·8	2·3	10·8	5·1	16·8	8·0
49	7 12·3	7 13·4	6 52·6	4·9	2·3	10·9	5·2	16·9	8·0
50	7 12·5	7 13·7	6 52·8	5·0	2·4	11·0	5·2	17·0	8·1
51	7 12·8	7 13·9	6 53·0	5·1	2·4	11·1	5·3	17·1	8·1
52	7 13·0	7 14·2	6 53·3	5·2	2·5	11·2	5·3	17·2	8·2
53	7 13·3	7 14·4	6 53·5	5·3	2·5	11·3	5·4	17·3	8·2
54	7 13·5	7 14·7	6 53·8	5·4	2·6	11·4	5·4	17·4	8·3
55	7 13·8	7 14·9	6 54·0	5·5	2·6	11·5	5·5	17·5	8·3
56	7 14·0	7 15·2	6 54·2	5·6	2·7	11·6	5·5	17·6	8·4
57	7 14·3	7 15·4	6 54·5	5·7	2·7	11·7	5·6	17·7	8·4
58	7 14·5	7 15·7	6 54·7	5·8	2·8	11·8	5·6	17·8	8·5
59	7 14·8	7 15·9	6 54·9	5·9	2·8	11·9	5·7	17·9	8·5
60	7 15·0	7 16·2	6 55·2	6·0	2·9	12·0	5·7	18·0	8·6

29m	SUN PLANETS	ARIES	MOON	v or d	Corrn	v or d	Corrn	v or d	Corrn
s	° ′	° ′	° ′	′	′	′	′	′	′
00	7 15·0	7 16·2	6 55·2	0·0	0·0	6·0	3·0	12·0	5·9
01	7 15·3	7 16·4	6 55·4	0·1	0·0	6·1	3·0	12·1	5·9
02	7 15·5	7 16·7	6 55·7	0·2	0·1	6·2	3·0	12·2	6·0
03	7 15·8	7 16·9	6 55·9	0·3	0·1	6·3	3·1	12·3	6·0
04	7 16·0	7 17·2	6 56·1	0·4	0·2	6·4	3·1	12·4	6·1
05	7 16·3	7 17·4	6 56·4	0·5	0·2	6·5	3·2	12·5	6·1
06	7 16·5	7 17·7	6 56·6	0·6	0·3	6·6	3·2	12·6	6·2
07	7 16·8	7 17·9	6 56·9	0·7	0·3	6·7	3·3	12·7	6·2
08	7 17·0	7 18·2	6 57·1	0·8	0·4	6·8	3·3	12·8	6·3
09	7 17·3	7 18·4	6 57·3	0·9	0·4	6·9	3·4	12·9	6·3
10	7 17·5	7 18·7	6 57·6	1·0	0·5	7·0	3·4	13·0	6·4
11	7 17·8	7 18·9	6 57·8	1·1	0·5	7·1	3·5	13·1	6·4
12	7 18·0	7 19·2	6 58·0	1·2	0·6	7·2	3·5	13·2	6·5
13	7 18·3	7 19·4	6 58·3	1·3	0·6	7·3	3·6	13·3	6·5
14	7 18·5	7 19·7	6 58·5	1·4	0·7	7·4	3·6	13·4	6·6
15	7 18·8	7 20·0	6 58·8	1·5	0·7	7·5	3·7	13·5	6·6
16	7 19·0	7 20·2	6 59·0	1·6	0·8	7·6	3·7	13·6	6·7
17	7 19·3	7 20·5	6 59·2	1·7	0·8	7·7	3·8	13·7	6·7
18	7 19·5	7 20·7	6 59·5	1·8	0·9	7·8	3·8	13·8	6·8
19	7 19·8	7 21·0	6 59·7	1·9	0·9	7·9	3·9	13·9	6·8
20	7 20·0	7 21·2	7 00·0	2·0	1·0	8·0	3·9	14·0	6·9
21	7 20·3	7 21·5	7 00·2	2·1	1·0	8·1	4·0	14·1	6·9
22	7 20·5	7 21·7	7 00·4	2·2	1·1	8·2	4·0	14·2	7·0
23	7 20·8	7 22·0	7 00·7	2·3	1·1	8·3	4·1	14·3	7·0
24	7 21·0	7 22·2	7 00·9	2·4	1·2	8·4	4·1	14·4	7·1
25	7 21·3	7 22·5	7 01·1	2·5	1·2	8·5	4·2	14·5	7·1
26	7 21·5	7 22·7	7 01·4	2·6	1·3	8·6	4·2	14·6	7·2
27	7 21·8	7 23·0	7 01·6	2·7	1·3	8·7	4·3	14·7	7·2
28	7 22·0	7 23·2	7 01·9	2·8	1·4	8·8	4·3	14·8	7·3
29	7 22·3	7 23·5	7 02·1	2·9	1·4	8·9	4·4	14·9	7·3
30	7 22·5	7 23·7	7 02·3	3·0	1·5	9·0	4·4	15·0	7·4
31	7 22·8	7 24·0	7 02·6	3·1	1·5	9·1	4·5	15·1	7·4
32	7 23·0	7 24·2	7 02·8	3·2	1·6	9·2	4·5	15·2	7·5
33	7 23·3	7 24·5	7 03·1	3·3	1·6	9·3	4·6	15·3	7·5
34	7 23·5	7 24·7	7 03·3	3·4	1·7	9·4	4·6	15·4	7·6
35	7 23·8	7 25·0	7 03·5	3·5	1·7	9·5	4·7	15·5	7·6
36	7 24·0	7 25·2	7 03·8	3·6	1·8	9·6	4·7	15·6	7·7
37	7 24·3	7 25·5	7 04·0	3·7	1·8	9·7	4·8	15·7	7·7
38	7 24·5	7 25·7	7 04·3	3·8	1·9	9·8	4·8	15·8	7·8
39	7 24·8	7 26·0	7 04·5	3·9	1·9	9·9	4·9	15·9	7·8
40	7 25·0	7 26·2	7 04·7	4·0	2·0	10·0	4·9	16·0	7·9
41	7 25·3	7 26·5	7 05·0	4·1	2·0	10·1	5·0	16·1	7·9
42	7 25·5	7 26·7	7 05·2	4·2	2·1	10·2	5·0	16·2	8·0
43	7 25·8	7 27·0	7 05·4	4·3	2·1	10·3	5·1	16·3	8·0
44	7 26·0	7 27·2	7 05·7	4·4	2·2	10·4	5·1	16·4	8·1
45	7 26·3	7 27·5	7 05·9	4·5	2·2	10·5	5·2	16·5	8·1
46	7 26·5	7 27·7	7 06·2	4·6	2·3	10·6	5·2	16·6	8·2
47	7 26·8	7 28·0	7 06·4	4·7	2·3	10·7	5·3	16·7	8·2
48	7 27·0	7 28·2	7 06·6	4·8	2·4	10·8	5·3	16·8	8·3
49	7 27·3	7 28·5	7 06·9	4·9	2·4	10·9	5·4	16·9	8·3
50	7 27·5	7 28·7	7 07·1	5·0	2·5	11·0	5·4	17·0	8·4
51	7 27·8	7 29·0	7 07·4	5·1	2·5	11·1	5·5	17·1	8·4
52	7 28·0	7 29·2	7 07·6	5·2	2·6	11·2	5·5	17·2	8·5
53	7 28·3	7 29·5	7 07·8	5·3	2·6	11·3	5·6	17·3	8·5
54	7 28·5	7 29·7	7 08·1	5·4	2·7	11·4	5·6	17·4	8·6
55	7 28·8	7 30·0	7 08·3	5·5	2·7	11·5	5·7	17·5	8·6
56	7 29·0	7 30·2	7 08·5	5·6	2·8	11·6	5·7	17·6	8·7
57	7 29·3	7 30·5	7 08·8	5·7	2·8	11·7	5·8	17·7	8·7
58	7 29·5	7 30·7	7 09·0	5·8	2·9	11·8	5·8	17·8	8·8
59	7 29·8	7 31·0	7 09·3	5·9	2·9	11·9	5·9	17·9	8·8
60	7 30·0	7 31·2	7 09·5	6·0	3·0	12·0	5·9	18·0	8·9

m 30	SUN PLANETS	ARIES	MOON	v or d	Corrn	v or d	Corrn	v or d	Corrn
s	° ′	° ′	° ′	′	′	′	′	′	′
00	7 30·0	7 31·2	7 09·5	0·0	0·0	6·0	3·1	12·0	6·1
01	7 30·3	7 31·5	7 09·7	0·1	0·1	6·1	3·1	12·1	6·2
02	7 30·5	7 31·7	7 10·0	0·2	0·1	6·2	3·2	12·2	6·2
03	7 30·8	7 32·0	7 10·2	0·3	0·2	6·3	3·2	12·3	6·3
04	7 31·0	7 32·2	7 10·5	0·4	0·2	6·4	3·3	12·4	6·3
05	7 31·3	7 32·5	7 10·7	0·5	0·3	6·5	3·3	12·5	6·4
06	7 31·5	7 32·7	7 10·9	0·6	0·3	6·6	3·4	12·6	6·4
07	7 31·8	7 33·0	7 11·2	0·7	0·4	6·7	3·4	12·7	6·5
08	7 32·0	7 33·2	7 11·4	0·8	0·4	6·8	3·5	12·8	6·5
09	7 32·3	7 33·5	7 11·6	0·9	0·5	6·9	3·5	12·9	6·6
10	7 32·5	7 33·7	7 11·9	1·0	0·5	7·0	3·6	13·0	6·6
11	7 32·8	7 34·0	7 12·1	1·1	0·6	7·1	3·6	13·1	6·7
12	7 33·0	7 34·2	7 12·4	1·2	0·6	7·2	3·7	13·2	6·7
13	7 33·3	7 34·5	7 12·6	1·3	0·7	7·3	3·7	13·3	6·8
14	7 33·5	7 34·7	7 12·8	1·4	0·7	7·4	3·8	13·4	6·8
15	7 33·8	7 35·0	7 13·1	1·5	0·8	7·5	3·8	13·5	6·9
16	7 34·0	7 35·2	7 13·3	1·6	0·8	7·6	3·9	13·6	6·9
17	7 34·3	7 35·5	7 13·6	1·7	0·9	7·7	3·9	13·7	7·0
18	7 34·5	7 35·7	7 13·8	1·8	0·9	7·8	4·0	13·8	7·0
19	7 34·8	7 36·0	7 14·0	1·9	1·0	7·9	4·0	13·9	7·1
20	7 35·0	7 36·2	7 14·3	2·0	1·0	8·0	4·1	14·0	7·1
21	7 35·3	7 36·5	7 14·5	2·1	1·1	8·1	4·1	14·1	7·2
22	7 35·5	7 36·7	7 14·7	2·2	1·1	8·2	4·2	14·2	7·2
23	7 35·0	7 37·0	7 15·0	2·3	1·2	8·3	4·2	14·3	7·3
24	7 36·0	7 37·2	7 15·2	2·4	1·2	8·4	4·3	14·4	7·3
25	7 36·3	7 37·5	7 15·5	2·5	1·3	8·5	4·3	14·5	7·4
26	7 36·5	7 37·7	7 15·7	2·6	1·3	8·6	4·4	14·6	7·4
27	7 36·8	7 38·0	7 15·9	2·7	1·4	8·7	4·4	14·7	7·5
28	7 37·0	7 38·3	7 16·2	2·8	1·4	8·8	4·5	14·8	7·5
29	7 37·3	7 38·5	7 16·4	2·9	1·5	8·9	4·5	14·9	7·6
30	7 37·5	7 38·8	7 16·7	3·0	1·5	9·0	4·6	15·0	7·6
31	7 37·8	7 39·0	7 16·9	3·1	1·6	9·1	4·6	15·1	7·7
32	7 38·0	7 39·3	7 17·1	3·2	1·6	9·2	4·7	15·2	7·7
33	7 38·3	7 39·5	7 17·4	3·3	1·7	9·3	4·7	15·3	7·8
34	7 38·5	7 39·8	7 17·6	3·4	1·7	9·4	4·8	15·4	7·8
35	7 38·8	7 40·0	7 17·9	3·5	1·8	9·5	4·8	15·5	7·9
36	7 39·0	7 40·3	7 18·1	3·6	1·8	9·6	4·9	15·6	7·9
37	7 39·3	7 40·5	7 18·3	3·7	1·9	9·7	4·9	15·7	8·0
38	7 39·5	7 40·8	7 18·6	3·8	1·9	9·8	5·0	15·8	8·0
39	7 39·8	7 41·0	7 18·8	3·9	2·0	9·9	5·0	15·9	8·1
40	7 40·0	7 41·3	7 19·0	4·0	2·0	10·0	5·1	16·0	8·1
41	7 40·3	7 41·5	7 19·3	4·1	2·1	10·1	5·1	16·1	8·2
42	7 40·5	7 41·8	7 19·5	4·2	2·1	10·2	5·2	16·2	8·2
43	7 40·8	7 42·0	7 19·8	4·3	2·2	10·3	5·2	16·3	8·3
44	7 41·0	7 42·3	7 20·0	4·4	2·2	10·4	5·3	16·4	8·3
45	7 41·3	7 42·5	7 20·2	4·5	2·3	10·5	5·3	16·5	8·4
46	7 41·5	7 42·8	7 20·5	4·6	2·3	10·6	5·4	16·6	8·4
47	7 41·8	7 43·0	7 20·7	4·7	2·4	10·7	5·4	16·7	8·5
48	7 42·0	7 43·3	7 21·0	4·8	2·4	10·8	5·5	16·8	8·5
49	7 42·3	7 43·5	7 21·2	4·9	2·5	10·9	5·5	16·9	8·6
50	7 42·5	7 43·8	7 21·4	5·0	2·5	11·0	5·6	17·0	8·6
51	7 42·8	7 44·0	7 21·7	5·1	2·6	11·1	5·6	17·1	8·7
52	7 43·0	7 44·3	7 21·9	5·2	2·6	11·2	5·7	17·2	8·7
53	7 43·3	7 44·5	7 22·1	5·3	2·7	11·3	5·7	17·3	8·8
54	7 43·5	7 44·8	7 22·4	5·4	2·7	11·4	5·8	17·4	8·8
55	7 43·8	7 45·0	7 22·6	5·5	2·8	11·5	5·8	17·5	8·9
56	7 44·0	7 45·3	7 22·9	5·6	2·8	11·6	5·9	17·6	8·9
57	7 44·3	7 45·5	7 23·1	5·7	2·9	11·7	5·9	17·7	9·0
58	7 44·5	7 45·8	7 23·3	5·8	2·9	11·8	6·0	17·8	9·0
59	7 44·8	7 46·0	7 23·6	5·9	3·0	11·9	6·0	17·9	9·1
60	7 45·0	7 46·3	7 23·8	6·0	3·1	12·0	6·1	18·0	9·2

m 31	SUN PLANETS	ARIES	MOON	v or d	Corrn	v or d	Corrn	v or d	Corrn
s	° ′	° ′	° ′	′	′	′	′	′	′
00	7 45·0	7 46·3	7 23·8	0·0	0·0	6·0	3·2	12·0	6·3
01	7 45·3	7 46·5	7 24·1	0·1	0·1	6·1	3·2	12·1	6·4
02	7 45·5	7 46·8	7 24·3	0·2	0·1	6·2	3·3	12·2	6·4
03	7 45·8	7 47·0	7 24·5	0·3	0·2	6·3	3·3	12·3	6·5
04	7 46·0	7 47·3	7 24·8	0·4	0·2	6·4	3·4	12·4	6·5
05	7 46·3	7 47·5	7 25·0	0·5	0·3	6·5	3·4	12·5	6·6
06	7 46·5	7 47·8	7 25·2	0·6	0·3	6·6	3·5	12·6	6·6
07	7 46·8	7 48·0	7 25·5	0·7	0·4	6·7	3·5	12·7	6·7
08	7 47·0	7 48·3	7 25·7	0·8	0·4	6·8	3·6	12·8	6·7
09	7 47·3	7 48·5	7 26·0	0·9	0·5	6·9	3·6	12·9	6·8
10	7 47·5	7 48·8	7 26·2	1·0	0·5	7·0	3·7	13·0	6·8
11	7 47·8	7 49·0	7 26·4	1·1	0·6	7·1	3·7	13·1	6·9
12	7 48·0	7 49·3	7 26·7	1·2	0·6	7·2	3·8	13·2	6·9
13	7 48·3	7 49·5	7 26·9	1·3	0·7	7·3	3·8	13·3	7·0
14	7 48·5	7 49·8	7 27·2	1·4	0·7	7·4	3·9	13·4	7·0
15	7 48·8	7 50·0	7 27·4	1·5	0·8	7·5	3·9	13·5	7·1
16	7 49·0	7 50·3	7 27·6	1·6	0·8	7·6	4·0	13·6	7·1
17	7 49·3	7 50·5	7 27·9	1·7	0·9	7·7	4·0	13·7	7·2
18	7 49·5	7 50·8	7 28·1	1·8	0·9	7·8	4·1	13·8	7·2
19	7 49·8	7 51·0	7 28·4	1·9	1·0	7·9	4·1	13·9	7·3
20	7 50·0	7 51·3	7 28·6	2·0	1·1	8·0	4·2	14·0	7·4
21	7 50·3	7 51·5	7 28·8	2·1	1·1	8·1	4·3	14·1	7·4
22	7 50·5	7 51·8	7 29·1	2·2	1·2	8·2	4·3	14·2	7·5
23	7 50·8	7 52·0	7 29·3	2·3	1·2	8·3	4·4	14·3	7·5
24	7 51·0	7 52·3	7 29·5	2·4	1·3	8·4	4·4	14·4	7·6
25	7 51·3	7 52·5	7 29·8	2·5	1·3	8·5	4·5	14·5	7·6
26	7 51·5	7 52·8	7 30·0	2·6	1·4	8·6	4·5	14·6	7·7
27	7 51·8	7 53·0	7 30·3	2·7	1·4	8·7	4·6	14·7	7·7
28	7 52·0	7 53·3	7 30·5	2·8	1·5	8·8	4·6	14·8	7·8
29	7 52·3	7 53·5	7 30·7	2·9	1·5	8·9	4·7	14·9	7·8
30	7 52·5	7 53·8	7 31·0	3·0	1·6	9·0	4·7	15·0	7·9
31	7 52·8	7 54·0	7 31·2	3·1	1·6	9·1	4·8	15·1	7·9
32	7 53·0	7 54·3	7 31·5	3·2	1·7	9·2	4·8	15·2	8·0
33	7 53·3	7 54·5	7 31·7	3·3	1·7	9·3	4·9	15·3	8·0
34	7 53·5	7 54·8	7 31·9	3·4	1·8	9·4	4·9	15·4	8·1
35	7 53·8	7 55·0	7 32·2	3·5	1·8	9·5	5·0	15·5	8·1
36	7 54·0	7 55·3	7 32·4	3·6	1·9	9·6	5·0	15·6	8·2
37	7 54·3	7 55·5	7 32·6	3·7	1·9	9·7	5·1	15·7	8·2
38	7 54·5	7 55·8	7 32·9	3·8	2·0	9·8	5·1	15·8	8·3
39	7 54·8	7 56·0	7 33·1	3·9	2·0	9·9	5·2	15·9	8·3
40	7 55·0	7 56·3	7 33·4	4·0	2·1	10·0	5·3	16·0	8·4
41	7 55·3	7 56·6	7 33·6	4·1	2·2	10·1	5·3	16·1	8·5
42	7 55·5	7 56·8	7 33·8	4·2	2·2	10·2	5·4	16·2	8·5
43	7 55·8	7 57·1	7 34·1	4·3	2·3	10·3	5·4	16·3	8·6
44	7 56·0	7 57·3	7 34·3	4·4	2·3	10·4	5·5	16·4	8·6
45	7 56·3	7 57·6	7 34·6	4·5	2·4	10·5	5·5	16·5	8·7
46	7 56·5	7 57·8	7 34·8	4·6	2·4	10·6	5·6	16·6	8·7
47	7 56·8	7 58·1	7 35·0	4·7	2·5	10·7	5·6	16·7	8·8
48	7 57·0	7 58·3	7 35·3	4·8	2·5	10·8	5·7	16·8	8·8
49	7 57·3	7 58·6	7 35·5	4·9	2·6	10·9	5·7	16·9	8·9
50	7 57·5	7 58·8	7 35·7	5·0	2·6	11·0	5·8	17·0	8·9
51	7 57·8	7 59·1	7 36·0	5·1	2·7	11·1	5·8	17·1	9·0
52	7 58·0	7 59·3	7 36·2	5·2	2·7	11·2	5·9	17·2	9·0
53	7 58·3	7 59·6	7 36·5	5·3	2·8	11·3	5·9	17·3	9·1
54	7 58·5	7 59·8	7 36·7	5·4	2·8	11·4	6·0	17·4	9·1
55	7 58·8	8 00·1	7 36·9	5·5	2·9	11·5	6·0	17·5	9·2
56	7 59·0	8 00·3	7 37·2	5·6	2·9	11·6	6·1	17·6	9·2
57	7 59·3	8 00·6	7 37·4	5·7	3·0	11·7	6·1	17·7	9·3
58	7 59·5	8 00·8	7 37·7	5·8	3·0	11·8	6·2	17·8	9·3
59	7 59·8	8 01·1	7 37·9	5·9	3·1	11·9	6·2	17·9	9·4
60	8 00·0	8 01·3	7 38·1	6·0	3·2	12·0	6·3	18·0	9·5

32m s	SUN PLANETS ° ′	ARIES ° ′	MOON ° ′	v or d ′	Corrn ′	v or d ′	Corrn ′	v or d ′	Corrn ′
00	8 00·0	8 01·3	7 38·1	0·0	0·0	6·0	3·3	12·0	6·5
01	8 00·3	8 01·6	7 38·4	0·1	0·1	6·1	3·3	12·1	6·6
02	8 00·5	8 01·8	7 38·6	0·2	0·1	6·2	3·4	12·2	6·6
03	8 00·8	8 02·1	7 38·8	0·3	0·2	6·3	3·4	12·3	6·7
04	8 01·0	8 02·3	7 39·1	0·4	0·2	6·4	3·5	12·4	6·7
05	8 01·3	8 02·6	7 39·3	0·5	0·3	6·5	3·5	12·5	6·8
06	8 01·5	8 02·8	7 39·6	0·6	0·3	6·6	3·6	12·6	6·8
07	8 01·8	8 03·1	7 39·8	0·7	0·4	6·7	3·6	12·7	6·9
08	8 02·0	8 03·3	7 40·0	0·8	0·4	6·8	3·7	12·8	6·9
09	8 02·3	8 03·6	7 40·3	0·9	0·5	6·9	3·7	12·9	7·0
10	8 02·5	8 03·8	7 40·5	1·0	0·5	7·0	3·8	13·0	7·0
11	8 02·8	8 04·1	7 40·8	1·1	0·6	7·1	3·8	13·1	7·1
12	8 03·0	8 04·3	7 41·0	1·2	0·7	7·2	3·9	13·2	7·2
13	8 03·3	8 04·6	7 41·2	1·3	0·7	7·3	4·0	13·3	7·2
14	8 03·5	8 04·8	7 41·5	1·4	0·8	7·4	4·0	13·4	7·3
15	8 03·8	8 05·1	7 41·7	1·5	0·8	7·5	4·1	13·5	7·3
16	8 04·0	8 05·3	7 42·0	1·6	0·9	7·6	4·1	13·6	7·4
17	8 04·3	8 05·6	7 42·2	1·7	0·9	7·7	4·2	13·7	7·4
18	8 04·5	8 05·8	7 42·4	1·8	1·0	7·8	4·2	13·8	7·5
19	8 04·8	8 06·1	7 42·7	1·9	1·0	7·9	4·3	13·9	7·5
20	8 05·0	8 06·3	7 42·9	2·0	1·1	8·0	4·3	14·0	7·6
21	8 05·3	8 06·6	7 43·1	2·1	1·1	8·1	4·4	14·1	7·6
22	8 05·5	8 06·8	7 43·4	2·2	1·2	8·2	4·4	14·2	7·7
23	8 05·8	8 07·1	7 43·6	2·3	1·2	8·3	4·5	14·3	7·7
24	8 06·0	8 07·3	7 43·9	2·4	1·3	8·4	4·6	14·4	7·8
25	8 06·3	8 07·6	7 44·1	2·5	1·4	8·5	4·6	14·5	7·9
26	8 06·5	8 07·8	7 44·3	2·6	1·4	8·6	4·7	14·6	7·9
27	8 06·8	8 08·1	7 44·6	2·7	1·5	8·7	4·7	14·7	8·0
28	8 07·0	8 08·3	7 44·8	2·8	1·5	8·8	4·8	14·8	8·0
29	8 07·3	8 08·6	7 45·1	2·9	1·6	8·9	4·8	14·9	8·1
30	8 07·5	8 08·8	7 45·3	3·0	1·6	9·0	4·9	15·0	8·1
31	8 07·8	8 09·1	7 45·5	3·1	1·7	9·1	4·9	15·1	8·2
32	8 08·0	8 09·3	7 45·8	3·2	1·7	9·2	5·0	15·2	8·2
33	8 08·3	8 09·6	7 46·0	3·3	1·8	9·3	5·0	15·3	8·3
34	8 08·5	8 09·8	7 46·2	3·4	1·8	9·4	5·1	15·4	8·3
35	8 08·8	8 10·1	7 46·5	3·5	1·9	9·5	5·1	15·5	8·4
36	8 09·0	8 10·3	7 46·7	3·6	2·0	9·6	5·2	15·6	8·5
37	8 09·3	8 10·6	7 47·0	3·7	2·0	9·7	5·3	15·7	8·5
38	8 09·5	8 10·8	7 47·2	3·8	2·1	9·8	5·3	15·8	8·6
39	8 09·8	8 11·1	7 47·4	3·9	2·1	9·9	5·4	15·9	8·6
40	8 10·0	8 11·3	7 47·7	4·0	2·2	10·0	5·4	16·0	8·7
41	8 10·3	8 11·6	7 47·9	4·1	2·2	10·1	5·5	16·1	8·7
42	8 10·5	8 11·8	7 48·2	4·2	2·3	10·2	5·5	16·2	8·8
43	8 10·8	8 12·1	7 48·4	4·3	2·3	10·3	5·6	16·3	8·8
44	8 11·0	8 12·3	7 48·6	4·4	2·4	10·4	5·6	16·4	8·9
45	8 11·3	8 12·6	7 48·9	4·5	2·4	10·5	5·7	16·5	8·9
46	8 11·5	8 12·8	7 49·1	4·6	2·5	10·6	5·7	16·6	9·0
47	8 11·8	8 13·1	7 49·3	4·7	2·5	10·7	5·8	16·7	9·0
48	8 12·0	8 13·3	7 49·6	4·8	2·6	10·8	5·9	16·8	9·1
49	8 12·3	8 13·6	7 49·8	4·9	2·7	10·9	5·9	16·9	9·2
50	8 12·5	8 13·8	7 50·1	5·0	2·7	11·0	6·0	17·0	9·2
51	8 12·8	8 14·1	7 50·3	5·1	2·8	11·1	6·0	17·1	9·3
52	8 13·0	8 14·3	7 50·5	5·2	2·8	11·2	6·1	17·2	9·3
53	8 13·3	8 14·6	7 50·8	5·3	2·9	11·3	6·1	17·3	9·4
54	8 13·5	8 14·9	7 51·0	5·4	2·9	11·4	6·2	17·4	9·4
55	8 13·8	8 15·1	7 51·3	5·5	3·0	11·5	6·2	17·5	9·5
56	8 14·0	8 15·4	7 51·5	5·6	3·0	11·6	6·3	17·6	9·5
57	8 14·3	8 15·6	7 51·7	5·7	3·1	11·7	6·3	17·7	9·6
58	8 14·5	8 15·9	7 52·0	5·8	3·1	11·8	6·4	17·8	9·6
59	8 14·8	8 16·1	7 52·2	5·9	3·2	11·9	6·4	17·9	9·7
60	8 15·0	8 16·4	7 52·5	6·0	3·3	12·0	6·5	18·0	9·8

33m s	SUN PLANETS ° ′	ARIES ° ′	MOON ° ′	v or d ′	Corrn ′	v or d ′	Corrn ′	v or d ′	Corrn ′
00	8 15·0	8 16·4	7 52·5	0·0	0·0	6·0	3·4	12·0	6·7
01	8 15·3	8 16·6	7 52·7	0·1	0·1	6·1	3·4	12·1	6·8
02	8 15·5	8 16·9	7 52·9	0·2	0·1	6·2	3·5	12·2	6·8
03	8 15·8	8 17·1	7 53·2	0·3	0·2	6·3	3·5	12·3	6·9
04	8 16·0	8 17·4	7 53·4	0·4	0·2	6·4	3·6	12·4	6·9
05	8 16·3	8 17·6	7 53·6	0·5	0·3	6·5	3·6	12·5	7·0
06	8 16·5	8 17·9	7 53·9	0·6	0·3	6·6	3·7	12·6	7·0
07	8 16·8	8 18·1	7 54·1	0·7	0·4	6·7	3·7	12·7	7·1
08	8 17·0	8 18·4	7 54·4	0·8	0·4	6·8	3·8	12·8	7·1
09	8 17·3	8 18·6	7 54·6	0·9	0·5	6·9	3·9	12·9	7·2
10	8 17·5	8 18·9	7 54·8	1·0	0·6	7·0	3·9	13·0	7·3
11	8 17·8	8 19·1	7 55·1	1·1	0·6	7·1	4·0	13·1	7·3
12	8 18·0	8 19·4	7 55·3	1·2	0·7	7·2	4·0	13·2	7·4
13	8 18·3	8 19·6	7 55·6	1·3	0·7	7·3	4·1	13·3	7·4
14	8 18·5	8 19·9	7 55·8	1·4	0·8	7·4	4·1	13·4	7·5
15	8 18·8	8 20·1	7 56·0	1·5	0·8	7·5	4·2	13·5	7·5
16	8 19·0	8 20·4	7 56·3	1·6	0·9	7·6	4·2	13·6	7·6
17	8 19·3	8 20·6	7 56·5	1·7	0·9	7·7	4·3	13·7	7·6
18	8 19·5	8 20·9	7 56·7	1·8	1·0	7·8	4·4	13·8	7·7
19	8 19·8	8 21·1	7 57·0	1·9	1·1	7·9	4·4	13·9	7·8
20	8 20·0	8 21·4	7 57·2	2·0	1·1	8·0	4·5	14·0	7·8
21	8 20·3	8 21·6	7 57·5	2·1	1·2	8·1	4·5	14·1	7·9
22	8 20·5	8 21·9	7 57·7	2·2	1·2	8·2	4·6	14·2	7·9
23	8 20·8	8 22·1	7 57·9	2·3	1·3	8·3	4·6	14·3	8·0
24	8 21·0	8 22·4	7 58·2	2·4	1·3	8·4	4·7	14·4	8·0
25	8 21·3	8 22·6	7 58·4	2·5	1·4	8·5	4·7	14·5	8·1
26	8 21·5	8 22·9	7 58·7	2·6	1·5	8·6	4·8	14·6	8·2
27	8 21·8	8 23·1	7 58·9	2·7	1·5	8·7	4·9	14·7	8·2
28	8 22·0	8 23·4	7 59·1	2·8	1·6	8·8	4·9	14·8	8·3
29	8 22·3	8 23·6	7 59·4	2·9	1·6	8·9	5·0	14·9	8·3
30	8 22·5	8 23·9	7 59·6	3·0	1·7	9·0	5·0	15·0	8·4
31	8 22·8	8 24·1	7 59·8	3·1	1·7	9·1	5·1	15·1	8·4
32	8 23·0	8 24·4	8 00·1	3·2	1·8	9·2	5·1	15·2	8·5
33	8 23·3	8 24·6	8 00·3	3·3	1·8	9·3	5·2	15·3	8·5
34	8 23·5	8 24·9	8 00·6	3·4	1·9	9·4	5·2	15·4	8·6
35	8 23·8	8 25·1	8 00·8	3·5	2·0	9·5	5·3	15·5	8·7
36	8 24·0	8 25·4	8 01·0	3·6	2·0	9·6	5·4	15·6	8·7
37	8 24·3	8 25·6	8 01·3	3·7	2·1	9·7	5·4	15·7	8·8
38	8 24·5	8 25·9	8 01·5	3·8	2·1	9·8	5·5	15·8	8·8
39	8 24·8	8 26·1	8 01·8	3·9	2·2	9·9	5·5	15·9	8·9
40	8 25·0	8 26·4	8 02·0	4·0	2·2	10·0	5·6	16·0	8·9
41	8 25·3	8 26·6	8 02·2	4·1	2·3	10·1	5·6	16·1	9·0
42	8 25·5	8 26·9	8 02·5	4·2	2·3	10·2	5·7	16·2	9·0
43	8 25·8	8 27·1	8 02·7	4·3	2·4	10·3	5·8	16·3	9·1
44	8 26·0	8 27·4	8 02·9	4·4	2·5	10·4	5·8	16·4	9·2
45	8 26·3	8 27·6	8 03·2	4·5	2·5	10·5	5·9	16·5	9·2
46	8 26·5	8 27·9	8 03·4	4·6	2·6	10·6	5·9	16·6	9·3
47	8 26·8	8 28·1	8 03·7	4·7	2·6	10·7	6·0	16·7	9·3
48	8 27·0	8 28·4	8 03·9	4·8	2·7	10·8	6·0	16·8	9·4
49	8 27·3	8 28·6	8 04·1	4·9	2·7	10·9	6·1	16·9	9·4
50	8 27·5	8 28·9	8 04·4	5·0	2·8	11·0	6·1	17·0	9·5
51	8 27·8	8 29·1	8 04·6	5·1	2·8	11·1	6·2	17·1	9·5
52	8 28·0	8 29·4	8 04·9	5·2	2·9	11·2	6·3	17·2	9·6
53	8 28·3	8 29·6	8 05·1	5·3	3·0	11·3	6·3	17·3	9·7
54	8 28·5	8 29·9	8 05·3	5·4	3·0	11·4	6·4	17·4	9·7
55	8 28·8	8 30·1	8 05·6	5·5	3·1	11·5	6·4	17·5	9·8
56	8 29·0	8 30·4	8 05·8	5·6	3·1	11·6	6·5	17·6	9·8
57	8 29·3	8 30·6	8 06·1	5·7	3·2	11·7	6·5	17·7	9·9
58	8 29·5	8 30·9	8 06·3	5·8	3·2	11·8	6·6	17·8	9·9
59	8 29·8	8 31·1	8 06·5	5·9	3·3	11·9	6·6	17·9	10·0
60	8 30·0	8 31·4	8 06·8	6·0	3·4	12·0	6·7	18·0	10·1

34m s	SUN PLANETS ° ′	ARIES ° ′	MOON ° ′	v or d ′	Corrn ′	v or d ′	Corrn ′	v or d ′	Corrn ′
00	8 30·0	8 31·4	8 06·8	0·0	0·0	6·0	3·5	12·0	6·9
01	8 30·3	8 31·6	8 07·0	0·1	0·1	6·1	3·5	12·1	7·0
02	8 30·5	8 31·9	8 07·2	0·2	0·1	6·2	3·6	12·2	7·0
03	8 30·8	8 32·1	8 07·5	0·3	0·2	6·3	3·6	12·3	7·1
04	8 31·0	8 32·4	8 07·7	0·4	0·2	6·4	3·7	12·4	7·1
05	8 31·3	8 32·6	8 08·0	0·5	0·3	6·5	3·7	12·5	7·2
06	8 31·5	8 32·9	8 08·2	0·6	0·3	6·6	3·8	12·6	7·2
07	8 31·8	8 33·2	8 08·4	0·7	0·4	6·7	3·9	12·7	7·3
08	8 32·0	8 33·4	8 08·7	0·8	0·5	6·8	3·9	12·8	7·4
09	8 32·3	8 33·7	8 08·9	0·9	0·5	6·9	4·0	12·9	7·4
10	8 32·5	8 33·9	8 09·2	1·0	0·6	7·0	4·0	13·0	7·5
11	8 32·8	8 34·2	8 09·4	1·1	0·6	7·1	4·1	13·1	7·5
12	8 33·0	8 34·4	8 09·6	1·2	0·7	7·2	4·1	13·2	7·6
13	8 33·3	8 34·7	8 09·9	1·3	0·7	7·3	4·2	13·3	7·6
14	8 33·5	8 34·9	8 10·1	1·4	0·8	7·4	4·3	13·4	7·7
15	8 33·8	8 35·2	8 10·3	1·5	0·9	7·5	4·3	13·5	7·8
16	8 34·0	8 35·4	8 10·6	1·6	0·9	7·6	4·4	13·6	7·8
17	8 34·3	8 35·7	8 10·8	1·7	1·0	7·7	4·4	13·7	7·9
18	8 34·5	8 35·9	8 11·1	1·8	1·0	7·8	4·5	13·8	7·9
19	8 34·8	8 36·2	8 11·3	1·9	1·1	7·9	4·5	13·9	8·0
20	8 35·0	8 36·4	8 11·5	2·0	1·2	8·0	4·6	14·0	8·1
21	8 35·3	8 36·7	8 11·8	2·1	1·2	8·1	4·7	14·1	8·1
22	8 35·5	8 36·9	8 12·0	2·2	1·3	8·2	4·7	14·2	8·2
23	8 35·8	8 37·2	8 12·3	2·3	1·3	8·3	4·8	14·3	8·2
24	8 36·0	8 37·4	8 12·5	2·4	1·4	8·4	4·8	14·4	8·3
25	8 36·3	8 37·7	8 12·7	2·5	1·4	8·5	4·9	14·5	8·3
26	8 36·5	8 37·9	8 13·0	2·6	1·5	8·6	4·9	14·6	8·4
27	8 36·8	8 38·2	8 13·2	2·7	1·6	8·7	5·0	14·7	8·5
28	8 37·0	8 38·4	8 13·4	2·8	1·6	8·8	5·1	14·8	8·5
29	8 37·3	8 38·7	8 13·7	2·9	1·7	8·9	5·1	14·9	8·6
30	8 37·5	8 38·9	8 13·9	3·0	1·7	9·0	5·2	15·0	8·6
31	8 37·8	8 39·2	8 14·2	3·1	1·8	9·1	5·2	15·1	8·7
32	8 38·0	8 39·4	8 14·4	3·2	1·8	9·2	5·3	15·2	8·7
33	8 38·3	8 39·7	8 14·6	3·3	1·9	9·3	5·3	15·3	8·8
34	8 38·5	8 39·9	8 14·9	3·4	2·0	9·4	5·4	15·4	8·9
35	8 38·8	8 40·2	8 15·1	3·5	2·0	9·5	5·5	15·5	8·9
36	8 39·0	8 40·4	8 15·4	3·6	2·1	9·6	5·5	15·6	9·0
37	8 39·3	8 40·7	8 15·6	3·7	2·1	9·7	5·6	15·7	9·0
38	8 39·5	8 40·9	8 15·8	3·8	2·2	9·8	5·6	15·8	9·1
39	8 39·8	8 41·2	8 16·1	3·9	2·2	9·9	5·7	15·9	9·1
40	8 40·0	8 41·4	8 16·3	4·0	2·3	10·0	5·8	16·0	9·2
41	8 40·3	8 41·7	8 16·5	4·1	2·4	10·1	5·8	16·1	9·3
42	8 40·5	8 41·9	8 16·8	4·2	2·4	10·2	5·9	16·2	9·3
43	8 40·8	8 42·2	8 17·0	4·3	2·5	10·3	5·9	16·3	9·4
44	8 41·0	8 42·4	8 17·3	4·4	2·5	10·4	6·0	16·4	9·4
45	8 41·3	8 42·7	8 17·5	4·5	2·6	10·5	6·0	16·5	9·5
46	8 41·5	8 42·9	8 17·7	4·6	2·6	10·6	6·1	16·6	9·5
47	8 41·8	8 43·2	8 18·0	4·7	2·7	10·7	6·2	16·7	9·6
48	8 42·0	8 43·4	8 18·2	4·8	2·8	10·8	6·2	16·8	9·7
49	8 42·3	8 43·7	8 18·5	4·9	2·8	10·9	6·3	16·9	9·7
50	8 42·5	8 43·9	8 18·7	5·0	2·9	11·0	6·3	17·0	9·8
51	8 42·8	8 44·2	8 18·9	5·1	2·9	11·1	6·4	17·1	9·8
52	8 43·0	8 44·4	8 19·2	5·2	3·0	11·2	6·4	17·2	9·9
53	8 43·3	8 44·7	8 19·4	5·3	3·0	11·3	6·5	17·3	9·9
54	8 43·5	8 44·9	8 19·7	5·4	3·1	11·4	6·6	17·4	10·0
55	8 43·8	8 45·2	8 19·9	5·5	3·2	11·5	6·6	17·5	10·1
56	8 44·0	8 45·4	8 20·1	5·6	3·2	11·6	6·7	17·6	10·1
57	8 44·3	8 45·7	8 20·4	5·7	3·3	11·7	6·7	17·7	10·2
58	8 44·5	8 45·9	8 20·6	5·8	3·3	11·8	6·8	17·8	10·2
59	8 44·8	8 46·2	8 20·8	5·9	3·4	11·9	6·8	17·9	10·3
60	8 45·0	8 46·4	8 21·1	6·0	3·5	12·0	6·9	18·0	10·4

35m s	SUN PLANETS ° ′	ARIES ° ′	MOON ° ′	v or d ′	Corrn ′	v or d ′	Corrn ′	v or d ′	Corrn ′
00	8 45·0	8 46·4	8 21·1	0·0	0·0	6·0	3·6	12·0	7·1
01	8 45·3	8 46·7	8 21·3	0·1	0·1	6·1	3·6	12·1	7·2
02	8 45·5	8 46·9	8 21·6	0·2	0·1	6·2	3·7	12·2	7·2
03	8 45·8	8 47·2	8 21·8	0·3	0·2	6·3	3·7	12·3	7·3
04	8 46·0	8 47·4	8 22·0	0·4	0·2	6·4	3·8	12·4	7·3
05	8 46·3	8 47·7	8 22·3	0·5	0·3	6·5	3·8	12·5	7·4
06	8 46·5	8 47·9	8 22·5	0·6	0·4	6·6	3·9	12·6	7·5
07	8 46·8	8 48·2	8 22·8	0·7	0·4	6·7	4·0	12·7	7·5
08	8 47·0	8 48·4	8 23·0	0·8	0·5	6·8	4·0	12·8	7·6
09	8 47·3	8 48·7	8 23·2	0·9	0·5	6·9	4·1	12·9	7·6
10	8 47·5	8 48·9	8 23·5	1·0	0·6	7·0	4·1	13·0	7·7
11	8 47·8	8 49·2	8 23·7	1·1	0·7	7·1	4·2	13·1	7·8
12	8 48·0	8 49·4	8 23·9	1·2	0·7	7·2	4·3	13·2	7·8
13	8 48·3	8 49·7	8 24·2	1·3	0·8	7·3	4·3	13·3	7·9
14	8 48·5	8 49·9	8 24·4	1·4	0·8	7·4	4·4	13·4	7·9
15	8 48·8	8 50·2	8 24·7	1·5	0·9	7·5	4·4	13·5	8·0
16	8 49·0	8 50·4	8 24·9	1·6	0·9	7·6	4·5	13·6	8·0
17	8 49·3	8 50·7	8 25·1	1·7	1·0	7·7	4·6	13·7	8·1
18	8 49·5	8 50·9	8 25·4	1·8	1·1	7·8	4·6	13·8	8·2
19	8 49·8	8 51·2	8 25·6	1·9	1·1	7·9	4·7	13·9	8·2
20	8 50·0	8 51·5	8 25·9	2·0	1·2	8·0	4·7	14·0	8·3
21	8 50·3	8 51·7	8 26·1	2·1	1·2	8·1	4·8	14·1	8·3
22	8 50·5	8 52·0	8 26·3	2·2	1·3	8·2	4·9	14·2	8·4
23	8 50·8	8 52·2	8 26·6	2·3	1·4	8·3	4·9	14·3	8·5
24	8 51·0	8 52·5	8 26·8	2·4	1·4	8·4	5·0	14·4	8·5
25	8 51·3	8 52·7	8 27·0	2·5	1·5	8·5	5·0	14·5	8·6
26	8 51·5	8 53·0	8 27·3	2·6	1·5	8·6	5·1	14·6	8·6
27	8 51·8	8 53·2	8 27·5	2·7	1·6	8·7	5·1	14·7	8·7
28	8 52·0	8 53·5	8 27·8	2·8	1·7	8·8	5·2	14·8	8·8
29	8 52·3	8 53·7	8 28·0	2·9	1·7	8·9	5·3	14·9	8·8
30	8 52·5	8 54·0	8 28·2	3·0	1·8	9·0	5·3	15·0	8·9
31	8 52·8	8 54·2	8 28·5	3·1	1·8	9·1	5·4	15·1	8·9
32	8 53·0	8 54·5	8 28·7	3·2	1·9	9·2	5·4	15·2	9·0
33	8 53·3	8 54·7	8 29·0	3·3	2·0	9·3	5·5	15·3	9·1
34	8 53·5	8 55·0	8 29·2	3·4	2·0	9·4	5·6	15·4	9·1
35	8 53·8	8 55·2	8 29·4	3·5	2·1	9·5	5·6	15·5	9·2
36	8 54·0	8 55·5	8 29·7	3·6	2·1	9·6	5·7	15·6	9·2
37	8 54·3	8 55·7	8 29·9	3·7	2·2	9·7	5·7	15·7	9·3
38	8 54·5	8 56·0	8 30·2	3·8	2·2	9·8	5·8	15·8	9·3
39	8 54·8	8 56·2	8 30·4	3·9	2·3	9·9	5·9	15·9	9·4
40	8 55·0	8 56·5	8 30·6	4·0	2·4	10·0	5·9	16·0	9·5
41	8 55·3	8 56·7	8 30·9	4·1	2·4	10·1	6·0	16·1	9·5
42	8 55·5	8 57·0	8 31·1	4·2	2·5	10·2	6·0	16·2	9·6
43	8 55·8	8 57·2	8 31·3	4·3	2·5	10·3	6·1	16·3	9·6
44	8 56·0	8 57·5	8 31·6	4·4	2·6	10·4	6·2	16·4	9·7
45	8 56·3	8 57·7	8 31·8	4·5	2·7	10·5	6·2	16·5	9·8
46	8 56·5	8 58·0	8 32·1	4·6	2·7	10·6	6·3	16·6	9·8
47	8 56·8	8 58·2	8 32·3	4·7	2·8	10·7	6·3	16·7	9·9
48	8 57·0	8 58·5	8 32·5	4·8	2·8	10·8	6·4	16·8	9·9
49	8 57·3	8 58·7	8 32·8	4·9	2·9	10·9	6·4	16·9	10·0
50	8 57·5	8 59·0	8 33·0	5·0	3·0	11·0	6·5	17·0	10·1
51	8 57·8	8 59·2	8 33·3	5·1	3·0	11·1	6·6	17·1	10·1
52	8 58·0	8 59·5	8 33·5	5·2	3·1	11·2	6·6	17·2	10·2
53	8 58·3	8 59·7	8 33·7	5·3	3·1	11·3	6·7	17·3	10·2
54	8 58·5	9 00·0	8 34·0	5·4	3·2	11·4	6·7	17·4	10·3
55	8 58·8	9 00·2	8 34·2	5·5	3·3	11·5	6·8	17·5	10·4
56	8 59·0	9 00·5	8 34·4	5·6	3·3	11·6	6·9	17·6	10·4
57	8 59·3	9 00·7	8 34·7	5·7	3·4	11·7	6·9	17·7	10·5
58	8 59·5	9 01·0	8 34·9	5·8	3·4	11·8	7·0	17·8	10·5
59	8 59·8	9 01·2	8 35·2	5·9	3·5	11·9	7·0	17·9	10·6
60	9 00·0	9 01·5	8 35·4	6·0	3·6	12·0	7·1	18·0	10·7

36m s	SUN PLANETS ° ′	ARIES ° ′	MOON ° ′	v or d ′	Corrⁿ ′	v or d ′	Corrⁿ ′	v or d ′	Corrⁿ ′
00	9 00·0	9 01·5	8 35·4	0·0	0·0	6·0	3·7	12·0	7·3
01	9 00·3	9 01·7	8 35·6	0·1	0·1	6·1	3·7	12·1	7·4
02	9 00·5	9 02·0	8 35·9	0·2	0·1	6·2	3·8	12·2	7·4
03	9 00·8	9 02·2	8 36·1	0·3	0·2	6·3	3·8	12·3	7·5
04	9 01·0	9 02·5	8 36·4	0·4	0·2	6·4	3·9	12·4	7·5
05	9 01·3	9 02·7	8 36·6	0·5	0·3	6·5	4·0	12·5	7·6
06	9 01·5	9 03·0	8 36·8	0·6	0·4	6·6	4·0	12·6	7·7
07	9 01·8	9 03·2	8 37·1	0·7	0·4	6·7	4·1	12·7	7·7
08	9 02·0	9 03·5	8 37·3	0·8	0·5	6·8	4·1	12·8	7·8
09	9 02·3	9 03·7	8 37·5	0·9	0·5	6·9	4·2	12·9	7·8
10	9 02·5	9 04·0	8 37·8	1·0	0·6	7·0	4·3	13·0	7·9
11	9 02·8	9 04·2	8 38·0	1·1	0·7	7·1	4·3	13·1	8·0
12	9 03·0	9 04·5	8 38·3	1·2	0·7	7·2	4·4	13·2	8·0
13	9 03·3	9 04·7	8 38·5	1·3	0·8	7·3	4·4	13·3	8·1
14	9 03·5	9 05·0	8 38·7	1·4	0·9	7·4	4·5	13·4	8·2
15	9 03·8	9 05·2	8 39·0	1·5	0·9	7·5	4·6	13·5	8·2
16	9 04·0	9 05·5	8 39·2	1·6	1·0	7·6	4·6	13·6	8·3
17	9 04·3	9 05·7	8 39·5	1·7	1·0	7·7	4·7	13·7	8·3
18	9 04·5	9 06·0	8 39·7	1·8	1·1	7·8	4·7	13·8	8·4
19	9 04·8	9 06·2	8 39·9	1·9	1·2	7·9	4·8	13·9	8·5
20	9 05·0	9 06·5	8 40·2	2·0	1·2	8·0	4·9	14·0	8·5
21	9 05·3	9 06·7	8 40·4	2·1	1·3	8·1	4·9	14·1	8·6
22	9 05·5	9 07·0	8 40·6	2·2	1·3	8·2	5·0	14·2	8·6
23	9 05·8	9 07·2	8 40·9	2·3	1·4	8·3	5·0	14·3	8·7
24	9 06·0	9 07·5	8 41·1	2·4	1·5	8·4	5·1	14·4	8·8
25	9 06·3	9 07·7	8 41·4	2·5	1·5	8·5	5·2	14·5	8·8
26	9 06·5	9 08·0	8 41·6	2·6	1·6	8·6	5·2	14·6	8·9
27	9 06·8	9 08·2	8 41·8	2·7	1·6	8·7	5·3	14·7	8·9
28	9 07·0	9 08·5	8 42·1	2·8	1·7	8·8	5·4	14·8	9·0
29	9 07·3	9 08·7	8 42·3	2·9	1·8	8·9	5·4	14·9	9·1
30	9 07·5	9 09·0	8 42·6	3·0	1·8	9·0	5·5	15·0	9·1
31	9 07·8	9 09·2	8 42·8	3·1	1·9	9·1	5·5	15·1	9·2
32	9 08·0	9 09·5	8 43·0	3·2	1·9	9·2	5·6	15·2	9·2
33	9 08·3	9 09·8	8 43·3	3·3	2·0	9·3	5·7	15·3	9·3
34	9 08·5	9 10·0	8 43·5	3·4	2·1	9·4	5·7	15·4	9·4
35	9 08·8	9 10·3	8 43·8	3·5	2·1	9·5	5·8	15·5	9·4
36	9 09·0	9 10·5	8 44·0	3·6	2·2	9·6	5·8	15·6	9·5
37	9 09·3	9 10·8	8 44·2	3·7	2·3	9·7	5·9	15·7	9·6
38	9 09·5	9 11·0	8 44·5	3·8	2·3	9·8	6·0	15·8	9·6
39	9 09·8	9 11·3	8 44·7	3·9	2·4	9·9	6·0	15·9	9·7
40	9 10·0	9 11·5	8 44·9	4·0	2·4	10·0	6·1	16·0	9·7
41	9 10·3	9 11·8	8 45·2	4·1	2·5	10·1	6·1	16·1	9·8
42	9 10·5	9 12·0	8 45·4	4·2	2·6	10·2	6·2	16·2	9·9
43	9 10·8	9 12·3	8 45·7	4·3	2·6	10·3	6·3	16·3	9·9
44	9 11·0	9 12·5	8 45·9	4·4	2·7	10·4	6·3	16·4	10·0
45	9 11·3	9 12·8	8 46·1	4·5	2·7	10·5	6·4	16·5	10·0
46	9 11·5	9 13·0	8 46·4	4·6	2·8	10·6	6·4	16·6	10·1
47	9 11·8	9 13·3	8 46·6	4·7	2·9	10·7	6·5	16·7	10·2
48	9 12·0	9 13·5	8 46·9	4·8	2·9	10·8	6·6	16·8	10·2
49	9 12·3	9 13·8	8 47·1	4·9	3·0	10·9	6·6	16·9	10·3
50	9 12·5	9 14·0	8 47·3	5·0	3·0	11·0	6·7	17·0	10·3
51	9 12·8	9 14·3	8 47·6	5·1	3·1	11·1	6·8	17·1	10·4
52	9 13·0	9 14·5	8 47·8	5·2	3·2	11·2	6·8	17·2	10·5
53	9 13·3	9 14·8	8 48·0	5·3	3·2	11·3	6·9	17·3	10·5
54	9 13·5	9 15·0	8 48·3	5·4	3·3	11·4	6·9	17·4	10·6
55	9 13·8	9 15·3	8 48·5	5·5	3·3	11·5	7·0	17·5	10·6
56	9 14·0	9 15·5	8 48·8	5·6	3·4	11·6	7·1	17·6	10·7
57	9 14·3	9 15·8	8 49·0	5·7	3·5	11·7	7·1	17·7	10·8
58	9 14·5	9 16·0	8 49·2	5·8	3·5	11·8	7·2	17·8	10·8
59	9 14·8	9 16·3	8 49·5	5·9	3·6	11·9	7·2	17·9	10·9
60	9 15·0	9 16·5	8 49·7	6·0	3·7	12·0	7·3	18·0	11·0

37m s	SUN PLANETS ° ′	ARIES ° ′	MOON ° ′	v or d ′	Corrⁿ ′	v or d ′	Corrⁿ ′	v or d ′	Corrⁿ ′
00	9 15·0	9 16·5	8 49·7	0·0	0·0	6·0	3·8	12·0	7·5
01	9 15·3	9 16·8	8 50·0	0·1	0·1	6·1	3·8	12·1	7·6
02	9 15·5	9 17·0	8 50·2	0·2	0·1	6·2	3·9	12·2	7·6
03	9 15·8	9 17·3	8 50·4	0·3	0·2	6·3	3·9	12·3	7·7
04	9 16·0	9 17·5	8 50·7	0·4	0·3	6·4	4·0	12·4	7·8
05	9 16·3	9 17·8	8 50·9	0·5	0·3	6·5	4·1	12·5	7·8
06	9 16·5	9 18·0	8 51·1	0·6	0·4	6·6	4·1	12·6	7·9
07	9 16·8	9 18·3	8 51·4	0·7	0·4	6·7	4·2	12·7	7·9
08	9 17·0	9 18·5	8 51·6	0·8	0·5	6·8	4·3	12·8	8·0
09	9 17·3	9 18·8	8 51·9	0·9	0·6	6·9	4·3	12·9	8·1
10	9 17·5	9 19·0	8 52·1	1·0	0·6	7·0	4·4	13·0	8·1
11	9 17·8	9 19·3	8 52·3	1·1	0·7	7·1	4·4	13·1	8·2
12	9 18·0	9 19·5	8 52·6	1·2	0·8	7·2	4·5	13·2	8·3
13	9 18·3	9 19·8	8 52·8	1·3	0·8	7·3	4·6	13·3	8·3
14	9 18·5	9 20·0	8 53·1	1·4	0·9	7·4	4·6	13·4	8·4
15	9 18·8	9 20·3	8 53·3	1·5	0·9	7·5	4·7	13·5	8·4
16	9 19·0	9 20·5	8 53·5	1·6	1·0	7·6	4·8	13·6	8·5
17	9 19·3	9 20·8	8 53·8	1·7	1·1	7·7	4·8	13·7	8·6
18	9 19·5	9 21·0	8 54·0	1·8	1·1	7·8	4·9	13·8	8·6
19	9 19·8	9 21·3	8 54·3	1·9	1·2	7·9	4·9	13·9	8·7
20	9 20·0	9 21·5	8 54·5	2·0	1·3	8·0	5·0	14·0	8·8
21	9 20·3	9 21·8	8 54·7	2·1	1·3	8·1	5·1	14·1	8·8
22	9 20·5	9 22·0	8 55·0	2·2	1·4	8·2	5·1	14·2	8·9
23	9 20·8	9 22·3	8 55·2	2·3	1·4	8·3	5·2	14·3	8·9
24	9 21·0	9 22·5	8 55·4	2·4	1·5	8·4	5·3	14·4	9·0
25	9 21·3	9 22·8	8 55·7	2·5	1·6	8·5	5·3	14·5	9·1
26	9 21·5	9 23·0	8 55·9	2·6	1·6	8·6	5·4	14·6	9·1
27	9 21·8	9 23·3	8 56·2	2·7	1·7	8·7	5·4	14·7	9·2
28	9 22·0	9 23·5	8 56·4	2·8	1·8	8·8	5·5	14·8	9·3
29	9 22·3	9 23·8	8 56·6	2·9	1·8	8·9	5·6	14·9	9·3
30	9 22·5	9 24·0	8 56·9	3·0	1·9	9·0	5·6	15·0	9·4
31	9 22·8	9 24·3	8 57·1	3·1	1·9	9·1	5·7	15·1	9·4
32	9 23·0	9 24·5	8 57·4	3·2	2·0	9·2	5·8	15·2	9·5
33	9 23·3	9 24·8	8 57·6	3·3	2·1	9·3	5·8	15·3	9·6
34	9 23·5	9 25·0	8 57·8	3·4	2·1	9·4	5·9	15·4	9·6
35	9 23·8	9 25·3	8 58·1	3·5	2·2	9·5	5·9	15·5	9·7
36	9 24·0	9 25·5	8 58·3	3·6	2·3	9·6	6·0	15·6	9·8
37	9 24·3	9 25·8	8 58·5	3·7	2·3	9·7	6·1	15·7	9·8
38	9 24·5	9 26·0	8 58·8	3·8	2·4	9·8	6·1	15·8	9·9
39	9 24·8	9 26·3	8 59·0	3·9	2·4	9·9	6·2	15·9	9·9
40	9 25·0	9 26·5	8 59·3	4·0	2·5	10·0	6·3	16·0	10·0
41	9 25·3	9 26·8	8 59·5	4·1	2·6	10·1	6·3	16·1	10·1
42	9 25·5	9 27·0	8 59·7	4·2	2·6	10·2	6·4	16·2	10·1
43	9 25·8	9 27·3	9 00·0	4·3	2·7	10·3	6·4	16·3	10·2
44	9 26·0	9 27·5	9 00·2	4·4	2·8	10·4	6·5	16·4	10·3
45	9 26·3	9 27·8	9 00·5	4·5	2·8	10·5	6·6	16·5	10·3
46	9 26·5	9 28·1	9 00·7	4·6	2·9	10·6	6·6	16·6	10·4
47	9 26·8	9 28·3	9 00·9	4·7	2·9	10·7	6·7	16·7	10·4
48	9 27·0	9 28·6	9 01·2	4·8	3·0	10·8	6·8	16·8	10·5
49	9 27·3	9 28·8	9 01·4	4·9	3·1	10·9	6·8	16·9	10·6
50	9 27·5	9 29·1	9 01·6	5·0	3·1	11·0	6·9	17·0	10·6
51	9 27·8	9 29·3	9 01·9	5·1	3·2	11·1	6·9	17·1	10·7
52	9 28·0	9 29·6	9 02·1	5·2	3·3	11·2	7·0	17·2	10·8
53	9 28·3	9 29·8	9 02·4	5·3	3·3	11·3	7·1	17·3	10·8
54	9 28·5	9 30·1	9 02·6	5·4	3·4	11·4	7·1	17·4	10·9
55	9 28·8	9 30·3	9 02·8	5·5	3·4	11·5	7·2	17·5	10·9
56	9 29·0	9 30·6	9 03·1	5·6	3·5	11·6	7·3	17·6	11·0
57	9 29·3	9 30·8	9 03·3	5·7	3·6	11·7	7·3	17·7	11·1
58	9 29·5	9 31·1	9 03·6	5·8	3·6	11·8	7·4	17·8	11·1
59	9 29·8	9 31·3	9 03·8	5·9	3·7	11·9	7·4	17·9	11·2
60	9 30·0	9 31·6	9 04·0	6·0	3·8	12·0	7·5	18·0	11·3

38m s	SUN PLANETS ° ′	ARIES ° ′	MOON ° ′	v or d ′	Corrn ′	v or d ′	Corrn ′	v or d ′	Corrn ′
00	9 30·0	9 31·6	9 04·0	0·0	0·0	6·0	3·9	12·0	7·7
01	9 30·3	9 31·8	9 04·3	0·1	0·1	6·1	3·9	12·1	7·8
02	9 30·5	9 32·1	9 04·5	0·2	0·1	6·2	4·0	12·2	7·8
03	9 30·8	9 32·3	9 04·7	0·3	0·2	6·3	4·0	12·3	7·9
04	9 31·0	9 32·6	9 05·0	0·4	0·3	6·4	4·1	12·4	8·0
05	9 31·3	9 32·8	9 05·2	0·5	0·3	6·5	4·2	12·5	8·0
06	9 31·5	9 33·1	9 05·5	0·6	0·4	6·6	4·2	12·6	8·1
07	9 31·8	9 33·3	9 05·7	0·7	0·4	6·7	4·3	12·7	8·1
08	9 32·0	9 33·6	9 05·9	0·8	0·5	6·8	4·4	12·8	8·2
09	9 32·3	9 33·8	9 06·2	0·9	0·6	6·9	4·4	12·9	8·3
10	9 32·5	9 34·1	9 06·4	1·0	0·6	7·0	4·5	13·0	8·3
11	9 32·8	9 34·3	9 06·7	1·1	0·7	7·1	4·6	13·1	8·4
12	9 33·0	9 34·6	9 06·9	1·2	0·8	7·2	4·6	13·2	8·5
13	9 33·3	9 34·8	9 07·1	1·3	0·8	7·3	4·7	13·3	8·5
14	9 33·5	9 35·1	9 07·4	1·4	0·9	7·4	4·7	13·4	8·6
15	9 33·8	9 35·3	9 07·6	1·5	1·0	7·5	4·8	13·5	8·7
16	9 34·0	9 35·6	9 07·9	1·6	1·0	7·6	4·9	13·6	8·7
17	9 34·3	9 35·8	9 08·1	1·7	1·1	7·7	4·9	13·7	8·8
18	9 34·5	9 36·1	9 08·3	1·8	1·2	7·8	5·0	13·8	8·9
19	9 34·8	9 36·3	9 08·6	1·9	1·2	7·9	5·1	13·9	8·9
20	9 35·0	9 36·6	9 08·8	2·0	1·3	8·0	5·1	14·0	9·0
21	9 35·3	9 36·8	9 09·0	2·1	1·3	8·1	5·2	14·1	9·0
22	9 35·5	9 37·1	9 09·3	2·2	1·4	8·2	5·3	14·2	9·1
23	9 35·8	9 37·3	9 09·5	2·3	1·5	8·3	5·3	14·3	9·2
24	9 36·0	9 37·6	9 09·8	2·4	1·5	8·4	5·4	14·4	9·2
25	9 36·3	9 37·8	9 10·0	2·5	1·6	8·5	5·5	14·5	9·3
26	9 36·5	9 38·1	9 10·2	2·6	1·7	8·6	5·5	14·6	9·4
27	9 36·8	9 38·3	9 10·5	2·7	1·7	8·7	5·6	14·7	9·4
28	9 37·0	9 38·6	9 10·7	2·8	1·8	8·8	5·6	14·8	9·5
29	9 37·3	9 38·8	9 11·0	2·9	1·9	8·9	5·7	14·9	9·6
30	9 37·5	9 39·1	9 11·2	3·0	1·9	9·0	5·8	15·0	9·6
31	9 37·8	9 39·3	9 11·4	3·1	2·0	9·1	5·8	15·1	9·7
32	9 38·0	9 39·6	9 11·7	3·2	2·1	9·2	5·9	15·2	9·8
33	9 38·3	9 39·8	9 11·9	3·3	2·1	9·3	6·0	15·3	9·8
34	9 38·5	9 40·1	9 12·1	3·4	2·2	9·4	6·0	15·4	9·9
35	9 38·8	9 40·3	9 12·4	3·5	2·2	9·5	6·1	15·5	9·9
36	9 39·0	9 40·6	9 12·6	3·6	2·3	9·6	6·2	15·6	10·0
37	9 39·3	9 40·8	9 12·9	3·7	2·4	9·7	6·2	15·7	10·1
38	9 39·5	9 41·1	9 13·1	3·8	2·4	9·8	6·3	15·8	10·1
39	9 39·8	9 41·3	9 13·3	3·9	2·5	9·9	6·4	15·9	10·2
40	9 40·0	9 41·6	9 13·6	4·0	2·6	10·0	6·4	16·0	10·3
41	9 40·3	9 41·8	9 13·8	4·1	2·6	10·1	6·5	16·1	10·3
42	9 40·5	9 42·1	9 14·1	4·2	2·7	10·2	6·5	16·2	10·4
43	9 40·8	9 42·3	9 14·3	4·3	2·8	10·3	6·6	16·3	10·5
44	9 41·0	9 42·6	9 14·5	4·4	2·8	10·4	6·7	16·4	10·5
45	9 41·3	9 42·8	9 14·8	4·5	2·9	10·5	6·7	16·5	10·6
46	9 41·5	9 43·1	9 15·0	4·6	3·0	10·6	6·8	16·6	10·7
47	9 41·8	9 43·3	9 15·2	4·7	3·0	10·7	6·9	16·7	10·7
48	9 42·0	9 43·6	9 15·5	4·8	3·1	10·8	6·9	16·8	10·8
49	9 42·3	9 43·8	9 15·7	4·9	3·1	10·9	7·0	16·9	10·8
50	9 42·5	9 44·1	9 16·0	5·0	3·2	11·0	7·1	17·0	10·9
51	9 42·8	9 44·3	9 16·2	5·1	3·3	11·1	7·1	17·1	11·0
52	9 43·0	9 44·6	9 16·4	5·2	3·3	11·2	7·2	17·2	11·0
53	9 43·3	9 44·8	9 16·7	5·3	3·4	11·3	7·3	17·3	11·1
54	9 43·5	9 45·1	9 16·9	5·4	3·5	11·4	7·3	17·4	11·2
55	9 43·8	9 45·3	9 17·2	5·5	3·5	11·5	7·4	17·5	11·2
56	9 44·0	9 45·6	9 17·4	5·6	3·6	11·6	7·4	17·6	11·3
57	9 44·3	9 45·8	9 17·6	5·7	3·7	11·7	7·5	17·7	11·4
58	9 44·5	9 46·1	9 17·9	5·8	3·7	11·8	7·6	17·8	11·4
59	9 44·8	9 46·4	9 18·1	5·9	3·8	11·9	7·6	17·9	11·5
60	9 45·0	9 46·6	9 18·4	6·0	3·9	12·0	7·7	18·0	11·6

39m s	SUN PLANETS ° ′	ARIES ° ′	MOON ° ′	v or d ′	Corrn ′	v or d ′	Corrn ′	v or d ′	Corrn ′
00	9 45·0	9 46·6	9 18·4	0·0	0·0	6·0	4·0	12·0	7·9
01	9 45·3	9 46·9	9 18·6	0·1	0·1	6·1	4·0	12·1	8·0
02	9 45·5	9 47·1	9 18·8	0·2	0·1	6·2	4·1	12·2	8·0
03	9 45·8	9 47·4	9 19·1	0·3	0·2	6·3	4·1	12·3	8·1
04	9 46·0	9 47·6	9 19·3	0·4	0·3	6·4	4·2	12·4	8·2
05	9 46·3	9 47·9	9 19·5	0·5	0·3	6·5	4·3	12·5	8·2
06	9 46·5	9 48·1	9 19·8	0·6	0·4	6·6	4·3	12·6	8·3
07	9 46·8	9 48·4	9 20·0	0·7	0·5	6·7	4·4	12·7	8·4
08	9 47·0	9 48·6	9 20·3	0·8	0·5	6·8	4·5	12·8	8·4
09	9 47·3	9 48·9	9 20·5	0·9	0·6	6·9	4·5	12·9	8·5
10	9 47·5	9 49·1	9 20·7	1·0	0·7	7·0	4·6	13·0	8·6
11	9 47·8	9 49·4	9 21·0	1·1	0·7	7·1	4·7	13·1	8·6
12	9 48·0	9 49·6	9 21·2	1·2	0·8	7·2	4·7	13·2	8·7
13	9 48·3	9 49·9	9 21·5	1·3	0·9	7·3	4·8	13·3	8·8
14	9 48·5	9 50·1	9 21·7	1·4	0·9	7·4	4·9	13·4	8·8
15	9 48·8	9 50·4	9 21·9	1·5	1·0	7·5	4·9	13·5	8·9
16	9 49·0	9 50·6	9 22·2	1·6	1·1	7·6	5·0	13·6	9·0
17	9 49·3	9 50·9	9 22·4	1·7	1·1	7·7	5·1	13·7	9·0
18	9 49·5	9 51·1	9 22·6	1·8	1·2	7·8	5·1	13·8	9·1
19	9 49·8	9 51·4	9 22·9	1·9	1·3	7·9	5·2	13·9	9·2
20	9 50·0	9 51·6	9 23·1	2·0	1·3	8·0	5·3	14·0	9·2
21	9 50·3	9 51·9	9 23·4	2·1	1·4	8·1	5·3	14·1	9·3
22	9 50·5	9 52·1	9 23·6	2·2	1·4	8·2	5·4	14·2	9·3
23	9 50·8	9 52·4	9 23·8	2·3	1·5	8·3	5·5	14·3	9·4
24	9 51·0	9 52·6	9 24·1	2·4	1·6	8·4	5·5	14·4	9·5
25	9 51·3	9 52·9	9 24·3	2·5	1·6	8·5	5·6	14·5	9·5
26	9 51·5	9 53·1	9 24·6	2·6	1·7	8·6	5·7	14·6	9·6
27	9 51·8	9 53·4	9 24·8	2·7	1·8	8·7	5·7	14·7	9·7
28	9 52·0	9 53·6	9 25·0	2·8	1·8	8·8	5·8	14·8	9·7
29	9 52·3	9 53·9	9 25·3	2·9	1·9	8·9	5·9	14·9	9·8
30	9 52·5	9 54·1	9 25·5	3·0	2·0	9·0	5·9	15·0	9·9
31	9 52·8	9 54·4	9 25·7	3·1	2·0	9·1	6·0	15·1	9·9
32	9 53·0	9 54·6	9 26·0	3·2	2·1	9·2	6·1	15·2	10·0
33	9 53·3	9 54·9	9 26·2	3·3	2·2	9·3	6·1	15·3	10·1
34	9 53·5	9 55·1	9 26·5	3·4	2·2	9·4	6·2	15·4	10·1
35	9 53·8	9 55·4	9 26·7	3·5	2·3	9·5	6·3	15·5	10·2
36	9 54·0	9 55·6	9 26·9	3·6	2·4	9·6	6·3	15·6	10·3
37	9 54·3	9 55·9	9 27·2	3·7	2·4	9·7	6·4	15·7	10·3
38	9 54·5	9 56·1	9 27·4	3·8	2·5	9·8	6·5	15·8	10·4
39	9 54·8	9 56·4	9 27·7	3·9	2·6	9·9	6·5	15·9	10·5
40	9 55·0	9 56·6	9 27·9	4·0	2·6	10·0	6·6	16·0	10·5
41	9 55·3	9 56·9	9 28·1	4·1	2·7	10·1	6·6	16·1	10·6
42	9 55·5	9 57·1	9 28·4	4·2	2·8	10·2	6·7	16·2	10·7
43	9 55·8	9 57·4	9 28·6	4·3	2·8	10·3	6·8	16·3	10·7
44	9 56·0	9 57·6	9 28·8	4·4	2·9	10·4	6·8	16·4	10·8
45	9 56·3	9 57·9	9 29·1	4·5	3·0	10·5	6·9	16·5	10·9
46	9 56·5	9 58·1	9 29·3	4·6	3·0	10·6	7·0	16·6	10·9
47	9 56·8	9 58·4	9 29·6	4·7	3·1	10·7	7·0	16·7	11·0
48	9 57·0	9 58·6	9 29·8	4·8	3·2	10·8	7·1	16·8	11·1
49	9 57·3	9 58·9	9 30·0	4·9	3·2	10·9	7·2	16·9	11·1
50	9 57·5	9 59·1	9 30·3	5·0	3·3	11·0	7·2	17·0	11·2
51	9 57·8	9 59·4	9 30·5	5·1	3·4	11·1	7·3	17·1	11·3
52	9 58·0	9 59·6	9 30·8	5·2	3·4	11·2	7·4	17·2	11·3
53	9 58·3	9 59·9	9 31·0	5·3	3·5	11·3	7·4	17·3	11·4
54	9 58·5	10 00·1	9 31·2	5·4	3·6	11·4	7·5	17·4	11·5
55	9 58·8	10 00·4	9 31·5	5·5	3·6	11·5	7·6	17·5	11·5
56	9 59·0	10 00·6	9 31·7	5·6	3·7	11·6	7·6	17·6	11·6
57	9 59·3	10 00·9	9 32·0	5·7	3·8	11·7	7·7	17·7	11·7
58	9 59·5	10 01·1	9 32·2	5·8	3·8	11·8	7·8	17·8	11·7
59	9 59·8	10 01·4	9 32·4	5·9	3·9	11·9	7·8	17·9	11·8
60	10 00·0	10 01·6	9 32·7	6·0	4·0	12·0	7·9	18·0	11·9

40m s	SUN PLANETS ° ′	ARIES ° ′	MOON ° ′	v or d ′	Corrn ′	v or d ′	Corrn ′	v or d ′	Corrn ′
00	10 00·0	10 01·6	9 32·7	0·0	0·0	6·0	4·1	12·0	8·1
01	10 00·3	10 01·9	9 32·9	0·1	0·1	6·1	4·1	12·1	8·2
02	10 00·5	10 02·1	9 33·1	0·2	0·1	6·2	4·2	12·2	8·2
03	10 00·8	10 02·4	9 33·4	0·3	0·2	6·3	4·3	12·3	8·3
04	10 01·0	10 02·6	9 33·6	0·4	0·3	6·4	4·3	12·4	8·4
05	10 01·3	10 02·9	9 33·9	0·5	0·3	6·5	4·4	12·5	8·4
06	10 01·5	10 03·1	9 34·1	0·6	0·4	6·6	4·5	12·6	8·5
07	10 01·8	10 03·4	9 34·3	0·7	0·5	6·7	4·5	12·7	8·6
08	10 02·0	10 03·6	9 34·6	0·8	0·5	6·8	4·6	12·8	8·6
09	10 02·3	10 03·9	9 34·8	0·9	0·6	6·9	4·7	12·9	8·7
10	10 02·5	10 04·1	9 35·1	1·0	0·7	7·0	4·7	13·0	8·8
11	10 02·8	10 04·4	9 35·3	1·1	0·7	7·1	4·8	13·1	8·8
12	10 03·0	10 04·7	9 35·5	1·2	0·8	7·2	4·9	13·2	8·9
13	10 03·3	10 04·9	9 35·8	1·3	0·9	7·3	4·9	13·3	9·0
14	10 03·5	10 05·2	9 36·0	1·4	0·9	7·4	5·0	13·4	9·0
15	10 03·8	10 05·4	9 36·2	1·5	1·0	7·5	5·1	13·5	9·1
16	10 04·0	10 05·7	9 36·5	1·6	1·1	7·6	5·1	13·6	9·2
17	10 04·3	10 05·9	9 36·7	1·7	1·1	7·7	5·2	13·7	9·2
18	10 04·5	10 06·2	9 37·0	1·8	1·2	7·8	5·3	13·8	9·3
19	10 04·8	10 06·4	9 37·2	1·9	1·3	7·9	5·3	13·9	9·4
20	10 05·0	10 06·7	9 37·4	2·0	1·4	8·0	5·4	14·0	9·5
21	10 05·3	10 06·9	9 37·7	2·1	1·4	8·1	5·5	14·1	9·5
22	10 05·5	10 07·2	9 37·9	2·2	1·5	8·2	5·5	14·2	9·6
23	10 05·8	10 07·4	9 38·2	2·3	1·6	8·3	5·6	14·3	9·7
24	10 06·0	10 07·7	9 38·4	2·4	1·6	8·4	5·7	14·4	9·7
25	10 06·3	10 07·9	9 38·6	2·5	1·7	8·5	5·7	14·5	9·8
26	10 06·5	10 08·2	9 38·9	2·6	1·8	8·6	5·8	14·6	9·9
27	10 06·8	10 08·4	9 39·1	2·7	1·8	8·7	5·9	14·7	9·9
28	10 07·0	10 08·7	9 39·3	2·8	1·9	8·8	5·9	14·8	10·0
29	10 07·3	10 08·9	9 39·6	2·9	2·0	8·9	6·0	14·9	10·1
30	10 07·5	10 09·2	9 39·8	3·0	2·0	9·0	6·1	15·0	10·1
31	10 07·8	10 09·4	9 40·1	3·1	2·1	9·1	6·1	15·1	10·2
32	10 08·0	10 09·7	9 40·3	3·2	2·2	9·2	6·2	15·2	10·3
33	10 08·3	10 09·9	9 40·5	3·3	2·2	9·3	6·3	15·3	10·3
34	10 08·5	10 10·2	9 40·8	3·4	2·3	9·4	6·3	15·4	10·4
35	10 08·8	10 10·4	9 41·0	3·5	2·4	9·5	6·4	15·5	10·5
36	10 09·0	10 10·7	9 41·3	3·6	2·4	9·6	6·5	15·6	10·5
37	10 09·3	10 10·9	9 41·5	3·7	2·5	9·7	6·5	15·7	10·6
38	10 09·5	10 11·2	9 41·7	3·8	2·6	9·8	6·6	15·8	10·7
39	10 09·8	10 11·4	9 42·0	3·9	2·6	9·9	6·7	15·9	10·7
40	10 10·0	10 11·7	9 42·2	4·0	2·7	10·0	6·8	16·0	10·8
41	10 10·3	10 11·9	9 42·4	4·1	2·8	10·1	6·8	16·1	10·9
42	10 10·5	10 12·2	9 42·7	4·2	2·8	10·2	6·9	16·2	10·9
43	10 10·8	10 12·4	9 42·9	4·3	2·9	10·3	7·0	16·3	11·0
44	10 11·0	10 12·7	9 43·2	4·4	3·0	10·4	7·0	16·4	11·1
45	10 11·3	10 12·9	9 43·4	4·5	3·0	10·5	7·1	16·5	11·1
46	10 11·5	10 13·2	9 43·6	4·6	3·1	10·6	7·2	16·6	11·2
47	10 11·8	10 13·4	9 43·9	4·7	3·2	10·7	7·2	16·7	11·3
48	10 12·0	10 13·7	9 44·1	4·8	3·2	10·8	7·3	16·8	11·3
49	10 12·3	10 13·9	9 44·4	4·9	3·3	10·9	7·4	16·9	11·4
50	10 12·5	10 14·2	9 44·6	5·0	3·4	11·0	7·4	17·0	11·5
51	10 12·8	10 14·4	9 44·8	5·1	3·4	11·1	7·5	17·1	11·5
52	10 13·0	10 14·7	9 45·1	5·2	3·5	11·2	7·6	17·2	11·6
53	10 13·3	10 14·9	9 45·3	5·3	3·6	11·3	7·6	17·3	11·7
54	10 13·5	10 15·2	9 45·6	5·4	3·6	11·4	7·7	17·4	11·7
55	10 13·8	10 15·4	9 45·8	5·5	3·7	11·5	7·8	17·5	11·8
56	10 14·0	10 15·7	9 46·0	5·6	3·8	11·6	7·8	17·6	11·9
57	10 14·3	10 15·9	9 46·3	5·7	3·8	11·7	7·9	17·7	11·9
58	10 14·5	10 16·2	9 46·5	5·8	3·9	11·8	8·0	17·8	12·0
59	10 14·8	10 16·4	9 46·7	5·9	4·0	11·9	8·0	17·9	12·1
60	10 15·0	10 16·7	9 47·0	6·0	4·1	12·0	8·1	18·0	12·2

41m s	SUN PLANETS ° ′	ARIES ° ′	MOON ° ′	v or d ′	Corrn ′	v or d ′	Corrn ′	v or d ′	Corrn ′
00	10 15·0	10 16·7	9 47·0	0·0	0·0	6·0	4·2	12·0	8·3
01	10 15·3	10 16·9	9 47·2	0·1	0·1	6·1	4·2	12·1	8·4
02	10 15·5	10 17·2	9 47·5	0·2	0·1	6·2	4·3	12·2	8·4
03	10 15·8	10 17·4	9 47·7	0·3	0·2	6·3	4·4	12·3	8·5
04	10 16·0	10 17·7	9 47·9	0·4	0·3	6·4	4·4	12·4	8·6
05	10 16·3	10 17·9	9 48·2	0·5	0·3	6·5	4·5	12·5	8·6
06	10 16·5	10 18·2	9 48·4	0·6	0·4	6·6	4·6	12·6	8·7
07	10 16·8	10 18·4	9 48·7	0·7	0·5	6·7	4·6	12·7	8·8
08	10 17·0	10 18·7	9 48·9	0·8	0·6	6·8	4·7	12·8	8·9
09	10 17·3	10 18·9	9 49·1	0·9	0·6	6·9	4·8	12·9	8·9
10	10 17·5	10 19·2	9 49·4	1·0	0·7	7·0	4·8	13·0	9·0
11	10 17·8	10 19·4	9 49·6	1·1	0·8	7·1	4·9	13·1	9·1
12	10 18·0	10 19·7	9 49·8	1·2	0·8	7·2	5·0	13·2	9·1
13	10 18·3	10 19·9	9 50·1	1·3	0·9	7·3	5·0	13·3	9·2
14	10 18·5	10 20·2	9 50·3	1·4	1·0	7·4	5·1	13·4	9·3
15	10 18·8	10 20·4	9 50·6	1·5	1·0	7·5	5·2	13·5	9·3
16	10 19·0	10 20·7	9 50·8	1·6	1·1	7·6	5·3	13·6	9·4
17	10 19·3	10 20·9	9 51·0	1·7	1·2	7·7	5·3	13·7	9·5
18	10 19·5	10 21·2	9 51·3	1·8	1·2	7·8	5·4	13·8	9·5
19	10 19·8	10 21·4	9 51·5	1·9	1·3	7·9	5·5	13·9	9·6
20	10 20·0	10 21·7	9 51·8	2·0	1·4	8·0	5·5	14·0	9·7
21	10 20·3	10 21·9	9 52·0	2·1	1·5	8·1	5·6	14·1	9·8
22	10 20·5	10 22·2	9 52·2	2·2	1·5	8·2	5·7	14·2	9·8
23	10 20·8	10 22·4	9 52·5	2·3	1·6	8·3	5·7	14·3	9·9
24	10 21·0	10 22·7	9 52·7	2·4	1·7	8·4	5·8	14·4	10·0
25	10 21·3	10 23·0	9 52·9	2·5	1·7	8·5	5·9	14·5	10·0
26	10 21·5	10 23·2	9 53·2	2·6	1·8	8·6	5·9	14·6	10·1
27	10 21·8	10 23·5	9 53·4	2·7	1·9	8·7	6·0	14·7	10·2
28	10 22·0	10 23·7	9 53·7	2·8	1·9	8·8	6·1	14·8	10·2
29	10 22·3	10 24·0	9 53·9	2·9	2·0	8·9	6·2	14·9	10·3
30	10 22·5	10 24·2	9 54·1	3·0	2·1	9·0	6·2	15·0	10·4
31	10 22·8	10 24·5	9 54·4	3·1	2·1	9·1	6·3	15·1	10·4
32	10 23·0	10 24·7	9 54·6	3·2	2·2	9·2	6·4	15·2	10·5
33	10 23·3	10 25·0	9 54·9	3·3	2·3	9·3	6·4	15·3	10·6
34	10 23·5	10 25·2	9 55·1	3·4	2·4	9·4	6·5	15·4	10·7
35	10 23·8	10 25·5	9 55·3	3·5	2·4	9·5	6·6	15·5	10·7
36	10 24·0	10 25·7	9 55·6	3·6	2·5	9·6	6·6	15·6	10·8
37	10 24·3	10 26·0	9 55·8	3·7	2·6	9·7	6·7	15·7	10·9
38	10 24·5	10 26·2	9 56·1	3·8	2·6	9·8	6·8	15·8	10·9
39	10 24·8	10 26·5	9 56·3	3·9	2·7	9·9	6·8	15·9	11·0
40	10 25·0	10 26·7	9 56·5	4·0	2·8	10·0	6·9	16·0	11·1
41	10 25·3	10 27·0	9 56·8	4·1	2·8	10·1	7·0	16·1	11·1
42	10 25·5	10 27·2	9 57·0	4·2	2·9	10·2	7·1	16·2	11·2
43	10 25·8	10 27·5	9 57·2	4·3	3·0	10·3	7·1	16·3	11·3
44	10 26·0	10 27·7	9 57·5	4·4	3·0	10·4	7·2	16·4	11·3
45	10 26·3	10 28·0	9 57·7	4·5	3·1	10·5	7·3	16·5	11·4
46	10 26·5	10 28·2	9 58·0	4·6	3·2	10·6	7·3	16·6	11·5
47	10 26·8	10 28·5	9 58·2	4·7	3·3	10·7	7·4	16·7	11·6
48	10 27·0	10 28·7	9 58·4	4·8	3·3	10·8	7·5	16·8	11·6
49	10 27·3	10 29·0	9 58·7	4·9	3·4	10·9	7·5	16·9	11·7
50	10 27·5	10 29·2	9 58·9	5·0	3·5	11·0	7·6	17·0	11·8
51	10 27·8	10 29·5	9 59·2	5·1	3·5	11·1	7·7	17·1	11·8
52	10 28·0	10 29·7	9 59·4	5·2	3·6	11·2	7·7	17·2	11·9
53	10 28·3	10 30·0	9 59·6	5·3	3·7	11·3	7·8	17·3	12·0
54	10 28·5	10 30·2	9 59·9	5·4	3·7	11·4	7·9	17·4	12·0
55	10 28·8	10 30·5	10 00·1	5·5	3·8	11·5	8·0	17·5	12·1
56	10 29·0	10 30·7	10 00·3	5·6	3·9	11·6	8·0	17·6	12·2
57	10 29·3	10 31·0	10 00·6	5·7	3·9	11·7	8·1	17·7	12·2
58	10 29·5	10 31·2	10 00·8	5·8	4·0	11·8	8·2	17·8	12·3
59	10 29·8	10 31·5	10 01·1	5·9	4·1	11·9	8·2	17·9	12·4
60	10 30·0	10 31·7	10 01·3	6·0	4·2	12·0	8·3	18·0	12·5

42m s	SUN PLANETS ° ′	ARIES ° ′	MOON ° ′	v or d ′	Corrn ′	v or d ′	Corrn ′	v or d ′	Corrn ′
00	10 30·0	10 31·7	10 01·3	0·0	0·0	6·0	4·3	12·0	8·5
01	10 30·3	10 32·0	10 01·5	0·1	0·1	6·1	4·3	12·1	8·6
02	10 30·5	10 32·2	10 01·8	0·2	0·1	6·2	4·4	12·2	8·6
03	10 30·8	10 32·5	10 02·0	0·3	0·2	6·3	4·5	12·3	8·7
04	10 31·0	10 32·7	10 02·3	0·4	0·3	6·4	4·5	12·4	8·8
05	10 31·3	10 33·0	10 02·5	0·5	0·4	6·5	4·6	12·5	8·9
06	10 31·5	10 33·2	10 02·7	0·6	0·4	6·6	4·7	12·6	8·9
07	10 31·8	10 33·5	10 03·0	0·7	0·5	6·7	4·7	12·7	9·0
08	10 32·0	10 33·7	10 03·2	0·8	0·6	6·8	4·8	12·8	9·1
09	10 32·3	10 34·0	10 03·4	0·9	0·6	6·9	4·9	12·9	9·1
10	10 32·5	10 34·2	10 03·7	1·0	0·7	7·0	5·0	13·0	9·2
11	10 32·8	10 34·5	10 03·9	1·1	0·8	7·1	5·0	13·1	9·3
12	10 33·0	10 34·7	10 04·2	1·2	0·9	7·2	5·1	13·2	9·4
13	10 33·3	10 35·0	10 04·4	1·3	0·9	7·3	5·2	13·3	9·4
14	10 33·5	10 35·2	10 04·6	1·4	1·0	7·4	5·2	13·4	9·5
15	10 33·8	10 35·5	10 04·9	1·5	1·1	7·5	5·3	13·5	9·6
16	10 34·0	10 35·7	10 05·1	1·6	1·1	7·6	5·4	13·6	9·6
17	10 34·3	10 36·0	10 05·4	1·7	1·2	7·7	5·5	13·7	9·7
18	10 34·5	10 36·2	10 05·6	1·8	1·3	7·8	5·5	13·8	9·8
19	10 34·8	10 36·5	10 05·8	1·9	1·3	7·9	5·6	13·9	9·8
20	10 35·0	10 36·7	10 06·1	2·0	1·4	8·0	5·7	14·0	9·9
21	10 35·3	10 37·0	10 06·3	2·1	1·5	8·1	5·7	14·1	10·0
22	10 35·5	10 37·2	10 06·5	2·2	1·6	8·2	5·8	14·2	10·1
23	10 35·8	10 37·5	10 06·8	2·3	1·6	8·3	5·9	14·3	10·1
24	10 36·0	10 37·7	10 07·0	2·4	1·7	8·4	6·0	14·4	10·2
25	10 36·3	10 38·0	10 07·3	2·5	1·8	8·5	6·0	14·5	10·3
26	10 36·5	10 38·2	10 07·5	2·6	1·8	8·6	6·1	14·6	10·3
27	10 36·8	10 38·5	10 07·7	2·7	1·9	8·7	6·2	14·7	10·4
28	10 37·0	10 38·7	10 08·0	2·8	2·0	8·8	6·2	14·8	10·5
29	10 37·3	10 39·0	10 08·2	2·9	2·1	8·9	6·3	14·9	10·6
30	10 37·5	10 39·2	10 08·5	3·0	2·1	9·0	6·4	15·0	10·6
31	10 37·8	10 39·5	10 08·7	3·1	2·2	9·1	6·4	15·1	10·7
32	10 38·0	10 39·7	10 08·9	3·2	2·3	9·2	6·5	15·2	10·8
33	10 38·3	10 40·0	10 09·2	3·3	2·3	9·3	6·6	15·3	10·8
34	10 38·5	10 40·2	10 09·4	3·4	2·4	9·4	6·7	15·4	10·9
35	10 38·8	10 40·5	10 09·7	3·5	2·5	9·5	6·7	15·5	11·0
36	10 39·0	10 40·7	10 09·9	3·6	2·6	9·6	6·8	15·6	11·1
37	10 39·3	10 41·0	10 10·1	3·7	2·6	9·7	6·9	15·7	11·1
38	10 39·5	10 41·3	10 10·4	3·8	2·7	9·8	6·9	15·8	11·2
39	10 39·8	10 41·5	10 10·6	3·9	2·8	9·9	7·0	15·9	11·3
40	10 40·0	10 41·8	10 10·8	4·0	2·8	10·0	7·1	16·0	11·3
41	10 40·3	10 42·0	10 11·1	4·1	2·9	10·1	7·2	16·1	11·4
42	10 40·5	10 42·3	10 11·3	4·2	3·0	10·2	7·2	16·2	11·5
43	10 40·8	10 42·5	10 11·6	4·3	3·0	10·3	7·3	16·3	11·5
44	10 41·0	10 42·8	10 11·8	4·4	3·1	10·4	7·4	16·4	11·6
45	10 41·3	10 43·0	10 12·0	4·5	3·2	10·5	7·4	16·5	11·7
46	10 41·5	10 43·3	10 12·3	4·6	3·3	10·6	7·5	16·6	11·8
47	10 41·8	10 43·5	10 12·5	4·7	3·3	10·7	7·6	16·7	11·8
48	10 42·0	10 43·8	10 12·8	4·8	3·4	10·8	7·7	16·8	11·9
49	10 42·3	10 44·0	10 13·0	4·9	3·5	10·9	7·7	16·9	12·0
50	10 42·5	10 44·3	10 13·2	5·0	3·5	11·0	7·8	17·0	12·0
51	10 42·8	10 44·5	10 13·5	5·1	3·6	11·1	7·9	17·1	12·1
52	10 43·0	10 44·8	10 13·7	5·2	3·7	11·2	7·9	17·2	12·2
53	10 43·3	10 45·0	10 13·9	5·3	3·8	11·3	8·0	17·3	12·3
54	10 43·5	10 45·3	10 14·2	5·4	3·8	11·4	8·1	17·4	12·3
55	10 43·8	10 45·5	10 14·4	5·5	3·9	11·5	8·1	17·5	12·4
56	10 44·0	10 45·8	10 14·7	5·6	4·0	11·6	8·2	17·6	12·5
57	10 44·3	10 46·0	10 14·9	5·7	4·0	11·7	8·3	17·7	12·5
58	10 44·5	10 46·3	10 15·1	5·8	4·1	11·8	8·4	17·8	12·6
59	10 44·8	10 46·5	10 15·4	5·9	4·2	11·9	8·4	17·9	12·7
60	10 45·0	10 46·8	10 15·6	6·0	4·3	12·0	8·5	18·0	12·8

43m s	SUN PLANETS ° ′	ARIES ° ′	MOON ° ′	v or d ′	Corrn ′	v or d ′	Corrn ′	v or d ′	Corrn ′
00	10 45·0	10 46·8	10 15·6	0·0	0·0	6·0	4·4	12·0	8·7
01	10 45·3	10 47·0	10 15·9	0·1	0·1	6·1	4·4	12·1	8·8
02	10 45·5	10 47·3	10 16·1	0·2	0·1	6·2	4·5	12·2	8·8
03	10 45·8	10 47·5	10 16·3	0·3	0·2	6·3	4·6	12·3	8·9
04	10 46·0	10 47·8	10 16·6	0·4	0·3	6·4	4·6	12·4	9·0
05	10 46·3	10 48·0	10 16·8	0·5	0·4	6·5	4·7	12·5	9·1
06	10 46·5	10 48·3	10 17·0	0·6	0·4	6·6	4·8	12·6	9·1
07	10 46·8	10 48·5	10 17·3	0·7	0·5	6·7	4·9	12·7	9·2
08	10 47·0	10 48·8	10 17·5	0·8	0·6	6·8	4·9	12·8	9·3
09	10 47·3	10 49·0	10 17·8	0·9	0·7	6·9	5·0	12·9	9·4
10	10 47·5	10 49·3	10 18·0	1·0	0·7	7·0	5·1	13·0	9·4
11	10 47·8	10 49·5	10 18·2	1·1	0·8	7·1	5·1	13·1	9·5
12	10 48·0	10 49·8	10 18·5	1·2	0·9	7·2	5·2	13·2	9·6
13	10 48·3	10 50·0	10 18·7	1·3	0·9	7·3	5·3	13·3	9·6
14	10 48·5	10 50·3	10 19·0	1·4	1·0	7·4	5·4	13·4	9·7
15	10 48·8	10 50·5	10 19·2	1·5	1·1	7·5	5·4	13·5	9·8
16	10 49·0	10 50·8	10 19·4	1·6	1·2	7·6	5·5	13·6	9·9
17	10 49·3	10 51·0	10 19·7	1·7	1·2	7·7	5·6	13·7	9·9
18	10 49·5	10 51·3	10 19·9	1·8	1·3	7·8	5·7	13·8	10·0
19	10 49·8	10 51·5	10 20·2	1·9	1·4	7·9	5·7	13·9	10·1
20	10 50·0	10 51·8	10 20·4	2·0	1·5	8·0	5·8	14·0	10·2
21	10 50·3	10 52·0	10 20·6	2·1	1·5	8·1	5·9	14·1	10·2
22	10 50·5	10 52·3	10 20·9	2·2	1·6	8·2	5·9	14·2	10·3
23	10 50·8	10 52·5	10 21·1	2·3	1·7	8·3	6·0	14·3	10·4
24	10 51·0	10 52·8	10 21·3	2·4	1·7	8·4	6·1	14·4	10·4
25	10 51·3	10 53·0	10 21·6	2·5	1·8	8·5	6·2	14·5	10·5
26	10 51·5	10 53·3	10 21·8	2·6	1·9	8·6	6·2	14·6	10·6
27	10 51·8	10 53·5	10 22·1	2·7	2·0	8·7	6·3	14·7	10·7
28	10 52·0	10 53·8	10 22·3	2·8	2·0	8·8	6·4	14·8	10·7
29	10 52·3	10 54·0	10 22·5	2·9	2·1	8·9	6·5	14·9	10·8
30	10 52·5	10 54·3	10 22·8	3·0	2·2	9·0	6·5	15·0	10·9
31	10 52·8	10 54·5	10 23·0	3·1	2·2	9·1	6·6	15·1	10·9
32	10 53·0	10 54·8	10 23·3	3·2	2·3	9·2	6·7	15·2	11·0
33	10 53·3	10 55·0	10 23·5	3·3	2·4	9·3	6·7	15·3	11·1
34	10 53·5	10 55·3	10 23·7	3·4	2·5	9·4	6·8	15·4	11·2
35	10 53·8	10 55·5	10 24·0	3·5	2·5	9·5	6·9	15·5	11·2
36	10 54·0	10 55·8	10 24·2	3·6	2·6	9·6	7·0	15·6	11·3
37	10 54·3	10 56·0	10 24·4	3·7	2·7	9·7	7·0	15·7	11·4
38	10 54·5	10 56·3	10 24·7	3·8	2·8	9·8	7·1	15·8	11·5
39	10 54·8	10 56·5	10 24·9	3·9	2·8	9·9	7·2	15·9	11·5
40	10 55·0	10 56·8	10 25·2	4·0	2·9	10·0	7·3	16·0	11·6
41	10 55·3	10 57·0	10 25·4	4·1	3·0	10·1	7·3	16·1	11·7
42	10 55·5	10 57·3	10 25·6	4·2	3·0	10·2	7·4	16·2	11·7
43	10 55·8	10 57·5	10 25·9	4·3	3·1	10·3	7·5	16·3	11·8
44	10 56·0	10 57·8	10 26·1	4·4	3·2	10·4	7·5	16·4	11·9
45	10 56·3	10 58·0	10 26·4	4·5	3·3	10·5	7·6	16·5	12·0
46	10 56·5	10 58·3	10 26·6	4·6	3·3	10·6	7·7	16·6	12·0
47	10 56·8	10 58·5	10 26·8	4·7	3·4	10·7	7·8	16·7	12·1
48	10 57·0	10 58·8	10 27·1	4·8	3·5	10·8	7·8	16·8	12·2
49	10 57·3	10 59·0	10 27·3	4·9	3·6	10·9	7·9	16·9	12·3
50	10 57·5	10 59·3	10 27·5	5·0	3·6	11·0	8·0	17·0	12·3
51	10 57·8	10 59·6	10 27·8	5·1	3·7	11·1	8·0	17·1	12·4
52	10 58·0	10 59·8	10 28·0	5·2	3·8	11·2	8·1	17·2	12·5
53	10 58·3	11 00·1	10 28·3	5·3	3·8	11·3	8·2	17·3	12·5
54	10 58·5	11 00·3	10 28·5	5·4	3·9	11·4	8·3	17·4	12·6
55	10 58·8	11 00·6	10 28·7	5·5	4·0	11·5	8·3	17·5	12·7
56	10 59·0	11 00·8	10 29·0	5·6	4·1	11·6	8·4	17·6	12·8
57	10 59·3	11 01·1	10 29·2	5·7	4·1	11·7	8·5	17·7	12·8
58	10 59·5	11 01·3	10 29·5	5·8	4·2	11·8	8·6	17·8	12·9
59	10 59·8	11 01·6	10 29·7	5·9	4·3	11·9	8·6	17·9	13·0
60	11 00·0	11 01·8	10 29·9	6·0	4·4	12·0	8·7	18·0	13·1

44ᵐ	SUN PLANETS	ARIES	MOON	v or d	Corrⁿ	v or d	Corrⁿ	v or d	Corrⁿ
s	° ′	° ′	° ′	′	′	′	′	′	′
00	11 00·0	11 01·8	10 29·9	0·0	0·0	6·0	4·5	12·0	8·9
01	11 00·3	11 02·1	10 30·2	0·1	0·1	6·1	4·5	12·1	9·0
02	11 00·5	11 02·3	10 30·4	0·2	0·1	6·2	4·6	12·2	9·0
03	11 00·8	11 02·6	10 30·6	0·3	0·2	6·3	4·7	12·3	9·1
04	11 01·0	11 02·8	10 30·9	0·4	0·3	6·4	4·7	12·4	9·2
05	11 01·3	11 03·1	10 31·1	0·5	0·4	6·5	4·8	12·5	9·3
06	11 01·5	11 03·3	10 31·4	0·6	0·4	6·6	4·9	12·6	9·3
07	11 01·8	11 03·6	10 31·6	0·7	0·5	6·7	5·0	12·7	9·4
08	11 02·0	11 03·8	10 31·8	0·8	0·6	6·8	5·0	12·8	9·5
09	11 02·3	11 04·1	10 32·1	0·9	0·7	6·9	5·1	12·9	9·6
10	11 02·5	11 04·3	10 32·3	1·0	0·7	7·0	5·2	13·0	9·6
11	11 02·8	11 04·6	10 32·6	1·1	0·8	7·1	5·3	13·1	9·7
12	11 03·0	11 04·8	10 32·8	1·2	0·9	7·2	5·3	13·2	9·8
13	11 03·3	11 05·1	10 33·0	1·3	1·0	7·3	5·4	13·3	9·9
14	11 03·5	11 05·3	10 33·3	1·4	1·0	7·4	5·5	13·4	9·9
15	11 03·8	11 05·6	10 33·5	1·5	1·1	7·5	5·6	13·5	10·0
16	11 04·0	11 05·8	10 33·8	1·6	1·2	7·6	5·6	13·6	10·1
17	11 04·3	11 06·1	10 34·0	1·7	1·3	7·7	5·7	13·7	10·2
18	11 04·5	11 06·3	10 34·2	1·8	1·3	7·8	5·8	13·8	10·2
19	11 04·8	11 06·6	10 34·5	1·9	1·4	7·9	5·9	13·9	10·3
20	11 05·0	11 06·8	10 34·7	2·0	1·5	8·0	5·9	14·0	10·4
21	11 05·3	11 07·1	10 34·9	2·1	1·6	8·1	6·0	14·1	10·5
22	11 05·5	11 07·3	10 35·2	2·2	1·6	8·2	6·1	14·2	10·5
23	11 05·8	11 07·6	10 35·4	2·3	1·7	8·3	6·2	14·3	10·6
24	11 06·0	11 07·8	10 35·7	2·4	1·8	8·4	6·2	14·4	10·7
25	11 06·3	11 08·1	10 35·9	2·5	1·9	8·5	6·3	14·5	10·8
26	11 06·5	11 08·3	10 36·1	2·6	1·9	8·6	6·4	14·6	10·8
27	11 06·8	11 08·6	10 36·4	2·7	2·0	8·7	6·5	14·7	10·9
28	11 07·0	11 08·8	10 36·6	2·8	2·1	8·8	6·5	14·8	11·0
29	11 07·3	11 09·1	10 36·9	2·9	2·2	8·9	6·6	14·9	11·1
30	11 07·5	11 09·3	10 37·1	3·0	2·2	9·0	6·7	15·0	11·1
31	11 07·8	11 09·6	10 37·3	3·1	2·3	9·1	6·7	15·1	11·2
32	11 08·0	11 09·8	10 37·6	3·2	2·4	9·2	6·8	15·2	11·3
33	11 08·3	11 10·1	10 37·8	3·3	2·4	9·3	6·9	15·3	11·3
34	11 08·5	11 10·3	10 38·0	3·4	2·5	9·4	7·0	15·4	11·4
35	11 08·8	11 10·6	10 38·3	3·5	2·6	9·5	7·0	15·5	11·5
36	11 09·0	11 10·8	10 38·5	3·6	2·7	9·6	7·1	15·6	11·6
37	11 09·3	11 11·1	10 38·8	3·7	2·7	9·7	7·2	15·7	11·6
38	11 09·5	11 11·3	10 39·0	3·8	2·8	9·8	7·3	15·8	11·7
39	11 09·8	11 11·6	10 39·2	3·9	2·9	9·9	7·3	15·9	11·8
40	11 10·0	11 11·8	10 39·5	4·0	3·0	10·0	7·4	16·0	11·9
41	11 10·3	11 12·1	10 39·7	4·1	3·0	10·1	7·5	16·1	11·9
42	11 10·5	11 12·3	10 40·0	4·2	3·1	10·2	7·6	16·2	12·0
43	11 10·8	11 12·6	10 40·2	4·3	3·2	10·3	7·6	16·3	12·1
44	11 11·0	11 12·8	10 40·4	4·4	3·3	10·4	7·7	16·4	12·2
45	11 11·3	11 13·1	10 40·7	4·5	3·3	10·5	7·8	16·5	12·2
46	11 11·5	11 13·3	10 40·9	4·6	3·4	10·6	7·9	16·6	12·3
47	11 11·8	11 13·6	10 41·1	4·7	3·5	10·7	7·9	16·7	12·4
48	11 12·0	11 13·8	10 41·4	4·8	3·6	10·8	8·0	16·8	12·5
49	11 12·3	11 14·1	10 41·6	4·9	3·6	10·9	8·1	16·9	12·5
50	11 12·5	11 14·3	10 41·9	5·0	3·7	11·0	8·2	17·0	12·6
51	11 12·8	11 14·6	10 42·1	5·1	3·8	11·1	8·2	17·1	12·7
52	11 13·0	11 14·8	10 42·3	5·2	3·9	11·2	8·3	17·2	12·8
53	11 13·3	11 15·1	10 42·6	5·3	3·9	11·3	8·4	17·3	12·8
54	11 13·5	11 15·3	10 42·8	5·4	4·0	11·4	8·5	17·4	12·9
55	11 13·8	11 15·6	10 43·1	5·5	4·1	11·5	8·5	17·5	13·0
56	11 14·0	11 15·8	10 43·3	5·6	4·2	11·6	8·6	17·6	13·1
57	11 14·3	11 16·1	10 43·5	5·7	4·2	11·7	8·7	17·7	13·1
58	11 14·5	11 16·3	10 43·8	5·8	4·3	11·8	8·8	17·8	13·2
59	11 14·8	11 16·6	10 44·0	5·9	4·4	11·9	8·8	17·9	13·3
60	11 15·0	11 16·8	10 44·3	6·0	4·5	12·0	8·9	18·0	13·4

45ᵐ	SUN PLANETS	ARIES	MOON	v or d	Corrⁿ	v or d	Corrⁿ	v or d	Corrⁿ
s	° ′	° ′	° ′	′	′	′	′	′	′
00	11 15·0	11 16·8	10 44·3	0·0	0·0	6·0	4·6	12·0	9·1
01	11 15·3	11 17·1	10 44·5	0·1	0·1	6·1	4·6	12·1	9·2
02	11 15·5	11 17·3	10 44·7	0·2	0·2	6·2	4·7	12·2	9·3
03	11 15·8	11 17·6	10 45·0	0·3	0·2	6·3	4·8	12·3	9·3
04	11 16·0	11 17·9	10 45·2	0·4	0·3	6·4	4·9	12·4	9·4
05	11 16·3	11 18·1	10 45·4	0·5	0·4	6·5	4·9	12·5	9·5
06	11 16·5	11 18·4	10 45·7	0·6	0·5	6·6	5·0	12·6	9·6
07	11 16·8	11 18·6	10 45·9	0·7	0·5	6·7	5·1	12·7	9·6
08	11 17·0	11 18·9	10 46·2	0·8	0·6	6·8	5·2	12·8	9·7
09	11 17·3	11 19·1	10 46·4	0·9	0·7	6·9	5·2	12·9	9·8
10	11 17·5	11 19·4	10 46·6	1·0	0·8	7·0	5·3	13·0	9·9
11	11 17·8	11 19·6	10 46·9	1·1	0·8	7·1	5·4	13·1	9·9
12	11 18·0	11 19·9	10 47·1	1·2	0·9	7·2	5·5	13·2	10·0
13	11 18·3	11 20·1	10 47·4	1·3	1·0	7·3	5·5	13·3	10·1
14	11 18·5	11 20·4	10 47·6	1·4	1·1	7·4	5·6	13·4	10·2
15	11 18·8	11 20·6	10 47·8	1·5	1·1	7·5	5·7	13·5	10·2
16	11 19·0	11 20·9	10 48·1	1·6	1·2	7·6	5·8	13·6	10·3
17	11 19·3	11 21·1	10 48·3	1·7	1·3	7·7	5·8	13·7	10·4
18	11 19·5	11 21·4	10 48·5	1·8	1·4	7·8	5·9	13·8	10·5
19	11 19·8	11 21·6	10 48·8	1·9	1·4	7·9	6·0	13·9	10·5
20	11 20·0	11 21·9	10 49·0	2·0	1·5	8·0	6·1	14·0	10·6
21	11 20·3	11 22·1	10 49·3	2·1	1·6	8·1	6·1	14·1	10·7
22	11 20·5	11 22·4	10 49·5	2·2	1·7	8·2	6·2	14·2	10·8
23	11 20·8	11 22·6	10 49·7	2·3	1·7	8·3	6·3	14·3	10·8
24	11 21·0	11 22·9	10 50·0	2·4	1·8	8·4	6·4	14·4	10·9
25	11 21·3	11 23·1	10 50·2	2·5	1·9	8·5	6·4	14·5	11·0
26	11 21·5	11 23·4	10 50·5	2·6	2·0	8·6	6·5	14·6	11·1
27	11 21·8	11 23·6	10 50·7	2·7	2·0	8·7	6·6	14·7	11·1
28	11 22·0	11 23·9	10 50·9	2·8	2·1	8·8	6·7	14·8	11·2
29	11 22·3	11 24·1	10 51·2	2·9	2·2	8·9	6·7	14·9	11·3
30	11 22·5	11 24·4	10 51·4	3·0	2·3	9·0	6·8	15·0	11·4
31	11 22·8	11 24·6	10 51·6	3·1	2·4	9·1	6·9	15·1	11·5
32	11 23·0	11 24·9	10 51·9	3·2	2·4	9·2	7·0	15·2	11·5
33	11 23·3	11 25·1	10 52·1	3·3	2·5	9·3	7·1	15·3	11·6
34	11 23·5	11 25·4	10 52·4	3·4	2·6	9·4	7·1	15·4	11·7
35	11 23·8	11 25·6	10 52·6	3·5	2·7	9·5	7·2	15·5	11·8
36	11 24·0	11 25·9	10 52·8	3·6	2·7	9·6	7·3	15·6	11·8
37	11 24·3	11 26·1	10 53·1	3·7	2·8	9·7	7·4	15·7	11·9
38	11 24·5	11 26·4	10 53·3	3·8	2·9	9·8	7·4	15·8	12·0
39	11 24·8	11 26·6	10 53·6	3·9	3·0	9·9	7·5	15·9	12·1
40	11 25·0	11 26·9	10 53·8	4·0	3·0	10·0	7·6	16·0	12·1
41	11 25·3	11 27·1	10 54·0	4·1	3·1	10·1	7·7	16·1	12·2
42	11 25·5	11 27·4	10 54·3	4·2	3·2	10·2	7·7	16·2	12·3
43	11 25·8	11 27·6	10 54·5	4·3	3·3	10·3	7·8	16·3	12·4
44	11 26·0	11 27·9	10 54·7	4·4	3·3	10·4	7·9	16·4	12·4
45	11 26·3	11 28·1	10 55·0	4·5	3·4	10·5	8·0	16·5	12·5
46	11 26·5	11 28·4	10 55·2	4·6	3·5	10·6	8·0	16·6	12·6
47	11 26·8	11 28·6	10 55·5	4·7	3·6	10·7	8·1	16·7	12·7
48	11 27·0	11 28·9	10 55·7	4·8	3·6	10·8	8·2	16·8	12·7
49	11 27·3	11 29·1	10 55·9	4·9	3·7	10·9	8·3	16·9	12·8
50	11 27·5	11 29·4	10 56·2	5·0	3·8	11·0	8·3	17·0	12·9
51	11 27·8	11 29·6	10 56·4	5·1	3·9	11·1	8·4	17·1	13·0
52	11 28·0	11 29·9	10 56·7	5·2	3·9	11·2	8·5	17·2	13·0
53	11 28·3	11 30·1	10 56·9	5·3	4·0	11·3	8·6	17·3	13·1
54	11 28·5	11 30·4	10 57·1	5·4	4·1	11·4	8·6	17·4	13·2
55	11 28·8	11 30·6	10 57·4	5·5	4·2	11·5	8·7	17·5	13·3
56	11 29·0	11 30·9	10 57·6	5·6	4·2	11·6	8·8	17·6	13·3
57	11 29·3	11 31·1	10 57·9	5·7	4·3	11·7	8·9	17·7	13·4
58	11 29·5	11 31·4	10 58·1	5·8	4·4	11·8	8·9	17·8	13·5
59	11 29·8	11 31·6	10 58·3	5·9	4·5	11·9	9·0	17·9	13·6
60	11 30·0	11 31·9	10 58·6	6·0	4·6	12·0	9·1	18·0	13·7

46^m	SUN PLANETS	ARIES	MOON	v or d	Corr^n	v or d	Corr^n	v or d	Corr^n
s	° ′	° ′	° ′	′	′	′	′	′	′
00	11 30·0	11 31·9	10 58·6	0·0	0·0	6·0	4·7	12·0	9·3
01	11 30·3	11 32·1	10 58·8	0·1	0·1	6·1	4·7	12·1	9·4
02	11 30·5	11 32·4	10 59·0	0·2	0·2	6·2	4·8	12·2	9·5
03	11 30·8	11 32·6	10 59·3	0·3	0·2	6·3	4·9	12·3	9·5
04	11 31·0	11 32·9	10 59·5	0·4	0·3	6·4	5·0	12·4	9·6
05	11 31·3	11 33·1	10 59·8	0·5	0·4	6·5	5·0	12·5	9·7
06	11 31·5	11 33·4	11 00·0	0·6	0·5	6·6	5·1	12·6	9·8
07	11 31·8	11 33·6	11 00·2	0·7	0·5	6·7	5·2	12·7	9·8
08	11 32·0	11 33·9	11 00·5	0·8	0·6	6·8	5·3	12·8	9·9
09	11 32·3	11 34·1	11 00·7	0·9	0·7	6·9	5·3	12·9	10·0
10	11 32·5	11 34·4	11 01·0	1·0	0·8	7·0	5·4	13·0	10·1
11	11 32·8	11 34·6	11 01·2	1·1	0·9	7·1	5·5	13·1	10·2
12	11 33·0	11 34·9	11 01·4	1·2	0·9	7·2	5·6	13·2	10·2
13	11 33·3	11 35·1	11 01·7	1·3	1·0	7·3	5·7	13·3	10·3
14	11 33·5	11 35·4	11 01·9	1·4	1·1	7·4	5·7	13·4	10·4
15	11 33·8	11 35·6	11 02·1	1·5	1·2	7·5	5·8	13·5	10·5
16	11 34·0	11 35·9	11 02·4	1·6	1·2	7·6	5·9	13·6	10·5
17	11 34·3	11 36·2	11 02·6	1·7	1·3	7·7	6·0	13·7	10·6
18	11 34·5	11 36·4	11 02·9	1·8	1·4	7·8	6·0	13·8	10·7
19	11 34·8	11 36·7	11 03·1	1·9	1·5	7·9	6·1	13·9	10·8
20	11 35·0	11 36·9	11 03·3	2·0	1·6	8·0	6·2	14·0	10·9
21	11 35·3	11 37·2	11 03·6	2·1	1·6	8·1	6·3	14·1	10·9
22	11 35·5	11 37·4	11 03·8	2·2	1·7	8·2	6·4	14·2	11·0
23	11 35·8	11 37·7	11 04·1	2·3	1·8	8·3	6·4	14·3	11·1
24	11 36·0	11 37·9	11 04·3	2·4	1·9	8·4	6·5	14·4	11·2
25	11 36·3	11 38·2	11 04·5	2·5	1·9	8·5	6·6	14·5	11·2
26	11 36·5	11 38·4	11 04·8	2·6	2·0	8·6	6·7	14·6	11·3
27	11 36·8	11 38·7	11 05·0	2·7	2·1	8·7	6·7	14·7	11·4
28	11 37·0	11 38·9	11 05·2	2·8	2·2	8·8	6·8	14·8	11·5
29	11 37·3	11 39·2	11 05·5	2·9	2·2	8·9	6·9	14·9	11·5
30	11 37·5	11 39·4	11 05·7	3·0	2·3	9·0	7·0	15·0	11·6
31	11 37·8	11 39·7	11 06·0	3·1	2·4	9·1	7·1	15·1	11·7
32	11 38·0	11 39·9	11 06·2	3·2	2·5	9·2	7·1	15·2	11·8
33	11 38·3	11 40·2	11 06·4	3·3	2·6	9·3	7·2	15·3	11·9
34	11 38·5	11 40·4	11 06·7	3·4	2·6	9·4	7·3	15·4	11·9
35	11 38·8	11 40·7	11 06·9	3·5	2·7	9·5	7·4	15·5	12·0
36	11 39·0	11 40·9	11 07·2	3·6	2·8	9·6	7·4	15·6	12·1
37	11 39·3	11 41·2	11 07·4	3·7	2·9	9·7	7·5	15·7	12·2
38	11 39·5	11 41·4	11 07·6	3·8	2·9	9·8	7·6	15·8	12·2
39	11 39·8	11 41·7	11 07·9	3·9	3·0	9·9	7·7	15·9	12·3
40	11 40·0	11 41·9	11 08·1	4·0	3·1	10·0	7·8	16·0	12·4
41	11 40·3	11 42·2	11 08·3	4·1	3·2	10·1	7·8	16·1	12·5
42	11 40·5	11 42·4	11 08·6	4·2	3·3	10·2	7·9	16·2	12·6
43	11 40·8	11 42·7	11 08·8	4·3	3·3	10·3	8·0	16·3	12·6
44	11 41·0	11 42·9	11 09·1	4·4	3·4	10·4	8·1	16·4	12·7
45	11 41·3	11 43·2	11 09·3	4·5	3·5	10·5	8·1	16·5	12·8
46	11 41·5	11 43·4	11 09·5	4·6	3·6	10·6	8·2	16·6	12·9
47	11 41·8	11 43·7	11 09·8	4·7	3·6	10·7	8·3	16·7	12·9
48	11 42·0	11 43·9	11 10·0	4·8	3·7	10·8	8·4	16·8	13·0
49	11 42·3	11 44·2	11 10·3	4·9	3·8	10·9	8·4	16·9	13·1
50	11 42·5	11 44·4	11 10·5	5·0	3·9	11·0	8·5	17·0	13·2
51	11 42·8	11 44·7	11 10·7	5·1	4·0	11·1	8·6	17·1	13·3
52	11 43·0	11 44·9	11 11·0	5·2	4·0	11·2	8·7	17·2	13·3
53	11 43·3	11 45·2	11 11·2	5·3	4·1	11·3	8·8	17·3	13·4
54	11 43·5	11 45·4	11 11·5	5·4	4·2	11·4	8·8	17·4	13·5
55	11 43·8	11 45·7	11 11·7	5·5	4·3	11·5	8·9	17·5	13·6
56	11 44·0	11 45·9	11 11·9	5·6	4·3	11·6	9·0	17·6	13·6
57	11 44·3	11 46·2	11 12·2	5·7	4·4	11·7	9·1	17·7	13·7
58	11 44·5	11 46·4	11 12·4	5·8	4·5	11·8	9·1	17·8	13·8
59	11 44·8	11 46·7	11 12·6	5·9	4·6	11·9	9·2	17·9	13·9
60	11 45·0	11 46·9	11 12·9	6·0	4·7	12·0	9·3	18·0	14·0

47^m	SUN PLANETS	ARIES	MOON	v or d	Corr^n	v or d	Corr^n	v or d	Corr^n
s	° ′	° ′	° ′	′	′	′	′	′	′
00	11 45·0	11 46·9	11 12·9	0·0	0·0	6·0	4·8	12·0	9·5
01	11 45·3	11 47·2	11 13·1	0·1	0·1	6·1	4·8	12·1	9·6
02	11 45·5	11 47·4	11 13·4	0·2	0·2	6·2	4·9	12·2	9·7
03	11 45·8	11 47·7	11 13·6	0·3	0·2	6·3	5·0	12·3	9·7
04	11 46·0	11 47·9	11 13·8	0·4	0·3	6·4	5·1	12·4	9·8
05	11 46·3	11 48·2	11 14·1	0·5	0·4	6·5	5·1	12·5	9·9
06	11 46·5	11 48·4	11 14·3	0·6	0·5	6·6	5·2	12·6	10·0
07	11 46·8	11 48·7	11 14·6	0·7	0·6	6·7	5·3	12·7	10·1
08	11 47·0	11 48·9	11 14·8	0·8	0·6	6·8	5·4	12·8	10·1
09	11 47·3	11 49·2	11 15·0	0·9	0·7	6·9	5·5	12·9	10·2
10	11 47·5	11 49·4	11 15·3	1·0	0·8	7·0	5·5	13·0	10·3
11	11 47·8	11 49·7	11 15·5	1·1	0·9	7·1	5·6	13·1	10·4
12	11 48·0	11 49·9	11 15·7	1·2	1·0	7·2	5·7	13·2	10·5
13	11 48·3	11 50·2	11 16·0	1·3	1·0	7·3	5·8	13·3	10·5
14	11 48·5	11 50·4	11 16·2	1·4	1·1	7·4	5·9	13·4	10·6
15	11 48·8	11 50·7	11 16·5	1·5	1·2	7·5	5·9	13·5	10·7
16	11 49·0	11 50·9	11 16·7	1·6	1·3	7·6	6·0	13·6	10·8
17	11 49·3	11 51·2	11 16·9	1·7	1·3	7·7	6·1	13·7	10·8
18	11 49·5	11 51·4	11 17·2	1·8	1·4	7·8	6·2	13·8	10·9
19	11 49·8	11 51·7	11 17·4	1·9	1·5	7·9	6·3	13·9	11·0
20	11 50·0	11 51·9	11 17·7	2·0	1·6	8·0	6·3	14·0	11·1
21	11 50·3	11 52·2	11 17·9	2·1	1·7	8·1	6·4	14·1	11·2
22	11 50·5	11 52·4	11 18·1	2·2	1·7	8·2	6·5	14·2	11·2
23	11 50·8	11 52·7	11 18·4	2·3	1·8	8·3	6·6	14·3	11·3
24	11 51·0	11 52·9	11 18·6	2·4	1·9	8·4	6·7	14·4	11·4
25	11 51·3	11 53·2	11 18·8	2·5	2·0	8·5	6·7	14·5	11·5
26	11 51·5	11 53·4	11 19·1	2·6	2·1	8·6	6·8	14·6	11·6
27	11 51·8	11 53·7	11 19·3	2·7	2·1	8·7	6·9	14·7	11·6
28	11 52·0	11 53·9	11 19·6	2·8	2·2	8·8	7·0	14·8	11·7
29	11 52·3	11 54·2	11 19·8	2·9	2·3	8·9	7·0	14·9	11·8
30	11 52·5	11 54·5	11 20·0	3·0	2·4	9·0	7·1	15·0	11·9
31	11 52·8	11 54·7	11 20·3	3·1	2·5	9·1	7·2	15·1	12·0
32	11 53·0	11 55·0	11 20·5	3·2	2·5	9·2	7·3	15·2	12·0
33	11 53·3	11 55·2	11 20·8	3·3	2·6	9·3	7·4	15·3	12·1
34	11 53·5	11 55·5	11 21·0	3·4	2·7	9·4	7·4	15·4	12·2
35	11 53·8	11 55·7	11 21·2	3·5	2·8	9·5	7·5	15·5	12·3
36	11 54·0	11 56·0	11 21·5	3·6	2·9	9·6	7·6	15·6	12·4
37	11 54·3	11 56·2	11 21·7	3·7	2·9	9·7	7·7	15·7	12·4
38	11 54·5	11 56·5	11 22·0	3·8	3·0	9·8	7·8	15·8	12·5
39	11 54·8	11 56·7	11 22·2	3·9	3·1	9·9	7·8	15·9	12·6
40	11 55·0	11 57·0	11 22·4	4·0	3·2	10·0	7·9	16·0	12·7
41	11 55·3	11 57·2	11 22·7	4·1	3·2	10·1	8·0	16·1	12·7
42	11 55·5	11 57·5	11 22·9	4·2	3·3	10·2	8·1	16·2	12·8
43	11 55·8	11 57·7	11 23·1	4·3	3·4	10·3	8·2	16·3	12·9
44	11 56·0	11 58·0	11 23·4	4·4	3·5	10·4	8·2	16·4	13·0
45	11 56·3	11 58·2	11 23·6	4·5	3·6	10·5	8·3	16·5	13·1
46	11 56·5	11 58·5	11 23·9	4·6	3·6	10·6	8·4	16·6	13·1
47	11 56·8	11 58·7	11 24·1	4·7	3·7	10·7	8·5	16·7	13·2
48	11 57·0	11 59·0	11 24·3	4·8	3·8	10·8	8·6	16·8	13·3
49	11 57·3	11 59·2	11 24·6	4·9	3·9	10·9	8·6	16·9	13·4
50	11 57·5	11 59·5	11 24·8	5·0	4·0	11·0	8·7	17·0	13·5
51	11 57·8	11 59·7	11 25·1	5·1	4·0	11·1	8·8	17·1	13·5
52	11 58·0	12 00·0	11 25·3	5·2	4·1	11·2	8·9	17·2	13·6
53	11 58·3	12 00·2	11 25·5	5·3	4·2	11·3	8·9	17·3	13·7
54	11 58·5	12 00·5	11 25·8	5·4	4·3	11·4	9·0	17·4	13·8
55	11 58·8	12 00·7	11 26·0	5·5	4·4	11·5	9·1	17·5	13·9
56	11 59·0	12 01·0	11 26·2	5·6	4·4	11·6	9·2	17·6	13·9
57	11 59·3	12 01·2	11 26·5	5·7	4·5	11·7	9·3	17·7	14·0
58	11 59·5	12 01·5	11 26·7	5·8	4·6	11·8	9·3	17·8	14·1
59	11 59·8	12 01·7	11 27·0	5·9	4·7	11·9	9·4	17·9	14·2
60	12 00·0	12 02·0	11 27·2	6·0	4·8	12·0	9·5	18·0	14·3

48m	SUN PLANETS	ARIES	MOON	v or d	Corrn	v or d	Corrn	v or d	Corrn
s	° ′	° ′	° ′	′	′	′	′	′	′
00	12 00·0	12 02·0	11 27·2	0·0	0·0	6·0	4·9	12·0	9·7
01	12 00·3	12 02·2	11 27·4	0·1	0·1	6·1	4·9	12·1	9·8
02	12 00·5	12 02·5	11 27·7	0·2	0·2	6·2	5·0	12·2	9·9
03	12 00·8	12 02·7	11 27·9	0·3	0·2	6·3	5·1	12·3	9·9
04	12 01·0	12 03·0	11 28·2	0·4	0·3	6·4	5·2	12·4	10·0
05	12 01·3	12 03·2	11 28·4	0·5	0·4	6·5	5·3	12·5	10·1
06	12 01·5	12 03·5	11 28·6	0·6	0·5	6·6	5·3	12·6	10·2
07	12 01·8	12 03·7	11 28·9	0·7	0·6	6·7	5·4	12·7	10·3
08	12 02·0	12 04·0	11 29·1	0·8	0·6	6·8	5·5	12·8	10·3
09	12 02·3	12 04·2	11 29·3	0·9	0·7	6·9	5·6	12·9	10·4
10	12 02·5	12 04·5	11 29·6	1·0	0·8	7·0	5·7	13·0	10·5
11	12 02·8	12 04·7	11 29·8	1·1	0·9	7·1	5·7	13·1	10·6
12	12 03·0	12 05·0	11 30·1	1·2	1·0	7·2	5·8	13·2	10·7
13	12 03·3	12 05·2	11 30·3	1·3	1·1	7·3	5·9	13·3	10·8
14	12 03·5	12 05·5	11 30·5	1·4	1·1	7·4	6·0	13·4	10·8
15	12 03·8	12 05·7	11 30·8	1·5	1·2	7·5	6·1	13·5	10·9
16	12 04·0	12 06·0	11 31·0	1·6	1·3	7·6	6·1	13·6	11·0
17	12 04·3	12 06·2	11 31·3	1·7	1·4	7·7	6·2	13·7	11·1
18	12 04·5	12 06·5	11 31·5	1·8	1·5	7·8	6·3	13·8	11·2
19	12 04·8	12 06·7	11 31·7	1·9	1·5	7·9	6·4	13·9	11·2
20	12 05·0	12 07·0	11 32·0	2·0	1·6	8·0	6·5	14·0	11·3
21	12 05·3	12 07·2	11 32·2	2·1	1·7	8·1	6·5	14·1	11·4
22	12 05·5	12 07·5	11 32·4	2·2	1·8	8·2	6·6	14·2	11·5
23	12 05·8	12 07·7	11 32·7	2·3	1·9	8·3	6·7	14·3	11·6
24	12 06·0	12 08·0	11 32·9	2·4	1·9	8·4	6·8	14·4	11·6
25	12 06·3	12 08·2	11 33·2	2·5	2·0	8·5	6·9	14·5	11·7
26	12 06·5	12 08·5	11 33·4	2·6	2·1	8·6	7·0	14·6	11·8
27	12 06·8	12 08·7	11 33·6	2·7	2·2	8·7	7·0	14·7	11·9
28	12 07·0	12 09·0	11 33·9	2·8	2·3	8·8	7·1	14·8	12·0
29	12 07·3	12 09·2	11 34·1	2·9	2·3	8·9	7·2	14·9	12·0
30	12 07·5	12 09·5	11 34·4	3·0	2·4	9·0	7·3	15·0	12·1
31	12 07·8	12 09·7	11 34·6	3·1	2·5	9·1	7·4	15·1	12·2
32	12 08·0	12 10·0	11 34·8	3·2	2·6	9·2	7·4	15·2	12·3
33	12 08·3	12 10·2	11 35·1	3·3	2·7	9·3	7·5	15·3	12·4
34	12 08·5	12 10·5	11 35·3	3·4	2·7	9·4	7·6	15·4	12·4
35	12 08·8	12 10·7	11 35·6	3·5	2·8	9·5	7·7	15·5	12·5
36	12 09·0	12 11·0	11 35·8	3·6	2·9	9·6	7·8	15·6	12·6
37	12 09·3	12 11·2	11 36·0	3·7	3·0	9·7	7·8	15·7	12·7
38	12 09·5	12 11·5	11 36·3	3·8	3·1	9·8	7·9	15·8	12·8
39	12 09·8	12 11·7	11 36·5	3·9	3·2	9·9	8·0	15·9	12·9
40	12 10·0	12 12·0	11 36·7	4·0	3·2	10·0	8·1	16·0	12·9
41	12 10·3	12 12·2	11 37·0	4·1	3·3	10·1	8·2	16·1	13·0
42	12 10·5	12 12·5	11 37·2	4·2	3·4	10·2	8·2	16·2	13·1
43	12 10·8	12 12·8	11 37·5	4·3	3·5	10·3	8·3	16·3	13·2
44	12 11·0	12 13·0	11 37·7	4·4	3·6	10·4	8·4	16·4	13·3
45	12 11·3	12 13·3	11 37·9	4·5	3·6	10·5	8·5	16·5	13·3
46	12 11·5	12 13·5	11 38·2	4·6	3·7	10·6	8·6	16·6	13·4
47	12 11·8	12 13·8	11 38·4	4·7	3·8	10·7	8·6	16·7	13·5
48	12 12·0	12 14·0	11 38·7	4·8	3·9	10·8	8·7	16·8	13·6
49	12 12·3	12 14·3	11 38·9	4·9	4·0	10·9	8·8	16·9	13·7
50	12 12·5	12 14·5	11 39·1	5·0	4·0	11·0	8·9	17·0	13·7
51	12 12·8	12 14·8	11 39·4	5·1	4·1	11·1	9·0	17·1	13·8
52	12 13·0	12 15·0	11 39·6	5·2	4·2	11·2	9·1	17·2	13·9
53	12 13·3	12 15·3	11 39·8	5·3	4·3	11·3	9·1	17·3	14·0
54	12 13·5	12 15·5	11 40·1	5·4	4·4	11·4	9·2	17·4	14·1
55	12 13·8	12 15·8	11 40·3	5·5	4·4	11·5	9·3	17·5	14·1
56	12 14·0	12 16·0	11 40·6	5·6	4·5	11·6	9·4	17·6	14·2
57	12 14·3	12 16·3	11 40·8	5·7	4·6	11·7	9·5	17·7	14·3
58	12 14·5	12 16·5	11 41·0	5·8	4·7	11·8	9·5	17·8	14·4
59	12 14·8	12 16·8	11 41·3	5·9	4·8	11·9	9·6	17·9	14·5
60	12 15·0	12 17·0	11 41·5	6·0	4·9	12·0	9·7	18·0	14·6

49m	SUN PLANETS	ARIES	MOON	v or d	Corrn	v or d	Corrn	v or d	Corrn
s	° ′	° ′	° ′	′	′	′	′	′	′
00	12 15·0	12 17·0	11 41·5	0·0	0·0	6·0	5·0	12·0	9·9
01	12 15·3	12 17·3	11 41·8	0·1	0·1	6·1	5·0	12·1	10·0
02	12 15·5	12 17·5	11 42·0	0·2	0·2	6·2	5·1	12·2	10·1
03	12 15·8	12 17·8	11 42·2	0·3	0·2	6·3	5·2	12·3	10·1
04	12 16·0	12 18·0	11 42·5	0·4	0·3	6·4	5·3	12·4	10·2
05	12 16·3	12 18·3	11 42·7	0·5	0·4	6·5	5·4	12·5	10·3
06	12 16·5	12 18·5	11 42·9	0·6	0·5	6·6	5·4	12·6	10·4
07	12 16·8	12 18·8	11 43·2	0·7	0·6	6·7	5·5	12·7	10·5
08	12 17·0	12 19·0	11 43·4	0·8	0·7	6·8	5·6	12·8	10·6
09	12 17·3	12 19·3	11 43·7	0·9	0·7	6·9	5·7	12·9	10·6
10	12 17·5	12 19·5	11 43·9	1·0	0·8	7·0	5·8	13·0	10·7
11	12 17·8	12 19·8	11 44·1	1·1	0·9	7·1	5·9	13·1	10·8
12	12 18·0	12 20·0	11 44·4	1·2	1·0	7·2	5·9	13·2	10·9
13	12 18·3	12 20·3	11 44·6	1·3	1·1	7·3	6·0	13·3	11·0
14	12 18·5	12 20·5	11 44·9	1·4	1·2	7·4	6·1	13·4	11·1
15	12 18·8	12 20·8	11 45·1	1·5	1·2	7·5	6·2	13·5	11·1
16	12 19·0	12 21·0	11 45·3	1·6	1·3	7·6	6·3	13·6	11·2
17	12 19·3	12 21·3	11 45·6	1·7	1·4	7·7	6·4	13·7	11·3
18	12 19·5	12 21·5	11 45·8	1·8	1·5	7·8	6·4	13·8	11·4
19	12 19·8	12 21·8	11 46·1	1·9	1·6	7·9	6·5	13·9	11·5
20	12 20·0	12 22·0	11 46·3	2·0	1·7	8·0	6·6	14·0	11·6
21	12 20·3	12 22·3	11 46·5	2·1	1·7	8·1	6·7	14·1	11·6
22	12 20·5	12 22·5	11 46·8	2·2	1·8	8·2	6·8	14·2	11·7
23	12 20·8	12 22·8	11 47·0	2·3	1·9	8·3	6·8	14·3	11·8
24	12 21·0	12 23·0	11 47·2	2·4	2·0	8·4	6·9	14·4	11·9
25	12 21·3	12 23·3	11 47·5	2·5	2·1	8·5	7·0	14·5	12·0
26	12 21·5	12 23·5	11 47·7	2·6	2·1	8·6	7·1	14·6	12·0
27	12 21·8	12 23·8	11 48·0	2·7	2·2	8·7	7·2	14·7	12·1
28	12 22·0	12 24·0	11 48·2	2·8	2·3	8·8	7·3	14·8	12·2
29	12 22·3	12 24·3	11 48·4	2·9	2·4	8·9	7·3	14·9	12·3
30	12 22·5	12 24·5	11 48·7	3·0	2·5	9·0	7·4	15·0	12·4
31	12 22·8	12 24·8	11 48·9	3·1	2·6	9·1	7·5	15·1	12·5
32	12 23·0	12 25·0	11 49·2	3·2	2·6	9·2	7·6	15·2	12·5
33	12 23·3	12 25·3	11 49·4	3·3	2·7	9·3	7·7	15·3	12·6
34	12 23·5	12 25·5	11 49·6	3·4	2·8	9·4	7·8	15·4	12·7
35	12 23·8	12 25·8	11 49·9	3·5	2·9	9·5	7·8	15·5	12·8
36	12 24·0	12 26·0	11 50·1	3·6	3·0	9·6	7·9	15·6	12·9
37	12 24·3	12 26·3	11 50·3	3·7	3·1	9·7	8·0	15·7	13·0
38	12 24·5	12 26·5	11 50·6	3·8	3·1	9·8	8·1	15·8	13·0
39	12 24·8	12 26·8	11 50·8	3·9	3·2	9·9	8·2	15·9	13·1
40	12 25·0	12 27·0	11 51·1	4·0	3·3	10·0	8·3	16·0	13·2
41	12 25·3	12 27·3	11 51·3	4·1	3·4	10·1	8·3	16·1	13·3
42	12 25·5	12 27·5	11 51·5	4·2	3·5	10·2	8·4	16·2	13·4
43	12 25·8	12 27·8	11 51·8	4·3	3·5	10·3	8·5	16·3	13·4
44	12 26·0	12 28·0	11 52·0	4·4	3·6	10·4	8·6	16·4	13·5
45	12 26·3	12 28·3	11 52·3	4·5	3·7	10·5	8·7	16·5	13·6
46	12 26·5	12 28·5	11 52·5	4·6	3·8	10·6	8·7	16·6	13·7
47	12 26·8	12 28·8	11 52·7	4·7	3·9	10·7	8·8	16·7	13·8
48	12 27·0	12 29·0	11 53·0	4·8	4·0	10·8	8·9	16·8	13·9
49	12 27·3	12 29·3	11 53·2	4·9	4·0	10·9	9·0	16·9	13·9
50	12 27·5	12 29·5	11 53·4	5·0	4·1	11·0	9·1	17·0	14·0
51	12 27·8	12 29·8	11 53·7	5·1	4·2	11·1	9·2	17·1	14·1
52	12 28·0	12 30·0	11 53·9	5·2	4·3	11·2	9·2	17·2	14·2
53	12 28·3	12 30·3	11 54·2	5·3	4·4	11·3	9·3	17·3	14·3
54	12 28·5	12 30·5	11 54·4	5·4	4·5	11·4	9·4	17·4	14·4
55	12 28·8	12 30·8	11 54·6	5·5	4·5	11·5	9·5	17·5	14·4
56	12 29·0	12 31·1	11 54·9	5·6	4·6	11·6	9·6	17·6	14·5
57	12 29·3	12 31·3	11 55·1	5·7	4·7	11·7	9·7	17·7	14·6
58	12 29·5	12 31·6	11 55·4	5·8	4·8	11·8	9·7	17·8	14·7
59	12 29·8	12 31·8	11 55·6	5·9	4·9	11·9	9·8	17·9	14·8
60	12 30·0	12 32·1	11 55·8	6·0	5·0	12·0	9·9	18·0	14·9

m 50	SUN PLANETS	ARIES	MOON	v or d	Corrn	v or d	Corrn	v or d	Corrn
s	° ′	° ′	° ′	′	′	′	′	′	′
00	12 30·0	12 32·1	11 55·8	0·0	0·0	6·0	5·1	12·0	10·1
01	12 30·3	12 32·3	11 56·1	0·1	0·1	6·1	5·1	12·1	10·2
02	12 30·5	12 32·6	11 56·3	0·2	0·2	6·2	5·2	12·2	10·3
03	12 30·8	12 32·8	11 56·5	0·3	0·3	6·3	5·3	12·3	10·4
04	12 31·0	12 33·1	11 56·8	0·4	0·3	6·4	5·4	12·4	10·4
05	12 31·3	12 33·3	11 57·0	0·5	0·4	6·5	5·5	12·5	10·5
06	12 31·5	12 33·6	11 57·3	0·6	0·5	6·6	5·6	12·6	10·6
07	12 31·8	12 33·8	11 57·5	0·7	0·6	6·7	5·6	12·7	10·7
08	12 32·0	12 34·1	11 57·7	0·8	0·7	6·8	5·7	12·8	10·8
09	12 32·3	12 34·3	11 58·0	0·9	0·8	6·9	5·8	12·9	10·9
10	12 32·5	12 34·6	11 58·2	1·0	0·8	7·0	5·9	13·0	10·9
11	12 32·8	12 34·8	11 58·5	1·1	0·9	7·1	6·0	13·1	11·0
12	12 33·0	12 35·1	11 58·7	1·2	1·0	7·2	6·1	13·2	11·1
13	12 33·3	12 35·3	11 58·9	1·3	1·1	7·3	6·1	13·3	11·2
14	12 33·5	12 35·6	11 59·2	1·4	1·2	7·4	6·2	13·4	11·3
15	12 33·8	12 35·8	11 59·4	1·5	1·3	7·5	6·3	13·5	11·4
16	12 34·0	12 36·1	11 59·7	1·6	1·3	7·6	6·4	13·6	11·4
17	12 34·3	12 36·3	11 59·9	1·7	1·4	7·7	6·5	13·7	11·5
18	12 34·5	12 36·6	12 00·1	1·8	1·5	7·8	6·6	13·8	11·6
19	12 34·8	12 36·8	12 00·4	1·9	1·6	7·9	6·6	13·9	11·7
20	12 35·0	12 37·1	12 00·6	2·0	1·7	8·0	6·7	14·0	11·8
21	12 35·3	12 37·3	12 00·8	2·1	1·8	8·1	6·8	14·1	11·9
22	12 35·5	12 37·6	12 01·1	2·2	1·9	8·2	6·9	14·2	12·0
23	12 35·8	12 37·8	12 01·3	2·3	1·9	8·3	7·0	14·3	12·0
24	12 36·0	12 38·1	12 01·6	2·4	2·0	8·4	7·1	14·4	12·1
25	12 36·3	12 38·3	12 01·8	2·5	2·1	8·5	7·2	14·5	12·2
26	12 36·5	12 38·6	12 02·0	2·6	2·2	8·6	7·2	14·6	12·3
27	12 36·8	12 38·8	12 02·3	2·7	2·3	8·7	7·3	14·7	12·4
28	12 37·0	12 39·1	12 02·5	2·8	2·4	8·8	7·4	14·8	12·5
29	12 37·3	12 39·3	12 02·8	2·9	2·4	8·9	7·5	14·9	12·5
30	12 37·5	12 39·6	12 03·0	3·0	2·5	9·0	7·6	15·0	12·6
31	12 37·8	12 39·8	12 03·2	3·1	2·6	9·1	7·7	15·1	12·7
32	12 38·0	12 40·1	12 03·5	3·2	2·7	9·2	7·7	15·2	12·8
33	12 38·3	12 40·3	12 03·7	3·3	2·8	9·3	7·8	15·3	12·9
34	12 38·5	12 40·6	12 03·9	3·4	2·9	9·4	7·9	15·4	13·0
35	12 38·8	12 40·8	12 04·2	3·5	2·9	9·5	8·0	15·5	13·0
36	12 39·0	12 41·1	12 04·4	3·6	3·0	9·6	8·1	15·6	13·1
37	12 39·3	12 41·3	12 04·7	3·7	3·1	9·7	8·2	15·7	13·2
38	12 39·5	12 41·6	12 04·9	3·8	3·2	9·8	8·2	15·8	13·3
39	12 39·8	12 41·8	12 05·1	3·9	3·3	9·9	8·3	15·9	13·4
40	12 40·0	12 42·1	12 05·4	4·0	3·4	10·0	8·4	16·0	13·5
41	12 40·3	12 42·3	12 05·6	4·1	3·5	10·1	8·5	16·1	13·6
42	12 40·5	12 42·6	12 05·9	4·2	3·5	10·2	8·6	16·2	13·6
43	12 40·8	12 42·8	12 06·1	4·3	3·6	10·3	8·7	16·3	13·7
44	12 41·0	12 43·1	12 06·3	4·4	3·7	10·4	8·8	16·4	13·8
45	12 41·3	12 43·3	12 06·6	4·5	3·8	10·5	8·8	16·5	13·9
46	12 41·5	12 43·6	12 06·8	4·6	3·9	10·6	8·9	16·6	14·0
47	12 41·8	12 43·8	12 07·0	4·7	4·0	10·7	9·0	16·7	14·1
48	12 42·0	12 44·1	12 07·3	4·8	4·0	10·8	9·1	16·8	14·1
49	12 42·3	12 44·3	12 07·5	4·9	4·1	10·9	9·2	16·9	14·2
50	12 42·5	12 44·6	12 07·8	5·0	4·2	11·0	9·3	17·0	14·3
51	12 42·8	12 44·8	12 08·0	5·1	4·3	11·1	9·3	17·1	14·4
52	12 43·0	12 45·1	12 08·2	5·2	4·4	11·2	9·4	17·2	14·5
53	12 43·3	12 45·3	12 08·5	5·3	4·5	11·3	9·5	17·3	14·6
54	12 43·5	12 45·6	12 08·7	5·4	4·5	11·4	9·6	17·4	14·6
55	12 43·8	12 45·8	12 09·0	5·5	4·6	11·5	9·7	17·5	14·7
56	12 44·0	12 46·1	12 09·2	5·6	4·7	11·6	9·8	17·6	14·8
57	12 44·3	12 46·3	12 09·4	5·7	4·8	11·7	9·8	17·7	14·9
58	12 44·5	12 46·6	12 09·7	5·8	4·9	11·8	9·9	17·8	15·0
59	12 44·8	12 46·8	12 09·9	5·9	5·0	11·9	10·0	17·9	15·1
60	12 45·0	12 47·1	12 10·2	6·0	5·1	12·0	10·1	18·0	15·2

m 51	SUN PLANETS	ARIES	MOON	v or d	Corrn	v or d	Corrn	v or d	Corrn
s	° ′	° ′	° ′	′	′	′	′	′	′
00	12 45·0	12 47·1	12 10·2	0·0	0·0	6·0	5·2	12·0	10·3
01	12 45·3	12 47·3	12 10·4	0·1	0·1	6·1	5·2	12·1	10·4
02	12 45·5	12 47·6	12 10·6	0·2	0·2	6·2	5·3	12·2	10·5
03	12 45·8	12 47·8	12 10·9	0·3	0·3	6·3	5·4	12·3	10·6
04	12 46·0	12 48·1	12 11·1	0·4	0·3	6·4	5·5	12·4	10·6
05	12 46·3	12 48·3	12 11·3	0·5	0·4	6·5	5·6	12·5	10·7
06	12 46·5	12 48·6	12 11·6	0·6	0·5	6·6	5·7	12·6	10·8
07	12 46·8	12 48·8	12 11·8	0·7	0·6	6·7	5·8	12·7	10·9
08	12 47·0	12 49·1	12 12·1	0·8	0·7	6·8	5·8	12·8	11·0
09	12 47·3	12 49·4	12 12·3	0·9	0·8	6·9	5·9	12·9	11·1
10	12 47·5	12 49·6	12 12·5	1·0	0·9	7·0	6·0	13·0	11·2
11	12 47·8	12 49·9	12 12·8	1·1	0·9	7·1	6·1	13·1	11·2
12	12 48·0	12 50·1	12 13·0	1·2	1·0	7·2	6·2	13·2	11·3
13	12 48·3	12 50·4	12 13·3	1·3	1·1	7·3	6·3	13·3	11·4
14	12 48·5	12 50·6	12 13·5	1·4	1·2	7·4	6·4	13·4	11·5
15	12 48·8	12 50·9	12 13·7	1·5	1·3	7·5	6·4	13·5	11·6
16	12 49·0	12 51·1	12 14·0	1·6	1·4	7·6	6·5	13·6	11·7
17	12 49·3	12 51·4	12 14·2	1·7	1·5	7·7	6·6	13·7	11·8
18	12 49·5	12 51·6	12 14·4	1·8	1·5	7·8	6·7	13·8	11·8
19	12 49·8	12 51·9	12 14·7	1·9	1·6	7·9	6·8	13·9	11·9
20	12 50·0	12 52·1	12 14·9	2·0	1·7	8·0	6·9	14·0	12·0
21	12 50·3	12 52·4	12 15·2	2·1	1·8	8·1	7·0	14·1	12·1
22	12 50·5	12 52·6	12 15·4	2·2	1·9	8·2	7·0	14·2	12·2
23	12 50·8	12 52·9	12 15·6	2·3	2·0	8·3	7·1	14·3	12·3
24	12 51·0	12 53·1	12 15·9	2·4	2·1	8·4	7·2	14·4	12·4
25	12 51·3	12 53·4	12 16·1	2·5	2·1	8·5	7·3	14·5	12·4
26	12 51·5	12 53·6	12 16·4	2·6	2·2	8·6	7·4	14·6	12·5
27	12 51·8	12 53·9	12 16·6	2·7	2·3	8·7	7·5	14·7	12·6
28	12 52·0	12 54·1	12 16·8	2·8	2·4	8·8	7·6	14·8	12·7
29	12 52·3	12 54·4	12 17·1	2·9	2·5	8·9	7·6	14·9	12·8
30	12 52·5	12 54·6	12 17·3	3·0	2·6	9·0	7·7	15·0	12·9
31	12 52·8	12 54·9	12 17·5	3·1	2·7	9·1	7·8	15·1	13·0
32	12 53·0	12 55·1	12 17·8	3·2	2·7	9·2	7·9	15·2	13·0
33	12 53·3	12 55·4	12 18·0	3·3	2·8	9·3	8·0	15·3	13·1
34	12 53·5	12 55·6	12 18·3	3·4	2·9	9·4	8·1	15·4	13·2
35	12 53·8	12 55·9	12 18·5	3·5	3·0	9·5	8·2	15·5	13·3
36	12 54·0	12 56·1	12 18·7	3·6	3·1	9·6	8·2	15·6	13·4
37	12 54·3	12 56·4	12 19·0	3·7	3·2	9·7	8·3	15·7	13·5
38	12 54·5	12 56·6	12 19·2	3·8	3·3	9·8	8·4	15·8	13·6
39	12 54·8	12 56·9	12 19·5	3·9	3·3	9·9	8·5	15·9	13·6
40	12 55·0	12 57·1	12 19·7	4·0	3·4	10·0	8·6	16·0	13·7
41	12 55·3	12 57·4	12 19·9	4·1	3·5	10·1	8·7	16·1	13·8
42	12 55·5	12 57·6	12 20·2	4·2	3·6	10·2	8·8	16·2	13·9
43	12 55·8	12 57·9	12 20·4	4·3	3·7	10·3	8·8	16·3	14·0
44	12 56·0	12 58·1	12 20·6	4·4	3·8	10·4	8·9	16·4	14·1
45	12 56·3	12 58·4	12 20·9	4·5	3·9	10·5	9·0	16·5	14·2
46	12 56·5	12 58·6	12 21·1	4·6	3·9	10·6	9·1	16·6	14·2
47	12 56·8	12 58·9	12 21·4	4·7	4·0	10·7	9·2	16·7	14·3
48	12 57·0	12 59·1	12 21·6	4·8	4·1	10·8	9·3	16·8	14·4
49	12 57·3	12 59·4	12 21·8	4·9	4·2	10·9	9·4	16·9	14·5
50	12 57·5	12 59·6	12 22·1	5·0	4·3	11·0	9·4	17·0	14·6
51	12 57·8	12 59·9	12 22·3	5·1	4·4	11·1	9·5	17·1	14·7
52	12 58·0	13 00·1	12 22·6	5·2	4·5	11·2	9·6	17·2	14·8
53	12 58·3	13 00·4	12 22·8	5·3	4·5	11·3	9·7	17·3	14·8
54	12 58·5	13 00·6	12 23·0	5·4	4·6	11·4	9·8	17·4	14·9
55	12 58·8	13 00·9	12 23·3	5·5	4·7	11·5	9·9	17·5	15·0
56	12 59·0	13 01·1	12 23·5	5·6	4·8	11·6	10·0	17·6	15·1
57	12 59·3	13 01·4	12 23·8	5·7	4·9	11·7	10·0	17·7	15·2
58	12 59·5	13 01·6	12 24·0	5·8	5·0	11·8	10·1	17·8	15·3
59	12 59·8	13 01·9	12 24·2	5·9	5·1	11·9	10·2	17·9	15·4
60	13 00·0	13 02·1	12 24·5	6·0	5·2	12·0	10·3	18·0	15·5

m 52	SUN PLANETS	ARIES	MOON	v or d	Corrn	v or d	Corrn	v or d	Corrn
s	° ′	° ′	° ′	′	′	′	′	′	′
00	13 00·0	13 02·1	12 24·5	0·0	0·0	6·0	5·3	12·0	10·5
01	13 00·3	13 02·4	12 24·7	0·1	0·1	6·1	5·3	12·1	10·6
02	13 00·5	13 02·6	12 24·9	0·2	0·2	6·2	5·4	12·2	10·7
03	13 00·8	13 02·9	12 25·2	0·3	0·3	6·3	5·5	12·3	10·8
04	13 01·0	13 03·1	12 25·4	0·4	0·4	6·4	5·6	12·4	10·9
05	13 01·3	13 03·4	12 25·7	0·5	0·4	6·5	5·7	12·5	10·9
06	13 01·5	13 03·6	12 25·9	0·6	0·5	6·6	5·8	12·6	11·0
07	13 01·8	13 03·9	12 26·1	0·7	0·6	6·7	5·9	12·7	11·1
08	13 02·0	13 04·1	12 26·4	0·8	0·7	6·8	6·0	12·8	11·2
09	13 02·3	13 04·4	12 26·6	0·9	0·8	6·9	6·0	12·9	11·3
10	13 02·5	13 04·6	12 26·9	1·0	0·9	7·0	6·1	13·0	11·4
11	13 02·8	13 04·9	12 27·1	1·1	1·0	7·1	6·2	13·1	11·5
12	13 03·0	13 05·1	12 27·3	1·2	1·1	7·2	6·3	13·2	11·6
13	13 03·3	13 05·4	12 27·6	1·3	1·1	7·3	6·4	13·3	11·6
14	13 03·5	13 05·6	12 27·8	1·4	1·2	7·4	6·5	13·4	11·7
15	13 03·8	13 05·9	12 28·0	1·5	1·3	7·5	6·6	13·5	11·8
16	13 04·0	13 06·1	12 28·3	1·6	1·4	7·6	6·7	13·6	11·9
17	13 04·3	13 06·4	12 28·5	1·7	1·5	7·7	6·7	13·7	12·0
18	13 04·5	13 06·6	12 28·8	1·8	1·6	7·8	6·8	13·8	12·1
19	13 04·8	13 06·9	12 29·0	1·9	1·7	7·9	6·9	13·9	12·2
20	13 05·0	13 07·1	12 29·2	2·0	1·8	8·0	7·0	14·0	12·3
21	13 05·3	13 07·4	12 29·5	2·1	1·8	8·1	7·1	14·1	12·3
22	13 05·5	13 07·7	12 29·7	2·2	1·9	8·2	7·2	14·2	12·4
23	13 05·8	13 07·9	12 30·0	2·3	2·0	8·3	7·3	14·3	12·5
24	13 06·0	13 08·2	12 30·2	2·4	2·1	8·4	7·4	14·4	12·6
25	13 06·3	13 08·4	12 30·4	2·5	2·2	8·5	7·4	14·5	12·7
26	13 06·5	13 08·7	12 30·7	2·6	2·3	8·6	7·5	14·6	12·8
27	13 06·8	13 08·9	12 30·9	2·7	2·4	8·7	7·6	14·7	12·9
28	13 07·0	13 09·2	12 31·1	2·8	2·5	8·8	7·7	14·8	13·0
29	13 07·3	13 09·4	12 31·4	2·9	2·5	8·9	7·8	14·9	13·0
30	13 07·5	13 09·7	12 31·6	3·0	2·6	9·0	7·9	15·0	13·1
31	13 07·8	13 09·9	12 31·9	3·1	2·7	9·1	8·0	15·1	13·2
32	13 08·0	13 10·2	12 32·1	3·2	2·8	9·2	8·0	15·2	13·3
33	13 08·3	13 10·4	12 32·3	3·3	2·9	9·3	8·1	15·3	13·4
34	13 08·5	13 10·7	12 32·6	3·4	3·0	9·4	8·2	15·4	13·5
35	13 08·8	13 10·9	12 32·8	3·5	3·1	9·5	8·3	15·5	13·6
36	13 09·0	13 11·2	12 33·1	3·6	3·2	9·6	8·4	15·6	13·7
37	13 09·3	13 11·4	12 33·3	3·7	3·2	9·7	8·5	15·7	13·7
38	13 09·5	13 11·7	12 33·5	3·8	3·3	9·8	8·6	15·8	13·8
39	13 09·8	13 11·9	12 33·8	3·9	3·4	9·9	8·7	15·9	13·9
40	13 10·0	13 12·2	12 34·0	4·0	3·5	10·0	8·8	16·0	14·0
41	13 10·3	13 12·4	12 34·2	4·1	3·6	10·1	8·8	16·1	14·1
42	13 10·5	13 12·7	12 34·5	4·2	3·7	10·2	8·9	16·2	14·2
43	13 10·8	13 12·9	12 34·7	4·3	3·8	10·3	9·0	16·3	14·3
44	13 11·0	13 13·2	12 35·0	4·4	3·9	10·4	9·1	16·4	14·3
45	13 11·3	13 13·4	12 35·2	4·5	3·9	10·5	9·2	16·5	14·4
46	13 11·5	13 13·7	12 35·4	4·6	4·0	10·6	9·3	16·6	14·5
47	13 11·8	13 13·9	12 35·7	4·7	4·1	10·7	9·4	16·7	14·6
48	13 12·0	13 14·2	12 35·9	4·8	4·2	10·8	9·5	16·8	14·7
49	13 12·3	13 14·4	12 36·2	4·9	4·3	10·9	9·5	16·9	14·8
50	13 12·5	13 14·7	12 36·4	5·0	4·4	11·0	9·6	17·0	14·9
51	13 12·8	13 14·9	12 36·6	5·1	4·5	11·1	9·7	17·1	15·0
52	13 13·0	13 15·2	12 36·9	5·2	4·6	11·2	9·8	17·2	15·1
53	13 13·3	13 15·4	12 37·1	5·3	4·6	11·3	9·9	17·3	15·1
54	13 13·5	13 15·7	12 37·4	5·4	4·7	11·4	10·0	17·4	15·2
55	13 13·8	13 15·9	12 37·6	5·5	4·8	11·5	10·1	17·5	15·3
56	13 14·0	13 16·2	12 37·8	5·6	4·9	11·6	10·2	17·6	15·4
57	13 14·3	13 16·4	12 38·1	5·7	5·0	11·7	10·2	17·7	15·5
58	13 14·5	13 16·7	12 38·3	5·8	5·1	11·8	10·3	17·8	15·6
59	13 14·8	13 16·9	12 38·5	5·9	5·2	11·9	10·4	17·9	15·7
60	13 15·0	13 17·2	12 38·8	6·0	5·3	12·0	10·5	18·0	15·8

m 53	SUN PLANETS	ARIES	MOON	v or d	Corrn	v or d	Corrn	v or d	Corrn
s	° ′	° ′	° ′	′	′	′	′	′	′
00	13 15·0	13 17·2	12 38·8	0·0	0·0	6·0	5·4	12·0	10·7
01	13 15·3	13 17·4	12 39·0	0·1	0·1	6·1	5·4	12·1	10·8
02	13 15·5	13 17·7	12 39·3	0·2	0·2	6·2	5·5	12·2	10·9
03	13 15·8	13 17·9	12 39·5	0·3	0·3	6·3	5·6	12·3	11·0
04	13 16·0	13 18·2	12 39·7	0·4	0·4	6·4	5·7	12·4	11·1
05	13 16·3	13 18·4	12 40·0	0·5	0·4	6·5	5·8	12·5	11·1
06	13 16·5	13 18·7	12 40·2	0·6	0·5	6·6	5·9	12·6	11·2
07	13 16·8	13 18·9	12 40·5	0·7	0·6	6·7	6·0	12·7	11·3
08	13 17·0	13 19·2	12 40·7	0·8	0·7	6·8	6·1	12·8	11·4
09	13 17·3	13 19·4	12 40·9	0·9	0·8	6·9	6·2	12·9	11·5
10	13 17·5	13 19·7	12 41·2	1·0	0·9	7·0	6·2	13·0	11·6
11	13 17·8	13 19·9	12 41·4	1·1	1·0	7·1	6·3	13·1	11·7
12	13 18·0	13 20·2	12 41·6	1·2	1·1	7·2	6·4	13·2	11·8
13	13 18·3	13 20·4	12 41·9	1·3	1·2	7·3	6·5	13·3	11·9
14	13 18·5	13 20·7	12 42·1	1·4	1·2	7·4	6·6	13·4	11·9
15	13 18·8	13 20·9	12 42·4	1·5	1·3	7·5	6·7	13·5	12·0
16	13 19·0	13 21·2	12 42·6	1·6	1·4	7·6	6·8	13·6	12·1
17	13 19·3	13 21·4	12 42·8	1·7	1·5	7·7	6·9	13·7	12·2
18	13 19·5	13 21·7	12 43·1	1·8	1·6	7·8	7·0	13·8	12·3
19	13 19·8	13 21·9	12 43·3	1·9	1·7	7·9	7·0	13·9	12·4
20	13 20·0	13 22·2	12 43·6	2·0	1·8	8·0	7·1	14·0	12·5
21	13 20·3	13 22·4	12 43·8	2·1	1·9	8·1	7·2	14·1	12·6
22	13 20·5	13 22·7	12 44·0	2·2	2·0	8·2	7·3	14·2	12·7
23	13 20·8	13 22·9	12 44·3	2·3	2·1	8·3	7·4	14·3	12·8
24	13 21·0	13 23·2	12 44·5	2·4	2·1	8·4	7·5	14·4	12·8
25	13 21·3	13 23·4	12 44·7	2·5	2·2	8·5	7·6	14·5	12·9
26	13 21·5	13 23·7	12 45·0	2·6	2·3	8·6	7·7	14·6	13·0
27	13 21·8	13 23·9	12 45·2	2·7	2·4	8·7	7·8	14·7	13·1
28	13 22·0	13 24·2	12 45·5	2·8	2·5	8·8	7·8	14·8	13·2
29	13 22·3	13 24·4	12 45·7	2·9	2·6	8·9	7·9	14·9	13·3
30	13 22·5	13 24·7	12 45·9	3·0	2·7	9·0	8·0	15·0	13·4
31	13 22·8	13 24·9	12 46·2	3·1	2·8	9·1	8·1	15·1	13·5
32	13 23·0	13 25·2	12 46·4	3·2	2·9	9·2	8·2	15·2	13·6
33	13 23·3	13 25·4	12 46·7	3·3	2·9	9·3	8·3	15·3	13·6
34	13 23·5	13 25·7	12 46·9	3·4	3·0	9·4	8·4	15·4	13·7
35	13 23·8	13 26·0	12 47·1	3·5	3·1	9·5	8·5	15·5	13·8
36	13 24·0	13 26·2	12 47·4	3·6	3·2	9·6	8·6	15·6	13·9
37	13 24·3	13 26·5	12 47·6	3·7	3·3	9·7	8·6	15·7	14·0
38	13 24·5	13 26·7	12 47·9	3·8	3·4	9·8	8·7	15·8	14·1
39	13 24·8	13 27·0	12 48·1	3·9	3·5	9·9	8·8	15·9	14·2
40	13 25·0	13 27·2	12 48·3	4·0	3·6	10·0	8·9	16·0	14·3
41	13 25·3	13 27·5	12 48·6	4·1	3·7	10·1	9·0	16·1	14·4
42	13 25·5	13 27·7	12 48·8	4·2	3·7	10·2	9·1	16·2	14·4
43	13 25·8	13 28·0	12 49·0	4·3	3·8	10·3	9·2	16·3	14·5
44	13 26·0	13 28·2	12 49·3	4·4	3·9	10·4	9·3	16·4	14·6
45	13 26·3	13 28·5	12 49·5	4·5	4·0	10·5	9·4	16·5	14·7
46	13 26·5	13 28·7	12 49·8	4·6	4·1	10·6	9·5	16·6	14·8
47	13 26·8	13 29·0	12 50·0	4·7	4·2	10·7	9·5	16·7	14·9
48	13 27·0	13 29·2	12 50·2	4·8	4·3	10·8	9·6	16·8	15·0
49	13 27·3	13 29·5	12 50·5	4·9	4·4	10·9	9·7	16·9	15·1
50	13 27·5	13 29·7	12 50·7	5·0	4·5	11·0	9·8	17·0	15·2
51	13 27·8	13 30·0	12 51·0	5·1	4·5	11·1	9·9	17·1	15·2
52	13 28·0	13 30·2	12 51·2	5·2	4·6	11·2	10·0	17·2	15·3
53	13 28·3	13 30·5	12 51·4	5·3	4·7	11·3	10·1	17·3	15·4
54	13 28·5	13 30·7	12 51·7	5·4	4·8	11·4	10·2	17·4	15·5
55	13 28·8	13 31·0	12 51·9	5·5	4·9	11·5	10·3	17·5	15·6
56	13 29·0	13 31·2	12 52·1	5·6	5·0	11·6	10·3	17·6	15·7
57	13 29·3	13 31·5	12 52·4	5·7	5·1	11·7	10·4	17·7	15·8
58	13 29·5	13 31·7	12 52·6	5·8	5·2	11·8	10·5	17·8	15·9
59	13 29·8	13 32·0	12 52·9	5·9	5·3	11·9	10·6	17·9	16·0
60	13 30·0	13 32·2	12 53·1	6·0	5·4	12·0	10·7	18·0	16·1

54^m	SUN PLANETS	ARIES	MOON	v or d	Corr^n	v or d	Corr^n	v or d	Corr^n
s	° ′	° ′	° ′	′	′	′	′	′	′
00	13 30·0	13 32·2	12 53·1	0·0	0·0	6·0	5·5	12·0	10·9
01	13 30·3	13 32·5	12 53·3	0·1	0·1	6·1	5·5	12·1	11·0
02	13 30·5	13 32·7	12 53·6	0·2	0·2	6·2	5·6	12·2	11·1
03	13 30·8	13 33·0	12 53·8	0·3	0·3	6·3	5·7	12·3	11·2
04	13 31·0	13 33·2	12 54·1	0·4	0·4	6·4	5·8	12·4	11·3
05	13 31·3	13 33·5	12 54·3	0·5	0·5	6·5	5·9	12·5	11·4
06	13 31·5	13 33·7	12 54·5	0·6	0·5	6·6	6·0	12·6	11·4
07	13 31·8	13 34·0	12 54·8	0·7	0·6	6·7	6·1	12·7	11·5
08	13 32·0	13 34·2	12 55·0	0·8	0·7	6·8	6·2	12·8	11·6
09	13 32·3	13 34·5	12 55·2	0·9	0·8	6·9	6·3	12·9	11·7
10	13 32·5	13 34·7	12 55·5	1·0	0·9	7·0	6·4	13·0	11·8
11	13 32·8	13 35·0	12 55·7	1·1	1·0	7·1	6·4	13·1	11·9
12	13 33·0	13 35·2	12 56·0	1·2	1·1	7·2	6·5	13·2	12·0
13	13 33·3	13 35·5	12 56·2	1·3	1·2	7·3	6·6	13·3	12·1
14	13 33·5	13 35·7	12 56·4	1·4	1·3	7·4	6·7	13·4	12·2
15	13 33·8	13 36·0	12 56·7	1·5	1·4	7·5	6·8	13·5	12·3
16	13 34·0	13 36·2	12 56·9	1·6	1·5	7·6	6·9	13·6	12·4
17	13 34·3	13 36·5	12 57·2	1·7	1·5	7·7	7·0	13·7	12·4
18	13 34·5	13 36·7	12 57·4	1·8	1·6	7·8	7·1	13·8	12·5
19	13 34·8	13 37·0	12 57·6	1·9	1·7	7·9	7·2	13·9	12·6
20	13 35·0	13 37·2	12 57·9	2·0	1·8	8·0	7·3	14·0	12·7
21	13 35·3	13 37·5	12 58·1	2·1	1·9	8·1	7·4	14·1	12·8
22	13 35·5	13 37·7	12 58·3	2·2	2·0	8·2	7·4	14·2	12·9
23	13 35·8	13 38·0	12 58·6	2·3	2·1	8·3	7·5	14·3	13·0
24	13 36·0	13 38·2	12 58·8	2·4	2·2	8·4	7·6	14·4	13·1
25	13 36·3	13 38·5	12 59·1	2·5	2·3	8·5	7·7	14·5	13·2
26	13 36·5	13 38·7	12 59·3	2·6	2·4	8·6	7·8	14·6	13·3
27	13 36·8	13 39·0	12 59·5	2·7	2·5	8·7	7·9	14·7	13·4
28	13 37·0	13 39·2	12 59·8	2·8	2·5	8·8	8·0	14·8	13·4
29	13 37·3	13 39·5	13 00·0	2·9	2·6	8·9	8·1	14·9	13·5
30	13 37·5	13 39·7	13 00·3	3·0	2·7	9·0	8·2	15·0	13·6
31	13 37·8	13 40·0	13 00·5	3·1	2·8	9·1	8·3	15·1	13·7
32	13 38·0	13 40·2	13 00·7	3·2	2·9	9·2	8·4	15·2	13·8
33	13 38·3	13 40·5	13 01·0	3·3	3·0	9·3	8·4	15·3	13·9
34	13 38·5	13 40·7	13 01·2	3·4	3·1	9·4	8·5	15·4	14·0
35	13 38·8	13 41·0	13 01·5	3·5	3·2	9·5	8·6	15·5	14·1
36	13 39·0	13 41·2	13 01·7	3·6	3·3	9·6	8·7	15·6	14·2
37	13 39·3	13 41·5	13 01·9	3·7	3·4	9·7	8·8	15·7	14·3
38	13 39·5	13 41·7	13 02·2	3·8	3·5	9·8	8·9	15·8	14·4
39	13 39·8	13 42·0	13 02·4	3·9	3·5	9·9	9·0	15·9	14·4
40	13 40·0	13 42·2	13 02·6	4·0	3·6	10·0	9·1	16·0	14·5
41	13 40·3	13 42·5	13 02·9	4·1	3·7	10·1	9·2	16·1	14·6
42	13 40·5	13 42·7	13 03·1	4·2	3·8	10·2	9·3	16·2	14·7
43	13 40·8	13 43·0	13 03·4	4·3	3·9	10·3	9·4	16·3	14·8
44	13 41·0	13 43·2	13 03·6	4·4	4·0	10·4	9·4	16·4	14·9
45	13 41·3	13 43·5	13 03·8	4·5	4·1	10·5	9·5	16·5	15·0
46	13 41·5	13 43·7	13 04·1	4·6	4·2	10·6	9·6	16·6	15·1
47	13 41·8	13 44·0	13 04·3	4·7	4·3	10·7	9·7	16·7	15·2
48	13 42·0	13 44·3	13 04·6	4·8	4·4	10·8	9·8	16·8	15·3
49	13 42·3	13 44·5	13 04·8	4·9	4·5	10·9	9·9	16·9	15·4
50	13 42·5	13 44·8	13 05·0	5·0	4·5	11·0	10·0	17·0	15·4
51	13 42·8	13 45·0	13 05·3	5·1	4·6	11·1	10·1	17·1	15·5
52	13 43·0	13 45·3	13 05·5	5·2	4·7	11·2	10·2	17·2	15·6
53	13 43·3	13 45·5	13 05·7	5·3	4·8	11·3	10·3	17·3	15·7
54	13 43·5	13 45·8	13 06·0	5·4	4·9	11·4	10·4	17·4	15·8
55	13 43·8	13 46·0	13 06·2	5·5	5·0	11·5	10·4	17·5	15·9
56	13 44·0	13 46·3	13 06·5	5·6	5·1	11·6	10·5	17·6	16·0
57	13 44·3	13 46·5	13 06·7	5·7	5·2	11·7	10·6	17·7	16·1
58	13 44·5	13 46·8	13 06·9	5·8	5·3	11·8	10·7	17·8	16·2
59	13 44·8	13 47·0	13 07·2	5·9	5·4	11·9	10·8	17·9	16·3
60	13 45·0	13 47·3	13 07·4	6·0	5·5	12·0	10·9	18·0	16·4

55^m	SUN PLANETS	ARIES	MOON	v or d	Corr^n	v or d	Corr^n	v or d	Corr^n
s	° ′	° ′	° ′	′	′	′	′	′	′
00	13 45·0	13 47·3	13 07·4	0·0	0·0	6·0	5·6	12·0	11·1
01	13 45·3	13 47·5	13 07·7	0·1	0·1	6·1	5·6	12·1	11·2
02	13 45·5	13 47·8	13 07·9	0·2	0·2	6·2	5·7	12·2	11·3
03	13 45·8	13 48·0	13 08·1	0·3	0·3	6·3	5·8	12·3	11·4
04	13 46·0	13 48·3	13 08·4	0·4	0·4	6·4	5·9	12·4	11·5
05	13 46·3	13 48·5	13 08·6	0·5	0·5	6·5	6·0	12·5	11·6
06	13 46·5	13 48·8	13 08·8	0·6	0·6	6·6	6·1	12·6	11·7
07	13 46·8	13 49·0	13 09·1	0·7	0·6	6·7	6·2	12·7	11·7
08	13 47·0	13 49·3	13 09·3	0·8	0·7	6·8	6·3	12·8	11·8
09	13 47·3	13 49·5	13 09·6	0·9	0·8	6·9	6·4	12·9	11·9
10	13 47·5	13 49·8	13 09·8	1·0	0·9	7·0	6·5	13·0	12·0
11	13 47·8	13 50·0	13 10·0	1·1	1·0	7·1	6·6	13·1	12·1
12	13 48·0	13 50·3	13 10·3	1·2	1·1	7·2	6·7	13·2	12·2
13	13 48·3	13 50·5	13 10·5	1·3	1·2	7·3	6·8	13·3	12·3
14	13 48·5	13 50·8	13 10·8	1·4	1·3	7·4	6·8	13·4	12·4
15	13 48·8	13 51·0	13 11·0	1·5	1·4	7·5	6·9	13·5	12·5
16	13 49·0	13 51·3	13 11·2	1·6	1·5	7·6	7·0	13·6	12·6
17	13 49·3	13 51·5	13 11·5	1·7	1·6	7·7	7·1	13·7	12·7
18	13 49·5	13 51·8	13 11·7	1·8	1·7	7·8	7·2	13·8	12·8
19	13 49·8	13 52·0	13 12·0	1·9	1·8	7·9	7·3	13·9	12·9
20	13 50·0	13 52·3	13 12·2	2·0	1·9	8·0	7·4	14·0	13·0
21	13 50·3	13 52·5	13 12·4	2·1	1·9	8·1	7·5	14·1	13·0
22	13 50·5	13 52·8	13 12·7	2·2	2·0	8·2	7·6	14·2	13·1
23	13 50·8	13 53·0	13 12·9	2·3	2·1	8·3	7·7	14·3	13·2
24	13 51·0	13 53·3	13 13·1	2·4	2·2	8·4	7·8	14·4	13·3
25	13 51·3	13 53·5	13 13·4	2·5	2·3	8·5	7·9	14·5	13·4
26	13 51·5	13 53·8	13 13·6	2·6	2·4	8·6	8·0	14·6	13·5
27	13 51·8	13 54·0	13 13·9	2·7	2·5	8·7	8·0	14·7	13·6
28	13 52·0	13 54·3	13 14·1	2·8	2·6	8·8	8·1	14·8	13·7
29	13 52·3	13 54·5	13 14·3	2·9	2·7	8·9	8·2	14·9	13·8
30	13 52·5	13 54·8	13 14·6	3·0	2·8	9·0	8·3	15·0	13·9
31	13 52·8	13 55·0	13 14·8	3·1	2·9	9·1	8·4	15·1	14·0
32	13 53·0	13 55·3	13 15·1	3·2	3·0	9·2	8·5	15·2	14·1
33	13 53·3	13 55·5	13 15·3	3·3	3·1	9·3	8·6	15·3	14·2
34	13 53·5	13 55·8	13 15·5	3·4	3·1	9·4	8·7	15·4	14·2
35	13 53·8	13 56·0	13 15·8	3·5	3·2	9·5	8·8	15·5	14·3
36	13 54·0	13 56·3	13 16·0	3·6	3·3	9·6	8·9	15·6	14·4
37	13 54·3	13 56·5	13 16·2	3·7	3·4	9·7	9·0	15·7	14·5
38	13 54·5	13 56·8	13 16·5	3·8	3·5	9·8	9·1	15·8	14·6
39	13 54·8	13 57·0	13 16·7	3·9	3·6	9·9	9·2	15·9	14·7
40	13 55·0	13 57·3	13 17·0	4·0	3·7	10·0	9·3	16·0	14·8
41	13 55·3	13 57·5	13 17·2	4·1	3·8	10·1	9·3	16·1	14·9
42	13 55·5	13 57·8	13 17·4	4·2	3·9	10·2	9·4	16·2	15·0
43	13 55·8	13 58·0	13 17·7	4·3	4·0	10·3	9·5	16·3	15·1
44	13 56·0	13 58·3	13 17·9	4·4	4·1	10·4	9·6	16·4	15·2
45	13 56·3	13 58·5	13 18·2	4·5	4·2	10·5	9·7	16·5	15·3
46	13 56·5	13 58·8	13 18·4	4·6	4·3	10·6	9·8	16·6	15·4
47	13 56·8	13 59·0	13 18·6	4·7	4·3	10·7	9·9	16·7	15·4
48	13 57·0	13 59·3	13 18·9	4·8	4·4	10·8	10·0	16·8	15·5
49	13 57·3	13 59·5	13 19·1	4·9	4·5	10·9	10·1	16·9	15·6
50	13 57·5	13 59·8	13 19·3	5·0	4·6	11·0	10·2	17·0	15·7
51	13 57·8	14 00·0	13 19·6	5·1	4·7	11·1	10·3	17·1	15·8
52	13 58·0	14 00·3	13 19·8	5·2	4·8	11·2	10·4	17·2	15·9
53	13 58·3	14 00·5	13 20·1	5·3	4·9	11·3	10·5	17·3	16·0
54	13 58·5	14 00·8	13 20·3	5·4	5·0	11·4	10·5	17·4	16·1
55	13 58·8	14 01·0	13 20·5	5·5	5·1	11·5	10·6	17·5	16·2
56	13 59·0	14 01·3	13 20·8	5·6	5·2	11·6	10·7	17·6	16·3
57	13 59·3	14 01·5	13 21·0	5·7	5·3	11·7	10·8	17·7	16·4
58	13 59·5	14 01·8	13 21·3	5·8	5·4	11·8	10·9	17·8	16·5
59	13 59·8	14 02·0	13 21·5	5·9	5·5	11·9	11·0	17·9	16·6
60	14 00·0	14 02·3	13 21·7	6·0	5·6	12·0	11·1	18·0	16·7

56m	SUN PLANETS	ARIES	MOON	v or d	Corrn	v or d	Corrn	v or d	Corrn
s	° ′	° ′	° ′	′	′	′	′	′	′
00	14 00·0	14 02·3	13 21·7	0·0	0·0	6·0	5·7	12·0	11·3
01	14 00·3	14 02·6	13 22·0	0·1	0·1	6·1	5·7	12·1	11·4
02	14 00·5	14 02·8	13 22·2	0·2	0·2	6·2	5·8	12·2	11·5
03	14 00·8	14 03·1	13 22·4	0·3	0·3	6·3	5·9	12·3	11·6
04	14 01·0	14 03·3	13 22·7	0·4	0·4	6·4	6·0	12·4	11·7
05	14 01·3	14 03·6	13 22·9	0·5	0·5	6·5	6·1	12·5	11·8
06	14 01·5	14 03·8	13 23·2	0·6	0·6	6·6	6·2	12·6	11·9
07	14 01·8	14 04·1	13 23·4	0·7	0·7	6·7	6·3	12·7	12·0
08	14 02·0	14 04·3	13 23·6	0·8	0·8	6·8	6·4	12·8	12·1
09	14 02·3	14 04·6	13 23·9	0·9	0·8	6·9	6·5	12·9	12·1
10	14 02·5	14 04·8	13 24·1	1·0	0·9	7·0	6·6	13·0	12·2
11	14 02·8	14 05·1	13 24·4	1·1	1·0	7·1	6·7	13·1	12·3
12	14 03·0	14 05·3	13 24·6	1·2	1·1	7·2	6·8	13·2	12·4
13	14 03·3	14 05·6	13 24·8	1·3	1·2	7·3	6·9	13·3	12·5
14	14 03·5	14 05·8	13 25·1	1·4	1·3	7·4	7·0	13·4	12·6
15	14 03·8	14 06·1	13 25·3	1·5	1·4	7·5	7·1	13·5	12·7
16	14 04·0	14 06·3	13 25·6	1·6	1·5	7·6	7·2	13·6	12·8
17	14 04·3	14 06·6	13 25·8	1·7	1·6	7·7	7·3	13·7	12·9
18	14 04·5	14 06·8	13 26·0	1·8	1·7	7·8	7·3	13·8	13·0
19	14 04·8	14 07·1	13 26·3	1·9	1·8	7·9	7·4	13·9	13·1
20	14 05·0	14 07·3	13 26·5	2·0	1·9	8·0	7·5	14·0	13·2
21	14 05·3	14 07·6	13 26·7	2·1	2·0	8·1	7·6	14·1	13·3
22	14 05·5	14 07·8	13 27·0	2·2	2·1	8·2	7·7	14·2	13·4
23	14 05·8	14 08·1	13 27·2	2·3	2·2	8·3	7·8	14·3	13·5
24	14 06·0	14 08·3	13 27·5	2·4	2·3	8·4	7·9	14·4	13·6
25	14 06·3	14 08·6	13 27·7	2·5	2·4	8·5	8·0	14·5	13·7
26	14 06·5	14 08·8	13 27·9	2·6	2·4	8·6	8·1	14·6	13·7
27	14 06·8	14 09·1	13 28·2	2·7	2·5	8·7	8·2	14·7	13·8
28	14 07·0	14 09·3	13 28·4	2·8	2·6	8·8	8·3	14·8	13·9
29	14 07·3	14 09·6	13 28·7	2·9	2·7	8·9	8·4	14·9	14·0
30	14 07·5	14 09·8	13 28·9	3·0	2·8	9·0	8·5	15·0	14·1
31	14 07·8	14 10·1	13 29·1	3·1	2·9	9·1	8·6	15·1	14·2
32	14 08·0	14 10·3	13 29·4	3·2	3·0	9·2	8·7	15·2	14·3
33	14 08·3	14 10·6	13 29·6	3·3	3·1	9·3	8·8	15·3	14·4
34	14 08·5	14 10·8	13 29·8	3·4	3·2	9·4	8·9	15·4	14·5
35	14 08·8	14 11·1	13 30·1	3·5	3·3	9·5	8·9	15·5	14·6
36	14 09·0	14 11·3	13 30·3	3·6	3·4	9·6	9·0	15·6	14·7
37	14 09·3	14 11·6	13 30·6	3·7	3·5	9·7	9·1	15·7	14·8
38	14 09·5	14 11·8	13 30·8	3·8	3·6	9·8	9·2	15·8	14·9
39	14 09·8	14 12·1	13 31·0	3·9	3·7	9·9	9·3	15·9	15·0
40	14 10·0	14 12·3	13 31·3	4·0	3·8	10·0	9·4	16·0	15·1
41	14 10·3	14 12·6	13 31·5	4·1	3·9	10·1	9·5	16·1	15·2
42	14 10·5	14 12·8	13 31·8	4·2	4·0	10·2	9·6	16·2	15·3
43	14 10·8	14 13·1	13 32·0	4·3	4·0	10·3	9·7	16·3	15·3
44	14 11·0	14 13·3	13 32·2	4·4	4·1	10·4	9·8	16·4	15·4
45	14 11·3	14 13·6	13 32·5	4·5	4·2	10·5	9·9	16·5	15·5
46	14 11·5	14 13·8	13 32·7	4·6	4·3	10·6	10·0	16·6	15·6
47	14 11·8	14 14·1	13 32·9	4·7	4·4	10·7	10·1	16·7	15·7
48	14 12·0	14 14·3	13 33·2	4·8	4·5	10·8	10·2	16·8	15·8
49	14 12·3	14 14·6	13 33·4	4·9	4·6	10·9	10·3	16·9	15·9
50	14 12·5	14 14·8	13 33·7	5·0	4·7	11·0	10·4	17·0	16·0
51	14 12·8	14 15·1	13 33·9	5·1	4·8	11·1	10·5	17·1	16·1
52	14 13·0	14 15·3	13 34·1	5·2	4·9	11·2	10·5	17·2	16·2
53	14 13·3	14 15·6	13 34·4	5·3	5·0	11·3	10·6	17·3	16·3
54	14 13·5	14 15·8	13 34·6	5·4	5·1	11·4	10·7	17·4	16·4
55	14 13·8	14 16·1	13 34·9	5·5	5·2	11·5	10·8	17·5	16·5
56	14 14·0	14 16·3	13 35·1	5·6	5·3	11·6	10·9	17·6	16·6
57	14 14·3	14 16·6	13 35·3	5·7	5·4	11·7	11·0	17·7	16·7
58	14 14·5	14 16·8	13 35·6	5·8	5·5	11·8	11·1	17·8	16·8
59	14 14·8	14 17·1	13 35·8	5·9	5·6	11·9	11·2	17·9	16·9
60	14 15·0	14 17·3	13 36·1	6·0	5·7	12·0	11·3	18·0	17·0

57m	SUN PLANETS	ARIES	MOON	v or d	Corrn	v or d	Corrn	v or d	Corrn
s	° ′	° ′	° ′	′	′	′	′	′	′
00	14 15·0	14 17·3	13 36·1	0·0	0·0	6·0	5·8	12·0	11·5
01	14 15·3	14 17·6	13 36·3	0·1	0·1	6·1	5·8	12·1	11·6
02	14 15·5	14 17·8	13 36·5	0·2	0·2	6·2	5·9	12·2	11·7
03	14 15·8	14 18·1	13 36·8	0·3	0·3	6·3	6·0	12·3	11·8
04	14 16·0	14 18·3	13 37·0	0·4	0·4	6·4	6·1	12·4	11·9
05	14 16·3	14 18·6	13 37·2	0·5	0·5	6·5	6·2	12·5	12·0
06	14 16·5	14 18·8	13 37·5	0·6	0·6	6·6	6·3	12·6	12·1
07	14 16·8	14 19·1	13 37·7	0·7	0·7	6·7	6·4	12·7	12·2
08	14 17·0	14 19·3	13 38·0	0·8	0·8	6·8	6·5	12·8	12·3
09	14 17·3	14 19·6	13 38·2	0·9	0·9	6·9	6·6	12·9	12·4
10	14 17·5	14 19·8	13 38·4	1·0	1·0	7·0	6·7	13·0	12·5
11	14 17·8	14 20·1	13 38·7	1·1	1·1	7·1	6·8	13·1	12·6
12	14 18·0	14 20·3	13 38·9	1·2	1·2	7·2	6·9	13·2	12·7
13	14 18·3	14 20·6	13 39·2	1·3	1·2	7·3	7·0	13·3	12·7
14	14 18·5	14 20·9	13 39·4	1·4	1·3	7·4	7·1	13·4	12·8
15	14 18·8	14 21·1	13 39·6	1·5	1·4	7·5	7·2	13·5	12·9
16	14 19·0	14 21·4	13 39·9	1·6	1·5	7·6	7·3	13·6	13·0
17	14 19·3	14 21·6	13 40·1	1·7	1·6	7·7	7·4	13·7	13·1
18	14 19·5	14 21·9	13 40·3	1·8	1·7	7·8	7·5	13·8	13·2
19	14 19·8	14 22·1	13 40·6	1·9	1·8	7·9	7·6	13·9	13·3
20	14 20·0	14 22·4	13 40·8	2·0	1·9	8·0	7·7	14·0	13·4
21	14 20·3	14 22·6	13 41·1	2·1	2·0	8·1	7·8	14·1	13·5
22	14 20·5	14 22·9	13 41·3	2·2	2·1	8·2	7·9	14·2	13·6
23	14 20·8	14 23·1	13 41·5	2·3	2·2	8·3	8·0	14·3	13·7
24	14 21·0	14 23·4	13 41·8	2·4	2·3	8·4	8·1	14·4	13·8
25	14 21·3	14 23·6	13 42·0	2·5	2·4	8·5	8·1	14·5	13·9
26	14 21·5	14 23·9	13 42·3	2·6	2·5	8·6	8·2	14·6	14·0
27	14 21·8	14 24·1	13 42·5	2·7	2·6	8·7	8·3	14·7	14·1
28	14 22·0	14 24·4	13 42·7	2·8	2·7	8·8	8·4	14·8	14·2
29	14 22·3	14 24·6	13 43·0	2·9	2·8	8·9	8·5	14·9	14·3
30	14 22·5	14 24·9	13 43·2	3·0	2·9	9·0	8·6	15·0	14·4
31	14 22·8	14 25·1	13 43·4	3·1	3·0	9·1	8·7	15·1	14·5
32	14 23·0	14 25·4	13 43·7	3·2	3·1	9·2	8·8	15·2	14·6
33	14 23·3	14 25·6	13 43·9	3·3	3·2	9·3	8·9	15·3	14·7
34	14 23·5	14 25·9	13 44·2	3·4	3·3	9·4	9·0	15·4	14·8
35	14 23·8	14 26·1	13 44·4	3·5	3·4	9·5	9·1	15·5	14·9
36	14 24·0	14 26·4	13 44·6	3·6	3·5	9·6	9·2	15·6	15·0
37	14 24·3	14 26·6	13 44·9	3·7	3·5	9·7	9·3	15·7	15·0
38	14 24·5	14 26·9	13 45·1	3·8	3·6	9·8	9·4	15·8	15·1
39	14 24·8	14 27·1	13 45·4	3·9	3·7	9·9	9·5	15·9	15·2
40	14 25·0	14 27·4	13 45·6	4·0	3·8	10·0	9·6	16·0	15·3
41	14 25·3	14 27·6	13 45·8	4·1	3·9	10·1	9·7	16·1	15·4
42	14 25·5	14 27·9	13 46·1	4·2	4·0	10·2	9·8	16·2	15·5
43	14 25·8	14 28·1	13 46·3	4·3	4·1	10·3	9·9	16·3	15·6
44	14 26·0	14 28·4	13 46·5	4·4	4·2	10·4	10·0	16·4	15·7
45	14 26·3	14 28·6	13 46·8	4·5	4·3	10·5	10·1	16·5	15·8
46	14 26·5	14 28·9	13 47·0	4·6	4·4	10·6	10·2	16·6	15·9
47	14 26·8	14 29·1	13 47·3	4·7	4·5	10·7	10·3	16·7	16·0
48	14 27·0	14 29·4	13 47·5	4·8	4·6	10·8	10·4	16·8	16·1
49	14 27·3	14 29·6	13 47·7	4·9	4·7	10·9	10·4	16·9	16·2
50	14 27·5	14 29·9	13 48·0	5·0	4·8	11·0	10·5	17·0	16·3
51	14 27·8	14 30·1	13 48·2	5·1	4·9	11·1	10·6	17·1	16·4
52	14 28·0	14 30·4	13 48·5	5·2	5·0	11·2	10·7	17·2	16·5
53	14 28·3	14 30·6	13 48·7	5·3	5·1	11·3	10·8	17·3	16·6
54	14 28·5	14 30·9	13 48·9	5·4	5·2	11·4	10·9	17·4	16·7
55	14 28·8	14 31·1	13 49·2	5·5	5·3	11·5	11·0	17·5	16·8
56	14 29·0	14 31·4	13 49·4	5·6	5·4	11·6	11·1	17·6	16·9
57	14 29·3	14 31·6	13 49·7	5·7	5·5	11·7	11·2	17·7	17·0
58	14 29·5	14 31·9	13 49·9	5·8	5·6	11·8	11·3	17·8	17·1
59	14 29·8	14 32·1	13 50·1	5·9	5·7	11·9	11·4	17·9	17·2
60	14 30·0	14 32·4	13 50·4	6·0	5·8	12·0	11·5	18·0	17·3

58ᵐ	SUN PLANETS	ARIES	MOON	v or d	Corrⁿ	v or d	Corrⁿ	v or d	Corrⁿ
s	° ′	° ′	° ′	′	′	′	′	′	′
00	14 30·0	14 32·4	13 50·4	0·0	0·0	6·0	5·9	12·0	11·7
01	14 30·3	14 32·6	13 50·6	0·1	0·1	6·1	5·9	12·1	11·8
02	14 30·5	14 32·9	13 50·8	0·2	0·2	6·2	6·0	12·2	11·9
03	14 30·8	14 33·1	13 51·1	0·3	0·3	6·3	6·1	12·3	12·0
04	14 31·0	14 33·4	13 51·3	0·4	0·4	6·4	6·2	12·4	12·1
05	14 31·3	14 33·6	13 51·6	0·5	0·5	6·5	6·3	12·5	12·2
06	14 31·5	14 33·9	13 51·8	0·6	0·6	6·6	6·4	12·6	12·3
07	14 31·8	14 34·1	13 52·0	0·7	0·7	6·7	6·5	12·7	12·4
08	14 32·0	14 34·4	13 52·3	0·8	0·8	6·8	6·6	12·8	12·5
09	14 32·3	14 34·6	13 52·5	0·9	0·9	6·9	6·7	12·9	12·6
10	14 32·5	14 34·9	13 52·8	1·0	1·0	7·0	6·8	13·0	12·7
11	14 32·8	14 35·1	13 53·0	1·1	1·1	7·1	6·9	13·1	12·8
12	14 33·0	14 35·4	13 53·2	1·2	1·2	7·2	7·0	13·2	12·9
13	14 33·3	14 35·6	13 53·5	1·3	1·3	7·3	7·1	13·3	13·0
14	14 33·5	14 35·9	13 53·7	1·4	1·4	7·4	7·2	13·4	13·1
15	14 33·8	14 36·1	13 53·9	1·5	1·5	7·5	7·3	13·5	13·2
16	14 34·0	14 36·4	13 54·2	1·6	1·6	7·6	7·4	13·6	13·3
17	14 34·3	14 36·6	13 54·4	1·7	1·7	7·7	7·5	13·7	13·4
18	14 34·5	14 36·9	13 54·7	1·8	1·8	7·8	7·6	13·8	13·5
19	14 34·8	14 37·1	13 54·9	1·9	1·9	7·9	7·7	13·9	13·6
20	14 35·0	14 37·4	13 55·1	2·0	2·0	8·0	7·8	14·0	13·7
21	14 35·3	14 37·6	13 55·4	2·1	2·0	8·1	7·9	14·1	13·7
22	14 35·5	14 37·9	13 55·6	2·2	2·1	8·2	8·0	14·2	13·8
23	14 35·8	14 38·1	13 55·9	2·3	2·2	8·3	8·1	14·3	13·9
24	14 36·0	14 38·4	13 56·1	2·4	2·3	8·4	8·2	14·4	14·0
25	14 36·3	14 38·6	13 56·3	2·5	2·4	8·5	8·3	14·5	14·1
26	14 36·5	14 38·9	13 56·6	2·6	2·5	8·6	8·4	14·6	14·2
27	14 36·8	14 39·2	13 56·8	2·7	2·6	0·7	8·5	14·7	14·3
28	14 37·0	14 39·4	13 57·0	2·8	2·7	8·8	8·6	14·8	14·4
29	14 37·3	14 39·7	13 57·3	2·9	2·8	8·9	8·7	14·9	14·5
30	14 37·5	14 39·9	13 57·5	3·0	2·9	9·0	8·8	15·0	14·6
31	14 37·8	14 40·2	13 57·8	3·1	3·0	9·1	8·9	15·1	14·7
32	14 38·0	14 40·4	13 58·0	3·2	3·1	9·2	9·0	15·2	14·8
33	14 38·3	14 40·7	13 58·2	3·3	3·2	9·3	9·1	15·3	14·9
34	14 38·5	14 40·9	13 58·5	3·4	3·3	9·4	9·2	15·4	15·0
35	14 38·8	14 41·2	13 58·7	3·5	3·4	9·5	9·3	15·5	15·1
36	14 39·0	14 41·4	13 59·0	3·6	3·5	9·6	9·4	15·6	15·2
37	14 39·3	14 41·7	13 59·2	3·7	3·6	9·7	9·5	15·7	15·3
38	14 39·5	14 41·9	13 59·4	3·8	3·7	9·8	9·6	15·8	15·4
39	14 39·8	14 42·2	13 59·7	3·9	3·8	9·9	9·7	15·9	15·5
40	14 40·0	14 42·4	13 59·9	4·0	3·9	10·0	9·8	16·0	15·6
41	14 40·3	14 42·7	14 00·1	4·1	4·0	10·1	9·8	16·1	15·7
42	14 40·5	14 42·9	14 00·4	4·2	4·1	10·2	9·9	16·2	15·8
43	14 40·8	14 43·2	14 00·6	4·3	4·2	10·3	10·0	16·3	15·9
44	14 41·0	14 43·4	14 00·9	4·4	4·3	10·4	10·1	16·4	16·0
45	14 41·3	14 43·7	14 01·1	4·5	4·4	10·5	10·2	16·5	16·1
46	14 41·5	14 43·9	14 01·3	4·6	4·5	10·6	10·3	16·6	16·2
47	14 41·8	14 44·2	14 01·6	4·7	4·6	10·7	10·4	16·7	16·3
48	14 42·0	14 44·4	14 01·8	4·8	4·7	10·8	10·5	16·8	16·4
49	14 42·3	14 44·7	14 02·1	4·9	4·8	10·9	10·6	16·9	16·5
50	14 42·5	14 44·9	14 02·3	5·0	4·9	11·0	10·7	17·0	16·6
51	14 42·8	14 45·2	14 02·5	5·1	5·0	11·1	10·8	17·1	16·7
52	14 43·0	14 45·4	14 02·8	5·2	5·1	11·2	10·9	17·2	16·8
53	14 43·3	14 45·7	14 03·0	5·3	5·2	11·3	11·0	17·3	16·9
54	14 43·5	14 45·9	14 03·3	5·4	5·3	11·4	11·1	17·4	17·0
55	14 43·8	14 46·2	14 03·5	5·5	5·4	11·5	11·2	17·5	17·1
56	14 44·0	14 46·4	14 03·7	5·6	5·5	11·6	11·3	17·6	17·2
57	14 44·3	14 46·7	14 04·0	5·7	5·6	11·7	11·4	17·7	17·3
58	14 44·5	14 46·9	14 04·2	5·8	5·7	11·8	11·5	17·8	17·4
59	14 44·8	14 47·2	14 04·4	5·9	5·8	11·9	11·6	17·9	17·5
60	14 45·0	14 47·4	14 04·7	6·0	5·9	12·0	11·7	18·0	17·6

59ᵐ	SUN PLANETS	ARIES	MOON	v or d	Corrⁿ	v or d	Corrⁿ	v or d	Corrⁿ
s	° ′	° ′	° ′	′	′	′	′	′	′
00	14 45·0	14 47·4	14 04·7	0·0	0·0	6·0	6·0	12·0	11·9
01	14 45·3	14 47·7	14 04·9	0·1	0·1	6·1	6·0	12·1	12·0
02	14 45·5	14 47·9	14 05·2	0·2	0·2	6·2	6·1	12·2	12·1
03	14 45·8	14 48·2	14 05·4	0·3	0·3	6·3	6·2	12·3	12·2
04	14 46·0	14 48·4	14 05·6	0·4	0·4	6·4	6·3	12·4	12·3
05	14 46·3	14 48·7	14 05·9	0·5	0·5	6·5	6·4	12·5	12·4
06	14 46·5	14 48·9	14 06·1	0·6	0·6	6·6	6·5	12·6	12·5
07	14 46·8	14 49·2	14 06·4	0·7	0·7	6·7	6·6	12·7	12·6
08	14 47·0	14 49·4	14 06·6	0·8	0·8	6·8	6·7	12·8	12·7
09	14 47·3	14 49·7	14 06·8	0·9	0·9	6·9	6·8	12·9	12·8
10	14 47·5	14 49·9	14 07·1	1·0	1·0	7·0	6·9	13·0	12·9
11	14 47·8	14 50·2	14 07·3	1·1	1·1	7·1	7·0	13·1	13·0
12	14 48·0	14 50·4	14 07·5	1·2	1·2	7·2	7·1	13·2	13·1
13	14 48·3	14 50·7	14 07·8	1·3	1·3	7·3	7·2	13·3	13·2
14	14 48·5	14 50·9	14 08·0	1·4	1·4	7·4	7·3	13·4	13·3
15	14 48·8	14 51·2	14 08·3	1·5	1·5	7·5	7·4	13·5	13·4
16	14 49·0	14 51·4	14 08·5	1·6	1·6	7·6	7·5	13·6	13·5
17	14 49·3	14 51·7	14 08·7	1·7	1·7	7·7	7·6	13·7	13·6
18	14 49·5	14 51·9	14 09·0	1·8	1·8	7·8	7·7	13·8	13·7
19	14 49·8	14 52·2	14 09·2	1·9	1·9	7·9	7·8	13·9	13·8
20	14 50·0	14 52·4	14 09·5	2·0	2·0	8·0	7·9	14·0	13·9
21	14 50·3	14 52·7	14 09·7	2·1	2·1	8·1	8·0	14·1	14·0
22	14 50·5	14 52·9	14 09·9	2·2	2·2	8·2	8·1	14·2	14·1
23	14 50·8	14 53·2	14 10·2	2·3	2·3	8·3	8·2	14·3	14·2
24	14 51·0	14 53·4	14 10·4	2·4	2·4	0·4	8·3	14·1	14·3
25	14 51·3	14 53·7	14 10·6	2·5	2·5	8·5	8·4	14·5	14·4
26	14 51·5	14 53·9	14 10·9	2·6	2·6	8·6	8·5	14·6	14·5
27	14 51·8	14 54·2	14 11·1	2·7	2·7	8·7	8·6	14·7	14·6
28	14 52·0	14 54·4	14 11·4	2·8	2·8	8·8	8·7	14·8	14·7
29	14 52·3	14 54·7	14 11·6	2·9	2·9	8·9	8·8	14·9	14·8
30	14 52·5	14 54·9	14 11·8	3·0	3·0	9·0	8·9	15·0	14·9
31	14 52·8	14 55·2	14 12·1	3·1	3·1	9·1	9·0	15·1	15·0
32	14 53·0	14 55·4	14 12·3	3·2	3·2	9·2	9·1	15·2	15·1
33	14 53·3	14 55·7	14 12·6	3·3	3·3	9·3	9·2	15·3	15·2
34	14 53·5	14 55·9	14 12·8	3·4	3·4	9·4	9·3	15·4	15·3
35	14 53·8	14 56·2	14 13·0	3·5	3·5	9·5	9·4	15·5	15·4
36	14 54·0	14 56·4	14 13·3	3·6	3·6	9·6	9·5	15·6	15·5
37	14 54·3	14 56·7	14 13·5	3·7	3·7	9·7	9·6	15·7	15·6
38	14 54·5	14 56·9	14 13·8	3·8	3·8	9·8	9·7	15·8	15·7
39	14 54·8	14 57·2	14 14·0	3·9	3·9	9·9	9·8	15·9	15·8
40	14 55·0	14 57·5	14 14·2	4·0	4·0	10·0	9·9	16·0	15·9
41	14 55·3	14 57·7	14 14·5	4·1	4·1	10·1	10·0	16·1	16·0
42	14 55·5	14 58·0	14 14·7	4·2	4·2	10·2	10·1	16·2	16·1
43	14 55·8	14 58·2	14 14·9	4·3	4·3	10·3	10·2	16·3	16·2
44	14 56·0	14 58·5	14 15·2	4·4	4·4	10·4	10·3	16·4	16·3
45	14 56·3	14 58·7	14 15·4	4·5	4·5	10·5	10·4	16·5	16·4
46	14 56·5	14 59·0	14 15·7	4·6	4·6	10·6	10·5	16·6	16·5
47	14 56·8	14 59·2	14 15·9	4·7	4·7	10·7	10·6	16·7	16·6
48	14 57·0	14 59·5	14 16·1	4·8	4·8	10·8	10·7	16·8	16·7
49	14 57·3	14 59·7	14 16·4	4·9	4·9	10·9	10·8	16·9	16·8
50	14 57·5	15 00·0	14 16·6	5·0	5·0	11·0	10·9	17·0	16·9
51	14 57·8	15 00·2	14 16·9	5·1	5·1	11·1	11·0	17·1	17·0
52	14 58·0	15 00·5	14 17·1	5·2	5·2	11·2	11·1	17·2	17·1
53	14 58·3	15 00·7	14 17·3	5·3	5·3	11·3	11·2	17·3	17·2
54	14 58·5	15 01·0	14 17·6	5·4	5·4	11·4	11·3	17·4	17·3
55	14 58·8	15 01·2	14 17·8	5·5	5·5	11·5	11·4	17·5	17·4
56	14 59·0	15 01·5	14 18·0	5·6	5·6	11·6	11·5	17·6	17·5
57	14 59·3	15 01·7	14 18·3	5·7	5·7	11·7	11·6	17·7	17·6
58	14 59·5	15 02·0	14 18·5	5·8	5·8	11·8	11·7	17·8	17·7
59	14 59·8	15 02·2	14 18·8	5·9	5·9	11·9	11·8	17·9	17·8
60	15 00·0	15 02·5	14 19·0	6·0	6·0	12·0	11·9	18·0	17·9

TABLES FOR INTERPOLATING SUNRISE, MOONRISE, ETC.

TABLE I—FOR LATITUDE

Tabular Interval			Difference between the times for consecutive latitudes															
10°	5°	2°	5m	10m	15m	20m	25m	30m	35m	40m	45m	50m	55m	60m	1h 05m	1h 10m	1h 15m	1h 20m
° ′	° ′	° ′	m	m	m	m	m	m	m	m	m	m	m	m	h m	h m	h m	h m
0 30	0 15	0 06	0	0	1	1	1	1	1	2	2	2	2	2	0 02	0 02	0 02	0 02
1 00	0 30	0 12	0	1	1	2	2	3	3	3	4	4	4	5	05	05	05	05
1 30	0 45	0 18	1	1	2	3	3	4	4	5	5	6	7	7	07	07	07	07
2 00	1 00	0 24	1	2	3	4	5	5	6	7	7	8	9	10	10	10	10	10
2 30	1 15	0 30	1	2	4	5	6	7	8	9	9	10	11	12	12	13	13	13
3 00	1 30	0 36	1	3	4	6	7	8	9	10	11	12	13	14	0 15	0 15	0 16	0 16
3 30	1 45	0 42	2	3	5	7	8	10	11	12	13	14	16	17	18	18	19	19
4 00	2 00	0 48	2	4	6	8	9	11	13	14	15	16	18	19	20	21	22	22
4 30	2 15	0 54	2	4	7	9	11	13	15	16	18	19	21	22	23	24	25	26
5 00	2 30	1 00	2	5	7	10	12	14	16	18	20	22	23	25	26	27	28	29
5 30	2 45	1 06	3	5	8	11	13	16	18	20	22	24	26	28	0 29	0 30	0 31	0 32
6 00	3 00	1 12	3	6	9	12	14	17	20	22	24	26	29	31	32	33	34	36
6 30	3 15	1 18	3	6	10	13	16	19	22	24	26	29	31	34	36	37	38	40
7 00	3 30	1 24	3	7	10	14	17	20	23	26	29	31	34	37	39	41	42	44
7 30	3 45	1 30	4	7	11	15	18	22	25	28	31	34	37	40	43	44	46	48
8 00	4 00	1 36	4	8	12	16	20	23	27	30	34	37	41	44	0 47	0 48	0 51	0 53
8 30	4 15	1 42	4	8	13	17	21	25	29	33	36	40	44	48	0 51	0 53	0 56	0 58
9 00	4 30	1 48	4	9	13	18	22	27	31	35	39	43	47	52	0 55	0 58	1 01	1 04
9 30	4 45	1 54	5	9	14	19	24	28	33	38	42	47	51	56	1 00	1 04	1 08	1 12
10 00	5 00	2 00	5	10	15	20	25	30	35	40	45	50	55	60	1 05	1 10	1 15	1 20

Table I is for interpolating the LMT of sunrise, twilight, moonrise, etc., for latitude. It is to be entered, in the appropriate column on the left, with the difference between true latitude and the nearest tabular latitude which is *less* than the true latitude; and with the argument at the top which is the nearest value of the difference between the times for the tabular latitude and the next higher one; the correction so obtained is applied to the time for the tabular latitude; the sign of the correction can be seen by inspection. It is to be noted that the interpolation is not linear, so that when using this table it is essential to take out the tabular phenomenon for the latitude *less* than the true latitude.

TABLE II—FOR LONGITUDE

Long. East or West	Difference between the times for given date and preceding date (for east longitude) or for given date and following date (for west longitude)																	
	10m	20m	30m	40m	50m	60m	1h + 10m	1h + 20m	1h + 30m	1h + 40m	1h + 50m	1h + 60m	2h 10m	2h 20m	2h 30m	2h 40m	2h 50m	3h 00m
°	m	m	m	m	m	m	m	m	m	m	m	m	h m	h m	h m	h m	h m	h m
0	0	0	0	0	0	0	0	0	0	0	0	0	0 00	0 00	0 00	0 00	0 00	0 00
10	0	1	1	1	1	2	2	2	2	3	3	3	04	04	04	04	05	05
20	1	1	2	2	3	3	4	4	5	6	6	7	07	08	08	09	09	10
30	1	2	2	3	4	5	6	7	7	8	9	10	11	12	12	13	14	15
40	1	2	3	4	6	7	8	9	10	11	12	13	14	16	17	18	19	20
50	1	3	4	6	7	8	10	11	12	14	15	17	0 18	0 19	0 21	0 22	0 24	0 25
60	2	3	5	7	8	10	12	13	15	17	18	20	22	23	25	27	28	30
70	2	4	6	8	10	12	14	16	17	19	21	23	25	27	29	31	33	35
80	2	4	7	9	11	13	16	18	20	22	24	27	29	31	33	36	38	40
90	2	5	7	10	12	15	17	20	22	25	27	30	32	35	37	40	42	45
100	3	6	8	11	14	17	19	22	25	28	31	33	0 36	0 39	0 42	0 44	0 47	0 50
110	3	6	9	12	15	18	21	24	27	31	34	37	40	43	46	49	0 52	0 55
120	3	7	10	13	17	20	23	27	30	33	37	40	43	47	50	53	0 57	1 00
130	4	7	11	14	18	22	25	29	32	36	40	43	47	51	54	0 58	1 01	1 05
140	4	8	12	16	19	23	27	31	35	39	43	47	51	54	0 58	1 02	1 06	1 10
150	4	8	13	17	21	25	29	33	38	42	46	50	0 54	0 58	1 03	1 07	1 11	1 15
160	4	9	13	18	22	27	31	36	40	44	49	53	0 58	1 02	1 07	1 11	1 16	1 20
170	5	9	14	19	24	28	33	38	42	47	52	57	1 01	1 06	1 11	1 16	1 20	1 25
180	5	10	15	20	25	30	35	40	45	50	55	60	1 05	1 10	1 15	1 20	1 25	1 30

Table II is for interpolating the LMT of moonrise, moonset and the Moon's meridian passage for longitude. It is entered with longitude and with the difference between the times for the given date and for the preceding date (in east longitudes) or following date (in west longitudes). The correction is normally *added* for west longitudes and *subtracted* for east longitudes, but if, as occasionally happens, the times become earlier each day instead of later, the signs of the corrections must be reversed.

INDEX TO SELECTED STARS, 2026

Name	No	Mag	SHA	Dec
			°	°
Acamar	**7**	3·2	315	S 40
Achernar	**5**	0·5	335	S 57
Acrux	**30**	1·3	173	S 63
Adhara	**19**	1·5	255	S 29
Aldebaran	**10**	0·9	291	N 17
Alioth	**32**	1·8	166	N 56
Alkaid	**34**	1·9	153	N 49
Alnair	**55**	1·7	28	S 47
Alnilam	**15**	1·7	276	S 1
Alphard	**25**	2·0	218	S 9
Alphecca	**41**	2·2	126	N 27
Alpheratz	**1**	2·1	358	N 29
Altair	**51**	0·8	62	N 9
Ankaa	**2**	2·4	353	S 42
Antares	**42**	1·0	112	S 26
Arcturus	**37**	0·0	146	N 19
Atria	**43**	1·9	107	S 69
Avior	**22**	1·9	234	S 60
Bellatrix	**13**	1·6	278	N 6
Betelgeuse	**16**	Var.*	271	N 7
Canopus	**17**	−0·7	264	S 53
Capella	**12**	0·1	280	N 46
Deneb	**53**	1·3	49	N 45
Denebola	**28**	2·1	182	N 14
Diphda	**4**	2·0	349	S 18
Dubhe	**27**	1·8	194	N 62
Elnath	**14**	1·7	278	N 29
Eltanin	**47**	2·2	91	N 51
Enif	**54**	2·4	34	N 10
Fomalhaut	**56**	1·2	15	S 29
Gacrux	**31**	1·6	172	S 57
Gienah	**29**	2·6	176	S 18
Hadar	**35**	0·6	149	S 61
Hamal	**6**	2·0	328	N 24
Kaus Australis	**48**	1·9	84	S 34
Kochab	**40**	2·1	137	N 74
Markab	**57**	2·5	13	N 15
Menkar	**8**	2·5	314	N 4
Menkent	**36**	2·1	148	S 37
Miaplacidus	**24**	1·7	222	S 70
Mirfak	**9**	1·8	308	N 50
Nunki	**50**	2·0	76	S 26
Peacock	**52**	1·9	53	S 57
Pollux	**21**	1·1	243	N 28
Procyon	**20**	0·4	245	N 5
Rasalhague	**46**	2·1	96	N 13
Regulus	**26**	1·4	208	N 12
Rigel	**11**	0·1	281	S 8
Rigil Kentaurus	**38**	−0·3	140	S 61
Sabik	**44**	2·4	102	S 16
Schedar	**3**	2·2	349	N 57
Shaula	**45**	1·6	96	S 37
Sirius	**18**	−1·5	258	S 17
Spica	**33**	1·0	158	S 11
Suhail	**23**	2·2	223	S 44
Vega	**49**	0·0	81	N 39
Zubenelgenubi	**39**	2·8	137	S 16

No	Name	Mag	SHA	Dec
			°	°
1	*Alpheratz*	2·1	358	N 29
2	*Ankaa*	2·4	353	S 42
3	*Schedar*	2·2	349	N 57
4	*Diphda*	2·0	349	S 18
5	*Achernar*	0·5	335	S 57
6	*Hamal*	2·0	328	N 24
7	*Acamar*	3·2	315	S 40
8	*Menkar*	2·5	314	N 4
9	*Mirfak*	1·8	308	N 50
10	*Aldebaran*	0·9	291	N 17
11	*Rigel*	0·1	281	S 8
12	*Capella*	0·1	280	N 46
13	*Bellatrix*	1·6	278	N 6
14	*Elnath*	1·7	278	N 29
15	*Alnilam*	1·7	276	S 1
16	*Betelgeuse*	Var.*	271	N 7
17	*Canopus*	−0·7	264	S 53
18	*Sirius*	−1·5	258	S 17
19	*Adhara*	1·5	255	S 29
20	*Procyon*	0·4	245	N 5
21	*Pollux*	1·1	243	N 28
22	*Avior*	1·9	234	S 60
23	*Suhail*	2·2	223	S 44
24	*Miaplacidus*	1·7	222	S 70
25	*Alphard*	2·0	218	S 9
26	*Regulus*	1·4	208	N 12
27	*Dubhe*	1·8	194	N 62
28	*Denebola*	2·1	182	N 14
29	*Gienah*	2·6	176	S 18
30	*Acrux*	1·3	173	S 63
31	*Gacrux*	1·6	172	S 57
32	*Alioth*	1·8	166	N 56
33	*Spica*	1·0	158	S 11
34	*Alkaid*	1·9	153	N 49
35	*Hadar*	0·6	149	S 61
36	*Menkent*	2·1	148	S 37
37	*Arcturus*	0·0	146	N 19
38	*Rigil Kentaurus*	−0·3	140	S 61
39	*Zubenelgenubi*	2·8	137	S 16
40	*Kochab*	2·1	137	N 74
41	*Alphecca*	2·2	126	N 27
42	*Antares*	1·0	112	S 26
43	*Atria*	1·9	107	S 69
44	*Sabik*	2·4	102	S 16
45	*Shaula*	1·6	96	S 37
46	*Rasalhague*	2·1	96	N 13
47	*Eltanin*	2·2	91	N 51
48	*Kaus Australis*	1·9	84	S 34
49	*Vega*	0·0	81	N 39
50	*Nunki*	2·0	76	S 26
51	*Altair*	0·8	62	N 9
52	*Peacock*	1·9	53	S 57
53	*Deneb*	1·3	49	N 45
54	*Enif*	2·4	34	N 10
55	*Alnair*	1·7	28	S 47
56	*Fomalhaut*	1·2	15	S 29
57	*Markab*	2·5	13	N 15

*0·1 — 1·2

App. Alt.	0°–4° Corrⁿ	5°–9° Corrⁿ	10°–14° Corrⁿ	15°–19° Corrⁿ	20°–24° Corrⁿ	25°–29° Corrⁿ	30°–34° Corrⁿ	App. Alt.
′	° ′	° ′	° ′	° ′	° ′	° ′	° ′	′
00	0 34·5	5 58·2	10 62·1	15 62·8	20 62·2	25 60·8	30 58·9	00
10	36·5	58·5	62·2	62·8	62·2	60·8	58·8	10
20	38·3	58·7	62·2	62·8	62·1	60·7	58·8	20
30	40·0	58·9	62·3	62·8	62·1	60·7	58·7	30
40	41·5	59·1	62·3	62·8	62·0	60·6	58·6	40
50	42·9	59·3	62·4	62·7	62·0	60·6	58·5	50
00	1 44·2	6 59·5	11 62·4	16 62·7	21 62·0	26 60·5	31 58·5	00
10	45·4	59·7	62·4	62·7	61·9	60·4	58·4	10
20	46·5	59·9	62·5	62·7	61·9	60·4	58·3	20
30	47·5	60·0	62·5	62·7	61·9	60·3	58·2	30
40	48·4	60·2	62·5	62·7	61·8	60·3	58·2	40
50	49·3	60·3	62·6	62·7	61·8	60·2	58·1	50
00	2 50·1	7 60·5	12 62·6	17 62·7	22 61·7	27 60·1	32 58·0	00
10	50·8	60·6	62·6	62·6	61·7	60·1	57·9	10
20	51·5	60·7	62·6	62·6	61·6	60·0	57·8	20
30	52·2	60·9	62·7	62·6	61·6	59·9	57·8	30
40	52·8	61·0	62·7	62·6	61·6	59·9	57·7	40
50	53·4	61·1	62·7	62·6	61·5	59·8	57·6	50
00	3 53·9	8 61·2	13 62·7	18 62·5	23 61·5	28 59·7	33 57·5	00
10	54·4	61·3	62·7	62·5	61·4	59·7	57·4	10
20	54·9	61·4	62·7	62·5	61·4	59·6	57·4	20
30	55·3	61·5	62·8	62·5	61·3	59·5	57·3	30
40	55·7	61·6	62·8	62·4	61·3	59·5	57·2	40
50	56·1	61·6	62·8	62·4	61·2	59·4	57·1	50
00	4 56·4	9 61·7	14 62·8	19 62·4	24 61·2	29 59·3	34 57·0	00
10	56·8	61·8	62·8	62·4	61·1	59·3	56·9	10
20	57·1	61·9	62·8	62·3	61·1	59·2	56·9	20
30	57·4	61·9	62·8	62·3	61·0	59·1	56·8	30
40	57·7	62·0	62·8	62·3	61·0	59·1	56·7	40
50	58·0	62·1	62·8	62·2	60·9	59·0	56·6	50

HP	L	U	L	U	L	U	L	U	L	U	L	U	L	U	HP
′	′	′	′	′	′	′	′	′	′	′	′	′	′	′	′
54·0	0·3	0·9	0·3	0·9	0·4	1·0	0·5	1·1	0·6	1·2	0·7	1·3	0·9	1·5	54·0
54·3	0·7	1·1	0·7	1·2	0·8	1·2	0·8	1·3	0·9	1·4	1·1	1·5	1·2	1·7	54·3
54·6	1·1	1·4	1·1	1·4	1·1	1·4	1·2	1·5	1·3	1·6	1·4	1·7	1·5	1·8	54·6
54·9	1·4	1·6	1·5	1·6	1·5	1·6	1·6	1·7	1·6	1·8	1·8	1·9	1·9	2·0	54·9
55·2	1·8	1·8	1·8	1·8	1·9	1·8	1·9	1·9	2·0	2·0	2·1	2·1	2·2	2·2	55·2
55·5	2·2	2·0	2·2	2·0	2·3	2·1	2·3	2·1	2·4	2·2	2·4	2·3	2·5	2·4	55·5
55·8	2·6	2·2	2·6	2·2	2·6	2·3	2·7	2·3	2·7	2·4	2·8	2·4	2·9	2·5	55·8
56·1	3·0	2·4	3·0	2·5	3·0	2·5	3·0	2·5	3·1	2·6	3·1	2·6	3·2	2·7	56·1
56·4	3·3	2·7	3·4	2·7	3·4	2·7	3·4	2·7	3·4	2·8	3·5	2·8	3·5	2·9	56·4
56·7	3·7	2·9	3·7	2·9	3·8	2·9	3·8	2·9	3·8	3·0	3·8	3·0	3·9	3·0	56·7
57·0	4·1	3·1	4·1	3·1	4·1	3·1	4·1	3·1	4·2	3·2	4·2	3·2	4·2	3·2	57·0
57·3	4·5	3·3	4·5	3·3	4·5	3·3	4·5	3·3	4·5	3·3	4·5	3·4	4·6	3·4	57·3
57·6	4·9	3·5	4·9	3·5	4·9	3·5	4·9	3·5	4·9	3·5	4·9	3·5	4·9	3·6	57·6
57·9	5·3	3·8	5·3	3·8	5·2	3·8	5·2	3·7	5·2	3·7	5·2	3·7	5·2	3·7	57·9
58·2	5·6	4·0	5·6	4·0	5·6	4·0	5·6	4·0	5·6	3·9	5·6	3·9	5·6	3·9	58·2
58·5	6·0	4·2	6·0	4·2	6·0	4·2	6·0	4·2	6·0	4·1	5·9	4·1	5·9	4·1	58·5
58·8	6·4	4·4	6·4	4·4	6·4	4·4	6·3	4·4	6·3	4·3	6·3	4·3	6·2	4·2	58·8
59·1	6·8	4·6	6·8	4·6	6·7	4·6	6·7	4·6	6·7	4·5	6·6	4·5	6·6	4·4	59·1
59·4	7·2	4·8	7·1	4·8	7·1	4·8	7·1	4·8	7·0	4·7	7·0	4·7	6·9	4·6	59·4
59·7	7·5	5·1	7·5	5·0	7·5	5·0	7·5	5·0	7·4	4·9	7·3	4·8	7·2	4·8	59·7
60·0	7·9	5·3	7·9	5·3	7·9	5·2	7·8	5·2	7·8	5·1	7·7	5·0	7·6	4·9	60·0
60·3	8·3	5·5	8·3	5·5	8·2	5·4	8·2	5·4	8·1	5·3	8·0	5·2	7·9	5·1	60·3
60·6	8·7	5·7	8·7	5·7	8·6	5·7	8·6	5·6	8·5	5·5	8·4	5·4	8·2	5·3	60·6
60·9	9·1	5·9	9·0	5·9	9·0	5·9	8·9	5·8	8·8	5·7	8·7	5·6	8·6	5·4	60·9
61·2	9·5	6·2	9·4	6·1	9·4	6·1	9·3	6·0	9·2	5·9	9·1	5·8	8·9	5·6	61·2
61·5	9·8	6·4	9·8	6·3	9·7	6·3	9·7	6·2	9·5	6·1	9·4	5·9	9·2	5·8	61·5

DIP

Ht. of Eye	Corrⁿ	Ht. of Eye	Ht. of Eye	Corrⁿ	Ht. of Eye
m	′	ft.	m	′	ft.
2·4		8·0	9·5		31·5
	−2·8			−5·5	
2·6		8·6	9·9		32·7
	−2·9			−5·6	
2·8		9·2	10·3		33·9
	−3·0			−5·7	
3·0		9·8	10·6		35·1
	−3·1			−5·8	
3·2		10·5	11·0		36·3
	−3·2			−5·9	
3·4		11·2	11·4		37·6
	−3·3			−6·0	
3·6		11·9	11·8		38·9
	−3·4			−6·1	
3·8		12·6	12·2		40·1
	−3·5			−6·2	
4·0		13·3	12·6		41·5
	−3·6			−6·3	
4·3		14·1	13·0		42·8
	−3·7			−6·4	
4·5		14·9	13·4		44·2
	−3·8			−6·5	
4·7		15·7	13·8		45·5
	−3·9			−6·6	
5·0		16·5	14·2		46·9
	−4·0			−6·7	
5·2		17·4	14·7		48·4
	−4·1			−6·8	
5·5		18·3	15·1		49·8
	−4·2			−6·9	
5·8		19·1	15·5		51·3
	−4·3			−7·0	
6·1		20·1	16·0		52·8
	−4·4			−7·1	
6·3		21·0	16·5		54·3
	−4·5			−7·2	
6·6		22·0	16·9		55·8
	−4·6			−7·3	
6·9		22·9	17·4		57·4
	−4·7			−7·4	
7·2		23·9	17·9		58·9
	−4·8			−7·5	
7·5		24·9	18·4		60·5
	−4·9			−7·6	
7·9		26·0	18·8		62·1
	−5·0			−7·7	
8·2		27·1	19·3		63·8
	−5·1			−7·8	
8·5		28·1	19·8		65·4
	−5·2			−7·9	
8·8		29·2	20·4		67·1
	−5·3			−8·0	
9·2		30·4	20·9		68·8
	−5·4			−8·1	
9·5		31·5	21·4		70·5

MOON CORRECTION TABLE

The correction is in two parts; the first correction is taken from the upper part of the table with argument apparent altitude, and the second from the lower part, with argument HP, in the same column as that from which the first correction was taken. Separate corrections are given in the lower part for lower (L) and upper(U) limbs. All corrections are to be **added** to apparent altitude, *but 30′ is to be subtracted from the altitude of the upper limb.*

For corrections for pressure and temperature see page A4.

For bubble sextant observations ignore dip, take the mean of upper and lower limb corrections and subtract 15′ from the altitude.

App. Alt. = Apparent altitude = Sextant altitude corrected for index error and dip.

ALTITUDE CORRECTION TABLES 35°–90°— MOON

App. Alt.	35°–39° Corrⁿ	40°–44° Corrⁿ	45°–49° Corrⁿ	50°–54° Corrⁿ	55°–59° Corrⁿ	60°–64° Corrⁿ	65°–69° Corrⁿ	70°–74° Corrⁿ	75°–79° Corrⁿ	80°–84° Corrⁿ	85°–89° Corrⁿ	App. Alt.
′	°	°	°	°	°	°	°	°	°	°	°	′
00	35 56′·5	40 53′·7	45 50′·5	50 46′·9	55 43′·1	60 38′·9	65 34′·6	70 30′·0	75 25′·3	80 20′·5	85 15′·6	00
10	56·4	53·6	50·4	46·8	42·9	38·8	34·4	29·9	25·2	20·4	15·5	10
20	56·3	53·5	50·2	46·7	42·8	38·7	34·3	29·7	25·0	20·2	15·3	20
30	56·2	53·4	50·1	46·5	42·7	38·5	34·1	29·6	24·9	20·0	15·1	30
40	56·2	53·3	50·0	46·4	42·5	38·4	34·0	29·4	24·7	19·9	15·0	40
50	56·1	53·2	49·9	46·3	42·4	38·2	33·8	29·3	24·5	19·7	14·8	50
00	36 56·0	41 53·1	46 49·8	51 46·2	56 42·3	61 38·1	66 33·7	71 29·1	76 24·4	81 19·6	86 14·6	00
10	55·9	53·0	49·7	46·0	42·1	37·9	33·5	29·0	24·2	19·4	14·5	10
20	55·8	52·9	49·5	45·9	42·0	37·8	33·4	28·8	24·1	19·2	14·3	20
30	55·7	52·8	49·4	45·8	41·9	37·7	33·2	28·7	23·9	19·1	14·2	30
40	55·6	52·6	49·3	45·7	41·7	37·5	33·1	28·5	23·8	18·9	14·0	40
50	55·5	52·5	49·2	45·5	41·6	37·4	32·9	28·3	23·6	18·7	13·8	50
00	37 55·4	42 52·4	47 49·1	52 45·4	57 41·4	62 37·2	67 32·8	72 28·2	77 23·4	82 18·6	87 13·7	00
10	55·3	52·3	49·0	45·3	41·3	37·1	32·6	28·0	23·3	18·4	13·5	10
20	55·2	52·2	48·8	45·2	41·2	36·9	32·5	27·9	23·1	18·2	13·3	20
30	55·1	52·1	48·7	45·0	41·0	36·8	32·3	27·7	22·9	18·1	13·2	30
40	55·0	52·0	48·6	44·9	40·9	36·6	32·2	27·6	22·8	17·9	13·0	40
50	55·0	51·9	48·5	44·8	40·8	36·5	32·0	27·4	22·6	17·8	12·8	50
00	38 54·9	43 51·8	48 48·4	53 44·6	58 40·6	63 36·4	68 31·9	73 27·2	78 22·5	83 17·6	88 12·7	00
10	54·8	51·7	48·3	44·5	40·5	36·2	31·7	27·1	22·3	17·4	12·5	10
20	54·7	51·6	48·1	44·4	40·3	36·1	31·6	26·9	22·1	17·3	12·3	20
30	54·6	51·5	48·0	44·2	40·2	35·9	31·4	26·8	22·0	17·1	12·2	30
40	54·5	51·4	47·9	44·1	40·1	35·8	31·3	26·6	21·8	16·9	12·0	40
50	54·4	51·2	47·8	44·0	39·9	35·6	31·1	26·5	21·7	16·8	11·8	50
00	39 54·3	44 51·1	49 47·7	54 43·9	59 39·8	64 35·5	69 31·0	74 26·3	79 21·5	84 16·6	89 11·7	00
10	54·2	51·0	47·5	43·7	39·6	35·3	30·8	26·1	21·3	16·4	11·5	10
20	54·1	50·9	47·4	43·6	39·5	35·2	30·7	26·0	21·2	16·3	11·4	20
30	54·0	50·8	47·3	43·5	39·4	35·0	30·5	25·8	21·0	16·1	11·2	30
40	53·9	50·7	47·2	43·3	39·2	34·9	30·4	25·7	20·9	16·0	11·0	40
50	53·8	50·6	47·0	43·2	39·1	34·7	30·2	25·5	20·7	15·8	10·9	50

HP	L	U	L	U	L	U	L	U	L	U	L	U	L	U	L	U	L	U	L	U	L	U	HP
′	′	′	′	′	′	′	′	′	′	′	′	′	′	′	′	′	′	′	′	′	′	′	′
54·0	1·1	1·7	1·3	1·9	1·5	2·1	1·7	2·4	2·0	2·6	2·3	2·9	2·6	3·2	2·9	3·5	3·2	3·8	3·5	4·1	3·8	4·5	54·0
54·3	1·4	1·8	1·6	2·0	1·8	2·2	2·0	2·5	2·2	2·7	2·5	3·0	2·8	3·2	3·1	3·5	3·3	3·8	3·6	4·1	3·9	4·4	54·3
54·6	1·7	2·0	1·9	2·2	2·1	2·4	2·3	2·6	2·5	2·8	2·7	3·0	3·0	3·3	3·2	3·5	3·5	3·8	3·8	4·0	4·0	4·3	54·6
54·9	2·0	2·2	2·2	2·3	2·3	2·5	2·5	2·7	2·7	2·9	2·9	3·1	3·2	3·3	3·4	3·5	3·6	3·8	3·9	4·0	4·1	4·3	54·9
55·2	2·3	2·3	2·5	2·4	2·6	2·6	2·8	2·8	3·0	2·9	3·2	3·1	3·4	3·3	3·6	3·5	3·8	3·7	4·0	4·0	4·2	4·2	55·2
55·5	2·7	2·5	2·8	2·6	2·9	2·7	3·1	2·9	3·2	3·0	3·4	3·2	3·6	3·4	3·7	3·5	3·9	3·7	4·1	3·9	4·3	4·1	55·5
55·8	3·0	2·6	3·1	2·7	3·2	2·8	3·3	3·0	3·5	3·1	3·6	3·3	3·8	3·4	3·9	3·6	4·1	3·7	4·2	3·9	4·4	4·0	55·8
56·1	3·3	2·8	3·4	2·9	3·5	3·0	3·6	3·1	3·7	3·2	3·8	3·3	4·0	3·4	4·1	3·6	4·2	3·7	4·4	3·8	4·5	4·0	56·1
56·4	3·6	2·9	3·7	3·0	3·8	3·1	3·9	3·2	3·9	3·3	4·0	3·4	4·1	3·5	4·3	3·6	4·4	3·7	4·5	3·8	4·6	3·9	56·4
56·7	3·9	3·1	4·0	3·1	4·1	3·2	4·1	3·3	4·2	3·3	4·3	3·4	4·3	3·5	4·4	3·6	4·5	3·7	4·6	3·8	4·7	3·8	56·7
57·0	4·3	3·2	4·3	3·3	4·3	3·3	4·4	3·4	4·4	3·4	4·5	3·5	4·5	3·5	4·6	3·6	4·7	3·6	4·7	3·7	4·8	3·8	57·0
57·3	4·6	3·4	4·6	3·4	4·6	3·4	4·6	3·5	4·7	3·5	4·7	3·5	4·7	3·6	4·8	3·6	4·8	3·6	4·8	3·7	4·9	3·7	57·3
57·6	4·9	3·6	4·9	3·6	4·9	3·6	4·9	3·6	4·9	3·6	4·9	3·6	4·9	3·6	4·9	3·6	5·0	3·6	5·0	3·6	5·0	3·6	57·6
57·9	5·2	3·7	5·2	3·7	5·2	3·7	5·2	3·7	5·2	3·7	5·1	3·6	5·1	3·6	5·1	3·6	5·1	3·6	5·1	3·6	5·1	3·6	57·9
58·2	5·5	3·9	5·5	3·8	5·5	3·8	5·4	3·8	5·4	3·7	5·4	3·7	5·3	3·7	5·3	3·6	5·2	3·6	5·2	3·5	5·2	3·5	58·2
58·5	5·9	4·0	5·8	4·0	5·8	3·9	5·7	3·9	5·6	3·8	5·6	3·8	5·5	3·7	5·5	3·6	5·4	3·6	5·3	3·5	5·3	3·4	58·5
58·8	6·2	4·2	6·1	4·1	6·0	4·1	6·0	4·0	5·9	3·9	5·8	3·8	5·7	3·7	5·6	3·6	5·5	3·5	5·4	3·5	5·3	3·4	58·8
59·1	6·5	4·3	6·4	4·3	6·3	4·2	6·2	4·1	6·1	4·0	6·0	3·9	5·9	3·8	5·8	3·6	5·7	3·5	5·6	3·4	5·4	3·3	59·1
59·4	6·8	4·5	6·7	4·4	6·6	4·3	6·5	4·2	6·4	4·1	6·2	3·9	6·1	3·8	6·0	3·7	5·8	3·5	5·7	3·4	5·5	3·2	59·4
59·7	7·1	4·7	7·0	4·5	6·9	4·4	6·8	4·3	6·6	4·1	6·5	4·0	6·3	3·8	6·1	3·7	6·0	3·5	5·8	3·3	5·6	3·2	59·7
60·0	7·5	4·8	7·3	4·7	7·2	4·5	7·0	4·4	6·9	4·2	6·7	4·0	6·5	3·9	6·3	3·7	6·1	3·5	5·9	3·3	5·7	3·1	60·0
60·3	7·8	5·0	7·6	4·8	7·5	4·7	7·3	4·5	7·1	4·3	6·9	4·1	6·7	3·9	6·5	3·7	6·3	3·5	6·0	3·2	5·8	3·0	60·3
60·6	8·1	5·1	7·9	5·0	7·7	4·8	7·6	4·6	7·3	4·4	7·1	4·2	6·9	3·9	6·7	3·7	6·4	3·4	6·2	3·2	5·9	2·9	60·6
60·9	8·4	5·3	8·2	5·1	8·0	4·9	7·8	4·7	7·6	4·5	7·3	4·2	7·1	4·0	6·8	3·7	6·6	3·4	6·3	3·2	6·0	2·9	60·9
61·2	8·7	5·4	8·5	5·2	8·3	5·0	8·1	4·8	7·8	4·5	7·6	4·3	7·3	4·0	7·0	3·7	6·7	3·4	6·4	3·1	6·1	2·8	61·2
61·5	9·1	5·6	8·8	5·4	8·6	5·1	8·3	4·9	8·1	4·6	7·8	4·3	7·5	4·0	7·2	3·7	6·9	3·4	6·5	3·1	6·2	2·7	61·5

LIST OF CONTENTS

Pages	
1 — 3	Title page, preface, etc.
4	Phases of the Moon
4 — 5	Calendars
5 — 7	Eclipses
8 — 9	Planet notes and diagram
10 — 253	Daily pages: Ephemerides of Sun, Moon, Aries and planets; sunrise, sunset, twilights, moonrise, moonset, etc.
254 — 261	Explanation
262 — 265	Standard times
266 — 267	Star charts
268 — 273	Stars: SHA and Dec of 173 stars, in order of SHA (accuracy 0.′1)
274 — 276	*Polaris* (Pole Star) tables
277 — 283	Sight reduction procedures; direct computation
284 — 318	Concise sight reduction tables
319	Form for use with concise sight reduction tables
320 — 321	Polar Phenomena
322	Semi-duration of sunlight and twilight
323 — 325	Semi-duration of moonlight
i	Conversion of arc to time
ii — xxxi	Tables of increments and corrections for Sun, planets, Aries, Moon
xxxii	Tables for interpolating sunrise, sunset, twilights, moonrise, moonset, Moon's meridian passage
xxxiii	Index to selected stars
xxxiv — xxxv	Altitude correction tables for the Moon

Auxiliary pages, preceding page 1

A2 — A3	Altitude correction tables for Sun, stars, planets
A4	Additional refraction corrections for non-standard conditions
Bookmark	Same as pages A2 and xxxiii

www.ingramcontent.com/pod-product-compliance
Ingram Content Group UK Ltd.
Pitfield, Milton Keynes, MK11 3LW, UK
UKHW051325020626
12860UKWH00026B/484

9 789797 784683